CAMBRIDGE
School
Dictionary

CAMBRIDGE UNIVERSITY PRESS
Cambridge, New York, Melbourne, Madrid, Cape Town, Singapore, São Paulo, Delhi

Cambridge University Press
The Edinburgh Building, Cambridge CB2 8RU, UK

http://www.cambridge.org
Information on this title: www.cambridge.org/9780521712637

First published 2008

Printed in Italy by L.E.G.O. S.p.A.

A catalogue record for this publication is available from the British Library

Library of Congress Cataloguing in Publishing data applied for.

ISBN 978-0-521-712644 paperback
ISBN 978-0-521-712637 paperback + CD-ROM

Contents

Cambridge School Dictionary

Managing Editor
Stella O'Shea

Commissioning Editors
Elizabeth Walter, Kate Woodford

Editor
Melissa Good

Science Advisor
Tina Brown

Illustrations
David Shenton, Corinne Burrows, Ray Burrows
Eikon Illustrators Ltd, Geoff Jones

Introduction

The **Cambridge School Dictionary** is a brand new dictionary designed to meet the needs of students studying through the medium of English, reflecting the growing popularity of CLIL (Content Language Integrated Learning) throughout the world. Particularly aimed at those taking International GCSE exams, the Cambridge School Dictionary gives you over 2000 curriculum based entries, from geography and anatomy to finance and literature, carefully selected by specialist teachers and checked by curriculum experts.

As well as having each word defined in clear, simple language, the Cambridge School Dictionary contains hundreds of illustrations and diagrams for when processes such as the nitrogen cycle or the digestion of food can be better understood in visual form. It also contains a unique Extra Help section, giving you tips on such matters as working with numbers, charts and graphs, and how to prepare for exams.

Also in the Extra Help section are ten pages of exercises focusing on school subject-based vocabulary and collocation, giving you the language you need to write or talk fluently and confidently about school subject areas such as photosynthesis, computing and the solar system. This helps you to reinforce your learning and to improve your English through your practice of subject-specific vocabulary.

All of the words relating to curriculum areas have been labelled with 'school subject' labels such as language, geology, religious studies and physics (see the inside front cover for a full list of these). The labels enable you to identify quickly and easily the words you need for any particular subject area.

The Cambridge School Dictionary does, of course, give you all the features you would expect from a good corpus-based learner's dictionary: clear, accurate definitions, extensive coverage of grammar and collocation, and examples of typical usage, enabling you to see how the word is really used in its natural contexts. It contains hundreds of Common Learner Errors boxes, thoroughly researched using the *Cambridge Learner Corpus* (a 30m word corpus of students' writing) helping you avoid the mistakes most frequently made by learners. Guidewords lead you to the meaning you need when the word has more than two senses. In addition, the dictionary contains hundreds of new words, enabling you to keep up with changes to the English language and keeping your own English up-to-date.

But this is not all: the CD-ROM comes with some really exciting features, including the unique SMART thesaurus, giving you alternatives to over-used words and helping you to find the exact word you need. It has recordings of every word in the dictionary with both British and American pronunciations - you can even record your own voice and play it back, comparing your own pronunciation with the standard. In addition to the exercises in the book, the CD-ROM contains hundreds of interactive vocabulary practice exercises. It is also searchable, so if you want to call up all the vocabulary relating to one topic area you can do this in a couple of clicks. And for when you're working at your computer, there is the QUICKfind facility, a mini pop-up version of the dictionary that gives you instant definitions of words while you are studying or surfing the Web.

This is the perfect companion for learners studying other subjects through the medium of English up to IGCSE level. In it you will find everything you need to help you study, revise for and pass those all-important exams.

Stella O'Shea

September 2008

How to use this dictionary

Finding a word

Each entry begins with the base form of the word.

language /ˈlæŋɡwɪdʒ/ *noun* **1 LANGUAGE** [U] communication between people, usually using words *She has done research into how children acquire language.* **2 LANGUAGE** [C] a type of communication used by the people of a particular country *How many* ***languages*** *do you* ***speak?*** **3 LANGUAGE** [U] words of a particular type, especially the words used by people in a particular job *legal language* ○ *the language of business* **4 COMPUTING** [C, U] a system of instructions that is used to write computer programs ➲See also: **body language, modern languages, second language, sign language**

Words which are made of two separate words (compounds) are found in alphabetical order. The stress marks (ˈ,ˌ) show you which part of the word to say strongly.

language laˌboratory *UK* (*US* **ˈlanguage ˌlaboratory**) *noun* [C] **EDUCATION** a room in a college or school where you can use equipment to help you practise listening to and speaking a foreign language

When a word can be spelled another way, or when there is another word for it, this is shown.

dialogue (*also US* **dialog**) /ˈdaɪəlɒɡ/ *noun* [C, U] **1** TALKING the talking in a book, play, or film **2** DISCUSSION a formal discussion between countries or groups of people

When two words have the same spelling but different parts of speech (e.g. a noun and an adjective), they have separate entries.

interface[1] /ˈɪntəfeɪs/ *noun* [C] **1 COMPUTING** a connection between two pieces of electronic equipment, or between a person and a computer *a simple* ***user interface*** **2** a situation, way, or place where two things can come together and have an effect on each other *the* ***interface between*** *technology and tradition*

interface[2] /ˈɪntəˌfeɪs/ *verb* [I, T] **COMPUTING** to communicate with people or electronic equipment, or to make people or electronic equipment communicate *We use email to* ***interface with*** *our customers.*

School subject labels show you what curriculum area the word belongs to.

Some words which are formed from the main word are shown at the end of an entry. If a word is not formed with a regular pattern, or if its meaning is not easy to guess, it has its own explanation. See Word beginnings and endings on page 873.

fluent /ˈfluːənt/ *adjective* **1** LANGUAGE able to use a language naturally without stopping or making mistakes *She is **fluent in** six languages.* **2** STYLE produced or done in a smooth, natural style *Hendrik speaks fluent English.* •**fluency** /ˈfluːənsi/ *noun* [U] •**fluently** *adverb*

Understanding an entry

Where a word has more than one meaning, the most frequent meaning is shown first.

Words which have several meanings have GUIDEWORDS to help you find the meaning you are looking for. Guidewords appear in black type with a black box around them.

voice¹ /vɔɪs/ *noun* **1** SOUNDS [C] the sounds that you make when you speak or sing *I could hear voices in the next room.* ○ *Jessie has a beautiful singing voice.* ○ *Could you please **keep your voices down*** (= speak more quietly)? ○ *He **raised his voice*** (= spoke more loudly) *so that everyone could hear.* **2** **lose your voice** HEALTH to become unable to speak, often because of an illness *She had a bad cold and was losing her voice.* **3** OPINION [C] someone's opinion about a particular subject *The programme gives people the opportunity to make their voices heard.* **4** PERSON [**no plural**] someone who expresses the opinions or wishes of a group of people *It's important that students have a voice on the committee.* ⊃See also: **the passive voice**

Each word has a part of speech label (e.g. *noun, verb, adj*) For a list of the parts of speech, see inside the front cover.

Grammar labels tell you how a word is used. See the grammar labels on page xiii.

Example sentences, based on the *Cambridge International Corpus*, show how words are used in typical situations.

say¹ /seɪ/ *verb* [T] **says** *past* **said** **1** WORDS to speak words *"I'd like to go home," she said.* ○ *I couldn't hear what they were saying.* ○ *How do you say this word?* **2** TELL to tell someone about a fact, thought, or opinion [+ **question word**] *Did she say where she was going?* [+ **(that)**] *The jury said that he was guilty.* **3** INFORMATION to give information in writing, numbers, or signs *My watch says one o'clock.* ○ *What do the papers say about the election?* **4** **say sth to yourself** to think something but not speak *"I hope she likes me," he said to himself.* **5** SHOW to show what

This symbol shows very frequent words which are important to learn.

Pronunciations use the International Phonetic Alphabet (IPA). There is a list of these symbols inside the back cover of the dictionary. The most difficult symbols are also explained at the bottom of each page.There is an explanation of the pronunciation system on page xvi.

Irregular inflections of words are clearly shown. There is a list of irregular verb inflections on page 870 and an explanation of regular inflections on page 868.

These labels show you when a word is used in British English or American English. See explanation of these labels on page xv.

These labels tell you how formal, informal, etc a word is. See explanation of all these labels on page xv.

o⁼speak /spiːk/ *verb past tense* **spoke**, *past participle* **spoken** **1** SAY WORDS [I] to say something using your voice *to speak loudly/quietly* ○ *There was complete silence - nobody spoke.* **2 speak to sb** *mainly UK* (*mainly US* **speak with sb**) to talk to someone *Could I speak to Mr Davis, please?* ○ *Have you spoken with your new neighbors yet?* **3 speak about/of sth** to talk about something *He refused to speak about the matter in public.* **4 speak English/French/German, etc** LANGUAGE to be able to communicate in English/French/German, etc *Do you speak English?* **5** IN PUBLIC [I] to make a speech to a large group of people *She was invited to speak at a conference in Madrid.* **6 speak for/on behalf of sb** to express the feelings, opinions, etc of another person or of a group of people *I've been chosen to speak on behalf of the whole class.* **7 generally/personally, etc speaking** used

o⁼chat[1] /tʃæt/ *verb* [I] **chatting** *past* **chatted** to talk with someone in a friendly and informal way *I wanted to* ***chat to*** *you* ***about*** *the party on Saturday.*
chat sb up *phrasal verb UK informal* to talk to someone in a way that shows them that you are sexually attracted to them

Learning more about a word

Cross references show you where you can find related information such as opposites, pictures, study pages, and idioms.

o⁼ask /ɑːsk/ *verb* **1** QUESTION [I, T] to say something to someone as a question which you want them to answer [+ **two objects**] *Can I* ***ask*** *you a few* ***questions***? ○ *I* ***asked*** *him* ***about*** his hobbies. [+ **question word**] *I asked why the plane was so late.* ➲See Common Learner Error at **question** **2** WANT SOMETHING [I, T] to say something to someone because you want them to give you something *He's* ***asked for*** *a bike for his birthday.* **3** REQUEST [I, T] to say something to some-

Words which are often used together, called **collocations** or **Word Partners** are shown in dark type in examples.

communicate /kəˈmjuːnɪkeɪt/ *verb* [I, T] **1** INFORMATION to share information with others by speaking, writing, moving your body, or using other signals *We can now **communicate** instantly **with** people on the other side of the world.* **2** FEELINGS to talk about your thoughts and feelings, and help other people to understand them *He can't **communicate with** his parents.*

Some words are used as part of a phrase. This is shown clearly at the start of the definition.

Phrasal verbs come after the entry for the verb in alphabetical order.

⊶ **spell**[1] /spel/ *verb past* **spelled**, *also UK* **spelt** **1** **LANGUAGE** [T] to write down or tell someone the letters which are used to make a word *How do you spell that?* ○ *Her name's spelt S-I-A-N.* **2** **LANGUAGE** [I] If you can spell, you know how to write the words of a language correctly. *My grammar's all right, but I can't spell.* **3** **spell disaster/trouble, etc** If something spells disaster, trouble, etc, you think it will cause something bad to happen in the future. *The new regulations could spell disaster for small businesses.*

spell sth out *phrasal verb* to explain something in a very clear way with details *They sent me a letter, **spelling out the details** of the agreement.*

Some words are used as part of an idiom. These are shown in dark type at the end of the entry.

⊶ **message**[1] /ˈmesɪdʒ/ *noun* [C] **1** a piece of written or spoken information which one person gives to another *Did you **get** my **message**?* ○ *I **left** her several **messages**, but she hasn't returned my call.* **2** the most important idea of a film, book, etc *The book conveys a complex message.* **3** **get the message** *informal* to understand what someone wants you to do by their actions *Don't return any of his calls - he'll soon get the message and leave you alone.*

All our definitions use very simple words. Where we have had to use a more difficult word than usual, that word is explained in brackets.

⊶ **express**[1] /ɪkˈspres/ *verb* [T] to show what you think or how you feel using words or actions *I'm simply expressing my opinion.* [**often reflexive**] *You're not expressing yourself* (= saying what you mean) *very clearly.*

The information in the boxes

These Word Partner boxes give you information on words that are often spoken or written together, called **collocations** or **Word Partners**. There are over 1000 of these boxes in this dictionary.

WORD PARTNERS FOR ***text message***

get/send a text message • a text message **saying** sth • a text message **from/to** sb

These thesaurus boxes show you all the different words which have the same or a similar meaning. There are 80 of these boxes in this dictionary.

OTHER WAYS OF SAYING ***talk***

The most common alternatives are **speak** and **say**: *Could you **speak** more quietly, please?* • *I couldn't hear what they were **saying**.*

The verb **chat** or the expression **have a chat** are often used if a person is talking with someone in a friendly, informal way: *We were just **chatting** about the party on Saturday.* • *Give me a call and we'll **have a chat**.*

If people talk for a long time about things that are not important, verbs such as **chatter**, **natter** (*UK, informal*), and the expression **have a natter** (*UK, informal*) are sometimes used: *She spent the morning **chattering** away to her friends.* • *We **had a** long **natter** over coffee.*

Common Learner Error notes based on the *Cambridge Learner Corpus* give extra information about words which often cause problems for learners.

COMMON LEARNER ERROR

mention

No preposition is normally needed after the verb **mention**.

He didn't mention the price.

~~*He didn't mention about the price.*~~

More information on using the dictionary

Grammar labels

When a word must *always* be used in a particular grammatical form, that form is shown at the beginning of the entry or the beginning of the meaning. Patterns which are common and typical, but are not *always* used, are given next to example sentences showing how they are used.

Nouns

Label	Meaning	Examples
C	countable noun	pencil, friend, house
U	uncountable noun, does not have a plural	water, advice, health
C, U	noun which can be countable or uncountable	ability, quantity, exercise ▶ *You should take some* ***exercise****.* ▶ *I do my* ***exercises*** *every morning.*
➡	see also Extra help page **Countable and uncountable nouns**, on page Centre 30	
group	noun which refers to a group of people or things and can be used with either a singular or a plural verb	government, class, team ▶ *The French* ***team are*** *European champions.* ▶ *His* ***team is*** *top of the league.*
plural	plural noun, used with a plural verb	trousers, scissors, pliers
no plural	noun which can be used with **a** and **an**, but does not have a plural	rush, vicious circle, wait ▶ *Sorry, I'm in* ***a rush****.*
usually plural	noun usually used in the plural form	statistics, resources, regulations
usually singular	noun usually used in the singular form	mess, range, world

Verbs

Label	Meaning	Examples
I	intransitive verb, does not have an object	sleep, glance, fall ▶ *Anna's* ***sleeping****.*
T	transitive verb, must have an object	cure, hit, catch ▶ *Fiona* ***hit*** *her* ***sister****.*
I, T	verb that can be intransitive or transitive	sing, explain, drive ▶ *I always* ***sing*** *in the bath.* ▶ *He* ***sang*** *a love* ***song****.*
+ two objects	ditransitive verb, that has two objects	give, send, lend ▶ *She* ***gave me*** *the* ***keys****.*

often passive	verb often used in the passive	allow ▶ *Smoking **is not allowed** in the restaurant.*
often reflexive	verb often used with a reflexive pronoun (myself, yourself, herself, etc)	defend ▶ *He can **defend himself**.*

If a verb or a meaning of a verb is ***always* passive** (e.g. inundate, demote, affiliate) or ***always* reflexive** (e.g. brace, ingratiate, steel), the whole grammar pattern is shown at the beginning of the entry.

Some verb or meanings of verbs are **always followed by an adverb or preposition** (e.g. creep, flick, trickle) . When this happens, common examples of adverbs and prepositions used are shown at the beginning of the entry or the meaning.

➡ see also Extra help page **Verb patterns**, on page Centre 25

Adjectives

always before noun	attributive adjective, always comes before the noun	major, basic, staunch ▶ *a **staunch** supporter*
never before noun	predicative adjective, used with verbs such as **be, seem, feel**	afraid, ready, done ▶ *She's **afraid** of water.*
always after noun	adjective always used directly after the noun	galore, personified, incarnate ▶ *the devil **incarnate***

Other grammar patterns

The following patterns can refer to nouns, adjectives, and verbs:

+ that	the word is followed by a **that clause**, and the word **that** must be included	boast, assertion, evident ▶ *It was **evident** from her voice **that** she was upset.*
+ (that)	the word is followed by a **that clause** but the word **that** does not have to be used	hope, amazed, doubt ▶ *I **hope that** the bus won't be late.* *I **hope** the bus won't be late.*
+ doing sth	the word is followed by a verb in the –ing form	enjoy, busy, difficulty ▶ *I **enjoy going** to the beach.*
+ to do sth	the word is followed by a verb in the infinitive	confidence, careful, decide ▶ *I didn't have the **confidence to speak up**.*
+ from/for/of, etc + doing sth	the word is followed by a preposition (e.g. from/for/of) then a verb in the –ing form	apologize, idea, guilty ▶ *He was **banned from** driving for two years.*
+ question word	the word is followed by a question word (e.g. who, what, how)	ask, certain, clue ▶ *I'm not **certain who** to ask.*
used in questions and negatives	the word is used in questions and negative sentences	mind, much, yet ▶ *Do you mind if I come in?* *I haven't seen him yet.*

Usage labels

Label	Meaning	Examples
informal	used when you are speaking, or communicating with people you know, but not usually in serious writing	brainy, freebie, cop
formal	used in serious writing or for communicating with people about things like law or business	examination, moreover, purchase
very informal	used when you are talking to people you know well, and not usually in writing. Some of these words may offend people, and this is explained in the entry.	dude, barf, innit
spoken	a way of writing a word which is used in conversation	yeah, hey, eh
humorous	used in order to be funny or to make a joke	couch potato, snail mail
literary	used in books and poems, not in ordinary conversation	beloved, slumber, weep
old-fashioned	not used in modern English – you might find these words in books, used by older people, or used in order to be funny	gramophone, spectacles, super
trademark	the name of a product that is made by one company. Sometimes a trademark is used as a general word.	Coke, iPod, Band-Aid

UK/US labels

The spelling used in definitions and examples in this dictionary is British English. However, American English is also explained, and where there is a difference between British and American English, this is shown.

Label	Meaning	Examples
UK	only used in British English	pavement, petrol station
US	only used in American English	sidewalk, gas station
mainly UK	mainly used in British English, but sometimes in American English	lecturer, rubbish, nightdress
mainly US	mainly used in American English, but sometimes in British English	movie, apartment, semester
also UK	another word that can also be used in British English	truck (*also UK* lorry) ■ **truck** is used in Britain and the US **lorry** is also used in Britain
also US	another word that can also be used in American English	railway (*also US* railroad) ■ **railway** is used in Britain and the US **railroad** is also used in the US

Pronunciation

All pronunciations use the International Phonetic Alphabet. There is a complete list of phonetic symbols inside the back cover.

Many phonetic symbols, e.g. /p/, /s/, /k/, sound exactly like the most common pronunciation of the letter they look like. Those that do not are explained at the bottom of every page of the dictionary.

Where more than one pronunciation is shown, the more common one is first, but both are often used.

British and American pronunciation

Most words are given only one pronunciation, which is acceptable in British and American English. There are some regular differences between British and American English which are not shown for every word.

The main ones are:

1 In American English, the **r** in words such as **hard** or **teacher** is pronounced, and in British English it is silent.

2 In American English, **t** and **tt** in words such as **later** and **butter**, are pronounced in a soft way, almost like a /d/ sound.

Where there is a big difference between British and American pronunciation, both forms are shown. The symbol Ⓤⓢ is shown before an American pronunciation, e.g. **schedule** /ˈʃedjuːl Ⓤⓢ ˈskedʒuːl/

Stress patterns

Stress patterns show you which parts of the word you should emphasize when you say them.

/ˈ/ shows the main emphasis on a word. For example, in the word **picture** /ˈpɪktʃəʳ/, you should emphasize the first part, and in the word **deny** /dɪˈnaɪ/ you should emphasize the second part.

/ˌ/ shows the second most important emphasis on the word. For example, in the word **submarine** /ˌsʌbmərˈiːn/, the main emphasis is on the last part of the word, but you should also emphasize the first part of the word slightly.

Compound words (words made of two or more separate words) have their stress patterns shown on them. For example in the word **deˌsigner ˈbaby**, the main emphasis is on the first part of the second word, but you should also emphasize the first part of the first word slightly.

Strong forms and weak forms

Some common words (e.g. and, them, of) have strong forms and weak forms. The weak forms are more common.

For example, in the sentence '*I saw them leave.*', the weak form /ðəm/ would be used.

The strong form is used when you want to emphasize the word. For instance, in the sentence '*They said they saw me, but I didn't see them.*', the strong form /ðem/ would be used.

Regular inflections

All inflections (e.g. plurals, past tenses) that are not regular (= are not formed in the usual way) are shown at the entry for the word. The regular way of forming inflections is shown below.

Nouns

Most nouns form their plurals by adding **–s**
▶ *chair, chairs* ▶ *plate, plates*

Nouns which end in **–s**, **–ss**, **–ch**, **–x**, and **–z**, make their plurals by adding **–es**
▶ *mass, masses* ▶ *match, matches*

Nouns which end in a consonant (e.g. m, t, p) + **–y**, form their plurals by taking away the **–y** and adding **–ies**
▶ *baby, babies* ▶ *university, universities*

Adjectives

The comparative form of adjectives is used to show that someone or something has more of a particular quality than someone or something else. To make the regular comparative form, you either add **–er** to the end of the adjective, or use the word **more** before it.

The superlative form of adjectives is used to show that someone or something has more of a particular quality than anyone or anything else. To make the regular superlative form, you either add **–est** to the end of the adjective, or use the word **most** before it.

One-syllable adjectives usually form their comparative and superlative with **–er** and **–est**
▶ *small, smaller, smallest*

Two-syllable adjectives can all form their comparative and superlative with **more** and **most**.
▶ *complex, more complex, most complex*

Some two-syllable adjectives can use **–er** and **–est** too. The most common of these are:

- adjectives ending in **–y** and **–ow**,
  ▶ *happy, noisy, shallow*
- adjectives ending in **–le**,
  ▶ *able, noble, simple*
- some other common two-syllable adjectives,
  ▶ *common, stupid, pleasant, polite, quiet, wicked*

Three-syllable adjectives usually form their comparative and superlative with **more** and **most**
▶ *beautiful, more beautiful, most beautiful*

When you are using the **–er**, **–est** forms, if the adjective ends in **–e**, take away the **–e** before adding the ending
▶ *pale, paler, palest*

If the adjective ends in **–y**, change this to **–i** before adding the ending
▶ *happy, happier, happiest*

Verbs

Regular verbs add the following endings:

for the **3rd person singular** add **–s**, or **–es** to verbs that end in **–s**, **–ss**, **–ch**, **–x**, and **–z**

for the **present participle** add **–ing**

for the **past tense** and the **past participle** add **–ed**
▶ *pack, packs, packing, packed*

For verbs ending in **–e**, take away the **–e** before adding the present participle, past tense, and past participle endings.
▶ *hate, hates, hating, hated*

For verbs ending in **–y**, for the third person singular take away the **–y** and add **–ies**, and for the past tense and past participle take away the **–y** and add **–ied**.
▶ *cry, cries, crying, cried*

Aa

A, a /eɪ/ the first letter of the alphabet

O⁻**a** (*also* **an**) *strong form* /eɪ/ *weak form* /ə/ *determiner* **1** BEFORE NOUN used before a noun to refer to a single thing or person but not a particular thing or person or not one that you have referred to before *I need a new car.* ○ *I saw a woman speaking to him.* **2** ONE one *a hundred dollars* ○ *a dozen eggs* **3** EVERY/EACH every or each *A child needs love.* ○ *Take one tablet three times a* (= each) *day.* **4** TYPE used to say what type of thing or person something or someone is *It's a guinea pig.* ○ *She's a doctor.* **5** AN ACTION used before some action nouns when referring to one example of the action *I'm just going to have a wash.* ○ *Take a look at this.* **6** TWO NOUNS used before the first of two nouns that are often used together *a cup and saucer* **7** AMOUNTS used before some phrases saying how much of something there is *a few days* ○ *a bit of sugar* **8** NAME used before a person's name when referring to someone you do not know *There's a Ms Leeming to see you.*

COMMON LEARNER ERROR

a or an?

Remember to use **an** in front of words which begin with a vowel sound. These are words which start with the letters a, e, i, o, u, or a sound like those letters.

*a car, **an** orange, **an** hour*

a- /eɪ/ *prefix* not, without *atypical* ○ *amoral*

aback /ə'bæk/ *adverb* **be taken aback** to be very surprised or shocked *I was rather taken aback by her honesty.*

abacus /'æbəkəs/ *noun* [C] **MATHEMATICS** a square object with small balls on wires, used for counting

WORD PARTNERS FOR ***abandon***

be **forced to** abandon sth • abandon an **attempt/effort/idea/plan/search**

abandon /ə'bændən/ *verb* [T] **1** LEAVE to leave someone or something somewhere, sometimes not returning to get them *They were **forced to abandon** the car.* **2** STOP DOING to stop doing something before it is finished, or to stop following a plan, idea, etc *The match was abandoned because of rain.* •**abandoned** *adjective* •**abandonment** *noun* [U]

abate /ə'beɪt/ *verb* [I] *formal* to become less strong *By the weekend, the storms had abated.*

abattoir /'æbətwɑːʳ/ *UK* (*UK/US* **slaughterhouse**) *noun* [C] **FARMING** a place where animals are killed for meat

abbey /'æbi/ *noun* [C] **RELIGION** a group of buildings that is a home for monks or nuns (= religious men or women who live separately from other people)

abbreviate /ə'briːvieɪt/ *verb* [T] **LANGUAGE** to make a word or phrase shorter *The word 'street' is often **abbreviated to** 'St'.*

abbreviation /əˌbriːvi'eɪʃən/ *noun* [C] **LANGUAGE** a shorter form of a word or phrase, especially used in writing *A doctor is often called a 'GP', an **abbreviation for** 'general practitioner'.*

abdicate /'æbdɪkeɪt/ *verb* **1** [I] If a king or queen abdicates, they choose to stop being king or queen. **2 abdicate responsibility** *formal* to decide not to be responsible for something any more •**abdication** /ˌæbdɪ'keɪʃən/ *noun* [C, U]

abdomen /'æbdəmən/ *noun* [C] *formal* **ANATOMY** the lower part of a person or animal's body, containing the stomach and other organs •**abdominal** /æb'dɒmɪnəl/ *adjective* to do with the abdomen *abdominal pains*

abduct /əb'dʌkt/ *verb* [T] to take someone away illegally *He was abducted by a terrorist group.* •**abduction** /əb'dʌkʃən/ *noun* [C, U]

aberration /ˌæbə'reɪʃən/ *noun* [C] *formal* a temporary change from what usually happens

abet /ə'bet/ *verb* **abetting**, *past* **abetted** ➲See: **aid**[2] and abet (sb)

abhor /əb'hɔːʳ/ *verb* [T] **abhorring**, *past* **abhorred** *formal* to hate something or someone very much •**abhorrence** /əb'hɒrəns/ *noun* [U] *formal*

abhorrent /əb'hɒrənt/ *adjective formal* morally very bad *an abhorrent crime*

abide /ə'baɪd/ *verb* **can't abide sb/sth** to strongly dislike someone or something *I can't abide rudeness.*
abide by sth *phrasal verb* to obey a rule *Staff who refused to **abide by the rules** were fired.*

abiding /ə'baɪdɪŋ/ *adjective* [**always before noun**] An abiding feeling or memory is one that you have for a long time. *My **abiding memory** is of him watering his plants in the garden.* ➲See also: **law-abiding**

WORD PARTNERS FOR ***ability***

have/lack/possess ability • **innate/remarkable/uncanny** ability

O⁻**ability** /ə'bɪləti/ *noun* [C, U] the physical or mental skill or qualities that you need to do something *athletic/academic ability* [+ **to do sth**] *He **had the ability** to explain things clearly.* ○ *The report questions the technical ability of the staff.* ➲Opposite **inability** ➲Compare **disability**

abject /'æbdʒekt/ *adjective* **1 abject misery/poverty/terror, etc** when someone is extremely unhappy, poor, afraid, etc **2** showing that you are very ashamed of what you have done *an **abject apology***

ablation /ə'bleɪʃən/ *noun* [U] **GEOGRAPHY** the loss of ice, snow or rock from melting or erosion (= being damaged and removed by wind, sea or rain)

ablaze /ə'bleɪz/ *adjective* [**never before noun**] burning strongly

O⁻**able** /'eɪbl/ *adjective* **1 be able to do sth** to have the ability to do something or the possibility of doing something *He'll be able to help you.* ➲Opposite be **unable** to do sth **2** clever or good at doing something *She's a very **able student**.*

A

•**ably** *adverb Robson,* ***ably assisted*** *by Anderson, has completely rebuilt the team.*

able-bodied /ˌeɪbl'bɒdɪd/ *adjective* **HEALTH** having all the physical abilities that most people have

abnormal /æb'nɔːməl/ *adjective* different from what is normal or usual, in a way which is strange or dangerous *abnormal behaviour/ weather* ○ *They found* ***abnormal levels*** *of lead in the water.* •**abnormally** *adverb*

abnormality /ˌæbnɔː'mæləti/ *noun* [**C, U**] **HEALTH** something abnormal, usually in the body *a* ***genetic abnormality***

aboard /ə'bɔːd/ *adverb, preposition* on or onto a plane, ship, bus, or train *Welcome aboard flight BA109 to Paris.*

abode /ə'bəʊd/ *noun* [**C**] *formal* a home

abolish /ə'bɒlɪʃ/ *verb* [**T**] **LAW** to officially end something, especially a law or system *National Service was abolished in Britain in 1962.* •**abolition** /ˌæbə'lɪʃən/ *noun* [**U**] *the abolition of slavery*

abominable /ə'bɒmɪnəbl/ *adjective* extremely bad *abominable behaviour* •**abominably** *adverb*

Aboriginal /ˌæbə'rɪdʒənəl/ *adjective* **SOCIETY** relating or belonging to the original race of people who lived in Australia •**Aborigine** /ˌæbə'rɪdʒəni/ *noun* [**C**] an Aboriginal person

abort /ə'bɔːt/ *verb* [**T**] **1** to stop a process before it has finished *The take-off was aborted due to bad weather.* **2 HEALTH** to end a pregnancy that is not wanted using a medical operation

abortion /ə'bɔːʃən/ *noun* [**C, U**] **HEALTH** a medical operation to end a pregnancy when the baby is still too small to live *She* ***had an abortion.***

abortive /ə'bɔːtɪv/ *adjective* [**always before noun**] An abortive attempt or plan fails before it is complete.

the ABO system /ˌeɪbiː'əʊsɪstəm/ *noun* **BIOLOGY, HEALTH** the system that divides human blood into four main groups called A, B, AB and O

abound /ə'baʊnd/ *verb* [**I**] *formal* to exist in large numbers ***Rumours abound*** *about a possible change of leadership.*

O-**about**[1] /ə'baʊt/ *preposition* **1** [SUBJECT] relating to a particular subject or person *a book about the Spanish Civil War* ○ *What was she talking about?* **2** [DIRECTION] *UK* (*US* **around**) to or in different parts of a place, often without purpose or order *We heard someone moving about outside.* **3 what/how about ...? a** [SUGGESTION] used to make a suggestion *How about France for a holiday?* **b** [OPINION] used to ask for someone's opinion on a particular subject *What about Ann - is she nice?*

O-**about**[2] /ə'baʊt/ *adverb* **1** [APPROXIMATELY] used before a number or amount to mean approximately *It happened about two months ago.* **2** [DIRECTION] *UK* (*US* **around**) to or in different parts of a place, often without purpose or order *She's always leaving her clothes lying about.* **3** [NEAR] *UK informal* (*US* **around**) If someone or something is about, they are near to the place where you are now. *Is Kate about?* **4 be about to do sth** to be going to do something very soon *I stopped her just as she was about to leave.*

O-**above**[1] /ə'bʌv/ *adverb, preposition* **1** [HIGHER POSITION] in or to a higher position than something else *There's a mirror above the washbasin.* ○ *I could hear music coming from the room above.* **2** [MORE] more than an amount or level *It says on the box it's for children aged three and above.* ○ *Rates of pay are above average.* **3** [RANK] in a more important or advanced position than someone else *Sally's a grade above me.* **4** [TOO IMPORTANT] too good or important for something *No one is above suspicion in this matter.* **5 above all** most importantly *Above all, I'd like to thank everyone.*

above[2] /ə'bʌv/ *adjective, adverb* higher on the same page *the above diagram* ○ *the address shown above*

aˌbove 'board *adjective* [**never before noun**] honest and legal *We hired a lawyer to make sure the agreement was all above board.*

aˌbove the line pro'motion *noun* [**U**] ways of advertising products that involve people outside the business, such as newspapers or TV

abrasive /ə'breɪsɪv/ *adjective* **1** [SUBSTANCE] An abrasive substance is rough and can be used for rubbing surfaces, to make them clean or smooth. **2** [PERSON] speaking or behaving in a rude and unpleasant way *an abrasive manner*

abreast /ə'brest/ *adverb* **1 keep (sb) abreast of sth** to make sure you or someone else knows about the most recent changes in a subject or situation *I'll keep you abreast of any developments.* **2 two/three/four, etc abreast** If people who are moving are two/three, etc abreast, that number of people are next to each other, side by side. *They were cycling four abreast, completely blocking the road.*

abridged /ə'brɪdʒd/ *adjective* An abridged book or other piece of writing has been made shorter. ⊃Opposite **unabridged** •**abridge** /ə'brɪdʒ/ *verb* [**T**]

WORD PARTNERS FOR ***abroad***

go/live/travel/work abroad • a **holiday/trip** abroad

O-**abroad** /ə'brɔːd/ *adverb* in or to a foreign country *He* ***goes abroad*** *a lot with his job.*

abrupt /ə'brʌpt/ *adjective* **1** [SUDDEN] sudden and not expected *Our conversation came to an* ***abrupt end.*** **2** [RUDE] dealing with people in a quick way that is unfriendly or rude *She has a rather* ***abrupt manner.*** •**abruptly** *adverb*

abscess /'æbses/ *noun* [**C**] **HEALTH** a painful, swollen area on the body which contains a yellow liquid

abscond /əb'skɒnd/ *verb* [**I**] *formal* to leave somewhere suddenly without permission because you want to escape, or because you have stolen something

WORD PARTNERS FOR ***absence***

a **lengthy/long/prolonged** absence • an absence **from** sth • **during/in** sb's absence

absence /'æbsəns/ *noun* **1** [NOT THERE] [**C, U**] a time when you are not in a particular place *Lisa* *will be acting as manager* ***in*** *Phil's* ***absence*** (= while Phil is not here). ○ *A large number of* ***absences from*** *work are caused by back problems.* **2** NOT EXIST **[U]** when something does not exist ***In the absence of*** *any proof, it is impossible to accuse her.*

absent /ˈæbsᵊnt/ *adjective* not in the place where you are expected to be, especially at school or work *He has been* ***absent from*** *school all week.*

absentee /ˌæbsᵊnˈtiː/ *noun* **[C]** someone who is not in a place where they should be •**absenteeism** *noun* **[U]** when someone is often absent from work or school

absently /ˈæbsəntli/ *adverb* without thinking about what you are doing *He stared absently at the television screen.*

absent-minded /ˌæbsᵊntˈmaɪndɪd/ *adjective* often forgetting things •**absent-mindedly** *adverb* •**absent-mindedness** *noun* **[U]**

absolute /ˈæbsəluːt/ *adjective* **[always before noun]** **1** COMPLETE complete *absolute power/control* ○ *The party was an absolute disaster.* **2** DEFINITE definite *There was no* ***absolute proof*** *of fraud.*

O-ᵚ**absolutely** /ˌæbsəˈluːtli/ *adverb* **1** completely *The food was absolutely delicious.* ○ *There's absolutely nothing* (= nothing at all) *left.* **2 Absolutely.** used to strongly agree with someone *"Do you think it helped his career?" "Absolutely."* **3 Absolutely not.** used to strongly disagree with someone or to agree with something negative *"Are you suggesting that we should just ignore the problem?" "No, absolutely not."*

ˌabsolute ˈzero *noun* **[U]** **PHYSICS, MEASURES** the lowest temperature that scientists think is possible

absolve /əbˈzɒlv/ *verb* **[T]** *formal* to formally say that someone is not guilty of something, or to forgive someone

absorb /əbˈzɔːb/ *verb* **[T]** **1** LIQUID If a substance absorbs a liquid, it takes it in through its surface and holds it. *The fabric absorbs all the moisture, keeping your skin dry.* **2 be absorbed in sth** to give all your attention to something that you are doing *Simon was so absorbed in his computer game, he didn't notice me come in.* **3** REMEMBER to understand and remember facts that you read or hear *It's hard to* ***absorb*** *so much* ***information***. **4** BECOME PART OF If something is absorbed into something else, it becomes part of it. *The drug is quickly* ***absorbed into*** *the bloodstream.* •**absorption** /əbˈzɔːpʃən/ *noun* **[U]**

absorbent /əbˈzɔːbənt/ *adjective* An absorbent substance can take liquids in through its surface and hold them. •**absorbency** /əbˈzɔːbəntsi/ *noun* **[U]**

absorbing /əbˈzɔːbɪŋ/ *adjective* very interesting *an absorbing book/game*

abstain /əbˈsteɪn/ *verb* **[I]** **1** NOT DO *formal* to not do something that you enjoy because it is bad or unhealthy *The doctor suggested that he* ***abstain from*** *alcohol.* **2** NOT VOTE to choose not to vote for or against something *63 members voted in favour, 39 opposed and 5 abstained.* •**abstention** /əbˈstenʃᵊn/ *noun* **[C, U]**

abstinence /ˈæbstɪnəns/ *noun* **[U]** *formal* when you do not do something that you enjoy because it is bad or unhealthy

abstract /ˈæbstrækt/ *adjective* **1** relating to ideas and not real things *an* ***abstract concept*** **2 ART** Abstract art involves shapes and colours and not images of real things or people.

absurd /əbˈzɜːd/ *adjective* very silly *an absurd situation/suggestion* •**absurdity** *noun* **[C, U]** •**absurdly** *adverb*

abundance /əˈbʌndəns/ *noun* **[U, no plural]** *formal* a lot of something *an abundance of flowers* ○ *There was food* ***in abundance*** (= a lot of food).

abundant /əˈbʌndənt/ *adjective* existing in large quantities *an* ***abundant supply*** *of food* •**abundantly** *adverb*

abuse¹ /əˈbjuːs/ *noun* **1** WRONG USE **[C, U]** when something is used for the wrong purpose in a way that is harmful or morally wrong ***drug/alcohol abuse*** ○ *abuse of public money* **2** VIOLENCE **[U]** violent, cruel treatment of someone ***child abuse*** ○ ***sexual abuse*** **3** LANGUAGE **[U]** rude and offensive words said to another person *Rival fans shouted abuse at each other.*

abuse² /əˈbjuːz/ *verb* **[T]** **1** VIOLENCE to treat someone cruelly and violently *He was* ***physically abused*** *by his alcoholic father.* **2** WRONG USE to use something for the wrong purpose in a way that is harmful or morally wrong *to abuse alcohol* **3** LANGUAGE to say rude and offensive words to someone *The crowd started abusing him.* •**abuser** *noun* **[C]**

abusive /əˈbjuːsɪv/ *adjective* saying rude and offensive words to someone *an abusive phone call*

abysmal /əˈbɪzmᵊl/ *adjective* very bad, especially of bad quality *the team's* ***abysmal performance*** *last season* •**abysmally** *adverb*

abyss /əˈbɪs/ *noun* **[C]** **1** SITUATION a very bad situation which will not improve **[usually singular]** *The country is sinking into an* ***abyss of*** *violence and bloodshed.* **2** HOLE *literary* a very deep hole

abyssal /əˈbɪsᵊl/ *adjective* **GEOGRAPHY** found at the bottom of deep oceans (= big seas)

AC /ˌeɪˈsiː/ *noun* **[U]** **PHYSICS** *abbreviation for* alternating current: electrical current which regularly changes the direction in which it moves ➲Compare **DC**

.ac /dɒtˈæk/ **COMPUTING, INTERNET** *internet abbreviation for* academic institution: used in some internet addresses for organizations such as universities

academia /ˌækəˈdiːmiə/ *noun* **[U]** **EDUCATION** the people and organizations, especially universities, involved in studying

academic¹ /ˌækəˈdemɪk/ *adjective* **1 EDUCATION** related to education, schools, universities, etc ***academic ability/standards*** ○ *It's the start of the* ***academic year***. **2** SUBJECTS related to subjects which involve thinking and studying and not technical or practical skills ***academic subjects*** **3** CLEVER clever and good at studying **4** NOT REAL If what someone says is

A

academic, it has no purpose because it relates to a situation that does not exist. *The whole discussion is academic since management won't even listen to us.* •**academically** *adverb*

academic² /ˌækəˈdemɪk/ *noun* [C] **EDUCATION** someone who teaches at a university or college, or is paid to study there

academy /əˈkædəmi/ *noun* [C] **1 EDUCATION** a college which teaches people the skills needed for a particular job *a military academy* **2** an organization whose purpose is to encourage and develop an art, science, language, etc *the Royal Academy of Music*

accelerate /əkˈseləreɪt/ *verb* **1** DRIVE [I] to start to drive faster **2** HAPPEN [I, T] to start to happen more quickly, or to make something start to happen more quickly *Inflation is likely to accelerate this year.* •**acceleration** /əkˌseləˈreɪʃᵊn/ *noun* [U]

accelerator /əkˈseləreɪtəʳ/ (*also US* **gas pedal**) *noun* [C] the part of a car which you push with your foot to make it go faster ➲See colour picture **Car** on page Centre 7

WORD PARTNERS FOR ***accent***

have/speak with a [local/northern/strong, etc] accent • **lose** your accent • a **heavy/ strong/thick** accent

accent /ˈæksᵊnt/ *noun* [C] **1 LANGUAGE** the way in which someone pronounces words, influenced by the country or area they come from, or their social class *an American accent* ○ *a French accent* **2 LANGUAGE** a mark above a letter to show you how to pronounce it, for example (â) and (é) **3 LANGUAGE** the word or part of a word that you emphasize when you are speaking *In the word 'impossible' the **accent** is **on** the second syllable.* **4 the accent on sth** particular importance or attention that you give to something *a wonderful menu with the accent on fresh fish*

accentuate /əkˈsentʃueɪt/ *verb* [T] to emphasize something so that people notice it *make-up to accentuate the eyes*

O-**accept** /əkˈsept/ *verb* **1** AGREE [I, T] to agree to take something that is offered to you *to **accept an invitation/offer*** ○ *He won't accept advice from anyone.* **2** ADMIT [T] to admit that something is true, often something unpleasant [+ **(that)**] *He refuses to accept that he's made a mistake.* **3** ALLOW TO JOIN [T] to allow someone to join an organization or become part of a group *She's been accepted by two universities.* **4 accept responsibility/blame** to admit that you caused something bad that happened *The company has now accepted responsibility for the accident.* **5** UNDERSTAND [T] to understand that you cannot change a very sad or unpleasant situation *The hardest part is **accepting the fact** that you'll never see that person again.*

COMMON LEARNER ERROR

accept or **agree?**

When you accept an invitation, job, or offer, you say yes to something which is offered. **Accept** is never followed by another verb.

They offered me the job and I've accepted it.

~~*They offered me the job and I've accepted to take it.*~~

When you **agree** to do something, you say that you will do something which someone asks you to do.

They offered me the job and I agreed to take it.

acceptable /əkˈseptəbl/ *adjective* **1** GOOD ENOUGH good enough *work of an **acceptable standard*** ○ *We still hope to find a solution which is **acceptable to** both sides.* **2** ALLOWED allowed or approved of *Smoking is less and less **socially acceptable**.* ➲Opposite **unacceptable** •**acceptability** /əkˌseptəˈbɪləti/ *noun* [U]

WORD PARTNERS FOR ***acceptance***

sb/sth **gains/wins** acceptance • **general/ growing/grudging/public** acceptance • acceptance **of** sth

acceptance /əkˈseptᵊns/ *noun* [C, U] when you accept something *his acceptance of the award* ○ *There is a growing **public acceptance of** alternative medicine.*

accepted /əkˈseptɪd/ *adjective* agreed or approved by most people *an accepted spelling*

access¹ /ˈækses/ *noun* [U] **1** OPPORTUNITY when you have the right or opportunity to use or see something *I don't **have access to** that kind of information.* ○ *Do you have Internet access?* **2** ENTRANCE the way in which you can enter a place or get to a place *The only **access to** the village is by boat.*

access² /ˈækses/ *verb* [T] **COMPUTING** to find or see information, especially using a computer *You can access the files over the Internet.*

accessible /əkˈsesəbl/ *adjective* **1** FIND easy to find or reach *Information such as this is freely **accessible to** the public.* ○ *The hotel is in a quiet but easily accessible part of the resort.* ➲Opposite **inaccessible 2** UNDERSTAND easy to understand *They are attempting to make opera **accessible to** a wider audience.* •**accessibility** /əkˌsesəˈbɪləti/ *noun* [U]

accessory /əkˈsesᵊri/ *noun* [C] **1** something extra which is not necessary but is attractive or useful *bathroom accessories* ○ *computer accessories* **2 LAW** *formal* someone who helps a criminal to commit a crime *an **accessory to** murder*

ˈaccess proˌvider *noun* [C] **COMPUTING, INTERNET** a company that makes you able to use the Internet, so that you can use email and see or show documents

WORD PARTNERS FOR ***accident***

have/be involved in an accident • an accident **happens/occurs** • a **fatal/serious/ tragic** accident • [killed, paralyzed, etc] **in** an accident • a **car/traffic** accident

O-**accident** /ˈæksɪdᵊnt/ *noun* [C] **1** something bad which happens that is not intended and which causes injury or damage *a **car/traffic accident*** ○ *She **had an accident** in the kitchen.* ○ *I didn't mean to spill his drink. It was an accident.* **2 by accident** without being intended *I deleted the wrong file by accident.*

A

accidental /ˌæksɪˈdentᵊl/ *adjective* not intended *accidental damage* •**accidentally** *adverb She accidentally knocked over a glass of red wine.*

accident-prone /ˈæksɪdᵊntˌprəun/ *adjective* Someone who is accident-prone often has accidents.

acclaim /əˈkleɪm/ *noun* [U] praise from a lot of people ***international/critical acclaim***

acclaimed /əˈkleɪmd/ *adjective* praised by a lot of people *the acclaimed singer and songwriter*

acclimatize (*also UK* **-ise**) /əˈklaɪmətaɪz/ *verb* [I, T] to start to feel happy with the weather, the way of life, etc in a new place, or to make someone do this •**acclimatization** /əˌklaɪmətaɪˈzeɪʃᵊn/ *noun* [U]

accolade /ˈækəleɪd/ *noun* [C] *formal* a prize or praise given to someone because they are very good at something

accommodate /əˈkɒmədeɪt/ *verb* [T] **1** HAVE SPACE FOR to have enough space somewhere for a number of things or people *We need more roads to accommodate the increase in traffic.* **2** HELP to do what someone wants, often by providing them with something *He requires special equipment and, where possible, we've accommodated those needs.* **3** GIVE A HOME to provide someone with a place to live or stay *The athletes will be accommodated in a special Olympic village.*

accommodating /əˈkɒmədeɪtɪŋ/ *adjective* willing to change your plans in order to help people

accommodation /əˌkɒməˈdeɪʃᵊn/ *noun* [U] **1** (*also US* **accommodations** [plural]) a place where you live or stay ***rented accommodation*** ○ *The price includes travel and accommodation.* **2** **BIOLOGY** the way the lens in the eye changes depending on on whether the thing it is looking at is close or far away

accompaniment /əˈkʌmpᵊnɪmənt/ *noun* **1** **FOOD** [C] *formal* something that is nice to eat or drink with a particular food or drink *salmon with an accompaniment of green salad* **2** **MUSIC** [C, U] music that is played with the main instrument or with a singing voice *a song with piano accompaniment*

accompany /əˈkʌmpəni/ *verb* [T] **1** GO WITH *formal* to go somewhere with someone *We accompanied her back to her hotel.* **2** HAPPEN TOGETHER to happen or exist at the same time as something else *The teachers' book is accompanied by a video cassette.* **3** **MUSIC** to play a musical instrument with someone else who is playing or singing

accomplice /əˈkʌmplɪs/ *noun* [C] **LAW** someone who helps a criminal to commit a crime

accomplish /əˈkʌmplɪʃ/ *verb* [T] to succeed in doing something good *I feel as if I've accomplished nothing all day.*

accomplished /əˈkʌmplɪʃt/ *adjective* having a lot of skill in art, music, writing, etc *an accomplished musician/painter*

accomplishment /əˈkʌmplɪʃmənt/ *noun* **1** ACHIEVEMENT [U] when you succeed in doing something good *Finishing the course gave me a great sense of accomplishment.* **2** SKILL [C] *formal* a skill in art, music, writing, etc

accord¹ /əˈkɔːd/ *noun* **1** **of your own accord** If you do something of your own accord, you choose to do it and no one else forces you. *Luckily, she left of her own accord.* **2** **POLITICS** [C] an official agreement, especially between countries *a peace/trade accord*

accord² /əˈkɔːd/ *verb* [T] *formal* to treat someone specially, usually by showing respect *the respect accorded to doctors*

accordance /əˈkɔːdᵊns/ *noun formal* **in accordance with sth** agreeing with a rule, law, or wish *Both companies have insisted that they were acting in accordance with the law.*

accordingly /əˈkɔːdɪŋli/ *adverb* in a way that is suitable *We'll wait until we hear the decision and **act accordingly**.*

O-- **according to** /əˈkɔːdɪŋtuː/ *preposition* **1** SAID BY as said by someone or shown by something *According to our records, she was absent last Friday.* **2** BASED ON based on a particular system or plan *Children are allocated to schools according to the area in which they live.*

accordion /əˈkɔːdiən/ *noun* [C] **MUSIC** a musical instrument with a folding centre part and keyboards at both ends, which you play by pushing the two ends together

accost /əˈkɒst/ *verb* [T] If someone you do not know accosts you, they move towards you and start talking to you in an unfriendly way.

WORD PARTNERS FOR ***account***

1 give an account of sth • a **brief/detailed/full** account • an **eye-witness/first-hand** account • an account **of** sth
2 close/open an account • **have** an account with [name of bank] • a **joint/personal/savings** account • an account **holder/number**

account¹ /əˈkaunt/ *noun* [C] **1** a written or spoken description of something that has happened *They **gave** conflicting **accounts** of the events.* **2** **FINANCE** (*also* **bank account**) an arrangement with a bank to keep your money there and to let you take it out when you need to *I paid the money into my account.* **3** **FINANCE** an agreement with a shop or company that allows you to buy things and pay for them later **4** **take sth into account; take account of sth** to consider something when judging a situation *You have to take into account the fact that he is less experienced when judging his performance.* **5** **on account of sth** *formal* because of something *He doesn't drink alcohol on account of his health.* **6** **by all accounts** as said by a lot of people *The party was, by all accounts, a great success.* **7** **on my account** just for or because of me *Please don't change your plans on my account.* **8** **on no account; not on any account** *UK* not for any reason or in any situation *On no account must these records be changed.* ⊃See also: **checking account, current account, deposit account**

account² /əˈkaunt/ *verb*
account for sth *phrasal verb* **1** BE PART OF to be part of a total number of something *Oil accounts for 40% of Norway's exports.* **2** EXPLAIN to be the reason for something, or to explain the reason for something *She was asked to account for the missing money.*

A

accountable /ə'kaʊntəbl/ *adjective* **[never before noun]** having to be responsible for what you do and able to explain your actions *Hospitals must be held **accountable for** their mistakes.* ○ *Politicians should be **accountable to** the public that elects them.* ➲Opposite **unaccountable** •**accountability** /əˌkaʊntə'bɪləti/ *noun* **[U]**

accountancy /ə'kaʊntənsi/ *UK* (*US* **accounting**) *noun* **[U]** **FINANCE** the job of being an accountant

accountant /ə'kaʊntənt/ *noun* **[C]** **FINANCE** someone whose job is to keep or examine the financial records of a company or organization

ac'counting ˌratio *noun* **[C]** **FINANCE** any of several kinds of calculation used to understand financial accounts, for instance comparing money received with money owed

accounts /ə'kaʊnts/ *noun* **[plural]** **FINANCE** an official record of all the money a company or organization has received or paid

accreditation /əˌkredɪ'teɪʃən/ *noun* **[U]** official approval of an organization •**accredited** /ə'kredɪtɪd/ *adjective* officially approved

accrual /ə'kruːəl/ *noun* **[U]** **FINANCE** when something increases in number or amount over a period of time

accrue /ə'kruː/ *verb* **[I]** **FINANCE** to increase in number or amount over a period of time *Interest accrues at a rate of 6%.* •**accrued** /ə'kruːd/ *adjective accrued interest*

accumulate /ə'kjuːmjəleɪt/ *verb* **[I, T]** to increase in amount over a period of time, or to make something increase over a period of time *The chemicals accumulate in your body.* •**accumulation** /əˌkjuːmjə'leɪʃən/ *noun* **[U]**

acˌcumulated 'fund *noun* **[C]** **FINANCE** the amount of money owned by an organization such as a club that does not sell things

accuracy /'ækjərəsi/ *noun* **[U]** how correct or exact something is *The new system should help to improve the accuracy of weather forecasts.*

accurate /'ækjərət/ *adjective* correct or exact ***accurate information/measurements*** ○ *She was able to give police a fairly **accurate description** of the man.* ➲Opposite **inaccurate** •**accurately** *adverb*

WORD PARTNERS FOR ***accusation***

make an accusation • **deny/dismiss/face/reject** an accusation • a **false/wild** accusation • accusations **of** sth • an accusation **against** sb • an accusation **by/from** sb

accusation /ˌækju'zeɪʃən/ *noun* **[C]** when you say that someone has done something bad *He **made** a number **of accusations against** his former colleagues.*

accusative /ə'kjuːzətɪv/ *noun* **[U]** **LANGUAGE** the form of a noun, pronoun or adjective which is used in some languages to show that the word is the direct object of a verb •**accusative** *adjective*

O‑ **accuse** /ə'kjuːz/ *verb* **[T]** to say that someone has done something bad *He was falsely **accused of** murder.* **[+ of + doing sth]** *She accused Andrew of lying to her.* •**accuser** *noun* **[C]**

the accused /ə'kjuːzd/ *noun formal* **LAW** the person or people who are accused of a crime in a court of law

accusing /ə'kjuːzɪŋ/ *adjective* showing that you think someone is responsible for something bad *Why are you giving me that **accusing look?*** •**accusingly** *adverb She looked at me accusingly.*

accustom /ə'kʌstəm/ *verb*
accustom yourself to sth/doing sth *phrasal verb* to experience something often enough for it to seem normal to you

accustomed /ə'kʌstəmd/ *adjective* **accustomed to sth/doing sth** If you are accustomed to something, you have experienced it often enough for it to seem normal to you. *I've worked nights for years now so I've **grown accustomed to** it.*

ace[1] /eɪs/ *noun* **[C]** **1** a playing card with one symbol on it, that has the highest or lowest value in many games **2** **SPORT** when the first shot by a tennis player is too good for the other player to hit back

ace[2] /eɪs/ *adjective informal* very good

acetic acid /əˌsiːtɪk'æsɪd/ *noun* **[U]** **CHEMISTRY** a colourless acid with a strong smell which is contained in vinegar

acetone /'æsɪtəʊn/ *noun* **[U]** **CHEMISTRY** a strong-smelling colourless liquid which is used in the production of various chemicals and is sometimes added to paint to make it thinner

acetylene /ə'setəliːn/ *noun* **[U]** **CHEMISTRY** a colourless gas which burns with a very hot bright flame, used in cutting and joining metal (formula C_2H_2)

ache[1] /eɪk/ *noun* **[C]** **HEALTH** a feeling of pain over an area of your body which continues for a long time *There's a **dull ache** in my right shoulder.* ➲See also: **stomach ache**

ache[2] /eɪk/ *verb* **[I]** **HEALTH** If a part of your body aches, it is painful. *My legs ache after all that exercise.*

O‑ **achieve** /ə'tʃiːv/ *verb* **[T]** to succeed in doing something good, usually by working hard *I've achieved my ambition* ○ *I've been working all day but I feel I've achieved nothing.* •**achievable** *adjective* possible to achieve ***achievable goals*** •**achiever** *noun* **[C]** *He's from a family of **high achievers*** (= very successful people).

WORD PARTNERS FOR ***achievement***

a **great/notable/outstanding/remarkable** achievement • sb's **crowning** achievement • a **sense of** achievement

achievement /ə'tʃiːvmənt/ *noun* **1** GOOD THING **[C]** something good that you achieve *This film is his **greatest achievement** to date.* **2** SUCCESS **[U]** when you succeed in doing something good, usually by working hard *You get such **a sense of achievement** when you finish the course.*

acid[1] /'æsɪd/ *noun* **[C, U]** **CHEMISTRY** one of several liquid substances with a pH of less than 7 which react with other substances, often burning or dissolving them *hydrochloric acid*

acid[2] /'æsɪd/ *adjective* **1** **CHEMISTRY** (*also* **acidic** /ə'sɪdɪk/) containing acid, or having similar qualities to an acid *acid soil* ○ *an acid smell/taste* **2 acid remark/comment, etc** an unkind remark that criticizes someone

acidify /əˈsɪdɪfaɪ/ *verb* [I, T] **CHEMISTRY** to become an acid or to make something become an acid

acidity /əˈsɪdɪti/ *noun* [U] **CHEMISTRY** the amount of acid in a substance or in your stomach

ˌacid ˈrain *noun* [U] **ENVIRONMENT** rain that contains chemicals from pollution and damages plants, etc

ˈacid ˌsalt *noun* [C] **CHEMISTRY** a chemical compound that is formed when an acid has reacted with another substance to produce salt and water

ˈacid ˌtest *noun* [C usually singular] a sure test of whether something is true or of good quality

WORD PARTNERS FOR ***acknowledge***

be **generally/widely/universally** acknowledged • acknowledge sb/sth **as/to be** sth

acknowledge /əkˈnɒlɪdʒ/ *verb* [T] **1** ACCEPT to accept that something is true or exists [+ (that)] *He acknowledged that there was a problem.* **2** LETTER to tell someone, usually in a letter, that you have received something they sent you *Send a letter acknowledging receipt of his application.* **3** SAY HELLO to let someone know that you have seen them, usually by saying hello *She didn't even acknowledge my presence.*

acknowledgement (*also* **acknowledgment**) /əkˈnɒlɪdʒmənt/ *noun* **1** ACCEPT [C, U] when you accept that something is true or exists *There was no acknowledgement of the extent of the problem.* **2** LETTER [C] a letter telling you that someone has received something that you sent them **3** BOOK [C] something written at the front of a book by the author to thank people who have helped them [usually plural] *His name appears in the acknowledgements.*

acne /ˈækni/ *noun* [U] **HEALTH** a skin problem that young people often have that causes spots on the face

acorn /ˈeɪkɔːn/ *noun* [C] **BIOLOGY** an oval nut which grows on oak trees

acoustic /əˈkuːstɪk/ *adjective* **1 MUSIC** [always before noun] An acoustic musical instrument does not use electricity. *an **acoustic guitar*** **2 PHYSICS** relating to sound and hearing

acoustics /əˈkuːstɪks/ *noun* [plural] **PHYSICS** the way in which the shape of a room affects the quality of sound *The acoustics of the hall were terrible.*

acquaintance /əˈkweɪntᵊns/ *noun* [C] someone who you know but do not know well *He's just a **business acquaintance**.*

acquainted /əˈkweɪntɪd/ *adjective* [never before noun] *formal* **1** If you are acquainted with someone, you have met them but do not know them well. *We're already acquainted - we met at Elaine's party.* **2 be acquainted with sth** to know about something *I'm afraid I'm not yet acquainted with the system.*

acquiesce /ˌækwiˈes/ *verb* [I] *formal* to agree to something, often when you do not want to •**acquiescence** *noun* [U] *formal*

acquire /əˈkwaɪəʳ/ *verb* [T] **1** GET to get something *I managed to acquire a copy of the report.* **2** LEARN to learn something *to **acquire knowledge/skills***

acquisition /ˌækwɪˈzɪʃᵊn/ *noun* **1** PROCESS [U] the process of learning or getting something *children's acquisition of language* **2** NEW THING [C] something that you get, usually by buying it *And the hat - is that a **recent acquisition**?*

acquit /əˈkwɪt/ *verb* [T] **acquitting**, *past* **acquitted LAW** If someone is acquitted of a crime, a court of law decides that they are not guilty. [often passive] *Both men were **acquitted of** murder.*

acquittal /əˈkwɪtᵊl/ *noun* [C, U] **LAW** when a court of law decides that someone is not guilty of a crime

acre /ˈeɪkəʳ/ *noun* [C] **MEASURES** a unit for measuring area, equal to 4047 square metres ➲See Extra help page **Numbers and measurements** on page Centre 24

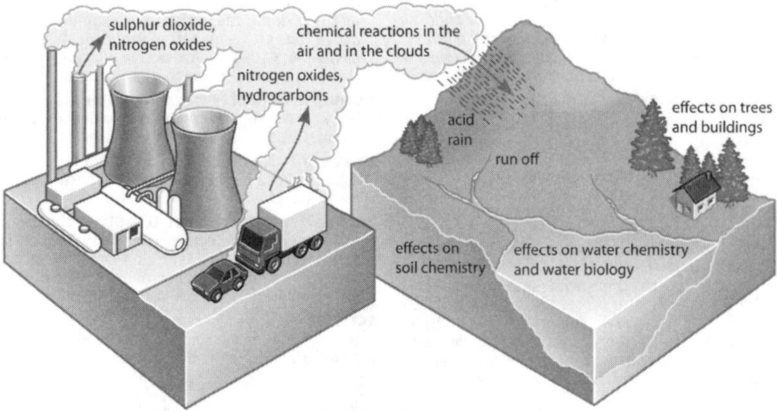

the formation of acid rain

A

acrid /ˈækrɪd/ *adjective* An acrid smell is unpleasant and causes a burning feeling in your throat.

acrimonious /ˌækrɪˈməʊniəs/ *adjective* involving a lot of anger, disagreement, and bad feelings *an **acrimonious divorce*** •**acrimony** /ˈækrɪməni/ *noun* [U] angry, bad feelings between people

acrobat /ˈækrəbæt/ *noun* [C] someone who entertains people by performing difficult physical acts, such as walking on a wire high above the ground •**acrobatic** /ˌækrəˈbætɪk/ *adjective* •**acrobatics** /ˌækrəˈbætɪks/ *noun* [plural] the actions of an acrobat

acronym /ˈækrəʊnɪm/ *noun* [C] **LANGUAGE** a word made from the first letters of other words *AIDS is the acronym for 'acquired immune deficiency syndrome'.*

across /əˈkrɒs/ *adverb, preposition* **1** [SIDES] from one side of something to the other *I was walking across the road.* ○ *They've built a new bridge across the river.* **2** [OPPOSITE] on the opposite side of *There's a library just across the street.* **3** [MEASURE] used after a measurement to show how wide something is *The window measures two metres across.*

acrylic /əˈkrɪlɪk/ *noun* **DT** **1** [U] a type of cloth or plastic produced by chemical processes **2** [C usually singular] a type of paint •**acrylic** *adjective acrylic paints*

act[1] /ækt/ *verb* **1** [BEHAVE] [I] to behave in a particular way *to act responsibly* ○ *Jeff's been acting strangely recently.* ○ *Stop **acting like** a child!* **2** [DO SOMETHING] [I] to do something, especially in order to solve a problem *We have to act now to stop the spread of this disease.* **3** [PERFORM] [I, T] to perform in a play or film *He's acted in a number of successful Hollywood films.*

act as sth *phrasal verb* **1** [JOB] to do a particular job, especially one you do not normally do *He was asked to act as an adviser on the project.* **2** [EFFECT] to have a particular effect *Caffeine acts as a stimulant.*

act sth out *phrasal verb* to perform the actions and words of a situation or story *The children acted out a verse from their favourite poem.*

act up *phrasal verb* If someone, especially a child, acts up, they behave badly.

WORD PARTNERS FOR ***act***

an act **of** sth • **commit** an act • a **barbaric/cowardly** act • a **criminal/terrorist** act

act[2] /ækt/ *noun* **1** [DO] [C] something that someone does *an **act of** terrorism/kindness* **2** **LAW** [C] a law made by a government *an act of Congress/Parliament* **3** **LITERATURE** [C] one of the parts a play is divided into *Her character doesn't appear until Act 2.* **4** [PERFORMERS] [C] one or several performers who perform for a short while in a show *a comedy **double act*** **5** [FALSE BEHAVIOUR] [no plural] behaviour which hides your real feelings or intentions *Was she really upset or was that just an act?* **6** **in the act (of doing sth)** doing something wrong *I caught him in the act of opening one of my letters.* **7** **get your act together** *informal* to organize your activities so that you can make progress **8** **get in on the act** *informal* to become involved in something successful that someone else has started

acting[1] /ˈæktɪŋ/ *adjective* **acting chairman/director, etc** someone who does a job for a short time while the person who usually does it is not there

acting[2] /ˈæktɪŋ/ *noun* [U] the job of performing in plays and films *He's trying to get into acting.*

action /ˈækʃᵊn/ *noun* **1** [DO] [C, U] something that you do *She has to accept the consequences of her actions.* ○ *We must **take action** (= do something) before the problem gets worse.* ○ *So what do you think is the best **course of action** (= way of dealing with the situation)?* ○ *It was the first time I'd seen firemen **in action** (= doing a particular activity).* **2** [ACTIVITY] [U] things which are happening, especially exciting or important things *He likes films with a lot of action.* ⊃Opposite **inaction** **3** **out of action** damaged or hurt and not able to operate or play sports *They've got three players out of action.* **4** **legal action** **LAW** a legal process in a court *They are planning to **take legal action against** the company.* **5** [FIGHTING] [U] fighting in a war *He was killed **in action** (= while fighting).* **6** [PROCESS] [no plural] a movement or natural process *The rocks are smoothed by the action of water.* ⊃See also: **industrial action**, be all **talk**[2] (and no action)

action-packed /ˈækʃᵊnˌpækt/ *adjective* An action-packed film or story has a lot of exciting events.

ˌaction ˈreplay *UK* (*US* **instant replay**) *noun* [C] when part of a film of a sporting event is shown again, often more slowly

activate /ˈæktɪveɪt/ *verb* [T] to make something start working *The alarm can be activated by a laser beam.*

active /ˈæktɪv/ *adjective* **1** [INVOLVED] very involved in an organization or planned activity *He played an **active role** in the campaign.* **2** [BUSY] doing a lot of things, or moving around a lot *Even at the age of 80 she's still very active.* **3** **LANGUAGE** An active verb or sentence is one in which the subject of the verb is the person or thing doing the action. For example 'Andy drove the car.' is an active sentence. ⊃Compare **passive** **4** **GEOLOGY** An active volcano could throw out rocks, fire, etc at any time.

ˌactive imˈmunity *noun* [U] **HEALTH** when the body produces its own antibodies (= substances in the blood that fight disease)

actively /ˈæktɪvli/ *adverb* in a way that causes something to happen *He **actively encourages** me to spend money.*

ˌactive ˈtransport *noun* [U] **BIOLOGY** the process by which molecules can pass through a membrane (= thin layer of tissue) from an area where there are not many of them into an area where there are a lot of them

activist /ˈæktɪvɪst/ *noun* [C] **POLITICS** someone who tries to cause social or political change *a **political activist*** •**activism** *noun* [U]

WORD PARTNERS FOR ***activity***

do/perform an activity • **frantic/strenuous** activity • **outdoor/leisure** activity • a **flurry** of activity

A

O-▪**activity** /æk'tɪvəti/ *noun* **1** EVENT [C] something which you do for enjoyment, especially an organized event *The centre offers a range of activities, such as cycling, swimming, and tennis.* **2** WORK [C, U] the work of a group or organization to achieve an aim ***criminal/terrorist activities*** **3** MOVEMENT [U] when a lot of things are happening or people are moving around *There was a sudden **flurry of activity*** (= short period of activity) *at the back of the hall.* ➲Opposite **inactivity**

O-▪**actor** /'æktəʳ/ *noun* [C] someone, especially a man, whose job is to perform in plays and films

O-▪**actress** /'æktrəs/ *noun* [C] a woman whose job is to perform in plays and films

O-▪**actual** /'æktʃuəl/ *adjective* **1** real, not guessed or imagined *We were expecting about fifty people, though the **actual number** was a lot higher.* **2 in actual fact** UK really *It was due to start at ten, but in actual fact, it didn't begin until nearly eleven.*

COMMON LEARNER ERROR

actual or current ?

Actual means 'real'. It does not mean 'happening now'.

His friends call him Jo-Jo, but his actual name is John.

Use **current** to talk about things which are happening or which exist now.

She started her current job two years ago.

O-▪**actually** /'æktʃuəli/ *adverb* **1** TRUTH used when you are saying what is the truth of a situation *He didn't actually say anything important.* **2** SURPRISE used when you are saying something surprising *She sounds English but she's actually Spanish.* ○ *Did you actually meet the President?* **3** MISTAKE *mainly UK* used when you are disagreeing with someone or saying no to a request *"You didn't tell me." "Actually, I did."* ○ *"Do you mind if I smoke?" "Actually, I'd rather you didn't."*

acumen /'ækjʊmən/ *noun* [U] the ability to make good judgments and decisions ***business/political acumen***

acupuncture /'ækjʊpʌŋktʃəʳ/ *noun* [U] **HEALTH** a way of treating pain or illness by putting thin needles into different parts of the body

acute /ə'kjuːt/ *adjective* **1** An acute problem or negative feeling is extreme. *There's an **acute shortage** of medical staff.* ○ ***acute pain*** ○ *acute anxiety* **2** **MATHEMATICS** An acute angle is less than 90 degrees. **3** quick to notice or understand things *an acute mind* ○ *Dogs rely on their acute sense of smell.*

acute angle

aˌcute 'accent *noun* [C] **LANGUAGE** a mark which is written above a letter in some languages, e.g. 'é', showing you how to pronounce the letter

acutely /ə'kjuːtli/ *adverb* very strongly *I was **acutely aware** of how Alex felt about the situation.*

AD /ˌeɪ'diː/ *abbreviation for* Anno Domini: used to show that a particular year came after the birth of Christ *1066 AD*

ad /æd/ *noun* [C] an advertisement ➲See also: **classified ad**

adagio /ə'dɑːdʒiəʊ/ *noun* [C] **MUSIC** a piece of classical music (= serious music by a composer such as Mozart) that should be played slowly

adamant /'ædəmənt/ *adjective* very sure of what you think and not willing to change your opinion [+ (that)] *They are adamant that they have not broken any rules.* •**adamantly** *adverb*

Adam's apple /ˌædəmz'æpl/ *noun* [C] **ANATOMY** the lump in a man's throat that you can see moving up and down when he speaks or swallows

adapt /ə'dæpt/ *verb* **1** CHANGE BEHAVIOUR [I] to change your behaviour so that it is suitable for a new situation *It takes time to **adapt to** a new working environment.* **2** CHANGE SOMETHING [T] to change something so that it is suitable for a different use or situation *Courses have to be **adapted for** different markets.* **3** BOOK [T] to change a book or play so that it can be made into a film or television programme *Both novels have been **adapted for** television.*

adaptable /ə'dæptəbl/ *adjective* able to change to suit different situations or uses •**adaptability** /əˌdæptə'bɪləti/ *noun* [U]

adaptation /ˌædæp'teɪʃᵊn/ *noun* **1** FILM [C] a film, television programme, or play which has been made from a book **2** CHANGE [C, U] the process or act of changing to suit a new situation *Evolution occurs as a result of **adaptation to** new environments.*

adapter (*also* **adaptor**) /ə'dæptəʳ/ *noun* [C] something that is used for connecting two or more pieces of electrical equipment to an electrical supply

O-▪**add** /æd/ *verb* **1** PUT WITH [T] to put something with something else ***Add** the eggs **to** the cream.* **2** INCREASE [I, T] to increase an amount or level *Then there's the service charge which **adds** another ten percent **to** the bill.* **3** SAY MORE [T] to say another thing [+ that] *She said she liked him but added that he was difficult to work with.* **4** **MATHEMATICS** [T] to put two or more numbers or amounts together to get a total ➲See also: add **insult**[2] to injury

add (sth) up *phrasal verb* **MATHEMATICS** to put numbers together in order to reach a total *When you add up everything we've spent, it's cost well over £200.*

not add up *phrasal verb informal* If something does not add up, you cannot believe it is true. *She gave me an explanation but somehow it doesn't add up.*

adder /'ædəʳ/ *noun* [C] a small, poisonous snake

addict /'ædɪkt/ *noun* [C] **1** **HEALTH** someone who cannot stop taking a drug *a heroin/**drug addict*** **2** *informal* someone who likes something very much and does it or has it very

A

often *a TV/computer game addict* ○ *She admits to being a crossword addict.*

addicted /əˈdɪktɪd/ *adjective* **1 HEALTH** not able to stop taking a drug *He later became* ***addicted to*** *heroin.* **2** *informal* liking something very much and doing or having it too often *He's* ***addicted to*** *chocolate/football.*

WORD PARTNERS FOR ***addiction***

fight/have/suffer from an addiction • **alcohol/drug/gambling** addiction • addiction **to** sth

addiction /əˈdɪkʃən/ *noun* **[C, U] HEALTH** when you cannot stop doing or taking something because you are addicted to it

addictive /əˈdɪktɪv/ *adjective* **HEALTH** If something is addictive, it makes you want more of it so that you become addicted. *Tobacco is* ***highly addictive.***

addition /əˈdɪʃən/ *noun* **1 in addition (to sth)** added to what already exists or happens, or more than you already do or have *In addition to teaching, she works as a nurse in the holidays.* **2 MATHEMATICS [U]** the process of adding numbers or amounts together in order to get a total **3 [C]** a new or extra thing which is added to something *Defender Matt Smith is the latest* ***addition to*** *the team.*

additional /əˈdɪʃənəl/ *adjective* extra to what already exists *We plan to take on an additional ten employees over the next year.* •**additionally** *adverb*

adˈdition reˌaction *noun* **[C] CHEMISTRY** a chemical reaction where two whole molecules join together to form one larger molecule

additive /ˈædɪtɪv/ *noun* **[C] FOOD** a chemical which is added to food in order to make it taste or look better or to keep it fresh

add-on /ˈædɒn/ *noun* **[C] COMPUTING** a piece of equipment that can be connected to a computer to give it an extra use

WORD PARTNERS FOR ***address***

give sb your address • your **business/home/work** address • a **change of** address

O┳**address¹** /əˈdres/ (US) /ˈædres/ *noun* **[C] 1** BUILDING DETAILS the details of where a building is, including the building number, road name, town, etc **2 INTERNET** a series of letters, signs, or numbers used to send email to someone or to reach a page of information on the Internet *an* ***email/web address*** **3** SPEECH a formal speech to a group of people ⊃See also: **forwarding address, public address system**

address² /əˈdres/ *verb* **[T] 1** BUILDING DETAILS to write a name or address on an envelope or parcel *A parcel arrived* ***addressed to*** *Emma.* **2** DEAL WITH to deal with a problem *We have to* ***address*** *the* ***issue/problem*** *before it gets worse.* **3** SPEAK *formal* to speak to someone, or to give a speech to an audience *Today she will be addressing a major conference in London.* **4 address sb as sth** *formal* to give someone a particular name or title when you speak or write to them *Do you think I should address him as 'Mr Benson' or 'Albert'?*

aˈddress ˌbook (*US* **ˈaddress ˌbook**) *noun* **[C] 1 COMPUTING** a computer document that keeps a list of names and email addresses **2** a book in which you keep a list of names and addresses

adept /ˈædept/ *adjective* good at doing something difficult *She's very* ***adept at*** *dealing with the media.*

adequate /ˈædɪkwət/ *adjective* **1** ENOUGH enough *I didn't have* ***adequate time*** *to prepare.* **2** QUITE GOOD good enough, but not very good *The sound quality isn't exceptional but it's* ***adequate for*** *everyday use.* ⊃Opposite **inadequate** •**adequately** *adverb Make sure you are adequately equipped for the journey.*

adhere /ədˈhɪəʳ/ *verb* **[I]** *formal* to stick to a surface

adhere to sth *phrasal verb* to obey a rule or principle *We always adhere strictly to the guidelines.*

adherence /ədˈhɪərəns/ *noun* **[U]** *formal* when someone obeys a set of rules or principles •**adherent** *noun* **[C]** *formal* someone who obeys a particular set of rules, principles, etc

adhesive /ədˈhiːsɪv/ *noun* **[C] DT** a substance used for sticking things together •**adhesive** *adjective*

ad hoc /ˌædˈhɒk/ *adjective* not regular or planned, but happening only when necessary *We meet* ***on an ad hoc basis.***

adipose /ˈædɪpəʊs/ *adjective* **[always before noun] BIOLOGY** of animal fat *adipose tissue*

adjacent /əˈdʒeɪsənt/ *adjective formal* If two things are adjacent, they are next to each other. *The fire started in an adjacent building.* ○ *They live in a house* ***adjacent to*** *the railway.*

adˌjacent ˈangle *noun* **[C] MATHEMATICS** one of two angles that are formed when one angle is divided by a straight line

O┳**adjective** /ˈædʒɪktɪv/ *noun* **[C] LANGUAGE** a word that describes a noun or pronoun. The words 'big', 'boring', 'purple', and 'obvious' are all adjectives. •**adjectival** /ˌædʒɪkˈtaɪvəl/ *adjective* containing or used like an adjective *an adjectival phrase*

adjoining /əˈdʒɔɪnɪŋ/ *adjective* next to and joined to something *an* ***adjoining room***

adjourn /əˈdʒɜːn/ *verb* **[I, T]** *formal* to stop a meeting, especially a legal process, for a period of time or until a later date *The judge* ***adjourned the case*** *until March 31.* •**adjournment** *noun* **[C]**

adjudicate /əˈdʒuːdɪkeɪt/ *verb* **[I, T]** *formal* **LAW** to make an official judgment or decision about a competition or disagreement *Occasionally, he has to* ***adjudicate on*** *a pensions matter.* •**adjudication** /əˌdʒuːdɪˈkeɪʃən/ *noun* **[U]** •**adjudicator** *noun* **[C]**

adjust /əˈdʒʌst/ *verb* **1** CHANGE **[T]** to change something slightly so that it works better, fits better, or is more suitable *You can adjust the heat using this switch here.* ○ *The figures need to be adjusted for inflation.* **2** BEHAVE **[I]** to change the way you behave or think in order to suit a new situation *They found it hard* ***adjusting to*** *life in a new country.*

adjustable /əˈdʒʌstəbl/ *adjective* able to be changed slightly in order to suit different people or situations *an adjustable seat*

adjustment /ə'dʒʌstmənt/ *noun* [C, U] a slight change that you make to something so that it works better, fits better, or is more suitable *We've **made** a few **adjustments to** the schedule.*

ad lib /ˌæd'lɪb/ *verb* [I, T] to speak in public without having planned what to say *I had no script so I had to ad lib.*

admin /'ædmɪn/ *noun* [U] *UK short for* administration

administer /əd'mɪnɪstər/ *verb* [T] **1** ORGANIZE to organize or arrange something *The fund is administered by the Economic Development Agency.* **2** HEALTH *formal* to give medicine or medical help to someone *to administer first aid*

administration /ədˌmɪnɪ'streɪʃən/ *noun* **1** [U] the work of organizing and arranging the operation of something, such as a company *The job involves a lot of administration.* **2** POLITICS [C] *mainly US* the President and politicians who govern a country at a particular time, or a period of government *the Bush administration*

administrative /əd'mɪnɪstrətɪv/ *adjective* relating to the organization and management of something *The work is largely administrative.*

administrator /əd'mɪnɪstreɪtər/ *noun* [C] someone who helps to manage an organization

admirable /'ædmərəbl/ *adjective* If something is admirable, you respect or approve of it. *He has many **admirable qualities**.* •**admirably** *adverb*

admiral /'ædmərəl/ *noun* [C] an officer of very high rank in the navy

WORD PARTNERS FOR ***admiration***

express/feel/have admiration • **enormous/great/grudging/profound** admiration • admiration **for** sb

admiration /ˌædmə'reɪʃən/ *noun* [U] when you admire someone or something *My **admiration for** him grows daily.*

admire /əd'maɪər/ *verb* [T] **1** RESPECT to respect or approve of someone or something *You have to **admire** him **for** being so determined.* **2** LOOK AT to look at something or someone, thinking how attractive they are *We stood for a few minutes, admiring the view.* •**admirer** *noun* [C]

admissible /əd'mɪsəbl/ *adjective formal* LAW allowed or acceptable, especially in a court of law *admissible evidence*

admission /əd'mɪʃən/ *noun* **1** MONEY [U] the money that you pay to enter a place *Art exhibition - admission free.* **2** TRUTH [C] when you agree that you did something bad, or that something bad is true *She is, **by her own admission**, lazy.* ○ *His departure was seen by many as an **admission of** guilt.* **3** PERMISSION [C, U] when someone is given permission to enter somewhere or to become a member of a club, university, etc *She's applied for **admission to** law school.*

OTHER WAYS OF SAYING ***admit***

If a person admits that something bad is true, the verbs **accept** and **acknowledge** may be used: *I **accept** that things should have been done differently.* • *He refuses to **acknowledge** the problem.*

If a person admits that they have done something bad, the verb **confess** is often used: *Rawlinson finally **confessed** to the murder.*

The phrasal verbs **own up** and (*informal*) **fess up**, and the idiom **come clean** can also be used when a person admits that they have done something bad: *I decided to **come clean** about the broken vase.* • *Come on, **own up** - who's eaten the last sandwich?*

O╼**admit** /əd'mɪt/ *verb* **admitting**, *past* **admitted** **1** SOMETHING BAD [I, T] to agree that you did something bad, or that something bad is true [+ **doing sth**] *Both men admitted taking illegal drugs.* [+ **to** + **doing sth**] *She **admitted to** stealing the keys.* ○ *I was wrong - I admit it.* [+ (**that**)] *He finally admitted that he couldn't cope.* **2** ALLOW [T] to allow someone to enter somewhere, especially to take someone who is ill into hospital *UK to be **admitted to** hospital/ US to be **admitted to** the hospital* ○ *It says on the ticket 'admits 2'.*

admittance /əd'mɪtəns/ *noun* [U] permission to enter a place

admittedly /əd'mɪtɪdli/ *adverb* used when you are agreeing that something is true although you do not want to *Admittedly I was partly to blame but it wasn't all my fault.*

admonish /əd'mɒnɪʃ/ *verb* [T] *formal* to gently tell someone that they have done something wrong

ado /ə'duː/ *noun* **without further/more ado** without waiting any more

adolescence /ˌædəl'esəns/ *noun* [U] the period of time in someone's life between being a child and an adult

adolescent /ˌædəl'esənt/ *noun* [C] a young person who is between being a child and an adult •**adolescent** *adjective*

adopt /ə'dɒpt/ *verb* **1** CHILD [I, T] to legally become the parents of someone else's child **2** START USING [T] to accept or start using something new *We've **adopted** a new **approach**.* •**adopted** *adjective an adopted son* •**adoption** /ə'dɒpʃən/ *noun* [C, U]

adorable /ə'dɔːrəbl/ *adjective* very attractive, often because of being small *an adorable little boy*

adore /ə'dɔːr/ *verb* [T] **1** LOVE to love someone and have a very good opinion of them *Sarah adored her father.* **2** LIKE to like something very much *I adore travelling.* •**adoration** /ˌædə'reɪʃən/ *noun* [U]

adorn /ə'dɔːn/ *verb* [T] *formal* to decorate something *The room was **adorned with** flowers.* •**adornment** *noun* [C, U]

adrenal gland /ə'driːnəlˌglænd/ *noun* [C] ANATOMY one of two body organs that produce adrenalin (= a substance the body produces when you are frightened)

A

adrenalin (*also* **adrenaline**) /ə'drenəlɪn/ *noun* [U] **BIOLOGY** a substance that your body produces when you are angry, excited, or frightened which makes your heart beat faster

adrift /ə'drɪft/ *adjective* **1** [**never before noun**] If a boat is adrift, it floats around in the water and is not tied to anything. **2 come adrift** to become loose and not joined to anything *A few bricks in the garden wall had come adrift.*

adsorb /æd'zɔːb/ *verb* [T] **PHYSICS** to cause a substance, usually a gas, to form a very thin layer on the surface of another substance •**adsorbent** /æd'zɔː.bənt/ *adjective* •**adsorption** /æd'zɔːpʃən/ *noun* [U]

adulation /ˌædjʊ'leɪʃən/ *noun* [U] great praise and admiration for someone, often which they do not deserve

O-**adult¹** /'ædʌlt, ə'dʌlt/ *noun* [C] a person or animal that has finished growing and is not now a child

adult² /'ædʌlt, ə'dʌlt/ *adjective* **1** NOT A CHILD having finished growing *an adult male rat* **2** RELATING TO ADULTS [**always before noun**] for or relating to adults ***adult education*** ○ *adult life* **3** SEXUAL Adult books, films, etc show naked people or sexual acts and are not for children.

adultery /ə'dʌltəri/ *noun* [U] sex between a married person and someone who is not their husband or wife •**adulterous** *adjective*

adulthood /'ædʌlthʊd/ (US) /ə'dʌlthʊd/ *noun* [U] the part of your life when you are an adult

WORD PARTNERS FOR ***advance***

medical/scientific/technological advances • a **major** advance • advances **in** sth

advance¹ /əd'vɑːns/ *noun* **1 in advance** before a particular time *You need to book your ticket at least 14 days in advance.* **2** PROGRESS [C, U] new discoveries and inventions ***technological/scientific advances*** **3 FINANCE** [C] a payment given to someone before work has been completed, or before the usual time **4** FORWARD [C] a movement forward, especially by an army

advance² /əd'vɑːns/ *verb* **1** PROGRESS [I, T] to develop or progress, or to make something develop or progress *He moved to New York with hopes of **advancing** his **career**.* **2** FORWARD [I] to move forward to a new position, especially while fighting *Rebel soldiers **advanced on** the capital.*

advance³ /əd'vɑːns/ *adjective* [**always before noun**] happening or ready before an event ***advance planning/warning*** ○ *an **advance booking***

advanced /əd'vɑːnst/ *adjective* **1** DEVELOPED having developed or progressed to a late stage ***advanced technology*** ○ *The disease was at an **advanced stage**.* **2** HIGH LEVEL at a higher, more difficult level *an advanced English course*

advancement /əd'vɑːnsmənt/ *noun* [C, U] progress ***career advancement*** ○ ***technological advancements***

advances /əd'vɑːnsɪz/ *noun* **sb's advances** things that someone says and does to try to start a sexual relationship with someone

WORD PARTNERS FOR ***advantage***

a **big/enormous/main/major** advantage • an **unfair** advantage • **take** advantage **of** sth • the advantage **of** sth

O-**advantage** /əd'vɑːntɪdʒ/ *noun* [C, U] **1** USEFUL THING something good about a situation that helps you *One of the **advantages of** living in town is having the shops so near.* **2** SUCCESS something that will help you to succeed *These new routes will give the airline a considerable **advantage over** its competitors.* ○ *If we could start early it would be **to our advantage*** (= help us to succeed). ➲Opposite **disadvantage** **3 take advantage of sth** to use the good things in a situation *I thought I'd take advantage of the sports facilities while I'm here.* **4 take advantage of sb/sth** to treat someone badly in order to get what you want

advantageous /ˌædvən'teɪdʒəs/ *adjective* helping to make you more successful

advent /'ædvent/ *noun* **1 the advent of sth** the start or arrival of something new *the advent of the Internet* **2 Advent RELIGION** the religious period before Christmas (= a Christian holiday) in the Christian year

WORD PARTNERS FOR ***adventure***

have an adventure • **be looking for** adventure • **a big/exciting** adventure • an adventure **holiday/playground**

O-**adventure** /əd'ventʃər/ *noun* [C, U] an exciting and sometimes dangerous experience *It's a film about the adventures of two friends travelling across Africa.* •**adventurer** *noun* [C]

adventurous /əd'ventʃərəs/ *adjective* **1** NEW THINGS willing to try new and often difficult things *I'm trying to be more adventurous with my cooking.* **2** EXCITING exciting and often dangerous *He led an adventurous life.*

O-**adverb** /'ædvɜːb/ *noun* [C] **LANGUAGE** a word that describes or gives more information about a verb, adjective, phrase, or other adverb. In the sentences 'He ate quickly.' and 'It was extremely good.', 'quickly' and 'extremely' are both adverbs.

adversary /'ædvəsəri/ *noun* [C] *formal* someone who you are fighting or competing against

adverse /'ædvɜːs/ *adjective formal* **1 adverse conditions/effects/impact** things that cause problems or danger *adverse weather conditions* ○ *Pollution levels like these will certainly have an adverse effect on health.* **2 adverse comment/publicity/reaction, etc** something negative that is said or written about someone or something •**adversely** *adverb*

adversity /əd'vɜːsəti/ *noun* [C, U] *formal* an extremely difficult situation *She showed a great deal of courage **in adversity**.*

advert /'ædvɜːt/ *noun* [C] *UK* an advertisement

advertise /'ædvətaɪz/ *verb* **1** TRY TO SELL [I, T] to tell people about a product or service, for example in newspapers or on television, in order to persuade them to buy it *Companies are not allowed to advertise cigarettes on television any more.* **2** ASK FOR [I] to put information in a newspaper or on the Internet, asking for someone or something that you need *The university is*

***advertising for** administrative staff.* •**advertiser** *noun* [C] a company that advertises things

advertisement /əd'vɜːtɪsmənt/ (US) /ˌædvər'taɪzmənt/ *noun* [C] a picture, short film, song, etc which tries to persuade people to buy a product or service *a newspaper/television advertisement*

O‑ **advertising** /'ædvətaɪzɪŋ/ *noun* [U] the business of trying to persuade people to buy products or services *an **advertising agency***

WORD PARTNERS FOR ***advice***

ask for/give/offer/provide/seek advice • **take** sb's advice • **bad/conflicting/expert/good** advice • advice **on/about** sth • a **piece** of advice

O‑ **advice** /əd'vaɪs/ *noun* [U] suggestions about what you think someone should do or how they should do something *She **asked** me **for advice** about writing a book.* ○ *There's a booklet **giving advice on** how to set up your own club.* ○ *I **took your advice*** (= did what you suggested) *and went home early.* ○ *Can I give you a **piece of advice**?*

COMMON LEARNER ERROR

advice

Remember that this word is not countable.

I need some advice.

~~*I need an advice.*~~

To make **advice** singular, say **a piece of advice**.

COMMON LEARNER ERROR

advice or **advise?**

Be careful not to confuse the noun **advice** with the verb **advise**.

I advise you to see a lawyer.

~~*I advice you to see a lawyer.*~~

advisable /əd'vaɪzəbl/ *adjective* [**never before noun**] If something is advisable, it will avoid problems if you do it. *It is advisable to book seats at least a week in advance.*

O‑ **advise** /əd'vaɪz/ *verb* **1** SUGGEST [**I, T**] to make a suggestion about what you think someone should do or how they should do something [+ **to do sth**] *His doctor advised him to take time off work.* ○ *They **advise** the government **on** environmental matters.* ○ *The government is **advising against** travelling in the area.* [+ **that**] *They're advising that children be kept out of the sun altogether.* **2** GIVE INFORMATION [**T**] *formal* to give someone official information about something *They were **advised of** their rights.*

adviser (*also* **advisor**) /əd'vaɪzəʳ/ *noun* [C] someone whose job is to give advice about a subject *a **financial adviser***

advisory¹ /əd'vaɪzəri/ *adjective* **advisory committee/panel/board, etc** a group of people whose purpose is to give advice

advisory² /əd'vaɪzəri/ *noun* [C] *US* an official announcement that contains advice, information, or a warning [**usually plural**] ***weather/travel advisories***

advocate¹ /'ædvəkeɪt/ *verb* [**T**] to express support for a particular idea or way of doing things *I certainly wouldn't advocate the use of violence.* •**advocacy** /'ædvəkəsi/ *noun* [**U**] when someone advocates something

advocate² /'ædvəkət/ *noun* [C] **1** someone who supports a particular idea or way of doing things *He has always been **an advocate of** stricter gun controls.* **2 LAW** *UK* a lawyer who defends someone in court

A&E /ˌeɪənd'iː/ *UK* (*US* **emergency room**) *noun* [**C, U**] **HEALTH** *abbreviation for* Accident and Emergency: the part of a hospital where people go when they are injured or ill and need treatment quickly

aeolian *UK* (*US* **eolian**) /iː'əʊliən/ *adjective* [**always before noun**] **GEOGRAPHY** produced or carried by the wind

aerial¹ /'eəriəl/ *UK* (*US* **antenna**) *noun* [C] a piece of metal that is used for receiving television or radio signals ➲See colour picture **Car** on page Centre 7

aerial² /'eəriəl/ *adjective* [**always before noun**] in or from the air, especially from an aircraft *an aerial photograph/view*

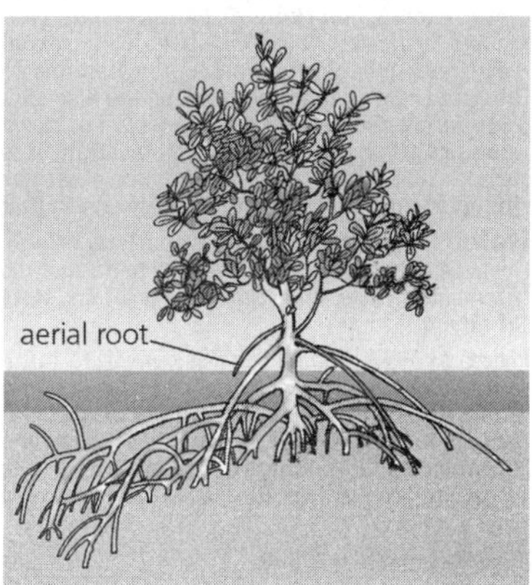

aerial root

ˌaerial 'root *noun* [C] **BIOLOGY** a plant root that grows down to the ground from above the ground

aerobic /eə'rəʊbɪk/ *adjective* **1 HEALTH** Aerobic exercise is intended to make your heart stronger. **2 BIOLOGY** needing or using oxygen

aeˌrobic respi'ration *noun* [U] **BIOLOGY** a chemical process in which energy is produced in the body from food by using oxygen

aerobics /eə'rəʊbɪks/ *noun* [U] **SPORT** physical exercises that you do to music, especially in a class *She goes to aerobics* (= to aerobics classes).

aerodynamic /ˌeərəʊdaɪ'næmɪk/ *adjective* **PHYSICS** having a shape that moves quickly through the air •**aerodynamics** *noun* [**U**] the study of how objects move through the air

A

aeroplane /ˈeərəpleɪn/ *UK* (*US* **airplane**) *noun* [C] a vehicle that flies and has an engine and wings

aerosol /ˈeərəsɒl/ *noun* [C] a metal container that forces a liquid out in small drops when you press a button ➲See picture at **CFC**

aerospace /ˈeərəʊspeɪs/ *noun* [U] the design and production of aircraft

aesthetic (*also US* **esthetic**) /esˈθetɪk/ *adjective* relating to beauty and the way something looks *the **aesthetic appeal** of cats* •**aesthetically** *adverb*

aesthetics (*also US* **esthetics**) /esˈθetɪks/ *noun* [U] **ART** the study of beauty, especially in art

aetiology *UK* (*US* **etiology**) /iː.tiˈɒlədʒi/ *noun* [U] **HEALTH** the study of the causes of a disease

AFAIK **INTERNET** *internet abbreviation for* as far as I know: used when you believe that something is true, but you are not completely certain

afar /əˈfɑːʳ/ *adverb literary* **from afar** from a long distance *He had admired her from afar.*

affable /ˈæfəbl/ *adjective* pleasant and friendly

affair /əˈfeəʳ/ *noun* **1** EVENTS [C] a situation or set of related events, especially bad ones *The government's handling of the affair has been widely criticized.* **2** RELATIONSHIP [C] a sexual relationship between two people when one or both of them is married to someone else *He's been **having an affair** with a woman at work.* **3 be sb's affair** If something is your affair, it is private and you do not want anyone else to be involved or know about it. ➲See also: **love affair**

affairs /əˈfeəz/ *noun* [plural] situations or subjects that involve you *He refused to discuss his financial affairs.* ➲See also: **current affairs, state of affairs**

O-**affect** /əˈfekt/ *verb* [T] **1** CAUSE CHANGE to influence someone or something, or cause them to change *It's a disease which affects many older people.* **2** CAUSE EMOTION to cause a strong emotion, especially sadness [**often passive**] *I was deeply affected by the film.* ➲See Common Learner Error at **effect**

COMMON LEARNER ERROR

affect someone or **something**

Remember that you do not need a preposition after the verb **affect**.

The problem affects everyone.

~~*The problem affects to everyone.*~~

affectation /ˌæfekˈteɪʃᵊn/ *noun* [C, U] a way of speaking or behaving that is not natural to someone

affected /əˈfektɪd/ *adjective* behaving or speaking in a way that is not natural or sincere

WORD PARTNERS FOR ***affection***

show affection • affection **for** sb • a **display/show** of affection

affection /əˈfekʃᵊn/ *noun* [C, U] a feeling of liking or loving someone *Ann's **affection for** her grandfather was obvious.*

affectionate /əˈfekʃᵊnət/ *adjective* showing that you like or love someone *an affectionate little girl* ○ *He's very affectionate.* •**affectionately** *adverb*

affiliate /əˈfɪlieɪt/ *verb* **be affiliated to/with sth** to be officially connected to, or a member of, a larger organization *a college affiliated to the University of London* •**affiliation** /əˌfɪliˈeɪʃᵊn/ *noun* [C, U]

affinity /əˈfɪnəti/ *noun* **1** FEELING [**no plural**] a feeling that you like and understand someone or something *She seems to have a natural **affinity for/with** water.* **2** SIMILARITY [C, U] a similarity *There are **affinities between** this poem and some of his earlier work.*

affirm /əˈfɜːm/ *verb* [T] *formal* to say that something is true *He gave a speech affirming the government's commitment to education.* •**affirmation** /ˌæfəˈmeɪʃᵊn/ *noun* [C, U]

affirmative /əˈfɜːmətɪv/ *adjective* **LANGUAGE** *formal* In language, an affirmative word or phrase expresses the meaning 'yes'. *an **affirmative answer***

affix /ˈæfɪks/ *noun* [C] **LANGUAGE** a group of letters that you add to the beginning or the end of a word to make another word. In the word 'non-alcoholic', 'non-' is an affix. ➲Compare **prefix, suffix**

afflict /əˈflɪkt/ *verb* [T] *formal* If an illness or problem afflicts you, it makes you suffer. [**often passive**] *a country afflicted by civil war* •**affliction** /əˈflɪkʃᵊn/ *noun* [C, U] something that makes you suffer

affluent /ˈæfluənt/ *adjective* having a lot of money *affluent families/neighbourhoods* •**affluence** /ˈæfluəns/ *noun* [U]

O-**afford** /əˈfɔːd/ *verb* [T] **1 can afford** to have enough money to buy something or enough time to do something *I can't afford a new computer.* [+ **to do sth**] Can we afford to go away? ○ I'd love to come out but I ***can't afford the time.*** **2 can afford to do sth** If you can afford to do something, it is possible for you to do it without causing problems. *We can't afford to take that risk.*

COMMON LEARNER ERROR

afford to do something

When **afford** is followed by a verb, it is always in the **to + infinitive** form.

We can't afford to go on holiday this year.

~~*We can't afford going on holiday this year.*~~

affordable /əˈfɔːdəbl/ *adjective* cheap enough for most people ***affordable housing/prices***

affront /əˈfrʌnt/ *noun* [C] something that is offensive or insulting to someone *He regarded the comments as an **affront to** his dignity.*

afield /əˈfiːld/ *adverb mainly UK* **far/further afield** away from the place where you are *We hired a car so we could travel further afield.*

afloat /əˈfləʊt/ *adjective* **1** floating on water **2 stay afloat** **FINANCE** to have enough money to continue a business *Many small business are struggling to stay afloat.*

A

afoot /əˈfʊt/ *adjective* [**never before noun**] being planned, or happening now *There are* ***plans afoot*** *to launch a new radio station.*

OTHER WAYS OF SAYING *afraid*

Other ways of saying 'afraid' are **frightened** and **scared**: *He's* ***frightened*** *that the other children will laugh at him.* • *Gerry has always been* ***scared*** *of heights.*

If someone is extremely afraid, then you can use adjectives such as **petrified**, **terrified**, **panic-stricken** or the informal phrase **scared to death**: *I'm* ***terrified*** *of flying.* • *She was* ***panic-stricken*** *when her little boy disappeared.* • *He's* ***scared to death*** *of having the operation.*

If someone is afraid because they are worrying about something, then you can use adjectives such as **anxious**, **concerned**, **nervous**, or **worried**: *I'm* ***worried*** *that something will go wrong.* • *All this waiting is making me feel* ***anxious****.*

If someone is afraid of something that might happen in the future, you can use the adjectives **apprehensive** or **uneasy**: *He's a bit* ***apprehensive*** *about living away from home.*

O-ᵥ**afraid** /əˈfreɪd/ *adjective* [**never before noun**] **1 I'm afraid** used to politely tell someone bad news or to politely disagree with someone *We haven't got any tickets left, I'm afraid.* [+ **(that)**] *I'm afraid that I've broken your vase.* **2** FRIGHTENED frightened *She's* ***afraid of*** *water.* **3** WORRIED worried that something bad might happen [+ **(that)**] *Many people are afraid that they might lose their jobs.* [+ **of** + **doing sth**] *He was* ***afraid of*** *upsetting Clare.*

afresh /əˈfreʃ/ *adverb* If you do something afresh, you do it again in a different way. *Juan tore up the letter he was writing and* ***started afresh****.*

African /ˈæfrɪkən/ *adjective* relating or belonging to Africa *African art/music* •**African** *noun* [**C**] someone from Africa

African-American /ˌæfrɪkənəˈmerɪkən/ (*also* **Afro-American** /ˌæfrəʊəˈmerɪkən/) *adjective* **SOCIETY** relating or belonging to American people whose families came from Africa in the past *the African-American community* •**African-American** (*also* **Afro-American**) *noun* [**C**] *a 25-year-old African-American*

Afro /ˈæfrəʊ/ *noun* [**C**] a way of arranging very curly hair, especially for black people, in a round shape

Afro-Caribbean /ˌæfrəʊkærɪˈbiːən/ *adjective UK* **SOCIETY** relating to people from the Caribbean whose families originally came from Africa *Afro-Caribbean art/music*

O-ᵥ**after**[1] /ˈɑːftəʳ/ *preposition* **1** TIME/EVENT when a time or event has happened *We went swimming after lunch.* ○ *Let's get the shopping.* ***After that****, we can have coffee.* **2** LIST following in order *H comes after G in the alphabet.* **3** TIME *US* (*UK/US* **past**) used to say how many minutes past the hour it is *It's five after three.* **4** BECAUSE OF because of something that happened *I'll never trust her again after what she did to me.* **5** DESPITE despite *I can't believe he was so unpleasant after you gave him so much help.* **6** FOLLOW following someone or something *We ran after him, but he escaped.* **7 after 5 minutes/2 weeks, etc** when five minutes, two weeks, etc have passed **8 day after day/year after year, etc** continuing for a long time, or happening many times *I'm bored with going to school day after day.* **9** NAMED FOR used when giving someone or something the same name as another person or thing *It was called the Biko building, after the famous South African.* **10 after all a** NOT EXPECTED used to say that something happened or was true although you did not expect it to happen or be true *Helen couldn't come to the party after all.* **b** EMPHASIZE TRUTH used to add information that shows that what you have just said is true *You can't expect to be perfect - after all, it was only your first lesson.* **11 be after sth** *informal* to be trying to get something *What type of job are you after?* **12 be after sb** *informal* to be looking for someone *The police are after him.*

O-ᵥ**after**[2] /ˈɑːftəʳ/ *conjunction* at a later time than something else happens *We arrived after the game had started.* ○ *After further discussion, we decided to call the police.*

O-ᵥ**after**[3] /ˈɑːftəʳ/ *adverb* later than someone or something else *He had the operation on Monday and I saw him the day after.*

afterbirth /ˈɑːftəbɜːθ/ *noun* [**U**] **BIOLOGY** the material, including the placenta (= organ that feeds a baby inside its mother) which is pushed out of a woman's or female animal's body soon after she has given birth

WORD PARTNERS FOR ***aftermath***

in the aftermath of sth • the **immediate** aftermath

aftermath /ˈɑːftəmɑːθ/ *noun* [**no plural**] a situation that is the result of an accident, crime, or other violent event *There are calls for tighter airport security* ***in the aftermath of*** *last week's bombing.*

O-ᵥ**afternoon** /ˌɑːftəˈnuːn/ *noun* **1** [**C, U**] the time between the middle of the day, and the evening *I played tennis on Saturday afternoon.* ○ *The train arrives at 3 o'clock in the afternoon.* ○ *What are you doing* ***this afternoon*** (= today in the afternoon)*?* **2 (Good) afternoon.** used to say hello to someone in the afternoon

COMMON LEARNER ERROR

afternoon

If you talk about what happens in the afternoon, use the preposition **in**.

In the afternoon I phoned my girlfriend.

~~*At the afternoon I phoned my girlfriend.*~~

If you say a day of the week before 'afternoon', use the preposition **on**.

I'm going to the dentist on Tuesday afternoon.

aftershave /ˈɑːftəʃeɪv/ *noun* [**C, U**] a liquid with a pleasant smell that men put on their faces after shaving (= removing hair)

aftertaste /ˈɑːftəteɪst/ *noun* [**C**] the taste that a food or drink leaves in your mouth when

A

you have swallowed it [usually no plural] *a bitter/sweet aftertaste*

afterthought /ˈɑːftəθɔːt/ *noun* [C] something that you say or do later [usually no plural] *She only asked me to the party* ***as an afterthought.***

afterwards /ˈɑːftəwədz/ (*also US* **afterward**) *adverb* at a later time, after something else has happened *I did my homework and went swimming afterwards.*

again /əˈgen/ *adverb* **1** REPEAT once more *I'll ask her again.* ○ *I'll see you again next week.* **2** AS BEFORE as before *Get some rest and you'll soon be well again.* **3 again and again** many times *He played the same song again and again.* **4 all over again** repeated from the beginning *We had to start all over again.* **5 then/there again** used when adding a fact to something you have just said *I failed my history test - but then again, I didn't do much studying for it.*

against /əˈgenst/ *preposition* **1** NOT AGREE disagreeing with a plan or activity *Andrew wants to change offices but I'm against it.* ○ *There were 70 votes for the new proposal and 30 against.* **2** COMPETE competing with or opposing someone or something *Liverpool is playing against AC Milan.* ○ *the fight against racism* **3** TOUCH touching something *Push the bed against the wall.* **4** PROTECT protecting you from something bad *Fresh fruit in the diet may protect against cancer.* **5** OPPOSITE DIRECTION in the opposite direction to the way something is moving *I was cycling against the wind.* **6 against the law/the rules** forbidden by a law or by rules *It's against the law to leave young children alone in the house.* **7 against sb's advice/wishes, etc** If you do something against someone's advice, wishes, etc, you do it although they have said you should not or must not. *He flew there against his doctor's advice.* **8 have sth against sb/sth** to have a reason not to like someone or something *I've got nothing against him personally, I just don't think he's the right man for the job.*

agar /ˈeɪgɑː/ *noun* [U] **CHEMISTRY** a thick clear substance used by scientists for growing microorganisms (= living things too small to see) or for making liquids thicker *agar jelly*

WORD PARTNERS FOR ***age***

reach the age of [18/60/75, etc] • **at/from** the age of [8/12/60, etc] • [8/25/70, etc] **years of** age • **at** sb's age • an age **limit**

age[1] /eɪdʒ/ *noun* **1** HOW OLD [C, U] the number of years that someone has lived, or that something has existed *The show appeals to people of all ages.* ○ *She left India* ***at the age of*** *12.* ○ *Children under 10* ***years of age*** *must be accompanied by an adult.* ➲See Common Learner Error at **year 2** HISTORY [C] a period of history *the Ice Age* ○ *We're living* ***in the age of*** *electronic communication.* **3** OLD [U] when something is old *Some wines improve* ***with age.*** **4 under age** too young to do something legally ➲See also: **the Middle Ages, old age**

age[2] /eɪdʒ/ *verb* [I, T] *UK* **ageing,** *US* **aging,** *past* **aged** to become older or to make someone seem older *Dad has aged a lot recently.*

aged[1] /eɪdʒd/ *adjective* having a particular age *They have one daughter, aged three.* ➲See also: **middle-aged**

aged[2] /ˈeɪdʒɪd/ *adjective* old *an aged dog* ○ *improved health care for the aged*

ˈage ˌgroup *noun* [C] **SOCIETY** people of a particular age *job training for people in the 16-24 age group*

ageing[1] *UK* (*US* **aging**) /ˈeɪdʒɪŋ/ *adjective* becoming older *an ageing population*

ageing[2] *UK* (*US* **aging**) /ˈeɪdʒɪŋ/ *noun* [U] the process of becoming older *the ageing process*

ˈage ˌlimit *noun* [C] **LAW** the age at which a person is allowed or not allowed to do something *Eighteen is the legal age limit for buying alcohol.*

agency /ˈeɪdʒənsi/ *noun* [C] **1** BUSINESS a business that provides a service *an advertising agency* **2** ORGANIZATION an international organization or government department *an international development agency* ➲See also: **travel agency**

WORD PARTNERS FOR ***agenda***

set (= decide) the agenda • be **off/on** the agenda • be **at the top of/high on** the agenda • the agenda **for** sth

agenda /əˈdʒendə/ *noun* [C] **1** MEETING a list of subjects that people will discuss at a meeting *There are several items* ***on the agenda.*** **2** IMPORTANT SUBJECTS important subjects that have to be dealt with *The issue of rail safety is back* ***on the*** *political* ***agenda.***

agent /ˈeɪdʒənt/ *noun* [C] **1** BUSINESS someone whose job is to deal with business for someone else *a literary agent* **2** GOVERNMENT (*also* **secret agent**) someone who tries to find out secret information, especially about another country ➲See also: **estate agent** *UK*, **real estate agent** *US*, **travel agent**

ages /ˈeɪdʒɪz/ *noun* [plural] *informal* a very long time *I've been waiting here* ***for ages.*** ○ *It* ***takes ages*** *to cook.*

aggravate /ˈægrəveɪt/ *verb* [T] **1** MAKE WORSE to make a situation or condition worse *His comments only* ***aggravated*** *the* ***problem.*** **2** ANNOY to annoy someone *She's starting to really aggravate me.* •**aggravating** *adjective* •**aggravation** /ˌægrəˈveɪʃən/ *noun* [C, U]

aggregate /ˈægrɪgət/ *noun* [C, U] **MATHEMATICS** a total *UK Liverpool won 2-0* ***on aggregate*** (= in total).

aggression /əˈgreʃən/ *noun* [U] angry or violent behaviour towards someone *an act of aggression*

aggressive /əˈgresɪv/ *adjective* **1** ANGRY behaving in an angry and violent way towards another person *aggressive behaviour* **2** DETERMINED using forceful methods and determined to succeed *an aggressive marketing campaign* •**aggressively** *adverb*

aggressor /əˈgresər/ *noun* [C] someone who starts a fight or war with someone else

aggrieved /əˈgriːvd/ *adjective* upset or angry because someone has treated you unfairly

aghast /əˈgɑːst/ *adjective* [never before noun] very shocked *She looked at him aghast.*

agile /ˈædʒaɪl/ (US) /ˈædʒəl/ *adjective* **1** MOVE able to move your whole body easily and quickly **2** MIND able to think quickly in an intelligent way *an agile mind* •**agility** /əˈdʒɪləti/ *noun* [U]

aging /ˈeɪdʒɪŋ/ *noun, adjective US spelling of* ageing

agitate /ˈædʒɪteɪt/ *verb* [I] **POLITICS** to argue strongly about something in order to achieve social or political changes *They continued to* ***agitate for*** *changes to the legal system.* •**agitator** *noun* [C]

agitated /ˈædʒɪteɪtɪd/ *adjective* very anxious or upset *He seemed agitated, as if something was worrying him.* •**agitation** /ˌædʒɪˈteɪʃən/ *noun* [U]

agitprop /ˈædʒɪtprɒp/ *noun* [U] **POLITICS** the spreading of strongly political ideas or arguments expressed especially through plays, art, books, etc.

AGM /ˌeɪdʒiːˈem/ *UK* (*US* **annual meeting**) *noun* [C] *abbreviation for* Annual General Meeting: a meeting that happens once every year in which an organization discusses the past year's activities and chooses the people who will be in charge of the organization

agnostic /æɡˈnɒstɪk/ *noun* [C] **RELIGION** someone who believes that we cannot know if God exists or not •**agnostic** *adjective*

O⁻ **ago** /əˈɡəʊ/ *adverb* **ten minutes/six years/a long time ago** used to refer to a time in the past *They moved to London ten years ago.*

agonist /ˈæɡənɪst/ *noun* [C] **ANATOMY** a muscle that is pulled in the opposite direction by another muscle

agonize (*also UK* **-ise**) /ˈæɡənaɪz/ *verb* [I] to spend a lot of time worrying about a decision *Lee* ***agonized over*** *what to buy his girlfriend.*

agonizing (*also UK* **-ising**) /ˈæɡənaɪzɪŋ/ *adjective* causing you a lot of pain or worry *an agonizing choice*

agony /ˈæɡəni/ *noun* [C, U] extreme suffering, either physical or mental *She lay on the bed* ***in agony.***

ˈ**agony** ˌ**aunt** *noun* [C] *UK* someone who gives advice on personal problems, in a newspaper or magazine

O⁻ **agree** /əˈɡriː/ *verb* **agreeing**, *past* **agreed** **1** SAME OPINION [I, T] to have the same opinion as someone *I* ***agree with*** *you.* ○ *"She's definitely the right person for the job." "I agree."* [+ (that)] *We all agreed that mistakes had been made.* ○ *We* ***agree about*** *most things.* **2** SAY YES [I] to say you will do something that someone asks you to do [+ to do sth] *She agreed to help him.* ➲See Common Learner Error at **accept** **3** DECIDE [I, T] to decide something with someone *We couldn't* ***agree on*** *what to buy.* [+ to do sth] *They agreed to meet on Sunday.* [+ (that)] *We agreed that they would deliver the sofa in the morning.* **4** DESCRIPTION [I] If two descriptions agree, they are the same. ➲Opposite **disagree**

agree with sth *phrasal verb* to think that something is morally acceptable *I don't agree with hunting.*

agreeable /əˈɡriːəbl/ *adjective formal* **1** pleasant or nice *an agreeable young man* ➲Opposite **disagreeable** **2 be agreeable to sth** to be willing to do or accept something *If Harvey is agreeable to the proposal, we'll go ahead.* •**agreeably** *adverb*

WORD PARTNERS FOR ***agreement***

reach/sign an agreement • a **draft/written** agreement • an agreement **between** sb

O⁻ **agreement** /əˈɡriːmənt/ *noun* **1** PROMISE [C] a promise or decision made between two or more people *an international agreement* ○ *It was difficult to* ***reach an agreement.*** **2** SAME OPINION [U] when people have the same opinion as each other *Not everyone was* ***in agreement.*** ➲Opposite **disagreement**

agriculture /ˈæɡrɪkʌltʃər/ *noun* [U] **FARMING** the work and methods of growing crops and looking after animals which are then used for food •**agricultural** /ˌæɡrɪˈkʌltʃərəl/ *adjective*

agritourism /ˌæɡrɪˈtʊərɪzm/ *noun* [U] the business of providing holidays for people on farms or in the countryside

aground /əˈɡraʊnd/ *adverb* **run aground** If a ship runs aground, it cannot move because the water is not deep enough.

ah /ɑː/ *exclamation* **1** SHOW FEELING used to show sympathy or to show pleasure at seeing a baby or attractive animal *Ah, you poor thing!* ○ *Ah, look at that little kitten!* **2** UNDERSTAND used to show that you have just understood something *Ah, now I see what you're saying!*

aha /əˈhɑː/ *exclamation* used when you suddenly understand or find something *Aha! That's where I left my keys!*

O⁻ **ahead** /əˈhed/ *adjective, adverb* **1** IN FRONT in front *The road ahead is very busy.* ○ *Rick walked* ***ahead of*** *us.* **2** FUTURE in the future *She has a difficult time* ***ahead of*** *her.* **3** MORE POINTS having more points than someone else in a competition *Barcelona was ahead after ten minutes.* **4** MORE PROGRESS making more progress than someone or something else *Sue is* ***ahead of*** *everyone else in French.* **5 go ahead** *informal* used to allow someone to do something *"Can I use your phone?" "Sure, go ahead."* **6 ahead of time/schedule** before the time that was planned *We finished the project ahead of schedule.* ➲See also: be one **step**[1] ahead (of sb), be streets (**street**) ahead (of sb/sth), be ahead of your **time**[1]

-aholic /-əˈhɒlɪk/ *suffix* unable to stop doing or taking something *chocaholic* (= someone who cannot stop eating chocolate)

aid[1] /eɪd/ *noun* **1** HELP [U] money, food, or equipment that is given to help a country or group of people *Emergency aid was sent to the flood victims.* ○ *aid workers* **2 in aid of sb/sth** *UK* in order to collect money for a group of people who need it *a concert in aid of famine relief* **3 with the aid of sth** using something to help you *She can walk with the aid of a stick.* **4 come/go to sb's aid** to go to someone and help them *Luckily a policeman came to my aid.* **5** EQUIPMENT [C] a piece of equipment that helps you to do something *teaching aids such as books and videos* ➲See also: **Band-Aid, first aid, visual aid**

aid[2] /eɪd/ *verb formal* **1** [T] to help someone **2 aid and abet (sb)** in law, to help someone do something that is illegal

aide /eɪd/ *noun* [C] **POLITICS** someone whose job is to help someone important, especially in the government *a former aide to the President*

AIDS, Aids /eɪdz/ *noun* [U] **HEALTH** *abbreviation for* acquired immune deficiency syndrome: a serious disease that destroys the body's ability to fight infection ➲Compare **HIV**

ailing /ˈeɪlɪŋ/ *adjective* weak or ill *an ailing company/economy*

ailment /ˈeɪlmənt/ *noun* [C] **HEALTH** an illness *Treat **minor ailments** yourself.*

WORD PARTNERS FOR ***aim***

achieve your aim • sb's/sth's **main/ultimate** aim • the aim **of** sth • **with** the aim of doing sth

aim[1] /eɪm/ *noun* **1** [C] the purpose of doing something, and what you hope to achieve *The **aim of** the film was to make people laugh.* [+ **of** + **doing sth**] *He went to Paris **with the aim** of improving his French.* **2 sb's aim** someone's ability to hit an object by throwing something or shooting at something **3 take aim** to point a weapon towards someone or something

aim[2] /eɪm/ *verb* **1 aim for/at sth; aim to do sth** to intend to achieve something *I aim to arrive at three o'clock.* ○ *We're aiming for a 10% increase in sales.* **2 be aimed at sb** to be intended to influence or affect a particular person or group *advertising aimed at students* **3 be aimed at doing sth** to be intended to achieve a particular thing *a plan aimed at reducing traffic* **4** [I, T] to point a weapon towards someone or something *He **aimed** the gun **at** the lion.*

aimless /ˈeɪmləs/ *adjective* with no purpose •**aimlessly** *adverb*

ain't /eɪnt/ *informal short for* am not, is not, are not, have not, or has not. This word is not considered correct by most people.

O-- **air**[1] /eəʳ/ *noun* **1** GAS [U] the mixture of gases around the Earth which we breathe *air pollution* ○ *He went outside to get some **fresh air*** (= clean, cool air). **2 the air** the space above and around things *He fired his gun into the air.* **3** TRAVEL [U] travel in an aircraft *I like travelling **by air**.* ○ *air safety* **4** QUALITY [**no plural**] a particular appearance or quality *He has **an air of** authority.* **5 be on air** to be broadcasting on television or radio **6 clear the air** If an argument or discussion clears the air, people feel less angry or upset after it. **7 disappear/vanish into thin air** to suddenly disappear in a mysterious way **8 be up in the air** If something is up in the air, no decision has been made. *Our plans for the summer are still up in the air.* ➲See also: a **breath** of fresh air, **mid-air**

air[2] /eəʳ/ *verb* **1** BROADCAST [T] to broadcast something on radio or television **2 air your opinions/views, etc** to say what your opinions are *The meeting will give everyone a chance to air their views.* **3** ROOM [T] to make a room smell better by opening a door or window **4** CLOTHES [I, T] If clothes air, or if you air them, you hang them up with a lot of air around them.

airbag /ˈeəbæg/ *noun* [C] a bag in the front of a car that protects people in an accident by filling with air *passenger/twin airbags*

airbase /ˈeəbeɪs/ *noun* [C] a military airport

ˈair ˌbladder *noun* [C] **BIOLOGY** a small bag of air or gas inside the body of a fish or inside a plant, that helps it to float or breathe

airborne /ˈeəbɔːn/ *adjective* moving in, or carried by the air *airborne troops* ○ *an airborne virus*

ˈair ˌcon *noun* [U] *UK abbreviation for* air conditioning

ˈair conˌditioner *noun* [C] a machine that keeps the air cool in a building or a car

ˈair conˌditioning *noun* [U] a system that keeps the air cool in a building or car •**air-conditioned** /ˈeəkənˌdɪʃənd/ *adjective* having air conditioning *an air-conditioned office*

O-- **aircraft** /ˈeəkrɑːft/ *noun* [C] *plural* **aircraft** a vehicle that can fly

ˈaircraft ˌcarrier *noun* [C] a ship on which aircraft can take off and land

airfare /ˈeəfeəʳ/ *noun* [C] the cost of a ticket to fly somewhere

airfield /ˈeəfiːld/ *noun* [C] a place where small or military aircraft can take off and land

ˈair ˌforce *noun* [C] the part of a country's military organization that uses aircraft to fight wars

ˈair hoˌstess *UK* (*UK/US* **flight attendant**) *noun* [C] someone whose job is to serve passengers on an aircraft and to make sure that safety rules are obeyed

ˈairing ˌcupboard *noun* [C] *UK* a warm cupboard where you keep sheets, clean clothes, etc

airless /ˈeələs/ *adjective* An airless room does not have enough fresh air.

airlift /ˈeəlɪft/ *noun* [C] when people or things are moved by aircraft because it is too difficult or too slow to travel by road *an airlift of medical supplies* •**airlift** *verb* [T] [**often passive**] *Three small children were airlifted to safety.*

airline /ˈeəlaɪn/ *noun* [C] a company that provides regular flights to places

airliner /ˈeəlaɪnəʳ/ *noun* [C] a large plane for carrying people

airmail /ˈeəmeɪl/ *noun* [U] the sending of letters or parcels by plane *an airmail letter*

airman /ˈeəmən/ *noun* [C] *plural* **airmen** a man who flies an aircraft in a country's air force

airplane /ˈeəpleɪn/ *US* (*UK* **aeroplane**) *noun* [C] a vehicle that flies and has an engine and wings

O-- **airport** /ˈeəpɔːt/ *noun* [C] a place where planes take off and land, with buildings for passengers to wait in

ˈair ˌraid *noun* [C] an attack by military planes

ˈair ˌsac *noun* [C] **1 BIOLOGY** a part of a bird or an insect used for breathing **2 ANATOMY** an alveolus (= small bag of air in the lung)

airship /ˈeə.ʃɪp/ *noun* [C] a large aircraft without wings and filled with a gas lighter than air, used especially in the past.

airspace /ˈeəspeɪs/ *noun* [U] the sky above a country that belongs to that country

airstrike /ˈeəstraɪk/ *noun* [C] an attack by military planes

airtight /ˈeətaɪt/ *adjective* An airtight container does not allow air in or out.

ˌair traffic conˈtroller *noun* [C] the person in an airport who tells pilots when to take off and land their aircraft

airway /ˈeəweɪ/ *noun* [C] **ANATOMY** the tube through the mouth and throat that carries air to the lungs

airy /ˈeəri/ *adjective* An airy room or building is pleasant because it has a lot of space and air.

aisle /aɪl/ *noun* [C] a passage between the lines of seats or goods in a plane, church, supermarket, etc

ajar /əˈdʒɑːʳ/ *adjective* [**never before noun**] If a door is ajar, it is slightly open.

aka /ˌeɪkeɪˈeɪ/ *adverb abbreviation for* also known as: used when giving the name that a person is generally known by, after giving their real name *Peter Parker, aka Spiderman*

akin /əˈkɪn/ *adjective formal* **be akin to sth** to be similar to something

à la carte /ˌæləˈkɑːt/ *adjective, adverb* **FOOD** choosing food as separate items from a menu (= list of food), not as a meal with a fixed price

alacrity /əˈlækrəti/ *noun* [U] *formal* If you do something with alacrity, you do it in a very quick and willing way.

WORD PARTNERS FOR ***alarm***

an alarm **goes off/sounds** • **set off/trigger** an alarm • a **burglar/fire/smoke** alarm • a **car** alarm • an alarm **system**

alarm¹ /əˈlɑːm/ *noun* **1** WARNING [C] a loud noise that warns you of danger *a fire alarm* ○ *to **set off** an **alarm*** **2** CLOCK [C] (*also* **alarm clock**) a clock that makes a noise to wake you **3** WORRY [U] a sudden feeling of fear or worry that something bad might happen *There's no need for alarm - it is completely safe.* **4 raise the alarm** to warn someone of a dangerous situation *Her parents raised the alarm when she failed to return home.* ➲See also: **burglar alarm, false alarm**

alarm² /əˈlɑːm/ *verb* [T] to make someone worried or frightened *I don't want to alarm you but he really should be here by now.*

aˈlarm ˌclock *noun* [C] a clock that makes a noise to wake you *I've **set the alarm clock for** six.*

alarmed /əˈlɑːmd/ *adjective* worried or frightened by something *I was a bit **alarmed at** the number of people in the audience.*

alarming /əˈlɑːmɪŋ/ *adjective* making you feel worried or frightened *alarming news*

alas /əˈlæs/ *exclamation literary* used to show sadness

albeit /ɔːlˈbiːɪt/ *conjunction formal* although *He tried, albeit without success.*

albino /ælˈbiːnəʊ/ ⓤⓢ /ælˈbaɪnəʊ/ *noun* [C] **BIOLOGY** a person or animal with white skin, white hair or fur, and pink eyes

album /ˈælbəm/ *noun* [C] **1 MUSIC** several songs or pieces of music on a CD, a record, etc **2** BOOK a book in which you keep photographs, stamps, etc

albumen /ˈælbjʊmən/ *noun* [U] **BIOLOGY, FOOD** the clear part inside an egg which is white when cooked and which is used as food by the bird or animal growing in the egg

alcohol /ˈælkəhɒl/ *noun* [U] **1 FOOD** drinks such as wine and beer that can make you drunk **2 CHEMISTRY, FOOD** a liquid that has no colour and is in drinks that make you drunk

alcoholic¹ /ˌælkəˈhɒlɪk/ *noun* [C] **HEALTH** someone who regularly drinks too much alcohol and cannot stop the habit

alcoholic² /ˌælkəˈhɒlɪk/ *adjective* **1 FOOD** containing alcohol *alcoholic drinks* **2 HEALTH** [**always before noun**] regularly drinking too much alcohol and unable to stop the habit *She lived with her alcoholic father.*

alcoholism /ˈælkəhɒlɪzᵊm/ *noun* [U] **HEALTH** the condition of being an alcoholic

alcove /ˈælkəʊv/ *noun* [C] a part of a wall in a room that is further back than the rest of the wall

ale /eɪl/ *noun* [C, U] **FOOD** a type of beer

alert¹ /əˈlɜːt/ *adjective* quick to notice and react to things around you *A young dog should be alert and playful.* ○ *Teachers need to be **alert to** sudden changes in students' behaviour.* •**alertness** *noun* [U]

alert² /əˈlɜːt/ *verb* [T] to warn someone of a possibly dangerous situation *Six hours later she still wasn't home so they alerted the police.*

alert³ /əˈlɜːt/ *noun* **1** [C] a warning about a possibly dangerous situation *a **bomb alert*** **2 be on full/red alert** to be expecting problems and ready to deal with them *Police in the region were on full alert against further attacks.*

ˈA ˌlevel *noun* [C] **EDUCATION** in England and Wales, an exam taken at the age of eighteen, or the qualification itself

algae /ˈældʒiː/ *noun* [U, group] **BIOLOGY** a plant with no stem or leaves that grows in or near water

algebra /ˈældʒɪbrə/ *noun* [U] **MATHEMATICS** a type of mathematics in which numbers and amounts are shown by letters and symbols

algorithm /ˈælgərɪðᵊm/ *noun* [C] **MATHEMATICS** a set of rules used to calculate an answer to a mathematical problem

alias¹ /ˈeɪliəs/ *noun* [C] a false name, especially one used by a criminal

alias² /ˈeɪliəs/ *preposition* used when giving the name that a person is generally known by, after giving their real name *Grace Kelly, alias Princess Grace of Monaco*

alibi /ˈælɪbaɪ/ *noun* [C] **LAW** proof that someone was not in the place where a crime happened and so cannot be guilty

alien¹ /ˈeɪliən/ *adjective* **1** STRANGE strange and not familiar *The custom was totally **alien to** her.* **2** ANOTHER PLANET [**always before noun**] relating to creatures from another planet *an alien spacecraft*

alien² /ˈeɪliən/ *noun* [C] **1** CREATURE a creature from another planet **2** FOREIGNER *formal* someone who does not legally belong to the country where they live or work

A

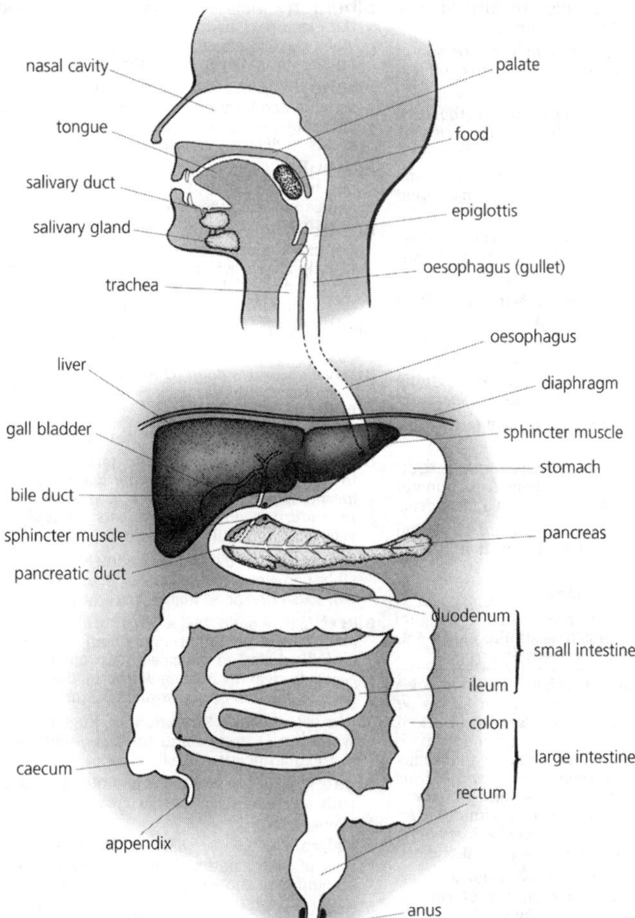

alimentary canal

alienate /ˈeɪliəneɪt/ *verb* [T] **1** LOSE SUPPORT to make someone stop supporting and liking you *The government's comments have alienated many teachers.* **2** NOT INCLUDE to make someone feel that they are different and do not belong to a group *Disagreements can* ***alienate*** *teenagers* ***from*** *their families.* •**alienation** /ˌeɪliəˈneɪʃən/ *noun* [U]

alight¹ /əˈlaɪt/ *adjective* [**never before noun**] *mainly UK* burning *Vandals* ***set*** *the car* ***alight*** (= made it burn).

alight² /əˈlaɪt/ *verb* [I] *formal* to get out of a bus, train, etc *He* ***alighted from*** *the taxi.*

align /əˈlaɪn/ *verb* **1** [T] to put things in an exact line or make them parallel **2 align yourself with sb; be aligned with sb** to support the opinions of a political group, country, etc *Many voters are not aligned with any party.* •**alignment** *noun* [C, U]

alike¹ /əˈlaɪk/ *adjective* [**never before noun**] similar *The children look so alike.*

alike² /əˈlaɪk/ *adverb* **1** SAME WAY in a similar way *We think alike.* **2** BOTH used to say that two people or groups are included *It is a disease which affects men and women alike.*

alimentary canal /ælɪˌmentərikəˈnæl/ *noun* [C] **ANATOMY** the parts of the body that food goes through as it is eaten and digested

alimony /ˈælɪməni/ *noun* [U] **FINANCE** money that someone must pay regularly to their wife or husband after the marriage has ended

O-■ **alive** /əˈlaɪv/ *adjective* [**never before noun**] **1** NOT DEAD living, not dead *Are your grandparents still alive?* **2** PLACE full of activity and excitement *The bar was* ***alive with*** *the sound of laughter.* ○ *The city* ***comes alive*** *at night.* **3** CONTINUING continuing to exist *Local people are fighting to* ***keep*** *the language* ***alive***. **4 be alive and kicking/well** to continue to be popular or successful *Despite rumours to the contrary, feminism is alive and kicking.*

alkali /ˈælkəlaɪ/ *noun* [**U, C**] **CHEMISTRY** a substance which has the opposite effect or chemical behaviour to an acid and has a pH (= measure of how acid something is) of more than 7 •**alkaline** /ˈælkəlaɪn/ *adjective* •**alkalinity** /ˌælkəˈlɪnəti/ *noun* [**U**]

ˌalkali ˈmetal *noun* [**C**] **CHEMISTRY** any of a group of metallic elements such as lithium, sodium and potassium that react very easily and have a positive electric charge

alkaloid /ˈælkəlɔɪd/ *noun* [**C**] **CHEMISTRY** a poisonous chemical found in plants that is sometimes used in medicines

alkane /ˈælkeɪn/ *noun* [**C**] **CHEMISTRY** any gas in a group of gases that contain carbon and hydrogen atoms *Alkanes, such as butane and methane, are very flammable.*

alkene /ˈælkiːn/ *noun* [**C**] **CHEMISTRY** any gas in a group that contains carbon and hydrogen atoms, with the carbon atoms joined together in a double bond (= connection)

O-■ **all**[1] /ɔːl/ *pronoun, determiner* **1** EVERY ONE every person or thing in a group *We were all dancing.* ○ *I've watched* ***all of*** *the programmes in the series.* **2** WHOLE AMOUNT the whole amount of something *Who's eaten all the cake?* ○ *He spends* ***all of*** *his money on clothes.* **3** WHOLE TIME the whole of a period of time *all week/month/year* ○ *He's been studying all day.* **4** ONLY THING the only thing *All I remember is waking up in hospital.* **5 at all** in any way *He hasn't changed at all.* ○ *UK Can I help at all?* **6 in all** in total *There were twenty people at the meeting in all.*

COMMON LEARNER ERROR

all + period of time

You do not say 'the' when you use **all** + a period of time.

all day/morning/week/year/summer

~~*all the day/morning/week/year/summer*~~

O-■ **all**[2] /ɔːl/ *adverb* **1** completely or very *You're all wet!* ○ *I'm all excited now.* **2 all over a** in every place *Lee has travelled all over the world.* **b** finished *It was all over very quickly.* **3 2/5/8, etc all SPORT** used to say that two players or teams have the same number of points in a game *It was 3 all at half time.* **4 all along** from the beginning of a period of time *I said all along that it was a mistake.* **5 all but** almost *The film was all but over by the time we arrived.* **6 all the better/easier/more exciting, etc** much better, easier, etc *The journey was all the more dangerous because of the bad weather.* **7 all in all** considering everything *All in all, I think she did well.*

Allah /ˈælə/ *noun* **RELIGION** the name of God for Muslims

allay /əˈleɪ/ *verb formal* **allay sb's concerns/fears/suspicions, etc** to make someone feel less worried or frightened, etc *I tried to allay his fears about the interview.*

WORD PARTNERS FOR ***allegation***

make/deny/face/investigate an allegation • a **serious** allegation • an allegation **of** sth • an allegation **against** sb

allegation /ˌælɪˈgeɪʃən/ *noun* [**C**] when you say that someone has done something wrong or illegal, without proof that this is true ***allegations of*** *corruption* [**+ that**] *He* ***denied allegations*** *that he had cheated.*

allege /əˈledʒ/ *verb* [**T**] to say that someone has done something wrong or illegal, but not prove it [**often passive**] *The teacher is alleged to have hit a student.* [**+ (that)**] *He alleges that Bates attacked him.*

alleged /əˈledʒd/ *adjective* [**always before noun**] believed to be true, but not proved *an alleged attack* •**allegedly** /əˈledʒɪdli/ *adverb He was arrested for allegedly stealing a car.*

allegiance /əˈliːdʒəns/ *noun* [**U**] loyalty and support *To become a citizen, you have to* ***pledge/swear allegiance to*** (= say you will be loyal to) *the United States.*

allegory /ˈælɪgəri/ *noun* [**C, U**] **LITERATURE** a story, poem, or painting that has a hidden meaning, especially a moral one •**allegorical** /ˌælɪˈgɒrɪkəl/ *adjective*

allele /əˈliːl/ *noun* [**C**] **BIOLOGY** one of two or more genes (= part of cell that controls characteristics) that is found in the same position in a chromosome (= part of a cell), and so produces a particular characteristic such as eye colour

allergen /ˈælədʒən/ *noun* [**C**] **HEALTH** a substance that can make some people ill if they eat it, touch it or breathe it in

allergic /əˈlɜːdʒɪk/ *adjective* **1 HEALTH** [**never before noun**] having an allergy *I'm* ***allergic to*** *eggs.* **2 HEALTH** [**always before noun**] caused by an allergy *an* ***allergic reaction***

allergy /ˈælədʒi/ *noun* [**C**] **HEALTH** a medical condition in which your body reacts badly to something that you eat, breathe, or touch *an* ***allergy to*** *dogs*

alleviate /əˈliːvieɪt/ *verb* [**T**] to make problems or suffering less extreme *She's been given some tablets to* ***alleviate*** *the* ***pain***. •**alleviation** /əˌliːviˈeɪʃən/ *noun* [**U**]

alley /ˈæli/ (*also* **alleyway** /ˈæliweɪ/) *noun* [**C**] **1** a narrow road between buildings **2 be right up sb's alley** *US informal* (*UK* **be right up sb's street**) to be exactly the type of thing that someone knows about or likes to do

WORD PARTNERS FOR ***alliance***

form an alliance • an alliance **between** sb and sb • an alliance **with** sb • **in** alliance with sb

alliance /əˈlaɪəns/ *noun* [**C**] **POLITICS** an agreement between countries or political parties to work together to achieve something *an* ***alliance between*** *France and Britain*

A

allied /ˈælaɪd/ *adjective* **1 POLITICS** [**always before noun**] joined by a formal agreement *the allied powers* **2 be allied to/with sth** to be related to something *a group closely allied with the Green Party*

alligator /ˈælɪgeɪtəʳ/ *noun* [**C**] a big reptile with a long mouth and sharp teeth, that lives in lakes and rivers

alliteration /əˌlɪtəˈreɪʃən/ *noun* [**U**] **LANGUAGE, LITERATURE** the use of the same sound or sounds at the beginning of several words that are close together

all-night /ˈɔːlnaɪt/ *adjective* lasting all night *Tom was tired after his **all-night party**.*

allocate /ˈæləkeɪt/ *verb* [**T**] to give some time, money, space, etc to be used for a particular purpose *The government has promised to **allocate** extra money **for** health care.* ○ *More police time should be **allocated to** crime prevention.*

allocation /ˌæləˈkeɪʃən/ *noun* **1** SHARE [**C**] an amount of money, time, space, etc that is allocated **2** PROCESS [**U**] when money, time, space, etc is allocated *the allocation of money*

allot /əˈlɒt/ *verb* [**T**] **allotting,** *past* **allotted** to give someone a particular amount of something [**often passive**] *They were allotted seats on the front row.*

allotment /əˈlɒtmənt/ *noun* **1** LAND [**C**] in Britain, a small area of land that people rent and grow vegetables and flowers on **2** SHARE [**C, U**] the process of sharing something, or the amount that you get

allotrope /ˈælətrəʊp/ *noun* [**C**] **CHEMISTRY** any of two or more forms of the same chemical substance

allotropy /æˈlɒtrəpiː/ *noun* [**U**] **CHEMISTRY** the existence of the same chemical substance in more than one form, each with different physical qualities •**allotropic** /ˌæləˈtrɒpɪk/ *adjective Diamond and graphite are allotropic forms of carbon.*

all-out /ˈɔːlˌaʊt/ *adjective* [**always before noun**] complete and with as much effort as possible *an all-out battle/effort*

O-- **allow** /əˈlaʊ/ *verb* [**T**] **1** GIVE PERMISSION to give someone permission for something [**often passive**] *Smoking is not allowed in the restaurant.* [**+ to do sth**] *You are not allowed to use calculators in the exam.* [**+ two objects**] *Patients are not allowed visitors after nine o'clock.* **2** NOT PREVENT to not prevent something from happening [**+ to do sth**] *They have allowed the problem to get worse.* **3** MAKE POSSIBLE to make it possible for someone to do something [**+ to do sth**] *The extra money will allow me to upgrade my computer.* **4** TIME/MONEY to plan to use a particular amount of money, time, etc for something *Allow three hours for the whole journey.*

allow for sth *phrasal verb* to consider or include something when you are making plans *The journey should take two hours, allowing for delays.*

COMMON LEARNER ERROR

allow or **let?**

Allow and **let** have similar meanings. **Allow** is used in more formal or official situations, especially when talking about rules and laws. Verb patterns - **allow someone to do something / allow something to happen**.

The new legislation allows companies to charge for this service.

We can't allow this situation to continue.

Let is used in more informal and spoken situations. Verb patterns - **let someone do something /let something happen**.

Dad never lets anyone else drive his car.

She let her hair grow longer.

allowance /əˈlaʊəns/ *noun* [**C**] **1** MONEY money that you are given regularly, especially to pay for a particular thing *a clothing allowance* **2** AMOUNT an amount of something that you are allowed *The luggage allowance is 25 kilos.* **3 make allowances for sb/sth** to remember that someone has a disadvantage which is not their fault when you are judging their behaviour or work *They made allowances for the fact that he was ill.*

alloy /ˈælɔɪ/ *noun* [**C**] **CHEMISTRY** a metal that is a mixture of two or more metals

O-- **ˌall ˈright¹** (*also* **alright**) *adjective* [**never before noun**], *adverb* **1** GOOD good enough, although not very good *The hotel wasn't brilliant but it was all right.* ○ *It's a cheap wine but it tastes all right.* **2** SAFE safe or well *I'm all right thanks. How are you?* ○ *Did you get home all right last night?* **3 that's all right a** THANKS used as an answer when someone thanks you *"Thanks for cleaning the kitchen." "That's all right."* **b** SORRY something you say when someone says sorry to show that you are not angry *"I'm sorry - I forgot all about it." "That's all right."*

ˌall ˈright² (*also* **alright**) *exclamation* used to agree to a suggestion or request *"How about going out for dinner?" "All right."*

all-time /ˌɔːlˈtaɪm/ *adjective* [**always before noun**] If something is at an all-time best/high/low, etc, it is the best/highest/lowest, etc it has ever been.

allude /əˈluːd/ *verb*

allude to sb/sth *phrasal verb formal* to refer to someone or something but not directly

allure /əˈljʊəʳ/ *noun* [**U**] an attractive or exciting quality *the allure of the city* •**alluring** *adjective* attractive or exciting *an alluring image*

allusion /əˈluːʒən/ *noun* [**C, U**] *formal* **LANGUAGE** when you refer to someone or something but not directly *a play full of **allusions to** Shakespeare*

alluvium /əˈluːviəm/ *noun* [**U**] **GEOLOGY** earth and sand that has been left by rivers, floods, etc. •**alluvial** /əˈluːviəl/ *adjective alluvial deposits*

ally¹ /ˈælaɪ/ *noun* [**C**] **1** someone who supports you, especially when other people are against you **2 POLITICS** a country that has agreed to help another country, especially in a war

ally² /əˈlaɪ/ *verb*

ally yourself to/with sb *phrasal verb* to join someone and support them

almighty /ɔːlˈmaɪti/ *adjective* **1** STRONG [**always before noun**] very strong or forceful *All of a* *sudden I heard an almighty bang in the kitchen.* **2** POWERFUL having the power to do everything, like a god ***Almighty God***

almond /'ɑːmənd/ *noun* [**C, U**] **FOOD** a flat, oval nut, often used in cooking

O─ **almost** /'ɔːlməʊst/ *adverb* **1** If something almost happens, it does not happen but it is very close to happening. *I almost missed the bus.* **2 almost always/everyone/half, etc** not always/everyone/half, etc but very close to it *He's almost always late.*

O─ **alone** /ə'ləʊn/ *adjective, adverb* **1** NO OTHER PEOPLE [**never before noun**] without other people *She lives alone.* **2** ONLY ONE [**always after noun**] used to emphasize that only one person or thing is involved *Last year alone the company made a million dollars.* **3 leave sb alone** to stop talking to someone or annoying them *Leave him alone, he's tired.* **4 leave sth alone** to stop touching something *Leave your hair alone!* ➲See also: **let** alone

COMMON LEARNER ERROR

alone or **lonely?**

Alone means without other people. If you feel sad because you are alone, you are **lonely**.

Sometimes I like to be alone to think.

She has been very lonely since her husband died.

O─ **along¹** /ə'lɒŋ/ *preposition* **1** DIRECTION from one part of a road, river, etc to another *a romantic walk along the beach* **2** NEXT TO in a line next to something long *a row of new houses along the river* **3** PARTICULAR PLACE at a particular place on a road, river, etc *Somewhere along this road there's a garage.*

O─ **along²** /ə'lɒŋ/ *adverb* **1** forward *We were just walking along, chatting.* **2 be/come along** to arrive somewhere *You wait ages for a bus and then three come along at once.* **3 bring/take sb along** to take someone with you to a place *She asked if she could bring some friends along to the party.* **4 along with sb/sth** in addition to someone or something else *California along with Florida is probably the most popular American holiday destination.*

alongside /əˌlɒŋ'saɪd/ *adverb, preposition* **1** NEXT TO next to someone or something *A car pulled up alongside ours.* **2** WITH together with someone *She enjoyed* ***working alongside*** *such famous actors.*

aloof /ə'luːf/ *adjective* **1** NOT FRIENDLY not friendly, especially because you think you are better than other people *He seems arrogant and aloof.* **2** NOT INVOLVED not involved in something *He tried to remain* ***aloof from*** *family arguments.*

aloud /ə'laʊd/ *adverb* in a way that other people can hear *to* ***laugh aloud*** ○ *The author* ***read aloud*** *from his new book.*

alphabet /'ælfəbet/ *noun* [**C**] **LANGUAGE** a set of letters used for writing a language *The English alphabet starts at A and ends at Z.*

alphabetical /ˌælfə'betɪkəl/ *adjective* **LANGUAGE** arranged in the same order as the letters of the alphabet *Put the names* ***in alphabetical order.*** ●**alphabetically** *adverb*

alphanumeric /ˌælfənjuː'merɪk/ *adjective* **LANGUAGE** containing or using letters of the alphabet and also numbers

alpha particle /'ælfəˌpɑːtɪkl/ *noun* [**C**] **PHYSICS** an extremely small piece of matter with a positive electrical charge, produced in a nuclear reaction

alphorn /'ælp.hɔːn/ *noun* [**C**] **MUSIC** a large, long musical instrument shaped like a horn, played in places like Switzerland

alpine /'ælpaɪn/ *adjective* [**always before noun**] **GEOGRAPHY** existing in, or relating to high mountains *an alpine village*

O─ **already** /ɔːl'redi/ *adverb* **1** BEFORE before now, or before a particular time in the past *I've already told him.* ○ *By the time we arrived, he'd already left.* **2** EARLIER used to say that something has happened earlier than you expected *I'm already full and I've only eaten one course.*

O─ **alright** /ɔːl'raɪt/ *adjective, adverb, exclamation* *another spelling of* all right

O─ **also** /'ɔːlsəʊ/ *adverb* in addition *She speaks French and also a little Spanish.* ○ *The book also has a chapter on grammar.*

altar /ˌɔːltəʳ/ *noun* [**C**] **RELIGION** a table used for religious ceremonies, especially in a Christian church

alter /ˌɔːltəʳ/ *verb* [**I, T**] to change, or to make someone or something change *We've had to alter our plans.*

WORD PARTNERS FOR ***alteration***

make alterations (**to** sth) ● a **major/minor/slight** alteration ● an alteration **in/to** sth

alteration /ˌɔːltəʳ'eɪʃən/ *noun* [**C, U**] a change, or the process of changing something *We've* ***made*** *a few* ***alterations to*** *the kitchen.*

alternate¹ /ɔːl'tɜːnət/ *adjective* **1 alternate days/weeks/years, etc** one out of every two days, weeks, years, etc *I work alternate Saturdays.* **2** REPEATING with first one thing, then another thing, and then the first thing again, etc *a dessert with alternate layers of chocolate and cream* **3** DIFFERENT [**always before noun**] *US* An alternate plan, method, etc is one that you can use if you do not want to use another one. ●**alternately** *adverb*

alternate² /'ɔːltəneɪt/ *verb* **1** [**I**] If two things alternate, one thing happens, then the other thing happens, then the first thing happens again, etc. *She* ***alternates between*** *cheerfulness and deep despair.* **2 alternate sth with sth** to use or do one thing then another thing and then the first thing again, etc *They alternate classical pieces with more modern works.* ●**alternating** *adjective alternating moods of anger and sadness*

alˌternate 'angle *noun* [**C**] **MATHEMATICS** one of two angles on opposite sides of a line that crosses two usually parallel (= always the same distance apart) lines ➲Compare **corresponding angle**

'alternating ˌcurrent *noun* [**C**] **PHYSICS** electrical current (= movement of electricity)

A

which regularly changes the direction in which it moves ⊃Compare **direct current**

alternative¹ /ɔːlˈtɜːnətɪv/ *noun* [C] one of two or more things that you can choose between *It's a low-fat* ***alternative to*** *butter.* ○ *After the public protests the government* ***had no alternative*** *but to change its policy.*

alternative² /ɔːlˈtɜːnətɪv/ *adjective* [**always before noun**] **1** INSTEAD (*also US* **alternate**) An alternative plan, method, etc is one that you can use if you do not want to use another one. *We can make* ***alternative arrangements*** *if necessary.* **2** UNUSUAL different to what is usual or traditional ***alternative comedy*** ○ *an alternative lifestyle*

alternatively /ɔːlˈtɜːnətɪvli/ *adverb* used to give a second possibility *We could go there by train or, alternatively, I could drive us.*

alˌternative ˈmedicine *noun* [U] **HEALTH** any way of trying to make an illness better that uses medicines or methods that are not normally used in Western medicine

O-**although** /ɔːlˈðəʊ/ *conjunction* **1** DESPITE despite the fact that *She walked home by herself, although she knew it was dangerous.* **2** BUT but *He's coming this evening, although I don't know exactly when.*

altitude /ˈæltɪtjuːd/ *noun* [C, U] **MEASURES** the height of something above sea level *flying at an altitude of 8000 metres*

Alt key /ˈæltkiː/ *noun* [**C usually singular**] **COMPUTING** a key on a computer keyboard that you press at the same time as another key to produce a particular result

alto /ˈæltəʊ/ *noun* [C] **MUSIC** a woman or boy with a low singing voice

altocumulus /ˌæltəʊˈkjuːmjələs/ *noun* [U] **GEOGRAPHY** a type of tall, round, white cloud with a flat base found at medium height

O-**altogether** /ˌɔːltəˈgeðəʳ/ *adverb* **1** COMPLETELY completely *The train slowed down and then stopped altogether.* ○ *I'm* ***not altogether*** *sure about the idea.* **2** TOTAL in total *There were twenty people there altogether.* **3** GENERALLY when you consider everything *Altogether, I'd say the party was a great success.*

altostratus /ˌæltəʊˈstrɑːtəs/ (US) /-ˈstreɪ-/ *noun* [U] **GEOGRAPHY** a type of flat, grey cloud formed in thin layers and found at medium height ⊃See picture at **cloud**

alum /ˈæləm/ *noun* [U] **CHEMISTRY** a chemical substance used for several purposes, including dyeing (= changing the colour of something) and some medicines

aluminium /ˌæljəˈmɪniəm/ *UK* (*US* **aluminum** /əˈluːmɪnəm/) *noun* [U] **CHEMISTRY** a light, silver-coloured metal used for making containers, cooking equipment, and aircraft parts (symbol **Al**) *aluminium cans/foil*

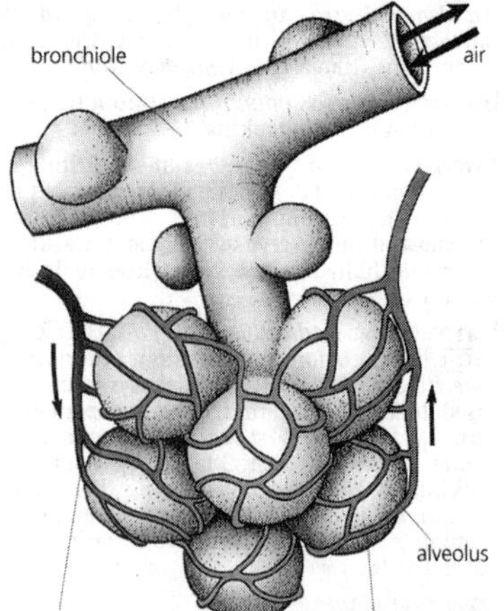

alveoli

alveolus /ˌælviˈəʊləs/ (US) /ˌæˈviː.ələs/ *noun* [C] *plural* **alveoli ANATOMY** one of the many very small air bags in the lungs, with thin walls that allow oxygen to enter the blood ⊃See picture at **circulation** ⊃See picture at **respiratory system**

OTHER WAYS OF SAYING *always*

If you are using **always** to mean 'again and again', then you could also use **constantly**, **continually**, **forever**, or the fixed expressions **time after time** or **all the time**: *He's constantly/forever losing his keys.* • *I'm fed up with you making excuses* ***all the time.***

The word **invariably** is sometimes used as a more formal way of saying **always**, especially when talking about something bad which happens: *The train is* ***invariably*** *late.*

The fixed expression **without fail** can be used to show that someone always does something, even when it is difficult: *He visited her every Sunday* ***without fail.***

O-**always** /ˈɔːlweɪz/ *adverb* **1** EVERY TIME every time, or at all times *I always walk to work.* **2** UNTIL NOW at all times in the past *We've always lived here.* **3** FOREVER forever *I will always remember you.* **4** MANY TIMES again and again, usually in an annoying way [**+ doing sth**] *He's always losing his keys.* **5 can/could always do sth** used to suggest something *You can always stay with us if you miss your train.*

Alzheimer's (disease) /ˈæltshaɪməzdɪˌziːz/ *noun* [U] **HEALTH** a brain disease mainly of old people which makes a person forget things and stops them from thinking clearly

O-**a.m.** (*also* **am**) /ˌeɪˈem/ used to refer to a time between 12 o'clock in the night and 12 o'clock in the day *We're open from 9 a.m. to 5 p.m. daily.*

AM /ˌeɪ'em/ *noun* [U] **PHYSICS** *abbreviation for* amplitude modulation; a system of radio signals used for broadcasting programmes

am *strong form* /æm/ *weak forms* /əm, m/ *present simple I of* be

amalgam /ə'mælgəm/ *noun* [U] **CHEMISTRY** a mixture of mercury (= a heavy, silver coloured metal) and another metal, especially one used by dentists to repair teeth

amalgamate /ə'mælgəmeɪt/ *verb* [I, T] If two or more organizations amalgamate, they join to become one, and if you amalgamate them, you make them do this. *a decision to* ***amalgamate with*** *another school* •**amalgamation** /əˌmælgə'meɪʃən/ *noun* [C, U]

amass /ə'mæs/ *verb* [T] *formal* to get a lot of money or information over a period of time *He* ***amassed a fortune*** *in the diamond trade.*

amateur¹ /'æmətəʳ/ *adjective* doing something as a hobby and not as your job *an amateur photographer*

amateur² /'æmətəʳ/ *noun* [C] **1** HOBBY someone who does something as a hobby and not as their job **2** NO SKILL someone who is not good at what they do *I won't be giving them any more work - they're a bunch of amateurs.*

amateurish /'æmətərɪʃ/ (US) /ˌæmə'tɜːrɪʃ/ *adjective* done without skill or attention

amaze /ə'meɪz/ *verb* [T] to make someone very surprised *It amazes me how much energy that woman has.*

amazed /ə'meɪzd/ *adjective* extremely surprised *I was* ***amazed at*** *the price.* [+ (that)] *I was amazed that Paul recognized me.*

amazement /ə'meɪzmənt/ *noun* [U] extreme surprise *Jana looked at him* ***in amazement.*** ○ ***To his amazement*** *they offered him the job.*

amazing /ə'meɪzɪŋ/ *adjective* very surprising [+ question word] *It's amazing how many people can't read.* •**amazingly** *adverb*

ambassador /æm'bæsədəʳ/ *noun* [C] **POLITICS** the main official sent by the government of a country to represent it in another country *the French ambassador to Britain*

amber /'æmbəʳ/ *noun* [U] **1** a colour between yellow and orange **2 GEOLOGY** a hard, clear yellowish-brown substance, used for making jewellery •**amber** *adjective an amber traffic light*

ambience (*also* **ambiance**) /'æmbiəns/ *noun* [U, no plural] the qualities of a place and the way it makes you feel *Lighting adds a lot to the ambience of a room.*

ambiguity /ˌæmbɪ'gjuːəti/ *noun* [C, U] when something has more than one possible meaning *Legal documents must be free of ambiguity.*

ambiguous /æm'bɪgjuəs/ *adjective* having more than one possible meaning *an ambiguous statement* •**ambiguously** *adverb*

WORD PARTNERS FOR ***ambition***

have an ambition • **achieve/fulfil/realize** an ambition • a **burning/lifelong** ambition

O‑**ambition** /æm'bɪʃən/ *noun* **1** HOPE [C] something you want to achieve in your life *My ambition is to retire at forty.* **2** FEELING [U] a strong feeling that you want to be successful or powerful *My sister always had more ambition than me.*

ambitious /æm'bɪʃəs/ *adjective* **1** PERSON wanting to be successful or powerful *an ambitious young lawyer* **2** PLAN An ambitious plan will need a lot of work and will be difficult to achieve. *This is our most ambitious project so far.*

ambivalent /æm'bɪvələnt/ *adjective* having two different feelings about something *He was* ***ambivalent about*** *moving to London.* •**ambivalence** /æm'bɪvələns/ *noun* [U]

amble /'æmbl/ *verb* **amble along/around/through, etc** to walk somewhere in a slow and relaxed way *We ambled home across the fields.*

ambulance /'æmbjələns/ *noun* [C] **HEALTH** a vehicle that takes people to hospital when they are ill or hurt

ambush /'æmbʊʃ/ *verb* [T] to attack a person or vehicle after hiding somewhere and waiting for them to arrive [often passive] *The bus was ambushed by a gang of youths.* •**ambush** *noun* [C] *Two men died in a terrorist ambush.*

ameba /ə'miːbə/ *noun* [C] **BIOLOGY** *US spelling of* amoeba

ameliorate /ə'miːliəreɪt/ *verb* [T] *formal* to make a problem or bad situation better

amen /ˌɑː'men/ *exclamation* **RELIGION** something that Christians say at the end of a prayer

amenable /ə'miːnəbl/ *adjective* willing to do or accept something *She may be more* ***amenable to*** *the idea now.*

amend /ə'mend/ *verb* [T] to slightly change the words of a document [often passive] *The contract has now been amended.*

amendment /ə'mendmənt/ *noun* [C, U] a change in the words of a document, or the process of doing this *to* ***make an amendment*** *to the human rights law*

amends /ə'mendz/ *noun* **make amends** to do something nice for someone to show that you are sorry for something that you have done *I want to* ***make amends for*** *the worry I've caused you.*

amenity /ə'miːnəti/ (US) /ə'menəti/ *noun* [C] a building, piece of equipment, or service that is provided for people's comfort or enjoyment [usually plural] *The campsite's amenities include a pool and three restaurants.*

American /ə'merɪkən/ *adjective* **1** relating to the United States of America *an American accent* **2 North/South American** relating to one or more of the countries of North/South America •**American** *noun* [C] someone who comes from the United States of America ➲See also: **Native American**

Aˌmerican 'football *UK* (*US* **football**) *noun* [U] **SPORT** a game for two teams of eleven players in which each team tries to kick, run with, or throw an oval ball across the opposing team's goal line ➲See colour picture **Sports 2** on page Centre 15

Aˌmerican 'Indian *adjective* **SOCIETY** relating or belonging to the original race of people who

A

lived in North America •**American Indian** *noun* [C]

amiable /ˈeɪmiəbl/ *adjective* pleasant and friendly *an amiable young man* •**amiably** *adverb*

amicable /ˈæmɪkəbl/ *adjective formal* done in a friendly way, without arguments *an amicable agreement/divorce* •**amicably** *adverb*

amid /əˈmɪd/ (*also* **amidst** /əˈmɪdst/) *preposition formal* **1** WHILE while something else is happening *Security was increased* ***amid fears*** *of further terrorist attacks.* **2** AMONG among *a village set amid the hills*

amino acid /əˌmiːnəʊˈæsɪd/ *noun* **BIOLOGY** any of the chemical substances found in plants and animals that combine to make protein (= substance necessary for the body to grow)

amiss[1] /əˈmɪs/ *adjective* [**never before noun**] If something is amiss, there is something wrong. *I knew something was amiss when he didn't answer the door.*

amiss[2] /əˈmɪs/ *adverb* **1 would not go amiss** *UK* If something would not go amiss, it would be useful or nice in a particular situation. *A cup of coffee wouldn't go amiss.* **2 take it amiss** *UK* to feel upset by what someone says or does *I think she might take it amiss if I left early.*

ammeter /ˈæmiːtəʳ/ *noun* [C] **PHYSICS** a device for measuring electric current

ammonia /əˈməʊniə/ *noun* [U] **CHEMISTRY** a liquid or gas with a strong smell, used in substances for cleaning things (formula NH_3) ➲See picture at **nitrogen cycle**

ammonite /ˈæmənaɪt/ *noun* [C] **BIOLOGY, GEOLOGY** an extinct (= no longer existing) sea creature often found as a fossil (= animal or plant turned into rock)

ammonium hydroxide /əˌməʊniəmhaɪˈdrɒksaɪd/ *noun* [U] **CHEMISTRY** a chemical mixture of water and ammonia used in cleaning materials and making some plastics (formula NH_4OH)

ammonium nitrate /əˌməʊniəmˈnaɪtreɪt/ *noun* [U] **CHEMISTRY** a chemical compound in the form of a white powder, often used as a fertilizer (= substance to make plants grow) and in explosives (formula $NH_4 NO_3$)

ammonium sulphate /əˌməʊniəmˈsʌlfeɪt/ *UK* (*US* **ammonium sulfate**) *noun* [U] **CHEMISTRY** a chemical compound often used as a fertilizer (= substance to make plants grow) (formula $NH_4 SO_4$)

ammunition /ˌæmjəˈnɪʃən/ *noun* [U] **1** GUN a supply of bullets and bombs to be fired from guns **2** INFORMATION facts that you can use to criticize someone

amnesia /æmˈniːʒə/ *noun* [U] **HEALTH** a medical condition that makes you forget things

amnesty /ˈæmnəsti/ *noun* **1 LAW** [C, U] a time when a government allows political prisoners to go free **2 LAW** [C] a time when people can give weapons or drugs to the police, or admit that they have done something illegal, without being punished

amnion /ˈæmniən/ *noun* [C] *plural* **amnions** or **amnia BIOLOGY** a bag made of thin skin which contains amniotic fluid and surrounds a baby growing inside its mother ➲See picture at **foetus**

amniotic fluid /ˌæmniɒtɪkˈfluːɪd/ *noun* [U] **BIOLOGY** the liquid that surrounds an embryo (= growing baby) inside its mother ➲See picture at **foetus**

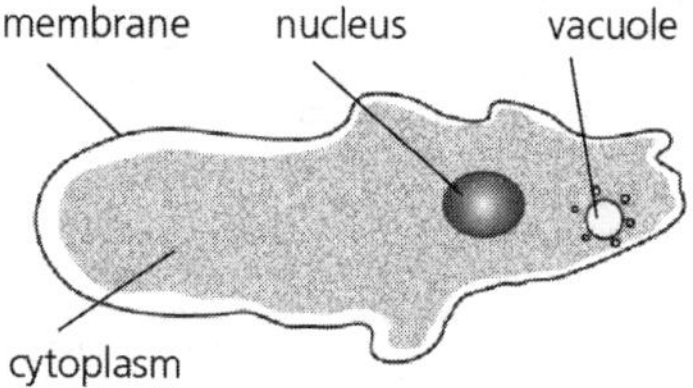

amoeba

amoeba /əˈmiːbə/ *UK* (*US* **ameba**) *noun* [C] *plural UK* **amoebas**, *US* **amebas**, *UK* **amoebae**, *US* **amebae BIOLOGY** a very small simple organism consisting of only one cell

O-- **among** /əˈmʌŋ/ (*also* **amongst** /əˈmʌŋst/) *preposition* **1** IN THE MIDDLE in the middle of something *He disappeared among the crowd.* **2** IN A GROUP in a particular group *The decision will not be popular among students.* ○ *I'm going to give you a minute to talk* ***amongst yourselves*** (= talk to each other). **3** ONE OF A GROUP to be one of a small group *He is among the top five tennis players in the country.* **4** DIVIDE to each one in a group *She divided the cake among the children.*

amoral /ˌeɪˈmɒrəl/ *adjective* not caring if what you are doing is morally wrong *an amoral person/act*

amorous /ˈæmərəs/ *adjective* full of love and sexual excitement *amorous adventures*

amortize (*UK* **-ise**) /əˈmɔːtaɪz/ *verb* [T] **FINANCE** to reduce a debt by paying small regular amounts •**amortization** (*UK* **-isation**) /əˌmɔːtɪˈzeɪʃən/ *noun* [U]

O-- **amount**[1] /əˈmaʊnt/ *noun* [C] how much there is of something *The project will take a huge* ***amount of*** *time and money.*

COMMON LEARNER ERROR

amount of or **number of?**

Amount of is used with uncountable nouns.

I should reduce the amount of coffee I drink.

Did you use the right amount of flour?

Number of is used with countable nouns.

We don't know the number of people involved yet.

They received a large number of complaints.

amount[2] /əˈmaʊnt/ *verb*

amount to sth *phrasal verb* **1** SAME to be the same as something, or to have the same effect as something *He gave what amounted to an apology on behalf of the company.* **2** TOTAL to have a particular total *goods amounting to $800*

A

amp /æmp/ (*also* **ampere** /ˈæmpeər/) *noun* [C] **PHYSICS** a unit for measuring the strength of an electric current

amperage /ˈæmpərɪdʒ/ *noun* [U] **PHYSICS** the strength of electrical current needed to make a piece of electric equipment work

ampersand /ˈæmpəsænd/ *noun* [C] **LANGUAGE** the sign (&) used for 'and'

amphibian /æmˈfɪbiən/ *noun* [C] **BIOLOGY** an animal, such as a frog, which lives both on land and in water but must lay its eggs in water

amphibious /æmˈfɪbiəs/ *adjective* **1 BIOLOGY** of or relating to a type of animal which lives both on land and in water *amphibious animals* **2** relating to vehicles which operate both on land or in water

amphoteric /ˌæmfəˈterɪk/ *adjective* **CHEMISTRY** able to act as a base (= substance with a pH of more than 7) or an acid

ample /ˈæmpl/ *adjective* **1** ENOUGH enough, or more than enough *She's had* ***ample time*** *to get the work done.* **2** LARGE large *her ample bosom* •**amply** *adverb*

amplifier /ˈæmplɪfaɪər/ *noun* [C] a piece of electronic equipment that makes sounds louder

amplify /ˈæmplɪfaɪ/ *verb* [T] **1** SOUND to make a sound louder using electronic equipment **2** OPINION *formal* to make a feeling or opinion stronger or clearer •**amplification** /ˌæmplɪfɪˈkeɪʃən/ *noun* [U]

amplitude /ˈæmplɪtjuːd/ *noun* [U] **PHYSICS** the greatest distance between the top or bottom of a curve, e.g. a sound wave, and its middle point

amputate /ˈæmpjəteɪt/ *verb* [I, T] **HEALTH** to cut off someone's leg, arm, finger, etc in a medical operation *His leg was amputated at the knee.* •**amputation** /ˌæmpjəˈteɪʃən/ *noun* [C, U]

amuse /əˈmjuːz/ *verb* [T] **1** HAPPY to make someone smile or laugh *I took him an article that I thought might amuse him.* **2** NOT BORED to keep someone interested and help them to have an enjoyable time [**often reflexive**] *I bought a magazine to amuse myself while I was on the train.*

amused /əˈmjuːzd/ *adjective* **1** showing that you think something is funny *an amused smile* ○ *She was very* ***amused by/at*** *your comments.* **2 keep sb amused** to keep someone interested and help them to have an enjoyable time *How do you keep an eight-year-old boy amused?*

amusement /əˈmjuːzmənt/ *noun* **1** FEELING [U] the feeling that you have when something makes you smile or laugh *I watched the performance* ***with*** *great* ***amusement.*** ○ ***To our amusement*** *the tent collapsed on top of them.* **2** ENJOYABLE [C, U] an enjoyable way of spending your time *I play the piano but just* ***for*** *my own* ***amusement.***

aˈmusement ˌpark *noun* [C] a large park where you can ride on exciting machines

amusing /əˈmjuːzɪŋ/ *adjective* making you laugh or smile *an amusing letter*

amylase /ˈæmɪleɪz/ *noun* [U] **CHEMISTRY** an enzyme (= substance that causes chemical change) that helps change starch into sugar

O‑ **an** *strong form* /æn/ *weak form* /ən/ *determiner* used instead of 'a' when the next word starts with a vowel sound *an apple* ○ *an hour* ⊃See Common Learner Error at **a**

anabolic steroid /ˌænəbɒlɪkˈsterɔɪd/ *noun* [C] **HEALTH** a hormone (= chemical substance produced by animals and plants) that causes muscle and bone growth. Anabolic steroids are sometimes used illegally by athletes competing in sports competitions

anaemia *UK* (*US* **anemia**) /əˈniːmiə/ *noun* [U] **HEALTH** a medical condition in which your blood does not contain enough red cells •**anaemic** *UK* (*US* **anemic**) /əˈniːmɪk/ *adjective*

anaerobic /ˌænəˈrəʊbɪk/ *adjective* **BIOLOGY** not needing, or without oxygen

ˌanaerobic respiˈration *noun* [U] **BIOLOGY** producing energy without the use of oxygen

anaesthetic *UK* (*US* **anesthetic**) /ˌænəsˈθetɪk/ *noun* [C, U] **HEALTH** a drug that makes you unable to feel pain during an operation *The operation is done* ***under anaesthetic*** (= using anaesthetic). ⊃See also: **general anaesthetic, local anaesthetic**

anaesthetist *UK* (*US* **anesthetist**) /əˈniːsθətɪst/ (US) /əˈnesθətɪst/ *noun* [C] **HEALTH** a doctor in a hospital who gives anaesthetics to people

anaesthetize /əˈniːsθətaɪz/ *UK* (*US* **anesthetize** /əˈnesθətaɪz/) *verb* [T] **HEALTH** to give someone drugs that make them unable to feel pain

anagram /ˈænəgræm/ *noun* [C] **LANGUAGE** a word or phrase made by putting the letters of another word or phrase in a different order *'Team' is an anagram of 'meat'.*

anal /ˈeɪnəl/ *adjective* **ANATOMY** relating to the anus (= hole where solid waste comes out of the body)

analogous /əˈnæləgəs/ *adjective formal* **1** similar in some ways *It's often said that life is* ***analogous to*** *a journey.* **2 BIOLOGY** Analogous organs or body parts have the same use but developed in different ways ⊃Compare **homologous**

analogue *UK* (*US* **analog**) /ˈænəlɒg/ *adjective* **1 PHYSICS** using signals that use continuously changing quantities of space, electrical current, etc to measure or store data *analogue data* **2 analogue clock/watch** a clock/watch which has hands (= narrow parts that point) that show what time it is

analogy /əˈnælədʒi/ *noun* [C, U] a comparison that shows how two things are similar *She* ***draws an analogy between*** *life's events and a game of chance.*

analyse *UK* (*US* **analyze**) /ˈænəlaɪz/ *verb* [T] to examine the details of something carefully, in order to understand or explain it *to analyse information* ○ *Blood samples were analysed in the laboratory.*

WORD PARTNERS FOR ***analysis***

do an analysis • a **detailed** analysis • an analysis **of** sth • send sth **for** analysis

analysis /əˈnæləsɪs/ *noun* [C, U] *plural* **analyses** /əˈnæləsiːz/ the process of analysing something *a* ***detailed analysis*** ○ *A sample of soil was sent* ***for analysis.***

A

analyst /ˈænəlɪst/ *noun* [C] someone whose job is to examine the details of a situation carefully, and give their opinion about it *a **financial/political analyst***

analytical /ˌænəˈlɪtɪkəl/ (*also* **analytic**) *adjective* examining the details of something carefully, in order to understand or explain it *analytical skills* ○ *an **analytical mind***

analyze /ˈænəlaɪz/ *verb* [T] *US spelling of* analyse

anapaest *UK* (*US* **anapest**) /ˈænəpest/ *noun* [C] **LITERATURE** in poetry, a unit of two short syllables and one long syllable

anarchist /ˈænəkɪst/ *noun* [C] **POLITICS** someone who thinks that society should not be controlled by a government and laws

anarchy /ˈænəki/ *noun* [U] **SOCIETY** when there is no law or government, or when people ignore them •**anarchic** /ænˈɑːkɪk/ *adjective*

anatomical /ˌænəˈtɒmɪkəl/ *adjective* **ANATOMY** connected with anatomy

anatomy /əˈnætəmi/ *noun* **1 ANATOMY** [U] the scientific study of the body and how its parts are arranged **2 ANATOMY** [C] the body of a person or living thing [**usually singular**] *the female anatomy* •**anatomical** /ˌænəˈtɒmɪkəl/ *adjective*

ancestor /ˈænsestəʳ/ *noun* [C] **SOCIETY** a relative who lived a long time ago *My ancestors came from Ireland.* •**ancestral** /ænˈsestrəl/ *adjective*

ancestry /ˈænsestri/ *noun* [C, U] **SOCIETY** your relatives who lived a long time ago, or the origin of your family *Americans of Japanese ancestry*

anchor[1] /ˈæŋkəʳ/ *noun* [C] **1** BOAT a heavy, metal object that is dropped into water to stop a boat from moving **2** JOB *US* someone who reads the news and announcements on a television or radio programme

anchor[2] /ˈæŋkəʳ/ *verb* **1** BOAT [I, T] to stop a boat from moving by dropping a heavy metal object into the water **2** FASTEN [T] to make something or someone stay in one position by fastening them firmly *We anchored ourselves to the rocks with a rope.* **3** PROGRAMME [T] *US* to read the news or announcements on television or radio as your job

ancient /ˈeɪnʃənt/ *adjective* **1** PAST [**always before noun**] from a long time ago *ancient Greece/Rome* ○ *an ancient building* **2** OLD *humorous* very old *This computer is ancient.*

O-ˣ **and** *strong form* /ænd/ *weak forms* /ənd, ən/ *conjunction* **1** JOIN used to join two words or two parts of a sentence *tea and coffee* ○ *We were tired and hungry.* **2** AFTER used to say that one thing happens after another thing *I got dressed and had my breakfast.* **3** SO so *The car wouldn't start and I had to get a taxi.* **4** AFTER VERB *mainly UK* used instead of 'to' after some verbs, such as 'try' and 'go' *Try and eat something.* **5** NUMBERS used when saying or adding numbers *It cost a hundred and twenty pounds. UK* ○ *Two and three equals five.* **6** EMPHASIZE used between two words that are the same to make their meaning stronger *The sound grew louder and louder.*

androgen /ˈændrədʒen/ *noun* [C] **BIOLOGY** a male hormone (= substance that influences growth and development)

androgynous /ænˈdrɒdʒɪnəs/ *adjective* **BIOLOGY** having both male and female features •**androgyny** /ænˈdrɒdʒəni/ *noun* [U]

anecdote /ˈænɪkdəʊt/ *noun* [C] a short story that you tell someone about something that happened to you or someone else *a speech full of anecdotes* •**anecdotal** /ˌænɪkˈdəʊtəl/ *adjective* consisting of things that people have said, and not facts ***anecdotal evidence***

anemia /əˈniːmiə/ *noun* [U] **HEALTH** *US spelling of* anaemia (= a medical condition in which your blood does not contain enough red cells)

anemic /əˈniːmɪk/ *adjective* **HEALTH** *US spelling of* anaemic (= having anemia)

anemometer /ˌænɪˈmɒmɪtər/ *noun* [C] **GEOGRAPHY** a device that measures the speed and force of wind

anesthetic /ˌænəsˈθetɪk/ *noun* [C, U] **HEALTH** *US spelling of* anaesthetic (= a drug that makes you unable to feel pain during an operation)

anesthetist /əˈnesθətɪst/ *noun* [C] **HEALTH** *US spelling of* anaesthetist (= a doctor who gives anaesthetics to people)

anew /əˈnjuː/ *adverb literary* If you do something anew, you do it again in a different way. *Moving to another city gave me the chance to **start anew**.*

angel /ˈeɪndʒəl/ *noun* [C] **1 RELIGION** a spiritual creature like a human with wings, who some people believe lives with God in heaven **2** a very good, kind person *Be an angel and get me a drink.* •**angelic** /ænˈdʒelɪk/ *adjective* very beautiful or good *an angelic child*

WORD PARTNERS FOR ***anger***

express/show anger • **be trembling with** anger • **in** anger • **public** anger • **mounting/growing** anger • anger **at/over** sth

O-ˣ **anger**[1] /ˈæŋgəʳ/ *noun* [U] a strong feeling against someone who has behaved badly, making you want to shout at them or hurt them *public anger at the terrorist killings* ○ ***anger at/over sth*** ○ *He never once raised his voice **in anger**.*

anger[2] /ˈæŋgəʳ/ *verb* [T] to make someone angry [**often passive**] *Students were angered by the college's decision.*

angle[1] /ˈæŋgl/ *noun* [C] **1 MATHEMATICS** a space between two lines or surfaces that meet at one point, which you measure in degrees *an angle of 90 degrees* **2 at an angle** not horizontal or vertical, but sloping *He wore his hat at an angle.* **3** WAY OF THINKING the way you think about a situation *Try looking at the problem **from my angle**.* **4** DIRECTION the direction from which you look at something *This is the same building photographed **from** different **angles**.* ➲See also: **right angle**

angle[2] /ˈæŋgl/ *verb* [T] to aim or turn something in a direction that is not horizontal or vertical *She angled a shot into the corner of the court.*
be angling for sth *phrasal verb* to try to get something without asking for it in a direct way *Is he angling for an invitation?*

angler /ˈæŋglər/ *noun* [C] **SPORT** someone who catches fish as a hobby or sport

Anglican /ˈæŋglɪkən/ *adjective* **RELIGION** belonging or relating to the Church of England (= the official church in England) •**Anglican** *noun* [C]

angling /ˈæŋglɪŋ/ *noun* [U] **SPORT** the sport or hobby of catching fish

Anglo- /æŋgləʊ-/ *prefix* of or connected with Britain or England *Anglo-Indian, Anglo-Saxon*

OTHER WAYS OF SAYING ***angry***

If someone is angry about something that has happened, you can say that they are **annoyed** or **irritated**: *He was a bit* ***annoyed*** *with her for being late.* • *I was* ***irritated*** *that he didn't thank me.*

If someone is extremely angry, you can use adjectives such as **furious**, **irate**, or **livid**: *My boss was* ***furious*** *with me.* • *Hundreds of* ***irate*** *passengers have complained to the airline.*

If you are angry with a child, you might describe yourself as **cross**: *I'm* ***cross*** *with you for not telling me where you were going.*

The expression **up in arms** is sometimes used when people are angry about something they think is unfair: *Local people are* ***up in arms*** *over plans to close the local swimming pool.*

If someone suddenly becomes very angry, you can use the informal expressions **go crazy/mad**: *Dad* ***went crazy/mad*** *when he found out we'd broken the window.*

O‒ **angry** /ˈæŋgri/ *adjective* having a strong feeling against someone who has behaved badly, making you want to shout at them or hurt them *He's really* ***angry at/with*** *me for upsetting Sophie.* ○ *I don't understand what he's* ***angry about****.* •**angrily** *adverb*

angst /æŋst/ *noun* [U] a strong feeling of worry and unhappiness *teenage angst*

anguish /ˈæŋgwɪʃ/ *noun* [U] extreme suffering, especially mental suffering *It's the anguish of knowing that I can do nothing to help.* •**anguished** *adjective* [**always before noun**] *anguished parents*

angular /ˈæŋgjʊlər/ *adjective* An angular shape or object has a lot of straight lines and sharp points. *an angular face*

anhydrous /ænˈhaɪdrəs/ *adjective* **CHEMISTRY** containing no water

O‒ **animal**[1] /ˈænɪməl/ *noun* [C] **1** [LIVING THING] something that lives and moves but is not a person, bird, fish, or insect *a wild animal* ○ *She's a real animal lover.* **2** **BIOLOGY** anything that lives and moves, including people, birds, etc *Are humans the only animals to use language?* **3** [CRUEL PERSON] *informal* a very cruel and violent person

animal[2] /ˈænɪməl/ *adjective* [**always before noun**] Animal qualities and feelings relate to your basic physical needs. *animal passion*

animate /ˈænɪmət/ *adjective formal* alive ➲Opposite **inanimate**

animated /ˈænɪmeɪtɪd/ *adjective* **1** [EXCITED] showing a lot of interest and excitement *an animated conversation* **2** [FILM] An animated film is one in which drawings and models seem to move.

animation /ˌænɪˈmeɪʃən/ *noun* **1** [EXCITEMENT] [U] interest and excitement *She spoke with great animation.* **2** [FILM] [C, U] an animated film, or the process of making animated films ***computer animation***

animosity /ˌænɪˈmɒsəti/ *noun* [C, U] when someone hates or feels angry towards someone else *There is no* ***animosity between*** *the two teams.*

anion /ˈænaɪən/ *noun* [C] **PHYSICS, CHEMISTRY** an ion (= type of atom) with a negative electrical charge ➲Compare **cation**

ankle /ˈæŋkl/ *noun* [C] **ANATOMY** the part of your leg that is just above your foot ➲See colour picture **The Body** on page Centre 13

annelid /ˈænəlɪd/ *noun* [C] **BIOLOGY** a type of worm whose body is divided into several parts

annex[1] /əˈneks/ *verb* [T] **POLITICS** to start to rule or control an area or country next to your own •**annexation** /ˌænekˈseɪʃən/ *noun* [C, U]

annex[2] (*also UK* **annexe**) /ˈæneks/ *noun* [C] a building that is joined to a larger one

annihilate /əˈnaɪɪleɪt/ *verb* [T] **1** [DESTROY] to destroy something completely *a city annihilated by an atomic bomb* **2** [DEFEAT] *informal* to defeat someone very easily •**annihilation** /əˌnaɪɪˈleɪʃən/ *noun* [U]

WORD PARTNERS FOR ***anniversary***

the [10th/50th/500th, etc] anniversary **of** sth • **commemorate/mark** an anniversary • sb's **wedding** anniversary • anniversary **celebrations**

anniversary /ˌænɪˈvɜːsəri/ *noun* [C] a date on which you remember or celebrate something that happened on that date one or more years ago *a* ***wedding anniversary*** ○ ***the 40th anniversary of*** *Kennedy's death* ➲See also: **silver wedding anniversary**

O‒ **announce** /əˈnaʊns/ *verb* [T] to tell people about something officially or with force or confidence *The company has* ***announced plans*** *to open six new stores.* [**+ (that)**] *Halfway through dinner, he announced that he was going out.*

COMMON LEARNER ERROR

announce or **advertise?**

Announce means to tell people about something. If you want to talk about telling people about a product or service so that they will buy it, for example in newspapers or on the television, you should use **advertise**.

WORD PARTNERS FOR ***announcement***

make an announcement • a **formal/official/public** announcement • an announcement **about/on** sth • an announcement **by/from** sb

O‒ **announcement** /əˈnaʊnsmənt/ *noun* **1** [INFORMATION] [C] something that someone says officially, giving information about something *The Prime Minister* ***made*** *an unexpected* ***announcement*** *this morning.* **2** [TELL] [**no plural**] when someone announces something

A

announcer /ə'naʊnsəʳ/ *noun* [C] someone who introduces programmes on the radio or television

annoy /ə'nɔɪ/ *verb* [T] to make someone slightly angry *He's always late and it's starting to annoy me.*

annoyance /ə'nɔɪəns/ *noun* [U] the feeling of being annoyed *He kept losing his keys,* ***much to the annoyance of*** (= which annoyed) *his wife.*

annoyed /ə'nɔɪd/ *adjective* slightly angry *I was a bit* ***annoyed with/at*** *Kathy for not coming.*

annoying /ə'nɔɪɪŋ/ *adjective* making you feel annoyed *an annoying habit/cough* ○ *It's very annoying to be kept waiting.*

⊶**annual**[1] /'ænjuəl/ *adjective* **1** EVERY YEAR happening or produced once a year *an* ***annual meeting/report*** **2** FOR A YEAR measured over a period of one year *annual rainfall* •**annually** *adverb*

annual[2] /'ænjuəl/ *noun* [C] **1** PLANT a plant which grows, produces seed, and dies within one year **2** BOOK a book produced every year containing new information about the same subject

annulment /ə'nʌlmənt/ *noun* [C, U] *formal* **LAW** when a court says officially that a marriage or agreement does not now exist and was never legal

anode /'ænəʊd/ *noun* [C] **PHYSICS** one of the electrodes (= object that electricity moves through) in a piece of electrical equipment; the negative electrode in a battery and the positive electrode in an electrolytic cell

anomaly /ə'nɒməli/ *noun* [C] *formal* something that is unusual or that does not seem right *There are some anomalies in the data.*

anonymity /ˌænə'nɪməti/ *noun* [U] when someone's name is not given or known *She agreed to speak to a journalist but* ***requested anonymity.***

anonymous /ə'nɒnɪməs/ *adjective* not giving a name *an anonymous phone call* ○ *The winner has asked to* ***remain anonymous.*** •**anonymously** *adverb*

anorak /'ænəræk/ *noun* [C] *UK* **1** a jacket with a hood (= part that covers your head) that protects you from rain and cold **2** *humorous* a boring person who is too interested in the details of a hobby and who is not good in social situations

anorexia /ˌænər'eksiə/ (*also* **anorexia nervosa** /ænərˌeksiənɜː'vəʊsə/) *noun* [U] **HEALTH** a mental illness in which someone refuses to eat and becomes very thin

anorexic /ˌænər'eksɪk/ *adjective* **HEALTH** having the illness anorexia •**anorexic** *noun* [C]

⊶**another** /ə'nʌðəʳ/ *pronoun, determiner* **1** ONE MORE one more person or thing, or an additional amount *Would you like another piece of cake?* ○ *We can fit another person in my car.* **2** DIFFERENT a different person or thing *I'm going to look for another job.* ○ *This one's slightly damaged - I'll get you another.*

COMMON LEARNER ERROR

another or **other?**

Another means 'one other' and is used with a singular noun. It is written as one word.

Would you like another cup of coffee?

~~*Would you like other cup of coffee?*~~

Other is used with a plural noun and means different things or people than the ones you are talking about.

She had other ambitions.

~~*She had another ambitions.*~~

⊶**answer**[1] /'ɑːnsəʳ/ *verb* **1** WORDS [I, T] to speak or write back to someone who has asked you a question or spoken to you *I asked when she was leaving but she didn't answer.* ○ *I must answer his letter.* **2** DOOR [I, T] to open the door when someone has knocked on it or rung a bell *I knocked several times but no one answered.* **3** TELEPHONE [I, T] to pick up the telephone receiver (= part that you hold to your ear) when it rings *Could someone* ***answer the phone?*** **4** TEST [T] to write or say something as a reply to a question in a test or competition **answer (sb) back** *phrasal verb* If a child answers back, they reply rudely to an adult. **answer for sth** *phrasal verb* **1** to be responsible for something, or punished for something *Do you think parents should have to answer for their children's behaviour?* **2 have a lot to answer for** to be the main cause of something bad which has happened *When it comes to violence, TV has a lot to answer for.*

WORD PARTNERS FOR ***answer***

get/give/know/provide an answer • a **correct/simple/wrong** answer • the answer **to** sth

⊶**answer**[2] /'ɑːnsəʳ/ *noun* [C] **1** WORDS what you say or write back to someone who has asked you a question or spoken to you *I asked him if he was going but I didn't hear his answer.* ○ *Please* ***give*** *me your* ***answer*** *by next week.* **2** DOOR/TELEPHONE when someone answers the telephone or the door [**usually singular**] *I rang the bell but there was no answer.* **3** SOLUTION a way of solving a problem *It's a difficult situation and I don't know what the answer is.* **4** TEST the correct number or information given as a reply to a question in a test or competition *Did you get the* ***answer to*** *Question 6 in the physics paper?*

answerphone /'ɑːnsəfəʊn/ *UK* (*UK/US* **answering machine**) *noun* [C] a machine that records your message if you telephone someone and they do not answer

ant /ænt/ *noun* [C] a small, black or red insect that lives in groups on the ground ➲See picture at **insect**

antacid /ˌæn'tæsɪd/ *noun* [C, U] **HEALTH** a substance used to reduce or prevent acid collecting in the body, especially in the stomach

antagonism /æn'tægənɪzəm/ *noun* [U] feelings of strong disagreement or hate *There's a history of* ***antagonism between*** *the two teams.*

antagonist /æn'tægənɪst/ *noun* [C] **1 ANATOMY** a muscle that is pulled in the opposite direction by another muscle **2 HEALTH** a drug that stops the effects of another drug

antagonistic /æn,tægᵊn'ɪstɪk/ *adjective* **1** strongly disagreeing with someone or something *He's* ***antagonistic towards*** *critics.* **2 ANATOMY** antagonistic muscles pull against each other

antagonize (*also UK* **-ise**) /æn'tægᵊnaɪz/ *verb* [**T**] to make someone angry or unfriendly towards you *He's antagonized colleagues by making changes without discussing them.*

the Antarctic /æn'tɑːktɪk/ *noun* the very cold area around the South Pole •**Antarctic** *adjective* [**always before noun**] *Antarctic wildlife*

antelope /'æntɪləʊp/ *noun* [**C**] an animal like a large deer with long horns

antenatal /,æntɪ'neɪtᵊl/ *UK* (*US* **prenatal**) *adjective* [**always before noun**] **HEALTH** relating to pregnant women before their babies are born *an* ***antenatal class***

antenna /æn'tenə/ *noun* [**C**] **1 BIOLOGY** *plural* **antennae** one of two long, thin parts on the head of an insect or sea creature, used for feeling things **2** *plural* **antennae** or **antennas** *US* (*UK* **aerial**) a piece of metal that is used for receiving television or radio signals ➲See colour picture **Car** on page Centre 7

anthem /'ænθəm/ *noun* [**C**] **MUSIC** a song chosen by a country or organization to be sung on special occasions ➲See also: **national anthem**

anther /'ænθəʳ/ *noun* [**C**] **BIOLOGY** the middle part of the stamen (= male part of plant) that produces pollen ➲See picture at **flower** ➲See picture at **pollen**

anthology /æn'θɒlədʒi/ *noun* [**C**] **LITERATURE** a book which includes stories or poems written by different people

anthropology /,ænθrə'pɒlədʒi/ *noun* [**U**] **SOCIETY** the scientific study of human development and society or different societies •**anthropologist** /,ænθrə'pɒlədʒɪst/ *noun* [**C**] •**anthropological** /,ænθrəpə'lɒdʒɪkᵊl/ *adjective*

anti- /æntɪ/ Ⓤⓢ /æntaɪ/ *prefix* **1** [AGAINST] opposed to or against *anti-terrorist laws, anti-American protesters* **2** [OPPOSITE] opposite of or preventing *anti-clockwise movement, anti-lock brakes, anti-depressant drugs* ➲Compare **pro-**

antibiotic /,æntɪbaɪ'ɒtɪk/ Ⓤⓢ /,æntaɪ-/ *noun* [**C**] **HEALTH** a medicine which cures infections by destroying harmful bacteria [**usually plural**] *He is* ***on antibiotics*** *for an ear infection.*

antibody /'æntɪ,bɒdi/ *noun* [**C**] **BIOLOGY, HEALTH** a substance produced in your blood to fight disease

anticipate /æn'tɪsɪpeɪt/ *verb* [**T**] to expect something, or to prepare for something before it happens *to* ***anticipate*** *a* ***problem*** [**+ that**] *We anticipate that prices will fall next year.*

anticipation /æn,tɪsɪ'peɪʃᵊn/ *noun* [**U**] **1** when you are waiting for something to happen, usually with excitement *The children were breathless* ***with anticipation.*** **2 in anticipation (of)** in preparation for something happening *She's even decorated the spare room in anticipation of your visit.*

anticlimax /,æntɪ'klaɪmæks/ Ⓤⓢ /,æntaɪ-/ *noun* [**C, U**] a disappointing experience, often one that you thought would be exciting before it happened or one that comes after a more exciting experience *After so much preparation, the party was a bit of an anticlimax.*

anticline /'æntɪklaɪn/ *noun* [**C**] **GEOLOGY** an upward curved fold in the layers of rock in the Earth's surface ➲Compare **syncline**

anti-clockwise /,æntɪ'klɒkwaɪz/ *UK* (*US* **counterclockwise**) *adjective, adverb* in the opposite direction to the way the hands (= parts that point to the numbers) of a clock move *Turn the knob anti-clockwise.* ➲See picture at **clockwise**

anti-competitive /,æntikəm'petɪtɪv/ Ⓤⓢ /,æntaɪ-/ *adjective* designed to stop businesses from competing with one another, for example by fixing prices, in a way that is not legal in some countries

antics /'æntɪks/ *noun* [**plural**] unusual or bad behaviour that entertains or annoys people *He's well known for his antics on and off the tennis court.*

anticyclone /,ænti'saɪkləʊn/ *noun* [**C**] **GEOGRAPHY** an area of high pressure in the air or atmosphere which causes calm weather

anti-depressant /,æntɪdɪ'presᵊnt/ Ⓤⓢ /,æntaɪ-/ *noun* [**C**] **HEALTH** a medicine for people who are depressed (= severely unhappy)

antidote /'æntɪdəʊt/ *noun* [**C**] **1 antidote to sth** an activity that stops something bad from harming you *Exercise is the* ***best antidote*** *to stress.* **2 HEALTH** a substance that stops another substance from damaging your body *a deadly poison with no antidote*

antigen /'æntɪdʒən/ *noun* [**C**] **BIOLOGY, HEALTH** a harmful substance that causes the body to produce antibodies (= substances that fight disease)

antimatter /'æntɪmætəʳ/ *noun* [**U**] **PHYSICS** particles (= small parts of atoms) that are the opposite to real particles in the universe, and which would destroy them if they came together

anti-oxidant /,ænti'ɒksɪdənt/ Ⓤⓢ /,æntaɪ-/ *noun* [**C**] **1 CHEMISTRY** a substance that slows down the rate at which something decays because of oxidization (= combining with oxygen) **2 FOOD** a substance, for example a vitamin in food, that protects your body from damage

antiparticle /,ænti'pɑːtɪkl/ Ⓤⓢ /,æntaɪ-/ *noun* [**C**] **PHYSICS** a particle that has the same mass as a normal particle, but the opposite electrical charge

antipathy /æn'tɪpəθi/ *noun* [**U**] *formal* a strong feeling of dislike for someone *He is a private man with a deep* ***antipathy to/towards*** *the press.*

antiperspirant /,æntɪ'pɜːspᵊrənt/ Ⓤⓢ /,æntaɪ-/ *noun* [**C, U**] a substance that prevents you from becoming wet under your arms when you are hot

antiquated /'æntɪkweɪtɪd/ *adjective* very old and not modern enough *an antiquated system*

A

antique /æn'tiːk/ *noun* [C] an object that is old, and often rare or beautiful *His home is full of* ***valuable antiques.*** ○ *an* ***antique*** *shop* •**antique** *adjective antique furniture/china*

antiquity /æn'tɪkwəti/ *noun* **1** TIME [U] *formal* the ancient past *the writers of antiquity* **2** OBJECT [C] an ancient object [**usually plural**] *priceless Egyptian antiquities*

anti-Semitism /ˌæntɪ'semɪtɪzᵊm/ US /ˌæntaɪ-/ *noun* [U] when someone hates Jewish people, or treats them in a cruel or unfair way •**anti-Semitic** /ˌæntɪsɪ'mɪtɪk/ *adjective*

antiseptic /ˌæntɪ'septɪk/ *noun* [C, U] **HEALTH** a substance that you put on an injury to prevent infection •**antiseptic** *adjective antiseptic cream*

anti-social /ˌæntɪ-/ US /ˌæntaɪ'səʊʃᵊl/ *adjective* **1** BEHAVIOUR Anti-social behaviour harms or upsets the people around you. *Increasingly, smoking is regarded as an anti-social habit.* **2** PERSON An anti-social person does not like being with other people.

anti-spam /ˌæntɪ'spæm/ US /ˌæntaɪ-/ *adjective* [**always before noun**] **COMPUTING, INTERNET** used to stop people sending or receiving emails that are not wanted, especially advertisements *anti-spam legislation*

anti-terrorist /ˌæntɪ'terᵊrɪst/ US /ˌæntaɪ-/ *adjective* intended to prevent or reduce terrorism (= the use of violence for political purposes) ***anti-terrorist laws/legislation***

antithesis /æn'tɪθəsɪs/ *noun* [C] *plural* **antitheses** /æn'tɪθəsiːz/ *formal* the exact opposite [**usually no plural**] *She is slim and shy - the* ***antithesis of*** *her sister.*

antitoxin /ˌæntɪ'tɒksɪn/ *noun* [C] **HEALTH** a substance that stops or reduces the effect of a toxin (= poisonous substance) in your body

anti-virus /ˌænti'vaɪərəs/ US /ˌæntaɪ-/ *adjective* [**always before noun**] **COMPUTING** produced and used to protect the main memory of a computer against infection by a virus *anti-virus software/programs*

antler /'æntlər/ *noun* [C] **BIOLOGY** a horn that looks like branches on the head of a male deer

antonym /'æntənɪm/ *noun* [C] **LANGUAGE** a word which means the opposite of another word

anus /'eɪnəs/ *noun* [C] **ANATOMY** a hole where solid waste comes out of the body ⊃See picture at **alimentary canal**

WORD PARTNERS FOR ***anxiety***

a **cause/source** of anxiety • **feelings/levels** of anxiety • anxiety **about/over** sth

anxiety /æŋ'zaɪəti/ *noun* [C, U] the feeling of being very worried *That explains his* ***anxiety about*** *her health.*

anxious /'æŋkʃəs/ *adjective* **1** WORRIED worried and nervous *She's very* ***anxious about*** *her exams.* **2** WANTING wanting to do something or wanting something to happen [**+ to do sth**] *He's anxious to get home.* [**+ that**] *I was anxious that no one else should know.* •**anxiously** *adverb We* ***waited anxiously*** *by the phone.*

o**any¹** *strong form* /'eni/ *weak form* /əni/ *pronoun, determiner* **1** SOME used in questions and negatives to mean 'some' *Is there any of that lemon cake left?* ○ *I haven't seen any of his films.* ○ *I asked Andrew for some change but he hasn't got any.* ⊃See Common Learner Error at **some** **2** NOT IMPORTANT WHICH one of or each of a particular kind of person or thing when it is not important which *Any advice that you can give me would be greatly appreciated.* ○ *Any of those shirts would be fine.*

o**any²** *strong form* /'eni/ *weak form* /əni/ *adverb* used in questions and negatives to emphasize a comparative adjective or adverb *Do you feel any better?* ○ *I can't walk any faster.* ○ *She couldn't wait* ***any longer***.

o**anybody** /'eniˌbɒdi/ *pronoun another word for* anyone

anyhow /'enihaʊ/ (*also* **anyway**) *adverb* **1** MORE IMPORTANTLY used to give a more important reason for something that you are saying *I don't need a car and I can't afford one anyhow.* **2** DESPITE despite that *He hates carrots but he ate them anyhow.* **3** IN CONVERSATION used when you are returning to an earlier subject *Anyhow, as I said, I'll be away next week.* **4** CHANGING STATEMENT used when you want to slightly change something that you have just said *Boys aren't horrible - not all of them anyhow!*

ˌ**any 'more** (*also* **anymore**) *adverb* If you do not do something or something does not happen any more, you have stopped doing it or it does not now happen. *This coat doesn't fit me any more.*

o**anyone** /'eniwʌn/ (*also* **anybody**) *pronoun* **1** A PERSON used in questions and negatives to mean 'a person or people' *I didn't know anyone at the party.* ○ *Does* ***anyone else*** (= another person/other people) *want to come?* **2** ANY PERSON any person or any people *Anyone can go - you don't have to be invited.*

anyplace /'enipleɪs/ *adverb US* anywhere

o**anything** /'eniθɪŋ/ *pronoun* **1** SOMETHING used in questions and negatives to mean 'something' *I haven't got anything to wear.* ○ *Was there* ***anything else*** (= another thing) *you wanted to say?* **2** ANY OBJECT/SITUATION any object, event, or situation *We can do anything you like.* ○ *Tom will eat anything.* **3 anything like** used in questions and negatives to mean 'at all similar to' *Does he look anything like his brother?*

o**anyway** /'eniweɪ/ (*also* **anyhow**) (*also US* **anyways** *spoken*) *adverb* **1** MORE IMPORTANTLY used to give a more important reason for something that you are saying *We can drive you to the station - we go that way anyway.* **2** DESPITE despite that *He hates carrots but he ate them anyway.* **3** IN CONVERSATION used when you are returning to an earlier subject *Anyway, as I said, I'll be away next week.* **4** CHANGING STATEMENT used when you want to slightly change something that you have just said *Boys aren't horrible - not all of them anyway!*

o**anywhere** /'eniweər/ (*also US* **anyplace**) *adverb* **1** IN ANY PLACE in or to any place *Just sit anywhere.* ○ *I couldn't find a post office anywhere.* **2** A PLACE used in questions and negatives to mean 'a place' *He doesn't have anywhere to stay.* ○ *Is there* ***anywhere else*** *you'd like to visit* *while you're here?* **3 anywhere near sth** used in questions and negatives to mean 'close to being or doing something' *The house isn't anywhere near ready.* **4 not get anywhere** *informal* to not make any progress *I tried discussing the problem with her but I didn't get anywhere.*

aorta /eɪ'ɔːtə/ *noun* [C] **ANATOMY** the main artery (= thick tube carrying blood from the heart) which takes blood to the other parts of the body ⊃See picture at **heart**

O-- **apart** /ə'pɑːt/ *adverb* **1** [SEPARATED] separated by a space or period of time *Stand with your feet wide apart.* ○ *Our kids were born just eighteen months apart.* **2** [INTO PIECES] into separate, smaller pieces *My jacket is **coming/falling apart**.* **3 apart from a** [EXCEPT] except for *Apart from Jodie, who hurt her leg, all the children were fine.* **b** [IN ADDITION] in addition to *He works a ten-hour day and that's apart from the work he does at the weekend.*

apartheid /ə'pɑːtaɪt/ *noun* [U] **POLITICS** in the past in South Africa, a political system in which white people had power over black people and made them live separately

O-- **apartment** /ə'pɑːtmənt/ *noun* [C] *mainly US* a set of rooms for someone to live in on one level of a building or house

a'partment ˌbuilding *noun* [C] *US* a building which is divided into apartments

apathetic /ˌæpə'θetɪk/ *adjective* not interested in anything or willing to change things *Young people today are so apathetic about politics.*

apathy /'æpəθi/ *noun* [U] when someone is not interested in anything or willing to change things

ape /eɪp/ *noun* [C] a hairy animal like a monkey but with no tail and long arms

aperitif /əˌperə'tiːf/ *noun* [C] **FOOD** a small alcoholic drink before a meal

aperture /'æpətʃəʳ/ *noun* [C] **ART** a small hole, especially one that allows light into a camera

apex /'eɪpeks/ *noun* [C] the highest part of a shape *the apex of a pyramid*

aphid /'eɪfɪd/ *noun* [C] **BIOLOGY** any of various small insects which suck the juices of plants for food

apiece /ə'piːs/ *adverb* each *Dolls from this period sell for £300 apiece.*

the apocalypse /ə'pɒkəlɪps/ *noun* **RELIGION** in some religions, the final destruction of the world

apocalyptic /əˌpɒkə'lɪptɪk/ *adjective* **RELIGION** showing or describing the destruction of the world *an apocalyptic vision of the future*

apologetic /əˌpɒlə'dʒetɪk/ *adjective* showing or saying that you are sorry about something *an apologetic smile* ○ *She was very **apologetic about** missing the meeting.*

apologize (*also UK* **-ise**) /ə'pɒlədʒaɪz/ *verb* [I] to tell someone that you are sorry about something you have done *The bank **apologized for** the error.* ○ *The pilot **apologized to** passengers for the delay.*

WORD PARTNERS FOR ***apology***

demand/make/owe sb/**receive** an apology • **accept** sb's apology • **make no** apology for (doing) sth • a **formal/full/public** apology • an apology **for** sth • an apology **to** sb

apology /ə'pɒlədʒi/ *noun* [C, U] something you say or write to say that you are sorry about something you have done *I have an **apology** to **make** to you - I opened your letter by mistake.*

apostle /ə'pɒsl/ *noun* [C] **RELIGION** one of the twelve men chosen by Jesus Christ to teach people about Christianity

apostrophe /ə'pɒstrəfi/ *noun* [C] **1 LANGUAGE** a mark (') used to show that letters or numbers are absent *I'm* (= I am) *hungry.* ○ *I graduated in '98* (= 1998). **2 LANGUAGE** a punctuation mark (') used before the letter 's' to show that something belongs to someone or something *I drove my brother's car.* ⊃See Extra help page **Punctuation** on page Centre 18.

appal *UK* (*US* **appall**) /ə'pɔːl/ *verb* [T] **appalling,** *past* **appalled** to make someone extremely shocked or upset *The amount of violence on television appals me.* ○ *We were **appalled at/by** her behaviour.* •**appalled** *adjective*

appalling /ə'pɔːlɪŋ/ *adjective* **1** [SHOCKING] shocking and very unpleasant *Many live in appalling conditions.* ○ *appalling injuries* **2** [BAD] very bad *appalling behaviour/weather* •**appallingly** *adverb*

apparatus /ˌæpər'eɪtəs/ (US) /ˌæpə'rætəs/ *noun* [C, U] *plural* **apparatus** or **apparatuses** a set of equipment or tools used for a particular purpose *The diver wore breathing apparatus.*

apparel /ə'pærəl/ *noun* [U] *mainly US* clothes *children's/women's apparel*

apparent /ə'pærənt/ *adjective* **1** [CLEAR] obvious or easy to notice [+ **that**] *It soon became apparent that she had lost interest in the project.* ○ *Suddenly, **for no apparent reason*** (= without a reason) *he started screaming and shouting.* **2** [SEEMS TRUE] [**always before noun**] seeming to exist or be true *I was a little surprised by her apparent lack of interest.*

O-- **apparently** /ə'pærəntli/ *adverb* **1** [OTHERS SAY] used to say that you have read or been told something although you are not certain it is true *Apparently it's going to rain today.* **2** [SEEMING TRUE] used to say that something seems to be true, although it is not certain *There were two apparently unrelated deaths.*

apparition /ˌæpər'ɪʃən/ *noun* [C] *literary* a ghost

WORD PARTNERS FOR ***appeal***

issue/launch/make an appeal • an appeal **for** sth

appeal¹ /ə'piːl/ *noun* **1** [REQUEST] [C] when a lot of people are asked to give money, information, or help *The appeal raised over £2 million for AIDS research.* **2** [QUALITY] [U] the quality in someone or something that makes them attractive or enjoyable *I've never understood the appeal of skiing.* **3 LAW** [C] a request to a court of law to change a previous legal decision *He won his **appeal against** his jail sentence.*

appeal² /ə'piːl/ *verb* [I] **1** [REQUEST] to strongly request something, often publicly *The police*

have **appealed for** more information. ○ They **appealed to** the commission to keep the hospital open. **2** ATTRACT to attract or interest someone *Cycling has never **appealed to** me.* **3** **LAW** to formally ask someone to change an official or legal decision *He is **appealing against** a ten year prison sentence.*

appealing /ə'piːlɪŋ/ *adjective* attractive or interesting *The idea of living in Paris is very appealing.* •**appealingly** *adverb*

O⁻**appear** /ə'pɪəʳ/ *verb* [I] **1** SEEM to seem to be a particular thing or have a particular quality *He appeared calm and relaxed.* ○ *She **appeared to be** crying.* [+ **(that)**] ***It appears** that we were wrong about him.* **2** BE SEEN to start to be seen *He suddenly appeared in the doorway.* ○ *Then a bright light appeared in the sky.* ➲Opposite **disappear** **3** BECOME AVAILABLE to start to exist or become available *Laptop computers first appeared in the 1990s.* ○ *The story appeared in all the major newspapers.* **4** **appear in/at/on, etc** to perform in a film, play, etc, or be seen in public *She appears briefly in the new Bond film.*

O⁻**appearance** /ə'pɪərᵊns/ *noun* **1** IN PUBLIC [C] an occasion when someone appears in public *a television/**public appearance*** ○ *He **made** two **appearances** during his brief visit.* **2** WAY YOU LOOK [**no plural**] the way a person or thing looks *She's very concerned with her appearance.* **3** ARRIVAL [**no plural**] when you arrive somewhere or can be seen somewhere *Her appearance at the party was a surprise.* ➲Opposite **disappearance** **4** BECOMING AVAILABLE [**no plural**] when something starts to exist or becomes available *The appearance of new products on the market has increased competition.*

appease /ə'piːz/ *verb* [T] to avoid more arguments by doing what someone wants •**appeasement** *noun* [U]

appendicitis /əˌpendɪ'saɪtɪs/ *noun* [U] **HEALTH** an illness in which your appendix becomes larger than usual and painful

appendix /ə'pendɪks/ *noun* [C] **1** **ANATOMY** *plural* **appendixes** a small tube-shaped part inside the body below the stomach, attached to the large intestine ➲See picture at **alimentary canal** **2** *plural* **appendices** a separate part at the end of a book, article, etc which contains extra information

WORD PARTNERS FOR ***appetite***

give sb /**have** an appetite • **lose** your appetite • a **good/healthy/huge** appetite • **loss of** appetite

appetite /'æpɪtaɪt/ *noun* [C, U] **1** the feeling that makes you want to eat *All that walking has **given** me an **appetite**.* **2** **an appetite for sth** when you want something very much *his appetite for adventure* **3** **whet sb's appetite** to make someone want more of something

appetizer /'æpɪtaɪzəʳ/ *US* (*UK* **starter**) *noun* [C] **FOOD** something that you eat as the first part of a meal

appetizing (*also UK* **-ising**) /'æpɪtaɪzɪŋ/ *adjective* If food is appetizing, it looks or smells as if it will taste good.

applaud /ə'plɔːd/ *verb* **1** CLAP [I, T] to clap your hands to show that you have enjoyed a performance, talk, etc *The audience applauded loudly.* **2** PRAISE [T] *formal* to approve of or admire something *Most people will surely applaud the decision.*

applause /ə'plɔːz/ *noun* [U] when people make a noise by clapping their hands to show they have enjoyed or approve of something *There was loud applause at the end of her speech.*

O⁻**apple** /'æpl/ *noun* [C] **FOOD** a hard, round fruit with a green or red skin ➲See colour picture **Fruit and Vegetables** on page Centre 10 ➲See also: **Adam's apple**

applet /'æplət/ *noun* [C] **COMPUTING** a small computer program that is automatically copied on to a computer when you look at a document that needs this program to make it work

appliance /ə'plaɪəns/ *noun* [C] a piece of electrical equipment with a particular purpose in the home *fridges, radios, and other **electrical appliances***

applicable /ə'plɪkəbl/ *adjective* affecting or relating to a person or situation *This law is only **applicable to** people living in Europe.*

applicant /'æplɪkənt/ *noun* [C] someone who asks for something officially, often by writing *There were over fifty **applicants for** the job.*

application /ˌæplɪ'keɪʃᵊn/ *noun* **1** REQUEST [C] an official request for something, usually in writing *an **application for** a bank loan* **2** USE [C, U] a way in which something can be used for a particular purpose *This technology has many practical applications.* **3** **COMPUTING** [C] a computer program designed for a particular purpose

appli'cation ˌform *noun* [C] a form that you use to officially ask for something, for example a job

appli'cation ˌsoftware *noun* [U] **COMPUTING** software that makes a computer do a process that the user wants ➲Compare **system software**

applied /ə'plaɪd/ *adjective* **EDUCATION** **applied mathematics/science, etc** mathematics, science, or another subject which is studied for a practical use

appliqué /ə'pliːkeɪ/ (US) /'æplɪkeɪ/ *noun* [U] **ART, DT** decorative work in which one piece of cloth is sewn or fixed onto another, or the activity of decorating cloth in this way

apply /ə'plaɪ/ *verb* **1** ASK [I] to ask officially for something, often by writing *I've **applied for** a job.* ○ *He has **applied to** several companies.* **2** AFFECT [I] to affect or relate to a particular person or situation *This law only **applies to** married people.* **3** USE [T] to use something in a particular situation *The same method can be **applied to** other situations.* **4** ON SURFACE [T] to spread a substance on a surface *Apply the cream daily until the symptoms disappear.* **5** **apply yourself** to work hard *If he doesn't apply himself, he'll never pass his exams.*

appoint /ə'pɔɪnt/ *verb* [T] to officially choose someone for a job *He was **appointed as** company director last year.*

appointed /ə'pɔɪntɪd/ *adjective* **appointed date/time/place, etc** the date, time, place, etc that has been chosen for something to happen

WORD PARTNERS FOR ***appointment***

have/make an appointment • **cancel/keep/miss** an appointment • an appointment **with** sb

O-ᵚ**appointment** /ə'pɔɪntmənt/ *noun* **1** TIME [C] a time you have arranged to meet someone or go somewhere *a doctor's/dental appointment* ○ *I **made** an **appointment** with my hairdresser for next Monday.* **2** JOB [C, U] when you officially choose someone for an important job, or the job itself *the appointment of three new teachers*

apportion /ə'pɔːʃən/ *verb* [T] *formal* **1** to choose how much of something a person or each person should have **2 apportion blame/responsibility** to say who was responsible for something bad that happened

appraisal /ə'preɪzəl/ *noun* [C, U] **1** when you examine someone or something and judge how good or successful they are *a critical appraisal* **2** a meeting where the manager of an employee talks to them about the quality of their work *an appraisal scheme*

appraise /ə'preɪz/ *verb* [T] to examine something and judge it *We need to stop and appraise the situation.*

appreciable /ə'priːʃəbl/ *adjective formal* large or important enough to be noticed *There's an **appreciable difference** in temperatures between the two regions.*

appreciate /ə'priːʃieɪt/ *verb* **1** VALUE [T] to understand how good something or someone is and be able to enjoy them *There's no point buying him expensive wines - he doesn't appreciate them.* **2** GRATEFUL [T] to feel grateful for something *I'd really appreciate your help.* **3** UNDERSTAND [T] to understand something about a situation, especially that it is complicated or difficult [+ **(that)**] *I appreciate that it is a difficult decision for you to make.* **4 FINANCE** [I] *formal* to increase in value *Houses and antiques generally appreciate with time.*

appreciation /əˌpriːʃi'eɪʃən/ *noun* [U] **1** VALUE when you understand how good something or someone is and are able to enjoy them *His **appreciation of** art increased as he grew older.* **2** FEEL GRATEFUL when you feel grateful for something *To show our appreciation, we've bought you a little gift.* **3** UNDERSTANDING when you understand something about a situation, especially that it is complicated or difficult *He has no **appreciation of** the size of the problem.* **4 FINANCE** *formal* an increase in value

appreciative /ə'priːʃiətɪv/ *adjective* showing that you understand how good something is, or are grateful for something *an appreciative audience* •**appreciatively** *adverb*

apprehend /ˌæprɪ'hend/ *verb* [T] *formal* If the police apprehend someone, they catch them and take them away to ask them about a crime which they might have committed.

apprehension /ˌæprɪ'henʃən/ *noun* [U] an anxious feeling about something that you are going to do *It's normal to feel a little apprehension before starting a new job.*

apprehensive /ˌæprɪ'hensɪv/ *adjective* feeling anxious about something that you are going to do *He's a bit **apprehensive about** living away from home.*

apprentice /ə'prentɪs/ *noun* [C] **EDUCATION** a person who is learning a job by working for someone who already has skills and experience

apprenticeship /ə'prentɪʃɪp/ *noun* [C, U] **EDUCATION** when someone learns the skills needed to do a job by working for someone who already has skills and experience

O-ᵚ**approach**¹ /ə'prəʊtʃ/ *noun* **1** METHOD [C] a way of doing something *Liam has a different **approach to** the problem.* ○ *We've decided to **adopt/take** a new **approach**.* **2** ASKING [C] when you speak or write to someone, often asking to buy something or offering them work **3** COMING CLOSER [U] when something or someone gets nearer, in distance or time *the approach of winter* **4** PATH [C] a path or route that leads to a place

O-ᵚ**approach**² /ə'prəʊtʃ/ *verb* **1** COME CLOSE [I, T] to come close in distance or time *The train now approaching platform 2 is the 5.35 to London, Kings Cross.* ○ *Christmas is fast approaching.* **2** DEAL WITH [T] to deal with something *I'm not sure how to approach the problem.* **3** SPEAK TO SOMEONE [T] to speak or write to someone, often asking to buy something or offering them work *She's been approached by a modelling agency.*

COMMON LEARNER ERROR

approach

The verb **approach** is not normally followed by a preposition.

He approached the door.

~~*He approached to the door.*~~

approachable /ə'prəʊtʃəbl/ *adjective* friendly and easy to talk to

O-ᵚ**appropriate**¹ /ə'prəʊpriət/ *adjective* suitable or right for a particular situation or person *Is this film **appropriate for** young children?* ➲Opposite **inappropriate** •**appropriately** *adverb appropriately dressed*

appropriate² /ə'prəʊprieɪt/ *verb* [T] *formal* to take or steal something •**appropriation** /əˌprəʊpri'eɪʃən/ *noun* [U]

appropri'ation ac,count *noun* [C] **FINANCE** a document that shows how the profit of a business is shared between the parters that own that business

WORD PARTNERS FOR ***approval***

gain/get/win/receive/seek approval • **formal/full** approval • approval **for** sth

approval /ə'pruːvəl/ *noun* [U] **1** GOOD OPINION when you think that something or someone is good or right *I don't need his approval.* ➲Opposite **disapproval** **2** PERMISSION official permission *The project has now **received approval** from the government.*

A

O-- **approve** /ə'pruːv/ *verb* **1** ALLOW [T] to allow or officially agree to something *The council has* ***approved plans*** *for a new shopping centre.* **2** GOOD OPINION [I] to think that something is good or right *I don't* ***approve of*** *smoking.* ⊃Opposite **disapprove**

approving /ə'pruːvɪŋ/ *adjective* showing that you think something is good or right *an approving smile* ⊃Opposite **disapproving** •**approvingly** *adverb*

approx *written abbreviation for* approximately

approximate[1] /ə'prɒksɪmət/ *adjective* not completely accurate but close *Do you have an approximate idea of when he's arriving?*

approximate[2] /ə'prɒksɪmeɪt/ (*also* **approximate to**) *verb* [T] *formal* to be almost the same as something •**approximation** /əˌprɒksɪ'meɪʃən/ *noun* [C, U]

approximately /ə'prɒksɪmətli/ *adverb* close to a particular number or time although not exactly that number or time *The college has approximately 700 students.*

Apr *written abbreviation for* April

apricot /'eɪprɪkɒt/ *noun* [C] **FOOD** a small, soft, orange fruit

O-- **April** /'eɪprəl/ (*written abbreviation* **Apr**) *noun* [C, U] the fourth month of the year

ˌApril 'Fool's Day *noun* 1 April, a day when people play tricks on people, then say 'April fool!'

apron /'eɪprən/ *noun* [C] a piece of clothing you wear when cooking to keep your clothes clean

apt /æpt/ *adjective* **1** suitable for a particular situation *an* ***apt description*** **2 be apt to do sth** to often do something *He's apt to forget his keys.* •**aptly** *adverb*

WORD PARTNERS FOR ***aptitude***

have/show an aptitude for (doing) sth • a **natural** aptitude • an aptitude **test**

aptitude /'æptɪtjuːd/ *noun* [C, U] a natural skill or an ability to do something well *He has an* ***aptitude for*** *learning languages.* ○ *an* ***aptitude test***

aquarium /ə'kweəriəm/ *noun* [C] **1** PLACE a building where fish and other water animals are kept for people to visit **2** CONTAINER a glass container filled with water that fish are kept in

Aquarius /ə'kweəriəs/ *noun* [C, U] the sign of the zodiac which relates to the period of 21 January - 19 February, or a person born during this period

aquatic /ə'kwætɪk/ *adjective* **BIOLOGY** living or growing in water, or related to water *aquatic animals*

aqueous /'eɪkwiəs/ *adjective* **CHEMISTRY** like or containing water *an aqueous solution*

ˌaqueous 'humour *noun* [U] **ANATOMY** a clear liquid that fills the space inside your eye between the cornea (= outer covering) and the lens (= part you see through)

aquifer /'ækwɪfər/ *noun* [C] **GEOLOGY** a layer of rock, sand or earth that contains water or allows water to pass through it

Arab /'ærəb/ *adjective* relating or belonging to the people of the Middle East or North Africa whose families came from Arabia in the past *Arab countries* •**Arab** *noun* [C] an Arab person

Arabic /'ærəbɪk/ *noun* the language used by Arab peoples •**Arabic** *adjective*

arable /'ærəbl/ *adjective* **FARMING** suitable for or used for growing crops *arable land/farming*

arachnid /ə'ræknɪd/ *noun* [C] **BIOLOGY** any of a group of small animals, similar to insects but with four pairs of legs, for example spiders

arbiter /'ɑːbɪtər/ *noun* [C] **1** someone who judges what is right or helps to solve an argument **2 arbiter of fashion/style/taste, etc** someone who decides what is beautiful or stylish

arbitrary /'ɑːbɪtrəri/ *adjective* not based on a system or principles and often seeming unfair *an arbitrary decision* •**arbitrarily** /ˌɑːbɪ'treərəli/ *adverb*

arbitrate /'ɑːbɪtreɪt/ *verb* [I, T] to officially help to solve an argument between two people or groups •**arbitrator** *noun* [C]

arbitration /ˌɑːbɪ'treɪʃən/ *noun* [U] the process of solving an argument between people by helping them to agree to an acceptable solution

arc /ɑːk/ *noun* [C] **MATHEMATICS** a curved line that looks like part of a circle

arcade /ɑː'keɪd/ *noun* [C] **1** GAMES a place where you can pay to play games on machines *an amusement arcade* **2** PASSAGE a passage, especially between shops, that is covered by a roof *a shopping arcade*

arch[1] /ɑːtʃ/ *noun* [C] **1** a curved structure that usually supports something, for example a bridge or wall **2 ANATOMY** the curved, middle part of your foot that does not touch the ground

arch[2] /ɑːtʃ/ *verb* [I, T] to be a curved shape or make something become a curved shape *The bridge arched over the river.*

archaeologist (*also US* **archeologist**) /ˌɑːki'ɒlədʒɪst/ *noun* [C] someone who studies archaeology

archaeology (*also US* **archeology**) /ˌɑːki'ɒlədʒi/ *noun* [U] the study of ancient cultures by looking for and examining their buildings, tools, and other objects •**archaeological** (*also US* **archeological**) /ˌɑːkiə'lɒdʒɪkəl/ *adjective*

archaic /ɑː'keɪɪk/ *adjective* very old and often not suitable for today *an archaic law*

archbishop /ˌɑːtʃ'bɪʃəp/ *noun* [C] **RELIGION** a priest of the highest rank in some Christian churches, responsible for a very large area *Archbishop Desmond Tutu*

archeologist /ˌɑːki'ɒlədʒɪst/ *noun* [C] *another US spelling of* archaeologist

archeology /ˌɑːki'ɒlədʒi/ *noun* [U] *another US spelling of* archaeology

archery /'ɑːtʃəri/ *noun* [U] **SPORT** a sport in which you shoot arrows

architect /'ɑːkɪtekt/ *noun* [C] someone who designs buildings

architecture /ˈɑːkɪtektʃəʳ/ *noun* [U] **1** STYLE the design and style of buildings ***modern architecture*** **2** BUILDINGS the skill of designing buildings •**architectural** /ˌɑːkɪˈtektʃərəl/ *adjective*

archive¹ /ˈɑːkaɪv/ *noun* [C] **1** a collection of historical documents that provides information about the past, or a place where they are kept *the national archives* **2** **COMPUTING** a place on a computer used to store information or documents that you do not need to use often

archive² /ˈɑːkaɪv/ *verb* [T] **COMPUTING** to store paper or electronic documents in an archive

the Arctic /ˈɑːktɪk/ *noun* the very cold area around the North Pole •**Arctic** *adjective*

WORD PARTNERS FOR ***ardent***

an ardent **admirer/fan/supporter**

ardent /ˈɑːdənt/ *adjective* [**always before noun**] enthusiastic or showing strong feelings *an* ***ardent supporter*** *of Arsenal* •**ardently** *adverb*

arduous /ˈɑːdjuəs/ *adjective* needing a lot of effort to do *an* ***arduous journey/task***

are *strong form* /ɑːʳ/ *weak form* /əʳ/ *present simple you/we/they of* be

O⊶**area** /ˈeəriə/ *noun* **1** REGION [C] a region of a country or city *an industrial area ○ a mountainous area ○ the London area* **2** PART [C] a part of a building or piece of land used for a particular purpose *a* ***play/picnic area*** **3** SUBJECT [C] a part of a subject or activity *Software is not really my area of expertise.* **4** **MATHEMATICS** [C, U] the size of a flat surface calculated by multiplying its width by its length ➲See also: **catchment area, no-go area**

ˈarea ˌcode *noun* [C] a set of numbers used at the beginning of all the telephone numbers in a particular area

arena /əˈriːnə/ *noun* [C] **1** **SPORT** a flat area with seats around where you can watch sports and other entertainments *an Olympic/sports arena* **2** **in the political/public, etc arena** involved in politics/the government, etc

aren't /ɑːnt/ **1** *short for* are not *We aren't going to the party.* **2** **aren't I?** *short for* am I not? *I am invited, aren't I?*

arete /ærˈet/ *noun* [C] **GEOGRAPHY** a high, thin, pointed area that separates two valleys (= low land between mountains)

argon /ˈɑːgɒn/ *noun* [U] **CHEMISTRY** a gas that does not react with any other substances, used in electric lights (symbol **Ar**)

arguable /ˈɑːgjuəbl/ *adjective* **1** **It is arguable that** it is possibly true that *It is arguable that the government has failed in this respect.* **2** If something is arguable, it is not certain if it is true. ***It is arguable whether*** *this method would even have succeeded.*

arguably /ˈɑːgjuəbli/ *adverb* possibly *He's arguably the greatest footballer in the world.*

O⊶**argue** /ˈɑːgjuː/ *verb* **arguing**, *past* **argued** **1** DISAGREE [I] to speak angrily to someone, telling them that you disagree with them *My parents are always* ***arguing about*** *money. ○ Kids, will you stop* ***arguing with*** *each other?* **2** GIVE REASONS [I, T] to give reasons to support or oppose an idea, action, etc [+ **that**] *He argued that cuts in military spending were necessary. ○ She* ***argued for/against*** *tax cuts.*

WORD PARTNERS FOR ***argument***

have an argument • an argument **about/over** sth • a **heated/violent** argument

O⊶**argument** /ˈɑːgjəmənt/ *noun* [C] **1** ANGRY DISCUSSION an angry discussion with someone in which you both disagree *They* ***had an argument*** *about who should do the cleaning.* **2** REASON a reason or reasons why you support or oppose an idea, action, etc *There are many* ***arguments for/against*** *nuclear energy.*

argumentative /ˌɑːgjəˈmentətɪv/ *adjective* often arguing or wanting to argue

aria /ˈɑːriə/ *noun* [C] **MUSIC** a song that one person sings in an opera

arid /ˈærɪd/ *adjective* **GEOGRAPHY** very dry and without enough rain for plants *an arid region/climate*

Aries /ˈeəriːz/ *noun* [C, U] the sign of the zodiac which relates to the period of 21 March - 20 April, or a person born during this period

arise /əˈraɪz/ *verb* [I] *past tense* **arose**, *past participle* **arisen** **1** START If a problem arises, it starts to happen. *The whole problem* ***arose from*** *a lack of communication.* **2** GET UP *literary* to get up, usually from a bed

aristocracy /ˌærɪˈstɒkrəsi/ *noun* [**group**] **SOCIETY** the highest social class, usually in countries which have or had a royal family

aristocrat /ˈærɪstəkræt/ *noun* [C] **SOCIETY** a member of the highest social class •**aristocratic** /ˌærɪstəˈkrætɪk/ *adjective an aristocratic family*

arithmetic /əˈrɪθmətɪk/ *noun* [U] **MATHEMATICS** when you calculate numbers, for example by multiplying or adding

O⊶**arm¹** /ɑːm/ *noun* [C] **1** **ANATOMY** the long part at each side of the human body, ending in a hand *He put his arms around her. ○ She was standing with her arms folded* (= with one arm crossed over the other). ➲See colour picture **The Body** on page Centre 13 **2** **arm in arm** with your arm gently supporting or being supported by someone else's arm **3** CLOTHES the part of a piece of clothing that you put your arm in **4** CHAIR the part of a chair where your arm rests **5** **twist sb's arm** *informal* to persuade someone to do something ➲See also: **arms**

arm² /ɑːm/ *verb* [T] to give weapons to someone *The terrorists had* ***armed*** *themselves* ***with*** *automatic rifles.* ➲Opposite **disarm**

armaments /ˈɑːməmənts/ *noun* [**plural**] military weapons and equipment *nuclear armaments*

armband /ˈɑːmbænd/ *noun* **1** [C] a strip of material worn around your upper arm *a black/reflective armband* **2** **armbands** *UK* two plastic tubes that you fill with air and wear round the top of your arms when you are learning to swim

armchair /ˈɑːmˌtʃeəʳ/ *noun* [C] a comfortable chair with sides that support your arms ➲See colour picture **The Living Room** on page Centre 4

armed /ɑːmd/ *adjective* **1** carrying or using weapons ***armed guards/police*** *○ an* ***armed robbery*** (= robbery where guns are used)

A

➲Opposite **unarmed** **2 armed with sth** carrying or knowing something that will be useful *I like to go to a meeting armed with the relevant facts.*

the ˌarmed ˈforces (*also* **the ˌarmed ˈservices**) *noun* [**plural**] a country's military forces, for example the army and the navy

armful /ˈɑːmfʊl/ *noun* [**C**] the amount that you can carry in your arms *an armful of books*

armistice /ˈɑːmɪstɪs/ *noun* [**C**] an agreement to stop fighting that is made between two countries

armour *UK* (*US* **armor**) /ˈɑːməʳ/ *noun* [**U**] metal clothing which soldiers wore in the past to protect them when fighting *a suit of armour*

armoured *UK* (*US* **armored**) /ˈɑːməd/ *adjective* covered with a protective layer of metal *an armoured vehicle*

armpit /ˈɑːmpɪt/ *noun* [**C**] **ANATOMY** the part of your body under your arm, where your arm meets your shoulder ➲See colour picture **The Body** on page Centre 13

arms /ɑːmz/ *noun* [**plural**] **1** weapons *the sale of arms* **2 be up in arms** to be very upset and angry about something *Local residents are up in arms over plans to close the swimming pool.*

WORD PARTNERS FOR ***army***

join the army • be **in** the army

O‑ **army** /ˈɑːmi/ *noun* [**C**] **1** MILITARY GROUP a military force that fights wars on the ground *the British Army* **2** ORGANIZED GROUP a group of people that is organized to do the same job *an army of cleaners/helpers*

aroma /əˈrəʊmə/ *noun* [**C**] a nice smell that usually comes from food or drink *the aroma of freshly baked bread* •**aromatic** /ˌærəʊˈmætɪk/ *adjective* having a nice smell ***aromatic herbs***

aromatherapy /əˌrəʊməˈθerəpi/ *noun* [**U**] **HEALTH** a way of making a person who is ill better by rubbing pleasant-smelling oils into the skin or allowing them to smell the oils

arose /əˈrəʊz/ *past tense of* arise

O‑ **around** /əˈraʊnd/ *adverb, preposition* **1** IN A CIRCLE (*also UK* **round**) on all sides of something *They sat around the table.* **2** DIRECTION (*also UK* **round**) to the opposite direction *He turned around and looked at her.* **3** CIRCULAR MOVEMENT (*also UK* **round**) in a circular movement *This lever turns the wheels around.* **4** ALONG OUTSIDE (*also UK* **round**) along the outside of something, not through it *You have to walk around the house to get to the garden.* **5** TO A PLACE (*also UK* **round**) to or in different parts of a place *I spent a year travelling around Australia.* **6** SEVERAL PLACES (*also UK* **round**) from one place or person to another *She passed a plate of biscuits around.* **7** HERE here, or near this place *Is Roger around?* **8** EXISTING present or available *Mobile phones have been around for years now.* **9** APPROXIMATELY used before a number or amount to mean 'approximately' *around four o'clock* ○ *around twenty thousand pounds* ➲See also: throw your **weight** around

arousal /əˈraʊzəl/ *noun* [**U**] when someone is sexually excited

arouse /əˈraʊz/ *verb* [**T**] **1** CAUSE REACTION to make someone have a particular feeling or reaction *It's a subject which has **aroused** a lot of **interest**.* **2** CAUSE SEXUAL FEELING to make someone sexually excited

O‑ **arrange** /əˈreɪndʒ/ *verb* [**T**] **1** ORGANIZE to make the necessary plans and preparations for something to happen *to arrange a meeting* ○ *I'll **arrange for** a car to come and pick you up.* [**+ to do sth**] *We've arranged to visit the house on Saturday afternoon.* **2** POSITION to put objects in a particular order or position *The books are arranged alphabetically by author.*

WORD PARTNERS FOR ***arrangement***

have/make an arrangement • arrangements **for** sth • **alternative/necessary** arrangements

O‑ **arrangement** /əˈreɪndʒmənt/ *noun* **1** PLANS [**C**] plans for how something will happen [**usually plural**] *We're meeting tomorrow to discuss **arrangements for** the competition.* [**+ to do sth**] *I've **made arrangements** to go home this weekend.* **2** AGREEMENT [**C, U**] an agreement between two people or groups *We have an arrangement whereby we share the childcare.* ○ *Viewing is **by prior arrangement**.* **3** POSITION [**C**] a group of objects in a particular order or position *a flower arrangement*

array /əˈreɪ/ *noun* [**C**] a large number of different things [**usually singular**] *There is **a** vast **array of** books on the subject.*

arrears /əˈrɪəz/ *noun* [**plural**] **FINANCE** money that is owed and should have been paid before *mortgage/rent arrears* ○ *He **is** already **in arrears** with the rent.*

O‑ **arrest¹** /əˈrest/ *verb* [**T**] **LAW** If the police arrest someone, they take them away to ask them about a crime which they might have committed. *He was **arrested for** possession of illegal drugs.*

WORD PARTNERS FOR ***arrest***

make an arrest • **resist** arrest • be **under** arrest • the arrest **of** sb • an arrest **for** [murder/drugs offences, etc]

arrest² /əˈrest/ *noun* [**C, U**] **LAW** when the police take someone away to ask them about a crime which they might have committed *Police **made** 20 **arrests** at yesterday's demonstration.* ○ *He's **under arrest*** (= has been arrested). ➲See also: **house arrest**

O‑ **arrival** /əˈraɪvəl/ *noun* **1** ARRIVING [**U**] when someone or something arrives somewhere *He first met Panos soon after his arrival in Greece.* ○ *There was a car waiting for him **on arrival**.* **2** BECOME AVAILABLE [**U**] when something new is discovered or created or becomes available *The town grew rapidly with **the arrival of** the railway.* **3** NEW PERSON/THING [**C**] a new thing or person that has arrived *Two teachers were there to greet the **new arrivals**.*

O‑ **arrive** /əˈraɪv/ *verb* [**I**] **1** REACH to get to a place *When he first **arrived in** New York, he didn't speak a word of English.* ○ *We were the last to **arrive at** the station.* ○ *A letter arrived for you this morning.* **2 arrive at an answer/decision/conclusion, etc** to find an answer to a problem or make a decision after a lot of discussion *We didn't arrive at any firm conclusions.* **3** HAPPEN to happen or start to exist *Summer had finally arrived.*

COMMON LEARNER ERROR

arrive somewhere

Be careful to choose the correct preposition after **arrive**. You **arrive at** a place such as a building.

We arrived at the hotel just after 12 o'clock.

You **arrive in** a town, city or country.

They arrived in Tokyo on Wednesday.

When did David arrive in Australia?

You **arrive** home, here, or there. You do not use a preposition when **arrive** is used before these words.

We arrived home yesterday.

I had a lot of problems when I first arrived here.

arrogant /ˈærəgənt/ *adjective* believing that you are better or more important than other people *I found him arrogant and rude.* •**arrogance** /ˈærəgəns/ *noun* [U] •**arrogantly** *adverb*

arrow /ˈærəʊ/ *noun* [C] **1** SIGN a symbol used on signs to show a direction **2** WEAPON a long, thin stick with a sharp point at one end which is fired from a bow (= curved piece of wood with a tight string fixed at both ends)

arsenal /ˈɑːsənəl/ *noun* [C] a large collection of weapons

arsenic /ˈɑːsənɪk/ *noun* [U] **CHEMISTRY** a chemical element that is a very strong poison (symbol **As**)

arson /ˈɑːsən/ *noun* [U] **LAW** the crime of intentionally burning something, such as a building •**arsonist** *noun* [C] someone who commits arson

O‑ **art** /ɑːt/ *noun* **1 ART** [U] the making or study of paintings, drawings, etc or the objects created *fine/modern art* ○ *an* ***art exhibition/gallery*** **2** [C, U] a skill in a particular activity *the art of conversation* ➲See also: **martial art, work of art**

artefact *UK* (*US* **artifact**) /ˈɑːtɪfækt/ *noun* [C] an object, especially something very old of historical interest

arteriole /ɑːˈtɪəriəʊl/ *noun* [C] **ANATOMY, BIOLOGY** a thin tube carrying blood that comes out from an artery (= large tube that carries blood) ➲See picture at **capillary**

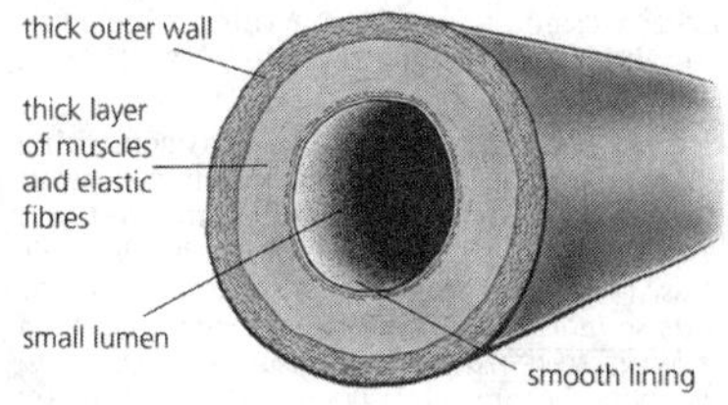

artery

artery /ˈɑːtəri/ *noun* [C] **1 ANATOMY, BIOLOGY** one of the tubes in your body that carries blood from your heart **2** an important route for traffic •**arterial** /ɑːˈtɪə.ri.əl/ *adjective*

artful /ˈɑːtfəl/ *adjective* [**always before noun**] showing skill *an artful use of colour* •**artfully** *adverb*

arthritis /ɑːˈθraɪtɪs/ *noun* [U] **HEALTH** an illness which causes the parts of the body where bones meet to become painful and often big •**arthritic** /ɑːˈθrɪtɪk/ *adjective an arthritic hip/knee*

arthropod /ˈɑːθrəpɒd/ *noun* [C] **BIOLOGY** a type of animal with no spine (= backbone), a hard outer skin, legs with bones joined together, and a body divided into sections, for example a spider, crab or ant

artichoke /ˈɑːtɪtʃəʊk/ *noun* [C, U] **FOOD** a round, green vegetable with thick, pointed leaves covering the outside

article /ˈɑːtɪkl/ *noun* [C] **1** WRITING a piece of writing in a magazine, newspaper, etc **2** OBJECT an object, especially one of many *an* ***article of clothing/furniture*** **3 LANGUAGE** in grammar, used to mean the words 'the', 'a', or 'an' ➲See also: **definite article, indefinite article**

ˌArticles of Associˈation *noun* [**plural**] **LAW** a legal document that is written when a limited company is formed and that says things like who controls the company and how the profits will be shared

articulate[1] /ɑːˈtɪkjələt/ *adjective* able to express ideas and feelings clearly in words *She's an intelligent and highly articulate young woman.* ➲Opposite **inarticulate**

articulate[2] /ɑːˈtɪkjəleɪt/ *verb* [T] *formal* to express ideas or feelings in words *He articulates the views and concerns of the local community.* •**articulation** /ɑːˌtɪkjəˈleɪʃən/ *noun* [U]

articulated /ɑːˈtɪkjəleɪtɪd/ *adjective* [**always before noun**] *mainly UK* An articulated vehicle is long and has two parts which are joined together to help it turn corners. *an* ***articulated*** *lorry*

artifact /ˈɑːtɪfækt/ *noun* [C] *US spelling of* artefact

artificial /ˌɑːtɪˈfɪʃəl/ *adjective* **1** NOT NATURAL not natural, but made by people *an artificial flower/lake* ○ *an artificial heart* **2** NOT SINCERE not sincere •**artificially** *adverb*

artificial insemination /ɑːtɪˌfɪʃəlɪnsemɪˈneɪʃən/ *noun* [U] **HEALTH** the process of putting sperm (= cell that joins an egg to make a baby) into a female using methods which do not involve sexual activity

ˌartificial inˈtelligence *UK* (*US* **artiˌficial inˈtelligence**) *noun* [U] **COMPUTING** the study and development of computer systems which do jobs that previously needed human intelligence

artillery /ɑːˈtɪləri/ *noun* [U] large guns, especially those fixed on wheels used by an army

artisan /ˌɑːtɪˈzæn/ (US) /ˈɑːrtəzən/ *noun* [C] *old-fashioned* someone who does skilled work with their hands

O‑ **artist** /ˈɑːtɪst/ *noun* [C] **ART** someone who creates art, especially paintings and drawings

artistic /ɑːˈtɪstɪk/ *adjective* **1** showing skill and imagination in creating things, especially in painting, drawing, etc *artistic talent* **2** ›

A

ART relating to art *the artistic director of the theatre* •**artistically** *adverb*

artistry /ˈɑːtɪstri/ *noun* [U] great skill in creating or performing something, such as in writing, music, sport, etc

arts /ɑːts/ *noun* **1 EDUCATION** [plural] (*also US* **liberal arts**) subjects of study which are not science, such as history, languages, etc *an arts subject/degree* **2 the arts** activities such as painting, music, film, dance, and literature *public interest in the arts* ⊃See also: **the performing arts**

artwork /ˈɑːtwɜːk/ *noun* [U] **ART** the pictures or patterns in a book, magazine, CD cover, etc

arty /ˈɑːti/ (*also US* **artsy** /ˈɑːtsi/) *adjective* knowing a lot about art, or wanting to appear as if you do

O-- **as** *strong form* /æz/ *weak form* /əz/ *preposition, conjunction* **1 as .... as** used to compare two things, people, amounts, etc *He's not as tall as his brother.* ○ *She earns three times as much as I do.* **2** [WHILE] used to describe two things happening at the same time or something happening at a particular time *He was shot in the back as he tried to escape.* ○ *I think your opinions change as you get older.* **3** [FOR THIS PURPOSE] used to describe the purpose, job, or appearance of something or someone *She **works as** a waitress.* ○ *It could be **used as** evidence against him.* **4** [LIKE] in the same way *This year, as in previous years, tickets sold very quickly.* **5** [IN THIS WAY] used to describe the way in which people see or think of something or someone *Most people think of nursing as a female occupation.* **6** [BECAUSE] because *You can go first as you're the oldest.* **7 as if/as though** used to describe how a situation seems to be *It looks as if it might rain.* **8 as for** used to talk about how another person or thing is affected by something *I was pleased. As for Emily, well, who cares what she thinks.* **9 as from/as of** *formal* starting from a particular time, date, etc *The new conditions are effective as of 15 May.* **10 as to** *formal* about *There's no decision as to when the work might start.*

asap /ˌeɪesefˈpiː/ *abbreviation for* as soon as possible

asbestos /æsˈbestɒs/ *noun* [U] a soft grey-white material which does not burn easily, once used in building

Asbo (**ASBO**) /ˈæzbəʊ/ **LAW** *UK abbreviation for* anti-social behaviour order: an official order that a person must stop doing something bad or they might go to prison

ascend /əˈsend/ *verb* [I, T] *formal* to move up or to a higher position

ascendancy (*also* **ascendency**) /əˈsendənsi/ *noun* [U] *formal* a position of power, strength, or success ***in the ascendancy***

ascending /əˈsendɪŋ/ *adjective* [**always before noun**] starting with the lowest or smallest and becoming greater or higher *They announced the results **in ascending order**.*

ascent /əˈsent/ *noun* **1** [CLIMB] [C] when someone climbs or moves up *his first ascent of the mountain* **2** [BECOMING SUCCESSFUL] [**no plural**] when someone starts to become successful *The book describes his rapid ascent from truck driver to film star.* **3** [PATH UP] [C] a path or road which goes up a hill or mountain *a steep ascent*

ascertain /ˌæsəˈteɪn/ *verb* [T] *formal* to discover something [**+ question word**] *We are still trying to ascertain whether the fire was started deliberately.*

ASCII /ˈæski/ *noun* **COMPUTING** *abbreviation for* American Standard Code for Information Interchange: a way of storing numbers, letters or symbols for exchanging information between computer systems

ascribe /əˈskraɪb/ *verb*

ascribe sth to sth *phrasal verb formal* to say that something is caused by something else *She ascribes her success to hard work.*

asexual reproduction /eɪˌseksjuəlriː.prəˈdʌk.ʃən/ *noun* [U] **BIOLOGY** a method of producing new young plants or animals from a single individual and without separate male and female cells joining together

ash /æʃ/ *noun* **1** [POWDER] [U] the soft, grey powder which remains when something has burnt *cigarette ash* **2** [TREE] [C] a forest tree

O-- **ashamed** /əˈʃeɪmd/ *adjective* **1** feeling guilty or embarrassed about something you have done *You've got nothing to be **ashamed of**.* [**+ to do sth**] *He was ashamed to admit his mistake.* **2 be ashamed of sb** to be angry and disappointed with a family member or friend because they have behaved badly *He was so rude to Phil - I was ashamed of him.*

ashes /ˈæʃɪz/ *noun* **sb's ashes** the powder that remains when a dead person's body has been burnt ***scatter** her **ashes***

ashore /əˈʃɔːʳ/ *adverb* onto land from the sea, a river, a lake, etc *We swam ashore.*

ashtray /ˈæʃˌtreɪ/ *noun* [C] a small, open container used to put cigarette ash and finished cigarettes in

Asian /ˈeɪʒᵊn/ *adjective* relating or belonging to Asia *Asian culture* •**Asian** *noun* [C] someone from Asia

aside¹ /əˈsaɪd/ *adverb* **1** [MOVE TO SIDE] in a direction to one side *I gave her a plate of food but she pushed it aside.* **2** [LATER] If you put or set something aside, you do not use it now, but keep it to use later. *We've put some money aside to pay for the children's education.* **3 aside from** except for

aside² /əˈsaɪd/ *noun* [C] something which you say quietly so that not everyone can hear it, often something funny

O-- **ask** /ɑːsk/ *verb* **1** [QUESTION] [I, T] to say something to someone as a question which you want them to answer [**+ two objects**] *Can I **ask** you a few **questions**?* ○ *I **asked** him **about** his hobbies.* [**+ question word**] *I asked why the plane was so late.* ⊃See Common Learner Error at **question** **2** [WANT SOMETHING] [I, T] to say something to someone because you want them to give you something *He's **asked for** a bike for his birthday.* **3** [REQUEST] [I, T] to say something to someone because you want them to do something [**+ to do sth**] *They've asked me to look after their dog while they're away.* **4** [INVITE] [T] to invite someone to do something *She **asked** him **out*** *to lunch the next day.* **5** WANT PERMISSION **[I, T]** to say something to someone because you want to know if you can do something *Bruce asked if he could stay with us for a few days.* **[+ to do sth]** *She asked to leave early.* **6** PRICE **[T]** to want a particular amount of money for something which you sell *How much are you* ***asking for*** *it?* **7 ask yourself sth** to think about something carefully *You've got to ask yourself whether it's what you really want.* **8 ask for it/trouble** *informal* to behave in a way that is likely to make something unpleasant happen to you or to cause you problems *Drinking and driving is asking for trouble.* **9 don't ask me** *informal* used to tell someone that you do not know the answer to a question and that you are surprised they have asked you *Don't ask me why you left your last job!* **10 you may well ask** said to someone who has asked you a question that would be difficult or interesting to answer

COMMON LEARNER ERROR

ask for

When you use **ask** with the meaning of saying you want someone to give you something, remember to use the preposition **for** before the thing that is wanted.

I'm writing to ask for information about your products.

~~*I'm writing to ask information about your products.*~~

askew /ə'skjuː/ *adjective* **[never before noun]** not straight *The picture was slightly askew.*

OTHER WAYS OF SAYING *asleep*

If someone starts to sleep, you can say that they **fall asleep**: ***I fell asleep*** *in front of the TV.*

If someone is completely asleep, you can say they are **fast asleep**: *You were* ***fast asleep*** *by the time I came to bed.*

The verbs **doze** and **snooze,** and the expression **have/take a nap** all mean 'to sleep, especially for a short time or during the day': *She's always* ***dozing*** *in front of the TV.* • *Granddad was* ***snoozing*** *in his chair.* • *Oliver is really tired so he's just* ***taking a nap.***

The phrasal verbs **doze off** and (*informal*) **nod off** mean to start to sleep, especially during the day: *I must have* ***nodded off*** *after lunch.* • *She* ***dozed off*** *during the lecture.*

O⊸**asleep** /ə'sliːp/ *adjective* **1 be asleep** to be sleeping *The children are asleep.* ○ *I was* ***fast/sound asleep*** (= sleeping deeply). **2 fall asleep** to start sleeping *He fell asleep in front of the TV.*

asparagus /ə'spærəgəs/ *noun* **[U]** **FOOD** a vegetable consisting of a long, green stem with a pointed end

aspect /'æspekt/ *noun* **1** **[C]** one part of a situation, problem, subject, etc *His illness affects almost every aspect of his life.* **2** **LANGUAGE** **[U, C]** the form of a verb which shows how the meaning of a verb is considered in relation to time

Asperger's syndrome /'æspɜːdʒəz,sɪndrəʊm/ *noun* **[U]** **HEALTH** a mental illness in which someone does not develop normal social abilities, and they are often very interested in one particular subject

asphalt /'æsfælt/ *noun* **[U]** a hard, black substance used to make roads and paths

asphyxiate /əs'fɪksieɪt/ *verb* **be asphyxiated** **HEALTH** to die because you cannot breathe •**asphyxiation** /əs,fɪksi'eɪʃᵊn/ *noun* **[U]**

WORD PARTNERS FOR *aspiration*

have aspirations to do sth/of doing sth • **high** aspirations • **dreams/hopes and** aspirations • aspirations **for** sth

aspiration /,æspᵊr'eɪʃᵊn/ *noun* **[C, U]** something you hope to achieve *The story is about the lives and aspirations of the Irish working classes.*

aspire /ə'spaɪəʳ/ *verb* **aspire to sth; aspire to do sth** to hope to achieve something *He has never aspired to a position of power.*

aspirin /'æspᵊrɪn/ *noun* **[C, U]** *plural* **aspirin, aspirins** **HEALTH** a common drug used to reduce pain and fever

aspiring /ə'spaɪərɪŋ/ *adjective* **an aspiring actor/politician/writer, etc** someone who is trying to become a successful actor/politician/writer, etc

ass /æs/ *noun* **[C]** **1** BOTTOM *US very informal* (*UK* **arse**) a person's bottom **2** PERSON *informal* a stupid person **3** ANIMAL *old-fashioned* a donkey (= animal like a small horse)

assailant /ə'seɪlənt/ *noun* **[C]** *formal* **LAW** a person who attacks someone

assassin /ə'sæsɪn/ *noun* **[C]** a person who kills someone important or famous, often for money

assassinate /ə'sæsɪneɪt/ *verb* **[T]** to kill someone important or famous •**assassination** /ə,sæsɪ'neɪʃᵊn/ *noun* **[C, U]**

assault /ə'sɔːlt/ *noun* **[C, U]** **LAW** an attack ***an assault on*** *a police officer* ○ ***sexual assault*** •**assault** *verb* **[T]**

assemble /ə'sembl/ *verb* **1** GROUP **[I, T]** to join other people somewhere to make a group, or to bring people together into a group *They assembled in the meeting room after lunch.* **2** BUILD **[T]** to build something by joining parts together

assembler /ə'sembləʳ/ *noun* **[C]** **COMPUTING** **1** a program that changes computer instructions into machine code (= a set of numbers that gives instructions to a computer) **2** assembly language (= the language used to write a computer program before it is turned into machine code)

assembly /ə'sembli/ *noun* **1** **EDUCATION** **[C, U]** *UK* a regular meeting of all the students and teachers at a school *morning assembly* **2** **POLITICS** **[C]** a group of people, such as a government, who meet to make decisions, laws, etc *the national assembly* **3** **[U]** when you build something by joining parts together

a'ssembly ,language *noun* **[C]** **COMPUTING** the language used to write a computer program before it is turned into machine code (= set of

A

numbers that gives instructions to a computer)

assent /ə'sent/ *noun* [U] *formal* agreement or approval *Has she **given** her **assent**?* •**assent** *verb* [I] *formal* to agree to something

assert /ə'sɜːt/ *verb* **1 assert yourself** to behave or speak in a strong, confident way *She has to learn to assert herself.* **2 assert your authority/control/independence, etc** to do something to show other people that you have power **3** [T] *formal* to say that something is certainly true [+ **that**] *He **asserts that** she stole money from him.*

assertion /ə'sɜːʃən/ *noun* [C, U] *formal* when you say that something is certainly true [+ **that**] *I don't agree with his assertion that men are safer drivers than women.*

assertive /ə'sɜːtɪv/ *adjective* behaving or speaking in a strong, confident way *You need to be much more assertive.* •**assertively** *adverb* •**assertiveness** *noun* [U]

assess /ə'ses/ *verb* [T] to make a judgment about the quality, size, value, etc of something *The tests are designed to assess a child's reading skills.* •**assessment** *noun* [C, U]

asset /'æset/ *noun* [C] **1** a person, skill, or quality which is useful or helps you to succeed *He'll be a great **asset to** the team.* **2 FINANCE** something which a person or company owns which has a value [**usually plural**] *The company has $70 billion in assets.*

assiduous /ə'sɪdjuəs/ *adjective formal* showing a lot of effort and determination •**assiduously** *adverb*

assign /ə'saɪn/ *verb* [T] to give someone a particular job or responsibility [+ **two objects**] *UN troops were assigned the task of rebuilding the hospital.* [**often passive**] *The case has been **assigned to** our most senior officer.*
assign sb to sth *phrasal verb* to give someone a particular job or place to work [**often passive**] *Which police officer has been assigned to this case?*

assignment /ə'saɪnmənt/ *noun* [C, U] a piece of work or job that you are given to do *a written assignment* ○ *He's **on assignment** in Brazil.*

assimilate /ə'sɪmɪleɪt/ *verb formal* **1** [T] to understand and remember new information **2 SOCIETY** [I, T] to become part of a group, society, etc, or to make someone or something become part of a group, society, etc *The refugees have now **assimilated into** the local community.* **3 BIOLOGY** to absorb food into the tissue of a living organism •**assimilation** /əˌsɪmɪ'leɪʃən/ *noun* [U]

assist /ə'sɪst/ *verb* [I, T] to help *The army arrived to **assist in** the search.* ○ *He's **assisting** the police **with** their investigation.*

assistance /ə'sɪstəns/ *noun* [U] *formal* help *financial/medical assistance* ○ *Can I **be of** any **assistance**?* (= Can I help you?)

assistant /ə'sɪstənt/ *noun* [C] **1** someone whose job is to help a person who has a more important job *an administrative assistant* ○ *assistant manager* **2 a sales/shop assistant** *mainly UK* someone who helps customers in a shop

associate¹ /ə'səʊʃieɪt/ *verb* [T] to relate two things, people, etc in your mind *Most people **associate** this brand **with** good quality.*
associate with sb *phrasal verb formal* to spend time with someone
be associated with sth *phrasal verb* to be related to something or caused by something *There are many risks associated with smoking.*

associate² /ə'səʊʃiət/ *noun* [C] someone who you know because of work or business *She's a business associate of mine.*

associate³ /ə'səʊʃiət/ *adjective* **associate director/editor/producer, etc** someone in a slightly less important position than the main person

association /əˌsəʊʃi'eɪʃən/ *noun* **1** ORGANIZATION [C] an organization of people with the same interests or with a particular purpose *the Football Association* **2** CONNECTION [C,U] a connection or relationship between two things or people **3 in association with** working together with *The event was organized in association with the Sports Council.* ⊃See also: **savings and loan association**

assonance /'æsənənts/ *noun* [U] **LANGUAGE, LITERATURE** using similar sounds several times close together

assorted /ə'sɔːtɪd/ *adjective* of different types *a box of assorted chocolates*

assortment /ə'sɔːtmənt/ *noun* [C] a group of different types of something *an assortment of vegetables*

assuage /ə'sweɪdʒ/ *verb* [T] *formal* to make unpleasant feelings less strong *The government tried to assuage the public's fears.*

O-ˉ**assume** /ə'sjuːm/ *verb* [T] **1** to think that something is likely to be true, although you have no proof [+ **(that)**] *Everything was quiet when I got home so I assumed that you had gone out.* **2 assume control/power/responsibility, etc** to take a position of control/power/responsibility, etc *He has assumed the role of spokesman for the group.* **3 assume an air/expression, etc** *formal* to pretend to have a feeling that you do not have **4 assume a false identity/name, etc** to pretend to be someone else *an assumed name*

WORD PARTNERS FOR ***assumption***

make an assumption • be **based on** an assumption • a **basic/common/false/underlying** assumption • do sth **under the** assumption that • an assumption **about** sth

assumption /ə'sʌmʃən/ *noun* [C] **1** something that you think is true without having any proof *People tend to **make assumptions about** you when you have a disability.* ○ *These calculations are based **on the assumption that** prices will continue to rise.* **2 the assumption of power/responsibility, etc** when someone takes a position of power, responsibility, etc

assurance /ə'ʃʊərəns/ *noun* **1** PROMISE [C] a promise [+ **that**] *He **gave** us **an assurance** that it would not happen again.* **2** CONFIDENCE [U] confidence *He spoke with calm assurance.*

assure /ə'ʃʊə/ *verb* [T] **1** PROMISE to tell someone that something is certainly true, especially so that they do not worry [+ **(that)**] *She assured them that she would be all right.* **2** MAKE CERTAIN to make something certain to happen *This loan should assure the company's future.*

assured /ə'ʃʊəd/ *adjective* **1** showing skill and confidence *an assured performance* **2 be assured of sth** to be certain to get or achieve something in the future *They are now assured of a place in the final.* ➲See also: **self-assured**

asterisk /'æstᵊrɪsk/ *noun* [C] **LANGUAGE** a written symbol in the shape of a star (*), often used to mark a particular word, phrase, etc

asteroid /'æstᵊrɔɪd/ *noun* [C] **ASTRONOMY** one of many large rocks that go around the sun

the asthenosphere /æs'θenəʊˌsfɪəʳ/ *noun* **GEOLOGY** the thin, almost liquid, layer under the hard rock that forms the outer layer of the Earth

asthma /'æsmə/ *noun* [U] **HEALTH** an illness which makes it difficult to breathe *She had an asthma attack.* •**asthmatic** /æs'mætɪk/ *adjective an asthmatic child*

astonish /ə'stɒnɪʃ/ *verb* [T] to make someone very surprised *Her quick recovery has astonished doctors.*

astonished /ə'stɒnɪʃt/ *adjective* very surprised *He was **astonished at** her behaviour.*

astonishing /ə'stɒnɪʃɪŋ/ *adjective* very surprising *It's astonishing that so many people believed his story.* •**astonishingly** *adverb*

astonishment /ə'stɒnɪʃmənt/ *noun* [U] extreme surprise *The others stared at him **in astonishment**.* ○ ***To my astonishment**, he started laughing.*

astound /ə'staʊnd/ *verb* [T] to make someone very surprised *The speed of her recovery has astounded doctors.*

astounded /ə'staʊndɪd/ *adjective* very surprised *I'm **astounded at/by** these prices.*

astounding /ə'staʊndɪŋ/ *adjective* very surprising *an astounding success* •**astoundingly** *adverb*

astray /ə'streɪ/ *adverb* **1 go astray** to get lost or go in the wrong direction *One of my bags went astray at the airport.* **2 lead sb astray** to encourage someone to do bad things that they should not do *He was led astray by his friends.*

astride /ə'straɪd/ *adverb* If you sit or stand astride something, you have one foot on each side of it.

astro- /æstrəʊ-/ *prefix* **ASTRONOMY** relating to stars or outer space *astronomer* ○ *astrophysics*

astrology /ə'strɒlədʒi/ *noun* [U] the study of the positions and movements of stars and planets to say how they might influence people's lives •**astrologer** *noun* [C] someone who studies astrology •**astrological** /ˌæstrə'lɒdʒɪkəl/ *adjective*

astronaut /'æstrənɔːt/ *noun* [C] someone who travels into space

astronomical /ˌæstrə'nɒmɪkᵊl/ *adjective* **1** An astronomical amount is extremely large. ***astronomical prices*** **2 ASTRONOMY** relating to astronomy •**astronomically** *adverb*

astronomy /ə'strɒnəmi/ *noun* [U] **ASTRONOMY** the scientific study of stars and planets •**astronomer** *noun* [C] a scientist who studies astronomy

astute /ə'stjuːt/ *adjective* good at judging situations and making decisions which give you an advantage *an astute businesswoman* ○ *politically astute* •**astutely** *adverb*

asylum /ə'saɪləm/ *noun* **1** [U] when someone is allowed to stay somewhere because they are escaping danger in another country **2 HEALTH** [C] *old-fashioned* a hospital for people with a mental illness ➲See also: **political asylum**

a'sylum ˌseeker *noun* [C] someone who leaves their country to escape from danger, and tries to get permission to live in another country

asymmetrical /ˌeɪsɪ'metrɪkᵊl/ *adjective* not being exactly the same shape and size on both sides •**asymmetry** /eɪ'sɪmɪtri/ *noun* [U]

O-■ **at** *strong form* /æt/ *weak form* /ət/ *preposition* **1** PLACE used to show the place or position of something or someone *We met at the station.* ○ *She's at the library.* **2** TIME used to show the time something happens *The meeting starts at three.* **3** DIRECTION towards or in the direction of *She threw the ball at him.* ○ *He's always shouting at the children.* **4** ABILITY used after an adjective to show a person's ability to do something *He's good at making friends.* **5** CAUSE used to show the cause of something, especially a feeling *We were surprised at the news.* **6** AMOUNT used to show the price, speed, level, etc of something *He denied driving at 120 miles per hour.* **7** ACTIVITY used to show a state or activity *a country at war* **8 INTERNET** the @ symbol, used in email addresses to separate the name of a person, department, etc from the name of the organization or company

ate /eɪt, et/ *past tense of* eat

atheist /'eɪθiɪst/ *noun* [C] **RELIGION** someone who believes that there is no god •**atheism** *noun* [U]

atheroma /ˌæθ.ə'rəʊ.mə/ *noun* [C] **BIOLOGY, HEALTH** a substance containing a lot of fat that forms on the inside wall of an artery (= tube that carries blood) and causes it to harden or become blocked

atherosclerosis /ˌæθərəʊsklə'rəʊsɪs/ *noun* [U] **HEALTH** a disease where the arteries (= large tubes that carry blood) are damaged or made too thin by fat collecting in them

athlete /'æθliːt/ *noun* [C] **SPORT** someone who is very good at a sport and who competes with others in organized events

athletic /æθ'letɪk/ *adjective* **1** strong, healthy, and good at sports **2 SPORT** [always before noun] relating to athletes or to the sport of athletics

athletics /æθ'letɪks/ *UK* (*US* **track and field**) *noun* [U] **SPORT** the sports which include running, jumping, and throwing ➲See colour picture **Sports 1** on page Centre 14

-athon /-əθɒn/ *suffix* an event or activity that lasts a long time, usually to collect money for charity *a walkathon* (= a long walk)

atlas /'ætləs/ *noun* [C] **GEOGRAPHY** a book of maps *a **road atlas*** ○ *a world atlas*

A

ATM /ˌeɪtiːˈem/ *noun* [C] *mainly US* **FINANCE** *abbreviation for* automated teller machine: a machine that you get money from using a plastic card

WORD PARTNERS FOR ***atmosphere***

create an atmosphere • an atmosphere **of** [fear/trust, etc]

atmosphere /ˈætməsfɪəʳ/ *noun* **1** FEELING [**no plural**] the feeling which exists in a place or situation *a **relaxed atmosphere*** **2 GEOGRAPHY the atmosphere** the layer of gases around the Earth ➲See picture at **Earth** **3** AIR [**no plural**] the air inside a room or other place *a smoky atmosphere*

atmospheric /ˌætməsˈferɪk/ *adjective* **1 GEOGRAPHY** [**always before noun**] relating to the air or to the atmosphere ***atmospheric conditions*** **2** FEELING creating a special feeling, such as mystery or romance ***atmospheric music/lighting***

ˌatmospheric ˈpressure *noun* [U] **PHYSICS** the pressure of the atmosphere on the Earth's surface, which gets less the higher the ground is

atom /ˈætəm/ *noun* [C] **PHYSICS, CHEMISTRY** the smallest unit that an element can be divided into

atomic /əˈtɒmɪk/ *adjective* **PHYSICS, CHEMISTRY** **1** [**always before noun**] relating to atoms *an atomic particle* **2** using the energy created when an atom is divided ***atomic power/weapons***

aˌtomic ˈbomb (*also* **ˈatom ˌbomb**) *noun* [C] a very powerful bomb which uses the energy created when an atom is divided

aˌtomic ˈenergy *noun* [U] **PHYSICS** energy which is produced by dividing atoms

aˌtomic ˈmass *noun* [U, C] **MEASURES** the mass of an atom of a particular chemical element

aˌtomic mass ˈunit *noun* [C] **MEASURES** a unit used for measuring atomic mass

aˌtomic ˈnumber *noun* [C] **CHEMISTRY** the number of protons found in the nucleus of an atom of a particular chemical, used as a way of listing the chemical elements in order in the periodic table

aˌtomic ˈweight *noun* [U] **MEASURES** atomic mass

atop /əˈtɒp/ *preposition US* on the top of

ATP /ˌeɪtiːˈpiː/ *noun* [U] **BIOLOGY** *abbreviation for* adenosine triphosphate: an important chemical in the cells of living organisms that stores energy and releases it when it is needed

atrium /ˈeɪtriəm/ *noun* [C] *plural* **atriums** or **atria** **1** a large, central room with a glass roof in an office building, restaurant, etc **2 ANATOMY, BIOLOGY** one of the two spaces in the top part of the heart which push blood around the body ➲See picture at **heart**

atrocious /əˈtrəʊʃəs/ *adjective* **1** BAD extremely bad *atrocious weather* **2** VIOLENT violent and shocking *an atrocious crime*

atrocity /əˈtrɒsəti/ *noun* [C, U] when someone does something extremely violent and shocking *Soldiers have been **committing atrocities against civilians.***

O-■**attach** /əˈtætʃ/ *verb* [T] **1** JOIN to join or fix one thing to another *She **attached** a photograph **to** her letter.* **2 attach importance/value, etc to sb/sth** to think that someone or something has importance/value, etc *You attach too much importance to money.* **3** INCLUDE to include something as part of something else *There were too many conditions **attached to** the deal.* ➲See also: no strings (**string**¹) (attached) **4** COMPUTER to add an attachment (= computer file) to an email message

attached /əˈtætʃt/ *adjective* **be attached to sb/sth** to like someone or something very much *I've become rather attached to my old car.*

attachment /əˈtætʃmənt/ *noun* **1** FEELING [C, U] a feeling of love or strong connection to someone or something *I wasn't aware of any **romantic attachments.*** **2 COMPUTING** [C] a computer file which is sent together with an email message *I wasn't able to **open** that **attachment.*** **3** EQUIPMENT [C] an extra part which can be added to a piece of equipment *There's a special attachment for cleaning in the corners.*

WORD PARTNERS FOR ***attack***

1 launch/mount an attack • be **under** attack • a **bomb/terrorist** attack • an attack **on** sb/sth
2 launch/mount an attack • be/come **under** attack • a **personal/scathing** attack • an attack **on** sb/sth

O-■**attack**¹ /əˈtæk/ *noun* **1** VIOLENCE [C, U] a violent act intended to hurt or damage someone or something *a terrorist **attack on** the capital* **2** CRITICISM [C, U] when you say something to strongly criticize someone or something *a scathing **attack on** the president* **3 HEALTH** [C] a sudden, short illness *a nasty **attack of** flu* **4 SPORT** [C, U] in games such as football, when the players in a team try to score points, goals, etc *I would have liked to see more attack in the second half.* ➲See also: **counter-attack**

O-■**attack**² /əˈtæk/ *verb* **1** VIOLENCE [I, T] to use violence to hurt or damage someone or something *He was attacked and seriously injured by a gang of youths.* **2** CRITICIZE [T] to strongly criticize someone or something *She attacked the government's new education policy.* **3** DISEASE [T] If a disease, chemical, etc attacks someone or something, it damages them. *The virus attacks the central nervous system.* **4 SPORT** [I, T] If players in a team attack, they move forward to try to score points, goals, etc. *Even at 3–0 up, they did not stop attacking.*

attacker /əˈtækəʳ/ *noun* [C] a person who uses violence to hurt someone *The police think she must have known her attackers.*

attain /əˈteɪn/ *verb* [T] to achieve something, especially after a lot of work *She's attained a high level of fitness.* •**attainable** *adjective* possible to achieve •**attainment** *noun* [C, U] when you achieve something

WORD PARTNERS FOR *attempt*

make an attempt • a **successful/unsuccessful** attempt • an attempt **at** sth/doing sth • **in an** attempt to do sth

O-- **attempt**[1] /ə'tempt/ *noun* [C] **1** when you try to do something *This is his second **attempt at** the exam.* [+ **to do sth**] *They closed the road **in an attempt** to reduce traffic in the city.* ○ *She **made no attempt*** (= did not try) *to be sociable.* **2 an attempt on sb's life** when someone tries to kill someone

O-- **attempt**[2] /ə'tempt/ *verb* [T] to try to do something, especially something difficult [+ **to do sth**] *He attempted to escape through a window.*

attempted /ə'temptɪd/ *adjective* LAW **attempted murder/robbery, etc** when someone tries to commit a crime but does not succeed

OTHER WAYS OF SAYING *attend*

Instead of the verb 'attend', people usually say **come/go to:** *How many people **came to** the meeting?* • *He **goes to** church regularly.*

The verb **make** is sometimes used when someone is talking about whether or not they are able to attend an event: *I'm afraid I can't **make** the meeting this afternoon (= I will not be able to attend).*

The expression **make it** is also used, meaning 'to get to a place, even when there are problems': *The traffic was so bad we only just **made it** in time for the start of the film.*

attend /ə'tend/ *verb* [I, T] *formal* **1** to go to an event *to attend a concert/meeting* **2 attend a church/school, etc** to go regularly to a particular church/school, etc

attend to sb/sth *phrasal verb formal* to deal with something or help someone

attendance /ə'tendəns/ *noun* [C, U] **1** NUMBER the number of people who go to an event, meeting, etc *falling attendance* **2** REGULARLY when you go somewhere such as a church, school, etc regularly *His attendance at school is very poor.* **3 in attendance** *formal* present at an event *They have doctors in attendance at every match.*

attendant /ə'tendənt/ *noun* [C] someone whose job is to help the public in a particular place *a parking attendant* ➲See also: **flight attendant**

WORD PARTNERS FOR *attention*

pay attention (**to** sth/sb)/**give** sth attention • **have/hold/keep** sb's attention • **careful/full/special/undivided** attention

O-- **attention** /ə'tenʃən/ *noun* [U] **1** INTEREST when you watch, listen to, or think about something carefully or with interest *Ladies and gentlemen, could I **have your attention**, please?* **2 pay attention (to sth)** to watch, listen to, or think about something carefully or with interest *You weren't paying attention to what I was saying.* **3 bring/draw (sb's) attention to sth/sb** to make someone notice something or someone *If I could just draw your attention to the second paragraph.* **4 attract/get (sb's) attention** to make someone notice you *I waved at him to get his attention.* **5** TREATMENT treatment to deal with a problem *medical attention* ○ *This old engine needs a lot of attention.*

COMMON LEARNER ERROR

attention

Attention is usually followed by the preposition **to**.

You should pay attention to what she tells you.

We want to draw people's attention to the risks involved.

attentive /ə'tentɪv/ *adjective* listening or watching carefully and showing that you are interested *an attentive student. The waiter was **attentive** all our needs.* •**attentively** *adverb We listened attentively to her speech.*

attest /ə'test/ *verb* [I, T] *formal* to show or prove that something is true *Several of her colleagues came forward to **attest** to her good character.*

attic /'ætɪk/ *noun* [C] a room at the top of a house under the roof

attire /ə'taɪəʳ/ *noun* [U] *old-fashioned* the clothes that you wear •**attired** *adjective* dressed in a particular way *suitably attired*

WORD PARTNERS FOR *attitude*

have/take a [positive/responsible, etc] attitude • a **casual/hostile/negative/positive** attitude • (sb's) attitude **to/towards** sth/sb

O-- **attitude** /'ætɪtjuːd/ *noun* [C, U] how you think or feel about something and how this makes you behave *a **positive attitude*** ○ *He has a very bad **attitude to/towards** work.*

attorney /ə'tɜːni/ *noun* [C] *US* LAW a lawyer *a defense attorney* ➲See Common Learner Error at **lawyer** ➲See also: **district attorney**

O-- **attract** /ə'trækt/ *verb* [T] **1** ENCOURAGE INTEREST to make people come to a place or do a particular thing by being interesting, enjoyable, etc *The castle attracts more than 300,000 visitors a year.* ○ *We need to **attract** more science graduates **to** teaching.* **2 attract attention/interest, etc** to cause people to pay attention/be interested, etc **3 be attracted to sb** to like someone, especially sexually, because of the way they look or behave *I was attracted to him straight away.* **4** PHYSICS If something attracts a substance or object, it causes it to move towards it. *Magnets attract metal.*

WORD PARTNERS FOR *attraction*

an **added**/a **big**/the **main**/a **major**/the **star** attraction • a **tourist** attraction • the attraction **of** sth • an attraction **for** sb

attraction /ə'trækʃən/ *noun* **1** GOOD THING [C] something that makes people come to a place or want to do a particular thing *a **tourist attraction*** ○ *The opportunity to travel is one of the main **attractions of** this job.* **2** FEELING [U] when you like someone, especially sexually, because of the way they look or behave *physical attraction* **3** PHYSICS when something causes an object or substance to move towards it

A

OTHER WAYS OF SAYING *attractive*

The adjectives **beautiful** and **lovely** are often used instead of 'attractive', and are used to describe both people and things: *His wife is very **beautiful**.* • *We drove through some really **beautiful/lovely** countryside.* • *You look **lovely**!*

If a person is attractive, we can say that they are **good-looking**. The adjective **handsome** is also sometimes used for men, and **pretty** for women: *He's certainly very **good-looking**.* • *Your daughter is very **pretty**.*

If someone is extremely attractive, you can say that they are **gorgeous** or **stunning**: *You look **gorgeous** in that dress!* • *Her daughter is absolutely **stunning**.*

If something is extremely attractive, you can say that it is **breathtaking**, **exquisite**, **stunning**, or **gorgeous**: *The views from the window were **breathtaking**.* • *These handmade decorations are **exquisite**.*

If a person or thing is attractive because of being small, you can say that they are **cute** or **sweet**: *He's got a really **cute** baby brother.* • *Look at that kitten - isn't she **sweet**?*

Adjectives such as **stylish** and **chic** can be used to describe something that has been made to look attractive and fashionable: *He took me to a very **chic** restaurant.* • *Their house is very **stylish**.*

O-ɯ **attractive** /ə'træktɪv/ *adjective* **1** BEAUTIFUL beautiful or pleasant to look at *an attractive woman* ○ *I **find** him very **attractive**.* **2** INTERESTING interesting or useful *We want to make the club **attractive to** a wider range of people.* ⊃Opposite **unattractive** •**attractively** *adverb* •**attractiveness** *noun* [U]

attributable /ə'trɪbjətəbl/ *adjective* **attributable to sth** caused by something *A lot of crime is attributable to the use of drugs.*

attribute[1] /ə'trɪbjuːt/ *verb*
attribute sth to sth *phrasal verb* to say that something is caused by something else *He attributes his success to hard work.*
attribute sth to sb *phrasal verb* to say that someone wrote, said, or made something *This drawing has been attributed to Picasso.*

attribute[2] /'ætrɪbjuːt/ *noun* [C] a quality or characteristic that someone or something has *Her hair is her best attribute.*

attributive /ə'trɪbjətɪv/ *adjective* **LANGUAGE** An attributive adjective comes before the noun it describes. ⊃Compare **predicative**

aubergine /'əʊbəʒiːn/ *UK* (*US* **eggplant**) *noun* [C, U] **FOOD** an oval, purple vegetable that is white inside ⊃See colour picture **Fruit and Vegetables** on page Centre 10

auburn /'ɔːbən/ *adjective* Auburn hair is red-brown.

auction /'ɔːkʃən/ *noun* [C, U] **FINANCE** a sale in which things are sold to the person who offers the most money •**auction** (*also* **auction off**) *verb* [T] to sell something at an auction

auctioneer /ˌɔːkʃən'ɪər/ *noun* [C] the person who is in charge of an auction

audacity /ɔː'dæsəti/ *noun* [U] showing too much confidence in your behaviour in a way that other people find shocking or rude *And then he **had the audacity to** blame me for his mistake!* •**audacious** /ɔː'deɪʃəs/ *adjective*

audible /'ɔːdəbl/ *adjective* If something is audible, you can hear it. *His voice was barely audible.* ⊃Opposite **inaudible** •**audibly** *adverb*

WORD PARTNERS FOR *audience*

1 be **in** the audience • a **member of** the audience
2 reach an audience • sth's **target** audience • a **wide** audience

O-ɯ **audience** /'ɔːdiəns/ *noun* **1** GROUP [group] the people who sit and watch a performance at a theatre, cinema, etc *There were a lot of children **in the audience**.* **2** TYPE [group] the type of people who watch a particular TV show, read a particular book, etc *This magazine is aimed at a teenage audience.* **3** MEETING [C] *formal* a formal meeting with an important person *an **audience with** the Queen*

audio /'ɔːdiəʊ/ *adjective* relating to the recording or playing of sound *audio equipment*

audio- /ɔːdiəʊ-/ *prefix* relating to hearing or sound *audiotape*

audit /'ɔːdɪt/ *noun* [C] **FINANCE** when an independent person examines all the financial records of a company to produce a report •**audit** *verb* [T] •**auditor** *noun* [C]

audition /ɔː'dɪʃən/ *noun* [C] when someone does a short performance to try to get a job as an actor, singer, etc •**audition** *verb* [I]

auditorium /ˌɔːdɪ'tɔːriəm/ *noun* [C] the part of a theatre, hall, etc where people sit to watch a performance

auditory nerve /'ɔːdɪtərɪˌnɜːv/ *noun* [C] **ANATOMY, BIOLOGY** a nerve in the ear that carries electrical signals to the brain

Aug *written abbreviation for* August

augment /ɔːg'ment/ *verb* [T] *formal* to increase the size or value of something by adding something to it

O-ɯ **August** /'ɔːgəst/ (*written abbreviation* **Aug**) *noun* [C, U] the eighth month of the year

O-ɯ **aunt** /ɑːnt/ (*also* **auntie, aunty** /'ɑːnti/) *noun* [C] the sister of your mother or father, or the wife of your uncle ⊃See also: **agony aunt**

au pair /ˌəʊ'peər/ *noun* [C] a young person who goes to live with a family in another country and looks after their children, does work in their house, etc

aura /'ɔːrə/ *noun* [C] a feeling which a person or place seems to have *an aura of mystery*

aural /'ɔːrəl/ *adjective* **BIOLOGY** relating to hearing

auricle /'ɔːrɪ.kəl/ *noun* [C] **ANATOMY, BIOLOGY** *old-fashioned* one of the two spaces in the top part of the heart which push blood around the body

auspices /'ɔːspɪsɪz/ *noun* **under the auspices of sb/sth** *formal* with the help or support of a person or organization *The conference was held under the auspices of the Red Cross.*

auspicious /ɔːˈspɪʃəs/ *adjective* If an event or time is auspicious, it makes you believe that something will be successful in the future. *an auspicious start*

austere /ɒsˈtɪəʳ/ *adjective* **1** SIMPLE plain, simple, and without unnecessary decorations or luxuries *an austere room* **2** STRICT strict or severe *an austere woman* •**austerity** /ɒsˈterəti/ *noun* [U]

authentic /ɔːˈθentɪk/ *adjective* If something is authentic, it is real, true, or what people say it is. *authentic Italian food* •**authentically** *adverb* •**authenticity** /ˌɔːθenˈtɪsəti/ *noun* [U]

O━**author** /ˈɔːθəʳ/ *noun* [C] **LITERATURE** someone who writes a book, article, etc *a popular author of children's fiction*

authoritarian /ˌɔːθɒrɪˈteəriən/ *adjective* very strict and not allowing people freedom to do what they want *an authoritarian leader/regime*

authoritative /ɔːˈθɒrɪtətɪv/ *adjective* **1** INFORMATION An authoritative book, report, etc is respected and considered to be accurate. *an authoritative guide* **2** PERSON confident and seeming to be in control of a situation *an authoritative manner/voice*

O━**authority** /ɔːˈθɒrəti/ *noun* **1** POWER [U] the official power to make decisions or to control other people *a **position of authority*** [+ **to do sth**] *The investigators have the authority to examine all the company's records.* ○ *We need the support of someone **in authority**.* **2 POLITICS** [C] an official group or government department with power to control particular public services *the local housing authority* **3** QUALITY [U] the quality of being confident and being able to control people *She has an **air of authority**.* **4 an authority on sth** someone who has a lot of knowledge about a particular subject *She is an authority on seventeenth-century English literature.* ➲See also: **local authority**

authorize (*also UK* **-ise**) /ˈɔːθəraɪz/ *verb* [T] **1** to give official permission for something **2 be authorized to do sth** to be officially allowed to do something *Only managers are authorized to sign expense forms.* •**authorization** /ˌɔːθəraɪˈzeɪʃən/ *noun* [U]

autistic /ɔːˈtɪstɪk/ *adjective* **HEALTH** Autistic children have a mental illness which causes problems with communicating and forming relationships. •**autism** /ˈɔːtɪzəm/ *noun* [U]

auto /ˈɔːtəʊ/ *adjective US* relating to cars *the auto industry*

auto- /ɔːtəʊ-/ *prefix* **1** WITHOUT HUMANS operating without being controlled by humans *autopilot* (= a comptuer that directs an aircraft) **2** SELF self *an autobiography* (= a book that someone writes about their own life)

autobiography /ˌɔːtəʊbaɪˈɒgrəfi/ *noun* [C] **LITERATURE** a book written by someone about their own life •**autobiographical** /ˌɔːtəʊbaɪəʊˈgræfɪkəl/ *adjective*

autograph /ˈɔːtəgrɑːf/ *noun* [C] a famous person's name, written by that person •**autograph** *verb* [T] *an autographed photo*

automate /ˈɔːtəmeɪt/ *verb* [T] to control something using machines and not people •**automated** *adjective a fully automated system* •**automation** /ˌɔːtəˈmeɪʃən/ *noun* [U]

automatic[1] /ˌɔːtəˈmætɪk/ *adjective* **1** MACHINE An automatic machine works by itself or with little human control. *automatic doors* **2** CERTAIN certain to happen as part of the normal process or system *You get an automatic promotion after two years.* **3** REACTION done as a natural reaction without thinking *My automatic response was to pull my hand away.* •**automatically** *adverb*

automatic[2] /ˌɔːtəˈmætɪk/ *noun* [C] a car in which you do not have to change the gears (= parts that control how fast the wheels turn)

automobile /ˈɔːtəməʊbiːl/ *noun* [C] *US* a car *the automobile industry*

automotive /ˌɔːtəˈməʊtɪv/ *adjective* [**always before noun**] relating to cars and car production *the automotive industry*

autonomous /ɔːˈtɒnəməs/ *adjective* independent and having the power to make your own decisions *an autonomous region/state*

autonomy /ɔːˈtɒnəmi/ *noun* [U] **POLITICS** the right of a country or group of people to govern itself *Local councils need more autonomy.*

autopsy /ˈɔːtɒpsi/ *noun* [C] **HEALTH** a medical examination of a dead body to discover the exact cause of death

autotroph /ˈɔːtːəʊtrəʊf/ *noun* [C] **BIOLOGY** a living thing that can make its own food from simple chemical substances such as carbon dioxide ➲Compare •**autotrophic** /ˌɔːtːəʊˈtrəʊfɪk/ *adjective autotrophic nutrition*

O━**autumn** /ˈɔːtəm/ (*also US* **fall**) *noun* [C, U] the season of the year between summer and winter, when leaves fall from the trees *I'm starting a new job **in the autumn**.* ○ *autumn leaves* •**autumnal** /ɔːˈtʌmnəl/ *adjective* typical of autumn

auxiliary /ɔːgˈzɪliəri/ *adjective* providing extra help or support *an auxiliary nurse*

auˌxiliary ˈverb *noun* [C] **LANGUAGE** a verb which is used with another verb to form tenses, negatives, and questions. In English the auxiliary verbs are 'be', 'have', and 'do'.

auxin /ˈɔːk.sɪn/ *noun* [U] **BIOLOGY** a chemical substance that controls growth in plants

avail /əˈveɪl/ *noun* **to no avail** without success, especially after a lot of effort *She sent more than 50 letters, but to no avail.*

WORD PARTNERS FOR ***available***

be/become available • **make** sth available • **easily/freely/readily/widely** available • be available **to** sb

O━**available** /əˈveɪləbl/ *adjective* **1** READY TO USE If something is available, you can use it or get it. *This information is available free on the Internet.* ○ *The new drug is not yet **available to the public**.* **2** NOT BUSY If someone is available, they are not busy and so are able to do something. *No one from the company was available to comment on the accident.* ➲Opposite **unavailable** •**availability** /əˌveɪləˈbɪləti/ *noun* [U]

A

avalanche /ˈævəlɑːnʃ/ *noun* [C] **1** when a large amount of snow falls down the side of a mountain **2 an avalanche of sth** a sudden, large amount of something, usually more than you can deal with *an avalanche of mail*

avant-garde /ˌævɒŋˈɡɑːd/ *adjective* If art, music, etc, is avant-garde, it is new and unusual in style.

avarice /ˈævərɪs/ *noun* [U] *formal* a strong feeling that you want a lot of money and possessions

avatar /ˈævətɑːr/ *noun* [C] **COMPUTING** an electronic image of a person that represents the computer user, especially in games ➲See Extra help page **The Web and the Internet** on page Centre 37.

Ave *written abbreviation for* avenue

avenge /əˈvendʒ/ *verb* [T] *literary* to punish someone for doing something bad to you, your family, etc *He swore he would avenge his brother's death.*

avenue /ˈævənjuː/ *noun* [C] **1** [ROAD] (*written abbreviation* **Ave**) a wide road in a town or city, often with trees along it **2** [POSSIBILITY] a possible way of doing or achieving something *We have exhausted all other avenues of treatment.*

O‑ **average¹** /ˈævərɪdʒ/ *adjective* **1** [USUAL] usual and like the most common type *an average person* ○ *an average day* **2 MATHEMATICS** [always before noun] An average amount is calculated by adding some amounts together and then dividing by the number of amounts. *an average age/temperature* **3** [NOT EXCELLENT] not excellent, although not bad *The food was pretty average.*

O‑ **average²** /ˈævərɪdʒ/ *noun* **1 MATHEMATICS** [C] an amount calculated by adding some amounts together and then dividing by the number of amounts *They work an average of 30.5 hours per week.* **2** [C, U] the usual or typical amount *well above/below average* **3 on average** usually, or based on an average *Female workers earn, on average, a third less than men.*

average³ /ˈævərɪdʒ/ *verb* [T] **MATHEMATICS** to reach a particular amount as an average *He averages about 20 points a game.*

averse /əˈvɜːs/ *adjective* **1 not be averse to sth** *UK humorous* to be happy or willing to do or have something *She's not averse to the occasional glass of champagne.* **2 be averse to sth** *formal* to strongly dislike something

aversion /əˈvɜːʒən/ *noun* **an aversion to sth** when you strongly dislike something

avert /əˈvɜːt/ *verb* **1 avert a crisis/disaster/war, etc** to prevent something bad from happening **2 avert your eyes/face/gaze** to turn your head away so that you do not see something

avian flu /ˌeɪviənˈfluː/ *noun* [U] **HEALTH** bird flu: an illness that kills birds and can sometimes pass from birds to people

aviary /ˈeɪviəri/ *noun* [C] a large cage for birds

aviation /ˌeɪviˈeɪʃən/ *noun* [U] flying aircraft or producing aircraft *the aviation industry*

avid /ˈævɪd/ *adjective* very interested and enthusiastic *an avid reader* •**avidly** *adverb*

avocado /ˌævəˈkɑːdəʊ/ *noun* [C, U] **FOOD** a dark green, oval fruit which is pale green inside and is not sweet

O‑ **avoid** /əˈvɔɪd/ *verb* [T] **1** [STAY AWAY] to stay away from a person, place, situation, etc *Try to avoid the city centre.* **2** [PREVENT] to prevent something from happening *Book early to avoid disappointment.* **3 avoid doing sth** to intentionally not do something *She managed to avoid answering my question.* •**avoidable** *adjective* possible to avoid ➲Opposite **unavoidable** •**avoidance** *noun* [U] when you avoid something

COMMON LEARNER ERROR

avoid doing something

When **avoid** is followed by a verb, the verb is always in the **-ing** form.

I avoided seeing him for several days.

~~*I avoided to see him for several days.*~~

await /əˈweɪt/ *verb* [T] *formal* **1** [WAIT FOR] to wait for something *We are awaiting the results of the tests.* **2** [IN FUTURE] If something awaits you, you will experience it in the future. *A surprise awaits her when she gets home.*

O‑ **awake¹** /əˈweɪk/ *adjective* **1 be/lie/stay, etc awake** to not be sleeping *Is Tom awake yet?* ○ *The noise from the party **kept** me **awake** all night.* **2 be wide awake** to be completely awake

awake² /əˈweɪk/ *verb* [I, T] *past tense* **awoke**, *past participle* **awoken** *literary* to wake up, or make someone wake up

awaken /əˈweɪkən/ *verb* **1** [FEELINGS] [T] *formal* to cause an emotion, feeling, etc *The song awakened painful memories.* **2** [WAKE] [I, T] *literary* to wake up, or make someone wake up

awakening /əˈweɪkənɪŋ/ *noun* [no plural] **1** when you start to be aware of something or feel something **2 a rude awakening** If you have a rude awakening, you have a shock when you discover the truth about a situation.

WORD PARTNERS FOR ***award***

present/receive/win an award • an award **for** sth • an awards **ceremony** • an award **winner**

award¹ /əˈwɔːd/ *noun* [C] **1** a prize given to someone for something they have achieved *the **award for** best actress* ○ *to **receive/win** an **award*** **2 FINANCE** money given to someone because of a legal decision

award² /əˈwɔːd/ *verb* [T] to officially give someone something such as a prize or an amount of money [+ **two objects, often passive**] *He was awarded the Nobel Prize for Physics.*

O‑ **aware** /əˈweər/ *adjective* **1 be aware of/that** to know about something *Are you aware of the risks involved?* ○ *She was **well aware** that he was married.* ➲Opposite **unaware** **2** interested in and knowing a lot about a particular subject ***politically**/socially **aware***

WORD PARTNERS FOR ***awareness***

create/increase/raise awareness • a **greater/growing/heightened/increased** awareness • **public** awareness • an awareness **about/of** sth • an awareness **among** [parents/students, etc]

A

awareness /əˈweənəs/ *noun* [U] when you know about something *Environmental awareness is increasing all the time.*

awash /əˈwɒʃ/ *adjective* **be awash with sth** *UK* (*US* **be awash in sth**) to have a lot of something, often too much *The sport is awash with money.*

O‑**away**[1] /əˈweɪ/ *adverb* **1** DIRECTION to or in a different place or situation *Go away and leave me alone.* ○ *We'd like to move* ***away from*** *the town centre.* **2** DISTANCE FROM at a particular distance from a place *The nearest town was ten miles away.* ○ *How far away is the station?* **3** NOT THERE not at the place where someone usually lives or works *Shirley's feeding the cat while we're away.* **4** SAFE PLACE into a usual or safe place *Can you put everything away when you've finished?* **5 two weeks/five hours, etc away** at a particular time in the future *My exam's only a week away now.* **6** CONTINUOUS ACTION used after a verb to mean 'continuously or repeatedly' *Chris was hammering away in the garden all day.* **7** GRADUALLY gradually disappearing until almost or completely gone *The snow has melted away.* **8 SPORT** *UK* If a sports team is playing away, the game is at the place where the other team usually plays. ➲See also: take your **breath** away, give the **game**[1] away

away[2] /əˈweɪ/ *adjective* [**always before noun**] **SPORT** *UK* In sports, an away game is played at the place where the other team usually plays.

awe /ɔː/ *noun* [U] **1** a feeling of great respect and sometimes fear *I was filled with awe at the sheer size of the building.* **2 be in awe of sb** to feel great respect for someone *As children we were rather in awe of our grandfather.*

awe-inspiring /ˈɔːɪnspaɪərɪŋ/ *adjective* causing people to feel great respect or admiration

awesome /ˈɔːsəm/ *adjective* very great, large, or special and making you feel respect and sometimes fear *an awesome challenge/responsibility* ○ *The scenery was awesome.*

O‑**awful** /ˈɔːfəl/ *adjective* **1** very bad, of low quality, or unpleasant *an awful place* ○ *The film was absolutely awful.* **2 an awful lot (of sth)** *informal* a large amount *It cost an awful lot of money.*

awfully /ˈɔːfəli/ *adverb* very *awfully difficult/good*

awhile /əˈwaɪl/ *adverb US* for a short time *Let's wait awhile and see what happens.*

O‑**awkward** /ˈɔːkwəd/ *adjective* **1** DIFFICULT difficult or causing problems *an awkward customer* ○ *an awkward question* **2** EMBARRASSING embarrassing and not relaxed *an awkward pause/silence* ○ *I'm in an awkward situation.* **3** NOT ATTRACTIVE moving in a way that is not attractive *His movements were slow and awkward.* •**awkwardly** *adverb* •**awkwardness** *noun* [U]

awoke /əˈwəʊk/ *past tense of* awake

awoken /əˈwəʊkən/ *past participle of* awake

awry /əˈraɪ/ *adverb* **go awry** to not happen in the correct way *Suddenly everything started to go awry.*

axe[1] (*also US* **ax**) /æks/ *noun* [C] a tool consisting of a wooden handle with a sharp piece of metal at one end, used for cutting trees or wood

axe[2] (*also US* **ax**) /æks/ *verb* [T] to get rid of something or someone suddenly *The company has announced plans to* ***axe 500 jobs.***

axes /ˈæksiːz/ *plural of* axis

axil /ˈæksɪl/ *noun* [C] **BIOLOGY** the angle between a branch or leaf stalk and the stem it is growing out from

axis /ˈæksɪs/ *noun* [C] *plural* **axes** /ˈæksiːz/ **MATHEMATICS** **1** an imaginary, central line around which an object turns **2** a line at the side or bottom of a graph (= picture showing measurements)

axle /ˈæksl/ *noun* [C] a long metal bar which connects two wheels on a vehicle

axon /ˈæksɒn/ *noun* [C] **BIOLOGY** a long thread that comes out of a nerve cell and carries signals from it

aye /aɪ/ *exclamation informal* yes, used especially in Scotland and the North of England

Bb

B

B, b /biː/ the second letter of the alphabet

BA /biːˈeɪ/ *noun* [C] **EDUCATION** *abbreviation for* Bachelor of Arts: a university or college qualification in an arts (= not science) subject which usually takes 3 or 4 years of study

baa /bɑː/ *noun* [C] the sound that a sheep makes

babble /ˈbæbl/ *verb* [I] **LANGUAGE** to talk quickly in a way which is confused, silly, or has no meaning •**babble** *noun* [U] *the babble of voices*

WORD PARTNERS FOR ***baby***

have/ be **expecting/give birth to** a baby • a baby is **born** • a **new/newborn** baby

O-★**baby** /ˈbeɪbi/ *noun* [C] **1** CHILD a very young child *a baby girl/boy* ○ *baby clothes* ○ *Liz has* ***had a baby***. ○ *Maria's* ***expecting a baby*** (= she is pregnant). **2** ANIMAL a very young animal *a baby bird*

ˈbaby ˌboom *noun* [C] **SOCIETY** a time when a lot of babies are born in a particular area *the postwar baby boom*

ˈbaby ˌcarriage *noun* [C] *US* a small vehicle with four wheels for carrying a baby

babyish /ˈbeɪbiɪʃ/ *adjective* Babyish behaviour is silly, like the behaviour of a young child.

babysit /ˈbeɪbɪsɪt/ *verb* [I, T] **babysitting,** *past* **babysat** to look after children while their parents are not at home •**babysitter** *noun* [C] *We'd like to come, but we can't get a babysitter.* •**babysitting** *noun* [U]

bachelor /ˈbætʃəlәr/ *noun* [C] **1** a man who is not married **2 Bachelor of Arts/Science/Education, etc EDUCATION** a university or college qualification which usually takes 3 or 4 years of study, or a person who has this qualification

bacillus /bəˈsɪləs/ *noun* [C] *plural* **bacilli** **BIOLOGY** a bacterium (= an extremely small organism) shaped like a very small rod (= thin, narrow pole), some types of which cause disease

O-★**back**[1] /bæk/ *adverb* **1** RETURNING where someone or something was before *When do you go back to college?* ○ *I put it back in the cupboard.* **2** BEHIND in a direction behind you *Anna stepped back.* ○ *Flint leaned back in his chair.* **3** REPLY as a reply or reaction to something *UK to ring back/ US to call back* ○ *I signalled to her and she waved back.* **4** STATE to the state something or someone was in before *Hopefully things will* ***get back to normal*** *again now.* ○ *I'm sure we can* ***put*** *it* ***back together*** *again* (= repair it). ○ *Try to go back to sleep.* **5** EARLIER at or to an earlier time *We first met* ***back in*** *1973.* ○ *Looking back, I think we did the right thing.* **6** AWAY FROM in a direction away from something *He pulled back the curtain.* **7 back and forth** (*also UK* **backwards and forwards**) in one direction, then the opposite way, then in the original direction again many times *He has to travel back and forth between London and Paris every week.*

COMMON LEARNER ERROR

back to

Remember to use the preposition **to** when you are talking about returning to a place.

I haven't seen her since she went back to Korea.

~~*I haven't seen her since she went back Korea.*~~

O-★**back**[2] /bæk/ *noun* [C] **1** NOT FRONT the part of something that is furthest from the front or in the opposite direction to the front *He wrote his number down on the back of an envelope.* ○ *I always keep a blanket in the back of the car.* **2** **ANATOMY** the part of your body from your shoulders to your bottom *back injuries/pain* ○ *He was lying on his back.* ⊃See colour picture **The Body** on page Centre 13 **3** SEAT the part of a seat that you lean against when you are sitting *the back of a chair* **4 back to front** *UK* with the back part of something where the front should be *You've got your trousers on back to front.* **5 in back of** *US* behind *They sat in back of us on the plane.* **6 at/in the back of your mind** If you have a thought or idea at the back of your mind, you are always thinking about it. **7 behind sb's back** If you do something behind someone's back, you do it without them knowing, often in an unfair way. *Have they been saying things about me behind my back?* **8 be glad/happy, etc to see the back of sb/sth** *UK* to be pleased when someone leaves or something ends because you did not like them **9 be on sb's back** to remind someone again and again to do something, or to criticize someone in an annoying way **10 turn your back on sb/sth** to decide to stop having contact with someone or something, or to refuse to help someone *She turned her back on Hollywood and went to live in Florida.* ⊃See also: a **pat**[2] on the back, be (like) **water**[1] off a duck's back

back[3] /bæk/ *verb* **1** SUPPORT [T] to give support or help to a person, plan, or idea *He backed Mr Clark in the recent election.* **2** MONEY [T] to risk money by saying that you think a horse, team, etc will win a race, game, or competition in order to win more money if they do *Many people are backing Holyfield to win the fight.* **3 back (sth) away/into/out, etc** to move backwards or drive backwards *She saw he had a gun and backed away.*

back away *phrasal verb* to show that you do not support a plan or idea any more and do not want to be involved with it *The government has backed away from plans to increase taxes.*

back down *phrasal verb* to admit that you were wrong, or agree not to do something *The council* ***backed down over*** *rent increases.*

back off *phrasal verb* **1** MOVE to move away from someone, usually because you are afraid *I saw the knife and backed off.* **2** STOP SUPPORTING *mainly US* to stop supporting a plan *The president has* ***backed off from*** *a threat to expel U.N. soldiers.*

back out *phrasal verb* to decide not to do something you had planned or agreed to do *Nigel backed out at the last minute, so we had a spare* *ticket.*

back sb up *phrasal verb* **1** SUPPORT to support or help someone *My family backed me up in my fight for compensation.* **2** SAY IS TRUE to say that someone is telling the truth *Honestly, that's exactly what happened - Claire'll back me up.*

back sth up *phrasal verb* **1** PROVE to prove that something is true [**often passive**] His claims are backed up by recent research. **2 COMPUTING** to make an extra copy of computer information

back (sth) up *phrasal verb* to drive backwards

O-w**back**[4] /bæk/ *adjective* **1** [**always before noun**] at or near the back of something *back door/garden/ page* ○ *I put it in the back pocket of my jeans.* **2 back road/street** a very small road or street that goes behind or between buildings ⊃See also: put sth on the back **burner**

backache /ˈbækeɪk/ *noun* [**C, U**] **HEALTH** a pain in your back

backbench /ˌbækˈbentʃ/ *adjective UK* **a backbench MP/politician, etc POLITICS** a member of the government who does not have an important position •**backbencher** *noun* [**C**] a backbench politician

the backbenches /ˌbækˈbentʃɪz/ *noun* [**plural**] *UK* **POLITICS** the place where backbench politicians sit *He prefers to remain* ***on the backbenches.***

backboard /ˈbækbɔːd/ *noun* [**C**] **SPORT** in basketball (= a sport), a board behind the metal ring that you have to throw the ball through to score ⊃See colour picture **Sports 2** on page Centre 15

backbone /ˈbækbəʊn/ *noun* [**C**] **1** the main or strongest part of something *The car industry remains* ***the backbone of*** *the area's economy.* **2 ANATOMY** the line of bones down the centre of your back ⊃See picture at **rib cage**

backdrop /ˈbækdrɒp/ *noun* [**C**] **1** SITUATION the situation that an event happens in [**usually singular**] *The attack took place* ***against a backdrop of*** *rising tensions between the two communities.* **2** CLOTH the painted cloth at the back of a stage in a theatre

backer /ˈbækəʳ/ *noun* [**C**] someone who supports a person or plan, especially by giving them money

backfire /ˌbækˈfaɪəʳ/ *verb* [**I**] If something that you do backfires, it has the opposite result of what you wanted.

WORD PARTNERS FOR ***background***

come from a [poor/different, etc] background
• sb's **family** background

background /ˈbækgraʊnd/ *noun* **1** SOUND [**no plural**] Sounds in the background are not the main sounds you can hear. ***background music/noise*** ○ *I could hear a baby crying* ***in the background.*** **2 SOCIETY** [**C**] a person's education, family, and experience of life *She* ***came from*** *a middle-class* ***background.*** **3 ART** [**C, U**] the parts at the back of a picture, view, etc which are not the main things you look at *gold stars* ***on*** *a black* ***background*** **4** SITUATION [**C**] the situation that an event happens in, or things which have happened in the past which affect it [**usually singular**] *The talks are taking place* ***against a background of*** *economic uncertainty.* **5 in the background** If a person stays in the background, they try not to be noticed.

ˌ**background radiˈation** *noun* [**U**] **PHYSICS** radiation found naturally on Earth, that comes from some soil and rocks, etc. and from the atmosphere

backhand /ˈbækhænd/ *noun* [**C**] **SPORT** when you hit a ball with your arm across your body, in sports such as tennis

backing /ˈbækɪŋ/ *noun* [**U**] support, especially money, for a person or plan *financial backing* ○ *The proposal has the full backing of the government.*

backlash /ˈbæklæʃ/ *noun* [**C**] when people react against an idea which was previously popular [**usually singular**] *a* ***backlash against*** *the royal family*

backlog /ˈbæklɒg/ *noun* [**C**] work that should have been done earlier

backpack /ˈbækpæk/ *noun* [**C**] a bag that you carry on your back •**backpacking** *noun* [**U**] *to go* ***backpacking*** •**backpacker** *noun* [**C**]

ˈ**back** ˌ**scatter** (*also* **back scattering**) *noun* [**U**] **PHYSICS 1** when radiation is scattered (= moved in different directions) by the atoms of the substance it is moving through **2** radiation that has been scattered this way

backside /ˌbækˈsaɪd/ (US) /ˈbækˌsaɪd/ *noun* [**C**] *informal* the part of your body that you sit on

backslash /ˈbækslæʃ/ *noun* [**C**] **COMPUTING** the symbol '\', used in computer programs ⊃Compare **forward slash**

backspace /ˈbækspeɪs/ *noun* [**C**] **COMPUTING** the key that you press on a computer keyboard to move the cursor (= symbol showing your place on the screen) backwards and delete (= get rid of) the character before it •**backspace** *verb* [**I**] to use the backspace key

backstage /ˌbækˈsteɪdʒ/ *adverb* in the area behind the stage in a theatre where performers get ready

backstroke /ˈbækstrəʊk/ *noun* [**U**] **SPORT** a style of swimming on your back

back-to-back /ˌbæktəˈbæk/ *adjective, adverb* **1** POSITION If two people or things are back-to-back, their backs are touching or facing each other. *They stood back-to-back.* **2** AFTER If two things happen back-to-back, one happens after the other without a pause. *back-to-back interviews*

backtrack /ˈbæktræk/ *verb* [**I**] to say that you did not mean something you said earlier *The government has* ***backtracked on*** *its promises.*

backup /ˈbækʌp/ *noun* **1** [**C,U**] extra help, support, or equipment which is available if you need it *Medical staff are on call to* ***provide backup*** *in case of an emergency.* **2 COMPUTING** [**C**] an extra copy of computer information *to make a backup*

backward /ˈbækwəd/ *adjective* **1** DIRECTION [**always before noun**] in the direction behind you *a* ***backward glance*** **2** DEVELOPMENT less developed or slower to develop than normal *a backward country*

B

O— **backwards** /ˈbækwədz/ (*also* **backward**) *adverb* **1** DIRECTION towards the direction behind you *She took a couple of steps backwards.* **2** EARLIER towards an earlier time or an earlier stage of development *Let's start with your most recent job and **work backwards**.* **3** OPPOSITE ORDER in the opposite order to what is usual *"Erehwon" is "nowhere" spelled backwards.* **4** WRONG WAY (*also UK* **back to front**) with the part that is usually at the front at the back *You've got your skirt on backwards.* **5 backwards and forwards** *UK* (*UK/US* **back and forth**) in one direction then the opposite way and back again many times *I have to drive backwards and forwards between here and Ipswich every day.* **6 bend over backwards** to try extremely hard to help or to please someone [+ **to do sth**] *She bent over backwards to help him.*

backyard /ˌbækˈjɑːd/ *noun* [C] *US* the area behind a house

bacon /ˈbeɪkᵊn/ *noun* [U] **FOOD** meat from a pig cut into long thin slices

bacteria /bækˈtɪəriə/ *noun* [plural] **BIOLOGY** very small living things that sometimes cause disease •**bacterial** *adjective* made from or caused by bacteria ***bacterial infections***

bacteriophage /bækˈtɪəriəʊfeɪdʒ/ (*also* **phage**) *noun* [C] **BIOLOGY** a virus (= organism that causes disease) that grows and divides inside a bacterium, destroying it

bacterium /bækˈtɪəriəm/ *noun* [C] *plural* **bacteria** **BIOLOGY** a very small organism that can sometimes cause disease

O— **bad** /bæd/ *adjective* **worse, worst** **1** NOT PLEASANT not pleasant ***bad weather*** ○ ***bad news*** ○ *My phone bill was even worse than I'd expected.* ○ *He's in a bad mood today.* **2** LOW QUALITY of low quality *bad behaviour* ○ *The service was really bad.* ○ *He's always been **bad at** maths.* **3** SEVERE very serious or severe *a bad injury* ○ *the worst flooding for years* **4** NOT LUCKY not lucky, not convenient, or not happening how you would like *It was just **bad luck** that she heard us.* ○ *Is this a bad time to ask?* **5 not bad** satisfactory *"There are about 10 people in a group." "Oh well, that's not bad."* ○ *That's **not bad for** such a small company.* **6 be bad for sb/sth** to be harmful for someone or something *Looking at a computer screen for too long can be bad for your eyes.* **7 feel bad about sth/doing sth** to feel guilty or sorry about something that has happened *I felt bad about letting her down.* **8 too bad a** SYMPATHY *mainly US informal* used to say that you are sorry about a situation *"He didn't get the job." "Oh, that's too bad."* **b** CANNOT CHANGE *informal* used to say that nothing can be done to change a situation *I know you don't want to go but it's too bad, we have to.* **9** EVIL evil *She's a really bad person.* **10** **FOOD** Bad food is not fresh and cannot be eaten. **11** PAINFUL [**always before noun**] If you have a bad arm, leg, heart, etc, there is something wrong with it and it is painful. ➲See also: bad **blood**, be in sb's good/bad books (**book**[1])

ˌbad ˈdebt *noun* [C] **ECONOMICS, FINANCE** a debt that is not likely to be paid

baddie /ˈbædi/ *noun* [C] *mainly UK informal* a bad person in a film, book, etc

bade /bæd/ *past tense of* bid[3]

badge /bædʒ/ *noun* [C] **1** NAME a piece of plastic, metal, etc which you wear on your clothes showing your name or the organization you work for **2** DECORATION *UK* (*US* **button**) a piece of plastic, metal, etc with words or pictures on it that you wear on your clothes for decoration

badger /ˈbædʒəʳ/ *noun* [C] a wild animal with thick black and white fur that lives under the ground and comes out at night

O— **badly** /ˈbædli/ *adverb* **worse, worst** **1** SERIOUSLY very seriously *badly damaged/injured* **2** UNPLEASANT in a way that is of low quality or in an unpleasant way *to behave badly* ○ *They played badly in the first half.*

badminton /ˈbædmɪntən/ *noun* [U] **SPORT** a sport for two or four people in which you hit a shuttlecock (= a light object with feathers) over a net

bad-tempered /ˌbædˈtempəd/ *adjective* a bad-tempered person gets angry or annoyed easily *'Sam's been bad-tempered recently, is something worrying him?'*

baffle /ˈbæfl/ *verb* [T] If something baffles you, you cannot understand it at all. [**often passive**] *The police were baffled by his disappearance.*

O— **bag**[1] /bæg/ *noun* [C] **1** CONTAINER a container made of paper, plastic, etc, used for carrying things *a paper/plastic bag* ○ *He **packed his bags** and left.* **2** FOR WOMAN (*also* **handbag**) *mainly UK* a bag with handles in which a woman carries her money, keys, etc **3** AMOUNT the amount a bag contains *It doesn't weigh more than a couple of bags of sugar.* **4 bags of sth** *mainly UK informal* a large amount of something *There's bags of room.* **5 bags** Bags under your eyes are areas of loose or dark skin. ➲See also: **carrier bag,** let the **cat** out of the bag, **shoulder bag, sleeping bag, tote bag**

bag[2] /bæg/ *verb* [T] **bagging,** *past* **bagged** *informal* to get something, especially before other people have a chance to take it *Bag us some decent seats.*

bagel /ˈbeɪgᵊl/ *noun* [C] **FOOD** a type of bread made in the shape of a ring

baggage /ˈbægɪdʒ/ *noun* [U] **1** BAGS all the cases and bags that you take with you when you travel *baggage reclaim* **2** FEELINGS feelings and experiences from the past that influence how you think and behave now *emotional baggage*

baggy /ˈbægi/ *adjective* Baggy clothes are big and loose.

bagpipes /ˈbægpaɪps/ *noun* [plural] **MUSIC** a Scottish musical instrument that is played by blowing air into a bag and forcing it through pipes

baguette /bægˈet/ *noun* [C] **FOOD** a French-style loaf of bread that is long and thin and white *a ham and cheese baguette*

bail[1] /beɪl/ *noun* [U] **LAW** when money is paid to a court so that someone can be released from prison until their trial *He was **released on bail**.* ○ *She was **granted bail**.*

bail[2] /beɪl/ *verb* **be bailed** **LAW** If someone is bailed until a particular time, they can leave prison until then if they pay money to the

court.
bail sb out *phrasal verb* **1** to help a person or organization by giving them money *Companies can't expect the government to keep bailing them out.* **2 LAW** to pay money to a court so that someone can be released from prison until their trial

bailiff /ˈbeɪlɪf/ *noun* [C] **1** *UK* someone whose job is to take away things people own when they owe money **2 LAW** *US* someone whose job is to guard prisoners in a court

bailout /ˈbeɪlaʊt/ *noun* [C] *mainly US* **FINANCE** when a company is given money to solve its financial problems

bait¹ /beɪt/ *noun* [U, no plural] **1 SPORT** food that is used to try to attract fish or animals so that you can catch them **2** something that you use to persuade someone to do something

bait² /beɪt/ *verb* [T] **1 SPORT** to put food in or on something to try to catch fish or animals *a mouse trap baited with cheese* **2** to try to make someone angry by laughing at them or criticizing them

bake /beɪk/ *verb* [I, T] **FOOD** to cook something such as bread or a cake with dry heat in an oven *a baked apple* ➲See picture at **cook**

ˌbaked ˈbeans *noun* [plural] **FOOD** beans cooked in a tomato (= soft, round, red fruit used like a vegetable) sauce and sold in tins (= metal containers)

ˌbaked poˈtato *noun* [C] **FOOD** a potato baked and served with the skin (= outer layer) still on

baker /ˈbeɪkəʳ/ *noun* [C] someone who makes and sells bread, cakes, etc *Can you call at the **baker's** and get a loaf of bread?*

bakery /ˈbeɪkəri/ *noun* [C] a shop where you can buy bread, cakes, etc

baking /ˈbeɪkɪŋ/ *adjective informal* Baking weather is very hot.

balalaika /ˌbæləˈlaɪkə/ *noun* [C] **MUSIC** a type of musical instrument with three strings, played especially in Russia

WORD PARTNERS FOR ***balance***

1 keep/lose your balance • **knock/throw** sb off balance • sb's **sense of** balance
2 find/maintain/strike a balance • **redress** the balance • a **delicate** balance • a balance **between** sth and sth

balance¹ /ˈbæləns/ *noun* **1** WEIGHT [U] when the weight of someone or something is spread in such a way that they do not fall over *I **lost my balance** and fell off the bike.* ○ *The force of the explosion threw him **off balance*** (= it was difficult for him to stay standing). **2** EQUAL [U, no plural] when the correct amount of importance is given to each thing so that a situation is successful *We hope to **strike a balance between** police powers and the protection of citizens.* ➲Opposite **imbalance** **3** FAIR [U] when you consider all the facts in a fair way *I felt his report lacked balance.* **4 on balance** used to give your opinion after you have considered all the facts about something *On balance, I'd prefer a woman dentist to a man.* **5 FINANCE** [C] the amount of money that you still have to pay, or that you have left to use [usually singular] *I always pay off the balance on my credit card each month.* **6 be/hang in the balance** If something hangs in the balance, nobody knows if it will continue to exist in the future or what will happen to it. *After a bad year, Judd's career hung in the balance.*

balance² /ˈbæləns/ *verb* **1** NOT FALL [I, T] to be in a position where you will not fall to either side, or to put something in this position *She was trying to balance a book on her head.* **2** IMPORTANCE [T] to give the correct amount of importance to each thing so that a situation is successful *I struggle to balance work and family commitments.* **3 balance the books/budget FINANCE** to make sure that you do not spend more money than you get
balance sth against sth *phrasal verb* to compare the advantages and disadvantages of something *The ecological effects of the factory need to be balanced against the employment it provides.*

balanced /ˈbælənst/ *adjective* **1** considering all the facts in a fair way *a balanced discussion of his work* **2 FOOD a balanced diet/meal** a healthy mixture of different kinds of food ➲See also: **well-balanced**

ˌbalanced eˈquation *noun* [C] **CHEMISTRY** a chemical equation that has the same number of each type of atom on the left and right sides

ˌbalance of ˈpayments *noun* [no plural] *mainly UK* **ECONOMICS** the difference between how much a country pays to other countries and how much it gets paid by other countries

ˌbalance of ˈpower *noun* [no plural] **POLITICS** the way in which power is divided between different people or groups *maintaining the balance of power in the European Union*

ˌbalance of ˈtrade *noun* [C usually singular] **ECONOMICS** the difference in value between exports (= goods sold abroad) and imports (= goods bought from abroad)

ˈbalance ˌsheet *noun* [C] **FINANCE** a document that shows what a company has earned and what it has spent

balcony /ˈbælkəni/ *noun* [C] **1** HOUSE a small area joined to the wall outside a room on a high level where you can stand or sit **2** THEATRE the seats in an upper area of a theatre

bald /bɔːld/ *adjective* **1** NO HAIR with little or no hair *John started to **go bald** at an early age.* ○ *I've got a **bald patch/spot**.* **2** INFORMATION [always before noun] Bald facts or ways of saying things are very clear and are not intended to comfort you. •**baldness** *noun* [U]

balding /ˈbɔːldɪŋ/ *adjective* becoming bald

baldly /ˈbɔːldli/ *adverb* If you say something baldly, you say it in a very clear way which may upset the person you are speaking to. *"I don't love you any more," he said baldly.*

bale /beɪl/ *noun* [C] a large amount of something such as paper, cloth, or hay (= dried grass), that is tied together so that it can be stored or moved

baleful /ˈbeɪlfəl/ *adjective formal* evil or angry *a baleful look*

B

balk (*also UK* **baulk**) /bɔːlk/ (US) /bɔːk/ *verb* [I] to not want to do something that is unpleasant or difficult *Most people **balk at** paying these kind of prices for clothes.*

B

O-w**ball** /bɔːl/ *noun* [C] **1** ROUND OBJECT a round object that you throw, kick, or hit in a game, or something with this shape *a tennis ball* ○ *a ball of string* **2** DANCE a large formal occasion where people dance **3 have a ball** *informal* to enjoy yourself very much **4 be on the ball** *informal* to be quick to understand and react to things **5 set/start the ball rolling** to begin an activity that involves a group of people *I've started the ball rolling by setting up a series of meetings.* ➲See also: **ball game, crystal ball**

ballad /ˈbæləd/ *noun* [C] **LITERATURE, MUSIC** a song that tells a story, especially about love

ballerina /ˌbæləˈriːnə/ *noun* [C] a female ballet dancer

ballet /ˈbæleɪ/ (US) /bælˈeɪ/ *noun* **1** DANCING [U] a type of dancing that is done in a theatre and tells a story, usually with music **2** PERFORMANCE [C] a particular story or performance of ballet dancing **3** DANCERS [C] a group of ballet dancers who work together *the Royal Ballet*

ˈball ˌgame *noun* [C] **1 SPORT** *US* a game of baseball (= where teams hit a ball and run round four fixed points), basketball (= where teams throw a ball through a high net), or American football **2 a whole new ball game** *informal* (*also* **a different ball game**) a completely different situation from how things were before *We'd been climbing in Scotland, but the Himalayas were a whole new ball game.*

ballistic /bəˈlɪstɪk/ *adjective* **go ballistic** *informal* to suddenly become very angry

balloon¹ /bəˈluːn/ *noun* [C] a small coloured rubber bag that you fill with air to play with or to use as a decoration *Could you help me to **blow up** some **balloons**?* ➲See also: **hot-air balloon**

balloon² /bəˈluːn/ *verb* [I] to suddenly become much larger *I ballooned to 14 stone when I had my second baby.*

WORD PARTNERS FOR ***ballot***

hold a ballot • a ballot **on** sth • be **on** a ballot • (*UK*) ballot **papers** • a ballot **box**

ballot¹ /ˈbælət/ *noun* [C, U] **POLITICS** a secret written vote *to **hold a ballot*** ○ *She was the only candidate **on the ballot*** (= available to vote for). ○ *UK **ballot papers*** ○ *a **ballot box*** (= box where votes are collected)

ballot² /ˈbælət/ *verb* [T] *mainly UK* **POLITICS** to ask people to vote in a ballot so that you can find out their opinion about something *In July he will **ballot** his members **on** how they want to proceed.*

ballpark /ˈbɔːlpɑːk/ *noun* **1 SPORT** [C] *US* a place where baseball (= game where teams hit a ball and run round four fixed points) is played and watched **2 ballpark estimate/figure** a number or amount that is not exact but should be near the correct number or amount *$3 million would be a ballpark figure for sales next year.*

ballpoint pen /ˌbɔːlpɔɪntˈpen/ *noun* [C] a pen with a very small ball in the end that rolls ink onto the paper

ballroom /ˈbɔːlruːm/ *noun* [C] a large room where dances are held

bamboo /bæmˈbuː/ *noun* [C, U] a tall plant with hard hollow stems, often used for making furniture

ban¹ /bæn/ *verb* [T] **banning**, *past* **banned** to officially say that someone must not do something *A lot of people think boxing should be banned.* [+ from + doing sth] *Ian's been banned from driving for 2 years.*

WORD PARTNERS FOR ***ban***

impose/introduce/lift a ban • a **blanket/complete/outright/total** ban • a ban **on** (doing) sth

ban² /bæn/ *noun* [C] an official rule that people must not do or use something *There is a **ban on** developing land around the city.*

banal /bəˈnɑːl/ *adjective* ordinary and not exciting *banal pop songs*

O-w**banana** /bəˈnɑːnə/ *noun* [C, U] **FOOD** a long, curved fruit with a yellow skin ➲See colour picture **Fruit and Vegetables** on page Centre 10

O-w**band¹** /bænd/ *noun* [C] **1 MUSIC** a group of musicians who play modern music together *a jazz band* **2** LINE a line of a different colour or design *The band of lighter coloured soil marks the position of the fort.* **3** CIRCLE a piece of material put around something *an **elastic band*** **4** PEOPLE a group of people who do something together *the Cathedral's band of regular worshippers* **5** PART *UK* one of the groups that something is divided into *the 20-25 age band* ➲See also: **elastic band, rubber band**

band² /bænd/ *verb*
band together *phrasal verb* to work with other people in order to achieve something *Companies banded together to keep prices high.* ➲Opposite **disband**

bandage¹ /ˈbændɪdʒ/ *noun* [C] **HEALTH** a long piece of soft cloth that you tie around an injured part of the body

bandage² /ˈbændɪdʒ/ *verb* [T] **HEALTH** to put a bandage around a wound or injury

Band-Aid /ˈbændeɪd/ *US trademark* (*UK* **plaster**) *noun* [C] **HEALTH** a small piece of cloth or plastic that sticks to your skin to cover and protect a small wound

bandit /ˈbændɪt/ *noun* [C] a thief who attacks people who are travelling in a wild place

bandwagon /ˈbændˌwægən/ *noun* **get/jump on the bandwagon** to become involved in an activity which is successful so that you can get the advantages of it yourself *Publishers are rushing to get on the CD-ROM bandwagon.*

bandwidth /ˈbændwɪtθ/ *noun* [usually no plural] **COMPUTING** the amount of information per second that can move between computers connected by a telephone wire

bang¹ /bæŋ/ *noun* [C] **1** NOISE a sudden loud noise *The door slammed with a deafening bang.* **2** HIT when you suddenly hit part of your body on something hard *a nasty bang on the head* **3 go out with a bang** *informal* If someone or something goes out with a bang, they stop existing or doing something in an exciting way. **4 more bang for your buck(s)** *US informal* the best result for the smallest effort

bang² /bæŋ/ *verb* [I, T] **1** NOISE to make a loud noise, especially by hitting something against something hard *We heard the door bang.* ○ *Ben banged his fist on the desk.* **2** HIT to hit part of your body against something hard *Ted fell and banged his head.* ➲See also: be banging your **head**¹ against a brick wall

bang³ /bæŋ/ *adverb UK informal* exactly *The books were piled up **slap bang** in the middle of the kitchen table.* ○ *The curtain rose **bang on time**.*

banger /ˈbæŋəʳ/ *noun* [C] *UK informal* **1** an old car that is in a bad condition **2** FOOD a sausage (= tube of meat and spices)

bangle /ˈbæŋgl/ *noun* [C] a circle of stiff plastic, metal etc that people wear around the arm as jewellery

bangs /bæŋz/ *noun* [plural] *US* (*UK* **fringe** [C]) hair that is cut short and straight at the top of someone's face

banish /ˈbænɪʃ/ *verb* [T] **1** LAW to send someone away from a place, often as a punishment [often passive] *He was **banished to** a remote Alaskan island.* **2** to make yourself stop thinking about something or feeling a particular way *Banish winter blues with a holiday in the sun!*

banister /ˈbænɪstəʳ/ *noun* [C] a long piece of wood that you can hold as you go up or down stairs

banjo /ˈbændʒəʊ/ *noun* [C] MUSIC a musical instrument like a guitar with a round body

O→**bank¹** /bæŋk/ *noun* [C] **1** FINANCE an organization or place where you can borrow money, save money, etc *Most banks are reluctant to lend money to new businesses.* **2** RIVER the land along the side of a river *We found a shady spot on the river bank.* **3** STORE a place where a supply of something can be kept until it is needed *a blood bank* **4** PILE a large pile of snow, sand, or soil ➲See also: **bottle bank, merchant bank, piggy bank**

bank² /bæŋk/ *verb* **1** FINANCE [I, T] to put or keep money in a bank *to bank a cheque* ○ *Who do you **bank with**?* ○ *I **bank at** the First National Bank.* **2** [I] When a plane banks, it flies with one wing higher than the other when turning.

bank on sb/sth *phrasal verb* to depend on someone doing something or something happening *Chrissie might arrive on time, but I wouldn't bank on it.*

ˈbank aˌccount *noun* [C] FINANCE an arrangement with a bank to keep your money there and take it out when you need to

ˈbank ˌbalance *noun* [C] FINANCE the amount of money in a bank account

ˈbank ˌcharges *noun* [usually plural] FINANCE sums of money paid by a customer for a bank's services

banker /ˈbæŋkəʳ/ *noun* [C] someone who has an important job in a bank

ˌbanker's ˈorder *noun* [C] FINANCE a standing order (= instruction to the bank to pay someone a regular amount of money)

ˌbank ˈholiday *noun* [C] *UK* an official holiday when all banks and most shops and offices are closed *Spring bank holiday*

banking /ˈbæŋkɪŋ/ *noun* [U] ECONOMICS, FINANCE the business of operating a bank

banknote /ˈbæŋknəʊt/ *mainly UK* (*US* **bill**) *noun* [C] ECONOMICS a piece of paper money

ˈbank ˌrate *noun* [C] ECONOMICS the amount of interest that a bank charges when it lends money

ˈbank reconciliˌation *noun* [C, U] FINANCE the process of checking a business's accounts (= financial records) against a bank statement (= record from the bank of money paid and received)

bankrupt¹ /ˈbæŋkrʌpt/ *adjective* FINANCE unable to continue in business because you cannot pay your debts *He **went bankrupt** after only a year in business.*

bankrupt² /ˈbæŋkrʌpt/ *verb* [T] FINANCE to make someone bankrupt

bankruptcy /ˈbæŋkrəptsi/ *noun* [C, U] FINANCE when a person or organization becomes bankrupt *Factories that continue to make losses could soon face bankruptcy.*

ˈbank ˌstatement *noun* [C] FINANCE a piece of paper that shows how much money you have put into your bank account and how much you have taken out

ˈbank ˌstatement *noun* [C] FINANCE a printed record of the money put into and removed from a bank account

banner /ˈbænəʳ/ *noun* [C] a long piece of cloth, often stretched between poles, with words or a sign written on it

ˈbanner ˌad *noun* [C] INTERNET an advertisement that appears across the top of a page on the Internet

banquet /ˈbæŋkwɪt/ *noun* [C] FOOD a large formal dinner for a lot of people

banter /ˈbæntəʳ/ *noun* [U] conversation which is funny and not serious

baptism /ˈbæptɪzᵊm/ *noun* [C, U] RELIGION a Christian ceremony in which water is put on someone to show that they are a member of the Church

Baptist /ˈbæptɪst/ *adjective* RELIGION belonging or relating to a Christian group which only believes in baptism for people who are old enough to understand what it means *the Baptist Church* •**Baptist** *noun* [C]

baptize (*also UK* **-ise**) /bæpˈtaɪz/ ⓤⓢ /ˈbæptaɪz/ *verb* [T] RELIGION to perform a baptism ceremony for someone

O→**bar¹** /bɑːʳ/ *noun* [C] **1** DRINKING a place where alcoholic drinks are sold and drunk, or the area behind the person serving the drinks *I met him in a bar in Soho.* **2** BLOCK a small block of something solid *a chocolate bar* ○ *gold bars* ➲See colour picture **Pieces and Quantities** on page Centre 1 **3** LONG PIECE a long, thin piece of metal or wood *There were bars on the downstairs windows.* **4** PREVENTING SUCCESS *UK* something that prevents you doing something or having something *Lack of money should not be* ***a bar to*** *a good education.* **5 MUSIC** one of the short, equal groups of notes that a piece of music is divided into *The band played the first few bars.* **6 GEOGRAPHY** a long area of sand, soil or stones in the sea but close to land or joining two pieces of land **7 the bar LAW** lawyers (= people whose job is to know about the law and deal with legal situations) thought of as a group *Haughey was* ***called to the bar*** (= became a lawyer) in 1949. **8 behind bars** in prison

bar² /bɑːʳ/ *verb* [T] **barring,** *past* **barred 1 LAW** to officially prevent someone doing something or going somewhere, or to prevent something happening [+ **from** + **doing sth**] *The court barred him from contacting his former wife.* **2** KEEP OUT to stop someone going into a place *A line of policemen barred the entrance to the camp.* **3** CLOSE to close and lock a door or gate

bar³ /bɑːʳ/ *preposition* **1** except *I've read all her books,* ***bar one.*** **2 bar none** used to emphasize that someone or something is the best *the best suspense writer going, bar none*

barbarian /bɑːˈbeəriən/ *noun* [C] someone who behaves in a way which shows they are not well educated and do not care about the feelings of others

barbaric /bɑːˈbærɪk/ *adjective* violent and cruel *a barbaric act of violence* •**barbarically** *adverb*

barbecue¹ /ˈbɑːbɪkjuː/ *noun* [C] **FOOD 1** a party at which you cook food over a fire outdoors **2** a metal frame for cooking food over a fire outdoors

barbecue² /ˈbɑːbɪkjuː/ *verb* [I, T] **barbecuing,** *past* **barbecued FOOD** to cook food on a barbecue *barbecued chicken wings*

barbed wire /ˌbɑːbdˈwaɪəʳ/ *noun* [U] strong wire with short, sharp points on it to keep people out of a place *a barbed wire fence*

barber /ˈbɑːbəʳ/ *noun* [C] someone whose job is to cut men's hair *Dad goes to* ***the barber's*** (= the barber's shop) *once a month.*

ˈbar ˌchart (*also* **bar graph**) *noun* [C] **MATHEMATICS** a graph (= mathematical picture showing measurements) in which different amounts are shown by thick lines of different heights or lengths ➲See Extra help page **Graphs and charts** on page Centre 21.

ISBN 978-0-521-35698-5

bar code

ˈbar ˌcode *noun* [C] **COMPUTING** a row of black lines on something you buy, that a computer reads to find the price

bare¹ /beəʳ/ *adjective* **1** NO CLOTHES not covered by clothes *a bare chest* ○ *She ran out into the road* ***in her bare feet.*** **2** NOT COVERED not covered by anything *bare floorboards* **3** EMPTY empty *a bare room* ○ *The cupboard was bare.* **4** BASIC including only the smallest amount that you need of something *The report just gave us the barest facts about the accident.* ○ *Tony's salary only covers* ***the bare essentials*** *for the family.* ➲See also: with your bare hands (**hand¹**)

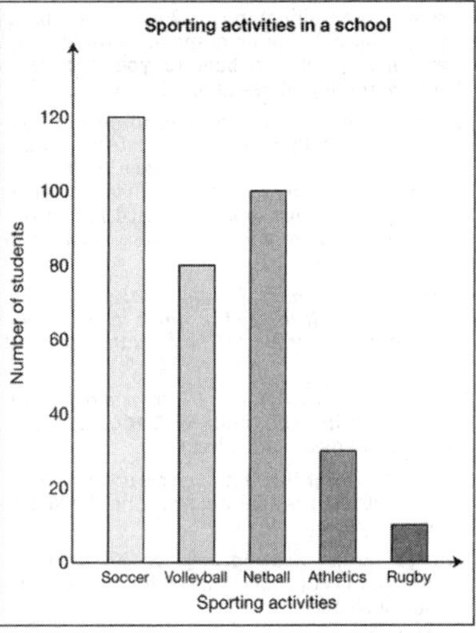

bar chart

bare² /beəʳ/ *verb* [T] to take away the thing that is covering something so that it can be seen *He bared his chest.* ○ *The dog bared its teeth.*

barefoot /beəˈfʊt/ *adjective, adverb* not wearing any shoes or socks *They ran barefoot along the wet beach.*

ˌbare inˈfinitive *noun* [C] **LANGUAGE** in grammar, the infinitive form of a verb without the word 'to'

barely /ˈbeəli/ *adverb* only just *He was barely alive when they found him.*

WORD PARTNERS FOR ***bargain***

get/pick up/snap up a bargain • a bargain price • bargain **hunting**

bargain¹ /ˈbɑːgɪn/ *noun* [C] **1 FINANCE** something that is sold for less than its usual price or its real value *At $8.95, it's a bargain.* **2** AGREEMENT when you agree to something someone else wants so that they will agree to something you want *They were prepared to* ***strike a bargain*** *to avoid more fighting.* **3 into the bargain** *mainly UK* as well as everything else *Caffeine has no good effects on health and is mildly addictive into the bargain.*

bargain² /ˈbɑːgɪn/ *verb* [I] to try to make someone agree to something better for you *Do not hesitate to* ***bargain over*** *the price.*

bargain for/on sth *phrasal verb* to expect or be prepared for something *We hadn't bargained on such a long wait.* ○ *The stormy weather proved to be* ***more than*** *anybody* ***bargained for.***

barge[1] /bɑːdʒ/ *noun* [C] a long, narrow boat with a flat bottom that is used to carry goods

barge[2] /bɑːdʒ/ *verb informal* **barge past/through/ahead, etc** to walk somewhere quickly, pushing people or things out of the way *Fred barged through the crowd.*
barge in/barge into sth *phrasal verb* to walk into a room quickly and without being invited

baritone /ˈbærɪtəʊn/ *noun* [C] **MUSIC** a man who sings in a voice that is quite low

barium /ˈbeəriəm/ *noun* [U] **CHEMISTRY** a soft, silver-white metal element (symbol **Ba**)

bark[1] /bɑːk/ *noun* **1 BIOLOGY** [U] the hard substance that covers the surface of a tree **2** [C] the sound that a dog makes

bark[2] /bɑːk/ *verb* **1** DOG [I] If a dog barks, it makes loud, short sounds. **2** SHOUT [I, T] to say something loudly and quickly *I'm sorry, I had no right to bark at you like that.*

barley /ˈbɑːli/ *noun* [U] **FOOD** a type of grain used for making food and alcoholic drinks

barmaid /ˈbɑːmeɪd/ *UK* (*US* **bartender**) *noun* [C] a woman who serves drinks in a bar

barman /ˈbɑːmən/ *UK* (*US* **bartender**) *noun* [C] *plural* **barmen** a man who serves drinks in a bar

bar mitzvah /ˌbɑːˈmɪtsvə/ *noun* [**usually no plural**] **RELIGION** a religious ceremony for a Jewish boy when he reaches the age of 13

barmy /ˈbɑːmi/ *adjective UK informal* crazy or silly *What a barmy idea!*

barn /bɑːn/ *noun* [C] **FARMING** a large building on a farm where crops or animals can be kept

barometer /bəˈrɒmɪtəʳ/ *noun* [C] **1** OPINION a way of showing what people think or what the quality of something is *Car sales are viewed as **a barometer of** consumer confidence.* **2** WEATHER a piece of equipment that measures air pressure (= the force of the air) and shows when the weather will change

baron /ˈbærᵊn/ *noun* [C] **1 SOCIETY** a man of high social rank in the UK and other parts of Europe **2** a man who owns or controls a lot of a particular industry *a wealthy media baron*

baroness /ˈbærᵊnes/ *noun* [C] **SOCIETY** a woman of the same rank as a baron or married to a baron, or a title given to a woman in the UK who has earned official respect *Baroness Thatcher*

baroque /bəˈrɒk/ *adjective* relating to the style of art, building, and music that was popular in Europe in the 17th and early 18th century, and which had a lot of decoration

barracks /ˈbærəks/ *noun* [C] *plural* **barracks** a group of buildings where soldiers live

barrage /ˈbærɑːdʒ/ (US) /bəˈrɑːdʒ/ *noun* **1 a barrage of sth** a lot of questions, complaints, or criticisms *He faced a barrage of questions about his decision to leave the show.* **2** [C] a continuous attack with several big guns

barrel /ˈbærᵊl/ *noun* [C] **1** LIQUIDS a large, round container for storing liquids such as oil or wine **2** GUN the tube in a gun that the bullet shoots out of

barren /ˈbærᵊn/ *adjective* **1 FARMING** Land that is barren does not produce crops. **2** *old-fashioned* A woman who is barren cannot have children. •**barrenness** *noun* [U]

barricade[1] /ˌbærɪˈkeɪd/ *noun* [C] something that is quickly put across a road or entrance to prevent people from going past

barricade[2] /ˌbærɪˈkeɪd/ *verb* [T] to build a barricade somewhere [**often reflexive**] *They barricaded themselves in the building* (= built a barricade so that nobody could get to them).

WORD PARTNERS FOR ***barrier***

act as/be/create/serve as a barrier **to sth** • **break through/overcome/remove** a barrier • **the biggest/the main/a major** barrier • [age/size, etc] is **no** barrier to sth •

barrier /ˈbæriəʳ/ *noun* [C] **1** FENCE a type of fence that prevents people from going into an area *Police erected barriers to hold back the crowd.* **2** LIMIT something that prevents people from doing what they want to do *Shyness is a big **barrier to** making friends.* ➲See also: **crash barrier**

barring /ˈbɑːrɪŋ/ *preposition* if something does not happen *We should arrive at about five o'clock, barring accidents.*

barrister /ˈbærɪstəʳ/ *noun* [C] **LAW** in the UK, a lawyer (= someone whose job is to know about the law and deal with legal situations) who can work in the highest courts ➲See Common Learner Error at **lawyer**

barrow /ˈbærəʊ/ *UK* (*UK/US* **wheelbarrow**) a big, open container with a wheel at the front and handles that is used to move things, especially around in a garden

bartender /ˈbɑːˌtendəʳ/ *US* (*UK* **barman/barmaid**) *noun* [C] someone who serves drinks in a bar

barter /ˈbɑːtəʳ/ *verb* [I, T] to exchange goods or services for other goods or services, without using money

basalt /ˈbæsɒlt/ *noun* [U] **GEOLOGY** a type of black rock that comes from a volcano (= mountain that explodes with hot, melted rock)

base[1] /beɪs/ *noun* [C] **1** BOTTOM the bottom part of something, or the part something rests on *I felt a sharp pain at the base of my thumb.* **2** MAIN PART the most important part of something, from which other things can develop *a solid economic base* **3** PLACE the main place where a person lives or works, or from where they do things *Keswick is an excellent base for exploring the Lake District.* **4** ARMY a place where people in the army or navy live and work *an American Air Force base* **5** ORGANIZATION the place where the main work of an organization is done *The company's European base is in Frankfurt.* **6** SUBSTANCE the main substance in a mixture *paints with an oil base* **7 SPORT** one of the four places in baseball that a player must run to in order to win a point **8 CHEMISTRY** a chemical substance with a pH (= measure of how acid something is) of more than 7 **9 MATHEMATICS** a number that is used as the most important unit in a system of counting *The binary system of counting uses*

B

base 2. **10 be off base** *US informal* to be wrong *In 1893, many of the forecasts about 1993 were way off base.* **11 touch/cover all the bases** *mainly US* to deal with every part of a situation or activity

base² /beɪs/ *verb* **be based at/in, etc** If you are based at/in, etc a particular place, that is the main place where you live or work. *The company is based in Geneva.*
base sth on/upon sth *phrasal verb* If you base something on facts or ideas, you use those facts or ideas to develop it. *Her latest TV serial is based on a true story.*

O-- **baseball** /ˈbeɪsbɔːl/ *noun* **SPORT 1** [U] a game in which two teams try to win points by hitting a ball and running around four fixed points **2** [C] the ball used in this game ➲See colour picture **Sports 2** on page Centre 15

ˈbaseball ˌcap *noun* [C] a type of hat with a long flat piece at the front to protect the eyes from the sun ➲See colour picture **Clothes** on page Centre 9

ˈbase ˌcamp *noun* [C] the place from which people go to climb mountains

basement /ˈbeɪsmənt/ *noun* [C] a room or set of rooms that is below ground level in a building

ˈbase ˌmetal *noun* [C] **CHEMISTRY** a common metal such as lead or copper which is not a precious metal (= valuable metal like gold)

ˈbase ˌrate *noun* [C] **ECONOMICS, FINANCE** a rate (= level of payment) decided by the Bank of England which banks use when deciding how much to charge for lending money

bases /ˈbeɪsiːz/ *plural of* basis

bash¹ /bæʃ/ *verb* [T] *informal* **1** to hit someone or something hard *I bashed my arm on the car door as I got out.* **2 immigrant-bashing/lawyer-bashing/union-bashing, etc** when particular groups are criticized strongly and unfairly

bash² /bæʃ/ *noun* [C] *informal* **1** [PARTY] a party **2** [HIT] a hard hit on something *a bash on the nose* **3 have a bash (at sth)** *UK informal* to try to do something *I've never been water-skiing but I'd love to have a bash at it.*

bashful /ˈbæʃfəl/ *adjective* shy and easily embarrassed •**bashfully** *adverb*

O-- **basic** /ˈbeɪsɪk/ *adjective* **1** [MAIN] [**always before noun**] being the main or most important part of something *basic ideas/principles* **2** [NECESSARY] including or providing only the things that are most necessary *basic training/services/skills* **3** [SIMPLE] very simple, with nothing special added *My software is pretty basic.*

O-- **basically** /ˈbeɪsɪkəli/ *adverb* **1** [MOST IMPORTANTLY] in the most important ways *Frazier's films are basically documentaries.* ○ *The two PCs are basically the same.* **2** [SIMPLY] used to introduce a short explanation about something *Basically, what he's saying is that we need more time.*

the basics /ˈbeɪsɪks/ *noun* the most important facts, skills, or needs *the basics of computer technology*

basil /ˈbæzəl/ (US) /ˈbeɪzəl/ *noun* [U] **FOOD** a herb with a sweet smell

basin /ˈbeɪsən/ *noun* [C] **1** [BOWL] *mainly UK* a bowl for liquids or food *a basin of water* **2** [BATHROOM] *UK* (*UK/US* **sink**) the bowl that is fixed to the wall in a bathroom, where you can wash your hands and face **3 GEOGRAPHY** a low area of land from which water flows into a river

O-- **basis** /ˈbeɪsɪs/ *noun* [C] *plural* **bases** /ˈbeɪsiːz/ **1 on a daily/monthly/regular, etc basis** how often something happens or is done *Meetings are held on a weekly basis.* **2 on a commercial/full-time/percentage, etc basis** the way something happens or is organized *We will consider claims for asylum on a case by case basis.* **3** [REASON] the reason for something *Marks are awarded* ***on the basis of*** *progress and performance.* ○ *There is no legal basis for his claim.* **4** [DEVELOPMENT] a situation, fact, or idea from which something can develop *Dani's essay can serve as* ***a basis for*** *our discussion.*

bask /bɑːsk/ *verb* [I] to sit or lie in a place that is warm *Seals basked on the rocks.*
bask in sth *phrasal verb* to enjoy the way other people admire you *They basked in the glory victory had brought them.*

O-- **basket** /ˈbɑːskɪt/ *noun* [C] **1** a container with a handle made of thin pieces of wood, wire, plastic, etc *a shopping basket* **2 SPORT** when a player throws the ball through the net in basketball ➲See also: **wastepaper basket**

O-- **basketball** /ˈbɑːskɪtbɔːl/ *noun* **SPORT 1** [U] a game in which two teams try to win points by throwing a ball through a high net **2** [C] the large ball used in the game of basketball ➲See colour picture **Sports 2** on page Centre 15

basmati (rice) /bəˌsmɑːtiˈraɪs/ *noun* [U] **FOOD** a type of South Asian rice with long grains

bass /beɪs/ *noun* **MUSIC 1** [C] a man who sings with a very low voice **2** [U] the lower half of the set of musical notes **3** [C, U] (*also* **double bass**) a large, wooden musical instrument with four strings that you play while standing up or sitting on a high chair **4** [C, U] (*also* **ˌbass guiˈtar**) an electric guitar that makes a low sound

bassoon /bəˈsuːn/ *noun* [C] **MUSIC** a long, wooden musical instrument that you blow through to make a low sound

bastard /ˈbɑːstəd/ *noun* [C] **1** [MAN] an offensive word for a man you do not like **2** [CHILD] *old-fashioned* an offensive word for a child whose parents are not married

bastion /ˈbæstiən/ *noun* [C] a place, organization, etc where particular ideas or ways of doing things are protected *the last bastion of male chauvinism*

bat¹ /bæt/ *noun* [C] **1 SPORT** a piece of wood used to hit the ball in some sports **2** a small animal like a mouse with wings that flies at night

bat² /bæt/ *verb* [I] **batting**, *past* **batted SPORT** to try to hit a ball with a bat *Rimmer batted well for Oxford.* ➲See also: not bat an **eyelid**

batch /bætʃ/ *noun* [C] a group of things or people that are dealt with at the same time or are similar in type *the university's first* ***batch of*** *students* ○ *Fry the aubergines in batches.*

ˈbatch ˌfile *noun* [C] **COMPUTING** a group of commands for a computer that are kept together in one file

ˌbatch ˈprocessing *noun* [U] **COMPUTING** when a computer does several jobs one after the other

ˈbatch proˌduction *noun* [U] in business, the production of a group of products together

bated /ˈbeɪtɪd/ *adjective* ➲See: with bated **breath**

O‑ **bath**[1] /bɑːθ/ *noun* [C] **1** CONTAINER *UK* (*US* **bathtub**) the container that you sit or lie in to wash your body ➲See colour picture **The Bathroom** on page Centre 3 **2** WASH when you wash your body in a bath, or the water in the bath [**usually singular**] *I'll just **have a** quick **bath**.* ○ *UK She **ran** herself **a bath*** (= filled a bath with water).

bath[2] /bɑːθ/ *verb* [I, T] *UK* to wash yourself or someone else in a bath *Emma usually baths the kids about seven o'clock.*

bathe /beɪð/ *verb* **1** WASH YOURSELF [I, T] to wash yourself or someone else in a bath *As a rule, I bathe every day.* **2** PART OF BODY [T] to wash part of someone's body, often because it is hurt *Bathe your eye with cool salty water.* **3** SWIM [I] *old-fashioned* to swim **4 be bathed in light** to look attractive in a beautiful light *The mountain was bathed in red-gold light from the setting sun.*

ˈbathing ˌsuit *noun* [C] a piece of clothing that you wear to swim in

bathrobe /ˈbɑːθrəʊb/ *noun* [C] a soft coat that you wear before or after a bath

O‑ **bathroom** /ˈbɑːθruːm/ *noun* [C] **1** a room with a bath, sink (= bowl for washing), and often a toilet ➲See colour picture **The Bathroom** on page Centre 3 **2 go to the bathroom** *US* to use the toilet ➲See Common Learner Error at **toilet**

bathtub /ˈbɑːθtʌb/ *US* (*UK* **bath**) *noun* [C] the container that you sit or lie in to wash your body ➲See colour picture **The Bathroom** on page Centre 3

batik /bætˈiːk/ *noun* [U] **ART** a method of printing patterns on cloth, in which wax is put on the cloth before it has colour put on it

bat mitzvah /ˌbætˈmɪtsvə/ *noun* [**usually singular**] **RELIGION** a religious ceremony for a Jewish girl when she reaches the age of 12 or 13

baton /ˈbætᵊn/ (US) /bəˈtɑːn/ *noun* [C] **1 MUSIC** a thin stick used to control the rhythm of a group of musicians **2** a thick stick that a police officer uses as a weapon **3 SPORT** a stick that a runner passes to the next person in a race

batsman /ˈbætsmən/ *noun* [C] *plural* **batsmen** *UK* **SPORT** the person who is trying to hit the ball in cricket ➲See colour picture **Sports 2** on page Centre 15

battalion /bəˈtæliən/ *noun* [C] a large group of soldiers made from several smaller groups

batter[1] /ˈbætəʳ/ *noun* **1 FOOD** [U] a mixture of flour, milk, and often eggs used to make cakes and pancakes (= thin fried cakes), and to cover fish, etc before it is fried **2 SPORT** [C] the person who is trying to hit the ball in baseball ➲See colour picture **Sports 2** on page Centre 15

batter[2] /ˈbætəʳ/ *verb* [I, T] to hit someone or something repeatedly very hard *If you don't open up we'll **batter** the door **down**.* ○ *Waves **battered against** the rocks.*

battered /ˈbætəd/ *adjective* old and not in very good condition *a battered copy of her favourite novel*

battering /ˈbætərɪŋ/ *noun* [C] when someone or something is hit repeatedly, criticized strongly, or damaged badly [**usually singular**] *The prime minister has **taken** quite **a battering** this week.*

O‑ **battery** /ˈbætᵊri/ *noun* **1** [C] an object that provides electricity for things such as radios, toys, or cars *My car has got **a flat battery*** (= one that has no electricity left). **2 LAW** [U] *formal* the crime of hitting someone *assault and battery*

battery

WORD PARTNERS FOR ***battle***

face/fight/lose/win a battle • a **bitter/long-running/uphill** battle • a **legal** battle • a battle **for** sth • a battle **with** sb **/between** sb and sb

battle[1] /ˈbætl/ *noun* **1** WAR [C, U] a fight between two armies in a war *the Battle of Waterloo* ○ *Her grandfather was killed **in battle*** (= while fighting). **2** POWER [C] when two people or groups compete against each other or have an argument about something *a **battle for** control in the boardroom* **3** PROBLEMS/ILLNESS [C] a fight against something that is hurting or destroying you *a long battle against cancer* **4 fight a losing battle** to try hard to do something when there is no chance that you will succeed *I try to control what my children watch on TV, but I think I'm fighting a losing battle.*

battle[2] /ˈbætl/ *verb* [I] to try very hard to do something that is difficult *Both teams **are battling for** a place in the Premier League.* ○ *Throughout the campaign Johnson was **battling against** severe health problems.*

baud /bɔːd/ *noun* [C] **MEASURES** a unit that measures how fast electronic data is sent

baulk /bɔːk, bɔːlk/ *UK* (*UK/US* **balk**) *verb* [I] to not want to do something that is unpleasant or difficult *Most people would **baulk at** paying these kind of prices for clothes.*

bauxite /ˈbɔːk.saɪt/ *noun* [U] **GEOLOGY** a type of rock from which aluminium is produced

bawl /bɔːl/ *verb* [I, T] *informal* to shout or cry loudly

bay /beɪ/ *noun* **1 GEOGRAPHY** [C] an area of coast where the land curves in *a sandy bay* **2** [C] a part of a building or place that is used for a particular purpose *a parking bay* **3 keep/hold sth at bay** to prevent something unpleasant from coming near you or from happening *Gunmen kept police at bay for almost four hours.*

bayonet /ˈbeɪənət/ *noun* [C] a knife that is fastened onto the end of a long gun

bazaar /bəˈzɑːʳ/ *noun* [C] **1** MARKET a market in Eastern countries **2** SALE a sale where goods are sold to raise money for a school, church, etc

B

B&B /ˌbiːənˈbiː/ *noun* [C] *abbreviation for* bed and breakfast (= a small hotel or private house where you pay for a room to sleep in for the night and a meal in the morning)

BBC /ˌbiːbiːˈsiː/ *noun abbreviation for* British Broadcasting Corporation: one of the main television and radio companies in the United Kingdom *a cookery programme on BBC2*

BC /biːˈsiː/ *abbreviation for* Before Christ: used to show that a particular year came before the birth of Christ *331 BC*

B-cell /ˈbiːsel/ (*also* **B lymphocyte**) *noun* [C] **BIOLOGY** a type of blood cell that produces antibodies (= substances in the blood that fight disease)

O‒**be**[1] *strong form* /biː/ *weak forms* /bi, bɪ/ *verb pres. participle* **being**, *past tense* **was**, *past participle* **been** **1** [DESCRIBE] used to describe or give information about someone or something *I'm sixteen.* ○ *I'm Andy.* ○ *Her mother is a teacher.* ○ *He's German.* ○ *They were very upset.* ○ *He was very ill last year.* ○ *I'm sorry I'm late.* ○ *They've been unlucky.* ○ *Be quiet!* **2** **there is/there are/there was, etc** used to show that someone or something exists *There were about fifty people at the party.* ○ *Is there a bank near here?* **3** [POSITION] used to show the position of someone or something *It's been in the cupboard for months.* ○ *She's in the kitchen.* **4** **it is/it was, etc** used to give a fact or your opinion about something *It's not surprising that she left him.* ○ *It's a good idea to keep a spare key somewhere safe.*

be[2] *strong form* /biː/ *weak forms* /bi, bɪ/ *auxiliary verb* **1** used with the present participle of other verbs to describe actions that are or were still continuing *Where are you going?* ○ *How long have you been sitting there?* ○ *He was standing by the window.* ○ *He's working at the moment.* **2** used with the present participle of other verbs, and sometimes after a modal verb, to describe actions that will happen in the future *I'm going to France next week.* ○ *I'll be coming back on Tuesday.* **3** used with the past participle of other verbs to form the passive *He was injured in a car crash.* ○ *The results will be announced next week.* **4** used in conditional sentences to say what might happen *If he were to offer me the job, I'd take it.* **5** used to say that someone must or should do something *You are not to see him again.* **6** *formal* used to show that something has been organized *They are to stay with us when they arrive.*

WORD PARTNERS FOR ***beach***

on the beach • a **sandy** beach • a beach **house**

O‒**beach** /biːtʃ/ *noun* [C] **GEOGRAPHY** an area of sand or rocks next to the sea

beacon /ˈbiːkᵊn/ *noun* [C] a light on a hill or in a tower that warns people of something or is a signal or guide

bead /biːd/ *noun* [C] **1** [JEWELLERY] a small, round ball of glass, plastic, or wood that is used for making jewellery *a necklace of coloured glass beads* **2** [LIQUID] a small drop of liquid on a surface *beads of sweat*

beak /biːk/ *noun* [C] **BIOLOGY** the hard part of a bird's mouth

beaker /ˈbiːkəʳ/ *noun* [C] *UK* a tall cup without a handle, usually made of plastic

beam[1] /biːm/ *noun* [C] **1** [LIGHT] a line of light shining from something *a laser beam* **2** [WOOD] a long, thick piece of wood, metal, or concrete that is used to support weight in a building or other structure **3** [SMILE] *UK* a big smile

beam[2] /biːm/ *verb* **1** [SMILE] [I] to smile very happily *The baby **beamed at** me.* **2** [SEND] [T] to send a television or radio signal [**often passive**] *The match was beamed live by satellite around the world.* **3** [SHINE] [I] If the sun or the moon beams, it shines brightly.

ˈ**beam** ˌ**balance** *noun* [C] **PHYSICS** a piece of equipment used by scientists to measure the mass of an object by hanging it from one end of a balanced bar

beamer /ˈbiːməʳ/ *noun* [C] a data projector: a machine that allows you to show words or images on a screen or wall

bean /biːn/ *noun* [C] **FOOD** **1** a seed of some climbing plants, that is used as food *soya beans* **2** a seed case of some climbing plants that is eaten as a vegetable *green beans* **3** a plant seed used to make coffee and chocolate *coffee beans* ➲See also: **baked beans, runner bean**

bean curd /ˈbiːnkɜːd/ *noun* [U] **FOOD** tofu (= a soft, pale food made from the soya bean plant)

bear[1] /beəʳ/ *verb* [T] *past tense* **bore**, *past participle* **borne** **1** [ACCEPT] to accept someone or something unpleasant *She **couldn't bear** the thought of him suffering.* ○ *I like her, but I **can't bear** her friends.* [+ **to do sth**] *How can you bear to watch?* ○ *The pain was too much to bear.* **2** **bear a resemblance/relation, etc to sb/sth** to be similar to someone or something *He bears a striking resemblance to his father.* **3** [CARRY] *formal* to carry something *He came in, bearing a tray of drinks.* **4** [WEIGHT] to support the weight of something *I don't think that chair will bear his weight.* **5** **bear the responsibility/cost, etc** to accept that you are responsible for something, you should pay for something, etc *He must bear some responsibility for the appalling conditions in the prison.* **6** [FEELING] to continue to have a bad feeling towards someone *They were rude to her in the past, but she's not the kind of woman who **bears grudges*** (= continues to be angry). **7** [HAVE CHILD] *formal* to give birth to a child *She has been told that she will never bear children.* **8** [NAME] to have or show a particular name, picture, or symbol *The shop bore his family name.* **9** **bear left/right** to turn left or right *Bear right at the next set of traffic lights.* ➲See also: bear **fruit**, **grin** and bear it

bear sb/sth out *phrasal verb* to prove that someone is right or that something is true *The facts do not bear out his claims.*

bear with sb *phrasal verb* to be patient and wait while someone does something *If you'll bear with me a moment, I'll just find your details.*

bear² /beəʳ/ *noun* [C] a large, strong, wild animal with thick fur ➲See also: **polar bear, teddy bear**

bearable /ˈbeərəbl/ *adjective* If an unpleasant situation is bearable, you can accept or deal with it. *Having her there* ***made*** *life at home more* ***bearable*** *for me.* ➲Opposite **unbearable**

beard /bɪəd/ *noun* [C] the hair that grows on a man's chin (= the bottom of his face) •**bearded** *adjective* with a beard

bearer /ˈbeərəʳ/ *noun* [C] a person who brings or carries something *I am sorry to be* ***the bearer of*** *bad news.*

bearing /ˈbeərɪŋ/ *noun* **have a bearing on sth** to have an influence on something or a relationship to something *What you decide now could have a considerable bearing on your future.*

bearings /ˈbeərɪŋz/ *noun* **1 get/find your bearings a** to find out where you are *She looked at the sun to find her bearings.* **b** to become confident in a new situation *When you start a new job, it can take some time to get your bearings.* **2 lose your bearings** to become confused about where you are

ˈbear ˌmarket *noun* [C] **ECONOMICS** a time when the price of shares (= parts of the value of a company that can be sold or bought) is falling and a lot of people are selling them

beast /biːst/ *noun* [C] **1** ANIMAL *formal* an animal, especially a large or wild one **2** PERSON *old-fashioned* an annoying or cruel person

beastly /ˈbiːstli/ *adjective old-fashioned* unkind or unpleasant

O⁻**beat¹** /biːt/ *verb past tense* **beat**, *past participle* **beaten**, *also US* **beat 1** DEFEAT [T] to defeat someone in a competition *Our team beat Germany 3-1.* ➲See Common Learner Error at **win 2** HIT [I, T] to hit a person or animal hard many times *She beat the dog with a stick.* ○ *She was beaten to death.* **3** SOUND [I, T] to hit against something hard, making a continuous or regular sound *soldiers beating drums* ○ *Rain beat against the windows.* **4** GET RID OF [T] to get rid of something bad *I'm determined to beat this illness.* **5 ANATOMY, BIOLOGY** [I] When your heart beats, it makes regular movements and sounds. *By the time the doctor arrived, his heart had stopped beating.* **6** BE BETTER [T] to be better than something [+ doing sth] *Being at the youth club beats sitting at home.* **7 you can't beat sth** used to emphasize that something is best *You can't beat Pedro's for a great pizza.* **8 take a lot of/some, etc beating** to be so good or enjoyable that it is hard to find anything better *This ice cream takes some beating.* **9 FOOD** [T] to mix food using hard, quick movements *Beat the egg whites until they are stiff.* **10 It beats me** *informal* something that you say when you do not understand a situation or someone's behaviour *It beats me why she goes out with him.* ➲See also: beat about the **bush**, beat/knock the (living) **daylights** out of sb, off the beaten **track¹**

beat down *phrasal verb* If the sun beats down, it is very hot and bright.

beat sb down *phrasal verb UK* to persuade someone to charge you less for something

beat sb/sth off *phrasal verb* to manage to defeat someone who is attacking you

beat sb to sth *phrasal verb* to do something before someone else does it *I was going to ask her to the party, but you beat me to it.*

beat sb up *phrasal verb* to attack someone by hitting or kicking them many times *He beat up one of the other prisoners.*

beat² /biːt/ *noun* [C] **1 ANATOMY** a regular sound that is made by your heart or by something hitting a surface *a heart beat* ○ *the beat of a drum* **2 MUSIC** the main rhythm of a piece of music *loud music with a repetitive beat* **3** the area of a town or city that a police officer walks around regularly *Having more police officers* ***on the beat*** (= walking around their beat) *should help to reduce crime.*

beating /ˈbiːtɪŋ/ *noun* **1** [C] when someone hits another person hard many times **2 take a beating** to be defeated, criticized, or damaged *Our team took a severe beating in the tournament.*

the Beaufort scale /ˈbəʊfət ˌskeɪl/ *noun* [no plural] **GEOGRAPHY** a set of numbers used for measuring and comparing wind speeds

beautician /bjuːˈtɪʃᵊn/ *noun* [C] someone whose job is to improve people's appearance by treatments to their hair, skin, etc

OTHER WAYS OF SAYING ***beautiful***

If a person (man or woman), is beautiful, we can say that they are **attractive** or **good-looking**. The adjective **handsome** is also sometimes used for men, and **pretty** for women: *Her husband is really* ***good-looking.*** • *Your daughter is very* ***pretty.***

If someone, especially a woman, is extremely beautiful, you can say that they are **gorgeous** or **stunning**: *You look* ***gorgeous*** *in that dress!* • *I think she's* ***stunning.***

The adjectives **breathtaking**, **lovely** and **gorgeous** are often used to describe scenery that is very beautiful. *The views from the window were* ***breathtaking.*** • *We drove through some* ***gorgeous*** *countryside.*

The adjective **exquisite** is sometimes used to describe objects which are very beautiful and often delicate: *They do the most* ***exquisite*** *hand-made decorations.*

O⁻**beautiful** /ˈbjuːtɪfᵊl/ *adjective* **1** ATTRACTIVE very attractive *a beautiful woman* ○ *beautiful scenery* **2** PLEASANT very pleasant *beautiful music* ○ *It's a beautiful day* (= the sun is shining). •**beautifully** *adverb a beautifully illustrated book* ○ *She sings beautifully.*

WORD PARTNERS FOR ***beauty***

great/sheer/stunning beauty • **natural** beauty • beauty **products**

O⁻**beauty** /ˈbjuːti/ *noun* **1** QUALITY [U] the quality of being beautiful *The whole area is famous for its* ***natural beauty.*** ○ *a beauty contest* (= competition to find the most beautiful woman) **2 the beauty of sth** the quality that makes something especially good or attractive *The beauty of the plan is that it won't cost anything.* **3 a beauty product/treatment** a product or treatment to make you more beautiful **4** EXCELLENT THING [C] *informal* something that is an excellent example of its type *That last goal was a* *beauty.* **5** WOMAN [C] *old-fashioned* a beautiful woman

ˈbeauty ˌsalon (*also US* **ˈbeautyˌparlor**) *noun* [C] a place where you can have beauty treatments

ˈbeauty ˌspot *noun* [C] **1** PLACE *UK* a place in the countryside that is very beautiful **2** MARK a small dark mark on someone's face

beaver /ˈbiːvəʳ/ *noun* [C] an animal with brown fur, a long, flat tail, and sharp teeth, which builds dams (= walls made of pieces of wood) across rivers

became /bɪˈkeɪm/ *past tense of* become

because /bɪˈkɒz, bɪˈkəz/ *conjunction* used to give a reason for something *I phoned because I needed to talk to you.* ○ *I can't come out tonight because I've got too much homework.*

because of /bɪˈkɒzəv, bɪˈkəzəv/ *preposition* as a result of someone or something *We got into all this trouble because of you.*

beck /bek/ *noun* **be at sb's beck and call** to be always ready and willing to do what someone wants

beckon /ˈbekᵊn/ *verb* **1** WAVE [I, T] to move your hand, head, etc to show someone that you would like them to come nearer *She* ***beckoned to*** *the waiter.* **2** BE LIKELY [I] to seem very likely to happen *A career as a lead guitarist beckoned.* **3** BE ATTRACTIVE [I] If a place beckons, it is very attractive to you, and you want to go there. *The bright lights of London beckoned.*

become /bɪˈkʌm/ *verb, past tense* **became** *past participle* **become** **1 become available/rich/a writer, etc** to begin to be something *They became great friends.* ○ *She wants to become a teacher when she leaves school.* ○ *This style of skirt is becoming fashionable.* **2 what/whatever became of sb/sth** something you say when you want to know what has happened to someone *Whatever became of your friend Harry?*

becquerel /ˌbekəˈrel/ *noun* [C] **MEASURES** a unit of measurement for radioactivity

WORD PARTNERS FOR ***bed***

go to bed • **be in /lie in/be tucked up in** bed • **get into/get out of** bed • **make** the bed • **be on** the bed • **share** a bed • a **double/single** bed

bed[1] /bed/ *noun* **1** FURNITURE [C, U] a piece of furniture that you sleep on *a* **single/double bed** ○ *What time did you* ***go to bed*** *last night?* ○ *She was lying* ***in bed*** *when I arrived.* ○ *He had only just* ***got out of bed.*** ○ *Have you* ***made the bed*** (= tidied the bed after you have slept in it)? **2** GROUND [C] a piece of ground that is used for growing plants, especially flowers *a flower bed* **3** BOTTOM [C] the ground at the bottom of the sea, a river, etc *the sea bed* ⊃See also: **bunk beds**

ˌbed and ˈbreakfast (*also* **B & B**) *noun* [C] a small hotel or private house where you pay for a room to sleep in for the night and a meal in the morning

bedclothes /ˈbedkləʊðz/ *noun* [plural] the sheets and other pieces of cloth that cover you and keep you warm in bed

bedding /ˈbedɪŋ/ *noun* [U] **1** the sheets and other pieces of cloth that cover you and keep you warm in bed **2 FARMING** material such as hay (= dried grass) that animals sleep on

bedraggled /bɪˈdrægld/ *adjective* untidy, and often wet and dirty

bedrock /ˈbedrɒk/ *noun* [U] *formal* a situation, idea, or principle that provides a strong base for something *Family life is* ***the bedrock of*** *a stable society.*

bedroom /ˈbedruːm/ *noun* [C] a room used for sleeping in

bedside /ˈbedsaɪd/ *noun* [no plural] **1** the area at the side of a bed *He was* ***at*** *her* ***bedside*** *in the hospital.* ○ *a* ***bedside table/lamp*** **2 bedside manner** a doctor's ability to make the people they are treating feel comfortable *My surgeon has a wonderful bedside manner.*

bedsit /ˈbedsɪt/ *noun* [C] *UK* a rented room where you live, sleep, and cook your meals

bedspread /ˈbedspred/ *noun* [C] a cloth cover that is put over a bed

bedtime /ˈbedtaɪm/ *noun* [C, U] the time that you usually go to bed

bee /biː/ *noun* [C] a flying insect that has a yellow and black body and makes honey (= sweet, sticky food) *the queen bee*

beech /biːtʃ/ *noun* [C, U] a large tree with a smooth grey trunk (= main, vertical part) that produces small nuts

beef[1] /biːf/ *noun* [U] **FOOD** the meat of a cow *roast beef* ⊃See also: **ground beef**

beef[2] /biːf/ *verb*

beef sth up *phrasal verb* to make something stronger or more important *The company wants to beef up its sales force by employing new graduates.*

beefburger /ˈbiːfˌbɜːgəʳ/ *UK* (*UK/US* **hamburger**) *noun* [C] **FOOD** very small pieces of meat that are pressed together into a round flat shape, cooked, and eaten between bread

beehive /ˈbiːhaɪv/ (*also* **hive**) *noun* [C] a special container where people keep bees

been /biːn, bɪn/ *verb* **have been to** to have gone to a place and come back *Have you ever been to Thailand?* ⊃Inflection of **be**

beep /biːp/ *verb* **1** MACHINE [I] If a machine beeps, it makes a short, high noise. **2** CAR [I, T] If a car horn (= part you press to make a warning sound) beeps or if you beep it, it makes a loud noise. *Beep the horn to let me know that you're here.* •**beep** *noun* [C]

beeper /ˈbiːpəʳ/ (*also UK* **bleeper**) *noun* [C] a small piece of electronic equipment that you carry which makes a short high sound when someone wants to talk to you

beer /bɪəʳ/ *noun* [C, U] **FOOD** an alcoholic drink made from grain, or a glass or container of this drink *a pint of beer*

beet /biːt/ *US* (*UK* **beetroot**) *noun* [C, U] **FOOD** a round, dark red vegetable, that is usually cooked and eaten cold

beetle /ˈbiːtl/ *noun* [C] an insect with a hard, usually black, shiny body

beetroot /ˈbiːtruːt/ *UK* (*US* **beet**) *noun* [C, U] **FOOD** a round, dark red vegetable, that is usually cooked and eaten cold

befall /bɪˈfɔːl/ *verb* [T] *past tense* **befell**, *past participle* **befallen** *formal* If something bad befalls you, it happens to you. *A dreadful misfortune has befallen the family.*

befit /bɪˈfɪt/ *verb* [T] **befitting**, *past* **befitted** *formal* to be suitable or right for someone or something *He was given a huge welcome, **as befits** such a hero.*

O‑ **before**[1] /bɪˈfɔːʳ/ *preposition* **1** EARLIER earlier than something or someone *a week before Christmas* ○ *She arrived before me.* [+ **doing sth**] *Think hard before accepting the offer.* **2** IN FRONT OF in a position in front of someone or something *I've never performed this before an audience.* ○ *He stood before her, shaking.* **3** PLACE at a place that you arrive at first when travelling towards another place *The hospital is just before the bridge.* **4** IN ORDER in front of someone or something in an order or a list *P comes before Q in the alphabet.* **5** IMPORTANCE treated as more important than someone or something *They always **put** the children's needs **before** their own.* **6** EXAMINATION being formally examined or considered by a group *He appeared before the court dressed in jeans.*

O‑ **before**[2] /bɪˈfɔːʳ/ *conjunction* **1** EARLIER earlier than the time when something happens *He was a teacher before he became famous.* ○ *Before I could warn him, he had fallen.* **2** TO AVOID STH in order to avoid something bad happening *Put that stick down before you hurt someone.* **3** UNTIL until *It took a few moments before I realized that he was lying.*

O‑ **before**[3] /bɪˈfɔːʳ/ *adverb* at an earlier time, or on a previous occasion *I've never seen her before.* ○ *We had spoken on the phone a few days before.*

beforehand /bɪˈfɔːhænd/ *adverb* before a particular time or event *Did you know beforehand what they had planned to do?*

befriend /bɪˈfrend/ *verb* [T] *formal* to be friendly to someone, especially someone who needs support or help

beg /beg/ *verb* **begging**, *past* **begged** **1** FOOD/MONEY [I] to ask someone for food or money, because you do not have any *Young children were begging on the streets.* **2** STRONG REQUEST [I, T] to make a very strong and urgent request *She **begged** him **for** help.* [+ **to do sth**] *I begged her not to go.* ⊃See also: I beg your **pardon**[2].

began /bɪˈgæn/ *past tense of* begin

beggar /ˈbegəʳ/ *noun* [C] a poor person who lives by asking other people for money and food

O‑ **begin** /bɪˈgɪn/ *verb* **beginning**, *past tense* **began**, *past participle* **begun** **1** START TO DO [I, T] to start to do something [+ **to do sth**] *The children began to cry.* [+ **doing sth**] *Have they begun building the wall yet?* ○ *She began her career as a journalist on a local newspaper.* **2** START TO HAPPEN [I] to start to happen *What time does the film begin?* **3 begin with sth** to have something at the start *Local phone numbers begin with 1223.* **4 to begin with a** AT THE START at the start of a situation *To begin with, the two girls got on well.* **b** GIVE REASON used to give the first important reason for something *To begin with, we can't leave the children alone.*

beginner /bɪˈgɪnəʳ/ *noun* [C] someone who is starting to do or learn something for the first time *I'm a **complete beginner** at yoga.*

O‑ **beginning** /bɪˈgɪnɪŋ/ *noun* [C] the first part of something or the start of something [**usually singular**] *We met **at the beginning of** 1998.* ○ *Things went well **in the beginning**.*

begrudge /bɪˈgrʌdʒ/ *verb* [T] **1** WANT SOMETHING to feel upset because someone has something that you would like [+ **two objects**] *I don't begrudge him his success.* **2** NOT WANT TO DO to feel upset because you have to spend money on something or spend time doing something *They begrudge every penny that they have to spend on him.*

beguile /bɪˈgaɪl/ *verb* [T] *formal* to attract someone very much, sometimes in order to deceive them [**often passive**] *I can see how people are beguiled by his charm.* ○ *a beguiling smile*

begun /bɪˈgʌn/ *past participle of* begin

behalf /bɪˈhɑːf/ *noun* **on sb's behalf** If you do something on someone's behalf, you do it for them or instead of them. *We are campaigning on behalf of thousands of refugees.* ○ *Will you accept the prize on my behalf?*

O‑ **behave** /bɪˈheɪv/ *verb* [I] **1** DO/SAY to do or say things in a particular way *to behave badly/stupidly* ○ *They are behaving like children.* **2** POLITELY (*also* **behave yourself**) to be polite and not make a situation difficult *Try to behave.* ○ *The children can only come if they promise to behave themselves.* ⊃Opposite **misbehave**

-behaved /bɪˈheɪvd/ *suffix* used after a word describing how someone behaves *a badly-behaved child* ⊃See also: **well-behaved**

WORD PARTNERS FOR ***behaviour***

anti-social/bad/disruptive/good/normal behaviour

O‑ **behaviour** *UK* (*US* **behavior**) /bɪˈheɪvjəʳ/ *noun* [U] the way that you behave ***good/bad behaviour*** ○ *Did you notice anything odd about his behaviour?*

behavioural *UK* (*US* **behavioral**) /bɪˈheɪvjərəl/ *adjective* relating to behaviour *behavioural changes/problems*

behead /bɪˈhed/ *verb* [T] to cut someone's head off

beheld /bɪˈheld/ *past of* behold

O‑ **behind**[1] /bɪˈhaɪnd/ *preposition* **1** BACK at or to the back of someone or something *Close the door behind you.* ○ *The pub is behind the train station.* **2** LESS SUCCESSFUL slower or less successful than someone or something *Our team is 3 points behind the winners.* ○ *The building work is already **behind schedule*** (= late). **3** CAUSING causing something, or responsible for something *What was the reason behind her decision to leave?* **4** SUPPORTING giving your help or support to someone *The group is 100 percent behind her.* **5** NOT AFFECTING If a bad experience or your own bad behaviour is behind you, it does not exist or affect your life now. *He's **put** his criminal past **behind** him.*

O‑ **behind**[2] /bɪˈhaɪnd/ *adverb* **1** BACK at or to the back of someone or something *Somebody grabbed me from behind.* **2** SLOWER slower or later than someone else, or than you should be *She's behind with the rent* (= is late to pay it). **3** PLACE in the place where someone or something was before *You go on ahead. I'll* ***stay behind*** *and tidy up.* ○ *When we got to the restaurant, I realized that I had* ***left*** *my purse* ***behind.***

B

behind³ /bɪˈhaɪnd/ *noun* [C] *informal* the part of your body that you sit on

behold /bɪˈhəʊld/ *verb* [T] *past* **beheld** *literary* to see something

beige /beɪʒ/ *noun* [U] a pale brown colour •**beige** *adjective* ➲See colour picture **Colours** on page Centre 12

being¹ /ˈbiːɪŋ/ *noun* **1** [C] a living person or imaginary creature *human beings* **2 come into being** to start to exist *The new law comes into being next month.* ➲See also: **well-being**

being² /ˈbiːɪŋ/ *present participle of* be

belated /bɪˈleɪtɪd/ *adjective* coming late, or later than expected *a* ***belated attempt*** *to win votes* •**belatedly** *adverb Supermarkets have belatedly realized the purchasing power of mothers.*

belch¹ /beltʃ/ *verb* **1** NOISE [I] to make a sudden noise as air from your stomach comes out through your mouth **2** SMOKE [T] (*also* **belch out**) to produce a lot of smoke, fire, gas, etc *tall chimneys belching smoke*

belch² /beltʃ/ *noun* [C] the noise you make when you belch

beleaguered /bɪˈliːgəd/ *adjective formal* having a lot of problems *the beleaguered farming industry*

belfry /ˈbelfri/ *noun* [C] the tower of a church where the bells are hung

belie /bɪˈlaɪ/ *verb* [T] **belying,** *past* **belied** *formal* to give a wrong idea about something *His shy manner belied his very sharp mind.*

WORD PARTNERS FOR ***belief***

a firm / mistaken / sincere / strong / widespread/widely-held belief • **have/hold** a belief • a belief **in** sth • **in the** belief **that**

O-■ **belief** /bɪˈliːf/ *noun* **1** TRUE [**U no plural**] when you believe that something is true or real *It is a* ***widely-held belief*** *that smoking helps you lose weight.* ○ *She married him* ***in the belief that*** *he would change.* ➲Opposite **disbelief 2** IDEA [C, U] an idea that you are certain is true ***religious/political beliefs*** **3** EFFECTIVE [**U, no plural**] the feeling that someone or something is effective or right *a* ***belief in*** *social justice* **4 beyond belief** too bad, good, difficult, etc to be real *The evil of this man is beyond belief.*

believable /bɪˈliːvəbl/ *adjective* If something is believable, you can believe that it could be true or real. ➲Opposite **unbelievable**

O-■ **believe** /bɪˈliːv/ *verb* **1** TRUE [T] to think that something is true, or that what someone says is true [+ (**that**)] *They believe that their health has suffered because of the chemicals.* ○ *Do you believe him?* ➲Opposite **disbelieve 2** THINK [T] to think something, without being completely sure *The murderer is believed to be in his thirties.* **3 RELIGION** [I] to have religious beliefs **4 not believe your eyes/ears** to be very surprised when you see someone or something, or when you hear what someone says *I couldn't believe my ears when Dan said they were getting married.* **5 believe it or not** used to say that something is true although it seems surprising *He even remembered my birthday, believe it or not.*

believe in sth *phrasal verb* to be certain that something exists *I believe in life after death.*

believe in sth/doing sth *phrasal verb* to be confident that something is effective or right *He believes in saying what he thinks.*

believer /bɪˈliːvəʳ/ *noun* [C] **1 RELIGION** a person who has a religious belief **2 a firm/great/strong, etc believer in sth/doing sth** someone who has confidence in a particular idea or way of doing things *She's a firm believer in freedom of speech.*

belittle /bɪˈlɪtl/ *verb* [T] *formal* to say that someone or something is not very important or not very good

O-■ **bell** /bel/ *noun* [C] **1** INSTRUMENT a hollow, metal object, shaped like a cup, that makes a ringing sound when you hit it *the sound of church bells ringing* **2** DOOR ETC an electrical object that makes a ringing sound when you press a switch *Please* ***ring the bell*** *for attention.* **3 give sb a bell** *UK informal* to telephone someone **4 ring a bell** If a word, especially a name, rings a bell, you think you have heard it before.

belligerent /bəˈlɪdʒərənt/ *adjective* wanting to fight or argue

bellow /ˈbeləʊ/ *verb* [**I, T**] to shout something in a loud voice •**bellow** *noun* [C]

belly /ˈbeli/ *noun* [C] *informal* your stomach (= organ where food is digested), or the front part of your body between your chest and your legs

ˈbelly ˌbutton *noun* [C] *informal* the small, round, and usually hollow place on your stomach, where you were connected to your mother before birth

O-■ **belong** /bɪˈlɒŋ/ *verb* **1 belong in/on/there, etc** to be in the right place *That chair belongs in the dining room.* **2** [I] to feel happy and comfortable in a place or with a group of people *I never felt that I belonged there.*

O-■ **belong to sb** *phrasal verb* If something belongs to you, you own it. *This necklace belonged to my grandmother.*

belong to sth *phrasal verb* to be a member of a group or organization *We belong to the same youth club.*

belongings /bɪˈlɒŋɪŋz/ *noun* [**plural**] the things that you own *I took a few* ***personal belongings*** *with me.*

beloved /bɪˈlʌvɪd/ *adjective literary* very much loved *in memory of our beloved son*

O-■ **below** /bɪˈləʊ/ *adverb, preposition* **1** POSITION in a lower position than someone or something else *Send your answers to the address below* (= lower on the page or on a later page). **2** LESS less than an amount or level *The temperature there rarely drops below 22°C.* ○ *His work is* ***below average.*** **3** RANK lower in rank *Monica is a grade below me.*

be͵low the line pro'motion *noun* [U] ways of persuading people to buy a product that a business can do itself, for example by offering low prices

O-ʷ**belt¹** /belt/ *noun* [C] **1** WAIST a long, thin piece of leather, cloth, or plastic that you wear around your waist ➲See colour picture **Clothes** on page Centre 9 **2 GEOGRAPHY** an area of a particular type of land, or an area where a particular group of people live *the **commuter belt*** ○ *a narrow belt of trees* **3** MACHINE part of a machine that moves in a circle to carry objects or to make a machine work *The car needs a new fan belt.* **4 have sth under your belt** to have already achieved, learnt, or done something important *At 18, she already has several victories under her belt.* **5 tighten your belt** to try to spend less money ➲See also: **conveyor belt, green belt, safety belt, seat belt**

belt² /belt/ *verb informal* **1 belt along/down/through, etc** *UK* to move very fast *He came belting down the street.* **2** [T] to hit someone or something very hard

belt sth out *phrasal verb* to sing something very loudly

belt up *phrasal verb UK informal* used to tell someone to stop talking or making a noise *Just belt up, would you? I'm trying to concentrate.*

belying /bɪ'laɪɪŋ/ *present participle of* belie

bemused /bɪ'mjuːzd/ *adjective* slightly confused *He seemed **bemused by** all the attention.*

bench /benʃ/ *noun* [C] **1** a long seat for two or more people, usually made of wood or metal *a park bench* **2 the bench a SPORT** in some sports, a place where players sit when they are not playing **b LAW** a judge in court, or judges as a group *Please address your comments to the bench.*

benchmark /'benʃmɑːk/ *noun* [C] a level of quality with which other things of the same type can be compared *Her performance set a new **benchmark for** ballet dancing.*

O-ʷ**bend¹** /bend/ *verb* [I, T] *past* **bent 1** BODY to move your body or part of your body so that it is not straight *He was **bending over** to tie his shoelaces.* ○ *Bend your knees when lifting heavy objects.* **2** OBJECT to become curved, or to make something become curved *The trees were bending in the wind.* ○ *The road bent sharply to the left.* ➲See also: bend over **backwards**, bend/stretch the rules (**rule¹**)

WORD PARTNERS FOR ***bend***

a **sharp/tight** bend • a bend **in** sth

bend² /bend/ *noun* [C] **1** a curved part of something *a bend in the road/river* **2 drive/send sb round the bend** *informal* to make someone very angry, especially by continuing to do something annoying ➲See also: **hairpin bend**

beneath¹ /bɪ'niːθ/ *adverb, preposition* **1** UNDER under something, or in a lower position than something *He hid the letter beneath a pile of papers.* ○ *She looked out of the window at the children playing beneath.* **2** NOT GOOD ENOUGH If someone or something is beneath you, you think they are not good enough for you. *He thinks housework is beneath him.*

benefactor /'benɪfæktəʳ/ *noun* [C] someone who gives money to help an organization or person

beneficial /͵benɪ'fɪʃəl/ *adjective* helpful or useful *Exercise is **beneficial to** almost everyone.*

beneficiary /͵benɪ'fɪʃəri/ *noun* [C] *formal* someone who receives money, help, etc from something or someone else *They were the **beneficiaries of** free education.*

WORD PARTNERS FOR ***benefit***

enjoy/have/offer/reap benefits • [the drawbacks/risks, etc] **outweigh** the benefits • **great/long-term/maximum/potential/tangible** benefit • **of** benefit **to** sb

benefit¹ /'benɪfɪt/ *noun* [C, U] **1** something that helps you or gives you an advantage *I've **had the benefit of** a happy childhood.* **2 SOCIETY** money that the government gives to people who are ill, poor, not working, etc *unemployment benefit* **3 for sb's benefit** in order to help someone *We bought the piano for the children's benefit.* **4 give sb the benefit of the doubt** to choose to believe what someone tells you even though it may be wrong or a lie ➲See also: **child benefit, fringe benefit**

benefit² /'benɪfɪt/ *verb* **benefiting,** *past* **benefited 1** BE HELPED [I] to be helped by something *The film **benefited from** the excellent acting by its stars.* **2** HELP [T] to help someone *The charity supports activities that directly benefit children.*

benevolent /bɪ'nevələnt/ *adjective formal* kind, generous, and helpful •**benevolence** /bɪ'nevələns/ *noun* [U]

benign /bɪ'naɪn/ *adjective* **1 HEALTH** not likely to kill you *a benign tumour* **2** kind, or not intending to harm anyone *a benign ruler*

bent¹ /bent/ *adjective* **1** CURVED curved and not now straight or flat *The metal bars were bent and twisted.* **2 bent on sth/doing sth** determined to do something or get something *Both parties are bent on destroying each other's chances of winning.* **3** NOT HONEST *UK informal* not honest *a bent policeman*

bent² /bent/ *past of* bend

benzene /'benziːn/ *noun* [U] **CHEMISTRY** a colourless liquid made from petroleum, from which plastics and many chemical products can be made (formula C_6H_6)

'benzene ͵ring *noun* [C] **CHEMISTRY** a connected ring of six carbon atoms, as found in a molecule of benzene

benzoic acid /ben͵zəʊɪk'æsɪd/ *noun* [U] **CHEMISTRY** a colourless substance found in various plant resins (= sticky substances), used for example in food preservatives (= substances used to keep food fresh) or medical products (formula C_6H_5COOH)

bequeath /bɪ'kwiːð/ *verb* [+ **two objects**] *formal* to formally arrange to give someone something after you die *He **bequeathed** his art collection **to** the city of Glasgow.*

bequest /bɪ'kwest/ *noun* [C] *formal* **LAW** money or property that you have arranged for someone to get after you die

berate /bɪ'reɪt/ *verb* [T] *formal* to speak angrily to someone *She **berated** him **for** being late.*

B

bereaved /bɪˈriːvd/ *adjective* If you have been bereaved, someone you loved has died. *bereaved parents* ○ *The minister spoke quietly with **the bereaved**.* •**bereavement** *noun* [**C, U**] *formal*

bereft /bɪˈreft/ *adjective formal* **1 bereft of sth** completely without something *They were bereft of new ideas.* **2** [**never before noun**] alone and extremely sad *She was left bereft by his death.*

beret /ˈbereɪ/ (US) /bəˈreɪ/ *noun* [**C**] a round, flat hat made of soft material

bergschrund /ˈbɜːɡʃrʊnd/ *noun* [**C**] **GEOLOGY** a deep crack near or at the top of a glacier (= large mass of ice)

berimbau /beˈrɪmbaʊ/ *noun* [**C**] **MUSIC** a musical instrument from Brazil, made from a long stick with a wire stretched between the ends

berry /ˈberi/ *noun* [**C**] **BIOLOGY, FOOD** a small, round fruit on some plants and trees

berserk /bəˈzɜːk/ *adjective* **go berserk** *informal* to become extremely angry or violent

berth /bɜːθ/ *noun* [**C**] **1** BED a bed on a boat or train **2** PORT a place for a boat to stay in a port

beryllium /bəˈrɪliəm/ *noun* [**U**] **CHEMISTRY** a hard, light, silver-grey metallic element, used to make strong alloys (= mixture of metals) (symbol **Be**)

beset /bɪˈset/ *verb* [**T**] *formal* If problems beset you, they cause you continuing difficulties. [**often passive**] *The project has been **beset by problems** from the start.*

beside /bɪˈsaɪd/ *preposition* **1** next to someone or something, or very near them *She knelt beside his bed.* **2 be beside yourself (with sth)** to experience a powerful emotion *He was beside himself with rage.*

besides¹ /bɪˈsaɪdz/ *preposition* in addition to something or someone *Do you play any other sports besides football?*

besides² /bɪˈsaɪdz/ *adverb* **1** ANOTHER REASON used to give another reason for something *She won't mind if you're late - besides, it's not your fault.* **2** ALSO in addition to *Besides looking after the children, she also runs a successful business.*

besiege /bɪˈsiːdʒ/ *verb* **1 be besieged by/with sb** to have lots of people asking you questions or making demands *The president was besieged by reporters.* **2 be besieged by/with sth** to receive many demands or criticisms *The radio station was besieged with calls from angry listeners.* **3** [**T**] to surround a place with an army in order to attack it

O-ᵚ**best¹** /best/ *adjective* (*superlative of* good) better than any other *She's one of our best students.* ○ *Give her my **best wishes**.* ○ *Susie's my **best friend*** (= the friend I like more than any other). ○ *What's the best way to get to Manchester from here?* ➲See also: **second best,** the best/ greatest **thing** since sliced bread

O-ᵚ**best²** /best/ *adverb* (*superlative of* well) **1** DEGREE most, or more than any other *Which of the songs did you like best?* **2** WAY in the most suitable or satisfactory way *I sleep best with the windows open.*

best³ /best/ *noun* **1 the best** someone or something that is better than any other *He's the best of the new players.* **2 at best** used to show that the most positive way of considering something is still not good *At best, only 50 per cent of babies born at 24 weeks will survive.* **3 at his/ its, etc best** at the highest level of achievement or quality *The article is an example of journalism at its best.* **4 do/try your best** to make the greatest effort possible *I did my best to persuade him.* **5 bring out the best in sb** to cause someone's best qualities to show **6 make the best of sth** to try to be positive about a situation you do not like but cannot change *Our hotel room is rather small, but we'll just have to make the best of it.* **7 for the best** If something is for the best, it seems unpleasant now, but will improve a situation in the future. *Divorce is always painful, but it really was for the best.* **8 at the best of times** used to show that something is not good when it is the best it can be *He's not exactly patient at the best of times.* **9 have the best of both worlds** to have the advantages of two different situations *Living in the country and working in the city you have the best of both worlds.*

ˌbest ˈman *noun* [**no plural**] a man who stands next to the man who is getting married at the marriage ceremony and helps him

bestow /bɪˈstəʊ/ *verb* [**T**] *formal* to give someone an important present or a public reward for their achievements *He won the Nobel Peace Prize, an honour also **bestowed on** his colleague.*

bestseller /ˌbestˈseləʳ/ *noun* [**C**] a very popular book that many people have bought •**best-selling** *adjective* [**always before noun**] *best-selling authors*

bet¹ /bet/ *verb* [**I, T**] **betting,** *past* **bet 1** to risk money on the result of a game, competition, etc *He lost all his money **betting on** horses.* [**+ two objects + (that)**] *I bet him a dollar that I was right.* **2 I bet** *informal* something that you say to show that you believe that something is true or will happen [**+ (that)**] I bet that he's forgotten my birthday again. **3 You bet!** *mainly US informal* used to say that you will do something with enthusiasm *"Are you going to Pam's party?" "You bet!"*

WORD PARTNERS FOR ***bet***

have/place a bet (on) sth • **put** a bet **on** sth • **lose/win** a bet

bet² /bet/ *noun* [**C**] **1** when you risk money on the result of a game, competition, etc *She **won** her **bet**.* ○ *He **put a bet on** Manchester United winning on Saturday.* **2 a good bet** something that would be useful, clever, or enjoyable to do *Putting your savings in a high-interest account would be a good bet.* **3 your best bet** the best decision or choice *Your best bet in terms of value would be the Regent Hotel.* **4 hedge your bets** to avoid choosing one particular thing or action when it is not certain which is the right choice *Journalists are hedging their bets on the likely outcome of the election.* **5 a safe bet** something that you are certain will happen *Wheeler is a safe bet for a place on the team.*

ˈbeta deˌcay *noun* [U] **PHYSICS** the process in which a neutron (= part with no electrical charge inside an atom) breaks up into a proton (= part with a positive electrical charge) and an electron (= part with a negative electrical charge)

ˈbeta ˌparticle *noun* [C] **PHYSICS** an extremely small piece of matter with a negative or sometimes positive electric charge, produced when an atom is broken down

betray /bɪˈtreɪ/ *verb* [T] **1** PERSON to behave in a dishonest or cruel way to someone who trusts you *When I heard what he had said about me, I felt betrayed.* **2** SECRETS If you betray your country or an organization, you give secret information to its enemies or to other organizations. **3** EMOTION to show an emotion that you were trying to hide *Her face was calm, but her hands betrayed her nervousness.*

betrayal /bɪˈtreɪəl/ *noun* [C, U] when you betray someone *a betrayal of trust*

O⁃**better¹** /ˈbetəʳ/ *adjective* **1** QUALITY (*comparative of* good) of a higher quality, more effective, or more enjoyable than something or someone else *Jeff's been offered a better job in the States.* ○ *The sales figures were **better than** expected.* ○ *Her English has **got** a lot **better*** (= improved) *recently.* **2** ILLNESS healthy, or less ill than before *I feel much better.* ○ *I hope you **get better** soon.* **3 the bigger/brighter/hotter, etc the better** used to say that the bigger, brighter, hotter, etc something is, the more pleased you will be

O⁃**better²** /ˈbetəʳ/ *adverb* **1** (*comparative of* well) to a greater degree, or in a more successful or effective way *I'd like to get to know you better.* ○ *Helen did much **better than** me in the exam.* **2 he/you, etc had better do sth** used in order to say what you think someone should do *You'd better hurry or you'll miss the train.* **3 know better** to have enough experience not to do something stupid or something that will not achieve anything *I thought she'd listen to me - I should have known better.*

better³ /ˈbetəʳ/ *noun* **1 for the better** If a situation changes for the better, it improves. *Their relationship has changed for the better.* **2 get the better of sb** If a feeling gets the better of you, it becomes too strong to control. *Curiosity finally got the better of her and she opened the letter.*

better⁴ /ˈbetəʳ/ *verb* [T] to do something better than it has been done before *He bettered his previous best time for a marathon.*

ˌbetter ˈoff *adjective* [never before noun] **1** RICHER richer *We're a lot better off now that Jane's started work again.* **2** BETTER SITUATION in a better situation *Simon's such an idiot - you'd be better off without him.* **3 you're better off doing sth** used to give advice *You're better off getting a taxi.*

O⁃**between¹** /bɪˈtwiːn/ *preposition* **1** SPACE in the space that separates two places, people, or things *The town lies halfway between Florence and Rome.* ○ *A narrow path runs between the two houses.* **2** TIME in the period of time that separates two events or times *The shop is closed for lunch between 12.30 and 1.30.* **3** INVOLVE involving two or more groups of people *Tonight's game is between the New Orleans Saints and the Los Angeles Rams.* **4** AMOUNT used to show the largest and smallest amount or level of something *Between 50 and 100 people will lose their jobs.* **5** CONNECT connecting two or more places or things *There is a regular train service between Glasgow and Edinburgh.* **6** SEPARATE separating two or more things or people *the gap between rich and poor* ○ *What's the **difference between** these two cameras?* **7** SHARE shared by a particular number of people *We drank two bottles of wine between four of us.* **8** AMOUNT If something is between two amounts, it is larger than the first amount but smaller than the second. *The temperature will be between 20 and 25 degrees today.* **9** CHOOSE If you choose between two things, you choose one thing or the other.

between² /bɪˈtwiːn/ (*also* **in between**) *adverb* **1** SPACE in the space that separates two places, people, or things *The wood is in neat piles with newspaper placed between.* **2** TIME in the period of time that separates two events or times *There's a train at 6.15 and one at 10.30 but nothing in between.*

beverage /ˈbevᵊrɪdʒ/ *noun* [C] *formal* **FOOD** a drink

beware /bɪˈweəʳ/ *verb* [I] used in order to warn someone to be careful ***Beware of** the dog.* [+ **of** + **doing sth**] *You should beware of spending too long in the sun.*

bewildered /bɪˈwɪldəd/ *adjective* very confused and not sure what to do *She looked bewildered.* •**bewilderment** *noun* [U] *He stared at me **in bewilderment**.*

bewildering /bɪˈwɪldᵊrɪŋ/ *adjective* making you feel confused *There was a bewildering range of subjects to choose from.*

bewitch /bɪˈwɪtʃ/ *verb* [T] If someone or something bewitches you, you find them extremely attractive and interesting. *a bewitching smile*

O⁃**beyond¹** /biˈjɒnd/ *preposition* **1** DISTANCE on the other side of something *Our house is just beyond the bridge.* **2** TIME continuing after a particular time or date *A lot of people now live beyond the age of 80.* **3 beyond belief/repair/recognition, etc** impossible to believe/repair/recognize, etc *Steven had changed beyond all recognition.* **4** NOT UNDERSTAND *informal* If something is beyond you, you cannot understand it. *It's beyond me why anyone would want to buy that house.* **5** EXCEPT except for *She said very little beyond the occasional 'yes' and 'no'.* **6** INVOLVING OTHERS involving or affecting other things or people than the ones you have talked about *You should try to develop interests beyond the family.*

beyond² /biˈjɒnd/ *adverb* **1** DISTANCE on the other side of something *From the top of the hill, we could see our house and the woods beyond.* **2** TIME continuing after a particular time or date *The strike looks set to continue into March and beyond.*

bhangra /ˈbæŋgrə/ *noun* [U] **MUSIC** a type of pop music based on traditional music from North India and Pakistan

B

bi- /baɪ-/ *prefix* two *bilingual* (= speaking two languages) ○ *bimonthly* (= happening twice in a month or once every two months)

biannual /baɪˈænjuəl/ *adjective* happening twice a year ➲Compare **biennial**

bias /ˈbaɪəs/ *noun* [C, U] when you support or oppose someone or something in an unfair way because you are influenced by your personal opinions *a* ***bias towards/against*** *private education* ○ *The news channel has been accused of* ***bias in favour of*** *the government.*

biased /ˈbaɪəst/ *adjective* showing unfair support for or opposition to someone or something because of your personal opinions *to be* ***biased against/towards*** *younger workers*

bib /bɪb/ *noun* [C] a piece of cloth or plastic that is worn by young children when they are eating in order to stop their clothes getting dirty

bible /ˈbaɪbl/ *noun* **1 the Bible** **RELIGION** the holy book of the Christian and Jewish religions **2** **RELIGION** [C] a copy of this book **3** [C] a book or magazine that gives important information and advice about a particular subject *'Vogue' was regarded as the fashion student's bible.*

biblical /ˈbɪblɪkəl/ *adjective* **RELIGION** relating to the Bible

bibliography /ˌbɪbliˈɒɡrəfi/ *noun* [C] a list of books and articles on a particular subject

bicentenary /ˌbaɪsenˈtiːnəri/ Ⓤⓢ /baɪˈsentəneri/ *UK* (*US* **bicentennial** /ˌbaɪsenˈteniəl/) *noun* [C] the day or year that is 200 years after an important event *the bicentenary of Schubert's birth* ○ *bicentennial celebrations*

biceps /ˈbaɪseps/ *noun* [C] *plural* **biceps** **ANATOMY** the large muscle at the front of your upper arm

bicker /ˈbɪkəʳ/ *verb* [I] to argue about something that is not very important *They were* ***bickering over*** *which channel to watch.*

bicuspid valve /baɪˈkʌspɪdˌvælv/ *noun* [C] **ANATOMY, BIOLOGY** a mitral valve

WORD PARTNERS FOR ***bicycle***

ride a bicycle • be **on** a bicycle • a bicycle **helmet**

O⟶**bicycle** /ˈbaɪsɪkl/ *noun* [C] a vehicle with two wheels that you sit on and move by turning the two pedals (= parts you press with your feet) ➲See colour picture **Sports 2** on page Centre 15

WORD PARTNERS FOR ***bid***

launch/mount a bid • **in a (desperate)** bid to do sth • a bid **for** sth

bid[1] /bɪd/ *noun* [C] **1** ATTEMPT an attempt to achieve something *a successful* ***bid for*** *re-election* [+ **to do sth**] *The council has banned cars from the city centre* ***in a bid*** *to reduce pollution.* **2** BUY an offer to pay a particular amount of money for something *I made a* ***bid*** *of $150* ***for*** *the painting.* **3** WORK an offer to do work for someone for a particular amount of money *We put in a* ***bid for*** *the stadium contract.*

bid[2] /bɪd/ *verb* **bidding**, *past* **bid** **1** **FINANCE** [I, T] to offer to pay an amount of money for something *They* ***bid*** *$500 million* ***for*** *the company.* **2 bid for sth; bid to do sth** to try to do or obtain something *Five firms have bid for the contract.*

bid[3] /bɪd/ *verb* **bidding**, *past* **bid** or **bade**, *past participle* **bid** or **bidden** **bid sb farewell/goodbye/good night, etc** *literary* to say goodbye, good night, etc *She bade her guests good night.*

bidder /ˈbɪdəʳ/ *noun* [C] **FINANCE** someone who offers to pay a particular amount of money for something *The house will be sold to* ***the highest bidder*** (= the person who offers to pay the most).

bidding /ˈbɪdɪŋ/ *noun* [U] **1** when people offer to pay a particular amount of money for something **2 do sb's bidding** *literary* to do what someone tells you to do

bide /baɪd/ *verb* ➲See: bide your **time**[1]

bidet /ˈbiːdeɪ/ Ⓤⓢ /bɪˈdeɪ/ *noun* [C] a small low bath that a person uses to wash their bottom and sex organs

biennial /baɪˈeniəl/ *adjective* happening every two years ➲Compare **biannual**

O⟶**big**[1] /bɪɡ/ *adjective* **bigger, biggest** **1** SIZE large in size or amount *I come from a big family.* ○ *We're looking for a bigger house.* **2** IMPORTANT important or serious *Tonight's big game is between Real Madrid and Manchester United.* ○ *Buying that car was a big mistake.* **3 your big brother/sister** *informal* your older brother/sister **4** SUCCESSFUL *informal* successful or popular *The programme's been* ***a big hit*** (= very popular) *with young children.* **5 make it big** *informal* to become very successful or famous

big[2] /bɪɡ/ *verb*

big sth/sb up *phrasal verb* [T] *informal* to praise someone or something a lot, sometimes more than they deserve

the ˌbig ˈbang *noun* **PHYSICS, ASTRONOMY** the large explosion that many scientists believe created the universe

ˌbig ˈbusiness *noun* [U] **ECONOMIC** **1** ACTIVITY an activity that makes a lot of money *Football has become big business.* **2** COMPANY large, powerful businesses

bigot /ˈbɪɡət/ *noun* [C] a bigoted person

bigoted /ˈbɪɡətɪd/ *adjective* A bigoted person has very strong, unfair opinions and refuses to consider different opinions. •**bigotry** /ˈbɪɡətri/ *noun* [U] when someone is bigoted

big-ticket /ˈbɪɡˌtɪkɪt/ *adjective* [**always before noun**] *US* Big-ticket items are expensive things to buy, such as cars or furniture.

O⟶**bike** /baɪk/ *noun* [C] **1** BICYCLE *informal short for* bicycle **2** MOTORCYCLE *informal short for* motorbike/motorcycle (= a vehicle with two wheels and an engine)

biker /ˈbaɪkəʳ/ *noun* [C] someone who rides a motorbike (= vehicle with two wheels and an engine)

bikini /bɪˈkiːni/ *noun* [C] a piece of clothing with two parts that women wear for swimming ➲See colour picture **Clothes** on page Centre 9

bilateral /baɪˈlætərəl/ *adjective* **POLITICS** involving two groups or countries *bilateral talks/agreements/trade*

bile /baɪl/ *noun* [U] **BIOLOGY** a bitter liquid made and stored in the body that helps to digest fat

ˈbile ˌduct *noun* [C] **ANATOMY, BIOLOGY** a tube from the liver and gall bladder through which

B

bile passes into the small intestine ➲See picture at **alimentary canal**

bilingual /baɪˈlɪŋgwəl/ *adjective* **LANGUAGE** using or able to speak two languages *a bilingual dictionary* ○ *She's bilingual.*

WORD PARTNERS FOR ***bill***

pay/settle a bill • a bill **comes to** [£100/$500, etc] • a bill **for** sth • an **electricity/gas/phone** bill

O‐**bill¹** /bɪl/ *noun* [C] **1 FINANCE** a piece of paper that tells you how much you must pay for something you have bought or for a service you have used *Have you **paid the** electricity **bill**?* **2 POLITICS** a written plan for a law *Parliament will vote today on whether to pass the reform bill.* **3 FINANCE** *US* (*UK* **note**) a piece of paper money *a five dollar bill* **4** *UK* what is on at a cinema or theatre **5 BIOLOGY** a bird's beak

bill² /bɪl/ *verb* **1 be billed as sth** to be advertised with a particular description *The film was billed as a romantic comedy.* **2 FINANCE** [T] to give or send someone a bill asking for money that they owe for a product or service *He **billed** us **for** the materials.*

billboard /ˈbɪlbɔːd/ (*also UK* **hoarding**) *noun* [C] a large board used for advertising, especially by the side of a road

billfold /ˈbɪlfəʊld/ *US* (*UK/US* **wallet**) *noun* [C] a small, flat container for carrying paper money and credit cards (= plastic cards used for paying with)

billiards /ˈbɪliədz/ *noun* [U] **SPORT** a game in which two people try to hit coloured balls into holes around the edge of a table using long, thin sticks

billing /ˈbɪlɪŋ/ *noun* [U] **1 FINANCE** when people are sent letters to ask for payments **2 star/top billing** when a particular performer is shown as the most important person in a performance

billion /ˈbɪliən/ the number 1,000,000,000

billow /ˈbɪləʊ/ *verb* [I] to be moved and spread out by a current of air *Smoke **billowed out of** the building.*

bimetallic strip /ˌbaɪmetælɪkˈstrɪp/ *noun* [C] **PHYSICS** a strip, used in a thermostat (= device to control temperature), made from two different metals which grow by different amounts when heated, causing it to bend and switch the thermostat on or off

O‐**bin** /bɪn/ *noun* [C] **1** WASTE *UK* (*US* **trash can**) a container that is used to put waste in *a **rubbish/wastepaper bin*** ○ *I threw it in the bin.* ➲See colour picture **The Office** on page Centre 5 **2** STORING a container for storing things *a storage bin*

binary /ˈbaɪnəri/ *adjective* **MATHEMATICS** The binary system expresses numbers using only 1 and 0, and is especially used for computers.

ˌbinary ˈcode *noun* [U] **COMPUTING** a code made of zeros and ones that represent numbers and letters

ˌbinary ˈfission *noun* [U] **BIOLOGY** when organisms with only one cell create new organisms by dividing

bind¹ /baɪnd/ *verb* [T] *past* **bound 1** TIE to tie something together with string, rope, etc *His hands were bound behind his back.* **2** KEEP PROMISE to force someone to keep a promise *His contract **binds** him **to** working a six-day week.* **3** UNITE to unite people *Culture and language **bind** people **together**.* **4** BOOK to fasten together pages to make a book

bind² /baɪnd/ *noun* [no plural] *informal* **1** SITUATION a difficult or unpleasant situation *a financial bind* **2** JOB *UK* a job which uses a lot of your time *Cleaning the bathroom is a bind.*

binder /ˈbaɪndəʳ/ *noun* [C] a strong cover for holding together pieces of paper

binding /ˈbaɪndɪŋ/ *adjective* A binding agreement, promise, etc cannot be broken or changed. *It's a **legally binding** contract.*

ˈbinding ˌsite *noun* [C] **BIOLOGY** an area on an enzyme, DNA or RNA to which particular molecules or ions attach

binge¹ /bɪndʒ/ *noun* [C] when you eat or drink too much or spend too much money in shops

binge² /bɪndʒ/ *verb* [I] **bingeing** to eat too much food at one time *I've been **bingeing on** chocolate.*

ˈbinge ˌdrinking *noun* [U] when someone drinks too much alcohol on one occasion •**ˈbinge ˌdrinker** *noun* [C]

bingo /ˈbɪŋgəʊ/ *noun* [U] a game in which people mark numbers on a card as they are called, and the person whose numbers are called first is the winner

binoculars /bɪˈnɒkjələz/ *noun* [plural] a piece of equipment for looking at things that are far away, made from two tubes with glass at the ends *a **pair of binoculars***

binomial /baɪˈnəʊmiəl/ *noun* [C] **MATHEMATICS** an expression that has two groups of numbers or letters, for example 4x + 3y

binomial system /ˌbaɪˈnəʊmiəlˌsɪstəm/ (*also* **binomial nomenclature**) *noun* [C] **BIOLOGY** the formal system for naming species (= groups of plants and animals that share characteristics)

bio- /baɪəʊ-/ *prefix* **BIOLOGY** relating to living things or human life *biodiversity* ○ *bioethics*

biochemical /ˌbaɪəʊˈkemɪkəl/ *adjective* **BIOLOGY, CHEMISTRY** relating to the chemistry of living things

biochemistry /ˌbaɪəʊˈkemɪstri/ *noun* [U] **BIOLOGY, CHEMISTRY** the study of the chemistry of living things such as plants, animals, or people •**biochemist** *noun* [C] a scientist who studies biochemistry

biodegradable /ˌbaɪəʊdɪˈgreɪdəbl/ *adjective* **ENVIRONMENT** Biodegradable substances decay naturally without damaging the environment.

biodiesel /ˈbaɪəʊˌdiːzl/ *noun* [U] **ENVIRONMENT** fuel used in the engines of some vehicles that is made from vegetable oil or animal fat

biodiversity /ˌbaɪəʊdaɪˈvɜːsɪti/ *noun* [U] **ENVIRONMENT** the number and types of plants and animals that exist in a particular area

bioethanol /ˌbaɪəʊˈeθənɒl/ *noun* [U] **ENVIRONMENT** fuel used in the engines of some vehicles that is partly made from ethanol (= a chemical that comes from sugar)

B

biofuel /ˈbaɪəʊˌfjʊəl/ *noun* [U] **ENVIRONMENT** fuel produced from plant material

biogas /ˈbaɪəʊˌgæs/ *noun* [U] **ENVIRONMENT** a gas produced by dead plants and animals that can be burned as a fuel

biographer /baɪˈɒgrəfəʳ/ *noun* [C] **LITERATURE** someone who writes the story of a particular person's life

biography /baɪˈɒgrəfi/ *noun* [C] **LITERATURE** the story of a person's life written by another person •**biographical** /ˌbaɪəʊˈgræfɪkəl/ *adjective* about someone's life *biographical information*

biological /ˌbaɪəˈlɒdʒɪkəl/ *adjective* **1 BIOLOGY** relating to the study of living things such as plants and animals *biological sciences* **2 BIOLOGY** using living things or poisons made from living things *biological weapons* •**biologically** *adverb*

bioˌlogical conˈtrol *noun* **ENVIRONMENT** the use of one plant or animal to control another, especially to prevent disease or damage

biology /baɪˈɒlədʒi/ *noun* [U] **BIOLOGY** the study of living things •**biologist** *noun* [C] a scientist who studies biology

biomass /ˈbaɪəʊˌmæs/ *noun* [U] **1 ENVIRONMENT** dead plant and animal material suitable for using as fuel **2** the total amount of living things in a particular area

biome /ˈbaɪəʊm/ *noun* [C] **ENVIRONMENT** a region of the Earth's surface and the particular combination of climate, plants and animals that are found in it

biometric /ˌbaɪəʊˈmetrɪk/ *adjective* using a person's characteristics, e.g. their voice or the pattern of their eyes, to prove who they are

biopsy /ˈbaɪɒpsi/ *noun* [C] **HEALTH** when a small number of cells are taken from a part of the body and examined to see if there is a disease

biosphere /ˈbaɪəʊsfɪəʳ/ *noun* [U] **GEOGRAPHY** the part of the Earth's environment where life exists

biotechnology /ˌbaɪəʊtekˈnɒlədʒi/ *noun* [U] **CHEMISTRY** the use of living cells and bacteria in chemical processes, especially in the food and medical industries

bioterrorism /ˌbaɪəʊˈterərɪzəm/ *noun* [U] when people use living things, such as bacteria, to hurt other people for political reasons •**bioterrorist** *noun* [C]

biotic /baɪˈɒtɪk/ *adjective* **ENVIRONMENT** involving, caused by, or relating to living things in the environment

biˌotic ˈindex *noun* [C] **ENVIRONMENT** a way of measuring the pollution (= dirty substances) in water, e.g. a river, by counting the organisms in it

bipartisan /baɪˈpɑːtɪzæn/ *adjective* **POLITICS** involving two political parties *a bipartisan agreement*

birch /bɜːtʃ/ *noun* [C, U] a tree that has thin, smooth branches

O⁃**bird** /bɜːd/ *noun* [C] an animal that has wings and feathers and is usually able to fly

ˈbird ˌflu (*also* **avian flu**) *noun* [U] **HEALTH** an illness that kills birds and can sometimes pass from birds to people

birdie /ˈbɜːdi/ *US* (*UK* **shuttlecock**) *noun* [C] **SPORT** a small object with feathers that is used like a ball in badminton (= a sport like tennis)

ˌbird of ˈprey *noun* [C] *plural* **birds of prey** a large bird that kills smaller animals for food

bird-watching /ˈbɜːdˌwɒtʃɪŋ/ *noun* [U] the hobby of looking at birds

biro /ˈbaɪərəʊ/ *noun* [C, U] *UK trademark* a type of pen that has a very small metal ball at its end and a thin tube of ink inside

O⁃**birth** /bɜːθ/ *noun* **1 give birth** When a woman or an animal gives birth, she produces a baby from her body. *She gave birth to twins.* **2** TIME [C, U] the time when a baby is born *a difficult birth* ○ *Write your* ***date of birth*** (= the date when you were born) *here.* **3** BEGINNING [U] *literary* the beginning of something ***the birth of*** *modern science* **4 American/Italian, etc by birth** born in a particular place or having parents with a particular nationality

ˈbirth caˌnal *noun* [C] **ANATOMY** the part of the female body which a baby travels through in order to be born

ˈbirth cerˌtificate *noun* [C] **LAW** an official document that records when and where a person was born

ˈbirth conˌtrol *noun* [U] **HEALTH** methods of limiting the number of children you have

WORD PARTNERS FOR ***birthday***

celebrate your birthday • **on** sb's [1st/50th/100th, etc] birthday • a birthday **cake/card/party/present**

O⁃**birthday** /ˈbɜːθdeɪ/ *noun* [C] the day on which someone was born, or the same date each year *She is* ***celebrating*** *her seventieth* ***birthday***. ○ ***Happy Birthday!*** ○ *a* ***birthday cake/party***

birthmark /ˈbɜːθmɑːk/ *noun* [C] **HEALTH** a mark on someone's skin that has been there since they were born

birthplace /ˈbɜːθpleɪs/ *noun* [C] the place where someone was born

ˈbirth ˌrate *noun* [C] **SOCIETY** a measurement of the number of babies born in a particular period

O⁃**biscuit** /ˈbɪskɪt/ *noun* [C] **1 FOOD** *UK* (*US* **cookie**) a thin, flat cake that is dry and usually sweet ➲See colour picture **Food** on page Centre 11 **2 FOOD** *US* a small, soft, round bread

bisect /baɪˈsekt/ *verb* [T] to divide something into two equal parts •**bisection** /baɪˈsekʃən/ *noun* [C, U]

bisector /baɪˈsektəʳ/ *noun* [C] **MATHEMATICS** a straight line that divides an angle or line into two equal parts

bisexual /baɪˈsekʃuəl/ *adjective* sexually attracted to both men and women

bishop /ˈbɪʃəp/ *noun* [C] **RELIGION** a priest of high rank in some Christian churches *the Bishop of Oxford*

bison /ˈbaɪsən/ *noun* [C] *plural* **bison** a large, wild animal similar to a cow with long hair

bistro /ˈbiːstrəʊ/ *noun* [C] an informal place to eat or drink, in a French style

O━**bit**[1] /bɪt/ *noun* [C] **1** SMALL AMOUNT a small amount or piece of something *I wrote it down on a bit of paper.* ○ *There's a little bit more pasta left.* ○ *My favourite bit of the film is right at the end.* ○ *The books are falling **to bits*** (= into separate parts). **2 a bit a** SLIGHTLY slightly *It's a bit cold in here.* ○ *It was a bit too expensive.* **b** SHORT TIME *informal* a short time *I'll see you **in a bit**.* ○ *She lived in Italy **for a bit**.* **3 a bit of a change/fool/problem, etc** a change, fool (= stupid person), problem, etc, but not an important or serious one *I am a bit of a romantic.* ○ *It was a bit of a shock.* **4 quite a bit** *informal* a lot *He does quite a bit of travelling.* ○ *She is quite a bit older than him.* **5 a bit much** *informal* more than is fair, or more than you can deal with *It's a bit much to expect me to tidy up their mess.* **6 bit by bit** gradually *She saved up the money, bit by bit.* **7 every bit as** used to emphasize that one thing is equally good, important, etc as something else *The gardens are every bit as impressive as the castle itself.* **8 bits and pieces** small things or jobs which are not connected or not very important *We've packed most of it up now, there are just a few bits and pieces left.* **9 COMPUTING** a unit of information in a computer **10 SPORT** a piece of metal which goes in the mouth of a horse to control it

bit[2] /bɪt/ *past tense of* bite

bitchy /ˈbɪtʃi/ *adjective* If someone is bitchy, they are unkind about other people. *a bitchy comment*

O━**bite**[1] /baɪt/ *verb past tense* **bit**, *past participle* **bitten 1** TEETH [I, T] to cut something using your teeth *She **bit into** an apple.* ○ *He bites his fingernails.* ○ *He was bitten by a dog.* **2** BAD EFFECT [I] to begin to have a bad effect *Higher mortgage rates are beginning to bite.* ➲See also: bite the **bullet**, bite the **dust**[1] **3 come back to bite you** If a problem will come back to bite you, it will causes more trouble for you in the future if you do not solve it now.

bite[2] /baɪt/ *noun* **1** PIECE OF FOOD [C] a piece taken from food when you bite it *She **took a bite** from her pizza.* **2** INJURY [C] an injury caused when an animal or insect bites you *mosquito bites* **3 a bite** a small meal *I just want to grab a bite to eat.*

biting /ˈbaɪtɪŋ/ *adjective* A biting wind or biting cold is extremely cold and hurts your skin.

bitmap /ˈbɪtmæp/ *noun* [C] **COMPUTING** a computer image formed from many small points on the screen

bitten /ˈbɪtən/ *past participle of* bite

bitter[1] /ˈbɪtəʳ/ *adjective* **1** ANGRY angry and upset because of something bad which has happened that you cannot forget *I feel very **bitter about** my childhood.* **2** HATE full of hate or anger *a bitter argument/dispute* **3 FOOD** having a strong, sour, usually unpleasant taste **4** COLD extremely cold *a bitter wind* **5 to/until the bitter end** until something is completely finished, usually something unpleasant *He was determined to stay right to the bitter end.* **6** DISAPPOINTED making you feel very disappointed *Losing the championship was a bitter disappointment.* •**bitterness** *noun* [U]

bitter[2] /ˈbɪtəʳ/ *noun* [U] *UK* **FOOD** a type of beer with a bitter taste

bitterly /ˈbɪtəli/ *adverb* **1** UPSET in a way which shows strong negative emotion such as anger or disappointment *We were **bitterly disappointed** about the decision.* **2** WEATHER If it is bitterly cold, the weather is extremely and unpleasantly cold.

bitumen /ˈbɪtʃʊmən/ *noun* [U] a black sticky substance used for making roads and roofs

bivalve /ˈbaɪvælv/ *noun* [C] **BIOLOGY** a type of mollusc that has its body inside two connected shells

bizarre /bɪˈzɑːʳ/ *adjective* very strange and surprising *bizarre behaviour* •**bizarrely** *adverb*

O━**black**[1] /blæk/ *adjective* **1** COLOUR being the colour of coal or of the sky on a very dark night *a black jacket* ➲See colour picture **Colours** on page Centre 12 **2** PERSON Someone who is black has the dark skin typical of people from Africa. *black athletes/Americans* **3** OF BLACK PEOPLE relating to black people *the black community* **4 FOOD** Black tea or coffee has no milk or cream added to it. **5** HUMOUR funny about unpleasant or frightening subjects *black comedy* **6** ANGRY angry *He gave her a black look.* **7** SITUATION If your situation or future is black, it is very bad. **8 black and blue** covered with bruises (= marks on your skin from being hit) **9 black and white** very clear or simple *The issue of nuclear weapons is not black and white.* •**blackness** *noun* [U] ➲See also: **jet-black, pitch-black**

O━**black**[2] /blæk/ *noun* **1** COLOUR [C, U] the colour of coal or of the sky on a very dark night *She always dresses **in black*** (= in black clothes). ➲See colour picture **Colours** on page Centre 6 **2** PERSON [C] a black person **3 in the black** If your bank account is in the black, it contains some money. **4 in black and white a** PRINT printed in a book, newspaper, or official document *Look at the contract - it's all there in black and white.* **b** NO COLOUR using or seeing no colours, but only black, white, and grey *I saw the original film in black and white.* ➲See also: **jet-black**

black[3] /blæk/ *verb*
black out *phrasal verb* **HEALTH** *informal* to suddenly become unconscious

blackberry /ˈblækbəri/ *noun* [C] **FOOD** a small, soft, dark purple fruit with seeds

BlackBerry /ˈblækbəri/ *noun* [C] *trademark* **COMPUTING** a computer with no wires that fits in your hand and that you can use for documents, email and Internet access •**BlackBerry** *verb* [I] to use a BlackBerry ➲See Extra help page **The Web and the Internet** on page Centre 37.

blackbird /ˈblækbɜːd/ *noun* [C] a bird with black feathers and a yellow beak

blackboard /ˈblækbɔːd/ (*also US* **chalkboard**) *noun* [C] **EDUCATION** a large board with a dark surface that teachers write on with chalk (= soft, white rock) ➲See colour picture **The Classroom** on page Centre 6

ˌblack ˈbox *noun* [C] a small machine on an aircraft that people use to discover the reason for an aircraft accident

B

blackcurrant /ˌblæk'kʌrᵊnt/ *noun* [C] *UK* **FOOD** a very small, round, sour, dark purple fruit *blackcurrant juice/jelly*

ˌblack 'dwarf *noun* [C] **ASTRONOMY** a small, cool star formed from a very old white dwarf (= small star that is not very bright but contains a lot of matter)

blacken /'blækᵊn/ *verb* **1** DARK [I, T] to become black or to make something become black *Storm clouds blackened the sky.* **2** BAD [T] If you blacken someone's name, you say bad things about them.

ˌblack 'eye *noun* [C] an eye that has a dark circle around it because it has been hit

ˌblack 'hole *noun* [C] **ASTRONOMY** an area in outer space that sucks material and light into it from which it cannot escape

blacklist /'blæklɪst/ *verb* [T] to include someone on a list of people you think are bad or you will not deal with [**often passive**] *He was blacklisted by the banks and credit card companies.*

ˌblack 'magic *noun* [U] magic used for evil

blackmail /'blækmeɪl/ *noun* [U] when someone forces you to do something, or to pay them money, by saying they will tell another person something that you want to keep secret •**blackmail** *verb* [T] [**+ into + doing sth**] *They used the photographs to blackmail her into spying for them.* •**blackmailer** *noun* [C]

ˌblack 'market *noun* [C] **ECONOMICS, LAW** illegal trading of goods that are not allowed to be bought and sold or that there are not enough of for everyone who wants them *the black market in heroin*

blackout /'blækaʊt/ *noun* [C] **1 HEALTH** when someone suddenly becomes unconscious **2** NO INFORMATION when information is kept from people [**usually singular**] *a **media/news blackout*** **3** NO ELECTRICITY a failure in the supply of electricity **4** NO LIGHTS a period during a war when no lights must show at night

blacksmith /'blæksmɪθ/ *noun* [C] someone whose job is to make things from metal, especially shoes for horses

bladder /'blædəʳ/ *noun* [C] **ANATOMY** the organ where waste liquid is stored before it leaves your body ⇨See also: **gall bladder**

blade /bleɪd/ *noun* [C] **1** the flat, sharp, metal part of a knife, tool, or weapon **2 BIOLOGY** a long, narrow leaf of grass or a similar plant *a **blade of grass*** ⇨See also: **razor blade, shoulder blade**

O→**blame¹** /bleɪm/ *verb* [T] **1** to say or think that someone or something is responsible for something bad which has happened *Many people **blame** him **for** Tony's death.* ○ *Poor housing **is to blame** for many of their health problems.* ○ *They apologized for the delay and **blamed** it **on** technical problems.* **2 I don't blame him/them/you, etc** used to say that you understand and accept the reason for what someone is doing *"I think I'll go home early." "I don't blame you - you look really tired."*

WORD PARTNERS FOR ***blame***

apportion blame • **get/shoulder/take** the blame **for** sth • **lay/put** the blame **on** sth

blame² /bleɪm/ *noun* [U] when people say that someone or something is responsible for something bad *The manager should **take the blame for** the team's defeat.* ○ *They **put the blame on** faulty equipment.*

blameless /'bleɪmləs/ *adjective* not responsible for anything bad *They concluded that Lucy was entirely blameless.*

blanch /blɑːntʃ/ *verb* [T] **FOOD** to put vegetables or similar foods into boiling water for a few minutes to make them white, remove the skins, get rid of strong flavours, or prepare them for freezing

bland /blænd/ *adjective* **1** not interesting or exciting *bland statements* **2 FOOD** If food is bland, it does not have much taste.

blank¹ /blæŋk/ *adjective* **1** EMPTY with no writing, pictures, or sound *a **blank page*** ○ *a blank tape* ○ *The space for the date was **left blank**.* **2 go blank** If your mind goes blank, you suddenly cannot remember or think of something. **3** NO FEELING showing no feeling or understanding *a **blank expression*** ⇨See also: **point-blank**

blank² /blæŋk/ *noun* **1** [C] an empty space on a piece of paper or form where information can be given *Just **fill in the blanks**.* **2 draw a blank** to be unable to get information, think of something, or achieve something *All their investigations have drawn a blank so far.*

ˌblank 'cheque *UK* (*mainly US* **ˌblank 'check**) *noun* [C] If you give someone a blank cheque, you allow them as much money as they want or need to do something.

blanket¹ /'blæŋkɪt/ *noun* [C] **1** COVER a thick, warm cover that you sleep under **2** LAYER a thick layer of something *a blanket of cloud/snow*

blanket² /'blæŋkɪt/ *adjective* [**always before noun**] including or affecting everything *a blanket ban*

blanket³ /'blæŋkɪt/ *verb* [T] to completely cover something *The ground was blanketed with snow.*

blankly /'blæŋkli/ *adverb* without showing any emotion or understanding *She just stared at me blankly.*

blare /bleəʳ/ (*also* **blare out**) *verb* [I] to make a very loud noise *There was **music blaring** from his room.*

blasphemy /'blæsfəmi/ *noun* [U] **RELIGION** something which you say or do that shows you do not respect God or a religion •**blasphemous** /'blæsfəməs/ *adjective* expressing blasphemy

blast² /blɑːst/ *verb* **1** NOISE [I, T] (*also* **blast out**) to make a very loud noise *rock music blasting from a stereo* **2** MOVE [I, T] to move through something or to hit something with force *Dixon blasted the ball past the goalkeeper.* **3** EXPLODE [T] to break through rock using explosives *They blasted a hole in the rock face.* **4** GUNS [T] to destroy a person or place with guns or bombs

blast off *phrasal verb* When a spacecraft blasts off, it leaves the ground to go into space.

blast³ /blɑːst/ *exclamation UK* used when you are annoyed at something *Blast! I forgot the keys.*

blast-off /ˈblɑːstɒf/ *noun* [U] when a spacecraft leaves the ground

WORD PARTNERS FOR ***blatant***

a blatant **attempt** to do sth • a blatant **disregard for** sth • a blatant **lie**

blatant /ˈbleɪtᵊnt/ *adjective* very obvious, with no attempt to be honest or behave well ***blatant lies****/racism* •**blatantly** *adverb*

blaze[1] /bleɪz/ *verb* [I] to burn or shine very brightly or strongly *The sun blazed down on the dry countryside.*

blaze[2] /bleɪz/ *noun* [C] **1** a large, strong fire *The blaze started in the hall.* **2 a blaze of colour/lights etc** very bright colour, lights, etc *The tulips provided a blaze of colour outside her window.* **3 a blaze of glory/publicity** a lot of public attention for a short time

blazer /ˈbleɪzəʳ/ *noun* [C] a type of jacket, often worn as part of a school uniform

blazing /ˈbleɪzɪŋ/ *adjective* [**always before noun**] **1** HOT very hot *a blazing log fire* **2** ANGRY *UK* very angry *a* ***blazing row***

bleach[1] /bliːtʃ/ *noun* [U] a strong chemical used for cleaning things or removing colour from things

bleach[2] /bliːtʃ/ *verb* [T] to remove the colour from something or make it lighter using chemicals *She's bleached her hair.*

bleak /bliːk/ *adjective* **1** NO HOPE If a situation is bleak, there is little or no hope for the future. *The future is looking bleak for small clubs struggling with debts.* **2** NOT INTERESTING If a place is bleak, it is cold, empty and not attractive. *a bleak landscape* •**bleakness** *noun* [U]

bleary /ˈblɪəri/ *adjective* If you have bleary eyes, you cannot see clearly because you are tired or have just woken up.

bleat /bliːt/ *verb* [I] **1** ANIMAL to make the noise of a sheep or goat **2** PERSON to speak or complain in a weak and annoying way *She keeps bleating about her lack of money.* •**bleat** *noun* [C]

bled /bled/ *past of* bleed

bleed /bliːd/ *verb* [I] *past* **bled** to have blood coming from a cut in your body •**bleeding** *noun* [U] *Try to stop the bleeding.*

bleep /bliːp/ *noun* [C] a short, high electronic noise •**bleep** *verb* [I]

bleeper /ˈbliːpəʳ/ *UK* (*UK/US* **beeper**) *noun* [C] a small piece of electronic equipment which you carry that makes a sound when someone wants to speak to you

blemish /ˈblemɪʃ/ *noun* [C] a mark which spoils the appearance of someone or something

blend[1] /blend/ *verb* **1** MIX [T] to mix two or more things together completely *Blend the ingredients into a smooth paste.* **2** COMBINE [I, T] to combine two or more things *The team blends new, young players with more mature, experienced ones.*

blend in *phrasal verb* If something or someone blends in, they look or seem the same as the people or things around them and so are not easily noticed.

blend[2] /blend/ *noun* [C] a combination of two or more things *Their music is a blend of jazz and African rhythms.*

blender /ˈblendəʳ/ *noun* [C] an electric machine for making soft foods into a smooth liquid ➲See colour picture **The Kitchen** on page Centre 2

B

bless /bles/ *verb* [T] **1** RELIGION to ask God to help or protect someone or something, or to make it holy *The priest blessed their marriage.* **2 be blessed with sth** to be lucky enough to have something good *He's blessed with a wonderful singing voice.* **3 Bless you!** something you say when someone sneezes **4 bless her/him/them, etc** *informal* used to show your affection for the person you are talking about *Peter, bless him, slept all the way through it.*

blessed /ˈblesɪd/ *adjective* [**always before noun**] **1** pleasant and wanted very much *The rain was a* ***blessed relief****.* **2** RELIGION holy *the Blessed Virgin Mary*

blessing /ˈblesɪŋ/ *noun* **1** LUCK [C] something which is lucky or makes you happy *It is a blessing that no one was hurt.* **2** APPROVAL [U] approval that someone gives to a plan or action *Mr Newton has* ***given*** *his* ***blessing*** *for the plan.* **3** RELIGION [C, U] protection or help from God, or a prayer to ask for this **4 a blessing in disguise** something that has a good effect, although at first it seemed that it would be bad **5 a mixed blessing** something which has both good and bad effects

blew /bluː/ *past tense of* blow

blight /blaɪt/ *noun* [**no plural**] something which has a very bad effect on something, often for a long time *the blight of poverty/unemployment* ○ *He became* ***a blight on*** *their lives.* •**blight** *verb* [T] to cause damage to or have a bad effect on something *Injury has blighted his career.*

O⁼**blind**[1] /blaɪnd/ *adjective* **1** not able to see *She* ***went blind*** *after an accident.* ○ *This project provides guide dogs for* ***the blind****.* **2 be blind to sth** to not notice something, or not want to notice something *Drivers who speed are often blind to the risks they cause.* **3 blind panic/rage/trust, etc** an extremely strong feeling that makes you do things without thinking **4 a blind corner/bend** *UK* a bend or corner on a road that is dangerous because you cannot see cars coming around it •**blindness** *noun* [U] ➲See also: **colour-blind,** turn a blind **eye**[1] (to sth)

blind[2] /blaɪnd/ *verb* **1** [T] to make someone blind, either for always or for a short time [**often passive**] *I was blinded by the car headlights.* **2 blind sb to sth** to make someone unable to understand the truth about someone or something *Love blinded her to all his faults.*

blind[3] /blaɪnd/ *noun* [C] a cover that you pull down over a window ➲See also: **venetian blind**

ˌblind ˈdate *noun* [C] a romantic meeting between a man and a woman who have not met before

blindfold /ˈblaɪndfəʊld/ *noun* [C] a piece of cloth that you put over someone's eyes so they cannot see •**blindfold** *verb* [T] to put a blindfold on someone

B

blinding /ˈblaɪndɪŋ/ *adjective* **1** A blinding light is extremely bright. **2 HEALTH** A blinding headache (= pain in the head) is extremely painful.

blindly /ˈblaɪndli/ *adverb* **1** NOT SEEING not able to see or not noticing what is around you *Carly reached blindly for the light switch.* **2** NOT THINKING not thinking about what you are doing *They just blindly followed orders.*

ˈblind ˌspot *noun* [C] **1** DIFFICULTY a difficulty in accepting or understanding a particular thing *She has a complete blind spot where relations with the press are concerned.* **2** ROAD the part of the road just behind you, that you cannot see when you are driving

blink /blɪŋk/ *verb* **1** EYES [I, T] to open and close both of your eyes quickly **2** LIGHT [I] If a light blinks, it goes on and off quickly. •**blink** *noun* [C]

blinkered /ˈblɪŋkəd/ *adjective* not willing to consider new or different ideas *a* ***blinkered attitude***

blip /blɪp/ *noun* [C] **1** CHANGE a small, temporary, and usually negative change from what usually happens *The rise in unemployment may just be a blip.* **2** SOUND/LIGHT a small spot of light on an electronic screen, sometimes with a short, high sound

bliss /blɪs/ *noun* [U] complete happiness *My idea of bliss is lying on a sunny beach.* •**blissful** *adjective* making you feel very happy *a blissful childhood* •**blissfully** *adverb She seemed* ***blissfully unaware*** *of the chaos she had caused.*

blister¹ /ˈblɪstəʳ/ *noun* [C] **HEALTH** a painful, raised area of skin with liquid inside, that you get if your skin has been rubbed or burned, or a similar area on a painted surface

blister² /ˈblɪstəʳ/ *verb* [I, T] **HEALTH** to get or cause blisters

blistering /ˈblɪstᵊrɪŋ/ *adjective* **1** CRITICISM using very strong criticism *a* ***blistering attack*** **2** HEAT extremely hot *blistering sunshine* **3** SPEED extremely fast *The economy has grown at a blistering pace.*

blithely /ˈblaɪðli/ *adverb* without thinking about what might happen *People were* ***blithely ignoring*** *warnings not to swim in the river.*

blitz¹ /blɪts/ *noun* [C] **1** a lot of activity to achieve something in a short time *We had a cleaning blitz before my parents came home.* **2 the Blitz** bomb attacks on British cities during the Second World War

blitz² /blɪts/ *verb* [T] **1** DEFEAT to defeat someone or something completely **2** BOMB to drop bombs on something

blitzkrieg /ˈblɪtskriːg/ *noun* [C] a sudden, very strong attack in a war which is intended to defeat the enemy quickly

blizzard /ˈblɪzəd/ *noun* [C] a storm with strong winds and snow

bloated /ˈbləʊtɪd/ *adjective* **1** SWOLLEN swollen because of air or liquid inside **2** TOO MUCH FOOD feeling uncomfortable because you have eaten too much

blob /blɒb/ *noun* [C] a small amount of a thick liquid *a blob of cream/glue* ➲See colour picture **Pieces and Quantities** on page Centre 1

bloc /blɒk/ *noun* [C] **POLITICS** a group of countries with similar political ideas, who work together *the communist bloc*

block¹ /blɒk/ *noun* [C] **1** PIECE a solid piece of something, usually in the shape of a square or rectangle *a block of ice/stone/wood* **2** DISTANCE *US* the distance along a street from where one road crosses it to the place where the next road crosses it *They only live two blocks away from the school.* **3** BUILDING a large building containing many apartments or offices *UK a* ***block of flats*** **4** GROUP OF BUILDINGS a square group of buildings or houses with roads on each side *Omar took the dog for a walk* ***round the block.*** **5** CANNOT THINK If you have a block about something, you cannot understand it or remember it. *I had a complete* ***mental block*** *about his name.* **6** STOP PROGRESS something that makes it difficult to move or make progress **7** AMOUNT an amount or group of something that is considered together *This block of seats is reserved.* ➲See also: be a **chip¹** off the old block, **stumbling block, tower block**

block² /blɒk/ *verb* [T] **1** CANNOT PASS (*also* **block up**) to prevent anyone or anything from passing through a place *A fallen tree blocked the road.* ○ *The sink is blocked up.* ○ *a blocked drain* **2** STOP PROGRESS to stop something from happening or making progress *The council's blocked plans for a new supermarket.* **3** CANNOT SEE to be between someone and the thing they are looking at, so that they cannot see *A pillar was blocking my view.*

block sth off *phrasal verb* to close a road, path, or entrance so that people cannot use it *Police blocked off the road where the body was found.*

block sth out *phrasal verb* **1** NOT THINK to try to stop yourself thinking about something unpleasant *I've blocked out memories of the accident.* **2** LIGHT/NOISE to stop light or noise passing through something *Most sunscreens block out UVB radiation.*

blockade /blɒkˈeɪd/ *noun* [C] when a government or soldiers stop goods or people from entering or leaving a place *The government* ***imposed a blockade on*** *oil trading.* •**blockade** *verb* [T]

blockage /ˈblɒkɪdʒ/ *noun* [C] something that stops something else passing through *His death was caused by a blockage in his arteries.*

blockbuster /ˈblɒkˌbʌstəʳ/ *noun* [C] *informal* a book, film, etc that is very popular and successful *a new blockbuster movie*

ˌblock ˈcapitals *noun* [plural] **LANGUAGE** letters in the form A, B, C, not a, b, c

ˈblock ˌgraph *noun* [C] **MATHEMATICS** a graph (= mathematical picture showing measurements) in which different amounts are shown by rectangular blocks

blog /blɒg/ (also **weblog**) *noun* [C] **INTERNET** a record of your thoughts that you put on the Internet for other people to read •**blog** *verb* [I] •**blogger** /ˈblɒgəʳ/ *noun* [C] a person who writes or reads a blog ➲See Extra help page **The Web and the Internet** on page Centre 36.

bloke /bləʊk/ *noun* [C] *UK informal* a man *Jake's a nice bloke.*

blonde[1] (*also* **blond**) /blɒnd/ *adjective* **1** HAIR Blonde hair is pale yellow. **2** PERSON Someone who is blonde has pale yellow hair.

blonde[2] (*also* **blond**) /blɒnd/ *noun* [C] someone, especially a woman, who has pale yellow hair

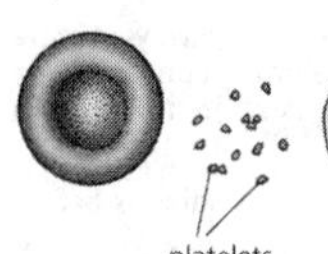

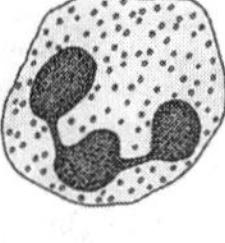

blood cells

WORD PARTNERS FOR ***blood***

donate/give blood (= allow blood to be taken from your body for someone else's body) • a **drop/pool/trickle** of blood • a blood **test**

O⁻**blood** /blʌd/ *noun* [U] **1** BIOLOGY the red liquid that flows around your body *a* ***blood test/sample*** **2** SOCIETY the family or place that you come from *I've got some Spanish blood in me.* **3 be in your blood** If something is in your blood, you and other people in your family are interested in it or good at it. *Sailing is in my blood.* **4 bad blood** feelings of hate between people because of things that have happened in the past **5 in cold blood** in a cruel way, without showing any emotion *He shot three policemen in cold blood.* **6 new blood** new people in an organization who will provide new ideas and energy ➲See also: your own **flesh** and blood

bloodbath /ˈblʌdbɑːθ/ *noun* [**no plural**] an extremely violent event in which many people are killed

blood-curdling /ˈblʌdˌkɜːdlɪŋ/ *adjective* extremely frightening *a* ***blood-curdling scream***

ˈblood ˌdonor *noun* [C] HEALTH someone who gives some of their blood for ill people who need it

ˈblood ˌgroup *UK* (*UK/US* **blood type**) *noun* [C] HEALTH, BIOLOGY one of the groups that human blood is divided into

bloodless /ˈblʌdləs/ *adjective* achieved without killing or violence *a bloodless coup*

ˈblood ˌpressure *noun* [U] HEALTH the force with which blood flows around your body ***high/low blood pressure***

bloodshed /ˈblʌdʃed/ *noun* [U] when people are killed or injured in fighting *Peace talks have failed to end the bloodshed in the region.*

bloodshot /ˈblʌdʃɒt/ *adjective* HEALTH Bloodshot eyes are red in the part that should be white.

ˈblood ˌsport *noun* [C] SPORT a sport in which animals are killed

bloodstained /ˈblʌdsteɪnd/ *adjective* Something that is bloodstained has blood on it.

bloodstream /ˈblʌdstriːm/ *noun* [**no plural**] BIOLOGY the flow of blood around your body

bloodthirsty /ˈblʌdˌθɜːsti/ *adjective* enjoying using or watching violence

ˈblood transˌfusion *noun* [C] HEALTH when blood is put into someone's body

ˈblood ˌtype (*also UK* **blood group**) *noun* [C] HEALTH, BIOLOGY one of the groups that human blood is divided into

ˈblood ˌvessel *noun* [C] ANATOMY, BIOLOGY one of the small tubes that blood flows through in your body

bloody[1] /ˈblʌdi/ *adjective* **1** BLOOD covered in blood *bloody hands* **2** VIOLENT violent and involving a lot of blood and injuries *a bloody war*

bloody[2] /ˈblʌdi/ *adjective, adverb UK very informal* used to show anger or to emphasize what you are saying in a slightly rude way *I can't find my bloody keys.* ○ *We were bloody lucky to win.*

bloom[1] /bluːm/ *noun* **1** [C] a flower *beautiful, pink blooms* **2 in bloom** with flowers that are open *In June the roses are in bloom.*

bloom[2] /bluːm/ *verb* [I] **1** BIOLOGY If a plant blooms, its flowers open. **2** to develop and become successful, happy, or healthy *Their romance bloomed while they were in Paris.*

blossom[1] /ˈblɒsᵊm/ *noun* [C, U] BIOLOGY a small flower, or the small flowers on a tree or plant *cherry blossom*

blossom[2] /ˈblɒsᵊm/ *verb* [I] **1** BIOLOGY If a tree blossoms, it produces flowers. **2** to develop and become successful or beautiful *She has* ***blossomed into*** *a world champion.*

blot[1] /blɒt/ *verb* [T] **blotting**, *past* **blotted** to dry wet marks using soft paper or a cloth

blot sth out *phrasal verb* **1** NOT THINK to stop yourself from thinking about something unpleasant *I've tried to blot out memories of my relationship with Dieter.* **2** CANNOT SEE If smoke or cloud blots out the sun, it prevents it from being seen.

blot[2] /blɒt/ *noun* **1** [C] a mark on something, made by ink or paint falling on it **2 a blot on sth** something that spoils something else *The financial scandal was a blot on his reputation.*

blotch /blɒtʃ/ *noun* [C] a mark on something, especially your skin •**blotchy** (*also* **blotched**) *adjective* having blotches

ˈblotting ˌpaper *noun* [U] thick paper used for drying wet ink

blouse /blaʊz/ (US) /blaʊs/ *noun* [C] a piece of clothing like a shirt that women wear

O⁻**blow**[1] /bləʊ/ *verb, past tense* **blew**, *past participle* **blown** **1** WIND [I] If the wind blows, it moves and makes currents of air. *A cool sea breeze was blowing.* **2** PERSON [I] to force air out through your mouth *She blew on her coffee before taking a sip.* **3 blow sth down/across/off, etc** If the wind blows something somewhere, it makes it move in that direction. *The storm blew trees across the road.* **4** MOVE [I] to move in the wind *branches blowing in the breeze* **5** INSTRUMENT [I, T] to make a sound by forcing air out of your mouth and through an instrument *Ann blew a few notes on the trumpet.* **6** ART [T] to make shapes out of something by blowing it *to blow bubbles* **7** SPEND [T] *informal*

B

to spend a lot of money quickly and without considering it seriously *Lou **blew** all her prize money **on** a diamond necklace.* **8 blow it/your chance(s)** *informal* If you blow it or blow your chance, you lose an opportunity to do something by doing or saying the wrong thing. *Tom blew his chances of getting the job by arriving late for the interview.* **9 blow your nose** to clear your nose by forcing air through it into a handkerchief (= piece of cloth or soft paper) **10** ELECTRICITY [I, T] If a piece of electrical equipment blows, it suddenly stops working because the electric current is too strong. ➲See also: blow your **mind**[1], blow/get sth out of **proportion**

blow sb away *phrasal verb mainly US informal* to surprise or please someone very much *a movie that will blow you away*

blow (sth) out *phrasal verb* If a flame blows out, or if you blow it out, it stops burning because you or the wind have blown it.

blow over *phrasal verb* If a storm or an argument blows over, it ends.

blow (sb/sth) up *phrasal verb* to destroy something or kill someone with a bomb, or to be destroyed by a bomb *Terrorists blew up an office building in the city.*

blow sth up *phrasal verb* to fill something with air *blow up a balloon*

blow up *phrasal verb* **1** START If a storm or an argument blows up, it starts suddenly. **2** BECOME ANGRY *informal* to suddenly become very angry

blow[2] /bləʊ/ *noun* [C] **1** DISAPPOINTMENT a shock or disappointment *Losing his job was a terrible **blow to** him.* **2** HIT a hard hit with a hand or heavy object *He suffered serious **blows to** the head during the attack.* **3** INSTRUMENT when you blow something or blow into an instrument or other object *a blow on the whistle* **4 come to blows** to fight or argue

blow-by-blow /ˌbləʊbaɪˈbləʊ/ *adjective* **a blow-by-blow account/description** a description of an event that gives all the details in the exact order that they happened

blow-dry /ˈbləʊdraɪ/ *verb* [T] to dry your hair in a particular style using a hairdryer (= electrical equipment for drying hair) •**blow-dry** *noun* [no plural] *I had a cut and blow-dry.*

ˈblow ˌmoulding *noun* [U] **DT** a method of making bottles and containers where air is blown into melted plastic

blown /ˈbləʊn/ *past participle of* blow

blowout /ˈbləʊaʊt/ *noun* [C] **1** TYRE when a tyre suddenly explodes while a vehicle is still moving **2** MEAL/PARTY *informal* an expensive meal or a big party **3 SPORT** *US informal* when one team or player beats another easily in a sport

bludgeon /ˈblʌdʒən/ *verb* [T] to hit someone several times with a heavy object [often passive] *She was bludgeoned to death with a hammer.*

O-**blue**[1] /bluː/ *adjective* **1** COLOUR being the same colour as the sky when there are no clouds *a dark blue jacket* ➲See colour picture **Colours** on page Centre 12 **2** SAD *informal* sad **3** SEX about sex *a blue joke/movie* ➲See also: **black**[1] and blue, once in a blue **moon**

O-**blue**[2] /bluː/ *noun* **1** [C, U] the colour of the sky when there are no clouds ➲See colour picture **Colours** on page Centre 6 **2 out of the blue** If something happens out of the blue, you did not expect it. *One day, completely out of the blue, I had a letter from her.*

bluebell /ˈbluːbel/ *noun* [C] a plant with small, blue flowers shaped like bells

blueberry /ˈbluːbəri/ *noun* [C] **FOOD** a small, sweet, dark blue fruit that grows on bushes

blue-chip /ˌbluːˈtʃɪp/ *adjective* [always before noun] **ECONOMICS** A blue-chip company or investment is considered certain to make a profit.

blue-collar /ˌbluːˈkɒləʳ/ *adjective* [always before noun] A blue-collar worker does physical work, especially in a factory.

blueprint /ˈbluːprɪnt/ *noun* [C] a plan that shows how someone will design, build, or achieve something *a blueprint for political reform*

blues /bluːz/ *noun* [plural] **1 MUSIC** a type of slow, sad music that was developed by African-Americans *jazz and blues* **2 have/get the blues** *informal* to feel or become sad

Bluetooth /ˈbluːtuːθ/ *noun* [U] *trademark* a technology that allows equipment such as computers and mobile phones to connect with no wires or cables *a Bluetooth headset*

bluff[1] /blʌf/ *verb* [I, T] to pretend you will do something or that you have knowledge, in order to force someone to do something *He won't really leave her - he's only bluffing.*

bluff[2] /blʌf/ *noun* **1** [C] an attempt to bluff **2 call sb's bluff** to tell someone to do the thing they say they will do, because you do not think they will do it

blunder[1] /ˈblʌndəʳ/ *noun* [C] a serious and often stupid mistake *a series of financial blunders*

blunder[2] /ˈblʌndəʳ/ *verb* **1** [I] to make a serious mistake **2 blunder around/into, etc** to move somewhere in a heavy way, as if you cannot see well *He blundered around, looking for the light switch.*

blunt[1] /blʌnt/ *adjective* **1** NOT SHARP not sharp *a blunt knife* **2** RUDE saying exactly what you think without caring about people's feelings *a blunt letter* •**bluntness** *noun* [U]

blunt[2] /blʌnt/ *verb* [T] **1** FEELING to make a feeling less strong *Mario's comments blunted everyone's enthusiasm.* **2** LESS SHARP to make something less sharp

bluntly /ˈblʌntli/ *adverb* saying exactly what you think without caring about people's feelings

blur[1] /blɜːʳ/ *verb* [I, T] **blurring**, *past* **blurred 1** LESS OBVIOUS to make the difference between two things less clear, or to make it difficult to see the exact truth about something *a book that blurs the distinction between reality and fiction* **2** DIFFICULT TO SEE to become difficult to see clearly, or to make something become difficult to see clearly *soft sunlight that blurred the edges of the mountains*

blur² /blɜːʳ/ *noun* [**no plural**] something that you cannot see or remember clearly *The accident happened so quickly that it's all a blur.*

blurb /blɜːb/ *noun* [**C**] a short description to advertise a product, especially a book

blurred /blɜːd/ *adjective* **1** NOT CLEAR (*also* **blurry** /ˈblɜːri/) not clear *a blurred photograph* ○ *blurred memories* **2** POOR SIGHT If your sight is blurred, you cannot see clearly. *blurred vision*

blurt /blɜːt/ (*also* **blurt out**) *verb* [**T**] to say something suddenly and without thinking, especially because you are excited or nervous *"Will you marry me?" he blurted.*

blush /blʌʃ/ *verb* [**I**] If you blush, your face becomes red, especially because you are embarrassed. *He* ***blushed with*** *shame.* •**blush** *noun* [**C**]

blusher /ˈblʌʃəʳ/ *UK* (*US* **blush**) *noun* [**U**] red powder or cream that women put on their faces in order to make them more attractive

bluster /ˈblʌstəʳ/ *verb* [**I, T**] to speak in a loud and angry way, often with little effect •**bluster** *noun* [**U**]

blustery /ˈblʌstəri/ *adjective* very windy *a cold, blustery day*

ˌB ˈlymphocyte (*also* **B-cell**) *noun* [**C**] **BIOLOGY** a type of blood cell that produces antibodies (= substances in the blood that fight disease)

boa constrictor /ˌbəʊəkənˈstrɪktəʳ/ *noun* [**C**] a large, strong snake, found in South and Central America, that kills animals and birds by wrapping itself around them and crushing them

boar /bɔːʳ/ *noun* [**C**] **1** FARM ANIMAL a male pig **2** WILD ANIMAL (*also* **wild boar**) a wild pig

board¹ /bɔːd/ *noun* **1** WOOD [**C**] a long, thin, flat piece of wood *He nailed some boards across the broken window.* **2** SURFACE [**C**] a flat piece of wood, plastic, etc used for a particular purpose *an* ***ironing board*** ○ *a* ***chopping board*** **3** INFORMATION [**C**] a piece of wood, plastic, etc on a wall, where information can be put *Have you seen the poster on the board?* **4 EDUCATION** [**C**] a surface on the wall of a school room that the teacher writes on *Copy down the sentences from the board.* **5** GAMES [**C**] a piece of wood, cardboard, etc for playing games on *a chess board* **6** ORGANIZATION [**group**] a group of people who officially control a company or organization, or a particular type of business activity *The board approved the sales plan.* ○ *the Gas/Tourist Board* **7 on board** on a boat, train, aircraft, etc **8** MEALS [**U**] meals that are provided when you stay in a hotel *bed and board* ○ *How much is a single room with* ***full board*** (= all meals)? **9 across the board** affecting everyone or every part of something *Jobs are likely to be lost across the board.* ⊃See also: **bulletin board, diving board, drawing board, full board, half board, ironing board**

board² /bɔːd/ *verb* **1** GET ON A VEHICLE [**I, T**] to get on a bus, boat, aircraft, etc *He boarded the train to London.* **2** TRAIN/AIRCRAFT ETC [**I**] If an aircraft, train, etc is boarding, passengers are getting onto it.

board sth up *phrasal verb* to cover a door or window with wooden boards

boarder /ˈbɔːdəʳ/ *noun* [**C**] **1 EDUCATION** *UK* a student who lives at school **2** *US* (*UK* **lodger**) someone who pays for a place to sleep and meals in someone else's house **3 SPORT** someone who goes snowboarding (= sport where you stand on a board to move over snow)

ˈboard ˌgame *noun* [**C**] a game such as chess that is played on a board

ˈboarding ˌhouse *noun* [**C**] a house where you pay for a room and meals

ˈboarding ˌpass (*also* **ˈboarding ˌcard**) *noun* [**C**] a piece of paper you must show to get on an aircraft

ˈboarding ˌschool *noun* [**C**] **EDUCATION** a school where students live and study

boardroom /ˈbɔːdruːm/ *noun* [**C**] a room where the people who control a company or organization have meetings

boast¹ /bəʊst/ *verb* **1** PRIDE [**I, T**] to talk with too much pride about what you have done or what you own *I wish she would stop* ***boasting about*** *her exam results.* [**+ that**] *Liam boasted that he owned two sports cars.* **2** HAVE [**T**] If a place boasts something good, it has it. *New York boasts some of the best museums in the world.*

boast² /bəʊst/ *noun* [**C**] something you are proud of and like to tell people about

boastful /ˈbəʊstfəl/ *adjective* talking with too much pride *boastful remarks*

O-ᵚ**boat** /bəʊt/ *noun* **1** [**C**] a vehicle for travelling on water *a fishing boat* **2 be in the same boat** to be in the same unpleasant situation as other people *She complains that she doesn't have enough money, but we're all in the same boat.* **3 miss the boat** to be too late to get what you want *I'm afraid you've missed the boat. All the tickets have been sold.* **4 push the boat out** *UK* to spend a lot of money, especially when you are celebrating **5 rock the boat** to do or say something that changes a situation in a way that causes problems ⊃See also: **rowing boat**

bob /bɒb/ *verb* [**I**] **bobbing,** *past* **bobbed** to move up and down quickly and gently *boats bobbing in the harbour*

bobby /ˈbɒbi/ *noun* [**C**] *UK informal old-fashioned* a police officer

ˈbobby ˌpin *US* (*UK* **hairgrip**) *noun* [**C**] a small, thin piece of metal, used to fasten a woman's hair in position

bode /bəʊd/ *verb literary* **bode ill/well** to be a bad or good sign for the future *These religious differences do not bode well for their marriage.*

bodily¹ /ˈbɒdɪli/ *adjective* [**always before noun**] **BIOLOGY** relating to a person's body ***bodily strength***

bodily² /ˈbɒdɪli/ *adverb* If you move someone bodily, you lift or push them. *He carried her bodily out of the room.*

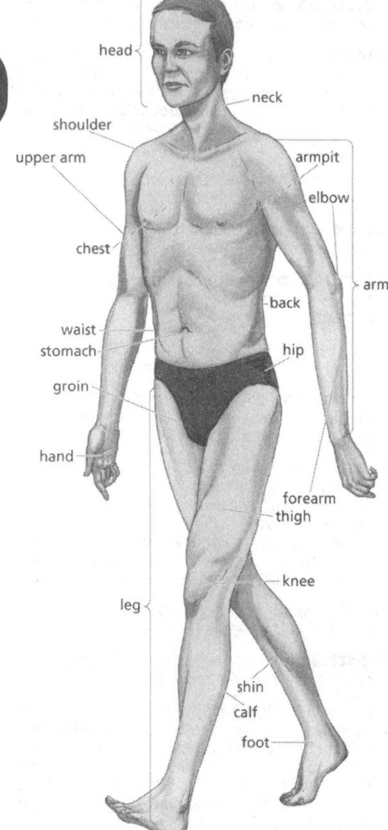

body

O-ᵐ**body** /ˈbɒdi/ *noun* **1 ANATOMY** [C] the whole physical structure of a person or animal *the* ***human body*** ➲See colour picture **The Body** on page Centre 13 **2** [DEAD] [C] a dead person *Police found the body in a field.* **3** [NOT ARMS/LEGS] [C] the main part of a person or animal's body, not the head, arms, or legs *a dog with a thin body and short legs* **4** [GROUP] [**group**] an official group of people who work together *the sport's regulatory body* **5** [MAIN PART] [**no plural**] the main part of something *The body of the book is about his childhood.* **6** [AMOUNT] [**no plural**] a large amount of information *a body of research into AIDS* **7** [VEHICLE] [C] the main part of a vehicle *The body of the ship was not damaged.*

bodybuilding /ˈbɒdibɪldɪŋ/ *noun* [U] **SPORT** doing exercises with heavy weights to make your muscles big •**bodybuilder** *noun* [C]

bodyguard /ˈbɒdigɑːd/ *noun* [C] someone whose job is to protect someone

ˈbody ˌlanguage *noun* [U] the way you move your body, that shows people what you are feeling

bog¹ /bɒg/ *noun* [C, U] **GEOGRAPHY** an area of soft, wet ground

bog² /bɒg/ *verb* **bogging**, *past* **bogged**
be bogged down *phrasal verb* to become so involved in something that you cannot do anything else *Try not to get too bogged down in details.*

boggle /ˈbɒgl/ *verb* **the mind boggles** *UK informal* (*US* **it boggles the mind** *informal*) something you say if something is difficult for you to accept, imagine, or understand *The mind boggles at the stupidity of some people.* ➲See also: **mind-boggling**

bogus /ˈbəʊgəs/ *adjective* pretending to be real *a bogus doctor* ○ *bogus documents*

bohemian /bəʊˈhiːmiən/ *adjective* typical of artists, musicians, etc, who live in a more informal way than most people

O-ᵐ**boil¹** /bɔɪl/ *verb* [I, T] **1 PHYSICS** If a liquid boils, or if you boil it, it reaches the temperature where bubbles rise up in it and it produces steam. *boiling water* **2** [CONTAINER] If a container of liquid boils, or if you boil it, the liquid inside it reaches the temperature where bubbles rise up in it and it produces steam. *I've boiled the kettle.* **3 FOOD** to cook food in water that is boiling *Boil the pasta for 10 minutes.* ➲See picture at **cook**
boil down to sth *phrasal verb* If a situation or problem boils down to something, that is the main reason for it. *The problem boils down to one thing - lack of money.*
boil over *phrasal verb* **1** [LIQUID] If a liquid that is being heated boils over, it flows over the side of the pan. **2** [SITUATION/FEELING] If a difficult situation or bad emotion boils over, it cannot be controlled any more and people start to argue or fight.

boil² /bɔɪl/ *noun* **1 bring sth to the boil FOOD** to heat something until it starts to produce bubbles and steam *Bring the water to the boil, then add the rice.* **2 HEALTH** [C] a red swollen area on the skin that is infected

boiler /ˈbɔɪləʳ/ *noun* [C] a piece of equipment that provides hot water for a house

boiling /ˈbɔɪlɪŋ/ (*also* **ˌboiling ˈhot**) *adjective informal* very hot *It's boiling in here!*

ˈboiling ˌpoint *noun* [C] **MEASURES, PHYSICS** the temperature that a liquid boils at

boisterous /ˈbɔɪstᵊrəs/ *adjective* noisy and full of energy *a boisterous child* •**boisterously** *adverb*

WORD PARTNERS FOR ***bold***

a bold **decision/move/plan/step**

bold¹ /bəʊld/ *adjective* **1** [NOT FRIGHTENED] not frightened of taking risks *It was a* ***bold decision*** *to go and live abroad.* **2** [COLOUR/SHAPE] strong in colour or shape ***bold colours*** ○ *a* ***bold design*** **3** [LETTERS] words that are printed in bold letters are darker and thicker than normal words •**boldly** *adverb* •**boldness** *noun* [U]

bold² /bəʊld/ *noun* [U] a style of printing in which the letters are darker and thicker than usual

bollard /ˈbɒlɑːd/ *noun* [C] *UK* a short thick post in a road, used to stop cars driving somewhere

Bolshevik /ˈbɒlʃəvɪk/ *noun* [C] **POLITICS** a supporter of the political system introduced by Lenin in Russia in 1917 •**Bolshevik** *adjective* •**Bolshevism** /ˈbɒlʃəvɪzm/ *noun* [U]

bolster /ˈbəʊlstəʳ/ *verb* [T] to make something stronger by supporting or encouraging it *Strong sales are bolstering the economy.*

bolt¹ /bəʊlt/ *noun* [C] **1** [FOR LOCKING] a metal bar that you push across a door or window to lock it **2** [FOR FASTENING] a small piece of metal that is used with a nut (= metal piece with a hole in the middle) to fasten pieces of wood or metal together ➲See also: the nuts (**nut**) and bolts

bolt² /bəʊlt/ *verb* [T] **1** [FASTEN] to fasten two things together with a bolt *The seats in the cinema were bolted to the floor.* **2** [LOCK] to lock a door or window with a bolt **3 bolt down/out/through, etc** to move suddenly and quickly *The cat bolted out of the door when it saw the dog.* **4** [EAT] (*also* **bolt down**) to eat something very quickly

ˌbolt ˈupright *adverb* sitting or standing with your back very straight

WORD PARTNERS FOR ***bomb***

plant a bomb • a bomb **explodes/goes off** • a bomb **attack/blast** • a bomb **scare/threat/warning**

O╍**bomb¹** /bɒm/ *noun* [C] a weapon that explodes and causes damage *The bomb destroyed several office buildings in the city.* ➲See also: **atomic bomb**

bomb² /bɒm/ *verb* **1** [T] to attack a place using bombs *The factories were bombed during the war.* **2 bomb along/down/through, etc** *UK informal* to move very quickly *A car came bombing down the road.*

bombard /bɒmˈbɑːd/ *verb* [T] to continuously attack a place using guns and bombs •**bombardment** *noun* [C, U] *an* ***aerial bombardment***
bombard sb with sth *phrasal verb* to give someone too much information, ask them too many questions, etc

bomber /ˈbɒməʳ/ *noun* [C] **1** [AIRCRAFT] an aircraft that drops bombs **2** [PERSON] someone who puts a bomb somewhere

bombshell /ˈbɒmʃel/ *noun* [C] *informal* a piece of usually bad news that surprises you very much *He* ***dropped a bombshell*** *by announcing that he was quitting the sport.*

bona fide /ˌbəʊnəˈfaɪdi/ *adjective* real and honest *Make sure you are dealing with a bona fide company.*

bonang /ˈbɒnæŋ/ *noun* [C] **MUSIC** a musical instrument from Indonesia, with several metal pots placed on strings over a wooden frame

bonanza /bəˈnænzə/ *noun* [C] a situation in which many people are successful and get a lot of money *The Internet is a bonanza for the computer industry.*

WORD PARTNERS FOR ***bond***

create/forge/form/strengthen a bond • a **close** bond • a bond **with** sb **/between** sb and sb

bond¹ /bɒnd/ *noun* [C] **1** an interest, experience, or feeling that makes two people feel connected *A love of opera created a* ***bond between*** *them.* **2 FINANCE** an official document from a government or company to show that you have given them money that they will pay back with a certain amount of extra money **3** (*also* **chemical bond**) **CHEMISTRY** the way two atoms are joined together in a chemical compound

bond² /bɒnd/ *verb* **1** [JOIN] [I, T] If two things bond, they stick together, or if you bond them, you make them stick together. *This glue bonds wood and metal in seconds.* **2** [RELATIONSHIP] [I] to develop a strong relationship with someone *Physical contact helps a mother* ***bond with*** *her baby.*

bondage /ˈbɒndɪdʒ/ *noun* [U] when someone is completely controlled by something or is a slave (= owned by the person they work for)

O╍**bone¹** /bəʊn/ *noun* **1 ANATOMY** [C, U] one of the hard pieces that make the structure inside a person or animal *He broke a bone in his hand.* **2 a bone of contention** something that people argue about **3 have a bone to pick with sb** *informal* to want to talk to someone because you are annoyed about something they have done **4 make no bones about sth/doing sth** to say what you think or feel, without being embarrassed *She made no bones about her reluctance to work with me.*

bone² /bəʊn/ *verb* [T] **FOOD** to remove the bones from meat or fish

ˈbone ˌmarrow *noun* [U] **ANATOMY, BIOLOGY** the soft substance inside bones

bonfire /ˈbɒnfaɪəʳ/ *noun* [C] a large fire outside, often used for burning waste

bonkers /ˈbɒŋkəz/ *adjective informal* crazy

bonnet /ˈbɒnɪt/ *noun* [C] **1** [CAR] *UK* (*US* **hood**) the metal cover of a car's engine ➲See colour picture **Car** on page Centre 7 **2** [HAT] a hat that you tie under your face

bonus /ˈbəʊnəs/ *noun* [C] **1 FINANCE** an extra amount of money that you are given, especially because you have worked hard *All employees received a bonus of £500.* **2** another pleasant thing in addition to something you were expecting *The sunny weather was an* ***added bonus.***

bony /ˈbəʊni/ *adjective* very thin, so that you can see or feel bones *bony elbows*

boo /buː/ *verb* [I, T] **booing,** *past* **booed** to shout the word "boo" to show that you do not like a speech, performance, etc •**boo** *noun* [C]

boob /buːb/ *noun* [C] *informal* **1** [BREAST] a woman's breast **2** [MISTAKE] a silly mistake

booby prize /ˈbuːbiˌpraɪz/ *noun* [C] a prize that you get if you finish last in a competition

booby trap /ˈbuːbiˌtræp/ *noun* [C] something dangerous, especially a bomb, that is hidden somewhere that looks safe •**booby-trap** *verb* [T] [**often passive**] His car was booby-trapped.

book[1] /bʊk/ *noun* **1** TEXT [C] a set of pages fastened together in a cover for people to read *a book about animals* **2 a book of stamps/tickets, etc** a set of stamps, tickets, etc that are fastened together inside a cover **3** FOR WRITING [C] a set of pages fastened together in a cover and used for writing on *an* ***address book*** **4 do sth by the book** to do something exactly as the rules tell you **5 be in sb's good/bad books** *UK informal* If you are in someone's good books, they are pleased with you, and if you are in their bad books, they are angry with you. ➲See also: **cookery book,** take a **leaf**[1] out of sb's book, **phone book, reference book**

book[2] /bʊk/ *verb* **1** ARRANGE [I, T] to arrange to use or do something at a particular time in the future *to book a ticket/hotel room* ○ *We've booked a trip to Spain for next month.* ○ *Sorry, the hotel is* ***fully booked*** (= has no more rooms). **2** CRIME [T] to officially accuse someone of a crime *Detectives* ***booked*** *him* ***for*** *resisting arrest.* **3 SPORT** [T] *UK* If a sports official books you, they write an official record of something you have done wrong. *The referee* ***booked*** *two players* ***for*** *fighting during the game.*

book in/book into sth *phrasal verb UK* to say that you have arrived when you get to a hotel

book sb in/book sb into sth *phrasal verb mainly UK* to arrange for someone to stay at a hotel

bookcase /ˈbʊkkeɪs/ *noun* [C] a piece of furniture with shelves for putting books on ➲See colour picture **The Living Room** on page Centre 4

ˈ**book** ˌ**club** *noun* [C] a group of people who meet regularly to talk about books they have read

bookie /ˈbʊki/ *noun* [C] *informal* someone whose job is to take and pay out money that people risk trying to guess the result of horse races, sports events, etc

WORD PARTNERS FOR ***booking***

accept/cancel/make/take a booking • an **advance** booking • a booking **for** sth • a booking **fee/form**

booking /ˈbʊkɪŋ/ *noun* [C, U] *mainly UK* an arrangement you make to have a hotel room, tickets, etc at a particular time in the future ***advance booking***

bookkeeping /ˈbʊkˌkiːpɪŋ/ *noun* [U] **FINANCE** recording the money that an organization or business spends and receives •**bookkeeper** *noun* [C]

booklet /ˈbʊklət/ *noun* [C] a small, thin book that contains information *The tourist office has booklets about the area.*

bookmaker /ˈbʊkˌmeɪkəʳ/ *noun* [C] a bookie

bookmark[1] /ˈbʊkmɑːk/ *noun* [C] **1** something you put in a book so you can findthe page you want **2 INTERNET** an address on the Internet that you record so that you can quickly find something again *Add this website to your bookmarks.*

bookmark[2] /ˈbʊkmɑːk/ *verb* [T] **INTERNET** to make a record of the address of an Internet document in your computer so that you can find it again easily

ˌ**book of prime** ˈ**entry** *noun* [C] **FINANCE** one of the books or computer files, for example the cash book, where a business's financial records are kept

books /bʊks/ *noun* [plural] **FINANCE** the written financial records of a business or organization

bookseller /ˈbʊkˌseləʳ/ *noun* [C] a person or company that sells books

bookshelf /ˈbʊkʃelf/ *noun* [C] *plural* **bookshelves** a shelf for holding books

bookshop /ˈbʊkʃɒp/ *UK* (*US* **bookstore** /ˈbʊkstɔːʳ/) *noun* [C] a shop that sells books

bookworm /ˈbʊkwɜːm/ *noun* [C] *informal* someone who enjoys reading very much

Boolean /ˈbuːliən/ *adjective* **COMPUTING** in a database, a Boolean field can have the values 'true' or 'false' *Boolean data* ○ *a Boolean search*

boom[1] /buːm/ *noun* [C] **1 ECONOMICS** a period when there is a big increase in sales or profits ***an economic boom*** ○ *The 1990's saw a* ***boom in*** *computer sales.* **2** a loud, deep sound ➲See also: **baby boom**

boom[2] /buːm/ *verb* [I] **1** INCREASE If something is booming, it is increasing or becoming more successful or popular very quickly. *House prices are booming.* **2** SOUND to make a loud, deep sound, or to speak in a loud, deep voice

boomerang /ˈbuːmᵊræŋ/ *noun* [C] a curved piece of wood that comes back to you when you throw it

boon /buːn/ *noun* [C] something helpful that improves your life [usually singular] *Microwaves are a boon for busy people.*

WORD PARTNERS FOR ***boost***

give sb/sth a boost • **receive** a boost • a **huge/major/massive/much-needed** boost • a **confidence/morale** boost • a boost **to** sth • a boost **for** sb

boost[1] /buːst/ *noun* [C] something that makes you feel more confident and happy, or that helps something increase or improve *Increased tourism was a major* ***boost to*** *the local economy.*

boost[2] /buːst/ *verb* [T] to increase or improve something *Getting the job has* ***boosted*** *my* ***confidence.***

booster /ˈbuːstəʳ/ *noun* **1 a confidence/morale, etc booster** something that makes you feel happier or more confident **2** [C] an engine on a spacecraft that gives extra power for the first part of a flight

boot[1] /buːt/ *noun* [C] **1** SHOE a strong shoe that covers your foot and part of your leg *a* ***pair of boots*** ➲See colour picture **Clothes** on pages Centre 8,9 **2** CAR *UK* (*US* **trunk**) a closed space at the back of a car for storing things in ➲See colour picture **Car** on page Centre 7 **3 get/be given the boot** *informal* to be told that you must leave your job **4 too big for your boots** *UK informal* (*US* **too big for your britches** *informal*) behaving as if you are more important or more clever than you really are ➲See also: **car boot sale**

boot[2] /buːt/ *verb* [T] *informal* to kick someone or something

boot sb out *phrasal verb informal* to make someone leave a place or job

bootcut /ˈbuːtkʌt/ *adjective* bootleg

booth /buːð/ *noun* [C] a small area that is separated from a larger public area, especially used for doing something privately *a telephone booth*

bootleg /ˈbuːtleg/ (*also* **bootcut**) *adjective* bootleg trousers are wider at the bottom than at the knee •**bootlegs** *noun* [plural]

booty /ˈbuːti/ *noun* [U] valuable things stolen by thieves or by an army in a war

booze¹ /buːz/ *noun* [U] *informal* alcoholic drinks

booze² /buːz/ *verb* [I] *informal* to drink alcohol

WORD PARTNERS FOR ***border***

cross the border • **across/on/over** the border • the border **between** [France and Spain/ Switzerland and Italy, etc] • [Germany's/Syria's, etc] border **with** [France/Lebanon, etc] • the [French/Mexican, etc] **side** of the border • border **controls /guards**

O━**border¹** /ˈbɔːdəʳ/ *noun* [C] **1** DIVIDE the line that separates two countries or states *the **border** **between** France and Spain* ○ *We **crossed the border** from Canada into the US.* **2** EDGE a strip around the edge of something for decoration *white plates with a blue border*

border² /ˈbɔːdəʳ/ *verb* [T] **1** EDGE to form a line around the edge of something [**often passive**] *The fields are bordered by tall trees.* **2** NEXT TO to have a border with another country [**often passive**] *Spain is bordered by France and Portugal.*

border on sth *phrasal verb* to almost be a more extreme thing *Her anger bordered on aggression.*

borderline¹ /ˈbɔːdᵊlaɪn/ *adjective* If something or someone is borderline, it is not clear if they are good enough or if they will succeed. ***Borderline cases** should take the exam again.*

borderline² /ˈbɔːdᵊlaɪn/ *noun* [**no plural**] the point where one feeling, quality, level, etc ends and another one begins *My work was **on the borderline between** two grades.*

bore¹ /bɔːʳ/ *verb* **1** MAKE BORED [T] to make someone feel bored *His war stories really bore me.* **2** MAKE A HOLE [I, T] to make a hole in something hard with a tool

bore² /bɔːʳ/ *noun* **1** PERSON [C] someone who talks too much about things that are not interesting **2** SITUATION [**no plural**] a situation or job that annoys you because it causes difficulties or is not interesting *It's a real bore not having a car.*

bore³ /bɔːʳ/ *past tense of* bear

O━**bored** /bɔːd/ *adjective* feeling tired and unhappy because something is not interesting or because you have nothing to do *I'm **bored with** doing homework.* ○ *We were **bored stiff*** (= extremely bored) *in her lessons.* •**boredom** /ˈbɔːdəm/ *noun* [U] when you are bored *I nearly died of boredom.*

OTHER WAYS OF SAYING ***boring***

We often use **bland** when describing food: *This sauce is really **bland**, it doesn't taste of anything.*

If a film, play, book, etc. or a person is boring, you can say that they are **dull**: *I find her writing a bit **dull**.*

Monotonous is often used about something that you listen to: *The teacher had a really **monotonous** voice and I almost fell asleep.*

When describing an activity, **tedious** is sometimes used: *You have to fill in various forms, which is a bit **tedious**.*

If speech or writing is boring because it is too long, we can describe it as **long-winded**: *He gave this really **long-winded** explanation about why he'd changed his mind.*

O━**boring** /ˈbɔːrɪŋ/ *adjective* not interesting or exciting *a boring job* ○ *The film was so boring, I fell asleep.*

COMMON LEARNER ERROR

bored or **boring?**

Bored is used to describe how someone feels about something.

He didn't enjoy the lesson because he was bored.

~~*He didn't enjoy the lesson because he was boring.*~~

If something or someone is **boring**, they make you feel bored.

The book was long and boring.

O━**born¹** /bɔːn/ *verb* **be born a** When a person or animal is born, they come out of their mother's body and start to exist. *She was born in London in 1973.* ○ *an American-born writer* (= born in America) **b** If an idea is born, it starts to exist.

born² /bɔːn/ *adjective* **a born actor/leader/ teacher, etc** someone who has a natural ability to act, lead, teach, etc

born-again /ˌbɔːnəˈgen/ *adjective* **a born-again Christian** RELIGION someone who has become a very enthusiastic member of the Christian religion

borne /bɔːn/ *past participle of* bear

boron /ˈbɔːrɒn/ *noun* [U] CHEMISTRY a hard, yellow-brown chemical element used in nuclear reactors and to make steel hard (symbol **B**)

borough /ˈbʌrə/ (US) /ˈbɜːrəʊ/ *noun* [C] a town or part of a city

O━**borrow** /ˈbɒrəʊ/ *verb* **1** USE [T] to use something that belongs to someone else and give it back later *Can I borrow a pen please?* ○ *I **borrowed** the book **from** my sister.* **2** ECONOMICS, FINANCE [I, T] to take money from a bank or financial organization and pay it back over a period of time **3** IDEA [T] to take and use a word or idea *The English word 'rucksack' is **borrowed from** German.*

borrower /ˈbɒrəʊəʳ/ *noun* [C] FINANCE someone who borrows money

B

bosom /ˈbʊzᵊm/ *noun* **1** [C] a woman's breasts **2 a bosom buddy/pal, etc** a very good friend

O‑**boss**[1] /bɒs/ *noun* [C] someone who is responsible for employees and tells them what to do *I'll ask my boss if I can leave work early tomorrow.*

boss[2] /bɒs/ (*also* **boss about/around**) *verb* [T] to tell someone what they should do all the time *My older brother is always bossing me about.*

bossy /ˈbɒsi/ *adjective* always telling other people what to do •**bossiness** *noun* [U]

botanist /ˈbɒtᵊnɪst/ *noun* [C] **BIOLOGY** someone who studies plants

botany /ˈbɒtᵊni/ *noun* [U] **BIOLOGY** the scientific study of plants •**botanical** /bəˈtænɪkəl/ (*also* **botanic** /bəˈtænɪk/) *adjective* relating to botany

botch /bɒtʃ/ (*also* **botch up**) *verb* [T] to spoil something by doing it badly *a botched robbery*

O‑**both** /bəʊθ/ *pronoun, determiner, quantifier* **1** used to talk about two people or things *The children both have red hair.* ○ ***Both of*** *my sisters are teachers.* ○ *Would you like cream, ice cream, or both?* **2 both...and...** used to emphasize that you are talking about two people or things *Both Jack and his wife are keen chess players.* ➲See also: have the **best**[3] of both worlds

bother[1] /ˈbɒðəʳ/ *verb* **1** ANNOY [T] to annoy someone by trying to get their attention when they do not want to see you or talk to you *Sorry to bother you, but could you spare any change?* **2** WORRY [T] to make someone feel worried or upset *Living on my own doesn't bother me at all.* **3** DO [I, T] to make the effort to do something [+ **doing** sth] *Don't bother making the bed - I'll do it later.* [+ **to do** sth] *He didn't even bother to call.* **4 can't be bothered** *informal* If you can't be bothered to do something, you are too lazy or tired to do it. [+ **to do** sth] *I can't be bothered to iron my clothes.* **5 not bothered** *UK informal* If you are not bothered about something, it is not important to you and does not worry you. *"Do you want tea or coffee?" "Either, I'm not bothered."*

bother[2] /ˈbɒðəʳ/ *noun* [U] trouble or problems *"Are you sure you don't mind taking me?" "No,* ***it's no bother****, really!"*

bothered /ˈbɒðəd/ *adjective* [**never before noun**] If you are bothered about something, it is important to you and you are worried about it. *He's very* ***bothered about*** *what other people think.*

Botox /ˈbəʊtɒks/ *noun* [U] *trademark* **HEALTH** Botulinum Toxin: a drug used in a person's face to make it look smooth and young •**Botox** *verb* [T]

O‑**bottle**[1] /ˈbɒtl/ *noun* [C] a container for liquids, usually made of glass or plastic, with a narrow top *an empty bottle* ○ *a bottle of wine* ➲See also: **hot-water bottle**

bottle[2] /ˈbɒtl/ *verb* [T] to put liquid into a bottle [**often passive**] *This wine was bottled in France.* ○ *bottled beer/water*

bottle sth up *phrasal verb* to not allow yourself to show or talk about your feelings

ˈ**bottle ˌbank** *noun* [C] *UK* **ENVIRONMENT** a large container outside, where you can put empty bottles so that the glass can be used again

bottleneck /ˈbɒtlnek/ *noun* [C] **1** PROBLEM something that causes a process to happen more slowly than it should **2** ROAD a narrow part of a road where traffic moves slowly

O‑**bottom**[1] /ˈbɒtəm/ *noun* **1** LOWEST PART [C] the lowest part of something [**usually singular**] *Click on the icon* ***at the bottom of*** *the page.* **2** FLAT SURFACE [C] the flat surface on the lowest side of something [**usually singular**] *There was a price tag on* ***the bottom of*** *the box.* **3** LOWEST POSITION [**no plural**] the lowest position in a group, organization, etc *He got bad exam marks and is* ***at the bottom of*** *the class.* **4** SEA/RIVER ETC [**no plural**] the ground under a river, lake, or sea *Divers found the wreck on* ***the bottom of*** *the ocean.* **5** FURTHEST PART [**no plural**] the part of a road or area of land that is furthest from where you are *Go to the bottom of the road and turn left.* **6 BIOLOGY, ANATOMY** [C] the part of your body that you sit on **7 be at the bottom of sth** to be the cause of a problem or situation **8 get to the bottom of sth** to discover the truth about a situation ➲See also: **rock bottom,** from **top**[1] to bottom

bottom[2] /ˈbɒtəm/ *adjective* [**always before noun**] in the lowest position *the bottom drawer*

bottomless /ˈbɒtəmləs/ *adjective* **a bottomless pit** a supply, especially of money, that has no limit

the ˌbottom ˈline *noun* the most important fact in a situation *The bottom line is that if you don't work, you'll fail the test.*

bough /baʊ/ *noun* [C] *literary* a large branch on a tree

bought /bɔːt/ *past of* buy

boulder /ˈbəʊldəʳ/ *noun* [C] **GEOLOGY** a very large rock

ˈ**boulder ˌclay** *noun* [U] **GEOLOGY** a type of heavy, sticky soil full of large rocks that is formed in and between large areas of ice

boulevard /ˈbuːləvɑːd/ *noun* [C] a wide road in a city, usually with trees along it

bounce[1] /baʊns/ *verb* **1** BALL [I, T] to hit a surface and then move quickly away, or to make something do this *The ball bounced high into the air.* **2** JUMP [I] to jump up and down several times on a soft surface *The children loved bouncing on the bed.* **3 bounce along/around/into, etc** to move somewhere in a happy and energetic way *Sarah bounced into the room with a big smile on her face.* **4 FINANCE** [I, T] If a cheque (= piece of printed paper you write on to pay for things) bounces, or a bank bounces it, the bank will not pay it because there is not enough money in the account.

bounce back *phrasal verb* **1** to be successful or happy again after a failure, disappointment, etc *After a terrible start the team bounced back and won the game.* **2 INTERNET** If an email bounces back, it is returned to you because the address is not correct or there is a computer problem.

bounce[2] /baʊns/ *noun* [C, U] when something bounces, or the quality that makes something able to bounce

bouncer /ˈbaʊnsəʳ/ *noun* [C] someone whose job is to stand at the door of a bar, party, etc and keep out people who are not wanted

bouncy /ˈbaʊnsi/ *adjective* **1** HAPPY happy and full of energy *She's very bouncy and confident.* **2** BOUNCE able to bounce *bouncy balls*

bound[1] /baʊnd/ *adjective* **1 bound to do sth** certain to do something, or certain to happen *You're bound to feel nervous before your driving test.* **2 bound up with sth** closely connected with something *A country's culture is bound up with its language and history.* **3** FORCED [**never before noun**] having a moral or legal duty to do something *The witness was **bound by** an oath to tell the truth.* **4** DIRECTION [**never before noun**] travelling towards a particular place *He was on a train **bound for** Berlin.*

bound[2] /baʊnd/ *verb* **bound across/down/into, etc** to move quickly with large steps or jumps *Guy bounded across the room to answer the phone.*

bound[3] /baʊnd/ *noun* [**C**] a big jump ➲See also: by/in leaps (**leap**[2]) and bounds

bound[4] /baʊnd/ *past of* bind

boundary /ˈbaʊndᵊri/ *noun* [**C**] **1** LINE a line that divides two areas or forms an edge around an area *The mountains mark the **boundary between** the two countries.* **2** LIMIT a limit *Such violence is beyond the boundaries of civilized conduct.*

boundless /ˈbaʊndləs/ *adjective* having no limit *He has **boundless energy/enthusiasm**.*

bounds /baʊndz/ *noun* **1** [**plural**] legal or social limits *They have overstepped **the bounds of** good taste.* **2 out of bounds** If a place is out of bounds, you are not allowed to go there. *The staff room is out of bounds to students.*

bounty /ˈbaʊnti/ *noun* **1** LARGE AMOUNT [**C, U**] a large or generous amount of something **2** REWARD [**C**] an amount of money paid as a reward

bouquet /bʊˈkeɪ/ *noun* [**C**] flowers that are tied together in an attractive way

bourbon /ˈbɜːbən/ *noun* [**C, U**] **FOOD** a type of American whisky (= strong alcoholic drink)

bourgeois /ˈbɔːʒwɑː/ *adjective* **SOCIETY** typical of middle class people who are too interested in money and correct social behaviour *bourgeois values* •**the bourgeoisie** /ˌbɔːʒwɑːˈziː/ *noun* [**group**] the middle class, that owns most of society's money

bout /baʊt/ *noun* [**C**] **1** a short period of activity or illness *a bout of depression* **2 SPORT** a fight in boxing

boutique /buːˈtiːk/ *noun* [**C**] a small shop that sells fashionable clothes

bovine /ˈbəʊvaɪn/ *adjective* relating to cows

bow[1] /baʊ/ *verb* [**I, T**] to bend your head or body forward in order to show respect or to thank an audience *The actors all bowed after the performance.* ○ *We **bowed** our **heads** in prayer.*

bow out *phrasal verb* to leave a job or stop doing an activity, usually after a long time *He **bowed out of** politics at the age of 70.*

bow to sth/sb *phrasal verb* to do what someone else wants you to do *The government are refusing to **bow to** public **pressure**.*

bow[2] /baʊ/ *noun* [**C**] **1** BEND when you bow *The actors came back on stage and **took a bow**.* **2** SHIP the front part of a ship

bow[3] /bəʊ/ *noun* [**C**] **1** KNOT a knot with two curved parts and two loose ends, that is used to tie shoes or as decoration **2 MUSIC** a long, thin piece of wood with hair stretched between the ends, used to play some musical instruments **3** WEAPON a piece of curved wood with string fixed to both ends, used for shooting arrows

bowel /baʊəl/ *noun* [**C**] **ANATOMY** the long tube that carries solid waste from your stomach out of your body [**usually plural**] *He's got trouble with his bowels.*

O⁻ **bowl**[1] /bəʊl/ *noun* [**C**] a round, deep dish used for holding soup and other food *a bowl of rice/soup*

bowl[2] /bəʊl/ *verb* [**I, T**] **SPORT** **1** to roll a ball along a surface as part of a game **2** in cricket, to throw a ball to the person who has to hit it

bowler /ˈbəʊləʳ/ *noun* [**C**] **SPORT** in cricket, the player who throws the ball so someone can hit it ➲See colour picture **Sports 2** on page Centre 15

ˌbowler ˈhat *UK* (*US* **derby**) *noun* [**C**] a round, hard, black hat worn by men, especially in the past

bowling /ˈbəʊlɪŋ/ *noun* [**U**] **SPORT** a game in which you roll a large ball along a wooden track in order to knock down bottle-shaped objects

bowls /bəʊlz/ *noun* [**U**] *UK* **SPORT** a game in which you roll large balls as close as possible to a smaller ball

ˌbow ˈtie *noun* [**C**] a piece of cloth around the neck in the shape of a bow that men sometimes wear, especially at formal events

O⁻ **box**[1] /bɒks/ *noun* **1** CONTAINER [**C**] a square or rectangular container *a cardboard box* ○ *a box of chocolates/matches* **2** SQUARE SPACE [**C**] a small square on a page that gives you information or where you write information *Tick the box if you would like more details.* **3** SMALL PLACE [**C**] a small area of a theatre, court, etc that is separate from where other people are sitting **4 the box** *informal* the television *What's **on the box** tonight?* ➲See also: **phone box, post box, witness box**

box[2] /bɒks/ *verb* **1 SPORT** [**I, T**] to do the sport of boxing **2** [**T**] (*also* **box up**) to put something in a box *We boxed up the old books.*

box sb/sth in *phrasal verb* to move so close to someone or something that they cannot move [**often passive**] *When I returned I found that my car had been boxed in.*

boxer /ˈbɒksəʳ/ *noun* [**C**] **SPORT** someone who does the sport of boxing

boxers /ˈbɒksəz/ (*also* **ˈboxer ˌshorts**) *noun* [**plural**] loose underwear worn by men ➲See colour picture **Clothes** on page Centre 9

boxing /ˈbɒksɪŋ/ *noun* [**U**] **SPORT** a sport in which two people hit each other while wearing big, leather gloves (= pieces of clothing for your hands) ➲See colour picture **Sports 1** on page Centre 14

ˈBoxing ˌDay *noun* [**C, U**] 26 December, a public holiday in Britain and Canada

ˈbox ˌoffice *noun* [**C**] the place in a theatre, cinema, etc where you buy tickets

B

boy[1] /bɔɪ/ *noun* **1** [C] a male child or young man *We've got three children - a boy and two girls.* **2 the boys** *informal* a group of male friends *Steve's gone out with the boys.*

boy[2] /bɔɪ/ (*also* **oh boy**) *exclamation* used when you are excited or pleased *Boy, that was good!*

ˈboy ˌband *noun* [C] **MUSIC** a pop music group made up of young men who sing and dance

boycott /ˈbɔɪkɒt/ *noun* [C] when someone refuses to buy, use, or do something because they do not approve of it *Environmental groups have called for a* ***boycott of*** *the company's products.* •**boycott** *verb* [T] *Several countries boycotted the international peace talks.*

boyfriend /ˈbɔɪfrend/ *noun* [C] a man or boy who someone is having a romantic relationship with

boyhood /ˈbɔɪhʊd/ *noun* [U] the part of a male's life when they are a boy

boyish /ˈbɔɪɪʃ/ *adjective* like a boy *boyish charm*

ˌBoy ˈScout *UK* (*US* **ˈBoy ˌScout**) *noun* [C] a boy who belongs to an organization that teaches boys practical skills

bra /brɑː/ *noun* [C] a piece of woman's underwear that supports the breasts ➲See colour picture **Clothes** on page Centre 5

brace[1] /breɪs/ *verb* **brace yourself** to prepare for something difficult or unpleasant *I* ***braced myself for*** *bad news.*

brace[2] /breɪs/ *noun* [C] **1** something that supports or holds something in the correct position *He wore a neck brace for months after the accident.* **2 HEALTH** a wire object that some children wear to make their teeth straight

bracelet /ˈbreɪslət/ *noun* [C] a piece of jewellery that you wear around your wrist

braces /ˈbreɪsɪz/ *UK* (*US* **suspenders**) *noun* [**plural**] two straps fixed to a pair of trousers that go over your shoulders and stop the trousers from falling down

bracing /ˈbreɪsɪŋ/ *adjective* Bracing weather or a bracing activity makes you feel cold but healthy and full of energy. *bracing sea air* ○ *a bracing walk*

bracket[1] /ˈbrækɪt/ *noun* [C] **1** GROUP a group of people whose ages, taxes, etc are between two limits *Most heart attack victims are in the 45-65 age bracket.* **2** SUPPORT a piece of metal, wood, etc, that is fixed to a wall to support something, especially a shelf

bracket[2] /ˈbrækɪt/ *verb* [T] **1 LANGUAGE** to put curved lines ( ) around words, phrases, numbers, etc to make them separate **2** to consider two or more people or things to be similar [**often passive**] *Canadian accents are often* ***bracketed with*** *American accents.*

brackets /ˈbrækɪts/ (*also* **parentheses**) *noun* [**plural**] *UK* **LANGUAGE** two curved lines ( ) used around extra information or information that should be considered as separate from the main part ➲See Extra help page **Punctuation** on page Centre 19.

bract /brækt/ *noun* [C] **BIOLOGY** a type of leaf that grows from the area just below a flower

brag /bræg/ *verb* [I] **bragging**, *past* **bragged** to talk with too much pride about what you have done or what you own *He's always* ***bragging about*** *how much money he earns.*

braid[1] /breɪd/ *noun* **1** HAIR [C] *US* (*UK* **plait**) a single piece of hair made by twisting three thinner pieces over and under each other **2** CLOTH [U] a thin piece of cloth or twisted threads used for decorating clothes

braid[2] /breɪd/ *US* (*UK* **plait**) *verb* [T] to twist three pieces of hair over and under each other

braille /breɪl/ *noun* [U] a system of printing for blind people, using raised patterns that they read by touching

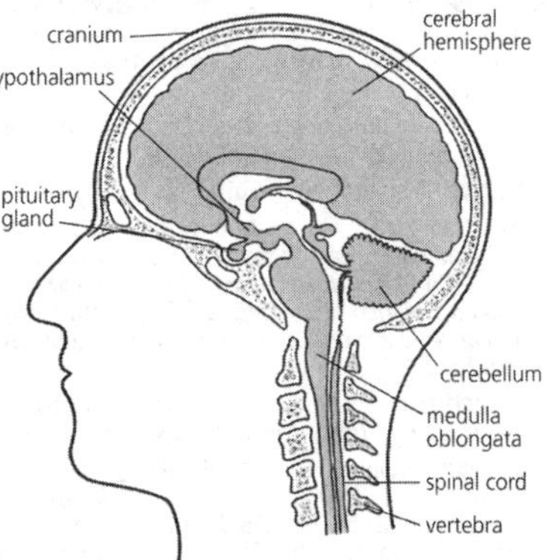

brain

brain /breɪn/ *noun* **1 ANATOMY** [C] the organ inside your head that controls your thoughts, feelings, and movements ***brain damage*** **2** [C] *informal* an extremely intelligent person [**usually plural**] *This university attracts some of the* ***best brains*** *in the country.* **3 brains** intelligence *He has brains and good looks.* **4 have sth on the brain** *informal* to think or talk about something all the time *You've got football on the brain!* **5 pick sb's brains** *informal* to ask someone for information *I want to pick your brains about keeping chickens.* **6 the brains behind sth** *informal* the person who has planned and organized something successful *Anthony is the brains behind the project.*

brainchild /ˈbreɪntʃaɪld/ *noun* **the brainchild of sb** someone's new and clever idea or invention *The project is the brainchild of a Japanese designer.*

brainstorm /ˈbreɪnstɔːm/ *US* (*UK* **brainwave**) *noun* [C] a sudden, clever idea

brainstorming /ˈbreɪnˌstɔːmɪŋ/ *noun* [U] when a group of people meet to develop new ideas *a* ***brainstorming session***

brainwash /ˈbreɪnwɒʃ/ *verb* [T] to make someone believe something by telling them that it is true many times [**+ into + doing sth**] *Advertising often brainwashes people into buying things they do not really need.* •**brainwashing** *noun* [U]

brainwave /ˈbreɪnweɪv/ *UK* (*US* **brainstorm**) *noun* [C] a sudden, clever idea

brainy /ˈbreɪni/ *adjective informal* clever

WORD PARTNERS FOR ***brake***

apply/hit/slam on the brakes • the brakes **fail**

brake¹ /breɪk/ *noun* [C] **1** VEHICLE the part of a vehicle that makes it stop or go more slowly **2** STOP PROGRESS something that stops or slows the progress of something *High inflation has **put the brakes on** economic growth.*

brake² /breɪk/ *verb* [I] to make a vehicle stop or move more slowly, using its brake

ˈbrake ˌpedal *noun* [C] the part of a car which you push with your foot to make it go more slowly ➲See colour picture **Car** on page Centre 7

O-m **branch¹** /brɑːnʃ/ *noun* [C] **1 BIOLOGY** one of the many parts of a tree that grows out from its trunk (= main, vertical part) **2** BUSINESS one of several shops, offices, etc that are part of a company or organization *a bank with branches all over the country* **3** SUBJECT a part of a subject *Neurology is a branch of medicine.*

branch² /brɑːnʃ/ (*also* **branch off**) *verb* [I] If a road, path, etc branches, it separates into two or more roads, paths, etc.

branch out *phrasal verb* to start to do something different from what you usually do, especially in your job *After working in publishing, she **branched out into** journalism.*

brand¹ /brænd/ *noun* [C] **1** PRODUCT a product that is made by a particular company *Which brand of toothpaste do you use?* **2** TYPE a particular type of something *a team that plays a distinctive brand of football*

brand² /brænd/ *verb* [T] **1** to describe someone or something in a way that makes them seem bad *The media branded him a liar.* **2 FARMING** to burn a mark on an animal to show who owns it

ˈbrand ˌequity *noun* [U] the value to a business of having products with a particular name or made by a particular company

ˈbrand exˌtension *noun* [U] in business, using a name for a new product that is already well known from other products

branding /ˈbrændɪŋ/ *noun* [U] the act of giving a company or a product a particular design or symbol in order to advertise it

brandish /ˈbrændɪʃ/ *verb* [T] to wave something in the air, especially a weapon *He came running into the room, brandishing a gun.*

ˈbrand ˌname *noun* [C] the special name that a company gives to a product

ˌbrand ˈnew *adjective* completely new

brandy /ˈbrændi/ *noun* [C, U] **FOOD** a strong alcoholic drink made from wine

brash /bræʃ/ *adjective* too confident *a brash young businessman*

brass /brɑːs/ *noun* [U] **1** a shiny yellow metal *a door with a brass handle* **2 MUSIC** the group of musical instruments made from brass *a brass band*

brat /bræt/ *noun* [C] a child who behaves badly *a spoilt brat*

bravado /brəˈvɑːdəʊ/ *noun* [U] behaviour that is intended to make people admire you for your bravery and confidence

O-m **brave¹** /breɪv/ *adjective* showing no fear of dangerous or difficult situations *He died after a brave fight against cancer.* •**bravely** *adverb*

brave² /breɪv/ *verb* [T] to deal with a dangerous or unpleasant situation in a brave way *Crowds braved the cold weather to watch the game.*

bravery /ˈbreɪvᵊri/ *noun* [U] when someone is brave

bravo /brɑːˈvəʊ/ *exclamation* something you shout to show that you approve of something, for example a performance

brawl /brɔːl/ *noun* [C] a noisy fight, usually in public *a drunken brawl in a bar* •**brawl** *verb* [I]

brazen /ˈbreɪzᵊn/ *adjective* not feeling at all ashamed about your bad behaviour *a brazen cheat* •**brazenly** *adverb*

BRB INTERNET *internet abbreviation for* be right back: used when you stop taking part in a discussion on the Internet

WORD PARTNERS FOR ***breach***

(a) breach **of** sth • be **in** breach of sth • a **flagrant** breach of sth

breach¹ /briːtʃ/ *noun* **1 LAW** [C, U] when someone breaks a rule, agreement, or law *a policy that is **in breach of** international law* ○ *He was sued for **breach of** contract.* **2** [C] *formal* a serious disagreement between two groups, countries, etc

breach² /briːtʃ/ *verb* [T] **LAW** to break a rule, law, or agreement

O-m **bread** /bred/ *noun* [U] **FOOD** a basic food made by mixing and baking flour, water, and sometimes yeast (= substance that makes it rise) *a **slice of bread*** ○ *a **loaf of** white bread* ➲See also: the best/greatest **thing** since sliced bread

breadcrumbs /ˈbredkrʌmz/ *noun* [plural] **FOOD** very small pieces of dry bread, used in cooking

breadth /bretθ/ *noun* [U, no plural] **1** the distance from one side of something to the other side *a swimming pool with a breadth of 10 metres and a length of 50 metres* **2 sb's breadth of experience/knowledge/interest, etc** the great number of different things that someone has done, knows, is interested in, etc ➲See also: the **length** and breadth of sth

breadwinner /ˈbredˌwɪnəʳ/ *noun* [C] the person who earns the money in a family

O-m **break¹** /breɪk/ *verb past tense* **broke**, *past participle* **broken** **1** SEPARATE [I, T] to separate into two or more pieces, or to make something separate into two or more pieces *The vase fell on the floor and broke.* ○ *They had to break a window to get in.* **2 break your arm/leg, etc HEALTH** to damage a bone in your arm/leg, etc *Carolyn broke her leg in a skiing accident.* **3** NOT WORK [I, T] If you break a machine, object, etc, or if it breaks, it stops working because it is damaged. *Who broke the video?* **4 break an agreement/promise/rule, etc** to not do what you should do according to an agreement/promise/rule, etc *Police stopped him for breaking the speed limit.* **5 break the law LAW** to do something illegal **6 break the news to sb** to tell someone about something unpleasant that has happened **7 break the silence** to make a noise, speak, etc and end a period of silence *The silence was broken by a sudden knock at the door.* **8 break a habit/routine, etc** to stop doing something that you usually do **9 break a record** to do something faster, better, etc than anyone else *He broke the world record for the 200m.* **10** REST [I, T] to stop the activity you are doing to have a short rest *Let's **break for** five minutes and have a drink.* **11** BECOME KNOWN [I, T] If news or a story breaks, or if someone breaks it, it becomes known by the public for the first time. **12** WEATHER [I] *UK* If the weather breaks, it changes suddenly, and usually becomes worse. **13** VOICE [I] When a boy's voice breaks, it becomes deeper and sounds like a man's voice. **14** WAVE [I] When a wave breaks, it reaches its highest point as it moves towards the land, and then becomes flat and white. **15** STORM [I] If a storm breaks, it starts suddenly. **16 break even** FINANCE to not make money but also not lose money **17 break free/loose** to suddenly escape or become separate from something **18 dawn/day breaks** When dawn (= early morning)/day breaks, the sky becomes lighter because the sun is rising. ⊃See also: break new **ground**[1], break sb's **heart**, break the **ice**[1], break the **mould**[1], break ranks (**rank**[1])

break away *phrasal verb* **1** ESCAPE to suddenly leave or escape from someone who is holding you **2** LEAVE GROUP to stop being part of a group because you disagree with them *Some members broke away to form a new political party.*

break down *phrasal verb* **1** MACHINE If a machine or vehicle breaks down, it stops working. *My car broke down on the way to work.* **2** COMMUNICATION If a system, relationship, or discussion breaks down, it fails because there is a problem or disagreement. *Their marriage broke down after only two years.* **3** CRY to become very upset and start crying

break sth down *phrasal verb* to divide something into smaller, simpler parts

break in *phrasal verb* to get into a building or car using force, usually to steal something

break sth in *phrasal verb* to wear something new, usually shoes, for short periods of time to make them more comfortable

break into sth *phrasal verb* **1** USE FORCE to get into a building or car using force, usually to steal something **2** START to suddenly start doing something *The crowd broke into a cheer when he came on stage.*

break (sth) off *phrasal verb* to separate a part from a larger piece, or to become separate from something *He broke off a piece of chocolate.*

break off *phrasal verb* to suddenly stop speaking or doing something *She broke off in the middle of a sentence.*

break sth off *phrasal verb* to end a relationship *She **broke off the engagement** just two weeks before the wedding.*

break out *phrasal verb* **1** START If a fire, war, disease, etc breaks out, it starts suddenly. *A fight broke out among the crowd.* **2** ESCAPE to escape from prison *to break out of jail* **3 break out in a rash/sweat, etc** HEALTH to suddenly have spots or sweat (= salty liquid) appear on your skin

break through sth *phrasal verb* to force your way through something that is holding you back *Protesters broke through the barriers.*

break (sth) up *phrasal verb* to divide into many pieces, or to divide something into many pieces *The company has been broken up and sold.*

break up *phrasal verb* **1** PEOPLE If people break up, they stop having a relationship or stop working together. *He's just **broken up with** his girlfriend.* **2** EDUCATION *UK* When schools or colleges break up, the classes end and the holidays begin.

break[2] /breɪk/ *noun* [C] **1** STOP when you stop an activity for a short time, usually to rest or to eat *a **coffee/tea break*** ○ ***Take a break** and come back after lunch.* **2** HOLIDAY a holiday or period of time away from work, school, etc *the spring break* ○ *a **weekend break** to Paris* **3** OPPORTUNITY a lucky opportunity *His **big break** came when he was offered a part in a TV series.* ○ *Meeting Tom was my **lucky break**.* **4** DAMAGE where something has separated in an accident *a break in the bone* **5 a break with sth** when you end a relationship, connection, or way of doing something *a break with tradition*

breakable /ˈbreɪkəbl/ *adjective* able to break easily *a breakable vase*

breakage /ˈbreɪkɪdʒ/ *noun* [C, U] when something has been broken *The delivery company must pay for any breakages.*

breakaway /ˈbreɪkəweɪ/ *adjective* **a breakaway group/republic/region, etc** a group/region, etc that has separated itself from a larger group or region because of a disagreement

break-bulk /ˈbreɪkˌbʌlk/ *noun* [U] FINANCE in business, the practice of dividing large amounts of goods that have been bought into smaller amounts to sell again

breakdown /ˈbreɪkdaʊn/ *noun* [C] **1** HEALTH (*also* **nervous breakdown**) a short period of mental illness when people are too ill to continue with their normal lives *to **have a breakdown*** **2** FAILURE when something such as communication or a relationship fails or ends *a breakdown in the peace talks* **3** EXPLANATION a short explanation of the details of something *I need a breakdown of the costs involved.* **4** NOT WORKING when a vehicle or machine stops working for a period of time

ˈbreak-even ˌpoint *noun* [C usually singular] FINANCE in business, the point at which you have sold enough so that you have not lost money but have not made any profit

breakfast /ˈbrekfəst/ *noun* [C] FOOD the food you eat in the morning after you wake up *She had breakfast in bed this morning.* •**breakfast** *verb* [I] ⊃See also: **bed and breakfast, continental breakfast, English breakfast**

break-in /ˈbreɪkɪn/ *noun* [C] when someone forces their way into a building or car, usually to steal something *There has been another break-in at the office.*

ˈbreaking ˌpoint *noun* [U] when a situation has become so bad that it cannot continue *Things had become so bad at work they'd almost **reached breaking point**.*

breakneck /ˈbreɪknek/ *adjective* **breakneck speed/growth, etc** dangerously fast speed/growth, etc

breakout /ˈbreɪkaʊt/ *noun* [C] an escape, usually from prison

WORD PARTNERS FOR ***breakthrough***

make/provide a breakthrough • a breakthrough **comes** • a **big/crucial/major/real** breakthrough • a **medical/scientific** breakthrough • a breakthrough **in** sth

breakthrough /ˈbreɪkθruː/ *noun* [C] an important discovery or development that helps solve a problem *a **major breakthrough in** the fight against cancer*

break-up /ˈbreɪkʌp/ *noun* [C] **1** END when a close relationship ends *He moved away after the break-up of his marriage.* **2** SEPARATION when a country, group, etc separates into several smaller parts

breast /brest/ *noun* **1 ANATOMY** [C] one of the two soft, round parts on a woman's chest **2** [C, U] the front part of a bird's body, or the meat from this area *chicken breast*

breastbone /ˈbrestbəʊn/ *noun* [C] **ANATOMY** the long, flat vertical bone in the centre of your chest

breast-feed /ˈbrestfiːd/ *verb* [I, T] *past* **breast-fed** If a woman breast-feeds, she gives a baby milk from her breast. •**breast-feeding** *noun* [U]

breaststroke /ˈbreststrəʊk/ *noun* [U] **SPORT** a way of swimming in which you push your arms forward and then to the side, while you kick your legs backwards

breath /breθ/ *noun* **1 BIOLOGY** [U] the air that comes out of your lungs *His breath smells of garlic.* **2** [C] when air goes into or out of your lungs *She **took a deep breath** before she started.* **3 be out of breath** to be breathing quickly because you have been running, walking fast, etc **4 catch your breath; get your breath back** to rest for a short time until you can breathe regularly again **5 under your breath** If you say something under your breath, you say it very quietly so that other people cannot hear it. **6 hold your breath** to keep air in your lungs and not let it out *How long can you hold your breath under water?* **7 don't hold your breath** *humorous* something that you say in order to tell someone that an event is not likely to happen *He said he'd phone, but don't hold your breath.* **8 a breath of fresh air** someone or something that is new, different, and exciting **9 take your breath away** If something takes your breath away, you feel surprise and admiration because it is so beautiful or exciting. *The view from the window took my breath away.* **10 with bated breath** in an excited or anxious way *I waited with bated breath as the results were read out.*

COMMON LEARNER ERROR

breath or **breathe?**

Be careful not to confuse the noun **breath** with the verb **breathe**.

I was so excited, I could hardly breathe.

breathalyser /ˈbreθəlaɪzəʳ/ *noun* [C] *UK* **LAW** a piece of equipment that tests your breath to measure how much alcohol you have had •**breathalyse** *verb* [T] *UK* to measure the alcohol in someone's body using a breathalyser

O-▪**breathe** /briːð/ *verb* [I, T] **BIOLOGY** to take air into and out of your lungs ***breathe in/out*** ○ ***breathe deeply*** ⊃See also: be breathing down sb's **neck**, not breathe a **word**[1]

breather /ˈbriːðəʳ/ *noun* [C] *informal* a short rest *If you start to feel tired, **take a breather**.*

breathing /ˈbriːðɪŋ/ *noun* [U] **BIOLOGY** when you take air into and out of your lungs *The doctor listened to my breathing.*

ˈ**breathing ˌspace** *noun* [U] an opportunity to stop, relax, or think about things

breathless /ˈbreθləs/ *adjective* not able to breathe enough •**breathlessly** *adverb*

breathtaking /ˈbreθˌteɪkɪŋ/ *adjective* very beautiful or surprising ***breathtaking views*** •**breathtakingly** *adverb*

bred /bred/ *past of* breed

breed[1] /briːd/ *noun* [C] **1 FARMING** a type of dog, sheep, pig, etc *a rare breed of cattle* **2** a type of person or thing *a **new breed** of bank*

breed[2] /briːd/ *verb past* **bred** /bred/ **1 BIOLOGY, FARMING** [I] If animals breed, they produce young animals. **2 breed chickens/horses/rabbits, etc FARMING** to keep animals in order to produce young animals **3 breed contempt/ignorance, etc** to cause something to develop, especially something bad

breeder /ˈbriːdəʳ/ *noun* [C] **FARMING** someone who keeps animals in order to produce young animals *a dog/horse breeder*

breeding /ˈbriːdɪŋ/ *noun* [U] **FARMING 1** when animals produce young animals *the **breeding season*** **2** when someone keeps animals in order to produce young animals *horse breeding*

ˈ**breeding ˌground** *noun* [C] **1** DEVELOP a place where something develops quickly, especially something bad *This estate is **a breeding ground for** crime.* **2** ANIMAL a place where animals breed

breeze[1] /briːz/ *noun* [C] a gentle wind *a cool breeze*

breeze[2] /briːz/ *verb informal* **breeze along/into/through, etc** to move somewhere quickly in a confident way and without worrying

breezy /ˈbriːzi/ *adjective* **1** WIND with a slight wind *a cool, breezy day* **2** HAPPY happy, confident, and enthusiastic *a cheerful, breezy style* •**breezily** *adverb*

brethren /ˈbreðrən/ *noun* [plural] **RELIGION** members of an organized group, especially a religious group of men

brevity /ˈbrevəti/ *noun* [U] *formal* **1** WORDS when speech or writing is short and contains few words **2** TIME when something lasts for a short time

brew[1] /bruː/ *verb* **1** [T] to make beer **2 FOOD** [I, T] If you brew tea or coffee, you make it by adding hot water, and if it brews, it gradually develops flavour in hot water. **3 be brewing** If something bad is brewing, it is beginning to develop. *There is a row brewing over the plans.*

brew² /bruː/ *noun* [C] **FOOD** *informal* a drink made by brewing, such as beer or tea

B

brewer /ˈbruːəʳ/ *noun* [C] a person or organization that makes beer

brewery /ˈbruːəri/ *noun* [C] a company that makes beer

WORD PARTNERS FOR ***bribe***

accept /take a bribe • **offer** sb/**pay** a bribe • a **cash** bribe

bribe /braɪb/ *noun* [C] **LAW** money or a present given to someone so that they will do something for you, usually something dishonest *The politician was accused of* ***accepting bribes*** *from businessmen.* •**bribe** *verb* [T] [+ **to do sth**] *He was bribed to give false evidence at the trial.*

bribery /ˈbraɪbəri/ *noun* [U] **LAW** when someone is offered money or a present so that they will do something, usually something dishonest ***bribery and corruption***

bric-a-brac /ˈbrɪkəˌbræk/ *noun* [U] a collection of small, decorative objects that have little value

brick /brɪk/ *noun* [C] a small, hard, rectangular block used for building walls, houses, etc *a* ***brick wall*** ➲See also: be banging your **head**¹ against a brick wall

bricklayer /ˈbrɪkˌleɪəʳ/ *noun* [C] someone whose job is to build houses, walls, etc with bricks

bridal /ˈbraɪdəl/ *adjective* [**always before noun**] relating to a woman who is getting married, or relating to a wedding *a bridal gown*

bride /braɪd/ *noun* [C] a woman who is getting married *the* ***bride and groom***

bridegroom /ˈbraɪdgruːm/ (*also* **groom**) *noun* [C] a man who is getting married

bridesmaid /ˈbraɪdzmeɪd/ *noun* [C] a woman or girl who helps the bride on her wedding day

O-- **bridge¹** /brɪdʒ/ *noun* **1** STRUCTURE [C] a structure that is built over a river, road, etc so that people or vehicles can go across it *to go across/over a bridge* ○ *Brooklyn Bridge* **2** CONNECTION [C] something that connects two groups, organizations, etc and improves the relationship between them *After the war they tried to* ***build bridges*** *with neighbouring countries.* **3 the bridge of your nose ANATOMY** the hard part of your nose between your eyes **4 the bridge** the raised area of a ship where the controls are **5** GAME [U] a card game for four players **6 I'll/We'll cross that bridge when I/we come to it.** something you say when you do not intend to worry about a possible problem now, but will deal with it if or when it happens

bridge² /brɪdʒ/ *verb* **bridge the gap/gulf, etc** to make the difference between two things smaller *This course is designed to* ***bridge the gap between*** *school and work.*

bridle /ˈbraɪdl/ *noun* [C] **SPORT** a set of straps that you put on a horse's head to control it

brief¹ /briːf/ *adjective* **1** TIME lasting only for a short time *a brief visit* **2** WORDS using only a few words *a brief description/statement* **3 in brief** using only a few words *world news in brief* •**briefly** *adverb They discussed the matter briefly.*

brief² /briːf/ *verb* [T] to give someone instructions or information [**often passive**] *At the meeting reporters were* ***briefed on*** *the plans.*

brief³ /briːf/ *noun* [C] a set of instructions or information [+ **to do sth**] *My brief was to improve the image of the city.*

briefcase /ˈbriːfkeɪs/ *noun* [C] a flat, rectangular case with a handle for carrying documents, books, etc

briefing /ˈbriːfɪŋ/ *noun* [C, U] a meeting when people are given instructions or information *a* ***press briefing***

briefs /briːfs/ *noun* [**plural**] underwear that you wear on your bottom *a pair of briefs* ➲See colour picture **Clothes** on page Centre 9

brigade /brɪˈgeɪd/ *noun* [C] **1** SOLDIER a large group of soldiers **2** GROUP *UK humorous* a group of people with a particular characteristic or interest *the anti-smoking brigade* ➲See also: **fire brigade**

brigadier /ˌbrɪgəˈdɪəʳ/ *noun* [C] a British army officer of high rank

O-- **bright** /braɪt/ *adjective* **1** COLOUR having a strong, light colour *bright yellow/blue* **2** LIGHT full of light or shining strongly *bright sunshine* **3** INTELLIGENT intelligent *He's a bright boy.* **4** HAPPY happy or full of hope *She's always so bright and cheerful.* •**brightly** *adverb* ***brightly coloured*** *flowers* •**brightness** *noun* [U]

brighten /ˈbraɪtən/ (*also* **brighten up**) *verb* [I, T] **1** LIGHT to become lighter or more colourful, or to make something become lighter or more colourful *A picture or two would brighten up the room.* **2** HAPPY to become happier, or to make someone become happier *She brightened up when she saw him.*

brilliant /ˈbrɪliənt/ *adjective* **1** GOOD *UK* very good *We saw a brilliant film.* **2** CLEVER extremely clever *a brilliant scholar* **3** LIGHT full of light or colour *The sky was a brilliant blue.* •**brilliantly** *adverb* •**brilliance** /ˈbrɪliəns/ *noun* [U]

brim¹ /brɪm/ *verb* **brimming**, *past* **brimmed be brimming with sth** to be full of something *Her eyes were brimming with tears.*

brim² /brɪm/ *noun* [C] **1** HAT the flat part around the bottom of a hat **2** TOP the top edge of a container *He* ***filled*** *my glass* ***to the brim.***

brine /braɪn/ *noun* [U] **FOOD** salty water, often used for keeping food from decaying *olives in brine*

O-- **bring** /brɪŋ/ *verb* [T] *past* **brought 1** to take someone or something with you when you go somewhere *Did you bring an umbrella with you?* [+ **two objects**] *He brought me some flowers.* **2 bring happiness/peace/shame, etc** to cause happiness/peace/shame, etc *Money does not always bring happiness.* **3 can not bring yourself to do sth** to not be willing to do something because it is so unpleasant *He couldn't bring* *himself to talk to her.* ➲See also: bring sb/sth to their knees (**knee**), bring sth to **light**[1]

COMMON LEARNER ERROR

bring or **take?**

Use **bring** to talk about moving something or someone towards the speaker or towards the place where you are now.

Did you bring any money?

I've brought you a present.

Use **take** to talk about moving something or someone away from the speaker or away from the place where you are now.

I can take you to the station.

Don't forget to take your umbrella.

bring sth about *phrasal verb* to make something happen *The Internet has **brought about** big **changes** in the way we work.*

bring sth back *phrasal verb* **1** FROM PLACE to return from somewhere with something [+ **two objects**] *Can you bring me back some milk from the shop, please?* **2** FROM PAST to make someone think about something from the past *The photos **brought back memories**.*

bring sb down *phrasal verb* to cause someone in a position of power to lose their job *This scandal could **bring down** the **government**.*

bring sth down *phrasal verb* to reduce the level of something *to **bring down prices***

bring sth forward *phrasal verb* to change the date or time of an event so that it happens earlier than planned *I've brought forward the meeting to this week.*

bring sth in *phrasal verb* **1** INTRODUCE to introduce something new, usually a product or a law *New safety regulations were brought in last year.* **2** EARN to earn or make money *The film has brought in millions of dollars.*

bring sb in *phrasal verb* to ask someone to do a particular job *We need to bring in an expert to sort out this problem.*

bring sth off *phrasal verb* to succeed in doing something difficult *How did he manage to bring that off?*

bring sth on *phrasal verb* to make something happen, usually something bad [**often passive**] *Headaches are often brought on by stress.*

bring sth out *phrasal verb* **1** PRODUCE to produce something to sell to the public *They have just brought out a new, smaller phone.* **2** MAKE NOTICEABLE to make a particular quality or detail noticeable *Salt can help to bring out the flavour of food.*

bring sb together *phrasal verb* to cause people to be friendly with each other *The disaster brought the community closer together.*

bring sb up *phrasal verb* to look after a child and teach them until they are old enough to look after themselves *She was brought up by her grandparents.*

bring sth up *phrasal verb* **1** TALK to start to talk about a particular subject *There are several points I'd like to bring up at tomorrow's meeting.* **2** VOMIT *UK* to vomit something

brink /brɪŋk/ *noun* **be on the brink of sth** to be in a situation where something bad is going to happen very soon *The two countries are on the brink of war.*

brisk /brɪsk/ *adjective* quick and energetic *a **brisk walk*** •**briskly** *adverb*

bristle[1] /ˈbrɪsl/ *verb* [**I**] to show that you are annoyed about something *She **bristled at** the suggestion that it was her fault.*

bristle[2] /ˈbrɪsl/ *noun* [**C, U**] a short, stiff hair •**bristly** *adjective*

Brit /brɪt/ *noun* [**C**] *informal* someone who comes from Great Britain

British /ˈbrɪtɪʃ/ *adjective* relating to Great Britain or the United Kingdom

the British /ˈbrɪtɪʃ/ *noun* [**plural**] the people of Great Britain or the United Kingdom

Briton /ˈbrɪtᵊn/ *noun* [**C**] someone who comes from Great Britain

brittle /ˈbrɪtl/ *adjective* hard but able to be broken easily *brittle bones*

broach /brəʊtʃ/ *verb* **broach an idea/subject/topic, etc** to begin to talk about something, usually something difficult or embarrassing *I don't know how to broach the subject of money with him.*

broad /brɔːd/ *adjective* **1** wide ***broad shoulders*** ○ *a **broad smile*** **2 a broad range/variety, etc** a group that includes many different things or people *a broad range of subjects* **3 a broad outline/picture, etc** a general description, without detail *This is just a broad outline of the proposal.* **4 LANGUAGE** A broad accent (= way of speaking from a region) is very noticeable. **5 in broad daylight** during the day when it is light and people can see *He was attacked in broad daylight.*

broadband /ˈbrɔːdbænd/ *noun* [**U**] **COMPUTING** a system that allows large amounts of information to be sent very quickly between computers or other electronic equipment

broadcast[1] /ˈbrɔːdkɑːst/ *noun* [**C**] a television or radio programme *a news broadcast* •**broadcast** *adjective* [**always before noun**] relating to television or radio *broadcast news*

broadcast[2] /ˈbrɔːdkɑːst/ *verb* [**I, T**] *past* **broadcast**, *also US* **broadcasted** to send out a programme on television or radio [**often passive**] *The concert will be **broadcast live** next week.* •**broadcaster** *noun* [**C**] someone who speaks on radio or television as a job •**broadcasting** *noun* [**U**]

broaden /ˈbrɔːdᵊn/ *verb* [**I, T**] **1** INCREASE to increase or make something increase and include more things or people *We need to broaden the range of services that we offer.* ○ *Travel **broadens your mind**.* **2** WIDER to become wider or make something become wider *Her smile broadened and she began to laugh.*

WORD PARTNERS FOR ***broadly***

broadly **in line with/similar** • broadly **welcome** sth

broadly /ˈbrɔːdli/ *adverb* in a general way and not including everything or everyone *The plans have been broadly accepted.*

broadsheet /ˈbrɔːdʃiːt/ *noun* [**C**] *UK* a large newspaper, usually considered to be more serious than smaller newspapers

B

broccoli /ˈbrɒkəli/ *noun* [U] **FOOD** a green vegetable with a thick stem

brochure /ˌbrəʊʃəʳ/ ⓤⓢ /brəʊˈʃʊr/ *noun* [C] a thin book with pictures and information, usually advertising something *a **holiday/travel brochure***

broil /brɔɪl/ *US* (*UK/US* **grill**) *verb* [T] **FOOD** to cook food using direct heat

broiler /ˈbrɔɪləʳ/ *US* (*UK/US* **grill**) *noun* [C] a piece of equipment used for cooking food under direct heat

broke[1] /brəʊk/ *adjective informal* **1 be broke** to not have any money **2 go broke** to lose all your money and have to end your business

broke[2] /brəʊk/ *past tense of* break

OTHER WAYS OF SAYING ***broken***

If a piece of equipment is broken (not working properly), you can use adjectives such as **dead**, **defunct**, or, informally, **bust** (*UK*): *You won't be able to watch the match, the telly's **bust**.* • *The phone's **dead**, there must be a problem with the line.*

If a piece of equipment or machinery in a public place is broken, you can say that it is **out of order**: *The coffee machine was **out of order**.*

If a piece of equipment has broken, in informal situations you can use expressions like **have had it** and **give up the ghost**: *The kettle's **had it**, you'll have to boil a pan of water.* • *I can't give you a lift - my car's **given up the ghost**.*

O-- **broken**[1] /ˈbrəʊkən/ *adjective* **1** DAMAGED damaged and separated into pieces *broken glass* ➲Opposite **unbroken** **2 a broken arm/leg, etc** **HEALTH** an arm/leg, etc with a damaged bone **3** NOT WORKING If a machine or piece of equipment is broken, it is not working. *The video's broken.* **4 a broken heart** when you are very sad because someone you love has ended a relationship with you **5 a broken home** a family in which the parents do not now live together **6 a broken promise** a promise that has not been kept **7 broken English/Spanish, etc** English/Spanish, etc that is spoken slowly and has a lot of mistakes in it

broken[2] /ˈbrəʊkən/ *past participle of* break

broken-down /ˌbrəʊkənˈdaʊn/ *adjective* not working or in bad condition *a broken-down vehicle*

broken-hearted /ˌbrəʊkənˈhɑːtɪd/ *adjective* very sad because someone you love has ended a relationship with you

broker[1] /ˈbrəʊkəʳ/ *noun* [C] **FINANCE** **1** (*also* **stockbroker**) someone whose job is to buy and sell shares (= equal parts of a company's total value) **2 an insurance/mortgage, etc broker** someone who makes other people's financial arrangements for them

broker[2] /ˈbrəʊkəʳ/ *verb* [T] to arrange an agreement *The peace deal was brokered by the US.*

brominate /ˈbrəʊmɪneɪt/ *verb* [T, I] **CHEMISTRY** to add bromine to something or to react with bromine •**bromination** /ˌbrəʊmɪnˈeɪʃən/ *noun* [U]

bromine /ˈbrəʊmiːn/ *noun* [U] **CHEMISTRY** a chemical element that is a strong-smelling, corrosive (= eats into other substances) dark red liquid that changes easily into a gas, used in photographic materials and other industries (symbol **Br**)

bronchiole /ˈbrɒŋkiəʊl/ *noun* [C] **BIOLOGY, ANATOMY** in the lungs, one of the very small tubes that come out from the bronchi (= two main tubes) and connect to the alveoli (= little air bags) ➲See picture at **respiratory system** ➲See picture at **alveoli**

bronchitis /brɒŋˈkaɪtɪs/ *noun* [U] **HEALTH** an illness in your lungs which makes you cough and have problems breathing

bronchus /ˈbrɒŋkəs/ *noun* [C] *plural* **bronchi** **BIOLOGY, ANATOMY** one of the two tubes that come from the trachea (= tube from your throat to your lungs) and carry air into the lungs ➲See picture at **respiratory system**

bronze[1] /brɒnz/ *noun* **1** METAL [U] a shiny orange-brown metal **2** COLOUR [U] an orange-brown colour **3** PRIZE [C] a bronze medal (= a small, round disc given to someone for finishing third in a competition) *He won a bronze in the 200m.*

bronze[2] /brɒnz/ *adjective* **1** METAL made of bronze *a bronze statue* **2** COLOUR being the colour of bronze

ˌbronze ˈmedal *noun* [C] a small, round disc given to someone for finishing third in a race or competition

brooch /brəʊtʃ/ *noun* [C] a piece of jewellery for women which is fastened onto clothes with a pin *a diamond brooch*

brood[1] /bruːd/ *noun* [C] a family of young birds or animals, all born at the same time

brood[2] /bruːd/ *verb* [I] to think for a long time about things that make you sad or angry *I wish he'd stop **brooding about** the past.*

brook /brʊk/ *noun* [C] a small stream

broom /bruːm/ *noun* [C] a brush with a long handle used for cleaning the floor

broth /brɒθ/ *noun* [U] **FOOD** soup, usually made with meat *chicken broth*

brothel /ˈbrɒθəl/ *noun* [C] a building where prostitutes (= people who have sex for money) work

O-- **brother** /ˈbrʌðəʳ/ *noun* [C] **1** a boy or man who has the same parents as you *an older/younger brother* ○ *my big/little brother* **2** a man who is a member of the same race, religious group, organization, etc **3** **RELIGION** (*also* **Brother**) a monk (= man who lives in a male religious group) *Brother Paul*

brotherhood /ˈbrʌðəhʊd/ *noun* **1** **RELIGION** [C] a group of men who have the same purpose or religious beliefs **2** [U] friendship and loyalty, like the relationship between brothers

brother-in-law /ˈbrʌðərɪnlɔː/ *noun* [C] *plural* **brothers-in-law** the man married to your sister, or the brother of your husband or wife

brotherly /ˈbrʌðəli/ *adjective* [**always before noun**] relating to or typical of brothers *brotherly love*

brought /brɔːt/ *past of* bring

brow /braʊ/ *noun* [C] **1 ANATOMY** the front part of your head between your eyes and your hair *He wiped the sweat from his brow.* **2 brow of a hill/slope** *UK* the top part of a hill or slope

O‑**brown** /braʊn/ *adjective* **1** COLOUR being the same colour as chocolate or soil *a brown leather bag ○ dark brown hair/eyes* ➲See colour picture **Colours** on page Centre 12 **2** SKIN having darker skin because you have been in the sun •**brown** *noun* [C, U] the colour brown

brownfield /ˈbraʊnfiːld/ *adjective UK* **ENVIRONMENT** describes land that was used for industry and where new buildings can be built *a brownfield site* ➲Compare **greenfield**

Brownian motion /ˌbraʊniənˈməʊʃᵊn/ (*also* **Brownian movement**) *noun* [U] **PHYSICS** the movement of particles in a liquid or gas, caused by being hit by molecules of that liquid or gas

brownie /ˈbraʊni/ *noun* [C] **FOOD** a small, square cake made with chocolate and nuts

browse /braʊz/ *verb* **1 INTERNET** [I, T] to look at information on the Internet *to browse the Internet/Web* **2** READ [I] to read a book, magazine, etc in a relaxed way and not in detail *She **browsed through** some travel brochures looking for ideas.* **3** SHOP [I] to walk around a shop and look at things without buying anything *I love **browsing around** bookshops.*

browser /ˈbraʊzəʳ/ *noun* [C] **1 INTERNET** a computer program which allows you to look at pages on the Internet **2** someone who browses

bruise /bruːz/ *noun* [C] **HEALTH** a dark area on your skin where you have been hurt *He suffered **cuts and bruises** after falling off his bike.* •**bruise** *verb* [T] to cause someone or something to have a bruise [**often passive**] He was badly bruised in the accident. •**bruising** *noun* [U]

brunette /bruːˈnet/ *noun* [C] a white woman with dark brown hair

brunt /brʌnt/ *noun* **bear/feel/take the brunt of sth** to experience the worst part of something *He took the brunt of the criticism.*

brush¹ /brʌʃ/ *noun* **1 ART** [C] an object made of short, thin pieces of plastic, wire, etc fixed to a handle and used to tidy hair, to clean, to paint, etc *a stiff wire brush* **2** [**no plural**] the action of using a brush *I need to **give** my hair a quick **brush**.* **3 the brush of sth** when something touches you lightly *She felt the brush of his lips against her cheek.* **4 a brush with sth** when you experience something, or almost experience something, especially something unpleasant *a brush with death*

brush² /brʌʃ/ *verb* [T] **1** to use a brush to clean or tidy something *to **brush your hair/teeth*** **2 brush sth away/off, etc** to move something somewhere using a brush or your hand *He brushed the snow off his coat.* **3 brush against/past sb/sth** to lightly touch someone or something as you move past *He brushed past me as he went up the stairs.*

brush sth aside/off *phrasal verb* to refuse to think about something seriously *He brushed aside her suggestion.*

brush up (on) sth *phrasal verb* to improve your skills in something *I'm trying to brush up on my French before I go to Paris.*

brush-off /ˈbrʌʃɒf/ *noun informal* **give sb the brush-off** to be unfriendly to someone by not talking to them

brusque /bruːsk/ (US) /brʌsk/ *adjective* dealing with people in a quick way that is unfriendly or rude *a **brusque manner*** •**brusquely** *adverb*

brussel sprout /ˌbrʌsᵊlˈspraʊt/ (US) /ˈbrʌsᵊlˌspraʊt/ *noun* [C] **FOOD** a small, green vegetable which is round and made of leaves

brutal /ˈbruːtᵊl/ *adjective* very violent or cruel *a **brutal murder*** •**brutally** *adverb brutally murdered ○ **brutally honest*** •**brutality** /bruːˈtæləti/ *noun* [C, U]

brute¹ /bruːt/ *noun* [C] someone who behaves in a very violent and cruel way •**brutish** /ˈbruːtɪʃ/ *adjective* like a brute

brute² /bruːt/ *adjective* **brute force/strength** great force or strength

BSc /ˌbiːesˈsiː/ *UK* (*US* **BS** /biːˈes/) *noun* [C] **EDUCATION** *abbreviation for* Bachelor of Science: a university or college qualification in a science subject which usually takes 3 or 4 years of study *He has a BSc in computer science.*

BSE /ˌbiːesˈiː/ *noun* [U] **HEALTH** *abbreviation for* bovine spongiform encephalopathy: a disease that kills cows by destroying their brains

BTW INTERNET *internet abbreviation for* by the way: used when you write some extra information that may or may not be related to what is being discussed

bubble¹ /ˈbʌbl/ *noun* [C] a ball of air or gas with liquid around it *an air bubble*

bubble² /ˈbʌbl/ *verb* [I] **1** If a liquid bubbles, balls of air or gas rise to its surface. *The soup was bubbling on the stove.* **2 bubble (over) with confidence/enthusiasm, etc** to be full of a positive emotion or quality

ˈ**bubble ˌgum** *noun* [U] **FOOD** a sweet that you chew and blow into a bubble

bubble-jet /ˈbʌbldʒet/ *adjective* **COMPUTING** A bubble-jet printer uses a very fast and quiet method of printing, in which ink is directed electronically onto the paper

bubbly /ˈbʌbli/ *adjective* **1** HAPPY happy and enthusiastic *a bubbly personality* **2** BUBBLES full of bubbles

Buchner funnel /ˈbuːxnəˌfʌnᵊl/ *noun* [C] **CHEMISTRY** a piece of equipment used by scientists for filtering (= passing liquids through a layer of material to remove solid pieces) ➲See picture at **filtrate**

buck¹ /bʌk/ *noun* [C] **1** MONEY *US informal* a dollar (= US unit of money) *It cost me twenty bucks to get a new bike lock.* **2** ANIMAL a male rabbit or deer **3 pass the buck** to blame someone or to make them responsible for a problem that you should deal with yourself

buck² /bʌk/ *verb* [I] If a horse bucks, it kicks its back legs into the air.

bucket /ˈbʌkɪt/ *noun* [C] a round, open container with a handle used for carrying liquids *a bucket of water*

B

buckle¹ /ˈbʌkl/ *noun* [C] a metal object used to fasten the ends of a belt or strap *a silver buckle*

buckle² /ˈbʌkl/ *verb* **1** FASTEN [I, T] to fasten a belt or strap with a buckle **2** BEND [I, T] to bend, or to cause something to bend because of too much weight, heat, etc *His **legs buckled** as he reached the finishing line.* **3** SUFFER [I] to suffer and stop working effectively because of too many problems or too much work
buckle down *phrasal verb* to start working hard *I must **buckle down to** some work this afternoon.*

buckminsterfullerene /ˌbʌkmɪnstəˈfʊləriːn/ *noun* [U] **CHEMISTRY** a form of pure carbon found in soot (= black powder formed when coal is burned) (symbol C_{60})

bud /bʌd/ *noun* [C] **1 BIOLOGY** a part of a plant that develops into a leaf or a flower *In spring the trees are covered in buds.* **2 nip sth in the bud** to stop a small problem from getting worse by stopping it soon after it starts ⇒See also: **taste buds**

Buddha /ˈbʊdə/ (US) /ˈbuːdə/ *noun* **RELIGION** the Indian holy man on whose life and teachings Buddhism is based

Buddhism /ˈbʊdɪzᵊm/ (US) /ˈbuːdɪzᵊm/ *noun* [U] **RELIGION** a religion based on the teachings of Buddha

Buddhist /ˈbʊdɪst/ (US) /ˈbuːdɪst/ *noun* [C] **RELIGION** someone who believes in Buddhism •**Buddhist** *adjective a Buddhist temple*

budding /ˈbʌdɪŋ/ *adjective* [always before noun] starting to develop well *a **budding romance***

buddy /ˈbʌdi/ *noun* [C] *informal* a friend *my best buddy*

budge /bʌdʒ/ *verb* [I, T] **1** MOVE If something will not budge, or you cannot budge it, it will not move. *I've tried to open the window, but it won't budge.* **2** CHANGE If someone will not budge, or you cannot budge them, they will not change their opinion.

budgerigar /ˈbʌdʒᵊrɪɡɑːʳ/ *noun* [C] *UK* a budgie

WORD PARTNERS FOR ***budget***

have a budget of [£30 000/$5000, etc] • be **on** a **tight** budget (= not have much money) • the budget **for** sth

O-■**budget¹** /ˈbʌdʒɪt/ *noun* [C] **1 FINANCE** a plan that shows how much money you have and how you will spend it **2 FINANCE** the amount of money you have for something *an **annual budget** of £30 million* **3 the Budget ECONOMICS, POLITICS** in the UK, when the government officially tells the public about its plans for taxes and spending •**budgetary** *adjective* [always before noun] relating to a budget

budget² /ˈbʌdʒɪt/ *verb* [I, T] **FINANCE** to plan how much money you will spend on something *An extra £20 million has been **budgeted for** schools this year.*

budget³ /ˈbʌdʒɪt/ *adjective* **a budget hotel/price, etc** a very cheap hotel, price, etc

budgie /ˈbʌdʒi/ *noun* [C] *UK* a small, brightly coloured bird often kept as a pet

buff¹ /bʌf/ *noun* [C] **a computer/film/wine, etc buff** someone who knows a lot about computers/films/wine, etc

buff² /bʌf/ *adjective informal* If someone's body is buff, it looks strong and attractive, as if they have had a lot of exercise

buffalo /ˈbʌfᵊləʊ/ *noun* [C] *plural* **buffaloes** or **buffalo** a large, wild animal, like a cow with horns *a herd of wild buffalo*

buffer /ˈbʌfəʳ/ *noun* [C] **1** something that helps protect someone or something from harm *I have some money saved to act as **a buffer against** unexpected bills.* **2 COMPUTING** an area in a computer memory where information can be stored for a short time

ˈbuffer ˌzone *noun* [C] an area created to separate two countries that are fighting

buffet¹ /ˈbʊfeɪ/ (US) /bəˈfeɪ/ *noun* [C] **FOOD** a meal in which dishes of food are arranged on a table and you serve yourself *a cold buffet ○ a buffet lunch*

buffet² /ˈbʌfɪt/ *verb* [T] If something is buffeted by the weather, sea, etc, it is hit repeatedly and with force. [often passive] *The little boat was buffeted by the waves.*

ˈbuffet ˌcar *noun* [C] *UK* the part of a train where you can buy something to eat or drink

buffoon /bəˈfuːn/ *noun* [C] *old-fashioned* someone who does silly things

bug¹ /bʌɡ/ *noun* [C] **1 HEALTH** a bacteria or virus, or the illness that it causes *a **flu/stomach bug*** **2 COMPUTING** a mistake in a computer program *This program is full of bugs.* **3** INSECT a small insect **4** EQUIPMENT a small, electronic piece of equipment used to secretly listen to people talking **5 be bitten by the bug/get the bug** *informal* to develop a strong interest or enthusiasm for a particular activity *He's been bitten by the tennis bug.*

bug² /bʌɡ/ *verb* [T] **bugging**, *past* **bugged 1** LISTEN to hide a piece of equipment somewhere in order to secretly listen to people talking [often passive] *Their hotel room had been bugged.* **2** ANNOY *informal* to annoy someone *He's been bugging me all morning.*

buggy /ˈbʌɡi/ *noun* [C] **1** CHAIR *UK* (*US* **stroller**) a chair on wheels which is used to move small children **2** VEHICLE a vehicle with two wheels that is pulled by a horse, especially in the past

bugle /ˈbjuːɡl/ *noun* [C] **MUSIC** a small, metal musical instrument that you play by blowing into it

O-■**build¹** /bɪld/ *verb past* **built 1** MAKE [I, T] to make something by putting materials and parts together *build a house/wall ○ The bridge **is built of** steel and aluminium.* **2** DEVELOP [T] to create and develop something over a long time *They have built a solid friendship over the years.*
build sth into sth *phrasal verb* to make something a part of something else *There are video screens built into the back of the seats.*
build on sth *phrasal verb* to use a success or achievement as a base from which to achieve more success
build (sth) up *phrasal verb* to increase or develop, or to make something increase or develop *Traffic usually builds up in the late afternoon.*

build² /bɪld/ *noun* [C, U] the size and shape of a person's body *He's of medium build with short brown hair.*

builder /ˈbɪldəʳ/ *noun* [C] someone who makes or repairs buildings as a job

O▬**building** /ˈbɪldɪŋ/ *noun* **1** STRUCTURE [C] a structure with walls and a roof, such as a house, school, etc *an office building* **2** ACTIVITY [U] the activity of putting together materials and parts to make structures *building materials* ⊃See also: **apartment building**

ˈ**building soˌciety** *UK* (*US* **savings and loan association**) *noun* [C] **FINANCE** an organization similar to a bank which lends you money to buy a house

build-up /ˈbɪldʌp/ *noun* [U] **1** when something slowly increases [**usually singular**] *the build-up of traffic* **2 the build-up to sth** *UK* the period of preparation before something happens *There was a lot of excitement in the build-up to the Olympics.*

built /bɪlt/ *past of* build

built-in /ˌbɪltˈɪn/ *adjective* [**always before noun**] included as part of the main structure of something *a computer with a built-in modem*

built-up /ˌbɪltˈʌp/ *adjective* a built-up area has a lot of buildings

bulb /bʌlb/ *noun* [C] **1** (*also* **light bulb**) a glass object containing a wire which produces light from electricity *an electric light bulb* **2 BIOLOGY** a round root that some plants grow from *daffodil bulbs*

bulbous /ˈbʌlbəs/ *adjective* large and round in an unattractive way *a **bulbous nose***

bulge¹ /bʌldʒ/ *verb* [I] to look larger and rounder or fuller than normal *Her bags were **bulging with** shopping.*

bulge² /bʌldʒ/ *noun* [C] a round, raised area on a surface

bulimia /buˈlɪmiə/ *noun* [U] **HEALTH** a mental illness in which someone eats too much and then forces themselves to vomit •**bulimic** *noun* [C], *adjective*

bulk /bʌlk/ *noun* **1 in bulk** in large amounts *to buy in bulk* **2 the bulk of sth** the largest part or most of something *He spends the bulk of his money on rent.* **3** [**no plural**] the large size of something or someone

bulky /ˈbʌlki/ *adjective* too big and taking up too much space

bull /bʊl/ *noun* [C] a male cow ⊃See also: be like a red **rag** to a bull

bulldog /ˈbʊldɒg/ *noun* [C] a short, strong dog with a large head and neck

bulldozer /ˈbʊlˌdəʊzəʳ/ *noun* [C] a heavy vehicle used to destroy buildings and make the ground flat •**bulldoze** *verb* [T]

WORD PARTNERS FOR ***bullet***

fire a bullet • a bullet **flies/lodges** swh • a **hail of** bullets • a bullet **hole/wound**

bullet /ˈbʊlɪt/ *noun* **1** [C] a small, metal object that is fired from a gun *a **bullet wound*** **2 bite the bullet** to make yourself do something or accept something difficult or unpleasant

bulletin /ˈbʊlətɪn/ *noun* [C] **1** PROGRAMME a short news programme on television or radio *the evening **news bulletin*** **2** NEWSPAPER a regular newspaper or report containing news about an organization

ˈ**bulletin ˌboard** *noun* [C] *US* (*UK* **noticeboard**) a board on a wall where you put advertisements and announcements ⊃See colour picture **The Classroom** on page Centre 6

ˈ**bullet ˌ(point)** *noun* [C] a small black circle used in writing to show separate items on a list

bulletproof /ˈbʊlɪtpruːf/ *adjective* made of material that a bullet cannot go through ***bulletproof vests***

ˈ**bullet ˌtrain** *noun* [C] a very fast Japanese train

bullion /ˈbʊliən/ *noun* [U] **ECONOMICS** blocks of gold or silver

ˈ**bull ˌmarket** *noun* [C] **ECONOMICS** a time when the prices of most shares (= parts of the value of a company that can be sold or bought) are rising

bullock /ˈbʊlək/ *noun* [C] a young bull (= male cow)

bully¹ /ˈbʊli/ *verb* [T] to intentionally frighten someone who is smaller or weaker than you *He was bullied at school by some older boys.* [+ **into** + **doing sth**] *She was bullied into leaving.* •**bullying** *noun* [U] *Bullying is a problem in many schools.*

bully² /ˈbʊli/ *noun* [C] someone who intentionally frightens a person who is smaller or weaker than them

bum¹ /bʌm/ *noun* [C] **1** BODY PART *UK informal* your bottom **2** PERSON *US informal* someone who has no home and no money

bumbag /ˈbʌmbæg/ *UK* (*US* **fanny pack**) *noun* [C] a small bag fixed to a belt that you wear around your waist

bumblebee /ˈbʌmblbiː/ *noun* [C] a large, hairy bee (= flying insect)

bumbling /ˈbʌmblɪŋ/ *adjective* [**always before noun**] confused and showing no skill *a **bumbling idiot***

bummer /ˈbʌməʳ/ *noun* **a bummer** *informal* something unpleasant or annoying *That last exam was a real bummer.*

bump¹ /bʌmp/ *verb* **1** [T] to hurt part of your body by hitting it against something hard *I bumped my head on the door.* **2 bump into/against sth** to hit your body, your car, etc against something by accident *He kept falling over and bumping into things.* **3 bump along/over sth** to move in a vehicle over a surface that is not smooth *The bus bumped along the country road.*

bump into sb *phrasal verb informal* to meet someone you know when you have not planned to meet them *I bumped into an old school friend in town today.*

bump sb off *phrasal verb informal* to murder someone

bump² /bʌmp/ *noun* [C] **1** SURFACE a round, raised area on a surface *My bike hit a bump in the road.* **2** BODY a raised area on your body where it has been hurt by hitting something hard *a nasty bump on the head* **3** MOVEMENT when something hits something hard *I heard a bump upstairs.*

B

bumper[1] /ˈbʌmpəʳ/ *noun* [C] a bar fixed along the front or back of a vehicle to protect it in an accident *a front/rear bumper*

bumper[2] /ˈbʌmpəʳ/ *adjective* [**always before noun**] bigger or better than usual *a **bumper year***

ˈbumper ˌsticker *noun* [C] a sign that you stick on a car, often with a funny message on it

bumpy /ˈbʌmpi/ *adjective* **1** SURFACE A bumpy road or surface is not smooth but has raised areas on it. **2** JOURNEY A bumpy journey is uncomfortable because the vehicle moves around a lot. **3** SITUATION full of problems or sudden changes *We had a **bumpy start**.*

bun /bʌn/ *noun* [C] **1 FOOD** *UK* a small, round cake *an iced bun* **2 FOOD** a small, round piece of bread *a hamburger/hot cross bun* **3** a hairstyle in which the hair is arranged in a small, round shape on the back of the head

WORD PARTNERS FOR ***bunch***

a bunch of **bananas/flowers/grapes/keys**

bunch[1] /bʌnʃ/ *noun* **1** THINGS TOGETHER [C] a number of things of the same type which are joined or held together *He handed me a **bunch of flowers**.* ➲See colour picture **Pieces and Quantities** on page Centre 1 **2** PEOPLE [C] *informal* a group of people [**usually singular**] *His friends are a nice bunch.* **3 a bunch of sth** *US informal* a large amount or number of something *There's a whole bunch of places I'd like to visit.*

bunch[2] /bʌnʃ/ *verb*

bunch (sb/sth) together/up *phrasal verb* to move close together so that you make a tight group, or to make someone or something do this [**often passive**] *We were all bunched up at the back of the room.*

bunch (sth) up *phrasal verb* If material bunches up, or if someone bunches it up, it moves into tight folds. [**often passive**] *My shirt's all bunched up at the back.*

bunches /ˈbʌntʃɪz/ *noun* [**plural**] *UK* a hairstyle in which the hair is tied together in two parts, one on each side of the head

bundle[1] /ˈbʌndl/ *noun* **1** [C] a number of things that are tied together *a bundle of letters/clothes* **2 a bundle of energy/nerves** *informal* a very energetic or nervous person

bundle[2] /ˈbʌndl/ *verb* **1 bundle sb into/out of/through sth** to push or carry someone somewhere quickly and roughly *He was bundled into the back of a car and driven away.* **2** to include an extra computer program or other product with something you sell

bundle sth up *phrasal verb* to tie a number of things together

bundle (sb) up *phrasal verb* to put warm clothes on yourself or someone else

bung /bʌŋ/ *verb* **bung sth in/on, etc** *UK informal* to put something somewhere in a quick, careless way *Shall I bung a chicken in the oven for dinner?*

bung sth up *phrasal verb UK informal* to cause something to be blocked so that it does not work in the way it should [**often passive**] *The toilet was bunged up with paper.*

bungalow /ˈbʌŋgələʊ/ *noun* [C] a house that has all its rooms on the ground floor

bungee jumping /ˈbʌndʒiˌdʒʌmpɪŋ/ (*also* **bungy jumping**) *noun* [U] **SPORT** the sport of jumping from a very high place while tied to a long elastic rope, so that the rope pulls you back before you hit the ground

bungle /ˈbʌŋgl/ *verb* [T] to do something wrong in a very careless or stupid way *a bungled robbery* •**bungling** *noun* [U]

bunk /bʌŋk/ *noun* [C] a narrow bed in a ship, train, etc

ˈbunk ˌbeds *noun* [**plural**] two beds fixed together with one on top of the other

bunker /ˈbʌŋkəʳ/ *noun* [C] **1** an underground room where people go to be protected, especially from bombs **2 SPORT** in golf, a hollow area filled with sand

bunny /ˈbʌni/ (*also* **ˈbunny ˌrabbit**) *noun* [C] a child's word for 'rabbit'

Bunsen burner /ˌbʌnsənˈbɜːnəʳ/ *noun* [C] **CHEMISTRY** a small device that burns gas to produce a flame which is used to heat things in scientific work ➲See picture at **laboratory**

buoy[1] /bɔɪ/ *noun* [C] a floating object used in water to mark dangerous areas for boats

buoy[2] /bɔɪ/ *verb* **be buoyed (up) by sth** to feel happy or confident because of something *The team was buoyed up by their win last week.*

buoyant /ˈbɔɪənt/ *adjective* **1** CONFIDENT happy and confident *in a **buoyant mood*** **2 ECONOMICS** successful or making a profit *a **buoyant economy*** **3** FLOATING floating or able to float •**buoyancy** /ˈbɔɪənsi/ *noun* [U]

WORD PARTNERS FOR ***burden***

be/become a burden **on/to** sb • **carry** the burden **of** sth • **ease/lighten/share** the burden • a **heavy** burden • the burden **of** (doing) sth

burden /ˈbɜːdᵊn/ *noun* [C] something difficult or unpleasant that you have to deal with or worry about *the **burden of** responsibility* ○ *I'd hate to **be a burden to** you when I'm older.* •**burden** *verb* [T] to give someone something difficult or unpleasant to deal with or worry about *Sorry to **burden** you **with** my problems.* •**burdensome** *adjective*

bureau /ˈbjʊərəʊ/ *noun* [C] *plural* **bureaux**, *US* **bureaus** **1** OFFICE a department or office **2** WRITING *UK* a piece of furniture with drawers and a sloping top used for writing **3** CLOTHES *US* (*UK* **chest of drawers**) a piece of furniture with drawers for keeping clothes in

bureaucracy /bjʊəˈrɒkrəsi/ *noun* **1** [U] complicated rules and processes used by an organization, especially when they do not seem necessary *government bureaucracy* **2 SOCIETY** [C, U] a government or organization in which there are a lot of officials in a lot of departments •**bureaucrat** /ˈbjʊərəʊkræt/ *noun* [C] someone working in a bureaucracy •**bureaucratic** /ˌbjʊərəʊˈkrætɪk/ *adjective*

burette /bjʊˈret/ *noun* [C] **CHEMISTRY** a glass tube with measurements marked on it and with a small tap at the bottom, used for adding small quantities of liquid to something ➲See picture at **laboratory**

burgeoning /ˈbɜːdʒənɪŋ/ *adjective* growing very quickly *a burgeoning population*

burger /ˈbɜːgər/ *noun* [C] **FOOD** a flat, round piece of food, usually made of meat, that is fried and served between pieces of bread *burger and fries ○ a veggie burger*

burglar /ˈbɜːglər/ *noun* [C] **LAW** someone who gets into buildings illegally and steals things

ˈburglar aˌlarm *noun* [C] something that makes a noise if someone tries to get into a building illegally

burglarize /ˈbɜːgləraɪz/ *verb US* **LAW** burgle

burglary /ˈbɜːgləri/ *noun* [C, U] **LAW** when someone gets into a building illegally and steals things

burgle /ˈbɜːgl/ *UK* (*US* **burglarize**) *verb* [T] **LAW** to get into a building illegally and steal things [**often passive**] *They've been burgled twice recently.*

burial /ˈberiəl/ *noun* [C, U] when a dead body is put into the ground

burly /ˈbɜːli/ *adjective* A burly man is large and strong.

O‑**burn**[1] /bɜːn/ *verb past* **burnt, burned 1** DESTROY [I, T] to destroy something with fire, or to be destroyed by fire *I burnt all his letters. ○ The factory burned to the ground. ○ He dropped his cigarette and **burnt a hole in** his jacket.* **2** FLAMES [I] to produce flames *The fire's burning well.* **3** COOK TOO LONG [I, T] If you burn something that you are cooking, you cook it too much and if something you are cooking burns, it cooks too much. *Check the pizza - I think it's burning!* **4 burn yourself/your fingers, etc** to be hurt by fire or heat *He burned his hand on the kettle.* **5** ENERGY [T] (*also* **burn up**) to use fuel to produce heat or energy *to burn calories/fuel* **6** COPY [T] to copy music, information or images onto a CD *He's **burnt** all his favourite records **onto** a CD.* **7** SKIN [I] to be very hot or sore *Her cheeks were burning.* **8 burn with anger/hatred, etc** to feel an emotion very strongly

burn (sth) down *phrasal verb* to destroy something, especially a building, by fire, or to be destroyed by fire *Their house burnt down while they were away on holiday.*

burn out *phrasal verb* If a fire burns out, it stops producing flames because nothing remains that can burn.

burn out *phrasal verb* to become ill or very tired from working too hard *If Olivia keeps working late every night, she will burn out.*

burn (sth) up *phrasal verb* to destroy something completely, or to be destroyed completely by fire or heat *The satellite will burn up when it enters the atmosphere.*

burn[2] /bɜːn/ *noun* [C] a place where fire or heat has damaged or hurt something *She has a nasty burn on her arm.*

burner /ˈbɜːnər/ *noun* **1** [C] a piece of equipment used to burn or heat something **2 put sth on the back burner** to not deal with something now, but intend to deal with it at a later time

burning /ˈbɜːnɪŋ/ *adjective* **1** very hot *the burning heat of the midday sun* **2 burning ambition/desire, etc** a very strong need to do something **3 a burning issue/question** a subject or question that must be dealt with or answered quickly

burnout /ˈbɜːnaʊt/ *noun* [U] *US* extreme tiredness, usually caused by working too much

burnt[1] /bɜːnt/ *adjective* destroyed or made black by fire or heat *burnt toast*

burnt[2] /bɜːnt/ *past of* burn

burnt-out /ˌbɜːntˈaʊt/ (*also* **burned-out** /bɜːndˈaʊt/) *adjective* **1** OBJECT A burnt-out car or building has been almost completely destroyed by fire. **2 HEALTH** *informal* tired and without enthusiasm because you have worked too hard *a burnt-out teacher*

burp /bɜːp/ *verb* [I] to let air from your stomach come out of your mouth in a noisy way •**burp** *noun* [C]

burrow[1] /ˈbʌrəʊ/ *verb* [I] When an animal burrows, it digs a hole or passage in the ground to live in. *There are rabbits burrowing under the building.*

burrow[2] /ˈbʌrəʊ/ *noun* [C] a hole or passage in the ground dug by an animal to live in

burst[1] /bɜːst/ *verb past* **burst 1** [I, T] If a container bursts, or if you burst it, it breaks suddenly, so that what is inside it comes out. *A water **pipe burst** and flooded the cellar.* **2 burst in/out/through, etc** to move somewhere suddenly and forcefully *Three masked men burst into the shop.* **3 burst into flames** to suddenly start burning **4 burst into laughter/tears, etc** to suddenly start laughing/crying, etc *She burst into tears and ran away.* **5 burst open** to open suddenly and with force **6 be bursting with confidence/joy, etc** to be full of an emotion or quality *She was bursting with pride.* **7 be bursting to do sth** *informal* to want to do something very much *I was bursting to tell him about the party.*

burst out *phrasal verb* **1** to suddenly say something loudly *'Don't go!' he burst out.* **2 burst out laughing/crying** to suddenly start laughing/crying *I walked in and everyone burst out laughing.*

burst[2] /bɜːst/ *noun* **1 a burst of sth** a sudden large amount of noise, activity, etc *a burst of applause/laughter* **2** [C] when something breaks open and what is inside it comes out

bury /ˈberi/ *verb* [T] **1** BODY to put a dead body into the ground [**often passive**] *He was buried next to his wife.* **2** HIDE to hide something in the ground or under something *buried treasure* [**often passive**] *Two climbers were buried in the snow.* **3 bury your face/head in sth** to move your face/head somewhere where it is hidden *She buried her face in her hands.* **4 bury yourself in sth** to give all your attention to something *He buried himself in his work.* ➲See also: bury the **hatchet**

WORD PARTNERS FOR *bus*

catch a bus • **miss** the bus • **on** a bus • **by** bus • a bus **route**

O‑**bus** /bʌs/ *noun* [C] *plural* **buses** a large vehicle that carries passengers by road, usually along a fixed route *a school bus ○ I'll go home **by bus**.*

B

•**bus** *verb* [T] *UK* **bussing,** *past* **bussed,** *US* **busing,** *past* **bused** to take a group of people somewhere in a bus

bush /bʊʃ/ *noun* **1** [C] a short, thick plant with a lot of branches *a rose bush* ○ *There was someone hiding in the bushes.* **2 the bush** GEOGRAPHY wild parts of Australia or Africa where very few people live **3 beat about the bush** to avoid talking about something difficult or embarrassing

bushy /ˈbʊʃi/ *adjective* If hair or a plant is bushy, it has grown very thick. ***bushy eyebrows***

busily /ˈbɪzɪli/ *adverb* in a busy, active way *He was busily writing notes.*

WORD PARTNERS FOR ***business***

be **in** business • **do** business • **go into** business • **go out of** business

O-- **business** /ˈbɪznɪs/ *noun* **1** TRADE [U] the buying and selling of goods or services *The shop closed last year, but now they're back* ***in business.*** ○ *We* ***do*** *a lot of* ***business with*** *China.* ○ *His company has* ***gone out of business*** (= failed). **2** ORGANIZATION [C] an organization that sells goods or services *My uncle* ***runs a*** *small decorating* ***business.*** **3** WORK [U] work that you do to earn money *She's in Vienna* ***on business*** (= working). **4 a nasty/strange, etc business** an unpleasant/strange, etc situation **5 be sb's (own) business** to be something private that other people do not need to know **6 be none of sb's business** If something is none of someone's business, they do not need to know about it, although they want to, because it does not affect them. **7 mind your own business** used to tell someone in a rude way that you do not want them to ask about something private ➲See also: **big business, show business**

ˈ**business** ˌ**class** *noun* [U] a more expensive way of travelling by aircraft in which you sit in a separate part of the aircraft and are given better service •**business class** *adjective, adverb*

businesslike /ˈbɪznɪslaɪk/ *adjective* working in a serious and effective way *a businesslike manner*

businessman, businesswoman /ˈbɪznɪsmən, ˈbɪznɪsˌwʊmən/ *noun* [C] *plural* **businessmen, businesswomen** someone who works in business, usually in a high position in a company

ˈ**business** ˌ**plan** *noun* [C] a detailed plan describing the future plans of a business

busk /bʌsk/ *verb* [I] *UK* to perform music in a public place to get money from people walking past •**busker** *noun* [C]

ˈ**bus** ˌ**station** (*also UK* **coach station**) *noun* [C] a building where a bus starts or ends its journey

ˈ**bus** ˌ**stop** *noun* [C] a place where buses stop to let passengers get on or off *I saw her waiting at the bus stop.* ➲See Common Learner Error at **station**

bust¹ /bʌst/ *verb* [T] *past* **bust,** *US* **busted** *informal* **1** BREAK to break or damage something *The cops had to bust the door down to get in.* **2** CATCH If the police bust someone, they catch them and accuse them of a crime. [**often passive**] *He was busted for selling drugs.*

bust² /bʌst/ *noun* [C] **1** a woman's breasts, or their size in relation to clothing *a 36-inch bust* **2** ART a model of someone's head and shoulders *a bronze bust of the Queen* **3 a drug bust** when the police catch people selling or using illegal drugs

bust³ /bʌst/ *adjective* **1 go bust** If a business goes bust, it stops trading because it does not have enough money. *His* ***company went bust,*** *leaving huge debts.* **2** *UK informal* (*US* **busted** /ˈbʌstɪd/) broken *My phone's bust - can I use yours?*

bustle¹ /ˈbʌsl/ *verb* **1 bustle about/around/in, etc** to move around and do things in a quick, busy way *There were lots of shoppers bustling about.* **2 bustle with sth** to be full of people or activity *The town centre was bustling with people.*

bustle² /ˈbʌsl/ *noun* [U] people and activity *We left the bustle of the city behind us.*

bustling /ˈbʌslɪŋ/ *adjective* full of people and activity *a bustling city/street*

bust-up /ˈbʌstʌp/ *noun* [C] *UK informal* a serious disagreement *He left home after a big bust-up with his dad.*

O-- **busy¹** /ˈbɪzi/ *adjective* **1** PERSON If you are busy, you are working hard, or giving your attention to a particular activity. *Mum was busy in the kitchen.* [+ **doing sth**] *I was busy mowing the lawn.* ○ *I've got plenty of jobs to* ***keep*** *you* ***busy.*** ○ *He was* ***too busy*** *talking* ***to*** *notice us come in.* **2** PLACE A busy place is full of activity or people. *a busy restaurant/road* **3** TIME In a busy period you have a lot of things to do. *I've had a very busy week.* **4** TELEPHONE *US* (*UK* **engaged**) If a telephone line is busy, someone is using it.

busy² /ˈbɪzi/ *verb* **busy yourself** to spend time working or doing something *We busied ourselves in the kitchen preparing dinner.*

O-- **but¹** *strong form* /bʌt/ *weak form* /bət/ *conjunction* **1** OPPOSITE INFORMATION used to introduce something new that you say, especially something which is different or the opposite from what you have just said *I'd drive you there, but I haven't got my car.* ○ *The tickets were expensive, but the kids really enjoyed it.* **2** EXPLAINING WHY used before you say why something did not happen or is not true *I was going to go to his party, but I was ill.* **3** SHOWING SURPRISE used to show that you are surprised about what someone has just said *'Tim is leaving.' 'But why?'* **4** CONNECTING PHRASES used to connect 'excuse me' or 'I'm sorry' with what you say next *Excuse me, but would you mind shutting the door?*

O-- **but²** *strong form* /bʌt/ *weak form* /bət/ *preposition* except *Everyone but Andrew knows.* ○ *Can you buy me a sandwich? Anything but ham.* ○ *This is the* ***last*** *programme* ***but one*** (= the programme before the last).

but³ *strong form* /bʌt/ *weak form* /bət/ *adverb formal* only *We can but try.*

butane /ˈbjuːˌteɪn/ *noun* [U] CHEMISTRY a gas obtained from petroleum used in its liquid form as a fuel (formula C_4H_{10})

butcher¹ /ˈbʊtʃəʳ/ *noun* [C] someone who prepares and sells meat

butcher² /ˈbʊtʃəʳ/ *verb* [T] **1** PERSON to kill someone in a very violent way **2** MEAT to cut an animal into pieces of meat

butcher's /ˈbʊtʃəz/ *UK* (*US* **ˈbutcherˌshop**) *noun* [C] a shop that prepares and sells meat *I went to the butcher's to buy some sausages.*

butler /ˈbʌtləʳ/ *noun* [C] a man who opens the door, serves dinner, etc in a large house as a job

butt¹ /bʌt/ *noun* **1** BOTTOM [C] *US informal* your bottom *He just sits on his butt all day long.* **2** CIGARETTE [C] the end of a cigarette that is left after it is smoked *There were* ***cigarette butts*** *all over the floor.* **3** GUN [C] the end of the handle of a gun *the butt of a rifle* **4 a head butt** when you hit someone with the top, front part of your head **5 kick sb's butt** *US informal* to punish someone or defeat someone with a lot of force

butt² /bʌt/ *verb* [T] to hit something with the top, front part of your head *He butted me in the stomach.*

butt in *phrasal verb* to interrupt or join in a conversation or activity when the other people do not want you to *The interviewer kept butting in and wouldn't let me answer the question.*

O-ᵚ**butter¹** /ˈbʌtəʳ/ *noun* **1** FOOD [U] a soft, pale yellow food made from cream that you put on bread and use in cooking ➲See colour picture **Food** on page Centre 11 **2 butter wouldn't melt in sb's mouth** used to say that someone looks as if they would never do anything wrong ➲See also: **peanut butter**

butter² /ˈbʌtəʳ/ *verb* [T] **FOOD** to put a layer of butter on something *hot buttered toast*

butter sb up *phrasal verb informal* to be very nice to someone so that they will do what you want them to do

buttercup /ˈbʌtəkʌp/ *noun* [C] a small, bright yellow flower

butterfly /ˈbʌtəflaɪ/ *noun* **1** [C] an insect with large, patterned wings ➲See picture at **insect** **2 have butterflies (in your stomach)** to feel very nervous about something that you are going to do

buttock /ˈbʌtək/ *noun* [C] **ANATOMY** one of the two sides of your bottom

button¹ /ˈbʌtᵊn/ *noun* [C] **1** CLOTHING a small, round object that you push through a hole to fasten clothing *to* ***do up/undo*** *your* ***buttons*** **2** CONTROL a switch that you press to control a piece of equipment *Press the play button to listen to your recording.* ➲See also: **belly button**

button² /ˈbʌtᵊn/ (*also* **button up**) *verb* [T] to fasten a piece of clothing with buttons *Jack buttoned up his jacket.* ➲Opposite **unbutton**

buttonhole /ˈbʌtᵊnhəʊl/ *noun* [C] **1** HOLE a hole that you push a button through on a piece of clothing **2** FLOWER *UK* a flower worn on a jacket or coat for a special occasion

buxom /ˈbʌksəm/ *adjective* A buxom woman has large breasts.

O-ᵚ**buy¹** /baɪ/ *verb* [T] *past* **bought FINANCE** to get something by paying money for it *I went to the shop to buy some milk.* ○ *They* ***bought*** *their house* ***for*** *£14,000.* [+ **two objects**] *He bought me a camera for my birthday.*

buy into sth *phrasal verb* to believe in something *I don't buy into all that dieting nonsense.*

buy sb/sth out *phrasal verb* **FINANCE** to buy part of a company or building from someone else so that you own all of it

buy sth up *phrasal verb* to quickly buy a lot of something, often all that is available

buy² /baɪ/ *noun* **a good buy** when you buy something good for a cheap price *This coat was a really good buy.*

buyer /ˈbaɪəʳ/ *noun* [C] **FINANCE** someone who buys something

buyout /ˈbaɪaʊt/ *noun* [C] **FINANCE** when a group of people buy the company that they work for

buzz¹ /bʌz/ *noun* **1** FEELING [**no plural**] *informal* a feeling of excitement, energy, or pleasure *He* ***gets a real buzz from*** *going to the gym.* **2** SOUND [C] a continuous sound like a bee makes

buzz² /bʌz/ *verb* [I] **1** SOUND to make a continuous sound like a bee *I can hear something buzzing.* **2** ACTIVITY to be full of activity or excitement *The crowd was* ***buzzing with*** *excitement.* **3 buzz about/around, etc** to move around in a quick and busy way

buzzer /ˈbʌzəʳ/ *noun* [C] a piece of electronic equipment that makes a long sound as a signal *to* ***press the buzzer***

buzzword /ˈbʌzwɜːd/ *noun* [C] **LANGUAGE** a word or expression that has become fashionable, usually in a particular subject or group of people *a new political buzzword*

O-ᵚ**by¹** *strong form* /baɪ/ *weak forms* /bɪ, bə/ *preposition* **1** DO used to show the person or thing that does something *She was examined by a doctor.* ○ *a painting by Van Gogh* **2** HOW through doing or using something *Can I pay by cheque?* ○ *We'll get there by car.* [+ **doing sth**] *Open the file by clicking on the icon.* **3** HOLDING holding a particular part of someone or something *She grabbed me by the arm.* **4** NEAR near or next to something or someone *I'll meet you by the post office.* ○ *A small child stood by her side.* **5** NOT LATER not later than a particular time or date *Applications have to be in by the 31st.* **6** ACCORDING TO according to *By law you must be eighteen to purchase alcohol.* **7** PAST past *He sped by me on a motorcycle.* **8** AMOUNT used to show measurements or amounts *twelve by ten metres of floor space* ○ *Interest rates have been increased by 0.25%.* ○ *I'm paid by the hour.* **9 by accident/chance/mistake, etc** as a result of an accident, chance, mistake, etc *I went to the wrong room by mistake.* **10 by day/night** during the day/night **11 day by day/little by little/one by one, etc** used in particular phrases to mean 'gradually' or 'in units of' *Day by day he grew stronger.*

O-ᵚ**by²** /baɪ/ *adverb* past *A motorcycle sped by.*

O-ᵚ**bye** /baɪ/ (*also* **bye-bye**) *exclamation* goodbye *Bye, see you tomorrow.*

by-election /ˈbaɪɪˌlekʃᵊn/ *noun* [C] **POLITICS** an election in the UK to choose a new member of parliament for an area because the old one has left or died

B

bygone /ˈbaɪgɒn/ *adjective literary* **bygone age/days/era, etc** a time in the past

bygones /ˈbaɪgɒnz/ *noun* **let bygones be bygones** something that you say to tell someone to forget about the unpleasant things in the past

bypass[1] /ˈbaɪpɑːs/ *noun* [C] **1** a road that goes around a town and not through it **2 HEALTH** a medical operation to make blood flow along a different route and avoid a damaged part of the heart *a* ***coronary/heart bypass***

bypass[2] /ˈbaɪpɑːs/ *verb* [T] **1** GO AROUND to go around a place or thing and not through it *I was hoping to bypass the city centre.* **2** AVOID to avoid dealing with someone or something by dealing directly with someone or something else *They bypassed him and went straight to his manager.*

by-product /ˈbaɪˌprɒdʌkt/ *noun* [C] something that is produced when you are making or doing something else *Carbon monoxide is a by-product of burning.*

bystander /ˈbaɪˌstændəʳ/ *noun* [C] someone who is near the place where an event happens, but not directly involved in it *The gunman began firing at* ***innocent bystanders.***

byte /baɪt/ *noun* [C] **COMPUTING** a unit for measuring the amount of information a computer can store, equal to 8 bits (= smallest unit of computer information)

Cc

C, c /siː/ the third letter of the alphabet

C **MEASURES** *written abbreviation for* Celsius or centigrade: measurements of temperature *30°C*

c *written abbreviation for* circa (= used before a number or date to show that it is not exact) *c. 1900*

cab /kæb/ *noun* [C] **1** CAR *informal* a taxi (= car that you pay to travel in) *We **took a cab** to the theatre.* ○ *a cab driver* **2** TRUCK the front part of a truck where the driver sits

cabaret /ˈkæbəreɪ/ *noun* [C, U] **MUSIC** when someone entertains people with songs, jokes, etc in a bar or restaurant *He's appearing **in cabaret** at the Cafe Royal.*

cabbage /ˈkæbɪdʒ/ *noun* [C, U] **FOOD** a large, round vegetable that consists of a lot of thick leaves

cabbie /ˈkæbi/ *noun* [C] *informal* someone who drives a taxi (= car that you pay to travel in)

cabin /ˈkæbɪn/ *noun* [C] **1** HOUSE a small, simple house made of wood *a log cabin* **2** SHIP a small room to sleep in on a ship **3** AIRCRAFT the area where passengers sit on an aircraft

ˈcabin ˌcrew *noun* [C] the people on an aircraft who take care of the passengers as their job

cabinet /ˈkæbɪnət/ *noun* **1 the Cabinet** **POLITICS** a group of people in a government who are chosen by and who advise the highest leader *a **Cabinet minister/member*** **2** [C] a cupboard with shelves or drawers to store or show things in *a **bathroom/medicine cabinet*** ➲See also: **filing cabinet**

cable¹ /ˈkeɪbl/ *noun* **1** WIRE [C, U] a wire covered by plastic that carries electricity, telephone signals, etc *overhead **power cables*** **2** ROPE [C, U] thick wire twisted into a rope **3** SYSTEM [U] the system of sending television programmes or telephone signals along wires under the ground ***cable TV*** ○ *This channel is only available **on cable**.*

ˈcable ˌcar *noun* [C] a vehicle that hangs from thick cables and carries people up hills and mountains

ˌcable (TˈV) (*also* **ˌcable ˈtelevision**) *noun* [U] a system of sending television pictures and sound along wires buried under the ground

cacao /kəˈkaʊ/ *noun* [U] the seeds of a tropical tree, from which chocolate and cocoa are made

cache /kæʃ/ *noun* [C] a secret supply of something *a **cache of weapons***

ˌcache ˈmemory *noun* [C, U] **COMPUTING** an area or type of computer memory in which information that is often used can be stored temporarily and got to quickly

cachet /ˈkæʃeɪ/ (US) /kæʃˈeɪ/ *noun* [U] when something is admired or respected

cacophony /kəˈkɒfəni/ *noun* [**no plural**] a loud, unpleasant mixture of sounds

cactus /ˈkæktəs/ *noun* [C] *plural* **cacti** /ˈkæktaɪ/, or **cactuses** a plant with thick leaves for storing water and often sharp points that grows in deserts

CAD /kæd/ *noun* [U] **COMPUTING** computer-aided design: the use of computers to design objects

caddie /ˈkædi/ *noun* [C] **SPORT** someone who carries the equipment for someone playing golf ➲See colour picture **Sports 2** on page Centre 15 •**caddie** *verb* [I] **caddying**, *past* **caddied** to be a caddie for someone

cadet /kəˈdet/ *noun* [C] a young person who is training to be in a military organization, the police, etc *an **army cadet***

cadmium /ˈkædmiəm/ *noun* [U] **CHEMISTRY** a poisonous soft, blue-white metallic element used for example in batteries and electroplating (= the process of using electricity to cover a metal object with a thin layer of another metal) (symbol **Cd**)

caecum *UK* (*US* **cecum**) /ˈsiːkəm/ *noun* [C] *plural UK* **caeca**, *US* **ceca** **ANATOMY, BIOLOGY** the bag-shaped part at the beginning of the large intestine (= lower part of the bowels) ➲See picture at **alimentary canal**

caesarean (*also US* **cesarean**) /sɪˈzeəriən/ *noun* [C] **HEALTH** an operation in which a baby is taken out of a woman through a cut in the front of her body

caesium *UK* (*US* **cesium**) /ˈsiːziəm/ *noun* [U] **CHEMISTRY** a soft silver-white metallic element that reacts strongly with other chemicals, used in photoelectric cells (symbol **Cs**)

O⁻ **cafe** (*also* **café**) /ˈkæfeɪ/ (US) /kæˈfeɪ/ *noun* [C] a small restaurant where you can buy drinks and small meals

cafeteria /ˌkæfəˈtɪəriə/ *noun* [C] a restaurant where you collect and pay for your food and drink before you eat it *a school cafeteria*

caffeine /ˈkæfiːn/ *noun* [U] **CHEMISTRY, FOOD** a chemical in coffee, tea, etc that makes you feel more awake

cage /keɪdʒ/ *noun* [C] a container made of wire or metal bars used for keeping birds or animals in *a bird cage* ➲See also: **rib cage**

cagey /ˈkeɪdʒi/ *adjective* If someone is cagey, they are not very willing to give information, and you may think they are not honest. *He's very **cagey about** his past.*

cajole /kəˈdʒəʊl/ *verb* [I, T] to persuade someone to do something by being friendly or by promising them something [**+ into + doing sth**] *She cajoled me into helping with the dinner.*

O⁻ **cake** /keɪk/ *noun* [C, U] **1** **FOOD** a sweet food made from flour, butter, sugar, and eggs mixed together and baked *a chocolate/fruit cake* ○ *a **piece/slice of cake*** ○ *to bake/make a cake* ➲See colour picture **Food** on page Centre 11 **2 have your cake and eat it** to have or do two things that it is usually impossible to have or do at the same time ➲See also: the **icing** on the cake, be a **piece¹** of cake

C

caked /keɪkt/ *adjective* **be caked in/with sth** to be covered with a thick, dry layer of something *His boots were caked in mud.*

CAL /kæl/ *noun* [U] **EDUCATION** *abbreviation for* computer-aided learning: the use of computers for teaching and learning

calamity /kəˈlæməti/ *noun* [C] a sudden, bad event that causes a lot of damage or unhappiness

calcium /ˈkælsiəm/ *noun* [U] **CHEMISTRY** a chemical element in teeth, bones, and chalk (= a soft, white rock) (symbol **Ca**)

calcium carbonate /ˌkælsiəmˈkɑːbəneɪt/ *noun* [U] **CHEMISTRY** a common, white chemical compound found in chalk, marble and other substances, and in bones and shells (formula $CaCO_3$)

calcium hydroxide /ˌkælsiəmhaɪˈdrɒksaɪd/ *noun* [U] **CHEMISTRY** a white alkaline chemical compound used to make cement and plaster and to reduce the acid in soil (formula $Ca(OH)_2$)

calcium sulphate *UK* (*US* **calcium sulfate**) /ˌkælsiəmˈsʌlfeɪt/ *noun* [U] **CHEMISTRY** a white chemical substance used to make some building materials, e.g. cement, and to make other substances drier (formula $CaSO_4$)

calculate /ˈkælkjəleɪt/ *verb* **1 MATHEMATICS** [T] to discover an amount or number using mathematics *to calculate a cost/percentage* **2 be calculated to do sth** to be intended to have a particular effect *His comments were calculated to embarrass the prime minister.*

calculated /ˈkælkjəleɪtɪd/ *adjective* based on careful thought or planning, not on emotion *a* ***calculated risk/decision***

calculating /ˈkælkjəleɪtɪŋ/ *adjective* Calculating people try to get what they want by thinking carefully and without emotion, and not caring about other people. *a cold, calculating criminal*

WORD PARTNERS FOR ***calculation***

do/perform a calculation • a **complex/precise/quick/rough** calculation

calculation /ˌkælkjəˈleɪʃən/ *noun* **1 MATHEMATICS** [C, U] when you use mathematics to discover a number or amount *I did some* ***quick calculations*** *to see if I could afford to buy it.* **2** [U] when someone thinks very carefully about something without any emotion

calculator /ˈkælkjəleɪtəʳ/ *noun* [C] an electronic device that you use to do mathematical calculations *a* ***pocket calculator***

calculus /ˈkælkjʊləs/ *noun* [U] **MATHEMATICS** an area of advanced mathematics in which continuously changing values are studied

caldera

caldera /kælˈdeərə/ *noun* [C] **GEOLOGY** a very large circular hole, sometimes containing a lake, that is made when the central part of a volcano falls in after an explosion

calendar /ˈkæləndəʳ/ *noun* **1** [C] something that shows all the days, weeks, and months of the year **2 the Christian/Jewish/Western, etc calendar** the system used to measure and arrange the days, weeks, months and special events of the year according to Christian/Jewish/Western, etc tradition **3 the political/school/sporting, etc calendar** the events that are arranged during the year for a particular activity or organization

calf /kɑːf/ *noun* [C] *plural* **calves** /kɑːvz/ **1** a young cow **2 ANATOMY** the back of your leg below your knee ➲See colour picture **The Body** on page Centre 13

calibre *UK* (*US* **caliber**) /ˈkælɪbəʳ/ *noun* [U] **1** the quality or level of ability of someone or something *The calibre of applicants was very high.* **2 MEASURES** the measurement across the inside of a gun, or across a bullet

CALL /kɔːl/ *abbreviation for* **COMPUTING, EDUCATION** computer aided language learning: a way of learning languages using computers

WORD PARTNERS FOR ***call***

make/get/take a call • **give** sb a call • a call **from/to** sb

O-ᵚ**call²** /kɔːl/ *noun* [C] **1** [TELEPHONE] (*also* **phone call**) when you use the telephone ***Give me a call*** *at the weekend.* ○ *I* ***got a call*** *from Sue this morning.* **2 a call for sth** a demand for something to happen *a call for action/peace* **3** [VISIT] a short visit *I thought I'd* ***pay*** *Gary* ***a call.*** **4** [SHOUT] when someone shouts something **5** [BIRD] a sound made by a bird or other animal **6 sb's call** *informal* when someone can decide something *I don't mind what we do - it's your call.* **7 call for sth** when people want or need a particular thing *There's not much call for interior designers round here.* **8 be on call** to be ready to go to work if you are needed, as part of your job **9 a close call** when something you do not want to happen nearly happens ➲See also: be at sb's **beck** and call, **wake-up call**

O-ᵚ**call¹** /kɔːl/ *verb* **1 be called sth** to have a particular name *a man called John* ○ *What's your dog called?* ○ *Their latest record is called "Ecstasy".* **2** [GIVE NAME] [+ two objects] to give someone or something a particular name *I want to call the baby Alex.* **3** [DESCRIBE] [+ two objects] to describe someone or something in a particular way *She called him a liar.* **4** [ASK TO COME] [T] to ask someone to come somewhere *She called me into her office.* **5** [SHOUT] [I, T] (*also*

call out) to shout or say something in a loud voice *I thought I heard someone calling my name.* **6** TELEPHONE [**I, T**] to telephone someone *He called me every night while he was away.* ○ *Has anyone called the police?* ➲See Common Learner Error at **phone** **7** VISIT [**I**] (*also* **call by/in/round**) *UK* to visit someone for a short time *John called round earlier.* **8 call an election/meeting, etc** to arrange for an election/meeting, etc to happen *The chairman has called an emergency meeting.* ➲See also: call sb's **bluff**², call it a **day**

call back *phrasal verb UK* to go back to a place in order to see someone or collect something *I'll call back later to pick up the books.*

call (sb) back *phrasal verb* to telephone someone again, or to telephone someone who telephoned you earlier *I can't talk now - I'll call you back in ten minutes.*

call for sth *phrasal verb* **1** SAY to demand that something happens *to call for a ban on guns* **2** NEED to need or deserve a particular action or quality *You passed your test? This calls for a celebration!*

call for sb *phrasal verb* to go to a place in order to collect someone *I'll call for you at eight.*

call sth off *phrasal verb* **1** NOT HAPPEN to decide that a planned event or activity will not happen because it is not possible, useful, or wanted now *The game has been called off because of the weather.* **2** STOP to decide to stop an activity *Police have called off the search.*

call on sb to do sth *phrasal verb* to ask someone in a formal way to do something *He called on the rebels to stop fighting.*

call (sb) up *phrasal verb mainly US* to telephone someone *My dad called me up to tell me the good news.*

call sth up *phrasal verb* **COMPUTING** to find and show information on a computer screen *I'll just call up your account details.*

be called up *phrasal verb* to be ordered to join a military organization or asked to join an official team *He was called up soon after the war started.*

'call ˌcentre *noun* [**C**] *UK* a place where people use telephones to provide information to customers, or to sell goods or services

caller /ˈkɔːləʳ/ *noun* [**C**] **1** TELEPHONE someone who makes a telephone call *an anonymous caller* **2** VISITOR *mainly UK* someone who visits for a short time

call-in /ˈkɔːlɪn/ *US* (*UK* **phone-in**) *noun* [**C**] a television or radio programme in which the public can ask questions or give opinions over the telephone

calling /ˈkɔːlɪŋ/ *noun* [**C**] a strong feeling that you should do a particular type of work *She found her true calling in teaching.*

callous /ˈkæləs/ *adjective* cruel and not caring about other people *a callous remark* •**callously** *adverb*

O-- **calm¹** /kɑːm/ *adjective* **1** PERSON relaxed and not worried, frightened, or excited *a calm voice/manner* ○ *Try to* ***stay calm*** *- the doctor will be here soon.* **2** SEA If the sea is calm, it is still and has no large waves. **3** WEATHER If the weather is calm, there are no storms or wind. •**calmness** *noun* [**U**]

calm² /kɑːm/ *noun* [**U**] when people or conditions are calm

calm³ /kɑːm/ *verb* [**T**] to make someone stop feeling upset, angry, or excited *The police tried to calm the crowd.* ○ *a calming effect*

calm (sb) down *phrasal verb* to stop feeling upset, angry, or excited, or to make someone stop feeling this way *Calm down and tell me what's wrong.*

calmly /ˈkɑːmli/ *adverb* in a relaxed way *He spoke slowly and calmly.*

calorie /ˈkælᵊri/ *noun* [**C**] **FOOD, MEASURES** a unit for measuring the amount of energy food provides *I try to eat about 2000 calories a day.*

calorimeter /ˌkæləˈrɪmɪtəʳ/ *noun* [**C**] **CHEMISTRY, PHYSICS** a piece of equipment for measuring the amount of heat produced in a chemical reaction

calves /kɑːvz/ *plural of* calf

calyx /ˈkeɪlɪks/ *noun* [**C**] *plural* **calyxes, calyces** **BIOLOGY** the outer part of a flower formed by the sepals (= separate outer parts), which covers and protects the flowers as they develop

CAM /kæm/ *noun* [**U**] **COMPUTING** *abbreviation for* computer-aided manufacture; the use of computers in producing goods

camaraderie /ˌkæməˈrɑːdᵊri/ *noun* [**U**] special friendship felt by people who work together or experience something together

cambium /ˈkæmbiəm/ *noun* [**C, U**] *plural* **cambiums, cambia** **BIOLOGY** a layer of cells in the roots and stems of plants that produce new tissue to make them thicker ➲See picture at **stem**

Cambrian /ˈkæmbriən/ *adjective* **GEOLOGY** from the period of time between about 543 and 490 million years ago, in which many different types of invertebrate (= without any back bone) animals first appeared

camcorder /ˈkæmˌkɔːdəʳ/ *noun* [**C**] a camera that you can hold in your hand and that takes moving pictures

came /keɪm/ *past tense of* come

camel /ˈkæmᵊl/ *noun* [**C**] a large animal that lives in the desert and has one or two humps (= raised parts on its back)

cameo /ˈkæmiəʊ/ *noun* [**C**] when someone famous appears for a short time in a film or play *a cameo role*

O-- **camera** /ˈkæmᵊrə/ *noun* [**C**] **ART** a piece of equipment used to take photographs or to make films *a digital camera* ○ *a television camera*

cameraman /ˈkæmᵊrəmæn/ *noun* [**C**] *plural* **cameramen** someone who operates a television camera or film camera as their job

camisole /ˈkæmɪsəʊl/ *noun* [**C**] a piece of women's underwear for the top half of the body, with thin straps that go over the shoulders *a lace camisole* ➲See colour picture **Clothes** at page Centre 9

camouflage /ˈkæməflɑːʒ/ *noun* [**U**] when the colour or pattern on something is similar to the area around it making it difficult to see *a camouflage jacket* •**camouflage** *verb* [**T**]

camp¹ /kæmp/ *noun* **1** [**C**] an area where people stay in tents for a short time, usually for a

C

holiday **2 an army/prison/refugee, etc camp** an area containing temporary buildings or tents used for soldiers/prisoners/refugees (= people forced to leave their home), etc ➲See also: **base camp, concentration camp**

C

camp² /kæmp/ (*also* **camp out**) *verb* [I] to stay in a tent or temporary shelter *We camped on the beach for two nights.*

WORD PARTNERS FOR *campaign*

launch/mount/run a campaign • a campaign **against/for** sth • an **advertising/election** campaign

campaign¹ /kæm'peɪn/ *noun* [C] **1** ACTIVITIES a series of organized activities or events intended to achieve a result *an **advertising/election campaign*** **2** WAR a series of military attacks *a bombing campaign*

campaign² /kæm'peɪn/ *verb* [I] to organize a series of activities to try to achieve something *to **campaign against/for** something* •**campaigner** *noun* [C] *an animal rights campaigner*

camper /'kæmpəʳ/ *noun* [C] **1** PERSON someone who stays in a tent on holiday **2** VEHICLE (*also* **'camper ˌvan**) a vehicle containing a bed, kitchen equipment, etc that you can live in

camping /'kæmpɪŋ/ *noun* [U] when you stay in a tent for a holiday *We're **going camping** in France this summer.* ○ *a camping trip*

COMMON LEARNER ERROR

camping or **campsite?**

Be careful not to use **camping**, the activity of staying in a tent, when you mean **campsite**, the area of ground where you do this.

campsite /'kæmpsaɪt/ (*also US* **campground** /'kæmpgraʊnd/) *noun* [C] an area where people can stay in tents for a holiday

campus /'kæmpəs/ *noun* [C, U] **EDUCATION** the land and buildings belonging to a college or university *I lived **on campus** in my first year.*

can¹ *strong form* /kæn/ *weak forms* /kən, kn/ *modal verb past* **could 1** ABILITY to be able to do something *We can't pay the rent.* ○ *Can you drive?* **2** PERMISSION to be allowed to do something *You can't park here.* ○ *Can I go now?* **3** ASK used to ask someone to do or provide something *Can you tell her to meet me outside?* ○ *Can I have a drink of water?* **4** OFFER used to politely offer to do something *Can I carry those bags for you?* **5** POSSIBLE used to talk about what is possible *You can buy stamps from the shop on the corner.* ○ *Smoking can cause cancer.* **6** TYPICAL used to talk about how someone often behaves or what something is often like *She can be really rude at times.* **7** SURPRISE used to show surprise or lack of belief *You can't possibly be hungry already!* ○ *Can you believe it?* ➲See Extra help page **Modal verbs** on page Centre 34.

can² /kæn/ *noun* [C] **1** a closed, metal container for food or liquids *a can of soup/beans* ○ *a can of paint* **2 a can of worms** a situation which causes a lot of trouble for you when you start to deal with it ➲See also: **trash can, watering can**

can³ /kæn/ *verb* [T] **canning,** *past* **canned** to put food or drink into metal containers in a factory *canned tomatoes*

Canadian /kə'neɪdiən/ *adjective* relating to Canada •**Canadian** *noun* [C] someone who comes from Canada

canal /kə'næl/ *noun* [C] an artificial river built for boats to travel along or to take water where it is needed

canary /kə'neəri/ *noun* [C] a small, yellow bird that sings

cancel /'kænsəl/ *verb* [T] *UK* **cancelling,** *past* **cancelled,** *US* **canceling,** *past* **canceled 1** EVENT to say that an organized event will not now happen [**often passive**] *The meeting has been cancelled.* **2** GOODS/SERVICES to stop an order for goods or services that you do not now want

cancel sth out *phrasal verb* If something cancels out another thing, it stops it from having any effect.

cancellation /ˌkænsəl'eɪʃən/ *noun* [C, U] when someone decides that an event will not now happen or stops an order for something *a last-minute cancellation*

Cancer /'kænsəʳ/ *noun* [C, U] the sign of the zodiac which relates to the period of 22 June - 22 July, or a person born during this period

WORD PARTNERS FOR *cancer*

get/have cancer • **breast/lung/prostate/skin** cancer • cancer **of the** [liver/stomach, etc] • cancer **patients/sufferers** • cancer **research/treatment**

cancer /'kænsəʳ/ *noun* [C, U] **HEALTH** a serious disease that is caused when cells in the body grow in a way that is uncontrolled and not normal ***breast/lung cancer*** ○ *His wife died of cancer.* •**cancerous** *adjective a cancerous growth*

candid /'kændɪd/ *adjective* honest, especially about something that is unpleasant or embarrassing *She was very candid about her personal life in the interview.* •**candidly** *adverb*

candidacy /'kændɪdəsi/ *noun* [U] **POLITICS** when someone is a candidate in an election

candidate /'kændɪdət/ *noun* [C] **1 POLITICS** one of the people taking part in an election or trying to get a job *a presidential candidate* **2 EDUCATION** *UK* someone who is taking an exam

candle /'kændl/ *noun* [C] a stick of wax with string going through it that you burn to produce light ➲See colour picture **The Living Room** on page Centre 4

candlelight /'kændllaɪt/ *noun* [U] light produced by a candle

candlestick /'kændlstɪk/ *noun* [C] an object that holds a candle

can-do /'kænˌduː/ *adjective informal* determined to deal with problems and achieve results *I really admire her **can-do attitude**.*

candour *UK* (*US* **candor**) /'kændəʳ/ *noun* [U] when you speak honestly, especially about something that is unpleasant or embarrassing

candy /'kændi/ *noun* [C, U] *US* **FOOD** a small piece of sweet food made from sugar, chocolate, etc *a box of candy* ○ *a candy bar*

cane¹ /keɪn/ *noun* **1** STEM [C, U] the long, hard, hollow stem of some plants, sometimes used to make furniture **2** WALK [C] a long stick used by people to help them walk **3** PUNISH [C] *UK* a long stick used in the past to hit children at school

cane² /keɪn/ *verb* [T] *UK* to hit someone, especially a school student, with a stick as a punishment

canine¹ /ˈkeɪnaɪn/ *adjective* relating to dogs

canine² /ˈkeɪnaɪn/ *noun* [C] **ANATOMY** one of four pointed teeth in a person's mouth ➲Compare **incisor, molar** ➲See picture at **skull**

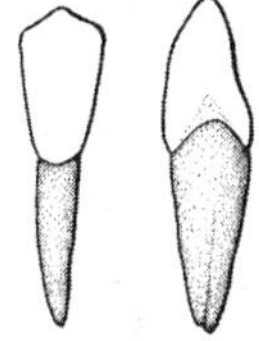

canine

canister /ˈkænɪstəʳ/ *noun* [C] a metal container for gases or dry things *a gas canister*

cannabis /ˈkænəbɪs/ *mainly UK* (*mainly US* **marijuana**) *noun* [U] **HEALTH** a drug that some people smoke for pleasure and that is illegal in many countries

canned /kænd/ (*also UK* **tinned**) *adjective* **FOOD** Canned food is sold in metal containers.

cannibal /ˈkænɪbəl/ *noun* [C] someone who eats human flesh •**cannibalism** *noun* [U]

cannon /ˈkænən/ *noun* [C] a very large gun, in the past one that was on wheels

O⁻**cannot** /ˈkænɒt/ *modal verb* the negative form of 'can' *I cannot predict what will happen.*

canny /ˈkæni/ *adjective* clever and able to think quickly, especially about money or business *a canny businessman*

canoe /kəˈnuː/ *noun* [C] a small, narrow boat with pointed ends that you move using a paddle (= stick with a wide, flat part) •**canoeing** *noun* [U] the activity of travelling in a canoe

canon /ˈkænən/ *noun* [C] **RELIGION** a Christian priest who works in a cathedral (= large, important church) *the Canon of Westminster*

ˈcan ˌopener (*also UK* **tin opener**) *noun* [C] a piece of kitchen equipment for opening metal food containers ➲See colour picture **The Kitchen** on page Centre 2

canopy /ˈkænəpi/ *noun* [C] a cover or type of roof for protection or decoration

can't /kɑːnt/ *modal verb* **1** CANNOT *short for* cannot *I can't find my keys.* **2** SUGGEST used to suggest that someone should do something *Can't you ask Jonathan to help?*

canteen /kænˈtiːn/ *noun* [C] a restaurant in an office, factory, or school

canter /ˈkæntəʳ/ *verb* [I] When a horse canters, it runs quite fast. •**canter** *noun* [**no plural**]

canvas /ˈkænvəs/ *noun* **1** [U] strong cloth used for making sails, tents, etc **2** **ART** [C] a piece of canvas used for a painting

canvass /ˈkænvəs/ *verb* **1** **POLITICS** [I, T] to try to persuade people to vote for someone in an election *He's* ***canvassing for*** *the Labour party.* **2** [T] to ask people their opinion about something *The study* ***canvassed the views*** *of over 9000 people.*

canyon /ˈkænjən/ *noun* [C] **GEOGRAPHY, GEOLOGY** a deep valley with very steep sides

cap¹ /kæp/ *noun* [C] **1** HAT a hat with a flat, curved part at the front *a baseball cap* ➲See colour picture **Clothes** on page Centre 9 **2** LID a small lid that covers the top or end of something

cap² /kæp/ *verb* [T] **capping**, *past* **capped** **1** END to be the last and the best or worst event in a series of events *The party capped a wonderful week.* **2** **ECONOMICS** to put a limit on an amount of money that can be borrowed, charged, etc [**often passive**] *The interest rate has been capped at 5%.* **3** COVER to cover the top of something [**often passive**] *The mountains were capped with snow.*

capability /ˌkeɪpəˈbɪləti/ *noun* [C, U] the ability or power to do something [+ **to do sth**] *Both players have the capability to win this match.*

capable /ˈkeɪpəbl/ *adjective* **1** able to do things effectively and achieve results *She's a very capable young woman.* **2** **capable of sth/doing sth** having the ability or qualities to be able to do something *She was capable of great cruelty.* ➲Opposite **incapable**

capacitance /kəˈpæsɪtənts/ *noun* [U] **1** the ability of a system to store electrical charge **2** **MEASURES** a measurement of this characteristic

capacitor /kəˈpæsɪtər/ *noun* [C] a device which collects and stores electricity, and is an important part of electronic equipment such as televisions and radios

capacity /kəˈpæsəti/ *noun* **1** CONTAIN [C, U] the largest amount or number that a container, building, etc can hold *The restaurant has* ***a capacity of*** *about 200.* ○ *The stadium was* ***filled to capacity*** (= completely full). **2** PRODUCE [U] the amount that a factory or machine can produce *The factory is operating* ***at full capacity*** (= producing as much as possible). **3** ABILITY [C] the ability to do, experience, or understand something *She has a great* ***capacity for*** *love.* **4** JOB [C] a position or job *He attended over 100 events last year* ***in his capacity as*** *mayor.*

cape /keɪp/ *noun* [C] **1** a loose coat without any sleeves that is fastened at the neck **2** **GEOGRAPHY** a large area of land that goes out into the sea

caper /ˈkeɪpəʳ/ *noun* [C] something that is done as a joke, or intended to entertain people *His new movie is a* ***comic caper***.

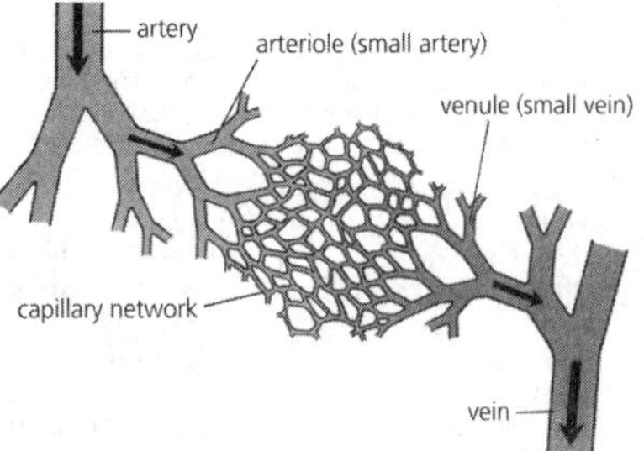

capillary

capillary /kəˈpɪləri/ (US) /ˈkæpəleri/ *noun* [C]

ANATOMY, BIOLOGY a very thin tube that carries blood around the body, connecting arteries to veins

O→**capital**[1] /ˈkæpɪtəl/ *noun* **1 GEOGRAPHY** [C] the most important city in a country or state, where the government is based *Paris is the capital of France.* **2 ECONOMICS, FINANCE** [U] an amount of money that you can use to start a business or to make more money **3 LANGUAGE** [C] (*also* ˌ**capital ˈletter**) a large letter of the alphabet used at the beginning of sentences and names ➲See Extra help page **Punctuation** on page Centre 18. ➲See also: **block capitals**

capital[2] /ˈkæpɪtəl/ *adjective* **a capital crime/offence LAW** a crime that can be punished by death

ˌ**capital ˈassets** *noun* [plural] **FINANCE** the buildings and machines owned by a business or other organization

ˌ**capital ˈgains** *noun* [plural] **FINANCE** profits made by selling property or an investment (= something bought hoping its value will increase) *They had to pay a lot of capital gains tax.*

ˌ**capital inˈtensive** *adjective* **FINANCE** A capital intensive business needs to spend a lot of money on buildings, equipment, etc before it can start.

ˌ**capital inˈvestment** *noun* [U] **FINANCE** money which is spent on buildings and equipment to make a business more effective

capitalism /ˈkæpɪtəlɪzəm/ *noun* [U] **ECONOMICS, POLITICS, SOCIETY** a political and economic system in which industry is owned privately for profit and not by the state

capitalist /ˈkæpɪtəlɪst/ *noun* [C] **POLITICS, SOCIETY** someone who supports capitalism •**capitalist** *adjective a capitalist society*

capitalize (*also UK* **-ise**) /ˈkæpɪtəlaɪz/ *verb* [T] **LANGUAGE** to write something using capital letters, or starting with a capital letter

capitalize on sth *phrasal verb* to use a situation to achieve something good for yourself *He failed to capitalize on his earlier success.*

ˌ**capital ˈpunishment** *noun* [U] **LAW** when someone is killed by the state for committing a serious crime

ˌ**capital reˈceipt** *noun* [C] **FINANCE** an amount of money received when fixed assets (= land, equipment, buildings, etc) are sold by a business

capitulate /kəˈpɪtjʊleɪt/ *verb* [I] to stop disagreeing or fighting with someone and agree to what they want •**capitulation** /kəˌpɪtjʊˈleɪʃən/ *noun* [C, U]

cappuccino /ˌkæpʊˈtʃiːnəʊ/ *noun* [C, U] **FOOD** coffee made with milk that has been heated with steam to produce a lot of small bubbles

capricious /kəˈprɪʃəs/ *adjective* likely to suddenly change your ideas or behaviour

Capricorn /ˈkæprɪkɔːn/ *noun* [C, U] the sign of the zodiac which relates to the period of 23 December - 20 January, or a person born during this period

capsize /kæpˈsaɪz/ *verb* [I, T] If a boat capsizes, or if it is capsized, it turns over in the water.

Caps lock (key) /ˈkæpslɒkˌkiː/ *noun* [C usually singular] **COMPUTING** a key on a computer keyboard that you press to make any letters you type appear as capital letters until you press it again

capsule /ˈkæpsjuːl/ *noun* [C] **1 HEALTH** a small container with medicine inside that you swallow **2** the part of a spacecraft that people live in

captain[1] /ˈkæptɪn/ *noun* [C] **1** [SHIP] the person in control of a ship or aircraft **2** [ARMY] an officer of middle rank in the army, navy, or air force **3** [SPORT] the leader of a team

captain[2] /ˈkæptɪn/ *verb* [T] to be the captain of a team, ship, or aircraft *He has captained the England cricket team three times.*

captaincy /ˈkæptɪnsi/ *noun* [U] when someone is the captain of a team

caption /ˈkæpʃən/ *noun* [C] words written under a picture to explain it

captivate /ˈkæptɪveɪt/ *verb* [T] to interest or attract someone very much *She captivated film audiences with her beauty and charm.* •**captivating** *adjective a captivating performance*

captive[1] /ˈkæptɪv/ *adjective* **1** A captive person or animal is being kept somewhere and is not allowed to leave. **2 a captive audience/market** a group of people who have to watch something or have to buy something because they do not have a choice **3 hold/take sb captive** to keep someone as a prisoner, or make someone a prisoner

captive[2] /ˈkæptɪv/ *noun* [C] someone who is kept as a prisoner

captivity /kæpˈtɪvəti/ *noun* [U] when a person or animal is kept somewhere and is not allowed to leave *lion cubs born **in captivity***

capture[1] /ˈkæptʃər/ *verb* [T] **1** [PRISONER] to catch someone and make them your prisoner *Two soldiers were captured by the enemy.* **2** [CONTROL] to get control of a place with force *Rebel troops have captured the city.* **3** [GET] to succeed in getting something when you are competing against other people *The Green Party has captured 12% of the vote.* **4** [DESCRIBE] to show or describe something successfully using words or pictures *His book really captures the spirit of the place.* **5 capture sb/sth on camera/film, etc** to record someone or something on camera/film, etc **6 capture sb's attention/imagination** to make someone very interested or excited *The campaign has really captured the public's imagination.* **7 capture sb's heart** to make someone love you *She captured the hearts of the nation.*

capture[2] /ˈkæptʃər/ *noun* [U] **1** [PRISONER] when someone is caught and made a prisoner *He shot himself to avoid capture.* **2** [CONTROL] when someone gets control of a place with force *the capture of the city by foreign troops*

WORD PARTNERS FOR ***car***

drive/park/start a car • a car **breaks down** • **by** car • a car **accident/crash** • a car **driver**

O→**car** /kɑːr/ *noun* [C] **1** [VEHICLE] a vehicle with an engine, four wheels, and seats for a small number of passengers *She goes to work **by car**.* ○ *Where did you **park** your **car**?* ➲See colour picture **Car** at page Centre 7 **2** [PART OF TRAIN] *US* a part of a train in which passengers sit, eat, sleep, etc *the dining car* ➲See also: **buffet car, cable car, estate car, sports car**

caramel /ˈkærəmᵊl/ *noun* [C, U] **FOOD** sugar that has been heated until it turns brown and that is used to add colour and flavour to food, or a sweet made from sugar, milk, and butter

carat (*also US* **karat**) /ˈkærət/ *noun* [C] **MEASURES** a unit for measuring how pure gold is, or how much jewels (= valuable stones) weigh *22 carat gold*

caravan /ˈkærəvæn/ *noun* [C] **1** VEHICLE *UK* a vehicle which people can live in on holiday and which is pulled by a car *a **caravan site*** **2** GROUP a group of people with animals or vehicles who travel together across a desert

carbohydrase /ˌkɑːbəʊˈhaɪdreɪz/ *noun* [U] **BIOLOGY** an enzyme (= substance that causes chemical reactions) which causes a chemical reaction that helps the body to digest carbohydrate

carbohydrate /ˌkɑːbəʊˈhaɪdreɪt/ *noun* [C, U] **BIOLOGY, FOOD** a substance in food such as sugar, potatoes, etc that gives your body energy

carbon /ˈkɑːbᵊn/ *noun* [U] **CHEMISTRY** a chemical element present in all animals and plants and in coal and oil (symbol **C**)

carbonate /ˈkɑːbᵊneɪt/ *noun* [C] **CHEMISTRY** a salt that contains carbon and oxygen and another chemical

carbonated /ˈkɑːbəneɪtɪd/ *adjective* **FOOD** Carbonated drinks contain a lot of small bubbles.

ˈcarbon ˌcapture *noun* [U] **ENVIRONMENT** a way of catching the carbon produced by machines so that it is not released into the air

ˈcarbon ˌchain *noun* [C] **CHEMISTRY** a line of connected carbon atoms

ˌcarbon ˈcopy *noun* [C] **1** WRITING a copy of a written document that is made using carbon paper (= thin paper covered in carbon) **2** PERSON an exact copy of something *He's a **carbon copy of** his father.*

ˈcarbon ˌcredits *noun* [plural] **ENVIRONMENT** a system that allows organizations the right to produce a certain amount of carbon, and allows them to buy or sell those rights

the ˈcarbon ˌcycle *noun* **ENVIRONMENT** the way carbon moves between living organisms and their environment, by being taken from the air by plants which are then eaten by animals, and being returned to the atmosphere by the respiration of plants and animals and by the burning of plant material

ˌcarbon ˈdating *noun* [U] **BIOLOGY** a method of calculating the age of extremely old objects by measuring the amount of a particular type of carbon in them

carbon dioxide /ˌkɑːbᵊndaɪˈɒksaɪd/ *noun* [U] **CHEMISTRY** a gas that is produced when people and animals breathe out, or when carbon is burned (formula CO_2)

ˈcarbon eˌmissions *noun* [plural] **ENVIRONMENT** carbon dioxide and carbon monoxide made by things such as factories or cars that burn carbon and cause pollution

carbonic /kɑːˈbɒnɪk/ *adjective* **CHEMISTRY** containing carbon

carbonic acid /kɑːˌbɒnɪkˈæsɪd/ *noun* [U] **CHEMISTRY** a weak acid made of carbon dioxide dissolved in water (formula H_2CO_3)

carboniferous /ˌkɑːbəˈnɪfərəs/ *adjective* **GEOLOGY** containing or producing carbon *carboniferous rocks*

carbon monoxide /ˌkɑːbᵊnməˈnɒksaɪd/ *noun* [U] **CHEMISTRY, ENVIRONMENT** a poisonous gas that is produced by burning some types of

C

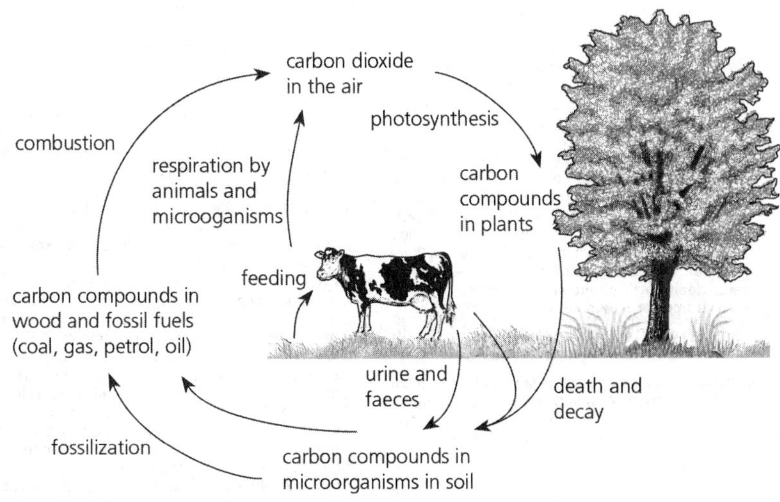

carbon cycle

fuel, especially petrol (= fuel for cars) (formula CO)

ˌcarbon ˈneutral *adjective* **ENVIRONMENT** not producing carbon emissions *a carbon-neutral fuel/home/lifestyle*

ˌcarbon offˈsetting *noun* [U] **ENVIRONMENT** trying to stop the damage caused by activities that produce carbon by doing other things to reduce it, such as planting trees

ˈcarbon ˌpaper *noun* [U] thin paper that is covered on one side with carbon (= a black substance) and is used for making copies of written documents

ˌcarbon ˈtax *noun* [C] **ENVIRONMENT** a tax on oil, coal and other things which produce greenhouse gases (= gases that harm the air around the Earth)

ˌcar ˈboot sale *noun* [C] *UK* an event where people sell things they no longer want from the backs of their cars

carburettor *UK* (*US* **carburetor**) /ˌkɑːbəˈretəʳ/ (US) /ˈkɑːbəreɪtər/ *noun* [C] the part of an engine that mixes fuel and air which are then burned to provide power

carcass /ˈkɑːkəs/ *noun* [C] the body of a dead animal

carcinogen /kɑːˈsɪnədʒən/ *noun* [C] **HEALTH** a substance that can cause cancer (= a disease when cells in your body grow in an uncontrolled way) •**carcinogenic** /ˌkɑːsɪnəʊˈdʒenɪk/ *adjective carcinogenic chemicals*

O-→**card** /kɑːd/ *noun* **1** [MESSAGE] [C] a folded piece of stiff paper with a picture on the front and a message inside that you send to someone on a special occasion *a **birthday card*** **2** [INFORMATION] [C] a piece of stiff paper or plastic that has information printed on it *a library card* **3** [GAME] [C] (*also* **playing card**) one of a set of 52 pieces of stiff paper with numbers and pictures used for playing games *UK a pack of cards/ US a deck of cards* ○ *We spent the evening **playing cards*** (= playing games using cards). **4** [PAPER] [U] *UK* thick, stiff paper **5** [WITHOUT ENVELOPE] [C] a postcard (= card with a picture on one side that you send without an envelope) **6 COMPUTING** a part inside a computer which controls how the computer operates *a graphics/sound card* **7 be on the cards** *UK* (*US* **be in the cards**) to be likely to happen *Do you think marriage is on the cards?* **8 put/lay your cards on the table** to tell someone honestly what you think or plan to do ⊃See also: **cash card, charge card, Christmas card, credit card, debit card, phone card, smart card, swipe card, trump card, wild card**

cardboard /ˈkɑːdbɔːd/ *noun* [U] thick, stiff paper that is used for making boxes

cardiac /ˈkɑːdiæk/ *adjective* [**always before noun**] **ANATOMY, BIOLOGY, HEALTH** relating to the heart *cardiac surgery* ○ ***cardiac arrest*** (= when the heart stops beating) ⊃See picture at **heart**

cardigan /ˈkɑːdɪgən/ *noun* [C] a piece of clothing, often made of wool, that covers the top part of your body and fastens at the front ⊃See colour picture **Clothes** on page Centre 8

cardinal¹ /ˈkɑːdɪnəl/ *noun* [C] **RELIGION** a priest with a high rank in the Catholic Church *Cardinal Basil Hume*

cardinal² /ˈkɑːdɪnəl/ *adjective* [**always before noun**] *formal* extremely important or serious *One of the **cardinal rules** of business is know what your customer wants.*

ˌcardinal ˈnumber (*also* **cardinal**) *noun* [C] **MATHEMATICS** a number such as 1, 2, 3, etc that shows the quantity of something

carding /ˈkɑːdɪŋ/ *noun* [U] **DT** using wire brushes to separate the threads of some materials such as wool before they can be used

O-→**care¹** /keəʳ/ *verb* **1** [IMPORTANT] [**I, T**] to think that something is important and to feel interested in it or worried about it *He **cares** deeply **about** the environment.* [**+ question word**] *I don't care how long it takes - just get the job done.* **2** [LOVE] [**I**] to love someone *Your parents are only doing this because they **care about** you.* ○ *I knew that Amy still **cared for** me.* **3 I/he, etc couldn't care less** *informal* used to emphasize that someone is not interested in or worried about something or someone [**+ question word**] *I couldn't care less what people think.* **4 Who cares?** *informal* used to emphasize that you do not think something is important *"Manchester United will be in the final if they win this match." "Who cares?"* **5 Would you care for sth/to do sth?** *formal* used to ask someone if they want something or want to do something *Would you care for a drink?* ○ *Would you care to join us for dinner?*

care for sb/sth *phrasal verb* to look after someone or something, especially someone who is young, old, or ill *The children are being cared for by a relative.*

not care for sth/sb *phrasal verb formal* to not like something or someone *I don't care for shellfish.*

WORD PARTNERS FOR ***care***

take care **of** sb • **need/provide/receive** care • **constant/long-term** care • **in/under** sb's care

O-→**care²** /keəʳ/ *noun* **1** [PROTECTION] [**U**] the process of looking after something or someone, especially someone who is young, old, or ill *skin/hair care* ○ *A small baby requires constant care.* **2** [ATTENTION] [**U**] If you do something with care, you give a lot of attention to it so that you do not make a mistake or damage anything. *She planned the trip with great care.* ○ *Fragile - please handle with care.* **3 take care** to give a lot of attention to what you are doing so that you do not have an accident or make a mistake *The roads are very icy so take care when you drive home.* **4 Take care!** *informal* used when saying goodbye to someone *See you soon, Bob - take care!* **5** [WORRY] [C] a feeling of worry *He was sixteen years old and **didn't have a care in the world*** (= had no worries). **6 in care** *UK* Children who are in care are looked after by government organizations because their parents cannot look after them. *She was **put/taken into care** at the age of twelve.* **7 take care of sb/sth** to look after someone or something *My parents are going to take care of the house while we're away.* **8 take care**

of sth/doing sth to be responsible for dealing with something *I did the cooking while Guy took care of the washing up.* ➲See also: **intensive care**

WORD PARTNERS FOR ***career***

begin/embark on/launch a career • **follow/pursue** a career • a career **in** sth • a career **change** • career **opportunities/prospects**

career¹ /kəˈrɪəʳ/ *noun* [C] **1** JOB a job that you do for a long period of your life and that gives you the chance to move to a higher position and earn more money *a successful career in marketing* **2** TIME the time that you spend doing a particular job *She began her acting career in TV commercials.* ➲See Common Learner Error at **work**

career² /kəˈrɪəʳ/ *verb* **career down/into/off, etc** *UK* to move quickly and in an uncontrolled way *The train careered off a bridge and plunged into the river.*

carefree /ˈkeəfriː/ *adjective* without any worries or problems *a carefree childhood*

OTHER WAYS OF SAYING ***careful***

If someone is careful to avoid risks or danger, you can describe them as **cautious**: *She's a very **cautious** driver.*

The expression **play (it) safe** also means 'to be careful to avoid risks': *I think I'll **play it safe** and get the earlier train.*

If someone does something in a very careful way, paying great attention to detail, you can use adjectives such as **meticulous**, **methodical**, and **painstaking**: *This book is the result of years of **meticulous/painstaking** research.*

O⊸**careful** /ˈkeəfᵊl/ *adjective* giving a lot of attention to what you are doing so that you do not have an accident, make a mistake, or damage something *careful planning/consideration* ○ ***Be careful**, Michael - that knife's very sharp.* [**+ to do sth**] *We were careful to avoid the midday sun.* •**carefully** *adverb a carefully prepared speech*

caregiver /ˈkeəˌgɪvəʳ/ *US* (*UK* **carer**) *noun* [C] someone who looks after a person who is young, old, or ill

careless /ˈkeələs/ *adjective* not giving enough attention to what you are doing *It was very **careless of** you to forget your passport.* ○ *He was fined £250 for **careless driving**.* •**carelessly** *adverb* •**carelessness** *noun* [U]

carer /ˈkeərəʳ/ *UK* (*US* **caregiver**) *noun* [C] someone who looks after a person who is young, old, or ill

caress /kəˈres/ *verb* [T] to touch someone in a gentle way that shows that you love them •**caress** *noun* [C]

caretaker /ˈkeəˌteɪkəʳ/ *noun* [C] **1** BUILDING someone whose job is to look after a large building, such as a school **2** PERSON *US* someone who looks after a person who is young, old, or ill

cargo /ˈkɑːgəʊ/ *noun* [C, U] *plural* **cargoes** goods that are carried in a vehicle *a cargo of oil* ○ *a cargo ship/plane*

caricature /ˈkærɪkətʃʊəʳ/ *noun* [C] **ART** a funny drawing or description of someone, especially someone famous, which makes part of their appearance or character more noticeable than it really is •**caricature** *verb* [T]

caring /ˈkeərɪŋ/ *adjective* kind and supporting other people *She's a very caring person.*

carnage /ˈkɑːnɪdʒ/ *noun* [U] *formal* when a lot of people are violently killed or injured

carnation /kɑːˈneɪʃᵊn/ *noun* [C] a small flower with a sweet smell that is usually white, pink, or red

carnival /ˈkɑːnɪvᵊl/ *noun* [C] **1** CELEBRATION a public celebration where people wear special clothes and dance and play music in the roads **2** ENTERTAINMENT *US* a place of outside entertainment where there are machines you can ride on and games that can be played for prizes

carnivore /ˈkɑːnɪvɔːʳ/ *noun* [C] an animal that eats meat ➲Compare **herbivore** •**carnivorous** /kɑːˈnɪvᵊrəs/ *adjective* eating meat

carol /ˈkærᵊl/ (*also* **Christmas carol**) *noun* [C] **MUSIC** a song that people sing at Christmas

carotid artery /kəˌrɒtɪdˈɑːtəri/ *noun* [C] **ANATOMY, BIOLOGY** one of the two large arteries (= large tubes that carry blood) in the neck that carry blood to the head

carousel /ˌkærəˈsel/ *noun* [C] **1** MOVING STRIP a moving strip where passengers collect their bags at an airport **2** ENTERTAINMENT *mainly US* a machine that goes round and round and has toy animals or cars for children to ride on

carp¹ /kɑːp/ *noun* [C, U] *plural* **carp FOOD** a large fish that lives in lakes and rivers, or the meat of this fish

carp² /kɑːp/ *verb* [I] to complain continually about things that are not important *He's always **carping about** how badly organized the office is.*

ˈcar ˌpark *UK* (*US* **parking lot**) *noun* [C] a place where vehicles can be parked

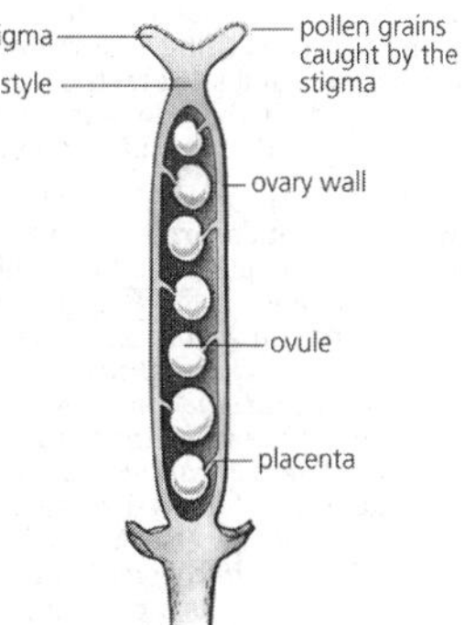

carpel

carpel /ˈkɑːpel/ *noun* [C] **BIOLOGY** the female reproductive (= producing young) part of a flower ➲See picture at **flower**

carpenter /ˈkɑːpᵊntəʳ/ *noun* [C] a person whose job is making and repairing wooden objects

carpentry /ˈkɑːpᵊntri/ *noun* [U] making and repairing wooden objects

carpet /ˈkɑːpɪt/ *noun* **1** [C, U] thick material for covering floors, often made of wool *a new living room carpet* ○ *UK fitted carpets* (= carpets that cover floors from wall to wall) **2 a carpet of sth** a thick layer of something that covers the ground *a carpet of snow* •**carpet** *verb* [T] to put carpet on the floor of a room *The stairs were carpeted.* ➲See also: **the red carpet**

carriage /ˈkærɪdʒ/ *noun* **1** TRAIN [C] *UK* one of the separate parts of a train where the passengers sit *The front carriage of the train is for first-class passengers only.* **2** WITH HORSE [C] a vehicle with wheels that is pulled by a horse **3** GOODS [U] *UK* the cost of transporting goods ➲See also: **baby carriage**

ˌcarriage ˈinwards *noun* [U] **FINANCE** the cost for a business of having goods sent to it

ˌcarriage ˈoutwards *noun* [U] **FINANCE** the cost for a business of sending goods to its customers

carriageway /ˈkærɪdʒweɪ/ *noun* [C] *UK* one of the two sides of a motorway or main road *the southbound carriageway* ➲See also: **dual carriageway**

carrier /ˈkæriəʳ/ *noun* [C] **1** TRANSPORT a person, vehicle, or machine that transports things from one place to another **2 HEALTH** a person who has a disease that they can give to other people without suffering from it themselves **3** COMPANY a company that operates aircraft ➲See also: **aircraft carrier, letter carrier**

ˈcarrier ˌbag *noun* [C] *UK* a large paper or plastic bag with handles that you are given in a shop to carry the things you have bought

carrot /ˈkærət/ *noun* **1 FOOD** [C, U] an orange-coloured vegetable that is long and thin and grows in the ground ➲See colour picture **Fruit and Vegetables** on page Centre 10 **2** [C] *informal* something that is offered to someone in order to encourage them to do something **3 carrot and stick** If you use a carrot-and-stick method, you offer someone rewards if they do something and say you will punish them if they do not.

O-- **carry** /ˈkæri/ *verb* **1** HOLD [T] to hold something or someone with your hands, arms, or on your back and take them from one place to another *He was carrying my bags.* **2** TRANSPORT [T] to move someone or something from one place to another *The plane was carrying 30 passengers.* ○ *Strong currents carried them out to sea.* **3** HAVE WITH YOU [T] to have something with you in a pocket, bag, etc *She still carries his photo in her purse.* **4 HEALTH** [T] to have a disease that you might give to someone else *Mosquitoes carry malaria and other infectious diseases.* **5** PART [T] to have something as a part or a result of something *All cigarette advertising must carry a government health warning.* ○ *Murder still carries the death penalty there.* **6** SOUND [I] If a sound or someone's voice carries, it can be heard a long way away. **7** SUPPORT [T] to support the weight of something *Is the ice thick enough to **carry my weight**?* **8 MATHEMATICS** [T] to put a number into another column when adding numbers **9** DEVELOP [T] to develop something in a particular way *She carried her diet to extremes.* **10 be carried** to be formally accepted by people voting at a meeting *The **motion was carried** by 210 votes to 160.* ➲See also: carry **weight**

be carried away *phrasal verb* to be so excited about something that you do not control what you say or do *There's far too much food - I'm afraid I got a bit carried away.*

carry sth forward/over *phrasal verb* **1** (in accounting) to move an amount from one page or column (= line of text) to the next **2** (in accounting) to move an amount into a period of time in the future

carry sth off *phrasal verb* to succeed in doing or achieving something difficult *It's not an easy part to act but he carried it off brilliantly.*

carry on *phrasal verb* to continue doing something [+ **doing** sth] *The doctors have warned him but he just carries on drinking.* ○ ***Carry on with** your work while I'm gone.*

carry out sth *phrasal verb* to do or complete something, especially something that you have said you would do or that you have been told to do *I was only **carrying out orders**.*

carryall /ˈkæriɔːl/ *US* (*UK* **holdall**) *noun* [C] a large bag for carrying clothes

cart[1] /kɑːt/ *noun* [C] **1** VEHICLE a vehicle with two or four wheels that is pulled by an animal and used for carrying goods **2** SHOP *US* (*UK* **trolley**) a metal structure on wheels that is used for carrying things ➲See also: **go-cart**

cart[2] /kɑːt/ *verb informal* **cart sb/sth around/away/off, etc** to take someone or something somewhere

carte blanche /ˌkɑːtˈblɑːnʃ/ *noun* [U] complete freedom to do what you want [+ **to do sth**] *She was **given carte blanche** to make whatever changes she wanted.*

cartel /kɑːˈtel/ *noun* [C] **ECONOMICS** a group of companies who join together to control prices and limit competition

cartilage /ˈkɑːtɪlɪdʒ/ *noun* [C, U] **ANATOMY, BIOLOGY** a strong elastic substance found where two bones connect in the human body

carton /ˈkɑːtᵊn/ *noun* [C] a container for food and drink that is made from strong, stiff paper or plastic *a carton of milk/fruit juice*

cartoon /kɑːˈtuːn/ *noun* [C] **1** a film made using characters that are drawn and not real *Mickey Mouse and other famous **cartoon characters*** **2 ART** a funny drawing, especially in a newspaper or magazine •**cartoonist** *noun* [C] someone whose job is to draw cartoons

cartridge /ˈkɑːtrɪdʒ/ *noun* [C] **1** CONTAINER a small container that is used in a larger piece of equipment and can be easily replaced *an ink cartridge* **2** GUN a tube containing an explosive substance and a bullet for use in a gun

carve /kɑːv/ *verb* [I, T] **1 ART** to make an object, a shape, or a pattern by cutting wood, stone, etc *The statue was **carved out of** stone.* ○ *They had **carved** their initials **into** the tree.*

2 FOOD to cut a large piece of cooked meat into smaller pieces **3 carve (out) a niche/career/role, etc for yourself** to be successful in a particular job or activity
carve sth up *phrasal verb* to divide something into smaller parts, in a way that people do not approve of *The countryside has been carved up and sold to property developers.*

carving /ˈkɑːvɪŋ/ *noun* **1 ART** [C] an object or a pattern that has been carved **2 ART** [U] the activity of carving an object or pattern *wood carving*

cascade /kæsˈkeɪd/ *verb* [I] to fall quickly and in large amounts *Water cascaded from the rocks above.* •**cascade** *noun* [C] *literary* a large amount of something, especially something falling or hanging *a cascade of golden hair*

O-• **case** /keɪs/ *noun* **1** SITUATION [C] a particular situation or example of something *People were imprisoned, and,* ***in some cases****, killed for their beliefs.* ○ *We usually ask for references, but in your case it will not be necessary.* ○ *The whole film is based on* ***a case of*** *mistaken identity.* **2 LAW** [C] something that is decided in a court of law *a libel/criminal/divorce case* ○ *He lost his case.* **3 LAW** [C] a crime that police are trying to solve *a murder case* ○ *Police in the town have investigated 50* ***cases of*** *burglary in the past month.* **4** ILLNESS [C] an illness, or somebody with an illness *4,000 new* ***cases of*** *the disease are diagnosed every year.* **5 be the case** to be true *Bad diet can cause tiredness, but I don't think that's the case here.* **6** REASONS [C] facts or reasons that prove a particular opinion [**usually singular**] *There is* ***a*** *strong* ***case for/against*** *bringing in the new legislation.* ○ mainly UK *He* ***put the case for*** *more funding very convincingly.* **7** CONTAINER [C] a container for storing or protecting something *a pencil case* ○ *a cigarette case* **8** BAG [C] *UK another word for* suitcase (= a rectangular bag or container with a handle which you use for carrying clothes in when you are travelling) **9 (just) in case** because something might happen, or might have happened *I don't think that it's going to rain, but I'll bring a raincoat just in case.* **10 in any case** used to give another reason for something that you are saying, or that you have done *I don't want to go skiing and, in any case, I can't afford it.* **11 in that case/in which case** because that is the situation/if that is the situation *"Peter's coming tonight." "Oh, in that case, I'll stay in."* **12 be a case of doing sth** to be necessary to do something *We know that we're right. It's just a case of proving it.* **13 in case of sth** *formal* when something happens, or in preparation for when something happens *We keep a bucket of water backstage, in case of fire.* **14 LANGUAGE** [C] any of the various types to which a noun can belong, depending on what it is doing in the sentence, usually shown by a particular ending **15 a case in point** a good example of something *Supermarkets often charge too much for goods. Bananas are a case in point.* **16 be/get on sb's case** *informal* to criticize someone in an annoying way because of something that they have done *She's always on my case about something.* **17 be on the case** *UK informal* to be doing what needs to be done ➲See also: **lower case, upper case**

ˌ**case ˈhistory** *noun* [C] a record of what happens to a particular person *The study used case histories from 500 teenage boys.*

ˈ**case ˌstudy** *noun* [C] a report about a particular person or thing, to show an example of a general principle

WORD PARTNERS FOR *cash*

pay (in) cash • [£50/$100, etc] **in** cash • a cash **machine** • cash **payments**

O-• **cash¹** /kæʃ/ *noun* [U] **1 FINANCE** money in the form of coins or notes (= paper money) *I'm taking £50* ***in cash.*** ○ *Are you* ***paying by cheque or cash?*** **2** *informal* money in any form *She's a bit short of cash at the moment.* ○ *a cash prize* ➲See also: **e-cash, hard cash**

cash² /kæʃ/ *verb* **cash a cheque FINANCE** to exchange a cheque (= piece of paper printed by a bank and used to pay for things) for coins or paper money
cash in on sth *phrasal verb* to get money or another advantage from an event or a situation, often in an unfair way *Her family have been accused of cashing in on her death.*

cashback /ˈkæʃbæk/ *noun* [U] *UK* **FINANCE** money that you can take from your bank account when you pay in a shop with a bank card *£50 cashback*

ˈ**cash ˌbook** *noun* [C] **FINANCE** a record that a business uses to record all money spent and received, either through the bank or as cash

ˈ**cash ˌcard** *noun* [C] *UK* **FINANCE** a plastic card that you use to get money from a machine

ˈ**cash ˌcrop** *noun* [C] **FARMING** a crop that is grown to be sold

ˈ**cash ˌdesk** *noun* [C] *UK* the place in a shop where you pay for the things that you buy

cashew /ˈkæʃuː, kəˈʃuː/ (*also* ˈ**cashew ˌnut**) *noun* [C] **FOOD** a curved nut that you can eat

cashflow /ˈkæʃfləʊ/ *noun* [U] **FINANCE** the movement of money in and out of a business or bank account

cashier /kæʃˈɪəʳ/ *noun* [C] someone whose job is to receive and pay out money in a shop, bank, etc

ˈ**cash maˌchine** (*also UK* **cashpoint**) *noun* [C] **FINANCE** a machine, usually in a wall outside a bank, that you can get money from using a plastic card

cashmere /ˈkæʃmɪəʳ/ (US) /ˈkæʒmɪr/ *noun* [U] a type of very soft, expensive wool

cashpoint /ˈkæʃpɔɪnt/ *UK* (*UK/US* **cash machine**) *noun* [C] **FINANCE** a machine, usually in a wall outside a bank, that you can get money from using a plastic card

ˈ**cash ˌregister** *noun* [C] a machine that is used in shops for keeping money in, and for recording everything that is sold

casino /kəˈsiːnəʊ/ *noun* [C] a place where card games and other games of risk are played for money

cask /kɑːsk/ *noun* [C] a strong, round, wooden container that is used for storing alcoholic drinks

C

casket /ˈkɑːskɪt/ *noun* [C] **1** FOR SMALL OBJECTS *UK* a small, decorated box that is used for keeping valuable objects **2** FOR DEAD BODY *US* (*UK/US* **coffin**) a box in which a dead body is buried

casserole /ˈkæsᵊrəʊl/ *noun* **FOOD 1** [C, U] a mixture of meat or beans with liquid and vegetables cooked for a long time in the oven **2** [C] (*also* ˈ**casserole** ˌ**dish**) a large, heavy container with a lid, that is used for cooking casseroles

cassette /kəˈset/ *noun* [C] a flat, plastic case containing a long piece of magnetic material that is used to record and play sound or pictures *a video cassette*

caˈssette ˌplayer *noun* [C] a machine that plays cassettes of music or sound

caˈssette reˌcorder *noun* [C] a machine that is used for playing cassettes of music or sound and for recording music or sound onto cassettes

cast¹ /kɑːst/ *verb* [T] *past* **cast 1** ACTOR to choose an actor for a particular part in a film or play [**often passive**] *Why am I always* **cast as** *the villain?* **2** THROW *literary* to throw something **3** LIGHT *literary* to send light or shadow (= dark shapes) in a particular direction *The moon cast a white light into the room.* **4 cast doubt/suspicion on sb/sth** to make people feel less sure about or have less trust in someone or something *A leading scientist has cast doubts on government claims that the drug is safe.* **5 cast a/your vote** to vote **6 cast a spell on sb a** ATTRACT to seem to use magic to attract someone *The city had cast a spell on me and I never wanted to leave.* **b** MAGIC to use magic to make something happen to someone **7** METAL to make an object by pouring hot metal into a container of a particular shape ➲See also: cast/run your/an **eye**¹ over sth, cast/shed **light**¹ on sth, cast a **pall**² over sth, cast a **shadow**¹ over sth

cast off *phrasal verb* If a boat casts off, it leaves.

WORD PARTNERS FOR ***cast***

[a play/film, etc] **features** a cast • the cast **includes** sb • the cast **of** sth • a **member of** the cast

cast² /kɑːst/ *noun* **1** [**group**] all the actors in a film or play *The cast are in rehearsal at the moment.* **2 HEALTH** [C] a hard cover used to keep a broken bone in the correct position until it gets better

castaway /ˈkɑːstəweɪ/ *noun* [C] someone who is left on an island, or in a place where there are few or no other people, after their ship has sunk

caste /kɑːst/ *noun* [C, U] **SOCIETY** a system of dividing Hindu society into social groups, or one of these groups *the caste system*

castigate /ˈkæstɪgeɪt/ *verb* [T] *formal* to criticize someone severely

casting /ˈkɑːstɪŋ/ *noun* [U] making an object by pouring liquid metal or plastic into a mould (= hollow shape)

cast-iron /ˈkɑːstˌaɪən/ *adjective* **1** NO DOUBT [**always before noun**] able to be trusted completely, or impossible to doubt *I need a cast-iron guarantee that the work will be finished on time.* **2** METAL made of cast iron

ˌ**cast ˈiron** *noun* [U] a type of very hard iron

O→**castle** /ˈkɑːsl/ *noun* [C] a large, strong building with towers and high walls, that was built in the past to protect the people inside from being attacked

cast-off /ˈkɑːstɒf/ *noun* [C] a piece of clothing or other item that you give to someone because you do not want it any more [**usually plural**] *This dress is another of my sister's cast-offs.*

castrate /kæsˈtreɪt/ ⓤⓢ /ˈkæstreɪt/ *verb* [T] to remove the testicles (= organs that produce sperm) of a man or male animal •**castration** /kæsˈtreɪʃᵊn/ *noun* [U]

casual /ˈkæʒjuəl/ *adjective* **1** NOT PLANNED [**always before noun**] not planned, or without particular meaning or importance *a casual remark/acquaintance/meeting* **2** RELAXED relaxed and not seeming very interested in someone or something *a casual manner/approach* ○ *She's much too casual about her work.* **3** CLOTHING Casual clothing is comfortable and not suitable for formal occasions. **4** WORK [**always before noun**] *mainly UK* Casual work is not regular or fixed. ***casual labour/workers***

casually /ˈkæʒjuəli/ *adverb* **1** RELAXED in a relaxed way, or not seeming to be interested in someone or something *I asked as casually as I could if she was going to be at the party.* **2** DRESS If you dress casually, you do not dress in a formal way.

casualty /ˈkæʒjuəlti/ *noun* **1** INJURED [C] someone who is injured or killed in an accident or war *Both sides in the conflict have promised to try to avoid civilian casualties.* **2** BADLY AFFECTED [C] someone or something that is badly affected by something that happens *The health service has been the biggest* ***casualty of*** *government cuts.* **3 HEALTH** [U] *UK* (*US* **emergency room**) the part of a hospital where people go when they have been injured or have urgent illnesses so that they can be treated immediately

O→**cat** /kæt/ *noun* [C] **1** PET a small animal with fur, four legs and a tail that is kept as a pet **2** WILD ANIMAL a large, wild animal that is related to the cat, such as the lion **3 let the cat out of the bag** to tell people secret information, often without intending to

cataclysmic /ˌkætəˈklɪzmɪk/ *adjective* sudden, shocking, and violent ***cataclysmic changes/events***

catalase /ˈkætæleɪz/ *noun* [C] **BIOLOGY** an enzyme found in living organisms that speeds up the breaking down of hydrogen peroxide into water and oxygen

catalogue¹ (*also US* **catalog**) /ˈkætᵊlɒg/ *noun* [C] **1** a book with a list of all the goods that you can buy from a shop, or of all the books, paintings, etc that you can find in a place *a clothing catalogue* **2 a catalogue of disasters/errors/failures, etc** a series of bad events

catalogue² (*also US* **catalog**) /ˈkætᵊlɒg/ *verb* [T] **cataloguing**, *past* **catalogued** to make a list of things, especially in order to put it in a catalogue

catalysis /kəˈtæləsɪs/ *noun* [U] **CHEMISTRY** the process of making a chemical reaction happen more quickly by using a catalyst •**catalytic** /ˌkætəˈlɪtɪk/ *adjective*

catalyst /ˈkætəlɪst/ *noun* [C] **1** someone or something that causes change *Recent riots and suicides have acted as* ***a catalyst for change*** *in the prison system.* **2 CHEMISTRY** a substance that makes a chemical reaction happen more quickly

cataˌlytic conˈverter *noun* [C] a device on a car that reduces the amount of poisonous gas that it produces

catalyze (*also UK* **-yse**) /ˈkætəlaɪz/ *verb* [T] **CHEMISTRY** to make a chemical reaction happen faster

catapult[1] /ˈkætəpʌlt/ *verb* **1 catapult sb/sth into/out/through, etc** to make someone or something move through the air very quickly and with great force [**often passive**] *When the two cars collided, he was catapulted out of his seat.* **2 catapult sb to stardom/into the lead, etc** to make someone suddenly very famous, successful, etc

catapult[2] /ˈkætəpʌlt/ *UK* (*US* **slingshot**) *noun* [C] a Y-shaped object with a piece of elastic used by children to shoot small stones

cataract /ˈkætərækt/ *noun* [C] **HEALTH** an area of someone's eye with a disease that gradually prevents them from seeing correctly

catarrh /kəˈtɑːr/ *noun* [U] *UK* **HEALTH** the thick substance that is produced in your nose and throat when you have a cold

catastrophe /kəˈtæstrəfi/ *noun* [C, U] an extremely bad event that causes a lot of suffering or destruction *After the drought, the country is facing environmental catastrophe.*

catastrophic /ˌkætəˈstrɒfɪk/ *adjective* causing a lot of suffering or destruction

O-ᵚ**catch**[1] /kætʃ/ *verb past* **caught** **1** GET HOLD [T] to stop someone or something that is moving through the air by getting hold of it *Try to catch the ball.* ○ *She fell backwards but he caught her in his arms.* **2** STOP ESCAPING [T] to find and stop a person or animal who is trying to escape *He ran after his attacker but couldn't catch him.* ○ *Did you catch many fish today?* **3** CRIMINAL [T] If the police catch a criminal, they find them and take them away. *These terrorists must be caught.* **4 HEALTH** [T] to get an illness or disease *I think I've caught a cold.* **5** TRANSPORT [T] to get on a bus, train, etc in order to travel somewhere *You can catch the bus from the top of the hill.* **6** DISCOVER [T] to discover someone who is doing something wrong or something secret [**+ doing sth**] *I caught her listening outside the door.* ○ *informal You* ***won't catch me*** *wearing* (= I never wear) *a tie.* **7** STICK [I, T] to stick somewhere, or to make something stick somewhere *My dress caught on the door handle as I was leaving.* **8** COLLECT [T] to collect something that is falling *I used a bucket to catch the drips.* **9** BE IN TIME [T] to manage to be in time to see or do something *I only caught the end of the programme.* **10** HEAR [T] to hear or understand something correctly *I'm sorry. I didn't catch your name.* **11 catch fire** to start burning **12 be/get caught** to be unable to avoid something unpleasant *I got caught in the rain.* **13 catch the sun** *UK* to burn your skin in the sun *You've caught the sun on your shoulders.* **14 catch sight of sth** to see something suddenly, often only for a short time *He caught sight of himself in the mirror.* **15** HIT [T] *UK* to hit something or someone *The ball flew across the garden, and caught me on the chin.* ➲See also: catch sb's **eye**[1], catch sb off **guard**[1]

catch on *phrasal verb* **1** BECOME POPULAR to become popular *I wonder if the game will* ***catch on with*** *young people?* **2** UNDERSTAND *informal* to understand something, especially after a long time *It took him a while to* ***catch on to*** *what we meant.*

catch sb out *phrasal verb UK* to trick someone so that they make a mistake

catch (sb/sth) up *phrasal verb* **1** REACH to reach someone or something that is in front of you, by going faster than them *We soon* ***caught up with*** *the car in front.* **2** QUALITY to reach the same level or quality as someone or something else *She's doing extra work to* ***catch up with*** *the rest of the class.*

catch up *phrasal verb* **EDUCATION** to learn or discuss the most recent news *Let's meet for a chat - I need to* ***catch up on*** *all the gossip.*

catch up on/with sth *phrasal verb* to do something that you did not have time to do earlier *After the exams, I need to catch up on some sleep.*

catch up with sb *phrasal verb* If something bad that you have done or that has been happening to you catches up with you, it begins to cause problems for you. *I can feel the stress of the last few weeks beginning to catch up with me.*

be/get caught up in sth *phrasal verb* to become involved in a situation, often without wanting to *How did the paper get caught up in a legal dispute?*

catch[2] /kætʃ/ *noun* [C] **1** WITH HANDS when someone catches something that is moving through the air *a brilliant catch* **2** FISH the amount of fish that someone has caught **3** PROBLEM a hidden problem or difficulty with something *He's offering us a free flight? There must be a catch.* **4** LOCK a part on something that fastens it and keeps it closed *a* ***safety catch***

Catch-22 /ˌkætʃtwentiˈtuː/ *noun* [C] an impossible situation: you cannot do one thing until you have done another thing, but you cannot do the other thing until you have done the first thing *a* ***Catch-22 situation***

catching /ˈkætʃɪŋ/ *adjective* [**never before noun**] **HEALTH** If an illness or a mood is catching, other people can get it from you.

catchment area /ˈkætʃməntˌeəriə/ *noun* [C] *UK* **EDUCATION** the area around a school or a hospital, where most of the students or patients come from

catchphrase /ˈkætʃfreɪz/ *noun* [C] **LANGUAGE** a phrase which is often repeated by a particular organization or person, and becomes connected with them

catchy /ˈkætʃi/ *adjective* A catchy song, tune, or phrase is easy to remember.

categorical /ˌkætəˈgɒrɪkəl/ *adjective* If someone is categorical about what they say, they say it with force and are completely certain about it. *a **categorical assurance/denial*** •**categorically** *adverb They have **denied categorically** that they were involved in the conspiracy.*

categorize (*also UK* **-ise**) /ˈkætəgᵊraɪz/ *verb* [T] to divide people or things into groups of similar types *The books are categorized according to subject.*

category /ˈkætəgᵊri/ *noun* [C] a group of people or things of a similar type *Our customers **fall into** two main **categories**: retired people and housewives.*

cater /ˈkeɪtəʳ/ *verb* [I, T] to provide and often serve food and drinks for a particular event *How many are we **catering for** at the wedding reception?*
cater for sb/sth *phrasal verb mainly UK* to provide what is wanted or needed by a particular group of people *The club caters for children between the ages of 4 and 12.*
cater to sb/sth *phrasal verb* to give people exactly what they want, usually something that people think is wrong *This legislation simply caters to unacceptable racist opinions.*

caterer /ˈkeɪtᵊrəʳ/ *noun* [C] a person or company that provides food and drinks for particular events, or for an organization

catering /ˈkeɪtərɪŋ/ *noun* [U] providing food and drinks for people *Who **did the catering** for the party?*

caterpillar /ˈkætəpɪləʳ/ *noun* [C] a small, long animal with many legs that eats leaves

cathartic /kəˈθɑːtɪk/ *adjective* A cathartic experience or event helps you to express and get rid of strong emotions.

cathedral /kəˈθiːdrᵊl/ *noun* [C] **RELIGION** the largest and most important church in a particular area

cathode /ˈkæθəʊd/ *noun* [C] **PHYSICS** one of the electrodes (= object that electricity moves through) in a piece of electrical equipment; the positive electrode in a battery and the negative electrode in an electrolytic cell ➲Compare **anode**

ˌcathode ˈray tube *noun* [C] **PHYSICS** a tube-shaped part in a television or computer screen, inside which a flow of electrons (= small piece of atom) is produced to create the images or text

Catholic /ˈkæθᵊlɪk/ (*also* **Roman Catholic**) *adjective* **RELIGION** belonging or relating to the part of the Christian religion that has the Pope (= a very important priest) as its leader *a Catholic priest/school* •**Catholic** *noun* [C] *I think he's a Catholic.*

the ˌCatholic ˈChurch *noun* **RELIGION** the Catholic religion and all the people who believe in it

Catholicism /kəˈθɒlɪsɪzᵊm/ (*also* **ˌRoman Caˈtholicism**) *noun* [U] **RELIGION** the beliefs of the Catholic religion

cation /ˈkætaɪən/ *noun* [C] **PHYSICS** an ion (= type of atom) with a positive electric charge ➲Compare **anion**

catsup /ˈkætsəp/ *noun* [U] **FOOD** *another US spelling of* ketchup (= a thick, red sauce that is eaten cold with food)

cattle /ˈkætl/ *noun* [**plural**] male and female cows, kept on a farm for their milk and meat

catty /ˈkæti/ *adjective informal* intending to hurt someone by saying unkind things *catty remarks*

catwalk /ˈkætwɔːk/ *noun* [C] the narrow, raised path that people walk along in a fashion show

Caucasian /kɔːˈkeɪʒən/ *adjective* **SOCIETY** belonging to a race of people with white or pale skin •**Caucasian** *noun* [C] a Caucasian person

caught /kɔːt/ *past of* catch

cauldron /ˈkɔːldrᵊn/ *noun* [C] *literary* a large, round metal pot that is used for cooking over a fire

cauliflower /ˈkɒlɪˌflaʊəʳ/ *noun* [C, U] **FOOD** a large, round, white vegetable with thick, green leaves around the outside ➲See colour picture **Fruit and Vegetables** on page Centre 10

WORD PARTNERS FOR ***cause***

a **common/leading/probable/root** cause • **discover/establish/identify** the cause **of** sth • the **main** cause

cause¹ /kɔːz/ *noun* **1** MAKES HAPPEN [C] someone or something that makes something happen *The police are still trying to **establish the cause of** the fire.* ○ *She died of **natural causes**.* **2** REASON [U] a reason to feel something or to behave in a particular way *He's never given me any **cause for** concern.* **3** PRINCIPLE [C] a principle or aim that a group of people support or fight for *The money will all go to a **good cause**.*

cause² /kɔːz/ *verb* [T] to make something happen *The hurricane caused widespread damage.* ○ *Most heart attacks are **caused by** blood clots.* [+ **two objects**] *I hope the children haven't caused you too much trouble.* [+ **to do sth**] *What caused the washing machine to blow up?*

causeway /ˈkɔːzweɪ/ *noun* [C] a raised path or road over a wet area

caustic /ˈkɔːstɪk/ *adjective* **1** A caustic remark is extremely unkind and intended to upset or criticize someone. **2 CHEMISTRY** Caustic chemicals can burn things.

ˌcaustic ˈsoda *noun* [U] **CHEMISTRY** the chemical sodium hydroxide used in soap and paper production and in powerful cleaning substances

WORD PARTNERS FOR ***caution***

advise/exercise/urge caution • **extreme/great** caution • do sth **with** caution • caution **in** doing sth

caution¹ /ˈkɔːʃᵊn/ *noun* **1** [U] great care and attention not to take risks or get into danger *Travellers have been advised to **exercise** great **caution** when passing through the region.* ○ *I would **treat** anything he says **with** extreme **caution** (= not be too quick to believe it).* **2 LAW** [C] *UK* when a police officer or other person in authority warns you that you will be punished if you do something bad again **3 throw caution to the wind** to take a risk ➲See also: err on the **side¹** of caution

caution² /ˈkɔːʃᵊn/ *verb* **1** WARN [I, T] *formal* to warn someone of something [**often passive**] *They were* ***cautioned against*** *buying shares in the company.* **2** POLICE [T] *UK* If police caution people, they are given a spoken warning that they will be punished next time.

cautionary /ˈkɔːʃᵊnᵊri/ *adjective* intended to warn or advise someone *a* ***cautionary tale***

cautious /ˈkɔːʃəs/ *adjective* taking care to avoid risks or danger *She is cautious about lending money to anyone.* •**cautiously** *adverb*

cavalier /ˌkævᵊlˈɪəʳ/ *adjective formal* without caring about other people or about a dangerous or serious situation *a* ***cavalier attitude***

the cavalry /ˈkævᵊlri/ *noun* [**U group**] soldiers who fight on horses

cave¹ /keɪv/ *noun* [C] **GEOLOGY** a large hole in the side of a cliff (= straight, high rock next to the sea), mountain, or under the ground

cave² /keɪv/ *verb*

cave in *phrasal verb* **1** FALL If a ceiling, roof, or other structure caves in, it breaks and falls into the space below. **2** AGREE to agree to something that you were against before, after someone has persuaded you or made you afraid *The company has finally* ***caved in to*** *the demands of the unions.*

caveat /ˈkæviæt/ *noun* [C] *formal* something you say which warns that there is a limit on a general announcement made earlier

cavern /ˈkævᵊn/ *noun* [C] **GEOLOGY** a large cave

caviar (*also* **caviare**) /ˈkæviɑːʳ/ *noun* [U] **FOOD** the eggs of a large fish, eaten as a food and usually very expensive

cavity /ˈkævəti/ *noun* [C] **1** HOLE a hole or a space inside something solid or between two surfaces **2** TOOTH a hole in a tooth

cavort /kəˈvɔːt/ *verb* [I] to jump, dance, or move about in an excited way

CBI /ˌsiːbiːˈaɪ/ *noun* **ECONOMICS** *abbreviation for* Confederation of British Industry; a large organisation that many British companies belong to

cc /ˌsiːˈsiː/ **1** *abbreviation for* carbon copy: used on a letter or email to show that you are sending a copy to other people **2** **MEASURES** *abbreviation for* cubic centimetre: a unit for measuring the volume of something *a 750cc motorcycle*

CCTV /ˌsiːsiːtiːˈviː/ *noun* [U] *abbreviation for* closed circuit television: a system of television cameras filming in shops and public places so that people can watch and protect those places *CCTV cameras*

O-★**CD** /ˌsiːˈdiː/ *noun* [C] *abbreviation for* compact disc: a small disc on which music or information is recorded ➲See colour picture **The Office** on page Centre 5

ˌCˈD ˌburner *noun* [C] **COMPUTING** a machine that can record information onto a CD

ˌCˈD ˌplayer *noun* [C] a machine that is used for playing music CDs

CD-R /ˌsiːdiːˈɑːʳ/ *noun* [C] **COMPUTING** *abbreviation for* compact disc recordable: an empty compact disc for recording information only once using special computer equipment

O-★**CD-ROM** /ˌsiːdiːˈrɒm/ *noun* [C] **COMPUTING** *abbreviation for* compact disc read-only memory: a CD that holds large amounts of information that can be read by a computer

CD-RW /ˌsiːdiːɑːˈdʌbljuː/ *noun* [C] **COMPUTING** *abbreviation for* compact disc rewritable: an empty compact disc for recording and changing information using special computer equipment

ˌCˈD ˌwriter *noun* [C] **COMPUTING** a CD burner

cease /siːs/ *verb* [I, T] *formal* to stop [+ **doing sth**] *He ordered his men to cease firing.* [+ **to do sth**] *Her behaviour never ceases to amaze me.*

ceasefire /ˈsiːsfaɪəʳ/ *noun* [C] an agreement between two armies or groups to stop fighting

ceaseless /ˈsiːsləs/ *adjective formal* continuous *the ceaseless movement of the sea* •**ceaselessly** *adverb*

cedar /ˈsiːdəʳ/ *noun* [C, U] a tall, evergreen (= with leaves that do not fall off in winter) tree, or the red wood of this tree

cede /siːd/ *verb* [T] *formal* to give something such as land or power to another country or person, especially because you are forced to

ceiling /ˈsiːlɪŋ/ *noun* [C] **1** ROOM the surface of a room which you can see when you look above you **2** AMOUNT a limit on the amount that can be paid for something *They have set* ***a ceiling on*** *pay rises.*

celeb /sɪˈleb/ *noun* [C] *informal* a celebrity (= famous person)

O-★**celebrate** /ˈseləbreɪt/ *verb* [I, T] to do something enjoyable because it is a special day, or because something good has happened *Do you celebrate Christmas in your country?*

celebrated /ˈseləbreɪtɪd/ *adjective* famous for a special ability or quality *She is* ***celebrated for*** *her wit.*

WORD PARTNERS FOR ***celebration***

anniversary/birthday/New Year celebrations • be a **cause for** celebration • sth **calls for** a celebration • a celebration **to mark/of** sth • **in** celebration **of** sth

celebration /ˌseləˈbreɪʃᵊn/ *noun* [C, U] when you celebrate a special day or event *Let's buy some champagne* ***in celebration of*** *her safe arrival.* ○ *You've passed? This* ***calls for a celebration.***

celebratory /ˌseləˈbreɪtᵊri/ (US) /ˈseləbrətɔːri/ *adjective* done to celebrate something or wanting to celebrate something *a celebratory dinner* ○ *in a* ***celebratory mood***

celebrity /səˈlebrəti/ *noun* [C] a famous person

celery /ˈselᵊri/ *noun* [U] **FOOD** a vegetable with long, pale green stems, often eaten in salads ➲See colour picture **Fruit and Vegetables** on page Centre 10

celestial /səˈlestiəl/ *adjective literary* relating to heaven or the sky

celibate /ˈseləbət/ *adjective* Someone who is celibate does not have sex. •**celibacy** /ˈseləbəsi/ *noun* [U] when you do not have sex

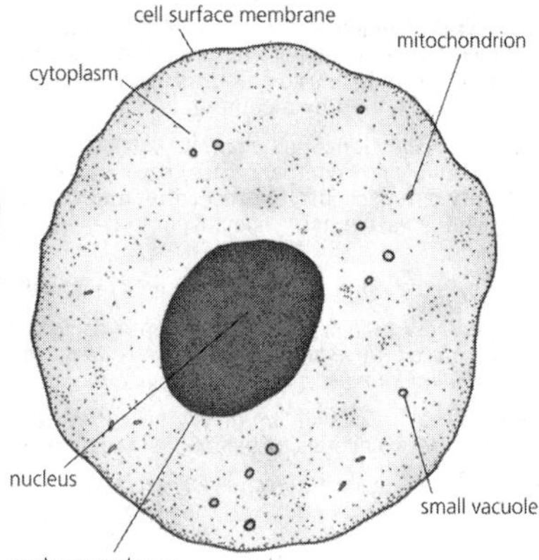

animal cell

cell /sel/ *noun* [C] **1 BIOLOGY** the smallest living part of an animal or a plant *brain/cancer cells* **2** a small room in a prison or police station where a prisoner is kept

cellar /'seləʳ/ *noun* [C] a room under the floor of a building ⊃See also: **salt cellar**

cellist /'tʃelɪst/ *noun* [C] **MUSIC** someone who plays the cello

cello /'tʃeləʊ/ *noun* [C] **MUSIC** a large, wooden musical instrument with four strings that you hold between your knees to play

Cellophane /'seləfeɪn/ *noun* [U] **DT** *trademark* thin, transparent material that is used for wrapping goods, especially flowers and food

cell phone /'selfəʊn/ (also **cellular phone**) *noun* [C] *US* a mobile phone

'cell ˌsap *noun* [U] **BIOLOGY** the liquid that is found in the vacuole (= place inside a cell) of plant cells

cellular /'seljələʳ/ *adjective* **1 BIOLOGY** relating to animal or plant cells *cellular damage* **2** [**always before noun**] relating to cellular phones *cellular companies/communications*

'cellular ˌphone (*also* **cell phone** /'selfəʊn/) *noun* [C] a mobile phone

cellulite /'seljəlaɪt/ *noun* [U] **BIOLOGY** fat that looks like small lumps below the skin, especially on the upper legs *I can't seem to get rid of my cellulite.*

celluloid /'seljʊlɔɪd/ *noun* [U] **1** *old-fashioned* films or the cinema generally **2** a type of plastic used to make many things, especially, in the past, photographic film

cellulose /'seljələʊs/ *noun* [U] **BIOLOGY** a substance in plants that is used to make some paper and plastics

Celsius /'selsiəs/ (*written abbreviation* **C**) *noun* [U] **MEASURES** a measurement of temperature in which water freezes at 0° and boils at 100°

Celtic /'keltɪk/ *adjective* relating to the people of Ireland, Scotland, and Wales *Celtic art/music*

cement¹ /sɪ'ment/ *noun* [U] **1** a grey powder used in building which is mixed with water and sand or stones to make a hard substance **2 ANATOMY, BIOLOGY** the substance that covers the roots of teeth ⊃See picture at **tooth**

cement² /sɪ'ment/ *verb* [T] **1** MAKE STRONGER to make something such as a relationship, a belief, or a position stronger *It was the holiday that really cemented our friendship.* **2** COVER (*also* **cement over**) to cover something with cement

cemetery /'semətri/ *noun* [C] a place where dead people are buried

censor /'sensəʳ/ *verb* [T] to examine books, documents, or films and remove parts of them that are offensive or not allowed by rules [**often passive**] *The book was heavily censored before publication.* •**censor** *noun* [C]

censorship /'sensəʃɪp/ *noun* [U] when a book, film, newspaper, or other information is censored *political/state censorship*

censure /'sensjəʳ/ *verb* [T] *formal* to criticize someone formally for something that they have done •**censure** *noun* [U] *formal*

census /'sensəs/ *noun* [C] **SOCIETY** when people in a country are officially counted and information is taken about them

O-- **cent** /sent/ *noun* [C] **FINANCE** a coin or unit of money with a value of 1/100 of a dollar (= US unit of money); ¢ *The newspaper costs sixty-five cents.*

centenary /sen'tiːnəri/ Ⓤⓢ /'sentəneri/ (*also US* **centennial** /sen'teniəl/) *noun* [C] the day or year that is 100 years after an important event *This year, there will be many concerts to mark **the centenary of** the composer's death.*

O-- **center** /'sentəʳ/ *noun, verb US spelling of* centre

centerpiece /'sentəpiːs/ *noun* [C] *US spelling of* centrepiece

centi-, cent- /senti-, sent-/ *prefix* hundred *a centimetre ○ a century*

centigrade /'sentɪgreɪd/ (*written abbreviation* **C**) *noun* [U] **MEASURES** a measurement of temperature in which water freezes at 0° and boils at 100°

centigram /'sentɪgræm/ *noun* [C] **MEASURES** a unit of weight equal to 0.01 of a gram

centilitre /'sentɪˌliːtəʳ/ *UK* (*US* **centiliter**) (*written abbreviation* **cl**) *noun* [C] **MEASURES** a unit for measuring liquid, equal to 0.01 litres

O-- **centimetre** *UK* (*US* **centimeter**) (*written abbreviation* **cm**) /'sentɪˌmiːtəʳ/ *noun* [C] **MEASURES** a unit for measuring length, equal to 0.01 metres

O-- **central** /'sentrəl/ *adjective* **1** POSITION in or near the centre of a place or object *central Africa/America ○ The roof is supported by a central column.* **2** ORGANIZATION [**always before noun**] controlled or organized in one main place *central authorities/government ○ the US central bank* **3** IMPORTANT main or most important *a central character/figure ○ Her role is **central to** the film.* **4** CITY in the main part of a town or city •**centrally** *adverb*

ˌcentral 'heating *noun* [U] a system of heating a building by warming air or water in one place and carrying it to different rooms in pipes

centralize (*also UK* **-ise**) /ˈsentrəlaɪz/ *verb* [T] **POLITICS** If a country or organization is centralized, it is controlled from one place. [often passive] *centralized control/government* •**centralization** /ˌsentrəlaɪˈzeɪʃən/ *noun* [U]

ˌcentral ˈnervous system *noun* **ANATOMY, BIOLOGY** the main system of nerve control in a living thing, consisting of the brain and the spinal cord

O-- **centre¹** *UK* (*US* **center**) /ˈsentəʳ/ *noun* **1** MIDDLE [C] the middle point or part of something *She stood **in the centre** of the room.* ○ *Cars are not allowed in the **town centre**.* **2** PLACE [C] a place or a building used for a particular activity *a **health/advice centre*** ○ *a **centre for** the homeless* **3** BUSINESS [C] a place where a lot of a particular activity or business takes place *an industrial centre* **4** **POLITICS** [no plural] (*also* **the centre**) a political position with opinions that are not extreme *His political views are left of centre.* **5** **be the centre of attention** to receive more attention than anyone or anything else ⊃See also: **community centre, garden centre, shopping centre**

centre² *UK* (*US* **center**) /ˈsentəʳ/ *verb* [T] to put something in the middle of an area

centre around/on sb/sth *phrasal verb* to have someone or something as the main part of a discussion or activity *The dispute centres on racial issues.*

ˌcentre of ˈgravity *noun* [C] *plural* **centres of gravity** **PHYSICS** the point in an object where its weight is balanced

centrepiece *UK* (*US* **centerpiece**) /ˈsentəpiːs/ *noun* [C] **1** IMPORTANT PART the most important or attractive part of something *The employment programme is **the centrepiece of** the government's economic strategy.* **2** DECORATION a decoration that is put in the middle of a dinner table

centrifugal /ˌsentrɪˈfjuːgəl/ *adjective* **PHYSICS** (of a turning object) moving away from the point around which it is turning *centrifugal force*

centrifuge /ˈsentrɪfjuːdʒ/ *noun* [C] **PHYSICS** a machine which turns a container round very quickly, causing the solids and liquids inside it to separate •**centrifugation** /ˌsentrɪfjuːˈgeɪʃən/ *noun* [U] when something is put in a centrifuge

centripetal /ˌsentrɪˈpiːtəl/ *adjective* **PHYSICS** (of a turning object) moving towards the point around which it is turning *centripetal force*

WORD PARTNERS FOR ***century***

in the [17th/21st, etc] century • the **early/mid/late** [15th/19th, etc] century • the **turn of the** century (= the time around the end of one century and the beginning of the next)

O-- **century** /ˈsenʃəri/ *noun* [C] a period of 100 years, especially used in giving dates *the twentieth century*

CEO /ˌsiːiːˈəʊ/ *noun* [C] *abbreviation for* chief executive officer: the person with the most important job in a company

cephalopod /ˈsefələʊpɒd/ *noun* [C] **BIOLOGY** an animal such as an octopus or squid, that has tentacles (= long parts like arms) joining directly on to a large head

ceramics /səˈræmɪks/ *noun* [plural] **ART** objects that are made by shaping and heating clay •**ceramic** *adjective* made by shaping and heating clay *a ceramic pot*

cereal /ˈsɪəriəl/ *noun* [C, U] **1** **FARMING, FOOD** a plant that is grown to produce grain for food *cereal crops* **2** **FOOD** a food that is made from grain and eaten with milk, especially in the morning ***breakfast cereals*** ⊃See colour picture **Food** on page Centre 11

cerebellum /ˌserəˈbeləm/ *noun* [C] *plural* **cerebellums** or **cerebella** **ANATOMY** a large part at the back of the brain that controls your muscles, movement and balance ⊃See picture at **brain**

cerebral /ˈserəbrəl/ *adjective formal* **1** Cerebral films, books, etc need a lot of thought to understand them, and cerebral people think a lot. **2** **ANATOMY, BIOLOGY** [always before noun] relating to the brain *cerebral arteries*

ˌcerebral ˈcortex *noun* [usually singular] **ANATOMY** the outer layer of the cerebrum (= front part of brain) responsible for language, thinking, creative skills, etc.

ˌcerebral ˈhemisphere *noun* [usually singular] **ANATOMY** one of the two halves of the cerebrum (= front part of brain), each of which controls the opposite side of the body ⊃See picture at **brain**

cerebral palsy /ˌserəbrəlˈpɔːlzi/ *noun* [U] **HEALTH** a medical condition caused by damage to the brain at birth

cerebrum /sɪˈriːbrəm/ *noun* [C] *plural* **cerebrums** or **cerebra** **ANATOMY** the front part of the brain, which is involved with thought, decision, emotion and character

ceremonial /ˌserɪˈməʊniəl/ *adjective* relating to a ceremony •**ceremonially** *adverb*

WORD PARTNERS FOR ***ceremony***

attend/hold a ceremony • **at** a ceremony • an **award/marriage/wedding** ceremony

ceremony /ˈserɪməni/ *noun* **1** EVENT [C] a formal event that is performed on important social or religious occasions *a **wedding/marriage ceremony*** ○ *an **award ceremony*** **2** BEHAVIOUR [U] formal behaviour, words, and actions that are part of a ceremony

O-- **certain** /ˈsɜːtən/ *adjective* **1** NO DOUBT [never before noun] completely sure of something, or knowing without doubt that something is true [+ (that)] *I feel absolutely certain that you're doing the right thing.* [+ question word] *Nobody was certain how the accident had happened.* ○ *He was quite **certain about/of** the thief's identity.* ⊃Opposite **uncertain** **2** **know/say for certain** to know something without doubt *We don't know for certain whether she's coming.* **3** SURE TO HAPPEN sure to happen, to do something, or to be true [+ (that)] *It now looks certain that she will resign.* [+ to do sth] *She is certain to do well in the exams.* ○ *How can we **make certain that*** (= do something to be sure that) *she sees the note?* **4** PARTICULAR [always before noun] used to refer to a particular person or thing without naming or describing them exactly *The museum is only open at certain times of the day.* **5 a certain** used before a noun to mean existing, but difficult to describe the exact quality or amount *He's got a certain charm.* **6 certain of** *formal* used to refer to some of a group of people or things *Certain of you already know the news.*

O-- **certainly** /'sɜːtənli/ *adverb* **1** WITHOUT DOUBT used to emphasize something and show that there is no doubt about it *Their team certainly deserved to win.* ○ *"Are your parents paying for dinner?" "I certainly hope so."* ○ *"Do you regret what you said?" "**Certainly not!**"* **2** OF COURSE used to agree to a request *"Could you pass the salt, please?" "Certainly."*

certainty /'sɜːtənti/ *noun* **1** FEELING [U] when you are completely sure about something *I can't say **with** any **certainty** what time she left.* **2** SURE THING [C] something that is very likely to happen or cannot be doubted *There are no absolute certainties in life.*

certificate /sə'tɪfɪkət/ *noun* [C] an official document that gives details to show that something is true *a **death/marriage certificate*** ○ *an **exam certificate*** ⊃See also: **birth certificate**

certify /'sɜːtɪfaɪ/ *verb* [T] **1** TRUTH *formal* to say in a formal or official way that something is true or correct [+ (that)] *I certify that the information I have given is true.* ○ *She was **certified dead** on arrival at the hospital.* **2 EDUCATION** to give someone a certificate to say that they have completed a course of study *a certified accountant* **3** HEALTH to say officially that someone has a mental illness

certitude /'sɜːtɪtjuːd/ *noun* [U] *formal* when you feel certain about something

cervix /'sɜːvɪks/ *noun* [C] **ANATOMY** the narrow entrance to a woman's womb •**cervical** /sə'vaɪkəl, 'sɜːvɪkəl/ *adjective cervical cancer*

cesarean /sɪ'zeəriən/ *noun* [C] **HEALTH** *US spelling of* caesarean

cessation /ses'eɪʃən/ *noun* [C, U] *formal* when something, especially violence, stops *the cessation of hostilities*

cetacean /sɪ'teɪʃən/ *noun* [C] **BIOLOGY** any of various types of mammal, such as the whale, that live in the sea like fish

cf used in writing when you want the reader to make a comparison between the subject being discussed and something else

CFC /ˌsiːef'siː/ *noun* [C] **CHEMISTRY, ENVIRONMENT** *abbreviation for* chlorofluorocarbon: a type of gas used in some fridges (= containers for keeping food cold) and aerosols (= containers for making liquids come out in small drops), which damages the layer of gases around the Earth

CGI /ˌsiːdʒiː'aɪ/ *noun* [U] **COMPUTING** *abbreviation for* computer generated imagery: the process of using computers to create pictures or characters in film and television

chafe /tʃeɪf/ *verb* **1** FEEL ANGRY [I] to feel angry because of rules and limits *He **chafed against/at** the narrow academic approach of his school.* **2** RUB [I, T] to make part of the body painful by rubbing, or to become painful because of being rubbed

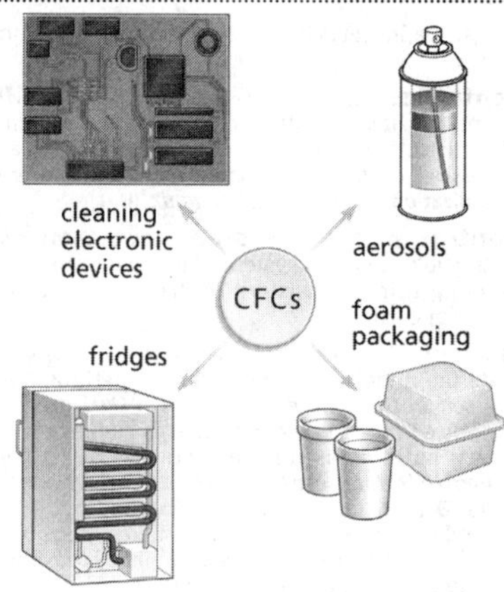

CFCs

chagrin /'ʃægrɪn/ (US) /ʃə'grɪn/ *noun* [U] anger or disappointment caused by something that does not happen the way you wanted it ***To** his parents' **chagrin**, he had no intention of becoming a lawyer.*

chain[1] /tʃeɪn/ *noun* **1** METAL RINGS [C, U] a line of metal rings connected together *a bicycle chain* ○ *She wore a gold chain around her neck.* ○ *The hostages were kept **in chains**.* **2** BUSINESS [C] a number of similar shops, restaurants, etc owned by the same company *a chain of hotels/supermarkets* **3** EVENTS [C] a series of things that happen one after the other *His arrival set off a surprising **chain of events**.*

chain[2] /tʃeɪn/ (*also* **chain up**) *verb* [T] to fasten someone or something to someone or something else using a chain *I **chained** my bike **to** a lamppost.* ○ *You shouldn't keep a dog **chained up** like that.*

the ˌchain of comˈmand *noun* the way a business or organization organizes what decisions can be taken and how much control people have at each level

ˌchain of proˈduction *noun* [C] all the businesses that are involved in making goods or providing services, from producing the materials to selling the product

ˌchain reˈaction *noun* [C] a series of events where each one causes the next one to happen

chain-smoke /'tʃeɪnsməʊk/ *verb* [I, T] to smoke cigarettes one after another •**chain smoker** *noun* [C]

ˈchain ˌstore *noun* [C] one of a group of similar shops owned by the same company

O-- **chair**[1] /tʃeər/ *noun* [C] **1** FURNITURE a seat for one person, with a back, usually four legs, and sometimes two arms ⊃See colour picture **The Office** on page Centre 5 **2** MEETING someone who controls a meeting or organization [**usually singular**] *All questions should be addressed to the chair.* **3 EDUCATION** a very important position in a university department, or the person who has this position ⊃See also: **the electric chair**

chair² /tʃeəʳ/ *verb* [T] to control a meeting or organization *I've been asked to chair the committee.*

chairman, chairwoman /ˈtʃeəmən, ˈtʃeə,wʊmən/ *noun* [C] *plural* **chairmen, chairwomen** a man/woman who controls a meeting, company, or other organization

chairperson /ˈtʃeə,pɜːsᵊn/ *noun* [C] someone who controls a meeting, company, or other organization

chalet /ˈʃæleɪ/ ⓤⓢ /ʃælˈeɪ/ *noun* [C] a small wooden house, often in a mountain area, or for people who are on holiday

chalk¹ /tʃɔːk/ *noun* **1** **GEOLOGY** [U] a type of soft, white rock **2** [C, U] a small stick of chalk that is used for writing and drawing *a piece of chalk* ➲See colour picture **The Classroom** on page Centre 6 **3 be like chalk and cheese** *UK* If two people are like chalk and cheese, they are completely different from each other.

chalk² /tʃɔːk/ *verb* [T] *UK* to write something with a piece of chalk
chalk sth up *phrasal verb* to achieve something *She's chalked up five goals this season.*

chalkboard /ˈtʃɔːkbɔːd/ *US* (*UK/US* **blackboard**) *noun* [C] **EDUCATION** a large board with a dark surface that teachers write on with chalk

chalky /ˈtʃɔːki/ *adjective* made of chalk, or similar to chalk

WORD PARTNERS FOR ***challenge***

face/pose/present/relish a challenge • a **big/formidable/serious/tough** challenge

O-ᵚ**challenge¹** /ˈtʃælɪndʒ/ *noun* **1** [DIFFICULT] [C, U] something that is difficult and that tests someone's ability or determination *Finding a decision that pleases everyone is the* ***challenge*** *which now* ***faces*** *the committee.* **2** [INVITATION] [C] an invitation to compete in a game or a fight *I'm sure Paul will race you. He never refuses a challenge.* **3** [DISAGREEMENT] [C] an expression of disagreement with ideas, rules, or someone's authority *a* ***challenge to*** *the authority of the President*

challenge² /ˈtʃælɪndʒ/ *verb* [T] **1** [DISAGREE] to express disagreement with ideas, rules, or someone's authority *The election results are being challenged.* **2** [INVITE] to invite someone to compete in a game or fight *He* ***challenged*** *Smith* ***to*** *a fight.*

challenger /ˈtʃæləndʒəʳ/ *noun* [C] someone who competes in a game, competition, or election, often to win a position that someone else has *There are five* ***challengers for*** *the title.*

challenging /ˈtʃæləndʒɪŋ/ *adjective* difficult to do in a way that tests your ability or determination *This has been a challenging time for us all.*

chamber /ˈtʃeɪmbəʳ/ *noun* [C] **1** [ROOM] a room used for an official or special purpose *a debating chamber* ○ *a burial chamber* **2** **POLITICS** one of the groups that a parliament is divided into *the* ***upper/lower chamber*** **3** [MACHINE/BODY] a closed space in a machine or in your body *the left chamber of the heart* ➲See also: **gas chamber**

chambermaid /ˈtʃeɪmbəmeɪd/ *noun* [C] a woman whose job is to clean and tidy hotel bedrooms

ˈ**chamber** ˌ**music** *noun* [U] **MUSIC** music that is written for a small group of musicians

ˌ**chamber of** ˈ**commerce** *noun* [C] *plural* **chambers of commerce** an organization of business people who work together to improve business in their local area

champ /tʃæmp/ *noun* [C] *informal short for* champion

champagne /ʃæmˈpeɪn/ *noun* [U] **FOOD** French white wine with lots of bubbles in it which people often drink to celebrate something

O-ᵚ**champion¹** /ˈtʃæmpiən/ *noun* [C] **1** [WINNER] a person, animal, or team that wins a competition *a boxing champion* ○ *the* ***world champions*** **2** [SUPPORT] someone who supports, defends, or fights for a person, belief, or principle ***a champion of*** *human rights* ➲See also: **reigning champion**

champion² /ˈtʃæmpiən/ *verb* [T] to support, defend, or fight for a person, belief, or principle *She* ***championed the cause*** *of free speech.*

championship /ˈtʃæmpiənʃɪp/ *noun* [C] **1** **SPORT** a competition to find the best team or player in a particular game or sport *The* ***world championship*** *will be held in this country next year.* **2** **SPORT** the position of being a champion *She is current holder of our tennis championship.*

WORD PARTNERS FOR ***chance***

a chance **of sth** • a **fifty-fifty** chance • a **fair/good/slim** chance

O-ᵚ**chance¹** /tʃɑːns/ *noun* **1** [POSSIBILITY] [C, U] the possibility that something will happen [+ **(that)**] *There's a chance that she'll still be there.* ○ *She has little* ***chance of*** *passing the exam.* ○ *Is there* ***any chance of*** *a drink?* **2** [OPPORTUNITY] [C] the opportunity to do something [+ **to do sth**] *I didn't* ***get a chance*** *to speak to you at the party.* ○ *I hope you've* ***had the chance*** *to look around the exhibition.* ○ ***Give*** *me* ***a chance*** *to prove that I can do the work.* ○ *Going on a world cruise is* ***the chance of a lifetime*** (= an opportunity which only comes once in your life). **3** [LUCK] [U] when something happens because of luck, or without being planned *I saw her* ***by chance*** *in the shop.* **4** [RISK] [C] a risk *I'm delivering my work by hand. I'm not* ***taking*** *any* ***chances.*** **5 by any chance** used to ask in a polite way whether something is possible or true *You're not Spanish by any chance, are you?* **6 stand a chance** to have a chance of success or of achieving something *He stands a good chance of winning the election.* **7 chances are** it is likely [+ **(that)**] *Chances are that he'll refuse.* **8 No chance!/ Not a chance!** used to emphasize that there is no possibility of something happening *"Do you think she'd go out with me?" "No chance!"* **9 fat chance** *informal* used to say that you do not think that something is likely to happen *"Do you think we'll win?" "Fat chance."* ➲See also: **off-chance, outside chance**

chance² /tʃɑːns/ *verb* [T] *informal* to take a risk by doing something

C

chance³ /tʃɑːns/ *adjective* [**always before noun**] A chance event is not planned or expected. *a chance meeting*

chancellor /ˈtʃɑːnsᵊləʳ/ *noun* [C] **1 POLITICS** the leader of the government in some countries *the German chancellor* **2 EDUCATION** the person with the highest position in some universities **3** MONEY (*also* ˌ**Chancellor of the Exˈchequer**) *UK* the person in the British government who makes decisions about taxes and government spending

chandelier /ˌʃændəˈlɪəʳ/ *noun* [C] a large light that hangs from the ceiling that is made of many small lights or candles and small pieces of glass

OTHER WAYS OF SAYING ***change***

The verb **alter** is a common alternative to 'change': *We've had to **alter** our plans.*

If you often change something that you do, you can use the verb **vary**: *Try to **vary** the children's diet a little.*

If someone changes the purpose or appearance of something, you can use the verb **convert**, or the phrasal verb **turn into**: *We're going to **convert** the spare bedroom into an office.* • *There are plans to **turn** his latest book **into** a film.*

If someone changes from doing or using one thing to doing or using another, the verb **switch** is sometimes used: *We've **switched** over to low fat milk.* • *Jack has just **switched** jobs.*

change¹ /tʃeɪndʒ/ *verb* **1** DIFFERENT [I, T] to become different, or to make someone or something become different *I hadn't seen her for twenty years, but she hadn't changed a bit.* ○ *The course changed my life.* ○ *She's **changed from** being a happy, healthy child **to** being ill all the time.* **2** FROM ONE THING TO ANOTHER [I, T] to stop having or using one thing, and start having or using another *The doctor has recommended changing my diet.* ○ *I'll have to ask them if they can change the time of my interview.* **3** CLOTHES [I, T] to take off your clothes and put on different ones *He **changed out of** his school uniform **into** jeans and a T-shirt.* ○ *Is there somewhere I can **get changed**?* **4** JOURNEY [I, T] to get off a bus, plane, etc and catch another, in order to continue a journey *I have to change trains at Bristol.* **5** IN SHOP [T] *UK* to take something you have bought back to a shop and exchange it for something else *If the dress doesn't fit, can I **change** it **for** a smaller one?* **6 FINANCE** [T] to get or give someone money in exchange for money of a different type *Where can I change my dollars?* ○ *Can you **change** a £20 note **for** two tens?* **7** BED [T] to take dirty sheets off a bed and put on clean ones *to change the bed/sheets* **8** BABY [T] to put a clean nappy (= thick cloth worn on a baby's bottom) on a baby ➲See also: **chop**¹ and change, change hands (**hand**¹), change your **tune**¹

change sth around/round *phrasal verb* to move objects such as furniture into different positions

change over *phrasal verb UK* to stop using or having one thing and start using or having something else *We've just **changed over from** gas central heating **to** electric.*

WORD PARTNERS FOR ***change***

bring about/implement/make/undergo change • change **occurs/takes place** • a **big/dramatic/fundamental/major/radical/sweeping** change • change **in/to** sth

change² /tʃeɪndʒ/ *noun* **1** DIFFERENCE [C, U] when something becomes different, or the result of something becoming different *We need to **make** a few **changes to** the design.* ○ *There is no **change in** the patient's condition* (= the illness has not got better or worse). ○ *How can we **bring about** social **change**?* **2** FROM ONE THING TO ANOTHER [C, U] when you stop having or using one thing and start having or using another *This country needs a **change of** government.* ○ *I've notified the school of our **change of address**.* **3** NEW EXPERIENCE [C] something that you enjoy because it is a new experience [**usually singular**] *Going abroad for our anniversary would **make a** lovely **change**.* ○ *It's nice to eat together as a family **for a change**.* **4 FINANCE** [U] the money that you get back when you pay more for something than it costs *There's your receipt and £3 change.* **5 FINANCE** [U] coins, not paper money *Have you got any change for the parking meter?* ○ *Have you got change for £5* (= can you give me £5 in coins in return for paper money)? **6 a change of clothes** a set of clean clothes that you can put on if you need to take off the ones you are wearing **7 a change of heart** If you have a change of heart, you change your opinion or feelings about something. ➲See also: **small change**

changeable /ˈtʃeɪndʒəbl/ *adjective* often changing, or likely to change

changeover /ˈtʃeɪndʒˌəʊvəʳ/ *noun* [C] a change from one system or situation to another [**usually singular**] *the **changeover from** the old computer system to the new one*

ˈ**changing** ˌ**room** *noun* [C] *UK* a room in a shop where you can try clothes, or a room where you change into clothes to do sport

channel¹ /ˈtʃænᵊl/ *noun* [C] **1** TELEVISION a television or radio station (= broadcasting company) **2** PASSAGE a long, narrow passage for water or other liquids to flow along *an irrigation channel* **3** COMMUNICATION a way of communicating with people or getting something done *a **channel of communication*** **4 the Channel** (*also* **the** ˌ**English** ˈ**Channel**) **GEOGRAPHY** the narrow area of water between England and France **5 GEOGRAPHY** a part of a river or sea that is deep and wide enough for ships to travel along *a navigable channel*

channel² /ˈtʃænᵊl/ *verb* [T] *UK* **channelling**, *past* **channelled**, *US* **channeling**, *past* **channeled** **1** WATER to direct water along a particular route *The waste water is channelled through this pipe.* **2** MONEY/ENERGY to use money or energy for a particular purpose *We've **channelled** all our resources **into** this project.*

the ˌ**Channel** ˈ**Tunnel** *noun* the three long passages under the English Channel between England and France

chant¹ /tʃɑːnt/ *verb* [I, T] **MUSIC** **1** to repeat or sing a word or phrase many times, often shouting *The demonstrators **chanted** anti-racist **slogans**.* **2** to sing a religious song or prayer using a very simple tune

chant² /tʃɑːnt/ *noun* [C] **1** a word or phrase that is repeated many times **2** **MUSIC** a religious song or prayer that is sung using a very simple tune

Chanukah /ˈhɑːnəkə/ *noun* [C, U] **RELIGION** Hanukkah

WORD PARTNERS FOR ***chaos***

cause chaos • **descend into/be thrown into** chaos • be **in** chaos • **total/utter** chaos

chaos /ˈkeɪɒs/ *noun* [U] a situation where there is no order at all and everyone is confused *The country's at war and everything is **in chaos**.*

chaotic /keɪˈɒtɪk/ *adjective* in a state of chaos *a chaotic situation*

chap /tʃæp/ *noun* [C] *UK informal* a man

chapel /ˈtʃæpᵊl/ *noun* [C] **RELIGION** a small church, or a room used as a church in a building

chaperone¹ (*also* **chaperon**) /ˈʃæpᵊrəʊn/ *noun* [C] an older person who goes somewhere with a younger person in order to make sure they behave well, especially a woman in the past who went with a younger woman who was not married

chaperone² (*also* **chaperon**) /ˈʃæpᵊrəʊn/ *verb* [T] to go somewhere with someone as their chaperone

chaplain /ˈtʃæplɪn/ *noun* [C] **RELIGION** a priest in the army, a school, a hospital, or a prison

chapter /ˈtʃæptəʳ/ *noun* [C] **1** [BOOK] one of the parts that a book is divided into **2** [PERIOD] a period of time when something happens in history or in someone's life *an interesting **chapter in** Spanish history*

WORD PARTNERS FOR ***character***

a **colourful/lovable/shady/strong/unsavoury** character • a **real** character

O⁃**character** /ˈkærəktəʳ/ *noun* **1** [QUALITIES] [C, U] the combination of qualities and personality that makes one person or thing different from others *It's **not in her character** to be jealous* (= she would not usually be jealous). ○ *It would be very **out of character*** (= not typical) *of her to lie.* ○ *The character of the village has changed since the road was built.* **2** **LITERATURE** [C] a person in a book, film, etc *a cartoon character* **3** [GOOD QUALITIES] [U] qualities that are interesting or unusual *a hotel of character* **4** [PERSON] [C] *informal* a particular kind of person *an unpleasant character* **5** [INTERESTING PERSON] [C] an interesting or funny person whose behaviour is different from most people's *Your granny's a **real character**.* **6** **LANGUAGE** [C] a letter, sign, or number that you use when you are writing or printing *Chinese characters*

characteristic¹ /ˌkærəktəˈrɪstɪk/ *noun* [C] a typical or obvious quality that makes one person or thing different from others *a national characteristic* ○ *Does he have any distinguishing physical characteristics?*

characteristic² /ˌkærəktəˈrɪstɪk/ *adjective* typical of someone or something *Grey stone is **characteristic of** buildings in that area.* ⊃Opposite **uncharacteristic** •**characteristically** *adverb*

characterization (*also UK* **-isation**) /ˌkærəktᵊraɪˈzeɪʃᵊn/ *noun* [U] **LITERATURE** the way that people are described in a play, book, etc

characterize (*also UK* **-ise**) /ˈkærəktᵊraɪz/ *verb* [T] **1** [TYPICAL] to be typical of someone or something [**often passive**] *Her behaviour in class has been characterized by rudeness and laziness.* **2** [DESCRIBE] to describe or show someone or something in a particular way *Historians have **characterized** the age **as** a period of great change.*

charade /ʃəˈrɑːd/ (US) /ʃəˈreɪd/ *noun* [C] a situation which is clearly false, but where people behave as if it is true or serious *The interview was just a charade.*

charcoal /ˈtʃɑːkəʊl/ *noun* [U] **ART** a hard, black substance that is produced by burning wood without much air, and that is used as fuel or for drawing

WORD PARTNERS FOR ***charge***

make a charge • **at no extra/free of/without** charge • a charge **for** sth • a charge **of** [£10/$12, etc] • a **small** charge

O⁃**charge¹** /tʃɑːdʒ/ *noun* **1** **FINANCE** [C, U] the amount of money that you have to pay for something, especially for an activity or a service *bank charges* ○ *There's no **charge for** children under 14.* ○ *He repaired the computer **free of charge*** (= it did not cost anything). **2** **be in charge** to be the person who has control of or is responsible for someone or something *She's **in charge of** a team of 20 people.* ○ *Who's in charge of organizing the music for the party?* **3** **take charge** to take control of or make yourself responsible for something *I was happy to let her take charge of paying all the bills.* **4** **LAW** [C] a formal police statement saying that someone is accused of a crime *to **bring/press charges*** ○ *She was **arrested on charges of** theft and forgery.* **5** [ACCUSE] [C] when you accuse someone of something *This is a **serious charge** to make against your colleagues.* **6** **PHYSICS** [C, U] the amount of electricity that an electrical device has in it or that a substance has in it **7** [ATTACK] [C] an attack in which people or animals run forward suddenly **8** **reverse the charges** *UK* (*US* **call collect**) to make a telephone call that is paid for by the person who receives it ⊃See also: **service charge**

O⁃**charge²** /tʃɑːdʒ/ *verb* **1** **FINANCE** [I, T] to ask someone to pay an amount of money for something, especially for an activity or a service [+ **two objects**] *They are going to charge motorists a tax to drive into the city centre.* ○ *How much do you **charge for** delivery?* **2** **LAW** [T] If the police charge someone, they accuse them officially of a crime. [**often passive**] *He was **charged with** assault.* **3** [ATTACK] [I, T] to attack someone or something by moving forward quickly *The bull looked as if it was about to charge.* **4** **charge around/into/through, etc** to run from one place to another *The children* *charged around the house.* **5 PHYSICS** [I, T] to put electricity into something

ˈcharge ˌcard *noun* [C] **FINANCE** a small plastic card that allows you to buy something and pay for it at a particular date in the future

C

charged /tʃɑːdʒd/ *adjective* A situation or a subject that is charged causes strong feelings or arguments. *a highly **charged debate***

chariot /ˈtʃæriət/ *noun* [C] a vehicle with two wheels that was used in races and fights in ancient times and was pulled by a horse

charisma /kəˈrɪzmə/ *noun* [U] a natural power which some people have to influence or attract people •**charismatic** /ˌkærɪzˈmætɪk/ *adjective*

charitable /ˈtʃærɪtəbl/ *adjective* **1** EVENT [always before noun] A charitable event, activity, or organization gives money, food, or help to people who need it. **2** KIND kind, and not judging other people in a severe way •**charitably** *adverb*

WORD PARTNERS FOR ***charity***

donate/give sth to charity • [money, etc] **goes to** charity • do sth **for** charity • a charity **for** [homeless people/sick children, etc] • a charity **event** (= an event to raise money for a charity)

charity /ˈtʃærɪti/ *noun* **1** ORGANIZATION [C, U] an official organization that gives money, food, or help to people who need it *The raffle will raise money **for charity**.* ○ *A percentage of the company's profits **go to charity**.* **2** MONEY/HELP [U] money, food, or other help that is given to people *I won't **accept charity**.* **3** KINDNESS [U] kindness towards other people *an act of charity*

ˈcharity ˌshop *UK* (*US* **thrift shop**) *noun* [C] a shop which sells goods given by the public, especially clothes, to make money for a particular charity

charlatan /ˈʃɑːlətᵊn/ *noun* [C] someone who pretends to have skills or knowledge that they do not have

charm¹ /tʃɑːm/ *noun* **1** QUALITY [C, U] a quality that makes you like someone or something *The building had a certain charm.* **2** LUCKY [C] an object that you keep or wear because you believe that it is lucky *a **lucky charm***

charm² /tʃɑːm/ *verb* [T] to attract someone or persuade someone to do something because of your charm [**often passive**] *We were charmed by his boyish manner.*

charmed /tʃɑːmd/ *adjective* very lucky, or managing to avoid danger *The young boy had led **a charmed life**.*

charmer /ˈtʃɑːməʳ/ *noun* [C] *informal* someone who knows how to be charming in order to attract people or persuade them to do things

charming /ˈtʃɑːmɪŋ/ *adjective* pleasant or attractive *a charming smile/place* •**charmingly** *adverb*

charred /tʃɑːd/ *adjective* black from having been burned *charred wreckage*

chart¹ /tʃɑːt/ *noun* **1** INFORMATION [C] a drawing which shows information in a simple way, often using lines and curves to show amounts *a sales chart* **2 the charts MUSIC** an official list of the most popular songs each week **3** MAP [C] a map of the sea or the sky

chart² /tʃɑːt/ *verb* [T] **1** INFORMATION to watch and record information about something over a period of time *The documentary **charted** the **progress** of the war.* **2** MAP to make a map of an area of land, sea, or sky

charter¹ /ˈtʃɑːtəʳ/ *noun* [C] a formal, written description of the principles, activities, and purpose of an organization

charter² /ˈtʃɑːtəʳ/ *verb* [T] to rent a vehicle, especially an aircraft *The holiday company chartered a plane to fly us all home.*

charter³ /ˈtʃɑːtəʳ/ *adjective* **a charter flight/company/plane, etc** using aircraft paid for by travel companies for their customers

chartered /ˈtʃɑːtəd/ *adjective* [**always before noun**] *UK* having the necessary qualifications to work in a particular profession *a **chartered accountant/surveyor***

chase¹ /tʃeɪs/ *verb* **1** CATCH [I, T] to run after someone or something in order to catch them *The dog was chasing a rabbit.* **2 chase sb/sth away/off/out, etc** to run after a person or animal to make them leave a place *I chased the cat away.* **3** TRY [T] *UK* to try very hard to get something *There are hundreds of graduates **chasing** very few **jobs**.*

chase² /tʃeɪs/ *noun* **1** [C] when you go after someone or something quickly in order to catch them *a high speed **car chase*** **2 give chase** to go after someone or something quickly in order to catch them

chasm /ˈkæzᵊm/ *noun* [C] **1 GEOGRAPHY** a long, deep, narrow hole in rock or ice **2** a very large difference between two opinions or two groups of people

chassis /ˈʃæsi/ *noun* [C] *plural* **chassis** /ˈʃæsiz/ the structure of a vehicle that the outer metal is fixed onto

chaste /tʃeɪst/ *adjective* not having had sex, or without sexual thoughts or intentions *a chaste relationship*

chasten /ˈtʃeɪsᵊn/ *verb* [T] *formal* to make someone feel ashamed by making them understand that they have failed or done something wrong [**often passive**] *The team were chastened by their defeat.* •**chastening** *adjective*

chastise /tʃæsˈtaɪz/ *verb* [T] *formal* to criticize or punish someone

chastity /ˈtʃæstəti/ *noun* [U] when someone does not have sex

O-ᵚ**chat¹** /tʃæt/ *verb* [I] **chatting** *past* **chatted** to talk with someone in a friendly and informal way *I wanted to **chat to** you **about** the party on Saturday.*

chat sb up *phrasal verb UK informal* to talk to someone in a way that shows them that you are sexually attracted to them

WORD PARTNERS FOR ***chat***

have a chat • a chat **about** sth • a **good/little/long/quick** chat • a chat **with** sb

O-ᵚ**chat²** /tʃæt/ *noun* [C, U] a friendly, informal conversation

chateau /ˈʃætəʊ/ (US) /ʃæˈtəʊ/ *noun* [C] *plural* **chateaux** a large house or castle in France

ˈchat ˌroom *noun* [C] **INTERNET** a place on the Internet where you can have discussions with other people ➲See Extra help page **The Web and the Internet on page Centre 37.**

ˈchat ˌshow *UK* (*US* **talk show**) *noun* [C] a television or radio programme where people are asked questions about themselves

chatter /ˈtʃætər/ *verb* [I] **1** TALK to talk for a long time about things that are not important **2** TEETH If your teeth chatter, they knock together because you are cold or frightened. •**chatter** *noun* [U]

chatty /ˈtʃæti/ *adjective* **1** PERSON liking to talk **2** WRITING A piece of writing that is chatty has a friendly and informal style. *a chatty letter*

chauffeur /ˈʃəʊfər/ (US) /ʃəʊˈfɜːr/ *noun* [C] someone whose job is to drive a car for someone else •**chauffeur** *verb* [T]

chauvinist /ˈʃəʊvənɪst/ *noun* [C] **1** MAN (*also* **male chauvinist**) a man who believes that men are better or more important than women **2** COUNTRY/RACE someone who believes that their country or race is better or more important than other countries or races •**chauvinism** *noun* [U] the beliefs and behaviour of chauvinists

chav /tʃæv/ *noun* [C] *UK informal* a young person who dresses in cheap clothes and jewellery that are intended to look expensive, and who does not look clever

OTHER WAYS OF SAYING ***cheap***

If something is cheap enough for most people to be able to buy, you can say that it is **affordable**, **inexpensive**, or **reasonable**: *There's very little* ***affordable*** *housing around here.* • *They sell* ***inexpensive*** *children's clothes.* • *I thought the food was very* ***reasonable****.*

The adjective **cut-price** is sometimes used to describe something that is cheaper than usual: *We managed to get* ***cut-price*** *tickets the day before the show.*

A piece of equipment that is cheap to use is often described as **economical**: *I need a car that's reliable and* ***economical****.*

O-- **cheap¹** /tʃiːp/ *adjective* **1** NOT EXPENSIVE not expensive, or costing less than usual *I got a cheap flight to Spain at the last minute.* ○ *It will be a lot cheaper to go by bus.* **2** PAY LESS where you have to pay less than usual or less than you expect *Are there any cheap restaurants around here?* **3** LOW QUALITY low in price and quality *cheap perfume* **4** PERSON *US* not willing to spend money

cheap² /tʃiːp/ *adverb informal* **1** for a low price *You'll* ***get*** *the table* ***cheap*** *if you buy the chairs too.* **2 be going cheap** *UK* to be offered for sale for less money than is usual **3 not come cheap** to be expensive *Good carpets don't come cheap.*

cheaply /ˈtʃiːpli/ *adverb* for a low price *You can buy some goods more cheaply in America.*

cheat¹ /tʃiːt/ *verb* [I, T] to behave in a way that is not honest or fair in order to win something or to get something *She was caught (UK)* ***cheating in*** *her French exam/ (US)* ***cheating on*** *her French exam.* ○ *He* ***cheats at*** *cards.*

cheat on sb *phrasal verb* to have a secret sexual relationship with someone who is not your usual sexual partner

cheat sb out of sth *phrasal verb* to get something that belongs to someone else by deceiving them

cheat² /tʃiːt/ *noun* [C] **1** someone who cheats **2** **COMPUTING** special instructions or information which someone can use to help them play a computer game more effectively

O-- **check¹** /tʃek/ *verb* **1** EXAMINE [I, T] to examine something in order to make sure that it is correct or the way it should be [+ **(that)**] *I went to check that I'd locked the door.* ○ *Have you* ***checked*** *your* ***facts****?* ○ *I knelt down beside the body and* ***checked for*** *a pulse.* **2** FIND OUT [I, T] to find out about something [+ **question word**] *I'll check whether Peter knows about the party.* **3** ASK [I] to ask someone for permission to do something *I'd like to stay overnight, but I need to* ***check with*** *my parents.* **4** STOP [T] to stop something bad from increasing or continuing *The government needs to find a way to check rising inflation.* **5** MARK [T] *US* (*UK* **tick**) to put a mark by an answer to show that it is correct, or by an item on a list to show that you have dealt with it **6** LEAVE [T] *US* to leave your coat, bags, or other possessions temporarily in someone's care ➲See also: **double-check**

check in *phrasal verb* **1** AIRPORT to go to the desk at an airport in order to say that you have arrived and to get the number of your seat *We have to check in three hours before the flight leaves.* **2** HOTEL to go to the desk at a hotel in order to say that you have arrived, and to get the key to your room

check sth off *phrasal verb US* (*UK* **tick sth off**) to put a mark next to a name or an item on a list to show that it is correct, or that it has been dealt with

check (up) on sb/sth *phrasal verb* to try to discover how something is progressing or whether someone is doing what they should be doing *My boss is always checking up on me.*

check out *phrasal verb* to leave a hotel after paying your bill

check sth out *phrasal verb* **1** INFORMATION *informal* to examine something or get more information about it in order to be certain that it is true, safe, or suitable *We'll need to check out his story.* **2** GO TO SEE *informal* to go to a place in order to see what it is like *Let's check out that new dance club.* **3** BOOKS *mainly US* to borrow books from a library

WORD PARTNERS FOR ***check***

do/make a check • a **rigorous** check • a **final/last-minute/random/routine** check • **safety/security** checks • a check **of/on** sth

check² /tʃek/ *noun* **1** EXAMINATION [C] an examination of something in order to make sure that it is correct or the way it should be *We* ***do safety checks on*** *all our equipment.* **2** **FINANCE** [C] *US spelling of* cheque (= a piece of paper printed by a bank that you use to pay for things) **3** [C] *US* (*UK* **bill**) a list that you are given in a restaurant showing how much your meal costs **4** MARK [C] *US* (*UK* **tick**) a mark (✓) that shows that an answer is correct, or that you have dealt with something on a list

5 [PATTERN] [C, U] a pattern of squares of different colours 6 **hold/keep sth in check** to control something that could increase too quickly or become too large or powerful *We need to keep our spending in check.* ➲See also: **rain check**

checkbook /'tʃekbʊk/ *noun* [C] **FINANCE** *US spelling of* chequebook (= a book of papers printed by a bank that you use to pay for things)

checked /tʃekt/ *adjective* with a pattern of squares of different colours *a checked shirt/tablecloth*

checkers /'tʃekəz/ *US* (*UK* **draughts**) *noun* [U] a game that two people play by moving flat, round objects around on a board of black and white squares

check-in /'tʃekɪn/ *noun* [C] the place at an airport where you go to say that you have arrived for your flight, or the act of going to the check-in to say that you have arrived for your flight *a* ***check-in counter/desk***

'checking ac,count *US* (*UK* **current account**) *noun* [C] **FINANCE** a bank account which you can take money out of at any time

checklist /'tʃeklɪst/ *noun* [C] a list of things that you should think about, or that you must do

checkmate /'tʃekmeɪt/ *noun* [U] the final position in the game of chess when your king cannot escape and you have lost the game

checkout /'tʃekaʊt/ *noun* [C] 1 (*also US* **'checkout ,counter**) the place in a large shop, especially a food shop, where you pay for your goods *a supermarket checkout* 2 **COMPUTING, INTERNET** the place on an Internet website where you order and pay for things *After you've chosen what you want, click here to go to checkout.*

checkpoint /'tʃekpɔɪnt/ *noun* [C] a place where people and vehicles are stopped and examined *a military/police checkpoint*

checksum /'tʃeksʌm/ *noun* [C] **COMPUTING** a number that is found from all the numbers in a piece of electronic data, in order to check that the data is correct

check-up /'tʃekʌp/ *noun* [C] **HEALTH** a general medical examination to see if you are healthy *I'm going to the doctor for a check-up.*

cheddar /,tʃedəʳ/ *noun* [U] **FOOD** a type of hard, yellow cheese

cheek /tʃiːk/ *noun* 1 **ANATOMY** [C] the soft part of your face below your eye *Tears ran down his cheeks.* ➲See colour picture **The Body** on page Centre 13 2 [U, no plural] *mainly UK* rude behaviour that shows that you do not respect someone [+ **to do sth**] *She* ***had the cheek to*** *ask me to pay for her!*

cheekbone /'tʃiːkbəʊn/ *noun* [C] **ANATOMY** one of the two bones below your eyes

cheeky /'tʃiːki/ *adjective UK* slightly rude or behaving without respect, but often in a funny way *He's got such a* ***cheeky grin.*** •**cheekily** *adverb*

cheer¹ /tʃɪəʳ/ *verb* 1 [I, T] to shout loudly in order to show your approval or to encourage someone *The crowd stood up and cheered at the end of the concert.* 2 **be cheered by sth** to feel happier or encouraged because of something

cheer sb on *phrasal verb* to shout loudly in order to encourage someone in a competition

cheer (sb) up *phrasal verb* to stop feeling sad, or to make someone feel happier *Cheer up. It's not the end of the world.*

cheer sth up *phrasal verb* to make a place look brighter or more attractive

cheer² /tʃɪəʳ/ *noun* [C] a shout of approval or encouragement

cheerful /'tʃɪəfᵊl/ *adjective* 1 [PERSON] happy *I'm not feeling very cheerful today.* 2 [ROOM ETC] bright and pleasant to look at *a bright and cheerful room* •**cheerfully** *adverb* •**cheerfulness** *noun* [U]

cheering¹ /'tʃɪərɪŋ/ *noun* [U] shouts of encouragement and approval

cheering² /'tʃɪərɪŋ/ *adjective* Something cheering encourages you and makes you feel happier. *We received some cheering news.*

cheerleader /'tʃɪə,liːdəʳ/ *noun* [C] a girl, especially in the United States, who leads the crowd in shouting encouragement to a team who are playing a sport

cheers /tʃɪəz/ *exclamation* 1 [DRINK] something friendly that you say before you start to drink alcohol with someone 2 [THANK YOU] *UK informal* thank you

cheery /'tʃɪəri/ *adjective* bright and happy *a* ***cheery wave/smile*** •**cheerily** *adverb*

O-- **cheese** /tʃiːz/ *noun* 1 **FOOD** [C, U] a food that is made from milk, is usually white or yellow, and can be either hard or soft *a cheese sandwich* ➲See colour picture **Food** on page Centre 11 2 **Say cheese!** something that you say to make someone smile when you are taking their photograph ➲See also: be like **chalk¹** and cheese, **cottage cheese, cream cheese**

cheesecake /'tʃiːzkeɪk/ *noun* [C, U] **FOOD** a sweet cake made with soft, white cheese on a biscuit base

cheesy /'tʃiːzi/ *adjective informal* 1 not fashionable and of low quality *cheesy music* 2 **a cheesy grin** a wide smile that is not always sincere

cheetah /'tʃiːtə/ *noun* [C] a large, wild cat that has black spots and can run very fast

chef /ʃef/ *noun* [C] someone who is the main cook (= person who cooks) in a hotel or a restaurant

chemical¹ /'kemɪkᵊl/ *adjective* **CHEMISTRY** relating to chemistry or chemicals *a chemical reaction* ○ *chemical weapons* •**chemically** *adverb*

O-- **chemical²** /'kemɪkᵊl/ *noun* [C] **CHEMISTRY** a basic substance that is used in chemistry or produced by chemistry

,chemical 'bond *noun* [C] **CHEMISTRY** the way two atoms are joined together in a chemical compound

,chemical 'element *noun* [C] **CHEMISTRY** a substance that cannot be broken down into any simpler chemical substances and is made of atoms all of the same type

ˌchemical eˈquation *noun* [C] **CHEMISTRY** a statement containing chemical symbols, used to show the changes that happen during a particular chemical reaction

ˌchemical ˈformula *noun* [C] **CHEMISTRY** the representation of a substance using the symbols of its elements

chemist /ˈkemɪst/ *noun* [C] **1** *UK* (*US* **pharmacist**) someone whose job is to prepare and sell drugs in a shop **2** **CHEMISTRY** a scientist who does work involving chemistry

chemistry /ˈkemɪstri/ *noun* [U] **CHEMISTRY** the scientific study of substances and how they change when they combine

chemist's /ˈkemɪsts/ *UK* (*US* **drugstore**) *noun* [C] a shop where you can buy drugs, soap, beauty products, etc

chemotherapy /ˌkiːməʊˈθerəpi/ (also **chemo**) *noun* [U] **HEALTH** the treatment of a disease using chemicals *Chemotherapy is often used to treat cancer.*

WORD PARTNERS FOR ***cheque***

pay by cheque • a cheque **bounces** • **write** a cheque • a cheque **for** [£50/£200, etc]

O→**cheque** *UK* (*US* **check**) /tʃek/ *noun* [C] **FINANCE** a piece of paper printed by a bank that you use to pay for things *a **cheque for** £1500* ○ *Are you **paying by cheque**?* ⊃See also: **blank cheque, traveller's cheque**

chequebook *UK* (*US* **checkbook**) /ˈtʃekbʊk/ *noun* [C] **FINANCE** a book of cheques

ˈcheque ˌcard *noun* [C] **FINANCE** a small plastic card from your bank which you show when you write a cheque

cherish /ˈtʃerɪʃ/ *verb* [T] **1** CARE FOR to love someone or something very much and take care of them **2** IMPORTANT If you cherish an idea, hope, memory, etc, it is very important to you.

cherry /ˈtʃeri/ *noun* **FOOD** [C] a small, round red or black fruit with a large seed inside

cherub /ˈtʃerəb/ *noun* [C] a small child with a beautiful, round face and wings who appears in religious paintings

chess /tʃes/ *noun* [U] a game that two people play by moving differently shaped pieces around a board of black and white squares *a **chess set***

chest /tʃest/ *noun* [C] **1** **ANATOMY** the front of your body between your neck and your waist *a hairy chest* ○ *chest pains* ⊃See colour picture **The Body** on page Centre 13 **2** a strong, usually wooden, container with a lid, used for keeping things in *a treasure chest* **3** **get sth off your chest** *informal* to tell someone about something that you have been worried or angry about for a long time

chestnut /ˈtʃesnʌt/ *noun* **1** **FOOD** [C] a nut that has a shiny, red-brown surface and is white inside, or the tree that produces these nuts *roasted chestnuts* **2** [C, U] a dark red-brown colour ⊃See also: **horse chestnut**

ˌchest of ˈdrawers *UK* (*US* **bureau**) *noun* [C] a piece of furniture with drawers for keeping clothes in

chew /tʃuː/ *verb* [I, T] **1** EAT to crush food between your teeth before you swallow it **2** BITE to repeatedly bite something without swallowing it *to chew gum*

chew sth over *phrasal verb* to think carefully about something, or to discuss it

ˈchewing ˌgum *noun* [U] **FOOD** a sweet substance that you chew but do not swallow

chewy /ˈtʃuːi/ *adjective* Chewy food needs to be chewed a lot before you can swallow it.

chic /ʃiːk/ *adjective* fashionable and attractive *a chic restaurant*

chick /tʃɪk/ *noun* [C] a baby bird, especially a baby chicken

O→**chicken¹** /ˈtʃɪkɪn/ *noun* **1** [C] **FARMING** a bird kept on a farm for its meat and eggs **2** **FOOD** [U] the meat of a chicken *a chicken sandwich*

chicken² /ˈtʃɪkɪn/ *verb*

chicken out *phrasal verb informal* to decide not to do something because you are too nervous

ˈchicken ˌpox *noun* [U] **HEALTH** a children's disease that causes a fever and red spots on the skin

ˈchick ˌflick *noun* [C] *humorous* a film about romantic relationships or other subjects that interest women

ˈchick ˌlit *noun* [C] *humorous* a book about romantic relationships or other subjects that interest women

chief¹ /tʃiːf/ *adjective* [**always before noun**] **1** MAIN most important *The wonderful weather was our **chief reason** for coming here.* **2** HIGH RANK highest in rank *chief economic adviser to the government*

chief² /tʃiːf/ *noun* [C] **1** GROUP LEADER the leader of a group of people *tribal chiefs* **2** ORGANIZATION a person who controls other people in an organization *police chiefs*

ˌchief exˈecutive (also **chief executive officer**) *noun* [C] the person with the most important job in a company

chiefly /ˈtʃiːfli/ *adverb* mainly *magazines intended chiefly for teenagers*

chieftain /ˈtʃiːftᵊn/ *noun* [C] **SOCIETY** the leader of a tribe (= group of people with the same language and customs)

chiffon /ˈʃɪfɒn/ (US) /ʃɪˈfɑːn/ *noun* [U] a soft, thin cloth used for making women's clothes

O→**child** /tʃaɪld/ *noun* [C] *plural* **children** **1** YOUNG PERSON a young person who is not yet an adult *an eight-year-old child* ○ *How many children are there in your class?* **2** SON/DAUGHTER someone's son or daughter, also when they are adults *Both our children have grown up and moved away.* ⊃See also: **only child**

ˈchild aˌbuse *noun* [U] when adults treat children in a cruel or violent way

ˌchild ˈbenefit *noun* [U] **SOCIETY** money that the British government pays every week to families with children

childbirth /ˈtʃaɪldbɜːθ/ *noun* [U] the process during which a baby is born *His mother died **in childbirth**.*

C

C

childcare /ˈtʃaɪldkeəʳ/ *noun* [U] when someone looks after children while their parents are working

WORD PARTNERS FOR ***childhood***

spend your childhood swh/doing sth • **early** childhood • **in** (sb's) childhood • a **happy/ lonely/unhappy** childhood • a childhood **friend/** sb's childhood **sweetheart** • childhood **memories**

childhood /ˈtʃaɪldhʊd/ *noun* [C, U] the part of your life when you are a child

childish /ˈtʃaɪldɪʃ/ *adjective* **1** SILLY Childish behaviour is silly, like that of a small child. *Don't be so childish!* **2** OF CHILD typical of a child *childish handwriting* •**childishly** *adverb* •**childishness** *noun* [U]

childless /ˈtʃaɪldləs/ *adjective* A childless person has no children.

childlike /ˈtʃaɪldlaɪk/ *adjective* Childlike people are like children in some ways, such as trusting people or behaving in a natural way.

childminder /ˈtʃaɪldˌmaɪndəʳ/ *noun* [C] *UK* someone whose job is to look after children while their parents are working

children /ˈtʃɪldrən/ *plural of* child

ˈchild supˌport *noun* [U] **FINANCE** money that someone gives the mother or father of their children when they do not live with them

chili /ˈtʃɪli/ *noun* **FOOD** *US spelling of* chilli

chill[1] /tʃɪl/ *verb* [I, T] to become cold, or to make someone or something become cold *Chill the wine before serving.*

chill out *phrasal verb informal* to relax completely, or not allow things to upset you *Chill out, Dad - if we miss this train there's always another one.*

chill[2] /tʃɪl/ *noun* **1** COLD [no plural] a cold feeling *There is a definite chill in the air.* **2** FEAR [C] a sudden frightened feeling *The scream **sent a chill down my spine.*** **3 HEALTH** [C] *UK* a cold (= common illness that makes you sneeze) that is not very bad

chilli *UK* (*US* **chili**) /ˈtʃɪli/ *noun plural* **chillies 1 FOOD** [C, U] a small, thin, red or green vegetable that tastes very hot *chilli powder* **2 FOOD** [U] a spicy dish of beans, meat, and chillies

chilling /ˈtʃɪlɪŋ/ *adjective* very frightening *a chilling tale*

chilly /ˈtʃɪli/ *adjective* **1** COLD unpleasantly cold *a chilly evening* **2** UNFRIENDLY unfriendly *He gave me a chilly look.*

chime /tʃaɪm/ *verb* [I, T] If a bell or clock chimes, it rings. •**chime** *noun* [C]

chime in *phrasal verb* to suddenly say something in order to add your opinion to a conversation *"Quite right too!" Tony chimed in.*

chimney /ˈtʃɪmni/ *noun* [C] a wide pipe that allows smoke from a fire to go out through the roof

ˈchimney ˌsweep *noun* [C] someone whose job is to clean inside a chimney, using long brushes

chimpanzee /ˌtʃɪmpənˈziː/ (*also* **chimp** /tʃɪmp/ *informal*) *noun* [C] an African animal like a large monkey

chin /tʃɪn/ *noun* [C] **ANATOMY** the bottom part of your face, below your mouth ⊃See colour picture **The Body** on page Centre 13

china /ˈtʃaɪnə/ *noun* [U] **1** SUBSTANCE the hard substance that plates, cups, bowls, etc are made from *a china teapot* **2** PLATES cups, plates, bowls, etc that are made from china

chink /tʃɪŋk/ *noun* [C] **1** OPENING a small, narrow opening in something **2** SOUND a short ringing sound that is made when glass or metal objects touch each other

chip[1] /tʃɪp/ *noun* [C] **1 FOOD** (*US* **french fry**) a long, thin piece of potato that is cooked in oil [**usually plural**] *fish and chips* ⊃See colour picture **Food** on page Centre 11 **2 FOOD** *US* (*UK* **crisp**) a very thin, dry, fried slice of potato [**usually plural**] *barbecue flavoured potato chips* ⊃See colour picture **Food** on page Centre 11 **3 COMPUTING** a microchip (= very small part of a computer that stores information) **4** SMALL PIECE a small piece that has broken off something *wood chips* **5** HOLE a place where a small piece has broken off something *This cup has a chip in it.* **6 be a chip off the old block** *informal* to be very similar to your mother or father **7 have a chip on your shoulder** *informal* to blame other people for something bad that has happened to you and continue to feel angry about it *She's always had a real chip on her shoulder because she didn't go to university.*

chip[2] /tʃɪp/ *verb* [T] **chipping,** *past* **chipped** to break a small piece off something *Henman may have chipped a bone in his wrist.* ○ *a chipped plate*

chip in *phrasal verb informal* to interrupt a conversation in order to say something *I'll start and you can all **chip in with** your comments.*

chip in (sth) *phrasal verb* If several people chip in, they each give money to buy something together. *We all chipped in to buy our teacher a present.*

ˌchip and ˈPIN *noun* [U] **FINANCE** a way to pay for goods and services using a credit card (= a small plastic card that allows you to buy things) and a secret number

chiropodist /kɪˈrɒpədɪst/ *UK* (*US* **podiatrist**) *noun* [C] **HEALTH** someone whose job is to treat problems with people's feet

chirp /tʃɜːp/ *verb* [I] If birds or insects chirp, they make short, high sounds. •**chirp** *noun* [C]

chirpy /ˈtʃɜːpi/ *adjective UK informal* happy and active *Why's Ben so chirpy this morning?*

chisel /ˈtʃɪzəl/ *noun* [C] a tool with a sharp end that you use for cutting and shaping wood or stone

chitin /ˈkaɪtɪn/ *noun* [U] **BIOLOGY** a tough substance in the outer protective covering of insects and animals such as lobsters, and in the cell walls of some fungi

chivalrous /ˈʃɪvəlrəs/ *adjective* A chivalrous man behaves very politely towards women. •**chivalry** *noun* [U] polite behaviour towards women

chives /tʃaɪvz/ *noun* [plural] **FOOD** a plant with long, thin leaves used in cooking to give a flavour similar to onions

chloride /ˈklɔːraɪd/ *noun* [C, U] **CHEMISTRY** a chemical compound that is a mixture of chlorine and another substance

chlorine /ˈklɔːriːn/ *noun* [U] **CHEMISTRY** a gas with a strong smell, used to make water safe to drink and swim in (symbol **Cl**) ➲See picture at **sodium chloride**

chlorofluorocarbon /ˌklɔːrəʊˌflɔː.rəʊˈkɑːbən/ *noun* [C, U] **CHEMISTRY** (a) CFC

chlorophyll /ˈklɒrəfɪl/ *noun* [U] **BIOLOGY** the green substance in plants, that allows them to use the energy from the sun for food ➲See picture at **photosynthesis**

chloroplast /ˈklɒrəplɑːst/ *noun* [C] **BIOLOGY** one of the parts in a plant cell that contain chlorophyll (= the green part in plant cells) and where the energy from the sun is turned into food by photosynthesis ➲See picture at **leaf**

O─**chocolate** /ˈtʃɒkᵊlət/ *noun* **1 FOOD** [U] a sweet, brown food that is usually sold in a block *a bar of chocolate* ○ *milk chocolate* ○ *a chocolate cake* **2 FOOD** [C] a small piece of sweet food covered in chocolate *a box of chocolates* **3 FOOD** [C, U] a sweet drink made with chocolate and hot milk

WORD PARTNERS FOR ***choice***

have/make a choice • **give/offer** sb a choice • **a good / informed / obvious / popular / stark/wide/wrong** choice • a choice **between** sth • **by** choice • **have (no)** choice

O─**choice¹** /tʃɔɪs/ *noun* **1** RIGHT [U, no plural] when you can choose between two or more things *If I **had a choice**, I'd give up work.* ○ *He **had no choice** but to accept their offer.* ○ *I'm single **by choice*** (= because I want to be). **2** DECISION [C] the decision to choose one thing or person and not someone or something else *In the past women had to **make a choice between** a career or marriage.* **3** THINGS TO CHOOSE FROM [U, no plural] the things or people you can choose from *The dress is available in a **choice of** colours.* ○ *The evening menu offers **a wide choice of** dishes.* **4** CHOSEN ONE [C] the person or thing that someone has chosen [usually no plural] *Harvard was not his **first choice**.* ○ *The winner got £1000 to give to the charity **of her choice**.* ➲See also: **multiple choice**

choice² /tʃɔɪs/ *adjective* [always before noun] of very good quality *the choicest cuts of meat*

choir /kwaɪəʳ/ *noun* [group] **MUSIC** a group of people who sing together *a school/church choir*

choke¹ /tʃəʊk/ *verb* **1 HEALTH** [I, T] If you choke, or if something chokes you, you stop breathing because something is blocking your throat. *Children can **choke on** peanuts.* **2** [T] (*also* **choke up**) to fill something such as a road or pipe so that nothing can pass through [often passive] *The roads were choked with traffic.*

choke sth back *phrasal verb* to try not to show how angry or upset you are *She ran to the door, choking back the tears.*

choke (sb) up *phrasal verb* to become unable to speak because you are starting to cry *I can't watch that movie without choking up.*

choke² /tʃəʊk/ *noun* [C] a piece of equipment that controls the amount of air going into a car engine

cholera /ˈkɒlᵊrə/ *noun* [U] **HEALTH** a serious disease that affects the stomach and bowels, usually caused by dirty water or food

cholesterol /kəˈlestᵊrɒl/ *noun* [U] **BIOLOGY, HEALTH** a type of fat in your body that can cause heart disease if you have too much

OTHER WAYS OF SAYING ***choose***

The verbs **pick** and **select** are often used when someone chooses someone or something after thinking carefully: *He's been **picked** for the school football team.* • *We've **selected** three candidates.*

In more informal situations, the phrasal verbs **go for**, **opt for**, or **decide on** are sometimes used: *I've **decided on** blue walls for the bathroom.* • *I think I'll **go for** the chocolate cake.* • *Mike's **opted for** early retirement.*

The verbs **opt** and **decide** can also be used when someone chooses to do something: *Most people **opt** to have the operation.* • *I've **decided** to take the job.*

O─**choose** /tʃuːz/ *verb past tense* **chose**, *past participle* **chosen 1** [I, T] to decide which thing you want *I helped my sister choose a name for her baby.* ○ *They have to **choose between** earning a living or getting an education.* ○ *There were lots of books to **choose from**.* [+ question word] *How did you choose which school to go to?* ○ *Adam was **chosen as** team captain.* **2 choose to do sth** to decide to do something *Manuela chose to take a job in Paris.*

choosy /ˈtʃuːzi/ *adjective* difficult to please because of being very exact about what you like *a choosy customer*

chop¹ /tʃɒp/ *verb* **chopping**, *past* **chopped 1** [T] (*also* **chop up**) to cut something into small pieces *Chop an onion finely.* **2 chop and change** *UK informal* to keep changing your opinions, activities, or job

chop sth down *phrasal verb* to cut through something to make it fall down

chop sth off *phrasal verb* to cut off part of something with a sharp tool

chop² /tʃɒp/ *noun* [C] **1 FOOD** a flat piece of meat with a bone in it *a lamb chop* **2** a quick, hard hit with a sharp tool or with the side of your hand

chopper /ˈtʃɒpəʳ/ *noun* [C] **1** AIRCRAFT *informal* a helicopter (= aircraft with turning parts on top) **2** TOOL a heavy tool with a sharp edge for cutting wood, meat, etc

choppy /ˈtʃɒpi/ *adjective* Choppy water has a lot of small waves.

chopsticks /ˈtʃɒpstɪks/ *noun* [plural] **FOOD** thin sticks used for eating food in East Asia

choral /ˈkɔːrᵊl/ *adjective* **MUSIC** Choral music is written for a choir (= group of people who sing).

chord /kɔːd/ *noun* **1 MUSIC** [C] two or more musical notes that are played at the same time **2 MATHEMATICS** a straight line connecting two points on a curve or a curved surface **3 strike**

a chord (with sb) If something strikes a chord with you, you like it or are interested in it because it is connected with your own life or opinions. ➲See also: **vocal cords**

chore /tʃɔːʳ/ *noun* [C] a boring job that you must do *I find cooking a real chore.*

choreograph /ˈkɒriəgrɑːf/ *verb* [T] **1** EVENT to arrange an event or series of events carefully *a carefully choreographed publicity stunt* **2** DANCE to design the dances for a performance •**choreographer** /ˌkɒriˌɒgrəfəʳ/ *noun* [C]

choreography /ˌkɒriˈɒgrəfi/ *noun* [U] the process of designing dances for a performance

choroid /ˈkɔː.rɔɪd/ *noun* [C] **ANATOMY** in the eye, the layer containing blood vessels between the retina and the sclera

chorus¹ /ˈkɔːrəs/ *noun* **1 MUSIC** [C] the part of a song that is repeated several times **2 MUSIC** [group] a large group of people who sing together **3 MUSIC** [group] a group of dancers and singers in a show who do not have the main parts **4 a chorus of approval/demands/protest, etc** something that a lot of people say at the same time

chorus² /ˈkɔːrəs/ *verb* [T] *UK* If two or more people chorus something, they say it at the same time.

chose /tʃəʊz/ *past tense of* choose

chosen /ˈtʃəʊzən/ *past participle of* choose

Christ /kraɪst/ (*also* **Jesus Christ**) *noun* **RELIGION** the Jewish holy man believed by Christians to be the Son of God, and on whose life and teachings Christianity is based

christen /ˈkrɪsᵊn/ *verb* [T] **RELIGION** to give a baby a name at a Christian ceremony and make them a member of the Christian Church [**often passive**] *She's being christened in June.*

christening /ˈkrɪsᵊnɪŋ/ *noun* [C] **RELIGION** a ceremony where someone is christened

Christian /ˈkrɪstʃən/ *noun* [C] **RELIGION** someone who believes in Christianity •**Christian** *adjective*

Christianity /ˌkrɪstiˈænəti/ *noun* [U] **RELIGION** a religion based on belief in God and the life and teachings of Jesus Christ, and on the Bible

ˈChristian ˌname *noun* [C] your first name, not your family name

O━ **Christmas** /ˈkrɪsməs/ *noun* [C, U] **RELIGION** the Christian period of celebration around 25 December, when Christians celebrate the birth of Jesus Christ and people give each other presents, or the day itself *We're going to my mother's for Christmas.* ○ ***Merry Christmas!*** ○ *Christmas dinner* ➲See also: **Father Christmas**

ˈChristmas ˌcard *noun* [C] a decorated card that you send to someone at Christmas

ˌChristmas ˈcarol *UK* (*US* **ˈChristmas ˌcarol**) *noun* [C] **MUSIC** a song that people sing at Christmas

ˌChristmas ˈcracker *noun* [C] a coloured paper tube with a small toy inside, that people in the UK pull open at Christmas

ˌChristmas ˈDay *noun* [C, U] **RELIGION** 25 December, the day on which Christians celebrate the birth of Jesus Christ

ˌChristmas ˈEve *noun* [C, U] **RELIGION** the day before Christmas Day

ˈChristmas ˌtree *noun* [C] a real or artificial tree that people decorate inside their home for Christmas

chromatid /krəʊˈmætɪd/ *noun* [C] **BIOLOGY** either of the parts into which a chromosome divides during mitosis (= when one cell divides into two identical cells)

chromatography /ˌkrəʊməˈtɒgrəfi/ *noun* [U] **CHEMISTRY** a method of finding what separate substances are in a mixture by making it flow, as a liquid or gas, through a material such as paper which different substances pass through at different speeds

chrome /krəʊm/ *noun* [U] a hard, shiny metal that is used to cover objects *chrome bath taps*

chromosome /ˈkrəʊməsəʊm/ *noun* [C] **BIOLOGY** the part of a cell found in the nucleus, that controls what an animal or plant is like •**chromosomal** /krəʊməˈsəʊməl/ *adjective*

chronic /ˈkrɒnɪk/ *adjective* **HEALTH** A chronic illness or problem continues for a long time. *a chronic shortage of nurses* ○ *chronic back pain* •**chronically** *adverb*

chronicle¹ /ˈkrɒnɪkl/ *noun* [C] **LITERATURE** a written record of things that happened in the past

chronicle² /ˈkrɒnɪkl/ *verb* [T] to make a record of something, or give details of something *The book chronicles his life as an actor.*

chronological /ˌkrɒnəˈlɒdʒɪkᵊl/ *adjective* arranged in the order in which events happened •**chronologically** *adverb*

chrysalis /ˈkrɪsəlɪs/ *noun* [C] **BIOLOGY** an insect covered by a hard case at the stage of development before it becomes a moth or butterfly with wings, or the case itself

chubby /ˈtʃʌbi/ *adjective* pleasantly fat *the baby's chubby legs*

chuck /tʃʌk/ *verb* [T] *informal* to throw something *Don't just chuck your coat on the floor!*

chuck sth away/out *phrasal verb informal* to throw something away *I chucked out all my old clothes.*

chuck sth in *phrasal verb UK informal* to stop doing something because it is boring

chuck sb out *phrasal verb informal* to force someone to leave a place *Pierre was chucked out of school for starting a fight.*

chuckle /ˈtʃʌkl/ *verb* [I] to laugh quietly •**chuckle** *noun* [C]

chug /tʃʌg/ *verb* **chugging,** *past* **chugged chug across/along/up, etc** If a vehicle chugs somewhere, it moves slowly, making a low, regular noise with its engine. *a boat chugging across the lake*

chum /tʃʌm/ *noun* [C] *informal* a friend •**chummy** *adjective* friendly

chunk /tʃʌŋk/ *noun* [C] **1** PIECE a large piece of something *a chunk of cheese* ➲See colour picture **Pieces and Quantities** on page Centre 1 **2** PART a large part of something *I spend a big* ***chunk*** *of my money on clothes.*

chunky /ˈtʃʌŋki/ *adjective* **1** PERSON A chunky person is short and heavy. **2** THING big, thick, and heavy *chunky shoes*

WORD PARTNERS FOR *church*

go to church • in church • a church service

O-■**church** /tʃɜːtʃ/ *noun* **1 RELIGION** [C, U] a building where Christians go to worship God *We used to **go to church** every Sunday morning.* **2 RELIGION** [C] (*also* **Church**) one of the different groups that make up the Christian religion *the Anglican Church* ➲See also: **the Catholic Church**

churchgoer /ˈtʃɜːtʃˌgəʊəʳ/ *noun* [C] **RELIGION** someone who goes to church regularly

churchyard /ˈtʃɜːtʃjɑːd/ *noun* [C] the land around a church, often where people are buried

churn[1] /tʃɜːn/ *verb* **1** SURFACE [T] (*also* **churn up**) to mix something, especially liquids, with great force *The sea was churned up by heavy winds.* **2** STOMACH [I] If your stomach is churning, you feel sick, usually because you are nervous. **3 FOOD** [T] to mix milk until it becomes butter
churn sth out *phrasal verb informal* to produce large quantities of something very quickly

churn[2] /tʃɜːn/ *noun* [C] **1 FARMING** a container that you fill with milk and mix to make butter **2 FARMING** *UK* a tall metal container for storing and transporting milk

chute /ʃuːt/ *noun* [C] **1** SLIDE a long thin structure that people or things can slide down *a water chute* **2** FOR FLOATING *informal short for* parachute

chutney /ˈtʃʌtni/ *noun* [U] **FOOD** a mixture of fruit, vegetables, sugar, and vinegar that you eat with meat or cheese

chyme /kaɪm/ *noun* [U] **BIOLOGY** the thick, wet mass of partly digested food that leaves the stomach

the CIA /ˌsiːaɪˈeɪ/ *noun* **POLITICS** *abbreviation for* Central Intelligence Agency: the department of the US government that collects secret information about people and organizations

the CID /ˌsiːaɪˈdiː/ *noun* **LAW** *abbreviation for* Criminal Investigation Department: the part of the British police force that deals with serious crimes

cider /ˈsaɪdəʳ/ *noun* [C, U] **1 FOOD** *UK* a drink made from apples that contains alcohol **2 FOOD** *US* a drink made from apples that contains no alcohol

cigar /sɪˈgɑːʳ/ *noun* [C] a thick tube made from rolled tobacco leaves, that people smoke

O-■**cigarette** /ˌsɪgᵊrˈet/ *noun* [C] a thin tube of paper filled with tobacco, that people smoke

cilantro /sɪˈlæntrəʊ/ *US* (*UK/US* **coriander**) *noun* [U] **FOOD** a herb that is used in cooking

ciliary muscle /ˈsɪliəriˌmʌsl/ *noun* [C] **ANATOMY** one of the muscles around the lens of the eye which are used to change the shape of the lens so that you can see clearly

cilium /ˈsɪliəm/ *noun* [C] *plural* **cilia** **BIOLOGY** one of the very small parts like hairs on the surface of a cell which move regularly and keep the surrounding liquid moving around it or help a organism with only one cell to move

CIM /ˌsiːaɪˈem/ *noun* [U] **COMPUTING** *abbreviation for* computer integrated manufacturing; a method of making goods that is controlled by computers

cinder /ˈsɪndəʳ/ *noun* [C] a small piece of coal, wood, etc that has been burned

O-■**cinema** /ˈsɪnəmə/ *noun* **1** BUILDING [C] *UK* (*US* **movie theater**) a building where you go to watch films **2** ART [U] the art or business of making films *an article about French cinema*

cinnamon /ˈsɪnəmən/ *noun* [U] **FOOD** a brown spice that is used in cooking

circa /ˈsɜːkə/ *formal* (*written abbreviation* **c**) *preposition* used before a date to show that something happened at about that time *Gainsborough's 'The Cottage Door' (circa 1780)*

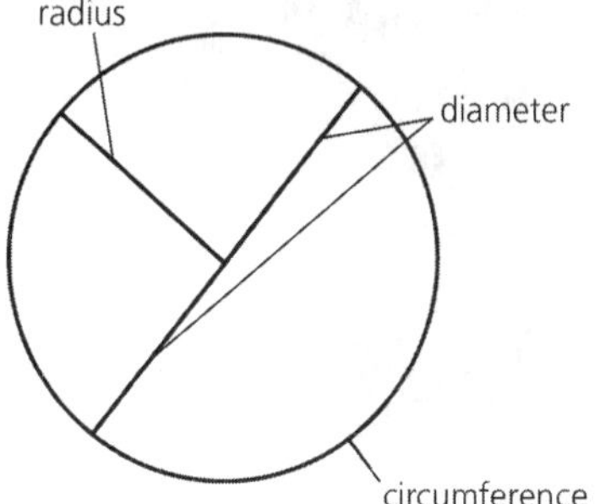

circle

O-■**circle**[1] /ˈsɜːkl/ *noun* **1** SHAPE [C] a round, flat shape like the letter O, or a group of people or things arranged in this shape *We all sat on the floor **in a circle**.* ➲See picture at **shape** **2** GROUP [C] a group of people with family, work, or social connections *a close circle of friends* ○ *It's a technical term used in medical circles.* **3 the circle** *UK* the seats in the upper area of a theatre ➲See also: **inner circle, traffic circle, vicious circle**

circle[2] /ˈsɜːkl/ *verb* **1** MOVE [I, T] to move in a circle, often around something *Birds circled above the trees.* **2** DRAW [T] to draw a circle around something *Circle the answer you think is correct.*

circuit /ˈsɜːkɪt/ *noun* [C] **1 SPORT** a path, route, or sports track that is shaped like a circle **2 PHYSICS** a complete circle that an electric current travels around **3** EVENTS a regular series of places or events that people involved in a particular activity go to [**usually singular**] *the tennis circuit* ➲See also: **short-circuit**

circular[1] /ˈsɜːkjələʳ/ *adjective* **1** CIRCLE shaped like a circle *a circular rug* **2** JOURNEY A circular journey takes you around in a circle, back to the place where you started. *a circular walk*

circular[2] /ˈsɜːkjələʳ/ *noun* [C] a letter or advertisement that is sent to a lot of people at the same time

circulate /ˈsɜːkjəleɪt/ *verb* **1** INFORMATION [I] If information circulates, a lot of people hear about it. ***Rumours are circulating** that the mayor is going to resign.* **2** SEND INFORMATION [T] to give or send information to a group of people *A copy of the report was circulated to each director.* **3** MOVE [**I, T**] to move around or through something, or to make something move around or through something *Hot water circulates through the pipes.*

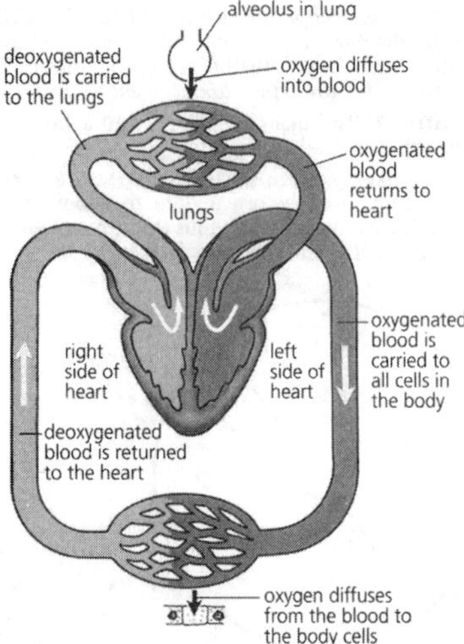

circulation

circulation /ˌsɜːkjəˈleɪʃən/ *noun* **1** **ANATOMY, BIOLOGY** [**U**] the movement of blood around your body *Exercise improves your circulation.* **2** INFORMATION [**U**] when something such as information, money, or goods pass from one person to another *Police have warned there are a lot of fake £50 notes* ***in circulation.*** **3** NEWSPAPERS [**no plural**] the number of copies of a newspaper or magazine that are sold each day, week, etc

circuˈlatory ˌsystem /ˌsɜːkjəˈleɪtəri ˌsistəm (UK) ˈsɜːkjələtɔːri sistəm (US)/ *noun* [**C**] **ANATOMY, BIOLOGY** the parts of the body that are involved in sending blood around it

circumcize (*also UK* **-ise**) /ˈsɜːkəmsaɪz/ *verb* [**T**] to cut off the skin at the end of a boy's or man's penis, or cut off part of a girl's sex organs •**circumcision** /ˌsɜːkəmˈsɪʒən/ *noun* [**C, U**] when someone is circumcised

circumference /səˈkʌmfərəns/ *noun* [**C, U**] **MATHEMATICS** the distance around the edge of a circle or round object *The lake is 250km* ***in circumference.*** ➲See picture at **circle**

circumflex /ˈsɜːkəmfleks/ *noun* [**C**] **LANGUAGE** a sign (^) over a letter, especially a vowel, in some languages

circumspect /ˈsɜːkəmspekt/ *adjective formal* careful about things you do or say

WORD PARTNERS FOR ***circumstances***

in/under [any/certain/difficult/normal, etc] circumstances • **in/under** the circumstances • the circumstances **of/surrounding** sth • **exceptional/normal/unforeseen** circumstances

circumstances /ˈsɜːkəmstænsɪz/ *noun* [**plural**] **1** facts or events that make a situation the way it is *I think they coped very well* ***under the circumstances.*** ○ *We oppose capital punishment* ***in/under*** *any* ***circumstances.*** **2 under no circumstances** used to say that something must never happen *Under no circumstances should you approach the man.*

circumstantial /ˌsɜːkəmˈstænʃəl/ *adjective* **circumstantial evidence LAW** information about a crime that makes you believe that something is true, but does not prove it

circumvent /ˌsɜːkəmˈvent/ *verb* [**T**] *formal* to find a way of avoiding something, especially a law or rule

circus /ˈsɜːkəs/ *noun* [**C**] a show in which a group of people and animals perform in a large tent

cirrhosis /sɪˈrəʊsɪs/ *noun* [**U**] **HEALTH** a serious disease of the liver, often caused by drinking too much alcohol

cirrostratus /ˌsɪrəʊˈstrɑːtəs/ ⓤⓢ /-ˈstreɪ-/ *noun* [**U**] **GEOGRAPHY** a type of flat white cloud formed in a very thin layer and seen high in the sky ➲See picture at **cloud**

cirrus /ˈsɪrəs/ *noun* [**U**] **GEOGRAPHY** a type of thin cloud that is very high up and is made of small pieces of ice ➲See picture at **cloud**

cistern /ˈsɪstən/ *noun* [**C**] a large container to store water, especially one that supplies water to a toilet ➲See colour picture **The Bathroom** on page Centre 3

citadel /ˈsɪtədəl/ *noun* [**C**] a strong castle that was used in the past to protect people when their city was attacked

cite /saɪt/ *verb* [**T**] *formal* **1** to mention something as an example or proof of something else *The doctor cited the case of a woman who had died after taking the drug.* **2 LAW** *US* to order someone to go to court because they have done something wrong [**often passive**] *A local farmer was* ***cited for*** *breaking environmental standards.*

WORD PARTNERS FOR ***citizen***

a citizen **of** [Paris/Tokyo, etc] • your **fellow** citizens • **decent/law-abiding** citizens

citizen /ˈsɪtɪzən/ *noun* [**C**] **SOCIETY** **1** someone who lives in a particular town or city *the citizens of Berlin* **2** someone who has a legal right to live in a particular country *My husband became a British citizen in 1984.* ➲See also: **senior citizen**

citizenship /ˈsɪtɪzənʃɪp/ *noun* [**U**] the legal right to be a citizen of a particular country *British/French citizenship*

citrus fruit /ˈsɪtrəsˌfruːt/ *noun* [**C, U**] **FOOD** an orange, lemon, or similar fruit

O-ᵯ**city** /ˈsɪti/ *noun* **1** [**C**] a large town *the city of Boston* ○ *the* ***city centre*** **2 the City** *UK* the part of London where the large financial organizations have their offices ➲See also: **inner city**

civic /ˈsɪvɪk/ *adjective* [**always before noun**] **POLITICS, SOCIETY** relating to a city or town and the people who live there ***civic leaders*** ○ *The opera house was a source of great* ***civic pride*** (= people in the city were proud of it).

civil /ˈsɪvᵊl/ *adjective* **1** SOCIETY **[always before noun]** relating to the ordinary people or things in a country and not to military or religious organizations *They married in a* ***civil ceremony.*** **2** LAW **[always before noun]** relating to private arguments between people and not criminal cases *a* ***civil court*** **3** polite in a formal way *He and his ex-wife can't even have a civil conversation.*

ˌcivil engiˈneering *noun* [U] the planning and building of roads, bridges, and public buildings

civilian /sɪˈvɪliən/ *noun* [C] SOCIETY someone who is not a member of a military organization or the police

civility /sɪˈvɪləti/ *noun* [U] polite behaviour

civilization (*also UK* **-isation**) /ˌsɪvᵊlaɪˈzeɪʃᵊn/ *noun* **1** SOCIETY [C, U] human society with its developed social organizations, or the culture and way of life of a society at a particular period of time *ancient civilizations* ○ *Nuclear war could mean the end of civilization.* **2** [U] when people have an advanced and comfortable way of life *modern civilization*

civilize (*also UK* **-ise**) /ˈsɪvᵊlaɪz/ *verb* [T] to educate a society so that it becomes more advanced and organized

civilized (*also UK* **-ised**) /ˈsɪvəlaɪzd/ *adjective* **1** [SOCIETY] A civilized society is advanced and has well-developed laws and customs. *A fair justice system is an important part of* ***civilized society.*** **2** [POLITE] polite and calm *Let's discuss this in a civilized manner.*

ˌcivil ˈliberties *noun* [plural] SOCIETY the freedom people have to do, think, and say what they want

ˌcivil ˈpartnership *noun* [C, U] in Britain, a legal relationship between two people of the same sex, which gives them the same rights as people who are married

ˌcivil ˈrights *noun* [plural] SOCIETY the rights that everyone in a country has

ˌcivil ˈservant *noun* [C] POLITICS someone who works in the Civil Service

the ˌCivil ˈService *noun* POLITICS the government departments and the people who work in them

ˌcivil ˈwar *noun* [C, U] a war between groups of people who live in the same country

cl MEASURES *written abbreviation for* centilitre (= a unit for measuring liquid) *a 75 cl bottle of wine*

clad /klæd/ *adjective literary* covered or dressed in something *He came to the door clad only in a towel.*

O-■ **claim¹** /kleɪm/ *verb* **1** [SAY] [T] to say that something is true, although you have not proved it [+ **(that)**] *She claimed that the dog attacked her.* [+ **to do sth**] *He claims to have seen a ghost.* **2 claim credit/responsibility/success, etc** to say that you have done or achieved something *No one has claimed responsibility for yesterday's bomb attack.* ➲Opposite **disclaim 3** [DEMAND] [I, T] to ask for something because it belongs to you or you have the right to have it *She claimed $2,500 in travel expenses.* ○ *If no one claims the watch, then you can keep it.* **4** [KILL] [T] If an accident, war, etc claims lives, people are killed because of it. *The floods claimed over 200 lives.*

WORD PARTNERS FOR ***claim***

make a claim • **deny/dismiss/reject** a claim • a **false** claim • a claim **by** sb

O-■ **claim²** /kleɪm/ *noun* [C] **1** [ANNOUNCEMENT] when someone says that something is true, although it has not been proved [+ **(that)**] *She* ***rejected claims*** *that she had lied.* **2** [DEMAND] an official demand for something you think you have a right to *a* ***claim for*** *compensation* **3** [RIGHT] a right to have something *You don't have any* ***claim to*** *the land.* **4 lay claim to sth** *formal* to say that something is yours or that you have done something **5 sb's/sth's claim to fame** a reason why someone or something is known *My main claim to fame is meeting the President.*

clam¹ /klæm/ *noun* [C] FOOD a small sea creature with a shell in two parts, that you can eat

clam² /klæm/ *verb* **clamming,** *past* **clammed**
clam up *phrasal verb informal* to suddenly stop talking, usually because you are embarrassed or nervous

clamber /ˈklæmbəʳ/ *verb* **clamber into/over/up, etc** to climb somewhere with difficulty, especially using your hands and feet *The children clambered into the boat.*

clammy /ˈklæmi/ *adjective* unpleasantly wet and sticky *clammy hands*

clamour¹ *UK* (*US* **clamor**) /ˈklæməʳ/ *verb* **clamour for sth; clamour to do sth** to ask for something continuously in a loud or angry way *Fans were clamouring for their autographs.*

clamour² *UK* (*US* **clamor**) /ˈklæməʳ/ *noun* [no plural] **1** [DEMAND] a demand for something, or a complaint about something that is made by a lot of people *the* ***public's clamour*** *for organic food* **2** [NOISE] a loud, continuous noise made by people talking or shouting *We heard the clamour of voices in the street outside.*

clamp¹ /klæmp/ *noun* [C] **1** DT a piece of equipment that is used for holding things together tightly **2** [CAR] *UK* a metal cover that is put on the wheel of a car so you cannot move it if you have parked in an illegal place

clamp² /klæmp/ *verb* **1 clamp sth around/over/to, etc** to put something in a particular position and hold it there tightly *He clamped his hand over her mouth.* **2 clamp sth onto/to/together, etc** to fasten two things together using a clamp **3** [T] *UK* to fasten a metal cover on the wheel of a car to stop it moving because it has been parked in an illegal place
clamp down *phrasal verb* to do something strict to try to stop or limit an activity *Local police have* ***clamped down on*** *teenage drinking.*

clampdown /ˈklæmpdaʊn/ *noun* [C] a strict attempt to stop or limit an activity [**usually singular**] *a* ***clampdown on*** *inner city pollution*

clan /klæn/ *noun* [C] SOCIETY a large group of families who are all related to each other, especially in Scotland

clandestine /klænˈdestɪn/ *adjective formal* secret and often illegal *a* ***clandestine meeting***

C

clang /klæŋ/ *verb* [I, T] If something metal clangs, it makes a loud ringing sound, or if you clang it, you make it do this. *The gate clanged shut behind me.* •**clang** *noun* [C]

clank /klæŋk/ *verb* [I] If metal objects clank, they make a low noise when they hit each other. *The bracelets on her arm clanked as she moved.* •**clank** *noun* [C]

clap¹ /klæp/ *verb* **clapping**, *past* **clapped** **1** [HANDS] [I, T] to hit your hands together, often repeatedly, especially in order to show that you enjoyed a performance *The crowd clapped and cheered for more.* **2 clap sb on the back/shoulder** to hit someone on the back or shoulder in a friendly way **3** [PUT] [T] to put something somewhere suddenly *She clapped her hands over her ears and refused to listen.*

clap² /klæp/ *noun* **1** [**no plural**] when you hit your hands together, often repeatedly *Let's give our winning contestant **a big clap**.* **2 a clap of thunder** a sudden, loud sound that is made by thunder

claret /ˈklærət/ *noun* [U] *UK* **FOOD** red wine from the area of France around Bordeaux

clarify /ˈklærɪfaɪ/ *verb* [T] to make something easier to understand by explaining it *The law aims to clarify building regulations.* •**clarification** /ˌklærɪfɪˈkeɪʃən/ *noun* [C, U]

clarinet /ˌklærɪˈnet/ *noun* [C] **MUSIC** a musical instrument like a long, black tube, that you play by blowing into it and pressing metal keys

clarity /ˈklærəti/ *noun* [U] the quality of being clear and easy to understand

clash¹ /klæʃ/ *verb* **1** [FIGHT] [I] to fight or argue *Government troops **clashed with** rebel soldiers.* ○ *Many young people **clash** with their parents **over** what time they must be home at night.* **2** [COLOUR] [I] If colours or styles clash, they do not look good together. *You can't wear pink lipstick - it **clashes with** your dress.* **3** [EVENT] [I] *UK* If two events clash, they happen at the same time so that you cannot go to them both. *Emma's party **clashes with** my brother's wedding.* **4** [NOISE] [I, T] to make a loud noise by hitting metal objects together

WORD PARTNERS FOR *clash*

be **involved in** a clash • **fierce/violent** clashes • clashes **between** sb and sb • a clash **with** sb • a clash **over** sth

clash² /klæʃ/ *noun* [C] **1** [FIGHT] a fight or argument *There were violent **clashes between** the police and demonstrators.* **2** [DIFFERENCE] when ideas or qualities are very different, and this causes problems *a clash of personalities* **3** [SOUND] a loud sound that is made when metal objects hit each other *the clash of pans in the sink*

clasp¹ /klɑːsp/ *verb* [T] to hold something or someone tightly *He clasped his daughter in his arms.*

clasp² /klɑːsp/ *noun* **1** [METAL OBJECT] [C] a small metal object that is used to fasten a bag, belt, or piece of jewellery **2** [HOLD] [**no plural**] a tight hold

O‒ **class¹** /klɑːs/ *noun* **1 EDUCATION** [C] a group of students who have lessons together *Katie and Sarah are in the same class at school.* **2 EDUCATION** [C, U] a period of time in which students are taught something *My first class starts at 8.30.* ○ *He was told off for talking **in class*** (= during the lesson). **3 SOCIETY** [C, U] one of the groups in a society with the same social and economic position, or the system of dividing people into these groups *She's from a working-class background.* **4** [QUALITY] [C] a group into which people or things are put according to their quality *When it comes to mathematics, he's in a different class to his peers.* ○ *second-class mail* **5** [SIMILARITY] [C] a group of similar or related things, especially plants and animals **6** [STYLE] [U] *informal* the quality of being stylish or fashionable *a player with real class* ⊃See also: **middle class, upper class, working class**

COMMON LEARNER ERROR

class or classroom?

A **class** is a group of students who have lessons together.

The whole class arrived late.

A **classroom** is a room where lessons happen.

There is a TV and video in every classroom.

class² /klɑːs/ *verb* **class sb/sth as sth** to put someone or something in a particular group according to their qualities *The tower is **classed as** a historic monument.*

classic¹ /ˈklæsɪk/ *adjective* **1** [POPULAR] A classic book, film, etc is one that has been popular for a long time and is considered to be of a high quality. *the classic film 'Gone with the Wind'* **2** [TRADITIONAL] having a traditional style that is always fashionable *a classic black jacket* **3** [TYPICAL] typical

classic² /ˈklæsɪk/ *noun* [C] **LITERATURE** a classic book, film, etc

classical /ˈklæsɪkəl/ *adjective* **1 classical music MUSIC** serious music by people like Mozart and Stravinsky *Do you prefer classical music or pop music?* **2** [TRADITIONAL] traditional in style *classical and modern dance* **3** [GREECE/ROME] relating to ancient Greece and Rome *classical literature*

classically /ˈklæsɪkəli/ *adverb* **1** [TRADITIONAL] in a traditional style *a **classically trained** actor* **2** [TYPICAL] in a typical style *a classically English tea room*

classics /ˈklæsɪks/ *noun* [U] **EDUCATION** the study of ancient Greece and Rome, especially the language, literature, and history

classification /ˌklæsɪfɪˈkeɪʃən/ *noun* [C, U] the process of putting people or things into groups by their type, size, etc, or one of these groups *the classification of plants*

classified /ˈklæsɪfaɪd/ *adjective* Classified information is officially kept secret by a government. ***classified documents/information***

ˌclassified ˈad *noun* [C] a small advertisement that you put in a newspaper if you want to buy or sell something

classify /ˈklæsɪfaɪ/ *verb* [T] to put people or things into groups by their type, size, etc [**often passive**] *A third of the population has been* ***classified as*** *poor.* ○ *The books are* ***classified by*** *subject.*

classmate /ˈklɑːsmeɪt/ *noun* [C] **EDUCATION** someone who is in your class at school or college

O-- **classroom** /ˈklɑːsruːm/ *noun* [C] **EDUCATION** a room in a school where students have lessons ➲See colour picture **The Classroom** on page Centre 6

classy /ˈklɑːsi/ *adjective informal* stylish and fashionable

clatter /ˈklætəʳ/ *verb* **1** [I] If something clatters, it makes a lot of noise when it hits something hard. **2 clatter about/around/down, etc** to move somewhere in a very noisy way *I could hear Sue clattering about upstairs.* •**clatter** *noun* [**no plural**] *He dropped his spoon* ***with a clatter***.

clause /klɔːz/ *noun* [C] **1 LAW** a part of a legal document *a clause in a contract* **2 LANGUAGE** a group of words containing a subject and a verb, that is usually only part of a sentence ➲See also: **relative clause, subordinate clause**

claustrophobia /ˌklɒstrəˈfəʊbiə/ *noun* [U] **HEALTH** fear of being in a small or crowded place

claustrophobic /ˌklɒstrəˈfəʊbɪk/ *adjective* **1 HEALTH** feeling very anxious when you are in a small or crowded place **2** PLACE A claustrophobic place makes you feel anxious because it is very small or crowded. *a claustrophobic room*

clavicle /ˈklævɪkəl/ *noun* [C] **ANATOMY** a bone between the base of the neck and the shoulder; collarbone

claw¹ /klɔː/ *noun* [C] **BIOLOGY** one of the sharp, curved nails on the feet of some animals and birds

claw² /klɔː/ *verb* [I, T] If a person or animal claws something, they try to get hold of it or damage it with their nails or claws. *He* ***clawed at*** *the rope, trying to free himself.*

claw sth back *phrasal verb mainly UK* to try to get back something that you had before *The party is desperately trying to claw back support.*

clay /kleɪ/ *noun* [U] **GEOLOGY** a type of heavy soil that becomes hard when dry, used for making things such as bricks and containers *a clay pot*

O-- **clean¹** /kliːn/ *adjective* **1** NOT DIRTY not dirty *clean hands* ○ *clean clothes* **2** NO SEX not about sex *a clean joke* **3** NO CRIME showing that you have not done anything illegal *a* ***clean driving licence*** **4** FAIR fair and honest *a clean election/fight* **5 come clean** *informal* to tell the truth about something that you have been keeping secret

O-- **clean²** /kliːn/ *verb* [I, T] to remove the dirt from something *I spent the morning cleaning the house.* ➲See also: **dry clean, spring clean**

clean sth out *phrasal verb* **1** CLEAN to take everything out of a room, car, container, etc and clean the inside of it **2** STEAL *informal* to steal everything from a place

clean (sb/sth) up *phrasal verb* to make a person or place clean and tidy *We have to clean up before we leave.*

clean³ /kliːn/ *adverb informal* used to emphasize that something is done completely *The bullet went clean through his helmet.*

clean-cut /ˌkliːnˈkʌt/ *adjective* Someone who is clean-cut has a tidy appearance.

cleaner /ˈkliːnəʳ/ *noun* **1** PERSON [C] someone whose job is to clean houses, offices, public places, etc **2** SUBSTANCE [C, U] a substance used for cleaning things *carpet/oven cleaner* **3 the cleaner's** a shop where clothes are cleaned with chemicals ➲See also: **vacuum cleaner**

cleanliness /ˈklenlɪnəs/ *noun* [U] the state of being clean, or the practice of keeping things clean

cleanly /ˈkliːnli/ *adverb* in a quick and tidy way *The branch broke cleanly away from the tree.*

cleanse /klenz/ *verb* [T] to clean your face or an injured part of your body

cleanser /ˈklenzəʳ/ *noun* [C, U] a substance for cleaning, especially your face

O-- **clear¹** /klɪəʳ/ *adjective* **1** UNDERSTAND easy to understand *clear instructions* **2** HEAR/SEE easy to hear, read, or see *These photos are very clear.* ○ *Can we make the sound any clearer?* **3** NO DOUBT not possible to doubt *The evidence against him was clear.* [+ **(that)**] *It was clear that Leif was angry.* ○ *Ella* ***made it clear that*** *she didn't like James.* **4** CERTAIN [**never before noun**] certain about something *Are you clear about how to get there?* [+ **question word**] *I'm not very clear why she phoned.* **5** NOT BLOCKED not covered or blocked by anything *a clear road* ○ *a clear desk* **6** WITHOUT CLOUDS A clear sky does not have any clouds. **7** TRANSPARENT easy to see through *clear water* ○ *clear glass* ➲See also: the **coast¹** is clear, **crystal clear**

clear² /klɪəʳ/ *verb* **1** EMPTY [T] to remove all the objects or people from a place *clear a room/shelf* ○ *Police cleared the building because of a bomb threat.* **2** WEATHER [I] If the sky or weather clears, the clouds and rain disappear. **3** NOT GUILTY [T] to prove that someone is not guilty of something that they were accused of *The jury* ***cleared*** *him* ***of*** *murder.* **4 FINANCE** [I] If a cheque (= printed paper used to pay for things) clears, the money goes from one person's bank account to another person's bank account. **5** GO OVER [T] to jump over something without touching it *The horse easily cleared the fence.* **6** GIVE PERMISSION [T] to give or get permission to do something *You have to* ***clear it with*** *the headteacher if you want a day off school.* ➲See also: clear the **air¹**

clear sth away *phrasal verb* to make a place tidy by removing things from it, or putting them where they should be *The children are not very good at clearing away their toys.*

clear off *phrasal verb UK informal* used to tell someone to go away immediately

clear sth out *phrasal verb* to tidy a place by getting rid of things that you do not want

clear (sth) up *phrasal verb* **1** MAKE TIDY *mainly UK* to make a place tidy by removing things from it or putting them where they should be *Dad was clearing up in the kitchen.* **2** GET BETTER to make an illness better *Antibiotics*

will clear up the infection.
clear sth up *phrasal verb* to give an explanation for something, or to deal with a problem or argument *Before we sign the contract, there are a few points we should clear up.*
clear up *phrasal verb informal* If the weather clears up, the cloud and rain disappears.

C

clear³ /klɪəʳ/ *adverb* **1** away from something so that you are not touching it *Stand **clear of** the doors, please.* **2 steer clear of sb/sth** to avoid someone or something because they are unpleasant or dangerous

clear⁴ /klɪəʳ/ *noun* **in the clear a** not responsible for a mistake or crime **b** *UK* not in a difficult situation or having problems any more

clearance /ˈklɪərᵊns/ *noun* [C, U] **1** PERMISSION permission from someone in authority *The company needs to get government clearance for the deal.* **2** DISTANCE the distance that is needed for one thing to avoid touching another thing **3** REMOVING THINGS when waste or things you do not want are removed from a place

clear-cut /ˌklɪəˈkʌt/ *adjective* very certain or obvious *The issue is not very clear-cut.*

clearing /ˈklɪərɪŋ/ *noun* [C] a small area in the middle of a forest, where there are no trees

clearly /ˈklɪəli/ *adverb* **1** EASY in a way that is easy to see, hear, read, or understand *He spoke very clearly.* **2** CERTAIN used to show that you think something is obvious or certain *Clearly he's very talented.* **3** NOT CONFUSED If you think clearly, you are not confused.

cleavage /ˈkliːvɪdʒ/ *noun* [C, U] the area between a woman's breasts

cleaver /ˈkliːvəʳ/ *noun* [C] a heavy knife with a large, square blade *a **meat cleaver***

clef /klef/ *noun* [C] **MUSIC** a sign written at the beginning of a line of music, that shows how high or low the notes are

clemency /ˈklemənsi/ *noun* [U] *formal* **LAW** when a judge, king, etc decides not to punish someone severely although they have committed a crime

clench /klenʃ/ *verb* [T] to close your hands or teeth very tightly, or to hold something tightly *Dan **clenched his fists**.*

clergy /ˈklɜːdʒi/ *noun* [plural] **RELIGION** priests or religious leaders *a member of the clergy*

clergyman /ˈklɜːdʒɪmən/ *noun* [C] *plural* **clergymen** **RELIGION** a man who is a member of the clergy

cleric /ˈklerɪk/ *noun* [C] **RELIGION** a member of the clergy

clerical /ˈklerɪkᵊl/ *adjective* **1** relating to work done in an office *a clerical assistant* **2** **RELIGION** relating to priests or religious leaders

clerk /klɑːk/ (US) /klɜːrk/ *noun* [C] **1** OFFICE someone who works in an office or bank, keeping records and doing general office work *a bank clerk* **2** SHOP *US* someone who sells things in a shop *a store/sales clerk*

OTHER WAYS OF SAYING *clever*

The adjectives **intelligent** and **smart** are common alternatives to 'clever': *She's a highly **intelligent** woman.* • *He's one of the **smartest** kids in the class.*

Young people who are clever are sometimes described as **bright**: *Jacob was a very **bright** boy.*

The adjective **brainy** is used in informal contexts, especially by young people when describing other young people: *Ask Louisa to help you - she's really **brainy**.*

Someone who is extremely clever is sometimes described as **brilliant** or **gifted**: *William was a **brilliant/gifted** scholar.*

clever /ˈklevəʳ/ *adjective* **1** INTELLIGENT able to learn and understand things quickly and easily *a clever student* **2** EFFECTIVE designed in an effective and intelligent way *a clever idea* ○ *a clever tool* •**cleverly** *adverb a cleverly designed toy* •**cleverness** *noun* [U]

cliché /ˈkliːʃeɪ/ (US) /kliːˈʃeɪ/ *noun* [C] **LANGUAGE** something that people have said or done so much that it has become boring or has no real meaning

click¹ /klɪk/ *verb* **1** SOUND [I, T] to make a short, sharp sound, or to use something to make this sound *The door clicked shut behind him.* **2** **COMPUTING** [I, T] to press on part of a computer mouse (= small computer control) to make the computer do something *To start the program, **click on** its icon.* **3** PEOPLE [I] *informal* If two people click, they like each other immediately. **4** IDEA [I] *informal* to suddenly understand something *Suddenly everything clicked and I realized where I'd met him.* ➲See also: **double-click**, snap your fingers (**finger¹**)

click² /klɪk/ *noun* [C] a short, sharp sound *the click of a switch*

client /klaɪənt/ *noun* [C] someone who pays someone else for services or advice

clientele /ˌkliːɒnˈtel/ *noun* [group, no plural] the regular customers of a business *The new bar aims to attract a younger clientele.*

client-server /ˌklaɪəntˈsɜːvər/ *adjective* [always before noun] **COMPUTING** using or consisting of several computers which are connected to a server (= large central computer) from which they get information *client-server applications*

cliff

cliff /klɪf/ *noun* [C] **GEOGRAPHY** an area of high, steep rocks beside the sea

climactic /klaɪˈmæktɪk/ *adjective* [always before noun] *literary* A climactic event or time is one in which important or exciting things happen.

WORD PARTNERS FOR *climate*

create a climate of [fear/trust, etc] • **in a** climate • **in the current/in the present** climate • the **political/social** climate

climate /ˈklaɪmət/ *noun* **1** [C, U] **GEOGRAPHY, ENVIRONMENT** the weather conditions that an area usually has *a hot, dry climate* **2** SITUATION [C] the situation, feelings, and opinions that exist at a particular time [usually singular] *the **political/social climate*** ○ *Terrorism **creates a climate of** fear.*

ˈclimate ˌchange *noun* [C, U] **ENVIRONMENT** the way the Earth's weather is changing

climatic /klaɪˈmætɪk/ *adjective formal* **GEOGRAPHY** relating to the weather conditions that an area usually has ***climatic change***

WORD PARTNERS FOR *climax*

build up to/come to/reach a climax • a **dramatic/exciting/fitting/thrilling** climax • the climax **of** sth

climax[1] /ˈklaɪmæks/ *noun* [C] the most exciting or important part of something [usually singular] *The **climax of** her career was winning a gold medal.* ➲Opposite **anticlimax**

climax[2] /ˈklaɪmæks/ *verb* [I, T] to reach the most important or exciting part *The festival **climaxed with/in** a huge fireworks display.*

O⁻**climb** /klaɪm/ *verb* **1** PERSON [I, T] (*also* **climb up**) to go up something, or onto the top of something ***climb a ladder/tree/mountain*** ○ *He climbed up on a chair to change the light bulb.* **2 climb into/out of/through, etc** to move somewhere using your hands and legs *The child climbed into the back of the car.* **3** NUMBER [I] If a price, number, or amount climbs, it increases. *Profits climbed 11% last quarter.* **4** MOVE HIGHER [I] to move to a higher position *The road climbs quite steeply.* •**climb** *noun* [C] *a long/steep/uphill climb*

climb down *phrasal verb UK informal* to change your opinion or admit that you are wrong *The government has been forced to **climb down over** the issue of increased taxes.*

climbdown /ˈklaɪmdaʊn/ *noun* [C] *UK* when someone admits that they were wrong about something or have changed their opinion *an embarrassing climbdown by the government*

climber /ˈklaɪməʳ/ *noun* [C] **SPORT** someone who climbs mountains, hills, or rocks as a sport

climbing /ˈklaɪmɪŋ/ *noun* [U] **SPORT** the sport of climbing mountains, hills, or rocks ***rock/mountain climbing*** ○ *climbing boots*

clinch /klɪnʃ/ *verb* [T] *informal* **1** to finally get or win something ***clinch a deal*** **2 clinch it** *informal* to make someone finally decide what to do *When he said the job was in Paris, that clinched it for me.*

cling /klɪŋ/ *verb* [I] *past* **clung** **1** HOLD TIGHT to hold someone or something tightly, especially because you are frightened *She was found **clinging to** the ledge.* ○ *I **clung on to** his hand in the dark.* **2** STICK to stick to something *His damp hair **clung to** his forehead.*

cling (on) to sth *phrasal verb* to try very hard to keep something *He clung on to power for ten more years.*

cling to sth *phrasal verb* to refuse to stop believing or hoping for something *He **clung to the belief** that his family were alive.*

clingfilm /ˈklɪŋfɪlm/ *UK trademark* (*US* **plastic wrap**) *noun* [U] thin, transparent plastic used for wrapping or covering food

clingy /ˈklɪŋi/ *adjective mainly UK* always wanting to be with someone and not wanting to do things alone *a clingy child*

clinic /ˈklɪnɪk/ *noun* [C] **HEALTH** a place where people go for medical treatment or advice *an eye/skin clinic*

clinical /ˈklɪnɪkəl/ *adjective* **1 HEALTH** [always before noun] relating to medical treatment and tests ***clinical trials/research*** **2** only considering facts and not influenced by feelings or emotions *a clinical approach/attitude* •**clinically** *adverb*

clinician /klɪˈnɪʃən/ *noun* [C] **HEALTH** a doctor who treats ill people and does not just study diseases

clink /klɪŋk/ *verb* [I, T] If pieces of glass or metal clink, they make a short ringing sound when they touch, and if you clink them, you make them do this. •**clink** *noun* [C]

clip[1] /klɪp/ *noun* [C] **1** FASTEN a small metal or plastic object used for holding things together **2** FILM a short part of a film or television programme that is shown at a different time *They showed clips from Spielberg's new movie.* **3 a clip round the ear/earhole** *UK informal* a quick hit on the side of someone's head ➲See also: **paper clip**

clip[2] /klɪp/ *verb* **clipping**, *past* **clipped** **1** FASTEN [I, T] to fasten things together with a clip, or to be fastened in this way ***Clip** the microphone **to** the collar of your jacket.* **2** CUT [T] to cut small pieces from something *Jamie was outside clipping the hedge.* **3** HIT [T] to hit something quickly and lightly *The plane clipped a telephone line and crashed.*

clipart /ˈklɪpɑːt/ *noun* [U] **COMPUTING** small pictures which are stored on a computer and can be easily added to a document

clipboard /ˈklɪpbɔːd/ *noun* [C] **1** a board with a clip at the top that holds paper in position for writing on **2 COMPUTING** an area for storing information in a computer when you are moving it from one document to another

clipped /klɪpt/ *adjective* If someone speaks in a clipped voice, their words sound quick, short, and not friendly.

clippers /ˈklɪpəz/ *noun* [plural] a tool used to cut small pieces off something *hedge clippers*

clipping /ˈklɪpɪŋ/ *noun* [C] **1** NEWSPAPER/MAGAZINE (*also UK* **cutting**) an article or picture that has been cut out of a newspaper or magazine *a collection of **newspaper clippings** about the princess* **2** SMALL PIECE a small piece that has been cut off something [usually plural] *grass clippings*

clique /kliːk/ *noun* [C] a small group of people who spend a lot of time together and are unfriendly to people who are not in the group

cloak /kləʊk/ *noun* **1** [C] a loose coat without sleeves that hangs down from your shoulders **2 a cloak of sth** *literary* something that is intended to cover or hide the truth of something else *a cloak of secrecy/mystery*

cloakroom /'kləʊkru:m/ *noun* [C] **1** COATS a room where you leave your coat at a theatre, school, etc **2** TOILET *UK old-fashioned* a toilet in a public building

C

clobber /'klɒbəʳ/ *verb* [T] *informal* **1** HIT to hit someone **2** AFFECT to affect someone very badly *a policy that has clobbered people on low incomes*

O-■ **clock¹** /klɒk/ *noun* [C] **1** TIME a piece of equipment that shows you what time it is, usually in a house or on a building *She could hear the hall clock ticking.* ➲See colour picture **The Living Room** on page Centre 4 **2** VEHICLE *UK* a piece of equipment in a vehicle for measuring how far it has travelled *a car with 63,000 kilometres* ***on the clock*** **3 around/round the clock** all day and all night *Rescue teams are* ***working round the clock*** *to search for survivors of the earthquake.* **4 race/work against the clock** to do something as fast as you can in order to finish before a particular time **5 turn/put the clock back** *UK* to make a situation the same as it was at an earlier time ➲See also: **alarm clock, grandfather clock**

clock² /klɒk/ *verb*

clock sth up *phrasal verb* to achieve a particular number or amount of something *Yuri has clocked up 5,500 flying hours.*

clockwise anti-clockwise *UK*, counterclockwise *US*

clockwise

clockwise /'klɒkwaɪz/ *adjective, adverb* in the same direction as the hands (= parts that point to the numbers) on a clock move ➲Opposite **anti-clockwise** *UK*, **counterclockwise** *US*

clockwork /'klɒkwɜ:k/ *noun* **1** [U] a system of machinery that starts when you turn a handle or key *a* ***clockwork toy*** **2 (as) regular as clockwork** extremely regularly *The bell rang at 8 a.m., regular as clockwork.* **3 run/go like clockwork** to happen exactly as planned, with no problems

clog /klɒg/ (*also* **clog up**) *verb* [I, T] **clogging**, *past* **clogged** to fill something so that nothing can pass through it, or to be filled in this way [**often passive**] *The plughole was* ***clogged with*** *hair.*

clogs /klɒgz/ *noun* [**plural**] shoes made from wood, or shoes with a wooden sole (= bottom part)

cloister /'klɔɪstəʳ/ *noun* [C] **RELIGION** a covered stone passage around the edges of a garden in a church or religious building

clone¹ /kləʊn/ *noun* [C] **1 BIOLOGY** an exact copy of a plant or animal that scientists make by removing one of its cells **2** *informal* someone or something that is very similar to someone or something else

clone² /kləʊn/ *verb* [T] **BIOLOGY** to create a clone of a plant or animal *Scientists have already cloned a sheep.* •**cloning** *noun* [U] *animal/human cloning*

O-■ **close¹** /kləʊz/ *verb* [I, T] **1** DOOR/WINDOW ETC If something closes, it moves so that it is not open, and if you close something, you make it move so that it is not open. *Jane closed the window.* ○ *Lie down and close your eyes.* ○ *Suddenly the door closed.* **2** PUBLIC PLACE If a shop, restaurant, public place, etc closes, people cannot go in it. *The supermarket closes at 8 p.m.* **3** ORGANIZATION (*also* **close down**) If a business or organization closes, or if someone or something closes it, it stops operating. *Many factories have closed in the last ten years.* **4** END to end, or to end something *She closed the meeting with a short speech.* ➲See Common Learner Error at **open**

close (sth) down *phrasal verb* If a business or organization closes down, or if someone or something closes it down, it stops operating.

close in *phrasal verb* If people close in, they gradually get nearer to someone, usually in order to attack them or stop them escaping. *Police* ***closed in on*** *the demonstrators.*

close sth off *phrasal verb* to put something across the entrance to a place in order to stop people entering it *Police quickly closed off the area.*

O-■ **close²** /kləʊs/ *adjective* **1** DISTANCE near in distance *His house is* ***close to*** *the sea.* **2** TIME near in time *It was* ***close to*** *lunchtime when we arrived.* **3** FRIENDLY If people are close, they know each other very well and like each other a lot. *close friends* ○ *I'm very* ***close to*** *my brother.* **4** RELATIVE [**always before noun**] A close relative is someone who is directly related to you, for example your mother, father, or brother. **5** RELATIONSHIP seeing or talking with someone a lot *Our school has* ***close links*** *with a school in China.* ○ *I'm still in* ***close contact*** *with my school friends.* **6 be/come close to doing sth** to almost achieve or do something *We are close to reaching an agreement.* **7 be close to sth** If someone or something is close to a particular state, they are almost in that state. *She was* ***close to tears.*** **8** COMPETITION A close game, competition, etc is one in which people's scores are nearly the same. **9** CAREFUL [**always before noun**] looking at or listening to someone or something very carefully *On* ***close inspection****, you could see that the painting was a fake.* ○ ***Keep a close watch on*** *the children* (= watch them carefully). **10** WEATHER Close weather is too warm and there is not enough fresh air. •**closeness** *noun* [U] ➲See also: a close **call**², a close **shave**²

O-■ **close³** /kləʊs/ *adverb* **1** DISTANCE near in distance *He stayed* ***close to*** *his mother.* ○ *Come a bit closer.* ○ *We walked close behind them.* ○ *There's a great beach* ***close by*** (= near). **2** TIME near in time *The time for change is coming closer.*

close⁴ /kləʊz/ *noun* END [**no plural**] the end of something *They finally reached an agreement*

***at the close of** a week of negotiations.* ○ *The year was **drawing to a close**.*

close⁵ /kləʊs/ *noun* [C] ROAD (*also* **Close**) used in the name of a road that cars can only enter from one end *They live at 7 Kingswear Close.*

O-ᵚ**closed** /kləʊzd/ *adjective* **1** BUSINESS/SHOP not open for business *We went to the library but it was closed.* **2** NOT OPEN not open *The door was closed.* ○ *Her eyes were closed.* **3** NOT ACCEPTING IDEAS not wanting to accept new ideas, people, customs, etc *a closed mind* ➲See Common Learner Error at **open**

ˌ**closed-circuit ˈtelevision** *noun* [C, U] a system of hidden cameras that take pictures of people in public places, used to help prevent crime

ˌ**closed ˈshop** *noun* [C usually singular] a place of work where you have to belong to a particular trade union (= organization of workers)

close-knit /ˌkləʊsˈnɪt/ *adjective* A close-knit group of people is one in which everyone helps and supports each other. *a **close-knit community***

closely /ˈkləʊsli/ *adverb* **1** CAREFULLY If you look at or listen to something closely, you look at it or listen to it very carefully. **2** CONNECTED If two things are closely connected, related, etc, they are very similar to each other or there is a relationship between them. *The two languages are **closely related**.* ○ *I saw a cat that closely resembles ours.* **3** VERY NEAR in a way that is very near in distance or time *Elke came into the room, closely followed by her children.* **4** WORK If you work closely with someone, you work together a lot. *Nurses **work closely** with other medical staff.*

closet¹ /ˈklɒzɪt/ *US* (*UK* **wardrobe**) *noun* [C] a large cupboard for keeping clothes in ➲See also: have a **skeleton** in the cupboard

closet² /ˈklɒzɪt/ *adjective* **a closet intellectual/liberal/socialist, etc** someone who hides their true opinions or way of life

close-up /ˈkləʊsʌp/ *noun* [C] a photograph of someone or something that is taken by standing very close to them

closing /ˈkləʊzɪŋ/ *adjective* [always before noun] The closing part of an event or period of time is the final part of it. *Owen scored a goal in the closing minutes of the game.*

WORD PARTNERS FOR ***closure***

face/be threatened with closure • **save** sth **from** closure • the closure **of** sth

closure /ˈkləʊʒəʳ/ *noun* **1** [C, U] when a business, organization, etc stops operating *factory closures* ○ *The company announced the **closure** of its Paris office.* **2** [U] the feeling that a sad or unpleasant experience has now finished so that you can think about and do other things

clot¹ /klɒt/ *noun* [C] **1** HEALTH a lump that forms when a liquid, especially blood, becomes almost solid **2** *UK informal* a stupid person

clot² /klɒt/ *verb* [I, T] **clotting** *past* **clotted** BIOLOGY to form clots, or to make clots form

cloth /klɒθ/ *noun* **1** MATERIAL [U] material made from cotton, wool, etc, and used, for example, to make clothes or curtains *a piece of cloth* **2** PIECE [C] a piece of cloth used for cleaning or drying things

COMMON LEARNER ERROR

cloth, clothes or **clothing?**

The most usual word for the things you wear is **clothes**. **Clothing** is slightly more formal, and often used for particular types of clothes. **Cloth** is the material that clothes are made from. Do not try to make a plural 'cloths' - it is an uncountable noun.

I put my clothes on.

~~*I put my cloth on.*~~

They gave us money for food and clothing.

~~*They gave us money for food and cloths.*~~

clothe /kləʊð/ *verb* [T] to supply clothes for someone

clothed /kləʊðd/ *adjective* wearing clothes *fully clothed*

WORD PARTNERS FOR ***clothes***

put on/take off/wear clothes • **change** your clothes

O-ᵚ**clothes** /kləʊðz/ *noun* [plural] items such as shirts and trousers that you wear on your body *She was **wearing** her sister's **clothes**.* ○ *to **put on/take off** your **clothes*** ➲See colour picture **Clothes** on pages Centre 8, 9

clothesline /ˈkləʊðzlaɪn/ *noun* [C] a rope for hanging wet clothes on until they dry

ˈ**clothes** ˌ**peg** *UK* (*US* **clothespin** /ˈkləʊðzpɪn/) *noun* [C] a short piece of wood or plastic that is used to hold clothes on a rope while they dry

clothing /ˈkləʊðɪŋ/ *noun* [U] clothes, especially of a particular type *outdoor/protective clothing*

cloud¹ /klaʊd/ *noun* **1** GEOGRAPHY [C, U] a white or grey mass that floats in the sky, made of small water drops ➲See picture **cloud** on next page **2** DIRTY AIR [C] a mass of gas or very small pieces of something floating in the air *a cloud of dust/smoke* **3 be under a cloud** If someone is under a cloud, they are not trusted or not popular because people think they have done something bad. •**cloudless** *adjective* without clouds

cloud² /klaʊd/ *verb* **1** NOT CLEAR [T] to make someone confused, or make something harder to understand *to **cloud** someone's **judgment/vision*** **2** NOT SEEING [I, T] If something transparent clouds, it becomes hard to see through, and if something clouds it, it makes it hard to see through.

cloud over *phrasal verb* to become covered with clouds

cloudy /ˈklaʊdi/ *adjective* **1** WEATHER When it is cloudy, there are clouds in the sky. **2** LIQUID A cloudy liquid is not transparent. *cloudy water*

clout /klaʊt/ *noun* **1** POWER [U] power and influence over other people *As mayor, he **has** political **clout**.* **2** BLOW [C] *UK informal* a heavy blow made with the hand

clove /kləʊv/ *noun* [C] **1** FOOD a small, dark-brown, dried flower that is used as a spice **2** one separate part in a root of garlic (= plant with a strong taste used in cooking)

C

C

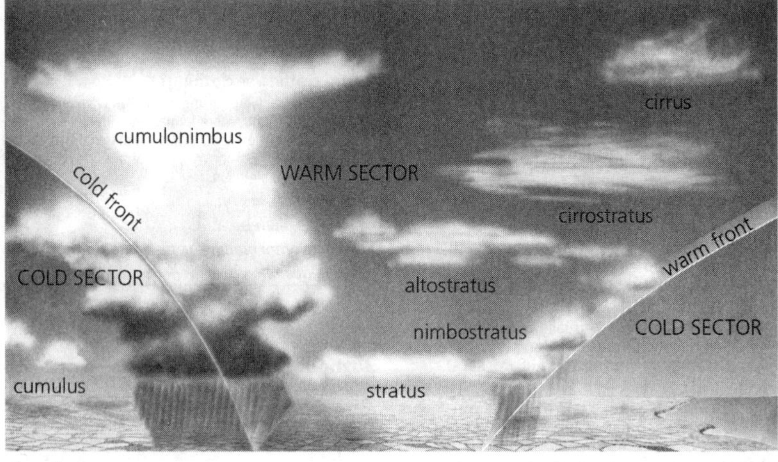

cloud

clover /ˈkləʊvəʳ/ *noun* [U] a small plant that has three round leaves and round flowers

clown¹ /klaʊn/ *noun* [C] **1** PERFORMER a performer who has special clothes and a painted face and makes people laugh **2** SILLY PERSON a silly person

clown² /klaʊn/ (*also* **clown around**) *verb* [I] to behave in a silly way in order to make people laugh

WORD PARTNERS FOR ***club***

belong to/join a club • a **member of** a club

O-- **club¹** /klʌb/ *noun* [C] **1** ORGANIZATION an organization for people who want to take part in a sport or social activity together, or the building they use for this *a fitness/football club* **2** **SPORT** (*also* **golf club**) a long, thin stick used to hit the ball in golf ➲See colour picture **Sports 2** on page Centre 15 **3** WEAPON a heavy stick used as a weapon **4** DANCE a place open late at night where people can dance **5** **clubs** playing cards with black shapes like three leaves on them *the ten of clubs* ➲See also: **fan club**

club² /klʌb/ *verb* **clubbing,** *past* **clubbed** **1** [T] to hit a person or animal with a heavy stick **2** **go clubbing** *mainly UK* to go to clubs where there is music and dancing

club together *phrasal verb UK* If a group of people club together to buy something, they share the cost of it.

clubhouse /ˈklʌbhaʊs/ *noun* [C] a building that the members of a club use for social activities or for changing their clothes

cluck /klʌk/ *verb* [I] to make the sound that a chicken makes •**cluck** *noun* [C]

clue /kluː/ *noun* [C] **1** a sign or a piece of information that helps you to solve a problem or answer a question *Police are searching the area for* ***clues to*** *the murder.* ○ *I can't remember who wrote it.* ***Give me a clue.*** **2** **not have a clue** *informal* to be completely unable to guess, understand, or deal with something [+ **question word**] *I haven't a clue what you're talking about.*

ˌclued ˈup *adjective UK* knowing all the most important information about something *He's very* ***clued up on*** *the law.*

clueless /ˈkluːləs/ *adjective informal* A clueless person does not know anything about a particular subject.

clump /klʌmp/ *noun* [C] a group of plants growing closely together *a clump of grass*

clumsy /ˈklʌmzi/ *adjective* **1** PERSON Clumsy people move in a way that is not controlled or careful enough, and often knock or damage things. **2** BEHAVIOUR If you behave in a clumsy way, you upset people because you are not careful about their feelings. ***a clumsy attempt*** *to be friendly* **3** OBJECT Clumsy objects are large, not attractive, and often difficult to use. •**clumsily** *adverb* •**clumsiness** *noun* [U]

clung /klʌŋ/ *past of* cling

cluster¹ /ˈklʌstəʳ/ *noun* a group of similar things that are close together *a cluster of galaxies*

cluster² /ˈklʌstəʳ/ *verb* **cluster around/round/together, etc** to form a close group *Photographers clustered round the film star.*

clutch¹ /klʌtʃ/ *verb* [T] to hold something tightly *She clutched a coin.*

clutch at sth *phrasal verb* to try very hard to hold something *She clutched wildly at the branch.*

clutch² /klʌtʃ/ *noun* **1** ENGINE [C] the part of a car or truck that you press with your foot when you change gear (= part that controls how fast the wheels turn) ➲See colour picture **Car** on page Centre 7 **2** HOLD [C, U] when someone holds or tries to hold something tightly **3** **sb's clutches** If you are in someone's clutches, they control you, often in an evil way.

clutter¹ /ˈklʌtəʳ/ (*also* **clutter up**) *verb* [T] to cover a surface, or to fill a place with things that are not tidy or well organized [**often passive**] *Every shelf is **cluttered with** ornaments.*

clutter² /ˈklʌtəʳ/ *noun* [U] a lot of objects that are not tidy or well organized *I've got too much clutter on my desk.*

cm **MEASURES** *written abbreviation for* centimetre (= a unit for measuring length)

CNS /ˌsiːenˈes/ *noun* [U] **ANATOMY, BIOLOGY** *abbreviation for* central nervous system

Co 1 COMPANY *written abbreviation for* Company (= name of business) *Williams & Co* **2** AREA OF COUNTRY *written abbreviation for* County (= area with own local government) *Co. Wexford*

co- /kəʊ-/ *prefix* with or together *a co-author* ○ *to coexist*

c/o *written abbreviation for* care of: used when you send a letter to someone who will give it to the person you are writing to

coach¹ /kəʊtʃ/ *noun* [C] **1** BUS *UK* a comfortable bus used to take groups of people on long journeys *a **coach trip*** **2** **EDUCATION, SPORT** someone whose job is to teach people to improve at a sport, skill, or school subject *a football/tennis coach* **3** OLD VEHICLE a vehicle with wheels that is pulled by horses

coach² /kəʊtʃ/ *verb* [T] **EDUCATION** to teach someone so they improve at a sport, skill, or in a school subject •**coaching** *noun* [U]

ˈcoach ˌstation *UK* (*UK/US* **bus station**) *noun* [C] a building where a bus starts or ends its journey

coal /kəʊl/ *noun* **1** **GEOLOGY** [U] a hard, black substance that is dug from under the ground and burnt as fuel *a lump of coal* **2** **coals** pieces of coal, usually burning

coalition /kəʊəˈlɪʃən/ *noun* [C] **POLITICS** two or more political parties that have joined together, usually to govern a country *to **form** a **coalition*** ○ *a **coalition government***

ˈcoal ˌmine *noun* [C] (*also UK* **colliery**) a place where people work digging coal from under the ground

coarse /kɔːs/ *adjective* **1** NOT SMOOTH rough and thick, or not in very small pieces *coarse cloth* ○ *coarse breadcrumbs* **2** RUDE not polite *coarse language* •**coarsely** *adverb*

O-ᵕ**coast¹** /kəʊst/ *noun* [C, U] **1** **GEOGRAPHY** the land beside the sea *The island lies **off the** North African **coast*** (= in the sea near North Africa). ○ *They live **on the** east **coast** of Scotland.* **2** **coast to coast** from one side of a country to the other **3** **the coast is clear** If the coast is clear, you can do something or go somewhere because there is nobody who might see you.

coast² /kəʊst/ *verb* [I] **1** NO DIFFICULTY to progress or succeed without any effort or difficulty *Pakistan **coasted to** a four-wicket victory over Australia.* **2** VEHICLE to move forward in a vehicle without using the engine, usually down a hill

coastal /ˈkəʊstəl/ *adjective* **GEOGRAPHY** situated on or relating to the coast *a coastal town/resort*

ˈcoastal deˌfence *noun* [U, C] **ENVIRONMENT** ways of protecting land from being flooded or worn away by the sea

coastguard /ˈkəʊstgɑːd/ *noun* [C] a person or the organization responsible for preventing accidents and illegal activities in the sea near a coast

coastline /ˈkəʊstlaɪn/ *noun* [C, U] **GEOGRAPHY** the part of the land along the edge of the sea *a rocky coastline*

O-ᵕ**coat¹** /kəʊt/ *noun* [C] **1** CLOTHES a piece of clothing with sleeves that you wear over your other clothes, especially when you go outside *a fur/winter coat* **2** FUR the fur that covers an animal's body **3** LAYER a layer of a substance such as paint *a coat of paint/varnish*

coat² /kəʊt/ *verb* [T] to cover something with a thin layer of something *Stir the rice until it is **coated with** butter.*

ˈcoat ˌhanger *noun* [C] a wire, wooden, or plastic object for hanging clothes on

coating /ˈkəʊtɪŋ/ *noun* [C] a thin layer that covers the surface of something *a protective/non-stick coating*

coax /kəʊks/ *verb* [T] to persuade someone in a gentle way [**+ into + doing sth**] *She coaxed me into joining the group.*

cobble¹ /ˈkɒbl/ *verb*
cobble sth together *phrasal verb* to make something quickly and not very carefully

cobble² /ˈkɒbl/ *noun* [C] a rounded stone used on the surface of an old-fashioned road •**cobbled** *adjective* made with cobbles ***cobbled streets***

cobbler /ˈkɒbləʳ/ *noun* [C] *mainly UK old-fashioned* someone whose job is to make or repair shoes

cobblestone /ˈkɒblstəʊn/ *noun* [C] a rounded stone that is used on the surface of an old-fashioned road

cobra /ˈkəʊbrə/ *noun* [C] a poisonous snake that makes the skin of its neck wide and flat when it is going to attack

cobweb /ˈkɒbweb/ *noun* [C] a structure of fine threads made by a spider (= insect with eight legs) to catch insects

Coca Cola /ˌkəʊkəˈkəʊlə/ *noun* [U] *trademark* **FOOD** a sweet, dark-brown drink with lots of bubbles

cocaine /kəʊˈkeɪn/ *noun* [U] **HEALTH** an illegal drug, often used in the form of white powder

cock¹ /kɒk/ *noun* [C] an adult male chicken

cock² /kɒk/ *verb* [T] to move part of the body up or to the side *to cock an ear/eyebrow*
cock sth up *phrasal verb UK informal* to do something wrong or badly *I really cocked up my exams.*

cockerel /ˈkɒkərəl/ *noun* [C] *UK* a young male chicken

cockney /ˈkɒkni/ *noun* **1** **LANGUAGE** [U] a type of English spoken in East London **2** [C] someone who speaks Cockney

cockpit /ˈkɒkpɪt/ *noun* [C] the part of an aircraft or racing car that contains the controls

C

cockroach /ˈkɒkrəʊtʃ/ *noun* [C] a large, brown or black insect that can live in houses and places where food is prepared

cocktail /ˈkɒkteɪl/ *noun* **1** [C] a mixture of powerful substances *a cocktail of drugs/chemicals* **2 FOOD** [C] an alcoholic drink made from two or more kinds of drink mixed together *a cocktail bar/party* **3 FOOD** [C, U] a cold dish containing small pieces of food mixed together *a prawn cocktail* ○ *fruit cocktail*

cocky /ˈkɒki/ *adjective* confident in an annoying way

cocoa /ˈkəʊkəʊ/ *noun* [U] **1 FOOD** a dark-brown powder produced from a type of bean, used to make chocolate **2 FOOD** a drink made by mixing cocoa powder with hot milk

coconut /ˈkəʊkənʌt/ *noun* [C] **FOOD** a very large nut with a hard, hairy shell, a white part that you eat, and liquid in the centre

cocoon /kəˈkuːn/ *noun* [C] **BIOLOGY** a cover that protects some insects as they develop into adults

cod /kɒd/ *noun* [C, U] *plural* **cod FOOD** a large sea fish which can be eaten as food

code /kəʊd/ *noun* **1** SECRET MESSAGE [C, U] a set of letters, numbers, or signs that are used instead of ordinary words to keep a message secret *It was written **in code**.* ○ *They were trying to **break*** (= understand) *the enemy's **code**.* **2** TELEPHONE [C] *UK* (*UK/US* **area code**) a set of numbers used at the beginning of all the telephone numbers in a particular area **3** RULES [C] a set of rules on how to behave or how to do things *a code of conduct/practice* ○ *The club has a strict **dress code*** (= rules about what you wear). ➲See also: **bar code, zip code**

coded /ˈkəʊdɪd/ *adjective* written or sent in code *a **coded message/warning***

codeine /ˈkəʊdiːn/ *noun* [U] **HEALTH** a medicine used to reduce pain

co-ed /ˌkəʊˈed/ (US) /ˈkəʊˌed/ *adjective* **EDUCATION** with both male and female students

coefficient /ˌkəʊɪˈfɪʃənt/ *noun* [C] **MATHEMATICS** a value that multiplies another value, e.g. the number 2 in '2x'

coelenterate /sɪˈlentəreɪt/ *noun* [C] **BIOLOGY** a type of sea animal that has a simple body with tentacles (= long arms) and a single opening at the centre, for example a jellyfish

coerce /kəʊˈɜːs/ *verb* [T] *formal* to make someone do something that they do not want to do [+ **into** + **doing sth**] *Employees said they were coerced into signing the agreement.* •**coercion** /kəʊˈɜːʃən/ *noun* [U]

coexist /ˌkəʊɪɡˈzɪst/ *verb* [I] If two things or groups coexist, they exist at the same time or together, although they may be very different. *Can science and religion coexist?* •**coexistence** *noun* [U]

O‑**coffee** /ˈkɒfi/ *noun* **1 FOOD** [C, U] a hot drink made from dark beans which are made into a powder, or a cup of this drink **2 FOOD** [U] the beans from which coffee is made, or the powder made from these beans *instant coffee*

ˈcoffee ˌtable *noun* [C] a low table in a room where people sit ➲See colour picture **The Living Room** on page Centre 4

coffers /ˈkɒfəz/ *noun* [plural] **FINANCE** a supply of money that a group or organization has and can spend *government/party coffers*

coffin /ˈkɒfɪn/ (*also US* **casket**) *noun* [C] a box in which a dead body is buried ➲See also: the final **nail**[1] in the coffin

cog /kɒɡ/ *noun* [C] a part shaped like a tooth on the edge of a wheel in a machine, that makes another wheel turn

cogent /ˈkəʊdʒənt/ *adjective* A cogent argument, reason, or explanation is one which people will believe because it is clear and careful.

cognac /ˈkɒnjæk/ *noun* [U] **FOOD** good quality French brandy (= strong alcoholic drink)

cognitive /ˈkɒɡnətɪv/ *adjective* [**always before noun**] *formal* relating to how people think, understand, and learn

cohabit /kəʊˈhæbɪt/ *verb* [I] *formal* If two people cohabit, they live together and are sexual partners but are not married. •**cohabitation** /kəʊˌhæbɪˈteɪʃən/ *noun* [U]

coherent /kəʊˈhɪərənt/ *adjective* **1** CAREFUL THOUGHT A coherent argument, plan, etc is clear, and each part of it has been carefully considered. **2** UNDERSTAND If someone is coherent, you can understand what they say. ➲Opposite **incoherent** •**coherence** /kəʊˈhɪərəns/ *noun* [U] •**coherently** *adverb*

cohesion /kəʊˈhiːʒən/ *noun* [U] when the members of a group or society are united *The country needs greater social cohesion.* •**cohesive** /kəʊˈhiːsɪv/ *adjective* united and working together effectively *a cohesive unit/group*

cohort /ˈkəʊhɔːt/ *noun* [C] someone who supports someone else, especially a political leader *the prime minister's cohorts*

coil[1] /kɔɪl/ *noun* [C] a long piece of wire, rope, etc curled into several circles *a coil of rope*

coil[2] /kɔɪl/ (*also* **coil up**) *verb* [I, T] to twist something into circles, or to become twisted into circles *Her hair was coiled in a bun on top of her head.*

coin[1] /kɔɪn/ *noun* **1 FINANCE** [C] a flat, usually round, piece of metal used as money *a pound coin* **2 toss a coin** to throw a coin into the air so that it turns over several times, and see which side it lands on, often in order to make a decision

coin[2] /kɔɪn/ *verb* [T] **1** to be the first person who uses a new word or phrase **2 to coin a phrase** something you say before using a common expression *Still, to coin a phrase, there is light at the end of the tunnel.*

coincide /ˌkəʊɪnˈsaɪd/ *verb* [I] **1** HAPPEN TOGETHER to happen at the same time as something else *The band's American tour **coincided with** the release of their second album.* **2** BE THE SAME When people's opinions or ideas coincide, they are the same.

WORD PARTNERS FOR ***coincidence***

by coincidence • an **amazing/happy/ remarkable/strange/unfortunate** coincidence • **mere/pure** coincidence • **it's no** coincidence **that**

coincidence /kəʊ'ɪnsɪdᵊns/ *noun* [C, U] when two very similar things happen at the same time but there is no reason for it *an* ***amazing/ strange coincidence*** ○ *It was* ***pure coincidence*** *that we both married dentists.* •**coincidental** /kəʊˌɪnsɪ'dentᵊl/ *adjective* happening by coincidence *The similarities are coincidental.* •**coincidentally** /kəʊˌɪnsɪ'dentᵊli/ *adverb*

Coke /kəʊk/ *noun* [C, U] *trademark* **FOOD** *short for* Coca Cola (= a sweet, dark-brown drink with lots of bubbles)

Col *written abbreviation for* Colonel (= an officer of high rank in the army or air force)

cola /'kəʊlə/ *noun* [U] **FOOD** a sweet, dark-brown drink with lots of bubbles ➲See also: **Coca Cola**

colander /'kɒləndəʳ/ *noun* [C] a bowl with small holes in it used for washing food or separating water from food after cooking ➲See colour picture **The Kitchen** on page Centre 2

OTHER WAYS OF SAYING ***cold***

If the weather outside or the temperature inside is very cold, you can use the adjectives **bitter** or **freezing**: *Wrap up warmly - it's* ***bitter*** *outside!* • *It's absolutely* ***freezing*** *in here!*

If the weather, especially the wind, is so cold that it is unpleasant to be in, the adjectives **biting** and **icy** are sometimes used: *A* ***biting/icy*** *wind blew in her face as she opened the door.*

The adjective **chilly** is often used to describe weather or temperatures that feel slightly cold and unpleasant: *It's a bit* ***chilly*** *in here - can you turn the heater on?*

If the temperature feels cold but pleasant, you can say that it is **cool**: *That's a nice* ***cool*** *breeze.*

Cold weather in autumn or winter that is dry and pleasant is sometimes described as **crisp**: *We walked through the forest on a* ***crisp*** *autumn day.*

O→**cold¹** /kəʊld/ *adjective* **1** TEMPERATURE having a low temperature *cold water/weather* ○ *This soup has* ***gone cold.*** ○ *My hands are* ***getting cold.*** **2** UNFRIENDLY unfriendly or showing no emotion *a cold stare/voice* ○ *She became quite cold and distant with me.* **3** FOOD served cold *cold roast beef* •**coldness** *noun* [U] ➲See also: in cold **blood**, get cold feet (**foot**¹)

WORD PARTNERS FOR ***cold***

catch/have a cold • a **bad/heavy/stinking** (= very bad) cold

cold² /kəʊld/ *noun* **1** **HEALTH** [C] a common illness which makes you sneeze and makes your nose produce liquid *I've got a cold.* ○ *He* ***caught a*** *bad* ***cold*** *at school.* **2 the cold** cold weather or temperatures **3 leave sb out in the cold** to not allow someone to be part of a group or activity

cold³ /kəʊld/ *adverb* **1 be out cold** *informal* to be unconscious *I hit my head and was out cold for two minutes.* **2** completely and immediately *I offered him £10 but he turned me down cold.*

cold-blooded /ˌkəʊld'blʌdɪd/ *adjective* showing no emotion or sympathy *a cold-blooded killer*

cold-hearted /ˌkəʊld'hɑːtɪd/ *adjective* feeling no kindness or sympathy towards other people

coldly /'kəʊldli/ *adverb* in a way that is not friendly or emotional *He looked at me coldly.*

colic /'kɒlɪk/ *noun* [U] **HEALTH** When a baby has colic, it has a bad pain in the stomach.

collaborate /kə'læbᵊreɪt/ *verb* [I] **1** WORK TOGETHER When two or more people collaborate, they work together to create or achieve the same thing. *Didn't you* ***collaborate with*** *him* ***on*** *one of your books?* **2** HELP ENEMY to help people who are an enemy of your country or government *He was accused of* ***collaborating with*** *the enemy.* •**collaborator** *noun* [C]

collaboration /kəˌlæbᵊ'reɪʃᵊn/ *noun* **1** WORK [C, U] when two or more people work together to create or achieve the same thing, or a product of this *The show was a result of* ***collaboration between*** *several museums.* **2** ENEMY [U] when someone helps an enemy country or government

collage /'kɒlɑːʒ/ *noun* [C, U] **ART** a picture made by sticking small pieces of paper or other materials onto a surface, or the process of making pictures like this

collagen /'kɒlədʒən/ *noun* [U] **BIOLOGY** a protein found especially in the joints (= places where two bones are connected) of humans and animals

collapse¹ /kə'læps/ *verb* **1** FALL [I] When someone collapses, they fall down, usually because they are ill or weak. **2** OBJECT [I, T] to fall down or towards the inside, or to make a structure or object fall down or towards its inside *The roof collapsed under the weight of snow.* **3** FAIL [I] to fail to work or succeed *The peace talks have collapsed.*

collapse² /kə'læps/ *noun* [C, U] **1** FAILURE the sudden failure of a system, organization, business, etc **2** FALL when a person or structure becomes too weak to stand and suddenly falls

collapsible /kə'læpsɪbl/ *adjective* able to be folded or made flat in order to be stored or carried *a collapsible table/boat*

collar¹ /'kɒləʳ/ *noun* [C] **1** CLOTHING the part of a shirt, coat, etc that is usually folded over and goes round your neck *a shirt collar* **2** ANIMAL a narrow piece of leather or plastic that you fasten round the neck of an animal

collar² /'kɒləʳ/ *verb* [T] *informal* to find someone and stop them going somewhere, often so that you can talk to them about something

collarbone /'kɒləbəʊn/ *noun* [C] **ANATOMY** a bone between the base of your neck and your shoulder

collateral /kə'lætᵊrᵊl/ *noun* [U] **FINANCE** things that you agree to give someone if you are not able pay back money you have borrowed from them *I used my car* ***as collateral*** *for a loan.*

C

O-- **colleague** /ˈkɒliːg/ *noun* [C] someone that you work with

O-- **collect¹** /kəˈlekt/ *verb* **1** BRING TOGETHER [T] to get things from different places and bring them together *Police collected a good deal of information during the investigation.* ○ *Would you* ***collect up*** *the books please, Joanne?* **2** KEEP [T] to get and keep things of one type such as stamps or coins as a hobby *She collects dolls.* **3** GO TO GET [T] *UK* to go to a place and bring someone or something away from it *She collects Anna* ***from*** *school at three o'clock.* **4** MONEY [I, T] to ask people to give you money for something, for example a charity (= organization that helps people) *I'm collecting on behalf of Oxfam.* **5** RECEIVE [T] to receive money that you are owed *You can begin to collect a pension at age 62.* **6** COME TOGETHER [I] to come together in a single place *Journalists collected outside the palace.* **7 collect yourself/your thoughts** to get control over your feelings and thoughts

collect² /kəlˈekt/ *adjective, adverb US* When you telephone collect or make a collect telephone call, the person you telephone pays for the call.

collected /kəˈlektɪd/ *adjective* **1** BOOK [**always before noun**] brought together in one book or series of books *His collected poems were published in 1928.* **2** CONTROL showing control over your feelings *Jane was very* ***calm and collected.***

colˈlecting ˌflask *noun* [C] **CHEMISTRY** a wide glass container with a flat base, used by scientists for collecting liquids

WORD PARTNERS FOR ***collection***

amass/display/have a collection • an **extensive/large/priceless/private** collection

O-- **collection** /kəˈlekʃən/ *noun* **1** OBJECTS [C] a group of objects of the same type that have been collected by one person or in one place *a* ***private art collection*** **2** TAKING AWAY [U] when something is taken away from a place *rubbish collection* **3** MONEY [C] an amount of money collected from several people *We* ***had a collection for*** *Emily's gift.* **4** GROUP [C] a group of things or people *There's quite a* ***collection of*** *toothbrushes in the bathroom.*

collective¹ /kəˈlektɪv/ *adjective* involving, felt by, or owned by everyone in a group *collective responsibility*

collective² /kəˈlektɪv/ *noun* [C] a business that is owned and controlled by the people who work in it

colˌlective ˈbargaining *noun* [U] the system in which employees talk as a group with their employers to try to agree on matters such as pay and working conditions

collectively /kəˈlektɪvli/ *adverb* as a group *She has a staff of four who collectively earn almost $200,000.*

collector /kəˈlektər/ *noun* [C] **1** JOB someone whose job is to collect tickets or money from people *a tax collector* **2** HOBBY someone who collects objects because they are interesting or beautiful *a collector of modern art*

WORD PARTNERS FOR ***college***

go to college • be **at** college • a college **course/lecturer/student**

O-- **college** /ˈkɒlɪdʒ/ *noun* **1 EDUCATION** [C, U] *UK* a place where students are educated when they are between 16 and 18 years old, or after they have finished school *a sixth-form college* ○ *a teacher-training college* **2 EDUCATION** [C, U] *US* a university **3 EDUCATION** [C] a part of a university that has its own teachers and students *Cambridge/Oxford colleges* ➲See also: **community college, junior college**

collegiate /kəˈliːdʒiət/ *adjective* **EDUCATION** relating to or belonging to a college or its students *collegiate sports*

collide /kəˈlaɪd/ *verb* [I] When two objects collide, they hit each other with force, usually while moving. *The car* ***collided with*** *a van.*

colliery /ˈkɒljəri/ *UK* (*UK/US* **coal mine**) *noun* [C] a place where people work digging coal from under the ground

WORD PARTNERS FOR ***collision***

avoid/be involved in a collision • [a car/train, etc] is **in a** collision with sth • a **head-on** collision • a collision **between** sth and sth

collision /kəˈlɪʒən/ *noun* **1** [C] an accident that happens when two vehicles hit each other with force **2 PHYSICS** when two or more objects or particles come together in a way that causes an exchange of energy and a change of direction **3 be on a collision course** If two people or groups are on a collision course, they are doing or saying things that are certain to cause a serious disagreement or fight between them.

collocation /ˌkɒləˈkeɪʃən/ *noun* [C] **1 LANGUAGE** a word or phrase that sounds natural and correct when it is used with another word or phrase *In the phrase 'a hard frost', 'hard' is a collocation of 'frost', and 'strong' would not sound natural.* **2 LANGUAGE** the combination of words formed when two or more words are frequently used together in a way that sounds natural *The phrase 'a hard frost' is a collocation.*

colloid /ˈkɒlɔɪd/ *noun* [C] **CHEMISTRY** a mixture in which particles of one substance are held inside another substance

colloquial /kəˈləʊkwiəl/ *adjective* **LANGUAGE** Colloquial words or expressions are informal. *colloquial speech* •**colloquially** *adverb*

collude /kəˈluːd/ *verb* [I] *formal* to do something secretly with another person or group, in order to deceive or cheat others *The company* ***colluded with*** *competitors to fix prices.* •**collusion** /kəˈluːʒən/ *noun* [U] *He was accused of being* ***in collusion with*** *the terrorists.*

colon /ˈkəʊlɒn/ *noun* [C] **1** a mark (:) used before a list, an example, an explanation, etc ➲See Extra help page **Punctuation** on page Centre 18. **2 ANATOMY** the large intestine (= lower part of a person's bowels) ➲See picture at **alimentary canal**

colonel /ˈkɜːnəl/ *noun* [C] an officer of high rank in the army or air force

colonial /kəˈləʊniəl/ *adjective* [**always before noun**] **POLITICS** relating to colonialism or a colony (= country controlled by another country) *colonial rule/government*

colonialism /kə'ləʊniəlɪzᵊm/ *noun* [U] **POLITICS** the system in which powerful countries control other countries

colonize (*also UK* **-ise**) /'kɒlənaɪz/ *verb* [T] **1 POLITICS** to send people to live in and govern another country [**often passive**] *Burundi was first colonized by the Germans.* **2** to start growing or living in large numbers in a place *Weeds quickly colonize areas of cleared ground.* •**colonist** /'kɒlənɪst/ *noun* [C] someone who goes to colonize a country •**colonization** /ˌkɒlənaɪ'zeɪʃᵊn/ *noun* [U]

colony /'kɒləni/ *noun* [C] **1 POLITICS** a country or area controlled in an official, political way by a more powerful country *a French/British colony* **2 BIOLOGY** a group of the same type of animals, insects, or plants living together in a particular place *a colony of ants* **3 SOCIETY** a group of people with the same interests or job who live together *an artists' colony*

O‑ **color** /'kʌlər/ *noun, verb US spelling of* colour

colored /'kʌləd/ *adjective US spelling of* coloured

colorful /'kʌləfəl/ *adjective US spelling of* colourful

coloring /'kʌlərɪŋ/ *noun* [U] *US spelling of* colouring

colorless /'kʌlələs/ *adjective US spelling of* colourless

colossal /kə'lɒsᵊl/ *adjective* extremely large *colossal amounts of money*

O‑ **colour¹** *UK* (*US* **color**) /'kʌlər/ *noun* **1** [RED/BLUE ETC] [C, U] red, blue, green, yellow, etc *Green is my favourite colour.* ○ *What colour shall I paint the kitchen?* ➲See colour picture **Colours** on page Centre 12 **2** [FILM/TV ETC] [U] using or showing all the colours, not only black and white *Why didn't he shoot the film **in colour**?* **3** [SKIN] [U] the colour of a person's skin, which shows their race **4** [FACE] [U] healthy pink skin on someone's face *The colour drained from her cheeks.* **5** [INTEREST] [U] interesting or exciting qualities or parts *We added your story for a bit of local colour.* **6 with flying colours** with a very high score or with great success *He passed the entrance exam with flying colours.* ➲See also: **primary colour**

colour² *UK* (*US* **color**) /'kʌlər/ *verb* **1** [ADD COLOUR] [I, T] to become a particular colour, or to make something a particular colour *He drew a heart and coloured it red.* ○ *Fry the onions until they start to colour.* **2** [AFFECT] [T] to affect what someone does, says, or feels [**often passive**] *Her views are coloured by her own bad experiences.*
colour sth in *phrasal verb* to fill an area with colour using paint, pens, etc

colour-blind *UK* (*US* **color-blind**) /'kʌləblaɪnd/ *adjective* **HEALTH** unable to see the difference between particular colours

coloured *UK* (*US* **colored**) /'kʌləd/ *adjective* **1** [THING] having or producing a colour or colours *coloured lights/cloth* **2** [PERSON] an old-fashioned way of describing someone from a race with dark skin that is now considered offensive

colourful *UK* (*US* **colorful**) /'kʌləfᵊl/ *adjective* **1** [BRIGHT] having bright colours *a colourful painting* **2** [INTERESTING] interesting and unusual *a **colourful character***

colouring *UK* (*US* **coloring**) /'kʌlərɪŋ/ *noun* [U] **1** [COLOUR] the colour of something, especially an animal or person's skin, hair, and eyes *The boys have their father's colouring.* **2** [SUBSTANCE] a substance that is used to colour something *food/artificial colouring*

colourless (*US* **colorless**) /'kʌlələs/ *adjective* **1** [COLOUR] without any colour *a colourless liquid* **2** [INTEREST] without the qualities that make someone or something interesting and unusual

ˈcolour sepaˌration *UK* (*US* **color separation**) *noun* [U] **DT** a method used for printing, where a colour image is divided into 4 images of a single colour which, when put together, make the complete colour image

ˈcolour ˌwheel *UK* (*US* **color wheel**) *noun* [C] **DT** a diagram showing colours in a circle so that you can see the relationship between them

colt /kəʊlt/ *noun* [C] a young male horse

column /'kɒləm/ *noun* [C] **1** [TALL POST] a tall, solid, usually stone post which is used to support a roof or as decoration in a building *a stone/marble column* **2** [NEWSPAPER] a regular article in a newspaper or magazine on a particular subject or by the same writer **3** [PRINT] one of the blocks of print into which a page of a newspaper, magazine, or dictionary is divided **4** [NUMBERS ETC] any block of numbers or words written one under the other **5 a column of sth** something with a tall, narrow shape *A column of smoke rose from the chimney.* **6** [PEOPLE MOVING] a long line of moving people or vehicles *a column of refugees* ➲See also: **gossip column**

columnist /'kɒləmnɪst/ *noun* [C] someone who writes a regular article for a newspaper or magazine *a **sports/gossip columnist***

.com /dɒt'kɒm/ **INTERNET** *internet abbreviation for* company: used in some Internet addresses which belong to companies or businesses *www.google.com*

coma /'kəʊmə/ *noun* [C] **HEALTH** when someone is not conscious for a long time [**usually singular**] *She has been **in a coma** for over a week.*

comb¹ /kəʊm/ *noun* [C] a flat piece of metal or plastic with a row of long, narrow parts along one side, that you use to tidy your hair

comb² /kəʊm/ *verb* [T] **1** [HAIR] to tidy your hair using a comb **2** [SEARCH] to search a place very carefully *Investigators **combed through** the wreckage.*

combat¹ /'kɒmbæt/ *noun* [C, U] a fight, especially during a war *The aircraft was shot down **in combat**.*

WORD PARTNERS FOR ***combat***

combat **crime/global warming/racism/terrorism** • combat **the effects** of sth • combat **a problem** • combat **the threat of** sth • combat **the rise in** [crime, etc]

combat² /ˈkɒmbæt/ *verb* [T] **combatting,** *past* **combatted** or **combating,** *past* **combated** to try to stop something unpleasant or harmful from happening or increasing *new measures to combat the rise in crime*

combatant /ˈkɒmbətᵊnt/ *noun* [C] *formal* someone who fights in a war

C

combative /ˈkɒmbətɪv/ *adjective formal* eager to fight or argue

O‐ **combination** /ˌkɒmbɪˈneɪʃᵊn/ *noun* **1** MIXTURE [C, U] a mixture of different people or things *Strawberries and cream - a perfect combination!* ○ *We won through a **combination of** luck and skill.* ○ *This drug can be safely used **in combination with** other medicines.* **2** LOCK [C] a set of numbers or letters in a particular order which is needed to open some types of locks *a combination lock*

O‐ **combine** /kəmˈbaɪn/ *verb* **1** JOIN TOGETHER [I, T] to become mixed or joined, or to mix or join things together *My wages **combined with** your savings should just pay for it.* ○ *The band combines jazz rhythms and romantic lyrics.* **2** DO BOTH [T] to do two or more activities at the same time *I don't know how she **combines** working **with** studying.*

combined /kəmˈbaɪnd/ *adjective* [always before noun] joined together *the **combined effects** of poverty and disease*

combine harvester /ˌkɒmbaɪnˈhɑːvɪstəʳ/ (*also* **combine**) *noun* [C] **FARMING** a large farm machine which cuts a crop and separates the grain from the stem

combustion /kəmˈbʌstʃᵊn/ *noun* [U] **PHYSICS** the process of burning ➲See picture at **carbon cycle**

O‐ **come** /kʌm/ *verb past tense* **came,** *past participle* **come 1** MOVE TOWARDS [I] to move or travel towards a person who is speaking or towards the place that they are speaking about *Come and see what I've done.* ○ *Can you come to my party?* ○ *The rain came down heavily.* ○ ***Here comes** Adam* (= Adam is coming). **2** ARRIVE [I] to arrive somewhere or go to a place *I'll come and see you later.* [+ **to do sth**] *I've come to see Mr Curtis.* ○ *Dad will **come for** you at six.* ○ *We **came to** a crossroads.* **3** GO WITH SOMEONE [I] to go somewhere with the person who is speaking *Come for a walk with us.* ○ *We're going to the cinema. Do you want to come?* **4 come after/first/last, etc** to have or achieve a particular position in a race, competition, list, etc *Our team came third.* ○ *Sunday comes after Saturday.* **5 come past/to/up to, etc** to reach a particular length, height, or depth *The water came up to my waist.* **6 come apart/off, etc** to become separated or removed from something *The book **came apart** in my hands.* ○ *The handle **came off**.* ○ *My shoelaces have **come undone**.* ○ *The door came open.* **7 come easily/easy/naturally** to be very easy for someone *Singing came naturally to Louise.* **8** HAPPEN [I] to happen *Spring has come early.* ○ *The worst problems are still **to come**.* **9 how come** *informal* used to ask why or how something has happened *How come you didn't go to the party?* **10 come and go** to exist or happen somewhere for a short time and then go away *The feeling of nausea comes and goes.* **11** BE AVAILABLE [I] to be available in a particular size, colour, etc *The table **comes in** three different sizes.* ○ *Furniture like this doesn't **come cheap**.* **12 come to do sth** to start to do something *I have come to rely on acupuncture.* ○ *This place has come to be known as 'Pheasant Corner'.* **13 when it comes to sth/doing sth** used to introduce a new idea that you want to say something about *When it comes to baking cakes, she's an expert.* **14 come to think of it** used to say that you have just thought of something *Come to think of it, I've got two batteries that you can have upstairs.* ➲See also: come to blows (**blow²**), I'll/We'll cross that **bridge¹** when I/we come to it., come **clean¹**, if/when it comes to the **crunch¹**, come (back) down to **earth**, come under **fire¹**, deliver/come up with the **goods**, come to **grief**, come/get to grips (**grip¹**) with sth, come to **light¹**, come into your/its **own¹**, not be/come up to **scratch²**, come to your senses (**sense¹**), come/turn up trumps (**trump**)

come about *phrasal verb* to happen, or start to happen *How did the idea for an arts festival come about?*

come across sb/sth *phrasal verb* to meet someone or discover something by chance *I came across a lovely little restaurant in the village.*

come across *phrasal verb* **1** SEEM to seem to be a particular type of person *He **came across as** shy.* **2** CLEAR If an idea or emotion comes across, it is expressed clearly and people understand it. *His bitterness comes across in his poetry.*

come along *phrasal verb* **1** ARRIVE to arrive or appear at a place *A taxi never comes along when you need one.* **2** GO WITH SOMEONE to go somewhere with someone *We're going to the cinema. Do you want to come along?* **3** EXIST to start to exist *I gave up climbing when my first child came along.* **4 be coming along** to be developing or making progress

come around *phrasal verb* **1** VISIT to visit someone at their house **2** AGREE to change your opinion about something, or agree to an idea or a plan that you were against *I'm sure she'll **come around to** our view eventually.* **3** EVENT If an event that happens regularly comes around, it happens, or is going to happen soon. *Thanksgiving has come around again.* **4 HEALTH** to become conscious again after an accident or medical operation

come back *phrasal verb* **1** RETURN to return to a place *I've just **come back from** the dentist's.* **2** BECOME POPULAR If a style or a fashion comes back, it becomes popular again. *Miniskirts are coming back into fashion.*

come back to sb *phrasal verb* If something comes back to you, you remember it. *Suddenly, the horror of the accident came back to me.*

come between sb *phrasal verb* to harm the relationship between two or more people *I won't let anything come between me and my children.*

come by sth *phrasal verb* to get something, especially something that is unusual or difficult to find *Cheap organic food is still **difficult to come by**.*

come down *phrasal verb* **1** FALL to break and fall to the ground *A lot of trees came down in the storm.* **2** BECOME LOWER If a price or a level comes down, it becomes lower. *Prices always come down after Christmas.* **3** to decide that you support a particular person or side in an argument, etc *The government has **come down on the side of** military action.*

come down on sb *phrasal verb* to punish or criticize someone *The police are **coming down hard on** people for not paying parking fines.*

come down to sth/doing sth *phrasal verb* If a situation, problem, decision, etc comes down to something, then that is the thing that will influence it most.

come down with sth *phrasal verb informal* to get an illness *I came down with the flu at Christmas.*

come forward *phrasal verb* to offer to help someone or to give information *We need witnesses to **come forward with** information about the attack.*

O‒**come from sth** *phrasal verb* to be born, obtained from, or made somewhere *She comes from Poland.* ○ *Milk comes from cows.*

come from sth/doing sth *phrasal verb* to be caused by something *"I feel awful." "That comes from eating too many sweets."*

O‒**come in** *phrasal verb* **1** ENTER to enter a room or building *Do you want to come in for a cup of tea?* **2** FASHION If a fashion or a product comes in, it becomes available or becomes popular. *Flared trousers came in during the seventies.* **3** BE RECEIVED If news, information, a report, etc comes in, it is received. *News is just coming in about the explosion.* **4 come in first/second, etc** to finish a race or a competition in first/second, etc position **5** SEA If the tide (= regular change in the level of the sea) comes in, the sea moves towards the beach or coast. **6** BE INVOLVED *informal* used to describe how someone is involved in a situation, story, or plan *We need people to help clean up, and that's where you come in.*

come in for sth *phrasal verb* If someone comes in for criticism, praise, etc, they are criticized, praised, etc.

come into sth *phrasal verb* **1** to get money from someone who has died *Just after I left university, I came into a bit of money.* **2 come into it** *UK informal* to influence a situation *Money doesn't come into it.*

come of sth/doing sth *phrasal verb* to happen as a result of something *Did anything come of all those job applications?*

come off *phrasal verb* **1** to happen successfully *His attempt to impress us all didn't quite come off.* **2 come off badly/best/well, etc** to be in a bad or good position at the end of a fight, argument, etc *She usually comes off best in an argument.* **3 Come off it!** *informal* used to tell someone that you do not agree with them or do not believe them *Oh, come off it! I saw you take it!*

come on *phrasal verb* **1** START to start to happen or work *The heating comes on at six in the morning.* ○ *I've got a cold coming on.* **2** MAKE PROGRESS to make progress *How's your new novel coming on?* **3 Come on!** *informal* **4** ENCOURAGEMENT used to encourage someone to do something, to hurry, to try harder, etc *Come on! We're going to be late.* **5** DISAGREEMENT used to tell someone that you do not agree with them, do not believe them, etc *Come on Bob! You made the same excuse last week.*

come out *phrasal verb* **1** BECOME AVAILABLE If a book, record, film, etc comes out, it becomes available for people to buy or see. *When does their new album come out?* **2** SUN If the sun, the moon, or a star comes out, it appears in the sky. **3** BECOME KNOWN to become known *The truth about him will come out in the end.* **4** SOCIAL EVENT *UK* to go somewhere with someone for a social event *Would you like to come out for a drink?* **5** RESULT If you describe how something comes out at the end of a process or activity, you say what it is like. *How did your chocolate cake come out?* **6** INFORMATION If results or information come out, they are given to people. *The exam results come out in August.* **7** BE REMOVED If dirt or a mark comes out of something, it disappears when you clean it. *Will this red wine stain come out?* **8** PHOTOGRAPH If a photograph comes out, the picture can be seen clearly. *The photos didn't come out very well.* **9** BE SAID If something that you say comes out in a particular way, you say it in that way. *I wanted to tell her that I loved her, but it came out all wrong.* **10** TELL to tell people that you are homosexual (= sexually attracted to people of the same sex) **11 come out against/in favour of sth** to say publicly that you oppose or support something

come out in sth *phrasal verb* If you come out in a skin disease, it appears on your skin.

come out of sth *phrasal verb* If something comes out of a process or event, it is one of the results. *I hope something good can come out of this mess.*

come out with sth *phrasal verb* to say something suddenly that is not expected

come over *phrasal verb* **1** MOVE TOWARDS to come to a place, move from one place to another, or move towards someone *Are your family **coming over from** Greece for the wedding?* **2** SEEM to seem to be a particular type of person *Henry **came over as** a real enthusiast.*

come over sb *phrasal verb* If a feeling comes over you, you suddenly experience it. *I don't usually get so angry. I don't know what came over me.*

come round *phrasal verb UK* **1** VISIT to visit someone at their house *You must come round to the flat for dinner some time.* **2** AGREE to change your opinion about something, or agree to an idea or a plan that you were against **3** EVENT If an event that happens regularly comes round, it happens, or is going to happen soon. *I can't believe that winter has come round already.* **4** BECOME CONSCIOUS to become conscious again after an accident or medical operation

come through *phrasal verb* **1** RECEIVE If information or a result comes through, you receive it. *Have the results of the tests come through yet?* **2** NOTICE If an emotion comes through, other people can notice it. *His nervousness came through when he spoke.*

come through (sth) *phrasal verb* to manage to get to the end of a difficult or dangerous situation *We've had some hard times, but we've come through them.*

come to *phrasal verb* **HEALTH** to become conscious again after an accident or medical operation

come to sb *phrasal verb* If a thought or idea

C

comes to you, you suddenly remember it or start to think about it.

come to sth *phrasal verb* **1** TOTAL to be a particular total when numbers or amounts are added together *That comes to £50, please.* **2 come to a decision/conclusion/arrangement, etc** to make a decision or decide what to think about something **3** REACH to reach a particular state or situation, especially a bad one *You won't **come to** any **harm**.*

come under sth *phrasal verb* **1 come under attack/criticism/scrutiny, etc** to be attacked, criticized, examined, etc **2** CONTROL to be controlled or dealt with by a particular authority *Water rates come under local government control.* **3** LIST to be in a particular part of a book, list, etc *Hairdressers come under 'beauty salons' in the Yellow Pages.*

come up *phrasal verb* **1** MOVE TOWARDS to move towards someone *After the concert, he **came up to** me to ask for my autograph.* **2** BE DISCUSSED to be discussed or suggested *The issue of security came up at the meeting yesterday.* **3** OPPORTUNITY If a job or opportunity comes up, it becomes available. **4** PROBLEM If a problem or difficult situation comes up, it happens. **5 be coming up** to be happening soon *My exams are coming up next month.* **6** SUN OR MOON When the sun or the moon comes up, it rises. **7 COMPUTING** If information comes up on a computer screen, it appears there.

come up against sb/sth *phrasal verb* to have to deal with a problem or difficulty *She came up against a lot of sexism in her first engineering job.*

come up to sth *phrasal verb* to reach the usual or necessary standard *This essay doesn't **come up to** your usual **standards**.*

come up with sth *phrasal verb* to think of a plan, an idea, or a solution to a problem *We need to come up with a good scheme to make money.*

comeback /ˈkʌmbæk/ *noun* [C] a successful attempt to become powerful, important, or famous again *She's **made a comeback** with her first new album for twenty years.*

comedian /kəˈmiːdiən/ *noun* [C] someone who entertains people by telling jokes

comedown /ˈkʌmdaʊn/ *noun* [C] *informal* a situation that is not as good as one you were in before [**usually singular**] *Cleaning windows is a bit of a comedown after his last job.*

comedy /ˈkɒmədi/ *noun* [C, U] entertainment such as a film, play, etc which is funny *The film is a **romantic comedy**.*

comet /ˈkɒmɪt/ *noun* [C] **ASTRONOMY** an object in space that leaves a bright line behind it in the sky

comfort¹ /ˈkʌmfət/ *noun* **1** NO PAIN [U] a pleasant feeling of being relaxed and free from pain *Now you can watch the latest films **in the comfort of** your sitting room.* **2** FOR SADNESS [U] when you feel better after being worried or sad *What she said brought me great comfort.* **3** ENOUGH MONEY [U] when you have a pleasant life with enough money for everything that you need *He can afford to retire and live **in comfort** for the rest of his life.* **4 a comfort to sb** someone or something that helps you when you are anxious or sad *The children have been a great comfort to me since his death.* **5** PLEASANT THING [C] something that makes your life easy and pleasant [**usually plural**] *Good chocolate is one of life's little comforts.* ➲Opposite **discomfort**

comfort² /ˈkʌmfət/ *verb* [T] to make someone feel better when they are anxious or sad •**comforting** *adjective He said a few comforting words.*

O▬ **comfortable** /ˈkʌmftəbl/ *adjective* **1** NOT CAUSING PAIN Comfortable furniture, clothes, rooms, etc make you feel relaxed and do not cause any pain. *comfortable shoes* ○ *We had a comfortable journey.* **2** PERSON If you are comfortable, you are relaxed and have no pain. ***Make yourself comfortable** while I fetch you a drink.* ➲Opposite **uncomfortable 3** WITHOUT WORRIES If you are comfortable in a situation, you do not have any worries about it. *I don't feel comfortable about leaving the children here alone.* **4** MONEY having enough money for everything that you need *a comfortable retirement* **5** WIN If you win a game or competition by a comfortable amount, you win easily. *a comfortable lead/victory* •**comfortably** *adverb*

comforter /ˈkʌmfətəʳ/ *US* (*UK* **duvet**) *noun* [C] a cover filled with feathers or warm material, that you sleep under

ˈcomfort ˌzone *noun* [C] a situation that you know well and in which you are relaxed and confident *Owen thought about deep-sea diving but decided it was beyond his comfort zone.*

comfy /ˈkʌmfi/ *adjective informal* comfortable

comic¹ /ˈkɒmɪk/ *adjective* funny *a comic actor*

comic² /ˈkɒmɪk/ *noun* [C] **1** MAGAZINE (*also* **ˈcomic ˌbook**) a magazine with stories told in pictures **2** PERSON someone who entertains people by telling jokes

comical /ˈkɒmɪkəl/ *adjective* funny in a strange or silly way *He looked so comical in that hat.* •**comically** *adverb*

ˈcomic ˌstrip *noun* [C] a set of pictures telling a story, usually in a newspaper

coming¹ /ˈkʌmɪŋ/ *noun* **1 the coming of sth** the arrival of something *the coming of spring* **2 comings and goings** people's movements to and from a particular place over a period of time

coming² /ˈkʌmɪŋ/ *adjective* [**always before noun**] a coming time or event will come or happen soon *the coming elections* ➲See also: **up-and-coming**

Comintern (**Komintern**) /ˈkɒmɪntɜːn/ *noun* **POLITICS** a communist organisation founded by Lenin and used by Stalin for controlling people

comma /ˈkɒmə/ *noun* [C] **LANGUAGE** a mark (,) used to separate parts of a sentence, or to separate the items in a list ➲See Extra help page **Punctuation** on page Centre 18. ➲See also: **inverted commas**

command¹ /kəˈmɑːnd/ *noun* **1** CONTROL [U] control over someone or something and responsibility for them *The soldiers were **under the command of** a tough sergeant-major.* ○ *Jones was **in command*** (= the leader). **2** ORDER [C] an order to do something **3** KNOWLEDGE [**no plural**] knowledge of a subject, especially a language *She **had** a good **command of** French.* **4 be at sb's command** to be ready to obey someone's orders **5 COMPUTING** [C] an instruction to a computer

command² /kə'mɑːnd/ *verb formal* **1** CONTROL [T] to control someone or something and tell them what to do *He commanded the armed forces.* **2** ORDER [I, T] to order someone to do something [+ to do sth] *The officer commanded his men to shoot.* **3 command attention/loyalty/respect, etc** to deserve and get attention, loyalty, respect, etc from other people

commandeer /ˌkɒmən'dɪəʳ/ *verb* [T] *formal* to take something, especially for military use *The ships were commandeered as naval vessels.*

commander /kə'mɑːndəʳ/ *noun* [C] an officer who is in charge of a military operation, or an officer of middle rank in the navy

commanding /kə'mɑːndɪŋ/ *adjective* [**always before noun**] in a very successful position and likely to win or succeed *He has a **commanding lead** in the championships.*

commandment /kə'mɑːndmənt/ *noun* [C] **RELIGION** one of the ten important rules of behaviour given by God in the Bible

commando /kə'mɑːndəʊ/ *noun* [C] a soldier who is part of a small group who make surprise attacks

commemorate /kə'meməreɪt/ *verb* [T] to do something to show you remember an important person or event in the past with respect *a ceremony to commemorate the battle* •**commemoration** /kəˌmemə'reɪʃᵊn/ *noun* [U] *a march **in commemoration of** the war of independence*

commemorative /kə'memᵊrətɪv/ *adjective* intended to commemorate a person or event *a commemorative coin*

commence /kə'mens/ *verb* [I, T] *formal* to begin something •**commencement** *noun* [C, U] *formal* the beginning of something

commend /kə'mend/ *verb* [T] *formal* to praise someone or something [**often passive**] *His courage was commended by the report.* •**commendation** /ˌkɒmen'deɪʃᵊn/ *noun* [C, U]

commendable /kə'mendəbl/ *adjective* deserving praise *She showed commendable modesty.*

commensalism /kə'mentsəlɪzᵊm/ *noun* [U] **BIOLOGY** a relationship between two species (= group of animals of the same type) in which one gets an advantage from living closely with the other and the other is not affected by it

WORD PARTNERS FOR ***comment***

make a comment • **make no** comment • do sth **without** comment • a comment **about/on** sth

O-ᵘ**comment¹** /'kɒment/ *noun* [C, U] **1** something that you say or write that shows what you think about something *He **made** negative **comments** to the press.* **2 No comment.** used to say that you do not want to answer someone's question

O-ᵘ**comment²** /'kɒment/ *verb* [I, T] to make a comment *My mum always **comments on** what I'm wearing.* [+ that] *He commented that the two essays were very similar.*

commentary /'kɒməntᵊri/ *noun* **1** RADIO/TELEVISION [C, U] a spoken description of an event on the radio or television while the event is happening *the football commentary* **2** DISCUSSION [U no plural] a discussion or explanation of something *a **commentary on** American culture*

commentator /'kɒmənteɪtəʳ/ *noun* [C] someone who describes an event on the radio or television while it is happening *a **sports commentator***

commerce /'kɒmɜːs/ *noun* [U] the activities involved in buying and selling things ⊃See also: **chamber of commerce, e-commerce**

commercial¹ /kə'mɜːʃᵊl/ *adjective* **1** BUY/SELL relating to buying and selling things **2** FOR PROFIT intended to make a profit *commercial television* •**commercially** *adverb*

commercial² /kə'mɜːʃᵊl/ *noun* [C] an advertisement on the radio or television

commercialism /kə'mɜːʃᵊlɪzᵊm/ *noun* [U] when making money is the most important aim of an activity

commercialized (*also UK* **-ised**) /kə'mɜːʃəlaɪzd/ *adjective* organized to make profits *Christmas has become so commercialized.* •**commercialization** /kəˌmɜːʃᵊlaɪ'zeɪʃᵊn/ *noun* [U]

commiserate /kə'mɪzᵊreɪt/ *verb* [I] to express sympathy to someone who is sad or has had bad luck

commission¹ /kə'mɪʃᵊn/ *noun* **1 POLITICS** [group] an official group of people who have been chosen to find out about something and say what they think should be done about it **2** PIECE OF WORK [C, U] when you arrange for someone to do a piece of work for you such as painting, writing, or making something **3 FINANCE** [C, U] money given to someone when they sell something *The staff receive 5% **commission on** everything that they sell.* ○ *Many salesmen work **on commission**.*

commission² /kə'mɪʃᵊn/ *verb* [T] to arrange for someone to do a piece of work [+ to do sth] *I've been commissioned to write a song for their wedding.*

commissioner /kə'mɪʃənəʳ/ *noun* [C] a member of a commission or someone with an important government job in a particular area

O-ᵘ**commit** /kə'mɪt/ *verb* [T] **committing**, *past* **committed 1** CRIME to do something that is considered wrong, or that is illegal *He was sent to prison for a **crime** that he didn't **commit**.* ○ *to **commit suicide/adultery*** **2** DECISION to make a firm decision that you will do something *He **committed himself to** helping others.* **3 not commit yourself** to refuse to express an opinion about a particular subject **4** MONEY/TIME If you commit money, time, energy, etc to something, you use it to try to achieve something. *The government has **committed** thousands of pounds **to** the research.*

WORD PARTNERS FOR ***commitment***

make a commitment • **fulfil/honour/meet** a commitment • a commitment **to** sth

O-ᵘ**commitment** /kə'mɪtmənt/ *noun* **1** PROMISE [C] a promise or firm decision to do something

*Players must **make a commitment to** daily training.* **2** LOYALTY [U] when you are willing to give your time and energy to something that you believe in *We are looking for someone with talent, enthusiasm, and commitment.* **3** ACTIVITY [C] something that you must do that takes your time *I've got too many commitments at the moment.*

C

committed /kəˈmɪtɪd/ *adjective* loyal and willing to give your time and energy to something that you believe in *a committed Christian* ○ *She's **committed to** the job.*

committee /kəˈmɪti/ *noun* [group] a group of people who have been chosen to represent a larger organization and make decisions for it

commodity /kəˈmɒdəti/ *noun* [C] **ECONOMICS** a product that you can buy or sell

O→**common¹** /ˈkɒmən/ *adjective* **1** USUAL happening often or existing in large numbers *Injuries are common in sports such as hockey.* ⊃Opposite **uncommon** **2** SHARED belonging to or shared by two or more people or things *a **common goal/interest*** ○ *English has some features **common to** many languages.* **3 common knowledge** something that a lot of people know [+ **that**] *It's common knowledge that he spent time in jail.* **4** ORDINARY [**always before noun**] not special in any way *The herbs all have **common names** and Latin names.* **5** LOW CLASS *UK* typical of a low social class *My mum thinks dyed blonde hair is really common.*

common² /ˈkɒmən/ *noun* **1 have sth in common** to share interests, experiences, or other characteristics with someone or something *Sue and I don't have much in common.* **2 in common with sb/sth** in the same way as someone or something *In common with many working mothers, she feels guilty towards her children.* **3** [C] a large area of grass in a town or village which everyone is allowed to use

ˌcommon deˈnominator *noun* [C] **MATHEMATICS** a number that can be divided exactly by all the denominators (=numbers under the lines) of a group of fractions

ˌcommon ˈfactor *noun* [C] **MATHEMATICS** a number that two or more other numbers can be divided by exactly

ˌcommon ˈfraction *noun* [C] **MATHEMATICS** a fraction written with one number above and one number below the line, not written as a number with a decimal point in it

ˌcommon ˈground *noun* [U] shared interests, beliefs, or ideas *It's difficult for me to **find** any **common ground** with my dad.*

common-law /ˌkɒmənˈlɔː/ *adjective* [**always before noun**] A common-law wife or husband is someone who is not married, but has lived with their partner for a long time as if they were married.

commonly /ˈkɒmənli/ *adverb* often or usually *These caterpillars are commonly found on nettles.*

ˌcommon ˈmultiple *noun* [C] **MATHEMATICS** a number that can be divided exactly by two or more different numbers

commonplace /ˈkɒmənpleɪs/ *adjective* [**never before noun**] happening often or existing in large numbers, and so not considered special or unusual

the Commons /ˈkɒmənz/ (*also* **the House of Commons**) *noun* **POLITICS** one of the two parts of the British parliament, with elected members who make laws

ˌcommon ˈsalt *noun* [U] **FOOD** sodium chloride, a substance used especially to make food taste better

ˌcommon ˈsense *noun* [U] the natural ability to be practical and to make good decisions *The children shouldn't be in any danger as long as they use their common sense.*

the Commonwealth /ˈkɒmənwelθ/ *noun* **POLITICS** Britain and the group of countries that used to be in the British Empire (= ruled by Britain)

commotion /kəˈməʊʃən/ *noun* [**U no plural**] a sudden period of noise and confused or excited movement *He looked up to see what all the commotion was about.*

communal /ˈkɒmjʊnəl/ (US) /kəˈmjuːnəl/ *adjective* belonging to or used by a group of people *a communal changing room*

commune /ˈkɒmjuːn/ *noun* [C] **SOCIETY** a group of people who live together, sharing the work and the things they own

communicate /kəˈmjuːnɪkeɪt/ *verb* [**I, T**] **1** INFORMATION to share information with others by speaking, writing, moving your body, or using other signals *We can now **communicate** instantly **with** people on the other side of the world.* **2** FEELINGS to talk about your thoughts and feelings, and help other people to understand them *He can't **communicate with** his parents.*

WORD PARTNERS FOR ***communication***

communication **between** sb and sb • **in** communication with sb • a **means of** communication • a **breakdown in** communication • communication **skills**

O→**communication** /kəˌmjuːnɪˈkeɪʃən/ *noun* **1** COMMUNICATING [U] the act of communicating with other people *The school is improving **communication between** teachers and parents.* ○ *We are **in direct communication with** Moscow.* **2** MESSAGE [C] *formal* a message sent to someone by letter, email, telephone, etc

communications /kəˌmjuːnɪˈkeɪʃənz/ *noun* [**plural**] the different ways of sending information between people and places, such as post, telephones, computers, and radio *the communications industry*

communicative /kəˈmjuːnɪkətɪv/ *adjective* willing to talk to people and give them information

communion /kəˈmjuːniən/ *noun* [U] **RELIGION** (*also* **Communion**) the Christian ceremony in which people eat bread and drink wine, as symbols of Christ's body and blood

communiqué /kəˈmjuːnɪkeɪ/ (US) /kəˌmjuːnɪˈkeɪ/ *noun* [C] an official announcement

communism, Communism /ˈkɒmjənɪzəm/ *noun* [U] **POLITICS** a political system in which the government controls the production of all goods, and where everyone is treated equally

communist, Communist /ˈkɒmjənɪst/ *noun* [C] **POLITICS** someone who supports communism •**communist** *adjective a communist country/leader*

community /kəˈmjuːnəti/ *noun* **1 SOCIETY** [C] the people living in a particular area *a rural/small community* **2 SOCIETY** [group] a group of people with the same interests, nationality, job, etc *the business/Chinese community* **3 BIOLOGY, ENVIRONMENT** a group of plants or animals living in the same area ➲See picture at **ecosystem**

comˈmunity ˌcentre *UK* (*US* **community center**) *noun* [C] a place where people who live in an area can meet together to play sport, go to classes, etc

comˌmunity ˈcollege *noun* [C, U] *US* **EDUCATION** a two-year college where students can learn a skill or prepare to enter a university

comˌmunity ˈservice *noun* [U] **LAW** work that someone who has committed a crime does to help other people instead of going to prison

commutative /kəˈmjuːtətɪv/ *adjective* **MATHEMATICS** a commutative calculation gives the same result whatever the order of the quantities in it

commutator /ˈkɒmjuteɪtəʳ/ *noun* [C] **1 PHYSICS** a device that changes the direction that electricity moves **2** a device for connecting a motor to an electricity supply

commute /kəˈmjuːt/ *verb* [I] to regularly travel between work and home •**commuter** *noun* [C]

compact¹ /kəmˈpækt/ *adjective* small and including many things in a small space

compact² /kəmˈpækt/ *verb* [T] to press something together so that it becomes tight or solid

ˌcompact ˈdisc *noun* [C] a CD (= a disc for recorded music or information)

companion /kəmˈpænjən/ *noun* [C] someone who you spend a lot of time with or go somewhere with *a travelling companion*

companionship /kəmˈpænjənʃɪp/ *noun* [U] the feeling of having friends around you

WORD PARTNERS FOR ***company***

establish/found/set up/start up a company

O‑ **company** /ˈkʌmpəni/ *noun* **1** BUSINESS [C] an organization which sells goods or services *a software/telephone company* **2** PEOPLE [U] when you have a person or people with you *I enjoy his company.* ○ *I didn't realize that you* ***had company***. **3 keep sb company** to stay with someone so that they are not alone **4 be good company** to be a pleasant or interesting person to spend time with **5** PERFORMERS [C] a group of performers such as actors or dancers *the Royal Shakespeare Company* ➲See also: **limited company**

ˌcompany ˈsecretary *noun* [C] *UK* a person in a business who has particular legal duties

comparable /ˈkɒmpᵊrəbl/ *adjective* similar in size, amount, or quality to something else *Our prices are* ***comparable to*** *those in other shops.*

comparative¹ /kəmˈpærətɪv/ *adjective* **1 comparative comfort/freedom/silence, etc** a situation which is comfortable/free/silent, etc when compared to another situation or to what is usual *I enjoyed the comparative calm of his flat after the busy office.* **2** comparing similar things *a comparative study of two poems*

comparative² /kəmˈpærətɪv/ *noun* [C] **LANGUAGE** the form of an adjective or adverb that is used to show that someone or something has more of a particular quality than someone or something else. For example 'better' is the comparative of 'good' and 'smaller' is the comparative of 'small'. ➲Compare **superlative**

comparatively /kəmˈpærətɪvli/ *adverb* **comparatively cheap/easy/little, etc** cheap/easy/little, etc when compared to something else or to what is usual

O‑ **compare** /kəmˈpeəʳ/ *verb* **1** EXAMINE [T] to examine the ways in which two people or things are different or similar *The teachers are always* ***comparing me with/to*** *my sister.* **2** AS GOOD [I] to be as good as something else *This product* ***compares well with*** *more expensive brands.* **3 compared to/with sb/sth** used when saying how one person or thing is different from another *This room is very tidy compared to mine.* ➲See also: compare notes (**note¹**)

compare sb/sth to sb/sth *phrasal verb* to say that someone or something is similar to someone or something else

WORD PARTNERS FOR ***comparison***

draw/make a comparison • a comparison **between** sth and sth • a comparison **of** sth **(with** sth) • **by/in** comparison **(with** sth)

O‑ **comparison** /kəmˈpærɪsᵊn/ *noun* [C, U] **1** when you compare two or more people or things *They published a* ***comparison of*** *schools in the area.* ○ *She's so tall that he looks tiny* ***by/in comparison***. **2 There's no comparison.** used to say that someone or something is much better than someone or something else

compartment /kəmˈpɑːtmənt/ *noun* [C] **1** VEHICLE one of the separate areas inside a vehicle, especially a train *The first class compartment is at the front of the train.* **2** CONTAINER a separate part of a container, bag, etc *a fridge with a small freezer compartment*

compass /ˈkʌmpəs/ *noun* [C] a piece of equipment which shows you which direction you are going in

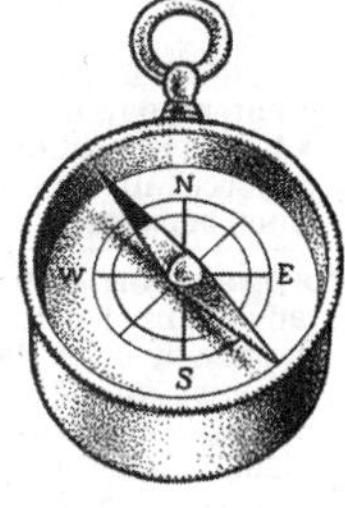

compass

compasses /ˈkʌmpəsɪz/ *noun* [plural] *UK* (*US* **compass** [C]) a piece of equipment which is used for drawing circles

compassion /kəmˈpæʃᵊn/ *noun* [U] a feeling of sympathy for people who are suffering

compassionate /kəmˈpæʃᵊnət/ *adjective* showing compassion

compatible /kəmˈpætɪbl/ *adjective* **1** EQUIPMENT compatible equipment can be used together *This keyboard is* ***compatible with*** *all of our computers.* **2** PEOPLE If people are compatible, they like each other and are happy to spend time together. **3** [IDEAS] *formal* compatible ideas or situations can exist together *Such policies are not **compatible with** democratic government.* **•compatibility** /kəm,pætə'bɪləti/ *noun* [U]

compatriot /kəm'pætriət/ *noun* [C] **SOCIETY** *formal* someone who comes from the same country

C

compel /kəm'pel/ *verb* **compelling** *past* **compelled** *formal* **compel sb to do sth** to force someone to do something [**often passive**] *He felt compelled to resign from his job.*

compelling /kəm'pelɪŋ/ *adjective* **1** [EXCITING] very exciting or interesting and making you want to watch, listen, etc *a compelling story* **2** [TRUE] If a reason, argument, etc is compelling, it makes you believe it or accept it because it is so strong. ***compelling evidence***

compensate /'kɒmpənseɪt/ *verb* **1** **FINANCE** [T] to pay someone money because you are responsible for injuring them or damaging something *Victims of the crash will be **compensated for** their injuries.* **2** [I, T] to reduce the bad effect of something, or make something bad become something good *Nothing will ever **compensate for** his lost childhood.*

compensation /,kɒmpən'seɪʃən/ *noun* **1** **FINANCE** [U] money that you pay to someone because you are responsible for injuring them or damaging something *Most of the workers have **won compensation for** losing their jobs.* **2** [C, U] something you get to make you feel better when you have suffered something bad *Free food was no **compensation for** a very boring evening.*

compete /kəm'piːt/ *verb* [I] **1** [COMPETITION] to take part in a race or competition *She's **competing for** a place in next year's Olympics.* **2** [SUCCESS] to try to be more successful than someone or something else *It's difficult for small shops to **compete with/against** the big supermarkets.*

competent /'kɒmpɪtənt/ *adjective* able to do something well *a competent swimmer/teacher* **•competence** /'kɒmpɪtəns/ *noun* [U] the ability to do something well **•competently** *adverb*

WORD PARTNERS FOR ***competition***

1 enter/go in for/take part in a competition • **hold** a competition • **win** a competition
2 fierce/intense/stiff competition • competition **between** sb and sb • competition **for** sth

O➔ **competition** /,kɒmpə'tɪʃən/ *noun* **1** [EVENT] [C] an organized event in which people try to win a prize by being the best, fastest, etc *to **enter a competition*** **2** [SITUATION] [U] when someone is trying to win something or be more successful than someone else *There's a lot of **competition between** computer companies.* ○ *Applicants face stiff **competition for** university places this year.* **3** **the competition** people you are competing against, especially in business

competitive /kəm'petɪtɪv/ *adjective* **1** [SITUATION] involving competition *competitive sports* ○ *a highly competitive industry* **2** [PERSON] wanting to win or to be more successful than other people *She's very competitive.* **3** **ECONOMICS** Competitive prices, services, etc are as good as or better than other prices, services, etc. **•competitively** *adverb* **•competitiveness** *noun* [U]

competitor /kəm'petɪtər/ *noun* [C] a person, team, or company that is competing with others

compilation /,kɒmpɪ'leɪʃən/ *noun* [C] a recording, book, or film containing a collection of things from many different recordings, books, or films

compile /kəm'paɪl/ *verb* [T] to collect information and arrange it in a book, report, or list

compiler /kəm'paɪlər/ *noun* [C] **COMPUTING** a computer program that changes instructions into machine language

complacent /kəm'pleɪsənt/ *adjective* feeling so satisfied with your own abilities or situation that you do not feel that you need to try any harder *We can't afford to become too complacent about our work.* **•complacency** *noun* [U] when someone is complacent **•complacently** *adverb*

OTHER WAYS OF SAYING ***complain***

The verbs **grumble**, **moan** and (*UK, informal*) **whinge** are sometimes used when someone is complaining about things which are not important: *She's always **grumbling** about something.* • *He's forever **moaning** about his work.* • *I hope you don't think I'm just **whingeing**.*

If someone, especially a child, complains in an annoying way, the verb **whine** is often used: *Stop **whining**, Tom - it's not that bad!*

The expression **kick up a fuss** is sometimes used in informal contexts, especially when someone is complaining that something has not happened in the way they wanted: *If the food doesn't come soon, I'm going to **kick up a fuss**.*

O➔ **complain** /kəm'pleɪn/ *verb* [I] to say that something is wrong or that you are annoyed about something *Lots of people have **complained about** the noise.* [**+ that**] *He's always complaining that nobody listens to him.*
complain of sth *phrasal verb* to tell other people that something is making you feel ill *She's been complaining of a headache all day.*

COMMON LEARNER ERROR

complain about something

Be careful to choose the correct preposition after **complain**.

*I am writing to **complain about** the trip.*

~~*I am writing to complain for the trip.*~~

~~*I am writing to complain on the trip.*~~

WORD PARTNERS FOR ***complaint***

make/investigate/receive a complaint • a complaint **about** sb/sth • a complaint **against** sb • a **formal/official/written** complaint • a **letter of** complaint • have **cause for/grounds for** complaint

O➔ **complaint** /kəm'pleɪnt/ *noun* **1** [NOT SATISFACTORY] [C, U] when someone says that something is wrong or not satisfactory *a letter of complaint* ○ *I wish to **make a complaint**.*

2 ANNOYING THING [C] something that makes you complain *My only complaint was the lack of refreshments.* **3** ILLNESS [C] an illness *a stomach complaint*

complement¹ /ˈkɒmplɪmənt/ *noun* [C] **1** MAKE GOOD something that makes something else seem good, attractive, or complete *This wine is the perfect* ***complement to*** *the meal.* **2** TOTAL NUMBER the total amount or number of something that is needed to complete a group *Do we have* ***a full complement of*** *players for Saturday's match?* **3** LANGUAGE a word or phrase which comes after the verb and gives more information about the subject of the verb **4** MATHEMATICS the angle that, when it is added to another angle, makes a right angle (= angle of 90°)

complement² /ˈkɒmplɪment/ *verb* [T] to make something else seem good or attractive *The music complements her voice perfectly.*

complementary /ˌkɒmplɪˈmentəri/ *adjective* **1** Things which are complementary are good or attractive together. *complementary colours/flavours* **2 complementary medicine/treatment, etc** HEALTH ways of treating medical problems which people use instead of or in addition to ordinary medicine *The clinic offers complementary therapies such as homeopathy.*

compleˌmentary ˈangle *noun* [C, usually plural] MATHEMATICS one of two angles which together add up to 90° ➲Compare **supplementary angle**

complete¹ /kəmˈpliːt/ *adjective* **1** WHOLE with all parts *the* ***complete works*** *of Oscar Wilde* ○ *The report comes* ***complete with*** (= including) *diagrams and colour photographs.* **2** TOTAL [always before noun] used to emphasize what you are saying *a complete waste of time* **3** FINISHED finished *Our report is almost complete.*

O⊸**complete²** /kəmˈpliːt/ *verb* [T] **1** FINISH to finish doing or making something *The palace took 15 years to complete.* **2** MAKE STH WHOLE to provide the last part needed to make something whole *Complete the sentence with one of the adjectives provided.* **3** WRITE to write all the details asked for on a form or other document

O⊸**completely** /kəmˈpliːtli/ *adverb* in every way or as much as possible *I completely forgot that you were coming.*

completion /kəmˈpliːʃən/ *noun* [U] when something that you are doing or making is finished *The stadium is due for completion in 2008.* ○ *They will be paid* ***on completion of*** *the job.*

O⊸**complex¹** /ˈkɒmpleks, kəmˈpleks/ *adjective* involving a lot of different but connected parts in a way that is difficult to understand *complex details/issues* ○ *The situation is very complex.* •**complexity** /kəmˈpleksəti/ *noun* [C, U] when something is complex *the complexities of life*

complex² /ˈkɒmpleks/ *noun* [C] **1** BUILDINGS a group of buildings or rooms that are used for a particular purpose *a sports/housing complex* **2** MENTAL a mental problem which makes someone anxious or frightened about something *an* ***inferiority complex***

ˌcomplex carboˈhydrate *noun* [C] BIOLOGY, FOOD a type of carbohydrate such as starch or cellulose that is is formed of many monosaccharides (= carbohydrates formed of molecules that cannot be broken down into a simpler form)

complexion /kəmˈplekʃən/ *noun* [C] **1** SKIN the colour and appearance of the skin on someone's face *a clear complexion* **2** GENERAL CHARACTER the way something seems to be *This new information* ***puts a*** *completely different* ***complexion on*** *the situation.*

ˌcomplex ˈnumber *noun* [C] MATHEMATICS a number that contains a real number and an imaginary number ➲Compare **imaginary number, real number**

compliance /kəmˈplaɪəns/ *noun* [U] *formal* when people obey an order, rule, or request *The work was done* ***in compliance with*** *planning regulations.*

compliant /kəmˈplaɪənt/ *adjective* Compliant people are willing to do what other people want them to.

complicate /ˈkɒmplɪkeɪt/ *verb* [T] to make something more difficult to deal with or understand *These new regulations just complicate matters further.*

O⊸**complicated** /ˈkɒmplɪkeɪtɪd/ *adjective* involving a lot of different parts, in a way that is difficult to understand *a complicated problem/process* ○ *The instructions were too complicated for me.*

complication /ˌkɒmplɪˈkeɪʃən/ *noun* [C] **1** something which makes a situation more difficult **2** HEALTH a new medical problem that develops when you are already ill *Eye problems can be a complication of diabetes.*

complicity /kəmˈplɪsəti/ *noun* [U] *formal* when someone is involved in doing something wrong

compliment¹ /ˈkɒmplɪmənt/ *noun* **1** [C] something that you say or do to show praise or admiration for someone *She was always* ***paying*** *him* ***compliments.*** **2 with the compliments of sb** *formal* used by someone to express good wishes when they give you something free, for example in a restaurant *Please accept this champagne with the compliments of the manager.*

compliment² /ˈkɒmplɪment/ *verb* [T] to praise or express admiration for someone *He* ***complimented*** *me* ***on*** *my writing.*

complimentary /ˌkɒmplɪˈmentəri/ *adjective* **1** PRAISING praising or expressing admiration for someone *a complimentary report* **2** FREE given free, especially by a business *a complimentary glass of wine*

comply /kəmˈplaɪ/ *verb* [I] to obey an order, rule, or request *The pilot* ***complied with*** *instructions to descend.*

component /kəmˈpəʊnənt/ *noun* [C] one of the parts of something, especially a machine

compose /kəmˈpəʊz/ *verb* **1** [T] to be the parts that something consists of [often passive] *The committee* ***was composed of*** *elected leaders and citizens.* **2** MUSIC [I, T] to write a piece of music **3 compose yourself** to make yourself calm again after being angry or upset **4** LANGUAGE [T] to write a speech, letter, etc, thinking carefully about the words to use *Laura was composing a letter of sympathy.*

composed /kəmˈpəʊzd/ *adjective* calm and in control of your emotions

composer /kəmˈpəʊzəʳ/ *noun* [C] **MUSIC** someone who writes music

C

composite /ˈkɒmpəzɪt/ *adjective* consisting of several different parts *a composite image of the killer*

composition /ˌkɒmpəˈzɪʃᵊn/ *noun* **1** PARTS [U] the parts, substances, etc that something consists of *the composition of the atmosphere* **2 MUSIC** [C] a piece of music that someone has written **3 MUSIC** [U] the process or skill of writing music *He taught composition at Yale.* **4 EDUCATION** [C, U] a short piece of writing about a particular subject, done by a student **5 ART** [U] the way that people or things are arranged in a painting or photograph

compost /ˈkɒmpɒst/ *noun* [U] **FARMING** a mixture of decayed leaves and plants that is added to the soil to improve its quality *a* ***compost heap***

composure /kəmˈpəʊʒəʳ/ *noun* [U] when you feel or look calm and confident *to* ***keep/lose your composure***

compound¹ /ˈkɒmpaʊnd/ *noun* [C] **1 BIOLOGY** a substance that is a combination of two or more elements *Water is a compound of hydrogen and oxygen.* **2** an area of land with a group of buildings surrounded by a fence or wall *a prison compound* **3 LANGUAGE** (*also* **compound noun/verb/adjective**) a noun, verb, or adjective that is made by two or more words used together. For example, 'golf club' is a compound.

compound² /kəmˈpaʊnd/ *verb* [T] to make a problem or difficult situation worse *Severe drought has compounded food shortages in the region.*

ˌcompound ˈeye *noun* [C] **BIOLOGY** a type of eye that some insects have, made of many separate parts ➲Compare **simple eye**

ˈcompound ˌleaf *noun* [C] **BIOLOGY** a type of leaf which is formed from a number of smaller leaves all joined to one stem ➲Compare **simple leaf**

compère /ˈkɒmpeəʳ/ *noun* [C] *UK* someone whose job is to introduce performers on television, radio, or in a theatre

comprehend /ˌkɒmprɪˈhend/ *verb* [I, T] *formal* to understand *I was too young to comprehend what was happening.*

comprehensible /ˌkɒmprɪˈhensəbl/ *adjective* easy to understand *Computer manuals should be easily comprehensible.*

comprehension /ˌkɒmprɪˈhenʃᵊn/ *noun* **1** [U] the ability to understand something *It's* ***beyond my comprehension*** (= I can't understand) *how anyone could be so cruel.* **2 EDUCATION** [C, U] *UK* a test to see how well students understand written or spoken language *a reading comprehension*

comprehensive¹ /ˌkɒmprɪˈhensɪv/ *adjective* including everything *a comprehensive study of the subject* •**comprehensively** *adverb* completely *We were comprehensively beaten in the finals.*

comprehensive² /ˌkɒmprɪˈhensɪv/ (*also* **compreˈhensive ˌschool**) *noun* [C] **EDUCATION** a school in Britain for students aged 11 to 18 of all levels of ability

compress /kəmˈpres/ *verb* [T] **1** to make something smaller, especially by pressing it, so that it uses less space or time *compressed air* ○ *The course* ***compresses*** *two years' training* ***into*** *six months.* **2 COMPUTING** to use a special program to make information on a computer use less space •**compression** /kəmˈpreʃᵊn/ *noun* [U]

comˈpression ˌmoulding *noun* [U] **DT** a method of making plastic shapes by pressing plastic between two shapes and heating it

comprise /kəmˈpraɪz/ *verb* [T] *formal* **1** CONSIST to consist of particular parts or members *The orchestra* ***was comprised of*** *amateur and professional musicians.* **2** FORM to form part of something, especially a larger group *Women comprise 15% of the police force.*

WORD PARTNERS FOR ***compromise***

accept/come to/find/reach a compromise • a compromise **between** sth and sth • a compromise **on** sth • a compromise **agreement/ deal/solution**

compromise¹ /ˈkɒmprəmaɪz/ *noun* [C, U] when you agree to something which is not exactly what you want *We need to* ***reach a compromise*** *over this issue.* ○ *Decorating is usually a* ***compromise between*** *taste and cost.*

compromise² /ˈkɒmprəmaɪz/ *verb* **1** AGREE [I] to agree to something that is not exactly what you want *The president may be willing to compromise in order to pass the bill.* ○ *I never* ***compromise on*** *fresh ingredients.* **2 compromise yourself** to do something dishonest or embarrassing that makes people stop admiring you **3** BELIEFS [T] to do something that does not agree with what you believe in *I refuse to compromise my principles.* **4** HARM [T] *formal* to have a harmful effect on something *The trial has been seriously compromised by sensational media coverage.*

compromising /ˈkɒmprəmaɪzɪŋ/ *adjective* A compromising situation, photograph, etc makes people think you have done something wrong. *The press printed compromising photographs of the princess and her bodyguard.*

compulsion /kəmˈpʌlʃᵊn/ *noun* **1** WISH [C] a strong wish to do something, often something that you should not do **2** FORCING [U] when you are forced to do something *We were* ***under no compulsion*** *to attend.*

compulsive /kəmˈpʌlsɪv/ *adjective* **1** HABIT A compulsive habit is something that you do a lot because you want to so much that you cannot control yourself. *a compulsive eating disorder* **2 a compulsive eater/gambler/liar, etc** someone who is unable to stop eating, lying, etc, despite knowing that they should stop **3** INTERESTING so interesting or exciting that you cannot stop reading, playing, or watching it *This documentary about life in prison makes* ***compulsive viewing.*** •**compulsively** *adverb*

compulsory /kəm'pʌlsəri/ *adjective* If something is compulsory, you must do it because of a rule or law.

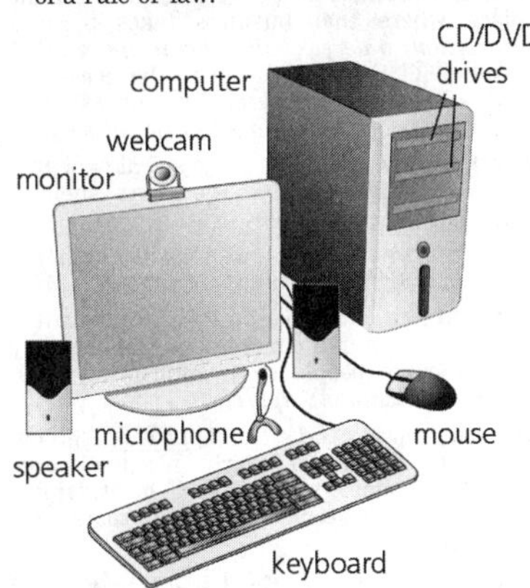

computer

O–■ **computer** /kəm'pjuːtər/ *noun* [C] **COMPUTING** an electronic machine that can store and arrange large amounts of information *We've put all our records **on computer**.* ○ *computer software* ➲See colour picture **The Office** on page Centre 5

com,puter aided de'sign ➲See: **CAD**

com,puter-aided 'learning (*also* **computer-assisted learning**) *noun* [U] **EDUCATION** the use of computers for teaching and learning

com,puter-aided manu'facture ➲See: **CAM**

computerize (*also UK* **-ise**) /kəm'pjuːtəraɪz/ *verb* [T] **COMPUTING** to use a computer to do something that was done by people or other machines before *a computerized accounts system* •**computerization** /kəm,pjuːtəraɪ'zeɪʃən/ *noun* [U]

com,puter 'literate *adjective* **COMPUTING** able to understand and use computer systems

com,puter 'science *noun* [U] **COMPUTING** the study of computers and how they can be used

computing /kəm'pjuːtɪŋ/ *noun* [U] **COMPUTING** the study or use of computers *a degree in computing*

comrade /'kɒmreɪd/ (US) /'kɑːmræd/ *noun* [C] **1** FRIEND *literary* a friend, especially someone who fights with you in a war **2** TITLE a word used by some members of trade unions (= organizations which represent people who do a particular job) or other Socialist organizations to talk to or about each other

comradeship /'kɒmreɪdʃɪp/ *noun* [U] the feeling of friendship between people who live or work together, especially in a difficult situation

con¹ /kɒn/ *verb* [T] **conning,** *past* **conned** *informal* to trick someone, especially in order to take money from them *Thieves **conned him out of** his life savings.* ○ *She felt she had been **conned into** buying the car.*

con² /kɒn/ *noun* [C] *informal* a trick to get someone's money, or make them do what you want

'con ,artist *noun* [C] someone who tricks people into giving them money or valuable things

concave /'kɒnkeɪv/ *adjective* **PHYSICS** A concave surface curves inwards. *a concave lens*

conceal /kən'siːl/ *verb* [T] to hide something *The listening device was concealed in a pen.* ○ *She could barely conceal her irritation.* •**concealment** *noun* [U] when something is hidden

concede /kən'siːd/ *verb* **1** ADMIT [T] to admit that something is true, even though you do not want to [+ **(that)**] *Even the company chairman concedes that the results are disappointing.* **2** GIVE [I, T] to allow someone to have something, even though you do not want to *The government will not **concede to** rebel demands.* **3 concede defeat** to admit that you have lost a fight, argument, game, etc

conceit /kən'siːt/ *noun* [U] when you are too proud of yourself and your actions

conceited /kən'siːtɪd/ *adjective* too proud of yourself and your actions •**conceitedly** *adverb*

conceivable /kən'siːvəbl/ *adjective* possible to imagine or to believe *every conceivable kind of fruit* [+ **(that)**] *It is just conceivable that the hospital made a mistake.* •**conceivably** *adverb*

conceive /kən'siːv/ *verb* **1 BIOLOGY** [I, T] to become pregnant **2** IMAGINE [I, T] to be able to imagine something *I cannot **conceive of** anything more horrible.* **3** IDEA [T] to think of an idea or plan *The original idea for the novel was conceived in Rome.*

O–■ **concentrate¹** /'kɒnsəntreɪt/ *verb* **1** [I] to think very carefully about something you are doing and nothing else *Be quiet - I'm trying to concentrate.* ○ *I can't **concentrate on** my work. It's too noisy here.* **2 be concentrated around/in/on, etc** to be present in large numbers or amounts in a particular area *Most of the fighting was concentrated in the mountains.*

concentrate on sth *phrasal verb* to use most of your time and effort to do something *She gave up her job to concentrate on writing a novel.*

concentrate² /'kɒnsəntreɪt/ *noun* [C, U] **CHEMISTRY** a substance that is strong because it has had water or other substances taken out of it

concentrated /'kɒnsəntreɪtɪd/ *adjective* **1** DETERMINED [**always before noun**] using a lot of effort to succeed at one particular thing *a **concentrated effort** to finish the work* **2** LIQUID A concentrated liquid has had most of the water removed. *concentrated tomato puree* ➲See picture at **diffusion**

WORD PARTNERS FOR ***concentration***

sth **demands/needs/requires** concentration • **lose** concentration • a **lapse in/of** concentration • your **powers of** concentration

concentration /,kɒnsən'treɪʃən/ *noun* **1** THINKING CAREFULLY [U] the ability to think carefully about something you are doing and nothing else **2** LARGE AMOUNT [C, U] a large number or amount of something in the same place ***high concentrations** of minerals* **3** [C, U] **CHEMISTRY** the amount of a substance in a liquid or other substance

C

concen'tration ˌcamp *noun* [C] a prison where large numbers of people are kept in very bad conditions, especially for political reasons

concentric /kən'sentrɪk/ *adjective* **MATHEMATICS** Concentric circles have the same centre but are different sizes.

concept /'kɒnsept/ *noun* [C] an idea or principle *the concept of free speech*

conception /kən'sepʃən/ *noun* **1** [C, U] an idea about what something is like or a way of understanding something **2 BIOLOGY** [U] when a woman or animal becomes pregnant

conceptual /kən'septʃuəl/ *adjective formal* based on ideas *a conceptual model*

concern¹ /kən'sɜːn/ *verb* [T] **1** INVOLVE to involve someone or be important to them *Environmental issues concern us all.* **2** WORRY to worry or upset someone *What really concerns me is her lack of experience.* **3** BE ABOUT If a story, film, etc concerns a particular subject, it is about that subject. **4 concern yourself** to become involved with doing something *You needn't concern yourself with the travel arrangements.*

WORD PARTNERS FOR ***concern***

cause concern • **express/raise/voice** concern • **grave/serious** concern • concerns **about/over** sth • a **matter of** concern • a **cause for** concern

concern² /kən'sɜːn/ *noun* **1** WORRY [C, U] a feeling of worry about something, or the thing that is worrying you *I have **concerns about** his health.* **2** IMPORTANT THING [C, U] something that involves or affects you or is important to you *Our primary concern is safety.* **3** BUSINESS [C] a company or business *The perfume factory was a family concern.*

O⁻**concerned** /kən'sɜːnd/ *adjective* **1** WORRIED worried [+ that] *I am very concerned that class sizes seem to be growing.* ○ *People are becoming more **concerned about** what they eat.* ➲Opposite **unconcerned 2** AFFECTED [never before noun] involved in something or affected by it *A letter will be sent out to everyone concerned.* **3 as far as sb is concerned** used to show what someone thinks about something *As far as our customers are concerned, price is the main consideration.* **4 as far as sth is concerned** used to tell someone what you are talking about *As far as college is concerned, everything is fine.*

concerning /kən'sɜːnɪŋ/ *preposition* about something *I've had a letter concerning my tax payments.*

O⁻**concert** /'kɒnsət/ *noun* [C] **MUSIC** a performance of music and singing *a pop concert*

concerted /kən'sɜːtɪd/ *adjective* [always before noun] done with a lot of effort, often by a group of people working together *Iceland has made **a concerted effort** to boost tourism.*

concerto /kən'tʃeətəʊ/ *noun* [C] **MUSIC** a piece of music for one main instrument and an orchestra (= large group of musicians) *a piano concerto*

concession /kən'seʃən/ *noun* **1** AGREEMENT [C, U] something that you agree to do or give to someone in order to end an argument *Both sides will have to **make concessions**.* **2** BUSINESS [C] a special right to use buildings or land or to sell a product in a particular area, or the place where that business takes place *a concession to develop oil fields in the north* **3 FINANCE** [C] *UK* a reduction in the price of a ticket for a particular group of people such as students, people without a job, or old people

conch /kɒntʃ/ *noun* [C] a large spiral (= with a curve turning round into the centre) shell, or the sea animal that lives in it

conciliation /kənˌsɪli'eɪʃən/ *noun* [U] *formal* the process of trying to end an argument

conciliatory /kən'sɪliətəri/ *adjective formal* If people behave in a conciliatory manner, they try to make people stop being angry with them. *a conciliatory approach*

concise /kən'saɪs/ *adjective* **1** FEW WORDS giving a lot of information clearly in a few words **2** BOOK A concise book is small. *a concise history of France* •**concisely** *adverb* •**conciseness** *noun* [U]

conclude /kən'kluːd/ *verb* **1** END [I, T] *formal* to end something such as a meeting, speech, or piece of writing by doing or saying one last thing *The concert **concluded with** a firework display.* ○ *I would like to **conclude by** thanking you all for attending.* **2** DECIDE [T] to decide something after studying all the information about it very carefully [+ that] *The report concluded that the drug was safe.* **3** COMPLETE [T] to complete something, especially an agreement or a business arrangement *talks aimed at concluding the peace treaty*

concluding /kən'kluːdɪŋ/ *adjective* [always before noun] last in a series of things *Don't miss tonight's **concluding episode**.*

WORD PARTNERS FOR ***conclusion***

draw/reach a conclusion • **come to** the conclusion that • sth **leads** you **to** the conclusion that

O⁻**conclusion** /kən'kluːʒən/ *noun* **1** OPINION [C] the opinion you have after considering all the information about something *I've **come to the conclusion that** we'll have to sell the car.* **2** END [C] the final part of something *the dramatic conclusion of the film* ○ *The case should finally **be brought to a conclusion** (= end) this week.* **3 in conclusion** used to introduce the last part of a speech or piece of writing *In conclusion, I would like to thank our guest speaker.* **4** ARRANGEMENT [U] when something is arranged or agreed formally *the conclusion of peace talks* **5 jump to conclusions** to guess the facts about a situation without having enough information ➲See also: **foregone conclusion**

conclusive /kən'kluːsɪv/ *adjective* proving that something is true ***conclusive evidence/proof*** •**conclusively** *adverb Tests have **proved conclusively** that the drugs are effective.*

concoct /kən'kɒkt/ *verb* [T] **1** INVENT to invent a story or explanation in order to deceive someone *He had concocted a web of lies.* **2** MIX to make something unusual, especially food, by mixing things together •**concoction** /kən'kɒkʃən/ *noun* [C] *a concoction of meringue, ice cream, and fresh strawberries*

concourse /'kɒŋkɔːs/ *noun* [C] a large room or open area inside a building such as an airport or station

concrete¹ /'kɒŋkriːt/ *noun* [U] a hard substance that is used in building and is made by mixing sand, water, small stones, and cement (= grey powder that is mixed with water and becomes hard when it dries) *concrete blocks*

concrete² /'kɒŋkriːt/ *adjective* **1** [CERTAIN] certain or based on facts ***concrete evidence/proof*** **2** [REAL] existing in a real form that can be seen or felt *concrete achievements/actions* ○ *concrete objects*

concrete³ /'kɒŋkriːt/ *verb* [T] *UK* to cover something with concrete

concur /kən'kɜːʳ/ *verb* [I] **concurring**, *past* **concurred** *formal* to agree *The new report* ***concurs with*** *previous findings.*

concurrent /kən'kʌrᵊnt/ *adjective* happening or existing at the same time *three concurrent prison sentences* •**concurrently** *adverb*

concussed /kən'kʌst/ *adjective* [never before noun] **HEALTH** If someone is concussed, they are suffering from concussion.

concussion /kən'kʌʃᵊn/ *noun* [C, U] **HEALTH** a slight injury to the brain that is caused by being hit on the head and makes you feel tired or sick

condemn /kən'dem/ *verb* [T] **1** [NOT APPROVE] to say very strongly that you think something is wrong or very bad *The Prime Minister was quick to condemn the terrorists.* **2** [BUILDING] to say that a building must be destroyed because it is not safe enough for people to use

condemn sb to sth *phrasal verb* **1** [PUNISHMENT] to say what the punishment of someone who is guilty of a serious crime will be *He* ***was condemned to death.*** **2** [MAKE SUFFER] to make someone suffer in a particular way *Poor education condemns many young people to low-paid jobs.*

condemnation /ˌkɒndem'neɪʃᵊn/ *noun* [C, U] when you say very strongly that you think something is wrong or very bad *widespread condemnation of the war*

condensation /ˌkɒnden'seɪʃᵊn/ *noun* [U] **PHYSICS** small drops of water that form when warm air touches a cold surface ➲See picture at **water cycle**

condense /kən'dens/ *verb* **1** **PHYSICS** [I, T] If hot air or a gas condenses, it changes into a liquid as it becomes colder. **2** [T] to make something such as a speech or piece of writing shorter *You need to* ***condense*** *your conclusion* ***into*** *a single paragraph.* **3** [T] to make a liquid thicker by taking some of the water out of it *condensed milk*

condenser /kən'densəʳ/ *noun* [C] **CHEMISTRY, PHYSICS** a piece of equipment that changes gases to their liquid or solid form ➲See picture at **distillation** ➲See picture at **laboratory**

condescend /ˌkɒndɪ'send/ *verb* **condescend to do sth** *humorous* to agree to do something even though you think you are too important to do it

condescend to sb *phrasal verb* to treat someone as though you are better or more important than them

condescending /ˌkɒndɪ'sendɪŋ/ *adjective* showing that you think that you are better or more important than someone else *a condescending smile* •**condescendingly** *adverb*

condescension /ˌkɒndɪ'senʃᵊn/ *noun* [U] when you behave as though you are better or more important than someone else

O⁻**condition¹** /kən'dɪʃᵊn/ *noun* **1** [STATE] [U, no plural] the state that something or someone is in *My bike's a few years old but it's* ***in really good condition.*** ○ *He's* ***in no condition*** (= not well enough) *to travel.* **2** [AGREEMENT] [C] something that must happen or be agreed before something else can happen *One of the conditions of the contract is that we can't keep pets.* **3** **on condition that** only if *Visitors are allowed in the gardens on condition that they don't touch the plants.* **4** **HEALTH** [C] an illness *a serious heart condition* **5** **conditions** the physical situation that people are in ***working/living conditions*** ○ *severe* ***weather conditions***

condition² /kən'dɪʃᵊn/ *verb* [T] **1** [INFLUENCE] to make a person or animal behave in a particular way by influencing the way they think [often passive + to do sth] *The boys were conditioned to be aggressive.* **2** [HAIR] to put a special liquid on your hair to make it soft and healthy

conditional /kən'dɪʃᵊnᵊl/ *adjective* **1** If an offer or agreement is conditional, it will only happen if something else is done first. *Their fee is* ***conditional on*** *the work being completed by January.* ➲Opposite **unconditional** **2** **LANGUAGE** A conditional sentence usually begins with 'if' and says that something must be true or happen before something else can be true or happen.

conditioner /kən'dɪʃᵊnəʳ/ *noun* [C, U] a liquid that you use when you wash your hair to make it soft

conditioning /kən'dɪʃᵊnɪŋ/ *noun* [U] when a person or animal is made to behave in a particular way *social/physical conditioning* ➲See also: **air conditioning**

condo /'kɒndəʊ/ *noun* [C] *US informal short for* condominium

condolence /kən'dəʊləns/ *noun* [C, U] *formal* sympathy for the family or friends of a person who has recently died *Please* ***offer my condolences*** *to your father.*

condom /'kɒndɒm/ ⓤⓢ /'kaːndəm/ *noun* [C] **HEALTH** a thin rubber covering that a man wears on his penis during sex to stop a woman becoming pregnant, or to protect against diseases

condominium /ˌkɒndə'mɪniəm/ *noun* [C] *US* a building containing apartments which are owned by the people living in them, or one of these apartments

condone /kən'dəʊn/ *verb* [T] to accept or allow behaviour that is wrong *His comments appeared to condone drug abuse.*

conducive /kən'djuːsɪv/ *adjective* making something possible or likely to happen *Such a noisy environment was not* ***conducive to*** *a good night's sleep.*

conduct¹ /'kɒndʌkt/ *noun* **1** [U] the way someone behaves *a code of conduct* (= rules about how to behave) **2 conduct of sth** the way someone organizes or does something *He was criticized for his conduct of the inquiry.*

WORD PARTNERS FOR ***conduct***

conduct an **experiment**/ an **interview**/ an **inquiry**/ an **investigation/research**/ a **survey**

C

conduct² /kən'dʌkt/ *verb* **1** DO [T] to organize or do something *They're **conducting a survey**.* **2 MUSIC** [I, T] to stand in front of a group of musicians and control their performance **3 PHYSICS** [T] If a substance conducts electricity or heat, it allows electricity or heat to go through it. **4 conduct yourself** to behave in a particular way *She conducted herself with great dignity.* **5** LEAD [T] *formal* to lead someone to a place *I was conducted to a side room.*

conduction /kən'dʌkʃən/ *noun* [U] **PHYSICS** the process by which heat or electricity goes through a substance

conductive /kən'dʌktɪv/ *adjective* **PHYSICS** A conductive substance allows heat or electricity to go through it. •**conductivity** /ˌkɒndʌk'tɪvɪti/ *noun* [U] *a high level of conductivity*

conductor /kən'dʌktəʳ/ *noun* [C] **1 MUSIC** someone who stands in front of a group of musicians or singers and controls their performance **2** BUS *UK* someone whose job is to sell or check tickets on a bus, train, etc **3** TRAIN *US* (*UK* **guard**) someone whose job is to be responsible for a train and the people who work on it **4 PHYSICS** a substance that allows electricity or heat to go through it

cone /kəʊn/ *noun* [C] **1 MATHEMATICS** a solid shape with a round or oval base which narrows to a point, or an object which has this shape *a row of **traffic cones*** **2 FOOD** a container for ice cream (= sweet, frozen food) that you can eat

confectionery /kən'fekʃᵊnᵊri/ *noun* [U] *mainly UK* **FOOD** sweet food like sweets and chocolate

confederacy /kən'fedᵊrəsi/ (*also* **confederation** /kənˌfedə'reɪʃᵊn/) *noun* [C] **POLITICS** an organization of smaller groups who have joined together for business or political purposes

confer /kən'fɜːʳ/ *verb* **conferring**, *past* **conferred** **1** DISCUSS [I] to discuss something with other people before making a decision *I'll need to **confer with** my lawyers.* **2** GIVE [T] *formal* to give someone something, especially an official title, an honour, or an advantage

WORD PARTNERS FOR ***conference***

attend/hold a conference • a conference **on** sth • **at** a conference • a conference **centre** • a **sales** conference

conference /'kɒnfᵊrᵊns/ *noun* [C] **1** LARGE MEETING a large, formal meeting, often lasting a few days, where people discuss their work, politics, subjects they are studying, etc *the annual **sales conference*** **2** SMALL MEETING a small, private meeting for discussion of a particular subject ➲See also: **press conference**

'conference ˌcall *noun* [C] a telephone call between three or more people in different places

confess /kən'fes/ *verb* [I, T] **1** to admit that you have done something wrong or something that you feel guilty about [**+ to + doing sth**] *The man has confessed to stealing the painting.* ○ *Rawlinson finally **confessed to** the murder.* **2 RELIGION** to tell a priest or God about all the wrong things that you have done

confession /kən'feʃᵊn/ *noun* [C, U] **1 LAW** when you admit that you have done something wrong or illegal *Sutcliffe has **made a full confession** to the police.* **2 RELIGION** when someone tells a priest all the wrong things they have done *to go to confession*

confetti /kən'feti/ *noun* [U] small pieces of coloured paper that you throw when celebrating something such as a marriage

confidant, confidante /'kɒnfɪdænt/ *noun* [C] a person you can talk to about your feelings and secrets

confide /kən'faɪd/ *verb* [I, T] to tell a secret to someone who you trust not to tell anyone else [**+ that**] *Holly **confided to** me that she was ill.*
confide in sb *phrasal verb* to tell someone who you trust about things that are secret or personal

WORD PARTNERS FOR ***confidence***

1 grow in/lack/lose confidence • sth **gives** you confidence • do sth **with** confidence • a **lack of** confidence
2 express/lose/restore confidence (in sth) • **have (complete/every/little/no)** confidence in sb/sth • **consumer/public** confidence • confidence **in** sth

O--**confidence** /'kɒnfɪdᵊns/ *noun* **1** ABILITY [U] when you are certain of your ability to do things well *He's a good student, but he **lacks confidence**.* [**+ to do sth**] *His training has **given** him the **confidence** to deal with any problem that arises.* **2** TRUST [U] trusting someone's ability or believing that something will produce good results *Kate's new to the job, but I've got **every confidence in** her.* **3** SECRET [C] something secret that you tell someone *to exchange confidences* **4 in confidence** If you tell something to someone in confidence, you do not want them to tell anyone else.

O--**confident** /'kɒnfɪdᵊnt/ *adjective* **1** ABILITY certain about your ability to do things well *a confident grin* ○ *He feels **confident of** winning.* **2** CERTAIN being certain that something will happen [**+ (that)**] *Doctors are confident that she'll recover.* •**confidently** *adverb* ➲See also: **self-confident**

confidential /ˌkɒnfɪ'denʃᵊl/ *adjective* secret, especially in an official situation *These documents are **strictly confidential**.* •**confidentially** *adverb* •**confidentiality** /ˌkɒnfɪdenʃi'æləti/ *noun* [U]

confine /kən'faɪn/ *verb* [T] to prevent someone from leaving a place or to prevent something from spreading [**often passive**] *He was **confined to** a prison cell for several days.*
be confined to sth/sb *phrasal verb* to only exist in a particular area or group of people *The flooding was confined to the basement.*
confine sb/sth to sth *phrasal verb* to limit an activity *Please confine your discussion to the topic.*

confined /kən'faɪnd/ *adjective* [**always before noun**] A confined space is very small.

confinement /kən'faɪnmənt/ *noun* [**U**] when someone is kept in a room or area, usually by force ➲See also: **solitary confinement**

confines /'kɒnfaɪnz/ *noun* [**plural**] the outer limits or edges of something

confirm /kən'fɜːm/ *verb* [**T**] **1** TRUE to say or show that something is true [+ **(that)**] *His wife confirmed that he'd left the house at 8.* **2** CERTAIN to make an arrangement certain *Flights should be confirmed 48 hours before departure.* **3 be confirmed RELIGION** to become a member of the Christian Church at a special ceremony

confirmation /ˌkɒnfə'meɪʃən/ *noun* [**C, U**] **1** an announcement or proof that something is true or certain *You'll receive* ***written confirmation of*** *your reservation within five days.* **2 RELIGION** a special ceremony in which someone becomes a full member of the Christian Church

confirmed /kən'fɜːmd/ *adjective* **a confirmed atheist/bachelor/pessimist, etc** someone who has behaved in a particular way for a long time and is not likely to change

confiscate /'kɒnfɪskeɪt/ *verb* [**T**] to take something away from someone, especially as a punishment •**confiscation** /ˌkɒnfɪ'skeɪʃən/ *noun* [**C, U**]

WORD PARTNERS FOR ***conflict***

resolve a conflict • **be in/come into** conflict with sb • a conflict **between** sb and sb • a conflict **over** sth • an **area of/source of** conflict

conflict[1] /'kɒnflɪkt/ *noun* [**C, U**] **1** DISAGREEMENT serious disagreement *The Government was* ***in conflict with*** *the unions over pay.* ○ *The peasants often* ***came into conflict with*** *the landowners.* **2** FIGHTING fighting between groups or countries ***armed conflict*** **3** DIFFERENCE when two or more different things cannot easily exist together *the conflict between science and religion* **4 a conflict of interest** a situation where someone cannot make fair decisions because they are influenced by something

conflict[2] /kən'flɪkt/ *verb* [**I**] If things such as beliefs, needs, or facts conflict, they are very different and cannot easily exist together or both be true. *Her views on raising children* ***conflict with*** *mine.* ○ *There were* ***conflicting accounts*** *of how the fight started.*

conflicted /kən'flɪktɪd/ *adjective* [**never before noun**] confused because you have two feelings or opinions about something that are opposite

confluence /'kɒnfluːənts/ *noun* [**C**] **GEOGRAPHY** the place where two rivers flow together and become one larger river

conform /kən'fɔːm/ *verb* [**I**] to behave in the way that most other people behave

conform to/with sth *phrasal verb* to obey a rule or to do things in a traditional way *All our toys conform with safety standards.*

conformity /kən'fɔːməti/ *noun* [**U**] **1** behaving in the way that most other people behave **2 conformity to/with sth** *formal* following rules or traditional ways of doing things

confound /kən'faʊnd/ *verb* [**T**] If something confounds someone, it makes them surprised and confused, because they cannot explain it. *The growth in the economy continues to confound the experts.*

confront /kən'frʌnt/ *verb* [**T**] **1** ACCUSE to tell someone something, or show them something to try to make them admit they have done something wrong ***Confronted with*** *the evidence, she broke down and confessed.* **2 be confronted by/with sth** to be in a difficult situation, or to be shown something which may cause difficulties *We are confronted by the possibility of war.* **3** FRIGHTEN to stand in front of someone in a frightening way *He was confronted by two masked men.* **4** DEAL WITH to see that a problem exists and try to deal with it *First, they must confront their addiction.*

confrontation /ˌkɒnfrʌn'teɪʃən/ *noun* [**C, U**] a fight or argument

confrontational /ˌkɒnfrʌn'teɪʃənəl/ *adjective* intentionally causing fighting or an argument *a confrontational style of management*

O━ **confuse** /kən'fjuːz/ *verb* [**T**] **1** NOT UNDERSTAND to make someone unable to think clearly or understand something *These advertisements simply confused the public.* **2** THINK SIMILAR to think that one person or thing is another person or thing *I don't see how anyone could* ***confuse*** *me* ***with*** *my mother!*

O━ **confused** /kən'fjuːzd/ *adjective* **1** UNCERTAIN unable to think clearly or to understand something *Sorry, I'm completely confused.* ○ *The politicians themselves are* ***confused about*** *what to do.* **2** NOT CLEAR not clear *The witnesses gave confused accounts of what happened.*

confusing /kən'fjuːzɪŋ/ *adjective* difficult to understand *I found the instructions very confusing.*

WORD PARTNERS FOR ***confusion***

sth **causes/creates/leads to** confusion • confusion **surrounds** sth • do sth **in** confusion • **widespread** confusion • confusion **about/over** sth

O━ **confusion** /kən'fjuːʒən/ *noun* **1** NOT UNDERSTAND [**C, U**] when people do not understand what is happening or what they should do *There was a lot of* ***confusion about*** *what was actually going on.* **2** THOUGHT [**U**] a feeling of not being able to think clearly *He could see the confusion on Marion's face.* **3** BETWEEN SIMILAR THINGS [**U**] when you think that one person or thing is another **4** SITUATION [**U**] a situation which is confusing because there is a lot of noise and activity *In the confusion, several prisoners tried to escape.*

congeal /kən'dʒiːl/ *verb* [**I**] If a liquid congeals, it becomes thick and almost solid. *congealed fat*

congenial /kən'dʒiːniəl/ *adjective formal* pleasant and friendly *congenial company*

congenital /kən'dʒenɪtəl/ *adjective* **HEALTH** Congenital diseases or problems are ones that people have from when they are born. *congenital heart defects*

congested /kən'dʒestɪd/ *adjective* full or blocked, especially with traffic *The roads are very congested.*

congestion /kən'dʒestʃən/ *noun* [U] when something is full or blocked, especially with traffic *traffic congestion*

C

conglomerate /kən'glɒmərət/ *noun* [C] **ECONOMICS** a large company that is made up of several smaller companies

conˌglomerate 'merger (*also* **diversifying merger**) *noun* [C] **ECONOMICS** when two companies that have completely different types of business join together

congratulate /kən'grætʃʊleɪt/ *verb* [T] to tell someone that you are happy because they have done something good or something good has happened to them *Did you* ***congratulate*** *Cathy* ***on*** *her engagement?*

congratulations /kənˌgrætʃʊ'leɪʃənz/ *exclamation* something that you say when you want to congratulate someone ***Congratulations on*** *doing an outstanding job.* ○ *I hear you're getting married. Congratulations!*

congregate /'kɒŋgrɪgeɪt/ *verb* [I] to come together in a group *Young people congregated on street corners.*

congregation /ˌkɒŋgrɪ'geɪʃən/ *noun* [group] **RELIGION** a group of people meeting to worship in church

congress /'kɒŋgres/ *noun* **1** [C] a large meeting of the members of one or more organizations *an international congress on art history* **2 Congress POLITICS** the group of people who make laws in the United States. Congress consists of the Senate and the House of Representatives.

congressional /kən'greʃənəl/ *adjective* [always before noun] **POLITICS** relating to the United States Congress *a congressional committee*

congressman, congresswoman /'kɒŋgresmən, 'kɒŋgresˌwʊmən/ *noun* [C] *plural* **congressmen, congresswomen POLITICS** a man or woman who is a member of the United States Congress

congruent /'kɒŋgruənt/ *adjective* **MATHEMATICS** congruent shapes have the same size and shape as another shape •**congruence** /'kɒŋgruənts/ *noun* [U]

conical /'kɒnɪkəl/ *adjective* Conical objects have a wide, round base, sloping sides and a pointed top.

ˌconical 'flask *noun* [C] **CHEMISTRY** a glass container with a flat base, a wide rounded body and a long neck, used by scientists ➲See picture at **laboratory**

conifer /'kɒnɪfər/ *noun* [C] **BIOLOGY** a tree with cones (= hard, brown, oval objects) and thin green leaves that stay green all winter •**coniferous** /kə'nɪfərəs/ *adjective a coniferous forest*

conjecture /kən'dʒektʃər/ *noun* [C, U] *formal* guessing about something without real evidence *Exactly what happened that night is still* ***a matter for conjecture.*** •**conjecture** *verb* [I, T] *formal* [+ (that)] Some people conjectured that it was an attempt to save money.

conjugal /'kɒndʒʊgəl/ *adjective formal* relating to marriage

conjugate /'kɒndʒʊgeɪt/ *verb* [T] **LANGUAGE** to add different endings to a verb in order to produce all its different forms •**conjugation** /ˌkɒndʒʊ'geɪʃən/ *noun* [C, U]

conjunction /kən'dʒʌŋkʃən/ *noun* **1 LANGUAGE** [C] A word that is used to connect phrases or parts of a sentence. For example the words 'and', 'because', and 'although' are conjunctions. **2 in conjunction with sth/sb** working, used, or happening with something or someone else

conjunctiva /ˌkɒndʒʌŋk'taɪvə/ *noun* [C usually singular] **ANATOMY** the transparent layer of mucous membrane that covers the inside of the eyelid and the front surface of the eye

conjure /'kʌndʒər/ *verb*

conjure sth up *phrasal verb* **1** PICTURE to make a picture or idea appear in someone's mind *Familiar tunes can help us conjure up memories of the past.* **2** MAKE to make something in a quick and clever way, especially food

conjurer /'kʌndʒərər/ *noun* [C] *another spelling of* conjuror

conjuring /'kʌndʒərɪŋ/ *noun* [U] performing magic to entertain people *a* ***conjuring trick***

conjuror /'kʌndʒərər/ *noun* [C] a person who performs magic to entertain people

conker /'kɒŋkər/ *noun* [C] the shiny brown poisonous nut of a large tree, used by children for playing a game

conman /'kɒnmæn/ *noun* [C] a man who tricks people into giving him money or valuable things

O‑‑**connect** /kə'nekt/ *verb* **1** JOIN [I, T] to join two things or places together *Ferries* ***connect*** *the mainland* ***with*** *the islands.* ○ ***Connect up*** *the printer* ***to*** *your computer.* **2** INVOLVE [T] to see or show that two or more people or things are involved with each other *There is no evidence to* ***connect*** *him* ***with*** *the crime.* **3** TRAVEL [I] If buses, trains, aircraft, etc connect, they arrive at a particular time so that passengers can get off one and onto another. *Can you get me a* ***connecting flight?*** **4** TELEPHONE [T] to make it possible for two people to talk to each other on the telephone ➲Opposite **disconnect**

connected /kə'nektɪd/ *adjective* **1** RELATIONSHIP If people or things are connected, there is a relationship between them. *The hospital is* ***connected to*** *the University of Rochester.* ○ *He remained closely* ***connected with*** *the museum until his death.* ➲Opposite **unconnected 2** JOINED If two things are connected, they are joined together. *The Red Sea is* ***connected to*** *the Mediterranean by the Suez Canal.* ➲Opposite **disconnected** ➲See also: **well-connected**

WORD PARTNERS FOR ***connection***

have a/no connection with sb/sth • a **close/direct** connection • a connection **between** sth and sth • a connection **with** sth

O‑‑**connection** /kə'nekʃən/ *noun* **1** RELATIONSHIP [C, U] a relationship between people or things *The* ***connection between*** *smoking and heart disease is well known.* ○ *He denied having any* ***connection with*** *the terrorists.* **2** JOINING THINGS [C, U] something that joins things together *Many companies now offer free* ***connection to*** *the Internet.* **3** TRAVEL [C] a train, bus, or aircraft that leaves a short time after another arrives, so that people can continue their journey *The train was half an hour late and I **missed my connection**.* **4 in connection with** used to say what something is about *A man has been arrested in connection with the murder.*

connections /kə'nekʃᵊnz/ *noun* [**plural**] important or powerful people who you know and who will help you *He has connections in Washington.*

connective tissue /kəˌnektɪv'tɪʃuː/ *noun* [U] **ANATOMY, BIOLOGY** the strong material in the body that supports and connect the organs in the body and is also found in the joints (= places where two bones are connected)

connectivity /ˌkɒnek'tɪvɪti/ *noun* [U] **COMPUTING** the ability of a computer, program, device or system to connect with one or more others

connive /kə'naɪv/ *verb* [I] to work secretly to do something wrong or illegal, or to allow something wrong or illegal to happen *They accused the government of **conniving in** drug smuggling.*

connoisseur /ˌkɒnə'sɜːʳ/ *noun* [C] someone who knows a lot about and enjoys good food, wine, art, etc

connotation /ˌkɒnə'teɪʃᵊn/ *noun* [C, U] **LANGUAGE** the feelings or ideas that words give in addition to their meanings *The word 'second-hand' has connotations of poor quality.*

conquer /'kɒŋkəʳ/ *verb* **1** LAND/PEOPLE [I, T] to take control of a country or to defeat people by war *Peru was conquered by the Spanish in 1532.* **2** PROBLEM [T] to succeed in stopping or dealing with a bad feeling or a difficult problem *He has finally conquered his fear of spiders.*

conqueror /'kɒŋkᵊrəʳ/ *noun* [C] someone who has conquered a country or its people

conquest /'kɒŋkwest/ *noun* [C, U] when someone takes control of a country, area, or situation *the Roman conquest of Britain*

conscience /'kɒnʃᵊns/ *noun* **1** [C, U] the part of you that makes you feel guilty when you have behaved badly *a guilty conscience* ○ *My **conscience is clear*** (= I do not feel guilty) *because I've done nothing wrong.* **2 be on your conscience** If something is on your conscience, it is making you feel guilty.

conscientious /ˌkɒnʃi'enʃəs/ *adjective* always doing your work with a lot of care *a conscientious student* ●**conscientiously** *adverb*

conscientious objector /kɒnʃiˌenʃəsəb'dʒektəʳ/ *noun* [C] someone who refuses to work in the armed forces because they think war is wrong

conscious /'kɒnʃəs/ *adjective* **1 be conscious of/that** to know that something is present or that something is happening *I'm very conscious that a lot of people disagree with me.* **2 a conscious decision/choice/effort, etc** a decision, choice, effort, etc that you make intentionally *Did you make a conscious decision to lose weight?* ➲Opposite **subconscious** **3** awake and able to think and notice things *He's still conscious but he's very badly injured.* ➲Opposite **unconscious** ●**consciously** *adverb* ➲See also: **self-conscious**

-conscious /'kɒnʃəs/ *suffix* used at the end of words to mean 'thinking that something is important' *a safety-conscious mother* ○ *fashion-conscious teenagers*

consciousness /'kɒnʃəsnəs/ *noun* **1 HEALTH** [U] when someone is awake and can think and notice things *He **lost consciousness*** (= stopped being conscious) *for several minutes.* ○ *I want to be here when she **regains consciousness*** (= becomes conscious again). **2** AWARE [**no plural**] when someone knows about something *There's a growing consciousness about environmental issues among young people.*

conscript¹ /'kɒnskrɪpt/ *noun* [C] someone who has been made to join the army

conscript² /kən'skrɪpt/ *verb* [T] to make someone join the army [**often passive**] *During World War I, he was **conscripted into** the Russian army.*

conscription /kən'skrɪpʃᵊn/ *noun* [U] a system in which people are made to join the army

consecrate /'kɒnsɪkreɪt/ *verb* [T] **RELIGION** to make a place or object holy in a religious ceremony ●**consecration** /ˌkɒnsɪ'kreɪʃᵊn/ *noun* [U] *a consecration ceremony*

consecutive /kən'sekjʊtɪv/ *adjective* Consecutive events, numbers, or periods of time come one after the other. *the third consecutive day of rain* ●**consecutively** *adverb*

consensus /kən'sensəs/ *noun* [U, **no plural**] when all the people in a group agree about something *to **reach a consensus*** ○ *The **general consensus** is that we should wait and see what happens.*

consent¹ /kən'sent/ *noun* [U] **1** permission for someone to do something *You can't come without your parents' consent.* **2 by common consent** UK used to say that everyone agrees about something *He is, by common consent, the most talented actor in Hollywood.*

consent² /kən'sent/ *verb* [I] to agree to do something, or to allow someone to do something [**+ to do sth**] *They eventually consented to let us enter.*

> WORD PARTNERS FOR ***consequence***
>
> **face/live with/suffer** the consequences • **as** a consequence (of sth) • a **direct** consequence • **devastating/dire/disastrous/serious** consequences • the consequences **of** sth

O⊶**consequence** /'kɒnsɪkwəns/ *noun* **1** [C] the result of an action or situation, especially a bad result *The ship capsized, with **disastrous consequences**.* ○ *If you make him angry, you'll have to **suffer the consequences**.* **2 of little/no consequence** *formal* not important *The money was of little consequence to Tony.*

consequent /'kɒnsɪkwənt/ *adjective* [**always before noun**] *formal* happening as a result of something *the closure of the factory and the consequent loss of 400 jobs*

consequently /'kɒnsɪkwəntli/ *adverb* as a result *She was the child of two models and, consequently, she was very tall.*

conservation /ˌkɒnsəˈveɪʃᵊn/ *noun* [U] **1** **ENVIRONMENT** the protection of nature *wildlife conservation* ○ *conservation groups* **2** **ENVIRONMENT** when you are careful not to waste energy, water, etc

conservationist /ˌkɒnsəˈveɪʃᵊnɪst/ *noun* [C] **ENVIRONMENT** someone who believes that people should protect nature

C

conservatism /kənˈsɜːvətɪzᵊm/ *noun* [U] conservative actions and beliefs

conservative /kənˈsɜːvətɪv/ *adjective* **1** not trusting sudden changes or new ideas *Older people tend to be very conservative.* **2** **a conservative estimate/guess** a guess about a number or amount that is probably lower than the true number or amount

Conservative /kənˈsɜːvətɪv/ *noun* [C] **POLITICS** someone who supports the Conservative Party in the UK *the Conservative candidate/MP*

the Conˈservative ˌParty *noun* [group] **POLITICS** one of the three main political parties in the UK

conservatory /kənˈsɜːvətri/ *noun* [C] a room attached to a house that has windows all around it and a glass roof

conserve /kənˈsɜːv/ *verb* [T] **1** NOT WASTE to use something in a way that does not waste it *Insulating the walls will help to conserve heat.* **2** NOT HARM to prevent harm or damage to animals or places

consider /kənˈsɪdəʳ/ *verb* **1** THINK [T] to think carefully about a decision or something you might do *Have you considered surgery?* [+ **doing sth**] *We're considering buying a new car.* **2** FACTS [T] to think about particular facts when you are making a decision about something *If you buy an old house, you have to consider the cost of repairs.* **3** **consider sb/sth (to be) sth; consider that** to have a particular opinion about someone or something [**often reflexive**] *I don't consider myself to be a great athlete.*

considerable /kənˈsɪdᵊrəbl/ *adjective* large or important enough to have an effect *a considerable amount of money* ○ *The damage has been considerable.* •**considerably** *adverb Rates of pay vary considerably.*

considerate /kənˈsɪdᵊrət/ *adjective* kind and helpful *a polite and considerate child* ➲Opposite **inconsiderate**

WORD PARTNERS FOR ***consideration***

1 an **important**/ the **main**/ a **major** consideration • **environmental/financial/political** considerations
2 **careful/serious** consideration • be **under** consideration • be **worthy of** consideration

consideration /kənˌsɪdᵊrˈeɪʃᵊn/ *noun* **1** IMPORTANT FACT [C] something that you have to think about when you make decisions or plans *Safety is our* ***main consideration.*** **2** CAREFUL THOUGHT [U] when you think about something very carefully *After* ***careful consideration,*** *we have decided to offer you the job.* ○ *Several options are* ***under consideration*** (= being considered). **3** KINDNESS [U] when you are kind to people or think about their feelings *They always treated me with consideration.* **4** **take sth into consideration** to think about something when you make a decision or plan

considered /kənˈsɪdəd/ *adjective* **1** [**always before noun**] A considered opinion or decision is based on careful thought. *It is our considered opinion that he should resign.* **2** **all things considered** used when you are giving your opinion about something after thinking carefully about all the facts *All things considered, I think we made the right choice.*

considering /kənˈsɪdərɪŋ/ *preposition, conjunction* used for saying that you have a particular opinion about something, because of a particular fact about it *She's fairly fit considering her age.* ○ *Considering she'd only been there once before, she did well to find the way.*

consign /kənˈsaɪn/ *verb*
consign sb/sth to sth *phrasal verb formal* to get rid of someone or something or to put them in an unpleasant place or situation *They were consigned to a life of poverty.*

consignment /kənˈsaɪnmənt/ *noun* [C] an amount of goods that is being sent somewhere *a ship carrying a small consignment of rice*

consist /kənˈsɪst/ *verb*
consist of sth *phrasal verb* to be formed or made from two or more things *a dessert consisting of fruit and cream*

consistency /kənˈsɪstənsi/ *noun* **1** NOT CHANGING [+ **(that)**] when someone always behaves or performs in a similar way or when something always happens in a similar way *The team has won a few matches but lacks consistency.* **2** LIQUID [**C, U**] how thick or smooth a liquid is *Beat the mixture to a smooth consistency.*

consistent /kənˈsɪstᵊnt/ *adjective* **1** always behaving or happening in a similar, usually positive, way *consistent effort/improvement* **2** **consistent with sth** *formal* having the same principles as something else, or agreeing with other facts *His account of events is entirely consistent with the video evidence.* •**consistently** *adverb The President has consistently denied the rumours.*

consolation /ˌkɒnsəˈleɪʃᵊn/ *noun* [**C, U**] something that makes you feel better about a bad situation *If it's any consolation, I failed my driving test too.*

console[1] /kənˈsəʊl/ *verb* [T] to make someone who is sad feel better *I tried to console her but she just kept crying.*

console[2] /ˈkɒnsəʊl/ *noun* [C] an object that contains the controls for a piece of equipment *a video game console*

consolidate /kənˈsɒlɪdeɪt/ *verb* **1** GET STRONGER [**I, T**] to make sure that you become more powerful, or that success and achievements continue strongly *It will take him some time to consolidate his position in the banking world.* **2** COMBINE [T] to combine several things, especially businesses, so that they become more effective, or to be combined in this way *He consolidated his businesses into one large company.* •**consolidation** /kənˌsɒlɪˈdeɪʃᵊn/ *noun* [U]

consonant /ˈkɒnsᵊnənt/ *noun* [C] **LANGUAGE** a letter of the alphabet that is not a vowel

consort /kən'sɔːt/ *verb*
consort with sb *phrasal verb* to spend time with a bad person *They claimed he had been consorting with drug dealers.*

consortium /kən'sɔːtiəm/ *noun* [C] *plural* **consortiums, consortia** an organization consisting of several businesses or banks *an international consortium of airlines*

conspicuous /kən'spɪkjuəs/ *adjective* very easy to notice *His army uniform made him very conspicuous.* •**conspicuously** *adverb His wife was **conspicuously absent**.*

conspiracy /kən'spɪrəsi/ *noun* [C, U] when a group of people secretly plan to do something bad or illegal [+ **to do sth**] *a conspiracy to overthrow the government*

conspirator /kən'spɪrətəʳ/ *noun* [C] someone who secretly plans with other people to do something bad or illegal

conspire /kən'spaɪəʳ/ *verb* **1** [I] to join with other people to secretly plan to do something bad or illegal [+ **to do sth**] *He was convicted of conspiring to blow up the World Trade Center.* ○ *The king accused his advisers of **conspiring against** him.* **2 conspire against sb; conspire to do sth** If events or a situation conspire against you, they cause problems for you. *Circumstances had conspired to ruin her plans.*

constable /'kɒnstəbl/ *noun* [C] a British police officer of the lowest rank

constant /'kɒnstənt/ *adjective* **1** FREQUENT happening a lot or all the time *machines that are in constant use* **2** SAME LEVEL staying at the same level *The temperature remained constant.* •**constantly** *adverb He's constantly changing his mind.*

constellation /ˌkɒnstə'leɪʃᵊn/ *noun* [C] **ASTRONOMY** a group of stars

consternation /ˌkɒnstə'neɪʃᵊn/ *noun* [U] a feeling of shock or worry

constipated /'kɒnstɪpeɪtɪd/ *adjective* **HEALTH** unable to empty your bowels as often as you should

constipation /ˌkɒnstɪ'peɪʃᵊn/ *noun* [U] **HEALTH** when you are constipated

constituency /kən'stɪtjuənsi/ *noun* [C] **POLITICS** an area of a country which elects someone to represent it in the government, or the people who live there

constituent /kən'stɪtjuənt/ *noun* [C] **1** one of the parts or substances that something is made of *Methane is the main **constituent of** natural gas.* **2 POLITICS** someone who lives in a particular constituency

constitute /'kɒnstɪtjuːt/ *verb* [T] to be or form something *This defeat constitutes a real setback for their championship hopes.*

constitution /ˌkɒnstɪ'tjuːʃᵊn/ *noun* [C] **1 POLITICS** the set of laws and principles that a country's government must obey *the US Constitution* **2** the state of someone's health *a **strong/weak constitution***

constitutional /ˌkɒnstɪ'tjuːʃᵊnᵊl/ *adjective* **POLITICS** relating to the constitution of a country *a constitutional crisis*

constrain /kən'streɪn/ *verb* [T] to control something by limiting it *regulations that constrain industry* [**often passive**] *I'm constrained by decisions made in the past.*

constraint /kən'streɪnt/ *noun* [C] something that limits what you can do *budget constraints* ○ *There are **constraints on** the medicines doctors can prescribe.*

constrict /kən'strɪkt/ *verb* **1** LIMIT [T] to limit someone's freedom to do what they want to or be the way they want to *His creativity was constricted by the political regime he lived under.* **2** MAKE NARROWER [I, T] to become narrower or tighter, or to make something narrower or tighter *The blood vessels constricted.* •**constriction** /kən'strɪkʃᵊn/ *noun* [U]

construct /kən'strʌkt/ *verb* [T] to build something from several parts *The building was constructed in 1930.*

construction /kən'strʌkʃᵊn/ *noun* **1** BUILDING WORK [U] the work of building houses, offices, bridges, etc *railway construction* ○ *construction work* **2** LARGE BUILDING [C] something large that is built *a large steel construction* **3 LANGUAGE** [C] The construction of a sentence or phrase is the way the words are arranged.

constructive /kən'strʌktɪv/ *adjective* helpful or useful ***constructive advice/criticism*** •**constructively** *adverb*

construe /kən'struː/ *verb* [T] **construing**, *past* **construed** to understand something in a particular way *Her comments could be **construed as** patronizing.*

consul /'kɒnsᵊl/ *noun* [C] **POLITICS** someone whose job is to work in a foreign country taking care of the people from their own country who go or live there

consular /'kɒnsjʊləʳ/ *adjective* [**always before noun**] **POLITICS** relating to a consul or a consulate *consular officials*

consulate /'kɒnsjʊlət/ *noun* [C] **POLITICS** the offices where a consul works *the Cuban consulate in Mexico City*

consult /kən'sʌlt/ *verb* [T] **1** GET INFORMATION to go to a particular person or book to get information or advice *For more information, consult your travel agent.* **2** DISCUSS to discuss something with someone before you make a decision *Why didn't you consult me about this?*

consultancy /kən'sʌltᵊnsi/ *noun* **1** COMPANY [C] a company that gives advice on subjects it knows a lot about *a **management/recruitment consultancy*** **2** ADVICE [U] the activity of giving advice on a particular subject

consultant /kən'sʌltᵊnt/ *noun* [C] **1** someone who advises people about a particular subject *a tax consultant* **2 HEALTH** *UK* a hospital doctor who is an expert in a particular area of medicine

consultation /ˌkɒnsᵊl'teɪʃᵊn/ *noun* **1** MEETING [C] a meeting to discuss something or to get advice *a medical consultation* **2** DISCUSSING [U] when you discuss something with someone in order to get their advice or opinion about it *After **consultation with** his lawyers, he decided to abandon the case.*

consultative /kən'sʌltətɪv/ *adjective* A consultative group or document gives advice about something.

consume /kən'sjuːm/ *verb* [T] **1** USE to use something such as a product, energy, or fuel *These lights don't consume much electricity.* **2** EAT OR DRINK *formal* to eat or drink something **3 be consumed with/by sth** to have so much of a feeling that it affects everything you do *a dancer consumed by ambition* **4** FIRE If fire consumes something, it completely destroys it.

WORD PARTNERS FOR ***consumer***

consumer **choice/confidence/demand/protection/spending**

consumer /kən'sjuːməʳ/ *noun* [C] **1 ECONOMICS** someone who buys or uses goods or services *These price cuts are good news for consumers.* **2 BIOLOGY** a person or animal that eats another

consumerism /kən'sjuːmərɪzᵊm/ *noun* [U] **ECONOMICS** buying and selling things, especially when this is an important part of a society's activities

conˌsumer 'price ˌindex *noun* [C usually singular] *US* **ECONOMICS** retail price index

conˌsumer 'spending *noun* [U] **ECONOMICS** the amount that people spend on goods *Consumer spending has risen in the last six months.*

consummate¹ /'kɒnsəmeɪt/ *verb* [T] to make a marriage or relationship complete by having sex •**consummation** /ˌkɒnsə'meɪʃᵊn/ *noun* [U]

consummate² /kən'sʌmət, 'kɒnsəmət/ *adjective* [always before noun] *formal* having great skill *a **consummate professional*** ○ ***consummate ease/skill***

consumption /kən'sʌmʃᵊn/ *noun* [U] **1** AMOUNT the amount of something that someone uses, eats, or drinks *China's total **energy consumption*** **2** USING when someone uses, eats, or drinks something *products sold for **personal consumption***

WORD PARTNERS FOR ***contact***

be in/get in/keep in/stay in contact **(with** sb) • **lose/make** contact (with sb) • **have no** contact **with sb** • **close/regular** contact

contact¹ /'kɒntækt/ *noun* **1** COMMUNICATION [U] when you communicate with someone, especially by speaking to them *We **keep in** close **contact** with our grandparents.* ○ *Jo and I are determined not to **lose contact**.* **2** TOUCH [U] when two people or things are touching each other *She dislikes any kind of **physical contact**.* ○ *Wash your hands if they **come into contact with** chemicals.* **3** PERSON [C] someone you know who may be able to help you because of their job or position ***business contacts*** **4** EYE [C] (*also* **contact lens**) a small piece of plastic that you put on your eye to make you see more clearly ➲See also: **eye contact**

contact² /'kɒntækt/ *verb* [T] to telephone, email or write to someone *I've been trying to contact you for days.*

'contact ˌlens *UK* (*US* ˌ**contact 'lens**) *noun* [C] **HEALTH** a small piece of plastic that you put on your eye to make you see more clearly

contagious /kən'teɪdʒəs/ *adjective* **1 HEALTH** A contagious disease is one that you can get if you touch someone who has it. **2** A contagious feeling spreads quickly amongst people. *Her excitement was contagious.*

contain /kən'teɪn/ *verb* [T] **1** INSIDE If one thing contains another, it has it inside it. *a box containing a diamond ring* **2** PART to have something as a part *Does this drink contain alcohol?* **3** CONTROL to control something by stopping it from spreading *The police were unable to contain the fighting.* **4** EMOTION to control your emotions *He could barely contain his anger.*

COMMON LEARNER ERROR

contain or **include?**

Use **contain** to talk about objects which have something else inside them.

This folder contains important letters.

This soup contains garlic and onions.

Use **include** to say that something or someone is a part of something else.

The team includes two new players.

The price of the ticket includes insurance and tax.

container /kən'teɪnəʳ/ *noun* [C] an object such as a box or a bottle that is used for holding something

contaminate /kən'tæmɪneɪt/ *verb* [T] to make something dirty or poisonous *contaminated drinking water* •**contamination** /kənˌtæmɪ'neɪʃᵊn/ *noun* [U]

contemplate /'kɒntəmpleɪt/ *verb* [T] to think about something for a long time or in a serious way [+ **doing sth**] *I'm contemplating changing my name.* ○ *He even contemplated suicide.* •**contemplation** /ˌkɒntəm'pleɪʃᵊn/ *noun* [U]

contemporary¹ /kən'tempᵊrᵊri, kən'tempəri/ *adjective* **1** PRESENT of the present time *contemporary music* **2** SAME TIME [always before noun] existing or happening at the same time as something *Most **contemporary accounts** of the event have been destroyed.*

contemporary² /kən'tempᵊrᵊri, kən'tempəri/ *noun* [C] Someone's contemporaries are the people who live at the same time as them. *Shakespeare and his contemporaries*

WORD PARTNERS FOR ***contempt***

treat sb/sth **with** contempt • **deep/open/utter** contempt • **have nothing but** contempt **for** sb/sth • sb's contempt **for** sb/sth

contempt /kən'tempt/ *noun* **1** [U] a strong feeling that you do not respect someone or something *He has utter **contempt for** anyone with power.* **2 contempt of court** behaviour that is illegal because it does not obey the rules of a law court

contemptible /kən'temptəbl/ *adjective* extremely bad, because of being dishonest or cruel

contemptuous /kənˈtemptʃuəs/ *adjective* showing contempt •**contemptuously** *adverb*

contend /kənˈtend/ *verb* **1** SAY [T] *formal* to say that something is true [+ **(that)**] *His lawyers contend that he is telling the truth.* **2** COMPETE [I] to compete with someone to try to win something *one of the groups* ***contending for*** *power*
contend with sth *phrasal verb* to have to deal with a difficult or unpleasant situation *I have enough problems of my own to contend with.*

contender /kənˈtendəʳ/ *noun* [C] someone who competes with other people to try to win something *a leading* ***contender for*** *an Oscar*

content¹ /ˈkɒntent/ *noun* [**no plural**] **1** MAIN IDEA the information or ideas that are talked about in a book, speech, film, etc *The* ***content of*** *the article was controversial.* **2** AMOUNT the amount of a particular substance that something contains *Most soft drinks have a high sugar content.*

content² /kənˈtent/ *adjective* happy or satisfied *Not* ***content with*** *second place, Jeff played only to win.* [+ **to do sth**] *I was content to stay home and read.*

content³ /kənˈtent/ *verb*
content yourself with sth *phrasal verb* to do something or have something although it is not exactly what you want *Since it rained we had to content ourselves with playing cards.*

contented /kənˈtentɪd/ *adjective* satisfied, or making you feel satisfied ⊃Opposite **discontented** •**contentedly** *adverb*

contention /kənˈtenʃən/ *noun* **1** OPINION [C] *formal* a belief or opinion *There's a general* ***contention that*** *too much violence is shown on TV.* **2** COMPETITION [U] when people or groups compete for something *Johnson is back* ***in contention for*** *the championships.* **3** DISAGREEMENT [U] arguments and disagreements ⊃See also: a **bone¹** of contention

contentious /kənˈtenʃəs/ *adjective* likely to make people argue *a contentious issue*

ˌcontent ˈmanagement ˌsystem *noun* [U] **COMPUTING** a computer system that allows you to organise large amounts of information, especially words and pictures to be shown on a website

contentment /kənˈtentmənt/ *noun* [U] the feeling of being happy or satisfied

contents /ˈkɒntents/ *noun* [**plural**] **1** THINGS INSIDE all of the things that are contained inside something *Please empty out* ***the contents of*** *your pockets.* **2** INFORMATION the information or ideas that are written in a book, letter, document, etc ***the contents of*** *his will* **3** BOOK a list in a book that tells you what different parts the book contains *a table of contents*

WORD PARTNERS FOR ***contest***

enter/be in a contest • **win** a contest • a **close** contest • a contest **between** sb and sb • a contest **for** sth

contest¹ /ˈkɒntest/ *noun* [C] a competition or election

contest² /kənˈtest/ *verb* [T] **1** SAY STH IS WRONG to say formally that something is wrong or unfair and try to have it changed *Mr Hughes went back to court to contest the verdict.* **2** COMPETE to compete for something

contestant /kənˈtestənt/ *noun* [C] someone who competes in a contest

context /ˈkɒntekst/ *noun* [C, U] **1** SITUATION all the facts, opinions, situations, etc relating to a particular thing or event *This small battle is important* ***in the context of*** *Scottish history.* **2** WORD other words that were said or written at the same time as the word or words you are talking about *Taken* ***out of context****, her remark sounded like an insult.*

O⁻**continent** /ˈkɒntɪnənt/ *noun* [C] **GEOGRAPHY** one of the seven main areas of land on the Earth, such as Asia, Africa, or Europe

the Continent /ˈkɒntɪnənt/ *noun UK* the main part of land in Europe, not including Britain

continental /ˌkɒntɪˈnentəl/ *adjective* **GEOGRAPHY** relating to a continent *the continental US*

Continental /ˌkɒntɪˈnentəl/ *adjective mainly UK* relating to Europe, but not Britain

ˌcontinental ˈbreakfast *noun* [C] **FOOD** a breakfast (= morning meal) consisting of fruit juice, coffee, and bread

ˌcontinental ˈcrust *noun* [U] **GEOLOGY** the part of the Earth's surface that includes the land and the rock underneath

ˌcontinental ˈplate *noun* [C] **GEOLOGY** one of the large sections of the surface of the Earth that move separately

ˌcontinental ˈshelf *noun* [**C usually singular**] **GEOLOGY** the area of the bottom of the sea near the coast of a continent, where the sea is not very deep

contingency /kənˈtɪndʒənsi/ *noun* [C] **1** an event or situation that might happen in the future, especially one which could cause problems *a* ***contingency fund/plan*** (= money or a plan that can be used if there are problems) **2 a contingency fee FINANCE** money that lawyers (= people who advise people about the law and deal with legal situations) charge, which is a share of what the person they represent has won

contingent¹ /kənˈtɪndʒənt/ *noun* [**group**] **1** SIMILAR PEOPLE a group of people from the same country, organization, etc who are part of a much larger group **2** MILITARY FORCES a group of soldiers who are part of a larger military group

contingent² /kənˈtɪndʒənt/ *adjective* **contingent on sth** depending on something else in order to happen *Buying the new house was contingent on selling the old one.*

continual /kənˈtɪnjuəl/ *adjective* happening again and again over a long period of time *I can't work with these continual interruptions.* •**continually** *adverb Dad continually complains about money.*

continuation /kənˌtɪnjuˈeɪʃən/ *noun* **1** COME AFTER [C] something that comes after an event, situation, or thing to make it continue or go further *Today's meeting will be* ***a continuation of*** *yesterday's talks.* **2** STILL EXIST [**U, no plural**] when something continues to exist, happen, or be used *the continuation of their partnership*

continue /kən'tɪnjuː/ *verb* **continuing,** *past* **continued 1** NEVER STOP [I, T] to keep happening, existing, or doing something [+ **to do sth**] *It continued to snow heavily for three days.* [+ **doing sth**] *Ann continued working part-time until June.* **2** BEGIN AGAIN [T] to start doing or saying something again, after stopping for a short period *We'll have to continue this discussion tomorrow.* **3 continue along/down/up, etc** to go further in a particular direction

C

continued /kən'tɪnjuːd/ *adjective* [**always before noun**] still happening, existing, or done *his continued success*

continuity /ˌkɒntɪ'njuːəti/ *noun* [U] the state of continuing for a long period of time without being changed or stopped

continuous¹ /kən'tɪnjuəs/ *adjective* **1** happening or existing without stopping *continuous pain* ○ *ten years of continuous service in the army* **2 LANGUAGE** The continuous form of a verb is used to show that an action is continuing to happen. The sentence 'He was eating lunch.' is in the continuous form. •**continuously** *adverb Their baby cried continuously all afternoon.*

the continuous /kən'tɪnjuəs/ *noun* **LANGUAGE** the continuous form of the verb

contort /kən'tɔːt/ *verb* [I, T] If your face or body contorts, or you contort it, you twist it into a different shape, often because you are experiencing a strong emotion. *His face was contorted with pain.*

contour /'kɒntʊəʳ/ *noun* [C] **1** SHAPE the shape of the outer edge of something *the contours of her body* **2 GEOGRAPHY** (*also* **'contour ˌline**) a line on a map joining places that are at the same height

contra- /kɒntrə-/ *prefix* against or opposite *to contradict* (= say the opposite) ○ *contraception* (= something that is used to prevent pregnancy)

contraband /'kɒntrəbænd/ *noun* [U] goods that are brought into or taken out of a country illegally

contraception /ˌkɒntrə'sepʃᵊn/ *noun* [U] **HEALTH** methods that prevent a woman from becoming pregnant

contraceptive /ˌkɒntrə'septɪv/ *noun* [C] **HEALTH** a drug or object that prevents a woman from becoming pregnant

WORD PARTNERS FOR ***contract***

enter into/negotiate/sign a contract • **breach/break/end/terminate** a contract • **in** a contract • the **terms of** a contract • a contract **between** sb and sb **/with** sb

contract¹ /'kɒntrækt/ *noun* [C] **LAW** a legal agreement between two people or organizations, especially one that involves doing work for a particular amount of money

contract² /kən'trækt/ *verb* **1** REDUCE [I, T] to become smaller or shorter, or to make something do this *The wood contracts in dry weather.* **2 HEALTH** [T] *formal* to get a serious disease *She contracted malaria while living abroad.* **3 LAW** [I, T] to make a legal agreement with someone to do work or to have work done for you [+ **to do sth**] *He's been contracted to perform in five shows.*

contract out sth *phrasal verb* to make a formal arrangement for other people to do work that you are responsible for *They've **contracted out** the cleaning **to** a private firm.*

contraction /kən'trækʃᵊn/ *noun* **1 HEALTH** [C] a strong, painful movement of the muscles that a woman has when she is having a baby *She was **having contractions** every ten minutes.* **2 LANGUAGE** [C] a short form of a word or group of words *'Won't' is a contraction of 'will not'.* **3** [U] when something becomes smaller or shorter

contractor /kən'træktəʳ/ *noun* [C] a person or company that supplies goods or does work for other people

contractual /kən'træktʃuᵊl/ *adjective* **LAW** relating to or stated in a contract (= legal agreement) *a contractual dispute*

contradict /ˌkɒntrə'dɪkt/ *verb* **1** DIFFERENT [T] If two things that are said or written about something contradict each other, they are so different that they cannot both be true. *His account of the accident contradicts the official government report.* **2** DISAGREE [I, T] to say that what someone else has just said is wrong

contradiction /ˌkɒntrə'dɪkʃᵊn/ *noun* **1** DIFFERENCE [C] a big difference between two things that are said or written about the same subject, or between what someone says and what they do *There is a clear **contradiction between** what she says and what she does.* **2** WRONG [U] when you say that what someone has just said is wrong **3 a contradiction in terms** a phrase that is confusing because it contains words that seem to have opposite meanings *An honest politician - isn't that a contradiction in terms?*

contradictory /ˌkɒntrə'dɪktᵊri/ *adjective* If two statements about the same subject or two actions by the same person are contradictory, they are very different.

'contra ˌentry *noun* [C] **FINANCE** an entry in a business's accounts where the letter 'c' is written to show that the other entry in the double entry bookkeeping system is on the other side of the same book

contraption /kən'træpʃᵊn/ *noun* [C] a machine or object that looks strange or complicated

contrary¹ /'kɒntrᵊri/ *noun* **1 to the contrary** saying or showing the opposite *She claimed she hadn't been involved, despite evidence to the contrary.* **2 on the contrary** used to show that the opposite of what has just been said is true *"You're a vegetarian, aren't you?" "On the contrary, I love meat."*

contrary² /'kɒntrᵊri/ *adjective* **1** opposite or very different *a contrary opinion/view* **2 contrary to sth a** opposite to what someone said or thought *Contrary to popular belief, bottled water is not always better than tap water.* **b** If something is contrary to a rule, it does not obey that rule.

WORD PARTNERS FOR *contrast*

1 a **complete/sharp/striking** contrast • the contrast **between** sth and sth
2 in **direct/marked/sharp/stark** contrast / **(to** sth)

contrast¹ /ˈkɒntrɑːst/ *noun* [C, U] **1** an obvious difference between two people or things *The **contrast between** their lifestyles couldn't be greater.* ○ *The busy north coast of the island is **in** sharp **contrast to** the peaceful south.* **2 by/in contrast** used to show that someone or something is completely different from someone or something else *She's quite petite, in contrast with her tall sister.*

contrast² /kənˈtrɑːst/ *verb* **1** COMPARE [T] to compare two people or things in order to show the differences between them *If you **contrast** his early novels **with** his later work, you can see how his writing has developed.* **2** DIFFERENCE [I] If one thing contrasts with another, it is very different from it. *The sharpness of the lemons **contrasts with** the sweetness of the honey.*

contrasting /kənˈtrɑːstɪŋ/ *adjective* very different *contrasting colours/styles*

contravene /ˌkɒntrəˈviːn/ *verb* [T] *formal* to do something that is forbidden by a law or rule •**contravention** /ˌkɒntrəˈvenʃən/ *noun* [C, U] *By accepting the money, she was **in contravention of** company rules.*

contribute /kənˈtrɪbjuːt, ˈkɒntrɪbjuːt/ *verb* [I, T] **1** MONEY to give something, especially money, in order to provide or achieve something together with other people *I **contributed** $20 **towards** Andrea's present.* **2** ARTICLE to write articles for a newspaper, magazine, or book *She **contributes to** several magazines.*

contribute to sth *phrasal verb* to be one of the causes of an event or a situation *Smoking contributed to his early death.*

contribution /ˌkɒntrɪˈbjuːʃən/ *noun* [C] **1** SUCCESS something that you do to help produce or develop something, or to help make something successful *She has **made** a major contribution **to** our work.* **2** MONEY an amount of money that is given to help pay for something *a generous contribution to charity*

contributor /kənˈtrɪbjʊtər/ *noun* [C] **1** ARTICLE someone who writes articles for a newspaper, magazine, or book **2** MONEY someone who gives something, especially money, together with other people **3** CAUSE one of the causes of something *Speeding is a major contributor to road accidents.*

contributory /kənˈtrɪbjʊtəri/ *adjective* helping to cause something

contrive /kənˈtraɪv/ *verb* [T] *formal* to manage to do something difficult, or to make something happen, by using your intelligence or by tricking people [+ **to do sth**] *They contrived to meet in secret.*

contrived /kənˈtraɪvd/ *adjective* Something that is contrived seems false and not natural.

control¹ /kənˈtrəʊl/ *noun* **1** POWER [U] the power to make a person, organization, or object do what you want *The new teacher has no **control over** the class.* ○ *The police are **in control of** the situation.* ○ *He **lost control of** the vehicle.* **2** RULE [U] the power to rule or govern an area *Soldiers **took control of** the airport.* **3 under control** being dealt with successfully *Don't worry - everything's under control.* ○ *I couldn't keep my drinking **under control**.* **4 out of control** If something or someone is out of control, you cannot influence, limit, or direct them. **5** RULE [C, U] a rule or law that limits something *The government has introduced tighter immigration controls.* **6** CALM [U] the ability to be calm *It took a lot of control to stop myself hitting him.* **7** EQUIPMENT [C] a switch or piece of equipment that you use to operate a machine or vehicle *Where's the volume control on your stereo?* **8** OFFICIAL PLACE [C, U] a place where something official, usually a document, is checked ***passport/immigration control*** **9** IN EXPERIMENT a person or thing that is used to compare with someone or something that is having an experiment done on them ➲See also: **birth control, remote control, self-control**

control² /kənˈtrəʊl/ *verb* [T] **controlling**, *past* **controlled** **1** MAKE SB DO STH to make a person, organization, or object do what you want *This switch controls the temperature.* ○ *Can't you control your dogs?* **2** LIMIT to limit the number, amount, or increase of something *Fire crews struggled to control the blaze.* **3** RULE to rule or govern an area *The whole area is controlled by rebel forces.* **4** EMOTION to stop yourself expressing strong emotions or behaving in a silly way *He can't control his temper.*

conˈtrol ˌfreak *noun* [C] *informal* someone who wants to control everything about a situation and does not want other people to be involved

conˈtrol ˌkey *noun* [C usually singular] **COMPUTING** the key on a computer keyboard thatis usually marked 'Ctrl' and is used together with other keys to do particular operations

controller /kənˈtrəʊlər/ *noun* [C] someone who directs the work of other people *a marketing controller*

controversial /ˌkɒntrəˈvɜːʃəl/ *adjective* causing a lot of disagreement or argument *a **controversial decision/issue***

WORD PARTNERS FOR *controversy*

sth **attracts /causes/provokes/sparks** controversy • the controversy **surrounding** sth • **bitter/continuing/furious** controversy • controversy **about/over** sth • be **at the centre of** a controversy

controversy /ˈkɒntrəvɜːsi/ *noun* [C, U] a lot of disagreement and argument about something *There is a lot of **controversy over** mobile phone towers.*

conundrum /kəˈnʌndrəm/ *noun* [C] a problem or question that is difficult to solve

conurbation /ˌkɒnəˈbeɪʃən/ *noun* [C] **GEOGRAPHY** a large city area formed by several towns growing and joining together

convalescence /ˌkɒnvəˈlesəns/ *noun* [U] **HEALTH** the period of time when you rest and get better after a serious illness •**convalesce** *verb* [I]

convection /kənˈvekʃən/ *noun* [U] **PHYSICS** the flow of heat through a gas or a liquid as the hotter part rises and the cooler part goes down •**convectional** /kənˈvekʃənəl/ *adjective*

con,vectional 'rainfall *noun* [U] **GEOGRAPHY** heavy rain caused by the surface of the atmosphere becoming hotter and causing damp (= slightly wet) air to rise

convene /kən'vi:n/ *verb* [I, T] *formal* to arrange a meeting, or to meet for a meeting *The committee convenes three times a year.*

C

convenience /kən'vi:niəns/ *noun* **1** QUALITY [U] when something is easy to use and suitable for what you want to do *the convenience of credit cards* **2** HELPFUL THING [C] something that makes life easier *Fortunately, the house has every **modern convenience**.*

con'venience ,food *noun* [C] **FOOD** food that can be prepared quickly and easily

con'venience ,store *noun* [C] *mainly US* a shop that sells food, drinks, etc, and is usually open late

convenient /kən'vi:niənt/ *adjective* **1** USEFUL easy to use or suiting your plans well *When would be a convenient time to meet?* **2** NEAR near or easy to get to *The new supermarket is very convenient for me.* •**conveniently** *adverb*

convent /'kɒnvənt/ *noun* [C] **RELIGION** a building where nuns (= religious women) live and pray together

convention /kən'venʃᵊn/ *noun* **1** MEETING [C] a large formal meeting of people with the same interest or work *the Democratic Party convention* **2** CUSTOM [C, U] a usual and accepted way of behaving or doing something *In many countries it is the convention to wear black at funerals.* **3 POLITICS** [C] a formal agreement between countries *an international convention on human rights*

conventional /kən'venʃᵊnᵊl/ *adjective* **1** TRADITIONAL Conventional people are traditional and not willing to try new ideas. **2** USUAL Conventional objects or ways of doing things are the usual ones which have been used for a long time. *conventional farming/medicine* **3 conventional arms/forces/warfare, etc** not involving the use of nuclear weapons **4 conventional wisdom** what most people believe ⊃Opposite **unconventional**

conventionally /kən'venʃᵊnᵊli/ *adverb* in a traditional way *He dressed conventionally in a suit and tie.*

converge /kən'vɜ:dʒ/ *verb* [I] **1** COME TOGETHER If lines, roads, or rivers converge, they meet at a particular point. **2** FORM GROUP to move towards a particular point and form a group there *The protesters **converged on** the town square.* **3** BECOME SIMILAR If ideas, interests, or systems converge, they become more similar to one another. •**convergence** *noun* [U]

WORD PARTNERS FOR ***conversation***

engage in/have/join in/strike up a conversation • **make** conversation • a **brief/casual/long/polite/private** conversation • a conversation **about** sth • a conversation **between** sb

conversation /,kɒnvə'seɪʃᵊn/ *noun* [C, U] a talk between two or more people, usually an informal one *a telephone conversation* ○ *We **had a conversation about** football.* •**conversational** *adjective* relating to or like a conversation *a conversational style*

converse /kən'vɜ:s/ *verb* [I] *formal* to talk with someone

conversely /'kɒnvɜ:sli/ *adverb* used to introduce something that is different to something you have just said *Dark lipsticks make your mouth look smaller. Conversely, light shades make it larger.*

conversion /kən'vɜ:ʒᵊn/ *noun* [C, U] **1** when the appearance, form, or purpose of something is changed *the country's **conversion to** democracy* **2 RELIGION** when someone changes to a new religion or belief *her **conversion to** Christianity*

convert[1] /kən'vɜ:t/ *verb* **1** CHANGE FORM [I, T] to change the appearance, form, or purpose of something *The old warehouse was **converted into** offices.* ○ *How do you convert miles into kilometres?* **2 RELIGION** [I, T] to change to a new religion, belief, etc, or to make someone do this *When did he **convert to** Islam?*

convert[2] /'kɒnvɜ:t/ *noun* [C] **RELIGION** someone who has been persuaded to change to a different religion or belief *a Catholic convert*

convertible[1] /kən'vɜ:təbl/ *adjective* able to be converted

convertible[2] /kən'vɜ:təbl/ *noun* [C] a car with a folding roof

convex /'kɒnveks/ *adjective* **PHYSICS** A convex surface curves out. *a convex mirror/lens*

convey /kən'veɪ/ *verb* [T] **1** COMMUNICATE to communicate information, feelings, or images to someone *She always conveys a sense of enthusiasm for her work.* **2** TRANSPORT to transport something or someone to a particular place

conveyor belt /kən'veɪə,belt/ *noun* [C] a continuous moving piece of rubber or metal used to transport objects from one place to another

convict[1] /kən'vɪkt/ *verb* [T] **LAW** to decide officially in a court of law that someone is guilty of a particular crime [**often passive**] *He was **convicted of** murder.* ○ *a convicted criminal*

convict[2] /'kɒnvɪkt/ *noun* [C] someone who is in prison because they are guilty of a particular crime

conviction /kən'vɪkʃᵊn/ *noun* **1 LAW** [C] when someone is officially found to be guilty of a particular crime *He already had two convictions for burglary.* **2** [C, U] a strong opinion or belief *religious/moral convictions*

convince /kən'vɪns/ *verb* [T] **1** CAUSE BELIEF to make someone believe that something is true [**+ that**] *He tried to convince me that I needed a new car.* ○ *She convinced the jury of her innocence.* **2** PERSUADE to persuade someone to do something [**+ to do sth**] *I convinced her to go to the doctor's.*

convinced /kən'vɪnst/ *adjective* completely certain about something [**+ (that)**] *I'm convinced that he's made a mistake.*

convincing /kən'vɪnsɪŋ/ *adjective* **1** able to make you believe that something is true or right *a convincing argument* **2 a convincing win/victory** a win or victory where the person or team that wins is much better than the people they are competing against •**convincingly** *adverb*

convoluted /ˈkɒnvəluːtɪd/ *adjective formal* extremely complicated and difficult to understand *a convoluted argument/story*

convoy /ˈkɒnvɔɪ/ *noun* [C] a group of vehicles or ships that travel together

convulsion /kənˈvʌlʃən/ *noun* [C] **HEALTH** a sudden uncontrollable movement of muscles in your body, caused by illness or drugs

coo /kuː/ *verb* [I] **cooing,** *past* **cooed 1** MAKE SOUND to make a soft, low sound, like a pigeon (= large, grey bird) **2** SPEAK to speak in a soft, low voice

cook

O⁻**cook¹** /kʊk/ *verb* **1** PREPARE [I, T] to prepare food and usually heat it *Who's cooking this evening?* ○ *She cooked the meat in oil and spices.* **2** HEAT [I] If food cooks, it is heated until it is ready to eat. *The rice is cooking.* ●**cooked** *adjective* not raw

cook sth up *phrasal verb informal* to invent a story, plan, etc, usually dishonestly

cook² /kʊk/ *noun* [C] someone who prepares and cooks food

cookbook /ˈkʊkbʊk/ (*also UK* **cookery book**) *noun* [C] a book containing instructions for preparing food

cooker /ˈkʊkər/ *UK* (*UK/US* **stove**) *noun* [C] a piece of equipment used to cook food *an electric cooker* ➲See also: **pressure cooker**

cookery /ˈkʊkəri/ *noun* [U] *UK* preparing or cooking food

ˈcookery ˌbook *UK* (*UK/US* **cookbook**) *noun* [C] a book containing instructions for preparing food

O⁻**cookie** /ˈkʊki/ *noun* [C] **1 FOOD** *US* (*also UK* **biscuit**) a thin, flat cake that is dry and usually sweet ➲See colour picture **Food** on page Centre11 **2 COMPUTING, INTERNET** a piece of information stored on your computer which contains information about Internet documents you have looked at

O⁻**cooking** /ˈkʊkɪŋ/ *noun* [U] **1** ACTIVITY preparing or cooking food *I do most of the cooking.* **2 FOOD** a style of preparing food *vegetarian/French cooking* ●**cooking** *adjective* [**always before noun**] suitable to cook with *cooking oil/apples*

O⁻**cool¹** /kuːl/ *adjective* **1** COLD slightly cold, but not too cold *a cool breeze/day* ○ *cool water* **2** GOOD *informal* good, stylish, or fashionable *He looks really cool in those sunglasses.* **3** CALM calm and not emotional *She seemed cool and confident.* **4** UNFRIENDLY unfriendly **5 be cool with sth** *informal* to be happy to accept a situation or suggestion *Yeah, we could leave later - I'm cool with that.* ●**coolness** *noun* [U]

cool² /kuːl/ *verb* [I, T] **1** LESS HOT to become less hot, or make something become less hot *Allow the bread to cool before slicing it.* **2** LESS STRONG If emotions or relationships cool, or if something cools them, they become less strong.

cool (sb/sth) down/off *phrasal verb* **1** LESS HOT to become less hot, or to make someone or something become less hot *We went for a swim to cool off.* **2** CALMER to become calmer, or to make someone become calmer

cool³ /kuːl/ *noun* **1 the cool** a cool temperature *the cool of the early morning* **2 keep your cool** to remain calm **3 lose your cool** to suddenly become very angry

cool⁴ /kuːl/ *exclamation informal* used when you like something or agree to something

coolly /ˈkuːlli/ *adverb* without showing emotion or interest *Her colleagues reacted coolly to the idea.*

coop¹ /kuːp/ *noun* [C] a cage for birds such as chickens

coop² /kuːp/ *verb*

coop sb up *phrasal verb* to keep a person or animal in a small area [**often passive**] We've been cooped up in a plane all day.

co-op /ˈkəʊɒp/ *noun* [C] *informal short for* cooperative²

cooperate (*also UK* **co-operate**) /kəʊˈɒpəreɪt/ *verb* [I] **1** WORK TOGETHER to work together with someone in order to achieve the same aim *Witnesses are* ***cooperating with*** *detectives.* ○ *Several countries are* ***cooperating in*** *the relief effort.* **2** HELP to help someone or do what they ask *We can get there early as long as the children will cooperate.*

cooperation (*also UK* **co-operation**) /kəʊˌɒpəˈreɪʃən/ *noun* [U] when you work together with someone or do what they ask you *international cooperation* ○ *The clubs work* ***in close cooperation with*** *the Football Association.*

cooperative¹ (*also UK* **co-operative**) /kəʊˈɒpərətɪv/ *adjective* **1** WILLING TO HELP willing to help or do what people ask *a cooperative and polite employee* **2** WORKING TOGETHER involving people working together to achieve the same aim *a cooperative relationship* ●**cooperatively** *adverb*

cooperative² (*also UK* **co-operative**) /kəʊˈɒpərətɪv/ *noun* [C] a business or organization owned and managed by the people who work in it

coordinate¹ (*also UK* **co-ordinate**) /kəʊˈɔːdɪneɪt/ *verb* [T] to make different people or things work together effectively, or to organize all the different parts of an activity *My manager is coordinating the new project.*

coordinate² /kəʊˈɔːdɪnət/ *noun* [C] **MATHEMATICS** of a pair of numbers and/or letters that show the exact position of a point on a map or graph

coordination (*also UK* **co-ordination**) /kəʊˌɔːdɪˈneɪʃən/ *noun* [U] **1** ORGANIZING when you organize the different parts of an activity or make people or things work together effectively *The President called for closer coordination between business and government.* **2** BODY the ability to make different parts of your body move together in a controlled way *Dancing helps develop balance and coordination.*

C

coordinator (*also UK* **co-ordinator**) /kəʊˈɔːdɪneɪtəʳ/ *noun* [C] someone who organizes the different parts of an activity or makes people or things work together effectively

cop /kɒp/ *noun* [C] *mainly US informal* a police officer

cope /kəʊp/ *verb* [I] to deal quite successfully with a difficult situation *How do you **cope with** stress?*

copier /ˈkɒpiəʳ/ *mainly US* (*UK/US* **photocopier**) *noun* [C] a machine which produces copies of documents by photographing them

copious /ˈkəʊpiəs/ *adjective* [**always before noun**] in large amounts *They drank **copious amounts** of wine.* •**copiously** *adverb*

coplanar /ˌkəʊˈplɒɪnəʳ/ *adjective* **MATHEMATICS** on the same plane (= flat surface) *coplanar lines*

copolymer /ˌkəʊˈpɒlɪməʳ/ *noun* **CHEMISTRY** a chemical compound with a high molecular weight, formed by joining the molecules of two or more compounds

copolymerize (*also UK* **-ise**) /ˌkəʊˈpɒlɪməraɪz/ *verb* [T, I] **CHEMISTRY** to form a copolymer or to make something form a copolymer •**copolymerization** (*also UK* **-isation**) /ˌkəʊpɒlɪməraɪˈzeɪʃən/ *noun* [U]

copper /ˈkɒpəʳ/ *noun* **1** **CHEMISTRY** [U] a soft, red-brown metal, used in electrical equipment and to make coins, etc. (symbol **Cu**) *copper wire* ➲See picture at **oxidation** **2** MONEY [C] *UK* a brown coin with a low value **3** POLICE [C] *UK informal* a police officer

O-■**copy¹** /ˈkɒpi/ *noun* [C] **1** SAME something that is made to look exactly like something else *Always **make copies of** important documents.* **2** PRODUCT a single book, newspaper, etc of which many have been produced *Four million copies of the book were sold in the first year.* ➲See also: **carbon copy**

O-■**copy²** /ˈkɒpi/ *verb* **1** PRODUCE [T] to produce something that is similar or exactly the same as something else *Copy the file onto disk.* ○ *The design was **copied from** the American model.* **2** BEHAVE [T] to behave like someone else *He likes to copy his older brother.* **3** CHEAT [I, T] to cheat by looking at and using someone else's work *She copied his answers.*

copy sth out *phrasal verb UK* If you copy out a piece of writing, you write it out again on a piece of paper.

copy sb in on sth *phrasal verb* If you copy somebody in on something, you give them a copy of something, usually an email, that you have written for somebody else. *Please copy me in on your email to Dr White.*

copyright /ˈkɒpiraɪt/ *noun* [C, U] **LAW** the legal right to control the use of an original piece of work such as a book, play, or song *The book **is protected by copyright**.*

coral /ˈkɒrəl/ *noun* [U] a hard, usually pink or white substance produced by a type of very small sea animal *a coral reef*

cord /kɔːd/ *noun* [C, U] **1** STRING thick string, or a piece of this **2** WIRE (*also UK* **flex**) a piece of wire covered in plastic, used to connect electrical equipment to a power supply *an electrical cord* ○ *a telephone cord* ➲See also: **umbilical cord**

cordial /ˈkɔːdiəl/ *adjective* polite and friendly *a cordial invitation* •**cordially** *adverb*

cordless /ˈkɔːdləs/ *adjective* able to operate without an electrical cord *a cordless phone*

cordon¹ /ˈkɔːdən/ *noun* [C] a line of police, soldiers, vehicles, etc around an area, protecting it or keeping people out

cordon² /ˈkɔːdən/ *verb*

cordon sth off *phrasal verb* If the police, army, etc cordon off an area, they stop people from entering it.

cords /kɔːdz/ *noun* [**plural**] *informal* trousers made from corduroy

corduroy /ˈkɔːdərɔɪ/ *noun* [U] thick, cotton cloth with raised parallel lines on the outside *a corduroy jacket*

core /kɔːʳ/ *noun* **1** IMPORTANT PART [**no plural**] the most important part of a system or principle *core values* ○ *Better health care was **at the core of** the senator's campaign.* **2** **BIOLOGY** [C] the hard, central part of certain fruits, such as apples, which contains the seeds **3** PLANET [**no plural**] the centre of a planet *the Earth's core* ➲See picture at **Earth** ➲See also: **hard core**

coriander /ˌkɒriˈændəʳ/ (*also US* **cilantro**) *noun* [U] **FOOD** a herb that is used in cooking

cork /kɔːk/ *noun* **1** MATERIAL [U] a light material obtained from the bark (= outer layer) of a particular type of tree **2** BOTTLE [C] a small cylindrical piece of this material put in the top of a bottle, especially a wine bottle, to close it

corkscrew /ˈkɔːkskruː/ *noun* [C] a piece of equipment used for pulling corks out of wine bottles

corn /kɔːn/ *noun* [U] **1** *mainly UK* a crop of grain, or the seed from this crop used to make flour or feed animals *fields of corn* **2** **FOOD** *US* (*UK* **sweetcorn**) a tall plant with yellow seeds that are cooked and eaten as a vegetable ➲See colour picture **Fruit and Vegetables** on page Centre 10

cornea /kɔːˈniə/ *noun* [C] **ANATOMY** the transparent outer part of the eye ➲See picture at **eye**

O-■**corner¹** /ˈkɔːnəʳ/ *noun* [C] **1** POINT the point or area where two lines, walls, or roads meet *There was a television **in the corner** of the room.* ○ *The pub is **on/at the corner** of Ross Street and Mill Road.* **2** PLACE a part of a larger area, often somewhere quiet or far away *He lives in a beautiful corner of northern California.* **3** **SPORT** a kick or hit taken from the corner of the field in some games, especially football **4 from/out of the corner of your eye** If you see something out of the corner of your eye, you just see it, but do not look at it directly. **5 around/round the corner** going to happen soon **6 cut corners** to do something in the quickest or cheapest way, often harming the quality of your work

corner² /ˈkɔːnəʳ/ *verb* **1** [T] to force a person or animal into a situation or place from which it is hard to escape *His attackers cornered him in a dark alley.* **2 corner the market** to become so successful at selling or making a particular product that almost no one else sells or makes it

cornerstone /ˈkɔːnəstəʊn/ *noun* [C] something very important that something else depends on *Freedom of speech is **the cornerstone of** democracy.*

cornflakes /ˈkɔːnfleɪks/ *noun* [plural] **FOOD** a food made from corn (= grain) and eaten with milk for breakfast (= morning meal)

corny /ˈkɔːni/ *adjective informal* repeated too often to be interesting or funny *a **corny** joke*

corolla /kəˈrɒlə/ *noun* [C] **BIOLOGY** all of the petals of a flower

coronary¹ /ˈkɒrənəri/ *adjective* **ANATOMY, HEALTH** relating to the heart *coronary heart disease*

coronary² /ˈkɒrənəri/ *noun* [C] **HEALTH** a heart attack (= when the heart stops working normally)

coronation /ˌkɒrəˈneɪʃən/ *noun* [C] a ceremony at which someone is officially made king or queen

coroner /ˈkɒrənəʳ/ *noun* [C] an official who examines the causes of someone's death, usually if it was violent or sudden

Corp *noun* [C] *written abbreviation for* corporation (=used after the name of a large company in the United States)

corporal /ˈkɔːpərəl/ *noun* [C] a soldier of low rank in the army or air force

ˌcorporal ˈpunishment *noun* [U] physical punishment, especially of children, usually by hitting with the hand or a stick

corporate /ˈkɔːpərət/ *adjective* [always before noun] relating to a large company or group *corporate finance*

corporation /ˌkɔːpərˈeɪʃən/ *noun* [C] a large company or group of companies

corpoˈration ˌtax *noun* [U] **FINANCE** tax paid by businesses on their profits

corps /kɔːʳ/ *noun* [C] *plural* **corps** **1** [GROUP] a group of people involved in the same job *the press/diplomatic corps* **2** [MILITARY] a special part of a military force *the Air Corps*

corpse /kɔːps/ *noun* [C] a dead person's body

corpuscle /ˈkɔːpʌsl/ *noun* [C] **BIOLOGY** any of the red or white cells in the blood

corpus luteum /ˌkɔːpəsˈluːtiːəm/ *noun* [U] *plural* **corpus lutea** **ANATOMY, BIOLOGY** a mass of yellow tissue that produces progesterone (= a hormone necessary for pregnancy) after a woman's egg is released

O→**correct¹** /kəˈrekt/ *adjective* **1** [NO MISTAKES] accurate, or having no mistakes *Check that you have the correct information.* ○ *Was that the correct answer?* **2** [SUITABLE] suitable for a particular situation *correct behaviour* ○ *Have you got the correct number of players for the match?* •**correctly** *adverb* •**correctness** *noun* [U] ➲See also: **politically correct**

correct² /kəˈrekt/ *verb* [T] **1** [MAKE RIGHT] to make a mistake or problem right or better *The new software finds and corrects any errors on the hard disk.* **2** [IMPROVE] to improve the quality of something *These contact lenses will help to correct your vision.* **3** [SHOW MISTAKE] to show someone the mistakes in something they have said or written *Our teacher normally corrects our pronunciation.*

WORD PARTNERS FOR ***correction***

make a correction • a **minor/small** correction • a correction **to** sth

O→**correction** /kəˈrekʃən/ *noun* [C, U] a change to make something right or better, or when you make such a change *She **made** some **corrections** before handing in the essay.*

corrective /kəˈrektɪv/ *adjective formal* intended to improve or correct something *corrective surgery/lenses*

correlate /ˈkɒrəleɪt/ *verb* [I, T] If facts or pieces of information correlate, they are connected to each other and influence each other, and if you correlate them, you show their connections.

WORD PARTNERS FOR ***correlation***

a **clear/close/direct/high/strong** correlation • a correlation **between** sth and sth

correlation /ˌkɒrəˈleɪʃən/ *noun* [C] a connection between two or more things, usually where one causes or influences the other *The research showed a **close correlation between** smoking and lung cancer.*

correspond /ˌkɒrɪˈspɒnd/ *verb* [I] **1** [BE SIMILAR] to be the same or very similar *The newspaper story does not **correspond with/to** what really happened.* **2** [WRITE] to communicate with someone by writing letters

correspondence /ˌkɒrɪˈspɒndəns/ *noun* **1** [LETTERS] [U] letters or emails from one person to another, or the activity of writing and receiving letters or emails *business correspondence* **2** [CONNECTION] [C, U] when there is a connection or similarity between two or more things

correspondent /ˌkɒrɪˈspɒndənt/ *noun* [C] **1** [NEWS] someone who reports news for newspapers, television, or radio, usually from another country **2** [LETTER WRITER] someone who writes letters, usually regularly

corresponding /ˌkɒrɪˈspɒndɪŋ/ *adjective* [always before noun] similar or related *Draw a line between the words with corresponding meanings.*

corresˌponding ˈangle *noun* [C] **MATHEMATICS** one of two equal angles on the same side of a line that crosses two parallel lines, and on the same side of each parallel line ➲Compare **alternate angle**

corridor /'kɒrɪdɔːʳ/ *noun* [C] a passage in a building or train with rooms on one or both sides

corrie /'kɒri/ *noun* [C] **GEOGRAPHY** a hollow round shape in the side of a mountain

corroborate /kə'rɒbəreɪt/ *verb* [T] *formal* to say something or provide information that supports what someone says *A witness corroborated his account of the accident.* •**corroboration** /kə,rɒbə'reɪʃən/ *noun* [U]

corrode /kə'rəʊd/ *verb* **1 CHEMISTRY** [I, T] If metal corrodes, or rain or chemicals corrode it, it is slowly damaged by them. *Rain corroded the metal pipes.* **2** [T] to slowly damage someone or something *He was corroded by guilt.* •**corrosion** /kə'rəʊʒən/ *noun* [U] •**corrosive** /kə'rəʊsɪv/ *adjective Acid rain is **highly corrosive**.*

corrugated /'kɒrəgeɪtɪd/ *adjective* [**always before noun**] Corrugated metal or cardboard has parallel rows of folds that look like waves. *a corrugated iron roof*

corrupt¹ /kə'rʌpt/ *adjective* **1** dishonest or illegal *a corrupt government* **2 COMPUTING** If information on a computer is corrupt, it has been damaged or spoiled. *corrupt files*

corrupt² /kə'rʌpt/ *verb* [T] **1** to make someone or something become dishonest or immoral [**often passive**] *He became corrupted by power and money.* **2 COMPUTING** to damage information on a computer

corruption /kə'rʌpʃən/ *noun* [U] **1** BAD BEHAVIOUR dishonest or immoral behaviour, usually by people in positions of power *He was arrested for corruption and bribery.* **2** MAKE DISHONEST when you cause someone or something to become dishonest or immoral *the corruption of innocent young children*

corset /'kɔːsət/ *noun* [C] a tight piece of underwear worn by women to make themselves look thinner, especially in the past

cortex /'kɔːteks/ *noun plural* **cortices 1 ANATOMY, BIOLOGY** the outer layer of an organ of the body, especially the brain **2 BIOLOGY** a layer of tissue in the stems and roots of plants ⊃See picture at **stem**

cosine /'kəʊsaɪn/ (*abbreviation* **cos**) *noun* [C] **MATHEMATICS** in a triangle that has one angle of 90°, the ratio of the length of the side next to an angle less than 90°, divided by the length of the hypotenuse (= the side opposite the 90° angle) ⊃Compare **sine, tangent**

cosmetic /kɒz'metɪk/ *adjective* **1** APPEARANCE intended to improve your appearance **2** SMALL CHANGE involving only small changes or improvements that will not solve a problem *Critics claimed that the changes were only cosmetic.*

cosmetics /kɒz'metɪks/ *noun* [**plural**] substances that you put on your face or body to improve your appearance

cos,metic 'surgery *noun* [U] **HEALTH** a medical operation to make someone more attractive

cosmic /'kɒzmɪk/ *adjective* relating to the whole universe *cosmic rays*

cosmopolitan /,kɒzmə'pɒlɪtən/ *adjective* **1** PLACE consisting of people and things from many different countries *London is a very cosmopolitan city.* **2** EXPERIENCE having experience of many different countries or cultures *a dynamic, cosmopolitan businesswoman*

the cosmos /'kɒzmɒs/ *noun* the whole universe

WORD PARTNERS FOR ***cost***

the cost **of** sth • **at a cost of** [£500/$1000, etc] • the **high/low** cost of sth • **cover** the cost **of** (doing) sth • **cut/reduce** costs • **at no extra** cost • the cost **of living**

cost¹ /kɒst/ *noun* **1 FINANCE** [C, U] the amount of money that you need to buy or do something *The cruise ship was built **at a cost of** $400 million.* ○ *Software is included at **no extra cost**.* ○ *The **cost of living*** (= the cost of food, clothes, etc) *has increased.* **2** [**no plural**] something that you give or lose, in order to get or achieve something else *He rescued four people **at the cost of** his own life.* **3 at all costs** If something must be done at all costs, it is very important that it is done. *We have to succeed at all costs.* **4 to your cost** *UK* because of a bad experience you have had *An ankle injury can last a long time, as I know to my cost.*

cost² /kɒst/ *verb past* **cost 1 FINANCE** [T] If something costs a particular amount of money, you have to pay that in order to buy or do it. *How much do these shoes cost?* [**+ to do sth**] ***It costs** $5 to send the package by airmail.* [**+ two objects**] *It's going to cost me a lot of money to buy a new car.* **2** [**+ two objects**] to make someone lose something *His lazy attitude cost him his job.*

cost³ /kɒst/ *verb* [T] **FINANCE** to calculate the amount of money needed to do or make something *The building work has been costed at $30,000.*

co-star¹ /'kəʊstɑːʳ/ *noun* [C] one of two famous actors who both have important parts in a particular film

co-star² /kəʊ'stɑːʳ/ (US) /'kəʊstɑːr/ *verb* **co-starring**, *past* **co-starred 1** FILM/PLAY [T] If a film, play, etc co-stars two or more famous actors, they are in it. **2** ACTOR [I] to be in a film, play, etc with another famous actor *Hugh Grant **co-stars with** Julia Roberts in 'Notting Hill'.*

cost-'benefit a,nalysis *noun* [C] **ECONOMICS** a method of deciding whether something is worth doing, especially by a government or a business, by comparing the cost with the benefits that will come from it

cost-cutting /'kɒst,kʌtɪŋ/ *noun* [U] **FINANCE** actions that reduce the amount of money spent on something ***cost-cutting measures**/**strategies***

cost-effective /,kɒstɪ'fektɪv/ *adjective* **FINANCE** If something is cost-effective, it achieves good results for little money.

costly /'kɒstli/ *adjective* **1** EXPENSIVE expensive [**+ to do sth**] *It would be too costly to build a swimming pool.* **2** CAUSING PROBLEMS causing a lot of problems, or causing you to lose something important *a costly mistake*

,cost of 'borrowing *noun* [U] **FINANCE** the amount of money that a person or business has to pay in order to borrow a sum of money

ˌcost of ˈsales *noun* [U] **FINANCE** the amount that it costs a business to produce and sell something

cost-plus pricing /ˌkɒstplʌsˈpraɪsɪŋ/ *noun* [U] **FINANCE** a method of deciding the price for a product by adding a particular amount to the cost of producing it

ˌcost ˈprice *noun* [C, U] **FINANCE** the price that it cost to make a product, without a profit being added

costume /ˈkɒstjuːm/ *noun* **1** PLAY [C, U] a set of clothes that someone wears to make them look like someone or something else, for example in a play *actors in costume* ○ *He arrived at the party dressed in a gorilla costume.* **2** TYPICAL CLOTHES [U] a set of clothes that are typical of a particular country or time in history *Japanese national costume* ➲See also: **swimming costume**

cosy *UK* (*US* **cozy**) /ˈkəʊzi/ *adjective* comfortable and warm

cot /kɒt/ *UK* (*US* **crib**) *noun* [C] a bed with high sides for a baby

ˈcot ˌdeath *UK* (*US* **SIDS**) *noun* [C, U] **HEALTH** the sudden death of a sleeping baby for no obvious reason

cottage /ˈkɒtɪdʒ/ *noun* [C] a small house, usually in the countryside

ˌcottage ˈcheese *noun* [U] **FOOD** a soft, white cheese with small lumps in it

cotton¹ /ˈkɒtᵊn/ *noun* [U] **1** CLOTH cloth or thread that is produced from the cotton plant *a cotton shirt/dress* **2** PLANT a plant that produces a soft, white substance used for making thread and cloth **3** FOR CLEANING *US* (*UK* **cotton wool**) a soft mass of cotton, usually used for cleaning your skin ➲See colour picture **The Bathroom** at page Centre 3

ˌcotton ˈwool *UK* (*US* **cotton**) *noun* [U] a soft mass of cotton, usually used for cleaning your skin ➲See colour picture **The Bathroom** on page Centre 3

cotyledon /ˌkɒtɪˈliːdən/ *noun* [C] **BIOLOGY** a type of leaf that is part of the developing plant inside a seed and either stores food or grows from the seed to produce food

couch¹ /kaʊtʃ/ *noun* [C] a long, comfortable piece of furniture that two or more people can sit on

couch² /kaʊtʃ/ *verb* **be couched in/as sth** to be expressed in a particular way *His explanation was* ***couched in*** *technical language.*

ˈcouch poˌtato *noun* [C] *UK humorous* a person who is not active and spends a lot of time watching television

O- **cough¹** /kɒf/ *verb* [I] **HEALTH** to make air come out of your throat with a short sound
cough sth up *phrasal verb* to make something come out of your lungs or throat by coughing *Doctors were worried when she started* ***coughing up blood.***
cough (sth) up *phrasal verb informal* to give money to someone although you do not want to

cough² /kɒf/ *noun* [C] **1 HEALTH** when you cough, or the sound this makes **2 HEALTH** an illness that makes you cough a lot *Uwe* ***has a nasty cough.*** ➲See also: **whooping cough**

O- **could** *strong form* /kʊd/ *weak form* /kəd/ *modal verb* **1** CAN used as the past form of 'can' to talk about what someone or something was able or allowed to do *I couldn't see what he was doing.* ○ *You said we could watch television when we'd finished our homework.* **2** POSSIBLE used to talk about what is possible or might happen *The baby could arrive any day now.* ○ *This kind of crime could easily be prevented.* ○ *She could have* (= might have) *been seriously injured.* **3** ASK used to ask someone politely to do or provide something *Could you lend me £5?* ○ *Could I have another drink?* **4** ASK PERMISSION used to ask politely for permission to do something *Could I speak to Mr Davis, please?* **5** SUGGEST used to make a suggestion *You could try painting it a different colour.* **6 I could (have)** used when you feel so happy, sad, angry, etc that you would like to do something *I was so grateful I could have kissed her!* ➲See Extra help page **Modal verbs** on page Centre 34.

O- **couldn't** /ˈkʊdᵊnt/ *short for* could not *I couldn't understand what he was saying.*

O- **could've** /ˈkʊdəv/ *short for* could have *It could've been much worse.*

coulomb /ˈkuːlɒm/ *noun* [C] **MEASURES** a unit of measurement for electric charge, representing the charge carried by one ampere (= unit of electric current) in one second

council, Council /ˈkaʊnsᵊl/ *noun* [C] **1 POLITICS** a group of people who are elected to control a town, city, or area *Edinburgh City Council* ○ *a council meeting* **2** a group of people who are elected or chosen to give advice or make decisions *the Medical Research Council* **3 a council house/flat** in the UK a house or flat that is owned by a city or town council and rented to people

ˈcouncil eˌstate *UK* (*US* **housing project**) *noun* [C] **SOCIETY** a part of a city with council houses and flats (= homes owned by a council and rented to people) *a Birmingham council estate*

councillor *UK* (*US* **councilor**) /ˈkaʊnsᵊlər/ *noun* [C] **POLITICS** a member of a town, city, or area council

counsel¹ /ˈkaʊnsᵊl/ *noun* **1 LAW** [C] a lawyer (= someone who advises people about the law and deals with legal situations) who speaks for someone in court **2** [U] *literary* advice

counsel² /ˈkaʊnsᵊl/ *verb* [T] *UK* **counselling,** *past* **counselled,** *US* **counseling,** *past* **counseled 1** ADVISE *formal* to advise someone to do something [+ **to do sth**] *Lawyers had counselled him not to say anything.* **2** ABOUT PROBLEMS to give advice to someone who has problems

counselling *UK* (*US* **counseling**) /ˈkaʊnsəlɪŋ/ *noun* [U] the job or process of listening to someone and giving them advice about their problems *a counselling service*

counsellor *UK* (*US* **counselor**) /ˈkaʊnsələr/ *noun* [C] someone whose job is to listen to people and give them advice about their problems

O- **count¹** /kaʊnt/ *verb* **1 MATHEMATICS** [T] to see how many people or things there are *I counted the money on the table.* **2 MATHEMATICS** [I] to say numbers in their correct order *Can you count* *to twenty in French?* **3** CONSIDER [T] to think of someone or something in a particular way *She* ***counted*** *Tim* ***as*** *her closest friend.* ○ *You should* ***count yourself lucky*** *you weren't hurt.* **4** IMPORTANT [I] to be important *I believe that health and happiness count more than money.* ○ *Doesn't my opinion* ***count for*** *anything?* **5** INCLUDE [T] to include something or someone in a calculation *There are 1500 people at my school, counting teachers.* **6** BE ACCEPTED [I] to be accepted or allowed as part of something *I've been to sixteen different countries, but I only spent half an hour in Luxembourg, so that doesn't really count.*

count against sb/sth *phrasal verb* to make someone or something more likely to fail *Her lack of experience will count against her.*

count sb in *phrasal verb* to include someone in an activity *If you're going for a pizza, you can count me in.*

count on sb *phrasal verb* to be confident that you can depend on someone *I can always count on my parents to help me.*

count on sth *phrasal verb* to expect something to happen and make plans based on it *I didn't count on so many people coming to the party.*

count sth out *phrasal verb* to count coins or pieces of paper money one by one as you put them down *She counted out five crisp $20 bills.*

count sb out *phrasal verb* to not include someone in an activity

count towards sth *phrasal verb* to be part of what is needed to complete something or achieve something *This essay counts towards my exam result.*

count up sb/sth *phrasal verb* to add together all the people or things in a group

count² /kaʊnt/ *noun* **1** NUMBER [C] when you count something, or the total number you get after counting [**usually singular**] *At the last count there were 410 club members.* **2 lose count** to forget how many of something there is *I've* ***lost count of*** *the number of times she's arrived late.* **3 on all/both/several, etc counts** in all, both, several, etc parts of a situation, argument, etc *I had been wrong* ***on both counts.*** **4** RANK [C] (*also* **Count**) a man of high social rank in some European countries **5** CRIME [C] one of the times that someone has been accused of a particular crime *He was charged with two counts of assault.* ➲See also: **pollen count**

countable noun /ˌkaʊntəbᵊl'naʊn/ (*also* **'count ˌnoun**) *noun* [C] **LANGUAGE** a noun that has both plural and singular forms ➲See Extra help page **Countable and uncountable nouns** on page Centre 30.

countdown /'kaʊntdaʊn/ *noun* [C] the time just before an important event when people are counting the time until it happens [**usually singular**] *The* ***countdown to*** *the Olympics has begun.*

countenance¹ /'kaʊntᵊnəns/ *noun* [C] *literary* the appearance or expression of someone's face

countenance² /'kaʊntᵊnəns/ *verb* [T] *formal* to accept that something should happen *They will not countenance building a new airport.*

counter¹ /'kaʊntəʳ/ *noun* [C] **1** IN A SHOP the place in a shop, bank, etc, where people are served *The woman* ***behind the counter*** *took his money.* **2** SURFACE *US* a flat surface in a kitchen on which food can be prepared **3** DISC a small disc used in some games that are played on a board

counter² /'kaʊntəʳ/ *verb* [T] **1** PREVENT to prevent something or reduce the bad effect that it has *This skin cream claims to counter the effects of sun damage.* **2** REACT to say something to show that what someone has just said is not true *"Of course I love him," Clare countered.*

counter³ /'kaʊntəʳ/ *adverb* **be/run counter to sth** to have the opposite effect to something else *The new road plans run counter to the government's aim of reducing pollution.*

counter- /kaʊntəʳ-/ *prefix* opposing or as a reaction to *a counter-attack* (= an attack on someone who has attacked you)

counteract /ˌkaʊntᵊr'ækt/ *verb* [T] to reduce the bad effect that something else has *drugs that counteract the side effects of sea sickness*

counter-attack /'kaʊntərəˌtæk/ *noun* [C] an attack that you make against someone who has attacked you in a sport, war, or argument •**counter-attack** *verb* [I, T]

counterclockwise /ˌkaʊntə'klɒkwaɪz/ *US* (*UK* **anti-clockwise**) *adjective, adverb* in the opposite direction to the way the hands (= parts that point to the numbers) of a clock move ➲See picture at **clockwise**

counterfeit /'kaʊntəfɪt/ *adjective* made to look like the real thing, in order to trick people *counterfeit money/jewellery*

counterpart /'kaʊntəpɑːt/ *noun* [C] someone or something that has the same job or position as someone or something in a different place or organization

counterproductive /ˌkaʊntəprə'dʌktɪv/ *adjective* having the opposite effect from the one you want

countess /'kaʊntɪs/ *noun* [C] a woman who has a high social rank in some European countries, especially the wife of an earl or count (= man of high social rank) *the Countess of Abingdon*

countless /'kaʊntləs/ *adjective* [**always before noun**] very many *The song has been played* ***countless times*** *on the radio.*

country¹ /'kʌntri/ *noun* **1** [C] **GEOGRAPHY** an area of land that has its own government, army, etc *European countries* **2 the country a** **GEOGRAPHY** the areas that are away from towns and cities **b** **SOCIETY** the people who live in a country *The country was shocked by the President's decision.*

COMMON LEARNER ERROR

country, land, nation, or **state?**

Country is the most general word which means 'an area of land'. It usually means an area of land with its own government and people.

China, Japan, and other countries in Asia

Nation is used to talk about a country, especially when you mean the people or the culture of that country.

The nation celebrated the 100th anniversary of independence.

State is used to talk about a country as a political or official area. Some countries are divided into political units that are also called **states**.

Belgium became an independent state in 1830.

America is divided into 50 states.

the State of Florida

Land means an area of ground, not an area with its own government.

We bought some land to build a house on.

country² /ˈkʌntri/ *adjective* [**always before noun**] **GEOGRAPHY** in or relating to the areas that are away from towns and cities *country roads/hotels*

countryman /ˈkʌntrɪmən/ *noun* [C] *plural* **countrymen** someone from the same country as you

ˌcountry ˈmusic (*also* **ˌcountry and ˈwestern**) *noun* [U] **MUSIC** a style of popular music from the southern and western US

countryside /ˈkʌntrɪsaɪd/ *noun* [U] land that is not in towns or cities and has farms, fields, forests, etc ⊃See Common Learner Error at **nature**

county /ˈkaʊnti/ *noun* [C] an area of Britain, Ireland, or the US that has its own local government

coup /kuː/ *noun* [C] **1 POLITICS** (*also* **coup d'état** /ˌkuːdeɪˈtɑː/) when a group of people suddenly takes control of a country using force *a **military coup*** **2** an important achievement, often one that was not expected *The award is a **major coup** for the university.*

o⁃**couple¹** /ˈkʌpl/ *noun* **1** A FEW [**no plural**] two or a few *I went to New York with **a couple of** friends.* ○ *The weather has improved over the last **couple of** weeks.* **2** TWO PEOPLE [C] two people who are married or having a romantic relationship *a **married couple***

couple² /ˈkʌpl/ *verb* **coupled with sth** combined with something else *Concern about farming methods, coupled with health awareness, have led to a fall in meat consumption.*

coupon /ˈkuːpɒn/ *noun* [C] **1 FINANCE** a piece of printed paper that you can use to buy something at a cheaper price or to get something free *Collect 10 coupons to get a free meal.* **2** a printed form in a magazine or newspaper, that you use to send for information, enter a competition, etc

WORD PARTNERS FOR ***courage***

have the courage to do sth • **show** courage • sth **takes** courage • **great/immense/personal** courage

courage /ˈkʌrɪdʒ/ *noun* [U] **1** the ability to deal with dangerous or difficult situations without being frightened [+ **to do sth**] *She didn't **have the courage** to tell him the truth.* **2 pluck up the courage (to do sth)** to decide to do something that you were too frightened to do before

courageous /kəˈreɪdʒəs/ *adjective* brave •**courageously** *adverb*

courgette /kɔːˈʒet/ *UK* (*US* **zucchini**) *noun* [C, U] **FOOD** a long, green vegetable which is white inside

courier /ˈkʊriəʳ/ *noun* [C] **1** DOCUMENTS someone whose job is to take and deliver documents and parcels **2** HOLIDAY *UK* someone whose job is to look after people who are on holiday

o⁃**course** /kɔːs/ *noun* **1 of course a** YES used to say 'yes' and emphasize your answer *"Can you help me?" "Of course!"* **b** OBVIOUS used to show that what you are saying is obvious or already known *Of course, the Olympics are not just about money.* **2 of course not** used to say 'no' and emphasize your answer *"Do you mind if I borrow your pen?" "Of course not."* **3 EDUCATION** [C] a series of lessons about a particular subject *She did a ten-week course in computing.* **4 FOOD** [C] a part of a meal *a three-course dinner* **5 SPORT** [C] an area used for horse races or playing golf *a golf course* **6 HEALTH** [C] *mainly UK* a fixed number of regular medical treatments *a course of antibiotics* **7** ROUTE [C, U] the direction in which a ship, aircraft, etc is moving *During the storm, the boat was blown **off course*** (= in the wrong direction). **8** ACTION [C] (*also* **ˌcourse of ˈaction**) something that you can do in a particular situation *I think the best course of action would be to write to him.* **9 during/in/over the course of sth** during a particular time or activity *In the course of the interview she mentioned her previous experience.* **10 in due course** at a suitable time in the future *The results will be sent to you in due course.* **11** DEVELOPMENT [**no plural**] the way something develops, usually over a long time *Nuclear weapons have changed **the course of** modern history.* **12 in the course of time** *UK* gradually, or over a period of time **13 be on course for sth/to do sth** *UK* to be very likely to succeed at something **14 run its course** If something runs its course, it continues naturally until it has finished. ⊃See also: be on a **collision** course, **crash course,** be **par** for the course

coursebook /ˈkɔːsbʊk/ *noun* [C] *UK* **EDUCATION** a book used by students when they do a particular course of study

coursework /ˈkɔːswɜːk/ *noun* [U] *UK* **EDUCATION** work done by students as part of their course of study

o⁃**court¹** /kɔːt/ *noun* [C, U] **1 LAW** the place where a judge decides whether someone is guilty of a crime *The suspect appeared **in court** charged with robbery.* ○ *You can **take them to court*** (= make them be judged in court) *if they don't pay.* **2 the court LAW** the judge and group of people at a trial who decide whether someone is guilty of a crime **3 SPORT** an area for playing particular sports *a tennis/basketball court* **4** ROYAL HOUSE the official home of a king or queen and the people who live with them ⊃See also: **High Court, the supreme court**

court² /kɔːt/ *verb* **1** PLEASE [T] to try to please someone because you want them to support you or join you *Adams is being courted by several football clubs.* **2** TRY TO GET [T] to try to get or achieve something *to court investment/publicity* **3** RELATIONSHIP [I, T] *old-fashioned* to have a romantic relationship with someone you hope to marry **4 court controversy/danger/disaster, etc** to behave in a way that risks bad results

courteous /ˈkɜːtiəs/ *adjective* polite and showing respect •**courteously** *adverb*

courtesy /ˈkɜːtəsi/ *noun* **1** [U] behaviour that is polite and shows respect, or a polite action or remark *The hotel treats all guests with courtesy.* [+ **to do sth**] *He didn't even **have the courtesy** to thank me.* **2 (by) courtesy of sb/sth** If you have something courtesy of someone, they have allowed you to have it. *The photograph is courtesy of the Natural History Museum.*

courthouse /ˈkɔːthaʊs/ *noun* [C] *plural* **courthouses** /ˈkɔːthaʊzɪz/ *mainly US* **LAW** a building with law courts inside it

courtier /ˈkɔːtiəʳ/ *noun* [C] someone who spent a lot of time in the home of a king or queen in the past

court-martial¹ /ˌkɔːtˈmɑːʃəl/ *noun* [C] a military court, or a trial in a military court

court-martial² /ˌkɔːtˈmɑːʃəl/ *verb* [T] to judge someone in a military court

ˈcourt ˌorder *noun* [C] **LAW** an instruction from a law court that someone must do or not do something

courtroom /ˈkɔːtrʊm/ *noun* [C] the room where a judge and other people decide whether someone is guilty of a crime

courtship /ˈkɔːtʃɪp/ *noun* [C, U] *formal* the time when people have a romantic relationship with the intention of getting married

courtyard /ˈkɔːtjɑːd/ *noun* [C] an open area by a building with walls or buildings around it

O-- **cousin** /ˈkʌzən/ *noun* [C] the child of your aunt or uncle

couture /kuːˈtjʊəʳ/ *noun* [U] **DT** the design, making, and selling of expensive and fashionable clothes

covalent bond /kəʊˌveɪləntˈbɒnd/ *noun* [C] **CHEMISTRY** a chemical bond in which two atoms share one or more pairs of electrons, which hold them together

cove /kəʊv/ *noun* [C] **GEOGRAPHY** a place on the coast where the land curves in

covenant /ˈkʌvənənt/ *noun* [C] **LAW** a formal written agreement

O-- **cover¹** /ˈkʌvəʳ/ *verb* [T] **1** [PUT] to put something over something else, in order to protect or hide it *They covered him with a blanket.* ○ *He covered his face with his hands.* ⊃Opposite **uncover 2** [LAYER] to form a layer on the surface of something *Snow covered the trees.* ○ *My legs were **covered in/with** mud.* **3** [DISTANCE] to travel a particular distance *We covered 700 kilometres in four days.* **4** [AREA] to be a particular size or area *The town covers an area of 10 square miles.* **5** [INCLUDE] to include or deal with a subject or piece of information *The book covers European history from 1789-1914.* **6** [REPORT] to report on an event for a newspaper, television programme, etc *Dave was asked to cover the Olympics.* **7** [MONEY] to be enough money to pay for something *£100 should cover the cost of the repairs.* **8 FINANCE** to provide financial protection if something bad happens *travel insurance that covers accident and injury* ⊃See also: touch/cover all the bases (**base**¹)

cover sth up *phrasal verb* to put something over something else, in order to protect or hide it

cover (sth) up *phrasal verb* to stop people from discovering the truth about something bad *She tried to cover up her mistakes.*

O-- **cover²** /ˈkʌvəʳ/ *noun* **1** [BOOK] [C] the outer part of a book, magazine, etc, that protects the pages *Her picture was **on the cover** of 'Vogue' magazine.* **2** [PROTECTION] [C] something you put over something else, usually to protect it *an ironing board cover* ○ *a lens cover* **3 FINANCE** [U] financial protection so that you get money if something bad happens *The policy provides £50,000 accidental damage cover.* **4** [FROM WEATHER/ATTACK] [U] protection from bad weather or an attack *They **took cover** under some trees until the rain stopped.* **5** [FOR ILLEGAL ACTIVITY] [C] something used to hide a secret or illegal activity *The club is used as a **cover for** a gang of car thieves.*

coverage /ˈkʌvərɪdʒ/ *noun* [U] **1** the way a newspaper, television programme, etc reports an event or subject *There is **live coverage** of the game on cable TV.* **2 FINANCE** *mainly US* financial protection so that you get money if something bad happens

coveralls /ˈkʌvərɔːlz/ *US* (*UK* **overalls**) *noun* [plural] a piece of clothing that you wear over your clothes to keep them clean while you are working

covering /ˈkʌvərɪŋ/ *noun* [C] a layer that covers something *a thick covering of snow*

ˌcovering ˈletter *UK* (*US* **ˈcover ˌletter**) *noun* [C] a letter that you send with something to explain what it is or to give more information about it

covers /ˈkʌvəz/ *noun* [plural] the sheets and other layers of cloth on your bed that keep you warm

covert /ˈkəʊvɜːt/ *adjective* done in a secret way *covert police operations* •**covertly** *adverb*

cover-up /ˈkʌvərʌp/ *noun* [C] an attempt to prevent people finding out the truth about a crime or a mistake *Police denied accusations of a cover-up.*

ˈcover ˌversion *noun* [C] **MUSIC** a recording of a song already recorded by someone else *a cover version of 'Let It Be'*

covet /ˈkʌvɪt/ *verb* [T] *formal* to want something very much, especially something that someone else has

O-- **cow** /kaʊ/ *noun* [C] **1** [ANIMAL] a large farm animal kept for milk or meat **2** [INSULT] *UK informal* an offensive word for a woman

coward /kaʊəd/ *noun* [C] someone who is not brave and tries to avoid dangerous or difficult situations

cowardice /ˈkaʊədɪs/ *noun* [U] behaviour that shows that someone is not brave

cowardly /ˈkaʊədli/ *adjective* behaving in a way that shows you are not brave

cowboy /ˈkaʊbɔɪ/ *noun* [C] **1** [ANIMAL WORKER] a man whose job is to look after cattle (= animals such as cows) in the US, and who usually rides a horse **2** [BAD WORKER] *UK informal* someone who does their job badly or who is dishonest in business *cowboy builders*

ˈcowboy ˌboots *noun* [C] a type of boots with pointed toes, first worn by cowboys ➲See colour picture **Clothes** on page Centre 9

ˈcowboy ˌhat *noun* [C] a type of hat with a hight top and a wide lower edge, first worn by cowboys

cower /kaʊəʳ/ *verb* [I] to bend down or move back because you are frightened

co-worker /ˌkəʊˈwɜːkəʳ/ *noun* [C] *mainly US* someone that you work with

coy /kɔɪ/ *adjective* **1** NO INFORMATION not wanting to give people information about something *Nigel's very coy about how much he earns.* **2** SHY pretending to be shy *a coy look* •**coyly** *adverb*

coyote /kaɪˈəʊti/ *noun* [C] a wild animal similar to a dog, that lives in North America

cozy /ˈkəʊzi/ *adjective US spelling of* cosy

CPU /ˌsiːpiːˈjuː/ *noun* [C] **COMPUTING** *abbreviation for* central processing unit: the part of a computer that controls all the other parts

Cr. FINANCE *written abbeviation for* credit: money going into an account

crab /kræb/ *noun* [C, U] **FOOD** a sea creature with ten legs and a round, flat body covered by a shell, or the meat from this animal

crack¹ /kræk/ *verb* **1** BREAK [I, T] to break something so that it does not separate, but very thin lines appear on its surface, or to become broken in this way *The concrete had started to crack.* ○ *cracked dishes* **2** EGG/NUT [T] to open an egg or nut by breaking its shell **3** HIT [T] to hit a part of your body against something hard, by accident *He cracked his head on the cupboard door.* **4** SOLVE [T] *informal* to solve a difficult problem *It took three months to crack the enemy's code.* **5 get cracking** *informal* to start doing something quickly **6** LOSE CONTROL [I] to lose control of your emotions and be unable to deal with a situation *He finally cracked after years of stress.* **7** NOISE [I, T] to make a sudden, short noise, or to cause something to make this noise **8 crack a joke** to tell a joke **9 not all it's cracked up to be** *informal* (*also* **not as good as it's cracked up to be** *informal*) not as good as people think or say *Being an actor isn't all it's cracked up to be.*

crack down *phrasal verb* to start dealing with bad or illegal behaviour in a more severe way *Police are* ***cracking down on*** *crime in the area.*

crack up *phrasal verb informal* to become mentally ill

crack (sb) up *phrasal verb informal* to suddenly laugh a lot, or to make someone suddenly laugh a lot

crack² /kræk/ *noun* **1** LINE [C] a line on the surface of something that is damaged *Several cups had cracks in them.* **2** NARROW SPACE [C] a narrow space between two parts of something or between two things *I could see sunlight through a crack in the curtains.* **3 HEALTH** [U] an illegal drug that is very harmful **4** NOISE [C] a sudden, short noise *a* ***crack of thunder*** **5** JOKE [C] an unkind joke or remark *He was always* ***making cracks about*** *my weight.* **6 have/take a crack at sth** *informal* to try to do something *I've never put up shelves before, but I'll have a crack at it.* **7 the crack of dawn** very early in the morning *He gets up at the crack of dawn.*

crack³ /kræk/ *adjective* [**always before noun**] of the highest quality *a crack regiment*

WORD PARTNERS FOR ***crackdown***

announce/call for/launch/order a crackdown • a crackdown **on** sth • a **tough** crackdown • a **government/police** crackdown

crackdown /ˈkrækdaʊn/ *noun* [C] when bad or illegal behaviour is dealt with in a very severe way, in order to stop it happening *The police are having* ***a crackdown on*** *speeding.*

cracker /ˈkrækəʳ/ *noun* **1 FOOD** [C] a dry biscuit that you eat with cheese **2** CHRISTMAS [C] (*also* **Christmas cracker**) a coloured paper tube with a small toy inside, that people pull open at Christmas (= a Christian holiday) in the UK **3** GOOD [**no plural**] *UK informal* someone or something that is very good

cracking /ˈkrækɪŋ/ *noun* [U] **CHEMISTRY** a process in which complex molecules are broken down into more simple molecules

crackle /ˈkrækl/ *verb* [I] to make a lot of short, dry noises *A fire crackled in the hearth.* •**crackle** *noun* [**no plural**]

cradle¹ /ˈkreɪdl/ *noun* **1** BED [C] a baby's bed, especially one that swings from side to side **2** TELEPHONE the part of a telephone that holds the receiver (= the part of a telephone that you hold in your hand and use to listen and speak) **3** MOBILE PHONE a small stand that holds a mobile phone **4 the cradle of sth** the place where something started *Massachusetts, the cradle of the American Revolution*

cradle² /ˈkreɪdl/ *verb* [T] to hold someone or something in a careful, gentle way *He* ***cradled*** *her* ***in*** *his arms.*

craft¹ /krɑːft/ *noun* **1 ART, DT** [C, U] an activity in which you make something using a lot of skill, especially with your hands *traditional crafts such as weaving* **2** [C] *plural* **craft** a boat

craft² /krɑːft/ *verb* [T] to make something using a lot of skill [**often passive**] *a bowl that was beautifully crafted from wood*

craftsman /ˈkrɑːftsmən/ *noun* [C] *plural* **craftsmen** someone who uses special skill to make things, especially with their hands •**craftsmanship** *noun* [U] skill at making things

crafty /ˈkrɑːfti/ *adjective* clever at getting what you want, especially by deceiving people •**craftily** *adverb*

crag /kræg/ *noun* [C] **GEOGRAPHY** a high, rough mass of rock that sticks up from the land around it

cram /kræm/ *verb* **cramming,** *past* **crammed** **1 cram sth between/in/into, etc** to force things into a small space *The refugees were crammed into the truck.* **2 EDUCATION** [I] to study a lot before an exam

crammed /kræmd/ *adjective* completely full of people or things *crammed commuter trains* ○ *The room was* ***crammed with*** *boxes.*

cramp¹ /kræmp/ *noun* [C, U] **HEALTH** a sudden, strong pain in a muscle that makes it difficult to move *I've got cramp in my legs.*

C

cramp² /kræmp/ *verb* ➲See: cramp sb's **style¹**

cramped /kræmpt/ *adjective* A cramped room, building, etc is unpleasant because it is not big enough.

cranberry /ˈkrænbəri/ *noun* [C] **FOOD** a small, red berry (= soft fruit) with a sour taste

crane¹ /kreɪn/ *noun* [C] **1** MACHINE a large machine used for lifting and moving heavy things **2** BIRD a bird with long legs and a long neck

crane² /kreɪn/ *verb* [I, T] to stretch your neck, in order to see or hear something

cranium /ˈkreɪniəm/ *noun* [C] *plural* **craniums** or **crania** **ANATOMY, BIOLOGY** the hard bone in animals and humans, which gives the head its shape and protects the brain ➲See picture at **brain** ➲See picture at **skull**

crank /kræŋk/ *noun* [C] **1** PERSON *informal* someone with strange ideas or behaviour **2** HANDLE a handle that you turn to make a machine work

cranny /ˈkræni/ *noun* ➲See: every **nook** and cranny

WORD PARTNERS FOR ***crash***

have/be involved in a crash • be **injured in/killed in** a crash • the **cause of** a crash • a crash **victim** • a **car/plane/train** crash

crash¹ /kræʃ/ *noun* [C] **1** VEHICLE an accident in which a vehicle hits something *a **car/plane crash*** **2** NOISE a sudden, loud noise made when something falls or breaks *I heard a crash and hurried into the kitchen.* **3** **COMPUTING** when a computer or computer system suddenly stops working **4** **ECONOMICS** when the value of a country's businesses suddenly falls by a large amount *He lost a lot of money in the stock market crash of 1929.*

crash² /kræʃ/ *verb* **1** VEHICLE [I, T] If a vehicle crashes, it hits something by accident, and if you crash a vehicle, you make it hit something by accident. *The van skidded and **crashed into** a tree.* ○ *Rick crashed his dad's car.* **2** **COMPUTING** [I] If a computer or computer system crashes, it suddenly stops working. **3** **crash against/on/through, etc** to hit something and make a loud noise *The waves crashed against the rocks.* **4** LOUD NOISE [I] to make a sudden, loud noise *Thunder crashed overhead.* **5** **ECONOMICS** [I] If a financial market crashes, prices suddenly fall by a large amount.

ˈcrash ˌbarrier *noun* [C] *UK* a fence along the middle or edge of a road for preventing accidents

ˈcrash ˌcourse *UK* (*US* ˌ**crash** ˈ**course**) *noun* [C] **EDUCATION** a course that teaches you a lot of basic facts in a very short time

ˈcrash ˌhelmet *noun* [C] a hard hat that protects your head when you ride a motorcycle

crass /kræs/ *adjective* showing that you do not understand or care about other people's feelings *a crass remark*

crate /kreɪt/ *noun* [C] a large box used for carrying or storing things

crater /ˈkreɪtəʳ/ *noun* [C] **1** **GEOLOGY** the round, open part at the top of a volcano ➲See picture at **volcano** **2** a big hole in the ground *The explosion left a crater in the road.*

ˈcrater ˌlake *noun* [C] **GEOLOGY** a round lake that has formed in the top of a volcano

crave /kreɪv/ *verb* [T] to want something very much *a child who craves affection* •**craving** *noun* [C] a strong feeling that you want or need a particular thing *She **had a craving for** chocolate.*

crawl¹ /krɔːl/ *verb* **1** PERSON [I] to move on your hands and knees *I crawled under the desk to plug the lamp in.* **2** ANIMAL [I] If an insect crawls, it uses its legs to move. *There's an ant crawling up your leg.* **3** TRAFFIC [I] If traffic crawls, it moves extremely slowly. *We were **crawling along** at 10 miles per hour.* **4** TRY TO PLEASE [I] *UK informal* to try to please someone because you want them to like you or help you *My brother is always **crawling to** Mum.* **5** **be crawling with sb/sth** to be full of insects or people in a way that is unpleasant *The kitchen's crawling with ants.*

crawl² /krɔːl/ *noun* **1** [**no plural**] a very slow speed *Traffic slowed to a crawl.* **2** **SPORT** [U] a style of swimming in which you move your arms over your head and kick with straight legs

crayon /ˈkreɪɒn/ *noun* [C] **ART** a stick of coloured wax used for drawing

craze /kreɪz/ *noun* [C] something that is very popular for a short time

crazed /kreɪzd/ *adjective* behaving in a dangerous and uncontrolled way *a crazed gunman*

O‒**crazy** /ˈkreɪzi/ *adjective* **1** STUPID stupid or strange *a crazy idea* ○ *I was crazy not to take that job.* **2** ANGRY annoyed or angry *The children are **driving me crazy*** (= making me annoyed). ○ *Dad **went crazy** when I told him what had happened.* **3** **be crazy about sb/sth** to love someone very much, or to be very interested in something *Mia's crazy about baseball.* **4** **go crazy** to become very excited about something *When he came on stage the audience went crazy.* **5** **like crazy** *informal* If you do something like crazy, you do a lot of it, or do it very quickly. *We worked like crazy to get everything finished.* •**crazily** *adverb* •**craziness** *noun* [U]

creak /kriːk/ *verb* [I] If something such as a door or a piece of wood creaks, it makes a long noise when it moves. *creaking floorboards* •**creak** *noun* [C] •**creaky** *adjective* A creaky door, stair, etc creaks.

O‒**cream¹** /kriːm/ *noun* **1** **FOOD** [U] a thick, yellowish-white liquid that is taken from milk *raspberries and cream* **2** FOR SKIN [C, U] a soft substance that you rub into your skin to make it softer or less painful *face/hand cream* **3** COLOUR [U] a yellowish-white colour **4** **the cream of sth** the best people or things in a particular group *the cream of Milan's designers* ➲See also: **ice cream**

cream² /kriːm/ *adjective* being a yellowish-white colour

cream³ /kriːm/ *verb*

cream sth/sb off *phrasal verb UK* to take away the best part of something, or the best people in a group, and use them for your own advantage

ˌcream ˈcheese *noun* [U] **FOOD** smooth, soft, white cheese

creamy /ˈkriːmi/ *adjective* **FOOD** like cream or containing cream *creamy sauce/soup*

crease¹ /kriːs/ *noun* [C] a line on cloth or paper where it has been folded or crushed

crease² /kriːs/ *verb* [I, T] If cloth, paper, etc creases, or if you crease it, it gets a line in it where it has been folded or crushed. *Cotton creases very easily.*

O‑**create** /kriˈeɪt/ *verb* [T] to make something happen or exist *The project will create more than 500 jobs.* ○ *The snow created further problems.*

creation /kriˈeɪʃᵊn/ *noun* **1** PROCESS [U] when someone makes something happen or exist *the creation of a new political party* **2** PRODUCT [C] something that someone has made *The museum contains some of his best creations.* **3** **RELIGION** [U] (*also* **Creation**) in many religions, when God made the universe and everything in it

creative /kriˈeɪtɪv/ *adjective* good at thinking of new ideas or using imagination to create new and unusual things *Her book is full of creative ways to decorate your home.* •**creatively** *adverb* •**creativity** /ˌkriːeɪˈtɪvəti/ *noun* [U] the ability to produce new ideas or things using skill and imagination

creator /kriˈeɪtəʳ/ *noun* **1** [C] someone who invents or makes something **2 the Creator** **RELIGION** God

creature /ˈkriːtʃəʳ/ *noun* [C] anything that lives but is not a plant *Dolphins are intelligent creatures.*

creche /kreʃ/ *noun* [C] *UK* a place where babies and young children are looked after while their parents do something else

credence /ˈkriːdᵊns/ *noun* **add/give/lend credence to sth** to make a story, theory, etc seem more likely to be true *The letters lend credence to the idea that he had an unhappy life.*

credentials /krɪˈdenʃᵊlz/ *noun* [plural] **1** SKILLS skills and experience that show you are suitable for a particular job or activity *academic credentials* **2** PAPERS documents that prove who you are

WORD PARTNERS FOR ***credibility***

gain/lose credibility • sth **damages/destroys/restores/undermines** sb's credibility • sb **lacks** credibility

credibility /ˌkredəˈbɪləti/ *noun* [U] when someone can be believed and trusted *This decision has* ***damaged*** *the President's* ***credibility****.*

credible /ˈkredəbl/ *adjective* able to be trusted or believed *credible evidence*

credit¹ /ˈkredɪt/ *noun* **1** **ECONOMICS, FINANCE** [U] a way of buying something in which you arrange to pay for it at a later time *We offer* ***interest-free credit*** *on all new cars.* ○ *He bought most of the furniture* ***on credit****.* **2** [U] praise that is given to someone for something they have done *I did most of the work but Dan* ***got all the credit!*** ○ *We should* ***give her credit for*** *her honesty.* ○ *I can't* ***take full credit for*** *this meal - Sam helped.* **3 be a credit to sb/sth** to do something that makes a person or organization proud of you *Giorgio is a credit to his family.* **4 to sb's credit** If something is to someone's credit, they deserve praise for it. *To his credit, Bill never blamed her for the incident.* **5 have sth to your credit** to have achieved something *By the age of 25, she had five novels to her credit.* **6 in credit** **FINANCE** having money in your bank account **7** **FINANCE** [C] an amount of money that you put into your bank account ⊃Opposite **debit** **8** **EDUCATION** [C] a unit that shows you have completed part of a college course

credit² /ˈkredɪt/ *verb* [T] **1** **FINANCE** to add money to someone's bank account **2** to believe that something is true *Dean's getting married! Who would have credited it?*

credit sth to sb *phrasal verb* to say that someone is responsible for something good *an idea credited to Isaac Newton*

credit sb with sth *phrasal verb* to believe that someone has a particular quality *Credit me with some intelligence!*

credit sb with sth/doing sth *phrasal verb* to say that someone is responsible for something good *She is credited with making the business a success.*

creditable /ˈkredɪtəbl/ *adjective* Something that is creditable deserves praise. *a creditable performance*

ˈcredit acˌcount *UK* (*US* **charge account**) *noun* [C] **FINANCE** a formal agreement between a shop or other business and a customer, in which the customer can take goods and pay the shop or business for them at a later time

ˈcredit ˌcard *noun* [C] **FINANCE** a small plastic card that allows you to buy something and pay for it later *He paid* ***by credit card****.*

ˈcredit conˌtrol *noun* [U] **FINANCE** a process or a group of people in a business that controls how much customers owe the business and how much they are allowed to owe it

ˈcredit ˌlimit *noun* [C] **FINANCE** the largest amount of money that a person can borrow with a credit card (= a small plastic card that allows you to buy something and pay for it later) *a £500 credit limit*

ˈcredit ˌnote *noun* [C] **1** **FINANCE** a piece of paper that a shop gives a customer who has returned goods, that allows them to have other goods of the same value **2** **FINANCE** a document that is sent by a business to a customer to reduce the amount the customer owes if there was a problem with the quality or amount of what they bought

creditor /ˈkredɪtəʳ/ *noun* [C] **FINANCE** a person or organization that someone owes money to

ˈcreditors ˌledger *noun* [C] **FINANCE** a record that a business keeps of how much it owes to each business that has supplied goods or services to it

ˈcredit ˌrating *noun* [C usually singular] **FINANCE** a calculation of someone's ability to pay back money which they have borrowed

the credits /ˈkredɪts/ *noun* [plural] a list of people who made a film or television programme

ˈcredit ˌterms *noun* [plural] **FINANCE** the arrangements made for giving a customer credit

C

(= allowing them to pay later), e.g. the amount of money, when they must pay it, etc.

ˈcredit ˌtransfer *noun* [C] **FINANCE** an arrangement where a bank pays a amount of money from someone's bank account directly into the bank account of a business

C

creed /kriːd/ *noun* [C] **RELIGION** a set of beliefs, especially religious beliefs that influence your life

creek /kriːk/ *noun* [C] **1 GEOGRAPHY** *UK* a narrow area of water that flows into the land from a sea or river **2 GEOGRAPHY** *mainly US* a stream or narrow river

creep[1] /kriːp/ *verb past* **crept 1 creep along/in/out, etc** to move very quietly and carefully *I crept out of the room.* **2 creep across/in/into, etc** to gradually start to exist or appear *Problems were beginning to creep into their relationship.* **3 creep along/down/through, etc** to move somewhere very slowly *The convoy crept along in the darkness.*

creep up on sb *phrasal verb* **1** SURPRISE to surprise someone by moving closer to them from behind *Don't creep up on me like that!* **2** FEELING/STATE If a feeling or state creeps up on you, it happens gradually so that you do not notice it. *Old age just creeps up on you.*

creep[2] /kriːp/ *noun* [C] **1** NOT SINCERE *UK* someone who you do not like because they are nice to people in a way that is not sincere **2** UNPLEASANT someone who you think is unpleasant

creeps /kriːps/ *noun* **give sb the creeps** *informal* to make someone feel frightened or nervous *These old buildings give me the creeps.*

creepy /ˈkriːpi/ *adjective informal* strange and frightening *a creepy story/person*

cremate /krɪˈmeɪt/ *verb* [T] to burn a dead body •**cremation** /krɪˈmeɪʃən/ *noun* [C, U] the ceremony where someone is cremated

crematorium /ˌkreməˈtɔːriəm/ (*also US* **crematory** /ˈkriːmətɔːri/) *noun* [C] a place where people are cremated

crept /krept/ *past of* creep

crescendo /krɪˈʃendəʊ/ *noun* [C] **MUSIC** when a noise or piece of music gradually gets louder

crescent /ˈkresənt/ *noun* **1** [C] a curved shape that is narrow at each end and wider in the middle *the pale crescent of the moon* **2 Crescent** used in the names of streets that have a curved shape *57 Park Crescent*

crest /krest/ *noun* [C] **1** TOP the highest part of a hill or wave **2** FEATHERS the feathers that point upwards on a bird's head **3** DESIGN a design used as the symbol of a school, important family, etc

crestfallen /ˈkrestˌfɔːlən/ *adjective* disappointed or sad

Cretacious /krɪˈteɪʃəs/ *adjective* **GEOLOGY** from the period of time between around 144 and 65 million years ago, in which plants with flowers first appeared

crevasse /krɪˈvæs/ *noun* [C] **GEOGRAPHY** a deep, wide crack, especially in ice

crevice /ˈkrevɪs/ *noun* [C] **GEOLOGY** a small, narrow crack, especially in a rock

crew /kruː/ *noun* [group] **1** SHIP/AIRCRAFT the people who work together on a ship, aircraft, or train *a crew member* **2** TEAM a team of people with special skills who work together *Fire and ambulance crews were at the scene.*

crewman /ˈkruːmæn/ *noun* [C] *plural* **crewmen** a member of the crew of a ship or aircraft

crib /krɪb/ *US* (*UK* **cot**) *noun* [C] a bed with high sides for a baby

cricket /ˈkrɪkɪt/ *noun* **1 SPORT** [U] a game in which two teams of eleven people try to score points by hitting a ball and running between two wickets (= sets of three wooden sticks) *a cricket ball/bat* ➲See colour picture **Sports 2** on page Centre 15 **2** [C] an insect that jumps and makes a noise by rubbing its wings together

cricketer /ˈkrɪkɪtəʳ/ *noun* [C] **SPORT** someone who plays cricket, especially as their job

WORD PARTNERS FOR ***crime***

commit a crime • **combat/reduce/fight** crime • a **minor/petty/terrible/violent** crime

O‑ **crime** /kraɪm/ *noun* **LAW 1** [U] illegal activities ***violent crime*** ○ *tough new measures to **fight crime*** **2** [C] something someone does that is illegal *He **committed** a serious **crime**.* ➲See also: **war crime**

criminal[1] /ˈkrɪmɪnəl/ *adjective* **1 LAW** [always before noun] relating to crime *criminal activity* ○ *He has a **criminal record*** (= the police have an official record of his crimes). **2** BAD *informal* very bad or morally wrong *It's criminal that people are having to wait so long for hospital treatment.* •**criminally** *adverb*

criminal[2] /ˈkrɪmɪnəl/ *noun* [C] **LAW** someone who has committed a crime *a **dangerous/violent criminal***

criminologist /ˌkrɪmɪˈnɒlədʒɪst/ *noun* [C] **LAW** someone who studies crime and criminals

crimson /ˈkrɪmzən/ *noun* [U] a dark red colour •**crimson** *adjective*

cringe /krɪndʒ/ *verb* [I] **1** EMBARRASSED to feel very embarrassed about something *Jan **cringed at** the sight of her father dancing.* **2** FRIGHTENED to move away from something because you are frightened

crinkle /ˈkrɪŋkl/ *verb* [I, T] to become covered in small lines or folds, or to make something become covered in small lines or folds •**crinkly** *adjective* Something that is crinkly has crinkles in it.

cripple[1] /ˈkrɪpl/ *verb* [T] **1** BODY to injure someone so that they cannot use their arms or legs [often passive] *His son was crippled by a riding accident.* **2** DAMAGE to damage something very badly and make it weak or not effective [often passive] *a country crippled by war*

cripple[2] /ˈkrɪpl/ *noun* [C] *old-fashioned* an offensive word for someone who cannot use their legs or arms in a normal way

crippling /ˈkrɪplɪŋ/ *adjective* **1** ILLNESS [always before noun] A crippling illness makes someone unable to use their arms or legs in a normal way. **2** DAMAGE causing great damage

O‑ **crisis** /ˈkraɪsɪs/ *noun* [C, U] *plural* **crises** /ˈkraɪsiːz/ a situation or time that is extremely dangerous or difficult *an economic/financial crisis* ○ *The country's leadership is **in crisis**.* ➲See also: **mid-life crisis**

crisp[1] /krɪsp/ *adjective* **1** FOOD Crisp food is pleasantly hard. *a crisp apple* ○ *crisp pastry* **2** MATERIAL Crisp cloth or paper money is clean and looks new, with no folds. *a crisp linen shirt* **3** WEATHER Crisp weather is pleasantly cold and dry. *a crisp autumn day* **4** QUICK A crisp way of talking or behaving is quick and confident. **5** IMAGE A crisp image is very clear.

crisp[2] /krɪsp/ *UK* (*US* **chip**) *noun* [C] **FOOD** a very thin slice of potato that has been cooked in oil and is eaten cold [**usually plural**] *a packet of crisps* ➲See colour picture **Food** on page Centre 11

crispy /ˈkrɪspi/ *adjective* Crispy food is pleasantly hard and easy to bite through. *crispy bacon*

criss-cross /ˈkrɪskrɒs/ *verb* [I, T] If something criss-crosses an area, it crosses it several times in different directions. [**often passive**] *The forest is criss-crossed with paths and tracks.*

criterion /kraɪˈtɪəriən/ *noun* [C] *plural* **criteria** a fact or level of quality that you use when making a choice or decision [+ **for** + **doing sth**] *We have strict criteria for deciding which students will receive a grant.*

critic /ˈkrɪtɪk/ *noun* [C] **1** NOT APPROVE someone who says that they do not approve of someone or something *an **outspoken critic** of the government* **2** JOB someone whose job is to give their opinion of a book, play, film, etc ***a theatre/film critic***

critical /ˈkrɪtɪkəl/ *adjective* **1** NOT PLEASED saying that someone or something is bad or wrong *a critical report* ○ *He is very **critical of** the way I work.* **2** IMPORTANT very important for the way things will happen in the future *a critical decision* **3** SERIOUS extremely serious or dangerous *The doctors said her condition was critical and she might not survive.* **4** OPINIONS giving judgments and opinions on books, plays, films, etc *a critical study of Tennyson's work* •**critically** *adverb*

ˌcritical ˈmass *noun* [**no plural**] **PHYSICS** the smallest amount of a substance that is needed to produce a nuclear reaction

WORD PARTNERS FOR ***criticism***

sth/sb **attracts/draws/faces/sparks** criticism • **deflect/dismiss** criticism • **fierce/stinging/strong** criticism • criticism **of** sb/sth • criticism **from** sb

O→**criticism** /ˈkrɪtɪsɪzəm/ *noun* **1** BAD [C, U] when you say that something or someone is bad *Plans to close the hospital **attracted** strong public **criticism**.* **2** OPINION [U] when someone gives their judgments and opinions on books, plays, films, etc *literary criticism*

criticize (*also UK* **-ise**) /ˈkrɪtɪsaɪz/ *verb* [I, T] to say that something or someone is bad [**often passive** + **for** + **doing sth**] *The film was criticized for being too violent.*

critique /krɪˈtiːk/ *noun* [C] a report that says what is good and bad about something

croak /krəʊk/ *verb* **1** VOICE [I, T] to talk or say something in a low, rough voice [I] *"I don't feel well," he croaked.* **2** SOUND [I] If a bird or frog (= green jumping animal) croaks, it makes a deep, low sound.

crochet /ˈkrəʊʃeɪ/ (US) /krəʊˈʃeɪ/ *verb* [I, T] to make clothes and other items using wool and a special needle with a hook at one end

crockery /ˈkrɒkəri/ *noun* [U] plates, cups, and other dishes, especially those made from clay

crocodile /ˈkrɒkədaɪl/ *noun* [C] a big reptile with a long mouth and sharp teeth, that lives in lakes and rivers ➲See picture at **reptile**

crocus /ˈkrəʊkəs/ *noun* [C] a small yellow, purple, or white spring flower

croissant /ˈkwæsɒŋ/ (US) /kwɑːˈsɒŋ/ *noun* [C] **FOOD** a soft, curved piece of bread, eaten for breakfast

crony /ˈkrəʊni/ *noun* [C] *informal* one of a group of friends who help each other, especially in a way that is not fair [**usually plural**] *He gave his cronies all the best jobs.*

crook /krʊk/ *noun* **1** [C] *informal* a criminal or someone who cheats people **2 the crook of your arm** the inside part of your arm where it bends

crooked /ˈkrʊkɪd/ *adjective* **1** NOT STRAIGHT not straight *crooked teeth* **2** DISHONEST *informal* not honest *a crooked politician*

croon /kruːn/ *verb* [I, T] **MUSIC** to sing in a soft, low, romantic voice

crop[1] /krɒp/ *noun* **1 FARMING** [C] a plant such as a grain, fruit, or vegetable that is grown in large amounts by farmers **2 FARMING** [C] the amount of plants of a particular type that are produced at one time *We had a record crop of grapes this year.* **3 a crop of sth** a group of the same type of things or people that exist at the same time *He's one of the current crop of young Italian artists.* ➲See also: **cash crop**

crop[2] /krɒp/ *verb* **cropping**, *past* **cropped 1** [T] to cut something so that it is short **2 COMPUTING** to cut pieces from the sides of a computer image so that it is the size you want **3 FARMING** [I] *UK* If a plant crops, it produces fruit, flowers, etc.

crop up *phrasal verb* to happen or appear suddenly *The same old problems **kept cropping up**.*

cropper /ˈkrɒpəʳ/ *noun* **come a cropper a** to fall over *The horse came a cropper at the first fence.* **b** to fail in an embarrassing way, or to make an embarrassing mistake

croquet /ˈkrəʊkeɪ/ (US) /krəʊˈkeɪ/ *noun* [U] **SPORT** a game played on grass, in which you hit a ball with a wooden hammer through curved wires pushed into the ground

O→**cross**[1] /krɒs/ *verb* **1** FROM ONE SIDE TO ANOTHER [I, T] to go from one side of something to the other side *It's not a good place to **cross the road**.* **2** LINE/BORDER [I, T] to travel over a border or line into a different area, country, etc *They **crossed from** Albania **into** Greece.* **3** MEET AND GO ACROSS [I, T] If two lines, roads, etc cross, they go over or across each other. **4 cross your arms/fingers/legs** to put one of your arms, fingers, or legs over the top of the other **5 cross yourself RELIGION** to touch your head, chest, and both shoulders as a sign to God **6 BIOLOGY, FARMING** [T] to mix two breeds of animal or plant to produce a new breed **7** MAKE SOMEONE ANGRY [T] to make someone angry by refusing to do what they want you to do ➲See also: I'll/We'll cross that **bridge**[1] when I/we come to it., **criss-cross, double-cross,** keep your fingers (**finger**[1]) crossed, cross your **mind**[1]

cross sth off (sth) *phrasal verb* to remove a word from a list by drawing a line through it *Did you cross her name off the guest list?*

cross sth out *phrasal verb* to draw a line through something that you have written, usually because it is wrong *Cross out that last sentence.*

O-- **cross²** /krɒs/ *noun* **1** WOOD [C] two pieces of wood that cross each other, on which people were left to die as a punishment in the past **2** **RELIGION** [C] an object in the shape of a cross, used as a symbol of the Christian religion **3** MARK [C] a written mark (x), used for showing where something is, or that something that has been written is wrong **4** **a cross between sth and sth** a mixture of two different things or people *The dog is a cross between a terrier and a rottweiler.* **5** **SPORT** [C] when someone kicks or hits the ball across the field in sport, especially football

cross³ /krɒs/ *adjective* annoyed or angry *Don't be* ***cross with*** *me!*

cross- /krɒs-/ *prefix* **1** across *cross-border* **2** including different groups or subjects *a cross-party committee* (= one formed from many political parties) ○ *cross-cultural*

crossbar /ˈkrɒsbɑːʳ/ *noun* [C] **1** **SPORT** the post at the top of a goal in games such as football **2** the metal tube that joins the front and back of a bicycle

cross-border /ˈkrɒsˌbɔːdəʳ/ *adjective* [**always before noun**] between different countries, or involving people from different countries *cross-border trade*

cross-Channel /ˌkrɒsˈtʃænəl/ *adjective* [**always before noun**] connecting or happening between England and France *a* ***cross-Channel ferry****/route*

cross-country /ˌkrɒsˈkʌntri/ *adjective* [**always before noun**], *adverb* **1** **SPORT** across fields and countryside *cross-country running/skiing* **2** from one side of a country to the other side

cross-examine /ˌkrɒsɪɡˈzæmɪn/ *verb* [T] **LAW** to ask someone a lot of questions about something they have said, in order to discover if it is true, especially in a court of law •**cross-examination** /ˌkrɒsɪɡˌzæmɪˈneɪʃən/ *noun* [U]

cross-eyed /krɒsˈaɪd/ *adjective* A cross-eyed person has both eyes looking in towards their nose.

crossfire /ˈkrɒsfaɪəʳ/ *noun* **1** [U] bullets fired towards you from different directions *Civilians died when a bus was* ***caught in crossfire*** *between government and rebel troops.* **2** **be caught in the crossfire** to be involved in a situation where people around you are arguing

crossing /ˈkrɒsɪŋ/ *noun* [C] **1** WHERE PEOPLE CROSS a place where people can go across a road, river, etc **2** SEA JOURNEY a journey across water **3** WHERE LINES CROSS a place where roads, railways, etc cross each other ➲See also: **grade crossing, level crossing, zebra crossing**

cross-legged /ˌkrɒsˈleɡɪd/ *adverb* **sit cross-legged** to sit on the floor with your knees wide apart and one foot over the other foot

cross-pollination /ˌkrɒspɒlɪˈneɪʃən/ *noun* [U] **BIOLOGY** when pollen is carried from one flower to another by wind, insects, etc

ˌcross ˈpurposes *noun* **at cross purposes** If two people are at cross purposes, they do not understand each other because they are talking about different things but do not know this.

ˌcross ˈreference *noun* [C] a note in a book that tells you to look somewhere else in the book for more information about something

crossroads /ˈkrɒsrəʊdz/ *noun* [C] *plural* **crossroads** **1** ROAD a place where two roads cross each other **2** DECISION a time when you have to make an important decision that will affect your future life *I felt I was* ***at a crossroads*** *in my life.*

cross-section /ˈkrɒssekʃən/ *noun* [C] **1** GROUP a small group of people or things that represents all the different types in a larger group *a* ***cross-section of society*** **2** VIEW something that has been cut in half so that you can see the inside, or a picture of this *a cross-section of a human heart*

crosswalk /ˈkrɒswɔːk/ *US* (*UK* **pedestrian crossing**) *noun* [C] a special place on a road where traffic must stop if people want to cross

crossword /ˈkrɒswɜːd/ (*also* **ˈcrossword ˌpuzzle**) *noun* [C] a game in which you write words which are the answers to questions in a pattern of black and white squares

crotch /krɒtʃ/ (*also UK* **crutch**) *noun* [C] **ANATOMY** the part of your body between the tops of your legs, or the part of a piece of clothing that covers this area

crouch /kraʊtʃ/ (*also* **crouch down**) *verb* [I] to move your body close to the ground by bending your knees *I crouched behind the chair to avoid being seen.*

crow¹ /krəʊ/ *noun* **1** [C] a large black bird that makes a loud noise **2** **as the crow flies** when measured in a straight line *It's about 50 miles from London to Cambridge as the crow flies.*

crow² /krəʊ/ *verb* [I] **1** SPEAK to talk in a proud and annoying way about something you have done *Donald wouldn't stop* ***crowing about*** *his exam results.* **2** LOUD NOISE If a cock (= male chicken) crows, it makes a loud noise, usually in the early morning.

WORD PARTNERS FOR ***crowd***

a crowd **gathers** • a crowd **of** [people/tourists, etc] • **in** a crowd

O-- **crowd¹** /kraʊd/ *noun* **1** LARGE GROUP [C] a large group of people who are together in one place *A large* ***crowd*** *had* ***gathered*** *to wait for the princess.* ○ *Shop early and avoid the crowds.* **2** PARTICULAR GROUP [**no plural**] *informal* a group of friends or people with similar interests *the art/theatre crowd*

crowd² /kraʊd/ *verb* [T] **1** TOGETHER to stand together in large numbers *Protesters crowded the streets.* **2** TOO CLOSE to stand too close to someone *Don't crowd me!*

crowd around/round (sb/sth) *phrasal verb* If a

group of people crowd around or crowd around someone or something, they stand very close all around them. *Everyone crowded around my desk.*

crowd in/crowd (sb) into sth *phrasal verb* If a large group of people crowd into somewhere, they all go there and fill the place.

crowd sb out *phrasal verb* to prevent someone or something from succeeding or existing by being much more successful than them or by being present in much larger numbers *Large national companies often crowd out smaller local businesses.*

crowded /'kraʊdɪd/ *adjective* very full of people *a crowded room/train*

crown¹ /kraʊn/ *noun* **1** KING/QUEEN [C] a round object made of gold and jewels (= valuable stones) that a king or queen wears on their head **2** TOP [C] the top of a hat, head, or hill **3 POLITICS the Crown** used to refer to the power or government of a king or queen *All this land belongs to the Crown.* **4** TOOTH [C] an artificial top that is put on a damaged tooth **5 ANATOMY** the top part of a tooth ➲See picture at **tooth**

crown² /kraʊn/ *verb* [T] **1** MAKE KING/QUEEN to put a crown on someone's head in an official ceremony that makes them a king or queen [**often passive**] *Queen Elizabeth II of England was crowned in 1952.* **2** ON TOP *literary* to be on top of something else *A large domed ceiling crowns the main hall.* **3** BEST PART to be the best or most successful part of something *a book that crowned his successful writing career*

crowning /'kraʊnɪŋ/ *adjective* [**always before noun**] more important, beautiful, etc than anything else *It was the **crowning achievement** of his political career.*

CRT /ˌsiːɑː'tiː/ *noun* [C] **PHYSICS** *abbreviation for* cathode ray tube

crucial /'kruːʃəl/ *adjective* extremely important or necessary *a crucial decision/question* ○ *Her work has been **crucial to** the project's success.* •**crucially** *adverb*

crucifix /'kruːsɪfɪks/ *noun* [C] **RELIGION** a model of a cross with Jesus Christ on it

crucifixion /ˌkruːsə'fɪkʃən/ *noun* [C, U] in the past, when someone was fastened to a cross and left to die *the crucifixion of Christ*

crucify /'kruːsɪfaɪ/ *verb* [T] **1** KILL in the past, to fasten someone to a cross and leave them to die **2** CRITICIZE *informal* to criticize someone or something in a cruel and damaging way [**often passive**] *The film has been crucified by the media.*

crude /kruːd/ *adjective* **1** WITHOUT SKILL made or done in a simple way and without much skill *a crude device/weapon* **2** RUDE rude and offensive *a crude comment/remark* •**crudely** *adverb*

ˌcrude 'oil (*also* **crude**) *noun* [U] **GEOLOGY** oil in its natural state before it has been treated

O⁻ **cruel** /'kruːəl/ *adjective* **crueller, cruellest** or **crueler, cruelest** extremely unkind, or causing people or animals to suffer *a cruel joke* ○ *Many people think hunting is **cruel to** animals.* •**cruelly** *adverb*

cruelty /'kruːəlti/ *noun* [C, U] cruel behaviour or a cruel action *laws against **cruelty to** animals*

cruise¹ /kruːz/ *noun* [C] a holiday on a ship, sailing from place to place

cruise² /kruːz/ *verb* **1** MOVE [I] to move in a vehicle at a speed that does not change *The plane is cruising at 500 miles per hour.* **2** SAIL [I] to go on a cruise **3 cruise to success/victory, etc** *informal* to win a competition easily

ˌcruise 'missile *UK* (*US* **'cruise ˌmissile**) *noun* [C] a weapon that flies through the air, and which often carries nuclear weapons

cruiser /'kruːzər/ *noun* [C] **1** WAR SHIP a large military ship used in wars **2** BOAT (*also* **'cabin ˌcruiser**) a motor boat with a room for people to sleep in

'cruise ˌship (*also* **'cruise ˌliner**) *noun* [C] a large ship like a hotel, which people travel on for pleasure

crumb /krʌm/ *noun* **1 FOOD** [C] a very small piece of bread, cake, etc **2 a crumb of sth** a very small amount of something

crumble /'krʌmbl/ *verb* **1** BREAK [I, T] to break into small pieces, or to make something break into small pieces *Buildings crumbled as the earthquake struck.* **2** FAIL [I] If a relationship, system, or feeling crumbles, it fails or ends. *His first marriage crumbled after only a year.*

crummy /'krʌmi/ *adjective informal* unpleasant, or of bad quality *a crummy job* ○ *a crummy hotel*

crumple /'krʌmpl/ *verb* **1** CRUSH [I, T] If something such as paper or cloth crumples, it becomes crushed, and if you crumple it, you crush it until it is full of folds. *a crumpled shirt* **2** LOOK SAD [I] If someone's face crumples, they suddenly look very sad or disappointed.

crumple sth up *phrasal verb* to crush a piece of paper until it is full of folds

crunch¹ /krʌnʃ/ *noun* **1** [C] the sound of something being crushed [**usually singular**] *the crunch of dried leaves under our feet* **2 if/when it comes to the crunch** if/when a situation becomes serious or you have to make an important decision

crunch² /krʌnʃ/ *verb* **1** FOOD [I, T] to make a noise by chewing hard food *She was **crunching on** an apple.* **2** CRUSH [I] to make a sound as if something is being crushed *The gravel crunched under our feet.*

crunchy /'krʌntʃi/ *adjective* Crunchy food is hard and makes a noise when you eat it.

WORD PARTNERS FOR ***crusade***

launch/mount a crusade • be **on** a crusade • a **moral/personal** crusade • a crusade **against/for** sth

crusade /kruː'seɪd/ *noun* [C] a determined attempt to change or achieve something that you believe in strongly •**crusader** *noun* [C] someone who is involved in a crusade

crush¹ /krʌʃ/ *verb* [T] **1** PRESS to press something so hard that it is made flat or broken into pieces *Her car was crushed by a falling tree.* **2** DEFEAT to defeat someone or something completely *government attempts to crush protests* ○ *a* ***crushing defeat***

crush² /krʌʃ/ *noun* **1** CROWD **[no plural]** a crowd of people forced to stand close together because there is not enough room *Many people fell over in the crush.* **2** LOVE **[C]** *informal* a strong temporary feeling of love for someone *Tim* ***has a crush on*** *Jennifer.*

C

crust /krʌst/ *noun* **[C, U]** **1** **FOOD** the hard outer surface of bread or other baked foods **2** a hard, dry layer on the surface of something ➲See picture at **Earth**

crustacean /krʌsˈteɪʃən/ *noun* **[C]** **BIOLOGY** any of various types of animal which live in water and have a hard outer shell

crusty /ˈkrʌsti/ *adjective* **1** unfriendly and becoming annoyed very easily **2** **FOOD** Something that is crusty has a hard outer layer. ***crusty bread***

crutch /krʌtʃ/ *noun* **[C]** **1** **HEALTH** a stick that you put under your arm to help you walk if you have injured your leg or foot **[usually plural]** *Charles was* ***on crutches*** (= walking with crutches) *for six weeks.* **2** *UK* (*UK/US* **crotch**) the part of your body between the tops of your legs, or the part of a piece of clothing that covers this area

crux /krʌks/ *noun* **the crux (of sth)** the main or most important part of a problem, argument, etc

O‑ **cry¹** /kraɪ/ *verb* **1** TEARS **[I]** to produce tears from your eyes, usually because you are sad, angry, or hurt *My baby brother cries all the time.* **2** SHOUT **[I, T]** to speak or say something loudly *"Look at this!" cried Raj.* ➲See also: cry your eyes (**eye**¹) out, a **shoulder**¹ to cry on

be crying out for sth *phrasal verb informal* to need something very much *a school that's crying out for more money*

cry out (sth) *phrasal verb* to shout or make a loud noise because you are frightened, hurt, etc *She* ***cried out*** *in terror.*

cry² /kraɪ/ *noun* **1** SHOUT **[C]** a shout, especially one that shows that someone is frightened, hurt, etc *a cry of horror/joy/pain* ○ *I could hear the cries of children playing in the street.* **2** ANIMAL/BIRD **[C]** a sound that a particular animal or bird makes *an eagle's cry* **3** **have a cry** to produce tears from your eyes, usually because you are sad, angry, or hurt **4** **be a far cry from sth** to be very different from something *Her luxury mansion is a far cry from the house she grew up in.*

crying /ˈkraɪɪŋ/ *adjective* **1** **a crying need for sth** *mainly UK* a need that is very urgent *There's a crying need for more nurses.* **2** **it's a crying shame** used to say that you think a situation is very wrong

cryogenics /ˌkraɪəʊˈdʒenɪks/ *noun* **[U]** **PHYSICS** the scientific study of very low temperatures and how to produce them •**cryogenic** /ˌkraɪəʊˈdʒenɪk/ *adjective*

cryolite /ˈkraɪəʊlaɪt/ *noun* **[U]** **GEOLOGY** a white or colourless mineral used in making aluminium, glass and other substances

crypt /krɪpt/ *noun* **[C]** a room under a church, especially one where people are buried

cryptic /ˈkrɪptɪk/ *adjective* mysterious and difficult to understand *a* ***cryptic comment/message*** •**cryptically** *adverb*

crystal /ˈkrɪstəl/ *noun* **1** **GEOLOGY** **[C, U]** a type of transparent rock **2** **[U]** a type of high quality glass *a crystal vase* **3** **GEOLOGY** **[C]** a piece of a substance that has become solid, with a regular shape *ice crystals*

ˌcrystal ˈball *noun* **[C]** a large, glass ball that some people believe you can look into to see what will happen in the future

ˌcrystal ˈclear *adjective* very obvious and easy to understand *She made her feelings crystal clear to me.*

crystallize (*mainly UK* **-ise**) /ˈkrɪstəlaɪz/ *verb* **[I, T]** **1** If something crystallizes your thoughts or opinions, or if they crystallize, they become clear and fixed **2** **CHEMISTRY** If a liquid crystallizes, it turns into crystals. •**crystallization** (*mainly UK* **-isation**) /ˌkrɪstəlaɪˈzeɪʃən/ *noun* **[U]**

Ctrl Key *noun* **[C usually singular]** **COMPUTING** *abbreviation for* control key (= on a computer keyboard)

CU **INTERNET** *internet abbreviation for* see you: used when saying goodbye at the end of an email or text message

cub /kʌb/ *noun* **[C]** a young bear, fox, lion, etc

cube¹ /kjuːb/ *noun* **1** **[C]** a solid object with six square sides of the same size *Cut the cheese into small cubes.* ➲See picture at **shape** **2** **the cube of sth** **MATHEMATICS** the number you get when you multiply a particular number by itself twice *The cube of 3 is 27.* ➲See also: **ice cube**

cube² /kjuːb/ *verb* **[T]** **1** **MATHEMATICS** to multiply a particular number by itself twice *5 cubed is 125.* **2** to cut something into cubes

ˌcube ˈroot *noun* **[C]** **MATHEMATICS** the cube root of a number is another number that, when multiplied by itself twice, makes the first number

cubic /ˈkjuːbɪk/ *adjective* **cubic centimetre/inch/metre, etc** **MEASURES** a unit of measurement that shows the volume (= length multiplied by width multiplied by height) of something *a reservoir that holds 22 million cubic metres of water*

cubicle /ˈkjuːbɪkl/ *noun* **[C]** a small space with walls around it, that is separate from the rest of a room *a shower cubicle*

cuboid¹ /ˈkjuːbɔɪd/ *noun* **[C]** **MATHEMATICS** a solid object with six rectangular sides

cuboid² /ˈkjuːbɔɪd/ *adjective* **MATHEMATICS** in the shape of a cube or a cuboid

cuckoo /ˈkʊkuː/ *noun* **[C]** a small bird that makes a sound like its name and puts its eggs into other birds' nests

cucumber /ˈkjuːkʌmbəʳ/ *noun* **[C, U]** **FOOD** a long, green vegetable that you eat raw in salads ➲See colour picture **Fruit and Vegetables** on page Centre 10

cuddle /ˈkʌdl/ *verb* **[I, T]** to put your arms around someone to show them that you love them *Her mother cuddled her until she stopped crying.* •**cuddle** *noun* **[C]**

cuddle up *phrasal verb* to sit or lie very close

to someone *The children* ***cuddled up to*** *me to keep warm.*

cuddly /ˈkʌdli/ *adjective* soft and pleasant to hold close to you

cue /kjuː/ *noun* **1** ACTION/EVENT [C] an action or event that is a sign that something should happen *The final goal was the* ***cue for*** *celebration.* **2** SIGNAL [C] a signal that tells someone to start speaking or doing something when acting in a play, film, etc **3 on cue** If something happens on cue, it happens at exactly the right time. *Then,* ***right on cue****, Andrew appeared at the door.* **4 take your cue from sb/sth** to copy what someone else does *I took my cue from the others and left.* **5 SPORT** [C] a long, straight stick used to hit the balls in games like snooker (= a game played with small coloured balls on a table)

cuff /kʌf/ *noun* [C] **1** the bottom part of a sleeve that goes around your wrist **2 off the cuff** If you speak off the cuff, you do it without having planned what you will say.

cuisine /kwɪzˈiːn/ *noun* [U] **FOOD** a style of cooking *French/international cuisine*

cul-de-sac /ˈkʌldəsæk/ *noun* [C] a short road with houses which is blocked at one end

culinary /ˈkʌlɪnəri/ *adjective* [**always before noun**] *formal* **FOOD** related to food and cooking *culinary equipment*

cull /kʌl/ *verb* [T] to kill some of the animals in a group, especially the weakest ones, to limit their numbers •**cull** *noun* [C]

cull sth from sth *phrasal verb* to collect ideas or information from several different places [**often passive**] *The book is culled from over 800 pages of his diaries.*

culminate /ˈkʌlmɪneɪt/ *verb formal* **1 culminate in/with sth** to finish with a particular event, or reach a final result after gradual development and often a lot of effort *His career culminated with the post of ambassador to NATO.* **2** [T] *US* to be the final thing in a series of events *The discovery of a body culminated two days of desperate searching.* •**culmination** /ˌkʌlmɪˈneɪʃən/ *noun* [**no plural**] *This discovery is* ***the culmination of*** *years of research.*

culpable /ˈkʌlpəbl/ *adjective formal* deserving to be blamed for something bad •**culpability** /ˌkʌlpəˈbɪləti/ *noun* [U]

culprit /ˈkʌlprɪt/ *noun* [C] **1** PERSON someone who has done something wrong **2** THING something that is responsible for a bad situation *In many of these illnesses, stress is the* ***main culprit****.*

cult /kʌlt/ *noun* [C] **1** someone or something which has become very popular with a particular group of people *a* ***cult figure/movie*** **2 RELIGION** a religious group whose ideas are considered strange by many people

cultivate /ˈkʌltɪveɪt/ *verb* [T] **1 FARMING** to prepare land and grow crops on it *This shrub is cultivated in Europe as a culinary herb.* **2** to try to develop or improve something *She has* ***cultivated an image*** *as a tough negotiator.* •**cultivation** /ˌkʌltɪˈveɪʃən/ *noun* [U]

cultivated /ˈkʌltɪveɪtɪd/ *adjective* A cultivated person has had a good education and knows a lot about art, books, music, etc.

cultural /ˈkʌltʃərəl/ *adjective* **1 SOCIETY** relating to the habits, traditions and beliefs of a society *cultural diversity/identity* **2** ARTS relating to music, art, theatre, literature, etc *cultural events* •**culturally** *adverb*

O‐ **culture** /ˈkʌltʃər/ *noun* **1 SOCIETY** [C, U] the habits, traditions, and beliefs of a country, society, or group of people *American/Japanese culture* ○ *It's a good opportunity for children to learn about other cultures.* **2** ARTS [U] music, art, theatre, literature, etc *popular culture* **3 BIOLOGY** [C, U] the process of growing things, especially bacteria (= very small living things that can cause disease), for scientific purposes, or the bacteria produced by this process

cultured /ˈkʌltʃəd/ *adjective* A cultured person knows a lot about music, art, theatre, etc.

ˈculture ˌmedium *noun* [C] **BIOLOGY** a substance that scientists use to grow cells or microorganisms (= extremely small life forms)

ˈculture ˌshock *noun* [U] the feeling of confusion someone has when they go to a new and very different place

-cum- /kʌm/ used between two nouns to describe something which combines the two things *a kitchen-cum-dining room* (= room which is used as a kitchen and a dining room)

cumbersome /ˈkʌmbəsəm/ *adjective* **1** LARGE large and difficult to move or use *cumbersome safety equipment* **2** NOT EFFECTIVE slow and not effective *cumbersome bureaucracy*

cumulative /ˈkjuːmjələtɪv/ *adjective* reached by gradually adding one thing after another *a cumulative score*

cumulonimbus /ˌkjuːmjələʊˈnɪmbəs/ *noun* [U] **GEOGRAPHY** a large, tall type of cloud that is often dark and brings heavy rain

cumulus /ˈkjuːmjʊləs/ *noun* [U] **GEOGRAPHY** a type of tall white cloud with a wide flat base and rounded shape ➲See picture at **cloud**

cunning /ˈkʌnɪŋ/ *adjective* clever at getting what you want, especially by tricking people *a* ***cunning plan/ploy*** •**cunning** *noun* [U] •**cunningly** *adverb*

O‐ **cup**[1] /kʌp/ *noun* [C] **1** CONTAINER a small, round container with a handle on the side, used to drink from *a cup of tea/coffee* **2** SPORT a prize given to the winner of a competition, or the name of the competition *the World Cup* **3 MEASURES** *mainly US* a measurement of amounts of food used in cooking ➲See also: **egg cup**

cup[2] /kʌp/ *verb* [T] **cupping**, *past* **cupped** to make your hands into the shape of a cup, or to hold something with your hands in this shape

O‐ **cupboard** /ˈkʌbəd/ *noun* [C] a piece of furniture with a door on the front and shelves inside, used for storing things ➲See colour picture **The Kitchen** on page Centre 2 ➲See also: have a **skeleton** in the cupboard

curate /ˈkjʊərət/ *noun* [C] **RELIGION** a person who works for the Church of England and whose job is to help the vicar (= priest in a particular area)

curator /kjʊəˈreɪtəʳ/ *noun* [C] a person who is in charge of a museum (= a building where you can look at objects, such as art or old things)

curb[1] /kɜːb/ *verb* [T] to limit or control something *to curb crime/inflation*

curb[2] /kɜːb/ *noun* [C] **1** LIMIT something which limits or controls something *They are proposing a **curb on** tobacco advertising.* **2** ROAD *US spelling of* kerb (= the line of stones at the edge of a path next to the road)

curdle /ˈkɜːdl/ *verb* [I, T] **FOOD** If a liquid curdles, or if you curdle it, it gets thicker and develops lumps. *Heat the sauce slowly or it will curdle.*

WORD PARTNERS FOR ***cure***

find/look for a cure • a cure **for** sth • **the search for** a cure

cure[1] /kjʊəʳ/ *noun* [C] **1 HEALTH** something that makes someone with an illness healthy again *They are trying to **find a cure for** cancer.* **2** SOLUTION a solution to a problem

cure[2] /kjʊəʳ/ *verb* [T] **1 HEALTH** to make someone with an illness healthy again *Getting a better chair completely cured my back problems.* **2** PROBLEM to solve a problem *the fight to cure social inequality* **3** to treat food with smoke or salt so that you can keep it for longer *cured meat*

curfew /ˈkɜːfjuː/ *noun* [C] **LAW** a time, especially at night, when people are not allowed to leave their homes

WORD PARTNERS FOR ***curiosity***

arouse/satisfy sb's curiosity • (do sth) **out of** curiosity • **mild/natural** curiosity • curiosity **about** sth

curiosity /ˌkjʊəriˈɒsəti/ *noun* **1** FEELING [U] the feeling of wanting to know or learn about something *My curiosity got the better of me and I opened the envelope.* ○ *Just **out of curiosity**, how did you get my address?* **2** STRANGE THING [C] something strange or unusual

curious /ˈkjʊəriəs/ *adjective* **1** INTERESTED wanting to know or learn about something *I was **curious about** his life in India.* ○ *I was **curious to know** what would happen next.* **2** STRANGE strange or unusual *The house was decorated in a curious style.* •**curiously** *adverb She looked at him curiously.*

curl[1] /kɜːl/ *noun* [C] something with a small, curved shape, especially a piece of hair *a child with blonde curls*

curl[2] /kɜːl/ *verb* [I, T] to make something into the shape of a curl, or to be this shape *The cat curled its tail around its body.*

curl up *phrasal verb* **1** SIT/LIE to sit or lie in a position with your arms and legs close to your body *She curled up and went to sleep.* **2** PAPER If something flat, such as a piece of paper, curls up, the edges start to curve up.

curly /ˈkɜːli/ *adjective* shaped like a curl, or with many curls *curly hair*

currant /ˈkʌrᵊnt/ *noun* [C] **FOOD** a small, black dried fruit used in cooking, especially in cakes

currency /ˈkʌrᵊnsi/ *noun* **1 ECONOMICS, FINANCE** [C, U] the units of money used in a particular country *foreign currency* **2** [U] when an idea is believed or accepted by many people *This view is **gaining currency** within the government.* ⊃See also: **hard currency**

O-ᵚ**current**[1] /ˈkʌrᵊnt/ *adjective* happening or existing now *What is your current address?* ⊃See Common Learner Error at **actual** •**currently** *adverb The factory currently employs 750 people.*

current[2] /ˈkʌrᵊnt/ *noun* **1** AIR/WATER [C] the natural flow of air or water in one direction *a current of air* ○ *dangerous/strong currents* **2 PHYSICS** [C, U] the flow of electricity through a wire *an electrical current*

ˌcurrent acˈcount *UK* (*US* **checking account**) *noun* [C] **FINANCE** a bank account which you can take money out of at any time

ˌcurrent afˈfairs *UK* (*US* **ˌcurrent eˈvents**) *noun* [plural] **POLITICS** important political or social events which are happening in the world at the present time

ˌcurrent ˈassets *noun* [plural] **ECONOMICS** everything of value that a business owns at a particular time

ˌcurrent liaˈbilities *noun* [plural] **ECONOMICS** everything that a business owes money for at a particular time

ˌcurrent ˈratio (*also* **working capital ratio**) *noun* [C usually singular] **ECONOMICS** a calculation that compares the assets (= things owned) of a business that will be changed into money within 12 months with the payments that have to be made in that time

curriculum /kəˈrɪkjələm/ *noun* [C] *plural* **curricula** or **curriculums EDUCATION** all the subjects taught in a school, college, etc or on an educational course *the school curriculum*

curry /ˈkʌri/ *noun* [C, U] **FOOD** a type of food from India, made of vegetables or meat cooked with hot spices

curse[1] /kɜːs/ *noun* [C] **1** MAGIC magic words which are intended to bring bad luck to someone *to **put a curse on** someone* **2** RUDE WORDS a rude or offensive word or phrase **3** PROBLEM something that causes harm or unhappiness, often over a long period of time *Traffic is one of the curses of modern living.*

curse[2] /kɜːs/ *verb* **1** RUDE WORDS [I] to use rude or offensive words *He cursed angrily under his breath.* **2** SHOW ANGER [T] to express anger towards someone or something *He cursed himself for not telling David about it earlier.* **3 be cursed by/with sth** to have something which causes problems over a long period of time

cursor /ˈkɜːsəʳ/ *noun* [C] **COMPUTING** a symbol on a computer screen which shows the place where you are working

cursory /ˈkɜːsᵊri/ *adjective* [always before noun] *formal* done quickly and without much care *a **cursory glance***

curt /kɜːt/ *adjective* If something you say or write is curt, it is short and not very polite. •**curtly** *adverb*

curtail /kɜːˈteɪl/ *verb* [T] *formal* to reduce, limit, or stop something *to curtail spending* •**curtailment** *noun* [U]

curtain /ˈkɜːtᵊn/ *noun* [C] a piece of material which hangs down to cover a window, stage, etc *to **draw the curtains*** (= open or close them) ○ *The **curtain goes up*** (= the performance starts) *at 8 o'clock* . ➲See colour picture **The Living Room** on page Centre 4

curtsey (*also* **curtsy**) /ˈkɜːtsi/ *noun* [C] a movement where a girl or woman puts one foot behind the other and bends her knees, especially to show respect to a king or queen •**curtsey** *verb* [I]

curve¹ /kɜːv/ *noun* [C] a line which bends round like part of a circle *a road with gentle curves*

curve² /kɜːv/ *verb* [I, T] to move in a curve, form a curve, or make something into the shape of a curve *The road curves to the left.* ○ *a chair with a curved back*

cushion¹ /ˈkʊʃᵊn/ *noun* [C] **1** SOFT THING a cloth bag filled with something soft which you sit on or lean against to make you comfortable ➲See colour picture **The Living Room** on page Centre 4 **2** PROTECTION something which protects you from possible problems *Overseas savings provide **a cushion against** tax rises at home.*

cushion² /ˈkʊʃᵊn/ *verb* [T] **1** MAKE BETTER to reduce the bad effects of something *attempts to cushion the impact of unemployment* **2** PROTECT to protect something, especially part of the body, with something soft *Soft grass cushioned his fall.*

cushy /ˈkʊʃi/ *adjective informal* very easy *a **cushy job***

custard /ˈkʌstəd/ *noun* **1** **FOOD** [U] a sweet, yellow sauce made from milk and eggs, usually eaten hot with sweet food *apple pie and custard* **2** **FOOD** [C, U] a soft baked mixture made from milk, eggs, and sugar *a custard pie/tart*

custodial /kʌsˈtəʊdiəl/ *adjective* **LAW** If someone is given a custodial sentence (= punishment), they are sent to prison.

custodian /kʌsˈtəʊdiən/ *noun* [C] **1** VALUABLE THING *formal* a person who takes care of something valuable or important *He's the grandson of Oscar Wilde and custodian of his private papers.* **2** BUILDING *US* someone whose job is to look after a building, especially a school

WORD PARTNERS FOR ***custody***

be **awarded/given** custody (**of** sb) • **have/win** custody (**of** sb)

custody /ˈkʌstədi/ *noun* [U] **1** **LAW** the legal right to look after a child, especially when parents separate *When they divorced, it was Nicola who **won custody of** their two children.* **2** **LAW** when someone is kept in prison, usually while they are waiting for a trial in court *He is being **held in custody** in Los Angeles charged with assault.* ○ *He was **taken into custody** by Mexican authorities.*

WORD PARTNERS FOR ***custom***

an **ancient/local/traditional** custom • the custom **of** doing sth

custom /ˈkʌstəm/ *noun* **1** **SOCIETY** [C, U] a habit or tradition **2** [U] when people buy things from shops or businesses *Free gifts are a good way of **attracting custom**.*

custom- /ˈkʌstəm/ *prefix* used before another word to mean 'specially designed for a particular person or purpose' *custom-built* ○ *custom-designed*

customary /ˈkʌstəmᵊri/ *adjective* normal or expected for a particular person, situation, or society [+ **to do** sth] *It is **customary for** the chairman to make the opening speech.* •**customarily** /ˌkʌstəˈmerᵊli/ *adverb*

O‑**customer** /ˈkʌstəməʳ/ *noun* [C] **ECONOMICS** a person or organization that buys goods or services from a shop or business *a **satisfied customer*** ○ *Mrs Wilson is one of our **regular customers**.*

customise *UK* (*US* **customize**) /ˈkʌstəmaɪz/ *verb* [T] to change something to make it suitable for a particular person or purpose *Our language courses are customised to each student.*

customs /ˈkʌstəmz/ *noun* [U] the place where your bags are examined when you are going into a country, to make sure you are not carrying anything illegal ***customs officials*** ○ ***to go through customs***

O‑**cut¹** /kʌt/ *verb* **cutting**, *past* **cut** **1** KNIFE [I, T] to use a knife or other sharp tool to divide something, remove part of something, or make a hole in something ***Cut** the meat **into** small pieces.* ○ *He **cut** the piece of wood **in half**.* ○ *I had my hair cut last week.* ○ *She **cut off** all the diseased buds.* **2** REDUCE [T] to reduce the size or amount of something *Prices have been cut by 25%.* ○ *The company is cutting 50 jobs.* **3** INJURE [T] to injure yourself on a sharp object which makes you bleed *She cut her finger on a broken glass.* **4** REMOVE [T] to remove part of a film or piece of writing *The film was too long so they cut some scenes.* ➲See also: cut corners (**corner**¹), cut it/things **fine**², have your **work**² cut out

cut across sth *phrasal verb* **1** AREA to go from one side of an area to the other instead of going round it *If we cut across this field, it will save time.* **2** GROUP If a problem or subject cuts across different groups of people, all of those groups are affected by it or interested in it.

cut back (sth) *phrasal verb* **FINANCE** to reduce the amount of money being spent on something *We have had to **cut back on** training this year.*

cut sth down *phrasal verb* to make a tree or other plant fall to the ground by cutting it near the bottom

cut down (sth) *phrasal verb* to eat or drink less of something, or to reduce the amount or number of something *My doctor says I should cut down on cigarettes.*

cut sb off *phrasal verb* to stop someone speaking by interrupting them or putting the telephone down *She cut me off in the middle of our conversation.*

cut sb/sth off *phrasal verb* **1** PLACE to prevent people from reaching or leaving a place, or to separate them from other people [**often passive**] *The whole village was cut off by flooding.* ○ *She lives abroad and feels very **cut off from** her family.* **2** STOP SUPPLY to stop providing something such as electricity or food supplies [**often**

passive] *If we don't pay the gas bill, we'll be cut off.*

cut sth out *phrasal verb* **1** SHAPE to remove something or form a shape by cutting, usually something made of paper or cloth *She cut out his picture from the magazine.* **2** STOP EATING to stop eating or drinking something, usually to improve your health *I've cut out red meat from my diet.* **3 Cut it out!** *informal* something you say to tell someone to stop doing something annoying **4 not be cut out to be sth/not be cut out for sth** to not have the right qualities for something *I'm not really cut out to be a nurse.*

cut out *phrasal verb* If an engine, machine, or piece of equipment cuts out, it suddenly stops working.

cut sth/sb out *phrasal verb* to not let someone share something or be included in something

cut sth up *phrasal verb* **1** to cut something into pieces **2 be cut up** *UK informal* to be very upset about something *He was very cut up when his brother died.*

cut² /kʌt/ *noun* [C] **1** INJURY an injury made when the skin is cut with something sharp *He suffered cuts and bruises in the accident.* **2** OPENING an opening made with a sharp tool *She **made a cut** in the material.* **3** REDUCTION a reduction in the number or amount of something ***tax/job cuts*** ○ *The workers were angry about the **cut in** pay.* **4 FOOD** a piece of meat from a particular part of an animal *an expensive cut of beef* **5** SHARE a share of something, usually money *My family owns the company, so we get a **cut of** the profits.* **6 an electricity/power, etc cut** when the supply of something is stopped **7** HAIR (*also* **haircut**) the style in which your hair has been cut ➲See also: **shortcut**

ˌcut and ˈpaste *verb* [I, T] **cutting and pasting,** *past* **cut and pasted COMPUTING** to move words or pictures from one place to another in a computer document

WORD PARTNERS FOR ***cutback***

make cutbacks • **drastic/severe/sharp** cutbacks • cutbacks **in** sth

cutback /ˈkʌtbæk/ *noun* [C] a reduction of something, usually to save money *The company has **made cutbacks** and closed one of its factories.*

cute /kjuːt/ *adjective* **1** ATTRACTIVE attractive *a cute baby* **2** RUDE *US informal* clever in a way that is annoying or rude *He thinks it's cute to tell dirty jokes.*

cuticle /ˈkjuːtɪkl/ *noun* [C] **1 ANATOMY, BIOLOGY** the thin skin at the bottom of the nails on the fingers and toes **2 BIOLOGY** the outer layer of a plant, that protects it ➲See picture at **leaf**

cutlery /ˈkʌtləri/ *UK* (*US* **silverware**) *noun* [U] knives, forks, and spoons

cutlet /ˈkʌtlət/ *noun* [C] **FOOD** a small piece of meat still joined to the bone *a lamb cutlet*

cut-price /ˈkʌtˌpraɪs/ *mainly UK* (*US* **cut-rate**) *adjective* [**always before noun**] cheaper than usual *cut-price tickets*

cutters /ˈkʌtəz/ *noun* [**plural**] a tool for cutting something *wire cutters*

cut-throat *mainly UK* (*also US* **cutthroat**) /ˈkʌtθrəʊt/ *adjective* a cut-throat business or other situation is where people will do anything to succeed and do not care if they hurt others *the cut-throat world of journalism*

cutting¹ /ˈkʌtɪŋ/ *noun* [C] **1** PLANT a piece cut from a plant and used to grow a new plant **2** NEWSPAPER *UK* (*UK/US* **clipping**) an article or picture that has been cut out of a newspaper or magazine

cutting² /ˈkʌtɪŋ/ *adjective* If something you say or write is cutting, it is unkind. *a **cutting remark***

cutting-edge /ˌkʌtɪŋˈedʒ/ *adjective* very modern and with all the newest developments ***cutting-edge design/technology***

CV /ˌsiːˈviː/ *UK* (*US* **résumé**) *noun* [C] a document which describes your qualifications and the jobs you have done, which you send to an employer that you want to work for

cwt MEASURES *written abbreviation for* hundredweight (= a unit for measuring weight, equal to 50.8 kilograms in the UK and 45.36 kilograms in the US)

cyanide /ˈsaɪənaɪd/ *noun* [U] a very strong poison

cyber- /saɪbəʳ/ *prefix* **INTERNET** relating to electronic communications, especially the Internet *cyberspace*

cybercafe /ˈsaɪbəˌkæfeɪ/ *noun* [C] **INTERNET** a place where customers can buy food and drink and use computers to search for information on the Internet

cyberspace /ˈsaɪbəˌspeɪs/ *noun* [U] **INTERNET** the Internet, considered as an imaginary area where you can communicate with people and find information

cycle¹ /ˈsaɪkl/ *noun* [C] **1** SERIES a series of events which happen in a particular order and are often repeated *the **life cycle** of a moth* **2** VEHICLE a bicycle ➲See also: **life cycle**

cycle² /ˈsaɪkl/ *verb* [I] to ride a bicycle •**cycling** *noun* [U] ➲See colour picture **Sports 2** on page Centre 15 •**cyclist** *noun* [C] someone who rides a bicycle

ˈcycle ˌhelmet *noun* [C] a hard hat that protects your head when you ride a bicycle ➲See colour picture **Clothes** on page Centre 9

cyclical /ˈsɪklɪkəl/ *adjective* happening in a regular and repeated pattern *the cyclical nature of the country's history*

cyclone /ˈsaɪkləʊn/ *noun* [C] a violent storm with very strong winds which move in a circle

cylinder /ˈsɪlɪndəʳ/ *noun* [C] **1** SHAPE a shape with circular ends and long, straight sides, or a container or object shaped like this *an oxygen cylinder* ➲See picture at **shape** **2** CAR PART a part in a car or machine's engine which is shaped like a tube, and where another part moves up and down

cylindrical /səˈlɪndrɪkəl/ *adjective* having the shape of a cylinder

cymbal /ˈsɪmbəl/ *noun* [C] **MUSIC** a musical instrument like a metal plate which is played by being hit with a stick or another cymbal

cynic /ˈsɪnɪk/ *noun* [C] a cynical person

cynical /ˈsɪnɪkəl/ *adjective* believing that people are only interested in themselves and are not sincere *Many people have become cynical about politicians.* •**cynically** *adverb* •**cynicism** /ˈsɪnɪsɪzəm/ *noun* [U] cynical beliefs

cyst /sɪst/ *noun* [C] **HEALTH** a small lump containing liquid that can grow under your skin

cystic fibrosis /ˌsɪstɪkfaɪˈbrəʊsɪs/ *noun* [U] **HEALTH** a serious disease which causes the lungs and other organs to become blocked

cytoplasm /ˈsaɪtəʊplæzəm/ *noun* [U] **BIOLOGY** the substance inside a cell which surrounds the cell's nucleus (= central part) ➲See picture at **cell** ➲See picture at **egg** ➲See picture at **leaf**

czar (*also UK* **tsar**) /zɑːr/ *noun* [C] **1** RULER a male Russian ruler before 1917 **2** OFFICIAL *informal* a powerful official who makes important decisions for the government about a particular activity *a drugs czar*

C

Dd

D

D, d /diː/ the fourth letter of the alphabet

dab /dæb/ *verb* [I, T] **dabbing,** *past* **dabbed** to touch something with quick, light touches, or to put a substance on something with quick, light touches *She **dabbed at** her eyes with a tissue.* •**dab** *noun* [C] a small amount of something *a **dab of** lipstick*

DAB /ˌdiːeɪ'biː/ *noun* [U] **PHYSICS** *abbreviation for* digital audio broadcasting: an electronic system for sending radio or television information using signals in the form of numbers

dabble /'dæbl/ *verb* [I] to try something or take part in an activity in a way that is not serious *I only **dabble in** politics.* ○ *He **dabbled with** drugs at university.*

dactyl /'dæktɪl/ *noun* **LITERATURE** a unit of poetry with one long syllable followed by two short syllables •**dactylic** /dæk'tɪlɪk/ *adjective*

O‑**dad** /dæd/ *noun* [C] *informal* father *Can I go to the park, Dad?*

daddy /'dædi/ *noun* [C] a word for 'father', used especially by children

daffodil /'dæfədɪl/ *noun* [C] a yellow flower that usually grows in spring

daft /dɑːft/ *adjective UK informal* silly *That's a **daft** idea.*

dagger /'dægəʳ/ *noun* [C] a short knife, used as a weapon

O‑**daily¹** /'deɪli/ *adjective* [**always before noun**], *adverb* **1** EVERY DAY happening or produced every day or once a day *a **daily newspaper*** ○ *The shop is open daily from 8 a.m. to 6 p.m.* **2** ONE DAY relating to one single day *They are paid on a **daily basis**.* **3 daily life** the usual things that happen to you every day *Shootings are **part of daily life** in the region.*

daily² /'deɪli/ *noun* [C] a newspaper that is published every day except Sunday

dainty /'deɪnti/ *adjective* small, attractive, and delicate *dainty feet* •**daintily** *adverb*

dairy¹ /'deəri/ *noun* [C] **1 FARMING** a place where milk is stored and cream and cheese are made **2 FARMING** a company which sells milk and products made of milk

dairy² /'deəri/ *adjective* [**always before noun**] **FOOD** relating to milk or products made using milk ***dairy products*** ○ ***dairy cattle***

daisy /'deɪzi/ *noun* [C] a small flower with white petals and a yellow centre that often grows in grass

dam /dæm/ *noun* [C] a strong wall built across a river to stop the water and make a lake •**dam** *verb* [T] **damming,** *past* **dammed** to build a dam across a river ➲See picture at **hydroelectric power station**

WORD PARTNERS FOR ***damage***

cause/inflict/repair/suffer damage • **extensive/permanent/serious/slight** damage • damage **to** sth

O‑**damage¹** /'dæmɪdʒ/ *noun* [U] harm or injury *He suffered **brain damage** in the car crash.* ○ *The strong wind caused serious **damage to** the roof.*

O‑**damage²** /'dæmɪdʒ/ *verb* [T] to harm or break something *Many buildings were damaged in the storm.* ○ *Smoking can seriously damage your health.* •**damaging** *adjective* harmful *the **damaging effects** of pollution*

WORD PARTNERS FOR ***damages***

award/claim/pay/seek/win damages • **substantial** damages • **[£400, $10,000, etc] in** damages

damages /'dæmɪdʒɪz/ *noun* [**plural**] **LAW** money that a person or organization pays to someone because they have harmed them or something that belongs to them *She was **awarded** £400 **in damages**.*

dame /deɪm/ *noun* [C] **1** TITLE a title used in the UK before the name of a woman who has been officially respected *Dame Agatha Christie* **2** WOMAN *US informal old-fashioned* a woman

damn¹ /dæm/ (*also* **damned** /dæmd/) *adjective* [**always before noun**] *informal* used to express anger *He didn't listen to a damn thing I said.*

damn² /dæm/ (*also* **damn it**) *exclamation* used to express anger or disappointment *Damn! I've forgotten the tickets.*

damn³ /dæm/ (*also* **damned** /dæmd/) *adverb informal* very *He worked damn hard to pass that exam.*

damn⁴ /dæm/ *noun* **not give a damn** *informal* to not be interested in or worried about someone or something *I don't give a damn what people think.*

damn⁵ /dæm/ *verb* **1 damn him/it/you, etc** used to express anger about someone or something *Stop complaining, damn you!* **2** [T] to strongly criticize someone or something *He was damned by the media.*

damning /'dæmɪŋ/ *adjective* criticizing someone or something very strongly, or showing clearly that someone is guilty ***damning evidence*** ○ *a **damning report** on education standards*

damp /dæmp/ *adjective* slightly wet, usually in an unpleasant way *damp clothes/grass* ○ *It was cold and damp outside.* •**damp** (*also* **dampness**) *noun* [U] when something is slightly wet

dampen /'dæmpən/ (*also* **damp**) *verb* [T] **1** REDUCE to make something less strong *Nothing you can say will **dampen** her **enthusiasm**.* **2** MAKE WET to make something slightly wet

damper /'dæmpəʳ/ *noun* **put a damper on sth** to stop an occasion from being enjoyable *The accident put a damper on their holiday.*

O‑**dance¹** /dɑːns/ *verb* [I, T] to move your feet and body to the rhythm of music *She's dancing with Steven.* ○ *Can you dance the tango?* •**dancer** *noun* [C] •**dancing** *noun* [U]

O‑**dance²** /dɑːns/ *noun* **1** MOVING [C] when you move your feet and body to music *I **had** a* *dance with my dad.* **2** STEPS [C] a particular set of steps or movements to music *My favourite dance is the tango.* **3** EVENT [C] a social event where people dance to music **4** ACTIVITY [U] the activity or skill of dancing *a dance school*

dandelion /ˈdændɪlaɪən/ *noun* [C] a yellow wild flower

dandruff /ˈdændrʌf/ *noun* [U] **HEALTH** small pieces of dead skin in someone's hair or on their clothes

WORD PARTNERS FOR ***danger***

face danger • **pose** a danger • **great/serious** danger • **be in** danger • **be in** danger **of** sth

O‑**danger** /ˈdeɪndʒəʳ/ *noun* **1** POSSIBILITY [C, U] the possibility that someone or something will be harmed or killed, or that something bad will happen *the dangers of rock climbing* ○ *The soldiers were* ***in serious danger.*** ○ *We were* ***in danger of*** *missing our flight.* **2** HARMFUL PERSON/THING [C] something or someone that may harm you *Icy roads are a* ***danger to*** *drivers.*

OTHER WAYS OF SAYING ***dangerous***

If something is extremely dangerous, you can use the adjectives **hazardous**, **perilous** or **treacherous**: *Ice had made the roads* ***treacherous.*** • *Heavy rain is causing* ***hazardous*** *driving conditions.* • *A* ***perilous*** *journey through the mountains was their only escape route.*

Substances which are dangerous are often described as **harmful** or **hazardous**: *Please be aware that these chemicals are* ***harmful/hazardous*** *to human health.*

If something is dangerous because something bad might happen, you can say that it is **risky**: *Surgery at his age would be too* ***risky.***

O‑**dangerous** /ˈdeɪndʒərəs/ *adjective* If someone or something is dangerous, they could harm you. *a dangerous chemical* •**dangerously** *adverb dangerously close to the edge*

dangle /ˈdæŋgl/ *verb* **1** HANG [I, T] to hang loosely, or to hold something so that it hangs loosely *Electrical wires were* ***dangling from*** *the ceiling.* **2** OFFER [T] to offer someone something they want in order to persuade them to do something *They dangled the possibility of a job in Paris in front of him.*

dank /dæŋk/ *adjective* wet, cold, and unpleasant *a dark, dank basement*

dapper /ˈdæpəʳ/ *adjective* A dapper man looks stylish and tidy.

dare[1] /deəʳ/ *verb* **1 dare (to) do sth** to be brave enough to do something *I didn't dare tell Dad that I'd scratched his car.* **2 dare sb to do sth** to try to make someone do something dangerous *She dared her friend to climb onto the roof.* **3 Don't you dare** *informal* used to tell someone angrily not to do something *Don't you dare hit your sister!* **4 How dare she/you, etc** used to express anger about something someone has done *How dare you talk to me like that!* **5 I dare say** (*also* **I daresay**) used when you think that something is probably true or will probably happen *I dare say she'll change her mind.*

dare[2] /deəʳ/ *noun* [C] something that you do to prove that you are not afraid [**usually singular**] *She climbed down the cliff for a dare.*

daredevil /ˈdeəˌdevəl/ *noun* [C] someone who enjoys doing dangerous things

daren't /deənt/ *UK short for* dare not *I daren't tell my wife how much it cost.*

daring /ˈdeərɪŋ/ *adjective* brave and taking risks *a daring escape* •**daring** *noun* [U]

O‑**dark**[1] /dɑːk/ *adjective* **1** NO LIGHT with no light or not much light *It's a bit dark in here.* ○ *It doesn't* ***get dark*** *until 9 o'clock in the evening.* **2** NOT PALE nearer to black than white in colour *dark blue/green* ○ *dark clouds* ○ *He's got dark hair and blue eyes.* **3** PERSON having black or brown hair or brown skin *A short, dark woman with glasses.* **4** BAD frightening or unpleasant *a dark period in human history*

O‑**dark**[2] /dɑːk/ *noun* **1 the dark** when there is no light somewhere *He's scared of the dark.* **2 before/after dark** before/after it becomes night *She doesn't let her children out after dark.* **3 be in the dark** to not know about something that other people know about *I'm completely in the dark about all this.* ➲See also: a **shot**[1] in the dark

darken /ˈdɑːkən/ *verb* [I, T] **1** DARK to become dark or make something dark *the darkening sky* ○ *a darkened room* **2** MOOD If someone's mood darkens, or if something darkens it, they suddenly feel less happy.

darkly /ˈdɑːkli/ *adverb* in a frightening or mysterious way *"He might not be what he seems," she said darkly.*

darkness /ˈdɑːknəs/ *noun* [U] when there is little or no light *He stumbled around in the darkness looking for the light switch.* ○ *There was a power cut and the house was* ***in darkness.***

darling[1] /ˈdɑːlɪŋ/ *noun* [C] used when you speak to someone you love *Would you like a drink, darling?*

darling[2] /ˈdɑːlɪŋ/ *adjective* [**always before noun**] loved very much *my darling daughter*

darn[1] /dɑːn/ *US informal* (*also* **darned** /dɑːnd/) *adjective* [**always before noun**], *adverb* used to emphasize what you are saying, or to show that you are annoyed *I'm too darn tired to care.*

darn[2] /dɑːn/ *verb* [I, T] to repair a piece of clothing by sewing across a hole with thread *to darn socks*

dart[1] /dɑːt/ *noun* [C] **SPORT** a small arrow used in the game of darts or as a weapon *a tranquilizer dart*

dart[2] /dɑːt/ *verb* **dart between/in/out, etc** to run or move somewhere quickly and suddenly *A cat darted across the street.*

darts /dɑːts/ *noun* [U] **SPORT** a game played by throwing small arrows at a round board

dash[1] /dæʃ/ *verb* **1** [I] to go somewhere quickly *She dashed downstairs when she heard the phone.* ○ *I must dash. I've got to be home by 7 p.m.* **2 dash sb's hopes** to destroy someone's hopes *Saturday's 2-0 defeat dashed their hopes of reaching the final.* **3 dash (sth) against/on, etc** *literary* to hit or throw something with great force, usually causing damage *Waves dashed against the cliffs.*

dash sth off *phrasal verb UK* to write something very quickly *She **dashed off a letter** to her solicitor.*

dash² /dæʃ/ *noun* **1** [RUN] [**no plural**] when you run somewhere very quickly *As the rain started, we **made a dash for** shelter.* **2** [AMOUNT] [**C**] a small amount of something, often food ***Add a dash** of milk to the sauce.* **3** [MARK] [**C**] a mark (–) used to separate parts of sentences ➲See Extra help page **Punctuation** on page Centre 19.

D

dashboard /ˈdæʃbɔːd/ *noun* [**C**] the part facing the driver at the front of a car with controls and equipment to show things such as speed and temperature ➲See colour picture **Car** on page Centre 7

dashing /ˈdæʃɪŋ/ *adjective* A dashing man is attractive in a confident and exciting way.

WORD PARTNERS FOR ***data***

analyse/collect data • data **on** sth

data /ˈdeɪtə/ *noun* [**U**] **1** information or facts about something *financial data* **2** **COMPUTING** information in the form of text, numbers, or symbols that can be used by or stored in a computer

database /ˈdeɪtəbeɪs/ *noun* [**C**] **COMPUTING** information stored in a computer in an organized structure so that it can be searched in different ways *a national database of missing people*

ˌdatabase ˈmanagement ˌsystem (*abbreviation* **DBMS**) *noun* [**C**] **COMPUTING** a system for organising large amounts of computer information

ˈdata ˌcapture *noun* [**U**] **COMPUTING** collecting data, especially using computers *They designed a new data capture form.*

dataglove /ˈdeɪtəglʌv/ *noun* [**C**] **COMPUTING** an electronic glove (= hand covering) which sends information about the hand movements of the person wearing it to a computer

ˈdata ˌprocessing *noun* [**U**] **COMPUTING** the use of a computer to do calculations on data (= information kept on a computer)

ˈdata proˌjector (*also* **beamer**) *noun* [**C**] a machine that allows you to show words or images on a screen or wall

WORD PARTNERS FOR ***date***

make/fix/set a date • **at a future/at a later** date • the date **of** sth • sb's date **of birth**

date¹ /deɪt/ *noun* [**C**] **1** [PARTICULAR DAY] a particular day of the month or year *"What's the date today?" "It's the fifth."* ○ *Please give your name, address and **date of birth**.* **2** [ARRANGED TIME] a time when something has been arranged to happen *Let's **make a date** to have lunch.* ○ *We agreed to finish the report **at a later date**.* **3 to date** *formal* up to the present time *This novel is his best work to date.* **4** [GOING OUT] a romantic meeting when two people go out somewhere, such as to a restaurant or to see a film *He's asked her out **on a date**.* **5** [PERSON] someone who you are having a romantic meeting with *Who's your date for the prom?* **6** **FOOD** a sticky brown fruit with a long seed inside ➲See also: **blind date, sell-by date**

date² /deɪt/ *verb* **1** [MEET] [**I, T**] to regularly spend time with someone you have a romantic relationship with *We've been dating for six months.* **2** [WRITE] [**T**] to write the day's date on something *a letter dated March 13th* **3** [TIME] [**T**] to say how long something has existed or when it was made *Scientists have dated the bones to 10,000 BC.* **4** [NOT MODERN] [**I, T**] to stop seeming modern, or to make something not seem modern *Clothes like these date really quickly.*

date back *phrasal verb* to have existed a particular length of time or since a particular time *This house **dates back to** 1650.*

date from sth *phrasal verb* to have existed since a particular time *The castle dates from the 11th century.*

dated /ˈdeɪtɪd/ *adjective* not modern *This film seems a bit dated today.*

ˈdate ˌrape *noun* [**C**] when someone is raped (= forced to have sex when they do not want to) by someone they know, or someone they have arranged to meet

daub /dɔːb/ *verb* [**T**] to put a lot of a substance like paint on a surface in a careless way, often to write words or draw pictures *The walls have been daubed with graffiti.*

daughter /ˈdɔːtəʳ/ *noun* [**C**] your female child

daughter-in-law /ˈdɔːtərɪnlɔː/ *noun* [**C**] *plural* **daughters-in-law** your son's wife

daunt /dɔːnt/ *verb* [**T**] If someone is daunted by something, they are worried because it is difficult or frightening. [**often passive**] *I was a bit daunted by the idea of cooking for so many people.*

daunting /ˈdɔːntɪŋ/ *adjective* If something is daunting, it makes you worried because it is difficult or frightening. *a daunting challenge/task*

dawdle /ˈdɔːdl/ *verb* [**I**] to walk very slowly, or do something very slowly in a way that wastes time *Stop dawdling! You'll be late for school!*

dawn¹ /dɔːn/ *noun* [**U**] **1** the early morning when light first appears in the sky *We woke **at dawn**.* **2 the dawn of sth** *literary* the time when something began ***the dawn of civilization*** ➲See also: the **crack²** of dawn

dawn² /dɔːn/ *verb* [**I**] If a day or a period of time dawns, it begins. *The day of her party dawned at last.*

dawn on sb *phrasal verb* If a fact dawns on you, you become aware of it after a period of not being aware of it. [+ **that**] *It suddenly dawned on them that Mary had been lying.*

day /deɪ/ *noun* **1** [24 HOURS] [**C**] a period of 24 hours *the days of the week* ○ *January has 31 days.* ○ *I saw her the day before yesterday.* **2** [LIGHT HOURS] [**C, U**] the period during the day when there is light from the sun *a bright, sunny day* ○ *We've been travelling all day.* **3** [WORK HOURS] [**C**] the time that you usually spend at work or school *She's had a very busy day at the office.* **4 the other day** a few days ago *I saw Terry the other day.* **5 day after day** every day for a long period of time *Day after day they marched through the mountains.* **6 one day** used to talk about something that happened in the past *One day, I came home to find my* *windows smashed.* **7 one day/some day/one of these days** used to talk about something you think will happen in the future *One of these days I'll tell her what really happened.* **8 days a** PERIOD used to talk about a particular period of time when something happened or existed ***in my younger days*** **b** LONG TIME a long time *I haven't seen Jack **for days**.* **9 these days** used to talk about the present time *I don't go out much these days.* **10 in those days** used to talk about a period in the past *In those days, boys used to wear short trousers.* **11 the old days** a period in the past **12 call it a day** *informal* to stop doing something, especially working *It's almost midnight - let's call it a day.* **13 it's early days** *UK* something that you say when it is too early to know what will happen *Both teams are at the bottom of the league, but it's early days yet.* **14 make sb's day** to make someone very happy *Go on, ask him to dance - it'll make his day!* **15 save the day** to do something that solves a serious problem ➲See also: **April Fool's Day, Boxing Day, Christmas Day,** at the **end**[1] of the day, **field day, Independence Day, Mother's Day, New Year's Day, open day, polling day, Valentine's Day**

daybreak /ˈdeɪbreɪk/ *noun* [U] the time in the morning when light first appears in the sky

daycare /ˈdeɪkeəʳ/ *noun* [U] care provided during the day for people who cannot look after themselves, especially young children or old people *a daycare centre*

daydream /ˈdeɪdriːm/ *verb* [I] to have pleasant thoughts about something you would like to happen •**daydream** *noun* [C]

daylight /ˈdeɪlaɪt/ *noun* **1** [U] the natural light from the sun **2 in broad daylight** used to emphasize that something happens when it is light and people can see *He was attacked in broad daylight.*

daylights /ˈdeɪlaɪts/ *noun* **1 beat/knock the (living) daylights out of sb** *informal* to hit someone very hard many times **2 scare/frighten the (living) daylights out of sb** *informal* to frighten someone very much

ˌday reˈturn *noun* [C] *UK* a ticket for a bus or train when you go somewhere and come back on the same day *a day return to Norwich*

daytime /ˈdeɪtaɪm/ *noun* [U] the period of the day when there is light from the sun, or the period when most people are at work ***daytime television*** ○ *a **daytime telephone number***

day-to-day /ˌdeɪtəˈdeɪ/ *adjective* [**always before noun**] happening every day as a regular part of your job or your life *day-to-day activities/problems*

daze /deɪz/ *noun* **in a daze** when you cannot think clearly because you are shocked or have hit your head *The survivors were walking around in a daze.*

dazed /deɪzd/ *adjective* not able to think clearly because you are shocked or have hit your head *a **dazed expression***

dazzle /ˈdæzl/ *verb* [T] **1** EXCITEMENT If you are dazzled by someone or something, you think they are extremely good and exciting. [**often passive**] *I was dazzled by his intelligence and good looks.* **2** LIGHT If light dazzles someone, it makes them unable to see for a short time.

dazzling /ˈdæzlɪŋ/ *adjective* **1** EXCITING extremely good and exciting *a **dazzling display/performance*** **2** BRIGHT A dazzling light is so bright that you cannot see for a short time after looking at it. *a dazzling white light*

DBMS /ˌdiːbiːemˈes/ *noun* [C] **COMPUTING** *abbreviation for* database management system; a system for organising large amounts of computer information

DC /diːˈsiː/ *noun* [C] **PHYSICS** *abbreviation for* direct current: electrical current that only moves in one direction ➲Compare **AC**

de- /di-/ *prefix* to take something away *deforestation* (= when the trees in an area are cut down)

deacon /ˈdiːkən/ *noun* [C] **RELIGION** an official in some Christian churches

O-- **dead**[1] /ded/ *adjective* **1** NOT ALIVE not now alive *She's been dead for 20 years now.* ○ *He was **shot dead** by a masked intruder.* ○ *There were three children among **the dead**.* ➲See Common Learner Error at **die** **2** EQUIPMENT If a piece of equipment is dead, it is not working. *a dead battery* ○ *The phone suddenly **went dead**.* **3** QUIET *informal* If a place is dead, it is too quiet and nothing interesting is happening there. **4** COMPLETE [**always before noun**] complete *We waited in dead silence as the votes were counted.* **5** BODY *mainly UK* If part of your body is dead, you cannot feel it. *My arm's **gone dead**.* **6 wouldn't be caught/seen dead** *informal* If someone wouldn't be caught dead in a place or doing something, they would never go there or do it, usually because it would be too embarrassing. [**+ doing sth**] *I wouldn't be caught dead wearing a bikini.* **7 drop dead** *informal* to die very suddenly

dead[2] /ded/ *adverb* **1** *informal* extremely or completely *UK The exam was dead easy.* ○ *US His advice was dead wrong.* **2 be dead set against sth/doing sth** to oppose something strongly *My parents were dead set against us getting married.* **3 stop dead** to suddenly stop moving or doing something

dead[3] /ded/ *noun* **the dead of night/winter** the middle of the night/winter

deadbeat /ˈdedbiːt/ *noun* [C] *US informal* someone who does not pay their debts *a deadbeat dad*

deaden /ˈdedᵊn/ *verb* [T] to make something less painful or less strong *She gave me an injection to **deaden** the **pain**.*

ˌdead ˈend *noun* [C] **1** ROAD a road which is closed at one end **2** SITUATION a situation in which it is impossible to make progress *The peace talks have **reached** a **dead end**.* •**dead-end** /ˌdedˈend/ *adjective* *a **dead-end job/relationship*** ○ *a **dead-end street***

ˌdead ˈheat *noun* [C] **SPORT** when two people finish a race at exactly the same time

WORD PARTNERS FOR ***deadline***

set a deadline • **meet/miss** a deadline • a **tight** deadline • the deadline **for** (doing) sth

deadline /ˈdedlaɪn/ *noun* [C] a time by which something must be done *to **meet/miss** a* *deadline* ○ *The **deadline for** entering the competition is tomorrow.*

deadlock /ˈdedlɒk/ *noun* [U] a situation in which it is impossible to make progress or to reach a decision *The talks have **reached deadlock**.* ○ *There have been several attempts to **break the deadlock**.* •**deadlocked** *adjective*

deadly¹ /ˈdedli/ *adjective* likely to cause death *a **deadly virus*** ○ *a **deadly weapon***

D

deadly² /ˈdedli/ *adverb* **deadly dull/serious, etc** extremely dull/serious, etc

deadpan /ˈdedpæn/ *adjective* looking or sounding serious when you are telling a joke *a deadpan expression*

deaf /def/ *adjective* **1** unable to hear *Many deaf people learn to lip read.* ○ *He goes to a school for **the deaf**.* **2** **be deaf to sth** to refuse to listen to something •**deafness** *noun* [U] ➲See also: fall on deaf ears (**ear**), **tone-deaf**

deafening /ˈdefᵊnɪŋ/ *adjective* extremely loud *a **deafening noise***

WORD PARTNERS FOR ***deal***

agree/do/make/strike a deal • **negotiate / sign** a deal • a deal **between** [two people/companies, etc] • a deal **with** sb

deal¹ /diːl/ *noun* **1** [C] an arrangement or an agreement, especially in business *a **business deal*** ○ *The police refused to **do/make/strike a deal** with the terrorists.* **2** **FINANCE** [C] the price you pay for something, and what you get for your money *I **got** a really **good deal on** my new car.* **3** **a good/great deal** a lot *A great deal of time and effort went into arranging this party.*

deal² /diːl/ *verb* [**I, T**] *past* **dealt** to give cards to players in a game *Whose turn is it to deal?*

deal in sth *phrasal verb* to buy and sell particular goods as a business *a shop dealing in rare books*

deal with sth *phrasal verb* **1** TAKE ACTION to take action in order to achieve something or to solve a problem *Can you deal with this gentleman's complaint?* **2** SUBJECT to be about a particular subject *The programme dealt with teenage pregnancy.*

deal with sb/sth *phrasal verb* to do business with a person or organization *I usually deal with the accounts department.*

deal with sb *phrasal verb* to meet or talk to someone, especially as part of your job *She's used to dealing with foreign customers.*

dealer /ˈdiːləʳ/ *noun* [C] **1** BUY/SELL a person or company that buys and sells things for profit *a **car dealer*** ○ *a **drug dealer*** **2** CARDS a person who gives out cards to players in a game

dealership /ˈdiːləʃɪp/ *noun* [C] a business that sells cars, usually cars made by a particular company *a Ford/Toyota dealership*

dealings /ˈdiːlɪŋz/ *noun* [**plural**] activities involving other people, especially in business *Have you **had** any **dealings with** their London office?*

dealt /delt/ *past of* deal

deaminate /ˌdiːˈæmɪneɪt/ *verb* [T] **CHEMISTRY** to remove one or more of the groups of atoms that contain nitrogen from a molecule •**deamination** /diːˌæmɪˈneɪʃᵊn/ *noun* [U]

dean /diːn/ *noun* [C] **1** **EDUCATION** an official in a college or university **2** **RELIGION** an official in charge of a large church or group of churches

O-- **dear¹** /dɪəʳ/ *adjective* **1** IN LETTERS used at the beginning of a letter, before the name of the person you are writing to *Dear Amy* ○ *Dear Mrs Simpson* ○ *Dear Sir/Madam* **2** LIKED [**always before noun**] A dear person is someone who you know and like very much. *my dear Peter* ○ *He's one of my dearest friends.* **3** EXPENSIVE *UK* expensive **4** **dear to sb/sb's heart** If something is dear to someone or dear to their heart, it is very important to them. *The charity was very dear to his heart.*

dear² /dɪəʳ/ *exclamation* **oh dear** used to express surprise and disappointment *Oh dear! I forgot my keys!*

dear³ /dɪəʳ/ *noun* [C] used to address someone in a friendly way, especially a child or someone you love *Don't cry, my dear.* ○ *Yes, dear?*

dearly /ˈdɪəli/ *adverb* very much *I would **dearly love** to visit Rome again.*

dearth /dɜːθ/ *noun formal* **a dearth of sth** when there are not many or not enough of something available *a dearth of new homes*

WORD PARTNERS FOR ***death***

bleed/choke/freeze/starve to death • be **beaten/crushed/stabbed/trampled** to death • sb's **premature/sudden/tragic/untimely** death • death **from** sth

O-- **death** /deθ/ *noun* **1** [C, U] the end of life *Do you believe in life after death?* ○ *We need to reduce the number of **deaths from** heart attacks.* ○ *a death threat* **2** **to death** until you die *He was beaten to death by a gang of youths.* **3** **put sb to death** to kill someone as a punishment [**often passive**] *She was put to death for her beliefs.* **4** **frightened/bored, etc to death** *informal* extremely frightened/bored, etc *She's scared to death of dogs.*

deathbed /ˈdeθbed/ *noun* **on your deathbed** very ill and going to die soon

deathly /ˈdeθli/ *adjective, adverb* extreme in a way which is unpleasant *a **deathly silence*** ○ *Her face turned **deathly pale**.*

ˈdeath ˌpenalty *noun* [C] **LAW** the legal punishment of death for a crime

ˌdeath ˈrow *noun* **LAW** **on death row** in prison and waiting to be killed as a punishment for a crime

ˈdeath ˌsentence *noun* [C] **LAW** a legal punishment of death for a crime

ˈdeath ˌtoll *noun* [C] the number of people who die because of an event such as a war or an accident *The death toll from the earthquake has risen to 1500.*

ˈdeath ˌtrap *noun* [C] something that is very dangerous and could cause death *That old factory across the road is a real death trap.*

debase /dɪˈbeɪs/ *verb* [T] *formal* to reduce the value or quality of something *They argue that money has debased football.*

debatable /dɪˈbeɪtəbl/ *adjective* If something is debatable, it is not certain if it is true or not. *It's **debatable whether** a university degree will help you in this job.*

debate¹ /dɪˈbeɪt/ *noun* [C, U] discussion or argument about a subject *a political debate* ○ *There has been a lot of public **debate on** the safety of food.*

debate² /dɪˈbeɪt/ *verb* **1** DISCUSS [I, T] to discuss a subject in a formal way *These issues need to be debated openly.* **2** DECIDE [T] to try to make a decision about something [+ **question word**] *I'm still debating whether to go out tonight or not.*

debenture /dɪˈbentʃəʳ/ *noun* [C] **FINANCE** an official document from a government or company to show that you have given them money that they will pay back with a certain amount of extra money

debilitating /dɪˈbɪlɪteɪtɪŋ/ *adjective formal* **HEALTH** A debilitating illness or problem makes you weak and unable to do what you want to do. *the debilitating effects of flu*

debit¹ /ˈdebɪt/ *noun* [C] **FINANCE** money taken out of a bank account, or a record of this ⊃Opposite **credit** ⊃See also: **direct debit**

debit² /ˈdebɪt/ *verb* [T] **FINANCE** to take money out of a bank account as a payment for something *Twenty pounds has been debited from my account.*

ˈdebit ˌcard *noun* [C] **FINANCE** a plastic card used to pay for things directly from your bank account

ˈdebit ˌnote *noun* [C] **FINANCE** a document that is sent by a business to a company supplying goods to record any problems with the quality or amount of what the business has received

debris /ˈdebriː/ ⓊⓈ /dəˈbriː/ *noun* [U] broken pieces of something *Debris from the aircraft was scattered over a wide area.*

WORD PARTNERS FOR ***debt***

be in/fall into/get into/run into debt • **get out of** debt • **clear/pay off/repay /settle** a debt

O-ᵚ**debt** /det/ *noun* **1 ECONOMICS, FINANCE** [C] an amount of money that you owe someone *She's working in a bar to try to **pay off her debts**.* **2 FINANCE** [U] when you owe money to someone *We don't want to **get into debt**.* ○ *He's heavily **in debt**.* **3 be in sb's debt** to feel grateful to someone who has helped you or given you something

debtor /ˈdetəʳ/ *noun* [C] **FINANCE** someone who owes money

ˈdebtors ˌledger (*also* **sales ledger**) *noun* [C] **FINANCE** a record that a business keeps of how much each customer owes

ˈdebt reˌlief *noun* [U] **ECONOMICS** when a bank tells a person, a company or a government that they do not have to pay back the money they owe the bank

debug /ˌdiːˈbʌg/ *verb* [T] **debugging**, *past* **debugged COMPUTING** to remove mistakes from a computer program

debut /ˈdeɪbjuː/ ⓊⓈ /deɪˈbjuː/ *noun* [C] when someone performs or presents something to the public for the first time *She **made her debut** as a pianist in 1975.* ○ *This is the band's **debut album**.*

Dec *written abbreviation for* December

O-ᵚ**decade** /ˈdekeɪd/ *noun* [C] a period of ten years

decadence /ˈdekədᵊns/ *noun* [U] when you do or have things only for your own pleasure or behave in an immoral way •**decadent** *adjective a decadent lifestyle*

decaf /ˈdiːkæf/ *noun* [C, U] *informal* **FOOD** *short for* decaffeinated coffee

decaffeinated /dɪˈkæfɪneɪtɪd/ *adjective* **FOOD** Decaffeinated tea or coffee is made by removing the caffeine (= chemical which makes you feel more awake).

decant /dɪˈkænt/ *verb* [T] to pour a liquid from one container into another •**decantation** /ˌdɪkænˈteɪʃᵊn/ *noun* [U]

decathlon /dɪˈkæθlɒn/ *noun* [C] **SPORT** a sports competition in which someone competes in ten events

decay /dɪˈkeɪ/ *verb* [I] **BIOLOGY** to gradually become bad or weak or be destroyed, often because of natural causes like bacteria or age *decaying leaves* ○ *Sugar makes your teeth decay.* •**decay** *noun* [U] when something decays ***tooth decay*** ○ *Many of the buildings had **fallen into decay**.*

deceased /dɪˈsiːst/ *adjective formal* **1** dead *the deceased man's belongings* **2 the deceased** someone who has died *The police have not yet informed the family of the deceased.*

deceit /dɪˈsiːt/ *noun* [U] when someone tries to make someone believe something that is not true •**deceitful** *adjective deceitful behaviour*

deceive /dɪˈsiːv/ *verb* [T] to make someone believe something that is not true *The company deceived customers by selling old computers as new ones.*

decelerate /ˌdiːˈselᵊreɪt/ *verb* [I] to move more slowly •**deceleration** /ˌdiːselᵊˈreɪʃᵊn/ *noun* [U]

O-ᵚ**December** /dɪˈsembəʳ/ (*written abbreviation* **Dec**) *noun* [C, U] the twelfth month of the year

decency /ˈdiːsᵊnsi/ *noun* [U] behaviour that is good, moral, and acceptable in society *a sense of decency* ○ *She didn't even **have the decency to** tell me she wasn't coming.*

decent /ˈdiːsᵊnt/ *adjective* **1** SATISFACTORY of a satisfactory quality or level *He earns a decent salary.* ○ *I haven't had a decent cup of coffee since I've been here.* **2** HONEST honest and morally good *Decent people have had their lives ruined by his behaviour.* ○ *She should **do the decent thing** and apologize.* **3** CLOTHES [**never before noun**] wearing clothes *Can I come in? Are you decent?* •**decently** *adverb*

decentralize (*also UK* **-ise**) /diːˈsentrəlaɪz/ *verb* [T] to move the control of an organization or a government from a single place to several smaller places •**decentralization** /diːˌsentrᵊlaɪˈzeɪʃᵊn/ *noun* [U]

deception /dɪˈsepʃᵊn/ *noun* [C, U] when someone makes someone believe something that is not true *He was found guilty of obtaining money by deception.*

deceptive /dɪˈseptɪv/ *adjective* If something is deceptive, it makes you believe something that is not true. *Appearances can be deceptive.* •**deceptively** *adverb*

decibel /ˈdesɪbel/ *noun* [C] **PHYSICS, MEASURES** a unit for measuring how loud a sound is

OTHER WAYS OF SAYING *decide*

If someone is deciding a time or an amount, especially an exact date or price, the verbs **fix** and **set** are often used: *The price has been **set/fixed** at $10.* • *Have you **set/fixed** a date for the wedding?*

If someone makes a final and certain decision about a plan, date, etc., the verb **finalize** is sometimes used: *We've chosen a venue, but we haven't **finalized** the details yet.*

The verb **settle** and the phrasal verb **settle on/upon** are also often used when someone is making a final decision: *Have you **settled on** a place to live yet?* • *Right then, we're going to Spain. That's **settled**.*

The fixed expression **make up your mind** is often used to mean 'to decide': *I like them both - I just can't **make up my mind** which one to pick.* • *Have you **made up your mind** whether you're going?*

If someone is unable to decide between two choices, in informal situations you can use the expression **be torn between** something **and** something else: *I'm **torn between** the fish pie **and** the beef.*

decide /dɪˈsaɪd/ *verb* **1** CHOOSE [I, T] to choose something after thinking about several possibilities [+ **question word**] *I haven't decided whether or not to tell him.* [+ **to do sth**] *She's decided to take the job.* [+ **(that)**] *The teachers decided that the school would take part in the competition.* **2** RESULT [T] to be the reason or situation that makes a particular result happen *This match will decide the tournament.* **3 deciding factor** the thing that helps to make the final decision

decide on sth/sb *phrasal verb* to choose something or someone after thinking carefully *I've decided on blue walls for the bathroom.*

decided /dɪˈsaɪdɪd/ *adjective* [**always before noun**] certain, obvious, or easy to notice *She had a decided advantage over her opponent.* •**decidedly** *adverb That exam was decidedly more difficult than the last one.*

deciduous /dɪˈsɪdjuəs/ *adjective* **BIOLOGY** A deciduous tree has leaves that drop off every autumn.

decimal¹ /ˈdesɪmᵊl/ *adjective* **MATHEMATICS** involving counting in units of 10 *a decimal system*

decimal² /ˈdesɪmᵊl/ *noun* [C] **MATHEMATICS** a number less than one that is written as one or more numbers after a point *The decimal 0.5 is the same as the fraction (= ½).* ➲See Extra help page **Numbers and measurements** on page Centre 22.

ˌdecimal ˈfraction *noun* [C] **MATHEMATICS** a fraction that is written using a decimal point

ˌdecimal ˈplace *UK* (*US* **ˈdecimal ˌplace**) *noun* [C] **MATHEMATICS** the position of a number after a decimal point *The number is accurate to three decimal places.*

deciduous

ˌdecimal ˈpoint *UK* (*US* **ˈdecimal ˌpoint**) *noun* [C] **MATHEMATICS** the point (.) that is used to separate a whole number and a decimal

decimate /ˈdesɪmeɪt/ *verb* [T] *formal* to destroy large numbers of people or things *Populations of endangered animals have been decimated.*

decipher /dɪˈsaɪfəʳ/ *verb* [T] to discover what something says or means *It's sometimes difficult to **decipher** his **handwriting**.*

WORD PARTNERS FOR *decision*

come to/make/reach a decision • a **big/difficult/final/important/unanimous/wise** decision • a decision **about/on** sth

decision /dɪˈsɪʒᵊn/ *noun* [C] a choice that you make about something after thinking about several possibilities *She has had to **make** some very difficult **decisions**.* [+ **to do sth**] *It was his decision to leave.* ○ *The committee should **come to/reach a** final **decision** by next week.*

decisive /dɪˈsaɪsɪv/ *adjective* **1** AFFECTING strongly affecting how a situation will progress or end *a **decisive goal/victory*** **2** MAKE DECISIONS making decisions quickly and easily *You need to be more decisive.* ➲Opposite **indecisive** •**decisively** *adverb* •**decisiveness** *noun* [U]

deck¹ /dek/ *noun* [C] **1** SHIP/BUS/PLANE one of the floors of a ship, bus, or aircraft *The children like to sit on the top deck of the bus.* **2 on deck** on the top floor of a ship that is not covered **3** CARDS *US* (*UK* **pack**) a collection of cards that you use to play a game **4** MACHINE a machine that you use to play records or tapes (= plastic cases containing magnetic material used to record sounds) *a tape deck*

deck² /dek/ *verb*
be decked out *phrasal verb* to be decorated with something, or dressed in something special *The bar was decked out with red and yellow flags.*

deckchair /ˈdektʃeəʳ/ *noun* [C] a folding chair that you use outside

declaration /ˌdekləˈreɪʃᵊn/ *noun* [C] an announcement, often one that is written and official *a declaration of independence*

declare /dɪˈkleəʳ/ *verb* [T] **1** SAY PUBLICLY to announce something publicly or officially *to declare war* [+ **that**] *Scientists have declared that this meat is safe to eat.* **2** TAX to officially tell someone the value of goods you have bought, or the amount of money you have earned because you might have to pay tax *Have you got anything to declare?*

WORD PARTNERS FOR ***decline***

be **in** decline • a **sharp/steady/steep** decline • a decline **in** sth

decline¹ /dɪˈklaɪn/ *noun* [C, U] when something becomes less in amount, importance, quality, or strength *a steady* ***decline in*** *sales/standards*

decline² /dɪˈklaɪn/ *verb* **1** REFUSE [I, T] *formal* If you decline something, you refuse it politely. *She* ***declined*** *his* ***offer*** *of a lift.* [+ **to do sth**] *He* ***declined to comment.*** **2** BECOME LESS [I] to become less in amount, importance, quality, or strength *Sales of records have declined steadily.*

decode /ˌdiːˈkəʊd/ *verb* [T] to discover the meaning of a message that is in code (= secret system of communication)

decoder /diːˈkəʊdəʳ/ *noun* [C] a piece of equipment that allows you to receive particular television signals

decompose /ˌdiːkəmˈpəʊz/ *verb* [I] **BIOLOGY** If a dead person, animal, or plant decomposes, it decays and is gradually destroyed. *a decomposing body* •**decomposition** /ˌdiːkɒmpəˈzɪʃᵊn/

decomposer /ˌdiːkəmˈpəʊzəʳ/ *noun* [C] **BIOLOGY** an organism such as a bacterium or fungus that makes dead plant and animal material decay

decor /ˈdeɪkɔːʳ/ ⓤⓢ /deɪˈkɔːr/ *noun* [U no plural] the style of decoration and furniture in a room or building

OTHER WAYS OF SAYING ***decorate***

The verbs **refurbish**, **renovate** and **revamp** are common alternatives to 'decorate' when you are talking about improving the appearance of a room or building: *The University library is currently being* ***refurbished.*** • *They were in the process of* ***renovating*** *an old barn.* • *The restaurant has recently been* ***revamped.***

Another alternative used in more informal situations is the phrasal verb **do up**: *He's bought an old cottage and is gradually* ***doing it up.***

O‒ **decorate** /ˈdekᵊreɪt/ *verb* **1** MAKE ATTRACTIVE [T] to make something look more attractive by putting things on it or around it *They decorated the room with balloons for her party.* **2** PAINT [I, T] to put paint or paper on the walls or other surfaces of a room or building *The whole house needs decorating.* **3 be decorated** to be given a medal (= small, metal disc) as official respect for military action *He was decorated for bravery.*

decoration /ˌdekᵊˈreɪʃᵊn/ *noun* **1** ATTRACTIVE THING [C, U] when you make something look more attractive by putting things on it or around it, or something that you use to do this ***Christmas decorations*** ○ *She hung some pictures around the room for decoration.* **2** PAINT [U] when the walls or other surfaces of rooms or buildings are covered with paint or paper *This place is badly in need of decoration.* **3** OFFICIAL RESPECT [C] an official sign of respect such as a medal (= small, metal disc)

decorative /ˈdekᵊrətɪv/ *adjective* making something or someone look more attractive *decorative objects*

decorator /ˈdekᵊreɪtəʳ/ *noun* [C] **1** SOMEONE WHO PAINTS *UK* someone whose job is to put paint or paper on the walls and other surfaces of rooms or buildings **2** SOMEONE WHO DESIGNS *US* someone whose job is to design the appearance of rooms in houses and buildings

decorum /dɪˈkɔːrəm/ *noun* [U] *formal* behaviour which is considered to be polite and correct

decoy /ˈdiːkɔɪ/ *noun* [C] someone or something used to lead a person or animal to a place so that they can be caught

OTHER WAYS OF SAYING ***decrease***

The verbs **lessen**, **lower**, and **reduce**, and the phrasal verb **bring down** are often used when someone decreases an amount or level: *They've just* ***lowered*** *the age at which you can join.* • *Exercise* ***reduces*** *the chance of heart disease.* • *They are* ***bringing down*** *their prices.*

The verbs **drop** and **fall**, and the phrasal verbs **go down** and **come down** are often used when a level or amount decreases: *Unemployment has* ***dropped/fallen*** *from 8% to 6% in the last year.* • *Prices always* ***come/go down*** *after Christmas.*

If a level or amount decreases very quickly, the verbs **plummet** and **plunge** are sometimes used: *Temperatures last night* ***plummeted/plunged*** *below zero.*

If the size of something decreases, the verb **shrink** is sometimes used. The verb **contract** is used in technical contexts: *Forests have* ***shrunk*** *to almost half the size they were 20 years ago.* • *As the metal cools, it* ***contracts.***

WORD PARTNERS FOR ***decrease***

a **marked/significant/slight** decrease • a decrease **in** sth • a decrease **of** [5%/1000, etc]

decrease /dɪˈkriːs/ *verb* [I, T] to become less, or to make something become less *During the summer months, rainfall decreases.* •**decrease** /ˈdiːkriːs/ *noun* [C, U] *There has been a* ***decrease in*** *the number of violent crimes.* ⊃Opposite **increase**

decree /dɪˈkriː/ *noun* [C] **POLITICS** an official order or decision from a government or leader *a presidential/royal decree* •**decree** *verb* [T] **decreeing**, *past* **decreed**

decrepit /dɪˈkrepɪt/ *adjective* old and in very bad condition *a decrepit building*

decrypt /dɪˈkrɪpt/ *verb* [T] **COMPUTING** to change electronic information from a secret system of letters, numbers, or symbols back into a form that people can understand

D

dedicate /ˈdedɪkeɪt/ *verb* **1 dedicate your life/yourself to sth** to give most of your energy and time to something *She has dedicated her life to helping others.* **2 dedicate sth to sb** to say that something you have made or done is to show your love or respect for someone [**often passive**] *This book is dedicated to my daughter.*

dedicated /ˈdedɪkeɪtɪd/ *adjective* **1** GIVING TIME/ENERGY believing that something is very important and giving a lot of time and energy to it *a dedicated teacher* **2** FOR PURPOSE designed to be used for a particular purpose *a dedicated word processor*

dedication /ˌdedɪˈkeɪʃᵊn/ *noun* **1** QUALITY [U] when you are willing to give a lot of time and energy to something because you believe it is very important *She thanked the staff for their dedication and enthusiasm.* **2** RESPECT [C] when someone says that something has been made or done to show love and respect for someone else *a dedication to the poet's mother*

deduce /dɪˈdjuːs/ *verb* [T] to decide that something is true using the available information [+ **(that)**] *From the contents of his shopping basket, I deduced that he was single.*

deduct /dɪˈdʌkt/ *verb* [T] **MATHEMATICS** to take an amount or a part of something away from a total *The company will* ***deduct*** *tax* ***from*** *your earnings.* ○ *Marks are deducted for spelling mistakes.*

deduction /dɪˈdʌkʃᵊn/ *noun* [C, U] **1 MATHEMATICS** when an amount or a part of something is taken away from a total, or the amount that is taken *tax deductions* **2** when you decide that something is true using the available information

deed /diːd/ *noun* [C] **1** *formal* something that you do *good deeds* ○ *I judge a person by their deeds, not their words.* **2 LAW** a legal document recording an agreement, especially saying who owns something [**usually plural**] *Where do you keep the deeds to the house?*

deem /diːm/ *verb* [T] *formal* to judge or consider something in a particular way *The book was deemed to be unsuitable for children.*

o- **deep**[1] /diːp/ *adjective* **1** TOP TO BOTTOM having a long distance from the top to the bottom *The water is a lot deeper than it seems.* **2** FRONT TO BACK having a long distance from the front to the back *How deep are the shelves?* **3 one metre/6ft, etc deep** one metre/6 ft, etc from the top to the bottom, or from the front the back *This end of the pool is two metres deep.* **4** FEELING A deep feeling is very strong. *deep affection/regret* **5** SOUND A deep sound is low. *a deep voice* **6** SERIOUS serious and difficult for most people to understand *a* ***deep and meaningful*** *conversation* **7 a deep sleep** when someone is sleeping in a way that makes it difficult to wake them up **8** COLOUR A deep colour is strong and dark. *deep brown eyes* **9 take a deep breath** to fill your lungs with air *Take a deep breath and relax.* **10 deep in thought/conversation** giving all of your attention to what you are thinking or talking about, and not noticing anything else ➲See also: throw sb in at the deep **end**[1], be in deep **water**[1]

o- **deep**[2] /diːp/ *adverb* **1** a long way into something from the top or outside *They travelled deep into the forest.* **2 deep down** If you know or feel something deep down, you are certain that it is true, or you feel it strongly although you do not admit it or show it. *Deep down, I knew that I was right.* **3 go/run deep** If a feeling or a problem goes deep, it is very strong or serious and has existed for a long time.

deepen /ˈdiːpᵊn/ *verb* [I, T] **1** DEEPER to become deeper, or to make something become deeper *The sky deepened to a rich, dark blue.* **2** WORSE to become worse, or to make something become worse *a* ***deepening crisis***

ˌdeep ˈfreeze *UK* (*US* **ˈdeep ˌfreeze**) *noun* [C] *another word for* freezer (= a large container in which food can be frozen and stored)

deep-fried /ˌdiːpˈfraɪd/ *adjective* **FOOD** fried in a lot of oil

deeply /ˈdiːpli/ *adverb* **1** very much *I have fallen deeply in love with her.* **2 breathe deeply** to fill your lungs with air

deep-seated /ˌdiːpˈsiːtɪd/ (*also* **deep-rooted**) *adjective* strongly felt or believed and difficult to change ***deep-seated fears/problems***

deer /dɪəʳ/ *noun* [C] *plural* **deer** a large, wild animal that is sometimes hunted for food and which has antlers (= long horns) if it is male

deface /dɪˈfeɪs/ *verb* [T] to spoil the appearance of something, especially by writing or painting on it *Several posters have been defaced with political slogans.*

default[1] /dɪˈfɔːlt/ *noun* **1** [**no plural**] what exists or happens usually if no changes are made **2 by default** If something happens by default, it happens only because something else does not happen. *No one else stood in the election, so he won by default.* •**default** *adjective* [**always before noun**] *The default font size is 10.*

default[2] /dɪˈfɔːlt/ *verb* [I] **FINANCE** to not do what you have made an agreement to do, especially paying back money you have borrowed *They have* ***defaulted on*** *their debt repayments.*

o- **defeat**[1] /dɪˈfiːt/ *verb* [T] **1** WIN to win against someone in a fight or competition *She was defeated by an Australian player in the first round of the tournament.* **2** MAKE FAIL to make someone or something fail *The bill was narrowly defeated in parliament.*

WORD PARTNERS FOR ***defeat***

admit/face/suffer defeat • a **comprehensive/crushing/humiliating/narrow** defeat

o- **defeat**[2] /dɪˈfiːt/ *noun* **1** LOSE [C, U] when someone loses against someone else in a fight or competition *The Chicago Cubs have* ***suffered*** *their worst* ***defeat*** *of the season.* **2** FAIL [**no**

plural] when someone or something is made to fail *the defeat of apartheid*

defeatism /dɪˈfiːtɪzᵊm/ *noun* [U] behaviour or thoughts that show that you do not expect to be successful

defeatist /dɪˈfiːtɪst/ *adjective* behaving in a way that shows that you do not expect to be successful *a **defeatist attitude*** •**defeatist** *noun* [C]

defect¹ /ˈdiːfekt/ *noun* [C] a fault or problem with someone or something *a birth defect* ○ *A mechanical defect caused the plane to crash.* •**defective** /dɪˈfektɪv/ *adjective* having a fault or problem ***defective goods***

defect² /dɪˈfekt/ *verb* [I] **POLITICS** to leave your country or organization and go to join an enemy country or competing organization *He **defected to** the West.* •**defection** /dɪˈfekʃᵊn/ *noun* [C, U] when someone defects •**defector** *noun* [C]

WORD PARTNERS FOR ***defence***

mount/put up a defence • an **effective/spirited/strong/vigorous** defence • defence **against** sth • [argue, etc] **in** defence **of** sth

O-**defence** *UK* (*US* **defense**) /dɪˈfens/ *noun* **1** MILITARY [U] the weapons and military forces that a country uses to protect itself against attack *Government spending on defence is increasing.* ○ *the defence minister/industry* **2** PROTECTION [C, U] protection, or something that provides protection against attack or criticism *the body's **defences against** infection* ○ *She argued strongly **in defence of** her actions.* **3 come to sb's defence** to support someone when they are being criticized **4 the defence LAW** [group] the lawyers in a court who work in support of the person who is accused of a crime *He was cross-examined by the defence.* ○ *a **defence lawyer*** **5 SPORT** [C, U] the part of a sports team which tries to prevent the other team from scoring points ➲See also: **self-defence**

defenceless *UK* (*US* **defenseless**) /dɪˈfensləs/ *adjective* weak and unable to protect yourself from attack *a small, defenceless child*

O-**defend** /dɪˈfend/ *verb* **1** PROTECT [T] to protect someone or something from being attacked, especially by fighting *The army was sent in to **defend** the country **against** enemy attack.* [**often reflexive**] *She tried to defend herself with a knife.* **2** SUPPORT [T] to support someone or something that is being criticized *The newspaper's editor **defended** his **decision** to publish the photos.* **3 LAW** [T] to try to show in a court that someone is not guilty of a crime *He has hired two lawyers to defend him in court.* **4 SPORT** [I, T] to try to stop the other sports team from scoring points **5 defend a championship/title, etc SPORT** to try to win a match or competition that you have won before •**defender** *noun* [C]

defendant /dɪˈfendənt/ *noun* [C] **LAW** the person in a court who is accused of a crime

O-**defense** /dɪˈfens/ *noun* **LAW, SPORT** *US spelling of* defence

defenseless /dɪˈfensləs/ *adjective US spelling of* defenceless

defensive¹ /dɪˈfensɪv/ *adjective* **1** CRITICISM quick to protect yourself from being criticized *He's very **defensive about** his weight.* **2 SPORT** *mainly US* A defensive player in a sports team tries to stop the other team scoring points. **3** ATTACK done or used to protect someone or something from attack •**defensively** *adverb*

defensive² /dɪˈfensɪv/ *noun* **on the defensive** ready to protect yourself because you are expecting to be criticized or attacked

defer /dɪˈfɜːʳ/ *verb* [T] **deferring**, *past* **deferred** to arrange for something to happen at a later time *The payments can be deferred for three months.*

deference /ˈdefᵊrᵊns/ *noun* [U] polite behaviour that shows that you respect someone or something •**deferential** /ˌdefᵊˈrenʃᵊl/ *adjective*

defiance /dɪˈfaɪəns/ *noun* [U] when you refuse to obey someone or something *an **act of defiance***

defiant /dɪˈfaɪənt/ *adjective* refusing to obey someone or something *a defiant child* •**defiantly** *adverb*

WORD PARTNERS FOR ***deficiency***

a **glaring/major/serious/severe** deficiency • a deficiency **in** sth

deficiency /dɪˈfɪʃᵊnsi/ *noun* [C, U] **1** NOT ENOUGH when you do not have enough of something *a **vitamin deficiency*** **2** FAULT a mistake or fault in something so that it is not good enough *Parents are complaining of serious **deficiencies in** the education system.*

deˈficiency diˌsease *noun* [C] **HEALTH** a disease caused by not getting enough vitamins or other substances that are important for the body

deficient /dɪˈfɪʃᵊnt/ *adjective* **1** NOT HAVING ENOUGH not having enough of something *If you have poor night vision you may be **deficient in** vitamin A.* **2** NOT GOOD ENOUGH not good enough *His theory is deficient in several respects.*

deficit /ˈdefɪsɪt/ *noun* [C] **FINANCE** the amount by which the money that you spend is more than the money that you receive *a **budget deficit***

defile /dɪˈfaɪl/ *verb* [T] *formal* to spoil someone or something that is pure, holy, or beautiful

define /dɪˈfaɪn/ *verb* [T] **1** MEANING to say exactly what something means, or what someone or something is like *Your duties are clearly defined in the contract.* **2** SHAPE to show the outer edges or shape of something *It has sharply defined edges.*

O-**definite** /ˈdefɪnət/ *adjective* **1** CERTAIN certain, fixed, and not likely to change *We need a definite answer by tomorrow.* **2** CLEAR clear and obvious *There has been a definite improvement in her behaviour.*

ˌdefinite ˈarticle *noun* [C] **LANGUAGE** in grammar, used to mean the word 'the' ➲Compare **indefinite article**

O-**definitely** /ˈdefɪnətli/ *adverb* without any doubt *This book is definitely worth reading.* ○ *"Do you want to come?" "Yes, definitely."*

definition /ˌdefɪˈnɪʃᵊn/ *noun* **1** [C] an explanation of the meaning of a word or phrase *a* *dictionary definition* **2 ART** [U] how clear an image of something is in a photograph or on a screen

definitive /dɪ'fɪnətɪv/ *adjective* **1** CERTAIN certain, clear, and not likely to change *a **definitive answer*** **2** BEST A definitive book or piece of work is the best of its type. *the definitive guide to London* •**definitively** *adverb*

D

deflate /dɪ'fleɪt/ *verb* **1** LOSE AIR [I, T] to let all the air or gas out of something, or to become emptied of air or gas *to deflate a balloon/tyre* **2** CONFIDENCE [T] to make someone lose confidence or feel less important [**often passive**] *They were totally deflated by losing the match.* **3 ECONOMICS** to reduce the supply of money in an economy

deflation /dɪ'fleɪʃᵊn/ *noun* [U] **ECONOMICS** a reduction of the supply of money in an economy, and because of this a reduction of economic activity, which is often part of an intentional government plan to reduce prices ⊃Compare **inflation**

deflationary /dɪ'fleɪʃᵊnᵊri/ *adjective* **ECONOMICS** causing deflation ⊃Compare **inflationary**

deflect /dɪ'flekt/ *verb* **1** [I, T] to make something change direction by hitting or touching it, or to change direction after hitting something *The ball was deflected into the corner of the net.* **2 deflect attention/blame/criticism, etc** to cause attention/blame/criticism, etc to be directed away from you •**deflection** /dɪ'flekʃᵊn/ *noun* [C, U]

deforestation /diːˌfɒrɪ'steɪʃᵊn/ *noun* [U] **ENVIRONMENT** when all the trees in a large area are cut down

deformed /dɪ'fɔːmd/ *adjective* **HEALTH** with a shape that has not developed normally *deformed hands* •**deform** /dɪ'fɔːm/ *verb* [T]

deformity /dɪ'fɔːməti/ *noun* [C, U] **HEALTH** when a part of the body has not developed in the normal way, or with the normal shape

defraud /dɪ'frɔːd/ *verb* [T] **FINANCE** to obtain money from someone illegally by being dishonest

defrost /ˌdiː'frɒst/ *verb* [I, T] **1 FOOD** If food defrosts, it becomes warmer after being frozen, and if you defrost it, you make it become warmer after being frozen. *You need to defrost the fish before you can cook it.* **2** If you defrost a fridge or freezer (= machines that keep food cold), you make them warmer and remove the ice, and if they defrost, they become warmer and the ice melts.

deft /deft/ *adjective* quick and showing great skill *a **deft movement/touch*** •**deftly** *adverb formal*

defunct /dɪ'fʌŋkt/ *adjective* not working or existing now

defuse /ˌdiː'fjuːz/ *verb* [T] **1** SITUATION to make a difficult or dangerous situation calmer *He made a joke to **defuse** the **tension**.* **2** BOMB to prevent a bomb from exploding by removing the fuse (= part that starts the explosion)

defy /dɪ'faɪ/ *verb* **1** [T] to refuse to obey someone or something *Some of these children openly defy their teachers.* **2 defy belief/description/explanation, etc** to be impossible to believe, describe, explain, etc *His attitude defies belief.* **3 defy sb to do sth** to tell someone to do something that you think will be impossible *I defy you to prove that I'm wrong.*

degenerate¹ /dɪ'dʒenᵊreɪt/ *verb* [I] to become worse *The protest soon **degenerated into** violence.* •**degeneration** /dɪˌdʒenə'reɪʃᵊn/ *noun* [U]

degenerate² /dɪ'dʒenᵊrət/ *adjective* having low moral principles

degrade /dɪ'greɪd/ *verb* [T] **1** NO RESPECT to treat someone without respect and as if they have no value *They think the advert degrades women.* **2** DAMAGE to damage the quality or condition of something **3 CHEMISTRY** to change into a more simple chemical substance •**degradation** /ˌdegrə'deɪʃᵊn/ *noun* [U]

degrading /dɪ'greɪdɪŋ/ *adjective* treating people without respect and as if they have no value *degrading work*

O-- **degree** /dɪ'griː/ *noun* **1 MEASURES** [C] a unit for measuring temperature, shown by the symbol ° written after a number **2 MATHEMATICS, MEASURES** [C] a unit for measuring angles, shown by the symbol ° written after a number **3 EDUCATION** [C] a qualification given for completing a university course *She has a **degree in** physics.* **4** [C, U] an amount or level of something *I agree with you **to a degree*** (= in some ways but not completely). ⊃See also: **Master's (degree)**

dehydrated /ˌdiːhaɪ'dreɪtɪd/ *adjective* **HEALTH** not having enough water in your body

dehydration /ˌdiːhaɪ'dreɪʃᵊn/ *noun* [U] **1 HEALTH** when you do not have enough water in your body **2** the process of removing water from something

deign /deɪn/ *verb* **deign to do sth** to do something that you think you are too important to do

deindustrialization (*also UK* **-isation**) /diːɪnˌdʌstriᵊlaɪ'zeɪʃᵊn/ *noun* [U] **ECONOMICS** the process by which a country or area stops having so much industry

deity /'deɪɪti/ (US) /'diːəti/ *noun* [C] **RELIGION** *formal* a god or goddess (= female god)

deja vu /ˌdeɪʒɑː'vuː/ *noun* [U] a feeling that you have already experienced exactly what is happening now *She suddenly had a strong **sense of deja vu**.*

dejected /dɪ'dʒektɪd/ *adjective* unhappy and disappointed *He looked tired and dejected.* •**dejection** /dɪ'dʒekʃᵊn/ *noun* [U]

O-- **delay¹** /dɪ'leɪ/ *verb* **1** CHANGE TIME [I, T] to make something happen at a later time than originally planned or expected *Can you delay your departure until next week?* **2** MAKE LATE [T] to cause someone or something to be slow or late [**often passive**] *I was delayed by traffic.*

WORD PARTNERS FOR ***delay***

a brief/short/slight delay • **a considerable/lengthy/long** delay • **cause** delays • **experience/face/suffer** delays

O-- **delay²** /dɪ'leɪ/ *noun* [C, U] when you have to wait longer than expected for something to happen, or the time that you have to wait *An accident **caused long delays** on the motorway.*

delayering /diːˈleɪərɪŋ/ *noun* [U] when a company or organization reduces the number of its managers

delectable /dɪˈlektəbl/ *adjective formal* extremely nice, especially to eat

delegate¹ /ˈdelɪgət/ *noun* [C] someone who is sent somewhere to represent a group of people, especially at a meeting

delegate² /ˈdelɪgeɪt/ *verb* [I, T] to give someone else part of your work or some of your responsibilities

delegation /ˌdelɪˈgeɪʃən/ *noun* **1** GROUP [C] a group of people who have been chosen to represent a much larger group of people *a delegation of Chinese officials* **2** WORK [U] when you give someone else part of your work or some of your responsibilities

delete /dɪˈliːt/ *verb* [T] **COMPUTING** to remove something, especially from a computer's memory *All names have been deleted from the report.* •**deletion** /dɪˈliːʃən/ *noun* [C, U]

deli /ˈdeli/ *noun* [C] *short for* delicatessen

deliberate¹ /dɪˈlɪbərət/ *adjective* **1** INTENTIONAL done intentionally, or planned *This was a **deliberate attempt** by them to deceive us.* **2** SLOW careful and without hurry *Her movements were calm and deliberate.*

deliberate² /dɪˈlɪbəreɪt/ *verb* [I, T] to consider something carefully before making a decision *They deliberated for ten hours before reaching a decision.*

O‑ **deliberately** /dɪˈlɪbərətli/ *adverb* intentionally, having planned to do something *He deliberately lied to the police.*

deliberation /dɪˌlɪbəˈreɪʃən/ *noun* [C, U] careful thought or talk about a subject before a decision is made *The jury began deliberations on Thursday.*

delicacy /ˈdelɪkəsi/ *noun* **1** **FOOD** [C] a special food, usually something rare or expensive **2** GENTLE QUALITY [U] the quality of being soft, light, or gentle **3** EASY TO DAMAGE [U] when something is easy to damage or break **4** NEEDING CARE [U] when something needs to be treated very carefully *You need to be very tactful because of the delicacy of the situation.* **5** ATTRACTIVE [U] when something has a thin, attractive shape

delicate /ˈdelɪkət/ *adjective* **1** GENTLE soft, light, or gentle *a delicate flavour* ○ *a delicate shade of pink* **2** EASY TO DAMAGE easy to damage or break *a delicate china cup* **3** NEEDING CARE needing to be dealt with very carefully *I need to discuss a very delicate matter with you.* **4** ATTRACTIVE having a thin, attractive shape *delicate hands* •**delicately** *adverb*

delicatessen /ˌdelɪkəˈtesən/ *noun* [C] a shop, or a part of a shop which sells cheeses, cooked meats, salads, etc

delicious /dɪˈlɪʃəs/ *adjective* If food or drink is delicious, it smells or tastes extremely good. *This soup is absolutely delicious.* •**deliciously** *adverb*

delight¹ /dɪˈlaɪt/ *noun* **1** PLEASURE [U] happiness and excited pleasure *The children screamed with delight.* **2** PERSON/THING [C] someone or something that gives you pleasure

delight² /dɪˈlaɪt/ *verb* [T] to make someone feel very pleased and happy *The new discovery has delighted scientists everywhere.*

delight in sth/doing sth *phrasal verb* to get a lot of pleasure from something, especially something unpleasant *She seems to delight in making him look stupid.*

delighted /dɪˈlaɪtɪd/ *adjective* very pleased [**+ to do sth**] *I'd be delighted to accept your invitation.* ○ *They are **delighted with** their new car.*

delightful /dɪˈlaɪtfəl/ *adjective* very pleasant, attractive, or enjoyable *We had a delightful evening.* •**delightfully** *adverb*

delinquency /dɪˈlɪŋkwənsi/ *noun* [U] **LAW** criminal or bad behaviour, especially by young people

delinquent /dɪˈlɪŋkwənt/ *noun* [C] **LAW** a young person who behaves badly, usually by committing crimes •**delinquent** *adjective delinquent behaviour*

deliquesce /ˌdelɪˈkwes/ *verb* [I] **CHEMISTRY** to dissolve in water from the air around •**deliquescence** /ˌdelɪˈkwesənts/ *noun* [U]

delirious /dɪˈlɪriəs/ *adjective* **1** **HEALTH** speaking or thinking in a confused way, often because of a fever or drugs **2** extremely happy *delirious fans* •**deliriously** *adverb*

deliver /dɪˈlɪvər/ *verb* **1** TAKE [I, T] to take things such as letters, parcels, or goods to a person or place *They can deliver the sofa on Wednesday.* **2** PROMISE [I, T] to achieve or do something that you have promised to do, or that people expect you to do *The company failed to deliver the high quality service that we expect.* **3** **deliver a speech/talk, etc** to speak formally to a group of people *She delivered the speech on national TV.* **4** **deliver a baby** to help take a baby out of its mother when it is being born ➲See also: deliver/come up with the **goods**

delivery /dɪˈlɪvəri/ *noun* [C, U] **1** LETTERS when someone takes things such as letters, parcels, or goods to a person or place *Is there a charge for delivery?* **2** BABY when a baby is born and comes out of its mother *Her husband was present at the delivery.*

delta /ˈdeltə/ *noun* [C] **GEOGRAPHY** a low, flat area of land where a river divides into smaller rivers and goes into the sea *the Nile delta*

delude /dɪˈluːd/ *verb* [T] to make someone believe something that is not real or true [**often reflexive + into + doing sth**] *She deluded herself into thinking she could win.* •**deluded** *adjective* believing things that are not real or true

deluge¹ /ˈdeljuːdʒ/ *noun* [C] **1** LARGE AMOUNT a very large amount of something that suddenly arrives *They have received a deluge of complaints.* **2** RAIN a sudden, large amount of rain, or a flood

deluge² /ˈdeljuːdʒ/ *verb* **be deluged with/by sth** to receive very large amounts of something suddenly *Our switchboard was deluged with calls last night.*

delusion /dɪˈluːʒən/ *noun* [C, U] when someone believes something that is not true [**+ (that)**]

*She is **under the delusion** that her debts will just go away.*

deluxe /də'lʌks/ *adjective* luxurious and of very high quality *a deluxe hotel*

delve /delv/ *verb* **delve in/into/inside, etc** to search in a container to try to find something *He delved in his pocket and pulled out a pen.* **delve into sth** *phrasal verb* to examine something carefully in order to discover more information about someone or something *I don't like to delve too deeply into his past.*

D

WORD PARTNERS FOR ***demand***

increase/meet/satisfy demand • **great/growing/high/steady** demand • be **in** demand • demand **for** sth

demand¹ /dɪ'mɑːnd/ *noun* **1 ECONOMICS** [**U, no plural**] a need for something to be sold or supplied *There's an increasing **demand for** cheap housing.* **2** [**C**] a strong request *They received a final **demand for** payment.* **3 in demand** wanted or needed in large numbers *Good teachers are always in demand.*

demand² /dɪ'mɑːnd/ *verb* [**T**] **1** ASK to ask for something in a way that shows that you do not expect to be refused *I demanded an explanation.* [+ **that**] *The survivors are demanding that the airline pays them compensation.* ⊃See Common Learner Error at **ask 2** NEED to need something such as time or effort *This job demands a high level of concentration.*

demanding /dɪ'mɑːndɪŋ/ *adjective* needing a lot of your time, attention, or effort *a very demanding job*

demands /dɪ'mɑːndz/ *noun* [**plural**] the difficult things that you have to do *the demands of modern life* ○ *His new job **makes** a lot of **demands on** him* (= he has to work very hard).

demarcation dispute /ˌdiːmɑː'keɪʃən-ˌdɪspjuːt/ *noun* [**C**] a disagreement between trade unions (= organizations of workers) about what types of work should be done by the members of each of them

demeaning /dɪ'miːnɪŋ/ *adjective* If something is demeaning, it makes you feel that you are not respected. *Some people consider beauty competitions **demeaning to** women.*

demeanour *UK* (*US* **demeanor**) /dɪ'miːnəʳ/ *noun* [**C**] the way that someone looks, seems, and behaves *a quiet, serious demeanour*

demented /dɪ'mentɪd/ *adjective* mentally ill, or behaving in a very strange way without any control

dementia /dɪ'menʃə/ *noun* [**U**] **HEALTH** a mental illness suffered especially by old people

demi- /demi-/ *prefix* half, partly *demitasse* (= a small coffee cup) ○ *demigod* (= a creature that is part god and part human)

demise /dɪ'maɪz/ *noun* **1** [**no plural**] when something ends, usually because it has stopped being popular or successful *the demise of apartheid* **2 sb's demise** someone's death

demo¹ /'deməʊ/ *noun* [**C**] **1** EXAMPLE an example of a product, given or shown to someone to try to make them buy it *a software demo* **2 POLITICS** *UK short for* demonstration (= political march) *a student demo*

demo² /'deməʊ/ *verb* [**T**] to show something and explain how it works *We need someone to demo a new piece of software.*

WORD PARTNERS FOR ***democracy***

an **emerging/new** democracy • **in** a democracy

democracy /dɪ'mɒkrəsi/ *noun* [**C, U**] **POLITICS** a system of government in which people elect their leaders, or a country with this system

democrat /'deməkræt/ *noun* [**C**] **1 POLITICS** someone who supports democracy **2 Democrat POLITICS** someone who supports the Democratic Party in the US *the Democrat candidate* ⊃See also: **Liberal Democrat**

democratic /ˌdemə'krætɪk/ *adjective* **1 POLITICS** following or supporting the political system of democracy *a democratic society/government* **2 POLITICS** where everyone has equal rights and can help to make decisions *a democratic discussion/debate* •**democratically** *adverb a democratically elected government*

the Demoˈcratic ˌParty *noun* [**group**] **POLITICS** one of the two main political parties in the US

demographics /ˌdemə'græfɪks/ *noun* [**plural**] **SOCIETY** the quantity and characteristics of the people who live in a particular area, for example their age, how much money they have, etc.

demography /dɪ'mɒgrəfi/ *noun* [**U**] **SOCIETY** the study of the characteristics of people in a particular area •**demographic** /ˌdemə'græfɪk/ *adjective*

demolish /dɪ'mɒlɪʃ/ *verb* [**T**] **1** DESTROY to destroy something such as a building *The factory is dangerous, and will have to be demolished.* **2** PROVE WRONG to show that an idea or argument is wrong *He completely demolished my argument.*

demolition /ˌdemə'lɪʃᵊn/ *noun* [**C, U**] when something such as a building is destroyed *the demolition of dangerous buildings*

demon /'diːmən/ *noun* [**C**] an evil spirit

demonic /dɪ'mɒnɪk/ *adjective* evil

demonstrable /dɪ'mɒnstrəbl/ *adjective* Something that is demonstrable can be shown to exist or be true. *a demonstrable fact* •**demonstrably** *adverb*

demonstrate /'demənstreɪt/ *verb* **1** PROVE [**T**] to show or prove that something exists or is true [+ **that**] *The survey clearly demonstrates that tourism can have positive benefits.* **2** SHOW HOW [**T**] to show someone how to do something, or how something works *She demonstrated how to use the new software.* **3** EXPRESS [**T**] to express or show that you have a feeling, quality, or ability *He has demonstrated a genuine interest in the project.* **4** MARCH [**I**] to march or stand with a group of people to show that you disagree with or support someone or something *Thousands of people gathered to **demonstrate against** the new proposals.*

WORD PARTNERS FOR ***demonstration***

hold/organize/stage a demonstration • **go on/take part in** a demonstration • a **mass** demonstration • a demonstration **against** sth

demonstration /ˌdemən'streɪʃᵊn/ *noun* **1** **POLITICS** [C] when a group of people march or stand together to show that they disagree with or support someone or something *They're taking part in a* ***demonstration against*** *the causes of climate change.* **2** SHOWING HOW [C, U] showing how to do something, or how something works *We asked the sales assistant to* ***give*** *us a* ***demonstration***. **3** PROOF [C, U] proof that something exists or is true *This disaster is a clear demonstration of the need for tighter controls.*

demonstrative /dɪ'mɒnstrətɪv/ *adjective* willing to show your feelings, especially your affection

demonstrator /'demənstreɪtəʳ/ *noun* [C] **POLITICS** a person who marches or stands with a group of people to show that they disagree with or support someone or something

demoralized (*also UK* **-ised**) /dɪ'mɒrəlaɪzd/ *adjective* having lost your confidence, enthusiasm, and hope *After the match, the players were tired and demoralized.* •**demoralizing** *adjective* making you lose your confidence, enthusiasm, and hope *a demoralizing defeat* •**demoralize** /dɪ'mɒrəlaɪz/ *verb* [T]

demote /dɪ'məʊt/ *verb* **be demoted** to be moved to a less important job or position, especially as a punishment •**demotion** /dɪ'məʊʃᵊn/ *noun* [C, U]

demotivated /ˌdiː'məʊtɪveɪtɪd/ *adjective* not having any enthusiasm for your work

demure /dɪ'mjʊəʳ/ *adjective* If a young woman is demure, she is quiet and shy. •**demurely** *adverb*

den /den/ *noun* [C] **1** ANIMAL'S HOME the home of some wild animals *a lions' den* **2** ILLEGAL ACTIVITY a place where secret and illegal activity happens *a gambling den* **3** ROOM *mainly US* a room in your home where you relax, read, watch television, etc

denature /diː'neɪtʃəʳ/ *verb* [T] **CHEMISTRY** to change the characteristics of a substance, for example by the action of heat or acid

dendrite /'dendraɪt/ *noun* [C] **BIOLOGY** the short parts like threads at the edge of a nerve cell that carry messages to the cell

WORD PARTNERS FOR ***denial***

issue a denial • a **categorical/emphatic/strenuous/vehement** denial • denial **of** sth

denial /dɪ'naɪəl/ *noun* **1** NOT TRUE [C, U] when you say that something is not true *a* ***denial of*** *his guilt* **2** NOT ALLOWING [U] not allowing someone to have or do something *the denial of medical treatment*

denigrate /'denɪgreɪt/ *verb* [T] to criticize and not show much respect for someone or something

denim /'denɪm/ *noun* [U] thick, strong, cotton cloth, usually blue, which is used to make clothes *a* ***denim jacket***

denitrify /di'naɪtrɪfaɪ/ *verb* [T] **CHEMISTRY** to break up nitrates (= chemicals containing nitrogen and oxygen), for example in soil, and so release nitrogen into the air *denitrifying bacteria* •**denitrification** /diˌnaɪtrɪ.fɪ'keɪʃᵊn/ *noun* [U] ➲See picture at **nitrogen cycle**

denomination /dɪˌnɒmɪ'neɪʃᵊn/ *noun* [C] **1** **RELIGION** a religious group which has slightly different beliefs from other groups which share the same religion **2** **ECONOMICS, FINANCE** the value of a particular coin, piece of paper money, or stamp

denominator /dɪ'nɒmɪneɪtəʳ/ *noun* [C] **MATHEMATICS** the number below the line in a fraction ➲Compare **numerator**

denote /dɪ'nəʊt/ *verb* [T] to be a sign of something *The colour red is used to denote passion or danger.*

denounce /dɪ'naʊns/ *verb* [T] to publicly criticize someone or something, or to publicly accuse someone of something *They've been* ***denounced as*** *terrorists.*

dense /dens/ *adjective* **1** CLOSE TOGETHER with a lot of people or things close together ***dense forest*** **2** THICK If cloud, smoke, etc is dense, it is thick and difficult to see through. ***dense fog*** **3** SUBSTANCE **PHYSICS** containing a lot of matter in a small space •**densely** *adverb a* ***densely populated*** *area*

density /'densɪti/ *noun* [C, U] **1** the number of people or things in a place when compared with the size of the place *The area has a high population density.* **2** **MEASURES, PHYSICS** the relationship between the weight of a substance and its size *bone density*

dent¹ /dent/ *noun* [C] **1** DAMAGE a hollow area in a hard surface where it has been hit *The car door had a dent in it.* **2** REDUCTION a reduction in something *The cost of repairs* ***made*** *a serious* ***dent in*** *my savings.*

dent² /dent/ *verb* [T] **1** DAMAGE to create a hollow area in the hard surface of something by hitting it *The side of the car was dented in the accident.* **2** REDUCE to reduce someone's confidence or positive feelings about something *The defeat did little to dent her enthusiasm.*

dental /'dentᵊl/ *adjective* **ANATOMY, BIOLOGY** relating to teeth ***dental treatment***

dental floss /'dentᵊlˌflɒs/ *noun* [U] **HEALTH** a thin thread which is used for cleaning between the teeth

dentine /'dentiːn/ *noun* [U] **ANATOMY, BIOLOGY** a hard substance which forms the main part of a tooth and has enamel (= shiny white substance) covering it ➲See picture at **tooth**

dentist /'dentɪst/ *noun* [C] **HEALTH** someone who examines and repairs teeth *I've got an appointment at the dentist's* (= where the dentist works) *tomorrow.* •**dentistry** *noun* [U] the subject or job of examining and repairing teeth

dentition /den'tɪʃᵊn/ *noun* [U] **ANATOMY, BIOLOGY** the number, type and arrangement of teeth in a person or animal

dentures /'dentʃəz/ *noun* [plural] **HEALTH** false teeth

denunciation /dɪˌnʌnsi'eɪʃᵊn/ *noun* [C, U] when you publicly criticize someone or something, or publicly accuse someone of something

o‑ **deny** /dɪ'naɪ/ *verb* [T] **1** NOT TRUE to say that something is not true, especially something that you are accused of [+ **(that)**] *He never denied that he said those things.* [+ **doing sth**] *He denies murdering his father.* **2** NOT ALLOW to not allow someone to have or do something [**often passive**] *These children are being denied access to education.*

deodorant /di'əʊdᵊrᵊnt/ *noun* [**C, U**] a substance that you put on your body to prevent or hide unpleasant smells

D

deoxygenate /diː'ɒksɪdʒəneɪt/ *verb* [**T**] **CHEMISTRY, BIOLOGY** to remove oxygen from a substance *deoxygenated blood* •**deoxygenation** /diːˌɒksɪdʒə'neɪʃən/ *noun* [**U**] ⇨See picture at **circulation**

depart /dɪ'pɑːt/ *verb* [**I**] *formal* to leave a place, especially to start a journey to another place *The train to Lincoln will* ***depart from*** *platform 9.* ○ *He* ***departed for*** *Paris on Tuesday.*

O‑ **department** /dɪ'pɑːtmənt/ *noun* [**C**] a part of an organization such as a school, business, or government which deals with a particular area of work *the sales department* ○ *head of the English department* ⇨See also: **police department**

departmental /ˌdiːpɑːt'mentᵊl/ *adjective* relating to a department *the departmental budget*

de'partment ˌstore *noun* [**C**] a large shop divided into several different parts which sell different types of things

O‑ **departure** /dɪˌpɑːtʃəʳ/ *noun* [**C, U**] **1** LEAVING when someone or something leaves a place, especially to start a journey to another place *the departure of flight BA117* ○ *This fare is valid for weekday* ***departures from*** *Manchester.* **2** CHANGE a change from what is expected, or from what has happened before *This film is a major* ***departure from*** *his previous work.*

O‑ **depend** /dɪ'pend/ *verb* **it/that depends** used to say that you are not certain about something because other things affect your answer [+ **question word**] *"Are you coming out tonight?" "It depends where you're going."*

depend on/upon sb/sth *phrasal verb* **1** NEED to need the help of someone or something in order to exist or continue as before *She depends on her son for everything.* ○ *The city's economy depends largely on the car industry.* **2** BE INFLUENCED BY If something depends on someone or something, it is influenced by them, or changes because of them. [+ **question word**] *The choice depends on what you're willing to spend.* **3** TRUST to be able to trust someone or something to help, or to do what you expect [+ **to do sth**] *You can always depend on Andy to keep his promises.*

COMMON LEARNER ERROR

depend on something

Be careful to choose the correct preposition after **depend**.

I might go on Friday, it depends on the weather.

~~*I might go on Friday, it depends of the weather.*~~

~~*I might go on Friday, it depends from the weather.*~~

dependable /dɪ'pendəbl/ *adjective* able to be trusted and very likely to do what you expect *the team's most dependable player*

dependant *UK* (*US* **dependent**) /dɪ'pendənt/ *noun* [**C**] someone, usually a child, who depends on you for financial support

dependence /dɪ'pendəns/ (*also* **dependency** /dɪ'pendəntsi/) *noun* [**U**] when you need someone or something all the time in order to exist or continue as before *Our society needs to reduce its* ***dependence on*** *the car.*

dependent¹ /dɪ'pendənt/ *adjective* **1** needing the help of someone or something in order to exist or continue as before *She's completely* ***dependent on*** *her parents for money.* **2 dependent on/upon sth** influenced by or decided by something *The amount of tax you pay is dependent on how much you earn.*

dependent² /dɪ'pendənt/ *noun* [**C**] *US spelling of* dependant

deˌpendent 'variable *noun* [**C**] **MATHEMATICS** a number or amount whose value depends on the value of another element in the same mathematical statement ⇨Compare **independent variable**

depict /dɪ'pɪkt/ *verb* [**T**] to represent someone or something in a picture or story *The cartoon* ***depicts*** *the president* ***as*** *a vampire.* •**depiction** /dɪ'pɪkʃᵊn/ *noun* [**C, U**]

deplete /dɪ'pliːt/ *verb* [**T**] to reduce the amount of something, especially a natural supply *Alcohol depletes the body of B vitamins.* •**depletion** /dɪ'pliːʃᵊn/ *noun* [**U**]

deplorable /dɪ'plɔːrəbl/ *adjective* very bad or morally wrong

deplore /dɪ'plɔːʳ/ *verb* [**T**] *formal* to feel or express strong disapproval of something *We deeply deplore the loss of life.*

deploy /dɪ'plɔɪ/ *verb* [**T**] to move soldiers or equipment to a place where they can be used when they are needed •**deployment** *noun* [**U**] *the deployment of nuclear weapons*

deport /dɪ'pɔːt/ *verb* [**T**] to force a foreign person to leave a country *Thousands of illegal immigrants are* ***deported from*** *the US every year.* •**deportation** /ˌdiːpɔː'teɪʃᵊn/ *noun* [**C, U**] *He now faces deportation back to his native country.*

depose /dɪ'pəʊz/ *verb* [**T**] **POLITICS** to remove a ruler or leader from their position of power •**deposed** *adjective the deposed president*

WORD PARTNERS FOR ***deposit***

pay/put down a deposit • a deposit **of** [£500/$300, etc] • a deposit **on** sth

deposit¹ /dɪ'pɒzɪt/ *noun* [**C**] **1** a payment that you make immediately when you decide to buy something, as proof that you will really buy it *They've* ***put down a deposit on*** *a house.* **2 FINANCE** an amount of money that you pay into a bank *to* ***make a deposit*** **3 GEOLOGY** a layer of a substance that has developed from a natural or chemical process *deposits of iron ore* **4 FINANCE** an amount of money that you pay when you rent something, and that is given back to you when you return it without any damage

deposit² /dɪ'pɒzɪt/ *verb* [**T**] **1** PUT DOWN to put something down somewhere *He deposited his books on the table.* **2 FINANCE** to put money into a bank or valuable things into a safe place *She* *deposited $150,000 in a Swiss bank account.* **3** SUBSTANCE to leave something lying on a surface, as a result of a natural or chemical process

de'posit ac,count *noun* [C] *UK* **FINANCE** a bank account that pays interest on the money you put into it and that you use for saving

deposition /ˌdepəˈzɪʃᵊn/ *noun* [U, C] **GEOLOGY** when a layer of a substance such as soil or rock is formed, or the substance that forms the layer

depot /ˈdepəʊ/ *noun* [C] **1** VEHICLES a place where trains, trucks, or buses are kept **2** GOODS a building where supplies of goods are stored **3** STATION *US* a small bus or train station

depraved /dɪˈpreɪvd/ *adjective* morally bad •**depravity** /dɪˈprævəti/ *noun* [U]

depreciate /dɪˈpriːʃieɪt/ *verb* [I] **FINANCE** to lose value over a period of time *New computers depreciate in value very quickly.* •**depreciation** /dɪˌpriːʃiˈeɪʃᵊn/ *noun* [U]

depress /dɪˈpres/ *verb* [T] **1** to make someone feel very unhappy, especially about the future *This place really depresses me.* **2 FINANCE** to reduce the value or level of something, especially in business *Competition between stores has depressed prices.*

depressed /dɪˈprest/ *adjective* **1** very unhappy, often for a long time *She has been feeling very depressed since her marriage broke up.* **2 ECONOMICS** A depressed country, area, or economy does not have enough jobs or business activity. *an economically depressed area*

depressing /dɪˈpresɪŋ/ *adjective* making you feel unhappy and without any hope for the future *The news is very depressing.*

depression /dɪˈpreʃᵊn/ *noun* [C, U] **1 HEALTH** when you feel very unhappy, or a mental illness that makes you feel very unhappy *Nearly three million people **suffer from depression** every year.* **2 ECONOMICS** a time when there is not much business activity *The stock market crash marked the start of a severe depression.* **3** WEATHER an area where the air pressure is low

deprive /dɪˈpraɪv/ *verb*
deprive sb/sth of sth *phrasal verb* to take something important or necessary away from someone or something *They were deprived of food for long periods.* •**deprivation** /ˌdeprɪˈveɪʃᵊn/ *noun* [C, U] ***sleep deprivation***

deprived /dɪˈpraɪvd/ *adjective* not having enough food, money, and the things that you need to have a normal life *children from **deprived backgrounds***

dept *written abbreviation for* department (= a part of an organization or government)

WORD PARTNERS FOR ***depth***

a depth **of** [6 metres/8 inches, etc] • [5cm/7 inches, etc] **in** depth • **at/to** a depth of [5 metres/6 inches, etc]

depth /depθ/ *noun* **1 MEASURES** [C, U] the distance from the top of something to the bottom *The lake reaches a maximum **depth of** 292 metres.* ○ *Dig a hole 10 cm **in depth**.* **2 MEASURES** [C, U] the distance from the front to the back of something **3** [U] how much someone knows or feels about something *She was amazed at the depth of his knowledge.* **4 in depth** giving all the details *With access to the Internet, students can do their homework in greater depth.* **5 be out of your depth** to not have the knowledge, experience or skills to deal with a particular subject or situation

depths /depθs/ *noun* [plural] **1** FAR BELOW a position far below the surface or far into something ***the depths of** the forest* **2** WORST PART the worst period of something *the **depths of** despair*

deputy /ˈdepjəti/ *noun* [C] someone who has the second most important job in an organization *the deputy Prime Minister*

derail /dɪˈreɪl/ *verb* **1** TRAIN [I, T] If a train derails, or is derailed, it comes off the railway tracks. **2** PREVENT [T] If you derail plans, you prevent them from happening. •**derailment** *noun* [C, U]

deranged /dɪˈreɪndʒd/ *adjective* behaving in a way that is not normal, especially when suffering from a mental illness

derby /ˈdɑːbi/ Ⓤⓢ /ˈdɜːrbi/ *noun* [C] **1 SPORT** *mainly UK* a type of sports competition *a fishing/motorcycle derby* **2 Derby SPORT** a type of horse race **3** *US* (*UK* **bowler hat**) a round, hard, black hat worn by men, especially in the past

deregulate /ˌdiːˈregjəleɪt/ *verb* [T] to remove national or local government controls from a business *The government plans to deregulate the banking industry.* •**deregulation** /ˌdiːregjəˈleɪʃᵊn/ *noun* [U]

derelict /ˈderəlɪkt/ *adjective* A derelict building or piece of land is not used any more and is in a bad condition. *a **derelict house***

deride /dɪˈraɪd/ *verb* [T] *formal* to talk about someone or something as if they are ridiculous and do not deserve any respect *Her novel, once derided by critics, is now a classic.*

derision /dɪˈrɪʒᵊn/ *noun* [U] when you talk about someone or something as if they are ridiculous and do not deserve respect *The novel was **greeted with derision**.*

derisive /dɪˈraɪsɪv/ *adjective* showing derision towards someone or something

derisory /dɪˈraɪsᵊri/ *adjective* **1** SMALL so small that it seems ridiculous *a **derisory sum** of money* **2** CRUEL cruel and making someone feel stupid *derisory remarks*

derivation /ˌderɪˈveɪʃᵊn/ *noun* [C, U] **LANGUAGE** the origin of something, such as a word, from which another form has developed, or the new form itself

derivative /dɪˈrɪvətɪv/ *noun* [C] **LANGUAGE** a form of something, such as a word, that has developed from another form

derive /dɪˈraɪv/ *verb*
derive (sth) from sth *phrasal verb* **1** to come from or be developed from something *The name derives from Latin.* **2 derive comfort/pleasure, etc from sth** to get a positive feeling or advantage from someone or something *I derive great pleasure from gardening.*

dermatitis /ˌdɜːməˈtaɪtɪs/ *noun* [U] **HEALTH** a condition which makes your skin red and painful

dermis /ˈdɜːmɪs/ *noun* [U] **ANATOMY, BIOLOGY** the thick layer of skin underneath the epidermis (thin outer layer)

derogatory /dɪˈrɒgətəri/ *adjective* showing strong disapproval and not showing any respect for someone *derogatory comments/remarks*

descale /ˌdiːˈskeɪl/ *verb* [T] to remove scale (= hard white substance) from something, for example a water pipe •**descaler** /ˌdiːˈskeɪləʳ/ a substance used for descaling things

descend /dɪˈsend/ *verb* [I, T] *formal* to move or go down *We descended four flights of stairs.*
be descended from sb/sth *phrasal verb* to be related to a person or creature that lived a long time ago

descendant /dɪˈsendənt/ *noun* [C] **SOCIETY** someone who is related to someone who lived a long time ago *She is a* ***descendant of*** *Queen Victoria.*

descent /dɪˈsent/ *noun* [C, U] **1** a movement down *The plane* ***began its descent*** *into Heathrow.* **2 SOCIETY of Irish/French, etc descent** being related to people who lived in the past in Ireland/France, etc

describe /dɪˈskraɪb/ *verb* [T] to say what someone or something is like *Neighbours* ***described*** *her* ***as*** *a shy, quiet girl.* [+ **question word**] *I tried to describe what I had seen.*

WORD PARTNERS FOR ***description***

give a description • an **accurate/detailed/short** description • a description **of** sth/sb

description /dɪˈskrɪpʃən/ *noun* **1** [C, U] something that tells you what someone or something is like *I gave the police a* ***description of*** *the stolen jewellery.* **2 of any/every/some description** of any/every/some type *They sell plants of every description.*

descriptive /dɪˈskrɪptɪv/ *adjective* describing something, especially in a detailed, interesting way

desert¹ /ˈdezət/ *noun* [C, U] **GEOGRAPHY** a large, hot, dry area of land with very few plants *the Sahara Desert*

desert² /dɪˈzɜːt/ *verb* **1** PERSON [T] to leave someone and never come back *He deserted his family.* **2** PLACE [T] to leave a place, so that it is empty *People are deserting the countryside to work in towns.* **3** ARMY [I, T] to leave the army without permission •**desertion** /dɪˈzɜːʃən/ *noun* [U]

deserted /dɪˈzɜːtɪd/ *adjective* If a place is deserted, it has no people in it. *a deserted street*

deserter /dɪˈzɜːtəʳ/ *noun* [C] someone who leaves the army without permission

desertification /dɪˌzɜːtɪfɪˈkeɪʃən/ *noun* [U] **ENVIRONMENT** the process of land that could once grow food becoming so dry that it turns into a desert

ˌdesert ˈisland *noun* [C] **GEOGRAPHY** a tropical island where no one lives, far from any other places

deserve /dɪˈzɜːv/ *verb* [T] If you deserve something good or bad, it should happen to you because of the way you have behaved. *The school deserves praise for the way it has raised standards.* [+ **to do sth**] *He deserves to be locked up for life.* •**deservedly** *adverb*

deserving /dɪˈzɜːvɪŋ/ *adjective* If something or someone is deserving, people should help or support them. *The children's charity is a* ***deserving cause.***

design¹ /dɪˈzaɪn/ *noun* **DT 1** [U] the way in which something is planned and made *There was a fault in the design of the aircraft.* **2** [C] a drawing which shows how an object, machine, or building will be made *Engineers are working on the new designs.* **3** [C] a pattern or decoration **4** [U] the process of making drawings to show how something will be made *a course in art and design* ➲See also: **interior design**

design² /dɪˈzaɪn/ *verb* [T] **DT 1** to draw or plan something before making it *She designs furniture.* **2 be designed to do sth** to have been planned or done for a particular purpose *The new law is designed to protect children.*

designate /ˈdezɪgneɪt/ *verb* [T] *formal* to choose someone or something for a particular purpose or duty *The area has been* ***designated*** *as a nature reserve.* •**designation** /ˌdezɪgˈneɪʃən/ *noun* [C, U]

designer¹ /dɪˈzaɪnəʳ/ *noun* [C] someone who draws and plans how something will be made *a* ***fashion designer***

designer² /dɪˈzaɪnəʳ/ *adjective* **designer jeans/sunglasses, etc** clothes or objects made by a fashionable designer

deˌsigner ˈbaby *noun* [C] a baby with some characteristics chosen by its parents and doctors using gene therapy (= the science of changing genes in order to stop or prevent a disease)

desirable /dɪˈzaɪərəbl/ *adjective* If something is desirable, it is very good or attractive and most people would want it. *A good education is highly desirable.* ➲Opposite **undesirable**

WORD PARTNERS FOR ***desire***

express/have a desire to do sth • a **burning/strong** desire • a desire **for** sth

desire¹ /dɪˈzaɪəʳ/ *noun* **1** WISH [C, U] a strong feeling that you want something [+ **to do sth**] *I have no desire to have children.* ○ *There is a strong* ***desire for*** *peace among the people.* **2** SEX [U] when you are sexually attracted to someone

desire² /dɪˈzaɪəʳ/ *verb* [T] *formal* to want something *You can have whatever you desire.*

desired /dɪˈzaɪəd/ *adjective* **the desired effect/result/shape, etc** the effect/result/shape, etc that is wanted *Her medicine seems to have had the desired effect.*

desk /desk/ *noun* [C] a table that you sit at to write or work, often with drawers ➲See also: **cash desk** ➲See colour picture **The Office** on page Centre 5

ˈdesk reˌsearch *noun* [U] market research (= finding out what customers want) that can be done from a desk, for example reading reports or looking for information on the Internet

desktop /ˈdesktɒp/ *noun* [C] **1 COMPUTING** a computer screen that contains icons (= symbols that represent programs, information or equipment) and which is usually used as a place to start and finish computer work **2 COMPUTING** (*also* **desktop computer**) a computer that is small enough to fit on a desk **3** the top of a desk

ˌdesktop ˈpublishing *noun* [U] **COMPUTING** producing finished designs for pages of books or documents using a small computer and printer (= machine for printing)

desolate /ˈdesəlɘt/ *adjective* **1** PLACE A desolate place is empty and makes you feel sad. *a desolate landscape* **2** PERSON lonely and unhappy *She felt desolate when he left.* •**desolation** /ˌdesəlˈeɪʃən/ *noun* [U]

WORD PARTNERS FOR ***despair***

abject/complete/utter despair • **in** despair

despair¹ /dɪˈspeər/ *noun* [U] a feeling of having no hope *She shook her head **in despair**.*

despair² /dɪˈspeər/ *verb* [I] to feel that you have no hope *Don't despair - things will improve.* [+ **of** + **doing sth**] *He had begun to despair of ever finding a job.* •**despairing** *adjective*

despatch¹ *UK* (*UK/US* **dispatch**) /dɪˈspætʃ/ *verb* [T] *formal* to send someone or something somewhere *They despatched a police car to arrest him.*

despatch² *UK* (*UK/US* **dispatch**) /dɪˈspætʃ/ *noun* **1** SENDING [U] when someone or something is sent somewhere *the despatch of troops* **2** REPORT [C] an official report that someone in a foreign country sends to their organization

desperate /ˈdespərət/ *adjective* **1** WITHOUT HOPE feeling that you have no hope and are ready to do anything to change the situation you are in *He was absolutely desperate and would have tried anything to get her back.* **2** NEEDING SOMETHING needing or wanting something very much *By two o'clock I was **desperate for** something to eat.* **3** BAD A desperate situation is very bad or serious. *The economy is in a really **desperate situation**.* •**desperately** *adverb* •**desperation** /ˌdespəˈreɪʃən/ *noun* [U]

despicable /dɪˈspɪkəbl/ *adjective* very unpleasant or cruel *a despicable act/crime*

despise /dɪˈspaɪz/ *verb* [T] to hate someone or something and have no respect for them *The two groups despise each other.*

O-■ **despite** /dɪˈspaɪt/ *preposition* **1** used to say that something happened or is true, although something else makes this seem not probable *I'm still pleased with the house despite all the problems we've had.* [+ **doing sth**] *He managed to eat lunch despite having had an enormous breakfast.* **2 despite yourself** If you do something despite yourself, you do it although you did not intend to.

despondent /dɪˈspɒndənt/ *adjective* unhappy and having no enthusiasm •**despondency** *noun* [U]

despot /ˈdespɒt/ *noun* [C] **POLITICS** a very powerful person, especially someone who treats people cruelly

dessert /dɪˈzɜːt/ *noun* [C, U] **FOOD** sweet food that is eaten after the main part of a meal *We had ice cream for dessert.*

dessertspoon /dɪˈzɜːtspuːn/ *noun* [C] *UK* a medium-sized spoon used for eating or measuring food, or the amount this spoon can hold

destabilize (*also UK* **-ise**) /ˌdiːˈsteɪbəlaɪz/ *verb* [T] **POLITICS** to cause change in a country or government so that it loses its power or control *a plot to destabilize the government*

destination /ˌdestɪˈneɪʃən/ *noun* [C] the place where someone or something is going *Spain is a very popular **holiday destination**.*

destined /ˈdestɪnd/ *adjective* **be destined for sth; be destined to do sth** to be certain to be something or do something in the future *She was destined for a brilliant future.*

destiny /ˈdestɪni/ *noun* **1** EVENTS [C] the things that will happen to someone in the future *At last she feels in control of her own destiny.* **2** POWER [U] a power that some people believe controls what will happen in the future *Nick said it was destiny that we met.*

destitute /ˈdestɪtjuːt/ *adjective* so poor that you do not have the basic things you need to live, such as food, clothes, or money •**destitution** /ˌdestɪˈtjuːʃən/ *noun* [U]

O-■ **destroy** /dɪˈstrɔɪ/ *verb* [T] to damage something so badly that it does not exist or cannot be used *Many works of art were destroyed in the fire.*

destroyer /dɪˈstrɔɪər/ *noun* [C] a small, fast ship that is used in a war

destruction /dɪˈstrʌkʃən/ *noun* [U] when something is destroyed *We are all responsible for the **destruction of** the forest.* •**destructive** /dɪˈstrʌktɪv/ *adjective* causing a lot of damage *the destructive power of nuclear weapons* ➲See also: **self-destructive**

detach /dɪˈtætʃ/ *verb* [T] to take a part of something off so that it is separate *Please complete and detach the form below and return it to the school.* •**detachable** *adjective*

detached /dɪˈtætʃt/ *adjective* **1** BUILDING *UK* A detached building is not joined to another building. **2** FEELINGS If someone is detached, they do not feel involved with someone or emotional about something. ➲See also: **semi-detached**

detachment /dɪˈtætʃmənt/ *noun* **1** FEELINGS [U] when someone does not feel involved in a situation *He spoke with cool detachment.* **2** SOLDIERS [C] a small group of soldiers with a particular job to do

WORD PARTNERS FOR ***detail***

disclose/discuss/divulge/reveal details • **exact/full/precise/relevant** details • details **about/of/on** sth

O-■ **detail¹** /ˈdiːteɪl/ (US) /dɪˈteɪl/ *noun* [C, U] **1** a fact or piece of information about something *Please send me **details of** your training courses.* ○ *She didn't include very much detail in her report.* **2 in detail** including every part of something *He explained it all in great detail.* **3 go into detail** to include all the facts about something

detail² /ˈdiːteɪl/ (US) /dɪˈteɪl/ *verb* [T] to describe something completely, giving all the facts

detailed /ˈdiːteɪld/ *adjective* giving a lot of information *a **detailed account/description***

D

detain /dɪˈteɪn/ *verb* [T] to keep someone somewhere and not allow them to leave, especially in order to ask them about a crime *Three men were detained by police for questioning.*

detect /dɪˈtekt/ *verb* [T] to discover or notice something, especially something that is difficult to see, hear, smell, etc *This special camera can detect bodies by their heat.*

detection /dɪˈtekʃᵊn/ *noun* [U] **1** NOTICING when someone notices or discovers something *the early detection of cancer* **2 LAW** when the police discover information about a crime

detective /dɪˈtektɪv/ *noun* [C] **LAW** someone, especially a police officer, whose job is to discover information about a crime

detector /dɪˈtektəʳ/ *noun* [C] a piece of equipment used to discover something, especially something that is difficult to see, hear, smell, etc *a **smoke detector***

detente /ˌdeɪˈtɒnt/ *noun* [U] *formal* **POLITICS** when countries become friendly with each other after a period of not being friendly

detention /dɪˈtenʃᵊn/ *noun* **1** [U] **LAW** when someone is officially kept somewhere and not allowed to leave **2 EDUCATION** [C, U] when a student is kept in school after the other students leave, as a punishment

deter /dɪˈtɜːʳ/ *verb* [T] **deterring,** *past* **deterred** to make someone less likely to do something, or to make something less likely to happen *We have introduced new security measures to deter shoplifters.* [+ **from** + **doing sth**] *Higher fuel costs could deter people from driving their cars.*

detergent /dɪˈtɜːdʒᵊnt/ *noun* [C, U] a liquid or powder that is used to clean things

deteriorate /dɪˈtɪəriᵊreɪt/ *verb* [I] to become worse *Her condition deteriorated rapidly.* •**deterioration** /dɪˌtɪəriəˈreɪʃᵊn/ *noun* [U]

WORD PARTNERS FOR ***determination***

demonstrate/show determination • **dogged/fierce/grim/steely** determination • **courage/grit/guts** and determination

determination /dɪˌtɜːmɪˈneɪʃᵊn/ *noun* [U] when someone continues trying to do something, although it is very difficult *Andy Murray will need great determination and skill to win this match.*

determine /dɪˈtɜːmɪn/ *verb* [T] **1** FIND to discover the facts or truth about something [+ **question word**] *The doctors are still unable to determine what is wrong.* **2** DECIDE to decide what will happen [+ **question word**] *Her exam results will determine which university she goes to.*

determined /dɪˈtɜːmɪnd/ *adjective* wanting to do something very much, and not letting anyone stop you [+ **to do sth**] *He's determined to win this match.*

determiner /dɪˈtɜːmɪnəʳ/ *noun* [C] **LANGUAGE** a word that is used before a noun or adjective to show which person or thing you are referring to. For example 'my' in 'my old car' and 'that' in 'that man' are determiners.

deterrent /dɪˈterᵊnt/ *noun* [C] something that stops people doing something because they are afraid of what will happen if they do *They've installed a security camera as a **deterrent to** thieves.* •**deterrent** *adjective a deterrent effect*

detest /dɪˈtest/ *verb* [T] to hate someone or something very much

detonate /ˈdetᵊneɪt/ *verb* [I, T] to explode or make something explode *The **bomb was detonated** safely by army officers and no one was hurt.* •**detonation** /ˌdetᵊnˈeɪʃᵊn/ *noun* [C, U]

detonator /ˈdetᵊneɪtəʳ/ *noun* [C] a piece of equipment that makes a bomb explode

detour /ˈdiːtʊəʳ/ *noun* [C] a different, longer route to a place that is used to avoid something or to visit something *Several roads were closed, so we had to **take a detour**.*

detox /ˈdiːtɒks/ *noun* [U] **HEALTH** *informal* treatment to clean out your blood, stomach, etc and get rid of bad substances such as drugs

detract /dɪˈtrækt/ *verb*

detract from sth *phrasal verb* to make something seem less good than it really is, or than it was thought to be

detriment /ˈdetrɪmənt/ *noun* **to the detriment of sth** causing damage to something *He was working very long hours, to the detriment of his health.* •**detrimental** /ˌdetrɪˈmentᵊl/ *adjective a **detrimental effect***

deuterium /djuːˈtɪəriəm/ *noun* [U] **CHEMISTRY** a type of hydrogen that is twice as heavy as normal hydrogen (symbol **D**)

devaluation /ˌdiːvæljuˈeɪʃᵊn/ *noun* [C, U] **ECONOMICS** when the value of something is reduced *the devaluation of the dollar*

devalue /ˌdiːˈvæljuː/ *verb* [T] **devaluing,** *past* **devalued 1 ECONOMICS** to make something less valuable, especially a country's money *to devalue the pound* **2** to make someone or something seem less important than they really are

devastate /ˈdevəsteɪt/ *verb* [T] to destroy or damage something very badly *A recent hurricane devastated the city.* •**devastation** /ˌdevəˈsteɪʃᵊn/ *noun* [U]

devastated /ˈdevəsteɪtɪd/ *adjective* **1** SHOCKED very shocked and upset *She was devastated when her husband died.* **2** DESTROYED completely destroyed

devastating /ˈdevəsteɪtɪŋ/ *adjective* **1** SHOCKING making someone very shocked and upset *Despite the devastating news, no one is giving up hope.* **2** DESTROYING causing a lot of damage or destruction *The fire has had a devastating effect on the local wildlife.*

devastatingly /ˈdevəsteɪtɪŋli/ *adverb* extremely *devastatingly funny/handsome*

develop /dɪˈveləp/ *verb* **1** CHANGE [I, T] to grow or change and become more advanced, or to make someone or something do this *The baby develops inside the mother for nine months.* ○ *He's **developing into** a very good tennis* *player.* **2** MAKE [T] to make something new such as a product *Scientists are developing new drugs all the time.* **3** ILLNESS [T] to start to have something, such as an illness, problem, or feeling *Shortly after take-off the plane developed engine trouble.* **4** HAPPEN [I] to start to happen or exist *Further problems may develop if you do not deal with this now.* **5** FILM [T] to use special chemicals on a piece of film to make photographs appear *I need to get my holiday photos developed.* **6** BUILD [T] to build houses, factories, shops, etc on a piece of land

developed /dɪˈveləpt/ *adjective* **ECONOMICS** a **developed country/nation, etc** a country with an advanced level of technology, industry, etc ➲Opposite **undeveloped**

developer /dɪˈveləpəʳ/ *noun* [C] a person or company that buys land and builds houses, factories, shops, etc

WORD PARTNERS FOR ***development***

encourage/monitor/restrict development • **dramatic/major/rapid** development • **in/under** development

O┘**development** /dɪˈveləpmənt/ *noun* **1** CHANGE [C, U] when someone or something grows or changes and becomes more advanced *The nurse will do some tests to check on your child's development.* ○ *There have been some* ***major developments*** *in technology recently.* **2** MAKE [C, U] when something new is made *the development of new drugs* **3** START [U] when something starts to happen or exist *Smoking encourages the development of cancer.* **4** BUILD [U] when new houses, factories, shops, etc, are built on an area of land *land suitable for development* **5** BUILDINGS [C] an area of land with new houses, factories, shops, etc on it *a new housing development* **6** EVENT [C] something new that happens and changes a situation *Have there been any more developments since I left?* **7** PHOTOGRAPH [U] when someone makes photographs from a film

developmental /dɪˌveləpˈmentəl/ *adjective* connected with the development of someone or something *developmental problems*

deviant /ˈdiːviənt/ *adjective* different to what most people think is normal or acceptable, usually relating to sexual behaviour •**deviant** *noun* [C]

deviate /ˈdiːvieɪt/ *verb* [I] to do something in a different way from what is usual or expected *The aircraft* ***deviated from*** *its original flight plan.*

deviation /ˌdiːviˈeɪʃən/ *noun* [C, U] when something is different to what is usual, expected, or accepted by most people ***sexual deviation***

device /dɪˈvaɪs/ *noun* **1** [C] a piece of equipment that is used for a particular purpose *A pager is a small, electronic device for sending messages.* **2 leave someone to their own devices** to leave someone to do what they want to do *With both parents out at work, the kids were often left to their own devices.*

devil /ˈdevəl/ *noun* **1 the Devil RELIGION** the most powerful evil spirit, according to the Christian and Jewish religions **2 RELIGION** [C] an evil spirit **3** PERSON [C] *informal* someone who behaves badly **4 lucky/poor, etc devil** *informal* used to describe a person **5 speak/talk of the devil** *informal* something that you say when someone you have been talking about suddenly appears

devilish /ˈdevəlɪʃ/ *adjective* evil or bad *a devilish smile* •**devilishly** *adverb* very ***devilishly difficult***

devious /ˈdiːviəs/ *adjective* clever in a way that is bad and not honest *a devious mind*

devise /dɪˈvaɪz/ *verb* [T] to design or invent something such as a system, plan, or piece of equipment

devoid /dɪˈvɔɪd/ *adjective* **devoid of sth** *formal* completely without a quality *His voice was devoid of emotion.*

devolution /ˌdiːvəˈluːʃən/ *noun* [U] **POLITICS** when power moves from a central government to local governments

devolve /dɪˈvɒlv/ *verb*

devolve sth to sb/sth *phrasal verb formal* to give power or responsibility to a person or organization at a lower or more local level

devote /dɪˈvəʊt/ *verb*

devote sth to sb/sth *phrasal verb* **1** TIME to use time, energy, etc for a particular purpose *She devotes most of her free time to charity work.* **2** AREA to use a space or area for a particular purpose [**often passive**] *Most of the magazine was devoted to coverage of the royal wedding.*

devoted /dɪˈvəʊtɪd/ *adjective* loving or caring very much about someone or something *She's absolutely* ***devoted to*** *her grandchildren.* •**devotedly** *adverb*

devotee /ˌdevəʊˈtiː/ *noun* [C] someone who likes something or someone very much *a* ***devotee of*** *classical music*

devotion /dɪˈvəʊʃən/ *noun* [U] **1** great love or loyalty for someone or something *She will always be remembered for her* ***devotion to*** *her family.* **2 RELIGION** strong religious belief or behaviour

devour /dɪˈvaʊəʳ/ *verb* [T] **1** FOOD to eat something quickly because you are very hungry **2** BOOK to read something quickly and enthusiastically

devout /dɪˈvaʊt/ *adjective* **RELIGION** extremely religious *a devout Catholic/Muslim* •**devoutly** *adverb*

dew /djuː/ *noun* [U] drops of water that form on surfaces outside during the night

ˈdew ˌpoint *noun* [U] **GEOGRAPHY** the point at which the air cannot hold any more water and dew (= drops of water) begins to form

dexterity /dekˈsterəti/ *noun* [U] skill at doing something, especially using your hands ***manual dexterity***

diabetes /ˌdaɪəˈbiːtiːz/ *noun* [U] **HEALTH** a serious medical condition in which your body cannot control the level of sugar in your blood •**diabetic** /ˌdaɪəˈbetɪk/ *adjective* •**diabetic** /ˌdaɪəˈbetɪk/ *noun* [C] someone who has diabetes

diabolical /ˌdaɪəˈbɒlɪkəl/ *adjective* extremely bad

D

diagnose /ˈdaɪəgnəʊz/ *verb* [T] **HEALTH** to say what is wrong with someone who is ill [**often passive**] *She was* ***diagnosed with/as having*** *cancer last year.*

WORD PARTNERS FOR ***diagnosis***

make a diagnosis • a diagnosis **of** [cancer, heart disease, etc]

diagnosis /ˌdaɪəgˈnəʊsɪs/ *noun* [C, U] *plural* **diagnoses HEALTH** when a doctor says what is wrong with someone who is ill

diagnostic /ˌdaɪəgˈnɒstɪk/ *adjective* **diagnostic methods/tests, etc** methods/tests, etc that help you discover what is wrong with someone or something

diagonal /daɪˈægᵊnᵊl/ *adjective* **1** SLOPING A diagonal line is straight and sloping and not horizontal or vertical. *a tie with diagonal stripes* **2** SQUARE going from the top corner of a square to the bottom corner on the other side •**diagonally** *adverb*

WORD PARTNERS FOR ***diagram***

draw a diagram • a diagram **of** sth • **in/on** a diagram

diagram /ˈdaɪəgræm/ *noun* [C] **ART, DT** a simple picture showing what something looks like or explaining how something works

dial[1] /daɪəl/ *noun* [C] **1** TIME/MEASUREMENT the round part of a clock, watch, or machine that shows you the time or other measurement **2** BUTTON a round part on a piece of equipment such as a television or radio that you turn to operate it, make it louder, etc **3** TELEPHONE the ring of holes with numbers that you turn on the front of an old telephone

dial[2] /daɪəl/ *verb* [I, T] *UK* **dialling,** *past* **dialled,** *US* **dialing,** *past* **dialed** to make a telephone call to a particular number *Dial 0 for the operator.*

dialect /ˈdaɪəlekt/ *noun* [C, U] **LANGUAGE** a form of a language that people speak in a particular part of a country

ˈdialog ˌbox *noun* [C] **COMPUTING** a window (= a separate area on a computer screen) that appears and asks the person using the computer for information

dialogue (*also US* **dialog**) /ˈdaɪəlɒg/ *noun* [C, U] **1** TALKING the talking in a book, play, or film **2 POLITICS** a formal discussion between countries or groups of people

dial-up /ˈdaɪəlʌp/ *adjective* [**always before noun**] **COMPUTING** Dial-up computer systems and equipment and Internet services use a telephone connection to reach them. ➲Compare **broadband**

dialysis /daɪˈæləsɪs/ *noun* [C] **HEALTH** a process for removing substances from liquid, especially for cleaning the blood of people whose kidneys do not work well

diameter /daɪˈæmɪtəʳ/ *noun* [C, U] **MATHEMATICS** a straight line that goes from one side of a circle to the other side and through the centre, or the length of this line *The cake was about 30 centimetres* ***in diameter***. ➲See picture at **circle**

diamond /ˈdaɪəmənd/ *noun* **1 GEOLOGY** [C, U] a very hard, transparent stone that is extremely valuable and is often used in jewellery *a diamond ring* **2** [C] a shape with four straight sides of equal length that join to form two large angles and two small angles **3 SPORT** [C] the field where baseball is played **4 diamonds** playing cards with red, diamond shapes on them *the queen of diamonds*

diaper /ˈdaɪəpəʳ/ *US* (*UK* **nappy**) *noun* [C] a thick piece of paper or cloth worn by a baby on its bottom

diaphragm /ˈdaɪəfræm/ *noun* [C] **ANATOMY** the large muscle between your lungs and your stomach that moves up and down to move air in and out of the lungs ➲See picture at **alimentary canal** ➲See picture at **respiratory system**

diarrhoea *UK* (*US* **diarrhea**) /ˌdaɪəˈrɪə/ *noun* [U] **HEALTH** an illness in which your solid waste is more liquid than usual, and comes out of your body more often

O-ᵯ **diary** /ˈdaɪəri/ *noun* [C] **1** a book containing spaces for all the days and months of the year, in which you write meetings and other things that you must remember **2 LITERATURE** a book in which you write each day about your personal thoughts and experiences *She* ***kept a diary*** *of her trip to Egypt.*

diastole /daɪˈæstᵊli/ *noun* [C] **BIOLOGY** the part of a heart's action where it fills with blood ➲Compare **systole** •**diastolic** /ˌdaɪəˈstɒlɪk/ *adjective*

diatomic /ˌdaɪəˈtɒmɪk/ *adjective* **CHEMISTRY** A diatomic molecule has two atoms of the same kind.

dice[1] /daɪs/ *noun* [C] *plural* **dice** a small object with six equal square sides, each with between one and six spots on it, used in games ***Roll the dice*** *to see who starts the game.*

dice[2] /daɪs/ *verb* [T] **FOOD** to cut food into small, square pieces *diced onions*

dicey /ˈdaɪsi/ *adjective informal* possibly dangerous or involving a risk

dichotomy /daɪˈkɒtəmi/ *noun* [C] *formal* the difference between two completely opposite ideas or things *the* ***dichotomy between*** *good and evil*

dicotyledon /ˌdaɪkɒtɪˈliːdᵊn/ *noun* [C] **BIOLOGY** a plant that produces flowers and has two cotyledons (= leaf parts inside the seed) •**dicotyledonous** /ˌdaɪkɒtɪˈliːdᵊnəs/ *adjective*

dictate /dɪkˈteɪt/ *verb* **1** SAY [I, T] to say or read something for someone to write down *Tony was busy* ***dictating*** *letters* ***to*** *his secretary.* **2** DECIDE [T] to decide or control what happens [**+ question word**] *The weather will dictate where we hold the party.*

dictate to sb *phrasal verb* to tell someone what to do, often in a way that annoys them *I'm 15 years old - you can't dictate to me any more.*

dictation /dɪkˈteɪʃᵊn/ *noun* **1** [U] when someone speaks or reads something for someone else to write down **2 EDUCATION** [C, U] when a teacher says or reads something for students to write down as a test

dictator /dɪk'teɪtəʳ/ *noun* [C] **POLITICS** a leader who has complete power in a country and has not been elected by the people •**dictatorial** /ˌdɪktə'tɔːriəl/ *adjective*

dictatorship /dɪk'teɪtəʃɪp/ *noun* [C, U] **POLITICS** a country or system of government with a dictator as leader

O‑ **dictionary** /'dɪkʃənəri/ *noun* [C] a book that contains a list of words in alphabetical order with their meanings explained or written in another language

O‑ **did** /dɪd/ *past tense of* do

didgeridoo /ˌdɪdʒəri'duː/ *noun* [C] **MUSIC** a long wooden wind instrument played by Australian Aborigines to produce a deep sound

O‑ **didn't** /'dɪdənt/ *short for* did not

O‑ **die** /daɪ/ *verb* **dying,** *past* **died 1** [I] to stop living *Many of the refugees* ***died of*** *hunger.* ○ *She* ***died from*** *brain injuries after a road accident.* **2 be dying for sth; be dying to do sth** *informal* to very much want to have, eat, drink, or do something *I'm dying for a drink.* **3 to die for** *informal* If something is to die for, it is extremely good. ⊃See also: die **hard**²

die away *phrasal verb* If something, especially a sound, dies away, it gradually becomes less strong and then stops.

die down *phrasal verb* If something, especially noise or excitement, dies down, it gradually becomes less loud or strong until it stops.

die off *phrasal verb* If a group of plants, animals, or people dies off, all of that group dies over a period of time.

die out *phrasal verb* to become more and more rare and then disappear completely *Dinosaurs died out about 65 million years ago.*

COMMON LEARNER ERROR

died or **dead?**

Be careful not to confuse the verb and adjective forms of these words. **Died** is the past of the verb 'to die', which means 'to stop living'.

My cat died last week.

Dead is an adjective and is used to talk about people or things which are not alive.

My cat is dead.

die-cast /'daɪkɑːst/ *verb* [T] **DT** to make something by pouring liquid metal, plastic, etc.into a mould (= hollow container) •**die-cast** *adjective die-cast toys*

ˈ**die** ˌ**cutting** *noun* [U] **DT** the process of cutting shapes from plastic by pressing with a sharp knife on one or more layers of plastic

diehard /'daɪhɑːd/ *adjective* [**always before noun**] supporting something in a very determined way and refusing to change *a* ***diehard fan***

diesel /'diːzəl/ *noun* **1** FUEL [U] fuel used in the engines of some vehicles, especially buses and trucks **2** VEHICLE [C] a vehicle that uses diesel in its engine

WORD PARTNERS FOR ***diet***

be on/go on a diet • **follow/stick to** a diet • a **special /strict** diet

diet¹ /daɪət/ *noun* **1 FOOD** [C, U] the type of food that someone usually eats **2** [C] when someone eats less food, or only particular types of food, because they want to become thinner, or because they are ill *No cake for me, thanks - I'm* ***on a diet.***

diet² /daɪət/ *verb* [I] to eat less food so that you become thinner

differ /'dɪfəʳ/ *verb* [I] **1** DIFFERENT to be different *How does the book* ***differ from*** *the film?* ○ *These computers* ***differ*** *quite a lot* ***in*** *price.* **2** OPINION to have a different opinion *Economists* ***differ on*** *the cause of inflation.*

WORD PARTNERS FOR ***difference***

know/tell the difference • a **big/fundamental/important/obvious** difference • a difference **between** [sth and sth]

O‑ **difference** /'dɪfərəns/ *noun* **1** WAY [C, U] the way in which two people or things are not the same *What's the* ***difference between*** *an ape and a monkey?* **2** QUALITY [U] when two people or things are not the same **3** AMOUNT [C, U] the amount by which one thing or person is different from another *There's a big* ***difference in*** *age between them.* **4** DISAGREEMENT [C] a disagreement or different opinion *They must try to resolve their differences peacefully.* **5 make a/ any difference** to have an effect on a situation *Painting the walls white has made a big difference to this room.*

COMMON LEARNER ERROR

difference

When you want to talk about how something or someone has changed, use the preposition **in**.

The graph shows the difference in sales this year.

~~*The graph shows the difference of sales this year.*~~

OTHER WAYS OF SAYING ***different***

If something is different from what people normally expect, you can say that it is **unusual**: *Carina - that's quite an* ***unusual*** *name.*

The adjective **alternative** is often used to describe something which is different to something else but can be used instead of it: *The hotel's being renovated, so we're looking for an* ***alternative*** *venue.*

If something is very different and separate from other things, you can describe it as **distinct** or **distinctive**: *She's got really* ***distinctive*** *handwriting.* • *The word has three* ***distinct*** *meanings.*

The preposition **unlike** is often used to compare people or things that are very different from each other: *Dan's actually quite nice,* ***unlike*** *his father.* • *The furniture was* ***unlike*** *anything she had ever seen.*

O‑ **different** /'dɪfərənt/ *adjective* **1** NOT THE SAME not the same as someone or something else *Jo's very* ***different from*** *her sister, isn't she? UK* ○ *The house is* ***different to*** *how I expected it to be.* **2** SEPARATE [**always before noun**] used to talk about separate things or people of the same type *I had to go to three different shops to find the book she wanted.* •**differently** *adverb* ⊃See also: a whole new **ball game**

COMMON LEARNER ERROR

different

Different is usually followed by the preposition **from**. In British English people also use **to**.

Anne is very different to her younger sister.

In American English people also use **than**, but teachers prefer students to use **from**.

D

differential /ˌdɪfəˈrenʃəl/ *noun* [C] **MATHEMATICS** a difference between amounts of things ***differentials in*** *pay/wealth*

diffeˌrential ˈcalculus *noun* [U] **MATHEMATICS** the branch of calculus in which rates of change and connected quantities are calculated

differentiate /ˌdɪfəˈrenʃieɪt/ *verb* **1** SEE DIFFERENCE [I, T] to understand or notice how two things or people are different from each other *He can't* ***differentiate between*** *blue and green.* **2** MAKE DIFFERENT [T] to make someone or something different *We need to* ***differentiate*** *ourselves* ***from*** *the competition.* •**differentiation** /ˌdɪfərenʃiˈeɪʃən/ *noun* [U]

OTHER WAYS OF SAYING *difficult*

Hard is very often used instead of **difficult** and means exactly the same: *The exam was really* ***hard****.* • *It must be* ***hard*** *to study with all this noise.*

If something is difficult to understand or do because it has a lot of different parts or stages, you can say that it is **complicated**: *The instructions were so* ***complicated*** *I just couldn't follow them.*

Tricky describes something difficult that needs skill or needs you to be very careful: *It's quite* ***tricky*** *getting the bits to fit together.* • *It's a* ***tricky*** *situation - I don't want to upset anyone.*

Fiddly (*UK*) describes something that you do with your hands which is difficult because the parts involved are so small: *Repairing a watch is very* ***fiddly****.*

Awkward describes something or someone that is difficult to deal with and could cause problems: *Dealing with* ***awkward*** *customers is just part of the job.* • *Luckily, she didn't ask any* ***awkward*** *questions.*

Demanding means 'needing a lot of your time, attention, or effort': *She has a very* ***demanding*** *job.* • *Like most young children, he's very* ***demanding****.*

A situation or piece of work that is **challenging** is difficult and needs all your skills and determination: *This has been a* ***challenging*** *time for us all.* • *I found the course very* ***challenging****.*

You say **easier said than done** about something that is impossible or very difficult to do: *I suppose I should stop smoking but it's* ***easier said than done****.*

O-ᵚ**difficult** /ˈdɪfɪkəlt/ *adjective* **1** NOT EASY not easy and needing skill or effort to do or understand *Japanese is a difficult language for Europeans to learn.* ○ *This game is too* ***difficult for*** *me.* [+ **to do sth**] *It's difficult to think with all that noise.* **2** PERSON not friendly or easy to deal with *a difficult teenager*

WORD PARTNERS FOR *difficulty*

create/experience/have difficulty • **great/ serious** difficulty • **with/without** difficulty

O-ᵚ**difficulty** /ˈdɪfɪkəlti/ *noun* **1** NOT EASY [U] when something is not easy to do or understand [+ **in + doing sth**] *He was* ***having difficulty in*** *breathing because of the smoke.* [+ **doing sth**] *I* ***had difficulty*** *finding somewhere to park.* ○ *She had twisted her ankle and was walking* ***with difficulty****.* **2** PROBLEM [C] something that is not easy to deal with *The company is having some* ***financial difficulties*** *at the moment.*

COMMON LEARNER ERROR

have difficulty doing something

You can say you **have difficulty doing** something or **have difficulty in doing** something.

She has difficulty walking.

She has difficulty in walking.

~~*I have difficulty to walk.*~~

diffident /ˈdɪfɪdənt/ *adjective* shy and without any confidence *a diffident young man* •**diffidence** /ˈdɪfɪdəns/ *noun* [U]

diffract /dɪˈfrækt/ *verb* [T] **PHYSICS** to break up light or sound waves by making them go through a narrow space or across an edge

diffraction /dɪˈfrækʃən/ *noun* [U] **PHYSICS** a change in the direction of light, water or sound waves or the pattern caused by this

diffuse /dɪˈfjuːz/ *verb* [I, T] **1** to spread, or to make something spread over a large area, or to a large number of people **2 PHYSICS** to cause a gas or liquid to spread through or into a surrounding substance by mixing with it

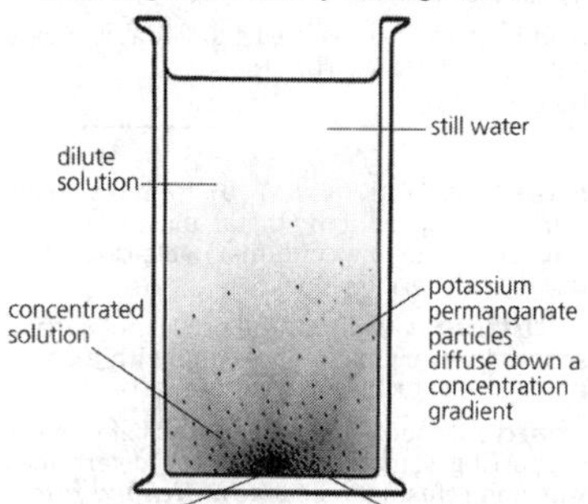

diffusion of potassium permanganate

diffusion /dɪˈfjuːʒən/ *noun* [U] **PHYSICS** the process of gases and liquids spreading into a surrounding substance

O‑**dig**[1] /dɪg/ *verb* **digging,** *past* **dug 1** [I, T] to break or move the ground with a tool, machine, etc *Digging the garden is good exercise.* **2 dig a hole/tunnel, etc** to make a hole in the ground by moving some of the ground or soil away *They've dug a huge hole in the road.* ➲See also: dig the/up **dirt**[1] on sb

dig in/dig into sth *phrasal verb informal* to start eating food *Dig in, there's plenty for everyone.*

dig (sth) into sb/sth *phrasal verb* to press or push hard into someone or something, or to press something hard into someone or something *A stone was digging into my heel.*

dig sb/sth out *phrasal verb* to get someone or something out of somewhere by digging

dig sth out *phrasal verb* to find something that you have not seen or used for a long time *Mum dug out some old family photographs to show me.*

dig sth up *phrasal verb* **1** [TAKE OUT] to take something out of the ground by digging *Could you dig up a few potatoes for dinner?* **2** [BREAK GROUND] to break the ground or make a hole in the ground with a tool, machine, etc *They're digging up the road outside my house.* **3** [INFORMATION] to discover information that is secret or forgotten by searching very carefully *See if you can dig up anything interesting about his past.*

dig[2] /dɪg/ *noun* **1** [REMARK] [C] something that you say to annoy or criticize someone *He was **having a dig at** me.* **2** [PLACE] [C] a place where people are digging in the ground looking for ancient things to study *an **archaeological dig*** **3** [PUSH] [no plural] *informal* a quick, hard push *a dig in the ribs*

digest /daɪˈdʒest/ *verb* [T] **1 BIOLOGY** to change food in your stomach into substances that your body can use **2** to read and understand new information *You need to give me time to digest this report.* •**digestible** *adjective* easy to digest

digestion /daɪˈdʒestʃən/ *noun* [U] **BIOLOGY** when your body changes food in your stomach into substances that it can use

digestive /daɪˈdʒestɪv/ *adjective* [always before noun] **BIOLOGY** relating to digestion *the **digestive system***

diˈgestive ˌsystem *noun* [C usually singular] **ANATOMY, BIOLOGY** the organs in your body that digest food

diˈgestive ˌtract *noun* [C usually singular] **ANATOMY, BIOLOGY** the tube that goes from your mouth through your body, along which food passes as it is being digested

digger /ˈdɪgər/ *noun* [C] a large machine that is used to lift and move soil, or a person who digs

Digibox /ˈdɪdʒɪbɒks/ *noun* [C] *trademark* a piece of electronic equipment that allows you to watch digital broadcasts (= television sounds and pictures sent as signals in the form of numbers) on an ordinary television

digit /ˈdɪdʒɪt/ *noun* [C] **MATHEMATICS** any of the numbers from 0 to 9, especially when they form part of a longer number *a seven digit telephone number*

digital /ˈdɪdʒɪtəl/ *adjective* **1 COMPUTING** using an electronic system that changes sounds or images into signals in the form of numbers before it stores them or sends them ***digital television*** **2** A digital clock or watch shows the time in the form of numbers.

ˌdigital ˈcamera *noun* [C] a type of camera that records images that you can use and store on a computer

ˌdigital ˈsignature *noun* [C] **COMPUTING** a way of putting a person's name on an electronic document that proves who they are

digitize (*also UK* **-ise**) /ˈdɪdʒɪtaɪz/ *verb* [T] **COMPUTING** to put information into the form of a series of the numbers 0 and 1, usually so that it can be processed by a computer •**digitizer** /ˌdɪdʒɪtaɪzər/ *noun* [C] a piece of software that digitizes information

dignified /ˈdɪgnɪfaɪd/ *adjective* calm, serious and behaving in a way that makes people respect you *a quiet, dignified woman*

dignitary /ˈdɪgnɪtəri/ *noun* [C] someone with an important, official position *a group of **visiting dignitaries***

dignity /ˈdɪgnəti/ *noun* [U] calm and serious behaviour that makes people respect you *He behaved with great dignity and courage.*

digress /daɪˈgres/ *verb* [I] to start talking about something that is not related to what you were talking about before •**digression** /daɪˈgreʃən/ *noun* [C, U]

digs /dɪgz/ *noun* [plural] *UK informal* a room in someone's house that you pay rent to live in

dike (*also* **dyke**) /daɪk/ *noun* **1** [WALL] a wall built to stop water from a sea or river going onto the land **2** [PASSAGE] *UK* a passage that has been dug to take water away from fields

diktat /ˈdɪktæt/ *noun* [C, U] an order which must be obeyed, or when you give such an order

dilapidated /dɪˈlæpɪdeɪtɪd/ *adjective* A dilapidated building or vehicle is old and in bad condition. •**dilapidation** /dɪˌlæpɪˈdeɪʃən/ *noun* [U]

dilate /daɪˈleɪt/ *verb* [I, T] If a part of your body dilates, or if you dilate it, it becomes wider or more open. *The drug causes your pupils to dilate.* •**dilation** /daɪˈleɪʃən/ *noun* [U]

WORD PARTNERS FOR ***dilemma***

face/have/be in a dilemma • sth **poses/presents** a dilemma • a **moral** dilemma • a dilemma **for** sb • a dilemma **about/over** sth

dilemma /dɪˈlemə/ *noun* [C] when you have to make a difficult choice between two things you could do *She's still **in a dilemma about** whether she should go or not.*

diligence /ˈdɪlɪdʒəns/ *noun* [U] when you work hard with care and effort

diligent /ˈdɪlɪdʒənt/ *adjective* working hard with care and effort *a diligent student* •**diligently** *adverb*

dilute /daɪˈluːt/ *verb* [T] **CHEMISTRY** to make a liquid thinner or weaker by adding water or another liquid to it •**dilute** *adjective dilute solution* ➲See picture at **diffusion**

D

dim¹ /dɪm/ *adjective* **dimmer, dimmest 1** NOT BRIGHT not bright or clear *He could hardly see her in the dim light.* **2 a dim memory/recollection, etc** when you can remember something slightly, but not very well **3** STUPID *UK informal* stupid *He's nice, but a bit dim.* •**dimly** *adverb a* ***dimly lit*** *room*

dim² /dɪm/ *verb* [I, T] **dimming,** *past* **dimmed** to become less bright, or to make something become less bright *He* ***dimmed*** *the* ***lights*** *and turned up the music.*

dime /daɪm/ *noun* [C] **1 ECONOMICS** a US or Canadian coin with a value of 10 cents **2 a dime a dozen** *mainly US informal* easy to find and very ordinary *Millionaires are now a dime a dozen.*

WORD PARTNERS FOR ***dimension***

add/give a [new/extra, etc] dimension **(to** sth) • an **added/extra/new** dimension

dimension /ˌdaɪˈmenʃᵊn/ *noun* [C] **1** PART a particular part of a situation, especially something that affects how you think or feel *Music has* ***added*** *a new* ***dimension to*** *my life.* **2** MEASUREMENT a measurement of the length, width, or height of something

dimensioning /daɪˈmentʃᵊnɪŋ/ *noun* [U] **1 DT** cutting or shaping something so that it is a particular size and shape **2 DT** marking particular measurements on something

diminish /dɪˈmɪnɪʃ/ *verb* [I, T] to become less, or to make something become less *Your pain should diminish gradually after taking these tablets.*

diminutive /dɪˈmɪnjətɪv/ *adjective formal* extremely small *a diminutive figure*

dimple /ˈdɪmpl/ *noun* [C] a small hollow place on your skin, often one that appears on your face when you smile •**dimpled** *adjective*

din /dɪn/ *noun* [**no plural**] a lot of loud, unpleasant noise

dine /daɪn/ *verb* [I] *formal* to eat dinner *On Saturday we dined with friends.*

dine out *phrasal verb formal* to eat your evening meal in a restaurant

diner /ˈdaɪnəʳ/ *noun* [C] **1** PERSON someone who is eating in a restaurant **2** RESTAURANT *mainly US* a small, informal restaurant

dinghy /ˈdɪŋi/ *noun* [C] a small boat *an inflatable dinghy*

dingy /ˈdɪndʒi/ *adjective* dirty and not bright *a dingy basement*

ˈdining ˌroom *noun* [C] a room where you eat your meals in a house or hotel

WORD PARTNERS FOR ***dinner***

eat/have dinner • **have** sth **for** dinner

O‑‑**dinner** /ˈdɪnəʳ/ *noun* [C, U] **FOOD** the main meal of the day that people usually eat in the evening *What's for dinner tonight?*

ˈdinner ˌjacket *UK* (*US* **tuxedo**) *noun* [C] a black or white jacket that a man wears on a very formal occasion

dinosaur /ˈdaɪnəsɔːʳ/ *noun* [C] a very large animal that used to live millions of years ago

diocese /ˈdaɪəsɪs/ *noun* [C] **RELIGION** the area controlled by a bishop (= an important Christian official)

diode /ˈdaɪəʊd/ *noun* [C] **PHYSICS** a device which controls an electric current so that it can only flow in one direction

dioxide /daɪˈɒksaɪd/ *noun* [U] **CHEMISTRY** a chemical substance consisting of two atoms of oxygen combined with one atom of another element

dioxin /daɪˈɒksɪn/ *noun* [C, U] **CHEMISTRY** a poisonous chemical of a type produced when substances used for killing plants are made

dip¹ /dɪp/ *noun* **1 FOOD** [C, U] a thick sauce that you can put pieces of food into before you eat them *a blue cheese dip* **2** SURFACE [C] a lower area on a surface *a sudden* ***dip in*** *the road* **3** AMOUNT [C] a sudden fall in the level or amount of something *a* ***dip in*** *profits* **4** SWIM [C] *informal* a short swim *Let's* ***have a*** *quick* ***dip*** *in the pool before breakfast.*

dip² /dɪp/ *verb* **dipping,** *past* **dipped 1** PUT INTO [T] to put something into a liquid for a short time *She* ***dipped*** *the brush* ***into*** *the paint.* **2** LOWER [I] to become lower in level or amount *The number of students taking sciences has dipped sharply.*

dip into sth *phrasal verb* **1** READ *UK* to read small parts of a book or magazine *It's the sort of book you can dip into now and then.* **2** SPEND to spend part of a supply of money that you have been keeping *I had to dip into my savings to pay for the repairs.*

dipeptide /ˌdaɪˈpeptaɪd/ *noun* [C] **CHEMISTRY** a compound formed of two linked amino acids

diphtheria /dɪpˈθɪəriə/ *noun* [U] **HEALTH** a very serious disease of the throat

diphthong /ˈdɪfθɒŋ/ *noun* [C] **LANGUAGE** a sound made by two vowels which are said together

diploid /ˈdɪplɔɪd/ *adjective* **BIOLOGY** a diploid cell has two sets of chromosomes, one from each parent ➲Compare **haploid**

diploma /dɪˈpləʊmə/ *noun* [C] **EDUCATION** a qualification from a school, college, or university, or an official document showing that someone has completed a course of study ***a diploma in*** *art and design*

diplomacy /dɪˈpləʊməsi/ *noun* [U] **1 POLITICS** dealing with the relationships between governments ***international diplomacy*** **2** skill in dealing with people well and not upsetting them *She showed great tact and diplomacy in the meeting.*

diplomat /ˈdɪpləmæt/ *noun* [C] **POLITICS** someone whose job is to live in another country and to keep a good relationship between their government and that country's government

diplomatic /ˌdɪpləˈmætɪk/ *adjective* **1 POLITICS** [**always before noun**] relating to diplomacy or diplomats *diplomatic relations* **2** good at dealing with people without upsetting them *That's a very diplomatic answer.* •**diplomatically** *adverb*

dire /daɪəʳ/ *adjective* very serious or bad *He's in* ***dire need*** *of help.*

O-- **direct**[1] /dɪˈrekt, daɪˈrekt/ *adjective* **1** STRAIGHT going straight from one place to another without turning or stopping *We went by the most direct route.* **2** NOTHING BETWEEN with no other person or thing involved or between *There is a **direct link** between smoking and cancer.* **3** CLEAR saying clearly and honestly what you think *a direct answer* ➲Opposite **indirect**

direct[2] /dɪˈrekt, daɪˈrekt/ *adverb* going straight from one place to another without turning or stopping *Several airlines now **fly direct** to Vancouver.*

direct[3] /dɪˈrekt, daɪˈrekt/ *verb* **1** FILM/PLAY [T] to tell the actors in a film or play what to do *a film directed by Alfred Hitchcock* **2 direct sth against/at/towards, etc sb/sth** to aim something at someone or something *The demonstrators' anger was directed at the police.* **3** ROUTE [T] to show or tell someone how to get to a place *Can you **direct** me **to** the manager's office please?* **4** ORGANIZE [T] to organize and control the way something is done *He directed the building of the new art gallery.* **5 direct sb to do sth** *formal* to officially order someone to do something *They directed us not to discuss the matter.*

ˌ**direct ˈaction** *noun* [U] **POLITICS** the use of action such as strikes (= refusing to work) or other forms of protest in order to try to make political or social changes in society

diˌrect ˈcurrent *noun* [U] **PHYSICS** electrical current that only moves in one direction ➲Compare **alternating current**

ˌ**direct ˈdebit** *noun* [C, U] **FINANCE** an arrangement that allows an organization to take money from your bank account at regular times to pay for goods or services *I pay my council tax by direct debit.*

ˌ**direct deˈposit** *noun* [U] *US* **FINANCE** an arrangement in which money is moved electronically into a bank account

WORD PARTNERS FOR ***direction***

change direction • **in the opposite/other** direction • **in the right/wrong** direction • **in the direction of sth** • **from all/in all** directions

O-- **direction** /dɪˈrekʃᵊn/ *noun* **1** WAY [C] the way that someone or something is going or facing *The car sped away **in the direction of** the airport.* ○ *I think we're going in the **wrong direction**.* **2 in sb's direction** towards someone *She keeps looking in my direction.* **3** DEVELOPMENT [C] the way that someone or something changes or develops *Our careers have gone in very different directions.* **4** CONTROL [U] control or instructions ***Under his direction** the company has doubled its profits.* **5** PURPOSE [U] knowing what you want to do *According to his teachers, he **lacks direction**.*

directions /dɪˈrekʃᵊnz/ *noun* [plural] instructions that tell you how to get to a place, or how to do something *We stopped to **ask for directions**.* ○ *Just **follow** the **directions** on the label.*

directive /dɪˈrektɪv/ *noun* [C] *formal* an official instruction *The government has **issued** new **directives** on food hygiene.*

ˌ**direct ˈlabour** *UK* (*US* **direct labor**) *noun* [U] **FINANCE** the cost of paying people who are employed directly to make products

directly /dɪˈrektli/ *adverb* **1** NOTHING BETWEEN with no other person or thing involved or between *Why don't you **speak to** him **directly**?* **2 directly after/behind/opposite, etc** exactly or immediately after/behind/opposite, etc *She was sitting directly opposite me.* **3** CLEAR clearly and honestly *Let me answer that question directly.*

ˌ**direct ˈmail** *noun* [U] when companies or organizations write to people to try to persuade them to buy their product or give money, etc.

directness /dɪˈrektnəs/ *noun* [U] when someone is clear and honest in their speech or behaviour *He liked her directness and simplicity.*

ˌ**direct ˈobject** *noun* [C] **LANGUAGE** the direct object of a transitive verb is the person or thing that is affected by the action of the verb. In the sentence 'I bought a new car yesterday.', 'a new car' is the direct object. ➲Compare **indirect object**

director /dɪˈrektəʳ/ *noun* [C] **1** MANAGER an important manager in an organization or company *Meet the new **sales director**.* **2** ACTORS someone who tells the actors in a film or play what to do *the famous film director, Alfred Hitchcock* ➲See also: **funeral director, managing director**

directorate /dɪˈrektᵊrət/ *noun* [C] **POLITICS** a part of a government or other organization with responsibility for a particular activity

directory /dɪˈrektᵊri/ *noun* [C] **1** a book or list of names, numbers, or other facts ➲See also: **telephone directory** **2 COMPUTING** (*also* **file directory**) a place on a computer for putting files and folders together

ˌ**direct ˈtax** *noun* [C] **FINANCE** tax that people must pay to the government themselves, especially income tax ➲Compare **indirect tax**

dirt[1] /dɜːt/ *noun* [U] **1** NOT CLEAN an unpleasant substance that makes something not clean *You've got some dirt on your trousers.* **2** GROUND soil or rough ground *a dirt road/track* **3 dig the/up dirt on sb** *informal* to try to discover bad things about someone to stop other people admiring them

dirt[2] /dɜːt/ *adverb* **dirt cheap/poor** extremely cheap/poor

O-- **dirty**[1] /ˈdɜːti/ *adjective* **1** NOT CLEAN not clean *dirty clothes* ○ *dirty dishes* **2** OFFENSIVE talking about sex in a way that some people find offensive *dirty books/jokes* **3** DISHONEST dishonest or unfair *a dirty business* ➲See also: do sb's dirty **work**[2]

OTHER WAYS OF SAYING ***dirty***

If something is extremely dirty, you can say it is **filthy**: *Wash your hands before supper - they're **filthy**!*

If someone or something looks dirty and untidy, you can say that they are **scruffy** or **messy**: *He's the typical **scruffy** student.* • *Ben's bedroom is always really **messy**.*

If something is covered in dirt and needs washing, the adjectives **grimy** and **grubby** are often used: *Don't wipe your **grimy** hands on that clean towel!* • *He was wearing an old pair of jeans and a **grubby** T-shirt.*

The adjective **soiled** is sometimes used to describe material that is dirty: ***Soiled** tablecloths should be soaked in detergent.*

If a place is extremely dirty and unpleasant, the adjective **squalid** is sometimes used: *The prisoners lived in **squalid** conditions.*

dirty² /ˈdɜːti/ *verb* [T] to make something dirty

dis- /dɪs-/ *prefix* not or the opposite of *dishonest* ○ *disbelief* ○ *to disagree*

disability /ˌdɪsəˈbɪləti/ *noun* [C, U] **HEALTH** an illness, injury, or condition that makes it difficult for someone to do the things that other people do

disable /dɪˈseɪbl/ *verb* [T] **1 HEALTH** If someone is disabled by an illness or injury, it makes it difficult for them to live in the way that most other people do. [**often passive**] *Some children were permanently disabled by the bomb.* **2** EQUIPMENT to stop a piece of equipment from working *The thieves must have disabled the alarm system.*

disabled /dɪˈseɪbld/ *adjective* **HEALTH** having an illness, injury, or condition that makes it difficult to do the things that other people do *They are demanding equal rights for **the disabled**.*

disaccharide /daɪˈsækəraɪd/ *noun* [C] **CHEMISTRY** a sugar that is formed of two simple sugar molecules

WORD PARTNERS FOR ***disadvantage***

have/face a disadvantage • a **big** / the **main**/ a **major**/a **serious** disadvantage • a disadvantage **of/to** (doing) sth • a disadvantage **for** sb • the **advantages** and disadvantages (**of** sth)

disadvantage /ˌdɪsədˈvɑːntɪdʒ/ *noun* **1** [C] something which makes a situation more difficult, or makes you less likely to succeed *One **disadvantage of** living in the country is the lack of public transport.* **2 at a disadvantage** having problems that other people do not have *Being shy puts him at a disadvantage.*

disadvantaged /ˌdɪsədˈvɑːntɪdʒd/ *adjective* Disadvantaged people are poor and do not have many opportunities. *disadvantaged children*

disaffected /ˌdɪsəˈfektɪd/ *adjective* disappointed with someone or something and not supporting them as you did before *disaffected voters* •**disaffection** /ˌdɪsəˈfekʃᵊn/ *noun* [U]

disagree /ˌdɪsəˈɡriː/ *verb* [I] **disagreeing**, *past* **disagreed** to have a different opinion from someone else about something *I **disagree with** most of what he said.* ○ *Experts **disagree about/on** the causes of the disease.*

disagreeable /ˌdɪsəˈɡriːəbl/ *adjective formal* unpleasant *a disagreeable old man*

disagreement /ˌdɪsəˈɡriːmᵊnt/ *noun* [C, U] when people have a different opinion about something or have an argument *They **had a disagreement about/over** money.* ○ *There is a lot of **disagreement among** doctors on this matter.*

disallow /ˌdɪsəˈlaʊ/ *verb* [T] to officially refuse to accept something because the rules have been broken *The goal was disallowed by the referee.*

disappear /ˌdɪsəˈpɪəʳ/ *verb* [I] **1** NOT SEE to become impossible to see *She watched him **disappear into** the crowd.* **2** GO to suddenly go somewhere else and become impossible to find *Her husband disappeared in 1991.* **3** STOP EXISTING to stop existing *These flowers are disappearing from our countryside.* •**disappearance** /ˌdɪsəˈpɪərᵊns/ *noun* [C, U] *Police are investigating the girl's disappearance.* See also: disappear/vanish into thin **air**¹

disappoint /ˌdɪsəˈpɔɪnt/ *verb* [T] to make someone feel unhappy because someone or something was not as good as they had expected *We don't want to disappoint the fans.*

OTHER WAYS OF SAYING ***disappointed***

If someone feels very disappointed about something that has happened, you can use the adjectives **disheartened** or, in informal situations, (*UK*) **gutted**: *He was very **disheartened** by the results of the test.* • *Nick's absolutely **gutted** that he's been dropped from the team.*

If a person disappoints someone by not doing what they agreed to do, then the phrasal verb **let down** is sometimes used: *John had promised to go but he **let** me **down** at the last minute.*

A situation which makes someone feel disappointed is often described as a **letdown**: *After all that planning the party was a bit of a **letdown**.*

An **anti-climax** is a disappointing experience, often one that you thought would be exciting before it happened or one that comes after a more exciting experience: *After so much preparation, the party itself was a bit of an **anticlimax**.*

disappointed /ˌdɪsəˈpɔɪntɪd/ *adjective* unhappy because someone or something was not as good as you hoped or expected, or because something did not happen [+ **(that)**] *I was very disappointed that he didn't come.* ○ *I'm really **disappointed in** you.*

disappointing /ˌdɪsəˈpɔɪntɪŋ/ *adjective* making you feel disappointed *a disappointing performance/result* •**disappointingly** *adverb a disappointingly small audience*

disappointment /ˌdɪsəˈpɔɪntmənt/ *noun* **1** FEELING [U] the feeling of being disappointed

She couldn't hide her disappointment when she lost. **2** PERSON/THING [C] someone or something that disappoints you *I'm sorry I'm such **a disappointment to** you.*

disapproval /ˌdɪsəˈpruːvᵊl/ *noun* [U] when you think that someone or something is bad or wrong

disapprove /ˌdɪsəˈpruːv/ *verb* [I] to think that someone or something is bad or wrong *Her family **disapproved of** the marriage.* •**disapproving** *adjective* showing that you think someone or something is bad or wrong *a disapproving look*

disarm /dɪˈsɑːm/ *verb* **1** WEAPONS [I, T] to give up your weapons, or to take away someone else's weapons *Both sides have agreed to disarm.* **2** FEELINGS [T] to make someone feel less angry *His smile disarmed her.*

disarmament /dɪˈsɑːməmənt/ *noun* [U] when a country or group gets rid of some or all of its weapons ***nuclear disarmament***

disarming /dɪˈsɑːmɪŋ/ *adjective* behaving in a way that stops people feeling angry with you or criticizing you *a **disarming smile***

disarray /ˌdɪsᵊrˈeɪ/ *noun* [U] when something is untidy and not organized *The house was **in** complete **disarray**.*

WORD PARTNERS FOR ***disaster***

bring/cause/prevent disaster • disaster **happens/strikes** • a **complete/major/terrible/unmitigated** disaster • a **natural** disaster

O─**disaster** /dɪˈzɑːstəʳ/ *noun* **1** DAMAGE [C] something that causes a lot of harm or damage *floods and other **natural disasters*** **2** FAILURE [C] a failure or something that has a very bad result *His idea was a total disaster.* **3** BAD SITUATION [U] an extremely bad situation *The holiday ended in disaster.*

disastrous /dɪˈzɑːstrəs/ *adjective* extremely bad ***disastrous consequences*** ○ *a disastrous week*

disband /dɪsˈbænd/ *verb* [I, T] *formal* to stop working together as a group, or to stop a group from working together

disbelief /ˌdɪsbɪˈliːf/ *noun* [U] when you do not believe that something is true or real *She shook her head **in disbelief**.*

disbelieve /ˌdɪsbɪˈliːv/ *verb* [T] to not believe someone or something

disc (*also US* **disk**) /dɪsk/ *noun* [C] **1** SHAPE a flat, round shape or object **2** RECORDING a record or CD **3 ANATOMY** a piece of cartilage (= strong material in the body) between the bones in your back ➲See also: **compact disc**

discard /dɪˈskɑːd/ *verb* [T] to throw something away *discarded food wrappers*

discern /dɪˈsɜːn/ *verb* [T] *formal* to see or recognize something •**discernible** *adjective There was no **discernible difference** between them.*

discerning /dɪˈsɜːnɪŋ/ *adjective* having or showing good judgment, especially about style and quality *a discerning customer/reader*

discharge¹ /dɪsˈtʃɑːdʒ/ *verb* [T] **1** PERSON to allow someone to leave a hospital or prison, or to order or allow someone to leave an organization such as the army [**often passive**] *She was **discharged from** the army yesterday.* **2** SUBSTANCE If a liquid or gas is discharged from something, it comes out of it.

discharge² /ˈdɪstʃɑːdʒ/ *noun* [C, U] **1** LEAVE when someone is officially allowed or ordered to leave somewhere such as a prison, hospital, or the army **2** COME OUT when a liquid or gas comes out of something *the discharge of carbon dioxide* **3** SUBSTANCE a liquid or gas that comes out of something

disciple /dɪˈsaɪpl/ *noun* [C] **RELIGION** someone who follows the ideas and teaching of someone, especially of a religious leader

disciplinarian /ˌdɪsəplɪˈneəriən/ *noun* [C] someone who is very strict and gives punishments when people break rules

disciplinary /ˌdɪsəˈplɪnᵊri / (US) /ˈdɪsəplɪneri/ *adjective* [**always before noun**] relating to punishment for someone who has broken rules ***disciplinary action***

WORD PARTNERS FOR ***discipline***

enforce/establish/restore discipline • **firm/harsh/rigorous** discipline • **lax/poor** discipline

discipline¹ /ˈdɪsəplɪn/ *noun* **1** CONTROL [U] when people's behaviour is controlled using rules and punishments *There should be better discipline in schools.* **2** SELF CONTROL [U] when you can control your own behaviour carefully *I don't have enough discipline to save money.* **3 EDUCATION** [C] *formal* a particular subject of study *the scientific disciplines* ➲See also: **self-discipline**

discipline² /ˈdɪsəplɪn/ *verb* [T] **1** PUNISH to punish someone [**often passive**] *He was disciplined for missing a training session.* **2** CONTROL to teach someone to behave in a controlled way [**often reflexive**] *You have to learn to discipline yourself.*

disciplined /ˈdɪsəplɪnd/ *adjective* behaving in a very controlled way *the most disciplined army in the world*

ˈdisc ˌjockey (*also* **DJ**) *noun* [C] **MUSIC** someone who plays music on the radio or at discos

disclaim /dɪsˈkleɪm/ *verb* [T] *formal* to say that you know nothing about something, or are not responsible for something *The terrorists **disclaimed responsibility** for the bomb.*

disclaimer /dɪsˈkleɪməʳ/ *noun* [C] when someone officially says that they are not responsible for something

disclose /dɪsˈkləʊz/ *verb* [T] *formal* to give new or secret information to someone *He refused to **disclose details** of the report.*

disclosure /dɪsˈkləʊʒəʳ/ *noun* [C, U] when someone gives people new or secret information

disco /ˈdɪskəʊ/ *noun* [C] **MUSIC** a place or event where people dance to pop music

discoloured *UK* (*US* **discolored**) /dɪsˈkʌləd/ *adjective* If something is discoloured, it has become a less attractive colour than it was originally. ***discoloured teeth***

D

discomfort /dɪ'skʌmfət/ *noun* **1** PAIN [U] slight pain *You may feel some discomfort for a few days.* **2** MENTAL FEELING [U] when you feel slightly embarrassed or anxious **3 HEALTH** [C, U] a physically uncomfortable situation

disconcert /ˌdɪskən'sɜːt/ *verb* [T] to make someone feel confused or anxious [**often passive**] *She was disconcerted by his questions.*

disconcerting /ˌdɪskən'sɜːtɪŋ/ *adjective* making you feel confused or anxious *a disconcerting silence* •**disconcertingly** *adverb*

D

disconnect /ˌdɪskə'nekt/ *verb* [T] to separate two things that are joined or connected, especially a piece of equipment and a power supply *Switch off the machine before* ***disconnecting*** *it* ***from*** *the power supply.*

disconnected /ˌdɪskə'nektɪd/ *adjective* not joined in any way *disconnected thoughts*

discontent /ˌdɪskən'tent/ *noun* [U] unhappiness about a situation *There is growing* ***discontent with*** *this government.* •**discontented** *adjective*

discontinue /ˌdɪskən'tɪnjuː/ *verb* [T] **discontinuing,** *past* **discontinued** to stop producing or providing something such as a product or service [**often passive**] *I'm afraid this model has been discontinued.*

discord /'dɪskɔːd/ *noun* [U] disagreement between people

discount[1] /'dɪskaʊnt/ *noun* [C, U] **FINANCE** a reduction in price *They offer a 10 percent* ***discount on*** *rail travel for students.*

discount[2] /dɪ'skaʊnt/ *verb* [T] **1** to ignore something because you do not believe that it is true or that it will happen *You shouldn't* ***discount the possibility*** *of him coming back.* **2 FINANCE** to reduce the price of something *discounted goods/rates*

ˌdiscount alˈlowed *noun* [U] **FINANCE** a discount (= lower price) given to customers who pay within a particular period of time

ˌdiscount reˈceived *noun* [U] **FINANCE** a discount (= lower price) a business receives when it pays for goods or services within a particular period of time

discourage /dɪ'skʌrɪdʒ/ *verb* **1 discourage sb from doing sth** to try to persuade someone not to do something *a campaign to discourage people from smoking* **2** PREVENT [T] to try to prevent something from happening *a campaign to discourage smoking* **3** LESS CONFIDENT [T] to make someone less confident or enthusiastic about something *I didn't mean to discourage her.* •**discouragement** *noun* [U] ⊃Opposite **encourage**

discouraged /dɪ'skʌrɪdʒd/ *adjective* having lost your confidence or enthusiasm for something

discouraging /dɪ'skʌrɪdʒɪŋ/ *adjective* making you feel less enthusiastic or confident about something *discouraging results*

O-- **discover** /dɪ'skʌvəʳ/ *verb* [T] **1** FIND to find something *The body was discovered in a ditch.* **2** FIRST to be the first person to find something important *Who discovered America?* **3** GET INFORMATION to get information about something for the first time [**+ (that)**] *She discovered that he had been married three times before.* [**+ question word**] *Have they discovered what was causing your headaches?*

discoverer /dɪ'skʌvərəʳ/ *noun* [C] someone who is the first person to find something important

WORD PARTNERS FOR ***discovery***

make a discovery • a **chance/new** discovery • the discovery **of** sth

discovery /dɪ'skʌvəri/ *noun* **1** FINDING [C, U] when someone discovers something *the* ***discovery of*** *bones in the garden* ○ *Scientists have* ***made*** *some important* ***discoveries*** *about genetics recently.* **2** THING/PERSON [C] something or someone that is discovered

discredit /dɪ'skredɪt/ *verb* [T] to make someone or something appear bad and lose the respect of other people *They're always looking for ways to discredit her.*

discreet /dɪ'skriːt/ *adjective* careful not to cause embarrassment or attract too much attention, especially by keeping something secret *Can I trust you to be discreet?* ⊃Opposite **indiscreet** •**discreetly** *adverb*

discrepancy /dɪ'skrepənsi/ *noun* [C, U] when two things that should be the same are different *There is a slight* ***discrepancy between*** *the two statements.*

discrete /dɪ'skriːt/ *adjective* separate and different *a word that has two discrete meanings*

discretion /dɪ'skreʃən/ *noun* [U] **1** CARE when someone is careful not to cause embarrassment or attract too much attention, especially by keeping something secret *You can rely on my discretion.* ⊃Opposite **indiscretion 2** RIGHT the right to decide something *Students can be expelled* ***at the discretion of*** *the head teacher* (= if the head teacher decides it).

discretionary /dɪ'skreʃənəri/ *adjective* decided by officials and not fixed by rules *Judges have great* ***discretionary powers.***

discriminate /dɪ'skrɪmɪneɪt/ *verb* [I] **1** TREAT UNFAIRLY to treat someone unfairly because of their sex, race, religion, etc *The company was accused of* ***discriminating against*** *people on the basis of age.* **2** NOTICE to notice a difference between two things *Police dogs are very good at* ***discriminating between*** *different smells.*

discriminating /dɪ'skrɪmɪneɪtɪŋ/ *adjective* good at judging what is good quality *a discriminating shopper*

WORD PARTNERS FOR ***discrimination***

face/suffer discrimination • **age/racial/sex** discrimination • discrimination **against** sb

discrimination /dɪˌskrɪmɪ'neɪʃən/ *noun* [U] when someone is treated unfairly because of their sex, race, religion, etc ***racial/sex discrimination*** ○ ***discrimination against*** *older workers*

discus /'dɪskəs/ *noun* [C] **SPORT** a round, flat, heavy object that people throw as a sport

O-- **discuss** /dɪ'skʌs/ *verb* [T] to talk about something with someone and tell each other your ideas or opinions *Have you discussed this matter with anyone else?*

COMMON LEARNER ERROR

discuss

Discuss is not followed by a preposition.

We discussed the plans for the wedding.

~~*We discussed about the plans for the wedding.*~~

You can **discuss something with someone**.

Can I discuss this report with you?

WORD PARTNERS FOR ***discussion***

have/hold a discussion • a **heated/lengthy** discussion • a discussion **about** sth • be **under** discussion

O➡**discussion** /dɪ'skʌʃən/ *noun* [**C, U**] when people talk about something and tell each other their ideas or opinions *They were **having a discussion about** football.* ○ *Several ideas are still **under discussion*** (= being discussed).

dis'cussion ˌgroup *noun* [**C**] **INTERNET** a group of people who use the Internet to discuss particular subjects ➲See Extra help page **The Web and the Internet** on page Centre 37.

disdain /dɪs'deɪn/ *noun* [**U**] when you dislike someone or something and think that they do not deserve any respect *His **disdain for** politicians is obvious.* •**disdainful** *adjective disdainful remarks* •**disdainfully** *adverb*

WORD PARTNERS FOR ***disease***

be affected by/have/suffer from a disease • **contract/develop** a disease • **cure/detect/diagnose/treat** a disease • a **chronic/deadly/hereditary/infectious** disease

O➡**disease** /dɪ'ziːz/ *noun* [**C, U**] **HEALTH** an illness caused by an infection or by a failure of health and not by an accident ***heart disease*** ○ ***an infectious disease*** •**diseased** *adjective* affected by a disease *a diseased lung*

disembark /ˌdɪsɪm'bɑːk/ *verb* [**I**] *formal* to leave a ship, boat, or aircraft *All passengers must disembark in Vancouver.* •**disembarkation** /ˌdɪsɪmbɑː'keɪʃən/ *noun* [**U**]

disembodied /ˌdɪsɪm'bɒdid/ *adjective* seeming not to have a body or not to be connected to a body *a disembodied voice*

disenchanted /ˌdɪsɪn'tʃɑːntɪd/ *adjective* disappointed with something that you thought was good in the past *He became **disenchanted with** politics.* •**disenchantment** *noun* [**U**]

disengage /ˌdɪsɪn'geɪdʒ/ *verb* [**I, T**] to become separated from something, or to make two things become separate from each other *He gently disengaged his hand from hers.*

disentangle /ˌdɪsɪn'tæŋgl/ *verb* [**T**] **1** SEPARATE to separate someone or something that is connected to something else in a complicated way *He **disentangled** himself **from** her arms.* **2** STRING/WIRE to separate things such as pieces of string, hair, or wire that have become twisted together

disfigure /dɪs'fɪgər/ *verb* [**T**] to spoil someone's or something's appearance [**often passive**] *Her face was disfigured by a huge scar.*

disgrace¹ /dɪs'greɪs/ *verb* [**T**] to make people stop respecting you or your family, team, etc by doing something very bad

disgrace² /dɪs'greɪs/ *noun* [**U**] **1** when someone does something very bad that makes people stop respecting them or their family, team, etc *They were sent home **in disgrace**.* **2 be a disgrace** to be very bad [**+ that**] *It's a disgrace that money is being wasted like this.* **3 be a disgrace to sb/sth** to be so bad or unacceptable that you make people stop respecting a particular group, activity, etc *You are a disgrace to your profession.*

disgraced /dɪs'greɪst/ *adjective* A disgraced person has lost other people's respect because they have done something very bad. *a disgraced politician*

disgraceful /dɪs'greɪsfəl/ *adjective* very bad *disgraceful behaviour* •**disgracefully** *adverb*

disgruntled /dɪs'grʌntld/ *adjective* angry and upset *Disgruntled workers have decided to go on strike.*

disguise¹ /dɪs'gaɪz/ *noun* [**C, U**] clothes and other things that you wear to change the way you look so that people cannot recognize you *She usually goes out **in disguise** to avoid being bothered by the public.* ➲See also: a **blessing** in disguise

disguise² /dɪs'gaɪz/ *verb* **1 disguise yourself/your voice, etc** to change your appearance/voice, etc so that people cannot recognize you *He managed to escape by **disguising** himself **as** a woman.* **2 be disguised as sb/sth** to be wearing clothes and other things that make you look like someone or something else **3** [**T**] to hide something such as a feeling or opinion *She couldn't disguise her disappointment.*

disgust¹ /dɪs'gʌst/ *noun* [**U**] a very strong feeling of dislike or disapproval *She walked out **in disgust**.*

disgust² /dɪs'gʌst/ *verb* [**T**] If something disgusts you, it makes you feel extreme dislike or disapproval. *These pictures disgust me.*

disgusted /dɪs'gʌstɪd/ *adjective* feeling extreme dislike or disapproval of something *I'm totally **disgusted with** your behaviour.*

disgusting /dɪs'gʌstɪŋ/ *adjective* extremely unpleasant *What's that disgusting smell?*

O➡**dish¹** /dɪʃ/ *noun* [**C**] **1** CONTAINER a curved container for eating or serving food from *a baking/serving dish* **2** FOOD food that is prepared in a particular way as part of a meal *a chicken/vegetarian dish* **3 the dishes** dirty plates, bowls, and other objects for cooking or eating food *Who's going to **wash the dishes**?*

dish² /dɪʃ/ *verb*

dish sth out *phrasal verb informal* to give or say things to people without thinking about them carefully

dishcloth /'dɪʃklɒθ/ *noun* [**C**] a cloth used for washing dirty dishes

disheartened /dɪs'hɑːtənd/ *adjective* disappointed or without hope *She was very disheartened by the results of the test.*

disheartening /dɪs'hɑːtənɪŋ/ *adjective* making you feel disappointed or without hope *a disheartening experience*

dishevelled *UK* (*US* **disheveled**) /dɪ'ʃevəld/ *adjective* very untidy *dishevelled hair*

dishonest /dɪˈsɒnɪst/ *adjective* not honest and likely to lie or do something illegal •**dishonestly** *adverb* •**dishonesty** *noun* [U] when someone is not honest

dishonour¹ *UK* (*US* **dishonor**) /dɪˈsɒnəʳ/ *noun* [U] when people stop respecting you because you have done something bad •**dishonourable** *adjective* bad or not deserving respect *dishonourable conduct*

D

dishonour² *UK* (*US* **dishonor**) /dɪˈsɒnəʳ/ *verb* [T] **1** to show no respect for someone or something by behaving badly *He felt that he had dishonoured his country.* **2** FINANCE to refuse to accept or pay a cheque or a bill (= amount charged)

ˈ**dish** ˌ**soap** *US* (*UK* **washing-up liquid**) *noun* [U] a thick liquid soap used to wash pans, plates, knives and forks etc.

dishtowel /ˈdɪʃtaʊəl/ *US* (*UK* **tea towel**) *noun* [C] a cloth that is used for drying plates, dishes, etc

dishwasher /ˈdɪʃˌwɒʃəʳ/ *noun* [C] a machine that washes plates, glasses and other kitchen equipment *I'll load the dishwasher.* ➲See colour picture **The Kitchen** on page Centre 2

disillusion /ˌdɪsɪˈluːʒən/ *verb* [T] to cause someone to discover that something they believed is not true

disillusioned /ˌdɪsɪˈluːʒənd/ *adjective* feeling disappointed because something is not as good as you thought it was *She says she's* ***disillusioned with*** *the music business.*

disillusionment /ˌdɪsɪˈluːʒənmənt/ (*also* **disillusion**) *noun* [U] the disappointment someone feels when they discover something is not as good as they thought it was *There's growing* ***disillusionment with*** *the government.*

disinfect /ˌdɪsɪnˈfekt/ *verb* [T] HEALTH to clean something with a chemical that destroys bacteria

disinfectant /ˌdɪsɪnˈfektənt/ *noun* [C, U] HEALTH a chemical substance that destroys bacteria

disintegrate /dɪˈsɪntɪgreɪt/ *verb* [I] **1** [BREAK] to break into a lot of small pieces **2** [GET WORSE] to become much worse *The situation* ***is disintegrating into*** *total chaos.* •**disintegration** /dɪˌsɪntɪˈgreɪʃən/ *noun* [U]

disinterested /dɪˈsɪntrəstɪd/ *adjective* not involved in a situation and so able to judge it without supporting a particular side *a* ***disinterested observer***

disjointed /dɪsˈdʒɔɪntɪd/ *adjective* having words or ideas that are not in a clear order *a disjointed conversation*

WORD PARTNERS FOR ***disk***

save/write sth to disk • on a disk • disk space

disk /dɪsk/ *noun* [C] **1** *another US spelling of* disc **2** COMPUTING a piece of computer equipment that records and stores information electronically *How much* ***disk space*** *is there ?* ➲See colour picture **The Office** on page Centre 5 ➲See also: **floppy disk, hard disk**

ˈ**disk** ˌ**drive** *noun* [C] COMPUTING the part of a computer that allows the person using the computer to store and read information from a disk

diskette /dɪˈsket/ *noun* [C] COMPUTING a small, flat, plastic object that you put in your computer to record and store information electronically

dislike¹ /dɪˈslaɪk/ *verb* [T] to not like someone or something *Why do you dislike her so much?* [+ doing sth] *I dislike ironing intensely.*

dislike² /dɪˈslaɪk/ *noun* [C, U] when you do not like someone or something *a dislike of cold weather* ○ *I* ***took an instant dislike to*** *her* (= disliked her immediately).

dislocate /ˈdɪsləʊkeɪt/ *verb* [T] HEALTH If you dislocate a part of your body, the bones move away from their correct position. *I think you've dislocated your shoulder.* ○ *a dislocated hip* •**dislocation** /ˌdɪsləʊˈkeɪʃən/ *noun* [U]

dislodge /dɪˈslɒdʒ/ *verb* [T] to move something away from a fixed position

disloyal /dɪˈslɔɪəl/ *adjective* not loyal or not supporting someone who you should support *I don't want to be* ***disloyal to*** *my friend.* •**disloyalty** *noun* [U] *They accused her of disloyalty.*

dismal /ˈdɪzməl/ *adjective* very bad or unpleasant and making you feel unhappy *What* ***dismal weather.*** ○ *That was a* ***dismal performance.*** •**dismally** *adverb I tried to cheer her up, but* ***failed dismally*** (= completely failed).

dismantle /dɪˈsmæntl/ *verb* [T] **1** [TAKE APART] to take something apart so that it is in several pieces *He's specially trained to dismantle bombs.* **2** [GET RID OF] to get rid of a system or organization

dismay /dɪˈsmeɪ/ *noun* [U] a feeling of unhappiness and disappointment ***To our dismay,*** *it started raining.*

dismayed /dɪˈsmeɪd/ *adjective* unhappy and disappointed [+ to do sth] *I was dismayed to discover that he'd lied to me.*

dismember /dɪˈsmembəʳ/ *verb* [T] to cut the arms and legs off the body of a person or animal *a* ***dismembered body***

dismiss /dɪˈsmɪs/ *verb* [T] **1** [NOT CONSIDER] to refuse to consider an idea or opinion *The committee* ***dismissed*** *the idea* ***as*** *rubbish.* **2** [MAKE LEAVE] to officially make someone leave their job [often passive] *Anyone who breaks company rules will be dismissed.* **3** [ALLOW TO LEAVE] to give someone official permission to leave *The bell rang and the teacher dismissed the class.*

dismissal /dɪˈsmɪsəl/ *noun* **1** [IDEA] [U] when someone refuses to consider an idea or opinion **2** [JOB] [C, U] when an employer officially makes someone leave their job

dismissive /dɪˈsmɪsɪv/ *adjective* treating something as if it is not important *He's so* ***dismissive of*** *all my suggestions.* •**dismissively** *adverb*

dismount /dɪˈsmaʊnt/ *verb* [I] *formal* to get off a horse or bicycle

disobedience /ˌdɪsəʊˈbiːdiəns/ *noun* [U] when someone refuses to do what someone in authority tells them to do

disobedient /ˌdɪsəʊ'biːdiənt/ *adjective* refusing to do what someone in authority tells you to do *a disobedient child*

disobey /ˌdɪsəʊ'beɪ/ *verb* [T] to not do what you are told to do by someone in authority *How dare you disobey me!*

disorder /dɪ'sɔːdəʳ/ *noun* **1 HEALTH** [C] a disease or mental problem *a blood disorder* **2** [BAD BEHAVIOUR] [U] uncontrolled, bad behaviour, especially by large groups of people *crime and disorder* **3** [NOT ORGANIZED] [U] when things are untidy or confused and not organized *His financial affairs are **in** complete **disorder**.* ➲See also: **eating disorder**

disordered /dɪ'sɔːdəd/ *adjective* confused and not organized *a disordered mind*

disorderly /dɪ'sɔːdᵊli/ *adjective* **1** [BADLY BEHAVED] behaving badly by being noisy or violent *He was charged with being **drunk and disorderly**.* **2** [UNTIDY] untidy

disorganized (*also UK* **-ised**) /dɪ'sɔːgənaɪzd/ *adjective* **1** [EVENT] not planned or organized well *The competition was completely disorganized.* **2** [PERSON] not good at planning or organizing things

disorient /dɪ'sɔːriənt/ (*also UK* **disorientate** /dɪ'sɔːriənteɪt/) *verb* [T] to make someone not know where to go or what to do

disoriented /dɪ'sɔːriəntɪd/ (*also UK* **disorientated** /dɪ'sɔːriənteɪtɪd/) *adjective* confused and not knowing where to go or what to do *Whales become disoriented in shallow water.*

disown /dɪ'səʊn/ *verb* [T] to say that you do not want to have any involvement or connection with someone *Even his parents have disowned him.*

disparage /dɪ'spærɪdʒ/ *verb* [T] to say that you think someone or something is not very good [**often passive**] *He is often disparaged by the critics.*

disparaging /dɪ'spærɪdʒɪŋ/ *adjective* criticizing someone or something ***disparaging remarks***

disparate /'dɪspᵊrət/ *adjective formal* completely different *people from disparate cultures*

disparity /dɪ'spærəti/ *noun* [C, U] *formal* difference, usually relating to the money people earn or their position

dispatch¹ (*also UK* **despatch**) /dɪ'spætʃ/ *verb* [T] *formal* to send someone or something somewhere *They dispatched a police car to arrest him.*

dispatch² (*also UK* **despatch**) /dɪ'spætʃ/ *noun* **1** [SENDING] [U] when someone or something is sent somewhere *the dispatch of troops* **2** [REPORT] [C] an official report that someone in a foreign country sends to their organization

dispel /dɪ'spel/ *verb* [T] **dispelling**, *past* **dispelled** to get rid of a feeling, thought, or belief *He appeared on TV to **dispel rumours** that he was dying.*

dispensary /dɪ'spensᵊri/ *noun* [C] **HEALTH** a place where medicines are given out

dispensation /ˌdɪspen'seɪʃᵊn/ *noun* [C, U] **LAW** special permission to do something [**+ to do sth**] *The court would not **grant** him a **dispensation** to visit his children.*

dispense /dɪ'spens/ *verb* [T] to give something out *a machine that dispenses drinks and snacks*
dispense with sth/sb *phrasal verb* to stop using something or someone, or to get rid of something or someone, usually because you do not need them

dispenser /dɪ'spensəʳ/ *noun* [C] a machine that you can get something from *a **cash/drink/soap dispenser***

disperse /dɪ'spɜːs/ *verb* [I, T] to separate and go in different directions, or to make something do this *We waited until the **crowds had dispersed**.* •**dispersal** *noun* [U]

dispersion /dɪ'spɜːʃᵊn/ *noun* [U] **PHYSICS** the separation of light into different colours

dispirited /dɪ'spɪrɪtɪd/ *adjective* unhappy and without hope

displace /dɪ'spleɪs/ *verb* [T] **1** [TAKE THE PLACE OF] to take the place of someone or something *Many of these workers will be displaced by modern technology.* **2** [MOVE] to make someone or something leave their usual place or position *The earthquake displaced thousands of people.* •**displacement** *noun* [U]

display¹ /dɪ'spleɪ/ *noun* **1** [ARRANGEMENT] [C] a collection of objects or pictures arranged for people to look at *a display of children's paintings* **2 on display** If something is on display, it is there for people to look at. *Many old aircraft are on display at the museum.* **3** [SHOW] [C] a performance or show for people to watch *a **firework display*** **4 COMPUTING** [C, U] when something is shown electronically such as on a computer screen *The display problems might be due to a shortage of disk space.* **5 a display of affection/anger, etc** when someone behaves in a way that shows they have a particular feeling

display² /dɪ'spleɪ/ *verb* **1** [ARRANGE] [T] to arrange something somewhere so that people can see it *There were some family photographs displayed on his desk.* **2 COMPUTING** [I, T] to show something electronically such as on a computer screen *The **text** can be **displayed** and edited on screen.* **3** [FEELING] [T] to show how you feel by your expression or behaviour *He never **displayed** any **interest** in girls.*

displease /dɪ'spliːz/ *verb* [T] *formal* to make someone annoyed or unhappy •**displeased** *adjective*

displeasure /dɪ'spleʒəʳ/ *noun* [U] *formal* when someone is annoyed or unhappy about something *She expressed great **displeasure at** his behaviour.*

disposable /dɪ'spəʊzəbl/ *adjective* intended to be used only once and then thrown away *a disposable camera/razor*

disˌposable 'income *UK noun* [C, U] **FINANCE** the amount of money that you have available to spend after tax, rent and other basic things that you must pay for

disposal /dɪ'spəʊzᵊl/ *noun* [U] **1** when you get rid of something, especially by throwing it away ***waste disposal*** ○ *the disposal of* *hazardous substances* **2 at sb's disposal** available for someone to use *We will have a car at our disposal for the whole trip.*

dispose /dɪˈspəʊz/ *verb*
dispose of sth *phrasal verb* to get rid of something, especially by throwing it away

disposed /dɪˈspəʊzd/ *adjective formal* **1 be disposed to do sth** to be willing or likely to do something *I tried to tell her but she didn't seem disposed to listen.* **2 be favourably/well, etc disposed towards sth** to like or approve of something *She seems well disposed towards the idea.*

D

disposition /ˌdɪspəˈzɪʃᵊn/ *noun* [C] the type of character someone has *a* ***cheerful/nervous disposition***

disproportionate /ˌdɪsprəˈpɔːʃᵊnət/ *adjective* too large or small in comparison to something else *There are a* ***disproportionate number*** *of girls in the class.* •**disproportionately** *adverb*

disprove /dɪˈspruːv/ *verb* [T] to prove that something is not true

WORD PARTNERS FOR ***dispute***

have/be involved in a dispute • **resolve/settle** a dispute • a **bitter/long-running** dispute • a dispute **about/over** sth

dispute[1] /ˈdɪspjuːt/ *noun* [C, U] a disagreement, especially one that lasts a long time *A man stabbed his neighbour in a* ***dispute over*** *noise.*

dispute[2] /dɪˈspjuːt/ *verb* [T] to disagree with something someone says [+ (that)] *I'm not disputing that the drug has benefits.*

disqualify /dɪˈskwɒlɪfaɪ/ *verb* [T] to stop someone from being in a competition or doing some other activity because they have done something wrong [often passive] *She was* ***disqualified from*** *the race after a drugs test.* •**disqualification** /dɪˌskwɒlɪfɪˈkeɪʃᵊn/ *noun* [U]

disquiet /dɪˈskwaɪət/ *noun* [U] *formal* when people are anxious or worried about something *His health has been causing disquiet.*

WORD PARTNERS FOR ***disregard***

blatant/callous/flagrant/total disregard • disregard **for/of** sb/sth

disregard[1] /ˌdɪsrɪˈɡɑːd/ *noun* [U, no plural] when someone does not care about or show any interest in someone or something *His behaviour shows a total* ***disregard for*** *other people.*

disregard[2] /ˌdɪsrɪˈɡɑːd/ *verb* [T] to ignore something *She chose to disregard my advice.*

disrepair /ˌdɪsrɪˈpeəʳ/ *noun* [U] when a building is in a bad condition because someone has not taken care of it *The house has* ***fallen into disrepair***.

disreputable /dɪsˈrepjətəbl/ *adjective* not respected or trusted by people *a disreputable company*

disrepute /ˌdɪsrɪˈpjuːt/ *noun* **bring sb/sth into disrepute** *formal* to cause people not to respect or trust someone or something *Corrupt policemen are bringing the law into disrepute.*

disrespect /ˌdɪsrɪˈspekt/ *noun* [U] when someone does not show any respect or behave politely towards someone or something *a* ***disrespect for*** *authority*

disrespectful /ˌdɪsrɪˈspektfᵊl/ *adjective* being rude and not showing any respect *Don't be* ***disrespectful to*** *your mother.* •**disrespectfully** *adverb*

disrupt /dɪsˈrʌpt/ *verb* [T] to interrupt something and stop it continuing as it should *He disturbs other children and disrupts the class.* •**disruption** /dɪsˈrʌpʃᵊn/ *noun* [C, U] *the disruption of services* •**disruptive** *adjective disruptive behaviour*

dissatisfaction /dɪsˌsætɪsˈfækʃᵊn/ *noun* [U] when you are not pleased or happy with something *He expressed his* ***dissatisfaction with*** *the legal system.*

dissatisfied /dɪsˈsætɪsfaɪd/ *adjective* not pleased or happy with something *a dissatisfied customer* ○ *Are you* ***dissatisfied with*** *our service?*

dissect /daɪˈsekt/ *verb* [T] to cut something into pieces for scientific study *We had to dissect a rat in biology.* •**dissection** /daɪˈsekʃᵊn/ *noun* [U]

disseminate /dɪˈsemɪneɪt/ *verb* [T] to spread information or ideas *They are using their website to disseminate political propaganda.* •**dissemination** /dɪˌsemɪˈneɪʃᵊn/ *noun* [U]

dissent /dɪˈsent/ *noun* [U] when someone does not agree with something *There is a lot of dissent within the Church about women priests.* •**dissent** *verb* [I] to not agree with other people about something •**dissenter** *noun* [C]

dissertation /ˌdɪsəˈteɪʃᵊn/ *noun* [C] **EDUCATION** a very long piece of writing done as part of a course of study *She's writing a* ***dissertation on*** *American poetry.*

disservice /ˌdɪsˈsɜːvɪs/ *noun* [no plural] when something causes harm to someone or something *Bad teaching* ***does a*** *great* ***disservice to*** *children.*

dissident /ˈdɪsɪdᵊnt/ *noun* [C] **POLITICS** someone who criticizes their government in a public way ***political dissidents***

dissimilar /ˌdɪsˈsɪmɪləʳ/ *adjective* different *Her hair is* ***not dissimilar to*** *yours* (= is similar to yours).

dissipate /ˈdɪsɪpeɪt/ *verb* [I, T] to disappear, or to make something disappear *The heat gradually dissipates into the atmosphere.*

dissociate /dɪˈsəʊʃieɪt/ *verb* **dissociate yourself from sb/sth** to say that you do not have any connection or involvement with someone or something *He's trying to dissociate himself from his former friends.*

dissolution /ˌdɪsəˈluːʃᵊn/ *noun* [U] when an organization or an official arrangement ends

dissolve /dɪˈzɒlv/ *verb* **1 CHEMISTRY** [I, T] If a solid dissolves, it becomes part of a liquid, and if you dissolve it, you make it become part of a liquid. *These tablets dissolve in water.* ⊃See picture at **diffusion** **2** [T] to end an organization or official arrangement [often passive] *Their marriage was dissolved in 1996.* **3 dissolve into laughter/tears, etc** to suddenly start to laugh/cry, etc

dissuade /dɪˈsweɪd/ *verb* [T] to persuade someone not to do something [+ from + doing sth] *We tried to dissuade him from leaving.*

WORD PARTNERS FOR *distance*

a **large/long/short/small/vast** distance • a (short/long, etc) distance **from** [a place] • the distance **between** sth **and** sth

O━**distance**[1] /ˈdɪstᵊns/ *noun* **1 MEASURES** [C, U] the length of the space between two places or things *We're only a short* ***distance from*** *my house.* ○ *He calculated the* ***distance between*** *the Earth and the Sun.* ○ *Are the shops* ***within walking distance****?* **2** [no plural] somewhere that is far away, but close enough for you to see or hear the things that are there *I could see Mary* ***in the distance.*** ○ ***From a distance****, it sounded like a bell ringing.*

distance[2] /ˈdɪstᵊns/ *verb* **distance yourself from sb/sth** to say or show that you are not connected or involved with someone or something *She has tried to distance herself from the book.*

distant /ˈdɪstᵊnt/ *adjective* **1** FAR AWAY far away in space or time *distant galaxies* ○ *the distant sound of traffic* ○ *We hope to see you in the* ***not too distant future.*** **2** RELATIVE A distant relative is not very closely related to you. *a distant cousin* **3** NOT FRIENDLY [never before noun] not friendly *She seemed cold and distant.* •**distantly** *adverb* ***distantly related***

distaste /dɪˈsteɪst/ *noun* [U] when you dislike something and think it is unpleasant *I have developed a* ***distaste for*** *meat.*

distasteful /dɪˈsteɪstfᵊl/ *adjective* unpleasant or offensive *I find this advertisement extremely distasteful.* •**distastefully** *adverb*

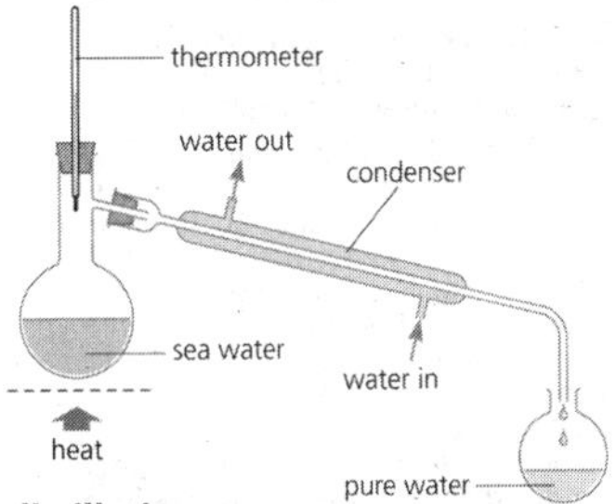

distillation

distil *UK* (*US* **distill**) /dɪˈstɪl/ *verb* [T] **distilling,** *past* **distilled CHEMISTRY** to make a liquid stronger or more pure by heating it until it changes into a gas and then changing it into a liquid again *distilled water* •**distillation** /ˌdɪstɪˈleɪʃᵊn/ *noun* [U] •**distillery** /dɪˈstɪlᵊri/ *noun* [C] a place where strong alcoholic drinks are produced

distillate /ˈdɪstɪlət/ *noun* [C] **CHEMISTRY** a substance that is formed by distilling a liquid

disˌtilled ˈwater *noun* [U] **CHEMISTRY** water that has been made purer by being heated until it becomes a gas and then cooled until it becomes a liquid again

distinct /dɪˈstɪŋkt/ *adjective* **1** DIFFERENT different and separate *This word has three distinct meanings.* **2** HEAR/SEE easy to hear, see, or smell *The voices gradually became louder and more distinct.* ⊃Opposite **indistinct** **3** CLEAR [always before noun] clear and certain *There's been a distinct improvement in your work.* •**distinctly** *adverb*

WORD PARTNERS FOR *distinction*

draw/make a distinction • a **clear** distinction • a distinction **between** sth **and** sth

distinction /dɪˈstɪŋkʃᵊn/ *noun* [C, U] **1** DIFFERENCE a difference between two similar things *the* ***distinction between*** *spoken and written language* **2** QUALITY a quality or fact that makes someone or something special or different *wines of distinction* ○ *He has* ***the distinction of*** *being the youngest player in the World Cup finals.*

distinctive /dɪˈstɪŋktɪv/ *adjective* Something that is distinctive is easy to recognize because it is different from other things. *a* ***distinctive style*** *of writing* •**distinctively** *adverb*

distinguish /dɪˈstɪŋgwɪʃ/ *verb* **1** RECOGNIZE DIFFERENCES [I, T] to recognize the differences between two people, ideas, or things *Children must learn to* ***distinguish between*** *right and wrong.* ○ *People have difficulty* ***distinguishing*** *Tracy* ***from*** *her twin sister Mary.* **2** SHOW DIFFERENCES [T] to make one person or thing seem different from another *His great skill* ***distinguishes*** *him* ***from*** *the rest of the team.* **3** SEE/HEAR [T] to be able to see, hear, or understand something **4 distinguish yourself** to do something so well that people notice and admire you •**distinguishable** *adjective*

distinguished /dɪˈstɪŋgwɪʃt/ *adjective* famous, praised, or admired *a distinguished writer*

distort /dɪˈstɔːt/ *verb* [T] **1** SHAPE/SOUND to change the shape, sound, or appearance of something so that it seems strange *It's a bad recording - the microphone distorted our voices.* **2** INFORMATION to change information so that it is not true or realistic *Newspapers* ***distorted the truth*** *about their marriage.* •**distorted** *adjective* •**distortion** /dɪˈstɔːʃᵊn/ *noun* [C, U] *a gross distortion of the facts*

distract /dɪˈstrækt/ *verb* [T] to make someone stop giving their attention to something *Stop distracting me - I'm trying to finish my essay.*

distracted /dɪˈstræktɪd/ *adjective* anxious and unable to think carefully

distraction /dɪˈstrækʃᵊn/ *noun* **1** [C, U] something that makes you stop giving your attention to something else *The phone calls were a* ***constant distraction.*** **2 drive sb to distraction** *UK* to make someone very annoyed

distraught /dɪˈstrɔːt/ *adjective* extremely upset and unhappy

WORD PARTNERS FOR *distress*

deep/great distress • **to** sb's distress • **be in** distress

distress[1] /dɪˈstres/ *noun* [U] **1** UPSET the feeling of being extremely upset or worried *The newspaper reports caused her a great deal of distress.* **2** DANGER when someone or something is in danger and needs help *an aircraft* ***in distress***

distress[2] /dɪˈstres/ *verb* [T] to make someone feel very upset or worried •**distressing** *adjective a distressing experience*

distribute /dɪ'strɪbjuːt/ *verb* [T] **1** GIVE OUT to give something out to people or places *The books will be* ***distributed*** *free* ***to*** *local schools.* **2** SUPPLY to supply goods to shops and companies *The company manufactures and distributes computer equipment worldwide.*

distribution /ˌdɪstrɪ'bjuːʃᵊn/ *noun* **1** SUPPLYING [U] when something is supplied or given out to people or places *the sale and distribution of videos* **2** SHARING [**U, no plural**] the way something is divided and shared in a group or area *the distribution of wealth*

D

distributor /dɪ'strɪbjətəʳ/ *noun* [C] a person or organization that supplies goods to shops and companies

district /'dɪstrɪkt/ *noun* [C] a part of a city or country, either an official area or one that is known for having a particular characteristic or business *the fashion district of New York*

ˌdistrict atˈtorney (*abbreviation* **DA**) *noun* [C] *US* **LAW** a lawyer who works for the government of a particular district

distrust /dɪ'strʌst/ *noun* [U] when you do not trust someone or something •**distrust** *verb* [T]

disturb /dɪ'stɜːb/ *verb* [T] **1** INTERRUPT to interrupt what someone is doing by making noise or annoying them *Don't disturb him, he needs to sleep.* **2** UPSET to make someone feel anxious or upset *Some scenes are violent and may disturb younger viewers.* **3** CHANGE to change something by touching it or moving it from its original position

disturbance /dɪ'stɜːbᵊns/ *noun* **1** INTERRUPTION [C, U] something that interrupts what you are doing, especially something loud or annoying **2** FIGHTING [C] when people fight or shout

disturbed /dɪ'stɜːbd/ *adjective* not thinking or behaving normally because of mental or emotional problems

disturbing /dɪ'stɜːbɪŋ/ *adjective* unpleasant in a way that makes people feel anxious or upset *disturbing images* •**disturbingly** *adverb*

disused /dɪ'sjuːzd/ *adjective* not used now *a disused warehouse* •**disuse** /dɪ'sjuːs/ *noun* [U] when something is not used *to* ***fall into disuse***

ditch¹ /dɪtʃ/ *noun* [C] a long, narrow hole in the ground next to a road or field, which water can flow through

ditch² /dɪtʃ/ *verb* [T] *informal* to get rid of someone or something that you do not need or want now *He ditched his girlfriend when she got pregnant.*

dither /'dɪðəʳ/ *verb* [I] to spend too much time trying to make a decision *Stop dithering and tell me which one you want!*

ditto¹ /'dɪtəʊ/ *adverb* used to agree with something that has been said, or to avoid repeating something that has been said

ditto² /'dɪtəʊ/ *noun* [C] **LANGUAGE** a mark (") used instead of words to show that you are repeating what is written above it

ditty /'dɪti/ *noun* [C] **MUSIC** a short, simple song

diva /'diːvə/ *noun* [C] **MUSIC** a successful and famous female singer

Divali /dɪ'vɑːli/ *noun* [U] **RELIGION** Diwali (= a Hindu festival)

dive¹ /daɪv/ *verb* [I] *past* **dived**, *also US* **dove**, *past participle* **dived** **1** JUMP IN to jump into water with your head and arms going in first *He dived off the side of the boat into the sea.* **2** SWIM to swim under water, usually with breathing equipment **3** **dive into/over/under, etc** to move somewhere quickly *He heard footsteps and dived under the table.* **4** FLY to fly down through the air very quickly *Suddenly the plane dived to the ground.* **5** VALUE If a value or price dives, it suddenly becomes less.

dive² /daɪv/ *noun* [C] **1** JUMP a jump into water with your arms and head going in first **2** MOVEMENT a quick movement somewhere **3** VALUE when the value or price of something suddenly becomes less *Share prices* ***took a dive*** *today.* **4** PLACE *informal* a place such as a bar which is considered to be dirty or of low quality

diver /'daɪvəʳ/ *noun* [C] someone who swims under water, usually with breathing equipment

diverge /daɪ'vɜːdʒ/ *verb* [I] **1** to be different, or to develop in a different way *Over the years our interests have diverged.* **2** to go in different directions *At that point, the paths diverged.* •**divergence** *noun* [C, U]

diverse /daɪ'vɜːs/ *adjective* including many different types *a diverse collection of music*

diversify /daɪ'vɜːsɪfaɪ/ *verb* [I, T] If a business diversifies, it starts making new products or offering new services. *Many designers are* ***diversifying into*** *casual wear.* •**diversification** /daɪˌvɜːsɪfɪ'keɪʃᵊn/ *noun* [U]

diˌversifying ˈmerger *noun* [C] when two companies that have completely different types of business join together

diversion /daɪ'vɜːʃᵊn/ *noun* **1** CHANGE [C, U] when something is sent somewhere different from where it was originally intended to go *the diversion of money to other projects* **2** ROUTE [C] *UK* (*US* **detour**) a different route that is used because a road is closed **3** ATTENTION [C] something that takes your attention away from something else *John* ***created a diversion*** *while the rest of us escaped.* **4** ENTERTAINMENT [C] an activity you do for entertainment or pleasure *Reading is a pleasant diversion.*

diversity /daɪ'vɜːsəti/ *noun* [U] when many different types of things or people are included in something *ethnic diversity*

divert /daɪ'vɜːt/ *verb* **1** [T] to send someone or something somewhere different from where they were expecting to go *The plane was* ***diverted to*** *Stansted because of engine trouble.* **2** **divert sb's attention/thoughts, etc** to take someone's attention away from something

O‑ **divide** /dɪ'vaɪd/ *verb* **1** SEPARATE [I, T] to separate into parts or groups, or to make something separate into parts or groups *We* ***divided up into*** *teams of six.* ○ *Each school year is divided into two semesters.* **2** **divide sth (up) among/between sb** to separate something into parts and give a part to each person in a group *The prize money will be divided equally among the winners.* **3** PLACE [T] to separate a place into two areas *An ancient wall divides the city.* **4** **MATHEMATICS** [I, T] to calculate how many times a number can go into another number *12* *divided by 6 equals 2.* **5** [DISAGREE] [T] to cause people to disagree about something [**often passive**] *Council members were* ***divided over*** *plans to build a new stadium.*

dividend /ˈdɪvɪdend/ *noun* [C] **FINANCE** an amount of money paid regularly to someone who owns shares in a company from the company's profits

dividers /dɪˈvaɪdəz/ *noun* [**plural**] **MATHEMATICS** a piece of equipment used in mathematics consisting of two parts which are joined at one end and have sharp points at the other and which are used for measuring lines and angles and for making marks to show positions along lines

divine /dɪˈvaɪn/ *adjective* **RELIGION** relating to or coming from God or a god

diving /ˈdaɪvɪŋ/ *noun* [U] **1** the activity or sport of swimming under water, usually using special breathing equipment **2 SPORT** the activity or sport of jumping into water with your arms and head going in first ⇨See also: **scuba diving**

ˈdiving ˌboard *noun* [C] **SPORT** a raised board next to a swimming pool that you jump from into the water

divisible /dɪˈvɪzəbl/ *adjective* **divisible by 2/7/50, etc MATHEMATICS** able to be divided by 2/7/50, etc

division /dɪˈvɪʒən/ *noun* **1** [SEPARATED] [U] when something is separated into parts or groups, or the way that it is separated *the equal division of labour among workers* **2** [ORGANIZATION] [C] one of the groups in a business or organization *the sales division* **3** [DISAGREEMENT] [C, U] when people disagree about something *a division over the issue of free medical care* **4 MATHEMATICS** [U] when you calculate how many times one number goes into another number

divisive /dɪˈvaɪsɪv/ *adjective* causing disagreements between people *a divisive issue*

divisor /dɪˈvaɪzər/ *noun* [C] **MATHEMATICS** a number by which another number is divided in a calculation

WORD PARTNERS FOR ***divorce***

get a divorce • a divorce **from** sb • divorce **proceedings/rate/settlement**

divorce /dɪˈvɔːs/ *noun* [C, U] **SOCIETY** when two people officially stop being married *My parents are* ***getting a divorce.*** •**divorce** *verb* [I, T] *She's divorcing her husband.*

divorced /dɪˈvɔːst/ *adjective* **1 SOCIETY** married before but not married now **2 get divorced SOCIETY** to officially stop being married *My parents got divorced when I was seven.* ⇨See Common Learner Error at **married**

divorcée /dɪˌvɔːˈsiː/ (US) /-seɪ/ *noun* [C] a person, usually a woman, who is divorced

divulge /daɪˈvʌldʒ/ *verb* [T] to give secret or private information to someone *He would not divulge how much the house cost.*

Diwali /dɪˈwɑːli/ (also **Divali**) *noun* [C, U] **RELIGION** a Hindu holiday in October/November that celebrates light and the new year

DIY /ˌdiːaɪˈwaɪ/ *noun* [U] *UK abbreviation for* do it yourself: when you do building, decorating, or repairs in your own home

dizygotic /ˌdaɪzaɪˈɡɒtɪk/ *adjective* **BIOLOGY** Dizygotic twins develop from two separate eggs. ⇨Compare **monozygotic**

dizzy /ˈdɪzi/ *adjective* **HEALTH** feeling like everything is turning round, so that you feel ill or as if you might fall

DJ /ˈdiːˌdʒeɪ/ (*also* **disc jockey**) *noun* [C] **MUSIC** someone who plays music on the radio or at discos

DNA /ˌdiːenˈeɪ/ *noun* [U] **BIOLOGY, CHEMISTRY** *abbreviation for* deoxyribonucleic acid; a chemical in the cells of living things which contains genetic information ⇨See picture at **helix**

O-**do**[1] *strong form* /duː/ *weak form* /də/ *auxiliary verb* **1** [QUESTIONS/NEGATIVES] used with another verb to form questions and negative phrases *Do you need any help?* ○ *When does the next bus leave?* ○ *I don't know.* **2** [MAKE QUESTION] used in a phrase at the end of a sentence to make it into a question *Sarah lives near here, doesn't she?* ○ *That doesn't make any sense, does it?* **3** [AVOID REPEATING] used to avoid repeating a verb that has just been used *"I hate that song." "So do I."* ○ *My sister reads a lot more than I do.* **4** [EMPHASIZE] used to emphasize the main verb *He does like you, he's just shy.* ○ *Do come and visit us soon.*

O-**do**[2] /duː/ *verb past tense* **did,** *past participle* **done** **1** [ACTION/JOB] [T] to perform an action or job *Go upstairs and do your homework.* ○ *What are you doing this weekend?* ○ *What does she do?* (= What is her job?) **2** [MAKE] [T] to make or prepare something *Our printer only does black and white copies.* ○ *Max's Cafe does great sandwiches.* **3 do badly/well, etc** to be unsuccessful/successful, etc *Sam did very well in her exams.* **4 do biology/French/history, etc** *UK* to study biology/French/history, etc **5 do your hair/make-up, etc** to make your hair/make-up, etc look nice **6 do sb good** to have a good effect on someone *A holiday would do you good.* **7 do damage/harm, etc** to cause damage/harm, etc *Luckily the fire didn't do much damage.* **8 will do** will be satisfactory *You don't have to pay now, next week will do.* **9** [SPEED] [T] to travel at a particular speed *For most of the journey we were doing 70 miles an hour.*

COMMON LEARNER ERROR

do or make?

Do usually means to perform an activity or job.

I should do more exercise.

~~*I should make more exercise.*~~

Make usually means to create or produce something.

Did you make the dress yourself ?

~~*Did you do the dress yourself?*~~

do away with sth *phrasal verb* to get rid of something, or to stop using something *We may do away with the school uniform soon.*

do away with sb *phrasal verb informal* to kill someone

do sb in *phrasal verb informal* **1** [MAKE TIRED] to

make someone extremely tired *All that exercise has done me in.* **2** ATTACK to attack or kill someone

do sth over *phrasal verb US* to do something again because you did not do it well the first time

do sth up *phrasal verb* **1** FASTEN *mainly UK* to fasten something *Do your coat up. It's cold outside.* **2** REPAIR to repair or decorate a building so that it looks attractive

do with sth *phrasal verb* used to ask where someone put something *What did you do with my keys?*

do with sb/sth *phrasal verb* **1 could do with sb/sth** to need or want someone or something *I could do with a few days off work.* **2 be/have to do with sb/sth** to be about or connected with someone or something *My question has to do with yesterday's homework.*

do without (sb/sth) *phrasal verb* to manage without having someone or something *Jack's the kind of player we can't do without.*

do³ /duː/ *noun* [C] *UK informal* a party *Are you going to the Christmas do?*

docile /ˈdəʊsaɪl/ (US) /ˈdɑːsᵊl/ *adjective* A docile person or animal is quiet and easily controlled.

dock¹ /dɒk/ *noun* **1** [C] the place where ships stop and goods are taken off or put on **2 the dock LAW** *UK* (*US* **the stand**) the place in a law court where the person who is accused of a crime sits

dock² /dɒk/ *verb* **1** [I, T] If a ship docks, it arrives at a dock. **2 dock sb's pay/wages** to take away part of the money you pay someone, usually as a punishment

WORD PARTNERS FOR ***doctor***

consult/see a doctor • **go to** the doctor's • a doctor's **appointment**

doctor¹ /ˈdɒktəʳ/ *noun* **1 HEALTH** [C] a person whose job is to treat people who have an illness or injury *I have to **go to the doctor's** for a check-up.* **2 Doctor of Philosophy/Divinity, etc EDUCATION** someone who has the most advanced type of qualification from a university ➲See also: **spin doctor**

doctor² /ˈdɒktəʳ/ *verb* [T] to change something, usually in a dishonest way *The photo in his passport had been doctored.*

doctorate /ˈdɒktᵊrət/ *noun* [C] **EDUCATION** the most advanced type of qualification from a university *He has a **doctorate in** physics from Cambridge.*

doctrine /ˈdɒktrɪn/ *noun* [C, U] **POLITICS, RELIGION** a belief or set of beliefs taught by a religious or political group *Christian doctrine*

WORD PARTNERS FOR ***document***

draw up/produce a document • **in** a document • a document **about/concerning/on** sth

document /ˈdɒkjəmənt/ *noun* [C] **1** PAPER a piece of paper with official information on it *Please sign and return the insurance documents enclosed.* **2 COMPUTING** a piece of text produced electronically on a computer *How do I create a new document?*

documentary /ˌdɒkjəˈmentᵊri/ *noun* [C] a film or television programme that gives facts about a real situation or real people *a TV documentary about the Russian Revolution*

documentation /ˌdɒkjəmenˈteɪʃᵊn/ *noun* [U] **1** OFFICIAL INFORMATION pieces of paper containing official information **2** INSTRUCTIONS the instructions written for a piece of computer software or equipment

docusoap /ˈdɒkjuːsəʊp/ *noun* [C] *UK* an entertaining television programme about the lives of real people who live in the same place or who do the same thing

doddle /ˈdɒdl/ *noun UK* **be a doddle** *informal* to be very easy *This computer's a doddle to use.*

dodecahedron /ˌdəʊdekəˈhiːdrən/ *noun* [C] *plural* **dodecahedrons, dodecahedra MATHEMATICS** a solid shape that has twelve flat surfaces of equal size with five sides

dodge¹ /dɒdʒ/ *verb* **1** MOVE [I, T] to move quickly to avoid someone or something *He managed to **dodge past** the security guard.* **2** NOT SAY/DO [T] to avoid talking about something or doing something you should do *The minister dodged questions about his relationship with the actress.*

dodge² /dɒdʒ/ *noun* [C] when you avoid something, usually in a dishonest way *a tax dodge*

dodgems /ˈdɒdʒəmz/ *noun* [plural] *trademark* a form of entertainment where people drive small electric cars on a special surface and try to hit each other

dodgy /ˈdɒdʒi/ *adjective UK informal* bad, or not able to be trusted *His friend's a bit dodgy.*

doe /dəʊ/ *noun* [C] a female deer

does *strong form* /dʌz/ *weak form* /dəz/ *present simple he/she/it of* do

doesn't /ˈdʌzᵊnt/ *short for* does not *Keith doesn't like mushrooms or garlic.*

dog¹ /dɒg/ *noun* [C] an animal with fur, four legs and a tail that is kept as a pet, or trained to guard buildings and guide blind people *Let's take the dog for a walk.* ➲See also: **guide dog, hot dog**

dog² /dɒg/ *verb* [T] **dogging**, *past* **dogged** to cause someone or something trouble for a long time [**often passive**] *His football career has been dogged by injury.*

dog-eared /ˈdɒgɪəd/ *adjective* If a piece of paper or a book is dog-eared, its corners are folded and torn from being touched a lot.

dogfight /ˈdɒgfaɪt/ *noun* [C] a fight between two military aircraft in which they fly very fast and very close to each other

dogged /ˈdɒgɪd/ *adjective* [**always before noun**] continuing to do or believe in something, although it is difficult ***dogged determination*** •**doggedly** *adverb*

doghouse /ˈdɒghaʊs/ *noun* **1** [C] *US* (*UK* **kennel**) a small building for a dog to sleep in **2 be in the doghouse** If you are in the doghouse, you have done something to make people angry or annoyed with you.

dogma /ˈdɒgmə/ *noun* [C, U] a belief or set of beliefs that people are expected to accept as the truth, without ever doubting them ***political dogma***

dogmatic /dɒg'mætɪk/ *adjective* not willing to accept other ideas or opinions because you think yours are right

dogsbody /'dɒgzbɒdi/ *noun* [C] *UK* someone who has to do boring jobs for someone else

doing /'duːɪŋ/ *noun* **1 be sb's doing** to have been done or caused by someone *The problem is not all his doing.* **2 take some/a lot of doing** *informal* to be difficult to do ***It took some doing*** *to convince him to come.*

doldrums /'dɒldrəmz/ *noun* **in the doldrums a** If a business or job is in the doldrums, it is not very successful and nothing new is happening in it. **b** *UK* sad and with no energy or enthusiasm

dole /dəʊl/ *verb*
dole sth out *phrasal verb* to give something, especially money, to several people or in large amounts

the dole /dəʊl/ *noun UK* money that the government gives someone when they are unemployed *He's been* ***on the dole*** *for years.*

doleful /'dəʊlfᵊl/ *adjective* very sad *doleful eyes*

doll /dɒl/ *noun* [C] a child's toy that looks like a small person

O⊸**dollar** /'dɒləʳ/ *noun* [C] **ECONOMICS** the unit of money used in the US, Canada, and some other countries; $ *a hundred dollars/$100* ○ ***a dollar bill***

dollop /'dɒləp/ *noun* [C] a lump or mass of a soft substance, usually food *a* ***dollop of*** *cream*

dolphin /'dɒlfɪn/ *noun* [C] an intelligent animal that lives in the sea, breathes air, and looks like a large, smooth, grey fish

domain /dəʊ'meɪn/ *noun* [C] AREA a particular area, activity, or subject that someone controls or deals with *The garden is his domain.* ○ *This information should be* ***in the public domain*** (= known by the public).

do'main ˌname *noun* [C] **INTERNET** the part of an email or website address that shows the name of the organization that the address belongs to

dome /dəʊm/ *noun* [C] a curved, round roof of a building •**domed** *adjective a domed roof*

domestic /də'mestɪk/ *adjective* **1 SOCIETY** relating to the home and family relationships ***domestic violence*** ○ *What are his* ***domestic arrangements?*** **2** COUNTRY inside one country and not international *a domestic flight* **3** ANIMAL A domestic animal is kept as a pet.

domesticated /də'mestɪkeɪtɪd/ *adjective* **1** ANIMAL A domesticated animal is kept as a pet or lives on a farm. **2** PERSON A domesticated person is able or willing to do cleaning, cooking, and other jobs in the home.

domesticity /ˌdɒmes'tɪsəti/ *noun* [U] life at home looking after a house and family

dominance /'dɒmɪnəns/ *noun* [U] power, influence, and control *the company's dominance in the software industry*

dominant /'dɒmɪnənt/ *adjective* **1** IMPORTANT main or most important *Her mother was the dominant influence in her life.* **2** STRONG strongest and wanting to take control *a dominant older brother* **3 BIOLOGY** a dominant gene will cause a particular characteristic even if it is only passed on by one parent ➲Compare **recessive**

dominate /'dɒmɪneɪt/ *verb* [I, T] **1** CONTROL to control or have power over someone or something *The US continues to dominate the world politically.* **2** BE IMPORTANT to be the largest, most important, or most noticeable part of something *The cathedral dominates the skyline.*

WORD PARTNERS FOR ***domination***

global/world domination • domination **of** sth • domination **over** sb/sth

domination /ˌdɒmɪ'neɪʃᵊn/ *noun* [U] great power and control over someone or something else ***world domination***

domineering /ˌdɒmɪ'nɪərɪŋ/ *adjective* trying to control people too much *a domineering mother*

dominion /də'mɪnjən/ *noun* [U] *formal* the power and right to control someone or something

domino /'dɒmɪnəʊ/ *noun* [C] *plural* **dominoes** a small, rectangular object that has spots on it, used in a game •**dominoes** *noun* [U] a game played using dominoes

don /dɒn/ *verb* [T] **donning,** *past* **donned** *formal* to put on a piece of clothing such as a coat or hat

donate /dəʊ'neɪt/ *verb* [T] **1** MONEY/GOODS to give money or goods to a person or organization that needs help *Four hundred new computers were* ***donated to*** *the college.* **2** BLOOD/ORGANS to allow some of your blood or part of your body to be used for medical purposes

WORD PARTNERS FOR ***donation***

make a donation • a donation **of** [$50/food/clothing, etc] • a donation **to** sb/sth

donation /dəʊ'neɪʃᵊn/ *noun* [C, U] when money or goods are given to help a person or organization *Would you like to* ***make a donation?***

O⊸**done**[1] /dʌn/ *adjective* **1** finished or completed *Did you* ***get*** *your essay* ***done*** *in time?* **2 FOOD** cooked enough *The potatoes aren't quite done yet.* ➲See also: easier (**easy**[2]) said than done, **well-done**

done[2] /dʌn/ *exclamation* something that you say to show that you accept someone's offer *"I'll give you 50 pounds for the whole lot." "Done!"*

done[3] /dʌn/ *past participle of* do

donkey /'dɒŋki/ *noun* [C] **1** an animal that looks like a small horse with long ears **2 for donkey's years** *UK informal* for a long time

'donkey ˌwork *noun* [U] *UK informal* the most boring or difficult parts of a job

donor /'dəʊnəʳ/ *noun* [C] **1 HEALTH** someone who gives some of their blood or part of their body to be used for medical purposes **2 FINANCE** someone who gives money or goods to a person or organization that needs help *Ten thousand dollars was given by an* ***anonymous donor.*** ➲See also: **blood donor**

don't /dəʊnt/ *short for* do not *Please don't talk during the exam.*

donut /ˈdəʊnʌt/ *noun* [C] **FOOD** *another US spelling of* doughnut (= a small, round, fried cake)

doodle /ˈduːdl/ *verb* [I, T] to draw little pictures or patterns on something without thinking about it •**doodle** *noun* [C]

D

doom /duːm/ *noun* [U] **1** death, destruction, and other unpleasant events that cannot be avoided *a horrible* ***sense of doom*** **2 doom and gloom** unhappiness and feeling no hope for the future *Life's* ***not all doom and gloom****, you know.*

doomed /duːmd/ *adjective* certain to fail, die, or have problems *Their marriage was doomed from the start.*

WORD PARTNERS FOR ***door***

close/open/shut/slam a door • **knock on** a door • be **at** the door

door /dɔːʳ/ *noun* [C] **1** THING YOU OPEN the part of a building, room, vehicle, or piece of furniture that you open or close to get inside it or out of it *Please* ***shut the door*** *behind you.* ○ *I can't* ***open the door****.* ○ *There's someone* ***at the door****.* **2** SPACE the space in a wall where you enter a building or room *He led us through the door to the rear of the building.* **3 behind closed doors** privately and not in public *Most of the deals were done behind closed doors.* **4 two/three, etc doors away** in a place that is two/three, etc houses away *We live just a few doors away from the Smiths.* ➲See also: **trap door**

doorbell /ˈdɔːbel/ *noun* [C] a button that you press next to a door that makes a noise to let someone know that you are there

doorknob /ˈdɔːnɒb/ *noun* [C] a round object on a door that you hold and turn to open or close it

doorman /ˈdɔːmən/ *noun* [C] *plural* **doormen** a man who stands near the doors of a large building such as a hotel to watch and help the visitors

doormat /ˈdɔːmæt/ *noun* [C] **1** MATERIAL a piece of thick material on the floor by a door used to clean your shoes before entering a building **2** PERSON *informal* someone who allows other people to treat them very badly

doorstep /ˈdɔːstep/ *noun* [C] **1** a step in front of the door of a building **2 on your doorstep** very near to where you live *They have the Rocky Mountains on their doorstep.*

door-to-door /ˌdɔːtəˈdɔːʳ/ *adjective* [**always before noun**], *adverb* **1** JOURNEY going from one house or building to another *The hotel offers a* ***door-to-door service*** *to the airport.* **2** EVERY HOUSE going to every house in an area *a* ***door-to-door salesman***

doorway /ˈdɔːweɪ/ *noun* [C] an entrance to a building or room through a door *She waited* ***in the doorway*** *while I ran back inside.*

dope¹ /dəʊp/ *noun informal* **1 HEALTH** [U] an illegal drug taken for pleasure, especially cannabis (= drug that you smoke) **2** [C] *US informal* a stupid or silly person

dope² /dəʊp/ *verb* **1 HEALTH** [T] to give a drug to a person or animal, usually so that they become sleepy **2 be doped up HEALTH** to have a lot of a drug in your body affecting your behaviour

dork /dɔːk/ *noun* [C] *mainly US informal* a stupid or silly person

dormant /ˈdɔːmənt/ *adjective* not active or developing now, but possibly active in the future *a dormant volcano*

dormitory /ˈdɔːmɪtᵊri/ (*also* **dorm** *informal*) *noun* [C] **1** BEDROOM a large bedroom with a lot of beds, especially in a school **2** BUILDING *US* (*UK* **hall of residence**) a large building at a college or university where students live

DOS /dɒs/ *noun* [U] *trademark* **COMPUTING** *abbreviation for* disk operating system: a type of operating system for computers

dosage /ˈdəʊsɪdʒ/ *noun* [C] **HEALTH** how much medicine you should take and how often you should take it *the recommended daily dosage*

WORD PARTNERS FOR ***dose***

a **high/low** dose • a **fatal/lethal** dose • a dose of sth

dose /dəʊs/ *noun* [C] **1 HEALTH** a measured amount of medicine that is taken at one time or during a period of time *What is the recommended dose?* ○ *a* ***lethal dose*** **2 a dose of sth** an amount of something, often something unpleasant *a dose of bad news* •**dose** *verb* [T] to give someone a drug or medicine

dosh /dɒʃ/ *noun* [U] *UK informal* money

doss /dɒs/ (*also* **doss down**) *verb* [I] *UK informal* to sleep somewhere temporarily, such as on the floor *Can I doss at your house tonight?*
doss about/around *phrasal verb UK informal* to spend your time doing very little

dossier /ˈdɒsieɪ/ *noun* [C] a set of documents that contain information about a particular person or subject *The officers* ***compiled*** *a* ***dossier*** *on the case.*

dot¹ /dɒt/ *noun* **1** [C] a small, round mark or spot *a pattern of blue and green dots* **2 INTERNET** [U] *spoken* the spoken form of '.' in an internet address *dot co dot uk* (= .co.uk) **3 on the dot** at that exact time *We have to leave at 7.30 on the dot.*

dot² /dɒt/ *verb* [T] **dotting**, *past* **dotted** **1** PUT to put a dot or dots on something **2** SPREAD (*also* **dot around**) to be spread across an area *The company has 43 hotels dotted around the UK.*

dot.com /ˌdɒtˈkɒm/ (also **dotcom**) *noun* [C] **INTERNET** a company that does most of its business on the Internet *a dot.com company/millionaire*

dote /dəʊt/ *verb*
dote on sb *phrasal verb* to love someone completely and believe that they are perfect *She absolutely dotes on that little boy.*

doting /ˈdəʊtɪŋ/ *adjective* [**always before noun**] extremely loving and caring *doting parents*

dot-matrix printer /ˌdɒtmeɪtrɪksˈprɪntər/ *noun* [C] **COMPUTING** a computer printer that forms letters, numbers and other symbols from dots (= very small marks)

ˌdotted ˈline *noun* **1** [C] a line of printed dots on a piece of paper **2 sign on the dotted line** to make an agreement official by writing your name on it

dotty /ˈdɒti/ *adjective UK* slightly crazy *a dotty old woman*

O— **double¹** /ˈdʌbl/ *adjective* **1** TWO PARTS having two parts of the same type or size *double doors* ○ *My number is four, two, six, double two, five* (= 426225). **2** TWICE THE SIZE twice the amount, number, or size of something *a double vodka* ○ *a double hamburger* **3** FOR TWO made to be used by two people *a* ***double bed/room***

double² /ˈdʌbl/ *verb* [I, T] to increase and become twice the original size or amount, or to make something do this *Our house has almost* ***doubled in*** *value.*

double (up) as sth *phrasal verb* If something doubles up as something else, it also has the purpose of that thing. *The school's gymnasium doubles up as a dining room.*

double back *phrasal verb* to turn and go back in the direction that you have come from

double (sb) over/up *phrasal verb* to suddenly bend your body forward, usually because of pain or laughter, or to make someone do this

double³ /ˈdʌbl/ *noun* **1** [C, U] something that is twice the usual amount, number, or size **2 sb's double** someone who looks exactly the same as someone else

double⁴ /ˈdʌbl/ *determiner* twice as much or as many *Our new house is double the size of our old one.*

double-barrelled *UK* (*US* **double-barreled**) /ˌdʌblˈbærəld/ *adjective* **1** GUN A double-barrelled gun has two of the cylindrical parts that bullets come out of. **2** NAME *UK* A double-barrelled name is two names joined together.

ˌdouble ˈbass *noun* [C] **MUSIC** a wooden musical instrument with four strings, like a very large violin (= instrument you hold against your neck), that you play while standing up or sitting on a high chair

ˌdouble ˈbed *noun* [C] a bed big enough for two people to sleep in

ˌdouble ˈbond *noun* [C] **CHEMISTRY** a chemical bond in which two atoms share two pairs of electrons, which hold them together

double-breasted /ˌdʌblˈbrestɪd/ *adjective* A double-breasted jacket or coat has two sets of buttons to fasten at the front.

double-check /ˌdʌblˈtʃek/ *verb* [I, T] to examine something again so that you are certain it is safe or correct

double-click /ˌdʌblˈklɪk/ *verb* [I, T] **COMPUTING** to quickly press a button twice on a mouse (= small computer control) to make something happen on a computer screen ***Double-click on*** *the icon to start the program.*

double-cross /ˌdʌblˈkrɒs/ *verb* [T] to deceive someone who you should be helping

double-decker /ˌdʌblˈdekəʳ/ *noun* [C] *UK* a tall bus with two levels *a* ***double-decker bus***

ˌdouble entry ˈbookkeeping *noun* [U] **FINANCE** a system that a business uses to record its financial situation, where each sum of money is shown as money received in one part and money spent in the other part

double-glazing /ˌdʌblˈgleɪzɪŋ/ *noun* [U] *UK* windows that have two layers of glass to keep a building warm or quiet

ˌdouble ˈhelix *noun* [C] **BIOLOGY** the structure of a DNA molecule that is made of two long thin pieces twisted together in a double spiral shape

doubles /ˈdʌblz/ *noun* [U] **SPORT** a game, especially tennis, in which two people play together against two other people

ˌdouble ˈstandard *noun* [C] when people are given different treatment in an unfair way [usually plural] *Critics accused the government of double standards in its policies.*

ˌdouble ˈtake *noun* [C] when you quickly look at someone or something a second time because you cannot believe you have seen something or heard something [usually singular] *He* ***did a double take*** *when he saw her.*

doubly /ˈdʌbli/ *adverb* twice as much, or very much more *It is doubly important to drink plenty of water when it's hot.*

WORD PARTNERS FOR ***doubt***

express/have/raise doubts • a **nagging/serious** doubt • doubts **about** sth

O— **doubt¹** /daʊt/ *noun* **1** [C, U] when you are not certain about something, or do not trust someone or something *I have some* ***doubts about*** *his ability to do the job.* **2 have no doubt** to be certain [+ (that)] *I have no doubt that I made the right decision.* **3 there's no doubt** it is certain [+ (that)] *There is no doubt that he's a good player.* **4 be in doubt** to not be certain *The future of the project is in doubt.* **5 cast doubt on sth** to make something seem uncertain *Witnesses have cast doubt on the suspect's innocence.* **6 without (a) doubt** certainly *She is without doubt a great musician.* **7 no doubt** used to say that something is very likely *No doubt she'll spend the money on new clothes.* ⮕See also: give sb the **benefit**¹ of the doubt, beyond/without a **shadow**¹ of a doubt

O— **doubt²** /daʊt/ *verb* [T] **1** FEEL UNCERTAIN to feel uncertain about something or think that something is not probable [+ (that)] *I doubt that I'll get the job.* ○ *I* ***doubt if/whether*** *he'll win.* **2** NOT BELIEVE to not believe someone or something *Do you have any reason to doubt her?*

doubtful /ˈdaʊtfəl/ *adjective* **1** NOT PROBABLE not probable *It's* ***doubtful if/whether*** *he'll be able to come.* [+ (that)] *It's doubtful that anyone survived the fire.* **2** NOT CERTAIN not feeling certain about something •**doubtfully** *adverb*

ˌdoubtful ˈdebt *noun* [C] **FINANCE** a debt that is not likely to be paid

doubtless /ˈdaʊtləs/ *adverb* probably *He will doubtless be criticized by journalists.*

dough /dəʊ/ *noun* [U] **FOOD** a thick mixture of flour and liquid used to make foods such as bread or pastry

doughnut (*also US* **donut**) /ˈdəʊnʌt/ *noun* [C] **FOOD** a small, round, fried cake, sometimes with a hole in the middle

dour /dʊəʳ, daʊəʳ/ *adjective* unfriendly and serious *a dour expression*

D

douse /daʊs/ *verb* [T] **1** POUR to pour a lot of liquid over someone or something *The dessert was doused with brandy and set alight.* **2** STOP BURNING to stop a fire burning by putting a lot of water on it *to douse the flames/fire*

dove¹ /dʌv/ *noun* [C] a white bird, sometimes used as a symbol of peace

dove² /dəʊv/ *US past tense of* dive

dowdy /ˈdaʊdi/ *adjective* plain and not fashionable

the Dow Jones /ˌdaʊˈdʒəʊnz/ *noun* [**no plural**] **ECONOMICS** a list of the prices of shares in the 30 most important companies on the New York Stock Exchange

O-ˉ**down¹** /daʊn/ *adverb, preposition* **1** LOWER PLACE towards or in a lower place *The kids ran down the hill to the gate.* ○ *I bent down to have a look.* **2** LEVEL/AMOUNT towards or at a lower level or amount *Can you turn the music down?* ○ *Slow down so they can see us.* **3** SURFACE moving from above and onto a surface *I sat down and turned on the TV.* ○ *Put that box down on the floor.* **4** DIRECTION in or towards a particular direction, usually south *Pete's moved down to London.* **5 down the road/river, etc** along or further along the road/river, etc *There's another pub further down the street.* **6 note/write, etc sth down** to write something on a piece of paper *Can I just take down your phone number?* **7** STOMACH inside your stomach *He's had food poisoning and can't keep anything down.* **8 be down to sb** *UK* to be someone's responsibility or decision *I've done all I can now, the rest is down to you.* **9 come/go down with sth** to become ill *The whole family came down with food poisoning.* **10 down under** *informal* Australia, or in Australia

down² /daʊn/ *adjective* [**never before noun**] **1** sad *What's the matter? You look a bit down today.* **2 COMPUTING** If a computer or machine is down, it is temporarily not working. *The network was down all morning.*

down³ /daʊn/ *noun* [U] soft feathers, often used as a warm filling for bed covers ➲See also: **ups and downs**

down⁴ /daʊn/ *verb* [T] *informal* to drink something quickly

down-and-out /ˌdaʊnənˈaʊt/ *adjective* If someone is down-and-out, they have no money, possessions, or opportunities. •**down-and-out** *noun* [C]

downcast /ˈdaʊnkɑːst/ *adjective* **1** SAD sad or disappointed **2** EYES If someone's eyes are downcast, they are looking down.

downgrade /ˌdaʊnˈgreɪd/ *verb* [T] to move someone or something to a less important position

downhearted /ˌdaʊnˈhɑːtɪd/ *adjective* sad or disappointed

downhill¹ /ˌdaʊnˈhɪl/ *adverb* **1** towards the bottom of a hill or slope *It's so much easier cycling downhill.* **2 go downhill** to gradually become worse *After his wife died, his health started to go downhill.*

downhill² /ˌdaʊnˈhɪl/ *adjective* **1** leading down towards the bottom of a hill or slope *downhill skiing* **2 be all downhill; be downhill all the way** to be much easier *From now on it will be all downhill.*

download¹ /ˌdaʊnˈləʊd/ (US) /ˈdaʊnˌləʊd/ *verb* [T] **COMPUTING** to copy computer programs, music or other information electronically using the Internet *You can **download** this software free **from** their website.* •**downloadable** *adjective* able to be downloaded ***downloadable files/images*** ➲See Extra help page **The Web and the Internet** on page Centre 36.

download² /ˈdaʊnləʊd/ *noun* [C] **COMPUTING** a computer program, music or other information that has been or can be downloaded

downmarket /ˌdaʊnˈmɑːkɪt/ *adjective UK* cheap and low quality

ˌdown ˈpayment *noun* [C] **FINANCE** the first amount of money that you pay when you buy something expensive and pay over a period of time *a **down payment on** a house*

downplay /ˌdaʊnˈpleɪ/ *verb* [T] to make something seem less important or bad than it really is *The report downplays the risks of nuclear power.*

downpour /ˈdaʊnpɔːʳ/ *noun* [C] when it suddenly rains a lot

downright /ˈdaʊnraɪt/ *adverb* **downright dangerous/rude/ugly, etc** extremely dangerous/rude/ugly, etc

downside /ˈdaʊnsaɪd/ *noun* [**no plural**] the disadvantage of a situation *The **downside of** living in a city is all the pollution.*

downsize /ˈdaʊnˌsaɪz/ *verb* [I, T] to make a company or organization smaller by reducing the number of people who work there •**downsizing** *noun* [U]

Down's syndrome /ˈdaʊnzˌsɪndrəʊm/ *noun* [U] **HEALTH** a condition that some babies are born with which affects their physical and mental development

downstairs /ˌdaʊnˈsteəz/ *adverb* on or to a lower level of a building *She **went downstairs** to see who was at the door.* •**downstairs** *adjective a downstairs bathroom*

downstream /ˌdaʊnˈstriːm/ *adverb* in the direction that the water in a river is moving in

down-to-earth /ˌdaʊntuˈɜːθ/ *adjective* practical and realistic

downtown /ˌdaʊnˈtaʊn/ *adjective* [**always before noun**], *adverb US* in or to the central part or main business area of a city *downtown Chicago*

downtrodden /ˈdaʊnˌtrɒdᵊn/ *adjective* treated badly and without respect from other people *downtrodden workers*

downturn /ˈdaʊntɜːn/ *noun* [C] **ECONOMICS** when a business or economy becomes less successful *There has been a sharp **downturn in** sales.*

downwards (*also US* **downward**) /ˈdaʊnwədz/ *adverb* towards a lower place or level *The road slopes downwards to the river.* •**downward** *adjective* ➲See also: a downward **spiral**

downwind /ˌdaʊnˈwɪnd/ *adjective, adverb* in the direction that the wind is blowing

dowry /ˈdaʊri/ *noun* [C] money that a woman's family gives to the man she is marrying in some cultures

doze /dəʊz/ *verb* [I] to sleep lightly *Grandma was dozing in front of the TV.*
doze off *phrasal verb* to gradually start sleeping, usually during the day *He dozed off during the film.*

dozen /ˈdʌzən/ *noun, determiner* **1** twelve, or a group of twelve *There were about a dozen people at the party.* **2 dozens** *informal* a lot *She's got **dozens of** friends.* ➲See also: a **dime** a dozen

O‑ **Dr** *written abbreviation for* doctor *Dr Paul Thomas*

Dr. **FINANCE** *written abbeviation for* debit: money taken out of an account

drab /dræb/ *adjective* without colour and boring to look at *drab, grey buildings*

draconian /drəˈkəʊniən/ *adjective* very severe *draconian laws*

draft[1] /drɑːft/ *noun* **1** [WRITING] [C] a piece of writing or a plan that is not yet in its finished form *He made several changes to the **first draft**.* **2 the draft** *US* when people are told that they must join the armed forces **3** [COLD AIR] [C] *US spelling of* draught (= a current of cold air in a room)

WORD PARTNERS FOR ***draft***

draft **a constitution/legislation/a letter/a proposal**

draft[2] /drɑːft/ *verb* [T] **1** [WRITE] to produce a piece of writing or a plan that you intend to change later *to **draft** a **letter*** **2** [MILITARY] to order someone to join the armed forces
draft sb in/draft sb into sth *phrasal verb UK* to bring someone somewhere to do a particular job *Extra police were drafted in to stop the demonstration.*

draftsman *US* (*UK* **draughtsman**) /ˈdrɑːftsmən/ *noun* [C] *plural* **draftsmen** **ART** someone who draws detailed drawings as plans for something

drafty /ˈdrɑːfti/ *adjective US spelling of* draughty

drag[1] /dræg/ *verb* **dragging**, *past* **dragged** **1 drag sth/sb across/along/over, etc** to pull something or someone along the ground somewhere, usually with difficulty *The table was too heavy to lift, so we had to drag it across the room.* **2 drag sb along/out/to, etc** to make someone go somewhere they do not want to go *I have to drag myself out of bed every morning.* **3** **COMPUTING** [T] to move something somewhere on a computer screen using a mouse (= small computer control) **4** [I] (*also* **drag on**) to continue for too much time in a boring way ➲See also: drag your feet (**foot**[1])
drag sb down *phrasal verb UK* If an unpleasant situation drags someone down, it makes them feel unhappy or ill.
drag sb into sth *phrasal verb* to force someone to become involved in an unpleasant or difficult situation *I don't want to be dragged into this argument.*
drag sth out *phrasal verb* to make something continue for more time than is necessary

drag[2] /dræg/ *noun* **1 in drag** *informal* If a man is in drag, he is wearing women's clothes. **2 be a drag** *informal* to be boring and unpleasant *Cleaning the house is such a drag.* **3** [C] when you breathe in smoke from a cigarette *He **took** a **drag** on his cigarette.*

ˌdrag and ˈdrop *verb* [I, T] **COMPUTING** to move something on a computer screen using a mouse

dragon /ˈdrægən/ *noun* [C] a big, imaginary creature which breathes out fire

dragonfly /ˈdrægənflaɪ/ *noun* [C] an insect with long wings and a thin, colourful body, often seen flying near water ➲See picture at **insect**

drain[1] /dreɪn/ *verb* **1** [REMOVE LIQUID] [T] to remove the liquid from something, usually by pouring it away *Drain the pasta and add the tomatoes.* **2** [FLOW AWAY] [I] If something drains, liquid flows away or out of it. **3** [MAKE TIRED] [T] to make someone very tired *The long journey drained him.* **4** [DRINK] [T] If you drain a glass or cup, you drink all the liquid in it.

drain[2] /dreɪn/ *noun* **1** [C] a pipe or hole that takes away waste liquids or water *She poured the dirty water **down** the **drain**.* **2 a drain on sth** something that uses or wastes a lot of money or energy **3 down the drain** *informal* If money or work goes down the drain, it is wasted.

drainage /ˈdreɪnɪdʒ/ *noun* [U] the system of water or waste liquids flowing away from somewhere into the ground or down pipes

ˈdrainage ˌbasin *noun* [C] **GEOGRAPHY** an area of land from which the rain flows into a particular river or lake, etc.

drained /dreɪnd/ *adjective* If someone is drained, they are extremely tired.

drainpipe /ˈdreɪnpaɪp/ *noun* [C] a pipe that carries waste water away from a building

WORD PARTNERS FOR ***drama***

a drama **unfolds** • **high** drama • **human** drama

drama /ˈdrɑːmə/ *noun* **1** **LITERATURE** [C] a play in a theatre or on television or radio *a historical drama* **2** [PLAYS/ACTING] [U] plays and acting generally *modern drama* **3** [EXCITEMENT] [C, U] when something exciting happens *There was a lot of drama in the courtroom.*

ˈdrama ˌqueen *noun* [C] *informal* someone who gets far too upset or angry over small problems

dramatic /drəˈmætɪk/ *adjective* **1** [SUDDEN] very sudden or noticeable *a **dramatic change/improvement*** **2** [EXCITING] full of action and excitement *a dramatic rescue* **3** [THEATRE] [**always before noun**] relating to plays and acting **4** [BEHAVIOUR] showing your emotions in a very obvious way because you want other people to notice you *Stop being so dramatic!* •**dramatically** *adverb*

dramatist /ˈdræmətɪst/ *noun* [C] **LITERATURE** someone who writes plays

dramatize (*also UK* **-ise**) /ˈdræmətaɪz/ *verb* [T] **LITERATURE** **1** to make an event or situation seem more exciting than it really is *The media tends to dramatize things.* **2** to change a story so that it can be performed as a play •**dramatization** /ˌdræmətaɪˈzeɪʃən/ *noun* [C, U]

drank /dræŋk/ *past tense of* drink

drape /dreɪp/ *verb* **1 drape sth across/on/over, etc** to put something such as cloth or a piece of clothing loosely over something *He draped his jacket over the chair and sat down to eat.* **2 be draped in/with sth** to be loosely covered with a cloth *The coffin was draped in a flag.*

drapes /dreɪps/ *noun* [**plural**] *mainly US* long, heavy curtains

drastic /ˈdræstɪk/ *adjective* Drastic action or change is sudden and extreme. *drastic reductions in price* •**drastically** *adverb*

draught[1] *UK* (*US* **draft**) /drɑːft/ *noun* [C] a current of cold air in a room

draught[2] *UK* (*US* **draft**) /drɑːft/ *adjective* **draught beer/lager, etc FOOD** a drink that comes from a large container and not from a can or bottle

draughts /drɑːfts/ *UK* (*US* **checkers**) *noun* [U] a game that two people play by moving flat, round objects around on a board of black and white squares

draughtsman *UK* (*US* **draftsman**) /ˈdrɑːftsmən/ *noun* [C] *plural* **draughtsmen DT** someone who draws detailed drawings as plans for something

draughty *UK* (*US* **drafty**) /ˈdrɑːfti/ *adjective* having currents of cold air blowing through *a draughty old building*

O-■ **draw**[1] /drɔː/ *verb past tense* **drew**, *past participle* **drawn 1 ART** [I, T] to produce a picture by making lines or marks, usually with a pen or pencil *She drew a picture of a tree.* **2 draw sth/sb across/back/over, etc** to pull something or someone gently in a particular direction *He took her hand and drew her towards him.* **3 draw into/out/away, etc** to move somewhere, usually in a vehicle *The train drew into the station.* **4 draw the curtains** to pull curtains open or closed **5 draw (sb's) attention to sth/sb** to make someone notice someone or something *I don't want to draw too much attention to myself.* **6** ATTRACT [T] to attract someone to a place or person *Thousands of tourists are* ***drawn to*** *the city every year.* **7 SPORT** [I, T] *UK* to finish a game or competition with each team or player having the same score *England drew 2-2 against Italy.* **8** TAKE OUT [T] to take something out of a container or your pocket, especially a weapon *He drew a knife and started threatening me.* **9 draw near/close** to become nearer in space or time *Her birthday's drawing nearer every day.* **10 draw (a) breath** to breathe in air *She drew a deep breath and started her speech.* **11 FINANCE** [T] (*also* **draw out**) to take money from your bank account **12 draw to a close/end** to be almost finished **13 draw conclusions** to make judgments after considering an subject or situation **14 draw a comparison/distinction** to say that there is a similarity or difference between two things ➲See also: draw a **blank**[2], draw the **line**[1] at sth, draw a **veil** over sth

draw back *phrasal verb* to move away from someone or something, usually because you are surprised or frightened

draw sb/sth into sth *phrasal verb* to make someone or something become involved in a difficult or unpleasant situation *I'm not going to be drawn into this argument.*

draw on sth *phrasal verb* to use information or your knowledge or experience of something to help you do something *His novels draw heavily on his childhood.*

draw sth up *phrasal verb* to prepare something, usually a plan, list, or an official agreement, by writing it

draw[2] /drɔː/ *noun* [C] **1 SPORT** *mainly UK* when a game or competition finishes with each player or team having the same score *The match ended in a draw.* **2** (*also US* **drawing**) a competition that is decided by choosing a particular ticket or number *the National Lottery draw* ➲See also: the **luck** of the draw

WORD PARTNERS FOR ***drawback***

have drawbacks • a **big/major** drawback • the **main/only** drawback • a drawback **of/to/with** sth

drawback /ˈdrɔːbæk/ *noun* [C] a problem or disadvantage *The only* ***drawback with*** *this camera is the price.*

drawer /drɔːʳ/ *noun* [C] a container like a box without a lid that is part of a piece of furniture and that slides in and out *She* ***opened*** *the* ***drawer*** *and took out a knife.* ➲See also: **chest of drawers**

drawing /ˈdrɔːɪŋ/ *noun* **1 ART** [C] a picture made with a pencil or pen *There were some children's drawings pinned up on the wall.* **2 ART** [U] the skill or activity of making pictures using a pencil or pen *Do you want to do some drawing?* **3** [C] *US* (*UK/US* **draw**) a competition that is decided by choosing a particular ticket or number

ˈdrawing ˌboard *noun* **back to the drawing board** If you go back to the drawing board, you have to start planning a piece of work again because the first plan failed.

ˈdrawing ˌpin *UK* (*US* **thumbtack**) *noun* [C] a pin with a wide, flat top, used for fastening pieces of paper to a wall

ˈdrawing ˌroom *noun* [C] *old-fashioned* a room in a large house used for sitting in and talking with guests

drawings /ˈdrɔːɪŋz/ *noun* [**plural**] **FINANCE** money that is taken out of a business, for example to pay the people who own the business

drawl /drɔːl/ *noun* [**no plural**] a lazy way of speaking that uses long vowel sounds •**drawl** *verb* [I]

drawn[1] /drɔːn/ *adjective* looking very tired or ill *She looked pale and drawn after the operation.* ➲See also: **horse-drawn**

drawn[2] /drɔːn/ *past participle of* draw

drawn-out /ˌdrɔːnˈaʊt/ *adjective* continuing for longer than you think is necessary *long, drawn-out negotiations*

dread[1] /dred/ *verb* **1** [T] to feel worried or frightened about something that has not happened yet *I'm dreading the first day at my new school.* [+ **doing sth**] *I dread seeing him again.* **2 I dread to think** *UK* used to say that you do not want to think about something because it is too worrying *I dread to think what could have happened if we hadn't been wearing seat belts.*

dread² /dred/ *noun* [**U, no plural**] a strong feeling of fear or worry [**+ of + doing sth**] *a dread of being lonely*

dreadful /ˈdredfəl/ *adjective* extremely bad or unpleasant *a dreadful mistake* ○ *a dreadful man*

dreadfully /ˈdredfəli/ *adverb* **1** VERY *mainly UK formal* very *I'm dreadfully sorry.* **2** VERY BADLY very badly *The children behaved dreadfully.*

dreadlocks /ˈdredlɒks/ *noun* [**plural**] a hairstyle in which the hair is twisted together in lengths and is never brushed

WORD PARTNERS FOR ***dream***

have a dream • **in** sb's dream • a **bad** dream • a **recurring** dream

O-- **dream¹** /driːm/ *noun* **1** SLEEP [**C**] a series of events and images that happen in your mind while you are sleeping *a **bad dream*** ○ *I had a very strange **dream** last night.* **2** HOPE [**C**] something that you want to happen although it is not very likely *It was his dream to become an actor.* **3 be in a dream** *UK* to not notice things that are around you because you are thinking about something else **4 beyond your wildest dreams** bigger or better than anything you could imagine or hope for **5 like a dream** If something or someone does something like a dream, they do it very well.

O-- **dream²** /driːm/ *verb past* **dreamed** or **dreamt** **1** SLEEP [**I, T**] to experience events and images in your mind while you are sleeping [**+ (that)**] *Last night I dreamed that I was flying.* **2** IMAGINE [**I, T**] to imagine something that you would like to happen [**+ of + doing sth**] *I dream of living on a desert island.* [**+ (that)**] *He **never dreamed** that one day he would become President.* **3 wouldn't dream of doing sth** used to say that you would not do something because you think it is wrong or silly

dream sth up *phrasal verb* to think of an idea or plan, usually using a lot of imagination *Who dreams up these new designs?*

dream³ /driːm/ *adjective* **dream house/job/car, etc** the perfect house/job/car, etc

dreamer /ˈdriːməʳ/ *noun* [**C**] someone who is not practical and thinks about things that are not likely to happen

dreamy /ˈdriːmi/ *adjective* **1** DREAMING seeming to be in a dream and thinking about pleasant things instead of what is happening around you *She had a dreamy look in her eyes.* **2** PLEASANT very pleasant *a dreamy dessert* •**dreamily** *adverb*

dreary /ˈdrɪəri/ *adjective* boring and making you feel unhappy *a rainy, dreary day* ○ *a dreary job*

dredge /dredʒ/ *verb* [**T**] to clean the bottom of a lake or river by removing dirt, plants, or rubbish

dredge sth up *phrasal verb* to talk about something bad or unpleasant that happened in the past

dregs /dregz/ *noun* **1** FOOD [**plural**] the part of a drink at the bottom of a glass or other container that usually contains small solid bits **2 the dregs of society/humanity** people who you think are extremely bad or unimportant

drench /drenʃ/ *verb* [**T**] to make something or someone completely wet [**often passive**] *He was completely drenched by the time he got home.*

O-- **dress¹** /dres/ *verb* **1** PUT ON CLOTHES [**I, T**] to put clothes on yourself or someone else *I usually get dressed before having breakfast.* ⊃Opposite **undress** **2** STYLE [**I**] to wear a particular type, style, or colour of clothes *Ali always dresses smartly for work.* [**often passive**] *She was **dressed in** black.* **3 dress a burn/cut/wound, etc** HEALTH to clean an injury and put a covering over it to protect it

dress up *phrasal verb* **1** FORMAL to put on formal clothes for a special occasion **2** SPECIAL to wear special clothes in order to change your appearance, usually for a game or party *He **dressed up as** Superman for the party.*

COMMON LEARNER ERROR

be/get dressed

Be careful to use the correct preposition. You do not always need one.

I got dressed and went to school.

Are you dressed yet?

*He was **dressed in** a black suit.*

~~*He was dressed with a black suit.*~~

O-- **dress²** /dres/ *noun* **1** CLOTHING [**C**] a piece of clothing for women or girls which covers the top of the body and hangs down over the legs *She was wearing a short, black dress.* ⊃See colour picture **Clothes** on page Centre 8 **2** STYLE [**U**] a particular style of clothes *casual/formal dress* ⊃See also: **fancy dress**

dresser /ˈdresəʳ/ *noun* [**C**] **1** BEDROOM *mainly US* a piece of bedroom furniture with a mirror and drawers for keeping clothes in **2** KITCHEN *UK* a piece of furniture consisting of a cupboard with shelves above for keeping plates, cups, and other kitchen equipment

dressing /ˈdresɪŋ/ *noun* **1** FOOD [**C, U**] a sauce, especially a mixture of oil and vinegar for salad **2** HEALTH [**C**] a covering that protects an injury

ˈdressing ˌgown *UK* (*US* **robe**) *noun* [**C**] a piece of clothing, like a long coat, that you wear at home when you are not dressed

ˈdressing ˌroom *noun* [**C**] a room where actors or sports teams get dressed before a performance or game

ˈdressing ˌtable *noun* [**C**] *mainly UK* a piece of bedroom furniture like a table with a mirror and drawers

dressy /ˈdresi/ *adjective* Dressy clothes are suitable for a formal occasion.

drew /druː/ *past tense of* draw

dribble /ˈdrɪbl/ *verb* **1** MOUTH [**I**] If someone dribbles, a small amount of liquid comes out of their mouth and goes down their face. *Babies dribble a lot.* **2** LIQUID [**I, T**] If a liquid dribbles, it falls slowly in small amounts, and if you dribble a liquid, you pour it so it falls slowly in small amounts. *Dribble some oil over the vegetables.* **3 SPORT** [I, T] to move a ball along by using your hand to hit it against the ground or kicking it several times •**dribble** *noun* [C, U]

dried /draɪd/ *past of* dry

drier /ˈdraɪəʳ/ *noun* [C] *another spelling of* dryer (= a machine for drying wet things)

D

drift[1] /drɪft/ *verb* **1 drift across/down/towards, etc** to be moved slowly somewhere by currents of wind or water *Smoke drifted across the rooftops.* **2 drift in/out/into, etc** to move somewhere slowly *Guests were drifting out onto the terrace.* **3** SITUATION [I] to get into a situation or job without having any particular plan *He **drifted into** acting after university.* **4** SNOW [I] If snow or leaves drift, they are blown into piles by the wind.

drift apart *phrasal verb* If two people drift apart, they gradually become less friendly and the relationship ends.

drift off *phrasal verb* to gradually start to sleep *I drifted off during the lecture.*

drift[2] /drɪft/ *noun* **1** MOVE [C] slow, gradual movement from one place to another *the drift of people into Western Europe* **2 catch/get sb's drift** to understand the general meaning of what someone is saying **3** PILE [C] a pile of snow or leaves that has been blown somewhere

drill[1] /drɪl/ *noun* **1** TOOL [C] a tool or machine for making holes in a hard substance *an electric drill* **2 EDUCATION** [C, U] a teaching method in which students repeat something several times to help them learn it *We do lots of drills to practise pronunciation.* **3 an emergency/fire, etc drill** when you practise what to do in an emergency/fire, etc **4** SOLDIERS [C, U] when soldiers do training for marching

drill[2] /drɪl/ *verb* **1** MAKE HOLE [I, T] to make a hole in a hard substance using a special tool *Billy drilled a hole in the wall.* ○ *The engineers were **drilling for** oil.* **2** PRACTISE [T] to make someone repeat something several times so that they learn it

drily /ˈdraɪli/ *adverb another spelling of* dryly (= in a serious voice but trying to be funny)

drink[1] /drɪŋk/ *verb past tense* **drank,** *past participle* **drunk 1** LIQUID [I, T] to put liquid into your mouth and swallow it *Would you like something to drink?* ○ *He was drinking a glass of milk.* **2** ALCOHOL [I] to drink alcohol, usually regularly *She doesn't smoke or drink.*

drink to sb/sth *phrasal verb* to hold your glass up before drinking from it, in order to wish someone or something good luck or success

drink (sth) up *phrasal verb* to finish your drink completely *Drink up! We've got to leave soon.*

WORD PARTNERS FOR ***drink***

have a drink • a drink **of** [water/milk, etc] • a **hot/cold** drink

drink[2] /drɪŋk/ *noun* **1 FOOD** [C] a liquid or an amount of liquid that you drink *a hot/cold drink* ○ *Can I **have a drink** of water please?* **2 FOOD** [C, U] alcohol, or an alcoholic drink *Do you fancy a drink tonight to celebrate?* ➲See also: **soft drink**

drink-driving /ˌdrɪŋkˈdraɪvɪŋ/ *UK* (*US* **drunk driving**) *noun* [U] **LAW** driving a vehicle after drinking too much alcohol *He was convicted of drink-driving.*

drinker /ˈdrɪŋkəʳ/ *noun* **1** [C] someone who regularly drinks alcohol *He's a **heavy drinker*** (= he drinks a lot of alcohol). **2 a coffee/tea/wine, etc drinker** someone who regularly drinks a particular drink

drinking /ˈdrɪŋkɪŋ/ *noun* [U] when someone drinks alcohol

ˈdrinking ˌwater *noun* [U] water that is safe for people to drink

drip[1] /drɪp/ *verb* **dripping,** *past* **dripped 1** FALL [I, T] If a liquid drips, it falls in drops or you make it fall in drops. *There was water **dripping from** the ceiling.* **2** PRODUCE [I] to produce drops of liquid *The candle's dripping.*

drip[2] /drɪp/ *noun* **1** DROP [C] a drop of liquid that falls from something **2** SOUND [**no plural**] the sound or action of a liquid falling in drops **3 HEALTH** [C] *UK* (*US* **IV**) a piece of medical equipment used for putting liquids into your body *The doctor's put him **on a drip**.*

drive[1] /draɪv/ *verb past tense* **drove,** *past participle* **driven 1** CONTROL VEHICLE [I, T] to make a car, bus, or train move, and control what it does *She's learning to drive.* ○ *He drives a red sports car.* **2** TRAVEL [I, T] to travel somewhere in a car, or to take someone somewhere in a car *My friend drove me home last night.* **3 drive sb out/away/from, etc** to force someone to leave a place *The supermarket has driven many small shops out of the area.* **4 drive sb crazy/mad/wild, etc** to make someone feel crazy, annoyed, or excited *That noise is driving me mad.* **5 drive sb to sth; drive sb to do sth** to make someone have a bad feeling or do something bad *The arguments and violence drove her to leave home.* **6 drive sth into/through/towards, etc** to push something somewhere by hitting it hard *He drove the nail into the wall with a hammer.* **7** MAKE WORK [T] to provide the power or energy that makes someone or something work [**often passive**] *She was driven by greed and ambition.* ➲See also: drive/send sb round the **bend**[2], drive sb up the **wall**

COMMON LEARNER ERROR

drive or ride?

You **drive** a car, truck, or bus.

She drives an expensive sports car.

You **ride** a bicycle, motorcycle, or horse.

My brother is learning to ride a bicycle.

~~*My brother is learning to drive a bicycle.*~~

be driving at sth *phrasal verb* used to ask what someone really means *Just what are you driving at?*

drive off *phrasal verb* to leave in a car

WORD PARTNERS FOR ***drive***

go for a drive

drive[2] /draɪv/ *noun* **1** JOURNEY [C] a journey in a car *The drive from Boston to New York took 4 hours.* **2** GROUND [C] the area of ground that you drive on to get from your house to the road

You can park on the drive. **3 COMPUTING** [C] a part of a computer thatcan read or store information *a DVD drive ○ Save your work on the C: drive.* **4** EFFORT [C] when someone makes a great effort to achieve something [**+ to do sth**] *The government started a drive to improve standards in schools.* **5** ENERGY [U] energy and determination to achieve things *She has drive and ambition.*

drive-by /ˈdraɪvbaɪ/ *adjective* describes something that someone does when they are inside a vehicle that is moving *a drive-by shooting*

drive-in /ˈdraɪvɪn/ *noun* [C] *mainly US* a cinema or restaurant that you can visit without getting out of your car

drivel /ˈdrɪvᵊl/ *noun* [U] nonsense *He was talking complete drivel.*

driven /ˈdrɪvᵊn/ *past participle of* drive

WORD PARTNERS FOR ***driver***

a **bus/taxi/train/truck** driver • the driver **of** sth

O--**driver** /ˈdraɪvəʳ/ *noun* [C] someone who drives a vehicle *a **bus/train driver*** ➲See also: **engine driver**

ˈ**driver's** ˌ**license** *US* (*UK* **driving licence**) *noun* [C] an official document that allows you to drive a car

drive-through /ˈdraɪvθruː/ *noun* [C] a place where you can get a type of service by driving through, without needing to get out of your car *a drive-through restaurant*

driveway /ˈdraɪvweɪ/ *noun* [C] the area of ground that you drive on to get from your house to the road

driving¹ /ˈdraɪvɪŋ/ *noun* [U] when you drive a car, or the way someone drives

driving² /ˈdraɪvɪŋ/ *adjective* **1 driving rain/snow** rain or snow that is falling very fast and being blown by the wind **2 the driving force** a person or thing that has a very strong effect and makes something happen *She was **the driving force behind** the project.*

ˈ**driving** ˌ**licence** *UK* (*US* **driver's license**) *noun* [C] an official document that allows you to drive a car

drizzle /ˈdrɪzl/ *noun* [U] light rain •**drizzle** *verb* [I]

drone¹ /drəʊn/ *verb* [I] to make a continuous, low sound, like an engine *I could hear traffic droning in the distance.*

drone on *phrasal verb* to talk for a long time in a very boring way *I wish he'd stop **droning on about** school.*

drool /druːl/ *verb* [I] If a person or animal drools, liquid comes out of the side of their mouth.

drool over sb/sth *phrasal verb* to look at someone or something in a way that shows you think they are very attractive

droop /druːp/ *verb* [I] to hang down, often because of being weak, tired, or unhappy *He was tired and his eyelids were starting to droop.*

O--**drop¹** /drɒp/ *verb* **dropping,** *past* **dropped 1** LET FALL [T] to let something you are carrying fall to the ground *She tripped and dropped the vase.* **2** FALL [I] to fall *The ball dropped to the ground.* **3** BECOME LESS [I] If a level or amount drops, it becomes less. *Unemployment has **dropped from** 8% to 6% in the last year.* **4** TAKE [T] (*also* **drop off**) to take someone or something to a place, usually by car as you travel somewhere else *I can drop you at the station on my way to work.* **5** STOP ACTIVITY [T] If you drop a plan, activity, or idea, you stop doing or planning it. *Plans for a new supermarket have been dropped.* ○ *When we heard the news, we **dropped everything*** (= stopped what we were doing) *and rushed to the hospital.* **6** STOP INCLUDING [T] to decide to stop including someone in a group or team *The coach **dropped** me **from** the team.* **7 drop it/the subject** to stop talking about something, especially because it is annoying or upsetting someone **8** VOICE [I, T] If your voice drops, or if you drop your voice, you talk more quietly. ➲See also: be dropping like flies (**fly²**)

drop by/in *phrasal verb* to visit someone for a short time, usually without arranging it before *I **dropped in on** George on my way home from school.*

drop sb/sth off *phrasal verb* to take someone or something to a place, usually by car as you travel somewhere else

drop off *phrasal verb* **1** SLEEP *informal* to start to sleep *She dropped off in front of the TV.* **2** BECOME LESS If the amount, number, or quality of something drops off, it becomes less. *The demand for mobile phones shows no signs of dropping off.*

drop out *phrasal verb* to stop doing something before you have completely finished *He **dropped out of** school at 14.*

WORD PARTNERS FOR ***drop***

a **big/dramatic/sharp/steep** drop • a drop **in** sth

O--**drop²** /drɒp/ *noun* **1** LIQUID [C] a small, round shaped amount of liquid *I felt a few drops of rain.* ➲See colour picture **Pieces and Quantities** on page Centre 1 **2** REDUCTION [**no plural**] when the level or amount of something becomes less *There has been a **drop in** crime recently.* **3** SMALL AMOUNT [**no plural**] a small amount of a liquid you can drink *Would you like a drop more milk?* **4 MEASURES** [**no plural**] a vertical distance down from somewhere to the ground *It's a drop of about 50 metres from the top of the cliff.*

ˈ**drop-down** ˌ**menu** *noun* [C] **COMPUTING** a pop-up menu: a list of choices on a computer screen which is hidden until you choose to look at it

droplet /ˈdrɒplət/ *noun* [C] a very small, round amount of liquid

dropout /ˈdrɒpaʊt/ *noun* [C] **1** STUDENT a student who leaves school or university before they have completely finished *a high-school dropout* **2** PERSON someone who does not want to have a job, possessions, etc because they do not want to be like everyone else

dropper /ˈdrɒpəʳ/ *noun* [C] a glass tube with a hollow rubber part on one end that you press to make small amounts of liquid come out

D

droppings /'drɒpɪŋz/ *noun* [plural] solid waste from birds and some small animals *rabbit droppings*

drought /draʊt/ *noun* [C, U] a long period when there is no rain and people do not have enough water *A severe drought ruined the crops.*

drove /drəʊv/ *past tense of* drive

droves /drəʊvz/ *noun* **in droves** If people do something in droves, they do it in large numbers.

drown /draʊn/ *verb* **1** DIE [I, T] to die because you are under water and cannot breathe, or to kill someone in this way *Two people drowned in a boating accident yesterday.* **2** COVER [T] (*also* **drown out**) If a loud noise drowns the sound of something else, it prevents that sound from being heard. *His voice was drowned out by the traffic.*

drowning /'draʊnɪŋ/ *noun* [C, U] when someone dies because they are under water and cannot breathe

drowsy /'draʊzi/ *adjective* feeling tired and wanting to sleep *The sun was making me drowsy.* •**drowsily** *adverb* •**drowsiness** *noun* [U]

drudgery /'drʌdʒəri/ *noun* [U] work that is very boring

WORD PARTNERS FOR ***drug***

be on/take/use drugs • drug **abuse/addiction** • a drug **addict/dealer/user**

drug¹ /drʌg/ *noun* [C] **1** HEALTH an illegal substance that people take to make them feel happy [usually plural] *He started* ***taking/using drugs*** *such as heroin and cocaine.* ○ *Greg is* ***on drugs*** (= he uses drugs regularly). ○ ***a drug dealer*** **2** HEALTH, CHEMISTRY a chemical substance used as a medicine *Scientists are developing a new drug to treat cancer.* ➲See also: **hard drugs**

drug² /drʌg/ *verb* [T] **drugging**, *past* **drugged** HEALTH to give someone a chemical substance that makes them sleep or stop feeling pain *He drugged his victims before robbing them.*

'drug ˌaddict *noun* [C] HEALTH someone who cannot stop taking drugs

drugstore /'drʌgstɔːr/ *US* (*UK* **chemist's**) *noun* [C] a shop that sells medicines and also things such as soap and beauty products

drum¹ /drʌm/ *noun* [C] **1** MUSIC a round, hollow, musical instrument that you hit with your hands or with sticks *Anna* ***plays the drums.*** **2** a large, round container for holding substances such as oil or chemicals

drum² /drʌm/ *verb* [I, T] **drumming**, *past* **drummed** to hit something several times and make a sound like a drum, or to make something do this *the sound of rain drumming on the roof* ○ *She drummed her fingers nervously on the desk.*

drum sth into sb *phrasal verb* to make someone remember or believe an idea or fact by repeating it to them many times [often passive] *The importance of good manners was drummed into me by my father.*

drum up sth *phrasal verb* to increase interest in something or support for something *He was trying to* ***drum up*** *some* ***enthusiasm*** *for his idea.*

drumlin /'drʌmlɪn/ *noun* [C] GEOGRAPHY a small hill formed by a glacier (= mass of ice), usually with an oval shape and found in groups

drummer /'drʌmər/ *noun* [C] MUSIC someone who plays a drum

drunk¹ /drʌŋk/ *adjective* unable to behave or speak normally because you have drunk too much alcohol *He usually* ***gets drunk*** *at parties.*

drunk² /drʌŋk/ *past participle of* drink

drunken /'drʌŋkən/ *adjective* [always before noun] drunk, or involving people who are drunk *a drunken man* ○ *drunken behaviour* •**drunkenly** *adverb* •**drunkenness** *noun* [U]

dry¹ /draɪ/ *adjective* **drier**, **driest** or **dryer**, **dryest** **1** NOT WET Something that is dry does not have water or liquid in it or on its surface. *dry paint* ○ *Is your hair dry yet?* **2** NO RAIN with no or not much rain *a dry summer* **3** HAIR/SKIN Dry skin or hair does not feel soft or smooth. *My lips feel really dry.* **4** FOOD Dry wine is not sweet. **5** BORING If a book, talk, or subject is dry, it is not interesting. **6** FUNNY saying something in a serious way but trying to be funny *a dry sense of humour* •**dryness** /'draɪnəs/ *noun* [U]

dry² /draɪ/ *verb* [I, T] to become dry, or to make something become dry *He dried his hands on a towel.* ➲See also: **blow-dry**

dry (sb/sth) off *phrasal verb* to make someone or something dry, or to become dry, especially on the surface [often reflexive] *I dried myself off with a towel and got dressed.*

dry (sth) out *phrasal verb* to become dry, or to make something become dry

dry (sth) up *phrasal verb mainly UK* to make plates, cups, etc dry with a cloth after they have been washed

dry up *phrasal verb* **1** END If a supply of something dries up, it ends. *The work dried up and he went out of business.* **2** WATER If a river or lake dries up, the water in it disappears.

ˌdry 'clean *verb* [T] to clean clothes using a special chemical and not with water •**dry cleaner's** *noun* [C] a shop where you can have your clothes cleaned this way •**dry cleaning** *noun* [U]

dryer (*also* **drier**) /'draɪər/ *noun* [C] a machine for drying wet things, usually clothes or hair ➲See also: **tumble dryer**

dryly (*also* **drily**) /'draɪli/ *adverb* If you say something dryly, you say it in a serious way but you are trying to be funny.

dual /'djuːəl/ *adjective* [always before noun] having two parts, or having two of something *dual nationality*

ˌdual 'carriageway *noun* [C] *UK* a road that consists of two parallel roads, so that traffic travelling in opposite directions is separated by a central strip of land

dub /dʌb/ *verb* [T] **dubbing**, *past* **dubbed** **1** NAME to give someone or something an unofficial or funny name [often passive] *He was dubbed 'Big Ears' by the media.* **2** LANGUAGE to change the language in a film or television programme into a different language [often passive] *The film was* ***dubbed into*** *English.*

dubious /'djuːbiəs/ *adjective* **1** NOT TRUE thought not to be completely true, honest, or legal *dubious evidence* ○ *a man with a dubious reputation* **2** [DOUBTING] not certain that something is good or true *He's* ***dubious about*** *the benefits of acupuncture.* •**dubiously** *adverb*

duchess /'dʌtʃɪs/ *noun* [C] **SOCIETY** a woman of very high social rank in some European countries *the Duchess of Windsor*

duck¹ /dʌk/ *noun* [C, U] **FOOD** a bird with short legs that lives in or near water, or the meat from this bird ⊃See also: be (like) **water¹** off a duck's back

duck² /dʌk/ *verb* **1** [MOVE] [I, T] to move your head or body down quickly to avoid being hit or seen *Billy ducked behind a car when he saw his teacher.* **2** [AVOID] [T] *informal* to avoid something that is difficult or unpleasant *He managed to* ***duck*** *the* ***issue.***

duck out of sth *phrasal verb* to avoid doing something that other people are expecting you to do [+ **doing sth**] She was trying to duck out of doing her homework.

duct /dʌkt/ *noun* [C] **1 ANATOMY, BIOLOGY** a tube in the body that a liquid substance can flow through *a* ***tear duct*** **2** a tube or passage for air or wires that is part of the structure of a building *a heating duct*

ductile /'dʌk.taɪl/ ⓤⓢ /-tɪl/ *adjective* **PHYSICS** Ductile metals bend easily. •**ductility** /dʌk'tɪləti/ *noun* [U]

dud /dʌd/ *noun* [C] something that does not work correctly •**dud** *adjective*

O-■ **due¹** /dju:/ *adjective* **1** [EVENT] [**never before noun**] expected or planned [+ **to do sth**] *He was due to fly back this morning.* ○ *Her book is* ***due out*** (= expected to be published) *next week.* ○ *When is the baby due* (= expected to be born)*?* **2 due to sth** because of something *The train was late due to snow.* **3 FINANCE** [**never before noun**] Money that is due is owed to someone and must be paid. *The rent is due today.* **4** [DESERVE] Something that is due to you is something that is owed to you or something you deserve. *He didn't get the praise and recognition that was* ***due to him.*** **5** [BEHAVIOUR] [**always before noun**] *formal* correct and suitable *He was fined for driving without due care and attention.* ⊃Opposite **undue 6 be due for sth** If you are due for something, it should happen very soon. *I'm due for a check-up at the dentist's.*

due² /dju:/ *noun* **give sb their due** something that you say when you want to describe someone's good qualities after they have done something wrong or after you have criticized them *Joe's a bit slow but, to give him his due, he does work hard.*

due³ /dju:/ *adverb* **due east/north/south/west, etc** directly east/north/south/west, etc *sail/fly due south*

duel /'dju:əl/ *noun* [C] **1** [FIGHT] a type of fight in the past between two people with weapons, used as a way of deciding an argument *He challenged him to a duel.* **2** [ARGUMENT/COMPETITION] an argument or competition between two people or groups

dues /dju:z/ *noun* [**plural**] **FINANCE** money that you must pay to be a member of an organization *annual dues*

duet /dju'et/ *noun* [C] **MUSIC** a piece of music for two people to perform together

dug /dʌg/ *past of* dig

duke /dju:k/ *noun* [C] **SOCIETY** a man of very high social rank in some parts of Europe *the Duke of Beaufort*

dull¹ /dʌl/ *adjective* **1** [BORING] not interesting *a dull place* ○ *a dull person* **2** [NOT BRIGHT] not bright *dull colours* ○ *dull weather* **3** [SOUND] A dull sound is not loud or clear. *a dull thud* **4** [PAIN] [**always before noun**] A dull pain is not strong. *a dull ache* •**dullness** *noun* [U] •**dully** *adverb*

dull² /dʌl/ *verb* [T] to make a feeling or quality become less strong *He's on morphine to dull the pain.*

duly /'dju:li/ *adverb formal* at the correct time, in the correct way, or as you would expect *I ordered it over the Internet and within a few days, it duly arrived.* ○ *I was duly impressed.*

dumb /dʌm/ *adjective* **1** [STUPID] *mainly US informal* stupid *a dumb idea/question* ○ *He's too dumb to understand.* **2** [UNABLE TO TALK] physically unable to talk **3 be struck dumb** to be unable to speak because you are so shocked or angry •**dumbly** *adverb*

dumbfounded /ˌdʌm'faʊndɪd/ *adjective* extremely surprised

ˌdumb 'terminal *noun* [C] **COMPUTING** a computer terminal that is used to enter or read information, but does not have many of the functions of a normal terminal and cannot work on its own

dummy¹ /'dʌmi/ *noun* [C] **1** [BABY EQUIPMENT] *UK* (*US* **pacifier**) a small, rubber object that a baby sucks to stop it crying **2** [STUPID PERSON] *mainly US informal* a stupid person *She's no dummy.* **3** [MODEL] a model of a person

dummy² /'dʌmi/ *adjective* [**always before noun**] not real but made to look real *dummy weapons*

dump¹ /dʌmp/ *verb* **1** [T] to put something somewhere to get rid of it, especially in a place where you should not put it *The company was fined for illegally dumping toxic chemicals.* **2 dump sth on/in/down, etc** to put something somewhere quickly and carelessly *Henri dumped his bag on the table and went upstairs.*

dump² /dʌmp/ (*also UK* **tip**) *noun* [C] **1** [WASTE] a place where people take things that they do not want *We took our old mattress to the dump.* **2** [UNTIDY PLACE] *informal* a place that is dirty and untidy *His room is a dump.*

dumpling /'dʌmplɪŋ/ *noun* [C] **FOOD** a round mixture of fat and flour that has been cooked in boiling liquid *stew and dumplings*

dumps /dʌmps/ *noun* **be down in the dumps** *informal* to be unhappy *He looks a bit down in the dumps.*

Dumpster /'dʌmpstəʳ/ *US trademark* (*UK* **skip**) *noun* [C] a very large, metal container for big pieces of rubbish

dumpy /'dʌmpi/ *adjective informal* short and fat

dune /dju:n/ (*also* **sand dune**) *noun* [C] **GEOGRAPHY** a hill of sand in the desert or on the coast

D

D

dung /dʌŋ/ *noun* [U] **FARMING** solid waste from a large animal

dungarees /ˌdʌŋɡəˈriːz/ *UK* (*US* **overalls**) *noun* [plural] trousers with a part that covers your chest and straps that go over your shoulders

dungeon /ˈdʌndʒᵊn/ *noun* [C] a dark, underground prison, used in the past

dunk /dʌŋk/ *verb* [T] to quickly put something into liquid and take it out again *He dunked the roll in his soup.*

dunno /dəˈnəʊ/ *informal* **I dunno** I do not know.

duo /ˈdjuːəʊ/ *noun* [C] **MUSIC** two people who perform together *a **comedy/pop duo***

duodecimal /ˌdjuːəʊˈdesɪməl/ *adjective* **MATHEMATICS** using a system of counting based on the number 12

duodenum /ˌdjuːəʊˈdiːnəm/ *noun* [C] *plural* **duodenums** or **duodena ANATOMY** the first part of the small intestine (= upper part of the bowels) just below the stomach ⊃See picture at **alimentary canal**

dupe /djuːp/ *verb* [T] to trick someone [**often passive + into + doing sth**] *He was duped into paying $4000 for a fake painting.*

duplicate¹ /ˈdjuːplɪkeɪt/ *verb* [T] **1** COPY to make an exact copy of something *The document has been duplicated.* **2** DO THE SAME to do something that has already been done, in exactly the same way *Ajax hope to duplicate last year's success.* •**duplication** /ˌdjuːplɪˈkeɪʃᵊn/ *noun* [U]

duplicate² /ˈdjuːplɪkət/ *noun* **1** [C] something that is an exact copy of something else *I lost my passport and had to get a duplicate.* **2 in duplicate** If a document is in duplicate, there are two copies of it. •**duplicate** *adjective a duplicate key*

duplicity /djʊˈplɪsəti/ *noun* [U] when you dishonestly tell different people different things

durable /ˈdjʊərəbl/ *adjective* remaining in good condition for a long time *durable goods* ○ *a fabric that is comfortable and durable* •**durability** /ˌdjʊərəˈbɪləti/ *noun* [U]

Duralumin /djʊəˈræljʊmɪn/ *noun* [U] *trademark* a strong, light metal containing aluminium, used to make aircraft

duration /djʊəˈreɪʃᵊn/ *noun* [U] *formal* the amount of time that something lasts *The singer remained in the hotel **for the duration of** his stay in the UK.*

duress /djʊˈres/ *noun formal* **under duress** If you do something under duress, you do it because someone is forcing you to. *a confession made under duress*

O‑‑**during** /ˈdjʊərɪŋ/ *preposition* **1** WHOLE TIME for the whole of a period of time *Emma's usually at home during the day.* **2** MOMENT IN TIME at a particular moment in a period of time *We'll arrange a meeting some time during the week.*

COMMON LEARNER ERROR

during or **for?**

Use **during** to talk about a period of time when something happens.

I'm at work during the day, so it's better to phone in the evening.

Please don't take photos during the performance.

Use **for** to say how long something happens or continues, for example 'for two hours', 'for three days'.

I've been in Cambridge for six months now.

We waited for an hour and then left.

~~*We waited during an hour and then left.*~~

dusk /dʌsk/ *noun* [U] the time in the evening when it starts to become dark *As **dusk fell**, we headed back to the hotel.*

dust¹ /dʌst/ *noun* [U] **1** a powder of dirt or soil that you see on a surface or in the air *He drove off in a cloud of dust.* **2 bite the dust** *informal* to die, fail, or stop existing **3 the dust settles** If the dust settles after an argument or big change, the situation becomes calmer. *Let the dust settle a bit before you make any decisions about the future.*

dust² /dʌst/ *verb* [I, T] to remove dust from something *I tidied and dusted the shelves.*

dustbin /ˈdʌstbɪn/ *UK* (*US* **garbage can**) *noun* [C] a large container for rubbish kept outside your house

duster /ˈdʌstəʳ/ *noun* [C] *UK* a cloth used for removing dust (= powder of dirt) from furniture and other objects

dustman /ˈdʌstmən/ *UK* (*US* **garbage man**) *noun* [C] *plural UK* **dustmen** someone whose job is to remove rubbish from containers outside people's houses

dustpan /ˈdʌstpæn/ *noun* [C] a flat container with a handle, used with a brush for removing dirt from a floor *Get the **dustpan and brush** and I'll sweep this up.*

dusty /ˈdʌsti/ *adjective* covered with dust (= powder of dirt) *a dusty old chair* ○ *dusty streets*

dutiful /ˈdjuːtɪfᵊl/ *adjective* doing everything that you should do in your position or job *a dutiful son* •**dutifully** *adverb*

WORD PARTNERS FOR ***duty***

have/neglect/perform a duty • a duty **to/towards** sb

O‑‑**duty** /ˈdjuːti/ *noun* [C, U] **1** RIGHT THING TO DO something you must do because it is morally or legally right *a **moral duty*** [**+ to do sth**] *Rail companies **have a duty** to provide safe transport.* **2** JOB something you do as part of your job or because of your position *professional/official duties* **3 on/off duty** If a doctor, police officer, etc is on duty, they are working, and if they are off duty, they are not working. **4 FINANCE** tax that you pay on something you buy

duty-free /ˌdjuːtiˈfriː/ *adjective* **FINANCE** Duty-free goods are things that you can buy and bring into a country without paying tax.

duvet /ˈdjuːveɪ/ Ⓤⓢ /duːˈveɪ/ *UK* (*US* **comforter**) *noun* [C] a cover filled with feathers or warm material that you sleep under

DVD /ˌdiːviːˈdiː/ *noun* [C] *abbreviation for* digital versatile disc: a small disc for storing music, films and information *a **DVD player/drive*** ○ *Is this film available **on DVD**?*

dwarf[1] /dwɔːf/ *noun* [C] **1** CREATURE an imaginary creature like a little man, in children's stories *Snow White and the Seven Dwarves* **2** PERSON an offensive word for someone who is very short •**dwarf** *adjective* A dwarf animal or plant is much smaller than the normal size.

dwarf[2] /dwɔːf/ *verb* [T] If something dwarfs other things, it is very big and makes them seem small. [**often passive**] *The hotel is dwarfed by skyscrapers.*

dwell /dwel/ *verb past* **dwelt** or **dwelled dwell in/among/with, etc** *literary* to live somewhere **dwell on/upon sth** *phrasal verb* to keep thinking or talking about something, especially something bad or unpleasant *I don't want to **dwell on the past**.*

dweller /ˈdweləʳ/ *noun* **an apartment/city/country, etc dweller** someone who lives in an apartment/city/the country, etc

dwelling /ˈdwelɪŋ/ *noun* [C] *formal* a house or place to live in

dwindle /ˈdwɪndl/ *verb* [I] to become smaller or less *The number of students in the school has **dwindled to** 200.* ○ *Our savings slowly **dwindled away**.* ○ ***dwindling supplies** of oil*

dye[1] /daɪ/ *noun* [C, U] **DT** a substance that is used to change the colour of something

dye[2] /daɪ/ *verb* [T] **DT dyeing,** *past* **dyed** to change the colour of something by using a dye *He dyed his hair pink last week.*

dying /ˈdaɪɪŋ/ *present participle of* die

dyke (*also* **dike**) /daɪk/ *noun* [C] **1** WALL a wall built to stop water from a sea or river going onto the land **2** PASSAGE *UK* a passage that has been dug to take water away from fields

dynamic /daɪˈnæmɪk/ *adjective* **1** ACTIVE full of ideas, energy, and enthusiasm *a dynamic, young teacher* ○ *dynamic leadership* **2** CHANGING continuously changing or moving *a dynamic economy* **3** PRODUCING MOVEMENT A dynamic force makes something move. •**dynamically** *adverb*

dyˌnamic equiˈlibrium *noun* [U] **CHEMISTRY** when two opposite chemical reactions happen at the same speed

dynamics /daɪˈnæmɪks/ *noun* **1** [**plural**] the way that parts of a situation, group, or system affect each other *political dynamics* ○ *The **dynamics of** family life have changed greatly.* **2 PHYSICS** [U] the scientific study of the movement of objects

dynamism /ˈdaɪnəmɪzᵊm/ *noun* [U] the quality of being dynamic

dynamite /ˈdaɪnəmaɪt/ *noun* [U] **1** EXPLOSIVE a type of explosive *a stick of dynamite* **2** PERSON/THING *informal* someone or something that is very exciting, powerful, or dangerous *an issue that is political dynamite*

dynamo /ˈdaɪnəməʊ/ *noun* [C] **PHYSICS** a device which changes energy of movement into electrical energy

dynasty /ˈdɪnəsti/ (US) /ˈdaɪnəsti/ *noun* [C] **POLITICS** a series of rulers who are all from the same family *the Ming dynasty*

dysentery /ˈdɪsᵊntᵊri/ *noun* [U] **HEALTH** an infectious disease which causes severe problems with the bowels, making solid waste become liquid

dysfunctional /dɪsˈfʌŋkʃᵊnᵊl/ *adjective formal* not behaving, working, or happening in the way that most people think is normal *a **dysfunctional family/childhood***

dyslexia /dɪˈsleksiə/ *noun* [U] **EDUCATION** a condition affecting the brain that makes it difficult for someone to read and write •**dyslexic** /dɪˈsleksɪk/ *adjective* having dyslexia

D

Ee

E, e /iː/ the fifth letter of the alphabet

e- /iː-/ *prefix* **INTERNET** electronic, usually relating to the Internet *an e-ticket* ○ *e-commerce*

O⊸**each** /iːtʃ/ *pronoun, determiner* every one in a group of two or more things or people when they are considered separately *A player from **each of** the teams volunteered to be captain.* ○ *The bill is £36 between the four of us, that's £9 each.*

ˌeach ˈother *pronoun* used to show that each person in a group of two or more people does something to the others *The kids are always arguing with each other.*

eager /ˈiːgəʳ/ *adjective* wanting to do or have something very much [**+ to do sth**] *Sam was eager to go home and play on his computer.* •**eagerly** *adverb an **eagerly awaited** announcement* •**eagerness** *noun* [U]

eagle /ˈiːgl/ *noun* [C] a large, wild bird with a big, curved beak, that hunts smaller animals

O⊸**ear** /ɪəʳ/ *noun* **1 ANATOMY** [C] one of the two organs on your head that you hear with *The child whispered something in her mother's ear.* ➲See colour picture **The Body** on page Centre 13 **2 BIOLOGY** [C] the top part of some crop plants, which produces grain *an ear of wheat/corn* **3 have an ear for sth** to be good at hearing, repeating, or understanding a particular type of sound *He has no ear for music.* **4 fall on deaf ears** If advice or a request falls on deaf ears, people ignore it. **5 play it by ear** to decide how to deal with a situation as it develops **6 play sth by ear** to play a piece of music by remembering the notes

earache /ˈɪəreɪk/ *noun* [C, U] **HEALTH** pain in your ear *I've got (UK) earache/ (US) an earache.*

eardrum /ˈɪədrʌm/ *noun* [C] **ANATOMY** a part inside your ear made of thin, tight skin that allows you to hear sounds

earl /ɜːl/ *noun* [C] **SOCIETY** a man of high social rank in the UK *the Earl of Northumberland*

earlobe /ˈɪələʊb/ *noun* [C] **ANATOMY** the soft part at the bottom of your ear

O⊸**early** /ˈɜːli/ *adjective, adverb* **earlier, earliest** **1** BEGINNING near the beginning of a period of time, process, etc *the early 1980s* ○ *It is too early to say whether he will recover completely.* **2** BEFORE before the usual time or the time that was arranged *early retirement* ○ *The plane arrived ten minutes early.* **3 at the earliest** used after a time or date to show that something will not happen before then *Building will not begin until July at the earliest.* **4 early on** in the first stage or part of something *I lost interest quite early on in the book.* ➲See also: it's early days (**day**)

earmark /ˈɪəmɑːk/ *verb* [T] to decide that something, especially money, will be used for a particular purpose [**often passive**] *More than $7 million has been **earmarked for** schools in the area.* ○ *The land is earmarked for development.*

O⊸**earn** /ɜːn/ *verb* **1 FINANCE** [I, T] to get money for doing work *She earns more than £40,000 a year.* **2 FINANCE earn a/your living** to work to get money for the things you need **3 FINANCE** [T] to get something that you deserve because of your work, qualities, etc *As a teacher you have to earn the respect of your students.* **4** PROFIT [T] to make a profit *an account that earns a high rate of interest*

WORD PARTNERS FOR ***earner***

high/low/top earners • **wage** earners

earner /ˈɜːnəʳ/ *noun* [C] **1** PERSON someone who earns money *a **high earner*** **2** PRODUCT *UK informal* a product or service that earns you money *She has a **nice little earner** making curtains.*

earnest /ˈɜːnɪst/ *adjective* **1** very serious and sincere *an earnest young man* ○ *an earnest effort* **2 in earnest** If something begins to happen in earnest, it really starts to happen in a serious way. *The research will **begin in earnest** early next year.* **3 be in earnest** to be very serious about something and mean what you are saying •**earnestly** *adverb* •**earnestness** *noun* [U]

earnings /ˈɜːnɪŋz/ *noun* [plural] **FINANCE** money that you get from working

earphones /ˈɪəfəʊnz/ *noun* [plural] a piece of electronic equipment that you put on your ears so that you can listen privately to radio, recorded music, etc

earring /ˈɪərɪŋ/ *noun* [C] a piece of jewellery that you wear on or through your ear [**usually plural**] *diamond earrings*

earshot /ˈɪəʃɒt/ *noun* **be out of/within earshot** If you are out of earshot, you are too far away to hear something, and if you are within earshot, you are close enough to hear something.

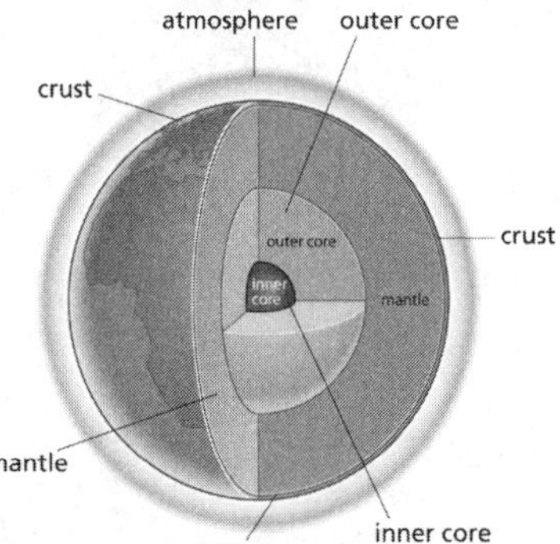

Earth

O⊸**earth** /ɜːθ/ *noun* **1 ASTRONOMY, GEOGRAPHY** [**no plural**] (*also* **the Earth**) the planet that we live on ➲See picture at **solar system** **2** SUBSTANCE [U] soil or ground *a mound of earth* **3 PHYSICS** [C] *UK* (*US* **ground**) a wire that makes electrical equipment safer **4 cost/charge, etc the earth** *UK informal* to cost/charge, etc an extremely large amount of money **5 come (back) down to earth** to start dealing with life and problems again after you have had a very exciting time **6 how/what/why, etc on earth?** *informal* used when you are extremely surprised, confused, or angry about something *Why on earth didn't you tell me before?*

earthly /ˈɜːθli/ *adjective* **1 no earthly doubt/reason/use, etc** used to emphasize that there is not any doubt/reason/use, etc *There's no earthly reason why you should feel guilty.* **2** *literary* relating to this world and not any spiritual life *earthly powers*

WORD PARTNERS FOR ***earthquake***

an earthquake **hits/strikes** [a place] • a **devastating/major/massive/powerful** earthquake

earthquake /ˈɜːθkweɪk/ *noun* [C] **GEOLOGY, GEOGRAPHY** a sudden movement of the Earth's surface, often causing severe damage *A powerful* ***earthquake struck*** *eastern Turkey last night.*

earthy /ˈɜːθi/ *adjective* **1** [DIRECT] referring to sex and the human body in a direct way *earthy jokes* **2** [LIKE SOIL] similar to soil in colour, smell, or taste

earwig /ˈɪəwɪg/ *noun* [C] a small dark-brown insect with two curved parts on its tail

ease¹ /iːz/ *noun* **1** [U] If you do something with ease, it is very easy for you to do it. *Gary passed his exams* ***with ease.*** ○ *I'm amazed at* ***the ease with which*** *he learnt the language.* **2 at ease** feeling relaxed and comfortable *I felt completely at ease with him.* **3 ill at ease** feeling anxious

ease² /iːz/ *verb* **1** [I, T] to become less severe, or to make something become less severe *The new road should ease traffic problems in the village.* **2 ease sb/sth back/out/up, etc** to move someone or something gradually and gently to another position [**often reflexive**] *Tom eased himself back in his chair.*

ease off/up *phrasal verb* **1** [STOP] to gradually stop or become less *The storm is easing off.* **2** [WORK LESS] to start to work less or do things with less energy *As he got older, he started to ease up a little.* **3** [TREAT LESS SEVERELY] to start to treat someone less severely *I wish his supervisor would* ***ease up on*** *him a bit.*

easel /ˈiːzᵊl/ *noun* [C] **ART** something used to support a painting while you paint it

O-■ **easily** /ˈiːzɪli/ *adverb* **1** [EASY] with no difficulty *She makes friends easily.* **2** [LIKELY] used to emphasize that something is likely *A comment like that could easily be misunderstood.* **3 easily the best/worst/biggest, etc** certainly the best/worst/biggest, etc

O-■ **east, East** /iːst/ *noun* **1** [U] the direction that you face to see the sun rise *Which way's east?* **2 the east** the part of an area that is further towards the east than the rest **3 the East** the countries of Asia, especially Japan and China •**east** *adjective New York is* ***east of*** *Chicago.* •**east** *adverb* towards the east *They sailed east.* ⊃See also: **the Middle East**

Easter /ˈiːstəʳ/ *noun* [C, U] **RELIGION** the Christian period of celebration around Easter Sunday (= the special Sunday in March or April on which Christians celebrate Jesus Christ's return to life) *the Easter holidays*

ˈEaster ˌegg *noun* [C] a chocolate egg that people give and receive at Easter

easterly /ˈiːstᵊli/ *adjective* **1** [DIRECTION] towards or in the east *The river flows in an easterly direction.* **2** [WIND] An easterly wind comes from the east. *a strong, easterly breeze*

O-■ **eastern, Eastern** /ˈiːstᵊn/ *adjective* [**always before noun**] **1** [AREA] in or from the east part of an area *eastern Europe* **2** [COUNTRIES] in or from the countries of Asia *Eastern philosophy*

easterner, Easterner /ˈiːstᵊnəʳ/ *noun* [C] *mainly US* someone from the east part of a country or area

ˌEaster ˈSunday (*also* **ˌEaster ˈDay**) *noun* [C, U] **RELIGION** the special Sunday in March or April on which Christians celebrate Jesus Christ's return to life

eastward, eastwards /ˈiːstwəd, ˈiːstwədz/ *adverb* towards the east •**eastward** *adjective an eastward direction*

OTHER WAYS OF SAYING ***easy***

If something is easy to do or understand, we often use the adjectives **simple** or **straightforward**: *The recipe is so* ***simple****, you just mix all the ingredients together.* • *It seems like a fairly* ***straightforward*** *task.*

If a machine or system is easy to use, we often describe it as **user-friendly**: *This latest version of the software is much more* ***user-friendly****.*

In informal situations there are also some fixed expressions you can use to say that something is very easy to do, for example: *(UK) This machine's* ***a doddle*** *to use.* • *My last exam was* ***a piece of cake****.* • *Once we reached the main road the journey was* ***plain sailing****.*

O-■ **easy¹** /ˈiːzi/ *adjective* **1** [NOT DIFFICULT] not difficult *an easy choice* ○ *He thought the exam was very easy.* [+ **to do sth**] *It's easy to see why he's so popular.* **2** [RELAXED] relaxed and comfortable *She has a very easy manner.* **3 I'm easy** *informal* used to say that you do not mind which choice is made *"Would you like pizza or curry?" "I'm easy. You choose."*

COMMON LEARNER ERROR

easy or **easily?**

Remember, **easy** is an adjective and usually describes a noun.

an easy question

The exam was easy.

Easily is an adverb and usually describes a verb.

You should pass the exam easily.

~~*You should pass the exam easy.*~~

easy² /ˈiːzi/ *adverb* **1 take it/things easy** to relax and not use too much energy *After his heart attack, he had to take things easy for a while.* **2 go easy on sb** *informal* to treat someone in a gentle way and not be so strict *Go easy on the boy - he's only young.* **3 go easy on sth** *informal* to not eat or use too much of something *Go easy on the chips, there aren't many left.* **4 easier said than done** used to say that something seems like a good idea but it would be difficult to do

easy-going /ˌiːziˈɡəʊɪŋ/ *adjective* relaxed and not easily upset or worried

OTHER WAYS OF SAYING **eat**

A more formal alternative is the verb **consume**: *He **consumes** vast quantities of bread with every meal.*

If someone eats something quickly because they are very hungry, the verb **devour** is sometimes used: *The children **devoured** a whole packet of biscuits.*

The phrasal verbs **bolt down**, **gobble up**, and **wolf down** are also used to describe the action of eating something very quickly: *He **gobbled up** his food before anyone else had started.* • *I gave her a plate of pasta and she **wolfed** it **down**.*

The verb **scoff** (**scarf** *US*) can be used in informal situations when someone eats a lot of something very quickly: *Who **scoffed/scarfed** all the cake?*

The verb **snack** means 'to eat a little food between main meals': *I've been **snacking** on biscuits and chocolate all afternoon.*

To **eat out** is to eat in a restaurant: *I thought we could **eat out** tonight.*

The phrasal verb **pick at** is sometimes used when someone eats only a little of something: *He didn't feel hungry, and sat at the table **picking at** his food.*

The phrasal verb **tuck into** means 'to start to eat something with enthusiasm': *I was just about to **tuck into** a huge bowl of ice cream.*

eat /iːt/ *verb past tense* **ate**, *past participle* **eaten** **1** SWALLOW [I, T] to put food into your mouth and then swallow it *Who ate all the cake?* ○ *I haven't eaten since breakfast.* ○ *Let's have **something to eat*** (= some food). **2** MEAL [I] to eat a meal *We usually eat in the kitchen.* ⊃See also: have your **cake** and eat it

eat away at sb *phrasal verb* If a memory or bad feeling eats away at someone, it makes them feel more and more unhappy.

eat away at sth *phrasal verb* to gradually damage or destroy something

eat into sth *phrasal verb* to use or take away a large part of something valuable, such as money or time

eat out *phrasal verb* to eat at a restaurant ⊃See colour picture **Phrasal Verbs** on page Centre 16

eat (sth) up *phrasal verb* to eat all the food you have been given *Be a good boy and eat up your spinach.*

eat up sth *phrasal verb* to use or take away a large part of something valuable, such as money or time *Cities are eating up more and more farmland.*

eater /ˈiːtəʳ/ *noun* **a big/fussy/meat, etc eater** someone who eats in a particular way or eats a particular food

eatery /ˈiːtᵊri/ *noun* [C] *informal* a restaurant

ˈeating diˌsorder *noun* [C] **HEALTH** a mental illness in which someone cannot eat normal amounts of food

eaves /iːvz/ *noun* [**plural**] the edges of a roof where it is wider than the walls

eavesdrop /ˈiːvzdrɒp/ *verb* [I] **eavesdropping**, *past* **eavesdropped** to secretly listen to a conversation *He stood outside the door **eavesdropping on** them.* •**eavesdropper** *noun* [C]

eBay /ˈiːbeɪ/ *noun* [U] **INTERNET** *trademark* a website that allows users to buy and sell things online

ebb¹ /eb/ *noun* **1 the ebb (tide) GEOGRAPHY** when the sea flows away from the land **2 be at a low ebb** If someone's enthusiasm, confidence, etc is at a low ebb, it is much less than before. *Staff morale is at a low ebb.* **3 ebb and flow** the way in which the level of something regularly becomes higher or lower in a situation *the ebb and flow of the economy*

ebb² /eb/ *verb* [I] **1** (*also* **ebb away**) to gradually disappear *She watched her father's life slowly ebbing away.* **2 GEOGRAPHY** When the tide ebbs, the sea flows away from the land.

ebony /ˈebᵊni/ *noun* [U] hard black wood

ebullient /ɪˈbuliənt/ *adjective* energetic, enthusiastic, and excited *an ebullient personality*

e-business /ˈiːbɪznɪs/ *noun* [C, U] **INTERNET, ECONOMICS** the business of buying and selling goods and services on the Internet, or a company which does this

e-cash /ˈiːkæʃ/ *noun* [U] **INTERNET, FINANCE** money in an electronic form, used for buying goods and services on the Internet

eccentric¹ /ɪkˈsentrɪk/ *adjective* behaving in a strange and unusual way *an eccentric professor* ○ *eccentric behaviour* •**eccentrically** *adverb* •**eccentricity** /ˌeksenˈtrɪsəti/ *noun* [U] when someone is eccentric

eccentric² /ɪkˈsentrɪk/ *noun* [C] someone who is eccentric *a harmless eccentric*

ecclesiastical /ɪˌkliːziˈæstɪkᵊl/ *adjective* **RELIGION** relating to the Christian Church *ecclesiastical law/history*

echelon /ˈeʃəlɒn/ *noun formal* **the lower/upper echelons SOCIETY** the people at the lower/upper level of a large organization or society *the upper echelons of government/management*

echinacea /ˌekɪˈneɪʃə/ *noun* [U] **HEALTH** a plant that is used as a medicine, especially to help your body fight illness

echinoderm /ɪˈkaɪnəʊdɜːm/ *noun* [C] **BIOLOGY** a type of sea animal with a body which has five equal parts arranged around a centre *A starfish is an example of an echinoderm.*

echo¹ /ˈekəʊ/ *verb* **echoing**, *past* **echoed** **1** SOUND [I] If a sound echoes, or a place echoes with a sound, you hear the sound again because you are in a large, empty space. *Their voices **echoed** around the room.* **2** REPEAT [T] to repeat something that someone else has said because you agree with it *This report echoes some of the earlier research I've read.*

echo² /ˈekəʊ/ *noun* [C] *plural* **echoes** **1** SOUND a sound that you hear more than once because you are in a big, empty space **2** EVENT/IDEA something that is very much like something else and makes you think of it [**usually plural**] *There are* ***echoes of*** *Shakespeare's work in the play.*

eclectic /ek'lektɪk/ *adjective* including many different styles and types *an* ***eclectic mix***

eclipse¹ /ɪ'klɪps/ *noun* [**C**] **ASTRONOMY** when the sun is covered by the moon, or the moon is covered by the Earth's shadow (= dark area) *a solar/lunar eclipse*

eclipse² /ɪ'klɪps/ *verb* [**T**] **1** to make another person or thing seem much less important, good, or famous [**often passive**] *Braque was somewhat eclipsed by Picasso.* **2 ASTRONOMY** to make an eclipse of the moon or sun

eco- /iːkəʊ-/ *prefix* **ENVIRONMENT** relating to the environment *eco-friendly cleaning products*

eco-friendly /ˌiːkəʊ'frendli/ *adjective* **ENVIRONMENT** describes a product that is designed so that it does not damage the environment *eco-friendly washing powder*

ecological /ˌiːkə'lɒdʒɪkəl/ *adjective* **ENVIRONMENT** relating to ecology or to the environment *an ecological disaster* •**ecologically** *adverb*

ecoˌlogical 'footprint *noun* [**C**] **ENVIRONMENT** the amount of the earth's energy that someone or something uses *You can reduce your ecological footprint by cycling more and driving less.*

ecology /iː'kɒlədʒi/ *noun* [**U, no plural**] **ENVIRONMENT** the relationship between living things and the environment, or the scientific study of this •**ecologist** *noun* [**C**] someone who studies ecology

e-commerce /'iːˌkɒmɜːs/ *noun* [**U**] **INTERNET** the buying and selling of goods and services on the Internet

econometrics /ɪˌkɒnə'metrɪks/ *noun* [**U**] **ECONOMICS** the use of mathematical methods to describe economic systems

O━**economic** /ˌiːkə'nɒmɪk, ˌekə'nɒmɪk/ *adjective* **1 ECONOMICS** [**always before noun**] relating to trade, industry, and money ***economic growth*** ○ ***economic policies*** **2** making a profit, or likely to make a profit *It's not economic to produce goods in small quantities.* ➲Opposite **uneconomic** •**economically** *adverb The country would benefit economically.*

economical /ˌiːkə'nɒmɪkəl, ˌekə'nɒmɪkəl/ *adjective* not using a lot of money, fuel, etc *I need a car that's economical and reliable.* •**economically** *adverb*

ˌeconomic 'migrant *noun* [**C**] a person who leaves their home country to live in another country with better work or living conditions

economics /ˌiːkə'nɒmɪks/ *noun* [**U**] **ECONOMICS** the study of the way in which trade, industry, and money are organized •**economist** /ɪ'kɒnəmɪst/ *noun* [**C**] someone who studies economics ➲See also: **home economics**

eˌconomies of 'scale *noun* [**plural**] **FINANCE** saving money by buying large amounts of things, especially in a business

economize (*also UK* **-ise**) /ɪ'kɒnəmaɪz/ *verb* [**I**] **FINANCE** to use less of something because you want to save money

WORD PARTNERS FOR ***economy***

a **booming/stable/strong/weak** economy • the **global/local/national economy** • the economy **grows/improves/recovers/slows**

O━**economy** /ɪ'kɒnəmi/ *noun* **1 ECONOMICS** [**C**] the system by which a country produces and uses goods and money *the German/US economy* ○ *a global economy* **2** [**C, U**] when someone or something does not use much money, fuel, etc *The car's design combines comfort with economy.* ○ *UK We'll need to* ***make*** *some* ***economies*** *when I stop work.*

e'conomy ˌclass *noun* [**U**] the cheapest and least comfortable seats on an aircraft •**e'conomy ˌclass** *adjective, adverb*

ecosystem /'iːkəʊˌsɪstəm/ *noun* [**C**] **ENVIRONMENT** all the living things in an area and the way they affect each other and the environment *Tourism is damaging the fragile ecosystem of the reef.* ➲See picture **ecosystem** on next page

ecotourism /'iːkəʊtʊərɪzəm/ *noun* [**U**] **ENVIRONMENT** the business of providing holidays for people so that they can help local people and not damage the environment

eco-warrior /'iːkəʊˌwɒriər/ *noun* [**C**] **ENVIRONMENT** someone who tries to stop activities which damage the environment

ecstasy /'ekstəsi/ *noun* [**U**] a feeling of extreme happiness *She danced about* ***in ecstasy***.

ecstatic /ɪk'stætɪk/ *adjective* extremely happy •**ecstatically** *adverb*

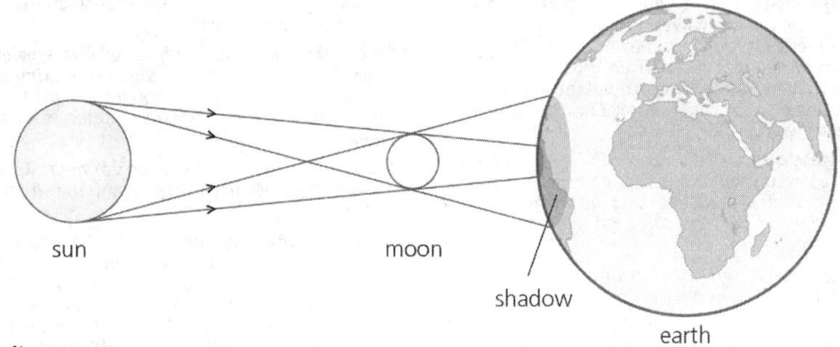

eclipse

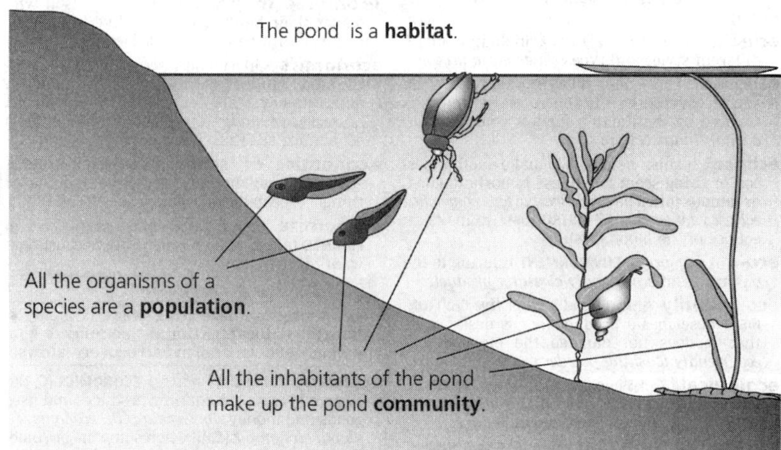
The pond and its inhabitants is an ecosystem.
The pond is a habitat.
All the organisms of a species are a population.
All the inhabitants of the pond make up the pond community.

ecosystem

ectoplasm /ˈektəplæzᵊm/ *noun* [U] **BIOLOGY** the outer layer of particular types of cell

ecumenical /ˌekjʊˈmenɪkᵊl/ *adjective* **RELIGION** encouraging different types of Christian churches to unite *an ecumenical service*

eczema /ˈeksmə/ *noun* [U] **HEALTH** a medical condition which makes areas of skin become red and dry

O━ **edge¹** /edʒ/ *noun* **1** OUTSIDE [C] the part around something that is furthest from the centre *Rick was sitting **on the edge of** the bed.* ○ *She ran down to the water's edge.* **2** SIDE [C] the part of a blade of a knife or tool that cuts *a sharp/cutting edge* **3 have the edge on/over sb/sth** to be slightly better than someone or something else **4 be on edge** to be nervous or worried *Sorry for shouting - I'm a bit on edge today.* **5 take the edge off sth** to make something unpleasant have less of an effect on someone *Have an apple. It'll **take the edge off** your **hunger**.*

edge² /edʒ/ *verb* **1 edge (sth) up/down/past, etc** to move somewhere gradually, or to make something move somewhere gradually *She edged her way through the crowd of reporters.* **2** [T] to put something around the edge of something else as a decoration *The cloth was edged with gold.*

edgeways /ˈedʒweɪz/ *UK* (*US* **edgewise** /ˈedʒwaɪz/) *adverb* with the narrowest part going first *We should be able to get the sofa through edgeways.* ➲See also: not get a **word**¹ in edgeways

edgy /ˈedʒi/ *adjective* nervous *David was starting to feel a bit edgy.*

EDI /ˌiːdiːˈaɪ/ *noun* [U] **INTERNET** *abbreviation for* electronic data interchange: a system for organizing information sent by computers that is often used by companies buying and selling things on the Internet

edible /ˈedɪbl/ *adjective* safe to eat and not harmful *edible berries* ➲Compare **inedible**

edict /ˈiːdɪkt/ *noun* [C] *formal* **POLITICS** an official order from someone in authority

edifice /ˈedɪfɪs/ *noun* [C] *formal* a very large building

edit /ˈedɪt/ *verb* [T] to prepare text, film, etc by deciding what to include and making mistakes correct

edition /ɪˈdɪʃᵊn/ *noun* [C] **1** BOOK a book, newspaper, etc that is one of several that are the same and were produced at the same time *a new edition* ○ *The paperback edition costs £7.95.* **2** PROGRAMME a radio or television programme that is one of a series

editor /ˈedɪtəʳ/ *noun* [C] **1** TEXT/FILM someone whose job is to prepare text, film, etc by deciding what to include and making mistakes correct **2** NEWSPAPER someone who is in charge of a newspaper or magazine

editorial¹ /ˌedɪˈtɔːriəl/ *adjective* [**always before noun**] **1** EDITOR relating to editors or editing *editorial skills* **2** OPINION written by or expressing the opinions of a newspaper editor *editorial pages*

editorial² /ˌedɪˈtɔːriəl/ (*US* **op-ed**) *noun* [C] an article in a newspaper expressing the editor's opinion

educate /ˈedʒʊkeɪt/ *verb* [T] **1 EDUCATION** to teach someone at a school or college [**often passive**] *She was educated at the Perse School.* **2** to give people information about something so that they understand it better *This is part of a campaign to **educate** people **about** the dangers of smoking.*

educated /ˈedʒʊkeɪtɪd/ *adjective* **1** Someone who is educated has learned a lot at school or university and has a good level of knowledge. **2 an educated guess** a guess that is probably correct because you have enough knowledge about something ➲See also: **well-educated**

WORD PARTNERS FOR ***education***

continue/have/provide/receive education • **compulsory/good** education

O-ш**education** /ˌedʒʊˈkeɪʃᵊn/ *noun* [**U, no plural**] **EDUCATION** the process of teaching and learning in a school or college, or the knowledge that you get from this *We expect a good standard of education for our children.* •**educational** *adjective* providing education, or relating to education *the **educational system*** •**educationally** *adverb* ➲See also: **further education, higher education**

educator /ˈedjʊkeɪtəʳ/ *mainly US noun* [**C**] **EDUCATION** a person who teaches people

eel /iːl/ *noun* [**C**] a long fish that looks like a snake

eerie /ˈɪəri/ *adjective* unusual and slightly frightening *an **eerie silence*** •**eerily** *adverb* •**eeriness** *noun* [**U**]

WORD PARTNERS FOR ***effect***

have/produce an effect • an **adverse/beneficial/devastating/harmful/profound** effect • an effect **on** sb/sth • the effects **of** sth

O-ш**effect¹** /ɪˈfekt/ *noun* **1** [**C, U**] a change, reaction, or result that is caused by something *The accident **had a** huge **effect on** her life.* ○ *We don't know the long-term **effects of** this drug.* **2 in effect** used to say what the real situation is *This means, in effect, that the plan has been scrapped.* **3 come/go into effect** to start being used *New food safety rules come into effect on Monday.* **4 take effect** to start to produce results or changes *The anaesthetic takes effect in about ten minutes.* **5 to that effect** used to say that you are giving the general meaning of something but not the exact words *He said he was bored with school or something to that effect.* **6 a sound/special/visual, etc effect** a sound, image, etc that is created artificially ➲See also: **side effect**

COMMON LEARNER ERROR

affect or effect?

Be careful not to confuse these two words.

Affect is a verb which means to cause a change.

Pollution seriously affects the environment.

Use the noun **effect** to talk about the change, reaction, or result caused by something.

Global warming is one of the effects of pollution.

effect² /ɪˈfekt/ *verb* [**T**] *formal* to make something happen *The civil rights movement **effected** a huge **change** in America.*

O-ш**effective** /ɪˈfektɪv/ *adjective* **1** ACHIEVING RESULT successful or achieving the result that you want *effective management* ○ *What is the most effective way of teaching grammar?* **2 become/be effective** If changes, laws, etc become effective, they officially start. **3** REAL [**always before noun**] used to say what the real situation is although officially it is different *She has effective control of the company.* ➲Opposite **ineffective** •**effectiveness** *noun* [**U**]

effectively /ɪˈfektɪvli/ *adverb* **1** WELL in a way that is successful and achieves what you want *Teachers need to be able to communicate ideas effectively.* **2** REALLY used when you describe what the real result of a situation is *His illness effectively ended his career.*

effector /ɪˈfektəʳ/ *noun* [**C**] **BIOLOGY** a body part or cell that changes or does something as a result of something that is outside the body *effector cells*

effects /ɪˈfekts/ *noun* [**plural**] *formal* possessions *my **personal effects***

effeminate /ɪˈfemɪnət/ *adjective* An effeminate man behaves or looks like a woman.

efficiency /ɪˈfɪʃᵊnsi/ *noun* [**U**] when someone or something uses time and energy well, without wasting any *fuel efficiency* ○ *We must improve the efficiency of the industry.*

efficient /ɪˈfɪʃᵊnt/ *adjective* working well and not wasting time or energy *an efficient person/organization* ○ *Email is a quick and efficient way of contacting people.* ➲Opposite **inefficient** •**efficiently** *adverb*

effigy /ˈefɪdʒi/ *noun* [**C**] a model of a person *Protesters burned effigies of the president.*

efflorescence /ˌef.lɔːˈresᵊnts/ *noun* [**U**] **CHEMISTRY** the powder that is left when a liquid has evaporated (= changed to a gas, epecially because of heating)

WORD PARTNERS FOR ***effort***

make an effort • **require/take** effort • a **big/brave/concerted/frantic/valiant** effort • **in** an effort to do sth

O-ш**effort** /ˈefət/ *noun* **1** ATTEMPT [**C, U**] an attempt to do something [**+ to do sth**] *We huddled together **in an effort** to keep warm.* ○ *He was **making an effort** to be sociable.* **2** ENERGY [**U**] the energy that you need to do something *I **put** a lot of **effort into** organizing the party.* [**+ to do sth**] *It would **take** too much **effort** to tidy my bedroom.* **3 PHYSICS** [**U**] the force that is used to make something move ➲See picture at **lever 4 to be an effort** to be difficult or painful *After his accident, walking was an effort.*

effortless /ˈefətləs/ *adjective* achieved without any special or obvious effort ***effortless grace/style*** •**effortlessly** *adverb*

effusive /ɪˈfjuːsɪv/ *adjective* showing a lot of enthusiasm or approval for someone or something, often too much

EFL /ˌiːefˈel/ *noun* [**U**] **EDUCATION** *abbreviation for* English as a Foreign Language: the teaching of English to students whose first language is not English

EFTPOS /ˈeftpɒz/ *noun* [**U**] **FINANCE** *abbreviation for* electronic funds transfer at point of sale; a method of paying money electronically

O-ш**e.g.** (*also* **eg**) /ˌiːˈdʒiː/ used to give an example of what you mean *crime writers, e.g. Agatha Christie and Ruth Rendell*

egalitarian /ɪˌgælɪ'teəriən/ *adjective formal* believing that everyone should have the same freedom and opportunities

egestion /ɪ'dʒestʃən/ *noun* [U] **BIOLOGY** the process by which solid waste leaves the body through the bottom

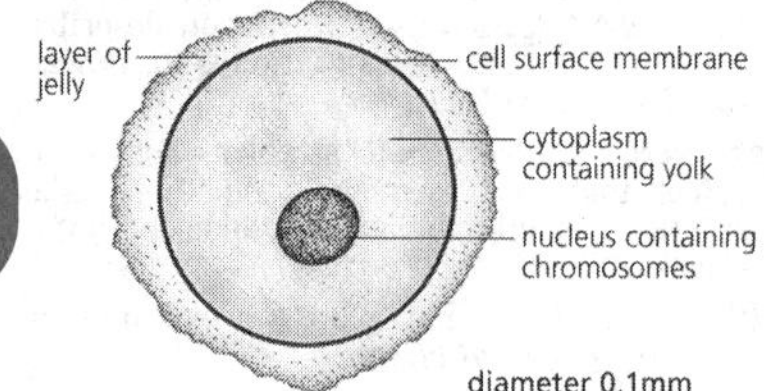

egg

O-- **egg¹** /eg/ *noun* **1 FOOD** [C, U] an oval object produced by a female chicken, that you eat as food ***a boiled/fried egg*** ➲See colour picture **Food** on page Centre 11 **2 BIOLOGY** [C] an oval object with a hard shell that contains a baby bird, insect, or other creature *The bird **lays** (= produces) **its eggs** in a nest.* **3 BIOLOGY** [C] a cell inside a female person or animal that can develop into a baby **4 have egg on your face** to seem stupid because of something you have done ➲See also: **Easter egg, scrambled eggs**

egg² /eg/ *verb*
egg sb on *phrasal verb* to encourage someone to do something, usually something that is wrong, stupid, or dangerous *Two girls were fighting outside the club, egged on by a group of friends.*

ˈegg ˌcup *noun* [C] a small container for holding a boiled egg while you eat it

eggplant /'egplɑːnt/ *US* (*UK* **aubergine**) *noun* [C, U] **FOOD** an oval, purple vegetable that is white inside ➲See colour picture **Fruit and Vegetables** on page Centre 10

ego /'iːgəʊ, 'egəʊ/ *noun* [C] your opinion of yourself *He has a huge ego.*

egocentric /ˌiːgəʊ'sentrɪk/ *adjective* interested only in yourself

egotism /'iːgəʊtɪzəm/ (*also* **egoism** /'iːgəʊɪzəm/) *noun* [U] when someone thinks that they are very important and is not interested in other people •**egotist** *noun* [C] •**egotistic** /ˌiːgəʊ'tɪstɪk/ (*also* **egotistical** /ˌiːgəʊ'tɪstɪkəl/) *adjective*

egregious /ɪ'griːdʒəs/ *adjective formal* extremely bad or shocking in an obvious way *an egregious example of racism*

eh? /eɪ/ *exclamation UK informal spoken* **1** REPEAT used to ask someone to repeat something because you did not hear or understand it *"You're looking tired." "Eh?" "I said, you're looking tired."* **2** REACT used to show interest or surprise at something *Sue's had a baby girl, eh?*

Eid /iːd/ *noun* **RELIGION** the name of two Muslim festivals. The more important one celebrates the end of Ramadan.

O-- **eight** /eɪt/ the number 8

O-- **eighteen** /ˌeɪ'tiːn/ the number 18 •**eighteenth** 18th written as a word

O-- **eighth¹** /eɪtθ/ 8th written as a word

eighth² /eɪtθ/ *noun* [C] one of eight equal parts of something; $^1/_8$

O-- **eighty** /'eɪti/ **1** the number 80 **2 the eighties** the years from 1980-1989 **3 be in your eighties** to be aged between 80 and 89 •**eightieth** 80th written as a word

either¹ /'aɪðər, 'iːðər/ *conjunction* **either... or** used when you are giving a choice of two or more things *Either call me tonight or I'll speak to you tomorrow.*

O-- **either²** /'aɪðər, 'iːðər/ *pronoun, determiner* **1** ONE OF TWO one of two people or things when it is not important which *"Would you like red or white wine?" - "Oh, either."* ○ *Ask Dom or Andrew, either of them will help you.* **2** BOTH both *People were smoking on either side* (= at both sides) *of me.* ○ *You can use the train or the bus, **either way** it'll take an hour.*

O-- **either³** /'aɪðər, 'iːðər/ *adverb* used in negative sentences to mean that something else is also true *The menu is boring and it's not cheap either.* ➲See Common Learner Error at **not**

ejaculate /ɪ'dʒækjʊleɪt/ *verb* [I] **BIOLOGY** If a man or male animal ejaculates, sperm (= many small cells, one of which joins an egg to make a baby) suddenly comes out from his penis. •**ejaculation** /ɪˌdʒækjʊ'leɪʃən/ *noun* [U] when a man or male animal ejaculates

eject /ɪ'dʒekt/ *verb* **1** LEAVE PLACE [T] *formal* to make someone leave a place, usually using force [**often passive**] *He was **ejected from** the courtroom for shouting.* **2** LEAVE MACHINE [I, T] to come out of a machine when a button is pressed, or to make something do this *How do you eject the tape?* **3** LEAVE AIRCRAFT [I] to leave an aircraft in an emergency by being pushed out while still in your seat

eke /iːk/ *verb*
eke sth out *phrasal verb* **1** to use something slowly or carefully because you only have a small amount of it **2 eke out a living/existence** to earn only just enough money to pay for things you need *He ekes out a living by cleaning windows.*

elaborate¹ /ɪ'læbərət/ *adjective* complicated, detailed, or made carefully from many parts *an elaborate system/scheme* ○ *an elaborate design* •**elaborately** *adverb*

elaborate² /ɪ'læbəreɪt/ *verb* [I, T] to explain something and give more details *He wouldn't **elaborate on** the details.* •**elaboration** /ɪˌlæbə'reɪʃən/ *noun* [U]

elapse /ɪ'læps/ *verb* [I] *formal* If time elapses, it passes. *Two years have elapsed since the attack.*

elastic¹ /ɪ'læstɪk/ *adjective* Something that is elastic can stretch and return to its original size. *Your skin is more elastic when you are young.* •**elasticity** /ˌɪlæs'tɪsəti/ *noun* [U] the quality of being elastic

elastic² /ɪ'læstɪk/ *noun* [U] a type of rubber that returns to its original size and shape after you stretch it

e,lastic 'band *UK* (*UK/US* **rubber band**) *noun* [C] a thin circle of rubber used to hold things together

elated /ɪ'leɪtɪd/ *adjective* extremely happy and excited *We were* ***elated by/at*** *the news.* •**elation** /ɪ'leɪʃᵊn/ *noun* [U]

elbow¹ /'elbəʊ/ *noun* [C] **ANATOMY** the part in the middle of your arm where it bends ➲See colour picture **The Body** on page Centre 13

elbow² /'elbəʊ/ *verb* [T] to push someone with your elbow, especially so you can move past them *He* ***elbowed his way through*** *the crowds of shoppers.*

'elbow ,room *noun* [U] space to move easily

elder¹ /'eldəʳ/ *adjective* **elder brother/daughter/sister, etc** the older of two brothers/daughters/sisters, etc ➲See Common Learner Error at **old**

elder² /'eldəʳ/ *noun* **1 the elder** the oldest of two people *He's the elder of two sons.* **2 your elders** people older than you *I was taught to respect my elders.* **3 SOCIETY** [C] an important, respected, older member of a group

elderly /'eldᵊli/ *adjective* a more polite word for 'old', used to describe people *an elderly man* ○ *Children should show respect for* ***the elderly****.*

eldest /'eldɪst/ *adjective* **eldest child/daughter/brother, etc** the oldest child/daughter/brother, etc *My eldest brother is a doctor.* ○ *Susan is* ***the eldest*** *of three sisters.*

e-learning /'iːlɜːnɪŋ/ *noun* [U] **INTERNET, EDUCATION** electronic learning: the business of providing courses online for students so that they can study and learn from home

elect /ɪ'lekt/ *verb* **1 POLITICS** [T] to choose someone for a particular job or position by voting [**often passive**] *She was* ***elected to*** *the US Senate in 2004.* ○ *He was elected president in 1997.* **2 elect to do sth** *formal* to choose to do something *The child elected to stay with his mother.* ➲See also: **re-elect**

WORD PARTNERS FOR ***election***

hold an election • **run for/stand for** election • **lose/win** an election • an election **campaign**

O-╌ **election** /ɪ'lekʃᵊn/ *noun* [C, U] **POLITICS** a time when people vote in order to choose someone for a political or official job *a presidential election* ○ *Who do you think will* ***win the election****?* ○ *Will you* ***stand/run for election*** *again this year?* ➲See also: **by-election, general election, re-election**

e'lection ,day *US* (*UK* **polling day**) *noun* [C] **POLITICS** the day when people vote in an election

electoral /ɪ'lektᵊrᵊl/ *adjective* [**always before noun**] **POLITICS** relating to elections *the* ***electoral system*** ○ ***electoral reform***

electorate /ɪ'lektᵊrət/ *noun* [**group**] **POLITICS** the people who are allowed to vote in an election *the British electorate*

O-╌ **electric** /ɪ'lektrɪk/ *adjective* **1 PHYSICS** Electric lights, tools, etc work using electricity. *an electric light/heater* **2 PHYSICS** supplying electricity *an electric socket* ○ *electric current* **3** EXCITING full of excitement and emotion *The atmosphere backstage was electric.*

electrical /ɪ'lektrɪkᵊl/ *adjective* **1 PHYSICS** Electrical goods or equipment work using electricity. ***electrical appliances/goods*** **2** SUPPLY relating to the production and supply of electricity *an electrical engineer*

the e,lectric 'chair *noun* a chair used in parts of the US to kill a criminal using electricity

electrician /ɪ,lek'trɪʃᵊn/ *noun* [C] someone whose job is to put in, check, or repair electrical wires and equipment

WORD PARTNERS FOR ***electricity***

generate/produce electricity • **be operated by/be powered by** electricity • an electricity **supply**

O-╌ **electricity** /ɪ,lek'trɪsəti/ *noun* [U] **PHYSICS** a type of energy that can produce light and heat, or make machines work *The electricity has been turned off.* ○ *an electricity bill*

e,lectric 'shock *noun* [C] a sudden, painful feeling that you get when electricity flows through your body

electrify /ɪ'lektrɪfaɪ/ *verb* [T] **1** MAKE EXCITED to make people who are watching something feel very excited *She electrified the crowd with her fantastic performance.* **2 PHYSICS** to supply something with electricity *an electrified railway*

electrocute /ɪ'lektrəkjuːt/ *verb* [T] to kill someone by causing electricity to flow through their body [**often passive**] *He was electrocuted while playing on a railway line.* •**electrocution** /ɪ,lektrə'kjuːʃᵊn/ *noun* [U]

electrode /ɪ'lektrəʊd/ *noun* [C] **PHYSICS** the point where an electric current enters or leaves something such as a battery (= object which provides electricity)

electrolysis /ɪ,lek'trɒləsɪs/ *noun* [U] **CHEMISTRY** the use of an electric current to cause chemical change in a liquid

electrolyte /ɪ'lektrəlaɪt/ *noun* [C] **CHEMISTRY** a liquid which electricity can go through or which breaks into its parts when electricity goes through it •**electrolytic** /ɪlektrə'lɪtɪk/ *adjective*

electrolytic cell /ɪlektrə,lɪtɪk'sel/ *noun* [C] **PHYSICS** a device which contains an electrolyte and through which an electrical current is passed in order to cause a reaction

electromagnet /ɪ,lektrəʊ'mægnət/ *noun* [C] **PHYSICS** a magnet (= piece of iron that makes metal move towards it) in which there is wire around the iron, and which only becomes magnetic when a current is passed through the wire

electromagnetism /ɪ,lektrəʊ'mægnətɪzᵊm/ *noun* [U] **PHYSICS** magnetism (= the power that makes metal move towards iron) that is produced by an electrical current •**electromagnetic** /ɪ,lektrəʊmæg'netɪk/ *adjective* *the electromagnetic spectrum*

electron /ɪ'lektrɒn/ *noun* [C] **PHYSICS, CHEMISTRY** an extremely small piece of an atom with a negative electrical charge

O-╌ **electronic** /ɪ,lek'trɒnɪk/ *adjective* **1 PHYSICS** Electronic equipment consists of things such as computers, televisions, and radios. **2** MUSIC/

E

GAMES Electronic music, games, etc use electronic equipment. •**electronically** *adverb*

ˌelectronic ˈbanking *noun* [U] **INTERNET, FINANCE** the use of the Internet to pay money into a bank account, take money out, etc. *electronic banking services*

electronics /ˌɪlekˈtrɒnɪks/ *noun* [U] **PHYSICS** the science of making electronic equipment *the electronics industry*

eˌlectron ˈmicroscope *noun* [C] **PHYSICS** a very powerful microscope (= device used for looking at very small things) which produces pictures by sending electrons through objects

E

electroplate /ɪˈlektrəʊpleɪt/ *verb* [T] **PHYSICS** to cover the surface of a metal object with a thin layer of a different metal, often silver, using electrolysis (= a method that uses electrical current)

electrostatic /ɪˌlektrəʊˈstætɪk/ *adjective* **PHYSICS** relating to electricity which does not move in a current but is attracted to the surface of some objects *an electrostatic charge*

electrovalent bond /ɪˌlektrəʊveɪləntˈbɒnd/ *noun* [C] **PHYSICS** the way two atoms are joined together when one atom loses an electron to form a positive ion and the other gains an electron to form a negative ion

elegance /ˈelɪgᵊns/ *noun* [U] when someone or something is stylish or attractive in their appearance or behaviour

elegant /ˈelɪgᵊnt/ *adjective* stylish or attractive in appearance or behaviour *an elegant dining room* ○ *She's a very elegant woman.* •**elegantly** *adverb*

element /ˈelɪmənt/ *noun* **1** PART [C] a part of something *This book has all the elements of a good detective story.* **2 an element of sth** a small amount of an emotion or quality *There's an element of truth in what she says.* **3** PEOPLE [C] a group of people of a particular type *The disruptive element on the committee voted against the proposal.* **4 CHEMISTRY** [C] a simple substance which cannot be reduced to smaller chemical parts *Iron is one of the elements of the Earth's crust.* **5 PHYSICS** [C] the part of a piece of electrical equipment which produces heat **6 be in your element** to be happy because you are doing what you like doing and what you are good at *I'm in my element at a children's party.*

elementary /ˌelɪˈmentᵊri/ *adjective* **1** basic *I only have an elementary knowledge of physics.* ○ *an elementary mistake* **2 EDUCATION** relating to the early stages of studying a subject *students at elementary level*

ˌelementary ˈparticle *noun* [C] **PHYSICS** any of the smallest and simplest parts that all physical things are made from, such as an electron, a proton or a neutron

eleˈmentary ˌschool *US* (*UK* **primary school**) *noun* [C] **EDUCATION** a school for children from the ages of five to eleven

elements /ˈelɪmənts/ *noun* **the elements** the weather, especially bad weather *Shall we **brave the elements** and go out for a walk?*

elephant /ˈelɪfənt/ *noun* [C] a very large, grey animal with big ears and a very long nose

elevate /ˈelɪveɪt/ *verb formal* **1 be elevated to sth** to be given a more important position *She has been elevated to deputy manager.* ○ *an elevated position* **2** [T] to move something to a higher level or height *High stress levels elevate blood pressure.* ○ *Try to keep your leg elevated.*

elevation /ˌelɪˈveɪʃᵊn/ *noun* **1 MEASURES** [C] the height of a place above the level of the sea *The hotel is situated at an elevation of 1000m.* **2** [U] *formal* when someone or something is given a more important position *his sudden **elevation to stardom***

elevator /ˈelɪveɪtəʳ/ *US* (*UK* **lift**) *noun* [C] a machine that carries people up and down in tall buildings

O⊷**eleven** /ɪˈlevᵊn/ the number 11 •**eleventh** 11th written as a word

elf /elf/ *noun* [C] *plural* **elves** a small person with pointed ears who has magic powers in children's stories

elicit /ɪˈlɪsɪt/ *verb* [T] *formal* to get information or a reaction from someone *You have to ask the right questions to **elicit** the **information** you want.*

eligible /ˈelɪdʒəbl/ *adjective* **1** ABLE TO DO If you are eligible to do something, you can do it because you are in the right situation. [+ **to do sth**] *Only people over 18 are eligible to vote.* ○ *You might be **eligible for** a grant for your studies.* ⊃Opposite **ineligible 2** MARRIAGE If someone who is not married is eligible, they would be a good husband or wife because they are rich, attractive, etc. *an eligible young bachelor* •**eligibility** /ˌelɪdʒəˈbɪləti/ *noun* [U]

eliminate /ɪˈlɪmɪneɪt/ *verb* [T] **1** REMOVE to remove something from something, or get rid of something *The doctor advised me to **eliminate** salt **from** my diet.* **2** DEFEAT to defeat someone so that they cannot go any further in a competition [**often passive**] *She was eliminated after the first round of the tournament.*

elimination /ɪˌlɪmɪˈneɪʃᵊn/ *noun* **1** [U] when you eliminate someone or something **2 a process of elimination** when you remove all possible answers to something until only one remains

elimiˈnation reˌaction *noun* [C] **CHEMISTRY** a chemical reaction where a substance separates from a molecule

elite /ɪˈliːt/ *noun* [**group**] **SOCIETY** the richest, most powerful, or best educated group in a society *a member of the elite* ○ *an elite group*

elitism /ɪˈliːtɪzᵊm/ *noun* [U] when a small group of rich, powerful, or educated people are given an advantage in a situation •**elitist** *adjective elitist attitudes*

elk /elk/ *UK* (*US* **moose**) *noun* [C] a large deer (= large, brown wild animal) which lives in northern US and Canada

elm /elm/ *noun* [C, U] a large tree which loses its leaves in winter

elocution /ˌeləˈkjuːʃᵊn/ *noun* [U] **LANGUAGE** the skill of speaking in a careful, clear way

elongated /ˈiːlɒŋgeɪtɪd/ (US) /ɪːˈlɒŋgeɪtɪd/ *adjective* longer and thinner than usual

elope /ɪˈləʊp/ *verb* [I] to leave home secretly with someone in order to get married

eloquent /ˈeləkwənt/ *adjective* expressing ideas clearly and in a way that influences people *the most eloquent speaker at the conference* •**eloquence** /ˈeləkwəns/ *noun* [U] when someone or something is eloquent •**eloquently** *adverb*

O‑**else** /els/ *adverb* **1** [IN ADDITION] in addition to someone or something *Would you like **anything else** to eat?* ○ ***What else** did he say?* **2** [DIFFERENT] different from someone or something *I don't like it here. Let's go **somewhere else**.* ○ *I didn't say that. It must have been **someone else**.* **3** [OTHER] other things or people *I forgot my toothbrush, but I remembered **everything else**.* **4 or else a** [COMPARE] used to compare two different things or situations *He talks to her all the time, or else he completely ignores her.* **b** [IF NOT] used to say what will happen if another thing does not happen *We must be there by six, or else we'll miss the beginning.* **5 if all else fails** if no other plan is successful *If all else fails, you're welcome to stay at our house.*

elsewhere /ˌelsˈweəʳ/ *adverb* in or to another place *The report studies economic growth in Europe and elsewhere.* ○ *If we can't find it here, we'll have to **go elsewhere**.*

ELT /ˌiːelˈtiː/ *noun* [U] **EDUCATION** *abbreviation for* English Language Teaching: the teaching of English to students whose first language is not English

elucidate /ɪˈluːsɪdeɪt/ *verb* [T] *formal* to explain something, or make it clear

elude /ɪˈluːd/ *verb* [T] *formal* **1** [NOT ACHIEVE] If something that you want eludes you, you do not succeed in achieving it. *The gold medal continues to elude her.* **2** [NOT BE CAUGHT] to not be caught by someone *He eluded the police for years before he was arrested.* **3** [NOT REMEMBER] If a piece of information eludes you, you cannot remember it.

elusive /ɪˈluːsɪv/ *adjective* difficult to describe, find, achieve, or remember *The answers to these questions remain as elusive as ever.*

elves /elvz/ *plural of* elf

'em /əm/ *informal spoken short for* them

emaciated /ɪˈmeɪsieɪtɪd/ *adjective* **HEALTH** very thin and weak because of being ill or not eating enough food

WORD PARTNERS FOR ***email***

get/send an email • **by** email • **in** an email • an email **address/attachment**

O‑**email** (*also* **e-mail**) /ˈiːmeɪl/ *noun* **1 INTERNET** [U] a system for sending messages electronically, especially from one computer to another using the Internet *You can contact me **by email**.* ○ *What's your **email address**?* **2 INTERNET** [C, U] a message sent electronically *I got an email from Danielle yesterday.* •**email** *verb* [T] to send a message using email

emanate /ˈeməneɪt/ *verb formal*

emanate from sth *phrasal verb* to come from something *Strange noises emanated from the room next door.*

emancipate /ɪˈmænsɪpeɪt/ *verb* [T] *formal* **POLITICS** to give people more freedom or rights by removing social, legal, or political controls that limit them *emancipated women* •**emancipation** /ɪˌmænsɪˈpeɪʃᵊn/ *noun* [U]

embalm /ɪmˈbɑːm/ *verb* [T] to use oils and chemicals to prevent a dead body from decaying

embankment /ɪmˈbæŋkmənt/ *noun* [C] an artificial slope built from soil or stones to stop floods, or to support a road or railway *a **railway embankment***

embargo /ɪmˈbɑːgəʊ/ *noun* [C] *plural* **embargoes POLITICS** an order by a government to stop trade with another country *an **arms/oil embargo*** ○ *We will not **lift*** (= stop) *the trade **embargo** until they end this war.*

embark /ɪmˈbɑːk/ *verb* [I] to get on a ship, boat, or aircraft to begin a journey ➲Opposite **disembark**

embark on/upon sth *phrasal verb* to start something new or important *You're never too old to embark on a new career.*

embarrass /ɪmˈbærəs/ *verb* [T] to make someone feel ashamed or shy *My dad's always embarrassing me in front of my friends.*

embarrassed /ɪmˈbærəst/ *adjective* feeling ashamed or shy *She felt **embarrassed about** undressing in front of the doctor.* [+ **to do sth**] *I was too embarrassed to admit that I was scared.*

embarrassing /ɪmˈbærəsɪŋ/ *adjective* making you feel embarrassed *an embarrassing defeat* ○ *What has been your most embarrassing moment?* •**embarrassingly** *adverb The play was embarrassingly bad.*

WORD PARTNERS FOR ***embarrassment***

acute/great/huge embarrassment • **a source of** embarrassment • **the** embarrassment **of doing sth**

embarrassment /ɪmˈbærəsmənt/ *noun* **1** [FEELING] [U] when you feel embarrassed *He blushed with embarrassment.* ○ *Her behaviour has caused great embarrassment to her family.* **2** [THING/PERSON] [C] something or someone that makes you feel embarrassed *He is becoming an **embarrassment to** the government.*

embassy /ˈembəsi/ *noun* [C] **POLITICS** the official group of people who live in a foreign country and represent their government there, or the building where they work

embedded /ɪmˈbedɪd/ *adjective* **1** [OBJECT] fixed into the surface of something *A small piece of glass was **embedded in** his finger.* **2** [ATTITUDE] If an emotion, attitude, etc is embedded in someone or something, it is a very strong and important part of them. *A sense of guilt was deeply **embedded in** my conscience.*

emˌbedded ˈsystem *noun* [C] **COMPUTING** a system used in a computer to do a particular thing that a general computer cannot do

embellish /ɪmˈbelɪʃ/ *verb* [T] to make something more beautiful or interesting by adding something to it *He embellished the story with lots of dramatic detail.* •**embellishment** *noun* [C, U]

embers /ˈembəz/ *noun* [**plural**] pieces of wood or coal that continue to burn after a fire has no more flames

embezzle /ɪm'bezl/ *verb* [T] to steal money that belongs to the company or organization that you work for •**embezzlement** *noun* [U]

embittered /ɪm'bɪtəd/ *adjective* very angry about unfair things that have happened to you

emblazoned /ɪm'bleɪzənd/ *adjective* decorated in a very obvious way with something such as a name or a design *Her T-shirt was* ***emblazoned with*** *the company logo.*

emblem /'embləm/ *noun* [C] a picture, object, or symbol that is used to represent a person, group, or idea *The rose is the national emblem of England.*

embodiment /ɪm'bɒdɪmənt/ *noun* **the embodiment of sth** If someone or something is the embodiment of a particular idea or quality, they express or represent it exactly. *The mother in the story is the embodiment of evil.*

embody /ɪm'bɒdi/ *verb* [T] to represent an idea or quality exactly *He embodies the values of hard work and fair play.*

emboss /ɪm'bɒs/ *verb* [T] to decorate an object, especially with letters, using special tools to make a mark on the surface of the object *The envelope was embossed with the company's logo.*

embrace¹ /ɪm'breɪs/ *verb* **1** HOLD [I, T] If you embrace someone, you put your arms around them, and if two people embrace, they put their arms around each other. **2** ACCEPT [T] to accept new ideas, beliefs, methods, etc in an enthusiastic way *We are always eager to embrace the latest technology.* **3** INCLUDE [T] *formal* to include a number of things *The report embraces a wide range of opinions.*

embrace² /ɪm'breɪs/ *noun* [C] when you put your arms around someone *a passionate embrace*

embroider /ɪm'brɔɪdər/ *verb* **1 ART, DT** [I, T] to decorate cloth by sewing small patterns or pictures onto it **2** [T] to add imaginary details to a story to make it more interesting *They accused him of embroidering the facts.*

embroidery /ɪm'brɔɪdəri/ *noun* [U] **1 ART** the activity of sewing small patterns or pictures onto things **2 ART** decoration on cloth made by sewing small patterns or pictures onto it

embroil /ɪm'brɔɪl/ *verb formal* **be embroiled in sth** to be involved in an argument or difficult situation *We don't want to become embroiled in a dispute over ownership.*

embryo /'embriəʊ/ *noun* [C] **BIOLOGY** a human or an animal that is starting to develop in its mother's uterus

embryonic /ˌembri'ɒnɪk/ *adjective* starting to develop *The project is still at an embryonic stage.*

emerald /'emərəld/ *noun* **1 GEOLOGY** [C] a bright green stone used in jewellery **2** [U] (*also* ˌ**emerald 'green**) a bright green colour •**emerald** *adjective*

emerge /ɪ'mɜːdʒ/ *verb* [I] **1** COME OUT to appear from somewhere or come out of somewhere *A figure* ***emerged from*** *the shadows.* **2** BECOME KNOWN to become known ***It emerged that*** *she had lied to her employers.* **3** DIFFICULT SITUATION to reach the end of a difficult situation *They emerged victorious from the fight.* •**emergence** *noun* [U]

WORD PARTNERS FOR ***emergency***

cope with/respond to an emergency • **a major/real** emergency • **in** an emergency

O⊸**emergency** /ɪ'mɜːdʒənsi/ *noun* [C] a serious or dangerous situation that needs immediate action *You should only ring this number* ***in an emergency.*** ○ *an* ***emergency exit***

e'mergency ˌbrake *US* (*UK* **handbrake**) *noun* [C] a stick inside a car that you can pull up to stop the car from moving ➲See colour picture **Car** on page Centre 7

e'mergency ˌroom *US* (*UK* **casualty**) *noun* [C] **HEALTH** the part of a hospital where people go when they have been injured or have urgent illnesses so that they can be treated immediately

eˌmergency 'services *noun* [plural] the organizations who deal with accidents and urgent problems such as fire, illness, or crime

emerging /ɪ'mɜːdʒɪŋ/ *adjective* [always before noun] starting to exist or develop ***emerging economies/markets***

emigrant /'emɪgrənt/ *noun* [C] **SOCIETY** someone who leaves their own country to go and live in another one

emigrate /'emɪgreɪt/ *verb* [I] **SOCIETY** to leave your own country to go and live in another one *We're thinking of* ***emigrating to*** *New Zealand.* •**emigration** /ˌemɪ'greɪʃən/ *noun* [U]

eminent /'emɪnənt/ *adjective* famous, respected, or important *an eminent historian* •**eminence** /'emɪnəns/ *noun* [U] ➲See also: **preeminent**

eminently /'emɪnəntli/ *adverb formal* very *He is eminently qualified for the job.*

emission /ɪ'mɪʃən/ *noun* [C, U] **ENVIRONMENT** when gas, heat, light, etc is sent out into the air, or an amount of gas, heat, light, etc that is sent out ***Carbon dioxide emissions*** *will be reduced by 20%.*

emit /ɪ'mɪt/ *verb* [T] **emitting**, *past* **emitted** to send out gas, heat, light, etc into the air *The machine emits a high-pitched sound when you press the button.*

emoticon /ɪ'məʊtɪkɒn/ *noun* [C] **INTERNET** an image such as :-) which looks like a face when you look at it from the side, made using keyboard symbols and used in emails to express emotions

WORD PARTNERS FOR ***emotion***

display/experience/feel/show emotion • **deep/powerful/strong** emotion

O⊸**emotion** /ɪ'məʊʃən/ *noun* [C, U] a strong feeling such as love or anger, or strong feelings in general *He finds it hard to* ***express his emotions.*** ○ *She was overcome with emotion and burst into tears.*

emotional /ɪ'məʊʃənəl/ *adjective* **1** EMOTIONS relating to emotions *a child's emotional development* **2** STRONG FEELINGS showing strong feelings, or making people have strong feelings *an emotional speech* ○ *After the argument, I was feeling confused and emotional.* **3** PERSON

An emotional person shows their emotions very easily or very often. •**emotionally** *adverb*

emotive /ɪ'məʊtɪv/ *adjective* making people feel strong emotions *Animal experimentation is a very* ***emotive issue.***

empathy /'empəθi/ *noun* [U] the ability to imagine what it must be like to be in someone's situation •**empathize** (*also UK* **-ise**) /'empəθaɪz/ *verb* [I] to feel empathy with someone *I think people find it easy to* ***empathize with*** *the main character.*

emperor /'empᵊrəʳ/ *noun* [C] **POLITICS** the male ruler of an empire (= group of countries ruled by one person or government) *Emperor Charlemagne*

emphasis /'emfəsɪs/ *noun* [C, U] *plural* **emphases** /'emfəsiːz/ **1** particular importance or attention that you give to something *Schools are starting to* ***place/put*** *greater* ***emphasis on*** *passing exams.* **2 LANGUAGE** the extra force that you give to a word or part of a word when you are saying it *The* ***emphasis*** *is* ***on*** *the final syllable.*

emphasize (*also UK* **-ise**) /'emfəsaɪz/ *verb* [T] to show that something is especially important or needs special attention *The government is* ***emphasizing*** *the* ***importance*** *of voting in the election.* [**+ that**] *He emphasized that the driver was not to blame for the accident.*

emphatic /ɪm'fætɪk/ *adjective* done or said in a strong way and without any doubt *an emphatic victory* •**emphatically** *adverb*

empire /'empaɪəʳ/ *noun* [C] **1 POLITICS** a group of countries that is ruled by one person or government **2** a large group of businesses that is controlled by one person or company *a publishing empire*

empirical /ɪm'pɪrɪkᵊl/ *adjective formal* based on experience or scientific experiments and not only on ideas ***empirical evidence*** •**empirically** *adverb*

O⁻**employ** /ɪm'plɔɪ/ *verb* [T] **1** WORK If a person or company employs someone, they pay that person to work for them. *The company employs 2500 staff.* [**+ to do sth**] *They employ her to look after their children.* **2** USE *formal* to use something *Companies employ clever tactics to persuade us to buy their products.*

employee /ɪm'plɔɪiː/ *noun* [C] someone who is paid to work for a person or company

O⁻**employer** /ɪm'plɔɪəʳ/ *noun* [C] a person or company that pays people to work for them

WORD PARTNERS FOR ***employment***

find/offer/provide/seek employment • **gainful/paid/full-time/part-time/temporary** employment • be **in** employment

O⁻**employment** /ɪm'plɔɪmənt/ *noun* [U] **1 ECONOMICS** when someone is paid to work for a person or company ***full-time/part-time employment*** ○ *It is not easy to* ***find employment*** *in the countryside.* ○ *employment opportunities/rights* ➲Compare **unemployment 2** USE *formal* the use of something

empower /ɪm'paʊəʳ/ *verb* **1** [T] to give someone the confidence, skills, freedom, etc to do something [**+ to do sth**] *Education empowers people to take control of their lives.* **2 be empowered to do sth** to have the legal or official right to do something

empress /'emprəs/ *noun* [C] **POLITICS** the female ruler, or the wife of a male ruler, of an empire (= group of countries ruled by one person or government) *Empress Josephine*

O⁻**empty¹** /'empti/ *adjective* **1** CONTAINING NOTHING If something is empty, it does not contain any things or people. *an empty house/street* ○ *empty bottles/glasses* ○ *The train was completely empty when it reached London.* **2** NO MEANING having no meaning or value *an* ***empty promise/threat*** •**emptiness** *noun* [U]

empty² /'empti/ *verb* **1** CONTAINER [T] (*also* **empty out**) If you empty a container, or if you empty the things inside it, you remove everything from it. *He* ***emptied*** *the dirty water* ***into*** *the sink.* **2** PLACE [I] to become empty *The room emptied rapidly when the fire started.*

empty-handed /ˌempti'hændɪd/ *adjective* without bringing or taking anything *We can't go to the party empty-handed.*

ˌempty 'set *noun* [C] **MATHEMATICS** a set (= group of numbers) that contains no elements

the EMS /ðiːˌiːem'es/ *noun* [**no plural**] **ECONOMICS** *abbreviation for* the European Monetary System: a system which limits changes in the values of the different types of money used in countries in the European Union

EMU /ˌiːem'juː/ *noun* [U] **ECONOMICS** *abbreviation for* Economic and Monetary Union; when several countries form a single market with one currency (= type of money)

emulate /'emjəleɪt/ *verb* [T] *formal* to try to be like someone or something that you admire or that is successful *They hope to* ***emulate*** *the* ***success*** *of other software companies.*

emulsifier /ɪ'mʌlsɪfaɪəʳ/ *noun* [C] **FOOD** a substance which is added to a mixture of food in order to stop the mixture from separating into different parts

emulsify /ɪ'mʌlsɪfaɪ/ *verb* [I, T] **CHEMISTRY** If two liquids emulsify or are emulsified, they combine and become a smooth mixture.

emulsion /ɪ'mʌlʃᵊn/ *noun* [U] paint used to cover walls, ceilings, etc

emulsion /ɪ'mʌlʃᵊn/ *noun* [C, U] **1** a liquid in which two liquids have been mixed together but neither liquid has dissolved into the other liquid **2** (*also* **emulsion paint**) a water-based paint which is not shiny when dry

enable /ɪ'neɪbl/ *verb* [T] to make someone able to do something, or to make something possible [**+ to do sth**] *This money has enabled me to buy a new computer.*

-enabled /ɪ'neɪbᵊld/ *suffix* **1 COMPUTING** having the necessary equipment or system to use something *Bluetooth-enabled mobile phones* **2** used or made possible by using a particular thing *voice-enabled software*

enact /ɪ'nækt/ *verb* [T] **1 LAW** to make something into a law [**often passive**] *When was this legislation enacted?* **2** PERFORM *formal* to perform a story or play •**enactment** *noun* [U]

enamel /ɪ'næm^əl/ *noun* [U] **1** **DT** a hard, shiny substance that is used to decorate or protect metal or clay **2** **ANATOMY** the hard, white substance that covers your teeth ➲See picture at **tooth**

enamoured /ɪ'næməd/ *UK* (*US* **enamored**) *formal adjective* **be enamoured of/with sb/sth** to like someone or something very much

enc (*also* **encl**) *written abbreviation for* enclosed: used at the end of a business letter to show that there is something else in the envelope

encapsulate /ɪn'kæpsjəleɪt/ *verb* [T] to express or show the most important facts about something *The film encapsulates the essence of that period.*

encase /ɪn'keɪs/ *verb formal* **be encased in sth** to be completely covered in something *The outside walls are encased in concrete.*

encephalitis /ˌenkefə'laɪtɪs/ (US) /enˌsefə'-/ *noun* [U] **HEALTH** a serious illness in which the brain swells (= becomes bigger), which is caused by an infection

enchanted /ɪn'tʃɑːntɪd/ *adjective* **1** LIKE If you are enchanted by something, you like it very much. *She was enchanted by the Scottish landscape.* **2** MAGICAL affected by magic *an enchanted forest*

enchanting /ɪn'tʃɑːntɪŋ/ *adjective* very nice *What an enchanting child!*

encircle /ɪn'sɜːkl/ *verb* [T] *formal* to form a circle around something [**often passive**] *The house is encircled by a high fence.*

enclave /'enkleɪv/ *noun* [C] a place which is different from the area that is around it because its people have a different language or culture *an Italian enclave in Switzerland*

enclose /ɪn'kləʊz/ *verb* [T] **1** SEND to send something in the same envelope or parcel as something else *I enclose a map of the area.* **2** BE ALL AROUND to be all around something and separate it from other things or places •**enclosed** *adjective He doesn't like* ***enclosed spaces***.

enclosure /ɪn'kləʊʒə^r/ *noun* [C] a small area of land that has a wall or fence around it

encompass /ɪn'kʌmpəs/ *verb* [T] to include a lot of things, ideas, places, etc *Their albums* ***encompass*** *a wide* ***range*** *of music.*

encore /'ɒŋkɔː^r/ *noun* [C] **MUSIC** an extra song or piece of music that is performed at the end of a show because the audience shout for it

encounter¹ /ɪn'kaʊntə^r/ *verb* [T] **1** EXPERIENCE to experience something unpleasant *We* ***encountered*** *quite a few* ***problems*** *at the beginning.* **2** MEET *literary* to meet someone, especially when you do not expect it

WORD PARTNERS FOR ***encounter***

have an encounter • a **chance** encounter • an encounter **with** sb

encounter² /ɪn'kaʊntə^r/ *noun* [C] a meeting, especially one that happens by chance

O⁃**encourage** /ɪn'kʌrɪdʒ/ *verb* [T] **1** MAKE DO/HAPPEN to make someone more likely to do something, or make something more likely to happen [+ **to do sth**] *My parents encouraged me to try new things.* ○ *Cutting back plants will encourage growth.* **2** GIVE CONFIDENCE/HOPE to give someone confidence or hope *My parents encouraged me when things weren't going well at school.* ➲Opposite **discourage** •**encouragement** *noun* [C, U] *Children need lots of encouragement from their parents.*

encouraged /ɪn'kʌrɪdʒd/ *adjective* having more confidence or hope about something *We were very encouraged by his exam results.*

encouraging /ɪn'kʌrɪdʒɪŋ/ *adjective* making you feel more hope and confidence *The team's performance was very encouraging.* ➲Opposite **discouraging** •**encouragingly** *adverb*

encroach /ɪn'krəʊtʃ/ *verb*

encroach on/upon sth *phrasal verb* to gradually take away someone's rights, power, etc, or get control of something, often without being noticed *My job is starting to encroach on my family life.*

encrusted /ɪn'krʌstɪd/ *adjective* covered with something hard, for example dirt or stones *My trousers were* ***encrusted with*** *mud.*

encrypt /ɪn'krɪpt/ *verb* [T] **COMPUTING** to change electronic information into a secret system of letters, numbers, or symbols •**encryption** *noun* [U]

encyclopedia (*also UK* **encyclopaedia**) /ɪnˌsaɪklə'piːdiə/ *noun* [C] a book or a set of books containing facts about a lot of subjects

WORD PARTNERS FOR ***end***

at the end (**of** sth) • **by** the end (**of** sth) • the **very** end

O⁃**end¹** /end/ *noun* **1** FINAL PART [**no plural**] the final part of something such as a period of time, activity, or story *I'll pay you* ***at the end*** *of next month.* ○ *I didn't meet him until the end of the course.* ○ *a film with a twist at the end* **2** FURTHEST PART [C] the furthest part or final part of a place or thing *They live* ***at the*** *other* ***end*** *of the street.* ○ *They were standing at* ***opposite ends*** *of the room.* **3** STOP [C] when something stops happening [**usually singular**] *They are calling for* ***an end to*** *the violence.* **4** **in the end** finally, after something has been thought about or discussed a lot **5** **come to an end** to finish **6** **put an end to sth** to make something stop happening or existing *He's determined to put an end to these rumours.* **7** **bring sth to an end** to make something finish *The stories in the newspaper brought her career to a sudden end.* **8** **no end** *informal* a lot *I've had* ***no end of*** *trouble finding a hotel room.* **9** **for hours/days, etc on end** for days, hours, etc without stopping *He waited by the telephone for hours on end.* **10** INTENTION [C] an intention or purpose *She only has one end in mind.* **11** **be at a loose end** to have nothing to do *Come and visit us if you're at a loose end over the weekend.* **12** **at the end of the day** *UK* something that you say before you give the most important fact of a situation *At the end of the day, what matters is that you're safe.* **13** **at the end of your tether** (*also US* **at the end of your rope**) so tired, annoyed, or worried by something that you do not feel that you can deal with it **14** **get (hold of) the wrong end of the stick** to not understand a situation correctly *My mum got the wrong end of the stick and thought that Jim was my boyfriend.* **15** **make ends meet** to have just enough money to pay for the things that you need *I've taken a second job in the evenings just to make ends meet.* **16 not be the end of the world** If something is not the end of the world, it will not cause very serious problems. *It won't be the end of the world if I don't get the job.* **17 be on/at the receiving end of sth** If you are on the receiving end of something, you suffer something unpleasant when you have done nothing to deserve it. *They are often on the receiving end of verbal abuse from angry customers.* **18 throw sb in at the deep end** to make someone start a new and difficult job or activity without helping them or preparing them for it ➲See also: **dead end, light**[1] at the end of the tunnel, **odds** and ends, the **tail**[1] end of sth, **the West End,** be at your **wits**' end

O-* **end**[2] /end/ *verb* [I, T] to finish or stop, or to make something finish or stop *What time does the concert end?* ○ *These talks do not look likely to end the war.*

end in/with sth *phrasal verb* to finish in a particular way *The evening ended in a big argument.*

end up *phrasal verb* to finally be in a particular place or situation *I never thought he'd end up in prison.* [+ doing sth] *He always ends up doing what Alan wants to do.* ○ *She'll end up unemployed.*

endanger /ɪn'deɪndʒəʳ/ *verb* [T] to put someone or something in a situation where they might be harmed or seriously damaged *He would never do anything to endanger the children's lives.*

endangered /ɪn'deɪndʒəd/ *adjective* **endangered birds/plants/species, etc ENVIRONMENT** animals or plants which may soon not exist because there are very few now alive

endear /ɪn'dɪəʳ/ *verb*

endear sb to sb *phrasal verb* If a quality in someone's character, or their behaviour endears them to you, it makes you like them.

endearing /ɪn'dɪərɪŋ/ *adjective* An endearing quality is one that makes people like you.

endeavour /ɪn'devəʳ/ *UK* (*US* **endeavor**) *formal verb* **endeavour to do sth** to try very hard to do something *I endeavoured to help her, but she wouldn't let me.* •**endeavour** *noun* [C, U] *human/artistic endeavour*

endemic /en'demɪk/ *adjective formal* If something unpleasant is endemic in a place or among a group of people, there is a lot of it there. *Corruption is endemic in some parts of the police force.*

ending /'endɪŋ/ *noun* [C] **1** the last part of a story *I hope this film has a* ***happy ending.*** **2 LANGUAGE** a part added to the end of a word *To make the plural of 'dog', you add the plural ending '-s'.*

endive /'endaɪv/ *noun* [C, U] **FOOD** a plant with bitter green leaves that are eaten in salads

endless /'endləs/ *adjective* continuing for a long time and never finishing, or never seeming to finish *He seems to think that I have an* ***endless supply*** *of money.* •**endlessly** *adverb*

endocrine gland /'endəkraɪn,glænd/ *noun* [C] **ANATOMY, BIOLOGY** any of the organs of the body which make hormones (= chemicals which make the body grow and develop) and put the hormones into the blood

endorse /ɪn'dɔːs/ *verb* [T] *formal* to say publicly that you support a person or action [**often passive**] *The idea was endorsed by a majority of members.* •**endorsement** *noun* [C, U]

endoscope /'endəskəʊp/ *noun* [C] **HEALTH** a very small camera on the end of a long, thin tube that can be pushed into the body so that doctors can see inside the body

endoscopy /en'dɒskəpi/ *noun* [C] **HEALTH** a medical operation using an endoscope

endoskeleton /,endəʊ'skelɪtᵊn/ *noun* [C] **ANATOMY, BIOLOGY** a set of bones inside a body, such as the bones that support the body of a vertebrate (= an animal with a back bone) ➲Compare **exoskeleton**

endosperm /'endəʊspɜːm/ *noun* [U] **BIOLOGY** the store of food inside a plant seed

endothermic reaction /endəʊ,θɜːmɪkri'ækʃən/ *noun* [C] **CHEMISTRY** a chemical reaction that needs heat in order to happen ➲Compare **exothermic reaction**

endow /ɪn'daʊ/ *verb formal* **1 be endowed with sth** to have a particular quality or characteristic *The country is richly endowed with natural resources.* **2 FINANCE** [T] to give a large amount of money to a college, hospital, etc

end-product /'end,prɒdʌkt/ *noun* [C] the thing that you get at the end of a process or activity

endurance /ɪn'djʊərᵊns/ *noun* [U] the ability to keep doing something difficult, unpleasant, or painful for a long time *a race to test athletes' endurance*

endure /ɪn'djʊəʳ/ *verb* [T] *formal* to suffer something difficult, unpleasant, or painful *She's already had to endure three painful operations on her leg.*

enduring /ɪn'djʊərɪŋ/ *adjective* existing for a long time *the enduring popularity of cartoons*

WORD PARTNERS FOR ***enemy***

have/make enemies • **arch/bitter/deadly** enemies

O-* **enemy** /'enəmi/ *noun* **1** PERSON [C] a person who you dislike or oppose *I try not to* ***make*** *any* ***enemies.*** **2** ARMY [**group**] a country or army that your country or army is fighting against in a war *enemy forces/territory*

energetic /,enə'dʒetɪk/ *adjective* having or involving a lot of energy *an energetic young woman* ○ *Aerobics is too energetic for me.* •**energetically** *adverb*

WORD PARTNERS FOR ***energy***

expend/have/save/waste energy • **boundless/high/restless/surplus** energy

O-* **energy** /'enədʒi/ *noun* [C, U] **1** the power and ability to be very active without becoming tired *Looking after children takes up a lot of time and energy.* [+ to do sth] *I didn't even have the energy to get out of bed.* **2 PHYSICS** the power that comes from electricity, gas, etc *nuclear energy* ○ *energy conservation* ➲See also: **atomic energy**

enforce /ɪn'fɔːs/ *verb* [T] **1 LAW** to make people obey a rule or law *It is the duty of the police to*

E

enforce the law. **2** SITUATION to make a particular situation happen, or to make people accept it *The new teacher failed to enforce discipline.* •**enforcement** *noun* [U] *law enforcement*

engage /ɪn'geɪdʒ/ *verb* [T] *formal* **1** INTEREST to interest someone in something and keep them thinking about it *The debate about food safety has engaged the whole nation.* **2** EMPLOY to employ someone [+ **to do sth**] *I have engaged a secretary to deal with all my paperwork.*

engage in sth *phrasal verb* to take part in something

engage sb in sth *phrasal verb* If you engage someone in conversation, you start a conversation with them.

engaged /ɪn'geɪdʒd/ *adjective* **1** RELATIONSHIP If two people are engaged, they have formally agreed to marry each other. *When did they get **engaged**?* **2** TELEPHONE *UK* If a telephone line or a toilet is engaged, it is already being used.

WORD PARTNERS FOR ***engagement***

announce/break off your engagement • your engagement **to** sb • an engagement **party/ring**

engagement /ɪn'geɪdʒmənt/ *noun* [C] **1** RELATIONSHIP an agreement to get married to someone *an **engagement ring*** **2** ARRANGEMENT an arrangement to meet someone or do something at a particular time

engaging /ɪn'geɪdʒɪŋ/ *adjective* pleasant, interesting, or attractive *She has a very engaging personality.*

engender /ɪn'dʒendəʳ/ *verb* [T] *formal* to make people have a particular feeling or make a situation start to exist *We want to engender loyalty to our products.*

WORD PARTNERS FOR ***engine***

start/switch on/switch off/turn off the engine

engine /'endʒɪn/ *noun* [C] **1** MACHINE the part of a vehicle that uses energy from oil, electricity, or steam to make it move *a diesel/petrol engine* **2** TRAIN the part of a train that pulls it along ➲See also: **fire engine, search engine**

'engine ˌdriver *UK* (*US* **engineer**) *noun* [C] someone whose job is to drive a train

engineer¹ /ˌendʒɪ'nɪəʳ/ *noun* [C] **1** MACHINES/BRIDGES ETC someone whose job is to design, build, or repair machines, engines, roads, bridges, etc *a **mechanical/structural engineer*** ○ *a **software engineer*** **2** TRAIN *US* someone whose job is to drive a train

engineer² /ˌendʒɪ'nɪəʳ/ *verb* [T] to arrange for something to happen, especially in a clever and secret way [**often passive**] *She was convinced that the accident had been engineered by his enemies.*

engineering /ˌendʒɪ'nɪərɪŋ/ *noun* [U] the work of an engineer, or the study of this work *mechanical engineering* ➲See also: **civil engineering, genetic engineering**

English¹ /'ɪŋglɪʃ/ *noun* **1** [U] **LANGUAGE** the language that is spoken in the UK, the US, and in many other countries *American/British English* ○ *Do you speak English?* **2 the English** [**plural**] the people of England

English² /'ɪŋglɪʃ/ *adjective* **1** **LANGUAGE** relating to the English language *an English teacher* **2** NATION relating to England *English law*

ˌEnglish 'breakfast *noun* [C] *UK* **FOOD** a dish including cooked meat and eggs, eaten as the first meal of the day

ˌEnglish 'muffin *US* (*UK* **muffin**) *noun* [C] **FOOD** a small, round, flat bread that is often eaten hot with butter

engrave /ɪn'greɪv/ *verb* [T] **ART** to cut words or pictures into the surface of metal, stone, etc *He gave her a silver pen engraved with her name.* •**engraver** *noun* [C]

engraving /ɪn'greɪvɪŋ/ *noun* [C] **ART** a picture printed from an engraved piece of metal or wood

engrossed /ɪn'grəʊst/ *adjective* giving all your attention to something *He was so **engrossed in** what he was doing that he didn't hear the bell.*

engrossing /ɪn'grəʊsɪŋ/ *adjective* very interesting, and needing all your attention *an engrossing book*

engulf /ɪn'gʌlf/ *verb* [T] **1** COVER to surround or cover someone or something completely [**often passive**] *The house **was** quickly **engulfed in** flames.* **2** AFFECT STRONGLY to affect a place or a group of people quickly and strongly *Panic is threatening to engulf the country.*

enhance /ɪn'hɑːns/ *verb* [T] *formal* to improve something *Winning that award greatly enhanced her reputation.* •**enhancement** *noun* [C, U] when something is improved

enigma /ɪ'nɪgmə/ *noun* [C] someone or something that is mysterious and difficult to understand *She is a complete enigma to me.*

enigmatic /ˌenɪg'mætɪk/ *adjective* mysterious and impossible to understand completely

OTHER WAYS OF SAYING ***enjoy***

A more formal way of saying 'enjoy' is **relish**: *Jonathan always **relishes** a challenge.*

When someone enjoys a situation or activity very much, you can use the phrasal verbs **lap up** or **revel in**: *He **lapped up** all the attention they gave him.* • *She **revelled in** her role as team manager.*

If someone enjoys doing something that other people think is unpleasant, the phrasal verb **delight in** is sometimes used: *She seems to **delight in** making other people look stupid.*

The verb **savour** (*UK*) (**savor** *US*) is sometimes used when someone enjoys something slowly so that they can appreciate it as much as possible: *It was the first chocolate he'd had for over a year, so he **savoured** every mouthful.*

When someone enjoys themselves very much, in informal situations you can use the expression **have a ball**: *We **had a ball** in Miami.*

enjoy /ɪn'dʒɔɪ/ *verb* [T] **1** LIKE If you enjoy something, it gives you pleasure. *I hope you enjoy your meal.* [+ **doing sth**] *I really enjoyed being with him.* **2 enjoy yourself** to get pleasure from something that you are doing *Everyone eventually relaxed and began to enjoy themselves.* **3** GOOD SITUATION *formal* to have or experience something good such as success *His play enjoyed great success on Broadway.*

COMMON LEARNER ERROR

enjoy doing something

When **enjoy** is followed by a verb, the verb must be in the **-ing** form.

My parents enjoy walking in the mountains.

~~*My parents enjoy to walk in the mountains.*~~

enjoyable /ɪn'dʒɔɪəbl/ *adjective* An enjoyable event or experience gives you pleasure. *We had a very enjoyable evening.*

enjoyment /ɪn'dʒɔɪmənt/ *noun* [U] when you enjoy something *She **gets** a lot of **enjoyment from** music.*

enlarge /ɪn'lɑːdʒ/ *verb* [I, T] to become bigger or to make something become bigger [**often passive**] *I want to get this photo enlarged.* ○ *an enlarged liver*

enlarge on/upon sth *phrasal verb formal* to give more details about something that you have said or written

enlargement /ɪn'lɑːdʒmənt/ *noun* [C, U] when something is enlarged, or something that has been enlarged *I'm going to get an enlargement of this wedding photo.*

enlighten /ɪn'laɪtᵊn/ *verb* [T] *formal* to give someone information about something, so that they understand a situation *He believes he has a duty to enlighten the public on these matters.*

enlightened /ɪn'laɪtᵊnd/ *adjective* having practical, modern ideas and ways of dealing with things *an **enlightened attitude***

enlightening /ɪn'laɪtᵊnɪŋ/ *adjective* giving you more information and understanding about something *an enlightening book*

enlist /ɪn'lɪst/ *verb* **1 enlist the help/support of sb** to ask for and get help or support from someone *They are hoping to enlist the support of local politicians.* **2** [I] to join the army, navy, etc

enliven /ɪn'laɪvᵊn/ *verb* [T] to make something more interesting *The children's arrival enlivened a boring evening.*

en masse /ɒn'mæs/ *adverb* If a group of people do something en masse, they do it together as a group. *They surrendered en masse.*

enmity /'enməti/ *noun* [U] *formal* a strong feeling of hate

enormity /ɪ'nɔːməti/ *noun* **the enormity of sth** how big or important something is *He hadn't realized the enormity of the problem.*

O→**enormous** /ɪ'nɔːməs/ *adjective* extremely large *This living room is enormous.*

enormously /ɪ'nɔːməsli/ *adverb* extremely *an enormously popular show*

O→**enough**[1] /ɪ'nʌf/ *pronoun, quantifier* **1** NECESSARY as much as is necessary *They had enough fuel for one week.* [**+ to do sth**] *Have you had enough to eat?* **2** WANTED as much as or more than you want *I've got enough work at the moment, without being given any more.* **3 have had enough** to want something to stop because it is annoying you *I've **had enough of** your excuses.* **4 that's enough** used to tell someone to stop behaving badly

O→**enough**[2] /ɪ'nʌf/ *adverb* **1** NECESSARY as much as is necessary [**+ to do sth**] *Are you old enough to vote?* ○ *You're not going fast enough.* **2** NOT VERY slightly, but not very *He's nice enough, but I don't really want to go out with him.* **3 funnily/oddly/strangely enough** although it may seem strange *I was dreading the party, but I really enjoyed it, funnily enough.*

enquire *UK* (*UK/US* **inquire**) /ɪn'kwaɪəʳ/ *verb* [I, T] to ask someone for information about something *"Are you staying long?" she enquired.* ○ *I'm **enquiring about** dentists in the area.* •**enquirer** *UK* (*UK/US* **inquirer**) *noun* [C]

enquire after sb *phrasal verb UK formal* to ask someone for information about someone else's health and what they are doing, in order to be polite

enquire into sth *phrasal verb formal* to try to discover the facts about something

enquiring *UK* (*UK/US* **inquiring**) /ɪn'kwaɪərɪŋ/ *adjective* [**always before noun**] **1** WANTING TO LEARN always wanting to learn new things *an **enquiring mind*** **2** EXPRESSION An enquiring expression on your face shows that you want to know something.

WORD PARTNERS FOR ***enquiry***

make/receive an enquiry • an enquiry **about** sth

enquiry *UK* (*UK/US* **inquiry**) /ɪn'kwaɪəri/ *noun* **1** QUESTION [C] *formal* a question that you ask when you want more information *We receive a lot of **enquiries about** tax issues.* **2** OFFICIAL PROCESS [C] an official process to discover the facts about something bad that has happened *The hospital is holding an **enquiry into** the accident.* **3** ASKING QUESTIONS [U] *formal* the process of asking questions in order to get information

enrage /ɪn'reɪdʒ/ *verb* [T] to make someone very angry [**often passive**] *Farmers are enraged by the government's refusal to help.*

enrich /ɪn'rɪtʃ/ *verb* [T] to improve the quality of something by adding something to it [**often passive**] *Our culture has been enriched by the many immigrants who live here.* •**enrichment** *noun* [U]

enrol *UK* (*US* **enroll**) /ɪn'rəʊl/ *verb* [I, T] **enrolling**, *past* **enrolled** to become or make someone become an official member of a course, college, or group *I've (UK) **enrolled on**/ (US) **enrolled in** a creative writing course.* •**enrolment** *UK* (*US* **enrollment**) *noun* [C, U]

en route /ˌɒn'ruːt/ *adverb* on the way to or from somewhere *We stopped in Monaco **en route to** Switzerland.*

ensemble /ɒn'sɒmbᵊl/ *noun* [C] **MUSIC** a small group of musicians or actors who regularly play or perform together

enshrined /ɪn'ʃraɪnd/ *verb formal* **be enshrined in sth** If a political or social right is enshrined in something, it is protected by being included in it. *These fundamental human rights are enshrined in the constitution.*

E

enslave /ɪn'sleɪv/ *verb* [T] *formal* to control someone and keep them in a bad situation [**often passive**] *These workers are enslaved by poverty.*

ensue /ɪn'sjuː/ *verb* [I] **ensuing**, *past* **ensued** *formal* to happen after something, often as a result of it •**ensuing** *adjective* [**always before noun**] *the ensuing hours/months*

en suite /ˌɒn'swiːt/ *adjective UK* An en suite bathroom is directly connected to a bedroom.

E

ensure /ɪn'ʃɔːʳ/ *verb* [T] *formal* to make certain that something is done or happens [+ **(that)**] *Please ensure that all examination papers have your name at the top.*

entail /ɪn'teɪl/ *verb* [T] to involve something *What exactly does the job entail?*

entangled /ɪn'tæŋgld/ *adjective* **1** INVOLVED involved with someone or something so that it is difficult to escape *I don't know how I ever got entangled in this relationship.* **2** CAUGHT caught in something such as a net or ropes *The dolphin had become entangled in the fishing net.*

entente cordiale /ˌɒntɒntˌkɔːdi'ɑːl/ *noun* [C **usually singular**, U] **POLITICS** a friendly agreement or relationship between two countries, especially that between the UK and France, agreed in 1904

enter /'entəʳ/ *verb* **1** PLACE [I, T] to come or go into a place *The police entered by the back door.* ○ *She is accused of entering the country illegally.* **2** **COMPUTING** [T] to put information into a computer, book, or document *You have to enter a password to access this information.* **3** COMPETITION [I, T] to take part in a competition, race, or exam, or to arrange for someone else to do this *Are you going to enter the photography competition?* **4** ORGANIZATION [T] to become a member of a particular organization, or start working in a particular type of job *She didn't enter the legal profession until she was 40.* **5** PERIOD OF TIME [T] to begin a period of time *The violence is now entering its third week.*

enter into sth *phrasal verb* to start to become involved in something, especially a discussion or agreement

COMMON LEARNER ERROR

enter a place

You do not need to use a preposition after **enter**.

I entered the classroom.

~~*I entered in the classroom.*~~

Be careful not to use **enter** with vehicles.

The children got on the bus.

~~*The children entered the bus.*~~

enterprise /'entəpraɪz/ *noun* **1** BUSINESS [C] a business or organization *a state-owned enterprise* **2** PLAN [C] a difficult and important plan *Putting on the concert will be a joint enterprise between the two schools.* **3** QUALITY [U] when someone is enthusiastic and willing to do something new and clever, although there are risks involved *The scheme shows imagination and enterprise.* ➲See also: **free enterprise**

enterprising /'entəpraɪzɪŋ/ *adjective* enthusiastic and willing to do something new, clever, and difficult *The film was made by an enterprising group of students.*

entertain /ˌentə'teɪn/ *verb* **1** INTEREST [T] to keep someone interested and help them to have an enjoyable time *We hired a clown to entertain the children.* **2** GUEST [I, T] to invite someone to be your guest and give them food, drink, etc *We don't entertain as much as we used to.* **3** THINK ABOUT [T] *formal* to consider or be willing to accept an idea or suggestion *He had never even **entertained** the **idea** of her returning.*

entertainer /ˌentə'teɪnəʳ/ *noun* [C] someone whose job is to entertain people by singing, telling jokes, etc

entertaining /ˌentə'teɪnɪŋ/ *adjective* interesting and helping someone to have an enjoyable time *an entertaining and informative book*

entertainment /ˌentə'teɪnmənt/ *noun* [C, U] shows, films, television, or other performances or activities that entertain people ***popular entertainment*** ○ *There is **live entertainment** in the bar every night.*

enthral *UK* (*US* **enthrall**) /ɪn'θrɔːl/ *verb* [T] **enthralling**, *past* **enthralled** to keep someone's interest and attention completely [**often passive**] *The children were enthralled by the circus.* •**enthralling** *adjective* keeping someone's interest and attention completely

enthuse /ɪn'θjuːz/ *verb* [I] to express excitement about something or great interest in it *She couldn't stop enthusing about the film.*

enthusiasm /ɪn'θjuːziæzᵊm/ *noun* [U] when you feel very interested in something and would very much like to be involved in it *She has always had a lot of **enthusiasm for** her work.*

enthusiast /ɪn'θjuːziæst/ *noun* [C] someone who is very interested in and involved with a particular activity or subject *a sports enthusiast*

enthusiastic /ɪnˌθjuːzi'æstɪk/ *adjective* showing enthusiasm *The teacher was very **enthusiastic about** my project.* •**enthusiastically** *adverb*

entice /ɪn'taɪs/ *verb* [T] to persuade someone to do something by offering them something pleasant [+ **to do sth**] *Supermarkets use all sorts of tricks to entice you to buy things.* •**enticing** *adjective* Something which is enticing attracts you by offering you something pleasant.

entire /ɪn'taɪəʳ/ *adjective* [**always before noun**] whole or complete *She spent her entire life caring for other people.*

entirely /ɪn'taɪəli/ *adverb* completely *I'm not entirely convinced that it will work.*

entirety /ɪn'taɪərəti/ *noun* **in its entirety** with all parts included *This is the first time that the book has been published in its entirety.*

entitle /ɪn'taɪtl/ *verb* **1** **entitle sb to (do) sth** to give someone the right to do or have something [**often passive**] I'm entitled to apply for citizenship. **2** [T] to give something a particular title *a lecture entitled "Language, Learning and Literacy"*

entitlement /ɪn'taɪtlmənt/ *noun* [C, U] when you have the right to do or have something

entity /'entɪti/ *noun* [C] something which exists apart from other things *They want the area recognized as a* ***separate*** *political* ***entity****.*

entourage /'ɒntʊrɑːʒ/ US /ɒntʊ'rɑːʒ/ *noun* [group] the group of people who travel with an important or famous person *She arrived with her usual entourage of dancers and musicians.*

WORD PARTNERS FOR ***entrance***

the **back/front/main** entrance • **at** the entrance • the entrance **to** sth

O‑ **entrance** /'entrəns/ *noun* **1** DOOR [C] a door or other opening which you use to enter a building or place *They must have used the back* ***entrance to*** *the building.* ○ *I'll meet you* ***at the*** *main* ***entrance****.* **2** COMING IN [C] when someone comes into or goes into a place, especially in a way that makes people notice them *The whole room went quiet when he* ***made his entrance****.* **3** RIGHT [U] the right to enter a place or to join an organization, college, etc *Entrance is free, but you have to pay for your drinks.*

entranced /ɪn'trɑːnst/ *adjective* If you are entranced by someone or something, you cannot stop watching them because they are very interesting or very beautiful. *The children were entranced by the puppet show.*

entrant /'entrənt/ *noun* [C] someone who enters a competition, organization, or examination

entreat /ɪn'triːt/ *verb* [T] *formal* to try very hard to persuade someone to do something

entrenched /ɪn'trenʃt/ *adjective* Entrenched ideas are so fixed or have existed for so long that they cannot be changed. *These* ***attitudes*** *are firmly* ***entrenched*** *in our culture.*

entrepreneur /ˌɒntrəprə'nɜːr/ *noun* [C] someone who starts their own business, especially when this involves risks •**entrepreneurial** *adjective*

entrust /ɪn'trʌst/ *verb* [T] to make someone responsible for doing something or looking after something [often passive] *I was* ***entrusted with*** *the task of organizing the party.*

WORD PARTNERS FOR ***entry***

allow/gain/refuse entry • entry **into/to** [a place]

O‑ **entry** /'entri/ *noun* **1** COMING IN [U] when you come into or go into a place *She was* ***refused*** *entry to the US.* ○ *Police* ***gained entry*** *by breaking a window.* **2** JOINING/TAKING PART [U] when you join an organization or take part in a competition *Are there lots of exams for* ***entry into*** *the legal profession?* ○ *an entry form* **3** COMPETITION WORK [C] a piece of work that you do to try to win a competition *The first ten correct entries will receive a prize.* **4** PIECE OF INFORMATION [C] one of the pieces of information or writing that is recorded in a book such as a dictionary, or in a computer system *a diary entry* **5** COMPUTING [U] when someone puts information into something such as a computer system ***data entry***

entwined /ɪn'twaɪnd/ *adjective* **1** TWISTED TOGETHER twisted together or twisted around something *Their arms were entwined.* **2** CONNECTED unable to be separated *My fate is entwined with his.*

enumerate /ɪ'njuːmərreɪt/ *verb* [T] *formal* to name each thing on a list

envelop /ɪn'veləp/ *verb* [T] to completely cover something [often passive] *The farm was enveloped in fog.*

envelope /'envələʊp/ *noun* [C] a flat paper container for a letter ➲See colour picture **The Office** on page Centre 5

enviable /'enviəbl/ *adjective* If someone is in an enviable situation, you wish that you were also in that situation. *She's in the* ***enviable position*** *of being able to choose who she works for.*

envious /'enviəs/ *adjective* wishing that you had what someone else has *She was* ***envious*** *of his successful career.* •**enviously** *adverb*

WORD PARTNERS FOR ***environment***

damage/harm/pollute/protect the environment

O‑ **environment** /ɪn'vaɪərənmənt/ *noun* **1 the environment** ENVIRONMENT the air, land, and water where people, animals, and plants live *The new road may cause damage to the environment.* ➲See Common Learner Error at **nature** **2** [C] the situation that you live or work in, and how it influences how you feel *We are working in a very competitive environment.*

environmental /ɪnˌvaɪərən'mentəl/ *adjective* ENVIRONMENT relating to the environment *environmental damage* ○ *an environmental disaster* •**environmentally** *adverb environmentally damaging chemicals*

environmentalist /ɪnˌvaɪərən'mentəlɪst/ *noun* [C] ENVIRONMENT someone who tries to protect the natural environment from being damaged

enˌvironmentally 'friendly *adjective* ENVIRONMENT not damaging the environment *environmentally-friendly washing powder*

envisage /ɪn'vɪzɪdʒ/ *mainly UK* (*mainly US* **envision** /ɪn'vɪʒən/) *verb* [T] to imagine something happening, or think that something is likely to happen *The police don't envisage any trouble at the festival.*

envoy /'envɔɪ/ *noun* [C] POLITICS someone who is sent to represent their government in another country

envy[1] /'envi/ *noun* **1** [U] the feeling that you wish you had something that someone else has *I watched with envy as he climbed into his brand new sports car.* **2 be the envy of sb** to be liked and wanted by someone *Her new office was the envy of the whole company.*

envy[2] /'envi/ *verb* [T] to wish that you had something that someone else has *I envy her good looks.* [+ two objects] *I don't envy him that job.*

enzyme /'enzaɪm/ *noun* [C] BIOLOGY a chemical substance produced by living cells which makes particular chemical reactions happen in animals and plants

eolian /iː'əʊ.li.ən/ *adjective* [always before noun] GEOGRAPHY *US spelling of* aeolian (= produced or carried by the wind)

ephemeral /ɪ'femᵊrᵊl/ *adjective formal* lasting for only a short time

epic /'epɪk/ *noun* [C] a story or film which is very long and contains a lot of action •**epic** *adjective an epic journey*

epicentre *UK* (*US* **epicenter**) /'epɪsentəʳ/ *noun* [C] **GEOLOGY** the point on the Earth's surface which is exactly above an earthquake (= a sudden, violent movement of the Earth's surface)

epidemic /ˌepɪ'demɪk/ *noun* [C] **HEALTH** when a large number of people get the same disease over the same period of time *the AIDS epidemic*

epidermis /ˌepɪ'dɜːmɪs/ *noun* [C, U] **1 ANATOMY, BIOLOGY** the thin outer layer of the skin **2** the outer layer of cells in plants ➲See picture at **leaf** ➲See picture at **stem**

epiglottis /ˌepɪ'glɒtɪs/ *noun* [C] **ANATOMY** a flat part at the back of the tongue which closes when you swallow to stop food from entering the tube that air goes down ➲See picture at **alimentary canal** ➲See picture at **respiratory system**

epilepsy /'epɪlepsi/ *noun* [U] **HEALTH** a brain disease which can make someone become unconscious and have fits (= when you shake in an uncontrolled way)

epileptic /ˌepɪ'leptɪk/ *noun* [C] **HEALTH** someone who suffers from epilepsy •**epileptic** *adjective*

epilogue /'epɪlɒg/ *noun* [C] **LITERATURE** a speech or piece of writing that is added to the end of a play or book

epiphany /ɪ'pɪfᵊni/ *noun* [U] *literary* a moment when you suddenly understand or become aware of something

epiphyte /'epɪfaɪt / *noun* [C] **BIOLOGY** a plant that grows on another plant, especially one that does not feed from it

episode /'epɪsəʊd/ *noun* [C] **1** PROGRAMME one programme of a series shown on television *Did you see last week's episode of The X-Files?* **2** EVENT a single event or period of time *an important **episode in** British history*

epitaph /'epɪtɑːf/ *noun* [C] words that are written to remember a dead person, usually on the stone where they are buried

epithelium /ˌˌep'ɪθiːliəm/ *noun* [usually singular] **BIOLOGY** a layer of cells that are tightly pressed together which covers the outside and inside surfaces of the body

epitome /ɪ'pɪtəmi/ *noun* **be the epitome of sth** to be a perfect example of a quality or type of thing *The hotel was the epitome of luxury.*

epitomize (*also UK* **-ise**) /ɪ'pɪtəmaɪz/ *verb* [T] to be a perfect example of a quality or type of thing *She epitomizes elegance and good taste.*

epoch /'iːpɒk/ Ⓤⓢ /'epək/ *noun* [C] *plural* **epochs** a long period of time in history

eponymous /ɪ'pɒnɪməs/ *adjective* [always before noun] *literary* An eponymous character in a play, book, etc, has the same name as the title.

EPOS /'iːpɒz/ *noun* [U] **FINANCE, COMPUTING** *abbreviation for* electronic point of sale; any electronic system used at the place where customers pay for their goods

O⊸**equal¹** /'iːkwəl/ *adjective* **1** the same in amount, number, or size *The sides are of equal length.* ○ *One metre is **equal to** 39.37 inches.* **2 equal opportunities/rights, etc SOCIETY** opportunities/rights, etc that are the same for everyone without anyone having an unfair advantage ➲Opposite **unequal**

equal² /'iːkwəl/ *verb* [T] *UK* **equalling,** *past* **equalled,** *US* **equaling,** *past* **equaled 1** SAME to have the same value, size, etc as something else, often shown using a symbol (=) *Two plus two equals four.* **2** AS GOOD AS to be as good as someone or something else *She equalled her own world record in the race.*

equal³ /'iːkwəl/ *noun* [C] someone who has the same ability, opportunities, or rights as someone else *The teacher treats us all as equals.*

WORD PARTNERS FOR ***equality***

racial/sexual/social equality • equality **between** sb and sb

equality /ɪ'kwɒləti/ *noun* [U] **SOCIETY** when everyone is equal and has the same opportunities, rights, etc ***racial/sexual equality*** ○ ***equality between** men and women* ➲Opposite **inequality**

equalize (*also UK* **-ise**) /'iːkwᵊlaɪz/ *verb* **1 SPORT** [I] *UK* to get the point in a game or competition that makes your score the same as the other team or player **2** [T] to make things or people equal

O⊸**equally** /'iːkwəli/ *adverb* **1** SAME DEGREE to the same degree or level *an equally important question* ○ *She did **equally well** in the competition last year.* **2** SAME AMOUNTS into amounts or parts that are the same size *She shared the money equally between the four children.* **3** SAME WAY If you treat people equally, you treat everyone in the same way so that no one has an unfair advantage.

'equal ˌsign (*also* **'equals ˌsign**) *noun* [C] **MATHEMATICS** the symbol =, used to show that two things are the same in value, size, meaning, etc

equanimity /ˌekwə'nɪməti/ *noun* [U] *formal* the ability to react calmly, especially in difficult situations

equate /ɪ'kweɪt/ *verb* [T] to consider one thing to be the same as or equal to another thing *Many people **equate** wealth **with** happiness.*

equation /ɪ'kweɪʒᵊn/ *noun* [C] **MATHEMATICS** when you show that two amounts are equal using mathematical symbols

equator /ɪ'kweɪtəʳ/ *noun* [U] the imaginary line around the Earth that divides it into equal north and south parts •**equatorial** /ˌekwə'tɔːriəl/ *adjective* relating to the equator

equestrian /ɪ'kwestriən/ *adjective* **SPORT** relating to riding horses

equi- /ekwɪ-/ *prefix* equal, equally *equidistant* (= the same distance from two or more places)

equidistant /ˌekwɪ'dɪstᵊnt/ *adjective formal* equally far or close *London is roughly equidistant from Oxford and Cambridge.*

equilateral /ˌiːkwɪ'lætᵊrᵊl/ /ˌekwɪ'-/ *adjective* **MATHEMATICS** describes a triangle whose sides are all the same length *an equilateral triangle* ➲Compare **isosceles triangle, scalene triangle**

equilibrium /ˌiːkwɪˈlɪbriəm/ *noun* [U] **1** a state of balance between forces or influences **2 PHYSICS** a state in which an object is not moving or is moving at the same speed all the time because there is a balance of forces acting on it

equip /ɪˈkwɪp/ *verb* **equipping,** *past* **equipped** **1 be equipped with sth** to include the things that are needed for a particular purpose *The new trains are equipped with all the latest technology.* **2** [T] to give someone the skills they need to do a particular thing [+ **to do sth**] *The course didn't really equip me to be a journalist.*

WORD PARTNERS FOR ***equipment***

install/operate/use equipment • **modern/necessary/specialist** equipment • equipment **for** sth

O–ʷ **equipment** /ɪˈkwɪpmənt/ *noun* **1** [U] the things that are used for a particular activity or purpose *kitchen/office equipment* ○ *electrical equipment* (= equipment that uses electricity) **2 a piece of equipment** a tool or object used for a particular activity or purpose

COMMON LEARNER ERROR

equipment

Remember you cannot make **equipment** plural. Do not say 'equipments'.

The computer room has all the equipment you need.

equitable /ˈekwɪtəbl/ *adjective formal* treating everyone in an equal way *a fair and equitable voting system* •**equitably** *adverb*

equity /ˈekwɪti/ *noun* [U] *formal* **1** when everyone is treated fairly and equally *pay equity* ➲Compare **inequity 2 FINANCE** [C, U] the value of a company, which is divided into many equal parts owned by the shareholders, or one of the equal parts into which the value of a company is divided *He sold his equity in the company last year.*

equivalent[1] /ɪˈkwɪvᵊlənt/ *adjective* equal in amount, value, importance, or meaning *The UK's Brit Awards are roughly **equivalent to** the Oscars.*

equivalent[2] /ɪˈkwɪvᵊlənt/ *noun* [C] something that has the same value, importance, size, or meaning as something else *She won **the equivalent of** $5 million.*

er /ɜːʳ/ *exclamation UK spoken* (*US* **uh**) something that you say while you are thinking what to say next *Well, er, I'm not too sure about that.*

ER /ˌiːˈɑːʳ/ *noun* [C] **HEALTH** *US abbreviation for* emergency room: the part of a hospital where people go when they have been injured or have urgent illnesses so that they can be treated immediately

era /ˈɪərə/ *noun* [C] a period of time in history that is special for a particular reason *the Victorian era* ○ *a new era of peace*

eradicate /ɪˈrædɪkeɪt/ *verb* [T] *formal* to destroy or completely get rid of something such as a social problem or a disease •**eradication** /ɪˌrædɪˈkeɪʃᵊn/ *noun* [U]

erase /ɪˈreɪz/ ⓤⓢ /ɪˈreɪs/ *verb* [T] **COMPUTING** to completely remove words, music, pictures, etc that are written or stored on a computer or other piece of equipment *I accidentally erased the tape she lent me.*

eraser /ɪˈreɪzəʳ/ ⓤⓢ /ɪˈreɪsər/ *US* (*UK* **rubber**) *noun* [C] **1** PENCIL a small object which is used to remove pencil marks from paper **2** BOARD an object which is used to remove marks from a blackboard (= a large dark board that teachers write on) ➲See colour picture **The Classroom** on page Centre 6

erect[1] /ɪˈrekt/ *adjective* straight and standing up *She stood very erect, with her hands behind her back.*

erect[2] /ɪˈrekt/ *verb* [T] *formal* to build or put up a structure *When was this building erected?*

erection /ɪˈrekʃᵊn/ *noun* **1 BIOLOGY** [C] when a penis becomes harder and bigger than usual **2** [C, U] *formal* when a structure is built or put up, or the building itself

erector muscle /ɪˈrektəˌmʌsl/ *noun* [C] **ANATOMY, BIOLOGY** a muscle that can pull something, such as the bone in a human's back, into an upright position

ergonomic /ˌɜːgəˈnɒmɪk/ *adjective* relating to the scientific study of people and their working conditions, especially the study of how well people work with their equipment, furniture, lighting, etc. *ergonomic design/features*

erode /ɪˈrəʊd/ *verb* **1 GEOGRAPHY, GEOLOGY** [I, T] If soil, stone, etc erodes or is eroded, it is gradually damaged and removed by the sea, rain, or wind. [**often passive**] *The coastline is slowly being eroded by the sea.* **2** [T] *formal* to gradually destroy a good quality or situation *Reports of corruption have eroded people's confidence in the police.* •**erosion** /ɪˈrəʊʒᵊn/ *noun* [U] *soil erosion*

erotic /ɪˈrɒtɪk/ *adjective* making you feel strong sexual feelings, or involving sexual love *an erotic film* •**erotically** *adverb*

err /ɜːʳ/ *verb* [I] *formal* to make a mistake or do something that is wrong ➲See also: err on the **side**[1] of caution

errand /ˈerənd/ *noun* [C] a short journey in order to buy or do something for someone *I've got to **run** a few **errands** this morning before we go.*

errant /ˈerənt/ *adjective* [**always before noun**] An errant person has behaved badly. *an errant husband*

erratic /ɪˈrætɪk/ *adjective* often changing suddenly and not regular *His behaviour is becoming more and more erratic.* •**erratically** *adverb*

erroneous /ɪˈrəʊniəs/ *adjective formal* not correct *an erroneous answer*

WORD PARTNERS FOR ***error***

make/correct an error • a **fundamental/glaring** error • do sth **in** error • **human** error

O–ʷ **error** /ˈerəʳ/ *noun* [C, U] a mistake, especially one that can cause problems *a computer error/human error* ○ *to **make** an **error*** ○ *The*

E

*documents were destroyed **in error** (= by mistake) by the police.*

ˈerror ˌmessage *noun* [C] **COMPUTING** a message that comes onto your computer screen when you have made a mistake

erupt /ɪˈrʌpt/ *verb* [I] **1 GEOLOGY** If a volcano erupts, it suddenly throws out smoke, fire, and melted rocks. **2** HAPPEN to happen suddenly or violently ***Violence erupted** in the city on Friday night.* **3** PERSON to suddenly become very excited or angry, or start to shout *The whole stadium erupted when he scored the second goal.* •**eruption** /ɪˈrʌpʃən/ *noun* [C, U] *a **volcanic eruption***

E

erythrocyte /ɪˈrɪθrəsaɪt/ *noun* [C] **BIOLOGY** a red blood cell

escalate /ˈeskəleɪt/ *verb* **1** GET WORSE [I, T] If a violent or bad situation escalates or is escalated, it quickly becomes worse or more serious. *The fight quickly **escalated into** a riot.* **2** INCREASE [I] to rise or increase quickly ***Airline prices escalate** during the holiday season.* •**escalation** /ˌeskəˈleɪʃən/ *noun* [C, U] *an **escalation** in violence*

escalator /ˈeskəleɪtəʳ/ *noun* [C] moving stairs that take people from one level of a building to another *We **took the escalator** down to the basement.*

escapade /ˌeskəˈpeɪd/ *noun* [C] an exciting and sometimes dangerous experience

escape[1] /ɪˈskeɪp/ *verb* **1** GET AWAY [I] to succeed in getting away from a place where you do not want to be *The two killers **escaped from** prison last night.* **2** AVOID [I, T] to avoid a dangerous or unpleasant situation *to **escape capture/injury*** **3** FORGET [T] If something such as a name escapes you, you cannot remember it. *The **name** of her book **escapes** me at the moment.* **4** NOT NOTICE [T] If something escapes your notice or attention, you do not notice or see it. *Nothing that goes on in this office escapes her **attention**.* **5** GAS/LIQUID [I] If a gas or liquid escapes from a pipe or container, it comes out, especially when it should not. •**escaped** *adjective an escaped prisoner*

WORD PARTNERS FOR ***escape***

attempt/make/plan an escape • a **lucky/remarkable** escape • an escape **from** sth/sb

escape[2] /ɪˈskeɪp/ *noun* **1** GETTING OUT [C, U] when someone succeeds in getting out of a place or a dangerous or bad situation **2 a narrow escape** when someone almost dies or almost has a very bad experience **3** FROM TROUBLE [U, no plural] something that helps you to forget about your usual life or problems *I love old movies, they're such an **escape from** the real world.* ➲See also: **fire escape**

esˈcape ˌ(key) (*written abbreviation* **Esc**) *noun* [C] **COMPUTING** the key on a computer keyboard which allows you to leave a particular screen or program *If you press the escape key, you will return to the main menu.*

escapism /ɪˈskeɪpɪzəm/ *noun* [U] entertainment or imagination that helps you to forget about your work and your problems •**escapist** *adjective*

escort[1] /ˈeskɔːt/ *noun* **1** GUARD [C, U] a person or vehicle that goes somewhere with someone to protect or guard them *She was driven to court **under** police **escort**.* **2** SOCIAL [C] a person who goes with someone else to a social event, sometimes for payment

escort[2] /ɪˈskɔːt/ *verb* [T] to go somewhere with someone, often to protect or guard them *He offered to escort me home.*

Eskimo /ˈeskɪməʊ/ *noun* [C, U] *plural* **Eskimos** or **Eskimo** *old-fashioned another word for* Inuit (= a group of people who live in the cold, northern areas of North America, Russia, and Greenland, or a member of this group) *an Eskimo village*

ESL /ˌiːesˈel/ *noun* [U] **EDUCATION** *abbreviation for* English as a Second Language: the teaching of English to students whose first language is not English, but who live in a country where it is the main language

esophagus *noun* [C] **ANATOMY** *US spelling of* oesophagus

especially /ɪˈspeʃəli/ *adverb* **1** MORE more than other things or people, or much more than usual *He's always making comments about her appearance, especially her weight.* ○ *She's especially interested in American poetry.* **2** ONLY for one particular person, purpose, or reason *I cooked this meal **especially for** you.* ➲See Common Learner Error at **specially**

espionage /ˈespiənɑːʒ/ *noun* [U] **POLITICS** the activity of discovering secret information about a country or company that is fighting or competing against you ***industrial espionage***

espouse /ɪˈspaʊz/ *verb* [T] *formal* to support a belief or way of life

espresso /esˈpresəʊ/ *noun* [C, U] **FOOD** strong, black coffee

WORD PARTNERS FOR ***essay***

do/write an essay • **in** an essay • an essay **on** sth

essay /ˈeseɪ/ *noun* [C] **EDUCATION** a short piece of writing about a particular subject, especially one written by a student *He wrote an **essay on** modern Japanese literature.*

essence /ˈesəns/ *noun* **1** BASIC QUALITY [U, no plural] the basic or most important idea or quality of something *The **essence of** his argument is that we should not eat meat.* **2** LIQUID [C, U] a strong liquid, usually made from a plant or flower, that is used to add a flavour or smell to something *vanilla essence*

essential /ɪˈsenʃəl/ *adjective* **1** NECESSARY very important and necessary *Computers are an **essential part** of our lives.* ○ *Fibre is **essential for** a healthy digestive system.* [+ **to do sth**] *It is essential to arrive early for the show.* [+ **(that)**] *It is absolutely essential that she gets this message.* **2** BASIC the most basic and important *There's one essential point I think you've forgotten.*

essentially /ɪˈsenʃəli/ *adverb* used when you are emphasizing the basic facts about something *What he is saying is essentially true.*

es͵sential ˈoil *noun* [C, U] a strong oil made from a plant which contains its smell or other special qualities

essentials /ɪˈsenʃəlz/ *noun* [plural] the most important or necessary things

establish /ɪˈstæblɪʃ/ *verb* **1** START [T] to start a company or organization that will continue for a long time [**often passive**] *The brewery was established in 1822.* **2 establish sb/sth as sth** to put someone or something into a successful and lasting position [**often reflexive**] He quickly established himself as a talented actor. **3 establish communication/relations, etc** to start having a relationship or communicating with another company, country, or organization *The two countries have only recently established diplomatic relations.* **4** DECIDE [T] to decide something *Our first step must be to establish priorities for the weeks ahead.* **5** DISCOVER [T] to find out information or prove something [+ **question word**] *The police are trying to establish how he died.* •**established** *adjective*

establishment /ɪˈstæblɪʃmənt/ *noun* **1** ORGANIZATION [C] an organization or business **2** STARTING [U] when an organization, school, business, etc is started *the establishment of a new national bank* **3 the Establishment** the people and organizations that have most power and influence in a country **4 the legal/medical, etc establishment** the group of people with most influence in a particular area of work or activity

estate /ɪˈsteɪt/ *noun* [C] **1** LAND a large area of land in the countryside that is owned by one person or organization *a country estate* **2** BUILDINGS *UK* an area with a lot of buildings of the same type *an **industrial estate*** **3** POSSESSIONS the possessions and money that someone owns when they die ➲See also: **housing estate, real estate**

esˈtate ͵agent *UK* (*US* **real estate agent**) *noun* [C] someone who sells buildings and land as their job

esˈtate ͵car *UK* (*US* **station wagon**) *noun* [C] a big car with a large space for bags behind the back seat

esteem /ɪˈstiːm/ *noun* [U] *formal* respect and admiration for someone *My father was **held in high esteem** by everyone who knew him.* ➲See also: **self-esteem**

esteemed /ɪˈstiːmd/ *adjective formal* respected and admired *a **highly esteemed** professor*

ester /ˈestəʳ/ *noun* [C] **CHEMISTRY** any of several compounds produced by a reaction between an acid and an alcohol

esthetic /esˈθetɪk/ *adjective another US spelling of* aesthetic (= relating to beauty and the way something looks) •**esthetically** *adverb*

esthetics /esˈθetɪks/ *noun* [U] *another US spelling of* aesthetics (= the study of beauty)

WORD PARTNERS FOR ***estimate***

an accurate/rough estimate • an estimate **of** sth • **give** sb an estimate

estimate¹ /ˈestɪmət/ *noun* [C] **1** a guess of what a size, value, amount, etc might be *a **rough estimate*** **2 FINANCE** a written document saying how much it will probably cost to do a job *Can you **give** me an **estimate** for the work?*

O‑ **estimate²** /ˈestɪmeɪt/ *verb* [T] to guess the cost, size, value, etc of something [+ **that**] *They estimate that a hundred people were killed in the accident.* ○ *The number of dead **is estimated at** a hundred.* •**estimated** *adjective an estimated cost*

estimation /͵estɪˈmeɪʃən/ *noun* [U] your opinion of someone or something *He is a total genius, **in my estimation**.*

estranged /ɪˈstreɪndʒd/ *adjective formal* **1** FRIEND not now communicating with a friend or a member of your family, because you have argued **2** HUSBAND/WIFE not now living with your husband or wife *his estranged wife* •**estrangement** *noun* [C, U]

estrogen /ˈiːstrədʒən/ Ⓤⓢ /ˈestrədʒən/ *noun* [U] **BIOLOGY** *US spelling of* oestrogen (= a chemical substance in a woman's body)

estuary /ˈestjʊəri/ *noun* [C] **GEOGRAPHY** the wide part of a river where it goes into the sea

O‑ **etc** /etˈsetərə/ *abbreviation for* et cetera: used at the end of a list to show that other things or people could also be added to it

etch /etʃ/ *verb* [I, T] **ART, DT** to cut lines on a hard surface to make a picture or words

eternal /ɪˈtɜːnəl/ *adjective* continuing forever, or seeming to continue forever ***eternal youth*** •**eternally** *adverb I will be **eternally grateful** to you.*

eternity /ɪˈtɜːnəti/ *noun* **1** [U] time that continues forever, especially after death **2 an eternity** *informal* a very long time *It **seemed like an eternity** until she came back.*

ethane /ˈiːθeɪn/ *noun* [U] **CHEMISTRY** a gas with no smell or colour, which burns easily and is found in natural gas and petroleum (= oil used as fuel) (formula C_2H_6)

ethanoic acid /eθə͵nəʊɪkˈæsɪd/ *noun* [U] **CHEMISTRY** (*also* **acetic acid**) a colourless acid with a strong smell that is contained in vinegar

ethanol /ˈeθənɒl/ (*also* **ethyl alcohol**) *noun* [U] **CHEMISTRY** a chemical compound which is the type of alcohol that is found in alcoholic drinks (formula CH_3CH_2OH)

ethereal /ɪˈθɪəriəl/ *adjective* very delicate and light and almost seeming not to be from this world •**ethereally** *adverb*

ethic /ˈeθɪk/ *noun* [**no plural**] a belief or idea that influences the way you think or behave

ethical /ˈeθɪkəl/ *adjective* **1** RIGHT/WRONG relating to what is right or wrong *The book raises some serious ethical questions.* **2** GOOD morally correct and good *He dealt with this case in a completely professional and ethical manner.* ➲Opposite **unethical** •**ethically** *adverb*

ethics /ˈeθɪks/ *noun* [plural] ideas and beliefs about what type of behaviour is morally right and wrong *a **code of ethics*** ○ *the ethics of genetic engineering*

ethnic /ˈeθnɪk/ *adjective* **SOCIETY** relating to a particular race of people ***ethnic minorities***

ethnic cleansing /ˌeθnɪk'klenzɪŋ/ *noun* [U] the use of violence to remove everyone of a particular race or religion from a country

ethos /'iːθɒs/ *noun* [no plural] the ideas and beliefs of a particular person or group

ethylene /'eθɪliːn/ (*also* **ethene**) *noun* [U] **CHEMISTRY** a colourless gas with a slightly sweet smell that burns easily and is often used in industry (formula C_2H_4)

e-ticket /'iːˌtɪkɪt/ *noun* [C] a ticket, usually for someone to travel on an aircraft, that is held on a computer and is not printed on paper

E

etiology /iiː.ti'ɒl.ə.dʒi/ *noun* [U] **HEALTH** *US spelling of* aetiology (= the study of the causes of a disease)

etiquette /'etɪket/ *noun* [U] rules about what is polite and correct behaviour

etymology /ˌetɪ'mɒlədʒi/ *noun* [U] **LANGUAGE** the study of the history and origin of words and their meanings •**etymological** /ˌetɪmə'lɒdʒɪkəl/ *adjective* •**etymologically** *adverb*

the EU /ˌiː'juː/ *noun* **POLITICS** *abbreviation for* the European Union: a European political and economic organization that encourages business and good relationships between the countries that are members

euphemism /'juːfəmɪzᵊm/ *noun* [C, U] **LANGUAGE** a polite word or phrase that is used to avoid saying something embarrassing or offensive *'Passed away' is a **euphemism for** 'died'.* •**euphemistic** /ˌjuːfə'mɪstɪk/ *adjective* •**euphemistically** *adverb*

euphoria /juː'fɔːriə/ *noun* [U] a feeling of extreme happiness and excitement •**euphoric** /juː'fɒrɪk/ *adjective*

euro /'jʊərəʊ/ *noun* [C] **ECONOMICS** a unit of money used in European countries that belong to the European Union (= a European political and economic organization); €

Euro- /jʊərəʊ-/ *prefix* **POLITICS** relating to Europe *Europop* (= pop music from Europe)

European /ˌjʊərə'piːən/ *adjective* relating or belonging to Europe *European countries/languages* ○ *the European Parliament* •**European** *noun* [C] *Many Europeans speak English.*

the ˌEuropean 'Union (*also* **the EU**) *noun* **POLITICS** a European political and economic organization that encourages business and good relationships between the countries that are members

Eustachian tube /juː'steɪʃənˌtjuːb/ *noun* [C] **ANATOMY** one of two tubes that connect the ear and the back of the nose, which open to keep the pressure equal on both sides of the eardrum (= thin piece of skin inside the ear)

euthanasia /ˌjuːθə'neɪziə/ *noun* [U] **HEALTH** when someone who is very old or very ill is killed so that they do not suffer any more ***voluntary euthanasia***

eutrophication /ˌjuːtrəfɪ'keɪʃᵊn/ *noun* [U] **BIOLOGY** when too many plants grow on the surface of a river, lake, etc, often because of chemicals that have come from farms that are near

evacuate /ɪ'vækjueɪt/ *verb* [T] to move people from a dangerous place to somewhere safer *The police quickly evacuated the area after the bomb threat.* •**evacuation** /ɪˌvækju'eɪʃᵊn/ *noun* [C, U] *the evacuation of civilians from the war zone*

evacuee /ɪˌvækju'iː/ *noun* [C] someone who is evacuated from a place to somewhere safer

evade /ɪ'veɪd/ *verb* **1** [T] to avoid something or someone, especially in a dishonest way *to **evade capture*** ○ *to evade paying tax* **2 evade the issue/question, etc** to intentionally not talk about something or not answer something

evaluate /ɪ'væljueɪt/ *verb* [T] *formal* to consider or study something carefully and decide how good or bad it is •**evaluation** /ɪˌvælju'eɪʃᵊn/ *noun* [C, U]

evangelical /ˌiːvæn'dʒelɪkᵊl/ *adjective* **RELIGION** Evangelical Christians believe that faith in Jesus Christ and studying the Bible are more important than religious ceremonies.

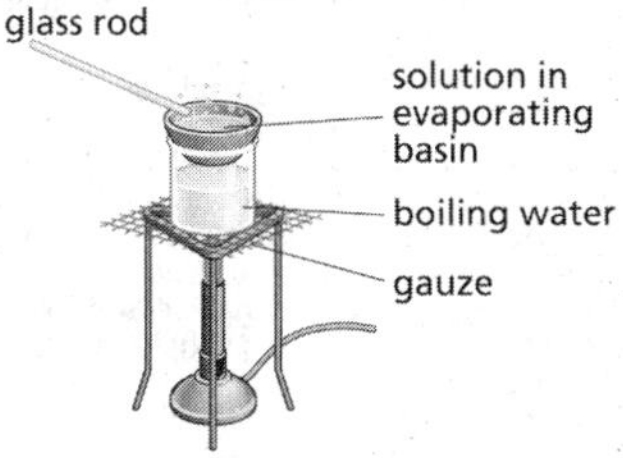

glass rod
solution in evaporating basin
boiling water
gauze

evaporation

evaporate /ɪ'væpᵊreɪt/ *verb* **1 CHEMISTRY** [I, T] If a liquid evaporates or is evaporated, it changes into gas or vapour (= very small drops of water). **2** [I] If feelings evaporate, they disappear. •**evaporation** /ɪˌvæpə'reɪʃᵊn/ *noun* [U] ➲See picture at **water cycle**

e'vaporating ˌdish *noun* [C] **CHEMISTRY** a small dish in which liquids are heated over fire so that they evaporate (= change to a gas), leaving a solid substance in the dish ➲See picture at **laboratory**

evasion /ɪ'veɪʒᵊn/ *noun* [C, U] when you avoid something, especially in a dishonest way ***tax evasion***

evasive /ɪ'veɪsɪv/ *adjective* **1** trying to avoid talking about something *He was very evasive about his past.* ○ *an **evasive answer*** **2 take evasive action** to do something to avoid an accident or bad situation •**evasively** *adverb* •**evasiveness** *noun* [U]

eve /iːv/ *noun* **1 Christmas Eve/New Year's Eve** the day or night before Christmas Day/New Year's Day **2 the eve of sth** the time just before something important happens *They were married in Washington on the eve of the Second World War.*

even[1] /'iːvᵊn/ *adjective* **1** FLAT flat, level, or smooth *Find an **even surface** to work on.* ➲Opposite **uneven** **2** NOT CHANGING An even temperature or rate is regular and does not change very much. **3 MATHEMATICS** An even number is a number which can be exactly divided by two, for example four, six, or eight. ➲Opposite

odd 4 MONEY *informal* not now owing someone money *If you pay for my cinema ticket, we'll be even.* **5** COMPETITION An even race or competition is one that both players, teams, or people involved have an equal chance of winning. **6 get even (with sb)** *informal* If you get even with someone who has done something bad to you, you do something bad to them.

O— **even²** /ˈiːvᵊn/ *adverb* **1** used to emphasize something that is surprising *Everyone danced, even Mick.* **2 even better/faster/smaller, etc** used when comparing things, to emphasize the difference *I think Alex is going to be even taller than his father.* **3 even if** used to emphasize that a particular situation would not change what you have just said *I would never eat meat, even if I was really hungry.* **4 even though** although *He still smokes, even though he's got asthma.* **5 even so** used to emphasize that something surprising is true despite what you have just said *Car prices have gone down a lot, but even so, we couldn't afford to buy one.*

even³ /ˈiːvᵊn/ *verb*
even (sth) out *phrasal verb* to become equal, or to make something equal *Sometimes I pay and sometimes Tom does - it usually evens out in the end.*

WORD PARTNERS FOR ***evening***

this/tomorrow/yesterday evening • **in the** evening

O— **evening** /ˈiːvnɪŋ/ *noun* **1** [C, U] the part of the day between the afternoon and the night *Are you doing anything **this evening**?* ○ *I go to band practice on Monday evenings.* ○ *We usually eat our main meal **in the evening**.* **2 (Good) evening.** something that you say when you meet someone in the evening

evenly /ˈiːvənli/ *adverb* **1** into equal amounts, or in a regular way *They decided to divide the prize money evenly between them.* **2 evenly matched** Two people or teams who are evenly matched are equally good, or have an equal chance of winning.

WORD PARTNERS FOR ***event***

an event **happens/occurs/takes place** • **witness** an event • a **dramatic/major/rare/tragic** event • **recent** events

O— **event** /ɪˈvent/ *noun* [C] **1** HAPPENING something that happens, especially something important or unusual *Local people have been shocked by **recent events** in the town.* **2** RACE a race, party, competition, etc that has been organized for a particular time *a **social/sporting event*** **3 in the event** *UK* used to emphasize what did happen when it was not what you had expected *In the event, we didn't need the extra money.* **4 in the event of sth** *formal* if something happens *An airbag could save your life in the event of an accident.* **5 in any event** whatever happens *I'm not sure if I'm coming on Friday, but in any event, I'll see you next week.* ➲See also: **non-event**

eventful /ɪˈventfᵊl/ *adjective* full of interesting or important events *a very eventful day/journey*

eventual /ɪˈventʃuəl/ *adjective* [**always before noun**] happening or existing at the end of a process or period of time *the eventual winner of the competition*

O— **eventually** /ɪˈventʃuəli/ *adverb* in the end, especially after a long time *We all hope that an agreement can be reached eventually.*

O— **ever** /ˈevəʳ/ *adverb* **1** at any time *Have you ever been skiing?* ○ *No one ever calls me any more.* **2 better/faster/happier, etc than ever** better/faster/happier, etc than at any time before **3 hardly ever** almost never *We hardly ever go out these days.* **4 ever since** always since that time *We met at school and have been friends ever since.* **5 ever so/ever such a** *UK* very/a very *She's ever so pretty.* **6 for ever** *UK* (*UK/US* **forever**) always in the future *I'm not going to live here for ever.* **7 ever-changing/growing/increasing, etc** always changing/growing/increasing, etc

evergreen /ˈevəgriːn/ *adjective* **BIOLOGY** An evergreen plant has green leaves that do not fall off in winter. •**evergreen** *noun* [C] a plant with leaves that do not fall off in winter

everlasting /ˌevəˈlɑːstɪŋ/ *adjective* continuing for a long time or always *everlasting love*

evermore /ˌevəˈmɔːʳ/ *adverb literary* always in the future

O— **every** /ˈevri/ *determiner* **1** EACH each one of a group of people or things *He knows the name of every child in the school.* ○ ***Every one** of the paintings was a fake.* **2** HOW OFTEN used to show that something is repeated regularly *He goes to Spain every summer.* **3** POSSIBLE as much as is possible *I'd like to wish you **every success** in your new job.* ○ ***Every effort** is being made to rectify the problem.* **4 every now and then/every so often** sometimes, but not often *We still meet up every now and then.* **5 one in every five/ten, etc** used to show how many people or things in a group are affected by or involved in something

COMMON LEARNER ERROR

every

When **every** is followed by **body**, **one**, **thing**, or **where**, you write the words together.

Everybody needs to bring something to eat.

Can everyone see that?

Have you got everything you need?

I've looked everywhere for it.

In other situations you use **every** as a separate word.

You have to take your membership card every time you go.

Do you go jogging every morning?

O— **everybody** /ˈevriˌbɒdi/ *pronoun another word for* everyone

everyday /ˈevrideɪ/ *adjective* [**always before noun**] normal, usual, or happening every day *Computers are now part of **everyday life**.*

O— **everyone** /ˈevriwʌn/ (*also* **everybody**) *pronoun* **1** every person *Everyone agreed with the decision.* **2 everyone else** every other person *Everyone else was wearing jeans.*

everyplace /ˈevripleɪs/ *adverb US another word for* everywhere

⊶**everything** /ˈevriθɪŋ/ *pronoun* **1** all things or each thing *They lost everything in the fire.* ○ *What's the matter Nick, is everything all right?* **2 everything else** all the other things *The meat tasted strange, but everything else was okay.* **3 be/mean everything** to be the most important part of someone's life *His children **mean everything to** him.* ○ *Money isn't everything.*

⊶**everywhere** /ˈevriweəʳ/ *adverb* in or to every place *I've looked everywhere, but I still can't find that letter.*

E

evict /ɪˈvɪkt/ *verb* [T] to legally force someone to leave the house they are living in *They were evicted after complaints from their neighbours.* •**eviction** /ɪˈvɪkʃᵊn/ *noun* [C, U]

WORD PARTNERS FOR ***evidence***

compelling/conclusive/hard/scientific/strong evidence • evidence **of** sth

⊶**evidence** /ˈevɪdᵊns/ *noun* [U] **1** FACTS something that makes you believe that something is true or exists ***evidence of*** *global warming* [+ **that**] *There is no **scientific evidence** that the drug is addictive.* **2 LAW** information that is given or objects that are shown in a court of law to help to prove if someone has committed a crime *He was arrested despite the lack of evidence against him.* **3 give evidence** *UK* to give information and answer questions in a court of law *She was called to give evidence at his trial.* **4 be in evidence** *formal* to be noticeable

evident /ˈevɪdᵊnt/ *adjective formal* obvious to everyone and easy to see or understand [+ **that**] *It was evident from his voice that he was upset.* ➲See also: **self-evident**

evidently /ˈevɪdᵊntli/ *adverb* **1** OBVIOUSLY used to say that something can easily be noticed *He evidently likes her.* **2** PROBABLY used to say that something seems probable from the information you have *The intruder evidently got in through an open window.*

evil¹ /ˈiːvᵊl/ *adjective* very cruel, bad, or harmful *an evil monster*

evil² /ˈiːvᵊl/ *noun* [C, U] something that is very bad and harmful *The theme of the play is the battle between **good and evil**.* ➲See also: the **lesser** of two evils

evocative /ɪˈvɒkətɪv/ *adjective* making you remember or imagine something that is pleasant *evocative music* ○ ***evocative of*** *the sea*

evoke /ɪˈvəʊk/ *verb* [T] to make someone remember something or feel an emotion *The story evoked memories of my childhood.*

evolution /ˌiːvəˈluːʃᵊn/ *noun* [U] **1 BIOLOGY** the way in which living things gradually change and develop over millions of years *Darwin's theory of evolution* **2** a gradual process of change and development *the evolution of language* •**evolutionary** *adjective*

evolve /ɪˈvɒlv/ *verb* **1 BIOLOGY** [I] to develop from other forms of life over millions of years **2** [I, T] to develop or make something develop, usually gradually *rapidly evolving technology*

ewe /juː/ *noun* [C] a female sheep

ex /eks/ *noun* [C] *informal* someone who used to be your husband, wife, or partner *My ex and his new wife live abroad.*

ex- /eks-/ *prefix* from before *an ex-boyfriend* ○ *an ex-boss*

exacerbate /ɪgˈzæsəbeɪt/ *verb* [T] to make something worse *Sunny weather exacerbates the effects of pollution.*

⊶**exact¹** /ɪgˈzækt/ *adjective* completely correct in every detail *I'm afraid I can't give you the exact details of the show yet.* ○ *They've lived here a long time - 25 years **to be exact**.* •**exactness** *noun* [U]

exact² /ɪgˈzækt/ *verb* [T] *formal* to demand and get something from someone

exacting /ɪgˈzæktɪŋ/ *adjective* needing a lot of effort and attention *an exacting training schedule*

⊶**exactly** /ɪgˈzæktli/ *adverb* **1** COMPLETELY CORRECT used when you are giving or asking for information that is completely correct *What exactly seems to be the problem?* ○ *The train got in at exactly ten o'clock.* **2** EMPHASIS used to emphasize what you are saying *I found a dress that's exactly the same colour as my shoes.* **3** AGREEMENT something you say when you agree completely with someone *"Surely they should have told us about this problem sooner?" "Exactly."* **4 not exactly** used to say that something is not completely true *"Do you live here?" "Not exactly, I'm staying with friends."* **5 not exactly easy/new/clear, etc** *informal* used to say that a description is completely untrue *Let's face it, we're not exactly rich, are we?*

exaggerate /ɪgˈzædʒᵊreɪt/ *verb* [I, T] to make something seem larger, better, worse, etc than it really is *Don't exaggerate - it didn't cost that much!*

WORD PARTNERS FOR ***exaggeration***

a **gross/slight** exaggeration • an exaggeration **of** sth

exaggeration /ɪgˌzædʒᵊrˈeɪʃᵊn/ *noun* [C, U] when you describe something as larger, better, worse, etc than it really is *a **gross exaggeration** of the facts*

exalted /ɪgˈzɔːltɪd/ *adjective formal* very highly respected, or with a very high position

WORD PARTNERS FOR ***exam***

do/(*UK*) **sit/take** an exam • **fail/pass** an exam • exam **results**

⊶**exam** /ɪgˈzæm/ *noun* [C] **1 EDUCATION** an official test of how much you know about something, or how well you can do something *a maths exam* ○ *to **fail/pass** an exam (UK)* ○ *to **sit/** (UK/US) to **take** (= do) an **exam*** **2** *US* a series of medical tests *an eye exam*

COMMON LEARNER ERROR

take/sit an exam

To **take an exam** means to do an official test. 'Sit' is slightly more formal than 'take' in this phrase and is only used in the UK.

We have to take an exam at the end of the course.

~~*We have to write an exam at the end of the course.*~~

If you **pass an exam**, you are successful because you get a good mark. If you **fail an exam**, you are not successful because you get a bad mark.

examination /ɪɡˌzæmɪˈneɪʃᵊn/ *noun* **1** [C, U] when someone looks at something very carefully *a **medical examination** ○ a **close examination** of the facts* **2** EDUCATION [C] *formal* an exam *a written examination*

examine /ɪɡˈzæmɪn/ *verb* [T] **1** LOOK AT to look at someone or something very carefully, especially to try to discover something *She picked up the knife and examined it closely. ○ He was examined by a doctor as soon as he arrived.* **2** TEST *formal* to test someone to see how much they know or how well they can do something *You'll be examined in three main areas: speaking, listening, and reading comprehension.* **3** CONSIDER to consider a plan or an idea carefully *They have called a special meeting to examine the proposal.* ➲See also: **cross-examine**

examiner /ɪɡˈzæmɪnəʳ/ *noun* [C] EDUCATION someone who tests how much you know about something, or how well you can do something

WORD PARTNERS FOR ***example***

a classic/good/prime example • an example **of** sth

O⊸ **example** /ɪɡˈzɑːmpl/ *noun* **1** TYPICAL [C] something that is typical of the group of things that you are talking about *This is a good **example of** medieval Chinese architecture.* **2 for example** used to give an example of what you are talking about *Some people, students for example, can get cheaper tickets.* **3** VERY GOOD [C] someone or something that is very good and should be copied *He is a very good example to the rest of the class.* **4 set an example** to behave in a way that other people should copy

exasperate /ɪɡˈzæspᵊreɪt/ *verb* [T] to annoy someone a lot

exasperated /ɪɡˈzæspᵊreɪtɪd/ *adjective* extremely annoyed *He's become increasingly exasperated with the situation.*

exasperating /ɪɡˈzæspᵊreɪtɪŋ/ *adjective* extremely annoying

exasperation /ɪɡˌzæspəˈreɪʃᵊn/ *noun* [U] when you feel extremely annoyed with someone or something

excavate /ˈekskəveɪt/ *verb* [I, T] to dig in the ground, especially with a machine, or to look for objects from the past *These Roman coins were excavated from a site in Cambridge.* •**excavation** /ˌekskəˈveɪʃᵊn/ *noun* [C, U]

exceed /ɪkˈsiːd/ *verb* **1** [T] to be more than a particular number or amount *Sales have exceeded $1 million so far this year.* **2 exceed the speed limit** to drive faster than you are allowed to according to the law

exceedingly /ɪkˈsiːdɪŋli/ *adverb formal* very *He was clever, attractive, and exceedingly rich.*

excel /ɪkˈsel/ *verb* **excelling**, *past* **excelled** *formal* **1** [I] to be very good at something *Paula always **excelled in** languages at school.* **2 excel yourself** to do something better than you usually do

O⊸ **excellent** /ˈeksᵊlᵊnt/ *adjective* very good, or of a very high quality *That was an excellent meal.* •**excellently** *adverb* •**excellence** /ˈeksᵊlᵊns/ *noun* [U]

O⊸ **except** /ɪkˈsept/ *preposition, conjunction* not including a particular fact, thing, or person *The boat sails from Oban every day except Sunday. ○ Everyone passed the exam **except for** Rory.* [+ (that)] *So nothing changed, except that Anna saw her son less and less.*

excepted /ɪkˈseptɪd/ *adjective* [always after noun] *formal* not included *Everybody who was asked, myself excepted, said no.*

excepting /ɪkˈseptɪŋ/ *preposition* not including

exception /ɪkˈsepʃᵊn/ *noun* **1** [C, U] someone or something that is not included in a rule, group, or list *There are **exceptions to** every rule. ○ I like all kinds of movies, **with the exception of** horror films. ○ All our pupils, **without exception**, have access to the Internet. ○ Her films are always popular and this one **is no exception**.* **2 make an exception** to not treat someone or something according to the usual rules *They don't usually take cheques, but they said they'd make an exception in my case.* **3 take exception to sth** *formal* to be annoyed or insulted by something

exceptional /ɪkˈsepʃᵊnᵊl/ *adjective* **1** GOOD extremely good *an exceptional student* **2** UNUSUAL very unusual and not likely to happen very often *Visitors are only allowed in exceptional circumstances.* •**exceptionally** *adverb an exceptionally gifted pianist*

excerpt /ˈeksɜːpt/ *noun* [C] a short piece from a book, film, piece of music, etc

excess¹ /ɪkˈses/ *noun* **1** [U, no plural] more of something than is usual or needed ***An excess of** oil on the markets has caused prices to fall sharply.* **2 in excess of sth** more than a particular amount or level *He earns in excess of £60,000 a year.* **3 do sth to excess** to do something too much *He occasionally has a beer, but he never drinks to excess.*

excess² /ɪkˈses/ *adjective* [always before noun] more than is usual or allowed *We had to pay £100 for **excess baggage**.*

excesses /ɪkˈsesɪz/ *noun* [plural] extreme, harmful, or immoral actions or behaviour

excessive /ɪkˈsesɪv/ *adjective* more than is necessary or wanted *They accused the police of using **excessive force**.* •**excessively** *adverb*

exchange¹ /ɪksˈtʃeɪndʒ/ *noun* **1** GIVING [C, U] when you give something to someone and they give you something else *an **exchange of ideas/information** ○ They were given food and shelter **in exchange for** work.* **2** STUDENTS [C] an arrangement by which students and teachers from one country go to stay with students and teachers in another **3** CONVERSATION [C] a short conversation or argument *There were **angry exchanges** between the police and demonstrators.* ➲See also: **the stock exchange**

exchange² /ɪksˈtʃeɪndʒ/ *verb* **1** GIVE [T] to give something to someone and receive something similar from them *It's traditional for the two*

E

teams to exchange shirts after the game. **2** SHOP [T] to take something back to the shop where you bought it and change it for something else *Could I **exchange** this shirt **for** a larger size?* **3 exchange looks/smiles/words, etc** If two people exchange looks, smiles, words, etc, they look at each other, smile at each other, talk to each other, etc.

ex'change ˌrate *noun* [C] **ECONOMICS** the amount of another country's money that you can buy with a particular amount of your own country's money

E

excise /'eksaɪz/ *noun* [U] **ECONOMICS** government taxes that must be paid on some things that are made or sold in a particular country

excitable /ɪk'saɪtəbl/ *adjective* easily becoming excited *a very excitable child/puppy*

excite /ɪk'saɪt/ *verb* [T] **1** EMOTION to make someone feel very happy and enthusiastic *Try not to excite the children too much.* **2** REACTION *formal* to cause a particular reaction in someone *This product has **excited** a great deal of **interest**.*

O⁻**excited** /ɪk'saɪtɪd/ *adjective* feeling very happy and enthusiastic *happy, excited faces* ○ *The children are getting really **excited about** the party.* •**excitedly** *adverb*

COMMON LEARNER ERROR

excited or **exciting**

Excited is used to describe how someone feels.

She was very excited about the visit.

~~*She was very exciting about the visit.*~~

Exciting is used to describe the thing that makes you excited.

I've had some exciting news!

WORD PARTNERS FOR ***excitement***

cause/feel excitement • excitement **mounts** • **great/wild** excitement • excitement **about/at/over** sth

O⁻**excitement** /ɪk'saɪtmənt/ *noun* [U] when people feel very happy and enthusiastic *The competition is causing a lot of excitement.*

OTHER WAYS OF SAYING ***exciting***

If something is so exciting that it holds your attention completely, you can say that it is **gripping** or **riveting**: *The book was **gripping** - I couldn't put it down.* • *I found the film absolutely **riveting**.*

Sports and outdoor activities which are exciting are often described as **exhilarating**: *I find skiing absolutely **exhilarating**.*

The adjective **action-packed** is often used to describe a story or period of time which is full of exciting events: *We had an **action-packed** weekend in Berlin.* • *The film is described as 'an **action-packed** thriller'.*

An exciting atmosphere is sometimes described as **electric**: *The atmosphere backstage was **electric**.*

Vibrant is often used to describe places which are exciting: *This is one of Europe's most **vibrant** cities.*

O⁻**exciting** /ɪk'saɪtɪŋ/ *adjective* making you feel very happy and enthusiastic *an exciting football match* ○ *You won? How exciting!*

exclaim /ɪks'kleɪm/ *verb* [I, T] to say something suddenly and loudly because you are surprised, annoyed, excited, etc *"How terrible!" she exclaimed.*

exclamation /ˌekskləˈmeɪʃən/ *noun* [C] something that you say loudly and suddenly because you are surprised, angry, excited, etc *an exclamation of delight*

excla'mation ˌmark (*also US* **excla'mation ˌpoint**) *noun* [C] **LANGUAGE** a mark (!) used at the end of a sentence that expresses surprise, excitement, or shock, or that is a greeting or an order ⊃See Extra help page **Punctuation** on page Centre 18.

exclude /ɪks'klu:d/ *verb* [T] **1** KEEP OUT to not allow someone or something to take part in an activity or enter a place [**often passive**] *Women are still **excluded from** the club.* **2** NOT INCLUDE to intentionally not include something *The insurance cover excludes particular medical conditions.* **3** POSSIBILITY to decide that something is certainly not true or possible *We can't **exclude** the **possibility** that he is dead.*

excluding /ɪks'klu:dɪŋ/ *preposition* not including *That's $600 per person for seven days, excluding travel costs.*

exclusion /ɪks'klu:ʒən/ *noun* **1** [C, U] when someone or something is not allowed to take part in an activity or to enter a place *the exclusion of disruptive pupils* ⊃Opposite **inclusion** **2 to the exclusion of sth** If you do something to the exclusion of something else, you do it so much that you have no time to do anything else.

exclusive¹ /ɪks'klu:sɪv/ *adjective* **1** EXPENSIVE expensive and only for people who are rich or of a high social class *an exclusive private club* **2 exclusive of sth** not including something *The price of the meal is exclusive of drinks.* ⊃Opposite **inclusive** **3** NOT SHARED not shared with another person, organization, newspaper, etc *an **exclusive interview***

exclusive² /ɪks'klu:sɪv/ *noun* [C] a news story that appears in only one newspaper or on one television programme

exclusively /ɪks'klu:sɪvli/ *adverb* only *an exclusively female audience*

excrement /'ekskrəmənt/ *noun* [U] *formal* solid waste that comes out of the bottom of a person or animal

excrete /ɪk'skri:t/ *verb* [I, T] **BIOLOGY** to get rid of waste substances from the body •**excretion** /ɪk'skri:ʃən/ *noun* [C, U]

excruciating /ɪk'skru:ʃieɪtɪŋ/ *adjective* very bad or painful *Her illness causes her **excruciating pain**.* •**excruciatingly** *adverb an **excruciatingly embarrassing** situation*

excursion /ɪk'skɜ:ʒən/ *noun* [C] a short journey made by a group of people for pleasure *We've booked to go on an **excursion to** Pompeii.*

excusable /ɪk'skju:zəbl/ *adjective* easy to forgive ⊃Opposite **inexcusable**

excuse¹ /ɪk'skju:z/ *verb* [T] **1** FORGIVE to forgive someone for something that is not very serious *Please excuse my appearance, I've been painting.* [+ **for** + **doing sth**] *She asked him to excuse her for being so rude.* **2** NOT DO to say that someone does not have to do something that they usually have to do *Could I be excused from football training today?* **3** EXPLAIN to be given as a reason for someone's bad behaviour, so that it does not seem so bad *Nothing can excuse what he did.* **4 excuse me a** ATTRACTING ATTENTION used to politely get someone's attention *Excuse me, does this bus go to Oxford Street?* **b** SAYING SORRY used to say sorry for something that you do without intending to *Oh, excuse me, did I take your seat?* •**excusable** *adjective*

WORD PARTNERS FOR ***excuse***

have/make/offer/think up an excuse • a **feeble/good** excuse

O-- **excuse²** /ɪk'skjuːs/ *noun* [C] **1** REASON a reason that you give to explain why you did something wrong [+ **for** + **doing sth**] *I hope he's got a good excuse for being so late.* **2** FALSE REASON a false reason that you give to explain why you do something *Nick was just looking for an excuse to call her.*

execute /'eksɪkjuːt/ *verb* [T] **1 LAW** to kill someone as a legal punishment *He was executed for murder.* **2** DO *formal* to do something, such as follow a plan or order *to **execute a deal/plan***

execution /ˌeksɪ'kjuːʃən/ *noun* **1 LAW** [C, U] when someone is killed as a legal punishment **2** DOING [U] when you do something, such as follow a plan or order *He was killed in **the execution of** his duties as a soldier.*

executioner /ˌeksɪ'kjuːʃənər/ *noun* [C] someone whose job is to execute criminals

executive¹ /ɪg'zekjətɪv/ *adjective* [**always before noun**] **1** OF MANAGEMENT relating to making decisions and managing businesses *an executive director* **2** FOR MANAGERS suitable for people who have important jobs in business *Peter always stays in the executive suite.*

executive² /ɪg'zekjətɪv/ *noun* **1** [C] someone who has an important job in a business *a company executive* **2 the executive** *mainly UK* the people who have the power to make decisions in an organization

exemplary /ɪg'zemplәri/ *adjective formal* very good and suitable to be copied by people *Sarah's behaviour is always exemplary.*

exemplify /ɪg'zemplɪfaɪ/ *verb* [T] *formal* to be or give a typical example of something

exempt¹ /ɪg'zempt/ *adjective* [**never before noun**] with special permission not to have to do something or pay something *The first £4,000 that you earn is **exempt from** tax.*

exempt² /ɪg'zempt/ *verb* [T] *formal* to officially say that someone does not have to do something or pay for something [**often passive**] *Students are **exempted from** payment.* •**exemption** /ɪg'zempʃən/ *noun* [C, U]

WORD PARTNERS FOR ***exercise***

do/get/take exercise • **daily/gentle/regular/strenuous** exercise • a **form of** exercise

O-- **exercise¹** /'eksәsaɪz/ *noun* **1 HEALTH** [C, U] physical activity that you do to make your body strong and healthy *Swimming is my favourite **form of exercise**.* ○ *Let's **do** some stretching **exercises** to start with.* **2 EDUCATION** [C] a piece of written work that helps you learn something *For your homework, please **do exercise** 3 on page 24.* **3** ACTIVITY WITH PURPOSE [C] an activity which is intended to achieve a particular thing *The whole **point of the exercise** was to get people to share their ideas.* ○ *a team-building exercise.* **4** MILITARY [C] a set of actions that a group of soldiers do to practise their skills *The cadets are out on military exercises.* **5** USE [U] *formal* the use of something such as a power or right

exercise² /'eksәsaɪz/ *verb* **1 HEALTH** [I, T] to do physical activities to make your body strong and healthy *I try to exercise every day.* **2** [T] *formal* to use a power, right, or ability *You should always **exercise** your **right** to vote.*

exert /ɪg'zɜːt/ *verb* **1** [T] to use something such as authority, power, influence, etc in order to make something happen *My parents **exerted** a lot of pressure **on** me to do well at school.* **2 exert yourself** to use a lot of physical or mental energy to do something *She was too ill to exert herself much.*

exertion /ɪg'zɜːʃən/ *noun* [C, U] when you use a lot of physical or mental energy to do something *I get out of breath with any kind of **physical exertion**.*

exhale /eks'heɪl/ *verb* [I, T] *formal* **BIOLOGY** to send air out of your lungs ➲Opposite **inhale**

exhaust¹ /ɪg'zɔːst/ *verb* [T] **1** SUPPLY to finish all of the supply of something *How long will it be before the world's fuel **supplies** are **exhausted**?* **2** TIRED to make someone very tired **3** SUBJECT to say everything possible about a subject *We seem to have exhausted that topic of conversation.*

exhaust² /ɪg'zɔːst/ *noun* **1** GAS [U] the waste gas from a vehicle's engine ***exhaust fumes*** **2** PIPE [C] (*also* **exhaust pipe**) *mainly UK* the pipe that waste gas from a vehicle's engine flows through ➲See colour picture **Car** on page Centre 7

exhausted /ɪg'zɔːstɪd/ *adjective* very tired

exhausting /ɪg'zɔːstɪŋ/ *adjective* making you feel very tired *What an exhausting day!*

exhaustion /ɪg'zɔːstʃən/ *noun* [U] when you are extremely tired *The tennis star was **suffering from exhaustion**.*

exhaustive /ɪg'zɔːstɪv/ *adjective* complete and including everything *an exhaustive account of the incident*

ex'haust ˌpipe *mainly UK* (*also US* **tailpipe**) *noun* [C] the pipe that waste gas from a vehicle's engine flows through

exhibit¹ /ɪg'zɪbɪt/ *verb* **1** SHOW OBJECTS [I, T] to show objects such as paintings to the public *She's exhibiting her roses at the local flower show.* **2** SHOW FEELINGS [T] *formal* to show a feeling, quality, or ability *The crew exhibited great courage when the plane crashed.*

exhibit² /ɪg'zɪbɪt/ *noun* [C] an object such as a painting that is shown to the public *a museum exhibit* •**exhibitor** *noun* [C] someone who shows something that they own or have made to the public

exhibition /ˌeksɪˈbɪʃᵊn/ *noun* **1** OBJECTS [C, U] when objects such as paintings are shown to the public *There's a new **exhibition of** sculpture on at the city gallery.* ○ *an exhibition centre* **2** SKILLS/QUALITIES [C] when someone shows a particular skill or quality that they have to the public

exhibitionist /ˌeksɪˈbɪʃᵊnɪst/ *noun* [C] someone who tries to attract attention to themselves with their behaviour •**exhibitionism** /ˌeksɪˈbɪʃᵊnɪzᵊm/ *noun* [U] behaviour which tries to attract attention

E

exhilarated /ɪɡˈzɪləreɪtɪd/ *adjective* very excited and happy

exhilarating /ɪɡˈzɪləreɪtɪŋ/ *adjective* making you feel very excited and happy *There's nothing more exhilarating than water-skiing.*

exhilaration /ɪɡˌzɪlᵊrˈeɪʃᵊn/ *noun* [U] when you feel very excited and happy

exhort /ɪɡˈzɔːt/ *verb* [T] *formal* to strongly encourage someone to do something •**exhortation** /ˌeɡzɔːˈteɪʃᵊn/ *noun* [C, U]

exile /ˈeksaɪl, ˈeɡzaɪl/ *noun* **1** **POLITICS** [U] when someone has to leave their home and live in another country, often for political reasons *He spent the war years **in exile** in New York.* ○ *The King was forced **into exile**.* **2** PERSON [C] someone who is forced to live in another country *She lived the rest of her life as an exile in the UK.* •**exile** *verb* [T] to force someone to leave their home and live in another country, often for political reasons •**exiled** *adjective*

O--**exist** /ɪɡˈzɪst/ *verb* [I] **1** BE REAL to be real or present *Poverty still exists in this country.* **2** LIVE to live in difficult conditions *You can't exist without water for more than a week.*

WORD PARTNERS FOR ***existence***

come into/go out of existence • be **in** existence • the existence **of** sth

existence /ɪɡˈzɪstᵊns/ *noun* **1** EXISTING [U] when something or someone exists *She never doubted **the existence of** God.* ○ *The theatre company that we started is still **in existence** today.* ○ *When did the Football League **come into existence*** (= begin to exist)? **2** LIFE [C] a particular way of life *We could have a much more peaceful existence in the countryside.*

existing /ɪɡˈzɪstɪŋ/ *adjective* [**always before noun**] which exist or are used at the present time *Existing schools will have to be expanded to accommodate the extra students.* ➲See also: **pre-existing**

O--**exit¹** /ˈeksɪt/ *noun* [C] **1** DOOR the door or gate which you use to leave a public building or place *a **fire exit*** ○ *an **emergency exit*** **2** LEAVING when someone leaves a place *Sue **made a** quick **exit** when she saw Mick come in.* **3** ROAD a road which you use to leave a motorway (= wide, fast road) or roundabout (= place where three or more main roads meet) ***Take** the third **exit** at the next roundabout.*

exit² /ˈeksɪt/ *verb* [I, T] **1** **COMPUTING** to stop using a program on a computer *Press escape to exit the game.* **2** *formal* to leave a place or a competition

ˈexit ˌstrategy *noun* [C] a plan that you use to get out of a difficult situation *A good politician will plan his exit strategy before announcing his retirement from office.*

exodus /ˈeksədəs/ *noun* [**no plural**] when a large number of people all leave a place together *There has been **a mass exodus** of workers from the villages to the towns.*

exonerate /ɪɡˈzɒnᵊreɪt/ *verb* [T] *formal* to say that someone is not guilty of doing something that they have been blamed for [**often passive**] *He was **exonerated of** all blame by the investigation.* •**exoneration** /ɪɡˌzɒnəˈreɪʃᵊn/ *noun* [U]

exorbitant /ɪɡˈzɔːbɪtᵊnt/ *adjective* Exorbitant prices or costs are much too high.

exorcism /ˈeksɔːsɪzᵊm/ *noun* [C, U] **RELIGION** when an evil spirit is exorcized

exorcize (*also UK* **-ise**) /ˈeksɔːsaɪz/ *verb* [T] **1** **RELIGION** to make evil spirits leave a person or place by saying special prayers and having a special ceremony **2** to get rid of something such as a bad memory *She moved to Paris to try to exorcize the past.*

exoskeleton /ˈeksəʊskelɪtᵊn/ *noun* [C] **ANATOMY, BIOLOGY** a hard outer layer that covers and protects the body of some animals, such as insects ➲Compare **endoskeleton**

exothermic reaction /eksəʊˌθɜːmɪkriˈækʃᵊn/ *noun* [C] **CHEMISTRY** a chemical reaction in which heat is produced ➲Compare **endothermic reaction**

exotic /ɪɡˈzɒtɪk/ *adjective* unusual, interesting, and often foreign *exotic fruits*

expand /ɪkˈspænd/ *verb* [I, T] to increase in size or amount, or to make something increase *We are hoping to **expand** our **range** of products.*
expand on sth *phrasal verb* to give more details about something that you have said or written *She mentioned a few ideas, but she didn't expand on them.*

exˌpanded polyˈstyrene *noun* [U] **DT** a type of polystyrene (= light white plastic substance) often used to protect goods when they are packed

expanse /ɪkˈspæns/ *noun* [C] a large, open area of land, sea, or sky *a vast expanse of water*

expansion /ɪkˈspænʃᵊn/ *noun* [U] when something increases in size or amount *the rapid expansion of the software industry*

expansive /ɪkˈspænsɪv/ *adjective formal* very happy to talk to people in a friendly way *He was in an **expansive mood** on the night of the party.*

expatriate /ɪkˈspætriət/ (*also UK* **expat** /ˌekˈspat/ *informal*) *noun* [C] someone who does not live in their own country •**expatriate** *adjective*

O--**expect** /ɪkˈspekt/ *verb* **1** SITUATION [T] to think that something will happen [+ **to do sth**] *He didn't expect to see me.* [+ **(that)**] *I expect that she'll be very angry about this.* **2** **be expecting sb/sth** to be waiting for someone or something to arrive *I'm expecting a letter from my sister.* **3** BEHAVIOUR [T] to think that someone should behave in a particular way or do a particular thing [+ **to do sth**] *You will be expected to work some weekends.* **4** **I expect** *mainly UK informal* used to show that you think that something is likely to be true *I expect Isabel's told you about me?* ○ *"Will you be coming to the party?" "**I expect so.**"* **5 be expecting** to be going to have a baby *I'm expecting my first baby in May.* ➲See Common Learner Error at **wait**

expectancy /ɪk'spektᵊnsi/ *noun* [U] when you think that something pleasant or exciting is going to happen *An air of expectancy filled the room.* ➲See also: **life expectancy**

expectant /ɪk'spektᵊnt/ *adjective* **1** thinking that something pleasant or exciting is going to happen *the children's expectant faces* **2 an expectant mother/father, etc** someone who is going to have a baby soon •**expectantly** *adverb*

WORD PARTNERS FOR ***expectation***

have high/have low expectations • **live up to/meet** (sb's) expectations • expectations **of** sth

expectation /ˌekspek'teɪʃᵊn/ *noun* **1** EXPECTING SOMETHING GOOD [C] when you expect good things to happen in the future [**usually plural**] *The holiday **lived up to** all our **expectations*** (= was as good as we expected). ○ *My parents **had high expectations** for me* (= expected me to be successful). **2** EXPECTING SOMETHING [C, U] when you expect something to happen *He had gone away and there was no **expectation of** his return.*

expedient¹ /ɪk'spiːdiənt/ *adjective formal* An expedient action achieves a useful purpose, although it may not be moral. *It might be expedient not to pay him until the work is finished.* •**expediency** /ɪk'spiːdiənsi/ *noun* [U] when something is expedient *an issue of political expediency*

expedient² /ɪk'spiːdiənt/ *noun* [C] *formal* a useful or clever action

expedite /'ekspɪdaɪt/ *verb* [T] *formal* to make an action or process happen more quickly

expedition /ˌekspɪ'dɪʃᵊn/ *noun* [C] an organized journey, especially a long one for a particular purpose *Peary **led** the first **expedition** to the North Pole.* ○ *a **shopping expedition***

expel /ɪk'spel/ *verb* [T] **expelling,** *past* **expelled** **1** MAKE SOMEONE LEAVE to make someone leave a school, organization, or country because of their behaviour [**often passive**] *He was **expelled from** school **for** hitting another student.* **2** FORCE SOMETHING OUT *formal* to force air, gas, or liquid out of something

expend /ɪk'spend/ *verb* [T] *formal* to use effort, time, or money to do something [+ **doing sth**] *You **expend** far too much **energy** doing things for other people.* ○ *Governments **expend** a lot of resources **on** war.*

expendable /ɪk'spendəbl/ *adjective* If someone or something is expendable, people can do something or deal with a situation without them. *He considers his staff as temporary and expendable.*

expenditure /ɪk'spendɪtʃəʳ/ *noun* [U] *formal* **1** FINANCE the total amount of money that a government or person spends *The government's annual **expenditure on** arms has been reduced.* **2** when you use energy, time, or money

O⁻**expense** /ɪk'spens/ *noun* **1** FINANCE [C, U] the money that you spend on something *You have to **pay** your own medical **expenses**.* ○ *He eventually found her the car she wanted, **at great expense*** (= it cost him a lot of money). **2 at the expense of sth** If you do one thing at the expense of another, doing the first thing harms the second thing. *He spent a lot of time at work, at the expense of his marriage.* **3 at sb's expense** **a** If you do something at someone's expense, they pay for it. *We went on holiday at my father's expense.* **b** in order to make someone look stupid *Stop making jokes at my expense.*

expenses /ɪk'spensɪz/ *noun* [**plural**] FINANCE money that you spend when you are doing your job, that your employer will pay back to you *travel expenses* ○ *They pay us two hundred pounds a week, plus expenses.*

O⁻**expensive** /ɪk'spensɪv/ *adjective* costing a lot of money *expensive jewellery* [+ **to do sth**] *It's too expensive to go out every night.* ➲Opposite **inexpensive** •**expensively** *adverb expensively dressed*

WORD PARTNERS FOR ***experience***

gain/have/lack experience • **good/previous/useful/wide** experience • experience **in/of** sth • **from** experience • **in my** experience

O⁻**experience¹** /ɪk'spɪəriəns/ *noun* **1** KNOWLEDGE [U] knowledge that you get from doing a job, or from doing, seeing, or feeling something *Do you have any **experience of** working with children?* ○ *He knows **from experience** not to play with fire.* ○ ***In my experience**, people smile back if you smile at them.* **2** SOMETHING THAT HAPPENS TO YOU [C] something that happens to you that affects how you feel *My trip to Australia was an experience I'll never forget.*

experience² /ɪk'spɪəriəns/ *verb* [T] If you experience something, it happens to you, or you feel it. *It was the worst pain I had ever experienced.* ○ *We experienced a lot of difficulty in selling our house.*

experienced /ɪk'spɪəriənst/ *adjective* having skill and knowledge because you have done something many times *Karsten's a very experienced ski instructor.* ➲Opposite **inexperienced**

WORD PARTNERS FOR ***experiment***

conduct/do/perform an experiment • an experiment **on** sth

O⁻**experiment¹** /ɪk'sperɪmənt/ *noun* [C] a test, especially a scientific one, that you do in order to learn something or discover if something is true *to **conduct/do/perform** an **experiment*** ○ *They're conducting **experiments on** hamster cells to test the effects of the drug.*

experiment² /ɪk'sperɪment/ *verb* [I] **1** TRY SOMETHING to try something in order to discover what it is like *Did he ever **experiment with** drugs?* **2** DO TESTS to do an experiment ***Experimenting on** mice can give us an idea of the effect of the disease in humans.* •**experimentation** /ɪkˌsperɪmen'teɪʃᵊn/ *noun* [U]

experimental /ɪkˌsperɪ'mentᵊl/ *adjective* relating to tests, especially scientific ones •**experimentally** *adverb*

O‑ **expert**[1] /ˈekspɜːt/ *noun* [C] someone who has a lot of skill in something or a lot of knowledge about something *He's **an expert on** Japanese literature.*

expert[2] /ˈekspɜːt/ *adjective* [always before noun] having a lot of skill in something or knowing a lot about something *I need some **expert advice** on investments.* ○ *What's your **expert opinion**?* •**expertly** *adverb He carved the roast expertly.*

E

expertise /ˌekspɜːˈtiːz/ *noun* [U] skill *the technical expertise of the engineers*

ˈ**expert** ˌ**system** *noun* [C] COMPUTING a computer system which asks questions and gives answers that have been thought of by a person who knows a lot about a subject

expiration /ekspɪˈreɪʃən/ *noun* [U, C] BIOLOGY the act of breathing out air, or a breath going out

expire /ɪkˈspaɪəʳ/ *verb* [I] **1** LAW If a legal document or agreement expires, you can no longer use it. *Your contract expired six months ago.* **2** BIOLOGY to breathe out air

expiry /ɪkˈspaɪəri/ *noun* [U] *UK* the end of a period when something can be used *What's **the expiry date** on your passport?*

OTHER WAYS OF SAYING ***explain***

If someone is explaining something in order to make it easier for someone else to understand, you can use the verb **clarify**: *Let me just **clarify** what I mean here.*

The verb **define** is sometimes used when explaining exactly what something means: *Your responsibilities are clearly **defined** in the contract.*

If something is being explained clearly in writing, the phrasal verb **set out** is sometimes used: *Your contract will **set out** the terms of your employment.*

If something is being explained in great detail, the phrasal verb **spell out** is often used: *They sent me a letter, **spelling out** the details of the agreement.*

O‑ **explain** /ɪkˈspleɪn/ *verb* [I, T] to make something clear or easy to understand by giving reasons for it or details about it [+ question word] *Can you explain why you did this?* ○ *Can you **explain to** me how this mobile phone works?* [+ (that)] *He explained that he was going to stay with his sister.* •**explaining** *noun* [U] when you have to explain or give a good reason for your actions *You'll **have** a lot of **explaining to do** when dad finds out what happened.*

COMMON LEARNER ERROR

explain something

Explain is followed by the thing you are explaining.

I'll explain the situation.

Remember to use the preposition **to** before a person.

I'll explain the situation to my parents.

~~*I'll explain the situation my parents.*~~

WORD PARTNERS FOR ***explanation***

demand/give/have/offer an explanation • a **clear/possible/satisfactory/simple** explanation • an explanation **for** sth

O‑ **explanation** /ˌekspləˈneɪʃən/ *noun* [C, U] the details or reasons that someone gives to make something clear or easy to understand *What's your **explanation for** the team's poor performance?* ○ *Could you give me a quick **explanation of** how it works?*

explanatory /ɪkˈsplænətəri/ *adjective* giving an explanation about something *There are **explanatory notes** with the diagram.* ⊃See also: **self-explanatory**

expletive /ɪkˈspliːtɪv/ (US) /ˈekspləṭɪv/ *noun* [C] *formal* a swear word (= word which people think is rude or offensive)

explicable /ɪkˈsplɪkəbl/ *adjective formal* Something that is explicable can be explained. ⊃Opposite **inexplicable**

explicit /ɪkˈsplɪsɪt/ *adjective* **1** CLEAR clear and exact *She was very **explicit about** her plans.* ○ *He made no **explicit references** to Tess.* **2** SHOWING SEX showing or talking about sex or violence in a very detailed way *a **sexually explicit** film* •**explicitly** *adverb She **explicitly stated** that she did not want her name to be revealed.*

O‑ **explode** /ɪkˈspləʊd/ *verb* **1** BOMB [I, T] If something such as a bomb explodes, it bursts (= breaks suddenly from inside) with noise and force, and if you explode it, you make it burst with noise and force. *One of the bombs did not explode.* **2** GET ANGRY [I] to suddenly start shouting because you are very angry

exploit[1] /ɪkˈsplɔɪt/ *verb* [T] **1** TREAT UNFAIRLY to not pay or reward someone enough for something [often passive] *I felt as though I was being exploited.* **2** USE to use or develop something for your advantage *We are not fully exploiting all the resources that we have.* •**exploitation** /ˌeksplɔɪˈteɪʃən/ *noun* [U] *the exploitation of child workers*

exploit[2] /ˈeksplɔɪt/ *noun* [C] something unusual, brave, or interesting that someone has done [usually plural] *Have you heard about her amazing exploits travelling in Africa?*

exploratory /ɪkˈsplɒrətəri/ *adjective* done in order to discover or learn about something *an exploratory expedition* ○ *an exploratory operation*

explore /ɪkˈsplɔːʳ/ *verb* **1** LOOK AROUND [I, T] to go around a place where you have never been in order to find out what is there *The children love exploring.* ○ *The best way to explore the countryside is on foot.* **2** THINK CAREFULLY [T] to think about something very carefully before you make a decision about it *We're **exploring the possibility** of buying a holiday home.* •**exploration** /ˌekspləˈreɪʃən/ *noun* [C, U] *She's always loved travel and exploration.*

explorer /ɪkˈsplɔːrəʳ/ *noun* [C] someone who travels to places where no one has ever been in order to find out what is there

O‑ **explosion** /ɪkˈspləʊʒən/ *noun* [C] **1** BOMB when something such as a bomb explodes *Forty people were killed in the explosion.* **2** INCREASE when something increases suddenly by a large amount *the recent **population explosion***

explosive¹ /ɪk'spləʊsɪv/ *adjective* **1** EQUIPMENT An explosive substance or piece of equipment can cause explosions. *The **explosive device** was hidden in a suitcase.* **2** SITUATION An explosive situation or subject causes strong feelings, and may make people angry or violent. *a highly explosive political issue*

explosive² /ɪk'spləʊsɪv/ *noun* [C] a substance or piece of equipment that can cause explosions

exponent /ɪk'spəʊnənt/ *noun* [C] **1** someone who supports a particular idea or belief, or performs a particular activity *The early **exponents of** votes for women suffered greatly.* **2** **MATHEMATICS** a number or sign which shows how many times another number is to be multiplied by itself

exponential /ˌekspəʊ'nentʃəl/ *adjective* **1** **MATHEMATICS** *formal* increasing extremely quickly *There has been an exponential increase in the world population in the last hundred years.* **2** **MATHEMATICS** containing an exponent (= number or sign which shows how many times you should multiply another number by itself)

export¹ /'ekspɔːt/ *noun* **ECONOMICS** **1** [C] a product that you sell in another country *Scottish beef exports to Japan* **2** [U] the business of sending goods to another country in order to sell them there *the export of industrial goods* ⊃Opposite **import**

export² /ɪk'spɔːt/ *verb* [I, T] **1** **ECONOMICS** to send goods to another country in order to sell them there *Singapore exports large quantities of rubber.* ⊃Opposite **import** **2** **COMPUTING** If you export information from a computer, you copy it to another place. ●**exporter** *noun* [C] *Brazil is the world's largest exporter of coffee.*

expose /ɪk'spəʊz/ *verb* [T] **1** HIDDEN THING to remove what is covering something so that it can be seen *Our bodies need to be exposed to sunlight in order to make vitamin D.* **2** BAD THING to make public something bad or something that is not honest *The review exposed widespread corruption in the police force.* **3** **be exposed to sth** to experience something or be affected by something because you are in a particular situation or place *It was the first time I'd been exposed to violence.* **4** PHOTOGRAPHY to allow light to reach a piece of camera film in order to produce a photograph

exposed /ɪk'spəʊzd/ *adjective* having no protection from bad weather *an exposed cliff*

exposure /ɪk'spəʊʒəʳ/ *noun* **1** EXPERIENCING [U] when someone experiences something or is affected by it because they are in a particular situation or place *There is a risk of **exposure to** radiation.* ○ *Many young children now have exposure to computers in the home.* **2** MAKING PUBLIC [C, U] when something bad that you have done is made public *She was threatened with exposure by a journalist.* **3** **HEALTH** [U] a serious medical condition that is caused by being outside in very cold weather **4** PHOTOGRAPH [C] a single photograph on a piece of film *This film has 24 exposures.*

expound /ɪk'spaʊnd/ *verb* [I, T] *formal* to give a detailed explanation of something *He's always **expounding on** what's wrong with the world.* ○ *She uses her newspaper column to **expound** her **views** on environmental issues.*

O→**express¹** /ɪk'spres/ *verb* [T] to show what you think or how you feel using words or actions *I'm simply expressing my opinion.* [**often reflexive**] *You're not expressing yourself* (= saying what you mean) *very clearly.*

express² /ɪk'spres/ *adjective* **1** **an express service/train, etc** a service, train, etc that is much faster than usual *an express train* ○ *an express service* **2** **an express aim/intention/purpose, etc** a clear and certain aim, intention, purpose, etc *You came here with the express purpose of causing trouble.*

express³ /ɪk'spres/ (*also* **ex'press ˌtrain**) *noun* [C] a fast train *I took the express to London.*

WORD PARTNERS FOR ***expression***

have a [pained, puzzled, etc] expression **on your face** • an expression **changes** • an **angry/dazed/pained/puzzled** expression • **facial** expression

O→**expression** /ɪk'spreʃən/ *noun* **1** LOOK [C] the look on someone's face showing what they feel or think *your **facial expression*** ○ *He had a sad expression on his face.* **2** PHRASE [C] a phrase that has a special meaning *'A can of worms' is an expression meaning a difficult situation.* **3** SHOWING THOUGHTS [C, U] when you say what you think or show how you feel using words or actions *As **an expression of** our disapproval, we will no longer use his shop.*

expressive /ɪk'spresɪv/ *adjective* showing your feelings *a very expressive face*

expressly /ɪk'spresli/ *adverb formal* **1** CLEARLY If you say something expressly, you say it in a clear way, so that your meaning cannot be doubted. *I **expressly stated** that I did not want any visitors.* **2** SPECIALLY If something is expressly for a particular reason or person, it is for that reason or person only. *The picture was painted expressly for me.*

expressway /ɪk'spresweɪ/ *US* (*UK* **motorway**) *noun* [C] a long, wide road, usually used by traffic travelling fast over long distances

expulsion /ɪk'spʌlʃən/ *noun* [C, U] when someone is made to leave their school, organization, or country because of their behaviour *They threatened him with **expulsion from** school.*

exquisite /ɪk'skwɪzɪt/ *adjective* very beautiful or perfect *a garden of exquisite flowers* ●**exquisitely** *adverb an exquisitely dressed woman*

extend /ɪk'stend/ *verb* **1** MAKE BIGGER [T] to make something bigger or longer *We're going to extend our kitchen.* **2** MAKE LAST [T] to make an activity, agreement, etc last for a longer time *They have extended the deadline by one week.* **3** **extend from/into/over, etc** to continue or stretch over a particular area of land or period of time *Will the building work extend into next week?* **4** STRETCH OUT [T] to stretch out a part of your body *She smiled and extended her hand.* **5** **extend an invitation/thanks, etc to sb** *formal* to give someone an invitation, thanks, etc *I'd like to extend a warm welcome to our guests.*

extension /ɪk'stenʃən/ *noun* [C] **1** PART OF A BUILDING a new room or rooms that are added to a building *You could build an extension onto the back of the house.* **2** EXTRA TIME extra time that you are given to do or use something *You might be able to get an extension on your visa.* **3** TELEPHONE a telephone that is connected to the main telephone in an office or other large building *Call me on extension 213.*

extensive /ɪk'stensɪv/ *adjective* large in amount or size *an **extensive** art **collection*** ○ *The hurricane caused **extensive damage**.* •**extensively** *adverb I have **travelled extensively** in Europe.*

extensor (muscle) /ɪk'stensəʳ/ *noun* [C] **ANATOMY, BIOLOGY** a muscle that allows you to make part of your body straight ➲Compare **flexor (muscle)**

WORD PARTNERS FOR ***extent***

the **full/true** extent of sth • **to such** an extent • the extent **of** sth

extent /ɪk'stent/ *noun* **1** [**no plural**] the size or importance of something *They are just beginning to realize the **full extent** of the damage.* ○ *Her face was injured **to such an extent*** (= so much) *that he didn't recognize her.* **2 to some extent/to a certain extent** in some ways *I was, to some extent, responsible for the accident.*

exterior /ɪk'stɪəriəʳ/ *noun* [C] the outside part of something or someone [**usually singular**] *The exterior of the house was painted white.* •**exterior** *adjective* [**always before noun**] *an exterior wall* ➲Opposite **interior**

exterminate /ɪk'stɜːmɪneɪt/ *verb* [T] to kill a large group of people or animals •**extermination** /ɪkˌstɜːmɪ'neɪʃən/ *noun* [**C, U**]

external /ɪk'stɜːnəl/ *adjective* **1** OUTSIDE relating to the outside part of something *the **external** walls of the house* ○ *The ointment is **for external use** only* (= it must not be put inside the body). **2** FROM ANOTHER PLACE coming from or relating to another country, group, or organization *All exams are marked by an **external examiner**.* ➲Opposite **internal** •**externally** *adverb*

extinct /ɪk'stɪŋkt/ *adjective* **BIOLOGY** If a type of animal is extinct, it does not now exist.

extinction /ɪk'stɪŋkʃən/ *noun* [U] **BIOLOGY** when a type of animal no longer exists *Many species of animal are **threatened with extinction**.*

extinguish /ɪk'stɪŋgwɪʃ/ *verb* [T] *formal* to stop something burning or giving out light *The fire took two hours to extinguish.*

extinguisher /ɪk'stɪŋgwɪʃəʳ/ (*also* **fire extinguisher**) *noun* [C] a piece of equipment shaped like a tube, which is used to spread a substance onto a fire to stop it burning

extol /ɪk'stəʊl/ *verb* [T] **extolling**, *past* **extolled** to say that you think that something is very good *He always **extols the virtues of*** (= praises) *French cooking.*

extort /ɪk'stɔːt/ *verb* [T] to get money from someone by saying that you will harm them •**extortion** /ɪk'stɔːʃən/ *noun* [U]

extortionate /ɪk'stɔːʃənət/ *adjective* Extortionate prices or costs are very high.

O— **extra¹** /'ekstrə/ *adjective* more, or more than usual *Can I invite a few extra people?* ○ *She's been babysitting to earn some extra cash.*

WORD PARTNERS FOR ***extra***

an **added/hidden/optional** extra

extra² /'ekstrə/ *noun* [C] **1** MORE something that costs more when you buy goods or pay for a service *The hi-fi comes with **optional extras** such as headphones and remote control.* **2** ACTOR an actor in a film who does not have a main part and usually plays someone in a crowd

extra³ /'ekstrə/ *adverb* more than usual *Do you get paid extra for working late?*

extra- /ekstrə-/ *prefix* outside of or in addition to *extracurricular activities* (= activities that are in addition to the usual school work)

extracellular /ˌekstrə'seljələʳ/ *adjective* **BIOLOGY** being or happening outside a cell

extract¹ /ɪk'strækt/ *verb* [T] *formal* **1** TAKE OUT to take something out, especially using force *He's going to the dentist's to have a tooth extracted.* **2** GET MONEY/INFORMATION to get the money, information, etc that you want from someone who does not want to give it to you *They were not able to extract a confession from her.*

extract² /'ekstrækt/ *noun* [C] **1** WRITING a particular part of a book, poem, etc that is chosen so that it can be used in a discussion, article, etc *The teacher read out **an extract from** 'Brave New World'.* **2** SUBSTANCE a substance taken from a plant, flower, etc and used especially in food or medicine *pure vanilla extract*

extraction /ɪk'strækʃən/ *noun* **1** [**C, U**] when something is taken out, especially using force **2 of Chinese/Italian, etc extraction** having a family whose origin is Chinese, Italian, etc

extradite /'ekstrədaɪt/ *verb* [T] to send someone back to the country where they are accused of a crime, so that a court there can decide if they are guilty [**often passive**] *The suspects were **extradited to** the UK.* •**extradition** /ˌekstrə'dɪʃən/ *noun* [**C, U**]

extraneous /ɪk'streɪniəs/ *adjective* not directly connected to something *extraneous information/noise*

extranet /'ekstrənet/ *noun* [C] **COMPUTING, INTERNET** a system of computers that makes it possible for organizations to communicate with each other and share information *The extranet will link the company with its customers and suppliers.*

extraordinary /ɪk'strɔːdənəri/ *adjective* very special, unusual, or strange *an extraordinary tale of courage* ○ *She was an extraordinary young woman.* •**extraordinarily** *adverb Their last album was extraordinarily successful.*

extravagant /ɪk'strævəgənt/ *adjective* **1** WASTING MONEY costing too much or spending a lot more money than you need to *the **extravagant lifestyle** of a movie star* **2** NOT ACCEPTABLE too unusual and extreme to be believed or controlled *the **extravagant claims** made by* *cosmetics companies* •**extravagance** /ɪk'strævəgəns/ *noun* [C, U] when someone or something is extravagant •**extravagantly** *adverb*

extravaganza /ɪkˌstrævə'gænzə/ *noun* [C] a large, exciting, and expensive event or entertainment *a three-hour extravaganza of country music*

extreme[1] /ɪk'striːm/ *adjective* **1** SERIOUS the most unusual or most serious possible *extreme weather conditions* ○ ***In extreme cases**, the disease can lead to blindness.* **2** VERY LARGE very large in amount or degree *extreme pain* ○ *extreme wealth* **3** OPINIONS having such strong opinions or beliefs that most people cannot agree with you *extreme views* ○ *the extreme right* **4** FURTHEST [always before noun] at the furthest point of something *in the extreme south of the island*

extreme[2] /ɪk'striːm/ *noun* [C] the largest possible amount or degree of something *Anna's moods went **from one extreme to another*** (= first she was very happy, then she was very unhappy). ○ *Coach Wilson **took** our training **to extremes*** (= made us train extremely hard).

O⁻ **extremely** /ɪk'striːmli/ *adverb* very, or much more than usual *extremely beautiful*

exˌtreme 'sports *noun* [C, U] **SPORT** a game or activity which people do that is dangerous *Extreme sports such as bungee jumping and snowboarding*

extremist /ɪk'striːmɪst/ *noun* [C] **POLITICS** someone who has such strong opinions or beliefs that most people cannot agree with them •**extremism** /ɪk'striːmɪzᵊm/ *noun* [U] •**extremist** *adjective*

extremities /ɪk'stremətiz/ *noun* [plural] **BIOLOGY** the end parts of your body such as your hands and feet

extremity /ɪk'streməti/ *noun formal* **1** FAR AWAY [C] the part of something that is furthest from the centre *at the north-west extremity of Europe* **2** FEELING/SITUATION [U] when a feeling is very strong or a bad situation very serious

extricate /'ekstrɪkeɪt/ *verb* **extricate yourself from sth** to get yourself out of a difficult situation or unpleasant place *I can't extricate myself from this embarrassing situation.*

extrovert /'ekstrəvɜːt/ *noun* [C] someone who is very confident and likes being with other people ➲Opposite **introvert** •**extrovert** *adjective an extrovert personality* ➲Opposite **introverted**

extrude /ɪk'struːd/ *noun* [T] **DT** to form something by forcing or pushing it out, especially through a small opening *extruded aluminium rods* •**extrusion** /ɪk'struːʒən/ *noun* [U]

exuberant /ɪg'zjuːbᵊrᵊnt/ *adjective* full of happiness, excitement, and energy *a warm and exuberant personality* •**exuberance** /ɪg'zjuːbᵊrᵊns/ *noun* [U]

exude /ɪg'zjuːd/ *verb* [T] If you exude love, confidence, pain, etc, you show that you have a lot of that feeling.

exult /ɪg'zʌlt/ *verb* [I] to show great pleasure, especially at someone else's defeat or failure *She seems to **exult in** her power.* •**exultation** /ˌegzʌl'teɪʃᵊn/ *noun* [U]

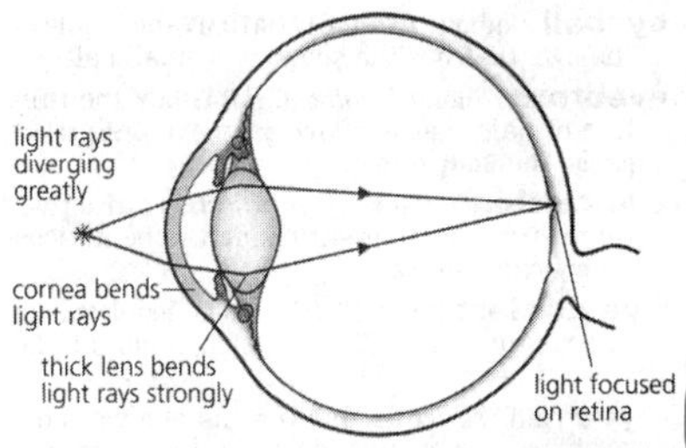

the eye: focusing on a nearby object

O⁻ **eye**[1] /aɪ/ *noun* **1 ANATOMY** [C] one of the two organs in your face, which you use to see with *Sara has black hair and brown eyes.* ○ *She **closed** her **eyes** and fell off to sleep.* **2** NEEDLE [C] the small hole at the end of a needle, that you put the thread through **3 have an eye for sth** to be good at noticing a particular type of thing *Your son has a very good eye for detail.* **4 keep your/an eye on sb/sth** to watch or look after someone or something *Could you keep an eye on this pan of soup for a moment?* **5 have your eye on sth** *informal* to want something and intend to get it *Jane's got her eye on that new advertising job.* **6 can't keep/take your eyes off sb/sth** to be unable to stop looking at someone or something because they are so attractive or interesting *He couldn't take his eyes off her all night.* **7 lay/set eyes on sb/sth** to see someone or something for the first time *They fell in love the moment they laid eyes on each other.* **8 look sb in the eye/eyes** to look at someone in a direct way, without showing fear or shame *Look me in the eye and say that you didn't steal it.* **9 in sb's eyes** in someone's opinion *In my parents' eyes, I'll always be a child.* **10 cast/run your/an eye over sth** *UK* to look at something quickly, often in order to give your opinion about it *Would you cast an eye over our work so far?* **11 catch sb's eye a** GET SOMEONE'S ATTENTION to get someone's attention by looking at them *I tried to catch her eye, but she had already turned away.* **b** BE NOTICED to be attractive or different enough to be noticed by people *It was the colour of his jacket that caught my eye.* **12 cry your eyes out** If someone cries their eyes out, they cry a lot about a problem or situation. **13 keep your eyes open/peeled (for sb/sth)** to watch carefully for someone or something *Keep your eyes peeled, he should be here any minute.* **14 keep an eye out for sb/sth** to watch carefully for someone or something to appear *Keep an eye out for the delivery van.* **15 see eye to eye (with sb)** If two people see eye to eye, they agree with each other. **16 turn a blind eye (to sth)** to choose to ignore something that you know is wrong or illegal **17 with your eyes open** knowing about all of the problems that could happen if you do something *I went into this marriage with my eyes open.* ➲See also: **black eye**

eye[2] /aɪ/ *verb* [T] **eyeing**, *also US* **eying**, *past* **eyed** to look at someone or something with interest *The two women eyed each other suspiciously.*

eyeball /ˈaɪbɔːl/ *noun* [C] **ANATOMY** the whole of the eye, that has the shape of a small ball

eyebrow /ˈaɪbraʊ/ *noun* [C] **ANATOMY** the thin line of hair that is above each eye ➲See colour picture **The Body** on page Centre 13

eye-catching /ˈaɪˌkætʃɪŋ/ *adjective* attractive, interesting, or different enough to be noticed *an eye-catching poster*

ˈeye ˌcontact *noun* [U] *UK* If two people make eye contact, they look at each other at the same time.

E

-eyed /aɪd/ *suffix* used at the end of a word describing a person's eyes *Both sisters are brown-eyed.* ➲See also: **cross-eyed, wide-eyed**

eyelash /ˈaɪlæʃ/ (*also* **lash**) *noun* [C] **ANATOMY** one of the short hairs that grow from the edge of your eyelids [**usually plural**] *false eyelashes*

eyelid /ˈaɪlɪd/ *noun* [C] **1 ANATOMY** the piece of skin that covers your eye when you close it **2 not bat an eyelid** to not react to something unusual

eyeliner /ˈaɪˌlaɪnəʳ/ *noun* [C, U] a coloured substance, usually contained in a pencil, which you put in a line above or below your eyes in order to make them more attractive

eye-opener /ˈaɪˌəʊpᵊnəʳ/ *noun* [C] something that surprises you and teaches you new facts about life, people, etc *Living in another country can be a **real eye-opener**.*

eyeshadow /ˈaɪʃædəʊ/ *noun* [C, U] a coloured cream or powder which you put above or around your eyes in order to make them more attractive

eyesight /ˈaɪsaɪt/ *noun* [U] **HEALTH, BIOLOGY** the ability to see *My eyesight is getting worse.*

eyesore /ˈaɪsɔːʳ/ *noun* [C] a building, area, etc that looks ugly compared to the things that are around it

eyewitness /ˌaɪˈwɪtnɪs/ (*also* **witness**) *noun* [C] someone who saw something such as a crime or an accident happen *Eyewitnesses saw two men running away from the bank.*

F, f /ef/ the sixth letter of the alphabet

F **MEASURES** *written abbreviation for* Fahrenheit (= a measurement of temperature) *a body temperature of 98.6 °F*

FA /ˌef'eɪ/ *noun* **SPORT** *abbreviation for* Football Association: the national organization for football in England *the FA Cup*

fable /'feɪbl/ *noun* [C] **LITERATURE** a short, traditional story, usually involving animals, which is intended to show people how to behave *Aesop's fables*

fabric /'fæbrɪk/ *noun* **1** [C, U] cloth *a light/woollen fabric* **2 the fabric of sth a** the basic way in which a society or other social group is organized *The family is part of* ***the fabric of society.*** **b** *UK* the walls, floor, and roof of a building

fabricate /'fæbrɪkeɪt/ *verb* [T] to invent facts, a story, etc in order to deceive someone *He claims that the police* ***fabricated evidence*** *against him.* •**fabrication** /ˌfæbrɪ'keɪʃən/ *noun* [C, U]

fabulous /'fæbjələs/ *adjective* extremely good *They've got a fabulous house.* ○ *We had an absolutely fabulous holiday.* •**fabulously** *adverb* extremely *Her family is* ***fabulously wealthy.***

facade (*also* **façade**) /fə'sɑːd/ *noun* [C] **1** APPEARANCE a false appearance ***Behind*** *that amiable* ***facade,*** *he's a deeply unpleasant man.* **2** BUILDING the front of a large building *the gallery's elegant 18th century facade*

O⊸**face**[1] /feɪs/ *noun* **1 ANATOMY** [C] the front part of the head where the eyes, nose, and mouth are, or the expression on this part *She's got a long, thin face.* ○ *I can't wait to see her face when she opens the present.* **2 make a face** (*also UK* **pull a face**) to show with your face that you do not like someone or something *The baby made a face every time I offered her some food.* **3 make faces** to make silly expressions with your face in order to try and make people laugh **4 sb's face falls/lights up** someone starts to look disappointed/happy *His face fell when I said that she wasn't coming.* **5 to sb's face** If you say something unpleasant to someone's face, you say it to them directly, when you are with them. *If you've got something to say, say it to my face.* **6** the front or surface of something *the north face of the cliff* ○ *a clock face* **7 in the face of sth** while having to deal with a difficult situation or problem *She refused to leave him, in the face of increasing pressure from friends and family.* **8 on the face of it** used when you are describing how a situation seems on the surface *On the face of it, it seems like a bargain, but I bet there are hidden costs.* **9 keep a straight face** to manage to stop yourself from smiling or laughing *I can never play jokes on people because I can't keep a straight face.* **10 lose/save face** to do something so that people stop respecting you/still respect you *He seemed more interested in saving face than telling the truth.* ⊃See also: have **egg**[1] on your face, a **slap**[2] in the face

O⊸**face**[2] /feɪs/ *verb* [T] **1** DIRECTION to be or turn in a particular direction *The room faces south.* ○ *She turned to face him.* **2** PROBLEM If you face a problem, or a problem faces you, you have to deal with it. [**often passive**] *This is one of the many problems faced by working mothers.* **3 can't face sth/doing sth** to not want to do something or deal with something because it is so unpleasant *I had intended to go for a run, but now I just can't face it.* **4** ACCEPT to accept that something unpleasant is true and start to deal with the situation *She's going to have to* ***face the fact that*** *he's not coming back to her.* **5 let's face it** something that you say before you say something that is unpleasant but true *Let's face it, none of us are getting any younger.* **6** PUNISHMENT If you face something unpleasant, especially a punishment, then it might happen to you. *If found guilty, the pair face fines of up to $40,000.* **7** DEAL WITH to deal with someone when the situation between you is difficult *How can I face him now that he knows what I've done?* **8** COMPETITION to play against another player or team in a competition, sport, etc *We face Spain in the semifinal.* ⊃See also: face the **music**

face up to sth *phrasal verb* to accept that a difficult situation exists

facelift /'feɪslɪft/ *noun* [C] **1** SKIN medical treatment which makes the skin of your face tighter so that you look younger *She looks like she's* ***had a facelift.*** **2** PLACE when you improve a place and make it look more attractive *The council is planning a £6 million facelift for the old harbour area.*

facet /'fæsɪt/ *noun* [C] one part of a subject, situation, etc that has many parts *She has many* ***facets to*** *her personality.*

facetious /fə'siːʃəs/ *adjective* trying to make a joke or a clever remark in a way that annoys people

face-to-face /ˌfeɪstə'feɪs/ *adjective, adverb* directly, meeting someone in the same place *We need to talk face-to-face.* ○ *She* ***came face-to-face with*** *the gunman as he strode into the playground.*

ˌface 'value *noun* **take sth at face value** to accept the way that something first appears without thinking about what it really means *You can't just take everything you read in the papers at face value.*

facial /'feɪʃəl/ *adjective* **ANATOMY** of or on the face ***facial expressions/hair***

facile /'fæsaɪl/ (US) /'fæsəl/ *adjective formal* A facile remark is too simple and has not been thought about enough.

facilitate /fə'sɪlɪteɪt/ *verb* [T] *formal* to make something possible or easier *I will do everything in my power to facilitate the process.*

WORD PARTNERS FOR ***facilities***

offer/provide facilities • facilities **for** sb/(doing) sth • **sports** facilities

facilities /fə'sɪlətiz/ *noun* [**plural**] buildings, equipment, or services that are provided for a particular purpose ***sports/washing facilities*** ○ *childcare facilities*

facility /fəˈsɪləti/ *noun* [C] **1** PART a part of a system or machine which makes it possible to do something *This phone has a memory facility.* **2** BUILDING a place where a particular activity happens *a new medical facility*

WORD PARTNERS FOR ***fact***

accept/face up to/establish/explain/ignore a fact • the fact **remains** • an **important/interesting/simple/undeniable** fact • the facts **about** sth • **know for a** fact

fact /fækt/ *noun* **1** TRUE THING [C] something that you know is true, exists, or has happened *I'm not angry that you drove my car, it's just* ***the fact that*** *you didn't ask me first.* ○ *No decision will be made until we know all the facts.* ○ *He* ***knew for a fact*** (= was certain) *that Natalie was lying.* **2** REAL THINGS [U] real events and experiences, not things that are imagined *It's hard to separate fact from fiction in what she says.* **3 in fact/in actual fact/as a matter of fact a** EMPHASIZING TRUTH used to emphasize what is really true *I was told there were some tickets left, but in actual fact they were sold out.* **b** MORE INFORMATION used when giving more information about something *"Is Isabel coming?" "Yes. As a matter of fact, she should be here soon."* **4 the fact (of the matter) is** used to tell someone that something is the truth *I wouldn't usually ask for your help, but the fact is I'm desperate.* **5 the facts of life** details about sexual activity and the way that babies are born

faction /ˈfækʃᵊn/ *noun* [C] a small group of people who are part of a larger group, and oppose the ideas of everyone else

factor /ˈfæktəʳ/ *noun* [C] **1** one of the things that has an effect on a particular situation, decision, event, etc *Money was an important* ***factor in*** *their decision to move.* **2** MATHEMATICS a number that another larger number can be divided by exactly *5 is a factor of 10.*

factoring /ˈfæktərɪŋ/ *noun* [U] ECONOMICS, FINANCE when a company buys the debts of another business for less than they are worth so that they make a profit and the business selling the debts gets money more quickly

factorize (*also UK* **-ise**) /ˈfæktᵊraɪz/ *verb* [T] MATHEMATICS If you factorize a number, you divide it into factors (= numbers that a larger number can be divided into).

factory /ˈfæktᵊri/ *noun* [C] a building or group of buildings where large amounts of products are made or put together *a textile factory*

factual /ˈfæktʃuəl/ *adjective* using or consisting of facts •**factually** *adverb factually correct/incorrect*

faculty /ˈfækᵊlti/ *noun* **1** [C] a natural ability to hear, see, think, move, etc **2 the English/law/science, etc faculty** EDUCATION a particular department at a college or university, or the teachers in that department **3 the faculty** EDUCATION *US* all of the teachers at a school or college

fad /fæd/ *noun* [C] something that is fashionable to do, wear, say, etc for a short period of time *the latest* ***health fad***

fade /feɪd/ *verb* **1** BECOME LESS [I, T] If a colour or a sound fades, or if something fades it, it become less bright or strong. *The music began to fade.* ○ *The walls had been faded by the sun.* **2** SLOWLY DISAPPEAR [I] (*also* **fade away**) to slowly disappear, lose importance, or become weaker *With time, memories of that painful summer would fade away.*

faeces *UK* (*US* **feces**) /ˈfiːsiːz/ *noun* [plural] BIOLOGY *formal* solid waste that comes out of the bottom of a person or animal

fag /fæg/ *noun* [C] *UK informal* a cigarette

Fahrenheit /ˈfærᵊnhaɪt/ (*written abbreviation* **F**) *noun* [U] MEASURES a measurement of temperature in which water freezes at 32° and boils at 212°

fail¹ /feɪl/ *verb* **1** NOT SUCCEED [I] to not be successful *Dad's business failed after just three years.* ○ *She keeps* ***failing in*** *her attempt to lose weight.* **2 fail to do sth** to not do what is necessary or expected *John failed to turn up for football practice yesterday.* **3** EXAM [I, T] to not pass a test or an exam, or to decide that someone has not passed *I'm worried about failing my driving test.* **4** STOP WORKING [I] to stop working normally, or to become weaker *Two of the plane's engines had failed.* **5** NOT HELPING [T] to stop being helpful or useful to someone when they need you *The government is failing the poor and unemployed.* **6 I fail to see/understand** used to show that you do not accept something [+ **question word**] *I fail to see why you cannot work on a Sunday.*

fail² /feɪl/ *noun* **without fail** If you do something without fail, you always do it, even when it is difficult. *I go to the gym every Monday and Thursday without fail.*

failing¹ /ˈfeɪlɪŋ/ *noun* [C] a bad quality or fault that someone or something has *Despite one or two failings, he's basically a nice guy.*

failing² /ˈfeɪlɪŋ/ *preposition* **failing that** if something is not possible or does not happen *Our goal is to move out by January, or failing that, by March.*

WORD PARTNERS FOR ***failure***

admit/end in failure • be **doomed to** failure • an **abject/complete/humiliating/total** failure

failure /ˈfeɪljəʳ/ *noun* **1** NO SUCCESS [U] when someone or something does not succeed *Their attempt to climb Everest* ***ended in failure.*** **2** PERSON/ACTION [C] someone or something that does not succeed *All my life I've felt like a failure.* **3 failure to do sth** when you do not do something that you must do or are expected to do *Failure to pay within 14 days will result in prosecution.* **4** NOT WORKING [C, U] when something does not work, or stops working as well as it should ***heart failure*** ○ *All trains were delayed due to a* ***power failure.***

faint¹ /feɪnt/ *adjective* **1** slight and not easy to notice, smell, hear, etc *a faint smell of smoke* ○ *faint laughter coming from next door* **2 feel faint** HEALTH to feel very weak and as if you might fall down *Seeing all the blood made me feel faint.* **3 faint hope/praise/chance, etc** very little hope, praise, chance, etc *a faint hope of winning the gold medal* **4 not have the faintest idea** used to emphasize that you do not know something [+ **question word**] I haven't the faintest idea what you're talking about.

faint² /feɪnt/ *verb* [I] **HEALTH** to suddenly become unconscious for a short time, usually falling down onto the floor *She fainted with exhaustion.*

faintly /ˈfeɪntli/ *adverb* slightly *faintly embarrassed*

O╼**fair¹** /feəʳ/ *adjective* **1** EQUAL treating everyone in the same way, so that no one has an advantage *a **fair trial*** ○ ***That's not fair.** You always go first!* **2** RIGHT acceptable or right *a fair deal* ○ *We'd like to move abroad, but it's just not **fair on** the children.* ➲Opposite **unfair 3** HAIR/SKIN having pale skin or a light colour of hair *a boy with fair hair and blue eyes* ➲Opposite **dark 4 a fair amount/distance/size, etc** quite a large amount, distance, size, etc *There's still a fair bit of work to be done on the house.* **5** WEATHER sunny and not raining *Tomorrow will be fair, with some early morning frost.* **6** AVERAGE not very good but not very bad *He has a **fair chance** of winning.* **7 fair enough** *UK informal* used to say that you agree, or think that something is acceptable *"He'll only work on Sunday if he gets paid extra." "Fair enough."* ➲See also: fair **play**², have your (fair) **share**² of sth

fair² /feəʳ/ *noun* [C] **1** ENTERTAINMENT an event outside where you can ride large machines for pleasure and play games to win prizes **2** SHOW OF GOODS/SERVICES an event where people show and sell goods or services relating to a particular business or hobby *a **trade fair***

fair³ /feəʳ/ *adverb* **1 play fair** to do something in a fair and honest way **2 fair and square** in an honest way and without any doubt *We won the match fair and square.*

fairground /ˈfeəgraʊnd/ *noun* [C] an outside area that is used for fairs

fair-haired /ˌfeəˈheəd/ *adjective* having a light colour of hair *a fair-haired child*

O╼**fairly** /ˈfeəli/ *adverb* **1** MORE THAN AVERAGE more than average, but less than very *a fairly big family* ○ *fairly quickly* **2** FAIR done in a fair way *treating people fairly*

fairness /ˈfeənəs/ *noun* [U] when you treat everyone in the same way, so that no one has an advantage

ˌ**fair ˈtrade** *noun* [U] a way of buying and selling products that makes certain that the original producer receives a fair price *fair trade coffee/chocolate* ➲Compare **free trade** •**fairly traded** *adverb*

fairy /ˈfeəri/ *noun* [C] a small, imaginary creature that looks like a person with wings, and has magic powers

fairytale /ˈfeəriteɪl/ *adjective* [**always before noun**] happy and beautiful, like something in a fairy tale *a **fairytale romance/wedding***

ˈ**fairy ˌtale** *noun* [C] **LITERATURE** a story told to children which involves magic, imaginary creatures, and a happy ending

WORD PARTNERS FOR ***faith***

have/lose faith • sb's faith **in** sb/sth

faith /feɪθ/ *noun* **1** [U] the belief that someone or something is good, right, and able to be trusted ***Have faith in** me. I won't let you down.* **2 RELIGION** [U] strong belief in a god or gods *Throughout her illness, she never **lost** her **faith in** God.* **3 RELIGION** [C] a religion *the Jewish and Christian faiths* **4 in good faith** If you act in good faith, you believe that what you are doing is good, honest, or legal.

faithful /ˈfeɪθfəl/ *adjective* **1** RELATIONSHIP If your husband, wife, or partner is faithful, they do not have a sexual relationship with anyone else. *a faithful husband* ○ *They remained **faithful to** each other throughout their long marriage.* **2** LOYAL always loyal *his trusted and faithful servant* **3** NOT CHANGED not changing any of the original details, facts, style, etc *Does the film adaptation stay **faithful to** the novel?* ➲Opposite **unfaithful** •**faithfulness** *noun* [U]

faithfully /ˈfeɪθfəli/ *adverb* **1** in a faithful way **2 Yours faithfully** used to end a formal letter to someone whose name you do not know

fake¹ /feɪk/ *adjective* not real, but made to look or seem real ***fake fur*** ○ *a fake passport*

fake² /feɪk/ *noun* [C] **1** COPY a copy of something that is intended to look real or valuable and deceive people *Experts say that the painting is a fake.* **2** PERSON someone who pretends to have particular skills or qualities so that they can deceive people or get their admiration

fake³ /feɪk/ *verb* [T] **1** COPY to copy something in order to deceive people *faked documents* **2** PRETEND to pretend that you have a particular feeling or emotion *He said he was feeling sick, but he was just **faking it**.*

falcon /ˈfɔːlkən/ *noun* [C] a large bird that eats small animals and is often taught to hunt by people

O╼**fall¹** /fɔːl/ *verb* [I] *past tense* **fell,** *past participle* **fallen 1** MOVE DOWN to move down towards the ground *Huge drops of rain were **falling from** the sky.* ○ *By winter, all the leaves had **fallen off** the trees.* **2** STOP STANDING to suddenly go down and hit the ground without intending to *She **fell off** her bike and broke her arm.* **3** BECOME LESS to become less in number or amount *Housing prices have **fallen by** 15% since last year.* ○ *Temperatures are expected to **fall from** 15°C **to** 9°C.* **4** BECOME WORSE to become worse, or start to be in a bad situation or condition *Education standards are continuing to fall.* ○ *Empty for 30 years, the building had **fallen into ruin*** (= become very damaged). **5 fall asleep/ill/still, etc** to start to sleep, become ill, become quiet, etc *I fell asleep on the sofa watching TV.* **6 darkness/night falls** *literary* used to say that it is becoming dark **7** LOSE POWER to lose power and start to be controlled by a different leader *In 1453 the city **fell to** the Turks.* **8** HANG DOWN to hang down *Her long blonde hair fell softly over her shoulders.* ➲See also: fall on deaf ears (**ear**), fall **flat**³, fall **foul**¹ of sb/sth, go/fall to pieces (**piece**¹), fall into **place**¹, fall **prey**¹ to sth, fall by the **wayside**

COMMON LEARNER ERROR

fall and **feel**

Be careful not to confuse the past forms of the verbs **fall** and **feel**.

The past tense of **fall** is **fell**.

Chris fell off the ladder and broke his arm.

The past tense of **feel** is **felt**.

I felt really happy and relaxed.

fall apart *phrasal verb* **1** BREAK to break into pieces *My poor old boots are falling apart.* **2** HAVE PROBLEMS to start having problems that you cannot deal with *Their relationship fell apart after they moved to Detroit.*
fall back on sb/sth *phrasal verb* to use someone or something when other things have failed, or when there are no other choices *We've been saving up the past few years, to have something to fall back on.*
fall behind *phrasal verb* to not do something fast enough, or not do something by a particular time *Lucy's been falling behind in her homework again.*
fall for sb *phrasal verb* to suddenly have strong, romantic feelings about someone
fall for sth *phrasal verb* to be tricked into believing something that is not true *He told me he owned a mansion in Spain and I fell for it.*
fall in *phrasal verb* If a roof or ceiling falls in, it drops to the ground because it is damaged.
fall off *phrasal verb* If the amount, rate, or quality of something falls off, it becomes smaller or lower. *Demand for new cars is falling off.*
fall on sth *phrasal verb* to happen on a particular day or date *New Year's Day* ***falls on*** *a Tuesday this year.*
fall out *phrasal verb UK* to argue with someone and stop being friendly with them *Have you and Sam* ***fallen out with*** *each other again?*
O─**fall over** *phrasal verb* If someone or something falls over, they fall to the ground or onto their side. *The fence fell over in the wind.* ⊃See colour picture **Phrasal Verbs** on page Centre 16
fall through *phrasal verb* If a plan or agreement falls through, it fails to happen.

WORD PARTNERS FOR ***fall***

a **dramatic/sharp/steep** fall • a fall **in** sth

O─**fall²** /fɔːl/ *noun* **1** AMOUNT [**C**] when the number or amount of something becomes smaller *There's been a sharp* ***fall in*** *prices.* **2** MOVEMENT [**C**] when someone or something moves down to the ground *a heavy fall of snow* **3** SEASON [**C, U**] *US* (*UK/US* **autumn**) the season of the year between summer and winter, when leaves fall from the trees *He started a new job* ***in the fall.*** **4** DEFEAT [**no plural**] when a city, government, leader, etc loses power or control *the fall of communism*

fallacy /ˈfæləsi/ *noun* [**C, U**] a belief that is not true or correct *It's a fallacy that problems will disappear if you ignore them.*

fallen /ˈfɔːlən/ *past participle of* fall

fallible /ˈfæləbl/ *adjective* able to make mistakes *We place our trust in doctors, but even they are fallible.* ⊃Opposite **infallible** •**fallibility** /ˌfæləˈbɪləti/ *noun* [**U**]

Fallopian tube /fəˌləʊpiənˈtjuːb/ *noun* [**C usually plural**] **ANATOMY, BIOLOGY** one of the two tubes in a woman's or female animal's body along which eggs travel, from the ovaries (= parts in which eggs are made) to the womb (= part in which the baby grows)

fallout /ˈfɔːlaʊt/ *noun* [**U**] **ENVIRONMENT** the radiation (= powerful and dangerous energy) from a nuclear explosion

fallow /ˈfæləʊ/ *adjective* **FARMING** If land is left fallow, it is not planted with crops, in order to improve the quality of the soil.

O─**false** /fɔːls/ *adjective* **1** NOT TRUE not true or correct *a false name* ○ *Many rumours about her life were later proved to be false.* **2** NOT REAL not real, but made to look or seem real ***false teeth*** ○ *false documents* **3** NOT SINCERE not sincere or expressing real emotions *false promises* •**falsely** *adverb*

ˌfalse aˈlarm *noun* [**C**] an occasion when people believe that something dangerous is happening, but it is not *Fire engines rushed to the scene, but it was a false alarm.*

falsehood /ˈfɔːlshʊd/ *noun* [**C**] *formal* a lie

ˌfalse ˈstart *noun* [**C**] an occasion when you try to start an activity, event, or process, but fail and have to stop *The after-school club finally opened this term, after several false starts.*

falsify /ˈfɔːlsɪfaɪ/ *verb* [**T**] to change important information, especially in documents, in order to deceive people

falter /ˈfɔːltəʳ/ *verb* [**I**] **1** STOP BEING SUCCESSFUL to stop being confident, powerful, or successful *In the late 1980s his career began to falter.* **2** MAKE MISTAKES to pause, make mistakes, or seem weak when you are talking or moving *Her voice didn't falter once during the ceremony.* ○ *a few* ***faltering steps***

fame /feɪm/ *noun* [**U**] when you are known by many people because of your achievements, skills, etc *fame and fortune* ○ *She first* ***rose to fame*** *as a pop star at the age of 16.* ⊃See also: sb's/sth's **claim²** to fame

famed /feɪmd/ *adjective* famous, especially for having particular qualities *It is a city* ***famed for*** *its ski slopes and casinos.*

O─**familiar** /fəˈmɪliəʳ/ *adjective* **1** EASY TO RECOGNIZE easy to recognize because of being seen, met, heard, etc before *It's nice to see a few* ***familiar faces*** (= people that I recognize) *around here.* ○ *This street doesn't look* ***familiar to*** *me.* **2 be familiar with sth** to know about something or have experienced it many times before *Anyone who's familiar with his poetry will find the course easy.* ⊃Opposite **unfamiliar** **3** FRIENDLY friendly and very informal *He doesn't like to be too familiar with his staff.*

familiarity /fəˌmɪliˈærəti/ *noun* [**U**] **1** KNOWLEDGE a good knowledge of something, or experience of doing or using it *Her* ***familiarity with*** *computers is very impressive.* **2** FRIENDLY BEHAVIOUR friendly and informal behaviour

familiarize (*also UK* **-ise**) /fəˈmɪliəraɪz/ *verb* **familiarize sb/yourself with sth** to teach someone more about something new, or try to understand more about it yourself *We spent a few minutes familiarizing ourselves with the day's schedule.*

WORD PARTNERS FOR ***family***

have/raise/start/support a family • a **big/close/happy** family • your **close/extended/immediate** family

O→**family** /ˈfæməli/ *noun* **1** **SOCIETY** [**group**] a group of people who are related to each other, such as a mother, a father, and their children *Her (UK) family are/ (US) family is originally from Ireland.* ○ *a family business* **2** [**C**] the children in a family [**usually singular**] *Single parents have to* ***raise a family*** *on their own.* ○ *Paul and Alison are hoping to* ***start a family*** *soon.* **3** **BIOLOGY** [**C**] a group of similar types of plants or animals that are related to each other

ˈ**family ˌname** *noun* [**C**] the name that is used by all the members of a family

ˌ**family ˈplanning** *noun* [**U**] **HEALTH** controlling how many children you have by using contraceptives (= pills or objects that prevent a woman from becoming pregnant)

ˌ**family ˈtree** *noun* [**C**] **SOCIETY** a drawing that shows the relationships between the different members of a family, especially over a long period of time

famine /ˈfæmɪn/ *noun* [**C, U**] when people living in a particular area do not have enough food for a long time causing suffering and death

O→**famous** /ˈfeɪməs/ *adjective* known or recognized by many people *a famous actress* ○ *New York is a city* ***famous for*** *its shopping and nightlife.* ➲See also: **world-famous**

famously /ˈfeɪməsli/ *adverb* **1** **get on famously (with sb)** to have a very friendly relationship with someone **2** in a way that is famous

WORD PARTNERS FOR ***fan***

a **big/huge** fan • a fan **of** sb/sth • **football/soccer** fans

O→**fan¹** /fæn/ *noun* [**C**] **1** PERSON someone who admires and supports a famous person, sport, type of music, etc *More than 15,000 Liverpool fans attended Saturday's game.* ○ *He's a big* ***fan of*** *country music.* **2** OBJECT something that is used to move the air around so that it feels cooler, such as a machine or an object that you wave with your hand *an electric fan*

fan² /fæn/ *verb* [**T**] **fanning**, *past* **fanned** to move the air around with a fan or something used like a fan, to make it feel cooler [**often reflexive**] *The spectators sat in the bright sun, fanning themselves with newspapers.*

fan out *phrasal verb* If a group of people fan out, they move out in different directions from a single point.

fanatic /fəˈnætɪk/ *noun* [**C**] someone whose interest in something or enthusiasm for something is extreme •**fanatical** *adjective* extremely enthusiastic about something *She's fanatical about football.* •**fanaticism** /fəˈnætɪsɪzəm/ *noun* [**U**]

fanciable /ˈfænsiəbl/ *adjective UK informal* sexually attractive

fanciful /ˈfænsɪfəl/ *adjective* Something that is fanciful comes from someone's imagination and so is probably not true or real. *a fanciful story*

ˈ**fan ˌclub** *noun* [**C**] an organization for the people who support and admire a particular singer, actor, sports team, etc

fancy¹ /ˈfænsi/ *verb* [**T**] **1** WANT *UK* to want to have or do something *Do you fancy a drink?* [**+ doing sth**] *We fancy going to the Caribbean for our holiday.* **2** PERSON *UK informal* to feel sexually attracted to someone *I fancied him the first time I saw him.* **3** **fancy (that)!** *UK informal* used to show that you are surprised or shocked by something [**+ doing sth**] Fancy seeing you here! **4** THINK *formal* to think that something is true [**+ (that)**] *I fancy that he was smiling, but I can't be sure.*

fancy² /ˈfænsi/ *adjective* **1** EXPENSIVE Fancy things and places are expensive and fashionable. *a fancy restaurant* **2** DECORATED with lots of decoration, or very complicated *fancy cakes*

fancy³ /ˈfænsi/ *noun* **1** **take a fancy to sb/sth** to start to like someone or something a lot *Marina had taken a fancy to her.* **2** **take sb's fancy** If something or someone takes your fancy, you find them interesting or attractive. *We can go anywhere that takes your fancy.*

ˌ**fancy ˈdress** *noun* [**U**] *UK* special clothes that people wear for a party, which make them look like a different person ***a fancy dress party***

fanfare /ˈfænfeəʳ/ *noun* [**C**] **MUSIC** a short, loud tune played on a trumpet (= metal musical instrument) to announce an important person or event

fang /fæŋ/ *noun* [**C**] **BIOLOGY** a long, sharp tooth of an animal such as a dog or a snake

ˈ**fanny ˌpack** *US* (*UK* **bumbag**) *noun* [**C**] a small bag fixed to a belt that you wear around your waist

fantasize (*also UK* **-ise**) /ˈfæntəsaɪz/ *verb* [**I, T**] to imagine something that you would like to happen, but is not likely to happen *We used to* ***fantasize about*** *becoming famous actresses.*

fantastic /fænˈtæstɪk/ *adjective* **1** GOOD *informal* very good *I've had a fantastic time.* **2** LARGE *informal* A fantastic amount or number of something is very large. *They're making fantastic amounts of money.* **3** STRANGE very strange and probably not true *fantastic stories about monsters and witches*

fantastically /fænˈtæstɪkəli/ *adverb* extremely *fantastically rich*

WORD PARTNERS FOR ***fantasy***

have fantasies **about /of** (doing) sth • a fantasy **world**

fantasy /ˈfæntəsi/ *noun* [**C, U**] a situation or event that you imagine, which is not real or true

FAQ /ˌefeɪˈkjuː/ *noun* [**C**] **COMPUTING, INTERNET** *abbreviation for* frequently asked question: something that many people ask when they use the Internet or a computer program, or a file (= collection) of these questions with their answers

O‑ **far**[1] /fɑːʳ/ *adverb* **farther** or **farthest**, **further**, **furthest** **1** DISTANCE used to talk about how distant something is *It's the first time I've been so* ***far away*** *from home.* ○ ***How far*** *is it to the supermarket?* ○ *Bournemouth is* ***not far from*** *Poole.* ○ *In the summer the herds move farther north.* **2** TIME a long time *How far back can you remember?* ○ *We need to plan further ahead.* **3 far better/cheaper/more, etc** much better, cheaper, more, etc *Young people are far more independent these days.* **4 far too difficult/expensive/late, etc** much too difficult, expensive, late, etc *His trousers were far too tight.* **5 as far as I know** *informal* used to say what you think is true, although you do not know all the facts *As far as I know, they haven't reached a decision yet.* **6 as far as sb is concerned** used to say what someone's opinion is *It's all over as far as I'm concerned.* **7 as far as sth is concerned** used to say what you are talking about *As far as sport's concerned, I like tennis and football.* **8 by far** used to emphasize that something is the biggest, the best, etc *This is his best film by far.* **9 far from sth** certainly not something *The situation is far from clear.* **10 far from doing sth** certainly not doing something *Far from being pleased, he was embarrassed by the praise.* **11 far from it** *informal* used to tell someone that something is certainly not true *He's not handsome - far from it.* **12 as far as possible** as much as is possible *We try to buy organic food as far as possible.* **13 go so far as to do sth** to take the extreme action of doing something *He even went so far as to stop her using the telephone.* **14 go too far** to behave in a way that upsets or annoys other people **15 how far** used to talk about how true something is *How far do politicians represent the views of ordinary people?* **16 so far** until now *So far, we haven't made much progress.* **17 so far so good** *informal* used to say that something has gone well until now **18 not go (very) far** If something such as money does not go far, you cannot do very much with it. *£1 doesn't go very far these days.*

O‑ **far**[2] /fɑːʳ/ *adjective* **farther**, **farthest** or **further**, **furthest** **1** [**always before noun**] describes the part of something that is most distant from you or from the centre *His office is at the far end of the corridor.* ○ *They live in the far south of the country.* **2 the far left/right** POLITICS used to describe political groups whose opinions are very extreme ➲See also: be a far **cry**[2] from sth

farad /ˈfærəd/ *noun* [**C**] MEASURES a unit for measuring capacitance (= the ability of a system to store electrical charge)

the Faraday constant /ˌfærədeɪˈkɒnstənt/ *noun* PHYSICS the amount of electric charge in a particular amount of electrons

faraway /ˌfɑːrəˈweɪ/ *adjective* **1** [**always before noun**] *literary* a long distance away ***faraway places*** **2 a faraway look/expression** an expression on someone's face that shows that they are not thinking about what is happening around them *He had a faraway look in his eyes.*

farce /fɑːs/ *noun* **1** SITUATION [**no plural**] a serious event or situation that becomes ridiculous because it is so badly organized *The meeting was a complete farce.* **2** LITERATURE [**C**] a funny play in which a lot of silly things happen •**farcical** /ˈfɑːsɪkəl/ *adjective* like a farce

WORD PARTNERS FOR ***fare***

a **return/single** fare • the fare **to** [Seattle/Moscow, etc]

fare[1] /feəʳ/ *noun* [**C**] the price that you pay to travel on an aircraft, train, bus, etc ***air/train fares***

fare[2] /feəʳ/ *verb formal* **fare well/badly/better, etc** used to say how well or badly someone or something does in a particular situation *All the children fared well in the exams.*

farewell /ˌfeəˈwel/ *exclamation old-fashioned* goodbye •**farewell** *noun* [**C**] when someone says goodbye *a sad farewell* ○ *a farewell party*

far-fetched /ˌfɑːˈfetʃt/ *adjective* difficult to believe and not likely to be true *The idea is not as far-fetched as it might sound.*

WORD PARTNERS FOR ***farm***

on a farm • farm **workers** • farm **animals**

O‑ **farm**[1] /fɑːm/ *noun* [**C**] FARMING an area of land with fields and buildings that is used for growing crops and keeping animals as a business *a dairy farm* ○ *farm animals/buildings*

farm[2] /fɑːm/ *verb* [**I, T**] FARMING to grow crops or keep animals as a business *Only 2% of the country's farmland is farmed organically.*

O‑ **farmer** /ˈfɑːməʳ/ *noun* [**C**] FARMING someone who owns or looks after a farm

farmhouse /ˈfɑːmhaʊs/ *noun* [**C**] *plural* **farmhouses** /ˈfɑːmhaʊzɪz/ the house on a farm where the farmer lives

farming /fɑːmɪŋ/ *noun* [**U**] FARMING working on a farm or organizing the work there

farmland /ˈfɑːmlænd/ *noun* [**U**] FARMING land which is used for or suitable for farming

farmyard /ˈfɑːmjɑːd/ *noun* [**C**] FARMING an area of ground with farm buildings around it

far-off /ˌfɑːrˈɒf/ *adjective literary* a long distance away or a long time in the past or future *far-off lands*

far-reaching /ˌfɑːˈriːtʃɪŋ/ *adjective* Far-reaching acts, events, or ideas have very big effects. ***far-reaching changes in the education system***

farsighted /ˈfɑːˌsaɪtɪd/ *US* (*UK* **long-sighted**) *adjective* HEALTH able to see objects which are far away, but not things which are near to you

farther /ˈfɑːðəʳ/ *adjective, adverb* (*comparative of* far) more distant *I couldn't walk any farther.*

farthest /ˈfɑːðɪst/ *adjective, adverb* (*superlative of* far) most distant *They walked to the farthest edge of the garden.*

fascinate /ˈfæsɪneɪt/ *verb* [**T**] to interest someone a lot *Science has always fascinated me.*

fascinated /ˈfæsɪneɪtɪd/ *adjective* extremely interested *They were absolutely fascinated by the game.*

fascinating /ˈfæsɪneɪtɪŋ/ *adjective* extremely interesting *I found the movie fascinating.*

fascination /ˌfæsɪˈneɪʃən/ *noun* [**U, no plural**] when you find someone or something fascinating *Her **fascination with** fashion started at an early age.*

fascism, Fascism /ˈfæʃɪzᵊm/ *noun* [U] **POLITICS** a political system in which the government is extremely powerful and controls people's lives

fascist /ˈfæʃɪst/ *noun* [C] **1 POLITICS** (*also* **Fascist**) someone who supports fascism **2** someone who you do not like because they try to control other people's behaviour •**fascist** *adjective a **fascist dictator/regime***

WORD PARTNERS FOR ***fashion***

be **in** fashion • **come into/go out of** fashion • a fashion **for** sth

O‑**fashion¹** /ˈfæʃᵊn/ *noun* **1** STYLE [C, U] the most popular style of clothes, appearance, or behaviour at a particular time *Long hair is back **in fashion** for men.* ○ *Fur coats have gone **out of fashion**.* **2** BUSINESS [U] making and selling clothes *the **fashion industry*** **3** WAY [no plural] *formal* the way in which someone does something *He told the story **in a** very amusing **fashion**.*

fashion² /ˈfæʃᵊn/ *verb* [T] *formal* to make something *jewellery **fashioned from** recycled metal*

fashionable /ˈfæʃᵊnəbl/ *adjective* popular at a particular time ***fashionable clothes*** [+ **to do** sth] *It's no longer fashionable to smoke.* ➲Opposite **unfashionable** •**fashionably** *adverb fashionably dressed*

OTHER WAYS OF SAYING ***fast***

If you want to use fast as an adjective, a very common alternative is **quick**: *I tried to catch him, but he was too **quick** for me.*

If something is done fast, without waiting, you can use the adjectives **prompt** or **speedy**: *A **prompt** reply would be very much appreciated.* • *He made a **speedy** recovery.*

If something is done too fast, without thinking carefully, the adjectives **hasty** and **hurried** are often used: *I don't want to make a **hasty** decision.* • *We left early after a **hurried** breakfast.*

A fast walk is often described as **brisk**: *We took a **brisk** walk through the park.*

The adjective **rapid** is often used to describe fast growth or change: *The 1990's were a period of **rapid** change/growth.*

If you want to use fast as an adverb, a very common alternative is **quickly**: *The problem needs to be sorted out as **quickly** as possible.*

If someone does something very fast, in informal situations you can use the expressions **in a flash** and **like a shot**: *I'll be back **in a flash**.* • *There was an almighty crash and he got up **like a shot**.*

O‑**fast¹** /fɑːst/ *adjective* **1** QUICK moving, happening, or doing something quickly *fast cars* ○ *a fast swimmer* ○ *Computers are getting faster all the time.* **2** TIME [never before noun] If a clock or watch is fast, it shows a time that is later than the correct time. ➲See also: a fast **track¹** (to sth)

O‑**fast²** /fɑːst/ *adverb* **1** QUICKLY moving or happening quickly *We ran as fast as we could.* ○ *You'll have to act fast.* **2 fast asleep** completely asleep (= sleeping) **3** FIRMLY in a firm or tight way *He tried to get away, but she **held** him **fast**.* ➲See also: **thick¹** and fast

COMMON LEARNER ERROR

fast

Remember that there is no adverb 'fastly'. Use the adverbs **fast** or **quickly** instead.

The situation is changing fast.

Alice got dressed very quickly.

fast³ /fɑːst/ *verb* [I] to eat nothing, or much less than you usually eat for a period of time •**fast** *noun* [C]

O‑**fasten** /ˈfɑːsᵊn/ *verb* **1** [I, T] to close or fix something together, or to become closed or fixed together *Fasten your seat belts.* ○ *This dress fastens at the side.* **2 fasten sth on/to/together, etc** to fix one thing to another *He fastened the rope to a tree.* ➲Opposite **unfasten**

fastener /ˈfɑːsᵊnəʳ/ *noun* [C] something that is used to close or fix things together

ˌ**fast ˈfood** *noun* [U] **FOOD** hot food that can be served very quickly in a restaurant because it is already prepared ***fast food restaurants***

fast-forward /ˌfɑːstˈfɔːwəd/ *verb* [I, T] If you fast-forward a recording, or if it fast-forwards, you make it play at very high speed so that you get to the end more quickly. •**fast-forward** *noun* [U]

fastidious /fæsˈtɪdiəs/ *adjective* Someone who is fastidious wants every detail of something to be correct and perfect.

O‑**fat¹** /fæt/ *adjective* **fatter, fattest 1** PERSON Someone who is fat weighs too much. *She eats all the time but never **gets fat**.* **2** THICK thick or large *a fat book* ➲See also: fat **chance¹**

fat² /fæt/ *noun* **1 BIOLOGY** [U] the substance under the skin of people and animals that keeps them warm *body fat* **2 FOOD** [C, U] a solid or liquid substance like oil that is taken from plants or animals and used in cooking ***animal/vegetable fat*** ➲See also: **saturated fat**

fatal /ˈfeɪtᵊl/ *adjective* **1** CAUSING DEATH A fatal accident or illness causes death. *a fatal car crash* **2** CAUSING PROBLEMS Fatal actions have very bad effects. *a **fatal error*** •**fatally** *adverb **fatally injured***

fatalism /ˈfeɪtᵊlɪzᵊm/ *noun* [U] the belief that people cannot change events, and that bad events cannot be avoided •**fatalistic** /ˌfeɪtᵊlˈɪstɪk/ *adjective*

fatality /fəˈtæləti/ *noun* [C] *formal* the death of a person caused by violence or an accident

ˈ**fat ˌcat** *noun* [C] someone who has a lot of money, especially someone in charge of a company

WORD PARTNERS FOR ***fate***

suffer a fate • **decide/seal** sb's fate

fate /feɪt/ *noun* **1** THINGS THAT HAPPEN [C] what happens to someone, especially when it is something bad *His fate is now in the hands of the jury.* **2** POWER [U] a power that some people believe decides what will happen *I believe it* *was fate that caused us to meet again.* ⊃See also: **quirk** of fate

fated /ˈfeɪtɪd/ *adjective* [**never before noun**] If something that happens or someone's actions are fated, they are decided by a power that controls events, and cannot be avoided. [+ **to do sth**] *I seem fated to meet him wherever I go.* ⊃See also: **ill-fated**

fateful /ˈfeɪtfᵊl/ *adjective* A fateful event has an important and usually bad effect on the future. *a **fateful** decision*

father¹ /ˈfɑːðəʳ/ *noun* **1** [**C**] your male parent **2 Father RELIGION** the title of some Christian priests *Father O'Brian* **3 the father of sth** the man who invented or started something *Descartes is known as the father of modern philosophy.*

F

father² /ˈfɑːðəʳ/ *verb* [**T**] *formal* to become a male parent *He fathered three children.*

ˌFather ˈChristmas *noun* [**no plural**] *UK* a kind, fat, old man in red clothes who people say brings presents to children at Christmas

ˈfather ˌfigure *noun* [**C**] an older man who gives you advice and support like a father

fatherhood /ˈfɑːðəhʊd/ *noun* [**U**] being a father

father-in-law /ˈfɑːðərɪnlɔː/ *noun* [**C**] *plural* **fathers-in-law** the father of your husband or wife

fathom¹ /ˈfæðəm/ (*also UK* **fathom out**) *verb* [**T**] to be able to understand something after thinking about it a lot [+ **question word**] *No one could fathom why she had left so early.*

fathom² /ˈfæðəm/ *noun* [**C**] **MEASURES** a unit for measuring the depth of water, equal to 1.8 metres

fatigue /fəˈtiːg/ *noun* [**U**] when you feel very tired •**fatigued** *adjective*

fatigues /fəˈtiːgz/ *noun* [**plural**] special clothes that soldiers wear when they are fighting or working

fatten /ˈfætᵊn/ *verb* [**T**] **FARMING** to make animals fatter so that they can be eaten

fatten sb/sth up *phrasal verb* to give a thin person or animal lots of food so that they become fatter

fattening /ˈfætᵊnɪŋ/ *adjective* Fattening food can make you fat. *I don't eat chips, they're too fattening.*

fatty /ˈfæti/ *adjective* **FOOD** Fatty foods contain a lot of fat.

ˌfatty ˈacid *noun* [**C**] **CHEMISTRY** any of a large group of acids, especially those found in fats and oils

fatuous /ˈfætjuəs/ *adjective* very stupid and not deserving your attention or respect *a **fatuous comment/remark***

faucet /ˈfɔːsɪt/ *US* (*UK/US* **tap**) *noun* [**C**] an object at the end of a pipe which you turn to control the flow of water ⊃See picture at **tap**

WORD PARTNERS FOR ***fault***

all/entirely sb's fault • it's sb's **own** fault

fault¹ /fɔːlt/ *noun* **1 sb's fault** If something bad that has happened is someone's fault, they are responsible for it. *She believes it was the doctor's fault that Peter died.* **2 at fault** responsible for something bad that has happened *I was at fault and I would like to apologize.* **3** [**C**] something that is wrong with something or with someone's character *The car has a serious **design fault**.* **4 find fault with sb/sth** to criticize someone or something, especially without good reasons **5 GEOLOGY** a place where the layers of rock under the surface of the Earth have broken and the pieces on either side can move

fault² /fɔːlt/ *verb* [**T**] to find a reason to criticize someone or something *I can't fault the way that they dealt with the complaint.*

faultless /ˈfɔːltləs/ *adjective* perfect, or without any mistakes *a **faultless performance***

faulty /ˈfɔːlti/ *adjective* not working correctly *faulty brakes/wiring*

fauna /ˈfɔːnə/ *noun* [**group**] **BIOLOGY** all the animals that live in a particular area *the **flora and fauna** of the area*

favour¹ *UK* (*US* **favor**) /ˈfeɪvəʳ/ *noun* **1** HELP [**C**] something that you do to help someone *Could you **do me a favour** please?* ○ *I wanted to **ask you a favour**.* **2 be in favour of sth** to agree with or approve of a plan or idea *Most people are in favour of reducing traffic in cities.* **3 in favour of sb/sth** If you refuse or get rid of someone or something in favour of someone or something else, you choose them instead. *They dropped him from the team in favour of a much younger player.* **4 in sb's favour a** ADVANTAGE If something is in your favour, it helps you to win or succeed. *Both sides have strong arguments in their favour.* **b** WINNING If a game, vote, or judgement is in someone's favour, they win. *The final score was 16-10 in England's favour.* **5** LIKE [**U**] *formal* when people like something or someone *Her work never **found favour** among the critics.* **6 be in favour/out of favour** to be popular/unpopular *He has fallen out of favour recently.*

favour² *UK* (*US* **favor**) /ˈfeɪvəʳ/ *verb* [**T**] **1** CHOOSE to choose or prefer one possibility [**often passive**] *These are the running shoes favoured by marathon runners.* **2** UNFAIRLY PREFER to act unfairly by treating one person better than another *She always felt that her parents favoured her brother.*

favourable *UK* (*US* **favorable**) /ˈfeɪvᵊrəbl/ *adjective* **1** JUDGMENT showing that you like or approve of someone or something, or making you like or approve of them *She made a very **favourable impression** on us.* **2** CONDITIONS making something more likely to be successful ***favourable weather conditions*** ⊃Opposite **unfavourable** •**favourably** *UK* (*US* **favorably**) *adverb*

favourite¹ *UK* (*US* **favorite**) /ˈfeɪvᵊrət/ *adjective* [**always before noun**] Your favourite person or thing is the one that you like best. *What's your favourite band?*

favourite² *UK* (*US* **favorite**) /ˈfeɪvᵊrət/ *noun* [**C**] **1** LIKE a person or thing that you like more than all others *These chocolates are my favourites.* **2** WIN the person or animal that is most likely to win a competition *The Dallas Cowboys are now favourites to win.*

favouritism *UK* (*US* **favoritism**) /ˈfeɪvᵊrətɪzᵊm/ *noun* [U] unfairly treating one person or group better than another

fawn¹ /fɔːn/ *noun* **1** [ANIMAL] [C] a young deer **2** [COLOUR] [U] a light brown colour

fawn² /fɔːn/ *verb*
fawn on/over sb *phrasal verb* to praise someone or be nice to someone in a way that is false in order to get something or to make them like you

fax¹ /fæks/ *noun* **1** [DOCUMENT] [C] a document that is sent or received using a special machine and a telephone line *I got a fax from them this morning.* **2** [SYSTEM] [U] the system of sending or receiving documents using a special machine and a telephone line *Some products can be ordered* ***by fax.*** **3** [MACHINE] [C] (*also* ˈ**fax ˌmachine**) a machine that is used to send and receive faxes ➲See colour picture **The Office** on page Centre 5

fax² /fæks/ *verb* [T] to send documents using a fax machine [+ **two objects**] *Can you fax me a price list?*

the FBI /ˌefbiːˈaɪ/ *noun* **LAW** *abbreviation for* the Federal Bureau of Investigation: one of the national police forces in the US that is controlled by the central government *He is wanted by the FBI for fraud.*

> WORD PARTNERS FOR ***fear***
>
> **allay/calm/cause/heighten** fear • **hold** no fear **for** sb • **great/morbid/widespread** fear • fear **of** sth

O-ᵂ **fear¹** /fɪəʳ/ *noun* **1** [C, U] a strong, unpleasant feeling that you get when you think that something bad, dangerous, or frightening might happen *She was trembling with fear.* ○ *Unlike the rest of us, Dave had no* ***fear of*** *snakes.* [+ **(that)**] *There are fears that the disease will spread to other countries.* **2 for fear of sth/doing sth** because you are worried about something/doing something *I didn't want to move for fear of waking her up.*

fear² /fɪəʳ/ *verb* [T] **1** [UNPLEASANT EVENT] to be worried or frightened that something bad might happen or might have happened [+ **(that)**] *Police fear that the couple may have drowned.* **2** [UNPLEASANT THING] to be frightened of something or someone unpleasant *Most older employees fear unemployment.* **3 fear the worst** If you fear the worst, you are frightened that an unpleasant situation will become much worse. *When there was no sign of the children, rescuers feared the worst.*
fear for sth/sb *phrasal verb* to be worried about something, or to be worried that someone is in danger *Her parents* ***fear for*** *her* ***safety*** (= worry that she may not be safe).

fearful /ˈfɪəfᵊl/ *adjective formal* **1** [FRIGHTENED] frightened or worried [+ **of** + **doing sth**] *Many women are fearful of travelling alone.* **2** [VERY BAD] [**always before noun**] *UK* very bad *Nigel has a fearful temper.* •**fearfully** *adverb*

fearless /ˈfɪələs/ *adjective* not frightened of anything *a fearless fighter* •**fearlessly** *adverb*

fearsome /ˈfɪəsəm/ *adjective* very frightening *a fearsome opponent*

feasible /ˈfiːzəbl/ *adjective* possible to do *a feasible plan* [+ **to do sth**] *It may be feasible to clone human beings, but is it ethical?* •**feasibility** /ˌfiːzəˈbɪləti/ *noun* [U]

feast¹ /ˈfiːst/ *noun* [C] **FOOD** a large meal, especially to celebrate something special *a wedding feast*

feast² /ˈfiːst/ *verb*
feast on sth *phrasal verb* to eat a lot of food and enjoy it very much *We feasted on fried chicken, ice cream, and chocolate cake.*

feat /ˈfiːt/ *noun* **1** [C] an act or achievement that shows great skill or strength *The Eiffel Tower is a remarkable* ***feat of*** *engineering.* **2 be no mean feat** used when you want to emphasize that an act or achievement is very difficult *Learning to ski at 60 is no mean feat!*

feather /ˈfeðəʳ/ *noun* [C] **BIOLOGY** one of the soft, light things that grow from and cover a bird's skin •**feathery** *adjective* like feathers *feathery leaves*

> WORD PARTNERS FOR ***feature***
>
> a **distinguishing/important/notable** feature • a **redeeming** feature • a feature **of** sth • a **new** feature

O-ᵂ **feature¹** /ˈfiːtʃəʳ/ *noun* [C] **1** [PART] a typical quality, or important part of something *This phone has several* ***new features.*** **2** [FACE] Someone's features are the parts of their face that you notice when you look at them. *His eyes are his* ***best feature.*** **3** [NEWSPAPER] a special article in a newspaper or magazine, or a special television programme *a double-page* ***feature on*** *global warming*

feature² /ˈfiːtʃəʳ/ *verb* [T] to include someone or something as an important part *a new movie featuring Bruce Willis*
feature in sth *phrasal verb* to be an important part of something

ˈ**feature ˌfilm** *noun* [C] a film that is usually 90 or more minutes long

O-ᵂ **February** /ˈfebruᵊri/ (*written abbreviation* **Feb**) *noun* [C, U] the second month of the year

feces /ˈfiːsiːz/ *noun* [**plural**] **BIOLOGY** *US spelling of* faeces

feckless /ˈfekləs/ *adjective* A feckless person is not willing to work or take responsibility for their actions.

fed /fed/ *past of* feed

federal /ˈfedᵊrᵊl/ *adjective* [**always before noun**] **1 POLITICS** relating to the central government, and not to the government of a region, of some countries such as the United States *the* ***federal government*** ○ *a federal agency/employee* **2 POLITICS** A federal system of government consists of a group of regions that is controlled by a central government.

ˌ**federal** ˈ**holiday** *US* (*UK/US* **national holiday**) *noun* [C] a day when most people in a country do not have to work

federalism /ˈfedᵊrᵊlɪzᵊm/ *noun* [U] **POLITICS** a political system in which separate states are organized under a central government •**federalist** *noun* [C] someone who supports federalism

federation /ˌfedᵊrˈeɪʃᵊn/ *noun* [C] **POLITICS** a group of organizations, countries, regions, etc that have joined together to form a larger organization or government *the International Tennis Federation*

ˌfed ˈup *adjective informal* [**never before noun**] annoyed or bored by something that you have experienced for too long *I'm* ***fed up with*** *my job.*

fee /fiː/ *noun* [C] **FINANCE** an amount of money that you pay to do something, to use something, or to get a service *an entrance fee* ○ *university fees*

F

feeble /ˈfiːbl/ *adjective* **1** WEAK extremely weak *She became too feeble to get out of bed.* **2** NOT GOOD not very good or effective *a* ***feeble argument/excuse*** •**feebly** *adverb*

feed[1] /fiːd/ *verb past* **fed 1** GIVE FOOD [T] to give food to a person, group, or animal *I fed Simone's cat while she was away.* **2** EAT FOOD [I] If an animal or a baby feeds, it eats. *The caterpillars* ***feed on*** *cabbage leaves.* **3** SUPPLY [T] to supply something such as information to a person or a machine, especially in a regular or continuous way *We fed them false information about our plans.* ➲See also: **breast-feed**

feed[2] /fiːd/ *noun* **1 FARMING** [U] food for animals that are not kept as pets *cattle/chicken feed* **2** [C] *UK* (*US* **feeding**) a meal for a baby or an animal *He has three feeds during the night.*

WORD PARTNERS FOR ***feedback***

get/give/provide feedback • **negative/positive** feedback • feedback **on** sth • feedback **from** sb

feedback /ˈfiːdbæk/ *noun* [U] an opinion from someone about something that you have done or made ***positive/negative feedback*** ○ *We've had lots of* ***feedback on*** *these new products* ***from*** *our customers.*

feedstock /ˈfiːdstɒk/ *noun* [U] the main material used for making a product

feel[1] /fiːl/ *verb past* **felt 1** EXPERIENCE [I, T] to experience an emotion or a physical feeling *You shouldn't feel embarrassed about making a mistake.* ○ *I felt a sharp pain in my side when I stood up.* ○ *"Are you feeling better?" "Yes, thanks, I feel fine now."* **2 feel better/different/strange, etc; feel like/as if** If you describe the way a place, situation, or object feels, you say how it seems to you, or what your experience of it is like. *It felt strange to see him again after so long.* ○ *The house feels empty without the children.* ○ *This shirt feels tight under my arms.* ○ *I feel as if I've known you for ages.* **3 feel like sb/sth** to seem to be similar to a type of person, thing, or situation *My feet feel like blocks of ice.* ○ *I felt like a fool when I saw what everyone else was wearing.* **4** OPINION [I, T] to think something or have an opinion [+ (**that**)] *I feel that he's the best person for the job.* ○ *Do you feel strongly* (= have strong opinions) *about it?* **5** TOUCH [I, T] to touch something, especially with your hands, in order to examine it *He felt her ankle to see if it was broken.* **6 feel like sth/doing sth** to want something, or want to do something *I feel like some chocolate.* ○ *Jane felt like crying.* **7** BE AWARE [T] to be aware of something *You could feel the tension in the room.* ○ *I could feel them watching me.* ➲See Common Learner Error at **fall** ➲See also: feel **free**[1], feel the **pinch**[2], be/feel under the **weather**[1]

feel for sb *phrasal verb* to feel sorry for someone because they are very unhappy, or in a difficult situation

feel[2] /fiːl/ *noun* **1** [**no plural**] the way that something seems, or feels when you touch it *I love the* ***feel of*** *silk against my skin.* ○ *His art has a very modern feel to it.* **2 a feel for sth** *informal* the ability to do something or use something well *Once you get a feel for it, using the mouse is easy.* ○ *Claire has a feel for this kind of work.*

feel-good /ˈfiːlgʊd/ *adjective* causing happy feelings about life *a feel-good story*

OTHER WAYS OF SAYING ***feeling***

A very common alternative to the noun 'feeling' is **emotion**: *He finds it hard to express his* ***emotions***.

The nouns **pang** or **stab** are sometimes used to describe a sudden, strong, bad feeling: *Amelia felt a sharp* ***pang*** *of jealousy when she saw her.* • *He felt a* ***stab*** *of regret as he looked at his son.*

A small amount of a sad feeling is often described as a **tinge**: *It was with a* ***tinge*** *of sadness that she finally said goodbye.*

feeling /ˈfiːlɪŋ/ *noun* **1** EMOTION [C, U] emotion *guilty feelings* ○ *a feeling of joy/sadness* ○ *Her performance was completely lacking in feeling.* **2** PHYSICAL [C, U] when you feel something physical *I had a tingling feeling in my fingers.* ○ *Pablo lost all feeling* (= could not feel anything) *in his feet.* **3** OPINION [C] an opinion or belief *My feeling is that we should wait until they come back.* **4 have/get a feeling (that)...** to think that something is likely *I had a feeling he'd be there.* ○ *I get the feeling that he doesn't like me.* **5 bad/ill feeling** when people are upset or angry with each other

WORD PARTNERS FOR ***feelings***

express/hide/show your feelings • **hurt** sb's feelings • **mixed/strong** feelings

feelings /ˈfiːlɪŋz/ *noun* **1** [**plural**] Your feelings are your beliefs and emotions. *You can't* ***hide*** *your* ***feelings*** *from me.* **2 hurt sb's feelings** to make someone feel unhappy

feet /fiːt/ *plural of* foot

feign /feɪn/ *verb* [T] *formal* If you feign an emotion, illness, etc, you pretend to have it. *He feigned illness to avoid having to work.*

feisty /ˈfaɪsti/ *adjective* active, confident and determined *a feisty young woman*

feldspar /ˈfeldspɑr/ *noun* [C, U] **GEOLOGY** a very common type of mineral (= substance that is dug out from the ground)

feline /ˈfiːlaɪn/ *adjective* relating to cats, or like a cat

fell[1] /fel/ *verb* [T] **1** CUT to cut down a tree **2** KNOCK to knock someone down *He was felled with a single punch.*

fell[2] /fel/ *past tense of* fall

fella (*also* **feller**) /ˈfelə/ *noun* [C] *informal* a man

fellow[1] /ˈfeləʊ/ *noun* [C] **1** MAN *old-fashioned* a man *a big fellow with broad shoulders* **2** **EDUCATION** someone whose job is to teach or study a particular subject at some colleges or universities *She's a research fellow at St Peter's college.* **3** MEMBER a member of an official organization for a particular subject or job

fellow[2] /ˈfeləʊ/ *adjective* **fellow countrymen/students, etc** used to describe people who share your interests or situation *She's earned enormous respect from her fellow artists.*

fellowship /ˈfeləʊʃɪp/ *noun* **1** **EDUCATION** [C] a job teaching or studying a particular subject at some colleges or universities *a research fellowship at Harvard* **2** FEELING [U] a friendly feeling among people **3** GROUP [C] a group of people who share the same interests or beliefs

felon /ˈfelən/ *noun* [C] **LAW** someone who is guilty of a serious crime in the US *a convicted felon*

felony /ˈfeləni/ *noun* [C, U] **LAW** a serious crime in the US *to* ***commit a felony***

felt[1] /felt/ *noun* [U] a soft, thick cloth that is made from wool, hair, or fur that has been pressed together

felt[2] /felt/ *past of* feel

ˌfelt-tip ˈpen *noun* [C] a pen with a point made of soft material, usually with brightly coloured ink for colouring pictures

O‿ **female**[1] /ˈfiːmeɪl/ *adjective* belonging to or relating to women, or to the sex that can produce eggs or have babies *a female athlete/employee* ○ *a female butterfly/elephant* ○ *Is it male or female?*

female[2] /ˈfiːmeɪl/ *noun* [C] a person or animal that belongs to the sex that can produce eggs or have babies *Our dog's just had puppies - three males and two females.*

feminine /ˈfemɪnɪn/ *adjective* **1** showing qualities that people generally think are typical of women *a feminine voice* ○ *feminine beauty* **2** **LANGUAGE** in some languages, belonging to a group of nouns or adjectives that have the same grammatical behaviour. The other groups are 'masculine' and 'neuter'.

femininity /ˌfemɪˈnɪnəti/ *noun* [U] when someone shows qualities that people generally think are typical of women

feminism /ˈfemɪnɪzᵊm/ *noun* [U] **POLITICS** the belief that women should have the same economic, social, and political rights as men •**feminist** *noun* [C] someone who supports feminism *a radical feminist* •**feminist** *adjective* *feminist literature*

fence[1] /fens/ *noun* [C] **1** a wood, wire, or metal structure that divides or goes around an area *a garden/electric fence* **2** **sit on the fence** to wait before you choose between two possibilities ➲See also: **picket fence**

fence[2] /fens/ *verb* [I] **SPORT** to take part in the sport of fencing

fence sth in *phrasal verb* to build a fence around an area

fence sth off *phrasal verb* to separate one area from another by building a fence

fencing /ˈfensɪŋ/ *noun* [U] **1** **SPORT** the sport of fighting with thin swords (= weapons like long knives) **2** fences, or the material that is used to make them

fend /fend/ *verb*

fend for yourself *phrasal verb* to take care of yourself without help

fend sb/sth off *phrasal verb* to defend yourself against someone or something that is attacking you or annoying you *They managed to fend off their attackers with rocks and sticks.*

fender /ˈfendəʳ/ *noun* [C] **1** CAR *US* (*UK* **wing**) one of the parts at each corner of a car above the wheels **2** BICYCLE *US* (*UK* **mudguard**) a curved piece of metal or plastic fixed above a wheel of a bicycle or motorcycle to prevent water or dirt from hitting the legs of the person who is riding it **3** FIREPLACE *UK* a low, metal structure around an open fireplace which stops the coal or wood from falling out

feng shui /fʌŋˈʃweɪ/ *noun* [U] an ancient Chinese belief that the way your house is built and the way that you arrange objects affects your success, health, and happiness

fennel /ˈfenᵊl/ *noun* [U] **FOOD** a plant whose base can be eaten, and whose leaves and seeds are used as a spice in cooking

ferment[1] /fəˈment/ *verb* [I, T] **CHEMISTRY** If food or drink ferments, or if you ferment it, the sugar in it changes into alcohol because of a chemical process. *wine fermenting in barrels* •**fermentation** /ˌfɜːmenˈteɪʃᵊn/ *noun* [U]

ferment[2] /ˈfɜːment/ *noun* [U] *formal* excitement or disagreement caused by change or a difficult situation

fermenter /fəˈmentəʳ/ *noun* [C] **CHEMISTRY** a substance that causes fermentation

fern /fɜːn/ *noun* [C] a green plant with long stems, narrow leaves like feathers, and no flowers

fern

ferocious /fəˈrəʊʃəs/ *adjective* extremely angry, violent, or forceful *a ferocious dog* ○ *a ferocious attack* •**ferociously** *adverb*

ferocity /fəˈrɒsəti/ *noun* [U] extreme violence or force *a storm of incredible ferocity*

ferret[1] /ˈferɪt/ *noun* [C] a small animal with a long, thin body that is sometimes used to hunt rabbits

ferret[2] /ˈferɪt/ *verb*

ferret sth out *phrasal verb* to find something after searching carefully for it

Ferris wheel /ˈferɪsˌwiːl/ *noun* [C] an entertainment consisting of a large wheel that turns slowly with seats for people to sit in

ferromagnetism /ˌferəʊˈmægnətɪzᵊm/ *noun* [U] **PHYSICS** the type of magnetism (= force that makes metal move towards it) that iron has •**ferromagnetic** /ˌferəʊmægˈnetɪk/ *adjective*

ferrous /ˈferəs / **CHEMISTRY** containing iron *ferrous metals/compounds*

ferry¹ /ˈferi/ *noun* [C] a boat that regularly carries passengers and vehicles across an area of water *a* ***car/passenger ferry***

ferry² /ˈferi/ *verb* [T] to regularly carry passengers or goods from one place to another in a vehicle

fertile /ˈfɜːtaɪl/ (US) /ˈfɜːrtᵊl/ *adjective* **1** **FARMING** Fertile land or soil produces a lot of healthy plants. **2** **BIOLOGY** If people or animals are fertile, they are able to have babies. **3** **fertile ground (for sth)** a situation or place where an idea, activity, etc is likely to succeed **4** **a fertile imagination** If someone has a fertile imagination, they have lots of interesting and unusual ideas. •**fertility** /fəˈtɪləti/ *noun* [U]

F

fertilize (*also UK* **-ise**) /ˈfɜːtɪlaɪz/ *verb* [T] **1** **BIOLOGY** to cause an egg to start to develop into a young animal or baby by combining it with a male cell *Once an egg is fertilized it becomes an embryo.* **2** **FARMING** to put a natural or chemical substance on land in order to make plants grow well •**fertilization** /ˌfɜːtɪlaɪˈzeɪʃᵊn/ *noun* [U]

fertilizer (*also UK* **-iser**) /ˈfɜːtɪlaɪzəʳ/ *noun* [C, U] **FARMING** a natural or chemical substance that you put on land in order to make plants grow well

fervent /ˈfɜːvᵊnt/ *adjective* showing sincere and enthusiastic beliefs or feelings *a* ***fervent supporter*** *of animal rights* •**fervently** *adverb*

fervour *UK* (*US* **fervor**) /ˈfɜːrvəʳ/ *noun* [U] extremely strong beliefs or feelings ***religious/patriotic fervour***

fess /fes/ *verb*

fess up *phrasal verb informal* to admit that you have done something bad *He eventually* ***fessed up to*** *having spilt coffee on it.*

fest /fest/ *noun* **a beer/film/jazz, etc fest** a special event where people can enjoy a particular activity or thing

fester /ˈfestəʳ/ *verb* [I] **1** [FEELING] If a bad feeling or situation festers, it becomes worse over a period of time. *Hatred between the two groups has festered for years.* **2** [INJURY] If an injury festers, it becomes infected. *a festering wound*

festival /ˈfestɪvᵊl/ *noun* [C] **1** a series of special events, performances, etc that often takes place over several days *a* ***dance/music festival*** ○ *the Berlin Film Festival* **2** **SOCIETY** a special day or period when people celebrate something, especially a religious event *the Jewish festival of Hanukkah*

festive /ˈfestɪv/ *adjective* happy and enjoyable because people are celebrating *a* ***festive mood/occasion*** ○ *What are you doing* ***for the festive season*** (= Christmas)*?* •**festivity** /fesˈtɪvəti/ *noun* [U] when people are happy and celebrating

festivities /fesˈtɪvətiz/ *noun* [plural] events that people organize in order to celebrate something

festoon /fesˈtuːn/ *verb* [T] to cover something with objects, especially decorations [**often passive**] *The balcony was* ***festooned with*** *flags and ribbons.*

fetch /fetʃ/ *verb* [T] **1** [GET] to go to another place to get something or someone and bring them back *Can you fetch my glasses from the bedroom?* **2** [SELL] If something fetches a particular amount of money, it is sold for that amount. *The painting is expected to fetch $50,000 in the auction.*

fetching /ˈfetʃɪŋ/ *adjective* attractive *That scarf looks rather fetching on you.*

fête /feɪt/ *noun* [C] **1** [ENTERTAINMENT] *UK* an event that is held outside and includes competitions, games, and things for sale *a* ***village fête*** **2** [CELEBRATION] *US* a special event to celebrate someone or something •**fête** *verb* [T] to publicly celebrate someone, often by having a special party [**often passive**] *She was fêted by audiences all over the world.*

fetish /ˈfetɪʃ/ *noun* [C] **1** [SEXUAL INTEREST] a strong sexual interest in something unusual *a rubber fetish* **2** [EXTREME INTEREST] something that someone spends too much time thinking about or doing *a fetish for cleanliness*

fetus /ˈfiːtəs/ *noun* [C] **BIOLOGY** *US spelling of* foetus (= a young human or animal that is still developing inside its mother) •**fetal** /ˈfiːtᵊl/ *adjective US spelling of* foetal

WORD PARTNERS FOR ***feud***

a **bitter/long-running** feud • a **family** feud • a feud **with** sb/**between** sb **and** sb

feud /fjuːd/ *noun* [C] a serious and sometimes violent argument between two people or groups that continues for a long period •**feud** *verb* [I] *The families have been feuding for years.*

feudal /ˈfjuːdᵊl/ *adjective* **POLITICS, SOCIETY** relating to a social system in the past in which people worked and fought for a lord (= a man of high rank) in exchange for land and protection •**feudalism** *noun* [U]

WORD PARTNERS FOR ***fever***

develop/have/run a fever • a **high** fever

fever /ˈfiːvəʳ/ *noun* **1** **HEALTH** [C, U] when someone's body temperature rises because they are ill *a* ***high/slight fever*** **2** [U] when people are very excited about something *Election fever has gripped the nation.* ➲See also: **glandular fever, hay fever**

feverish /ˈfiːvᵊrɪʃ/ *adjective* **1** **HEALTH** having a fever *I feel a bit feverish.* **2** Feverish activity is done quickly, often because of excitement or fear. *The rescuers worked at a* ***feverish pace.*** •**feverishly** *adverb They worked feverishly to put out the fire.*

ˈfever ˌpitch *noun* **reach fever pitch** If emotions reach fever pitch, they become so strong that they are difficult to control.

O-ₘ **few** /fjuː/ *quantifier* **1** **a few** some, or a small number of *It'll be here in a few minutes.* ○ *I met* ***a few of*** *the other employees at my interview.* **2** **quite a few/a good few** quite a large number of *Quite a few people have had the same problem.* **3** not many, or only a small number of *We get few complaints.* ○ ***Few of*** *the children can read or write yet.* ○ ***Very few*** *people can afford to pay those prices.* ➲See Common Learner Error at **less** **4** **few and far between** not happening or existing very often *Opportunities like this are few and far between.*

fiancé /fiˈɑːnseɪ/ *noun* [C] A woman's fiancé is the man that she has promised to marry.

fiancée /fiˈɑːnseɪ/ *noun* [C] A man's fiancée is the woman that he has promised to marry.

fiasco /fiˈæskəʊ/ *noun* [C] a complete failure, especially one that embarrasses people *My last dinner party was a complete fiasco.*

fib /fɪb/ *noun* [C] *informal* a small lie that is not very important *Don't **tell fibs**.* •**fib** *verb* [I] **fibbing**, *past* **fibbed** to say something that is not true

fibre *UK* (*US* **fiber**) /ˈfaɪbəʳ/ *noun* **1** CLOTH [C, U] cloth made from thin threads twisted together *Man-made fibres like nylon are easy to wash.* **2** THIN THREAD [C] one of the thin threads that forms a substance such as cloth *The fibres are woven into fabric.* **3 FOOD** [U] the substance in plants which cannot be digested and helps food pass through your body *Broccoli is a good source of fibre.* **4 ANATOMY, BIOLOGY** [C] a structure like a thread in your body *muscle/nerve fibres*

fibreglass *UK* (*US* **fiberglass**) /ˈfaɪbəglɑːs/ *noun* [U] **DT** a strong, light material made by twisting together glass or plastic threads

ˌfibre ˈoptics (*US* **fiber optics**) *noun* [U] **PHYSICS** the use of long, very thin pieces of glass or plastic to carry light signals, used in telephone, television and computer systems

fibrin /ˈfɪbrɪn/ *noun* [U] **BIOLOGY** a substance that forms in the blood to stop the blood from flowing, for example when the body is injured

fibrinogen /fɪˈbrɪnəʊdʒən/ *noun* [U] **BIOLOGY** a substance in the blood from which fibrin is produced

fibula /ˈfɪbjələ/ *noun* [C] **ANATOMY** the thin outer bone in a person's leg, between the knee and the foot

fickle /ˈfɪkl/ *adjective* Someone who is fickle often changes their opinion about things.

fiction /ˈfɪkʃən/ *noun* **1 LITERATURE** [U] literature and stories about imaginary people or events *What's the best-selling children's fiction title?* ➲Opposite **nonfiction** **2** NOT TRUE [U, **no plural**] something that is not true or real ➲See also: **science fiction**

fictional /ˈfɪkʃənəl/ *adjective* existing only in fiction *a **fictional character***

fictitious /fɪkˈtɪʃəs/ *adjective* invented and not real or true *a **fictitious name***

fiddle¹ /ˈfɪdl/ *verb* [T] *UK informal* to change something dishonestly in order to get money *She was fired for fiddling her travel expenses.*
fiddle (about/around) with sth *phrasal verb* **1** MOVE THINGS to touch or move things with your fingers because you are nervous or bored *Stop fiddling with your hair!* **2** MAKE CHANGES to make small changes to something to try to make it work *He fiddled with the wires to get the radio working again.*

fiddle² /ˈfɪdl/ *noun* [C] **1 MUSIC** *informal* a violin (= a wooden musical instrument with strings) **2** *UK* a dishonest way to get money *a tax fiddle*

fiddler /ˈfɪdləʳ/ *noun* [C] **MUSIC** someone who plays the violin (= a wooden musical instrument with strings)

fiddly /ˈfɪdli/ *adjective UK* difficult to do because the parts involved are small *Repairing a watch is very fiddly.*

fidelity /fɪˈdeləti/ *noun* [U] loyalty, especially to a sexual partner ➲Opposite **infidelity**

fidget /ˈfɪdʒɪt/ *verb* [I] to keep making small movements with your hands or feet because you are nervous or bored *She fidgeted all the way through the interview.* •**fidgety** *adjective*

O➡ **field¹** /fiːld/ *noun* **1 FARMING** [C] an area of land used for growing crops or keeping animals *a wheat field* **2 SPORT** [C] an area of grass where you can play a sport *a football field* **3** [C] an area of study or activity *He's an expert **in the field of** biochemistry.* **4 SPORT** [**no plural**] the people who are competing in a race, activity, or business *We **lead the field** in genetic research.* **5 COMPUTING** [C] a part of a computer screen which is for a particular type of information, or a piece of information in a database *There's a field for you to enter your name and address.* **6 a gas/oil field** an area of land containing gas or oil **7 a gravitational/magnetic field PHYSICS** an area affected by a particular physical force ➲See also: **paddy field, playing field**

field² /fiːld/ *verb* **1 SPORT** [I, T] to try to catch or stop a ball after it has been hit in a game such as cricket or baseball *Are we fielding or batting?* **2 SPORT** [T] to send out a team or player to play in a game *Brazil fielded a strong team in the World Cup.* **3 field questions/telephone calls** to answer or deal with questions/telephone calls

ˈfield ˌday *noun* **have a field day** to have the opportunity to do a lot of something you want to do, especially to criticize someone *The press had a field day when they found out about the scandal.*

fielder /ˈfiːldəʳ/ *noun* [C] **SPORT** a player who tries to catch or stop the ball in games such as cricket or baseball

ˈfield ˌhockey *US* (*UK* **hockey**) *noun* [U] **SPORT** a team game played on grass where you hit a small ball with a long, curved stick

ˌfield ˈmarshal *UK* (*US* **ˈfield ˌmarshal**) *noun* [C] an officer of the highest rank in the British army

fiend /fiːnd/ *noun* [C] **1** EVIL PERSON an evil or cruel person **2** ENTHUSIASTIC PERSON someone who is very interested in a particular thing

fiendish /ˈfiːndɪʃ/ *adjective* **1** EVIL evil or cruel *a fiendish attack* **2** DIFFICULT very difficult or complicated *a fiendish crossword* •**fiendishly** *adverb mainly UK* extremely ***fiendishly clever/difficult***

fierce /fɪəs/ *adjective* **1** VIOLENT violent or angry ***a fierce attack*** ○ ***a fierce dog*** **2** POWERFUL very strong or powerful ***fierce winds/storms*** ○ *There is **fierce competition** between car manufacturers.* •**fiercely** *adverb*

fiery /ˈfaɪəri/ *adjective* **1** EMOTION showing strong emotion, especially anger ***a fiery temper*** **2** LIKE FIRE bright or burning like a fire *a fiery sunset*

O➡ **fifteen** /ˌfɪfˈtiːn/ the number 15 •**fifteenth** 15th written as a word

fifth[1] /fɪfθ/ 5th written as a word

fifth[2] /fɪfθ/ *noun* [C] one of five equal parts of something; $^1/_5$

O⁔**fifty** /ˈfɪfti/ **1** the number 50 **2 the fifties** the years from 1950 to 1959 **3 be in your fifties** to be aged between 50 and 59 •**fiftieth** 50th written as a word

fifty-fifty /ˌfɪftiˈfɪfti/ *adjective, adverb informal* **1** shared equally between two people *Let's divide the bill fifty-fifty.* **2 a fifty-fifty chance** If something has a fifty-fifty chance, it is equally likely to happen or not to happen. *We have a fifty-fifty chance of winning the match.*

fig /fɪg/ *noun* [C] **FOOD** a dark, sweet fruit with lots of seeds, that is often eaten dried

fig. *written abbreviation for* figure (= a picture or drawing in a book or document, usually with a number) *See fig. 1.*

O⁔**fight**[1] /faɪt/ *verb past* **fought 1** [USE FORCE] [I, T] When people fight, they use physical force to try to defeat each other. *Two men were arrested for fighting outside a bar.* ○ *Sam's always* ***fighting with*** *his little brother.* **2** [JOIN WAR] [I, T] to take part in a war *Millions of young men fought in World War I.* **3** [ARGUE] [I] to argue *We've got to stop fighting in front of the children.* **4** [TRY TO STOP] [I, T] to try hard to stop something bad happening *He* ***fought against*** *racism.* ○ *New measures have been introduced to* ***fight crime.*** **5** [TRY TO ACHIEVE] [I] to try hard to achieve something you want or think is right *They are* ***fighting for*** *their freedom.* [+ **to do sth**] *He had to fight very hard to keep his job.* **6 be fighting for your life** to be trying very hard to stay alive when you are very ill or badly injured ➲See also: fight a losing **battle**[1]

fight back *phrasal verb* to defend yourself when someone or something attacks you or causes problems for you

WORD PARTNERS FOR ***fight***

a fight **with** sb • **have/get into/pick/start** a fight • **lose/win** a fight

O⁔**fight**[2] /faɪt/ *noun* [C] **1** [PHYSICAL FORCE] when people use physical force to hurt or attack others *He's always* ***getting into fights.*** **2** [EFFORT] a determined effort to achieve or stop something *She was very active in the* ***fight against*** *drugs.* ○ *Join us in our* ***fight for*** *freedom!* [+ **to do sth**] *This year has brought some good news in the fight to save the whales.* **3** [ARGUMENT] an argument *I don't want to have a fight over this.* **4** **SPORT** a boxing competition

fighter /ˈfaɪtəʳ/ *noun* [C] **1** (*also* ˈ**fighter ˌplane**) a fast military aircraft that can attack other aircraft *a* ***fighter pilot*** **2** **SPORT** someone who fights in a war or as a sport

fighting /ˈfaɪtɪŋ/ *noun* [U] when people fight, usually in a war *Thousands of civilians were killed in the fighting.*

figment /ˈfɪgmənt/ *noun* **a figment of sb's imagination** something that someone believes is real but that only exists in their imagination

figurative /ˈfɪgjʳətɪv/ *adjective* **1** **LANGUAGE** A figurative meaning of a word or phrase is a more imaginative meaning developed from the usual meaning. **2** Figurative art shows people, places, or things in a similar way to how they look in real life. •**figuratively** *adverb*

WORD PARTNERS FOR ***figure***

a **key /leading/major/prominent** figure • a **public** figure

O⁔**figure**[1] /ˈfɪgəʳ/ *noun* [C] **1** **MATHEMATICS** a symbol for a number *Write down the amount in words and figures.* ○ *He's now being paid a six-figure salary.* **2 single/double, etc figures** numbers from 0 to 9/numbers from 10 to 99, etc **3** [AMOUNT] a number that expresses an amount, especially in official documents ***Government figures*** *show a rise in unemployment.* **4** [TYPE OF PERSON] a particular type of person, often someone important or famous *a mysterious figure* ○ *Lincoln was a major figure in American politics.* **5** [PERSON] a person that you cannot see clearly *I could see two figures in the distance.* **6** [BODY SHAPE] the shape of someone's body, usually an attractive shape *She's got a good figure for her age.* **7** [PICTURE] (*written abbreviation* **fig.**) a picture or drawing in a book or document, usually with a number *Look at the graph shown in Figure 2.* ➲See also: **father figure**

figure[2] /ˈfɪgəʳ/ *verb* **1** [BE PART] [I] to be a part of something, or to appear in something *Love* ***figures in*** *most pop songs.* **2** [THINK] [T] to decide something after thinking about it [+ **(that)**] *I figured that it was time to tell her the truth.* **3 that/it figures** *informal* something you say when you expected something to happen *"I've run out of money, Mum." "That figures."*

figure sth/sb out *phrasal verb* to finally understand something or someone after a lot of thought [+ **question word**] *I never could figure out what she saw in him.*

figurehead /ˈfɪgəhed/ *noun* [C] a leader who has no real power

ˌ**figure of** ˈ**speech** *noun* [C] *plural* **figures of speech** **LANGUAGE** words that are used together in an imaginative way to mean something different from their usual meaning

filament /ˈfɪləmənt/ *noun* [C] **1** **PHYSICS** a thin wire, especially one which lights up inside an electric light bulb **2** **BIOLOGY** the long, thin stem that carries the anther (= part that produces pollen) of a flower ➲See picture at **flower** ➲See picture at **pollen**

WORD PARTNERS FOR ***file***

1 **hold/keep** a file on sb/sth
2 **close/create/download/open/save** a file

O⁔**file**[1] /faɪl/ *noun* **1** [INFORMATION] [C] a collection of information and documents about someone or something *The school* ***keeps files on*** *all its pupils.* **2** **COMPUTING** [C] a piece of text, a picture, or a computer program stored on a computer *Do you want to* ***download*** *all these* ***files?*** **3** [CONTAINER] [C] a box or folded piece of thick paper used to put documents in *He keeps all his bank statements in a file.* ➲See colour picture **The Office** on page Centre 5, **The Classroom** on page Centre 6 **4 on file** If information is on file, it is recorded and stored somewhere. **5** [TOOL] [C] a small tool with a rough edge that is used to make a surface smooth *a* ***nail file*** **6 in single file** in a line with one person following the other ➲See also: the **rank**[1] and file

file² /faɪl/ *verb* **1** PAPER [T] (*also* **file away**) to put documents into an ordered system of boxes or files where you can easily find them again *She filed all her tax returns under T.* **2** **LAW** [T] (*also* **file for**) to officially state that you are going to take someone to court *The police **filed charges** against the suspect.* **3** RUB [T] to rub something with a rough tool in order to make it smooth **4 file along/into/through, etc** to walk somewhere in a line, one behind the other *The audience slowly filed back to their seats.*

ˈfile diˌrectory *noun* [C] **COMPUTING** a place on a computer for putting files and folders together

ˈfile exˌtension *noun* [C] **COMPUTING** a dot followed by three letters, such as .doc or .jpg, that forms the end of the name of a computer document and shows what sort of document it is

filename /ˈfaɪlneɪm/ *noun* [C] **COMPUTING** a name given to a computer file

ˈfile ˌsharing *noun* [U] **COMPUTING** the activity of putting a file onto a special place on your computer so that many other people can copy it, look at it, or use it by using the Internet ➲See Extra help page **The Web and the Internet** on page Centre 36

filet /fɪˈleɪ/ *noun* [C] **FOOD** *another US spelling of* fillet (= a piece of meat or fish with the bones taken out)

ˈfiling ˌcabinet (*also US* **ˈfile ˌcabinet**) *noun* [C] a piece of office furniture with deep drawers for storing documents ➲See colour picture **The Office** on page Centre 5

O-ꟷ**fill¹** /fɪl/ *verb* **1** MAKE FULL [I, T] (*also* **fill up**) to make a container or space full, or to become full *He filled the bucket with water.* ○ *I made a drink while the bath was filling.* **2** TAKE SPACE [T] If people or things fill a place, there are a lot of them in it. *The streets were **filled with** tourists.* ○ *Dark clouds filled the sky.* **3** BE NOTICEABLE [T] If light, sound, or a smell fills a place, you can easily notice it. *The smell of smoke filled the room.* **4 fill sb with anger/joy/pride, etc** to make someone feel very angry/happy/proud, etc *The thought of losing him filled her with fear.* **5 fill a post/position/vacancy** to take a new job *They still haven't found anyone to fill the vacancy.* **6 fill a need/gap/demand** to provide something that people need or want

fill sth in/out *phrasal verb* to write the necessary information on an official document *to **fill in** a **form/questionnaire***

fill (sth) up *phrasal verb* to become full, or to make something become full *The restaurant soon filled up with people.*

fill² /fɪl/ *noun* **your fill** as much of something as you want or need *I've **had my fill of** living in the city.*

fillet (*also US* **filet**) /ˈfɪlɪt/ Ⓤⓢ /fɪˈleɪ/ *noun* [C] **FOOD** a piece of meat or fish with the bones taken out

filling¹ /ˈfɪlɪŋ/ *noun* **1** [C, U] food that is put inside things such as cakes, pastry, pieces of bread, etc *What sort of filling do you want in your sandwich?* **2** **HEALTH** [C] a hard substance that fills a hole in a tooth

filling² /ˈfɪlɪŋ/ *adjective* Food that is filling makes your stomach feel full. *This soup is very filling.*

ˈfilling ˌstation *noun* [C] a petrol station (= place where you can buy fuel for your car)

> WORD PARTNERS FOR ***film***
>
> **make** a film • a film **about** sb/sth • **in** a film • a **horror** film • a **classic** film • the film **industry**

O-ꟷ**film¹** /fɪlm/ *noun* **1** PICTURES [C] (*also US* **movie**) a story shown in moving pictures, shown at the cinema or on television *'Titanic' was one of the most popular Hollywood **films** ever **made**.* **2** MATERIAL [C, U] special thin plastic used for making photographs or moving pictures, or a length of this *I need to buy another **roll of film**.* **3** LAYER [**no plural**] a thin layer of something on a surface *a thick film of dust.*

film² /fɪlm/ *verb* [I, T] to record moving pictures with a camera, usually to make a film for the cinema or television *Most of the scenes were filmed in a studio.* •**filming** *noun* [U]

film-maker *UK* (*US* **filmmaker**) /ˈfɪlmmeɪkəʳ/ *noun* [C] someone who makes films for the cinema or television

ˈfilm ˌstar *noun* [C] a famous cinema actor or actress

filter¹ /ˈfɪltəʳ/ *verb* **1** [T] to pass a liquid or gas through a piece of equipment in order to remove solid pieces or other substances *The water was filtered to remove any impurities.* **2 filter down/in/through, etc** to gradually appear or become known *News is filtering in of an earthquake in Mexico.*

filter sth out *phrasal verb* to remove a particular substance from a liquid or gas

filter² /ˈfɪltəʳ/ *noun* [C] a piece of equipment that you pass a liquid or gas through in order to remove particular substances *a coffee filter*

ˈfilter ˌpaper *noun* [U] **CHEMISTRY** thick paper used for filtering substances ➲See picture at **filtrate**

filth /fɪlθ/ *noun* [U] **1** DIRT thick and unpleasant dirt *His clothes were covered in filth and mud.* **2** OFFENSIVE offensive language or pictures, usually relating to sex

filthy /ˈfɪlθi/ *adjective* **1** DIRTY extremely dirty *Wash your hands, they're filthy!* **2** OFFENSIVE rude or offensive *filthy language/jokes* ○ *Smoking is a **filthy habit**.*

filtrate /ˈfɪltreɪt/ *noun* [C] **CHEMISTRY** a liquid, gas or other substance that has passed through a filter (= piece of equipment that removes substances that are not wanted) ➲See picture **filtrate** on next page

filtration /fɪlˈtreɪʃᵊn/ *noun* [U] **CHEMISTRY, PHYSICS** the act of passing a liquid or gas through a filter (= piece of equipment that removes substances that are not wanted)

fin /fɪn/ *noun* [C] **BIOLOGY** a thin, triangular part on a fish, which helps it to swim

O-ꟷ**final¹** /ˈfaɪnᵊl/ *adjective* **1** LAST [**always before noun**] last in a series or coming at the end of something *the final paragraph* ○ *They scored a goal in the final minute.* **2** NO MORE DISCUSSION If a decision, agreement, or answer is final, it will not be changed or discussed any more. *The committee's decision is final.* ➲See also: the final **nail**¹ in the coffin, the final/last **straw**

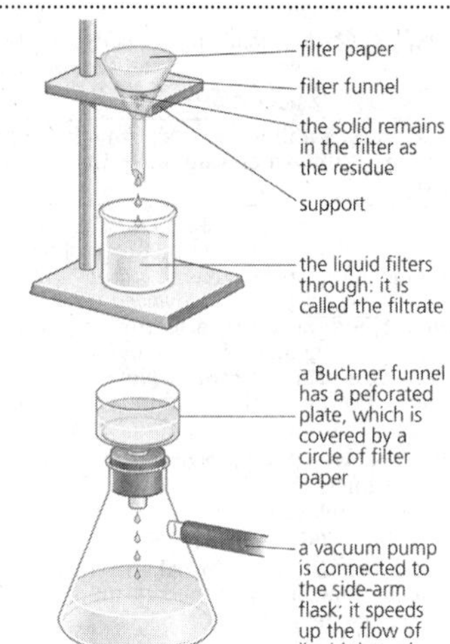
filter paper
filter funnel
the solid remains in the filter as the residue
support
the liquid filters through: it is called the filtrate
a Buchner funnel has a peforated plate, which is covered by a circle of filter paper
a vacuum pump is connected to the side-arm flask; it speeds up the flow of liquid through the funnel
filtrate

final² /ˈfaɪnəl/ *noun* **1** [C] the last part of a competition to decide which person or team will be the winner *the European Cup Final* ○ *The finals will be shown on TV.* **2 finals EDUCATION** exams taken at the end of a university course

ˌfinal acˈcounts *noun* [plural] **FINANCE** the accounts produced by a business, usually at the end of each year, that show the financial situation of the business

finale /fɪˈnɑːli/ *noun* [C] the last part of a show, event, or piece of music

finalist /ˈfaɪnəlɪst/ *noun* [C] a person or team in the last part of a competition

finalize (*also UK* **-ise**) /ˈfaɪnəlaɪz/ *verb* [T] to make a final and certain decision about a plan, date, etc *to **finalize arrangements/details***

O‑ **finally** /ˈfaɪnəli/ *adverb* **1** AFTER A LONG TIME after a long time or some difficulty *After months of looking, he finally found a job.* **2** LAST POINT used to introduce the last point or idea *Finally, I'd like to thank everyone for coming this evening.* **3** CERTAINLY in a way that will not be changed *The date of the wedding hasn't been finally decided yet.*

finance¹ /ˈfaɪnæns/ *noun* **1 FINANCE, ECONOMICS** [U] the control of how large amounts of money should be spent **2 FINANCE, ECONOMICS** [U] the money that is needed to support a business *Who **put up** the **finance** for the project?* **3 sb's finances FINANCE** the money which a person, company, or country has *You must learn how to manage your own finances.*

finance² /ˈfaɪnæns/ *verb* [T] **FINANCE** to provide the money needed to do something *Who's financing the project?*

O‑ **financial** /faɪˈnænʃəl/ *adjective* **FINANCE** relating to money or how money is managed *a **financial adviser*** ○ *She's having some financial difficulties at the moment.* •**financially** *adverb Many students are still financially dependent on their parents.*

fiˌnancial ˈyear *noun* [C] **FINANCE** (*also UK* **tax year**) the period of twelve months when a person or company's finances and taxes are calculated

finch /fɪnʃ/ *noun* [C] a small singing bird with a short beak

OTHER WAYS OF SAYING *find*

A very common alternative to 'find' is the verb **discover**: *The victim's wallet was **discovered** in a ditch.* • *I finally **discovered** the letters in a drawer.*

If someone finds the exact position of someone or something, in formal situations the verb **locate** is sometimes used: *Police are still trying to **locate** the suspect.*

If someone finds something that has been secret or hidden, then the verbs **uncover** or **unearth** are sometimes used: *Reporters **uncovered/unearthed** evidence of corruption.*

The phrasal verbs **come across** and **stumble across/on** are used when someone finds something by chance: *I **stumbled on** these photographs when I was cleaning out my desk.* • *We **came across** a lovely little restaurant in the village.*

If someone finds something or someone after looking carefully in different places, you can use the verb **trace** or the phrasal verb **track down**: *Police have so far failed to **trace/track down** the missing woman.*

O‑ **find¹** /faɪnd/ *verb* [T] *past* **found 1** DISCOVER WHEN SEARCHING to discover something or someone that you have been searching for *I can't find my glasses and I've looked everywhere.* ○ *Police found the missing girl at a London railway station.* [+ two objects] *Has he found himself a place to live yet?* **2** DISCOVER BY CHANCE to discover something or someone by chance *The body was found by a man walking his dog.* **3** BECOME AWARE to become aware that something exists, or has happened *I came home to find that my cat had had kittens.* **4 find the energy/money/time, etc** to have or get enough energy/money/time, etc to do something *Where do you find the energy to do all these things?* **5 find sb/sth easy/boring/funny, etc** to think or feel a particular way about someone or something *I still find exams very stressful.* **6 find yourself somewhere/doing sth** to become aware that you have gone somewhere or done something without intending to *I suddenly found myself making everyone's lunch.* **7 be found** to exist or be present somewhere *Vitamin C is found in oranges and other citrus fruit.* **8 find sb guilty/not guilty** to judge that someone is guilty or not guilty in a law court [often passive] She was ***found guilty of*** *murder.*

find (sth) out *phrasal verb* to get information about something, or to learn a fact for the first time *I must find out the train times.* [+ question word] *Peter was shocked when he found out what we had done.* ➲See Common Learner Error at **know**

find[2] /faɪnd/ *noun* [C] something or someone valuable, interesting, or useful that you discover [**usually singular**] *This hotel was a real find.*

finding /ˈfaɪndɪŋ/ *noun* [C] a piece of information that has been discovered as a result of an official study [**usually plural**] *The findings of this research will be published next year.*

O- **fine**[1] /faɪn/ *adjective* **1** WELL well, healthy, or happy *"How are you?" "I'm* ***fine thanks.*** *And you?"* ○ *I had a cold last week, but I'm fine now.* **2** GOOD good or good enough *"Is the soup hot enough?" "Yes, it's fine."* **3** EXCELLENT excellent, or of very good quality *fine wines* ○ *He's a fine musician.* **4 (that's) fine** used to agree with a suggestion, idea, decision, etc *"Shall we meet at 8 o'clock?" "Yes, that's* ***fine by me.****"* **5** THIN thin or made of very small pieces *fine, brown hair* ○ *fine sand* **6** SUNNY *mainly UK* sunny and not raining *If it's fine, we could have a picnic.* **7 the finer details/points, etc of sth** the more detailed or more difficult parts of an argument, idea, etc

fine[2] /faɪn/ *adverb informal* **1** very well or without any problems *"How did your exam go?" "It went fine thanks."* **2 cut it/things fine** to leave yourself only just enough time to do something *Twenty minutes to get to the station? That's cutting it a bit fine!*

fine[3] /faɪn/ *verb* [T] to make someone pay an amount of money as a punishment for breaking a law or rule [**often passive**] *He was* ***fined*** *£500* ***for*** *dangerous driving.*

WORD PARTNERS FOR ***fine***

face/get/receive a fine • **pay** a fine • a **heavy/hefty/stiff** fine • a **parking** fine

fine[4] /faɪn/ *noun* [C] an amount of money that you must pay for breaking a law or rule *a* ***parking fine*** ○ *The court gave her two weeks to* ***pay*** *the* ***fine.***

finely /ˈfaɪnli/ *adverb* **1** SMALL PIECES into small pieces ***Finely chop*** *the garlic.* **2** EXACTLY very exactly *a finely tuned machine*

O- **finger**[1] /ˈfɪŋgəʳ/ *noun* **1 ANATOMY** [C] one of the five, long, separate parts at the end of your hand, including your thumb ⊃See colour picture **The Body** on page Centre 13 **2 have green fingers** *UK* (*US* **have a green thumb**) to be good at gardening and making plants grow well **3 keep your fingers crossed** *informal* to hope that things will happen in the way that you want them to *Let's keep our fingers crossed that it doesn't rain.* **4 not lift a finger** *informal* to not help someone do something, usually because you are too lazy *He never lifts a finger to help with the housework.* **5 put your finger on sth** to understand exactly why a situation is the way it is *Something was wrong, but I couldn't put my finger on it.* **6 snap your fingers** (*also UK* **click your fingers**) to press your thumb and middle finger together until the finger hits your hand and makes a short sound ⊃See also: **index finger**

finger[2] /ˈfɪŋgəʳ/ *verb* [T] to touch or feel something with your fingers

fingernail /ˈfɪŋgəneɪl/ *noun* [C] **ANATOMY** the hard, thin part on the top of the end of your finger

fingerprint /ˈfɪŋgəprɪnt/ *noun* [C] the mark made on something by the pattern of curved lines on the end of someone's finger *The police found fingerprints all over the murder weapon.*

fingertip /ˈfɪŋgətɪp/ *noun* **1 ANATOMY** [C] the end of your finger **2 at your fingertips** If you have something at your fingertips, you can get it and use it very easily. *He had all the information he needed at his fingertips.*

OTHER WAYS OF SAYING ***finish***

The verb **end** is a common alternative to 'finish' when it means 'stop': *What time does the concert* ***end?***

When someone finishes doing or making something, the verb **complete** is sometimes used: *Have you* ***completed*** *all the questions?* • *The project took 5 years to* ***complete.***

If someone finishes something quickly and easily, especially food or a piece of work, in informal situations you can use the phrasal verb **polish off**: *He's just* ***polished off*** *two huge bowls of pasta.*

The phrasal verb **wind up** is sometimes used when an activity is gradually finishing: *It's time to* ***wind up*** *the game now.*

O- **finish**[1] /ˈfɪnɪʃ/ *verb* **1** COMPLETE [I, T] to complete something, or come to the end of an activity *When I finish my homework, can I watch TV?* [**+ doing sth**] *Have you finished reading that book yet?* **2** END [I] to end *The meeting should finish at five o'clock.* **3** USE COMPLETELY [T] (*also* **finish off**) to eat, drink, or use something completely *They finished their drinks and left the bar.* **4 finish first/second, etc** to be in the first/second, etc winning position at the end of a race or competition

finish sth off *phrasal verb* **1** COMPLETE to complete the last part of something that you are doing *I have to finish off this report by Friday.* **2** EAT/DRINK to eat, drink, or use the last part of something *Would you like to finish off the pizza?*

finish up *phrasal verb mainly UK* to finally be in a particular place, state, or situation, usually without having planned it *I only went for two days, but finished up staying for a week.*

finish with sth *phrasal verb* to stop using or needing something *Have you finished with the newspaper?*

finish with sb *phrasal verb UK* to stop having a romantic relationship with someone

finish[2] /ˈfɪnɪʃ/ *noun* [C] **1** END the end of a race, or the last part of something *a* ***close/exciting finish*** ○ *I enjoyed the film* ***from start to finish.*** **2** SURFACE the way the surface of something feels or looks *The table has a smooth, shiny finish.*

finished /ˈfɪnɪʃt/ *adjective* **1** completed *How much does the* ***finished product*** *cost?* ⊃Opposite **unfinished 2 be finished** If you are finished, you have completed something. *I hope I'll be finished before 5 p.m.*

F

fir /fɜːʳ/ (*also* **ˈfir ˌtree**) *noun* [C] a tree with thin, straight leaves shaped like needles that do not fall in winter

WORD PARTNERS FOR ***fire***

put out/start a fire • a fire **breaks out/burns/rages** • be **on** fire • **catch** fire

fire[1] /faɪəʳ/ *noun* **1** FLAME [U] heat, light, and flames that are produced when something burns **2 catch fire** to start burning *The car crashed and caught fire.* **3 on fire** burning *That house is on fire.* **4 set fire to sth; set sth on fire** to make something start burning, usually to cause damage *Enemy troops set fire to the village.* **5** EVENT [C] when something burns in a way that causes damage and cannot be controlled *Three people were killed in the fire.* ○ *It took the firefighters two hours to* ***put the fire out*** (= stop it burning). **6** NATURAL HEAT [C] a pile of wood, coal, etc that is burning to produce heat *We sat by the fire.* ○ *They put up the tents and* ***lit a fire.*** **7 an electric/gas fire** *UK* a piece of equipment that uses electricity/gas to heat a room **8** SHOOTING [U] the shooting of guns and other weapons *The soldiers* ***opened fire*** (= started shooting). **9 come under fire** to be criticized *The government has come under fire for closing the hospital.*

fire[2] /faɪəʳ/ *verb* **1** GUN [I, T] to shoot a bullet from a gun *She* ***fired*** *three shots* ***at*** *him.* **2** JOB [T] *informal* to tell someone they must leave their job [**often passive**] *I was fired for being late.* **3 fire sb's imagination** to make someone very excited or interested in something **4 fire questions at sb** to ask someone questions quickly one after the other

fire sb up *phrasal verb* to make someone excited or angry

ˈfire aˌlarm *noun* [C] a device such as a bell that warns the people in a building that the building is on fire *If you hear the fire alarm, you must leave the building immediately.*

firearm /ˈfaɪərɑːm/ *noun* [C] a gun that you can carry easily

ˈfire briˌgade *UK* (*US* **ˈfire deˌpartment**) *noun* [C] an organization of people whose job is to stop fires burning

ˈfire ˌengine *noun* [C] a vehicle for carrying firefighters and equipment for stopping large fires

ˈfire esˌcape *noun* [C] a set of metal stairs on the outside of a building which allows people to leave if there is an emergency

ˈfire exˌtinguisher *noun* [C] a piece of equipment kept inside buildings which is used to stop small fires

firefighter /ˈfaɪəfaɪtəʳ/ *noun* [C] someone whose job is to stop fires burning

fireman /ˈfaɪəmən/ *noun* [C] *plural* **firemen** a man whose job is to stop fires burning

fireplace /ˈfaɪəpleɪs/ *noun* [C] a space in the wall of a room where you can have a fire, or the structure around this space ⊃See colour picture **The Living Room** on page Centre 4

fireside /ˈfaɪəsaɪd/ *noun* [U] the area next to a fireplace

ˈfire ˌstation *noun* [C] the building where fire engines are kept, and firefighters wait for emergencies

firewall /ˈfaɪəwɔːl/ *noun* [C] **COMPUTING** a system that controls what information can be sent from your computer using the Internet

firewood /ˈfaɪəwʊd/ *noun* [U] wood that is used for burning on a fire

WORD PARTNERS FOR ***firework***

let off/set off a firework • a firework(s) **display**

firework /ˈfaɪəwɜːk/ *noun* [C] a small object that explodes to produce a loud noise and bright colours and is often used to celebrate special events ***a firework display***

ˈfiring ˌsquad *noun* [C] a group of soldiers who are ordered to shoot and kill a prisoner

firm[1] /fɜːm/ *adjective* **1** NOT SOFT not soft, but not completely hard *A firm bed is better for your back.* **2** FIXED [**always before noun**] certain or fixed and not likely to change *We don't have any* ***firm plans*** *for the weekend yet.* ○ *I'm a* ***firm believer*** *in equal rights.* **3** STRONG strong and tight *a* ***firm handshake/grip*** **4** STRICT strict and making certain that people do what you want *You've got to be firm with children.* •**firmly** *adverb* •**firmness** *noun* [U]

WORD PARTNERS FOR ***firm***

run/set up a firm • a firm **of** [solicitors, accountants, etc]

firm[2] /fɜːm/ *noun* [C] a company that sells goods or services *a law firm*

first[1] /ˈfɜːst/ *adjective* **1** BEFORE coming before all others *Who was the first person to arrive at the party?* ○ *He was nervous on his first day at school.* ○ *They went abroad last year* ***for the first time*** *since having children.* **2** NUMBER 1st written as a word **3** IMPORTANT most important *Sheila won first prize in the photo competition.* ⊃See also: in the first **place[1]**

first[2] /ˈfɜːst/ *adverb* **1** BEFORE before everything or everyone else *I can go to the cinema, but I've got to do my homework first.* ○ *Jason* ***came first*** *in the 400 metres* (= he won). **2** FIRST TIME for the first time *I first heard the song on the radio.* ○ *He first started playing the piano at school.* **3 at first** at the beginning of a situation or period of time *At first I thought she was unfriendly, but actually she is just shy.* **4 first; first of all a** BEGINNING SENTENCE used to introduce the first idea, reason, etc in a series *First, I think we have to change our marketing strategy.* **b** BEFORE EVERYTHING before doing anything else *First of all check you have all the correct ingredients.* **5 come first** to be the most important person or thing *Her career always comes first.* **6 put sb/sth first** to consider someone or something to be the most important thing *Most couples put their children first when sorting out their problems.* **7 First come, first served.** something you say when there is not enough of something for everyone and only the first people who ask for it will get it

first[3] /ˈfɜːst/ *noun, pronoun* **1 the first** the first person, people, thing, or things *Hillary and Norgay were the first to climb Everest.* **2 be a**

first to be something that has never happened before *Man walking on the moon was a first in space history.* **3 EDUCATION** [C] the highest exam result that you can achieve at the end of a university course in the UK

ˌfirst ˈaid *noun* [U] **HEALTH** basic medical treatment that you give someone who is ill or injured in an emergency *The policeman **gave** him **first aid** before the ambulance arrived.*

first-class /ˌfɜːstˈklɑːs/ *adjective* **1** BEST relating to the best and most expensive available service, especially when travelling or sending something somewhere *a **first-class ticket*** ○ *a **first-class stamp*** **2** VERY GOOD of very good quality *It was a first-class restaurant.* •**first class** *adverb How much is it to **send** this letter **first class**?*

ˌfirst ˈfloor *noun* [no plural] **1** ABOVE GROUND *UK* the level of a building directly above the ground level **2** ON GROUND *US* (*UK* **ground floor**) the level of a building on the same level as the ground

firsthand /ˌfɜːstˈhænd/ *adjective, adverb* experienced, seen, or learnt directly *Police heard **firsthand accounts** of the accident from witnesses.* ○ ***firsthand experience***

ˈfirst ˌlanguage *noun* [C] **LANGUAGE** the language that someone learns to speak first *Madeleine's first language is French, but she also knows English and German.*

firstly /ˈfɜːstli/ *adverb* used to introduce the first idea, reason, etc in a series *The aim of this activity is firstly to have fun, and secondly to keep fit.*

ˈfirst ˌname *noun* [C] the name that people who know you call you and that comes before your family name

the ˌfirst ˈperson *noun* **LANGUAGE** the form of a verb or pronoun that is used when people are speaking or writing about themselves. For example, 'I' and 'we' are first person pronouns.

first-rate /ˌfɜːstˈreɪt/ *adjective* extremely good *a first-rate team/writer*

fiscal /ˈfɪskəl/ *adjective* **ECONOMICS, FINANCE** relating to government money, especially taxes

ˌfiscal ˈyear *noun* [C] **ECONOMICS, FINANCE** the period of twelve months when a person or company's finances and taxes are calculated

O⁻**fish¹** /fɪʃ/ *noun plural* **fish** or **fishes** **1** [C] an animal that lives only in water and swims using its tail and fins (= thin, triangular parts) *Are there any fish in the pond?* **2 FOOD** [U] fish eaten as food *fish and chips* ➲See colour picture **Food** on page Centre 11

COMMON LEARNER ERROR

fish or **fishes?**

Fish is the usual plural of **fish**.

I caught six fish in the river.

~~*I caught six fishes in the river.*~~

Fishes is sometimes used to talk about different types of fish.

fish² /fɪʃ/ *verb* [I] **SPORT** to try to catch fish *They're **fishing for** tuna.*

fish sth out *phrasal verb informal* to pull or take something out of a bag or pocket, especially after searching

fisherman /ˈfɪʃəmən/ *noun* [C] *plural* **fishermen** **SPORT** someone who catches fish as a job or as a hobby

fishing /ˈfɪʃɪŋ/ *noun* [U] **SPORT** the sport or job of catching fish *Dad loves to **go fishing**.*

ˈfish ˌslice *noun* [C] *UK* a kitchen tool with a wide, flat end used for lifting and serving food ➲See colour picture **The Kitchen** on page Centre 2

fishy /ˈfɪʃi/ *adjective* **1 FOOD** smelling or tasting like fish **2** making you feel that someone is lying or something dishonest is happening *His story sounds a bit fishy to me.*

fission /ˈfɪʃən/ *noun* [U] **1 PHYSICS** (**nuclear fission**) when the nucleus (= centre part) of an atom is divided, creating a very large amount of energy **2 BIOLOGY** when cells divide to form new cells

fist /fɪst/ *noun* [C] a hand closed into a ball with the fingers and thumb curled tightly together *He banged his fist down angrily on the table.*

O⁻**fit¹** /fɪt/ *verb* **fitting**, *past* **fitted** **1** RIGHT SHAPE [I, T] to be the right shape or size for someone or something *These trousers don't fit any more.* ○ *I can't find a lid to fit this jar.* **2 fit (sth) in/through/under, etc** If people or things fit somewhere, or if you can fit them somewhere, that place is big enough for them. *How many people can you fit in your car?* ○ *This radio is small enough to fit into my pocket.* **3** PUT [T] *mainly UK* to put or fix something somewhere *You ought to fit a smoke alarm in the kitchen.* **4** SAME [I, T] to be the same as or like something *She seems to fit the police description.* **5** SUITABLE [T] to be suitable for something *The punishment should fit the crime.*

COMMON LEARNER ERROR

fit or **suit?**

Remember that the verb **fit** means to be the right shape or size.

This jacket doesn't fit me. It's too tight.

Use the verb **suit** when you want to say that something is right for someone or makes them look more attractive.

That dress looks lovely. Red really suits you.

Life in the big city didn't suit him.

~~*Life in the big city didn't fit him.*~~

fit in *phrasal verb* to feel that you belong to a particular group and are accepted by them *He doesn't **fit in with** the other pupils in his class.*

fit sb/sth in *phrasal verb* to find the time to see someone or do something *The dentist can fit you in on Tuesday morning.*

fit in with sth *phrasal verb* If one activity or event fits in with another, they exist or happen together in a way that is convenient. *The party is in early June. How does that fit in with your holiday plans?*

fit² /fɪt/ *adjective* **fitter**, **fittest** **1** of a good enough quality or suitable type for a particular purpose [+ **to do sth**] *Is this water fit to drink?* ○ *She's not in a **fit state** to drive.* **2 HEALTH** healthy, especially because you exercise regularly *He's very fit for his age.* ➲Opposite **unfit** **3 do sth as you see/think fit** to do something that you feel is the right thing to do, although other people might disapprove *You must spend the money as you see fit.*

fit³ /fɪt/ *noun* **1 a good/loose/tight, etc fit** when something fits someone or somewhere well, loosely, tightly, etc *These shoes are a perfect fit.* **2** [C] a sudden, uncontrolled period of doing something or feeling something *a coughing fit* ○ *I hit him **in a fit of** anger.* **3 HEALTH** [C] a short period of illness when someone cannot control their movements and becomes unconscious *to have an epileptic fit* **4 have a fit** *informal* to become extremely angry

F

fitful /ˈfɪtfᵊl/ *adjective* stopping and starting and not happening in a regular or continuous way ***fitful sleep*** •**fitfully** *adverb*

WORD PARTNERS FOR ***fitness***

improve your fitness • sb's fitness **level(s)** • a fitness **programme/regime/test** • **physical** fitness

fitness /ˈfɪtnəs/ *noun* [U] **1 HEALTH** the condition of being physically strong and healthy ***physical fitness*** **2** the quality of being suitable for a particular purpose, job, course of study, etc *The purpose of the exercise is to judge a soldier's **fitness for** combat.*

fitted /ˈfɪtɪd/ *adjective* **1** FURNITURE *UK* made or cut to fill a particular space exactly ***fitted carpets/kitchens*** **2** CLOTHES Fitted clothes fit tightly to your body. *a fitted jacket*

fitting /ˈfɪtɪŋ/ *adjective* suitable or right for a particular situation *The promotion was a fitting reward for all his hard work.*

ˈfitting ˌroom *noun* [C] a room in a shop where you can put on clothes to check that they fit before you buy them

fittings /ˈfɪtɪŋz/ *noun* [plural] *mainly UK* **1** ON FURNITURE parts that are fixed to a piece of furniture or equipment *a circular bath with gold fittings* **2** IN HOUSE things that are fixed to the walls, floors, and ceilings inside a house but that can be moved

O‑ **five** /faɪv/ the number 5

fiver /ˈfaɪvəʳ/ *noun* [C] *UK informal* a piece of paper money worth £5 *You owe me a fiver.*

five-star /faɪvˈstɑːʳ/ *adjective* describes a hotel or resort of very high quality

O‑ **fix¹** /fɪks/ *verb* [T] **1** REPAIR to repair something *My watch is broken - can you fix it?* **2** DECIDE to decide a certain and exact date, price, plan, etc *Let's fix a day to have lunch together.* ○ *The price has been fixed at $10.* **3 fix sth onto/to/under, etc** to fasten something in a particular place *They fixed the bookcase to the wall.* **4** PREPARE to prepare a drink or meal [+ two objects] *I'll fix you a sandwich.* **5** CHEAT to do something dishonest to make certain that a competition, race, or election is won by a particular person [often passive]

fix sth up *phrasal verb* **1** ARRANGE *UK* to arrange a meeting, date, event, etc *Can we fix up a date for the next meeting?* **2** REPAIR to repair or change something in order to improve it *Nick loves fixing up old cars.*

fix sb up *phrasal verb* to provide someone with something that they need *My uncle has **fixed** me **up with** a summer job.*

fix² /fɪks/ *noun* **1 a quick fix** a way of solving a problem easily *There is no quick fix for unemployment.* **2 be in a fix** to be in a difficult situation *I'm in a fix and need your help.* **3** [C] *informal* an amount of an illegal drug or something that you want very much *Cath needs her **fix of** chocolate every day.*

fixation /fɪkˈseɪʃᵊn/ *noun* [C] a very strong interest in a particular person or thing *She's got an unhealthy **fixation with** her weight.*

fixed /fɪkst/ *adjective* **1** NOT CHANGING decided already and not able to be changed ***a fixed price*** ○ *Is the date of the wedding fixed yet?* **2** FASTENED fastened somewhere and not able to be moved

ˌfixed ˈassets *noun* [plural] **ECONOMICS** the equipment, buildings and land that a business owns

ˌfixed ˈcosts *noun* [plural] **FINANCE, ECONOMICS** the things that a company must pay for in order to keep working, that do not depend on the amount of work the company gets ⊃Compare **variable costs**

fixture /ˈfɪkstʃəʳ/ *noun* [C] **1** a piece of furniture or equipment that is fixed inside a house or building and is usually sold with it [usually plural] *It comes with the usual **fixtures and fittings**.* **2 SPORT** *UK* a sports event that is arranged for a particular day

fizz /fɪz/ *noun* [U] bubbles of gas in a liquid or the sound that they make •**fizz** *verb* [I]

fizzle /ˈfɪzl/ *verb*

fizzle out *phrasal verb* to gradually end in a disappointing way *Their relationship soon fizzled out when they got back from holiday.*

fizzy /ˈfɪzi/ *adjective* **FOOD** A fizzy drink has lots of bubbles of gas in it.

flabbergasted /ˈflæbəgɑːstɪd/ *adjective informal* extremely surprised

flabby /ˈflæbi/ *adjective* having too much loose fat on your body *flabby arms/thighs*

flaccid /ˈflæsɪd/ *adjective formal* soft and not firm

flag¹ /flæg/ *noun* [C] a piece of cloth with a special design and colours, that is fixed to a pole as the symbol of a country or group *the French flag* ○ *There was a flag flying above the castle.*

flag² /flæg/ *verb* [I] **flagging**, *past* **flagged** to become tired or less interested in something *The players started to flag towards the end of the game.*

flag sth down *phrasal verb* to make a vehicle stop by waving at the driver

flagrant /ˈfleɪgrənt/ *adjective* shocking because of being so obviously wrong or bad *a flagrant disregard for the law* •**flagrantly** *adverb*

flagship /ˈflægʃɪp/ *noun* [C] a product or service that is the best and most admired that a company has

flail /fleɪl/ (*also* **flail about/around**) *verb* [I, T] to wave or move your arms and legs about energetically and in an uncontrolled way *The wasp came towards us and Howard started flailing his arms around.*

flair /fleəʳ/ *noun* **1** ABILITY [no plural] a natural ability to do something well *She has a **flair***

for languages. **2** STYLE [U] when you do something in an exciting and interesting way *He played with great imagination and flair.*

flak /flæk/ *noun* [U] *informal* criticism *The government* ***took*** *a lot of* ***flak for*** *breaking its election promises.*

flake¹ /fleɪk/ *noun* [C] a small, flat, thin piece of something *flakes of paint/snow*

flake² /fleɪk/ *verb* [I] to come off in small, flat, thin pieces *The paint was* ***flaking off*** *the walls.* •**flaky** *adjective* coming off easily in small, flat, thin pieces *dry, flaky skin*

flamboyant /flæmˈbɔɪənt/ *adjective* **1** PERSON A flamboyant person is loud, stylish, and confident. *a flamboyant pop star* **2** CLOTHES Flamboyant clothes or colours are very bright and noticeable. •**flamboyance** /flæmˈbɔɪəns/ *noun* [U]

WORD PARTNERS FOR ***flame***

be in flames • **burst into/go up in** flames • flames **spread**

flame¹ /fleɪm/ *noun* [C, U] **1** hot, bright, burning gas produced by something on fire *Smoke and flames were pouring out of the burning factory.* ○ *The whole building was soon* ***in flames*** (= burning). ○ *The car crashed and* ***burst into flames*** (= suddenly started burning). **2 COMPUTING, INTERNET** an angry email or message in a chat room, etc.

flame² /fleɪm/ *verb* [I, T] **COMPUTING, INTERNET** to send an angry email to someone

ˈ**flame** ˌ**test** *noun* [C] **CHEMISTRY** a method used by scientists to discover whether a substance contains metal ions

flaming /ˈfleɪmɪŋ/ *adjective* [**always before noun**] **1** BURNING burning with a bright light *a flaming building* **2** BRIGHT very bright in colour or light *flaming red hair* **3** ANNOYED *UK informal* used to emphasize something when you are annoyed *What a flaming idiot!*

flamingo /fləˈmɪŋgəʊ/ *noun* [C] a large bird with long, thin legs and pink feathers that lives near water in some hot countries

flammable /ˈflæməbl/ (*also* **inflammable**) *adjective* Flammable liquids, gases, or materials burn very easily.

flan /flæn/ *noun* [C, U] **FOOD** a round, open pastry base filled with something such as fruit, or cheese and vegetables *cheese and onion flan*

flank¹ /flæŋk/ *verb* **be flanked by sb/sth** to have someone or something at the side or at each side *The President was flanked by police officers.*

flank² /flæŋk/ *noun* [C] **1 ANATOMY** the side of the body of an animal or person from the chest to the hips **2** the side of an army when it is ready to fight

flannel /ˈflænəl/ *noun* **1** CLOTHES MATERIAL [U] soft, warm cloth for making clothes *flannel pyjamas* **2** WASHING CLOTH [C] *UK* (*US* **washcloth**) a small cloth that you use to wash your face and body ➲See colour picture **The Bathroom** on page Centre 3

flap¹ /flæp/ *noun* **1** CLOTH [C] a piece of cloth or material fixed along one edge to cover or close an opening **2** EXCITEMENT [C, U] *US* when someone is worried or excited, or a situation that causes them to feel this way *The President's remarks caused a huge flap.* **3 be/get in a flap** *mainly UK informal* to be or become worried or excited

flap² /flæp/ *verb* **flapping**, *past* **flapped** **1** WINGS [T] If a bird flaps its wings, it moves them up and down. **2** MOVE [I] If something such as cloth or paper flaps, the side that is not fixed to something moves around, especially in the wind. *The curtains were flapping around in the breeze.* **3** WORRY [I] *UK informal* to become worried or excited about something *Don't flap! We've got plenty of time to get to the airport.*

flare¹ /fleəʳ/ (*also* **flare up**) *verb* [I] **1** START If something bad such as anger or pain flares or flares up, it suddenly starts or gets worse. *Violence flared up between football fans yesterday.* **2** BURN to suddenly burn brightly, usually for a short time *The rocket flared in the sky and disappeared into space.*

flare² /fleəʳ/ *noun* [C] **1** SAFETY EQUIPMENT a piece of safety equipment that produces a bright signal when you are lost or injured **2** LIGHT a sudden, bright light

flared /fleəd/ *adjective* wide at the bottom *flared trousers*

flash¹ /flæʃ/ *verb* **1** SHINE [I, T] to shine brightly and suddenly, or to make something shine in this way *The doctor flashed a light into my eye.* ○ *Lightning flashed across the sky.* **2** APPEAR [I, T] (*also* **flash up**) to appear for a short time, or to make something appear for a short time *An icon flashed up on the screen.* **3 flash by/past/through, etc** to move somewhere fast *The motorcycle flashed past us and around the corner.* **4 flash (sb) a look/smile, etc** to look, smile, etc at someone quickly *She flashed him a smile as he came in.*

flash back *phrasal verb* If your mind or thoughts flash back to something that happened in the past, you suddenly remember it.

flash² /flæʃ/ *noun* **1** BRIGHT LIGHT [C] a sudden bright light *The bomb exploded in a* ***flash of*** *yellow light.* **2** CAMERA [C, U] a piece of camera equipment that produces a bright light when you take a photograph in a dark place **3** SUDDEN EXPERIENCE [C] a sudden experience of something such as a feeling or idea *a flash of anger* ○ *I had a* ***flash of inspiration.*** **4 in a flash** immediately, or very quickly *I'll be back in a flash.* **5 a flash in the pan** a sudden success that does not continue

flashback /ˈflæʃbæk/ *noun* [C] **1** MEMORY when you suddenly remember something that happened in the past, usually something bad **2** STORY part of a film or book that goes back in time to something that happened before the main story began

flashlight /ˈflæʃlaɪt/ *US* (*UK* **torch**) *noun* [C] an electric light that you can hold in your hand

flash-mob /ˈflæʃmɒb/ *noun* [C] *informal* a group of people who agree to come together suddenly in a place and do something funny or silly and then move away

flashpoint /ˈflæʃpɔɪnt/ *noun* [C] **PHYSICS** The flashpoint of a liquid is the lowest temperature at which its vapour (= small drops of water in the air) will burn in the air.

flashy /ˈflæʃi/ *adjective* looking too bright, big, and expensive, in a way that is intended to get attention *flashy gold jewellery*

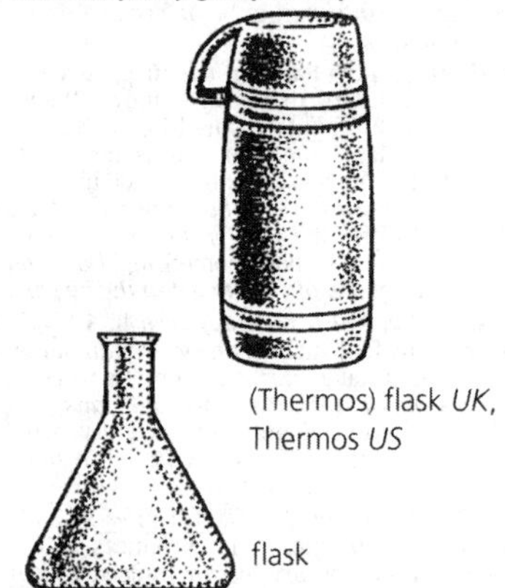

flask

flask /flɑːsk/ *noun* [C] **1** HOT DRINKS *UK* (*UK/US* **Thermos**) a special container that keeps drinks hot or cold *a flask of coffee* **2** ALCOHOL a flat bottle that is used to carry alcohol in your pocket **3** SCIENCE a glass container with a wide base and a narrow opening used in science ➲See picture at **filtrate**

WORD PARTNERS FOR ***flat***

in a flat • a **block of** flats • a **one-bedroom/two-bedroom** flat • a **basement** flat

O-- **flat¹** /flæt/ *mainly UK* (*mainly US* **apartment**) *noun* [C] a set of rooms to live in, with all the rooms on one level of a building *a large **block of flats***

O-- **flat²** /flæt/ *adjective* **flatter, flattest 1** SMOOTH smooth and level, with no curved, high, or hollow parts *a flat surface* ○ *The countryside around here is very flat.* **2** WITHOUT EMOTION without any energy, interest, or emotion *Her voice sounded very flat.* **3** WITHOUT AIR If a tyre is flat, it does not contain enough air. **4 FOOD** If a drink is flat, it does not contain enough bubbles of gas. **5** WITHOUT POWER *UK* If a battery (= object which provides electricity) is flat, it does not contain any more electrical power. **6 a flat price/rate, etc FINANCE** a price/rate, etc which is the same for everyone and does not change *He charges a flat rate of £15 an hour.* **7 B flat/E flat, etc MUSIC** the musical note that is between the note B/E, etc and the note below it **8 MUSIC** A flat musical note sounds unpleasant because it is slightly lower than it should be. **9** LOW Flat shoes do not raise your feet far from the ground.

flat³ /flæt/ *adverb* **flatter, flattest 1** in a horizontal or level position on a surface *She spread the cloth flat across the kitchen table.* **2 flat out** using all your energy or effort *We've all been working flat out to finish the project on time.* **3 in 5 minutes/30 seconds, etc flat** in exactly and only 5 minutes, 30 seconds, etc *He showered and got dressed in 10 minutes flat.* **4 fall flat** If an event or joke falls flat, it fails to have the effect that you wanted, such as making people laugh.

flat-bed scanner /ˌflætbedˈskænəʳ/ *noun* [C] **COMPUTING** a flat piece of computer equipment that turns words, pictures or objects into digital images

flatly /ˈflætli/ *adverb* **1 flatly deny/refuse, etc** to say something in a direct and certain way *He flatly refused to answer our questions.* **2** without showing any emotion or interest *"He's gone," she said flatly.*

flatmate /ˈflætmeɪt/ *mainly UK* (*US* **roommate**) *noun* [C] someone who you share a flat with

flatpack /ˈflætpæk/ *adjective* used to describe furniture that is sold in pieces inside a flat box, ready to be put together *a flatpack table*

flat-screen TV

ˈflat ˌscreen *noun* [C] a computer screen or a television that is thin and flat

ˌflat-screen TˈV *noun* [C] a type of television with a screen that is very thin and shows a very clear picture

flatten /ˈflætᵊn/ *verb* [I, T] to become flat or to make something become flat *Roll out the dough into balls and flatten them slightly.*

flatter /ˈflætəʳ/ *verb* **1** SAY NICE THINGS [T] to say nice things to someone in order to make them feel attractive or important, sometimes in a way that is not sincere *The interviewer flattered him about his recent work.* **2 be flattered** to feel very pleased and proud *She was flattered by his attention.* **3** LOOK ATTRACTIVE [T] to make someone look more attractive than usual *That new hairstyle really flatters you.* **4 flatter yourself** to believe something good about yourself, although it might not be true *He flatters himself that he's a good driver.*

flattering /ˈflætərɪŋ/ *adjective* making you look more attractive than usual *a flattering picture*

flattery /ˈflætᵊri/ *noun* [U] when you say nice things to someone, often because you want something from that person

flaunt /flɔːnt/ *verb* [T] to make your success, money, beauty, etc very obvious so that people notice it and admire you *Although he's a millionaire, he doesn't flaunt his wealth.*

WORD PARTNERS FOR ***flavour***

have a [mild/spicy/strong, etc] flavour • a delicate/delicious flavour

flavour¹ *UK* (*US* **flavor**) /ˈfleɪvəʳ/ *noun* **1** TASTE [C, U] the taste of a particular type of food or drink *We sell 50 different flavours of ice cream.* ○ *Add some salt to give the soup more flavour.* **2** QUALITY [no plural] a particular quality or style that something has *London has a very international flavour.*

flavour² *UK* (*US* **flavor**) /ˈfleɪvəʳ/ *verb* **1** [T] to give a particular taste to food or drink [often passive] *This sauce is flavoured with garlic and herbs.* **2 cheese/chocolate, etc -flavoured** tasting of cheese/chocolate, etc *lemon-flavoured sweets*

flavouring *UK* (*US* **flavoring**) /ˈfleɪvərɪŋ/ *noun* [C, U] **FOOD** something that is added to food or drink to give it a particular taste

flaw /flɔː/ *noun* [C] a mistake or bad characteristic that stops someone or something from being perfect *There's a **flaw in** your reasoning.* •**flawed** *adjective a **flawed argument***

flawless /ˈflɔːləs/ *adjective* with no mistakes or bad characteristics *a flawless complexion* •**flawlessly** *adverb*

flea /fliː/ *noun* [C] a small, jumping insect that lives on animals or people and drinks their blood

ˈflea ˌmarket *noun* [C] a market where you can buy old or used things cheaply

fleck /flek/ *noun* [C] a mark, or a very small piece of something *His shirt was covered in **flecks of** paint.*

fledgling /ˈfledʒlɪŋ/ *adjective* [always before noun] A fledgling company, country, or organization is new and not yet developed. *a fledgling democracy*

flee /fliː/ *verb* [I, T] **fleeing**, *past* **fled** to leave a place quickly because you are in danger or are afraid *Police think the suspect has now fled the country.*

fleece /fliːs/ *noun* [C, U] **1** CLOTHING a warm, soft, light jacket, or the material used to make it ➲See colour picture **Clothes** on page Centre 8 **2** WOOL the thick covering of wool on a sheep

fleet /fliːt/ *noun* [C] **1** SHIPS a group of ships, or all of the ships in a country's navy **2** VEHICLES a group of vehicles that are owned and controlled by one person or organization *a **fleet of** aircraft/cars*

flesh /fleʃ/ *noun* [U] **1 ANATOMY** the soft part of a person's or animal's body between the skin and bones **2 in the flesh** in real life and not on television or in a film *She looks much taller in the flesh.* **3 FOOD** the soft part of a fruit or vegetable which you can eat **4 your own flesh and blood** a member of your family •**fleshy** *adjective* fat or thick, or with a lot of flesh

flew /fluː/ *past tense of* fly

flex¹ /fleks/ *verb* [T] to bend a part of your body so that the muscle becomes tight

flex² /fleks/ *UK* (*UK/US* **cord**) *noun* [C, U] a piece of wire covered in plastic, that is used to connect electrical equipment to a power supply

flexible /ˈfleksɪbl/ *adjective* **1** ABLE TO CHANGE able to change or be changed easily according to the situation *I'd like a job with more flexible working hours.* **2** ABLE TO BEND A flexible substance can bend easily without breaking. •**flexibility** /ˌfleksɪˈbɪləti/ *noun* [U]

flexography /fleksˈɒɡrəfi/ *noun* [U] **DT** a method of printing using flexible (= able to bend) printing plates, often used for printing on plastic or foil (= very thin sheets of metal)

flexor (muscle) /ˈfleksəʳ/ *noun* [C] **ANATOMY, BIOLOGY** a muscle that allows you to bend part of your body ➲Compare **extensor (muscle)**

flick¹ /flɪk/ *verb* **1 flick sth into/off/over, etc** to move something somewhere suddenly and quickly through the air, usually with your fingers *He quickly flicked the crumbs off the table.* **2 flick down/out/towards, etc** to make a sudden, quick movement somewhere *His eyes flicked between her and the door.* **3 flick a switch** to move a switch in order to make electrical equipment start or stop working

flick sth on/off *phrasal verb* to move a switch in order to make electrical equipment start/stop working

flick through sth *phrasal verb* to look quickly at the pages of a magazine, book, etc

flick² /flɪk/ *noun* [C] a sudden, quick movement *With **a flick of** her wrist, she threw the pebble into the water.*

flicker¹ /ˈflɪkəʳ/ *verb* [I] **1** SHINE to shine with a light that is sometimes bright and sometimes weak *a candle flickering in the window* **2** APPEAR to appear for a short time or make a sudden movement somewhere *A smile flickered across her face.*

flicker² /ˈflɪkəʳ/ *noun* [no plural] **1** LIGHT when a light is sometimes bright and sometimes weak *the soft flicker of candlelight* **2** EMOTION a slight, brief feeling or expression of an emotion *a **flicker of hope***

flier (*also* **flyer**) /ˈflaɪəʳ/ *noun* [C] **1** ADVERTISEMENT a small piece of paper advertising a business, show, event, etc **2** PERSON someone who flies, especially a passenger on an aircraft

flies /flaɪz/ *UK* (*UK/US* **fly**) *noun* [plural] the part where trousers open and close at the front

WORD PARTNERS FOR ***flight***

on a flight • a flight from/to [Paris/Tokyo, etc] • a long-haul/short-haul flight

O‑ **flight** /flaɪt/ *noun* **1** JOURNEY [C] a journey in an aircraft *The **flight to** Chicago took 4 hours.* **2** AIRCRAFT [C] an aircraft that carries passengers from one place to another *Flight 102 is ready for boarding at Gate 3.* **3** MOVEMENT [U] when something flies or moves through the air *an eagle in flight* **4 a flight of stairs/steps** a set of stairs

ˈflight atˌtendant *noun* [C] someone whose job is to look after passengers on an aircraft

flimsy /ˈflɪmzi/ *adjective* **1** THIN thin and not solid or strong *a flimsy cardboard box* **2** WEAK A flimsy argument, excuse, etc is weak and difficult to believe. *I'm sick of his **flimsy excuses** for being late.*

flinch /flɪnʃ/ *verb* [I] **1** MOVE BACKWARDS to make a sudden movement backwards because you are afraid or in pain *She didn't flinch when the nurse cleaned the wound.* **2** AVOID DOING to avoid doing something that is unpleasant *Nick never* ***flinches from*** *difficult decisions.*

fling[1] /flɪŋ/ *verb past* **flung fling sth around/across/down, etc** to throw or move something suddenly and with a lot of force *She flung her arms around his neck.*

fling[2] /flɪŋ/ *noun* [C] **1** RELATIONSHIP a sexual relationship that is short and not serious *She* ***had a fling with*** *someone last summer.* **2** ENJOYMENT a short period of time when you have a lot of enjoyment or pleasure *This is my last fling before the exams.*

F

flint /flɪnt/ *noun* [C, U] **GEOLOGY** a very hard, grey stone that can be used to produce a flame

flip /flɪp/ *verb* **flipping**, *past* **flipped 1** TURN OVER [I, T] to turn or make something turn onto a different side, or so that it is the wrong way up *to flip a coin/pancake* ○ *The boat* ***flipped*** *right* ***over***. **2** LOSE CONTROL [I] *informal* to become uncontrollably angry, crazy, or excited *Dad completely flipped when he saw the car.*

flip through sth *phrasal verb* to look quickly at the pages of a magazine, book, etc

ˈflip ˌchart *noun* [C] large pieces of paper attached to a board on legs, which you write or draw on when you are talking to a group of people

flip-flop /ˈflɪpˌflɒp/ (US also **thong**) *noun* [**usually plural**] a type of shoe, often made of rubber, with a V-shaped strap in between the big toe and the toe next to it ➲See colour picture **Clothes** on page Centre 9

flippant /ˈflɪpᵊnt/ *adjective* without respect or not serious *a* ***flippant remark*** •**flippantly** *adverb* •**flippancy** /ˈflɪpᵊnsi/ *noun* [U]

flipper /ˈflɪpəʳ/ *noun* [C] **1 BIOLOGY** a part like a wide, flat arm without fingers that some sea animals use for swimming **2 SPORT** a long, flat, rubber shoe that you use when swimming under water

flipping /ˈflɪpɪŋ/ *adjective* [**always before noun**] *UK informal* used to emphasize something, or to show slight anger *Where are my flipping keys?*

the ˈflip ˌside *noun* the opposite, less good, or less popular side of something

flirt[1] /flɜːt/ *verb* [I] to behave as if you are sexually attracted to someone, usually not in a very serious way *She was* ***flirting with*** *a guy at the bar.*

flirt with sth *phrasal verb* **1** to be interested in an idea, activity, etc but not seriously, or for only a short time *He* ***flirted with the idea*** *of becoming a priest.* **2 flirt with danger/disaster, etc** to risk experiencing something bad •**flirtation** /flɜːˈteɪʃᵊn/ *noun* [C, U]

flirt[2] /flɜːt/ *noun* [C] someone who often flirts with people

flirtatious /flɜːˈteɪʃəs/ *adjective* behaving as if you are sexually attracted to someone, usually not in a very serious way

flit /flɪt/ *verb* **flitting**, *past* **flitted flit about/around/in and out, etc** to fly or move quickly from one place to another *Birds were flitting from tree to tree.*

float[1] /fləʊt/ *verb* **1 PHYSICS** [I, T] to stay on the surface of a liquid instead of sinking, or to make something do this *I like floating on my back in the pool.* **2** [I] to stay in the air, or move gently through the air *A balloon floated across the sky.* **3 FINANCE** [I, T] to start selling a company's shares to the public **4 float sb's boat** *informal* to interest someone *Georgia likes William, but he just doesn't float my boat.*

float[2] /fləʊt/ *noun* [C] **1** a large, decorated vehicle that is used in public celebrations **2 SPORT** an object that floats on water, used in fishing or when learning to swim **3 FINANCE**- when you float a business **4 FINANCE** [C] *mainly UK* a small amount of money which you have before you sell things so that you can give people change (= money which you give to people if they give you more money than the price of something)

flock[1] /flɒk/ *noun* [**group**] **1** BIRD/SHEEP a group of birds or sheep *a flock of geese* **2** PEOPLE a group of people led by one person *a flock of children/visitors*

flock[2] /flɒk/ *verb* [I] to move or come together in large numbers *Tourists are* ***flocking to*** *the beaches.* [**+ to do sth**] *People flocked to hear him speak.*

flog /flɒg/ *verb* [T] **flogging**, *past* **flogged 1** PUNISH to hit someone repeatedly as a punishment with something such as a stick **2** SELL *UK informal* to sell something quickly or cheaply *I had to flog the car to pay my bills.* •**flogging** *noun* [C, U]

flood[1] /flʌd/ *verb* [I, T] **1 GEOGRAPHY** If a place floods or is flooded, it becomes covered in water. [**often passive**] *The town was flooded when the river burst its banks.* ○ *I left the taps running and flooded the bathroom.* **2** to fill or enter a place in large numbers or amounts *Light flooded the room.* ○ *Shoppers* ***flooded into*** *the store.* •**flooding** *noun* [U] *There is widespread flooding in the South.*

be flooded with sth *phrasal verb* to receive so many letters, telephone calls, etc that you cannot deal with them

WORD PARTNERS FOR ***flood***

catastrophic/devastating floods • flood damage/victims/warnings

O‐ **flood**[2] /flʌd/ *noun* **1 GEOGRAPHY** [C] when a lot of water covers an area that is usually dry, especially when a river becomes too full **2** [C] a large number or amount of things or people that arrive at the same time *a flood of letters/calls* **3 in floods of tears** *UK* crying a lot

floodgates /ˈflʌdgeɪts/ *noun* **open the floodgates** to make it possible for a lot of people to do something

floodlights /ˈflʌdlaɪts/ *noun* [**plural**] powerful lights used to light up sports fields or the outside of buildings at night •**floodlit** /ˈflʌdlɪt/ *adjective* lit up by floodlights

ˈflood ˌplain *noun* [C] **GEOGRAPHY** an area of low, flat land near a river that often floods when the river becomes too full

O┅ **floor** /flɔːʳ/ *noun* **1** SURFACE [C] a surface that you walk on inside a building *a wooden/tiled floor* ○ *I must sweep the kitchen floor.* **2** BUILDING [C] a particular level of a building *the second/third floor* **3** BOTTOM [**no plural**] the ground or surface at the bottom of something *the forest/sea floor* **4** AREA [C] an area where a particular activity happens *a dance floor* ➲See also: **first floor, ground floor, shop floor**

floorboard /ˈflɔːbɔːd/ *noun* [C] a long, narrow, flat board that forms part of a wooden floor in a building

flooring /flɔːrɪŋ/ *noun* [U] the material used to make or cover a floor *vinyl flooring*

flop¹ /flɒp/ *verb* [I] **flopping**, *past* **flopped 1 flop down/into/onto, etc** to fall or sit somewhere suddenly in a heavy or relaxed way *He flopped down on the sofa.* **2** HANG to hang loosely *Her hair kept flopping in her eyes.* **3** NOT SUCCESSFUL *informal* If a film, product, plan, etc flops, it is not successful.

flop² /flɒp/ *noun* [C] *informal* **1** FAILURE something that is not a success *The party was a bit of a flop.* **2** MOVEMENT a movement towards the ground, or the noise someone or something makes as they fall down *She fell onto the bed with a flop.*

floppy /ˈflɒpi/ *adjective* soft and loose or hanging down loosely *floppy hair* ○ *a floppy hat*

ˌ**floppy** ˈ**disk** (*also* **floppy**) *noun* [C] **COMPUTING** a small disk inside a flat, square piece of plastic used in the past for storing information from a computer

flora /ˈflɔːrə/ *noun* [U, group] **BIOLOGY** the plants that grow naturally in a particular area *Scotland's **flora and fauna***

floral /ˈflɔːrəl/ *adjective* [**always before noun**] made from flowers or relating to flowers *a floral arrangement/pattern*

florist /ˈflɒrɪst/ *noun* [C] **1** PERSON someone who sells and arranges flowers in a shop **2** SHOP (*also* **florist's**) a shop that sells flowers

flotation /fləʊˈteɪʃən/ *noun* **1 FINANCE** [C, U] when a company's shares are sold to the public for the first time **2** [U] when something or someone floats on or in liquid

flounder /ˈflaʊndəʳ/ *verb* [I] **1** MOVEMENT to make wild movements with your arms or body, especially because you are trying not to sink **2** NOT KNOW to not know what to do or say *When he resigned, the team was left floundering.* **3** FAIL If a relationship, organization, or plan flounders, it fails or begins to experience problems. *By 1993 his marriage was floundering.*

flour /flaʊəʳ/ *noun* [U] **FOOD** a powder made from grain that is used to make bread, cakes, and other food

flourish¹ /ˈflʌrɪʃ/ *verb* **1** SUCCEED [I] to grow or develop well *a flourishing tourist industry* **2** HOLD [T] to wave something around in the air

flourish² /ˈflʌrɪʃ/ *noun* [**no plural**] when someone does something in a special and noticeable way *The waiter handed me the menu **with a flourish**.*

flout /flaʊt/ *verb* [T] to intentionally not obey or accept something *to **flout** the **law/rules***

flow¹ /fləʊ/ *verb* [I] **1** MOVEMENT If something such as a liquid flows, it moves somewhere in a smooth, continuous way. *The river flows from the Andes to the ocean.* **2** TALK If words, ideas, or conversations flow, they continue in an easy and relaxed way without stopping. *At dinner, the **conversation flowed** freely.*

flow² /fləʊ/ *noun* **1** [**no plural**] when something such as a liquid moves somewhere in a smooth, continuous way *the flow of blood* ○ *the flow of information* **2 go with the flow** *informal* to do or accept what other people are doing because it is the easiest thing to do *Just relax and go with the flow!* ➲See also: **ebb¹** and flow

flowchart /ˈfləʊtʃɑːt/ (**flow diagram**) *noun* **MATHEMATICS** a diagram which shows the stages of a process

WORD PARTNERS FOR ***flower***

a bouquet of /bunch of flowers • **wild** flowers • **cut/fresh** flowers • **wild** flowers

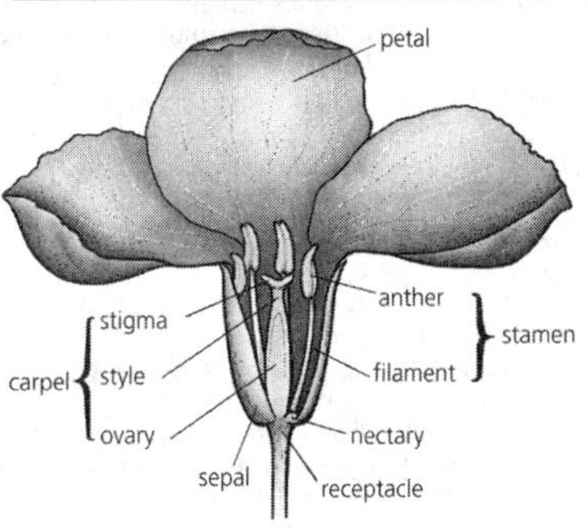

flower

O┅ **flower¹** /flaʊəʳ/ *noun* **1 BIOLOGY** [C] the attractive, coloured part of a plant where the seeds grow *a **bunch of flowers*** **2** [C] a type of plant that produces flowers *spring/wild flowers* **3 be in flower BIOLOGY** When plants are in flower, they have flowers on them. **4 the flower of sth** *literary* the best part of something *the flower of our nation's youth*

flower² /flaʊəʳ/ *verb* [I] **BIOLOGY** to produce flowers *These pansies flower all summer.*

ˈ**flower** ˌ**bed** *noun* [C] an area of soil in a garden that you grow flowers in

flowery /ˈflaʊəri/ *adjective* **1** PATTERN (*also* **flowered** /flaʊəd/) decorated with a pattern of flowers *a flowery dress* **2** WORDS Flowery language contains unnecessarily complicated and unusual words.

flowing /ˈfləʊɪŋ/ *adjective* **1** LONG AND LOOSE hanging down in a long, loose way *flowing robes/hair* **2** STYLE produced in a smooth, continuous, or relaxed style *flowing lines*

flown /fləʊn/ *past participle of* fly

ˈ**flow pro**ˌ**duction** *noun* [U] in business, the continuous production of a single product

fl oz MEASURES *written abbreviation for* fluid ounce (= a unit for measuring liquid)

F

flu /fluː/ *noun* [U] **HEALTH** an illness like a very bad cold, that makes you feel hot and weak *I **had the flu** last week.*

fluctuate /ˈflʌktʃueɪt/ *verb* [I] to keep changing, especially in level or amount *Oil **prices** have **fluctuated** wildly in recent weeks.* •**fluctuation** /ˌflʌktʃuˈeɪʃᵊn/ *noun* [C, U] ***fluctuations** in house prices*

fluent /ˈfluːənt/ *adjective* **1** ABILITY able to use a language naturally without stopping or making mistakes *She is **fluent in** six languages.* **2** STYLE produced or done in a smooth, natural style *Hendrik speaks fluent English.* •**fluency** /ˈfluːənsi/ *noun* [U] •**fluently** *adverb*

fluff¹ /flʌf/ *noun* [U] small, loose bits of wool or other soft material *There's a piece of fluff on your jacket.*

fluff² /flʌf/ *verb* [T] *informal* to fail to do something successfully *I had a great chance to score but I fluffed it.*
fluff sth out/up *phrasal verb* to make something appear bigger or fuller by hitting or shaking it so that it contains more air *I'll fluff up your pillows for you.*

fluffy /ˈflʌfi/ *adjective* made or covered with soft fur or cloth *a fluffy toy*

fluid¹ /ˈfluːɪd/ *noun* [C, U] a liquid *cleaning fluid* ○ *Drink plenty of fluids.*

fluid² /ˈfluːɪd/ *adjective* **1** **PHYSICS** able to flow easily like liquid **2** CHANGING likely or able to change *a fluid situation* **3** SMOOTH smooth and continuous *fluid movements*

ˌfluid ˈounce (*written abbreviation* **fl oz**) *noun* [C] **MEASURES** a unit for measuring liquid, equal to 0.0284 litres in the UK and 0.0296 litres in the US ➲See Extra help page **Numbers and measurements** on page Centre 24.

fluke /fluːk/ *noun* [C, U] something good that happens only because of luck or chance *That first goal was just a fluke.*

flume /fluːm/ *noun* [C] **SPORT** a large tube for people to slide down at a swimming pool

flung /flʌŋ/ *past of* fling

fluorescent /flɔːˈresᵊnt/ *adjective* **1** LIGHT Fluorescent lights are very bright, tube-shaped, electric lights, often used in offices. **2** COLOUR Fluorescent colours, clothes, etc are very bright and can be seen in the dark. *fluorescent pink* ○ *a fluorescent jacket*

fluoride /ˈflɔːraɪd/ *noun* [U] **CHEMISTRY, HEALTH** a chemical that helps to prevent tooth decay

fluorocarbon /ˌflʊərəˈkɑːbᵊn / *noun* [C] **CHEMISTRY** one of a group of chemical compounds which has many uses but which causes damage to the environment

flurry /ˈflʌri/ *noun* [C] **1** ACTIVITY a sudden, short period of activity, interest, or excitement *a flurry of phone calls* **2** SNOW a sudden, short period of snow and wind

flush¹ /flʌʃ/ *verb* **1** TOILET [I, T] If you flush a toilet, or if it flushes, its contents empty and it fills with water again. **2 flush sth away/down/out, etc** to get rid of something by pushing it somewhere with lots of water, such as down a toilet **3** FACE [I] If you flush, your face becomes red and hot, usually because you are embarrassed or angry.
flush sb/sth out *phrasal verb* to force a person or animal to come out from where they are hiding

flush² /flʌʃ/ *noun* [C] **1** when your face becomes hot and red *a **hot flush*** **2 a flush of excitement/pleasure, etc** a sudden feeling of excitement/pleasure, etc

flush³ /flʌʃ/ *adjective* [**never before noun**] **1** LEVEL at the same level as another surface *I want the door **flush with** the wall.* **2** RICH *informal* rich *flush with cash*

flustered /ˈflʌstəd/ *adjective* upset and confused *She arrived very late, looking flustered.*

flute /fluːt/ *noun* [C] **MUSIC** a musical instrument in the shape of a tube that is held out to the side and played by blowing across a hole near one end

flutter¹ /ˈflʌtəʳ/ *verb* **1** [I, T] to move quickly and gently up and down or from side to side in the air, or to make something move in this way *The flag was fluttering in the breeze.* **2 flutter about/around/down, etc** to move somewhere quickly and gently, usually without any particular purpose *There were several moths fluttering around the light.*

flutter² /ˈflʌtəʳ/ *noun* [C] **1** MOVEMENT a quick, gentle movement *the flutter of wings* **2** EMOTION a state of excitement or worry *a flutter of excitement* **3** RISK MONEY *UK informal* when you risk money on the result of a game, competition, etc

flux /flʌks/ *noun* [U] continuous change *The housing market is still **in a state of flux**.*

O⁔**fly¹** /flaɪ/ *verb past tense* **flew**, *past participle* **flown** **1** MOVE THROUGH AIR [I] When a bird, insect, aircraft, etc flies, it moves through the air. *The robin flew up into a tree.* ○ *The plane was flying at 5000 feet.* **2** TRAVEL [I] to travel through the air in an aircraft *I'm flying to Delhi tomorrow.* **3** CONTROL AIRCRAFT [I, T] to control an aircraft *She learned to fly at the age of 18.* **4** TAKE/SEND [T] to take or send people or goods somewhere by aircraft [**often passive**] *She was flown to hospital by helicopter.* **5 fly along/down/past, etc** to move somewhere very quickly *He grabbed some clothes and flew down the stairs.* **6 send sb/sth flying** to cause someone or something to move through the air suddenly, usually in an accident **7** LEAVE [I] *UK* to leave suddenly *I must fly - I'm late for work.* **8 let fly (at sb/sth)** *mainly UK informal* to start shouting angrily or attacking someone **9** TIME [I] If time flies, it passes very quickly. **10** FLAG [I, T] If you fly a flag, or a flag is flying, it is fixed to a rope or pole and raised in the air. •**flying** *noun* [U] *Ben's afraid of flying.* ➲See also: as the **crow**¹ flies, fly off the **handle**²
fly about/around *phrasal verb* If ideas or remarks are flying about, they are being passed quickly from one person to another and causing excitement. *All kinds of **rumours are flying around** about the school closing.*
fly into a rage/temper *phrasal verb* to suddenly become very angry

fly² /flaɪ/ *noun* **1** INSECT [C] a small insect with two wings *There was a fly buzzing around in the kitchen.* ➲See picture at **insect** **2** TROUSERS

[C] (*also UK* **flies** [**plural**]) the part where trousers open and close at the front *a **button/zip fly*** **3 fly on the wall** If you say that you would like to be a fly on the wall in a certain situation, you mean that you would like to be there secretly to see and hear what happens. **4 a fly-on-the-wall documentary/film** a television programme or film in which people do not act but are recorded in real situations, sometimes without knowing **5 be dropping like flies** to be dying or becoming ill in large numbers **6 wouldn't hurt a fly** If you say that someone wouldn't hurt a fly, you mean that they are very gentle and would never do anything to injure or upset anyone.

flyer (*also* **flier**) /ˈflaɪəʳ/ *noun* [C] **1** ADVERTISEMENT a small piece of paper advertising a business, show, event, etc *She's handing out flyers in the shopping centre.* **2** PERSON someone who flies, especially a passenger on an aircraft *a frequent flyer* ➲See also: **high-flyer**

flying /ˈflaɪɪŋ/ *adjective* [**always before noun**] **1** A flying creature or object moves or is able to move through the air. *flying ants* **2 a flying visit** *UK* a very brief visit ➲See also: with flying colours (**colour**[1])

ˌflying ˈsaucer *noun* [C] *old-fashioned* a UFO (= an object in the sky which some people think is a spacecraft from another planet)

flyover /ˈflaɪˌəʊvəʳ/ *UK* (*US* **overpass**) *noun* [C] a bridge that carries a road over another road

FM /ˌefˈem/ *noun* [U] **PHYSICS** *abbreviation for* frequency modulation; a system of radio signals used for broadcasting programmes

foal /fəʊl/ *noun* [C] a young horse

foam /fəʊm/ *noun* [U] **1** BUBBLES a mass of small, white bubbles on the surface of a liquid **2** PRODUCT a thick substance of small, white bubbles used as a cleaning or beauty product ***shaving foam*** **3** FILLING a soft substance used to fill furniture and other objects

foamboard /ˈfəʊmbɔːd/ *noun* [U] **DT** a type of very light board made of a plastic substance full of small bubbles between two sheets of paper or card, often used to attach documents to in order to display them

focal point /ˈfəʊkəlˌpɔɪnt/ *noun* [**no plural**] the thing that attracts most of your attention or interest in a place, picture, etc *The fireplace is the focal point of the room.*

focus[1] /ˈfəʊkəs/ *verb* **focusing**, *past* **focused** **1** [T] If you focus a camera or something else that you look through, you make small changes to it until you can see something clearly. **2 BIOLOGY** [I, T] If you focus your eyes, or your eyes focus, they change so that you can see clearly. *Give your eyes time to focus in the darkness.* ➲See picture at **eye**

focus (sth) on sth *phrasal verb* to give a lot of attention to one particular subject or thing *The research focused on men under thirty.*

WORD PARTNERS FOR ***focus***

be **the focus of** sth • the focus is **on** (doing) sth

focus[2] /ˈfəʊkəs/ *noun* **1 the focus of sth** the person or thing that is getting most attention in a situation or activity *the focus of our attention* ○ *He is the focus of a police investigation.* **2** [U] when you give special attention to something *Their main **focus** must be **on** reducing crime.* **3 in focus** If an image is in focus, you are able to see it clearly. **4 out of focus** If an image is out of focus, you are not able to see it clearly.

ˈfocus ˌgroup *noun* [**group**] a group of people who are brought together to discuss what they think about something such as a new product

fodder /ˈfɒdəʳ/ *noun* [U] **FARMING** food such as dried grass for animals that are kept on farms *cattle fodder*

foe /fəʊ/ *noun* [C] *literary* an enemy

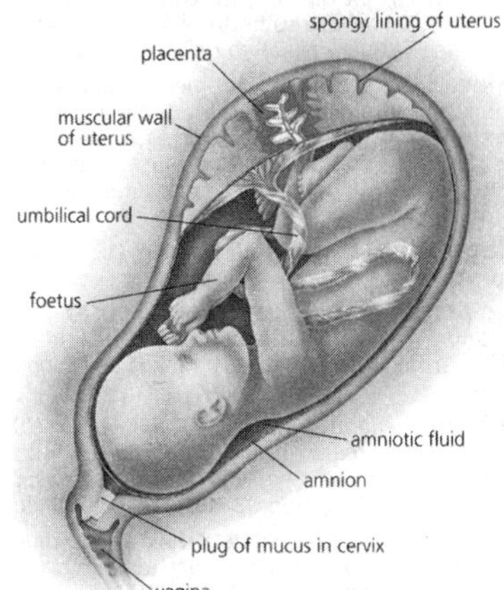

foetus

foetus *UK* (*US* **fetus**) /ˈfiːtəs/ *noun* [C] **BIOLOGY** a young human or animal that is still developing inside its mother •**foetal** *UK* (*US* **fetal**) /ˈfiːtəl/ *adjective* ***foetal development***

WORD PARTNERS FOR ***fog***

fog **descends** • fog **clears/lifts** • **dense/heavy/thick** fog

fog /fɒg/ *noun* [U] thick cloud just above the ground or sea that makes it difficult to see

foggy /ˈfɒgi/ *adjective* **1** with fog *a foggy day* **2 not have the foggiest (idea)** *informal* to not know anything about something [+ **question word**] I haven't the foggiest idea what you're talking about.

foible /ˈfɔɪbl/ *noun* [C] a slightly unusual or annoying habit [**usually plural**] *Married couples must learn to accept each other's **little foibles**.*

foil[1] /fɔɪl/ *noun* **1** [U] metal made into very thin sheets like paper and used mainly for covering food *(UK) aluminium foil/ (US) aluminum foil* **2 a foil for sb/sth** a person or thing that shows or emphasizes how different someone or something else is

foil[2] /fɔɪl/ *verb* [T] to stop a crime, plan, etc from succeeding, or to stop someone doing what they want to do [**often passive**] *The plot was foiled by undercover police officers.*

O→ **fold¹** /fəʊld/ *verb* **1** [MATERIAL] [T] If you fold paper, cloth, etc, you bend it so that one part of it lies flat on top of another part. *He **folded** the letter **in half**.* **2** [FURNITURE] [I, T] (*also* **fold up**) to make something such as a chair or table smaller or flatter by closing it or bending it together *a folding chair* ⊃Opposite **unfold** **3** [BUSINESS] [I] *informal* If a business folds, it fails and is unable to continue. *The magazine folded last year.* **4 fold your arms** to bend your arms across your chest, with one crossing over the other *He sat with his arms folded.*

fold² /fəʊld/ *noun* [C] **1** [MARK] a line or mark where paper, cloth, etc was or is folded *Make a fold across the centre of the card.* **2** [THICK PART] a thick part where something folds or hangs over itself [**usually plural**] *folds of skin/fabric*

folder /ˈfəʊldəʳ/ *noun* [C] **1** a piece of plastic or thick paper folded down the middle and used to store loose papers ⊃See colour picture **The Office** on page Centre 5 **2 COMPUTING** a place on a computer where particular files (= documents, pictures, etc) are kept

foliage /ˈfəʊliɪdʒ/ *noun* [U] **BIOLOGY** the leaves on a plant

folic acid /ˌfəʊlɪkˈæsɪd/ *noun* [U] **BIOLOGY** a B vitamin found in the leaves of plants and in liver, from which the body makes red blood cells

folk¹ /fəʊk/ *noun* **1** [**plural**] *UK informal* (*US* **folks**) people *country folk ○ old folk* **2 sb's folks** *informal* someone's parents *We always spend Christmas with my folks.* **3 MUSIC** [U] folk music

folk² /fəʊk/ *adjective* **SOCIETY** **folk art/dancing, etc** the traditional style of art, dancing, etc among a particular group of people

ˈfolk ˌmusic *noun* [U] **MUSIC** music written and played in a traditional style

follicle /ˈfɒlɪkl/ *noun* [C] **ANATOMY, BIOLOGY** one of the many very small holes in the skin from which hairs grow

O→ **follow** /ˈfɒləʊ/ *verb* **1** [GO] [I, T] to move behind someone or something and go where they go, sometimes secretly *She followed me into the kitchen.* **2** [HAPPEN] [I, T] to happen or come after something *There was a bang, **followed by** a cloud of smoke.* **3 follow a path/road, etc** to travel along a path, road, etc *Follow the main road down to the traffic lights.* **4 follow instructions/orders/rules, etc** to do what the instructions, orders, rules, etc say you should do *I followed your advice and stayed at home.* **5 follow sb's example/lead** to copy someone's behaviour or ideas **6** [UNDERSTAND] [I, T] to understand something *Could you say that again? I didn't quite follow.* **7** [BE INTERESTED] [T] to be interested in an event or activity *I followed the trial closely.* **8 as follows** used to introduce a list or description **9 it follows that** used to say that if one thing is true, another thing will also be true *He's big, but it doesn't follow that he's strong.* ⊃See also: follow in sb's footsteps (**footstep**), follow **suit¹**

follow on *phrasal verb mainly UK* to happen or exist as the next part of something *This report **follows on from** my earlier study.*

follow sth through *phrasal verb* to do something as the next part of an activity or period of development, usually to make certain that it is completed or successful

follow sth up *phrasal verb* to discover more about a situation or take further action in connection with it

follower /ˈfɒləʊəʳ/ *noun* [C] someone who believes in a particular person or set of ideas *a follower of Jesus*

following¹ /ˈfɒləʊɪŋ/ *adjective* **1 the following day/morning, etc** the next day, morning, etc **2 the following** what comes next, often used to introduce a list, report, etc *The following is an extract from her diary: Today I stayed in bed all day.*

following² /ˈfɒləʊɪŋ/ *noun* [**no plural**] a group of people who follow a leader, sport, etc, or admire a particular performer *He has a large and loyal following.*

following³ /ˈfɒləʊɪŋ/ *preposition* after or as a result of *He died on October 23rd, following several years of illness.*

follow-up /ˈfɒləʊʌp/ *noun* [C] something that is done to continue or complete something that was done before *a follow-up meeting*

fond /fɒnd/ *adjective* **1 be fond of sb/sth** to like someone or something *to be fond of animals/music* [**+ doing sth**] He's not very fond of dancing. **2** [**always before noun**] expressing or causing happy feelings *fond memories* **3 a fond hope/belief, etc** something that you wish were true, but probably is not •**fondly** *adverb* •**fondness** *noun* [C, U] *We both **have a fondness for** cricket.*

fondle /ˈfɒndl/ *verb* [T] to touch and rub part of someone's body, in a loving or sexual way

font /fɒnt/ *noun* [C] **1** a set of letters and symbols that are printed in a particular design and size *What size font are you using?* **2 RELIGION** a container in a church which holds the water for a baptism (= Christian ceremony)

WORD PARTNERS FOR ***food***

cold/hot/savoury/sweet food • **baby/cat/dog** food • **canned/frozen/organic/processed** food

O→ **food** /fuːd/ *noun* [C, U] **FOOD** something that people and animals eat, or plants absorb, to keep them alive *baby/dog food ○ His favourite food is pizza.* ⊃See colour picture **Food** on page Centre 11 ⊃See also: **fast food, junk food**

ˈfood ˌchain *noun* [C] **BIOLOGY** a series of living things which are connected because each group of things eats the group below it in the series ⊃See picture **food chain** on next page

foodie /ˈfuːdi/ *noun* [C] *informal* someone who loves food and knows a lot about it

ˈfood ˌmile *noun* [C] **ENVIRONMENT** a unit for measuring how far food travels from where it is made or grown to where it is eaten *People are becoming more concerned about how many food miles their produce has travelled.*

ˈfood ˌpoisoning *noun* [U] **HEALTH** an illness caused by eating food containing harmful bacteria

ˈfood ˌprocessor *noun* [C] a piece of electrical equipment with a sharp blade, for cutting and

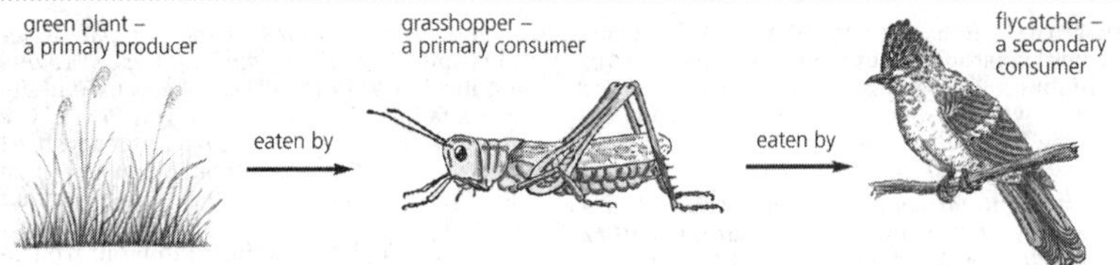

food chain

mixing food ⊃See colour picture **The Kitchen** on page Centre 2

foodstuff /ˈfuːdstʌf/ *noun* [C] *formal* a substance used as food or to make food [**usually plural**] *They need **basic foodstuffs** like rice and corn*

ˈfood techˌnology *noun* [U] **FOOD** (the study of) using science in preparing and storing food

ˈfood ˌweb *noun* [C] **BIOLOGY** the relationship between all the animals and organisms in a particular area when thinking about how they eat each other

fool[1] /fuːl/ *noun* **1** [C] a stupid person *I was a fool to trust him.* **2 make a fool (out) of sb** to try to make someone look stupid intentionally *She was always trying to make a fool out of me in front of my friends.* **3 make a fool of yourself** to behave in a silly or embarrassing way *I got drunk and started singing and making a fool of myself.* **4 act/play the fool** *UK* to behave in a silly way, usually in order to make people laugh *Joe is always playing the fool in class.*

fool[2] /fuːl/ *verb* **1** [T] to trick someone *Don't be fooled by his appearance.* [**+ into + doing sth**] *He fooled the old man into giving him the money.* **2 you could have fooled me** *informal* something that you say when you do not believe what someone says about something that you saw or experienced yourself *"I wasn't cross." "Really? You could have fooled me."*

fool around/about *phrasal verb* to behave in a silly way or have a good time

fool with sb/sth *phrasal verb mainly US* to deal with someone or something that could be dangerous in a stupid or careless way

foolhardy /ˈfuːlˌhɑːdi/ *adjective* taking or involving silly and unnecessary risks *a foolhardy decision*

foolish /ˈfuːlɪʃ/ *adjective* silly and not wise [**+ to do sth**] *It would be foolish to ignore his advice.* •**foolishly** *adverb* •**foolishness** *noun* [U]

foolproof /ˈfuːlpruːf/ *adjective* A foolproof method, plan, or system is certain to succeed and not fail.

O⁻**foot**[1] /fʊt/ *noun* **1 ANATOMY** [C] *plural* **feet** one of the two flat parts on the ends of your legs that you stand on *bare feet* ○ *He stepped on my foot.* ⊃See colour picture **The Body** on page Centre 13 **2 MEASURES** [C] *plural* **foot** or **feet** (*written abbreviation* **ft**) a unit for measuring length, equal to 0.3048 metres or 12 inches *Alex is about 6 feet tall.* ⊃See Extra help page **Numbers and measurements** on page Centre 24. **3 LITERATURE** [C] *plural* **feet** a part of a line of poetry which contains one strong beat and one or two weaker ones **4 the foot of sth** the bottom of something such as stairs, a hill, a bed, or a page *Put the notes at the foot of the page.* **5 on foot** If you go somewhere on foot, you walk there. ⊃See Common Learner Error at **walk 6 be on your feet** to be standing and not sitting *I'm exhausted, I've been on my feet all day.* **7 put your feet up** to relax, especially by sitting with your feet supported above the ground **8 set foot in/on sth** to go into a place or onto a piece of land *He told me never to set foot in his house again.* **9 get/rise to your feet** to stand up after you have been sitting *The audience rose to their feet.* **10 drag your feet** to deal with something slowly because you do not really want to do it **11 get cold feet** to suddenly become too frightened to do what you had planned to do, especially something important **12 get/start off on the wrong foot** to start a relationship or activity badly *He got off on the wrong foot with my parents by arriving late.* **13 not put a foot wrong** *UK* to not make any mistakes **14 put your foot down** to tell someone in a strong way that they must do something or must stop doing something **15 put your foot in it** *UK* (*US* **put your foot in your mouth**) to say something silly or embarrassing, without intending to **16 stand on your own two feet** to do things for yourself without wanting or needing anyone else to help you

foot[2] /fʊt/ *verb* **foot the bill** to pay for something *Why should taxpayers have to foot the bill?*

footage /ˈfʊtɪdʒ/ *noun* [U] film of an event *news/TV footage*

WORD PARTNERS FOR ***football***

play football • a football **club/match/player/team** • **a game of** football

O⁻**football** /ˈfʊtbɔːl/ *noun* **1 SPORT** [U] *UK* (*UK/US* **soccer**) a game in which two teams of players kick a round ball and try to score goals *a game of football* ○ *a **football match/team*** ⊃See colour picture **Sports 2** on page Centre 15 **2 SPORT** [U] *US* (*UK* **American football**) a game in which two teams of players try to kick, run with, or throw an oval ball across each other's goal line ⊃See colour picture **Sports 2** on page Centre 15 **3 SPORT** [C] a large ball for kicking, especially in football •**footballer** *noun* [C] *UK* someone who plays football, especially as their job •**footballing** *adjective* [**always before noun**] relating to or playing football *his **footballing career***

footer /ˈfʊt.əʳ/ *noun* [C] **COMPUTING** a word or words that appear at the bottom of every page in a book or document ⊃Compare **header**

foothills /ˈfʊthɪlz/ *noun* [plural] **GEOGRAPHY** the lower hills next to a mountain or line of mountains

foothold /ˈfʊthəʊld/ *noun* [C] **1** CLIMBING a place where it is safe to put your foot when you are climbing **2** PROGRESS a safe position from which you can make more progress, for example in business *We are still trying to* ***gain a foothold*** *in the Japanese market.*

footing /ˈfʊtɪŋ/ *noun* **1** [**no plural**] when you are standing on a surface firmly *I* ***lost my footing*** *and fell.* **2 be on an equal/firm, etc footing** to be in an equal/safe, etc position or situation

footnote /ˈfʊtnəʊt/ *noun* [C] extra information that is printed at the bottom of a page

footpath /ˈfʊtpɑːθ/ *noun* [C] *mainly UK* a path or track for people to walk along, especially in the countryside *a* ***public footpath***

F

footprint /ˈfʊtprɪnt/ *noun* [C] **1** a mark made by a foot or shoe [**usually plural**] *The police found some footprints in the mud.* **2 COMPUTING** the amount of space on a surface that something needs, especially a computer ➲Compare **ecological footprint**

footstep /ˈfʊtstep/ *noun* **1** [C] the sound of a foot hitting the ground when someone walks [**usually plural**] *I heard footsteps behind me and quickly turned round.* **2 follow in sb's footsteps** to do the same job or the same things in your life as someone else, especially a member of your family *He followed in his father's footsteps and became an actor.*

footwear /ˈfʊtweəʳ/ *noun* [U] shoes, boots, and other things that you wear on your feet

o‒**for**[1] *strong form* /fɔːʳ/ *weak form* /fəʳ/ *preposition* **1** GIVEN/USED intended to be given to or used by someone or something *I've bought a few clothes for the new baby.* ○ *parking for residents only* **2** PURPOSE having a particular purpose *a cream for dry skin* ○ *What are those large scissors for?* **3** BECAUSE OF because of or as a result of something [+ **doing sth**] *I got fined for travelling without a ticket.* ○ *Scotland is famous for its spectacular countryside.* **4** TIME/DISTANCE used to show an amount of time or distance *We drove for miles before we found a phone box.* ○ *I've been living with my parents for a few months.* ➲See Common Learner Error at **during** **5** GET in order to get or achieve something *I've sent off for an application form.* ○ *We had to wait for a taxi.* **6** HELP in order to help someone *I'll carry those bags for you.* **7** OCCASION on the occasion of *We're having a party for Jim's 60th birthday.* **8** AT A TIME at a particular time *I've booked a table for 9 o'clock.* **9** IN EXCHANGE in exchange for something, especially an amount of money *How much did you pay for your computer?* ○ *I'd like to change it for a smaller one.* **10** SUPPORT supporting or agreeing with someone or something *Who did you vote for?* ○ *There were 16 people for the motion and 14 against.* **11** REPRESENT representing or working with a country, organization, etc *He plays football for Cambridge United.* ○ *She works for a charity.* **12** TOWARDS towards or in the direction of *Just follow the signs for the airport.* **13** COMPARE when compared to a particular fact *She's quite tall for her age.* **14** MEANING meaning or representing something *What's the German word for 'cucumber'?* **15** RESPONSIBILITY used to say whose responsibility something is *I can't tell you whether you should go or not - that's for you to decide.* **16 for all** despite *For all her qualifications, she's useless at the job.* **17 for all I care/know** used to say that a fact is not important to you *He could be married by now, for all I care.* **18 for now** used to say that something should happen or be done now but can be changed later *Just put everything on the table for now.* **19 be for it** UK *informal* (*UK/US* **be in for it**) to be in trouble *If Hilary finds out I'll be for it!*

forage /ˈfɒrɪdʒ/ *verb* [I] to move about searching for things you need, especially food *Chimpanzees spend most of the day* ***foraging for*** *fruit, leaves, and insects.*

foray /ˈfɒreɪ/ *noun* [C] when you try to do something that is not familiar to you, or go somewhere different, for a short time *In 2004, she* ***made her first foray into*** *politics.*

forbid /fəˈbɪd/ *verb* [T] **forbidding**, *past tense* **forbade**, *past participle* **forbidden** **1** to order someone not to do something, or to say that something must not happen [+ **to do sth**] *I forbid you to see that boy again.* [**often passive + from + doing sth**] *He is forbidden from leaving the country.* **2 God/Heaven forbid!** something you say when you hope that something will not happen [+ **(that)**] God forbid that he should die during the operation. •**forbidden** *adjective* not allowed by an official rule *Smoking is* ***strictly forbidden*** *in this area.*

forbidding /fəˈbɪdɪŋ/ *adjective* looking unpleasant, unfriendly, or frightening *a cold and forbidding landscape*

WORD PARTNERS FOR ***force***

exert/use force • **brute/sheer** force • do sth **by** force • the force **of** sth

o‒**force**[1] /fɔːs/ *noun* **1** POWER [U] physical power or strength *The force of the explosion shattered every window in the street.* ○ *The army has seized power* ***by force***. **2** ORGANIZED GROUP [C] a group of people organized to work together for a particular purpose, for example in military service *the Royal Air Force* ○ *a skilled* ***work force*** **3** INFLUENCE [C, U] power and influence, or a person or thing that has it *the forces of good/evil* **4 in/into force** If a law, rule, etc is in force, it is being used, and if it comes into force, it starts to be used. *The new law came into force in April.* **5 be out in force** to be somewhere in large numbers *Photographers were out in force at the palace today.* **6 a force to be reckoned with** a very powerful person or organization **7 join forces** When two people or groups join forces, they act or work together. [+ **to do sth**] She ***joined forces with*** *her sister-in-law to set up a restaurant.* ➲See also: **air force, the armed forces, market forces, police force, task force**

o‒**force**[2] /fɔːs/ *verb* [T] **1** PERSON to make someone do something that they do not want to do [+ **to do sth**] *The hijacker forced the pilot to fly to New York.* [**often passive**] *She was* ***forced out of*** *the race by a knee injury.* **2** OBJECT to make an object move or open by physical strength or effort *They had to force the lock.* ○ *She forced the window open.*

force-feed /ˈfɔːsfiːd/ *verb* [T] to make a person or animal eat, often by putting food in the stomach through a pipe in the mouth *Eventually, the hunger strikers were force-fed.*

forceful /'fɔːsfᵊl/ *adjective* expressing opinions strongly and demanding attention or action *a forceful manner/personality* •**forcefully** *adverb to **argue forcefully***

forcible /'fɔːsəbl/ *adjective* A forcible action is done using force. *forcible entry/arrest* •**forcibly** *adverb Thousands of people were **forcibly removed** from their homes.*

fore /fɔːʳ/ *noun* **to the fore** in or to an important or popular position *The band first **came to the fore** in the late 1990s.*

forearm /'fɔːrɑːm/ *noun* [C] **ANATOMY** the lower part of your arm between your hand and your elbow (= the place where it bends) ➲See picture at **body**

foreboding /fɔː'bəʊdɪŋ/ *noun* [U, no plural] a feeling that something very bad is going to happen *a **sense of foreboding***

WORD PARTNERS FOR ***forecast***

a forecast **of** sth • an **economic** forecast • a **gloomy** forecast

forecast[1] /'fɔːkɑːst/ *noun* [C] a report saying what is likely to happen in the future ***economic forecasts*** ➲See also: **weather forecast**

forecast[2] /'fɔːkɑːst/ *verb* [T] *past* **forecast, forecasted** to say what you expect to happen in the future *In 2001 a serious earthquake was forecast for the area.* •**forecaster** *noun* [C] *a **weather forecaster***

forecourt /'fɔːkɔːt/ *noun* [C] *UK* a large area with a hard surface at the front of a building *a **garage forecourt***

forefather /'fɔːˌfɑːðəʳ/ *noun formal* **sb's forefathers** **SOCIETY** someone's relatives who lived a long time ago

forefinger /'fɔːˌfɪŋgəʳ/ *noun* [C] **ANATOMY** the finger next to your thumb

forefront /'fɔːfrʌnt/ *noun* **be at/in the forefront of sth** to have an important position or job in an area of activity *The company is at the forefront of developing new technology.*

forego /fɔː'gəʊ/ *verb* [T] **foregoing**, *past tense* **forewent**, *past participle* **foregone** *another spelling of* forgo (= to decide not to have or do something you want)

ˌforegone conˈclusion *noun* [no plural] a result that is obvious before it happens [+ **(that)**] *It was a foregone conclusion that he'd go into politics.*

the foreground /fɔːgraʊnd/ *noun* **1** **ART** the area of a view or picture which seems closest to you *There's a seated figure in the foreground of the painting.* **2** the subject or person that people give most attention to *Environmental issues have recently moved to the foreground.*

forehand /'fɔːhænd/ *noun* [C] **SPORT** when you hit the ball in sports such as tennis with your arm held out on the side that you hold the racket (= object to hit balls with) ***a forehand volley***

forehead /'fɔːhed/ *noun* [C] **ANATOMY** the part of your face between your eyes and your hair ➲See colour picture **The Body** on page Centre 13

O⁻ **foreign** /'fɒrɪn/ *adjective* **1** FROM ANOTHER COUNTRY belonging to or coming from another country, not your own *a foreign language/student ○ foreign cars/films* **2** OTHER COUNTRIES [**always before noun**] relating to or dealing with countries that are not your own ***foreign policy*** *○ the **Foreign Minister*** **3** **be foreign to sb** to be something you know nothing about or do not understand *The concept of loyalty is completely foreign to him.*

foreigner /'fɒrɪnəʳ/ *noun* [C] someone from another country

foreman /'fɔːmən/ *noun* [C] *plural* **foremen** someone who leads a group of workers *a factory foreman*

foremost /'fɔːməʊst/ *adjective, adverb formal* most important *He's one of the country's **foremost experts** on military law.*

forename /'fɔːneɪm/ *noun* [C] *UK formal* your first name, which comes before your family name

forensic /fə'rensɪk/ *adjective* [**always before noun**] relating to scientific methods of solving crimes ***forensic evidence/medicine*** *○ **a forensic scientist***

forerunner /'fɔːˌrʌnəʳ/ *noun* [C] an earlier, less developed example *the forerunner of the modern car*

foresee /fɔː'siː/ *verb* [T] **foreseeing**, *past tense* **foresaw**, *past participle* **foreseen** to expect a future situation or event *I don't **foresee** any **problems** in the future.*

foreseeable /fɔː'siːəbl/ *adjective* **for/in the foreseeable future** as far in the future as you can imagine *Prices will remain high for the foreseeable future.*

foreshadow /fɔː'ʃædəʊ/ *verb* [T] *formal* to show or warn that something bigger, worse, or more important is coming

foresight /'fɔːsaɪt/ *noun* [U] when you know or can judge what will happen or what you will need in the future *She **had the foresight to** book her flight early.*

foreskin /'fɔːskɪn/ *noun* [C, U] **ANATOMY** the loose skin that covers the end of a penis

O⁻ **forest** /'fɒrɪst/ *noun* [C, U] a large area of trees growing closely together *pine forest* •**forested** *adjective* covered by forest *heavily forested areas*

forestall /fɔː'stɔːl/ *verb* [T] to prevent something from happening by taking action before it does *to forestall an attack/crisis*

forestry /'fɒrɪstri/ *noun* [U] the work of looking after or making forests

foretell /fɔː'tel/ *verb* [T] *past* **foretold** *formal* to say what is going to happen in the future

forever /fə'revəʳ/ *adverb* **1** IN FUTURE for all time in the future *I'll love you forever.* **2** A LONG TIME *informal* used to emphasize that something takes a long time *The journey home took forever.* **3** OFTEN used to emphasize that something happens often *She is forever helping people.*

foreword /ˈfɔːwɜːd/ *noun* [C] **LITERATURE** a short piece of writing at the front of a book that introduces the book or its writer

forfeit /ˈfɔːfɪt/ *verb* [T] to lose the right to do something or have something because you have done something wrong *They have **forfeited the right** to live in society.*

forgave /fəˈgeɪv/ *past tense of* forgive

forge¹ /fɔːdʒ/ *verb* [T] **1 LAW** to make an illegal copy of something in order to deceive people *a **forged passport*** **2** DEVELOP to develop a good relationship with someone or something *The group **forged friendships** that have lasted more than twenty years.*
forge ahead *phrasal verb* to suddenly make a lot of progress with something *The organizers are **forging ahead with** a programme of public events.*

forge² /fɔːdʒ/ *noun* [C] a place where metal objects are made by heating and shaping metal

forgery /ˈfɔːdʒəri/ *noun* **LAW** **1** [C] an illegal copy of a document, painting, etc **2** [U] the crime of making an illegal copy of something

OTHER WAYS OF SAYING ***forget***

The expression **slip someone's mind** is often used informally when someone forgets to do something: *I meant to tell you that he'd phoned, but it completely **slipped my mind**.*

If a word is **on the tip of your tongue**, you have forgotten it but think that you will very soon remember it: *Oh, what was that film called? - it's **on the tip of my tongue**.*

If something such as a name **escapes** you, you cannot remember it: *The name of her book **escapes** me at the moment.*

forget /fəˈget/ *verb* **forgetting**, *past tense* **forgot**, *past participle* **forgotten** **1** NOT REMEMBER [I, T] to be unable to remember a fact, something that happened, or how to do something *I've forgotten his name.* [+ (that)] *Don't forget that Lucy and John are coming this weekend.* ○ *He'd completely **forgotten about** their quarrel.* [+ question word] *You never forget how to ride a bike.* **2** NOT DO [I, T] to not remember to do something [+ to do sth] *Dad's always forgetting to take his pills.* **3** NOT BRING [T] to not bring something with you because you did not remember it *Oh no, I've forgotten my passport.* **4** STOP THINKING [T] (*also* **forget about**) to stop thinking about someone or something *I'll never forget him for as long as I live.* **5 forget it** used to tell someone not to worry about something as it is not important **6 I forget** used instead of 'I have forgotten' *I forget when we last saw him.* **7 forget yourself** to do or say something that is not acceptable in a particular situation *She completely forgot herself and started screaming at him.*

forgetful /fəˈgetfəl/ *adjective* often forgetting things *She's 84 now and getting a bit forgetful.* •**forgetfulness** *noun* [U]

forgive /fəˈgɪv/ *verb past tense* **forgave**, *past participle* **forgiven** **1** [I, T] to decide not to be angry with someone or not to punish them for something they have done *I've apologized, but I don't think she'll ever forgive me.* [often reflexive] *Mike would never forgive himself if anything happened to the children.* [+ for + doing sth] *Jane never forgave her mother for lying to her.* **2 forgive me** used before you ask or say something that might seem rude *Forgive me for asking, but how much did you pay for your bag?* **3 sb could be forgiven for doing sth** used to say that you can understand if someone might think, believe, or do something

WORD PARTNERS FOR ***forgiveness***

ask (for)/beg (for) forgiveness • forgiveness for sth

forgiveness /fəˈgɪvnəs/ *noun* [U] when you forgive someone for something they have done

forgiving /fəˈgɪvɪŋ/ *adjective* ready to forgive someone for something they have done

forgo /fɔːˈgəʊ/ *verb* [T] **forgoing**, *past tense* **forwent**, *past participle* **forgone** *formal* to decide not to have or do something, although you want to have it or do it *She had to forgo her early ambition to be a writer.*

forgot /fəˈgɒt/ *past tense of* forget

forgotten /fəˈgɒtən/ *past participle of* forget

fork¹ /fɔːk/ *noun* [C] **1** FOOD a small object with three or four points and a handle, that you use to pick up food and eat with *a **knife and fork*** **2** DIGGING a tool with a long handle and three or four points, used for digging and breaking soil into pieces *a garden fork* **3** ROAD a place where a road or river divides into two parts *Turn right when you reach a **fork in the road**.*

fork² /fɔːk/ *verb* [I] If a road or river forks, it divides into two parts.
fork sth out *phrasal verb UK* (*US* **fork sth over**) *informal* to pay or give money for something, especially when you do not want to

forlorn /fəˈlɔːn/ *adjective* lonely and unhappy *The captured soldiers looked forlorn and helpless.* •**forlornly** *adverb*

form¹ /fɔːm/ *noun* **1** TYPE [C] a type of something or way of doing something *Swimming is the best **form of** exercise.* **2** PAPER [C] a printed document with spaces for you to write information *Please **fill in/out the form** using black ink.* **3 the form of sth** the particular way in which something exists *The novel is written **in the form of** a series of letters.* **4 SPORT** [U] In sport, someone's form is how well or badly they are performing. *The team seems to have **lost its form** lately.* **5 be in/on/off form** *UK* If someone is in form or on form, they are feeling or performing well, and if they are off form they are not feeling or performing well. *Harry was **on good form** last night.* **6 EDUCATION** [C] *UK* (*US* **grade**) a school class or group of classes for students of the same age or ability *He's in the third form.* **7** SHAPE [C] the body or shape of someone or something **8 LANGUAGE** [C] a way of writing or saying a word that shows if it is singular or plural, past or present, etc *The plural form of 'sheep' is 'sheep'.* See also: **application form, sixth form**

form² /fɔːm/ *verb* **1** BEGIN [I, T] to begin to exist, or to make something begin to exist [often passive] *We are learning more about how stars are* *formed.* **2** SHAPE [**I, T**] to take or to make something take a particular shape ***Form** the dough **into** little balls.* **3** COMBINE [**T**] to make something by combining different parts *In English you form the present participle by adding -ing to the verb.* **4** START [**T**] to start an organization or business *Brown formed her own company eleven years ago.* **5** BE [**T**] to be the thing talked about or be part of it *The Alps form a natural barrier between Italy and Switzerland.* **6 form an opinion/impression, etc** to begin to have a particular opinion or idea about something because of the information you have

O-ꟷ **formal** /ˈfɔːməl/ *adjective* **1** SERIOUS used about clothes, language, and behaviour that are serious and not friendly or relaxed *a formal dinner party* **2** OFFICIAL [**always before noun**] public or official *a **formal announcement/apology*** **3 EDUCATION** [**always before noun**] Formal education, training, etc happens in a school or college. *Tom had little **formal schooling**.*

formality /fɔːˈmæləti/ *noun* **1** OFFICIAL THING [**C**] something that the law or an official process says must be done *There are certain **legal formalities** to be completed.* **2** BEHAVIOUR [**U**] formal and polite behaviour *the formality of a royal funeral*

formally /ˈfɔːməli/ *adverb* **1** OFFICIALLY officially *The deal will be **formally announced** on Tuesday.* **2** POLITELY in a polite way *They shook hands formally.*

format[1] /ˈfɔːmæt/ *noun* [**C**] the way something is designed, arranged, or produced *This year's event will have a new format.*

format[2] /ˈfɔːmæt/ *verb* [**T**] **formatting**, *past* **formatted 1 COMPUTING** to prepare a computer disk so that information can be stored on it **2** to organize and design the words on a page or document

formation /fɔːˈmeɪʃən/ *noun* **1** DEVELOPMENT [**U**] the development of something into a particular thing or shape *the formation of a crystal* **2** SHAPE [**C, U**] when something has a particular shape or things are arranged in a particular way *rock/cloud formations* ○ *The planes flew overhead **in formation*** (= in a pattern).

formative /ˈfɔːmətɪv/ *adjective* relating to the time when your character and opinions are developing *She spent **her formative years** in New York.*

former /ˈfɔːməʳ/ *adjective* [**always before noun**] happening, existing, or true in the past but not now *the former Soviet Union* ○ *former President Bill Clinton*

the former /ˈfɔːməʳ/ *noun* the first of two people or things that have just been talked about

formerly /ˈfɔːməli/ *adverb* in the past *The European Union was formerly called the European Community.*

formidable /ˈfɔːmɪdəbl/ *adjective* **1** PERSON Someone who is formidable is strong and a bit frightening. *a formidable woman* **2** DIFFICULT difficult and needing a lot of effort or thought *a **formidable task***

formula /ˈfɔːmjələ/ *noun* [**C**] *plural* **formulas** or **formulae 1** METHOD a plan or method that is used to achieve something *There's no magic **formula for success**.* **2 MATHEMATICS** a set of letters, numbers, or symbols that are used to express a mathematical or scientific rule **3** LIST a list of the substances that something is made of

formulate /ˈfɔːmjəleɪt/ *verb* [**T**] **1** PLAN to develop all the details of a plan for doing something *They **formulated a plan** to save the company.* **2** SAY to say what you think or feel after thinking carefully *to **formulate an answer/reply*** •**formulation** /ˌfɔːmjəˈleɪʃən/ *noun* [**C, U**]

forsake /fəˈseɪk/ *verb* [**T**] *past tense* **forsook**, *past participle* **forsaken** *formal* **1** LEAVE to leave someone, especially when they need you *He felt he couldn't forsake her when she was so ill.* **2** STOP to stop doing or having something *He decided to forsake politics for journalism.*

fort /fɔːt/ *noun* [**C**] a strong building that soldiers use to defend a place

forth /fɔːθ/ *adverb literary* out of a place or away from it *The knights rode forth into battle.*

forthcoming /ˌfɔːθˈkʌmɪŋ/ *adjective* **1** SOON [**always before noun**] *formal* going to happen soon *the forthcoming election/visit* **2** OFFERED [**never before noun**] If money or help is forthcoming, it is offered or given. *He insisted that no more money would be forthcoming.* **3** WILLING [**never before noun**] willing to give information *Elaine wasn't very forthcoming about her love life.*

forthright /ˈfɔːθraɪt/ *adjective* saying what you think honestly and clearly *They dealt with all our questions in a very **forthright manner**.*

forthwith /ˌfɔːθˈwɪθ/ *adverb formal* immediately *to cease forthwith*

fortifications /ˌfɔːtɪfɪˈkeɪʃənz/ *noun* [**plural**] strong walls, towers, etc that are built to protect a place

fortify /ˈfɔːtɪfaɪ/ *verb* [**T**] **1** PLACE to build strong walls, towers, etc around a place to protect it *a fortified city/town* **2** PERSON to make someone feel stronger physically or mentally *She had a sandwich to fortify herself before going on.* **3 FOOD** to add something, especially vitamins, to food •**fortification** /ˌfɔːtɪfɪˈkeɪʃən/ *noun* [**U**]

fortitude /ˈfɔːtɪtjuːd/ *noun* [**U**] *formal* when you are brave and do not complain about pain or problems

fortnight /ˈfɔːtnaɪt/ *noun* [**C**] *UK* two weeks [**usually singular**] *a fortnight's holiday* ○ *We usually get together about once a fortnight.* •**fortnightly** *adverb UK* happening every two weeks *a fortnightly meeting*

fortress /ˈfɔːtrəs/ *noun* [**C**] a castle or other strong building built to defend a place

fortunate /ˈfɔːtʃənət/ *adjective* lucky [**+ to do sth**] *I'm very fortunate to be alive.* [**+ (that)**] *It was fortunate that someone was available to take over.* ➲Opposite **unfortunate**

O-ꟷ **fortunately** /ˈfɔːtʃənətli/ *adverb* happening because of good luck *Fortunately, no one was hurt in the accident.* ➲Opposite **unfortunately**

WORD PARTNERS FOR ***fortune***

cost/earn/make/spend a fortune • a **personal** fortune • **the family** fortune

fortune /ˈfɔːtʃuːn/ *noun* **1** MONEY [C] a lot of money *She **made a fortune** selling her story to the newspapers.* **2** LUCK [C, U] the good or bad things that happen to you [**usually plural**] *The family's fortunes changed almost overnight.* **3 tell sb's fortune** to say what is going to happen to someone in the future

ˈfortune ˌcookie *noun* [C] **FOOD** a biscuit containing a piece of paper with a message about your future written on it, eaten especially in Chinese restaurants

fortune-teller /ˈfɔːtʃuːnˌteləʳ/ *noun* [C] someone who tells you what will happen to you in the future

F

O-■**forty** /ˈfɔːti/ the number 40 •**fortieth** 40th written as a word

forum /ˈfɔːrəm/ *noun* [C] **1** a situation or meeting in which people can exchange ideas and discuss things *a forum for debate/discussion* **2** **INTERNET** an area of a website where people go to discuss things ⊃See Extra help page **The Web and the Internet** on page Centre 37.

O-■**forward**[1] /ˈfɔːwəd/ (*also* **forwards**) *adverb* **1** DIRECTION towards the direction that is in front of you *She leaned forward to make sure I could hear her.* **2** FUTURE towards the future *I always **look forward**, not back.* **3** PROGRESS used to say that something is making good progress *This is a big **step forward** for democracy.*

forward[2] /ˈfɔːwəd/ *adjective* **1 forward motion/movement, etc** movement towards the direction that is in front of you **2 forward planning/thinking, etc** when you plan or think about something for the future **3** Someone who is forward is too confident or too friendly with people they do not know.

forward[3] /ˈfɔːwəd/ *verb* [T] to send a letter, email, etc that you have received to someone else *Could you forward my mail to me while I'm away?* ⊃See also: **fast-forward**

forward[4] /ˈfɔːwəd/ *noun* [C] **SPORT** a player in a sport such as football who plays near the front and tries to score goals

ˌforwarding aˈddress *noun* [C] a new address that letters and parcels should be sent to

forward-looking /ˈfɔːwədlʊkɪŋ/ *adjective* planning for the future and using new ideas or technology *a forward-looking plan/policy*

forwards /ˈfɔːwədz/ *adverb another word for* forward

ˈforward ˌslash (*also* **slash**) *noun* [C] **COMPUTING** the symbol '/', a symbol used in Internet addresses and used to show where on a computer files are kept ⊃Compare **backslash**

forwent /fɔːˈwent/ *past tense of* forgo

fossil /ˈfɒsəl/ *noun* [C] **GEOLOGY** part of an animal or plant from thousands of years ago, preserved in rock

ˈfossil ˌfuel *noun* [C, U] **GEOLOGY, ENVIRONMENT** a fuel such as coal or oil that is obtained from under the ground ⊃See picture at **greenhouse effect**

fossilize (*also UK* **-ise**) /ˈfɒsɪlaɪz/ *verb* [I] **GEOLOGY** to become a fossil •**fossilization** (*also UK* **-isation**) /ˌfɒsɪlaɪˈzeɪʃən/ *noun* [U]

foster[1] /ˈfɒstəʳ/ *verb* [T] **1** to encourage a particular feeling, situation, or idea to develop *The growth of the Internet could foster economic development worldwide.* **2** **SOCIETY** to look after a child as part of your family for a time, without becoming their legal parent

foster[2] /ˈfɒstəʳ/ *adjective* **1 foster home/mother/parent, etc** **SOCIETY** the home where a child who is fostered lives, or the person or people who foster a child **2 foster child/daughter/son, etc** **SOCIETY** a child who is fostered

fought /fɔːt/ *past of* fight

foul[1] /faʊl/ *adjective* **1** DIRTY very dirty, or with an unpleasant smell *the foul smell of rotting fish* **2** BAD very bad or unpleasant *foul weather* ○ *She's in a foul mood.* **3 foul language/words** very rude and offensive words **4 fall foul of sb/sth** *UK* to do something which causes you to be in trouble

foul[2] /faʊl/ *verb* **1** [T] to make something very dirty *The beaches had been fouled by dogs.* **2** **SPORT** [I, T] to do something that is against the rules in a sport *He was fouled as he was about to shoot at goal.*

foul sth up *phrasal verb informal* to spoil something completely *The travel company completely fouled up our holiday.*

WORD PARTNERS FOR ***foul***

commit a foul • a foul **against/on** sb

foul[3] /faʊl/ *noun* [C] **SPORT** something that someone does in a sport that is not allowed by the rules

ˌfoul ˈplay *noun* [U] **LAW** when someone's death is caused by a violent crime

found[1] /faʊnd/ *verb* [T] **1** START to start an organization, especially by providing money *The company was founded in 1861.* **2** BASE to base something on a set of ideas or beliefs [**often passive**] *a society **founded on** principles of equality*

found[2] /faʊnd/ *past of* find

foundation /faʊnˈdeɪʃən/ *noun* **1** IDEA [C] the idea or principle that something is based on *Jefferson's document **formed the foundation of** a new nation.* **2** STARTING [U] when an organization, state, or country is established *the foundation of a new state* **3** ORGANIZATION [C] an organization that gives money for a particular purpose *the Mental Health Foundation* **4 foundations** [**plural**] *UK* (*US* **foundation** [C]) the part of a building, road, bridge, etc that is under the ground and supports it *concrete foundations* **5** MAKE-UP [U] make-up that is worn all over the face to give it a smooth appearance **6 be without foundation; have no foundation** If something is without foundation, there is no proof that it is true. *The allegations are completely without foundation.* **7 lay the foundation(s) for/of sth** to provide the conditions that make it possible for something to happen *His reforms laid the foundation of future greatness.*

founˈdation ˌcourse *UK* (*US* **introductory course**) *noun* [C] **EDUCATION** a college or university course on a subject that students take to prepare them for a more advanced course on that subject

founder /ˈfaʊndəʳ/ *noun* [C] someone who establishes an organization

foundry /ˈfaʊndri/ *noun* [C] a place where metal or glass is melted and made into objects

fountain /ˈfaʊntɪn/ *noun* [C] a structure that forces water up into the air as a decoration

ˈfountain ˌpen *noun* [C] a pen that you fill with ink

O⁻ **four** /fɔːʳ/ the number 4

four-by-four /ˌfɔːbaɪˈfɔːʳ/ a four-wheel drive

fours /fɔːz/ *noun* **on all fours** with your hands and knees on the ground

foursome /ˈfɔːsəm/ *noun* [C] a group of four people *We could go out as a foursome.*

O⁻ **fourteen** /ˌfɔːˈtiːn/ the number 14 •**fourteenth** 14th written as a word

fourth[1] /fɔːθ/ 4th written as a word

fourth[2] /fɔːθ/ *US* (*UK/US* **quarter**) *noun* [C] one of four equal parts of something; $^1/_4$

ˌFourth of Juˈly (*also* **Independence Day**) *noun* [U] 4 July, a national holiday in the US to celebrate the country's freedom from Great Britain in 1776

ˌfour-wheel ˈdrive (*written abbreviation* **4WD**) *noun* [C] a vehicle with an engine that supplies power to all four wheels so that it can drive easily over rough ground •**ˌfour-wheel ˈdrive** *adjective a four-wheel drive car*

fovea /ˈfɒviə/ *noun* [C] **ANATOMY** a small part at the back of the retina (= part of the eye that sends pictures to the brain) that is the area with the clearest sight

fowl /faʊl/ *noun* [C] *plural* **fowl** or **fowls** **FOOD** a bird that is kept for its eggs and meat, especially a chicken

fox /fɒks/ *noun* [C] a wild animal like a dog with red-brown fur, a pointed nose, and a long thick tail

foyer /ˈfɔɪeɪ/ (US) /ˈfɔɪər/ *noun* [C] a room at the entrance of a hotel, theatre, cinema, etc

fracas /ˈfrækɑː/ (US) /ˈfreɪkəs/ *noun* [**no plural**] a noisy fight or argument

WORD PARTNERS FOR ***fraction***

a **minute/small/tiny** fraction of sth • a fraction of sth

fraction /ˈfrækʃᵊn/ *noun* [C] **1** **MATHEMATICS** a number less than 1, such as $^1/_2$ or $^3/_4$ ➲See Extra help page **Numbers and measurements** on page Centre 22. **2** a very small number or amount *a fraction of a second* •**fractionally** *adverb* by a very small amount *Harry is fractionally taller than Ben.*

fractional distillation /ˌfrækʃᵊnᵊlˌdɪstɪˈleɪʃᵊn/ *noun* [U] **CHEMISTRY** the process of separating parts of a liquid by heating it gradually so that different parts become gas, rise up, then turn back into liquid that can be collected as they cool

fracture /ˈfræktʃəʳ/ *verb* [T] **HEALTH** to break something hard such as a bone, or a piece of rock *She's fractured her ankle.* •**fracture** *noun* [C]

fragile /ˈfrædʒaɪl/ (US) /ˈfrædʒᵊl/ *adjective* **1** [BREAK] easily broken, damaged, or destroyed *a fragile china cup* ○ *a fragile economy* **2** [PERSON] physically or emotionally weak *a fragile little girl* •**fragility** /frəˈdʒɪləti/ *noun* [U]

fragment[1] /ˈfrægmənt/ *noun* [C] a small piece of something *fragments of pottery*

fragment[2] /frægˈment/ *verb* [I, T] to break something into small parts, or to be broken in this way *The opposition has fragmented into a number of small groups.* •**fragmented** *adjective a fragmented society*

fragrance /ˈfreɪgrəns/ *noun* [C, U] **1** [SMELL] a pleasant smell *the delicate fragrance of roses* **2** [SUBSTANCE] a substance which people put on their bodies to make themselves smell nice

fragrant /ˈfreɪgrənt/ *adjective* with a pleasant smell *fragrant flowers*

frail /freɪl/ *adjective* not strong or healthy *a frail old lady*

frailty /ˈfreɪlti/ *noun* [C, U] when someone is physically or morally weak

frame[1] /freɪm/ *noun* [C] **1** [PICTURE] a structure that goes around the edge of something such as a door, picture, window, or mirror ***a picture frame*** ○ ***a window frame*** **2** [STRUCTURE] the basic structure of a building, vehicle, or piece of furniture that other parts are added onto *a bicycle frame* **3** [BODY] the shape of someone's body *his large/small frame* **4** **frame of mind** the way someone feels at a particular time *She was in a more positive frame of mind today.*

frame[2] /freɪm/ *verb* [T] **1** [PICTURE] to put something such as a picture into a frame *I'm going to frame this and put it on the wall.* **2** [EDGE] to form an edge to something in an attractive way *Dark hair framed her face.* **3** [CRIME] to intentionally make it seem as if someone is guilty of a crime [**often passive**] *He claimed he had been framed by the police.* **4** [EXPRESS] *formal* to express something choosing your words carefully *I tried to frame a suitable reply.*

frames /freɪmz/ *noun* [**plural**] the plastic or metal structure that holds together a pair of glasses

WORD PARTNERS FOR ***framework***

create/develop/establish/provide a framework • a framework **for** (doing) sth

framework /ˈfreɪmwɜːk/ *noun* [C] **1** [SYSTEM] a system of rules, ideas, or beliefs that is used to plan or decide something *a legal* ***framework for*** *resolving disputes* **2** [STRUCTURE] the basic structure that supports something such as a vehicle or building and gives it its shape

franchise /ˈfrænʃaɪz/ *noun* **1** **ECONOMICS** [C] the right to sell a company's products or services in a particular area using the company's name *a fast food franchise* **2** **POLITICS** [U] the legal right to vote in elections

franchisee /ˌfræntʃaɪˈziː/ *noun* [C] **ECONOMICS** a person or company that has the right to sell a company's products or services in a particular area using the company's name

franchiser /ˈfræntʃaɪzər/ *noun* [C] **ECONOMICS** a business that sells the right to sell a company's products or services in a particular area using the company's name

frank /fræŋk/ *adjective* speaking honestly and saying what you really think *a full and frank*

F

discussion ○ ***To be frank,*** *I don't really want to see him.* •**frankness** *noun* [U]

frankfurter /'fræŋkfɜːtəʳ/ *noun* [C] **FOOD** a long, thin sausage (= tube of meat and spices), often eaten with bread

frankly /'fræŋkli/ *adverb* in an honest and direct way ***Quite frankly,*** *I think you're making a big mistake.*

frantic /'fræntɪk/ *adjective* **1** FAST done in a fast and excited way and not calm or organized *a frantic search* **2** WORRIED very worried or frightened *frantic calls for help* ○ *I got home to find Joe* ***frantic with*** *worry.* •**frantically** *adverb Laura was searching frantically for her keys.*

F

fraternal /frə'tɜːnəl/ *adjective* like or relating to a brother

fraternity /frə'tɜːnəti/ *noun* **1** [U] a feeling of friendship between people **2 EDUCATION** [C] in the US, a social organization of male college students

WORD PARTNERS FOR ***fraud***

commit fraud • a fraud **case/charge/investigation**

fraud /frɔːd/ *noun* **1 LAW** [U] when someone does something illegal in order to get money *credit card fraud* **2** [C] someone who deceives people by pretending to be someone or something that they are not

fraudulent /'frɔːdjələnt/ *adjective formal* dishonest and illegal *fraudulent insurance claims* •**fraudulently** *adverb*

fraught /frɔːt/ *adjective* **1 fraught with danger/difficulties, etc** full of danger/difficulties, etc *The present situation is fraught with danger.* **2** *mainly UK* causing worry, or feeling worried *a fraught silence*

fray¹ /freɪ/ *verb* **1** CLOTH [I, T] If material or clothing frays, or if it is frayed, the threads at the edge break and become loose. **2** ANNOYED [I] If your temper (= mood) frays or your nerves fray, you gradually become annoyed or upset. *After hours of waiting,* ***tempers*** *were beginning to* ***fray.***

fray² /freɪ/ *noun* **enter/join, etc the fray** to start taking part in an argument or fight *The time had come for the US to enter the fray.*

freak¹ /friːk/ *noun* [C] **1** INTEREST *informal* someone who is very interested in a particular subject or activity *My brother's a bit of a computer freak.* **2** STRANGE someone who looks strange or behaves in a strange way *They made me feel like a freak.*

freak² /friːk/ *adjective* **a freak accident/storm, etc** A freak event is one that is very unusual.

freak³ /friːk/ (*also* **freak out**) *verb* [I, T] *informal* to suddenly become very angry, frightened, or surprised, or to make someone do this *I hated that film, it totally freaked me out.*

freckle /'frekl/ *noun* [C] a very small, brown spot on your skin from the sun •**freckled** *adjective*

O⁃**free¹** /friː/ *adjective* **1** NOT CONTROLLED able to live, happen, or exist without being controlled by anyone or anything *free trade* ○ *a free society* [**+ to do sth**] *People should be free to say what they think.* **2** NO COST not costing any money *a free sample of perfume* ○ *Entry is free for children under 12.* ○ *The unemployed get their prescriptions* ***free of charge.*** **3** NOT A PRISONER not in prison or in a cage *He opened the cage and* ***set*** *the birds* ***free.*** **4** NOT BUSY not busy doing anything *Are you free this evening?* ○ *I don't have much* ***free time.*** **5** NOT USED not being used by anyone *Is this seat free?* **6 CHEMISTRY** If an element is free, it is not combined with anything else or attached to anything else. **7 free from/of sth** not containing or having anything harmful or unpleasant *a life free from pain* **8 feel free** something that you say in order to tell someone that they are allowed to do something [**+ to do sth**] *Please feel free to ask questions.* ➲See also: **duty-free,** a free **hand¹**, free **rein, tax-free, toll-free**

free² /friː/ *adverb* **1** NO COST without cost or payment *Children under five travel free.* ○ *He offered to do it* ***for free.*** **2** NOT CONTROLLED in a way that is not tied, limited, or controlled *She* ***broke free*** *from his grasp and ran away.*

O⁃**free³** /friː/ *verb* [T] **freeing,** *past* **freed 1** ALLOW TO LEAVE to allow someone to leave a prison or place where they have been kept *The last hostages were finally freed yesterday.* **2** GET OUT to get someone out of a situation or place that they cannot escape from *Firefighters worked for two hours to* ***free*** *the driver* ***from*** *the wreckage.* **3** TAKE AWAY to help someone by taking something unpleasant away from them *The book's success* ***freed*** *her* ***from*** *her financial worries.* **4** MAKE AVAILABLE (*also* **free up**) to make something available for someone to use *I need to free up some space for these files.*

-free /friː/ *suffix* used at the end of words to mean 'without' or 'not containing' *sugarfree gum* ○ *an interest-free loan*

freebie /'friːbi/ *noun* [C] *informal* something that you are given, usually by a company, and do not have to pay for

ˌfree collective ˈbargaining *noun* [U] when workers and their employers talk formally about pay, working hours, etc. in a way that is not limited by the law or government

Freecycle /'friːsaɪkl/ *verb* [T, I] *trademark* to use a local Freecycle email group to give away things that you do not want now •**freecycler** *noun* [C]

WORD PARTNERS FOR ***freedom***

be given/have the freedom to do sth • freedom **of choice/of expression/of movement/of speech**

O⁃**freedom** /'friːdəm/ *noun* **1** RIGHT [C, U] the right to live in the way you want, say what you think, and make your own decisions without being controlled by anyone else *religious freedom* ○ ***freedom of choice/speech*** [**+ to do sth**] *You have the freedom to do what you want to do.* **2 freedom from sth** a situation in which you are not suffering because of something unpleasant or harmful *freedom from fear/poverty* **3** STATE [U] when someone is no longer a prisoner

ˌfree ˈenterprise *noun* [U] **ECONOMICS** when trade and business is allowed to operate without much control from the government

freehand /ˈfriːhænd/ *adjective, adverb* **ART** describes a drawing which has been done only by hand, without using any special equipment

ˌfree ˈkick *noun* [C] **SPORT** a kick that a player in a football match is allowed to take after a player from the other team has broken the rules

freelance /ˈfriːlɑːns/ *adjective, adverb* working for several different organizations, and paid according to the hours you work *a freelance photographer* ○ *Most of our producers work freelance.* •**freelance** *verb* [I] •**freelancer** *noun* [C]

freely /ˈfriːli/ *adverb* **1** NOT CONTROLLED without being controlled or limited *For the first time in months she could move freely.* ○ *Exotic foods are **freely available** in supermarkets.* **2** WILLINGLY If you freely admit something, you are very willing to agree that it is true. *I **freely admit** that I was wrong about him.*

ˌfree ˈmarket *noun* [no plural] **ECONOMICS** when the government does not control prices and trade *a free-market economy*

freephone /ˈfriːfəʊn/ *UK* (*US* **toll-free**) *adjective* [always before noun] A freephone number is a telephone number that you can connect to without paying.

ˌfree ˈradical *noun* [C usually plural] **PHYSICS, CHEMISTRY** an atom or molecule that is missing one electron (= small piece of atom with a negative electrical charge) and is therefore very quick to react with other atoms and molecules

free-range /ˌfriːˈreɪndʒ/ *adjective* **FOOD, FARMING** relating to or produced by farm animals that are allowed to move around outside and are not kept in cages ***free-range eggs***

freesheet /ˈfriːʃiːt/ *noun* [C] a free newspaper

ˌfree ˈspeech *noun* [U] **POLITICS** the right to express your opinions in public

ˌfree ˈtrade *noun* [C] **ECONOMICS** a way to buy and sell products between countries, without limits on the amount of goods that can be bought and sold, and without special taxes on the goods ➲Compare **fair trade**

freeware /ˈfriːweəʳ/ *noun* [U] **COMPUTING** computer software that you do not have to pay for, for example from the Internet

freeway /ˈfriːweɪ/ *US* (*UK* **motorway**) *noun* [C] a long, wide road, usually used by traffic travelling fast over long distances

ˌfree ˈwill *noun* **1** [U] when people choose and decide what they want to do in their own lives **2 do sth of your own free will** to do something because you want to, not because someone forces you to *She had gone there of her own free will.*

O-m**freeze¹** /friːz/ *verb past tense* **froze**, *past participle* **frozen 1** ICE [I, T] If something freezes or is frozen, it becomes hard and solid because it is very cold. *The river had frozen overnight.* ○ *Water freezes at 0° Celsius.* **2 FOOD** [I, T] to make food last a long time by making it very cold and hard *You can freeze any cakes that you have left over.* **3** PERSON [I] to feel very cold *One of the climbers **froze to death** on the mountain.* **4** NOT MOVE [I] to suddenly stop moving, especially because you are frightened *She saw someone outside the window and froze.* **5** - **ECONOMICS** [T] to fix the level of something such as a price or rate so that it does not increase

freeze² /friːz/ *noun* **1** LEVEL [C] when the level of something such as a price or rate is fixed so that it does not increase *a pay freeze* **2** PROCESS [C] when a process is stopped for a period of time *an immediate freeze on all new building in the city* **3** COLD [no plural] *informal* a period of extremely cold weather

freezer /ˈfriːzəʳ/ *noun* [C] a large container operated by electricity in which food can be frozen and stored ➲See colour picture **The Kitchen** on page Centre 2

freezing¹ /ˈfriːzɪŋ/ *adjective informal* very cold *It's absolutely freezing in here.*

freezing² /ˈfriːzɪŋ/ *noun* [U] **MEASURES, PHYSICS** the temperature at which water freezes *It was five degrees **below/above freezing**.*

ˈfreezing ˌpoint *noun* [C, U] **MEASURES, PHYSICS** the temperature at which a liquid freezes

freight /freɪt/ *noun* [U] goods that are carried by trains, trucks, ships, or aircraft

freighter /ˈfreɪtəʳ/ *noun* [C] a large ship or aircraft that carries goods

ˈfrench ˌfries *US* (*UK* **chips**) *noun* [plural] **FOOD** long, thin pieces of potato that have been cooked in hot oil ➲See colour picture **Food** on page Centre 11

ˌFrench ˈknickers *noun* [plural] women's loose underwear that covers all the bottom ➲See colour picture **Clothes** on page Centre 9

ˌFrench ˈwindows (*also* **ˌFrench ˈdoors**) *noun* [plural] a pair of glass doors that usually open into a garden

frenetic /frəˈnetɪk/ *adjective* fast and exciting in an uncontrolled way *a **frenetic pace*** ○ ***frenetic activity***

frenzied /ˈfrenzɪd/ *adjective* wild and uncontrolled *a frenzied dance*

frenzy /ˈfrenzi/ *noun* [U, no plural] when you are so excited, nervous, or anxious that you cannot control what you are doing *She hit him in a frenzy of rage.*

frequency /ˈfriːkwənsi/ *noun* [C, U] **1** the number of times something happens in a particular period, or the fact that something happens often or a large number of times *The **frequency of** attacks seems to have increased recently.* **2 PHYSICS** the rate at which a sound wave or radio wave is repeated *the very high frequencies of a television signal*

O-m**frequent¹** /ˈfriːkwənt/ *adjective* happening often *He is a frequent visitor to the US.*

frequent² /frɪˈkwent/ (US) /ˈfriːkwent/ *verb* [T] to go to a place often *a bar frequented by criminals*

O-m**frequently** /ˈfriːkwəntli/ *adverb formal* often *a frequently asked question*

O-m**fresh** /freʃ/ *adjective* **1** DIFFERENT new or different from what was there before *We're looking for fresh ideas.* ○ *They decided to move abroad and **make a fresh start**.* **2 FOOD** Fresh food has been produced or collected recently and has not been frozen, dried, etc. *fresh fruit/vegetables* ○ *fresh bread* **3** CLEAN/COOL smelling clean or feeling pleasantly cool *a fresh breeze* ○ *a fresh smell* **4 fresh air** air outside buildings that is clean and cool *Let's go outside and get some fresh air.* **5 fresh water** water from lakes, rivers, etc that has no salt in it **6** [NOT TIRED] having a lot of energy and not feeling tired *We got up the next day feeling fresh and relaxed.* **7** [SKIN] Fresh skin looks healthy. *a fresh complexion* **8** [RECENT] recently made or done and not yet changed by time *The memory of the accident is still very fresh in my mind.* **9 fresh from/out of sth** having just left a place *The new French teacher's fresh out of college.* •**freshness** *noun* [U] ⊃See also: a **breath** of fresh air

F

freshen /ˈfreʃᵊn/ *verb*
freshen up *phrasal verb* to quickly wash yourself so that you feel clean *Would you like to freshen up before dinner?*
freshen sth up *phrasal verb* to make something look cleaner and more attractive *A coat of paint would help to freshen this place up.*

fresher /ˈfreʃəʳ/ *noun* [C] *UK informal* **EDUCATION** a student in the first year of university

freshly /ˈfreʃli/ *adverb* recently ***freshly baked*** *bread*

freshman /ˈfreʃmən/ *noun* [C] *plural* **freshmen** *US* **EDUCATION** a student in the first year of a course at a US college, university, or high school (= school for students aged 15 to 18)

freshwater /ˈfreʃwɔːtəʳ/ *adjective* relating to water that is not salty *freshwater fish*

fret /fret/ *verb* [I] **fretting**, *past* **fretted** to be anxious or worried *There's no point in* ***fretting about*** *what you cannot change.* •**fretful** *adjective* anxious and unhappy

Fri *written abbreviation for* Friday

friar /fraɪəʳ/ *noun* [C] **RELIGION** a member of a religious group of men

friction /ˈfrɪkʃᵊn/ *noun* [U] **1 PHYSICS** when a surface rubs against something, often making movement more difficult **2** when people argue or disagree, often over a long period of time *There's a lot of* ***friction between*** *my wife and my mother.*

O-■**Friday** /ˈfraɪdeɪ/ (*written abbreviation* **Fri**) *noun* [C, U] the day of the week after Thursday and before Saturday ⊃See also: **Good Friday**

fridge /frɪdʒ/ *noun* [C] a large container that uses electricity to keep food cold ⊃See colour picture **The Kitchen** on page Centre 2 ⊃See picture at **CFC**

fridge-freezer /ˌfrɪdʒˈfriːzəʳ/ *noun* [C] a piece of equipment for storing food that has two parts: a fridge (= a container that keeps food cold) and a freezer (= a container that keeps food frozen)

fried /fraɪd/ *adjective* **FOOD** cooked in hot oil or fat *a fried egg* ⊃See also: **deep-fried**

WORD PARTNERS FOR ***friend***

sb's **best** friend • a **close/good** friend • a **family** friend • an **old** friend • a friend **of mine**

O-■**friend** /frend/ *noun* [C] **1** someone who you know well and like *Sarah's my* ***best friend*** (= the friend I like most). ○ *Gordon is* ***a friend of mine.*** **2 an old friend** someone who you have known and liked for a long time **3 be friends (with sb)** to know and like someone *I have been friends with Jo for years.* **4 make friends (with sb)** to begin to know and like someone *He's shy and finds it difficult to make friends.* **5 INTERNET** a person you write to on an Internet site

OTHER WAYS OF SAYING ***friend***

The words **chum**, **mate** (*UK*), and **pal** are all informal words for 'friend': *Pete was there with a couple of his* ***mates.***

An **old friend** is someone you have known and liked for many years: *Rachel is one of my* ***oldest friends.***

An **acquaintance** is someone you know, but do not know well: *He had a few business* ***acquaintances.***

A **confidant** is a friend whom you can talk to about your feelings and secrets: *Sarah was my* ***confidant*** *throughout this period and I told her everything.*

A group of friends with similar interests are sometimes described informally as a **crowd**: *"Who was there?" "Oh, you know, Dave, Fiona and all that* ***crowd."***

The informal word **crony** is sometimes used disapprovingly to describe one of a group of friends who help each other in an unfair way: *He always gives his* ***cronies*** *all the best jobs.*

O-■**friendly**¹ /ˈfrendli/ *adjective* **1** behaving in a pleasant, kind way towards someone *a* ***friendly face/smile*** ○ *The other students have been very* ***friendly to*** *us.* ⊃Opposite **unfriendly** **2 be friendly with sb** to know and like someone •**friendliness** *noun* [U]

friendly² /ˈfrendli/ *noun* [C] *UK* **SPORT** a sports match that is not part of an official competition

-friendly /ˈfrendli/ *suffix* **1** [NOT HARMFUL] used at the end of words to mean 'not harmful' ***environmentally-friendly*** *detergent* **2** [SUITABLE] used at the end of words to mean 'suitable for particular people to use' *a family-friendly restaurant* ⊃See also: **user-friendly**

WORD PARTNERS FOR ***friendship***

strike up a friendship • a **close** friendship • sb's friendship **with** sb • a friendship **between sb and** sb

friendship /ˈfrendʃɪp/ *noun* [C, U] when two people are friends *a close friendship*

fries /fraɪz/ *mainly US* (*also UK* **chips**) *noun* [plural] **FOOD** long, thin pieces of potato that have been cooked in hot oil

frieze /friːz/ *noun* [C] **ART** an area of decoration along a wall

frigate /ˈfrɪgət/ *noun* [C] a small, fast military ship

fright /fraɪt/ *noun* [U, no plural] a sudden feeling of shock and fear *That dog* ***gave me a*** *terrible* ***fright.*** ○ *She screamed* ***in fright*** *when she saw him.*

O-■**frighten** /ˈfraɪtᵊn/ *verb* [T] to make someone afraid or nervous *It frightens me when he drives so fast.* ⊃See also: scare/frighten the (living) **daylights** out of sb, scare/frighten sb out of their **wits**

frighten sb away/off *phrasal verb* to make a person or animal afraid or nervous so that they go away

OTHER WAYS OF SAYING *frightened*

The adjectives **afraid** and **scared** are common alternatives to 'frightened': *She's very **afraid** of dogs.* • *Gerry has always been **scared** of heights.*

If someone is extremely frightened, then you can use adjectives like **petrified**, **terrified**, **panic-stricken**, or the informal phrase **scared to death**: *I'm **terrified** of flying.* • *She was **panic-stricken** when her little boy disappeared.* • *He's **scared to death** of having the operation.*

If someone is frightened because they are worrying about something, then you can use the adjectives **afraid** and **worried**: *I'm **afraid/worried** that something will go wrong.*

If someone is frightened about something that might happen in the future, you can use the adjectives **apprehensive** or **uneasy**: *He's a bit **apprehensive** about living away from home.*

O-■ **frightened** /'fraɪtᵊnd/ *adjective* afraid or nervous *I've always been **frightened of** going to the dentist.* [+ (that)] *Gerry was frightened that people would laugh at him.*

O-■ **frightening** /'fraɪtᵊnɪŋ/ *adjective* making you feel afraid or nervous *a very frightening film* •**frighteningly** *adverb*

frightful /'fraɪtfᵊl/ *adjective UK old-fashioned* very bad *The house was in a frightful mess.*

frightfully /'fraɪtfᵊli/ *adverb UK old-fashioned* very *They're frightfully rich, you know.*

frigid /'frɪdʒɪd/ *adjective* **1** SEX not enjoying sexual activity, usually said about a woman **2** UNFRIENDLY *literary* not friendly or emotional

frill /frɪl/ *noun* **1** [C] a strip of material with a lot of folds which is used to decorate the edge of cloth **2 frills** extra things that are added to something to make it nicer or more attractive, but that are not really necessary *a cheap, **no frills** airline service*

frilly /'frɪli/ *adjective* with a lot of frills *a frilly dress*

fringe¹ /frɪndʒ/ *noun* [C] **1** HAIR *UK* (*US* **bangs** [plural]) hair that is cut short and straight at the top of someone's face **2** DECORATION loose threads that hang along the edge of cloth as a decoration **3** EDGE the outside edge of an area, group, or subject and not the main part

fringe² /frɪndʒ/ *verb* **be fringed with sth** If a place or object is fringed with something, that thing forms a border along the edge. *The river is fringed with wild flowers.*

fringe³ /frɪndʒ/ *adjective* [always before noun] not belonging to the main part of a group, activity, or subject *fringe politics/theatre*

ˌ**fringe 'benefit** *noun* [C] something extra that you get from your employer in addition to money [usually plural] *fringe benefits such as private health care*

Frisbee /'frɪzbi/ *noun* [C] *trademark* **SPORT** a circular piece of plastic with a curved edge which people throw to each other as a game

frisk /frɪsk/ *verb* **1** TOUCH [T] to move your hands over someone's body to discover if they are hiding something such as a weapon *There were guards frisking people as they went into the building.* **2** MOVE [I] to run and jump happily like a young animal

frisky /'frɪski/ *adjective* energetic and wanting to be active or play *a frisky puppy*

fritter /'frɪtəʳ/ *verb*

fritter sth away *phrasal verb* to waste money or time on something that is not important

frivolity /frɪ'vɒləti/ *noun* [C, U] when people are being silly and not being serious

frivolous /'frɪvᵊləs/ *adjective* silly and not serious •**frivolously** *adverb*

frizzy /'frɪzi/ *adjective* Frizzy hair has a lot of very small, tight curls.

fro /frəʊ/ *adverb* ⇒See: **to³** and fro

frog /frɒg/ *noun* [C] a small, green animal with long back legs for jumping that lives in or near water

frogman /'frɒgmən/ *noun* [C] *plural* **frogmen** someone whose job is to swim under water wearing a rubber suit and using special breathing equipment ***Police frogmen** are searching the lake.*

O-■ **from** *strong form* /frɒm/ *weak form* /frəm/ *preposition* **1** STARTING PLACE used to show the place, time, or level that someone or something started at *Did you walk all the way from Bond Street?* ○ *The museum is open from 9.30 to 6.00, Tuesday to Sunday.* ○ *Prices start from £5,595.* **2** HOME used to say where someone was born, or where someone lives or works *His mother's originally from Poland.* ○ *Our speaker tonight is from the BBC.* **3** DISTANCE used to say how far away something is *Their holiday cottage is about 15 kilometres from the coast.* **4** GIVING used to say who gave or sent something to someone *Have you had a Christmas card from Faye yet?* **5** REMOVING If you take something from a person, place, or amount, you take it away. *Two from ten leaves eight.* ○ *We had to borrow some money from my father to pay the bill.* **6** PRODUCED used to say where something was produced or grown *These vegetables are fresh from the garden.* **7** MATERIAL used to say what something is made of *juice made from oranges* **8** AVOID used to show something that you want to avoid or prevent *There's a bar across the front to prevent you from falling out.* **9** POSITION used to show where you are when you look at something or how you see something *The view from the top was absolutely breathtaking.* **10** REASON used to say why you think or believe something *I guessed from her accent that she must be French.* ○ *From what I've heard, the new exam is going to be a lot more difficult.* **11** CAUSE used to say what causes something *Deaths from heart disease continue to rise every year.* ○ *He was rushed to hospital **suffering from** severe burns.* **12** COMPARE used when you are saying how similar or different two things, people, or places are *University is very different from school.* **13 a week/**

six months/ten years, etc from now a week/six months/ten years, etc after the time when you are speaking *Who knows what we'll all be doing five years from now?* **14 from now/then, etc on** starting now/then, etc and continuing into the future *They were good friends from that day on.*

front¹ /frʌnt/ *noun* **1 the front a** MOST IMPORTANT SIDE the side of something that is most important or most often seen because it faces forward *You need to write the address clearly* ***on the front of*** *the envelope.* ○ *There was blood on the front of his shirt.* **b** FORWARD PART the part of something that is furthest forward *We asked to sit* ***in the front of*** *the plane.* ○ *He was standing right* ***at the front.*** **2 in front a** FURTHER FORWARD further forward than someone or something else *She started a conversation with the man sitting* ***in front of*** *her.* **b** WINNING winning in a game or competition *By half time the Italians were well in front.* **3 in front of a** NEAR close to the front part of something *He parked the car in front of the house.* **b** SEEING/HEARING where someone can see or hear you *Please don't swear in front of the children.* **4** BEHAVIOUR **[C]** when someone behaves in a way that hides how they really feel **[usually singular]** Many parents decide to stay together, ***putting up a front*** *for the children's sake.* **5** ILLEGAL ACTIVITY **[C]** an organization or activity that is used to hide a different, illegal activity **[usually singular]** Police discovered the restaurant was just a front for a drugs operation. **6 the front** an area of land where soldiers fight during a war *Thousands of young men were sent to the front to fight.* **7 on the business/jobs/politics, etc front** in a particular area of activity *How are things on the work front at the moment?* **8** WEATHER **[C]** a line where warm air meets cold air affecting the weather *A cold front is moving across the Atlantic.*

front² /frʌnt/ *adjective* **[always before noun]** in or at the front of something *the front door/garden* ○ *the front page of the newspaper*

frontal /ˈfrʌntᵊl/ *adjective* **1** relating to the front of something **2 a frontal attack/assault** when you criticize or attack someone or something in a very strong and direct way

frontier /frʌnˈtɪəʳ/ *noun* **1 [C] GEOGRAPHY** a line or border between two countries **2 the frontiers of sth** the limits of what is known or what has been done before in an area of knowledge or activity *the frontiers of science and technology*

ˌfront ˈline *noun* **the front line a** the place where soldiers fight in a war **b** a position of direct and important influence *doctors working* ***in the front line*** *of medicine* **•front-line** /ˈfrʌntlaɪn/ *adjective* **[always before noun]** *front-line troops*

front-page /ˈfrʌntˌpeɪdʒ/ *adjective* **front-page news/story, etc** news that is very important and suitable for the front page of a newspaper

front-runner /ˌfrʌntˈrʌnəʳ/ (US) /ˈfrʌntˌrʌnəʳ/ *noun* **[C]** the person or organization that will most probably win something

frost¹ /frɒst/ *noun* **1** SUBSTANCE **[U]** a thin, white layer of ice that forms on surfaces, especially at night, when it is very cold **2** COLD **[C]** when the temperature is cold and water freezes *We're expecting a* ***hard frost*** *tonight.*

frost² /frɒst/ *US* (*UK/US* **ice**) *verb* **[T] FOOD** to cover a cake with frosting (= sweet mixture used to cover cakes)

frostbite /ˈfrɒstbaɪt/ *noun* **[U] HEALTH** when extreme cold injures your fingers and toes

frosted /ˈfrɒstɪd/ *adjective* Frosted glass has a special surface so that you cannot see through it.

frosting /ˈfrɒstɪŋ/ *US* (*UK/US* **icing**) *noun* **[U] FOOD** a sweet mixture used to cover or fill cakes, made from sugar and water or sugar and butter

frosty /ˈfrɒsti/ *adjective* **1** COLD very cold, with a thin layer of white ice covering everything *a frosty morning* **2** NOT FRIENDLY not friendly *She gave me a very frosty look.*

froth /frɒθ/ *noun* **[U]** small, white bubbles such as on the surface of a liquid **•froth** *verb* **[I]** **•frothy** *adjective* ***frothy coffee***

frown¹ /fraʊn/ *verb* **[I]** to make your face show that you are annoyed or worried by moving your eyebrows (= lines of hair above your eyes) *She frowned when I mentioned his name.* **frown on/upon sth** *phrasal verb* to think that something is wrong and that you should not do it **[often passive]** *Smoking is frowned upon in many public places.*

frown² /fraʊn/ *noun* **[C]** the expression on your face when you frown *He looked at me with a puzzled frown.*

froze /frəʊz/ *past tense of* freeze

frozen¹ /ˈfrəʊzᵊn/ *adjective* **1 FOOD** Frozen food has been made so that it will last a long time by freezing. *frozen peas* **2** WATER turned into ice *The pond was frozen and people were skating on it.* **3** PERSON *informal* extremely cold *Is there any heating in here? I'm frozen!*

frozen² /ˈfrəʊzᵊn/ *past participle of* freeze

fructose /ˈfrʊktəʊs/ *noun* **[U] CHEMISTRY, BIOLOGY** a type of sugar that you find in honey and many fruits

frugal /ˈfruːgᵊl/ *adjective* careful not to spend very much money

WORD PARTNERS FOR ***fruit***

dried/fresh fruit • a **piece of** fruit • fruit **juice** • **citrus/tropical** fruit

fruit /fruːt/ *noun* **1 BIOLOGY, FOOD [C, U]** something such as an apple or orange that grows on a tree or a bush, contains seeds, and can be eaten as food ***dried/fresh fruit*** ○ *fruit juice* ➲See colour picture **Fruit and Vegetables** on page Centre 10 **2 the fruit(s) of sth** the good result of someone's work or actions *This book is the fruit of 15 years' research.* **3 bear fruit** If something that someone does bears fruit, it produces successful results. *Our decision is just beginning to bear fruit.* ➲See also: **citrus fruit**

fruitful /ˈfruːtfᵊl/ *adjective* producing good or useful results *We had a very fruitful discussion.*

fruition /fruˈɪʃᵊn/ *noun* **[U]** *formal* when a plan or an idea really begins to happen, exist, or be successful *The plan never really **came to fruition**.*

fruitless /ˈfruːtləs/ *adjective* not successful or achieving good results *a long and **fruitless** search*

fruity /ˈfruːti/ *adjective* **FOOD** smelling or tasting of fruit *a fruity wine/taste*

frustrate /frʌsˈtreɪt/ ⓊⓈ /ˈfrʌstreɪt/ *verb* [T] **1** ANNOY to make someone feel annoyed because things are not happening in the way that they want, or in the way that they should *It really frustrates me when she arrives late for meetings.* **2** PREVENT to prevent someone from achieving something, or to prevent something from happening *They have frustrated all our attempts to find a solution to this problem.*

frustrated /frʌsˈtreɪtɪd/ ⓊⓈ /ˈfrʌstreɪtɪd/ *adjective* annoyed because things are not happening in the way that you want, or in the way that they should *I'm very **frustrated at/with** my lack of progress.*

frustrating /frʌsˈtreɪtɪŋ/ ⓊⓈ /ˈfrʌstreɪtɪŋ/ *adjective* making you feel frustrated *a frustrating situation*

WORD PARTNERS FOR ***frustration***

sheer frustration • **in** frustration • frustration **at** (doing) sth

frustration /frʌsˈtreɪʃᵊn/ *noun* [C, U] the feeling of being annoyed because things are not happening in the way that you want, or in the way that they should *I could sense his **frustration at** not being able to help.*

frustum /ˈfrʌstəm/ *noun* [C] **MATHEMATICS** the part of a solid shape such as a cone that is between the base of the shape and parallel plane (= layer) through the shape or between two parallel layers through the shape

fry /fraɪ/ *verb* [I, T] **FOOD** to cook something in hot oil or fat or to be cooked in hot oil or fat *Fry the onions in a little butter.* ➲See picture at **cook**

ˈ**frying ˌpan** *noun* [C] a flat, metal pan with a long handle that is used for frying food ➲See colour picture **The Kitchen** on page Centre 2

ft MEASURES *written abbreviation for* foot (= a unit for measuring length)

the FTSE 100 Index /ˌfʊtsiwʌnˌhʌndrədˈɪn.deks/ (*trademark, informal* **the Footsie**) *noun* [**no plural**] **ECONOMICS** a number which shows the value of the share prices of the hundred most important British companies, which is published by the Financial Times, a British newspaper *The FTSE 100 Index closed 31.6 points down at 2459.3 in today's trading.*

fudge¹ /fʌdʒ/ *noun* [U] **FOOD** a soft sweet food made from butter, sugar, and milk

fudge² /fʌdʒ/ *verb informal* **1** AVOID ANSWER [T] *UK* to avoid making a decision or giving a clear answer about something *The government continues to **fudge** the **issue**.* **2** SLIGHTLY CHEAT [I, T] *US* to slightly cheat, often by not telling the exact truth *He **fudged on** his income tax return.*

WORD PARTNERS FOR ***fuel***

fuel **bills/consumption/prices/supplies** • fuel **efficiency**

O⊸**fuel¹** /ˈfjuːəl/ *noun* [C, U] a substance that is burned to provide heat or power *The plane ran out of fuel and had to land at sea.*

fuel² /ˈfjuːəl/ *verb* [T] *UK* **fuelling**, *past* **fuelled**, *US* **fueling**, *past* **fueled** to make people's ideas or feelings stronger, or to make a situation worse *Newspaper reports are **fuelling fears** about GM foods.*

fugitive /ˈfjuːdʒətɪv/ *noun* [C] someone who is escaping or hiding from the police or from a dangerous situation

fulcrum /ˈfʊlkrəm/ *noun* [C **usually singular**] **PHYSICS** the point at which a bar, or something that is balancing, is supported or turns ➲See picture at **lever**

fulfil *UK* (*US* **fulfill**) /fʊlˈfɪl/ *verb* **fulfilling**, *past* **fulfilled 1 fulfil a duty/promise/responsibility, etc** to do something that you have promised to do or that you are expected to do *He has failed to fulfil his duties as a father.* **2 fulfil an ambition/dream/goal, etc** to do something that you really wanted to do **3 fulfil a function/need/role, etc** to do something that is necessary or useful *You seem to fulfil a very useful role in the organization.* **4 fulfil criteria/requirements/qualifications, etc** to have all the qualities that are wanted or needed for something *You have to fulfil certain requirements to qualify for the competition.*

fulfilled /fʊlˈfɪld/ *adjective* feeling happy that you are receiving everything that you want from your life ➲Opposite **unfulfilled**

fulfilling /fʊlˈfɪlɪŋ/ *adjective* If something is fulfilling, it satisfies you and makes you happy. *a fulfilling job*

fulfilment *UK* (*US* **fulfillment**) /fʊlˈfɪlmənt/ *noun* [U] **1** PLEASURE a feeling of pleasure because you are receiving or achieving what you want *I hope that you'll find happiness and fulfilment in your life together.* **2** SOMETHING DONE when someone does something necessary or something that they have wanted or promised to do *Being here is the **fulfilment of** a lifelong ambition.*

O⊸**full¹** /fʊl/ *adjective* **1** NO MORE POSSIBLE If a container or a space is full, it contains as many things or people as possible or as much of something as possible. *We couldn't get in, the cinema was full.* ○ *The shelves were **full of** books.* **2** A LOT containing a lot of things or people or a lot of something *The room was **full of** people.* ○ *His face was full of anger.* **3** COMPLETE [**always before noun**] complete and including every part *Please give your full name and address.* **4 full speed/strength/volume, etc** the greatest speed, strength, volume, etc possible *We were driving at full speed.* ○ *She got full marks in the test.* **5 be full of yourself** to think that you are very important **6 be full of sth** to be talking or thinking a lot about a particular thing *He's full of stories about his holiday.* **7** FOOD *informal* (*also UK* **full up**) having eaten enough food *No more for me, thanks, I'm full.* **8 a full face/figure** a face or body shape that is large and round ➲See also: have your hands (**hand**[1]) full, be in full **swing**[2]

full[2] /fʊl/ *noun* **1 in full** completely and with nothing missing *The speech will be published in full in tomorrow's newspaper.* **2 to the full** *mainly UK* as much or as well as possible *She certainly **lived life to the full**.*

full-blown /ˈfʊlˌbləʊn/ *adjective* completely developed *a full-blown crisis* ○ *a full-blown disease*

ˌfull ˈboard *noun* [U] *UK* when all your meals are provided in a hotel

fullerene /ˈfʊləriːn/ *noun* [C] **CHEMISTRY** any of several carbon compounds with molecules arranged in a round, hollow shape

full-fledged /ˌfʊlˈfledʒd/ *US* (*UK* **fully-fledged**) *adjective* [**always before noun**] having finished developing, studying, or establishing yourself

full-grown /ˌfʊlˈgrəʊn/ *adjective* A full-grown person, animal, or plant has developed completely, and is not expected to grow more. *a full-grown man*

ˌfull ˈhouse *noun* [C] when all the seats in a place such as a theatre or cinema are full

full-length /ˌfʊlˈleŋθ/ *adjective* **1 a full-length book/film, etc** a book or film that is the usual length and not shorter *a full-length feature film* **2 a full-length mirror/photograph, etc** a mirror or image that shows a person's whole body from the head to the feet **3 a full-length coat/dress/skirt, etc** a long piece of clothing that reaches to your feet

ˌfull ˈmoon *noun* [**no plural**] **ASTRONOMY** the moon when it appears as a complete circle

full-on /fʊlˈɒn/ *adjective* **1** GREAT very great or to the greatest degree *full-on luxury* **2** ENTHUSIASTIC very serious and enthusiastic, often in a way which annoys other people

full-page /ˌfʊlˈpeɪdʒ/ *adjective* [**always before noun**] filling a complete page in a newspaper or magazine *a **full-page ad***

full-scale /ˌfʊlˈskeɪl/ *adjective* [**always before noun**] **1** LARGE very large or serious and involving everything that is possible or expected *The violence has developed into a full-scale war.* **2** MODEL A full-scale model is the same size as the original thing that it is representing.

ˌfull ˈstop *UK* (*US* **period**) *noun* [C] **LANGUAGE** a mark (.) used at the end of a sentence, or to show that the letters before it are an abbreviation ➲See Extra help page **Punctuation** on page Centre 18.

full-time /ˌfʊlˈtaɪm/ *adjective* happening or working for the whole of the working week and not only part of it *a **full-time job/course*** •**full-time** *adverb She works full-time.*

O⊸**fully** /ˈfʊli/ *adverb* completely *The restaurant was **fully booked**.* ○ *He is **fully aware** of the dangers involved.*

fully-fledged /ˌfʊliˈfledʒd/ *UK* (*US* **full-fledged**) *adjective* [**always before noun**] having finished developing, studying, or establishing yourself *I won't be a fully-fledged doctor until after the exams.*

fumble /ˈfʌmbl/ *verb* [I] to use your hands with difficulty to try to get hold of something or find something *She fumbled in her bag for her glasses.*

fume /fjuːm/ *verb* [I] to be extremely angry, especially in a quiet way *A week later, she was still fuming about his behaviour.*

fumes /fjuːmz/ *noun* [**plural**] strong, unpleasant, and often dangerous gas or smoke *car exhaust fumes*

WORD PARTNERS FOR ***fun***

have fun • **good/great** fun • **be no** fun • **for** fun

O⊸**fun**[1] /fʌn/ *noun* [U] **1** enjoyment or pleasure, or something that gives you enjoyment or pleasure *She's **great fun** to be with.* ○ ***Have fun!*** (= enjoy yourself) ○ *It's **no fun** having to work late every night.* **2 for fun/for the fun of it** for pleasure and not for any other reason **3 make fun of sb/sth** to make a joke about someone or something in an unkind way *The other children at school used to make fun of his hair.*

fun[2] /fʌn/ *adjective* enjoyable or entertaining *There are lots of fun things to do here.*

WORD PARTNERS FOR ***function***

a **basic/important/primary/vital** function • **carry out/fulfil/provide/serve** a function

O⊸**function**[1] /ˈfʌŋkʃᵊn/ *noun* [C] **1** PURPOSE the purpose of something or someone *Each button has a different function.* **2** EVENT a large, formal party or ceremony *a charity function* **3** **MATHEMATICS** a quantity whose value depends on another value and changes with that value

function[2] /ˈfʌŋkʃᵊn/ *verb* [I] to work or operate *The operation should help his lungs to function properly again.*
function as sth *phrasal verb* to have a particular purpose *The spare bedroom also functions as a study.*

functional /ˈfʌŋkʃᵊnᵊl/ *adjective* **1** PRACTICAL designed to be practical or useful and not only attractive *functional clothing* **2** WORKING operating or working correctly *The system is not yet fully functional.*

ˈfunction ˌkey (*written abbreviation* **F**) *noun* [C] **COMPUTING** one of the keys on a computer keyboard which has the letter F and a number on it and that makes the computer do particular jobs *Press F4 to print.*

O⊸**fund** /fʌnd/ *noun* **1** **FINANCE** [C] an amount of money collected, saved, or provided for a purpose *a **pension fund*** **2 funds** **FINANCE** [**plural**] money needed or available to spend on something *The charity closed down due to **lack of funds**.* •**fund** *verb* [T] to provide money for an event, activity, or organization *Who is the project funded by?*

fundamental /ˌfʌndəˈmentᵊl/ *adjective* relating to the most important or main part of something *a fundamental change/difference* ○ *Training is **fundamental to** success.* •**fundamentally** *adverb The world has changed fundamentally over the last century.*

fundamentalism /ˌfʌndəˈmentᵊlɪzᵊm/ *noun* [U] **RELIGION** the belief that the traditions and rules of a religion should be followed exactly

fundamentalist /ˌfʌndəˈmentəlɪst/ *noun* [C] **RELIGION** someone who believes that the rules of their religion should be followed exactly •**fundamentalist** *adjective*

fundamentals /ˌfʌndəˈmentəlz/ *noun* [plural] the main principles, or most important parts of something

funding /ˈfʌndɪŋ/ *noun* [U] **FINANCE** money given by a government or organization for an event or activity *The company received state funding for the project.*

fundraiser /ˈfʌndˌreɪzəʳ/ *noun* [C] **FINANCE** a person or an event that collects money for a particular purpose

fundraising /ˈfʌndˌreɪzɪŋ/ *noun* [U] **FINANCE** when you collect money for a particular purpose *a **fundraising event***

O‒**funeral** /ˈfjuːnərəl/ *noun* [C] a ceremony for burying or burning the body of a dead person

ˈ**funeral** ˌ**director** *UK* (*US* ˈ**funeral director**) *noun* [C] someone whose job is to organize funerals and prepare dead bodies to be buried or burned

fungus /ˈfʌŋgəs/ *noun* [C, U] *plural* **fungi** or **funguses** **BIOLOGY** a type of plant without leaves and without green colouring which gets its food from other living or decaying things

funk /fʌŋk/ *noun* [U] **MUSIC** a style of popular music with a strong rhythm that is influenced by African and jazz music

funky /ˈfʌŋki/ *adjective informal* **1** fashionable in an unusual and noticeable way *She's got some very funky clothes.* **2** **MUSIC** Funky music has a strong rhythm, and is good to dance to.

funnel /ˈfʌnəl/ *noun* [C] **1** LIQUID a tube with a wide part at the top that you use to pour liquid or powder into something that has a small opening ⊃See picture at **filtrate** **2** SMOKE a metal pipe on the top of a ship or train which smoke comes out of

funnel

funnily /ˈfʌnɪli/ *adverb* *UK* **funnily enough** although it seems strange and surprising *Funnily enough, I was just thinking about you when you called.*

O‒**funny** /ˈfʌni/ *adjective* **1** MAKING YOU LAUGH making you smile or laugh *a funny story* ○ *It's not funny. Don't laugh!* **2** STRANGE strange or unusual and not what you expect *This chicken tastes a bit funny.*

COMMON LEARNER ERROR

fun or **funny?**

Use **fun** to talk about something which you enjoy doing.

Going to the cinema is fun.

Use **funny** to describe something which makes you laugh.

The film was really funny.

OTHER WAYS OF SAYING *funny*

The adjective **amusing** is a more formal alternative to 'funny': *I gave her an article that I thought she would find **amusing**.*

If something is extremely funny, you can use the adjectives **hilarious** or (*informal*) **hysterical**: *I've just read his autobiography - it's absolutely **hilarious/hysterical**.*

If someone talks in a way that is clever and funny, you can use the adjective **witty**: *He was a very **witty** man.*

The adjective **comical** is sometimes used if someone or something looks funny: *She looked so **comical** in that hat!*

If you want to describe a person as very funny, in informal situations you can use the expressions **be a good laugh** (*UK*) and **be a scream**. *You'd like Amanda - she's **a scream/good laugh**.*

O‒**fur** /fɜːʳ/ *noun* **1** **BIOLOGY** [U] the thick hair that covers the bodies of some animals like cats and rabbits **2** [C, U] the skin of an animal covered in thick hair and used for making clothes, or a piece of clothing made from this

furious /ˈfjʊəriəs/ *adjective* **1** ANGRY extremely angry *He's **furious at** the way he's been treated.* ○ *My boss was **furious with** me.* **2** ENERGETIC very energetic or fast *a furious attack* •**furiously** *adverb*

furlong /ˈfɜːlɒŋ/ *noun* [C] **MEASURES, SPORT** a unit of length used in horse races equal to 201 metres

furnace /ˈfɜːnɪs/ *noun* [C] a container which is heated to a very high temperature and used to heat buildings, melt metal, or burn things

furnish /ˈfɜːnɪʃ/ *verb* [T] to put furniture into a room or building *They have furnished the room very simply.*
furnish sb with sth *phrasal verb formal* to provide someone with something *Can you furnish me with any further information?*

furnished /ˈfɜːnɪʃt/ *adjective* If a room or building is furnished, there is furniture in it.

furnishings /ˈfɜːnɪʃɪŋz/ *noun* [plural] the furniture, curtains and other decorations in a room or building

WORD PARTNERS FOR ***furniture***

a **piece of** furniture • **garden/office** furniture • **antique** furniture

O‒**furniture** /ˈfɜːnɪtʃəʳ/ *noun* [U] objects such as chairs, tables, and beds that you put into a room or building *antique furniture*

furore /fjʊəˈrɔːri/ *UK* (*US* **furor** /ˈfjʊrɔːr/) *noun* [no plural] a sudden, excited, or angry reaction to something by a lot of people *The book **caused a furore** when it was published.*

furrow¹ /ˈfʌrəʊ/ *noun* [C] **1** **FARMING** a deep line cut into a field that seeds are planted in **2** FACE a deep line on someone's face, especially above their eyes

furrow² /ˈfʌrəʊ/ *verb* **furrow your brow** to make deep lines appear on your face above your eyes *He furrowed his brow as he struggled to think of a solution.*

furry /ˈfɜːri/ *adjective* covered with fur or with something that feels like fur

further¹ /ˈfɜːðəʳ/ *adverb* **1** [MORE] more *He refused to discuss the matter further.* ○ *Have you* ***got any further*** (= achieved any more) *with your research?* **2** [PLACE/TIME] (*comparative of* far) at or to a place or time that is a longer distance away *Let's walk a bit further down the road.*

further² /ˈfɜːðəʳ/ *adjective* [**always before noun**] more or extra *For further details about the offer, call this number.* ○ *We will let you know if there are any further developments.*

further³ /ˈfɜːðəʳ/ *verb* [T] to make something develop or become more successful *He'll do anything to* ***further*** *his* ***career***.

ˌfurther eduˈcation *noun* [U] *UK* **EDUCATION** education at a college for people who have left school but are not at a university

furthermore /ˌfɜːðəˈmɔːʳ/ (US) /ˈfɜːrðərmɔːr/ *adverb* in addition to what has just been said

furthest /ˈfɜːðɪst/ *adjective, adverb* (*superlative of* far) most distant

furtive /ˈfɜːtɪv/ *adjective* doing something secretly, or done secretly, so that people do not notice *He gave her a* ***furtive glance*** *as soon as his wife left the room.* •**furtively** *adverb*

fury /ˈfjʊəri/ *noun* [**U, no plural**] extreme anger *He could hardly control his fury.*

fuse¹ /fjuːz/ *noun* [C] **1 PHYSICS** a small object that stops electrical equipment working if there is too much electricity going through it *The* ***fuse*** *has* ***blown***. *You'll have to change it.* ○ *a* ***fuse box*** **2** [BOMB] the part of a bomb or other explosive object that starts the explosion ***Light*** *the* ***fuse***, *and then stand back.*

fuse² /fjuːz/ *verb* [**I, T**] **1 PHYSICS** *UK* If a piece of electrical equipment fuses, or if you fuse it, it stops working because there is too much electricity going through it. *You've* ***fused*** *the* ***lights***. **2** to join or become combined *The bones of the skull are not properly fused at birth.*

fuselage /ˈfjuːzəlɑːʒ/ *noun* [C] the main body of an aircraft

fusion /ˈfjuːʒən/ *noun* [**C, U**] **1 PHYSICS** when two or more things join or become combined *nuclear fusion* ○ *She describes her music as a fusion of folk and rock.* **2 PHYSICS** the process of joining two nuclei (= central parts of atoms) to produce energy

fuss¹ /fʌs/ *noun* **1** [**U, no plural**] when people become excited, annoyed, or anxious about something, especially about something unimportant *What's all the fuss about?* ○ *They were* ***making*** *a big* ***fuss*** *over nothing.* **2 kick up/make a fuss** to complain about something *If they don't bring our food soon, I'll have to kick up a fuss.* **3 make a fuss of/over sb** to give someone a lot of attention and treat them well *My uncle always makes a big fuss of the children.*

fuss² /fʌs/ *verb* [I] to worry too much or get too excited, especially about unimportant things *Please don't fuss, Mum. Everything's under control.*

fuss over sb/sth *phrasal verb* to give someone or something too much attention because you want to show that you like them

fussy /ˈfʌsi/ *adjective* **1** [NOT LIKING] only liking particular things and very difficult to please *She's a very* ***fussy eater***. **2** [CAREFUL] too careful about unimportant details **3** [TOO COMPLICATED] If something is fussy, it is too complicated in design and has too many details.

futile /ˈfjuːtaɪl/ (US) /ˈfjuːtəl/ *adjective* certain not to have a successful effect or result *a futile attempt to escape* •**futility** /fjuːˈtɪləti/ *noun* [U] when something is futile

futon /ˈfuːtɒn/ *noun* [C] a flat bed filled with soft material that can be used on the floor or on a wooden base, or folded into a seat

WORD PARTNERS FOR ***future***

the **distant/foreseeable/near** future • **plan for/predict** the future • **in the** future

O‑ **future¹** /ˈfjuːtʃəʳ/ *noun* **1 the future a** [TIME TO COME] the time which is to come *He likes to* ***plan for the future***. ○ *They hope to get married* ***in the near future*** (= soon). **b LANGUAGE** In grammar, the future is the form of the verb used to talk about something that will happen. **2 in future** *UK* (*mainly US* **in the future**) beginning from now *In future, I'll be more careful about who I lend my bike to.* **3** [WHAT WILL HAPPEN] [C] what will happen to someone or something in the time which is to come *We need to discuss the future of the company.* **4** [SUCCESS] [**U, no plural**] the chance of continuing to exist or succeed *She's got a very promising future ahead of her.*

O‑ **future²** /ˈfjuːtʃəʳ/ *adjective* [**always before noun**] **1** happening or existing in the time which is to come *future plans* ○ *in future years* ○ *What will we leave for future generations?* **2 future tense LANGUAGE** the form of the verb which is used to talk about something that will happen

the ˌfuture ˈperfect *noun* **LANGUAGE** the form of the verb which is used to show that an action will have been completed before a particular time in the future. The sentence 'I'll probably have left by then.' is in the future perfect.

futuristic /ˌfjuːtʃəˈrɪstɪk/ *adjective* very modern and strange and seeming to come from some imagined time in the future *a futuristic steel building*

fuzzy /ˈfʌzi/ *adjective* **1** [NOT CLEAR] confused and not clear *We could only get a fuzzy picture on the television.* **2** [WITH HAIRS] covered in soft, short hairs, or material like this *a fuzzy kitten* ○ *fuzzy slippers*

ˌfuzzy ˈlogic *noun* [U] a way of solving questions in which statements or opinions are formed from information which is not clear or definite

FYI *internet abbreviation for* for your information: used when you send someone a document or tell them something you think they should know about

Gg

G, g /dʒiː/ the seventh letter of the alphabet

g MEASURES *written abbreviation for* gram (= a unit for measuring weight)

gabble /ˈɡæbl/ *verb* [I, T] *UK informal* to talk quickly or in a way that people cannot understand *He gabbled something in Italian.*

gable /ˈɡeɪbl/ *noun* [C] the top end of a wall of a building where two sloping parts of a roof meet at a point

gadget /ˈɡædʒɪt/ *noun* [C] a small piece of equipment that does a particular job, especially a new type *a **kitchen gadget***

Gaelic /ˈɡeɪlɪk, ˈɡælɪk/ *noun* [U] **LANGUAGE** a language spoken in parts of Scotland and Ireland •**Gaelic** *adjective* relating to Gaelic or to the Gaelic culture of Scotland and Ireland

gaffe /ɡæf/ *noun* [C] when someone says or does something embarrassing without intending to *The minister has **made** a series of embarrassing **gaffes**.*

gag¹ /ɡæɡ/ *verb* **gagging**, *past* **gagged** 1 COVER MOUTH [T] to fasten something over someone's mouth so that they cannot speak *The owners of the house were found **bound and gagged** in the cellar.* 2 STOP INFORMATION [T] to prevent someone from giving their opinion or giving information about something *The government is trying to gag the press over the issue.* 3 ALMOST VOMIT [I] to feel that you are going to vomit *The sight of the body made him gag.* 4 **be gagging for sth** *UK informal* to want something or want to do something very much *I'm gagging for a coffee.*

gag² /ɡæɡ/ *noun* [C] 1 JOKE *informal* a joke or funny story 2 COVER something that is fastened over someone's mouth to stop them speaking

gaggle /ˈɡæɡl/ *noun* [C] a group of people, especially when they are noisy *a gaggle of newspaper reporters*

gaiety /ˈɡeɪəti/ *noun* [U] *old-fashioned* happiness or excitement

gaily /ˈɡeɪli/ *adverb old-fashioned* in a happy way

O-■ **gain¹** /ɡeɪn/ *verb* 1 GET [T] to get something useful or positive *The country gained independence in 1948.* ○ *You'll gain a lot of experience working there.* 2 **gain by/from sth** to get an advantage or something valuable from something *Who stands to gain from the will?* 3 INCREASE [T] to increase in something such as size, weight, or amount *He's gained a lot of weight in the last few months.* 4 CLOCK [I, T] If a clock or a watch gains, it works too quickly and shows a time that is later than the real time. ➲See also: gain/lose **ground**¹, get/gain the upper **hand**¹

gain on sb/sth *phrasal verb* to get nearer to someone or something that you are chasing *Quick! They're gaining on us.*

gain² /ɡeɪn/ *noun* [C, U] 1 POSITIVE THING when you get something useful or positive ***financial gain*** 2 INCREASE an increase in something such as size, weight, or amount

gait /ɡeɪt/ *noun* [C] someone's particular way of walking *I recognized his gait from a distance.*

gala /ˈɡɑːlə/ (US) /ˈɡeɪlə/ *noun* [C] a special social event, performance, or sports competition *a gala concert*

galaxy /ˈɡæləksi/ *noun* [C] **ASTRONOMY** a very large group of stars held together in the universe

gale /ɡeɪl/ *noun* [C] a very strong wind

gall¹ /ɡɔːl/ *noun* **have the gall to do sth** to be rude enough to do something that is not considered acceptable *I can't believe he had the gall to complain.*

gall² /ɡɔːl/ *verb* [T] to annoy someone *What galls me is that he escaped without punishment.* •**galling** *adjective* annoying *It's particularly galling for me that she gets paid more than I do.*

gallant /ˈɡælənt/ *adjective literary* 1 BRAVE brave *a gallant attempt to rescue a drowning man* 2 POLITE polite and kind, especially to women •**gallantly** *adverb* •**gallantry** *noun* [U] when someone is gallant

ˈgall ˌbladder *noun* [C] **ANATOMY, BIOLOGY** an organ in the body that contains a substance that helps you to digest food ➲See picture at **alimentary canal**

gallery /ˈɡælᵊri/ *noun* [C] 1 **ART** a room or building that is used for showing paintings and other art to the public *a museum and **art gallery*** 2 HIGH FLOOR a floor at a higher level that looks over a lower floor inside a large room or building *The courtroom has a **public gallery**.*

galley /ˈɡæli/ *noun* [C] a kitchen in a ship or aircraft

gallon /ˈɡælən/ *noun* [C] **MEASURES** a unit for measuring liquid, equal to 4.546 litres in the UK and 3.785 litres in the US ➲See Extra help page **Numbers and measurements** on page Centre 24.

gallop /ˈɡæləp/ *verb* [I] If a horse gallops, it runs very fast. •**gallop** *noun* [**no plural**]

gallows /ˈɡæləʊz/ *noun* [C] *plural* **gallows** a wooden structure used in the past to hang criminals from to kill them

galore /ɡəˈlɔːʳ/ *adjective* [**always after noun**] in large amounts or numbers *There are bargains galore at the new supermarket.*

galvanize (*also UK* **-ise**) /ˈɡælvənaɪz/ *verb* [T] 1 to make someone suddenly decide to do something *His words **galvanized** the team **into action**.* 2 to cover the metals iron or steel with a thin layer of zinc (= blue-white metal) in order to protect them •**galvanization** (*also UK* **-isation**) *noun* [U]

galvanized (*also UK* **-ised**) /ˈɡælvənaɪzd/ *adjective* describes metal, or something made of metal, that is covered with a thin layer of zinc (= blue-white metal)

gamble¹ /ˈɡæmbl/ *verb* [I, T] to risk money on the result of a game, race, or competition *He gambled away all of our savings.* •**gambler** *noun* [C] •**gambling** *noun* [U]

G

gamble on sth *phrasal verb* to take a risk that something will happen

WORD PARTNERS FOR ***gamble***

take a gamble • a gamble **backfires/pays off** • a gamble **on** sth

gamble² /ˈɡæmbl/ *noun* [C] a risk that you take that something will succeed *Buying this place was a big* ***gamble****, but it seems to have* ***paid off****.*

WORD PARTNERS FOR ***game***

play a game • **lose/win** a game • a game **of** [chess/football, etc] • a **computer** game

game¹ /ɡeɪm/ *noun* **1** ACTIVITY [C] an entertaining activity or sport that people play, usually needing some skill and played according to rules *a* ***computer game*** ○ *Do you want to* ***play*** *a different* ***game****?* **2** OCCASION [C] a particular competition, match, or occasion when people play a game *Would you like a game of chess?* ○ *Who won yesterday's game?* **3 games** *UK* organized sports that children do at school *I always hated games at school.* ○ *a games teacher* **4 the European/Commonwealth, etc Games SPORT** a special event where there are lots of competitions for different sports **5** SECRET PLAN [C] *UK informal* a secret plan *What's your game?* **6 FOOD** [U] wild animals and birds that are hunted for food or sport **7 give the game away** *UK* to spoil a surprise or joke by letting someone know something that should have been kept secret **8 play games** to not deal with a situation seriously or honestly *Someone's life is in danger here - we're not playing games.* ➲See also: **ball game, board game, the Olympic Games, video game**

game² /ɡeɪm/ *adjective* willing to do new things, or things that involve a risk *She's* ***game for*** *anything.*

Gameboy /ˈɡeɪmbɔɪ/ *noun* [C] *trademark* **COMPUTING** a small machine that you play computer games on and that you can carry with you

gamekeeper /ˈɡeɪmˌkiːpəʳ/ *noun* [C] someone whose job is to look after wild animals and birds that are going to be hunted

gamepad /ˈɡeɪmpæd/ *noun* [C] **COMPUTING** a device that you hold in your hands and use to control a computer game or video game (= a game in which you make pictures move on a screen)

gamer /ˈɡeɪməʳ/ *noun* [C] someone who plays games, especially computer games

ˈgame ˌshow *noun* [C] a programme on television in which people play games to try to win prizes

gamete /ˈɡæmiːt/ *noun* [C] **BIOLOGY** in sexual reproduction, a male or female cell that combines with a cell of the opposite sex to produce a zygote (= the cell which will develop into a person or animal)

gamma globulin /ˌɡæməˈɡlɒbjʊlɪn/ *noun* [U] **BIOLOGY** a natural substance in the blood that protects the body against disease

ˌgamma radiˈation (**gamma rays**) *noun* [U] **PHYSICS** a type of radiation (= form of energy that can be dangerous) which goes through most solid objects

gammon /ˈɡæmən/ *noun* [U] *UK* **FOOD** a type of meat from a pig, usually cut in thick slices

gamut /ˈɡæmət/ *noun* [**no plural**] the whole group of things that can be included in something *The film explores* ***the whole gamut*** *of emotions from despair to joy.*

WORD PARTNERS FOR ***gang***

in a gang • a gang **of** sth • a gang **leader/member**

gang¹ /ɡæŋ/ *noun* [C] **1** YOUNG PEOPLE a group of young people who spend time together, usually fighting with other groups and behaving badly *a* ***member*** *of a* ***gang*** ○ *gang violence* **2** CRIMINALS a group of criminals who work together *a* ***gang of*** *armed robbers* **3** FRIENDS *informal* a group of young friends

gang² /ɡæŋ/ *verb*

gang up against/on sb *phrasal verb* to form a group to attack or criticize someone, usually unfairly *Some older girls have been ganging up on her at school.*

gangly /ˈɡæŋɡli/ (*also* **gangling**) *adjective* tall and thin *a gangly youth*

gangrene /ˈɡæŋɡriːn/ *noun* [U] **HEALTH** the death and decay of a part of the body because blood is not flowing through it

gangster /ˈɡæŋstəʳ/ *noun* [C] a member of a group of violent criminals

gangway /ˈɡæŋweɪ/ *noun* [C] **1** SPACE *UK* a space that people can walk down between two rows of seats in a vehicle or public place **2** SHIP a board or stairs for people to get on and off a ship

gaol /dʒeɪl/ *noun* [C, U] *another UK spelling of* jail (= a place where criminals are kept as a punishment)

WORD PARTNERS FOR ***gap***

bridge/close/narrow the gap • the gap **between** sth **and** sth

gap /ɡæp/ *noun* [C] **1** SPACE an empty space or hole in the middle of something, or between two things *There's quite a big* ***gap between*** *the door and the floor.* ○ *The sun was shining through a* ***gap in*** *the curtains.* **2** DIFFERENCE a difference between two groups of people, two situations, etc *an* ***age gap*** ○ *This course* ***bridges the gap*** *between school and university.* **3** ABSENT THING something that is absent and stops something from being complete *There are huge gaps in my memory.* **4 a gap in the market** an opportunity for a product or service that does not already exist **5** TIME a period of time when nothing happens, or when you are doing something different from usual *I decided to go back to teaching after a gap of 10 years.* ➲See also: **the generation gap**

gape /ɡeɪp/ *verb* [I] **1** LOOK to look at someone or something with your mouth open because you are so surprised *We stood there* ***gaping*** *in wonder* ***at*** *the beautiful landscape.* **2** OPEN to be wide open

gaping /ˈɡeɪpɪŋ/ *adjective* **a gaping hole/wound, etc** a hole/wound, etc that is open very wide

ˈgap ˌyear *noun* [C] *UK* **EDUCATION** a year between leaving school and starting university which you usually spend travelling or working

O⁻ **garage** /ˈgærɑːʒ/ (US) /gəˈrɑːʒ/ *noun* [C] **1** BUILDING a small building, often built next to a house, that you can put a car in **2** BUSINESS a business that repairs or sells cars, and sometimes also sells fuel

garbage /ˈgɑːbɪdʒ/ *US* (*UK* **rubbish**) *noun* [U] **1** THINGS NOT WANTED things that you throw away because you do not want them **2** BAD THINGS something that you think is nonsense, wrong, or very bad quality *How can you listen to that garbage on the radio!*

ˈgarbage ˌcan *US* (*UK* **dustbin**) *noun* [C] a large container for waste kept outside your house

ˈgarbage colˌlector *US* (*UK* **dustman**) *noun* [C] someone whose job is to remove the waste from containers left outside houses

ˈgarbage ˌman *noun* [C] *US another word for* garbage collector

garbled /ˈgɑːbəld/ *adjective* Garbled words or messages are not clear and are very difficult to understand.

O⁻ **garden** /ˈgɑːdᵊn/ *noun* **1** [C] *UK* (*US* **yard**) an area of ground belonging to a house, often containing grass, flowers, or trees *the **front/back garden*** ○ *Dad's outside **in the garden**.* **2 gardens** [plural] a park or large public area where plants and flowers are grown •**garden** *verb* [I] to work in a garden, growing plants and making it look attractive

ˈgarden ˌcentre *noun* [C] *UK* a place that sells things for gardens such as plants and tools

gardener /ˈgɑːdᵊnəʳ/ *noun* [C] someone who works in a garden, growing plants and making it look attractive

gardening /ˈgɑːdᵊnɪŋ/ *noun* [U] the job or activity of growing a garden and keeping it attractive

gargle /ˈgɑːgl/ *verb* [I] **HEALTH** to move liquid or medicine around in your throat without swallowing, especially to clean it or stop it feeling painful

garish /ˈgeərɪʃ/ *adjective* unpleasantly bright in colour, or decorated too much *a garish red jacket*

garlic /ˈgɑːlɪk/ *noun* [U] **FOOD** a vegetable like a small onion with a very strong taste and smell *a **clove of garlic*** ➲See colour picture **Fruit and Vegetables** on page Centre 10

garment /ˈgɑːmənt/ *noun* [C] *formal* a piece of clothing

garnish /ˈgɑːnɪʃ/ *verb* [T] **FOOD** to decorate food with something such as herbs or pieces of fruit *salmon **garnished with** herbs and lemon* •**garnish** *noun* [C]

garrison /ˈgærɪsᵊn/ *noun* [C] a group of soldiers living in a particular area or building to defend it

garter /ˈgɑːtəʳ/ *noun* [C] a piece of elastic that holds up a woman's stockings (= very thin pieces of clothing that cover a woman's foot and leg)

O⁻ **gas**[1] /gæs/ *noun* **1 PHYSICS** [C, U] a substance in a form like air and not solid or liquid *poisonous gases* **2** FUEL [U] a substance in a form like air used as a fuel for heating and cooking *(UK) a gas cooker/ (US) a gas stove* **3** CAR FUEL [U] *US* (*UK* **petrol**) a liquid fuel used in cars *half a tank of gas* **4 HEALTH** [U] *US* (*UK* **wind**) gas or air in your stomach that makes you feel uncomfortable and sometimes makes noises **5 the gas** *US informal* the part of a car which you push with your foot to make it go faster *We'd better **step on the gas** (= drive faster).* ➲See also: **natural gas, tear gas**

gas[2] /gæs/ *verb* [T] **gassing**, *past* **gassed** to poison or kill someone with gas

ˈgas ˌchamber *noun* [C] a room that is filled with poisonous gas to kill people

gash /gæʃ/ *noun* [C] a long, deep wound or cut •**gash** *verb* [T]

ˈgas ˌmask *noun* [C] a cover you wear over your face to protect you from breathing poisonous gas

gasohol /ˈgæsəhɒl/ *noun* [U] a fuel made of alcohol and petrol

gasoline /ˈgæsᵊliːn/ *US* (*UK* **petrol**) *noun* [U] *another word for* gas (= a liquid fuel used in cars)

gasp /gɑːsp/ *verb* [I] **1** MAKE NOISE to make a noise by suddenly breathing in because you are shocked or surprised *She gasped in horror as the car spun out of control.* **2** BREATHE WITH DIFFICULTY to breathe loudly and with difficulty trying to get more air *He clutched his heart, **gasping for breath**.* •**gasp** *noun* [C] *a gasp of surprise*

ˈgas ˌpedal *US* (*UK/US* **accelerator**) *noun* [C] the part of a car which you push with your foot to make it go faster

ˈgas ˌstation *US* (*UK* **petrol station**) *noun* [C] a place where you can buy petrol (= fuel for cars)

gastric /ˈgæstrɪk/ *adjective* **ANATOMY, BIOLOGY** relating to the stomach

ˌgastric ˈjuice *noun* [U] **BIOLOGY** the acid in your stomach that helps to digest food

gastrointestinal /ˌgæstrəʊˌɪntesˈtaɪnᵊl/ *adjective* **ANATOMY, BIOLOGY** relating to the stomach and the intestines (= long tube that food passes through after the stomach)

gastronomic /ˌgæstrəˈnɒmɪk/ *adjective* **FOOD** relating to good food and cooking

gastropod /ˈgæstrəʊpɒd/ *noun* [C] **BIOLOGY** a type of animal with a soft, flat body, no legs and often a shell, for example a snail or a slug

O⁻ **gate** /geɪt/ *noun* [C] **1** DOOR the part of a fence or outside wall that opens and closes like a door *Please **shut the gate**.* **2** AIRPORT the part of an airport where passengers get on or off an aircraft *The flight to Dublin is now boarding at gate 8.*

gateau /ˈgætəʊ/ (US) /gæˈtəʊ/ *noun* [C, U] *plural* **gateaux** *UK* **FOOD** a large cake, usually filled and decorated with cream

gatecrash /ˈgeɪtkræʃ/ *verb* [I, T] to go to a party or private event without an invitation •**gatecrasher** *noun* [C] someone who gatecrashes

G

gateway /ˈgeɪtweɪ/ *noun* **1** [C] an opening in a fence or outside wall that is closed with a gate **2 the gateway to sth** the way to get into something or somewhere *the gateway to the North*

gather /ˈgæðəʳ/ *verb* **1** MAKE A GROUP [I, T] to join other people somewhere to make a group, or to bring people together into a group *Crowds of fans gathered at the stadium for the big match.* **2** COLLECT [T] to collect several things together, often from different places or people *They interviewed 1000 people to gather data on TV viewing habits.* ○ *She* ***gathered*** *her things* ***together*** *and left.* **3** THINK [T] to think something is true because you have heard or seen information about it *From what I can gather, they haven't sold their house yet.* **4 gather speed/strength/support, etc** to increase in speed/strength/support, etc

G

WORD PARTNERS FOR ***gathering***

at a gathering • a gathering **of** [teachers/world leaders, etc] • a **family** gathering

gathering /ˈgæðərɪŋ/ *noun* [C] a party or a meeting when many people get together as a group *a* ***family gathering***

GATT /gæt/ *noun* [U] **ECONOMICS** *abbreviation for* General Agreement on Tariffs and Trade: an international agreement (1948-94) between over 100 countries to end rules that limit trade between them

gaudy /ˈgɔːdi/ *adjective* unpleasantly bright in colour or decoration *a gaudy pink sweatshirt with gold embroidery*

gauge¹ /geɪdʒ/ *verb* [T] **1** JUDGMENT to make a judgment about a situation or about what someone thinks or feels [+ **question word**] *It's impossible to gauge what her reaction will be.* **2** MEASURE to measure a distance, size, or amount

gauge² /geɪdʒ/ *noun* [C] **1** JUDGING a way of judging something such as a situation or what someone thinks or feels *Street interviews aren't an accurate* ***gauge of*** *public opinion.* **2** MEASURING a method or piece of equipment that you use to measure something *a* ***fuel gauge***

gaunt /gɔːnt/ *adjective* very thin, especially because of being ill or old *a pale, gaunt face*

gauntlet /ˈgɔːntlət/ *noun* **1** [C] a long, thick glove (= piece of clothing for your hand) **2 run the gauntlet** to have to deal with a lot of people who are criticizing or attacking you **3 throw down the gauntlet** to invite someone to argue, fight, or compete with you

gauze /gɔːz/ *noun* [U] **1 HEALTH** thin, transparent cloth, especially used to cover injuries **2 CHEMISTRY** a flat square made of wires, used by scientists to put under containers that are being heated by a flame

gave /geɪv/ *past tense of* give

gawp /gɔːp/ *UK* (*US* **gawk** /gɔːk/) *verb* [I] to look at someone or something with your mouth open because you are shocked or surprised *He just stood there* ***gawping at*** *me.*

gay¹ /geɪ/ *adjective* **1** HOMOSEXUAL homosexual *Have you told your parents you're gay yet?* ○ *a gay bar/club* **2** HAPPY *old-fashioned* very happy and enjoying yourself

gay² /geɪ/ *noun* [C] someone who is homosexual, especially a man *equal rights for gays and lesbians*

gaze /geɪz/ *verb* **gaze at/into, etc** to look for a long time at someone or something or in a particular direction *They gazed into each other's eyes.* •**gaze** *noun* [**no plural**]

GB COMPUTING *written abbreviation for* gigabyte (= a unit for measuring the amount of information a computer can store) *a 4 GB hard drive*

GCSE /ˌdʒiːsiːesˈiː/ *noun* [C] **EDUCATION** *abbreviation for* General Certificate of Secondary Education: in the UK, an exam taken by students at the age of sixteen, or the qualification itself *Mary's got nine GCSEs.*

GDP /ˌdʒiːdiːˈpiː/ *noun* [U] **ECONOMICS** *abbreviation for* Gross Domestic Product: the total value of goods and services that a country produces in a year ⊃Compare **GNP**

gear¹ /gɪəʳ/ *noun* **1** VEHICLE [C] a set of parts in a motor vehicle or bicycle that control how fast the wheels turn [**usually plural**] *a mountain bike with 21 gears* ○ *to* ***change gear*** **2 first/second/third, etc gear** a particular position of the gears in a motor vehicle or bicycle that controls how fast the wheels turn *The lights turned green, but I couldn't* ***get into first gear****.* **3** CLOTHES/EQUIPMENT [U] the clothes and equipment used for a particular purpose *sports/swimming gear*

gear² /gɪəʳ/ *verb*

gear sth to/towards sb/sth *phrasal verb* to design or organize something so that it is suitable for a particular purpose, situation, or group of people [**often passive**] These advertisements are geared towards a younger audience.

gear (sb/sth) up *phrasal verb* to prepare for something that you have to do, or to prepare someone else for something [**often reflexive**] I'm trying to ***gear myself up for*** *the exams.*

gearbox /ˈgɪəbɒks/ *noun* [C] the set of gears in a motor vehicle and the metal box that contains them

gearing /ˈgɪərɪŋ/ *noun* [U] **FINANCE** the amount of a company's money that has been borrowed

ˈ**gear ˌlever** *UK* (*US* **gearshift** /ˈgɪəʃɪft/) *noun* [C] a stick with a handle that you move to change gear in a vehicle ⊃See colour picture **Car** on page Centre 7

gearstick /ˈgɪərstɪk/ *noun* [C] *UK another word for* gear lever ⊃See colour picture **Car** on page Centre 7

GED /ˌdʒiːiːˈdiː/ *noun* [C] **EDUCATION** *abbreviation for* General Equivalency Diploma: an official document in the US that is given to someone who did not complete high school (= school for students aged 15 to 18) but who has passed a government exam instead

geek /giːk/ *noun* [C] *informal* a man who is boring and not fashionable •**geeky** *adjective informal a geeky guy with a beard and glasses*

geese /giːs/ *plural of* goose

gel /dʒel/ *noun* [**C, U**] a thick, clear, liquid substance, especially a product used to style hair ***hair gel*** ○ ***shower gel***

gelatine /ˈdʒelətiːn/ *UK* (*US* **gelatin** /ˈdʒelətɪn/) *noun* [**U**] **FOOD** a clear substance made from animal bones, often used to make food thicker

gem /dʒem/ *noun* [**C**] **1 GEOLOGY** a valuable stone, especially one that has been cut to be used in jewellery **2** *informal* someone or something that you like very much and think is very special

Gemini /ˈdʒemɪnaɪ/ *noun* [**C, U**] the sign of the zodiac which relates to the period of 23 May - 21 June, or a person born during this period

gender /ˈdʒendəʳ/ *noun* [**C, U**] **1 SOCIETY** the state of being male or female **2 LANGUAGE** the division of nouns, pronouns and adjectives into masculine, feminine and neuter types

WORD PARTNERS FOR ***gene***

carry/have a gene • a gene **(responsible) for** sth • gene **therapy**

gene /dʒiːn/ *noun* [**C**] **BIOLOGY** a part of a cell that is passed on from a parent to a child and that controls particular characteristics

O┘**general¹** /ˈdʒenᵊrᵊl/ *adjective* **1** NOT DETAILED not detailed, but including the most basic or necessary information *These leaflets contain some general information about the school.* ○ *I've got a general idea of how it works.* **2** MOST PEOPLE [**always before noun**] relating to or involving all or most people, things, or places *There seems to be general agreement on this matter.* **3** NOT LIMITED [**always before noun**] including a lot of things or subjects and not limited to only one or a few *general knowledge* **4 in general a** CONSIDERING EVERYTHING considering the whole of someone or something, and not just a particular part of them *I still have a sore throat, but I feel much better in general.* **b** USUALLY usually, or in most situations *In general, the weather here stays sunny.*

general² /ˈdʒenᵊrᵊl/ *noun* [**C**] an officer of very high rank in the army or air force

ˌgeneral anaesˈthetic *UK* (*US* **general anesthetic**) *noun* [**C, U**] **HEALTH** a substance that is used to stop someone being conscious when they have an operation so that they do not feel any pain

ˌgeneral eˈlection *noun* [**C**] **POLITICS** a big election in which the people living in a country vote to decide who will represent them in the government

WORD PARTNERS FOR ***generalization***

make a generalization • a **broad/gross/sweeping** generalization

generalization (*also UK* **-isation**) /ˌdʒenᵊrᵊlaɪˈzeɪʃᵊn/ *noun* [**C, U**] when someone says something very basic that is often true but not always true

generalize (*also UK* **-ise**) /ˈdʒenᵊrᵊlaɪz/ *verb* [**I**] to say something very basic that is often true but not always true

ˌgeneral ˈledger (*also* **nominal ledger**) *noun* [**C**] **FINANCE** a record that a business keeps of its sales, things it has bought, things it owns, things it has to pay regular amounts for, etc.

O┘**generally** /ˈdʒenᵊrᵊli/ *adverb* **1** USUALLY usually, or in most situations *I generally wake up early.* **2** AS A WHOLE considering the whole of someone or something, and not just a particular part of them *The police said that the crowd was generally well-behaved.* **3** BY MOST PEOPLE by most people, or to most people *He is generally believed to be their best player.*

ˌgeneral pracˈtitioner (*also* **GP**) *noun* [**C**] **HEALTH** a doctor who sees people in the local area and treats illnesses that do not need a hospital visit

ˌgeneral ˈstrike *noun* [**C**] **POLITICS** a strike (= time when people stop working because they want more money, etc.) in which most people in a country take part

generate /ˈdʒenᵊreɪt/ *verb* [**T**] **1** CAUSE to cause something to exist *to **generate income/profit*** ○ *This film has **generated** a lot of **interest**.* **2 PHYSICS** to produce energy *Many countries use nuclear fuels to generate electricity.*

generation /ˌdʒenəˈreɪʃᵊn/ *noun* **1 SOCIETY** [**C**] all the people in a society or family who are approximately the same age *the **older/younger generation*** ○ *This is the story of three generations of women.* **2** TIME [**C**] a period of about 25 to 30 years, the time it takes for a child to become an adult and take the place of their parents in society *Our family has lived in this village **for generations**.* **3** PRODUCT [**C**] a product when it is at a particular stage of development *a new generation of computers* **4** ENERGY [**U**] the production of energy *the generation of electricity*

the generˈation ˌgap *noun* **SOCIETY** when young people and old people do not understand each other because of their age difference

generator /ˈdʒenᵊreɪtəʳ/ *noun* [**C**] a machine that produces electricity ➲See picture at **wind turbine**

generic /dʒəˈnerɪk/ *adjective* **1** TYPE relating to a whole group of things or type of thing **2 ECONOMICS** A generic product such as a drug is not sold with the name of the company that produced it.

generosity /ˌdʒenᵊˈrɒsəti/ *noun* [**U**] the quality of being generous

O┘**generous** /ˈdʒenᵊrəs/ *adjective* **1** GIVING giving other people a lot of money, presents, or time in a kind way *a very generous man* **2** LARGE larger than usual or than expected *a generous discount for students* ○ *a generous portion* •**generously** *adverb*

ˈgene ˌtherapy *noun* [**U**] **BIOLOGY, HEALTH** the science of changing genes (= parts of cells which control particular characteristics) in order to stop or prevent a disease

genetic /dʒəˈnetɪk/ *adjective* **BIOLOGY** relating to genes *a rare **genetic disorder*** ○ ***genetic research*** •**genetically** *adverb*

geˌnetically ˈmodified *adjective* **BIOLOGY** Genetically modified plants or animals have had some of their genes (= parts of cells which control particular characteristics) changed.

geˌnetic ˈcode *noun* [C] **BIOLOGY** the pattern of chemicals inside the genes (= cells which are passed from parent to child) which controls the characteristics and qualities of a living thing

geˌnetic engiˈneering *noun* [U] **BIOLOGY** when scientists change the genes (= parts of cells which control particular characteristics) in the cells of plants or animals

geˌnetic ˈfingerprint *noun* [C] **BIOLOGY** the pattern of someone's genes, which make each person different

G

geˌnetic modifiˈcation *noun* [U] **BIOLOGY** when the genes (= cells which are passed from parent to child) of a living thing are changed in order to make it healthier or more useful to humans

genetics /dʒəˈnetɪks/ *noun* [U] **BIOLOGY** the scientific study of genes (= parts of cells which control particular characteristics)

genial /ˈdʒiːniəl/ *adjective* kind and friendly

genitals /ˈdʒenɪtᵊlz/ *noun* [plural] **ANATOMY, BIOLOGY** the sexual organs

genius /ˈdʒiːniəs/ *noun* **1** PERSON [C] someone who is extremely intelligent or extremely good at doing something *Einstein was a genius.* **2** QUALITY [U] the quality of being extremely intelligent or extremely good at doing something *Einstein's genius*

genocide /ˈdʒenəsaɪd/ *noun* [U] the intentional killing of a large group of people who belong to a particular race or country

genotype /ˈdʒenəʊtaɪp/ *noun* [C] **BIOLOGY** the type and arrangement of genes (= cells which are passed from parent to child) that each living thing has

genre /ˈʒɒnrə/ *noun* [C] **LITERATURE, MUSIC, ART** a type of art or writing with a particular style *a literary/musical genre*

gent /dʒent/ *noun* [C] *informal short for* gentleman

genteel /dʒenˈtiːl/ *adjective* very polite, especially in an artificial way **•gentility** /ˌdʒenˈtɪləti/ *noun* [U]

o-gentle /ˈdʒentl/ *adjective* **1** KIND kind and careful not to hurt or upset anyone or anything *My mother was such a gentle, loving person.* **2** NOT STRONG not strong or severe *a mild soap that is gentle on your skin* ○ *a gentle breeze* **3** SLOPE A gentle slope or climb is not steep. **•gently** *adverb* **•gentleness** *noun* [U]

gentleman /ˈdʒentlmən/ *noun* [C] *plural* **gentlemen** **1** POLITE MAN a man who behaves politely and treats people with respect *He was a perfect gentleman.* **2** MAN a polite word for 'man', used especially when talking to or about a man you do not know *There's a gentleman here to see you.*

the gents /ðədʒents/ *noun* [group] *UK informal* a toilet in a public place for men See Common Learner Error at **toilet**

o-genuine /ˈdʒenjuɪn/ *adjective* **1** SINCERE If a person or their feelings are genuine, they are sincere and honest. *He shows a genuine concern for the welfare of his students.* **2** REAL If something is genuine, it is really what it seems to be. *a genuine gold necklace* **•genuinely** *adverb*

genus /ˈdʒiːnəs, ˈdʒenəs/ *noun* [C] *plural* **genera** **BIOLOGY** a group of animals or plants that have the same characteristics

geo- /dʒiːəʊ-/ *prefix* relating to the earth *geothermal* (= of or connected with the heat inside the Earth)

geography /dʒiˈɒgrəfi/ *noun* [U] **GEOGRAPHY** the study of all the countries of the world, and of the surface of the Earth such as the mountains and seas **•geographer** *noun* [C] someone who studies geography **•geographical** /ˌdʒiːəʊˈgræfɪkəl/ (*also* **geographic** /dʒiːəʊˈgræfɪk/) *adjective* **•geographically** *adverb*

geology /dʒiˈɒlədʒi/ *noun* [U] **GEOLOGY** the study of rocks and soil and the physical structure of the Earth **•geological** /ˌdʒiːəʊˈlɒdʒɪkəl/ *adjective* **•geologist** *noun* [C] someone who studies geology

geomagnetism /ˌdʒiːəʊˈmægnɪtɪzᵊm/ *noun* [U] **GEOLOGY, PHYSICS** (the study of) the magnetic characteristics of the Earth **•geomagnetic** /ˌdʒiːəʊmægˈnetɪk/ *adjective*

geometric /ˌdʒiːəʊˈmetrɪk/ (*also* **geometrical**) *adjective* **1** **MATHEMATICS** having a regular shape such as a circle or triangle, or having a pattern made of regular shapes **2** **MATHEMATICS** relating to geometry

geometry /dʒiˈɒmɪtri/ *noun* [U] **MATHEMATICS** a type of mathematics that deals with points, lines, angles and shapes

geomorphic /ˌdʒiːəʊˈmɔːfɪk/ *adjective* **GEOLOGY** like or relating to the Earth's surface

geothermal /ˌdʒiːəʊˈθɜːməl/ *adjective* **GEOGRAPHY** relating to the heat that is produced inside the Earth *geothermal energy/power*

geotropism /ˌdʒiːəʊˈtrəʊpɪzm/ *noun* [U] **BIOLOGY** the way plants or plant parts react to gravity (= the force that pulls objects towards planets)

geriatric /ˌdʒeriˈætrɪk/ *adjective* relating to very old people *geriatric patients* ○ *a geriatric hospital* **•geriatrics** *noun* [U] care and medical treatment for very old people

germ /dʒɜːm/ *noun* **1** [C] a very small living thing that causes disease *Wash your hands before cooking so that you don't spread germs.* **2 the germ of sth** the beginning of something *the germ of a brilliant idea*

ˌGerman ˈmeasles (*also* **rubella**) *noun* [U] **HEALTH** a disease which causes red spots on your skin

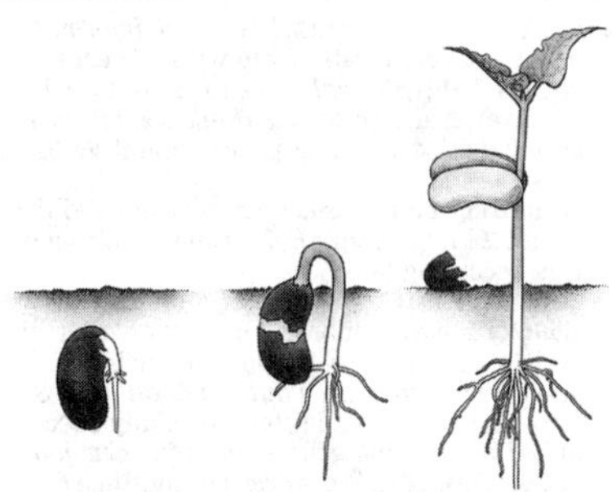

germination

germinate /ˈdʒɜːmɪneɪt/ *verb* [I, T] **BIOLOGY** If a seed germinates or is germinated, it begins to grow. •**germination** /ˌdʒɜːmɪˈneɪʃᵊn/ *noun* [U]

gerund /ˈdʒerᵊnd/ *noun* [C] **LANGUAGE** a noun made from the form of a verb that ends with -ing, for example 'fishing' in 'John loves fishing.'

gestation /dʒesˈteɪʃᵊn/ *noun* [U] **BIOLOGY** the development of a baby child or animal inside its mother's body *Elephants have a long **gestation period**.*

gesticulate /dʒesˈtɪkjəleɪt/ *verb* [I] to move your hands and arms around to emphasize what you are saying or to express something

WORD PARTNERS FOR ***gesture***

a **grand/token** gesture • a gesture **of** [friendship/goodwill, etc] • a **nice** gesture

gesture¹ /ˈdʒestʃəʳ/ *noun* [C] **1** MOVEMENT a movement you make with your hand, arm, or head to express what you are thinking or feeling *He **made** a rude **gesture** at the crowd.* **2** ACTION something you do to show people how you feel about a person or situation *It would be a **nice gesture** to invite her to dinner.*

gesture² /ˈdʒestʃəʳ/ *verb* [I] to point at something or express something using your hand, arm, or head *He **gestured towards** the window.*

O⁻**get¹** /get/ *verb* **getting**, *past tense* **got**, *past participle* **got**, *US* **gotten** **1** OBTAIN [T] to obtain or buy something *I need to get some bread on the way home.* [+ **two objects**] *I'll try to get you a ticket.* **2** BRING [T] to go somewhere and bring back someone or something *Wait here while I get the car.* **3** RECEIVE [T] to receive something or be given something *Did you get anything nice for your birthday?* ○ *Guy still hasn't got my email yet.* **4** UNDERSTAND [T] to understand something *He never gets any of my jokes.* **5 get into/off/through, etc** to move somewhere *Get over here right now!* **6 get sth into/down/out, etc** to move something somewhere *Could you get that bowl down from the shelf for me?* **7 get here/there/to the bank, etc** to arrive somewhere *What time do you normally get home from work?* **8 get sb/sth to do sth** to make someone or something do something *Sorry, I couldn't get the window to shut properly.* **9 get to do sth** to have an opportunity to do something *I never get to sit in the front seat.* **10 get ill/rich/wet, etc** to become ill/rich/wet, etc *We should go. It's getting late.* **11 get caught/killed/married, etc** to have something done to you **12 get sth painted/repaired, etc** to arrange for someone to do something for you, usually for money *I need to get my hair cut.* **13 get cancer/flu/malaria, etc** to become ill or develop an illness *I feel like I'm getting a cold.* **14 get a bus/train, etc** to travel somewhere on a bus/train, etc *Maybe we should get a taxi home.* **15 get the phone/door** *informal* to answer someone calling on the telephone or waiting at the door *Can you get the phone?*

COMMON LEARNER ERROR

got or **gotten?**

The past participle of the verb 'get' is **got** in British English and **gotten** in American English.

Have you got my email yet? (UK)

Have you gotten my email yet? (US)

get about *phrasal verb UK* (*US* **get around**) **1** TRAVEL to travel to a lot of places **2** MOVE to be able to go to different places without difficulty, especially if you are old or ill **3** INFORMATION If news or information gets about, a lot of people hear about it.

get sth across *phrasal verb* to successfully communicate information to other people *This is the message that we want to **get across to** the public.*

get ahead *phrasal verb* to be successful in the work that you do *It's tough for any woman who wants to **get ahead in** politics.*

get along *phrasal verb mainly US* (*mainly UK* **get on**) **1** BE FRIENDS If two or more people get along, they like each other and are friendly to each other. *I don't really **get along with** my sister's husband.* **2** DEAL WITH to deal with a situation, especially successfully *I wonder how Michael's getting along in his new job?*

get around sth *phrasal verb* (*also UK* **get round sth**) to find a way of dealing with or avoiding a problem *Our lawyer found a way of getting around the adoption laws.*

get around to sth *phrasal verb* (*also UK* **get round to sth**) to do something that you have intended to do for a long time *I finally got around to calling her yesterday.*

get at sb *phrasal verb UK informal* to criticize someone in an unkind way

be getting at sth *phrasal verb informal* If you ask someone what they are getting at, you are asking them what they really mean.

get at sth *phrasal verb* to be able to reach or get something

get away *phrasal verb* **1** LEAVE to leave or escape from a place or person, often when it is difficult to do this *We walked to the next beach to **get away from** the crowds.* **2** HOLIDAY to go somewhere to have a holiday, especially because you need to rest *We decided to go up to Scotland to **get away from it all*** (= have a relaxing holiday).

get away with sth *phrasal verb* to succeed in doing something bad or wrong without being punished or criticized *He shouldn't treat you like that. Don't let him get away with it.*

get back *phrasal verb* to return to a place after you have been somewhere else *By the time we*

G

got back to the hotel, Lydia had already left.

get sth back *phrasal verb* If you get something back, something that you had before is given to you again. *I wouldn't lend him anything, you'll never get it back.*

get sb back *phrasal verb informal* to do something unpleasant to someone because they have done something unpleasant to you

get back to sb *phrasal verb* to talk to someone, usually on the telephone, to give them some information they have asked for or because you were not able to speak to them before

get back to sth *phrasal verb* to start doing or talking about something again *Anyway, I'd better get back to work.*

get behind *phrasal verb* **FINANCE** If you get behind with work or payments, you have not done as much work or paid as much money as you should by a particular time.

get by *phrasal verb* to be able to live or deal with a situation with difficulty, usually by having just enough of something you need, such as money *I don't know how he* ***gets by on*** *so little money.*

get sb down *phrasal verb* to make someone feel unhappy *All this uncertainty is really getting me down.*

get sth down *phrasal verb* to write something, especially something that someone has said

get down to sth *phrasal verb* to start doing something seriously and with a lot of attention and effort *Before we get down to business, I'd like to thank you all for coming today.*

get in *phrasal verb* **1** [ENTER] to succeed in entering a place, especially a building *They must have got in through the bathroom window.* **2** [PERSON ARRIVING] to arrive at your home or the place where you work *What time did you get in last night?* **3** [VEHICLE ARRIVING] If a train or other vehicle gets in at a particular time, that is when it arrives. *Our flight's getting in later than expected.* **4** [BE CHOSEN] to succeed in being chosen or elected for a position in a school or other organization *He wanted to go to Oxford but he didn't get in.*

get into sth *phrasal verb* **1** [BE CHOSEN] to succeed in being chosen or elected for a position in a school or other organization **2** [BE INTERESTED] to become interested in an activity or subject, or start being involved in an activity *How did you get into journalism?*

get into sb *phrasal verb* If you do not know what has got into someone, you do not understand why they are behaving strangely.

O-ᵚ**get off (sth)** *phrasal verb* **1** [LEAVE BUS/TRAIN] to leave a bus, train, aircraft, or boat *We should get off at the next stop.* ➲See colour picture **Phrasal Verbs** on page Centre 16 **2** [LEAVE WORK] to leave the place where you work, usually at the end of the day *What time do you get off work?*

Get off! *phrasal verb UK informal* something that you say in order to tell someone to stop touching someone or something

get (sb) off (sth) *phrasal verb* to avoid being punished for something you have done wrong, or to help someone avoid getting punished for something they have done wrong *He got off with a £20 fine.*

get off on sth *phrasal verb informal* If you get off on something, it makes you feel very excited, especially in a sexual way.

O-ᵚ**get off with sb** *phrasal verb UK informal* to begin a sexual relationship with someone

O-ᵚ**get on (sth)** *phrasal verb* to go onto a bus, train, aircraft, or boat *I think we got on the wrong bus.* ➲See colour picture **Phrasal Verbs** on page Centre 16

be getting on *phrasal verb informal* **1** [OLD] to be old **2** [LATE] *mainly UK* If time is getting on, it is becoming late.

get on *phrasal verb mainly UK* (*mainly US* **get along**) **1** If two or more people get on, they like each other and are friendly to each other. *I never knew that Karen didn't* ***get on with*** *Sue.* **2** to deal with a situation, especially successfully *How's Frank getting on in his new job?*

get on with sth *phrasal verb* to continue doing something, especially work *Get on with your homework.*

get onto sth *phrasal verb* to start talking about a subject after discussing something else *How did we get onto this subject?*

get out *phrasal verb* **1** [MOVE OUT] to move out of something, especially a vehicle *I'll get out when you stop at the traffic lights.* **2** [DIFFERENT PLACES] to go out to different places and meet people in order to enjoy yourself *She doesn't get out so much now that she's got the baby.* **3** [NEWS] If news or information gets out, people hear about it although someone is trying to keep it secret.

get (sb) out *phrasal verb* to escape from or leave a place, or to help someone do this *I left the door open and the cat got out.*

get out of sth *phrasal verb* to avoid doing something that you should do, often by giving an excuse *You're just trying to get out of doing the housework!*

get sth out of sb *phrasal verb* to persuade or force someone to tell or give you something *He was determined to get the truth out of her.*

get sth out of sth *phrasal verb* to enjoy something or think that something is useful *It was an interesting course but I'm not sure I got much out of it.*

get over sth *phrasal verb* **1** to begin to feel better after being unhappy or ill *It took her months to get over the shock of Richard leaving.* **2 can't/couldn't get over sth** *informal* to be very shocked or surprised about something *I can't get over how different you look with short hair.*

get sth over with *phrasal verb* to do and complete something difficult or unpleasant that must be done *I'll be glad to get these exams over with.*

get round *phrasal verb UK* (*US* **get around**) If news or information gets round, a lot of people hear about it.

get round sth *phrasal verb UK* (*US* **get around sth**) to find a way of dealing with or avoiding a problem

get round sb *phrasal verb UK* to persuade someone to do what you want by being kind to them

get through *phrasal verb* to manage to talk to someone on the telephone *I tried to ring earlier, but I couldn't get through.*

get through to sb *phrasal verb* to succeed in making someone understand or believe something *I just don't seem to be able to get through to him these days.*

get through sth *phrasal verb* **1** [DEAL WITH] to

deal with a difficult or unpleasant experience successfully, or to help someone do this *If I can just get through my exams I'll be so happy.* **2** FINISH *mainly UK* to finish doing or using something *We got through a whole jar of coffee last week.*

get to sb *phrasal verb informal* to make someone feel upset or angry *I know he's annoying, but you shouldn't let him get to you.*

get together *phrasal verb* **1** MEET to meet in order to do something or spend time together *Jan and I are getting together next week for lunch.* **2** RELATIONSHIP to begin a romantic relationship *She got together with Phil two years ago.*

O→**get (sb) up** *phrasal verb* to wake up and get out of bed, or to make someone do this *I had to get up at five o'clock this morning.* ⊃See colour picture **Phrasal Verbs** on page Centre 16

get up *phrasal verb* to stand up *The whole audience got up and started clapping.*

get up to sth *phrasal verb UK* to do something, especially something that other people think is wrong *She's been getting up to all sorts of mischief lately.*

getaway /ˈgetəweɪ/ *noun* [C] when someone leaves a place quickly, especially after committing a crime *They had a car waiting outside so they could **make** a quick **getaway**.*

get-together /ˈgettəgeðə/ *noun* [C] an informal meeting or party *We have a big family get-together every year.*

geyser /ˈgiːzəʳ/ (US) /ˈgaɪzər/ *noun* [C] **GEOGRAPHY** a hole in the ground that hot water and steam come out of

ghastly /ˈgɑːstli/ *adjective* very bad or unpleasant *a ghastly mistake* ○ *a ghastly man*

ghetto /ˈgetəʊ/ *noun* [C] *plural* **ghettos** or **ghettoes SOCIETY** an area of a city where people of a particular race or religion live, especially a poor area

ghost /gəʊst/ *noun* **1** [C] the spirit of a dead person which appears to people who are alive *Do you believe in ghosts?* ○ *a **ghost story*** **2 give up the ghost** *UK humorous* If a machine gives up the ghost, it stops working completely. •**ghostly** *adverb a ghostly figure*

ˈghost ˌtown *noun* [C] a town where few or no people now live

ghoul /guːl/ *noun* [C] an evil spirit

GI /ˌdʒiːˈaɪ/ *noun* [C] a soldier in the US army

giant¹ /ˈdʒaɪənt/ *adjective* [**always before noun**] extremely big, or much bigger than other similar things *a giant spider*

giant² /ˈdʒaɪənt/ *noun* [C] **1** IMAGINARY MAN an imaginary man who is much bigger and stronger than ordinary men **2** ORGANIZATION a very large and important company or organization *a media/software giant*

gibberish /ˈdʒɪbᵊrɪʃ/ *noun* [U] something that someone says that has no meaning or that cannot be understood

gibe /dʒaɪb/ *noun* [C] *another spelling of* jibe (= an insulting remark)

giddy /ˈgɪdi/ *adjective* **HEALTH** feeling as if you cannot balance and are going to fall

O→**gift** /gɪft/ *noun* [C] **1** PRESENT something that you give to someone, usually for a particular occasion *a birthday/wedding gift* **2** ABILITY a natural ability or skill *She **has a gift for** design.*

gifted /ˈgɪftɪd/ *adjective* A gifted person has a natural ability or is extremely intelligent. *a gifted athlete* ○ *a school for gifted children*

ˈgift ˌtoken/ˌvoucher *UK* (*US* **gift certificate**) *noun* [C] a card with an amount of money printed on it which you exchange in a shop for goods that cost that amount of money *a £20 gift voucher*

gig /gɪg/ *noun* [C] *informal* a performance of pop or rock music

gigabyte /ˈgɪgəbaɪt/ (*written abbreviation* **GB**) *noun* [C] **COMPUTING** a unit for measuring the amount of information a computer can store, equal to 1,000,000,000 bytes

gigantic /dʒaɪˈgæntɪk/ *adjective* extremely big *a gigantic teddy bear*

giggle /ˈgɪgl/ *verb* [I] to laugh in a nervous or silly way *She started giggling and couldn't stop.* •**giggle** *noun* [C]

gilded /ˈgɪldɪd/ *adjective* covered with a thin layer of gold or gold paint *a gilded frame/mirror*

gill /gɪl/ *noun* [C] **BIOLOGY** an organ on each side of a fish or other water creature which it uses to breathe

gilt /gɪlt/ *noun* [U] a thin covering of gold or gold paint •**gilt** *adjective*

gimmick /ˈgɪmɪk/ *noun* [C] something that is used only to get people's attention, especially to make them buy something *a **marketing/publicity gimmick*** •**gimmicky** *adjective*

gin /dʒɪn/ *noun* [C, U] **FOOD** a strong alcoholic drink which has no colour

ginger¹ /ˈdʒɪndʒəʳ/ *noun* [U] **FOOD** a pale brown root with a strong taste used as a spice in cooking *ginger cake*

ginger² /ˈdʒɪndʒəʳ/ *adjective UK* Ginger hair is an orange-brown colour. *She's got ginger hair and freckles.*

ginger³ /ˈgɪŋəʳ/ *noun* [C] *UK informal* an offensive word for a person with red hair

gingerly /ˈdʒɪndʒᵊli/ *adverb* slowly and carefully *He lowered himself gingerly into the water.*

gipsy /ˈdʒɪpsi/ *noun* [C] **SOCIETY** *another UK spelling of* gypsy (= a member of a race of people who travel from place to place, especially in Europe)

giraffe /dʒɪˈrɑːf/ *noun* [C] a large African animal with a very long neck and long, thin legs

girder /ˈgɜːdəʳ/ *noun* [C] a long, thick piece of metal that is used to support bridges or large buildings

O→**girl** /gɜːl/ *noun* **1** [C] a female child or young woman *We have three children - a boy and two girls.* **2 the girls** a group of female friends *I'm going out with the girls tonight.*

O→**girlfriend** /ˈgɜːlfrend/ *noun* [C] **1** RELATIONSHIP a woman or girl who someone is having a romantic relationship with *Have you met Steve's*

G

new girlfriend? **2** [FRIEND] a female friend, especially of a woman

girth /gɜːθ/ *noun* [**C, U**] the measurement around something round, such as someone's waist

gist /dʒɪst/ *noun* **the gist of sth** the main point or meaning of something without the details

OTHER WAYS OF SAYING *give*

Very common alternatives to 'give' are verbs such as **offer**, **provide**, and **supply**: *This booklet **provides** useful information about local services.* • *Your doctor should be able to **offer** advice.* • *The lake **supplies** the whole town **with** water.*

The verb **donate** is often used when someone gives money or goods to an organisation that needs help: *Four hundred pounds has been **donated** to the school book fund.*

If one of many people gives something, especially money, in order to provide or achieve something, the verb **contribute** is used: *I **contributed** twenty dollars towards Jamie's present.*

If you put something from your hand into someone else's hand, you can use verbs such as **pass** and **hand**: *Could you **hand** me that book, please?* • *He **passed** a note to her during the meeting.*

The phrasal verb **hand in** is sometimes used when you give something to someone in a position of authority: *Have you **handed in** your history essay yet?*

The phrasal verb **pass on** is often used when you ask someone to give something to someone else: *Could you **pass** this **on** to Laura when you've finished reading it?*

If something like a prize or an amount of money is given in an official way, you can use verbs like **award** or **present**: *She was **presented** with a bouquet of flowers and a cheque for £500.* • *He was **awarded** the Nobel Prize for Physics.*

O-■ **give**[1] /gɪv/ *verb past tense* **gave**, *past participle* **given 1** [PROVIDE] [**+ two objects**] to provide someone with something *Her parents gave her a car for her birthday.* ○ *Do you **give** money **to** charity?* ○ *Could you give me a lift to the station, please?* **2** [PUT NEAR] [**+ two objects**] to put something near someone or in their hand so that they can use it or look at it *Can you give me that pen?* ○ *He poured a cup of coffee and **gave** it **to** Isabel.* **3** [ALLOW] [**+ two objects**] to allow someone to have a right or an opportunity *We didn't really give him a chance to explain.* **4** [TELL] [**T**] to tell someone something *The woman refused to give her name.* [**+ two objects**] *Can you give Jo a message?* **5** [CAUSE] [**+ two objects**] to cause someone to have or feel something *I hope he hasn't given you any trouble.* ○ *This news will **give** hope **to** thousands of sufferers.* **6** [ALLOW TIME] [**+ two objects**] to allow someone or something a particular amount of time *I'm nearly ready - just give me a few minutes.* **7** [PAY MONEY] [**+ two objects**] to pay someone a particular amount of money for something *I gave him £20 for his old camera.* **8** [DO] [**T**] to perform an action *to give a cry/shout* [**+ two objects**] *He gave her a kiss on the cheek.* **9 give sb a call/ring** to telephone someone *Why don't you just give him a call?* **10 give a performance/speech, etc** to perform or speak in public *Tony gave a great speech.* **11 give a party** to have a party *Claire's giving a birthday party for Eric.* **12** [MOVE] [**I**] to bend, stretch, or break because of too much weight **13 give way** *UK* (*US* **yield**) to stop in order to allow other vehicles to go past before you drive onto a bigger road

give sth away *phrasal verb* **1** [NO MONEY] to give something to someone without asking for any money *They're giving away a CD with this magazine.* **2** [SECRET] to let someone know a secret, often without intending to *The party was meant to be a surprise, but Caroline gave it away.*

give sth back *phrasal verb* to return something to the person who gave it to you *Has she given you those books back yet?*

give in *phrasal verb* **1** [AGREE] to finally agree to what someone wants after a period when you refuse to agree *We will never **give in to** terrorists' demands.* **2** [STOP] to accept that you have been beaten and agree to stop competing or fighting

give sth in *phrasal verb UK* to give a piece of written work or a document to someone for them to read, judge, or deal with *I have to give my essay in on Monday.*

give off sth *phrasal verb* to produce heat, light, a smell, or a gas *The fire was giving off a lot of smoke.*

give sth out *phrasal verb* to give something to a large number of people *He gave out copies of the report at the end of the meeting.*

give out *phrasal verb* If a machine or part of your body gives out, it stops working correctly. *She read until her eyes gave out.*

give up (sth) *phrasal verb* **1** [STOP HABIT] If you give up a habit such as smoking, or give up something unhealthy such as alcohol, you stop doing it or having it. *I gave up smoking two years ago.* **2** [TOO DIFFICULT] to stop doing something before you have completed it, usually because it is too difficult [**+ doing sth**] *I've given up trying to help her.*

give up sth *phrasal verb* to stop doing a regular activity or job *Are you going to give up work when you have your baby?*

give up *phrasal verb* to stop trying to think of the answer to a joke or question *Do you give up?*

give it up for sb *phrasal verb* used to ask people to clap their hands to show that they like a performance *Ladies and gentlemen, give it up for the star of our show, Amy Jones!*

give yourself up *phrasal verb* to allow the police or an enemy to catch you

give up on sb *phrasal verb* to stop hoping that someone will do what you want them to do *The doctors have given up on him.*

give up on sth *phrasal verb* to stop hoping that something will achieve what you want it to achieve

give[2] /gɪv/ *noun* **1** [**U**] when something can bend or move from its normal shape to take extra weight or size **2 give and take** when people reach agreement by letting each person have part of what they want

giveaway /ˈgɪvəweɪ/ *noun* **1** FREE [C] something that is given to people free **2** EASY TO GUESS [**no plural**] something that makes it easy for people to guess something

given¹ /ˈgɪvᵊn/ *adjective* **1** [**always before noun**] already arranged or agreed *They can only stay for a given amount of time.* **2 any given day/time/week, etc** any day/time/week, etc *About 4 million women are pregnant in the US at any given time.*

given² /ˈgɪvᵊn/ *preposition* when you consider *Given the force of the explosion, it's a miracle they survived.*

given³ /ˈgɪvᵊn/ *past participle of* give

glacial /ˈgleɪsiəl/ (US) /ˈgleɪʃᵊl/ *adjective* [**always before noun**] relating to glaciers or ice *glacial lakes*

glaciation /ˌgleɪsiˈeɪʃᵊn/ *noun* [U] **GEOGRAPHY** when land becomes covered with glaciers

glacier /ˈglæsiəʳ/ (US) /ˈgleɪʃər/ *noun* [C] **GEOGRAPHY** a large mass of ice that moves very slowly, usually down a slope or valley

O‑ **glad** /glæd/ *adjective* [**never before noun**] **1** HAPPY happy about something [+ **(that)**] *She's very glad that she left.* [+ **to do sth**] *I'm so glad to see you.* **2** WILLING very willing to do something [+ **to do sth**] *She's always glad to help.* **3 be glad of sth** *formal* to be grateful for something *I was glad of a few days off before going back to work.*

gladly /ˈglædli/ *adverb* willingly or happily *I would gladly pay extra for better service.*

glamorize (*also UK* **-ise**) /ˈglæmᵊraɪz/ *verb* [T] to make something seem glamorous

glamorous /ˈglæmᵊrəs/ *adjective* attractive in an exciting and special way *a glamorous woman* ○ *a glamorous lifestyle*

glamour (*also US* **glamor**) /ˈglæməʳ/ *noun* [U] the quality of being attractive, exciting and special *the glamour of Hollywood*

glance¹ /glɑːns/ *verb* **1 glance at/around/towards, etc** to look somewhere for a short time *He glanced at his watch.* **2 glance at/over/through, etc** to read something quickly *She glanced through the newspaper.*

WORD PARTNERS FOR ***glance***

cast/give/have a glance [at/around, etc] sb/sth • **exchange** glances • a **cursory/quick** glance

glance² /glɑːns/ *noun* **1** [C] a quick look *She* ***had a quick glance*** *around the restaurant.* **2 at a glance** If you see something at a glance, you see it very quickly or immediately.

gland /glænd/ *noun* [C] **ANATOMY, BIOLOGY** an organ in the body that produces a particular chemical substance or liquid

glandular fever /ˌglændjʊləˈfiːvəʳ/ *UK* (*US* **mononucleosis**) *noun* [U] **HEALTH** an infectious disease that makes your glands swell and makes you feel tired

glare¹ /gleəʳ/ *noun* **1** LIGHT [U] strong, bright light that hurts your eyes *I get a lot of glare from my computer screen.* **2** LOOK [C] a long, angry look **3 the glare of publicity/the media, etc** when someone gets too much attention from newspapers and television

glare² /gleəʳ/ *verb* [I] to look at someone in an angry way

glaring /ˈgleərɪŋ/ *adjective* **1 a glaring error/mistake/omission, etc** a very noticeable mistake or problem **2 glaring light/sun, etc** light which is too strong and bright

glasnost /ˈglæsnɒst/ *noun* [U] **POLITICS** a government policy of greater political freedom and information, especially in the former Soviet Union

WORD PARTNERS FOR ***glass***

a **pane/sheet** of glass • **broken** glass

O‑ **glass** /glɑːs/ *noun* **1** SUBSTANCE [U] a hard, transparent substance that objects such as windows and bottles are made of ***broken glass*** ○ *glass jars* **2** DRINKING CONTAINER [C] a container made of glass that is used for drinking *Would you like* ***a glass of*** *water?* ➲See also: **magnifying glass, stained glass**

glasses /ˈglɑːsɪz/ *noun* [**plural**] **HEALTH** a piece of equipment with two transparent parts that you wear in front of your eyes to help you see better *a* ***pair of glasses*** ○ *She was* ***wearing glasses.***

glassy /ˈglɑːsi/ *adjective* **1** SURFACE A glassy surface is smooth and shiny like glass. **2** EYES Glassy eyes show no expression and seem not to see anything.

glaze¹ /gleɪz/ *verb* **1** EYES [I] (*also* **glaze over**) If someone's eyes glaze or glaze over, they stop showing any interest or expression because they are bored or tired. **2 ART** [T] to cover the surface of objects made of clay with a liquid that makes them hard and shiny when they are baked **3 FOOD** [T] to put a liquid on food to make it shiny and more attractive **4** GLASS [T] to put glass in a window or door

glaze² /gleɪz/ *noun* [C, U] **1 ART** a liquid that is put on objects made of clay to make them hard and shiny when they are baked **2 FOOD** a liquid that is put on food to make it shiny and attractive

gleam¹ /gliːm/ *verb* [I] to shine in a pleasant, soft way *a gleaming new car*

gleam² /gliːm/ *noun* [**no plural**] **1** LIGHT when something shines in a pleasant, soft way *the gleam of sunlight on the frozen lake* **2** EXPRESSION an expression in someone's eyes *She had a strange gleam in her eye.*

glean /gliːn/ *verb* [T] to discover information slowly or with difficulty [**often passive**] *Some useful information can be* ***gleaned from*** *this study.*

glee /gliː/ *noun* [U] a feeling of great happiness, usually because of your good luck or someone else's bad luck *Rosa began laughing with glee.* •**gleeful** *adjective* •**gleefully** *adverb*

glib /glɪb/ *adjective* using words in a way that is clever and confident, but not sincere

glide /glaɪd/ *verb* **glide along/into/over, etc** to move somewhere smoothly and quietly *The train slowly glided out of the station.*

glider /ˈglaɪdəʳ/ *noun* [C] an aircraft that has no engine and flies on air currents •**gliding** *noun*

[U] the activity of flying in a glider ⊃See also: **hang glider, hang gliding**

glimmer¹ /ˈglɪməʳ/ *noun* **1 a glimmer of happiness/hope, etc** a small sign of something good **2** [C] when a light shines in a weak way

glimmer² /ˈglɪməʳ/ *verb* [I] to shine in a weak way

WORD PARTNERS FOR ***glimpse***

catch/get a glimpse • a **brief/fleeting** glimpse • a glimpse **of** sb/sth

glimpse /glɪms/ *noun* [C] when you see something or someone for a very short time *He **caught/got a glimpse of** her as she got into the car.* •**glimpse** *verb* [T] to see something or someone for a very short time *She glimpsed him out of the corner of her eye.*

G

glint /glɪnt/ *noun* [no plural] **1** EYE when your eyes shine with excitement or because you are going to do something bad *She had a wicked glint in her eye.* **2** LIGHT when something shines or reflects light for a short time •**glint** *verb* [I]

glisten /ˈglɪsᵊn/ *verb* [I] If something glistens, it shines, often because it is wet. *Their faces were **glistening with** sweat.*

glitch /glɪtʃ/ *noun* [C] *informal* a mistake or problem that stops something from working correctly ***technical glitches***

glitter¹ /ˈglɪtəʳ/ *verb* [I] to shine with small flashes of light *Snow glittered on the mountains.*

glitter² /ˈglɪtəʳ/ *noun* [U] **1** SUBSTANCE very small, shiny pieces of metal used for decoration **2** EXCITEMENT when something seems exciting and attractive

glittering /ˈglɪtᵊrɪŋ/ *adjective* **1** SHINY shining with small flashes of light *glittering jewels* **2** EXCITING successful and exciting *a glittering party/career*

glitz /glɪts/ *noun* [U] when something is attractive, exciting and shows money in an obvious way •**glitzy** *adjective a glitzy nightclub*

gloat /gləʊt/ *verb* [I] to show pleasure at your success or at someone else's failure *His enemies were **gloating over** his defeat.*

global /ˈgləʊbᵊl/ *adjective* relating to the whole world *the global problem of nuclear waste* •**globally** *adverb*

globalization /ˌgləʊbᵊlaɪˈzeɪʃᵊn/ *noun* [U] **1** ECONOMICS the increase of business around the world, especially by big companies operating in many countries **2** when things all over the world become more similar *the globalization of fashion*

ˌglobal ˈwarming *noun* [U] ENVIRONMENT when the air around the world becomes warmer because of pollution

globe /gləʊb/ *noun* **1 the globe** the world *This event is being watched by 200 million people around the globe.* **2** [C] a model of the world shaped like a ball with a map of all the countries on it

globule /ˈglɒbjuːl/ *noun* [C] a small, round mass or lump of a liquid substance *a globule of oil*

gloom /gluːm/ *noun* [U] **1** UNHAPPINESS a feeling of unhappiness and of not having any hope *an atmosphere of gloom* **2** DARK when it is dark, but not completely dark

gloomy /ˈgluːmi/ *adjective* **1** NEGATIVE very negative about a situation *a gloomy report* **2** DARK dark in an unpleasant way *a small, gloomy room* **3** UNHAPPY unhappy and without hope *a gloomy face* •**gloomily** *adverb*

glorify /ˈglɔːrɪfaɪ/ *verb* [T] **1** MAKE BETTER to describe or represent something in a way that makes it seem better or more important than it really is *films that glorify violence* **2** PRAISE to praise someone, especially God

glorious /ˈglɔːriəs/ *adjective* **1** BEAUTIFUL beautiful or wonderful *We had four days of glorious sunshine.* ○ *glorious colours* **2** DESERVING PRAISE deserving praise and respect *a glorious career* •**gloriously** *adverb*

glory¹ /ˈglɔːri/ *noun* [U] **1** PRAISE when people praise and respect you for achieving something important **2** GREAT BEAUTY great beauty *The castle has been restored to its **former glory**.*

glory² /ˈglɔːri/ *verb*

glory in sth *phrasal verb* to enjoy something and be very proud of it

gloss¹ /glɒs/ *noun* **1** PAINT [U] paint that creates a shiny surface **2** SHINE [U] shine on a surface **3** EXPLANATION [C] a short explanation of a word or phrase in a text

gloss² /glɒs/ *verb* [T] to give a short explanation of a word or phrase

gloss over sth *phrasal verb* to avoid discussing something, or to discuss something without any details in order to make it seem unimportant

glossary /ˈglɒsᵊri/ *noun* [C] LANGUAGE a list of difficult words with their meanings like a small dictionary, especially at the end of a book

glossy /ˈglɒsi/ *adjective* **1** SMOOTH smooth and shiny *glossy hair* **2** PAPER Glossy magazines and pictures are printed on shiny paper.

glottis /ˈglɒtɪs/ *noun* [C] ANATOMY, BIOLOGY the part of the throat that contains the vocal cords (= muscles that make the voice) and the opening between the vocal cords

glove /glʌv/ *noun* [C] a piece of clothing which covers your fingers and hand *a pair of gloves* ⊃See colour picture **Clothes** on page Centre 9

ˈglove comˌpartment (also **glove box**) *noun* [C] a small cupboard in the front of a car, used to hold small things

glow¹ /gləʊ/ *noun* [no plural] **1** LIGHT a soft, warm light *the warm glow of the moon* **2** HEALTH when your face feels or appears warm and healthy *Sam's face had lost its rosy glow.* **3 a glow of happiness/pride, etc** a strong feeling of being happy/proud, etc

glow² /gləʊ/ *verb* [I] **1** PRODUCE LIGHT to produce a soft, warm light *toys which glow in the dark* **2** LOOK HEALTHY to have a warm and healthy appearance *Her eyes were bright and her cheeks were glowing.* **3 glow with happiness/pride, etc** to feel very happy, proud, etc *Glowing with pride, she showed me her painting.*

glower /glaʊəʳ/ *verb* [I] to look at someone in a very angry way *The woman glowered at her husband.*

WORD PARTNERS FOR ***glowing***

a glowing **reference/report/tribute** • **in** glowing terms

glowing /ˈgləʊɪŋ/ *adjective* praising someone a lot *She got a* ***glowing report*** *from her teacher.*

glucagon /ˈgluːkəgɒn/ *noun* [U] **BIOLOGY** a hormone produced in the pancreas that helps glucose (= a type of sugar) to get into the blood

glucose /ˈgluːkəʊs/ *noun* [U] **CHEMISTRY, BIOLOGY** a type of sugar

glue¹ /gluː/ *noun* [U] a substance used to stick things together *Put a bit of glue on both edges and hold them together.* ➲See colour picture **The Classroom** on page Centre 6

glue² /gluː/ *verb* [T] **glueing** or **gluing**, *past* **glued** to stick something to something else with glue *Do you think you can* ***glue*** *this vase back* ***together?***

be glued to sth *phrasal verb* to be watching something, especially television *The kids were glued to the TV all morning.*

glum /glʌm/ *adjective* unhappy *Why are you looking so glum today?* •**glumly** *adverb*

glut /glʌt/ *noun* [C] **ECONOMICS** more of something than is needed [**usually singular**] *There is* ***a glut of*** *houses for sale in this area.*

gluten /ˈgluːtᵊn / *noun* [U] **FOOD** a substance which is found in wheat and some other food. Some people become ill if they eat it. *a gluten-free diet*

glutton /ˈglʌtᵊn/ *noun* **1** [C] someone who eats too much **2 be a glutton for punishment** to enjoy doing things that are unpleasant or difficult

gluttony /ˈglʌtᵊni/ *noun* [U] when someone eats too much

glycerol /ˈglɪsᵊrɒl/ (*also* **glycerine**) *noun* [U] **CHEMISTRY** a clear, thick liquid which is used in making many things, including explosives and medicines

glycogen /ˈglaɪkəʊdʒən/ *noun* [U] **BIOLOGY** a substance that is found in the liver and the muscles, which stores carbohydrate (= substance which gives energy) and helps to control the level of sugar in the blood

gm MEASURES *written abbreviation for* gram (= a unit for measuring weight)

GM /dʒiːˈem/ *adjective* **BIOLOGY** *abbreviation for* genetically modified: genetically modified plants or animals have had some of their genes (= parts of cells which control particular characteristics) changed. ***GM foods***

GMO /ˌdʒiːemˈəʊ/ *noun* [U] **BIOLOGY** *abbreviation for* genetically modified organism: a plant or animal in which scientists have changed the genes (= parts of cells which control particular characteristics)

GMT /ˌdʒiːemˈtiː/ *noun* [U] *abbreviation for* Greenwich Mean Time: the time at Greenwich in London, which is used as an international measurement for time

gnarled /nɑːld/ *adjective* rough and twisted, usually because of being old *a gnarled tree trunk*

gnat /næt/ *noun* [C] a small flying insect that can bite you

gnaw /nɔː/ *verb* [I, T] to bite something with a lot of small bites *He was gnawing on a bone.*

gnaw at sb *phrasal verb* to make someone feel more and more anxious or annoyed *Doubt kept gnawing at him.*

gneiss /naɪs/ *noun* [U] **GEOLOGY** a type of rock formed deep under the ground by high temperature and high pressure

gnome /nəʊm/ *noun* [C] an imaginary little man with a pointed hat *a garden gnome*

GNP /ˌdʒiːenˈpiː/ *noun* [U] **ECONOMICS** *abbreviation for* gross national product: the total value of goods and services produced in a country in a year, including the profits made in foreign countries ➲Compare **GDP**

O-★**go¹** /gəʊ/ *verb* [I] **going**, *past tense* **went**, *past participle* **gone 1** MOVE to move or travel somewhere *I'd love to go to America.* ○ *We went into the house.* ○ *Are you* ***going by*** *train?* **2** DO SOMETHING to move or travel somewhere in order to do something *Let's* ***go for*** *a walk.* [**+ doing sth**] *We're going camping tomorrow.* **3** DISAPPEAR to disappear or no longer exist *When I turned round the man had gone.* **4 go badly/well, etc** to develop in a particular way *My exams went really badly.* **5** CONTINUE to continue to be in a particular state *We won't let anyone go hungry.* **6** WORKING to work correctly *Did you manage to get the car going?* **7** STOP WORKING to stop working correctly *Her hearing is going, so speak loudly.* **8** MATCH If two things go, they match each other. *That jumper doesn't* ***go with*** *those trousers.* **9** TIME If time goes, it passes. *The day went very quickly.* **10** SONG to have a particular tune or words *I can't remember how it goes.* **11** SOUND/MOVEMENT to make a particular sound or movement *My dog goes like this when he wants some food.* **12 not go there** to not think or talk about a subject that makes you feel bad *"Then there's the guilt I feel about leaving my child with another woman." "Don't even go there!"*

COMMON LEARNER ERROR

go, gone, and **been**

Gone is the usual past participle of the verb **go**. Sometimes you use the past participle **been** when you want to say that you have gone somewhere and come back, or to say that you have visited somewhere.

Paul has gone to the hospital this morning (= he is still there).

Paul has been to the hospital this morning (= he went and has come back).

He has gone to New York (= he is still there).

Have you ever been to New York? (= Have you ever visited New York?)

go about sth *phrasal verb* to start to do something or deal with something *What's the best way to go about this?*

G

go after sb *phrasal verb* to chase or follow someone in order to catch them *He ran away, but the police went after him.*
go against sth *phrasal verb* If something goes against a rule or something you believe in, it does not obey it or agree with it. *It goes against my principles to lie.*
go against sb *phrasal verb* If a decision or vote goes against someone, they do not get the result that they needed. *The judge's decision went against us.*
go ahead *phrasal verb* **1** [START] to start to do something *We have permission to go ahead with the project.* **2** [PERMISSION] something that you say to someone to give them permission to do something *"Can I borrow your book?" "Yes, go ahead."* •**go-ahead** *noun* ***get/give the go-ahead***
G
go along *phrasal verb* **1** [GO SOMEWHERE] *UK* to go to a place or event, usually without much planning *I might go along to the party after work.* **2** [CONTINUE] to continue doing something *I'll tell you the rules as we go along.*
go along with sth/sb *phrasal verb* to support an idea, or to agree with someone's opinion *She'll never go along with this idea.*
go around *phrasal verb* (*also UK* **go round**) **1** to be enough for everyone in a group *There aren't enough chairs to go around.* **2 go around doing sth** to spend your time behaving badly or doing something that is unpleasant for other people *She's been going around telling people I'm stupid.*
go at sth *phrasal verb UK informal* to start doing something with a lot of energy and enthusiasm *There were a lot of dishes to wash so we went at it straight away.*
go away *phrasal verb* **1** [LEAVE] to leave a place *Go away - I'm busy.* **2** [HOLIDAY] to leave your home in order to spend time in a different place, usually for a holiday *They're going away for a few weeks in the summer.* **3** [DISAPPEAR] to disappear *That smell seems to have gone away.*
go back *phrasal verb* to return to a place where you were or where you have been before *When are you going back to London?*
go back on sth *phrasal verb* to not do something that you promised you would do *I never go back on my word* (= not do what I said I would do).
go back to sb *phrasal verb* to start a relationship again with a person who you had a romantic relationship with in the past *Jim's gone back to his ex-wife.*
go back to sth *phrasal verb* to start doing something again that you were doing before *It's time to go back to work now.*
go by *phrasal verb* **1** [TIME] If time goes by, it passes. *The days went by really slowly.* **2** [MOVE PAST] to move past *A green sports car went by.*
go by sth *phrasal verb* to use information about something to help you make a decision about the best thing to do *You can't go by anything she says.*
go down *phrasal verb* **1** [BECOME LESS] to become lower in level *Interest rates are going down at the moment.* **2** [SUN] When the sun goes down, it moves down in the sky until it cannot be seen any more. **3 COMPUTING** If a computer goes down, it stops working. **4** [REMEMBER] to be considered or remembered in a particular way *This will **go down as** one of the most exciting soccer matches ever played.* ○ *UK I don't think my plan will go down well at all.*
go down with sth *phrasal verb UK informal* **HEALTH** to become ill, usually with an illness that is not very serious *Our whole class went down with the flu.*
go for sth *phrasal verb* **1** [CHOOSE] to choose something *What sort of printer are you going to go for?* **2** [HAVE] *informal* to try to have or achieve something *He'll be going for his third straight Olympic gold medal in the 200-meter dash.* ○ *If you want it, go for it* (= do what you need to do in order to have or achieve it). **3** [GET] to try to get something *He tripped as he was going for the ball.* **4** [MONEY] If something goes for a particular amount of money, it is sold for that amount.
go for sb *phrasal verb* to attack someone *He suddenly went for me with a knife.*
go in *phrasal verb* to enter a place *I looked through the window, but I didn't actually go in.*
go in for sth *phrasal verb* to like a particular activity *I don't really go in for sports.*
go into sth *phrasal verb* **1** [START] to start to do a particular type of work *What made you decide to go into politics?* **2** [DESCRIBE] to describe, discuss, or examine something in a detailed way *She didn't go into any detail about the job.* **3** [BE USED] If an amount of time, money, or effort goes into a product or activity, it is used or spent creating that product or doing that activity. *A lot of effort has gone into producing this play.*
go off *phrasal verb* **1** [LEAVE] to leave a place and go somewhere else *She's gone off to the pub with Tony.* **2** [FOOD] *UK informal* If food goes off, it is not good to eat any more because it is too old. **3** [STOP] If a light or machine goes off, it stops working. *The heating goes off at 10 o'clock.* **4** [EXPLODE] If a bomb or gun goes off, it explodes or fires. **5** [MAKE NOISE] If something that makes a noise goes off, it suddenly starts making a noise. *His car alarm goes off every time it rains.* **6 go off on one** *informal* to react angrily to something
go off sb/sth *phrasal verb UK* to stop liking someone or something *I've gone off fish recently.*
go on *phrasal verb* **1** [LAST] to last for a particular period of time *The film seemed to go on forever.* **2** [CONTINUE] to continue doing something [+ **doing sth**] *We can't go on living like this.* **3 go on to do sth** to do something else in the future *He went on to win the final.* **4** [HAPPEN] to happen *What's going on?* **5** [TALK] *UK* to talk in an annoying way about something for a long time *I wish she'd stop **going on about** her boyfriend.* **6** [TALK AGAIN] to start talking again after stopping for a short time *He paused and then went on with his story.* **7 Go on** *informal* something that you say to encourage someone to do something *Go on, what happened next?*
go on sth *phrasal verb* to use a piece of information to help you discover or understand something *Her first name was all we had to go on.*
go out *phrasal verb* **1** [LEAVE] to leave a place in order to go somewhere else *Are you going out tonight?* **2** [LIGHT/FIRE] If a light or something that

is burning goes out, it stops producing light or heat. *It took ages for the fire to go out.* **3** RELATIONSHIP If two people go out together, they have a romantic relationship with each other. *I've been **going out with** him for a year.*

go over *phrasal verb US* to be thought of in a particular way *I wonder how my speech will go over this afternoon.*

go over sth *phrasal verb* to talk or think about something in order to explain it or make certain that it is correct *Let's go over the plan one more time.*

go round *phrasal verb UK* (*UK/US* **go around**) **1** to be enough for everyone in a group *There aren't enough chairs to go round.* **2 go round doing sth** to spend your time behaving badly or doing something that is unpleasant for other people *She's been going round telling people I'm stupid.*

go through sth *phrasal verb* **1** EXPERIENCE to experience a difficult or unpleasant situation *She's going through a difficult time with her job.* **2** EXAMINE to carefully examine the contents of something or a collection of things in order to find something *A customs officer went through my suitcase.* **3** USE to use a lot of something *I've gone through two boxes of tissues this week.*

go through *phrasal verb* If a law, plan, or deal goes through, it is officially accepted or approved.

go through with sth *phrasal verb* to do something unpleasant or difficult that you have planned or promised to do *He was too scared to go through with the operation.*

go under *phrasal verb* If a company or business goes under, it fails financially.

go up *phrasal verb* **1** INCREASE to become higher in level *House **prices** keep **going up**.* **2** BE FIXED If a building or sign goes up, it is fixed into position. **3** EXPLODE to suddenly explode *There was a loud bang, and then the building **went up in flames**.*

go without (sth) *phrasal verb* to not have something that you usually have *They went without food for four days.*

go² /gəʊ/ *noun* [C] *plural* **goes 1** TRY *UK* when someone tries to do something *I **had a go at** catching a fish.* ○ *If you think you might like skiing, why don't you **give it a go*** (= try to do it)*?* **2** TURN *mainly UK* someone's turn to do something *Throw the dice Jane, it's your go.* **3 have a go at sb** *UK* to criticize someone angrily *My mother's always having a go at me about my hair.* **4 make a go of sth** to try to make something succeed, usually by working hard

goad /gəʊd/ *verb* [T] to make someone angry or annoyed so that they react in the way that you want [+ **into** + **doing sth**] *They tried to goad us into attacking the police.*

WORD PARTNERS FOR ***goal***

1 **score** a goal • the **winning** goal
3 **set yourself** a goal • **achieve** a goal

O‑ **goal** /gəʊl/ *noun* [C] **1** SPORT a point scored in sports such as football when a player sends a ball or other object into a particular area, such as between two posts *He **scored** two **goals** in the second half.* **2** SPORT in some sports, the area between two posts where players try to send the ball ➲See colour picture **Sports 2** on page Centre 15 **3** something you want to do successfully in the future *Andy's goal is to run in the New York Marathon.*

goalie /ˈgəʊli/ *noun* [C] SPORT *informal short for* goalkeeper

goalkeeper /ˈgəʊlˌkiːpəʳ/ (*also US* **goaltender** /ˈgəʊlˌtendəʳ/) *noun* [C] SPORT the player in a sport such as football who tries to stop the ball going into the goal ➲See colour picture **Sports 2** on page Centre 15

goalpost /ˈgəʊlpəʊst/ *noun* [C] SPORT either of the two posts that are each side of the area where goals are scored in sports such as football ➲See colour picture **Sports 2** on page Centre 15

goat /gəʊt/ *noun* [C] an animal with horns which is kept for the milk it produces

gobble /ˈgɒbl/ (*also* **gobble up/down**) *verb* [T] *informal* to eat food very quickly

gobbledygook (*also* **gobbledegook**) /ˈgɒbldiˌguːk/ *noun* [U] LANGUAGE *informal* nonsense or very complicated language that you cannot understand

go-between /ˈgəʊbɪˌtwiːn/ *noun* [C] someone who talks and gives messages to people who will not or cannot talk to each other

goblet cell /ˈgɒblətˌsel/ *noun* [C] BIOLOGY a simple cell that produces mucus (= thick liquid produced by the body)

goblin /ˈgɒblɪn/ *noun* [C] a short, ugly, imaginary creature who behaves badly

go-cart (*also UK* **go-kart**) /ˈgəʊkɑːt/ *noun* [C] SPORT a small, low racing car with no roof or windows

O‑ **god** /gɒd/ *noun* **1 God** RELIGION in Jewish, Christian, or Muslim belief, the spirit who created the universe and everything in it, and who rules over it **2** RELIGION [C] a spirit, especially a male one, that people pray to and who has control over parts of the world or nature *the ancient Greek gods and goddesses* **3 (Oh) (my) God!** *informal* used to emphasize how surprised, angry, shocked, etc you are *Oh my God! The car has been stolen.* **4 thank God** *informal* something you say when you are happy because something bad did not happen

godchild /ˈgɒdtʃaɪld/ *noun* [C] *plural* **godchildren** RELIGION a child who has godparents (= people who take responsibility for the child's moral and religious development)

goddess /ˈgɒdes/ *noun* [C] RELIGION a female spirit that people pray to and who has control over parts of the world or nature

godfather /ˈgɒdfɑːðəʳ/ *noun* [C] RELIGION a man who is responsible for the moral and religious development of another person's child

godforsaken /ˈgɒdfəˌseɪkᵊn/ *adjective* [**always before noun**] *informal* A godforsaken place is very unpleasant and usually far from other places.

godlike /ˈgɒdlaɪk/ *adjective* having qualities that make someone admired and respected as if they were a god or God

godmother /ˈgɒdˌmʌðəʳ/ *noun* [C] RELIGION a woman who is responsible for the moral and

G

religious development of another person's child

godparent /ˈgɒdˌpeərᵊnt/ *noun* [C] **RELIGION** a person who is responsible for the moral and religious development of another person's child

godsend /ˈgɒdsend/ *noun* [**no plural**] something good which happens unexpectedly, usually when you really need it *The lottery win was a godsend for her.*

goes /gəʊz/ *present simple he/she/it of* go

goggles /ˈgɒglz/ *noun* [**plural**] special glasses which fit close to your face to protect your eyes ***a pair of goggles*** ➲See colour picture **Sports 1** on page Centre 14

WORD PARTNERS FOR ***going***

hard/heavy/slow/tough going

going¹ /ˈgəʊɪŋ/ *noun* **1** DIFFICULTY [U] how easy or difficult something is *I found the exam quite **hard going**.* **2** GROUND [U] the condition of the ground for walking, riding, etc **3** LEAVING [**no plural**] when someone leaves somewhere *His going came as a big surprise.*

going² /ˈgəʊɪŋ/ *adjective* **the going price/rate, etc** the usual amount of money you would expect to pay for something *What's the going rate for babysitting these days?* ➲See also: **easy-going**

going³ /ˈgəʊɪŋ/ *present participle of* go

ˌgoing conˈcern *noun* [C] a business that is able to continue successfully *He sold the business **as a going concern**.*

goings-on /ˌgəʊɪŋzˈɒn/ *noun* [**plural**] *informal* unusual events or activities ***strange goings-on***

go-kart /ˈgəʊkɑːt/ *noun* [C] **SPORT** *another UK spelling of* go-cart (= a small, low racing car with no roof or windows)

gold¹ /gəʊld/ *noun* **1** **CHEMISTRY** [U] a valuable, shiny, yellow metal used to make coins and jewellery (symbol **Au**) **2** [C, U] a gold medal (= a small, round disc given to someone for winning a race or competition)

gold² /gəʊld/ *adjective* **1** METAL made of gold *gold coins* **2** COLOUR being the colour of gold *gold paint*

golden /ˈgəʊldᵊn/ *adjective* **1** COLOUR being a bright yellow colour *bright golden hair* **2** METAL *literary* made of gold or like gold *a golden ring* **3 a golden opportunity** a very exciting and valuable opportunity

ˌgolden ˈwedding *noun* [C] the day when two people have been married for 50 years

goldfish /ˈgəʊldfɪʃ/ *noun* [C] *plural* **goldfish** or **goldfishes** a small, orange fish that is often kept as a pet

ˌgold ˈmedal *noun* [C] a small, round disc given to someone for winning a race or competition *to win an Olympic gold medal*

ˈgold ˌmine *noun* [C] **1** GOLD a place where gold is taken from the ground **2** MONEY something that provides you with a lot of money

golf /gɒlf/ *noun* [U] **SPORT** a game on grass where players try to hit a small ball into a series of holes using a long, thin stick •**golfer** *noun* [C] ➲See colour picture **Sports 2** on page Centre 15

ˈgolf ˌball *noun* [C] **SPORT** a small hard white ball used for playing golf

ˈgolf ˌclub *noun* [C] **1 SPORT** a place where people can play golf **2 SPORT** a long, thin stick used to play golf ➲See colour picture **Sports 2** on page Centre 15

ˈgolf ˌcourse *noun* [C] **SPORT** an area of land used for playing golf

gone /gɒn/ *past participle of* go

gong /gɒŋ/ *noun* [C] a metal disc which makes a loud sound when you hit it with a stick

gonna /ˈgᵊnə/ *informal short for* going to

goo /guː/ *noun* [U] a thick, sticky substance

good¹ /gʊd/ *adjective* **better**, **best** **1** PLEASANT enjoyable, pleasant, or interesting *a good book* ○ *Did you have a **good time** at the party?* **2** HIGH QUALITY of a high quality or level *She speaks good French.* ○ *The food at this restaurant is very good.* **3** SUCCESSFUL successful, or able to do something well *Anne's a good cook.* ○ *She's very **good at** geography.* **4** KIND kind or helpful *a good friend* ○ *My granddaughter is very **good to** me.* **5** HEALTHY something that you say when a person asks how you are *'Hi, how are you?' 'I'm good, thanks.'* **6** POSITIVE having a positive or useful effect *Exercise is **good for** you.* **7** SUITABLE suitable or satisfactory *When would be a **good time** to phone?* **8** BEHAVIOUR A good child or animal behaves well. **9** MORALLY RIGHT morally right *a good person* ○ *He sets a **good example** to the rest of the class.* **10** COMPLETE complete and detailed *She got a good look at the robbers.* **11** LARGE used to emphasize the number, amount, quality, etc of something *There's a **good chance** he'll pass the exam.* **12** SATISFACTION something you say when you are satisfied or pleased about something or when you agree with something *Oh good, he's arrived at last.* **13 Good God/grief/heavens!, etc** used to express surprise or shock *Good heavens! It's already 11 p.m.* **14 a good 20 minutes/30 miles, etc** not less than 20 minutes/30 miles, etc and probably a bit more ➲See also: be in sb's good/bad books (**book¹**), it's a good **job**, for good **measure²**, stand sb in good **stead** **15 good to go** *informal* be ready to go *I'll get my coat and then I'm good to go.*

COMMON LEARNER ERROR

good or **well?**

Good is an adjective and is used to describe nouns.

*She's a **good** cook.*

*Her children had a **good** education.*

Well is an adverb and is used to describe verbs.

*She cooks **well**.*

*Her children were **well** educated.*

good² /gʊd/ *noun* **1** ADVANTAGE [U] something that is an advantage or help to a person or situation *It's hard work, but it's for your own good.* **2 be no good/not any good** to not be useful, helpful, or valuable **3 do sb good** to be useful or helpful to someone *A holiday will do you good.* **4** MORALLY RIGHT [U] what people think is morally right *Children don't always understand the difference between* ***good and bad.*** **5 for good** forever *When he was 20, he left home for good.* ➲See also: do sb a/the **world**[1] of good

ˌ**good afterˈnoon** *exclamation* something you say to greet someone when you meet them in the afternoon

WORD PARTNERS FOR ***goodbye***

kiss/say/wave goodbye • a **final** goodbye

O-■ **goodbye** /gʊdˈbaɪ/ *exclamation* something you say when you leave someone or when they leave you *Goodbye Vicki! See you next week.*

ˌ**good ˈevening** *exclamation* something you say to greet someone in the evening

ˌ**Good ˈFriday** *noun* [C, U] **RELIGION** the Friday before Easter (= a Christian holiday), a day when Christians remember the death of Jesus Christ

good-humoured *UK* (*US* **good-humored**) /ˌgʊdˈhjuːməd/ *adjective* pleasant and friendly

goodies /ˈgʊdiz/ *noun* [plural] *informal* special or nice things that you will enjoy *She gave the children some sweets and other goodies.*

good-looking /ˌgʊdˈlʊkɪŋ/ *adjective* If someone is good-looking, they have an attractive face. *a good-looking woman*

ˌ**good ˈlooks** *noun* [plural] an attractive face

O-■ ˌ**good ˈmorning** *exclamation* something you say to greet someone when you meet them in the morning

good-natured /ˌgʊdˈneɪtʃəd/ *adjective* pleasant and friendly *a good-natured smile/crowd*

goodness /ˈgʊdnəs/ *noun* **1** [U] the quality of being good *She believes in the goodness of human nature.* **2 my goodness** *informal* something you say when you are surprised *My goodness, he's a big baby, isn't he?* **3 thank goodness** *informal* something you say when you are happy because something bad did not happen *Thank goodness that dog didn't bite you.* **4 for goodness sake** used when you are annoyed or when you want something to happen quickly *For goodness sake, come in out of the rain.*

O-■ ˌ**good ˈnight** *exclamation* something you say when you leave someone or when they leave you in the evening or when someone is going to bed

O-■ **goods** /gʊdz/ *noun* **1** [plural] items which are made to be sold *radios, stereos and other electrical goods* **2 deliver/come up with the goods** If you deliver the goods, you do what people hope you will do.

goodwill /gʊdˈwɪl/ *noun* [U] **1** kind, friendly, or helpful feelings towards other people *He gave them a thousand pounds as a* ***gesture of goodwill.*** **2 FINANCE** the positive feelings of customers for a business, which has a money value if a business is sold

goody-goody /ˈgʊdiˌgʊdi/ *noun* [C] *informal* someone who tries too hard to be good, usually to parents or teachers

gooey /ˈguːi/ *adjective* soft and sticky *a sweet, gooey sauce*

goof /guːf/ (*also* **goof up**) *verb* [I] *US informal* to make a silly mistake
goof around *phrasal verb US* to spend your time doing silly or unimportant things
goof off *phrasal verb US* to avoid doing any work

goofy /ˈguːfi/ *adjective mainly US* silly *a goofy sense of humour*

Google[1] /ˈguːgl/ *noun trademark* **INTERNET** a popular Internet search engine (= a computer program which finds things on the Internet by looking for words which you have typed in)

Google[2] /ˈguːgl/ *verb* [T] to use the Google® search engine

goose /guːs/ *noun* [C, U] *plural* **geese** a large water bird similar to a duck, or the meat from this bird

gooseberry /ˈgʊzbᵊri/ (US) /ˈguːsberi/ *noun* [C] **FOOD** a small, sour, green fruit with a hairy skin

ˈ**goose ˌpimples** (*also* ˈ**gooseˌbumps**) *noun* [plural] small, raised lumps that appear on your skin when you are cold or frightened

gore[1] /gɔːʳ/ *noun* [U] blood, usually from a violent injury

gore[2] /gɔːʳ/ *verb* [T] If an animal gores someone, it injures them with its horn.

gorge[1] /gɔːdʒ/ *noun* [C] **GEOGRAPHY** a narrow and usually steep valley

gorge[2] /gɔːdʒ/ *verb* **gorge (yourself) on sth** to eat food until you cannot eat any more *She gorged herself on chocolate biscuits.*

gorgeous /ˈgɔːdʒəs/ *adjective* very beautiful or pleasant *You look gorgeous in that dress.*

gorilla /gəˈrɪlə/ *noun* [C] a big, black, hairy animal, like a large monkey

gorse /gɔːs/ *noun* [U] a bush with yellow flowers and sharp, pointed leaves

gory /ˈgɔːri/ *adjective* involving violence and blood *a gory murder*

gosh /gɒʃ/ *exclamation* used to express surprise or shock *Gosh! I didn't realize it was that late.*

gosling /ˈgɒzlɪŋ/ *noun* [C] a young goose (= large water bird)

gospel /ˈgɒspᵊl/ *noun* **1 RELIGION** [no plural] the teachings of Jesus Christ *to* ***preach the gospel*** **2 RELIGION** [C] one of the four books in the Bible that tells the life of Jesus Christ **3 the gospel truth** something that is completely true **4 MUSIC** [U] a style of Christian music, originally sung by black Americans

WORD PARTNERS FOR ***gossip***

a bit of/piece of gossip • **juicy** gossip

gossip[1] /ˈgɒsɪp/ *noun* **1** [CONVERSATION] [U] conversation or reports about other people's private lives that might or might not be true *an interesting* ***piece of gossip*** **2** [PERSON] [C] someone who likes to talk about other people's private lives

gossip[2] /ˈgɒsɪp/ *verb* [I] to talk about other people's private lives *They were* ***gossiping about*** *her boss.*

G

ˈgossip ˌcolumn *noun* [C] an article appearing regularly in a newspaper giving information about famous people's private lives

got /gɒt/ *past of* get

gotta /ˈgɒtə/ *informal short for* got to

gotten /ˈgɒtᵊn/ *US past participle of* get

gouge /gaʊdʒ/ *verb* [T] to make a hole or long cut in something
gouge sth out *phrasal verb* to remove something by digging or cutting it out of a surface, often violently

gourmet¹ /ˈgʊəmeɪ/ *noun* [C] **FOOD** someone who enjoys good food and drink and knows a lot about it

gourmet² /ˈgʊəmeɪ/ *adjective* [**always before noun**] **FOOD** relating to good food and drink *a gourmet meal*

G

govern /ˈgʌvᵊn/ *verb* **1 POLITICS** [I, T] to officially control a country *The country is now governed by the Labour Party.* ○ *a governing body* **2** [T] to influence or control the way something happens or is done *There are rules that govern how teachers treat children.*

governess /ˈgʌvᵊnəs/ *noun* [C] **EDUCATION** a woman employed to teach the children in a family at home

WORD PARTNERS FOR ***government***

bring down/elect/form/overthrow a government • a **democratic/elected** government • be **in** government

O-- **government** /ˈgʌvᵊnmənt/ *noun* **1 POLITICS** [group] the group of people who officially control a country *The Government has cut taxes.* **2 POLITICS** [U] the method or process of governing a country *a new style of government* •**governmental** /ˌgʌvᵊnˈmentᵊl/ *adjective* relating to government

governor /ˈgʌvᵊnəʳ/ *noun* [C] **POLITICS** someone who is officially responsible for controlling a region, city, or organization *a prison/school governor* ○ *the Governor of Texas*

gown /gaʊn/ *noun* [C] **1** DRESS a woman's dress, usually worn on formal occasions *a silk gown* **2** LOOSE CLOTHING a loose piece of clothing like a coat worn for a particular purpose *a hospital gown* ⊃See also: **dressing gown**

GP /ˌdʒiːˈpiː/ *noun* [C] **HEALTH** *abbreviation for* general practitioner: a doctor who sees people in the local area and treats illnesses that do not need a hospital visit

GPS /ˌdʒiːpiːˈes/ *noun* [U] **COMPUTING** *abbreviation for* Global Positioning System: a system of computers and satellites (= equipment that is sent into space around the Earth to receive and send signals) that work together to tell a user where they are

O-- **grab¹** /græb/ *verb* [T] **grabbing**, *past* **grabbed** **1** TAKE SUDDENLY to take hold of something or someone suddenly *He grabbed my arm and pulled me away.* **2** DO QUICKLY *informal* to eat, do, or get something quickly because you do not have much time *I grabbed a sandwich on the way to the station.* **3 grab sb's attention** *informal* to attract someone's attention **4** TAKE OPPORTUNITY If someone grabs a chance or opportunity, they take it quickly and with enthusiasm.
grab at sb/sth *phrasal verb* to try to get hold of someone or something quickly, with your hand

grab² /græb/ *noun* **1 make a grab for sth/sb** to try to take hold of something or someone suddenly *He made a grab for the gun.* **2 up for grabs** *informal* If something is up for grabs, it is available to anyone who wants to try to get it. *Ten free concert tickets are up for grabs.*

grace¹ /greɪs/ *noun* [U] **1** MOVEMENT the quality of moving in a smooth, relaxed, and attractive way *She moved* ***with grace*** *and elegance.* **2** POLITENESS the quality of being pleasantly polite *He* ***had the grace to*** *apologize for his mistake the next day.* **3 with good grace** in a willing and happy way *He accepted the failure with good grace.* **4 a month's/week's, etc grace** an extra month/week, etc you are given before something must be paid or done **5 RELIGION** a prayer of thanks said before or after a meal ***to say grace***

grace² /greɪs/ *verb* [T] When a person or object graces a place or thing, they make it more attractive. *Her face has graced the covers of magazines across the world.*

graceful /ˈgreɪsfᵊl/ *adjective* **1** MOVEMENT/SHAPE moving in a smooth, relaxed, and attractive way, or having a smooth, attractive shape *graceful movements* ○ *a graceful neck* **2** POLITE behaving in a polite and pleasant way •**gracefully** *adverb*

gracious /ˈgreɪʃəs/ *adjective* **1** PLEASANT behaving in a pleasant, polite, calm way *He was gracious enough to thank me.* **2** COMFORTABLE comfortable and with a good appearance and quality *gracious homes/living* **3 Good/Goodness gracious!** used to express polite surprise •**graciously** *adverb*

grade¹ /greɪd/ *noun* [C] **1 EDUCATION** a number or letter that shows how good someone's work or performance is *Steve never studies, but he always* ***gets*** *good* ***grades***. ○ *(UK) Carla got a grade A in German.* **2** a level of quality, size, importance, etc *I applied for a position a grade higher than my current job.* **3 EDUCATION** *US* a school class or group of classes for students of the same age or ability *My son is in fifth grade.* **4 make the grade** to perform well enough to succeed *He wanted to get into the team but he didn't make the grade.*

grade² /greɪd/ *verb* [T] **1** LEVEL to separate people or things into different levels of quality, size, importance, etc *The fruit is washed and then* ***graded by*** *size.* **2 EDUCATION** *US* (*UK* **mark**) to give a score to a student's piece of work *to grade work/papers*

ˈgrade ˌcrossing *US* (*UK* **level crossing**) *noun* [C] a place where a railway crosses a road

ˈgrade ˌschool *noun* [C, U] *US* **EDUCATION** a school for the first six to eight years of a child's education

gradient /ˈgreɪdiənt/ *noun* [C] how steep a slope is *a steep/gentle gradient*

O-- **gradual** /ˈgrædʒuəl/ *adjective* happening slowly over a period of time *a gradual change/improvement*

O⁻ **gradually** /ˈgrædʒuəli/ *adverb* slowly over a period of time *Gradually he began to get better.*

graduate¹ /ˈgrædʒuət/ *noun* [C] **1 EDUCATION** *UK* someone who has studied for and received a degree (= qualification) from a university *a science graduate* **2 EDUCATION** *US* someone who has studied for and received a degree (= qualification) from a school, college, or university *a high-school graduate*

graduate² /ˈgrædjueɪt/ *verb* **1 EDUCATION** [I] to complete your education successfully at a university, college, or, in the US, at school *He* ***graduated from*** *Cambridge University in 2006.* **2 graduate to sth** to move up to something more advanced or important

graduated /ˈgrædjueɪtɪd/ *adjective* divided into levels or stages *a graduated scale*

graduation /ˌgrædʒuˈeɪʃᵊn/ *noun* [C, U] **EDUCATION** when you receive your degree (= qualification) for completing your education or a course of study *a* ***graduation ceremony***

graffiti /grəˈfiːti/ *noun* [U] **LANGUAGE** writing or pictures painted on walls and public places, usually illegally

graft¹ /grɑːft/ *noun* **1 HEALTH** [C] a piece of skin or bone taken from one part of a body and joined to another part *a* ***skin/bone graft*** **2 BIOLOGY** [C] a piece cut from one plant and joined onto another plant **3** [U] *UK informal* work ***hard graft***

graft² /grɑːft/ *verb* **1 HEALTH** [T] to join a piece of skin or bone taken from one part of the body to another part **2 BIOLOGY** [T] to join a piece cut from one plant onto another plant **3** [WORK] [I] *UK informal* to work hard

grain /greɪn/ *noun* **1 FARMING, FOOD** [C, U] a seed or seeds from types of grass which are eaten as food *grains of wheat/rice* **2** [PIECE] [C] a very small piece of something *a grain of sand/sugar* **3** [QUALITY] [no plural] a very small amount of a quality *There isn't* ***a grain of truth*** *in her story.* **4 the grain** the natural direction and pattern of lines which you can see in wood or material *to cut something along/against the grain* **5 go against the grain** If something goes against the grain, you would not normally do it because it would be unusual or morally wrong. ➲See also: take sth with a pinch of **salt¹**

gram (*also UK* **gramme**) (*written abbreviation* **g, gm**) /græm/ *noun* [C] **MEASURES** a unit for measuring weight, equal to 0.001 kilograms

grammage /ˈgræmɪdʒ/ *noun* [U] **MEASURES, DT** a measurement of paper weight

O⁻ **grammar** /ˈgræməʳ/ *noun* **1 LANGUAGE** [U] the way you combine words and change their form and position in a sentence, or the rules or study of this **2** [C] *mainly UK* a book of grammar rules

ˈ**grammar** ˌ**school** *noun* [C, U] **1 EDUCATION** in the UK, a school which clever children over 11 years old can go to if they pass a special exam **2 EDUCATION** *US another way of saying* elementary school (= a school for children from the ages of five to eleven in the US)

grammatical /grəˈmætɪkᵊl/ *adjective* **LANGUAGE** relating to grammar, or obeying the rules of grammar *grammatical rules* ○ *a grammatical sentence* •**grammatically** *adverb*

gramme /græm/ *noun* [C] **MEASURES** *another UK spelling of* gram

gramophone /ˈgræməfəʊn/ *noun* [C] **MUSIC** *old-fashioned* a machine for playing music

gran /græn/ *noun* [C] *UK informal short for* grandmother

grand¹ /grænd/ *adjective* **1** [LARGE] very large and special *a grand hotel* ○ *the Grand Canal* **2** [IMPORTANT] rich and important, or behaving as if you are *a grand old lady* **3** [GOOD] *informal* very good or enjoyable

grand² /grænd/ *noun* [C] *plural* **grand** *informal* one thousand dollars or pounds *The holiday cost me two grand.*

grandad /ˈgrændæd/ *noun* [C] *another UK spelling of* granddad

grandchild /ˈgrændtʃaɪld/ *noun* [C] *plural* **grandchildren** the child of your son or daughter

granddad /ˈgrændæd/ *noun* [C] *mainly UK informal* grandfather

granddaughter /ˈgrændˌdɔːtəʳ/ *noun* [C] the daughter of your son or daughter

grandeur /ˈgrændjəʳ/ *noun* [U] the quality of being very large and special or beautiful *the grandeur of the hills*

O⁻ **grandfather** /ˈgrændˌfɑːðəʳ/ *noun* [C] the father of your mother or father

ˌ**grandfather** ˈ**clock** *noun* [C] a clock in a very tall, wooden case

grandiose /ˈgrændiəʊs/ *adjective* large or detailed and made to appear important, often in an unnecessary and annoying way ***grandiose plans***

grandly /ˈgrændli/ *adverb* in a very important way, or as if you are very important

grandma /ˈgrændmɑː/ *noun* [C] *informal another word for* grandmother

O⁻ **grandmother** /ˈgrændˌmʌðəʳ/ *noun* [C] the mother of your mother or father

grandpa /ˈgrændpɑː/ *noun* [C] *informal another word for* grandfather

grandparent /ˈgrændˌpeərᵊnt/ *noun* [C] the parent of your mother or father

ˌ**grand pi**ˈ**ano** *noun* [C] **MUSIC** a very large piano, usually used in public performances

grand prix /ˌgrɒnˈpriː/ *noun* [C] *plural* **grands prix SPORT** one of a series of important international races for very fast cars *the Italian Grand Prix*

ˌ**grand** ˈ**slam** *noun* [C] **SPORT** when you win all the important competitions that are held in one year for a particular sport

grandson /ˈgrændsʌn/ *noun* [C] the son of your son or daughter

grandstand /ˈgrændstænd/ *noun* [C] **SPORT** a large, open structure containing rows of seats, used for watching sporting events

granite /ˈgrænɪt/ *noun* [U] **GEOLOGY** a type of very hard, grey rock

granny /ˈgræni/ *noun* [C] *informal another word for* grandmother

grant¹ /grɑːnt/ *verb* **1** GIVE [T] *formal* to give or allow someone something, usually in an official way [+ **two objects**] *to grant someone a licence/visa* **2** ADMIT [T] *formal* to admit or agree that something is true *She's a good-looking woman, I grant you.* **3 take sb/sth for granted** to not show that you are grateful for someone or something, and forget that you are lucky to have them *Most of us take our freedom for granted.* **4 take it for granted** to believe that something is true without checking or thinking about it [+ **(that)**] *I took it for granted that we'd be invited.*

WORD PARTNERS FOR ***grant***

apply for/get/receive a grant • a grant **for/towards** sth • a **research** grant

G

grant² /grɑːnt/ *noun* [C] **FINANCE** an amount of money provided by a government or organization for a special purpose *They received a **research grant** for the project.*

granule /ˈgrænjuːl/ *noun* [C] a small, hard piece of a substance *coffee granules* •**granulated** /ˈgrænjəleɪtɪd/ *adjective* ***granulated sugar***

grape /greɪp/ *noun* [C] **FOOD** a small, round, green, purple or red fruit that grows in large, close groups and is often used to make wine *a **bunch of grapes*** See colour picture **Fruit and Vegetables** on page Centre 10

grapefruit /ˈgreɪpfruːt/ *noun* [C, U] *plural* **grapefruit** or **grapefruits** **FOOD** a large, round, yellow fruit with a sour taste

grapevine /ˈgreɪpvaɪn/ *noun* **hear sth on/through the grapevine** to hear news from someone who heard the news from someone else

WORD PARTNERS FOR ***graph***

draw a graph • a graph **indicates/shows** sth • a graph **of** sth

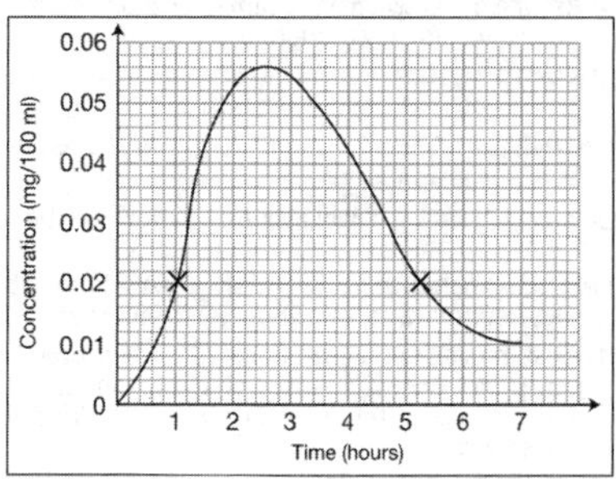

graph

graph /grɑːf/ *noun* [C] **MATHEMATICS** a picture with measurements marked on it as lines or curves, used to compare different things or show the development of something See Extra help page **Graphs and Charts** on page Centre 20.

graphic¹ /ˈgræfɪk/ *adjective* A graphic description or image is extremely clear and detailed. *The film contains **graphic violence**.* •**graphically** *adverb*

graphic² /ˈgræfɪk/ *noun* [C] **COMPUTING** an image, especially on a computer or in a newspaper or book *I want to add a graphic here.*

ˌgraphical user ˈinterface *noun* [C] **COMPUTING** a way of arranging information on a computer screen that is easy to understand because it uses pictures and symbols as well as words

ˌgraphic deˈsign *noun* [U] **ART, DT** the art of designing pictures and text for books, magazines, advertisements, etc

graphics /ˈgræfɪks/ *noun* [plural] **COMPUTING** images shown on a computer screen

ˈgraphics ˌcard *noun* [C] **COMPUTING** the part inside a computer that allows it to receive and show pictures and video

ˈgraphics ˌtablet *noun* [C] **COMPUTING** a flat device that is connected to a computer, that you draw on with a stylus (= electronic pen) to make an image on the computer screen

graphite /ˈgræfaɪt/ *noun* [U] **GEOLOGY** a soft, grey-black form of carbon used in pencils

ˈgraph ˌpaper *noun* [U] paper with small squares on it, used for drawing graphs

grapple /ˈgræpl/ *verb*

grapple with sth *phrasal verb* to try to deal with or understand something difficult

grapple with sb *phrasal verb* to hold onto someone and fight with them

grasp¹ /grɑːsp/ *verb* [T] **1** HOLD to take hold of something or someone firmly *He **grasped** my **hand** enthusiastically.* **2** UNDERSTAND to understand something *I find these mathematical problems difficult to grasp.*

grasp at sth *phrasal verb* to quickly try to get hold of something

WORD PARTNERS FOR ***grasp***

have a [**good/poor**, etc] grasp **of** sth

grasp² /grɑːsp/ *noun* [no plural] **1** UNDERSTAND when you understand something *He **has an** excellent **grasp** of English.* **2** HOLD when you hold onto someone or something *I tried to pull him out but he slipped from my grasp.* **3** ABILITY the ability to obtain or achieve something *Victory is **within** our **grasp**.*

grasping /ˈgrɑːspɪŋ/ *adjective* wanting much more of something than you need, especially money *a grasping, greedy man*

grass /grɑːs/ *noun* **1** PLANT [U] a common plant with narrow green leaves that grows close to the ground in gardens and fields *to **mow/cut** the **grass*** ○ *We lay on the grass in the sunshine.* **2** TYPE OF GRASS [C] a particular type of grass *ornamental grasses*

grasshopper /ˈgrɑːsˌhɒpəʳ/ *noun* [C] a green insect which jumps about using its long back legs

ˌgrass ˈroots *noun* [plural] **SOCIETY** ordinary people in a society or political organization and not the leaders

grassy /ˈgrɑːsi/ *adjective* covered with grass

grate¹ /greɪt/ *verb* **1 FOOD** [T] to break food such as cheese into small, thin pieces by rubbing it against a grater (= kitchen tool with holes) *grated cheese/carrot* **2** [I] to make an unpleasant noise when rubbing against something

grate on sb/sth *phrasal verb* If someone's

voice or behaviour grates on you, it annoys you.

grate² /greɪt/ *noun* [C] a metal structure for holding the wood or coal in a fireplace

OTHER WAYS OF SAYING ***grateful***

The adjective **appreciative** is sometimes used to show that someone is grateful, or you can use the verb **appreciate** to express the same idea: *I'm really* ***appreciative*** *of all the help you've given me.* • *I really* ***appreciate*** *all the help you've given me.*

The expression **be glad of** is another alternative: *We* ***were*** *very* ***glad of*** *some extra help.*

The expression **be indebted to** is a more formal way of saying that someone is very grateful for something: *I'm* ***indebted to*** *my parents for all their love and support.*

The adjectives **thankful** or **relieved** are often used when a person is grateful that something bad did not happen: *I'm just* ***thankful/relieved*** *that she's safe and well.*

If a person is grateful that someone has done something kind, the adjective **touched** is sometimes used: *She was really* ***touched*** *that he remembered her birthday.*

O→**grateful** /ˈgreɪtfəl/ *adjective* feeling or showing thanks *I'm really* ***grateful to*** *you* ***for*** *all your help.* ➲Opposite **ungrateful** •**gratefully** *adverb All donations* ***gratefully received.***

grater /ˈgreɪtəʳ/ *noun* [C] a kitchen tool with a surface full of holes with sharp edges, used to grate (= break into small pieces) foods such as cheese ➲See colour picture **The Kitchen** on page Centre 2

gratify /ˈgrætɪfaɪ/ *verb* [T] *formal* to please someone or satisfy their wishes or needs *I was gratified by their decision.* ○ *a gratifying result* •**gratification** /ˌgrætɪfɪˈkeɪʃən/ *noun* [U]

grating /ˈgreɪtɪŋ/ *noun* [C] a flat structure made of long, thin pieces of metal crossing each other over a hole in the ground or a window

gratitude /ˈgrætɪtjuːd/ *noun* [U] the feeling or quality of being grateful *I would like to express my deep gratitude to all the hospital staff.*

gratuitous /grəˈtjuːɪtəs/ *adjective* unnecessary and done without a good reason ***gratuitous violence***

gratuity /grəˈtjuːəti/ *noun* [C] *formal* **FINANCE** an extra amount of money given to someone to thank them for providing a service

O→**grave¹** /greɪv/ *noun* [C] a place in the ground where a dead body is buried

grave² /greɪv/ *adjective* very serious ***grave doubts*** ○ ***a grave mistake*** •**gravely** *adverb*

gravel /ˈgrævəl/ *noun* [U] small pieces of stone used to make paths and road surfaces

gravestone /ˈgreɪvstəʊn/ *noun* [C] a stone that shows the name of a dead person who is buried under it

graveyard /ˈgreɪvjɑːd/ *noun* [C] an area of land where dead bodies are buried, usually next to a church

gravitate /ˈgrævɪteɪt/ *verb*
gravitate to/towards sth/sb *phrasal verb* to be attracted to something or someone, or to move in the direction of something or someone

gravitational /ˌgrævɪˈteɪʃənəl/ *adjective* **PHYSICS** relating to gravity ***gravitational force***

gravity /ˈgrævəti/ *noun* [U] **1 PHYSICS** the force that makes objects fall to the ground or that pulls objects towards a planet or other body *the laws of gravity* **2** SERIOUS PROBLEM *formal* when something is very serious *You don't seem to realize the gravity of the situation.* ➲See also: **centre of gravity**

gravure /grəˈvjʊəʳ/ *noun* [U] a method of printing using a surface with many small cuts in it *a gravure press*

gravy /ˈgreɪvi/ *noun* [U] **FOOD** a warm, brown sauce made from the fat and liquid that comes from meat when it is being cooked

O→**gray** /greɪ/ *noun*, [C, U] *adjective US spelling of* grey

graying /ˈgreɪɪŋ/ *adjective US spelling of* greying (= having hair that is becoming grey or white)

graze¹ /greɪz/ *verb* **1 FARMING** [I] When cows or other animals graze, they eat grass. *Cattle grazed in the meadow.* **2** INJURE [T] *UK* (*UK/US* **skin**) to injure your skin by rubbing it against something rough *I fell and grazed my knee.* **3** TOUCH [T] to touch or move lightly along the surface or edge of something *A bullet grazed his cheek.*

graze² /greɪz/ *noun* [C] *mainly UK* **HEALTH** an injury on the surface of your skin caused by rubbing against something *She has a nasty* ***graze on*** *her elbow.*

grease¹ /griːs/ *noun* [U] **1 FOOD** a substance such as oil or fat **2** a substance like thick oil that is put on parts in an engine or machine to make them move more smoothly

grease² /griːs/ *verb* [T] **FOOD** to put fat or oil on or in something

greasy /ˈgriːsi/ *adjective* containing or covered with fat or oil *greasy food/fingers*

O→**great** /greɪt/ *adjective* **1** EXCELLENT very good *We had a great time.* ○ *I've had a great idea!* **2** IMPORTANT important or famous *a great statesman/novelist* **3** LARGE large in amount, size, or degree *a great crowd of people* **4** EXTREME extreme *great success/difficulty* **5 great big/long, etc** very big/long, etc *I gave her a great big hug.* **6 a great many** a large number •**greatness** *noun* [U] ➲See also: go to great lengths (**length**) to do sth, set great **store**¹ by sth, the best/greatest **thing** since sliced bread

great- /greɪt/ *prefix* **1 great-grandfather/-grandmother** the father/mother of your grandfather or grandmother **2 great-aunt/-uncle** the aunt/uncle of your mother or father **3 great-grandchild/-granddaughter, etc** the child/daughter, etc of your grandson or granddaughter **4 great-niece/-nephew** the daughter/son of your niece or nephew

greatly /ˈgreɪtli/ *adverb* very much *I greatly admire your paintings.* ○ *We will miss her greatly.*

greed /griːd/ *noun* [U] when you want a lot more food, money, etc, than you need

greedy /ˈgriːdi/ *adjective* wanting a lot more food, money, etc, than you need *greedy, selfish people* ○ *They were* ***greedy for*** *money.* •**greedily** *adverb* •**greediness** *noun* [U]

Greek /griːk/ *adjective* relating to the culture, language, or people of Greece or ancient Greece

green¹ /griːn/ *adjective* **1** COLOUR being the same colour as grass *The traffic lights turned green.* ⊃See colour picture **Colours** on page Centre 12 **2 ENVIRONMENT** [always before noun] relating to nature and protecting the environment *a green activist/campaigner* **3** GRASS covered with grass or other plants ***green spaces*** **4** NOT EXPERIENCED *informal* having little experience or understanding *I was very green when I joined the company.* **5 be green with envy** to wish very much that you had something that another person has ⊃See also: have green fingers (**finger¹**), **green light**

green² /griːn/ *noun* **1** COLOUR [C, U] the colour of grass ⊃See colour picture **Colours** on page Centre 6 **2 SPORT** [C] a special area of very short, smooth grass on a golf course *the 18th green* **3** VILLAGE [C] an area of grass in the middle of a village

ˈ**green** ˌ**belt** *noun* [C] an area of land around a city or town where no new building is allowed

ˌ**green** ˈ**card** *noun* [C] **LAW** an official document allowing a foreigner to live and work in the US permanently

greenery /ˈgriːnᵊri/ *noun* [U] green leaves, plants, or branches

greenfield /ˈgriːfiːld/ *adjective UK* **ENVIRONMENT** describes land where there were no buildings before, or buildings on land that have never had buildings *a* ***greenfield site*** ⊃Compare **brownfield**

greengrocer /ˈgriːnˌgrəʊsəʳ/ *noun* [C] *UK* **1 greengrocer's** a shop where you buy fruit and vegetables **2** someone who sells fruit and vegetables

greenhouse /ˈgriːnhaʊs/ *noun* [C] *plural* **greenhouses** /ˈgriːnhaʊzɪz/ a building made of glass for growing plants in

the ˈ**greenhouse ef**ˌ**fect** *noun* **ENVIRONMENT** the gradual warming of the Earth's surface caused by an increase in pollution and gases in the air

ˌ**greenhouse** ˈ**gas** *noun* [C] **ENVIRONMENT** a gas which causes the greenhouse effect, especially carbon dioxide (= a gas produced when carbon is burned)

ˌ**green** ˈ**light** *noun* [no plural] permission to do something [+ to do sth] *They've been* ***given the green light*** *to build two new supermarkets.*

the ˈ**Green** ˌ**Party** *noun* [group] **POLITICS** a political party whose main aim is to protect the environment

greens /griːnz/ *noun* [plural] **FOOD** green leaves that are cooked and eaten as a vegetable

greet /griːt/ *verb* [T] **1** WELCOME to welcome someone *He greeted me at the door.* **2** REACT to react to something in a particular way [often passive] *His story was* ***greeted with*** *shrieks of laughter.*

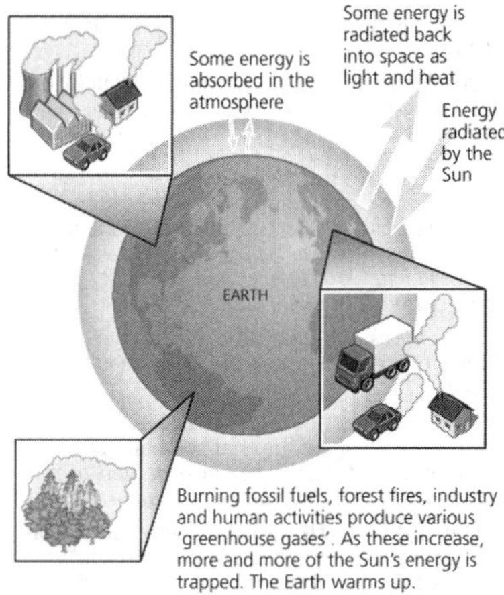
Some energy is radiated back into space as light and heat
Some energy is absorbed in the atmosphere
Energy radiated by the Sun
EARTH
Burning fossil fuels, forest fires, industry and human activities produce various 'greenhouse gases'. As these increase, more and more of the Sun's energy is trapped. The Earth warms up.

greenhouse effect

greeting /ˈgriːtɪŋ/ *noun* [C] *formal* something friendly or polite that you say or do when you meet or welcome someone

gregarious /grɪˈgeəriəs/ *adjective* If you are gregarious, you enjoy being with other people.

grenade /grəˈneɪd/ *noun* [C] a small bomb that is thrown or fired from a weapon

grew /gruː/ *past tense of* grow

grey¹ *UK* (*US* **gray**) /greɪ/ *adjective* **1** COLOUR being a colour that is a mixture of black and white *grey clouds* ⊃See colour picture **Colours** on page Centre 12 **2** HAIR having hair that has become grey or white *She* ***went grey*** *in her thirties.* **3** WEATHER cloudy and not bright *a cold, grey morning* **4** BORING not interesting or attractive *Life was grey and tedious.* **5 grey area** something which people are not certain about, usually because there are no clear rules for it

grey² *UK* (*US* **gray**) /greɪ/ *noun* [C, U] a colour that is a mixture of black and white ⊃See colour picture **Colours** on page Centre 12

greyhound /ˈgreɪhaʊnd/ *noun* [C] a thin dog with short hair that runs very fast, sometimes in races

greying *UK* (*US* **graying**) /ˈgreɪɪŋ/ *adjective* having hair that is becoming grey or white

grid /grɪd/ *noun* **1** PATTERN [C] a pattern or structure made from horizontal and vertical lines crossing each other to form squares **2** POWER [no plural] a system of connected wires used to supply electrical power to a large area *the National Grid* **3 GEOGRAPHY** [C] a pattern of squares with numbers or letters used to find places on a map

gridlock /ˈgrɪdlɒk/ *noun* [U] when the traffic cannot move in any direction because all of the roads are blocked with cars

grief /griːf/ *noun* **1** [U] great sadness, especially caused by someone's death **2 Good grief!**

informal something that you say when you are surprised or annoyed **3 come to grief** *informal* to suddenly fail or have an accident **4 cause/give sb grief** *informal* to annoy someone or cause trouble or problems for them

grievance /ˈgriːvᵊns/ *noun* [C] *formal* a complaint, especially about unfair behaviour

ˈgrievance proˌcedure *noun* [C] a set of rules that a company has to deal with a situation when an employee is upset or angry about something

grieve /griːv/ *verb* **1** FEEL SAD [I] to feel or express great sadness, especially when someone dies *He is still* ***grieving for*** *his wife.* **2** MAKE SAD [T] *formal* to make someone feel very sad

grievous /ˈgriːvəs/ *adjective formal* very serious ***grievous injuries*** •**grievously** *adverb*

grill¹ /grɪl/ *noun* [C] **1** KITCHEN (*also US* **broiler**) a piece of equipment which cooks food using direct heat from above ➲See colour picture **The Kitchen** on page Centre 2 **2** FIRE a flat, metal structure used to cook food over a fire

grill² /grɪl/ *verb* [T] **1 FOOD** (*also US* **broil**) to cook food using direct heat *Grill the fish for 2 to 3 minutes on each side.* ➲See picture at **cook 2** to ask someone questions continuously and for a long time *I was grilled by the police for two days.*

grille /grɪl/ *noun* [C] a metal structure of bars built across something to protect it

grim /grɪm/ *adjective* **grimmer, grimmest 1** BAD worrying and bad ***grim news*** ○ *The future looks grim.* **2** SERIOUS sad and serious *a grim expression* **3** UNPLEASANT A grim place is ugly and unpleasant. •**grimly** *adverb*

grimace /ˈgrɪməs/ *verb* [I] to make your face show an expression of pain or unhappiness *He grimaced at the bitter taste.* •**grimace** *noun* [C]

grime /graɪm/ *noun* [U] dirt that covers a surface *The walls were covered in grime.* •**grimy** *adjective* covered in dirt *grimy hands*

grin /grɪn/ *verb* **grinning**, *past* **grinned 1** [I] to smile a big smile *He* ***grinned at*** *me from the doorway.* **2 grin and bear it** to accept an unpleasant or difficult situation because there is nothing you can do to improve it •**grin** *noun* [C] *She had a big grin on her face.*

grind¹ /graɪnd/ *verb* [T] *past* **ground 1 FOOD** to keep rubbing something between two rough, hard surfaces until it becomes a powder *to grind coffee* **2** to rub a blade against a hard surface to make it sharp **3 grind your teeth** to rub your teeth together, making an unpleasant sound

grind sb down *phrasal verb* to gradually make someone lose hope, energy, or confidence

grind² /graɪnd/ *noun* [no plural] *informal* work or effort that is boring and unpleasant and makes you tired because it does not change *the* ***daily grind***

grinder /ˈgraɪndəʳ/ *noun* [C] a machine used to rub or press something until it becomes a powder *a* ***coffee grinder***

WORD PARTNERS FOR ***grip***

loosen/release/tighten your grip • sb's grip **on** sth

grip¹ /grɪp/ *noun* [no plural] **1** HOLDING when you hold something tightly *She* ***tightened*** *her* ***grip on*** *my arm.* **2** CONTROL control over something or someone *He has a firm* ***grip on*** *the economy.* **3 come/get to grips with sth** to understand and deal with a problem or situation *It's a difficult subject to get to grips with.* **4 get a grip (on yourself)** to make an effort to control your emotions and behave more calmly

grip² /grɪp/ *verb* [T] **gripping**, *past* **gripped 1** HOLD to hold something tightly *She gripped his arm.* **2** INTEREST to keep someone's attention completely *This trial has gripped the whole nation.* **3** EMOTION When an emotion grips you, you feel it very strongly. [**often passive**] *He was gripped by fear.*

gripe /graɪp/ *verb* [I] *informal* to complain, often in an annoying way •**gripe** *noun* [C]

gripping /ˈgrɪpɪŋ/ *adjective* If something is gripping, it is so interesting that it holds your attention completely. *a gripping story*

grisly /ˈgrɪzli/ *adjective* very unpleasant, especially because death or blood is involved *a grisly murder*

grit¹ /grɪt/ *noun* [U] **1** STONE very small pieces of stone or sand *I've got a bit of grit in my eye.* **2** CHARACTER the quality of being brave and determined

grit² /grɪt/ *verb* [T] **gritting**, *past* **gritted** to put grit onto a road surface when the road has ice on it ➲See also: grit your teeth (**teeth**)

gritty /ˈgrɪti/ *adjective* **1** UNPLEASANT showing unpleasant details about a situation in a way that seems very real *a* ***gritty drama*** ○ ***gritty realism*** **2** BRAVE brave and determined ***gritty determination***

groan /grəʊn/ *verb* [I] to make a long, low sound such as when expressing pain, unhappiness, etc *He collapsed, groaning with pain.* •**groan** *noun* [C]

grocer /ˈgrəʊsəʳ/ *noun* **1 grocer's** *UK* a shop that sells food and other products used in the home **2** [C] someone who owns or works in a grocer's

groceries /ˈgrəʊsᵊriz/ *noun* [plural] goods bought to be used in the home such as food and cleaning products

grocery /ˈgrəʊsᵊri/ (*also US* **ˈgroceryˌstore**) *noun* [C] a shop that sells food and products used in the home

groggy /ˈgrɒgi/ *adjective informal* unable to think or act quickly because you have just woken up, been ill, etc *I felt a bit groggy after the operation.*

groin /grɔɪn/ *noun* [C] **ANATOMY** the area where the legs join the rest of the body near the sexual organs *He pulled a muscle in his groin.* ➲See picture at **body**

groom¹ /gruːm/ *verb* [T] **1** PREPARE to prepare someone carefully for a special position or job *He's being* ***groomed for*** *stardom.* **2** CLEAN to clean and brush an animal's fur

groom² /gruːm/ *noun* [C] **1** MARRIAGE (*also* **bridegroom**) a man who is getting married **2** HORSE someone who cleans and looks after horses

groove /gruːv/ *noun* [C] a long, narrow line that has been cut into a surface

groovy /ˈgruːvi/ *adjective old-fashioned informal* fashionable and stylish *groovy clothes*

grope /grəʊp/ *verb* **1** [I, T] to try to get hold of something with your hand, usually when you cannot see it *I* ***groped*** *in my bag* ***for*** *my keys.* **2 grope your way along/through, etc** to move somewhere with difficulty, feeling with your hands because you cannot see clearly *We groped our way through the smoke to the exit.*
grope for sth *phrasal verb* to try to think of the right words or the right way to express something *He groped for the words to tell her.*

gross¹ /grəʊs/ *adjective* **1 FINANCE** A gross amount of money has not had taxes or other costs taken from it. ***gross earnings/profit*** **2** SERIOUS [always before noun] *formal* very serious or unacceptable ***gross misconduct*** **3** UNPLEASANT *informal* very unpleasant *Oh, yuck. That's really gross.*

gross² /grəʊs/ *verb* [T] **FINANCE** to earn a particular amount of money as a total before tax or other costs are taken from it *The film grossed $250 million.*

grossly /ˈgrəʊsli/ *adverb* extremely ***grossly unfair/exaggerated***

grotesque /grəʊˈtesk/ *adjective* strange and unpleasant, especially in a ridiculous or slightly frightening way *a grotesque image* •**grotesquely** *adverb*

grotto /ˈgrɒtəʊ/ *noun* [C] a small cave

ground¹ /graʊnd/ *noun* **1 the ground GEOLOGY** the surface of the Earth *I sat down on the ground.* **2** SOIL [U] the soil in an area *soft/stony ground* **3 SPORT** [C] an area of land used for a particular purpose or activity *a football ground* **4** KNOWLEDGE [U] an area of knowledge, information, interest, or experience *He had to* ***go over the same ground*** *several times before I understood it.* **5 break new ground** to do something that is different to anything that has been done before **6 gain/lose ground** to become more/less popular and accepted *The idea is gradually gaining ground.* **7 get (sth) off the ground** If a plan or activity gets off the ground, or if you get it off the ground, it starts or succeeds. *He worked hard at getting the project off the ground.* **8 stand your ground** to refuse to change your opinion or move your position despite attempts to make you **9 suit sb down to the ground** *UK* to be exactly right or suitable for someone *That job would suit you down to the ground.* **10 be thin on the ground** *UK* to exist only in small numbers or amounts ➲See also: **breeding ground, common ground**

ground² /graʊnd/ *verb* **1 be grounded** If a vehicle that travels on water or in the air is grounded, it cannot or may not leave the ground. *The aircraft was* ***grounded by*** *fog.* **2 be grounded in sth** *formal* to be based firmly on something *Fiction should be grounded in reality.*

ground³ /graʊnd/ *past of* grind

ˌground ˈbeef *US* (*UK* **mince**) *noun* [U] **FOOD** beef (= meat from a cow) that has been cut into very small pieces by a machine

groundbreaking /ˈgraʊndˌbreɪkɪŋ/ *adjective* based on or containing completely new ideas ***groundbreaking research***

grounded /ˈgraʊndɪd/ *adjective* **1** Someone who is grounded does not say or do stupid things and generally behaves well and makes good decisions. *He seems remarkably grounded considering his background.* **2** describes an aircraft that is prevented from flying, or a ship that cannot move because it has hit solid ground

ˌground ˈfloor *UK* (*US* **first floor**) *noun* [C] the level of a building which is on the ground

grounding /ˈgraʊndɪŋ/ *noun* [no plural] knowledge of the basic facts and principles of a subject *The course gave me a good* ***grounding in*** *bookkeeping.*

groundless /ˈgraʊndləs/ *adjective* Groundless fears, worries, etc have no reason or facts to support them.

ˈground ˌrules *noun* [plural] the basic rules or principles for doing something

grounds /graʊndz/ *noun* [plural] **1** REASON the reason for doing or believing something *He resigned* ***on*** *medical* ***grounds.*** ○ *I refused* ***on the grounds that*** (= because) *it was too risky.* **2** LAND the land around and belonging to a particular building or organization *We strolled around the hospital grounds.*

groundwork /ˈgraʊndwɜːk/ *noun* [U] work or events that prepare for something that will be done or produced in the future *The project is* ***laying the groundwork for*** *a new approach to research.*

ˌground ˈzero *noun* [U] **1** the exact place where a nuclear bomb explodes **2** the place in New York City where the World Trade Center stood before it was destroyed in an attack on September 11, 2001

WORD PARTNERS FOR ***group***

form/join a group • **divide/split** sth into groups • a **large/small** group • a group **of** sth

group¹ /gruːp/ *noun* [C] **1** a number of people or things that are together in one place or are connected *She went camping with a small* ***group of*** *friends.* **2 MUSIC** a few musicians or singers who perform together, usually playing popular music *a* ***pop group*** **3 CHEMISTRY** a set of chemical elements with similar characteristics, that are arranged under one another on the Periodic Table ➲See also: **age group, blood group, focus group, peer group, pressure group**

group² /gruːp/ *verb* [I, T] to form a group or put people or things into a group or groups *The children are grouped according to their ability.*

grouping /ˈgruːpɪŋ/ *noun* [C] a group of people or things that have the same aims or qualities *regional groupings*

groupwork /ˈgruːpwɜːk/ *noun* [U] **EDUCATION** work in class done by groups of students together

grouse¹ /graʊs/ *noun* [C] **1 FOOD** *plural* **grouse** a small, fat, brown bird that some people hunt for food **2** a small complaint about something

grouse² /graʊs/ *verb* [I] to complain about something

grove /grəʊv/ *noun* [C] a small group of trees *an olive grove*

grovel /ˈgrɒvəl/ *verb* [I] *UK* **grovelling**, *past* **grovelled**, *US* **groveling**, *past* **groveled** **1** TRY to try very hard to be nice to someone important so that they will be nice to you or forgive you *She grovelled to the producer to get that part.* **2** MOVE to move around on your hands and knees *He was grovelling around on the floor.*

O⁃**grow** /grəʊ/ *verb past tense* **grew**, *past participle* **grown** **1** DEVELOP [I] to develop and become bigger or taller as time passes *Children grow very quickly.* **2** PLANT [I, T] If a plant grows, or you grow it, it develops from a seed to a full plant. *These shrubs grow well in sandy soil.* **3** INCREASE [I] to increase *The number of people living alone grows each year.* **4** **grow tired/old/calm, etc** to gradually become tired/old/calm, etc *The music grew louder and louder.* **5** HAIR [I, T] If your hair or nails grow, or if you grow them, they get longer.

grow into sb/sth *phrasal verb* to develop into a particular type of person or thing

grow into sth *phrasal verb* If a child grows into clothes, they gradually become big enough to wear them.

grow on sb *phrasal verb* If someone or something grows on you, you start to like them. *I didn't like her at first but she's grown on me over the years.*

grow out of sth *phrasal verb* **1** CLOTHES If children grow out of clothes, they gradually become too big to wear them. *Adam's grown out of his shoes.* **2** STOP to stop doing something as you get older *He still bites his nails, but hopefully he'll grow out of it.*

O⁃**grow up** *phrasal verb* **1** BECOME ADULT to become older or an adult *She grew up in New York.* **2** DEVELOP to develop or become bigger or stronger *A close friendship had grown up between them.*

grower /ˈgrəʊəʳ/ *noun* [C] **FARMING** someone who grows fruit or vegetables to sell to people

growing /ˈgrəʊɪŋ/ *adjective* increasing *A growing number of people are choosing to live alone.*

growl /graʊl/ *verb* [I] If a dog or similar animal growls, it makes a deep, angry noise in its throat. •**growl** *noun* [C]

grown¹ /grəʊn/ *adjective* **a grown man/woman** an adult, used especially when they are not behaving like an adult

grown² /grəʊn/ *past participle of* grow

grown-up¹ /ˈgrəʊnʌp/ *noun* [C] an adult, used especially when talking to children *Ask a grown-up to cut the shape out for you.*

grown-up² /ˌgrəʊnˈʌp/ *adjective* with the physical and mental development of an adult *Jenny has a grown-up son of 24.*

WORD PARTNERS FOR ***growth***

encourage/slow/stimulate/stunt growth • **healthy/long-term/low/rapid/slow/steady** growth • a growth **in** sth

O⁃**growth** /grəʊθ/ *noun* **1** [U, no plural] when something grows, increases, or develops *population growth* ○ *A balanced diet is essential for healthy growth.* **2** **HEALTH** [C] something that grows on your skin or inside your body, that should not be there

ˈgrowth ˌhormone *noun* [C] **HEALTH** a hormone (= chemical made by living cells) that helps an animal or plant to grow

grub /grʌb/ *noun* **1** FOOD [U] *informal* food **2** CREATURE [C] a young, developing insect which has a fat, white tube shape

grubby /ˈgrʌbi/ *adjective* quite dirty *a grubby little boy*

grudge¹ /grʌdʒ/ *noun* [C] a feeling of dislike or anger towards someone because of something they have done in the past *He is not the type of person to* ***bear a grudge against*** *anyone.*

grudge² /grʌdʒ/ *verb* [T] to not want to spend time or money or to give something to someone *He grudged the time he spent in meetings.*

grudging /ˈgrʌdʒɪŋ/ *adjective* done against your will, in a way that shows you do not want to do it *He treated her with* ***grudging respect.*** •**grudgingly** *adverb*

gruelling *UK* (*US* **grueling**) /ˈgruːəlɪŋ/ *adjective* Gruelling activities are very difficult and make you very tired. *a gruelling bicycle race*

gruesome /ˈgruːsəm/ *adjective* very unpleasant or violent, usually involving injury or death *a* ***gruesome murder***

gruff /grʌf/ *adjective* sounding unfriendly *a* ***gruff voice*** •**gruffly** *adverb*

grumble /ˈgrʌmbl/ *verb* [I] to complain about something in a quiet but angry way *She's always* ***grumbling about*** *something.* •**grumble** *noun* [C]

grumpy /ˈgrʌmpi/ *adjective* easily annoyed and often complaining *a* ***grumpy old man*** •**grumpily** *adverb* •**grumpiness** *noun* [U]

grunt /grʌnt/ *verb* **1** PERSON [I, T] to make a short, low sound instead of speaking, usually when you are angry or in pain **2** PIG [I] If a pig grunts, it makes short, low sounds. •**grunt** *noun* [C]

guarantee¹ /ˌgærənˈtiː/ *verb* [T] **guaranteeing**, *past* **guaranteed** **1** PROMISE to promise that something is true or will happen *Every child is guaranteed a place at a local school.* [+ **(that)**] *We can't guarantee that it will arrive in time.* **2** PRODUCT If a company guarantees its products, it makes a written promise to repair them or give you a new one if they have a fault.

guarantee² /ˌgærənˈtiː/ *noun* [C, U] **1** **LAW** a written promise made by a company to repair one of its products or give you a new one if it has a fault *a three-year guarantee* ○ *I'm afraid this camera is no longer* ***under guarantee.*** **2** a promise that something will be done or will happen [+ **(that)**] *There's no guarantee that it actually works.*

guard¹ /gɑːd/ *noun* **1** PROTECT [C] someone whose job is to make certain someone does not escape or to protect a place or another person *a* ***security guard*** ○ ***prison guards*** **2** SOLDIERS [**no plural**] a group of soldiers or police officers who are protecting a person or place **3** TRAIN [C] (*also* **conductor**) someone who is in charge of a train **4** THING [C] something that covers or protects someone or something *a fire guard*

5 be on guard; stand guard to be responsible for protecting a place or a person *Armed police stood guard outside the house.* **6 be under guard** to be kept in a place by a group of people who have weapons *The suspect is now under guard in the local hospital.* **7 catch sb off guard** to surprise someone by doing something when they are not ready to deal with it **8 be on (your) guard** to be ready to deal with something difficult that might happen *Companies were warned to be **on their guard for** suspicious packages.*

guard² /gɑːd/ *verb* [T] **1** PROTECT to protect someone or something from being attacked or stolen *Soldiers guarded the main doors of the embassy.* **2** PREVENT ESCAPE to watch someone and make certain that they do not escape from a place *Five prison officers guarded the prisoners.*

guard against sth *phrasal verb* to try to make certain that something does not happen by being very careful *Regular exercise helps guard against heart disease.*

ˈguard ˌcell *noun* [C] **BIOLOGY** on a leaf, one of two cells that are around each stoma (= small hole in the surface) which open the hole to let out gases or close it to stop water from leaving ➲See picture at **leaf**

guarded /ˈgɑːdɪd/ *adjective* careful not to give too much information or show how you really feel *a guarded response* •**guardedly** *adverb*

guardian /ˈgɑːdiən/ *noun* [C] **1** FOR CHILD someone who is legally responsible for someone else's child *The consent form must be signed by the child's parent or guardian.* **2** PROTECTING LAWS a person or organization that protects laws, principles, etc •**guardianship** *noun* [U]

guerrilla /gəˈrɪlə/ *noun* [C] **POLITICS** a member of an unofficial group of soldiers fighting to achieve their political beliefs *guerrilla warfare*

O⊷**guess¹** /ges/ *verb* **1** SAY WITHOUT KNOWING [I, T] to give an answer or opinion about something without having all the facts *Can you guess how old he is?* **2** SAY CORRECTLY WITHOUT KNOWING [I, T] to give a correct answer without having all the facts *"You've got a promotion!" "Yes, how did you guess?"* [+ (that)] *I'd never have guessed that you two were related.* **3 I guess** used when you think that something is probably true or likely *I've known her for about 12 years, I guess.* **4 I guess so/not** used when you agree/disagree but are not completely certain about something **5 Guess what?** something you say when you have some surprising news for someone *Guess what? I'm pregnant.*

WORD PARTNERS FOR ***guess***

have/hazard/make/take a guess • **a rough** guess • **at** a guess • a guess **as to/at** sth

guess² /ges/ *noun* [C] **1** ATTEMPT an attempt to give the right answer when you are not certain what it is *How old do you think John is? Go on, (UK) **have a guess**/ (US) **take a guess**.* ○ ***At a guess**, I'd say there were about 70 people there.* **2** OPINION an opinion that you have formed by guessing *My guess is they'll announce their engagement soon.* **3 be anybody's guess** *informal* to be something that no one can be certain about *What happens after the election is anybody's guess.*

guesswork /ˈgeswɜːk/ *noun* [U] when you try to find an answer by guessing

WORD PARTNERS FOR ***guest***

entertain/invite/welcome guests • a **frequent/honoured/special/uninvited** guest

O⊷**guest** /gest/ *noun* [C] **1** VISITOR someone who comes to visit you in your home, at a party, etc *We've got some guests coming this weekend.* **2** HOTEL someone who is staying in a hotel *The hotel has accommodation for 200 guests.* **3** TV a famous person who takes part in a television programme or other entertainment *Our special guest tonight is George Michael.* **4 Be my guest.** something you say when you give someone permission to use something or do something

guesthouse /ˈgesthaʊs/ *noun* [C] a small cheap hotel

GUI /ˈguːi/ *noun* [C] **COMPUTING** graphical user interface: a way of arranging information on a computer screen that is easy to understand because it uses pictures and symbols as well as words

guidance /ˈgaɪdᵊns/ *noun* [U] help or advice *Students make choices about their future, with the guidance of their teachers.*

guide¹ /gaɪd/ *noun* [C] **1** PERSON someone whose job is to show interesting places to visitors, or to help people get somewhere *a **tour guide*** **2** BOOK a book that gives information about something or tells you how to do something *a hotel/restaurant guide* ○ *a user's guide* **3** PLAN something that helps you plan or decide what to do [**usually singular**] *Parents use this report as a guide when choosing schools for their children.* **4 Guide** (*also* ˌ**Girl** ˈ**Guide**) a girl who belongs to an organization in the UK that teaches practical things like living outside, and how to work as part of a team **5 the Guides** an organization in the UK that teaches girls practical skills and how to work as part of a team

guide² /gaɪd/ *verb* [T] **1** GO to help someone or something go somewhere *He gently guided her back to her seat.* **2** ADVISE to tell someone what they should do *She had no one to guide her as a teenager.*

guidebook /ˈgaɪdbʊk/ *noun* [C] a book that gives visitors information about a particular place

ˈguide ˌdog (*also US* **seeing eye dog**) *noun* [C] a dog that is trained to help blind people

WORD PARTNERS FOR ***guidelines***

draw up/issue/lay down/produce guidelines • guidelines **on** sth

guidelines /ˈgaɪdlaɪnz/ *noun* [**plural**] advice about how to do something *government **guidelines on** tobacco advertising*

guild /gɪld/ *noun* [C] an organization of people who have the same job or interests *the Designers' Guild*

guile /gaɪl/ *noun* [U] *formal* clever but sometimes dishonest behaviour that you use to deceive someone

guillotine /ˈgɪlətiːn/ *noun* [C] a piece of equipment used to cut off criminals' heads in the past •**guillotine** *verb* [T]

guilt /gɪlt/ *noun* [U] **1** FEELING the strong feeling of shame that you feel when you have done something wrong *He was overcome with guilt over what he had done.* **2** ILLEGAL the fact that someone has done something illegal *The prosecution must convince the jury of his guilt.* **3** WRONG the responsibility for doing something bad

guilt-ridden /ˈgɪltrɪdᵊn/ *adjective* feeling very guilty

O-w **guilty** /ˈgɪlti/ *adjective* **1** ASHAMED ashamed because you have done something wrong [+ **about** + **doing sth**] *I feel so guilty about not going to see them.* **2** LAW having broken a law *The jury **found her guilty*** (= decided that she was guilty of a crime). ○ *They found him **guilty of** rape.* •**guiltily** *adverb* •**guiltiness** *noun* [U]

guinea pig /ˈgɪni,pɪg/ *noun* [C] **1** ANIMAL a small animal with fur and no tail that people sometimes keep as a pet **2** PERSON *informal* someone who is used in a test for something such as a new medicine or product

guise /gaɪz/ *noun* [C] *formal* what something seems to be, although it is not *Banks are facing new competition **in the guise of** supermarkets.*

guitar /gɪˈtɑːʳ/ *noun* [C] **MUSIC** a musical instrument with strings that you play by pulling the strings with your fingers or a piece of plastic *an **electric guitar***

guitarist /gɪˈtɑːrɪst/ *noun* [C] **MUSIC** someone who plays the guitar, especially as their job

gulf /gʌlf/ *noun* [C] **1 GEOGRAPHY** a large area of sea that has land almost all the way around it *the Arabian Gulf* **2** an important difference between the opinions or situations of two groups of people *There is a growing **gulf between** the rich and the poor.*

gull /gʌl/ (*also* **seagull**) *noun* [C] a white or grey bird that lives near the sea and has a loud cry

gullible /ˈgʌlɪbl/ *adjective* Someone who is gullible is easily tricked because they trust people too much. *How could you be so gullible?*

gully /ˈgʌli/ *noun* [C] **GEOGRAPHY** a narrow valley which is usually dry except after a lot of rain

gulp /gʌlp/ *verb* **1** DRINK/EAT [T] (*also* **gulp down**) to drink or eat something quickly *I just had time to gulp down a cup of coffee before I left.* **2** BREATHE [I, T] to breathe in large amounts of air **3** SWALLOW [I] to swallow suddenly, sometimes making a noise, because you are nervous or surprised •**gulp** *noun* [C] *He took a large gulp of tea.*

gum¹ /gʌm/ *noun* **1 ANATOMY** [C] the hard, pink part inside your mouth that your teeth grow out of [**usually plural**] *Protect your teeth and gums by visiting your dentist regularly.* ○ ***gum disease*** ➲See picture at **tooth 2 FOOD** [U] (*also* **chewing gum**) a sweet substance that you chew (= bite repeatedly) but do not swallow *a stick of gum* **3** [U] a sticky substance like glue, used for sticking papers together ➲See also: **bubble gum**

gum² /gʌm/ *verb* [T] **gumming**, *past* **gummed** *UK* to stick things together using glue

WORD PARTNERS FOR ***gun***

point a gun at sb/sth • **fire** a gun

O-w **gun¹** /gʌn/ *noun* **1** [C] a weapon that you fire bullets out of **2 jump the gun** to do something too soon, before you have thought about it carefully **3 stick to your guns** *informal* to refuse to change your ideas although other people try to make you ➲See also: **machine gun**

gun² /gʌn/ *verb* **gunning**, *past* **gunned**
gun sb down *phrasal verb* to shoot someone and kill them or injure them badly

gunboat /ˈgʌnbəʊt/ *noun* [C] a small ship used during a war

gunfire /ˈgʌnfaɪəʳ/ *noun* [U] when guns are fired, or the noise that this makes

gunman /ˈgʌnmən/ *noun* [C] *plural* **gunmen** a criminal with a gun

gunner /ˈgʌnəʳ/ *noun* [C] a soldier or sailor whose job is to fire a large gun

gunpoint /ˈgʌnpɔɪnt/ *noun* **at gunpoint** with someone aiming a gun towards you *The hostages are being **held at gunpoint**.*

gunpowder /ˈgʌn,paʊdəʳ/ *noun* [U] an explosive powder

gunshot /ˈgʌnʃɒt/ *noun* [C] when a gun is fired *I heard a gunshot and rushed into the street.* ○ ***gunshot wounds** to the chest*

gurgle /ˈgɜːgl/ *verb* [I] to make a sound like bubbling liquid *The baby was gurgling happily.* •**gurgle** *noun* [C]

guru /ˈguːruː/ *noun* [C] **1** someone whose opinion you respect because they know a lot about a particular thing **2 RELIGION** a teacher or leader in the Hindu religion

gush¹ /gʌʃ/ *verb* [I, T] **1** LIQUID If liquid gushes from an opening, it comes out quickly and in large amounts. *He ran down the street, blood gushing from a wound in his neck.* **2** PRAISE to praise someone so much that they do not believe you are sincere *"Darling! I'm so excited!" she gushed.*

gush² /gʌʃ/ *noun* [C] **1** LIQUID/GAS a large amount of liquid or gas that flows quickly **2** FEELING a sudden feeling of a particular emotion

gust /gʌst/ *verb* [I] If winds gust, they blow strongly. *Winds gusting to 50 mph brought down power cables.* •**gust** *noun* [C] *a gust of air* •**gusty** *adjective*

gusto /ˈgʌstəʊ/ *noun* **with gusto** with a lot of energy and enthusiasm *Everyone joined in the singing with great gusto.*

gut¹ /gʌt/ *noun* [C] **ANATOMY** the tube in your body that takes food from your stomach to be passed out as waste

gut² /gʌt/ *adjective* **gut reaction/feeling/instinct** a reaction, feeling, etc that you feel certain is right, although you have no reason to think so *I had a gut feeling that he was going to come back.*

gut[3] /gʌt/ *verb* [T] **gutting**, *past* **gutted** **1** **FOOD** to remove the organs from inside a fish or other animal **2** to completely destroy or remove the inside of a building *A fire gutted the bookshop last week.*

guts /gʌts/ *noun* [**plural**] *informal* **1** the bravery and determination that is needed to do something difficult or unpleasant *It **took guts** to stand up and tell the boss how she felt.* **2** **ANATOMY** the organs inside a person or animal's body **3** **hate sb's guts** *informal* to dislike someone very much

gutsy /ˈgʌtsi/ *adjective* brave and determined *a gutsy performance*

gutted /ˈgʌtɪd/ *adjective UK informal* very disappointed and upset [+ **(that)**] *Neil's absolutely gutted that he's been dropped from the team.*

G

gutter /ˈgʌtəʳ/ *noun* [C] **1** PIPE a long, open pipe that is fixed to the edge of a roof to carry water away **2** ROAD the edge of a road where water flows away

O━**guy** /gaɪ/ *noun informal* **1** [C] a man *What a nice guy!* **2** **guys** used when you are talking to or about two or more people *Come on, you guys, let's go home.*

guzzle /ˈgʌzl/ *verb* [I, T] *informal* to eat or drink a lot of something quickly *Who's guzzled all the beer?*

gym /dʒɪm/ *noun* **1** **SPORT** [C] a building with equipment for doing exercises *Nick goes to the gym three times a week.* **2** **SPORT** [U] exercises done inside, especially as a school subject

gymnasium /dʒɪmˈneɪziəm/ *noun* [C] **SPORT** a gym

gymnast /ˈdʒɪmnæst/ *noun* [C] **SPORT** someone who does gymnastics *an Olympic gymnast*

gymnastics /dʒɪmˈnæstɪks/ *noun* [U] **SPORT** a sport in which you do physical exercises on the floor and on different pieces of equipment, often in competitions

gynaecologist *UK* (*US* **gynecologist**) /gaɪnəˈkɒlədʒɪst/ *noun* [C] **HEALTH** a doctor who treats medical conditions that only affect women

gynaecology *UK* (*US* **gynecology**) /gaɪnəˈkɒlədʒi/ *noun* [U] **HEALTH** the study and treatment of diseases and medical conditions that only affect women •**gynaecological** /ˌgaɪnəkəˈlɒdʒɪkəl/ *adjective*

gypsy (*also UK* **gipsy**) /ˈdʒɪpsi/ *noun* [C] **SOCIETY** a member of a race of people who travel from place to place, especially in Europe *a gypsy caravan*

H, h /eɪtʃ/ the eighth letter of the alphabet

ha /hɑː/ *exclamation* something you say when you are surprised or pleased

the Haber process /ˈhɑːbːəˌprəʊses/ *noun* **CHEMISTRY** a method used in industry for producing ammonia (= a strong-smelling substance used in cleaning materials)

WORD PARTNERS FOR ***habit***

get into/get out of the habit of doing sth • **have/kick** a habit • an **annoying/bad/good** habit • do sth **from/out of/through** habit

O⁃**habit** /ˈhæbɪt/ *noun* **1** [C, U] something that you do regularly, almost without thinking about it *He's just eating **out of habit** - he's not really hungry.* **2 be in/get into the habit of doing sth** to be used/get used to doing something regularly *We don't want the children to get into the habit of watching a lot of TV.* **3 HEALTH** [C, U] something that you often do that is bad for your health or is annoying *He has some really nasty habits.* ○ *We offer help to alcoholics who want to **kick the habit**.* **4 RELIGION** [C] a long, loose piece of clothing worn by some religious groups *a monk's habit*

habitable /ˈhæbɪtəbl/ *adjective* A habitable building is in good enough condition to live in.

habitat /ˈhæbɪtæt/ *noun* [C] **BIOLOGY, ENVIRONMENT** the natural environment of an animal or plant ➲See picture at **ecosystem**

habitation /ˌhæbɪˈteɪʃᵊn/ *noun* [U] when people live in a place *This place is not fit for **human habitation**.*

habitual /həˈbɪtʃuəl/ *adjective* **1** USUAL usual or typical *an habitual expression/gesture* **2** PERSON doing something often because it is a habit *a habitual drug user* •**habitually** *adverb*

hack¹ /hæk/ *verb* [I, T] **1** to cut something roughly into pieces *The victim had been **hacked to death**.* **2 COMPUTING** to use a computer to illegally get into someone else's computer system and read the information that is kept there *Two British youths were caught **hacking into** government computers.*

hack² /hæk/ *noun* [C] *informal* someone who produces low quality writing for books, newspapers, etc

hacker /ˈhækəʳ/ *noun* [C] **COMPUTING** someone who illegally gets into someone else's computer system

O⁃**had** *strong form* /hæd/ *weak forms* /həd, əd, d/ *verb* **1** *past of* have **2 be had** *informal* to be tricked or made to look silly *I think I've been had - this camera doesn't work.*

haddock /ˈhædək/ *noun* [C, U] *plural* **haddock** **FOOD** a fish that lives in northern seas and is eaten as food

O⁃**hadn't** /ˈhædᵊnt/ *short for* had not *I hadn't seen Megan since college.*

haematite *UK* (*US* **hematite**) /ˈhiːmətaɪt/ *noun* [U] **GEOLOGY** a common dark red rock from which we get iron

haemoglobin *UK* (*US* **hemoglobin**) /ˌhiːməˈgləʊbɪn/ *noun* [U] **BIOLOGY** a red substance in the blood which carries oxygen (= gas that we need to live) around the body

haemophilia *UK* (*US* **hemophilia**) /ˌhiːməˈfɪliə/ *noun* [U] **HEALTH** a serious disease in which the flow of blood from someone's body cannot be stopped when they are hurt •**haemophiliac** *UK* (*US* **hemophiliac**) *noun* [C] someone who has haemophilia

haemorrhage *UK* (*US* **hemorrhage**) /ˈhemᵊrɪdʒ/ *noun* [C, U] **HEALTH** when someone suddenly loses a lot of blood *a **brain haemorrhage***

haemorrhoids *UK* (*US* **hemorrhoids**) /ˈhemərɔɪdz/ *noun* [plural] **HEALTH** painful swollen tissue around the opening of a person's bottom

haggard /ˈhægəd/ *adjective* Someone who is haggard has a thin face with dark marks around their eyes because they are ill or tired.

haggle /ˈhægl/ *verb* [I] **FINANCE** to argue, especially about the price of something *I spent 20 minutes **haggling over** the price of a leather bag.*

ˌha ˈha *exclamation* used in writing to represent the sound someone makes when they laugh

haiku /ˈhaɪkuː/ *noun* [C] **LITERATURE** a short Japanese poem which has only 17 syllables (= words or parts of word with one vowel sound)

hail¹ /heɪl/ *noun* **1** [U] small, hard pieces of frozen rain that fall from the sky **2 a hail of bullets/stones/bottles, etc** a lot of bullets/stones/bottles, etc that are fired or thrown at the same time

hail² /heɪl/ *verb* **1** [T] to call or wave to someone to get their attention *She stepped into the road and **hailed a taxi**.* **2 it hails** If it hails, small, hard pieces of frozen rain fall from the sky.

hail sb/sth as sth *phrasal verb* to say publicly and enthusiastically that someone or something is something very good

hail from *phrasal verb* to come from a particular place

O⁃**hair** /heəʳ/ *noun* **1** [U] the thin, thread-like parts that grow on your head *a girl with long, fair hair* **2 BIOLOGY** [C] one of the thin thread-like parts that grow on a person's or animal's skin *My black skirt was covered in cat hairs.* **3 let your hair down** *informal* to relax and enjoy yourself **4 pull/tear your hair out** to be very anxious about something *When they still weren't home by midnight, I was pulling my hair out.* **5 split hairs** to argue about small details that are not important ➲See also: **pubic hair**

hairbrush /ˈheəbrʌʃ/ *noun* [C] a brush that you use to make your hair look tidy

haircut /ˈheəkʌt/ *noun* [C] **1** CUTTING when someone cuts your hair *I really need a haircut.* **2** STYLE the style in which your hair has been cut

hairdo /ˈheəduː/ *noun* [C] *informal* the style in which someone arranges their hair

hairdresser /ˈheəˌdresəʳ/ *noun* **1** [C] someone whose job is to wash, cut, colour, etc people's hair **2 hairdresser's** the place where you go to have your hair washed, cut, coloured, etc

hairdryer /ˈheəˌdraɪəʳ/ *noun* [C] a piece of electrical equipment for drying your hair with hot air

-haired /-ˈheəd/ *suffix* used after a word describing someone's hair *a red-haired woman* ○ *a short-haired cat* ⊃See also: **fair-haired**

hairgrip /ˈheəgrɪp/ *UK* (*US* **bobby pin**) *noun* [C] a small, thin piece of metal, used to fasten a woman's hair in position

hairline /ˈheəlaɪn/ *noun* **1** [C] the place at the top of your face where your hair starts growing **2 a hairline crack/fracture HEALTH** a very thin line where something hard such as a bone or cup is broken

H

hairpin /ˈheəpɪn/ *noun* [C] a piece of metal shaped like a U, used to fasten a woman's hair in position

ˌhairpin ˈbend *UK* (*US* **ˌhairpin ˈturn**) *noun* [C] a bend shaped like a U on a steep road

hair-raising /ˈheəˌreɪzɪŋ/ *adjective* frightening but in an enjoyable way *It was a rather **hair-raising journey** down the mountain road.*

hairstyle /ˈheəstaɪl/ *noun* [C] the style in which someone arranges their hair *Do you like my new hairstyle?*

hairy /ˈheəri/ *adjective* **1** [WITH HAIR] covered in hair *a **hairy chest*** ○ ***hairy legs*** **2** [FRIGHTENING] *informal* frightening or dangerous *There were some rather **hairy moments** during the race.* •**hairiness** *noun* [U]

hajj (also **haj**) /hædʒ/ *noun* [C] *plural* **hajjes** or **hajes RELIGION** the religious journey to Mecca which all Muslims try to make at least once in their life

halal /hælˈæl/ *adjective* **RELIGION, FOOD** Halal meat is prepared according to Islamic law.

hale /heɪl/ *adjective* **hale and hearty** healthy and full of life

O-- **half**[1] /hɑːf/ *noun, determiner plural* **halves 1** [C, U] one of two equal parts of something; ½ *Rice is eaten by **half of** the world's population.* ○ *Cut the lemons into halves.* ○ *It'll take **half an hour** to get there.* ○ *Jenny lived in Beijing for a year and a half.* **2 break/cut/split sth in half** to divide something into two equal parts *Divide the dough in half and roll it out into two circles.* **3 decrease/increase, etc sth by half** to make something smaller/larger, etc by half its size *The drug reduces the risk of stroke by half.* **4 half past one/two/three, etc** *mainly UK* 30 minutes past one o'clock/two o'clock/three o'clock, etc *We got back to our hotel at half past seven.* **5 half one/two/three, etc** *UK informal* 30 minutes past one o'clock/two o'clock/three o'clock, etc *"What time does it start?" "About half six."* **6 go halves with sb** *informal* to divide the cost of something with someone *Shall we go halves on a present for Laura?* **7 half the fun/time/pleasure, etc** *informal* a large part of the enjoyment/time, etc *Kids today - parents don't know where they are half the time.* **8 not half as good/bad/exciting, etc** *informal* to be much less good/bad/exciting, etc than something else *Her new book's not half as good as the last one.*

half[2] /hɑːf/ *adverb* partly, but not completely *half empty/full* ○ *Sophia is half Greek and half Spanish* (= she has one Greek parent and one Spanish parent). ○ *She was only half aware of what was happening.*

ˌhalf ˈboard *noun* [U] *mainly UK* the price for a room in a hotel, which includes breakfast and dinner

half-brother /ˈhɑːfˌbrʌðəʳ/ *noun* [C] **SOCIETY** a brother who is the son of only one of your parents

half-hearted /ˌhɑːfˈhɑːtɪd/ *adjective* without much effort or interest *a **half-hearted attempt*** •**half-heartedly** *adverb*

half-life /ˈhɑːflaɪf/ *noun* [C] **PHYSICS** the amount of time that is needed for the radioactivity (= harmful form of energy produced during a nuclear reaction) of a radioactive substance to be reduced by half

half-sister /ˈhɑːfˌsɪstəʳ/ *noun* [C] **SOCIETY** a sister who is the daughter of only one of your parents

half-term /hɑːfˈtɜːm/ *noun* [C, U] *UK* **EDUCATION** a short holiday in the middle of a school term (= one of the periods the school year is divided into)

half-time /ˌhɑːfˈtaɪm/ *noun* [U] **SPORT** a short period of rest between the two halves of a game

halfway /ˌhɑːfˈweɪ/ *adjective, adverb* at an equal distance between two places, or in the middle of a period of time *the **halfway point*** ○ *He was released **halfway through** his prison sentence.*

O-- **hall** /hɔːl/ *noun* [C] **1** [ENTRANCE] (*also* **hallway** /ˈhɔːlweɪ/) a room or passage in a building, which leads to other rooms **2** [LARGE ROOM] a large room or building where meetings, concerts, etc are held *The Albert Hall* ○ *The disco will be held in the school hall.* ⊃See also: **town hall**

hallmark /ˈhɔːlmɑːk/ *noun* [C] **1** [OFFICIAL] an official mark that is put on something made of silver or gold to prove that it is real **2** [TYPICAL] a quality or method that is typical of a particular type of person or thing *Simplicity is a **hallmark of** his design.*

hallo *UK* (*UK/US* **hello**) /həˈləʊ/ *exclamation* **1** [GREET] used to greet someone *Hallo, Chris, how are things?* **2** [TELEPHONE] used to start a conversation on the telephone *Hallo, this is Alex.*

ˌhall of ˈresidence *UK* (*US* **dormitory**) *noun* [C] *plural* **halls of residence EDUCATION** a building where university or college students live

hallowed /ˈhæləʊd/ *adjective* **1** respected and considered important *a **hallowed tradition*** **2 RELIGION** made holy by a priest *the **hallowed ground** of the churchyard*

Halloween /ˌhæləʊˈiːn/ *noun* [U] the night of 31 October when children dress in special clothes and people try to frighten each other

hallucinate /həˈluːsɪneɪt/ *verb* [I] **HEALTH** to see things that are not really there, because you are ill or have taken an illegal drug

hallucination /hə,luːsɪ'neɪʃən/ *noun* [C, U] **HEALTH** when you see things that are not really there because you are ill or have taken an illegal drug

halo /'heɪləʊ/ *noun* [C] a gold circle of light that is shown around the head of a holy person in a painting

halogen /'hælədʒen/ *noun* [C] **CHEMISTRY** any of a group of five chemical elements which combine with hydrogen to make compounds from which salts can be made *Chlorine and iodine are halogens.* ○ *halogen lighting*

halothane /'hæləθeɪn/ *noun* [U] **HEALTH** a chemical that is used as an anaesthetic (= drug to stop pain) that is breathed in

WORD PARTNERS FOR ***halt***

bring sth to/come to a halt • an **abrupt/grinding/sudden** halt

halt¹ /hɒlt/ *noun* **1** [**no plural**] when something stops moving or happening *The car **came to a halt** just inches from the edge of the cliff.* ○ *News of the accident **brought** the party **to a halt**.* **2 call a halt to sth** to officially order something to stop *The government has called a halt to all new building in the area.*

halt² /hɒlt/ *verb* [I, T] *formal* to stop or make something stop *The council ordered that work on the project should be halted immediately.*

halting /'hɒltɪŋ/ *adjective* stopping often while you are saying or doing something, especially because you are nervous *He spoke quietly, in halting English.*

halve /hɑːv/ *verb* **1** DIVIDE [T] to divide something into two equal parts *Peel and halve the potatoes.* **2** REDUCE [I, T] If you halve something, or if it halves, it is reduced to half the size it was before. *They have almost halved the price of flights to New York.*

ham /hæm/ *noun* [C, U] **FOOD** meat from a pig's back or upper leg *a ham sandwich*

hamburger /'hæm,bɜːgər/ *noun* **1 FOOD** [C] a round, flat shape of meat which is cooked in hot oil and eaten between round pieces of bread *a hamburger and fries* **2 FOOD** [U] *US* (*UK* **mince**) beef (= meat from a cow) that is cut into very small pieces

hamlet /'hæmlət/ *noun* [C] a very small village

hammer¹ /'hæmər/ *noun* [C] a tool with a heavy, metal part at the top that you use to hit nails into something

hammer² /'hæmər/ *verb* [I, T] to hit something with a hammer

hammer sth into sb *phrasal verb* to repeat something to someone a lot of times until they remember it

hammer on sth *phrasal verb* to hit something many times, making a lot of noise *They were woken up by someone **hammering on** the door.*

hammer sth out *phrasal verb* to finally agree on a plan, business agreement, etc after arguing about the details for a long time

hammering /'hæmərɪŋ/ *noun* **1** NOISE [U] the noise made by hitting something with a hammer or hitting something hard with your hands **2** DEFEAT [**no plural**] *UK informal* a very bad defeat

hammock /'hæmək/ *noun* [C] a large piece of cloth or strong net that you hang between two trees or poles to sleep on

hamper¹ /'hæmpər/ *verb* [T] to make it difficult for someone to do something *The police investigation was hampered by a lack of help from the community.*

hamper² /'hæmpər/ *noun* [C] a large basket (= container made of thin pieces of wood) with a lid *a **picnic hamper***

hamster /'hæmstər/ *noun* [C] a small animal with soft fur and no tail that is often kept as a pet

hamstring¹ /'hæmstrɪŋ/ *noun* [C] **ANATOMY** a tendon (= part that connects a muscle to a bone) at the back of the upper part of your leg *a hamstring injury*

hamstring² /'hæmstrɪŋ/ *verb* [T] *past* **hamstrung** to make it difficult for a person, team, or organization to do something

O╼**hand¹** /hænd/ *noun* **1 ANATOMY** [C] the part of your body on the end of your arm that has fingers and a thumb *Take your hands out of your pockets.* ⊃See colour picture **The Body** on page Centre 13 **2 take sb by the hand** to get hold of someone's hand *Bill took her by the hand and led her into the garden.* **3 hand in hand** holding each other's hand *The young couple walked hand in hand by the lake.* **4 hold hands** to hold each other's hand **5 at hand** near in time or space *Teachers are always close at hand to give help to any child who needs it.* **6 by hand** done or made by a person instead of a machine *This sweater has to be washed by hand.* **7 in hand** being worked on or dealt with now *Despite the pressures we are determined to get on with the job in hand.* **8 be in sb's hands** to be in someone's control or care *The matter is now in the hands of my solicitor.* **9 on hand** (*also UK* **to hand**) near to someone or something, and ready to help or be used when necessary *Extra supplies will be on hand, should they be needed.* **10 at the hands of sb** If you suffer at the hands of someone, they hurt you or treat you badly. **11** CLOCK [C] one of the long, thin pieces that point to the numbers on a clock or watch **12** CARDS [C] the set of playing cards that one player has been given in a game **13 a hand** some help, especially to do something practical *Could you **give me a hand with** these suitcases?* ○ *I think Matthew might **need a hand with** his homework.* **14 on the one hand ... on the other hand** used when you are comparing two different ideas or opinions *On the one hand, computer games develop many skills, but on the other, they mean kids don't get enough exercise.* **15 hands off** *informal* used to tell someone not to touch something *Hands off - that's mine!* **16 change hands** to be sold by someone and bought by someone else *The hotel has changed hands twice since 1982.* **17 a free hand** permission to make your own decisions about how you want to do something **18 get out of hand** to become difficult to control *It was the end of term and the children were getting a little out of hand.* **19 go hand in hand** If two things go hand in hand, they exist together and are connected with each other. **20 have your hands full** to be very busy

H

Shelley has her hands full with three kids under 5. **21 get/lay your hands on sth** to find something **22 get/gain the upper hand** to get into a stronger position than someone else so that you are controlling a situation *Government troops are gradually gaining the upper hand over the rebels.* **23 with your bare hands** without using a weapon or tool **24 wring your hands** to press your hands together because you are upset or worried about something

hand² /hænd/ *verb* **1** [+ **two objects**] to give something to someone *Could you hand me that book, please?* **2 you have to hand it to sb** *informal* used when you want to show that you admire someone *You have to hand it to Mick, he's done a good job on that kitchen.*

hand sth back *phrasal verb* to return something to the person who gave it to you

hand sth down *phrasal verb* **1** [CHILDREN] to give toys, clothes, books, etc to children who are younger than you in your family **2** [TRADITIONS] to pass traditions from older people to younger ones *a custom handed down through the generations*

hand sth in *phrasal verb* to give something to someone in a position of authority *Have you handed your history essay in yet?*

hand sth out *phrasal verb* to give something to all the people in a group *A girl was handing out leaflets at the station.*

hand sb/sth over *phrasal verb* to give someone or something to someone else *The hijacker was handed over to the French police.*

-hand /hænd/ ⊃See: **left-hand, right-hand, second-hand**

handbag /ˈhændbæg/ *mainly UK* (*mainly US* **purse**) *noun* [C] a bag carried by a woman with her money, keys, etc inside

handball /ˈhændbɔːl/ *noun* **1 SPORT** [U] in the US, a game in which players hit a small rubber ball against a wall with their hands **2 SPORT** [C, U] in football, when a player breaks a rule by touching the ball with their hand or arm

handbook /ˈhændbʊk/ *noun* [C] a book that contains information and advice about a particular subject *a teacher's handbook*

handbrake /ˈhændbreɪk/ *UK* (*US* **emergency brake**) *noun* [C] a stick inside a car that you can pull up to stop the car from moving ⊃See colour picture **Car** on page Centre 7

handcuffs /ˈhændkʌfs/ *noun* [**plural**] two metal rings that are joined by a chain and are put on a prisoner's wrists (= lower arms)

-handed /ˈhændɪd/ *suffix* ⊃See: **empty-handed, heavy-handed, left-handed, red-handed, right-handed, single-handed**

handful /ˈhændfʊl/ *noun* **1** [C] the amount of something that you can hold in one hand **2 a handful of sth** a small number of people or things *Only a handful of people came to the meeting.* **3 a handful** *informal* someone who is difficult to control, especially a child

handgun /ˈhændgʌn/ *noun* [C] a small gun that you can hold in one hand

hand-held /ˈhændheld/ *adjective* describes something that is designed to be held and used easily with one or two hands *a hand-held computer/device*

handicap /ˈhændɪkæp/ *noun* [C] *old-fashioned* **1** [MIND/BODY] something that is wrong with your mind or body permanently *a* ***mental/physical handicap*** **2** [DISADVANTAGE] something that makes it more difficult for you to do something *I found not having a car quite a handicap in the countryside.*

handicapped /ˈhændɪkæpt/ *adjective old-fashioned* not able to use part of your body or your mind because it has been damaged in some way ***mentally/physically handicapped***

handicraft /ˈhændɪkrɑːft/ *noun* **ART, DT 1** [C] an activity that involves making things with your hands and that needs skill and artistic ability **2 handicrafts** things that people make with their hands *a sale of handicrafts*

handiwork /ˈhændɪwɜːk/ *noun* [U] something that someone makes or does *She put down the brush and stood back to* ***admire*** *her* ***handiwork.***

handkerchief /ˈhæŋkətʃiːf/ *noun* [C] a small piece of cloth or soft paper that you use to dry your eyes or nose

O⊶**handle¹** /ˈhændl/ *verb* [T] **1** [DEAL WITH] to deal with something *He handled the situation very well.* ○ *This office handles thousands of enquiries every day.* **2** [TOUCH] to touch, hold, or pick up something *You must wash your hands before handling food.* **3** [BUY] to buy and sell goods *He's been charged with* ***handling stolen goods.***

handle² /ˈhændl/ *noun* **1** [C] the part of something that you use to hold it or open it *a* ***door handle*** ○ *the handle on a suitcase* **2 fly off the handle** *informal* to suddenly become very angry

handlebars /ˈhændlbɑːz/ *noun* [**plural**] the metal bars at the front of a bicycle or motorcycle that you hold onto to control direction

handler /ˈhændləʳ/ *noun* [C] someone whose job is to deal with or control a particular type of thing *a police dog handler*

ˈhand ˌluggage *noun* [U] small bags that you can carry onto an aircraft with you when you travel

handmade /ˌhændˈmeɪd/ *adjective* made by hand instead of by machine

handout /ˈhændaʊt/ *noun* [C] **1** [MONEY] money or food that is given to people who are poor *Increasing numbers of people are dependent on government handouts.* **2** [PAPER] a copy of a document that is given to all the people in a class or meeting

handpicked /ˌhændˈpɪkt/ *adjective* carefully chosen for a particular purpose or job *a handpicked audience*

handset /ˈhændset/ *noun* [C] **1** the outer part of a mobile phone **2** the part of a telephone that you hold in front of your mouth and against your ear

ˌhands ˈfree *adjective* describes a piece of equipment, especially a telephone, that you can use without needing to hold it in your hand

handshake /ˈhændʃeɪk/ *noun* [C] the action of taking someone's right hand and shaking it when you meet or leave each other

handshaking /ˈhændʃeɪkɪŋ/ *noun* [U] **COMPUTING** the processes that happen so that two pieces of computer equipment can send information to each other

handsome /ˈhændsəm/ *adjective* **1** A handsome man is attractive. *tall, dark and handsome* **2 a handsome profit/sum, etc** a large amount of money

hands-on /ˌhændzˈɒn/ *adjective* physically doing something and not only studying it or watching someone else do it ***hands-on experience***

handwriting /ˈhændˌraɪtɪŋ/ *noun* [U] the way that someone forms the letters when they write with a pen or pencil

handwritten /ˌhændˈrɪtᵊn/ *adjective* written with a pen or pencil *a **handwritten letter***

handy /ˈhændi/ *adjective* **1** [USEFUL] useful or easy to use *a handy container/tool* **2 come in handy** *informal* to be useful at some time in the future *Don't throw those jars away - they might come in handy.* **3** [NEAR] *UK informal* near to a place *It's a nice house and it's **handy for** the station.* **4 be handy with sth** to be good at using something, usually a tool *He's very handy with a paintbrush.*

handyman /ˈhændimæn/ *noun* [C] *plural* **handymen** someone who is good at making things or repairing them

O‑**hang**[1] /hæŋ/ *verb* **hung 1** [FASTEN] [I, T] to fasten something so that the top part is fixed but the lower part is free to move, or to be fastened in this way *He **hung** his coat **on** the hook behind the door.* **2** *past also* **hanged** [KILL] [I, T] to kill someone by putting a rope around their neck and making them drop, or to die in this way **3** [IN AIR] [I] to stay in the air for a long time *Thick fog hung over the town.* ➲See also: be/hang in the **balance**[1], hang your **head**[1] (in shame)

hang around *phrasal verb informal* (*also UK* **hang about**) **1** to spend time somewhere, usually without doing very much *There's nowhere for teenagers to go, so they just **hang around** on street corners.* **2 hang around with sb** to spend time with someone

hang on *phrasal verb* **1** [WAIT] *informal* to wait for a short time *Hang on - I'm almost finished.* **2** [HOLD] to hold something tightly *Hang on, we're going over a big bump here.*

hang onto sth *phrasal verb informal* to keep something *You should hang onto that - it might be worth something.*

hang out *phrasal verb informal* to spend a lot of time in a particular place or with a particular group of people

hang up *phrasal verb* to finish a conversation on the telephone by putting the phone down

hang sth up *phrasal verb* to put something such as a coat somewhere where it can hang *You can hang up your jacket over there.*

hang[2] /hæŋ/ *noun* **get the hang of sth** *informal* to gradually learn how to do or use something

hangar /ˈhæŋgəʳ/ *noun* [C] a large building where aircraft are kept

hanger /ˈhæŋəʳ/ (*also* **coat hanger**) *noun* [C] a wire, wooden, or plastic object for hanging clothes on

ˈhang ˌglider *noun* [C] a structure covered in cloth that you hold onto and float through the air

ˈhang ˌgliding *noun* [U] **SPORT** the sport of flying using a structure covered in cloth that you hang from

ˌhanging ˈvalley *noun* [C] **GEOGRAPHY** a valley that ends suddenly where it meets the side of a larger, deeper valley

hangover /ˈhæŋəʊvəʳ/ *noun* [C] **HEALTH** If you have a hangover, you feel ill because you drank too much alcohol the evening before.

hanker /ˈhæŋkəʳ/ *verb*

hanker after/for sth *phrasal verb* to want something very much, especially over a long period of time

hankie (*also* **hanky**) /ˈhæŋki/ *noun* [C] *informal short for* handkerchief

Hanukkah (*also* **Chanukah**) /ˈhɑːnəkə/ *noun* [C, U] **RELIGION** a Jewish religious holiday lasting for eight days in December

haphazard /ˌhæpˈhæzəd/ *adjective* not planned, organized, controlled, or done regularly *The whole examination process seemed completely haphazard.* •**haphazardly** *adverb*

hapless /ˈhæpləs/ *adjective literary* having bad luck

haploid /ˈhæplɔɪd/ *adjective* **BIOLOGY** a haploid cell has only one set of chromosomes, from one parent ➲Compare **diploid**

O‑**happen** /ˈhæpᵊn/ *verb* [I] **1** [EXIST] If an event or situation happens, it exists or starts to be done, usually by chance. *Were you anywhere nearby when the accident happened?* ○ *We can't let a mistake like this happen again.* **2** [RESULT] to be the result of an action, situation, or event that someone or something experiences *Did you hear what **happened to** Jamie last night?* ○ *What happens if we can't get enough tickets?* **3 happen to do sth** to do something by chance *If you happen to see Peter, say "hi" for me.* ○ *You don't happen to know her phone number, do you?* **4 as it happens; it so happens** something that you say in order to introduce a surprising fact *As it happens, her birthday is the day after mine.*

happen on/upon sth/sb *phrasal verb* to find something or meet someone without planning to

happening /ˈhæpᵊnɪŋ/ *noun* [C] something that happens, often a strange event that is difficult to explain

happily /ˈhæpɪli/ *adverb* **1** [HAPPY] in a happy way ***happily married*** **2** [WILLING] in a way that is very willing *I'd happily drive you to the airport.* **3** [LUCKY] having a good or lucky result *Happily, the operation was a complete success.*

WORD PARTNERS FOR ***happiness***

find happiness

happiness /ˈhæpɪnəs/ *noun* [U] the feeling of being happy

OTHER WAYS OF SAYING *happy*

A person who seems happy may be described as **cheerful**: *She's always very **cheerful**.*

If someone is happy because of something, they may be described as **pleased** or **glad**, and if they are extremely happy because of something, they may be described as **delighted**: *He was **pleased** that she had come back.* • *I was so **glad** to see her.* • *They are **delighted** with their new car.*

If someone is extremely happy and excited, they may be described as **ecstatic** or **elated**: *The new president was greeted by an **ecstatic** crowd.* • *We were **elated** at the news.*

O━**happy** /ˈhæpi/ *adjective* **1** [PLEASED] pleased and in a good mood, especially because something good has happened *I'm glad you've finally found someone who **makes** you **happy**.* ○ *Jean seems much happier now that she's moved out.* **2 happy to do sth** to be willing to do something *I'd be very happy to help, if you need a hand.* **3** [SHOWING HAPPINESS] making you feel happy, or expressing happiness *Did the book have a **happy ending**?* **4** [SATISFIED] satisfied and not worried *Are you **happy with** your exam results?* ○ *I'm not very **happy about** you travelling alone at night.* **5 Happy Birthday/New Year, etc** something friendly that you say to someone on a special day or holiday *Happy Christmas!* ➲Opposite **unhappy**

happy-go-lucky /ˌhæpigəʊˈlʌki/ *adjective* not worried and not having any responsibilities

ˈhappy ˌhour *noun* [**usually singular**] a period of time, usually in the early evening, when a bar (= a place where alcoholic drinks are sold and drunk) sells drinks more cheaply than usual

ˌhappy ˈslapping *noun* [**U**] when a group of young people attack someone and photograph their attack with mobile phones

harass /ˈhærəs, həˈræs/ *verb* [**T**] to continue to annoy or upset someone over a period of time

harassed /ˈhærəst/ *adjective* tired and feeling anxious *harassed passengers*

WORD PARTNERS FOR *harassment*

be subjected to/suffer harassment • **racial/sexual** harassment • harassment **of** sb

harassment /ˈhærəsmənt/ *noun* [**U**] behaviour that annoys or upsets someone ***sexual harassment***

harbour¹ *UK* (*US* **harbor**) /ˈhɑːbəʳ/ *noun* [**C**] an area of water near the coast where ships are kept and are safe from the sea

harbour² *UK* (*US* **harbor**) /ˈhɑːbəʳ/ *verb* [**T**] **1** [FEEL/THINK] If you harbour doubts, hopes, thoughts, etc, you feel or think about them for a long time. *He harboured dreams of one day becoming a professional footballer.* **2** [HIDE] to hide someone or something bad *to **harbour** a **criminal***

O━**hard¹** /hɑːd/ *adjective* **1** [FIRM] firm and stiff, and not easy to press or bend *a hard surface* ○ *The seats in the waiting room were hard and uncomfortable.* **2** [DIFFICULT] difficult to do or understand [**+ to do sth**] *It must be hard to study with all this noise.* ○ *Quitting my job was the hardest decision I ever had to make.* **3** [WITH EFFORT] using or done with a lot of effort *the long, **hard struggle*** ○ *With a bit of **hard work** and determination we might still finish on time.* **4** [UNPLEASANT] full of problems and difficult to deal with *My grandparents had a very **hard life**.* **5** [NOT KIND] not gentle or kind *She had a cold, hard look in her eyes.* **6 be hard on sb a** [CRITICIZE] to criticize someone too much or treat them unfairly *You shouldn't be so hard on yourself.* **b** [MAKE UNHAPPY] to make someone unhappy by causing them problems *Our divorce has been particularly hard on the children.* **7 be hard on sth** to damage something or make it have problems *Stress can be hard on any relationship.* **8 do/learn sth the hard way** to do or learn something by experiencing a lot of problems or difficulty **9 give sb a hard time** *informal* to criticize someone or to treat them unfairly *He gave me a hard time about losing his keys.*

O━**hard²** /hɑːd/ *adverb* **1** [WITH EFFORT] with a lot of effort *She **tried** very **hard** but she wasn't quite fast enough.* ○ *You'll have to **work harder**, if you want to pass this exam.* **2** [WITH FORCE] with a lot of force *It's been raining hard all day.* ○ *She kicked the ball as hard as she could.* **3 die hard** If a belief, custom, or habit dies hard, it is very difficult to change. *I'm afraid that **old habits die hard**.* **4 hit sb hard** *UK* If a situation or experience hits you hard, it makes you so upset that you have difficulty dealing with it.

hardback /ˈhɑːdbæk/ *noun* [**C**] a book that has a thick, stiff cover

hard-boiled /ˌhɑːdˈbɔɪld/ *adjective* **FOOD** A hard-boiled egg has been boiled with its shell on, until the inside is solid.

ˌhard ˈcash *noun* [**U**] **FINANCE** coins and paper money

ˌhard ˈcopy *UK* (*US* **ˈhardˌcopy**) *noun* [**C, U**] **COMPUTING** information from a computer that has been printed on paper

hardcore (*also* **hard-core**) /ˈhɑːdˌkɔː/ *adjective* **1** [EXTREMELY LOYAL] extremely loyal to someone or something, and not willing to change *a **hard-core following*** **2** [SEXUAL] Hardcore magazines, films, etc show very active or offensive sexual acts. ***hardcore pornography***

ˌhard ˈcore *noun* [**no plural**] a small group of people in society or an organization who are very active and determined not to change *a hard core of activists*

ˌhard ˈcurrency *noun* [**U**] **ECONOMICS** money that is valuable and can be exchanged easily because it comes from a powerful country

ˌhard ˈdisk *noun* [**C**] **COMPUTING** a hard drive

ˈhard ˌdrive (also **hard disk**) *noun* [**C**] **COMPUTING** the part inside a computer that is not removed and stores very large amounts of information

ˌhard ˈdrugs *noun* [**plural**] **HEALTH** very strong, illegal drugs

harden /ˈhɑːdᵊn/ *verb* [**I, T**] **1** [BECOME HARD] to become hard and stiff, or to make something become hard and stiff *This island is formed from volcanic lava that has hardened into rock.*

2 STOP FEELING EMOTIONS to stop feeling emotions about someone or something, so that you seem less kind, gentle, or weak ***hardened criminals***

hard-headed /ˌhɑːdˈhedɪd/ *adjective* very determined, and not willing to be influenced by your emotions *a hard-headed manager*

hard-hearted /ˌhɑːdˈhɑːtɪd/ *adjective* not caring how other people feel

hard-hitting /ˌhɑːdˈhɪtɪŋ/ *adjective* A hard-hitting speech, report, article, etc is very severe or criticizes someone or something a lot.

ˌhard ˈline *noun* [**no plural**] when someone is very strict and severe *Judge Tucker has a reputation for **taking a hard line on** criminals.* •**hardline** /ˌhɑːdˈlaɪn/ *adjective a **hardline policy** on illegal immigrants*

O‑ **hardly** /ˈhɑːdli/ *adverb* **1** NOT MUCH almost not, or only a very small amount *I was so tired that I could hardly walk.* ○ *We've **hardly ever** spoken to each other.* ○ *There's **hardly any** food left in the fridge.* **2** NOT LIKELY used to emphasize that you think something is not likely, true, possible, etc *I hardly think she'll want to talk to me now that I have a new girlfriend.*

COMMON LEARNER ERROR

hardly or **hard**

When you mean 'with a lot of effort or force', you should use the adverb **hard**, not 'hardly'.

We worked very hard.

~~*We worked very hardly.*~~

hard-nosed /ˌhɑːdˈnəʊzd/ *adjective* very determined, and not willing to be influenced by your emotions *a hard-nosed lawyer*

ˌhard ˈpalate *noun* [**C**] **ANATOMY** the hard bony part that forms the top of the mouth, behind the front teeth ➲Compare **soft palate** ➲See picture at **respiratory system**

hard-pressed /ˌhɑːdˈprest/ *adjective* **1 be hard-pressed to do sth** to not be able to do something, or have difficulty doing something *You'd be hard-pressed to find a better worker than Jeff.* **2** having problems because you are poor *hard-pressed farmers*

WORD PARTNERS FOR ***hardship***

suffer hardship • **economic/financial/physical** hardship

hardship /ˈhɑːdʃɪp/ *noun* [**C, U**] a problem or situation that makes you suffer a lot, especially because you are very poor *They have suffered years of **financial hardship**.*

ˌhard ˈshoulder *UK* (*US* **shoulder**) *noun* [**C**] the area on the edge of a main road where a car can stop in an emergency

ˌhard ˈup *adjective informal* not having enough money

hardware /ˈhɑːdweəʳ/ *noun* [**U**] **1 COMPUTING** the machines or equipment that your computer system is made from, not the programs **2** tools and strong equipment, such as those used in the home or garden

hard-wired /hɑːdˈwaɪəd/ *adjective* **COMPUTING** If something that a computer or electronic device does is hard-wired, it cannot be changed.

hardwood /ˈhɑːdwʊd/ *noun* [**C, U**] **DT** hard heavy wood from a tree with wide leaves *tropical hardwoods, such as mahogany and teak*

hard-working /ˌhɑːdˈwɜːkɪŋ/ *adjective* doing a job seriously and with a lot of effort

hardy /ˈhɑːdi/ *adjective* strong enough to deal with bad conditions or difficult situations

hare /heəʳ/ *noun* [**C**] an animal like a large rabbit that can run very fast and has long ears

harem /ˈhɑːriːm/ (US) /ˈherəm/ *noun* [**C**] **SOCIETY** a group of women who live with or are married to one man in some Muslim societies, or the place where these women live

WORD PARTNERS FOR ***harm***

cause/do (sb/sth) harm • **not come to any** harm • **great/serious/untold** harm • harm **to** sb

O‑ **harm¹** /hɑːm/ *noun* **1** [**U**] hurt or damage *Smoking can **cause** serious **harm to** the lungs.* ○ *Alan would never **do** anyone any **harm**.* **2 not come to any harm** to not be hurt or damaged **3 not do any harm** to not be a bad thing to do and possibly be a good thing [+ **to do sth**] ***It wouldn't do any harm** to have another look.* **4 there's no harm in doing sth** used to say that something is not a bad thing to do and could possibly have a good effect *I suppose there's no harm in trying.* **5 not mean any harm** to not intend to hurt someone or damage something *I never meant him any harm, I just wanted him to leave me alone.* **6 out of harm's way** safe from a dangerous place or situation

O‑ **harm²** /hɑːm/ *verb* [**T**] to hurt someone or damage something *Thankfully no one was harmed in the accident.*

harmful /ˈhɑːmfəl/ *adjective* causing or likely to cause harm *Doctors believe that smoking is **harmful to** your health.*

harmless /ˈhɑːmləs/ *adjective* **1** NOT CAUSING DAMAGE not able or not likely to cause any hurt or damage *Taken in small doses, this drug is completely harmless.* **2** NOT UPSETTING not likely to shock or upset people *Their jokes seemed harmless enough.* •**harmlessly** *adverb*

harmonica /hɑːˈmɒnɪkə/ *noun* [**C**] **MUSIC** a small musical instrument that you blow into as you move it across your mouth

harmonious /hɑːˈməʊniəs/ *adjective* **1** PEACEFUL friendly and peaceful *a harmonious business relationship* **2** SOUND having or making a pleasant sound

harmonize (*also UK* **-ise**) /ˈhɑːmənaɪz/ *verb* [**I, T**] **1** to be suitable together, or to make different people, plans, situations, etc suitable for each other *The gardens had been designed to **harmonize with** the natural landscape.* **2 MUSIC** to sing or play music in harmony

harmony /ˈhɑːməni/ *noun* **1** [**U**] when people are peaceful and agree with each other, or when different things seem right or suitable together *living together **in peace and harmony*** **2 MUSIC** [**C, U**] a pleasant sound in music, made

H

by playing or singing a group of different notes together

harness¹ /ˈhɑːnɪs/ *noun* [C] **1** FOR HORSES a set of straps fastened around a horse's body and connecting it to a vehicle that it will pull **2** FOR PEOPLE a set of strong, flat ropes that fasten equipment to your body or fasten you to a vehicle to prevent you from moving too much *All climbers must wear safety harnesses and helmets.*

harness² /ˈhɑːnɪs/ *verb* [T] **1** HORSES to put a harness on a horse, or to connect a horse to a vehicle using a harness **2** CONTROL to control something so that you can use its power or qualities for a particular purpose

harp¹ /hɑːp/ *noun* [C] **MUSIC** a large wooden musical instrument with many strings that you play with your fingers

harp² /hɑːp/ *verb*
harp on (about sb/sth) *phrasal verb* to talk about someone or something too much

harpoon /ˌhɑːˈpuːn/ *noun* [C] a weapon with a sharp point, used especially for hunting whales (= large sea animals)

harrowing /ˈhærəʊɪŋ/ *adjective* making you feel extremely frightened or upset *a harrowing experience*

harsh /hɑːʃ/ *adjective* **1** CRUEL cruel, unkind, or unpleasant in a way that seems unfair ***harsh criticism/punishment*** ○ *Taking him out of the game was bit harsh.* **2** DIFFICULT very cold, dangerous, or unpleasant and difficult to live in ***harsh conditions*** **3** STRONG too strong, bright, loud, etc ***harsh chemicals*** ○ ***harsh lighting*** •**harshly** *adverb* •**harshness** *noun* [U]

harvest¹ /ˈhɑːvɪst/ *noun* **1** **FARMING** [C, U] when crops are cut and collected from fields **2** **FARMING** [C] the quality or amount of crops that are collected

harvest² /ˈhɑːvɪst/ *verb* [I, T] **FARMING** to cut and collect crops when they are ready

⊶**has** *strong form* /hæz/ *weak forms* /həz, əz, z/ *present simple he/she/it of* have

has-been /ˈhæzbiːn/ *noun* [C] *informal* someone who was famous or important in the past but is now ignored

hash /hæʃ/ *noun* **make a hash of sth** *UK informal* to do something very badly

hashish /hæʃˈiːʃ/ (*also* **hash**) *noun* [U] **HEALTH** an illegal drug that is usually smoked for pleasure

⊶**hasn't** /ˈhæzᵊnt/ *short for* has not *It hasn't rained for three weeks.*

hassle¹ /ˈhæsl/ *noun* [C, U] **1** PROBLEM something that is annoying because it is difficult or unpleasant to do *I don't want to drive - it's such a hassle finding a place to park.* **2** ARGUMENT an argument or fight *They aren't giving you any hassle, are they?*

hassle² /ˈhæsl/ *verb* [T] to annoy someone, especially by asking them something again and again *He's always hassling me about money.*

WORD PARTNERS FOR ***haste***

indecent/undue haste • **in** sb's haste • do sth **in** haste

haste /heɪst/ *noun* [U] when you are in a hurry and do something more quickly than you should ***In their haste*** *to escape, they left behind all their belongings.*

hasten /ˈheɪsᵊn/ *verb* **1** [T] to make something happen faster than usual **2** **hasten to do sth** to hurry to do or say something *I was not, I hasten to add, the only male there.*

hasty /ˈheɪsti/ *adjective* done very quickly, usually too quickly and without thinking enough *a* ***hasty decision/remark*** •**hastily** *adverb*

⊶**hat** /hæt/ *noun* [C] something you wear to cover your head, for fashion or protection *a cowboy hat* ➲See also: **bowler hat, top hat**

hatch¹ /hætʃ/ *verb* **1** **BIOLOGY** [I, T] If an egg hatches or is hatched, it is broken open by a baby creature such as a bird, fish, or snake being born. **2** **hatch a plan/plot, etc** to plan something secretly, especially something bad *He hatched a plot to kill his wife.*

hatch² /hætʃ/ *noun* [C] a small door or opening, especially in a ship, aircraft, or spacecraft *an escape hatch*

hatchback /ˈhætʃbæk/ *noun* [C] a car that has a large door at the back, which you lift up to open

hatchet /ˈhætʃɪt/ *noun* **1** [C] a small axe (= tool for cutting wood) **2** **bury the hatchet** to forget about your arguments and become friends with someone again

⊶**hate¹** /heɪt/ *verb* [T] **1** DISLIKE to dislike someone or something very much *They've hated each other since they were kids.* [+ **doing sth**] *He hates going to the dentist's.* [+ **to do sth**] *I hate to see you look so upset.* **2** SORRY used to emphasize that you are sorry you have to do something *I hate to interrupt, John, but we need to leave.* ➲See also: hate sb's **guts**

hate² /heɪt/ *noun* [U] when you dislike someone or something very much ➲See also: **pet hate**

hateful /ˈheɪtfᵊl/ *adjective* extremely unpleasant or unkind *She called me the most hateful names.*

WORD PARTNERS FOR ***hatred***

deep/intense hatred • **racial** hatred • hatred **of** sb/sth

hatred /ˈheɪtrɪd/ *noun* [U] when you dislike someone or something very much *He developed an* ***intense hatred*** *of all women.*

ˈhat ˌtrick *noun* [C] **SPORT** when a player or team has three successes, one after the other, especially three goals in a game

haughty /ˈhɔːti/ *adjective* showing that you think you are much better or more important than other people *a haughty young actress* •**haughtily** *adverb*

haul¹ /hɔːl/ *verb* [T] to pull something somewhere slowly and with difficulty *They hauled the piano into the living room.*

haul² /hɔːl/ *noun* **1** [C] an amount of something that has been stolen or that is owned illegally *a haul of arms/drugs* **2** **be a long haul** to be difficult and take a long time

haulage /ˈhɔːlɪdʒ/ *noun* [U] *UK* the business of moving things by road or railway *a road haulage firm*

haunt¹ /hɔːnt/ *verb* [T] **1** GHOST If a ghost haunts a place, it appears there often. *a **haunted house*** **2** UNPLEASANT MEMORY If an unpleasant memory or feeling haunts you, you think about or feel it often. [**often passive**] *He was haunted by memories of the war.*

haunt² /hɔːnt/ *noun* [C] a place that someone visits often *Regents Park is one of my **favourite haunts** in London.*

haunting /ˈhɔːntɪŋ/ *adjective* beautiful, but in a sad way *the haunting beauty of Africa*

O⊸**have¹** *strong form* /hæv/ *weak forms* /həv, əv, v/ *auxiliary verb* used with the past participle of another verb to form the present and past perfect tenses *Have you seen Roz?* ○ *I've passed my test.* ○ *He hasn't visited London before.* ○ *It would have been better to tell the truth.* ○ *He's been working in France for two years now.* ○ *I had met his wife before.*

O⊸**have²** /hæv/ *modal verb* **1 have to do sth; have got to do sth** to need to do something or be forced to do something *I have to go to Manchester tomorrow.* ○ *Do we have to finish this today?* ○ *They've had to change their plans.* **2** used when you are telling someone how to do something *You've got to type in your name, then your password.* **3** used to say that you feel certain that something is true or will happen *Interest rates have to come down at some point.* ○ *There's* (= there has) *got to be a better way of doing this.* ➲See Extra help page **Modal verbs** on page Centre 34.

O⊸**have³** *strong form* /hæv/ *weak forms* /həv, əv, v/ *verb past* **had** **1** OWN [T] (*also* **have got**) to own something *I have two horses.* ○ *Laura has got beautiful blue eyes.* **2** HOLD [T] used to say that someone is holding something, or that someone or something is with them *He had a pen in his hand.* ○ *She had a baby with her.* **3** BE ILL [T] (*also* **have got**) If you have a particular illness, you are suffering from it. *Have you ever had the measles?* **4** EAT/DRINK [T] to eat or drink something *We are having dinner at 7 o'clock.* ○ *Can I have a drink of water?* **5 have a bath/sleep/walk, etc** used with nouns to say that someone does something *Can I have a quick shower?* ○ *Let Mark have a try.* **6 have difficulty/fun/problems, etc** used with nouns to say that someone experiences something *We had a great time in Barcelona.* **7 have a baby** to give birth to a baby **8 have sth done** If you have something done, someone does it for you. *I'm having my hair cut tomorrow.* ○ *We had the carpets cleaned.* **9 have had it** to be broken or not working well *I think the car engine's had it.* **10 have it in for sb** to dislike someone and want to cause problems for them *She really has it in for me - I don't know what I've done to offend her.* **11 have it out (with sb)** to talk to someone about something they have done which made you angry, in order to try to solve the problem

have (got) sth on *phrasal verb* to be wearing something *She only had a bikini on.*

have sb on *phrasal verb UK* to make someone think that something is true, as a joke *He's not really angry - he's just having you on.*

have sth out *phrasal verb* to have something removed from your body *I'm having two teeth out next week.*

haven /ˈheɪvᵊn/ *noun* [C] a safe place *a haven for wildlife*

O⊸**haven't** /ˈhævᵊnt/ *short for* have not *I haven't finished eating.*

WORD PARTNERS FOR ***havoc***

cause/create/wreak havoc • **play** havoc with sth

havoc /ˈhævək/ *noun* [U] a very confused and possibly dangerous situation *The snow has **caused havoc** on Scotland's roads today.*

hawk /hɔːk/ *noun* [C] a large hunting bird

hay /heɪ/ *noun* [U] **FARMING** dried grass for animals to eat

ˈhay ˌfever *noun* [U] **HEALTH** an illness caused by a bad reaction to plants that some people get in the summer, especially affecting the nose and eyes

haystack /ˈheɪstæk/ *noun* [C] **FARMING** a large pile of hay

hazard¹ /ˈhæzəd/ *noun* **1** [C] something that is dangerous *a **fire hazard*** ○ *a **health hazard*** **2 an occupational hazard** something unpleasant that sometimes happens to people who do a particular job

hazard² /ˈhæzəd/ *verb* **hazard a guess** to risk guessing something *I don't know where he is, but I'd be willing to hazard a guess.*

hazardous /ˈhæzədəs/ *adjective* dangerous ***hazardous chemicals***

haze /heɪz/ *noun* [U] when the air is not very clear because of something such as heat or smoke, making it difficult to see well

hazel /ˈheɪzᵊl/ *adjective* green-brown in colour *hazel eyes*

hazy /ˈheɪzi/ *adjective* **1** NOT CLEAR If the air is hazy, it is not very clear because of something such as heat or smoke, making it difficult to see well. *a hazy day* **2** CONFUSED not remembering things clearly *He has only a hazy recollection of what happened.*

HCF /ˌeɪtʃsiːˈef/ **MATHEMATICS** *abbreviation for* highest common factor: the highest number that a set of two or more different numbers can be divided by exactly

HCFC /ˌeɪtʃsiˈefsiː/ *noun* [U, C] **CHEMISTRY** *abbreviation for* hydrochlorofluorocarbon: a type of gas used especially in aerosols (= containers that force out liquids in very small drops)

HCI /ˌeɪtʃsiːˈaɪ/ *noun* [C] **COMPUTING** *abbreviation for* human-computer interface; the part of a computer system, for example what you see on the screen, that allows a person to use a computer

O⊸**he** *strong form* /hiː/ *weak form* /hi/ *pronoun* used as the subject of the verb when referring to someone male who has already been talked about *"When is Paul coming?" "He'll be here in a minute."*

H

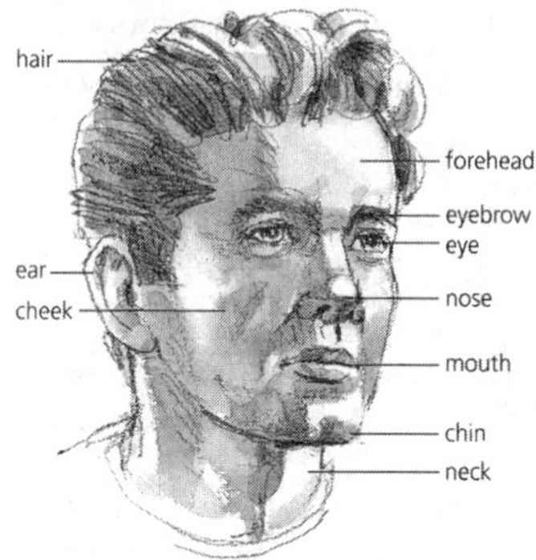

head

head[1] /hed/ *noun* [C] **1 ANATOMY** the part of your body above your neck which contains your brain, eyes, ears, mouth, nose, etc and on which your hair grows *He fell and hit his head on the table.* ➲See colour picture **The Body** on page Centre 13 **2** MIND your mind *All these thoughts were going round in my head.* **3** ORGANIZATION the person who is in charge of an organization *Her father is the head of an oil company.* **4 EDUCATION** (*also* ˌ**head 'teacher**) *UK* the person in charge of a school *You'll have to ask the head if you can have a day off school.* **5** FRONT/TOP the front or top part of something *Who is that **at the head of** the table?* **6 £10/$6, etc a head** costing £10/$6, etc for each person *The meal costs £20 a head.* **7 heads** the side of a coin that has a picture of someone's head on it *Heads or tails?* **8 be banging your head against a brick wall** to do, say, or ask for something repeatedly but to be unable to change a situation **9 come to a head** If a problem or disagreement comes to a head, it becomes so bad that you have to start dealing with it. **10 go over sb's head** to be too difficult for someone to understand *All this talk about philosophy went right over my head.* **11 go to your head** If something that you have achieved goes to your head, it makes you too proud. *Fame and fortune had gone to his head.* **12 hang your head (in shame)** to look ashamed or embarrassed **13 keep your head** to stay calm in a difficult situation **14 lose your head** to stop being calm in a difficult situation **15 raise/rear its ugly head** If a problem or something unpleasant raises its ugly head, it becomes a problem that people have to deal with. **16 laugh/shout/scream, etc your head off** to laugh/shout/scream, etc very much and very loudly ➲See also: hit the **nail**[1] on the head, a **roof** over your head, off the **top**[1] of your head

head[2] /hed/ *verb* **1 head back/down/towards, etc** to move in a particular direction *They headed back to the shore.* **2** LEAD [T] to lead an organization or group [**often passive**] *The company is headed by a young entrepreneur.* **3** FRONT/TOP [T] to be at the front or top of something *Jo headed a very short list of candidates.* **4 SPORT** [T] to hit a ball with your head *Owen headed the ball straight into the back of the net.*
be heading for sth *phrasal verb* to be likely to get or experience something soon *Those children are heading for trouble.*
head off *phrasal verb* to start a journey or leave a place

headache /'hedeɪk/ *noun* [C] **HEALTH** pain inside your head *I've got a bad headache.* ➲See also: **splitting headache**

header /'hedəʳ/ *noun* [C] a word or words that appear at the top of every page in a book or document ➲Compare **footer**

headhunt /'hedhʌnt/ *verb* [T] to persuade someone to leave their job for a job with a different company *She was headhunted by a rival firm.* •**headhunter** *noun* [C]

heading /'hedɪŋ/ *noun* [C] words at the top of a piece of writing that tell you what it is about

headland /'hedlənd/ *noun* [C] **GEOGRAPHY** a piece of land that sticks out into the sea

headlight /'hedlaɪt/ *noun* [C] one of the two large lights on the front of a car

headline /'hedlaɪn/ *noun* **1** [C] the title of a newspaper story that is printed in large letters above it *a **front-page headline*** **2 the headlines** the main stories in newspapers, on television, etc *That story **made headlines** all over the world.*

headlong /'hedlɒŋ/ *adverb* quickly and directly *The plane **plunged headlong** into the sea.*

headmaster /ˌhed'mɑːstəʳ/ *UK* (*US* **principal**) *noun* [C] **EDUCATION** a man who is in charge of a school

headmistress /ˌhed'mɪstrəs/ *UK* (*US* **principal**) *noun* [C] **EDUCATION** a woman who is in charge of a school

ˌ**head 'office** *noun* [**usually singular**] the most important office of a company, or the people who work there *Head office handles all complaints made against the company.*

ˌ**head 'on** *adverb* **1** MOVING FORWARDS If two vehicles hit each other head on, the front parts hit each other as they are moving forward. **2** DIRECTLY If you deal with something head on, you deal with it directly, although it is difficult. •**head-on** /ˌhed'ɒn/ *adjective a **head-on collision***

headphones /'hedfəʊnz/ *noun* [**plural**] a piece of equipment that you wear over your ears so that you can listen to music without anyone else hearing it *a pair of headphones*

headquarters /'hedˌkwɔːtəz/ *noun* [**group**] *plural* **headquarters** the place from where an organization is controlled *police headquarters*

headset /'hedset/ *noun* [C] a piece of equipment that you wear over your ears so that you can hear things, especially one with a microphone (= a piece of equipment that you speak into) attached to it *a mobile phone headset*

ˌ**head 'start** *noun* [C] an advantage that someone has over other people *Caroline's language skills should **give** her a **head start** over/on other people applying for the job.*

headstone /'hedstəʊn/ *noun* [C] a stone that shows the name of a dead person who is buried under it

headstrong /ˈhedstrɒŋ/ *adjective* extremely determined *a headstrong young girl*

heads-up /ˈhedzʌp/ *noun* [**usually singular**] *informal* a warning that something is going to happen, usually so that you can prepare for it

headteacher /ˌhedˈtiːtʃəʳ/ *UK* (*US* **principal**) *noun* [C] **EDUCATION** the person in charge of a school

headway /ˈhedweɪ/ *noun* **make headway** to make progress in what you are doing *The builders aren't* ***making*** *much* ***headway*** *with our new house.*

heady /ˈhedi/ *adjective* having a powerful effect on the way you feel, for example by making you feel excited *a heady experience*

heal /hiːl/ (*also* **heal up**) *verb* [**I, T**] **HEALTH** If a wound or broken bone heals, it becomes healthy again, and if something heals it, it makes it healthy again. *The wound on his head had begun to heal.* •**healer** *noun* [C] someone who makes ill people well again using something such as prayer or magic

WORD PARTNERS FOR ***health***

damage/improve sb's health • **excellent/good/ill/poor** health • be **in** [good/bad, etc] health

O⁃**health** /helθ/ *noun* [U] **1** BODY the condition of your body *to be* ***in good/poor health*** ○ *Regular exercise is good for your health.* **2** SUCCESS how successful and strong something is *the financial health of the business* ➲See also: **the National Health Service**

ˌ**health and** ˈ**safety** *noun* [U] making sure that people are safe and healthy, for instance at work or in public places *health and safety regulations*

health-care /ˈhelθˌkeəʳ/ *noun* [U] **HEALTH** the set of services provided by a country or an organization for treating people who are ill

ˈ**health** ˌ**service** *noun* [C] *UK* **HEALTH** the National Health Service: the system providing free medical service in the UK

O⁃**healthy** /ˈhelθi/ *adjective* **1** PHYSICALLY STRONG physically strong and well *Sue is a normal healthy child.* **2** GOOD good for your health *a* ***healthy diet*** **3** SUCCESSFUL successful and strong *a* ***healthy economy*** ➲Opposite **unhealthy**

COMMON LEARNER ERROR

healthy or **health?**

Remember not to use 'healthy' as a noun. If you need a noun, use **health**.

She has some health problems.

~~*She has some healthy problems.*~~

WORD PARTNERS FOR ***heap***

a heap **of** sth • **in** a heap

heap¹ /hiːp/ *noun* **1** [C] an untidy pile of things *a* ***heap of rubbish*** **2 heaps of sth** *informal* a lot of something *He's got heaps of money.*

heap² /hiːp/ *verb informal* **1** [T] to put things into an untidy pile *He heaped more food onto his plate.* **2 heap criticism/insults/praise, etc on sb** to criticize/insult/praise, etc someone a lot

O⁃**hear** /hɪəʳ/ *verb past* **heard 1** SOUND [**I, T**] to be aware of a sound through your ears *I could hear his voice in the distance.* ○ *I can't hear - can you turn the sound up?* **2** INFORMATION [**I, T**] to be told some information *When did you first* ***hear about*** *this?* ○ *Have you heard the news? Jane's back.* [+ **(that)**] *I hear that you're leaving.* **3** LAW [T] If a judge hears a case, they listen to it in a law court, to decide if someone is guilty or not. **4 will not hear of sth** If someone will not hear of something, they will not allow it. *I wanted to pay for her meal but she wouldn't hear of it.*

hear from sb *phrasal verb* to receive a letter, telephone call, or other message from someone *Have you heard from Sue recently?*

have heard of sb/sth *phrasal verb* to know that someone or something exists *I've never heard of her.*

hearing /ˈhɪərɪŋ/ *noun* **1 BIOLOGY** [U] the ability to hear sounds *He lost his hearing when he was a child.* **2** [C] **LAW** a meeting in a law court when a judge hears the facts of a case *The preliminary hearing will take place next week.* **3 a fair hearing** If you get a fair hearing, someone listens to your opinion.

hearing-impaired /ˈhɪərɪŋɪmˌpeəd/ *adjective* **HEALTH** A person who is hearing-impaired cannot hear or cannot hear well. ➲Compare **deaf**

hearsay /ˈhɪəseɪ/ *noun* [U] things that people have told you and that may or may not be true

hearse /hɜːs/ *noun* [C] a large car that is used to take a dead body to a funeral

WORD PARTNERS FOR ***heart***

your heart **beats** • heart **disease/failure** • a heart **condition/problem**

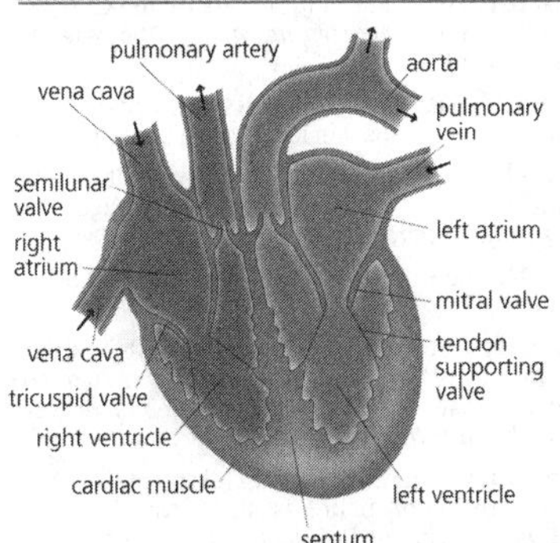

heart

O⁃**heart** /hɑːt/ *noun* **1 ANATOMY** [C] the organ inside your chest that sends blood around your body *Isabel's* ***heart was beating fast.*** ○ ***heart disease/failure*** ➲See picture at **respiratory system 2** CENTRE [**no plural**] the centre of something *Her office is* ***in the heart of*** *Tokyo.* **3 the heart of sth** the most important part of something *We need to get to the heart of the matter.* **4** FEELINGS [**C, U**] someone's deepest feelings and true character *She has a kind heart.* **5** SHAPE [C] a shape that is used to mean love ➲See picture at **shape 6 hearts** playing cards with red, heart shapes on them **7 at heart** used to say what someone is really like *I'm just a kid at heart.* **8 in your heart** used to say what you really think *In his heart he felt they were wrong.* **9 with all your heart** used to say that you feel something very strongly *I thank you with all my heart.* **10 not have the heart to do sth** to decide not to do something that would make someone unhappy **11 learn/know, etc sth by heart** to be able to remember all of something **12 break sb's heart** to make someone very unhappy **13 heart and soul** used to say that you give all your attention and enthusiasm to something *She threw herself into teaching heart and soul.* ➲See also: a **change**[2] of heart

heartache /'hɑːteɪk/ *noun* [C, U] extreme sadness

'heart at,tack *noun* [C] **HEALTH** when someone's heart suddenly stops working correctly, sometimes causing death *I think he's had a heart attack.*

heartbeat /'hɑːtbiːt/ *noun* [C, U] **BIOLOGY, ANATOMY** the regular movement of the heart as it moves blood around the body

heartbreaking /'hɑːt,breɪkɪŋ/ *adjective* causing extreme sadness *heartbreaking news*

heartbroken /'hɑːt,brəʊkᵊn/ *adjective* If you are heartbroken, you feel extremely sad about something that has happened.

-hearted /-'hɑːtɪd/ ➲See: **broken-hearted, cold-hearted, half-hearted, hard-hearted, light-hearted**

heartened /'hɑːtᵊnd/ *adjective* feeling happier because of something *We all felt heartened by the news.* ➲Opposite **disheartened**

heartening /'hɑːtᵊnɪŋ/ *adjective* making you feel happier *heartening news* ➲Opposite **disheartening**

'heart ,failure *noun* [U] **HEALTH** when someone's heart stops working, often causing death

heartfelt /'hɑːtfelt/ *adjective* Heartfelt feelings and words are strong and sincere. ***heartfelt thanks/gratitude***

hearth /hɑːθ/ *noun* [C] the floor around a fireplace

heartily /'hɑːtɪli/ *adverb* **1** WITH ENTHUSIASM with a lot of enthusiasm *We all* ***laughed heartily*** *at the joke.* **2** COMPLETELY completely or very much *I am* ***heartily sick*** *of the situation.*

heartland /'hɑːtlænd/ *noun* [C] the place where an activity or belief is strongest *the* ***traditional heartland*** *of the motor industry*

heartless /'hɑːtləs/ *adjective* cruel and not caring about other people

heart-to-heart /,hɑːttə'hɑːt/ *noun* [C] a serious conversation between two people in which they talk honestly about their feelings

hearty /'hɑːti/ *adjective* **1** ENERGY friendly and full of energy *a* ***hearty laugh/welcome*** **2** FOOD Hearty meals are large and satisfy you.

WORD PARTNERS FOR ***heat***

generate/give out heat • **intense/searing** heat

O╼**heat**[1] /hiːt/ *noun* **1** HOT [U] the quality of being hot or warm *the heat of summer* **2 the heat** when it is very hot *I don't really like the heat.* **3** TEMPERATURE [U no plural] the temperature of something *Cook on a low heat.* **4 the heat** *US* (*UK* **the heating**) the system that keeps a building warm *Could you turn the heat up a little.* **5 SPORT** [C] a competition, especially a race, which decides who will be in the final event **6 in the heat of the moment** If you do or say something in the heat of the moment, you do or say it without thinking because you are angry or excited. ➲See also: **dead heat**

heat[2] /hiːt/ (*also* **heat up**) *verb* [I, T] to make something become hot or warm, or to become hot or warm *I'll just heat up some soup.*

heated /'hiːtɪd/ *adjective* **1** made warm or hot **2 a heated argument/debate, etc** an angry or excited argument

heater /'hiːtəʳ/ *noun* [C] a machine that heats air or water

heath /hiːθ/ *noun* [C] **GEOGRAPHY** an open area of land covered with wild plants and rough grass

heather /'heðəʳ/ *noun* [C, U] a small plant with purple or white flowers that grows on hills

heating /'hiːtɪŋ/ *UK* (*US* **heat**) *noun* [U] the system that keeps a building warm ➲See also: **central heating**

heatwave /'hiːtweɪv/ *noun* [C] a period of time, usually a few days or weeks, when the weather is much hotter than usual

heave /hiːv/ *verb* **1** SOMETHING HEAVY [I, T] to move something heavy using a lot of effort *He heaved the bag on to his shoulder.* **2** UP AND DOWN [I] to move up and down *Her chest heaved as she started to cry.* **3 heave a sigh of relief** to breathe out loudly because you are pleased that something bad has not happened •**heave** *noun* [C]

heaven /'hevᵊn/ *noun* [U] **1 RELIGION** according to some religions, the place where good people go when they die **2** *informal* something very nice that gives you great pleasure *This cake is absolute heaven.*

heavenly /'hevᵊnli/ *adjective* **1 RELIGION** [always before noun] relating to heaven *the heavenly kingdom* **2** *informal* very nice *a heavenly day*

heavens /'hevᵊnz/ *noun* **1 the heavens** *literary* the sky **2 (Good) Heavens!** used when you are surprised or annoyed *Heavens, what's the matter?*

heavily /'hevɪli/ *adverb* **1** A LOT a lot or to a great degree *She's heavily involved in politics.* **2 drink/smoke heavily** to drink/smoke a lot **3 rain/snow heavily** to rain/snow a lot **4** FORCE using a lot of force *to breathe heavily*

O╼**heavy** /'hevi/ *adjective* **1** WEIGHING A LOT Heavy objects weigh a lot. *heavy bags* ○ *heavy machinery/equipment* **2** HOW MUCH used to say how much someone or something weighs *How heavy are you?* ○ *Oxygen is sixteen times heavier than hydrogen.* **3** A LOT large in amount or degree ***heavy traffic*** ○ *heavy costs* **4 a heavy drinker/smoker** someone who drinks/smokes a lot **5 heavy snow/rain** when a lot of snow/rain falls **6** FORCE using a lot of force *a heavy blow*

○ *heavy breathing* **7** SERIOUS *informal* serious *The discussion got a bit too heavy.* **8 heavy going** *mainly UK* too serious or difficult *I found the book very heavy going.*

heavy-handed /ˌheviˈhændɪd/ *adjective* using too much force in dealing with people

ˌheavy ˈmetal *noun* [U] **MUSIC** a type of very loud, modern music

heavyweight /ˈheviweɪt/ *noun* [C] **1 SPORT** a fighter such as a boxer who is in the heaviest weight group *the **heavyweight champion** of the world* **2** someone who is powerful and important *a political heavyweight*

Hebrew /ˈhiːbruː/ *noun* [U] the language used in the Jewish religion and in Israel •**Hebrew** *adjective*

hectare /ˈhekteəʳ/ *noun* [C] **MEASURES** a unit for measuring area, equal to 10,000 square metres

hectic /ˈhektɪk/ *adjective* extremely busy and full of activity *a hectic day/week*

O⁻**he'd** /hiːd/ **1** HE HAD *short for* he had *We knew he'd taken the money.* **2** HE WOULD *short for* he would *No one thought he'd get the job.*

hedge¹ /hedʒ/ *noun* [C] a row of bushes growing close together, often used to divide land into separate areas

hedge² /hedʒ/ *verb* [I, T] to avoid giving a direct answer ➲See also: hedge your bets (**bet²**)

hedgehog /ˈhedʒhɒg/ *noun* [C] a small animal whose body is covered with sharp points

hedgerow /ˈhedʒrəʊ/ *noun* [C] *UK* a row of bushes and small trees along the edge of a field or road

heed¹ /hiːd/ *verb* [T] *formal* to pay attention to some advice or a warning *Officials failed to **heed** his **warning**.*

heed² /hiːd/ *noun formal* **take heed of sth** to pay attention to something, especially some advice or a warning

heel /hiːl/ *noun* [C] **1** FOOT the back part of your foot ➲See colour picture **The Body** on page Centre 13 **2** SHOE the part of a shoe that is under your heel *high heels*

hefty /ˈhefti/ *adjective informal* very large *a **hefty bill/fine*** ○ *a hefty woman with dyed hair*

WORD PARTNERS FOR ***height***

grow to/reach a height of sth • be [3 metres, etc] **in** height

O⁻**height** /haɪt/ *noun* **1** HOW TALL [C, U] how tall or high something or someone is *a man of average height* ○ *The tower measures 27.28 metres **in height**.* **2** HOW FAR UP [C, U] how far above the ground something is *The aircraft was flying at a height of about 6000 metres.* **3** TALL [U] being tall *People always make comments about his height.* **4 the height of sth** the strongest or most important part of something *I met him when he was at the height of his fame.*

heighten /ˈhaɪtᵊn/ *verb* [I, T] to increase or make something increase ***heightened awareness*** [**often passive**] *The book's success was heightened by the scandal.*

heights /haɪts/ *noun* **1** [**plural**] high places *I've always been afraid of heights.* **2 new heights** when something is better or more successful than ever before *Our athletes have reached new heights of sporting glory.*

heinous /ˈheɪnəs/ *adjective formal* very bad and shocking ***heinous crimes***

heir /eəʳ/ *noun* [C] **SOCIETY** a person who will have the legal right to someone's money and possessions when they die *He is the **heir to a** huge fortune.*

heiress /ˈeəres/ *noun* [C] **SOCIETY** a woman who will have the legal right to someone's money and possessions when they die

held /held/ *past of* hold

helicopter /ˈhelɪkɒptəʳ/ *noun* [C] an aircraft which flies using long, thin parts on top of it that turn round and round very fast

helium /ˈhiːliəm/ *noun* [U] **CHEMISTRY** a gas that is lighter than air and that will not burn (formula **He**) *a **helium balloon***

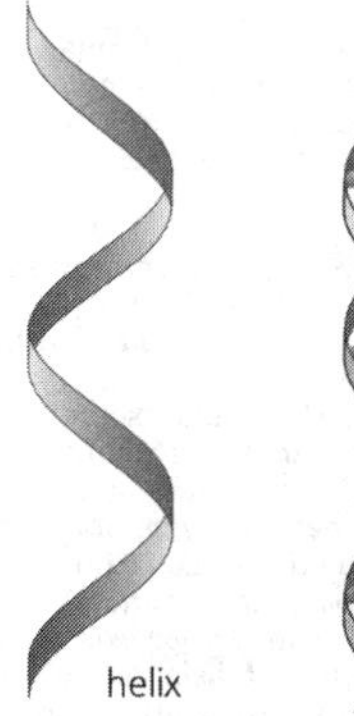

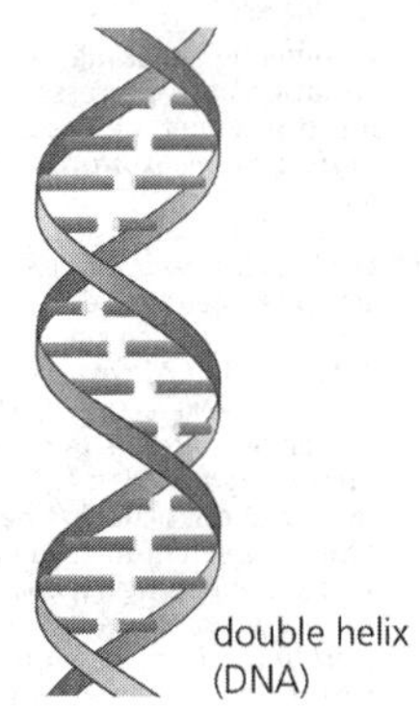

helix

helix /ˈhiːlɪks/ *noun* [C] **MATHEMATICS** a line that goes around a central tube or cone shape in the form of a spiral

he'll /hiːl/ *short for* he will *He'll be home soon.*

O⁻**hell** /hel/ *noun* **1 RELIGION** [U] according to some religions, the place where bad people go when they die **2** [U] *informal* an experience that is very unpleasant *It's been hell working with him.* **3 the hell** *informal* used to emphasize something in a rude or angry way *What the hell are you doing here?* **4 a/one hell of a** *informal* used to say that someone or something is very good, big, etc *a hell of a noise* ○ *He's one hell of a tennis player.* **5 from hell** *informal* used to say that someone or something is extremely bad *We had the holiday from hell.* **6 like hell** *informal* very much *It's raining like hell out there.*

hellish /ˈhelɪʃ/ *adjective informal* extremely bad or unpleasant *a hellish place/journey*

O⁻**hello** (*also UK* **hallo**) /helˈəʊ/ *exclamation* **1** GREET used to greet someone *Hello, Chris, how are things?* **2** TELEPHONE used to start a conversation on the telephone *Hello, this is Alex.*

helm /helm/ *noun* **1** [C] the part that you use to direct a boat or ship **2 at the helm** controlling a group or organization *With Lewis at the helm we are certain of success.*

helmet /'helmət/ *noun* [C] a hard hat that protects your head *a cycling helmet* ➲See also: **crash helmet** ➲See colour picture **Sports 2** on page Centre 15

OTHER WAYS OF SAYING *help*

The verbs **aid** and **assist** are more formal alternatives to 'help': *The army arrived to **assist** in the search.* • *The project is designed to **aid** poorer countries.*

If two or more people help each other in order to achieve the same thing, verbs such as **collaborate** or **cooperate** are sometimes used: *Several countries are **collaborating/cooperating** in the relief effort.*

The verb **benefit** is sometimes used when someone is helped by something: *The children have **benefited** greatly from the new facilities.*

If someone is asking for help, in informal situations the expression **give** someone **a hand** is sometimes used: *Do you think you could **give** me **a hand** with these heavy boxes?*

help¹ /help/ *verb* **1** GIVE HELP [I, T] to make it easier for someone to do something *Thank you for helping.* [+ **(to) do sth**] *Shall I help you to set the table?* ○ *Dad always **helps** me **with** my homework.* **2** MAKE EASIER [I, T] to make something easier or better [+ **to do sth**] *When you're nervous or frightened, it helps to breathe slowly and deeply.* **3 can't/couldn't help sth** to be unable to stop yourself doing something or to stop something happening [+ **doing sth**] *I couldn't help thinking about what had happened.* ○ *He couldn't help it, he slipped.* **4 help yourself (to sth)** to take something, especially food or drink, without asking *Please help yourself to some coffee.*

help (sb) out *phrasal verb* to help someone, especially by giving them money or working for them *Carol's been helping out in the shop this week.*

WORD PARTNERS FOR *help*

ask for/need/offer/provide/refuse help • **a big/great** help • **extra/professional** help

help² /help/ *noun* **1** ACTION [U] when someone helps another person *I was too embarrassed to **ask for help**.* ○ *Do you want any help?* **2** PERSON/THING [no plural] something or someone that helps *Dave has been a great help to me.* **3 with the help of sth** using something *We assembled the computer with the help of the manual.*

help³ /help/ *exclamation* something that you shout when you are in danger

'help ˌdesk *noun* [C] **COMPUTING** a service which provides help to the people who use a computer network (= a group of computers that share information and programs)

helper /'helpəʳ/ *noun* [C] someone who helps another person to do something

helpful /'helpfᵊl/ *adjective* **1** USEFUL useful *helpful advice/comments* **2** PERSON willing to help *The staff here are very helpful.* ➲Opposite **unhelpful** •**helpfully** *adverb* •**helpfulness** *noun* [U]

helping /'helpɪŋ/ *noun* [C] **FOOD** an amount of food given to one person at one time *She gave me a very large helping of pasta.*

helpless /'helpləs/ *adjective* not able to defend yourself or do things without help *a helpless animal/child* •**helplessly** *adverb*

helpline /'helplaɪn/ *noun* [C] *UK* a telephone number that you can ring for help or information *If you have any questions about any of our products, just **call** our **helpline**.*

hem /hem/ *noun* [C] the edge of a piece of clothing or cloth that has been folded under and sewn •**hem** *verb* [T] **hemming**, *past* **hemmed** to sew a hem on a piece of clothing or cloth

hem sb in *phrasal verb* to prevent someone from moving, or from doing what they want to do

hemisphere /'hemɪsfɪəʳ/ *noun* [C] **GEOGRAPHY** one half of the Earth *birds of the northern hemisphere*

hemophilia /ˌhiːmə'fɪliə/ *noun* [U] **HEALTH** *US spelling of* haemophilia (= a serious disease in which the flow of blood from someone's body cannot be stopped when they are hurt)

hemophiliac /ˌhiːmə'fɪliæk/ *noun* [C] **HEALTH** *US spelling of* haemophiliac (= someone who has haemophilia)

hemorrhage /'hemᵊrɪdʒ/ *noun* [C, U] **HEALTH** *US spelling of* haemorrhage (= when someone suddenly loses a lot of blood)

hemorrhoids /'hemərɔɪdz/ *noun* [plural] **HEALTH** *US spelling of* haemorrhoids (= painful swollen tissue around the opening of a person's bottom)

hemp /hemp/ *noun* [U] a plant that is used for making rope, cloth, and the drug cannabis

hen /hen/ *noun* [C] a female bird, especially a chicken

hence /hens/ *adverb* **1** for this reason *He's got an interview today, hence the suit.* **2 three weeks/two months, etc hence** *formal* three weeks/two months, etc from this time

henceforth /ˌhens'fɔːθ/ *adverb formal* from this time *Henceforth only English may be spoken in this classroom.*

henchman /'henʃmən/ *noun* [C] *plural* **henchmen** someone who does unpleasant jobs for a powerful person

'hen ˌnight (also **'hen ˌparty**) *noun* [C] a party for women only, usually one held for a woman before she gets married ➲Compare **stag night**

hepatic /hep'ætɪk/ *adjective* **ANATOMY, BIOLOGY** relating to the liver (= organ in the body that cleans the blood)

heˌpatic 'portal ˌvein (*also* **portal vein**) *noun* [C] **ANATOMY, BIOLOGY** a vein which carries blood to the liver from the stomach and other organs

hepatitis /ˌhepə'taɪtɪs/ *noun* [U] **HEALTH** a serious disease that affects your liver (= the organ that cleans your blood)

heptagon /'heptəgᵊn/ *noun* [C] **MATHEMATICS** a flat shape which has seven straight sides

her¹ *strong form* /hɜːʳ/ *weak forms* /həʳ, əʳ/ *pronoun* **1** FEMALE used after a verb or preposition to refer to someone female who has already been talked about *Where's Kath - have you seen her?* **2** COUNTRY/SHIP used to refer to a country or ship *God bless HMS Victoria and all who sail in her.*

O‑ **her²** *strong form* /hɜːʳ/ *weak form* /həʳ/ *determiner* belonging to or relating to someone female who has already been talked about *That's her house on the corner.* ○ *It's not her fault.*

herald¹ /ˈherəld/ *verb* [T] to be a sign that a particular event will happen soon *Thick black clouds heralded rain.*

herald² /ˈherəld/ *noun* [C] a sign that a particular event will happen soon *A fall in unemployment was the **herald of** economic recovery.*

herb /hɜːb/ (US) /ɜːrb/ *noun* [C] **FOOD** a plant that is used in cooking to add flavour to food or used in medicines •**herbal** /ˈhɜːbᵊl/ *adjective* *herbal medicine*

herbaceous /hɜːˈbeɪʃəs/ *adjective* **BIOLOGY** describes plants which are soft and not woody *a herbaceous border*

herbivore /ˈhɜː.bɪ.vɔːʳ/ *noun* [C] **BIOLOGY** an animal that eats only plants *Cows and sheep are herbivores.* ➲Compare **carnivore**

herd¹ /hɜːd/ *noun* [C] a large group of animals such as cows that live and eat together *a herd of cattle/deer*

herd² /hɜːd/ *verb* [T] If people or animals are herded somewhere, they are moved there in a group. [**often passive**] *The passengers were quickly herded onto a bus.*

O‑ **here** /hɪəʳ/ *adverb* **1** IN THIS PLACE in the place where you are *Does Jane live near here?* ○ *Come here!* **2** GETTING ATTENTION used to bring someone's attention to someone or something *Look, here's our bus.* ○ *Here, put this on.* **3 here you are/ here he is, etc** used when you see someone or something you have been looking for or waiting for *Here she is at last.* ○ *Here we are, this is the place.* **4** GIVING used when you are giving someone something *Here's a present for you.* **5 Here you are.** used when you are giving someone something *"Have you got the paper?" "Here you are."* **6** AT THIS POINT at this point in a discussion *I don't have time here to go into all the arguments.* **7** ON THE TELEPHONE used when saying who you are on the telephone *Hello, it's Tim here.* **8 here and there** in several different places but without any pattern *Tall trees were growing here and there.*

hereafter /ˌhɪərˈɑːftəʳ/ *adverb formal* from now or after this time

hereby /ˌhɪəˈbaɪ/ *adverb formal* with these words or this action *I hereby declare you the winner.*

hereditary /hɪˈredɪtᵊri/ *adjective* **1 BIOLOGY** passed to a child from its parents before birth *Depression is often hereditary.* **2 SOCIETY** passed from parent to child as a right *a **hereditary title***

heredity /hɪˈredəti/ *noun* [U] **BIOLOGY** the way in which mental or physical qualities pass from parent to child

heresy /ˈherəsi/ *noun* [C, U] **RELIGION** a belief which is against what a group or society generally believe to be right or good

heretic /ˈherətɪk/ *noun* [C] **RELIGION** someone with a belief which is against what a group or society generally believe to be right or good •**heretical** /həˈretɪkᵊl/ *adjective*

heritage /ˈherɪtɪdʒ/ *noun* [U] **SOCIETY** the buildings, paintings, customs, etc which are important in a culture or society because they have existed for a long time *our architectural/cultural heritage*

hermaphrodite /hɜːˈmæfrədaɪt/ *noun* [C] **BIOLOGY** a plant, animal or person with both male and female sex organs

hermit /ˈhɜːmɪt/ *noun* [C] someone who chooses to live alone and away from other people

hernia /ˈhɜːniə/ *noun* [C] **HEALTH** a medical condition in which an organ pushes through the muscle which is around it

WORD PARTNERS FOR ***hero***

a **local/national** hero • an **unsung** hero

O‑ **hero** /ˈhɪərəʊ/ *noun* [C] *plural* **heroes 1** someone who does something brave or good which people respect or admire them for *He became a **national hero** for his part in the revolution.* **2 LITERATURE** the main male character in a book or film who is usually good *the hero of her new novel*

heroic /hɪˈrəʊɪk/ *adjective* **1** BRAVE very brave *a **heroic figure*** ○ *a **heroic act/deed*** **2** TRYING HARD If someone makes a heroic effort to do something, they work very hard to try to do it. *In spite of England's **heroic efforts**, they lost the match.* •**heroically** *adverb*

heroics /hɪˈrəʊɪks/ *noun* [**plural**] actions which seem brave but are stupid because they are dangerous

heroin /ˈherəʊɪn/ *noun* [U] **HEALTH** a very strong drug which some people use illegally for pleasure *a **heroin addict***

heroine /ˈherəʊɪn/ *noun* [C] **1 LITERATURE** the main female character in a book or film, who is usually good *the heroine of the film 'Alien'* **2** a woman who does something brave or good which people respect or admire her for

heroism /ˈherəʊɪzᵊm/ *noun* [U] very brave behaviour *an act of heroism*

herring /ˈherɪŋ/ *noun* [C, U] **FOOD** a small, silver-coloured fish which lives in the sea and is eaten as food ➲See also: **red herring**

O‑ **hers** /hɜːz/ *pronoun* the things that belong or relate to someone female who has already been talked about *That's Ann's coat over there - at least I think it's hers.* ○ *I borrowed it from a friend of hers.*

O‑ **herself** /həˈself/ *pronoun* **1** REFLEXIVE the reflexive form of the pronoun 'she' *She kept telling herself that nothing was wrong.* **2** EMPHASIZE used to emphasize the pronoun 'she' or the particular female person you are referring to *She decorated the cake herself.* **3 (all) by herself** alone or without anyone else's help *She managed to put her shoes on all by herself.* **4 (all) to herself** for her use only *Mum's got the house to herself this weekend.*

H

hertz /hɜːts/ (*written abbreviation* **Hz**) *noun* [C] *plural* **hertz** MEASURES a unit for measuring the frequency (= how often the wave is repeated of) a sound wave

he's /hiːz/ **1** HE IS *short for* he is *He's my best friend.* **2** HE HAS *short for* he has *Sam must be tired - he's been dancing all night!*

hesitant /ˈhezɪtᵊnt/ *adjective* If you are hesitant, you do not do something immediately or quickly because you are nervous or not certain. *She was hesitant about returning to her home town.* •**hesitantly** *adverb* •**hesitancy** *noun* [U]

hesitate /ˈhezɪteɪt/ *verb* **1** [I] to pause before doing something, especially because you are nervous or not certain *Richard hesitated before answering.* **2 not hesitate to do sth** to be very willing to do something because you are certain it is right *They would not hesitate to call the police at the first sign of trouble.*

WORD PARTNERS FOR ***hesitation***

without hesitation • a **brief/momentary/moment's/slight** hesitation

hesitation /ˌhezɪˈteɪʃᵊn/ *noun* **1** [C, U] when you pause before doing something, especially because you are nervous or not certain *After a **moment's hesitation**, he unlocked the door.* **2 have no hesitation in doing sth** when you are very willing to do something because you know it is the right thing to do *He had no hesitation in signing for the team.*

heterogeneous /ˌhetᵊrəʊˈdʒiːniəs/ *adjective formal* consisting of parts or things of different types *a heterogeneous sample of people*

heterosexual /ˌhetᵊrəʊˈsekʃuᵊl/ *adjective* sexually attracted to people of the opposite sex •**heterosexual** *noun* [C]

heterotroph /ˈheterəʊtrəʊf/ *noun* [C] BIOLOGY a living thing that gets its food from other plants or animals •**heterotrophic** /ˌheterəʊˈtrəʊfɪk/ *adjective*

heterozygous /ˌhetᵊrəʊˈzaɪɡəs/ *adjective* BIOLOGY having two different forms of a gene (= part of a cell passed from a parent to a child) that controls one characteristic, and therefore able to pass either form to the young *a heterozygous cell* ➲Compare **homozygous**

het up /hetˈʌp/ *adjective* [never before noun] *UK informal* worried and upset *Why are you getting so **het up** about this?*

hexagon /ˈheksəɡən/ *noun* [C] MATHEMATICS a flat shape with six sides of the same length •**hexagonal** /hekˈsæɡᵊnᵊl/ *adjective* shaped like a hexagon

hey /heɪ/ *exclamation spoken* used to get someone's attention or to show that you are interested, excited, angry, etc *Hey, Helen, look at this!* ○ *Hey, wait a minute!*

heyday /ˈheɪdeɪ/ *noun* [no plural] the time when something or someone was most successful or popular ***In its heyday**, the company employed over a thousand workers.*

HFC /ˌeɪtʃefˈsiː/ *noun* [U, C] CHEMISTRY *abbreviation for* hydrofluorocarbon: a type of gas used especially in aerosols (= containers that force out liquids in very small drops)

hi /haɪ/ *exclamation* hello *Hi! How's it going?*

hiatus /haɪˈeɪtəs/ *noun* [no plural] *formal* a short pause in which nothing happens or is said

hibernate /ˈhaɪbəneɪt/ *verb* [I] BIOLOGY If an animal hibernates, it goes to sleep for the winter. •**hibernation** /ˌhaɪbəˈneɪʃᵊn/ *noun* [U] *Bears **go into hibernation** in the autumn.*

hiccup (*also* **hiccough**) /ˈhɪkʌp/ *noun* [C] **1** NOISE a quick noise you make in your throat when a muscle in your chest moves suddenly [usually plural] *I **got hiccups** from drinking too quickly.* **2** PROBLEM a small, temporary problem *I'm afraid there's been a slight hiccup.*

hide¹ /haɪd/ *verb past tense* **hid**, *past participle* **hidden** **1** THING [T] to put something in a place where it cannot be seen or found *I hid the money in a vase.* [often passive] *She kept the diary hidden in a drawer.* **2** PERSON [I] (*also* **hide yourself**) to go to a place where you cannot be seen or found *She ran off and hid behind a tree.* **3** FEELING/INFORMATION [T] to keep a feeling or information secret *He couldn't hide his embarrassment.* ○ *There's something about her past that she's trying to **hide from** me.*

hide² /haɪd/ *noun* [C, U] the skin of an animal which is used for making leather

hide-and-seek /ˌhaɪdənˈsiːk/ *noun* [U] a children's game in which one child hides and the others try to find them

hideaway /ˈhaɪdəweɪ/ *noun* [C] a place where you go to hide or to be alone

hideous /ˈhɪdiəs/ *adjective* very ugly *a hideous monster* •**hideously** *adverb*

hideout /ˈhaɪdaʊt/ *noun* [C] a place where you go to hide, especially from the police or if you are in danger

hiding /ˈhaɪdɪŋ/ *noun* **be in hiding; go into hiding** to hide in a place, especially from the police or if you are in danger

WORD PARTNERS FOR ***hierarchy***

in a hierarchy • a hierarchy **of** sth

hierarchy /ˈhaɪərɑːki/ *noun* [C] SOCIETY a system or organization in which people or things are arranged according to their importance •**hierarchical** /ˌhaɪəˈrɑːkɪkəl/ *adjective a **hierarchical structure***

hieroglyphics /ˌhaɪərəʊˈɡlɪfɪks/ *noun* [plural] LANGUAGE a system of writing which uses pictures instead of words, especially used in ancient Egypt

hi-fi /ˈhaɪfaɪ/ *noun* [C] a set of electronic equipment for playing music, consisting of a CD player, radio, etc

high¹ /haɪ/ *adjective* **1** TALL having a large distance from the bottom to the top *a high building/mountain* **2** ABOVE GROUND a large distance above the ground or the level of the sea *a high shelf/window* ○ *The village was **high up** in the mountains.* **3** MEASUREMENT used to say how big the distance is from the top of something to the bottom, or how far above the ground something is *How high is it?* ○ *It's ten metres high.* **4** AMOUNT great in amount, size, or level *a high temperature* ○ *high prices/costs* ○ *The car sped away **at high speed**.* **5** VERY GOOD very good *high standards/quality* **6** IMPORTANT important, powerful, or at the top level of something *a high rank* ○ *Safety is our highest priority.* **7 HEALTH** If someone is high, they are behaving in an unusual way because they have taken an illegal drug. **8 MUSIC** A high sound or note is near the top of the set of sounds that people can hear. **9 high in sth** If a food is high in something, it contains a lot of it.

O-- **high²** /haɪ/ *adverb* **1** ABOVE GROUND at or to a large distance above the ground *We flew high above the city.* ○ *He threw the ball high into the air.* **2** AMOUNT/LEVEL at or to a large amount or level *Temperatures rose as high as 40 degrees.*

WORD PARTNERS FOR ***high***

hit/reach a high • an **all-time/new/record** high

high³ /haɪ/ *noun* [C] **1** LARGE AMOUNT/LEVEL the top amount or level which something reaches *Computer ownership has **reached** an **all-time high*** (= more people own computers than ever before). **2** EXCITEMENT a feeling of excitement or happiness [**usually singular**] *The players are still **on a high** from their last match.*

highbrow /ˈhaɪbraʊ/ *adjective* A highbrow book, film, etc is serious and intended for very intelligent or well-educated people.

high-class /ˌhaɪˈklɑːs/ *adjective* of very good quality *a high-class hotel*

ˌHigh ˈCourt *noun* [C] **LAW** the most important law court in some countries *a High Court judge*

ˌhigher eduˈcation *noun* [U] **EDUCATION** education at a college or university

ˌhighest common ˈfactor (*abbreviation* **HCF**) *noun* [C] **MATHEMATICS** the highest number that a set of two or more different numbers can be divided by exactly

high-flyer (*also* **high-flier**) /ˌhaɪˈflaɪəʳ/ *noun* [C] someone who is very successful or who is likely to be very successful, especially in business •**high-flying** *adjective*

ˌhigh ˈheels (also **heels**) *noun* [**plural**] women's shoes with heels raised high off the ground •**high-heeled** *adjective*

the ˈhigh ˌjump *noun* **SPORT** a sports event in which people try to jump over a bar which gets higher and higher during the competition ➲See colour picture **Sports 1** on page Centre 14

highlands /ˈhaɪləndz/ *noun* [**plural**] **GEOGRAPHY** an area with a lot of mountains *the Scottish highlands* •**highland** /ˈhaɪlənd/ *adjective* in or relating to the highlands *a highland village*

high-level /ˌhaɪˈlevᵊl/ *adjective* involving important or powerful people ***high-level meetings/talks***

ˌhigh-level ˈlanguage *noun* [C] **COMPUTING** a language for writing computer programs which looks like a human language and is therefore easier to understand

WORD PARTNERS FOR ***highlight***

highlight a **danger/need/issue/problem** • highlight **the need for** sth

highlight¹ /ˈhaɪlaɪt/ *verb* [T] **1** EMPHASIZE to emphasize something or make people notice something *to **highlight** a **problem/danger*** ○ *The report **highlights the need for** stricter regulations.* **2** COLOUR to make something a different colour so that it is more easily noticed, especially written words

highlight² /ˈhaɪlaɪt/ *noun* [C] the best or most important part of something *The boat trip was one of the **highlights of** the holiday.*

highlighter /ˈhaɪˌlaɪtəʳ/ *noun* [C] a pen with bright, transparent ink which is used to emphasize words in a book, article, etc ➲See colour picture **The Office** on page Centre 5

O-- **highly** /ˈhaɪli/ *adverb* **1** VERY very or to a large degree *a highly effective treatment* ○ *It is highly unlikely that they will succeed.* **2** HIGH LEVEL at a high level *a highly paid worker* **3 to speak/think highly of sb/sth** to have or express a very good opinion of someone or something

Highness /ˈhaɪnəs/ *noun* **Her/His/Your Highness** used when you are speaking to or about a royal person *Thank you, Your Highness.*

high-pitched /haɪˈpɪtʃt/ *adjective* **1** VOICE A voice that is high-pitched is higher than usual. **2** NOISE describes a noise that is high and sometimes also loud or unpleasant *a high-pitched whine*

high-powered /ˌhaɪˈpaʊəd/ *adjective* very important or responsible *a high-powered executive/job*

high-profile /ˌhaɪˈprəʊfaɪl/ *adjective* A high-profile person or event is known about by a lot of people and receives a lot of attention from television, newspapers, etc. *a **high-profile campaign/case***

high-rise /ˈhaɪˌraɪz/ *adjective* A high-rise building is very tall and has a lot of floors.

ˈhigh ˌschool *noun* [C, U] **EDUCATION** a school in the US which children go to between the ages of 14 and 18 *I played violin when I was **in high school.*** ○ *a high-school student/teacher*

ˈhigh ˌstreet *noun* [C] *UK* the main road in the centre of a town where there are a lot of shops

high-tech (*also UK* **hi-tech**) /ˌhaɪˈtek/ *adjective* using or involved with the most recent and advanced electronic machines, computers, etc *high-tech companies/industry* ➲Compare **low-tech**

highway /ˈhaɪweɪ/ *noun* [C] *mainly US* a main road, especially between two towns or cities

hijack /ˈhaɪdʒæk/ *verb* [T] to take control of an aircraft during a journey, especially using violence [**often passive**] *The plane was hijacked by terrorists.* •**hijacker** *noun* [C] •**hijacking** *noun* [C, U]

hike¹ /haɪk/ *noun* [C] **SPORT** a long walk, usually in the countryside

hike² /haɪk/ *verb* [I] **SPORT** to go for a long walk in the countryside •**hiker** *noun* [C] •**hiking** *noun* [U] *to go hiking in the mountains*

hilarious /hɪˈleəriəs/ *adjective* extremely funny *They all thought the film was hilarious.* •**hilariously** *adverb* ***hilariously funny***

hilarity /hɪˈlærəti/ *noun* [U] when people laugh very loudly and think something is very funny

O-- **hill** /hɪl/ *noun* [C] **GEOGRAPHY** a raised area of land, smaller than a mountain *They climbed up the hill to get a better view.*

hillside /ˈhɪlsaɪd/ *noun* [C] **GEOGRAPHY** the sloping side of a hill

hilly /ˈhɪli/ *adjective* **GEOGRAPHY** having a lot of hills *hilly countryside*

hilt /hɪlt/ *noun* **to the hilt** very much or as much as is possible *Mark borrowed to the hilt to pay for his new car.*

hilum /ˈhaɪləm/ *noun* [C] **BIOLOGY** the mark on the surface of a seed from where it was attached to its stalk

O-- **him** *strong form* /hɪm/ *weak form* /ɪm/ *pronoun* used after a verb or preposition to refer to someone male who has already been talked about *Where's Serge - have you seen him?*

O-- **himself** /hɪmˈself/ *pronoun* **1** REFLEXIVE the reflexive form of the pronoun 'he' *John always cuts himself when he's shaving.* **2** EMPHASIZE used to emphasize the pronoun 'he' or the particular male person you are referring to *Do you want to speak to Dr Randall himself or his secretary?* ○ *He made the bookcase himself.* **3 (all) by himself** alone or without anyone else's help *Joe made that snowman all by himself.* **4 (all) to himself** for his use only *Tim wants a desk all to himself.*

hind /haɪnd/ *adjective* **a hind foot/leg** a foot/leg at the back of an animal

hinder /ˈhɪndəʳ/ *verb* [T] to make it difficult to do something or for something to develop [**often passive**] *His performance at the Olympics was hindered by a knee injury.*

hindrance /ˈhɪndrəns/ *noun* [C] something or someone that makes it difficult for you to do something *Large class sizes are a **hindrance** to teachers.*

hindsight /ˈhaɪndsaɪt/ *noun* [U] the ability to understand an event or situation only after it has happened ***With hindsight**, I should have taken the job.*

Hindu /ˈhɪnduː/ *noun* [C] **RELIGION** someone who believes in Hinduism •**Hindu** *adjective a Hindu temple*

Hinduism /ˈhɪnduːɪzᵊm/ *noun* [U] **RELIGION** the main religion of India, based on belief in many gods and the belief that when someone dies their spirit returns to life in another body

hinge¹ /hɪndʒ/ *noun* [C] a metal fastening that joins the edge of a door, window, or lid to something else and allows you to open or close it

hinge² /hɪndʒ/ *verb*
hinge on sth *phrasal verb* to depend completely on something *Her career hinges on the success of this project.*

WORD PARTNERS FOR ***hint***

drop a hint • a broad/heavy/subtle hint

hint¹ /hɪnt/ *noun* **1** SUGGESTION [C] when you say something that suggests what you think or want, but not in a direct way *He **dropped** (= made) several **hints** that he wanted a CD player for his birthday.* **2** ADVICE [C] a small piece of advice *The magazine gives lots of **useful hints** on how to save money.* **3 a hint of sth** a small amount of something *There was a hint of anger in her voice.*

hint² /hɪnt/ *verb* [I, T] to suggest something, but not in a direct way [+ **(that)**] *He hinted that he wants to retire next year.* ○ *She **hinted at** the possibility of moving to America.*

hip¹ /hɪp/ *noun* [C] **ANATOMY** one of the two parts of your body above your leg and below your waist ➲See colour picture **The Body** on page Centre 13

hip² /hɪp/ *adjective informal* fashionable

hip-hop /ˈhɪphɒp/ *noun* [U] **MUSIC** a type of pop music with songs about problems in society and words that are spoken and not sung

hippie /ˈhɪpi/ (*also UK* **hippy**) *noun* [C] someone who believes in peace and love and has long hair, especially someone who was young in the 1960s

hippo /ˈhɪpəʊ/ *noun* [C] *short for* hippopotamus

hippopotamus /ˌhɪpəˈpɒtəməs/ *noun* [C] *plural* **hippopotamuses** or **hippopotami** a very large animal with a thick skin that lives near water in parts of Africa

O-- **hire¹** /haɪəʳ/ *verb* [T] **1** PAY TO USE SOMETHING *UK* (*US* **rent**) to pay money in order to use something for a short time *They hired a car for a few weeks.* ➲See Common Learner Error at **rent** **2** EMPLOY to begin to employ someone *We hired a new secretary last week.*
hire sth out *phrasal verb UK* to allow someone to borrow something from you in exchange for money *The shop hires out electrical equipment.*

hire² /haɪəʳ/ *noun* [U] *UK* when you arrange to use something by paying for it *The price includes flights and **car hire**.* ○ *Do you have bikes **for hire**?*

ˌhire ˈpurchase *noun* [U] *UK* **FINANCE** a method of paying for something in which you pay part of the money owed immediately and then the rest in small regular amounts until the whole amount is paid

O-- **his¹** *strong form* /hɪz/ *weak form* /ɪz/ *determiner* belonging to or relating to someone male who has already been talked about *Alex is sitting over there with his daughter.* ○ *It's not his fault.*

O-- **his²** /hɪz/ *pronoun* the things that belong or relate to someone male who has already been talked about *That's Frank's coat over there - at least I think it's his.* ○ *I borrowed them from a friend of his.*

Hispanic /hɪˈspænɪk/ *adjective* **SOCIETY** relating or belonging to people whose families came from Spain or Latin America in the past •**Hispanic** *noun* [C] a Hispanic person

hiss /hɪs/ *verb* **1** MAKE NOISE [I] to make a long noise like the letter 's' *The gas hissed through the pipes.* **2** SPEAK [T] to speak in an angry or urgent way *"Will you be quiet," she hissed.* •**hiss** *noun* [C] a sound like the letter 's'

hissy (fit) /ˈhɪsiˌfɪt/ *noun* [C] *informal* a sudden strong feeling of anger that someone cannot control *David, of course, **threw a hissy fit** when he found out.*

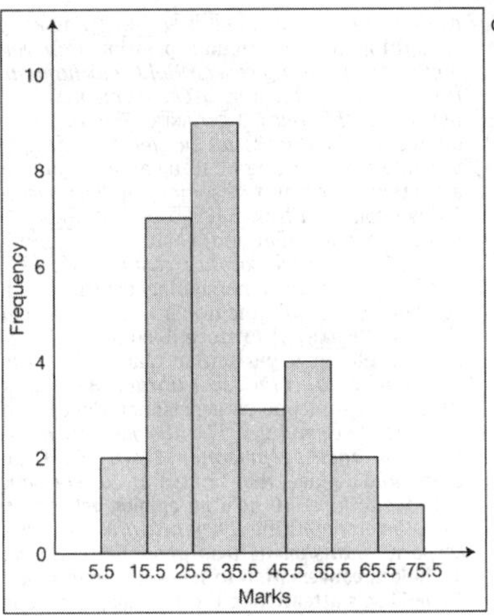

histogram

histogram /ˈhɪstəgræm/ *noun* [C] **MATHEMATICS** a graph (= mathematical picture showing measurements) in which different amounts are shown by thick lines of different heights, lengths or widths

historian /hɪˈstɔːriən/ *noun* [C] someone who studies or writes about history

historic /hɪˈstɒrɪk/ *adjective* important in history or likely to be important in history ***historic buildings*** ○ ***a historic day/moment***

historical /hɪˈstɒrɪkəl/ *adjective* relating to events or people in the past, or the study of history *a historical novel* ○ *historical documents* •**historically** *adverb*

WORD PARTNERS FOR ***history***

in sth's history • recent history

O⁻**history** /ˈhɪstəri/ *noun* **1** PAST [U] the whole series of events in the past which relate to the development of a country, subject, or person *The Civil War was a terrible time in American history.* **2** SUBJECT [U] the study of events in the past *He's very interested in modern European history.* ○ *a history book* **3 a history of sth** If you have a history of a particular problem or illness, you have already suffered from it. *a man with a history of drug addiction* **4** DESCRIPTION [C] a description or record of events in the past relating to someone or something *The doctor read through his **medical history**.* ➲See also: **case history, natural history**

COMMON LEARNER ERROR

history or **story?**

History is events that happened in the past.

He's studying history at university.

A **story** is a description of real or imaginary events, often told to entertain people.

The story is about two friends travelling across India.

O⁻**hit**[1] /hɪt/ *verb* **hitting**, *past* **hit 1** HAND [T] to touch something quickly and with force using your hand or an object in your hand *She hit him on the head with her tennis racket.* **2** TOUCH [T] to touch someone or something quickly and with force, usually causing injury or damage *The car skidded and hit a wall.* ○ *As she fell, she hit her head on the pavement.* **3** AFFECT [I, T] to affect something badly [**often passive**] *The economy has been hit by high unemployment.* **4** REACH [T] to reach a place, position, or state *Our profits have already hit $1 million.* **5** THINK [T] *informal* If an idea or thought hits you, you suddenly think of it. *The idea for the book hit me in the middle of the night.* **6 hit it off** *informal* If people hit it off, they like each other and become friendly immediately. ➲See also: hit sb **hard**[2], hit the **jackpot**, hit the **nail**[1] on the head, hit the **roof**

hit back *phrasal verb* to criticize or attack someone who has criticized or attacked you *The President **hit back at** journalists who said he was a liar.*

hit on/upon sth *phrasal verb* to have a good idea, especially one which solves a problem *We **hit upon the idea** of writing to the mayor to ask for his help.*

WORD PARTNERS FOR ***hit***

a big/massive/smash hit • a hit CD/single

hit[2] /hɪt/ *noun* [C] **1** SONG/FILM a very successful song, film, book, etc *The film 'Titanic' was a **big hit**.* **2** PERSON/THING a popular person or thing *The chocolate cake was a **big hit** with the children.* **3** TOUCH when you touch something or when something touches you quickly and with force **4 INTERNET** a request to see a document on the Internet that is then counted to calculate the number of people looking at the page

hit-and-miss /ˌhɪtənˈmɪs/ *UK* (*US* **hit or miss**) *adjective* not planned, but happening by chance

hit-and-run /ˌhɪtənˈrʌn/ *adjective* A hit-and-run accident is when the driver of a vehicle hits and injures someone, but then drives away without helping.

hitch[1] /hɪtʃ/ *noun* [C] a small problem *The ceremony **went without a hitch**.*

hitch[2] /hɪtʃ/ *verb* **1 hitch a lift/ride** to get a free ride in someone's vehicle, by standing next to the road and waiting for someone to pick you up **2** [T] (*also US* **hitch up**) to fasten something to an object or vehicle *They hitched the caravan to the car.*

hitch sth up *phrasal verb* to pull up a piece of clothing

hitchhike /ˈhɪtʃhaɪk/ *verb* [I] to get free rides in people's vehicles by standing next to the road and waiting for someone to pick you up •**hitchhiker** *noun* [C]

hi-tech *UK* (*UK/US* **high-tech**) /ˌhaɪˈtek/ *adjective* using or involved with the most recent and advanced electronic machines, computers, etc

hitherto /ˌhɪðəˈtuː/ *adverb formal* until now, or until a particular point in time

HIV /ˌeɪtʃaɪˈviː/ *noun* [U] **HEALTH** *abbreviation for* human immunodeficiency virus: a virus which causes AIDS (= a serious disease that destroys the body's ability to fight infection.)

hive /haɪv/ *noun* **1** [C] (*also* **beehive**) a special container where people keep bees **2 a hive of activity** a place where people are busy and working hard

HIV-positive /ˌeɪtʃaɪviːˈpɒzətɪv/ *adjective* **HEALTH** If a person is HIV-positive, they are infected with HIV although they might not have AIDS.

hiya /ˈhaɪjə/ *exclamation informal* a way to say hello to someone you know well *Hiya, Mike, how are you doing?*

hm (*also* **hmm**) /həm/ *spoken* something you say when you pause while talking or when you are uncertain *"Which one do you like best?" "Hmm. I'm not sure."*

hoard /hɔːd/ *verb* [T] to collect and store a large supply of something, often secretly *He hoarded antique books in the attic.* •**hoard** *noun* [C] a large, secret supply or collection of something *Police found a hoard of stolen jewellery in the car.*

hoarding /ˈhɔːdɪŋ/ *UK* (*UK/US* **billboard**) *noun* [C] a large board used for advertising, especially by the side of a road

hoarse /hɔːs/ *adjective* If you are hoarse, your voice sounds rough when you speak, often because you are ill. *The teacher was hoarse from shouting.* •**hoarsely** *adverb*

hoax /həʊks/ *noun* [C] when someone tries to make people believe something which is not true *The police said the bomb threat was a hoax.*

hob /hɒb/ *noun* [C] *UK* the flat part on top of an oven where you heat food in pans ➲See colour picture **The Kitchen** on page Centre 2

hobble /ˈhɒbl/ *verb* [I] to walk with small, uncomfortable steps, especially because your feet hurt

hobby /ˈhɒbi/ *noun* [C] an activity that you enjoy and do regularly when you are not working *Do you have any hobbies?*

hockey /ˈhɒki/ *noun* [U] **1 SPORT** *UK* (*US* **field hockey**) a team game played on grass where you hit a small ball with a long, curved stick **2 SPORT** *US* (*UK/US* **ice hockey**) a team game played on ice where you hit a small, hard object with a long, curved stick ➲See colour picture **Sports 1** on page Centre 14

hoe /həʊ/ *noun* [C] **FARMING** a garden tool with a long handle used for removing weeds (= plants you do not want)

hog¹ /hɒg/ *noun* [C] *mainly US* a large pig

hog² /hɒg/ *verb* [T] **hogging**, *past* **hogged** *informal* to use or keep all of something for yourself *Stop hogging the newspaper! I want to read it too.*

hoist /hɔɪst/ *verb* [T] to raise something, sometimes using a rope or machine *They slowly hoisted the flag.*

O-- **hold¹** /həʊld/ *verb past* **held 1** [IN HAND] [T] to have something in your hand or arms *He was holding a glass of wine.* ○ *They were holding hands and kissing.* **2** [KEEP IN POSITION] [T] to keep something in a particular position *Can you hold the door open please?* ○ *Hold your hand up if you know the answer.* ○ *The frame was held together with screws.* **3** [ORGANIZE] [T] to organize an event *to hold talks/an election* **4** [CONTAIN] [T] to contain something or to be able to contain a particular amount of something *The bucket holds about 10 litres.* **5** [JOB OR QUALIFICATION] [T] to have a particular job, position, or qualification *She held the post of treasurer.* **6** [COMPETITION] [T] to have a particular position in a competition *to hold the world record* ○ *to hold the lead* **7** [STORE] [T] to store documents, information, etc in a particular place *The documents are held in the local library.* **8** [PRISONER] [T] to keep someone as a prisoner *Police held the suspect overnight.* ○ *The hijackers are **holding** them **hostage/prisoner**.* **9** [ARMY] [T] If soldiers hold a place, they control it. *Rebel troops held the village.* **10 hold an opinion/belief/view** to believe something *They held the view that corporal punishment was good for children.* **11 hold a conversation** to have a conversation **12 hold sb's attention/interest** to keep someone interested in something *The film held my attention from beginning to end.* **13** [TELEPHONE] [I, T] to wait on the telephone until someone can speak to you *Her line's busy. Would you like to hold?* ○ ***Hold the line**, please.* **14** [NOT BREAK] [I] to not break *The rope held.* **15 Hold it!** *informal* used to tell someone to wait or stop doing something *Hold it! I've forgotten my coat.* **16 hold shares FINANCE** to own shares (= small, equal parts of the value of a company) **17 hold your breath a** [STOP BREATHING] to intentionally stop breathing for a time **b** [WAIT] to wait for something to happen, often feeling anxious **18 hold your nose** to close your nose with your fingers to avoid smelling something unpleasant ➲See also: hold your **own**¹

hold sth against sb *phrasal verb* to like someone less because they have done something wrong or behaved badly *It was his mistake, but I won't hold it against him.*

hold sb/sth back *phrasal verb* **1** [PREVENT MOVEMENT] to prevent someone or something from moving forward *The police held back the protesters.* **2** [PREVENT PROGRESS] to prevent someone or something from making progress *She felt that having children would hold her back.*

hold sth back *phrasal verb* **1** [CONTROL EMOTION] to stop yourself showing an emotion *She couldn't hold back the tears.* **2** [NOT SAY] to not give information to someone

hold sth/sb down *phrasal verb* **1** [PREVENT ESCAPING] to stop someone moving or escaping *It took three officers to hold down the suspect.* **2** [KEEP LOW] to keep the cost of something at a low level *to hold down prices/wages* **3 hold down a job** to keep a job *It's difficult for mothers to hold down a full-time job.*

hold off (sth/doing sth) *phrasal verb* to wait before doing something *They are holding off making a decision until next week.*

hold on *phrasal verb informal* **1** [WAIT] to wait *Hold on! I'll just check my diary.* **2** [HOLD] to hold something or someone firmly with your hands or arms *Hold on tight!*

hold onto sth/sb *phrasal verb* to hold

something or someone firmly with your hands or arms *Hold onto the rope and don't let go.*
hold onto/on to sth *phrasal verb* to keep something you have *It was a tough election, but they held onto their majority.*
hold sth out *phrasal verb* to move your hand or an object in your hand towards someone *She held out her glass for some more wine.*
hold out *phrasal verb* **1** BE ENOUGH If a supply of food or money holds out, you have enough for a particular period of time. **2** DEFEND to continue to defend yourself against an attack *The city is still* ***holding out against*** *rebel troops.*
hold out for sth *phrasal verb* to wait until you get what you want *I decided to hold out for a better offer.*
hold sth up *phrasal verb* to prevent something from falling down *The tent was held up by ropes.*
hold sth/sb up *phrasal verb* to make something or someone slow or late *Sorry I'm late. I got held up in traffic.*
hold up sth *phrasal verb* to try to steal money from a bank, shop, or vehicle using force

hold² /həʊld/ *noun* **1** WITH HANDS [C] when you hold something or someone, or the way you do this ***Keep*** *a tight* ***hold on*** *your tickets.* **2 catch/grab/take, etc hold of sth/sb** to start holding something or someone *He tried to escape, but I grabbed hold of his jacket.* **3 get hold of sth/sb** to obtain something, or to manage to speak to someone *I got hold of a copy at the local library.* ○ *I rang three times, but couldn't get hold of her.* **4 on hold a** DO IN FUTURE If a plan or activity is on hold, it will not be done until a later time. *The project is on hold until we get more money.* **b** TELEPHONE waiting to speak to someone on the telephone *His secretary* ***put*** *me* ***on hold.*** **5 keep hold of sth** to keep something *Keep hold of this. You might need it later.* **6 hold on/over sth/sb** power or control over something or someone *Their company has a strong hold on the computer market.* **7** SPACE [C] an area on a ship or aircraft for storing things *a cargo hold* ➲See also: get (hold of) the wrong **end**¹ of the stick

holdall /ˈhəʊldɔːl/ *UK* (*US* **carryall**) *noun* [C] a large bag for carrying clothes

holder /ˈhəʊldəʳ/ *noun* [C] someone who officially owns something *the world record holder* ○ *passport holders* ➲See also: **title-holder**

holding /ˈhəʊldɪŋ/ *noun* [C] **FINANCE** part of a company which someone owns

hold-up *UK* (*US* **holdup**) /ˈhəʊldʌp/ *noun* [C] **1** MAKES YOU LATE something that slows you down or makes you late *There were several hold-ups on the motorway.* **2** CRIME when someone steals money from a bank, shop, or vehicle using force

O- **hole¹** /həʊl/ *noun* **1** [C] a hollow space in something, or an opening in a surface *a bullet hole* ○ *There's a* ***hole in*** *the roof.* ○ *We* ***dug*** *a* ***hole*** *to plant the tree.* **2 a rabbit/mouse, etc hole** a hollow space where a rabbit/mouse, etc lives **3 SPORT** a small, hollow space in the ground that you try to hit a ball into in a game of golf

WORD PARTNERS FOR ***hole***

dig/fill/make a hole • a hole **in** sth • a **deep** hole

hole² /həʊl/ *verb*
hole up *phrasal verb informal* (*also* **be holed up**) to stay or hide somewhere

WORD PARTNERS FOR ***holiday***

book/go on/have a holiday • a **summer** holiday • be **on** holiday

O- **holiday¹** /ˈhɒlədeɪ/ *noun* **1** NO WORK [C, U] *UK* (*US* **vacation**) a time when you do not have to go to work or school *My aunt looks after us during the* ***school holidays.*** **2** VISIT [C, U] *UK* (*US* **vacation**) a long visit to a place away from where you live, for pleasure *a skiing/walking holiday* ○ *Are you* ***going on holiday*** *this year?* **3** DAY [C] an official day when you do not have to go to school or work *a* ***public holiday*** ➲See also: **bank holiday, federal holiday, national holiday, package holiday, summer holiday**

holiday² /ˈhɒlədeɪ/ *UK* (*US* **vacation**) *verb* [I] to have your holiday somewhere *We usually holiday in Spain.*

holidaymaker /ˈhɒlədeɪˌmeɪkəʳ/ *noun* [C] *UK* someone who is away from home on holiday

holiness /ˈhəʊlɪnəs/ *noun* [U] **RELIGION** the quality of being holy

holistic /həʊˈlɪstɪk/ *adjective* dealing with or treating the whole of something or someone and not just some parts

holler /ˈhɒləʳ/ *verb* [I] *US informal* to shout or call loudly •**holler** *noun* [C]

hollow¹ /ˈhɒləʊ/ *adjective* **1** NOTHING INSIDE having a hole or empty space inside *a hollow shell/tube* **2** WITHOUT MEANING without meaning or real feeling *a* ***hollow victory*** ○ *a* ***hollow laugh*** **3 hollow cheeks/eyes** If someone has hollow cheeks/eyes, their face seems to curve in around these areas.

hollow² /ˈhɒləʊ/ *noun* [C] a hole or empty space in something, or a low area in a surface

hollow³ /ˈhɒləʊ/ *verb*
hollow sth out *phrasal verb* to make an empty space inside something

holly /ˈhɒli/ *noun* [U] a green bush with sharp, pointed leaves and small, red fruit

Hollywood /ˈhɒliwʊd/ *noun* the centre of the US film industry

holocaust /ˈhɒləkɔːst/ *noun* [C] when a very large number of people are killed and things destroyed, such as in a war or fire *a nuclear holocaust*

hologram /ˈhɒləgræm/ *noun* [C] **ART** a photograph or image which appears to be solid and have depth when light shines on it in a particular way

holster /ˈhəʊlstəʳ/ *noun* [C] a leather container for carrying a gun on your body

holy /ˈhəʊli/ *adjective* **1 RELIGION** relating to a religion or a god *the holy city of Jerusalem* **2 RELIGION** very religious or pure *a holy man*

H

homage /ˈhɒmɪdʒ/ *noun* **pay homage to sb** to show your respect for someone, especially by praising them in public *Fans paid homage to the actress who died yesterday.*

WORD PARTNERS FOR ***home***

go home • be **at** home

O‑**home**[1] /həʊm/ *noun* **1** LIVE [C, U] the place where you live or feel you belong *I tried to ring him, but he wasn't **at home**. ○ He **left home*** (= stopped living with his family) *when he was eighteen.* **2** CARE [C] a place where people who need special care live *a **children's home** ○ My grandmother lives in a home now.* **3 feel at home** to feel happy and confident in a place or situation *After a month she felt at home in her new job.* **4 make yourself at home** to behave in a relaxed way in a place, as if it was your own home *Take off your coat and make yourself at home.* **5 the home of sth/sb** the place where you usually find something or someone, or where they come from *France, the home of good food* ➲See also: **nursing home, stately home**

COMMON LEARNER ERROR

home

When you use verbs of movement with **home**, for example 'go' or 'come', you do not need to use a preposition.

What time did you go home?

I'll call you as soon as I get home.

When you use the verbs **be** or **stay** with **home**, you can use the preposition **at**.

I was at home all afternoon.

I'll stay at home to look after the children.

Let's stay home and watch a movie. (mainly US)

O‑**home**[2] /həʊm/ *adverb* **1** TO PLACE to the place where you live *He didn't **come home** until midnight. ○ I **went home** to visit my parents.* **2** AT/IN PLACE at or in the place someone lives *Will you be home tomorrow evening?*

home[3] /həʊm/ *adjective* **1 sb's home address/phone number, etc** an address/telephone number, etc for the place where someone lives **2** FOR/FROM HOME made or used in the place where someone lives ***home cooking** ○ a home computer* **3 SPORT** relating to the place where a sporting event happens *The home team won 2-0.* **4** COUNTRY relating to things in your own country *home affairs*

home[4] /həʊm/ *verb*

home in on sth/sb *phrasal verb* to give a lot of attention to something or someone *The report only homes in on the negative points.*

homeboy /ˈhəʊmbɔɪ/ (*also* **homey**) *noun* [C] *mainly US informal* a boy or man who is a close friend or who is from your own town

homecoming /ˈhəʊmˌkʌmɪŋ/ *noun* [C, U] when someone returns home, usually after being away for a long time

ˌ**home ecoˈnomics** *noun* [U] **EDUCATION** a school subject in which you learn how to cook and sew

the ˌ**home** ˈ**front** *noun* [**no plural**] the people who stay in their own country when some of its people are fighting a war in another country

home-grown /ˌhəʊmˈgrəʊn/ *adjective* **1 FOOD** from your own garden *home-grown vegetables* **2** If someone or something is home-grown, they belong to or were developed in your own country. *Our football team has many home-grown players.*

homeland /ˈhəʊmlænd/ *noun* [C] the country where you were born

homeless /ˈhəʊmləs/ *adjective* **SOCIETY** without a place to live *10,000 people were made homeless by the floods. ○ They're opening a new shelter for **the homeless**.* •**homelessness** *noun* [U]

homely /ˈhəʊmli/ *adjective* **1** COMFORTABLE *UK* A homely place is simple, but comfortable and pleasant. *It's a small restaurant with a homely atmosphere.* **2** NOT ATTRACTIVE *US* Someone who is homely is not very attractive.

homemade (*also UK* **home-made**) /ˌhəʊmˈmeɪd/ *adjective* made at home and not bought from a shop *homemade bread/cookies*

homeopathy /ˌhəʊmiˈɒpəθi/ *noun* [U] **HEALTH** a way of treating illnesses using very small amounts of natural substances •**homeopathic** /ˌhəʊmiəʊˈpæθɪk/ *adjective a **homeopathic remedy***

homeostasis /ˌhəʊmiəʊˈsteɪsɪs/ *noun* [U] **BIOLOGY** the process by which a living thing or a cell keeps the conditions inside it the same despite any changes in the conditions around it

homeothermic /ˌhəʊmiəʊˈθɜːmɪk/ *adjective* **BIOLOGY** able to keep a body temperature the same even when the temperature outside the body changes

homeowner /ˈhəʊmˌəʊnəʳ/ *noun* [C] someone who owns the house that they live in

ˈ**home** ˌ**page** *noun* [C] **INTERNET** the first page that you see when you look at a website on the Internet ➲See Extra help page **The Web and the Internet** on page Centre 36.

ˌ**home** ˈ**shopping** *noun* [U] when someone buys goods from a magazine, a television programme or a website

homesick /ˈhəʊmsɪk/ *adjective* feeling sad because you are away from your home •**homesickness** *noun* [U]

homestead /ˈhəʊmsted/ *noun* [C] *mainly US* a house and area of land usually used as a farm

hometown *US* (*UK/US* ˌ**home** ˈ**town**) /ˌhəʊmˈtaʊn/ *noun* [C] the town or city that you come from

homeward /ˈhəʊmwəd/ *adjective, adverb* towards home *the **homeward journey***

O‑**homework** /ˈhəʊmwɜːk/ *noun* [U] **1 EDUCATION** work which teachers give students to do at home *Have you **done your homework** yet?* **2 do your homework** to prepare carefully for a situation *It was clear that she had done her homework before the meeting.*

homey[1] /ˈhəʊmi/ *US* (*UK* **homely**) *adjective* A homey place is simple, but comfortable and pleasant.

homey[2] /ˈhəʊmi/ (*also* **homeboy**) *noun* [C] *mainly US informal* a boy or man who is a close friend or who is from your own town

homicide /ˈhɒmɪsaɪd/ *noun* [C, U] US **LAW** the crime of killing someone *There were over 400 homicides in Chicago last year.* •**homicidal** /ˌhɒmɪˈsaɪdᵊl/ *adjective* likely to murder someone *a* ***homicidal maniac***

homogeneous /ˌhɒməˈdʒiːniəs, ˌhəʊməˈdʒiːniəs/ *adjective formal* **1** consisting of parts or members that are all the same *The village was a fairly homogeneous community.* **2 CHEMISTRY** A homogeneous substance has the same characteristics, for example density, all the way through.

homologous /həˈmɒləgəs/ *adjective* **1** If two things are homologous, they have a similar position or appearance **2 BIOLOGY** Homologous body parts developed from the same thing but now have different uses. ➲Compare **analogous**

hoˌmologous ˈchromosomes *noun* [plural] **BIOLOGY** two chromosomes (= cells that control what an animal or plant is like), one from the father and one from the mother, that look exactly the same and join together

hoˌmologous ˈseries *noun* [C] **CHEMISTRY** a series of organic compounds with similar characteristics

homophobia /ˌhəʊməˈfəʊbiə/ *noun* [U] hate of homosexual people •**homophobic** *adjective* hating homosexual people

homosexual /ˌhəʊməˈsekʃuᵊl/ *adjective* sexually attracted to people of the same sex •**homosexual** *noun* [C] someone who is homosexual •**homosexuality** /ˌhəʊməʊˌsekʃuˈæləti/ *noun* [U] the quality of being homosexual

homozygous /ˌhɒməˈzaɪgəs/ *adjective* **BIOLOGY** having two of the same form of gene (= part of a cell passed from a parent to a child) that controls one characteristic and therefore able to pass on one form only to the young ➲Compare **heterozygous**

hone /həʊn/ *verb* [T] to improve something and make it perfect *This is an opportunity for you to* ***hone your skills.***

O— **honest** /ˈɒnɪst/ *adjective* **1** TRUTH sincere and telling the truth *If you want my* ***honest opinion****, I think your hair looks awful.* **2** NOT CHEAT not likely to lie, cheat, or steal *an honest man* ➲Opposite **dishonest** **3 to be honest** *informal* used to express your real opinion *To be honest, I didn't really enjoy the party.*

honestly /ˈɒnɪstli/ *adverb* **1** EMPHASIZE used to emphasize that you are telling the truth *Thanks, but I honestly couldn't eat another piece of cake.* **2** HONEST in an honest way **3** ANNOYED used to show that you are annoyed or do not approve of something *Honestly! He should have been here hours ago.*

honesty /ˈɒnɪsti/ *noun* **1** [U] the quality of being honest **2 in all honesty** used when you are saying what you really think or feel about something *In all honesty, I'd rather not go.* ➲Opposite **dishonesty**

honey /ˈhʌni/ *noun* **1 FOOD** [U] a sweet, sticky food that is made by bees ➲See colour picture **Food** on page Centre 11 **2** [C] *mainly US* a name that you call someone you love or like very much

> WORD PARTNERS FOR ***honeymoon***
>
> be **on** (your) honeymoon • a honeymoon **couple**

honeymoon /ˈhʌnimuːn/ *noun* [C] a holiday taken by two people who have just got married *We went to Paris* ***on our honeymoon.*** •**honeymooner** *noun* [C]

honk /hɒŋk/ *verb* [I, T] to make a short sound with your car's horn (= part you press to make a warning noise) *The lorry driver* ***honked his horn*** *at me.*

honor /ˈɒnəʳ/ *noun, verb US spelling of* honour

honorable /ˈhɒnᵊrəbl/ *adjective US spelling of* honourable

honorary /ˈɒnᵊrəri/ *adjective* **1** GIVEN given as a reward to show respect *He was given an* ***honorary degree*** *from Cambridge University.* **2** NOT PAID If you have an honorary job, you are not paid for it. *the honorary chairman*

honour[1] *UK* (*US* **honor**) /ˈɒnəʳ/ *noun* **1** RESPECT [U] when people respect you because you have done what you believe is honest and right, or the quality of doing this *a man of honour* ○ *The soldiers fought for the honour of their country.* ➲Opposite **dishonour** **2 in honour of sb/sth** in order to celebrate or show great respect for someone or something *a banquet in honour of the President* **3** PRIDE [no plural] something which makes you feel proud and pleased [+ to do sth] *It's an honour to be team captain.* [+ of + doing sth] *I had the great honour of meeting the King.* **4** REWARD [C] something that you give to someone in public to show respect for them and their achievements *She was granted the Order of Merit - one of the nation's highest honours.* **5 Her/His/Your Honour** used when you are speaking to or about a judge **6 honours EDUCATION** A qualification or university course with honours is of a very high level. *an honours degree*

honour[2] *UK* (*US* **honor**) /ˈɒnəʳ/ *verb* **1** [T] to show great respect for someone or something, usually in public [often passive] *He was* ***honoured for*** *his bravery.* ○ *She was* ***honoured with*** *an Oscar.* **2 honour an agreement/contract/promise, etc** to do what you agreed or promised to do ➲Opposite **dishonour**

honourable /ˈɒnᵊrəbl/ *adjective UK* **1** (*US* **honorable**) honest and fair, or deserving praise and respect *a decent, honourable man* ➲Opposite **dishonourable** **2 the Honourable a** a title used before the name of some important government officials **b** a title used in the UK before the name of certain people of high social rank •**honourably** *adverb*

hood /hʊd/ *noun* [C] **1** HEAD a part of a coat or jacket that covers your head and neck *a waterproof jacket with a hood* ➲See colour picture **Clothes** on page Centre 8 **2** CAR *US* (*UK* **bonnet**) the metal part that covers a car engine ➲See colour picture **Car** on page Centre 7

hooded /ˈhʊdɪd/ *adjective* having or wearing a hood *a hooded sweatshirt* ○ *hooded figures*

hoodie (also **hoody**) /ˈhʊdi/ *noun* [C] a sweatshirt (= a piece of clothing made of soft cotton which covers the top of your body) with a hood

(= part which covers your head) See colour picture **Clothes** on page Centre 8

hoof /huːf/ *noun* [C] *plural* **hooves** or **hoofs** **BIOLOGY** the hard part on the foot of a horse and some other large animals

hook¹ /hʊk/ *noun* **1** [C] a curved piece of metal or plastic used for hanging something on, or a similar object used for catching fish *His coat was hanging from a hook on the door.* **2 off the hook** If a telephone is off the hook, the part you speak into is not in its correct position, so the telephone will not ring. **3 a left/right hook** **SPORT** when you hit someone hard with your left/right hand **4 get/let sb off the hook** *informal* to allow someone to escape from a difficult situation or to avoid doing something that they do not want to do

H

hook² /hʊk/ *verb* **1** [T] to fasten something with a hook, hang something on a hook, or catch something with a hook **2 be/get hooked on sth** **a** to like or start to like doing something very much and want to do it all the time *He's completely hooked on computer games.* **b** If you are hooked on a drug, you cannot stop taking it. •**hooked** *adjective* shaped like a hook *a hooked nose*

hook sth/sb up *phrasal verb* to connect a machine to a power supply or to another machine, or to connect someone to a piece of medical equipment

hooligan /ˈhuːlɪgᵊn/ *noun* [C] someone who behaves badly or violently and causes damage in a public place •**hooliganism** *noun* [U]

hoop /huːp/ *noun* [C] a ring made of metal, plastic, or wood

hooray (*also* **hurrah**) /hʊˈreɪ/ *exclamation* something that you shout when you are happy, excited, etc or when you approve of someone or something ***Hip, hip, hooray!***

hoot¹ /huːt/ *noun* **1** SOUND [C] a short sound made by an owl (= bird) or by a car horn (= warning equipment) **2 a hoot of laughter** when someone laughs loudly **3** FUNNY [**no plural**] *informal* something or someone that is very funny *The film was an absolute hoot.*

hoot² /huːt/ *verb* **1** CAR [I, T] *mainly UK* to make a short sound with your car's horn (= part you press to make a warning noise) *The van driver hooted his horn impatiently.* **2** BIRD [I] If an owl (= bird) hoots, it makes a low 'oo' sound. **3 hoot with laughter** to laugh a lot very loudly

Hoover /ˈhuːvəʳ/ *mainly UK trademark* (*UK/US* **vacuum cleaner**) *noun* [C] an electric machine which cleans floors by sucking up dirt •**hoover** *verb* [I, T]

hooves /huːvz/ *plural of* hoof

hop¹ /hɒp/ *verb* [I] **hopping**, *past* **hopped** **1** ONE FOOT to jump on one foot or to move about in this way **2** ANIMAL If a small animal, bird, or insect hops, it moves by jumping on all of its feet at the same time. *Rabbits were hopping across the field.* **3** MOVE QUICKLY *informal* to go somewhere quickly or get into or out of a vehicle quickly *to hop on a plane/train*

hop² /hɒp/ *noun* **1** [C] a short jump, especially on one leg **2 a short hop** *informal* a short journey or distance *London to Paris is only a short hop by plane.*

hope¹ /həʊp/ *verb* **1** [I, T] to want something to happen or be true [+ **(that)**] *I hope that the bus won't be late.* ○ *We had* ***hoped for*** *better weather than this.* ○ *"Do you think it's going to rain?"* ***"I hope not!"*** ○ *"Is he coming?"* ***"I hope so."*** **2 hope to do sth** to intend to do something *Dad hopes to retire next year.*

WORD PARTNERS FOR ***hope***

bring / give / give up / hold out / lose / offer hope • **fresh/great/renewed/vain** hope • hope **of** sth/doing sth

hope² /həʊp/ *noun* **1** [C, U] a positive feeling about the future, or something that you want to happen *a message full of hope* ○ *What are your* ***hopes*** *and dreams* ***for*** *the future?* [+ **of + doing sth**] *Young people are growing up in our cities without any hope of getting a job.* **2 sb's best/last/only hope** the best/last/only person or thing that can help you and make you succeed *Doctors say his only hope is a transplant.* **3 in the hope of/that** because you want something good to happen [+ **doing sth**] *She went to Paris in the hope of improving her French.* **4 pin your hopes on sb/sth** to hope that someone or something will help you achieve what you want

hopeful /ˈhəʊpfᵊl/ *adjective* **1** SOMEONE feeling positive about a future event or situation *Many teenagers do not feel* ***hopeful about*** *the future.* [+ **(that)**] *Police are still hopeful that they will find the missing family.* **2** SOMETHING If something is hopeful, it makes you feel that what you want to happen will happen. *There are* ***hopeful signs*** *that she will make a full recovery.* •**hopefulness** *noun* [U] •**hopeful** *noun* [C] someone who hopes to succeed, especially in the entertainment business ***a young hopeful***

hopefully /ˈhəʊpfᵊli/ *adverb* **1** EXPRESS WISH used, often at the start of a sentence, to express what you would like to happen *Hopefully it won't rain.* **2** HOPING in a hopeful way *"Are there any tickets left?" she asked hopefully.*

hopeless /ˈhəʊpləs/ *adjective* **1** VERY BAD very bad and not likely to succeed or improve ***a hopeless situation*** ○ *They searched for survivors, but it was hopeless.* **2** NOT ABLE very bad at a particular activity *Dad's a hopeless cook.* ○ *I'm* ***hopeless at*** *sports.* **3** NOT POSITIVE feeling no hope *She was depressed and felt totally hopeless about the future.* •**hopelessness** *noun* [U]

hopelessly /ˈhəʊpləsli/ *adverb* extremely, or in a way that makes you lose hope *hopelessly lost* ○ *They met at university and fell* ***hopelessly in love.***

hops /hɒps/ *noun* [**plural**] **FOOD** the flowers of a plant that are used to make beer

hopscotch /ˈhɒpskɒtʃ/ *noun* [U] a children's game in which the player throws a stone onto one of a set of squares drawn on the ground and then jumps and hops (= jumps on one leg) into each square in turn to pick up the stone

horde /hɔːd/ *noun* [C] a large group of people *There was a* ***horde of*** *tourists outside Buckingham Palace.*

horizon /həˈraɪzᵊn/ *noun* **1** [C] the line in the distance where the sky seems to touch the land or sea **2 broaden/expand/widen your horizons** to increase the number of things that you know about, have experienced, or can do *Travelling certainly broadens your horizons.* **3 on the horizon** likely to happen soon *Economic recovery is on the horizon.*

horizontal /ˌhɒrɪˈzɒntᵊl/ *adjective* level and flat, or parallel to the ground or to the bottom of a page *a horizontal line/stripe* •**horizontally** *adverb*

hoˌrizontal ˈaxis *noun* [no plural] **MATHEMATICS** the line of figures or letters along the bottom of a graph or map; the x-axis ➲Compare **vertical axis** ➲See Extra help page **Graphs and charts** on page Centre 20.

hoˌrizontal ˈmerger *noun* [C] **FINANCE, ECONOMICS** when two companies that have the same type of business join together

hormone /ˈhɔːməʊn/ *noun* [C] **BIOLOGY** one of several chemicals produced in your body that influence its growth and development •**hormonal** /hɔːˈməʊnᵊl/ *adjective a **hormonal** imbalance*

horn /hɔːn/ *noun* [C] **1 BIOLOGY** one of the two hard, pointed growths on the heads of cows, goats, and some other animals **2** a piece of equipment used to make a loud sound as a warning or signal *a car horn* ○ *The taxi driver **hooted his horn**.* **3 MUSIC** a curved musical instrument that you blow into to make a sound *the French horn*

horoscope /ˈhɒrəskəʊp/ *noun* [C] a description of what someone is like and what might happen to them in the future, based on the position of the stars and planets when they were born

horrendous /hərˈendəs/ *adjective* extremely unpleasant or bad *She suffered horrendous injuries in the accident.* •**horrendously** *adverb* extremely or extremely badly *horrendously expensive*

horrible /ˈhɒrəbl/ *adjective* very unpleasant or bad *What's that horrible smell?* ○ *That was a horrible thing to say to your sister.* •**horribly** *adverb* extremely, or in a very bad or unpleasant way *His plan went horribly wrong.*

horrid /ˈhɒrɪd/ *adjective* very unpleasant or unkind

horrific /hɒrˈɪfɪk/ *adjective* very bad and shocking *a **horrific accident/crime*** ○ ***horrific injuries*** •**horrifically** *adverb*

horrify /ˈhɒrɪfaɪ/ *verb* [T] to make someone feel very shocked [often passive] *I was horrified to hear about your accident.* •**horrifying** *adjective*

horror /ˈhɒrəʳ/ *noun* **1** [C, U] a strong feeling of shock or fear, or something that makes you feel shocked or afraid *She watched **in horror** as the car skidded across the road.* **2 a horror film/movie/story** a film or story that entertains people by shocking or frightening them

O‑ **horse** /hɔːs/ *noun* [C] a large animal with four legs, which people ride or use to pull heavy things

horseback /ˈhɔːsbæk/ *noun* **1 on horseback** riding a horse *police on horseback* **2 horseback riding SPORT** *US* (*UK* **horse riding**) the sport or activity of riding a horse ➲See colour picture **Sports 1** on page Centre 14

ˌhorse ˈchestnut *noun* [C] a tree that produces shiny, brown nuts in thick green shells with sharp points, or one of these nuts

horse-drawn /ˈhɔːsdrɔːn/ *adjective* [always before noun] A horse-drawn vehicle is pulled by a horse.

horseman, horsewoman /ˈhɔːsmən, ˈhɔːsˌwʊmən/ *noun* [C] *plural* **horsemen, horsewomen SPORT** a man/woman who rides horses well

horsepower /ˈhɔːsˌpaʊəʳ/ (*written abbreviation* **hp**) *noun* [U] **MEASURES** a unit for measuring the power of an engine

ˈhorse ˌracing *noun* [U] **SPORT** the sport where people race on horses, usually to win money

ˈhorse ˌriding *UK* (*US* **ˈhorseback ˌriding**) *noun* [U] **SPORT** the sport or activity of riding a horse ➲See colour picture **Sports 1** on page Centre 14

horseshoe /ˈhɔːsʃuː/ *noun* [C] a U-shaped piece of metal that is nailed to a horse's foot

horticulture /ˈhɔːtɪkʌltʃəʳ/ *noun* [U] **FARMING** the study or activity of growing plants •**horticultural** /ˌhɔːtɪˈkʌltʃᵊrᵊl/ *adjective* relating to gardening

hose /həʊz/ *noun* **1** PIPE [C] (*also UK* **hosepipe** /ˈhəʊzpaɪp/) a long pipe made of rubber or plastic and used for directing water somewhere, usually onto a garden or fire **2** CLOTHES [plural] (*also* **pantyhose**) *US* a piece of women's clothing made of very thin material that covers the legs and bottom

hospice /ˈhɒspɪs/ *noun* [C] **HEALTH** a place where people who are dying live and are cared for

hospitable /hɒsˈpɪtəbl/ *adjective* A hospitable person or place is friendly, pleasant, and welcomes visitors.

WORD PARTNERS FOR ***hospital***

be **admitted to/discharged from** hospital • be (UK) **in**/(US) **in the** hospital

O‑ **hospital** /ˈhɒspɪtᵊl/ *noun* [C, U] **HEALTH** a place where ill or injured people go to be treated by doctors and nurses *He was (UK) **in hospital**/(US) **in the hospital** for two weeks.*

hospitalize (*also UK* **-ise**) /ˈhɒspɪtᵊlaɪz/ *verb* [T] **HEALTH** to take someone to hospital and keep them there for treatment [often passive] *My wife was often hospitalized for depression.*

host¹ /həʊst/ *noun* **1** PARTY [C] someone who organizes a party and invites the guests **2** TELEVISION [C] someone who introduces the guests on a radio or television programme *a **talk show host*** **3** PLACE [C] a country or city that provides the place and equipment for an organized event *Australia **played host to** the Olympics in 2000.* **4 INTERNET** a company that hosts websites on the Internet **5 a host of sth** a large number of people or things *I've got a whole host of questions to ask you.*

host² /həʊst/ *verb* [T] **1** to be the host of an event *to **host a party/dinner*** **2 INTERNET** to provide the computer equipment and programs that allow a website to operate on the Internet

hostage /ˈhɒstɪdʒ/ *noun* **1** [C] someone who is kept as a prisoner and may be hurt or killed

H

in order to force other people to do something **2 take/hold sb hostage** to catch or keep someone as a prisoner *Two tourists were held hostage by terrorists.*

hostel /ˈhɒstᵊl/ *noun* [C] a place like a cheap hotel, where you can live when you are away from home or have no home *a hostel for the homeless* ○ *a **student hostel*** ➲See also: **youth hostel**

hostess /ˈhəʊstɪs/ *noun* [C] **1** PARTY a woman who organizes a party and invites the guests **2** TELEVISION a woman who introduces the guests on a television programme ➲See also: **air hostess**

hostile /ˈhɒstaɪl/ *adjective* **1** UNFRIENDLY unfriendly and not liking or agreeing with something *Some politicians were very **hostile to** the idea.* **2** DIFFICULT unpleasant or not suitable for living or growing *a hostile climate*

WORD PARTNERS FOR ***hostility***

arouse/provoke hostility • **open** hostility • hostility **to/towards** sb

hostility /hɒsˈtɪləti/ *noun* **1** UNFRIENDLY BEHAVIOUR [U] unfriendly, angry behaviour that shows that you dislike someone ***hostility towards** outsiders* **2** DISAGREEMENT [U] when you strongly disagree with something or someone *There is still open **hostility to** the idea.* **3 hostilities** [plural] *formal* fighting in a war

⊶**hot¹** /hɒt/ *adjective* **hotter, hottest 1** VERY WARM having a high temperature *a hot summer's day* ○ *a hot drink/meal* ○ *I'm too hot in this jacket.* **2 FOOD** Hot food contains strong spices which cause a burning feeling in your mouth. *Be careful. The chilli sauce is very hot.* **3** EXCITING *informal* exciting or interesting *Hollywood's hottest new actress* **4 a hot issue/topic** a subject which people discuss and have strong feelings about *The legalization of drugs is a hot topic.* ➲See also: **piping hot, red-hot**

hot² /hɒt/ *verb* **hotting**, *past* **hotted**

hot up *phrasal verb UK informal* If a situation or event hots up, it becomes more exciting and more things start to happen.

hot-ˈair balˌloon *noun* [C] a very large balloon filled with hot air, that has a container below it where people can travel

hotbed /ˈhɒtbed/ *noun* [C] a place where there is a lot of a particular activity, usually something bad *The government was **a hotbed of** corruption.*

ˌhot ˈchocolate *noun* [C, U] **FOOD** a hot, sweet drink with a chocolate flavour

ˈhot ˌdog *noun* [C] **FOOD** a cooked sausage (= tube of meat and spices) that you usually eat inside bread

WORD PARTNERS FOR ***hotel***

at/in a hotel • a hotel **guest/room** • a **luxury** hotel

⊶**hotel** /həʊˈtel/ *noun* [C] a place where you pay to stay when you are away from home *We spent our honeymoon **in a** luxury **hotel**.* ○ *a **hotel room***

hotelier /həʊˈtelieɪ/ (US) /həʊˈtəljər/ *noun* [C] someone who owns or is in charge of a hotel

ˈhot ˌkey *noun* [C] **COMPUTING** a key that starts a particular computer program or causes a series of actions to be performed, sometimes used with other keys; a shortcut (key)

hotline /ˈhɒtlaɪn/ *noun* [C] a telephone number that you can ring for help or information *Ring our 24-hour hotline for advice.*

hotly /ˈhɒtli/ *adverb* **1** in an angry or excited way *He **hotly denied** the rumours.* **2 hotly contested** If a race, election or other competition is hotly contested, everyone is trying very hard to win it.

ˌhot-ˈwater bottle *noun* [C] a flat, rubber container that you fill with hot water to keep you warm

hound¹ /haʊnd/ *noun* [C] a dog that is used when people hunt animals

hound² /haʊnd/ *verb* [T] to follow someone and annoy them by asking questions or taking photographs [**often passive**] *She is always being hounded by photographers.*

⊶**hour** /aʊəʳ/ *noun* **1** 60 MINUTES [C] a period of time equal to 60 minutes *half an hour* ○ *It's a six-hour flight.* ○ *The job pays $5 an hour.* **2** PERIOD OF TIME [C] the period of time when a particular activity happens or when a shop or public building is open [**usually plural**] ***working hours*** ○ *Our **opening hours** are from 8 to 6.* ○ *I've got to go to the bank (UK)* in my ***lunch hour**/ (US)* on my lunch hour. **3 hours** *informal* a long time *I **spent hours** doing my homework.* **4 the hour** the point when a new hour begins *The train leaves at two minutes past the hour.* ○ *My watch beeps **on the hour**.* **5 all hours** very late at night, until early morning, or almost all the time *Our neighbours are up till all hours every night, playing loud music.* **6 the early/small hours** the hours between midnight and the time that the sun rises ➲See also: **rush hour**

COMMON LEARNER ERROR

hour or **time?**

An **hour** is a period of 60 minutes.

The journey takes about three hours.

We went for a 2-hour walk.

Time is measured in hours and minutes. We use **time** to refer to a particular point during the day or night, or to say when something happens.

What time do you get up in the morning?

There's only one bus at that time of night.

Remember to use **time** not 'hour' when you are talking about what time it is.

"What time is it?" "2 o'clock".

~~*"What hour is it?" "2 o'clock".*~~

hourly /ˈaʊəli/ *adjective, adverb* **1** EVERY happening every hour *There is an hourly bus service.* **2** EACH for each hour *an hourly rate/wage*

WORD PARTNERS FOR ***house***

build/buy/rent/sell a house • a **detached/semi-detached/terraced** house

⊶**house¹** /haʊs/ *noun plural* **houses** /ˈhaʊzɪz/ **1** BUILDING [C] a building where people live, usually one family or group *a three-bedroomed house* ○ *We went to my aunt's house for dinner.*

2 PEOPLE [no plural] the people who live in a house *The baby's screaming woke the **whole house** up.* 3 PLACE FOR ACTIVITY [C] the place where a particular business or activity happens *an opera house* ○ *a publishing house* **4 the House POLITICS** a group of people which makes a country's laws, or the place where they meet *the House of Commons/Representatives* ○ *The House voted on the proposals.* 5 THEATRE [C] the people watching a performance or the area where they sit [usually singular] *The actors played to a **full house**.* **6 on the house** If food or drink is on the house in a bar or restaurant, it is free. ➲See also: **boarding house, full house, row house, terraced house, the White House**

house² /haʊz/ *verb* [T] **1** GIVE HOME to give a person or animal a place to live *This development will house over 100 families.* **2** PROVIDE SPACE to provide space for something *The museum houses a huge collection of paintings.*

ˌhouse arˈrest *noun* **LAW under house arrest** when you are kept as a prisoner in your own home

houseboat /ˈhaʊsbəʊt/ *noun* [C] a boat that people can live on

housebound /ˈhaʊsbaʊnd/ *adjective* unable to leave your home because you are too ill or old

household¹ /ˈhaʊshəʊld/ *noun* [C] **SOCIETY** a family or group of people who live together in a house *Many households own more than one television.*

household² /ˈhaʊshəʊld/ *adjective* **1** [always before noun] connected with or belonging to a home ***household bills/expenses*** ○ ***household products/goods*** **2 a household name** someone or something that everyone knows *Her TV roles made her a household name in the UK.*

householder /ˈhaʊshəʊldəʳ/ *noun* [C] *UK* someone who owns or rents a house

ˈhouse ˌhusband *noun* [C] a man who takes care of the house and children while his wife or partner earns money for the family

housekeeper /ˈhaʊsˌkiːpəʳ/ *noun* [C] someone who is paid to clean and cook in someone else's house

housekeeping /ˈhaʊsˌkiːpɪŋ/ *noun* [U] the cleaning and cooking that you do in your home

ˈhouse ˌ(music) *noun* [U] **MUSIC** a type of electronic pop music with a strong beat for dancing

ˌHouse of ˈCommons *noun* [no plural] **POLITICS** one of the two parts of the British parliament, with elected members who make laws

ˌHouse of ˈLords *noun* [no plural] **POLITICS** one of the two parts of the British parliament, with members who are chosen by the government

ˌHouse of Repreˈsentatives *noun* [no plural] **POLITICS** a group of politicians elected by people in the US to make laws

ˌHouses of ˈParliament *noun* [plural] **POLITICS** the House of Commons and the House of Lords, or the building in London where they meet

ˈhouse ˌwarming *noun* [C] a party to celebrate moving into a new house

housewife /ˈhaʊswaɪf/ *noun* [C] *plural* **housewives** /ˈhaʊswaɪvz/ a woman who stays at home to cook, clean, and take care of her family

housework /ˈhaʊswɜːk/ *noun* [U] the work that you do to keep your house clean *I can't stand **doing housework**.*

housing /ˈhaʊzɪŋ/ *noun* [U] buildings for people to live in *a shortage of local housing*

ˈhousing eˌstate *UK* (*US* **ˈhousing development**) *noun* [C] an area with a large number of houses that were built at the same time

hover /ˈhɒvəʳ/ *verb* [I] **1** IN AIR to stay up in the air but without moving anywhere *A helicopter hovered overhead.* **2** WAIT If you hover, you stand and wait near someone or something. *A waiter hovered at the table ready to take our order.*

hovercraft /ˈhɒvəkrɑːft/ *noun* [C] a boat that moves across the surface of water or land supported by a large cushion (= soft container) of air

H

O‑ **how¹** /haʊ/ *adverb* **1** WAY used to ask about the way something happens or is done *How did he die?* ○ *How does she manage to keep the house so tidy?* **2** QUANTITY used to ask about quantity, size, or age *How big is the house?* ○ *How old are they?* ○ *How much* (= what price) *was that dress?* **3** EMPHASIZE used before an adjective or adverb to emphasize it *I was amazed at how quickly she finished.* **4** HEALTH used to ask about someone's health *How are you feeling today?* **5** SITUATION used to ask about the success or progress of a situation *How's everything going?* ○ *How was the exam?* **6 How are you?** used to ask someone if they are well and happy *"How are you Jane?" - "Oh, not so bad thanks."* **7 How about..?** used to make a suggestion *How about a drink?* [+ doing sth] *How about going to the cinema?* **8 How come?** *informal* used to ask about the reason for something, especially when you feel surprised about it *"Kate's gone to the party on her own." "How come?"* **9 How strange/stupid/weird, etc. is that?** said to mean that something is strange/stupid, etc. ➲See also: **know-how**

COMMON LEARNER ERROR

how or **what?**

In these expressions we use **what**. Be careful not to use 'how'.

what something is called

I don't know what it's called in English.

~~*I don't know how it's called in English.*~~

what something/someone looks like

I'd like to see what it looks like before I buy it.

What does your brother look like?

how² /haʊ/ *conjunction* used to talk about the way that something happens or is done [+ to do sth] *I don't know how to turn the video on.*

O‑ **however¹** /haʊˈevəʳ/ *adverb* **1 however cold/difficult/slowly, etc** used to say that it does not make any difference how cold/difficult/slowly, etc *We're not going to get there in time, however fast we drive.* **2** COMPARING used when you are about to say something which is surprising compared with what you have just said *He had always been a successful businessman. Recently, however, things have not been going well for him.* **3** ASKING *UK* used to ask about how something happened when the person asking feels surprised *However did you manage to persuade her?*

however² /haʊˈevəʳ/ *conjunction* in any way *However you look at it, it's still a mess.* ○ *You can do it however you like.*

howl /haʊl/ *verb* [I] **1** ANIMAL If a dog or wolf (= wild animal like a dog) howls, it makes a long, sad sound. **2** MAKE SOUND to make a loud sound, usually to express pain, sadness, or another strong emotion *He **howled in** pain.* ○ *The audience was **howling with** laughter.* **3** WIND If the wind howls, it blows hard and makes a lot of noise. •**howl** *noun* [C]

H

hp MEASURES *written abbreviation for* horsepower (= a unit for measuring the power of an engine)

HQ /ˌeɪtʃˈkjuː/ *noun* [C, U] *abbreviation for* headquarters (= the place from where an organization is controlled)

hr *written abbreviation for* hour

HRH /ˌeɪtʃɑːrˈeɪtʃ/ *abbreviation for* His/Her Royal Highness: used when speaking to or about a royal person

HTH INTERNET *internet abbreviation for* hope this helps: used when you send someone information you think is useful, especially when you answer a question

HTML /ˌeɪtʃtiːemˈel/ COMPUTING, INTERNET *abbreviation for* hypertext markup language: a way of marking text so that it can be seen on the Internet

http /ˌeɪtʃtiːtiːˈpiː/ COMPUTING, INTERNET *abbreviation for* hypertext transfer protocol: a set of instructions made by a computer program that allows your computer to connect to an Internet document

hub /hʌb/ *noun* [C] **1** OF ACTIVITY a place that is the centre of a particular activity [usually singular] *Silicon Valley has become the **hub of** the electronics industry.* **2** WHEEL the round part in the centre of a wheel

huddle¹ /ˈhʌdl/ (*also* **huddle together/up**) *verb* [I] to move closer to other people, or to hold your arms and legs close to your body, usually because you are cold or frightened *They huddled around the fire to keep warm.*

huddle² /ˈhʌdl/ *noun* [C] a group of people or things that are standing close together

hue /hjuː/ *noun* [C] *literary* a colour

huff¹ /hʌf/ *verb* **huff and puff** *informal* to breathe loudly, especially because you have been exercising

huff² /hʌf/ *noun* **in a huff** *informal* angry with someone *Mum's in a huff because I didn't call yesterday.*

hug¹ /hʌg/ *verb* **hugging**, *past* **hugged** **1** HOLD SOMEONE [I, T] to put your arms around someone and hold them tightly, usually because you love them *They hugged and kissed each other.* **2** BE CLOSE [T] to stay very close to the edge of something *The road hugs the coast for several miles.*

hug² /hʌg/ *noun* [C] when you put your arms around someone and hold them tightly *She **gave** me a big **hug** before she left.*

huge /hjuːdʒ/ *adjective* extremely large *a huge house*

hugely /ˈhjuːdʒli/ *adverb* extremely ***hugely popular/successful***

huh /hʌ/ *exclamation informal* used to ask a question, or to express surprise, anger, etc *So, you're leaving, huh?*

Hula Hoop /ˈhuːləhuːp/ *noun* [C] *trademark* a large plastic ring that you put around your waist and move your body so that it goes round and round

hull /hʌl/ *noun* [C] the main part of a ship that is mostly under water

hullo *UK* (*UK/US* **hello**) /həˈləʊ/ *exclamation* **1** GREET used to greet someone *Hullo, Chris, how are things?* **2** TELEPHONE used to start a conversation on the telephone *Hullo, this is Alex.*

hum¹ /hʌm/ *verb* **humming**, *past* **hummed** **1** MUSIC [I, T] to sing without opening your mouth *She hummed to herself as she walked to school.* **2** [I] to make a continuous, low sound *The computers were humming in the background.* **3** **be humming** If a place is humming, it is busy and full of activity. •**hum** *noun* [C] a low, continuous sound *the **hum of traffic***

human¹ /ˈhjuːmən/ *adjective* **1** relating to people or their characteristics *the human body* ○ *human behaviour* ○ *The accident was caused by **human error*** (= a person's mistake). **2** **be only human** to not be perfect *Of course Tom makes mistakes - he's only human.*

human² /ˈhjuːmən/ (*also* ˌ**human ˈbeing**) *noun* [C] a man, woman, or child *The disease affects both humans and animals.*

humane /hjuːˈmeɪn/ *adjective* kind, especially towards people or animals that are suffering *They fought for more humane treatment of prisoners of war.* ➲Opposite **inhumane** •**humanely** *adverb*

ˌ**human ˈgeography** *noun* [U] GEOGRAPHY the part of geography that studies the way in which human behaviour affects the Earth's surface, or the way in which the Earth affects human behaviour

humanism /ˈhjuːmənɪzᵊm/ *noun* [U] a belief system based on human needs and values and not on a god or religion •**humanist** *noun* [C] •**humanistic** /ˌhjuːməˈnɪstɪk/ *adjective*

humanitarian /hjuːˌmænɪˈteəriən/ *adjective* connected with improving people's lives and reducing suffering *The UN is sending **humanitarian aid** to the refugees.*

humanities /hjuːˈmænətiz/ *noun* [plural] EDUCATION subjects that you study which are not connected with science, such as literature and history

humanity /hjuːˈmænəti/ *noun* [U] **1** SOCIETY all people *The massacre was a **crime against humanity**.* **2** KINDNESS kindness and sympathy towards others ➲Opposite **inhumanity** **3** BEING HUMAN the condition of being human

humankind /ˌhjuːmənˈkaɪnd/ *noun* [U] **SOCIETY** all the people in the world

humanly /ˈhjuːmənli/ *adverb* **humanly possible** able to be done by people *Doctors did everything humanly possible to save her life.*

ˌhuman ˈnature *noun* [U] feelings, qualities, and behaviour that are typical of most people *It's human nature to want to be loved.*

the ˌhuman ˈrace *noun* [no plural] **SOCIETY** all the people in the world

ˌhuman reˈsources *UK* (*US* **ˌhuman ˈresources**) *noun* [U] the department of an organization that deals with finding new people to work there, keeping records about all the organization's employees, and helping them with any problems

ˌhuman ˈrights *noun* [plural] **SOCIETY** the basic rights that every person should have, such as justice and the freedom to say what you think *international laws protecting human rights*

humble¹ /ˈhʌmbl/ *adjective* **1** NOT PROUD not proud or not believing that you are important *He's very humble about his success.* **2** POOR poor or of a low social rank *She rose from **humble beginnings** to become Prime Minister.* •**humbly** *adverb*

humble² /ˈhʌmbl/ *verb* [T] to make someone understand that they are not as important or special as they think they are *She was humbled by the unexpected defeat.* •**humbling** *adjective a **humbling experience***

humdrum /ˈhʌmdrʌm/ *adjective* boring and ordinary *a **humdrum existence***

humerus /ˈhjuːmᵊrəs/ *noun* [C] *plural* **humeri** **ANATOMY** the large bone at the top of the arm, between the shoulder and the elbow

humid /ˈhjuːmɪd/ *adjective* Humid air or weather is hot and slightly wet. *a hot and humid climate*

humidity /hjuːˈmɪdəti/ *noun* [U] **GEOGRAPHY** a measurement of how much water there is in the air

humiliate /hjuːˈmɪlieɪt/ *verb* [T] to make someone feel stupid or ashamed *How could you humiliate me in front of all my friends!* •**humiliated** *adjective Sue felt completely humiliated.* •**humiliation** /hjuːˌmɪliˈeɪʃᵊn/ *noun* [C, U]

humiliating /hjuːˈmɪlieɪtɪŋ/ *adjective* making you feel stupid or ashamed

humility /hjuːˈmɪləti/ *noun* [U] the quality of not being proud or not thinking that you are better than other people

hummingbird /ˈhʌmɪŋbɜːd/ *noun* [C] a very small brightly coloured bird with a long thin beak whose wings move very fast, making a continuous, low noise

humor /ˈhjuːmə^r/ *noun, verb US spelling of* humour

humorless /ˈhjuːmələs/ *adjective US spelling of* humourless

humorous /ˈhjuːmᵊrəs/ *adjective* funny, or making you laugh *a humorous book* •**humorously** *adverb*

WORD PARTNERS FOR ***humour***

a sense of humour • a dry/wry humour

humour¹ *UK* (*US* **humor**) /ˈhjuːmə^r/ *noun* [U] **1** ABILITY the ability to laugh and recognize that something is funny *He's got a great **sense of humour**.* **2** FUNNY QUALITY the quality of being funny, or things that are funny *His speech was full of humour.* **3** MOOD *formal* the way you are feeling, or your mood ***good humour***

humour² *UK* (*US* **humor**) /ˈhjuːmə^r/ *verb* [T] to do what someone wants so that they do not become annoyed or upset *Carol applied for the job just to humour me.*

humourless *UK* (*US* **humorless**) /ˈhjuːmələs/ *adjective* unable to laugh and recognize when something is funny, or being without funny qualities

hump /hʌmp/ *noun* [C] **1** ON SURFACE a round, raised area on a road or other surface **2** HARD PART a round, hard part on an animal's or person's back *a camel's hump*

humus /ˈhjuːməs/ *noun* [U] dark earth made of dead leaves and plants

hunch¹ /hʌnʃ/ *noun* [C] a feeling or guess that something might be true, when there is no proof *I **had a hunch** that he would get the job.*

hunch² /hʌnʃ/ *verb* [I] to stand or sit with your shoulders and back curved forward *Sitting **hunched over** a computer all day can cause back problems.*

hunchback /ˈhʌnʃbæk/ *noun* [C] someone with a large lump on their back, which makes them lean forward

O‑ **hundred** /ˈhʌndrəd/ **1** the number 100 **2 hundreds** *informal* a lot ***Hundreds of** people wrote in to complain.*

hundredth¹ /ˈhʌndrədθ/ 100th written as a word

hundredth² /ˈhʌndrədθ/ *noun* [C] one of a hundred equal parts of something; 1/100, .01 *a hundredth of a second*

hundredweight /ˈhʌndrədweɪt/ (*written abbreviation* **cwt**) *noun* [C] *plural* **hundredweight** **MEASURES** a unit for measuring weight, equal to 50.8 kilograms in the UK and 45.36 kilograms in the US ⊃See Extra help page **Numbers and measurements** on page Centre 24.

hung /hʌŋ/ *past of* hang

hunger /ˈhʌŋgə^r/ *noun* **1** FEELING [U] the feeling you have when you need to eat *The children were almost crying with hunger by the time we got home.* **2** NOT ENOUGH FOOD [U] when you do not have enough food *Many of the refugees **died of hunger**.* **3** WISH [no plural] a strong wish for something *a **hunger for** success/knowledge*

ˈhunger ˌstrike *noun* [C, U] when someone refuses to eat in order to show that they strongly disagree with something *The prisoners **went on hunger strike**.*

hungover /ˌhʌŋˈəʊvə^r/ *adjective* **HEALTH** feeling ill after drinking too much alcohol the day before

O‑ **hungry** /ˈhʌŋgri/ *adjective* **1** wanting or needing food *I'm hungry. What's for supper?* **2 go hungry** to not have enough food to eat *In an ideal world, nobody should go hungry.* **3 be**

hungry for sth to have a strong wish for something *The journalists were hungry for more details of the accident.* •**hungrily** *adverb*

hunk /hʌŋk/ *noun* [C] **1** MAN *informal* an attractive man who is often young and has a strong body **2** PIECE a piece of something, usually large and not flat or smooth *a hunk of bread* ➲See colour picture **Pieces and Quantities** on page Centre 1

hunt[1] /hʌnt/ *verb* [I, T] **1** **SPORT** to chase and kill wild animals *to hunt deer/rabbits* **2** to search for something *The children **hunted for** sea shells on the beach.* •**hunter** *noun* [C] a person who hunts wild animals

hunt sb/sth down *phrasal verb* to search everywhere for someone or something until you find them

WORD PARTNERS FOR ***hunt***

launch a hunt • a hunt **for** sb/sth

H

hunt[2] /hʌnt/ *noun* [C] **1** a search for something or someone *a **job hunt*** ○ *The detective leading **the hunt for** the killer spoke at the news conference.* **2** **SPORT** when people chase and kill wild animals *a fox/deer hunt* ➲See also: **witch-hunt**

hunting /ˈhʌntɪŋ/ *noun* [U] **SPORT** the sport of chasing and killing animals *fox-hunting*

hurdle[1] /ˈhɜːdl/ *noun* [C] **1** **SPORT** a bar or fence that people or horses jump over in a race **2** a problem or difficulty that you have to deal with in order to be able to make progress *Getting a work permit was the **first hurdle** to overcome.*

hurdle[2] /ˈhɜːdl/ *verb* [I, T] **SPORT** to jump over something, such as a bar or a fence, when you are running •**hurdler** *noun* [C]

hurl /hɜːl/ *verb* **1** [T] to throw something with a lot of force, usually in an angry or violent way *The demonstrators **hurled** stones **at** police.* **2** **hurl abuse/insults, etc at sb** to shout something at someone in a rude or angry way

hurrah (*also* **hooray**) /həˈrɑː/ *exclamation* something that you shout when you are happy, excited, etc, or when you approve of someone or something *Hurrah! Ian's won!*

hurricane /ˈhʌrɪkən/ *noun* [C] a violent storm with very strong winds

hurried /ˈhʌrid/ *adjective* done more quickly than normal *a hurried explanation/meeting* •**hurriedly** *adverb*

O→**hurry**[1] /ˈhʌri/ *verb* [I, T] to move or do things more quickly than normal or to make someone do this *to hurry away/home* ○ *Please hurry, the train is about to leave.* [+ **to do sth**] *We had to hurry to get there on time.*

hurry up *phrasal verb* to start moving or doing something more quickly *Hurry up! We're going to be late.*

hurry[2] /ˈhʌri/ *noun* **1** **be in a hurry** If you are in a hurry, you want or need to do something quickly. *If you're in a hurry, it's better to take a taxi.* **2** **be in no hurry; not be in any hurry** If you are in no hurry to do something, either you do not need to do it soon or you do not really want to do it . [+ **to do sth**] *They are in no hurry to sign a contract.*

O→**hurt**[1] /hɜːt/ *verb past* **hurt** **1** CAUSE PAIN [T] to cause someone pain or to injure them *Simon hurt his knee playing football.* [**often reflexive**] *She hurt herself when she slipped on an icy step.* **2** BE PAINFUL [I] If a part of your body hurts, it is painful. *My eyes really hurt.* [+ **to do sth**] *It hurts to walk on it.* **3** UPSET [I, T] to cause emotional pain to someone *Her comments about my work really hurt.* **4** AFFECT [T] to have a harmful effect on something *His chances of re-election were hurt by allegations of corruption.* **5** **it won't/wouldn't hurt (sb) to do sth** *informal* used to say that someone should do something *It wouldn't hurt to get there a bit earlier than usual.* ➲See also: wouldn't hurt a **fly**[2]

hurt[2] /hɜːt/ *adjective* [**never before noun**] **1** INJURED injured or in pain *Several people were **seriously hurt** in the accident.* ○ *Put that knife away before someone **gets hurt**.* **2** UPSET upset or unhappy *She was deeply hurt by what he said.*

hurt[3] /hɜːt/ *noun* [U] emotional pain *She has **caused** a lot of **hurt**.*

hurtful /ˈhɜːtfəl/ *adjective* Hurtful behaviour or remarks make someone feel upset. ***hurtful comments/remarks***

hurtle /ˈhɜːtl/ *verb* [I] to move very quickly in a way which is not controlled and may be dangerous *The explosion sent pieces of glass and metal hurtling through the air.*

O→**husband** /ˈhʌzbənd/ *noun* [C] **SOCIETY** the man you are married to *Janet's husband is in the Navy.*

hush[1] /hʌʃ/ *exclamation* used to tell someone to be quiet, especially if they are crying *It's okay. Hush now and wipe your eyes.*

WORD PARTNERS FOR ***hush***

a hush **descends/falls** • a **deathly** hush

hush[2] /hʌʃ/ *noun* [**no plural**] a period of silence *A **hush fell** over the room.* •**hushed** *adjective a hushed atmosphere/crowd*

hush[3] /hʌʃ/ *verb* [T] to make someone be quiet

hush sth up *phrasal verb* to keep something secret, especially from the public, because it could cause embarrassment or trouble *The whole affair was hushed up by the management.*

hush-hush /ˌhʌʃˈhʌʃ/ *adjective informal* If something is hush-hush, it is kept secret. *The project's **all very hush-hush**.*

husky[1] /ˈhʌski/ *adjective* **1** VOICE A husky voice is low and rough but usually sounds attractive. **2** MAN *US* A husky man or boy is big and strong.

husky[2] /ˈhʌski/ *noun* [C] a large, strong dog that is used to pull heavy things across snow

hustle[1] /ˈhʌsl/ *verb* **1** PUSH [T] to make someone move somewhere, especially by pushing them quickly *The security men hustled him out of the back door.* **2** PERSUADE [I, T] *informal* to try to persuade someone, especially to buy something, often illegally *to hustle for business/customers*

hustle[2] /ˈhʌsl/ *noun* **hustle and bustle** busy movement and noise, especially where there

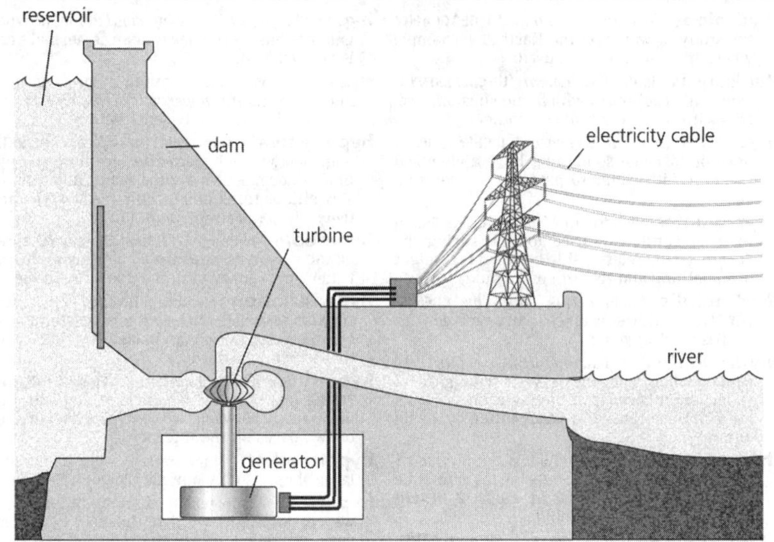

hydroelectric power station

are a lot of people *He wanted to escape the hustle and bustle of city life.*

hustler /ˈhʌsləʳ/ *noun* [C] someone who tries to persuade people to give them what they want, especially in order to make money illegally

hut /hʌt/ *noun* [C] a small, simple building, often made of wood *a mountain hut*

hybrid /ˈhaɪbrɪd/ *noun* [C] **1 BIOLOGY** a plant or animal that is produced from two different types of plant or animal **2** THING something, for example a machine, which is made using ideas or parts from two different things **3** CAR (*also* **hybrid car**) a vehicle with an engine that uses both petrol (= a liquid fuel made from oil) and another type of energy, usually electricity •**hybrid** *adjective*

hydrant /ˈhaɪdrᵊnt/ *noun* [C] a pipe, especially at the side of the road, which is connected to the water system and is used to get water to stop fires ***a fire hydrant***

hydrate¹ /haɪˈdreɪt/ *verb* [I] to make something absorb water •**hydration** /haɪˈdreɪʃᵊn/ *noun* [U]

hydrate² /ˈhaɪdreɪt/ *noun* [C] **CHEMISTRY** a chemical compound that contains water

hydraulic /haɪˈdrɔːlɪk/ *adjective* **PHYSICS** operated using the force of water or another liquid

hydro- /haɪdrəʊ-/ *prefix* relating to water *hydroponic* (= a method of growing plants in water)

hydrocarbon /ˌhaɪdrəʊˈkɑːbᵊn/ *noun* [C] **CHEMISTRY** a chemical combination of hydrogen (= a gas) and carbon (= element found in all animals and plants), found in oil and petrol *hydrocarbon emissions*

hydrochloric acid /ˌhaɪdrəklɒrɪkˈæsɪd/ *noun* [U] **CHEMISTRY** an acid containing hydrogen (= a gas) and chlorine (= gas with a strong smell) (formula **HCl**)

hydrochlorofluorocarbon /ˈhaɪdrəʊˌklɔːrəʊˌflʊərəʊˌkɑːbən/ (*abbreviation* **HCFC**) *noun* [U, C] **CHEMISTRY** a type of gas used especially in aerosols (= containers that force out liquids in very small drops)

hydroelectric /ˌhaɪdrəʊɪˈlektrɪk/ *adjective* **PHYSICS** using the force of water to create electricity ***hydroelectric power***

hydroelectricity /ˌhaɪdrəʊɪlekˈtrɪsɪti/ *noun* [U] **PHYSICS** electricity produced by the force of fast moving water such as rivers or waterfalls

hydrofluorocarbon /ˈhaɪdrəʊˌflʊərəʊˌkɑːbən/ (*abbreviation* **HFC**) *noun* [U, C] **CHEMISTRY** a type of gas used especially in aerosols (= containers that force out liquids in very small drops)

hydrofoil /ˈhaɪdrəʊfɔɪl/ *noun* [C] a large boat which travels quickly above the surface of the water on structures which are the shape of wings

hydrogen /ˈhaɪdrədʒən/ *noun* [U] **CHEMISTRY** a gas that combines with oxygen to form water (formula **H**)

hydrogenated /haɪˈdrɒdʒɪneɪtɪd/ *adjective* **FOOD** Hydrogenated substances, for example fats, have had hydrogen added to them. •**hydrogenation** /haɪˌdrɒdʒɪˈneɪʃᵊn/ *noun* [U]

ˌhydrogen peˈroxide (*also* **peroxide**) *noun* [U] **CHEMISTRY** a colourless liquid that is used to kill bacteria and to make hair very pale (formula H_2O_2)

hydrograph /ˈhaɪdrəʊgrɑːf/ *noun* [C] a graph (= mathematical picture showing measurements) showing the amount of water at different times, for example in a lake

hydrology /haɪˈdrɒlədʒi/ *noun* [U] **GEOGRAPHY** the study of water on the Earth, for example where it is and how it is used

hydrolysis /haɪˈdrɒləsɪs/ *noun* [U] **CHEMISTRY** a chemical reaction in which one substance reacts with water to produce another

hydrolyze (*also UK* **-ise**) *verb* [T, I] **CHEMISTRY** to have or to make something have a chemical reaction with water to produce another substance

hydrometer /haɪˈdrɒmɪtəʳ/ *noun* [C] **PHYSICS** a piece of equipment used for measuring the density (= the relationship between the weight of something and its size) of a liquid

hydrophilic /ˌhaɪdrəʊˈfɪlɪk/ *adjective* **CHEMISTRY** Hydrophilic substances can be mixed with or dissolved in water.

hydrophobia /ˌhaɪdrəʊˈfəʊbiə/ *noun* [U] **HEALTH** when someone is very frightened of water, often because of having rabies (= a serious disease caused by being bitten by a wild animal)

hydrophobic /ˌhaɪdrəʊˈfəʊbɪk/ *adjective* **1 CHEMISTRY** Hydrophobic substances cannot be mixed with or dissolved in water. **2 HEALTH** suffering from hydrophobia

hydroponics /ˌhaɪdrəʊˈpɒnɪks/ *noun* [U] **FARMING** a way of growing plants in water with special chemicals added, and not in earth

hydrosphere /ˈhaɪdrəʊsfɪəʳ/ *noun* [C] **GEOGRAPHY** all of the water on the Earth's surface, such as the seas, lakes and ice. This sometimes includes water above the Earth's surface, such as clouds.

hydroxide /haɪˈdrɒksaɪd/ *noun* [C] **CHEMISTRY** a chemical compound that contains the hydroxyl ion, or a compound of an oxide with water

hydroxyl ion /haɪˌdrɒksɪlˈaɪən/ *noun* [C] **CHEMISTRY** an ion with a negative charge, which is made of an oxygen atom and a hydrogen atom

WORD PARTNERS FOR ***hygiene***

standards of hygiene • **dental/personal** hygiene

hygiene /ˈhaɪdʒiːn/ *noun* [U] **HEALTH** the process of keeping things clean, especially to prevent disease ***dental/personal hygiene*** •**hygienic** /haɪˈdʒiːnɪk/ *adjective* very clean, so that bacteria cannot spread

hygrometer /haɪˈgrɒmɪtəʳ/ *noun* [C] a piece of equipment used to measure how much water there is in the air

hymn /hɪm/ *noun* [C] **MUSIC** a song sung by Christians in church to praise God

hype¹ /haɪp/ *noun* [U] when people talk a lot about something, especially in newspapers, on television, etc, and make it seem more important or exciting than it really is ***media hype*** ○ *There's been a lot of **hype about/surrounding** his latest film.*

hype² /haɪp/ (*also* **hype up**) *verb* [T] to make something seem more important or exciting than it really is by talking about it a lot, especially in newspapers, on television, etc *It's being **hyped as** the musical event of the year.* •**hyped** *adjective*

hyper /ˈhaɪpəʳ/ *adjective informal* Someone who is hyper has more energy than is normal and is very excited.

hyper- /haɪpəʳ/ *prefix* having a lot of or too much of a quality *hyperactive* ○ *hypersensitive* (= more than normally sensitive)

hyperactive /ˌhaɪpərˈæktɪv/ *adjective* **HEALTH** Someone who is hyperactive has more energy than is normal, gets excited easily, and cannot stay still or think about their work. •**hyperactivity** /ˌhaɪpəʳrækˈtɪvəti/ *noun* [U]

hyperbole /haɪˈpɜːbəli/ *noun* [U] *formal* **LANGUAGE** when you describe something as much better, more important, etc than it really is

hyperinflation /ˌhaɪpərɪnˈfleɪʃən/ *noun* [U] **ECONOMICS** when the price of everything increases very quickly and suddenly, in a way that is not controlled

hyperlink /ˈhaɪpəlɪŋk/ *noun* [C] **COMPUTING, INTERNET** text that you can click on that lets you move easily between two computer documents or two pages on the Internet

hypermarket /ˈhaɪpəˌmɑːkɪt/ *noun* [C] a very large shop, usually outside the centre of town

hypertext /ˈhaɪpətekst/ *noun* [U] **INTERNET** a way of joining a word or image to another page, document, etc on the Internet or in another computer program so that you can move from one to the other easily

hypha /ˈhaɪfə/ *noun* [C] *plural* **hyphae** /ˈhaɪfiː/ **BIOLOGY** any of the parts like threads that form the body of a fungus (= plant such as a mushroom)

hyphen /ˈhaɪfən/ *noun* [C] **LANGUAGE** a mark (-) used to join two words together, or to show that a word has been divided and continues on the next line ➲See Extra help page **Punctuation** on page Centre 19. •**hyphenated** *adjective* written with a hyphen

hypnosis /hɪpˈnəʊsɪs/ *noun* [U] a mental state like sleep, in which a person's thoughts can be easily influenced by someone else *Police placed witnesses **under hypnosis** in an effort to gain additional information.* •**hypnotic** /hɪpˈnɒtɪk/ *adjective*

hypnotize (*also UK* **-ise**) /ˈhɪpnətaɪz/ *verb* [T] to place someone in a mental state like sleep, in which their thoughts can be easily influenced •**hypnotist** *noun* [C] someone who hypnotizes people •**hypnotism** /ˈhɪpnətɪzəm/ *noun* [U] when someone is hypnotized

hypochondriac /ˌhaɪpəˈkɒndriæk/ *noun* [C] someone who worries about their health more than is normal, although they are not really ill •**hypochondria** /ˌhaɪpəʊˈkɒndriə/ *noun* [U]

hypocrisy /hɪˈpɒkrəsi/ *noun* [C, U] when someone pretends to believe something that they do not really believe or that is the opposite of what they do or say at another time

hypocrite /ˈhɪpəkrɪt/ *noun* [C] someone who pretends to believe something that they do not really believe or that is the opposite of what they do or say at another time •**hypocritical** /ˌhɪpəʊˈkrɪtɪkəl/ *adjective* •**hypocritically** *adverb*

hypotenuse /haɪˈpɒtənjuːz/ *noun* [C] **MATHEMATICS** the longest side of any triangle which has one angle of 90°

hypothalamus /ˌhaɪpəʊˈθæləməs/ *noun* [C usually singular] **ANATOMY, BIOLOGY** a small part in the front of the brain that controls body temperature and tells your body if you are hungry or thirsty ➲See picture at **brain**

hypothermia /ˌhaɪpəʊˈθɜːmiə/ *noun* [U] **HEALTH** a serious illness caused by someone's body becoming too cold

hypothesis /haɪˈpɒθəsɪs/ *noun* [C] *plural* **hypotheses** /haɪˈpɒθəsiːz/ a suggested explanation for something which has not yet been proved to be true

hypothetical /ˌhaɪpəˈθetɪkəl/ *adjective* A hypothetical situation or idea has been suggested but does not yet really exist or has not been proved to be true.

hysteria /hɪˈstɪəriə/ *noun* [U] extreme fear, excitement, anger, etc which cannot be controlled ***mass hysteria***

hysterical /hɪˈsterɪkəl/ *adjective* **1** NO CONTROL If someone is hysterical, they cannot control their feelings or behaviour because they are extremely frightened, angry, excited, etc. ***hysterical laughter*** ○ *As soon as Wendy saw the blood, she became hysterical.* **2** FUNNY *informal* extremely funny •**hysterically** *adverb They all thought it was **hysterically funny**.*

hysterics /hɪˈsterɪks/ *noun* **1** [plural] uncontrolled behaviour **2 in hysterics** *informal* laughing so much that you cannot stop

Hz **MEASURES** *written abbreviation for* hertz (= a unit of measurement used in electronics)

H

I, i /aɪ/ the ninth letter of the alphabet

I /aɪ/ *pronoun* used when the person speaking or writing is the subject of the verb *I had lunch with Glen yesterday.* ○ *Chris and I have been married for twelve years.* ➲See Common Learner Error at **me**

iambus /aɪˈæmbəs/ (*also* **iamb** /ˈaɪæm/) *noun* [C] *plural* **iambuses** or **iambi** **LITERATURE** a rhythm in poetry with one short or weak syllable followed by one strong or long syllable •**iambic** /aɪˈæmbɪk/ *adjective*

ice¹ /aɪs/ *noun* [U] **1** water that has frozen and become solid *Gerry slipped on the ice and broke his arm.* ○ *I've put a couple of bottles of champagne **on ice*** (= in a bucket of ice to get cold). **2 break the ice** to make people who have not met before feel relaxed with each other, often by starting a conversation

ice² /aɪs/ (*also US* **frost**) *verb* [T] **FOOD** to cover a cake with icing (= sweet mixture of mainly sugar) *an iced bun*

iceberg /ˈaɪsbɜːg/ *noun* [C] **GEOGRAPHY** a very large piece of ice that floats in the sea ➲See also: be the **tip**¹ of the iceberg

ˈice ˌcap *noun* [C] **GEOGRAPHY** a thick layer of ice that permanently covers an area of land

ˌice ˈcream *UK* (*US* **ˈice ˌcream**) *noun* [C, U] **FOOD** a sweet food made from frozen milk or cream and sugar *chocolate/vanilla ice cream*

ˈice ˌcube *noun* [C] a small block of ice that you put into drinks to make them cold

ˈice ˌhockey (*also US* **hockey**) *noun* [U] **SPORT** a game played on ice in which two teams try to hit a small hard object into a goal using long curved sticks ➲See colour picture **Sports 1** on page Centre 14

ˌice ˈlolly /aɪsˈlɒli/ *UK* (*US* **Popsicle** *trademark*) *noun* [C] **FOOD** a sweet, fruit-flavoured piece of ice on a small stick

ˈice ˌrink *noun* [C] **SPORT** an area of ice, usually inside a building, which is prepared for people to ice skate on

ˈice ˌsheet *noun* [C] **GEOGRAPHY** a thick layer of ice that covers a large area of land for a long time

ˈice ˌskate *noun* [C] **SPORT** a boot with a metal part on the bottom, used for moving across ice •**ice skate** *verb* [I] to move across ice using ice skates •**ice skating** *noun* [U] the activity or sport of moving across ice using ice skates ➲See colour picture **Sports 1** on page Centre 14

icicle /ˈaɪsɪkl/ *noun* [C] a long, thin piece of ice that hangs down from something

icing /ˈaɪsɪŋ/ *noun* [U] **1 FOOD** (*also US* **frosting**) a sweet mixture used to cover or fill cakes, made from sugar and water or sugar and butter *chocolate butter icing* **2 the icing on the cake** something that makes a good situation better *He was delighted to get the article published and the £100 payment was the icing on the cake.*

icon /ˈaɪkɒn/ *noun* [C] **1 COMPUTING** a small picture on a computer screen that you choose in order to make the computer do something ***Click on the print icon.*** **2** a person or thing that is famous because it represents a particular idea or way of life *a **cultural/fashion/national icon***

ICT /ˌaɪsiːˈtiː/ *noun* [U] **COMPUTING** *abbreviation for* information and communication technology: the use of computers and other electronic equipment to store and send information

icy /ˈaɪsi/ *adjective* **1** WITH ICE covered in ice ***icy conditions/roads*** **2** COLD extremely cold *an icy wind* ○ *icy water* **3** WITHOUT EMOTION without showing any emotion *an **icy look**/stare* •**icily** *adverb*

I'd /aɪd/ **1** I HAD *short for* I had *Everyone thought I'd gone.* **2** I WOULD *short for* I would *I'd like to buy some stamps, please.*

ID /ˌaɪˈdiː/ *noun* [C, U] **LAW** *abbreviation for* identification: an official document that shows or proves who you are *You'll need to show some form of ID, such as a passport or driving licence.*

I.ˈD. ˌcard *noun* [C] **LAW** an identity card

OTHER WAYS OF SAYING *idea*

An idea about how to do something is often described as a **plan**, **thought** or **suggestion**: *The **plan** is to hire a car when we get there.* • *Have you got any **suggestions** for improvements?* • *Have you had any **thoughts** on presents for your mother?*

A sudden, clever idea is sometimes described as a **brainwave** in the UK and a **brainstorm** in the US: *I wasn't sure what to do and then I had a **brainwave** - I could ask Anna for help.*

The noun **theory** is sometimes used to describe a set of ideas intended to explain something: *He was giving a lecture on Darwin's **theory** of evolution.*

WORD PARTNERS FOR *idea*

come up with/have an idea • a **bad/bright/brilliant/good/stupid** idea

idea /aɪˈdɪə/ *noun* **1** SUGGESTION [C] a suggestion or plan *"Why don't we ask George?" "That's **a good idea.**"* [+ for + doing sth] *Stevens explained his ideas for improving production.* [+ to do sth] *It was Kate's idea to hire a car.* **2** THOUGHT [U, no plural] an understanding, thought, or picture in your mind [+ of + doing sth] *Clive soon got used to the idea of having children around the house again.* [+ (that)] *I don't want them to **get the idea** that we're not interested.* **3 have no idea** to not know *Beth had no idea where he'd gone.* **4** OPINION [C] an opinion or belief *My husband and I have very different **ideas about** school discipline.* **5** AIM [no plural] the aim or purpose of something *The idea is to give local people a chance to voice their opinions.* ➲See also: not have the foggiest (**foggy**) (idea)

ideal¹ /aɪˈdɪəl/ *adjective* perfect, or the best possible *an ideal candidate/solution* ○ *The book is **ideal for** children aged 4 to 6.* ○ ***In an ideal***

world, you wouldn't need to use a keyboard at all.

ideal² /aɪ'dɪəl/ *noun* **1** BELIEF [C] a belief about the way you think something should be *democratic ideals* ○ *They are committed to the ideal of equality.* **2** PERFECT [no plural] a perfect thing or situation *The ideal would be to have a house in the country and a flat in the city too.*

idealism /aɪ'dɪəlɪzᵊm/ *noun* [U] the belief that your ideals can be achieved, often when this does not seem likely to others •**idealist** *noun* [C] a person who believes that it is possible to achieve your ideals •**idealistic** /aɪˌdɪə'lɪstɪk/ *adjective*

ideally /aɪ'dɪəli/ *adverb* **1** PERFECT SITUATION used to describe how something would be in a perfect situation *Ideally, I'd like to work at home.* **2** PERFECTLY in a perfect way *She seemed **ideally suited** for the job.*

identical /aɪ'dentɪkᵊl/ *adjective* exactly the same *The two rooms were almost/virtually identical.* ○ *She found a dress **identical to** the one in the picture.* •**identically** *adverb*

iˌdentical 'twin *noun* [C] one of two babies who are born at the same time from the same egg, and look exactly the same

identifiable /aɪˌdentɪ'faɪəbl/ *adjective* If someone or something is identifiable, you can recognize them and say or prove who or what they are. *clearly/readily identifiable*

WORD PARTNERS FOR ***identification***

a form/a means/proof of identification

identification /aɪˌdentɪfɪ'keɪʃᵊn/ *noun* [U] **1** when you recognize and can name someone or something *Most of the bodies were badly burned, making identification almost impossible.* **2** LAW an official document that shows or proves who you are *an identification card/number*

O-ᵐ **identify** /aɪ'dentɪfaɪ/ *verb* [T] **1** RECOGNIZE to recognize someone or something and say or prove who or what they are *The gunman in Wednesday's attack has been identified as Lee Giggs, an unemployed truck driver.* **2** NAME to tell people who someone is *My informant asked not to be identified.* **3** DISCOVER to find a particular thing or all the things of a particular group *You need to identify your priorities.*

identify sb/sth with sb/sth *phrasal verb* to connect one person or thing with another *As a politician he was identified with liberal causes.*

identify with sb/sth *phrasal verb* to feel that you are similar to someone, and can understand them or their situation because of this

WORD PARTNERS FOR ***identity***

cultural/national/personal identity • **a sense of** identity

identity /aɪ'dentəti/ *noun* [C, U] **1** PERSON who someone is *Police are trying to **establish the identity** of a woman seen walking away from the accident.* **2** DIFFERENT FROM the things that make one person or group of people different from others ***cultural/national identity***

i'dentity ˌcard *noun* [C] LAW a piece of paper or a card that shows your name, photograph and information to prove who you are

ideological /ˌaɪdiə'lɒdʒɪkᵊl/ *adjective* based on or relating to a particular set of ideas or beliefs *ideological conflicts/disagreements* •**ideologically** *adverb*

ideology /ˌaɪdi'ɒlədʒi/ *noun* [C, U] a set of ideas or beliefs, especially about politics *socialist ideology*

idiom /'ɪdiəm/ *noun* [C] LANGUAGE a group of words used together with a meaning that you cannot guess from the meanings of the separate words •**idiomatic** /ˌɪdiəʊ'mætɪk/ *adjective idiomatic language*

idiosyncratic /ˌɪdiəʊsɪŋ'krætɪk/ *adjective* An idiosyncratic quality or way of behaving is typical of only one person and is often strange or unusual. •**idiosyncrasy** /ˌɪdiəʊ'sɪŋkrəsi/ *noun* [C] an idiosyncratic habit or way of behaving

idiot /'ɪdiət/ *noun* [C] a stupid person or someone who is behaving in a stupid way *Like an idiot, I believed him.* •**idiocy** /'ɪdiəsi/ *noun* [C, U] stupid behaviour •**idiotic** /ˌɪdi'ɒtɪk/ *adjective* stupid *an idiotic grin/idea* •**idiotically** *adverb*

idle¹ /'aɪdl/ *adjective* **1** NOT WORKING not working or being used *The factory has **stood idle** for over a year.* **2** NOT SERIOUS [always before noun] not serious or having no real purpose ***idle gossip*** ○ *This is no **idle threat**.* **3** LAZY lazy and not willing to work *He knows what has to be done, he's just **bone idle*** (= extremely lazy). •**idleness** *noun* [U] •**idly** *adverb We cannot **stand idly by*** (= not do anything) *and let this plan go ahead.*

idle² /'aɪdl/ *verb* **1** ENGINE [I] If an engine or machine idles, it runs slowly but does not move or do any work. **2** STOP WORKING [T] *US* to stop someone or something working or being used, often because there is not enough work to do *The closure of the plant idled about 300 workers.* **3** TIME [I] to spend time doing nothing *We saw her idling in the school grounds.*

idle sth away *phrasal verb* to waste time doing nothing *I idled away a few hours watching TV.*

idol /'aɪdᵊl/ *noun* [C] **1** someone that you admire and respect very much *a **pop/sporting idol*** **2** RELIGION a picture or object that people pray to as part of their religion •**idolize** (*also UK* **-ise**) *verb* [T] to admire and respect someone very much

idyllic /ɪ'dɪlɪk/ *adjective* An idyllic place or experience is extremely pleasant, beautiful, or peaceful. *an **idyllic childhood*** ○ *an **idyllic existence***

i.e. (*also* **ie**) /ˌaɪ'iː/ used to explain exactly what you are referring to or what you mean *The price must be more realistic, i.e. lower.*

O-ᵐ **if¹** /ɪf/ *conjunction* **1** DEPEND used to say that something will happen only after something else happens or is true *We'll have the party in the garden if the weather's good.* ○ *If you eat up all your dinner you can have some chocolate.* **2** MIGHT used to talk about something that might happen or be true *What will we do if this doesn't work?* **3** WHETHER whether *I wonder if he'll get the job.* **4** ALWAYS used to mean always or every time *If you mention his mother, he always cries.*

if² /ɪf/ *noun* [C] *informal* something which is not certain or not yet decided *There are still a lot* *of ifs.* ○ *There are* ***no ifs and buts*** (= no doubts or excuses) *about it - we'll have to start again.*

iffy /ˈɪfi/ *adjective informal* **1** NOT SUITABLE not completely good, honest, or suitable *The milk smells a bit iffy.* **2** NOT CERTAIN not certain or decided *Simon's still kind of iffy about going to Colombia.*

igloo /ˈɪgluː/ *noun* [C] a house made of blocks of hard snow

igneous /ˈɪgniəs/ *adjective* **GEOLOGY** Igenous rocks are made from magma (= liquid rock that has cooled.) ➲Compare **metamorphic, sedimentary**

ignite /ɪgˈnaɪt/ *verb formal* **1** BURN [I, T] to start to burn or make something start to burn *A spark ignited the fumes.* **2** FIGHT [T] to start an argument or fight

ignition /ɪgˈnɪʃᵊn/ *noun* **1** CAR [no plural] the part of a car that starts the engine *He turned the key in the ignition.* ➲See colour picture **Car** on page Centre 7 **2** BURN [U] *formal* when something makes something start to burn

ignominious /ˌɪgnəʊˈmɪniəs/ *adjective formal* making you feel embarrassed or ashamed *an* ***ignominious defeat*** •**ignominiously** *adverb*

ignorance /ˈɪgnᵊrᵊns/ *noun* [U] when someone does not have enough knowledge, understanding, or information about something *There is still widespread* ***ignorance about*** *the disease.* ○ *I was shocked by her total* ***ignorance of*** *world history.*

ignorant /ˈɪgnᵊrᵊnt/ *adjective* **1** NOT HAVING KNOWLEDGE not having enough knowledge, understanding, or information about something *He was a newcomer to Formula One and* ***ignorant of*** *many of the circuits.* **2** NOT POLITE UK not polite or showing respect *an ignorant lout*

ignore /ɪgˈnɔːʳ/ *verb* [T] to pay no attention to something or someone *They just ignored him and carried on with the game.* ○ *We cannot afford to ignore the fact that the world's population is increasing rapidly.*

IIRC **INTERNET** *internet abbreviation for* if I remember correctly

il- /ɪl-/ *prefix* not *illegal* ○ *illegible*

ileum /ˈɪliəm/ *noun* [C usually singular] **ANATOMY, BIOLOGY** the last and narrowest part of the small intestine (= upper part of the bowels), where substances from food are absorbed ➲See picture at **alimentary canal**

OTHER WAYS OF SAYING *ill*

A common alternative is the adjective **sick**: *He was off work* ***sick*** *last week.*

In informal situations in the UK, you can also use the adjectives **poorly** and **rough**: *What's the matter, Sophie - are you feeling* ***poorly****?* • *I felt really* ***rough*** *after eating that curry.*

A more formal adjective meaning 'ill' is **unwell**: *I've felt a little* ***unwell*** *all week.*

If you want to say that someone feels slightly ill, in informal situations you can also use the expressions **be/feel under the weather** and **be/feel below par**: *I don't think I'll be coming to the party - I'm a bit* ***under the weather***.

ill[1] /ɪl/ *adjective* **1** **HEALTH** not feeling well, or suffering from a disease *critically/seriously ill* ○ *Mark had been* ***feeling ill*** *for a couple of days.* ➲See Common Learner Error at **sick 2** [always before noun] *formal* bad ***ill health*** ○ *He suffered no* ***ill effects*** *from his fall.* ➲See also: ill at **ease**[1]

ill[2] /ɪl/ *noun* [C] *formal* a problem [usually plural] *social and economic ills*

ill[3] /ɪl/ *adverb formal* **1** badly *Many of the nurses were* ***ill prepared*** *to deal with such badly burned patients.* **2 can ill afford (to do) sth** If you can ill afford to do something, it is likely to make things difficult for you if you do it. *This is a match United can ill afford to lose.* **3 speak ill of sb** *formal* to say bad things about someone

I'll /aɪl/ *short for* I shall/I will *I'll be there at 6:00.*

ill- /ɪl-/ *prefix* in a way which is bad or not suitable *ill-prepared* ○ *an ill-judged remark*

ill-advised /ˌɪlədˈvaɪzd/ *adjective* not wise, and likely to cause problems in the future

ill-conceived /ˌɪlkənˈsiːvd/ *adjective* badly planned or not wise

illegal /ɪˈliːgᵊl/ *adjective* **LAW** not allowed by law ***illegal drugs/weapons*** [+ to do sth] *It is illegal to sell cigarettes to anyone under 16.* •**illegally** *adverb an illegally parked car*

ilˌlegal ˈimmigrant (*also US* **iˌllegal ˈalien**) *noun* [C] someone who goes to live or work in another country when they do not have the legal right to

illegible /ɪˈledʒəbl/ *adjective* Illegible writing is difficult or impossible to read.

illegitimate /ˌɪlɪˈdʒɪtəmət/ *adjective* **1** CHILD An illegitimate child is born to parents who are not married to each other. **2** NOT LEGAL not legal, honest, or fair *an illegitimate use of council funds* •**illegitimacy** /ˌɪlɪˈdʒɪtəməsi/ *noun* [U]

ill-equipped /ˌɪlɪˈkwɪpt/ *adjective* **1** EQUIPMENT not having the necessary equipment **2** ABILITY not having the necessary ability or qualities to do something [+ to do sth] *These teachers were ill-equipped to deal with rowdy students.*

ill-fated /ˌɪlˈfeɪtɪd/ *adjective* unlucky and often unsuccessful *an ill-fated expedition to the South Pole*

ill-fitting /ˌɪlˈfɪtɪŋ/ *adjective* Ill-fitting clothes do not fit well.

ill-gotten /ˌɪlˈgɒtᵊn/ *adjective literary* obtained in a dishonest or illegal way *He deposited his* ***ill-gotten gains*** *in foreign bank accounts.*

illicit /ɪˈlɪsɪt/ *adjective* not legal or not approved of by society *an illicit love affair*

ill-informed /ˌɪlɪnˈfɔːmd/ *adjective* without enough knowledge or information *an ill-informed decision*

illiterate /ɪˈlɪtᵊrət/ *adjective* not able to read or write

WORD PARTNERS FOR ***illness***

cause / develop / have / recover from / treat an illness • a **critical/minor/rare/serious/ terminal** illness

O-ᵐ**illness** /ˈɪlnəs/ *noun* **1 HEALTH** [C] a disease of the body or mind *a **serious/terminal illness** ○ He died at the age of 83 after a long illness.* **2 HEALTH** [U] when you are ill

illogical /ɪˈlɒdʒɪkᵊl/ *adjective* not based on careful thought *It would be illogical for them to stop at this stage.*

illuminate /ɪˈluːmɪneɪt/ *verb* [T] **1** LIGHT to shine lights on something *The paintings and sculptures are illuminated by spotlights.* **2** EXPLAIN to explain something clearly or make it easier to understand •**illumination** /ɪˌluːmɪˈneɪʃᵊn/ *noun* [C, U] *formal*

illuminating /ɪˈluːmɪneɪtɪŋ/ *adjective* giving you new information about something or making it easier to understand *a most illuminating discussion*

illusion /ɪˈluːʒᵊn/ *noun* **1** FALSE IDEA [C, U] an idea or belief that is not true *He **had no illusions about** his talents as a singer. ○ We are not **under any illusion** - we know the work is dangerous.* **2** DIFFERENT [C] something that is not really what it seems to be *There is a large mirror at one end to **create the illusion of** more space.* ➲See also: **optical illusion**

illustrate /ˈɪləstreɪt/ *verb* [T] **1** to give more information or examples to explain or prove something *to illustrate a point/problem* [+ **question word**] *This new discovery illustrates how little we know about early human history.* **2 ART** to draw pictures for a book, magazine, etc *an illustrated children's book*

illustration /ˌɪləˈstreɪʃᵊn/ *noun* **1 ART** [C] a picture in a book, magazine, etc *a full-page colour illustration* **2** [C, U] an example that explains or proves something *This is another **illustration of** the power of the media.*

illustrator /ˈɪləstreɪtəʳ/ *noun* [C] **ART** a person whose job is to draw or paint pictures for books

illustrious /ɪˈlʌstriəs/ *adjective formal* famous and well respected *an **illustrious career***

ˌill ˈwill *noun* [U] bad feelings between people because of things that happened in the past

O-ᵐ**I'm** /aɪm/ *short for* I am

im- /ɪm-/ *prefix* not *impossible ○ immortal*

WORD PARTNERS FOR ***image***

create/project an image • sb's/sth's **public** image • an **image of** sth

O-ᵐ**image** /ˈɪmɪdʒ/ *noun* **1** PUBLIC [C, U] the way that other people think someone or something is *The aim is to improve the **public image of** the police.* **2** PICTURE [C] a picture, especially on film or television or in a mirror ***television images** of starving children* **3** IDEA [C] a picture in your mind or an idea of how someone or something is *I have an image in my mind of the way I want the garden to look.*

imagery /ˈɪmɪdʒᵊri/ *noun* [U] **LANGUAGE, LITERATURE** the use of words or pictures in books, films, paintings, etc to describe ideas or situations

imaginable /ɪˈmædʒɪnəbl/ *adjective* possible to think of *ice cream of every imaginable flavour* ➲Opposite **unimaginable**

imaginary /ɪˈmædʒɪnᵊri/ *adjective* not real but imagined in your mind *The story takes place in an imaginary world.*

iˌmaginary ˈnumber *noun* [C] **MATHEMATICS** a number that is the square root (= number you multiply by itself to get a particular number) of a negative number (= number less than zero), especially the square root of -1 ➲Compare **complex number, real number**

WORD PARTNERS FOR ***imagination***

have/lack/show imagination • **use** your imagination • **capture** sb's imagination • a **fertile/vivid** imagination

O-ᵐ**imagination** /ɪˌmædʒɪˈneɪʃᵊn/ *noun* **1** MIND [C] the part of your mind that creates ideas or pictures of things that are not real or that you have not seen [**usually singular**] *There's nothing out here - it's just your imagination.* **2** ABILITY [U] the ability to create ideas or pictures in your mind *The job needs someone with creativity and imagination.* ➲See also: not by any **stretch**[2] of the imagination

imaginative /ɪˈmædʒɪnətɪv/ *adjective* **1** THING Something which is imaginative is new or clever and often unusual. *an imaginative use of colour* **2** PERSON Someone who is imaginative is able to create new and interesting ideas or things. *a highly imaginative poet* •**imaginatively** *adverb*

O-ᵐ**imagine** /ɪˈmædʒɪn/ *verb* [T] **1** CREATE to create an idea or picture of something in your mind [+ **doing sth**] *Imagine being able to do all your shopping from your armchair.* [+ **question word**] *You can imagine how pleased I was when the letter arrived.* **2** BELIEVE to believe that something is probably true *I imagine he must be under a lot of pressure at the moment.* **3** NOT REAL to think that you hear or see something which does not really exist *I can't hear anything - you must be imagining it.*

imaging /ˈɪmɪdʒɪŋ/ *noun* [U] **COMPUTING** the process of producing an exact picture of something, especially on a computer screen ***computer/digital imaging***

imbalance /ˌɪmˈbæləns/ *noun* [C] when two things which should be equal or are normally equal are not *There is a huge economic **imbalance between** the two countries.*

imbue /ɪmˈbjuː/ *verb* **imbuing**, *past* **imbued**
imbue sb/sth with sth *phrasal verb formal* to fill someone or something with a particular feeling, quality, or idea *His poetry is imbued with deep religious feeling.*

the IMF /ðiˌaɪemˈef/ *noun* [**no plural**] **ECONOMICS** *abbreviation for* the International Monetary Fund: a part of the United Nations which encourages international trade and gives money to poor countries

IMHO **INTERNET** *internet abbreviation for* in my humble opinion: used when you tell someone your opinion

imitate /ˈɪmɪteɪt/ *verb* [T] to copy the way someone or something looks, sounds, or behaves *She tried to imitate the way the models walked.* •**imitator** *noun* [C]

WORD PARTNERS FOR ***imitation***

a **cheap/convincing/good/pale** imitation • an imitation **of** sb/sth

imitation /ˌɪmɪˈteɪʃᵊn/ *noun* **1** COPY [C] a copy of something that is made to look like the real thing *It wasn't a genuine Gucci handbag, just **a cheap imitation**.* ○ ***imitation leather/fur*** **2** BEHAVIOUR [C, U] when someone copies the way another person speaks or behaves *He does a very good **imitation of** the Prime Minister.*

immaculate /ɪˈmækjələt/ *adjective* **1** CLEAN perfectly clean and tidy or in perfect condition *an immaculate garden/room* **2** NO MISTAKES perfect and without any mistakes *an **immaculate performance*** •**immaculately** *adverb*

immaterial /ˌɪməˈtɪəriəl/ *adjective* If something is immaterial, it is not important because it does not affect a situation.

immature /ˌɪməˈtjʊəʳ/ *adjective* **1** BEHAVIOUR not behaving in a way which is as wise and calm as people expect from someone your age *Some of the boys are quite immature for their age.* **2** NOT DEVELOPED not completely developed *immature cells* •**immaturity** *noun* [U]

immeasurable /ɪˈmeʒᵊrəbl/ *adjective* very large or extreme and so impossible to measure *the immeasurable pain of losing a child* •**immeasurably** *adverb His confidence has grown immeasurably since he got the job.*

immediate /ɪˈmiːdiət/ *adjective* **1** WITHOUT WAITING happening or done without waiting or very soon after something else *The government has promised to take **immediate action**.* ○ *The drugs will have an **immediate effect**.* **2** IMPORTANT NOW important now and needing attention *Our **immediate concern** is getting food and water to the refugees.* **3** CLOSEST [always before noun] closest to something or someone *Police cleared people from the **immediate area** following the bomb warning.* **4 the immediate future** the period of time that is coming next **5 sb's immediate family** someone's closest relatives, such as their parents, children, husband, or wife

immediately[1] /ɪˈmiːdiətli/ *adverb* **1** NOW now or without waiting or thinking about something *The cause of the problem wasn't **immediately obvious**.* **2** NEXT next to something, or close to something in time *There are fields immediately behind the house.* ○ *Cole scored again **immediately after** half-time.*

immediately[2] /ɪˈmiːdiətli/ *conjunction UK* as soon as *Immediately I saw her I knew something terrible had happened.*

immense /ɪˈmens/ *adjective* extremely big *immense pressure/value* ○ *Health care costs the country **an immense amount of** money.*

immensely /ɪˈmensli/ *adverb* extremely *immensely powerful/popular*

immerse /ɪˈmɜːs/ *verb* **1 be immersed in sth; immerse yourself in sth** to be or become completely involved in something, so that you do not notice anything else **2** [T] to put something in a liquid so that it is completely covered •**immersion** /ɪˈmɜːʃᵊn/ *noun* [U]

immigrant /ˈɪmɪɡrənt/ *noun* [C] **SOCIETY** someone who comes to live in a different country ➲See also: **illegal immigrant**

immigration /ˌɪmɪˈɡreɪʃᵊn/ *noun* [U] **SOCIETY** **1** when someone comes to live in a different country ***immigration policy*** **2** the place where people's official documents are checked when they enter a country at an airport, port, border, etc ***immigration control*** •**immigrate** /ˈɪmɪɡreɪt/ *verb* [I] to come to live in a different country

imminent /ˈɪmɪnənt/ *adjective* coming or happening very soon ***imminent danger***

immiscible /ɪˈmɪsəbᵊl/ *adjective* **CHEMISTRY** An immiscible liquid cannot be mixed with another liquid without separating from it. ➲Opposite **miscible**

immobile /ɪˈməʊbaɪl/ (US) /ɪˈməʊbᵊl/ *adjective* not moving or not able to move •**immobility** /ˌɪməʊˈbɪləti/ *noun* [U]

immoral /ɪˈmɒrᵊl/ *adjective* morally wrong *immoral behaviour* •**immorality** /ˌɪməˈræləti/ *noun* [U]

immortal /ɪˈmɔːtᵊl/ *adjective* **1** LIFE living or lasting forever *an immortal soul/God* **2** MEMORY famous or remembered for a very long time *Then he uttered the **immortal line** - "My name is Bond".* •**immortality** /ˌɪmɔːˈtæləti/ *noun* [U]

immortalize (*also UK* **-ise**) /ɪˈmɔːtᵊlaɪz/ *verb* [T] to make someone or something famous for a long time

immune /ɪˈmjuːn/ *adjective* **1 HEALTH** [never before noun] If you are immune to a disease, you will not get it. *Once you've had the virus, you are **immune to it**.* **2 HEALTH** [always before noun] relating to the way your body fights disease *an **immune deficiency/response*** **3** NOT AFFECTED [never before noun] not affected by a particular type of behaviour or emotion *He is **immune to** flattery.* **4** NOT PUNISHED [never before noun] not able to be punished or damaged by something *His diplomatic passport makes him **immune from** prosecution.*

imˈmune ˌsystem *noun* [C] **HEALTH** the cells and tissues in your body that fight against infection [usually singular] *Vitamins help **boost*** (= make stronger) *your **immune system**.*

immunity /ɪˈmjuːnəti/ *noun* [U] **HEALTH** when you are immune, especially to disease or from legal action ***diplomatic immunity*** ○ *The vaccine gives you lifelong **immunity to the virus**.*

immunize (*also UK* **-ise**) /ˈɪmjənaɪz/ *verb* [T] **HEALTH** to make a person or animal immune by giving them special medicine *He was **immunized against** measles as a child.* •**immunization** /ˌɪmjənaɪˈzeɪʃᵊn/ *noun* [C, U] *a programme of mass immunization*

immunosuppression /ˌɪmjənəʊsəˈpreʃᵊn/ *noun* [U] **HEALTH** when the body's immune system (= system that fights disease) is intentionally stopped from working, or is made less effective, usually by drugs, especially in order to help the body accept an organ which has been taken from another person's body •**immunosuppressant** /ˌɪmjənəʊsə'presənt/ *noun* [C] a drug that stops the body's immune system from working

IMO **INTERNET** *internet abbreviation for* in my opinion: used when you want to give an opinion

WORD PARTNERS FOR ***impact***

have/make an impact • a **major/negative/significant** impact • an impact **on** sth

impact¹ /'ɪmpækt/ *noun* **1** [**no plural**] the effect that a person, event, or situation has on someone or something *Latino singers **have had a** major **impact on** pop music this year.* **2** **PHYSICS** [U] the force or action of one object hitting another *The missile explodes **on impact*** (= when it hits another object).

impact² /ɪm'pækt/ (*also* **impact on/upon**) *verb* [T] *mainly US* to affect something or someone *Rising interest rates are sure to **impact on** the housing market.*

impair /ɪm'peəʳ/ *verb* [T] *formal* to harm something and make it less good [**often passive**] *When you're tired your **judgment is impaired**.* •**impairment** *noun* [C, U] when something is impaired ***mental/physical impairment***

impaired /ɪm'peəd/ *adjective* **visually/hearing impaired** unable to see or hear as well as most people

impale /ɪm'peɪl/ *verb* [T] to push a sharp object through something or someone

impart /ɪm'pɑːt/ *verb* [T] *formal* **1** COMMUNICATE to communicate information or knowledge to someone *I have disappointing **news to impart**.* **2** GIVE to give something a particular feeling, quality, or taste *Preservatives can impart colour and flavour to a product.*

impartial /ɪm'pɑːʃəl/ *adjective* not supporting or preferring any person, group, plan, etc more than others ***impartial advice*** ○ *A trial must be fair and impartial.* •**impartiality** /ɪmˌpɑːʃi'æləti/ *noun* [U] when someone or something is impartial

impassable /ɪm'pɑːsəbl/ *adjective* If roads or paths are impassable, vehicles cannot move along them.

WORD PARTNERS FOR ***impasse***

break/reach an impasse • an impasse **in** sth

impasse /'æmpæs/ (US) /'ɪmpæs/ *noun* [U] a situation in which it is impossible to make any progress *He is determined to **break** (= end) **the impasse** in the peace process.*

impassioned /ɪm'pæʃənd/ *adjective* showing and expressing strong emotion *an **impassioned plea/speech***

impassive /ɪm'pæsɪv/ *adjective* An impassive person or face shows no emotion. •**impassively** *adverb*

impatience /ɪm'peɪʃəns/ *noun* [U] when someone is impatient

impatient /ɪm'peɪʃənt/ *adjective* **1** EASILY ANNOYED easily annoyed by someone's mistakes or because you have to wait *I do get **impatient with** the children when they won't do their homework.* **2** WANTING ACTION [**never before noun**] wanting something to happen as soon as possible *People are increasingly **impatient for** change in this country.* •**impatiently** *adverb We waited impatiently for the show to begin.*

impeccable /ɪm'pekəbl/ *adjective* perfect and with no mistakes *She speaks impeccable English.* •**impeccably** *adverb **impeccably dressed***

impede /ɪm'piːd/ *verb* [T] *formal* to make it difficult or impossible for someone or something to move or make progress *A broken-down car is impeding the flow of traffic.*

impediment /ɪm'pedɪmənt/ *noun* [C] **1** NO PROGRESS *formal* something that makes it difficult or impossible for someone or something to move or make progress *Cramped classrooms are an **impediment to** learning.* **2** SPEECH/HEARING a problem that makes speaking, hearing, or moving difficult *a **speech impediment***

impel /ɪm'pel/ *verb* [T] **impelling**, *past* **impelled** *formal* to make you feel that you must do something [+ **to do sth**] *Harry felt impelled to tell the truth.*

impending /ɪm'pendɪŋ/ *adjective* [**always before noun**] An impending event will happen soon and is usually bad or unpleasant. ***impending disaster/doom*** ○ *I've just heard about the **impending departure** of our chairman.*

impenetrable /ɪm'penɪtrəbl/ *adjective* **1** CANNOT UNDERSTAND impossible to understand *impenetrable jargon* **2** CANNOT SEE/GO THROUGH impossible to see through or go through *impenetrable fog*

imperative¹ /ɪm'perətɪv/ *adjective* **1** *formal* When an action or process is imperative, it is extremely important that it happens or is done. [+ **(that)**] *It is imperative that I speak with him at once.* **2** **LANGUAGE** An imperative form of a verb is used to express an order. In the sentence 'Stop the machine!', the verb 'stop' is an imperative verb.

imperative² /ɪm'perətɪv/ *noun* [C] **1** something that must happen, exist, or be done *a moral/political imperative* **2** **LANGUAGE** the imperative form of a verb

imperceptible /ˌɪmpə'septəbl/ *adjective* not able to be noticed or felt *She heard a faint, almost imperceptible cry.* •**imperceptibly** *adverb*

imperfect /ɪm'pɜːfɪkt/ *adjective* not perfect and with some mistakes *an imperfect solution* •**imperfectly** *adverb*

the imperfect /ɪm'pɜːfɪkt/ (*also* **the imˌperfect 'tense**) *noun* **LANGUAGE** the form of the verb that is used to show an action in the past which has not been completed. In the sentence 'We were crossing the road', 'were crossing' is in the imperfect.

imperfection /ˌɪmpə'fekʃən/ *noun* [C, U] when something or someone is not perfect *Make-up can hide small skin imperfections.*

imperial /ɪm'pɪəriəl/ *adjective* **1** **POLITICS** [**always before noun**] relating or belonging to an empire (= group of countries ruled by one person or government) or the person who rules it *imperial rule* ○ *the imperial family* **2** **MEASURES** The imperial system of measurement uses units based on measurements such as inches, pints, and ounces.

imperialism /ɪmˈpɪəriəlɪzᵊm/ *noun* [U] **1 POLITICS** when one government or person rules a group of other countries *the age of imperialism* **2 POLITICS** when one country has a lot of power or influence over others ***cultural/economic imperialism*** •**imperialist** *adjective* relating to imperialism

imperil /ɪmˈperᵊl/ *verb* [T] *UK* **imperilling**, *past* **imperilled**, *US* **imperiling**, *past* **imperiled** *formal* to put someone or something in a dangerous situation

imperious /ɪmˈpɪəriəs/ *adjective formal* showing that you think that you are important and expect others to obey you *an* ***imperious manner***

impermeable /ɪmˈpɜːmiəbl/ *adjective* **PHYSICS, BIOLOGY, GEOLOGY** If a substance is impermeable, it does not allow liquids or gases to go through it. ⊃Opposite **permeable**

impersonal /ɪmˈpɜːsᵊnᵊl/ *adjective* not being friendly towards people or showing any interest in them *a cold and impersonal letter*

impersonate /ɪmˈpɜːsᵊneɪt/ *verb* [T] to copy the way someone looks and behaves in order to pretend to be them or to make people laugh *Impersonating a police officer is a serious offence.* •**impersonation** /ɪmˌpɜːsᵊnˈeɪʃᵊn/ *noun* [C, U] *He* ***did*** *an* ***impersonation*** *of Bill Clinton.* •**impersonator** *noun* [C] *an Elvis impersonator*

impertinent /ɪmˈpɜːtɪnənt/ *adjective formal* rude or not showing respect *an* ***impertinent remark***

impervious /ɪmˈpɜːviəs/ *adjective* **1** [EFFECT] not affected by something *She was* ***impervious to*** *the pain.* **2** [LIQUID] *formal* Impervious material does not let liquid into or through it. *impervious rock*

impetuous /ɪmˈpetʃuəs/ *adjective* done or acting quickly and without thinking carefully *an impetuous outburst*

WORD PARTNERS FOR ***impetus***

give/provide [new, fresh, added, etc] impetus **to** sth • the impetus **behind/for** sth

impetus /ˈɪmpɪtəs/ *noun* [U] **1** something that makes an activity or process happen or continue with more speed and energy *His visit* ***gave*** *new* ***impetus to*** *the peace process.* **2 PHYSICS** a physical force that makes an object start or continue to move

impinge /ɪmˈpɪndʒ/ *verb formal*
impinge on/upon sb/sth *phrasal verb* to affect or limit someone or something *How does your religious commitment impinge upon your professional life?*

implacable /ɪmˈplækəbl/ *adjective formal* determined not to change the strong feelings you have against someone or something ***implacable opposition/hostility***

implant¹ /ˈɪmplɑːnt/ *noun* [C] **HEALTH** an object placed inside part of your body in an operation, to improve your appearance or treat a medical condition ***breast implants***

implant² /ɪmˈplɑːnt/ *verb* [T] **HEALTH** to place something into someone's body in a medical operation *Two embryos were implanted in her womb.*

implausible /ɪmˈplɔːzəbl/ *adjective* difficult to believe or imagine *an implausible explanation*

implement¹ /ˈɪmplɪment/ *verb* [T] *formal* to make a law, system, plan, etc start to happen or operate *Our new computerized system will soon be fully implemented.* •**implementation** /ˌɪmplɪmenˈteɪʃᵊn/ *noun* [U]

implement² /ˈɪmplɪmənt/ *noun* [C] a tool *a garden/farm implement*

implicate /ˈɪmplɪkeɪt/ *verb* [T] to show that someone or something is involved in something bad, especially a crime [**often passive**] *Two senior officers are* ***implicated in*** *the latest drugs* ***scandal.***

WORD PARTNERS FOR ***implication***

have implications **for** sth • **far-reaching/profound/serious** implications • the implications **of** sth

implication /ˌɪmplɪˈkeɪʃᵊn/ *noun* **1** [EFFECT] [C] a result or effect that seems likely in the future [**usually plural**] *financial/health implications* ○ *This scheme* ***has*** *serious* ***implications for*** *the local economy.* **2** [SUGGESTION] [C, U] when you seem to suggest something without saying it directly *The* ***implication*** *was* ***that*** *the school had to do much better or it would be closed.* **3** [INVOLVEMENT] [U] when something or someone is implicated in something bad

implicit /ɪmˈplɪsɪt/ *adjective* **1** [SUGGESTED] suggested but not stated directly *an implicit threat* ○ *We interpreted his silence as implicit agreement.* **2** [COMPLETE] complete ***implicit faith/trust*** •**implicitly** *adverb I* ***trust*** *him* ***implicitly.***

implore /ɪmˈplɔːʳ/ *verb* [T] *literary* to ask for something in a serious and emotional way [**+ to do sth**] *I implored him to let the child go.*

imply /ɪmˈplaɪ/ *verb* [T] to suggest or show something, without saying it directly [**+ (that)**] *Are you implying that I'm fat?* ○ *an* ***implied criticism***

impolite /ˌɪmpᵊlˈaɪt/ *adjective formal* not polite

import¹ /ɪmˈpɔːt/ *verb* [T] **1 ECONOMICS** to bring something into your country from another country for people to buy *We import about 20 percent of our food.* **2 COMPUTING** to copy information from one computer or computer program to another *to* ***import data*** ○ *imported files* ⊃Opposite **export** •**importation** /ˌɪmpɔːˈteɪʃᵊn/ *noun* [U] •**importer** *noun* [C]

import² /ˈɪmpɔːt/ *noun* **ECONOMICS 1** [C] a product which is imported from another country [**usually plural**] *Japanese/American imports* **2** [U] when you import goods *a ban on the import of beef* ⊃Opposite **export**

WORD PARTNERS FOR ***importance***

central/great/major/paramount/the utmost/vital importance • **emphasize/stress** the importance **of** sth • **attach** (great) importance **to** sth • the importance **of** sth

O⊸ **importance** /ɪmˈpɔːtᵊns/ *noun* [U] how important someone or something is *He emphasized* *the importance of following safety procedures.* ○ *She* ***attaches*** *a lot of* ***importance to*** *personal possessions* (= she thinks they are important).

OTHER WAYS OF SAYING ***important***

Adjectives such as **big**, **major** and **significant** are often used to mean 'important' in this sense: *This is a* ***big*** *game tonight - if Manchester lose, they're out of the championship.* • *This is a* ***major*** *decision so we'd better get it right.* • *Did he make any* ***significant*** *changes to my suggestions?*

Someone or something **of note** is important or famous: *Did she say anything* ***of note*** *at the meeting?*

A person who is important and famous is sometimes described as **eminent**, **prominent**, or **great**: *Her father was an* ***eminent*** *historian.*

O-- **important** /ɪm'pɔːtᵊnt/ *adjective* **1** [VALUABLE] valuable, useful, or necessary *My family is very* ***important to*** *me.* [+ **to do sth**] *Listen, Donna has something important to say.* **2** [POWERFUL] having a lot of power, influence, or effect *an important person/decision* ⊃Opposite **unimportant** •**importantly** *adverb They provided hot showers and, more importantly, clean clothes.*

impose /ɪm'pəʊz/ *verb* [T] **1** [ORDER OFFICIALLY] to officially order that a rule, tax, punishment, etc will happen *to* ***impose*** *a* ***ban/tax*** ○ *The judge* ***imposed*** *the death penalty* ***on*** *both men.* **2** [FORCE TO ACCEPT] to force someone to accept a belief or way of living *I don't want them to* ***impose*** *their religious beliefs* ***on*** *my children.*
impose on sb *phrasal verb* to ask or expect someone to do something that may give them extra work or trouble *I hate to impose on you, but could I stay the night?*

imposing /ɪm'pəʊzɪŋ/ *adjective* looking big and important in a way that people admire *He was an* ***imposing figure*** *- tall and broad-chested.*

imposition /ˌɪmpə'zɪʃᵊn/ *noun* **1** [ORDER OFFICIALLY] [U] when you impose something *the imposition of a fine* **2** [WORK/TROUBLE] [C] the cause of extra work or trouble for someone else *It's a bit of an imposition, but could you take me to the airport?*

O-- **impossible**[1] /ɪm'pɒsəbl/ *adjective* **1** [CANNOT HAPPEN] If an action or event is impossible, it cannot happen or be done. *an impossible task* ○ *He finds walking almost impossible.* [+ **to do sth**] *It was impossible to sleep because of the noise.* **2** [DIFFICULT] very difficult to deal with *You're putting me in an impossible position.* •**impossibility** /ɪmˌpɒsə'bɪləti/ *noun* [C, U] when something is impossible [**usually singular**] I can't do it - it's a ***physical impossibility***.

the impossible /ɪm'pɒsəbl/ *noun* something that it is not possible to have or achieve

impossibly /ɪm'pɒsəbli/ *adverb* extremely, in a way that is very difficult to achieve or deal with *a picture of an impossibly pretty woman*

impostor (*also* **imposter**) /ɪm'pɒstəʳ/ *noun* [C] someone who pretends to be someone else in order to deceive people

impotent /'ɪmpətənt/ *adjective* **1** [SEX] An impotent man is unable to have sex because his penis does not become or stay hard. **2** [POWER] not having the power or strength to do anything to change a situation *When your child is ill, you feel so impotent.* •**impotence** /'ɪmpətəns/ *noun* [U]

impound /ɪm'paʊnd/ *verb* [T] If the police or someone in authority impounds something that belongs to you, for example your car, they take it away because you have broken the law.

impoverished /ɪm'pɒvᵊrɪʃt/ *adjective formal* **1** [POOR] poor or made poor *an impoverished country/family* **2** [WEAK] made worse or weaker *culturally/emotionally impoverished*

impractical /ɪm'præktɪkᵊl/ *adjective* **1** [METHOD/IDEA] Impractical ideas, methods, etc cannot be used or done easily. **2** [PERSON] Impractical people are not good at making, repairing, or planning things. **3** [MATERIAL/CLOTHING] not suitable for using in normal situations *I love high heels but they're rather impractical.*

imprecise /ˌɪmprɪ'saɪs/ *adjective* not accurate or exact *an imprecise description*

impress /ɪm'pres/ *verb* [T] to make someone admire or respect you *I was impressed by her professionalism.* ○ *Sarah was hoping to* ***impress*** *him* ***with*** *her cooking.*
impress sth on sb *phrasal verb* to make someone understand the importance of something *He tried to impress the importance of hygiene on them.*

WORD PARTNERS FOR ***impression***

convey/create/give/make an impression • **get** an impression • be **under** an impression • a **distinct** / **false** / **favourable** / **indelible** / **lasting/misleading** impression

O-- **impression** /ɪm'preʃᵊn/ *noun* **1** [OPINION] [**no plural**] an idea, feeling, or opinion about something or someone [+ **(that)**] *I* ***got/had the impression*** *that he was bored.* ○ *Monica* ***gives the impression*** *of being shy.* ○ *Remember that it* ***makes a*** *bad* ***impression*** *if you're late.* ○ *I think Mick* ***was under the impression that*** (= thought that) *we were married.* **2** [COPY] [C, U] when you copy the way a particular person or animal speaks or behaves, often to make people laugh *He* ***does a*** *brilliant* ***impression of*** *the president.* **3** [MARK] [C] a mark left when an object is pressed into something soft

impressionable /ɪm'preʃᵊnəbl/ *adjective* easy to influence *impressionable young people*

impressive /ɪm'presɪv/ *adjective* Someone or something that is impressive makes you admire and respect them. *an impressive performance/view* •**impressively** *adverb*

imprest /'ɪmprest/ *noun* [C] **FINANCE** an amount of money used by part of a business to pay for small things

imprest system /'ɪmprestˌsɪstəm/ *noun* [**C usually singular**] **FINANCE** a method of keeping an amount of cash (= money in the form of coins and notes) in a business for paying small amounts, where a certain amount of money is kept and replaced to the same level at the beginning of each new period

imprint /'ɪmprɪnt/ *noun* **1** [MARK] [C] a mark left when an object is pressed into something soft *The steps showed the imprint of his boots in the* *snow.* **2** EFFECT [**no plural**] the effect that something leaves behind *Much of the house still **bears the imprint of** her personality.*

imprison /ɪm'prɪzᵊn/ *verb* [T] to put someone in prison or keep them as a prisoner [**often passive**] *Taylor was imprisoned in 1969 for burglary.* •**imprisonment** *noun* [U]

improbable /ɪm'prɒbəbl/ *adjective* **1** NOT LIKELY not likely to be true or to happen **2** SURPRISING surprising *Shirley seemed an improbable choice for a supermodel.* •**improbably** *adverb*

impromptu /ɪm'prɒmptjuː/ *adjective, adverb* not planned or prepared *an impromptu performance/party*

improper /ɪm'prɒpəʳ/ *adjective formal* not correct, suitable, honest, or acceptable *improper conduct* •**improperly** *adverb The court ruled that he had **acted improperly**.*

im,proper 'fraction *noun* [C] **MATHEMATICS** a fraction where the number above the line is bigger than the number below the line ➲Compare **proper fraction**

impropriety /,ɪmprə'praɪəti/ *noun* [U] *formal* behaviour that is not correct, suitable, or honest *The enquiry found no evidence of financial impropriety.*

OTHER WAYS OF SAYING ***improve***

If something improves after a period of doing badly, you can use the verbs **rally** and **recover**: *The team played badly in the first half but **rallied** in the second.* • *We are still waiting for the economy to **recover**.*

The phrasal verbs **look up** and **pick up** can be used informally to say that a situation is improving: *Our financial situation is **looking up**.* • *Business is really beginning to **pick up**.*

The phrasal verb **work on** means 'to try to improve something': *You need to **work on** your technique.*

The verb **refine** can be used when someone improves something by making small changes: *A team of experts spent several months **refining** the software.*

O━ **improve** /ɪm'pruːv/ *verb* [I, T] to get better or to make something better *Scott's behaviour has improved a lot lately.* ○ *Every year thousands of students come to London to improve their English.* ○ *improved earnings/productivity*

improve on sth *phrasal verb* to do something in a better way or with better results than before *I hope our team can improve on last Saturday's performance.*

WORD PARTNERS FOR ***improvement***

a **continuous/dramatic/gradual/significant/slight** improvement • **bring about/notice/produce** an improvement • an improvement **in/to** sth

O━ **improvement** /ɪm'pruːvmənt/ *noun* [C, U] when something gets better or when you make it better ***home improvements*** ○ *There's been a noticeable **improvement in** her work this term.* ○ *He's a definite **improvement on** her last boyfriend.* ○ *Sadly, her health has **shown** no **improvement**.*

improvise /'ɪmprəvaɪz/ *verb* [I, T] **1** to make or do something without any preparation, using only the things that are available *For a football, we improvised with some rolled-up socks.* **2** **MUSIC** to play music or say words that you are inventing, not reading or remembering •**improvisation** /,ɪmprəvaɪ'zeɪʃᵊn/ *noun* [C, U]

WORD PARTNERS FOR ***impulse***

resist an impulse • sb's **first** impulse

impulse /'ɪmpʌls/ *noun* **1** FEELING [C] a sudden feeling that you must do something, without thinking about the results [**usually singular**] *Her **first impulse** was to run away.* **2 on impulse** suddenly and without thinking first *I tend to act on impulse.* **3** SIGNAL [C] **BIOLOGY** a short signal that carries information through a system, for example an electrical system or the nerves in your body

impulsive /ɪm'pʌlsɪv/ *adjective* Impulsive people do things suddenly, without planning or thinking carefully, but because they want to. •**impulsively** *adverb*

impunity /ɪm'pjuːnəti/ *noun formal* **with impunity** without being punished *Criminal gangs are terrorizing the city with apparent impunity.*

impure /ɪm'pjʊəʳ/ *adjective* not pure, but mixed with other substances •**impurity** *noun* [C, U] when something is impure or a substance that is impure

O━ **in¹** /ɪn/ *preposition* **1** POSITION inside or towards the inside of a container, place, or area *There's milk in the fridge.* ○ *a shop in South London* ○ *He put his hand in his pocket.* **2** DURING during part or all of a period of time *We're going to Italy in April.* ○ *I started working here in 1993.* **3** USING TIME needing or using no more than a particular amount of time *I'll be ready in a few minutes.* **4** PART OF part of something *Who's the woman in the painting?* ○ *There's a few spelling mistakes in your essay.* **5** JOB involved in a particular kind of job *a career in publishing/politics* **6** SUBJECT connected with a particular subject *a degree in philosophy* ○ *advances in medical science* **7** WEARING wearing *Do you know that man in the grey suit?* **8** EXPRESSED expressed or written in a particular way *Complete the form in black ink.* ○ *She spoke to him in Russian.* **9** ARRANGED arranged in a particular way *We sat down in a circle.* ○ *Is this list in alphabetical order?* **10** EXPERIENCE experiencing an emotion or condition *She's in a bad mood this morning.* ○ *The kitchen's in a terrible state.* **11 in all** used to show the total amount of something *Some of the children came, so there were 15 of us in all.*

O━ **in²** /ɪn/ *adverb* **1** INTO A SPACE into an area or space from the outside of it *He rushed in halfway through the meeting.* ○ *Annie opened the car door and threw her luggage in.* **2** AT A PLACE at the place where a person usually lives or works *I phoned, but she wasn't in.* ○ *Could you ask him to ring me when he **gets in**?* **3** TRAIN/PLANE If a train, plane, etc is in, it has arrived at the place it was going to. *My train gets in at 17.54.* **4** SENT given or sent to someone official in order to be read *Applications must be in by 28th February.* **5** TOWARDS LAND used when the sea or a ship moves close to land *Let's go*

- *the tide is **coming in**.* **6 be in for sth** *informal* If someone is in for a surprise, treat, shock, etc, it will happen to them soon. *If he thinks looking after a baby is easy, he's in for a shock.* **7 be in on sth** *informal* If you are in on something, you know about it or are involved in it. *Were you in on the surprise?* ○ *Please **let me in on*** (= tell me) *the secret.* **8 SPORT** *UK* In cricket and similar sports, if a person or team is in, they are taking a turn to play. **9 be in for it** (*also UK* **be for it**) to be in trouble

in³ /ɪn/ *adjective informal* fashionable or popular *Pink is in this season.*

in⁴ /ɪn/ *noun* **the ins and outs of sth** the details of a particular subject *the ins and outs of the legal system*

in⁵ (*also* **in.**) **MEASURES** *written abbreviation for* inch (= a unit for measuring length)

in- /ɪn-/ *prefix* not *inaccurate* ○ *insensitive*

inability /ˌɪnəˈbɪləti/ *noun* [**no plural**] when you are unable to do something

inaccessible /ˌɪnəkˈsesəbl/ *adjective* impossible or extremely difficult to get to *The plane crashed in a mountain area that was totally **inaccessible to** vehicles.*

inaccurate /ɪnˈækjərət/ *adjective* not correct or exact *inaccurate information/figures* •**inaccuracy** /ɪnˈækjərəsi/ *noun* [**C, U**] when something is not correct or exact *His book contains historical inaccuracies.*

inaction /ɪnˈækʃən/ *noun* [**U**] when people do not take any action, especially about a problem *This announcement follows months of inaction and delay.*

inactive /ɪnˈæktɪv/ *adjective* not active or working *Beetle grubs stay inactive underground until spring.* •**inactivity** /ˌɪnækˈtɪvəti/ *noun* [**U**] when something or someone is not active or working *a **period of inactivity***

inadequacy /ɪˈnædɪkwəsi/ *noun* **1** QUALITY [**C, U**] when something or someone is not good enough or not of a high enough quality *feelings of inadequacy* ○ *He pointed out several **inadequacies in** the present system.* **2** AMOUNT [**U**] when there is not enough of something *The basic problem is the inadequacy of our school budget.*

inadequate /ɪˈnædɪkwət/ *adjective* **1** QUALITY not good enough or too low in quality *inadequate facilities/training* ○ *Our equipment is totally **inadequate for** a job like this.* **2** AMOUNT not enough *inadequate funds* •**inadequately** *adverb*

inadvertent /ˌɪnədˈvɜːtənt/ *adjective* not done intentionally *an inadvertent error* •**inadvertently** *adverb I had inadvertently picked up the wrong keys.*

inadvisable /ˌɪnədˈvaɪzəbl/ *adjective* likely to cause problems *It is inadvisable for women to travel alone in this region.*

inane /ɪˈneɪn/ *adjective* very silly and annoying *an inane question*

inanimate /ɪˈnænɪmət/ *adjective* not alive *an **inanimate object***

inappropriate /ˌɪnəˈprəʊpriət/ *adjective* not suitable *inappropriate behaviour* ○ *It would **be inappropriate for** me to comment, without knowing the facts.* •**inappropriately** *adverb*

inarticulate /ˌɪnɑːˈtɪkjələt/ *adjective* unable to express clearly what you feel or mean in words

inasmuch as /ɪnəzˈmʌtʃˌəz/ *conjunction formal* used to introduce a phrase which explains the degree to which something you have just said is true *They were strict about our appearance inasmuch as we weren't allowed to wear jewellery or make-up.*

inattentive /ˌɪnəˈtentɪv/ *adjective* not giving attention to someone or something

inaudible /ɪˈnɔːdəbl/ *adjective* impossible to hear *His voice was almost inaudible.*

inaugural /ɪˈnɔːgjərəl/ *adjective* [**always before noun**] An inaugural speech, meeting, etc is the first one of a new organization or leader. *the President's inaugural address*

inaugurate /ɪˈnɔːgjəreɪt/ *verb* [**T**] **1** CEREMONY to have a ceremony to celebrate an important person starting a new job, a new building opening, etc *Ronald Reagan was inaugurated in 1981.* **2** START *formal* to start a new system or organization *He inaugurated a programme to fight tuberculosis.* •**inauguration** /ɪˌnɔːgjəˈreɪʃən/ *noun* [**C, U**] *the inauguration of the Lord Mayor*

in-box (*also* **inbox**) /ˈɪnbɒks/ *noun* [**C**] **1 INTERNET** the place on a computer where email messages are sent **2** *US* (*UK* **in-tray**) a container where you keep letters and documents that need to be dealt with

Inc. *written abbreviation for* incorporated (= used after the name of some companies) *Macmillan Inc.*

incalculable /ɪnˈkælkjələbl/ *adjective* too big to measure *The cost in human terms is incalculable.*

incapable /ɪnˈkeɪpəbl/ *adjective* **incapable of sth/doing sth** not able to do something or to feel a particular emotion *He's incapable of controlling his temper.*

incapacitate /ˌɪnkəˈpæsɪteɪt/ *verb* [**T**] *formal* to make someone too ill or weak to work or do things normally [**often passive**] *He was incapacitated by illness.* •**incapacity** /ˌɪnkəˈpæsəti/ *noun* [**U**] when you cannot do something because you do not have the ability or you are too weak

incarcerate /ɪnˈkɑːsəreɪt/ *verb* [**T**] *formal* to put and keep someone in prison [**often passive**] *Marks was incarcerated for robbery.* •**incarceration** /ɪnˌkɑːsərˈeɪʃən/ *noun* [**U**]

incarnate /ɪnˈkɑːnət/ *adjective* [**always after noun**] in human form *He was acting like **the devil incarnate**.*

incarnation /ˌɪnkɑːˈneɪʃən/ *noun* **1** FORM [**C**] a particular form of something or someone that is changing or developing *In their new incarnation, the band have acquired a female singer.* **2 the incarnation of sth** the physical form of a god or quality *the incarnation of evil/freedom* **3** LIFE [**C**] a particular life, in religions which believe we have many lives

I

incendiary /ɪnˈsendiᵊri/ *adjective* [**always before noun**] designed to cause a fire *an **incendiary** **bomb/device***

incense /ˈɪnsens/ *noun* [**U**] a substance which burns with a strong, sweet smell, often used in religious ceremonies

incensed /ɪnˈsenst/ *adjective* extremely angry

WORD PARTNERS FOR ***incentive***

have/provide an incentive • an **added/powerful/strong** incentive • an incentive **for** sb

incentive /ɪnˈsentɪv/ *noun* [**C, U**] something that encourages you to act in a particular way [**+ to do sth**] *People had little incentive to save.* ○ *The government should **provide incentives for** young people to stay in school.*

inception /ɪnˈsepʃᵊn/ *noun* [**no plural**] *formal* the time when an organization or official activity began *He has directed the project since its inception.*

incessant /ɪnˈsesᵊnt/ *adjective* continuous, especially in a way that is annoying or unpleasant *incessant rain/noise* •**incessantly** *adverb*

incest /ˈɪnsest/ *noun* [**U**] sex that is illegal because it is between closely related people, for example a father and daughter

incestuous /ɪnˈsestjuəs/ *adjective* **1** [SEX] involving sex between people who are closely related **2** [GROUP] involving a group of people who are not interested in people or things outside the group *Universities can be very incestuous places.*

O-- **inch**¹ /ɪnʃ/ *noun* [**C**] **1 MEASURES** (*written abbreviation* **in.**) a unit for measuring length, equal to 2.54 centimetres ➲See Extra help page **Numbers and measurements** on page Centre 24. **2 not budge/give an inch** *informal* to refuse to change your opinions **3 to be every inch sth** to be a particular kind of person in every way *He is every inch a gentleman.*

inch² /ɪnʃ/ *verb* **inch closer/forward/up, etc** to move somewhere slowly or by very small amounts

WORD PARTNERS FOR ***incidence***

a **high/increased/low** incidence • the incidence **of** sth

incidence /ˈɪnsɪdᵊns/ *noun* [**C**] how often something happens, especially something bad [**usually singular**] *There's a high **incidence of** crime in the area.*

WORD PARTNERS FOR ***incident***

an incident **happens/occurs** • an **isolated** incident

incident /ˈɪnsɪdᵊnt/ *noun* [**C**] *formal* an event, especially one that is bad or unusual *Police are investigating the incident.*

incidental /ˌɪnsɪˈdentᵊl/ *adjective* less important than the thing something is connected with or part of *The lyrics here are **incidental to** the music.*

incidentally /ɪnsɪˈdentᵊli/ *adverb* used when you say something that is not as important as the main subject of conversation but is connected to it *Incidentally, talking of Stephen, have you met his girlfriend?*

ˈ**incident ˌray** *noun* [**C**] **PHYSICS** a ray of light which hits a surface ➲Compare **reflected ray**

incinerate /ɪnˈsɪnᵊreɪt/ *verb* [**T**] to burn something completely •**incineration** /ɪnˌsɪnᵊrˈeɪʃᵊn/ *noun* [**U**]

incinerator /ɪnˈsɪnᵊreɪtəʳ/ *noun* [**C**] a machine that is used to burn waste, especially harmful materials

incipient /ɪnˈsɪpiənt/ *adjective* [**always before noun**] *formal* just beginning *incipient wrinkles*

incision /ɪnˈsɪʒᵊn/ *noun* [**C**] **HEALTH** *formal* an opening that is made in something with a sharp tool, especially in someone's body during an operation

incisive /ɪnˈsaɪsɪv/ *adjective* showing an ability to think quickly and clearly and deal with situations effectively *incisive questions*

incisor /ɪnˈsaɪzəʳ/ *noun* [**C**] **ANATOMY** one of the sharp teeth at the front of the mouth which cut food when you bite into it ➲Compare **canine, molar** ➲See picture at **skull**

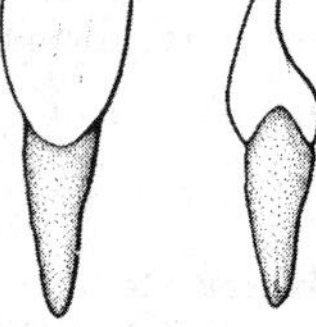

incisor

incite /ɪnˈsaɪt/ *verb* [**T**] to do or say something that encourages people to behave violently or illegally *They denied **inciting** the crowd **to** violence.* •**incitement** *noun* [**C, U**] when someone does or says something that incites people

incl *written abbreviation for* including or inclusive

inclination /ˌɪnklɪˈneɪʃᵊn/ *noun* [**C, U**] a feeling that you want to do something [**+ to do sth**] *She **showed** little **inclination** to leave.*

incline¹ /ɪnˈklaɪn/ *verb* [**T**] *formal* If you incline your head, you bend your neck so that your face bends down.

incline to/towards sth *phrasal verb formal* to think that a belief or opinion is probably correct *I incline to the view that peace can be achieved.*

incline² /ˈɪnklaɪn/ *noun* [**C**] *formal* a slope *a steep/gentle incline*

inclined /ɪnˈklaɪnd/ *adjective* [**never before noun**] **1 be inclined to think/believe/agree, etc** to have an opinion, but not a strong opinion *I'm inclined to agree with you.* **2 inclined to do sth a** often behaving in a particular way *Tom is inclined to be forgetful.* **b** wanting to do something *No one seemed inclined to help.* **3 artistically/technically, etc inclined** having natural artistic/technical, etc ability *She's very bright, but not academically inclined.*

O-- **include** /ɪnˈkluːd/ *verb* [**T**] **1** [BE PART OF] to have something or someone as part of something larger or more general, such as a group, price, or process *His books include the best-selling novel 'The Foundling'.* ○ *The price includes flights and three nights' accommodation.* ➲See Common Learner Error at **contain 2** [ALLOW] to allow someone to take part in an activity [**often passive**] *Local residents were **included in** the initial planning discussions.* ➲Opposite **exclude**

O━ **including** /ɪnˈkluːdɪŋ/ *preposition* used to show that someone or something is part of a larger group, amount, or process *Fourteen people, including a prison warden, were killed.* ○ *It's £24.99, including postage and packing.*

inclusion /ɪnˈkluːʒᵊn/ *noun* [C, U] when you include someone or something, especially in a group, amount, or event *Her self-portrait was chosen for inclusion in the exhibition.* ➲Opposite **exclusion**

inclusive /ɪnˈkluːsɪv/ *adjective* **1** COST An inclusive price or amount includes everything. *Prices are **inclusive of** flights and accommodation.* **2** NUMBERS [**always after noun**] including the first and last date or number stated *The course will run from October 19 to November 13, inclusive.* **3** PEOPLE Inclusive groups try to include many different types of people. *Our aim is to create a fairer, more inclusive society.* ➲Opposite **exclusive**

incoherent /ˌɪnkəʊˈhɪərᵊnt/ *adjective* not using clear words or ideas, and difficult to understand *His statement to the police was rambling and incoherent.* ●**incoherence** /ˌɪnkəʊˈhɪərᵊns/ *noun* [U]

WORD PARTNERS FOR *income*

an **average/good/high/low/steady** income ● **earn/have/provide** an income ● be **on** a (high/low, etc) income

O━ **income** /ˈɪŋkʌm/ *noun* [C, U] **FINANCE** money that you earn by working, investing, or producing goods *families on **low incomes*** ○ *Tourism accounts for 25% of the country's national income.* ➲See Common Learner Error at **pay**

ˈ**income supˌport** *noun* [U] **FINANCE, SOCIETY** in the UK, money that is paid by the government to people who have very little or no income

ˈ**income ˌtax** *noun* [C, U] **FINANCE** tax that you have to pay on your income

incoming /ˈɪnˌkʌmɪŋ/ *adjective* [**always before noun**] coming into a place or starting a job ***incoming phone calls/mail*** ○ *the incoming government*

incomparable /ɪnˈkɒmpᵊrəbl/ *adjective* too good to be compared with anything or anyone else *incomparable beauty*

incompatible /ˌɪnkəmˈpætəbl/ *adjective* **1** DIFFERENT too different to exist or live together *He regarded being a soldier as **incompatible with** his Christian faith.* **2** EQUIPMENT If equipment or software is incompatible with other equipment or software, it will not work with it. ●**incompatibility** /ˌɪnkəmˌpætəˈbɪləti/ *noun* [U] when two people or things are incompatible

incompetent /ɪnˈkɒmpɪtᵊnt/ *adjective* not able to do your job, or things that you are expected to do, successfully *incompetent managers* ●**incompetence** /ɪnˈkɒmpɪtᵊns/ *noun* [U]

incomplete /ˌɪnkəmˈpliːt/ *adjective* not finished, or having one or more parts missing *Decisions were made on the basis of incomplete information.* ●**incompleteness** *noun* [U]

incomprehensible /ɪnˌkɒmprɪˈhensəbl/ *adjective* impossible to understand *The instructions are almost incomprehensible.* ○ *His behaviour is quite **incomprehensible to** me.*

incomprehension /ɪnˌkɒmprɪˈhenʃᵊn/ *noun* [U] *formal* when you do not understand something *She looked at him in total incomprehension.*

inconceivable /ˌɪnkənˈsiːvəbl/ *adjective* impossible to imagine [+ **that**] *I find it inconceivable that she could be a killer.*

inconclusive /ˌɪnkənˈkluːsɪv/ *adjective* not leading to a definite decision or result ***inconclusive evidence/results*** ○ *The battle was inconclusive.*

incongruous /ɪnˈkɒŋgruəs/ *adjective formal* strange or not suitable for a particular situation *Bill was an incongruous sight, standing on the beach in his suit.*

inconsequential /ɪnˌkɒnsɪˈkwenʃᵊl/ *adjective formal* not important *inconsequential remarks*

inconsiderate /ˌɪnkənˈsɪdᵊrət/ *adjective* not caring about other people's situations or the way they feel *It was very **inconsiderate of** you to keep us all waiting.*

WORD PARTNERS FOR *inconsistency*

(an) **apparent/glaring** inconsistency ● (an) inconsistency **in** sth

inconsistency /ˌɪnkənˈsɪstᵊnsi/ *noun* [C, U] when something is inconsistent *The report was full of errors and inconsistencies.*

inconsistent /ˌɪnkənˈsɪstənt/ *adjective* **1** CHANGING not staying the same in quality or behaviour *His homework is very inconsistent.* **2** NOT AGREEING not having the same principles as something else, or not agreeing with other facts *The story Robert told his mother is totally **inconsistent with** what he told me.*

inconspicuous /ˌɪnkənˈspɪkjuəs/ *adjective* not noticeable or attracting attention *Emma tried to make herself as inconspicuous as possible.*

incontinent /ɪnˈkɒntɪnənt/ *adjective* **HEALTH** not able to control when urine or faeces come out of your body

incontrovertible /ˌɪnˌkɒntrəˈvɜːtəbl/ *adjective formal* certainly true ***incontrovertible evidence/proof***

inconvenience /ˌɪnkənˈviːniəns/ *noun* [C, U] when something is inconvenient, or something that is inconvenient *The Director apologized for any **inconvenience caused**.* [**usually singular**] *Having to wait for ten minutes was a minor inconvenience.* ●**inconvenience** *verb* [T] *There were complaints from travellers inconvenienced by delays and cancellations.*

inconvenient /ˌɪnkənˈviːniənt/ *adjective* involving or causing difficulty, such as unexpected changes or effort *I'm sorry, I seem to have called at an **inconvenient time**.*

incorporate /ɪnˈkɔːpᵊreɪt/ *verb* [T] to include something as part of another thing *He began to **incorporate** dance and mime **into** his plays.* ●**incorporation** /ɪnˌkɔːpᵊrˈeɪʃᵊn/ *noun* [U]

Incorporated /ɪnˈkɔːpᵊreɪtɪd/ (*written abbreviation* **Inc.**) *adjective* used after the name of companies which have been organized in a particular legal way *They formed their own company, Broadcast Music Incorporated.*

incorrect /ˌɪnkᵊrˈekt/ *adjective* not correct *His answers were incorrect.* •**incorrectly** *adverb My name is spelled incorrectly on your list.*

incorrigible /ɪnˈkɒrɪdʒəbl/ *adjective* having particular faults and impossible to change

OTHER WAYS OF SAYING *increase*

The verbs **grow** and **rise** are common alternatives to 'increase': *The number of people living alone **grows** each year.* • *Prices **rose** by ten percent.*

The phrasal verb **go up** is often used when prices increase: *House prices keep **going up**.* • *The price of fuel has **gone up** by 5p a litre.*

If something suddenly increases by a large amount, you can use verbs such as **escalate**, **rocket**, or **soar**: *Crime in the city has **escalated** in recent weeks.* • *Building costs have **rocketed** by seventy percent.* • *House prices have **soared** this year.*

If someone makes something increase in size or amount, you can use verbs like **expand** or **extend**: *We're hoping to **expand/extend** our range of products.*

The verb **maximize** is sometimes used when someone tries to increase something as much as possible: *We need to **maximize** profits.*

O-ᵚ**increase¹** /ɪnˈkriːs/ *verb* [I, T] to get bigger or to make something bigger in size or amount *Eating fatty food increases the risk of heart disease.* ○ *Exports of computers have **increased by** 15% since January.* ○ *increased demand/competition* ➲Opposite **decrease**

WORD PARTNERS FOR *increase*

a **dramatic/sharp/significant/slight/substantial** increase • an increase **in** sth

O-ᵚ**increase²** /ˈɪnkriːs/ *noun* **1** [C, U] when the number, size, or amount of something gets bigger *a price/tax increase* ○ *We are seeing **an increase in** standards of living.* **2 on the increase** If something is on the increase, it is happening more often. *Violent crime is on the increase.* ➲Opposite **decrease**

COMMON LEARNER ERROR

increase in or **increase of?**

Use **increase in** before the thing which is increasing.

an increase in profits/sales

an increase in the number of AIDS cases

Use **increase of** before the size of the increase.

an increase of 30%

increasingly /ɪnˈkriːsɪŋli/ *adverb* more and more *increasingly important* ○ *Increasingly, education is seen as a right, not a privilege.*

O-ᵚ**incredible** /ɪnˈkredɪbl/ *adjective* **1** GOOD OR LARGE *informal* very good, exciting, or large *We had an incredible time that summer.* ○ *an incredible noise* **2** STRANGE too strange to be believed *an incredible story*

incredibly /ɪnˈkredɪbli/ *adverb* **1** EXTREMELY *informal* extremely *The team played incredibly well.* **2** DIFFICULT TO BELIEVE in a way that is difficult to believe *Incredibly, no one was hurt.*

incredulous /ɪnˈkredjələs/ *adjective* not able to believe something *He looked incredulous when I told him the results.* •**incredulity** /ˌɪnkrəˈdjuːləti/ *noun* [U] •**incredulously** *adverb*

increment /ˈɪnkrəmənt/ *noun* [C] *formal* one of a series of increases ***pay increments***

incremental /ˌɪnkrəˈmentᵊl/ *adjective formal* increasing by small amounts ***incremental changes***

incriminate /ɪnˈkrɪmɪneɪt/ *verb* [T] to make someone seem guilty of a crime or to show that they are guilty [**often reflexive**] *He refused to answer questions on the grounds that he might incriminate himself.*

incriminating /ɪnˈkrɪmɪneɪtɪŋ/ *adjective* Something that is incriminating makes someone seem guilty of a crime. ***incriminating evidence/remarks***

incubate /ˈɪŋkjʊbeɪt/ *verb* [T, I] **1 BIOLOGY** If eggs are incubating, or being incubated, they are being kept warm until the baby birds come out **2 HEALTH** If a disease is incubating, or you are incubating a disease, the germs are inside you although you do not seem ill yet. •**incubation** /ˌɪŋkjʊˈbeɪʃən/ *noun* [U] *a long incubation period*

incubator /ˈɪŋkjʊbeɪtəʳ/ *noun* [C] **HEALTH, FARMING** a heated container that provides the right conditions for a baby born too early, or for very young birds, animals, or eggs

incumbent¹ /ɪnˈkʌmbənt/ *noun* [C] *formal* someone who has an official job, especially a political one *the previous incumbent*

incumbent² /ɪnˈkʌmbənt/ *adjective* **1 be incumbent on/upon sb to do sth** *formal* to be someone's duty or responsibility to do something **2** [**always before noun**] holding an official job, especially a political one *the incumbent president*

incur /ɪnˈkɜːʳ/ *verb* [T] **incurring**, *past* **incurred** *formal* to experience something unpleasant as a result of something you have done *to **incur** debts* ○ *I am sorry to have incurred his anger.*

incurable /ɪnˈkjʊərəbl/ *adjective* **HEALTH** impossible to cure *an **incurable disease***

incursion /ɪnˈkɜːʃᵊn/ *noun* [C] *formal* a sudden attack or entry into an area that belongs to other people ***incursions into** enemy territory*

incus /ˈɪŋkəs/ *noun* [**C, usually singular**] *plural* **incudes ANATOMY** one of three very small bones that carry sound into the inner ear ➲Compare **malleus, stapes**

indebted /ɪnˈdetɪd/ *adjective* **1 be indebted to sb** to be very grateful to someone *I'm indebted to my parents for all their support.* **2 FINANCE** having a debt to pay *indebted countries* •**indebtedness** *noun* [U]

indecent /ɪnˈdiːsᵊnt/ *adjective* showing or consisting of sexual behaviour, language, etc which is unacceptable to most people *indecent photographs* •**indecency** /ɪnˈdiːsᵊnsi/ *noun* [U] indecent behaviour, or when something is indecent •**indecently** *adverb*

indecision /ˌɪndɪ'sɪʒᵊn/ *noun* [U] when you cannot make a decision *a moment of indecision*

indecisive /ˌɪndɪ'saɪsɪv/ *adjective* not good at making decisions, or not producing a decision *She was weak and indecisive.*

indeed /ɪn'diːd/ *adverb* **1** EMPHASIS used to add emphasis after 'very' followed by an adjective or adverb *For a four-year-old, her vocabulary is very good indeed.* ○ *Thank you very much indeed.* **2** REACTION used when someone has said something that surprises, interests, or annoys you *"She asked if you were married." "Did she, indeed? "* **3** TRUE used to emphasize that something is true or that you agree with it *"He sounds a very interesting man." "He is indeed."* **4** MORE *formal* used when you say more to support or develop what has already been said *For such creatures speed is not important, indeed it is counterproductive.*

indefatigable /ˌɪndɪ'fætɪgəbl/ *adjective formal* never becoming tired *She was indefatigable in promoting her cause.*

indefensible /ˌɪndɪ'fensəbl/ *adjective* completely wrong, and so impossible to defend or support *Racism is **morally indefensible**.*

indefinable /ˌɪndɪ'faɪnəbl/ *adjective* difficult to describe or explain *an indefinable atmosphere of tension*

indefinite /ɪn'defɪnət/ *adjective* with no fixed time, size, end, or limit *an **indefinite period***

inˌdefinite 'article *noun* [C] **LANGUAGE** in grammar, a phrase used to mean the words 'a' or 'an' ⊃Compare **definite article**

indefinitely /ɪn'defɪnətli/ *adverb* for a period of time for which no end has been fixed *His visit has been **postponed indefinitely**.*

indelible /ɪn'deləbl/ *adjective* **1** MEMORY impossible to forget *an indelible impression/image* **2** MARK impossible to wash away or remove ***indelible ink***

indemnity /ɪn'demnəti/ *noun formal* **1 LAW** [U] protection against possible damage or punishment **2 FINANCE** [C, U] money paid or promised to you if something valuable to you is lost or damaged *indemnity insurance*

indentation /ˌɪnden'teɪʃᵊn/ *noun* [C] a mark, cut, or hole in the surface of something

WORD PARTNERS FOR ***independence***

achieve/gain independence • independence **from** sth

⁻**independence** /ˌɪndɪ'pendəns/ *noun* [U] **1** when someone looks after themselves and does not need money, help, or permission from other people *My parents gave me a lot of independence.* ○ *Many old people are afraid of **losing their independence**.* **2 POLITICS** when a country has its own government and is not ruled by another country *Mexico **gained** its **independence from** Spain in 1821.*

Indeˈpendence ˌDay (*also* **Fourth of July**) *noun* 4 July, a national holiday in the US to celebrate the country's freedom from Great Britain in 1776

⁻**independent¹** /ˌɪndɪ'pendənt/ *adjective* **1** RULE not controlled or ruled by anyone else *an independent state/company* ○ *The group is independent of any political party.* **2** NEED not wanting or needing anyone else to help you or do things for you *She's a proud, independent woman.* **3** INFLUENCE not influenced by anyone or anything else *an independent expert/study* •**independently** *adverb to operate independently*

independent² /ˌɪndɪ'pendənt/ *noun* [C] **POLITICS** a politician who does not belong to a political party

ˌindependent 'variable *noun* [U] **MATHEMATICS** a number or amount in a mathematical statement that can change and which decides the value of the dependent variable

in-depth /'ɪnˌdepθ/ *adjective* [**always before noun**] involving or considering all the details of something ***in-depth knowledge***

indescribable /ˌɪndɪ'skraɪbəbl/ *adjective* so good, bad, large, etc that it is impossible to describe *an indescribable feeling* ○ *indescribable agony*

indestructible /ˌɪndɪ'strʌktəbl/ *adjective* impossible to destroy or break

indeterminate /ˌɪndɪ'tɜːmɪnət/ *adjective* impossible to know *a large woman of **indeterminate age***

index¹ /'ɪndeks/ *noun* [C] **1** *plural* **indexes** an alphabetical list of subjects or names at the end of a book, showing on what page they are found in the text *Look up 'heart disease' **in the index**.* **2 COMPUTING** *plural* **indexes** a collection of information stored on a computer or on cards in alphabetical order **3 FINANCE, ECONOMICS** *plural* **indices** or **indexes** a system for comparing different values and recording changes, especially in financial markets *the retail price index*

index² /'ɪndeks/ *verb* [T] **COMPUTING** to make an index for text or information, or arrange it in an index

'index ˌfinger *noun* [C] **ANATOMY** the finger next to your thumb

'index ˌform *noun* [U] **MATHEMATICS** a way of writing a very large number with one number before the decimal point, multiplied by a power of 10. For example, 280,000 is 2.8 x 10^5

Indian /'ɪndiən/ *noun* [C] **1** someone from India **2** an American Indian (= one of the original race of people who lived in North America) ⊃See also: **West Indian**

indicate /'ɪndɪkeɪt/ *verb* **1** SHOW [T] to show that something exists or is likely to be true [+ **(that)**] *Recent evidence indicates that the skeleton is about 3 million years old.* **2** SAY [T] to say something or give a signal to show what you mean or what you intend to do *He has indicated his intention to resign.* **3** POINT [T] to point to someone or something *He indicated a man in a dark coat.* **4** SIGNAL [I, T] *UK* to show that you intend to turn left or right when you are driving *The driver turned right without indicating.*

WORD PARTNERS FOR ***indication***

a **clear/good/strong** indication • an indication **of** sth

indication /ˌɪndɪ'keɪʃᵊn/ *noun* [C, U] **1** EXIST a sign showing that something exists or is likely to be true [+ **(that)**] *There are **strong***

indications that the case will be referred to the Court of Appeal. **2** INTENTION a sign showing what someone means or what they intend to do *Helen's face* ***gave*** *no* ***indication of*** *what she was thinking.*

indicative¹ /ɪn'dɪkətɪv/ *adjective formal* **1 be indicative of sth** to be a sign that something exists, is true, or is likely to happen *These statistics are indicative of a widespread problem.* **2 LANGUAGE** An indicative form of a verb is used to express a fact or action.

indicative² /ɪn'dɪkətɪv/ *noun* [**no plural**] **LANGUAGE** the indicative form of a verb

WORD PARTNERS FOR ***indicator***

a **good/reliable/useful** indicator • an indicator **of** sth

indicator /'ɪndɪkeɪtəʳ/ *noun* [**C**] **1** FACT a fact, measurement, or condition that shows what something is like or how it is changing *With some goods, cost is the most reliable* ***indicator of*** *quality.* **2** LIGHT *UK* (*US* **turn signal**) a light that flashes on a vehicle to show that the driver intends to turn right or left ➲See colour picture **Car** on page Centre 7 **3 CHEMISTRY** a substance that shows if another substance is acid or alkaline

indict /ɪn'daɪt/ *verb* [**T**] *formal* **LAW** to accuse someone officially of a crime [**often passive**] *Pound was* ***indicted for*** *treason.*

indictment /ɪn'daɪtmənt/ *noun* **1** [**C**] something which shows the bad things which a person or system is responsible for *The novel is a scathing* ***indictment of*** *the slave trade.* **2 LAW** [**C, U**] when someone is legally indicted, or the official document or process for doing this

indie /'ɪndi/ *noun* [**C, U**] *informal* **MUSIC** a small independent music company or film producer ***indie music/bands***

WORD PARTNERS FOR ***indifference***

callous/casual/cold indifference • indifference **to/towards** sth

indifference /ɪn'dɪfᵊrᵊns/ *noun* [**U**] when you do not care about something or have any particular opinions about it *an air of indifference*

indifferent /ɪn'dɪfᵊrᵊnt/ *adjective* **1** NOT CARING not caring about or interested in someone or something *They are* ***indifferent to*** *the plight of the unemployed.* **2** NOT GOOD neither good nor bad *an indifferent performance*

indigenous /ɪn'dɪdʒɪnəs/ *adjective* **GEOGRAPHY** having always lived or existed in a place ***indigenous peoples*** ○ *The kangaroo is* ***indigenous to*** *Australia.*

indigestion /ˌɪndɪ'dʒestʃᵊn/ *noun* [**U**] **HEALTH** pain which you feel when your stomach is unable to digest food correctly

indignant /ɪn'dɪgnənt/ *adjective* angry because you have been treated badly or unfairly *Consumers are* ***indignant at/about*** *the high prices charged by car dealers.* •**indignantly** *adverb*

indignation /ˌɪndɪg'neɪʃᵊn/ *noun* [**U**] when someone is indignant *His voice was trembling with indignation.*

indignity /ɪn'dɪgnəti/ *noun* [**C, U**] a situation which makes you lose respect or look silly, or the feeling of shame and embarrassment it gives you [**+ of + doing sth**] *They* ***suffered the indignity*** *of being searched like common criminals.*

indigo /'ɪndɪgəʊ/ *noun* [**U**] a blue-purple colour •**indigo** *adjective*

indirect /ˌɪndɪ'rekt/ *adjective* **1** NOT CONNECTED not directly caused by or connected with something ***Indirect effects*** *of the fighting include disease and food shortages.* **2** NOT OBVIOUS hidden, or not taken or given in a way that is obvious ***indirect taxes/costs*** ○ *an indirect criticism* **3** NOT STRAIGHT not going straight from one place or person to another *an indirect route* •**indirectly** *adverb*

ˌindirect 'object *noun* [**C**] **LANGUAGE** The indirect object of a verb with two objects is the person or thing that is affected by the result of the action of the verb. In the sentence 'Give Val some cake.', 'Val' is the indirect object. ➲Compare **direct object**

ˌindirect 'tax *noun* [**C**] **FINANCE** a tax charged on goods and services rather than on the money that people earn ➲Compare **direct tax**

indiscreet /ˌɪndɪ'skriːt/ *adjective* saying or doing things which let people know things that should be secret ***indiscreet remarks*** •**indiscretion** /ˌɪndɪ'skreʃᵊn/ *noun* [**C, U**]

indiscriminate /ˌɪndɪ'skrɪmɪnət/ *adjective* not planned or controlled in a responsible or careful way *the indiscriminate use of pesticides* •**indiscriminately** *adverb The gunman* ***fired indiscriminately*** *into the crowd.*

indispensable /ˌɪndɪ'spensəbl/ *adjective* completely necessary *an* ***indispensable tool/guide*** ○ *She quickly became* ***indispensable to*** *him.*

indisputable /ˌɪndɪ'spjuːtəbl/ *adjective* obviously and certainly true *an* ***indisputable fact***

indistinct /ˌɪndɪ'stɪŋkt/ *adjective* not clear *His words became indistinct.*

indistinguishable /ˌɪndɪ'stɪŋgwɪʃəbl/ *adjective* impossible to see or hear as different or separate *Many toy pistols are* ***indistinguishable from*** *real guns.*

individual¹ /ˌɪndɪ'vɪdʒuəl/ *adjective* **1** SEPARATE [**always before noun**] considered separately from other things in a group *Read out the individual letters of each word.* **2** FOR ONE given to or relating to one particular person or thing *We deal with each case on an* ***individual basis.***

individual² /ˌɪndɪ'vɪdʒuəl/ *noun* [**C**] **1** SEPARATE a person, especially when considered separately and not as part of a group *We try to treat our students as individuals.* **2** SPECIAL *informal* a person with a special characteristic, usually one you dislike *a ruthless individual*

individualism /ˌɪndɪ'vɪdʒuəlɪzᵊm/ *noun* [**U**] the quality of being different from other people

individualist /ˌɪndɪ'vɪdʒuəlɪst/ *noun* [**C**] someone who likes to behave or do things differently from other people •**individualistic** /ˌɪndɪˌvɪdʒuə'lɪstɪk/ *adjective* behaving or doing things differently from other people

individuality /ˌɪndɪˌvɪdʒuˈæləti/ *noun* [U] the quality of being different from others *The houses had no character and no individuality.*

individually /ˌɪndɪˈvɪdʒuəli/ *adverb* separately and not as a group *He apologized to each person individually.*

Indo-China /ˌɪndəʊˈtʃaɪnə/ *noun* [U] the area of land between India and China that includes countries like Vietnam

indoctrinate /ɪnˈdɒktrɪneɪt/ *verb* [T] to make someone accept your ideas and beliefs by repeating them so often that they do not consider any others *They try to indoctrinate young people with their religious beliefs.* •**indoctrination** /ɪnˌdɒktrɪˈneɪʃᵊn/ *noun* [U] ***political indoctrination***

indoor /ˌɪnˈdɔːʳ/ *adjective* [always before noun] happening, used, or existing in a building *an indoor swimming pool*

indoors /ˌɪnˈdɔːz/ *adverb* into or inside a building *If you're feeling cold, we can go indoors.*

induce /ɪnˈdjuːs/ *verb* [T] **1** PERSUADE *formal* to persuade someone do something [+ to do sth] *Nothing would induce me to marry that man!* **2** CAUSE *formal* to cause a particular condition *High doses of the drug may induce depression.* **3 HEALTH** to give a woman a drug to make her have a baby earlier than she would naturally

inducement /ɪnˈdjuːsmənt/ *noun* [C, U] *formal* something that someone offers you to try to persuade you to do something *They offered me more money as an inducement to stay.*

induct /ɪnˈdʌkt/ *verb* [T] *formal* to accept someone officially as a member of an organization *He was **inducted into** the army in 1943.*

induction /ɪnˈdʌkʃᵊn/ *noun* [C, U] **1** when someone is officially accepted into a new job or an organization *a two-week **induction course*** **2 PHYSICS** the process by which electrical or magnetic forces are passed from one object to another without them touching

indulge /ɪnˈdʌldʒ/ *verb* **1** YOURSELF [I, T] to let yourself do or have something that you enjoy but which may be bad for you *They **indulged in** a bit of gossip.* [often reflexive] *Go on, indulge yourself! Have another chocolate.* **2** SOMEONE ELSE [T] to let someone do or have anything they want *Their children are dreadfully indulged.*

indulgence /ɪnˈdʌldʒəns/ *noun* **1** STATE [U] when you eat or drink too much or do anything you want **2** THING [C] something that you do or have because you want to, not because you need it *Silk sheets are one of my indulgences.*

indulgent /ɪnˈdʌldʒənt/ *adjective* If you are indulgent to someone, you give them anything they want and do not mind if they behave badly. *an indulgent father* •**indulgently** *adverb She **smiled indulgently** at her son.* ➲See also: **self-indulgent**

O-ɯ **industrial** /ɪnˈdʌstriəl/ *adjective* **1 ECONOMICS** connected with industry *the **industrial revolution*** **2 GEOGRAPHY** with a lot of factories *an industrial city such as Sheffield*

inˌdustrial ˈaction *noun* [U] **POLITICS** *UK* when workers stop working or do less work because they want better pay or conditions

inˌdustrial esˈtate *UK* (*US* **industrial park**) *noun* [C] an area where there are a lot of factories and businesses

industrialist /ɪnˈdʌstriəlɪst/ *noun* [C] someone who owns or has an important position in a large industrial company

industrialization /ɪnˌdʌstriəlaɪˈzeɪʃᵊn/ *noun* [U] **ECONOMICS** the process of developing industries in a country

industrialized (*also UK* **-ised**) /ɪnˈdʌstriəlaɪzd/ *adjective* **ECONOMICS, GEOGRAPHY** Industrialized countries have a lot of industry. *the **industrialized nations***

inˈdustrial ˌpark *US* (*UK* **industrial estate**) *noun* [C] an area where there are a lot of factories and businesses

inˌdustrial triˈbunal *noun* [C] **LAW** in the UK, a type of law court that decides on disagreements between companies and their workers

industrious /ɪnˈdʌstriəs/ *adjective formal* Industrious people work hard. •**industriously** *adverb*

WORD PARTNERS FOR ***industry***

an **important/major/thriving** industry • an industry **booms/grows**

O-ɯ **industry** /ˈɪndəstri/ *noun* **ECONOMICS** **1** [U] the production of goods in factories *heavy industry* **2** [C] all the companies involved in a particular type of business *the entertainment industry*

inedible /ɪˈnedɪbl/ *adjective* not suitable for eating *The meat was inedible.*

ineffective /ˌɪnɪˈfektɪv/ *adjective* If something is ineffective, it does not work well. •**ineffectively** *adverb* •**ineffectiveness** *noun* [U]

ineffectual /ˌɪnɪˈfektʃuᵊl/ *adjective* Ineffectual people or actions do not achieve much. *a weak and ineffectual president* •**ineffectually** *adverb*

inefficient /ˌɪnɪˈfɪʃᵊnt/ *adjective* Inefficient people or things waste time, money, or effort, and do not achieve as much as they should. *an inefficient heating system* •**inefficiently** *adverb* •**inefficiency** /ˌɪnɪˈfɪʃᵊnsi/ *noun* [C, U]

ineligible /ɪˈnelɪdʒəbl/ *adjective* not allowed to do something or have something [+ to do sth] *Foreign residents are ineligible to vote.* ○ *Non-graduates are **ineligible for** this position.* •**ineligibility** /ɪˌnelɪdʒəˈbɪləti/ *noun* [U]

inept /ɪˈnept/ *adjective* unable to do something well *socially inept* ○ *She was totally **inept at** telling jokes.* •**ineptly** *adverb* •**ineptitude** /ɪˈneptɪtjuːd/ *noun* [U]

WORD PARTNERS FOR ***inequality***

gender/racial/social inequality • inequality **between** sb **and** sb

inequality /ˌɪnɪˈkwɒləti/ *noun* [C, U] **SOCIETY** when some groups in a society have more advantages than others ***inequality between** the sexes*

inequity /ɪˈnekwəti/ *noun* [C, U] when something is unfair, or something that is unfair *inequities in the health care system*

inert /ɪ'nɜːt/ *adjective formal* **1** **CHEMISTRY** Inert substances do not produce a chemical reaction when another substance is added. *inert gases* **2** not moving *Vanessa **lay inert** on the sofa.* •**inertly** *adverb*

inertia /ɪ'nɜːʃə/ *noun* [U] **1** [NO CHANGE] when a situation remains the same or changes very slowly *the inertia of larger organizations* **2** [LAZY] when you are too lazy to do anything *International inertia could lead to a major disaster in the war zone.* **3** **PHYSICS** the physical force that keeps something in the same position or moving in the same direction

inescapable /ˌɪnɪ'skeɪpəbl/ *adjective* An inescapable fact cannot be ignored. *Racial discrimination is an **inescapable fact** of life for some people.* •**inescapably** *adverb*

inevitable /ɪ'nevɪtəbl/ *adjective* **1** If something is inevitable, you cannot avoid or prevent it. [+ **(that)**] *It was inevitable that his crime would be discovered.* **2** **the inevitable** something that cannot be prevented *Eventually the inevitable happened and he had a heart attack.* •**inevitably** *adverb Inevitably, there was a certain amount of fighting between the groups.* •**inevitability** /ɪˌnevɪtə'bɪləti/ *noun* [U]

inexcusable /ˌɪnɪk'skjuːzəbl/ *adjective* Inexcusable behaviour is too bad to be forgiven. *His rudeness was inexcusable.* •**inexcusably** *adverb*

inexhaustible /ˌɪnɪg'zɔːstəbl/ *adjective* existing in very large amounts that will never be finished *The Internet is an **inexhaustible source** of information.*

inexorable /ɪ'neksᵊrəbl/ *adjective formal* continuing without any possibility of being stopped *the inexorable progress of civilization* •**inexorably** *adverb These events **led inexorably** to war.*

inexpensive /ˌɪnɪk'spensɪv/ *adjective* cheap but of good quality *inexpensive children's clothes*

inexperience /ˌɪnɪk'spɪəriəns/ *noun* [U] when you do not know how to do something because you have not done it or experienced it much before *The accident was probably caused by the driver's inexperience.*

inexperienced /ˌɪnɪk'spɪəriənst/ *adjective* without much experience or knowledge of something *Kennedy was young and inexperienced.*

inexplicable /ˌɪnɪk'splɪkəbl/ *adjective* so strange or unusual that you cannot understand or explain it *To me his behaviour was quite inexplicable.* •**inexplicably** *adverb*

inextricably /ˌɪnɪk'strɪkəbli/ *adverb* If things are inextricably connected, they are so closely connected that you cannot separate them. *His story is **inextricably linked** with that of his brother.*

infallible /ɪn'fæləbl/ *adjective* always right, true, or correct *infallible evidence of guilt* ○ *They're experts, but they're not infallible.* •**infallibility** /ɪnˌfælə'bɪləti/ *noun* [U]

infamous /'ɪnfəməs/ *adjective* famous for being bad *The area became infamous for its slums.*

infancy /'ɪnfənsi/ *noun* **1** [U] when you are a baby or a very young child *Their fourth child died **in infancy**.* **2** **in its infancy** Something that is in its infancy has only just begun to develop. *In the 1950s, space travel was in its infancy.*

infant /'ɪnfənt/ *noun* [C] *formal* a baby or very young child

infantile /'ɪnfəntaɪl/ *adjective* behaving like a young child in a way that seems silly *Don't be so infantile.*

infantry /'ɪnfəntri/ *noun* [U, group] soldiers who fight on foot

infatuated /ɪn'fætjueɪtɪd/ *adjective* If you are infatuated with someone, you feel extremely strongly attracted to them. *As the weeks passed he became totally **infatuated with** her.* •**infatuation** /ɪnˌfætju'eɪʃᵊn/ *noun* [C, U]

infect /ɪn'fekt/ *verb* [T] **1** **HEALTH** to give someone a disease [**often passive**] *Thousands of people were **infected with** the virus.* **2** **HEALTH** If a place, wound, or substance is infected, it contains bacteria or other things that can cause disease. [**often passive**] *The wound became infected.* ○ *infected water/meat* ➲Compare **disinfect** **3** to make other people feel the same way as you do [**often passive**] *They became infected by the general excitement.*

O‒**infection** /ɪn'fekʃᵊn/ *noun* [C, U] **HEALTH** a disease in a part of your body that is caused by bacteria or a virus *an ear/throat infection*

infectious /ɪn'fekʃəs/ *adjective* **1** **HEALTH** An infectious disease can be passed from one person to another. **2** Infectious laughter or feelings quickly spread from one person to another. ***infectious enthusiasm***

infer /ɪn'fɜːʳ/ *verb* [T] **inferring**, *past* **inferred** *formal* to guess that something is true because of the information that you have [+ **(that)**] *I **inferred from** the number of cups that he was expecting visitors.*

inference /'ɪnfᵊrᵊns/ *noun* [C] *formal* a fact that you decide is true because of the information that you have *What **inferences** can we **draw** from this?*

inferior¹ /ɪn'fɪəriəʳ/ *adjective* not good, or not so good as someone or something else *I've never felt **inferior to** anyone.* ○ *They're selling inferior products at inflated prices.* •**inferiority** /ɪnˌfɪəri'ɒrəti/ *noun* [U] when something is not as good as another thing, or when someone feels they are not as good as other people

inferior² /ɪn'fɪəriəʳ/ *noun* [C] someone who is considered to be less important than other people

inferno /ɪn'fɜːnəʊ/ *noun* [C] *literary* a very large hot fire

infertile /ɪn'fɜːtaɪl/ Ⓤⓢ /ɪn'fɜːrtᵊl/ *adjective* **1** **BIOLOGY** An infertile person or animal cannot have babies. **2** **FARMING** Infertile land is not good enough for plants to grow well there. •**infertility** /ˌɪnfə'tɪləti/ *noun* [U] when a person or piece of land is infertile

infest /ɪn'fest/ *verb* [T] If insects, animals, weeds (= plants you do not want), etc infest a place, they cause problems by being there in large numbers. [**often passive**] *The hotel was **infested with** cockroaches.*

infidelity /ˌɪnfɪˈdeləti/ *noun* [C, U] when someone who is married or in a relationship has sex with someone who is not their wife, husband, or regular partner

infighting /ˈɪnˌfaɪtɪŋ/ *noun* [U] arguments between the members of a group ***political infighting***

infiltrate /ˈɪnfɪltreɪt/ *verb* [T] to secretly join a group or organization so that you can learn more about them *A journalist managed to infiltrate the gang of drug dealers.* •**infiltration** /ˌɪnfɪlˈtreɪʃᵊn/ *noun* [C, U] •**infiltrator** *noun* [C]

infinite /ˈɪnfɪnət/ *adjective* **1** GREAT extremely large or great *She took infinite care with the painting.* **2** NO END without limits or without an end *God's power is infinite.*

infinitely /ˈɪnfɪnətli/ *adverb* very or very much *Travel is infinitely more comfortable now than it used to be.*

infinitive /ɪnˈfɪnətɪv/ *noun* [C] **LANGUAGE** the basic form of a verb that usually follows 'to'. In the sentence 'She decided to leave.', 'to leave' is an infinitive.

infinity /ɪnˈfɪnəti/ *noun* [U] **1** time or space that has no end **2 MATHEMATICS** a number that is larger than all other numbers

infirm /ɪnˈfɜːm/ *adjective formal* weak or ill, especially because of being old

infirmary /ɪnˈfɜːmᵊri/ *noun* [C] **1 HEALTH** *UK formal* used in the name of some hospitals *Leicester Royal Infirmary* **2 HEALTH** *mainly US* a room in a school, prison, etc where people go when they are ill

infirmity /ɪnˈfɜːməti/ *noun* [C, U] *formal* **HEALTH** when someone is weak and unhealthy, or the illness they have

inflame /ɪnˈfleɪm/ *verb* [T] to cause or increase strong emotions *These brutal attacks have **inflamed passions** in a peaceful country.*

inflamed /ɪnˈfleɪmd/ *adjective* **HEALTH** If part of your body is inflamed, it is red and often painful and swollen.

inflammable /ɪnˈflæməbl/ *adjective* Inflammable liquids, gases, or materials burn very easily.

inflammation /ˌɪfləˈmeɪʃᵊn/ *noun* [C, U] **HEALTH** a red, painful, and often swollen area in or on a part of your body

inflammatory /ɪnˈflæmətᵊri/ *adjective* intended or likely to cause anger or hate ***inflammatory statements/speeches***

inflatable /ɪnˈfleɪtəbl/ *adjective* An inflatable object has to be filled with air before you can use it. *an inflatable boat*

inflate /ɪnˈfleɪt/ *verb* **1** [I, T] to fill something with air or gas, or to become filled with air or gas **2 ECONOMICS** [T] to make something such as a number, price, etc larger

inflated /ɪnˈfleɪtɪd/ *adjective* Inflated prices, costs, numbers, etc are higher than they should be.

O⊸**inflation** /ɪnˈfleɪʃᵊn/ *noun* [U] **ECONOMICS** the rate at which prices increase, or a continuing increase in prices *low/rising inflation*

inflationary /ɪnˈfleɪʃᵊnᵊri/ *adjective* **ECONOMICS** likely to make prices rise

inflection /ɪnˈflekʃᵊn/ *noun* [C, U] **1 LANGUAGE** the way the end of a word changes to show tense, plural forms, etc **2 LANGUAGE** the way that your voice goes up and down when you speak, for example to show that you are asking a question

inflexible /ɪnˈfleksəbl/ *adjective* **1** NOT CHANGING Inflexible rules, opinions, beliefs, etc do not change easily. *a cold and inflexible man* **2** STIFF Inflexible materials do not bend easily. •**inflexibility** /ɪnˌfleksəˈbɪləti/ *noun* [U]

inflict /ɪnˈflɪkt/ *verb* [T] to make someone suffer by doing something unpleasant to them *I would never have **inflicted** such suffering **on** you.*

in-flight /ˈɪnˌflaɪt/ *adjective* [**always before noun**] happening or available during a flight ***in-flight entertainment***

inflorescence /ˌɪflɔːˈresᵊnts/ *noun* **1 BIOLOGY** [C] in a plant, a flower or group of flowers on the stem, or the way they are arranged **2 BIOLOGY** [U] the formation of buds and flowers on a plant

inflow /ˈɪfləʊ/ *noun* [C] **FINANCE** an amount of money coming into a business

WORD PARTNERS FOR ***influence***

exert/have/wield influence • **bad/considerable / disruptive / good / powerful** influence • influence **on/over** sb/sth • be **under** the influence **of** sb/sth

O⊸**influence**[1] /ˈɪnfluəns/ *noun* **1** POWER [C, U] the power to affect how someone thinks or behaves, or how something develops *The drug companies have a lot of **influence on** doctors.* **2** PERSON/THING [C] someone or something that has an effect on another person or thing *His grandfather was a strong **influence on** him.*

O⊸**influence**[2] /ˈɪnfluəns/ *verb* [T] to affect or change how someone or something develops, behaves, or thinks *Many factors influence a film's success.* [**often passive**] *Were you influenced by anybody when you were starting your career?*

influential /ˌɪnfluˈenʃᵊl/ *adjective* having a lot of influence *an **influential figure** in modern jazz*

influenza /ˌɪnfluˈenzə/ *noun* [U] *formal* **HEALTH** flu (= an illness like a very bad cold, that makes you feel hot and weak)

influx /ˈɪnflʌks/ *noun* [C] the arrival of a lot of people or things at the same time [**usually no plural**] *The 1990s saw an **influx of** foreign players into British football.*

info /ˈɪnfəʊ/ *noun* [U] *informal short for* information

inform /ɪnˈfɔːm/ *verb* [T] **1** TELL to tell someone about something *If he calls me again, I shall inform the police.* [+ **(that)**] *He informed us that we would have to leave.* **2** GIVE INFORMATION to give someone information about something [**often passive**] *Patients should be **informed about** the risks.* ○ *He keeps his parents **informed of** his whereabouts.*
inform against/on sb *phrasal verb* to tell the

police about something illegal that someone has done

informal /ɪnˈfɔːməl/ *adjective* **1** FRIENDLY relaxed and friendly *an* ***informal discussion/meeting*** **2** ORDINARY suitable for normal situations *informal clothes* •**informality** /ˌɪnfɔːˈmæləti/ *noun* [U] •**informally** *adverb*

informant /ɪnˈfɔːmənt/ *noun* [C] someone who gives information to another person *Our survey is based on over 200 informants.*

OTHER WAYS OF SAYING ***information***

The plural noun **details** is often used to describe facts or pieces of information grouped together: *Please send me* ***details*** *of your training courses.*

The plural nouns **directions** and **instructions** are often used to talk about information which describes how to do something: *Just follow the* ***directions/instructions*** *on the label.*

The plural noun **directions** is also used to mean 'information about how to get to a place': *We had to stop and ask for* ***directions.***

The noun **data** is sometimes used to describe information in the form of facts and numbers: *Our consultants have been collecting financial* ***data.***

Written information about a subject is sometimes described as **literature**: *Some* ***literature*** *on our current policy is enclosed.*

WORD PARTNERS FOR ***information***

accurate/confidential/detailed/further/useful information • **access/exchange/gather/give/need/provide** information • information **about/on** sth

information /ˌɪnfəˈmeɪʃən/ *noun* [U] facts about a situation, person, event, etc *a vital* ***piece of information*** ○ *Police are urging anyone with* ***information about*** *the crime to contact them.*

COMMON LEARNER ERROR

information

Remember you cannot make **information** plural. Do not say 'informations'.

Could you send me some information about your courses?

For more information contact our office.

That's the only piece of information we've been able to find out.

inforˌmation techˈnology *noun* [U] **COMPUTING** (*abbreviation* **IT**) the use of computers and other electronic equipment to store and send information

informative /ɪnˈfɔːmətɪv/ *adjective* containing a lot of useful facts *a very informative lecture*

informed /ɪnˈfɔːmd/ *adjective* having a lot of information or knowledge about something *an* ***informed choice/decision*** ⊃See also: **well-informed**

informer /ɪnˈfɔːməʳ/ *noun* [C] someone who secretly gives information to the police about a crime

infraction /ɪnˈfrækʃən/ *noun* [C, U] *formal* **LAW** when someone breaks a rule or the law

infrared /ˌɪnfrəˈred/ *adjective* **PHYSICS** Infrared light feels warm but cannot be seen.

infrastructure /ˈɪnfrəˌstrʌktʃəʳ/ *noun* [C] **ECONOMICS** the basic systems, such as transport and communication, that a country or organization uses in order to work effectively [**usually singular**] *The country's infrastructure is in ruins.*

infrequent /ɪnˈfriːkwənt/ *adjective* not happening very often •**infrequently** *adverb*

infringe /ɪnˈfrɪndʒ/ *verb* [T] **1** BREAK LAW *formal* to break a law or rule *They infringed building regulations.* **2** LIMIT (*also* **infringe on**) to limit someone's rights or freedom *This law infringes on a citizen's right to bear arms.* •**infringement** *noun* [C, U] *an infringement of copyright*

infuriate /ɪnˈfjʊərieɪt/ *verb* [T] to make someone very angry *What really infuriated me was the fact that he'd lied.* •**infuriating** *adjective* extremely annoying

infuse /ɪnˈfjuːz/ *verb* **1** [T] *formal* to fill someone or something with a lot of a particular emotion or quality [**often passive**] *His work is* ***infused with*** *a love for tradition.* **2 FOOD** [I, T] to put something into a liquid so that its taste goes into the liquid

infusion /ɪnˈfjuːʒən/ *noun* [C, U] *formal* when one thing is added to another thing to make it stronger or better *an infusion of cash*

ingenious /ɪnˈdʒiːniəs/ *adjective* very clever and involving new ideas, equipment, or methods *an* ***ingenious idea/scheme/solution*** •**ingeniously** *adverb*

ingenuity /ˌɪndʒɪˈnjuːəti/ *noun* [U] skill at inventing things or finding new ways to solve problems

ingest /ɪnˈdʒest/ *verb* [T] *formal* to eat or drink something •**ingestion** *noun* [U]

ingrained /ɪnˈgreɪnd/ *adjective* **1** BELIEFS Ingrained beliefs, behaviour, problems, etc have existed for a long time and are difficult to change. *For most of us, watching television is a deeply* ***ingrained habit.*** **2** DIRT Ingrained dirt has got under the surface of something and is difficult to remove.

ingratiate /ɪnˈgreɪʃieɪt/ *verb* **ingratiate yourself (with sb)** to try to make people like you by doing things to please them •**ingratiating** *adjective* Ingratiating behaviour is done to try to make people like you. *an* ***ingratiating smile/manner***

ingratitude /ɪnˈgrætɪtjuːd/ *noun* [U] when someone is not grateful for something

WORD PARTNERS FOR ***ingredient***

a **basic/essential/vital** ingredient • an ingredient **in/of** sth

ingredient /ɪnˈgriːdiənt/ *noun* [C] **1 FOOD** one of the different foods that a particular type of food is made from **2** one of the parts of something successful *Trust is an* ***essential ingredient*** *in a successful marriage.*

inhabit /ɪn'hæbɪt/ *verb* [T] *formal* to live in a place [**often passive**] *an area inhabited by artists and writers*

inhabitant /ɪn'hæbɪtᵊnt/ *noun* [C] someone who lives in a particular place *a city with 10 million inhabitants*

inhabited /ɪn'hæbɪtɪd/ *adjective* An inhabited place or building has people living in it. *Is the island inhabited?*

inhale /ɪn'heɪl/ *verb* [I, T] *formal* **1 BIOLOGY** to breathe air, smoke, or gas into your lungs **2** *US informal* to eat something very quickly *Slow down, you're inhaling that pizza!*

inherent /ɪn'herᵊnt/ *adjective* existing as a natural and basic part of something *The desire for freedom is **inherent in** all people.* •**inherently** *adverb There's nothing inherently wrong with his ideas.*

inherit /ɪn'herɪt/ *verb* [T] **1** FROM DEAD PERSON to receive possessions or money from someone who has died *In 1842 he inherited a small estate near Liverpool.* **2 BIOLOGY** to have the same physical or mental characteristics as one of your parents or grandparents *Miranda has inherited her father's red hair.* **3** PROBLEM If you inherit a problem, situation, or belief, it is passed on to you by someone who had it before. *The mayor will inherit a city hopelessly in debt.*

inheritance /ɪn'herɪtᵊns/ *noun* [C, U] money or possessions that someone gives you when they die *Nick has sold off much of his inheritance.*

inhibit /ɪn'hɪbɪt/ *verb* [T] **1** SLOW GROWTH to make the progress or growth of something slower *a product which inhibits the growth of harmful bacteria* **2** PERSON to make it more difficult for someone to do something *Their threats **inhibited** witnesses **from** giving evidence.*

inhibited /ɪn'hɪbɪtɪd/ *adjective* not confident enough to say or do what you want

WORD PARTNERS FOR ***inhibition***

have no inhibitions about doing sth • **lose** your inhibitions

inhibition /ˌɪnhɪ'bɪʃᵊn/ *noun* [C, U] a feeling of embarrassment or worry that prevents you from saying or doing what you want *The whole point about dancing is to **lose all your inhibitions**.*

inhospitable /ˌɪnhɒs'pɪtəbl/ *adjective* **1** PLACE An inhospitable place is not pleasant or easy to live in because it is too hot, cold, etc. *the world's most inhospitable deserts* **2** PERSON not friendly towards people who are visiting you

in-house /ˌɪn'haʊs/ *adjective, adverb* done in the offices of a company or organization by employees of that company *in-house training of staff*

inhuman /ɪn'hju:mən/ *adjective* extremely cruel *the inhuman treatment of prisoners*

inhumane /ˌɪnhju:'meɪn/ *adjective* treating people or animals in a cruel way *inhumane experiments on monkeys* •**inhumanely** *adverb*

inhumanity /ˌɪnhju:'mænəti/ *noun* [U] extremely cruel behaviour *the inhumanity of war*

initial[1] /ɪ'nɪʃᵊl/ *adjective* [**always before noun**] first, or happening at the beginning *My initial reaction was one of anger.*

initial[2] /ɪ'nɪʃᵊl/ *noun* [C] **LANGUAGE** the first letter of a name [**usually plural**] *His initials are S.G.M.*

initial[3] /ɪ'nɪʃᵊl/ *verb* [T] *UK* **initialling**, *past* **initialled**, *US* **initialing**, *past* **initialed** to write your initials on something

initialize /ɪ'nɪʃᵊlaɪz/ *verb* [T] **COMPUTING** to make a computer program ready to use

initially /ɪ'nɪʃᵊli/ *adverb* at the beginning *The situation was worse than they initially thought.*

initiate /ɪ'nɪʃieɪt/ *verb* [T] **1** START to make something begin [**often passive**] *The reforms were initiated by Gorbachev.* **2** JOIN to make someone a member of a group or organization in a special ceremony, or to show someone how to do an activity *At the age of 50, he was **initiated into** the priesthood.* •**initiation** /ɪˌnɪʃi'eɪʃᵊn/ *noun* [C, U]

initiative /ɪ'nɪʃətɪv/ *noun* **1** ACTION [C] a plan or activity that is done to solve a problem or improve a situation *a **new** government **initiative** to reduce crime* **2** ABILITY [U] the ability to make decisions and do things without needing to be told what to do *We need someone who can work **on their own initiative*** (= without anyone telling them what to do). **3 take the initiative** to be the first person to do something that solves a problem or improves a situation *Jackson had taken the initiative and prepared a report.*

inject /ɪn'dʒekt/ *verb* [T] **1 HEALTH** to put a drug into someone's body using a needle *Phil's diabetic and has to **inject** himself **with** insulin every day.* **2** IMPROVE to add a good quality to something *The new teacher has **injected** a bit of enthusiasm **into** the school.* **3** MONEY to provide a large amount of money for a plan, service, organization, etc *The government plans to **inject** £100 million **into** schools.*

injection /ɪn'dʒekʃᵊn/ *noun* **1 HEALTH** [C, U] when someone puts a drug into your body using a needle *an injection of insulin* **2** [C] when a large amount of money is provided for a plan, service, organization, etc *The university has welcomed the $5 million **cash injection**.*

in'jection ˌmoulding *UK* (*US* **injection molding**) *noun* [U] **DT** a process used for making plastic objects, in which melted plastic is forced into metal shapes and left until it is hard

injunction /ɪn'dʒʌŋkʃᵊn/ *noun* [C] **LAW** an official order from a court that prevents someone from doing something *The courts have **issued an injunction** to prevent the book from being published.*

O- **injure** /'ɪndʒəʳ/ *verb* [T] to hurt a person, animal, or part of your body *She injured her ankle when she fell.*

injured /'ɪndʒəd/ *adjective* hurt *Fortunately, no one was **seriously injured** in the accident.*

WORD PARTNERS FOR ***injury***

a **fatal/major/minor/serious** injury • **cause/prevent/receive/recover from/suffer** an injury • an injury **to** sth

O-- **injury** /ˈɪndʒəri/ *noun* [C, U] damage to someone's body in an accident or attack *head injuries* ○ *The passenger in the car escaped with **minor injuries**.* ➲See also: add **insult**[2] to injury

injustice /ɪnˈdʒʌstɪs/ *noun* [C, U] a situation or action in which people are treated unfairly *the fight against racial injustice*

ink /ɪŋk/ *noun* [C, U] a coloured liquid that you use for writing, printing, or drawing

ink-jet printer

ink-jet printer /ˈɪŋkdʒetˌprɪntəʳ/ *noun* [C] **COMPUTING** an electronic printer which blows ink onto paper using very small jets (= small openings which push out liquid)

inkling /ˈɪŋklɪŋ/ *noun* **have an inkling** to think that something might be true or might happen *She **had** absolutely **no inkling** that we were planning the party.*

inland[1] /ˈɪnlənd/ *adjective* [always before noun] **GEOGRAPHY** Inland areas, lakes, towns, etc are a long way from the coast.

inland[2] /ˈɪnlænd/ *adverb* **GEOGRAPHY** towards the middle of a country and away from the coast

in-laws /ˈɪnlɔːz/ *noun* [plural] *informal* the parents of your husband or wife, or other people in their family

inlet /ˈɪnlet/ *noun* [C] **GEOGRAPHY** a narrow part of a sea, river, or lake where it flows into a curve in the land

ˌin-line ˈskate *noun* [C] **SPORT** (*also* **rollerblades** [plural]) a boot with a single line of wheels on the bottom, used for moving across the ground ➲See colour picture **Sports 1** on page Centre 14

inmate /ˈɪnmeɪt/ *noun* [C] someone who lives in a prison or in a hospital for people with mental illnesses

inn /ɪn/ *noun* [C] a small hotel in the countryside

innate /ɪˈneɪt/ *adjective* An innate quality or ability is one that you were born with, not one you have learned. *He has an innate desire to win.* •**innately** *adverb*

inner /ˈɪnəʳ/ *adjective* [always before noun] **1** [INSIDE] on the inside, or near the middle of something *The monastery is built around an inner courtyard.* ➲Opposite **outer 2** [PRIVATE] Inner feelings, thoughts, etc are ones that you do not show or tell other people. *a profound sense of inner peace*

ˌinner ˈcircle *noun* [C] the small group of people who control an organization, political party, etc *The statement was made by a member of the President's inner circle.*

ˌinner ˈcity *noun* [C] **SOCIETY** the part of a city that is closest to the centre, often where buildings are in a bad condition and there are social problems *a plan to tackle rising crime in inner cities* •**inner-city** /ˈɪnəˌsɪti/ *adjective* [always before noun] *inner-city schools*

innermost /ˈɪnəməʊst/ *adjective* [always before noun] **1** [FEELINGS] Your innermost feelings, thoughts, etc are the most private ones that you do not want other people to know about. **2** [INSIDE] *formal* closest to the middle of something

inning /ˈɪnɪŋ/ *noun* [C] **SPORT** one of the nine playing periods in a baseball game

innings /ˈɪnɪŋz/ *noun* [C] *plural* **innings SPORT** the period of time in a game of cricket when one player or one team hits the ball

WORD PARTNERS FOR ***innocence***

proclaim/protest/prove sb's **innocence**

innocence /ˈɪnəsəns/ *noun* [U] **1** [NOT GUILTY] when someone is not guilty of a crime *She fought to **prove** her son's **innocence**.* **2** [NOT EXPERIENCED] when someone does not have much experience of life and does not know about the bad things that happen *the innocence of childhood*

O-- **innocent** /ˈɪnəsənt/ *adjective* **1** [NOT GUILTY] not guilty of committing a crime *He claims to be **innocent of** the crime.* **2** [NO EXPERIENCE] not having much experience of life and not knowing about the bad things that happen *an innocent young woman* **3** [NOT DESERVED] used to emphasize that someone who was hurt had done nothing wrong *Several innocent civilians were killed in the bombing.* **4** [NOT INTENDED TO HARM] not intended to harm or upset anyone *It was an innocent mistake.* •**innocently** *adverb*

innocuous /ɪˈnɒkjuəs/ *adjective* not likely to upset or harm anyone *The parcel looked innocuous enough.* •**innocuously** *adverb*

innovation /ˌɪnəʊˈveɪʃən/ *noun* [C, U] a new idea or method that is being tried for the first time, or the use of such ideas or methods *the latest innovations in education*

innovative /ˈɪnəvətɪv/ (US) /ˈɪnəveɪtɪv/ *adjective* using new methods or ideas *an **innovative approach** to programme making*

innovator /ˈɪnəveɪtəʳ/ *noun* [C] someone who uses or designs new methods or products

innuendo /ˌɪnjuˈendəʊ/ *noun* [C, U] *plural* **innuendoes** or **innuendos** a remark that intentionally suggests something about sex, or something unpleasant about someone, without saying it directly *The advertisement was criticized for its **sexual innuendo**.*

innumerable /ɪˈnjuːmərəbl/ *adjective* very many, or too many to count *innumerable problems*

inoffensive /ˌɪnəˈfensɪv/ *adjective* not likely to upset anyone or make them angry *an inoffensive colour*

inordinate /ɪˈnɔːdɪnət/ *adjective formal* much more than is usual or suitable *James seems to spend an **inordinate amount** of time on his computer.* •**inordinately** *adverb*

inorganic /ˌɪnɔːˈgænɪk/ *adjective* **CHEMISTRY** not being or consisting of living things *inorganic waste*

ˌinorganic ˈchemistry *noun* [U] **CHEMISTRY** the scientific study of chemical substances which do not contain carbon

in-patient /ˈɪnˌpeɪʃᵊnt/ *noun* [C] **HEALTH** someone who stays in hospital for one or more nights while they are receiving treatment

input¹ /ˈɪnpʊt/ *noun* **1** IDEAS [C, U] ideas, money, effort, etc that you put into an activity or process in order to help it succeed *Input from students is used to develop new and exciting courses.* **2** ELECTRICAL [C, U] electrical energy that is put into a machine to make it work **3** **COMPUTING** [U] information that is put into a computer

input² /ˈɪnpʊt/ *verb* [T] **inputting**, *past* **inputted** or **input** **COMPUTING** to put information into a computer

WORD PARTNERS FOR ***inquest***

hold an inquest • an inquest **into** sth

inquest /ˈɪŋkwest/ *noun* [C] **LAW** a legal process to discover the cause of an unexpected death *There will be an **inquest into** the deaths of the three men.*

inquire *formal* (*also UK* **enquire**) /ɪnˈkwaɪəʳ/ *verb* [I, T] to ask someone for information about something *If you like languages, why don't you **inquire about** French classes in your area?* [+ **question word**] *Vronsky inquired whether the picture was for sale.* •**inquirer** (*also UK* **enquirer**) *noun* [C]

inquire after sb *phrasal verb UK formal* to ask someone for information about someone else's health and what they are doing, in order to be polite *Jane inquired after your mother.*

inquire into sth *phrasal verb formal* to try to discover the facts about something *a report inquiring into the causes of the region's housing problem*

inquiring (*also UK* **enquiring**) /ɪnˈkwaɪərɪŋ/ *adjective* [**always before noun**] **1** INTERESTED always wanting to learn new things *an **inquiring mind*** **2** EXPRESSION An inquiring expression on your face shows that you want to know something. •**inquiringly** *adverb*

WORD PARTNERS FOR ***inquiry***

make/receive an inquiry • an inquiry **about** sth

inquiry (*also UK* **enquiry**) /ɪnˈkwaɪəri/ *noun* **1** QUESTION [C] *formal* a question that you ask when you want more information *The company has received a lot of **inquiries about** its new Internet service.* **2** **POLITICS** [C] an official process to discover the facts about something bad that has happened *There will be an official **inquiry into** the train crash.* **3** ASKING QUESTIONS [U] *formal* the process of asking questions in order to get information

inquisitive /ɪnˈkwɪzətɪv/ *adjective* wanting to discover as much as you can about things *an inquisitive child* •**inquisitively** *adverb* •**inquisitiveness** *noun* [U]

inroads /ˈɪnrəʊdz/ *noun* **make inroads (into/on sth)** to start to become successful by getting sales, power, votes, etc that someone else had before *Women have made great inroads into the male-dominated legal profession.*

the ˌins and ˈouts *noun* all the details and facts about something *Tolya is someone who knows **the ins and outs of** the music industry.*

insane /ɪnˈseɪn/ *adjective* **1** ILL seriously mentally ill *a hospital for the **criminally insane*** **2** STUPID very silly or stupid *an insane decision* •**insanely** *adverb*

insanity /ɪnˈsænəti/ *noun* [U] **1** **HEALTH** when someone is seriously mentally ill **2** STUPID when something is extremely stupid *It would be insanity to expand the business at the moment.*

insatiable /ɪnˈseɪʃəbl/ *adjective* always wanting more of something *There was an **insatiable demand** for pictures of Princess Diana.* •**insatiably** *adverb*

inscribe /ɪnˈskraɪb/ *verb* [T] *formal* to write words in a book or cut them on an object [**often passive**] *The child's bracelet was inscribed with the name 'Amy'.*

inscription /ɪnˈskrɪpʃᵊn/ *noun* [C, U] words that are written or cut in something *The inscription on the gravestone was almost illegible.*

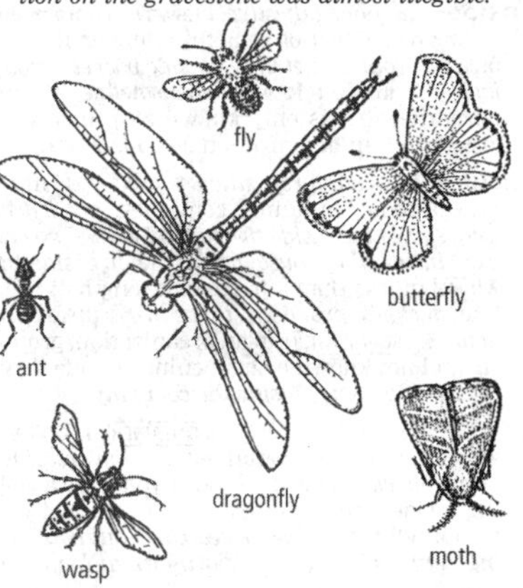

insects

O⊷**insect** /ˈɪnsekt/ *noun* [C] **BIOLOGY** a small creature with six legs, for example a bee or a fly

insecticide /ɪnˈsektɪsaɪd/ *noun* [C, U] **FARMING** a chemical that is used for killing insects

insecure /ˌɪnsɪˈkjʊəʳ/ *adjective* **1** WORRIED having no confidence in yourself and what you can do *a shy, insecure teenager* **2** NOT SAFE not safe or protected *Many of our staff are worried because their jobs are insecure.* •**insecurely** *adverb* •**insecurity** /ˌɪnsɪˈkjʊərəti/ *noun* [U]

insensitive /ɪnˈsensətɪv/ *adjective* **1** PEOPLE not noticing or not caring about other people's feelings *an **insensitive remark*** ○ *He was completely **insensitive to** Maria's feelings.* **2** PAIN not able to feel something, or not affected by it *She was **insensitive to** the pain.* •**insensitively** *adverb* •**insensitivity** /ɪnˌsensəˈtɪvəti/ *noun* [U]

inseparable /ɪnˈsepᵊrəbl/ *adjective* **1** THINGS *formal* Two things that are inseparable are so closely connected that you cannot consider them separately. *Rossetti's work was **insepa-rable from** his life.* **2** FRIENDS People who are inseparable are always together because they are such good friends. •**inseparably** *adverb*

insert[1] /ɪnˈsɜːt/ *verb* [T] *formal* **1** PUT INTO to put something into something else *Insert the coin in the slot.* **2** ADD TO WRITING to add something to the middle of a document or piece of writing *He inserted a new paragraph.* •**insertion** /ɪnˈsɜːʃən/ *noun* [C, U]

insert[2] /ˈɪnsɜːt/ *noun* [C] something that is made to go inside or into something else *The leaflet is designed as an insert for a magazine.*

inshore /ˌɪnˈʃɔːr/ *adjective, adverb* **GEOGRAPHY** near or towards the coast *inshore waters*

O-**inside[1]** /ˌɪnˈsaɪd/ *noun* **1 the inside** the part of something that is under its surface *I cleaned the inside of the oven.* **2 inside out** If a piece of clothing is inside out, the part that is usually outside is on the inside. *Harry, you've got your sweater on inside out again.* **3 know sth inside out** to know everything about something

inside[2] /ˌɪnˈsaɪd/ *adjective* **1** [**always before noun**] in or on the part of something under its surface *Put your wallet in the inside pocket of your jacket.* **2 inside information/knowledge, etc** information that is only known by people who are part of an organization, group, etc

O-**inside[3]** /ˌɪnˈsaɪd/ *preposition* **1** CONTAINER in or into a room, building, container, etc *There were some keys inside the box.* ○ *Luckily, no one was inside the house when the fire started.* **2** TIME in less than a particular length of time *The doctor's promised to be here inside an hour.* **3** ORGANIZATION in an organization, group, etc and not known or happening outside it *rumours of disputes inside the company*

O-**inside[4]** /ˌɪnˈsaɪd/ *adverb* **1** CONTAINER in or into a room, building, container, etc *I'm freezing, let's go back inside.* **2** FEELING If you have a feeling inside, people do not know about it if you do not tell them. *She looked calm but was feeling nervous inside.* **3** PRISON *informal* in prison

insider /ɪnˈsaɪdər/ *noun* [C] someone who knows about a business or organization because they are part of it *Industry insiders say they are surprised by the company's success.* ⊃Compare **outsider**

insides /ˌɪnˈsaɪdz/ *noun* [**plural**] *informal* your stomach

insidious /ɪnˈsɪdiəs/ *adjective* having harmful effects that happen gradually so you do not notice them for a long time *the **insidious effects** of pollution* •**insidiously** *adverb* •**insidiousness** *noun* [U]

WORD PARTNERS FOR ***insight***

gain/give/provide an insight **into** sth • a **fascinating/rare/unique/valuable** insight

insight /ˈɪnsaɪt/ *noun* [C, U] the ability to understand what something is really like, or an example of this *The book **provides** a fascinating **insight into** the world of art.*

insignia /ɪnˈsɪgniə/ *noun* [C] *plural* **insignia** a piece of cloth or a symbol that shows someone's military rank or official position

insignificant /ˌɪnsɪgˈnɪfɪkənt/ *adjective* not important or large enough to consider or worry about *insignificant differences* •**insignificance** /ˌɪnsɪgˈnɪfɪkəns/ *noun* [U] •**insignificantly** *adverb*

insincere /ˌɪnsɪnˈsɪər/ *adjective* pretending to feel something that you do not really feel, or not meaning what you say *an insincere apology* •**insincerely** *adverb* •**insincerity** /ˌɪnsɪnˈserəti/ *noun* [U]

insinuate /ɪnˈsɪnjueɪt/ *verb* [T] to suggest that something bad is true without saying it directly [+ **that**] *She insinuated that Perez had lied.* •**insinuation** /ɪnˌsɪnjuˈeɪʃən/ *noun* [C, U]

insipid /ɪnˈsɪpɪd/ *adjective* not interesting, exciting, or colourful *a dull, insipid man* ○ *The soup was rather insipid.* •**insipidly** *adverb*

O-**insist** /ɪnˈsɪst/ *verb* [I, T] **1** SAY to say firmly that something is true, especially when other people do not believe you [+ (**that**)] *Mia insisted that she and Carlo were just friends.* **2** DEMAND to demand that something must be done or that you must have a particular thing *The school **insists on** good behaviour from its students.* [+ **on** + **doing sth**] *Frank insisted on doing all the work himself.* [+ (**that**)] *Gerlinde insisted that I stay for dinner.*

insistence /ɪnˈsɪstəns/ *noun* [U] **1** DEMAND when you demand that something must be done or that you must have a particular thing [+ **that**] *his insistence that his children should have a good education* ○ *Clare's **insistence on** a vegetarian diet caused arguments with her mother.* **2** SAYING SOMETHING IS TRUE when you say firmly that something is true, especially when other people do not believe you [+ **that**] *Jane was in trouble despite her insistence that she had done nothing wrong.*

insistent /ɪnˈsɪstənt/ *adjective* firmly saying that something is true or must be done [+ **that**] *Pedro is absolutely insistent that Sinda should be invited too.* •**insistently** *adverb*

insofar as /ɪnsəʊˈfɑːrˌəz/ *conjunction formal* to the degree that *The story is based insofar as possible on notes made by Scott himself.*

insolation /ˌɪnsəʊˈleɪʃən/ *noun* [U] **BIOLOGY, ASTRONOMY** the amount of sun falling on an object or a planet

insolent /ˈɪnsələnt/ *adjective formal* rude and not showing respect *an insolent reply* •**insolence** /ˈɪnsələns/ *noun* [U] •**insolently** *adverb*

insoluble /ɪnˈsɒljəbl/ *adjective* **1** An insoluble problem, mystery, etc is impossible to solve. **2 CHEMISTRY** An insoluble substance does not dissolve when you put it in liquid.

insomnia /ɪnˈsɒmniə/ *noun* [U] **HEALTH** when you find it difficult to sleep •**insomniac** /ɪnˈsɒmniæk/ *noun* [C] someone who often finds it difficult to sleep

inspect /ɪnˈspekt/ *verb* [T] **1** OFFICIALLY VISIT to officially visit a building or organization, in order to check that everything is correct and legal *Schools will be inspected regularly to maintain standards.* **2** LOOK AT to look at something very carefully *Clara inspected her make-up in the mirror.*

WORD PARTNERS FOR ***inspection***

carry out an inspection • an inspection **of** sth

inspection /ɪn'spekʃᵊn/ *noun* [C, U] **1** OFFICIAL an official visit to a building or organization to check that everything is correct and legal *Fire officers **carried out an inspection** of the building.* **2** EXAMINATION when you look at something carefully ***On closer inspection*** (= when looked at more carefully), *the painting was discovered to be a fake.*

inspector /ɪn'spektəʳ/ *noun* [C] **1** OFFICIAL someone whose job is to check that things are being done correctly *a factory inspector* **2 LAW** a police officer of middle rank

inspiration /ˌɪnspᵊr'eɪʃᵊn/ *noun* **1** GIVES IDEAS [C, U] someone or something that gives you ideas for doing something *Africa has long been a source of **inspiration for** his painting.* **2** GOOD IDEA [C] a sudden good idea about what you should do **3 be an inspiration to sb** to be so good that someone else admires you and is encouraged by your behaviour *The way she has dealt with her illness is an inspiration to us all.* **4** [U] **BIOLOGY** the act of breathing in

inspire /ɪn'spaɪəʳ/ *verb* [T] **1** ENCOURAGE to make someone feel that they want to do something and can do it [+ **to do sth**] *A drama teacher at school had inspired Sam to become an actor.* **2** FEELING to make someone have a particular feeling or reaction *Robson's first task will be to **inspire** his team **with** some confidence.* ○ *He **inspires** great loyalty **in** his staff.* **3** PROVIDE IDEA to give someone an idea for a book, play, painting, etc [**often passive**] *a television drama that was inspired by a true story* •**inspiring** *adjective* giving you new ideas and making you feel you want to do something *an inspiring teacher* ○ *an inspiring book*

inspired /ɪn'spaɪəd/ *adjective* showing a lot of skill and good ideas *an inspired performance*

instability /ˌɪnstə'bɪləti/ *noun* [U] when a situation or someone's behaviour changes a lot and you do not know what will happen next

install (*also UK* **instal**) /ɪn'stɔːl/ *verb* **1** [T] EQUIPMENT to put a piece of equipment somewhere and make it ready to use *The school has installed a burglar alarm.* **2** [T] PERSON to give someone an important and powerful job *She will be **installed as** Managing Director in May.* **3 COMPUTING** [T, I] to put software onto a computer •**installation** /ˌɪnstə'leɪʃᵊn/ *noun* [C, U]

instalment *UK* (*US* **installment**) /ɪn'stɔːlmənt/ *noun* [C] **1 FINANCE** a regular payment that you make, for example each month, in order to pay for something *You can pay for your computer in six monthly **instalments**.* **2** one of the parts of a story that you can see every day or week in a magazine or on television *Don't miss next week's exciting instalment.*

instance /'ɪnstəns/ *noun* **1 for instance** for example *Many teenagers earn money, for instance by babysitting or cleaning cars.* **2** [C] an example of a particular type of event, situation, or behaviour *There have been several **instances of** violence in the school.*

O-- **instant¹** /'ɪnstənt/ *adjective* **1** happening immediately *The book was an **instant success** in the US.* **2 FOOD** Instant food or drink is dried, usually in the form of a powder, and can be made quickly by adding hot water. ***instant coffee*** ⇒See also: **instant replay**

instant² /'ɪnstənt/ *noun* [C] a moment *Take a seat, I'll be with you in an instant.*

instantaneous /ˌɪnstən'teɪniəs/ *adjective* happening immediately *The Internet offers almost instantaneous access to vast amounts of information.* •**instantaneously** *adverb*

instantly /'ɪnstəntli/ *adverb* immediately *A car hit them, killing them both instantly.*

instant messaging /ˌɪnstənt 'mesɪdʒɪŋ/ *noun* [U] **INTERNET** a system on the Internet which makes it possible to send messages quickly between two people using the system

ˌinstant ˈreplay *US* (*UK* **action replay**) *noun* [C] when part of a film of a sporting event is shown again, often more slowly

O-- **instead** /ɪn'sted/ *adverb* in the place of someone or something else *If you don't want pizza, we can have pasta instead.* ○ *I'm going swimming on Monday **instead of** Friday now.* [+ **of** + **doing sth**] *Why don't you help instead of just complaining?*

instigate /'ɪnstɪgeɪt/ *verb* [T] *formal* to make something start to happen *Carolyn had instigated divorce proceedings.* •**instigation** /ˌɪnstɪ'geɪʃᵊn/ *noun* [U] •**instigator** *noun* [C]

instil *UK* (*US* **instill**) /ɪn'stɪl/ *verb* [T] **instilling**, *past* **instilled** to make someone have a particular feeling or idea *He's a manager with great skill at **instilling** confidence **in/into** his players.*

WORD PARTNERS FOR ***instinct***

follow/trust your instincts • instinct **tells** sb sth • sb's **first/gut** instinct

instinct /'ɪnstɪŋkt/ *noun* [C, U] the way someone naturally reacts or behaves, without having to think or learn about it [+ **to do sth**] *a mother's instinct to protect her children*

instinctive /ɪn'stɪŋktɪv/ *adjective* behaving or reacting naturally and without thinking *Her **instinctive response** was to fight back.* •**instinctively** *adverb*

institute¹ /'ɪnstɪtjuːt/ *noun* [C] **EDUCATION** an organization where people do a particular kind of scientific, educational, or social work *the Massachusetts Institute of Technology*

institute² /'ɪnstɪtjuːt/ *verb* [T] *formal* to start a plan, law, system, etc *Major reforms were instituted in the company's finance department.*

institution /ˌɪnstɪ'tjuːʃᵊn/ *noun* [C] **1** ORGANIZATION a large and important organization, such as a university or bank *one of the country's top medical institutions* **2** PLACE a building where people are sent so they can be looked after, for example a prison or hospital **3** TRADITION a custom that has existed for a long time *the institution of marriage* •**institutional** *adjective* relating to an institution

instruct /ɪn'strʌkt/ *verb* [T] **1** ORDER to officially tell someone to do something [+ **to do sth**] *Staff are instructed not to use the telephones for personal calls.* **2** TEACH *formal* to teach someone about something *She is there to **instruct** people **in** the safe use of the gym equipment.*

O‑**instruction** /ɪnˈstrʌkʃᵊn/ *noun* **1** ORDER/DEMAND [C] something that you have been told to do [+ **to do sth**] *I had **strict instructions** to call them as soon as I arrived home.* **2** TEACHING [U] *formal* the activity of teaching or training someone, or the information you are being taught *religious instruction*

WORD PARTNERS FOR ***instructions***

follow the instructions • **give** instructions • **detailed/full** instructions • instructions **on** sth

instructions /ɪnˈstrʌkʃᵊnz/ *noun* [**plural**] information that explains how to do or use something *Are there any **instructions on** how to load the software?* ○ *I just **followed the instructions**.*

inˈstruction ˌset *noun* [C] **COMPUTING** a list of all the instructions that a computer processor (= part that controls all the other parts) can do

instructive /ɪnˈstrʌktɪv/ *adjective* providing useful information *an instructive discussion* •**instructively** *adverb*

instructor /ɪnˈstrʌktəʳ/ *noun* [C] **EDUCATION** someone who teaches a particular sport or activity *a **driving instructor***

O‑**instrument** /ˈɪnstrəmənt/ *noun* [C] **1** TOOL a tool that is used for doing something *scientific instruments* **2 MUSIC** an object that is used for playing music, for example a piano or drum **3** EQUIPMENT a piece of equipment that is used for measuring speed, light, fuel level, etc **4** FOR ACHIEVING SOMETHING someone or something that is used for achieving something *The Internet is a very powerful instrument of communication.* ➲See also: **wind instrument**

instrumental /ˌɪnstrəˈmentᵊl/ *adjective* **1 be instrumental in sth/doing sth** to be one of the main people or things that make something happen *Mikan was instrumental in establishing professional basketball in the US.* **2 MUSIC** involving only musical instruments, and no singing

insubordinate /ˌɪnsəˈbɔːdᵊnət/ *adjective* not willing to obey rules or people in authority •**insubordination** /ˌɪnsəˌbɔːdɪˈneɪʃᵊn/ *noun* [U]

insubstantial /ˌɪnsəbˈstænʃᵊl/ *adjective* not very large, strong, or good *The meal was rather insubstantial.*

insufferable /ɪnˈsʌfᵊrəbl/ *adjective* extremely annoying or unpleasant *insufferable arrogance* •**insufferably** *adverb*

insufficient /ˌɪnsəˈfɪʃᵊnt/ *adjective* not enough *insufficient information* [+ **to do sth**] *Her income is insufficient to support a family.* •**insufficiently** *adverb*

insular /ˈɪnsjələʳ/ *adjective* only interested in your own country, life, etc and not willing to accept new ideas or people •**insularity** /ˌɪnsjəˈlærəti/ *noun* [U]

insulate /ˈɪnsjəleɪt/ *verb* [T] **1** COVER to cover something with a special material so that heat, electricity, or sound cannot escape through it **2** PROTECT to protect someone from unpleasant experiences or bad influences *parents who want to insulate their children from real life*

insulation /ˌɪnsjəˈleɪʃᵊn/ *noun* [U] **1** MATERIAL a special material used for insulating something such as a wall, roof, or building **2** PROCESS/CONDITION when you insulate something, or when something is insulated

insulator /ˈɪnsjəleɪtəʳ/ *noun* [C] material or a device that stops heat, electricity or sound coming through

insulin /ˈɪnsjəlɪn/ *noun* [U] **BIOLOGY** a substance produced by the body that controls the amount of sugar in your blood

insult¹ /ɪnˈsʌlt/ *verb* [T] to say or do something to someone that is rude and offensive *How dare you insult me in front of my friends!* •**insulting** *adjective* rude and offensive *an insulting remark*

insult² /ˈɪnsʌlt/ *noun* [C] **1** a rude and offensive remark or action *They were shouting insults at each other.* ○ *His comments are **an insult to** the victims of the war.* **2 add insult to injury** to make someone's bad situation worse by doing something else to upset them

insupportable /ˌɪnsəˈpɔːtəbl/ *adjective formal* too bad or unpleasant to deal with or accept

WORD PARTNERS FOR ***insurance***

take out insurance • insurance **against** [sickness/fire, etc] • an insurance **company/policy/premium** • **car/travel** insurance

insurance /ɪnˈʃʊərᵊns/ *noun* [U] **FINANCE** an agreement in which you pay a company money and they pay your costs if you have an accident, injury, etc ***car/travel insurance*** ○ *an **insurance policy***

insure /ɪnˈʃʊəʳ/ *verb* [T] **FINANCE** to buy insurance from a company, or to provide insurance for someone *I need to **get** my car **insured**.* ○ *The policy **insures** you **against** damage and theft.*

insurmountable /ˌɪnsəˈmaʊntəbl/ *adjective formal* impossible to deal with *an **insurmountable problem/task***

insurrection /ˌɪnsᵊrˈekʃᵊn/ *noun* [C, U] **POLITICS** when a group of people use force to try to get control of a government

intact /ɪnˈtækt/ *adjective* not damaged or destroyed *Many of the old buildings are **still intact**.*

intaglio printing /ɪnˈtɑːliəʊˌprɪntɪŋ/ *noun* [U] **DT** a method of printing using a surface with lines cut into it

intake /ˈɪnteɪk/ *noun* [C] **1** FOOD/AIR the amount of food or drink that you take into your body [**usually singular**] ***Reducing** your **salt intake** can help to lower blood pressure.* **2** PEOPLE *UK* the group of people who start working or studying somewhere at the same time ***a new intake** of students*

intangible /ɪnˈtændʒəbl/ *adjective* An intangible feeling or quality exists but you cannot describe or prove it.

integer /ˈɪntɪdʒər/ *noun* [C] **MATHEMATICS** a whole number

integral /ˈɪntɪgrəl/ *adjective* necessary and important as part of something *The Internet has become an **integral part of** modern life.*

integrate /ˈɪntɪgreɪt/ *verb* **1** PEOPLE [**I, T**] to become part of a group or society, or to help someone do this *After a few weeks of training he was fully **integrated into** the team.* **2** THINGS/IDEAS [**T**] to combine two or more things to make something more effective *plans to integrate the two schools* •**integration** /ˌɪntɪˈgreɪʃᵊn/ *noun* [**U**]

ˌintegrated ˈcircuit *noun* [**C**] **COMPUTING** a lot of small electronic parts on one microchip, used for doing jobs where separate parts would take much more space

integrity /ɪnˈtegrəti/ *noun* [**U**] **1** honesty and the ability to do or know what is morally right *a woman of great integrity* **2** **COMPUTING** The integrity of computer data is the state of being correct and well organized.

intellect /ˈɪntᵊlekt/ *noun* [**C, U**] the ability to learn and understand something, and to form ideas, judgments, and opinions about what you have learned *His energy and intellect are respected by many people.*

intellectual¹ /ˌɪntᵊlˈektjuəl/ *adjective* **1** THINKING using or relating to your ability to think and understand things *intellectual work* ○ *intellectual and physical development* **2** INTERESTED IN IDEAS interested in learning and in thinking about complicated ideas *She's very intellectual.* •**intellectually** *adverb*

intellectual² /ˌɪntᵊlˈektjuəl/ *noun* [**C**] someone who enjoys studying and thinking about complicated ideas

WORD PARTNERS FOR ***intelligence***

average/great/high/low intelligence • **have/show/use** intelligence

O-ꟷ**intelligence** /ɪnˈtelɪdʒᵊns/ *noun* [**U**] **1** the ability to learn, understand, and think about things *a child of **low intelligence*** **2** **POLITICS** secret information about the governments of other countries, or the group of people who get this information *military intelligence* ➲See also: **artificial intelligence**

O-ꟷ**intelligent** /ɪnˈtelɪdʒᵊnt/ *adjective* able to learn and understand things easily *a highly intelligent young woman* •**intelligently** *adverb*

intelligible /ɪnˈtelɪdʒəbl/ *adjective* able to be understood ➲Opposite **unintelligible**

O-ꟷ**intend** /ɪnˈtend/ *verb* **1** [**T**] to want and plan to do something [**+ to do sth**] *How long are you intending to stay in Paris?* [**+ doing sth**] *I don't intend seeing him again.* **2 be intended for sb; be intended as sth** to be made, designed, or provided for a particular person or purpose *The book is intended for anyone who wants to learn more about the Internet.*

intense /ɪnˈtens/ *adjective* **1** EXTREME extreme or very strong *intense heat/pain* **2** SERIOUS Intense people are very serious, and usually have strong emotions or opinions. •**intensely** *adverb Clare disliked him intensely.* •**intensity** *noun* [**U**]

intensify /ɪnˈtensɪfaɪ/ *verb* [**I, T**] to become greater, more serious, or more extreme, or to make something do this *The fighting has intensified in the past week.*

intensive /ɪnˈtensɪv/ *adjective* involving a lot of work in a short period of time *ten weeks of **intensive training*** •**intensively** *adverb*

inˌtensive ˈcare *noun* [**U**] **HEALTH** the part of a hospital used for treating people who are seriously ill or very badly injured

intent¹ /ɪnˈtent/ *noun* [**U, no plural**] *formal* **1** when you want and plan to do something [**+ to do sth**] *It had not been his intent to hurt anyone.* **2 to/for all intents (and purposes)** in all the most important ways *To all intents and purposes, the project was a disaster.*

intent² /ɪnˈtent/ *adjective* **1 be intent on sth/doing sth** to be determined to do or achieve something *She seems intent on winning this year's tennis tournament.* **2** giving a lot of attention to something *She had an intent look on her face.* •**intently** *adverb*

WORD PARTNERS FOR ***intention***

announce/declare/signal your intention • **have no** intention of doing sth

O-ꟷ**intention** /ɪnˈtenʃᵊn/ *noun* [**C, U**] something that you want and plan to do [**+ to do sth**] *She announced her intention to resign.* [**+ of + doing sth**] *I **have no intention** of seeing him again.*

intentional /ɪnˈtenʃᵊnᵊl/ *adjective* planned or intended *I'm sorry if I said something that offended you. It really wasn't intentional.* •**intentionally** *adverb*

inter- /ɪntəʳ-/ *prefix* between or among *international* ○ *an interdepartmental meeting*

interact /ˌɪntərˈækt/ *verb* [**I**] **1** TALK/BEHAVE to talk and do things with other people *At school, teachers say he **interacted** well **with** other students.* **2** HAVE AN EFFECT If two things interact, they have an effect on each other. *We are looking at how these chemicals interact.*

interaction /ˌɪntərˈækʃᵊn/ *noun* [**C, U**] **1** PEOPLE the activity of talking and doing things with other people, or the way you do this *Our work involves a lot of **interaction with** the customers.* **2** THINGS when two or more things combine and have an effect on each other

interactive /ˌɪntərˈæktɪv/ *adjective* **1** **COMPUTING** Interactive computer programs, games, etc involve the person using them by reacting to the way they use them. **2** involving communication between people

intercept /ˌɪntəˈsept/ *verb* [**T**] to stop someone or something before they are able to reach a particular place *Johnson intercepted the pass and went on to score the third goal.* •**interception** /ˌɪntəˈsepʃᵊn/ *noun* [**C, U**]

interchangeable /ˌɪntəˈtʃeɪndʒəbl/ *adjective* If things are interchangeable, you can exchange them because they can be used in the same way. *interchangeable words* •**interchangeably** *adverb*

intercom /ˈɪntəkɒm/ *noun* [**C**] an electronic system used for communicating with people in different parts of a building, aircraft, ship, etc *A stewardess asked **over the intercom** if there was a doctor on board.*

intercontinental /ˌɪntəˌkɒntɪˈnentəl/ *adjective* in or between two continents *an intercontinental flight*

intercostal /ˌɪntəˈkɒstəl/ *adjective* **ANATOMY, BIOLOGY** between the ribs (= bones around the chest) *intercostal muscles* ⊃See picture at **rib cage** ⊃See picture at **respiratory system**

intercourse /ˈɪntəkɔːs/ (*also* **sexual intercourse**) *noun* [U] *formal* when a man puts his penis into a woman's vagina

WORD PARTNERS FOR ***interest***

develop/generate/have/show/take an interest • a **genuine/keen/passionate/strong** interest • an interest **in** sth • be **of** interest

interest¹ /ˈɪntrəst/ *noun* **1** FEELING [U, no plural] the feeling of wanting to give attention to something or discover more about it *Mark **had an interest in** the media and wanted to become a journalist.* ○ *After a while he simply **lost interest in*** (= stopped being interested) *his studies.* ○ *Bindi felt that her father didn't **take** much of **an interest in** her* (= he was not very interested). **2** ACTIVITY/SUBJECT [C] something you enjoy doing, studying, or experiencing *We **share** a lot of the same **interests**, particularly music and football.* **3 FINANCE** [U] the extra money that you must pay to a bank, company, etc which has lent you money *low **interest rates*** **4 FINANCE** [U] the money you earn from keeping your money in a bank account **5** QUALITY [U] a quality that makes you think something is interesting *Would this book **be of** any **interest to** you?* **6** ADVANTAGE [C, U] something that gives someone or something an advantage *A union looks after the interests of its members.* **7 be in sb's interest(s)** to help someone and give them an advantage *It may not be in your interests to change jobs so soon.* **8 in the interest(s) of sth** in order to achieve a particular situation or quality *In the interest of safety, passengers are advised to wear their seat belts at all times.* **9** LEGAL RIGHT [C] *formal* the legal right to own or receive part of a building, company, profits, etc ⊃See also: **self-interest, vested interest**

interest² /ˈɪntrəst/ *verb* [T] If someone or something interests you, you want to give them your attention and discover more about them. *History doesn't really interest me.*

interested /ˈɪntrəstɪd/ *adjective* **1** GIVING ATTENTION [**never before noun**] wanting to give your attention to something and discover more about it *Sarah's only **interested in** boys, CDs, and clothes.* [**+ to do sth**] *I'd be interested to find out more about the course.* ⊃Opposite **uninterested** **2** WANTING SOMETHING [**never before noun**] wanting to do, get, or achieve something [**+ in + doing sth**] *Mark said he's interested in buying your bike.* **3 interested parties/groups** people who will be affected by a situation ⊃Opposite **disinterested**

interesting /ˈɪntrəstɪŋ/ *adjective* Someone or something that is interesting keeps your attention because they are unusual, exciting, or have lots of ideas. *an interesting person* ○ *The museum was really interesting.* [**+ to do sth**] *It'll be interesting to see what Mum thinks of John's new girlfriend.*

OTHER WAYS OF SAYING ***interesting***

You can use **absorbing** or **gripping** to describe a game, book, film, etc. which is so interesting that it keeps your attention completely: *I found the book absolutely **gripping** - I couldn't put it down.* • *It was a very **absorbing** film.*

A game, book, TV programme, etc. which is so interesting that you cannot stop playing, reading, or watching it, may be described as **compulsive**: *I found the whole series **compulsive** viewing.*

Fascinating is often used to describe someone or something you have seen or heard that you have found extremely interesting: *The history of the place was absolutely **fascinating**.* • *He's **fascinating** on the subject.*

If something or someone is interesting because they seem mysterious and make you want to know more about them, you can say that they are **intriguing**: *It's a very **intriguing** situation.*

COMMON LEARNER ERROR

interesting or **interested?**

Interested is used to describe how someone feels about a person or thing.

I'm interested in theatre.

~~*I'm interesting in theatre.*~~

If a person or thing is **interesting**, they make you feel interested.

It was an interesting film.

ˈinterest ˌrate *noun* [C] **ECONOMICS, FINANCE** the per cent of an amount of money which is charged by a bank or other financial company

interface¹ /ˈɪntəfeɪs/ *noun* [C] **1 COMPUTING** a connection between two pieces of electronic equipment, or between a person and a computer *a simple **user interface*** **2** a situation, way, or place where two things can come together and have an effect on each other *the **interface between** technology and tradition*

interface² /ˈɪntəˌfeɪs/ *verb* [I, T] **COMPUTING** to communicate with people or electronic equipment, or to make people or electronic equipment communicate *We use email to **interface with** our customers.*

interfere /ˌɪntəˈfɪəʳ/ *verb* [I] to try to control or become involved in a situation, in a way that is annoying *I know he's worried about us, but I wish he wouldn't interfere.* ○ *You shouldn't **interfere in** other people's business.*

interfere with sth *phrasal verb* **1** CAUSE PROBLEMS to prevent something from working effectively or from developing successfully *I try not to let my dancing classes interfere with my schoolwork.* **2** RADIO SIGNALS If something interferes with radio or television signals, it stops you from getting good pictures or sound.

WORD PARTNERS FOR ***interference***

interference **in** sth • interference **from** sb

interference /ˌɪntəˈfɪərəns/ *noun* [U] **1** SITUATION when someone tries to interfere in a situation

*There have been claims of too much political **interference** in education.* **2** ELECTRONIC SIGNAL noise or other electronic signals that stop you from getting good pictures or sound on a television or radio

interferon /ˌɪntəˈfɪərɒn/ *noun* [U] **BIOLOGY** a substance produced in the body to fight against viruses (= organisms that cause disease)

interglacial /ˌɪntəˈɡleɪsiəl/ *adjective* **GEOGRAPHY** happening between two periods where glaciers (= large masses of ice) covered the land

interim¹ /ˈɪntᵊrɪm/ *adjective* [**always before noun**] temporary and intended to be used or accepted until something permanent exists *an interim solution* ○ *an **interim government***

interim² /ˈɪntᵊrɪm/ *noun* **in the interim** in the time between two particular periods or events

interior /ɪnˈtɪəriəʳ/ *noun* [C] the inside part of something *the grand interior of the hotel* ➲Opposite **exterior**

inˌterior deˈsign *noun* [U] the job of choosing colours, designs, etc for the inside of a house or room •**interior designer** *noun* [C] someone whose job is to do interior design

interjection /ˌɪntəˈdʒekʃᵊn/ *noun* [C] **LANGUAGE** an exclamation or sudden expression of your feelings. For example 'Hey' in 'Hey you!' is an interjection.

interlude /ˈɪntəluːd/ *noun* [C] a period of time between two events, activities, etc *a **brief interlude** of peace*

intermediary /ˌɪntəˈmiːdiəri/ *noun* [C] someone who works with two people or groups to help them agree on something important

intermediate /ˌɪntəˈmiːdiət/ *adjective* **1** **EDUCATION** between the highest and lowest levels of knowledge or skill *intermediate students* **2** between two different stages in a process ***intermediate steps** towards achieving our goal*

interminable /ɪnˈtɜːmɪnəbl/ *adjective* lasting a very long time, in a way that is boring *an interminable train journey* •**interminably** *adverb*

intermission /ˌɪntəˈmɪʃᵊn/ *noun* [C] a short period between the parts of a play, performance, etc

intermittent /ˌɪntəˈmɪtᵊnt/ *adjective* stopping and starting again for short periods of time *intermittent rain* •**intermittently** *adverb*

inter-molecular /ˌɪntəməˈlekjələʳ/ *adjective* **PHYSICS** happening among or between molecules

intern¹ /ˈɪntɜːn/ *noun* [C] *US* **1** **HEALTH** a young doctor who works in a hospital to finish their medical education **2** a student who learns about a particular job by doing it for a short period of time •**internship** *noun* [C] the time when someone is an intern

intern² /ɪnˈtɜːn/ *verb* [T] **POLITICS** to put someone in prison for political reasons, especially during a war •**internment** *noun* [U] when someone is interned

internal /ɪnˈtɜːnᵊl/ *adjective* **1** INSIDE A PLACE happening or coming from inside a particular country, group, or organization *an internal report* ○ *internal disputes* **2** BODY inside your body *internal injuries* **3** PLACE inside a country, building, area, etc *an internal flight* ○ *internal walls* ➲Opposite **external** •**internally** *adverb*

O→**international¹** /ˌɪntəˈnæʃᵊnᵊl/ *adjective* relating to or involving two or more countries *international politics* ○ *an international team of scientists* •**internationally** *adverb*

international² /ˌɪntəˈnæʃᵊnᵊl/ *noun* [C] *UK* **SPORT** a game of sport involving two or more countries, or a player in one of these games *a one-day international in South Africa*

the interˌnational comˈmunity *noun* **POLITICS** countries of the world considered or acting together as a group *The international community expressed shock at the attacks.*

WORD PARTNERS FOR ***the Internet***

browse/surf the Internet • **on** the Internet • **download** sth **from** the Internet • Internet **access** • an Internet **provider/service provider**

O→**the Internet** /ˈɪntənet/ *noun* **INTERNET** (*also* **the Net**) the system that connects computers all over the world and allows people who use computers to look at websites (= electronic documents) *She found a lot of information **on the Internet**.* ○ *a company that provides cheap **Internet access*** ➲See Extra help page **The Web and the Internet** on page Centre 36.

ˈinternet ˌcafe *noun* [C] a place where customers can buy food and drink and use computers to search for information on the Internet

ˈInternet ˌdating *noun* [U] **INTERNET** a way to meet people for possible romantic relationships, in which you look at descriptions of people on a website and arrange to meet them if you like them

interpersonal /ˌɪntəˈpɜːsᵊnᵊl/ *adjective* **SOCIETY** connected with relationships between people

interplay /ˈɪntəpleɪ/ *noun* [U] the effect that two or more things have on each other *I'm interested in the **interplay between** Latin and English.*

interpret /ɪnˈtɜːprɪt/ *verb* **1** [T] to explain or decide what you think a particular phrase, performance, action, etc means *His comments were **interpreted as** an attack on the government.* **2** **LANGUAGE** [I, T] to change what someone has said into another language *We had to ask the guide to interpret for us.*

interpretation /ɪnˌtɜːprɪˈteɪʃᵊn/ *noun* **1** EXPLANATION [C, U] an explanation or opinion of what something means *traditional interpretations of the Bible* **2** STORY/MUSIC [C] the way someone performs a particular play, piece of music, etc *a beautiful interpretation of Swan Lake*

interpreter /ɪnˈtɜːprɪtəʳ/ *noun* [C] **1** **LANGUAGE** someone whose job is to change what someone else is saying into another language **2** **COMPUTING** a computer program that changes the instructions in another program into a form that can be easily understood by a computer

interquartile range /ɪntəˌkwɔːtaɪl ˈreɪndʒ/ *noun* [**C usually singular**] **MATHEMATICS** in statistics, the numbers that are above the lowest 25% and below the top 25%

interrogate /ɪnˈterəgeɪt/ *verb* [T] to ask someone a lot of questions, often with great force *Police have arrested and interrogated the two suspects.* •**interrogation** /ɪnˌterəˈgeɪʃən/ *noun* [C, U] *twelve hours of brutal interrogation* •**interrogator** *noun* [C]

interrogative /ˌɪntəˈrɒgətɪv/ *noun* [C] **LANGUAGE** a word or sentence used when asking a question. For example 'Who' and 'Why' are interrogatives. •**interrogative** *adjective*

O→**interrupt** /ˌɪntəˈrʌpt/ *verb* **1** [STOP SOMEONE] [I, T] to stop someone while they are talking or doing something, by saying or doing something yourself *I was trying to work but the children were interrupting me.* **2** [STOP FOR PERIOD] [T] to stop an action or activity, usually for a short period of time *In 1998, a leg injury interrupted his sporting career.*

WORD PARTNERS FOR ***interruption***

a **brief/short** interruption • **without** interruption • an interruption **in/of** sth

interruption /ˌɪntəˈrʌpʃən/ *noun* [C, U] when an action or activity is interrupted, or something that interrupts someone or something

intersect /ˌɪntəˈsekt/ *verb* [I, T] If two things such as lines or roads intersect, they go across each other at a particular point.

intersection /ˌɪntəˈsekʃən/ *noun* [C] **1** *US* (*UK* **junction**) the place where two roads meet or cross each other **2 MATHEMATICS** the place where two lines cross each other **3 MATHEMATICS** the group of items that belong to two different sets

interspersed /ˌɪntəˈspɜːst/ *adjective* **interspersed with sth** having something in several places among something else *farmland interspersed with forests and lakes*

interstate /ˈɪntəˌsteɪt/ *adjective* [**always before noun**] relating to, or involving two or more US states *interstate commerce/travel* ○ *an interstate highway*

interval /ˈɪntəvəl/ *noun* **1** [TIME] [C] a period of time between two actions, activities, or events *After an interval of three days the peace talks resumed.* **2 at intervals** repeated after a particular period of time or particular distance *Patients were injected with the drug at four-hour intervals* (= every four hours). **3** [PERFORMANCE] [C] *UK* (*UK/US* **intermission**) a short period of time between the parts of a play, performance, etc

intervene /ˌɪntəˈviːn/ *verb* [I] **1** [BECOME INVOLVED] to become involved in a situation in order to try to stop a fight, argument, problem, etc *Government officials refused to **intervene in** the recent disputes.* [+ **to do sth**] *Harris intervened to stop the attack.* **2** [INTERRUPT] to interrupt someone who is talking *"Mr Lawrence," the judge intervened, "please be silent".* **3** [PREVENT] If something intervenes, it stops something or prevents it from happening. *She was going to marry Barratt but tragedy intervened.*

intervening /ˌɪntəˈviːnɪŋ/ *adjective* **the intervening months/period/years, etc** the time between two events *In the intervening years, his illness had become a lot worse.*

intervention /ˌɪntəˈvenʃən/ *noun* [C, U] when someone intervenes, especially to prevent something from happening *Without **medical intervention**, the child would have died.*

WORD PARTNERS FOR ***interview***

an **exclusive/frank/in-depth** interview • **conduct/do/give/have** an interview • an interview **with** sb

O→**interview**[1] /ˈɪntəvjuː/ *noun* [C] **1** [JOB/COURSE] a meeting in which someone asks you questions to see if you are suitable for a job or course *I **had an interview** last week for a job in London.* **2** [NEWS] a meeting in which someone is asked questions for a newspaper article, television show, etc *an **exclusive interview** with Madonna* **3 LAW** a meeting in which the police ask someone questions to see if they have committed a crime

interview[2] /ˈɪntəvjuː/ *verb* [T] to ask someone questions in an interview *Police are interviewing a 43-year-old man in connection with the murder.* ○ *So far we've **interviewed** five applicants **for** the Managing Director's job.* •**interviewer** *noun* [C]

interviewee /ˌɪntəvjuˈiː/ *noun* [C] someone who is being interviewed

intestine /ɪnˈtestɪn/ *noun* [C] **ANATOMY** a long tube that carries food from your stomach •**intestinal** /ˌɪntesˈtaɪnəl, ɪnˈtestɪnəl/ *adjective* relating to your intestine

intimacy /ˈɪntɪməsi/ *noun* [U] when you have a very special friendship or sexual relationship with someone

intimate[1] /ˈɪntɪmət/ *adjective* **1** [PRIVATE] private and personal ***intimate details** of her family life* ○ *intimate conversations* **2** [RELATIONSHIP] having a special relationship with someone who you like or love very much *an intimate friend* **3** [SMALL] If a place or event is intimate, it is small in a way that feels comfortable or private. *an intimate hotel* **4 an intimate knowledge/understanding of sth** when you know all of the facts about something or about how it works •**intimately** *adverb*

intimate[2] /ˈɪntɪmeɪt/ *verb* [T] *formal* to suggest that something is true without saying it directly

intimidate /ɪnˈtɪmɪdeɪt/ *verb* [T] to intentionally frighten someone, especially so that they will do what you want •**intimidation** /ɪnˌtɪmɪˈdeɪʃən/ *noun* [U]

intimidated /ɪnˈtɪmɪdeɪtɪd/ *adjective* frightened or nervous because you are not confident in a situation *Older people can feel very intimidated by computers.* •**intimidating** *adjective* making you feel intimidated *I find speaking in front of a crowd very intimidating.*

O→**into** /ˈɪntə, ˈɪntu/ *preposition* **1** [IN] towards the inside or middle of something *Stop running around and get into bed!* ○ *He's gone into a shop across the road.* **2** [CHANGE] used to show when a person or thing changes from one form or condition to another *We're planning to **turn** the smallest bedroom **into** an office.* ○ *Her last novel was translated into nineteen languages.* **3** [ABOUT] involving or about something *an investigation into the cause of the fire* **4** [TOWARDS] in the direction of something or someone *She was looking straight into his eyes.* **5** HIT moving towards something or someone and hitting them *I backed the car into the garden wall.* **6 be into sth** *informal* to be very interested in something *Kate's really into classical music.* **7** DIVIDE used when dividing one number by another *What's 5 into 125?*

intolerable /ɪn'tɒlᵊrəbl/ *adjective* too bad or unpleasant to deal with or accept *an intolerable situation* •**intolerably** *adverb*

intolerance /ɪn'tɒlᵊrᵊns/ *noun* [U] when someone is intolerant ***religious intolerance***

intolerant /ɪn'tɒlᵊrᵊnt/ *adjective* refusing to accept any opinions, beliefs, customs, etc that are different from your own

intonation /ˌɪntəʊ'neɪʃᵊn/ *noun* [C, U] **LANGUAGE** the way your voice goes up and down when you speak

intoxicated /ɪn'tɒksɪkeɪtɪd/ *adjective* **1** DRUNK *formal* drunk **2** VERY EXCITED *literary* very excited or enthusiastic about someone or something •**intoxicating** *adjective* making you intoxicated •**intoxication** /ɪnˌtɒksɪ'keɪʃᵊn/ *noun* [U]

intra- /ɪntrə-/ *prefix* within *an intranet*

intra-molecular /ˌɪntrəmə'lekjələʳ/ *adjective* **PHYSICS** happening inside a molecule or molecules

intranet /'ɪntrənet/ *noun* [C] **COMPUTING** a system that connects the computers in a company or organization so that people can share information and send messages

intransitive /ɪn'trænsətɪv/ *adjective* **LANGUAGE** An intransitive verb does not have an object. In the sentence 'John arrived first.', 'arrived' is an intransitive verb. ⊃See Extra help page **Verb patterns** on page Centre 25. ⊃Compare **transitive**

intravenous /ˌɪntrə'viːnəs/ *adjective* **HEALTH, BIOLOGY** Intravenous medicines or drugs are put directly into your veins (= tubes that carry your blood). •**intravenously** *adverb*

in-tray /'ɪntreɪ/ *UK* (*US* **in-box**) *noun* [C] a container where you keep letters and documents that need to be dealt with ⊃See colour picture **The Office** on page Centre 5

intrepid /ɪn'trepɪd/ *adjective* brave and willing to do dangerous things *intrepid travellers*

intricacy /'ɪntrɪkəsi/ *noun* **1 the intricacies of sth** the complicated details of something *a booklet explaining the intricacies of the game's rules* **2** [U] the quality of being intricate *the intricacy of the stone carvings*

intricate /'ɪntrɪkət/ *adjective* having many small or complicated parts and details ***an intricate pattern*** •**intricately** *adverb*

intrigue[1] /ɪn'triːg/ *verb* [T] **intriguing**, *past* **intrigued** If someone or something intrigues you, they interest you very much. *Ancient Egyptian art has always intrigued me.*

intrigue[2] /'ɪntriːg/ *noun* [C, U] a secret, clever plan to deceive someone or do something bad *a tale of romance, intrigue, and betrayal*

intriguing /ɪn'triːgɪŋ/ *adjective* very interesting *an intriguing story*

intrinsic /ɪn'trɪnsɪk/ *adjective* [**always before noun**] An intrinsic quality or thing forms part of the basic character of something or someone. *Drama is an **intrinsic part** of the school's curriculum.* •**intrinsically** *adverb*

⊶**introduce** /ˌɪntrə'djuːs/ *verb* [T] **1** SOMETHING NEW to make something exist, happen, or be used for the first time *CD players were first introduced in 1983.* ○ *We have introduced a new training schedule for employees.* **2** MEETING PEOPLE to tell someone another person's name the first time that they meet *He took me round the room and **introduced** me **to** everyone.* [**often reflexive**] *Emma introduced herself and they shook hands.* **3** TO AN AUDIENCE to tell an audience who is going to speak to them or perform for them *I'd like to introduce Rachel Elliott who is our speaker this evening.*

introduce sb to sth *phrasal verb* to help someone experience something for the first time *His father introduced him to the pleasures of good food.*

⊶**introduction** /ˌɪntrə'dʌkʃᵊn/ *noun* **1** SOMETHING NEW [U] when you make something exist, happen, or be used for the first time *the introduction of a minimum wage* **2** BOOK [C] the first part of a book or speech **3** BASIC KNOWLEDGE [C] a book or course which provides basic knowledge about a subject *an introduction to psychology* **4** FIRST EXPERIENCE [**no plural**] the first time someone experiences something *It was our first **introduction to** great poetry.* **5** FIRST MEETING [C] when you tell someone another person's name the first time that they meet [**usually plural**] *Can you do the introductions?* **6** TO AN AUDIENCE [C, U] when you tell an audience who is going to speak to them or perform for them *My next guest **needs no introduction**.*

introductory /ˌɪntrə'dʌktᵊri/ *adjective* **1 an introductory chapter/essay/message, etc** a part that comes at the beginning of a piece of writing or a speech and explains what will come later **2 an introductory book/course/lesson, etc** something that provides basic information about a subject *an introductory course in economics* **3 an introductory discount/fare/offer, etc** something that you get when you start buying something or using a service

introspective /ˌɪntrəʊ'spektɪv/ *adjective* thinking a lot about your own thoughts and feelings, in a way that is not always good for you •**introspection** /ˌɪntrəʊ'spekʃᵊn/ *noun* [U]

introvert /'ɪntrəʊvɜːt/ *noun* [C] someone who is quiet and shy and prefers to be alone •**introverted** *adjective an introverted child* ⊃Opposite **extrovert**

intrude /ɪn'truːd/ *verb* [I] to become involved in a situation which people want to be private *They should not have **intruded on** the family's grief.*

intruder /ɪn'truːdəʳ/ *noun* [C] someone who enters a place where they are not allowed to be, often to commit a crime

WORD PARTNERS FOR ***intrusion***

an **unwarranted/unwelcome** intrusion • an intrusion **into/on** sth

intrusion /ɪn'truːʒᵊn/ *noun* [C, U] when someone becomes involved in a situation which people want to be private *She could not bear the **intrusion into** her private life.*

intrusive /ɪnˈtruːsɪv/ *adjective* If something or someone is intrusive, they become involved in things which should be private. *The magazine published intrusive pictures of the princess's family.*

intuition /ˌɪntjuˈɪʃᵊn/ *noun* [C, U] the feeling that you know something without being able to explain why *Her approach to childcare is based on intuition.*

intuitive /ɪnˈtjuːɪtɪv/ *adjective* using intuition *He has an intuitive understanding of animals.* •**intuitively** *adverb*

Inuit /ˈɪnuɪt/ *noun* [C, U] *plural* **Inuit** or **Inuits** SOCIETY a group of people who live in the cold, northern areas of North America, Russia, and Greenland, or a member of this group

inundate /ˈɪnʌndeɪt/ *verb* **be inundated with/by sth** to receive so much of something that you cannot deal with it *Laura was inundated with flowers, cards, and other gifts.*

I

invade /ɪnˈveɪd/ *verb* **1** COUNTRY [I, T] to enter a country by force in order to take control of it *Portugal was invaded by the French in 1807.* **2** PLACE [T] to enter a place in large numbers *Every summer the town is invaded by tourists.* **3 invade sb's privacy** to become involved in someone's private life when they do not want you to

invader /ɪnˈveɪdəʳ/ *noun* [C] someone who enters a country by force in order to take control of it

invalid[1] /ˈɪnvəlɪd/ *noun* [C] HEALTH someone who is so ill that they have to be looked after by other people

invalid[2] /ɪnˈvælɪd/ *adjective* **1** LAW An invalid document, ticket, law, etc is not legally or officially acceptable. **2** An invalid argument is not correct.

invaluable /ɪnˈvæljuəbl/ *adjective* extremely useful *Her contacts in government **proved invaluable** to the company.*

invariably /ɪnˈveəriəbli/ *adverb* always *The train is invariably packed.*

invasion /ɪnˈveɪʒᵊn/ *noun* **1** [C, U] when an army enters a country by force in order to take control of it **2 an invasion of privacy** becoming involved in someone's private life when they do not want you to

O-ꟷ**invent** /ɪnˈvent/ *verb* [T] **1** NEW to design or create something that has never existed before *We've invented a new game.* **2** DECEIVE to think of a story or explanation in order to deceive someone *She invented an excuse to leave.*

O-ꟷ**invention** /ɪnˈvenʃᵊn/ *noun* **1** NEW THING [C] something that has been designed or created for the first time **2** MAKING NEW THINGS [U] when someone designs or creates something new *the invention of printing*

inventive /ɪnˈventɪv/ *adjective* full of clever and interesting ideas *inventive designs* •**inventively** *adverb* •**inventiveness** *noun* [U]

inventor /ɪnˈventəʳ/ *noun* [C] someone who designs and makes new things

inventory /ˈɪnvᵊntri, ɪnˈventᵊri/ *noun* [C] a list of all the things that are in a place

inverse /ɪnˈvɜːs/ *adjective* [never before noun] opposite in relation to something else *Their standard of living was in inverse proportion to the number of children they had.*

ˌinverse ˈfunction *noun* [C] MATHEMATICS a function (= quantity that depends on another value) that does the opposite of a particular function

ˌinverse proˈportion *noun* [U] MATHEMATICS when the proportion of different amounts changes so that when one gets bigger, the other gets smaller

invert /ɪnˈvɜːt/ *verb* [T] *formal* to turn something upside-down, or put something in the opposite order from how it usually is

invertase /ɪnˈvɜːteɪz/ (*also* **sucrase**) *noun* [U] BIOLOGY an enzyme (= substance in the body that makes chemical reactions happen) found in the intestines that breaks down sucrose to fructose and glucose

invertebrate /ɪnˈvɜːtɪbrət/ *noun* [C] BIOLOGY an animal with no spine (= bones in the back) ➲Compare **vertebrates** •**invertebrate** *adjective*

inverted commas /ɪnˌvɜːtɪdˈkɒməz/ *noun* [plural] *UK* LANGUAGE a pair of marks (" ") or (' ') used before and after a group of words to show that they are spoken or that someone else originally wrote them ➲See Extra help page **Punctuation** on page Centre 19.

invest /ɪnˈvest/ *verb* **1** FINANCE [I, T] to give money to a bank, business, etc, or buy something, because you hope to get a profit *He's **invested** over a million pounds **in** the city's waterfront restoration project.* **2** [T] to use a lot of time, effort, or emotions because you want to succeed *I think she **invests** too much time and energy **in** her career.*

invest in sth *phrasal verb* FINANCE to buy something because you think it will be useful *Dad's decided to invest in a computer.*

investigate /ɪnˈvestɪgeɪt/ *verb* [I, T] to try to discover all the facts about something, especially a crime or accident *He was questioned by detectives investigating the murder.*

WORD PARTNERS FOR ***investigation***

carry out/conduct/launch an investigation • a **detailed/full/thorough** investigation • an investigation **into** sth • be **under** investigation

investigation /ɪnˌvestɪˈgeɪʃᵊn/ *noun* [C, U] when officials try to discover all the facts about something, especially a crime or an accident *Police have begun an **investigation into** his death.* ○ *The cause of the fire is still **under investigation*** (= being investigated).

investigative /ɪnˈvestɪgətɪv/ (US) /ɪnˈvestɪgeɪtɪv/ *adjective* trying to discover all the facts about something ***investigative journalists***

investigator /ɪnˈvestɪgeɪtəʳ/ *noun* [C] someone who tries to discover all the facts about something, especially as their job

investment /ɪnˈvestmənt/ *noun* **1** ECONOMICS, FINANCE [C, U] the money that you put in a bank, business, etc in order to make a profit, or the act of doing this *Businesses need to increase their **investment in** new technology.*

2 [C] something that you do or have, in order to have more in the future *Going to college is an **investment in** the future.*

investor /ɪnˈvestəʳ/ *noun* [C] **FINANCE** someone who puts money in a bank, business, etc in order to make a profit

inveterate /ɪnˈvetərət/ *adjective* **an inveterate liar/gambler/reader, etc** someone who does something very often

invigorating /ɪnˈvɪɡəreɪtɪŋ/ *adjective* making you feel very healthy and energetic *a long, invigorating walk* •**invigorate** *verb* [T] to make you feel very healthy and energetic

invincible /ɪnˈvɪnsəbl/ *adjective* If someone or something is invincible, it is impossible to defeat or destroy them. *The French army seemed invincible.*

invisible /ɪnˈvɪzəbl/ *adjective* Someone or something that is invisible cannot be seen. *invisible particles called electrons* ○ *The house was invisible from the road.* •**invisibility** /ɪnˌvɪzəˈbɪləti/ *noun* [U]

WORD PARTNERS FOR ***invitation***

accept/decline/turn down an invitation • an invitation **to** sth

O⁃ **invitation** /ˌɪnvɪˈteɪʃən/ *noun* **1** [INVITING SOMEONE] [C, U] when someone invites you to do something or go somewhere *an **invitation to** dinner* [+ **to do sth**] *He has **accepted** their **invitation** to visit China.* **2** [PIECE OF PAPER] [C] a piece of paper or card that invites someone to an event **3** [CAUSE RESULT] [**no plural**] something that is likely to cause a particular result, especially a bad one *It is **an invitation to** violence.*

O⁃ **invite¹** /ɪnˈvaɪt/ *verb* [T] **1** [SOCIAL EVENT] to ask someone to come to a social event *They've **invited** us **to** the wedding.* **2** [ASK OFFICIALLY] to officially ask someone to do something [+ **to do sth**] *I was invited to appear on television.* **3** [REACTION] to do something that is likely to cause a particular reaction or result, especially a bad one *Unconventional ideas often invite attack.*

invite sb in *phrasal verb* to ask someone to come into your house *The neighbours **invited** us **in for** coffee.*

invite sb over *phrasal verb* (*also UK* **invite sb round**) to invite someone to come to your house

COMMON LEARNER ERROR

invite someone **to** something

If you are talking about a social event, use the preposition **to**.

She invited me to the party.

~~*She invited me for the party.*~~

~~*She invited me at the party.*~~

If you are talking about a meal, you can use **to** or **for**.

He invited me for dinner/to dinner.

If you are talking about a particular type of food, or inviting someone for a particular activity, use **for**.

I was invited for an interview.

They invited her for a pizza.

invite² /ˈɪnvaɪt/ *noun* [C] *informal* an invitation

inviting /ɪnˈvaɪtɪŋ/ *adjective* pleasant and attractive *an inviting smile* ○ *The room looked cosy and inviting.* •**invitingly** *adverb*

in vitro fertilization /ɪnˌviːtrəʊfɜːtɪlaɪˈzeɪʃən/ (*also* **IVF**) *noun* [U] **HEALTH** a treatment where a woman's egg is fertilized outside her body and put back in her body for the baby to grow

invoice¹ /ˈɪnvɔɪs/ *noun* [C] **FINANCE** a list that shows you how much you owe someone for work they have done or for goods they have supplied

invoice² /ˈɪnvɔɪs/ *verb* [T] **FINANCE** to send someone an invoice

invoke /ɪnˈvəʊk/ *verb* [T] *formal* to use a law, rule, etc to support what you are saying or doing *The President may **invoke** federal **law** to stop the strike.*

involuntary /ɪnˈvɒləntəri/ *adjective* An involuntary movement or action is something you do but cannot control. *an involuntary shudder* •**involuntarily** *adverb*

O⁃ **involve** /ɪnˈvɒlv/ *verb* [T] **1** [NECESSARY PART] If a situation or activity involves something, that thing is a necessary part of it. *The trips often involve a lot of walking.* ○ *There are a lot of risks involved.* **2** [AFFECT/INCLUDE] to affect or include someone or something in an activity *an event involving hundreds of people* **3** [TAKE PART] to make someone be part of an activity or process *I prefer teaching methods that actively **involve** students **in** learning.*

O⁃ **involved** /ɪnˈvɒlvd/ *adjective* **1 be/get involved (in/with sth)** to do things and be part of an activity or event *How did you get involved in acting?* **2 be/get involved with sb** to have a sexual or romantic relationship with someone *She got involved with a boy from college.* **3** complicated *a long and involved story*

WORD PARTNERS FOR ***involvement***

close/direct/personal involvement • involvement **in** sth

O⁃ **involvement** /ɪnˈvɒlvmənt/ *noun* [U] when someone or something is involved in an activity or event *He denies any **involvement in** the attack.*

inward¹ /ˈɪnwəd/ *adjective* **1** [MOVEMENT] [**always before noun**] towards the centre or the inside of something **2 inward investment ECONOMICS, FINANCE** *UK* money from foreign companies that is put into businesses in your own country **3** [INSIDE YOURSELF] [**always before noun**] inside your mind and not shown to other people *inward feelings* ⊃Opposite **outward**

inward² /ˈɪnwəd/ (*also UK* **inwards**) *adverb* towards the inside or the centre *The door slowly opened inward.*

inwardly /ˈɪnwədli/ *adverb* in your mind without anyone else seeing or knowing *She smiled inwardly.* ⊃Opposite **outwardly**

in-your-face (*also* **in-yer-face**) /ˌɪnjəˈfeɪs/ *adjective informal* describes something that is done in a forceful way that intends to shock people *in-your-face television advertising*

I

iodide /ˈaɪəʊdaɪd/ *noun* [C] **CHEMISTRY** a chemical compound of iodine with another element

iodine /ˈaɪədiːn/ *noun* [U] **CHEMISTRY** a chemical element found in sea water, and used in some medicines (symbol **I**)

ion /ˈaɪɒn/ *noun* [C] **PHYSICS, CHEMISTRY** an atom or small group of atoms which has an electrical charge because it has added or lost one or more electrons •**ionic** /aɪˈɒnɪk/ *adjective*

iˌonic ˈbond *noun* [C] **CHEMISTRY** a chemical bond in which two ions are joined together because one has a positive charge and the other a negative charge

ionize (*also UK* **-ise**) /ˈaɪənaɪz/ *verb* [T, I] **CHEMISTRY** to form an ion or to make something form an ion

the ionosphere /ˌaɪˈɒnəˌsfiːr/ *noun* **GEOGRAPHY** part of the Earth's atmosphere, from about 60 kilometres to about 1000 kilometres above the surface, in which there are many ions

I

IOU /ˌaɪəʊˈjuː/ *noun* [C] **FINANCE** *abbreviation for* I owe you: a piece of paper saying that you will pay back money you owe

IOW **INTERNET** *internet abbreviation for* in other words: used when you want to express something in a different way in order to explain it clearly

IPA /ˌaɪpiːˈeɪ/ *noun* [U] **LANGUAGE** *abbreviation for* International Phonetic Alphabet: a system of symbols for showing how words are spoken

iPod /ˈaɪpɒd/ *noun* [C] *trademark* one of a group of small electronic devices for storing and playing music

IQ /ˌaɪˈkjuː/ *noun* [C, U] *abbreviation for* intelligence quotient: a person's intelligence when measured by a special test *a high/low IQ*

ir- /ɪr-/ *prefix* not *irregular*

irate /aɪˈreɪt/ *adjective* extremely angry *Hundreds of irate passengers have complained to the airline.*

iridium /ɪˈrɪdiəm/ *noun* [U] **CHEMISTRY** a hard, yellow-white metal (formula **Ir**)

iris /ˈaɪərɪs/ *noun* [C] **1** a tall plant with purple, yellow, or white flowers **2** **ANATOMY** the coloured part of your eye

Irish[1] /ˈaɪərɪʃ/ *adjective* relating to Ireland *Irish music/culture* ○ *Irish whisky*

Irish[2] /ˈaɪərɪʃ/ *noun* **1** [U] the language that is spoken in some parts of Ireland **2 the Irish** [plural] the people of Ireland

O-ᵐ**iron**[1] /aɪən/ *noun* **1** **CHEMISTRY** [U] a dark grey metal used to make steel (= very strong metal) and found in small amounts in blood and food (formula **Fe**) *an iron bar/gate* **2** [C] a piece of electrical equipment that you use for making clothes flat and smooth ➲See also: **cast iron, wrought iron**

iron[2] /aɪən/ *verb* [I, T] to make clothes flat and smooth using an iron *I need to iron a shirt to wear tomorrow.*

iron sth out *phrasal verb* to solve a problem or difficulty *We're still trying to* ***iron out*** *a few* ***problems*** *with the computer system.*

iron[3] /aɪən/ *adjective* [**always before noun**] extremely strong and determined *a man of* ***iron will*** ➲See also: **cast-iron**

ironic /aɪəˈrɒnɪk/ *adjective* **1** HUMOUR saying something that you do not mean, as a joke *ironic comments* **2** SITUATION An ironic situation is strange because it is the opposite of what you expected. [+ **that**] *It's ironic that she was hurt by the very person she's trying to help.* •**ironically** *adverb*

ironing /ˈaɪənɪŋ/ *noun* [U] **1** ACTIVITY the activity of making clothes flat and smooth using an iron (= a piece of electrical equipment) *John was* ***doing the ironing****.* **2** CLOTHES the clothes that are waiting to be ironed, or those that have just been ironed *a basket full of ironing*

ˈironing ˌboard *noun* [C] a narrow table that you use for ironing

irony /ˈaɪərᵊni/ *noun* **1** SITUATION [C, U] a situation that is strange because it is the opposite of what you expected *The irony is that now he's retired, he's busier than ever.* **2** HUMOUR [U] a type of humour in which people say something they do not mean

irradiate /ɪˈreɪdieɪt/ *verb* [T] **FOOD** to treat with radiation, especially food to keep it fresh •**irradiation** *noun* [U]

irrational /ɪˈræʃᵊnᵊl/ *adjective* Irrational feelings and actions are based on your emotions and not on good reasons. ***irrational behaviour*** ○ *an* ***irrational fear*** *of flying* •**irrationality** /ɪˌræʃᵊnˈæləti/ *noun* [U] •**irrationally** *adverb*

iˌrrational ˈnumber *noun* [C] **MATHEMATICS** a number that cannot be expressed as the ratio (= relationship expressed in numbers showing how much bigger one thing is than the other) of two whole numbers

irreconcilable /ˌɪrekᵊnˈsaɪləbl/ *adjective formal* Irreconcilable beliefs, opinions, etc are so different that no agreement is possible. ***Irreconcilable differences*** *led to their divorce.*

irregular /ɪˈregjələʳ/ *adjective* **1** TIME Irregular actions or events happen with a different amount of time between each one. *an irregular heartbeat* ○ *They met at irregular intervals.* **2** SHAPE not smooth or straight, or having parts that are different sizes *an irregular coastline* **3** **LANGUAGE** not following the general rules in grammar *irregular verbs/plurals* **4** BEHAVIOUR *UK formal* slightly illegal, or not done in the usual and acceptable way *He led a very irregular life.* •**irregularity** /ɪˌregjəˈlærəti/ *noun* [C, U] •**irregularly** *adverb*

irrelevant /ɪˈreləvᵊnt/ *adjective* not important in a particular situation *The car had faults but these were* ***irrelevant to*** *the crash.* •**irrelevance** /ɪˈreləvᵊns/ *noun* [C, U] something that is irrelevant, or the quality of being irrelevant •**irrelevantly** *adverb*

irreparable /ɪˈrepᵊrəbl/ *adjective* Irreparable damage, harm, injury, etc is so bad that it can never be repaired. •**irreparably** *adverb*

irreplaceable /ˌɪrɪˈpleɪsəbl/ *adjective* Someone or something that is irreplaceable is so valuable or special that you could not get another one like them.

irrepressible /ˌɪrɪˈpresəbl/ *adjective* **1** PERSON always happy and energetic **2** FEELINGS An irrepressible feeling is impossible to control. *an irrepressible urge to travel* •**irrepressibly** *adverb*

irresistible /ˌɪrɪˈzɪstəbl/ *adjective* **1** ATTRACTIVE extremely attractive and impossible not to like or want *an irresistible smile* **2** STRONG too powerful to control or ignore *irresistible pressure* ○ *an irresistible desire to run away* •**irresistibly** *adverb*

irrespective /ˌɪrɪˈspektɪv/ *adverb* **irrespective of sth** used to say that something does not affect a situation *Everyone should be treated equally, irrespective of skin colour.*

irresponsible /ˌɪrɪˈspɒnsəbl/ *adjective* not thinking about the possible bad results of what you are doing *an irresponsible attitude* •**irresponsibility** /ˌɪrɪˌspɒnsəˈbɪləti/ *noun* [U] •**irresponsibly** *adverb*

irreverent /ɪˈrevᵊrᵊnt/ *adjective* not showing any respect for people or traditions that are usually respected *irreverent humour* •**irreverence** /ɪˈrevᵊrᵊns/ *noun* [U] when someone or something is irreverent •**irreverently** *adverb*

irreversible /ˌɪrɪˈvɜːsəbl/ *adjective* Something that is irreversible cannot be changed back to how it was before. *Smoking has caused **irreversible damage** to his lungs.* •**irreversibly** *adverb*

irrevocable /ɪˈrevəkəbl/ *adjective formal* impossible to change or stop ***irrevocable decisions*** •**irrevocably** *adverb*

irrigate /ˈɪrɪgeɪt/ *verb* [T] **FARMING** to provide water for an area of land so that crops can be grown •**irrigation** /ˌɪrɪˈgeɪʃᵊn/ *noun* [U]

irritable /ˈɪrɪtəbl/ *adjective* becoming annoyed very easily *Jack's been irritable all day.* •**irritability** /ˌɪrɪtəˈbɪləti/ *noun* [U] •**irritably** *adverb*

irritant /ˈɪrɪtᵊnt/ *noun* [C] **1** ANNOYING someone or something that makes you feel annoyed **2** **HEALTH** a substance that makes part of your body hurt

irritate /ˈɪrɪteɪt/ *verb* [T] **1** ANNOY to annoy someone *His comments really irritated me.* **2** **HEALTH** to make a part of your body hurt *The smoke irritated her eyes.* •**irritation** /ˌɪrɪˈteɪʃᵊn/ *noun* [C, U]

irritated /ˈɪrɪteɪtɪd/ *adjective* annoyed *Ben began to get increasingly **irritated by/at** her questions.* [+ **that**] *I was irritated that he didn't thank me.*

irritating /ˈɪrɪteɪtɪŋ/ *adjective* making you feel annoyed *an irritating habit* •**irritatingly** *adverb*

O→**is** *strong form* /ɪz/ *weak form* /z/ *present simple he/she/it of* be

Islam /ˈɪzlɑːm/ *noun* [U] **RELIGION** a religion based on belief in Allah, on the Koran, and on the teachings of Mohammed *The followers of Islam are called Muslims.*

Islamic /ɪzˈlæmɪk/ *adjective* **RELIGION** related to Islam *Islamic art* ○ *an Islamic country*

O→**island** /ˈaɪlənd/ *noun* [C] **GEOGRAPHY** an area of land that has water around it *the Caribbean island of Grenada* ○ *the Hawaiian Islands* •**islander** *noun* [C] someone who lives on an island ➲See also: **desert island**

isle /aɪl/ *noun* [C] **GEOGRAPHY** an island, often used in the name of a particular island *the British Isles*

islets of Langerhans /ˌaɪlɪtsəvˈlæŋgəhænz/ *noun* [**plural**] **ANATOMY** a group of cells in the pancreas that produce the hormones insulin and glucagon

O→**isn't** /ˈɪzᵊnt/ *short for* is not *Mike isn't coming with us.*

isobar /ˈaɪsəʊbɑːʳ/ *noun* [C] **GEOGRAPHY** a line drawn on a weather map joining all the places which have the same air pressure

isohyet /ˌaɪsəʊˈhaɪɪt/ *noun* [C] **GEOGRAPHY** a line on a map that connects places that have the same amount of rain

isolate /ˈaɪsəleɪt/ *verb* [T] to separate someone or something from other people or things *Scientists have been able to isolate the gene responsible for causing the illness.* ○ *He had been **isolated from** other prisoners.*

isolated /ˈaɪsəleɪtɪd/ *adjective* **1** FAR AWAY a long way from other places *an isolated village in the mountains* **2** ALONE alone and not having help or support from other people *Kazuo felt very isolated at his new school.* **3** **an isolated case/example/incident, etc** an event, action, etc that happens only once

isolation /ˌaɪsᵊlˈeɪʃᵊn/ *noun* **1** SEPARATE [U] the state of being separate from other people, places, or things *the country's economic isolation from the rest of the world* **2** **in isolation** alone, or separately from other people, places, or things *These poems cannot be considered in isolation.* **3** LONELY [U] a feeling of being lonely *I had this awful sense of isolation.*

isomer /ˈaɪsəməʳ/ *noun* [C] **CHEMISTRY** any one of a group of chemical substances which all have the same number and type of atoms but in which the arrangement of the atoms is slightly different between each substance

isomerism /ˈaɪsəmərɪzm/ *noun* [U] **CHEMISTRY** when two or more compounds have the same type of molecule but a different arrangement of atoms in the molecule

isometric /ˌaɪsəʊˈmetrɪk/ *adjective* **ART, DT** isometric drawing uses a method of drawing a shape with three dimensions using two dimensions *isometric projection*

isosceles triangle /aɪˌsɒsəliːzˈtraɪæŋgl/ *noun* [C] **MATHEMATICS** a triangle with two sides of equal length ➲Compare **equilateral, scalene triangle**

isotope /ˈaɪ.sə.təʊp/ *noun* [C] **CHEMISTRY** a form of an atom which has a different atomic weight from other forms of the same atom but the same chemical structure •**isotopic** /aɪsəˈtɒpɪk/ *adjective*

ISP /ˌaɪesˈpiː/ *noun* [C] **COMPUTING, INTERNET** *abbreviation for* Internet service provider: a company that connects your computer to the Internet, and lets you use email and other services

WORD PARTNERS FOR ***issue (noun)***

a **contentious / important / key / major / thorny** issue • **address/discuss/raise/resolve** an issue • the issue **of** sth

issue¹ /ˈɪʃuː/ *noun* **1** PROBLEM [C] an important subject or problem that people are discussing *the issues of race and social class* ○ *political issues* ○ *Chris has* ***raised*** *a very important* ***issue.*** **2** NEWSPAPER OR MAGAZINE [C] the newspaper, magazine, etc that is produced on a particular day *Have you seen the latest issue of Computer World?* **3 at issue** most important in what is being discussed *The point at issue is what is best for the child.* **4 take issue (with sb/sth)** to disagree with what someone says or writes *I would take issue with you on that.* **5 have issues with sth** to often be sad, anxious or angry because of something *A very high proportion of women diet frequently and have issues with their bodies.*

WORD PARTNERS FOR ***issue (verb)***

issue an **order/statement/warning** • issue **guidelines/instructions**

issue² /ˈɪʃuː/ *verb* [T] **issuing**, *past* **issued** **1** SAY PUBLICLY to say something officially *The Prime Minister will* ***issue a statement*** *tomorrow.* ○ *Police* ***issued*** *a* ***warning*** *about the dangers of playing near water.* **2** GIVE OFFICIALLY to officially give something to someone *to* ***issue*** *a* ***passport/ticket/invitation*** ○ *All members will be* ***issued with*** *a membership card.*

IT /ˌaɪˈtiː/ *noun* [U] **COMPUTING** *abbreviation for* information technology: the use of computers and other electronic equipment to store and send information

it /ɪt/ *pronoun* **1** THING used to refer to the thing, situation, or idea that has already been talked about *"Have you seen my bag?" "It's in the hall."* **2** DESCRIPTION used before certain adjectives, nouns, or verbs to introduce an opinion or description of a situation *It's unlikely that she'll arrive on time.* **3** SUBJECT/OBJECT used with certain verbs that need a subject or object but do not refer to a particular noun *It costs less if you travel at the weekend.* ○ *I liked it in Scotland.* **4** TIME/WEATHER used with the verb 'be' in sentences giving the time, date, weather or distances *It rained all day.* ○ *What time is it?* **5** SEEM used as the subject of verbs such as 'seem', 'appear' and 'look' *It seemed unfair to leave her at home.* **6** EMPHASIZE used to emphasize one part of a sentence *It's the children I'm concerned about, not me.* **7 it's sb/sth** used to say the name of a person or thing when the person you are speaking to does not know *It's your Dad on the phone.*

italics /ɪˈtælɪks/ *noun* [plural] **LANGUAGE** a style of writing or printing in which the letters slope to the right •**italic** *adjective* written in italics

itch¹ /ɪtʃ/ *verb* **1** **HEALTH** [I] If a part of your body itches, it feels uncomfortable and you want to rub it with your nails. *Woollen sweaters make my arms itch.* **2 be itching to do sth** *informal* to want to do something very much *You could tell that they were itching to leave.*

itch² /ɪtʃ/ *noun* [C] **HEALTH** an uncomfortable feeling on your skin that makes you want to rub it with your nails *I've* ***got an itch*** *in the middle of my back.*

itching /ˈɪtʃɪŋ/ *noun* [U] **HEALTH** when a part of your body itches *a lotion to stop itching*

itchy /ˈɪtʃi/ *adjective* **HEALTH** If a part of your body is itchy, it feels uncomfortable and you want to rub it with your nails. *an itchy nose* •**itchiness** *noun* [U]

it'd /ˈɪtəd/ **1** IT WOULD *short for* it would *It'd be great if we could meet next week.* **2** IT HAD *short for* it had *It'd taken us an hour to find Bruce's house.*

item /ˈaɪtəm/ *noun* [C] **1** SINGLE THING a single thing in a set or on a list *the last item on the list* ○ *Various stolen items were found.* **2** PIECE OF NEWS a piece of news on television or radio, or in a newspaper *a small item on the back page of the local newspaper*

itemize (*also UK* **-ise**) /ˈaɪtəmaɪz/ *verb* [T] to list things separately, often including details about each thing *an* ***itemized*** *phone* ***bill***

iteration /ˌɪtəˈreɪʃən/ *noun* [C] **COMPUTING** a new version of a piece of software

itinerant /aɪˈtɪnərənt/ *adjective* [always before noun] *formal* travelling from one place to another *an itinerant preacher*

itinerary /aɪˈtɪnərəri/ *noun* [C] a list of places that you plan to visit on a journey *The President's itinerary includes visits to Boston and New York.*

it'll /ˈɪtəl/ *short for* it will *It'll take about twenty minutes to get there.*

it's /ɪts/ **1** IT IS *short for* it is *"What time is it?" "It's one o'clock."* **2** IT HAS *short for* it has *It's been a long day and I'm tired.*

its /ɪts/ *determiner* belonging to or relating to the thing that has already been talked about *The house has its own swimming pool.*

itself /ɪtˈself/ *pronoun* **1** REFLEXIVE the reflexive form of the pronoun 'it' *The cat licked itself clean.* **2** EMPHASIS used to emphasize the particular thing you are referring to *The garden is enormous but the house itself is very small.* **3 (all) by itself a** ALONE alone *The dog was in the house by itself for several days.* **b** AUTOMATIC automatically *The heating comes on by itself.* **4 in itself** as the only thing being talked about and nothing else *You've managed to complete the course - that in itself is an achievement.*

ITV /ˌaɪtiːˈviː/ *noun abbreviation for* Independent Television: one of the main television companies in the United Kingdom *There's a good film on ITV tonight.*

IV /ˌaɪˈviː/ *US* (*UK* **drip**) *noun* [C] **HEALTH** a piece of medical equipment used for putting liquids into your body

I've /aɪv/ *short for* I have *I've decided not to go.*

IVF /ˌaɪviːˈef/ *noun* [U] **HEALTH** *abbreviation for* in vitro fertilization: a treatment where a woman's egg is fertilized outside her body and put back in her body for the baby to grow

ivory /ˈaɪvəri/ *noun* [U] a hard, white substance from the tusks (= long teeth) of some animals, such as elephants (= large, grey animals)

ivy /ˈaɪvi/ *noun* [U] a dark green plant that often grows up walls

J, j /dʒeɪ/ the tenth letter of the alphabet

jab¹ /dʒæb/ *verb* [I, T] **jabbing**, *past* **jabbed** to push something quickly and hard into or towards another thing *He **jabbed** a finger **into** her back.*

jab² /dʒæb/ *noun* [C] **1** a quick, hard push into or towards something **2** HEALTH *UK informal* an injection (= when a drug is put in your body with a needle) *a flu jab*

jack¹ /dʒæk/ *noun* [C] **1** EQUIPMENT a piece of equipment for lifting a heavy object such as a car **2** PLAYING CARD a playing card that comes between a ten and a queen *the jack of diamonds*

jack² /dʒæk/ *verb*
jack sth in *phrasal verb UK informal* to stop doing something, especially a job *She's **jacked in** her **job**.*
jack sth up *phrasal verb informal* to increase a price or rate suddenly and by a large amount

jackal /ˈdʒækᵊl/ *noun* [C] a wild dog that hunts in groups

O⊷**jacket** /ˈdʒækɪt/ *noun* [C] a short coat *a leather jacket* ⊃See colour picture **Clothes** on page Centre 8 ⊃See also: **dinner jacket, life jacket, strait-jacket**

ˌjacket poˈtato *noun* [C] *plural* **jacket potatoes** *UK* FOOD a potato that has been baked in the oven with its skin on

jack-knife¹ /ˈdʒæknaɪf/ *noun* [C] *plural* **jack-knives** a knife with a blade that can be folded away into the handle

jack-knife² /ˈdʒækˌnaɪf/ *verb* [I] If a large truck jack-knifes, the front part turns round to face the back in a way that is not controlled.

jackpot /ˈdʒækpɒt/ *noun* **1** [C] an amount of money that is the largest prize anyone can win in a competition **2 hit the jackpot** to be very successful, especially by winning or earning a lot of money

Jacuzzi /dʒəˈkuːzi/ *noun* [C] *trademark* a bath or pool that produces bubbles in the water

jade /dʒeɪd/ *noun* [U] GEOLOGY a green stone used in making jewellery

jaded /ˈdʒeɪdɪd/ *adjective* tired or bored with something, especially because you have done it too much

jagged /ˈdʒægɪd/ *adjective* very rough and sharp ***jagged rocks***

jaguar /ˈdʒægjuəʳ/ *noun* [C] a large, wild cat that lives in Central and South America

WORD PARTNERS FOR ***jail***

be released from/be sent to jail • **in** jail • **a** jail **sentence**

jail¹ (*also UK* **gaol**) /dʒeɪl/ *noun* [C, U] a place where criminals are kept as a punishment *He ended up **in jail**.*

jail² /dʒeɪl/ *verb* [T] to put someone in a jail [**often passive**] *He was jailed for two years.*

jailer /ˈdʒeɪləʳ/ *noun* [C] someone who guards prisoners in a jail

jam¹ /dʒæm/ *noun* **1** FOOD [C, U] (*also US* **jelly**) a sweet food made from fruit that you spread on bread *a jar of strawberry jam* ⊃See colour picture **Food** on page Centre 11 **2** [C] (*also* **traffic jam**) a line of cars, trucks, etc that are moving slowly or not moving *We were stuck **in a jam** for hours.*

jam² /dʒæm/ *verb* **jamming**, *past* **jammed 1 jam sth in/into/on, etc** to push something somewhere firmly and tightly *She jammed her hands into her pockets.* **2** STUCK [I, T] to get stuck or make something get stuck *The machine keeps jamming.* **3** FILL [T] to fill a place completely [**often passive**] *The streets were **jammed with** cars.* **4** STOP RADIO [T] to send a signal that stops a radio being able to broadcast

jamboree /ˌdʒæmbᵊrˈiː/ *noun* [C] a big celebration or party

Jan *written abbreviation for* January

jangle /ˈdʒæŋgl/ *verb* [I, T] If small metal objects jangle, they hit together making a ringing noise, and if you jangle them, you make them make this noise. *He was jangling his keys.* •**jangle** *noun* [C]

janitor /ˈdʒænɪtəʳ/ *noun* [C] *US* someone whose job is to look after a building *the school janitor*

O⊷**January** /ˈdʒænjuᵊri/ (*written abbreviation* **Jan**) *noun* [C, U] the first month of the year

jar¹ /dʒɑːʳ/ *noun* [C] a glass container used for storing food *a jar of jam*

jar² /dʒɑːʳ/ *verb* **jarring**, *past* **jarred** HIT [I, T] to move suddenly, hitting something and causing pain or damage *The movement jarred his injured leg.*
jar on sb *phrasal verb UK* to annoy someone *Her voice jars on me.*

jargon /ˈdʒɑːgən/ *noun* [U] LANGUAGE words and phrases used by particular groups of people that are difficult for other people to understand *legal jargon*

jaundice /ˈdʒɔːndɪs/ *noun* [U] HEALTH a disease that makes your eyes and skin yellow

jaundiced /ˈdʒɔːndɪst/ *adjective* having a negative opinion of something because of bad things that have happened to you ***a jaundiced view** of marriage*

jaunt /dʒɔːnt/ *noun* [C] a short, enjoyable journey

jaunty /ˈdʒɔːnti/ *adjective* happy and confident *a **jaunty walk***

javelin /ˈdʒævᵊlɪn/ *noun* **1** SPORT [C] a long, pointed stick that you throw as a sport **2 the javelin** SPORT a sport in which you throw a javelin as far as you can ⊃See colour picture **Sports 1** on page Centre 14

jaw /dʒɔː/ *noun* [C] **1** ANATOMY either of the two bones in your mouth that contain your teeth ⊃See colour picture **The Body** on page Centre 13 ⊃See picture at **skull 2 sb's jaw drops** If someone's jaw drops, their mouth opens because they are very surprised.

jazz /dʒæz/ *noun* [U] MUSIC music with a strong beat that is often played without written music *a **jazz band***

J

WORD PARTNERS FOR ***jealous***

make sb jealous • **insanely/madly** jealous • jealous **of** sb/sth

jealous /ˈdʒeləs/ *adjective* **1** WANTING SOMETHING unhappy and angry because you want something that someone else has *His new bike was **making** his friends **jealous**.* ○ *Steve has always been **jealous of** his brother's good looks.* **2** LOVE upset and angry because someone you love seems too interested in another person *a jealous husband* •**jealously** *adverb*

jealousy /ˈdʒeləsi/ *noun* [U] jealous feelings

O-→**jeans** /dʒiːnz/ *noun* [plural] trousers made from denim (= a strong, usually blue, material) *a **pair of jeans*** ➲See colour picture **Clothes** on page Centre 8

Jeep /dʒiːp/ *noun* [C] *trademark* a strongly built vehicle with big wheels that is used for driving over rough ground

jeer /dʒɪəʳ/ *verb* [I, T] to laugh and shout insults at someone *The crowd outside his house jeered as he left.* •**jeer** *noun* [C]

J

Jell-O /ˈdʒeləʊ/ *noun* [U] *US trademark* **FOOD** jelly

jelly /ˈdʒeli/ *noun* [C, U] **1 FOOD** *UK* (*US* **Jell-O**) a soft but solid sweet food that shakes when you move it *jelly and ice cream* **2 FOOD** *US* (*UK/US* **jam**) a sweet food made from fruit that you spread on bread **3** any substance that looks or feels like jelly *The egg is surrounded by a layer of jelly.*

jellyfish /ˈdʒelifɪʃ/ *noun* [C] *plural* **jellyfish** a sea creature with a clear body that may sting you (= put poison into your skin)

jelutong /ˈdʒeljətɒŋ/ *noun* [U] **DT** a type of soft wood often used to make models

jeopardize (*also UK* **-ise**) /ˈdʒepədaɪz/ *verb* [T] to put something in a situation where there is a risk of failing or being harmed *Bad weather could jeopardize all our plans.*

jeopardy /ˈdʒepədi/ *noun* **in jeopardy** in danger of failing or being harmed *If the factory closes, local jobs will be in jeopardy.*

jerk¹ /dʒɜːk/ *verb* [I, T] to move very quickly and suddenly, or to make something move like this *The truck jerked forward.*

jerk² /dʒɜːk/ *noun* [C] **1** MOVEMENT a quick, sudden movement *a sudden jerk of the head* **2** STUPID PERSON *mainly US informal* a stupid or annoying person

jerky /ˈdʒɜːki/ *adjective* Jerky movements are quick and sudden. •**jerkily** *adverb*

jersey /ˈdʒɜːzi/ *noun* **1** PIECE OF CLOTHING [C] a piece of clothing which covers the top of your body and is pulled on over your head **2** CLOTH [U] soft wool or cotton cloth used for making clothes

jest /dʒest/ *noun* **in jest** said as a joke

Jesus Christ /ˌdʒiːzəsˈkraɪst/ *noun* **RELIGION** the Jewish holy man believed by Christians to be the Son of God, and on whose life and teachings Christianity is based

jet¹ /dʒet/ *noun* [C] **1** AIRCRAFT an aircraft that flies very fast ➲See also: **jumbo jet** **2** WATER OR GAS water or gas that is forced out of something in a thin, strong line

jet² /dʒet/ *verb* [I] **jetting**, *past* **jetted jet in/off, etc** to fly somewhere in an aircraft *She jetted off to Athens for a week.*

jet-black /ˌdʒetˈblæk/ *noun* [U] a very dark black colour •**jet-black** *adjective jet-black hair*

ˈ**jet ˌengine** *noun* [C] an engine that makes an aircraft fly very fast

ˈ**jet ˌlag** *noun* [U] when you feel tired because you have just travelled a long distance on an aircraft

jettison /ˈdʒetɪsᵊn/ *verb* [T] **1** NOT WANT/NEED to get rid of something you do not want or need *The station has jettisoned educational broadcasts.* **2** MAKE LIGHTER If an aircraft or a ship jettisons something, it throws it off to make itself lighter.

jetty /ˈdʒeti/ *noun* [C] a wooden structure at the edge of the sea or a lake where people can get on and off boats

Jew /dʒuː/ *noun* [C] **RELIGION, SOCIETY** someone whose religion is Judaism, or who is related to the ancient people of Israel

jewel /ˈdʒuːəl/ *noun* [C] a valuable stone that is used to make jewellery

jeweller *UK* (*US* **jeweler**) /ˈdʒuːələ/ *noun* [C] someone whose job is to sell or make jewellery

jewellery *UK* (*US* **jewelry**) /ˈdʒuːəlri/ *noun* [U] objects made from gold, silver, and valuable stones that you wear for decoration

Jewish /ˈdʒuːɪʃ/ *adjective* **RELIGION, SOCIETY** relating or belonging to the Jews *Jewish history/law*

jibe (*also* **gibe**) /dʒaɪb/ *noun* [C] an insulting remark *He kept making **jibes at** me about my weight.*

jig /dʒɪg/ *noun* [C] **1 MUSIC** a traditional, quick dance, or the music it is danced to **2 DT** a piece of equipment that guides a tool for cutting and holds the object being cut

jiggle /ˈdʒɪgl/ *verb* [I, T] to make quick, short movements from side to side or to make something else move like this

jigsaw /ˈdʒɪgsɔː/ (*also* ˈ**jigsaw ˌpuzzle**) *noun* [C] a picture in many small pieces that you put together as a game

jingle¹ /ˈdʒɪŋgl/ *noun* [C] **1 MUSIC** a short song that is used to advertise a product on the radio or television **2** a sound made when small metal objects hit against each other

jingle² /ˈdʒɪŋgl/ *verb* [I, T] to make the sound of small metal objects hitting against each other *a pocket full of jingling coins*

jinx /dʒɪŋks/ *noun* [C] someone or something that brings bad luck *There seems to be **a jinx on** the school.* •**jinx** *verb* [T]

JIT /ˌdʒeɪaɪˈtiː/ *adjective* [always before noun] *abbreviation for* just-in-time

jitters /ˈdʒɪtəz/ *noun* [plural] a nervous feeling *Hospitals give me **the jitters**.*

jittery /ˈdʒɪtᵊri/ *adjective* nervous *She gets quite **jittery about** exams.*

Jnr *UK* (*UK/US* **Jr**) *written abbreviation for* junior (= the younger of two men in a family with the same name)

OTHER WAYS OF SAYING *job*

A more formal alternative is the noun **occupation**: *Please fill in your name, age and **occupation**.*

The nouns **post** and **position** are often used to talk about a particular job within an organisation: *She's applied for a part-time teaching **post/position**.*

The noun **career** is sometimes used to describe a job that a person does for a long period in their life: *She's had a very successful **career** in marketing.*

A **placement** (*UK*) (**internship** *US*) is a job that someone does for a short time in order to learn more about a particular kind of work: *He's got a year's **placement** in the medical labs.*

WORD PARTNERS FOR *job*

a **dead-end/full-time/good/part-time/temporary** job • **apply for/create/do/find/get/lose** a job • a job **as** sth

o-- **job** /dʒɒb/ *noun* [C] **1** PAID EMPLOYMENT the regular work that you do in order to earn money *She **got a job** in publishing.* ○ *Hundreds of workers could **lose** their **jobs**.* ○ *Why don't you **apply for a** part-time **job**?* ➲See Common Learner Error at **work** **2** PIECE OF WORK a piece of work that you have to do *cooking, cleaning and other household jobs* **3** RESPONSIBILITY something that is your responsibility *It's my job to water the plants.* **4 make a bad/good, etc job of sth** *UK* to do sth badly/well, etc **5 do a good/excellent, etc job** to do something well/very well, etc *She did a great job of organizing the event.* **6 out of a job** without a job *How long have you been out of a job?* **7 do the job** If something does the job, it is suitable for a particular purpose. *Here, this knife should do the job.* **8 it's a good job** *UK informal* If it is a good job that something happened, it is lucky that it happened. [+ (that)] *It's a good job that Jo was there to help you.* **9 just the job** *UK* If something is just the job, it is exactly what you want or need.

ˈjob deˌscription *noun* [C] a list of the things you must do in your work

jobless /ˈdʒɒbləs/ *adjective* **SOCIETY** without a job *young jobless people*

ˈjob proˌduction *noun* [U] in business, the production of single products for different customers

ˈjob satisˌfaction *noun* [U] the amount of pleasure and achievement your job makes you feel

ˈjob seˌcurity *noun* [U] If you have job security, your job is likely to be permanent.

jobshare /ˈdʒɒbʃeəʳ/ *verb* [I] *UK* If two people jobshare, they do one job between them, working at different times. •**jobshare** *noun UK*

jockey /ˈdʒɒki/ *noun* [C] **SPORT** someone who rides horses in races ➲See also: **disc jockey**

jog /dʒɒg/ *verb* **jogging**, *past* **jogged** **1 SPORT** [I] to run slowly for exercise *I jog through the park every morning.* **2** [T] to hit something gently by mistake *He jogged her arm.* **3 jog sb's memory** to cause someone to remember something *They hoped the photographs would jog his memory.* •**jog** *noun* [no plural] *Let's go for a jog.* •**jogging** *noun* [U]

jogger /ˈdʒɒgəʳ/ *noun* [C] **SPORT** someone who runs for exercise

o-- **join**[1] /dʒɔɪn/ *verb* **1** BECOME MEMBER [T] to become a member of a group or organization *He joined the army when he was eighteen.* **2** DO WITH OTHERS [T] to do something or go somewhere with someone *Would you like to join us for dinner?* **3** FASTEN [T] to fasten or connect things together ***Join** the ends **together** with strong glue.* **4** MEET [I, T] to meet at a particular point *The Mississippi River and the Missouri join near St Louis.* **5 join a line** (*also UK* **join a queue**) to go and stand at the end of a row of people waiting for something ➲See also: join forces (**force**[1])

COMMON LEARNER ERROR

join

Join is not followed by a preposition when it is used in expressions such as 'join a company'.

He joined the team in 1998.

~~*He joined to the team in 1998.*~~

o-- **join in (sth)** *phrasal verb* to become involved in an activity with other people *We're playing cards. Would you like to join in?*

join up *phrasal verb* to become a member of the army or other military group

join[2] /dʒɔɪn/ *noun* [C] *UK* the place where two or more things are fastened together

joined-up /ˌdʒɔɪnˈdʌp/ *adjective UK* **1 joined-up writing** a style of writing where each letter in a word is connected to the next one **2 joined-up thinking** thinking about a complicated problem in an intelligent and original way, and considering everything that is connected with it

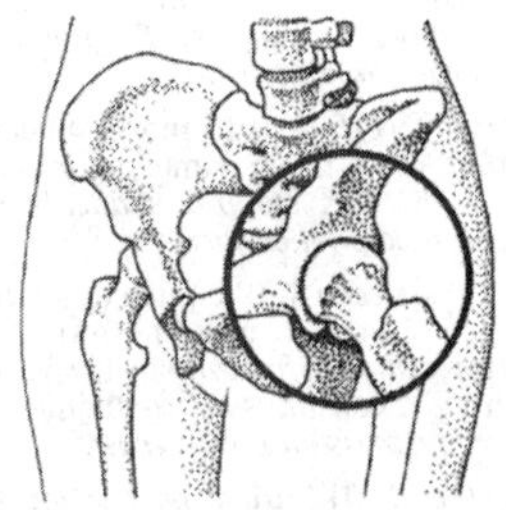

joint

joint[1] /dʒɔɪnt/ *adjective* [always before noun] belonging to or done by two or more people *a **joint** statement* ○ *The project was a **joint** effort by all the children in the class.* •**jointly** *adverb*

joint[2] /dʒɔɪnt/ *noun* [C] **1 ANATOMY** a place in your body where two bones meet *the knee joint* **2 FOOD** *UK* a large piece of meat, usually cooked in the oven *a joint of beef* **3** CONNECTION a place where parts of a structure or machine are connected **4** PLACE *informal* a place where something is sold, especially a restaurant or bar *a pizza joint*

joint-stock company /ˌdʒɔɪntstɒkˈkʌmpəni/ *noun* [C] a business which is owned by the group of people who have shares (= parts of a business) in the company

ˌjoint ˈventure *noun* [C] a business activity that is done by two separate companies working together

WORD PARTNERS FOR ***joke***

crack/make/tell a joke • a **dirty/sick** joke • a joke **about** sth

O—**joke¹** /dʒəʊk/ *noun* **1** [C] something which someone says to make people laugh, usually a short story with a funny ending *to **tell/make** a joke* **2 be a joke** *informal* to not be serious or not deserve respect *The investigation was a joke.* **3 be no joke** to be serious or difficult *It's no joke driving on icy roads.* **4 take a joke** to understand and accept a trick without becoming angry or upset ➲See also: **practical joke**

joke² /dʒəʊk/ *verb* **1** [I] to say funny things, or not be serious *She always **jokes about** her husband's cooking.* **2 You must be joking!/You're joking!** *informal* something you say to show that you are surprised by what someone has said, or do not believe it is true •**jokingly** *adverb*

joker /ˈdʒəʊkəʳ/ *noun* [C] **1** PERSON someone who likes saying or doing funny things **2** CARD one of a set of playing cards which can be used instead of another card in some games

jolly¹ /ˈdʒɒli/ *adjective* happy or enjoyable *We had a jolly evening.*

jolly² /ˈdʒɒli/ *adverb old-fashioned* very *a jolly good idea*

jolt¹ /dʒəʊlt/ *noun* [C] **1** SUDDEN MOVEMENT a sudden, violent movement *With a **sudden jolt** the train started moving again.* **2** SHOCK an unpleasant shock or surprise *The reminder that he was dead **gave** her **a jolt**.*

jolt² /dʒəʊlt/ *verb* [I, T] to move suddenly and forcefully, or to make someone or something do this *The bus stopped suddenly and the passengers were jolted forward.*

jostle /ˈdʒɒsl/ *verb* [I, T] to push other people in order to get somewhere in a crowd

jostle for sth *phrasal verb* to try hard to get something *Thousands of companies are jostling for business on the Internet.*

jot /dʒɒt/ *verb* [T] **jotting**, *past* **jotted** to write something quickly *She **jotted** a note to Sue.*

jot sth down *phrasal verb* to write something quickly on a piece of paper so that you remember it *I **jotted down** some **notes** during his speech.*

joule /dʒuːl/ (*abbreviation* **J**) *noun* [C] **MEASURES, PHYSICS** a unit of energy or work done

journal /ˈdʒɜːnəl/ *noun* [C] **1** MAGAZINE a magazine containing articles about a particular subject *a medical journal* **2** BOOK a book in which you regularly write about what has happened to you **3 FINANCE** a book in which financial records of different types are kept

journalism /ˈdʒɜːnəlɪzəm/ *noun* [U] the work of writing articles for newspapers, magazines, television, or radio

O—**journalist** /ˈdʒɜːnəlɪst/ *noun* [C] someone whose job is journalism

journalistic /ˌdʒɜːnəlˈɪstɪk/ *adjective* relating to journalism or typical of journalism

WORD PARTNERS FOR ***journey***

an **arduous/long/perilous/short** journey • **begin/complete/embark on/go on/make** a journey

O—**journey** /ˈdʒɜːni/ *noun* [C] when you travel from one place to another *a car/train journey* ○ *We take games for the children when we **go on** long **journeys**.* ➲See Common Learner Error at **travel**

jovial /ˈdʒəʊviəl/ *adjective* happy and friendly *a jovial man*

joy /dʒɔɪ/ *noun* **1** HAPPINESS [U] a feeling of great happiness *the joy of winning* **2** PLEASURE [C] something or someone that makes you feel very happy *She's a joy to work with.* **3** SUCCESS [U] *UK informal* success *I tried ringing for a plumber, but had **no joy**.*

joyful /ˈdʒɔɪfəl/ *adjective* very happy, or making people feel very happy *joyful news* •**joyfully** *adverb*

joyous /ˈdʒɔɪəs/ *adjective literary* extremely happy, or making people extremely happy •**joyously** *adverb*

joypad /ˈdʒɔɪpæd/ *noun* [C] **COMPUTING** a gamepad

joyriding /ˈdʒɔɪˌraɪdɪŋ/ *noun* [U] stealing cars and driving them fast and dangerously •**joyride** /ˈdʒɔɪraɪd/ *noun* [C] *They took the car for a joyride.* •**joyrider** *noun* [C]

joystick /ˈdʒɔɪstɪk/ *noun* [C] **COMPUTING** a vertical handle you move to control a computer game, machine, or aircraft

JP /ˌdʒeɪˈpiː/ *noun* [C] **LAW** *abbreviation for* Justice of the Peace: a judge in a small or local court of law

JPEG /ˈdʒeɪpeg/ *noun* **1 COMPUTING** [U] *abbreviation for* joint photographics experts group: a system for making electronic pictures use less space **2 COMPUTING** [C] a type of computer file (= collection of information) that contains pictures or photographs

Jr (*also UK* **Jnr**) *written abbreviation for* junior (= the younger of two men in a family with the same name) *John F. Kennedy, Jr.*

jubilant /ˈdʒuːbɪlənt/ *adjective* feeling or showing great happiness, usually because of a success *jubilant United supporters* •**jubilation** /ˌdʒuːbɪˈleɪʃən/ *noun* [U] a feeling of great happiness and success

jubilee /ˈdʒuːbɪliː/ *noun* [C] a celebration of an important event in the past, usually one which happened 25 or 50 years ago *a **golden jubilee*** (= 50 years) ○ *a **silver jubilee*** (= 25 years)

Judaism /ˈdʒuːdeɪɪzəm/ *noun* [U] **RELIGION** the religion of the Jewish people, based on belief in one God and on the laws contained in the Torah

judge¹ /dʒʌdʒ/ *noun* [C] **1** **LAW** someone who controls a trial in court, decides how criminals should be punished, and makes decisions about legal things *Judge Moylan* ○ *The judge ruled that they had acted correctly.* **2** someone who decides which person or thing wins a competition *the Olympic judges* **3** **a bad/good, etc judge of sth** someone who is usually wrong, usually right, etc when they judge something *a good judge of character*

O⸻**judge²** /dʒʌdʒ/ *verb* **1** DEVELOP OPINION [I, T] to have or develop an opinion about something or someone, usually after thinking carefully [+ **question word**] *I can't judge whether he's telling the truth or not.* ○ *You shouldn't* ***judge*** *people* ***on*** *their appearances.* ○ *He was judged guilty/insane.* **2** **judging by/from** used to express the reasons why you have a particular opinion *She must be popular judging by the number of letters that she receives.* **3** COMPETITION [I, T] to decide the winner or results of a competition *I've been asked to judge the art contest.* **4** BAD OPINION [I, T] to have a bad opinion of someone's behaviour, often because you think you are better than them *What gives you the right to judge people?* **5** GUESS [T] to try to guess something, especially a measurement *I find it difficult to judge distances.*

WORD PARTNERS FOR ***judgment***

make/pass/reserve judgment • **poor/good** judgment • a **harsh/subjective** judgment • an **error/lapse** of judgment

O⸻**judgment** (*also* **judgement**) /ˈdʒʌdʒmənt/ *noun* **1** OPINION [C, U] an opinion about someone or something that you decide on after thinking carefully *The inspector needs to* ***make a judgment*** *about how the school is performing.* **2** ABILITY [U] the ability to make good decisions or to be right in your opinions *to have good/bad judgment* **3** LEGAL DECISION [C, U] an official legal decision, usually made by a judge

judgmental (*also UK* **judgemental**) /dʒʌdʒˈmentᵊl/ *adjective* quick to criticize people

judicial /dʒuːˈdɪʃᵊl/ *adjective* **LAW** relating to a court of law or the legal system *a* ***judicial inquiry***

the judiciary /dʒuːˈdɪʃᵊri/ *noun* **LAW** all the judges in a country

judicious /dʒuːˈdɪʃəs/ *adjective* done or decided carefully and with good judgment

judo /ˈdʒuːdəʊ/ *noun* [U] **SPORT** a sport from Japan in which two people try to throw each other to the ground

jug /dʒʌg/ *noun* [C] a container with a handle used for pouring out liquids *a jug of water*

juggle /ˈdʒʌgl/ *verb* **1** MANAGE MANY THINGS [T] to try to do several things at once, when it is difficult to have enough time *Many women have to juggle work and family.* **2** THROW AND CATCH [I, T] to keep two or more objects such as balls in the air by throwing them repeatedly, usually in order to entertain people

juggler /ˈdʒʌgləʳ/ *noun* [C] someone who juggles objects to entertain people

O⸻**juice** /dʒuːs/ *noun* [C, U] **FOOD** the liquid that comes from fruit or vegetables ➲See also: **orange juice**

juices /ˈdʒuːsɪz/ *noun* [plural] **FOOD** the liquid that comes from cooked meat

juicy /ˈdʒuːsi/ *adjective* **1** **FOOD** full of juice *juicy apples* **2** interesting because of shocking or personal information ***juicy gossip***

jukebox /ˈdʒuːkbɒks/ *noun* [C] **MUSIC** a machine, usually in a bar, which plays a song when you put money into it

O⸻**July** /dʒʊˈlaɪ/ *noun* [C, U] the seventh month of the year ➲See also: **Fourth of July**

jumble¹ /ˈdʒʌmbl/ *noun* [no plural] a confused mixture or group of things *Her handbag is* ***a jumble of*** *pens, make-up, and keys.*

jumble² /ˈdʒʌmbl/ (*also* **jumble up**) *verb* [T] to mix things together in an untidy way [**often passive**] *Her clothes were all jumbled up in the suitcase.*

ˈjumble ˌsale *UK* (*US* **rummage sale**) *noun* [C] a sale of old items, especially clothes, usually to make money for an organization

jumbo /ˈdʒʌmbəʊ/ *adjective* [**always before noun**] extra large *a jumbo bag of sweets*

ˌjumbo ˈjet *noun* [C] a very large aircraft for carrying passengers

O⸻**jump¹** /dʒʌmp/ *verb* **1** INTO AIR [I] to push your body up and away from the ground using your feet and legs *The children were* ***jumping up and down*** *with excitement.* ○ *I jumped over the log.* ○ *They jumped into the water.* **2** **jump into/up, etc** to move somewhere suddenly and quickly *She jumped into a taxi and rushed to the station.* **3** GO OVER [T] to move over something by moving up into the air *The horse jumped the last fence.* **4** INCREASE [I, T] to suddenly increase by a large amount *House prices have jumped by 20%.* **5** FEAR [I] to make a sudden movement because you are frightened or surprised *Her scream* ***made me jump.*** ➲See also: get/jump on the **bandwagon**, jump to conclusions (**conclusion**), jump the **gun**¹, jump the **queue**

jump at sth *phrasal verb* to take an opportunity to have or do something in a very willing and excited way *He jumped at the chance to join the band.*

jump² /dʒʌmp/ *noun* [C] **1** MOVEMENT when you push your body up into the air using your feet and legs *He won with a jump of 8.5 metres.* **2** INCREASE a sudden increase in the amount of something *a jump in profits* ➲See also: **the high jump, the long jump**

jumper /ˈdʒʌmpəʳ/ *noun* [C] **1** WARM CLOTHING *UK* (*UK/US* **sweater**) a warm piece of clothing which covers the top of your body and is pulled on over your head ➲See colour picture **Clothes** on page Centre 5 **2** DRESS *US* (*UK* **pinafore**) a loose dress with no sleeves that is worn over other clothes such as a shirt

ˈjump ˌrope *US* (*UK* **skipping rope**) *noun* [C] **SPORT** a rope that you move over your head and then jump over as you move it under your feet

jumpy /ˈdʒʌmpi/ *adjective* nervous or anxious

J

WORD PARTNERS FOR ***junction***

the junction **of** sth **and** sth • a **railway/road** junction • a **busy** junction

junction /ˈdʒʌŋkʃᵊn/ *noun* [C] *UK* the place where two roads or railway lines meet or cross each other *The accident happened at a busy road junction.* ➲See also: **T-junction**

juncture /ˈdʒʌŋktʃəʳ/ *noun* [C] *formal* a particular point in an event or period of time

June /dʒuːn/ *noun* [C, U] the sixth month of the year

jungle /ˈdʒʌŋgl/ *noun* [C, U] an area of land, usually in tropical countries, where trees and plants grow close together

junior¹ /ˈdʒuːniəʳ/ *adjective* **1** LOW RANK low or lower in rank *a junior minister/senator* **2** YOUNG PEOPLE for or relating to young people *a junior tennis tournament* **3** NAME *mainly US* (*written abbreviation* **Jr**) used at the end of a man's name to show that he is the younger of two men in the same family who have the same name *Hello, I'd like to speak to Mr Anderson Junior, please.*

J

junior² /ˈdʒuːniəʳ/ *noun* **1 be 10/20, etc years sb's junior** to be 10, 20, etc years younger than someone *My wife is 8 years my junior.* **2** EDUCATION [C] a student in their third year of study at an American college or high school (= school for 15-18 year olds) **3** EDUCATION [C] *UK* a child who goes to a junior school

ˈjunior ˌcollege *noun* [C, U] EDUCATION a two-year college in the US where students can learn a skill or prepare to enter a university

ˌjunior ˈhigh school (*also* **ˌjunior ˈhigh**) *noun* [C, U] EDUCATION a school in the US or Canada for children who are 12 to 15 years old

ˈjunior ˌschool *noun* [C, U] EDUCATION a school in the UK for children who are 7 to 11 years old

junk /dʒʌŋk/ *noun* [U] *informal* old things which have little value

ˈjunk ˌfood *noun* [U] FOOD food which is unhealthy but is quick and easy to eat

junkie /ˈdʒʌŋki/ *noun* [C] *informal* **1** DRUGS someone who cannot stop taking illegal drugs **2** WANTING SOMETHING someone who wants something or wants to do something very much *a publicity junkie*

ˈjunk ˌmail *noun* [U] letters sent by companies to advertise their goods and services

junta /ˈdʒʌntə/ *noun* [C] POLITICS a military government that has taken power in a country by force

Jupiter /ˈdʒuːpɪtəʳ/ *noun* [no plural] ASTRONOMY the planet that is fifth from the Sun, after Mars and before Saturn ➲See picture at **solar system**

Jurassic /dʒʊəˈræsɪk/ *adjective* BIOLOGY, GEOLOGY from a period of time between around 208 and 146 million years ago, in which the first birds appeared and the single piece of land broke up into separate continents

jurisdiction /ˌdʒʊərɪsˈdɪkʃᵊn/ *noun* [U] LAW the legal power to make decisions and judgments *The school is **under the jurisdiction of** the local council.*

juror /ˈdʒʊərəʳ/ *noun* [C] LAW a member of a jury

WORD PARTNERS FOR ***jury***

be **on** a jury

jury /ˈdʒʊəri/ *noun* [group] **1** LAW a group of people in a court of law who decide if someone is guilty or not **2** a group of people who decide the winner of a competition

just¹ *strong form* /dʒʌst/ *weak form* /dʒəst/ *adverb* **1** ONLY only *I'll just have a small piece.* ○ *He just wants to win.* ○ *The film is not just about love.* **2** RECENTLY a very short time ago *I've just been on a trip to France.* ○ *We've only just begun.* **3** EMPHASIS used to emphasize something you say *I just can't bear it!* **4** ALMOST NOT *UK* almost not *This dress **only just** fits.* **5** EXACTLY exactly *Tim looks **just like** his father.* ○ *This carpet would be **just right** for my bedroom.* **6** ALMOST NOW now or very soon *I'm just coming!* **7 just before/over/under, etc** a little before/over/under, etc something else *It costs just over $10.* ○ *She left just before Michael.* **8 just about** almost *I think I've remembered just about everything.* **9 be just about to do sth** to be going to do something very soon *I was just about to phone you.* **10 just as bad/good/tall, etc (as sb/sth)** equally bad/good/tall, etc *He's just as talented as his brother.* **11 I/you/we, etc will just have to do sth** used to say that there is nothing else someone can do *You'll just have to wait.* **12 just as** at the same time as *She woke up just as we got there.* **13 it's just as well** used to say that it is lucky that something happened *It's just as well we brought an umbrella.* ➲See also: just the **job**

just² /dʒʌst/ *adjective* fair or morally right *a just society* ➲Opposite **unjust** •**justly** *adverb*

WORD PARTNERS FOR ***justice***

fight for/seek justice • justice **for** sb

justice /ˈdʒʌstɪs/ *noun* **1** FAIR BEHAVIOUR [U] behaviour or treatment that is fair and morally correct *She tried to bring about fairness and **justice for all**.* ➲Opposite **injustice** **2** LAW [U] the system of laws which judges or punishes people *the **criminal justice system*** **3** LAW [C] *US* someone who judges in a court of law **4** LAW **bring sb to justice** to catch a criminal and decide if they are guilty or not **5 do sb/sth justice; do justice to sb/sth** to show the best or real qualities of something or someone *This postcard doesn't do justice to the wonderful scenery.*

ˌJustice of the ˈPeace *noun* [C] LAW someone who acts as a judge in a small or local court of law

justifiable /ˈdʒʌstɪfaɪəbl/ *adjective* having a good reason *justifiable anger* •**justifiably** *adverb*

justification /ˌdʒʌstɪfɪˈkeɪʃᵊn/ *noun* [C, U] a reason for something *There's no **justification for** treating her so badly.*

justified /ˈdʒʌstɪfaɪd/ *adjective* fair or having a good reason *justified criticism* ○ *He's perfectly **justified in** asking for a larger salary.* ➲Opposite **unjustified**

justify /ˈdʒʌstɪfaɪ/ *verb* [T] **1** MAKE ACCEPTABLE to give a good enough reason to make something seem acceptable *I don't know how they can justify those ticket prices.* **2** PRINTING in printing, to arrange the spaces between words so that lines are the correct length, usually to form a straight line at the edges

just-in-time /ˌdʒʌstɪnˈtaɪm/ *adjective* [**always before noun**] A just-in-time system of manufacturing (= producing goods) is based on preventing waste by producing only the amount of goods needed at a particular time, and not paying to produce and store more goods than are needed.

jut /dʒʌt/ *verb* **jutting**, *past* **jutted jut into/out, etc** If something juts out, it comes out further than the edge or surface around it. *The rocks jutted out into the sea.*

juvenile[1] /ˈdʒuːvᵊnaɪl/ *adjective* **1** YOUNG [**always before noun**] by, for, or relating to young people ***juvenile crime*** **2** SILLY behaving in a silly way as if you were a young child

juvenile[2] /ˈdʒuːvᵊnaɪl/ *noun* [C] **LAW** especially in law, a young person

ˌjuvenile deˈlinquent *noun* [C] **LAW** a young criminal

juxtapose /ˌdʒʌkstəˈpəʊz/ *verb* [T] *formal* to place very different things or people close to each other *The exhibition **juxtaposes** paintings **with** black and white photographs.* •**juxtaposition** /ˌdʒʌkstəpəˈzɪʃᵊn/ *noun* [C, U]

J

Kk

K, k /keɪ/ the eleventh letter of the alphabet

K /keɪ/ **COMPUTING** *abbreviation for* kilobyte: a unit for measuring the amount of information a computer can store

kaizen /ˈkaɪzen/ *noun* [U] a Japanese way of running a company by always trying to improve the way people work and what they do

kaleidoscope /kəˈlaɪdəskəʊp/ *noun* **1** TOY [C] a tube-shaped toy you look through which contains mirrors and pieces of coloured glass that make patterns **2** MIXTURE [**no plural**] a mixture of different things *The fashion show was a kaleidoscope of colours.*

kangaroo /ˌkæŋgəˈruː/ *noun* [C] a large Australian animal that moves by jumping on its back legs ➲See picture at **marsupials**

karat /ˈkærət/ *noun* [C] **MEASURES** *another US spelling of* carat (= a unit for measuring how pure gold is, or how much valuable stones weigh)

K

karate /kəˈrɑːti/ *noun* [U] **SPORT** a sport from Japan in which people fight using fast, hard hits with the hands or feet

karma /ˈkɑːmə/ *noun* [U] **RELIGION** in some religions, the actions of a person in this life or earlier lives, which influence their future

kayak /ˈkaɪæk/ *noun* [C] **SPORT** a light, narrow boat, usually for one person, which you move using a paddle (= stick with a wide, flat part) •**kayaking** *noun* [U] the activity of travelling in a kayak

kebab /kɪˈbæb/ (*also* **shish kebab**) *noun* [C] **FOOD** small pieces of meat or vegetables cooked on a long, thin stick

keel[1] /kiːl/ *noun* [C] a long piece of wood or metal at the bottom of a boat that helps it to balance

keel[2] /kiːl/ *verb*
keel over *phrasal verb* to fall over suddenly

O**keen** /kiːn/ *adjective* **1** INTERESTED very interested or enthusiastic *a keen golfer/photographer* ○ *He's very* ***keen on*** *travelling.* **2** WANTING TO DO wanting to do something very much [+ **to do sth**] *The shop is keen to attract new customers.* **3** VERY GOOD very good or well developed *a keen sense of smell* •**keenness** *noun* [U] •**keenly** *adverb*

O**keep**[1] /kiːp/ *verb past* **kept** **1** HAVE [T] to have something permanently or for the whole of a period of time *You can keep that dress if you like it.* ○ *He borrowed my bike and kept it all week.* **2 keep sth in/on, etc** to regularly store something in a particular place *I think he keeps his keys in the desk drawer.* ○ *We'll keep your application on file.* **3 keep doing sth** to continue to do something, or to do something repeatedly *I keep telling her not to leave her clothes on the floor.* ○ *He keeps hitting me.* **4 keep (sb/sth) awake/clean/safe, etc** to remain in a particular state or make someone or something remain in a particular state *He goes jogging twice a week to keep fit.* ○ *He keeps his car spotlessly clean.* **5 keep sb/sth in/inside, etc** to make someone or something stay in the same place *They will keep her at home for a few more days.* **6** MAKE DO STH [T] to make someone do something that stops them doing something else [+ **doing sth**] *She kept me talking for ages.* ○ *Sorry to* ***keep you waiting.*** ○ *Don't let me* ***keep you from*** *your work.* **7 keep a secret** to not tell anyone a secret **8 keep a promise/your word, etc** to do what you have promised to do **9 keep an appointment** to meet someone when you have arranged to meet them **10** MAKE LATE [T] to make someone arrive later than they planned *I was expecting you at six - what kept you?* **11** WRITE [T] to write down something in order to remember it *to keep records/notes* **12** FOOD [I] If food or drink keeps, it remains fresh. **13** PROVIDE MONEY [T] to provide enough money for someone to live *I can't keep a family on that salary.* **14** ANIMALS [T] to have and look after animals *Our neighbours keep pigs.* **15 keep sb going** to provide what someone needs for a short period of time *Dinner is at eight, but I had an apple to keep me going.* ➲See also: keep your **cool**[3], keep a straight **face**[1], keep your fingers (**finger**[1]) crossed, put/keep sb in the **picture**[1], keep a low **profile**[1], keep a tight **rein** on sb/sth, keep tabs (**tab**) on sb/sth, keep sb on their toes (**toe**[1])

OTHER WAYS OF SAYING ***keep***

If someone keeps something somewhere until they need it, the verb **store** is sometimes used: *I've* ***stored*** *all Helen's books in the attic.*

The verb **stash** (*informal*) and the phrasal verb **stash away** (*informal*) are sometimes used if someone keeps a lot of something in a secret place: *His money was* ***stashed (away)*** *in a cupboard.*

The verb **save** is often used when someone keeps something to use in the future: *I have some really good chocolates that I've been* ***saving*** *for a special occasion.*

The phrasal verbs **hang onto** and **hold onto** are also often used when someone keeps something that they might need in the future: *You should* ***hang/hold onto*** *that picture - it might be worth something.*

keep at sth *phrasal verb* to continue working hard at something difficult *Learning a language is hard but you've just got to keep at it.*
keep (sb/sth) away *phrasal verb* to not go somewhere or near something, or to prevent someone from going somewhere or near something *I told them to keep away from the edge of the cliff.*
keep (sb/sth) back *phrasal verb* to not go near something, or to prevent someone or something from going past a particular place *Barriers were built to keep back the flood water.*
keep sth back *phrasal verb* to not tell someone everything you know about a situation or an event *I was sure she was keeping something back.*
keep sth down *phrasal verb* **1** NO INCREASE to

stop the number, level, or size of something from increasing *I have to exercise to keep my weight down.* **2** **HEALTH** to be able to eat or drink without vomiting

keep sb/sth from doing sth *phrasal verb* to prevent someone or something from doing something

keep sth from sb *phrasal verb* to not tell someone about something *Is there something you're keeping from me?*

keep sb in *phrasal verb* to make a child stay inside as a punishment, or to make someone stay in hospital

keep (sb/sth) off sth *phrasal verb* to not go onto an area, or to stop someone or something going onto an area *Keep off the grass.*

keep sth off (sb/sth) *phrasal verb* to stop something touching or harming someone or something *He put a cloth over the salad to keep the flies off.*

O━ **keep on doing sth** *phrasal verb* to continue to do something, or to do something again and again *She kept on asking me questions the whole time.*

keep on *phrasal verb UK* to continue to talk in an annoying way about something *I wish he wouldn't* ***keep on about*** *how much he earns.*

keep (sb/sth) out *phrasal verb* to not go into a place, or to stop someone or something from going into a place *He locked the room and put up a sign asking people to keep out.*

keep to sth *phrasal verb* **1** STAY SOMEWHERE to stay in one particular area *We kept to main roads all the way.* **2** NOT CHANGE PLANS to do what you have promised or planned to do *I think we should keep to our original plan.*

keep sth to sth *phrasal verb* If you keep something to a particular number or amount, you make sure it does not become larger than that. *I'm trying to keep costs to a minimum.*

keep sth to yourself *phrasal verb* to keep something secret and not tell anyone else about it

keep up *phrasal verb* **1** SAME SPEED to move at the same speed as someone or something that is moving forward so that you stay level with them *She was walking so fast I couldn't* ***keep up with*** *her.* **2** MAKE PROGRESS to increase or make progress at the same speed as something or someone else so that you stay at the same level as them *Prices have been rising very fast and wages haven't kept up.* **3** UNDERSTAND to be able to understand or deal with something that is happening or changing very fast *I feel it's important to* ***keep up with*** *current events.*

keep sth up *phrasal verb* to not allow something that is at a high level to fall to a lower level *Make sure you eat properly - you've got to keep your strength up.*

keep (sth) up *phrasal verb* to continue without stopping or changing or to continue something without allowing it to stop or change *People are having difficulties keeping up the repayments on their loans.*

keep² /kiːp/ *noun* [**no plural**] the money needed to pay for someone to eat and live in a place *He* ***earns his keep*** *working in a garage.*

keeper /ˈkiːpəʳ/ *noun* [**C**] **1** someone who looks after a place and the things, people, or animals there *a park keeper* **2** **SPORT** *informal short for* goalkeeper (= the player in a sport such as football who tries to stop the ball going into the goal)

keeping /ˈkiːpɪŋ/ *noun* **1** **for safe keeping** in order to keep something safe *She put the money into a bank for safe keeping.* **2** **in keeping with sth** suitable or right for a situation, style, or tradition *The antique desk was in keeping with the rest of the furniture in the room.*

keg /keg/ *noun* [**C**] a large, round container used for storing beer

keks /keks/ *noun* [**plural**] *informal* men's shorts (= short trousers) or pants (= underwear)

kelvin /ˈkelvɪn/ (*abbreviation* **K**) *noun* [**C**] **MEASURES** a standard unit of temperature

kennel /ˈkenᵊl/ *noun* [**C**] **1** STRUCTURE a small building for a dog to sleep in **2** PLACE *US* (*UK* **kennels**) a place where dogs are cared for while their owners are away

kept /kept/ *past of* keep

keratin /ˈkerətɪn/ *noun* [**U**] **BIOLOGY** the main substance that forms hair, nails, hooves, horns, feathers, etc

kerb *UK* (*US* **curb**) /kɜːb/ *noun* [**C**] the line of stones at the edge of a pavement (= raised path that people walk on) next to the road

kernel /ˈkɜːnᵊl/ *noun* [**C**] **BIOLOGY** the part of a nut or seed inside the hard shell which you can usually eat

kerning /ˈkɜːnɪŋ/ *noun* [**U**] **DT** in printing, the amount of space between letters and lines of words

kerosene /ˈkerəsiːn/ *US* (*UK* **paraffin**) *noun* [**U**] oil used for heating and in lamps (= equipment that produces light)

ketchup /ˈketʃʌp/ *noun* [**U**] **FOOD** a thick sauce made from tomatoes (= round, red fruit) that is eaten cold with food

kettle /ˈketl/ *noun* [**C**] a metal or plastic container with a lid, used for boiling water *Charlotte* ***put the kettle on*** *to make some tea.* ➲See colour picture **The Kitchen** on page Centre 2

WORD PARTNERS FOR ***key***

a **bunch of/set of** keys • the key **for/to** sth • a **car** key

O━ **key¹** /kiː/ *noun* [**C**] **1** FOR LOCKS a piece of metal cut into a particular shape and used for locking things such as doors, or for starting an engine *I've lost my car keys.* **2** METHOD a way of explaining or achieving something *Hard work is the key to success.* **3** **MUSIC** one of the parts you press with your fingers on a keyboard or musical instrument to produce letters, numbers, or to make a sound **4** **MUSIC** a set of musical notes based on one particular note *the key of D major* **5** SYMBOLS a list which explains the symbols on a map or picture **6** ANSWERS a list of answers to an exercise or game ➲See also: under **lock²** and key

key² /kiː/ *adjective* very important in influencing or achieving something *a* ***key factor***

key³ /kiː/ *verb*

key sth in *phrasal verb* **COMPUTING** to put information into a computer or machine using a keyboard

keyboard /'kiːbɔːd/ *noun* [C] **1 COMPUTING** a set of keys on a computer, which you press to make it work, or the rows of keys on a piano ➲See colour picture **The Office** on page Centre 5 **2 MUSIC** an electrical musical instrument similar to a piano

'key ˌfield *noun* [C] **COMPUTING** a field (= area for a particular kind of information) or fields in a computer database that identifies a particular record (= collection of pieces of information treated as one unit)

keyhole /'kiːhəʊl/ *noun* [C] a hole in a lock where you put a key

keynote /'kiːnəʊt/ *noun* [C] the most important part of an event, idea, or speech, or something that is emphasized strongly *the **keynote speech/speaker***

keypad /'kiːpæd/ *noun* [C] **COMPUTING** a set of buttons with numbers on them used to operate a television, telephone, etc

'key ˌring *noun* [C] a metal ring used for keeping keys together

kg MEASURES *written abbreviation for* kilogram (= a unit for measuring weight)

khaki /'kɑːki/ *noun* [U] a pale green-brown colour, often worn by soldiers •**khaki** *adjective* ➲See colour picture **Colours** on page Centre 12

kibbutz /kɪ'bʊts/ *noun* [C] **SOCIETY** *plural* **kibbutzim** a place in Israel where people live and work together, often a farm or a factory

O⁻**kick¹** /kɪk/ *verb* **1** HIT [I, T] to hit or move something or someone with your foot *The boys were **kicking a ball** back and forth.* ○ *They tried to kick the door down.* **2** MOVE LEGS [I] to move your feet and legs forwards or backwards quickly and with force *I kicked at them and screamed for help.* **3 kick yourself** *informal* to be very annoyed with yourself for doing something stupid or wrong *I could have kicked myself for saying that.* ➲See also: be **alive** and kicking/well

be kicking about/around *phrasal verb informal* If something is kicking about, it is in a particular place, but nobody is using it or paying attention to it. *We've probably got a copy of the document kicking around the office.*

kick in *phrasal verb informal* to start to be effective or to happen *The new tax rate kicks in next month.*

kick off *phrasal verb* **1 SPORT** When a football match or other event kicks off, it starts. **2** *informal* to start to get angry or complain

kick (sth) off *phrasal verb informal* When you kick off a discussion or activity, you start it.

kick sb out *phrasal verb informal* to force someone to leave a place or organization *His wife kicked him out.*

kick² /kɪk/ *noun* **1** HIT [C] when you kick something with your foot *He **gave her a kick** in the ribs.* **2** FEELING [C] *informal* a special feeling of excitement and energy *She **gets a kick out of** performing live.* **3 a kick in the teeth** used when someone treats you badly or unfairly, especially when you need or expect support *This latest pay award amounts to a kick in the teeth.* ➲See also: **free kick**

kickback /'kɪkbæk/ *noun* [C] *US* money given to someone, especially illegally, for providing help, a job, or a piece of business

kickboxing /'kɪkˌbɒksɪŋ/ *noun* [U] **SPORT** a sport in which two people fight by hitting each other with their hands and kicking each other with their feet

kick-off /'kɪkɒf/ *noun* [C, U] **SPORT** the time when a football match begins

O⁻**kid¹** /kɪd/ *noun* [C] **1** CHILD *informal* a child or young person *school kids* **2** GOAT a young goat

kid² /kɪd/ *verb* [I, T] **kidding**, *past* **kidded 1** JOKE to make a joke, or to trick someone with a joke **2** DECEIVE to deceive or trick someone into believing something [**often reflexive**] *You've got to stop kidding yourself. She's not coming back.*

kiddie /'kɪdi/ *noun* [C] *informal* a child

kidnap /'kɪdnæp/ *verb* [T] **kidnapping**, *past* **kidnapped** to take someone away using force, usually to obtain money in exchange for releasing them •**kidnap** *noun* [C] *a kidnap victim/attempt* •**kidnapper** *noun* [C]

kidnapping /'kɪdnæpɪŋ/ *noun* [C, U] when someone is kidnapped

kidney /'kɪdni/ *noun* [C] **ANATOMY** one of the two organs in your body which remove waste from the blood and produce urine

O⁻**kill¹** /kɪl/ *verb* **1** DEATH [I, T] to cause someone or something to die *Sunday's bomb killed 19 people.* ○ *Their son was killed in a road accident.* **2 sb will kill sb** *informal* used to say that someone will be very angry with someone else *Dad will kill me for being late.* **3** END [T] to stop an activity or experience completely *His remark killed the conversation.* **4** CAUSE PAIN [T] *informal* to cause you a lot of pain or effort *My feet are killing me.* ○ *It wouldn't kill you to tidy up occasionally.* ➲See also: kill **time¹**

kill sth/sb off *phrasal verb* to stop something or someone from existing any more *Lack of funding is killing off local theatres.*

kill² /kɪl/ *noun* **1** [**no plural**] when an animal is killed **2 go/move in for the kill** to prepare to defeat someone completely or to kill them

killer /'kɪləʳ/ *noun* [C] someone who kills, or a disease, substance, or animal that kills *Cancer and heart disease are the UK's biggest killers.* ➲See also: **serial killer**

killing /'kɪlɪŋ/ *noun* **1** [C] a murder, or when someone or something is killed *the killing of civilians* **2 make a killing** *informal* to make a lot of money very quickly

kiln /kɪln/ *noun* [C] **ART** a large oven for baking bricks and other clay objects until they are hard

kilo /'kiːləʊ/ *noun* [C] **MEASURES** *short for* kilogram

kilo- /kɪlə-/ *prefix* **MEASURES** a thousand *a kilometre* ○ *a kilogram*

kilobyte /'kɪləʊbaɪt/ (*written abbreviation* **K**) *noun* [C] **COMPUTING, MEASURES** a unit for measuring the amount of information a computer can store, equal to 1024 bytes

kilogram (*also UK* **kilogramme**) (*written abbreviation* **kg**) /'kɪləʊgræm/ *noun* [C] **MEASURES** a unit for measuring weight, equal to 1000 grams

kilohertz /'kɪləhɜːts/ (*written abbreviation* **kHz**) *noun* [C] *plural* **kilohertz MEASURES** a unit of measurement of sound waves which is equal to 1000 hertz

O⁃**kilometre** *UK* (*US* **kilometer**) (*written abbreviation* **km**) /kɪˈlɒmɪtəʳ, ˈkɪləˌmiːtəʳ/ *noun* [C] **MEASURES** a unit for measuring distance, equal to 1000 metres

kilowatt /ˈkɪləʊwɒt/ (*written abbreviation* **kW**) *noun* [C] **MEASURES** a unit for measuring electrical power, equal to 1000 watts

kilt /kɪlt/ *noun* [C] a traditional Scottish skirt for men, made of heavy material with close vertical folds at the back

kin /kɪn/ *noun* [plural] *formal* **SOCIETY** the members of your family ➲See also: **next of kin**

O⁃**kind¹** /kaɪnd/ *noun* **1** [C] a type of thing or person *What **kind of** music do you like?* ○ ***All kinds of** people come to our church.* ○ *Older kids like board games and that **kind of thing**.* ○ *Her travel company was the first **of its kind*** (= the first one like it). **2 some kind of** used to talk about something when you are not sure of its exact type *She has some kind of disability.* **3 kind of** *informal* used when you are trying to explain or describe something, but you cannot be exact *It's kind of unusual.* **4 of a kind** used to describe something that exists but is not very good *The school had a swimming pool of a kind, but it was too small for most classes to use.*

OTHER WAYS OF SAYING ***kind***

The adjectives **nice** and **sweet** are common alternatives to 'kind': *It was really **nice** of you to come.* • *Wasn't it **sweet** of Heidi to call?*

If someone is **good to** you, they do things to help you: *Jay's mother has been very **good to** us.*

If someone is very willing to help, you can describe them as **helpful**: *The staff here are very **helpful**.*

Someone who is **caring** is kind to other people and tries to make them happy and well: *I've always thought of Mary as a very **caring** person.*

The expression **mean well** is sometimes used to describe a person who tries to be kind and help but who does not improve a situation: *I know my parents **mean well**, but I do wish they wouldn't interfere.*

O⁃**kind²** /kaɪnd/ *adjective* Kind people do things to help others and show that they care about them. *Your mother was very **kind to** us.* ○ *It was very **kind of** you to come and see me.* ➲Opposite **unkind**

kinda /ˈkaɪndə/ *mainly US informal short for* kind of *I'm kinda busy right now.*

kindergarten /ˈkɪndəˌɡɑːtᵊn/ *noun* [C, U] **1** **EDUCATION** in the UK, a school for children under five **2** **EDUCATION** in the US, a class in school for children aged five

kind-hearted /ˌkaɪndˈhɑːtɪd/ *adjective* having a kind character *a kind-hearted family man*

kindly¹ /ˈkaɪndli/ *adverb* **1** KIND WAY in a kind or generous way *She **kindly offered** to cook me lunch.* **2** PLEASE *formal* used in instructions to mean 'please', usually when you are annoyed *Would you kindly get out of my car?* **3 not take kindly to sth** to not like something that someone says or does *He doesn't take kindly to criticism.*

kindly² /ˈkaɪndli/ *adjective old-fashioned* kind *a kindly old gentleman*

kindness /ˈkaɪndnəs/ *noun* [C, U] when someone is kind *Thanks for all your kindness this morning.*

kinetic /kɪˈnetɪk/ *adjective* [always before noun] **PHYSICS** involving or producing movement *kinetic energy*

O⁃**king** /kɪŋ/ *noun* [C] **1** RULER a male ruler in some countries *King Richard II* ○ *the kings and queens of England* **2** BEST PERSON the best or most important person in a particular activity *He's the new king of pop music.* **3** PLAYING CARD a playing card with a picture of a king on it *the king of spades*

kingdom /ˈkɪŋdəm/ *noun* **1** [C] **POLITICS** a country with a king or queen *the Kingdom of Belgium* **2 the animal/plant kingdom** all animals or plants considered together

kingfisher /ˈkɪŋˌfɪʃəʳ/ *noun* [C] a small, brightly coloured bird which catches fish from rivers and lakes

king-size (*also* **king-sized**) /ˈkɪŋsaɪz/ *adjective* very big *a **king-size** bed*

kink /kɪŋk/ *noun* [C] a bend in something long and thin *There was a kink in the cassette tape.*

kinky /ˈkɪŋki/ *adjective informal* involving strange or unusual sexual behaviour

kiosk /ˈkiːɒsk/ *noun* [C] a small building with a window where things like tickets or newspapers are sold

kip /kɪp/ *noun* [C, U] *UK informal* a short period of sleep •**kip** *verb* [I] **kipping**, *past* **kipped**

kipper /ˈkɪpəʳ/ *noun* [C] *UK* **FOOD** a type of fish that has been cut open and dried over smoke

O⁃**kiss¹** /kɪs/ *verb* [I, T] to press your lips against another person's lips or skin to show love or affection *He kissed her cheek.* ○ *Len **kissed** Samantha **goodbye** at the front gate.*

WORD PARTNERS FOR ***kiss***

give sb a kiss • **plant** a kiss **on** sb's [lips/cheek, etc] • a **lingering/passionate** kiss

O⁃**kiss²** /kɪs/ *noun* [C] **1** an act of kissing someone *She ran up and **gave** me **a** big **kiss**.* **2 give sb the kiss of life** *UK* **HEALTH** to help to keep someone who has stopped breathing alive by blowing into their mouth

kit /kɪt/ *noun* **1** COLLECTION [C] a collection of things kept in a container ready for a particular use *a **first-aid/tool kit*** **2** CLOTHES [C, U] *UK* a set of clothes worn for sport or military service *a football kit* **3** PARTS [C] a set of parts which you put together to make something *He's making a model car from a kit.*

O⁃**kitchen** /ˈkɪtʃɪn/ *noun* [C] a room used to prepare and cook food in ➲See colour picture **The Kitchen** on page Centre 2

kite /kaɪt/ *noun* [C] a toy made of paper or cloth which flies in the air on the end of a long string

kitsch /kɪtʃ/ *noun* [U] decorative objects or pieces of art that are ugly, silly, or have little value

kitten /ˈkɪtᵊn/ *noun* [C] a young cat

kitty /ˈkɪti/ *noun* [C] **FINANCE** an amount of money consisting of a share from everyone in a group, used for a special purpose [**usually singular**] *We all put money into a kitty to pay for drinks.*

kiva /ˈkiːvə/ *noun* [C] **RELIGION** a large room built under the ground in a Native American village for religious ceremonies

kiwi /ˈkiːwiː/ (*also* **ˈkiwi ˌfruit**) *noun* [C] **FOOD** a small, green fruit with black seeds and brown, hairy skin

km MEASURES *written abbreviation for* kilometre (= a unit for measuring distance)

WORD PARTNERS FOR ***knack***

have/lose the knack **of** doing sth • an **uncanny** knack • a knack **for** doing sth

knack /næk/ *noun* [**no plural**] a special skill, or the ability to use or do something easily *a **knack for** remembering faces* ○ *She **has** the **knack** of making people feel comfortable.*

knackered /ˈnækəd/ *adjective UK informal* extremely tired

knead /niːd/ *verb* [T] **FOOD** to press and shape the mixture for making bread firmly and repeatedly with your hands

knee /niː/ *noun* [C] **1 ANATOMY** the middle part of your leg where it bends *a knee injury* ➲See colour picture **The Body** on page Centre 13 **2** the part of a pair of trousers that covers the knee **3 bring sb/sth to their knees** to destroy or defeat someone or something *The war brought the country to its knees.*

kneecap /ˈniːkæp/ *noun* [C] **ANATOMY** the round bone at the front of your knee

knee-deep /ˌniːˈdiːp/ *adjective* **1** reaching as high as someone's knees *knee-deep in cold water* **2 be knee-deep in sth** to have a lot of something to deal with *I'm knee-deep in paperwork.*

knee-jerk /ˈniːdʒɜːk/ *adjective* **a knee-jerk reaction/response, etc** an immediate reaction that does not allow you time to consider something carefully

kneel /niːl/ *verb* [I] *past* **knelt, kneeled** to go down into or stay in a position where one or both of your knees are on the ground *She **knelt down** beside the child.*

knew /njuː/ *past tense of* know

knickers /ˈnɪkəz/ *UK* (*US* **panties**) *noun* [**plural**] women's underwear that covers the bottom ➲See Common Learner Error at **underwear** ➲See colour picture **Clothes** on page Centre 9

knife¹ /naɪf/ *noun* [C] *plural* **knives** a sharp tool or weapon for cutting, usually with a metal blade and a handle *a **knife and fork***

knife² /naɪf/ *verb* [T] to attack someone using a knife ➲See also: **jack-knife**

knight¹ /naɪt/ *noun* [C] **1** a man of high social rank who fought as a soldier on a horse in the past **2 SOCIETY** a man who has been given the title 'Sir' by the King or Queen in the UK

knight² /naɪt/ *verb* **be knighted SOCIETY** to be given a knighthood

knighthood /ˈnaɪthʊd/ *noun* [C] **SOCIETY** the title of 'Sir' given to someone by the King or Queen in the UK

knit /nɪt/ *verb* [I, T] **knitting**, *past tense* **knitted**, *past participle* **knit** to make clothes using wool and two long needles to join the wool into rows *She was knitting him a jumper.*

knitting /ˈnɪtɪŋ/ *noun* [U] when something is being knitted or the thing that is being knitted *She put down her knitting.*

knitwear /ˈnɪtweəʳ/ *noun* [U] knitted clothes

knob /nɒb/ *noun* **1** [C] a round handle, or a round button on a machine *a door knob* ○ ***Turn** the black **knob** to switch on the radio.* **2 a knob of butter** *UK* a small lump of butter

knock¹ /nɒk/ *verb* **1** MAKE NOISE [I] to make a noise by hitting something, especially a door, with your closed hand in order to attract someone's attention *There's someone **knocking at/on** the door.* ○ *Please knock before entering.* **2** HIT [T] to hit something or someone and make them move or fall down *He accidentally knocked the vase off the table.* ○ *I **knocked over** the mug.* **3** CRITICIZE [T] *informal* to criticize someone or something, often unfairly *She knocks every suggestion I make.* **4 Knock it off!** *informal* something you say when you want someone to stop doing something that is annoying you ➲See also: beat/knock the (living) **daylights** out of sb

COMMON LEARNER ERROR

knock

Be careful to use the correct prepositions. You do not always need one.

*The policeman **knocked on/knocked at** the door.*

~~*Listen! There is someone knocking to the door.*~~

Knock before you come in.

knock sth back *phrasal verb UK informal* to drink alcohol very quickly

knock sb down *phrasal verb UK* to hit someone with a vehicle and injure or kill them [**often passive**] *She was knocked down by a bus.*

knock sb/sth down *phrasal verb US* to cause someone or something to fall to the ground by hitting them

knock sth down *phrasal verb* to destroy a building or part of a building

knock off *phrasal verb informal* to stop working, usually at the end of a day *I don't knock off until six.*

knock sth off (sth) *phrasal verb* to take a particular amount away from something, usually a price *The manager knocked $5 off because it was damaged.*

knock sb out *phrasal verb* **1 HEALTH** to make someone become unconscious, usually by hitting them on the head *He was knocked out halfway through the fight.* **2** DEFEAT to defeat a person or team in a competition so they cannot take part any more [**often passive**] *The French team were knocked out in the semifinal.*

WORD PARTNERS FOR **knock**

a **sharp** knock • a knock **at/on** [the door/window, etc.]

knock² /nɒk/ *noun* [C] **1** NOISE a sudden short noise made when something or someone hits a surface *a* ***knock at/on*** *the door* **2** HIT when someone or something is hit, sometimes causing damage or injury *a knock on the head*

knocker /ˈnɒkəʳ/ *noun* [C] a metal object fixed to the outside of a door which visitors use to knock

knock-on /ˌnɒkˈɒn/ *adjective UK* **a knock-on effect** When an event or situation has a knock-on effect, it causes another event or situation. *Cutting schools' budgets will have a knock-on effect on teachers' jobs.*

knockout /ˈnɒkaʊt/ *noun* **SPORT** [C] in boxing, when one person hits the other hard and they become unconscious

WORD PARTNERS FOR **knot**

tie a knot **(in** sth**)** • **undo/untie** a knot

knot¹ /nɒt/ *noun* **1** [C] a place where pieces of string, rope, etc have been tied together **2** **MEASURES** [C] a unit for measuring the speed of the wind, ships, or aircraft **3 tie the knot** *informal* to get married

knot² /nɒt/ *verb* [T] **knotting**, *past* **knotted** to tie knots in pieces of string, rope, etc

O‑‑ **know¹** /nəʊ/ *verb past tense* **knew**, *past participle* **known** **1** HAVE INFORMATION [I, T] to have knowledge or information about something in your mind *"How old is she?" "I don't know."* ○ *Andrew* ***knows*** *a lot* ***about*** *computers.* [+ **question word**] *Do you know where the station is?* [+ **(that)**] *He knew that she was lying.* **2** BE FAMILIAR WITH [T] to be familiar with a person, place, or thing because you have met them, been there, used it, etc before *I've known Tim since primary school.* ○ *I grew up in Brussels so I know it well.* ○ *Since moving to London, I've* ***got to know*** (= become familiar with) *some nice people.* **3** BE ABLE [T] to be able to do something [+ **question word**] *Do you know how to ski?* ○ *I only know* (= understand and speak) *a little Spanish.* **4 let sb know** to tell someone something *Let me know if you're going to the party.* **5** GUESS CORRECTLY [T] to guess something correctly *I knew she'd arrive late.* ○ *I* ***should have known*** *he wouldn't come.* **6** UNDERSTAND [I, T] to understand and agree with someone *I know what you mean about Pete - I wouldn't trust him at all.* **7 be known as sth** to be called something *California is also known as the Sunshine State.* **8 have known sth** to have had experience of something *I've never known the weather be so hot.* **9 know better (than to do sth)** to have the intelligence or judgment not to do something *She should have known better than to eat so much. No wonder she feels sick now.* **10 I know a** AGREEING used when you agree with something someone has just said *"It's a lovely day, isn't it?" "I know - let's hope it lasts."* **b** NEW IDEA used when you have an idea *I know - let's go to Helen's house.* **11 you know a** used to emphasize that someone does know what you are referring to *You know, he's the one with curly hair.* **b** something that you say while you are thinking what to say next *It's, you know, supposed to be a surprise.* **c** used to emphasize what you are saying *I'm not an idiot, you know.* **12 as far as I know** used to say that you think something is true, but cannot be sure *As far as I know, he's never been in prison.* **13 you never know** used to say that something could be possible although it does not seem likely *You never know - you might win the lottery.* **14 before you know it** very soon *We'll be there before you know it.* ➲See also: know sth **inside**[1] out, learn/know the ropes (**rope**[1]), know your **stuff**[1]

COMMON LEARNER ERROR

meet, get to know and **know**

When you **meet someone**, you see or speak to them for the first time. When you **get to know someone**, you learn more about them and after this you can say that you **know** them.

I met Nick on holiday.

~~I know Nick on holiday.~~

We got to know each other and became good friends.

~~We knew each other and became friends.~~

How long have you known Nick?

~~How long have you got to know Nick?~~

COMMON LEARNER ERROR

know or **find out?**

To **know** something means to already have information about something.

Kelly knows what time the train leaves.

His parents already know about the problem.

To **find out** something means to learn new information for the first time.

Can you find out what time the train leaves?

His parents were angry when they found out about the problem.

know of sth/sb *phrasal verb* to have heard of something or someone and have a little information about them *I know of a good restaurant near the station.*

know² /nəʊ/ *noun* **be in the know** to have knowledge about something which not everyone knows *People in the know were sure the film would win an Oscar.*

know-how /ˈnəʊhaʊ/ *noun* [U] practical skill and knowledge ***technical know-how***

knowing /ˈnəʊɪŋ/ *adjective* A knowing smile, look, etc shows that you know what another person is really thinking. *He gave me a knowing wink.*

knowingly /ˈnəʊɪŋli/ *adverb* **1** INTENTIONALLY If you knowingly do something, you mean to do it although it is wrong. **2** SHOWING KNOWLEDGE showing that you know what another person is really thinking *He smiled knowingly.*

WORD PARTNERS FOR **knowledge**

common/detailed/firsthand/poor/thorough knowledge • knowledge **about/of** sth • **have/gain/impart** knowledge

K

O⊸**knowledge** /ˈnɒlɪdʒ/ *noun* **1** [U, no plural] information and understanding that you have in your mind *He has **a** detailed **knowledge of** naval history.* ○ *He took the car **without my knowledge*** (= I did not know). **2 to (the best of) sb's knowledge** used to say that someone thinks that something is true, but cannot be sure *To the best of my knowledge, she's never worked abroad.*

knowledgeable /ˈnɒlɪdʒəbl/ *adjective* knowing a lot *He's very **knowledgeable about** art.*

known¹ /nəʊn/ *adjective* recognized or known about by most people *He's a member of a known terrorist organization.* ➲Opposite **unknown** ➲See also: **well-known**

known² /nəʊn/ *past participle of* know

knuckle¹ /ˈnʌkl/ *noun* [C] **ANATOMY** one of the parts of your finger where it bends ➲See also: a **rap¹** on/across/over the knuckles

knuckle² /ˈnʌkl/ *verb*
knuckle down *phrasal verb* to start to work or study hard

koala /kəʊˈɑːlə/ (*also* **koˈala ˌbear**) *noun* [C] an Australian animal like a small bear with grey fur which lives in trees and eats leaves ➲See picture at **marsupials**

the Koran /kɒrˈɑːn/ Ⓤⓢ /kəˈræn/ *noun* **RELIGION** the holy book of Islam

kosher /ˈkəʊʃəʳ/ *adjective* **FOOD, RELIGION** Kosher food is prepared according to Jewish law.

kph **MEASURES** *written abbreviation for* kilometres per hour: a unit for measuring speed *a car travelling at 100 kph*

krypton /ˈkrɪptɒn/ *noun* [U] **CHEMISTRY** a gas which is used in particular types of lights and lasers (formula **Kr**)

kudos /ˈkjuːdɒs/ *noun* [U] praise and respect for what you have done

kung fu /kʌŋˈfuː/ *noun* [U] **SPORT** a sport from China in which people fight using their hands and feet

Kurdish /ˈkɜːdɪʃ/ *adjective* **SOCIETY** belonging or relating to a Muslim people living in parts of Turkey, Iran, Iraq, etc •**Kurd** /kɜːd/ *noun* [C] a Kurdish person

kW (*also* **kw**) **MEASURES** *written abbreviation for* kilowatt (= a unit for measuring electrical power)

kwashiorkor /ˌkwæʃiˈɔːkɔːʳ/ *noun* [U] **HEALTH** a serious disease caused by eating too little protein

K

L, l /el/ the twelfth letter of the alphabet

l **MEASURES** *written abbreviation for* litre (= a unit for measuring liquid)

lab /læb/ *noun* [C] *short for* laboratory (= a room used for scientific work)

label¹ /ˈleɪbᵊl/ *noun* [C] **1** INFORMATION a small piece of paper or other material which gives information about the thing it is fixed to *There should be washing instructions on the label.* **2** WORD a word or phrase that is used to describe the qualities of someone or something, usually in a way that is not fair *He seems to be stuck with the label of 'troublemaker'.* **3** MUSIC (*also* **record label**) a company that records and sells music *They've just signed a deal with a major record label.*

label² /ˈleɪbᵊl/ *verb* [T] *UK* **labelling**, *past* **labelled**, *US* **labeling**, *past* **labeled** **1** INFORMATION to fix a small piece of paper or other material to something which gives information about it *All food has to be labelled with 'best before' or 'use by' dates.* **2** DESCRIBE to describe the qualities of someone or something using a word or phrase, usually in a way that is not fair [**often passive**] *They've been unfairly* ***labelled as*** *criminals.*

labor /ˈleɪbəʳ/ *noun, verb US spelling of* labour

laboratory /ləˈbɒrətᵊri/ (US) /ˈlæbrətɔːri/ *noun* [C] a room used for scientific work *research laboratories* ○ *a computer laboratory* ➲See also: **language laboratory**

laborer /ˈleɪbᵊrəʳ/ *noun* [C] *US spelling of* labourer

laborious /ləˈbɔːriəs/ *adjective* Laborious work is very difficult and needs a lot of effort. *a* ***laborious task***

labors /ˈleɪbəz/ *noun* [**plural**] *US spelling of* labours

ˈlabor ˌunion *US* (*UK/US* **trade union**) *noun* [C] an organization that represents people who do a particular job

labour¹ *UK* (*US* **labor**) /ˈleɪbəʳ/ *noun* **1** WORK [U] work, especially the type of work that needs a lot of physical effort ***manual labour*** **2** **ECONOMICS** [U] people who work ***cheap/skilled labour*** **3** **HEALTH** [C, U] the stage of pregnancy when a woman has pain in the lower part of her body because the baby is coming out *to be* ***in labour/go into labour*** ○ ***labour pains*** **4** **Labour** **POLITICS** [**group**] *short for* the Labour Party *I voted Labour* (= for the Labour party) *at the last election.* ○ *a Labour MP* **5** **a labour of love** work that you do because you like it, not because you are paid for it

labour² *UK formal* (*US* **labor**) /ˈleɪbəʳ/ *verb* [I] to work hard *He laboured night and day to get the house finished on time.*

labourer *UK* (*US* **laborer**) /ˈleɪbᵊrəʳ/ *noun* [C] a worker who uses a lot of physical effort in their job *a farm labourer*

the ˈLabour ˌParty *noun* [**group**] **POLITICS** one of the three main political parties in the UK

labours (*US* **labors**) /ˈleɪbəz/ *noun* [**plural**] **sb's labours** work done with a lot of effort *He earned a mere $15 for his labours.*

lace¹ /leɪs/ *noun* **1** CLOTH [U] a delicate cloth with patterns of holes *a lace curtain* **2** STRING [C] a string used to tie shoes *to tie/untie your laces*

lace² /leɪs/ *verb*
lace sth up *phrasal verb* to fasten something with laces *He laced up his boots.*
be laced with sth *phrasal verb* **FOOD** If food or drink is laced with alcohol or a drug, a small amount has been added to it. *coffee laced with brandy*

lacerate /ˈlæsᵊreɪt/ *verb* [T] *formal* to make deep cuts in someone's skin *a lacerated arm* •**laceration** /ˌlæsᵊrˈeɪʃᵊn/ *noun* [C] *formal* a cut

WORD PARTNERS FOR ***lack***

a **complete/distinct/marked/total** lack **of** sth • an **apparent** lack **of** sth

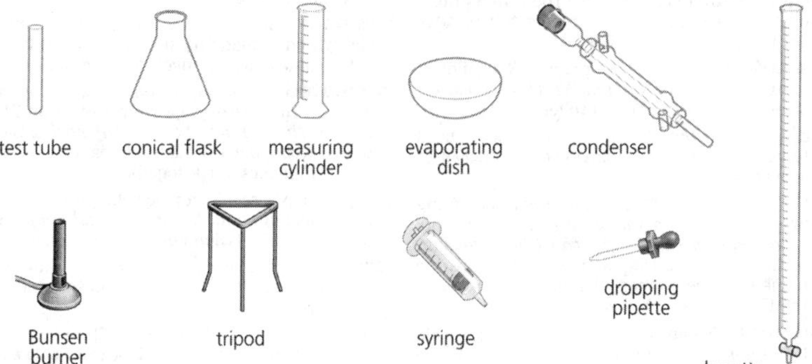

laboratory

O-- **lack**[1] /læk/ *noun* **lack of sth** not having something, or not having enough of something *a lack of food/money*

O-- **lack**[2] /læk/ *verb* **1** [T] to not have something, or not have enough of something *She really lacks confidence.* **2 be lacking** If something that you need is lacking, you do not have enough of it. *Enthusiasm has been sadly lacking these past few months at work.* **3 be lacking in sth** to not have a quality *He's totally lacking in charm of any sort.*

lacklustre *UK* (*US* **lackluster**) /ˈlækˌlʌstəʳ/ *adjective* without energy or excitement *a* ***lacklustre performance***

laconic /ləˈkɒnɪk/ *adjective formal* using very few words to express yourself *laconic humour/wit*

lacquer /ˈlækəʳ/ *noun* [U] **DT** a clear, hard substance which is painted on wood or metal to protect it

lactate /lækˈteɪt/ *verb* [I] **BIOLOGY** (of a woman or female mammal) to produce milk •**lactation** /lækˈteɪʃᵊn/ *noun* [U]

lacteal /ˈlæktiəl/ *adjective* **BIOLOGY** like or connected to milk

lactic /ˈlæktɪk/ *adjective* **BIOLOGY** relating to milk

ˌ**lactic** ˈ**acid** *noun* [U] **BIOLOGY** an acid that exists in old milk and is produced in muscles after a lot of exercise

lactose /ˈlæktəʊs/ *noun* [U] **BIOLOGY** a type of sugar which is found in milk

lad /læd/ *noun* [C] *UK* a boy or young man *a nice young lad informal* ○ *He's having a night out* ***with the lads*** (= his male friends).

ladder /ˈlædəʳ/ *noun* [C] a piece of equipment which is used to reach high places, consisting of short steps fixed between two long sides ➲See also: the first/highest/next, etc **rung**[1] of the ladder

laddish /ˈlædɪʃ/ *adjective UK* rude, noisy and typical of the way that young men behave in groups

laden /ˈleɪdᵊn/ *adjective* **be laden with sth** to be holding a lot of something *She staggered home, laden with shopping.*

ˈ**ladies'** ˌ**room** *noun* [C] *US* a room in a public place where there are women's toilets ➲See Common Learner Error at **toilet**

the ladies /ˈleɪdiz/ *noun* [group] *UK* a toilet in a public place for women *Where's the ladies?* ➲See Common Learner Error at **toilet**

ladle /ˈleɪdl/ *noun* [C] a large, deep spoon, used to serve soup ➲See colour picture **The Kitchen** on page Centre 2

O-- **lady** /ˈleɪdi/ *noun* **1** [C] a polite way of saying 'woman' *There's a young lady here to see you.* ○ ***Ladies and gentlemen****, can I have your attention please?* **2 Lady** a title used before the name of some women of high social rank in the UK *Lady Alison Weir*

ladybird /ˈleɪdibɜːd/ *UK* (*US* **ladybug** /ˈleɪdibʌg/) *noun* [C] a small flying insect which is usually red with black spots

lag[1] /læg/ (*also* **time lag**) *noun* [C] a period of time between two things happening *You have to allow for a time* ***lag between*** *order and delivery.* ➲See also: **jet lag**

lag[2] /læg/ *verb* **lagging**, *past* **lagged**

lag behind (sb/sth) *phrasal verb* **1** MOVE SLOWLY to move more slowly than someone or something else so that you are behind them **2** ACHIEVE LESS to achieve less than someone or something else *Britain is lagging far behind the rest of Europe on this issue.*

lager /ˈlɑːgəʳ/ *noun* [C, U] **FOOD** a pale yellow beer *A pint of lager, please.*

lagoon /ləˈguːn/ *noun* [C] **GEOGRAPHY** a lake that contains sea water

lahar /ləˈhɑː/ *noun* [C] **GEOLOGY** a large stream of mud, rocks and water from a volcano that becomes hard when it stops moving

laid /leɪd/ *past of* lay

laid-back /ˌleɪdˈbæk/ *adjective informal* very relaxed and not seeming worried about anything *a laid-back style of teaching* ○ *He's very laid-back.*

lain /leɪn/ *past participle of* lie[1]

laissez-faire /ˌleɪseɪˈfeəʳ/ *adjective* allowing things to happen and not trying to control them *a laissez-faire attitude*

O-- **lake** /leɪk/ *noun* [C] **GEOGRAPHY** a large area of water which has land all around it *Lake Windermere*

lamb /læm/ *noun* **1** [C] a young sheep *a newborn lamb* ○ *a lamb's-wool sweater* **2 FOOD** [U] meat from a young sheep *grilled lamb chops* ○ *roast leg of lamb* ➲See also: **mutton** dressed as lamb

lame /leɪm/ *adjective* **1** A lame excuse or explanation is one that you cannot believe. *He said he didn't go because it was raining, which is a pretty* ***lame excuse*** *if you ask me.* **2 HEALTH** A lame animal or person cannot walk because they have an injured foot or leg. *a lame horse*

lament /ləˈment/ *verb* [I, T] *formal* to say that you are disappointed about a situation *He was lamenting the fact that so few people read fiction nowadays.*

lamentable /ˈlæməntəbl/ *adjective formal* extremely bad *a lamentable performance*

lamina /ˈlæmɪnə/ *noun* [C] **BIOLOGY** the flat part of a leaf or petal

laminate /ˈlæmɪnət/ *noun* [C, U] **DT** any material which is made by sticking several layers of the same material together *a laminate finish*

laminated /ˈlæmɪneɪtɪd/ *adjective* **1** covered with a thin layer of plastic for protection *They gave us sheets of laminated cardboard.* **2** Laminated wood, plastic, glass, etc. is made of several thin layers stuck together.

lamp /læmp/ *noun* [C] a piece of equipment that produces light *a table lamp* ○ *an oil lamp* ➲See colour picture **The Living Room** on page Centre 4

lamppost /ˈlæmppəʊst/ *noun* [C] a tall post with a light at the top, which you see on roads where there are houses

lampshade /ˈlæmpʃeɪd/ *noun* [C] a decorative cover for an electric light ➲See colour picture **The Living Room** on page Centre 4

LAN /læn, ˌeleɪˈen/ *noun* [C] **COMPUTING** *abbreviation for* local area network: a system that

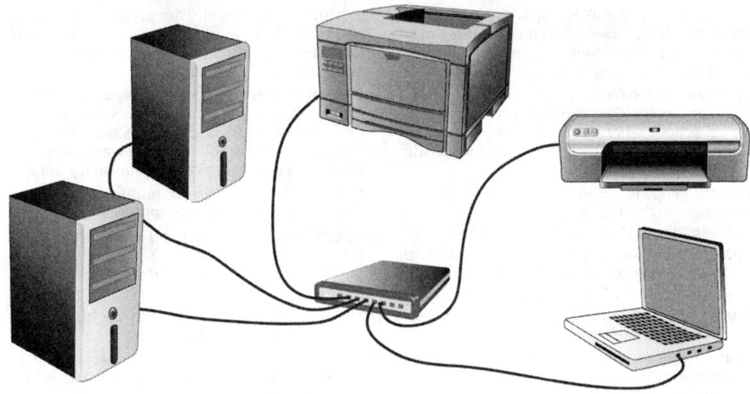

LAN

connects the computers of people who work in the same building ➲Compare **WAN**

land¹ /lænd/ *noun* **1** AREA [U] an area of ground *agricultural land* ○ *undeveloped land* ➲See Common Learner Error at **country 2 GEOGRAPHY** [U] the surface of the Earth that is not sea *to travel over land and sea* **3** COUNTRY [C] *literary* a country *a land of ice and snow* ➲See also: **no-man's land**

land² /lænd/ *verb* **1** ARRIVE [I, T] If an aircraft lands, it arrives on the ground after a journey, and if you land it, you make it arrive on the ground. *We should* ***land in*** *Madrid at 7 a.m.* ○ *He managed to* ***land*** *the helicopter* ***on*** *the cliff.* **2 land in/on, etc** If an object or person lands somewhere, they fall to the ground there. *She landed flat on her back.* **3** ACHIEVE [T] to get something, usually something good *He's just landed a new job at an agency in London.*
land sb in sth *phrasal verb* to cause someone to be in a difficult situation *His remarks have landed him in a lot of trouble with the association.*
land sb with sth *phrasal verb* If something lands you with problems, it causes problems for you. *The project's failure has landed him with debts of over £50,000.*

landfill /ˈlændfɪl/ *noun* [C] **ENVIRONMENT** a place where waste is buried in the ground *a* ***landfill site***

landform /ˈlændfɔːm/ *noun* [C] **GEOGRAPHY** a natural shape on the Earth's surface, such as a mountain or a valley

landing /ˈlændɪŋ/ *noun* [C] **1** ARRIVAL an arrival on the ground, usually of an aircraft or boat *They had to make an* ***emergency landing*** *in Chicago.* **2** FLOOR the area of floor at the top of a set of stairs

landlady /ˈlændˌleɪdi/ *noun* [C] a woman who you rent a room or house from

landline /ˈlændlaɪn/ *noun* [C] a telephone that is not a mobile phone

landlord /ˈlændlɔːd/ *noun* [C] a man who you rent a room or house from

landmark /ˈlændmɑːk/ *noun* [C] **1** BUILDING a building that you can easily recognize, especially one that helps you to know where you are *a historic landmark* **2** EVENT an event which is famous or important in the history of something *His speech was a* ***landmark in*** *the history of civil rights.*

landmine /ˈlændmaɪn/ *noun* [C] a bomb which is hidden in the ground

landowner /ˈlændəʊnəʳ/ *noun* [C] someone who owns a lot of land *a wealthy landowner*

landscape /ˈlændskeɪp/ *noun* [C] the appearance of an area of land, especially in the countryside *The cathedral dominates the landscape for miles around.*

landslide /ˈlændslaɪd/ *noun* [C] **1 GEOGRAPHY** when rocks and soil slide down a mountain or hill **2 POLITICS** an easy victory in an election *a* ***landslide defeat/victory***

WORD PARTNERS FOR ***lane***

in the [inside/fast, etc] lane • the **fast/slow** lane

lane /leɪn/ *noun* [C] **1 SPORT** part of a road or track that is separated from the other parts, usually by a painted line *the inside/middle/outside lane* ○ *the* ***fast/slow lane*** **2** ROAD a narrow road, usually in the countryside *We drove down a winding country lane.* **3** BOATS/AIRCRAFT a route that is regularly used by boats or aircraft *It's one of the world's busiest shipping lanes.*

WORD PARTNERS FOR ***language***

learn/speak a language • **foreign** languages • **foul/native/official/strong** language

language /ˈlæŋgwɪdʒ/ *noun* **1 LANGUAGE** [U] communication between people, usually using words *She has done research into how children acquire language.* **2 LANGUAGE** [C] a type of communication used by the people of a particular country *How many* ***languages*** *do you* ***speak?*** **3 LANGUAGE** [U] words of a particular type, especially the words used by people in a particular job *legal language* ○ *the language of*

L

business **4 COMPUTING** [C, U] a system of instructions that is used to write computer programs ➲See also: **body language, modern languages, second language, sign language**

ˈlanguage laˌboratory *UK* (*US* **ˈlanguage ˌlaboratory**) *noun* [C] **EDUCATION** a room in a college or school where you can use equipment to help you practise listening to and speaking a foreign language

languid /ˈlæŋgwɪd/ *adjective literary* moving or speaking slowly and with little energy, often in an attractive way *a languid manner/voice*

languish /ˈlæŋgwɪʃ/ *verb* [I] *formal* **languish at/in, etc sth** to stay in an unpleasant or difficult situation for a long time *to languish in jail*

lanky /ˈlæŋki/ *adjective informal* A lanky person is very tall and thin.

lantern /ˈlæntən/ *noun* [C] a light that can be carried, usually with a candle inside it *a paper lantern*

lanthanide /ˈlæntθənaɪd/ *noun* [U] **CHEMISTRY** any chemical element in the group that have the atomic numbers 57 to 71 in the periodic table

lap[1] /læp/ *noun* [C] **1** Your lap is the top part of your legs when you are sitting down. *Sit on my lap and I'll read you a story.* **2 SPORT** one journey around a circular race track *He's two laps behind the leaders.*

L

lap[2] /læp/ *verb* **lapping**, *past* **lapped lap against/on, etc sth** If water laps against something, it touches it gently in waves.

lap sth up *phrasal verb informal* to enjoy something very much *He loved all the attention - he was lapping it up!*

lapel /ləˈpel/ *noun* [C] the part of a collar that is folded against the front of a shirt or jacket *wide lapels* ➲See picture at **jacket**

WORD PARTNERS FOR ***lapse***

a **momentary** lapse • a lapse **in/of** sth

lapse[1] /læps/ *noun* [C] **1** FAILURE a period of time when something fails to happen as it should *a memory lapse* ○ *It is thought that the accident was caused by a* ***lapse of*** *concentration.* **2** TIME a period of time passing between two things happening *a* ***time lapse****/a* ***lapse of time*** ○ *He turned up again after a lapse of two years.*

lapse[2] /læps/ *verb* [I] If an arrangement lapses, it stops existing because of the amount of time that has passed. *I've allowed my membership to lapse.*

lapse into sth *phrasal verb* If you lapse into something, you change to a different, and usually bad, condition. *to lapse into silence*

laptop /ˈlæptɒp/ *noun* [C] **COMPUTING** a computer that is small enough to be carried around and used where you are sitting

larch /lɑːtʃ/ *noun* [C] a tall tree which grows in cold northern countries and has leaves that are shaped like needles

O-■ **large** /lɑːdʒ/ *adjective* **1** big in size or amount *a large number of people* ○ *a large amount of money* ○ *She comes from quite a large family.* ○ *The shirt was a bit too large.* ➲Opposite **small** **2 be at large** If someone dangerous is at large, they are not in prison. **3 sb/sth at large** people or things in general *This group is not representative of the population at large.* **4 by and large** in most situations *By and large, people have welcomed the changes.*

ˌlarge inˈtestine *noun* [C, usually singular] **ANATOMY** the lower part of the bowels in which water is removed from digested food before it is passed out of the body as solid waste ➲Compare **small intestine** ➲See picture at **alimentary canal**

largely /ˈlɑːdʒli/ *adverb* mainly *Their complaints have been largely ignored.*

large-scale /ˈlɑːdʒˌskeɪl/ *adjective* involving a lot of people or happening in big numbers *a large-scale development* ○ *large-scale redundancies*

lark /lɑːk/ *noun* [C] a small brown bird that is known for its beautiful singing

larva /ˈlɑːvə/ *noun* [C] *plural* **larvae** /ˈlɑːviː/ **BIOLOGY** the form of some creatures, for example insects, before they develop into a different form *insect larvae*

larynx /ˈlærɪŋks/ *noun* [C] *plural* **larynxes** or **larynges ANATOMY** (*informal* **voice box**) an organ between the nose and the lungs which contains the muscles that move very quickly to create the human voice and many animal sounds ➲See picture at **respiratory system**

lasagne *UK* (*US* **lasagna**) /ləˈzænjə/ (US) /ləˈzɑːnjə/ *noun* [U] **FOOD** a type of Italian food consisting of flat pieces of pasta with layers of meat and sauce in between

laser /ˈleɪzəʳ/ *noun* [C] **PHYSICS** a strong beam of light that has medical and technical uses *a* ***laser beam*** ○ ***laser surgery***

ˈlaser ˌprinter *noun* [C] **COMPUTING** a printer (= a machine which is connected to a computer and which produces writing or pictures) which uses a laser (= a strong beam of light) to produce very clear writing or pictures

lash[1] /læʃ/ *verb* **1** [I, T] If wind or rain lashes against something, the wind or rain is very strong and hits or blows hard against it. ***Rain lashed*** *against the window.* **2 lash sth down/together, etc** to tie something firmly to something else

lash out *phrasal verb* **1** HIT to suddenly hit someone *He lashed out and caught her on the side of the face.* **2** CRITICIZE to criticize someone angrily *He* ***lashed out at*** *the government for refusing to take action.*

lash[2] /læʃ/ *noun* [C] a hit with a whip (= long, thin piece of leather) *He was given forty lashes.*

lashes /ˈlæʃɪz/ *noun* [plural] **ANATOMY** the small hairs on the edges of your eye

lass /læs/ *noun* [C] *UK informal* a girl or a young woman *a young lass*

O-■ **last[1]** /lɑːst/ *adjective, determiner* **1** MOST RECENT [**always before noun**] the most recent *What was the last film you saw?* ○ *It's rained for the last three days.* **2** ONE BEFORE PRESENT [**always before noun**] The last book, house, job, etc is the one before the present one. *I liked his last book but I'm not so keen on this latest one.* **3** FINAL happening or coming at the end *It's the last room on the left.* ○ *That's the last programme of the series.* ○ *I was the last one to arrive.* ○ *"How did she get on in her race?" "She was last."*

4 REMAINING [**always before noun**] only remaining *Who wants the last piece of cake?* **5 the last person/thing, etc** the least expected or wanted person or thing *Three extra people to feed - that's the last thing I need!* ○ *He's the last person you'd expect to see at an aerobics class.* ➲Opposite **first** ➲See also: be on its last legs (**leg**), the final/last **straw**, have the last **word**[1]

O╍**last**[2] /lɑːst/ *adverb* **1** AFTER ALL OTHERS after everything or everyone else *I wasn't expecting to win the race but I didn't think I'd come last!* ○ *We've still got to check the figures but we'll do that last.* **2** MOST RECENT used to talk about the most recent time you did something *When did you last see her?* **3 last but not least** something that you say to introduce the last person or thing on a list *This is Jeremy, this is Cath and, last but not least, this is Eva.* ➲Opposite **first**

O╍**last**[3] /lɑːst/ *noun, pronoun* **1 the last** a person or thing that comes after all the others [**+ to do sth**] We were the last to get there. **2 the last of sth** the only part of something that remains *We've just finished the last of the wine.* **3 the day/week/year before last** the day, week, or year before the one that has just finished **4 at (long) last** finally *At last, I've found a pair of jeans that actually fit.* **5 the last I heard** used before saying a piece of information about someone that you previously heard *The last I heard, they were selling their house.*

O╍**last**[4] /lɑːst/ *verb* [**I, T**] **1** CONTINUE to continue to happen, exist, or be useful *How long will the meeting last?* ○ *We don't get much sun - **enjoy it while it lasts!*** ○ *The batteries only last about five hours.* **2** BE ENOUGH to be enough for a period of time *I've only got £30 to last me till the end of the month.* ○ *We've got enough food to last another week.*

last-ditch /ˌlɑːstˈdɪtʃ/ *adjective* **a last-ditch attempt/effort** a final attempt to solve a problem that you have failed to solve several times before *a last-ditch effort to prevent war*

lasting /ˈlɑːstɪŋ/ *adjective* continuing to exist for a long time ***lasting damage*** ○ *a lasting friendship*

lastly /ˈlɑːstli/ *adverb* finally *And lastly, I'd like to thank everyone who took part in the event.*

last-minute /ˌlɑːstˈmɪnɪt/ *adjective* done at the last possible time *I was just doing some **last-minute preparations**.*

ˈlast ˌname *noun* [**C**] the name that you and other members of your family all have

latch[1] /lætʃ/ *noun* [**C**] **1** BAR a small piece of metal on a door that you move down so that the door will stay closed **2** LOCK a type of lock for a door that you need a key to open from the outside

latch[2] /lætʃ/ *verb*

latch on *phrasal verb informal* to begin to understand something *It took me ages to **latch on** to what she was saying.*

O╍**late** /leɪt/ *adjective, adverb* **1** AFTER THE USUAL TIME after the usual time or the time that was arranged *I was late for work this morning.* ○ *We got there too late and all the tickets had been sold.* ○ *We had a late lunch.* **2** NEAR END OF PERIOD near the end of a period of time *It was built in the late nineteenth century.* ○ *It was late at night.* ○ *Marsha is in her late twenties.* **3 it's late** something that you say when it is near the end of a day *It's late - I really should be going.* ○ *It's **getting late** and I'm a bit tired.* **4** DEAD [**always before noun**] not now alive *the late Mrs Walker* **5 of late** *formal* recently *We've scarcely seen him of late.*

lately /ˈleɪtli/ *adverb* recently *I haven't been feeling so well lately.* ○ *Lately, I've been walking to work.*

latent /ˈleɪtᵊnt/ *adjective* A feeling or quality that is latent exists now but is hidden or not yet developed. *latent hostility/racism*

ˌlatent ˈheat *noun* [**U**] **PHYSICS** the heat that is absorbed or released by a substance when it changes state, for example from a liquid to a gas, while the temperature of the substance remains unchanged

later /ˈleɪtəʳ/ *adjective* **1** AFTER SOME TIME after some time *I might arrange it for a later date.* **2** MORE RECENT more recent *I'm not so familiar with his later work.*

lateral /ˈlætᵊrᵊl/ *adjective formal* relating to the sides of an object or to sideways movement *Trim the lateral shoots of the plant.*

ˌlateral ˈmerger *noun* [**C**] **ECONOMICS** when two companies that produce similar goods but who do not compete with each other join together

laterite /ˈlætᵊraɪt/ *noun* [**U**] **GEOLOGY** a type of red clay soil containing iron and aluminium, often found in hot areas

later (on) *adverb* after some time *I'm off now - see you later.* ○ *If you're busy now we could do it later on.*

latest[1] /ˈleɪtɪst/ *adjective* [**always before noun**] most recent *the latest fashions/news/technology*

latest[2] /ˈleɪtɪst/ *noun* **1 the latest in sth** the most recent of its type *This is the latest in a series of terrorist attacks in the region.* **2 at the latest** If you tell someone to do something by a particular time at the latest, you mean they must do it before that time. *She said to be there by 8 o'clock at the latest.*

lathe /leɪð/ *noun* [**C**] **DT** a machine for changing the shape of a piece of wood, metal, etc. which works by turning the material while a sharp tool is pressed against it

lather /ˈlɑːðəʳ/ *noun* **1** [**U**] small white bubbles that are produced when soap is used with water **2 get into a lather** *informal* to become anxious or upset about something

Latin /ˈlætɪn/ *noun* [**U**] the language used by ancient Romans •**Latin** *adjective*

ˌLatin Aˈmerican *adjective* **SOCIETY** relating or belonging to the countries of South and Central America, and Mexico •**Latin American** *noun* [**C**] a Latin American person

Latino /ləˈtiːnəʊ/ *noun* [**C**] *US* **SOCIETY** someone who lives in the US whose family came from Latin America

latitude /ˈlætɪtjuːd/ *noun* **1** DISTANCE [**C, U**] **GEOGRAPHY** the distance of a place north or south of the Equator (= imaginary line around the Earth's middle), measured in degrees *The latitude of Helsinki is approximately 60 degrees*

L

north. **2** FREEDOM [U] *formal* freedom to do what you want *She should be allowed the latitude to choose the people she wants.*

latte /ˈlæteɪ/ (US) /ˈlɑːteɪ/ *noun* [C, U] **FOOD** a drink of coffee made from espresso (= strong coffee) and milk

latter /ˈlætəʳ/ *adjective* [**always before noun**] *formal* near the end of a period *the **latter half** of the twentieth century* ○ *She had moved to California in the **latter part** of the year.* ○ *She is now in the **latter stages** of the disease.*

latterly /ˈlætəli/ *adverb UK formal* recently *She started her career in radio, but latterly she has been working in television.*

the latter /ˈlætəʳ/ *noun* the second of two people or things that have just been talked about *She offered me more money or a car, and I chose the latter.*

laudable /ˈlɔːdəbl/ *adjective formal* A laudable idea or action deserves admiration, even if it is not successful. ***a laudable aim/ambition/goal***

O-■ **laugh**[1] /lɑːf/ *verb* [I] to smile while making sounds with your voice that show you are happy or think something is funny *You never **laugh at** my jokes.* ○ *She really **makes** me **laugh**.* ○ *It's very rare that a book is so good you **laugh out loud**.* ○ *It was so funny, we **burst out laughing*** (= laughed suddenly and loudly). ⊃See also: be no laughing **matter**[1]
laugh at sb/sth *phrasal verb* to show that you think someone or something is stupid *I can't go into work looking like this - everyone will laugh at me.*
laugh sth off *phrasal verb* to laugh about something unpleasant so that it seems less important *He was upset by the criticism though he tried to laugh it off at the time.*

laugh[2] /lɑːf/ *noun* [C] **1** the act or sound of laughing *a loud/nervous laugh* ○ *At the time, I was embarrassed, but I **had a good laugh*** (= laughed a lot) *about it later.* **2 be a (good) laugh** *UK informal* to be funny *You'd like David - he's a good laugh.* **3 for a laugh** *informal* If you do something for a laugh, you do it because you think it will be funny. *Just for a laugh, I pretended that I'd forgotten it was his birthday.*

laughable /ˈlɑːfəbl/ *adjective* If something is laughable, it is stupid and you cannot believe it or respect it. *Most people thought his suggestions were laughable.*

ˈlaughing ˌstock *noun* [**no plural**] someone who does something very stupid which makes other people laugh at them *If I wear this hat, I'll be the laughing stock of the party!*

WORD PARTNERS FOR ***laughter***

burst into laughter • **roar** with laughter • **be in fits of** laughter

O-■ **laughter** /ˈlɑːftəʳ/ *noun* [U] the sound or act of laughing *I heard the sound of laughter in the room next door.* ○ *The crowd **roared with laughter*** (= laughed very loudly).

launch[1] /lɔːnʃ/ *verb* [T] **1** SEND to send a spacecraft or bomb into the sky, or a ship into the water *to **launch** a **rocket/satellite*** ○ *to **launch** a **boat/fleet*** **2** BEGIN to begin an important activity *to **launch** an **attack/inquiry/investigation*** **3** NEW PRODUCT If a company launches a product or service, it makes it available for the first time. *The book was launched last February.* ○ *The airline will launch its new transatlantic service next month.*
launch into sth *phrasal verb* to start saying or criticizing something with a lot of anger or energy *Then he launched into a verbal attack on her management of the situation.*

launch[2] /lɔːnʃ/ *noun* [C] **1** SENDING the launching of a spacecraft, ship, or weapon *Poor weather delayed the space shuttle's launch.* **2** BEGINNING the beginning of an activity *The campaign's launch was a well-publicized event.* **3** NEW PRODUCT the time when a new product or service becomes available *The film's launch attracted a lot of Hollywood stars.* **4** BOAT a large boat with a motor *a police launch*

launder /ˈlɔːndəʳ/ *verb* [T] to hide the fact that an amount of money has been made illegally by putting the money into legal bank accounts or businesses *to **launder** drug **money*** •**laundering** *noun* [U] ***money laundering***

launderette /ˌlɔːndᵊrˈet/ *UK* (*US* **laundromat** /ˈlɔːndrəmæt/ *trademark*) *noun* [C] a place where you pay to use machines that wash and dry your clothes

laundry /ˈlɔːndri/ *noun* [U] clothes, sheets, etc that need to be washed *to **do the laundry*** ○ ***a laundry basket***

ˈlaundry deˌtergent *noun* [C, U] *US* washing powder

laurels /ˈlɒrᵊlz/ *noun* [**plural**] **rest on your laurels** to be so satisfied with what you have achieved that you make no effort to improve *Just because you've passed your exams, that's no reason to rest on your laurels.*

lava /ˈlɑːvə/ *noun* [U] **GEOLOGY** hot melted rock that comes out of a volcano ⊃See picture at **volcano**

lavatory /ˈlævətᵊri/ *noun* [C] *formal mainly UK* a toilet *to go to the lavatory* ○ *public lavatories* ⊃See Common Learner Error at **toilet**

lavender /ˈlævᵊndəʳ/ *noun* [U] a plant with purple flowers and a strong, pleasant smell *lavender oil*

lavish[1] /ˈlævɪʃ/ *adjective* showing that a lot of money has been spent *a lavish meal/party* •**lavishly** *adverb a lavishly illustrated book*

lavish[2] /ˈlævɪʃ/ *verb*
lavish sth on sb/sth *phrasal verb* to give a large amount of money, presents, attention, etc to someone or something *They have lavished more than £6 million on the new stadium.*

WORD PARTNERS FOR ***law***

break/enforce/obey/pass a law • the law **forbids/prohibits/requires** sth • a law **against** sth • **be against the law**

O-■ **law** /lɔː/ *noun* **1 LAW the law** the system of official rules in a country *You're **breaking the*** *law.* ○ *It's **against the law*** (= illegal) not to wear seat belts. ○ It's their job to ***enforce** the **law**.* **2** LAW **by law** If you have to do something by law, it is illegal not to do it. *They have to provide a contract by law.* **3** LAW [C] an official rule in a country *There are **laws against** drinking in the street.* ○ *They led the fight to impose **laws on** smoking.* **4** LAW **law and order** the obeying of laws in society *a breakdown in law and order* **5** EDUCATION [U] the subject or job of understanding and dealing with the official laws of a country *to study/practise law* ○ *a law school/firm* ○ *a specialist in civil/criminal law* **6** ALWAYS TRUE [C] something that is always true in science, mathematics, etc. *the **laws of** nature/physics* ○ *the law of averages/gravity* **7 lay down the law** to repeatedly tell people what they should do, without caring about how they feel *People are fed up with him laying down the law the whole time.* ➲See also: **brother-in-law, common-law, daughter-in-law, father-in-law, in-laws, martial law, mother-in-law, sister-in-law, son-in-law**

law-abiding /ˈlɔːəˌbaɪdɪŋ/ *adjective* A law-abiding person always obeys the law. *a **law-abiding citizen***

lawful /ˈlɔːfəl/ *adjective* LAW allowed by the law *He was going about his lawful business as a press photographer.*

lawmaker /ˈlɔːˌmeɪkər/ *noun* [C] *US* LAW someone who makes laws *state lawmakers*

lawn /lɔːn/ *noun* [C] an area of grass that is cut *to mow the lawn*

ˈlawn ˌmower *noun* [C] a machine that you use to cut grass

lawsuit /ˈlɔːsuːt/ *noun* [C] LAW a legal complaint against someone that does not usually involve the police *The tenants have **filed a lawsuit against** their landlord.*

O⁻**lawyer** /ˈlɔɪər/ *noun* [C] LAW someone whose job is to understand the law and deal with legal situations *I want to see my lawyer before I say anything else.*

> **COMMON LEARNER ERROR**
>
> **lawyer, solicitor, barrister, attorney**
>
> In Britain, **lawyers** are divided into two types, **solicitors** and **barristers**. **Solicitors** give advice on legal subjects and work in the lower courts of law. **Barristers** can represent people in the higher courts of law. In America, there is only one type of lawyer, who is sometimes called an **attorney**.

lax /læks/ *adjective* not careful enough or not well controlled *They seem to have a very lax attitude towards security.*

O⁻**lay¹** /leɪ/ *verb past* **laid 1 lay sth down/in/on, etc** to put something down somewhere carefully *She laid the baby on the bed.* ○ *He laid the tray down on the table.* **2** [T] to put something into its correct position *to lay a carpet* ○ *to lay bricks* **3 lay eggs** If an animal lays eggs, it produces them out of its body. **4 lay the blame on sb** to blame someone, usually when this is not fair *You always lay the blame on me!* **5 lay the table** *UK* to put plates, knives, forks, etc on the table to prepare for a meal ➲See also: put/lay your cards (**card**) on the table, lay the **foundation**(s) for/of sth, get/lay your hands (**hand**¹) on sth, lay down the **law**

> **COMMON LEARNER ERROR**
>
> **lay and lie**
>
> Be careful not to confuse these verbs.
>
> **Lay** means 'put down carefully' or 'put down flat'. This verb is always followed by an object. **Laying** is the present participle. **Laid** is the past simple and the past participle.
>
> *She laid the papers on the desk.*
>
> **Lie** means 'be in a horizontal position' or 'be in a particular place'. This verb is irregular and is never followed by an object. **Lying** is the present participle. **Lay** is the past simple and **lain** is the past participle.
>
> *The papers were lying on the desk.*
>
> ~~*The papers were laying on the desk.*~~
>
> *I lay down and went to sleep.*
>
> ~~*I laid down and went to sleep.*~~
>
> The regular verb **lie** means 'not say the truth'.
>
> *He lied to me about his age.*

lay sth down *phrasal verb* **1** MAKE RULES to officially make new rules, or to officially say how something must be done *The committee has **laid down guidelines** for future cases.* **2** STOP FIGHTING If someone lays down their weapons, they stop fighting. *It is hoped the two sides will lay down their arms and return to peace.*

lay into sb *phrasal verb informal* to attack or criticize someone *They started laying into me for no reason.*

lay sb off *phrasal verb* to stop employing someone, usually because there is no more work for them [**often passive**] *Thirty more people were laid off last week.*

lay sth on *phrasal verb* to provide something for a group of people *They're laying on free buses to and from the concert.*

lay sth out *phrasal verb* **1** ARRANGE to arrange something on a surface *He'd laid his tools out all over the kitchen floor.* **2** EXPLAIN to explain something clearly, usually in writing *I've just laid out some proposals.*

lay² /leɪ/ *adjective* [**always before noun**] **1** RELIGION involved in religious activities, but not trained as a priest *a **lay preacher*** **2** not having special or detailed knowledge of a subject *a lay person/audience*

lay³ /leɪ/ *past tense of* lie¹

lay-by /ˈleɪbaɪ/ *noun* [C] *UK* a small area where cars can stop at the side of a road

> WORD PARTNERS FOR ***layer***
>
> a layer **of** sth • an **outer/top** layer • a **thick** layer of sth

O⁻**layer** /leɪər/ *noun* [C] an amount of a substance covering a surface, or one of several amounts of substance, each on top of the other *the **outer/top layer*** ○ *Place alternate **layers of** pasta and meat sauce in a shallow dish.* ○ *The shelf was covered in a thick layer of dust.* •**layer** *verb* [T] [**often passive**] The potatoes are ***layered with** onion.* ➲See also: **the ozone layer**

layman /ˈleɪmən/ (*also* **layperson**) *noun* [C] *plural* **laymen** someone who does not have special knowledge of a subject *Could you please explain that **in layman's terms*** (= in a simple way) *?*

layoff /ˈleɪɒf/ *noun* [C] the ending of someone's job by an employer, usually because there is no more work [**usually plural**] *Several hundred more layoffs are planned next month.*

layout /ˈleɪaʊt/ *noun* [C] the way that something is arranged *Do you like the* ***layout of*** *the kitchen?*

⊶**lazy** /ˈleɪzi/ *adjective* **1** [WORK] Someone who is lazy does not like working or using any effort. *You lazy thing!* ○ *He's too lazy to make his bed in the morning.* **2** [RELAXED] slow and relaxed *a lazy morning/weekend* •**lazily** *adverb* •**laziness** *noun* [U]

lb **MEASURES** *written abbreviation for* pound (= a unit for measuring weight)

LCD /ˌelsiːˈdiː/ *noun* [C] *abbreviation for* liquid crystal display: a screen for showing words or pictures which uses a liquid and an electric current *LCD TV*

LCM /ˌelsiːˈem/ *noun* [C] **MATHEMATICS** *abbreviation for* lowest common multiple: the lowest number that can be divided exactly by a particular group of numbers

leach /liːtʃ/ *verb* [T, I] **GEOGRAPHY** (of a substance) to come out of or to be removed from another substance, especially soil, by passing water through it

⊶**lead**[1] /liːd/ *verb past* **led** /led/ **1** [TAKE SOMEONE] [I, T] to show someone where to go, usually by taking them to a place or by going in front of them *She led them down the hall.* ○ *We followed a path that led us up the mountain.* ○ *You lead and we'll follow.* ○ *I'll* ***lead the way*** (= go first to show the route). **2** **lead into/to/towards, etc** If a path or road leads somewhere, it goes there. *That path leads to the beach.* **3** [BE WINNING] [I, T] to be winning a game *They were* ***leading by*** *11 points at half-time.* ○ *The Lions lead the Hawks 28-9.* **4** [BE THE BEST] [T] to be better than anyone else *I still believe that we lead the world in acting talent.* **5** [CONTROL] [T] to be in control of a group, country, or situation *to lead a discussion* ○ *Is this man really capable of leading the country?* ○ *Shearer* ***led*** *his team* ***to*** *victory.* **6** **lead sb to do sth** to cause someone to do or think something *What led you to think that?* ○ *I was* ***led to believe*** *that breakfast was included.* **7** **lead a busy/normal/quiet, etc life** to live in a particular way *He was able to lead a normal life despite his illness.* **8** **lead sb to a conclusion** to cause you to think that something is probably true *So you thought I was leaving, did you? What led you to that conclusion?*

lead to sth *phrasal verb* to cause something to happen or exist *A poor diet can lead to health problems in later life.*

lead up to sth *phrasal verb* to happen before an event *The shops are always busy in the weeks leading up to Christmas.*

WORD PARTNERS FOR ***lead (noun)***

take the lead • **increase/stretch** your lead • be **in** the lead

⊶**lead**[2] /liːd/ *noun* **1** [WINNING] [**no plural**] a winning position during a race or other situation where people are competing *She's* ***in the lead*** (= winning). ○ *France has just* ***taken the lead*** (= started to win). ○ *a three-goal lead* **2** [FILM/PLAY] [C] the main person in a film or play *She* ***plays the lead*** *in both films.* **3** [DOG] [C] *UK* (*US* **leash**) a chain or piece of leather fixed to a dog's collar so that it can be controlled *Dogs must be kept* ***on a lead*** *at all times.* **4** [ELECTRICITY] [C] *UK* (*US* **cord**) the wire that connects a piece of electrical equipment to the electricity supply **5** [INFORMATION] [C] information about a crime that police are trying to solve *Police are chasing up a new lead.*

lead[3] /liːd/ *adjective* [**always before noun**] The lead performer or lead part in a performance is the main performer or part. *the* ***lead singer*** ○ *Who played the* ***lead role****?*

lead[4] /led/ *noun* **1** **CHEMISTRY** [U] a soft, heavy, grey, poisonous metal used for roofs, pipes, etc (formula **Pb**) *a lead pipe* ○ *lead-free petrol/gasoline* **2** [C, U] the black part inside a pencil

⊶**leader** /ˈliːdər/ *noun* [C] **1** [PERSON IN CONTROL] a person in control of a group, country, or situation *a religious leader* ○ *Who's the* ***leader of*** *the Democratic Party in the Senate?* **2** [WINNER] someone or something that is winning during a race or other situation where people are competing *He's fallen two laps behind the leaders.* ○ *Microsoft is a world leader in software design.*

WORD PARTNERS FOR ***leadership***

leadership **of** sth • **under** sb's leadership • leadership **skills/qualities** • a leadership **contest**

leadership /ˈliːdəʃɪp/ *noun* **1** [JOB] [U] the job of being in control of a group, country, or situation *the* ***leadership of*** *the Conservative party* ○ ***leadership skills/qualities*** ○ ***a leadership contest*** **2** [PEOPLE] [**group**] the people in control of a group, country, or situation *There is growing discontent with the leadership.*

leading /ˈliːdɪŋ/ *adjective* [**always before noun**] very important or most important *He's a leading Hollywood producer.*

⊶**leaf**[1] /liːf/ *noun* [C] *plural* **leaves** /liːvz/ **1** **BIOLOGY** a flat, green part of a plant that grows from a stem or branch *an oak leaf* ○ *a lettuce leaf* ○ *the falling leaves* ➲See picture on **next page** **2** **take a leaf out of sb's book** *mainly UK* to copy something good that someone else does **3** **turn over a new leaf** to start to behave in a better way

leaf[2] /liːf/ *verb*

leaf through sth *phrasal verb* to turn the pages of a book or magazine and look at them quickly *She lay on the sofa, leafing through glossy magazines.*

leaflet /ˈliːflət/ *noun* [C] a piece of folded paper or a small book which contains information *I picked up a useful* ***leaflet on*** *how to fill in tax forms.*

leafy /ˈliːfi/ *adjective* [**always before noun**] A leafy place is pleasant and quiet with a lot of trees. *a* ***leafy lane/suburb***

league /liːg/ *noun* **1** **SPORT** [C] a group of teams which compete against each other in a sport *top/bottom of the league* ○ ***major/minor league baseball*** ○ *Who won the league championship this year?* **2** **be in league with sb** to be secretly working or planning something with

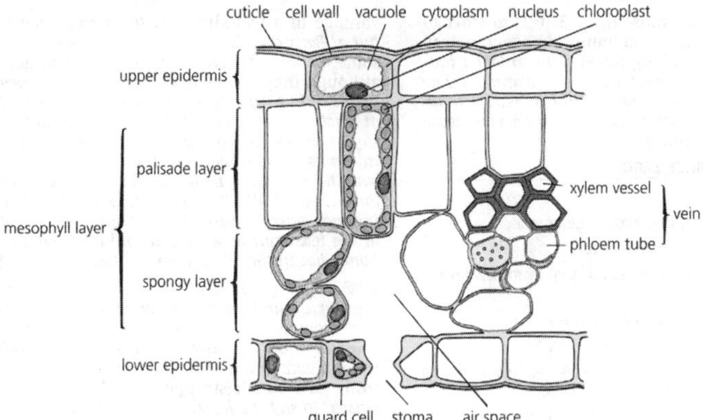

transverse section through part of leaf

someone, usually to do something bad **3 not be in the same league as sb/sth** *informal* to not be as good as someone or something *It's a nice enough restaurant but it's not in the same league as Rossi's.*

the ˌLeague of ˈNations *noun* **POLITICS** an organization of several countries formed to try to keep world peace, that existed from 1920 to 1946

leak¹ /liːk/ *verb* **1** LIQUID/GAS **[I, T]** If a liquid or gas leaks, it comes out of a hole by accident, and if a container leaks, it allows liquid or gas to come out when it should not. *Water had leaked all over the floor.* ○ *The bottle must have leaked because the bag's all wet.* **2** SECRETS **[T]** If someone leaks secret information, they intentionally tell people about it. *Details of the report had been **leaked to** the press.*
leak out *phrasal verb* If secret information leaks out, people find out about it.

leak² /liːk/ *noun* **[C]** **1** HOLE a hole in something that a liquid or gas comes out of, or the liquid or gas that comes out *I think we may have a leak in the roof.* ○ *a **gas leak*** **2** SECRET the act of intentionally telling people a secret

leakage /ˈliːkɪdʒ/ *noun* **[U]** the problem of a liquid or gas coming out of something when it should not

leaky /ˈliːki/ *adjective informal* Something that is leaky has a hole in it and liquid or gas can get through. *a leaky boat/roof*

O⊸**lean¹** /liːn/ *verb past* **leaned,** *(also UK)* **leant** /lent/ **lean (sth) back/forward/out, etc** to move the top part of your body in a particular direction *She leaned forward and whispered in my ear.* ○ *Lean your head back a bit.*
lean (sth) against/on sth *phrasal verb* to sit or stand with part of your body touching something as a support *He leaned against the wall.* ○ *She leaned her head on his shoulder.*
lean sth against/on sth *phrasal verb* to put something against a wall or other surface so that it is supported *Lean the ladder against the wall.*
lean on sb/sth *phrasal verb* to use someone or something to help you, especially in a difficult situation *Her mother had always leaned on her for support.*

lean² /liːn/ *adjective* **1** thin and healthy *lean and fit* **2 FOOD** Lean meat has very little fat on it.

leaning /ˈliːnɪŋ/ *noun* **[C]** a belief or idea **[usually plural]** *I don't know what his **political leanings** are.*

leap¹ /liːp/ *verb past* **leapt** /lept/ or **leaped** **1 leap into/out of/up, etc** to suddenly move somewhere *He leapt out of his car and ran towards the house.* ○ *I leapt up to answer the phone.* **2 leap off/over/into, etc** to jump somewhere *She leapt over the wall and disappeared down the alley.*
leap at sth *phrasal verb* to accept the chance to have or do something with enthusiasm *I'd **leap at the opportunity** to work in Japan.*

WORD PARTNERS FOR ***leap***

a leap **in** sth • a leap **of** [75%/5 million, etc] • a leap **forward**

leap² /liːp/ *noun* **[C]** **1** CHANGE a sudden improvement or increase *There was a big **leap in** profits last year.* ○ *This represents a great **leap forward** in technology.* **2** JUMP a big jump *He finished third in the long jump with a leap of 26 feet.* **3 by/in leaps and bounds** If progress or growth happens in leaps and bounds, it happens very quickly. ⊃See also: **quantum leap**

ˈleap ˌyear *noun* **[C]** a year that happens every four years, in which February has 29 days instead of 28

O⊸**learn** /lɜːn/ *verb past* **learned,** *(also UK)* **learnt** /lɜːnt/ **1 EDUCATION [I, T]** to get knowledge or skill in a new subject or activity *I learned Russian at school.* ○ *"Can you drive?" "I'm learning."* ○ *She's **learned** a lot **about** computers in the last three months.* **[+ to do sth]** *I'm learning to play the piano.* **2 EDUCATION [T]** to make yourself remember a piece of writing by reading or repeating it many times *I don't know how* *actors learn all those lines.* **3** [**I, T**] to start to understand that you must change the way you behave [**+ (that)**] *She'll have to learn that she can't have everything she wants.* ○ *The good thing is, he's not afraid to* ***learn from his mistakes***. See also: learn your **lesson**, learn/know the ropes (**rope**[1])

COMMON LEARNER ERROR

learn, teach, or **study?**

To **learn** is to get new knowledge or skills.

I want to learn how to drive.

When you **teach** someone, you give them new knowledge or skills.

My dad taught me how to drive.

~~*My dad learnt me how to drive.*~~

When you study, you go to classes, read books, etc to try to understand new ideas and facts.

He is studying biology at university.

learn about/of sth *phrasal verb* to hear facts or information that you did not know *We only learned about the accident later.*

learned /ˈlɜːnɪd/ *adjective formal* Someone who is learned has a lot of knowledge from reading and studying. *He was a very learned man.*

learner /ˈlɜːnəʳ/ *noun* [**C**] someone who is getting knowledge or a new skill *learners of English*

learning /ˈlɜːnɪŋ/ *noun* [**U**] the process of getting knowledge or a new skill *language learning*

ˈlearning ˌcurve *noun* [**C**] **EDUCATION** how quickly or slowly someone learns a new skill *I've been on a* ***steep learning curve*** *since I started my new job.*

WORD PARTNERS FOR ***lease***

renew/sign/take a lease • a lease **of/on** sth

lease[1] /liːs/ *noun* [**C**] **1 LAW** a legal agreement in which you pay money in order to use a building or a piece of land for a period of time *We* ***signed*** *a three-year* ***lease*** *when we moved into the house.* **2 give sb/sth a new lease of life** *UK* (*also US* **give sb/sth a new lease on life**) **a** HAPPY/HEALTHY AGAIN to make someone feel happy or healthy after a period of illness or sadness *The operation has given her a new lease of life.* **b** IMPROVE to improve something that was old so that it works much better

lease[2] /liːs/ *verb* [**T**] **LAW** to use a building or piece of land, or to allow someone to use a building or piece of land, in exchange for money *We want to lease some office space in the centre of town.* ○ *The council eventually* ***leased*** *the land* ***to*** *a local company.*

leash /liːʃ/ (*also UK* **lead**) *noun* [**C**] a chain or piece of leather fixed to a dog's collar so that it can be controlled

least[1] /liːst/ *adverb* **1** less than anyone or anything else *Which car costs least?* ○ *I chose the least expensive dish on the menu.* ○ *No one,* ***least of all*** (= especially not) *James, is going to be angry with you.* **2 at least a** as much as, or more than, a number or amount *You'll have to wait at least an hour.* **b** something that you say when you are telling someone about an advantage in a bad situation *It's a small house but at least there's a garden.* **c** used to say that someone should give a small amount of help although they do not intend to give a lot *Even if you didn't want to send a present, you could at least have sent a card.* **d** something that you say in order to correct something you said that was wrong *I've seen that film. At least, I saw the beginning then I fell asleep.* **3 not least** *formal* especially *The whole trip was fascinating, not least because of the people I met.* **4 not in the least** not at all *I don't mind staying at home, not in the least.* See also: **last**[2] but not least

least[2] /liːst/ *quantifier* **1** the smallest amount *She earns the least money of all of us.* ○ *Jake had more experience than anyone else and I probably had the least.* **2 to say the least** used to emphasize that you could have said something in a much stronger way *We were surprised, to say the least.*

leather /ˈleðəʳ/ *noun* [**U**] the skin of animals that is used to make things such as shoes and bags *a leather jacket*

leave[1] /liːv/ *verb past* **left** /left/ **1** GO AWAY [**I, T**] to go away from a place or a situation, either permanently or for a temporary period *I'm leaving work early this afternoon.* ○ *What time does the bus leave?* ○ *They* ***left for*** *Paris last night.* ○ *"Does Trevor still work there?" "No, he left."* (= he does not work there now). ○ *She left school at 16.* **2** END RELATIONSHIP [**I, T**] to end a relationship with a husband, wife, or partner and stop living with them *I'll never leave you.* ○ *She* ***left*** *him* ***for*** *a younger man.* **3** NOT TAKE [**T**] to not take something with you when you go away from a place, either intentionally or by accident *Why don't you leave your jacket in the car?* ○ *She'd left a note for him in the kitchen.* ○ *That's the second umbrella I've left on the train!* **4** NOT USE ALL [**T**] to not use all of something *They'd drunk all the wine but they'd left some food.* ○ *Are there any biscuits left?* **5** REMAIN [**T**] to make a permanent mark *The operation may leave a scar.* **6 leave sth open/on/off, etc** to cause something to stay in a particular condition *Who left the window open?* **7** DO LATER [**T**] to do something later that you could do immediately *Don't leave your packing till the night before you go.* **8** GIVE [**T**] to arrange for someone to receive something after you die *His aunt left him a lot of money.* ○ *He* ***left*** *the house* ***to*** *Julia.* **9 leave sb alone** to stop speaking to or annoying someone *Leave me alone! I'm trying to work.* **10 leave sth alone** to stop touching something *Leave your hair alone!* See also: leave someone to their own devices (**device**), leave/make your **mark**[1]

leave sb/sth behind *phrasal verb* to leave a place without taking something or someone with you *We were in a hurry and I think I must have left my keys behind.*

leave behind sth; leave sth behind (sb) *phrasal verb* to cause a situation to exist after you have left a place *The army left a trail of destruction behind them.*

leave sth for/to sb *phrasal verb* to give someone the responsibility for dealing with something *I've left the paperwork for you.*

leave sb/sth out *phrasal verb* to not include someone or something *I've made a list of*

names - I hope I haven't left anyone out.
be left out *phrasal verb* If someone feels left out, they are unhappy because they have not been included in an activity. *The older children had gone upstairs to play and she felt left out.*
be left over *phrasal verb* If an amount of money or food is left over, it remains when the rest has been used or eaten. *There was a lot of food left over from the party.*

WORD PARTNERS FOR ***leave***

annual/maternity/paternity/sick leave • **on** leave • leave **from** [work/your job, etc]

leave[2] /liːv/ *noun* [U] a period of time when you do not go to work *She's **on** maternity/sick **leave**.*

leaves /liːvz/ *plural of* leaf

lecherous /ˈletʃᵊrəs/ *adjective* A lecherous man shows too much interest in sex, in a way that is unpleasant.

lecithin /ˈlesɪθɪn/ *noun* [U] **BIOLOGY** a substance found in plant and animal tissue which is often used in food products to help the different parts mix together well

lecture[1] /ˈlektʃəʳ/ *noun* [C] **1 EDUCATION** a formal talk given to a group of people in order to teach them about a subject *We went to a **lecture on** Italian art.* ○ *Do you know who's **giving the lecture** this afternoon?* **2** an angry or serious talk given to someone in order to criticize their behaviour *My dad **gave** me **a lecture on** smoking last night.*

lecture[2] /ˈlektʃəʳ/ *verb* **1 EDUCATION** [I] to give a formal talk to a group of people, often at a university *She travelled widely throughout North America **lecturing on** women's rights.* ○ *For ten years she **lectured in** law.* **2** [T] to talk angrily to someone in order to criticize their behaviour *Stop lecturing me!* ○ *His parents used to **lecture** him **on** his table manners.*

lecturer /ˈlektʃᵊrəʳ/ *noun* [C] *mainly UK* **EDUCATION** someone who teaches at a university or college *a **lecturer in** psychology* ○ *a senior lecturer*

COMMON LEARNER ERROR

lecturer or **teacher?**

In American English, **lecturer** is formal, and **teacher** or **professor** is usually used instead.

led /led/ *past of* lead

ledge /ledʒ/ *noun* [C] a long, flat surface that comes out under a window or from the side of a mountain *The birds landed on a ledge about halfway up the cliff.*

ledger /ˈledʒəʳ/ *noun* [C] **FINANCE** a book in which things are regularly recorded, especially business activities and money received or paid

leech /liːtʃ/ *noun* [C] a type of fat worm that drinks the blood of people and animals

leek /liːk/ *noun* [C, U] **FOOD** a long white and green vegetable that smells and tastes similar to an onion

leer /lɪəʳ/ *verb* [I] to look at someone in an unpleasant and sexually interested way *He was always **leering at** female members of staff.* •**leer** *noun* [C]

leery /ˈlɪəri/ *adjective US* worried and not able to trust someone *I've gotten more **leery of** the media.*

leeway /ˈliːweɪ/ *noun* [U] freedom to do what you want *My current boss **gives** me much more **leeway**.*

O⁻ **left**[1] /left/ *adjective, adverb* on or towards the side of your body that is to the west when you are facing north [**always before noun**] *Step forward on your left leg.* ○ *She had a diamond earring in her left ear.* ○ ***Turn left** at the end of the corridor.* ⊃Opposite **right**

WORD PARTNERS FOR ***left (noun)***

on the left • the left **of** sth • be **to** sb's left

O⁻ **left**[2] /left/ *noun* **1** [**no plural**] the left side *Ned's the man sitting **on** my **left** in that photo.* ○ *Jean's house is last **on the left**.* **2 the Left/left POLITICS** political groups which believe that power and money should be shared more equally among people *The proposals were sharply criticized by the Left.* ⊃Opposite **right**

left[3] /left/ *past of* leave

ˌ**left** ˈ**click** *verb* [I] **COMPUTING** to press the button on the left of a computer mouse (= a small piece of equipment that you move with your hand to control what the computer does)

ˌ**left** ˈ**field** *noun US informal* **in/from/out of left field** strange and not expected *His question came out of left field, and I didn't know what to say.*

left-hand /ˌleftˈhænd/ *adjective* [**always before noun**] on the left *a left-hand drive car* (= car which you drive sitting on the left-hand side) ○ *The swimming pool is on **the left-hand side** of the road.*

left-handed /ˌleftˈhændɪd/ *adjective* Someone who is left-handed uses their left hand to do most things. *Are you left-handed?*

leftist /ˈleftɪst/ *adjective* **POLITICS** supporting the ideas of parties on the political left *leftist politics/ideas*

leftover /ˈleftˌəʊvəʳ/ *adjective* [**always before noun**] Leftover food remains after a meal. *If there's any leftover food we can take it home with us.* •**leftovers** *noun* [**plural**] food which remains after a meal *We've been eating up the leftovers from the party all week.*

left-wing /ˌleftˈwɪŋ/ *adjective* **POLITICS** supporting the ideas of parties on the political left *a left-wing newspaper* •**left-winger** *noun* [C]

O⁻ **leg** /leg/ *noun* [C] **1 ANATOMY** one of the parts of the body of a human or animal that is used for standing and walking *He broke his leg in the accident.* ○ *There were cuts on her arms and legs.* ○ *She had bare legs and wore only a light summer dress.* ⊃See colour picture **The Body** on page Centre 13 **2 FOOD** the meat of an animal's leg eaten as food *a chicken leg* **3** FURNITURE one of the vertical parts of a chair, table, etc that is on the floor *a **chair/table leg*** **4** CLOTHES the part of a pair of trousers that covers one of your legs *He rolled up his **trouser legs** and* *waded into the water.* **5** PART OF JOURNEY one part of a journey or competition *the first/second/third leg of the journey* **6 not have a leg to stand on** to have no chance of proving that something is true *If you don't have a witness, you don't have a leg to stand on.* **7 be on its last legs** *informal* If a machine is on its last legs, it will stop working soon because it is so old. *We've had the same oven for twenty years now and it really is on its last legs.* **8 stretch your legs** *informal* to go for a walk

legacy /ˈlegəsi/ *noun* [C] **1** SITUATION a situation that was caused by something from an earlier time *The war has left a* ***legacy of*** *hatred.* **2** MONEY money or buildings, etc that you receive after someone dies

O-■**legal** /ˈliːgəl/ *adjective* **1** LAW relating to the law *legal action/advice ○ the legal profession/system* **2** LAW allowed by law *Is it legal to carry a handgun?* ➲Opposite **illegal** •**legally** *adverb Children under sixteen are not legally allowed to buy cigarettes.*

ˌ**legal ˈaid** *noun* [U] LAW a system that provides free advice about the law to people who are too poor to pay for it

legality /liːˈgæləti/ *noun* [U] LAW the legal quality of a situation or action *Some board members have questioned the legality of the proposal.*

legalize /ˈliːgəlaɪz/ *verb* [T] LAW to make something legal *How many Americans want to legalize drugs?* •**legalization** /ˌliːgəlaɪˈzeɪʃən/ *noun* [U] *the legalization of abortion*

legend /ˈledʒənd/ *noun* **1** LITERATURE [C, U] an old story or set of stories from ancient times *the legends of King Arthur ○ She's writing a book on Greek legend.* **2** FAMOUS PERSON [C] a famous person *a living legend ○ Jazz legend, Ella Fitzgerald, once sang in this bar.*

legendary /ˈledʒəndəri/ *adjective* **1** OLD from a legend (= old story) *a legendary Greek hero* **2** FAMOUS very famous *He became editor of the legendary Irish journal, 'The Bell'.*

leggings /ˈlegɪŋz/ *noun* [plural] tight trousers which are made of soft material that stretches and are worn mainly by women *a pair of leggings*

legible /ˈledʒəbl/ *adjective* If writing is legible, you can read it easily. ➲Opposite **illegible**

legion /ˈliːdʒən/ *noun* [C] a large group of soldiers that forms part of an army

legions /ˈliːdʒənz/ *noun* [plural] **legions of sb** large numbers of people *He failed to turn up for the concert, disappointing the legions of fans waiting outside.*

legislate /ˈledʒɪsleɪt/ *verb* [I] POLITICS, LAW If a government legislates, it makes a new law. *We believe it is possible to* ***legislate against*** *racism. ○ It's hard to* ***legislate for*** (= make a law that will protect) *the ownership of an idea.*

WORD PARTNERS FOR ***legislation***

introduce/pass legislation • a **piece of** legislation • legislation **on** sth

legislation /ˌledʒɪˈsleɪʃən/ *noun* [U] POLITICS, LAW a law or a set of laws *Most people want tougher environmental legislation but large corporations continue to oppose it. ○ They're relaxing the legislation.*

legit /ləˈdʒɪt/ *adjective informal short for* legitimate

legitimate /lɪˈdʒɪtəmət/ *adjective* **1** LAW allowed by law *Sales of illegal CDs now exceed those of legitimate recordings.* ➲Opposite **illegitimate** **2** CAN BE UNDERSTOOD A legitimate complaint or fear can be understood or believed. *People have expressed* ***legitimate fears*** *about the spread of the disease. ○ It's a legitimate criticism.* •**legitimately** *adverb*

leisure /ˈleʒər/ (US) /ˈliːʒər/ *noun* [U] **1** the time when you are not working ***leisure activities*** *○ Try to spend your* ***leisure time*** *doing activities you really enjoy.* **2 at your leisure** If you do something at your leisure, you do it when you have the time. *Take it home and read it at your leisure.*

ˈ**leisure** ˌ**centre** *noun* [C] *UK* SPORT a building with a swimming pool and places where you can play sports *She goes to aerobic classes at the local leisure centre.*

leisurely /ˈleʒəli/ (US) /ˈliːʒərli/ *adjective* in a relaxed way without hurrying *a* ***leisurely stroll***

lemon /ˈlemən/ *noun* [C, U] FOOD an oval, yellow fruit that has sour juice *a* ***slice of lemon*** *○* ***lemon juice*** ➲See colour picture **Fruit and Vegetables** on page Centre 10

lemonade /ˌleməˈneɪd/ *noun* [C, U] **1** FOOD *UK* a cold drink with a lemon flavour that is sweet and has bubbles **2** FOOD *mainly US* a cold drink that is made from lemon juice, water, and sugar

O-■**lend** /lend/ *verb past* **lent** /lent/ **1** [+ two objects] to give something to someone for a period of time, expecting that they will then give it back to you *She lent me her car for the weekend. ○ I do have a bike but I've* ***lent*** *it* ***to*** *Sara. ○ I've lent my copy of the book to Celia.* **2** ECONOMICS, FINANCE [I, T] If a bank lends money, it gives money to someone who then pays the money back in small amounts over a period. *The bank refused to lend us money for another mortgage.*
lend itself to sth *phrasal verb formal* to be suitable for a particular purpose *The old system doesn't lend itself to mass production.*
lend sth to sb/sth *phrasal verb formal* to add a quality to something or someone *We will continue to lend support to our allies.*

lender /ˈlendər/ *noun* [C] FINANCE a person or organization that lends money to people *mortgage lenders*

WORD PARTNERS FOR ***length***

the length **of** sth • [20m/3cm, etc] **in** length

O-■**length** /leŋθ/ *noun* **1** MEASURES [C, U] the measurement or distance of something from one end to the other *The carpet is over three metres* ***in length.*** *○ The length of the bay is roughly 200 miles.* ➲See Extra help page **Numbers and measurements** on page Centre 24. **2** TIME [C, U] the amount of time something takes *the length of* *a film/play/speech* ○ *Sitting still for any length of time is quite hard for most children.* **3** WRITING **[C, U]** the amount of writing in a book or document *He's written books of various lengths on the subject.* **4 at length** If you talk about something at length, you talk for a long time. *We discussed both topics at length.* **5** PIECE **[C]** a long piece of something *a length of cloth/cord/rope* **6 go to great lengths to do sth** to try very hard to achieve something *He'll go to great lengths to get what he wants.* **7 the length and breadth of sth** in every part of a place *They travelled the length and breadth of Scotland together.*

lengthen /'leŋθən/ *verb* **[I, T]** to become longer or to make something longer *lengthening waiting lists*

lengthy /'leŋθi/ *adjective* continuing for a long time *a **lengthy discussion/process***

lenient /'liːniənt/ *adjective* A lenient punishment is not severe. *He asked the judge to pass a lenient sentence.*

lens /lenz/ *noun* **[C] 1 PHYSICS** a curved piece of glass in cameras, glasses, and scientific equipment used for looking at things ⊃See also: **contact lens, zoom lens 2 ANATOMY** the part of the eye behind the pupil (= dark hole) that helps you see well ⊃See picture at **eye**

lens

lens

lent /lent/ *past of* lend

Lent /lent/ *noun* **[U] RELIGION** the religious period before Easter (= a Christian holiday), in which some Christians do not allow themselves something that they usually enjoy *She's given up chocolate for Lent.*

lentil /'lentᵊl/ *noun* **[C] FOOD** a very small dried bean which is cooked and eaten *lentil soup*

Leo /'liːəʊ/ *noun* **[C, U]** the sign of the zodiac which relates to the period of 23 July - 22 August, or a person born during this period

leopard /'lepəd/ *noun* **[C]** a large, wild animal of the cat family, with yellow fur and dark spots

leper /'lepəʳ/ *noun* **[C] HEALTH** a person who has leprosy

leprosy /'leprəsi/ *noun* **[U] HEALTH** a serious skin disease which can destroy parts of the body

lesbian /'lezbiən/ *noun* **[C]** a woman who is sexually attracted to other women *a lesbian affair*

O-m**less**[1] /les/ *adverb* **1** not as much *I'm trying to exercise more and eat less.* ○ *Plastic bottles are less expensive to produce.* **2 less and less** If something happens less and less, it gradually becomes smaller in amount or not so frequent. *I find I'm eating less and less red meat.*

O-m**less**[2] /les/ *quantifier* a smaller amount *She gets about £50 a week or less.* ○ *I was driving at **less than** 20 miles per hour.* ○ *Tuberculosis is **less of** a threat these days.* ○ *I prefer my coffee with a little less sugar.*

COMMON LEARNER ERROR

less or **fewer?**

Less is used before uncountable nouns.

I should eat less fat.

Fewer is used before countable nouns.

I should smoke fewer cigarettes.

-less /-ləs/ *suffix* changes a noun into an adjective meaning 'without' *homeless people* ○ *a meaningless statement* ○ *a hopeless situation*

lessen /'lesᵊn/ *verb* **[I, T]** to become less or to make something less *Exercise and a healthy diet lessen the chance of heart disease.*

lesser /'lesəʳ/ *adjective* **1** not as large, important, or of such good quality *The price increase was due to labour shortages and, **to a lesser extent**, the recent earthquake.* ○ *He faces the lesser charge of assault.* **2 the lesser of two evils** the less bad of two bad things *I suppose I regard the Democratic candidate as the lesser of two evils.*

lesser-known /ˌlesə'nəʊn/ *adjective* not as popular or famous as something else *We stayed on one of the lesser-known Greek islands.*

WORD PARTNERS FOR ***lesson***

have/take lessons • **give** sb a lesson

O-m**lesson** /'lesᵊn/ *noun* **[C] 1 EDUCATION** a period of time when a teacher teaches people *The best way to improve your game is to **take lessons**.* ○ *She **gives** French **lessons**.* ○ *Lessons start at 9 a.m.* **2** an experience which teaches you how to behave better in a similar situation in the future *My parents made me pay back all the money, and it was a lesson I never forgot.* **3 learn your lesson** to decide not to do something again because it has caused you problems in the past *I'm not going out without my umbrella again - I've learnt my lesson!* **4 teach sb a lesson** to punish someone so that they will not behave badly again *The next time she's late, go without her. That should teach her a lesson.*

O-m**let** /let/ *verb* **[T] letting**, *past* **let 1** ALLOW to allow someone to do something, or to allow something to happen *Let them play outside.* ○ *Don't let the camera get wet.* ○ *We let a whole year go by before we tried again.* ⊃See Common Learner Error at **allow 2 let sb/sth in/past/through, etc** to allow someone or something to move to a particular place *They won't let us past the gate.* ○ *I won't let him near my children.* ○ *The roof lets in a lot of rain.* **3 let's** something that you say when you are making a suggestion *Let's eat out tonight.* **4 let me/us** something that you say when you are offering to help someone *Let me carry your cases.* **5** BUILDING If you let a building or part of a building, you allow someone to live there and they give you money. *I **let** the top floor of my house **to** a student.* **6 Let's see/Let me see** something that you say when you are trying to remember something or calculate something *Let's see - there are five people and only three beds.* ○ *It must have been - let me see - three years ago.* **7 Let's say** something that you say when you are suggesting a possible situation or action *Let's say we'll meet back here in an hour.* **8 let sb know (sth)** to tell

L

someone something [+ **question word**] *I'll let you know when we've fixed a date for the meeting.* **9 let (sth) go** to stop holding something *I let go of the rope.* **10 let yourself go a** LESS ATTRACTIVE to allow yourself to become less attractive or healthy **b** RELAX to relax completely and enjoy yourself *It's a party - let yourself go!* **11 let's face it** something that you say when the truth is unpleasant but must be accepted *Let's face it, we're not getting any younger.* **12 let alone** used to emphasize that something is more impossible than another thing *You couldn't trust her to look after your dog, let alone your child.* ➲See also: let the **cat** out of the bag, let your **hair** down, get/let sb off the **hook**[1], let off **steam**[1]

let sb down *phrasal verb* to disappoint someone by failing to do what you agreed to do *I promised to go to the party with Jane and I can't let her down.*

let sb in *phrasal verb* to allow someone to enter a room or building, often by opening the door *Could you go down and let Darren in?*

let yourself in for sth *phrasal verb* to become involved in an unpleasant situation without intending to *Do you realize how much work you're letting yourself in for?*

let sb off *phrasal verb* to not punish someone who has done something wrong, or to not punish them severely *I'll let you off this time, but don't ever lie to me again.* ○ *The judge **let** her **off with*** (= only punished her with) a fine.

let on *phrasal verb* to tell someone about something secret *She **let on to** a friend that she'd lied in court.*

let sb/sth out *phrasal verb* to allow a person or animal to leave somewhere, especially by opening a locked or closed door

let up *phrasal verb* If bad weather or an unpleasant situation lets up, it stops or improves. *I hope the rain lets up for the weekend.*

letdown /ˈletdaʊn/ *noun* [**no plural**] *informal* a disappointment *After all I'd heard about the film it was a bit of a letdown when I finally saw it.*

lethal /ˈliːθəl/ *adjective* able to cause death

lethargic /ləˈθɑːdʒɪk/ *adjective* When you feel lethargic, you have no energy and you do not want to do anything. •**lethargy** /ˈleθədʒi/ *noun* [**U**] the feeling of being tired and having no energy

WORD PARTNERS FOR ***letter***

get/receive/send/write a letter • **in** a letter • a letter **from/to** sb

O-m **letter** /ˈletəʳ/ *noun* [**C**] **1** a written message that you send to someone, usually by post *I got a **letter** from Paul this morning.* **2** LANGUAGE a symbol that is used in written language and that represents a sound in that language *the letter K* ➲See also: **covering letter**

letterbox /ˈletəbɒks/ *noun* [**C**] *UK* **1** IN DOOR a small hole in a door that letters are put through **2** IN PUBLIC PLACE (*US* **mailbox**) a large, metal container in a public place where you can post letters

ˈletter ˌcarrier *US* (*UK* **postman**) *noun* [**C**] someone who takes and brings letters and parcels as a job

letterpress /ˈletəpres/ *noun* [**U**] **DT** a method of printing in which raised surfaces covered with ink are pressed onto paper

lettuce /ˈletɪs/ *noun* [**C**] **FOOD** a plant with green leaves, which is eaten in salads ➲See colour picture **Fruit and Vegetables** on page Centre 10

leucocyte /ˈljuːkəʊsaɪt/ *noun* [**C**] **BIOLOGY** a white blood cell

leukaemia *UK* (*US* **leukemia**) /luːˈkiːmiə/ *noun* [**U**] **HEALTH** a serious disease in which a person's body produces too many white blood cells

levee /ˈlevi/ *noun* [**C**] a wall made of land or other materials that is built next to a river to stop the river from flooding (= covering everywhere in water)

WORD PARTNERS FOR ***level***

the level **of** sth • **at** a (high/low, etc) level

O-m **level**[1] /ˈlevəl/ *noun* [**C**] **1** HEIGHT the height of something *the water level* **2** AMOUNT the amount or number of something *Chess requires a high level of concentration.* **3** ABILITY someone's ability compared to other people *Students at this level need a lot of help.* **4** FLOOR a floor in a building *The store had three levels.* ➲See also: **A level,** a level **playing field, sea level**

level[2] /ˈlevəl/ *adjective* **1** HEIGHT [**never before noun**] at the same height *I got down till my face was **level** with his.* **2** FLAT flat or horizontal *Make sure the camera is level before you take the picture.*

level[3] /ˈlevəl/ *verb* [**T**] *UK* **levelling,** *past* **levelled,** *US* **leveling,** *past* **leveled 1** MAKE FLAT to make something flat *He levelled the wet cement before it set.* **2** DESTROY to completely destroy a building *Artillery fire levelled the town.*

level sth against/at sb *phrasal verb* to say that someone has done something wrong [**often passive**] *Charges of corruption have been levelled against him.*

level sth at sb *phrasal verb* to aim a gun at someone or something *He levelled the gun at my head.*

level off/out *phrasal verb* to stop rising or falling and stay at the same level *Road deaths have levelled off since the speed limit was lowered.*

ˌlevel ˈcrossing *UK* (*US* **grade crossing**) *noun* [**C**] a place where a railway crosses a road

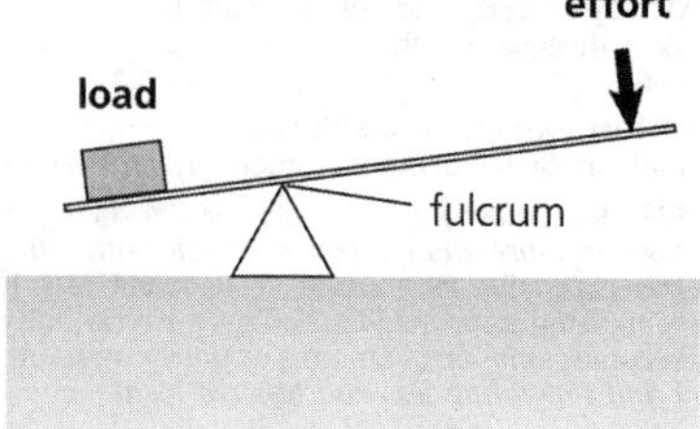

lever

lever /ˈliːvəʳ/ (US) /ˈlevər/ *noun* [**C**] **1** HANDLE a handle that you push or pull to make a machine work **2** [LIFTING] a long bar that you use to lift or move something by pressing one end

leverage /ˈliːvᵊrɪdʒ/ Ⓤ /ˈlevərɪdʒ/ *noun* **[U]** the power to influence people in order to get what you want

levy /ˈlevi/ *verb* **levy a charge/fine/tax, etc FINANCE** to officially demand money **[often passive]** *A new tax was* ***levied on*** *consumers of luxury goods.*

lewd /luːd/ *adjective* sexual in a way that is unpleasant *lewd comments/gestures*

liability /ˌlaɪəˈbɪləti/ *noun* **1** [RESPONSIBILITY] **[U]** when you are legally responsible for something *They have* ***admitted liability for*** *the damage caused.* **2** [TROUBLE] **[no plural]** someone or something that is likely to cause you a lot of trouble *Wherever we go she upsets someone - she's a real liability.* **3 FINANCE [usually plural]** a debt of a business

liable /ˈlaɪəbl/ *adjective* **1 be liable to do sth** to be likely to do something *He's liable to make a fuss if you wake him.* **2** legally responsible *Corporate officials are* ***liable for*** *the safety of their employees.*

liaise /liˈeɪz/ *verb* **[I]** to speak to other people at work in order to exchange information with them *Our head office will* ***liaise with*** *the suppliers to ensure delivery.*

liaison /liˈeɪzᵊn/ *noun* **1** [COMMUNICATION] **[U]** communication between people or groups that work with each other **2** [PERSON] **[C]** *US* someone who helps groups to communicate effectively with each another *She served as an informal liaison between employees and management.* **3** [RELATIONSHIP] **[C]** a short sexual relationship between people who are not married

liana /liˈɑːnə/ *noun* **[C]** a woody plant that grows in tropical (= in very hot parts of the world) forests

liar /ˈlaɪəʳ/ *noun* **[C]** someone who tells lies

Lib Dem /lɪbˈdem/ *noun* **[C] POLITICS** *short for* Liberal Democrat

libel /ˈlaɪbᵊl/ *noun* **[U]** writing which contains bad information about someone which is not true *Tabloid magazines are often sued for libel.*

liberal /ˈlɪbᵊrᵊl/ *adjective* **1** accepting beliefs and behaviour that are new or different from your own *a* ***liberal attitude*** **2 POLITICS** Liberal political ideas emphasize the need to make new laws as society changes and the need for government to provide social services. **•liberal** *noun* **[C]** someone who is liberal

ˌliberal ˈarts *US* (*UK/US* **arts**) *noun* **[plural] EDUCATION** subjects of study which are not science, such as history, languages, etc

ˌLiberal ˈDemocrat *noun* **[C] 1 the Liberal Democrats POLITICS** one of the three main political parties in the UK *He's the leader of the Liberal Democrats.* **2 POLITICS** someone who supports the Liberal Democrats

liberally /ˈlɪbᵊrᵊli/ *adverb* in large amounts *fruit liberally sprinkled with sugar*

liberate /ˈlɪbᵊreɪt/ *verb* **[T]** to help someone or something to be free *Troops liberated the city.* **•liberation** /ˌlɪbᵊrˈeɪʃᵊn/ *noun* **[U]** *the invasion and liberation of France*

liberated /ˈlɪbəreɪtɪd/ *adjective* not following traditional ways of behaving or old ideas *a liberated woman*

liberating /ˈlɪbəreɪtɪŋ/ *adjective* making you feel that you can behave in exactly the way that you want to *Taking all your clothes off can be a very* ***liberating experience.***

liberty /ˈlɪbəti/ *noun* **[C, U] 1** the freedom to live, work, and travel as you want to *Many would willingly fight to preserve their liberty.* **2 be at liberty to do sth** *formal* to be allowed to do something *I'm not at liberty to discuss the matter at present.* **3 take the liberty of doing sth** *formal* to do something that will have an effect on someone else, without asking their permission *I took the liberty of booking theatre seats for us.* ➲See also: **civil liberties**

Libra /ˈliːbrə/ *noun* **[C, U]** the sign of the zodiac which relates to the period of 23 September - 22 October, or a person born during this period

librarian /laɪˈbreəriən/ *noun* **[C]** someone who works in a library

O⁻ **library** /ˈlaɪbrᵊri/ *noun* **[C]** a room or building that contains a collection of books and other written material that you can read or borrow

lice /laɪs/ *plural of* louse

WORD PARTNERS FOR ***licence***

apply for/hold/issue a licence • a licence **for** sth

licence *UK* (*US* **license**) /ˈlaɪsᵊns/ *noun* **[C] LAW** an official document that allows you to do or have something *a hunting licence* ○ *a marriage licence* ➲See also: **driving licence, off-licence**

license /ˈlaɪsᵊns/ *verb* **[T] LAW** to give someone official permission to do or have something **[often passive + to do sth]** *Undercover agents are licensed to carry guns.*

licensed /ˈlaɪsᵊnst/ *adjective* **1** [APPROVED] *mainly US* officially approved *a licensed physician* **2** [ALCOHOL] A licensed bar or restaurant is officially allowed to serve alcoholic drinks.

ˈlicense ˌplate *US* (*UK* **number plate**) *noun* **[C]** an official metal sign with numbers and letters on the front and back of a car ➲See colour picture **Car** on page Centre 7

lick[1] /lɪk/ *verb* **[T]** to move your tongue across the surface of something *to* ***lick your lips*** ○ *We licked the chocolate off our fingers.*

lick[2] /lɪk/ *noun* **1 [C]** when you lick something **[usually singular]** *Here, have a lick of my ice cream.* **2 a lick of paint** *UK informal* If you give a wall or other surface a lick of paint, you paint it.

lid /lɪd/ *noun* **[C]** the top part of a container that can be removed in order to put something in or take something out

O⁻ **lie**[1] /laɪ/ *verb* **[I] lying**, *past tense* **lay**, *past participle* **lain 1 lie in/on, etc** to be in a horizontal or flat position on a surface *to lie in bed* ○ *to lie on a beach* ○ *to lie on your side* ○ *The pen lay on the desk.* ○ *She had lain where she fell until morning.* **2 lie below/in/on/to, etc** to be in a particular place *The river lies 30 km to the south of the city.* ➲See Common Learner Error at **lay**

lie around *phrasal verb* **1** [REST] *informal* to

spend time lying down and doing very little *We spent a week by the sea, lying around on the beach.* **2** UNTIDY If things are lying around, they are left in an untidy way in places where they should not be. *He's always leaving money lying around.*

lie back *phrasal verb* to lower the top half of your body from a sitting position to a lying position *Lie back and relax.*

lie down *phrasal verb* to move into a position in which your body is flat, usually in order to sleep or rest *I'm not feeling well - I'm going to lie down.* ⊃See colour picture **Phrasal Verbs** on page Centre 16

lie in *phrasal verb UK* to stay in bed in the morning later than usual *I lay in till eleven o'clock this morning.*

lie in sth *phrasal verb* to exist or be found in something *Her strength lies in her faith.*

lie with sb *phrasal verb* If the responsibility or blame for something lies with someone, it is their responsibility. *The final decision lies with me.*

⊶**lie²** /laɪ/ *verb* [I] **lying**, *past* **lied** to say or write something that is not true in order to deceive someone *Are you **lying to** me?* ○ *He **lied about** his qualifications for the job.*

⊶**lie³** /laɪ/ *noun* [C] something that you say or write which you know is not true *I **told a lie** when I said I liked her haircut.* ⊃See also: **white lie**

L

lie-in /ˈlaɪˌɪn/ *noun* [**no plural**] *UK* when you stay in bed in the morning longer than usual *I **had a long lie-in** this morning.*

lieu /luː/ *noun* **in lieu of sth** *formal* instead of something *She took the money in lieu of the prize.*

lieutenant /lefˈtenənt/ (US) /luːˈtenənt/ *noun* [C] an officer of middle rank in the army, navy, or air force *first/second lieutenant*

WORD PARTNERS FOR ***life***

have/lead/live a [charmed/normal, etc] life • **spend** your life (doing sth) • an **aspect/part** of sb's life

⊶**life** /laɪf/ *noun plural* **lives** /laɪvz/ **1** ANIMALS/PLANTS [U] living things and their activities *human/marine life* ○ *Is there life in outer space?* **2** PERSON'S EXISTENCE [C] the existence of a person *How many lives will be lost to AIDS?* **3** TIME [C, U] the time between a person's birth and their death *I'm not sure I want to **spend** the rest of my **life** with him.* ○ ***Life's too short** to worry about stuff like that.* ○ *Unfortunately, accidents are **part of life**.* ○ *He **had** a happy **life**.* **4** WAY OF LIVING [C, U] a way of living *You **lead** an exciting **life**.* **5 family/private/sex, etc life** one part of someone's existence *My private life is nobody's business but mine.* **6** ACTIVITY [U] energy and activity *She was always bubbly and **full of life**.* ○ *I looked through the window but couldn't see any **signs of life*** (= people moving). **7** ACTIVE PERIOD [**no plural**] the amount of time that a machine, system, etc exists or can be used *Careful use will prolong the life of your machine.* **8 bring sth to life/come to life** to make something more real or exciting, or to become more real or exciting **9 That's life.** something you say which means bad things happen and you cannot prevent them *You don't get everything you want but that's life, isn't it?* **10 Get a life!** *informal* something you say to a boring person when you want them to do more exciting things *Surely you're not cleaning the house on Saturday night? Get a life!* ⊃See Common Learner Error at **live** ⊃See also: the facts (**fact**) of life, give sb the **kiss**² of life, give sb/sth a new **lease**¹ of life, **shelf life, walk**² of life

lifeboat /ˈlaɪfbəʊt/ *noun* [C] a small boat that is used to help people who are in danger at sea

ˈlife ˌcoach *noun* [C] someone whose job is to teach people how to solve problems and make decisions in their daily life

ˈlife ˌcycle *noun* [C] BIOLOGY the changes that happen in the life of an animal or plant

ˈlife exˌpectancy *noun* [C, U] the number of years that someone is likely to live

lifeguard /ˈlaɪfgɑːd/ *noun* [C] SPORT someone at a swimming pool or beach whose job is to help people who are in danger in the water

ˈlife inˌsurance (*also UK* **ˈlife aˌssurance**) *noun* [U] FINANCE a system of payments to an insurance company (= a company that will pay money) that will pay money to your family when you die

ˈlife ˌjacket *noun* [C] a piece of equipment that you wear on the upper part of your body to help you float if you fall into water

lifeless /ˈlaɪfləs/ *adjective* **1** DEAD without life *his lifeless body* **2** WITHOUT ENERGY without energy or feeling *a lifeless performance*

lifelike /ˈlaɪflaɪk/ *adjective* If something is lifelike, it looks real. *a lifelike portrait/sculpture*

lifeline /ˈlaɪflaɪn/ *noun* [C] something that helps you when you are in a difficult or dangerous situation *For a lot of old people who live on their own, the telephone is a lifeline.*

lifelong /ˌlaɪfˈlɒŋ/ *adjective* [**always before noun**] for all of your life *a **lifelong friend/interest***

ˌlife ˈpeer *noun* [C] POLITICS someone who has been officially respected in the UK by being given an important title, for example 'Lord', 'Lady' or 'Baroness'

ˈlife ˌsentence (*informal* **life**) *noun* [C] LAW the punishment of spending a very long time, or the rest of your life, in prison

lifespan /ˈlaɪfspæn/ *noun* [C] the amount of time that a person lives or a thing exists

lifestyle /ˈlaɪfstaɪl/ *noun* [C] the way that you live *a **healthy lifestyle***

life-threatening /ˈlaɪfθretᵊnɪŋ/ *adjective* likely to cause death ***life-threatening conditions/diseases***

lifetime /ˈlaɪftaɪm/ *noun* [C] the period of time that someone is alive [**usually singular**] *We'll see such huge changes **in our lifetime**.*

⊶**lift¹** /lɪft/ *verb* **1** UP [T] to put something or someone in a higher position *Could you help me lift this table, please?* ○ *She **lifted** the baby **up** and put him in his chair.* **2** WEATHER [I] If fog lifts, it disappears. *By noon the fog had lifted and the day turned hot.* **3** RULES [T] to stop a rule *The government had already **lifted the ban** on beef imports.* **4** STEAL [T] *informal* to steal or copy something *Entire paragraphs of his thesis* *were lifted from other sources.* ➲See also: not lift a **finger**

O‒ **lift²** /lɪft/ *noun* [C] **1** MACHINE *UK* (*US* **elevator**) a machine that carries people up and down in tall buildings *Shall we use the stairs or **take the lift**?* **2** RIDE a free ride somewhere, usually in a car [**usually singular**] *Can you **give me a lift** to the airport?* **3** MOVE when you move someone or something up to a higher position

lift-off /ˈlɪftɒf/ *noun* [C] the moment when a spacecraft leaves the ground

ligament /ˈlɪɡəmənt/ *noun* [C] **ANATOMY, BIOLOGY** a piece of strong tissue in the body that holds bones together *ankle/knee ligaments* ○ *torn ligaments*

WORD PARTNERS FOR ***light***

light **shines** • a **beam/ray/shaft** of light • **bright** light

O‒ **light¹** /laɪt/ *noun* **1** BRIGHTNESS [U] the brightness that shines from the sun, from fire, or from electrical equipment, allowing you to see things ***bright/dim light*** ○ *fluorescent/ultraviolet light* ○ *a **beam/ray** of light* ○ *Light was streaming in through the open door.* **2** DEVICE [C] a device which produces light *car lights* ○ *to switch/turn the light on* ○ *They must be in bed - I can't see any **lights on** anywhere.* **3 a light** a flame from a match, etc used to make a cigarette start burning *Have you got a light, please?* **4 set light to sth** *UK* to make something start burning **5 in the light of sth** (*also US* **in light of sth**) If something is done or happens in the light of facts, it is done or happens because of those facts. *The drug has been withdrawn in the light of new research.* **6 bring sth to light** If information about something bad is brought to light, it is discovered. *The trial brought to light numerous contradictions in his story.* **7 cast/shed light on sth** to help people understand a situation *We were hoping you might be able to shed some light on the matter.* **8 come to light** If information about something bad comes to light, it is discovered. **9 light at the end of the tunnel** something which makes you believe that an unpleasant situation will soon end ➲See also: **green light, street light, tail light, traffic light**

O‒ **light²** /laɪt/ *adjective* **1** NOT HEAVY not heavy *light clothing/machinery* ○ *I can carry both bags - they're quite light.* **2** NOT MUCH small in amount *light rain/snow* ○ *I only had a light lunch.* **3** NOT STRONG not strong or not forceful *a light breeze* ○ *a light embrace* **4** PALE Light colours are pale. *light brown/green* ○ *a light blue cardigan* **5** NOT SERIOUS easy to understand and not serious ***light entertainment*** ○ *I'm taking some **light reading** on holiday.* **6 make light of sth** to talk or behave as if you do not think a problem is serious **7 it is light** bright from the sun *Let's go now while it's still light.* •**lightness** *noun* [U]

light³ /laɪt/ *verb past* **lit** *or* **lighted 1** BURN [I, T] to start to burn, or to make something start to burn *to **light** a **candle/cigarette/fire*** ○ *The wood was damp and wouldn't light.* **2** BRIGHT [T] to produce light somewhere so that you can see things [**often passive**] *The room was lit by a single light bulb.* ○ *Burning buildings **lit up** the sky.*

light up *phrasal verb* If your face or your eyes light up, you suddenly look happy or excited. *His **eyes lit up** when you mentioned her name.*

light (sth) up *phrasal verb* to make a cigarette, etc start burning *He made himself a coffee and **lit up** a **cigarette**.*

ˈ**light ˌbulb** *noun* [C] a glass object containing a wire which produces light from electricity

light bulb

lighten /ˈlaɪtᵊn/ *verb* **1** LESS SERIOUS [I, T] If a serious situation lightens, it becomes less serious, and if something or someone lightens it, they make it less serious. *Her **mood lightened** a bit when I asked about her holiday.* ○ *He tried to **lighten** the **atmosphere** by telling a joke.* **2 lighten the burden/load** to reduce the amount of work or trouble someone has to deal with **3** LESS DARK [I, T] to become less dark, or to make something less dark *The sun had lightened her hair.*

lighten up *phrasal verb informal* to become more relaxed and less serious *I wish she'd lighten up a bit.*

lighter /ˈlaɪtəʳ/ *noun* [C] a small object that produces a flame and is used to make cigarettes start burning

light-hearted /ˌlaɪtˈhɑːtɪd/ *adjective* not serious *a light-hearted remark*

lighthouse /ˈlaɪthaʊs/ *noun* [C] *plural* **lighthouses** /ˈlaɪthaʊzɪz/ a tall building on the coast containing a large light which warns ships that there are rocks

lighting /ˈlaɪtɪŋ/ *noun* [U] the light created by electrical equipment, candles, etc *soft lighting*

lightly /ˈlaɪtli/ *adverb* **1** GENTLY gently *He kissed her lightly on the cheek.* **2** NOT MUCH not much ***lightly cooked*** *vegetables* **3 not do sth lightly** to think carefully about something before you do it, knowing that it is serious *It's not a decision that I take lightly.* **4 get off lightly** (*also UK* **escape lightly**) to have less trouble or punishment than you expected

WORD PARTNERS FOR ***lightning***

be **struck by** lightning • a **bolt/flash** of lightning • **thunder and** lightning

lightning /ˈlaɪtnɪŋ/ *noun* [U] a sudden flash of light in the sky during a storm ***thunder and lightning*** ○ *He was **struck by lightning** and killed.* ➲See picture at **nitrogen cycle**

ˈ**light ˌpen** *noun* [C] **COMPUTING** a device like a pen that is used for reading bar codes (= thin lines on products that tell their price)

lights /laɪts/ (*also* ˈ**traffic ˌlights**) *noun* [**plural**] a set of red, green, and yellow lights that is used to stop and start traffic

lightweight /ˈlaɪtweɪt/ *adjective* not weighing much *a lightweight jacket for the summer* •**lightweight** *noun* [C] a sportsman such as a boxer who is not in the heaviest weight group

lignified /ˈlɪɡnɪfaɪd/ *adjective* **BIOLOGY** hard and like wood, because of containing lignin

lignin /ˈlɪgnɪn/ *noun* [U] **BIOLOGY** a substance found in the edges of some plant cells that makes the plant hard like wood

like[1] /laɪk/ *preposition* **1** SIMILAR similar to or in the same way as someone or something *They were acting like children.* ○ *He looks like his father.* ○ *It sounded like Harry.* **2 What is sb/sth like?** something you say when you want someone to describe someone or something *I haven't met him - what's he like?* ○ *So what's your new dress like?* **3 What are you like?** *UK* used when someone has said or done something silly *You've bought another jacket? What are you like?* **4** TYPICAL If behaviour is like someone, it is typical of the way that they behave. *It's **just like** Anita to miss her train.* ○ *It's not like Tim to be late.* **5** FOR EXAMPLE for example *She looks best in bright colours, like red and pink.*

OTHER WAYS OF SAYING ***like***

If a person likes someone or something very much, you can use the verbs **love** and **adore**: *I **adore/love** seafood.* ● *Oliver **loves** animals.* ● *Kate **adored** her grandfather.*

The expressions **think the world of** someone and **have a soft spot for** someone can also be used when a person likes someone very much: *I've always **had a soft spot for** Rebecca ever since she was tiny.* ● *Annabel's like a daughter to him, he **thinks the world of** her.*

The expression **be fond of** is sometimes used to talk about someone or something that someone likes: *She's very **fond of** Chinese food.* ● *I think she's very **fond of** you.*

The phrasal verbs **grow on** and **take to/ warm to** can be used when someone starts to like someone or something: *I wasn't sure about the colour at first, but it's **growing on** me.* ● *For some reason, I just didn't **take/warm to** him.*

The expressions **take a shine to** or **take a liking to** are sometimes used when someone immediately likes a person: *I think he's **taken a** bit of a **shine to** you.*

like[2] /laɪk/ *verb* [T] **1** to enjoy something or feel that someone or something is pleasant [+ **doing sth**] *I just like playing with my computer.* [+ **to do sth**] *I like to paint in my spare time.* ○ *He really likes her.* ○ *What do you **like about** him?* ➲Opposite **dislike 2 not like to do sth/not like doing sth** to not usually do something because you think it is wrong *I don't like to criticize her too much.* **3 would like sth** to want something [+ **to do sth**] *I'd like to think about it.* ○ *I'd like some chips with that, please.* **4 Would you like...?** used to offer someone something *Would you like a drink?* [+ **to do sth**] Would you like to eat now? **5 if you like a** used to say 'yes' when someone suggests a plan *"Shall I come?" "If you like."* **b** used when you offer someone something *If you like I could drive you there.* **6 How do you like sb/sth?** used to ask someone for their opinion *How do you like my new shoes?*

like[3] /laɪk/ *conjunction* **1** SAME WAY *informal* in the same way as *Do it exactly like I told you to.* **2** AS IF *US informal* as if *He acted like he didn't hear me.*

like[4] /laɪk/ *noun* **1** [**no plural**] *formal* someone or something that is similar to someone or something else *Economists are predicting a depression, **the like of which** the world has never seen.* **2 and the like** *informal* and similar things *There's a gym that they use for dance and aerobics and the like.* **3 sb's likes and dislikes** the things that someone thinks are pleasant and not pleasant

-like /-laɪk/ *suffix* changes a noun into an adjective meaning 'typical of or similar to' *childlike trust* ○ *a cabbage-like vegetable*

likeable /ˈlaɪkəbl/ *adjective* If you are likeable, you are pleasant and easy to like. *a likeable character*

WORD PARTNERS FOR ***likelihood***

increase/reduce the likelihood **of** sth ● a **real/strong** likelihood ● the likelihood **of** (doing) sth

likelihood /ˈlaɪklihʊd/ *noun* [U] the chance that something will happen *There's not much **likelihood of** that happening.*

likely[1] /ˈlaɪkli/ *adjective* **1** EXPECTED expected [+ **to do sth**] *Do remind me because I'm likely to forget.* [+ **(that)**] *It's likely that he'll say no.* **2** TRUE probably true *the most likely explanation* ➲Opposite **unlikely**

likely[2] /ˈlaɪkli/ *adverb* **1** probably *She'll most likely come without him.* **2 Not likely!** *UK informal* used to say that you will certainly not do something *"So are you coming running with me?" "Not likely!"*

liken /ˈlaɪkən/ *verb*
liken sth/sb to sth/sb *phrasal verb formal* to say that two people are similar or two things are similar *She's been likened to a young Elizabeth Taylor.*

likeness /ˈlaɪknəs/ *noun* [**C, U**] being similar in appearance *There's a definite **family likeness** around the eyes.*

likewise /ˈlaɪkwaɪz/ *adverb formal* in the same way *Water these plants twice a week and likewise the ones in the bedroom.* ○ *Watch what she does and then **do likewise**.*

liking /ˈlaɪkɪŋ/ *noun* **1** [**no plural**] a feeling that you like someone or something *He has **a liking for** young women.* **2 take a liking to sb** to like someone immediately *He obviously took a liking to her.* **3 be too bright/sweet, etc for your liking** to be brighter/sweeter, etc than you like **4 be to sb's liking** *formal* to be the way that someone prefers something *Is the wine to your liking, sir?*

lilac /ˈlaɪlək/ *noun* [**C, U**] a small tree that has sweet-smelling purple, pink, or white flowers

lily /ˈlɪli/ *noun* [C] a plant with large, bell-shaped flowers that are often white

limb /lɪm/ *noun* [C] **1 ANATOMY** a leg or an arm of a person **2** a large branch of a tree

lime /laɪm/ *noun* **1 FOOD** [**C, U**] a small, green fruit that is sour like a lemon **2** TREE [C] (*also* **ˈlime ˌtree**) a large tree that has pale green leaves and yellow flowers **3 FARMING** [U] a white substance that is found in water and soil and is used to improve the quality of soil **4** COLOUR [U] (*also* ˌ**lime** ˈ**green**) a bright colour that is a mixture of yellow and green ➲See colour picture **Colours** on page Centre 12 ●**lime** (*also* **lime-green**) *adjective*

the limelight /ˈlaɪmlaɪt/ *noun* attention from the public *She's been* ***in the limelight*** *for most of her career.*

limerick /ˈlɪmᵊrɪk/ *noun* [C] **LITERATURE** a funny poem with five lines

limescale /ˈlaɪmskeɪl/ *noun* [U] a hard white layer that forms on the sides of pipes or containers that heat water

limestone /ˈlaɪmstəʊn/ *noun* [U] **GEOLOGY** a white or light grey rock formed from the bones of sea animals, often used in building materials

limewater /ˈlaɪmwɔːtə/ *noun* [U] **CHEMISTRY** a liquid containing calcium hydroxide that is used by scientists to test whether substances contain carbon dioxide

WORD PARTNERS FOR ***limit***

an **age/height/speed/time** limit ● a **legal/maximum/strict/upper** limit ● **exceed/impose** a limit ● a limit **on/to** sth

O━**limit¹** /ˈlɪmɪt/ *noun* [C] **1** the largest amount of something that is possible or allowed *a time limit* ○ *Is there a* ***limit on*** *the amount of money you can claim?* ○ *There's a* ***limit to*** *how much time we can spend on this.* **2 be over the limit** *UK* to have more alcohol in your blood than is legally allowed while driving **3 within limits** avoiding behaviour that is extreme or silly *You can wear what you want, within limits.* **4 off limits** If an area is off limits, you are not allowed to enter it. ➲See also: **speed limit**

O━**limit²** /ˈlɪmɪt/ *verb* [T] to control something so that it is less than a particular amount or number *We'll have to limit the number of guests.*

be limited to sth *phrasal verb* to only exist in a particular area *Racial problems are certainly not limited to the south.*

limit sb to sth *phrasal verb* to only allow someone a particular amount or number of something [**often passive**] *We're limited to two pieces of luggage each.* [**often reflexive**] *I try to limit myself to two cups of coffee a day.*

limitation /ˌlɪmɪˈteɪʃᵊn/ *noun* [C, U] when something is controlled so that it is less than a particular amount or number *the limitation of free speech* ○ *You can't write everything you want to because of space limitations.*

limitations /ˌlɪmɪˈteɪʃᵊnz/ *noun* [**plural**] things that someone is not good at doing *Both films show her limitations as an actress.*

limited /ˈlɪmɪtɪd/ *adjective* small in amount or number *a* ***limited choice*** ○ *limited resources* ➲Opposite **unlimited**

ˌ**limited** ˈ**company** *noun* [C] a company, especially one in the UK, whose owners only have to pay part of the money they owe if the company fails financially

ˌ**limited lia**ˈ**bility** *noun* [U] A business with limited liability only has to pay part of its debts if the business fails.

limousine /ˌlɪməˈziːn/ (*also* **limo** /ˈlɪməʊ/) *noun* [C] a large, expensive car, usually for rich or important people *a chauffeur-driven limousine*

limp¹ /lɪmp/ *adjective* soft and weak *a* ***limp handshake*** ○ *a limp lettuce*

limp² /lɪmp/ *verb* [I] to walk with difficulty because one of your legs or feet is hurt ●**limp** *noun* [**no plural**] *She walks with a limp.*

WORD PARTNERS FOR ***line***

draw a line ● a **diagonal/horizontal/straight/vertical** line

O━**line¹** /laɪn/ *noun* **1** MARK [C] a long, thin mark *a horizontal/straight/vertical line* ○ *Sign your name on the dotted line.* ○ ***Draw*** *a* ***line*** *around your hand.* **2** ROW [C] a row of people or things *a line of trees* ○ *We formed two lines, men on one side and women on the other.* **3** ROPE ETC [C] a piece of rope or wire with a particular purpose *a clothes/fishing line* **4** TELEPHONE [C] the connection between two telephones *I've got Neil* ***on the line*** *for you* (= waiting to speak to you). ○ *I'll be with you in a moment - could you* ***hold the line*** (= wait), *please?* **5** WAITING [C, U] *US* (*UK* **queue**) a row of people waiting for something, one behind the other *We were* ***standing in line*** *for hours to get tickets.* **6** SONG/POEM [C] a row of words on a page, for example in a song or poem *The same line is repeated throughout the poem.* **7 lines** the words spoken by an actor in a performance *I don't know how actors remember all their lines.* **8** OPINION [C] the official opinion of an organization [**usually singular**] *the government's* ***line on*** *immigration* **9 along the lines of sth** based on and similar to something *He gave a talk along the lines of the one he gave in Oxford.* **10 sb's line of reasoning/thinking, etc** your reasons for

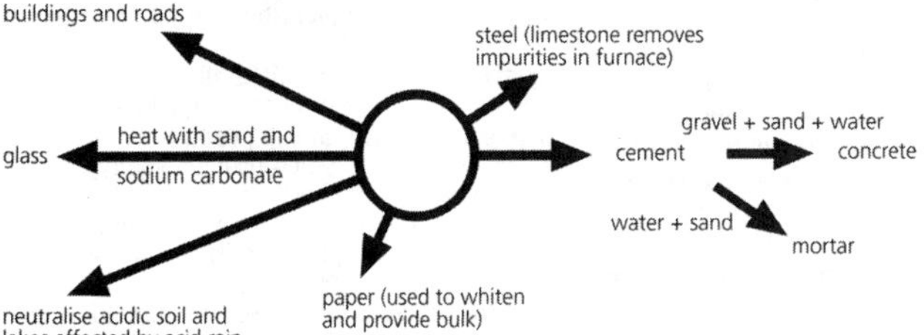

uses of limestone

believing that something is true or right **11** PRODUCT [C] a type of product that a company sells *They're advertising a new **line** in garden furniture.* **12** DIRECTION [C] the direction that something moves in *He can't kick the ball in a **straight line**.* **13 lines** the marks that older people have on their faces, when the skin is loose **14** BORDER [C] *US* a border between two areas *the New York state line* **15 be on the line** If someone's job is on the line, they may lose it. **16 be in line for sth** to be likely to get something good, especially a job **17 be in line with sth** to be similar to and suitable for something *a pay increase in line with inflation* **18 draw the line at sth** to never do something because you think it is wrong *I swear a lot but even I draw the line at certain words.* **19 toe the (party) line** to do what someone in authority tells you to do although you may not agree with it ➲See also: **the bottom line, dotted line, front line, hard line**

line² /laɪn/ *verb* [T] **1** to form a row along the side of something *Trees and cafes lined the street.* **2 be lined with sth** If a piece of clothing is lined with a material, its inside is covered with it. *a jacket lined with fur*

line (sb/sth) up *phrasal verb* to stand in a row, or to arrange people or things in a row *Books were neatly lined up on the shelves.*

line sb/sth up *phrasal verb* to plan for something to happen *What future projects have you lined up?*

linear /ˈlɪniəʳ/ *adjective* **1** to do with lines **2** **MEASURES** relating to length, not volume *linear measurement*

ˌlinear eˈquation *noun* [C] **MATHEMATICS** an equation which makes a straight line if it is drawn on a graph

ˈline ˌmanager *noun* [C] *mainly UK* the person who manages another person in a company or business

linen /ˈlɪnɪn/ *noun* [U] **1** CLOTH an expensive cloth that is like rough cotton *a linen jacket* **2** SHEETS ETC pieces of cloth that you use to cover tables and beds *bed linen*

liner /ˈlaɪnəʳ/ *noun* [C] a large ship like a hotel, which people travel on for pleasure *a cruise/ocean liner*

linesman /ˈlaɪnzmən/ *noun* [C] *plural* **linesmen** **SPORT** in a sport, someone who watches to see if a ball goes into areas where it is not allowed

linger /ˈlɪŋgəʳ/ *verb* [I] to stay somewhere for a long time *The smell from the fire still lingered hours later.*

lingerie /ˈlɒnʒəri/ ⓤⓢ /ˌlɑːnʒəˈreɪ/ *noun* [U] women's underwear

lingering /ˈlɪŋgərɪŋ/ *adjective* [always before noun] lasting a long time ***lingering doubts***

linguist /ˈlɪŋgwɪst/ *noun* [C] **LANGUAGE** someone who is good at learning foreign languages, or someone who studies or teaches linguistics

linguistic /lɪŋˈgwɪstɪk/ *adjective* [always before noun] **LANGUAGE** relating to language or linguistics

linguistics /lɪŋˈgwɪstɪks/ *noun* [U] **LANGUAGE** the scientific study of languages

lining /ˈlaɪnɪŋ/ *noun* [C, U] a material or substance that covers the inside of something *a coat/jacket lining* ○ *the lining of the stomach*

WORD PARTNERS FOR ***link***

discover/establish/find a link • a **close/direct/strong** link • a link **between** sth **and** sth • a link **with** sth

O— **link¹** /lɪŋk/ *noun* [C] **1** CONNECTION a connection between two people, things, or ideas *There's a direct **link between** diet and heart disease.* ○ *Their **links with** Britain are still strong.* **2** CHAIN one ring of a chain **3** **COMPUTING, INTERNET** (*also* **hyperlink**) a connection between documents or areas on the Internet *Click on this link to visit our online bookstore.* ➲See Extra help page **The Web and the Internet** on page Centre 36.

link² /lɪŋk/ *verb* [T] to make a connection between two or more people, things, or ideas [often passive] *Both men have been **linked with** the robberies.* ○ *The drug has been **linked to** the deaths of several athletes.*

link (sb/sth) up *phrasal verb* If two or more things or people link up, or if you link them up, they form a connection so that they can operate or work together. *Each house will be linked up with the communications network.*

lion /laɪən/ *noun* [C] a large, wild animal of the cat family, with light brown fur ➲See also: **sea lion**

O— **lip** /lɪp/ *noun* [C] **1** **ANATOMY, BIOLOGY** one of the two soft, red edges of the mouth *He licked his lips.* ➲See colour picture **The Body** on page Centre 13 **2** the edge of a container that liquid is poured from

lipase /ˈlaɪpeɪz/ ⓤⓢ /ˈlɪpeɪs/ *noun* [U] **BIOLOGY** an enzyme that is produced mainly in the pancreas and helps the body to digest lipids (= fats and oils)

lipid /ˈlɪpɪd/ *noun* [C] **BIOLOGY** a substance that is an important part of living cells, mainly in the form of fat or oil

liposome /ˈlɪpəʊsəʊm/ *noun* [C] **HEALTH, BIOLOGY** an extremely small artificial sac (= bag) made of a type of fat, used in medicine to carry a drug or other substance to particular cells in the body

lip-read /ˈlɪpriːd/ *verb* [I, T] *past* **lip-read** to understand what someone is saying by looking at the way their mouth moves **•lip-reading** *noun* [U]

lip-service /ˈlɪpsɜːvɪs/ *noun* [no plural] **give/pay lip-service to sth** *informal* to say that you support an idea or plan, but not do anything to help it succeed

lipstick /ˈlɪpstɪk/ *noun* [C, U] a coloured substance that women put on their lips

liqueur /lɪˈkjʊəʳ/ *noun* [C] **FOOD** a strong, sweet alcoholic drink which people usually drink a little of at the end of a meal

O— **liquid¹** /ˈlɪkwɪd/ *noun* [C, U] **PHYSICS** a substance, for example water, that is not solid and that can be poured easily

liquid² /ˈlɪkwɪd/ *adjective* **1** **PHYSICS** in a form that is not solid and can be poured easily **2** **FINANCE** in the form of money, or able to be changed into money easily *liquid assets*

liquidate /ˈlɪkwɪdeɪt/ *verb* [T] to close a business because it has no money left •**liquidation** /ˌlɪkwɪˈdeɪʃᵊn/ *noun* [C, U] *The store **went into liquidation**.*

liquid-crystal display /ˌlɪkwɪdˌkrɪstᵊldɪˈspleɪ/ *noun* [C] LCD

liquidity /lɪˈkwɪdɪti/ *noun* [U] **FINANCE** (of a business) owning enough money or things that can be sold to be able to pay its debts

liquor /ˈlɪkəʳ/ *noun* [U] *US* **FOOD** a strong alcoholic drink

ˈliquor ˌstore *US* (*UK* **off-licence**) *noun* [C] a shop that sells alcoholic drink

lisp /lɪsp/ *noun* [C] **LANGUAGE** a way of speaking where 's' and 'z' sound like 'th' •**lisp** *verb* [I]

WORD PARTNERS FOR ***list***

compile/draw up/make/write a list • a list of sth • **on** a list • a **shopping** list

O⁻ **list¹** /lɪst/ *noun* [C] a series of names, numbers, or items that are written one below the other *a **shopping list** ○ Is your name **on the list**? ○ **Make a list** of everything you need.* ⊃See also: **mailing list, waiting list**

list² /lɪst/ *verb* [T] to make a list, or to include something in a list *All participants' names are listed alphabetically.*

O⁻ **listen** /ˈlɪsᵊn/ *verb* [I] **1** HEAR to give attention to someone or something in order to hear them *What kind of music do you **listen to**? ○ She does all the talking - I just sit and listen. ○ You haven't listened to a word I've said. ○ Listen, if you need money, I'm happy to lend you some.* **2** TAKE ADVICE to accept someone's advice *I told you she wouldn't like it but you wouldn't listen to me!*
listen (out) for sth *phrasal verb* to try to hear something *Could you listen out for the phone while I'm upstairs?*
listen in *phrasal verb* to secretly listen to a conversation, especially a telephone conversation
Listen up! *phrasal verb mainly US* something you say to tell people to listen to you *Okay, everyone, listen up! I have an announcement to make.*

COMMON LEARNER ERROR

listen, listen to, or **hear?**

Use **hear** when you want to say that sounds, music, etc come to your ears. You can **hear** something without wanting to.

I could hear his music through the wall.

Use **listen** to say that you pay attention to sounds or try to hear something.

The audience listened carefully.

Ssh! I'm listening!

Use **listen to** when you want to say what it is that you are trying to hear.

The audience listened to the speaker.

Ssh! I'm listening to the radio!

listener /ˈlɪsᵊnəʳ/ *noun* [C] someone who listens *The new radio station already has twelve million listeners. ○ She's a **good listener** (= she gives you all her attention when you speak).*

lit /lɪt/ *past of* light

liter /ˈliːtəʳ/ *noun* [C] **MEASURES** *US spelling of* litre

literacy /ˈlɪtᵊrəsi/ *noun* [U] the ability to read and write

literal /ˈlɪtᵊrᵊl/ *adjective* The literal meaning of a word or phrase is its real or original meaning. *the **literal meaning/sense***

literally /ˈlɪtᵊrᵊli/ *adverb* **1** ORIGINAL MEANING having the real or original meaning of a word or phrase *They were responsible for literally millions of deaths.* **2** EMPHASIZING *informal* used to emphasize what you are saying *He missed that kick literally by miles!*

literary /ˈlɪtᵊrᵊri/ *adjective* **LITERATURE** relating to literature, or typical of the type of language that is used in literature ***literary criticism***

literate /ˈlɪtᵊrət/ *adjective* able to read and write ⊃Opposite **illiterate**

O⁻ **literature** /ˈlɪtrətʃəʳ/ *noun* [U] **1 LITERATURE** books, poems, etc that are considered to be art *classical/modern literature* **2** written information about a subject *There is very little literature on the disease.*

lithium /ˈlɪθiəm/ *noun* [U] **CHEMISTRY** a soft, silver metal that is lighter than other metals (formula **Li**)

the lithosphere /ˈlɪθəʊˌsfɪəʳ/ *noun* **GEOLOGY** the rock that forms the outer layer of the Earth

litmus /ˈlɪtməs/ *noun* [U] **CHEMISTRY** a powder which is turned red by acid and blue by alkali

ˈlitmus ˌpaper *noun* [U] **CHEMISTRY** a type of paper that is used for testing whether a substance is acid or alkali

ˈlitmus ˌtest *noun* [C] **CHEMISTRY** a test of a chemical substance using litmus paper

O⁻ **litre** *UK* (*US* **liter**) (*written abbreviation* **l**) /ˈliːtəʳ/ *noun* [C] **MEASURES** a unit for measuring liquid

WORD PARTNERS FOR ***litter***

drop litter • a **piece of** litter • a litter **bin**

litter¹ /ˈlɪtəʳ/ *noun* **1** WASTE [U] pieces of paper and other waste that are left in public places **2** ANIMALS [C] a group of baby animals that are from the same mother and born at the same time *a litter of kittens/puppies*

litter² /ˈlɪtəʳ/ *verb* [T] If things litter an area, they cover parts of it in an untidy way. *Clothes littered the floor.*
be littered with sth *phrasal verb* to contain a lot of something *The whole book is littered with errors.*

O⁻ **little¹** /ˈlɪtl/ *adjective* **1** SMALL small in size or amount *a little bag/box/town ○ She's so little. ○ It costs **as little as** one dollar. ○ I might have **a little bit of** cake.* **2** SHORT [**always before noun**] short in time or distance *Sit down **for a little while**. ○ Let's have a little break.* **3** NOT IMPORTANT [**always before noun**] not important *It's only a little problem. ○ I'm having a little trouble with my back.* **4** YOUNG [**always before noun**] young and small *She was my little sister and I looked after her.* ⊃See Common Learner Error at **small**

O⁻ **little²** /ˈlɪtl/ *quantifier* **1** not much or not enough *He has little chance of winning.*

L

○ *There's so little choice.* **2 a little sth** a small amount of something *It just needs a little effort.*

COMMON LEARNER ERROR

little

When **little** is used as a quantifier, it can only be used with uncountable nouns.

O-■**little³** /ˈlɪtl/ *pronoun* **1** not much, or not enough *We did* ***very little*** *on Sunday.* **2 a little** a small amount *I only know a little about my grandparents.* ○ *"More dessert?" "Just a little, please."*

O-■**little⁴** /ˈlɪtl/ *adverb* not much or not enough *She ate very little at dinner.* ○ *a little-known fact*

O-■**live¹** /lɪv/ *verb* **1** ALIVE [I] to be alive *She only lived a few days after the accident.* ○ *I hope I live to see my grandchildren.* **2 live at/in/near, etc** to have your home somewhere *They live in New York.* ○ *We live near each other.* ○ *Where do you live?* **3** WAY OF LIVING [I, T] to spend your life in a particular way *Many people are living in poverty.* **4 I'll never live it down!** *humorous* something you say about an embarrassing experience that other people will not forget

live for sth/sb *phrasal verb* to have something or someone as the most important thing in your life *I love dancing - I just live for it.*

live on *phrasal verb* to continue to live *She lived on well into her nineties.*

live on sth *phrasal verb* **1** MONEY Money that you live on is the money you use to buy the things that you need. *We lived on very little when we were students.* **2** FOOD to only eat a particular type of food *All summer we live on hamburgers and hot dogs.*

live together *phrasal verb* If two people live together, they live in the same home and have a sexual relationship, but are not married.

live up to sth *phrasal verb* to be as good as someone hopes *Did the trip* ***live up to*** *your* ***expectations****?*

live with sb *phrasal verb* to live in the same home as someone and have a sexual relationship with them although you are not married

live with sth *phrasal verb* to accept a difficult or unpleasant situation *It's a problem she's going to have to live with.*

O-■**live²** /laɪv/ *adjective* **1** LIFE having life *Millions of live animals are shipped around the world each year.* **2** ELECTRICITY A live wire has electricity in it. **3** BROADCAST A live radio or television programme is seen or heard as it happens. *live coverage* ○ *a live broadcast* **4** AUDIENCE A live performance or recording of a performance is done with an audience. *a live concert* **5** BOMB A live bomb has not yet exploded.

live³ /laɪv/ *adverb* broadcast at the same time that something happens *We'll be bringing the match to you live on Wednesday.*

COMMON LEARNER ERROR

live or **life**

Live cannot be used as a noun. The correct noun to use is **life**.

It was the best day of my life.

livelihood /ˈlaɪvlihʊd/ *noun* [C, U] **FINANCE** the way that you earn the money you need for living *The farm is his livelihood.*

lively /ˈlaɪvli/ *adjective* full of energy and interest *a lively conversation/debate* ○ *a lively child* •**liveliness** *noun* [U]

liver /ˈlɪvəʳ/ *noun* **1 ANATOMY** [C] a large organ in your body that cleans your blood **2 FOOD** [U] the liver of an animal that is eaten by people ➲See picture at **alimentary canal**

lives /lɪvz/ *plural of* life

livestock /ˈlaɪvstɒk/ *noun* [U] **FARMING** animals that are kept on a farm

livid /ˈlɪvɪd/ *adjective* very angry

living¹ /ˈlɪvɪŋ/ *noun* **1** [C] the money that you earn from your job [**usually singular**] *to* ***earn/make a living*** ○ *What does he* ***do for a living*** (= how does he earn money)*?* **2 country/healthy, etc living** the way in which you live your life ➲See also: **standard of living**

living² /ˈlɪvɪŋ/ *adjective* [**always before noun**] **1** ALIVE NOW alive now *He's probably the best known living photographer.* **2** ALIVE alive *living organisms* ○ ***living things*** ➲See also: beat/knock the (living) **daylights** out of sb, scare/frighten the (living) **daylights** out of sb

ˈ**living ˌroom** (*also UK* **sitting room**) *noun* [C] the room in a house where people sit to relax and, for example, watch television ➲See colour picture **The Living Room** on page Centre 4

lizard /ˈlɪzəd/ *noun* [C] a small animal with thick skin, a long tail, and four short legs ➲See picture at **reptile**

load¹ /ləʊd/ *noun* **1** [C] something that is carried, often by a vehicle *We were behind a truck carrying a load of coal.* ➲See picture at **lever 2 a load/loads** *informal* a lot of something *There were loads of people there.* ○ *Have some more food - there's loads.* **3 a load of rubbish/nonsense, etc** *UK informal* nonsense

load² /ləʊd/ *verb* **1** VEHICLE/MACHINE [I, T] (*also* **load up**) to put a lot of things into a vehicle or machine *Bring the car up to the door and I'll start loading up.* ○ *to load the dishwasher/washing machine* ➲Opposite **unload 2** CAMERA/GUN [T] to put film in a camera or bullets in a gun

be loaded down with sth *phrasal verb* to have too much to carry, or too much work to do *I was loaded down with shopping.*

be loaded with sth *phrasal verb* to contain a lot of something *Most fast foods are loaded with fat.*

-load /ləʊd/ *suffix* used at the end of a word to describe an amount of something that is being carried *a truckload of soldiers*

loaded /ˈləʊdɪd/ *adjective* **1** WEAPON A loaded gun, or similar weapon, has a bullet in it. **2** RICH [**never before noun**] *informal* very rich

ˌ**loaded** ˈ**question** *noun* [C] a question which makes you answer in a particular way

loaf /ləʊf/ *noun* [C] *plural* **loaves** /ləʊvz/ **FOOD** bread that has been baked in one large piece so that it can be cut into smaller pieces ***a loaf of bread***

WORD PARTNERS FOR ***loan***

apply for/repay/take out a loan • a **bank** loan

O-ᵚ **loan**[1] /ləʊn/ *noun* **1** **ECONOMICS, FINANCE** [C] money that someone has borrowed *a* ***bank loan*** ○ *He* ***repaid the loan*** *within two years.* **2** **be on loan** **FINANCE** If something is on loan, someone is borrowing it. *Both paintings are on loan from the city museum.*

loan[2] /ləʊn/ *verb* [+ two objects] **ECONOMICS** to lend something to someone *I was glad to* ***loan*** *my old books* ***to*** *her.* ○ *My dad loaned me the money.*

loath /ləʊθ/ *adjective* **be loath to do sth** *formal* to not want to do something because it will cause problems *I'm loath to spend it all.*

loathe /ləʊð/ *verb* [T] to hate someone or something •**loathing** *noun* [U] a feeling of hating someone or something

loaves /ləʊvz/ *plural of* loaf

lobby[1] /ˈlɒbi/ *noun* [C] **1** a room at the main entrance of a building, often with doors and stairs that lead to other parts of the building *a hotel lobby* **2** **POLITICS** a group of people who try to persuade the government to do something *the anti-smoking lobby*

lobby[2] /ˈlɒbi/ *verb* [I, T] **POLITICS** to try to persuade the government to do something *They're* ***lobbying for*** *changes to the law.*

lobster /ˈlɒbstəʳ/ *noun* [C, U] **FOOD** a sea creature that has two claws (= sharp, curved parts) and eight legs, or the meat of this animal

O-ᵚ **local**[1] /ˈləʊkəl/ *adjective* relating to an area near you *the* ***local school/newspaper****/radio station* •**locally** *adverb locally grown vegetables*

local[2] /ˈləʊkəl/ *noun* [C] **1** someone who lives in the area you are talking about **2** **sb's local** *UK informal* a bar that is near someone's home

ˌ**local anaesˈthetic** *UK* (*US* **local anesthetic**) *noun* [C, U] **HEALTH** a substance that is put into a part of your body so that you do not feel pain there *The procedure is carried out* ***under local anaesthetic.***

ˌ**local auˈthority** *noun* [group] **POLITICS** the group of people who govern a small area of a country *Local authorities are looking for new ways to promote investment.*

ˈ**local ˌtime** *noun* [U] the official time in an area or country *We will shortly be landing in London, where the local time is 3.15.*

locate /ləʊˈkeɪt/ *verb* [T] *formal* **1** to find the exact position of someone or something *Police are still trying to locate the suspect.* **2** **be located in/near/on, etc** to be in a particular place *Both schools are located in the town.*

WORD PARTNERS FOR ***location***

at/in a [remote/secret, etc] location • the location **of** sth

location /ləʊˈkeɪʃən/ *noun* **1** [C] a place or position *They haven't yet decided on* ***the location of*** *the new store.* **2** **on location** If a film or television programme is made on location, it is made at a place suitable to the story.

loch /lɒk, lɒx/ *noun* [C] **GEOGRAPHY** a lake in Scotland *Loch Lomond*

O-ᵚ **lock**[1] /lɒk/ *verb* **1** FASTEN [I, T] to fasten something with a key, or to be fastened with a key *Did you lock the door?* ○ *If you shut the door it will lock automatically.* ⊃Opposite **unlock** **2** **lock sth/sb away/in, etc** to put something or someone in a place or container that is fastened with a key *She locked herself in her bedroom.* ○ *Most of my jewellery is locked away in a safe.* **3** FIXED [I] to become fixed in one position *I tried to move forward but the wheels had locked.*

lock sb in/out *phrasal verb* to prevent someone from entering/leaving a room or building by locking the door

lock (sth) up *phrasal verb* to lock all the doors and windows of a building when you leave it

lock sb up *phrasal verb* to put someone in prison or a hospital for people who are mentally ill

WORD PARTNERS FOR ***lock (noun)***

fit a lock • a lock **on** sth • a **safety** lock

O-ᵚ **lock**[2] /lɒk/ *noun* [C] **1** IN DOOR the thing that is used to close a door, window, etc, and that needs a key to open it *I heard someone turn a key in the lock.* ○ ***safety locks*** **2** WATER a place on a river with gates to allow boats to move to a different water level **3** **under lock and key** kept safely in a room or container that is locked *I tend to keep medicines under lock and key because of the kids.*

locker /ˈlɒkəʳ/ *noun* [C] a small cupboard in a public area where your personal possessions can be kept *a gym/luggage/school locker*

ˈ**locker ˌroom** *noun* [C] a room where you change your clothes and leave those and other personal possessions in a locker

locomotive /ˌləʊkəˈməʊtɪv/ *noun* [C] the part of a train that makes it move *a steam locomotive*

locus /ˈləʊkəs/ *noun* [C] *plural* **loci** **MATHEMATICS** a set of points or lines whose position is decided by a particular rule or statement *The locus of points equidistant from a given point is a circle.*

lodge[1] /lɒdʒ/ *noun* [C] a small house in the country that is used especially by people on holiday *a hunting/mountain/ski lodge*

lodge[2] /lɒdʒ/ *verb* **1** **lodge in/on, etc** to become stuck somewhere *The bullet had lodged near his heart.* ⊃Compare **dislodge** **2** **lodge at/with, etc** to live in someone's home and give them money for it **3** **lodge a claim/complaint/protest, etc** to officially complain about something *He lodged an official complaint against the officers responsible.*

lodger /ˈlɒdʒəʳ/ *UK* (*US* **boarder**) *noun* [C] someone who pays for a place to sleep and meals in someone else's house

lodgings /ˈlɒdʒɪŋz/ *noun* [plural] *mainly UK* a room in someone's home that you pay money to live in *temporary lodgings*

loess /ˈləʊes/ *noun* [U] **GEOLOGY** small pieces of light-brown or grey soil which is blown and left behind by the wind

L

loft /lɒft/ *noun* [C] **1** HOUSE the space under the roof of a house or other building **2** FACTORY *US* space where someone lives or works in a building that used to be a factory

log¹ /lɒg/ *noun* [C] **1** WOOD a thick piece of wood that has been cut from a tree **2** WRITTEN RECORD a written record of events, often on a ship or aircraft

log² /lɒg/ *verb* [T] **logging**, *past* **logged** to make a written record of events, often on a ship or aircraft

login/on *phrasal verb* **COMPUTING** to connect a computer to a system of computers by typing your name and often a password, usually so that you can start working

log off/out *phrasal verb* **COMPUTING** to stop a computer being connected to a computer system, usually when you want to stop working

logarithm /ˈlɒgərɪðəm/ *noun* [C] **MATHEMATICS** the number which shows how many times a number, called the base, has to be multiplied by itself to produce another number

loggerheads /ˈlɒgəhedz/ *noun* **be at loggerheads (with sb)** If two people or groups are at loggerheads, they disagree strongly about something. *He is at loggerheads with the Prime Minister over public spending.*

WORD PARTNERS FOR *logic*

the logic **behind/in/of** sth

logic /ˈlɒdʒɪk/ *noun* [U] the use of reason, or the science of using reason *It was difficult to understand the **logic behind** his argument.*

logical /ˈlɒdʒɪkəl/ *adjective* using reason *a logical choice/conclusion* ➲Opposite **illogical** •**logically** *adverb*

ˈlogic ˌgate *noun* [C] **COMPUTING** an electronic switch used in computers, that reacts in one of two ways to information given to it

login /ˈlɒgɪn/ *noun* [C, U] **COMPUTING** a box that appears on your computer screen when you start to use a computer which is connected to a computer system

logistics /ləˈdʒɪstɪks/ *noun* **the logistics of sth/doing sth** the practical arrangements for something *We could all use the one car but I'm not sure about the logistics of it.*

logo /ˈləʊgəʊ/ *noun* [C] a design or symbol used by a company to advertise its products *a corporate logo*

loiter /ˈlɔɪtər/ *verb* [I] to stand in a place or walk slowly around without any purpose *A gang of youths were loitering outside the cinema.*

LOL **INTERNET** *internet abbreviation for* laughing out loud: used when you think something is very funny

lollipop /ˈlɒlipɒp/ (*also UK* **lolly** /ˈlɒli/) *noun* [C] **FOOD** a large, hard sweet on a stick

lone /ləʊn/ *adjective* [**always before noun**] alone *lone parents* ○ *the lone survivor*

lonely /ˈləʊnli/ *adjective* **1** PERSON unhappy because you are not with other people *She gets lonely now that the kids have all left home.* ➲See Common Learner Error at **alone** **2** PLACE A lonely place is a long way from where people live. •**loneliness** *noun* [U]

loner /ˈləʊnər/ *noun* [C] someone who likes to be alone *He was always a bit of a loner at school.*

lonesome /ˈləʊnsəm/ *adjective US* lonely

long¹ /lɒŋ/ *adjective* **1** DISTANCE having a large distance from one end to the other *long, brown hair* ○ *a long dress* ○ *It's a long way to travel to work.* **2** TIME continuing for a large amount of time *a long film/meeting* ○ *Have you been waiting a long time?* **3** HOW LONG used when asking for or giving information about the distance or time of something *It's about three metres long.* ○ *Most of the concerts are over three hours long.* ○ *Do you know how long the film is?* **4** BOOK A long book or other piece of writing has a lot of pages or words. *a long article/letter* ➲See also: in the long/short **run²**

long² /lɒŋ/ *adverb* **1** for a long time *We didn't have to **wait long** for the train.* ○ *The band played long into the night.* **2 as long as** used when you are talking about something that must happen before something else can happen *You can play football as long as you do your homework first.* **3 before long** soon *He'll be home before long.* **4 long ago** If something happened long ago, it happened a great amount of time ago. **5 no longer/not any longer** not now *He no longer works here.*

long³ /lɒŋ/ *noun* [U] a large amount of time *She won't be away for long.*

long⁴ /lɒŋ/ *verb formal* **long for sth; long to do sth** to want something very much *She longed to see him again.*

longboat /ˈlɒŋbəʊt/ *noun* [C] a long, narrow, open boat, moved with oars (= long poles with flat ends)

long-distance /ˌlɒŋˈdɪstəns/ *adjective* travelling or communicating between two places that are a long way apart *a long-distance race* ○ *a long-distance phone call*

ˌlong diˈvision *noun* [U] **MATHEMATICS** when you divide one large number by another large number

long-haul /ˈlɒŋˌhɔːl/ *adjective* [**always before noun**] travelling a long distance *a **long-haul flight***

longhouse /ˈlɒŋhaʊs/ *noun* [C] a long house where many families live together

longing /ˈlɒŋɪŋ/ *noun* [U, **no plural**] a feeling of wanting something or someone very much *He gazed at her, his eyes full of longing.* ○ *a **longing for** his homeland* •**longingly** *adverb She looked longingly at the silk dresses.*

longitude /ˈlɒndʒɪtjuːd/ *noun* [U] **GEOGRAPHY** the distance of a place east or west of an imaginary line from the top to the bottom of the Earth, measured in degrees

longitudinal /ˌlɒndʒɪˈtjuːdɪnəl/ *adjective* **GEOGRAPHY** relating to longitude

longiˌtudinal ˈwave *noun* [C] **PHYSICS** in physics, a wave moving in the same direction as the vibrations (= fast movements backwards and forwards) of the particles of the substance through which it is moving ➲Compare **transverse wave**

the ˈlong ˌjump *noun* **SPORT** a sports event where people try to jump as far as possible

long-life /ˌlɒŋˈlaɪf/ *adjective UK* **FOOD** Long-life drink or food has been treated so that it will last a long time. *long-life milk*

long-lost /ˈlɒŋˌlɒst/ *adjective* **long-lost friend/ cousin, etc** a friend or relative that you have not seen for a long time

long-range /ˌlɒŋˈreɪndʒ/ *adjective* [**always before noun**] **1** TIME relating to a time in the future *a* ***long-range*** *weather* ***forecast*** **2** DISTANCE able to be sent long distances *a* ***long-range*** *bomber/****missile***

longshore drift /ˌlɒŋʃɔːˈdrɪft/ *noun* [**U**] **GEOGRAPHY** the movement of sand and small stones, etc. along the coast caused by waves travelling parallel or at an angle to the coast

ˈ**long** ˌ**shot** *noun* [**C**] *informal* something that is not likely to succeed *It's a long shot, but you could try phoning him at home.*

long-sighted /ˌlɒŋˈsaɪtɪd/ *UK* (*US* **farsighted**) *adjective* **HEALTH** able to see objects which are far away but not things which are near to you

long-standing /ˌlɒŋˈstændɪŋ/ *adjective* having existed for a long time *a* ***long-standing relationship***

long-suffering /ˌlɒŋˈsʌfərɪŋ/ *adjective* A long-suffering person has been very patient for a long time about all the trouble that someone has caused them. *Bill and his long-suffering wife*

long-term /ˌlɒŋˈtɜːm/ *adjective* continuing a long time into the future *long-term unemployment*

ˌ**long-term liaˈbility** *noun* [**C**] **FINANCE** an amount owed by a business that does not have to be paid in the next 12 months

long-winded /ˌlɒŋˈwɪndɪd/ *adjective* If what someone says or writes is long-winded, it is boring because it is too long. *a* ***long-winded explanation***

loo /luː/ *noun* [**C**] *UK informal* toilet *I'll just go to the loo.* ➲See Common Learner Error at **toilet**

O━**look[1]** /lʊk/ *verb* **1** SEE [**I**] to turn your eyes in the direction of something or someone so that you can see them ***Look at*** *the picture on page two.* ○ *He was looking out of the window.* ○ *I looked around and there she was.* **2** SEARCH [**I**] to try to find someone or something *I'm* ***looking for*** *my keys.* ○ *I've looked everywhere but I can't find my bag.* **3 look nice/strange, etc; look like/as if** used to describe the appearance of a person or thing *That food looks nice.* ○ *You look tired, my love.* ○ *Do I look silly in this hat?* ○ *He looked like a drug addict.* **4 it looks like; it looks as if** used to say that something is likely to happen *It looks like there'll be three of us.* ○ *It looks as if he isn't coming.* **5 be looking to do sth** to plan to do something *I'm looking to start my own business.* **6 Look!** something you say when you are annoyed and you want people to know that what you are saying is important *Look, I've had enough of your complaints.* ➲See also: look the **part**[1]

COMMON LEARNER ERROR

look, see, or **watch?**

See means to notice people and things with your eyes.

She saw a big spider and screamed.

Did you see anyone you knew at the party?

Look (at) is used when you are trying to see something or someone. **Look** cannot be followed by an object.

I've looked everywhere, but can't find my keys.

He looked at the map to find the road.

~~*He looked the photographs.*~~

Watch means to look at something for a period of time, usually something which moves or changes.

He watched television all evening.

I watched them playing football.

O━**look after sb/sth** *phrasal verb* to take care of someone or something by keeping them healthy or in a good condition *Could you look after the children while I'm out?*

look ahead *phrasal verb* to think about something that will happen in the future and plan for it

look at sth *phrasal verb* **1** THINK to think about a subject carefully so that you can make a decision about it *Management is looking at ways of cutting costs.* **2** READ to read something *Can you look at my essay sometime?* **3** EXPERT If an expert looks at something, they examine it. *Did you get the doctor to look at your knee?* **4** OPINION to consider something in a particular way *If I'd been a mother I might have looked at things differently.*

look back *phrasal verb* to remember something in the past *He* ***looked back on*** *his childhood with affection.*

look down on sb *phrasal verb* to think that someone is less important than you

O━**look forward to sth/doing sth** *phrasal verb* to feel happy and excited about something that is going to happen *I'm really looking forward to seeing him.*

COMMON LEARNER ERROR

look forward to

Remember always to use the preposition **to** when you use this verb.

We are looking forward to your visit.

~~*We are looking forward your visit.*~~

look into sth *phrasal verb* to examine the facts about a situation *They are looking into the causes of the accident.*

look on *phrasal verb* to watch something happen but not become involved in it

look on sb/sth *phrasal verb* to think about someone or something in a particular way *We look on him almost as our own son.*

Look out! *phrasal verb* something you say when someone is in danger *Look out - there's a car coming!*

look out for sb/sth *phrasal verb* to try to notice someone or something *Look out for Anna while you're there.*

look over sth *phrasal verb* to examine something quickly *I'm just looking over what you've written.*

look through sth *phrasal verb* to read something quickly *I've looked through a few catalogues.*

look up *phrasal verb* to become better *Our financial situation is looking up.*

look sth up *phrasal verb* to look at a book or

L

computer in order to find information *I looked it up in the dictionary.*
look up to sb *phrasal verb* to respect and admire someone

WORD PARTNERS FOR ***look (noun)***

have/take a look • a **close/good** look • a look **at** sb/sth

O-- **look²** /lʊk/ *noun* **1** SEE [C] when you look at someone or something [**usually singular**] ***Take a look*** *at these pictures.* ○ *You've got your photos back - can I* ***have a look?*** **2 have/take a look** when you try to find something *I've had a look in the drawer but I can't find your passport.* **3** FACE [C] an expression on someone's face *She had a worried look about her.* ○ *She* ***gave me a*** *questioning* ***look.*** **4** FASHION [**no plural**] a style or fashion *the* ***new look*** *for the summer* **5 the look of sb/sth** the appearance of someone or something *I like the look of that new music programme they're advertising.* **6 sb's looks** a person's appearance, especially how attractive they are ⇒See also: **good looks**

lookalike /ˈlʊkəlaɪk/ *noun* [C] *informal* someone who looks very similar to a famous person *an Elvis lookalike*

look-in /ˈlʊkɪn/ *noun UK informal* **not get a look-in** to get no chance to achieve what you want or to succeed in something *He played so well, nobody else got a look-in.*

lookout /ˈlʊkaʊt/ *noun* **1** [C] a person who watches for danger and warns other people **2 be on the lookout** to be continuing to search for something or someone *I'm always on the lookout for interesting new recipes.*

loom¹ /luːm/ *verb* [I] **1** APPEAR to appear as a large, sometimes frightening shape *Dark storm clouds loomed on the horizon.* **2** WORRY If an unpleasant event looms, it is likely to happen soon. *The threat of closure* ***looms over*** *the workforce.*

loom² /luːm/ *noun* [C] **DT** a machine for making cloth by weaving together (= crossing over) threads

loony /ˈluːni/ *noun* [C] *informal* someone who behaves in a crazy way *The man's a complete loony.* •**loony** *adjective informal* crazy *loony ideas*

loop¹ /luːp/ *noun* [C] a circle of something long and thin, such as a piece of string or wire

loop² /luːp/ *verb* **loop sth around/over, etc sth** to make something into the shape of a loop *Loop the rope around your waist.*

WORD PARTNERS FOR ***loophole***

a loophole **in** sth • a **legal** loophole

loophole /ˈluːphəʊl/ *noun* [C] a mistake in an agreement or law which gives someone the chance to avoid having to do something

O-- **loose** /luːs/ *adjective* **1** NOT FIXED not firmly fixed *There were some loose wires hanging out of the wall.* ○ *One of my buttons is loose.* **2** CLOTHES large and not fitting tightly *a loose dress/sweater* **3** FREE An animal that is loose is free to move around. *Two lions escaped and are still loose.* **4** NOT EXACT not exact *It's only a loose translation of the poem.* •**loosely** *adverb The film is* ***based*** *very* ***loosely*** (= not exactly) on the novel. ⇒See also: be at a loose **end**¹

COMMON LEARNER ERROR

loose or **lose?**

Be careful, these two words look and sound similar but have completely different meanings.
Loose is an adjective, meaning not fixed or not tight.

These trousers are a bit loose.

Be careful not to use **loose** when you really mean the verb **lose**.

I hope he doesn't lose his job.

~~*I hope he doesn't loose his job.*~~

loosen /ˈluːsᵊn/ *verb* [I, T] to become loose or make something loose *He loosened his tie.*
loosen up *phrasal verb* to become more relaxed with other people *After a while he loosened up.*

loot¹ /luːt/ *verb* [I, T] to steal from shops and houses during a war or period of fighting *Rioters looted the capital.*

loot² /luːt/ *noun* [U] goods which have been stolen

lop /lɒp/ *verb* **lopping**, *past* **lopped**
lop sth off *phrasal verb* to cut off something in one quick movement *I lopped off the biggest branches.*

lopsided /ˌlɒpˈsaɪdɪd/ (US) /ˈlɒpsaɪdɪd/ *adjective* with one side lower than the other *a lopsided grin*

loquacious /ləʊˈkweɪʃəs/ *adjective formal* talking a lot

lord /lɔːd/ *noun* **1** SOCIETY [C, U] (*also* **Lord**) a man of high social rank, or a title given to a man who has earned official respect, in the UK *Lord Lichfield* **2 the Lord** RELIGION God or Christ **3 Good Lord!** *informal* something you say when you are surprised or angry *Good Lord! Is that the time?* ⇒See also: **House of Lords**

the Lords /lɔːdz/ (*also* **House of Lords**) *noun* [**group**] **POLITICS** one of the two parts of the British parliament, with members who are chosen by the government

lorry /ˈlɒri/ *UK* (*UK/US* **truck**) *noun* [C] a large road vehicle for carrying goods from place to place

O-- **lose** /luːz/ *verb past* **lost** **1** NOT FIND [T] to not be able to find someone or something *I've lost my passport.* ○ *She's always losing her car keys.* **2** NOT HAVE [T] to stop having someone or something that you had before *She lost a leg in a car accident.* ○ *I hope he doesn't lose his job.* ○ *He lost his mother* (= his mother died) *last year.* **3** HAVE LESS [T] to have less of something than you had before *She's lost a lot of weight.* ○ *He's losing his hair.* ○ *to lose your memory* **4** NOT WIN [I, T] If you lose a game, the team or person that you are playing against wins. *Chelsea lost by a goal.* ○ *They're losing 3-1.* ○ *They hadn't lost an election in 15 years.* **5 lose faith/interest/patience, etc** to stop feeling something good *I'm rapidly losing interest in the whole subject.* ○ *He kept on crying and I lost my patience.* **6** TIME [T] If you lose a number of hours or days, you cannot work during this time. *Four million hours were lost last year* *through stress-related illnesses.* **7** CLOCK [T] If a clock loses time, it goes slower than it should. **8** CONFUSE [T] *informal* to confuse someone so that they do not understand something *No, you've lost me there - can you explain that again?* **9** GET RID OF *informal* to take something away, usually because it looks bad. *Lose the belt, Andrea, it looks ridiculous with that dress.* **10 lose your balance** to fall because you are leaning too much to one side **11 lose count of sth** to forget the exact number *I've lost count of how many times I've called her.* **12 lose your life** to die *Millions of young men lost their lives in the war.* **13 be losing it** *informal* to start to become crazy *I can't even remember my own telephone number - I think I must be losing it.* **14 lose it** *informal* to stop being able to control your emotions and suddenly start to laugh, shout or cry *I was trying so hard to stay calm but in the end I just lost it.* ➲See Common Learner Error at **loose** ➲See also: fight a losing **battle**[1], lose your **cool**[3], lose/save **face**[1], gain/lose **ground**[1], lose **sight**[1] of sth, lose **sleep**[2] over sth

COMMON LEARNER ERROR

lose or **miss?**

Usually you **miss** something which happens, such as an event, a train leaving, or an opportunity.

I do not want to miss my class.

~~*I do not want to lose my class.*~~

Usually you **lose** a thing.

I've lost my umbrella.

lose out *phrasal verb* to not have an advantage that someone else has

loser /ˈluːzəʳ/ *noun* [C] **1** NOT WINNING someone who does not win a game or competition *The losers of both games will play each other for third place.* **2** NOT SUCCESSFUL *informal* someone who is not successful in anything they do

WORD PARTNERS FOR ***loss***

make/suffer a loss • a loss **of** [$50,000/£3 million, etc]

O⁃**loss** /lɒs/ *noun* **1** NOT HAVING [C, U] when you do not have someone or something that you had before, or when you have less of something than before *loss of income/memory* ○ *blood/hair/weight loss* ○ *job losses* **2** FINANCE [C, U] when a company spends more money than it earns *Both companies* ***suffered losses*** *this year.* **3** DISADVANTAGE [**no plural**] a disadvantage caused by someone leaving an organization *It would be a great* ***loss to*** *the department if you left.* **4 be at a loss** to not know what to do or say [+ **to do sth**] *I'm at a loss to explain his disappearance.* **5 a sense of loss** sadness because someone has died or left **6** DEATH [C, U] the death of a person *They never got over the loss of their son.*

O⁃**lost**[1] /lɒst/ *adjective* **1** PERSON not knowing where you are or where you should go *I* ***got lost*** *on the way.* **2** OBJECT If something is lost, no one knows where it is. *Things tend to* ***get lost*** *when you move house.* ○ *Lost: black cat with white paws.* **3** NEW SITUATION not knowing what to do in a new situation *It was his first day in the office and he seemed a bit lost.* **4 be lost without sb/sth** *informal* to be unable to live or work without someone or something *She's lost without her computer.* **5 be lost on sb** If a joke or remark is lost on someone, they do not understand it. *I wouldn't bother telling your joke to Sean – it will be lost on him.* **6 Get lost!** *informal* an impolite way of telling someone to go away ➲See also: **long-lost**

lost[2] /lɒst/ *past of* lose

ˌ**lost ˈproperty** *noun* [U] *UK* things that people have left in public places which are kept somewhere until the owners can collect them *Have you had a look in lost property?*

O⁃**lot** /lɒt/ *noun* **1 a lot; lots** a large number or amount of people or things *There were* ***a lot of*** *people outside the building.* ○ *He earns* ***lots of*** *money.* ○ *I've got a lot to do this morning.* ○ *He has lots of friends* ○ *She has caused an awful lot of trouble.* ➲See Common Learner Error at **many** **2 a lot better/older/quicker, etc** much better/older/quicker, etc *It's a lot better than the old system.* ○ *It's a lot quicker by train.* ○ *She looks a lot older now.* **3 the lot** *UK informal* all of an amount or number *I made enough curry for three people and he ate the lot.* **4** GROUP [C] *UK* a group of people or things that you deal with together *I've already done one lot of washing.* **5** AREA [C] *US* an area of land *a parking lot* ○ *an empty lot* **6** SALE [C] something being sold at an auction (= sale where things are sold to the people who pay the most) *Lot 3: a Victorian chest.* **7 sb's lot** the quality of someone's life and the type of experiences they have *They've done much to improve the lot of working people.*

COMMON LEARNER ERROR

a lot of sth

Remember to use the preposition **of** before the thing that there is a large number of.

A lot of people enjoy travelling to other countries.

~~*A lot people enjoy travelling to other countries.*~~

lotion /ˈləʊʃᵊn/ *noun* [C, U] a liquid that you put on your skin to make it soft or healthy *suntan lotion* ○ *body lotion*

lottery /ˈlɒtᵊri/ *noun* [C] a way of making money by selling numbered tickets to people who then have a chance of winning a prize if their number is chosen *the national lottery* ○ *What would you do if you* ***won*** *the* ***lottery****?*

O⁃**loud**[1] /laʊd/ *adjective* **1** NOISE making a lot of noise *a loud noise* ○ *a* ***loud voice*** ○ *a loud explosion* **2** CLOTHES Loud clothes are too bright or have too many colours. •**loudly** *adverb She was speaking very loudly.*

loud[2] /laʊd/ *adverb* **1** loudly *Can you speak a bit louder?* **2 out loud** If you say or read something out loud, you say or read it so that other people can hear you.

loudspeaker /ˌlaʊdˈspiːkəʳ/ (US) /ˈlaʊdˌspiːkəʳ/ *noun* [C] a piece of equipment used for making voices or sounds louder

lounge[1] /laʊndʒ/ *noun* [C] **1** HOME *UK* the room in a home where you sit and relax **2** HOTEL *US*

L

a room in a hotel, theatre, airport, etc where people can relax or wait

lounge² /laʊndʒ/ *verb*
lounge about/around (sth) *phrasal verb* to spend your time in a relaxed way, doing very little *Most days were spent lounging around the pool.*

louse /laʊs/ *noun* [C] *plural* **lice** /laɪs/ a very small insect that lives on the bodies or in the hair of people or animals

lousy /ˈlaʊzi/ *adjective informal* very bad *lousy food/service* ○ *I* ***felt lousy*** *when I woke up this morning.*

lout /laʊt/ *noun* [C] a man who behaves in a rude or violent way

lovable (*also* **loveable**) /ˈlʌvəbl/ *adjective* A person or animal that is lovable has qualities which make them easy to love.

love¹ /lʌv/ *verb* [T] **1** ROMANCE/SEX to like someone very much and have romantic or sexual feelings for them *Last night he told me he loved me.* ○ *I've only ever loved one woman.* **2** FRIENDS/FAMILY to like a friend or a person in your family very much *I'm sure he loves his kids.* **3** ENJOY to enjoy something very much or have a strong interest in something *He loves his music.* ○ *She loves animals.* [+ **doing sth**] *I love eating out.* **4 I'd love to** used to say that you would very much like to do something that someone is offering *"I wondered if you'd like to meet up sometime?" "I'd love to."*

WORD PARTNERS FOR *love*

in love **with** sb • **fall** in love • **madly** in love • **brotherly/unconditional** love

love² /lʌv/ *noun* **1** ROMANCE/SEX [U] when you like someone very much and have romantic or sexual feelings for them *He's madly* ***in love with*** (= he loves) *her.* ○ *I was 20 when I first* ***fell in love*** (= started to love someone). ○ *a love song/story* **2 make love** to have sex **3** PERSON [C] someone who you like very much and have a romantic or sexual relationship with *He was my first love.* **4** FRIENDS/FAMILY [U] when you like a friend or person in your family very much *Nothing is as strong as the love you have for your kids.* **5** INTEREST [C, U] something that interests you a lot *his love of books* **6 Love from; All my love** something you write at the end of a letter to a friend or someone in your family *Love from Mum.* ○ *All my love, Louise.* **7** SPEAKING TO SOMEONE *mainly UK* You call someone 'love' to show affection or to be friendly. *"Margot?" "Yes, love."* ○ *Two portions of chips please, love.* **8 SPORT** [U] in games such as tennis, a score of zero *She's leading by two sets to love.* ➲See also: a **labour¹** of love

ˈlove afˌfair *noun* [C] a romantic or sexual relationship

loveless /ˈlʌvləs/ *adjective* without love *She was trapped in a* ***loveless marrage.***

ˈlove ˌlife *noun* [C] the romantic relationships in a person's life *How's your love life these days?*

lovely /ˈlʌvli/ *adjective* **1** ENJOYABLE pleasant or enjoyable *We had a lovely day together.* ○ *What lovely weather.* **2** ATTRACTIVE very attractive *a lovely dress/house/village* ○ *You look lovely!*

lover /ˈlʌvəʳ/ *noun* **1** [C] If two people are lovers, they have a sexual relationship but they are not married. *She had a string of lovers before her marriage finally broke up.* **2 a book/cat/dog, etc lover** someone who is very interested in books/cats/dogs, etc *She's a real cat lover.*

loving /ˈlʌvɪŋ/ *adjective* showing a lot of affection and kindness towards someone *a loving relationship* ○ *a loving father* •**lovingly** *adverb*

low¹ /ləʊ/ *adjective* **1** NOT HIGH near the ground, not high *low aircraft* ○ *a low fence* **2** LEVEL below the usual level *a low income* ○ *low temperatures/prices* ○ *a low number* ○ *Fish is very* ***low in*** (= has little) *fat.* **3** SOUND deep or quiet *a low voice* ○ *a low note* **4** LIGHTS If lights are low, they are not bright. *We have very low lighting in the main room.* **5** UNHAPPY unhappy and without energy *Illness of any sort can leave you feeling low.* ➲See also: be at a low **ebb¹**, keep a low **profile¹**

low² /ləʊ/ *adverb* **1** in or to a low position or level *low-paid workers* ○ *Turn the oven on low.* **2 MUSIC** with deep notes *You can sing lower than me.*

low³ /ləʊ/ *noun* **a new/record/all-time, etc low** the lowest level *Temperatures in the region hit a record low yesterday.*

low-alcohol /ˌləʊˈælkəhɒl/ *adjective* **FOOD** A low-alcohol drink has less alcohol in it than the normal type. *low-alcohol beer*

low-calorie /ˌləʊˈkælᵊri/ (*abbreviation* **low-cal, lo-cal**) *adjective* **FOOD** A low-calorie food or drink will not make you fat because it has fewer calories (= units for measuring the amount of energy a food provides) than normal food or drink.

low-cut /ˌləʊˈkʌt/ *adjective* describes a piece of clothing that does not cover the top part of a woman's chest *a low-cut dress*

the lowdown /ˈləʊdaʊn/ *noun informal* the most important information about something *Jenny will* ***give you the lowdown on*** *what happened at yesterday's meeting.*

lower¹ /ˈləʊəʳ/ *adjective* being the bottom part of something *I've got a pain in my lower back.* ○ *She bit her lower lip.*

lower² /ˈləʊəʳ/ *verb* [T] **1** MOVE to move something to a low position *They lowered the coffin into the grave.* **2** REDUCE to reduce the amount of something *I'll join if they lower the entrance fee.*

ˌlower ˈcase *noun* [U] letters of the alphabet which are not written as capital letters, for example a, b, c

ˌlowest common deˈnominator *noun* [C] **MATHEMATICS** the smallest number that can be exactly divided by all the bottom numbers in a group of fractions

ˌlowest common ˈmultiple (*abbreviation* **LCM**) *noun* [C] **MATHEMATICS** the lowest number that can be divided exactly by a particular group of numbers

low-fat /ˌləʊˈfæt/ *adjective* **FOOD** Low-fat foods do not contain much fat. *low-fat cheese* ○ *a low-fat diet*

low-key /ˌləʊˈkiː/ *adjective* not attracting attention *The reception itself was surprisingly low-key.*

lowland /ˈləʊlənd/ *noun* [C, usually singular] **GEOGRAPHY** flat land that is at the same level as the sea

ˌlow-level ˈlanguage *noun* [C] **COMPUTING** a language for writing computer programs which is similar to machine code (= a set of numbers that gives instructions to a computer)

lowly /ˈləʊli/ *adjective* not important or respected *He took a lowly job in an insurance firm.*

low-rise /ˈləʊˌraɪz/ *adjective* describes trousers in which the top part of the trousers ends below the person's waist

low-tech /ˌləʊˈtek/ *adjective* Something that is low-tech does not use the most recent technology. ➲Compare **high-tech**

loyal /ˈlɔɪəl/ *adjective* always liking and supporting someone or something, sometimes when other people do not *a **loyal supporter*** ○ *She's very **loyal to** her friends.* ➲Opposite **disloyal** •**loyally** *adverb*

loyalties /ˈlɔɪəltiz/ *noun* [plural] a feeling of support for someone *My loyalties to my family come before work.*

loyalty /ˈlɔɪəlti/ *noun* [U] the quality of being loyal *Your **loyalty to** the company is impressive.* ➲Opposite **disloyalty**

lozenge /ˈlɒzɪndʒ/ *noun* [C] **FOOD, HEALTH** a sweet which you suck to make your throat feel better

LP /ˌelˈpiː/ *noun* [C] a record that has about 25 minutes of music on each side

LPG /ˌelpiːˈdʒiː/ *noun* [U] *abbreviation for* liquid petroleum gas: a type of fuel used for heating, cooking and in some vehicles

L-plate /ˈelpleɪt/ *noun* [C] *UK* a red and white 'L' symbol on the car of someone learning to drive

Ltd *written abbreviation for* limited company (= used after the name of some companies) *Pinewood Supplies Ltd*

lubricant /ˈluːbrɪkənt/ *noun* [C, U] a liquid, such as oil, which is used to make the parts of an engine move smoothly together

lubricate /ˈluːbrɪkeɪt/ *verb* [T] to put a lubricant on something •**lubrication** /ˌluːbrɪˈkeɪʃən/ *noun* [U]

lucid /ˈluːsɪd/ *adjective* **1** [CLEAR] clear and easy to understand *a lucid account* **2** [MIND] able to think and speak clearly *In a lucid moment, she spoke about her son.* •**lucidly** *adverb*

WORD PARTNERS FOR ***luck***

bad/beginner's/good/rotten luck • **bring/wish** sb luck • **curse** your luck • a **stroke** of luck

O- **luck** /lʌk/ *noun* [U] **1** [BY CHANCE] good and bad things caused by chance and not by your own actions *It was just luck that I asked for a job at the right time.* ○ *Then I met this gorgeous woman and I **couldn't believe my luck**.* ○ *He seems to have had a lot of **bad luck** in his life.* **2** [SUCCESS] success *Have you **had** any **luck** (= succeeded in) finding your bag?* ○ *He's been trying to find work but with no luck so far.* **3 be in luck** *informal* to be able to have or do what you want *"Do you have any tuna sandwiches?" "You're in luck - there's one left."* **4 Good luck!** something you say to someone when you hope that they will be successful *Good luck with your exam!* **5 Bad/Hard luck!** used to show sympathy when someone is unsuccessful or unlucky *"They've run out of tickets." "Oh, bad luck!"* **6 the luck of the draw** If something is the luck of the draw, it is the result of chance and you have no control over it. ➲See also: a **stroke**[1] of luck

O- **lucky** /ˈlʌki/ *adjective* **1** [HAVING GOOD LUCK] having good things happen to you *"I'm going on holiday." "Lucky you!"* ○ *The **lucky winner** will be able to choose from three different holidays.* [+ to do sth] *You're lucky to have such a nice office to work in.* **2** [GIVING LUCK] If an object is lucky, some people believe that it gives you luck. *I chose six - it's my lucky number.* ➲Opposite **unlucky** •**luckily** *adverb Luckily I had some money with me.* ➲See also: **happy-go-lucky**

lucrative /ˈluːkrətɪv/ *adjective* If something is lucrative, it makes a lot of money. *a lucrative contract/job/offer*

ludicrous /ˈluːdɪkrəs/ *adjective* stupid *a ludicrous idea/suggestion* •**ludicrously** *adverb*

lug /lʌg/ *verb* [T] **lugging**, *past* **lugged** *informal* to carry or pull a heavy object *You don't want to lug your suitcase across London.*

luggage /ˈlʌgɪdʒ/ *noun* [U] bags and cases that you carry with you when you are travelling ➲See also: **hand luggage**

lukewarm /ˌluːkˈwɔːm/ *adjective* **1** [LIQUID] A liquid which is lukewarm is only slightly warm. *Dissolve yeast and one tablespoon of sugar in lukewarm water.* **2** [LITTLE INTEREST] showing little interest or enthusiasm *She seemed rather lukewarm about the idea.*

lull[1] /lʌl/ *verb* [T] to make someone feel calm and make them want to sleep *Soft music **lulled** him **to sleep**.*

lull sb into sth/doing sth *phrasal verb* to make someone feel safe so that you can then trick them

lull[2] /lʌl/ *noun* [C] a short period of calm in which little happens *a **lull in** the conversation/traffic*

lullaby /ˈlʌləbaɪ/ *noun* [C] **MUSIC** a song which you sing to children to make them sleep

lumber[1] /ˈlʌmbər/ *verb* **lumber along/around/off, etc** to move slowly with heavy steps *The bear lumbered off into the forest.*

be lumbered with sth/sb *phrasal verb mainly UK* to have to deal with something or someone that you do not want to *I've been lumbered with my neighbours' cat while they're away.*

lumber[2] /ˈlʌmbər/ *US* (*UK* **timber**) *noun* [U] wood that is used for building

lumberjack /ˈlʌmbədʒæk/ *noun* [C] a person whose job is to cut down trees in a forest

lumen /ˈluːmɪn/ *noun* [C] **1 MEASURES** (*abbreviation* **lm**) a unit for measuring the flow of light **2 BIOLOGY** a small space inside a plant cell **3** **BIOLOGY** a hollow area inside a body part, for example inside an artery (= tube that carries blood) ➲See picture at **artery** ➲See picture at **vein**

luminary /ˈluːmɪnəri/ *noun* [C] *formal* a famous person who is respected for their skills or knowledge

luminous /ˈluːmɪnəs/ *adjective* Something that is luminous shines in the dark.

lump[1] /lʌmp/ *noun* [C] **1** a piece of a solid substance with no particular shape *a lump of coal* ○ *You don't want lumps in the sauce.* ➲See colour picture **Pieces and Quantities** on page Centre 1 **2** **HEALTH** a hard piece of tissue under the skin caused by injury or illness *She found a lump in her breast.*

lump[2] /lʌmp/ *verb*
lump sth/sb together *phrasal verb* to put different groups together and think about them or deal with them in the same way *American and Canadian authors tend to be lumped together.*

ˌlump ˈsum *noun* [C] **FINANCE** a large amount of money given as a single payment *She received a tax-free lump sum on leaving the company.*

lumpy /ˈlʌmpi/ *adjective* covered with or containing lumps (= bits of solid substance) *a lumpy sauce*

L

lunacy /ˈluːnəsi/ *noun* [U] stupid behaviour that will have bad results *It was lunacy spending all that money.*

lunar /ˈluːnər/ *adjective* [**always before noun**] **ASTRONOMY** relating to the moon

lunatic /ˈluːnətɪk/ *noun* [C] someone who behaves in a crazy way *He drives like a lunatic.*

WORD PARTNERS FOR ***lunch***

eat/have lunch • **have** sth **for** lunch • **a light** lunch

O‑**lunch[1]** /lʌnʃ/ *noun* [C, U] **FOOD** a meal that you eat in the middle of the day ➲See also: **packed lunch**

lunch[2] /lʌnʃ/ *verb* [I] to eat lunch

luncheon /ˈlʌnʃən/ *noun* [C] *formal* lunch

lunchtime /ˈlʌnʃtaɪm/ *noun* [C, U] the time when lunch is eaten

lung /lʌŋ/ *noun* [C] **ANATOMY** one of the two organs inside your chest that are used for breathing *lung cancer* ➲See picture at **circulation** ➲See picture at **respiratory system** ➲See picture at **rib cage**

lurch /lɜːtʃ/ *verb* **lurch forward/towards, etc** to suddenly move in a way that is not controlled *The car lurched forward before hitting the tree.*

lure[1] /lʊər/ *verb* [T] to persuade someone to go somewhere or do something by offering them something exciting *It seems that he was **lured into** a trap.* ○ *They had been **lured to** the big city by the promise of high wages.*

lure[2] /lʊər/ *noun* [U] the power to attract people *the lure of fame/power/money*

lurid /ˈlʊərɪd/ *adjective* **1** SHOCKING shocking in a way that involves sex or violence *lurid details/stories* **2** COLOUR too brightly coloured *a lurid green miniskirt*

lurk /lɜːk/ *verb* [I] **1** to wait somewhere secretly, especially before doing something bad *Someone was lurking in the shadows.* **2** **INTERNET** to enter a place on the Internet and read what other people have written without them knowing you are there ➲See Extra help page **The Web and the Internet** on page Centre 37. •**lurker** *noun* [C]

lush /lʌʃ/ *adjective* A lush area has a lot of healthy grass, plants, or trees.

lust[1] /lʌst/ *noun* [U] **1** SEX a strong feeling of sexual attraction to someone **2** WANTING SOMETHING when you want something very much *a lust for power*

lust[2] /lʌst/ *verb*
lust after sb *phrasal verb* to feel strong sexual attraction for someone
lust after sth *phrasal verb* to want something very much *to lust after fame/power*

Lutheran /ˈluːθərən/ *adjective* **RELIGION** belonging or relating to a Christian group based on the teachings of Martin Luther •**Lutheran** *noun* [C]

luxurious /lʌgˈʒʊəriəs/ *adjective* very comfortable and expensive *a luxurious hotel* ○ *luxurious fabrics*

luxury /ˈlʌkʃəri/ *noun* **1** COMFORT/PLEASURE [U] great comfort or pleasure from expensive or beautiful things *to live in luxury* ○ *a luxury apartment/car* **2** NOT NECESSARY [C] something expensive that you enjoy but do not need *It's nice to buy people the little luxuries that they wouldn't buy themselves.* **3** RARE PLEASURE [**U, no plural**] something which gives you a lot of pleasure but which you cannot often do *A day off work is such a luxury.*

lying /ˈlaɪɪŋ/ *present participle of* lie[1,2]

lymph /lɪmpf/ *noun* [U] **BIOLOGY** a colourless liquid which takes waste matter away from body tissue in order to prevent infection •**lymphatic** *adjective lymphatic system*

ˈlymph ˌgland (*also* **lymph node**) *noun* [C] **ANATOMY, BIOLOGY** one of many small organs in the body which produce the white blood cells needed for the body to fight infection

lymphocyte /ˈlimpfəʊsaɪt/ *noun* [C] **BIOLOGY** a type of blood cell that fights disease in the body ➲See picture at **blood cells**

ˈlymph ˌvessel *noun* [C] **ANATOMY, BIOLOGY** any of the thin tubes in the body through which lymph flows

lyrical /ˈlɪrɪkəl/ *adjective* **LITERATURE** expressing the writer's emotions in a beautiful way *lyrical poetry/verse*

lyrics /ˈlɪrɪks/ *noun* [**plural**] **MUSIC** the words of a song

Mm

M, m /em/ the thirteenth letter of the alphabet

m **MEASURES** *written abbreviation for* metre (= a unit of length)

MA /ˌem'eɪ/ *noun* [C] **EDUCATION** *abbreviation for* Master of Arts: a higher university qualification in an arts (= not science) subject

ma'am /mæm, mɑːm/ *US short for* madam *Can I help you, Ma'am?*

mac /mæk/ *noun* [C] *UK* a coat that you wear in the rain ➲See colour picture **Clothes** on page Centre 8

macabre /mə'kɑːbrə/ *adjective* strange and frightening, and often connected with death *a macabre story*

macaroni /ˌmækᵊr'əʊni/ *noun* [U] **FOOD** pasta that is shaped like small tubes

machete /mə'ʃeti/ *noun* [C] a large knife with a wide blade

machinations /ˌmæʃɪ'neɪʃᵊnz/ *noun* [plural] complicated and secret plans and activities *political machinations*

WORD PARTNERS FOR ***machine***

operate/use a machine • **turn off/turn on** a machine • do sth **by machine** • a machine **for** doing sth

O‑ **machine** /mə'ʃiːn/ *noun* [C] **1** EQUIPMENT a piece of equipment with moving parts that uses power to do a particular job *a fax machine* ○ *a coffee machine* ○ *Clothes are generally sewn **by machine** these days.* **2** GROUP a group of people all working together to achieve the same result *a political/war machine* **3** **COMPUTING** a computer ➲See also: **answering machine, cash machine, sewing machine, slot machine, vending machine, washing machine**

ma'chine ˌcarding *noun* [U] **DT** using machines with wire brushes to separate the threads of some materials such as wool before they can be used

ma'chine ˌcode *noun* [U] **COMPUTING** a set of numbers that gives instructions to a computer

ma'chine ˌgun *noun* [C] a gun that fires a lot of bullets very quickly

machine-readable /məˌʃiːn'riːdəbl/ *adjective* **COMPUTING** able to be understood by a computer *a machine-readable dictionary*

machinery /mə'ʃiːnᵊri/ *noun* [U] **1** EQUIPMENT machines, often large machines *industrial/farm machinery* **2** SYSTEM the system that a group of people uses to achieve something *the machinery of government*

ma'chine ˌtool *noun* [C] **DT** a tool that uses power for cutting and shaping wood, metal, etc

macho /'mætʃəʊ/ (US) /'mɑːtʃəʊ/ *adjective informal* Men who are macho emphasize their traditional male qualities, such as physical strength, and do not show emotion.

mackerel /'mækrᵊl/ *noun* [C, U] *plural* **mackerel** or **mackerels** **FOOD** a type of sea fish, or the meat from this fish

mackintosh /'mækɪntɒʃ/ *noun* [C] *old-fashioned* a mac

macramé /mə'krɑːmeɪ/ (US) /'mæk.re.mei/ *noun* [U] **DT** the art of twisting pieces of string together in knots to form a decorative pattern

macro /'mækrəʊ/ *noun* [C] **COMPUTING** a single instruction given to a computer which produces a set of instructions for the computer to perform a particular piece of work

macro- /mækrəʊ-/ *prefix* large or on a large scale *macroeconomics* (= the study of financial systems at a national level)

macromolecule /'mækrəʊˌmɒlɪkjuːl/ *noun* [C] **PHYSICS, CHEMISTRY** a large molecule, for example a protein

O‑ **mad** /mæd/ *adjective* **1** CRAZY *informal* stupid or crazy [+ **to do sth**] *You're mad to walk home alone at night.* **2** ANGRY *mainly US* angry *Were your parents **mad at** you when you came home late?* **3** **go mad a** ANGRY to become very angry *Dad'll go mad when he finds out you took the car.* **b** EXCITED to suddenly become very excited *When the band arrived on stage, the crowd went mad.* **4** **be mad about sb/sth** *informal* to love something or someone *Jo's mad about skiing.* **5** ILL mentally ill **6** NOT CONTROLLED not controlled *We made a **mad dash** for the exit.* **7** **like mad a** QUICKLY If you run, work, etc like mad, you do it very quickly and with a lot of energy. **b** PAIN If something hurts like mad, it hurts a lot.

COMMON LEARNER ERROR

mad or **mentally ill?**

If someone has mental health problems, it is not polite to say that they are **mad**, use **mentally ill** instead.

madam /'mædəm/ *noun formal* **1** (*also* **Madam**) You call a woman 'madam' when you are speaking to her politely. *This way, madam.* **2** **Madam** You write 'Madam' at the beginning of a formal letter to a woman when you do not know her name. *Dear Madam, I am writing to...*

made /meɪd/ *past of* make

-made /meɪd/ *suffix* ➲See: **man-made, ready-made, self-made, tailor-made**

madhouse /'mædhaʊs/ *noun* [C] *informal* a place where there is a lot of uncontrolled noise and activity

madly /mædli/ *adverb* **1** with a lot of energy and enthusiasm *We cheered madly as the team came out onto the field.* **2** **be madly in love** to love someone very much

madman, madwoman /'mædmən, 'mædˌwʊmən/ *noun* [C] *plural* **madmen, madwomen** a crazy person *He was running around **like a madman**.*

madness /'mædnəs/ *noun* [U] **1** DANGER stupid or dangerous behaviour *It would be madness to give up your job when you've just bought a house.* **2** ILLNESS mental illness

M

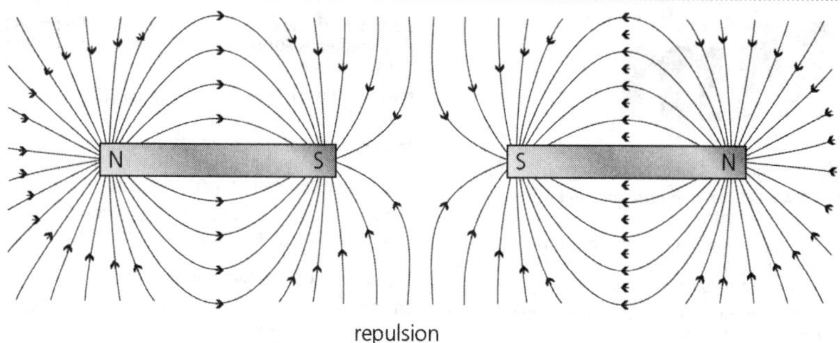

repulsion

magnet

maestro /ˈmaɪstrəʊ/ *noun* [C] **MUSIC** someone who is very good at something, especially playing music

the mafia /ˈmæfiə/ (US) /ˈmɑːfiə/ *noun* a large group of organized criminals *Drug-smuggling activities have been linked to the Mafia.*

O-ᵚ**magazine** /ˌmæɡəˈziːn/ *noun* [C] a thin book published every week or month, that has shiny, colourful pages with articles and pictures *a fashion/news magazine*

maggot /ˈmæɡət/ *noun* [C] a small insect with a soft body and no legs that often lives in decaying food

O-ᵚ**magic¹** /ˈmædʒɪk/ *noun* [U] **1** SPECIAL POWERS special powers that can make things happen that seem impossible *Do you believe in magic?* **2** ENTERTAINMENT clever actions intended to entertain people, often making objects appear and disappear **3** SPECIAL QUALITY a quality that makes something or someone seem special or exciting *No one could fail to be charmed by **the magic of** this beautiful city.* **4 as if by magic** in a way that is surprising and impossible to explain *Food would appear on the table every day, as if by magic.* ➲See also: **black magic**

magic² /ˈmædʒɪk/ *adjective* **1** SPECIAL POWERS with special powers *a **magic spell/wand*** **2** ENTERTAINMENT relating to magic *a **magic trick*** **3 magic moments** special and exciting experiences

magical /ˈmædʒɪkəl/ *adjective* **1** SPECIAL POWERS with special powers *Diamonds were once thought to have **magical powers**.* **2** EXCITING special or exciting *It was a magical night.* •**magically** *adverb I knew my problems would not just magically disappear.*

magician /məˈdʒɪʃən/ *noun* [C] **1** ENTERTAINMENT someone who entertains people by performing magic tricks **2** PERSON a character in old stories who has magic powers

magistrate /ˈmædʒɪstreɪt/ *noun* [C] a type of judge (= person who decides what punishments should be given) who deals with less serious crimes

maglev train /ˈmæɡlevˌtreɪn/ *noun* [C] a fast train that uses magnetic force to hold it just above the ground

magma /ˈmæɡmə/ *noun* [U] **GEOLOGY** hot liquid rock found just below the surface of the Earth ➲See picture at **volcano**

magnate /ˈmæɡneɪt/ *noun* [C] someone who is rich and successful in business *a media magnate*

magnesium /mæɡˈniːziəm/ *noun* [U] **CHEMISTRY** a metallic element that burns very brightly, used to make fireworks (= explosives used to entertain people) (symbol **Mg**)

magnet /ˈmæɡnət/ *noun* **1 PHYSICS** [C] an iron object that makes pieces of iron or steel (= metal made with iron) move towards it **2 be a magnet for sb** If a place or event is a magnet for people, a lot of people go there. *Airports are a magnet for thieves.*

magnetic /mæɡˈnetɪk/ *adjective* **1 PHYSICS** with the power of a magnet *a **magnetic field*** **2 magnetic tape/disk/storage, etc COMPUTING** equipment used in the past for storing information from a computer **3** having a character that attracts people to you

magˌnetic ˈfield *noun* [C] **PHYSICS** the area around a magnet that is affected by its force

magnetism /ˈmæɡnətɪzəm/ *noun* [U] **PHYSICS** the force produced by some metals that pulls objects towards each other or pushes them away from each other

magnificent /mæɡˈnɪfɪsənt/ *adjective* very good or very beautiful *a magnificent view* •**magnificently** *adverb*

magnify /ˈmæɡnɪfaɪ/ *verb* [T] **1 PHYSICS** to make an object look larger than it is by looking through special equipment *The cells are first magnified under a microscope.* **2** to make a bad situation worse *All your problems are magnified when you're ill.*

ˈmagnifying ˌglass *noun* [C] a piece of curved glass which makes objects look larger than they are

magnitude /ˈmæɡnɪtjuːd/ *noun* [U] *formal* the large size or importance of something *People were still unaware of **the magnitude of** the problem.*

mahogany /məˈhɒɡəni/ *noun* [U] a dark, red-brown wood used to make furniture

maid /meɪd/ *noun* [C] a woman who works as a servant in a hotel or in someone's home

maiden¹ /ˈmeɪdən/ *noun* [C] *literary old-fashioned* a young woman who is not married

maiden² /ˈmeɪdən/ *adjective* **a maiden flight/voyage** the first journey of a new aircraft or ship

ˈmaiden ˌname *noun* [C] the family name that a woman has before she gets married

O‑‑ **mail¹** /meɪl/ *noun* [U] **1** LETTERS letters and parcels that are brought by post **2** SYSTEM *mainly US* the system by which letters and parcels are taken and brought *Send it* ***by mail.*** ○ *The letter is* ***in the mail.*** ➲See also: **email, junk mail, snail mail, surface mail, voice mail**

mail² /meɪl/ *verb* [T] *mainly US* to send a letter or parcel or email something *Could you* ***mail*** *it to me?*

mailbox /ˈmeɪlbɒks/ *noun* [C] *US* **1** AT HOME a small box outside your home where letters are delivered **2** IN PUBLIC PLACE (*UK* **letterbox, post box**) a large, metal container in a public place where you can post letters

ˈmailing ˌlist *noun* [C] a list of names and addresses that an organization uses in order to send information to people

mailman /ˈmeɪlmæn/ *US* (*UK* **postman**) *noun* [C] *plural* **mailmen** a man who takes and brings letters and parcels as a job

ˈmail ˌmerge *noun* [U] **COMPUTING** using a computer to produce many copies of a letter with each copy with a different name and address stored on file, or a computer program that does this

ˈmail ˌorder *noun* [U] a way of buying goods by ordering them from a catalogue (= book) and receiving them by post

maim /meɪm/ *verb* [T] to injure someone permanently *Thousands of innocent people have been killed or maimed by landmines.*

O‑‑ **main¹** /meɪn/ *adjective* [**always before noun**] **1** most important or largest *the main problem/reason* ○ *The main airport is 15 miles from the capital.* **2 the main thing** the most important fact in a situation *You're happy and that's the main thing.*

main² /meɪn/ *noun* [C] **1 gas/water main** a pipe that carries gas or water to a building **2 in the main** generally or mostly *Her friends are teachers in the main.*

ˈmain ˌcourse *noun* [C] **FOOD** the largest or most important part of a meal

mainframe /ˈmeɪnfreɪm/ *noun* [C] **COMPUTING** a large, powerful computer which many people can use at the same time

mainland /ˈmeɪnlənd/ *noun* **the mainland GEOGRAPHY** the main part of a country, not including the islands around it *A daily ferry links the islands to the mainland.* •**mainland** *adjective* [**always before noun**] *mainland Britain*

O‑‑ **mainly** /ˈmeɪnli/ *adverb* mostly or to a large degree *The waitresses are mainly French.*

ˌmain ˈroad *noun* [C] a large road which leads from one town to another *Stay on the main road for about three miles and you'll be there.*

mainstay /ˈmeɪnsteɪ/ *noun* **a/the mainstay of sth** the most important thing or activity *Cattle farming is the mainstay of the country's economy.*

the mains /meɪnz/ *noun* [**group**] *UK* **1** PIPES the system of pipes or wires that carries gas, water, or electricity to a building *The house isn't connected to the mains yet.* **2** ELECTRICITY the place inside a building where you can connect a machine to a supply of electricity *Is the cooker turned off* ***at the mains?***

mainstream /ˈmeɪnstriːm/ *noun* **the mainstream SOCIETY** the beliefs or way of living accepted by most people *The party is now* ***in the mainstream of*** *politics.* •**mainstream** *adjective* [**always before noun**] *mainstream culture/politics*

maintain /meɪnˈteɪn/ *verb* [T] **1** NOT CHANGE to make a situation or activity continue in the same way *The army has been brought in to maintain order in the region.* **2** CONDITION to keep a building or area in good condition *A large house is very expensive to maintain.* **3** SPEAK TRUTH *formal* to say that you are certain something is true [**+ (that)**] *He has always maintained that he is innocent.*

WORD PARTNERS FOR ***maintenance***

carry out maintenance • **high/low** maintenance • maintenance **of** sth

maintenance /ˈmeɪntənəns/ *noun* [U] **1** WORK the work that is done to keep something in good condition *car maintenance* ○ *I want a garden that's very* ***low maintenance*** (= easy to look after). **2 FINANCE** *UK* regular amounts of money that someone must pay after they have left their family so that the family still has money to live ***child maintenance***

maize /meɪz/ *UK* (*US* **corn**) *noun* [U] **FOOD** a tall plant with yellow seeds that are eaten as food

majestic /məˈdʒestɪk/ *adjective* very beautiful or powerful in a way that people admire *majestic scenery*

majesty /ˈmædʒəsti/ *noun* **1** [U] the quality of being majestic *the majesty of the pyramids* **2 His/Her/Your Majesty** used when you are speaking to or about a king or queen *His Majesty King Edward VII*

O‑‑ **major¹** /ˈmeɪdʒər/ *adjective* **1** [**always before noun**] more important or more serious than other things or people of a similar type *a* ***major problem/issue*** ○ *a major city* ○ *America has played a major role in the peace process.* **2 MUSIC** in music, belonging to a key (= set of musical notes) which often produces a happy sound ➲Opposite **minor**

major² /ˈmeɪdʒər/ *noun* [C] **1 EDUCATION** *US* the most important subject that a college or university student studies, or the student who is studying *What's your major?* ○ *Diane's an English major.* **2** an officer of middle rank in the army or air force

major³ /ˈmeɪdʒər/ *verb*

major in sth *phrasal verb* **EDUCATION** If you major in a subject, it is the most important part of your course at a college or university.

O‑‑ **majority** /məˈdʒɒrəti/ *noun* **1** [**no plural**] more than half of a group of people or things ***The majority of*** *people in this country own their houses.* ○ *The* ***vast majority*** *of smokers claim they would like to give up.* **2 be in a/the majority** to be larger than other similar groups *Women*

M

are in the majority in the publishing world. **3** **POLITICS** [C] in an election, the difference between the number of votes for the winner, and the votes for the party that came second *Labour has a **strong majority**.* ⊃Opposite **minority**

WORD PARTNERS FOR ***majority***

a **narrow/outright/overwhelming/tiny/vast** majority • the majority **of** sth • **in** the majority

O-- **make¹** /meɪk/ *verb* [T] *past* **made** **1** CREATE to produce or create something *Shall I make some coffee?* ○ *They've made a film about her life.* ⊃See Common Learner Error at **do** **2** **make a promise/remark/mistake, etc** to promise something, to say something, to do something wrong, etc *We have to make a decision today.* ○ *You're making a big mistake.* ○ *She made some useful suggestions.* **3** **make sb do sth** to force someone to do something *You can't make me go.* **4** **make sb/sth happy/sad/difficult, etc** to cause someone or something to become happy, sad, difficult, etc *You've made me very happy.* ○ *This is the song that made her a star.* **5** GO TO to be able to go to an event *I'm afraid I can't make the meeting this afternoon.* **6** EARN MONEY If you make an amount of money, you earn it. *He makes £20,000 a year.* **7** NUMBERS If two or more numbers make a particular amount, that is the amount when they are added together. *That makes $40 altogether.* **8** PERSONAL QUALITIES [T] to have the right qualities to become a father or mother or to do a particular job *Andy would make a good teacher.* **9** GIVE A JOB [+ **two objects**] to give someone a particular job *They made her a director of the company.* **10** **make an appointment** to arrange to do something at a particular time *I've made an appointment with the doctor.* **11** **make the bed** to make the sheets and covers on a bed tidy **12** **make time** to leave enough time to do something although you are busy [+ **to do sth**] *You must make time to do your homework.* **13** **make do (with)** to accept that something is less good than you would like *If we can't get a bigger room we'll have to make do with this.* **14** **make it a** ARRIVE to manage to arrive at a place *Will we make it in time for the film?* **b** SUCCEED to be successful *Very few actors actually make it.*

make for sth *phrasal verb* to move towards a place *He got up and made for the exit.*

make sth into sth *phrasal verb* to change something into something else *We're going to make the spare room into an office.*

make of sb/sth *phrasal verb* If you ask someone what they make of someone or something, you want to know their opinion about that person or thing. *What do you make of this letter?*

make off with sth *phrasal verb informal* to steal something

make sth/sb out *phrasal verb* to be able to see, hear, or understand something or someone *We could just make out a building through the trees.*

make out sth *phrasal verb* to say something that is not true [+ **(that)**] *He made out that he'd been living in Boston all year.*

make out *phrasal verb US informal* **1** BE SUCCESSFUL to deal with a situation, usually in a successful way *How is Jake **making out in** his new school?* **2** KISS to kiss and touch someone in a sexual way

make it up to sb *phrasal verb* to do something good for someone because you have done something bad to them in the past *I'm sorry I missed your birthday. I'll make it up to you, I promise.*

make sth up *phrasal verb* to say or write something that is not true *I made up some story about having to go and see my sick mother.*

make up sth *phrasal verb* to form the whole of an amount *Women make up nearly 50% of medical school entrants.*

make up *phrasal verb* to become friendly with someone again after you have argued with them *Have you **made up with** Daryl yet?*

make up for sth *phrasal verb* to reduce the bad effect of something, or make something bad become something good *I hope this money will make up for the inconvenience.*

make² /meɪk/ *noun* [C] the name of a company that makes a particular product *I like your stereo. What make is it?*

make-believe /ˈmeɪkbɪˌliːv/ *noun* [U] when you pretend that something is real *Disneyland creates a world of make-believe.*

makeover /ˈmeɪkˌəʊvəʳ/ *noun* [C] when you suddenly improve your appearance by wearing better clothes, cutting your hair, etc *to **have a makeover***

maker /ˈmeɪkəʳ/ *noun* [C] the person or company that makes a product *makers of top quality electrical products*

makeshift /ˈmeɪkʃɪft/ *adjective* [**always before noun**] temporary and low quality *makeshift shelters*

make-up, makeup /ˈmeɪkʌp/ *noun* [U] coloured substances that a woman puts on her face in order to make herself more attractive *to **put on/take off make-up*** ○ *She doesn't wear much **make-up**.*

making /ˈmeɪkɪŋ/ *noun* [U] **1** the process of making or producing something *There's an article on **the making of** a television series.* ○ *the art of film making* **2** **be a sth/sb in the making** to be likely to develop into a particular thing or type of person *What we're seeing is a disaster in the making.* **3** **have the makings of sth** to seem likely to develop into something *She has the makings of a great violinist.*

malaria /məˈleəriə/ *noun* [U] **HEALTH** a serious disease that you can get in hot countries if a mosquito (= small insect) bites you

O-- **male¹** /meɪl/ *adjective* belonging to or relating to the sex that cannot have babies *a male colleague* ⊃Opposite **female**

male² /meɪl/ *noun* [C] a male person or animal *In 1987, 27 percent of adult males smoked.*

ˌmale ˈchauvinist *noun* [C] a man who believes that men are better or more important than women

malice /ˈmælɪs/ *noun* [U] when you want to harm or upset someone *There was no malice in her comments.*

malicious /məˈlɪʃəs/ *adjective* intended to harm or upset someone *malicious gossip*

malignant /məˈlɪgnənt/ *adjective* **HEALTH** A malignant tumour (= group of diseased cells) is one that could cause death.

mall /mɔːl/ (*also* **shopping mall**) *noun* [C] a large, covered shopping area

malleable /ˈmæliəbl/ *adjective* **1** SOFT easy to bend or make into a different shape **2** INFLUENCE *formal* easily influenced and controlled •**malleability** /ˌmæliəˈbɪlɪti/ *noun* [U]

mallet /ˈmælɪt/ *noun* [C] a tool like a hammer with a large, flat end made of wood or rubber

malleus /ˈmæliəs/ *noun* [C **usually singular**] *plural* **mallei** **ANATOMY** one of three very small bones that carry sound into the inner ear ➲Compare **incus, stapes**

malnutrition /ˌmælnjuːˈtrɪʃᵊn/ *noun* [U] **HEALTH** a serious illness caused by too little food

malpractice /ˌmælˈpræktɪs/ *noun* [U] when a doctor, lawyer, etc does not do one of their duties or makes a mistake at work *medical malpractice*

malt /mɔːlt/ *noun* [U] **FOOD** a substance made from grain that is used to make drinks, for example beer and whisky (= strong alcoholic drink)

maltase /ˈmɒlteɪz/ *noun* [U] **BIOLOGY** an enzyme (= substance that causes chemical change) that helps maltose change to glucose

maltose /ˈmɔːltəʊz/ *noun* [U] **BIOLOGY** a type of sugar made in the body from starch by enzymes (= substances that cause chemical change)

mama /məˈmɑː/ *noun* [C] *mainly US* a child's word for 'mother'

mammal /ˈmæmᵊl/ *noun* [C] **BIOLOGY** an animal that feeds its babies on milk from its body

mammoth /ˈmæməθ/ *adjective* very large *a mammoth task/project*

O⁻ **man¹** /mæn/ *noun plural* **men** **1** MALE [C] an adult male human *a young/tall man* ○ *men and women* **2** PEOPLE [U] used to refer to both men and women *Man is still more intelligent than the cleverest robot.* ➲See also: **best man, garbage man, no-man's land,** the man/person, etc in the **street**

man² /mæn/ *verb* [T] **manning**, *past* **manned** to be present somewhere, especially in order to operate a machine *The emergency room is manned 24 hours a day.*

O⁻ **manage** /ˈmænɪdʒ/ *verb* **1** DO SUCCESSFULLY [I, T] to do something or deal with something successfully *Will you be able to manage on your own?* [+ **to do sth**] *Anyway, we managed to get there on time.* **2** CONTROL [T] to be in control of an office, shop, team, etc *He used to manage the bookshop on King Street.* **3** USE TIME/MONEY [T] to use or organize your time or money *He's no good at managing his money.* **4** HAVE ENOUGH MONEY [I] to have enough money to live *How can anyone **manage on** such a low income?*

manageable /ˈmænɪdʒəbl/ *adjective* easy to control *Are they going to reduce classes to a more **manageable size**?*

> WORD PARTNERS FOR ***management***
>
> management **of** sth • management **skills** • **middle/senior** management

O⁻ **management** /ˈmænɪdʒmənt/ *noun* **1** CONTROL [U] being in control of an office, shop, team, etc *management skills/training* **2** PEOPLE [**group**] the people who are in control of an office, shop, team, etc ***middle/senior management***

O⁻ **manager** /ˈmænɪdʒəʳ/ *noun* [C] someone in control of an office, shop, team, etc *a sales manager* ○ *She's the manager of the local sports club.*

managerial /ˌmænəˈdʒɪəriəl/ *adjective* relating to a manager or management ***managerial skills***

ˌmanaging diˈrector *noun* [C] *mainly UK* the main person in control of a company

mandate /ˈmændeɪt/ *noun* [C] *formal* **POLITICS** support for action given to someone by the people voting for them *The electorate have **given** them a clear **mandate** for social reform.*

mandatory /ˈmændətᵊri/ *adjective formal* If something is mandatory, it must be done.

mandible /ˈmændɪbᵊl/ *noun* [C] **1 ANATOMY** in a person or animal, the lower jaw bone **2 BIOLOGY** in insects, one of the two parts of the mouth used for biting and cutting food

mane /meɪn/ *noun* [C] **BIOLOGY** the long, thick hair that grows on the necks of animals such as horses or lions

maneuver¹ *US* (*UK* **manoeuvre**) /məˈnuːvəʳ/ *noun* [C] **1** MOVEMENT a movement that needs care or skill **2** ACTION a clever action, usually done to trick someone *a **political/tactical maneuver***

maneuver² *US* (*UK* **manoeuvre**) /məˈnuːvəʳ/ *verb* [I, T] to move with care or skill *I find big cars difficult to maneuver.*

mangled /ˈmæŋgld/ *adjective* badly crushed and damaged *a mangled body*

mango /ˈmæŋgəʊ/ *noun* [C] *plural* **mangoes** or **mangos** **FOOD** a tropical fruit that has a green skin and is orange inside

manhood /ˈmænhʊd/ *noun* [U] the qualities related to being a man and not a boy

mania /ˈmeɪniə/ *noun* [U] extreme enthusiasm or interest *football mania*

maniac /ˈmeɪniæk/ *noun* [C] *informal* someone who behaves in an extreme or uncontrolled way *a **sex maniac*** ○ *He drives like a maniac.*

manic /ˈmænɪk/ *adjective* behaving in an excited and uncontrolled way

manicure /ˈmænɪkjʊəʳ/ *noun* [C, U] when someone makes your hands look attractive by cleaning and cutting your nails, etc

manifest¹ /ˈmænɪfest/ *verb* [T] *formal* to show a quality or condition [**often reflexive**] *Grief manifests itself in a number of different ways.*

manifest² /ˈmænɪfest/ *adjective* [**always before noun**] *formal* obvious *her manifest lack of interest*

manifestation /ˌmænɪfesˈteɪʃᵊn/ *noun* [C, U] *formal* something which shows that a quality or condition exists *one of the manifestations of the disease*

manifesto /ˌmænɪˈfestəʊ/ *noun* [C] **POLITICS** when a political group says publicly what it intends to do

manipulate /məˈnɪpjəleɪt/ *verb* [T] to control someone or something in a clever way so that they do what you want them to do *She knows how to manipulate the press.* •**manipulation** /məˌnɪpjəˈleɪʃᵊn/ *noun* [U]

manipulative /məˈnɪpjələtɪv/ *adjective* A manipulative person controls people in a clever and unpleasant way. *a devious, manipulative little boy*

mankind /mænˈkaɪnd/ *noun* [U] **SOCIETY** all people, considered as a group *the history of mankind*

manly /ˈmænli/ *adjective* having the qualities and appearance that people think a man should have *a deep, manly voice*

man-made /ˌmænˈmeɪd/ *adjective* not natural, but made by people *man-made fibres* ○ *a man-made lake*

manned /mænd/ *adjective* A place or vehicle that is manned has people working in it. *a manned space flight*

WORD PARTNERS FOR ***manner***

in a [similar/traditional/professional, etc] manner • the manner **of** sth

manner /ˈmænəʳ/ *noun* [no plural] **1** PERSONALITY the way in which a person talks and behaves with other people *an aggressive/friendly manner* **2** WAY the way something happens or something is done *They dealt with the problem* ***in a*** *very efficient* ***manner.***

mannerism /ˈmænᵊrɪzᵊm/ *noun* [C] something strange that someone often does with their face, hands, or voice, and that is part of their personality

manners /ˈmænəz/ *noun* [plural] **SOCIETY** polite ways of behaving with other people ***bad/good manners*** ○ ***table manners***

WORD PARTNERS FOR ***manoeuvre (noun)***

carry out/perform a manoeuvre

manoeuvre¹ *UK* (*US* **maneuver**) /məˈnuːvəʳ/ *noun* [C] **1** MOVEMENT a movement that needs care or skill **2** ACTION a clever action, usually done to trick someone *a* ***political/tactical manoeuvre***

manoeuvre² *UK* (*US* **maneuver**) /məˈnuːvəʳ/ *verb* [I, T] to move with care or skill *I find big cars difficult to manoeuvre.*

manpower /ˈmænˌpaʊəʳ/ *noun* [U] the people needed or available to do a job *a manpower shortage*

mansion /ˈmænʃᵊn/ *noun* [C] a very large house

manslaughter /ˈmænˌslɔːtəʳ/ *noun* [U] **LAW** the crime of killing someone without intending to kill them

mantelpiece /ˈmæntᵊlpiːs/ (*also US* **mantel**) *noun* [C] the shelf above a fireplace (= place in a room where wood, etc is burned) *There was an old family photo* ***on the mantelpiece.*** See colour picture **The Living Room** on page Centre 4

mantle /ˈmæntl/ *noun* [C] **GEOGRAPHY** the part of the Earth that surrounds the part in the centre See picture at **Earth**

mantra /ˈmæntrə/ *noun* [C] an idea or belief that people often say but do not think about *the mantra of 'democratic reform'*

manual¹ /ˈmænjuəl/ *adjective* using your hands *manual labour/work* ○ *a manual control/gearbox* •**manually** *adverb*

manual² /ˈmænjuəl/ *noun* [C] a book that tells you how to use something or do something

manufacture /ˌmænjəˈfæktʃəʳ/ *verb* [T] to produce something, usually in large numbers in a factory *Local industries manufacture plastic products, boats, and clothing.* •**manufacture** *noun* [U] *the manufacture of computers/margarine*

manufacturer /ˌmænjəˈfæktʃᵊrəʳ/ *noun* [C] a company that manufactures something *a shoe manufacturer*

manufacturing /ˌmænjəˈfæktʃᵊrɪŋ/ *noun* [U] the production of something, usually in large numbers in a factory *car/food manufacturing*

manure /məˈnjʊəʳ/ *noun* [U] **FARMING** solid waste from animals that is used to make plants grow well *cow/horse manure*

manuscript /ˈmænjəskrɪpt/ *noun* [C] **MUSIC** a piece of writing or music that has been written, but not published

many /ˈmeni/ *pronoun, quantifier* **1** used mainly in negative sentences and questions to mean 'a large number of' *I don't have many clothes.* ○ *Were there many cars on the road?* ○ *I've got* ***so many*** *things to do this morning.* ○ *You've given me* ***too many*** *potatoes* (= more than I want). ○ *There aren't* ***as many*** *people here* ***as*** *last year.* **2 how many** used in questions to ask about the number of something *How many hours a week do you work?* ○ *How many do you want?* **3 as many as** used before a number or amount to show that the number or amount is large *As many as 6000 people may have been infected with the disease.*

COMMON LEARNER ERROR

many, much, or **a lot of?**

Many is used with countable nouns in negative sentences and questions. **Much** is used with uncountable nouns in negative sentences and questions.

Do you have many friends?

I don't earn much money.

A lot of can be used to mean **much** or **many**. In positive sentences it sounds formal to use **much** or **many**. You can use **a lot of** instead.

~~*There was much enthusiasm for the project.*~~

There was a lot of enthusiasm for the project.

Maori /ˈmaʊəri/ *adjective* **SOCIETY** relating or belonging to the original group of people who lived in New Zealand *Maori culture* •**Maori** *noun* [C] a Maori person

WORD PARTNERS FOR ***map***

read a map • a **detailed** map • a map **of** sth • be **(marked) on** a map • a **road** map

map /mæp/ *noun* [C] a picture that shows where countries, towns, roads, rivers, etc are *a **road map*** ○ *a large-scale **map of** Europe*

maple /ˈmeɪpl/ *noun* [C, U] a tree that has colourful leaves in the autumn and that produces a substance like sugar *a **maple leaf*** ○ ***maple syrup***

Mar *written abbreviation for* March

mar /mɑːʳ/ *verb* [T] **marring**, *past* **marred** *formal* to spoil something [**often passive**] *The evening was marred by Meg's appalling behaviour.*

marathon /ˈmærəθᵊn/ *noun* [C] **1** **SPORT** a race in which people run for about 26 miles/42 km *the London marathon* ○ *a marathon runner* **2** a very long event *a dance marathon*

marble /ˈmɑːbl/ *noun* [U] **GEOLOGY** hard, smooth stone which is often used for decoration *green/pink marble* ○ *a marble statue*

marbling /ˈmɑːblɪŋ/ *noun* [U] **DT** decorating something such as paper or wood with a pattern that looks like marble

march¹ /mɑːtʃ/ *noun* [C] **1** [SHOWING DISAGREEMENT] an organized walk by a group to show that they disagree with something *to **go on** a **march*** **2** [SOLDIERS' WALK] the special type of walking that soldiers do

march² /mɑːtʃ/ *verb* [I] **1** [SHOW DISAGREEMENT] to walk somewhere as a group to show that you disagree with something *They marched to London to protest against health cuts.* **2** [SOLDIERS' WALK] When soldiers march, they walk together with regular steps. **3 march off/up/down, etc** to walk somewhere fast, often because you are angry

O‑ **March** /mɑːtʃ/ (*written abbreviation* **Mar**) *noun* [C, U] the third month of the year

mare /meəʳ/ *noun* [C] a female horse

margarine /ˌmɑːdʒəˈriːn/ (US) /ˈmɑːrdʒərɪn/ *noun* [U] **FOOD** a yellow substance made from vegetable oil which you put on bread and use in cooking

margin /ˈmɑːdʒɪn/ *noun* [C] **1** the difference between two amounts of time, money, etc, usually between people in a competition *to win by a **narrow/wide margin*** ○ *He took third place **by a margin of** seven minutes.* **2** an empty space down the side of a page of writing *You can make notes **in the margin**.* **3 a margin of error MATHEMATICS** the amount by which a calculation can be wrong but still produce a good result *a margin of error of 5 percent* **4 FINANCE** the amount of profit that is made by a business after costs have been taken off

marginal /ˈmɑːdʒɪnᵊl/ *adjective* small and not important *a marginal effect/improvement*

ˌmarginal ˈcost *noun* [U] **FINANCE** the amount by which the total cost of producing a group of goods increases if a business makes one more of that thing

marginalize (*also UK* **-ise**) /ˈmɑːdʒɪnᵊlaɪz/ *verb* [T] to treat someone or something as if they are not important [**often passive**] *The poorest countries are increasingly marginalized from the world economy.*

marginally /ˈmɑːdʒɪnᵊli/ *adverb* by a small amount *marginally more expensive*

marijuana /ˌmærɪˈwɑːnə/ *mainly US* (*mainly UK* **cannabis**) *noun* [U] **HEALTH** a drug that some people smoke for pleasure and that is illegal in many countries

marina /məˈriːnə/ *noun* [C] an area of water where people keep their boats

marinate /ˈmærɪneɪt/ (*also* **marinade** /ˌmærɪˈneɪd/) *verb* [T] **FOOD** to add a mixture of oil, wine, herbs, etc to food before cooking it •**marinade** /ˌmærɪˈneɪd/ *noun* [C, U]

marine¹ /məˈriːn/ *adjective* [**always before noun**] found in the sea, or relating to the sea *marine creatures/life* ○ *marine biology*

marine² /məˈriːn/ *noun* [C] a soldier who has been trained to fight at sea and on land *the Marine Corps*

marital /ˈmærɪtᵊl/ *adjective* [**always before noun**] **SOCIETY** relating to marriage *marital problems*

ˈmarital ˌstatus *noun* [U] **SOCIETY** whether or not someone is married *The form asks for personal information such as name, date of birth and marital status.*

maritime /ˈmærɪtaɪm/ *adjective* [**always before noun**] relating to ships and sea travel *a maritime museum*

WORD PARTNERS FOR ***mark***

leave/make a mark • a mark **on** sth • **dirty** marks

O‑ **mark¹** /mɑːk/ *noun* **1** [AREA] [C] an area of dirt, damage, etc that is left on something *You've got a black mark on your nose.* ○ *He's **left** dirty **marks** all over the carpet.* **2 EDUCATION** [C] a number or letter that is written on a piece of work, saying how good the work is *She always gets good marks in English.* **3** [LEVEL] [**no plural**] a particular level, degree, distance, etc *They've just passed **the** 5000m **mark**.* ○ *Interest rates are somewhere around the seven percent mark.* **4 a mark of sth** a sign or proof that something exists *a mark of genius* ○ *There was a minute's silence everywhere **as a mark of respect**.* **5 leave/make your mark** to do something that makes you successful or makes people notice you **6 On your marks. Get set. Go!** something that you say to start a running race **7 be wide of the mark** to not be correct or accurate ➲See also: **punctuation mark, quotation marks**

O‑ **mark²** /mɑːk/ *verb* **1** [HAPPEN] [T] If an event marks the beginning, end, etc of something, it causes it, or happens at the same time as it. *His death marks the end of an era in television.* **2** [CELEBRATE] [T] If you mark an occasion, you do something to celebrate it. *They've declared Tuesday a national holiday to mark the 10th anniversary of Independence.* **3** [SHOW A PLACE] [T] to show where something is by drawing or putting something somewhere *I've marked my street on the map for you.* **4 EDUCATION** [I, T] to check a piece of work or an exam, showing mistakes and giving a letter or number to say how good it is *to **mark** essays* **5** [DIRTY] [T] to leave an area of dirt on something

mark sth out *phrasal verb* to show the shape or position of something by drawing a line around it

marked /mɑːkt/ *adjective* very noticeable *There has been a* ***marked improvement*** *since last year.* •**markedly** *adverb*

marker /ˈmɑːkəʳ/ *noun* [C] **1** PEN (*also* ˈ**marker** ˌ**pen**) a thick pen used especially for writing on boards *a black felt marker* ➲See colour picture **The Classroom** on page Centre 6 **2** SIGN a sign that shows where something is

WORD PARTNERS FOR ***market***

the market **is booming/is growing** • a market **collapses** • the market **in** sth

market¹ /ˈmɑːkɪt/ *noun* [C] **1** SELLING PLACE a place where people go to buy or sell things, often outside *a cattle/fish/flower market* ○ *a market stall* **2** SHOP *US* a supermarket (= large shop that sells food) **3** **ECONOMICS** the buying and selling of something *the insurance/personal computer market* **4** **ECONOMICS** all the people who want to buy a particular product, or the area where they live *South America is our largest market.* ○ *Is there* ***a market for*** (= will people buy) *second-hand jewellery?* **5 on the market** available to buy *His house has been on the market for over a year.* ➲See also: **black market, flea market, free market, niche market, the stock market**

market² /ˈmɑːkɪt/ *verb* [T] to try to sell products using advertising or other ways of making people want to buy them *Their products are very cleverly marketed.*

marketable /ˈmɑːkɪtəbl/ *adjective* Marketable products or skills are easy to sell because people want them.

ˌ**market** ˈ**forces** *noun* [plural] **ECONOMICS** the way that prices and wages are influenced by how many people want to buy a particular product and how much is available

marketing /ˈmɑːkɪtɪŋ/ *noun* [U] the work of encouraging people to buy a product or service *a career in marketing/****sales and marketing***

ˈ**marketing** ˌ**mix** *noun* [C] all the things connected with selling a product, such as what the product is like, how it is advertised, and how much it costs

market-led /ˌmɑːkɪtˈled/ *adjective* **ECONOMICS** Market-led businesses find out what customers want and offer it to them.

ˌ**market** **pene**ˈ**tration** *noun* [U] **ECONOMICS** getting customers, for example by having low prices or attracting customers away from other businesses

marketplace /ˈmɑːkɪtpleɪs/ *noun* **1 the marketplace** **ECONOMICS** in business, the buying and selling of products *We have to learn to compete* ***in the*** *international* ***marketplace****.* **2** [C] an area in a town where there is a market

ˌ**market re**ˈ**search** *noun* [U] the activity of finding out what people like about products and what new things they want to buy *a market research company*

ˌ**market** ˈ**segment** *noun* [U] **ECONOMICS** a group of customers or possible customers that have a particular characteristic *Our largest regional market segment is in Spain.*

ˈ**market** ˌ**share** *noun* [C] **ECONOMICS** the number of things that a company sells compared with the number of things of the same type that other companies sell

marking ˈ**out** ˌ**tool** *noun* [C] **DT** a tool used for putting a design onto a piece of wood or metal before cutting or shaping it

markings /ˈmɑːkɪŋz/ *noun* [plural] the shapes and colours on an animal or bird

mark-up /ˈmɑːkʌp/ *noun* [C] **FINANCE** the amount by which the price of something is increased before it is sold again *The usual mark-up on clothes is around 20%.*

marmalade /ˈmɑːməleɪd/ *noun* [U] **FOOD** a sweet, soft food made with oranges or lemons and often eaten on toast (= cooked bread)

maroon¹ /məˈruːn/ *noun* [U] a dark red-purple colour •**maroon** *adjective* ➲See colour picture **Colours** on page Centre 12

maroon² /məˈruːn/ *verb* **be marooned** to be left somewhere where you cannot get away

marquee /mɑːˈkiː/ *noun* [C] *UK* **1** TENT a large tent used for parties, shows, etc **2** SIGN *US* a large sign over a cinema or theatre that says what films or shows are playing

WORD PARTNERS FOR ***marriage***

sb's marriage **breaks up/fails** • sb's marriage **to** sb • a **happy** marriage

marriage /ˈmærɪdʒ/ *noun* **1** **SOCIETY** [C, U] the legal relationship of a man and a woman being a husband and a wife *a* ***happy marriage*** **2** **SOCIETY** [C] the ceremony where people become a husband and a wife *a marriage ceremony/certificate*

married /ˈmærid/ *adjective* **1** **SOCIETY** A married man or woman has a wife or husband. ***a married couple*** ○ *She's been* ***married to*** *David for nearly ten years.* ○ *As far as I know, they're very* ***happily married.*** ➲Opposite **unmarried** **2 get married** **SOCIETY** to begin a legal relationship with someone as their husband or wife *We got married last year.*

marrow /ˈmærəʊ/ *noun* *UK* **1** **FOOD** [C, U] a large vegetable which has dark green skin and is white on the inside **2** **ANATOMY, BIOLOGY** [U] (*also* **bone marrow**) the soft substance inside bones

marry /ˈmæri/ *verb* **1** **SOCIETY** [I, T] to begin a legal relationship with someone as their husband or wife ***Will you marry me?*** ○ *He never married.* **2** **SOCIETY** [T] to officially make people become a husband and a wife in a ceremony *We were married by our local vicar.*

Mars /mɑːz/ *noun* [no plural] **ASTRONOMY** the planet that is fourth from the Sun, after the Earth and before Jupiter ➲See picture at **solar system**

marsh /mɑːʃ/ *noun* [C, U] **GEOGRAPHY** an area of soft, wet land

marshal /ˈmɑːʃəl/ *noun* [C] **1** PERSON ORGANIZING someone who helps to organize or control a large public event *race marshals* **2** POLICE/FIRE OFFICER an important officer in police or fire departments in the US ➲See also: **field marshal**

marshmallow /ˌmɑːʃˈmæləʊ/ (US) /ˈmɑːrʃˌmæləʊ/ *noun* [C, U] **FOOD** a soft, white food made from sugar

PIECES AND QUANTITIES

a piece of . . .
tart
wood
paper
material
a slice of . . .
bread
meat
cake
a bunch of . . .
grapes
bananas
keys
flowers
a bar of . . .
soap
chocolate
a drop of . . .
oil
lumps
sugar lumps
lumps of coal
chunks of . . .
vegetables
a hunk of . . .
bread
cheese
a blob of . . .
cream

THE KITCHEN

chopping board

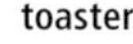

toaster

bread bin UK, bread box US

tin opener UK, can opener US

food processor

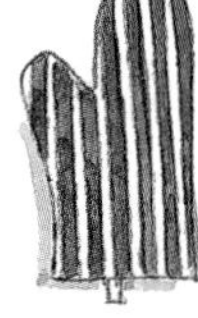

grater

oven glove

kettle

blender

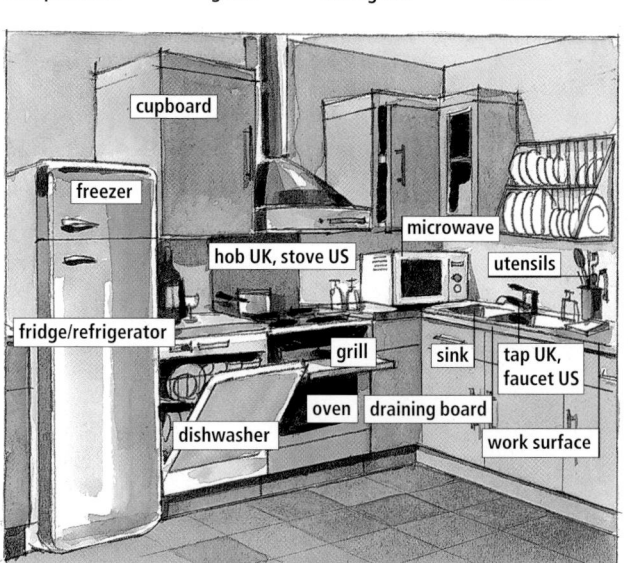

coffee maker

teapot

sieve

colander

cake tin UK, cake pan US

baking tray UK, baking pan US

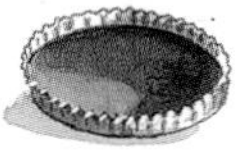

flan dish

rolling pin

saucepan

frying pan

whisk

ladle

fish slice UK, spatula US

scales UK, scal

measuring spo

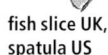

THE BATHROOM

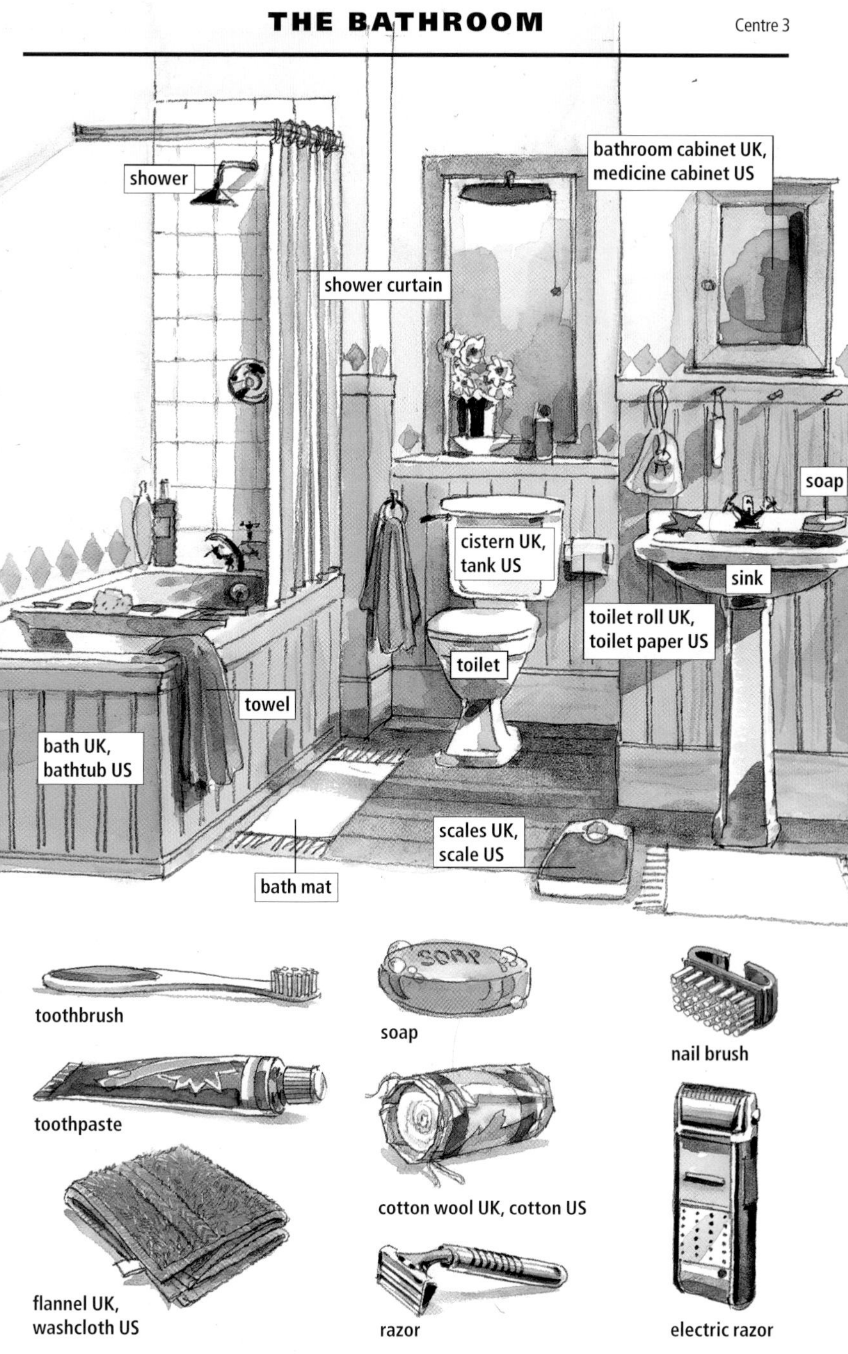
shower
shower curtain
bathroom cabinet UK,
medicine cabinet US
soap
cistern UK,
tank US
sink
toilet roll UK,
toilet paper US
toilet
towel
bath UK,
bathtub US
scales UK,
scale US
bath mat
SOAP
toothbrush
soap
nail brush
toothpaste
cotton wool UK, cotton US
flannel UK,
washcloth US
razor
electric razor

THE LIVING ROOM

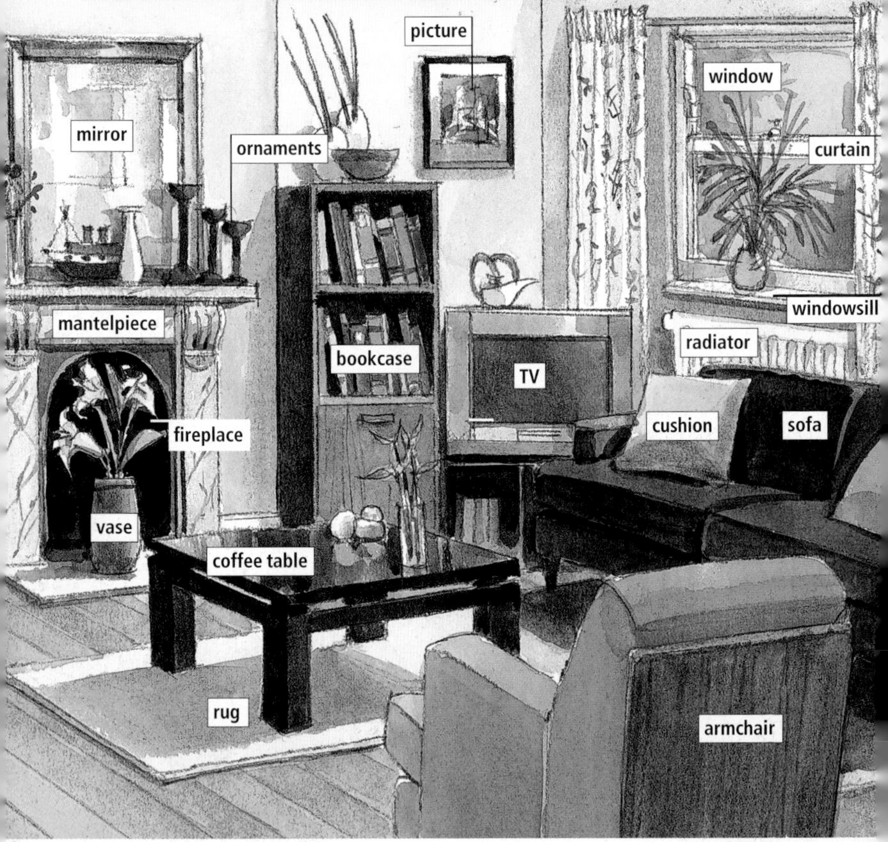

picture
window
mirror
ornaments
curtain
mantelpiece
windowsill
radiator
bookcase
TV
fireplace
cushion
sofa
vase
coffee table
rug
armchair

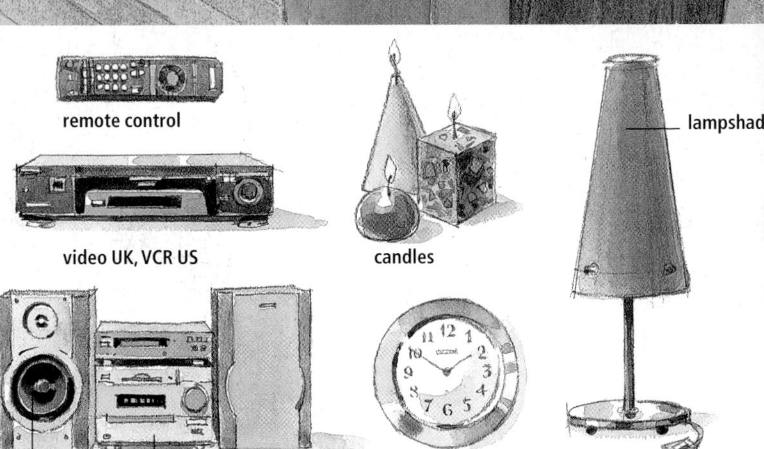

THE OFFICE

fax
photocopier
monitor
screen
desk tidy UK
desk organizer US
in-tray
computer
paper clips
envelope
file
mouse
telephone
CD
keyboard
disk
desk
folder
filing cabinet
highlighter
bin UK, trash can US
hanging files
chair

THE CLASSROOM

timetable UK, schedule US
board rubber UK, eraser US
blackboard
chalk
whiteboard
whiteboard mark
noticeboard UK, bulletin board US
teacher
pupil
pen
ruler
exercise book
textbook
file
chair
glue
Sellotape UK, Scotch tape US
rubber UK, eraser US
satchel
pencil
scissors
pencil sharpener
desk

CAR

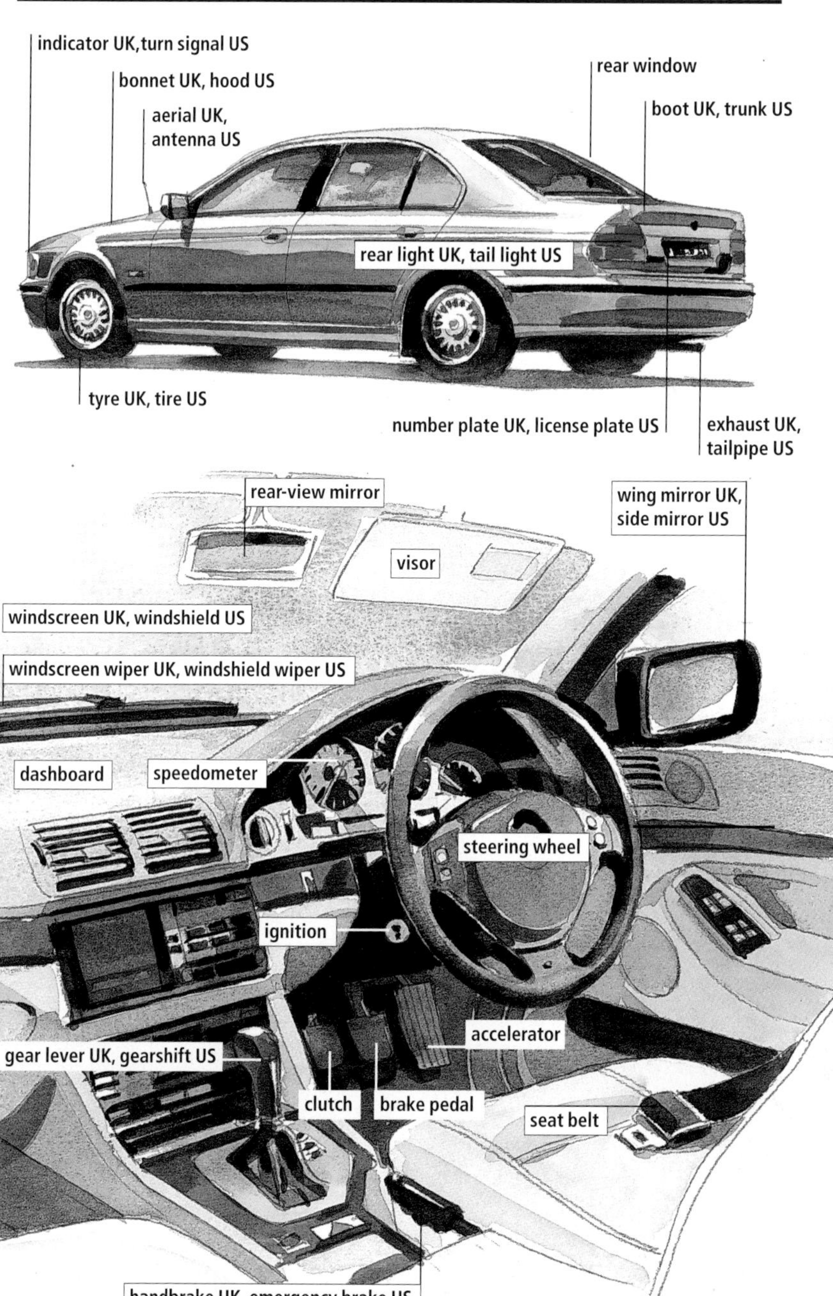
indicator UK,turn signal US
bonnet UK, hood US
aerial UK,
antenna US
rear window
boot UK, trunk US
rear light UK, tail light US
tyre UK, tire US
number plate UK, license plate US
exhaust UK,
tailpipe US
rear-view mirror
wing mirror UK,
side mirror US
visor
windscreen UK, windshield US
windscreen wiper UK, windshield wiper US
dashboard
speedometer
steering wheel
ignition
accelerator
gear lever UK, gearshift US
clutch
brake pedal
seat belt
handbrake UK, emergency brake US

CLOTHES

jacket
trousers UK
pants US
suit
cardigan
jeans
sweater
skirt
halter top
miniskirt
t-shirt
shorts
pyjamas
slippers
salwar kameez
dress
sweatshirt
fur collar
coat
boots
mac UK
raincoat US
jacket
hood
hoodie

CLOTHES

tie
waistcoat UK
vest US
sweatshirt
shirt
gloves
scarves
(one scarf)
trousers UK
pants US
cycling shorts
shoes
bra
tracksuit UK
sweats US
boxers
briefs
bikini
swimming
trunks UK
swimsuit US
trunks
French knickers
pants UK panties US
swimming
costume UK
swimsuit US
briefs
underpants
socks
cycle helmet
camisole
sunglasses
sun visor
tights UK
belt
flip-flops
mules
trainers UK sneakers US
baseball cap
ankle
boots
sun hat
cowboy boots
sandals
boots

FRUITS AND VEGETABLES

apples
bananas
grapes
pears
oranges
pineapples
lemons
melons
sweetcorn UK, corn US
carrots
tomatoes
potatoes
garlic
celery
lettuce
cucumbers
onions
cauliflower
mushrooms
aubergines UK, eggplants US
peppers

FOOD

roll UK, sandwich US

sandwich UK & US

soup

salad

biscuits UK, cookies US

cake

vegetables

pizza

cereal

rice

chips UK, french fries US

pasta

peanuts

crisps UK, chips US

honey

jam

fish

butter

egg

yoghurt

cheese

meat

COLOURS

red
blue
green
yellow
brown
black
grey
white
purple
pink
orange
navy blue
lime green
beige
maroon
khaki

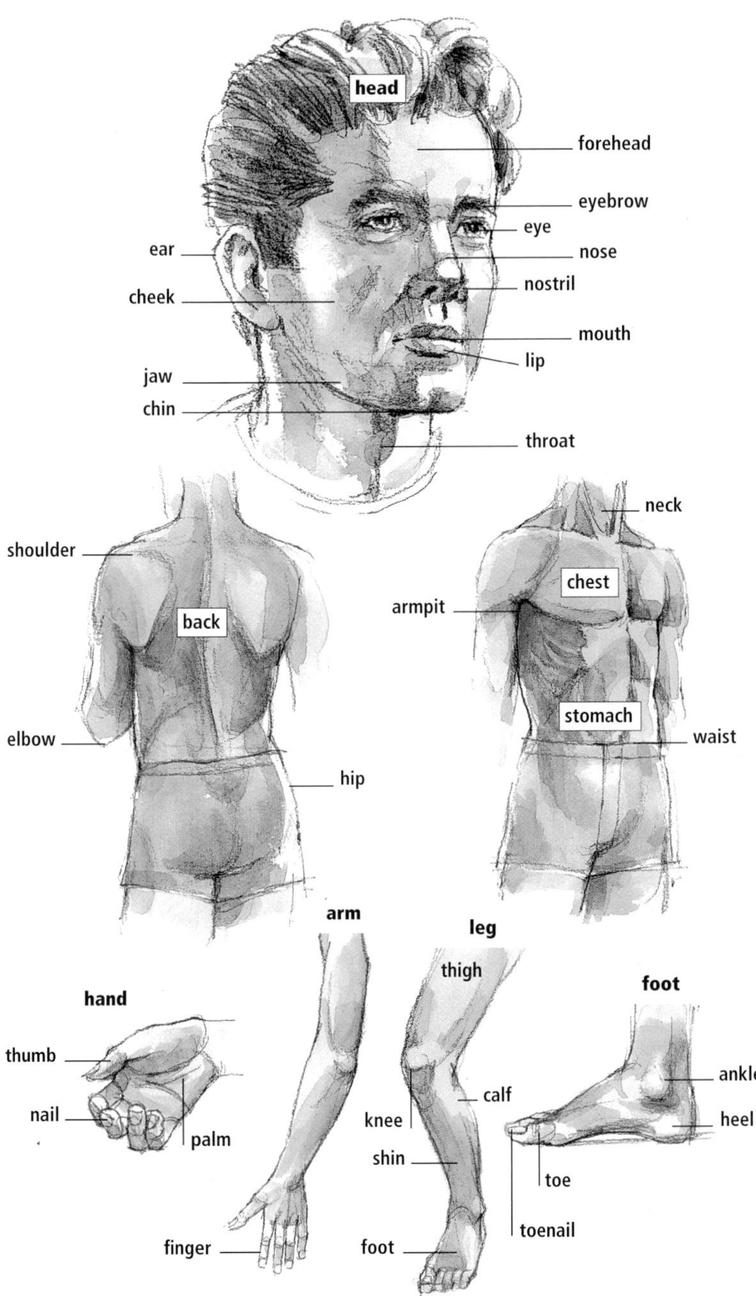
head
forehead
eyebrow
eye
ear
nose
nostril
cheek
mouth
lip
jaw
chin
throat
neck
shoulder
chest
armpit
back
stomach
waist
elbow
hip
arm
leg
thigh
foot
hand
thumb
ankle
calf
nail
knee
heel
palm
shin
toe
toenail
finger
foot

SPORTS

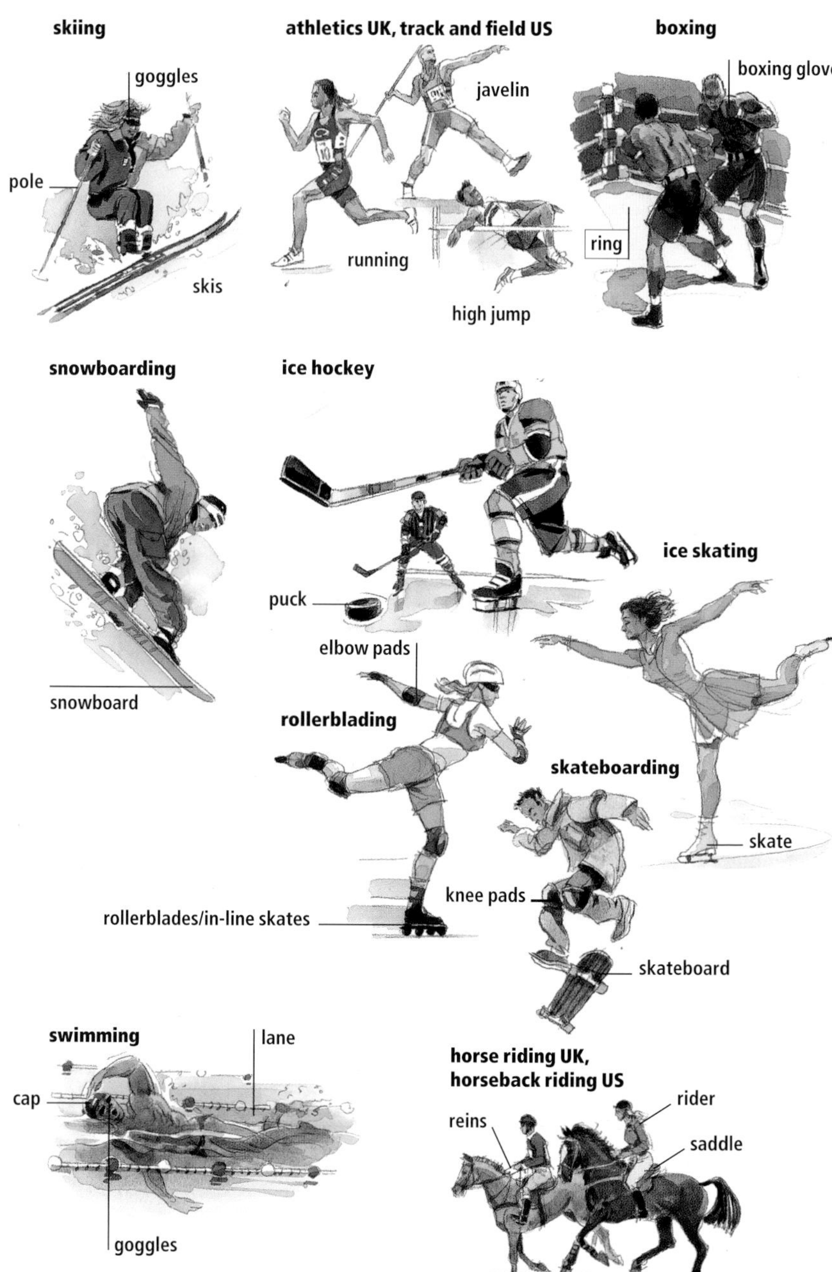
skiing
goggles
pole
skis
athletics UK, track and field US
javelin
running
high jump
boxing
boxing glove
ring
snowboarding
snowboard
ice hockey
puck
ice skating
skate
elbow pads
rollerblading
rollerblades/in-line skates
skateboarding
knee pads
skateboard
swimming
lane
cap
goggles
horse riding UK,
horseback riding US
rider
reins
saddle

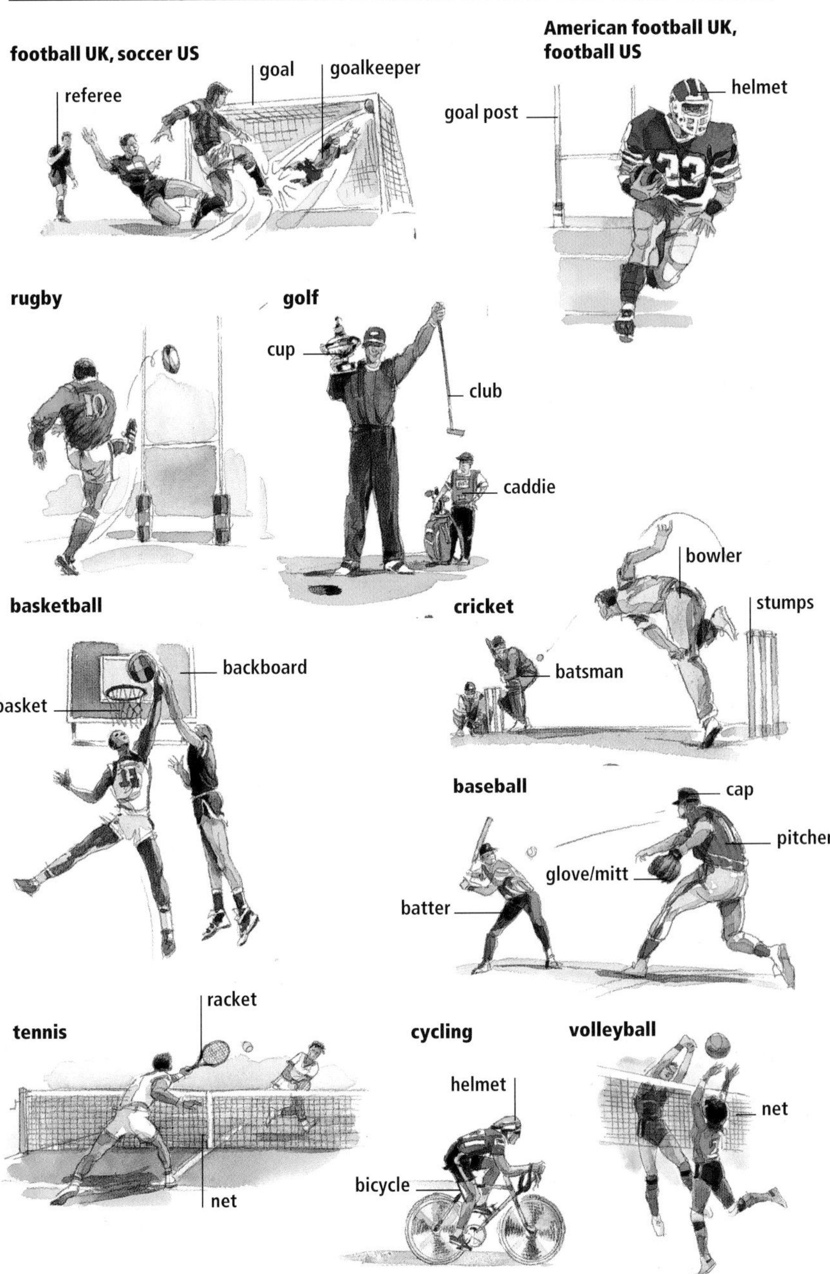
football UK, soccer US
referee
goal
goalkeeper
American football UK, football US
goal post
helmet
rugby
golf
cup
club
caddie
basketball
backboard
basket
cricket
bowler
stumps
batsman
baseball
cap
pitcher
glove/mitt
batter
tennis
racket
net
cycling
helmet
bicycle
volleyball
net

PHRASAL VERBS

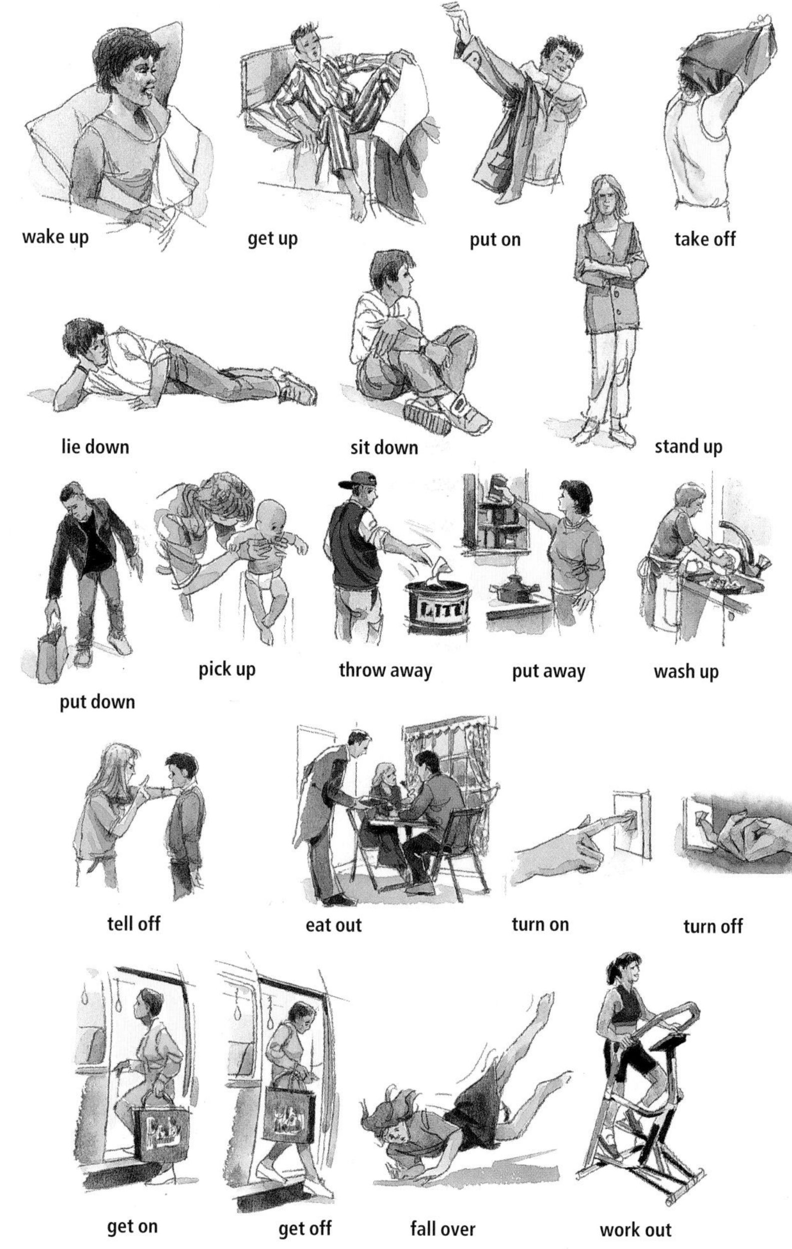

wake up

get up

put on

take off

lie down

sit down

stand up

put down

pick up

throw away

put away

wash up

tell off

eat out

turn on

turn off

get on

get off

fall over

work out

Extra help pages

Punctuation

	Uses	Examples
capital letter	■ the first letter of a sentence ■ for people's names and titles ■ for countries, nationalities, languages, places, religions ■ for organizations, trademarks ■ for days, months ■ for titles of books, films, etc. ■ for most abbreviations ■ for the personal pronoun 'I'	*Hydrogen is a chemical element.* *Sven • Mary Jones • Lord Rose* *China • French • London • Hindu* *Oxfam • the World Bank • Nike* *Monday • June* *Macbeth • Gone with the Wind* *UK • BBC* *I opened the book.*
full stop (UK) period (US) [.]	■ at the end of a sentence ■ after some abbreviations ■ to separate parts of an email or website address ■ as a decimal point in numbers NOTE: full stops are *not* usually used after abbreviations of measurements	*Wind and rain cause erosion.* *Marton Rd. • Mrs. White* *info@cambridge.org* *23.4* *cm • g • km*
question mark [?]	■ after a direct question	*How many sides does a hexagon have?*
exclamation mark [!]	■ at the end of a sentence to express surprise, shock, etc. ■ to emphasize what you have said ■ to indicate a loud sound	*I can't believe it!* *I want this mess tidied up – fast!* *Ouch! • Bang!*
comma [,]	■ between items in a list ■ to show a pause in a long sentence ■ when you add extra information ■ in direct speech ■ in a list of adjectives before a noun ■ before question tags (e.g. isn't it?, don't you?) ■ in large numbers, to separate groups of numbers	*You will need paper, pens, a ruler and a calculator.* *We heated the substance in a flame, then cooled it in water.* *Our teacher, who is very strict, always gives us a lot of homework.* *'I will tell you,' he said.* *It is a heavy, green substance.* *We've met before, haven't we?* *2,583,000*
apostrophe [']	■ for missing letters ■ for possessives (showing that something belongs to someone) NOTE: for plural words ending in 's', the apostrophe goes after the 's', but there is no need to add another 's'	*don't • I'll • it's (= it is)* *Paul's bike* *the boys' homework*
colon [:]	■ to introduce a list ■ to introduce writing that follows	*You need the following: paint, brushes, water, cloths.* *Read the following poem by Larkin:*

	Uses	Examples
semicolon [;]	■ to separate two parts of a sentence	*We repeated the experiment three times; the results were always the same.*
	■ to separate items on a list where the items are long, or where commas have already been used	*You can do the following combinations of subjects: maths, physics and music; maths, English and geography; English, geography and biology.*
hyphen [-]	■ in some compound words (words made from two or more words)	*drop-down menu*
	■ to join two words together	*a blue-green colour*
	■ when you have to divide a word at the end of a line	*This process helps to deoxygen-ate the blood.*
	■ sometimes for adding prefixes	*pro-democracy*
	■ often for compound numbers	*seventy-three*
dash [–]	■ to separate parts of a sentence	*Get the book – the one with the blue cover – and give it to John.*
	■ near the end of a sentence as a short way of repeating the most important part of what you have said	*Make sure you read the instructions, the questions, the text – everything.*
	■ to show that speech has been interrupted	*'Be careful not to – oh, too late!' he said as the vase crashed to the floor.*
quotation/ quote marks *also* inverted commas (UK) [' or ""]	■ to show that words are spoken	*'I'm tired,' she said.*
	■ to show someone's thoughts	*'I must remember to phone Mum,' he thought.*
	■ to show that someone else said or wrote the words	*She had described the school as 'not attracting the best students'.*
	■ To show a word that is new or unusual	*He called his invention the "robocat".*
	NOTE: double quotation marks are used in US English.	
brackets (UK) parentheses (US) [() or []]	■ to add extra information but keep it separate from the rest of the sentence	*You will need suitable clothing (waterproof coat, strong shoes) and a picnic lunch.*
	■ after numbers or letters in a list	*These are my favourite foods:* *1) cheese* *2) pizza* *3) tomatoes*

Graphs and charts

Graphs

This graph shows the speed of a vehicle over a period of 18 seconds. The line at the bottom is called the **horizontal axis**, and shows the time in seconds. The line at the side is called the **vertical axis** and shows the vehicle's speed in metres per second.

The speed of the vehicle has been **plotted** on the graph.

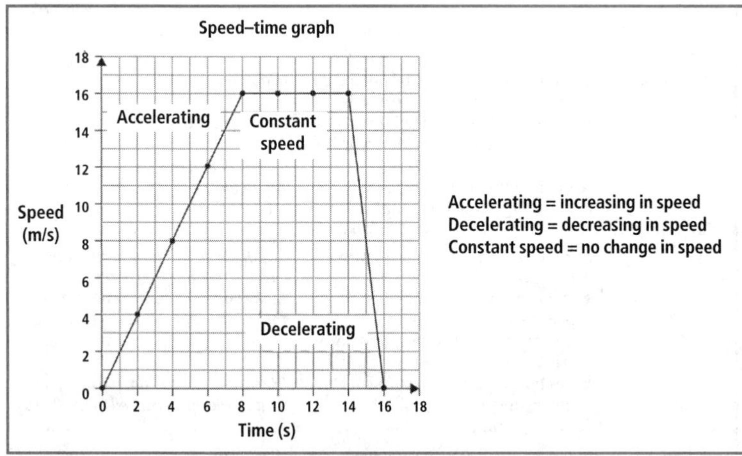

1 Look at the graph and fill in the gaps in the sentences below.

1 From 0 seconds (rest) to 8 seconds, the vehicle increases its speed from 0 metres per second to ..... metres per second.

2 From ..... seconds to ..... seconds, the vehicle maintains a constant speed of ..... metres per second.

3 From 14 seconds to ..... seconds, the vehicle decreases its speed from ..... metres per second to ..... metres per second.

2 Use the words in the box to fill in the gaps.

rate	sharply	maintains	increases	reaches

The vehicle ..... its speed at a constant ..... until it ..... its top speed of 16 metres per second. It ..... that speed for six seconds. The speed then decreases ..... over the next two seconds until the vehicle has stopped.

Bar charts

Ninety people were asked to name their favourite fruit. On this bar chart, the number of people (the **frequency**) goes on the vertical axis and the type of fruit (the **category**) goes on the horizontal axis.

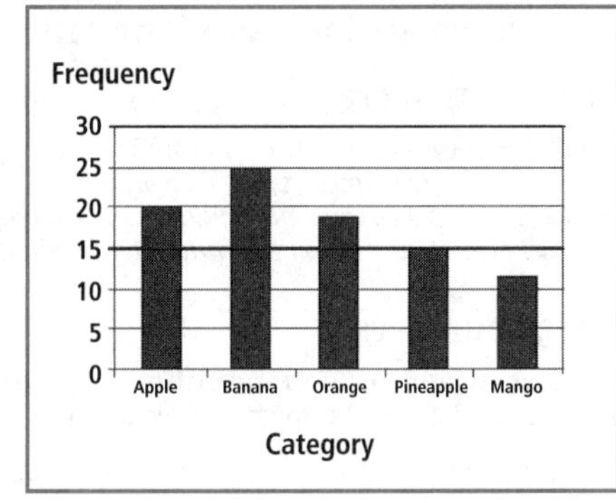

3 Look at the bar chart and answer the following questions.

1. Which is the most popular fruit?
2. How many people like apples best?
3. Do more people like oranges or pineapples?

Pie charts

This pie chart shows the same information as the bar chart above, but drawn in a different way. The data is shown as sectors of a circle. The larger the sector, the more people like that fruit.

The following formula can be used to calculate the sector angle:

$$\text{angle} = \frac{\text{amount}}{\text{total}} \times 360^\circ$$

For instance $= \frac{20}{90} \times 360 = 80^\circ$

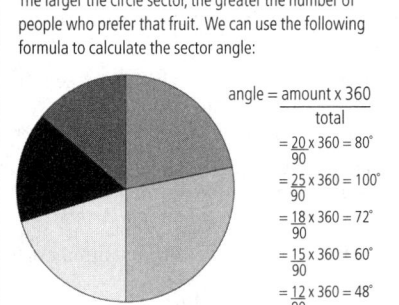

The larger the circle sector, the greater the number of people who prefer that fruit. We can use the following formula to calculate the sector angle:

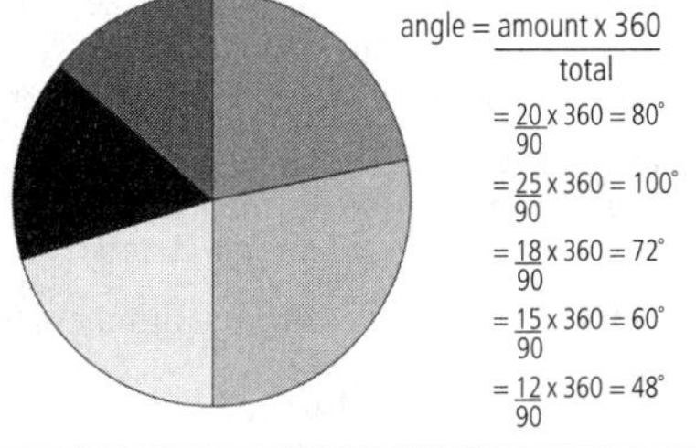

Pictograms

The amount in each category is shown as a **symbol** or picture. In this pictogram each drawing of a person **represents** two people, so for banana and pineapple, half symbols have been used. Every pictogram must have a **key** to explain what the symbols mean.

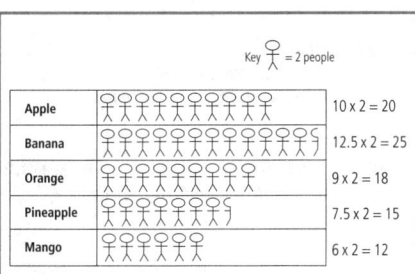

Key (one person symbol) = 2 people

Apple		10 x 2 = 20
Banana		12.5 x 2 = 25
Orange		9 x 2 = 18
Pineapple		7.5 x 2 = 15
Mango		6 x 2 = 12

Numbers and measurements

Saying numbers

Don’t forget to say ‘and’ after hundreds:

- 569 *five hundred and sixty-nine*
- 7,892 *seven thousand, eight hundred and ninety-two*
- 4,680,022 *four million, six hundred and eighty thousand and twenty-two*

Large numbers

When **thousand**, **million** and **billion** are used after a particular number, they are used in the singular form and without 'of'.

Don't say 'five/ten/fifteen millions of something', say five/ten/fifteen **million** something:
The house cost two million dollars.

When **million** is used without a particular number, it is used in the plural form and is sometimes followed by 'of':
The house cost millions (of dollars).

Parts of numbers: decimals and fractions

For decimals, you say each number separately after the decimal point (.):

- 2.5 *two point five*
- 3.65 *three point six five*
- 22.33 *twenty-two point three three*

When you use fractions, if you are talking about a half or quarters, you say:

- 2 ¼ *two and a quarter*
- 4 ½ *four and a half*
- 5 ¾ *five and three quarters*

For other fractions, use ordinal numbers for the second number:

- 6/8 *six eighths*
- 3 ⅔ *three and two thirds*
- 1/12 *a twelfth/one twelfth*

For complicated fractions in maths, say ‘over’:

- 19/53 *nineteen over fify-three*

Saying amounts of money

- £2.50 *two fifty* or *two pounds fifty* or *two pounds and fifty pence*
- £12.95 *twelve ninety-five* or *twelve pounds ninety-five* or *twelve pounds and ninety-five pence*
- $2.50 *Two fifty* or *two dollars and fifty cents*
- $12.95 *Twelve ninety-five* or *twelve dollars and ninety-five cents*

Writing and saying dates

In UK English: write: *18 August 2007* or *18th August 2007* or *18/08/07*
say: *the eighteenth of August, two thousand and seven*
In US English: write: *August 18, 2007* or *08/18/07*
say: *August eighteenth, two thousand and seven*

- ▶ 1800 *eighteen hundred*
- ▶ 1803 *eighteen oh three* or *eighteen hundred and three*
- ▶ 1878 *eighteen seventy-eight*
- ▶ 2000 *two thousand* or *the year two thousand*
- ▶ 2010 *two thousand and ten* or *twenty ten*
- ▶ 2030 *two thousand and thirty* or *twenty thirty*
- ▶ 2031 *two thousand and thirty-one* or *twenty thirty-one*

Saying the time

Say **o'clock** only with whole hours:
- ▶ 2:00 *two o'clock*

For other times:
- ▶ 4:30 *four thirty* or *half past four*
- ▶ 2:15 *two fifteen* or *(a) quarter past two* (UK), *(a) quarter after two* (US)
- ▶ 3:45 *three forty-five* or *(a) quarter to four* (UK & US), *(a) quarter of four* (US)
- ▶ 8:10 *eight ten* or *ten past eight* (UK), *ten after eight* (US)
- ▶ 9:35 *nine thirty-five* or *twenty-five to ten* (UK & US), *twenty-five of ten* (US)

Saying phone numbers

You should say all the numbers separately. Say əʊ for 0. In UK English, when two numbers next to each other are the same, you can also say 'double'.
- ▶ (01223) 91259 *oh one double two three, nine one two five nine.*

Maths symbols used with numbers

1+2 = 3	*one plus two equals three* or *one add two is three* (UK)
3-1 = 2	*three minus one is two* or *three take away one equals two*
2 x 3 = 6	*two times three equals six* or *two threes are six* or *two multiplied by three is six*
6 ÷ 2 = 3	*six divided by two equals three* or *two into six is three*
3^2	*three squared*
2^3	*two cubed*
5^{10}	*five to the power of ten*
x > 2	*x is greater than two*
x < 2	*x is less than two*
53%	*fifty-three per cent*
180°	*one hundred and eighty degrees*

Metric and imperial measurements

The international system of metric units of measurement is not used in the US. It is used in the UK, but many people still use the older system of imperial units such as pounds, feet and gallons.

Some units have the same name but mean different amounts in the UK and the US. Some spellings are different in UK and US English too. For example, note the difference between the endings of the words **metre** and **litre** in British English, and the same words spelled in American English - **meter** and **liter**.

	Metric		**Imperial**
Length and Distance	1 centimetre (cm)	= 10 millimetres (mm)	0.394 inch
	1 metre (m)	= 100 centimetres	39.4 inches
	1 kilometre (km)	= 1000 metres	.6214 miles
Area	1 hectare (ha)		2.471 acres
	1 square kilometre	= 100 hectares	0.386 square mile
Weight	1 gram (g)	= 100 milligrams (mg)	.033 ounce
	1 kilogram (kg)	= 1000 grams	2.205 pounds
	1 tonne	= 1000 kilograms	19.688 hundredweight
Volume	1 centilitre (cl)	= 10 millilitres (ml)	0.018 UK pint 0.021 US pint
	1 litre (l)	= 100 centilitres	1.76 UK pints 2.1 US pints

	Imperial		**Metric**
Length and Distance	1 inch (in)		2.54 centimetres
	1 foot (ft)	= 12 inches	30.48 centimetres
	1 yard (yd)	= 3 feet	0.914 metre
	1 mile	= 1760 yards	1.609 kilometres
Area	1 square inch		6.452 square centimetres
	1 acre	= 4840 square yards	0.405 hectare
Weight	1 ounce (oz)		28.35 grams
	1 pound (lb)	= 16 ounces	0.545 kilogram
	1 stone	= 14 pounds	6.356 kilograms
	1 hundredweight	= 8 stone	50.8 kilograms
	1 ton	= 20 hundredweight	1016.04 kilograms
Volume (UK)	1 fluid ounce (fl oz)		0.028 litre
	1 pint (pt)	= 20 fluid ounces	0.568 litre
	1 gallon	= 8 pints	4.546 litres
Volume (US)	1 fluid ounce		0.029 litre
	1 pint	= 16 fluid ounces	0.473 litre
	1 gallon	= 8 pints	3.785 litres

Verb patterns

Some verbs must have something (an object) after them. These verbs are **transitive** verbs and are marked [T] in the dictionary:

- *He **bought** shares in the company.*
- *They **sacked** a lot of staff.*

Other verbs do not need anything after them. These verbs are **intransitive** verbs. They are marked [I] in the dictionary:

- *She started to **laugh**.*
- *Production costs have **fallen**.*

Some verbs can be both transitive and intransitive:

- *We have to **pay tax** on this income.* [T]
- *Have you **paid** yet?* [I]
- *We **sold three cars** today.* [T]
- *Our new range of clothing is **selling** very well.* [I]

1 Look at the underlined verbs in the sentences below. Write 'I' after those that are used as intransitive verbs and 'T' after those that are used as transitive verbs.

1. We advertise in local newspapers.
2. They decided to computerize their accounts.
3. The price of printing has increased a lot.
4. We plan to increase production of DVD players.
5. We employ over a thousand staff.

Sometimes a verb must be followed by other grammar patterns, for example an infinitive verb, or a verb ending '-ing'. These patterns are shown in the dictionary entries, at the beginning of the entry if they are *always* used, and in example sentences if they are *often* used.

[+ to do sth]	*They **promised to increase** our wages.*
[+ doing sth]	*They **started using** cheaper materials.*
[+ (that)]	*Statistics **show that** our products work better.*
	*Statistics **show** our products work better.*
[+ two objects]	*The bank **lent us the money**.*
[+ question word]	*He wouldn't **tell** me **why** his business failed.*

Some verbs are often followed by particular prepositions. These are shown in **bold type** in the example sentences in this dictionary.

2 Fill in the correct prepositions in the sentences below.

1. He updated me ..... the latest sales figures.
2. We are searching ..... the missing files.
3. The company relocated ..... Paris.
4. All our offices are equipped ..... air conditioning.
5. We spent a lot of money ..... new computers.

Phrasal verbs

What are phrasal verbs?

A phrasal verb is a verb followed by one or two adverbs or prepositions, which together make a meaning that is usually impossible to guess from the meanings of the words on their own.

Look at the meanings of these common phrasal verbs:

break down	If a machine or vehicle breaks down, it stops working.
look forward to something	to feel happy and excited about something that is going to happen
pick sth up	to lift something by using your hands

Of course, verbs are often used with their normal meanings with adverbs and prepositions too, e.g.:

- *I **went into** the classroom.*
- *He **put** the book **on** the desk.*

These are not phrasal verbs. They are just the normal meanings explained at the entries for the verbs, adverbs and prepositions.

Finding phrasal verbs

In this dictionary, phrasal verbs follow the entry for the main verb, and are in alphabetical order. For instance, the phrasal verb 'mark sth out' comes after all the meanings of the verb 'mark'.

1 Look at the dictionary entries for the following verbs. Which phrasal verbs are formed with these verbs?

1 draw 2 help 3 kill 4 move 5 round

2 Use the dictionary to help you fill in the gaps in the sentences below to make phrasal verbs.

1 Carefully measure ..... the amount of sulphur you need.
2 The steel is melted ..... in a furnace.
3 Could you read ..... the answers to the whole class, please?
4 Have you all given ..... your homework?
5 Tick each question ..... as you finish it.

Phrasal verbs with more than one meaning

A phrasal verb can have more than one meaning. Often the meanings are not related:

- *I **grew up** in Nigeria.* (**grow up** = become an adult)
- *A great friendship has* **grown up** *between them.* (**grow up** = develop)

3 Look at the way the phrasal verbs are used in the sentences below, and underline the correct meaning.

1 Make sure you **back up** all your files.
make a copy/prove that something is true
2 We should **clear up** the classroom before our teacher comes back.
tidy up/make an illness better
3 Our physics teacher explains everything so quickly, I can't **keep up**.
move at the same speed/understand
4 I think I'll **take** Friday **off** to prepare for the exam.
remove something/spend time away from work

The grammar of phrasal verbs

Some phrasal verbs have objects, some do not, and some sometimes have objects and sometimes do not. This is shown in the way the phrasal verb is written in the dictionary. The dictionary also shows you whether the object is a person, a thing or an action.

Phrasal verbs that do not need an object are shown like this in the dictionary:

hurry up ▶ ***Hurry up**, or we'll be late!*

If a phrasal verb needs an object, the dictionary shows whether the object is 'something' (sth) or 'somebody' (sb). Here are some examples:

go over sth ▶ *Let's **go over** the figures one more time.*
look up to sb ▶ *He really **looks up to** his brother.*
make sb/sth out ▶ *I could just **make** Julie **out** at the back of the room.*
▶ *I could **make out** a faint mark on the wood.*
set about sth/doing sth ▶ *We **set about** the cleaning.*

If the phrasal verb is followed by a verb ending in '-ing', the dictionary shows it like this:

▶ *We **set about** emptying the boxes.*

Phrasal verbs that sometimes use an object and sometimes do not use an object are shown like this:

give up (sth) ▶ *I really want to **give up** smoking.*
▶ *I smoke, but I'm trying to **give up**.*

Some phrasal verbs have two objects. They are shown like this:

put sth down to sth ▶ *We **put** his bad temper **down to** tiredness.*

Prepositions following phrasal verbs

When phrasal verbs are often followed by a particular preposition, this is shown in **bold type** in an example.

4 Fill in the gaps in these sentences with the correct preposition.

1 Can you think back ..... the lesson on photosynthesis?
2 She got told off ..... not handing in her homework on time.
3 I've been slogging away ..... this essay for hours.
4 We all paired up ..... a friend for the project work.

Word formation

Prefixes

Prefixes are added to the beginning of words to change their meaning. There is a list of common prefixes in the appendices at the end of this book.

Here are some common prefixes that are used to make opposite and often negative meanings. They are all used with adjectives, and **dis-** and **un-** are used with some verbs too.

dis-	*dissimilar, disappear*	**in-**	*inaccurate, inexpensive*
il-	*illegal, illogical*	**ir-**	*irregular, irresponsible*
im-	*impossible, impatient*	**un-**	*uncertain, uncover*

1 Use the prefixes **im-**, **in-**, and **un-** to make the opposites of these science words. Use the dictionary to help you choose the correct prefix.

1 saturated 2 permeable 3 organic 4 miscible 5 soluble

Prefixes are often used to show numbers, especially in science.

mono-, uni-	one	*monosaccharide, monozygotic, unicellular, unify*
bi-, di-	two	*bimetallic, bisect, dioxide, disaccharide*
centi-	a hundred	*centigrade, centilitre, centimetre*
kilo-	a thousand	*kilobyte, kilogram, kilowatt*
milli-	a thousandth	*millimetre, millilitre, millisecond*
multi-, poly-	many	*multicellular, polygon, polymer*

2 There are many other prefixes used in English. Look at the prefixes used in the words below and match them to the meanings on the right.

1 **hydro**electric	relating to living things
2 **inter**glacial	relating to water
3 **bio**diversity	preventing or destroying
4 **haemo**globin	between
5 **anti**septic	relating to blood

3 Now use those prefixes to complete the words in **bold letters** in the examples below.

1 I have installed some new ..... **virus** software.
2 Measure the angle at the ..... **section** of the two lines.
3 One sign of the disease of rabies is ..... **phobia**.
4 After the operation, he began to ..... **rrhage** severely.
5 We would like to be able to run our car on ..... **fuel**.

Suffixes

Suffixes are added at the end of words to change their meaning. There is a list of common suffixes in the appendices at the end of this book.

The following suffixes are often used to make verbs:

-ify	*nitrify, magnify*	**-ize**	*computerize, oxidize*
-ate	*hydrogenate, pollinate*		

The suffix –**tion** is often used to form nouns from these and other verbs, but be careful with this ending:

You may need to add **-ication**, e.g. magnify → magnifi**cation**.
You may need to change the verb ending, or take a bit off, e.g. absorb → absor**ption**, oxidize → oxid**ation**.

If you are not sure, check in the dictionary.

4 Make nouns from the following verbs, using the suffix –**tion**. Use the dictionary to help you choose the correct form.

1 pollinate 2 nitrify 3 circulate 4 computerize

Other suffixes that are often used to make nouns are:

-ness	*happiness, sickness*	**-ist**	*chemist, scientist*
-ment	*development, improvement*	**-er/-or**	*browser, conductor*

NOTE: Adding a suffix to a word sometimes changes its pronunciation. Look at how the stress changes in these words:

ac**cel**erate → accele**ra**tion **fil**ter → fil**tra**tion dis**til** → distil**la**tion

Suffixes that are often used to make adjectives include:

-al	*biological, digital*	**-ful**	*hopeful, careful*
-ous	*famous, androgynous*	**-y**	*dirty, happy*

Adjectives ending in –**able** or –**ible** describe things that can have a certain thing done to them.

5 Match the two parts of each sentence.

1 Biodegrad**able** packaging
2 Malle**able** substances
3 The number nine is
4 Substances that cannot be mixed together
5 If a layer of something is perme**able**

a divis**ible** by three.
b other substances can pass through it.
c can be bent into a different shape.
d decays naturally over time.
e are immisc**ible**.

Countable and uncountable nouns

Countable nouns can have *a/an* or *the* before them and can be used both in the singular and the plural: ▶ *A **meal** with lots of **vegetables** will give you the **vitamins** you need.*	**Uncountable nouns** cannot have *a/an* before them and cannot be used in the plural: ▶ ***Food** is mixed with **saliva** before it is swallowed.*

In this dictionary, countable nouns have the symbol [C], and uncountable nouns have the symbol [U].

1 Underline the uncountable nouns in the sentences below. Some sentences have more than one. Use the dictionary to help you.

1 All plant cells are surrounded by a cell wall made of cellulose.
2 We all need to eat plenty of fibre to help our digestion.
3 In photosynthesis, plants convert energy from sunlight into food.
4 The lungs are supplied with air through the windpipe.

2 Some of these sentences need 'a' or 'an' in the gaps. Put them in if necessary.

1 We drew the diagram on ..... graph paper.
2 Can you write 0.8 as ..... fraction?
3 Draw ..... line from the centre of the circle to ..... point on the circumference.
4 We have been studying ..... algebra today.
5 I can't remember how to do ..... long division.

Top 10 uncountable noun errors

In the *Cambridge Learner Corpus* these are the ten most common uncountable nouns that intermediate students try to make plural by adding an 's'. Try to remember that these nouns cannot be used in the plural.

1 information
2 equipment
3 advice
4 furniture
5 transport
6 homework
7 paper (material used for writing on)
8 knowledge
9 countryside
10 stuff

Some and **any**

You can use **some** and **any** with *plural* countable nouns. ▶ *There were **some** black **clouds** in the sky.* ▶ *Are there **any animals** in the desert?*	You can use **some** and **any** with uncountable nouns. ▶ *There is still **some snow** on the mountains.* ▶ *Is there **any water** in the river?*

Many, a few, much, a lot of

You can use **many** and **a few** with *plural* countable nouns:	You can use **much** with uncountable nouns:
▶ *There aren't **many** plants in the desert.* ▶ *There are **a few** good beaches near here.*	▶ *Has there been **much** erosion in this area?*

You can use **a lot of** with both *plural* countable nouns and with uncountable nouns:
▶ *There have been **a lot of** earthquakes recently.*
▶ *There was **a lot of** rain in the night.*
NOTE: **Many** and **much** are used especially in questions and negatives.

3 Which of the underlined parts of these sentences is right? Put a circle round the correct part.

1 There is many/a lot of chalk in the soil.
2 I didn't see many/much whales on my trip.
3 This far south we don't get much/many snow.
4 Cars cause many/a lot of pollution.
5 Are there much/many active volcanoes in this area?

Nouns which can be both countable and uncountable

Some nouns can be countable or uncountable, depending on how they are used.

You can use them as *countable* nouns to talk about particular things:	You can use them as *uncountable* nouns to talk about the thing in general.
▶ Argon is **a gas.** ▶ Rabies and cholera are terrible **diseases.**	▶ I think I can smell **gas.** ▶ Dirty water is causing **disease.**

4 Write two sentences for each word in the box, one using it as a countable noun and one as an uncountable noun.

fertilizer	liver	acid	liquid	fuel

It is important to check the symbols [C], [U] and [C, U] for every meaning of a word, because the same word can be countable for some meanings and uncountable for others. For example, look at these entries for 'thread' and 'fibre'.

fibre *UK* (*US* **fiber**) /'faɪbəʳ/ *noun* **1** CLOTH [C, U] cloth made from thin threads twisted together *Man-made fibres like nylon are easy to wash.* **2** THIN THREAD [C] one of the thin threads that forms a substance such as cloth *The fibres are woven into fabric.* **3 FOOD** [U] the substance in plants which cannot be digested and helps food pass through your body *Broccoli is a good source of fibre.* **4 ANATOMY, BIOLOGY** [C] a structure like a thread in your body *muscle/nerve fibres*

thread[1] /θred/ *noun* **1** MATERIAL [C, U] a long, thin piece of cotton, wool, etc that is used for sewing *a needle and thread* **2** CONNECTION [C] the connection between different events or different parts of a story or discussion *By that point I'd **lost the thread** of the conversation.* **3 INTERNET** a group of pieces of writing on the Internet in which people discuss one subject

thread[2] /θred/ *verb* [T] **1 thread a needle** to push thread through the hole in a needle **2 thread your way through, between, etc** to move carefully through a crowded place, changing direction in order to avoid people or things

Pronunciation

Pronouncing words in English can be very difficult. Often, words are not written the way they are pronounced. The phonetic symbols after each word in the dictionary show you how to say each word. There is an explanation of all these symbols inside the back cover.

Some of the symbols are pronounced in the same way as the letter they look like, e.g. /b/ sounds like 'b' in 'bad'. All the others are explained at the bottom of every page in the dictionary.

1 All these words are parts of the eye. Match them to their pronunciations.

1	pupil	a	/kɔː'niːə/
2	lens	b	/'retinə/
3	cornea	c	/lenz/
4	iris	d	/'pjuːpəl/
5	retina	e	/'aɪərɪs/

2 All these words are chemical elements. What are they?

1 'klɔːriːn 2 'kɑːbən 3 mæg'niːziəm
4 'naɪtrədʒən 5 'haɪdrədʒən 6 'hiːliəm

Word stress

Probably the most important thing about pronunciation is to make sure that you put the stress (emphasis) on the right part of the word.

The symbol /'/ shows you where to put the main stress. Some words have another, less important stress too, and that is shown with the symbol /ˌ/.

> **lime**stone /'laɪmˌstəʊn envi**ron**ment /ɪn'vaɪrənmənt
> environ**men**tal /ɪn'vaɪrənˌmentəl

3 Look at these geography words and underline the part with the main stress.

1 climate 2 ecosystem 3 deciduous
4 erosion 5 demography 6 demographics

Compound words

Compound words are made from two or more separate words. Their stress is shown in the headword, e.g. '**credit** ˌ**card**.

4 Look at these finance words and underline the parts with the main stress.

1 deposit account 2 electronic banking 3 direct debit
4 fixed assets 5 petty cash 6 bank account

Vowels

Short vowels are ones like /ɪ/ in d**i**sk or /æ/ in gr**a**phic, which you say quickly. As you can tell from the name, long vowels take longer to say. Examples of long vowels are /uː/ in reb**oo**t, /iː/ in k**ey**board and /3ː/ in c**ur**sor.

5 In each of these pairs of computing words, the letters in **bold type** have the same pronunciation. Try to find the correct phonetic symbol for each pair. Remember that letters are not always pronounced the way they look.

1 deb**u**g, datagl**o**ve
2 disk**e**tte, h**ea**der
3 s**u**percomputer, t**oo**lbar
4 b**i**tmap, encr**y**pt
5 sp**ea**ker, spreadsh**ee**t
6 dial**o**g box, anal**o**gue

Diphthongs

Diphthongs are made by two vowel sounds said together. These are some of the most common ones:

/eɪ/ ur**a**nium	/aɪ/ d**i**rect current	/əʊ/ isot**o**pe	/aʊ/ comp**ou**nd eye

6 Match the diphthongs in the box above to the parts of these science words in **bold type**.

1 hydr**o**electric
2 m**i**croscope
3 ultras**ou**nd
4 x-r**ay**
5 Fahrenh**ei**t
6 osm**o**sis

Other sounds

Here are some other symbols that do not look like letters.

/θ/ **th**eorem	/ð/ logari**th**m	/dʒ/ al**g**ebra	/ʒ/ equa**ti**on
/ʃ/ frac**ti**on	/tʃ/ exponen**ti**al		

7 Look at these maths words, and say whether they contain the sound /dʒ/, /ʒ/ or /ʃ/.

1 adjacent
2 integer
3 ratio
4 division
5 intersection
6 percentage

8 Look at these maths words, and say whether the 'c' in **bold type** should be pronounced /s/ or /k/.

1 **c**ircumference
2 spheri**c**al
3 surfa**c**e
4 **c**osine
5 de**c**imal
6 **c**ylinder

Modal verbs

A modal verb is a verb that is used before another verb to express meanings such as ability, permission, possibility, necessity or advice. These pages will show you some of the uses of modal verbs. Look at their their dictionary entries for more information.

These are the main modal verbs in English:

modal verb	short form	negative	short form
can		cannot	can't
could		could not	couldn't
may		may not	mayn't (UK)
might		might not	mightn't
must		must not	mustn't
ought to		ought not to	oughtn't to
shall		shall not	shan't (UK)
should		should not	shouldn't
will	'll	will not	won't
would	'd	would not	wouldn't

You can also use ***need*** and ***have to*** as modal verbs.

Saying how certain you think something is

This is an important use of some modal verbs. Look at the sentences below:

The speaker is sure that the angle is 90°.
► *It is a square, so the angle in the corner* ***must*** *be 90°.*

The speaker is sure that Harry will be there.
► *If Harry promised to come, he* ***will*** *come.*

The speaker thinks the metal might be gold, but is not sure.
► *It* ***might/could*** *be gold, but it's too dark to tell.*

The speaker thinks it is not possible that the metal is real silver.
► *It* ***can't*** be real silver – it's too cheap.

The speaker thinks it is possible that the rain will stop later.
► *Let's wait a bit – the rain* ***may*** *stop later.*

1 Fill in the gaps with a word from the box.

may	**will**	**mustn't**	**can't**	**might not**

1 If we don't hurry, we ..... get there on time.
2 Don't worry. Everything ..... be fine.
3 You ..... forget to lock the door.
4 He ..... have failed his exams – he's always top of the class.
5 We ..... have to catch a later train – I'm not sure.

Here are some other common uses of modal verbs:

Asking someone to do something	Offering to do something
▶ ***Can** you pass me a ruler?* ▶ ***Could** you help me with my homework, please?* ▶ ***Will** you explain how to do these fractions?* ▶ ***Would** you mind checking my answers?*	▶ ***Shall** I explain these figures again?* ▶ ***Can** I help you at all?* ▶ ***Would** you like me to lend you a calculator?*

Asking for permission	Giving someone permission
▶ ***Can** we use our dictionaries?* ▶ ***Could** I finish this work at home?* ▶ ***May** I borrow your pen?* (formal)	▶ *You **can** discuss your answers with your neighbour.* ▶ *He said we **could** go outside.* ▶ *You **may** leave the room.* (formal)

Making suggestions

2 Use the words ‘could’, ‘shall’ or ‘might’ to complete the suggestions below.

1 If you are cold, you ..... shut the window.
2 ..... we do our homework now?
3 .....n't you try asking your teacher?
4 You ..... like to do some more reading on the subject.
5 ..... we meet up this evening?

Same word, different use

Each modal verb has more than one meaning. This dictionary tells you what they are.

3 Look at the modal verb **can** in these sentences, and match each use to a word on the right. Use the dictionary to help you.

1 **Can** you hand out these books for me, please?	possible
2 You **can** leave early today.	offerings
3 I **can't** speak Russian.	permission
4 **Can** you get to work by train?	asking
5 **Can** I help you with those bags?	ability

The Web and the Internet

The Web or the World Wide Web (www) refers to all the websites (= electronic documents) that you can look at using the Internet. The Internet or the Net is the system that connects computers all over the world and allows computer users to look at websites. The Internet is now a very important part of many people's lives – both working and social – and has generated a lot of new words and phrases. Here are some important ones:

Online

To be online is to be connected to the Internet or to be available on the Internet. To go online is to start to connect your computer to the Internet.

Modems

A modem is a piece of equipment that allows you to send information from a computer through a cable or telephone line.

Moving around on the Web

You can use your mouse to click on links (= connections between the documents or areas on the Internet), to go to a different website, or to move from one part of a website to another.

Websites

Websites consist of a series of web pages. The main page on a website is called the home page. If you know the web address or URL of a website you can type it in at the top of the screen. Otherwise, you can use a search engine. A search engine is the software which allows you to search for information on the Internet by typing in one or two words. To surf or surf the Web is to look at many different websites, often without knowing where you are going next.

Blogs

A blog is a part of a website where someone describes what they do every day or what they think about different subjects. A blogger is someone who writes a blog.

Podcasts

A podcast is a recording from the Internet that you can listen to on your computer or MP3 player. You can also sign up to (= say that you want to receive) a podcast which is then updated (= new information is added to it) through the Internet when you plug your MP3 player into your computer.

Downloading and uploading

If you download an image, video, music, etc., you copy it onto your computer from the Internet. To upload something is to copy something from your computer onto a website or other place where, through the Internet, many people can copy it, look at it, or use it.

File sharing

File sharing is the activity of putting a file from your computer onto a special place on your computer so that other people can, through the Internet, copy it, look at it, or use it.

BlackBerry ®

A BlackBerry® is a combination of a small computer and a mobile phone that fits in your hand and can be used for documents, email, and Internet access.

Chat room

A chat room is a place on the Internet where you can discuss subjects with other people.

Social networking

Social networking is the use of a website to communicate with friends and get to know new people. To start you need to register, which means choosing a user name, a password and possibly an avatar. Then you create a profile of yourself and search for people you know, who have already joined the same site – people from your old school, for example. With any luck, you might make new friends who will read what you have written and write something to you. You can then exchange messages with them, and share photos, videos or music.

There are other ways of communicating on the Web. You can join a forum or discussion group and discuss a subject that interests you. You may choose to lurk for a while first and find out what the forum is like. Then you can start posting messages. You might look at existing threads or start a new thread if there is something else you want to discuss.

Glossary

avatar *noun* [C] an image which represents you in online games, chat rooms, etc. and which you can move around the screen

forum *noun* [C] (*also* discussion group) a place on the Internet where people can leave messages or discuss a subject with other people, or the people who discuss that particular subject

friend *noun* [C] a person who you write to on a social networking website and who writes back to you

lurk *verb* [I] to enter a chat room and read other people's messages without other people knowing you are doing this

post *verb* [T] to leave a message on a website

profile *noun* [C] a description of yourself and your interests on a social networking website

thread (*also* topic) *noun* [C] a group of pieces of writing on the Internet, in which people discuss one subject

user name *noun* [C] a name or other word that you sometimes need to type together with a password so that you are allowed to use a computer or the Internet

Writing letters

Formal letters

47 Abrahams Rd
Cambridge
CB4 3AL

20 September 2008

Ms R Perry
Evening News
107 Wolfs Way
Newtown
NT7 OPE

Dear Ms Perry ❶

I am ❷ writing to inquire about ❸ the possibility of vacation work with your company this summer. I am very interested in gaining some experience working for a newspaper.

For the last two years I have been editor of the student magazine at my school. Next year I am planning to do a one-year course in newspaper journalism.

I have good computer skills and accurate written English.

I very much hope you have a vacancy for me. I enclose a copy of my CV and look forward to hearing from you soon. ❹

Yours sincerely, ❶

Anna Thompson

❶ If you know the name of the person you are writing to, but the letter is formal, end the letter: *Yours sincerely.*

If you do not know the name of the person you are writing to, begin the letter: *Dear Sir/Madam* and end it: *Yours faithfully.*

❷ You should not use contractions (e.g. *I'm, I'd*) in a formal letter.

❸ Other ways of beginning a formal letter:

- *I am writing to inform you of/that ...*
- *I am writing to complain about ...*
- *I am writing regarding your advertisement ...*
- *Please send me ...*
- *Further to my letter of June 1st ...*

❹ Other ways of ending a formal letter:

- *Thank you in advance for your help.*
- *Wishing you all the best for the future.*

Informal letters

47 Abrahams Rd
Cambridge
CB4 3AL

20 September 2008

Dear Julia,

It was lovely to chat to you the other day. ❶ It seems ages since we last met. We're so excited that you're finally coming over to see us. In fact, John's going to take those two weeks off work so he can spend more time with us.

By the way, could you bring some photos of your family? I'd love to see them.

We're both really looking forward to seeing you again. ❷

Love, ❸

Anna

❶ Other ways of starting an informal letter:

- *Thanks for your letter.*
- *How are you?*
- *I hope you're well.*
- *Sorry it's been so long since I last wrote.*
- *It was lovely to hear from you.*

❷ Other ways of ending an informal letter:

- *Drop me a line soon.*
- *Write soon.*
- *Take care.*
- *Keep in touch.*
- *Give my love to Paul.*
- *Hope to hear from you soon.*

❸ Before your name, you can write:
to close friends:

- *Love from*
- *All my love*
- *Lots of love*

to less close friends:

- *Best wishes*
- *All the best*
- *Best*
- *Kind regards*

Checking your work

There are a lot of ways that this dictionary can help you avoid common mistakes.

Common Learner Error Notes

Words that often cause difficulty for learners of English have special notes explaining how to use them correctly. These are all based on the *Cambridge Learner Corpus*.

1 Correct the following sentences by looking at the Common Learner Error notes for the underlined word.

1. The temperature in the laboratory may effect the result of your experiment.
2. Where can I find informations about volcanoes?
3. I had a trouble with my maths homework.
4. He did an interesting speech about African animals.

Grammar

Always check the grammar of words you want to use. There is an explanation of all the grammar labels on page xiv, and the Extra help pages on **Countable and uncountable nouns** and **Verb patterns** will help you too.

It is important to use the correct preposition. In this dictionary, when a particular preposition is very common with a word, this is shown in **bold type** in an example sentence, e.g. *She is **fluent in** six languages.*

2 Fill in the correct prepositions in the following sentences.

1. There has been a drop ..... the birth rate recently.
2. They were campaigning ..... slavery.
3. He is ..... trial ..... murder.
4. Your offer is still ..... discussion.

Spelling

Spelling is one of the most difficult parts of learning English. Often words are not spelled the way they sound, and words that sound the same can be spelled differently.

3 Match the pairs of words that sound the same.

hour	cell	through	witch	write
which	right	our	sell	threw

Make sure you know how to make the different forms of verbs (e.g. *start, starts, starting, started*). There is information on regular verb tenses on page 868. There is a list of irregular verbs on page 870, and these are also shown in the dictionary. Irregular plurals are also shown in the dictionary.

4 There are six mistakes in the paragraph below. Try to correct them.

Ancient tribes moved to the area hundreds of years ago, bringing sheep and cattles with them. They also hunted deer and catched fish, and learned to grind wheat to make loafs of bread. They builded simple houses with mud walls and roofs made of sticks, and in the evenings, they sung songs and told storys around the fire.

Preparing for exams

Nobody likes exams, but if you stay calm and take the advice below, you can be sure you have prepared in the best possible way.

Make a revision timetable

Revision is the studying you have to do to prepare for an exam. A revision **timetable** or **schedule** is a plan of what you will study and the times when you will study. Be sure to remember the following points:

- Plan your time carefully. See how much work you need to do and make sure you have enough time to finish everything.
- Be realistic. Don't plan to work every moment of your spare time.
- Revise your least favorite subjects first. If you get them done, you can feel pleased with yourself, but if you leave them until last, you might not do them at all.
- Plan your timetable so that you finish your revision a few days before the exam. That way, you will have extra time if you need it.

Find a good place to work

You can't prepare effectively with the TV on or your brothers and sisters chatting near you.

- Find a place which is quiet and where you have enough room for your books and papers.
- It might be best to go to the library sometimes, or even to someone else's house where it will be quiet.
- Make sure you have all the materials you need to study what is on your revision timetable.

Other ways to revise

Learning your notes isn't the only way to revise.

- You can buy revision guides that help you learn the most important points of each subject. Ask your teacher to recommend one – you only need one for each subject.
- Ask your teacher to let you see the questions that have been asked in exams before so that you have a good idea of what to expect. You can try doing those questions yourself.
- Try recording your notes – then you can listen to them anywhere.

Ways of remembering things

Everyone is different so choose the memory tricks that suit you best. Here are some ideas:

- Write down the most important points in your notes on postcards or pieces of paper to stick on your wall.
- If you remember things by writing, write down the most important points from memory.
- If you remember things by looking at them, make patterns with your notes – turn them into diagrams or pictures.

- If you remember things by sound, try reading your notes aloud, recording them, or making up songs.
- If you are an active person, try moving around the room and chanting your notes in a strong rhythm.

Get help from other people

Everyone wants you to do well in your exams. Ask people to help you!

- Put a copy of your revision timetable on the wall so your family know what you are doing and can help you.
- Ask them to test you on what you have learned.
- Try studying with a friend sometimes – it's more fun.
- If you are having trouble with a particular subject, ask your teacher for help.

And finally – be kind to yourself!

You will not do your best in your exam if you are tired and unhappy.

- Take a short break from your revision every hour – go for a short walk or have a good stretch.
- Too much caffeine, for example in coffee or fizzy drinks, can make you anxious and stop you sleeping properly.
- Take some exercise – it will give you more energy and help you concentrate better.

Taking exams

You have done all your studying, and now it's the day of the exam. Here is some advice to help you do your best.

Before the exam

You may be feeling a bit nervous, but if you prepare well it will make things easier.

- Get everything ready the night before.
- Make sure you know what you're allowed to have in the exam, for example a dictionary or calculator.
- Make sure you have everything you need, including extra pens and pencils.
- Take a watch or small clock in case you can't see the clock in the exam room.
- Don't work all night before your exam – you won't do well if you're tired.
- Have a good breakfast.

If you feel nervous

Exam nerves can make it difficult to concentrate.

- Remember that it is perfectly natural to be a little nervous.
- Leave plenty of time to get to the exam – if you're late, you'll feel more anxious.
- Be confident that you have prepared well and that this is your opportunity to show the examiners what you know.
- Take a few deep breaths and try to relax.
- Remember that everyone else is probably as nervous as you!

At the beginning of the exam

At last you are in the exam room.

- Listen very carefully to all the instructions you are given.
- If there is anything you don't understand, do ask before the papers are given out.
- Make sure you have all the question papers, answer papers and extra pieces of paper that you need.

Planning your answers

It can be easy to spoil your work with careless mistakes. Be very careful to do everything you are asked to do.

- Read the instructions slowly and carefully. For instance, the question might ask you to answer *either* one thing *or* another – if you answer both, you will be wasting time.
- Read through all the questions before you start. Don't forget to turn the paper over and check if there are questions on the back.
- Look at how many marks you can get for each question and plan how much time to spend on each one.
- Choose the questions that will best show what you have learned. However, remember that you will need to answer *all* the parts of each question. If a question has four parts and you can only answer two of them, you can only get 50% of the marks.
- Remember to allow time for checking at the end.

Writing your answers

Now you are ready to start writing.

- Write as neatly as you can – it is difficult to mark untidy writing.
- For long answers, plan your answer on another piece of paper before you start writing.
- Do the questions that you think you can do well first – that will make you feel more confident, and you may remember other things as you work.
- Write what you know, but not necessarily *everything* you know – make sure that you are answering the question.
- If you are doing a maths question, always show how you have worked out your answer. Even if your answer is wrong, you may get some marks if some of what you did was correct.
- For multiple choice questions (questions where you are given a few answers to choose from), use a pencil in case you want to change your answer.

After the exam

Now it's all over and you've done your best.

- Don't compare your answers with your friends' answers – you can't change anything now, and it may make you feel more nervous about your next exam.
- Think about what you did well and what you were not so happy with, and see if you can learn any lessons for your next exam.

Good luck!

Writing essays

These pages give advice on writing the type of essays that ask you to discuss a subject or give an opinion on a subject.

Some general advice

Writing an essay in your own language can be hard enough but writing one in English is even harder. However, there are things that you can do to help yourself. Much of the advice that you will read here is on the type of English that people use when writing essays. 'Essay English' is often more formal than the English that is used for speaking and there are particular words and phrases that are often used. First, here is some practical advice that you should try to keep in mind when you are writing an essay.

Read the essay title

Do not start writing immediately. Read the essay title carefully three or four times until you are sure that you know exactly what it means. Then start thinking about what you are going to write.

Plan your essay

Plan your essay before you start to write it. A good idea is to write a list of your main points or arguments. Each point in the list will become a paragraph in your essay.

Answer the essay title

Always keep in mind the essay title and write only about those parts of a subject that relate to the title. Do not write everything you know on the subject.

Use paragraphs

Remember to separate your ideas into paragraphs, each new idea or point starting a new line. This makes your essay much clearer to read.

Use essay language

Essays should not contain slang or informal language. (In this dictionary you will see the labels *informal* and *very informal* at the entries for such words.)

You should also avoid using contractions, such as *don't*, *can't*, and *shouldn't*, in your essays.

The different parts of an essay

The introduction

A well-written essay will start with an introduction. Your introduction should describe briefly the main ideas that you will be discussing in the rest of the essay. Do not give details and do not give your opinion on the subject. Introductions should be short.

There are a number of ways to start an essay. You might:

- say why the subject is so important, or
- write about some new facts that have recently been discovered about the subject

You might use these words and phrases to start your introduction:

> *Recently ...*
> *Nowadays ...*
> *It is certainly true that ...*

The 'body' (= main part) of the essay

This is the part of the essay where you explain and develop the ideas that you described briefly in the introduction. The words and phrases below will help you to do this.

You may want to give some **facts**. Start your sentence with:

> *Recent research shows/suggests ...*
> *A recent report/survey showed ...*
> *There is evidence to suggest ...*

You may want to give **possible reasons** for something:

> *Perhaps this is because ...*
> *This may be a result of ...*
> *This may be due to ...*

The word 'also' at the start of a sentence is too informal for an essay. There are some more formal ways of saying 'also', which sound better in an essay, such as:

> *Furthermore, ...*
> *More importantly, ...*
> *What is more, ...*
> *In addition, ...*

You might want to say what the **result** of something is:

> *Thus ...*
> *As a result ...*
> *Consequently ...*
> *As a consequence ...*
> *This has the effect of ...*
> *Therefore ...*

You will probably need to show that you are aware of **different opinions** on the subject:

> *However ...*
> *Nevertheless ...*
> *On the other hand ...*

The conclusion

The conclusion is the final paragraph of your essay. In your conclusion you should describe briefly the main ideas in the essay and give your opinion of all of the points you have made. Try to answer any questions that you might have put in the introduction. Here are some useful phrases to start your conclusion:

> *To conclude ...*
> *To sum up ...*
> *In conclusion ...*

Other useful phrases

Here are some other phrases that you may find useful in your essay writing. They are put in groups with similar meaning.

Saying things that are generally true

On the whole …
Generally …
As a general rule …
For the most part …

Saying when something is happening now

Today …
Currently …
Nowadays …
These days …
Recently …
In recent years …
In the past few years …

Saying when something happened in the past

In the past …
In previous years …
Previously …
In those days …

Giving your opinion

I believe that …
I feel that …
It is my feeling that …
It is my opinion that …
In my opinion …
In my view …

Giving other people's opinions

According to x …
In x's opinion …
In x's view …
Many people argue …
Many experts agree …
As x explains/says/writes …

Saying that something might not be true

It is not always true …
It is not necessarily true …
Not everyone agrees that …

Saying that something is certainly true

Undoubtedly …
Without a doubt …
Unquestionably …

Practising collocations

A collocation is a combination of two or more words which are often used together in a language. For example, in English you say:

*He **made** a **mistake**.*

Not:

*He **did** a **mistake**.*

In the main part of this dictionary collocations are shown at many entries in boxes called 'Word partners'. If you can use collocations or 'word partners' correctly, your English will sound more natural and it will be easier to understand.

The exercises on the next pages give you help with the type of collocations that you find when you are studying different subjects. For example, if you are studying finance, you will already know that **capital** is 'an amount of money that you need to start a business'. In addition to knowing the word 'capital' you should also know that companies **raise capital**. They do not 'get' or 'make' capital. **Raise** is therefore an important collocation of **capital**. The exercises below will help you to practise the most important collocations in a variety of subject areas.

In the exercises below, fill in the gaps with the correct form of the verbs in the boxes. Each verb should only be used once.

Business Studies

Limited companies

submit	influence	set up	elect	raise	divide up	audit	recover

1
1 The ownership of a limited company is ..... into equal parts called shares.
2 Private limited companies are quite easy and cheap to .....
3 The more shares a shareholder owns, the more he or she can ..... the company.
4 To become a limited company, applicants have to ..... a Memorandum of Association which describes the business's name, address and main purpose.
5 The owners of a limited company are not involved in the day-to-day running of the business, unless they have been ..... to the Board of Directors.
6 A public limited company ..... capital by selling its shares to the public on the stock market.
7 Public limited companies and private limited companies must both ..... their accounts.
8 The abbreviations plc and Ltd in the names of companies mean that debts cannot be ..... from the personal funds of the company shareholders.

Public ownership or privatization

fund	provide	run	return	take over	maintain	improve

2
1 An industry that has been ..... by the government is called a nationalized industry.
2 The industries that are ..... by the government are different from country to country.
3 The main aim of public ownership is to ..... essential services for the whole population of a country.
4 The cost of public ownership is ..... by taxation.
5 Nationalizing large industries with a lot of employees can be a way of ..... levels of employment.
6 It is often said that privatization reduces costs and ..... efficiency.
7 In many countries nationalized industries have recently been ..... to private ownership.

Branding and packaging

differentiate	stand out	attract	target	package	carry
associate with	stick to	encourage	identify		

3
1 Shape, size and colour are important factors when ..... a product.
2 One important aim of a product's package design is to ..... that product from the competitors.
3 A brand name will enable customers to ..... a particular brand when purchasing a product.
4 If we have not tried a product before, it is often the packaging and advertising that will first ..... us to it.
5 Giving a successful product a brand name can ..... customer loyalty and repeat buying.
6 By law, the packaging of many products must ..... specific information about ingredients.
7 There are some brands which everyone ..... quality.
8 A lot of products are ..... at particular groups of people, for example young people.
9 Consumers tend to ..... products that they know they like.
10 Distinctive packaging will make a product ..... against the competitors.

The product life cycle

launch	expand	promote	maintain	decline	exceed	respond

4
1 Businesses have to ..... to changes in the markets.
2 In a changing market, demand for some products increases and for others demand ..... .
3 To make a market aware of a new product, it is important to ..... it.
4 A company may consider ..... a product's distribution in order to reach more consumers.
5 If many similar products are launched by other companies, supply may eventually ..... demand.
6 The introduction phase of a product is when the new product is ..... .

History/politics

sign	come	declare	go	overthrow	nationalize	lift	impose	abolish	form

1 Leaders gathered to ..... the treaty.
2 Lenin ..... to power in 1917.
3 Because of the invasion, Britain was obliged to ..... war.
4 The United Nations decided to ..... sanctions on their country.
5 The government was ..... in a coup.
6 More and more workers started to ..... unions.
7 The blockade of Berlin was ..... in May 1949.
8 The new revolutionary government ..... the monarchy.
9 Many British workers ..... on strike in 1926.
10 The government decided to ..... the railways.

hold	stand	present	make	lose	take up	cast	introduce

1 The prime minister was forced to ..... a general election.
2 She decided to ..... for Parliament.
3 He ..... his vote in favour of the new law.
4 He was accused of lying, and ..... his seat at the next election.
5 The government has promised to ..... a new bill to deal with Internet crime.
6 In 1965, he ..... his first speech in Parliament.
7 After the election, she travelled to London to ..... her seat in the House of Lords.
8 The chancellor ..... his budget to Parliament.

Literature – drama

develop/progress	convey	set	open	perform/put on/stage	close

1 The play ..... on board a ship.
2 As the plot ..... we learn more about the main character's past.
3 This play was first ..... at the National Theatre in 1987.
4 Through his characters, the playwright ..... the complex emotions that people in this situation experience.
5 This play is ..... in Baltimore in 1962.
6 By the time the play..... all the main characters have been killed.

Literature – novels

evoke	publish	narrate/tell	develop/progress
recur/run	express	portray	explore

1 The novel was first ..... in 1897.
2 The story is ..... in the first person by Travis, the main character.
3 As the story ..... we start to understand the reason for the main character's unhappiness.
4 The theme of jealousy..... throughout the whole of the novel.
5 In the novel, the father is..... as a very kind, sympathetic character.
6 The author ..... the atmosphere of the prison very effectively.
7 She used her novels to..... her anger at the way women were being treated at the time.
8 One idea that the author ..... in his writing is: what makes a man?

Geography

Climate change

shrink	release	rise	fell/chop down	retain	contribute	reduce

1
1. It is thought that the average temperature of the Earth has ..... by 0.6 °C in the last 100 years.
2. It is generally believed that the build-up of carbon dioxide in the atmosphere is ..... to global warming.
3. Many glaciers are now ....
4. When fossil fuels are burnt, carbon dioxide is ..... into the atmosphere.
5. Large areas of tropical rainforest have been ...... , increasing the problem.
6. Greenhouse gases cause the atmosphere to ..... more radiation from the sun.
7. In Kyoto, Japan, in 1997, many governments promised to ..... emissions of greenhouse gases.

Energy sources (renewable and non-renewable)

run out	generate	replenish	harness	reduce	derive	convert	invest

2
1. Fossil fuels are non-renewable energy sources which means that one day they will ....
2. Renewable energy sources are sources of energy that quickly ..... themselves and can be used repeatedly.
3. The burning of fossil fuels ..... greenhouse gases.
4. Energy from sunlight can be captured in solar panels and ..... into electricity.
5. Energy can be ..... from the movement of water through rivers, lakes and dams.
6. The government wants to ..... its carbon dioxide emissions.
7. The UK intends to ..... 10% of its electricity from renewable sources by 2010.
8. UK power companies are ..... huge sums of money in renewable power.

Coasts

blow	crash	erode	shape	meet	deposit	dissolve

3
1. A coast is where the land ..... the sea.
2. Coasts are ..... by the sea and the action of waves.
3. Destructive waves ..... the coastline.
4. Waves are created when the wind ..... over the surface of the sea.
5. Waves ..... on the shore have the effect of damaging the shore.
6. Acids found in the sea water ..... some types of rock.
7. The sea ..... particles of rock and stones that it has been carrying on the shore.

Glaciers

cover	advance	erode	retreat	break off	melt	rise	compress	accumulate

4
1 Glaciers currently ..... one tenth of the Earth's surface.
2 A glacier starts to form when snowflakes ..... in a hollow in the side of a mountain.
3 As more snow falls on the snowflakes, it ..... them into a compact substance.
4 The now heavy glacier moves slowly downhill, ... the landscape under it.
5 Glaciers that are increasing in size are said to be ..... .
6 Glaciers that are decreasing in size are said to be ..... .
7 A glacier ..... in the summer and freezes again in the winter.
8 Where an ice sheet meets the sea, enormous pieces of it ..... as icebergs.
9 If glaciers melt, global sea levels will ..... .

Biology

The circulatory system

carry	tire	clot	pump	take away	leave	flow	fight	beat	return

1
1 The circulatory system ..... food and oxygen to the cells.
2 The circulatory system also ..... waste products from the cells.
3 The heart ..... blood to the body and lungs.
4 The heart ..... about 70 times a minute in the average adult.
5 The heart never ....
6 The functions of blood are to ..... disease and to carry substances around the body.
7 Blood ..... the heart in the arteries.
8 Blood ..... to the heart in the veins.
9 Blood in the veins ..... smoothly.
10 The blood will ..... at the site of a small injury.

Bones and muscles

contract	attach	relax	fuse	pull	allow	stretch	hold

2
1 Bones play a vital part in ..... up the body structure and giving it shape.
2 The bones of the skull are ..... together to provide protection for the brain.
3 Muscles ..... but never push.
4 When muscles ..... they get shorter.
5 When they return to their original length, they ..... .
6 Muscles are ..... to bones by tendons.
7 Tendons never ..... .
8 A hinge joint, such as the knee, ... movement in one plane only.

Diet

store control come from build up obtain put on miss out on use up

3 1 In general men ..... more energy that women.
2 The energy that we use ..... the food that we eat.
3 If we eat too much food, some of the extra food is ..... as fat.
4 If we ..... important vitamins, our bodies do not function properly.
5 We ..... weight when we eat more food than our bodies need.
6 If we do not eat enough we may not be able to ..... the energy that we need.
7 You can ..... your weight by eating well-balanced meals and taking regular exercise.
8 Fat deposits may ..... on the inside of arteries, slowing down the flow of blood.

Digestion

absorb dissolve pass through convert digest roll pass out secrete break down

4 1 Food is ..... in the mouth, the stomach and the small intestine.
2 In the colon, water and salts are ..... .
3 The tongue ..... the food into balls.
4 Some food is ..... into other substances.
5 The stomach wall ..... gastric juice.
6 Waste matter is ..... through the anus.
7 Digested food molecules ..... the wall of the small intestine and into our bloodstream.
8 Food is ..... into simple, soluble molecules which can be used as a source of energy.
9 Food is ..... in the blood plasma and then taken to other parts of the body where it may become part of the cells.

Sexual reproduction

fuse connect diffuse deposit fertilize mix embed form contract reach release

5 1 Eggs start to be ..... inside a girl's ovaries before she is even born.
2 The sperm are ..... near the cervix of the female.
3 The egg is ..... by the sperm.
4 Fertilization happens when a sperm ..... with an egg cell.
5 Each ovary ..... one ovum every eight weeks.
6 When a girl ..... puberty, some of her eggs will start to develop.
7 The embryo ..... itself into the spongy lining of the uterus.
8 The placenta is ..... to the foetus by the umbilical cord.
9 Oxygen and nutrients in the mother's blood ..... across the placenta into the foetus's blood.
10 The blood of the mother and the foetus does not ..... .
11 The process of birth starts when the muscles in the uterus begin to ..... .

Photosynthesis

trap	absorb	build	take in	produce	obtain	give off	convert

6 1 Photosynthesis is the process by which plants use the energy from sunlight to ..... sugar.
2 Green plants use small molecules around them to ..... large organic molecules of glucose.
3 During photosynthesis, carbon dioxide and water are ..... into glucose and oxygen.
4 Oxygen is ..... during photosynthesis.
5 In photosynthesis, plants ..... simple substances such as carbon dioxide and water.
6 Carbon dioxide is ..... from the air.
7 Energy from the sunlight is ..... in a plant by chlorophyll.
8 Roots ..... the water necessary for photosynthesis from the soil.

Chemistry

Acids, bases and salts

react	measure	change	produce	neutralize	give	turn	dissolve	form

1 1 The pH of a solution can be ..... in many ways.
2 Salts are made when an acid ..... with a base, carbonate or metal.
3 The oxides of non-metals mainly ..... acidic solutions.
4 The more acidic solutions ..... universal indicator bright red.
5 The most alkaline solutions ..... a violet colour.
6 Bases are substances that can react with acids and ..... them to make a salt and water.
7 Bases that ..... in water are called alkalis.
8 Neutral solutions do not ..... the colour of litmus paper.
9 When acids dissolve in water they ..... hydrogen ions.

Enzymes

break down	proceed	speed up	convert	bind	work	denature

2 1 An enzyme is a protein molecule that ..... chemical reactions.
2 Enzymes are proteins, and are usually ..... above about 45°C.
3 The job of an enzyme is to ..... a large molecule into smaller molecules.
4 Enzymes ..... temporarily to one or more of the substances that are reacting with each other.
5 This enzyme is used in some diet foods to ..... glucose syrup into fructose syrup.
6 Every enzyme has an optimum temperature at which the reaction that it causes ..... at its fastest rate.
7 Enzymes in the stomach ..... best in acidic conditions.

Chemical reactions

take in	break down	gain	reverse	react with	lose	give out

3 1 Exothermic reactions ..... energy, usually in the form of heat.
2 Endothermic reactions ..... energy from their surroundings.
3 Decomposition is when a compound ..... into two or more substances.
4 Oxidation happens when substances ..... oxygen.
5 Reduction happens when substances ..... oxygen.
6 When acids ..... bases or alkalis, their acidity is destroyed.
7 In a chemical reaction, generally the process is not easily ..... .

Physics

Energy

create	absorb	waste	conduct	release
reduce	convert	transfer	emit/radiate	

1 1 Different types of energy can be ..... from one form to another.
2 Dark surfaces ..... more heat energy than light surfaces.
3 Sound energy is ..... by vibrating objects.
4 An electric light bulb ..... electrical energy into light energy.
5 Energy is not ..... or destroyed. It is transferred from one form to another or moved.
6 Energy can be ..... during energy transfers, for example the heat energy from an electric light bulb.
7 There are many ways to ..... heat loss from buildings, such as insulation and double-glazed windows.
8 Heat energy is ..... from a hot area of an object to a cold area.
9 A hotter object will ..... more infrared radiation than a cooler one.

The solar system

exert	hold	decrease	complete	increase	orbit	pull	attract

2 1 Planets ..... the sun in circles with the sun near the centre.
2 Gravity is a force that ..... objects towards each other.
3 The force of gravity between two objects ..... as the objects move further apart.
4 Any object with mass ..... a force of gravity.
5 It takes one year for a planet to ..... a single orbit around the sun.
6 The speed of a comet ..... as it gets nearer to the sun.
7 Gravity ..... objects on Earth towards the centre of the planet.
8 Gravity also has the effect of ..... the Earth's atmosphere in place.

Radiation

penetrate	absorb	give out	deflect	stop	detect	decay	emit

3
1. Radiation can be ..... using a Geiger-Muller tube.
2. Radioactive materials ..... radiation the whole time.
3. There are three types of radiation. Each type ..... materials in different ways.
4. Gamma radiation is the most penetrating type of radiation and can only be ..... by lead or thick concrete.
5. Each time the Geiger-Muller tube ..... radiation, it transmits an electrical pulse to a counting machine.
6. Alpha particles are ..... from the nuclei of radioactive atoms.
7. Some forms of radiation can be ..... by electric and magnetic fields.
8. The half-life of a radioactive isotope is the time taken for half its radioactive atoms to ......

Answer key

Graphs and charts

1 **1** 8 **2** 8, 14, 16 **3** 16, 16, 0
2 increases, rate, reaches, maintains, sharply
3 **1** banana **2** 20 **3** oranges

Verb patterns

1 1 I **2** T **3** I **4** T **5** T
2 1 on **2** for **3** to **4** with **5** on

Phrasal verbs

1 **1** draw back, draw sb/sth into sth, draw on sth, draw sth up
2 help (sb) out
3 kill sth/sb off
4 move in, move on, move out, move over
5 round sth down, round sth off, round sb/sth up, round sth up
2 **1** out **2** down **3** out **4** in **5** off
3 **1** make a copy **2** tidy up **3** understand
4 spend time away from work
4 **1** to **2** for **3** at **4** with

Word formation

1 **1** unsaturated **2** impermeable
3 inorganic **4** immiscible **5** insoluble
2 **1** relating to water
2 between
3 relating to living things
4 relating to blood
5 preventing or destroying
3 **1** antivirus **2** intersection **3** hydrophobia
4 haemorrhage **5** biofuel
4 **1** pollination **2** nitrification **3** circulation
4 computerization
5 **1** d **2** c **3** a **4** e **5** b

Countable and uncountable nouns

1 **1** cellulose **2** fibre, digestion
3 photosynthesis, energy, sunlight, food
4 air
2 **1-2** a **3** a, a **4** – **5** –
3 **1** a lot of **2** many **3** much
4 a lot of **5** many
4 Student's own sentences using words listed.

Pronunciation

1 **1** d **2** c **3** a **4** c **5** b
2 **1** chlorine **2** carbon **3** magnesium
4 nitrogen **5** hydrogen **6** helium
3 **1** <u>cli</u>mate **2** <u>e</u>cosystem **3** de<u>cid</u>uous
4 e<u>ro</u>sion **5** de<u>mog</u>raphy **6** demo<u>graph</u>ics
4 **1** de<u>pos</u>it account **2** electronic <u>bank</u>ing
3 direct <u>de</u>bit **4** fixed <u>as</u>sets **5** petty <u>cash</u>
6 <u>bank</u> account
5 **1** /ʌ/ **2** /e/ **3** /uː/ **4** /ɪ/ **5** /iː/
6 /ɒ/
6 **1** /əʊ/ **2** /aɪ/ **3** /aʊ/ **4** /eɪ/ **5** /aɪ/
6 /əʊ/
7 **1** /dʒ/ **2** /dʒ/ **3** /ʃ/ **4** /ʒ/ **5** /ʃ/
6 /dʒ/
8 **1** /s/ **2** /k/ **3** /s/ **4** /k/ **5** /s/
6 /s/

Modal verbs

1 **1** might not **2** will **3** mustn't **4** can't
5 may
2 **1** could **2** Shall **3** Could **4** might
5 Shall
3 **1** asking **2** permission **3** ability
4 possible **5** offering

Checking your work

1 **1** The temperature in the laboratory may **affect** the result of your experiment.
2 Where can I find **information** about volcanoes?
3 I had **trouble** with my maths homework.
4 He **made** an interesting speech about African animals.
2 **1** in **2** against **3** on, for **4** under
3 hour/our cell/sell through/threw witch/which write/right
4 Ancient tribes moved to the area hundreds of years ago, bringing sheep and **cattle** with them. They also hunted deer and **caught** fish, and learned to grind wheat to make **loaves** of bread. They **built** simple houses with mud walls and roofs made of sticks, and in the evenings, they **sang** songs and told **stories** around the fire.

Practising collocations

Business studies

1 **1** divided up **2** set up **3** influence **4** submit **5** elected **6** raises **7** audit **8** recovered

2 **1** taken over **2** run **3** provide **4** funded **5** maintaining **6** improves **7** returned

3 **1** packaging **2** differentiate **3** identify **4** attract **5** encourage **6** carry **7** associates with **8** targeted **9** stick to **10** stand out

4 **1** respond **2** declines **3** promote **4** expanding **5** exceed **6** launched

History/Politics

1 sign **2** came **3** declare **4** impose **5** overthrown **6** forming **7** lifted **8** abolished **9** went **10** nationalize

Literature – drama

1 opens **2** develops/progresses **3** performing/put on/staged **4** conveys **5** set **6** closes

Literature – novels

1 published **2** narrated/told **3** develops/progresses **4** recurs/runs **5** portrayed **6** evokes **7** express **4** explores

Geography

1 **1** risen **2** contributing **3** shrinking **4** released **5** felled/chopped down **6** retain **7** reduce

2 **1** run out **2** replenish **3** generates **4** converted **5** harnessed **6** reduce **7** derive **8** investing

3 **1** meets **2** shaped **3** erode **4** blows **5** crashing **6** dissolve **7** deposits

4 **1** cover **2** accumulate **3** compresses **4** eroding **5** advancing **6** retreating **7** melts **8** break off **9** rise

Biology

1 **1** carries **2** takes away **3** pumps **4** beats **5** tires **6** fight **7** leaves **8** returns **9** flows **10** clot

2 **1** holding **2** fused **3** pull **4** contract **5** relax **6** attached **7** stretch **8** allows

3 **1** use up **2** comes from **3** stored **4** miss out on **5** put on **6** obtain **7** control **8** build up

4 **1** digested **2** absorbed **3** rolls **4** converted **5** secretes **6** passed out **7** pass through **8** broken down **9** dissolved

5 **1** formed **2** deposited **3** fertilized **4** fuses **5** releases **6** reaches **7** embeds **8** connected **9** diffuse **10** mix **11** contract

6 **1** produce **2** build **3** converted **4** given off **5** take in **6** obtained **7** trapped **8** absorb

Chemistry

1 **1** measured **2** reacts **3** form **4** turn **5** give **6** neutralize **7** dissolve **8** change **9** produce

2 **1** speeds up **2** denatured **3** break down **4** bind **5** convert **6** proceeds **7** work

3 **1** give out **2** take in **3** breaks down **4** gain **5** lose **6** react with **7** reversed

Physics

1 **1** transferred **2** absorb **3** released **4** converts **5** created **6** wasted **7** reduce **8** conducted **9** emit/radiate

2 **1** orbit **2** attracts **3** decreases **4** exerts **5** complete **6** increases **7** pulls **8** holding

3 **1** detected **2** give out **3** penetrates **4** stopped **5** absorbs **6** emitted **7** deflected **8** decay

Notes

marsupial /mɑːˈsuːpiəl/ *noun* [C] **BIOLOGY** a type of mammal from Australasia or South or Central America which is not completely developed when it is born and is carried around in a pocket on the mother's body

martial art /ˌmɑːʃəlˈɑːt/ *noun* [C] **SPORT** traditional Japanese or Chinese skills of fighting, done as sports in western countries

martial law /ˌmɑːʃəlˈlɔː/ *noun* [U] **POLITICS** the control of a country by its army instead of by its usual leaders *to declare martial law*

Martian /ˈmɑːʃən/ *noun* [C] in stories, someone from the planet Mars

martyr /ˈmɑːtər/ *noun* [C] someone who dies for their beliefs *a Catholic martyr* •**martyrdom** *noun* [U]

marvel¹ /ˈmɑːvəl/ *noun* [C] something really surprising, exciting, or good *a marvel of modern technology*

marvel² /ˈmɑːvəl/ *verb* [I] *UK* **marvelling**, *past* **marvelled**, *US* **marveling**, *past* **marveled** to admire something very much *I'm just* ***marvelling at*** *your skills.*

marvellous *UK* (*US* **marvelous**) /ˈmɑːvələs/ *adjective* extremely good *What a marvellous idea!* •**marvellously** *UK* (*US* **marvelously**) *adverb*

Marxism /ˈmɑːksɪzəm/ *noun* [U] **POLITICS** the political and economic ideas of Karl Marx

Marxist /ˈmɑːksɪst/ *adjective* **POLITICS** relating to Marxism *Marxist ideology* •**Marxist** *noun* [C] someone who supports Marxism

mascara /mæsˈkɑːrə/ *noun* [U] a dark substance that you put on your eyelashes (= hairs that grow above and below your eyes) to make them look longer and thicker

mascot /ˈmæskɒt/ *noun* [C] a toy or a child that a person or a team takes with them to bring them luck *He's our* ***lucky mascot.***

masculine /ˈmæskjəlɪn/ *adjective* **1** having qualities that are typical of men *a masculine appearance/voice* **2 LANGUAGE** in some languages, belonging to a group of nouns or adjectives that have the same grammatical behaviour. The other groups are 'feminine' and 'neuter'.

masculinity /ˌmæskjəˈlɪnəti/ *noun* [U] the qualities that are typical of men

mash /mæʃ/ *verb* [T] **FOOD** to crush food until it is soft *(UK) mashed potato/ (US) mashed potatoes*

mask¹ /mɑːsk/ *noun* [C] a covering for the face that protects, hides, or decorates the person wearing it ⊃See also: **gas mask**

mask² /mɑːsk/ *verb* [T] to prevent something from being noticed *I've had to put some flowers in there to* ***mask the smell.***

masked /mɑːskt/ *adjective* wearing a mask *a* ***masked gunman***

masochism /ˈmæsəkɪzəm/ *noun* [U] when people get pleasure from being hurt •**masochist** *noun* [C] someone who gets pleasure from being hurt

masochistic /ˌmæsəˈkɪstɪk/ *adjective* getting pleasure from being hurt *masochistic behaviour*

masonry /ˈmeɪsənri/ *noun* [U] the parts of a building that are made of bricks or stone

masquerade /ˌmæskərˈeɪd/ *verb*
masquerade as sb/sth *phrasal verb* to pretend to be someone or something *She's just a teacher masquerading as an academic.*

mass¹ /mæs/ *noun* **1** [C] a solid lump with no clear shape *The sauce was now a sticky mass in the bottom of the pan.* **2 a mass of sth** a large amount or number of something *She had a mass of blond curls.* **3 MEASURES** [U] in physics, the amount of substance that something contains *One litre of water has a mass of one*

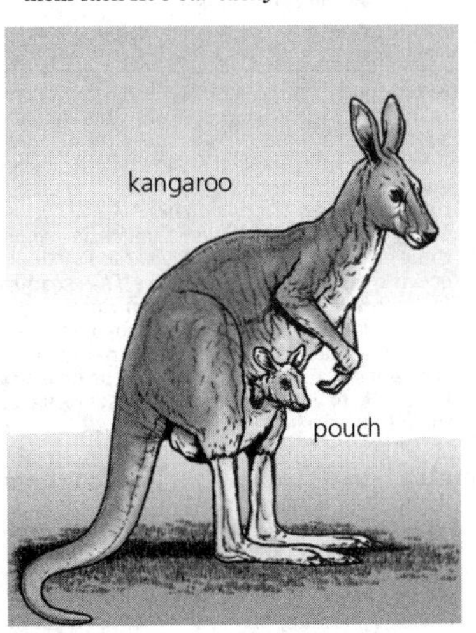

marsupials

kilogram. **4 masses** *informal* a large amount or number of something *I've got **masses of** work to do.* **5 the masses** the ordinary people who form the largest part of society *He failed to win the support of the masses.*

mass² /mæs/ *adjective* [**always before noun**] involving a lot of people ***mass destruction/unemployment*** ○ *a **mass murderer***

mass³ /mæs/ *verb* [**I, T**] *formal* to come together somewhere in large numbers, or make people or things do this *Over 20,000 demonstrators massed in the town's main square.*

Mass, mass /mæs/ *noun* [**C, U**] **RELIGION** a religious ceremony in some Christian churches in which people eat bread and drink wine *to go to Mass*

massacre /ˈmæsəkəʳ/ *noun* [**C**] the killing of a lot of people *He ordered the massacre of over 2,000 women and children.* •**massacre** *verb* [**T**] *Hundreds of civilians were massacred in the raid.*

massage /ˈmæsɑːdʒ/ (US) /məˈsɑːdʒ/ *noun* [**C, U**] **HEALTH** the activity of rubbing or pressing parts of someone's body in order to make them relax or to stop their muscles hurting *to **have a massage*** ○ *She **gave** me a foot **massage**.* •**massage** *verb* [**T**] *Would you massage my shoulders?*

massive /ˈmæsɪv/ *adjective* very big *a massive building* ○ *massive debts*

M

mass-market /ˌmæsˈmɑːkɪt/ *adjective* describes something that is made to be sold to as many people as possible •**ˈmass ˌmarket** *noun* [**C**]

the ˌmass ˈmedia *noun* [**group**] newspapers, television, and radio

ˈmass ˌnumber *noun* [**C**] **PHYSICS, CHEMISTRY** the total number of protons and neutrons in an atom

mass-produce /ˌmæs.prəˈdjuːs/ *verb* [**T**] to produce a lot of goods cheaply using machines in a factory •**ˌmass proˈduction** *noun* [**U**]

mass spectrometer /ˌmæsspekˈtrɒmɪtəʳ/ (*also* **spectroscope**) *noun* [**C**] **PHYSICS** a piece of equipment used by scientists to separate ions into groups to measure and compare their mass and charge (= amount of electricity)

mass spectrometry /ˌmæsspekˈtrɒmətri/ *noun* [**U**] **PHYSICS** a method used by scientists to measure and compare the mass and the charge (= amount of electricity) of ions

mast /mɑːst/ *noun* [**C**] **1** BOAT a tall pole on a boat that supports its sails **2** SIGNALS a tall metal pole that sends out television, radio or mobile phone signals

master¹ /ˈmɑːstəʳ/ *noun* [**C**] **1** IN CHARGE In the past, a servant's master was the man that they worked for. **2 EDUCATION** *old-fashioned* a male teacher *the Latin master* **3** SKILL someone who does something very well *He was a **master of** disguise.* **4** FOR COPYING a document or recording from which copies can be made **5 Master of Arts/Science, etc EDUCATION** a higher university qualification which usually takes 1 or 2 more years of study after your first qualification, or a person who has this qualification **6 Master's (degree) EDUCATION** a higher university qualification *to study for a Master's degree* **7 Master** *formal* a title for a boy, used before his family name or full name *Master Thomas Mills*

master² /ˈmɑːstəʳ/ *verb* [**T**] to learn how to do something well *to **master** a **technique*** ○ *He lived for several years in Italy but never quite **mastered** the **language**.*

master³ /ˈmɑːstəʳ/ *adjective* [**always before noun**] having the skills for a particular job *a **master chef/craftsman***

masterful /ˈmɑːstəfəl/ *adjective* done with great skill *a **masterful display** of golf*

mastermind /ˈmɑːstəmaɪnd/ *verb* [**T**] to plan every detail of a complicated event or activity and make sure that it happens *He allegedly masterminded both bomb attacks in the region.* •**mastermind** *noun* [**C**] *It is thought he was the **mastermind behind*** (= the person who planned) last year's bombing campaign.

masterpiece /ˈmɑːstəpiːs/ *noun* [**C**] a painting, book, or film that is generally considered to be of excellent quality *'Mona Lisa' is widely regarded as Leonardo da Vinci's masterpiece.*

mastery /ˈmɑːstᵊri/ *noun* **1 mastery of sth** great skill or understanding of something *his mastery of the Japanese language* **2 mastery of/over sth** control over something *The two countries battled for mastery over the region.*

masturbate /ˈmæstəbeɪt/ *verb* [**I**] to make yourself feel sexually excited by touching your sexual organs •**masturbation** /ˌmæstəˈbeɪʃᵊn/ *noun* [**U**]

mat /mæt/ *noun* [**C**] **1** FLOOR a piece of thick material that you put on the floor, often in order to protect it *There's a mat by the door for you to wipe your feet on.* **2** TABLE a small piece of plastic or other material that you put on a table so that hot plates and liquid will not damage it

WORD PARTNERS FOR ***match***

play/lose/win a match • a match **against** sb • **in** a match

match¹ /mætʃ/ *noun* **1 SPORT** [**C**] a sports competition in which two people or teams compete against each other *a football/tennis match* **2** FIRE [**C**] a thin, wooden stick which produces a flame when you rub one end of it against a rough surface *a box of matches* **3** ATTRACTIVE [**no plural**] If something is a good match for something else, it looks attractive next to it, usually because it is the right colour. *The curtains look nice - they're a perfect **match for** the sofa.* **4** RELATIONSHIP [**no plural**] If two people who are having a relationship are a good match, they are very suitable for each other. **5 be no match for sb/sth** to not be as good as someone or something else *Gibson ran well but was no match for the young Italian.*

match² /mætʃ/ *verb* **1** BE THE SAME [**I, T**] If two things match, they are the same colour or type. *I can't find anything to match my green shirt.* ○ *Your socks don't match.* ○ *Traces of blood found on Walker's clothing matched the victim's blood type.* **2** CHOOSE [**T**] to choose someone or something that is suitable for a particular person, activity, or purpose *In the first exercise, you have to **match** the famous person* *to their country of origin.* **3** BE AS GOOD AS [T] to be as good as someone or something else *It would be difficult to match the service this airline gives to its customers.*

match up *phrasal verb* If two pieces of information match up, they are the same. *Their accounts of what happened that evening didn't match up.*

match sb/sth up *phrasal verb* to choose someone or something that is suitable for a particular person, activity, or purpose *They look at your interests and try to* ***match you up with*** *someone suitable.*

match up to sth *phrasal verb* to be as good as something else *Nothing that he wrote after this point ever matched up to his early work.*

matchbox /ˈmætʃbɒks/ *noun* [C] a small box containing matches

matching /ˈmætʃɪŋ/ *adjective* [always before noun] having the same colour or pattern as something else *She wore purple shorts and a matching T-shirt.*

ˈmatching (ˌconcept) *noun* [C] **FINANCE** a method used in a business's accounts where the money it receives in a certain period is compared with its costs for the same period

mate[1] /meɪt/ *noun* [C] **1** FRIEND *UK informal* a friend *She's my* ***best mate.*** ○ *Pete was there with a couple of mates.* **2** TALKING TO A MAN *UK informal* You call a man 'mate' when you are speaking to him informally. *Thanks, mate.* **3** **BIOLOGY** an animal's sexual partner

mate[2] /meɪt/ *verb* [I] **BIOLOGY** When animals mate, they have sex in order to produce babies.

O-w **material[1]** /məˈtɪəriəl/ *noun* **1** SUBSTANCE [C, U] a solid substance from which things can be made *building materials* ○ *Crude oil is used as the* ***raw material*** *for making plastics.* **2** CLOTH [C, U] cloth for making clothes, curtains, etc *Her dress was made of a soft, silky material.* **3** INFORMATION [U] the facts or ideas in a piece of writing *I'm collecting material for an article that I'm writing.*

material[2] /məˈtɪəriəl/ *adjective* relating to money and possessions and not emotions or thoughts *the* ***material world***

materialism /məˈtɪəriəlɪzəm/ *noun* [U] the belief that having money and possessions is the most important thing in life •**materialistic** /məˌtɪəriəˈlɪstɪk/ *adjective* believing in materialism

materialize (*also UK* **-ise**) /məˈtɪəriəlaɪz/ *verb* [I] If something does not materialize, it does not happen. *She was promised a promotion but it never materialized.*

materials /məˈtɪəriəlz/ *noun* [plural] the equipment that you need for a particular activity *teaching/writing materials*

maternal /məˈtɜːnəl/ *adjective* **1** like a mother *I've never had much of a* ***maternal instinct*** (= wish to have children). **2** **SOCIETY** [always before noun] A maternal relation is part of your mother's family. *He's my maternal grandfather.*

maternity /məˈtɜːnəti/ *adjective* [always before noun] **HEALTH** related to pregnancy and birth ***maternity clothes***

maternity leave /məˈtɜːnətiˌliːv/ *noun* [U] a period of weeks or months that a mother spends away from her usual job so that she can look after a new baby

math /mæθ/ *noun* [U] **MATHEMATICS** *US short for* mathematics

mathematical /ˌmæθəmˈætɪkəl/ *adjective* **MATHEMATICS** relating to mathematics *a mathematical formula/equation* •**mathematically** *adverb*

mathematician /ˌmæθəməˈtɪʃən/ *noun* [C] **MATHEMATICS** someone who studies mathematics

mathematics /mæθəmˈætɪks/ *noun* [U] *formal* **MATHEMATICS** the study or science of numbers and shapes

maths /mæθs/ *noun* [U] **MATHEMATICS** *UK short for* mathematics

matinée /ˈmætɪneɪ/ (US) /mætəˈneɪ/ *noun* [C] an afternoon performance of a play or film

matrimony /ˈmætrɪməni/ *noun* [U] *formal* **SOCIETY** the state of being married

matrix /ˈmeɪtrɪks/ *noun* [C] *plural* **matrixes** or **matrices** **MATHEMATICS** a group of numbers or other symbols arranged in a rectangle which can be used together to solve particular mathematical problems

matron /ˈmeɪtrən/ *noun* [C] **1** **HEALTH** *UK old-fashioned* a female nurse in a school, or a female nurse who is in charge of other nurses in a hospital **2** WOMAN *US* a married woman, especially one who is old or a widow (= woman whose husband has died) **3** PRISON/SCHOOL *US* a woman who is a manager at some hospitals, schools, prisons, etc

matt *UK* (*US* **matte**) /mæt/ *adjective* not shiny *a matt photograph* ○ *matt paint*

WORD PARTNERS FOR ***matter***

consider/discuss/pursue/raise/resolve a matter • **on** the matter (of sth)

O-w **matter[1]** /ˈmætəʳ/ *noun* **1** SUBJECT [C] a subject or situation that you need to think about, discuss, or deal with *I've been thinking about this matter for a long time.* ○ *He denied any knowledge of the matter.* ○ ***To make matters worse,*** *our car broke down!* **2** **PHYSICS** [U] the physical substances that exist in the universe **3** TYPE OF THING [U] a particular type of substance or thing *vegetable matter* ○ *printed matter* **4** **what's the matter** used to ask or talk about the reason for a problem *What's the matter with your leg?* **5** **there's something/nothing the matter** used to say that there is/is not a problem ***There's something the matter with*** *the washing machine.* **6** **a matter of days/weeks/feet, etc** used in expressions describing how small an amount or period of time is *The aircraft missed each other by a matter of feet.* **7** **a matter of confidence/luck/waiting, etc** If something is a matter of confidence/luck/waiting, etc, that is what you need for it to happen. *Learning languages is just a matter of hard work.* **8** **no matter how/what/when, etc** used to emphasize that something cannot be changed

M

I never manage to lose any weight, no matter how hard I try. **9 as a matter of fact** used to emphasize that something is true, especially when it is surprising *As a matter of fact, I used to live next door to him.* **10 a matter of course** If something happens as a matter of course, it always happens as part of the normal process or system. *Babies were tested for the disease as a matter of course.* **11 a matter of life and/or death** a serious situation where people could die *Getting water to these people is a matter of life and death.* **12 it's only a matter of time** If you say that it is only a matter of time before something happens, you are sure it will happen but you do not know when. **13 be no laughing matter** If a subject is no laughing matter, it is serious and not something that people should joke about. ➲See also: **subject matter**

O━**matter²** /ˈmætəʳ/ *verb* [I] to be important, or to affect what happens *It doesn't **matter to** me whether he comes or not.* ○ *"I've forgotten to bring your book back." "It doesn't matter - there's no hurry."*

matter-of-fact /ˌmætərəvˈfækt/ *adjective* not showing emotion when you talk about something *a **matter-of-fact tone/manner*** ●**matter-of-factly** *adverb*

matting /ˈmætɪŋ/ *noun* [U] strong, rough material for covering floors

mattress /ˈmætrəs/ *noun* [C] the soft, comfortable part of a bed that you lie on

M

mature¹ /məˈtjʊəʳ/ *adjective* **1** [AGE] completely grown or developed *sexually mature* ○ *mature trees* **2** [BEHAVIOUR] Mature people behave like adults in a way which shows they are well developed emotionally. *She seems very mature for thirteen.* ➲Opposite **immature**

mature² /məˈtjʊəʳ/ *verb* [I] **1** [AGE] to become completely grown or developed **2** [BEHAVIOUR] to start to behave in a more mature way *Girls mature sooner than boys.* **3 FINANCE** If an investment (= money you have given to a bank or a company in order to make a profit) matures, you receive the money you have made from it.

maˌture ˈstudent *noun* [C] **EDUCATION** a college or university student who is older than the usual age

maturity /məˈtjʊərəti/ *noun* [U] **1** [BEHAVIOUR] the quality of behaving like an adult, in a way which shows that you are well developed emotionally *She shows remarkable maturity for a child of 13.* **2** [AGE] when someone or something is completely grown or developed *Penguins **reach maturity** in late summer.*

maul /mɔːl/ *verb* [T] **1** [INJURE] If you are mauled by an animal, you are injured by its teeth or claws (= the sharp parts of its feet). [**often passive**] *He was mauled by a lion.* **2** [CRITICIZE] to criticize someone or something very badly [**often passive**] *His film was mauled by critics.*

mausoleum /ˌmɔːsəˈliːəm/ *noun* [C] a building where dead people are buried

mauve /məʊv/ *noun* [U] a pale purple colour ●**mauve** *adjective*

maverick /ˈmævᵊrɪk/ *noun* [C] someone who thinks and behaves in an unusual way *a maverick cop/politician*

max¹ /mæks/ *adjective* **1** [AMOUNT] *informal* maximum (= the largest amount allowed or possible), often used after numbers *The trip should take 30 minutes max.* **2 to the max** *informal* as much as possible *He lived life to the max.*

max² *verb*

max out *phrasal verb informal* to use all that is available of something, especially money *We maxed out our credit cards when we bought all that new furniture.*

maxim /ˈmæksɪm/ *noun* [C] **LANGUAGE** a phrase which gives advice *Our company works on the maxim that small is beautiful.*

maximize (*also UK* **-ise**) /ˈmæksɪmaɪz/ *verb* [T] to increase something as much as you can *to maximize profits*

O━**maximum¹** /ˈmæksɪməm/ *adjective* [**always before noun**] The maximum amount of something is the largest amount that is allowed or possible. *the maximum temperature/speed* ➲Opposite **minimum**

> WORD PARTNERS FOR ***maximum***
>
> **reach** a maximum ● a maximum **of** [10/50%, etc] ● **up to** a maximum [of 10/50%, etc]

maximum² /ˈmæksɪməm/ *noun* [**no plural**] the largest amount that is allowed or possible *The school has **a maximum of** 30 students per class.*

O━**may** /meɪ/ *modal verb* **1** [POSSIBLE] used to talk about what is possibly true or will possibly happen *There may be other problems that we don't know about.* ○ *I think I may have a cold.* **2** [PERMISSION] *formal* used to ask or give permission *May I be excused, please?* ○ *You may begin.* **3 may (well) ... but** used to show that the first thing you say is not important when compared to another fact *It may be cheap but it's not very good.* ➲See Extra help page **Modal verbs** on page Centre 34.

> **COMMON LEARNER ERROR**
>
> **may be** or **maybe?**
>
> **May be** is written as two separate words when **be** is used as a verb. Here **may** is being used as a modal verb.
>
> *I may be late this evening.*
>
> ~~*I maybe late this evening.*~~
>
> **Maybe** is an adverb, and is written as one word.
>
> *Maybe we should do it tomorrow.*
>
> ~~*May be we should do it tomorrow.*~~

O━**May** /meɪ/ *noun* [C, U] the fifth month of the year

O━**maybe** /ˈmeɪbi/ *adverb* **1** [POSSIBLY] possibly *Maybe we're too early.* ○ *It could take a month, or maybe more, to complete.* **2** [SUGGEST] used to suggest something *Maybe Ted would like to go.*

mayhem /ˈmeɪhem/ *noun* [U] a situation in which there is no order or control *With five kids running around, it was complete mayhem.*

mayonnaise /ˌmeɪəˈneɪz/ *noun* [U] **FOOD** a thick, cold, white sauce that is made from eggs and oil

mayor /meəʳ/ *noun* [C] **POLITICS** the person who is elected to be the leader of the group that governs a town or city

maze /meɪz/ *noun* [C] a complicated system of paths where you can easily become lost

MB COMPUTING *written abbreviation for* megabyte (= a unit for measuring the amount of information a computer can store) *This program needs 8 MB of hard-disk space.*

MBA /ˌembiːˈeɪ/ *noun* [C] **EDUCATION** *abbreviation for* Master of Business Administration: an advanced degree in business, or a person who has this degree *a Harvard MBA*

McCoy /məˈkɔɪ/ *noun* **the real McCoy** *informal* the real thing, and not a copy or something similar *Cheap sparkling wines cannot be labelled 'champagne' - it has to be the real McCoy.*

MD /ˌemˈdi/ **EDUCATION** *abbreviation for* Doctor of Medicine

O─ **me** /miː/ *pronoun* used after a verb or preposition to refer to the person who is speaking or writing *She gave me some money.* ○ *She never gave it to me.* ○ *Lydia is three years younger than me.* ○ *It wasn't me!*

COMMON LEARNER ERROR

me or **I?**

Me is used after 'than', 'as', or 'be'. It would sound very formal if you used **I**.

She's taller than me.

David is not as tall as me.

"Who's there?" "It's me."

~~*"Who's there?" "It's I."*~~

Sometimes **me** is used with another noun as the subject of a sentence, especially in informal English.

Jane and me went to the cinema yesterday. (informal)

Jane and I went to the cinema yesterday.

meadow /ˈmedəʊ/ *noun* [C] **FARMING** a field of grass, often with flowers

meagre *UK* (*US* **meager**) /ˈmiːgəʳ/ *adjective* not enough in amount *a meagre ration/salary*

WORD PARTNERS FOR ***meal***

cook/eat/have/prepare a meal • a [two/three, etc.] **course** meal

O─ **meal** /miːl/ *noun* [C] **1** when you eat, or the food that you eat at that time *a three-course meal* **2 make a meal of sth** *UK* to spend more time and energy doing something than is necessary *A simple apology will do. There's no need to make a meal of it!* ➲See also: a **square²** meal

mealtime /ˈmiːltaɪm/ *noun* [C] when you eat *These days I only see him at mealtimes.*

O─ **mean¹** /miːn/ *verb* [T] *past* **meant** /ment/ **1** MEANING to have a particular meaning *What does 'perpendicular' mean?* ○ *The red light means stop.* **2** EXPRESS to intend to express a fact or opinion *I didn't* ***mean*** *that* ***as*** *a criticism.* ○ *What exactly do you* ***mean by*** *'old-fashioned'?* **3 mean to do sth** to intend to do something *I didn't mean to hurt her.* **4** RESULT to have a particular result *These changes will mean better health care for everyone.* [+ **(that)**] *It doesn't mean that you can stop working.* **5** SERIOUS to be serious about something that you have said *I'll take that sandwich away if you don't eat it properly - I* ***mean it!*** **6** IMPORTANT to have an important emotional effect on someone *You don't know what it* ***means to*** *me to get this letter.* ○ *Their support has* ***meant a lot*** *to us.* **7 have been meaning to do sth** to have been wanting and planning to do something *I've been meaning to call you for weeks.* **8 be meant to do sth** If you are meant to do something, that is what you should do in order to behave correctly. *You're meant to shake the bottle first.* **9 mean well** to intend to behave in a kind way *I know my parents mean well, but I wish they wouldn't interfere.* **10 I mean a** CONTINUING SENTENCE something that people often say before they continue their sentence *I mean, I don't dislike her.* **b** CORRECTING YOURSELF something that you say in order to correct yourself *We went there in May - I mean June.*

mean² /miːn/ *adjective* **1** UNKIND unkind and unpleasant *I thought my sister was being* ***mean to*** *me.* **2** NOT GENEROUS *mainly UK* A mean person does not like spending money, especially on other people. *He's too mean to buy her a ring.* **3** VIOLENT *mainly US* A mean person or animal is strong and violent, and makes people frightened. *He's a big, mean guy.* **4** GOOD [**always before noun**] *informal* very good *I make a mean spaghetti.* **5 MATHEMATICS** [**always before noun**] In maths, a mean number is an average number. *Their mean age at death was 84.6.* **6 no mean** used to describe something very difficult *Setting up a business in two days was* ***no mean feat*** (= was a difficult thing to do).

mean³ /miːn/ *noun* [**no plural**] *formal* **MATHEMATICS** the average

meander /miˈændəʳ/ *verb* **1 meander along/around/through, etc** If a river, a road, or a line of something meanders, it has many curves. *The coast road meanders along the beach for miles.* ➲See picture at **oxbow lake** **2 meander around/from/off, etc** to move around with no clear purpose *We meandered around town for a couple of hours.*

WORD PARTNERS FOR ***meaning***

different/hidden/precise/real/true meaning • **convey/explain/grasp/understand** the meaning of sth

O─ **meaning** /ˈmiːnɪŋ/ *noun* **1** EXPRESS [**C, U**] The meaning of words, signs, or actions is what they express or represent. *The word 'squash' has several meanings.* ○ *The meaning of her gesture was clear.* **2** PURPOSE [**U, no plural**] purpose or emotional importance *She felt that her life had no meaning.*

meaningful /ˈmiːnɪŋfəl/ *adjective* **1** USEFUL useful, serious, or important *a meaningful discussion* **2** WITH MEANING having a clear meaning which people can understand *a meaningful comparison/conclusion* **3** LOOK intended to show a meaning, often secretly *a* ***meaningful look*** •**meaningfully** *adverb*

meaningless /ˈmiːnɪŋləs/ *adjective* without any meaning or purpose *He produced yet another set of meaningless statistics.*

M

WORD PARTNERS FOR *means*

(as) a means of (doing) sth • the means **by which** sth happens/sb does sth

O-- **means** /miːnz/ *noun* **1** METHOD [C] *plural* **means** a way of doing something *We had no **means of** communication.* ○ *It was a means of making money.* **2** MONEY [**plural**] money *We don't have the means to buy the house.* **3 by no means; not by any means** not at all *I'm not an expert by any means.* **4 by all means** something that you say when you are agreeing to let someone do something *I have a copy of the report on my desk. By all means have a look at it.*

means-tested /ˈmiːnztestɪd/ *adjective mainly UK* If an amount of money or an activity such as education is means-tested, it is only given to people who are poor enough. *means-tested benefits*

meant /ment/ *past of* mean

meantime /ˈmiːnˌtaɪm/ *noun* **in the meantime** in the time between two things happening, or while something else is happening *Your computer won't be arriving till Friday. In the meantime, you can use Julie's.*

O-- **meanwhile** /ˈmiːnˌwaɪl/ *adverb* in the time between two things happening, or while something else is happening *The mother is ill. The child, meanwhile, is living with foster parents.*

measles /ˈmiːzlz/ *noun* [U] **HEALTH** an infectious disease which covers your skin in small, red spots ➲See also: **German measles**

M

measurable /ˈmeʒᵊrəbl/ *adjective* If something is measurable, it is big enough to be measured. *Extra training has led to measurable improvements in performance.* ➲Opposite **immeasurable**

O-- **measure**[1] /ˈmeʒəʳ/ *verb* **1** JUDGE [T] to judge the quality, effect, importance, or value of something *We will soon be able to measure the results of these policy changes.* ○ *They measured the performance of three different engines.* **2** FIND SIZE [T] to find the size, weight, amount, or speed of something *I've measured all the windows.* ○ *The distances were **measured in** kilometres.* **3** BE SIZE [I] to be a certain size *a whale measuring around 60 feet in length*

measure sth out *phrasal verb* to weigh or measure a small amount of something and remove it from a larger amount *Use a hot spoon to measure out honey into a bowl.*

measure up *phrasal verb* to be good enough, or as good as something or someone else *He did not **measure up to** the requirements of the job.*

O-- **measure**[2] /ˈmeʒəʳ/ *noun* **1** METHOD [C] a way of achieving something or dealing with a situation *This arrangement is only a **temporary measure**.* ○ *We must **take** preventative **measures** to stop the spread of the disease.* ○ ***security measures*** **2 a measure of sth** a good way of judging something *Ticket sales are not necessarily a measure of the show's popularity.* **3 a/some measure of sth** *formal* an amount of something *Bulletproof vests give some measure of protection.* **4** SIZE [U] a way of measuring something *The basic units of measure we use are distance, time, and mass.* **5 for good measure** as well as something you have already done or given to someone *They stole his passport and wallet, and for good measure beat him unconscious.* ➲See also: **tape measure**

O-- **measurement** /ˈmeʒəmənt/ *noun* **1** PROCESS [U] the process of measuring something **2** SIZE [C] the size and shape of something *I've **taken measurements** of all the rooms.* **3** WAY OF MEASURING [U] a way of measuring something *SI units are the standard **units of measurement** used all over the world.*

O-- **meat** /miːt/ *noun* [U] **FOOD** muscles and other soft parts of animals, used as food *I don't eat meat.* ○ ***red/white meat*** ➲See colour picture **Food** on page Centre 11

mecca /ˈmekə/ *noun* [**no plural**] a place where particular groups of people like to go because they feel happy there *His Indiana bookstore became **a mecca for** writers and artists.*

mechanic /mɪˈkænɪk/ *noun* [C] someone whose job is to repair machines *a car mechanic*

mechanical /mɪˈkænɪkᵊl/ *adjective* **1** MACHINE relating to or operated by machines *a mechanical engineer* ○ *a mechanical device* **2** BEHAVIOUR If you do something in a mechanical way, you do it without emotion or without thinking about it. *a mechanical performance* •**mechanically** *adverb*

meˌchanical diˈgestion *noun* [U] **BIOLOGY** the parts of the process of digestion where food is broken up by being bitten and chewed

mechanics /mɪˈkænɪks/ *noun* [U] **PHYSICS** the study of physical forces on objects and their movement

mechanism /ˈmekənɪzᵊm/ *noun* [C] **1** PART OF EQUIPMENT a part of a piece of equipment that does a particular job *The clock's winding mechanism had broken.* **2** SYSTEM a system for achieving something, or the way that a system works *We need a **mechanism for** resolving this sort of dispute.*

mechanized (*also UK* **-ised**) /ˈmekənaɪzd/ *adjective* A mechanized organization or activity uses machines. *mechanized farming/production*

medal /ˈmedᵊl/ *noun* [C] a metal disc given as a prize in a competition or given to someone who has been very brave *a bronze medal* ○ *an **Olympic medal*** ➲See also: **gold medal, silver medal**

medallist *UK* (*US* **medalist**) /ˈmedᵊlɪst/ *noun* [C] **SPORT** someone who has received a medal in a sports event *an **Olympic medallist***

meddle /ˈmedl/ *verb* [I] to try to influence people or change things that are not your responsibility *He's always **meddling in** other people's business.*

the media /ˈmiːdiə/ *noun* [**group**] television, newspapers, magazines, and radio considered as a group ***media coverage/attention*** ○ *The issue has been much discussed **in the media**.* ➲See also: **the mass media**

mediaeval /mediˈiːvᵊl/ *adjective another spelling of* medieval (= relating to the period in Europe between about AD 500 and AD 1500)

median /ˈmiːdiən/ *adjective* [**always before noun**] **MATHEMATICS** relating to the middle number or amount in a series *the median age/income*

mediate /ˈmiːdieɪt/ *verb* [I, T] to try to find a solution between two or more people who disagree about something *Negotiators were called in to **mediate between** the two sides.* •**mediation** /ˌmiːdiˈeɪʃᵊn/ *noun* [U]

mediator /ˈmiːdieɪtəʳ/ *noun* [C] someone who mediates between people who disagree about something

medic /ˈmedɪk/ *noun* [C] *informal* **1 HEALTH** a medical student or doctor **2 HEALTH** *US* someone who does medical work in a military organization

O-■ **medical¹** /ˈmedɪkᵊl/ *adjective* **HEALTH** relating to medicine and different ways of curing illness ***medical treatment*** ○ *a **medical student*** ○ *She has a **medical condition** that makes it hard for her to work.* •**medically** *adverb*

medical² /ˈmedɪkᵊl/ *UK* (*US* **physical**) *noun* [C] **HEALTH** an examination of your body by a doctor to find out if you are healthy

medicated /ˈmedɪkeɪtɪd/ *adjective* **HEALTH** A medicated substance contains medicine. *medicated soap*

medication /ˌmedɪˈkeɪʃᵊn/ *noun* [C, U] **HEALTH** medicine that is used to treat an illness *He's **on medication** to control his depression.*

medicinal /məˈdɪsɪnᵊl/ *adjective* **HEALTH** Medicinal substances are used to cure illnesses. *I keep some brandy for **medicinal purposes**.*

WORD PARTNERS FOR ***medicine***

take medicine • a medicine for sth

O-■ **medicine** /ˈmedɪsᵊn/ *noun* **1 HEALTH** [C, U] a substance used to cure an illness or injury *cough medicine* ○ *Have you **taken** your **medicine** today?* **2 HEALTH** [U] the science of curing and preventing illness and injury *to study medicine* ○ *western/Chinese medicine*

medieval (*also* **mediaeval**) /ˌmediˈiːvᵊl/ *adjective* relating to the period in Europe between about AD 500 and AD 1500 *medieval literature/art*

mediocre /ˌmiːdiˈəʊkəʳ/ *adjective* not good in quality *The acting was mediocre.* •**mediocrity** /ˌmiːdiˈɒkrəti/ *noun* [U]

meditate /ˈmedɪteɪt/ *verb* [I] **1** RELAX to think calm thoughts for a long period in order to relax or as a religious activity *I meditate twice a day.* **2** THINK *formal* to think seriously about something *He **meditated on** the consequences of his decision.* •**meditation** /ˌmedɪˈteɪʃᵊn/ *noun* [U] *Let's spend a few moments **in quiet meditation**.*

the Mediterranean /ˌmedɪtᵊrˈeɪniən/ *noun* the sea that has southern Europe, northern Africa, and the Middle East around it, or the countries around this sea •**Mediterranean** *adjective a Mediterranean climate/island*

O-■ **medium¹** /ˈmiːdiəm/ *adjective* **MATHEMATICS** in the middle of a group of different amounts or sizes *people of medium weight* ○ *She bought a **medium-sized** car.* ○ *The shirt comes in small, medium, and large.*

medium² /ˈmiːdiəm/ *noun* [C] *plural* **media** or **mediums** a way of communicating or expressing something *the medium of television/radio* ○ *The Internet has become yet another **medium** for marketing.*

medium-term /ˈmiːdiəmˌtɜːm/ *adjective* continuing into the future for a time that is neither short nor long *The medium-term outlook remains favourable.*

medley /ˈmedli/ *noun* [C] **MUSIC** a mixture of different items, especially songs *She sang **a medley of** show tunes.*

medulla oblongata /meˌdʌləɒblɒŋˈgɑːtə/ *noun* [C usually singular] *plural* **medulla oblongatas** or **medullae oblongatae** **ANATOMY** the lowest part of the brain, that controls the way the heart works, breathing, etc. ➲See picture at **brain**

meek /miːk/ *adjective* Someone who is meek is quiet and does not argue with others. •**meekly** *adverb*

O-■ **meet¹** /miːt/ *verb past* **met** /met/ **1** COME TOGETHER [I, T] to come to the same place as someone else by arrangement or by chance *We met for coffee last Sunday.* ○ *I met my old English teacher while trekking in the Alps.* ○ *Each student **meets with** an adviser at the start of the school year.* **2** INTRODUCE [I, T] to see and speak to someone for the first time *I've always wanted to meet a movie star.* ○ *"This is Helen." "Pleased to meet you."* ➲See Common Learner Error at **know** **3** GROUP [I] If a group of people meet, they come to a place in order to do something. *The shareholders meet once a year to discuss profits.* **4** PLACE [T] to wait at a place for someone or something to arrive *They met me at the airport.* **5** ENOUGH [T] to be a big enough amount or of a good enough quality for something *This old building will never meet the new fire regulations.* ○ *Can your product **meet the needs** of a wide range of consumers?* **6** ACHIEVE [T] to be able to achieve something *He **met** every **goal** he set for himself.* ○ *to **meet** a **deadline*** **7** JOIN [I, T] to join something *There's a large crack where the ceiling meets the wall.* ➲See also: make ends (**end¹**) meet

meet up *phrasal verb* **1** MEET SOMEONE to meet another person in order to do something together *I **met up with** a few friends yesterday.* **2** ROADS/PATHS JOIN If roads or paths meet up, they join at a particular place. *This path **meets up with** the main road.*

meet with sth *phrasal verb* to cause a particular reaction or result *Both proposals have met with fierce opposition.* ○ *formal* I trust the arrangements ***meet with your approval*** (= I hope that you like them).

meet² /miːt/ *noun* [C] **SPORT** *US* a sports competition *a swim/track meet* ○ *His final jump set a new **meet record**.*

WORD PARTNERS FOR ***meeting***

arrange/attend/chair/convene/have/hold a meeting • an **emergency/private/recent/urgent** meeting • a meeting **between** sb • **be in** a meeting

O-■ **meeting** /ˈmiːtɪŋ/ *noun* [C] **1** an event where people come together for a reason, usually to discuss something *We're **having a meeting** on Thursday to discuss the problem.* ○ *He's **in a meeting** - I'll ask him to call you back later.* **2** **SPORT** *UK* a sporting competition *an international meeting*

M

mega- /megə-/ *prefix* **1** *informal* extremely *megarich* (= extremely rich) **2 MEASURES** one million *40 megabytes*

megabyte /ˈmegəbaɪt/ (*written abbreviation* **MB**) *noun* [C] **COMPUTING** a unit for measuring the amount of information a computer can store, equal to 1,000,000 bytes

megahertz /ˈmegəhɜːts/ (*written abbreviation* **MHz**) *noun* [C] *plural* **megahertz MEASURES** a unit of measurement of sound waves which is equal to a million hertz

megaphone /ˈmegəfəʊn/ *noun* [C] a thing that you hold in your hand and speak into to make your voice louder

megapixel /ˈmegəˌpɪksᵊl/ *noun* [C] **COMPUTING** one million pixels (= small points that form part of the image on a computer screen), used to describe the amount of detail in images made by a digital camera, computer screen, etc

megawatt /ˈmegəwɒt/ *noun* [C] **MEASURES** a unit for measuring electrical power, equal to 1,000,000 watts

meiosis /maɪˈəʊsɪs/ *noun* [U] **BIOLOGY** the type of cell division in which one cell divides into four gametes (= male or female cells that join to form an organism), each with a different mixture of chromosomes and half the number contained in the original cell ➲Compare **mitosis**

M

melancholy /ˈmelənkɒli/ *adjective formal* sad *a melancholy expression* •**melancholy** *noun* [U] *formal* a feeling of sadness

melanin /ˈmelənɪn/ *noun* [U] **BIOLOGY** a substance in the skin and hair that makes the skin go darker in the sun

melanoma /ˌmeləˈnəʊmə/ *noun* [C] **HEALTH** a type of skin cancer (= a serious disease) that appears as a coloured mark on the skin

melatonin /meləˈtəʊnɪn/ *noun* [U] **BIOLOGY** a hormone (= chemical that controls the body's growth and development) in the body which produces changes in skin colour

melee /ˈmeleɪ/ *noun* [C] a situation where many people are behaving in a noisy, confused, and sometimes violent way ***In the melee*** *his jaw was broken.*

mellow¹ /ˈmeləʊ/ *adjective* **1** PLEASANT pleasant and soft *a mellow voice* ○ *a mellow flavour/wine* **2** CALM calm and relaxed *After a few drinks, he became very mellow.*

mellow² /ˈmeləʊ/ *verb* [I, T] to become more relaxed and gentle, or to make someone become more relaxed and gentle *Age has mellowed him.*

melodic /məˈlɒdɪk/ *adjective* **MUSIC** Melodic music has a pleasant tune, and melodic sounds are pleasant and like music.

melodrama /ˈmeləʊˌdrɑːmə/ *noun* [C, U] **LITERATURE** a story in which the characters show much stronger emotions than in real life

melodramatic /ˌmeləʊdrəˈmætɪk/ *adjective* showing much stronger emotions than are necessary for a situation *Don't be so melodramatic! It's only a scratch.*

melody /ˈmelədi/ *noun* [C] **MUSIC** a song or tune

melon /ˈmelən/ *noun* [C, U] **FOOD** a large, round, sweet fruit with a thick, green or yellow skin and a lot of seeds ➲See colour picture **Fruit and Vegetables** on page Centre 10

O-ꟸ**melt** /melt/ *verb* **1 PHYSICS** [I, T] If something melts, it changes from a solid into a liquid because of heat and if you melt something, you heat it until it becomes liquid. *The sun soon melted the ice on the pond.* ○ *The chocolate had melted in my pocket.* ○ *melted cheese* **2** [I] to start to feel love or sympathy, especially after feeling angry *When he smiles at me, I just melt.* ➲See also: **butter¹** wouldn't melt in sb's mouth

melt away *phrasal verb* to disappear *Then I saw her and all my fears just melted away.*

melt sth down *phrasal verb* If you melt something down, especially a metal object, you heat it until it changes to liquid.

meltdown /ˈmeltdaʊn/ *noun* [C, U] **1** FAILURE *informal* a situation of complete failure and no control ***economic meltdown*** **2** NUCLEAR POWER a serious accident in which nuclear fuel melts through its container and escapes into the environment

ˈmelting ˌpoint *noun* [C usually singular] **MEASURES** the temperature at which a substance melts

ˈmelting ˌpot *noun* [C] a place where people of many different races and from different countries live together

meltwater /ˈmeltwɔːtəʳ/ *noun* [U] **GEOGRAPHY** water made from melted snow or ice

O-ꟸ**member** /ˈmembəʳ/ *noun* [C] a person who belongs to a group or an organization ***family/staff members*** ○ *He was a member of the university rowing club.*

ˌMember of ˈParliament *noun* [C] *plural* **Members of Parliament POLITICS** a person who has been elected to represent people in their country's parliament

WORD PARTNERS FOR ***membership***

apply for membership • membership **of/in** sth • a membership **card/fee**

membership /ˈmembəʃɪp/ *noun* **1** BELONGING [C, U] the state of belonging to a group or an organization *I've* ***applied for membership*** *of the union.* ○ *a* ***membership card/fee*** **2** PEOPLE [group] the people who belong to a group or an organization *Union membership is now over three million and rising.*

membrane /ˈmembreɪn/ *noun* [C] **ANATOMY, BIOLOGY** a thin sheet of tissue that covers some parts inside the body in order to protect, connect or separate them ➲See picture at **cell** ➲See picture at **egg**

memento /mɪˈmentəʊ/ *noun* [C] *plural* **mementos** or **mementoes** an object that you keep to remember a person, place, or event

memo /ˈmeməʊ/ *noun* [C] a written message sent from one member of an organization to another

memoirs /ˈmemwɑːz/ *noun* [plural] a written story of a person's own life and experiences

memorabilia /ˌmemᵊrəˈbɪliə/ *noun* [plural] objects relating to famous people or events that people collect *an auction of pop memorabilia*

memorable /ˈmemᵊrəbl/ *adjective* If an occasion is memorable, you will remember it for a long time because it is so good. *a memorable performance* •**memorably** *adverb*

memorandum /ˌmemᵊrˈændəm/ *noun plural* **memoranda** *formal* a memo

memorial /məˈmɔːriəl/ *noun* [C] an object, often made of stone, that is built to help people remember an important person or event *a **war memorial** ○ a **memorial service***

memorize (*also UK* **-ise**) /ˈmemᵊraɪz/ *verb* [T] to learn something so that you remember it exactly *I've memorized all my friends' birthdays.*

WORD PARTNERS FOR ***memory***

have a bad /good memory • **have** a [good, amazing, etc] memory **for** sth • a **photographic** memory

O— **memory** /ˈmemᵊri/ *noun* **1** ABILITY [C, U] your ability to remember *John has an amazing **memory for** historical facts. ○ She had a **photographic memory*** (= was able to remember every detail). **2** THOUGHT [C] something that you remember [**usually plural**] *I have fond **memories of** my childhood.* **3** MIND [C, U] the part of your mind that stores what you remember *He recited the poem **from memory**.* **4 in memory of sb** If you do something in memory of a dead person, you do it to show your respect or love for them. *They built a statue in memory of those who died in the fire.* **5 COMPUTING** [C, U] the part of a computer where information and instructions are stored, or the amount of information that can be stored there *You need 32 megabytes of memory to run this software.*

ˈ**memory** ˌ**card** *noun* [C] **COMPUTING** a device for storing information in computers or digital cameras

ˈ**Memory** ˌ**Stick** *noun* [C] *trademark* **COMPUTING** a small electronic device designed to store information that can be put into a computer, mobile phone, etc

men /men/ *plural of* man

menace¹ /ˈmenɪs/ *noun* **1** DANGER [C] something that is likely to cause harm [**usually singular**] *Drunk drivers are **a menace to** everyone.* **2** QUALITY [U] a dangerous quality that makes you think someone is going to do something bad *His eyes were cold and filled with menace.*

menace² /ˈmenɪs/ *verb* [T] *formal* to cause harm to someone or something, or be likely to cause harm *Hurricane Bonnie continues to menace the east coast.*

menacing /ˈmenɪsɪŋ/ *adjective* making you think that someone is going to do something bad *a menacing gesture/voice*

mend¹ /mend/ *verb* [T] to repair something that is broken, torn, or not working correctly *I've mended that hole in your skirt for you.*

mend² /mend/ *noun* **be on the mend HEALTH** *informal* If you are on the mend, your health is improving after an illness.

mendacious /menˈdeɪʃəs/ *adjective formal* not telling the truth

menial /ˈmiːniəl/ *adjective* Menial work is boring, and not well paid or respected. *a **menial job/task***

meninges /məˈnɪndʒiːz/ *noun* [**plural**] **ANATOMY, BIOLOGY** the three membranes (= thin layers) that surround the brain and the spinal cord (= nerves inside the spine that connect to the brain)

meningitis /ˌmenɪnˈdʒaɪtɪs/ *noun* [U] **HEALTH** a serious infectious disease that affects a person's brain and spinal cord (= the nerves in your back)

meniscus /məˈnɪskəs/ *noun* [C] *plural* **meniscuses** or **menisci** **1 ANATOMY, BIOLOGY** a curved piece of cartilage (= strong elastic substance) inside a place where two bones are connected in the body such as the knee **2** on a liquid, a surface that curves either out or in as a result of surface tension (= the way the surface is held tight) ⊃See picture at **potometer**

menopause /ˈmenəʊpɔːz/ *noun* [U] **HEALTH** the time, usually between the ages of 45 and 55, when a woman gradually stops having periods (= monthly blood from the uterus)

Menshevik /ˈmenʃəvɪk/ *noun* [C] **POLITICS** a supporter of a political group formed in Russia in 1903 when it broke away from Lenin and the Bolsheviks •**Menshevik** *adjective*

ˈ**men's** ˌ**room** *noun* [C] *US* a room in a public place where there are men's toilets ⊃See Common Learner Error at **toilet**

menstrual /ˈmenstruəl/ *adjective* [**always before noun**] *formal* **BIOLOGY** relating to menstruating *a **menstrual cycle***

menstruate /ˈmenstrueɪt/ *verb* [I] *formal* **BIOLOGY** to have a monthly flow of blood from the uterus •**menstruation** /ˌmenstruˈeɪʃᵊn/ *noun* [U]

mensuration /ˌmenʃᵊrˈeɪʃᵊn/ *noun* [U] *formal* **MEASURES** the act or process of measuring

O— **mental** /ˈmentᵊl/ *adjective* [**always before noun**] relating to the mind, or involving the process of thinking ***mental health/illness*** •**mentally** *adverb a **mentally ill** person*

mentality /menˈtæləti/ *noun* [C] a person's opinions or way of thinking *I can't understand the mentality of people who hunt animals for fun.*

O— **mention¹** /ˈmenʃᵊn/ *verb* [T] **1** to briefly speak or write about something or someone *I'll mention your ideas to Caroline. ○ She didn't mention her daughter.* [+ (**that**)] *He mentioned that he liked skydiving.* **2 not to mention** used to emphasize the importance of something that you are adding to a list *The resort has great hotels and restaurants, not to mention some of the best skiing in the region.*

COMMON LEARNER ERROR

mention

No preposition is normally needed after the verb **mention**.

He didn't mention the price.

~~*He didn't mention about the price.*~~

WORD PARTNERS FOR ***mention (noun)***

deserve/get/be worth a mention • **make no** mention **of** sth • a **brief/passing/special** mention • mention **of** sth

M

mention² /ˈmenʃᵊn/ *noun* [C] a brief remark *The report **made no mention of** the problem.*

mentor /ˈmentɔːʳ/ *noun* [C] *formal* an experienced person who gives help and advice to someone with less experience

O-- **menu** /ˈmenjuː/ *noun* [C] **1** a list of food and drinks that you can order in a restaurant *a lunch/dinner menu* ○ *I ordered the most expensive thing **on the menu*** (= available in the restaurant). **2** **COMPUTING** a list that appears on a computer screen of the choices available in a computer program *a **pop-up menu***

ˈmenu ˌbar *noun* [C] **COMPUTING** a long, narrow area, usually at the top of a computer screen, that contains computer menus

ˈmenu ˌoption *noun* [C] **COMPUTING** one of the choices on a computer menu

meow /miːˈaʊ/ *noun* [C] *US spelling of* miaow (= the sound that a cat makes)

MEP /ˌemiːˈpiː/ *noun* [C] **POLITICS** *abbreviation for* Member of European Parliament: a person who represents an area of a European country in the European Parliament *the MEP for Glasgow*

mercenary¹ /ˈmɜːsᵊnᵊri/ *noun* [C] a soldier who fights for any country or organization who pays them

mercenary² /ˈmɜːsᵊnᵊri/ *adjective* interested only in getting money or an advantage from a situation

merchandise /ˈmɜːtʃᵊndaɪz/ *noun* [U] *formal* goods that are traded, or sold in shops *We stock a broad range of merchandise.*

merchandising /ˈmɜːtʃᵊndaɪzɪŋ/ *noun* [U] the selling of products relating to films, television programmes, and famous people

merchant¹ /ˈmɜːtʃᵊnt/ *noun* [C] *formal* someone whose job is buying and selling goods, usually in large amounts *a wine/grain merchant*

merchant² /ˈmɜːtʃᵊnt/ *adjective* [**always before noun**] relating to trading of large amounts of goods *a merchant ship/seaman*

ˌmerchant ˈbank *noun* [C] **ECONOMICS** a bank that organizes investments in companies or lends money to them •**merchant banker** *noun* [C]

mercifully /ˈmɜːsɪfᵊli/ *adverb informal* used to show that you are pleased that something unpleasant has been avoided *Her illness was mercifully short.*

merciless /ˈmɜːsɪləs/ *adjective* cruel, or showing no kindness *a merciless attack* ○ *She was merciless in her criticism of his work.* •**mercilessly** *adverb*

Mercury /ˈmɜːkjᵊri/ *noun* [**no plural**] **ASTRONOMY** the planet that is closest to the Sun, before Venus ➲See picture at **solar system**

mercury /ˈmɜːkjᵊri/ *noun* [U] **CHEMISTRY** a heavy, silver-coloured metal that is liquid at ordinary temperatures (formula **Hg**)

WORD PARTNERS FOR ***mercy***

ask for/beg for/plead for mercy • **show (no)** mercy

mercy /ˈmɜːsi/ *noun* [U] **1** kindness that makes you forgive someone, usually someone that you have authority over *The judge **showed no mercy**.* **2** **be at the mercy of sth/sb** to not be able to protect yourself from something or someone that you cannot control *Farmers are often at the mercy of the weather.*

mere /mɪəʳ/ *adjective* [**always before noun**] **1** used to emphasize that something is not large or important *It costs a mere twenty dollars.* ○ *The **mere thought of*** (= Just thinking about) *eating octopus makes me feel sick.* **2** **the merest** used to emphasize that something is small, often when it has an important effect *She's upset by **the merest hint of** criticism.*

merely /ˈmɪəli/ *adverb* **1** [WHAT YOU SAY] used to emphasize that you mean exactly what you are saying and nothing more *I'm not arguing with you - I'm merely explaining the problem.* **2** [NOT LARGE] used to emphasize that something is not large, important, or effective when compared to something else *The medicine doesn't make you better, it merely stops the pain.*

merge /mɜːdʒ/ *verb* [**I, T**] If two or more things merge, they combine or join, and if you merge two or more things, you combine or join them. *The two companies merged, forming the largest brewery in Canada.* ○ *The city's smaller libraries will be **merged into** a large, central one.*

merger /ˈmɜːdʒəʳ/ *noun* [**C, U**] when two or more companies or organizations join together

meringue /məˈræŋ/ *noun* [**C, U**] **FOOD** a light, sweet food that is made by baking the white part of an egg mixed with sugar

meristem /ˈmeristem/ *noun* [C] **BIOLOGY** a tissue (= substance plants and animals are made of) with cells that divide, found in the parts of plants where growth happens

merit¹ /ˈmerɪt/ *noun* [**C, U**] *formal* good qualities which deserve praise *His ideas **have merit**.* ○ *We debated **the merits of** using television in the classroom.* ○ *Every application has to be judged **on its own merits*** (= judged by considering the qualities of each).

merit² /ˈmerɪt/ *verb* [T] *formal* to be important enough to receive attention or punishment *Her crimes were serious enough to merit a prison sentence.*

mermaid /ˈmɜːmeɪd/ *noun* [C] an imaginary creature that lives in the sea and has the upper body of a woman and the tail of a fish

merry /ˈmeri/ *adjective* showing enjoyment and happiness *a merry laugh* ○ ***Merry Christmas!*** •**merrily** *adverb*

mesh¹ /meʃ/ *noun* [**C, U**] material that is like a net and is made of wire, plastic, or thread *a wire mesh fence*

mesh² /meʃ/ *verb* [I] If two or more things mesh, they are suitable for each other. *Her ideas **mesh** well **with** our plans for the future.*

mesophyll /ˈmesəʊfɪl/ *noun* [U] **BIOLOGY** the part of a leaf between the two thin surface layers, containing the cells responsible for photosynthesis (= making food from the sun)

the mesosphere /ˈmesəʊsfɪər/ *noun* [**no plural**] **GEOGRAPHY** the layer of gases surrounding the Earth at a height of between 50 and 100 kilometres, above the stratosphere and below the thermosphere

WORD PARTNERS FOR ***mess***

make a mess • **clean up/clear up** a mess • be **in** a mess

O⊸**mess¹** /mes/ *noun* [**C**] **1** UNTIDY Someone or something that is a mess, or is in a mess, is dirty or untidy. [**usually singular**] *My hair's such a mess!* ○ *The house is* ***in a mess****.* ○ *Don't* ***make a mess*** *in the kitchen!* **2** DIFFICULT a confused or difficult situation [**usually singular**] *She told me that her life was a mess.* ○ *If he hadn't lied, he wouldn't be* ***in this mess*** *now.* **3 make a mess of sth** to damage or spoil something *He made a mess of his first marriage.* **4** MILITARY a place where members of the armed forces eat [**usually singular**] *the officers' mess*

mess² /mes/ *verb*
mess about/around *phrasal verb informal* **1** WASTE TIME to waste time, often by doing things that are not important *Stop messing around and do your homework!* **2** PLAY to spend time playing and doing things with no particular purpose *I can spend hours* ***messing around with*** *my computer.*
mess sb about/around *phrasal verb UK informal* to treat someone badly, often by not doing something that you have promised
mess about/around with sth *phrasal verb informal* to use or treat something in a careless or harmful way *Who's been messing around with my computer?*
mess sth up *phrasal verb* **1** MAKE UNTIDY to make something untidy or dirty *I hate wearing hats - they always mess up my hair.* **2** SPOIL to spoil something, or to do something badly *Don't try to cook lunch by yourself - you'll only mess it up.*
mess with sb/sth *phrasal verb informal* to become involved with someone or something dangerous *If you mess with drugs, you're asking for trouble.*

WORD PARTNERS FOR ***message***

get/leave/send/take a message • a message **for/from** sb

O⊸**message¹** /ˈmesɪdʒ/ *noun* [**C**] **1** INFORMATION a piece of written or spoken information which one person gives to another *Did you* ***get*** *my* ***message****?* ○ *I* ***left*** *her several* ***messages****, but she hasn't returned my call.* **2** IDEA the most important idea of a film, book, etc *The book conveys a complex message.* **3 get the message** *informal* to understand what someone wants you to do by their actions *Don't return any of his calls - he'll soon get the message and leave you alone.*

message² /ˈmesɪdʒ/ *verb* [**T**] **COMPUTING, INTERNET** to send someone an email or text message (= a written message sent from one mobile phone to another)

ˈ**message** ˌ**board** *noun* [**C**] **COMPUTING, INTERNET** a place on a website where you can leave messages for other people to read

messenger /ˈmesɪndʒəʳ/ *noun* [**C**] someone who takes a message between two people

the Messiah /məˈsaɪə/ *noun* **1 RELIGION** Jesus Christ **2 RELIGION** the leader that Jews believe God will send them

Messrs /ˈmesəz/ *noun formal* a title used before the names of two or more men *Messrs Davis and Dixon led the discussion on tax reform.*

messy /ˈmesi/ *adjective* **1** UNTIDY untidy or dirty *messy hair* ○ *a messy house/car* ○ *My son's bedroom is always messy.* **2** UNPLEASANT unpleasant and complicated *Ian's just gone through a* ***messy divorce****.*

met /met/ *past of* meet

metabolism /məˈtæbəlɪzəm/ *noun* [**C**] **BIOLOGY** all the chemical processes in your body, especially the ones that use food

O⊸**metal** /ˈmetəl/ *noun* [**C, U**] **PHYSICS** a usually hard, shiny material such as iron, gold, or silver which heat and electricity can travel through *scrap metal* ○ *Metals are used for making machinery and tools.* ○ *a metal sheet/bar* •**metallic** /məˈtælɪk/ *adjective* having a quality that is similar to metal *a metallic paint/taste* ⊃See also: **heavy metal**

metalloid /ˈmetəlɔɪd/ *noun* [**C**] **CHEMISTRY** a chemical element with some of the properties of a metal and some of a non-metal, for example silicon and arsenic

metamorphic /ˌmetəˈmɔːfɪk/ *adjective* **GEOLOGY** (of rock) changed into a new form and structure by very great heat and pressure ⊃Compare **igneous, sedimentary**

metamorphosis /ˌmetəˈmɔːfəsɪs/ *noun plural* **metamorphoses** /metəˈmɔːfəsiːz/ **1** [**C**] a gradual change into something very different *The past year has seen a complete metamorphosis of the country's economy.* **2 BIOLOGY** [**U**] in biology, the process by which the young forms of some animals, such as insects, develop into very different adult forms *Caterpillars changing into butterflies is an example of metamorphosis.*

metaphor /ˈmetəfəʳ/ *noun* [**C, U**] **LANGUAGE, LITERATURE** a way of describing something by comparing it with something else which has some of the same qualities *She used a computer metaphor to explain how the human brain works.* •**metaphorical** /ˌmetəˈfɒrɪkəl/ *adjective* using a metaphor

mete /miːt/ *verb* **meting**, *past* **meted**
mete sth out *phrasal verb formal* to punish someone [**often passive**] *Long jail sentences are* ***meted out to*** *drug smugglers.*

meteor /ˌmiːtiəʳ/ *noun* [**C**] **ASTRONOMY** a rock from outer space which becomes very hot and burns brightly in the sky at night as it enters Earth's atmosphere (= air surrounding Earth)

meteoric /ˌmiːtiˈɒrɪk/ *adjective* If the development of something is meteoric, it happens very quickly or causes great success. *a meteoric career* ○ *The band's rise to fame was meteoric.*

meteorite /ˈmiːtiəraɪt/ *noun* [**C**] **ASTRONOMY** a piece of rock from outer space which has fallen on Earth's surface

M

meteorological /ˌmiːtiərəˈlɒdʒɪkəl/ *adjective* [always before noun] GEOGRAPHY relating to the scientific study of weather

meteorologist /ˌmiːtiərˈɒlədʒɪst/ *noun* [C] GEOGRAPHY someone who studies weather, especially to say how it will be in the near future •**meteorology** *noun* [U] the scientific study of weather

meter /ˈmiːtər/ *noun* [C] **1** a piece of equipment for measuring the amount of something such as electricity, time, or light *a gas/water meter* ○ *a parking/taxi meter* **2** MEASURES *US spelling of* metre

methadone /ˈmeθədəʊn/ *noun* [U] HEALTH a drug for treating people who want to stop using heroin (= an illegal drug)

methane /ˈmiːθeɪn/ (US) /ˈmeθeɪn/ *noun* [U] CHEMISTRY a gas that has no colour or smell, used for cooking and heating (formula CH_4)

methanol /ˈmeθənɒl/ *noun* [U] CHEMISTRY a poisonous chemical substance which is the simplest type of alcohol (formula CH_3OH)

WORD PARTNERS FOR *method*

an **alternative/new/reliable/simple/traditional** method • **develop/devise/use** a method

method /ˈmeθəd/ *noun* [C] a way of doing something, often one that involves a system or plan *What's the best **method of/for** solving this problem?* ○ *traditional teaching methods*

methodical /məˈθɒdɪkəl/ *adjective* careful and well organized, using a plan or system *a methodical researcher* •**methodically** *adverb*

Methodist /ˈmeθədɪst/ *adjective* RELIGION belonging or relating to a Christian group that was started by John Wesley •**Methodist** *noun* [C]

methodological /ˌmeθədəlˈɒdʒɪkəl/ *adjective* relating to a methodology *methodological problems*

methodology /ˌmeθəˈdɒlədʒi/ *noun* [C, U] the system of methods used for doing, teaching, or studying something

methyl orange /ˌmeθəlˈɒrɪndʒ/ *noun* [U] CHEMISTRY a substance used by scientists to show the amount of acid in a substance

meticulous /məˈtɪkjələs/ *adjective* very careful, and giving great attention to detail *This book is the result of meticulous research.* •**meticulously** *adverb*

me time /ˈmiːtaɪm/ *noun* [U] *informal* time when you can do exactly what you want

metre *UK* (*US* **meter**) /ˈmiːtər/ *noun* **1** MEASURES [C] (*written abbreviation* **m**) a unit for measuring length, equal to 100 centimetres *Our bedroom is five metres wide.* ○ *She finished third in the women's 400 metres* (= running race). **2** LITERATURE [C, U] a pattern of rhythm in poetry

metric /ˈmetrɪk/ *adjective* MEASURES The metric system of measurement uses units based on the gram, metre, and litre.

ˌmetric ˈton *noun* [C] MEASURES a unit for measuring weight, equal to 1000 kilograms

metro[1] /ˈmetrəʊ/ *noun* [C] an underground railway system in a large city *the Paris metro*

COMMON LEARNER ERROR

metro, subway, or **underground?**

All these words mean an underground railway system in a large city. **Metro** is the most general word. The usual word in British English is **underground**. In American English it is **subway**.

the Paris metro

the London underground

the New York subway

metro[2] /ˈmetrəʊ/ *adjective* [always before noun] *US informal* relating to a large city and the towns around it *the New York metro area*

metropolis /məˈtrɒpəlɪs/ *noun* [C] a very large city, often the capital of a country or region

metropolitan /ˌmetrəˈpɒlɪtən/ *adjective* [always before noun] relating to a large city *a metropolitan area/council*

mew /mjuː/ *verb* [I] to make the sound that a cat makes

mg MEASURES *written abbreviation for* milligram (= a unit for measuring weight)

miaow *UK* (*US* **meow**) /ˌmiːˈaʊ/ *noun* [C] the sound that a cat makes

mice /maɪs/ *plural of* mouse

mickey /ˈmɪki/ **take the mickey (out of sb)** *UK informal* to laugh at someone and make them seem silly

micro- /maɪkrəʊ-/ *prefix* very small *a microchip* ○ *microscopic* (= very small)

microbe /ˈmaɪkrəʊb/ *noun* [C] BIOLOGY a very small organism, often a bacterium that causes disease

microchip /ˈmaɪkrəʊtʃɪp/ *noun* [C] COMPUTING a very small part of a computer or machine which does calculations or stores information

microclimate /ˈmaɪkrəʊklaɪmɪt/ *noun* [C] GEOGRAPHY an area in which the weather is usually different from the areas around it

microcomputer /ˈmaɪkrəʊkəmˌpjuːtər/ *noun* [C] COMPUTING a small computer or personal computer containing a microprocessor (= part which controls operations)

microcosm /ˈmaɪkrəʊˌkɒzəm/ *noun* [C] *formal* a place, group of people, or situation that has the same characteristics as a larger one *The town is a microcosm of French culture.*

microfibre *UK* (*US* **microfiber**) /ˈmaɪkrəʊˌfaɪbər/ *noun* [C] DT a soft, light material made from very thin artifical threads

microorganism /ˌmaɪkrəʊˈɔːgənɪzəm/ *noun* [C] BIOLOGY a living thing which on its own is too small to be seen without a microscope

microphone /ˈmaɪkrəfəʊn/ *noun* [C] a piece of electrical equipment for recording or broadcasting sounds, or for making sounds louder ➲See picture at **computer**

microprocessor /ˌmaɪkrəʊˈprəʊsesər/ (US) /ˈmaɪkrəʊˌprɑːsesər/ *noun* [C] COMPUTING the part of a computer that controls all the other parts

micropyle /ˈmaɪkrəʊpaɪl/ *noun* [C] BIOLOGY a very small opening in the cover of a plant's ovule (= part that contains the female sex cell)

WORD PARTNERS FOR ***microscope***

under a microscope • **through** a microscope

microscope /ˈmaɪkrəskəʊp/ *noun* [C] a piece of scientific equipment which uses lenses (= pieces of curved glass) to make very small objects look bigger

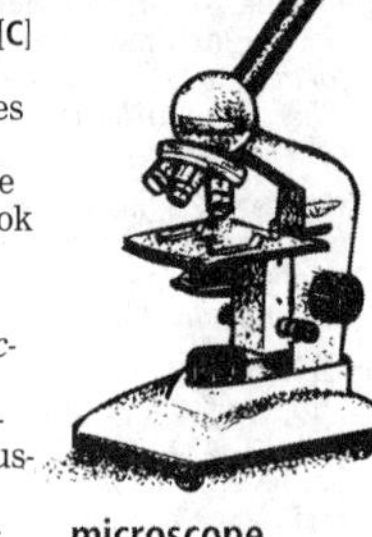
microscope

microscopic /ˌmaɪkrəˈskɒpɪk/ *adjective* extremely small and needing a microscope to be seen, or using a microscope to see something *microscopic organisms/particles*

microwave¹ /ˈmaɪkrəʊweɪv/ *noun* [C] **1** OVEN (*also* **microwave ˈoven**) an electric oven that uses waves of energy to cook or heat food ⊃See colour picture **The Kitchen** on page Centre 2 **2** **PHYSICS** a very short wave similar to a radio wave that is used for sending information and cooking

microwave² /ˈmaɪkrəʊweɪv/ *verb* [T] to cook or heat food using a microwave oven

mid- /mɪd-/ *prefix* among or in the middle of *mid-March* ○ *mid-afternoon*

mid-air /ˌmɪdˈeəʳ/ *noun* **in mid-air** in the air or sky *She jumped up and caught the ball in mid-air.* •**mid-air** *adjective* [**always before noun**] *a* ***mid-air collision***

midday /ˌmɪdˈdeɪ/ *noun* [U] 12 o'clock in the middle of the day, or the period around this time *the heat of the midday sun*

O‑ **middle¹** /ˈmɪdl/ *noun* **1 the middle** the central part, position, or point in time *We used to live just outside Boston but now we live right* (= exactly) ***in the middle.*** ○ *The letter should arrive by the middle of next week.* **2 be in the middle of doing sth** to be busy *I can't talk now - I'm in the middle of cooking a meal.* **3 your middle** *informal* your waist, or your waist and stomach *He wrapped the towel round his middle.* **4 in the middle of nowhere** a long way from places where people live *His car broke down in the middle of nowhere.*

O‑ **middle²** /ˈmɪdl/ *adjective* [**always before noun**] **1** CENTRAL in a central position *The middle layer is made of plastic.* ○ *Our company rents the middle warehouse.* **2** NEITHER HIGH NOR LOW neither high nor low in importance or amount *middle managers*

middle-aged /ˌmɪdlˈeɪdʒd/ *adjective* in the middle of your life before you are old *a middle-aged couple/man/woman*

the ˌMiddle ˈAges *noun* the period in European history between the end of the Roman Empire and the start of the Renaissance

ˌmiddle ˈclass *noun* [**group**] **SOCIETY** a social group that consists of well-educated people, such as doctors, lawyers, and teachers, who have good jobs and are neither very rich nor very poor •**middle-class** /ˌmɪdlˈklɑːs/ *adjective* belonging or relating to the middle class *a middle-class suburb*

the ˌMiddle ˈEast *noun* a group of countries in the area where Africa, Asia, and Europe meet •**Middle Eastern** *adjective* relating to the Middle East *Middle Eastern cuisine*

middleman /ˈmɪdlmæn/ *noun* [C] *plural* **middlemen** someone who buys goods from one person and sells them to someone else for a higher price *Selling direct from the factory* ***cuts out the middleman.***

ˈmiddle ˌname *noun* [C] an extra name between someone's first and family names

ˈmiddle ˌschool *noun* [C] **EDUCATION** a school in the US for children usually between the ages of 11 and 14

midget /ˈmɪdʒɪt/ *noun* [C] someone who is very small

MIDI /ˈmɪdi/ *noun* **COMPUTING, MUSIC** *abbreviation for* Musical Instrument Digital Interface: a system for allowing electronic musical instruments to communicate with each other

the Midlands /ˈmɪdləndz/ *noun* the central area of England which includes several large industrial cities

ˌmid-life ˈcrisis *noun* [C] *plural* **mid-life crises** a period in the middle of your life when you lose confidence in your abilities and worry about the future

midnight /ˈmɪdnaɪt/ *noun* [U] 12 o'clock at night *He died shortly after midnight.*

midriff /ˈmɪdrɪf/ *noun* [C] the front of your body between your chest and waist

midst /mɪdst/ *noun* **1 in the midst of sth** in the middle of something, usually an event or activity [**+ of + doing sth**] *Can I phone you back? I'm in the midst of cooking dinner.* **2 in your midst** among the group of people that you belong to *Residents are protesting about a convicted murderer living in their midst.*

midsummer /ˌmɪdˈsʌməʳ/ *noun* [U] the longest day of the year, or the period around this

midway /ˌmɪdˈweɪ/ *adverb* **1 midway between sth and sth** at the middle point between two places or things *Leeds is midway between London and Edinburgh.* **2 midway through sth** at the middle point of an activity or a period of time *He scored the third goal midway through the second half.*

midweek /ˌmɪdˈwiːk/ *noun* [U] the middle of the week, usually from Tuesday to Thursday •**midweek** *adjective, adverb* [**always before noun**] in the middle of the week *a midweek game/match* ○ *Flights are cheaper if you travel midweek.*

the Midwest /ˌmɪdˈwest/ *noun* the northern central area of the United States •**Midwestern** *adjective* [**always before noun**] relating to the Midwest

midwife /ˈmɪdwaɪf/ *noun* [C] *plural* **midwives** /ˈmɪdwaɪvz/ **HEALTH** a nurse who has had special training to help women give birth

midwifery /mɪdˈwɪfᵊri/ *noun* [U] **HEALTH** the work of a midwife

midwinter /ˌmɪdˈwɪntəʳ/ *noun* [U] the shortest day of the year, or the period around this

M

might¹ /maɪt/ *modal verb* **1** HAPPEN used to talk about what will possibly happen *She might not come.* **2** TRUE used to talk about what is possibly true *I think Isabel might be pregnant.* ○ *The rain might have stopped by now.* **3 you might like/want to** *UK formal* used to politely suggest something *You might want to try a different approach next time.* ➲See Extra help page **Modal verbs** on page Centre 34.

might² /maɪt/ *noun* [U] *formal* great strength or power ***economic/military might*** ○ *She pushed the door **with all her might*** (= with as much force as possible).

mightn't /ˈmaɪtᵊnt/ *mainly UK formal short for* might not *It mightn't be true.*

might've /ˈmaɪtəv/ *short for* might have *The children might've seen her in the park.*

mighty¹ /ˈmaɪti/ *adjective* very powerful or successful *In their next game they're playing the mighty Redskins.*

mighty² /ˈmaɪti/ *adverb mainly US informal* very *It's mighty tempting to stay in bed on a rainy morning.*

migraine /ˈmaɪgreɪn/ *noun* [C, U] **HEALTH** a very bad pain in the head, often one that makes you vomit

migrant /ˈmaɪgrᵊnt/ *noun* [C] **SOCIETY** someone who goes to live in a different place in order to find work *migrant labour/workers*

migrate /maɪˈgreɪt/ Ⓤⓢ /ˈmaɪgreɪt/ *verb* [I] **1** ANIMALS When birds, fish, or animals migrate, they travel from one place to another at the same time each year. *Many birds migrate from Europe to African forests for the winter.* **2 SOCIETY** When people migrate, they move to another place, often a different country, in order to find work and a better life. *Between 1900 and 1914, 3.1 million people **migrated to** the US from central Europe.* •**migration** /maɪˈgreɪʃᵊn/ *noun* [C, U]

migratory /ˈmaɪgreɪtᵊri/ Ⓤⓢ /ˈmaɪgrətɔːri/ *adjective* [**always before noun**] **BIOLOGY** relating to birds, fish, or animals that migrate

mike /maɪk/ *noun* [C] *informal short for* microphone

mild /maɪld/ *adjective* **1** WEATHER When weather is mild, it is less cold than you would expect. *a **mild winter*** **2 HEALTH** When an illness is mild, it is not as serious as it could be. *a mild form of pneumonia* **3** WEAK not having a strong effect *a mild taste* ○ *a mild detergent* **4** KIND calm and gentle *He has a very mild manner.*

mildly /ˈmaɪldli/ *adverb* **1** slightly *I find his films mildly amusing.* **2 to put it mildly** something you say when an opinion is not expressed as strongly as it should be *The building is unsafe, to put it mildly.*

mile /maɪl/ *noun* [C] **1 MEASURES** a unit for measuring distance, equal to 1609 metres or 1760 yards *The nearest station is two miles from here.* ○ *It's a five-mile walk to the next village.* ○ *The latest high-speed trains can travel at 140 **miles per hour**.* ➲See Extra help page **Numbers and measurements** on page Centre 24. **2 miles** a very long distance *We drove **for miles** along dusty roads.* ○ *Her cottage is **miles from** the nearest village.*

mileage /ˈmaɪlɪdʒ/ *noun* **1** DISTANCE [C, U] the number of miles that a vehicle has travelled since it was new ***low mileage*** **2** FUEL [C, U] the number of miles a vehicle can travel using a particular amount of fuel **3** ADVANTAGE [U] *informal* an advantage got from something *There's no **mileage in** taking your employer to court.*

milestone /ˈmaɪlstəʊn/ *noun* [C] an important event in the history or development of something or someone *Passing my driving test was an important milestone for me.*

militant¹ /ˈmɪlɪtᵊnt/ *adjective* expressing strong support for a political or social idea, and willing to use extreme or violent methods to achieve it *a **militant group/organization*** •**militancy** /ˈmɪlɪtᵊnsi/ *noun* [U] when someone is militant

militant² /ˈmɪlɪtᵊnt/ *noun* [C] a militant person

military¹ /ˈmɪlɪtri/ *adjective* relating to the army, navy, or air force ***military action/service***

the military² /ˈmɪlɪtri/ *noun* a country's army, navy, and air force

militia /mɪˈlɪʃə/ *noun* [C] a group of people who have been trained as soldiers but are not part of a country's official army •**militiaman** *noun* [C] *plural* **militiamen** a member of a militia

milk¹ /mɪlk/ *noun* [U] **BIOLOGY, FOOD** a white liquid produced by women and other female animals, such as cows, for feeding their babies *a carton of milk* ○ *breast milk* ➲See also: **skimmed milk**

milk² /mɪlk/ *verb* [T] **1** to get as much money or as many advantages as possible from a person or situation *She **milked** her grandfather **for** all his savings.* **2 FARMING** to take milk from a cow using your hands or a machine

milkman /ˈmɪlkmən/ *noun* [C] *plural* **milkmen** a man whose job is bringing milk to people's homes early in the morning

milkshake /ˈmɪlkʃeɪk/ *noun* [C, U] **FOOD** a sweet drink made of milk and chocolate or fruit *a banana milkshake*

milky /ˈmɪlki/ *adjective* **1** CONTAINING MILK containing milk, often a lot of it *milky coffee/tea* **2** LIKE MILK similar to milk *a milky liquid*

the Milky Way /ˌmɪlkiˈweɪ/ *noun* **ASTRONOMY** the group of very many stars which includes the sun

mill¹ /mɪl/ *noun* [C] **1** FLOUR a machine for crushing grain into flour, or a building with this machine *a flour mill* **2** POWDER a small machine used in the kitchen for crushing things such as coffee beans into a powder *a coffee/pepper mill* **3** MATERIAL a factory where one material or substance is made *a cotton/woollen mill* ○ *a paper/steel mill*

mill² /mɪl/ *verb* [T] to use a machine to crush something into a powder *freshly milled black pepper*

mill about/around (sth) *phrasal verb* When people mill around, they come together in a place, usually to wait for someone or something.

millennium /mɪˈleniəm/ *noun* [C] *plural* **millennia 1** a period of 1000 years, often calculated from the date when Christ is thought to have been born **2 the Millennium** the change from the year 1999 to 2000 in the Western calendar *Where did you celebrate the Millennium?*

milli- /mɪli-/ *prefix* **MEASURES** a thousandth *a millisecond*

milligram /ˈmɪlɪgræm/ (*written abbreviation* **mg**) *noun* [C] **MEASURES** a unit for measuring weight, equal to 0.001 grams

millilitre *UK* (*US* **milliliter**) (*written abbreviation* **ml**) /ˈmɪlɪˌliːtəʳ/ *noun* [C] **MEASURES** a unit for measuring liquid, equal to 0.001 litres

millimetre *UK* (*US* **millimeter**) (*written abbreviation* **mm**) /ˈmɪlɪˌmiːtəʳ/ *noun* [C] **MEASURES** a unit for measuring length, equal to 0.001 metres

O-ᵡ**million** /ˈmɪljən/ **1** the number 1,000,000 **2 millions** *informal* a lot *I've seen that film millions of times.*

millionaire /ˌmɪljəˈneəʳ/ *noun* [C] a very rich person who has money and possessions to the value of at least one million pounds or dollars

millionth[1] /ˈmɪljənθ/ 1,000,000th written as a word

millionth[2] /ˈmɪljənθ/ *noun* [C] one of a million equal parts of something; $^1/_{1,000,000}$; .000001

mime /maɪm/ *verb* [I, T] to act or tell a story without speaking, using movements of your hands and body, and expressions on your face *Pop stars often mime* (= pretend to sing while their song is played) *on TV.* •**mime** *noun* [C, U] ***a mime artist***

mimic[1] /ˈmɪmɪk/ *verb* [T] **mimicking**, *past* **mimicked 1** COPY to copy the way someone talks and behaves, usually to make people laugh *He's always getting into trouble for mimicking his teachers.* **2** BE THE SAME to have the same behaviour or qualities as something else *The drug **mimics the effects** of a natural hormone.*

mimic[2] /ˈmɪmɪk/ *noun* [C] someone who is good at mimicking other people

mince[1] /mɪns/ *UK* (*US* **ground beef**) *noun* [U] **FOOD** meat, usually from a cow, which has been cut into very small pieces by a machine

mince[2] /mɪns/ *verb* [T] **FOOD** to cut food into small pieces in a machine *minced beef/onions*

mincemeat /ˈmɪnsmiːt/ *noun* [U] **1 FOOD** a spicy, sweet mixture of apples, dried fruit, and nuts, which have been cut into small pieces **2 make mincemeat of sb** *informal* to defeat someone very easily

ˌmince ˈpie *noun* [C] *UK/US* **FOOD** a small pastry filled with mincemeat that is eaten mainly at Christmas

O-ᵡ**mind**[1] /maɪnd/ *noun* [C] **1** someone's memory or their ability to think, feel emotions, and be aware of things *For some reason her words **stuck in** my **mind**.* ○ *She has a very logical mind.* **2 have sth on your mind** to think or worry about something *Jim has a lot on his mind at the moment.* **3 bear/keep sb/sth in mind** to remember someone or something that may be useful in the future *I'll keep you in mind if another job comes up.* [+ **(that)**] *Bear in mind that there's a bank holiday next week.* **4 make your mind up** to make a decision [+ **question word**] *I haven't made up my mind whether to go yet.* **5 change your mind** to change a decision or opinion *We've changed our minds about selling the house.* **6 come/spring to mind** If an idea comes to mind, it is the first thing you think of. *I was thinking about who might be suitable for this job, and your name came to mind.* **7 put your mind to sth** to give your full attention to something *You could win if you put your mind to it.* **8 be out of your mind** *informal* to be crazy or very stupid **9 be out of your mind with worry/grief, etc** to be very worried or upset **10 blow your mind** *informal* If something blows your mind, you are very excited or surprised by it. *There was one scene in the film that really blew my mind.* **11 cross your mind** If an idea crosses your mind, you think about it for a short time. [+ **(that)**] *It never crossed my mind* (= I never thought) *that she might be married.* **12 be in two minds** *UK* (*US* **be of two minds**) to have difficulty making a decision *I'm in two minds about accepting his offer.* **13 put/set sb's mind at rest** to say something to someone to stop them worrying *I was really worried about the tests, but talking to the doctor put my mind at rest.* **14 read sb's mind** to know what someone is thinking **15 slip your mind** If something slips your mind, you forget it. **16 speak your mind** to say exactly what you think without worrying if it will upset anyone *She has very strong opinions and she's not afraid to speak her mind.* **17 take your mind off sth** to stop you thinking about something unpleasant *Talking to him took my mind off the pain.* ⊃See also: at/in the **back**[2] of your mind, **frame**[1] of mind, give sb a **piece**[1] of your mind, a **weight** off your mind

O-ᵡ**mind**[2] /maɪnd/ *verb* **1** BE ANNOYED [I, T] to be annoyed or worried by something *Do you think he'd mind if I borrowed his book?* [+ **doing sth**] *Tim won't mind lending you his car.* ○ *He doesn't seem to mind doing all the driving.* ○ *I don't mind taking her* (= I am willing to take her) *if you're too busy.* **2** LOOK AFTER [T] to look after someone or something *Who's minding the baby?* **3 do you mind/would you mind** something you say when politely asking someone to do something *Do you mind not smoking in here, please?* ○ *Would you mind if I borrowed your phone?* **4** BE CAREFUL [T] something you say when telling someone to be careful with something dangerous *Mind the iron - it's still very hot!* **5 never mind a** DO NOT WORRY something that you say to tell someone that something is not important *"I forgot to bring any money." "Never mind, you can pay me next week."* **b** IMPOSSIBLE something you say to emphasize that something is impossible *I can't afford to buy a bike, never mind a car!* **6 mind you** something you say before saying the opposite of what you have just said *We had a lovely holiday in France. Mind you, the weather was appalling.*

Mind out! *phrasal verb UK* something you say to warn someone about a danger or to tell them to move *Mind out - this plate's very hot!*

mind-boggling /ˈmaɪndˌbɒglɪŋ/ *adjective informal* difficult to accept, imagine, or understand

M

-minded /'maɪndɪd/ ⊃See: **absent-minded, narrow-minded, open-minded, single-minded**

minder /'maɪndəʳ/ *noun* [C] *UK* someone who physically protects a famous, important, or very rich person

mindless /'maɪndləs/ *adjective* stupid and done without a good reason ***mindless violence***

O-**mine¹** /maɪn/ *pronoun* the things that belong or relate to the person who is speaking or writing *I borrowed them from a friend of mine.* ○ *"Whose book is this?" "It's mine."* ○ *Can I use your pen? Mine's not working.*

O-**mine²** /maɪn/ *noun* [C] **1** UNDERGROUND an underground system of holes and passages where people dig out coal or other minerals **2** BOMB a bomb hidden in the ground or water which explodes when it is touched ⊃See also: **gold mine**

mine³ /maɪn/ *verb* **1** DIG [I, T] to dig out of the ground minerals such as coal, metals, and valuable stones *Tin was mined in this area for hundreds of years.* ○ *He made his fortune **mining for** gold and diamonds.* **2** BOMB [T] to put mines (= bombs) in the ground or water *The southern coast was heavily mined during the war.*

minefield /'ma phon_'_ɑfiːld/ *noun* [C] **1** PROBLEMS a situation with many complicated problems *a **legal minefield*** **2** BOMBS an area of land or sea where bombs have been hidden

miner /'maɪnəʳ/ *noun* [C] someone who works in a mine *a coal miner*

mineral /'mɪnᵊrᵊl/ *noun* [C] **1 GEOLOGY** a valuable or useful substance that is dug out of the ground *The region's rich mineral deposits include oil, gold, and aluminium.* **2 FOOD** a chemical that your body needs to stay healthy

'mineral ˌwater *noun* [C, U] water which is taken from the ground and contains chemicals that are good for your health

mingle /'mɪŋgl/ *verb* **1** MIX [I, T] to mix, or be mixed *The smell of fresh coffee **mingled with** cigarette smoke.* **2** TALK [I] to meet and talk to a lot of people at a party or similar event *The party will be a good opportunity to **mingle with** the other students.*

mini- /mɪni-/ *prefix* small *a miniskirt* (= very short skirt) ○ *a minibus*

miniature¹ /'mɪnətʃəʳ/ *adjective* [**always before noun**] extremely small *a miniature camera*

miniature² /'mɪnətʃəʳ/ *noun* **1** [C] a very small copy of an object *You can buy miniatures of the statue in the museum shop.* **2 in miniature** If something is in miniature, it is a very small copy of something else.

mini-break /'mɪnibreɪk/ *noun* [C] a very short holiday

minibus /'mɪnɪbʌs/ *noun* [C] a small bus with seats for about ten people

minicomputer /'mɪnikəmˌpjuːtəʳ/ *noun* [C] **COMPUTING** a computer that is smaller than a mainframe (= large, powerful computer that many people can use) but larger and faster than a microcomputer

MiniDisk /'mɪnɪdɪsk/ *noun* [C] *trademark* a very small plastic disc on which high-quality sound, especially music, is recorded

minimal /'mɪnɪmᵊl/ *adjective* very small in amount *Damage to the building was minimal.* •**minimally** *adverb*

minimize (*also UK* **-ise**) /'mɪnɪmaɪz/ *verb* [T] to make the amount of something that is unpleasant or not wanted as small as possible *Airport staff are trying to minimize the inconvenience caused to passengers.*

O-**minimum¹** /'mɪnɪməm/ *adjective* [**always before noun**] The minimum amount of something is the smallest amount that is allowed, needed, or possible. *How much is the **minimum wage**?* ○ *There is a **minimum charge** of $5 for postage.* ⊃Opposite **maximum**

WORD PARTNERS FOR ***minimum***

a minimum **of** [5/2%, etc] • **keep** sth **to** a minimum • an **absolute/bare** minimum • **with the** minimum **of** sth

O-**minimum²** /'mɪnɪməm/ *noun* [**no plural**] the smallest amount that is allowed, needed, or possible *The judge sentenced him to a minimum of five years in prison.* ○ *Please **keep** noise **to** an absolute **minimum**.*

mining /'maɪnɪŋ/ *noun* [U] the industrial process of digging coal or other minerals out of the ground

miniscule /'mɪnɪskjuːl/ *adjective* a common spelling of 'minuscule' that is not correct

miniskirt /'mɪnɪˌskɜːt/ *noun* [C] a very short skirt ⊃See colour picture **Clothes** on page Centre 8

minister /'mɪnɪstəʳ/ *noun* [C] **1 POLITICS** a politician who is responsible for a government department or has an important position in it *a finance/health minister* **2 RELIGION** a priest in some Christian churches *a Baptist/Methodist minister* ⊃See also: **prime minister**

ministerial /ˌmɪnɪ'stɪəriəl/ *adjective* **POLITICS** relating to a government minister ***a ministerial job/post***

ministry /'mɪnɪstri/ *noun* **1 POLITICS** [C] a government department which is responsible for a particular subject *the Ministry of Defence* ○ *a Foreign Ministry spokesman* **2 the ministry RELIGION** the job of being a priest

minivan /'mɪnivæn/ *noun* [C] *US* a people carrier (= large, high car for many people)

mink /mɪŋk/ *noun* [C, U] a small animal with valuable fur which is used to make expensive coats, or the fur from this animal *a mink coat*

minor¹ /'maɪnəʳ/ *adjective* **1** not important or serious *a minor offence* ○ *Most of the passengers suffered only minor injuries.* **2 MUSIC** [**always before noun**] in music, belonging to a key (= set of musical notes) that often produces a sad sound ⊃Opposite **major**

minor² /'maɪnəʳ/ *noun* [C] *formal* **LAW** someone who is too young to have the legal responsibilities of an adult

WORD PARTNERS FOR ***minority***

be **in** a minority • a **sizeable/small/substantial/tiny** minority • a minority **of** sth

O⁃ **minority** /maɪˈnɒrəti/ *noun* **1** [**no plural**] a part of a group which is less than half of the whole group, often much less *The violence was caused by a* ***small minority*** *of football supporters.* ○ *I voted to accept the proposal, but I was* ***in the minority****.* ⊃Opposite **majority** **2** **SOCIETY** [**C**] a group of people whose race is different from the race of most of the people where they live [**usually plural**] ***ethnic minorities***

mint¹ /mɪnt/ *noun* **1** **FOOD** [**C**] a sweet with a fresh, strong taste **2** **FOOD** [**U**] a plant whose leaves are used to add flavour to food and drinks **3** [**C**] a factory which produces coins for the government

mint² /mɪnt/ *verb* [**T**] to produce a coin for the government

minus¹ /ˈmaɪnəs/ *preposition* **1** **MATHEMATICS** used when the second of two numbers should be taken away from the first *Five minus three is two.* **2** *informal* without something that should be there *She arrived at the meeting minus her briefcase.*

minus² /ˈmaɪnəs/ *adjective* **1** **MATHEMATICS** [**always before noun**] A minus number is less than zero. *The temperature last night was minus ten.* **2** **A minus/B minus, etc** **EDUCATION** used with scores given to written work meaning 'slightly lower than' *I got an A minus for my last essay.*

minus³ /ˈmaɪnəs/ *noun* [**C**] **1** **MATHEMATICS** (*also* **ˈminus ˌsign**) the sign which shows that the second of two numbers should be taken away from the first, or that a number is less than zero, shown by the symbol '–' **2** a problem or difficulty *It isn't easy having a child but the pluses outweigh the minuses.*

minuscule /ˈmɪnəskjuːl/ *adjective* extremely small *The cost of vaccination is minuscule compared to the cost of treating the disease.*

O⁃ **minute¹** /ˈmɪnɪt/ *noun* [**C**] **1** 60 SECONDS a period of time equal to 60 seconds *She was ten minutes late for her interview.* ○ *"Did you have a good holiday?" "Yes, thanks. I enjoyed every minute of it."* ○ *a thirty-minute journey* **2** SHORT TIME a very short period of time *It'll only* ***take a minute*** *to call him.* ○ *I'll be with you* ***in a minute****.* ○ *She died* ***within minutes of*** (= very soon after) *the attack.* **3** **(at) any minute** very soon *Her train should be arriving any minute.* **4** **the last minute** the latest time possible *The concert was cancelled at the last minute.* **5** **the minute (that)** as soon as *I'll tell you the minute we hear any news.* **6** **Wait/Just a minute; Hold on a minute.** **a** WAIT used when asking someone to wait for a short time *Just a minute - I've left my coat in the restaurant.* **b** DISAGREEING used when you disagree with something that someone has said or done *Hold on a minute, Pete! I never said you could borrow my car.*

minute² /maɪˈnjuːt/ *adjective* **1** SMALL extremely small *a minute amount/quantity* **2** EXACT [**always before noun**] done in great detail *He explained everything* ***in minute detail****.*

the minutes /ˈmɪnɪts/ *noun* [**plural**] an official record of what is said and decided during a meeting *Michael has kindly agreed to* ***take the minutes*** (= write them down).

miracle /ˈmɪrəkl/ *noun* [**C**] **1** SURPRISING something that is very surprising or difficult to believe *an economic miracle* [**+ (that)**] *It's a miracle that he's still alive.* ○ ***a miracle cure*** **2** IMPOSSIBLE an event which should be impossible and cannot be explained by science

miraculous /mɪˈrækjələs/ *adjective* very surprising or difficult to believe *John's made a* ***miraculous recovery*** *from his illness.* •**miraculously** *adverb*

mirage /ˈmɪrɑːʒ/ (US) /mɪˈrɑːʒ/ *noun* [**C**] when hot air produces an image of water in a desert or on a road

O⁃ **mirror¹** /ˈmɪrəʳ/ *noun* [**C**] a piece of glass with a shiny metallic material on one side which produces an image of anything that is in front of it *a bathroom mirror* ○ *He looked at his reflection* ***in the mirror****.* ⊃See colour picture **The Living Room** on page Centre 4 ⊃See also: **rear-view mirror, wing mirror**

mirror² /ˈmɪrəʳ/ *verb* [**T**] to be similar to or represent something *Our newspaper mirrors the opinions of ordinary people.*

mirth /mɜːθ/ *noun* [**U**] *formal* laughter or happiness

mis- /mɪs-/ *prefix* not or badly *mistrust* ○ *to misbehave*

misadventure /ˌmɪsədˈventʃəʳ/ *noun* **1** **LAW** [**U**] *UK formal* when someone is killed by accident and no one is legally responsible for the death *The coroner recorded a verdict of* ***death by misadventure****.* **2** [**C**] an unlucky event

misanthrope /ˈmɪsənθrəʊp/ *noun* [**C**] *formal* someone who hates people in general and avoids being with them

misapprehension /ˌmɪsæprɪˈhenʃən/ *noun* [**C**] *formal* a idea or opinion about someone or something that is wrong [**+ that**] *He was* ***labouring under the misapprehension*** (= wrongly believed) *that she loved him.*

misbehave /ˌmɪsbɪˈheɪv/ *verb* [**I**] to behave badly •**misbehaviour** *UK* (*US* **misbehavior**) *noun* [**U**] bad behaviour

misc *written abbreviation for* miscellaneous

miscalculate /mɪsˈkælkjəleɪt/ *verb* [**I, T**] **1** CALCULATE BADLY to make a mistake when calculating something *I think I've miscalculated how much wine we'll need for the party.* **2** DECIDE BADLY to make a bad decision because you do not completely understand a situation *If she thinks Mike will support her plan, then she's seriously miscalculated.* •**miscalculation** /ˌmɪskælkjəˈleɪʃən/ *noun* [**C, U**]

miscarriage /ˈmɪsˌkærɪdʒ/ *noun* [**C, U**] **1** **HEALTH** when a baby is born too early and dies because it has not developed enough *She* ***had a miscarriage*** *after her car accident.* **2** **miscarriage of justice** when a court makes a wrong or unfair decision

miscarry /mɪˈskæri/ *verb* [**I, T**] **HEALTH** to give birth to a baby too early so that it dies

miscellaneous /ˌmɪsəlˈeɪniəs/ *adjective* [**always before noun**] consisting of a mixture of several different things *The plumber tried to charge me fifty pounds for miscellaneous items.*

M

mischief /ˈmɪstʃɪf/ *noun* [U] behaviour, usually of a child, which is slightly bad but not serious

mischievous /ˈmɪstʃɪvəs/ *adjective* behaving in a way that is slightly bad but not serious *a* ***mischievous grin*** ○ *a mischievous five-year-old* •**mischievously** *adverb*

miscible /ˈmɪsɪbəl/ *adjective* **CHEMISTRY** A miscible liquid can be mixed with another liquid without separating from it. ➲Opposite **immiscible**

misconceived /ˌmɪskənˈsiːvd/ *adjective* If a plan is misconceived, it is not suitable or has not been thought about carefully.

WORD PARTNERS FOR ***misconception***

be **based on** a misconception • a **common/popular** misconception • a misconception **about** sth

misconception /ˌmɪskənˈsepʃən/ *noun* [C] when your understanding of something is wrong [+ **that**] *It's a* ***common misconception*** *that older workers cannot learn to use new technology.*

misconduct /mɪˈskɒndʌkt/ *noun* [U] *formal* when someone in a position of responsibility behaves in a way that is morally wrong or breaks rules while doing their job ***professional misconduct***

misdemeanour *UK* (*US* **misdemeanor**) /ˌmɪsdɪˈmiːnər/ *noun* [C] **1** [BAD BEHAVIOUR] behaviour that is bad or not moral *political/sexual misdemeanours* **2** [CRIME] *US* a crime which is not serious

misdirect /ˌmɪsdɪˈrekt/ *verb* [T] to use money or people's skills in a way that is not suitable [**often passive**] *Large quantities of money and expertise have been misdirected.*

miserable /ˈmɪzərəbl/ *adjective* **1** [SAD] unhappy *I just woke up feeling miserable.* **2** [NOT PLEASANT] very unpleasant or bad, and causing someone to feel unhappy *Some families are living in miserable conditions.* **3** [NOT ENOUGH] *informal* A miserable amount is too small to be acceptable. *She offered me a miserable £50 for my old computer.*

miserably /ˈmɪzərəbli/ *adverb* **1** [DISAPPOINTING] in a way that causes disappointment or suffering *miserably low wages* ○ *Every job application that I've made has* ***failed miserably*** (= has been extremely unsuccessful). **2** [SAD] in a very unhappy way *"I feel so ill," said Rachel miserably.*

misery /ˈmɪzəri/ *noun* [C, U] **1** great suffering or unhappiness *The war brought misery to millions of people.* ○ *Her husband's drinking is* ***making her life a misery.*** **2 put sb out of their misery** to stop someone worrying by telling them what they want to know

misfire /mɪsˈfaɪər/ *verb* [I] When something that you do misfires, it does not have the result that you intended. *His joke misfired badly, and he was forced to make a public apology.*

misfit /ˈmɪsfɪt/ *noun* [C] someone with strange or unusual behaviour who is not accepted by other people *a* ***social misfit***

misfortune /mɪsˈfɔːtʃuːn/ *noun* [C, U] bad luck, or an unlucky event [+ **to do sth**] *He* ***had the misfortune*** *to fall in love with a married woman.*

WORD PARTNERS FOR ***misgiving***

express/have misgivings • **grave/serious/strong** misgivings • misgivings **about** sth

misgiving /mɪsˈɡɪvɪŋ/ *noun* [C] a feeling of doubt or worry about a future event [**usually plural**] *She* ***has*** *serious* ***misgivings about*** *giving birth at home.*

misguided /mɪsˈɡaɪdɪd/ *adjective* not likely to succeed because of a bad judgment or understanding of a situation *The government's policy seems to me completely misguided.*

mishandle /mɪsˈhændl/ *verb* [T] to deal with a problem or situation badly *The murder investigation was mishandled from the beginning.*

mishap /ˈmɪshæp/ *noun* [C, U] an accident or unlucky event which usually is not serious *They suffered a series of mishaps during the trip.*

misinform /ˌmɪsɪnˈfɔːm/ *verb* [T] to give someone false information [**often passive**] *I'm afraid you've been misinformed about your exam results.*

misinterpret /ˌmɪsɪnˈtɜːprɪt/ *verb* [T] to understand something in the wrong way [**often passive**] *He claims his speech was deliberately misinterpreted by journalists.*

misjudge /mɪsˈdʒʌdʒ/ *verb* [T] **1** [OPINION] to form a wrong opinion about a person or situation *We believe that the government has seriously misjudged the public mood.* **2** [GUESS] to guess an amount or distance wrongly

misjudgment (*also UK* **misjudgement**) /mɪsˈdʒʌdʒmənt/ *noun* [C, U] when you form a wrong opinion or make a wrong guess *Her outspoken criticism of her boss was a serious misjudgment.*

mislay /mɪˈsleɪ/ *verb* [T] *past* **mislaid** /mɪˈsleɪd/ *formal* to lose something for a short time by forgetting where you put it *I seem to have mislaid my car keys.*

mislead /mɪˈsliːd/ *verb* [T] *past* **misled** /mɪˈsled/ to make someone believe something that is untrue by giving them information that is wrong or not complete [**often passive**] *She claims the public was misled by the government.*

misleading /mɪˈsliːdɪŋ/ *adjective* making someone believe something that is untrue *misleading information/statements*

mismanage /ˌmɪsˈmænɪdʒ/ *verb* [T] to control or organize something badly *He accused the government of mismanaging the crisis.* •**mismanagement** *noun* [U] when something is badly organized or controlled

misnomer /mɪˈsnəʊmər/ *noun* [C] a name which is not suitable for the person or thing that it refers to [**usually singular**] *It's a misnomer to call young car thieves 'joyriders'.*

misogynist /mɪˈsɒdʒənɪst/ *noun* [C] a man who dislikes women very much •**misogynistic** /mɪˌsɒdʒənˈɪstɪk/ (*also* **misogynist**) *adjective* expressing a great dislike of women *a misogynistic attitude/writer*

misogyny /mɪˈsɒdʒɪni/ *noun* [U] a great dislike of women

misplaced /mɪˈspleɪst/ *adjective* If you have a misplaced feeling or belief, it is wrong because you have not understood the situation correctly. ***misplaced loyalty/trust***

misprint /ˈmɪsprɪnt/ *noun* [C] a mistake made in the printing of a newspaper or book *The article is full of misprints.*

misread /mɪsˈriːd/ *verb* [T] *past* **misread** /mɪsˈred/ **1** READING to make a mistake when you are reading something *He misread the cooking instructions on the packet.* **2** UNDERSTANDING to not understand something correctly *She completely* ***misread*** *the* ***situation****.*

misrepresent /ˌmɪsreprɪˈzent/ *verb* [T] to say things that are not true about someone or something *He claims that the article misrepresented his views.* •**misrepresentation** /ˌmɪsreprɪzenˈteɪʃən/ *noun* [C, U]

O‐ **miss¹** /mɪs/ *verb* **1** FEEL SAD [T] to feel sad about someone that you do not see now or something that you do not have or do now *I'll miss you when you go.* [+ **doing sth**] *He misses having a room of his own.* **2** NOT GO TO [T] to not go to something *I missed my class this morning.* **3** NOT SEE/HEAR [T] to not see or hear something or someone *Sorry, I missed that, could you repeat it please?* ○ *We missed the first five minutes of the film.* **4** NOT HIT [I, T] to not hit or catch something as you intended *It should have been such an easy goal and he missed.* **5** TOO LATE [T] to arrive too late to get on a bus, train, or aircraft *If I don't leave now, I'll miss my train.* ➲See Common Learner Error at **lose** **6** NOT NOTICE [T] to not notice someone or something *It's the big house on the corner - you can't miss it.* **7** **miss a chance/opportunity** to not use an opportunity to do something *You can't afford to miss a chance like this.* **8** **miss the point** to not understand something correctly ➲See also: miss the **boat**

miss sb/sth out *phrasal verb UK* to not include someone or something

miss out *phrasal verb* to not do or have something that you would enjoy or something that other people do or have *I got there late and* ***missed out on*** *all the fun.*

miss² /mɪs/ *noun* **1** [C] when you do not hit or catch something as you intended **2** **give sth a miss** *UK informal* to not do an activity *I think I'll give aerobics a miss this evening.* **3** **a near miss** something bad which does not happen but almost happens

O‐ **Miss** /mɪs/ *noun* a title for a girl or woman who is not married, used before her family name or full name *Miss Olivia Allenby* ○ *Tell Miss Russell I'm here.* ➲See Common Learner Error at **Mr**

misshapen /mɪsˈʃeɪpən/ *adjective* not the correct or normal shape

missile /ˈmɪsaɪl/ (US) /ˈmɪsəl/ *noun* [C] **1** WEAPON an explosive weapon which can travel long distances through the air *nuclear missiles* ○ *a missile attack* **2** OBJECT an object which is thrown through the air to hit someone or something

WORD PARTNERS FOR ***missing***

go missing • **report** sb missing • missing **from** sth

O‐ **missing** /ˈmɪsɪŋ/ *adjective* **1** LOST If someone or something is missing, you cannot find them because they are not in their usual place. *Have you found those missing documents?* ○ *Her daughter* ***went missing*** *a week ago.* **2** NOT INCLUDED not included in something *There are a couple of things* ***missing from*** *the list.*

mission /ˈmɪʃən/ *noun* [C] **1** JOB an important job, usually travelling somewhere *I'll be going* ***on a*** *fact-finding* ***mission*** *to Paris next week.* **2** GROUP an official group of people who are sent somewhere, usually to discover information about something *a trade mission* **3** JOURNEY an important journey which a spacecraft or military aircraft goes on **4** PURPOSE someone's duty or purpose in life *Her* ***mission in life*** *was to help the poor.*

missionary /ˈmɪʃənəri/ *noun* [C] **RELIGION** someone who travels to another country to teach people about the Christian religion

ˈmission ˌstatement *noun* [C] a short written description of the aims of a business or other organization

missive /ˈmɪsɪv/ *noun* [C] *literary* a letter or message

misspell /mɪsˈspel/ *verb* [T] *past* **misspelled** or *UK* **misspelt** **LANGUAGE** to spell something wrongly

mist¹ /mɪst/ *noun* [C, U] small drops of water in the air which make it difficult to see objects which are not near *Gradually the mist cleared and the sun began to shine.*

mist² /mɪst/ *verb*

mist over/up *phrasal verb* If a glass surface mists over, it becomes covered with very small drops of water so that you cannot see through it easily.

WORD PARTNERS FOR ***mistake***

correct/make/repeat a mistake • a **big/costly/fatal/serious/terrible** mistake • **by** mistake

O‐ **mistake¹** /mɪˈsteɪk/ *noun* [C] **1** something that you do or think which is wrong *a spelling mistake* ○ *He* ***made*** *a lot of* ***mistakes*** *in his written test.* [+ **to do sth**] *It would be a* ***big mistake*** *to leave school.* [+ **of** + **doing sth**] *She* ***made the mistake of*** *giving him her phone number.* **2** **by mistake** If you do something by mistake, you do it without intending to. *I picked up someone else's book by mistake.*

COMMON LEARNER ERROR

mistake

Remember to use the correct verb with this word.

I always ***make mistakes*** *in my essays.*

~~*I always do mistakes in my essays.*~~

mistake² /mɪˈsteɪk/ *verb* [T] *past tense* **mistook**, *past participle* **mistaken** to not understand something correctly *I think you mistook my meaning.*

mistake sb/sth for sb/sth *phrasal verb* to confuse someone or something with someone or

M

something else *People sometimes mistake him for a girl.*

OTHER WAYS OF SAYING **mistake**

A common alternative is the noun **error**: *He admitted that he'd made an* ***error***. • *The letter contained a number of typing* ***errors***.

A stupid mistake is sometimes described as a **blunder**: *The company was struggling after a series of financial* ***blunders***.

A mistake which causes confusion is often described as a **mix-up**: *There was a* ***mix-up*** *with the bags at the airport.*

An embarrassing mistake that someone makes when they are talking is sometimes described as a **gaffe**: *I made a real* ***gaffe*** *by calling her 'Emma' which is the name of his previous girlfriend.*

The noun **oversight** is sometimes used to describe a mistake which someone makes by forgetting to do something: *The payment was delayed because of an* ***oversight*** *in the accounts department.*

mistaken /mɪˈsteɪkᵊn/ *adjective* If you are mistaken, or you have a mistaken belief, you are wrong about something. *If you think you can behave like that, you are mistaken.* •**mistakenly** *adverb I* ***mistakenly*** (= wrongly) ***thought*** *he had left.*

Mister /ˈmɪstəʳ/ *noun* [U] *US informal* used when calling or talking to a man that you do not know *Hey Mister, you forgot your suitcase!*

mistletoe /ˈmɪsltəʊ/ *noun* [U] a plant with white berries (= small, round fruit) which is often used as a decoration at Christmas

mistook /mɪˈstʊk/ *past tense of* mistake

mistreat /mɪsˈtriːt/ *verb* [T] to treat a person or animal in a bad or cruel way *A local farmer has been accused of mistreating horses.* •**mistreatment** *noun* [U] when people or animals are badly or cruelly treated

mistress /ˈmɪstrəs/ *noun* [C] a woman who has a sexual relationship with a man who is married to someone else

mistrust /mɪˈstrʌst/ *noun* [U] when you do not believe or have confidence in someone or something *They have a deep mistrust of strangers.* •**mistrust** *verb* [T]

misty /ˈmɪsti/ *adjective* If the weather is misty, there is a cloud of small drops of water in the air, which makes it difficult to see objects which are not near. *a cold and misty morning*

misunderstand /ˌmɪsʌndəˈstænd/ *verb* [T] *past* **misunderstood 1** to not understand someone or something correctly *He misunderstood the question completely.* **2 be misunderstood** If someone is misunderstood, other people do not understand that they have good qualities.

misunderstanding /ˌmɪsʌndəˈstændɪŋ/ *noun* **1** NOT UNDERSTAND [C, U] when someone does not understand something correctly *There must have been a misunderstanding.* **2** DISAGREE [C] a slight disagreement

misuse /ˌmɪsˈjuːz/ *verb* [T] to use something in the wrong way or for the wrong purpose *He misused his position to obtain money dishonestly.* •**misuse** /ˌmɪsˈjuːs/ *noun* [C, U] *the misuse of drugs/power*

mite /maɪt/ *noun* [C] **1** INSECT an extremely small insect with eight legs *dust mites* **2** CHILD *informal* a small child *You're so cold, you poor little mite!* **3 a mite** *mainly UK informal* slightly *He seemed a mite embarrassed.*

mitigate /ˈmɪtɪgeɪt/ *verb* [T] to reduce the harmful effects of something •**mitigation** /ˌmɪtɪˈgeɪʃᵊn/ *noun* [U]

mitigating /ˈmɪtɪgeɪtɪŋ/ *adjective* **mitigating circumstances/factors** facts that make something bad that someone has done seem less bad or less serious

mitochondrion /ˌmaɪtəʊˈkɒndriən/ *noun* [C] *plural* **mitochondria BIOLOGY** in a cell, a long or round piece found in the cytoplasm (= substance surrounding the nucleus) that produces energy for the cell by breaking down food ➲See picture at **cell**

mitosis /maɪˈtəʊsɪs/ *noun* [U] **BIOLOGY** the type of cell division in which one cell divides into two identical cells, each with the same number of chromosomes as the original cell ➲Compare **meiosis**

mitral valve /ˈmaɪtrəlˌvælv/ *noun* [C] **ANATOMY** the valve (= part that opens and closes) in the heart which stops blood from returning into the atrium (= upper space) ➲See picture at **heart**

mitt /mɪt/ *noun* [C] **SPORT** a thick leather glove (= cover for the hand) used for catching a baseball ➲See colour picture **Sports 2** on page Centre 15

mix¹ /mɪks/ *verb* **1** COMBINE SUBSTANCES [I, T] If two or more substances mix, they combine to make one substance, and if you mix two or more substances, you combine them to make one substance. ***Mix*** *the powder* ***with*** *water to form a paste.* ○ *Put the chocolate, butter, and egg in a bowl and* ***mix*** *them all* ***together***. ○ *Oil and water don't mix.* **2** COMBINE QUALITIES ETC [I, T] to have or do two or more qualities, styles, activities, etc at the same time *a feeling of anger mixed with sadness* **3** MEET [I] to meet and talk to people *She enjoys going to parties and* ***mixing with*** *people.*

mix sth/sb up *phrasal verb* to confuse two people or things by thinking that one person or thing is the other person or thing *People often mix them up because they look so similar.*

mix sth up *phrasal verb* to cause a group of things to be untidy or badly organized *The books were all mixed up in a box.*

WORD PARTNERS FOR ***mix***

a mix **of** sth • an **ethnic/racial/social** mix

mix² /mɪks/ *noun* **1** COMBINATION [C] a combination of things or people, often in a group [**usually singular**] *There's a good* ***mix of*** *nationalities in the class.* **2** POWDER [C, U] a powder to which you add liquid in order to make something *cake mix*

mixed /mɪkst/ *adjective* **1** made of a combination of different people or things *a racially mixed area* ○ *a mixed salad* **2 mixed feelings** If you have mixed feelings about something, you are pleased and not pleased at the same time. ➲See also: a mixed **blessing**

ˌmixed eˈconomy *noun* [C] **ECONOMICS** an economic system in which some industries are controlled privately and some by the government

ˌmixed ˈfraction *noun* [C] **MATHEMATICS** a combination of a whole number and a fraction

mixed-race /mɪkstˈreɪs/ *adjective* describes a person whose parents are of different races (= the groups that people are divided into according to their physical characteristics)

ˌmixed ˈup *adjective informal* **1** confused *I got a bit mixed up and thought we were supposed to be there at eight.* **2 be mixed up in sth** to be involved in an activity that is bad or illegal **3 be mixed up with sb** to be involved with someone who has a bad influence on you *Her son got mixed up with the wrong people.*

mixer /ˈmɪksəʳ/ *noun* [C] a machine that mixes things *an electric mixer*

O-➡**mixture** /ˈmɪkstʃəʳ/ *noun* **1** [SUBSTANCE] [C, U] a substance made of other substances that have been combined *Add milk to the mixture and stir until smooth.* **2** [STYLES/IDEAS] [no plural] when there is a combination of two or more ideas, qualities, styles, etc *Their house is decorated in a mixture of styles.*

mix-up /ˈmɪksʌp/ *noun* [C] *informal* when there is a mistake because things are confused [usually singular] *There was a mix-up with the bags at the airport.*

ml **MEASURES** *written abbreviation for* millilitre (= a unit for measuring liquid)

mm **MEASURES** *written abbreviation for* millimetre (= a unit for measuring length)

moan /məʊn/ *verb* [I] **1** [COMPLAIN] to complain or speak in a way that shows you are unhappy *She's always **moaning about** something.* **2** [SOUND] to make a low sound, especially because you are in pain *He lay on the floor moaning.* •**moan** *noun* [C]

mob¹ /mɒb/ *noun* [C] a large group of people that is often violent or not organized *an angry mob*

mob² /mɒb/ *verb* [T] **mobbing**, *past* **mobbed** If a group of people mob someone, they get close to them, often to get their photograph or signature. [often passive] *She was mobbed by photographers.*

mobile¹ /ˈməʊbaɪl/ (US) /ˈməʊbəl/ *adjective* able to move or be moved easily *a mobile home* ➲Opposite **immobile**

O-➡**mobile²** /ˈməʊbaɪl/ (US) /ˈməʊbiːl/ *noun* [C] **1** [TELEPHONE] a mobile phone **2** [DECORATION] a decoration made of objects on threads that hang down and move in the air

O-➡**ˌmobile ˈphone** *noun* [C] a telephone that you can carry everywhere with you

mobilize (*also UK* **-ise**) /ˈməʊbɪlaɪz/ *verb* **1** [POLITICS] [T] to organize a group of people so that they support or oppose something or someone *He's trying to **mobilize support** for the strike.* **2** [WAR] [I, T] *formal* to prepare for a war *The forces were fully mobilized for action.* •**mobilization** /ˌməʊbɪlaɪˈzeɪʃᵊn/ *noun* [U]

mock¹ /mɒk/ *verb* [I, T] to laugh at someone or something in an unkind way *The older kids mocked him whenever he made a mistake.*

mock² /mɒk/ *adjective* [always before noun] not real but appearing or pretending to be exactly like something *a **mock exam** ○ mock leather*

mockery /ˈmɒkᵊri/ *noun* [U] **1** when someone laughs at someone or something in an unkind way **2 make a mockery of sth** to make something seem stupid *The latest outbreak of fighting makes a mockery of the peace process.*

modal verb /ˈməʊdəlˌvɜːb/ (*also* **modal**) *noun* [C] **LANGUAGE** a verb, for example 'can', 'might', or 'must', that is used before another verb to show that something is possible, necessary, etc ➲See Extra help page **Modal verbs** on page Centre 34.

mode /məʊd/ *noun* [C] *formal* **1** a way of doing something *a mode of transport* **2** **MATHEMATICS** the number or value which appears most often in a particular set

O-➡**model¹** /ˈmɒdᵊl/ *noun* [C] **1** [PERSON] someone whose job is to wear fashionable clothes, be in photographs, etc in order to advertise things *a fashion model* **2** [COPY] a smaller copy of a real object, often used to show how something works or what it looks like **3** [EXAMPLE] someone or something that is an example for others to copy *a model of good behaviour* **4** [DESIGN] a design of machine or car that is made by a particular company *I think her car is a slightly older model.* ➲See also: **role model**

model² /ˈmɒdᵊl/ *verb* [I, T] *UK* **modelling**, *past* **modelled**, *US* **modeling**, *past* **modeled** to wear clothes in fashion shows, magazines, etc as a model

be modelled on sth *phrasal verb* to be based on the design of something else *The house is modelled on a 16th century castle.*

model yourself on sb *phrasal verb* to try to make yourself very similar to someone else

modelling /ˈmɒdᵊlɪŋ/ *noun* [U] **1** the job of being a fashion model **2** making models of objects, for example when designing them

modem /ˈməʊdem/ *noun* [C] **COMPUTING** a piece of equipment that is used to send information from a computer through a telephone line, cable or other link ➲See Extra help page **The Web and the Internet** on page Centre 36.

moderate¹ /ˈmɒdᵊrət/ *adjective* **1** average in size or amount and not too much *Eating a moderate amount of fat is healthy.* **2** **POLITICS** not extreme, especially relating to political opinions *a moderate political group* •**moderately** *adverb*

moderate² /ˈmɒdᵊrət/ *noun* [C] **POLITICS** someone who does not have extreme political opinions

moderate³ /ˈmɒdᵊreɪt/ *verb* [T] to make something less extreme *He's trying to moderate his drinking.*

moderation /ˌmɒdᵊrˈeɪʃᵊn/ *noun* **1 in moderation** If you do something in moderation, you do not do it too much. *I only drink alcohol in moderation now.* **2** [U] when you control your feelings or actions and stop them from becoming extreme

M

O‒ **modern** /ˈmɒdᵊn/ *adjective* **1** NOW relating to the present time and not to the past *modern society* ○ *the stresses of **modern life*** **2** NEW using the newest ideas, design, technology, etc and not traditional *modern art/architecture* ○ *modern medicine* •**modernity** /mɒdˈɜːnəti/ *noun* [U] *formal* when something is modern

modern-day /ˈmɒdᵊndeɪ/ *adjective* [**always before noun**] relating to the present time and not to the past *a modern-day version of Shakespeare*

modernize (*also UK* **-ise**) /ˈmɒdᵊnaɪz/ *verb* [I, T] to make something more modern or to become more modern *We really need to modernize our image.* •**modernization** /ˌmɒdᵊnaɪˈzeɪʃᵊn/ *noun* [U]

ˌmodern ˈlanguages *noun* [plural] **LANGUAGE** languages that are spoken now such as Spanish or German

modest /ˈmɒdɪst/ *adjective* **1** NOT LARGE not large in size or amount, or not expensive *a modest amount of money* ○ *Their house is quite modest in size.* **2** NOT PROUD If you are modest, you do not talk in a proud way about your skills or successes. *He's very modest about his achievements.* •**modestly** *adverb*

modesty /ˈmɒdɪsti/ *noun* [U] when you do not talk in a proud way about your skills or successes

modicum /ˈmɒdɪkəm/ *noun formal* **a modicum of sth** a small amount of something *a modicum of success*

M

modification /ˌmɒdɪfɪˈkeɪʃᵊn/ *noun* [C, U] a small change to something *We've **made** a few **modifications to** the system.*

modifier /ˈmɒdɪfaɪəʳ/ *noun* [C] **LANGUAGE** in grammar, a word that describes or limits the meaning of another word

modify /ˈmɒdɪfaɪ/ *verb* [T] **1** to change something in order to improve it [**often passive**] *The plans will have to be modified to reduce costs.* ○ *genetically modified food* **2** **LANGUAGE** In grammar, a word that modifies another word describes or limits the meaning of that word. *Adjectives modify nouns.*

module /ˈmɒdjuːl/ *noun* [C] **1** **EDUCATION** *UK* a part of a university or college course **2** a part of an object that can operate alone, especially a part of a spacecraft

mogul /ˈməʊgᵊl/ *noun* [C] an important, powerful person ***media/movie moguls***

Mohammed /məˈhæmɪd/ *noun* **RELIGION** the Arab holy man on whose life and teachings Islam is based

moist /mɔɪst/ *adjective* slightly wet *Keep the soil moist but not wet.* •**moisten** /ˈmɔɪsᵊn/ *verb* [I, T] to make something slightly wet, or to become slightly wet

moisture /ˈmɔɪstʃəʳ/ *noun* [U] very small drops of water in the air or on a surface

moisturizer (*also UK* **-iser**) /ˈmɔɪstʃəraɪzəʳ/ *noun* [C, U] a substance which you put on your skin to make it less dry •**moisturize** (*also UK* **-ise**) /ˈmɔɪstʃᵊraɪz/ *verb* [T] to put moisturizer on your skin

molar¹ /ˈməʊləʳ/ *noun* [C] **ANATOMY** one of the large teeth at the back of the mouth used for crushing food ➲Compare **incisor, canine** ➲See picture at **skull**

molar

molar² /ˈməʊləʳ/ *adjective* **MEASURES** contained in one mole (= unit of measurement of the amount of a substance) *molar mass/volume*

molasses /məʊˈlæsɪz/ (*also UK* **treacle**) *noun* [U] **FOOD** a sweet, thick, dark liquid used in sweet dishes

mold /məʊld/ *noun, verb US spelling of* mould

moldy /ˈməʊldi/ *adjective US spelling of* mouldy

mole /məʊl/ *noun* [C] **1** **HEALTH** a small, dark mark on the skin **2** ANIMAL a small animal with black fur that digs holes in the soil and lives under the ground **3** PERSON *informal* someone who gives other organizations or governments secret information about the organization where they work **4** **MEASURES** a unit of measurement of the amount of a substance

molecular /məˈlekjʊləʳ/ *adjective* **PHYSICS, CHEMISTRY** made from or relating to molecules

moˌlecular ˈweight *noun* [U] **PHYSICS, CHEMISTRY** the weight of a molecule, found by adding together the atomic masses of all the atoms it contains

molecule /ˈmɒlɪkjuːl/ *noun* [C] **PHYSICS, CHEMISTRY** the smallest unit of a substance, consisting of one or more atoms

molehill /ˈməʊlhɪl/ *noun* [C] ➲See: make a **mountain** out of a molehill

molest /məʊˈlest/ *verb* [T] to hurt or attack someone in a sexual way *He was accused of molesting children.* •**molestation** /ˌməʊlesˈteɪʃən/ *noun* [U]

mom /mɒm/ *US* (*UK* **mum**) *noun* [C] *informal* mother *My mom phoned last night.* ○ *Can we go now, Mom?*

O‒ **moment** /ˈməʊmənt/ *noun* **1** SHORT TIME [C] a very short period of time *I'll be back **in a moment**.* ○ ***For a moment** I thought it was Anna.* ○ *Could you **wait a moment**?* **2** POINT IN TIME [C] a point in time ***Just at that moment**, the phone rang.* **3 at the moment** now *I'm afraid she's not here at the moment.* **4 for the moment** If you do something for the moment, you are doing it now but might do something different in the future. **5 the moment (that)** as soon as *I'll call you the moment I hear anything.* **6 have a senior, blond etc moment** *informal* to behave, for a short time, in a way which shows you are old, silly, etc *I've just had a senior moment - I couldn't remember why I'd gone into the kitchen.* ➲See also: on the **spur²** of the moment

momentarily /ˈməʊməntᵊrᵊli/ *adverb* for a very short time *I momentarily forgot his name.*

momentary /ˈməʊməntᵊri/ *adjective* lasting for a very short time *a **momentary lapse** of memory*

momentous /məʊˈmentəs/ *adjective* A momentous decision, event, etc is very important because it has a big effect on the future.

WORD PARTNERS FOR **momentum**

gain/gather/lose momentum • **keep up/maintain** the momentum • the momentum **for/of** sth

momentum /məʊˈmentəm/ *noun* [U] **1** when something continues to move, increase, or develop *to **gain/gather momentum*** ○ *The players seemed to **lose momentum** halfway through the game.* **2** **PHYSICS** in science, the force that makes something continue to move

momma /ˈmɒmə/ *noun* [C] *US another word for* mommy

mommy /ˈmɒmi/ *US* (*UK* **mummy**) *noun* [C] *informal* a word for 'mother', used especially by children *I want my mommy!* ○ *Can I have some candy, Mommy?*

Mon *written abbreviation for* Monday

monarch /ˈmɒnək/ *noun* [C] a king or queen

monarchy /ˈmɒnəki/ *noun* **1** **POLITICS** [U, no plural] when a country is ruled by a king or queen **2** **POLITICS** [C] a country that is ruled by a king or queen

monastery /ˈmɒnəstᵊri/ *noun* [C] **RELIGION** a building where men live as a religious group

monastic /məˈnæstɪk/ *adjective* **RELIGION** relating to a monk (= religious man) or a monastery

O⇀**Monday** /ˈmʌndeɪ/ (*written abbreviation* **Mon**) *noun* [C, U] the day of the week after Sunday and before Tuesday

monetary /ˈmʌnɪtᵊri/ *adjective* **ECONOMICS** relating to money

WORD PARTNERS FOR **money**

borrow/earn/lend/pay/raise/save/spend money

O⇀**money** /ˈmʌni/ *noun* [U] **ECONOMICS, FINANCE** the coins or banknotes (= pieces of paper with values) that are used to buy things *How much money have you got?* ○ *He **spends** all his **money** on clothes and CDs.* ○ *The company's not **making*** (= earning) *any money at the moment.* ➲See also: **pocket money**

ˈ**money** ˌ**order** *US* (*UK* **postal order**) *noun* [C] **FINANCE** an official piece of paper bought at a post office that you can send instead of money

ˈ**money sup**ˌ**ply** *noun* [C usually singular] **ECONOMICS** all the money which is in use in a country

mongrel /ˈmʌŋgrᵊl/ *noun* [C] a dog that is a mix of different breeds

monies /ˈmʌniz/ *noun* [plural] *formal* **FINANCE** amounts of money

monitor¹ /ˈmɒnɪtəʳ/ *noun* [C] **1** **COMPUTING** a screen that shows information or pictures, usually connected to a computer *a colour monitor* ➲See colour picture **The Office** on page Centre 5 **2** MACHINE a machine, often in a hospital, that measures something such as the rate that your heart beats *a **heart monitor*** **3** PERSON someone who watches something to make certain that it is done correctly or fairly *a human rights monitor*

monitor² /ˈmɒnɪtəʳ/ *verb* [T] to watch something carefully and record your results *to monitor progress*

monk /mʌŋk/ *noun* [C] **RELIGION** a member of a group of religious men living apart from other people

monkey /ˈmʌŋki/ *noun* [C] a hairy animal with a long tail that lives in hot countries and climbs trees

mono- /mɒnəʊ-/ *prefix* one or single *monolingual* ○ *a monologue*

monochrome /ˈmɒnəkrəʊm/ *adjective* A monochrome image is only in black, white, and grey and not in colour.

monocotyledon /ˌmɒnəʊˌkɒtɪˈliːdən/ *noun* [C] **BIOLOGY** a plant that produces flowers and has only one cotyledon (= leaf part inside the seed) •**monocotyledonous** /ˌmɒnəʊˌkɒtɪˈliːdənəs/ *adjective*

monogamy /məˈnɒgəmi/ *noun* [U] **SOCIETY** when someone has a sexual relationship with only one person •**monogamous** *adjective* relating to monogamy *a **monogamous relationship***

monolingual /ˌmɒnəʊˈlɪŋgwᵊl/ *adjective* **LANGUAGE** using only one language *monolingual dictionaries*

monolithic /ˌmɒnəʊˈlɪθɪk/ *adjective* large and powerful

monologue (*also US* **monolog**) /ˈmɒnᵊlɒg/ *noun* [C] a long speech by one person, often in a performance

M

monomer /ˈmɒnəʊməʳ/ *noun* [C] **CHEMISTRY** a chemical compound whose simple molecules can join together to form polymers

mononucleosis /ˌmɒnəʊˌnjuːkliˈəʊsɪs/ *US* (*UK* **glandular fever**) *noun* [U] **HEALTH** an infectious disease that makes your glands (= small organs in your body) swell and makes you feel tired

monopolize (*also UK* **-ise**) /məˈnɒpᵊlaɪz/ *verb* [T] to control a situation by being the only person or organization involved in it

monopoly /məˈnɒpᵊli/ *noun* [C] **1** SYSTEM when a company or organization is the only one in an area of business or activity and has complete control of it *They **have a monopoly on** the postal service.* **2** COMPANY a company or other organization that has a monopoly in a particular industry

monosaccharide /ˌmɒnəʊˈsækᵊraɪd/ *noun* [C] **CHEMISTRY** a simple type of carbohydrate, such as glucose and fructose, formed of molecules that cannot be broken down into any simpler form ➲Compare **polysaccharide**

monosyllabic /ˌmɒnəʊsɪˈlæbɪk/ *adjective* using only short words such as 'yes' or 'no', usually because you do not want to talk

monotonous /məˈnɒtᵊnəs/ *adjective* If something is monotonous, it is boring because it stays the same. *a **monotonous voice*** ○ ***monotonous work*** •**monotonously** *adverb*

monozygotic /ˌmɒnəʊzaɪˈgɒtɪk/ *adjective* **BIOLOGY** Monozygotic twins develop from the same egg and are often called identical twins. ➲Compare **dizygotic**

monsoon /mɒn'su:n/ *noun* [C] **GEOGRAPHY** the season when there is heavy rain in Southern Asia

monster /'mɒnstəʳ/ *noun* [C] an imaginary creature that is large, ugly, and frightening

monstrous /'mɒnstrəs/ *adjective* **1** BAD very bad or cruel *a **monstrous crime*** **2** MONSTER like a monster

O— **month** /mʌnθ/ *noun* [C] **1** PART OF YEAR one of the twelve periods of time that a year is divided into *last/next month* ○ *Your birthday's this month, isn't it?* **2** FOUR WEEKS a period of approximately four weeks *I saw him about three months ago.*

monthly /'mʌnθli/ *adjective, adverb* happening or produced once a month *a monthly meeting* ○ *a monthly magazine*

monument /'mɒnjəmənt/ *noun* [C] **1** REMEMBER a building or other structure that is built to make people remember an event in history or a famous person *a national monument* ○ *They built the statue as **a monument to** all the soldiers who died.* **2** OLD PLACE an old building or place that is important in history *an ancient monument*

monumental /ˌmɒnjə'mentᵊl/ *adjective* very large *a **monumental task***

moo /mu:/ *noun* [C] the sound that a cow makes •**moo** *verb* [I] **mooing**, *past* **mooed**

WORD PARTNERS FOR ***mood***

be **in** a [bad/confident/foul/good, etc] mood • mood **changes/swings** • a **bad/foul/good** mood

O— **mood** /mu:d/ *noun* **1** [C, U] the way someone feels at a particular time *to be in a **good/bad mood*** ○ *The **public mood** changed dramatically after the bombing.* **2 be in a mood** to not be friendly to other people because you are feeling angry **3 be in the mood for sth/to do sth** to want to do or have something *I'm not really in the mood for shopping at the moment.* **4 be in no mood for sth/to do sth** to not want to do something with someone else, often because you are angry with them **5 LANGUAGE** [C] in grammar, one of the different ways a sentence is being used, for example to give an order, express a fact, etc *the indicative/imperative mood*

moody /'mu:di/ *adjective* If someone is moody, they are often unfriendly because they feel angry or unhappy. •**moodily** *adverb* •**moodiness** *noun* [U]

O— **moon** /mu:n/ *noun* **1 the moon ASTRONOMY** the round object that shines in the sky at night and moves around the Earth **2 crescent/full/new moon ASTRONOMY** the shape made by the amount of the moon that you can see at a particular time **3 ASTRONOMY** [C] a round object like the moon that moves around another planet **4 once in a blue moon** rarely *We only go out once in a blue moon.* **5 be over the moon** *UK* to be very pleased about something *"I bet she was pleased with her results." "She was over the moon."*

'moon ˌbuggy *noun* [C] a vehicle used for driving on the moon

moonlight /'mu:nlaɪt/ *noun* [U] light that comes from the moon *In the moonlight she looked even more beautiful.* •**moonlit** *adjective* [**always before noun**] with light from the moon

moor /mɔ:ʳ/ *noun* [C] **GEOGRAPHY** an open area in the countryside that is covered with rough grass and bushes [**usually plural**] *the Yorkshire Moors*

moose /mu:s/ *noun* [C] *plural* **moose** a large deer that comes from North America

moot point /ˌmu:t'pɔɪnt/ *noun* [C] a subject that people cannot agree about

mop[1] /mɒp/ *noun* [C] a piece of equipment used for cleaning floors that has a long handle and thick strings at one end

mop[2] /mɒp/ *verb* [T] **mopping**, *past* **mopped** to use a mop *to **mop the floor***
mop sth up *phrasal verb* to use a cloth or mop to remove liquid from a surface

moraine /mɒr'eɪn/ *noun* [C] **GEOGRAPHY** a large mass of rocks and soil that is carried along with a glacier (= large mass of ice) and remains when the glacier melts

O— **moral**[1] /'mɒrᵊl/ *adjective* **1** RIGHT AND WRONG [**always before noun**] relating to beliefs about what is right or wrong ***moral standards/values*** ○ *a **moral issue*** **2** GOOD CHARACTER behaving in a way that most people think is correct and honest *He's a very moral person.* ➲Opposite **immoral** ➲Compare **amoral** •**morally** *adverb morally wrong*

moral[2] /'mɒrᵊl/ *noun* [C] something you learn from a story or event about how to behave *The **moral of the story** is never lie.*

WORD PARTNERS FOR ***morale***

boost/damage/improve/raise/undermine morale • **high/low** morale

morale /mə'rɑ:l/ *noun* [U] the amount of confidence or hope for the future that people feel *The pay increase should help to **improve** staff **morale**.*

morality /mə'ræləti/ *noun* [U] ideas and beliefs about what is right or wrong

morals /'mɒrəlz/ *noun* [**plural**] principles of good behaviour *He doesn't care what he does, he has no morals at all.*

ˌmoral su'pport *noun* [U] help and encouragement *Roz has said she'll come with me for moral support.*

morbid /'mɔ:bɪd/ *adjective* showing too much interest in unpleasant things such as death *a **morbid fascination** with death*

O— **more**[1] /mɔ:ʳ/ *quantifier* **1** IN ADDITION something in addition to what you already have *Would anyone like some more food?* ○ *I need a bit more money.* **2** GREATER AMOUNT a greater number or amount of people or things *There are a lot more people here today than yesterday.* ○ *He knows more about computers than I do.* **3 more and more** an increasing number *More and more people are choosing not to get married.* ➲See also: **any more**

COMMON LEARNER ERROR

more

The opposite of **more** is **fewer** for countable nouns and **less** for uncountable nouns.

He takes more exercise now.

He takes less exercise now.

He smokes fewer cigarettes.

more² /mɔːʳ/ *adverb* **1 more beautiful/difficult/interesting, etc** used to show that someone or something has a greater amount of a quality than someone or something else *It's* ***more*** *expensive* ***than*** *the others.* ○ *She's far more intelligent than her sister.* **2** used to show that something happens a greater number of times than before *We eat out a lot* ***more than*** *we used to.* **3 more or less** almost *We've more or less finished work on the house.* **4 more and more** more as time passes *It's becoming more and more difficult to pass the exam.* ➲See also: **any more**

COMMON LEARNER ERROR

more

More is used to form the comparative of many adjectives and adverbs that have two or more syllables.

a more expensive hotel

Could you drive more slowly please?

~~*an expensiver hotel*~~

The opposite of the adverb **more** is **less**.

a less expensive hotel

moreover /mɔːr'əʊvəʳ/ *adverb formal* also *It is a cheap and, moreover, effective way of dealing with the problem.*

morgue /mɔːg/ *noun* [C] a building or room where dead bodies are prepared and kept before a funeral

Mormon /'mɔːmən/ *adjective* **RELIGION** belonging or relating to a Christian group that was started in the US by Joseph Smith •**Mormon** *noun* [C]

morning /'mɔːnɪŋ/ *noun* [C, U] **1** the first half of the day, from the time when the sun rises or you wake up until the middle of the day *Friday morning* ○ ***tomorrow morning*** ○ *I got up late* ***this morning***. **2 in the morning a** during the early part of the day *I listen to the radio in the morning.* **b** tomorrow morning *I'll pack my bags in the morning.* **3 3/4/, etc o'clock in the morning** 3/4, etc o'clock in the night *My car alarm went off at 3 o'clock in the morning.* **4 (Good) morning.** used to say hello to someone in the morning

moron /'mɔːrɒn/ *noun* [C] *informal* a very stupid person •**moronic** /mɔː'rɒnɪk/ *adjective informal* stupid

morose /mə'rəʊs/ *adjective* If someone is morose, they are not friendly or happy and they talk very little.

morphine /'mɔːfiːn/ *noun* [U] **HEALTH** a powerful drug that is used to reduce pain

morsel /'mɔːsᵊl/ *noun* [C] a small piece of something *a morsel of food*

mortal¹ /'mɔːtᵊl/ *adjective* **1** not living forever ➲Opposite **immortal 2 mortal danger/fear/terror, etc** extreme danger/fear/terror, etc, because you could die •**mortally** *adverb* ***mortally wounded***

mortal² /'mɔːtᵊl/ *noun* [C] *literary* a human being

mortality /mɔː'tæləti/ *noun* [U] **1** NUMBER the number of deaths at a particular time or in a particular place ***infant mortality*** ○ ***the mortality rate*** **2** NOT LIVING FOREVER the way that people do not live forever *Her death made him more aware of his own mortality.*

mortar /'mɔːtəʳ/ *noun* **1** WEAPON [C] a heavy gun that fires explosives high into the air ***a mortar attack/bomb*** **2** MIXTURE [U] a mixture of substances, for example sand and water, that is used between bricks or stones to keep them together

WORD PARTNERS FOR ***mortgage***

get/have/pay off/take out a mortgage • a mortgage **payment**

mortgage /'mɔːgɪdʒ/ *noun* [C] **FINANCE** money that you borrow to buy a home *a monthly mortgage payment*

mortified /'mɔːtɪfaɪd/ *adjective* very embarrassed

mortify /'mɔːtɪfaɪ/ *verb* **be mortified** to feel very embarrassed or upset about something *I told her she'd upset John and she was mortified.*

mortuary /'mɔːtʃuᵊri/ *noun* [C] a building or room where dead bodies are prepared and kept before a funeral

mosaic /məʊ'zeɪɪk/ *noun* [C, U] **ART** a picture or pattern that is made with small pieces of coloured stone, glass, etc

Moslem /'mɒzləm/ *noun* [C] **RELIGION** *another spelling of* Muslim (= someone who believes in Islam) •**Moslem** *adjective*

mosque /mɒsk/ *noun* [C] **RELIGION** a building where Muslims say their prayers

mosquito /mɒ'skiːtəʊ/ *noun* [C] *plural* **mosquitoes** a small flying insect that sucks your blood, sometimes causing malaria (= a serious disease) ***mosquito bites***

moss /mɒs/ *noun* [C, U] a very small, green plant that grows on the surface of rocks, trees, etc

most¹ /məʊst/ *adverb* **1 the most attractive/important/popular, etc** used to show that someone or something has the greatest amount of a quality *She's the most beautiful girl I've ever seen.* ○ *There are various reasons but this is the most important.* **2** more than anyone or anything else *Which subject do you like most?* ○ *Sam enjoyed the swings* ***most of all***.

COMMON LEARNER ERROR

most

The adverb **most** is used to form the superlative of many adjectives and adverbs.

the most beautiful actress in the world

most² /məʊst/ *quantifier* **1** ALMOST ALL almost all of a group of people or things *Most people think he's guilty.* ○ ***Most of*** *our students walk to school.* **2** MORE THAN a larger amount than anyone or anything else *This one costs the most.* ○ *Which of you earns most?* **3 the most**

M

the largest number or amount possible *That's the most I can pay you.* **4 make the most of sth** to take full advantage of something because it may not last long *We should make the most of this good weather.* **5 at (the) most** not more than a particular amount or number *The journey will take an hour at the most.*

mostly /ˈməʊstli/ *adverb* mainly or most of the time *She reads mostly romantic novels.*

motel /məʊˈtel/ *noun* [C] a hotel for people who are travelling by car

moth /mɒθ/ *noun* [C] an insect with large wings that often flies at night and is attracted to light ➲See picture at **insect**

mother /ˈmʌðəʳ/ *noun* [C] **1** your female parent *a single mother* ○ *My mother and father are divorced.* **2 Mother RELIGION** the title of an important nun (= woman who lives in a female religious group) *Mother Teresa* ➲See also: **surrogate mother**

motherhood /ˈmʌðəhʊd/ *noun* [U] when someone is a mother

mother-in-law /ˈmʌðərɪnˌlɔː/ *noun* [C] *plural* **mothers-in-law** the mother of your husband or wife

motherly /ˈmʌðəli/ *adjective* A motherly woman is like a mother, usually because she is kind and looks after people.

ˈMother's ˌDay *noun* [C, U] a Sunday in the spring when people give their mothers presents to show their love

ˈmother ˌtongue *noun* [C] **LANGUAGE** the first language that you learn when you are a child

motif /məʊˈtiːf/ *noun* [C] a small design used as a decoration on something *a floral motif*

motion¹ /ˈməʊʃən/ *noun* **1** MOVEMENT [U] when or how something moves *The motion of the boat made him feel sick.* **2** ACTION [C] a single action or movement *She made a motion with her hand.* **3** SUGGESTION [C] a suggestion that you make in a formal meeting or court of law *to **propose/oppose** a **motion*** **4 set sth in motion** to make something start to happen **5 go through the motions** to do something that you have to do without enthusiasm ➲See also: **slow motion**

motion² /ˈməʊʃən/ *verb* **motion (for/to) sb to do sth** to make a movement as a sign for someone to do something *She motioned him to sit down.*

motionless /ˈməʊʃənləs/ *adjective* not moving *He stood motionless in the middle of the road.*

motivate /ˈməʊtɪveɪt/ *verb* [T] **1** ENTHUSIASTIC to make someone enthusiastic about doing something [+ **to do sth**] *Teaching is all about motivating people to learn.* **2** CAUSE to cause someone to behave in a particular way [**often passive**] *Some people are motivated by greed.* •**motivated** *adjective a racially motivated crime* ○ *a very motivated student* (= one who works hard and wants to succeed)

WORD PARTNERS FOR ***motivation***

sb's **main/primary** motivation • the motivation **behind/for** sth

motivation /ˌməʊtɪˈveɪʃən/ *noun* **1** ENTHUSIASM [U] enthusiasm for doing something *There is a lack of motivation among the staff.* **2** REASON [C] the need or reason for doing something *What was the **motivation for** the attack?*

motivational /ˌməʊtɪˈveɪʃənəl/ *adjective* [**always before noun**] giving you encouragement to do something *a **motivational speaker***

WORD PARTNERS FOR ***motive***

have a motive • an **ulterior/underlying** motive • the motive **behind/for** sth

motive /ˈməʊtɪv/ *noun* [C] a reason for doing something *The police don't yet know the **motive for** the killing.*

motor¹ /ˈməʊtəʳ/ *noun* [C] the part of a machine or vehicle that changes electricity or fuel into movement and makes it work *an electric motor*

motor² /ˈməʊtəʳ/ *adjective* [**always before noun**] relating to cars *motor racing*

motorbike /ˈməʊtəbaɪk/ *noun* [C] a vehicle with two wheels and an engine

motorcycle /ˈməʊtəˌsaɪkl/ *noun* [C] a motorbike

motoring /ˈməʊtərɪŋ/ *adjective* [**always before noun**] *UK* relating to driving *a motoring offence*

motorist /ˈməʊtərɪst/ *noun* [C] someone who drives a car

ˌmotor ˈneuron *noun* [C] **ANATOMY, BIOLOGY** a nerve cell that sends messages to muscles or glands (= organs that produce chemical substances in the body)

ˈmotor ˌracing *noun* [U] **SPORT** the sport of driving extremely fast and powerful cars around a track

motorway /ˈməʊtəweɪ/ *UK* (*US* **freeway, expressway, interstate**) *noun* [C] a long, wide road, usually used by traffic travelling fast over long distances

mottled /ˈmɒtld/ *adjective* A mottled pattern has a mixture of dark and light areas. *mottled skin*

motto /ˈmɒtəʊ/ *noun* [C] **LANGUAGE** a short phrase that expresses someone's purpose or beliefs *Her motto is, "Work hard, play hard".*

mould¹ *UK* (*US* **mold**) /məʊld/ *noun* **1 BIOLOGY** [U] a green or black substance that grows in wet places or on old food **2** [C] a container that is used to make something in a particular shape *a chocolate mould* **3 break the mould** to do something differently after it has been done in the same way for a long time

mould² *UK* (*US* **mold**) /məʊld/ *verb* [T] to make a soft substance a particular shape *moulded plastic*

moulding /ˈməʊldɪŋ/ *noun* [U] a piece of wood, plastic, stone, etc. which has been made into a particular shape to decorate the top or bottom of a wall, or a door, window or piece of furniture

mouldy *UK* (*US* **moldy**) /ˈməʊldi/ *adjective* covered with mould *mouldy cheese*

mound /maʊnd/ *noun* [C] **1** PILE a large pile of something *a mound of clothes waiting to be ironed* **2** HILL a higher area of soil, like a small hill *an ancient burial mound*

Mount /maʊnt/ *noun* [C] used in the names of mountains *Mount Everest*

mount /maʊnt/ *verb* **1 mount a campaign/challenge/protest, etc** to arrange a series of organized activities that will achieve a particular result **2** [INCREASE] [I] to increase in amount or level *Tension in the room was mounting.* **3 mount sth on/to, etc** to fix an object onto something *They've mounted a camera on the wall by the door.* **4** [GO UP] [T] to go up something *to mount the stairs* **5** [RIDE] [T] to get on a horse or bicycle ⊃Opposite **dismount**

mount up *phrasal verb* to gradually become a large amount *My homework is really mounting up this week.*

O‑ **mountain** /ˈmaʊntɪn/ *noun* [C] **1 GEOGRAPHY** a very high hill *to* ***climb*** *a* ***mountain*** ○ *a* ***mountain range*** **2** *informal* a large pile of something *There's a* ***mountain of*** *papers on my desk.* **3 make a mountain out of a molehill** to deal with a small problem as if it were a big problem

ˈ**mountain ˌbike** *noun* [C] **SPORT** a bicycle with thick tyres, originally made for people to ride on hills and rough ground

mountainous /ˈmaʊntɪnəs/ *adjective* **GEOGRAPHY** A mountainous area has a lot of mountains.

mourn /mɔːn/ *verb* [I, T] to feel very sad because someone has died *He* ***mourned for*** *his dead son every day.*

mourner /ˈmɔːnəʳ/ *noun* [C] someone at a funeral

mournful /ˈmɔːnfəl/ *adjective* very sad *a mournful voice* •**mournfully** *adverb*

mourning /ˈmɔːnɪŋ/ *noun* [U] when someone mourns the death of someone else *a* ***period of mourning*** ○ *She's* ***in mourning*** *for her husband.*

mouse /maʊs/ *noun* [C] *plural* **mice 1 COMPUTING** a small piece of equipment connected to a computer that you move with your hand to control what the computer does ⊃See colour picture **The Office** on page Centre 5 **2** a small animal with fur and a long, thin tail

ˈ**mouse ˌmat** *noun* [C] **COMPUTING** a flat piece of material on which you move the mouse of your computer

mousse /muːs/ *noun* [C, U] **1 FOOD** a soft, cold food that is often sweet and usually has eggs or cream in it ***chocolate mousse*** **2** a substance that you put in your hair so that it stays in a particular shape

moustache (*also US* **mustache**) /məˈstɑːʃ/ (US) /ˈmʌstæʃ/ *noun* [C] a line of hair that some men grow above their mouths

mousy (*also* **mousey**) /ˈmaʊsi/ *adjective* **1** [HAIR] Mousy hair is light brown. **2** [PERSON] A mousy person is shy and not very interesting.

WORD PARTNERS FOR ***mouth***

close/open your mouth • **in** your mouth

O‑ **mouth** /maʊθ/ *noun* [C] **1 ANATOMY** the part of the face that is used for eating and speaking ⊃See colour picture **The Body** on page Centre 13 **2 mouth of a cave/tunnel, etc** the opening or entrance of a cave/tunnel, etc **3 mouth of a river GEOGRAPHY** where a river goes into the sea ⊃See also: **butter**[1] wouldn't melt in sb's mouth

mouthful /ˈmaʊθfʊl/ *noun* [C] the amount of food or drink that you can put into your mouth at one time

mouthpiece /ˈmaʊθpiːs/ *noun* [C] a person, newspaper, etc that expresses the opinions of the government or a political group

mouthwash /ˈmaʊθwɒʃ/ *noun* [U] a liquid used to make your mouth clean and fresh

movable /ˈmuːvəbl/ *adjective* able to be moved

O‑ **move**[1] /muːv/ *verb* **1** [CHANGE PLACE] [I] If a person or an organization moves, they go to a different place to live or work. *Eventually, he* ***moved to*** *Germany.* ○ *She's* ***moving into*** *a new apartment.* ○ *Our children have all* ***moved away****.* **2** [POSITION] [I, T] to change place or position, or to make something change place or position *We* ***moved*** *the chairs* ***to*** *another room.* ○ *Someone was* ***moving around*** *upstairs.* **3 move ahead/along/forward, etc** to make progress with something that you have planned to do *The department is moving ahead with changes to its teaching programme.* **4** [ACTION] [I] to take action [**+ to do sth**] *The company moved swiftly to find new products.* **5** [TIME] [T] to change the time or order of something *We need to move the meeting back a few days.* **6** [FEELING] [T] to make someone have strong feelings of sadness or sympathy [**often passive**] *I was deeply moved by his speech.* ○ *Many people were* ***moved to tears*** (= were so sad they cried). ⊃Compare **unmoved** **7 move house** *UK* to leave your home in order to live in a new one **8 get moving** *informal* to hurry

COMMON LEARNER ERROR

move or travel?

Move means to change position or put something in a different position.

Could you ***move*** *back a bit, please?*

Why don't you ***move*** *the table over there?*

Travel means to go from one place to another, usually in a vehicle.

Most people ***travel*** *to work by car.*

move in *phrasal verb* to begin living in a new home *She's just* ***moved in with*** *her boyfriend.* ○ *They want to* ***move in together*** *before they get married.*

move out *phrasal verb* to stop living in a particular home

move on *phrasal verb* **1** [NEW PLACE] to leave the place where you are staying and go somewhere else *After three days in Madrid we thought we'd move on.* **2** [NEW ACTIVITY] to start doing a new activity *I'd done the same job for ten years and felt it was time to move on.* **3** [NEW SUBJECT] to change from one subject to another when you are talking or writing *Let's* ***move on to*** *the next topic.*

move over *phrasal verb* to change the place where you are sitting or standing so that there is space for someone else to sit or stand

move[2] /muːv/ *noun* [C] **1** [ACTION] something that you do in order to achieve something or to make progress in a situation *"I've told her she's got to find somewhere else to live." "****Good move****!"* ○ *The latest policies are clearly* ***a move towards*** *democracy.* ○ *a good* ***career move***

M

2 [NEW HOME/OFFICE] when you go to live or work in a different place *The move will cost us a lot of money.* **3 make a move a** [MOVE] to change from one place or position to another *He made a move as if to leave.* **b** [LEAVE] *UK informal* to leave somewhere *I'd better make a move or I'll be late.* **4 get a move on** *informal* to hurry *Come on, get a move on!*

O-- **movement** /ˈmuːvmənt/ *noun* **1** [GROUP] [C] a group of people with the same beliefs who work together to achieve something *the women's movement ○ the labour movement* **2** [CHANGE] [C] a change or development in the way people think or behave *a movement towards democracy* **3** [POSITION] [C, U] a change of position or place *His movements were rather clumsy.* **4 MUSIC** [C] a part of a piece of music *The symphony opens with a slow movement.* **5 sb's movements** what someone is doing during a particular period of time *I don't know his movements this week.*

WORD PARTNERS FOR ***movie***

make/see/watch a movie • **in** a movie

O-- **movie** /ˈmuːvi/ *noun* [C] *US* **1** a film **2 the movies** *US* (*UK* **the cinema**) a cinema, or group of cinemas *What's playing at the movies? ○ Why don't we **go to the movies** tonight?*

ˈ**movie** ˌ**star** *noun* [C] a famous movie actor or actress

ˈ**movie** ˌ**theater** *US* (*UK* **cinema**) *noun* [C] a building where you go to watch films

moving /ˈmuːvɪŋ/ *adjective* **1** [FEELING] causing strong feelings of sadness or sympathy ***a moving tribute*** **2** [NOT STILL] [**always before noun**] A moving object is one that moves. *a moving target*

mow /məʊ/ *verb* [T] *past tense* **mowed**, *past participle* **mown** or **mowed** to cut grass using a machine *to **mow the lawn***

mower /ˈməʊəʳ/ (*also* **lawn mower**) *noun* [C] a machine that you use to cut grass

MP /ˌemˈpiː/ *noun* [C] **POLITICS** *abbreviation for* Member of Parliament: someone who has been elected to the government of the United Kingdom

MP3 /empiːˈθriː/ *noun* [C, U] **COMPUTING** a computer file (= collection of information) which stores good-quality sound in a small amount of space, or the technology that makes this possible

MPˈ**3** ˌ**player** *noun* [C] **COMPUTING** a piece of electronic equipment or a computer program for playing music that has been stored as MP3 files (= collections of information)

mph **MEASURES** *written abbreviation for* miles per hour: a unit for measuring speed *a 30 mph speed limit*

MPV /ˌempiːˈviː/ *UK* (*US* **minivan**) *noun* [C] *abbreviation for* multi-purpose vehicle: a large, high car which can carry more people than a normal car

O-- **Mr** /ˈmɪstəʳ/ *noun* a title for a man, used before his family name or full name *Good morning, Mr Smith. ○ This package is addressed to Mr Gordon Harper.*

COMMON LEARNER ERROR

Mr, Mrs, Ms, Miss

All these titles are used before someone's name.

Mr is used for men. **Mrs** is used for women who are married. **Miss** is used for girls or for women who are not married. **Ms** is used for women and does not show if a woman is married. Many women prefer to use this title to **Miss** or **Mrs**.

We do not use these titles on their own as a way of speaking to someone. Usually, we use no name.

Can I help you?

~~*Can I help you, Mrs?*~~

MRI /ˌemɑːrˈaɪ/ *noun* [C] **HEALTH** *abbreviation for* magnetic resonance imaging: a system that produces electronic pictures of the organs inside a person's body

O-- **Mrs** /ˈmɪsɪz/ *noun* a title for a married woman, used before her family name or full name *Hello, Mrs. Jones. ○ Please send your application to the finance director, Mrs Laura Fox.*

MRSA /ˌemɑːresˈeɪ/ *noun* **HEALTH** *abbreviation for* Methicillin Resistant Staphylococcus Aureus: a type of bacteria (= very small living things that causes disease) that is often found in hospitals and can make people very ill

O-- **Ms** /mɪz/ *noun* a title for a woman, used before her family name or full name *Ms Holly Fox*

MS /ˌemˈes/ *noun* [U] **HEALTH** *abbreviation for* multiple sclerosis (= a serious disease that gradually makes it difficult for a person to see, speak, or move)

MSc *UK* (*US* **MS**) /ˌemesˈsiː/ *noun* [C] **EDUCATION** *abbreviation for* Master of Science: a higher university qualification in a science subject

MTV® /ˌemtiːˈviː/ *noun* [U] *abbreviation for* Music Television: an organization that broadcasts pop music around the world

O-- **much**[1] /mʌtʃ/ *quantifier* **1** [QUESTION] In questions, 'much' is used to ask about the amount of something. *Was there much food there? ○ **How much** money will I need for the taxi?* **2** [NEGATIVE] In negative sentences, 'much' is used to say that there is not a large amount of something. *She doesn't earn much money. ○ Pete didn't say much at dinner. ○ "Is there any coffee left?" "Not much."* **3 too much/so much** a large amount of something, often more than you want *I'd love to come, but I've got too much work. ○ We were having so much fun, I didn't want to go home.* **4** [A LOT OF] *formal* a lot of *Much work remains to be done. ○ Much of his evidence was unreliable.* **5 not much of a sth** used when you want to say that a person or thing is a bad example of something *I'm not much of a cook.* **6 not be up to much** *UK informal* to be of bad quality *Her latest novel isn't up to much.* ➲See Common Learner Error at **many**

O-- **much**[2] /mʌtʃ/ *adverb* **more**, **most** **1** [A LOT] often or a lot *Do you go to London much? ○ I don't like curry very much.* **2** [WITH ADJECTIVES] used before comparative adjectives (= adjectives like 'better' and 'smaller', that are used to compare things) to mean 'a lot' *Their old house was much bigger. ○ That's a much more sensible idea. ○ "Is her new car faster than her old one?" "Oh yes, much."*

M

muck¹ /mʌk/ *noun* [U] *informal* dirt *You've got muck on your shoes.*

muck² /mʌk/ *verb*
muck about/around *phrasal verb mainly UK informal* to behave stupidly and waste time *Stop mucking around, will you!*
muck sth up *phrasal verb informal* to do something badly, or to spoil something *I mucked up the interview.*

mucous membrane /ˌmjuːkəs'membreɪn/ *noun* [C] **ANATOMY, BIOLOGY** a thin layer of skin that produces mucus, for example inside the nose

mucus /'mjuːkəs/ *noun* [U] **BIOLOGY** a thick liquid produced inside the nose and other parts of the body

O‑ **mud** /mʌd/ *noun* [U] a thick liquid mixture of soil and water, or this mixture after it has dried *He'd been playing football and was covered in mud.*

WORD PARTNERS FOR ***muddle***

be/get **in** a muddle • a muddle **over/with** sth

muddle¹ /'mʌdl/ *noun* [C, U] a situation of confusion or bad organization *There was a big muddle over who was buying the tickets.* ○ *I'm* ***in such a muddle*** *with these bills.*

muddle² /'mʌdl/ *verb* **get sb/sth muddled up** to think that a person or thing is someone or something else *I often get Jonathan and his brother muddled up.*
muddle through (sth) *phrasal verb* to manage to do something although you do not know how to do it well *None of us has any formal training but somehow we muddle through.*
muddle sth up *phrasal verb* to arrange things in the wrong order *Please don't muddle up those books - I've just sorted them out.*

muddled /'mʌdld/ *adjective* **1** CONFUSED A person who is muddled is confused. *He became increasingly muddled as he grew older.* **2** NOT ORGANIZED Things that are muddled are badly organized. *He left his clothes in a muddled pile in the corner.*

muddy /'mʌdi/ *adjective* covered by or containing mud (= mixture of soil and water) *a muddy stream* ○ *muddy boots*

mudguard /'mʌdgɑːd/ *UK* (*US* **fender**) *noun* [C] a curved piece of metal or plastic fixed above a wheel of a bicycle or motorcycle to prevent water or dirt from hitting the person's legs

muesli /'mjuːzli/ *noun* [U] **FOOD** a mixture of grains, dried fruit and nuts that people eat with milk as part of the first meal of the day

muffin /'mʌfɪn/ *noun* [C] **1 FOOD** a small, sweet cake *a blueberry muffin* **2 FOOD** *UK* (*US* **English muffin**) a small, round, flat bread that is often eaten hot with butter *toasted muffins*

muffle /'mʌfl/ *verb* [T] to make a noise quieter and less clear *The pillow muffled her screams.* •**muffled** *adjective* Muffled sounds cannot be heard clearly. *a* ***muffled sound/voice*** ○ *a* ***muffled scream/cry***

muffler /'mʌflər/ *US* (*UK* **silencer**) *noun* [C] a part of a vehicle that reduces noise

mug¹ /mʌg/ *noun* [C] **1** CUP a large cup with straight sides usually used for hot drinks *a coffee mug* ○ *a steaming mug of tea* **2** PERSON *informal* someone who is stupid and easily deceived *I was such a mug to think he'd pay me back.*

mug² /mʌg/ *verb* [T] **mugging**, *past* **mugged** to attack and rob someone in a public place [**often passive**] *He was mugged as he walked across the park.* •**mugger** *noun* [C] someone who mugs people

mugging /'mʌgɪŋ/ *noun* [C, U] when someone is attacked in a public place and money, etc stolen from them

muggy /'mʌgi/ *adjective* When the weather is muggy, it is unpleasantly warm and the air contains a lot of water. *a muggy afternoon*

Muhammad /mə'hæmɪd/ *noun* **RELIGION** *another spelling of* Mohammed (= the Arab holy man on whose life and teachings Islam is based)

mule /mjuːl/ *noun* [C] an animal whose mother is a horse and whose father is a donkey (= animal like a small horse)

mules /mjuːlz/ *noun* [**plural**] women's shoes that have no back ⊃See colour picture **Clothes** on page Centre 9

mull /mʌl/ *verb*
mull sth over *phrasal verb* to think carefully about something for a long time, often before you make a decision

mullah /'mʌlə/ *noun* [C] **RELIGION** a Muslim religious teacher or leader

multi- /mʌlti-/ *prefix* many *a multi-millionaire* ○ *a multi-storey car park*

multicellular /ˌmʌlti'seljələr/ *adjective* **BIOLOGY** made of many cells

multicultural /ˌmʌlti'kʌltʃərəl/ *adjective* **SOCIETY** including people of different races and religions *a* ***multicultural society***

multilingual /ˌmʌlti'lɪŋgwəl/ *adjective* **LANGUAGE** using or speaking more than two languages

multimedia /ˌmʌlti'miːdiə/ *adjective* [**always before noun**] **COMPUTING** Multimedia computers and programs use sound, pictures, film, and text. *multimedia software/technology*

multinational¹ /ˌmʌlti'næʃənəl/ *adjective* active in several countries, or involving people from several countries *a* ***multinational company/corporation***

multinational² /ˌmʌlti'næʃənəl/ *noun* [C] a large company that produces and sells goods in many different countries

multiple¹ /'mʌltɪpl/ *adjective* with several parts ***multiple injuries***

multiple² /'mʌltɪpl/ *noun* [C] **MATHEMATICS** a number that can be divided by another number an exact number of times *Nine is* ***a multiple of*** *three.*

ˌmultiple 'choice *adjective* **EDUCATION** A multiple choice exam or question gives you different answers and you choose the correct one.

multiple sclerosis /ˌmʌltɪplsklə'rəʊsɪs/ *noun* [U] **HEALTH** a serious disease that gradually makes it difficult for a person to see, speak, or move

M

multiplex /ˈmʌltipleks/ *noun* [C] a cinema which has separate screens and shows different films at the same time

multiplication /ˌmʌltɪplɪˈkeɪʃᵊn/ *noun* [U] **MATHEMATICS** the process of multiplying a number with other numbers

multiply /ˈmʌltɪplaɪ/ *verb* **1** [I, T] to increase by a large number, or to cause something to increase by a large number *In warm weather, germs multiply rapidly.* **2** **MATHEMATICS** [T] to add one number to itself a particular number of times *Three* ***multiplied by*** *six equals eighteen.*

multi-purpose /ˌmʌltiˈpɜːpəs/ *adjective* describes something that can be used in many different ways

multiracial /ˌmʌltiˈreɪʃᵊl/ *adjective* **SOCIETY** involving people from different races *a* ***multiracial society***

multi-storey /ˌmʌltiˈstɔːri/ *UK* (*US* **multistory**) *adjective* describes a building with many floors *(UK) a multi-storey car park/(US) a multistory office building*

multitasking /ˌmʌltiˈtɑːskɪŋ/ *noun* [U] **1** the ability of a person to do more than one thing at a time *Women are often very good at multitasking.* **2** **COMPUTING** when a computer does several processes at the same time

multitude /ˈmʌltɪtjuːd/ *noun* [C] *formal* a large number of people or things *a multitude of problems/questions*

O-- **mum** /mʌm/ *UK* (*US* **mom**) *noun* [C] *informal* mother *I asked my mum but she said no.* ○ *Can we go now, Mum?*

mumble /ˈmʌmbl/ *verb* [I, T] to speak too quietly and not clearly enough for someone to understand you *He* ***mumbled something about*** *it being a waste of time.*

mummy /ˈmʌmi/ *noun* [C] **1** [MOTHER] *UK informal* (*US* **mommy**) a word for 'mother', used especially by children *Come here, Mummy!* ○ *My mummy and daddy came too.* **2** [DEAD BODY] a dead body covered in cloth, especially from ancient Egypt

mumps /mʌmps/ *noun* [U] **HEALTH** an illness that children get which makes the throat and neck swell *to have mumps*

munch /mʌnʃ/ *verb* [I, T] to eat something in a noisy way *She was sitting on the lawn munching an apple.*

mundane /mʌnˈdeɪn/ *adjective* ordinary, or not interesting *a mundane task/life*

municipal /mjuːˈnɪsɪpᵊl/ *adjective* [**always before noun**] **POLITICS** relating to the government of a town or city *a municipal council/election*

munitions /mjuːˈnɪʃᵊnz/ *noun* [**plural**] bombs, guns, and other military equipment *a* ***munitions factory***

mural /ˈmjʊərᵊl/ *noun* [C] **ART** a picture that is painted on a wall

WORD PARTNERS FOR ***murder***

commit (a) murder • the murder **of** sb • a murder **charge / investigation / victim / weapon**

O-- **murder¹** /ˈmɜːdəʳ/ *noun* [C, U] **1** the crime of intentionally killing someone *to* ***commit murder*** ○ *She was charged with* ***attempted murder.*** ○ *a murder charge/trial* **2 be murder** *informal* to be unpleasant or cause difficulty *Driving in Chicago at rush hour is murder.*

O-- **murder²** /ˈmɜːdəʳ/ *verb* [T] to kill someone intentionally and illegally [**often passive**] *He was murdered by a former employee.*

murderer /ˈmɜːdᵊrəʳ/ *noun* [C] someone who has committed murder *a convicted murderer*

murderous /ˈmɜːdᵊrəs/ *adjective* [**always before noun**] likely to kill someone, or wanting to kill them *a murderous dictator/regime*

murky /ˈmɜːki/ *adjective* **1** [SECRET] secret, and involving dishonest or illegal activities *He has a* ***murky past*** *as an arms dealer.* ○ *the* ***murky world*** *of drug dealing* **2** [DIRTY] dirty and dark *murky water*

murmur¹ /ˈmɜːməʳ/ *verb* [I, T] to speak quietly so that you can only be heard by someone near you *"Go to sleep now," she murmured.* ○ *He murmured a few words of sympathy.*

murmur² /ˈmɜːməʳ/ *noun* [C] the sound of something being said quietly *I could hear the low* ***murmur of voices*** *from behind the door.*

O-- **muscle¹** /ˈmʌsl/ *noun* **1** **ANATOMY, BIOLOGY** [C, U] one of many pieces of tissue in the body that are connected to bones and which produce movement by becoming longer or shorter *aching joints and muscles* ○ *stomach/thigh muscles* ○ *I think I may have* ***pulled*** (= injured) ***a muscle.*** **2** [U] the ability to control or influence people *political/military muscle*

muscle² /ˈmʌsl/ *verb*

muscle in *phrasal verb* to force yourself into an activity in which other people do not want you to be involved *How can we stop him* ***muscling in on*** *this project?*

muscular /ˈmʌskjələʳ/ *adjective* **1** having firm, strong muscles *muscular legs/arms* **2** **ANATOMY, BIOLOGY** relating to muscles *muscular aches/pains*

muse /mjuːz/ *verb* [I] *formal* to think carefully about something for a long time *I was just* ***musing about*** *relationships.*

O-- **museum** /mjuːˈziːəm/ *noun* [C] a building where you can look at important objects connected with art, history, or science *a museum of modern art*

mush /mʌʃ/ *noun* [U] *informal* food that is unpleasantly soft and wet, usually because it has been cooked for too long

mushroom¹ /ˈmʌʃruːm/ *noun* [C] **BIOLOGY, FOOD** a type of fungus (= organism like a plant) with a short stem and a round top, some types of which can be eaten *pasta with wild mushrooms*

mushroom² /ˈmʌʃruːm/ *verb* [I] to increase or develop very quickly *mushrooming costs*

WORD PARTNERS FOR ***music***

compose/listen to/play music • a **piece of** music • **dance/pop/classical** music • **put on some** music

O-- **music** /ˈmjuːzɪk/ *noun* [U] **1** **MUSIC** a pattern of sounds that is made by playing instruments or singing, or a recording of this ***pop/dance music*** ○ ***classical music*** ○ *He likes **listening to music**.* ○ *Could you **put on some music**?* ○ *a music festival* ○ *a music lesson/teacher* **2** **MUSIC** written signs which represent sounds that can be sung or played with instruments *I never learnt to **read music*** (= understand written music). **3 face the music** to accept punishment or criticism for something bad that you have done ⊃See also: **chamber music, country music, folk music**

musical[1] /'mju:zɪkᵊl/ *adjective* **1** **MUSIC** [**always before noun**] relating to music *a **musical instrument*** **2** **MUSIC** good at playing music *She comes from a very musical family.* •**musically** *adverb*

musical[2] /'mju:zɪkᵊl/ *noun* [**C**] a play or film in which singing and dancing tell part of the story *a Broadway/Hollywood musical*

musician /mju:'zɪʃᵊn/ *noun* [**C**] **MUSIC** someone who plays a musical instrument, often as a job *a talented jazz/classical musician*

Muslim (*also* **Moslem**) /'mʊzlɪm/ ⓤⓢ /'mʌzləm/ *noun* [**C**] **RELIGION** someone who believes in Islam •**Muslim** *adjective a Muslim family*

muslin /'mʌzlɪn/ *noun* [**U**] a very thin cotton cloth

mussel /'mʌsᵊl/ *noun* [**C**] **FOOD** a small sea creature that has a black shell in two parts and that can be eaten

O⊸**must**[1] *strong form* /mʌst/ *weak forms* /məst, məs/ *modal verb* **1** NECESSARY used to say that it is necessary that something happens or is done *The meat must be cooked thoroughly.* ○ *You mustn't show this letter to anyone else.* ○ *I must get some sleep.* **2** LIKELY used to show that you think something is very likely or certain to be true *You must be exhausted.* ○ *She must be very wealthy.* **3** SUGGEST used to show that you think it is a good idea for someone to do something *You must come and stay with us some time.* ⊃See Extra help page **Modal verbs** on page Centre 34.

must[2] /mʌst/ *noun* **be a must** *informal* If something is a must, it is very important to have or do it. *The restaurant has become so popular that reservations are a must.*

mustache /mə'stɑ:ʃ/ ⓤⓢ /'mʌstæʃ/ *noun* [**C**] *another US spelling of* moustache (= a line of hair above the mouth)

mustard /'mʌstəd/ *noun* [**U**] **FOOD** a thick, spicy, yellow or brown sauce often eaten in small amounts with meat *a teaspoon of mustard*

muster /'mʌstəʳ/ (*also* **muster up**) *verb* [**T**] to get enough support, bravery, or energy to do something difficult *I hope she **musters** the **courage** to invite him for dinner.*

O⊸**mustn't** /'mʌsᵊnt/ *short for* must not *You mustn't let her know I'm coming.*

musty /'mʌsti/ *adjective* smelling old and slightly wet in an unpleasant way *a musty room* ○ *the **musty smell** of old books*

mutant /'mju:tᵊnt/ *noun* [**C**] **BIOLOGY** an organism or cell that is different from others of the same type because of a change in its genes *a mutant virus*

mutation /mju:'teɪʃᵊn/ *noun* [**C, U**] **BIOLOGY** a permanent change in the genes of an organism, or an organism with such a change *The disease is caused by a mutation in a single gene.*

mute /mju:t/ *adjective* **1** THOUGHT expressed in thoughts but not in speech or writing *The president has **remained mute** about whether he will resign.* ○ *I gazed at her in **mute admiration**.* **2** NOT SPEAKING unable to speak for physical or mental reasons *a school for deaf and mute children*

muted /'mju:tɪd/ *adjective* **1** FEELING not strongly expressed *a **muted response/reaction*** ○ ***muted criticism*** **2** SOUND A muted sound is quieter than usual. ***muted voices*** **3** COLOUR [**always before noun**] A muted colour is not bright or easily noticed.

mutilate /'mju:tɪleɪt/ *verb* [**T**] to damage someone's body violently and severely, often by cutting off a part of it *a **mutilated body/corpse*** •**mutilation** /ˌmju:tɪ'leɪʃᵊn/ *noun* [**C, U**]

mutiny /'mju:tɪni/ *noun* [**C, U**] when a group of people, usually soldiers or sailors, refuse to obey orders, often because they want to be in control themselves •**mutiny** *verb* [**I**] to take part in a mutiny

mutt /mʌt/ *noun* [**C**] *informal* a dog that is a mixture of different breeds (= types)

mutter /'mʌtəʳ/ *verb* [**I, T**] to speak quietly so that your voice is difficult to hear, often when complaining about something *She walked past me, **muttering to herself**.* ○ *He muttered **something about** the restaurant being too expensive.* •**mutter** *noun* [**C**]

mutton /'mʌtᵊn/ *noun* [**U**] **1** **FOOD** meat from an adult sheep *a leg/shoulder of mutton* **2 mutton dressed as lamb** *UK informal* an older woman who wears clothes that would be more suitable for a young woman

mutual /'mju:tʃuəl/ *adjective* **1** OPINION When two or more people have a mutual feeling, they have the same opinion about each other. ***mutual admiration/respect*** ○ *He doesn't like her, and I suspect **the feeling's mutual**.* **2** FRIEND/INTEREST When two or more people have a mutual friend or interest, they have the same one. *Andrew and Jean were introduced to each other by a **mutual friend**.*

mutualism /'mju:tʃuəlɪzᵊm/ *noun* [**U**] **BIOLOGY** when two organisms live together and get advantages from each other

mutually /'mju:tʃuəli/ *adverb* You use mutually before an adjective when the adjective describes all sides of a situation. *a **mutually dependent** relationship* ○ *Being attractive and intelligent are not **mutually exclusive*** (= someone can be attractive and intelligent).

muzak /'mju:zæk/ *noun* [**U**] *trademark* **MUSIC** recorded music that is played quietly and continuously in public places such as airports, hotels and shops

muzzle[1] /'mʌzl/ *noun* [**C**] **1** **BIOLOGY** the mouth and nose of a dog, or a covering put over these to prevent the dog biting **2** the open end of the long cylindrical part of a gun

M

muzzle² /ˈmʌzl/ *verb* [T] **1** PREVENT BITE to put a muzzle on a dog **2** PREVENT OPINION to prevent someone expressing their own opinions

O-■ **my** /maɪ/ *determiner* belonging to or relating to the person who is speaking or writing *Tom's my older son.* ○ *It's not my fault.* ○ *My house is near the station.*

mycelium /maɪˈsiːliəm/ *noun* [U] *plural* **mycelia** **BIOLOGY** the main part of a fungus (= plant such as a mushroom)

myelin /ˈmaɪəlɪn/ *noun* [U] **ANATOMY, BIOLOGY** a substance containing a lot of fat that covers nerves to protect them, and helps them to send signals •**myelination** /maɪəlɪnˈeɪʃən/ *noun* [C]

MYOB *informal* **INTERNET** *internet abbreviation for* mind your own business: used in emails and text messages to say rudely that you do not want to talk about something

myriad /ˈmɪriəd/ *adjective literary* very many ***myriad problems*** •**myriad** *noun* [C] *literary Digital technology resulted in **a myriad of*** (= many) new TV channels.

O-■ **myself** /maɪˈself/ *pronoun* **1** REFLEXIVE the reflexive form of the pronouns 'me' or 'I' *I've bought myself a new coat.* ○ *I looked at myself in the mirror.* **2** EMPHASIZE used to emphasize the pronoun 'I', especially when the speaker wants to talk about their actions and not someone else's *I'll tell her myself.* ○ *Jack always drinks red wine but I prefer white myself.* **3 (all) by myself** alone or without anyone else's help *I live by myself in a small flat.* ○ *Mummy, I got dressed all by myself.* **4 (all) to myself** for my use only *I'll have the flat all to myself this weekend.*

mysterious /mɪˈstɪəriəs/ *adjective* **1** NOT KNOWN strange or unknown, and not explained or understood *a mysterious stranger* ○ *the mysterious death of her son* **2** NOT TALKING refusing to talk about something and behaving in a secretive way *Nick is being very **mysterious about** where he's going on holiday.* •**mysteriously** *adverb to **disappear/vanish mysteriously***

WORD PARTNERS FOR ***mystery***

explain/solve/unravel a mystery • the mystery **surrounding** sth • an **unexplained/unsolved** mystery • the mystery **of** sth • be a mystery **to** sb

mystery¹ /ˈmɪstəri/ *noun* **1** STRANGE EVENT [C, U] something strange or unknown that cannot be explained or understood *an **unsolved mystery*** ○ *He never gave up hope that he would **solve the mystery of** his son's disappearance.* ○ *He's out of work, so how he pays his rent is **a mystery to** me* (= I cannot explain it). **2** **LITERATURE** [C] a story, often about a crime, in which the strange events that happen are explained at the end *a **murder mystery***

mystery² /ˈmɪstəri/ *adjective* [**always before noun**] A mystery person or thing is one who is unknown. *I saw her with a **mystery man** in a restaurant last night.*

mystic /ˈmɪstɪk/ *noun* [C] **RELIGION** someone who attempts to be united with God through prayer

mystical /ˈmɪstɪkəl/ (*also* **mystic**) *adjective* **1** **RELIGION** relating to the religious beliefs and activities of mystics **2** involving magical or spiritual powers that are not understood

mysticism /ˈmɪstɪsɪzəm/ *noun* [U] **RELIGION** the religious beliefs and activities of mystics

mystify /ˈmɪstɪfaɪ/ *verb* [T] If something mystifies someone, they cannot understand or explain it because it is confusing or complicated. [**often passive**] *I was mystified by the decision.*

mystique /mɪˈstiːk/ *noun* [U] a mysterious quality that makes a person or thing seem interesting or special *the mystique of the princess*

WORD PARTNERS FOR ***myth***

debunk/dispel/explode a myth (= show that an idea is not true) • a **common/popular** myth • the myth **of** sth

myth /mɪθ/ *noun* [C] **1** **LITERATURE** an ancient story about gods and brave people, often one that explains an event in history or the natural world *a Greek myth* **2** IDEA an idea that is not true but is believed by many people *It's a myth that men are better drivers than women.*

mythical /ˈmɪθɪkəl/ (*also* **mythic**) *adjective* **1** FROM ANCIENT STORY existing in a myth *a mythical character* **2** FALSE imaginary or not true

mythology /mɪˈθɒlədʒi/ *noun* [U] myths, often those relating to a single religion or culture ***classical mythology*** ○ *the mythology of the ancient Greeks* •**mythological** /ˌmɪθəlˈɒdʒɪkəl/ *adjective*

Nn

N, n /en/ the fourteenth letter of the alphabet

N/A (*also US* **NA**) *written abbreviation for* not applicable: used on official forms to show that you do not need to answer a question

naff /næf/ *adjective UK informal* silly and not fashionable *naff lyrics*

NAFTA /ˈnæftə/ *noun* **ECONOMICS** *abbreviation for* North American Free Trade Agreement: an agreement between the US, Canada and Mexico about how they do business between them

nag /næg/ *verb* [I, T] **nagging**, *past* **nagged** to keep criticizing or giving advice to someone in an annoying way *They keep nagging me about going to university.*
nag (away) at sb *phrasal verb* If doubts or worries nag at you, you think about them all the time. *The same thought has been nagging away at me since last week.*

nagging /ˈnægɪŋ/ *adjective* [always before noun] Nagging doubts or worries make you worried and you cannot forget them. *a **nagging doubt***

O━**nail¹** /neɪl/ *noun* [C] **1** a thin piece of metal with a sharp end, used to join pieces of wood together *a hammer and nails* ➲See picture at **tools** **2 ANATOMY** the hard surface at the end of your fingers and toes *fingernails/toenails* ○ *to **cut** your **nails*** ○ ***nail clippers/scissors*** ○ *Stop **biting** your **nails**.* **3 hit the nail on the head** to describe exactly what is causing a situation or problem **4 the final nail in the coffin** an event which causes the failure of something that had already started to fail *This latest evidence could be the final nail in the coffin for Jackson's case.*

nail² /neɪl/ *verb* **1 nail sth down/on/to, etc** to fasten something with nails *There was a 'private property' sign nailed to the tree.* **2** [T] *mainly US informal* to catch someone who has committed a crime *They eventually **nailed** him **for** handling stolen goods.*
nail sb down *phrasal verb* to make someone give you exact details or a decision about something
nail sth down *phrasal verb US* to understand something completely, or to describe something correctly *We haven't been able to nail down the cause of the fire yet.*

ˈnail ˌbrush *noun* [C] a small brush, used for cleaning your nails ➲See colour picture **The Bathroom** on page Centre 3

ˈnail ˌpolish (*also UK* **ˈnail ˌvarnish**) *noun* [U] paint that you put on your nails

naive /naɪˈiːv/ *adjective* If someone is naive, they believe things too easily and do not have enough experience of the world. *I was much younger then, and very naive.* •**naively** *adverb I naively believed that we would be treated as equals.* •**naivety** /naɪˈiːvəti/ *noun* [U] the quality of being naive

WORD PARTNERS FOR ***naked***

(US) **buck** /(UK/US) **stark** naked • **half** naked

O━**naked** /ˈneɪkɪd/ *adjective* **1** [WITHOUT CLOTHES] not wearing clothes or not covered by anything *a naked thigh/shoulder* ○ *He was **stark naked*** (= completely naked). **2** [NOT HIDDEN] [always before noun] A naked feeling or quality is not hidden, although it is bad. ***naked aggression*** **3 the naked eye** If something can be seen by the naked eye, it is big enough to be seen without special equipment.

O━**name¹** /neɪm/ *noun* **1** [C] the word or group of words that is used to refer to a person, thing, or place *What's your name?* ○ *My name's Alexis.* ○ *I can't remember the name of the street he lives on.* ○ *He didn't mention her **by name*** (= he did not say her name). **2 in the name of sth** If bad things are done in the name of something, they are done in order to help that thing succeed. *So much blood has been spilt in the name of religion.* **3 a bad/good name** If things or people have a bad/good name, people have a bad/good opinion of them. *Their behaviour gives us all a bad name.* **4 call sb names** to use impolite or unpleasant words to describe someone **5 make a name for yourself** to become famous or respected by a lot of people **6 the name of the game** the main purpose or most important part of an activity *Popularity is the name of the game in television.* ➲See also: **brand name, Christian name, family name, first name, last name, maiden name, middle name**

O━**name²** /neɪm/ *verb* [T] **1** [GIVE A NAME] to give someone or something a name [+ two objects] *We named our first son Mike.* ○ *A young boy named Peter answered the phone.* **2** [SAY NAME] to say what the name of someone or something is [often passive] *The dead man has been **named as** John Kramer.* ○ *She cannot be named for legal reasons.* **3** [ANNOUNCE] to announce who has got a new job or won a prize [+ two objects] *She has been named manager of the new Edinburgh branch.* **4 you name it** something that you say which means anything you say or choose *I've never seen such a wide selection. You name it, they've got it.* **5 name and shame** *UK* to publicly say that a person or business has done something wrong
name sb after sb *phrasal verb* to give someone the same name as someone else *We named him after my wife's brother.*

ˈname ˌday *noun* [C] **RELIGION** the day that is celebrated by some Christians with the same name as a saint who is also celebrated on that day

nameless /ˈneɪmləs/ *adjective* If someone or something is nameless, they have no name or their name is not known. *a nameless soldier* ➲Compare **unnamed**

namely /ˈneɪmli/ *adverb* a word used when you are going to give more detail about something you have just said *She learned an important lesson from failing that exam, namely that nothing is ever certain.*

namesake /ˈneɪmseɪk/ *noun* [C] **your namesake** someone who has the same name as you

nan /næn/ *noun* [C] *UK informal* grandmother

N

nanny /ˈnæni/ *noun* [C] someone whose job is to look after a family's children

nano- /nænəʊ/ *prefix* **1** extremely small *nanotechnology* **2** MEASURES one billionth (= a thousand millionth) *a nanosecond*

nap /næp/ *noun* [C] a short sleep *He likes to **have/take a nap** after lunch.* •**nap** *verb* [I] **napping**, *past* **napped**

nape /neɪp/ *noun* [C] ANATOMY the back of your neck

napkin /ˈnæpkɪn/ (*also UK* **serviette**) *noun* [C] a piece of cloth or paper used when you eat to keep your clothes clean and to clean your mouth and hands *a paper napkin*

nappy /ˈnæpi/ *UK* (*US* **diaper**) *noun* [C] a thick piece of paper or cloth worn by a baby on its bottom ***disposable nappies*** ○ *to **change** a **nappy***

narcissism /ˈnɑːsɪsɪzᵊm/ *noun* [U] *formal* great interest in and pleasure at your own appearance and qualities •**narcissistic** /ˌnɑːsɪˈsɪstɪk/ *adjective* If people or their actions are narcissistic, they show narcissism.

narcotic /nɑːˈkɒtɪk/ *noun* [C] HEALTH a drug that stops you feeling pain or makes you sleep, and that is addictive (= difficult to stop using)

narrate /nəˈreɪt/ *verb* [T] *formal* LITERATURE to tell the story in a book, film, play, etc *'Peter and the Wolf,' narrated by actress Glenn Close* •**narration** /nəˈreɪʃᵊn/ *noun* [U] *formal*

narrative /ˈnærətɪv/ *noun* [C] LITERATURE *formal* a story or description of a series of events

narrator /nəˈreɪtəʳ/ *noun* [C] LITERATURE the person who tells the story in a book, film, play, etc

O-ᵚ**narrow**¹ /ˈnærəʊ/ *adjective* **1** NOT WIDE Narrow things measure a small distance from one side to the other. *a narrow lane/street* ○ *a narrow tie* **2** FEW including only a small number *He has very narrow interests.* **3 a narrow defeat/victory** If you have a narrow defeat/victory, you only just lose/win. **4 a narrow escape** If you have a narrow escape, you only just avoid danger.

narrow² /ˈnærəʊ/ *verb* [I, T] **1** MAKE SMALLER to become less wide or to make something less wide *The road has been narrowed to one lane.* **2** BECOME LESS to become less or to make something become less

narrow sth down *phrasal verb* to make something, for example a list or a choice, smaller and clearer by removing the things that are less important *We've managed to narrow the list down to four.*

narrowly /ˈnærəʊli/ *adverb* only by a small amount *A tile fell off the roof, **narrowly missing** my head.*

narrow-minded /ˌnærəʊˈmaɪndɪd/ *adjective* not willing to accept new ideas or opinions different from your own

nasal /ˈneɪzᵊl/ *adjective* ANATOMY, BIOLOGY relating to the nose *the **nasal passages***

nascent /ˈnæsᵊnt, ˈneɪsᵊnt/ *adjective formal* starting to develop *a nascent democracy*

nasty /ˈnɑːsti/ *adjective* **1** BAD very bad *a nasty shock/surprise* ○ *a nasty smell/taste* ○ *a nasty cut/burn* **2** UNKIND unkind *She's always being **nasty to** her little brother.* **3** ANGRY very angry or violent *When I asked for the money, he turned really nasty.* •**nastiness** *noun* [U]

WORD PARTNERS FOR ***nation***

a **civilized/industrialized/poor/powerful** nation • **govern/lead** a nation • **across** the nation • a nation **of** sth

O-ᵚ**nation** /ˈneɪʃᵊn/ *noun* [C] a country or the people living in a country *Asian nations* ○ *industrial nations* ○ *The entire nation mourned her death.* ○ *a nation of dog lovers.* ➲See Common Learner Error at **country** ➲See also: **the United Nations**

O-ᵚ**national**¹ /ˈnæʃᵊnᵊl/ *adjective* **1** WHOLE COUNTRY relating to the whole of a country *to threaten **national security*** ○ *a sense of national identity* ○ *a national newspaper* ○ ***national elections*** ○ *His income is way above the **national average**.* ○ *Gambling is a **national pastime*** (= many people do it) *here.* **2** TRADITION [**always before noun**] connected with the traditions of a particular nation *national dress/customs* •**nationally** *adverb*

national² /ˈnæʃᵊnᵊl/ *noun* [C] POLITICS someone who officially belongs to a particular country *a British/Chinese national*

ˌnational ˈanthem *noun* [C] MUSIC the official song of a country, played at public events

the ˌNational ˈHealth Service *noun* HEALTH the system providing free medical services in the UK

ˌnational ˈholiday (*also US* **federal holiday**) *noun* [C] a day when most people in a country do not have to work

ˌNational Inˈsurance *noun* [U] ECONOMICS the system in the UK in which people regularly pay money to the government in order to help people who are ill or have no work

nationalism /ˈnæʃᵊnᵊlɪzᵊm/ *noun* [U] POLITICS **1** a feeling of pride in your own country **2** the belief that a particular area should have its own government *Welsh nationalism*

nationalist /ˈnæʃᵊnᵊlɪst/ *noun* [C] POLITICS someone who wants a particular area to have its own government

nationalistic /ˌnæʃᵊnᵊlˈɪstɪk/ *adjective* POLITICS having a lot of pride, often too much pride, in your own country *nationalistic fervour*

nationality /ˌnæʃᵊnˈæləti/ *noun* [C, U] SOCIETY If you have American/British/Swiss, etc nationality, you are legally a member of that country. *What nationality is she?* ○ *She has **dual nationality*** (= nationality of two countries).

nationalize /ˈnæʃᵊnᵊlaɪz/ *verb* [T] POLITICS, ECONOMICS If private companies are nationalized, the government takes control of them. •**nationalization** /ˌnæʃᵊnᵊlaɪˈzeɪʃᵊn/ *noun* [U]

ˌnational ˈpark *noun* [C] ENVIRONMENT a large area of park for use by the public, usually an area of special beauty

ˌnational ˈservice *noun* [U] the period of time young people in some countries have to spend in the army

nationwide /ˌneɪʃᵊnˈwaɪd/ *adjective, adverb* including all parts of a country ***a nationwide campaign*** ○ *Surveys have been carried out nationwide.*

native¹ /ˈneɪtɪv/ *adjective* **1** BORN IN **[always before noun]** Your native town or country is the place where you were born. *It was a custom in his native Algeria.* ○ *She is a **native-born** Texan.* **2** LANGUAGE **[always before noun]** Your native language is the first language you learn. **3** SOCIETY **[always before noun]** relating to the people who lived in a country first, before other people took control of it *the **native inhabitants/population*** **4** ANIMALS AND PLANTS Native animals or plants live or grow naturally in a place, and have not been brought from somewhere else. *a large bird **native to** Europe*

native² /ˈneɪtɪv/ *noun* **[C]** **1** BORN someone who was born in a particular place *He's **a native of** Texas.* **2** ORIGINAL PEOPLE an old-fashioned and often offensive word for a person who lived in a country, for example an African country, before Europeans went there

ˌNative Aˈmerican *adjective* **SOCIETY** relating or belonging to the original group of people who lived in North America •**Native American** *noun* **[C]**

ˌnative ˈspeaker *noun* **[C]** **LANGUAGE** someone who speaks a language as their first language

NATO (*also UK* **Nato**) /ˈneɪtəʊ/ *noun* **POLITICS** *abbreviation for* North Atlantic Treaty Organization: an international military organization formed in 1949 to improve the defence of Western Europe

natter /ˈnætəʳ/ *verb* **[I]** *mainly UK informal* to talk about things that are not important •**natter** *noun* **[no plural]** *UK to **have a natter***

O‒ **natural** /ˈnætʃᵊrᵊl/ *adjective* **1** NATURE Something that is natural exists or happens because of nature, not because it was made or done by people. ***natural gas/resources*** ○ ***natural beauty*** ○ *to die of **natural causes*** (= because you are ill or old) ○ *This product contains only **natural ingredients**.* **2** NORMAL normal or expected *a **natural impulse/instinct*** ○ *It's perfectly natural to feel nervous.* ➲Opposite **unnatural** **3** FROM BIRTH If you have a natural characteristic, it is something you have been born with. *a natural talent* ○ *She's a natural athlete/blonde.* •**naturalness** *noun* **[U]**

ˌnatural ˈgas *noun* **[U]** **CHEMISTRY, GEOLOGY** a gas that is found under the ground and is used for cooking and heating

ˌnatural ˈhistory *noun* **[U]** the study of animals and plants

naturalist /ˈnætʃᵊrᵊlɪst/ *noun* **[C]** someone who studies animals and plants

naturalistic /ˌnætʃᵊrᵊlˈɪstɪk/ *adjective* Naturalistic art, writing, or acting tries to show things as they really are.

naturalize /ˈnætʃᵊrᵊlaɪz/ *verb* **POLITICS** **be naturalized** to officially become a member of another country *a naturalized US citizen* •**naturalization** /ˌnætʃᵊrᵊlaɪˈzeɪʃᵊn/ *noun* **[U]**

naturally /ˈnætʃᵊrᵊli/ *adverb* **1** AS EXPECTED as you would expect *Naturally, he was very disappointed.* **2** NORMALLY in a normal way *Relax and try to behave naturally.* **3** FROM BIRTH having been born with a characteristic *naturally aggressive/funny/slim* **4** NATURE Something that exists or happens naturally is part of nature and not made or done by people. *Organic tomatoes are grown naturally without chemical fertilizers.*

ˌnatural ˈsciences *noun* **[plural]** **EDUCATION** sciences that relate to the physical world such as biology, chemistry, and physics

ˌnatural seˈlection *noun* **[U]** **BIOLOGY** the way that plants and animals die when they are weak or not suitable for the place where they live, while stronger ones continue to exist

WORD PARTNERS FOR ***nature***

2 in sb's nature • [happy/optimistic, etc.] **by** nature

O‒ **nature** /ˈneɪtʃəʳ/ *noun* **1** PLANTS AND ANIMALS **[U]** all the plants, creatures, substances, and forces that exist in the universe, which are not made by people *the laws of nature* ○ *I like to get out and enjoy nature.* ○ *a nature trail* **2** CHARACTER **[no plural]** someone's character *I didn't think it was **in his nature** to behave like that.* **3** TYPE **[no plural]** *formal* type *What exactly is **the nature of** your business?* ○ *I don't like hunting and things **of that nature**.* ➲See also: **human nature, second nature**

COMMON LEARNER ERROR

nature, the environment and **countryside**

Nature means all the things in the world which exist naturally and were not created by people.

He's interested in wildlife and anything to do with nature.

The environment means the land, water, and air that animals and plants live in. It is usually used when talking about the way people use or damage the natural world.

The government has introduced new policies to protect the environment.

Countryside means land where there are no towns or cities.

I love walking in the countryside.

ˈnature reˌserve *noun* **[C]** **ENVIRONMENT** a place where animals and plants live and are protected

naught *old-fashioned* (*also UK* **nought**) /nɔːt/ *noun* **[U]** nothing

naughty /ˈnɔːti/ *adjective* **1** BEHAVIOUR If a child is naughty, they behave badly. *a **naughty** little **boy/girl*** **2** SEXUAL a word used humorously to describe things that are sexual *naughty films/magazines*

nausea /ˈnɔːziə/ *noun* **[U]** **HEALTH** the unpleasant feeling of wanting to vomit *She was hit by a sudden **wave of nausea**.*

nauseating /ˈnɔːsieɪtɪŋ/ *adjective* **HEALTH** If something is nauseating, it makes you want to vomit. *a nauseating smell*

N

nauseous /ˈnɔːsiəs/ *adjective* **HEALTH** If you feel nauseous, you feel like you might vomit, and if something is nauseous, it makes you want to vomit.

nautical /ˈnɔːtɪkəl/ *adjective* relating to boats or sailing *a **nautical mile***

naval /ˈneɪvəl/ *adjective* [**always before noun**] relating to the navy *a **naval base/officer***

navel /ˈneɪvəl/ *noun* [C] **ANATOMY** the small, round, and usually hollow place on your stomach, where you were connected to your mother before birth

navigable /ˈnævɪgəbl/ *adjective* If an area of water is navigable, it is wide, deep, and safe enough to sail a boat on.

navigate /ˈnævɪgeɪt/ *verb* **1** WITH MAP [I, T] to find the right direction to travel by using maps or other equipment *He navigated the ship back to Plymouth.* ○ *We navigated using a map and compass.* ○ *I drive and he navigates.* **2** BOAT [T] to successfully sail along an area of water **3** DIFFICULT JOURNEY [T] to find your way through a difficult place *We had to navigate several flights of stairs.* **4** SYSTEM [T] to successfully use a complicated system *to navigate a website* ●**navigation** /ˌnævɪˈgeɪʃən/ *noun* [U] ●**navigator** *noun* [C] a person who navigates

navy /ˈneɪvi/ *noun* **1 the Navy** ships and soldiers used for fighting wars at sea *to be **in the navy*** **2** [U] (*also* ˌ**navy** ˈ**blue**) a very dark blue colour ➲See colour picture **Colours** on page Centre 12

Nazi /ˈnɑːtsi/ *noun* [C] **POLITICS** someone who supported the ideas of Hitler in Germany in the 1930s and 1940s *Nazi propaganda*

N

nb, NB /ˌenˈbiː/ used to tell the reader that a particular piece of information is very important

née /neɪ/ *adjective* [**always before noun**] a word used to introduce the family name that a woman had before she got married *Margaret Hughes, née Johnson*

o**near¹** /nɪəʳ/ *adverb, preposition* **1** DISTANCE not far away in distance *Could you come a bit nearer, please?* ○ *I stood near the window.* ○ *Are you going anywhere near the post office?* **2 be/come near to doing sth** to almost achieve or do something *This is the nearest I've ever got to winning anything.* ○ *He came near to punching him.* **3** STATE If something or someone is near a particular state, they are almost in that state. *She looked near exhaustion.* ○ *She was **near to tears*** (= almost crying) *when I told her.* **4** TIME not far away in time *She shouldn't be partying so near her exams.* ○ *We can decide **nearer the time**.* **5** SIMILAR similar *The feelings I had were near hysteria.* ○ *He is Russia's **nearest thing to** a rock legend.* **6 nowhere near** not close in distance, amount, time, or quality *It wasn't me - I was nowhere near him.* ○ *That's nowhere near enough for six people.* ○ *It was nowhere near as difficult as I thought it would be.* **7 near enough** almost *The books were ordered near enough alphabetically.*

o**near²** /nɪəʳ/ *adjective* **1** not far away in distance or time *The school's very near.* ○ *The nearest garage is 10 miles away.* ○ *The baby's due date was getting nearer.* **2 in the near future** at a time that is not far away *Space travel may become very common in the near future.* ➲See also: a near **miss²**

near³ /nɪəʳ/ *verb* [T] to get close to something in distance or time *The building work is **nearing completion** at last.*

nearby /ˌnɪəˈbaɪ/ *adjective, adverb* not far away *a nearby town/village*

o**nearly** /ˈnɪəli/ *adverb* **1** almost *It's nearly three weeks since I last saw her.* ○ *Nearly all the food had gone when I arrived.* ○ *She nearly drowned when she was eight.* ○ *I'll be with you in a minute - I've nearly finished.* **2 not nearly (as/so)** a lot less *It's not nearly as expensive as I thought.*

nearsighted /ˌnɪəˈsaɪtɪd/ *US* (*UK* **short-sighted**) *adjective* **HEALTH** If you are nearsighted, you cannot see things very well if they are too far away.

neat /niːt/ *adjective* **1** TIDY tidy and clean *He always looks very **neat and tidy**.* **2** GOOD *US informal* good *That's really neat.* ○ *What a neat idea.* **3** ALCOHOL A neat alcoholic drink is drunk on its own, and not mixed with any other liquid.

neatly /ˈniːtli/ *adverb* in a tidy way *neatly dressed* ○ *a neatly folded pile of clothes*

necessarily /nesəˈserəli/ *adverb* **not necessarily** not for certain *That's not necessarily true.* ○ *I know she doesn't say much, but it doesn't necessarily mean she's not interested.*

OTHER WAYS OF SAYING *necessary*

The verbs **need** and **require** and the modal verb **must** are very commonly used to show that something is necessary: *The meat **must** be cooked thoroughly.* ● *Does she have the skills **needed/required** for work of that sort?*

If something is very important and necessary, you can use adjectives such as **essential**, **fundamental**, and **indispensable**: *Some understanding of grammar is **essential/fundamental** to learning a language.* ● *This book is an **indispensable** resource for teachers.*

The expression **be a must** is sometimes used in informal situations to describe things that are necessary to have or do: *If you live in the country a car **is a must**.*

o**necessary** /ˈnesəsəri/ *adjective* needed in order to achieve something [+ **to do sth**] *Is it really necessary to give so much detail?* ○ *Does he have the necessary skills and experience?* ○ *The police are prepared to use force, **if necessary**.* ➲Opposite **unnecessary**

necessitate /nəˈsesɪteɪt/ *verb* [T] *formal* to make something necessary

WORD PARTNERS FOR *necessity*

out of necessity ● the necessity **for/of** sth ● **financial** necessity

necessity /nəˈsesəti/ *noun* **1** NEED [U] the need for something *There's no **financial necessity** for her to work.* ○ *Sewing is something I do **out of necessity**, not for pleasure.* **2** SOMETHING NEEDED [C] something you need *Most people seem to consider a car a necessity, not a luxury.*

O‑**neck** /nek/ *noun* [C] **1 ANATOMY** the part of the body between your head and your shoulders *He was wearing a gold chain **around** his **neck**.* ⊃See colour picture **The Body** on page Centre 13 **2** the part of a piece of clothing that goes around your neck *a polo-neck/V-neck jumper* **3 be breathing down sb's neck** to watch what someone does all the time in a way that annoys them *The last thing I want is a boss breathing down my neck.* **4 neck and neck** If two people who are competing are neck and neck, they are very close and either of them could win. **5 be up to your neck (in sth)** to be very busy ⊃See also: **polo neck,** by the **scruff** of the/your neck

necklace /ˈnekləs/ *noun* [C] a piece of jewellery that you wear around your neck *a pearl necklace*

neckline /ˈneklaɪn/ *noun* [C] the shape made by the edge of a dress or shirt at the front of the neck *a low neckline*

nectar /ˈnektəʳ/ *noun* [U] a sweet liquid produced by plants and collected by bees

nectarine /ˈnektəriːn/ *noun* [C] **FOOD** a soft, round fruit which is sweet and juicy and has a smooth red and yellow skin

nectary /ˈnektəri/ *noun* [C] **BIOLOGY** the part of a flower that produces nectar ⊃See picture at **flower**

O‑**need¹** /niːd/ *verb* [T] **1** NECESSARY If you need something, you must have it, and if you need to do something, you must do it. *I need some new shoes.* ○ *The country still desperately needs help.* [+ **to do sth**] *If there's anything else you need to know, just give me a call.* ○ *We need you to look after the children for us.* **2 don't need to do sth/ needn't do sth** used in order to say that someone does not have to do something or should not do something *You didn't need to come all this way.* ○ *You don't need to be frightened.* ○ *She needn't have taken him to the hospital.* **3** NECESSARY ACTION If something needs something to be done to it, that thing should be done in order to improve it. *Do the clothes on this chair need washing?* ○ *The car needs to be serviced.* **4 There needs to be sth** used to say that something is necessary *There needs to be more funding for education in this country.*

COMMON LEARNER ERROR

needed or **necessary?**

It is not usual to use 'needed' as an adjective. We usually say **necessary** instead.

He gave us the necessary information.

~~*He gave us the needed information.*~~

WORD PARTNERS FOR ***need** (noun)*

identify a need • **meet** a need (= provide what is needed) • a need **for** sth

O‑**need²** /niːd/ *noun* **1** [**no plural**] something that is necessary to have or do *There's an urgent **need for** more medical supplies.* [+ **to do sth**] *Is there any need to change the current system?* ○ *There's really **no need for** that sort of behaviour.* **2 be in need of sth** to need something *My car's in desperate need of repair.*

needle /ˈniːdl/ *noun* [C] **1 HEALTH** the thin, sharp, metal part of a piece of medical equipment used to take blood out of the body, or to put medicine or drugs in **2** SEWING a thin, pointed metal object with a small hole at one end for thread, used in sewing *a needle and thread* **3** MEASURING a thin, pointed piece of metal or plastic that moves to point to numbers on equipment used for measuring things ⊃See also: **pins and needles**

needless /ˈniːdləs/ *adjective* not necessary *a **needless expense*** ○ ***Needless to say*** (= as you would expect), *it rained the whole time we were there.* •**needlessly** *adverb*

O‑**needn't** /ˈniːdᵊnt/ *short for* need not *You needn't have come.*

needs /niːdz/ *noun* [**plural**] the things you need in order to have a good life *her emotional needs* ○ *The city is struggling to **meet the needs of** its homeless people.*

needy /ˈniːdi/ *adjective* Needy people do not have enough money. *The mayor wants to establish permanent housing for **the needy**.*

negate /nɪˈgeɪt/ *verb* [T] *formal* to make something lose its effect or value •**negation** /nɪˈgeɪʃᵊn/ *noun* [U] *formal*

O‑**negative¹** /ˈnegətɪv/ *adjective* **1** NO ENTHUSIASM not having enthusiasm or positive opinions about something ***negative feelings*** ○ *Many people have a **negative attitude** towards ageing.* **2** BAD A negative effect is bad and causes damage to something. *Terrorist threats have had a very **negative impact** on tourism.* **3 HEALTH** If the result of a test to prove if someone is pregnant or ill is negative, that person is not pregnant or ill. **4 MATHEMATICS** A negative number is less than zero. **5 LANGUAGE** In language, a negative word or phrase expresses the meaning 'no' or 'not'. **6 PHYSICS** of the type of electrical charge which is carried by electrons

negative² /ˈnegətɪv/ *noun* [C] **1** PHOTOGRAPH a piece of film from which a photograph can be produced, where dark areas look light and light areas look dark **2** GRAMMAR a word or phrase which expresses the meaning 'no' or 'not'

negatively /ˈnegətɪvli/ *adverb* **1** WITHOUT ENTHUSIASM without enthusiasm or positive opinions *to **react/respond negatively*** **2** WITH A BAD EFFECT with a bad effect ***negatively affected***

negativity /ˌnegəˈtɪvəti/ *noun* [U] when you do not feel enthusiastic or positive about things

neglect¹ /nɪˈglekt/ *verb* [T] **1** to not give enough care or attention to something or someone *to neglect your appearance/the garden* [**often passive**] *Some of these kids have been badly neglected in the past.* ○ *neglected children* **2 neglect to do sth** to not do something, often intentionally *He neglected to mention the fact that we could lose money on the deal.*

neglect² /nɪˈglekt/ *noun* [U] when you do not give enough care or attention to something or someone *to suffer years of neglect*

negligence /ˈneglɪdʒəns/ *noun* [U] when you are not careful enough in something you do, especially in a job where your actions affect

N

other people *Her parents plan to sue the surgeon for medical negligence.*

negligent /ˈneglɪdʒənt/ *adjective* not giving enough care or attention to a job or activity, especially where your actions affect someone else *The report found him negligent in his duties.*

negligible /ˈneglɪdʒəbl/ *adjective* small and not important *a* ***negligible effect/result***

negotiable /nɪˈgəʊʃiəbl/ *adjective* If something is negotiable, it is not completely fixed, and can be changed after discussion. *The January deadline is not negotiable.*

negotiate /nɪˈgəʊʃieɪt/ *verb* **1** DISCUSS [I, T] to try to make or change an agreement by discussion *to negotiate with employers about working conditions* **2** MOVE THROUGH [T] to successfully move around, through, or past something *to negotiate your way around/through a city* •**negotiator** *noun* [C] *a peace negotiator*

WORD PARTNERS FOR ***negotiation***

enter into/be in negotiations • negotiations **break down/fail** • negotiations **about/on/over** sth • negotiations **with** sb • negotiations **between** sb **and** sb

negotiation /nɪˌgəʊʃiˈeɪʃᵊn/ *noun* [C] when people try to make or change an agreement by discussion ***Peace negotiations*** *are due to start.*

Negro /ˈniːgrəʊ/ *noun* [C] *plural* **Negroes** *old-fashioned* a word that means a black person, which some people think is offensive

N

neighbour *UK* (*US* **neighbor**) /ˈneɪbəʳ/ *noun* [C] **1** LIVING NEAR someone who lives very near you, especially in the next house *Our* ***next-door neighbours*** *are always arguing.* **2** POSITION someone or something that is near or next to someone or something else *The French make more films than their European neighbours.*

neighbourhood *UK* (*US* **neighborhood**) /ˈneɪbəhʊd/ *noun* [C] an area of a town or city that people live in *I grew up in a very poor neighbourhood.* ○ *Are there any good restaurants* ***in the neighbourhood*** (= in this area)*?*

neighbouring *UK* (*US* **neighboring**) /ˈneɪbᵊrɪŋ/ *adjective* [**always before noun**] near or next to somewhere *neighbouring countries/villages*

neither[1] /ˈnaɪðəʳ, ˈniːðəʳ/ *adverb* used to say that a negative fact is also true of someone or something else *Jerry doesn't like it, and neither do I.* ○ *Her family wouldn't help her and neither would anyone else.* ○ *She's not very tall and neither is her husband.*

neither[2] /ˈnaɪðəʳ, ˈniːðəʳ/ *pronoun, determiner* not either of two people or things *Luckily, neither child was hurt in the accident.* ○ ***Neither of*** *us had ever been to London before.* ○ *They gave us two keys, but neither worked.*

neither[3] /ˈnaɪðəʳ, ˈniːðəʳ/ *conjunction* **neither ... nor** used when a negative fact is true of two people or things or when someone or something does not have either of two qualities *Neither he nor his mother would talk to the police.* ○ *Their performance was neither entertaining nor educational.*

COMMON LEARNER ERROR

Neither...nor

This expression can be used with a singular or plural verb.

Neither Jack nor Philip likes/like football.

nematode /ˈnemətəʊd/ *noun* [C] **BIOLOGY** a thin worm that is not divided into sections

neo- /niːəʊ-/ *prefix* new *neo-facists*

neologism /niˈɒlədʒɪzᵊm/ *noun* [C] *formal* **LANGUAGE** a new word or phrase, or a new meaning for a word that already exists

neon /ˈniːɒn/ *noun* [U] **CHEMISTRY** a gas that produces bright, colourful light when electricity passes through it, often used in signs (formula Ne) ***neon lights/signs***

nephew /ˈnefjuː/ *noun* [C] the son of your brother or sister, or the son of your husband's or wife's brother or sister

nephron /ˈnefrɒn/ *noun* [C] **ANATOMY, BIOLOGY** one of the very small tubes that form the kidney and which produce urine

Neptune /ˈneptjuːn/ *noun* [**no plural**] **ASTRONOMY** the planet that is eighth from the Sun, after Uranus and before Pluto ➲See picture at **solar system**

nerd /nɜːd/ *noun* [C] *informal* someone, especially a man, who is not fashionable and who is interested in boring things •**nerdy** *adjective informal* boring and not fashionable

nerve /nɜːv/ *noun* **1** **ANATOMY, BIOLOGY** [C] one of the threads in your body which carry messages between your brain and other parts of the body *the optic nerve* ○ ***nerve cells/endings*** **2** BEING BRAVE [**no plural**] the quality of being brave [**+ to do sth**] *I* ***haven't got the nerve*** *to tell him I'm leaving.* ○ *He* ***lost his nerve*** *and couldn't go through with it.* **3** RUDENESS [**no plural**] the rudeness necessary to do something you know will upset someone *You've* ***got a nerve****, coming here!* [**+ to do sth**] *I can't believe she* ***had the nerve*** *to talk to me after what happened.* **4 hit/touch a (raw) nerve** to upset someone by talking about a particular subject

ˈnerve ˌcell *noun* [C] **ANATOMY, BIOLOGY** a neuron (= cell that carries information between the brain and other parts of the body)

nerve-racking /ˈnɜːvˌrækɪŋ/ *adjective* If an experience is nerve-racking, it makes you very nervous. *a nerve-racking experience*

WORD PARTNERS FOR ***nerves***

suffer from nerves • **calm/settle/steady** your nerves

nerves /nɜːvz/ *noun* [**plural**] **1** the state of being nervous *I need something to* ***calm my nerves****.* ○ *I always* ***suffer from nerves*** *before a match.* **2 steady/strong nerves** the ability to be calm in difficult situations *You need a cool head and steady nerves for this job.* **3 get on sb's nerves** to annoy someone, especially by doing something again and again *If we spend too much time together we end up getting on each other's nerves.*

nervous /ˈnɜːvəs/ *adjective* **1** worried and anxious *a* ***nervous cough/laugh*** ○ *She's very* ***nervous about*** *her driving test.* **2** **ANATOMY,**

BIOLOGY [**always before noun**] relating to the nerves in the body *a nervous disorder*

COMMON LEARNER ERROR

nervous, agitated or **irritable?**

Nervous means 'worried or frightened'. It does not mean 'angry' or 'upset'.

I get very nervous if I have to speak in public.

If you want to describe someone who cannot control their voice and movements because they are anxious and upset, use **agitated**.

He was very agitated and aggressive.

If you want to describe someone who becomes annoyed easily, use **irritable** or **bad-tempered**.

She was tired and irritable.

ˌnervous ˈbreakdown *noun* [C] **HEALTH** a short period of mental illness when people are too ill to continue with their normal lives

nervously /ˈnɜːvəsli/ *adverb* in a worried and anxious way *to **giggle/laugh** nervously* •**nervousness** *noun* [U]

ˈnervous ˌsystem *noun* [C] **ANATOMY, BIOLOGY** your brain and all the nerves in your body which control your feelings and actions *a disease of the central nervous system*

nest¹ /nest/ *noun* [C] a home built by birds for their eggs and by some other creatures to live in *a **birds'/wasps' nest***

nest² /nest/ *verb* [I] to live in a nest or build a nest

nestle /ˈnesl/ *verb* **1 nestle (sth) against/in/on, etc** to rest yourself or part of your body in a comfortable, protected position *The cat was nestling in her lap.* **2 nestle beneath/between/in, etc** If a building, town, or object nestles somewhere, it is in a protected position, with bigger things around it. *a village nestled in the Carpathian mountains*

net¹ /net/ *noun* **1** [U] material made of crossed threads with holes between them **2 SPORT** [C] something made with a piece of net, for example for catching fish or insects, or for sports *a fishing net ○ a tennis/basketball net* **3 the Net INTERNET** *short for* the Internet ⊃See also: **safety net**

net² (*also UK* **nett**) /net/ *adjective* **FINANCE** A net amount of money has had costs such as tax taken away from it. *a **net income/profit** of £10,000*

net³ /net/ *verb* [T] **netting**, *past* **netted 1 FINANCE** to get an amount of money as profit *One trader netted a bonus of £1 million.* **2 SPORT** to hit, throw, or kick a ball into a net *He netted a great penalty.*

netball /ˈnetbɔːl/ *noun* [U] **SPORT** a game usually played by teams of women, where a ball is thrown from player to player and goals are scored by throwing the ball through a high net

ˌnet ˈprofit *noun* [C, U] **FINANCE** the money that a business makes after it has paid all the money it owes

netting /ˈnetɪŋ/ *noun* [U] material made of crossed threads or wires with holes between them *wire netting*

nettle /ˈnetl/ *noun* [C] a wild plant whose leaves hurt you if you touch them

WORD PARTNERS FOR ***network***

build/create/establish/form a network • a network **of** sth • a **rail/road** network

network¹ /ˈnetwɜːk/ *noun* [C] **1 COMPUTING** a system or group of connected parts *a **rail/road network** ○ a **network of** cables/tunnels* **2 SOCIETY** a group of people who know each other or who work together *a large network of friends* **3** COMPANY a large television or radio company that broadcasts programmes in many areas

network² /ˈnetwɜːk/ *verb* **1** [I] to use social events to meet people who might be useful for your business **2 COMPUTING** [T] to connect computers together so that they can share information and programs

networking /ˈnetwɜːkɪŋ/ *noun* [U] **1** when you use social events to meet people who might be useful for your business **2 COMPUTING** when you connect computers together so that they can share programs and information

neural /ˈnjʊərəl/ *adjective* [**always before noun**] **ANATOMY, BIOLOGY** relating to the nerves in your body *neural activity*

neurology /njʊəˈrɒlədʒi/ *noun* [U] **BIOLOGY** the study of the system of nerves in people's bodies •**neurological** /ˌnjʊərəˈlɒdʒɪkəl/ *adjective* Neurological illnesses affect the nerves in people's bodies. •**neurologist** /njʊəˈrɒlədʒɪst/ *noun* [C] a doctor who deals with neurological illnesses

neuron /ˈnjʊərɒn/ (*also* **neurone**) *noun* [C] **ANATOMY, BIOLOGY** a nerve cell which carries messages between your brain and other parts of your body

neurosis /njʊəˈrəʊsɪs/ *noun* [C] **HEALTH** *plural* **neuroses** /njʊəˈrəʊsiːz/ a mental illness, often causing you to worry too much about something

neurotic /njʊəˈrɒtɪk/ *adjective* If you are neurotic, you worry about things too much.

neuter /ˈnjuːtəʳ/ *adjective* **LANGUAGE** in some languages, belonging to a group of nouns or adjectives that have the same grammatical behaviour. The other groups are 'masculine' and 'feminine'.

neutral¹ /ˈnjuːtrəl/ *adjective* **1** INDEPENDENT independent and not supporting any side in an argument, fight, or competition ***neutral ground/territory*** *○ He decided to remain neutral on the issue.* **2** COLOUR Neutral colours are not strong or bright. **3 CHEMISTRY** neither acid nor alkaline

neutral² /ˈnjuːtrəl/ *noun* [U] In driving, neutral is the position of the gears (= parts of a vehicle that control how fast the wheels turn) when they are not connected. *to be **in neutral***

neutrality /njuːˈtræləti/ *noun* [U] the state of being independent and not supporting any side in an argument, war, etc

neutralize (*also UK* **-ise**) /ˈnjuːtrəlaɪz/ *verb* [T] **1** to stop something from having an effect *This spray will help to neutralize unpleasant odours.* **2 CHEMISTRY** to make something

N

neutral (= neither an acid nor an alkali) •**neutralization** /ˌnjuːtrəlaɪˈzeɪʃᵊn/ *noun* [U]

neutron /ˈnjuːtrɒn/ *noun* [C] **PHYSICS, CHEMISTRY** a part of an atom which has no electrical charge (= the electricity something stores or carries)

⊶**never** /ˈnevəʳ/ *adverb* **1** NOT EVER not ever, not one time *"Have you ever been to Australia?" "No, never."* ○ *I've never even thought about that before.* ○ *She'll never be able to have children.* ○ *He just walked out of the door one day and never came back.* **2** NOT used to emphasize something negative *I never knew you lived around here.*

never-ending /ˌnevᵊrˈendɪŋ/ *adjective* If something is never-ending, it continues for ever. *The housework in this place is just never-ending.*

nevertheless /ˌnevəðəˈles/ *adverb* despite that *I knew a lot about the subject already, but her talk was interesting nevertheless.*

⊶**new** /njuː/ *adjective* **1** DIFFERENT different from before *I need some new shoes.* ○ *Have you met Fiona's new boyfriend?* ○ *He's starting his new job on Monday.* ○ *We're always looking for new ways to improve our services.* **2** RECENTLY MADE recently made *Their house is quite new - it's about five years old.* ○ *The factory will provide hundreds of new jobs for the area.* **3** NOT KNOWN BEFORE not known before *to discover a new gene/star* **4 be new to sb** If a situation or activity is new to you, you have not had experience of it before. **5 be new to sth** If you are new to a situation or activity, you have only recently started experiencing it. *I'm new to the job.* ➲See also: a whole new **ball game**, new **blood**, **brand new**, break new **ground**[1], new **heights**, turn over a new **leaf**[1], give sb/sth a new **lease**[1] of life

newborn /ˌnjuːˈbɔːn/ *adjective* [**always before noun**] A newborn baby has just been born. •**newborn** *noun* [C] a newborn baby

newcomer /ˈnjuːˌkʌməʳ/ *noun* [C] someone who has only recently arrived or started doing something *He's a relative* ***newcomer to*** *the area.*

new-found /ˈnjuːˌfaʊnd/ *adjective* [**always before noun**] A new-found quality or ability has started recently. *This success is a reflection of their new-found confidence.*

newly /ˈnjuːli/ *adverb* recently *a* ***newly married*** *couple* ○ *newly-built houses*

WORD PARTNERS FOR ***news***

the latest news • **hear/listen to/see/watch** the news • **in/on** the news

⊶**news** /njuːz/ *noun* [U] **1 the news** the announcement of important events on television, radio, and in newspapers *the* ***local/national news*** ○ *to* ***watch*** *the 6 o'clock* ***news*** ○ *Did you see that report about child labour* ***on the news*** *last night?* ○ *a* ***news bulletin/report*** **2** new information *Have you* ***had*** *any* ***news*** *about your job yet?* ○ *I've got some* ***good news*** *for you.* ○ *Any news from John?* **3 be news to sb** *informal* to be a surprise to someone *He's leaving? Well that's certainly news to me.* **4 be bad/good news for sb** to affect someone badly/well *This weather is bad news for farmers.*

newsagent /ˈnjuːzˌeɪdʒᵊnt/ *noun* [C] *UK* **1 newsagent's** a shop that sells newspapers, magazines, and things like sweets and cigarettes **2** someone who owns or works in a newsagent's

newscast /ˈnjuːzkɑːst/ *noun* [C] *US* a television or radio broadcast of the news *the evening newscast*

newscaster /ˈnjuːzkɑːstəʳ/ *noun* [C] someone who reads the news on the radio or television

newsgroup /ˈnjuːzgruːp/ *noun* [**group**] **INTERNET** a collection of messages on the Internet that people write about a particular subject *a political newsgroup*

newsletter /ˈnjuːzˌletəʳ/ *noun* [C] a regular report with information for people who belong to an organization or who are interested in a particular subject *a monthly newsletter about business and the environment*

⊶**newspaper** /ˈnjuːsˌpeɪpəʳ/ Ⓤⓢ /ˈnuːzˌpeɪpəʳ/ *noun* **1** NEWS [C] large, folded sheets of paper which are printed with the news and sold every day or every week *a* ***local/national newspaper*** ○ *I read about his death* ***in the newspaper.*** ○ *a* ***newspaper article/headline*** **2** PAPER [U] paper from newspapers *The cups were wrapped in newspaper.*

newsprint /ˈnjuːzprɪnt/ *noun* [U] cheap, low quality paper used to print newspapers

newsreader /ˈnjuːzˌriːdəʳ/ *noun* [C] *UK* someone who reads the news on the radio or television

newsstand /ˈnjuːzstænd/ *noun* [C] *US* a small shop in a public area of a building or station, or part of a bigger shop, where newspapers and magazines are sold

newsworthy /ˈnjuːzˌwɜːði/ *adjective* interesting or important enough to be included in the news

the ˌNew ˈTestament *noun* **RELIGION** the part of the Bible (= holy book) written after the birth of Jesus Christ

newton /ˈnjuːtᵊn/ (*abbreviation* **N**) *noun* [C] **MEASURES** a unit used to measure force. One newton is equal to the force which moves a mass of one kilogram one metre in one second

ˈnew ˌtown *noun* [C] a British town which was planned by the government and built after 1946 *Milton Keynes is a new town which was founded in 1967.*

ˌnew ˈwave *noun* [C] people who are doing activities in a new and different way *the new wave of wine producers*

ˌnew ˈyear (*also* **New Year**) *noun* [C] the period in January when another year begins ***Happy New Year!*** ○ *We're going away* ***in the new year.***

ˌNew ˌYear's ˈDay *noun* [C, U] 1 January, the first day of the year and a public holiday in many countries

ˌNew ˌYear's ˈEve *noun* [C, U] 31 December, the last day of the year

⊶**next**[1] /nekst/ *adjective* **1 next week/year/Monday, etc** the week/year/Monday, etc that follows the present one *I'm planning to visit California next year.* ○ *Are you doing anything next*

Wednesday? ○ *Next time, ask my permission before you borrow the car.* **2** AFTER The next time, event, person, or thing is the one nearest to now or the one that follows the present one. *What time's the next train to London?* ○ *We're going to be very busy for the next few months.* **3** NEAR The next place is the one nearest to the present one. *She only lives in the next village.* ○ *Turn left at the next roundabout.* **4 the next best thing** the thing that is best, if you cannot have or do the thing you really want *Coaching football is the next best thing to playing.* **5 the next thing I knew** used to talk about part of a story that happens in a sudden and surprising way *A car came speeding round the corner, and the next thing I knew I was lying on the ground.*

O–■ **next²** /nekst/ *adverb* **1** AFTER immediately after *You'll never guess what happened next.* ○ *Where shall we go next?* **2** AGAIN The time when you next do something is the first time you do it again. *Could you get some coffee when you next go to the supermarket?*

O–■ **next³** /nekst/ *preposition* **next to sth/sb** very close to something or someone, with nothing in between *Come and sit next to me.* ○ *The factory is right next to a residential area.*

O–■ **next⁴** /nekst/ *pronoun* **1** the person or thing that follows the present person or thing *Who's next to see the nurse?* ○ *Blue roses? **Whatever next?*** (= What other strange things might happen?) **2 the weekend/week/Thursday, etc after next** the weekend/week/Thursday, etc that follows the next one

ˌnext ˈdoor *adjective, adverb* in the next room, house, or building *What are your **next-door neighbours** like?* ○ *That's the old man who lives **next door to** Paul.*

ˌnext of ˈkin *noun* [C] *plural* **next of kin** *formal* **SOCIETY** the person you are most closely related to *The names of the dead cannot be released until their next of kin have been notified.*

the NHS /ˌeneɪtʃˈes/ *noun* **HEALTH** *abbreviation for* the National Health Service: the system providing free medical services in the UK *Did she get it done privately or **on the NHS**?*

niacin /ˈnaɪəsɪn/ *noun* [U] **FOOD** a B vitamin which you find in foods such as wheat, meat and milk, which is important for making energy from food

nib /nɪb/ *noun* [C] the pointed end of a pen, where the ink comes out

nibble /ˈnɪbl/ *verb* [I, T] to eat something by taking very small bites or to bite something gently *He was nibbling a biscuit.* ○ *She **nibbled** playfully **at** his ear.*

O–■ **nice** /naɪs/ *adjective* **1** PLEASANT pleasant *They live in a nice old house on Market Street.* ○ *We could go to the coast tomorrow, if the weather's nice.* [**+ to do sth**] *It was very nice to meet you.* [**+ doing sth**] *Nice talking to you.* **2** KIND kind and friendly *He seems like a really nice guy.* ○ *She's always been very **nice to** me.* **3 nice and sth** *informal* used to emphasize a positive quality *nice and clean* ○ *This chair's nice and comfy.*

OTHER WAYS OF SAYING *nice*

If a person is nice because they are kind to other people, you can say that they are **kind** or **sweet**: *She's a very **kind** person.* • *Thank you so much for the card - it was very **sweet** of you!*

If something that you do is nice, you can describe it as **fun**, **enjoyable**, or **lovely**: *We had a really **lovely** day at the beach.* • *You'd have liked the party - it was **fun**.*

If something is nice to look at, then adjectives such as **attractive**, **beautiful**, **pleasant**, **lovely**, and **pretty** are often used: *There's some **beautiful** countryside in Yorkshire.* • *That's a **pretty** dress you're wearing.*

If food tastes nice, then we can say that it is **delicious** or **tasty**: *This chicken soup is absolutely **delicious**.*

nicely /ˈnaɪsli/ *adverb* **1** WELL well *That table would fit nicely in the bedroom.* ○ *His business is **doing very nicely**.* **2** PLEASANTLY in a pleasant way *nicely dressed*

niche /niːʃ/ (US) /nɪtʃ/ *noun* [C] **1** ACTIVITY a job or activity that is very suitable for someone *After years of job dissatisfaction, he's at last **found his niche in** financial services.* **2** HOLE a hollow space cut into a wall

ˈniche ˌmarket *noun* [C] **ECONOMICS** a small number of people who buy a particular product or service, especially an unusual or expensive one *They make luxury cars for a small but significant niche market.*

nick¹ /nɪk/ *verb* [T] **1** STEAL *UK informal* to steal something *She got caught nicking CDs from Woolworth's.* **2** CATCH *UK informal* If the police nick someone, they catch that person because they have committed a crime. [**often passive**] *He got nicked for handling stolen goods.* **3** CUT to make a small cut in something without intending to *He nicked himself shaving.*

nick² /nɪk/ *noun* **1** PRISON [C] *mainly UK informal* a prison or police station *They spent the night **in the nick**.* **2** CUT [C] a small cut *He has a little nick on his cheek.* **3 in bad/good nick** *UK informal* in bad/good condition **4 in the nick of time** just before it was too late *The ambulance arrived in the nick of time.*

nickel /ˈnɪkl/ *noun* **1 FINANCE** [C] a US or Canadian coin with a value of 5 cents **2 CHEMISTRY** [U] a silver-white metal that is often mixed with other metals (formula **Ni**)

nickname /ˈnɪkneɪm/ *noun* [C] a name used informally instead of your real name *His behaviour has earned him the nickname 'Mad Dog'.* •**nickname** *verb* [**+ two objects**] *They nicknamed her 'The Iron Lady'.*

nicotine /ˈnɪkətiːn/ *noun* [U] **CHEMISTRY, HEALTH** a poisonous chemical substance in tobacco

niece /niːs/ *noun* [C] the daughter of your brother or sister, or the daughter of your husband's or wife's brother or sister

nifty /ˈnɪfti/ *adjective informal* well-designed and effective *a nifty piece of software*

nigger /ˈnɪgəʳ/ *noun* [C] a very offensive word for a black person

niggle /ˈnɪgl/ *verb* **1** [I, T] to worry or annoy someone slightly for a long time ***a niggling injury*** **2 niggle about/over, etc** *UK* to complain about things which are not very important *She kept niggling about the extra work.* •**niggle** *noun* [C]

nigh /naɪ/ *adverb* **1** *literary* near *The end of the world is nigh.* **2 well nigh/nigh on** *old-fashioned* almost *Our family has lived here well nigh two hundred years.*

WORD PARTNERS FOR ***night***

spend the night • **at** night • **in** the night • the **middle of** the night • **last** night

O━**night** /naɪt/ *noun* [C, U] **1** DARK the time in every 24 hours when it is dark and people usually sleep *I didn't get any sleep* ***last night.*** ○ *It's warm during the day, but it can get quite cold* ***at night.*** ○ *The phone rang in the* ***middle of the night.*** ○ *We stayed up almost all night talking.* ○ *Tim's working nights this week.* **2** EVENING the period from the evening to the time when you go to sleep *Did you have a good time* ***last night?*** ○ *Are you doing anything* ***on*** *Friday night?* **3** SAYING THE TIME used to describe the hours from the evening until just after 12 midnight *They're open from 7 in the morning until 10 o'clock at night.* **4 have an early/a late night** to go to bed early/late **5 a night out** an evening spent away from home doing something enjoyable *a night out at the theatre* **6 Good night.** You say 'Good night' to someone who is going to bed. *Good night, sleep well.* ➲See also: the **dead**[3] of night/winter

nightclub /ˈnaɪtklʌb/ *noun* [C] a place where you can dance and drink at night

nightdress /ˈnaɪtdres/ *noun* [C] *mainly UK* a loose dress that women wear in bed

nightfall /ˈnaɪtfɔːl/ *noun* [U] the time in the evening when it gets dark

nightgown /ˈnaɪtgaʊn/ *noun* [C] a loose dress that women wear in bed

nightie /ˈnaɪti/ *noun* [C] a loose dress that women wear in bed

nightingale /ˈnaɪtɪŋgeɪl/ *noun* [C] a small brown bird which sings very well

nightlife /ˈnaɪtlaɪf/ *noun* [U] entertainment for the night such as bars, restaurants, and theatres *What's the nightlife like around here?*

nightly /ˈnaɪtli/ *adjective* [always before noun], *adverb* happening every night *the nightly news* ○ *The show, lasting ninety minutes, will be broadcast nightly from Monday to Friday.*

WORD PARTNERS FOR ***nightmare***

an **absolute/complete/living/total** nightmare • be sb's **worst** nightmare • the nightmare **of** (doing) sth • a nightmare **for** sb

nightmare /ˈnaɪtmeəʳ/ *noun* [C] **1** EXPERIENCE a very unpleasant experience *The traffic can be a real nightmare after 4.30.* **2** DREAM a frightening dream

ˈ**night** ˌ**school** *noun* [U] **EDUCATION** classes for adults that are taught in the evening

nightstick /ˈnaɪtstɪk/ *US* (*UK* **truncheon**) *noun* [C] a short stick that police officers carry to use as a weapon

night-time /ˈnaɪttaɪm/ *noun* [U] the period of time when it is dark at night

nil /nɪl/ *noun* [U] **1 SPORT** *UK* In sports results, nil means 'zero'. *Germany beat England three nil* (= 3-0). **2** NOT EXISTING not existing *The chances of that happening are virtually nil.*

nimble /ˈnɪmbl/ *adjective* able to move quickly and easily ***nimble fingers***

nimbostratus /nɪmbəʊˈstrɑːtəs/ *noun* [U] **GEOGRAPHY** a thick grey cloud which forms at a low level, from which rain or snow often falls ➲See picture at **cloud**

O━**nine** /naɪn/ the number 9

O━**nineteen** /ˌnaɪnˈtiːn/ the number 19 •**nineteenth** 19th written as a word

nine-to-five /ˌnaɪntəˈfaɪv/ *adj, adv* describes work that begins at nine o'clock in the morning and ends at five o'clock, which are the hours that people work in many offices from Monday to Friday *She's tired of working nine-to-five.* •**nine-to-five** *noun* [C]

O━**ninety** /ˈnaɪnti/ **1** the number 90 **2 the nineties** the years from 1990 to 1999 **3 be in your nineties** to be aged between 90 and 99 •**ninetieth** 90th written as a word

ninth[1] /naɪnθ/ 9th written as a word

ninth[2] /naɪnθ/ *noun* [C] one of nine equal parts of something; $^1/_9$

nip /nɪp/ *verb* **nipping**, *past* **nipped 1 nip down/out/up, etc** *UK informal* to go somewhere quickly and for a short time *I'm just nipping down the road to get a paper.* **2** [T] If something nips you, it gives you a small, sharp bite. *His parrot nipped him on the nose.* ➲See also: nip sth in the **bud**

nipple /ˈnɪpl/ *noun* [C] **ANATOMY** the small, circular area of slightly darker, harder skin in the centre of each breast in women, or on each side of the chest in men

nirvana /nɪəˈvɑːnə/ *noun* [U] a state of perfection

nitrate /ˈnaɪtreɪt/ *noun* [C, U] **CHEMISTRY** a chemical containing nitrogen and oxygen that is used on crops to make them grow better ➲See picture at **nitrogen cycle**

nitric acid /ˌnaɪtrɪkˈæsɪd/ *noun* [U] **CHEMISTRY** a clear, colourless liquid which is used in making many chemicals, especially explosives and fertilizers (= substances that help plants to grow) (formula HNO_3)

nitrify /ˈnaɪtrɪfaɪ/ *verb* [T] **CHEMISTRY** to add nitrogen or a nitrogen compound (= two or more substances combined) to something •**nitrification** /ˌnaɪtrɪfɪˈkeɪʃᵊn/ *noun* [U] the process by which bacteria in the soil use oxygen to change dead plants into nitrates. The nitrates can then be used by plants as food.

ˌ**nitrifying bac**ˈ**teria** *noun* [plural] **BIOLOGY** bacteria in the soil that change the nitrogen in dead plants into a form that is good for the soil and which growing plants can use for food

nitrogen /ˈnaɪtrədʒən/ *noun* [U] **CHEMISTRY** a gas that has no colour or smell and is the main part of air (symbol **N**)

the ˈ**nitrogen** ˌ**cycle** *noun* [no plural] **PHYSICS, BIOLOGY, CHEMISTRY** the way that nitrogen is

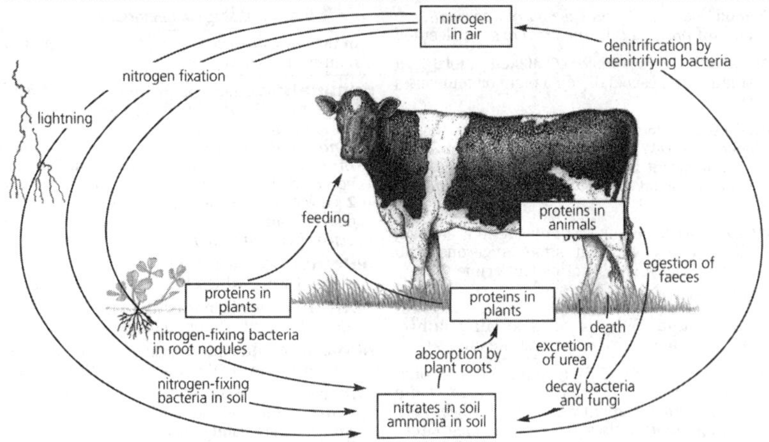

nitrogen cycle

exchanged between different living organisms on Earth and between living organisms and the environment, for instance when plants take it from the air and animals eat the plants

ˌnitrogen diˈoxide *noun* [U] **CHEMISTRY** a poisonous brown gas, formed when some metals dissolve in nitric acid (formula NO²)

ˈnitrogen fixˌation *noun* [U] **CHEMISTRY** the process by which nitrogen from the atmosphere is changed either naturally or in industry into compounds that are used in several processes ⊃See picture **nitrogen cycle**

nitrogenous /naɪˈtrɒdʒɪnəs/ *adjective* **CHEMISTRY** containing nitrogen

nitroglycerine (*also US* **nitroglycerin**) /ˌnaɪtrəʊˈglɪsəriːn/ *noun* [U] **CHEMISTRY** a very powerful liquid explosive

nitrous oxide /ˌnaɪtrəsˈɒksaɪd/ *noun* [U] **CHEMISTRY** a type of gas with a sweet smell which is used as a weak anaesthetic (= substance which stops pain) (formula N_2O)

the nitty-gritty /ˌnɪtiˈgrɪti/ *noun* the important details of a subject or activity *English teachers should concentrate on **the nitty-gritty of** teaching grammar.*

no¹ /nəʊ/ *exclamation* **1** DISAGREE something that you say in order to disagree, give a negative answer, or say that something is not true *"Have you seen Louise?" "No, I haven't."* ○ *"Have you ever been to Ireland?" "No."* ○ *"Can I have some more cake?" "No, you'll be sick."* ○ *"He's really ugly." "No he isn't!"* **2** AGREE something that you say to agree with something that is negative *"He's not very bright, is he?" "No, I'm afraid not."* **3 Oh no!** something that you say when you are shocked and upset *Oh no! It's gone all over the carpet!*

no² /nəʊ/ *determiner* **1** NOT ANY not any *There were no signposts anywhere.* ○ *I had no difficulty getting work.* ○ *There was no mention of money.* **2** FORBID a word used to say that something is forbidden *No smoking.* ○ *There was no talking in her classes.* **3 There's no doing sth** something that you say when an action is impossible *There's no pleasing some people* (= nothing that you do will make them happy).

no³ /nəʊ/ *adverb* **no ... than** not any *The work should be done no later than Friday.* ○ *There were no more than ten people there.*

no. *written abbreviation for* number

nobility /nəʊˈbɪləti/ *noun* **1 SOCIETY the nobility** [group] the people from the highest social group in a society **2** [U] the quality of being noble

noble¹ /ˈnəʊbl/ *adjective* **1** honest, brave, and kind *a noble gesture* **2 SOCIETY** belonging to the highest social group of a society

noble² /ˈnəʊbl/ *noun* [C] **SOCIETY** a person of the highest social group in some countries

ˌnoble ˈgas *noun* [C] **CHEMISTRY** any of a group of gases, such as helium, that do not react with other chemicals

nobleman, noblewoman /ˈnəʊblmən, ˈnəʊblˌwʊmən/ *noun* [C] *plural* **noblemen** or **noblewomen SOCIETY** someone belonging to the highest social group in some countries

nobly /ˈnəʊbli/ *adverb* in a brave or generous way *She nobly offered to sell her jewellery.*

nobody /ˈnəʊbədi/ *pronoun* no person *There was nobody I could talk to.* ○ *Nobody's listening.* ○ *Sally helped me, but **nobody else** bothered.*

no-brainer /ˌnəʊˈbreɪnəʳ/ *noun* [C] *informal* something that is very simple to do or to understand, or a decision that is very easy to take

nocturnal /nɒkˈtɜːnəl/ *adjective* **1** ANIMALS Nocturnal animals and birds are active at night. **2** ACTIVITIES happening at night *nocturnal activities/habits*

nod /nɒd/ *verb* [I, T] **nodding**, *past* **nodded** to move your head up and down as a way of agreeing, to give someone a sign, or to point to something *They nodded enthusiastically at the proposal.* ○ *Barbara nodded in approval.*

•**nod** *noun* [C] *He gave a **nod** of approval.*
nod off *phrasal verb informal* to start sleeping

nodule /ˈnɒdjuːl/ *noun* [C] **HEALTH, BIOLOGY** a small lump, especially on a plant or someone's body

no-fault /ˈnəʊfɔːlt/ *adjective* [**always before noun**] *US* **LAW** No-fault laws or systems are ones where it is not important who is responsible for what has happened. *no-fault insurance*

ˌno-go ˈarea *noun* [C] *mainly UK* an area, usually in a city, where it is too dangerous to go because there is a lot of violent crime there

WORD PARTNERS FOR ***noise***

background noise • a **deafening/faint/loud/strange** noise • **hear/make** a noise

O→**noise** /nɔɪz/ *noun* [C, U] a sound, often a loud, unpleasant sound *a deafening/loud noise* ○ *Stop **making** so much **noise**!* ○ *The engine's making funny noises.* ○ *There is some **background noise** on the recording.* ○ *I had to shout above the noise of the party.*

ˈnoise pollˌution *noun* [U] **ENVIRONMENT** noise, often from traffic, which upsets people where they live or work

O→**noisy** /ˈnɔɪzi/ *adjective* Noisy people or things make a lot of noise. *A crowd of noisy protesters gathered in the square.* ○ *We've had problems with noisy neighbours.* •**noisily** *adverb*

N

nomad /ˈnəʊmæd/ *noun* [C] **SOCIETY** a member of a group of people who move from one place to another instead of living in the same place all the time •**nomadic** /nəʊˈmædɪk/ *adjective* Nomadic people move from place to place.

ˈno-man's ˌland *noun* [U, **no plural**] an area of land which no one owns or controls, especially in a war

nomenclature /nəˈmeŋklətʃər/ *noun* [U] *formal* a system of naming things, especially in science

nominal /ˈnɒmɪnəl/ *adjective* **1** NOT REAL existing officially, but not in reality *a nominal leader* **2** MONEY A nominal sum of money is a small amount of money. *a **nominal charge/fee***

ˌnominal ˈledger (*also* **general ledger**) *noun* [C] **FINANCE** the main financial record of a company that uses double entry bookkeeping (= a system where each amount is shown as money spent in one part and money received in the other part)

nominally /ˈnɒmɪnəli/ *adverb* officially but not in reality *nominally Catholic areas*

nominate /ˈnɒmɪneɪt/ *verb* [T] **1** SUGGEST to officially suggest a person for a job or a position in an organization, or to suggest a person or their work for a prize [**often passive**] *Judges are nominated by the governor.* ○ *The film was **nominated for** an Academy Award.* ○ *He was **nominated as** best actor.* **2** CHOOSE to choose someone for a job or to do something *He has **nominated** his brother **as** his heir.* [**+ to do sth**] *Two colleagues were nominated to attend the conference.*

WORD PARTNERS FOR ***nomination***

make/receive/seek/win a nomination • a nomination **as/for** sth

nomination /ˌnɒmɪˈneɪʃən/ *noun* [C, U] **1** SUGGESTION the act of officially suggesting a person for a job or their work for a prize *to **seek/win** a **nomination*** ○ *He won the Democratic **nomination for** mayor of Chicago.* ○ *She has just **received** her fourth Oscar **nomination**.* **2** CHOICE the choice of someone for a job or to do something *They did everything they could to defeat his nomination to be surgeon general.*

nominee /ˌnɒmɪˈniː/ *noun* [C] a person or a piece of work which has been nominated

non- /nɒn-/ *prefix* not or the opposite of *non-alcoholic drinks* ○ *non-smokers*

non-alcoholic /ˌnɒnælkəˈhɒlɪk/ *adjective* **FOOD** describes a drink that does not contain alcohol

nonchalant /ˈnɒnʃələnt/ (US) /ˌnɑːnʃəˈlɑːnt/ *adjective* calm and not worried *a nonchalant shrug* •**nonchalantly** *adverb*

noncommittal /ˌnɒnkəˈmɪtəl/ *adjective* not showing your opinion about something *a noncommittal expression/response*

nondescript /ˈnɒndɪskrɪpt/ *adjective* not interesting *a nondescript building/man*

O→**none** /nʌn/ *quantifier* **1** not any ***None of** them smoke.* ○ *In 1992, the company had 2,700 part-time workers. Today it has none.* ○ *There were only three births here in March and **none at all** in April.* ○ *He asked if there was any hope. I told him frankly that there was none.* **2 none too clean/clever/pleased, etc** not at all clean/clever/pleased, etc *His handkerchief was none too clean.* **3 none the happier/poorer/wiser, etc** not any happier/poorer/wiser, etc than before *She must have explained the theory three times, but I'm still none the wiser.*

nonetheless /ˌnʌnðəˈles/ *adverb* despite what has just been said *He was extremely rude in meetings. Nonetheless, his arguments found some support.*

non-event /ˌnɒnɪˈvent/ *noun* [**no plural**] *informal* an event that was not as exciting or interesting as you expected it to be *Her party was a bit of a non-event.*

non-existent /ˌnɒnɪɡˈzɪstənt/ *adjective* not existing *We knew our chances of success were non-existent.*

nonfiction /ˌnɒnˈfɪkʃən/ *noun* [U] **LITERATURE** writing about things which are true *nonfiction books/titles*

non-metal /ˌnɒnˈmetəl/ *noun* **CHEMISTRY** a chemical element that is not a metal

no-no /ˈnəʊnəʊ/ *noun* [C] *informal* something that is forbidden or not socially acceptable *Cardigans are a fashion no-no this season.*

no-nonsense /ˌnəʊˈnɒnsəns/ *adjective* [**always before noun**] not having or allowing others to have any silly ideas or behaviour *a **no-nonsense approach** to child rearing*

nonplussed /ˌnɒnˈplʌst/ *adjective* extremely surprised

non-profit-making /ˌnɒnˈprɒfɪtˌmeɪkɪŋ/ *UK* (*US* **nonprofit**) *adjective* **FINANCE** A non-profit-making organization does not make money from its activities.

WORD PARTNERS FOR ***nonsense***

talk nonsense • **absolute/complete/utter** nonsense • a **load of** nonsense

nonsense /ˈnɒnsᵊns/ *noun* [U] **1** SPEECH AND WRITING If something someone has said or written is nonsense, it is silly and not true. *She talks such nonsense sometimes.* ○ *That's* ***a load of nonsense.*** ○ *It's nonsense to suggest they could have cheated.* **2** BEHAVIOUR silly behaviour *Will you stop this childish nonsense!* **3 make a nonsense of sth** *UK* to spoil something or make it seem stupid *Cuts to the text made a nonsense of the play.*

non-smoker /ˌnɒnˈsməʊkəʳ/ *noun* [C] a person who does not smoke

non-smoking /ˌnɒnˈsməʊkɪŋ/ *adjective* A non-smoking area is one where people are not allowed to smoke.

non-starter /ˌnɒnˈstɑːtəʳ/ *noun* [C] *informal* something that will not be successful *The amount of money needed makes his project a non-starter.*

non-stop /ˌnɒnˈstɒp/ *adjective, adverb* without stopping or resting ***non-stop flights*** *from Britain to the West Indies* ○ *We've been* ***talking non-stop*** *the whole way.*

non-violent /ˌnɒnˈvaɪələnt/ *adjective* not using violent methods *non-violent action/protests* ○ *non-violent crimes/offenders*

noodles /ˈnuːdlz/ *noun* [plural] **FOOD** thin pieces of pasta (= food made from flour, eggs, and water)

nook /nʊk/ *noun* **every nook and cranny** every part of a place *I know every nook and cranny of this place.*

noon /nuːn/ *noun* [U] 12 o'clock in the middle of the day *He has until noon to act.* ○ *The service will be held at 12 noon.*

O-ᵾ**ˈno ˌone** *pronoun* no person *No one bothered to read the report.* ○ *No one knows where he is now.* ○ *There was no one there.* ○ ***No one else*** *makes puddings like my Mum.*

noose /nuːs/ *noun* [C] a piece of rope tied in a circle, used to catch animals or to hang (= kill) people

O-ᵾ**nor** /nɔːʳ/ *adverb, conjunction* **1 neither...nor...** used after 'neither' to introduce the second thing in a negative sentence *Strangely, neither James nor Emma saw what happened.* ○ *He neither spoke nor moved.* **2 nor can I/nor do you, etc** *mainly UK* used after something negative to say that the same thing is true for someone or something else *"I don't like cats." "Nor do I."* ○ *"I won't get to see him tomorrow." "Nor will Tom."* ○ *She couldn't speak a word of Italian and nor could I.*

Nordic /ˈnɔːdɪk/ *adjective* **SOCIETY** from or relating to the North European countries of Sweden, Denmark, Norway, Finland, and Iceland

norm /nɔːm/ *noun* **1 the norm** the usual way that something happens *Short-term job contracts are the norm nowadays.* **2** [C] **SOCIETY** an accepted way of behaving in a particular society [usually plural] ***cultural/social norms***

WORD PARTNERS FOR ***normal***

be back to/return to normal • **perfectly** normal

O-ᵾ**normal** /ˈnɔːmᵊl/ *adjective* usual, ordinary, and expected *to lead a* ***normal life*** ○ *It's perfectly normal to feel some degree of stress at work.* ○ *It's normal for couples to argue now and then.* ○ *Now that trains are running again things are* ***back to normal.***

normality /nɔːˈmæləti/ (*also US* **normalcy** /ˈnɔːmᵊlsi/) *noun* [U] a situation in which everything is happening normally *a* ***return to normality***

O-ᵾ**normally** /ˈnɔːməli/ *adverb* **1** USUALLY usually *Normally, I start work around nine o'clock.* **2** ORDINARY in the ordinary way that you would expect *Both lungs are now functioning normally.*

O-ᵾ**north, North** /nɔːθ/ *noun* [U] **1** the direction that is on your left when you face towards the rising sun *The stadium is to the north of the city.* **2 the north** the part of an area that is further towards the north than the rest *She's from the north of England.* •**north** *adjective a north wind* •**north** *adverb* towards the north *I live north of the river.* ○ *We're going to visit Paul's family* ***up north.***

northbound /ˈnɔːθbaʊnd/ *adjective* going or leading towards the north

northeast, Northeast /ˌnɔːθˈiːst/ *noun* [U] **1** the direction between north and east **2 the northeast** the northeast part of a country •**northeast, Northeast** *adjective, adverb*

northeastern, Northeastern /ˌnɔːθˈiːstən/ *adjective* in or from the northeast

northerly /ˈnɔːðᵊli/ *adjective* **1** DIRECTION towards or in the north *Canada's most* ***northerly point*** **2** WIND A northerly wind comes from the north.

O-ᵾ**northern, Northern** /ˈnɔːðᵊn/ *adjective* in or from the north part of an area *Northern England* ○ *a northern accent*

northerner, Northerner /ˈnɔːðᵊnəʳ/ *noun* [C] someone from the north part of a country

northernmost /ˈnɔːðənməʊst/ *adjective* The northernmost part of an area is the part furthest to the north.

north-facing /ˈnɔːθˌfeɪsɪŋ/ *adjective* [always before noun] positioned towards the north *a north-facing slope*

the ˌNorth ˈPole *noun* **GEOGRAPHY** the point on the Earth's surface which is furthest north

northward, northwards /ˈnɔːθwəd, ˈnɔːθwədz/ *adverb* towards the north •**northward** *adjective a northward direction*

northwest, Northwest /ˌnɔːθˈwest/ *noun* [U] **1** the direction between north and west **2 the northwest** the northwest part of a country •**northwest, Northwest** *adjective, adverb*

northwestern, Northwestern /ˌnɔːθˈwestən/ *adjective* in or from the northwest

O-ᵾ**nose¹** /nəʊz/ *noun* [C] **1 ANATOMY** the part of your face through which you breathe and smell *a big/broken nose* ○ *She paused to* ***blow her nose*** (= breathe out hard to empty it into

N

a piece of cloth). ➲See colour picture **The Body** on page Centre 13 **2 get up sb's nose** *UK informal* to annoy someone **3 poke/stick your nose into sth** *informal* to show too much interest in a situation that does not involve you *You shouldn't go sticking your nose into other people's business!* **4 thumb your nose at sth/sb** to show that you do not respect rules, laws, or powerful people **5 turn your nose up at sth** *informal* to not accept something because you do not think it is good enough for you *He turned his nose up at my offer of soup, saying he wanted a proper meal.* **6 under your nose** If something bad happens under your nose, it happens close to you but you do not notice it.

nose[2] /nəʊz/ *verb*
nose about/around (sth) *phrasal verb informal* to look around a place, often in order to find something *I caught him nosing around in my office.*

nosebleed /ˈnəʊzbliːd/ *noun* [C] **have a nosebleed HEALTH** to have blood coming from your nose

nosedive /ˈnəʊzdaɪv/ *verb* [I] to fall very quickly in value *The economy nosedived after the war.* •**nosedive** *noun* [C]

nosey /ˈnəʊzi/ *another spelling of* nosy

nostalgia /nɒsˈtældʒə/ *noun* [U] a feeling of happiness mixed with sadness when you think about things that happened in the past *his nostalgia for his college days*

nostalgic /nɒsˈtældʒɪk/ *adjective* feeling both happy and sad when you think about things that happened in the past *Talking about those holidays has made me feel quite nostalgic.*

N

nostril /ˈnɒstrəl/ *noun* [C] **ANATOMY** one of the two holes at the end of your nose ➲See colour picture **The Body** on page Centre 13 ➲See picture at **respiratory system**

nosy /ˈnəʊzi/ *adjective* always trying to find out private things about other people ***nosy neighbours*** ○ *Don't be so nosy!*

O━ **not** /nɒt/ *adverb* **1** used to form a negative phrase after verbs like 'be', 'can', 'have', 'will', 'must', etc, usually used in the short form 'n't' in speech *I won't tell her.* ○ *I can't go.* ○ *He hasn't eaten yet.* ○ *Don't you like her?* ○ *It isn't difficult* (= It is easy). ○ *The service isn't very good* (= it is bad). ○ *You're coming, aren't you?* ○ *I will not tolerate laziness.* **2** used to give the next word or group of words a negative meaning *I told you not to do that.* ○ *I like most vegetables but not cabbage.* ○ *"Come and play football, Dad." "Not now, Jamie."* ○ *"Whose are these?" "Not mine."* **3** used after verbs like 'be afraid', 'hope', 'suspect', etc in short, negative replies *"Do you think it's going to rain?" "I hope not."* ○ *"Have you finished?" "I'm afraid not."* **4 certainly/hopefully not** used after an adverb in short, negative replies *"She's not exactly poor, is she?" "Certainly not."* ○ *"We won't need much money, will we?" "Hopefully not."* **5 not at all** used instead of 'no' or 'not' to emphasize what you are saying *"I hope this won't cause you any trouble." "No, not at all."* ○ *I'm not at all happy about it.* **6 Not at all.** used as a polite reply after someone has thanked you *"Thanks for all your help." "Not at all."* **7 if not** used to say what the situation will be if something does not happen *I hope to see you there but, if not, I'll call you.* **8 or not** used to express the possibility that something might not happen *Are you coming or not?* **9 not a/one** used to emphasize that there is nothing of what you are talking about *Not one person came to hear him talk.* ○ *"You haven't heard from Nick, have you?" "Not a word."*

COMMON LEARNER ERROR

not ... either

The words **not ... either** are used to add another piece of negative information.

I'd forgotten my credit card and I didn't have any cash either.

~~*I'd forgotten my credit card and I didn't have any cash neither.*~~

Helen didn't enjoy it either.

~~*Helen didn't enjoy it too.*~~

notable /ˈnəʊtəbl/ *adjective* If someone or something is notable, they are important or interesting.

notably /ˈnəʊtəbli/ *adverb* used to emphasize an important example of something *Florida is well known for many of its fruits, notably oranges and avocados.*

notation /nəʊˈteɪʃən/ *noun* [U] **MATHEMATICS, MUSIC** a system of written symbols used especially in mathematics or to represent musical notes

notch[1] /nɒtʃ/ *noun* [C] **1** [LEVEL] a level of quality or amount *Interest rates have moved up another notch.* **2** [CUT] a cut in the shape of the letter V on the edge or surface of something

notch[2] /nɒtʃ/ *verb*
notch up sth *phrasal verb* to achieve something *He has notched up a total of 34 goals this season.*

WORD PARTNERS FOR ***note (noun)***

leave/scribble/send/write a note • a note **for/from** sb • **get** sb's note

O━ **note**[1] /nəʊt/ *noun* **1** [LETTER] [C] a short letter *He left a **note** on her desk.* ○ *Did you **get** my **note**?* **2** [INFORMATION] [C] words that you write down to help you remember something *She studied her notes before the exam.* ○ *Let me **make a note of*** (= write) *your phone number.* ○ *The doctor **took notes*** (= wrote information) *while I described my symptoms.* **3** [EXPLANATION] [C] a short explanation or an extra piece of information that is given at the bottom of a page or at the back of a book *See note 3, page 37.* **4** [FEELING] [**no plural**] a particular feeling or mood *a **sad/serious/positive note*** ○ *His speech had just the **right note** of sympathy.* **5 MUSIC** [C] a single musical sound or the symbol that represents it **6 FINANCE** [C] *UK* (*US* **bill**) a piece of paper money *a ten-pound note* **7 take note (of sth)** to pay careful attention to something *Make sure you take note of what she says.* **8 sb/sth of note** *formal* someone or something famous or important *A medieval church is the only monument of note in the town.* **9 compare notes** If two people compare notes, they tell each other what they think about something that they have both done. *We compared notes about our experiences in China.*

note² /nəʊt/ *verb* [T] **1** NOTICE to notice something *She noted a distinct chill in the air.* [+ **(that)**] *We noted that their idea had never been tried.* **2** SAY OR WRITE to say or write something *In the article, she notes several cases of medical incompetence.*

note down sth *phrasal verb* to write something so that you do not forget it *I noted down the telephone number for the police.*

notebook /ˈnəʊtbʊk/ *noun* [C] **1** a book with empty pages that you can write in **2** COMPUTING a small computer that can be carried around and used anywhere

noted /ˈnəʊtɪd/ *adjective* important or famous *a noted artist* ○ *He was* ***noted for*** *his modern approach to architecture.*

ˈnotepad (comˌputer) *noun* [C] COMPUTING a very small computer which you can carry easily

notepaper /ˈnəʊtˌpeɪpəʳ/ *noun* [U] paper that you write letters on

noteworthy /ˈnəʊtˌwɜːði/ *adjective* If someone or something is noteworthy, they are important or interesting. *a* ***noteworthy example***

O━**nothing** /ˈnʌθɪŋ/ *pronoun* **1** NOT ANYTHING not anything *I've had nothing to eat since breakfast.* ○ *He claimed that he did nothing wrong.* ○ *He had nothing in his pockets.* ○ *There was* ***nothing else*** (= no other thing) *I could do to help.* ○ *She did* ***nothing but*** *criticize* (= criticized a lot). **2** NOT IMPORTANT not something important or of value *He's a dangerous person - human life means nothing to him.* ○ *A thousand pounds is nothing to a woman of her wealth.* **3 for nothing** without a successful result *I've come all this way for nothing.* **4 be nothing to do with sb** If something is or has nothing to do with you, you have no good reason to know about it or be involved with it. *I wish he wouldn't offer advice on my marriage - it's nothing to do with him.* **5 have nothing to do with sb/sth** to have no connection or influence with someone or something *He made his own decision - I had nothing to do with it.* **6 to say nothing of sth** used to emphasize other problems you have not talked about *Most wild otters have disappeared from populated areas, to say nothing of wilderness areas.* **7 nothing of the sort** used to emphasize that something is not true *He said that he was a legitimate businessman - in fact, he was nothing of the sort.* **8 It was nothing.** a polite reply to someone who has thanked you for doing something **9 be nothing if not sth** used to emphasize a quality *The senator was nothing if not honest* (= he was very honest). **10 stop at nothing** to be willing to do anything in order to achieve something *He will stop at nothing to get what he wants.*

nothingness /ˈnʌθɪŋnəs/ *noun* [U] a state where nothing exists

O━**notice¹** /ˈnəʊtɪs/ *verb* [I, T] to see something and be aware of it *If the sign's too small, no one will notice it.* [+ **(that)**] *I noticed that he walked with a limp.*

WORD PARTNERS FOR ***notice (noun)***

display/put up a notice • a notice **says** sth • a notice **about** sth • **on** a notice

notice² /ˈnəʊtɪs/ *noun* **1** SIGN [C] a sign giving information about something *The notice said that the pool was closed for repairs.* ○ *Have you seen any* ***notices about*** *the new sports club?* **2** WARNING [U] a warning that something will happen *I had to give my landlord a month's notice before moving.* **3 at short notice** *UK* (*US* **on short notice**) only a short time before something happens **4** ATTENTION [U] attention *I didn't* ***take any notice of*** (= give attention to) *his advice.* ○ *It has* ***come to our notice*** (= we became aware) *that you are being overcharged for your insurance.* **5 hand/give in your notice** to tell your employer that you are going to stop working for them *I handed in my notice yesterday.*

noticeable /ˈnəʊtɪsəbl/ *adjective* easy to see or be aware of *There was a noticeable difference in his behaviour after the injury.* •**noticeably** *adverb*

noticeboard /ˈnəʊtɪsbɔːd/ *UK* (*US* **bulletin board**) *noun* [C] a board on a wall where you put advertisements and announcements *I saw the ad on the noticeboard.* ➲See colour picture **The Classroom** on page Centre 6

notify /ˈnəʊtɪfaɪ/ *verb* [T] *formal* to officially tell someone about something *You should notify the police if you are involved in a road accident.* [+ **(that)**] *The court notified her that her trial date had been postponed.* •**notification** /ˌnəʊtɪfɪˈkeɪʃᵊn/ *noun* [C, U]

notion /ˈnəʊʃᵊn/ *noun* [C] an idea or belief *The notion of sharing is unknown to most two-year-olds.*

notoriety /ˌnəʊtᵊrˈaɪəti/ *noun* [U] when someone is famous for something bad *He* ***gained notoriety*** *for his racist speeches.*

notorious /nəʊˈtɔːriəs/ *adjective* famous for something bad *a notorious criminal* ○ *She was* ***notorious for*** her bad temper. •**notoriously** *adverb Mount Everest is a notoriously difficult mountain to climb.*

notwithstanding /ˌnɒtwɪθˈstændɪŋ/ *adverb, preposition formal* despite *Injuries notwithstanding, he won the semi-final match.*

nought /nɔːt/ *noun* [C, U] **1** NUMBER *UK* the number 0 **2** NOTHING *old-fashioned* (*mainly US* **naught**) nothing

O━**noun** /naʊn/ *noun* [C] LANGUAGE a word that refers to a person, place, object, event, substance, idea, feeling, or quality. For example the words 'teacher', 'book', 'development', and 'beauty' are nouns. ➲See also: **countable noun, proper noun, uncountable noun**

nourish /ˈnʌrɪʃ/ *verb* [T] *formal* FOOD, HEALTH to provide living things with food in order to make them grow or stay healthy *Mammals provide milk to nourish their young.*

nourishing /ˈnʌrɪʃɪŋ/ *adjective* FOOD, HEALTH Nourishing food makes you healthy.

nourishment /ˈnʌrɪʃmənt/ *noun* [U] *formal* FOOD the food that you need to stay alive and healthy

N

Nov *written abbreviation for* November

nova /'nəʊvə/ *noun* [C] *plural* **novas** or **novae** **ASTRONOMY** a type of star that shines much more brightly for a few months as a result of a nuclear explosion

WORD PARTNERS FOR ***novel***

read/write a novel • a novel **by** sb • a novel **about** sth • **in** a novel

novel¹ /'nɒvᵊl/ *noun* [C] **LITERATURE** a book that tells a story about imaginary people and events *Have you **read** any good **novels** lately?* •**novelist** *noun* [C] someone who writes novels

novel² /'nɒvᵊl/ *adjective* new or different from anything else

novelty /'nɒvᵊlti/ *noun* **1** QUALITY [U] the quality of being new or unusual *The fashion industry relies on novelty, and photographers are always looking for new faces.* **2** NEW THING [C] an object, event, or experience that is new or unusual *Tourists are still a novelty on this remote island.* **3** CHEAP TOY [C] a cheap toy or unusual object, often given as a present

O‑**November** /nəʊ'vembəʳ/ (*written abbreviation* **Nov**) *noun* [C, U] the eleventh month of the year

novice /'nɒvɪs/ *noun* [C] someone who is beginning to learn how to do something *I've never used a computer before - I'm a complete novice.*

O‑**now¹** /naʊ/ *adverb* **1** AT PRESENT at the present time *She's finished her degree and now she teaches English.* ○ *Do you know where Eva is **right now*** (= at this moment)*?* **2** IMMEDIATELY immediately *Come on, Andreas, we're going home now.* ○ *I don't want to wait - I want it now!* **3** LENGTH OF TIME used to show the length of time that something has been happening, from the time it began until the present *I've lived in Cambridge for two years now.* **4** IN SPEECH used when you start to tell someone something *Now, I have been to Glasgow many times before.* ○ ***Now then**, would anyone else like to ask a question?* **5 just now** a very short time ago *When I came in just now, everyone was laughing.* ○ *Who was that woman who was speaking just now?* **6 (every) now and then/again** If something happens now and then, it happens sometimes but not very often. *I love chocolate, but I only eat it now and then.* **7 any day/minute/time, etc now** used to say that something will happen very soon *We're expecting our second child any day now.*

O‑**now²** /naʊ/ (*also* **now that**) *conjunction* as a result of a new situation *Now that I've got a car I can visit her more often.* ○ *You should help in the house more, now you're older.*

O‑**now³** /naʊ/ *pronoun* the present time or moment *Now isn't a good time to speak to him.* ○ *She'd kept calm until now.* ○ *I'll be more careful **from now on*** (= from this moment and always in the future).

nowadays /'naʊədeɪz/ *adverb* at the present time, especially when compared to the past *Everything seems more expensive nowadays.*

O‑**nowhere** /'nəʊweəʳ/ *adverb* **1** not anywhere *The room was very crowded - there was nowhere to sit.* ○ *We had **nowhere else** to go.* **2 out of nowhere** If someone or something appears out of nowhere, it appears suddenly or unexpectedly. *The car came out of nowhere and we had to swerve to miss it.* **3 get/go nowhere** *informal* to fail to make any progress or achieve anything *They're getting nowhere on this project.* **4 get you nowhere** If something gets you nowhere, it does not help you to succeed. *Bad manners will get you nowhere.*

noxious /'nɒkʃəs/ *adjective* [always before noun] *formal* poisonous or harmful *noxious fumes/gases*

nozzle /'nɒzl/ *noun* [C] a narrow, hollow object which is fixed to a tube and which helps you to control the liquid or air that comes out

O‑**n't** /ənt/ *short for* not *She isn't* (= is not) *going.* ○ *I can't* (= cannot) *hear you.* ○ *They didn't* (= did not) *believe me.*

nuance /'njuːɑːns/ *noun* [C] a very slight difference in meaning, appearance, sound, etc *a **subtle nuance*** ○ *Linguists explore the nuances of language.*

O‑**nuclear** /'njuːkliəʳ/ *adjective* [always before noun] **PHYSICS** **1** relating to the energy that is released when the nucleus (= central part) of an atom is divided ***nuclear weapons/waste*** ○ *a **nuclear power** plant* **2** relating to the nucleus (= central part) of an atom ***nuclear physics***

ˌnuclear 'fission *noun* [U] **PHYSICS** when the nucleus (= centre part) of an atom is divided, creating a very large amount of energy

ˌnuclear 'fusion *noun* [U] **PHYSICS** the process of joining two nuclei (= central parts of atoms) to produce energy

ˌnuclear re'actor *noun* [C] **PHYSICS** a large machine which uses nuclear fuel to produce power

nucleic acid /njuːˌkleɪɪk'æsɪd/ *noun* [C, U] **CHEMISTRY** a type of acid that is found in all living cells

nucleotide /'njuːkliəʊtaɪd/ *noun* [C] **CHEMISTRY** one of a group of chemical compounds found in living cells in nucleic acids such as DNA and RNA

nucleus /'njuːkliəs/ *noun* [C] *plural* **nuclei** /'njuːkliaɪ/ **1** **BIOLOGY, PHYSICS, CHEMISTRY** the central part of an atom or cell ➲See picture at **cell** ➲See picture at **leaf** **2** the central or most important part of a group or idea *Senior coaches handpicked the nucleus of the team.*

nude¹ /njuːd/ *adjective* not wearing any clothes *Our children were running around the garden **in the nude*** (= not wearing any clothes).

nude² /njuːd/ *noun* [C] **ART** a painting or other piece of art that shows a nude person

nudge /nʌdʒ/ *verb* [T] to gently push someone or something *She nudged me towards the door.* •**nudge** *noun* [C] *I gave him a nudge.*

nudism /'njuːdɪzᵊm/ *noun* [U] when someone wears no clothes when they are outside with other people, etc •**nudist** *noun* [C] someone who practices nudism

nudity /'njuːdəti/ *noun* [U] when you are wearing no clothes *Some people are offended by nudity.*

nugget /'nʌgɪt/ *noun* [C] **1** GOOD THING a small amount of something good ***nuggets of wisdom***

2 PIECE a small, round piece of a solid substance *gold nuggets*

nuisance /ˈnjuːsᵊns/ *noun* [C] **1** a person, thing, or situation that annoys you or causes problems for you *Not being able to use my computer is a real nuisance.* **2 make a nuisance of yourself** to annoy someone or cause problems for them

nullify /ˈnʌlɪfaɪ/ *verb* [T] *formal* **1** to make something lose its effect *Advances in medicine have nullified the disease's effect.* **2 LAW** to say officially that something has no legal power *The judge could nullify the entire trial.*

numb /nʌm/ *adjective* **1** BODY PART If a part of your body is numb, you cannot feel it. *My fingers and toes were* ***numb with cold****.* **2** EMOTION If you are numb with a bad emotion, you are so shocked that you are not able to think clearly. *I was* ***numb with*** *grief after his death.*

O⁃**number¹** /ˈnʌmbəʳ/ *noun* **1 MATHEMATICS** [C] a symbol or word used in a counting system or used to show the position or order of something *Think of a number smaller than 100.* ○ *The Prime Minister lives at number 10, Downing Street.* ○ *Look at item number three on your agenda.* **2** GROUP OF NUMBERS [C] a group of numbers that represents something *What's your* ***phone number****?* ○ *Each person receives a membership number when they join.* **3** AMOUNT [C] an amount *a* ***small number*** *of* (= a few) ○ *a* ***large number*** *of* (= many) ○ *There were* ***a number of*** (= several) *soldiers present at the rally.* ○ *Scientists have noticed a drop in the number of song birds in Britain.* ➲See Common Learner Error at **amount** ➲See also: **cardinal number, ordinal number, phone number, telephone number**

COMMON LEARNER ERROR

number

We use the adjectives **large** and **small** with the word **number**, not 'big' and 'little'.

A large number of people attended the concert.

~~*A big number of people attended the concert.*~~

number² /ˈnʌmbəʳ/ *verb* [T] **1** GIVE A NUMBER to give something a number [**often passive**] *Each volume was numbered and indexed.* **2** BE AN AMOUNT If people or things number a particular amount, there are that many of them. *Our company's sales force numbered over 5,000.*

ˈnumber ˌplate *UK* (*US* **license plate**) *noun* [C] an official metal sign with numbers and letters on the front and back of a car ➲See colour picture **Car** on page Centre 7

numeral /ˈnjuːmᵊrᵊl/ *noun* [C] **MATHEMATICS** a symbol used to represent a number ➲See also: **Roman numeral**

numerator /ˈnjuːməreɪtəʳ/ *noun* [C] **MATHEMATICS** the number above the line in a fraction ➲Compare **denominator**

numerical /njuːˈmerɪkl/ *adjective* [**always before noun**] **MATHEMATICS** relating to or expressed by numbers *The exams were filed in numerical order.*

numerous /ˈnjuːmᵊrəs/ *adjective formal* many *He is the author of numerous articles.*

nun /nʌn/ *noun* [C] **RELIGION** a member of a group of religious women living apart from other people

O⁃**nurse¹** /nɜːs/ *noun* [C] **HEALTH** someone whose job is to care for ill and injured people

nurse² /nɜːs/ *verb* [T] **1 HEALTH** to care for a person or animal that is ill *We nursed the injured sparrow back to health.* **2 FOOD** *US* to feed a baby milk from its mother's breast *She nursed her son until he was a year old.* **3 HEALTH** to try to cure an illness or injury by resting *He was nursing a broken nose.* **4** EMOTION to think about an idea or an emotion for a long time *She nursed a great hatred towards her older sister.*

nursery /ˈnɜːsᵊri/ *noun* [C] **1** CHILDREN a place where babies and young children are looked after without their parents **2 FARMING** a place where plants are grown and sold

ˈnursery ˌrhyme *noun* [C] **LITERATURE** a short poem or song for young children

ˈnursery ˌschool *noun* [C] **EDUCATION** a school for very young children

nursing /ˈnɜːsɪŋ/ *noun* [U] **HEALTH** the job of being a nurse

ˈnursing ˌhome *noun* [C] **HEALTH** a place where old people live to receive medical care

nurture /ˈnɜːtʃəʳ/ *verb* [T] *formal* **1** ENCOURAGE to encourage or support the development of someone or something *He was an inspiring leader who* ***nurtured*** *the* ***talents*** *of his colleagues.* **2** LOOK AFTER to look after, feed, and protect young children, animals, or plants *The rains nurtured the newly planted crops.*

O⁃**nut** /nʌt/ *noun* [C] **1 BIOLOGY, FOOD** the dry fruit of some trees which grows in a hard shell, and can often be eaten *a brazil/cashew nut* **2** METAL a piece of metal with a hole in it through which you put a bolt (= metal pin) to hold pieces of wood or metal together **3** KEEN *informal* a person who is keen on a particular subject or hobby *She's a real sports nut.* **4 the nuts and bolts** the basic parts of a job or an activity *Law school can teach you theory, but it can't teach you the nuts and bolts of the profession.*

nutrient /ˈnjuːtriənt/ *noun* [C] *formal* **BIOLOGY** any substance that animals need to eat and plants need from the soil in order to live and grow *A healthy diet should provide all your* ***essential nutrients****.*

nutrition /njuːˈtrɪʃᵊn/ *noun* [U] **BIOLOGY** the food that you eat and the way that it affects your health *Good nutrition is essential for growing children.* •**nutritional** *adjective* relating to nutrition *Some snacks have little* ***nutritional value****.*

nutritionist /njuːˈtrɪʃᵊnɪst/ *noun* [C] **HEALTH** someone who gives advice on the subject of nutrition

nutritious /njuːˈtrɪʃəs/ *adjective* **FOOD** Nutritious food contains substances that your body needs to stay healthy. *a nutritious meal*

nuts /nʌts/ *adjective informal* **1** crazy *They thought I was nuts to go parachuting.* **2 go nuts** to become very excited, angry, or upset *If I don't have a holiday soon, I'll go nuts.*

nutshell /ˈnʌtʃel/ *noun* **in a nutshell** something that you say when you are describing something using as few words as possible *The answer, in a nutshell, is yes.*

nutty /ˈnʌti/ *adjective* **1** *informal* crazy *nutty ideas* **2 FOOD** Something nutty tastes of nuts.

nylon /ˈnaɪlɒn/ *noun* [U] **DT** a strong, artificial material used to make clothes, ropes, etc *nylon stockings* ○ *a nylon shirt/bag*

nymph /nɪmf/ *noun* [C] in Greek and Roman stories, a spirit in the form of a young girl who lives in trees, rivers, mountains, etc

N

Oo

O, o /əʊ/ the fifteenth letter of the alphabet

oak /əʊk/ *noun* [C, U] a large tree found in northern countries, or the wood of this tree

OAP /ˌəʊeɪ'piː/ *noun* [C] *UK abbreviation for* old-age pensioner: a person who regularly receives money from the state because they are too old to work

oar /ɔːʳ/ *noun* [C] **1** a long pole with a wide, flat end that you use to move a boat through water **2 stick/put your oar in** *UK informal* to involve yourself in a discussion or situation when other people do not want you to

oasis /əʊ'eɪsɪs/ *noun* [C] *plural* **oases** /əʊ'eɪsiːz/ **1 GEOGRAPHY** a place in the desert where there is water and where plants grow **2** a place that is much calmer and more pleasant than what is around it *The cafe was an oasis in the busy, noisy city.*

oath /əʊθ/ *noun* **1** [C] a formal promise *an oath of allegiance* ○ *They refused to **take an oath** of* (= to promise) *loyalty to the king.* **2 under oath LAW** If someone is under oath, they have promised to tell the truth in a law court. *He denied under oath that he was involved in the crime.*

oats /əʊts/ *noun* [plural] **FOOD, FARMING** grain which people eat or feed to animals

obedience /əʊ'biːdiəns/ *noun* [U] when someone is willing to do what they are told to do *He demanded complete obedience from his soldiers.* ➲Opposite **disobedience** •**obedient** /əʊ'biːdiənt/ *adjective* willing to do what you are told to do *an obedient child/dog* ➲Opposite **disobedient**

obese /əʊ'biːs/ *adjective* **HEALTH** extremely fat •**obesity** *noun* [U] when someone is obese

O→**obey** /əʊ'beɪ/ *verb* [I, T] to do what you are told to do by a person, rule, or instruction *He gave the command, and we obeyed.* ➲Opposite **disobey**

obfuscate /'ɒbfʌskeɪt/ *verb* [T] *formal* to make something harder to understand or less clear

obituary /əʊ'bɪtʃʊəri/ *noun* [C] a report in a newspaper that gives details about a person who has recently died

O→**object¹** /'ɒbdʒɪkt/ *noun* **1** [C] a thing that you can see or touch but that is usually not alive *a bright, shiny object* **2 the object of sth** the purpose of something *The object of the game is to score more points than the opposing team.* **3 the object of sb's affection/desire, etc** the cause of someone's feelings *He's the object of my affection.* **4 LANGUAGE** in grammar, the person or thing that is affected by the action of the verb ➲See also: **direct object, indirect object**

object² /əb'dʒekt/ *verb* [I] to feel or say that you do not like or do not approve of something or someone *We **objected to** his unreasonable demands.* ○ *Would anyone object if I were to leave early?* ➲See also: **conscientious objector**

WORD PARTNERS FOR ***objection***

lodge/make/raise/voice an objection • **have no** objections • a **serious/strong** objection • an objection **to** sth

objection /əb'dʒekʃən/ *noun* [C, U] when someone says that they do not like or approve of something or someone *Our main **objection to** the new factory is that it's noisy.* ○ *I **have** no **objections**, if you want to stay an extra day.*

objectionable /əb'dʒekʃənəbl/ *adjective formal* very unpleasant

objective¹ /əb'dʒektɪv/ *noun* [C] something that you are trying to achieve *His main objective was to increase profits.*

objective² /əb'dʒektɪv/ *adjective* only influenced by facts and not by feelings *I try to be objective when I criticize someone's work.*

WORD PARTNERS FOR ***obligation***

feel/have an obligation to do sth • **carry out/ fulfil/meet** an obligation • be **under** an obligation

obligation /ˌɒblɪ'geɪʃən/ *noun* [C, U] something that you do because it is your duty or because you feel you have to *a **moral/legal obligation*** ○ *to **fulfil** an **obligation*** ○ *He was **under no obligation** to answer any questions.* [+ to do sth] *Parents have an obligation to make sure their children receive a proper education.*

obligatory /ə'blɪgətəri/ *adjective* If something is obligatory, you must do it because of a rule, or because everyone else does it. *obligatory military service*

oblige /ə'blaɪdʒ/ *verb* **1 be obliged to do sth** to be forced to do something *Sellers are not legally obliged to accept the highest offer.* **2** [I, T] *formal* to be helpful *The manager was only too happy to oblige.*

obliged /ə'blaɪdʒd/ *adjective* **1 feel obliged to do sth** to think that you must do something *They helped us when we moved so I feel obliged to do the same.* **2** *formal old-fashioned* grateful or pleased *Thank you, I'm much obliged to you.*

oblique /əʊ'bliːk/ *adjective formal* **1** not expressed in a direct way *an oblique comment* **2 MATHEMATICS** describes an angle which is either more or less than 90° but not 90° •**obliquely** *adverb formal*

obliterate /ə'blɪtəreɪt/ *verb* [T] to destroy something completely [often passive] *The town was obliterated by bombs.*

oblivion /ə'blɪviən/ *noun* [U] **1** [NOT REMEMBERED] when someone or something is not remembered *to disappear into oblivion* **2** [NOT AWARE] when you are not aware of what is happening around you *He drank himself **into oblivion**.*

oblivious /ə'blɪviəs/ *adjective* not aware of something *She seemed completely **oblivious to** what was happening around her.*

obnoxious /əb'nɒkʃəs/ *adjective* very unpleasant or rude *He was loud and obnoxious.*

obscene /əb'siːn/ *adjective* **1** [SEX] relating to sex in a way that is unpleasant or shocking *an **obscene gesture*** ○ ***obscene language*** **2** [MORALLY WRONG] An obscene amount of something is

O

morally wrong because it is too large. ***obscene profits***

obscenity /əbˈsenəti/ *noun* **1** SEX [U] when something is sexually shocking *obscenity laws/trials* **2** SPEECH [C] a sexually shocking word or expression [**usually plural**] *He was shouting obscenities at people walking by.*

obscure[1] /əbˈskjʊəʳ/ *adjective* **1** NOT KNOWN not known by many people *an obscure figure/writer* **2** NOT CLEAR difficult to understand *His answers were obscure and confusing.*

obscure[2] /əbˈskjʊəʳ/ *verb* [T] **1** NOT SEE to prevent something from being seen or heard [**often passive**] *The moon was partially obscured by clouds.* **2** NOT UNDERSTAND to make something difficult to understand *He deliberately obscured details of his career in the army.*

obscurity /əbˈskjʊərəti/ *noun* [U] when something or someone is not known by many people *to fade into obscurity* ○ *He rose from relative obscurity to worldwide recognition.*

obsequious /əbˈsiːkwiəs/ *adjective formal* too willing to praise or obey someone

observance /əbˈzɜːvᵊns/ *noun* [C, U] *formal* when someone obeys a law or follows a religious custom *strict observance of the law* ○ ***religious observances***

observant /əbˈzɜːvᵊnt/ *adjective* good or quick at noticing things *He's very observant.*

WORD PARTNERS FOR ***observation***

careful/close observation • observation **of** sth • **under** observation • **powers of** observation

observation /ˌɒbzəˈveɪʃᵊn/ *noun* **1** WATCHING [U] when someone watches someone or something carefully *The doctor wants to keep him* ***under observation*** *for a week.* ○ *to have good* ***powers of observation*** (= to be good at noticing things) **2** REMARK [C] a remark about something that you have noticed *He* ***made an*** *interesting* ***observation.***

observatory /əbˈzɜːvətri/ *noun* [C] **ASTRONOMY** a building that is used by scientists to look at stars and planets

observe /əbˈzɜːv/ *verb* [T] **1** WATCH to watch someone or something carefully *Children learn by observing adults.* **2** NOTICE *formal* to notice something **3** SAY *formal* to make a remark about something you have noticed *"It's still raining," he observed.* **4** OBEY to obey a law, rule, or religious custom *to observe the law*

observer /əbˈzɜːvəʳ/ *noun* [C] **1** JOB someone who watches people and events as a job *a UN observer* ○ *a political observer* **2** SEE someone who sees something *a* ***casual observer***

obsess /əbˈses/ *verb* [I, T] If something or someone obsesses you, or if you obsess about something or someone, you think about them all the time. *She used to obsess about her weight.*

obsessed /əbˈsest/ *adjective* **be obsessed by/with sb/sth** to think about someone or something all the time *to be obsessed with money/sex*

obsession /əbˈseʃᵊn/ *noun* [C, U] someone or something that you think about all the time *an* ***unhealthy obsession*** *with death* ○ *a life-long/national obsession*

obsessive /əbˈsesɪv/ *adjective* thinking too much about something, or doing something too much *obsessive behaviour* ○ *He's obsessive about his health.* **•obsessively** *adverb*

obsolete /ˈɒbsᵊliːt/ *adjective* not used now *obsolete equipment* ○ *Will books become obsolete because of computers?*

WORD PARTNERS FOR ***obstacle***

face/overcome an obstacle • **the biggest/the main/a major** obstacle • an obstacle **to** sth

obstacle /ˈɒbstəkl/ *noun* [C] something that makes it difficult for you to go somewhere or to succeed at something *to* ***overcome*** *an* ***obstacle*** ○ *His refusal to talk is the main* ***obstacle*** ***to*** *peace.*

obstetrician /ˌɒbstəˈtrɪʃᵊn/ *noun* [C] **HEALTH** a doctor who looks after pregnant women and helps in the birth of children

obstinate /ˈɒbstɪnət/ *adjective* not willing to change your ideas or behaviour although you are wrong *He's a very rude and obstinate man.*

obstruct /əbˈstrʌkt/ *verb* [T] **1** STOP MOVING/SEEING to be in a place that stops someone or something from moving or stops someone from seeing something *to* ***obstruct the traffic*** ○ *There was a pillar* ***obstructing*** *our* ***view.*** **2** STOP HAPPENING to try to stop something from happening or developing *to obstruct a police investigation* **•obstruction** /əbˈstrʌkʃᵊn/ *noun* [C, U] *Your car's* ***causing an obstruction.*** ○ *the obstruction of justice*

obtain /əbˈteɪn/ *verb* [T] *formal* to get something *to obtain permission* ○ *He obtained a law degree from the University of California.* **•obtainable** *adjective* If something is obtainable, you can get it. *This information is easily obtainable on the Internet.*

obtuse /əbˈtjuːs/ *adjective* **MATHEMATICS** describes an angle which is more than 90° and less than 180°

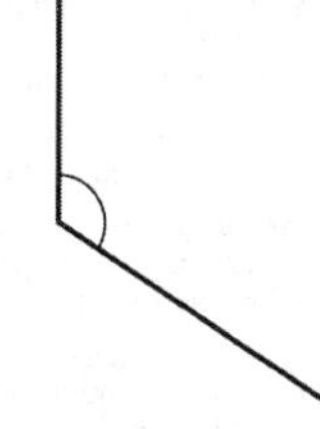

obtuse angle

O-- **obvious** /ˈɒbviəs/ *adjective* easy to understand or see *an obvious choice/answer* [+ **(that)**] ***It's obvious*** *that he doesn't really care about her.*

O-- **obviously** /ˈɒbviəsli/ *adverb* in a way that is easy to understand or see *They're obviously in love.* ○ *Obviously we want to start as soon as possible.*

O-- **occasion** /əˈkeɪʒᵊn/ *noun* **1** TIME [C] a time when something happens *a previous/separate occasion* ○ *We met* ***on*** *several* ***occasions*** *to discuss the issue.* ➲See Common Learner Error at **possibility** **2** EVENT [C] an important event or ceremony *a* ***special occasion*** ○ *She bought a new dress for the occasion.* **3 on occasion(s)** sometimes, but not often *I only drink alcohol on occasion.*

occasional /ə'keɪʒᵊnᵊl/ *adjective* not happening often *He still plays the occasional game of football.* •**occasionally** *adverb They only meet occasionally.*

occlusion /ə'kluːʒᵊn/ *noun* [C, U] **1 HEALTH** (in medicine), when a tube or opening in the body is blocked by something or is closed **2 GEOGRAPHY** a situation in the weather when two masses of air meet, especially when a mass of cold air reaches warm air and pushes the warm air up off the Earth's surface

the occult /'ɒkʌlt/ *noun* the study of magic or mysterious powers

occupant /'ɒkjəpənt/ *noun* [C] *formal* someone who lives or works in a room or building *the occupant of No. 46*

occupation /ˌɒkjə'peɪʃᵊn/ *noun* **1** JOB [C] *formal* your job *You have to give your name, age, and occupation on the application form.* ⊃See Common Learner Error at **work 2** CONTROL [U] when an army moves into a place and takes control of it *a **military occupation*** **3** HOBBY [C] *formal* something that you do in your free time

occupational /ˌɒkjə'peɪʃᵊnᵊl/ *adjective* relating to your job *an **occupational hazard***

occupied /'ɒkjəpaɪd/ *adjective* **1** USED being used by someone *All of these seats are occupied.* ⊃Opposite **unoccupied 2** BUSY busy doing something or thinking about something *There was enough **to keep** us **occupied**.*

occupier /'ɒkjəpaɪəʳ/ *noun* [C] *UK* someone who lives or works in a room or building

occupy /'ɒkjəpaɪ/ *verb* [T] **1** FILL to fill a place or period of time *His book collection occupies most of the room.* ○ *The baby seems to **occupy** all our **time**.* **2** LIVE to live or work in a room or building *They occupy the second floor of the building.* **3** CONTROL to move into a place and take control of it *The troops eventually occupied most of the island.*

O⊸**occur** /ə'kɜːʳ/ *verb* [I] **occurring**, *past* **occurred 1** *formal* to happen, often without being planned *According to the police, the shooting occurred at about 12.30 a.m.* **2 occur in/among, etc sth/sb** to exist or be present in a particular place or group of people *Minerals occur naturally in the Earth's crust.* ○ *The disease mainly occurs in women over 40.*

occur to sb *phrasal verb* to suddenly think of something [+ **(that)**] ***It had never occurred to** me that he might be lying.*

WORD PARTNERS FOR ***occurrence***

a **common/everyday/rare/regular** occurrence

occurrence /ə'kʌrᵊns/ *noun* [C] something that happens *a **common/everyday occurrence***

ocean /'əʊʃᵊn/ *noun* **GEOGRAPHY 1** [no plural] the sea *to swim in the ocean* **2** [C] one of the five main areas that the sea is divided into *the Pacific Ocean*

oceanic /ˌəʊʃi'ænɪk/ *adjective* **GEOGRAPHY** *formal* related to the ocean

ˌ**oceanic** ˈ**crust** *noun* [C usually singular] **GEOGRAPHY** the part of the outer rocky layer of the Earth that is under the oceans and is thinner than the layer under the land

O⊸**o'clock** /ə'klɒk/ *adverb* **one/two/three, etc o'clock** used after the numbers one to twelve to mean exactly that hour when you tell the time *It was ten o'clock when we got home.*

OCR /ˌəʊsiː'ɑːʳ/ *noun* [U] **COMPUTING** *abbreviation for* optical character recognition: software that allows computers to read printed or written words and store them in the computer

Oct *written abbreviation for* October

octagon /'ɒktəgən/ *noun* [C] **MATHEMATICS** a flat shape with eight equal sides

octahedron /ˌɒktə'hiːdrᵊn/ *noun* [C] **MATHEMATICS** a solid shape that has eight flat triangular surfaces of the same size

octave /'ɒktɪv/ *noun* [C] **MUSIC** the space between two musical notes that are eight notes apart

O⊸**October** /ɒk'təʊbəʳ/ (*written abbreviation* **Oct**) *noun* [C, U] the tenth month of the year

octopus /'ɒktəpəs/ *noun* [C] a sea creature with eight long arms

odd /ɒd/ *adjective* **1** STRANGE strange or unusual *I always thought there was something odd about her.* ○ *It's a bit odd that he didn't come.* **2** NOT OFTEN [**always before noun**] not happening often *He does **odd jobs** here and there.* **3** SEPARATED [**always before noun**] being one of a pair when the other item is missing *an **odd sock*** **4** APPROXIMATELY used after a number to mean approximately *There are thirty odd kids in the class.* **5 MATHEMATICS** An odd number does not produce a whole number when it is divided by two.

oddity /'ɒdɪti/ *noun* [C] someone or something that is strange or unusual

oddly /'ɒdli/ *adverb* in a strange way *He's been **behaving** very **oddly** lately.* ○ ***Oddly enough**, business was good during the bad weather months.*

WORD PARTNERS FOR ***odds***

the odds **of/on** sth happening • the odds are **(stacked) against** sb

odds /ɒdz/ *noun* [**plural**] **1** the probability that something will happen *What are the odds of winning the top prizes?* ○ *I'm afraid the odds are against us.* **2 against all (the) odds** If you do or achieve something against all the odds, you succeed although you were not likely to. *We won the game against all odds.* **3 be at odds with sb/sth** to not agree with someone or something *His remark was at odds with our report.* **4 odds and ends** *informal* a group of small objects of different types which are not valuable or important

odious /'əʊdiəs/ *adjective formal* very unpleasant *an odious little man*

odour *UK* (*US* **odor**) /'əʊdəʳ/ *noun* [C] a smell, often one that is unpleasant ***body odour***

odyssey /'ɒdɪsi/ *noun* [C] *literary* a long, exciting journey

oedema *UK* (*US* **edema**) /ɪ'diːmə/ *noun* [U] **HEALTH** (in medicine) a condition in which there is too much liquid in the body tissues between the cells

O

oesophagus (*US* **esophagus**) /ɪˈsɒfəgəs/ *noun* [**C usually singular**] **ANATOMY** the tube in the body which takes food from the mouth to the stomach ➲See picture at **alimentary canal** ➲See picture at **respiratory system**

oestrogen *UK* (*US* **estrogen**) /ˈiːstrəʊdʒᵊn/ Ⓤⓢ /ˈestrədʒən/ *noun* [**U**] **BIOLOGY, HEALTH** a chemical substance in a woman's body which prepares her eggs for fertilization (= joining with the male seed to make a baby)

O⊸**of** *strong form* /ɒv/ *weak form* /əv/ *preposition* **1** [BELONG] belonging or relating to someone or something *a friend of mine* ○ *the colour of her hair* ○ *part of the problem* **2** [AMOUNT] used after words which show an amount *a kilo of apples* ○ *both of us* ○ *a handful of raisins* **3** [NUMBER] used with numbers, ages and dates *a boy of six* ○ *a decrease of 10%* ○ *the 14th of February 2005* **4** [CONTAIN] containing *a glass of milk* ○ *sacks of rubbish* **5** [MADE] made or consisting of *dresses of lace and silk* **6** [ADJECTIVE/VERB] used to connect particular adjectives and verbs with nouns *frightened of spiders* ○ *smelling of garlic* **7** [SHOW] showing someone or something *a map of the city centre* **8** [CAUSE] showing a reason or cause *He died of a heart attack.* **9** [POSITION] showing position or direction *the front of the queue* ○ *a small town north of Edinburgh* **10** [ACTION/FEELING] used after nouns describing actions or feelings to mean 'done to' or 'experienced by' *the destruction of the rain forest* ○ *the suffering of millions* **11** [WRITTEN] written or made by *the collected works of William Shakespeare*

O⊸**of course** /əvˈkɔːs/ *adverb* **1** [YES] used to say 'yes' and emphasize your answer *'can you help me?' 'Of course!'* **2** [OBVIOUS] used to show that what you are saying is obvious or already known *The rain meant, of course, that the match was cancelled.* ○ *Of course, the Olympics are not just about money.* **3 of course not** used to say 'no' and emphasize your answer *'Do you mind if I borrow your pen?' 'Of course not.'*

O⊸**off**[1] /ɒf/ *adverb, preposition* **1** [NOT TOUCHING] not touching or connected to something or not on a surface *Keep off the grass!* ○ *A button came off my coat.* **2** [AWAY] away from a place or position *He ran off to find his friend.* ○ *I'll* ***be off*** (= will go) *soon.* **3** [NOT OPERATING] not operating or being used *Make sure you switch your computer off.* **4** [NEAR] near to a building or place *an island off the coast of Spain* **5 FINANCE** If a price has a certain amount of money off, it costs that much less than the usual price. *These jeans were $10 off.* **6** [DISTANCE/TIME] far in distance or time *My holidays seem a long way off.* **7 go off sth/sb** *UK* to stop liking something or someone *I've gone off meat.* **8** [NOT AT WORK] not at work *I had 6 months off when my son was born.* ➲See also: off the **cuff**, **on**[2] and off

off[2] /ɒf/ *adjective* [**never before noun**] **1** [NOT CORRECT] not correct *Our sales figures were off by ten percent.* **2 FOOD** If food or drink is off, it is not now fresh and good to eat or drink. *This milk smells off.* **3** [NOT AT WORK] not at work *He's off today - I think he's ill.* ➲See also: **off-chance**

offal /ˈɒfᵊl/ *noun* [**U**] **FOOD** organs from the inside of animals that are killed for food

ˌ**off ˈbalance** *adjective, adverb* If someone or something is off balance, they are in a position where they are likely to fall or be knocked down. *to knock/throw someone off balance*

off-chance /ˈɒftʃɑːns/ *noun UK informal* **on the off-chance** hoping that something may be possible, although it is not likely *I went to the station on the off-chance that she'd be there.*

ˌ**off ˈduty** *adjective* When an official such as a police officer is off duty, they are not working.

WORD PARTNERS FOR ***offence***

cause/give/take offence • **grave** offence

O⊸**offence** *UK* (*US* **offense**) /əˈfens/ *noun* **1** [UPSET] [**U**] when something rude makes someone upset or angry *to* ***cause/give offence*** ○ *Many people* ***take offence*** *at swearing.* **2 LAW** [**C**] a crime *a* ***criminal offence*** ○ *He* ***committed*** *several serious* ***offences***.

O⊸**offend** /əˈfend/ *verb* **1** [UPSET] [**T**] to make someone upset or angry [**often passive**] *I was deeply offended by her comments.* **2 LAW** [**I**] *formal* to commit a crime *If she offends again, she'll go to prison.*

offender /əˈfendəʳ/ *noun* [**C**] **LAW** someone who has committed a crime *a young offender*

O⊸**offense** /əˈfens/ *noun* **LAW** *US spelling of* offence

offensive[1] /əˈfensɪv/ *adjective* **1** [UPSETTING] likely to make people angry or upset *an* ***offensive remark*** ➲Opposite **inoffensive 2** [ATTACKING] used for attacking *an* ***offensive weapon*** •**offensively** *adverb*

offensive[2] /əˈfensɪv/ *noun* [**C**] an attack *It's time to launch a major* ***offensive against*** *terrorism.*

O⊸**offer**[1] /ˈɒfəʳ/ *verb* **1** [ASK] [**+ two objects**] to ask someone if they would like something *They offered me a job.* **2** [SAY YOU WILL DO] [**I, T**] to say that you are willing to do something [**+ to do sth**] *He offered to get me a cab.* **3 FINANCE** [**T**] to say that you will pay a particular amount of money [**+ two objects**] *I offered him £500 for the car.* ○ *Police have offered a $1,000 reward for information.* **4** [PROVIDE] [**T**] to give or provide something *to offer advice* ○ *The hotel offers a wide range of facilities.*

WORD PARTNERS FOR ***offer***

accept/make/receive/turn down an offer • a **generous/tempting** offer • an offer **of** sth

O⊸**offer**[2] /ˈɒfəʳ/ *noun* [**C**] **1** [ASK] when you ask someone if they would like something *an* ***offer*** *of* ***help*** ○ *a job offer* ○ *to* ***accept/refuse*** *an* ***offer*** **2 FINANCE** an amount of money that you say you will pay for something *The highest* ***offer*** *anyone has* ***made*** *so far is £150.* **3 FINANCE** a cheap price or special arrangement for something you are buying *This* ***special offer*** *ends on Friday.* **4 on offer a FINANCE** at a cheaper price than usual *Are these jeans still on offer?* **b** [AVAILABLE] available to do or have *We were amazed at the range of products on offer.*

offering /ˈɒfᵊrɪŋ/ *noun* [**C**] something that you give to someone *a* ***peace offering***

offhand[1] /ˌɒfˈhænd/ *adjective* not friendly or polite *He was a bit offhand with me.*

O

offhand² /ˌɒfˈhænd/ *adverb* immediately, without thinking about something *I don't know offhand how much it will cost.*

O⊸**office** /ˈɒfɪs/ *noun* **1** PLACE [C] a room or building where people work *an **office worker*** ○ *I never get to the office before nine.* ➲See colour picture **The Office** on page Centre 5 **2** INFORMATION [C] a room or building where you can get information, tickets, or a particular service *a **ticket office*** ○ *the **tourist office*** **3** JOB [U] an important job in an organization *Some people think he has been **in office** for too long.* ○ *She **held the office** of mayor for eight years.* ➲See also: **box office, the Oval Office, post office, register office, registry office**

ˈ**office** ˌ**building** (*also UK* **office block**) *noun* [C] a large building which contains offices

ˈ**office** ˌ**hours** *noun* [plural] the hours during the day when people who work in offices are usually at work

officer /ˈɒfɪsəʳ/ *noun* [C] **1** MILITARY someone with an important job in a military organization *an **army/naval officer*** **2** **POLITICS** someone who works for a government department *a customs officer* ○ *a prison officer* **3** POLICE a police officer *a uniformed officer* ➲See also: **probation officer**

O⊸**official¹** /əˈfɪʃəl/ *adjective* **1** APPROVED approved by the government or someone in authority *the **official language** of Singapore* ○ *an **official document*** **2** JOB [always before noun] relating to the duties of someone in a position of authority *the **official residence** of the ambassador* ○ *an **official visit*** **3** KNOWN known by the public *It's official - they're getting married!* **4** NOT TRUE [always before noun] An official explanation or statement is one that is given, but which may not be true. *The **official reason** for the delay is bad weather.* ➲Opposite **unofficial** •**officially** *adverb The new hospital was officially opened yesterday.*

official² /əˈfɪʃəl/ *noun* [C] **POLITICS** someone who has an important position in an organization such as the government *a senior official* ○ *a UN official*

ofˌ**ficial re**ˈ**ceiver** *noun* [C] **FINANCE** *UK* a person who deals officially with the money problems of a company that has gone bankrupt (= has no money and cannot now pay the money that it owes)

offing /ˈɒfɪŋ/ *noun* **be in the offing** If something is in the offing, it will happen or be offered soon. *He thinks there might be a promotion in the offing.*

off-licence /ˈɒfˌlaɪsəns/ *UK* (*US* **liquor store**) *noun* [C] a shop that sells alcoholic drink

offline /ɒfˈlaɪn/ (*also* **off-line**) *adjective, adverb* **COMPUTING** A computer is offline when it is not connected to a central system, or not connected to the Internet.

off-peak /ˌɒfˈpiːk/ *adjective* not at the most popular and expensive time *an off-peak phone call*

offset /ˌɒfˈset/ *verb* [T] **offsetting**, *past* **offset** If one thing offsets another thing, it has the opposite effect and so creates a more balanced situation. [**often passive**] *The costs have been offset by savings in other areas.*

offset lithography /ˌɒfsetlɪˈθɒgrəfi/ *noun* [U] **DT** a method of printing in which an image is put on a rubber sheet before going on to the paper or object being printed

offsetting /ɒfˈsetɪŋ/ *noun* [U] **ENVIRONMENT** trying to stop the damage caused by activities that produce carbon by doing other things to reduce it, such as planting trees

offshore /ˌɒfˈʃɔːʳ/ *adjective* [**always before noun**] **1** **GEOGRAPHY** in the sea and away from the coast *an offshore island* **2** **ECONOMICS** An offshore bank or bank account is based in another country and so less tax has to be paid. *an **offshore account/trust***

offside /ˌɒfˈsaɪd/ (*also US* **offsides**) *adjective* [**always before noun**] **SPORT** In sports such as football, a player who is offside is in a position that is not allowed.

offspring /ˈɒfsprɪŋ/ *noun* [C] *plural* **offspring** *formal* the child of a person or animal *to produce offspring*

off-the-cuff /ˌɒfðəˈkʌf/ *adjective* An off-the-cuff remark is one that is not planned.

off-the-job /ˈɒfðəˌdʒɒb/ *adjective* Off-the-job training happens away from the place of work.

O⊸**often** /ˈɒfən, ˈɒftən/ *adverb* **1** MANY TIMES many times or regularly *I often see her there.* ○ *He said I could visit as often as I liked.* ○ ***How often*** (= How many times) *do you go to the gym?* ○ *I don't see her **very often**.* **2** NORMALLY If something often happens or is often true, it is normal for it to happen or it is usually true. *Headaches are often caused by stress.* ○ *Brothers and sisters often argue.*

ogre /ˈəʊgəʳ/ *noun* [C] an unpleasant, frightening person

O⊸**oh** /əʊ/ *exclamation* **1** PAUSE used before you say something, often before replying to what someone has said *"Ian's going." "Oh, I didn't realize."* ○ *"I'm so sorry." "Oh, don't worry."* **2** EMOTION used to show an emotion or to emphasize your opinion about something *Oh, no! I don't believe it!* ○ *"I don't think I can come." "Oh, that's a shame."* ○ *Oh, how sweet of you!*

ohm /əʊm/ *noun* [C] **PHYSICS** a unit used for measuring electrical resistance (= how much or little a substance allows electricity to flow through it)

O⊸**oil** /ɔɪl/ *noun* [U] **1** **GEOLOGY, GEOGRAPHY** a thick liquid that comes from under the Earth's surface that is used as a fuel and for making parts of machines move smoothly *an oil company* ○ *an oil well* **2** **FOOD** a thick liquid produced from plants or animals that is used in cooking *vegetable oil* ➲See also: **crude oil, olive oil**

oilfield /ˈɔɪlˌfiːld/ *noun* [C] **GEOLOGY** an area under the ground where oil is found *an offshore oilfield*

ˈ**oil** ˌ**painting** *noun* [C] **ART** a picture made using paint which contains oil

ˈ**oil** ˌ**spill** *noun* [C] **ENVIRONMENT** when oil has come out of a ship and caused pollution

oily /ˈɔɪli/ *adjective* containing a lot of oil or covered with oil ***oily fish*** ○ *oily hands*

oink /ɔɪnk/ *noun* [C] the sound that a pig makes

ointment /ˈɔɪntmənt/ *noun* [C, U] **HEALTH** a smooth, thick substance that is used on painful or damaged skin

okapi /əʊˈkɑːpi/ *noun* [C] an African animal of the giraffe family which is brown with stripes of black and white around its legs and back part

okay¹ (*also* **OK**) /əʊˈkeɪ/ *exclamation* **1** AGREEING used when agreeing to do something or when allowing someone to do something *"Let's meet this afternoon." "Okay."* ○ *"Can I use the car?" "Okay."* **2** BEFORE SPEAKING used before you start speaking, especially to a group of people *Okay, I'm going to start by showing you a few figures.*

O-ᵐ**okay²** *informal* (*also* **OK**) /əʊˈkeɪ/ *adjective, adverb* **1** GOOD good or good enough *Is your food okay?* ○ *It was okay, but it wasn't as good as his last film.* **2** SAFE safe or healthy *Is your grandmother okay now?* **3** ALLOWED allowed or acceptable *Is it okay if I leave early today?* [+ **to do sth**] *Is it okay to smoke in here?*

O-ᵐ**old** /əʊld/ *adjective* **1** LIVED LONG having lived or existed for a long time *an old man/woman* ○ *an old house* ○ *We're all **getting older**.* ○ *Children should show some respect for **the old**.* **2** USED A LOT having been used or owned for a long time *You might get dirty so wear some old clothes.* **3** AGE used to describe or ask about someone's age ***How old** are you?* ○ *She'll be 3 **years old** this month.* ➲See Common Learner Error at **year 4 an old friend/enemy, etc** someone who has been your friend/enemy, etc for a long time *I met an old friend who I was at college with.* **5** BEFORE [**always before noun**] used before or in the past *I think the old system was better in many ways.*

COMMON LEARNER ERROR

older, oldest, elder, eldest

Older and **oldest** are the comparative and superlative forms of the adjective 'old'.

I'm four years older than my sister.

Pedro is the oldest student in the class.

The adjectives **elder** and **eldest** are only used before nouns. They are usually used when you are comparing members of a family.

My elder brother is a doctor.

Mary has three sons. Her eldest boy is called Mark.

ˌold ˈage *noun* [U] the period of time when you are old

ˌold-age ˈpension *noun* [U] *UK* money that people receive regularly from the government when they are old and have stopped working

ˌold-age ˈpensioner *noun* [C] *UK* someone who gets an old-age pension

olden /ˈəʊldᵊn/ *adjective* **in the olden days/in olden times** a long time ago

O-ᵐ**old-fashioned** /ˌəʊldˈfæʃᵊnd/ *adjective* not modern *old-fashioned clothes/furniture*

oldie /ˈəʊldi/ *noun* [C] *informal* an old song or film, or an old person *a **golden oldie***

old-style /ˈəʊldstaɪl/ *adjective* [**always before noun**] used or done in the past *old-style politics*

the ˌOld ˈTestament *noun* **RELIGION** the part of the Bible (= holy book) written before the birth of Jesus Christ

the ˈOld ˌWorld *noun* Asia, Africa, and Europe

olive /ˈɒlɪv/ *noun* **1 FOOD** [C] a small green or black fruit with a bitter taste that is eaten or used to produce oil **2** [U] (*also* ˌ**olive ˈgreen**) a colour that is a mixture of green and yellow •**olive** (*also* **olive-green**) *adjective*

ˈolive ˌoil *noun* [U] **FOOD** oil produced from olives, used for cooking or on salads

-ology /-ɒlədʒi/ *suffix* makes a noun meaning 'the study of something' *psychology* (= the study of the mind) ○ *sociology* (= the study of society)

the Olympic Games /əˈlɪmpɪkˌgeɪmz/ (*also* **the Olympics**) *noun* [**plural**] **SPORT** an international sports competition that happens every four years •**Olympic** *adjective* [**always before noun**] relating to the Olympic Games *She broke the **Olympic record**.*

ombudsman /ˈɒmbʊdzmən/ *noun* [C] *plural* **ombudsmen LAW** someone who deals with complaints that people make against the government or public organizations

omelette /ˈɒmlət/ (*also US* **omelet**) *noun* [C] **FOOD** a food made with eggs that have been mixed and fried, often with other foods added *a cheese omelette*

WORD PARTNERS FOR ***omen***

a **bad/good/lucky** omen • an omen **of** [death/disaster/good fortune,etc] • an omen **for** sb/sth

omen /ˈəʊmən/ *noun* [C] a sign of what will happen in the future *a **good/bad omen***

ominous /ˈɒmɪnəs/ *adjective* making you think that something bad is going to happen *an **ominous sign*** ○ *ominous clouds*

WORD PARTNERS FOR ***omission***

a **glaring/serious/surprising** omission • sb/sth's omission **from** sth • the omission **of** sb/sth

omission /əʊˈmɪʃᵊn/ *noun* [C, U] when something has not been included but should have been *There are some **serious omissions** in the book.*

omit /əʊˈmɪt/ *verb* **omitting**, *past* **omitted 1** [T] to not include something [**often passive**] *He was **omitted from** the team because of his behaviour.* **2 omit to do sth** *mainly UK formal* to not do something *She omitted to mention where she was going.*

O-ᵐ**on¹** /ɒn/ *preposition* **1** SURFACE on a surface of something *We put all of our medicine on a high shelf.* **2** PLACE in a particular place *the diagram on page 22* ○ *I met her on a ship.* **3** RECORDING/PERFORMANCE used to show the way in which something is recorded or performed *What's on television tonight?* **4** TOUCHING used to show what happens as a result of touching something *I cut myself on a knife.* **5** SUBJECT about *a book on pregnancy* **6** MONEY/TIME used to show what money or time is used for *I've wasted too* *much time on this already.* ○ *She refuses to spend more than £20 on a pair of shoes.* **7** NEXT TO next to or along the side of *The post office is on Bateman Street.* **8** DATE/DAY used to show the date or day when something happens *He's due to arrive on 14 February.* ○ *I'm working on my birthday.* **9** USING using something *I spoke to Mum on the phone.* **10** AFTER happening after something and often because of it *The Prince was informed on his return to the UK.* **11** TRANSPORT used to show some methods of travelling *Did you go over on the ferry?* ○ *Sam loves travelling on buses.* **12** FOOD/FUEL/DRUGS used to show something that is used as food, fuel, or a drug *This radio runs on batteries.* ○ *I can't drink wine because I'm on antibiotics.* **13 be on a committee/panel, etc** to be a member of a group or organization *She's on the playgroup committee.* **14 have/carry sth on you** to have something with you *Do you have your driving licence on you?* **15 be on me/him, etc** *informal* used to show who is paying for something *This meal is on me.*

O⊸**on²** /ɒn/ *adverb* **1** CONTINUE used to show that an action or event continues *The old tradition lives on.* ○ *It was a complicated situation that dragged on for weeks.* **2** WEAR If you have something on, you are wearing it. *She's got a black coat on.* ○ *Why don't you* ***put*** *your new dress* ***on****?* **3** WORKING working or being used *The heating has been on all day.* **4** TRAVEL into a bus, train, plane, etc *Amy got on in Stamford.* **5** HAPPENING happening or planned *I've got a lot on at the moment.* ○ *Have you checked what's on at the cinema?* **6 on and off** (*also* **off and on**) If something happens on and off during a period of time, it happens sometimes. *They've been seeing each other on and off since Christmas.*

O⊸**once¹** /wʌns/ *adverb* **1** ONE TIME one time *It's only snowed once or twice this year.* ○ *I go swimming* ***once a week*** (= one time every week). **2** NOT NOW in the past, but not now *This house once belonged to my grandfather.* **3 once again** again *Once again I'm left with all the washing up.* **4 all at once** suddenly *All at once he stood up and walked out of the room.* **5 at once a** IMMEDIATELY immediately *I knew at once that I would like it here.* **b** AT SAME TIME at the same time *They all started talking at once.* **6 once in a while** sometimes but not often *He plays tennis once in a while.* **7 once and for all** If you do something once and for all, you do it now so that it does not have to be dealt with again. *Let's get to the bottom of this matter once and for all!* **8 once more** one more time *If you say that once more, I'm going to leave.* **9 for once** used to mean that something is happening that does not usually happen *For once, I think I have good news for him.* **10 LITERATURE once upon a time** used at the beginning of a children's story to mean that something happened a long time ago ➲See also: once in a blue **moon**

O⊸**once²** /wʌns/ *conjunction* as soon as *Once I've found somewhere to live, I'll send you my new address.* ○ *We'll send your tickets once we've received your cheque.*

oncoming /ˈɒnˌkʌmɪŋ/ *adjective* [**always before noun**] Oncoming vehicles are coming towards you.

O⊸**one¹** /wʌn/ the number 1 ➲See also: back to **square¹** one

O⊸**one²** /wʌn/ *pronoun* **1** PARTICULAR PERSON/THING used to refer to a particular person or thing in a group that has already been talked about *I've just made some scones, do you want one?* ○ *Throw those gloves away and get some new ones.* ○ *Chris is* ***the one*** *with glasses.* **2** GENERAL *formal* any person in general *One ought to respect one's parents.* **3 one at a time** separately *Eat them one at a time.* **4 one by one** separately, with one thing happening after another *One by one the old buildings have been demolished.* **5 one another** each other *How can they reach an agreement if they won't talk to one another?* **6 (all) in one** combined into a single thing *It's a CD player and cassette deck all in one.*

O⊸**one³** /wʌn/ *determiner* **1** PARTICULAR PERSON/THING used to refer to a particular person or thing in a group *One drawback is the cost of housing in the area.* ○ ***One of*** *our daughters has just got married.* **2** FUTURE TIME used to refer to a time in the future which is not yet decided *We must have a drink together one evening.* **3** TIME IN PAST at a particular time in the past *I first met him one day in the park.* **4** ONLY only *He's the one person you can rely on in this place.* **5** WITH ADJECTIVE *mainly US* used to emphasize an adjective *That's one big ice cream you've got there!* **6 one or two** a few *I'd like to make one or two suggestions.* ➲See also: put sth to one **side¹**, be one **step¹** ahead (of sb)

one-man /ˌwʌnˈmæn/ *adjective* [**always before noun**] with only one person doing something *a His* ***one-man show*** *has been a fantastic success.*

one-off /ˌwʌnˈɒf/ *adjective* [**always before noun**] *UK* only happening once *a* ***one-off payment*** •**one-off** *noun* [C] *UK* something that only happens once *His Olympic victory was not just a one-off.*

one-on-one /ˌwʌnɒnˈwʌn/ *adjective, adverb mainly US* only including two people

onerous /ˈəʊnᵊrəs/ *adjective formal* difficult and needing a lot of effort *an* ***onerous task***

oneself /wʌnˈself/ *pronoun formal* the reflexive form of the pronoun 'one' when it refers to the person speaking or people in general *How else should one protect oneself and one's family?*

one-sided /ˌwʌnˈsaɪdɪd/ *adjective* **1** BETTER If a competition is one-sided, one team or player is much better than the other. *a one-sided contest/game* **2** UNFAIR only considering one opinion in an argument in a way that is unfair *a one-sided view*

one-time /ˈwʌntaɪm/ *adjective* [**always before noun**] A one-time position or job is one that you had or did in the past, but not now. *a one-time friend/minister*

one-to-one /ˌwʌntəˈwʌn/ *adjective, adverb mainly UK* only including two people *She's having private lessons on a one-to-one basis.*

one-way /ˌwʌnˈweɪ/ *adjective* If a road is one-way, you can only drive on it in one direction. *a* ***one-way street***

O

ˌone-way ˈticket *US* (*UK* **single**) *noun* [C] A one-way ticket for a journey can only be used to travel in one direction and not to return.

ongoing /ˈɒnˌɡəʊɪŋ/ *adjective* [**always before noun**] still happening *an ongoing process/investigation*

onion /ˈʌnjən/ *noun* [C, U] **FOOD** a round vegetable with layers that has a strong taste and smell ➲See colour picture **Fruit and Vegetables** on page Centre 10 ➲See also: **spring onion**

O-ᵚ**online** /ˌɒnˈlaɪn/ *adjective, adverb* **COMPUTING** connected to a system of computers, especially the Internet *online services* ○ *to **go online*** (= start using the Internet) ○ *Most newspapers are now available online.* ➲See Extra help page **The Web and the Internet** on page Centre 36.

onlooker /ˈɒnˌlʊkəʳ/ *noun* [C] someone who watches something happening without becoming involved in it *a crowd of onlookers*

O-ᵚ**only¹** /ˈəʊnli/ *adverb* **1** [NOT MORE] not more than a particular size or amount *It'll only take a few minutes.* ○ *She's only fifteen.* **2** [NO ONE/NOTHING ELSE] not anyone or anything else *The offer is available to UK residents only.* **3** [RECENTLY] used to mean that something happened very recently *She's **only just** finished writing it.* **4 not only ... (but) also** used to say that one thing is true and another thing is true too, especially a surprising thing *Not only did he turn up late, he also forgot his books.*

O-ᵚ**only²** /ˈəʊnli/ *adjective* [**always before noun**] used to mean that there are not any others *This could be our only chance.* ○ *You're the only person here I know.*

only³ /ˈəʊnli/ *conjunction* used to introduce a statement which explains why something you have just said cannot happen or is not completely true *I'd phone him myself only I know he's not there at the moment.*

ˈonly ˌchild *noun* [C] *plural* **only children** someone who has no brothers or sisters

onomatopoeia /ˌɒnəʊˌmætəˈpiːə/ *noun* [U] **LANGUAGE, LITERATURE** the use of words which have sounds in them that are like the noises that the words refer to *'Pop!' is an example of onomatopoeia.*

on-screen /ˈɒnskriːn/ *adjective, adverb* appearing on a computer or television screen

onset /ˈɒnset/ *noun* **the onset of sth** the beginning of something, usually something unpleasant *the onset of cancer*

WORD PARTNERS FOR ***onslaught***

launch/mount an onslaught • an onslaught **against/on** sb

onslaught /ˈɒnslɔːt/ *noun* [C] when someone attacks or criticizes someone or something

on-the-job /ˈɒnðəˌdʒɒb/ *adjective* on-the-job training happens while you are at work

O-ᵚ**onto** (*also* **on to**) /ˈɒntuː/ *preposition* **1** [MOVING] used to show movement into or on a particular place *The sheep were loaded onto trucks.* ○ *Can you get back onto the path?* **2 hold/grip, etc onto sth** to hold something *Hold onto my hand before we cross the road.* **3** [TALKING] used to show that you are starting to talk about a different subject *Can we move onto the next item on the agenda?* **4 be onto sb** to know that someone has done something wrong or illegal *She knows we're onto her and she's trying to get away.* ○ *Who **put** the police **onto*** (= told the police about) her? **5 be onto sth** to know or discover something useful or important *Researchers think they may be onto something big.* ○ *Can you **put** me **onto*** (= tell me about) *a good dentist?*

the onus /ˈəʊnəs/ *noun formal* the responsibility for doing something *The **onus is on** parents to make sure their children attend school.*

onward /ˈɒnwəd/ (*also* **onwards**) *adverb* **1 from the 1870s/March/6.30 pm, etc onwards** beginning at a time and continuing after it **2** If you move onwards, you continue to go forwards.

oops /uːps/ *exclamation* something you say when you make a mistake or have a slight accident *Oops! I've spilled my coffee.*

ooze /uːz/ *verb* **1** [FLOW] [I, T] If a liquid oozes from something or if something oozes a liquid, the liquid comes out slowly. *Blood was oozing out of the wound.* **2** [SHOW] [T] *informal* to show a lot of a quality *to **ooze charm***

opal /ˈəʊpəl/ *noun* [C, U] **GEOLOGY** a precious stone whose colour changes when the position of the person looking at it changes

opaque /əʊˈpeɪk/ *adjective* **1** [NOT SEE] If an object or substance is opaque, you cannot see through it. **2** [NOT UNDERSTAND] *formal* difficult to understand

op-ed /ɒpˈed/ *US* (*UK* **editorial**) *adjective* [**always before noun**] describes a piece of writing in a newspaper in which a writer gives an opinion about a subject *an op-ed article/page*

O-ᵚ**open¹** /ˈəʊpᵊn/ *adjective* **1** [NOT CLOSED] not closed or fastened *an **open** door/window* ○ *Someone had left the gate **wide open**.* ○ *Is there a bottle of wine already open?* ○ *A magazine was lying open on her lap.* **2** [DOING BUSINESS] A shop or business is open during the time it is available for business or serving customers. *Most shops are open on Sundays now.* **3 COMPUTING** If a computer document or program is open, it is ready to be read or used. **4** [WITHOUT BUILDINGS] [**always before noun**] An open area of land has no buildings on it or near it. *large **open spaces*** **5** [NOT COVERED] [**always before noun**] without a roof or cover *an open courtyard* **6** [FOR EVERYONE] If a place or event is open, everyone can go to it or become involved in it. *an **open debate*** ○ *Are the gardens **open to** the public?* **7** [HONEST] An open person is honest and does not hide their feelings. **8** [NOT HIDDEN] [**always before noun**] Open feelings, usually negative ones, are not hidden. ***open hostility/rivalry*** **9** [NOT DECIDED] If a decision or question is open, it has not yet been decided. *We don't have to make a firm arrangement now. Let's **leave it open**.* **10 have/keep an open mind** to wait until you know all the facts before you form an opinion about something or judge someone *The cause of the fire is still unclear and we are keeping an open mind.* **11 open to discussion/suggestions, etc** willing to consider a discussion/suggestions, etc *This is only a proposal. I'm open to suggestions.* **12 open to abuse/criticism, etc** likely to be abused/criticized, etc *The system is wide open to abuse.* ➲See also: with your eyes (**eye¹**) open

COMMON LEARNER ERROR

open and close

Be careful not to confuse the adjective and verb forms of these words.

The adjectives are **open** and **closed**.

Is the supermarket open on Sunday?

The museum is closed today.

The verbs are **open** and **close**.

The supermarket opens at 8 a.m.

The museum closes at 5 p.m. today.

open² /'əʊpᵊn/ *verb* **1** NOT CLOSED [I, T] If something opens, it changes to a position that is not closed, and if you open it, you make it change to a position that is not closed. *to open a door/ window* ○ *The gate won't open.* ○ *Don't open your eyes yet.* **2** REMOVE COVER [T] to remove part of a container or parcel so that you can see or use what it contains *Karen opened the box and looked inside.* ○ *Why don't you open the envelope?* ○ *I can't open this bottle.* **3** PREPARE FOR USE [I, T] If an object opens, the parts that are folded together move apart, and if you open it, you make the parts that are folded together move apart. *Shall I open the umbrella?* ○ *Open your books at page 22.* **4** START WORK [I] If a shop or office opens at a particular time of day, it starts to do business at that time. *What time does the bank open?* **5 COMPUTING** [T] to make a computer document or program ready to be read or used **6** START OFFICIALLY [I, T] If a business or activity opens, it starts officially for the first time, and if you open it, you make it start officially for the first time. *That restaurant's new - it only opened last month.* ○ *Several shops have* ***opened up*** *in the last year.* **7** MAKE AVAILABLE [T] to allow people to use a road or area *They* ***opened up*** *the roads again the day after the flooding.* **8 open an account FINANCE** to make an arrangement to keep your money with a bank *Have you opened a bank account yet?* ➲See also: open the **floodgates**

open (sth) up *phrasal verb* **1** CREATE OPPORTUNITY to create a new opportunity or possibility *A teaching qualification can* ***open up*** *many more career* ***opportunities.*** **2** OPEN LOCK to open the lock on the door of a building *The caretaker opens up the school every morning at seven.*

open up *phrasal verb* to start to talk more about yourself and your feelings *I've tried to get him to* ***open up to*** *me, but with no success.*

the open /'əʊpᵊn/ *noun* **1 in the open** outside *We spent the night in the open.* **2 bring sth out into the open** to tell people information that was secret [**often passive**] *It's time this issue was brought out into the open.*

open-air /ˌəʊpən'eəʳ/ *adjective* [**always before noun**] An open-air place does not have a roof. *an* ***open-air swimming pool***

'open ˌday *noun* [C] **EDUCATION** *UK* a day when people can visit a school or organization to see what happens there

open-ended /ˌəʊpən'endɪd/ *adjective* An open-ended activity or situation does not have a planned ending. *We are not willing to enter into* ***open-ended discussions.***

opener /'əʊpənəʳ/ *noun* [C] **1 bottle/can/tin, etc opener** a piece of kitchen equipment used to open bottles/cans, etc **2** someone or something that begins a series of events, usually in sports ➲See also: **eye-opener**

opening¹ /'əʊpənɪŋ/ *noun* [C] **1** HOLE a hole or space that something or someone can pass through *We found an opening in the fence and climbed through.* **2** START the beginning of something *The opening of the opera is quite dramatic.* **3** CEREMONY a ceremony at the beginning of an event or activity *I've been invited to the opening of the new exhibition on Tuesday.* **4** OPPORTUNITY a job or an opportunity to do something *There's* ***an opening for*** *an editorial assistant in our department.*

opening² /'əʊpənɪŋ/ *adjective* [**always before noun**] happening at the beginning of an event or activity *the* ***opening night*** ○ *her* ***opening remarks***

openly /'əʊpᵊnli/ *adverb* without hiding any of your thoughts or feelings *He* ***talks*** *quite* ***openly*** *about his feelings.*

open-minded /ˌəʊpən'maɪndɪd/ *adjective* willing to consider ideas and opinions that are new or different to your own

openness /'əʊpᵊnnəs/ *noun* [U] when someone is honest about their thoughts and feelings *I appreciated his openness.*

open-plan /ˌəʊpᵊn'plæn/ *adjective* describes a room or a building without many walls *an* ***open-plan office***

open-source /ˌəʊpən'sɔːs/ *adjective* **COMPUTING** Open-source software is free to use, and the original program can be changed by anyone.

opera /'ɒpᵊrə/ *noun* [C, U] **MUSIC** a musical play in which most of the words are sung *to go to the opera* ○ ***opera singers*** ○ *an* ***opera house*** (= building for opera) •**operatic** /ˌɒpᵊr'ætɪk/ *adjective* relating to opera *an operatic society*

operate /'ɒpᵊreɪt/ *verb* **1** ORGANIZATION [I, T] If an organization or business operates, it is working, and if you operate it, you manage it and make it work. *Our company is operating under very difficult conditions at present.* **2** MACHINE [I, T] If a machine operates, it does what it is designed to do, and if you operate it, you make it do what it is designed to do. *You have to be trained to operate the machinery.* **3 HEALTH** [I] to treat an illness or injury by cutting someone's body and removing or repairing part of it *Did they have to* ***operate on*** *him?*

'operating ˌroom *US* (*UK* **operating theatre**) *noun* [C] **HEALTH** a room in a hospital where doctors do operations

'operating ˌsystem *noun* [C] **COMPUTING** computer software that controls how different parts of a computer work together

'operating ˌtheatre *UK* (*US* **operating room**) *noun* [C] **HEALTH** a room in a hospital where doctors do operations

WORD PARTNERS FOR ***operation***

have/undergo an operation • **do/perform** an operation • an operation **on** sb/sb's [knee/ hand,etc] • a **major/minor** operation

O

O-ᵚ**operation** /ˌɒpᵊrˈeɪʃᵊn/ *noun* [C] **1 HEALTH** when a doctor cuts someone's body to remove or repair part of it *a heart/lung operation* ○ *a **major/minor operation*** ○ *My son's got to **have an operation**.* **2** ORGANIZATION an organization or business *a large commercial operation* **3** ACTIVITY an activity that is intended to achieve a particular purpose *a military/peacekeeping operation* ○ *a joint operation by French and Spanish police* **4 in operation** If a machine or system is in operation, it is working or being used. *The new rail link is now in operation.* ○ *Most of the machines are now back in operation.*

operational /ˌɒpᵊrˈeɪʃᵊnᵊl/ *adjective* **1** WORKING If a system is operational, it is working. *The service becomes **fully operational** next June.* **2** ACTIVITY [**always before noun**] relating to a particular activity *operational control/responsibility*

operative[1] /ˈɒpᵊrətɪv/ *adjective formal* working or being used *The agreement will not become operative until all members have signed.*

operative[2] /ˈɒpᵊrətɪv/ *noun* [C] *mainly US* someone who does secret work for a government or other organization *a former CIA operative*

operator /ˈɒpəreɪtəʳ/ *noun* [C] **1** TELEPHONE someone who helps to connect people on a telephone system *Why don't you call the operator?* **2** MACHINE someone whose job is to use and control a machine or vehicle *a computer operator* **3** BUSINESS a company that does a particular type of business *a tour operator*

WORD PARTNERS FOR ***opinion***

express/hold/voice an opinion • a **favourable/low/personal/poor/strong** opinion • **in** sb's opinion • sb's opinion **about/on** sth

O-ᵚ**opinion** /əˈpɪnjən/ *noun* **1** [C] a thought or belief about something or someone *What's your **opinion about/on** the matter?* ○ *He **has** fairly strong **opinions** on most subjects.* ○ ***In my opinion*** (= I think) *he's the best football player we have in this country.* **2 POLITICS public opinion** the thoughts and beliefs that most people have about a subject *Eventually, the government will have to take notice of public opinion.* **3 have a high/low opinion of sb/sth** to think that someone or something is good/bad *He has a low opinion of doctors.*

opinionated /əˈpɪnjəneɪtɪd/ *adjective* being too certain that your strong opinions are correct

oˈpinion ˌpoll *noun* [C] **POLITICS** when people are asked questions to discover what they think about a subject *The latest opinion poll shows that the president's popularity has improved.*

opium /ˈəʊpiəm/ *noun* [U] **HEALTH** a drug made from the seeds of a poppy (= a red flower)

opponent /əˈpəʊnənt/ *noun* [C] **1** COMPETE someone who you compete against in a game or competition *He beat his opponent six games to two.* **2** DISAGREE someone who disagrees with an action or belief and tries to change it *an opponent of slavery* ○ *a **political opponent***

opportune /ˈɒpətjuːn/ *adjective formal* **an opportune moment/time** a good time for something to happen *His letter arrived at an opportune moment.*

opportunist /ˌɒpəˈtjuːnɪst/ *noun* [C] someone who tries to get power or an advantage in every situation •**opportunistic** /ˌɒpətjuːˈnɪstɪk/ *adjective* using a situation to get power or an advantage

WORD PARTNERS FOR ***opportunity***

create/have/miss/offer/provide/seize an opportunity • a **golden/good/great/unique/wasted** opportunity • **at every** opportunity • an opportunity **for** sth

O-ᵚ**opportunity** /ˌɒpəˈtjuːnəti/ *noun* **1** POSSIBILITY [C, U] a situation in which it is possible for you to do something, or a possibility of doing something *a **unique opportunity*** ○ *a **golden*** (= very good) ***opportunity*** [+ **to do sth**] *Everyone will **have an opportunity** to comment.* ○ *There are plenty of **opportunities for** research.* ○ *Don't **miss** this **opportunity** to win a million pounds.* ○ *She talks about her boyfriend **at every opportunity**.* **2** JOB [C] the chance to get a job [**usually plural**] *opportunities for young graduates* ○ ***job/employment opportunities*** **3 take the opportunity to do sth** to use an occasion to do or say something *I'd like to take this opportunity to thank all of you.* ➲See Common Learner Error at **possibility**

opporˈtunity ˌcost *noun* [C, U] **FINANCE** the cost to a business of not being able to do something, for example because available money is being used for something else

O-ᵚ**oppose** /əˈpəʊz/ *verb* [T] to disagree with a plan or activity and to try to change or stop it *The committee opposed a proposal to allow women to join the club.*

opposed /əˈpəʊzd/ *adjective* **1 be opposed to sth** to disagree with a plan or activity *We're not opposed to tax increases.* **2 as opposed to** used to say that two things are very different *I'm talking about English football, as opposed to European football.*

opposing /əˈpəʊzɪŋ/ *adjective* **1 SPORT opposing teams/players, etc** Opposing teams/players, etc are competing against each other. **2 opposing ideas/beliefs, etc** Opposing ideas/beliefs, etc are completely different. *The book presents two opposing views.*

O-ᵚ**opposite**[1] /ˈɒpəzɪt/ *adjective* **1** OTHER SIDE in a position facing something or someone but on the other side *on the **opposite page*** ○ *in the **opposite corner*** ○ *We live on **opposite sides** of the city.* ○ *I noticed a gate at the **opposite end** of the courtyard.* **2** DIFFERENT completely different *Police attempts to calm the violence had completely the **opposite effect**.*

O-ᵚ**opposite**[2] /ˈɒpəzɪt/ *adverb, preposition* in a position facing something or someone but on the other side *The couple sat down opposite her.* ○ *UK* She lives opposite (= on the other side of the road). ○ *Is there a bakery opposite your house?*

O-ᵚ**opposite**[3] /ˈɒpəzɪt/ *noun* [C] someone or something that is completely different from another person or thing *They're **complete opposites**.* ○ *He's **the exact opposite of** my father.*

the ˌopposite ˈsex *noun* someone who is male if you are female, or female if you are male *It's not always easy to meet* ***members of the opposite sex.***

O-■ **opposition** /ˌɒpəˈzɪʃən/ *noun* **1** [U] strong disagreement *Is there much* ***opposition to*** *the proposed changes?* ○ *There has been strong* ***opposition from*** *local residents.* **2 the Opposition/opposition POLITICS** political parties that are not in power

oppress /əˈpres/ *verb* [T] **1** LIMIT FREEDOM to treat a group of people in an unfair way, often by limiting their freedom [**often passive**] *Women were oppressed by a society which considered them inferior.* **2** MAKE ANXIOUS to make someone feel anxious

oppressed /əˈprest/ *adjective* treated in an unfair way ***oppressed minorities***

oppression /əˈpreʃən/ *noun* [U] when people are treated in a way that is unfair and that limits their freedom ***political oppression*** ○ *the oppression of women*

oppressive /əˈpresɪv/ *adjective* **1** UNFAIR cruel and unfair *an* ***oppressive government/regime*** **2** HOT If the weather or heat is oppressive, it is too hot and there is no wind. ***oppressive heat*** **3** NOT RELAXING not relaxing or pleasant *an oppressive silence*

oppressor /əˈpresər/ *noun* [C] someone who treats people in an unfair way, often by limiting their freedom

opt /ɒpt/ *verb* **opt for sth; opt to do sth** to choose something or to decide to do something *Mike opted for early retirement.* ○ *Most people opt to have the operation.*

opt out *phrasal verb* to choose not to be part of an activity or to stop being involved in it *He's decided to* ***opt out of*** *the company's pension scheme.*

optical /ˈɒptɪkəl/ *adjective* **HEALTH, BIOLOGY, PHYSICS** relating to light or the ability to see *optical equipment/instruments*

ˌoptical ˈcharacter recogˌnition (*abbreviation* **OCR**) *noun* [U] **COMPUTING** software that allows computers to read printed or written words and store them in the computer

ˌoptical ˈfibre *UK* (*US* **optical fiber**) *noun* [C, U] **COMPUTING, PHYSICS** a very thin glass or plastic thread which is used for telephones and computers to carry information in the form of light *optical fibre transmission*

ˌoptical iˈllusion *noun* [C] something that you think you see, but which is not really there

optician /ɒpˈtɪʃən/ *noun* [C] **HEALTH 1** someone whose job is to make eye glasses **2** *UK* a shop where you can have your eyes tested and have your glasses made

ˌoptic ˈnerve *noun* [C] **ANATOMY** the nerve that passes signals to the brain from the retina (= eye part that sends images to the brain) at the back of each eye

WORD PARTNERS FOR ***optimism***

express optimism • **cautious/renewed** optimism • **cause for/grounds for/reason for** optimism • optimism **about** sth

optimism /ˈɒptɪmɪzəm/ *noun* [U] when you believe good things will happen *a mood/spirit of optimism* ○ *There is* ***cause/reason for*** *optimism.* ○ *He expressed cautious* ***optimism about*** *the future.* ➲Opposite **pessimism**

optimist /ˈɒptɪmɪst/ *noun* [C] someone who always believes that good things will happen

optimistic /ˌɒptɪˈmɪstɪk/ *adjective* always believing that good things will happen *We're* ***optimistic about*** *our chances of success.* [+ **(that)**] *I'm not optimistic that we'll reach an agreement.* ➲Opposite **pessimistic**

optimum /ˈɒptɪməm/ *adjective* [**always before noun**] *formal* best or most suitable *the optimum temperature*

WORD PARTNERS FOR ***option***

consider/examine the options • **be given/have** the option **of** doing sth • an **attractive/viable** option • an option **for** sb

O-■ **option** /ˈɒpʃən/ *noun* **1** [C] a choice *That's an option you might like to consider.* ○ *We don't have many options.* [+ **of + doing sth**] *You always have the* ***option of*** *not attending.* **2 have no option (but to do sth)** to not have the possibility of doing something else *We didn't want to dismiss him, but we had no option.* **3 keep/leave your options open** to wait and not make a decision or choice yet ➲See also: **soft option**

optional /ˈɒpʃənəl/ *adjective* If something is optional, it is available but you do not have to have it. *an* ***optional extra***

opulent /ˈɒpjələnt/ *adjective* Opulent things are expensive and give a feeling of luxury. *an opulent bathroom*

O-■ **or** *strong form* /ɔːr/ *weak form* /ər/ *conjunction* **1** BETWEEN POSSIBILITIES used between possibilities, or before the last in a list of possibilities *Would you like toast or cereal?* ○ *Is that a boy or a girl?* ○ *You can have beer, wine, or mineral water.* ○ *The house will take two or three years to complete.* **2** CHANGE used to change or correct something you have said *We told the truth, or most of it.* **3** REASON used to give a reason for something you have said *She must love him or she wouldn't have stayed with him all these years.* **4** NOT EITHER used after a negative verb between a list of things to mean not any of those things or people *Tim doesn't eat meat or fish.*

oral[1] /ˈɔːrəl/ *adjective* **1** spoken *an* ***oral examination*** ○ *an* ***oral agreement*** **2 ANATOMY** relating to or using the mouth ***oral medication*** •**orally** *adverb*

oral[2] /ˈɔːrəl/ *noun* [C] **EDUCATION** an examination that is spoken, usually in a foreign language

O-■ **orange**[1] /ˈɒrɪndʒ/ *adjective* being a colour that is a mixture of red and yellow *a deep orange sunset* ➲See colour picture **Colours** on page Centre 12

O-■ **orange**[2] /ˈɒrɪndʒ/ *noun* **1 FOOD** [C] a round, sweet fruit with a thick skin and a centre that is divided into many equal parts *orange juice* ➲See colour picture **Fruit and Vegetables** on page Centre 10 **2** [C, U] a colour that is a mixture of red and yellow ➲See colour picture **Colours** on page Centre 6 **3 FOOD** [U] *UK* a drink made with oranges *Would you like some orange?*

O

ˈorange ˌjuice *noun* [U] **FOOD** a drink made from the juice of oranges

orang-utan /ɔːˈræŋutæŋ/ *noun* [C] a large ape (= animal like a large monkey with no tail) with reddish brown hair and long arms which lives in the forests of Sumatra and Borneo

orator /ˈɒrətəʳ/ *noun* [C] **LANGUAGE** *formal* someone who gives good speeches *a brilliant orator*

oratory /ˈɒrətəri/ *noun* [U] **LANGUAGE** *formal* when people give good speeches *political oratory*

orbit /ˈɔːbɪt/ *noun* [C, U] **1 ASTRONOMY** the circular journey that a spacecraft or planet makes around the sun, the moon, or another planet *the Earth's orbit* ○ *Two satellites are already **in orbit**.* ○ *It was the first spacecraft to **go into orbit** around Jupiter.* **2 ANATOMY** the hole in the skull (= bone in the head) that contains the eye ➲See picture at **skull** ●**orbit** *verb* [I, T] *The moon orbits the Earth.*

orchard /ˈɔːtʃəd/ *noun* [C] **FARMING** a piece of land where fruit trees are grown *an apple/cherry orchard*

orchestra /ˈɔːkɪstrə/ *noun* [C] **1 MUSIC** a large group of musicians who play different instruments together *a symphony orchestra* ○ *a youth orchestra* **2** *US* (*UK* **the stalls**) the seats on the main floor near the front of a theatre or cinema ●**orchestral** /ɔːˈkestrəl/ *adjective* [always before noun] Orchestral music is played by or written for an orchestra.

orchestrate /ˈɔːkɪstreɪt/ *verb* [T] to intentionally organize something in order to achieve what you want

orchid /ˈɔːkɪd/ *noun* [C] a plant with flowers which are an unusual shape and beautiful colours

O

ordain /ɔːˈdeɪn/ *verb* [T] **RELIGION** to officially make someone a Christian priest [often passive] *Dr Coker was ordained by the Bishop of London in 1986.*

ordeal /ɔːˈdiːl/ *noun* [C] a very unpleasant experience *a terrible ordeal* ○ *They feared he would not **survive** the **ordeal**.* ○ *She **went through** the **ordeal** of being interviewed by a panel of ten people.*

WORD PARTNERS FOR ***order***

follow/give/ignore/issue/obey orders • **clear/strict** orders

O-ɯ**order¹** /ˈɔːdəʳ/ *noun* **1** ARRANGEMENT [C, U] the arrangement of a group of people or things in a list from first to last *in alphabetical order* ○ *in **the right/wrong order*** ○ *We ranked the tasks **in order of** importance.* **2** INSTRUCTION [C] an instruction that someone must obey *to **obey orders*** ○ *to **give orders*** **3 under orders** If you are under orders, someone has told you to do something. [+ to do sth] Team members are under orders to behave well. ○ *They claimed they were under orders from the president.* **4** REQUEST [C] a request for food or goods in return for payment *Can I **take** your **order** now?* **5** TIDINESS [U] a situation in which everything is in its correct place *It's nice to see some order around here for a change.* ○ *I want to put all my things **in order** before I go away.* ➲Opposite **disorder** **6 out of order a** MACHINE If a machine or system is out of order, it is not working as it should. *The coffee machine's out of order.* **b** BEHAVIOUR If someone's behaviour is out of order, it is not acceptable. *What he did was completely out of order.* **7 in order to do/for sth to do sth** with the purpose of achieving something *She worked all summer in order to save enough money for a holiday.* **8** NO TROUBLE [U] a situation in which people obey laws and there is no trouble *The army was brought in to **restore order** to the troubled province.* ➲Opposite **disorder** **9 economic/political/social order** the way that the economy, politics, or society is organized *a threat to the established social order* **10 RELIGION** [C] a religious group who live together and have the same rules *an order of nuns* ○ *a **monastic order*** ➲See also: **mail order, postal order, standing order**

O-ɯ**order²** /ˈɔːdəʳ/ *verb* **1** TELL [T] to give someone an instruction that they must obey [+ to do sth] *He ordered them to leave.* **2** REQUEST [I, T] to ask for food, goods, etc *to order a drink/pizza* ○ *to order tickets* ○ *We've ordered new lights for the kitchen.* [+ two objects] *Can I order you a drink?* **3** ARRANGE [T] to arrange a group of people or things in a list from first to last *Have you ordered the pages correctly?*

order sb about/around *phrasal verb* to tell someone what they should do all the time *You can't just come in here and start ordering people around.*

orderly¹ /ˈɔːdəli/ *adjective* tidy or organized *an orderly pile* ○ *Please form an **orderly queue**.* ➲Opposite **disorderly**

orderly² /ˈɔːdəli/ *noun* [C] **HEALTH** a hospital worker who has no special skills or training

ordinal number /ˌɔːdɪnəlˈnʌmbəʳ/ (*also* **ordinal**) *noun* [C] **MATHEMATICS** a number such as 1st, 2nd, 3rd, etc that shows the order of things in a list

ordinance /ˈɔːdɪnəns/ *noun* [C] *mainly US* **LAW** a law or rule which limits or controls something *a tax ordinance*

ordinarily /ˈɔːdənərəli/ *adverb* usually *These are people who would not ordinarily carry guns.*

O-ɯ**ordinary** /ˈɔːdənəri/ *adjective* **1** NOT UNUSUAL not special, different, or unusual in any way *ordinary life* ○ *an ordinary day* ○ *I had a very ordinary childhood.* **2** NOT FAMOUS Ordinary people are not rich or famous and do not have special skills. *ordinary people/citizens* ○ *an ordinary man/woman* **3 out of the ordinary** unusual or different *Their relationship was a little out of the ordinary.* ○ *The investigation revealed **nothing out of the ordinary**.*

ore /ɔːʳ/ *noun* [U] **GEOLOGY** rock or soil from which metal can be obtained *iron ore*

.org /dɒtˈɔːg/ **INTERNET** *internet abbreviation for* organization: used in some Internet addresses *You can search Cambridge dictionaries online at www.dictionary.cambridge.org*

organ /ˈɔːgən/ *noun* [C] **1 ANATOMY, BIOLOGY** a part of an animal or plant that has a special purpose *reproductive/sexual organs* ○ *The liver is a **vital organ*** (= you need it to stay alive). ○ *an **organ donor/transplant*** **2 MUSIC** a large musical instrument that has keys like a piano and produces different notes when air is blown through pipes of different lengths *a church organ*

organelle /ˌɔːgᵊnˈel/ *noun* [C] **ANATOMY, BIOLOGY** any of the parts inside a living cell that have a particular purpose, such as a nucleus or a chloroplast

organic /ɔːˈgænɪk/ *adjective* **1 FARMING, FOOD** not using artificial chemicals when keeping animals or growing plants for food ***organic farming/farmers*** ○ ***organic food/vegetables*** **2 CHEMISTRY** In chemistry, 'organic' describes chemicals that contain carbon. *organic compounds* **3 BIOLOGY** from a living organism *organic matter/material* ➲Opposite **inorganic** •**organically** *adverb We have a weekly delivery of* ***organically grown*** *vegetables.*

organism /ˈɔːgᵊnɪzᵊm/ *noun* [C] **BIOLOGY** a living thing, often one that is extremely small *Plants, animals, bacteria, and viruses are organisms.*

organist /ˈɔːgᵊnɪst/ *noun* [C] **MUSIC** someone who plays the organ (= an instrument like a piano) *His childhood ambition was to be a church organist.*

WORD PARTNERS FOR ***organization***

a **charitable/international/voluntary** organization • **join/set up** an organization

O━**organization** (*also UK* **-isation**) /ˌɔːgᵊnaɪˈzeɪʃᵊn/ *noun* **1** GROUP [C] an official group of people who work together for the same purpose *a* ***charitable/voluntary organization*** **2** ARRANGEMENT [U] the way that parts of something are arranged *Better organization of the office would improve efficiency.* **3** PLAN [U] the planning of an activity or event *Who was responsible for the organization of the conference?* •**organizational** *adjective* ***organizational skills***

O━**organize** (*also UK* **-ise**) /ˈɔːgᵊnaɪz/ *verb* [T] to plan or arrange something *to organize a meeting/wedding*

organized (*also UK* **-ised**) /ˈɔːgᵊnaɪzd/ *adjective* **1** PERSON An organized person plans things well and does not waste time or effort. ➲Opposite **disorganized** **2** GROUP [**always before noun**] involving a group of people who have planned to do something together ***organized crime/religion*** ➲See also: **well-organized**

organizer (*also UK* **-iser**) /ˈɔːgᵊnaɪzəʳ/ *noun* [C] someone who plans an event or activity *conference/exhibition organizers*

orgy /ˈɔːdʒi/ *noun* [C] **an orgy of sth** a period when there is too much of an often bad activity *an orgy of destruction*

the Orient /ˈɔːriənt/ *noun old-fashioned* the countries of east Asia

Oriental /ˌɔːriˈentᵊl/ *adjective* relating or belonging to the countries of east Asia *Oriental art*

orientated /ˈɔːriənteɪtɪd/ *UK* (*UK/US* **oriented**) *adjective* directed towards or interested in something

orientation /ˌɔːrienˈteɪʃᵊn/ *noun* **1** BELIEFS [C, U] the type of beliefs that a person has *He's very secretive about his political orientation.* **2** TRAINING [U] training or preparation for a new job or activity *an orientation session*

oriented /ˈɔːrientɪd/ (*also UK* **orientated**) *adjective* directed towards or interested in something *His new TV series is* ***oriented towards*** *teenage viewers.* ○ *He's very family oriented.*

WORD PARTNERS FOR ***origin***

sth **has** its origins **in** sth • the origin(s) **of** sth • be [Chinese/French, etc] **in** origin

origin /ˈɒrɪdʒɪn/ *noun* [C, U] **1** the cause of something, or where something begins or comes from ***the origin of*** *the universe* ○ *This dish is Greek* ***in origin.*** **2 SOCIETY** the country, race, or social class of a person's family ***ethnic origin*** ○ *She's* ***of*** *Irish* ***origin.***

O━**original**[1] /əˈrɪdʒᵊnᵊl/ *adjective* **1** INTERESTING special and interesting because of not being the same as others *Her essay was full of* ***original ideas.*** ○ *He's a highly* ***original thinker.*** **2** FIRST [**always before noun**] existing since the beginning, or being the earliest form of something *His original plan was to stay for a week, but he ended up staying for a month.* ○ *Does the committee still have the original version of this document?*

original[2] /əˈrɪdʒᵊnᵊl/ *noun* [C] something that is in the form in which it was first created and has not been copied or changed *If the painting were an original, it would be very valuable.*

originality /əˌrɪdʒᵊnˈæləti/ *noun* [U] the quality of being interesting and different from everyone or everything else *The judges were impressed by the originality of his work.*

O━**originally** /əˈrɪdʒᵊnᵊli/ *adverb* at the beginning or before any changes *The bathroom was originally a bedroom.*

originate /əˈrɪdʒᵊneɪt/ *verb* [I] **originate from/in/with, etc** to come from a particular place or person, or to begin during a particular period *Citrus fruits originated in China and Southeast Asia.*

originator /əˈrɪdʒᵊneɪtəʳ/ *noun* [C] *formal* The originator of an idea is the person who first thought of it.

ornament /ˈɔːnəmənt/ *noun* [C] an attractive object that is used as a decoration in a home or garden ➲See colour picture **The Living Room** on page Centre 4

ornamental /ˌɔːnəˈmentᵊl/ *adjective* used for decoration and having no other purpose

ornate /ɔːˈneɪt/ *adjective* decorated with a lot of complicated patterns *ornate wooden doors*

ornithology /ˌɔːnɪˈθɒlədʒi/ *noun* [U] **BIOLOGY** the scientific study of birds •**ornithologist** *noun* [C] a scientist who studies birds

orographic /ɒrəˈgræfik/ *adjective formal* **GEOGRAPHY** relating to mountains, their shape and how they were formed, etc

orography /ɒrˈɒgrəfi/ *noun* [U] **GEOGRAPHY** the height of land and the way this is shown on maps •**orographic** /ɒrəˈgræfɪk/ *adjective*

orphan[1] /ˈɔːfᵊn/ *noun* [C] **1 SOCIETY** a child whose parents are dead **2** in printing, the first line of a paragraph, separated from the rest which is on the next page

orphan² /ˈɔːfᵊn/ *verb* **be orphaned** SOCIETY When a child is orphaned, both their parents die. *She was orphaned at the age of six.*

orphanage /ˈɔːfᵊnɪdʒ/ *noun* [C] a home for children whose parents are dead

orthodox /ˈɔːθədɒks/ *adjective* **1** RELIGION keeping the traditional beliefs and customs of Judaism or some types of Christianity *an orthodox Jewish family* ○ *the Russian/Greek Orthodox Church* **2** If ideas or methods are orthodox, most people think they are correct, usually because they have existed for a long time. ***orthodox medicine*** ⊃Opposite **unorthodox**

orthodoxy /ˈɔːθədɒksi/ *noun* [C, U] *formal* RELIGION an idea of a society, religion, political party, or subject that most people believe is correct, or a set of such ideas

orthopaedic *UK* (*US* **orthopedic**) /ˌɔːθəˈpiːdɪk/ *adjective* [always before noun] HEALTH relating to the treatment or study of bones that have been injured or have not grown correctly *an orthopaedic surgeon*

Oscar /ˈɒskəʳ/ *noun* [C] *trademark* one of several prizes given to actors and people who make films every year in Hollywood in the US *Who **won the Oscar** for best actress this year?*

oscillate /ˈɒsɪleɪt/ *verb* [I] *formal* to move repeatedly between two positions or opinions *an oscillating fan* ○ *The story **oscillates between** comedy and tragedy.* •**oscillation** /ˌɒsɪˈleɪʃᵊn/ *noun* [C, U]

oscilloscope /əˈsɪləskəʊp/ *noun* [C] PHYSICS a piece of equipment that shows changes in electrical currents as waves on a screen

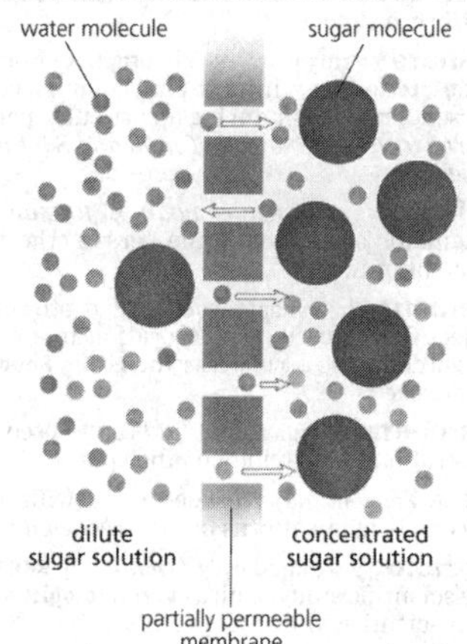

osmosis

osmosis /ɒzˈməʊsɪs/ *noun* [U] BIOLOGY the way that water moves from one part of a body or a plant to another part through a membrane (= thin layer) *Fluid flows back into the tiny blood vessels by osmosis.* •**osmotic** /ɒzˈmɒtɪk/ *adjective*

ostensibly /ɒsˈtensɪbli/ *adverb* If something is ostensibly the reason for something else, people say it is the reason, although you do not believe it. *He was discharged from the army, ostensibly for medical reasons.*

ostentatious /ˌɒstenˈteɪʃəs/ *adjective* intended to attract attention or admiration, often by showing money or power *an **ostentatious display** of wealth* •**ostentatiously** *adverb*

osteopath /ˈɒstiəʊpæθ/ *noun* [C] HEALTH someone who treats injuries to bones and muscles by moving and rubbing them •**osteopathy** *noun* [C]

osteoporosis /ˌɒstiəʊpəˈrəʊsɪs/ *noun* [U] HEALTH a disease which makes bones weak and makes them break easily

ostracize (*also UK* **-ise**) /ˈɒstrəsaɪz/ *verb* [T] SOCIETY When a group of people ostracizes someone, they refuse to talk to or do things with that person. [often passive] *He was ostracized by the other children at school.*

ostrich /ˈɒstrɪtʃ/ *noun* [C] a very large bird from Africa which cannot fly but can run very fast

O‑‑**other¹** /ˈʌðəʳ/ *adjective, determiner* **1** MORE used to refer to people or things which are similar to or in addition to those you have talked about *I don't like custard - do you have **any other** desserts?* ○ *I don't think he's funny, but other people do.* **2** PART OF SET used to talk about the remaining members of a group or items in a set *Mario and Anna sat down to watch the other dancers.* ○ *I found one shoe - have you seen **the other one**?* **3** DIFFERENT different from a thing or person which you have talked about *Ask me some other time, when I'm not so busy.* ⊃See Common Learner Error at **another** **4 the other side/end (of sth)** the opposite side/end of something *Our house is on the other side of town.* **5 the other day/week, etc** used to mean recently, without giving a particular date *I asked Kevin about it just the other day.* **6 every other day/week, etc** happening one day/week, etc but not the next *Alice goes to the gym every other day.* **7 other than** except *The form cannot be signed by anyone other than the child's parent.* [+ to do sth] *They had no choice other than to surrender.* **8 other than that** *informal* except for the thing you have just said *My arm was a bit sore - other than that I was fine.*

O‑‑**other²** /ˈʌðəʳ/ *pronoun* **1** used to refer to a person or thing which belongs to a group or set that you have already talked about *Hold the racket in one hand, and the ball in the other.* ○ *Some of the pieces were damaged, others were missing.* **2 others** used to refer to people or things that are similar to people or things you have already talked about *This is broken - do you have **any others**?* ⊃See also: **each other**

O‑‑**others** /ˈʌðəz/ *pronoun* [plural] other people *Don't expect others to do your work for you.*

otherwise¹ /ˈʌðəwaɪz/ *adverb* **1** EXCEPT except for what has just been referred to *She hurt her arm in the accident, but otherwise she was fine.* **2** DIFFERENT different to what has just been stated *I'll meet you there at 6 o'clock unless I **hear otherwise**.* ○ *I'd like to help you with any problems, financial **or otherwise**.*

otherwise² /ˈʌðəwaɪz/ *conjunction* used when saying what will happen if someone does not obey an order or do what has been suggested *You'd better phone home, otherwise your parents will start to worry.* ○ *They had to leave early, otherwise the children would have been up too late.*

otter /ˈɒtəʳ/ *noun* [C] a small animal with short, brown fur and a long body that swims well

ouch /aʊtʃ/ *exclamation* something you say when you experience sudden physical pain *Ouch! This radiator's really hot.*

O⊸**ought** /ɔːt/ *modal verb* **1 ought to do sth** used to say or ask what is the correct or best thing to do *You ought to see a doctor.* ○ *He ought to have told her the truth.* ○ *Ought I to phone her?* **2 ought to be/do sth** used to say that you expect something to be true or that you expect something to happen *He ought to pass the exam this time.* ➲See Extra help page **Modal verbs** on page Centre 34.

oughtn't /ˈɔːtᵊnt/ *formal short for* ought not *He* ***oughtn't to*** *have shouted at us.*

ounce /aʊns/ *noun* **1 MEASURES** [C] (*written abbreviation* **oz**) a unit for measuring weight, equal to 28.35 grams ➲See Extra help page **Numbers and measurements** on page Centre 24. ➲See also: **fluid ounce 2 not have an ounce of sth** to not have any of a quality or emotion *His new novel doesn't have an ounce of originality.* **3 every ounce of sth** all of a quality or emotion that is available *He deserves every ounce of support that we can give him.*

O⊸**our** /aʊəʳ/ *determiner* belonging to or relating to the person who is speaking and one or more other people *Janice is our youngest daughter.* ○ *There's no point in our buying a new car this year.*

O⊸**ours** /aʊəz/ *pronoun* the things that belong or relate to the person who is speaking and one or more other people *Matt's a friend of ours.* ○ *That's their problem - not ours.*

O⊸**ourselves** /ˌaʊəˈselvz/ *pronoun* **1** REFLEXIVE the reflexive form of the pronoun 'we' *We've promised ourselves a holiday abroad this year.* **2** EMPHASIZE used for emphasis with the pronoun 'we' or when referring to yourself and at least one other person *John and I arranged the wedding reception ourselves.* **3 (all) by ourselves** alone or without anyone else's help *It's a big garden but we manage to look after it by ourselves.* **4 (all) to ourselves** for our use only *We had the swimming pool all to ourselves.*

oust /aʊst/ *verb* [T] to force someone to leave a position of power or responsibility [**often passive**] *He was* ***ousted from*** *power by a military coup.*

O⊸**out** /aʊt/ *adjective, adverb* **1** AWAY FROM used to show movement away from the inside of a place or container *He dropped the bag and all the apples fell out.* ○ *She opened the window and stuck her head out.* **2** OUTSIDE outside a building or room *Would you like to wait out here?* ○ *It's bitterly cold out today.* **3** NOT THERE not in the place where you usually live or work, especially for a short time *I came round to see you this morning but you were out.* **4** FIRE/LIGHT A fire or light that is out is not burning or shining. *Bring some more wood, the fire's gone out.* **5** AVAILABLE available to buy or see *When's the new Spielberg film out?* **6** FASHION no longer fashionable or popular *Trousers like that* ***went out*** *years ago.* **7** NOT ACCURATE not accurate *Your figures are out by £300.* **8 SPORT** no longer able to play or take part in a game or competition *Two of the best players were out after ten minutes.* **9** APPEAR able to be seen *After a few minutes the sun came out.* **10** NOT POSSIBLE not possible or not acceptable *Next weekend is out because we're going away.* **11 be out of sth** to have no more of something left *We're nearly out of petrol.* **12 be out for sth; be out to do sth** to intend to do something, especially for an unpleasant reason *He's only out to impress the boss.* ➲See also: **out of**

out- /aʊt-/ *prefix* more than or better than *to outgrow something* ○ *to outnumber* ○ *to outdo someone* (= to show that you are better than someone)

out-and-out /ˌaʊtᵊnˈaʊt/ *adjective* [**always before noun**] complete or in every way *an out-and-out lie*

the outback /ˈaʊtbæk/ *noun* **GEOGRAPHY** the areas of Australia where few people live, especially the central desert areas

outbid /ˌaʊtˈbɪd/ *verb* [T] **outbidding**, *past* **outbid** **FINANCE** to offer to pay more for something than someone else *She had to outbid two rivals to buy the business.*

out-box /ˈaʊtbɒks/ (*also* **outbox**) *noun* [C] **1** **INTERNET** the place on a computer which keeps copies of email messages which you have sent **2** *US* (*UK* **out-tray**) a container where you keep letters and documents that you want to send to someone else

outbreak /ˈaʊtbreɪk/ *noun* [C] when something unpleasant and difficult to control starts, such as a war or disease *an outbreak of flu/fighting*

outburst /ˈaʊtbɜːst/ *noun* [C] a sudden, forceful expression of emotion in words or actions *an* ***angry outburst***

outcast /ˈaʊtkɑːst/ *noun* [C] **SOCIETY** someone who is not accepted by society because they are different to most other people *a* ***social outcast***

WORD PARTNERS FOR ***outcome***

announce/await/determine the outcome • the **eventual/final** outcome • the outcome **of** sth

outcome /ˈaʊtkʌm/ *noun* [C] the final result of an activity or process ***the outcome of*** *an election*

outcrop /ˈaʊtkrɒp/ (*also US* **outcropping**) *noun* [C] **GEOLOGY** a rock or group of rocks that sticks out above the surface of the ground *a rocky outcrop*

WORD PARTNERS FOR ***outcry***

cause/provoke/spark an outcry • an **international /national/public** outcry • an outcry **against/over** sth

outcry /ˈaʊtkraɪ/ *noun* [C] a strong public expression of anger and disapproval about a recent event or decision *There has been a public* ***outcry against*** *the new road.*

outdated /ˌaʊtˈdeɪtɪd/ *adjective* not modern enough *outdated equipment* ○ *an outdated idea*

outdo /ˌaʊtˈduː/ *verb* [T] *past tense* **outdid**, *past participle* **outdone** to do something better than someone else *They are always trying to outdo each other with their jokes and funny stories.*

outdoor /ˌaʊtˈdɔːʳ/ *adjective* [**always before noun**] happening, used, or in a place that is outside and not inside a building ***outdoor activities*** ○ *an* ***outdoor concert*** ○ *an* ***outdoor swimming pool*** ○ ***outdoor clothing*** ➲Opposite **indoor**

outdoors /ˌaʊtˈdɔːz/ *adverb* not inside a building *If it's warm this evening, we could eat outdoors.* ➲Opposite **indoors**

the outdoors /ˌaʊtˈdɔːz/ *noun* countryside *He enjoys hunting, fishing, and the outdoors.*

outer /ˈaʊtəʳ/ *adjective* [**always before noun**] on the edge or surface of something *Remove the* ***outer layers*** *of the onion.* ➲Opposite **inner**

ˌouter ˈspace *noun* [U] **ASTRONOMY** the universe outside the Earth and its gases where other planets and stars are

the outfield /ˈaʊtfiːld/ *noun* **SPORT** the outer area of the playing field in sports such as cricket and baseball •**outfielder** *noun* [C] a baseball player who stands in the outfield

outfit¹ /ˈaʊtfɪt/ *noun* [C] **1** CLOTHES a set of clothes for a particular event or activity *a cowboy outfit* **2** GROUP *informal* an organization, company, or any group of people who work together

outfit² /ˈaʊtfɪt/ *verb* [T] **outfitting**, *past* **outfitted** *US* to provide equipment for something [**often passive**] *My hotel room was small and outfitted with cheap wooden furniture.*

outflow /ˈaʊtfləʊ/ *noun* [C] **FINANCE** an amount of money going out of a business

outgoing /ˌaʊtˈgəʊɪŋ/ Ⓤⓢ /ˈaʊtgəʊɪŋ/ *adjective* **1** FRIENDLY Someone who is outgoing is friendly, talks a lot, and enjoys meeting people. **2** LEAVING POWER [**always before noun**] leaving a position of power or responsibility *the outgoing president* **3** LEAVING A PLACE [**always before noun**] going to another place ***outgoing calls/messages***

outgoings /ˈaʊtˌgəʊɪŋz/ *noun* [**plural**] *UK* **FINANCE** money that you have to spend on rent, food, etc

outgrow /ˌaʊtˈgrəʊ/ *verb* [T] *past tense* **outgrew**, *past participle* **outgrown** **1** TOO BIG to grow too big for something *He's already outgrown these shoes.* **2** NOT SUITABLE to develop so that something is not now suitable *She's outgrown her current job and needs a new challenge.*

outing /ˈaʊtɪŋ/ *noun* [C] when a group of people go on a short journey for pleasure or education *a* ***family/school outing*** ○ ***to go on an outing***

outlandish /ˌaʊtˈlændɪʃ/ *adjective* very strange and unusual *an outlandish story/idea* ○ ***outlandish behaviour/clothes***

outlast /ˌaʊtˈlɑːst/ *verb* [T] to continue for longer than someone or something else

outlaw¹ /ˈaʊtlɔː/ *verb* [T] **LAW** to make something officially illegal *I think all handguns should be outlawed.*

outlaw² /ˈaʊtlɔː/ *noun* [C] **LAW** *old-fashioned* a criminal *a dangerous outlaw*

outlay /ˈaʊtleɪ/ *noun* [C] **FINANCE** an amount of money spent by a business or government *The project requires an* ***initial outlay*** *of $450,000.*

outlet /ˈaʊtlet/ *noun* [C] **1** SHOP In business, an outlet is a shop that sells one type of product or the products of one company. **2** CHEAP SHOP *US* a shop that sells goods for a lower price than usual **3** EXPRESS a way for someone to express an emotion, idea, or ability *She needs a job that will provide* ***an outlet for*** *her creative talent.* **4** WAY OUT a place where a liquid or gas can flow out of something **5 PHYSICS** *US* a place where you can connect a wire on a piece of electrical equipment *an electrical outlet*

outline¹ /ˈaʊtlaɪn/ *verb* [T] to describe only the most important ideas or facts about something *He outlined the department's plans for next year.*

outline² /ˈaʊtlaɪn/ *noun* [C] **1** DESCRIPTION a short description of the most important ideas or facts about something *He gave us a* ***brief outline*** *of the town's history.* **2** SHAPE the shape made by the outside edge of something

outlive /ˌaʊtˈlɪv/ *verb* [T] to continue living or existing after someone or something else has died or stopped existing *She outlived both her children.*

outlook /ˈaʊtlʊk/ *noun* **1** FUTURE [**no plural**] the likely future situation *The* ***outlook for*** *the economy next year is bleak.* **2** THINKING [C] the way a person thinks about something *Despite her illness, she has a very positive* ***outlook on*** *life.*

outlying /ˈaʊtˌlaɪɪŋ/ *adjective* [**always before noun**] **GEOGRAPHY** far from towns and cities, or far from the centre of a place *outlying farms/villages*

outmanoeuvre *UK* (*US* **outmaneuver**) /ˌaʊtməˈnuːvəʳ/ *verb* [T] to do something clever that gives you an advantage over someone you are competing against *She outmanoeuvred her opponents throughout the election campaign.*

outmoded /ˌaʊtˈməʊdɪd/ *adjective* not modern enough *outmoded equipment*

outnumber /ˌaʊtˈnʌmbəʳ/ *verb* [T] to be larger in number than another group *Women now far outnumber men on language courses.*

out of /aʊt əv/ *preposition* **1** AWAY FROM used to show movement away from the inside of a place or container *A bunch of keys fell out of her bag.* ○ *She stepped out of the car and walked towards me.* **2** NO LONGER IN no longer in a place or situation *He's out of the country until next month.* ○ *I've been out of work for the past year.* **3** MADE FROM used to show what something is made from *The statue was carved out of a single block of stone.* **4** BECAUSE OF used to show the reason why someone does something *I only gave her the job out of pity.* **5** FROM AMONG from among an amount or number *Nine out of ten people said they preferred it.* **6** NOT INVOLVED no longer involved in something *He missed the practice session and now he's out of the team.*

out-of-court /ˌaʊtəv'kɔːt/ *adjective* [**always before noun**] **LAW** agreed without involving a law court *an* ***out-of-court settlement***

out-of-date /ˌaʊtəv'deɪt/ *adjective* old and not useful or correct any more *I do have a road map but I think it's out-of-date.*

out-of-town /ˌaʊtəv'taʊn/ *adjective* [**always before noun**] positioned or happening in the countryside or on the edge of a town *an out-of-town supermarket*

outpace /ˌaʊt'peɪs/ *verb* [**T**] to move or develop more quickly than someone or something else

outpatient /'aʊtˌpeɪʃənt/ *noun* [**C**] **HEALTH** someone who is treated in a hospital but does not sleep there at night

outperform /ˌaʊtpə'fɔːm/ *verb* [**T**] to do something better than someone or something else *Girls are consistently outperforming boys at school.*

outplay /ˌaʊt'pleɪ/ *verb* [**T**] **SPORT** to play a game or sport better than another player or team

outpost /'aʊtpəʊst/ *noun* [**C**] **GEOGRAPHY** a small place that is far from large towns or cities, often where a government or company is represented

outpouring /'aʊtˌpɔːrɪŋ/ *noun* [**C**] when an emotion is expressed a lot in public *His death provoked a national* ***outpouring of*** *grief.*

output[1] /'aʊtpʊt/ *noun* [**U**] **1** AMOUNT the amount of something that is produced *Over the past year the factory's output has fallen by 15%.* **2 COMPUTING** information produced by a computer *You can look at the output on screen before you print it out.* **3** POWER the power or energy produced by an electrical or electronic system

WORD PARTNERS FOR ***outrage***

cause/express/provoke/spark outrage • **moral/public** outrage • outrage **at/over** sth

outrage[1] /'aʊtreɪdʒ/ *noun* **1** ANGER [**U**] a strong feeling of anger or shock ***moral outrage*** ○ *The scandal caused* ***public outrage.*** **2** SHOCKING THING [**C**] something that causes great anger or shock *a terrorist outrage* [+ **(that)**] *It's an outrage that these children don't have enough to eat.*

outrage[2] /'aʊtreɪdʒ/ *verb* [**T**] to make someone feel very angry or shocked [**often passive**] *Local people were* ***outraged at*** *the bombing.*

outrageous /ˌaʊt'reɪdʒəs/ *adjective* shocking or extreme *outrageous behaviour/clothes* ○ *The prices in that restaurant were outrageous.* •**outrageously** *adverb outrageously expensive*

outran /ˌaʊt'ræn/ *past tense of* outrun

outreach /'aʊtriːtʃ/ *noun* [**U**] *mainly US* when an organization helps people with their social, medical, or educational problems *an* ***outreach programme*** ○ *an* ***outreach worker***

outright /'aʊtraɪt/ *adjective* [**always before noun**] total, clear, and certain *an* ***outright ban*** *on smoking* ○ *an* ***outright victory*** •**outright** /ˌaʊt'raɪt/ *adverb She needs 51% of the vote to* ***win outright.*** ○ *He was* ***killed outright*** (= immediately) when the car hit him.

outrun /ˌaʊt'rʌn/ *verb* [**T**] **outrunning**, *past tense* **outran**, *past participle* **outrun** to move or develop faster or further than someone or something

outscore /ˌaʊt'skɔːʳ/ *verb* [**T**] *mainly US* **SPORT** to score more points than another player or team

outset /'aʊtset/ *noun* **at/from the outset** at or from the beginning of something *I made my views clear at the outset.*

outshine /ˌaʊt'ʃaɪn/ *verb* [**T**] *past* **outshone** to be much better than someone else *She easily outshone the other students on the course.*

O─ **outside**[1] /ˌaʊt'saɪd/ (*also US* **outside of**) *preposition* **1** NEAR not in a particular building or room, but near it *She waited outside his room for nearly two hours.* **2** NOT IN not in *a flat just outside Blackpool* ○ *You have to phone a different number outside office hours.*

O─ **outside**[2] /ˌaʊt'saɪd/ *adverb* **1** NOT INSIDE not inside a building *Go and play outside for a while.* ○ *It's cold outside today.* **2** NEAR not in a particular building or room, but near it *She knocked on his bedroom door and left the tray outside.*

outside[3] /ˌaʊt'saɪd/ *adjective* [**always before noun**] **1** NOT INSIDE not in a building *an outside light* ○ *outside activities* **2** DIFFERENT from a different organization or group of people ***outside help*** ○ ***outside influences*** ⊃See also: **the outside world**

O─ **the outside**[4] /ˌaʊt'saɪd/ *noun* the outer part or surface of something *The pie was cooked on the outside but cold in the middle.*

ˌoutside 'chance *noun* [**no plural**] when something is not likely to happen *She has an outside chance of reaching the final.*

outsider /ˌaʊt'saɪdəʳ/ *noun* [**C**] **SOCIETY** someone who does not belong to a particular group, organization, or place *The villagers are very suspicious of outsiders.* ⊃Compare **insider**

the ˌoutside 'world *noun* other people in other places *When he was in prison, his radio was his only contact with the outside world.*

outsize /ˌaʊt'saɪz/ (*also* **outsized**) *adjective* [**always before noun**] larger than usual *an outsize jumper*

the outskirts /'aʊtskɜːts/ *noun* **GEOGRAPHY** the outer area of a city, town, or village *There are plans to build a new stadium* ***on the outskirts of*** *Liverpool.*

outspoken /ˌaʊt'spəʊkən/ *adjective* expressing an opinion forcefully and not worrying about what other people think ***outspoken comments*** ○ *He's an* ***outspoken critic*** *of nuclear energy.*

outstanding /ˌaʊt'stændɪŋ/ *adjective* **1** EXCELLENT excellent and much better than most *an* ***outstanding achievement*** **2** NOT DONE waiting to be paid or dealt with *an outstanding debt*

outstandingly /ˌaʊt'stændɪŋli/ *adverb* used to emphasize how good something is *outstandingly successful*

outstay /ˌaʊt'steɪ/ *verb* ⊃See: outstay/overstay your **welcome**[4]

outstretched /ˌaʊt'stretʃt/ *adjective* When a part of your body is outstretched, it is

O

reaching out as far as possible. *He ran towards me with his arms outstretched.*

outstrip /ˌaʊt'strɪp/ *verb* [T] **outstripping**, *past* **outstripped** When one amount outstrips another amount, it is much greater than it. ***Demand** for the toys far **outstrips supply**.*

outta /'aʊtə/ *informal short for* out of *Let's get outta here!*

out-take /'aʊtteɪk/ *noun* [C] a short part of a film, television programme or music recording that was removed, usually because it contains mistakes *They showed a video with funny out-takes from famous films.*

outward¹ /'aʊtwəd/ *adjective* [**always before noun**] **1** showing on the outside *He had a serious illness, but there was no **outward sign** of it.* **2 outward flight/journey, etc** when you travel away from a place that you will return to ➲Opposite **inward**

outward² /'aʊtwəd/ (*also UK* **outwards**) *adverb* towards the outside or away from the centre

outwardly /'aʊtwədli/ *adverb* If someone is outwardly calm, confident, etc, they seem to be calm, confident, etc, although they may not feel that way. *She was very nervous, but she remained **outwardly calm**.* ➲Opposite **inwardly**

outweigh /ˌaʊt'weɪ/ *verb* [T] to be greater or more important than something else *The benefits of this treatment far outweigh the risks.*

outwit /ˌaʊt'wɪt/ *verb* [T] **outwitting**, *past* **outwitted** to get an advantage over someone by doing something clever and deceiving them *She outwitted her kidnappers and managed to escape.*

O

oval /'əʊvᵊl/ *adjective* in the shape of an egg or a slightly flat circle *an oval face* ○ *an oval table* •**oval** *noun* [C] an oval shape ➲See picture at **shape**

the ˈOval ˌOffice *noun* **POLITICS** the office of the president of the United States

ovary /'əʊvᵊri/ *noun* [C] **ANATOMY, BIOLOGY** the part of a woman or female animal that produces eggs, or the part of a plant that produces seeds ➲See picture at **carpel** ➲See picture at **flower** •**ovarian** /əʊ'veəriən/ *adjective* [**always before noun**] relating to the ovaries *ovarian cancer*

ovation /əʊ'veɪʃᵊn/ *noun* [C] when a group of people clap for a long time to show that they approve of someone or something ➲See also: **standing ovation**

oven /'ʌvᵊn/ *noun* [C] a piece of kitchen equipment with a door which is used for cooking food *an electric oven* ○ *a microwave oven* ➲See colour picture **The Kitchen** on page Centre 2

O-ᵚ**over¹** /'əʊvəʳ/ *adverb, preposition* **1** [ABOVE] above or higher than something *The sign over the door said "Private, No Entry".* ○ *A fighter plane flew over.* **2** [SIDE TO SIDE] If you walk, jump, climb, etc over an object or place, you go from one side of it to the other side. *We had to climb over large rocks to get to the beach.* **3** [AMOUNT] more than a particular amount, number, or age *Over 5,000 Internet users contact our website every year.* ○ *Suitable for children aged 5 and over.* **4** [OPPOSITE SIDE] on or to the opposite side of a road, bridge, path, etc *The station is over the bridge.* **5** [COVER] covering someone or something *She placed the quilt over the bed.* **6** [DOWN] down from a higher to a lower position *The little boy fell over and started to cry.* ○ *She tripped over the rug.* **7** [PLACE] to a particular place *Could you bring the plates **over here*** (= bring them to this place). ○ *He was sent **over there** during the war.* **8** [TIME] during a particular period of time *I was in Seattle over the summer.* **9** [ABOUT] connected with or about *It's stupid arguing over something so trivial.* **10** [NOT USED] not used *There's some food **left over** from the party.* **11** [USING] using the radio or telephone *I made the booking over the phone.* **12 be/get over sth** to feel better after being ill or feeling unhappy about something *It took him months to get over splitting up with his girlfriend.* **13 do sth over** *US* to do something again from the beginning because you did not do it well the first time *You've ruined it! - Now I'll have to do it over.* **14 (all) over again** again from the beginning *It looks all messy. I'm going to have to do it all over again.* **15 over and over (again)** repeatedly *He was whistling the same tune over and over.* **16 roll/turn, etc (sth) over** to move so that a different part is showing, or to make something do this *She turned the page over.* **17** [CONTROL] in control of someone or something *Her husband has a lot of influence over her.*

O-ᵚ**over²** /ˌəʊvəʳ/ *adjective* **1** [**never before noun**] finished *The exams will be over next week.* ○ *It was **all over** very quickly.* **2 get sth over (and done) with** to do something difficult or unpleasant as soon as you can so that you do not have to worry about it any more

over- /əʊvəʳ/ *prefix* too much *to overeat* ○ *overpopulated*

overall /'əʊvᵊrɔːl/ *adjective* [**always before noun**] considering everything or everyone *the overall cost of the holiday* ○ *the **overall** effect* •**overall** /ˌəʊvᵊr'ɔːl/ *adverb How would you rate the school overall?*

overalls /'əʊvᵊrɔːlz/ *noun* [**plural**] **1** [KEEP CLEAN] *UK* (*US* **coveralls**) a piece of clothing that you wear over your clothes to keep them clean while you are working **2** [TROUSERS] *US* (*UK* **dungarees**) trousers with a part that covers your chest and straps that go over your shoulders

over-anxious /ˌəʊvə'ræŋkʃəs/ *adjective* worrying too much

overbearing /ˌəʊvə'beərɪŋ/ *adjective* trying to have too much control over other people *an overbearing mother*

overblown /ˌəʊvə'bləʊn/ *adjective* If something is overblown, it is made to seem more important or serious than it really is.

overboard /'əʊvəbɔːd/ *adverb* **1** over the side of a boat and into the water *to **fall overboard*** **2 go overboard** *informal* to do something too much, or to be too excited about something *I think people go overboard at Christmas.*

overburdened /ˌəʊvə'bɜːdᵊnd/ *adjective* having too much to deal with *overburdened with work*

overcame /ˌəʊvə'keɪm/ *past tense of* overcome

overcast /'əʊvəkɑːst/ *adjective* cloudy and dark *an overcast sky/day*

overcharge /ˌəʊvəˈtʃɑːdʒ/ *verb* **[I, T] FINANCE** to charge someone too much money for something *The shop overcharged me by £5.*

overcoat /ˈəʊvəkəʊt/ *noun* **[C]** a long, warm coat

overcome /ˌəʊvəˈkʌm/ *verb past tense* **overcame**, *past participle* **overcome 1 [T]** to deal with and control a problem or feeling *He's trying to overcome his drug addiction and find a job.* ○ *Let's hope she overcomes her shyness.* **2 be overcome by excitement/fear/sadness, etc** to suddenly have too much of a feeling *She was overcome by emotion.* **3 be overcome by smoke/fumes, etc** to become ill or weak because you have been breathing smoke or poisonous gas *One worker died when he was overcome by chemical fumes.*

overcrowded /ˌəʊvəˈkraʊdɪd/ *adjective* containing too many people or things *an overcrowded classroom/prison* •**overcrowding** *noun* **[U]**

overdo /ˌəʊvəˈduː/ *verb* **[T]** *past tense* **overdid**, *past participle* **overdone** to do or use too much of something *I went to the gym yesterday, but I think I* ***overdid it*** *a bit.*

overdone /ˌəʊvəˈdʌn/ *adjective* **FOOD** cooked for too long

overdose /ˈəʊvədəʊs/ *noun* **[C] HEALTH** too much of a drug taken at one time *Her daughter died of a* ***drug overdose.*** •**overdose** /ˌəʊvəˈdəʊs/ *verb* **[I]**

overdraft /ˈəʊvədrɑːft/ *noun* **[C] FINANCE** If you have an overdraft, you have taken more money out of your bank account than you had in it. *a £250 overdraft*

overdrawn /ˌəʊvəˈdrɔːn/ *adjective* **FINANCE** If you are overdrawn, you have taken more money out of your bank account than you had in it. *We've* ***gone*** *£200* ***overdrawn!***

overdue /ˌəʊvəˈdjuː/ *adjective* happening later than expected *This decision is* ***long overdue.***

overestimate /ˌəʊvərˈestɪmeɪt/ *verb* **[I, T]** to guess or think that something is bigger or better than it really is *They overestimated her ability to do the job.* ⊃Opposite **underestimate**

over-fishing /ˌəʊvəˈfɪʃɪŋ/ *noun* **[U] ENVIRONMENT** catching so many fish in a part of the sea that there are not many fish left there *low fish stocks caused by over-fishing*

overflow /ˌəʊvəˈfləʊ/ *verb* **1** CONTAINER **[I]** If a container or a place overflows, the thing that is inside it starts coming out because it is too full. *The bath overflowed, and there's water all over the floor!* ○ *The bin was* ***overflowing with*** *rubbish.* **2** CONTENTS **[I, T]** to come out of a container or a place because it is too full *The river overflowed its banks after the heavy rainfall.* **3 overflow with confidence/happiness/love, etc** to have a lot of a quality or emotion •**overflow** /ˈəʊvəfləʊ/ *noun* **[C, U]**

overgrown /ˌəʊvəˈgrəʊn/ *adjective* covered with plants that have become too big *an overgrown garden*

overhang /ˌəʊvəˈhæŋ/ *verb* **[T]** *past* **overhung** to hang over something ***overhanging branches***

overhaul /ˌəʊvəˈhɔːl/ *verb* **[T]** to examine a machine or a system carefully and improve it or repair it *to overhaul an engine* •**overhaul** /ˈəʊvəhɔːl/ *noun* **[C]**

overhead /ˌəʊvəˈhed/ *adjective, adverb* above you, usually in the sky *overhead power cables* ○ *A police helicopter was hovering overhead.*

overheads /ˈəʊvəhedz/ *UK* (*US* **overhead**) *noun* **[plural] FINANCE** money that a company spends on its regular and necessary costs, for example rent and heating

overhear /ˌəʊvəˈhɪər/ *verb* **[T]** *past* **overheard** to hear what someone is saying when they are not talking to you **[+ doing sth]** *I overheard him telling her he was leaving.*

overheat /ˌəʊvəˈhiːt/ *verb* **[I]** to become too hot *The engine keeps overheating.*

overhung /ˌəʊvəˈhʌŋ/ *past of* overhang

overjoyed /ˌəʊvəˈdʒɔɪd/ *adjective* very happy **[+ to do sth]** *He was overjoyed to hear from his old friend.*

overkill /ˈəʊvəkɪl/ *noun* **[U]** when something is done too much *Should I add an explanation or would that be overkill?*

overlap /ˌəʊvəˈlæp/ *verb* **[I, T] overlapping**, *past* **overlapped 1** SAME If two subjects or activities overlap, they are the same in some way. *Although our job titles are different, our responsibilities overlap quite a lot.* **2** COVER If two objects overlap, part of one covers part of the other. •**overlap** /ˈəʊvəlæp/ *noun* **[C, U]**

overload /ˌəʊvəlˈəʊd/ *verb* **[T] 1** VEHICLE to put too many people or things into or onto a vehicle **[often passive]** *The coach was overloaded with passengers.* **2** WORK to give someone more work or problems than they can deal with

overlook /ˌəʊvəˈlʊk/ *verb* **[T] 1** VIEW to have a view of something from above *a balcony overlooking the sea* **2** NOT NOTICE to not notice or consider something *Two important facts have been overlooked in this case.* **3** FORGIVE to forgive or ignore someone's bad behaviour

overly /ˈəʊvəli/ *adverb* in a way that is extreme or too much *overly optimistic* ○ *It wasn't overly expensive.*

overnight /ˌəʊvəˈnaɪt/ *adverb* **1** NIGHT for or during the night *Sometimes we would* ***stay overnight*** *at my grandmother's house.* **2** QUICKLY very quickly or suddenly *Change does not happen overnight.* •**overnight** *adjective* **[always before noun]** *overnight rain* ○ *an* ***overnight*** (= sudden) ***success***

overpass /ˈəʊvəpɑːs/ *US* (*UK* **flyover**) *noun* **[C]** a bridge that carries a road over another road

overpower /ˌəʊvəˈpaʊər/ *verb* **[T] 1** DEFEAT to defeat someone by being stronger than they are **[often passive]** *The gunman was overpowered by two security guards.* **2** MAKE WEAK If a feeling, smell, etc overpowers you, it is very strong and makes you feel weak.

overpowering /ˌəʊvəˈpaʊərɪŋ/ *adjective* unpleasantly strong or powerful *an* ***overpowering smell***

overpriced /ˌəʊvəˈpraɪst/ *adjective* too expensive

overran /ˌəʊvərˈæn/ *past tense of* overrun

overrated /ˌəʊvᵊrˈeɪtɪd/ *adjective* If something is overrated, it is considered to be better or more important than it really is.

overreact /ˌəʊvᵊriˈækt/ *verb* [I] to react in a way that is more extreme than you should *She tends to **overreact to** criticism.*

override /ˌəʊvᵊrˈaɪd/ *verb* [T] *past tense* **overrode**, *past participle* **overridden 1** NOT ACCEPT If someone in authority overrides a decision or order, they officially decide that it is wrong. *I don't have the power to **override** his **decision**.* **2** MORE IMPORTANT to be more important than something else *His desire for money seems to override anything else.*

overriding /ˌəʊvᵊrˈaɪdɪŋ/ *adjective* [always before noun] more important than others *an **overriding concern***

overrule /ˌəʊvᵊrˈuːl/ *verb* [T] **LAW** If someone in authority overrules a decision or order, they officially decide that it is wrong. *Does the judge have the power to overrule the jury?*

overrun /ˌəʊvᵊrˈʌn/ *verb* **overrunning**, *past tense* **overran**, *past participle* **overrun 1** FILL [T] If something unpleasant overruns a place, it fills it in large numbers. [often passive] *The house was overrun by rats.* ○ *Troops overran the city.* **2** CONTINUE [I] *UK* to continue for a longer time than planned *Sorry I'm late, but the meeting overran by 20 minutes.*

overseas /ˌəʊvəˈsiːz/ *adjective* [always before noun] in, to, or from another country *an **overseas student*** •**overseas** *adverb to live/work overseas*

oversee /ˌəʊvəˈsiː/ *verb* [T] **overseeing**, *past tense* **oversaw**, *past participle* **overseen** to watch work as it is done in order to make certain that it is done correctly *A committee has been set up to oversee the project.*

overshadow /ˌəʊvəˈʃædəʊ/ *verb* [T] **1** SPOIL to cause something to be less enjoyable [often passive] *The party was overshadowed by a family argument.* **2** BE BETTER THAN to cause someone or something to seem less important or successful

oversight /ˈəʊvəsaɪt/ *noun* [C, U] a mistake that you make by not noticing something or by forgetting to do something

oversleep /əʊvəˈsliːp/ *verb* [I] *past* **overslept** to sleep longer than you had intended *Sorry I'm late, I overslept.*

overstate /ˌəʊvəˈsteɪt/ *verb* [T] to talk about something in a way that makes it seem more important than it really is

overstep /ˌəʊvəˈstep/ *verb* **overstepping**, *past* **overstepped overstep the mark** to behave in a way that is not allowed or not acceptable

overt /əʊˈvɜːt/ *adjective* done or shown publicly and not hidden ***overt criticism*** •**overtly** *adverb overtly racist remarks*

overtake /ˌəʊvəˈteɪk/ *verb past tense* **overtook**, *past participle* **overtaken 1** MORE SUCCESSFUL [T] to become more successful than someone or something else *Tobacco has overtaken coffee to become the country's leading export.* **2** GO PAST [I, T] to go past a vehicle or person that is going in the same direction

over-the-counter /ˌəʊvəðəˈkaʊntəʳ/ *adjective* [always before noun] **HEALTH** Over-the-counter medicines can be bought in a shop without first visiting a doctor. •**over-the-counter** *adverb Most of these tablets can be **bought over-the-counter**.*

overthrow /ˌəʊvəˈθrəʊ/ *verb* [T] *past tense* **overthrew**, *past participle* **overthrown POLITICS** to remove someone from power by using force *They were accused of plotting to **overthrow the government**.* •**overthrow** /ˈəʊvəθrəʊ/ *noun* [no plural]

overtime /ˈəʊvətaɪm/ *noun* [U] extra time that you work after your usual working hours *unpaid overtime* •**overtime** *adverb*

overtones /ˈəʊvətəʊnz/ *noun* [plural] ideas that seem to be expressed but that are not stated directly *His speech had political overtones.*

overtook /ˌəʊvəˈtʊk/ *past tense of* overtake

overture /ˈəʊvətjʊəʳ/ *noun* [C] **MUSIC** a piece of classical music that introduces another longer piece such as an opera

overturn /ˌəʊvəˈtɜːn/ *verb* **1 overturn a conviction/ruling/verdict, etc LAW** to officially change a legal decision **2** [I, T] If something overturns or if you overturn something, it turns over onto its top or onto its side. *She overturned her car in the accident.*

WORD PARTNERS FOR ***overview***

give/provide an overview • a **brief/broad/comprehensive/general** overview • an overview **of** sth

overview /ˈəʊvəvjuː/ *noun* [C] a short description giving the most important facts about something *I'll just **give** you **an overview** of the job.*

overweight /ˌəʊvəˈweɪt/ *adjective* too heavy or too fat *He's still a few pounds overweight.* ⊃Opposite **underweight**

overwhelm /ˌəʊvəˈwelm/ *verb* [T] If a feeling or situation overwhelms someone, it has an effect that is too strong or extreme. [often passive] *She was overwhelmed by the excitement of it all.*

overwhelming /ˌəʊvəˈwelmɪŋ/ *adjective* very strong in effect or large in amount *an **overwhelming feeling** of sadness* ○ *They won by an **overwhelming majority**.* •**overwhelmingly** *adverb*

overworked /ˌəʊvəˈwɜːkt/ *adjective* Someone who is overworked has to work too much. *We're **overworked and underpaid**.*

overwrite /ˌəʊvəˈraɪt/ *verb* [T] **COMPUTING** If you overwrite a computer file, you replace it with a different one.

oviduct /ˈəʊvɪdʌkt/ *noun* [C] **ANATOMY, BIOLOGY** in the female body, the tube that an egg passes through after it leaves the ovary (= part that makes eggs) *In a woman's body the oviduct is either of the two fallopian tubes.*

ovulate /ˈɒvjəleɪt/ *verb* [I] **BIOLOGY** When a woman ovulates, her body produces eggs. •**ovulation** /ˌɒvjəˈleɪʃᵊn/ *noun* [U]

ovule /ˈɒvjuːl/ *noun* [C] **ANATOMY, BIOLOGY** in plants, the part inside the ovary (= organ that makes eggs) that contains the female sex cell and will develop into a seed

ovum /ˈəʊvəm/ *noun* [C] *plural* **ova** **ANATOMY, BIOLOGY** an egg in a female animal or plant that can grow into a baby or new plant

O━**owe** /əʊ/ *verb* [T] **1 FINANCE** to have to pay money back to someone [+ **two objects**] *You still owe me money.* ○ *He* **owes** *about £5000* **to** *the bank.* **2 owe sb an apology/favour/drink, etc** to have to give something to someone because they deserve it *I think I owe you an apology.* **3 owe your existence/success, etc to sb/sth** to have something or achieve something because of someone or something else *The museum owes much of its success to the present generation of young British artists.*

owing to /əʊɪŋ tuː/ *preposition* because of *The concert has been cancelled owing to lack of support.*

owl /aʊl/ *noun* [C] a bird that has large eyes and hunts small animals at night

O━**own**[1] /əʊn/ *adjective, pronoun, determiner* **1** belonging to or done by a particular person or thing *Each student has their own dictionary.* ○ *Petra makes all her own clothes.* ○ *"Is that your mum's car?" "No, it's my own* (= it belongs to me)*."* **2 of your own** belonging to someone or something *I'll have a home of my own* (= home belonging only to me) someday. **3 (all) on your own a** alone *Jessica lives on her own.* **b** If you do something on your own, you do it without any help from other people. *She's raised three kids on her own.* **4 come into your/its own** to be very useful or successful *By the 1970s, Abrams was starting to come into his own as a soloist.* **5 get your own back (on sb)** *UK* to do something unpleasant to someone because they have done something unpleasant to you **6 hold your own** to be as successful as other people or things *She could always hold her own in political debates.*

O━**own**[2] /əʊn/ *verb* [T] to have something that legally belongs to you *The University owns a lot of the land around here.*

own up *phrasal verb* to admit that you have done something wrong [+ **to** + **doing sth**] *No one has owned up to breaking that window.*

WORD PARTNERS FOR ***owner***

the **current/original/previous** owner • the owner **of** sth

O━**owner** /ˈəʊnəʳ/ *noun* [C] someone who legally owns something *a property owner* •**ownership** *noun* [U] when you own something

ox /ɒks/ *noun* [C] *plural* **oxen** a large, male cow, used especially in the past to pull farm vehicles

oxbow lake /ˌɒksbəʊˈleɪk/ *noun* [C] **GEOGRAPHY** a c-shaped lake that was in the past a bend in a river but became separated when the river stopped flowing round the bend and started flowing in a straight line

oxide /ˈɒksaɪd/ *noun* [C, U] **CHEMISTRY** a chemical combination of oxygen and one other element *iron oxide*

oxidize (*also UK* **-ise**) /ˈɒksɪdaɪz/ *verb* [T, I] **CHEMISTRY** If a substance oxidizes, it combines with oxygen and forms another substance, and if something oxidizes a substance, it causes it to do this. •**oxidation** /ˌɒksɪˈdeɪʃᵊn/ *noun* [U]

oxygen /ˈɒksɪdʒən/ *noun* [U] **CHEMISTRY** a gas that is in the air and that animals need to live (formula **O**)

oxygenate /ˈɒksɪdʒəneɪt/ *verb* [T] **PHYSICS, BIOLOGY, CHEMISTRY** to get oxygen into a substance *oxygenated blood* •**oxygenation** /ˌɒksɪdʒəˈneɪʃᵊn/ *noun* [U] ⊃See picture at **circulation**

ˈoxygen ˌdebt *noun* [C] **BIOLOGY** the extra oxygen that the body uses during exercise, which must be replaced when resting

oxyhaemoglobin *UK* (*US* **oxyhemoglobin**) /ˌɒksiˌhiːməʊˈgləʊbɪn/ *noun* [U] **BIOLOGY** the bright red form of haemoglobin (= substance in red blood cells) that contains oxygen

oxymoron /ˌɒksɪˈmɔːrɒn/ *noun* [C] **LANGUAGE** two words used together, which mean two different or opposite things, such as 'bitter-sweet' or 'smart casual'

oyster /ˈɔɪstəʳ/ *noun* [C] **FOOD** a sea creature that lives in a flat shell and is eaten as food

oz MEASURES *written abbreviation for* ounce (= a unit for measuring weight) *an 8 oz steak*

ozone /ˈəʊzəʊn/ *noun* [U] **CHEMISTRY** a form of oxygen that has a powerful smell (formula **Oz**)

the ˈozone ˌlayer *noun* **ENVIRONMENT** the layer of ozone high above the Earth's surface that prevents the sun from harming the Earth

O

Pp

P, p /piː/ the sixteenth letter of the alphabet

p. **1** *written abbreviation for* page *See diagram on p.135.* **2** **ECONOMICS** *abbreviation for* penny or pence (= units of British money) *a 20p coin* ➲See Common Learner Error at **pence**

PA /piːˈeɪ/ *UK abbreviation for* personal assistant: a person who organizes letters, meetings and telephone calls for someone with an important job

WORD PARTNERS FOR ***pace***

quicken/slow your pace • **at** a [blistering/brisk/leisurely, etc] pace • the pace **of** sth

pace¹ /peɪs/ *noun* **1** SPEED [**no plural**] the speed at which someone or something moves or does something *We started to walk at a much faster pace.* ○ *the* ***pace of*** *life* **2** STEP [**C**] a step *Every few paces I stopped to listen.* **3 keep pace with sb/sth** to move or develop at the same speed as someone or something else *We have to keep pace with the changing times.* ➲See also: at a **snail**'s pace

pace² /peɪs/ *verb* **1 pace about/up and down, etc** to walk around because you are worried or excited about something *He kept pacing up and down, glancing at his watch.* **2 pace yourself** to be careful not to do something too quickly so that you do not get too tired to finish it

pacemaker /ˈpeɪsˌmeɪkəʳ/ *noun* [**C**] **HEALTH** a small piece of medical equipment in someone's heart that makes it work at the correct speed

pachyderm /ˈpækɪdɜːm/ *noun* [**C**] **BIOLOGY** a type of large animal with thick skin and hooves (= hard parts on the feet), for example an elephant

pacifier /ˈpæsɪfaɪəʳ/ *US* (*UK* **dummy**) *noun* [**C**] a small rubber object that you give to a baby to suck in order to make it calm

pacifism /ˈpæsɪfɪzᵊm/ *noun* [**U**] **POLITICS** the belief that war or fighting of any type is wrong •**pacifist** /ˈpæsɪfɪst/ *noun* [**C**] someone who believes in pacifism

pacify /ˈpæsɪfaɪ/ *verb* [**T**] to do something in order to make someone less angry or upset *She smiled at Jamie to pacify him.*

O-■ **pack¹** /pæk/ *verb* **1** THINGS IN BAGS [**I, T**] to put your things into bags or boxes when you are going on holiday or leaving the place where you live *I've got to go home and pack.* ○ *to* ***pack your bags*** ➲Opposite **unpack** **2** CROWD [**T**] If people pack a place, there are so many of them in it that it is very crowded. *Thousands of fans packed the club.*

pack sth in *phrasal verb* **1** STOP *informal* to stop doing something *If this job doesn't get any better I'm going to* ***pack it in.*** **2** A LOT to manage to do a lot of things in a short period of time *We were only there four days but we packed so much in.*

pack sb off *phrasal verb informal* to send someone away *We were* ***packed off to*** *our grandparents' for the summer holidays.*

pack (sth) up *phrasal verb* to collect all your things together when you have finished doing something *I'm about to* ***pack*** *my* ***things up*** *and go home.*

pack² /pæk/ *noun* [**C**] **1** BOX *mainly US* a small box that contains several of the same thing *a pack of cigarettes* **2** BAG *mainly US* a bag that you carry on your back **3** ANIMALS a group of animals that live together, especially those of the dog family *a* ***pack of wolves*** **4** CARDS (*also US* **deck**) a set of playing cards ➲See also: **fanny pack**

package¹ /ˈpækɪdʒ/ *noun* [**C**] **1** PARCEL an object that is covered in paper, inside a box, etc, especially so that it can be sent somewhere **2** GROUP OF THINGS a group of objects, plans, or arrangements that are sold or considered together *a computer package* ○ *This ski package includes hotel, transport, and four days of skiing.* **3** BOX *US* a box or container in which something is put to be sold *a package of raisins/cookies*

package² /ˈpækɪdʒ/ *verb* [**T**] **1** IN A BOX to put something into a box or container so that it can be sold *It's neatly packaged in a blue and white box.* **2** SHOW to show someone or something in an attractive way so that people will like or buy them *What's important is the way we package the programme.*

ˌpackage ˈholiday *UK* (*UK/US* **ˈpackage ˌtour**) *noun* [**C**] a holiday that is arranged for you by a travel company and for which you pay a fixed price before you go

packaging /ˈpækɪdʒɪŋ/ *noun* [**U**] the paper, box, etc that something is inside so that it can be sold or sent somewhere ➲See picture at **CFC**

packed /pækt/ (*also UK* **packed out**) *adjective* very crowded *The hall was packed.*

ˌpacked ˈlunch *noun* [**C**] *UK* food that you put in a bag or box and take to eat at work, school, etc

packet /ˈpækɪt/ *UK* (*US* **pack**) *noun* [**C**] a small container that contains several of the same thing *a packet of cigarettes/sweets*

packing /ˈpækɪŋ/ *noun* [**U**] **1** THINGS IN BAGS when you put things into bags or boxes in order to take them somewhere *I've got to* ***do my packing*** *because I'm going tomorrow.* **2** PROTECTION paper, material, etc that you put around an object in a box so that it does not get damaged

WORD PARTNERS FOR ***pact***

have/make/sign a pact • a pact **between** sb **and** sb • a pact **with** sb

pact /pækt/ *noun* [**C**] an agreement between two people or groups *We* ***have a pact*** *never to talk about each other.*

pad¹ /pæd/ *noun* [**C**] **1** PAPER (*also US* **tablet**) sheets of paper that have been fastened together at one edge, used for writing or drawing *There's a pad and pencil by the phone.* **2** SOFT MATERIAL a small piece of soft material used to protect something or to make something more comfortable *knee/shin pads*

pad² /pæd/ *verb* **padding**, *past* **padded 1 pad about/around/down, etc** to walk somewhere with small, quiet steps *He padded downstairs and out of the front door.* **2** [T] to protect something or make something more comfortable by filling or surrounding it with soft material

pad sth out *phrasal verb* to make a piece of writing or a speech longer by adding more information to it

padding /'pædɪŋ/ *noun* [U] soft material that is used to fill or cover something to protect it or make it more comfortable

paddle¹ /'pædl/ *noun* **1** BOAT [C] a short pole with one flat end that you use to make a small boat move through the water **2** WALK [no plural] *UK* when you walk in water that is not deep *to go for a paddle*

paddle² /'pædl/ *verb* **1** BOAT [I, T] to move a small boat through water with a paddle **2** WALK [I] *UK* (*US* **wade**) to walk in water that is not deep **3** SWIM [I] *US* to swim using short, quick movements with your arms and legs

paddock /'pædək/ *noun* [C] **FARMING** a small field where animals are kept, especially horses

paddy field /'pædi,fi:ld/ *UK* (*UK/US* **rice paddy**) *noun* [C] **FARMING** a field in which rice is grown

padlock /'pædlɒk/ *noun* [C] a metal lock with a U-shaped part that is used for fastening bicycles, doors, etc •**padlock** *verb* [T]

paediatrician *UK* (*US* **pediatrician**) /,pi:diə'trɪʃən/ *noun* [C] **HEALTH** a children's doctor

pagan /'peɪgən/ *adjective* **RELIGION** relating to religious beliefs that do not belong to any of the main religions of the world *a pagan festival* •**pagan** *noun* [C] someone who has pagan religious beliefs

WORD PARTNERS FOR ***page***

turn a page • the **back/front** page • **on** page [25/36, etc.]

O★**page¹** /peɪdʒ/ *noun* [C] **1** a piece of paper in a book, magazine, etc, or one side of a piece of paper *The article is **on page** 36.* ○ *I've only read 50 pages so far.* **2 COMPUTING, INTERNET** (*also* **web page**) one part of a website that you can see or print separately ➲See also: **home page, the Yellow Pages**

page² /peɪdʒ/ *verb* [T] **1** ANNOUNCEMENT to call someone using a sound system in a public place **2** ELECTRONIC MESSAGE to send a message to someone's pager (= small piece of electronic equipment)

pageant /'pædʒənt/ *noun* [C] a show that happens outside in which people dress and act as if they are from a time in history

pageantry /'pædʒəntri/ *noun* [U] ceremonies in which there are a lot of people in special clothes

pager /'peɪdʒər/ *noun* [C] a small piece of electronic equipment that you carry which makes a noise or movement when someone sends a message

pagoda /pə'gəʊdə/ *noun* [C] **RELIGION** a tall religious building in Asia with many levels, each of which has a curved roof

paid /peɪd/ *past of* pay

pail /peɪl/ *noun* [C] a container with an open top and a handle used for carrying liquids

WORD PARTNERS FOR ***pain***

excruciating/severe/sharp/unbearable pain • **ease/inflict/relieve/suffer** pain • **in** pain

O★**pain¹** /peɪn/ *noun* **1** HURT [C, U] an unpleasant physical feeling caused by an illness or injury *chest/stomach pains* ○ *Are you **in pain**?* ○ *I felt a **sharp pain** in my foot.* **2** SADNESS [U] sadness or mental suffering caused by an unpleasant event *I can't describe the pain I suffered when he died.* **3 be a pain (in the neck)** *informal* to be annoying *My brother can be a real pain in the neck sometimes.* **4 be at pains to do sth; take pains to do sth** to make a lot of effort to do something *He was at great pains to explain the reasons for his decision.*

pain² /peɪn/ *verb* [T] *formal* If something pains you, it makes you feel sad or upset. [+ **to do sth**] *It pained him to see animals being treated so cruelly.*

pained /peɪnd/ *adjective* appearing to be sad or upset *a **pained expression***

O★**painful** /'peɪnfəl/ *adjective* **1** HURT causing physical pain *Recovery from the operation is a slow and painful process.* **2** SAD making you feel sad or upset *a painful memory*

painfully /'peɪnfəli/ *adverb* **1** WITH PAIN in a painful way *He landed painfully on his elbow.* **2 painfully clear/obvious, etc** If a problem is painfully clear/obvious, etc, it is embarrassing because it is so clear/obvious, etc. *It was painfully obvious that she didn't like him.* **3** VERY used to emphasize an unpleasant situation or quality *She's **painfully thin**.*

painkiller /'peɪn,kɪlər/ *noun* [C] **HEALTH** a drug which reduces pain

painless /'peɪnləs/ *adjective* **1** NO PAIN causing no physical pain *a painless death* **2** NO PROBLEMS causing no problems or difficulties *There is no painless way of learning a language.* •**painlessly** *adverb*

painstaking /'peɪnz,teɪkɪŋ/ *adjective* done with a lot of care *It took months of **painstaking research** to write the book.* •**painstakingly** *adverb*

O★**paint¹** /peɪnt/ *noun* [C, U] **DT** a coloured liquid that you put on a surface to decorate it *a gallon of blue paint* ○ *The door needs another **coat*** (= layer) ***of paint**.*

O★**paint²** /peɪnt/ *verb* **1** [T] **DT** to cover a surface with paint in order to decorate it *We've painted the kitchen yellow.* **2 ART, DT** [I, T] to produce a picture of something or someone using paint *These pictures were all painted by local artists.* ➲See also: paint a bleak/rosy, etc **picture**[1] of sth

paintbrush /'peɪntbrʌʃ/ *noun* [C] **ART, DT** a brush that is used for painting pictures or for painting surfaces such as walls and doors

painter /'peɪntər/ *noun* [C] **1 ART, DT** someone who paints pictures **2** someone whose job is to

P

paint surfaces, such as walls and doors *a painter and decorator*

WORD PARTNERS FOR ***painting***

do a painting • a painting **of** sth/sb • a painting **by** sb

painting /ˈpeɪntɪŋ/ *noun* **ART** **1** [C] a picture that someone has painted **2** [U] the activity of painting pictures or painting surfaces ➲See also: **oil painting**

pair¹ /peəʳ/ *noun* [C] **1** TWO THINGS two things that look the same and that are used together *a pair of socks/shoes* **2** TWO PARTS something that is made of two parts that are joined together *a pair of scissors* ○ *a new pair of jeans/trousers* **3** TWO PEOPLE two people who are doing something together *For the next exercise, you'll need to work **in pairs**.*

pair² /peəʳ/ *verb*

pair off *phrasal verb* If two people pair off, they begin a romantic or sexual relationship.

pair sb off with sb *phrasal verb* to introduce one person to another because you hope they will begin a romantic relationship *Caroline tried to pair me off with her sister.*

pair up *phrasal verb* to join another person for a short time in order to do something *I **paired up with** Chris for the last dance.*

pajamas /pəˈdʒɑːməz/ *noun* [**plural**] *US spelling of* pyjamas (= shirt and trousers that you wear in bed)

pal /pæl/ *noun* [C] *informal* a friend *He's an old pal of mine.*

palace /ˈpælɪs/ *noun* [C] a large house where a king or queen lives *Buckingham Palace*

palatable /ˈpælətəbl/ *adjective formal* **1** **FOOD** If food or drink is palatable, it has a pleasant taste. *a palatable local wine* **2** IDEA If an idea or plan is palatable, it is acceptable. *They need to make the project more palatable to local people.* ➲Opposite **unpalatable**

palate /ˈpælət/ *noun* [C] **1** **ANATOMY** the top part of the inside of your mouth ➲See picture at **alimentary canal** **2** the ability to judge and enjoy good food and drink

pale /peɪl/ *adjective* **1** **pale blue/green/red, etc** light blue/green/red, etc *a pale yellow dress* **2** If your face is pale, it has less colour than usual because you are ill or frightened.

palisade layer /ˌpælɪseɪdˈleɪəʳ/ *noun* [C] **BIOLOGY** a layer of long cells between two thin surface layers of a leaf, that contains a lot of chloroplasts (= parts of a cell where energy from the sun is turned into food) ➲See picture at **leaf**

pall¹ /pɔːl/ *verb* [I] to become less interesting and enjoyable *The pleasure of not having to work soon began to pall.*

pall² /pɔːl/ *noun* **1** **a pall of dust/smoke, etc** a thick cloud of dust/smoke, etc **2** **cast a pall over sth** If an unpleasant situation or piece of news casts a pall over an event, it spoils it. *The news of Nick's accident cast a pall over the celebrations.*

palm¹ /pɑːm/ *noun* [C] **1** **ANATOMY** the inside surface of your hand ➲See colour picture **The Body** on page Centre 13 **2** a palm tree

palm² /pɑːm/ *verb*

palm sb off *phrasal verb* to tell someone something that is not true so that they will stop asking questions *He **palmed** me **off with** an excuse about why he couldn't pay.*

palm sth off as sth *phrasal verb* to deceive people by saying that something has a particular quality or value that it does not have

palm sth off on sb *phrasal verb* to give or sell something to someone because you want to get rid of it *He palmed his old computer off on me.*

Palm /pɑːm/ *noun* [C] *trademark* **COMPUTING** a small computer that you can carry with you

palmate /ˈpælmeɪt/ *adjective* **BIOLOGY** describes leaves which all grow from the same point at the end of a stalk, in a hand-shape

palmtop /ˈpɑːmtɒp/ *noun* [C] **COMPUTING** a type of computer which is small enough to fit in your hand

ˈpalm ˌtree *noun* [C] a tall tree with long leaves at the top which grows in hot countries

palpable /ˈpælpəbl/ *adjective* very obvious *There was a palpable sense of tension in the crowd.*

paltry /ˈpɔːltri/ *adjective* A paltry amount of something, especially money, is very small. *a **paltry sum** of money*

pamper /ˈpæmpəʳ/ *verb* [T] to treat someone in a kind way and give them everything they want *She pampered herself with a trip to the beauty salon.*

pamphlet /ˈpæmflɪt/ *noun* [C] a very thin book with a paper cover that gives information about something *The tourist office gave me a pamphlet about places to visit in the city.*

pan¹ /pæn/ *noun* [C] a metal container with a handle that is used for cooking food in ➲See also: a **flash²** in the pan, **frying pan**

pan² /pæn/ *verb* [T] **panning**, *past* **panned** *informal* to criticize something severely [**often passive**] *His last novel was panned by the critics.*

pan out *phrasal verb* to develop in a particular way *Not all his ideas had panned out in the way he would have liked.*

panacea /ˌpænəˈsiːə/ *noun* [C] something that people believe can solve all their problems

panache /pəˈnæʃ/ *noun* [U] a confident and attractive way of doing things *The orchestra played with great panache.*

pancake /ˈpænkeɪk/ *noun* [C] **FOOD** a thin, flat food made from flour, milk, and egg mixed together and cooked in a pan

pancreas /ˈpæŋkriəs/ *noun* [C] **ANATOMY** an organ in the body that makes insulin (= a substance that controls the amount of sugar in the blood) and other substances which help to change food into a form that the body can use ➲See picture at **alimentary canal**

pancreˈaticˌ duct *noun* [**C usually singular**] **ANATOMY** in the human body, a tube in the pancreas that takes pancreatic juice into the small intestine (= upper tube of the bowels) ➲See picture at **alimentary canal**

pancreˈaticˌjuice *noun* [U] **BIOLOGY, ANATOMY** a watery liquid made in the pancreas which helps to change food into a form that the body can use

panda /ˈpændə/ *noun* [C] a large, black and white animal that lives in forests in China

pandemonium /ˌpændəˈməʊniəm/ *noun* [U] when there is a lot of noise and confusion because people are angry or excited about something that has happened ***Pandemonium broke out** in the courtroom as they took him away.*

pander /ˈpændəʳ/ *verb*
pander to sb/sth *phrasal verb* to do what someone wants although it is wrong *He said he would not pander to public pressure.*

P&P /ˌpiːənˈpiː/ *noun* [U] *UK abbreviation for* postage and packing

pane /peɪn/ *noun* [C] a flat piece of glass in a window or door

panel /ˈpænəl/ *noun* [C] **1** [PIECE] a flat, rectangular piece of wood, metal, etc that forms the surface of a door, wall, etc **2** [PEOPLE] a group of people who are chosen to discuss something or make a decision about something *a panel of experts* **3** [CONTROLS] the part of a car, aircraft, etc that the controls are fixed to ⊃See also: **solar panel**

panelling *UK* (*US* **paneling**) /ˈpænəlɪŋ/ *noun* [U] flat, rectangular pieces of wood that form the surface of walls, doors, etc *carved oak panelling*

panellist *UK* (*US* **panelist**) /ˈpænəlɪst/ *noun* [C] one of a group of people who are chosen to discuss something or make a decision about something

pang /pæŋ/ *noun* [C] a sudden, strong feeling of an unpleasant emotion *Bernard felt a sharp pang of jealousy.*

panhandle /ˈpænˌhændl/ *verb* [I] *US* to ask people for money in a public place •**panhandler** *noun* [C] *US*

WORD PARTNERS FOR ***panic***

be **in a** panic • panic **breaks out** • **absolute/blind** panic • panic **about/over** sth • do sth **in** panic • a panic **attack**

panic¹ /ˈpænɪk/ *noun* [C, U] a sudden, strong feeling of worry or fear that makes you unable to think or behave calmly *He was **in a panic** about his exams.* ○ *She had a **panic attack*** (= suddenly felt extreme panic) *in the supermarket.*

panic² /ˈpænɪk/ *verb* [I, T] **panicking**, *past* **panicked** to suddenly feel so worried or frightened that you cannot think or behave calmly, or to make someone feel this way *Don't panic, we've got plenty of time.*

panicky /ˈpænɪki/ *adjective* feeling worried or frightened

panic-stricken /ˈpænɪkˌstrɪkən/ *adjective* extremely frightened

panorama /ˌpænərˈɑːmə/ *noun* [C] a view of a wide area

panoramic /ˌpænərˈæmɪk/ *adjective* A panoramic view is very wide. *a **panoramic view** of the city*

pansy /ˈpænzi/ *noun* [C] a small garden flower with round petals which can be many different colours

pant /pænt/ *verb* [I] to breathe quickly and loudly because it is hot or because you have been running, etc

panther /ˈpænθəʳ/ *noun* [C] a large, black, wild cat

panties /ˈpæntiz/ *mainly US* (*UK* **knickers**) *noun* [**plural**] women's underwear that covers the bottom ⊃See Common Learner Error at **underwear** ⊃See colour picture **Clothes** on page Centre 9

pantomime /ˈpæntəmaɪm/ *noun* [C, U] a funny play performed in the UK around Christmas, based on traditional children's stories

pantry /ˈpæntri/ *noun* [C] **FOOD** a small room where food is kept

pants /pænts/ *noun* [**plural**] **1** [TROUSERS] *US* (*UK/US* **trousers**) a piece of clothing that covers the legs and has a separate part for each leg ⊃See colour picture **Clothes** on page Centre 8 **2** [UNDERWEAR] *UK* (*US* **underpants**) underwear that covers the bottom ⊃See Common Learner Error at **underwear**

ˈpant ˌsuit *US* (*UK* **trouser suit**) *noun* [C] a woman's jacket and trousers made of the same material

pantyhose /ˈpæntihəʊz/ *US* (*UK* **tights**) *noun* [**plural**] a piece of women's clothing made of very thin material that covers the legs and bottom

papa /pəˈpɑː/ *noun* [C] *old-fashioned another word for* father

the papacy /ˈpeɪpəsi/ *noun* **RELIGION** the position or authority of the Pope (= leader of the Roman Catholic Church)

papal /ˈpeɪpəl/ *adjective* **RELIGION** relating to the Pope (= leader of the Roman Catholic Church)

paparazzi /ˌpæpəˈrætsi/ *noun* [**plural**] photographers whose job is to follow famous people and take photographs of them for newspapers and magazines

O‒ **paper¹** /ˈpeɪpəʳ/ *noun* **1** [MATERIAL] [U] thin, flat material used for writing on, covering things in, etc *a piece/sheet of paper* **2** [NEWSPAPER] [C] a newspaper **3 EDUCATION** [C] *UK* an examination *Candidates must answer two questions from each paper.* **4** [WRITING] [C] a piece of writing about a particular subject written by someone who has been studying that subject *She's just published a paper on language acquisition.* ⊃See also: **blotting paper, carbon paper, toilet paper, White Paper, wrapping paper**

paper² /ˈpeɪpəʳ/ *verb* [T] to decorate the walls of a room by covering them with paper

paperback /ˈpeɪpəbæk/ *noun* [C] a book that has a soft paper cover

ˈpaper ˌclip *noun* [C] a small piece of metal used to hold several pieces of paper together ⊃See colour picture **The Office** on page Centre 5

ˈpaper ˌround *noun* [C] When someone does a paper round, they deliver newspapers to all the houses in a particular area.

papers /ˈpeɪpəz/ *noun* [**plural**] official documents *I keep all my papers safely locked away.*

ˈpaper ˌweight *noun* [C] a small, heavy object that you put on top of pieces of paper to stop them from moving

P

paperwork /ˈpeɪpəwɜːk/ *noun* [U] the part of a job that involves writing letters, organizing information, etc

par /pɑːʳ/ *noun* **1 be on a par with sb/sth** to be the same as or equal to someone or something **2 below par** not as good as usual *I'm feeling a bit below par today.* **3 be par for the course** If a type of behaviour, event, or situation is par for the course, it is not good but it is normal or as you would expect. *"Simon was late." "That's just par for the course, isn't it?"*

parable /ˈpærəbl/ *noun* [C] **LITERATURE, RELIGION** a short story, especially in the Bible, that shows you how you should behave

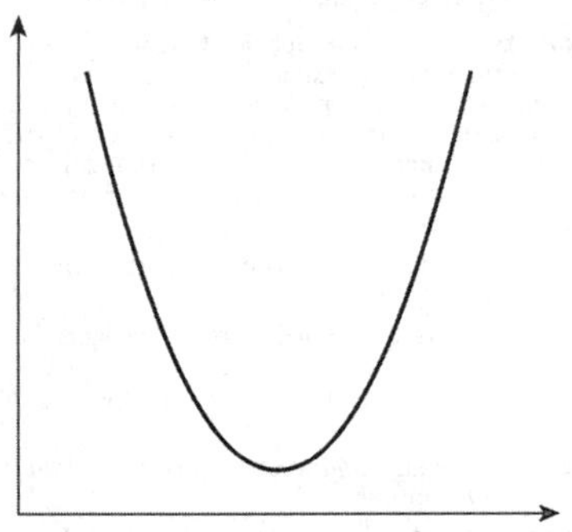

parabola

parabola /pəˈræbᵊlə/ *noun* [C] **MATHEMATICS** a type of curve such as that made by an object that is thrown up in the air and falls to the ground in a different place

paracetamol /ˌpærəˈsiːtəmɒl/ *noun* [C, U] **HEALTH** a common drug used to reduce pain and fever

parachute /ˈpærəʃuːt/ *noun* [C] a large piece of cloth which is fixed to your body by strings and helps you to drop safely from an aircraft •**parachute** *verb* [I] to jump from an aircraft using a parachute

parade¹ /pəˈreɪd/ *noun* [C] a line of people or vehicles that moves through a public place as a way of celebrating an occasion ***a victory parade***

parade² /pəˈreɪd/ *verb* **1 parade down/past/through sth** to walk as a group, usually to show disagreement about something *Thousands of workers paraded through the streets.* **2 parade around/up and down, etc** to walk somewhere so that people will see and admire you *The kids were parading around in their new clothes.* **3** [T] to try to make someone notice something that you are proud of, especially how rich you are or how much you know

paradigm /ˈpærədaɪm/ *noun* [C] *formal* a typical example or model of something *Career women are establishing a new paradigm of work and family life.*

paradise /ˈpærədaɪs/ *noun* **1 RELIGION** [no plural] in some religions, a place where good people go after they die **2** [C, U] a perfect place or situation *a tropical paradise* ○ *a shoppers' paradise*

paradox /ˈpærədɒks/ *noun* [C] a situation that seems very strange or impossible because of two opposite qualities or facts •**paradoxical** /ˌpærəˈdɒksɪkᵊl/ *adjective* involving a paradox •**paradoxically** *adverb*

paraffin /ˈpærəfɪn/ *UK* (*US* **kerosene**) *noun* [U] oil used for heating and lights

paragraph /ˈpærəgrɑːf/ *noun* [C] **LANGUAGE** a part of a text that contains at least one sentence and starts on a new line

parallel¹ /ˈpærəlel/ *adjective* **1 MATHEMATICS** If two or more lines are parallel, the distance between them is the same along all their length. *The streets are parallel.* **2** SIMILAR similar and happening at the same time *Parallel experiments are being conducted in both countries.*

WORD PARTNERS FOR ***parallel (noun)***

draw a parallel • a **clear/close/strong** parallel • a parallel **between** sth **and** sth • a parallel **with** sth

parallel² /ˈpærəlel/ *noun* [C] a similarity *There are a number of* ***parallels between*** *our two situations.* ○ *People are* ***drawing parallels*** (= describing similarities) *between the two cases.*

ˌparallel ˈcircuit *noun* [C] **PHYSICS** a circuit (= closed system of wires) in which the electric current passes through two or more connected parts at the same time before it combines again ➲Compare **series circuit**

parallelism /ˈpærəlelɪzm/ *noun* [no plural] **LANGUAGE** (in language) repeating the same pattern of words in different sentences

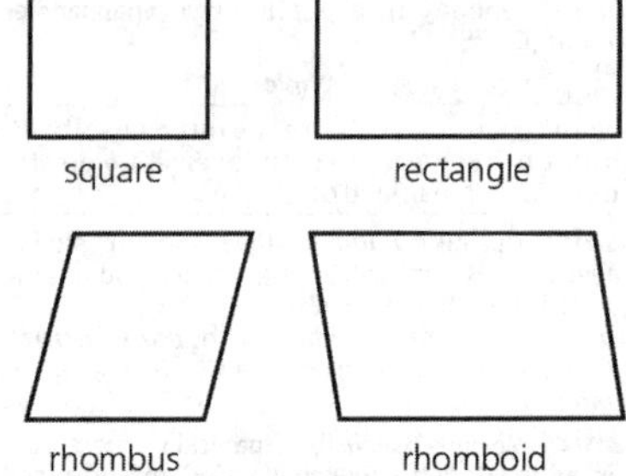

parallelograms

parallelogram /ˌpærəˈleləgræm/ *noun* [C] **MATHEMATICS** a flat shape which has four sides. The two sets of opposite sides are parallel and the same length as each other.

ˈparallel ˌport *noun* [C] **COMPUTING** a part of a computer where wires from other pieces of equipment such as a printer can be connected to it, sending information eight bits (= units of information) at a time ➲Compare **serial port**

the Paralympic Games /ðəˌpærəˌlɪmpɪkˈgeɪmz/ (also **Paralympics**) *noun* [plural] **SPORT** an international sports competition for people who have a disability (= a condition that makes it difficult for a person to do the things that other people do) **•Paralympic** *adjective* **•Paralympian** *noun* [C]

paralyse *UK* (*US* **paralyze**) /ˈpærəlaɪz/ *verb* [T] **1** **HEALTH** to make someone unable to move all or part of their body [**often passive**] *He was paralysed from the waist down by polio.* **2** to make something stop working *Rail strikes have paralysed the city's transport system.*

paralysed *UK* (*US* **paralyzed**) /ˈpærəlaɪzd/ *adjective* **1** **HEALTH** unable to move all or part of your body because of an injury or illness **2** unable to move or speak because you are so frightened *to be paralysed with fear*

paralysis /pəˈræləsɪs/ *noun* [U] **1** **HEALTH** being unable to move all or part of your body because of injury or illness *muscular paralysis* **2** not being able to take action *political paralysis*

paralyze /ˈpærəlaɪz/ *verb* [T] **HEALTH** *US spelling of* paralyse

paramedic /ˌpærəˈmedɪk/ *noun* [C] **HEALTH** someone who is trained to give medical treatment to people who are injured or very ill, but who is not a doctor or nurse

parameter /pəˈræmɪtəʳ/ *noun* [C] a limit that controls the way that you can do something [**usually plural**] *Before we can start the research we need to **set** some **parameters*** (= decide some limits).

paramilitaries /ˌpærəˈmɪlɪtəriz/ *noun* [**plural**] people who belong to paramilitary organizations

paramilitary /ˌpærəˈmɪlɪtəri/ *adjective* [**always before noun**] organized like an army, but not belonging to an official army *a **paramilitary** organization/group*

paramount /ˈpærəmaʊnt/ *adjective formal* more important than anything else *Safety, of course, is paramount.* ○ *Communication is **of paramount importance**.*

paranoia /ˌpærəˈnɔɪə/ *noun* [U] **1** FEAR when you wrongly think that other people do not like you and are always criticizing you *Do you think his boss really hates him or is it just paranoia?* **2** **HEALTH** a mental illness that makes people wrongly think that other people are trying to harm them **•paranoid** /ˈpærənɔɪd/ *adjective* when you have paranoia *Stop being so paranoid - no one's talking about you.*

paraphernalia /ˌpærəfəˈneɪliə/ *noun* [U] all the objects used in a particular activity *the painter's paraphernalia of brushes, paints, and pencils*

paraphrase /ˈpærəfreɪz/ *verb* [I, T] **LANGUAGE** to express something that has been said or written in a different way, usually so that it is clearer **•paraphrase** *noun* [C]

parasite /ˈpærəsaɪt/ *noun* [C] **1** **BIOLOGY** a plant or animal that lives on or inside another plant or animal in order to get food **2** a lazy person who expects other people to give them money and food

paratrooper /ˈpærətru:pəʳ/ *noun* [C] a soldier who is trained to be dropped from an aircraft using a parachute (= large piece of cloth fixed to the body by strings)

O⊸**parcel** /ˈpɑ:səl/ *noun* [C] something that is covered in paper so that it can be sent by post ➲See also: **part**[1] and parcel

parched /pɑ:tʃt/ *adjective* **1** **be parched** *informal* to be very thirsty *I'm going to get a drink - I'm parched.* **2** very dry *a parched desert/land*

pardon[1] /ˈpɑ:dən/ *exclamation* **1** (*also US* **pardon me**) a polite way of asking someone to repeat what they have just said *"You'll need an umbrella." "Pardon?" "I said you'll need an umbrella."* **2** **Pardon me.** used to say 'sorry' after you have done something rude, for example after burping (= letting air from your stomach out of your mouth)

pardon[2] /ˈpɑ:dən/ *noun* **1** [C] **LAW** when someone who has committed a crime is officially forgiven and allowed to be free **2** **I beg your pardon.** *formal spoken* **a** SORRY used for saying 'sorry' when you have made a mistake or done something wrong *I beg your pardon - I thought you were speaking to me.* **b** DISAGREEMENT/ANGER used to show that you strongly disagree or that you are angry about something that someone has said *I beg your pardon, young man - I don't want to hear you speak like that again!*

pardon[3] /ˈpɑ:dən/ *verb* [T] **LAW** to officially forgive someone who has committed a crime and allow them to be free

O⊸**parent** /ˈpeərənt/ *noun* [C] your mother or father *Her parents live in Oxford.* **•parental** /pəˈrentəl/ *adjective* relating to a parent *parental responsibility*

COMMON LEARNER ERROR

parents or **relations/relatives?**

Your **parents** are only your mother and father. The other people in your family are **relations** or **relatives**.

We spent the holidays visiting all our relatives.

~~*We spent the holidays visiting all our parents.*~~

ˈparent ˌcompany *noun* [C] **ECONOMICS** a company which controls other smaller companies

parentheses /pəˈrenθəsi:z/ (*also UK* **brackets**) *noun* [**plural**] **LANGUAGE** two curved lines ( ) used around extra information or information that should be considered as separate from the main part *The age of each student is listed **in parentheses**.* ➲See Extra help page **Punctuation** on page Centre 19.

parenthood /ˈpeərənthʊd/ *noun* [U] **SOCIETY** being a parent *the demands of parenthood*

parenting /ˈpeərəntɪŋ/ *noun* [U] **SOCIETY** the things that you do during the time when you take care of your baby or child

parish /ˈpærɪʃ/ *noun* [C] **RELIGION** an area that has its own church

parishioner /pəˈrɪʃənəʳ/ *noun* [C] **RELIGION** someone who lives in a parish and often goes to church

parity /ˈpærəti/ *noun* [U] *formal* equality, usually relating to the money people earn or their position *The union has also asked for wage **parity** with similar public-sector workers.* ➲Opposite **disparity**

O⊸**park**[1] /pɑ:k/ *noun* [C] a large area of grass, often in a town, where people can walk and enjoy themselves *We went for a walk in the park.*

P

⊃See also: **amusement park, car park, industrial park, national park, theme park, trailer park**

⊶**park²** /pɑːk/ *verb* [I, T] to leave a vehicle in a particular place for a period of time *I parked the car near the old bridge.* ○ *You can park outside the school.*

parking /ˈpɑːkɪŋ/ *noun* [U] leaving a vehicle in a particular place for a period of time *free/underground parking*

ˈparking ˌlot *US* (*UK* **car park**) *noun* [C] a place where vehicles can be parked

ˈparking ˌmeter *noun* [C] a device next to a road that you pay so that you can park your vehicle on that road

ˈparking ˌticket *noun* [C] a piece of paper that tells you that you must pay money because you have parked your car where you should not

WORD PARTNERS FOR ***parliament***

dissolve/elect a parliament • **enter** parliament • **in** parliament

⊶**parliament** /ˈpɑːləmənt/ *noun* [C, U] **POLITICS** in some countries, a group of people who make the laws for the country *the Russian parliament* •**parliamentary** /ˌpɑːləˈmentᵊri/ *adjective* [always before noun] relating to a parliament *a parliamentary candidate/election* ⊃See also: **Houses of Parliament, Member of Parliament**

parlour *UK* (*US* **parlor**) /ˈpɑːləʳ/ *noun* [C] a shop that provides a particular type of goods or services *a beauty/pizza parlour*

parody /ˈpærədi/ *noun* [C, U] a film, book, etc that copies someone else's style in a way that is funny *It's a parody of a low-budget 1950's horror movie.* •**parody** *verb* [T]

parole /pəˈrəʊl/ *noun* [U] **LAW** when someone is allowed to leave prison early but is only allowed to remain free if they behave well *He's hoping to get released **on parole**.*

parrot /ˈpærət/ *noun* [C] a tropical bird with a curved beak and colourful feathers that can be taught to copy what people say

parsimonious /ˌpɑːsɪˈməʊniəs/ *adjective formal* not willing to spend money or give something

parsley /ˈpɑːsli/ *noun* [U] **FOOD** a herb that is added to food to give it flavour

parsnip /ˈpɑːsnɪp/ *noun* [C] **FOOD** a long, cream-coloured root that is eaten as a vegetable

⊶**part¹** /pɑːt/ *noun* **1** NOT ALL [C, U] one of the things that, with other things, makes the whole of something ***Part of** this form seems to be missing.* ○ *I did French **as part of** my degree course.* ○ *It's **all part of** growing up.* ○ *You're part of the family.* **2 take part (in sth)** to be involved in an activity with other people *She doesn't usually take part in any of the class activities.* **3** FILM/PLAY [C] a person in a film or play *He **plays** the **part** of the father.* **4 have/play a part in sth** to be one of the people or things that are involved in an event or situation *Alcohol plays a part in 60 percent of violent crime.* **5** MACHINE [C] a piece of a machine or vehicle *aircraft parts* ○ ***spare parts*** **6** HAIR [C] *US* (*UK* **parting**) the line on your head made by brushing your hair in two different directions **7 the best/better part of sth** most of a period of time *It took the better part of the afternoon to put those shelves up.* **8 in part** *formal* partly *He is in part to blame for the accident.* **9 for the most part** mostly or usually *I enjoyed it for the most part.* **10 look the part** to look suitable for a particular situation *If you're going to be a successful businesswoman, you've got to look the part.* **11 part and parcel** If something is part and parcel of an experience, it is a necessary part of that experience and cannot be avoided. *Stress is part and parcel of the job.*

part² /pɑːt/ *adverb* not completely *She's part Irish and part English.*

part³ /pɑːt/ *verb* **1** SEPARATE [I, T] If two sides of something part, they become separated, and if you part them, you make them separate. *Slowly her lips parted and she smiled.* **2** LEAVE [I, T] *formal* If two people part, or if one person parts from another, they leave each other. *That summer, after six years of marriage, we parted.* ○ *Even after we **parted company**, we remained in contact.* **3** HAIR [T] to brush your hair in two directions so that there is a straight line showing on your head *In my school days, I had long hair parted in the middle.*

part with sth *phrasal verb* to give something to someone else, often when you do not want to *You know how hard it is to get Simon to part with his money.*

partial /ˈpɑːʃᵊl/ *adjective* **1** not complete *He made a partial recovery.* **2 be partial to sth** If you are partial to something, you like it. *I'm rather partial to red wine myself.*

partially /ˈpɑːʃᵊli/ *adverb* not completely *partially cooked*

WORD PARTNERS FOR ***participant***

an **active/unwilling** participant • a participant **in** sth

participant /pɑːˈtɪsɪpᵊnt/ *noun* [C] someone who is involved in an activity *All participants finishing the race will receive a medal.*

participate /pɑːˈtɪsɪpeɪt/ *verb* [I] to be involved with other people in an activity *She rarely **participates in** any of the discussions.* •**participation** /pɑːˌtɪsɪˈpeɪʃᵊn/ *noun* [U] *Both shows encourage **audience participation**.*

participle /pɑːˈtɪsɪpl/ ⓤⓢ /ˈpɑːtɪsɪpl/ *noun* [C] **LANGUAGE** the form of a verb that usually ends with '-ed' or '-ing' and is used in some verb tenses or as an adjective ⊃See also: **past participle, present participle**

particle /ˈpɑːtɪkl/ *noun* [C] **1** a very small piece of something *particles of dust* **2 PHYSICS, CHEMISTRY** a very small part of an atom, for example an electron or a proton

⊶**particular** /pəˈtɪkjələʳ/ *adjective* **1** ONE PERSON/THING [always before noun] used to talk about one thing or person and not others *Is there any particular restaurant you'd like to go to?* ○ *"Why did you ask?" "No particular reason."* **2** SPECIAL [always before noun] special *"Was anything important said at the meeting?" "Nothing of particular interest."* **3** NOT EASILY SATISFIED [never before noun] choosing things carefully and not easily satisfied *Teenagers are very* *particular about the clothes they'll wear.* **4 in particular** especially *Are you looking for anything in particular?*

O-- **particularly** /pə'tɪkjələli/ *adverb* especially *She didn't seem particularly interested.* ○ *"Was the food good?" "**Not particularly.**"*

particulars /pə'tɪkjələz/ *noun* [**plural**] *formal* details about something or someone *There's a form for you to note down all your particulars.*

parting[1] /'pɑːtɪŋ/ *noun* **1** SEPARATION [**C, U**] *formal* when you are separated from another person, often for a long time *The pain of parting gradually lessened over the years.* **2** HAIR [**C**] *UK* (*US* **part**) the line on your head made by brushing your hair in two different directions

parting[2] /'pɑːtɪŋ/ *adjective* **parting glance/words, etc** something that you do or say as you leave

partisan[1] /ˌpɑːtɪ'zæn/ (US) /'pɑːrtɪzən/ *adjective* **POLITICS** showing support for a particular political system or leader *partisan politics* ○ *a partisan crowd*

partisan[2] /ˌpɑːtɪ'zæn/ (US) /'pɑːrtɪzən/ *noun* [**C**] **POLITICS 1** someone who supports a particular political system or leader **2** a member of a group that secretly fights against soldiers who are controlling their country

partition /pɑː'tɪʃən/ *noun* **1** [**C**] a wall that divides a room into two parts **2 POLITICS** [**U**] when a country divides into two or more countries or areas of government •**partition** *verb* [**T**]

O-- **partly** /'pɑːtli/ *adverb* used to show that something is true to some degree but not completely *The house is partly owned by her father.* ○ *He was partly responsible.*

O-- **partner**[1] /'pɑːtnər/ *noun* [**C**] **1 SOCIETY** someone that you are married to or having a sexual relationship with *sexual partners* ○ *Are partners invited to the office dinner?* **2** SPORTS/DANCING someone that you are dancing or playing a sport or game with **3 ECONOMICS** someone who owns a business with another person *a **junior/senior partner*** ○ *He's a **partner in** a law firm.* **4 ECONOMICS, POLITICS** a country that has an agreement with another country *a **trading partner*** ○ *Britain and its European partners*

partner[2] /'pɑːtnər/ *verb* [**T**] to be someone's partner in a dance, sport, or game *He looks certain to partner him again in the finals.*

WORD PARTNERS FOR ***partnership***

enter into/go into partnership • be **in** partnership with sb • a partnership **between** sb and sb

partnership /'pɑːtnəʃɪp/ *noun* **1** WORKING TOGETHER [**C, U**] when two people or organizations work together to achieve something *She's **gone into partnership*** (= started to work together) *with an ex-colleague.* **2 ECONOMICS** [**C**] a company which is owned by two or more people

part-time /ˌpɑːt'taɪm/ *adjective, adverb* working or studying only for part of the day or the week *a **part-time job*** ○ *He **works part-time** as a waiter.*

WORD PARTNERS FOR ***party***

go to/have/throw a party • a **birthday/Christmas** party • be **at** a party

O-- **party**[1] /'pɑːti/ *noun* [**C**] **1** EVENT an event where people enjoy themselves by talking, eating, drinking, and dancing *a **birthday party*** ○ *We're **having a party** to celebrate the occasion.* **2 POLITICS** an organization that shares the same political beliefs and tries to win elections *a **political party*** **3** GROUP a group of people who are working or travelling together *a party of tourists* **4 LAW** one of the sides in a legal agreement or disagreement *the guilty party* ○ *We hope to provide a solution that is acceptable to both parties.* ⊃See also: **the Conservative Party, the Democratic Party, the Green Party, the Labour Party,** toe the (party) **line**[1], **the Republican Party, search party, slumber party, third party**

party[2] /'pɑːti/ *verb* [**I**] to enjoy yourself by talking, eating, drinking, and dancing with a group of people *They were out partying till five o'clock in the morning.*

O-- **pass**[1] /pɑːs/ *verb* **1** GO PAST [**I, T**] (*also* **pass by**) to go past something or someone *She passed me this morning in the corridor.* ○ *Cars kept passing us on the motorway.* **2 pass (sth) over/through, etc** to go in a particular direction, or to cause something to go in a particular direction *Another plane passed over our heads.* ○ *We pass through your village on the way home.* **3** GIVE [**T**] to give something to someone *Could you pass the salt, please?* ○ *He **passed** a note **to** her in the meeting.* **4** TIME [**I**] If a period of time passes, it happens. *Four years have passed since that day.* **5 pass (the) time** to spend time doing something *She was eating only to pass the time.* **6 EDUCATION** [**I, T**] to succeed at a test or an exam, or to decide that someone has been successful *I passed my driving test the first time.* **7** BE MORE THAN [**T**] to be more than a particular level *Donations have passed the one million mark.* **8 SPORT** [**I, T**] in sports, to throw or kick a ball to someone else *Edwards **passes to** Brinkworth.* **9 pass a law/motion, etc LAW** to officially approve of something and make it into a law or rule *They passed a law banning the sale of alcohol.* **10** GO AWAY [**I**] If a feeling passes, it goes away. *I know he's angry now but it'll pass.* **11 pass judgment** to judge someone's behaviour **12 pass sentence LAW** If a judge passes sentence, they state what the criminal's punishment will be. **13 let sth pass** to decide not to criticize someone when they say something unpleasant or they make a mistake ⊃See also: pass the **buck**[1]

pass sth around/round *phrasal verb* to offer something to each person in a group of people *Take a copy for yourself and pass the rest around.*

pass as/for sth/sb *phrasal verb* If someone or something passes as or for someone or something else, they appear like that person or thing. *She's fifteen but could easily pass for eighteen.*

pass away *phrasal verb* to die *She passed away peacefully in her sleep.*

pass sth down *phrasal verb* to teach or give something to someone who will be alive after you have died [**often passive**] *Folk tales have*

P

been passed down from generation to generation.

pass sth/sb off as sth/sb *phrasal verb* to pretend that something or someone is different from what they really are *He tried to pass himself off as some sort of expert.*

pass on *phrasal verb* to die

pass sth on *phrasal verb* **1** TELL to tell someone something that someone else has told you *Did you pass on my message to him?* **2** GIVE to give something to someone else *Could you pass it on to Laura when you've finished reading it?* **3 HEALTH** to give a disease to another person *The virus can be passed on through physical contact.*

pass out *phrasal verb* **HEALTH** to become unconscious *I don't remember any more because I passed out at that point.*

pass sth up *phrasal verb* to not use an opportunity to do something interesting *It's a great opportunity - you'd be a fool to pass it up.*

pass² /pɑːs/ *noun* [C] **1 EDUCATION** a successful result in a test or a course *A pass is above 60%.* **2** DOCUMENT an official document that allows you to do something *a bus/rail pass* ○ *You need a pass to get into the building.* **3 SPORT** in sports, when you throw or kick a ball to someone else **4 GEOGRAPHY** a narrow path between two mountains *a mountain pass* ➲See also: **boarding pass**

passage /ˈpæsɪdʒ/ *noun* **1** SPACE [C] (*also* **passageway** /ˈpæsɪdzweɪ/) a long, narrow space that connects one place to another *There's a passage to the side of the house, leading to the garden.* **2 MUSIC, LITERATURE** [C] a short part of a book, speech, or piece of music *She can quote whole passages from the novel.* **3 ANATOMY, BIOLOGY** [C] a tube in your body that allows air, liquid, etc to pass through it *the nasal/respiratory passages* **4** PROGRESS [**U, no plural**] the movement or progress from one stage or place to another *It's a difficult passage from boyhood to manhood.* **5 the passage of time** *literary* the way that time passes *Love changes with the passage of time.*

passenger /ˈpæsəndʒəʳ/ *noun* [C] someone who is travelling in a vehicle, but not controlling the vehicle *a front-seat passenger*

passer-by /ˌpɑːsəˈbaɪ/ *noun* [C] *plural* **passers-by** someone who is walking past something by chance *Police were alerted by a passer-by who saw the accident.*

passing¹ /ˈpɑːsɪŋ/ *adjective* [**always before noun**] lasting only for a short time and not important ***a passing interest***

passing² /ˈpɑːsɪŋ/ *noun* **1 the passing of time/years** the way that time passes *With the passing of time their love had changed.* **2 in passing** If you say something in passing, you talk about one thing briefly while talking mainly about something else. *She mentioned in passing that she'd seen Stuart.*

passion /ˈpæʃən/ *noun* **1** SEX [U] a strong, sexual feeling for someone *She saw the passion in his eyes.* **2** BELIEF [C, U] a strong belief in something or a strong feeling about a subject *She spoke with passion about the injustice.* **3 a passion for sth** when you like something very much *a passion for football*

passionate /ˈpæʃənət/ *adjective* **1** SEX having a strong, sexual feeling for someone *a passionate affair/lover* **2** BELIEF showing a strong belief in something or a strong feeling about a subject *a passionate speaker* •**passionately** *adverb*

passive /ˈpæsɪv/ *adjective* **1** letting things happen to you and not taking action *Women at that time were expected to be passive.* **2 LANGUAGE** A passive verb or sentence is one in which the subject does not do or cause the action but is affected by it. For example 'He was released from prison.' is a passive sentence.

the passive /ˈpæsɪv/ (*also* **the ˌpassive ˈvoice**) *noun* **LANGUAGE** the passive form of a verb

ˌpassive imˈmunity *noun* [U] **HEALTH** when people or animals get antibodies (= substances in the blood that fight disease) from someone else, for example from the mother's milk

ˌpassive ˈsmoking *noun* [U] **HEALTH** breathing in smoke from other people's cigarettes

Passover /ˈpɑːsˌəʊvəʳ/ *noun* [U] **RELIGION** the Jewish period of religious celebration held in March or April

WORD PARTNERS FOR ***passport***

apply for a passport • **have/hold** a [British/Japanese, etc] passport • a **valid** passport

O➡**passport** /ˈpɑːspɔːt/ *noun* **1 LAW** [C] an official document, often a small book, that you need to enter or leave a country *a British passport* **2 a passport to sth** something that allows you to achieve something else *Education is a passport to a better life.*

WORD PARTNERS FOR ***password***

enter /put in your password • a **secret** password • **forget** a password • **change** a password

password /ˈpɑːswɜːd/ *noun* [C] **COMPUTING** a secret word that allows you to do something, such as use your computer

O➡**past¹** /pɑːst/ *adjective* **1** BEFORE NOW [**always before noun**] having happened or existed before now *past relationships* ○ *I know this from past experience.* **2** UNTIL NOW [**always before noun**] used to refer to a period of time before and until the present *It's been raining for the past three days.* **3** FINISHED [**never before noun**] Something that is past has now finished. *My student days are past.* **4 past tense LANGUAGE** the form of the verb which is used to show what happened in the past

O➡**past²** /pɑːst/ *noun* **1 the past a** the time before the present and all the things that happened then ***In the past*** *people would bathe once a month.* **b LANGUAGE** the form of the verb which is used to show what happened in the past **2 sb's past** all of the things that someone has done in their life *I knew nothing about his past.*

O➡**past³** /pɑːst/ *adverb, preposition* **1** FURTHER further than *I live on Station Road, just past the Post Office.* **2** UP TO AND FURTHER up to and further than someone or something *Three boys went past us on mountain bikes.* ○ *I've just seen the bus go past.* **3** AFTER HOUR used to say 'after' the hour when you are saying what time it is *It's five past three.* **4** AFTER LIMIT after a particular time or age limit *This bacon is past its sell-by date.* **5 past it** *informal* too old to do something **6 I wouldn't put it past sb (to do sth)** *informal* used to say that you would not be surprised if someone did something, especially something bad, because it is a typical thing for them to do *I wouldn't put it past him to sell her jewellery.*

pasta /ˈpæstə/ (US) /ˈpɑːstə/ *noun* [U] **FOOD** a food that is made from flour, water, and sometimes eggs and is made in many different shapes ➲See colour picture **Food** on page Centre 11

paste¹ /peɪst/ *noun* [C, U] **1 DT** a soft, wet, sticky substance that is used to stick things together *wallpaper paste* **2 FOOD** a soft food that spreads easily *tomato/almond paste*

paste² /peɪst/ *verb* **1** [T] **DT** to stick a piece of paper to another piece of paper *The cuttings had been pasted into a scrapbook.* **2 COMPUTING** [I, T] to move a piece of text to a particular place in a computer document ➲See also: **cut and paste**

pastel /ˈpæstᵊl/ (US) /pæsˈtel/ *adjective* A pastel colour is light. ***pastel colours/shades*** ○ *pastel pink* •**pastel** *noun* [C] *The bedroom is decorated in pastels* (= pale colours).

pastime /ˈpɑːstaɪm/ *noun* [C] an activity that you enjoy doing when you are not working *Shopping is one of her **favourite pastimes**.*

pastor /ˈpɑːstəʳ/ *noun* [C] **RELIGION** a priest in some Protestant churches

pastoral /ˈpɑːstᵊrᵊl/ *adjective* **1 SOCIETY** related to giving advice and looking after people *the teacher's **pastoral role*** **2** [always before noun] *literary* relating to life in the country *a pastoral song/tradition*

ˌpast parˈticiple *UK* (*US* **ˌpast ˈparticiple**) *noun* [C] **LANGUAGE** the form of a verb that usually ends with '-ed' and can be used in the perfect tense, the passive tense, or as an adjective. For example 'baked' is the past participle of 'bake'.

the ˌpast ˈperfect (*also* **the pluperfect**) *noun* **LANGUAGE** the form of a verb that is used to show that an action had already finished when another action happened. In English, the past perfect is made with 'had' and a past participle.

pastry /ˈpeɪstri/ *noun* **1 FOOD** [U] a mixture of flour, fat, and water that is cooked, usually used to cover or contain other food **2 FOOD** [C] a small cake that is made with pastry

pasture /ˈpɑːstʃəʳ/ *noun* [C] **FARMING** an area of land with grass where animals can feed

pat¹ /pæt/ *verb* [T] **patting**, *past* **patted** to touch a person or animal with a flat hand in a gentle, friendly way *She stopped to pat the dog.*

pat² /pæt/ *noun* **1** [C] when you pat a person or animal *He gave her an encouraging **pat on** the shoulder.* **2 a pat on the back** praise for something good that someone has done *I got a pat on the back for all my hard work.*

patch¹ /pætʃ/ *noun* [C] **1** AREA a small area that is different from the area around it *a **bald patch**.* ○ *There are **icy patches** on the road.* **2** MATERIAL a piece of material that you use to cover a hole in your clothes or in other material *He had leather patches sewn on the elbows of his jacket.* **3 HEALTH** a small piece of material used to cover an injured eye **4** LAND a small area of land used for a particular purpose *a cabbage/vegetable patch* **5 a bad/rough, etc patch** a difficult time *I think their marriage is going through a bad patch.* **6 not be a patch on sb/sth** *UK informal* to not be as good as someone or something else *Her cooking is okay but it's not a patch on yours.*

patch² /pætʃ/ *verb* [T] to repair a hole in a piece of clothing or other material by sewing a piece of material over it *to patch your trousers*

patch sth up *phrasal verb* to try to improve your relationship with someone after you have had an argument *Has he managed to patch things up with her?*

patchwork /ˈpætʃwɜːk/ *noun* **1** [U] **DT** a type of sewing in which a lot of small pieces of different material are sewn together *a **patchwork quilt*** **2 a patchwork of sth** something that seems to be made of many different pieces *We flew over a patchwork of fields.*

patchy /ˈpætʃi/ *adjective* **1** NOT COMPLETE not complete or not good in every way *a **patchy knowledge** of Spanish* **2** IN SOME AREAS existing only in some areas ***patchy clouds/fog***

patent¹ /ˈpeɪtᵊnt, ˈpætᵊnt/ *noun* [C] **LAW** a legal right that a person or company receives to make or sell a particular product so that others cannot copy it •**patent** *verb* [T] to get a patent for something

patent² /ˈpeɪtᵊnt, ˈpætᵊnt/ *adjective formal* **patent lie/nonsense** something that is obviously false *The explanation he gave - that was patent nonsense.* •**patently** *adverb formal Her claims are patently* (= obviously) *false.*

paternal /pəˈtɜːnᵊl/ *adjective* **1** like a father *paternal affection* **2 SOCIETY** [always before noun] A paternal relative is part of your father's family. *He was my paternal grandfather.*

paternity /pəˈtɜːnəti/ *noun* [U] **SOCIETY** the state of being a father

paˈternity ˌleave *noun* [U] a period of weeks or months that a father spends away from his usual job so that he can look after his baby or child

path /pɑːθ/ *noun* [C] **1** GROUND a long, narrow area of ground for people to walk along *There's a path through the forest.* ○ *a **garden path*** **2** DIRECTION the direction that a person or vehicle moves in *a **flight path*** **3** CHOOSING a particular way of doing something over a period of time *a **career path*** ○ *Whichever path we choose, we'll have difficulties.*

pathetic /pəˈθetɪk/ *adjective* **1** BAD *informal* showing no skill, effort, or bravery *He made a rather **pathetic attempt** to apologize.* ○ *You're too frightened to speak to her? Come on, that's pathetic!* ○ *It was a pathetic performance.* **2** SAD sad and weak *Four times the pathetic little creature fell to the ground.* •**pathetically** *adverb a pathetically small amount of money*

paˌthetic ˈfallacy *noun* [U, no plural] **LANGUAGE** (in art and literature) when animals and things are described as if they have human emotions or qualities

P

pathogen /ˈpæθədʒən/ *noun* [C] **BIOLOGY** any small living thing that can cause disease *a dangerous pathogen*

pathological /ˌpæθəˈlɒdʒɪkəl/ *adjective* **1** Pathological behaviour or feelings are extreme and cannot be controlled. *a **pathological liar** ○ **pathological hatred*** **2** **HEALTH** relating to pathology (= the study of disease)

pathologist /pəˈθɒlədʒɪst/ *noun* [C] **HEALTH** a doctor who has studied pathology, especially one who tries to find out why people have died

pathology /pəˈθɒlədʒi/ *noun* [U] **HEALTH** the scientific study of disease and causes of death

pathos /ˈpeɪθɒs/ *noun* [U] *literary* a quality in a situation that makes you feel sympathy and sadness

WORD PARTNERS FOR ***patience***

have/run out of patience • **lose** (your) patience • **test/try** sb's patience • sth **takes** patience • patience **with** sb/sth

O‑**patience** /ˈpeɪʃəns/ *noun* [U] **1** BEHAVIOUR the quality of being able to stay calm and not get angry, especially when something takes a long time *Finally, I **lost** my **patience** and shouted at her. ○ Making small scale models **takes a lot of patience**.* ⊃Opposite **impatience** **2** CARD GAME *UK* (*US* **solitaire**) a card game for one person

O‑**patient**[1] /ˈpeɪʃənt/ *adjective* having patience *You need to be **patient with** children.* •**patiently** *adverb* ⊃Opposite **impatient**

O‑**patient**[2] /ˈpeɪʃənt/ *noun* [C] **HEALTH** someone who is being treated by a doctor, nurse, etc *a cancer patient*

patio /ˈpætiəʊ/ *noun* [C] an outside area with a stone floor next to a house, where people can sit to eat and relax

patriot /ˈpeɪtriət/ *noun* [C] **POLITICS** someone who loves their country and is proud of it

patriotic /ˌpeɪtriˈɒtɪk/ *adjective* **POLITICS** showing love for your country and pride in it *patriotic duty ○ a patriotic song* •**patriotism** /ˈpeɪtriətɪzəm/ *noun* [U] when you love your country and are proud of it

patrol[1] /pəˈtrəʊl/ *noun* **1** ACT [C, U] the act of looking for trouble or danger around an area or building *We passed a group of soldiers **on patrol**. ○ a patrol boat/car* **2** SOLDIERS [C] a group of soldiers or vehicles that patrol an area or building *a border patrol ○ an armed patrol*

patrol[2] /pəˈtrəʊl/ *verb* [I, T] **patrolling**, *past* **patrolled** to look for trouble or danger in an area or around a building *Police patrol the streets night and day.*

patron /ˈpeɪtrən/ *noun* [C] **1** SUPPORTER someone who supports and gives money to artists, writers, musicians, etc *a generous patron ○ a patron of the arts* **2** CUSTOMER a customer at a bar, restaurant, or hotel

patronize (*also UK* **-ise**) /ˈpætrənaɪz/ *verb* [T] **1** BEHAVIOUR to speak or behave towards someone as if you were better than them *Don't patronize me! I know what I'm doing.* **2** GO OFTEN *formal* to go to a store, business, etc, especially if you go regularly

ˌpatron ˈsaint *noun* [C] **RELIGION** a saint (= a special, famous Christian) who is believed to help a particular place, person, or activity *St. Christopher is the patron saint of travellers.*

WORD PARTNERS FOR ***pattern***

alter/establish/fall into/follow a pattern • a **consistent/familiar/traditional** pattern

O‑**pattern** /ˈpætən/ *noun* [C] **1** a particular way that something is often done or repeated *behaviour patterns* **2** **ART** a design of lines, shapes, colours, etc **3** **ART** a drawing or shape that helps you to make something *a dress pattern*

O‑**pause** /pɔːz/ *verb* [I] to stop doing something for a short time *She **paused for** a moment and looked around her.* •**pause** *noun* [C] *There was a short pause before he spoke.*

pave /peɪv/ *verb* [T] to cover a path or road with flat stones, bricks, concrete, etc

pavement /ˈpeɪvmənt/ *noun* [C] **1** PATH *UK* (*US* **sidewalk**) a path by the side of a road that people walk on *It's illegal to park on the pavement.* **2** HARD SURFACE *US* the hard surface of a road

pavilion /pəˈvɪljən/ *noun* [C] **1** TENT a large tent that is used for outside events **2** **SPORT** *UK* a building next to a sports field where players can change their clothes **3** BUILDING *US* one of a group of related buildings, such as a hospital

paw /pɔː/ *noun* [C] **BIOLOGY** the foot of certain animals, such as cats and dogs •**paw** (*also* **paw at**) *verb* [T] to touch something with a paw *I could hear the dog pawing at the door.*

pawn[1] /pɔːn/ *noun* [C] **1** CHESS in the game of chess, the smallest piece and the one that has the lowest value **2** PERSON someone who does not have power and is used by other people

pawn[2] /pɔːn/ *verb* [T] **FINANCE** to leave something with a pawnbroker, who gives you money for it and will sell it if you do not pay the money back *She pawned her wedding ring to pay the rent.*

pawnbroker /ˈpɔːnˌbrəʊkər/ *noun* [C] **FINANCE** someone who lends you money in exchange for items that they will sell if you cannot pay the money back

O‑**pay**[1] /peɪ/ *verb past* **paid** **1** BUY [I, T] to give money to someone because you are buying something from them, or because you owe them money *Helen **paid for** the tickets. ○ Did you **pay** the telephone **bill**? ○ You can pay by cash or credit card.* **2** WORK [I, T] to give someone money for the work that they do *She **gets paid** twice a month. ○ People work for them because they pay well.* [+ **two objects**] *We **paid** them £600 **for** the work. ○ a paid job* **3** ADVANTAGE [I] to be a good thing to do because it gives you money or an advantage *Crime doesn't pay.* **4** SUFFER [I, T] to suffer because of something bad you have done *He's certainly **paying for** his mistakes.* **5** **pay attention** to look at or listen to someone or something carefully *I missed what she was saying because I wasn't paying attention.* **6** **pay sb a compliment** to tell someone that you admire something about them **7** **pay tribute to sb/sth** to thank someone or say that you admire someone or something, especially in public *He paid tribute to his former teacher.*

8 pay sb/sth a visit; pay a visit to sb/sth to visit a place or a person, usually for a short time

COMMON LEARNER ERROR

pay for something

Remember that when **pay** means give money to buy something, it is usually followed by the preposition **for**.

Rachel paid for the meal.

~~*Rachel paid the meal.*~~

pay sb/sth back *phrasal verb* **FINANCE** to pay someone the money that you owe them *Only borrow money if you're sure you can pay it back.* ○ *I lent him £10 last month and he still hasn't paid me back.*

pay sth off *phrasal verb* **FINANCE** to pay all of the money that you owe *I'm planning to pay off my bank loan in five years.*

pay (sth) out *phrasal verb* **FINANCE** to spend a lot of money on something, or to pay a lot of money to someone *I've just paid out £700 to get the car fixed.*

pay up *phrasal verb informal* **FINANCE** to give someone all of the money that you owe them, especially when you do not want to *Come on, pay up!*

WORD PARTNERS FOR ***pay***

a pay **cheque/cut/raise/rise** • **rates of** pay

pay² /peɪ/ *noun* [U] **FINANCE** the money you receive from your employer for doing your job *(UK) a **pay rise**/ (US) a **pay raise*** ○ *good **rates of pay***

COMMON LEARNER ERROR

pay, wage, salary, or **income?**

Pay is a general word which means the money that you receive for working.

Doctors usually get more pay than teachers.

A **wage** is an amount of money you receive each day or week. It is often paid in cash (= notes and coins).

His weekly wage is $400.

A **salary** is the money you receive each month. A person's **salary** is often expressed as the total amount in a year.

His salary is £20,000.

Your **income** is the total amount of money that you earn by working or investing money.

She has a monthly income of £1,300.

payable /ˈpeɪəbl/ *adjective* **1 FINANCE** describes something to be paid *Rent is payable monthly.* **2 FINANCE** If a cheque (= a piece of paper printed by a bank that you use to pay for things) is payable to a person, that person's name is written on the cheque and the money will be paid to them.

pay-as-you-go /ˌpeɪəzjəˈɡəʊ/ *adjective* [always before noun] **FINANCE** describes a system in which you pay for a service before you use it *a pay-as-you-go mobile phone* •**pay-as-you-go** *noun* [U]

ˈpay ˌchannel *noun* [C] a television channel (= a broadcasting company) that you pay money to watch *Most of the best football matches are on the pay channels.*

ˈpay ˌcheck *noun* [C] *US* **FINANCE** pay cheque

ˈpay ˌcheque *noun* [C] **FINANCE** the amount of money a person earns

payday /ˈpeɪdeɪ/ *noun* [C] **FINANCE** the day on which a worker is paid

WORD PARTNERS FOR ***payment***

make/receive payment • a **form/method** of payment • payment **for/of** sth

O‑**payment** /ˈpeɪmənt/ *noun* **1 FINANCE** [U] the act of paying *They will accept payment by credit card.* **2 FINANCE** [C] the amount of money that is paid *monthly payments* ⊃See also: **balance of payments, down payment**

pay-per-view /ˌpeɪpəˈvjuː/ *noun* [U] a system in which you choose particular television programmes and then pay to watch them ***pay-per-view television/channels***

ˈpay ˌphone *noun* [C] a telephone in a public place that you pay to use

PC¹ /ˌpiːˈsiː/ *noun* [C] **1 COMPUTING** a personal computer **2** *UK abbreviation for* police constable (= a police officer of the lowest rank)

PC² /ˌpiːˈsiː/ *adjective* **POLITICS** *abbreviation for* politically correct (= careful to speak or behave in a way which is not offensive to women, people of a particular race, or people who have physical or mental problems)

PDA /ˌpiːdiːˈeɪ/ *noun* [C] **COMPUTING** *abbreviation for* personal digital assistant: a small computer that you can carry with you

PDF /ˌpiːdiːˈef/ *abbreviation* **COMPUTING 1** [U] portable document format: a system for storing and moving documents between computers that usually only allows them to be looked at or printed **2** [C] a document using the PDF system

PE /ˌpiːˈiː/ *noun* [U] **SPORT** *abbreviation for* physical education: classes at school where children do exercise and play sport

pea /piː/ *noun* [C] **FOOD** a small, round, green seed that people eat as a vegetable

WORD PARTNERS FOR ***peace***

bring about/establish/restore peace • **keep** the peace • the peace **process** • a peace **agreement/initiative/treaty**

O‑**peace** /piːs/ *noun* [U] **1** NO VIOLENCE when there is no war, violence, or arguing ***peace talks*** ○ *a **peace agreement/treaty*** ○ *There seems little hope for world peace.* ○ *The UN sent troops to the region to **keep the peace**.* **2** QUIET when there is quiet and calm *a feeling of peace* ○ *After a busy day, all I want is **peace and quiet**.* ○ *I wish you'd stop complaining and **leave me in peace**!* **3 peace of mind** a feeling that you do not need to worry about anything *We lock our doors and windows at night for peace of mind.* ⊃See also: **Justice of the Peace**

O‑**peaceful** /ˈpiːsfᵊl/ *adjective* **1** NO VIOLENCE without violence *a peaceful protest* **2** QUIET quiet and calm *The churchyard was empty and peaceful.* •**peacefully** *adverb He died peacefully at home.*

peacekeeping /ˈpiːsˌkiːpɪŋ/ *adjective* [always before noun] **POLITICS** relating to the activity of preventing war and violence ***peacekeeping forces****/troops* ○ *a **peacekeeping effort/***

P

operation •**peacekeeper** /ˈpiːsˌkiːpəʳ/ *noun* [C] someone, usually a soldier, who tries to prevent war and violence in countries where there is trouble *UN peacekeepers*

peacetime /ˈpiːstaɪm/ *noun* [U] a time when a country is not at war

peach /piːtʃ/ *noun* [C] **FOOD** a soft, sweet, round fruit with red and yellow skin

peacock /ˈpiːkɒk/ *noun* [C] a large, male bird with long tail feathers that it can lift up to show a lot of colours

peak[1] /piːk/ *noun* [C] **1** the highest level or value of something *Here we see an athlete* ***at the peak of*** *fitness.* ○ *The price of gold* ***reached its peak*** *during the last recession.* ○ ***peak travel times*** **2 GEOGRAPHY** the top of a mountain, or the mountain itself ***snow-covered/mountain peaks***

peak[2] /piːk/ *verb* [I] to reach the highest level or value of something *Her singing career peaked in the 1990s.*

peanut /ˈpiːnʌt/ *noun* [C] **FOOD** an oval-shaped nut with a soft, brown shell *salted peanuts* ○ *peanut oil* ➲See colour picture **Food** on page Centre 11

ˌpeanut ˈbutter *UK* (*US* **ˈpeanut ˌbutter**) *noun* [U] **FOOD** a pale brown food made by crushing peanuts *a peanut butter and jelly sandwich*

pear /peəʳ/ *noun* [C] **FOOD** an oval-shaped, pale green or yellow fruit ➲See colour picture **Fruit and Vegetables** on page Centre 10

pearl /pɜːl/ *noun* [C] a hard, white, round object that is made inside the shell of an oyster (= a sea creature) and that is used to make jewellery *a string of pearls* ○ *a pearl necklace* ○ *pearl earrings*

pear-shaped /ˈpeəʃeɪpt/ *adjective* **go pear-shaped** *UK informal* If a plan goes pear-shaped, it fails.

peasant /ˈpezᵊnt/ *noun* [C] **SOCIETY** a poor person who works on the land, usually in a poor country *a peasant farmer*

peat /piːt/ *noun* [U] **FARMING** a dark brown soil made from decaying plants that you can burn as fuel or that you can put around living plants to help them grow

pebble /ˈpebl/ *noun* [C] **GEOLOGY** a small stone

pecan /ˈpiːkæn/ Ⓤⓢ /pɪˈkɑːn/ *noun* [C] **FOOD** a nut that grows on a tree, or the tree itself *chopped pecans* ○ *pecan pie*

peck[1] /pek/ (*also* **peck at**) *verb* [T] If a bird pecks something, it lifts or hits it with its beak. *chickens pecking at corn*

peck[2] /pek/ *noun* [C] **1 give sb a peck on the cheek** to give someone a quick, gentle kiss on the face **2** when a bird pecks something

peckish /ˈpekɪʃ/ *adjective UK* slightly hungry

ˈpectoralˌ fin *noun* [C] **BIOLOGY** one of the fins (= parts used for swimming) on each side of a fish near the front of its body

peculiar /pɪˈkjuːliəʳ/ *adjective* **1** strange, often in an unpleasant way *The wine had a peculiar, musty smell.* **2 peculiar to sb/sth** belonging to or relating to a particular person or thing *Her accent is peculiar to the region.*

peculiarity /pɪˌkjuːliˈærəti/ *noun* [C] **1** [TYPICAL THING] something that is typical of a person, place, or thing *Each college has its own traditions and peculiarities.* **2** [STRANGE THING] a strange or unusual characteristic *My mother always hummed - it was one of her little peculiarities.*

peculiarly /pɪˈkjuːliəli/ *adverb* **1** [TYPICAL] in a way that is typical of someone or something *a peculiarly American sense of humour* **2** [STRANGE] in a strange way *The birds were peculiarly quiet just before the earthquake.*

pedagogue /ˈpedəgɒg/ *noun* [C] *formal* **EDUCATION** a teacher, usually a very strict one

pedal /ˈpedᵊl/ *noun* [C] a part of a machine that you press with your foot to operate or move the machine *bicycle pedals* ○ *a* ***gas/brake pedal***

pedant /ˈpedᵊnt/ *noun* [C] someone who thinks too much about details and rules •**pedantic** /pɪˈdæntɪk/ *adjective* thinking too much about details and rules *I hate to be pedantic, but Freud was actually Austrian, not German.*

peddle /ˈpedl/ *verb* [T] to sell things, especially drugs or things of bad quality *The shops on the pier peddled cheap souvenirs to the tourists.* ○ *He was arrested for peddling drugs.*

pedestal /ˈpedɪstᵊl/ *noun* [C] **1** the base for a statue (= model of a person or animal) **2 put sb on a pedestal** to believe that someone is perfect

pedestrian[1] /pɪˈdestriən/ *noun* [C] a person who is walking and not travelling in a vehicle *Many streets are reserved for cyclists and pedestrians.* ○ *a pedestrian precinct/crossing*

pedestrian[2] /pɪˈdestriən/ *adjective formal* ordinary or not interesting *pedestrian ideas* ○ *a pedestrian speech*

peˌdestrian ˈcrossing *UK* (*US* **crosswalk**) *noun* [C] a special place on a road where traffic must stop if people want to cross

pediatrician /ˌpiːdiəˈtrɪʃᵊn/ *noun* [C] **HEALTH** *US spelling of* paediatrician

pedicure /ˈpedɪkjʊəʳ/ *noun* [C, U] when someone makes your feet look attractive by cleaning and cutting your nails ➲Compare **manicure**

pedigree[1] /ˈpedɪgriː/ *noun* [C] **1** [LIST] a list of the parents and other relatives of an animal **2 SOCIETY** someone's family history, or their education and experience

pedigree[2] /ˈpedɪgriː/ *adjective* [**always before noun**] A pedigree animal has parents and other relatives all from the same breed and is thought to be of high quality. *a pedigree dog*

pee /piː/ *verb* [I] **peeing**, *past* **peed** *informal* to urinate •**pee** *noun* [**no plural**] *informal Do I have time for a pee before we go?*

peek[1] /piːk/ *verb* [I] to look at something for a short time, often when you do not want other people to see you *I peeked out the window to see who was there.*

peek[2] /piːk/ *noun* **have/take a peek** to look at something for a short time

peel¹ /piːl/ *verb* **1 FOOD** [T] to remove the skin of fruit or vegetables *Peel and chop the onions.* **2** [I, T] If you peel something from a surface, you remove it and if something peels, it comes away from a surface. *The paint is starting to* ***peel off*** *where the wall is damp.* ⊃See also: keep your eyes (**eye**¹) open/peeled (for sb/sth)
peel sth off *phrasal verb* to take off clothes, especially wet or tight clothes *We peeled off our muddy socks and left them outside.*

peel² /piːl/ *noun* [U] **FOOD** the skin of fruit or vegetables, especially after it has been removed *Combine nuts, sugar, and orange peel in a small bowl.*

peep /piːp/ *verb* [I] **1 peep at/ through/out, etc** to look at something for a short time, often when you do not want other people to see you *She peeped at them through the fence.* **2 peep through/over/out from, etc** to appear but not be seen completely *The sun peeped out from behind the clouds.* •**peep** *noun* [no plural] *She* ***took a peep*** *at herself in the mirror.*

peer¹ /pɪəʳ/ *noun* [C] **1 SOCIETY** someone who is the same age, or who has the same social position or abilities as other members of a group *Most teenagers want to be accepted by their peers.* **2 POLITICS** in the UK, a person who has a title and a high social position

peer² /pɪəʳ/ *verb* **peer at/into/through, etc** to look carefully or with difficulty *She peered at me over her glasses.*

ˈpeer ˌgroup *noun* [C] **SOCIETY** a group of people of about the same age, social position, etc *He was the first of his peer group to get married.*

ˈpeer ˌpressure *noun* [U] **SOCIETY** strong influence on a member of a group to behave in the same way as other members in the group, although that behaviour is not good *Many teenagers take drugs because of boredom or peer pressure.*

peg¹ /peg/ *noun* [C] **1** ON WALL an object on a wall or door that you hang things on **2** ON ROPE (*also* **clothes peg**) *UK* a short piece of wood, plastic, etc that is used to hold clothes on a rope while they dry **3** STICK a stick made of metal or wood that has a sharp end and which is used to fix something somewhere *a tent peg*

peg² /peg/ *verb* [T] **pegging**, *past* **pegged ECONOMICS** to fix the cost of borrowing money or the value of a country's money at a particular level [**often passive**] *Interest rates were* ***pegged at*** *8.2 %.*

pellet /ˈpelɪt/ *noun* [C] a small, hard ball of metal, grain, etc *shotgun/feed pellets*

pelvic /ˈpelvɪk/ *adjective* [**always before noun**] **ANATOMY** relating to the area below your waist and above your legs

pelvis /ˈpelvɪs/ *noun* [C] **ANATOMY** the group of bones that forms the area below your waist and above your legs and to which your leg bones are joined

O-- **pen¹** /pen/ *noun* [C] **1** WRITING TOOL a long, thin object that you use to write or draw in ink ⊃See colour picture **The Classroom** on page Centre 6 **2 FARMING** a small area with a fence around it that you keep animals in *a pig/sheep pen* ⊃See also: **ballpoint pen, felt-tip pen, fountain pen**

pen² /pen/ *verb* [T] **penning**, *past* **penned** *literary* to write something *sonnets penned by Shakespeare*
pen sb/sth in/up *phrasal verb* to keep people or animals in a small area [**often passive**] *The soldiers were penned up in their barracks.*

penal /ˈpiːnᵊl/ *adjective* [**always before noun**] **LAW** relating to the punishment of criminals *a* ***penal code/system***

penalize (*also UK* **-ise**) /ˈpiːnᵊlaɪz/ *verb* [T] **1** CAUSE DISADVANTAGE to cause someone a disadvantage *The present tax system penalizes poor people.* **2 LAW** to punish someone for breaking a law or a rule *He was penalized early in the match for dangerous play.*

WORD PARTNERS FOR ***penalty***

face a penalty • a **heavy/severe/stiff** penalty • a penalty **for** (doing) sth

penalty /ˈpenᵊlti/ *noun* [C] **1 LAW** a punishment for doing something which is against a law or rule *There's a £50* ***penalty for*** *late cancellation of tickets.* **2 SPORT** in sports, an advantage given to a team when the opposing team has broken a rule *They won a penalty in the first five minutes of the game.* ○ *a* ***penalty goal/kick*** ⊃See also: **death penalty**

penance /ˈpenəns/ *noun* [C, U] **RELIGION** an act that shows you are sorry for something that you have done

pence /pens/ *noun* **ECONOMICS** plural of British penny; p

COMMON LEARNER ERROR

pence, pennies, or **p?**

Pence is the usual plural of penny (UK) and is used to talk about amounts of money. In informal UK English you can also say **p**.

Can you lend me 50 pence?

Can you lend me 50p?

The plural form **pennies** is only used to talk about the coins as objects.

He found some pennies in his pocket.

penchant /ˈpɒnʃɒŋ/ (US) /ˈpentʃənt/ *noun* **have a penchant for sth** *formal* to like something very much *Miguel has a penchant for fast cars.*

O-- **pencil** /ˈpensᵊl/ *noun* [C, U] **ART** a long, thin wooden object with a black or coloured point that you write or draw with ⊃See colour picture **The Classroom** on page Centre 6

ˈpencil ˌsharpener *noun* [C] a tool that you use to make pencils sharp ⊃See colour picture **The Classroom** on page Centre 6

pendant /ˈpendənt/ *noun* [C] a piece of jewellery on a chain that you wear around your neck

pending¹ /ˈpendɪŋ/ *preposition formal* used to say that one thing must wait until another thing happens *Several employees have been suspended pending an investigation.*

pending² /ˈpendɪŋ/ *adjective formal* not decided or finished *Their court case is still pending.*

P

pendulum /ˈpendjələm/ *noun* [C] a heavy object on a chain or stick that moves from side to side, especially inside a large clock

penetrate /ˈpenɪtreɪt/ *verb* **1** MOVE INTO [I, T] If something penetrates an object, it moves into that object. *The bullet penetrated his skull.* **2** SUCCEED IN MOVING [T] If someone penetrates a place or a group, they succeed in moving into or joining it. *No one in our industry has successfully penetrated the Asian market.* •**penetration** /ˌpenɪˈtreɪʃən/ *noun* [U]

penetrating /ˈpenɪtreɪtɪŋ/ *adjective* **1** INTELLIGENT intelligent and full of careful thought *a penetrating discussion/mind* ○ *She wrote a penetrating analysis of Shakespeare's Hamlet.* **2 a penetrating gaze/look/stare, etc** If someone gives you a penetrating look, you feel as if they know what you are thinking. **3** STRONG If a sound is penetrating, it is very strong and unpleasant. *a penetrating voice/scream*

peneˈtration ˌpricing *noun* [U] **FINANCE** when a business gives a low price to its product so that people start to buy it, often increasing it later

penguin /ˈpeŋgwɪn/ *noun* [C] a large, black and white sea bird that swims and cannot fly

penicillin /ˌpenɪˈsɪlɪn/ *noun* [U] **HEALTH** a type of medicine that kills bacteria and is used to treat illness

peninsula /pəˈnɪnsjələ/ *noun* [C] **GEOGRAPHY** a long, thin piece of land which has water around most of it *the Korean peninsula*

penis /ˈpiːnɪs/ *noun* [C] **ANATOMY** the part of a man's or male animal's body that is used for urinating and having sex

penitentiary /ˌpenɪˈtenʃəri/ *noun* [C] **LAW** a prison in the US

pennant /ˈpenənt/ *noun* [C] a long, pointed flag

penniless /ˈpeniləs/ *adjective* having no money

penny /ˈpeni/ *noun* [C] *plural* **pence** or **p** or **pennies 1 ECONOMICS** a coin or unit of money with a value of 1/100 of a pound (= UK unit of money); p *There are 100 pence in a pound.* ○ *fifty pence/50p* ➲See Common Learner Error at **pence 2 ECONOMICS** a coin with a value of one cent (= 1/100 of a dollar) *My dad always let us have his pennies to buy candy.* **3 every penny** all of an amount of money *He seemed intent on spending every penny of his salary.*

WORD PARTNERS FOR ***pension***

get/be on/receive a pension • a pension **fund/plan/scheme** • a **state/private** pension

pension¹ /ˈpenʃən/ *noun* [C] **FINANCE** money that is paid regularly by the government or a private company to a person who has stopped working because they are old or ill *a state/private pension* ○ *a pension plan/scheme* •**pensioner** *noun* [C] *mainly UK* someone who receives a pension ➲See also: **old-age pension, old-age pensioner**

pension² /ˈpenʃən/ *verb*
pension sb off *phrasal verb* **FINANCE** *mainly UK* If an organization pensions someone off, it forces that person to leave their job but pays them a pension.

pentagon /ˈpentəgən/ *noun* [C] **MATHEMATICS** a shape with five sides and five angles

the Pentagon /ˈpentəgɒn/ *noun* **POLITICS** the department of the US government that controls the army, navy, etc, or the building where it is *The Pentagon refused to comment on potential military targets.*

penthouse /ˈpenthaʊs/ *noun* [C] *plural* **penthouses** /ˈpenthaʊzɪz/ an expensive apartment at the top of a building

pent-up /ˌpentˈʌp/ *adjective* [**always before noun**] Pent-up feelings are feelings that you have not expressed for a long time. *pent-up anger*

penultimate /pəˈnʌltɪmət/ *adjective* [**always before noun**] *formal* next to the last *Y is the penultimate letter of the alphabet.*

O-- **people¹** /ˈpiːpl/ *noun* **1** [**plural**] more than one person *Our company employs over 400 people.* ○ *People live much longer than they used to.* **2 the people SOCIETY** all the ordinary people in a country *The rebels have gained the support of the people.* **3 SOCIETY** [C] *formal* all the people of a race *Europe is made up of many different peoples.*

people² /ˈpiːpl/ *verb*
be peopled by/with sb *phrasal verb literary* to be filled with a particular kind of person *His novels are peopled with angry young men.*

ˈpeople ˌcarrier *UK* (*US* **minivan**) *noun* [C] a large, high car which can carry more people than a normal car

pepper¹ /ˈpepəʳ/ *noun* **FOOD 1** [U] a black, grey, or red powder that is made from crushed seeds, used to give food a slightly spicy flavour *salt and pepper* **2** [C] a hollow green, red, or yellow vegetable *green/red pepper* ➲See colour picture **Fruit and Vegetables** on page Centre 10

pepper² /ˈpepəʳ/ *verb*
pepper sth with sth *phrasal verb* to include a lot of something [**often passive**] *His speech was peppered with quotations.*

peppermint /ˈpepəmɪnt/ *noun* **FOOD 1** [U] oil from a plant that is added to food to give it a strong, fresh taste, or the taste itself *peppermint tea* **2** [C] a small, hard sweet that tastes like peppermint

pepsin /ˈpepsɪn/ *noun* [U] **CHEMISTRY** an enzyme (= substance made by living cells) in the stomach that helps to change protein (= substance found in meat, cheese, eggs, etc.) to a form that the body can use

peptide /ˈpeptaɪd/ *noun* [C] **CHEMISTRY** a chemical that is made of two or more amino acids (= the substances which combine to form protein)

per *strong form* /pɜːʳ/ *weak form* /pəʳ/ *preposition* for each *Our hotel room costs $60 per night.* ○ *The speed limit is 100 kilometres per hour.* ○ *The wedding dinner will cost £30* ***per head*** (= for each person).

per annum /pɜːrˈænʌm/ *adverb formal* every year *a salary of $19,000 per annum*

per capita /pɜːˈkæpɪtə/ *adjective, adverb formal* for each person *This county has the lowest per capita income in the country.* ○ *Belgians eat* *more chocolate per capita than any other nation in Europe.*

perceive /pə'siːv/ *verb* [T] *formal* **1** THINK to think of something or someone in a particular way [**often passive**] *The British are often perceived as being very formal.* **2** NOTICE to notice something that is not easy to notice *We perceived a faint light in the distance.*

O━ **percent** (*also* **per cent**) /pə'sent/ *adjective, adverb* **MATHEMATICS** for or out of every 100, shown by the symbol % *a 40 percent increase in prices* •**percent** (*also* **per cent**) *noun* [C] *Nearly 70 percent of all cars in the UK are less than five years old.*

WORD PARTNERS FOR ***percentage***

a **high/large/small** percentage • the percentage **of** sth

percentage /pə'sentɪdʒ/ *noun* [C] **MATHEMATICS** an amount of something, expressed as a number out of 100 *The **percentage of** women who work has risen steadily.* ○ *The **percentage of** people who are left-handed is small - only about 10%.*

perceptible /pə'septəbl/ *adjective formal* just able to be noticed *a **perceptible difference** in colour* ○ *His pulse was barely perceptible.*

perception /pə'sepʃᵊn/ *noun* **1** BELIEF [C] what you think or believe about someone or something *The **public perception** of him as a hero is surprising.* **2** NOTICE [U] the ability to notice something *Alcohol reduces your perception of pain.*

perceptive /pə'septɪv/ *adjective* quick to notice or understand things *a perceptive writer*

perch[1] /pɜːtʃ/ *verb* **1 perch (sth) on/in/above, etc** to be in a high position or in a position near the edge of something, or to put something in this position [**often passive**] *The village was perched on the side of a mountain.* ○ *She wore glasses perched on the end of her nose.* **2 perch on/in, etc** to sit near the edge of something *The children perched on the edges of their seats.*

perch[2] /pɜːtʃ/ *noun* [C] a place where a bird sits, especially a stick inside a cage

percolate /'pɜːkᵊleɪt/ *verb* [I] If a liquid percolates, it moves slowly through a substance that has very small holes. *Sea water percolates down through the rocks.*

percussion /pə'kʌʃᵊn/ *noun* [U] **MUSIC** musical instruments that make a sound when you hit them with a stick or your hand *Drums, tambourines, and cymbals are percussion instruments.*

perennial[1] /pᵊr'eniəl/ *adjective* happening again and again, or continuing for a long time *the perennial problem of unemployment*

perennial[2] /pᵊr'eniəl/ *noun* [C] a plant that lives for several years

perestroika /ˌperə'strɔɪkə/ *noun* [U] **POLITICS** the political, social and economic changes which happened in the USSR during the late 1980s

OTHER WAYS OF SAYING ***perfect***

If something is perfect because it has no mistakes or anything bad, then you can use adjectives such as **faultless**, **flawless**, **immaculate**, and **impeccable**: *They gave a **faultless/immaculate** performance.* • *His English is **impeccable**.* • *She has a **flawless** complexion.*

The adjectives **ideal** and **tailor-made** are sometimes used to describe something that is perfect for a particular purpose: *The book is **ideal** for children aged between four and six.* • *It sounds as if she's **tailor-made** for the job.*

In informal situations, if you want to describe something such as a job, house, etc, which is perfect for you, you can use the expression **dream job**, **dream home**, etc: *A pretty cottage in the Suffolk countryside - that would be my **dream home**.*

O━ **perfect**[1] /'pɜːfɪkt/ *adjective* **1** WITHOUT FAULT without fault, or as good as possible *James is a perfect husband and father.* ○ *Her performance was perfect.* **2** SUITABLE exactly right for someone or something *You'd be **perfect for** the job.* ○ *The weather's just perfect for a picnic.* **3** TO EMPHASIZE [**always before noun**] used to emphasize a noun *His suggestion makes perfect sense.*

perfect[2] /pə'fekt/ *verb* [T] to make something as good as it can be *I've spent hours perfecting my speech.*

perfection /pə'fekʃᵊn/ *noun* [U] when someone or something is perfect *She strives for perfection in everything she does.* ○ *chicken legs cooked to perfection*

perfectionist /pə'fekʃənɪst/ *noun* [C] someone who wants everything to be perfect

O━ **perfectly** /'pɜːfɪktli/ *adverb* **1** TO EMPHASIZE used to emphasize the word that follows it *To be perfectly honest, I don't care any more.* ○ *I made it perfectly clear to him what I meant.* **2** VERY WELL in a perfect way *The jacket fits perfectly, the skirt not so well.*

the perfect /'pɜːfɪkt/ (*also* **the ˌperfect 'tense**) *noun* **LANGUAGE** the form of the verb that is used to show an action that has happened in the past or before another time or event. In English, the perfect is made with 'have' and a past participle. ⊃See also: **the future perfect, the past perfect, the present perfect**

perforated /'pɜːfəreɪtɪd/ *adjective* **1** WITH HOLES Perforated materials such as paper have small holes in them so that they can be torn or liquid can pass through them. **2** **HEALTH** If an organ of your body is perforated, it has a hole in it. *a perforated eardrum* •**perforate** *verb* [T]

O━ **perform** /pə'fɔːm/ *verb* **1** ENTERTAIN [**I, T**] to entertain people by acting, singing, dancing, etc *She has performed all over the world.* ○ *The orchestra will perform music by Mozart.* **2** DO [T] *formal* to do a job or a piece of work *In the future, many **tasks** will be **performed** by robots.* ○ *Surgeons **performed** the **operation** in less than two hours.* **3 perform well/badly, etc** If something performs well, badly, etc, it works that way. *These cars perform poorly at high speeds.*

WORD PARTNERS FOR *performance*

give/put on a performance • a **brilliant/virtuoso/wonderful** performance

performance /pə'fɔːməns/ *noun* **1** ENTERTAINMENT [C] acting, singing, dancing, or playing music to entertain people *a performance of Shakespeare's Hamlet* **2** SUCCESS [U] how successful someone or something is *The company's performance was poor for the first two years.* ○ *Some athletes take drugs to improve their performance.*

performer /pə'fɔːməʳ/ *noun* [C] someone who entertains people

the per,forming 'arts *noun* [plural] **EDUCATION** types of entertainment that are performed in front of people, such as dancing, singing, and acting

perfume /'pɜːfjuːm/ *noun* [C, U] a liquid with a pleasant smell that women put on their skin •**perfumed** *adjective* containing perfume

perhaps /pə'hæps/ *adverb* **1** POSSIBLY possibly *Perhaps I'll go to the gym after work.* ○ *Ben won't be coming but perhaps it's better that way.* **2** USED TO SUGGEST used when you want to suggest or ask someone something *Perhaps you should leave now.*

pericarp /'perɪkɑːp/ *noun* [C usually singular] **BIOLOGY** the layer which grows around the seed of a plant and forms the skin and flesh of the fruit

peril /'perᵊl/ *noun* [C, U] *formal* extreme danger *A shortage of firefighters is putting lives **in peril**.* ○ *His book describes **the perils of** war.*

perilous /'perᵊləs/ *adjective formal* very dangerous *a perilous journey* •**perilously** *adverb*

perimeter /pə'rɪmɪtəʳ/ *noun* [C] **MATHEMATICS** the outer edge of an area *the perimeter of the airport*

period /'pɪəriəd/ *noun* [C] **1** a length of time *a 24-hour period* ○ *a period of four months* **2** **EDUCATION** one of the equal parts of time that a school day or sports game is divided into **3** **BIOLOGY** when blood comes out of a woman's uterus each month **4** **LANGUAGE** US (UK **full stop**) a mark (.) used at the end of a sentence, or to show that the letters before it are an abbreviation ➲See Extra help page **Punctuation** on page Centre 18.

periodic /,pɪəri'ɒdɪk/ *adjective* happening regularly *Our sales team makes periodic trips to Asia.* •**periodically** *adverb*

periodical /,pɪəri'ɒdɪkᵊl/ *noun* [C] a magazine about a particular subject

the ,Periodic 'Table *noun* [no plural] **CHEMISTRY** a list of the symbols of all the chemical elements arranged in rows and columns down a page

peripheral¹ /pə'rɪfᵊrᵊl/ *adjective* not as important as someone or something else

peripheral² /pə'rɪfᵊrᵊl/ *noun* [C] **COMPUTING** a piece of equipment, such as a printer, that can be connected to a computer

periphery /pə'rɪfᵊri/ *noun* [C] the outer edge of an area *The soldiers were camped **on the periphery** of the village.*

perish /'perɪʃ/ *verb* [I] *literary* to die *Hundreds of people perished in the flood.*

perishable /'perɪʃəbl/ *adjective* **FOOD** Food that is perishable goes bad very quickly.

peristalsis /,perɪ'stælsɪs/ *noun* [U] **BIOLOGY** the repeated movements made in the tube that carries food away from the stomach, which push food and waste through the body

perjury /'pɜːdʒᵊri/ *noun* [U] **LAW** the crime of telling a lie in a court of law *The witness was accused of **committing perjury**.*

perk¹ /pɜːk/ *noun* [C] an advantage, such as money or a car, that you are given because of your job [usually plural] *A mobile phone is one of the perks of the job.*

perk² /pɜːk/ *verb*

perk (sb) up *phrasal verb* to start to feel happier, or to make someone feel happier *A cup of coffee always perks me up in the morning.*

perm /pɜːm/ *noun* [C] the use of chemicals on someone's hair to make it have curls for several months, or the hair style that is made in this way *I'm thinking of **having a perm**.* •**perm** *verb* [T]

permanence /'pɜːmᵊnəns/ *noun* [U] when something continues forever or for a long time

permanent /'pɜːmᵊnənt/ *adjective* continuing forever or for a long time *permanent damage* ○ *a permanent job* •**permanently** *adverb He moved here permanently in 1992.*

permeable /'pɜːmiəbl/ *adjective* **PHYSICS, BIOLOGY, GEOLOGY** If a substance is permeable, it allows liquids or gases to go through it. ➲Opposite **impermeable**

permeate /'pɜːmieɪt/ *verb* [T] *formal* to move gradually into every part of something *The pungent smell of vinegar permeated the air.* ○ *Drug dealers have permeated every level of society.*

permissible /pə'mɪsəbl/ *adjective formal* allowed by the rules [+ **to do sth**] *It is not permissible to smoke inside the building.*

WORD PARTNERS FOR *permission*

ask for/give/grant/obtain/receive/refuse/seek permission • permission **for** sth

permission /pə'mɪʃᵊn/ *noun* [U] when you allow someone to do something *She **gave** him **permission** without asking any questions.* [+ **to do sth**] *He has permission to stay in the country for one more year.* ○ *They even have to **ask for permission** before they go to the toilet.* ○ *He took the car **without permission**.*

permissive /pə'mɪsɪv/ *adjective* allowing people to behave in ways which other people may not approve of *permissive attitudes*

permit¹ /pə'mɪt/ *verb* **permitting**, *past* **permitted** **1** ALLOW [T] *formal* to allow something [**often passive**] *Photography is not permitted inside the museum.* [+ **to do sth**] *He permitted them to leave.* **2** MAKE POSSIBLE [I] to make something possible *The match starts at 3 p.m., **weather permitting**.*

permit² /'pɜːmɪt/ *noun* [C] an official document that allows you to do something *a **work permit*** ○ *You need a permit to park your car here.*

pernicious /pə'nɪʃəs/ *adjective formal* very harmful

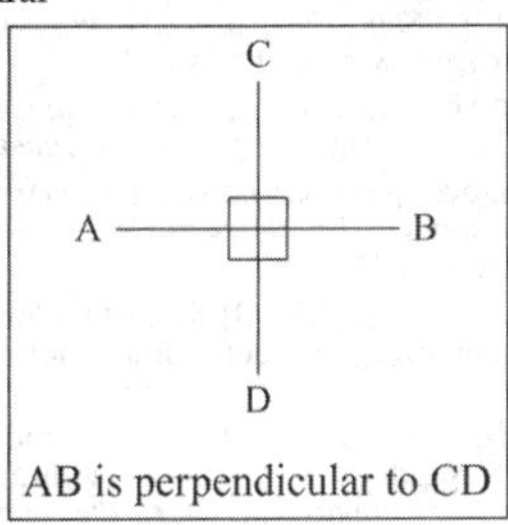

perpendicular

perpendicular /ˌpɜːpᵊn'dɪkjʊləʳ/ *adjective* **MATHEMATICS** at an angle of 90 degrees to something

perpetrate /'pɜːpɪtreɪt/ *verb* [T] *formal* to do something very bad [**often passive**] *They heard of torture perpetrated by the army.*

perpetrator /'pɜːpɪtreɪtəʳ/ *noun* [C] *formal* someone who has done something very bad *There is great public pressure to bring the **perpetrators of** these crimes to justice.*

perpetual /pə'petʃuəl/ *adjective* never ending *He seems to be in a **perpetual state** of confusion.* •**perpetually** *adverb*

perpetuate /pə'petʃueɪt/ *verb* [T] *formal* to make something continue, especially something bad *People think of him as a cruel man, an image perpetuated by the media.*

perplexed /pə'plekst/ *adjective* confused *He seemed a little perplexed by the question.* •**perplex** *verb* [T]

perplexing /pə'pleksɪŋ/ *adjective* confusing *a perplexing problem*

persecute /'pɜːsɪkjuːt/ *verb* [T] to treat someone unfairly or cruelly because of their race, religion, or beliefs [**often passive**] *He was persecuted for his religious beliefs.* •**persecution** /ˌpɜːsɪ'kjuːʃᵊn/ *noun* [U] ***political/religious persecution***

persecutor /'pɜːsɪkjuːtəʳ/ *noun* [C] someone who persecutes people

perseverance /ˌpɜːsɪ'vɪərᵊns/ *noun* [U] when you persevere *Hard work and perseverance do pay off in the end.*

persevere /ˌpɜːsɪ'vɪəʳ/ *verb* [I] to continue to try to do something although it is difficult *Despite the difficulties, I decided to **persevere with** the project.*

persist /pə'sɪst/ *verb* [I] **1** CONTINUE TO EXIST If an unpleasant feeling or situation persists, it continues to exist. *If symptoms persist, consult a doctor.* **2** CONTINUE TO DO to continue to do something although it is annoying other people *He **persists in** calling me Jane, even though I've corrected him twice.*

persistence /pə'sɪstᵊns/ *noun* [U] when someone or something persists

persistent /pə'sɪstᵊnt/ *adjective* **1** THING Something unpleasant that is persistent continues for a long time or is difficult to get rid of. *a persistent cough* **2** PERSON A persistent person continues to do something although other people do not want them to. *He can be very persistent sometimes.* •**persistently** *adverb He has persistently lied to us.*

O‒**person** /'pɜːsᵊn/ *noun plural* **people** **1** [C] a human being *You're the only person I know here.* ○ *He is a very dangerous person.* **2 in person** If you do something in person, you go somewhere to do it yourself. *If you can't be there in person the next best thing is watching it on TV.* ➲See also: **the first person, the second person, the third person**

persona /pə'səʊnə/ *noun* [C] *plural* **personae** or **personas** the way your character seems to other people *He's trying to improve his **public persona**.*

O‒**personal** /'pɜːsᵊnᵊl/ *adjective* **1** RELATING TO A PERSON [**always before noun**] relating to or belonging to a particular person *I can only speak from my own **personal experience.*** ○ *Please ensure you take all **personal belongings** with you when you leave the train.* ○ *This is a personal view and not that of the government.* **2** PRIVATE relating to the private parts of someone's life, including their relationships and feelings *He's got a few **personal problems** at the moment.* ○ *She prefers to keep her personal and professional lives separate.* **3** FOR ONE PERSON [**always before noun**] designed for or used by one person *a personal computer/stereo* ○ *a personal loan/pension* **4** RUDE rude about or offensive towards someone *I know you're upset, but there's no need to **get personal*** (= start making offensive remarks). **5** BODY [**always before noun**] relating to your body ***personal hygiene***

ˌpersonal comˈputer (*abbreviation* **PC**) *noun* [C] **COMPUTING** a computer designed for one person to use

ˌpersonal ˌdigital aˈssistant (*abbreviation* **PDA**) *noun* [C] **COMPUTING** a small computer that you can carry with you

WORD PARTNERS FOR ***personality***

a **bubbly/forceful/outgoing/warm** personality

O‒**personality** /ˌpɜːsᵊn'æləti/ *noun* **1** CHARACTER [C] the way you are as a person *She's got a lovely, **bubbly personality**.* **2** FAMOUS [C] a famous person *a well-known TV personality* **3** INTERESTING [U] the quality of having a very strong or interesting character *Sales people need a lot of personality.*

personalized (*also UK* **-ised**) /'pɜːsənᵊlaɪzd/ *adjective* A personalized object has someone's name on it, or has been made for a particular person. *a personalized fitness plan* •**personalize** *verb* [T]

personally /'pɜːsənᵊli/ *adverb* **1** BY YOU done by you and not someone else *I'd like to personally apologize for the delay.* **2** OPINION used when you are going to give your opinion *Personally, I'd rather stay at home and watch TV.* **3 take sth personally** to think that someone is criticizing you when they are not *You mustn't take everything so personally.*

ˌpersonal ˈorganizer *noun* [C] **COMPUTING** a small book or computer containing a calendar, address book, etc ➲See: **PDA**

ˌpersonal ˈpronoun *noun* [C] **LANGUAGE** a word that is used to refer to a person in speech or in writing. For example the words 'I', 'you', and 'they' are personal pronouns.

ˌpersonal ˈstereo *noun* [C] a small machine that plays music and which has headphones (= small parts that go in the ears) so that you can listen to music while you are walking

ˌpersonal ˈtrainer *noun* [C] **SPORT** a person whose job is to help you improve the shape of your body by showing you what exercises to do

personify /pəˈsɒnɪfaɪ/ *verb* [T] If someone personifies a particular quality, they are a perfect example of that quality. *She seems to personify honesty and goodness.* •**personified** *adjective* [**always after noun**] *Tom has always been laziness personified.* •**personification** /pəˌsɒnɪfɪˈkeɪʃən/ *noun* [U]

personnel /ˌpɜːsənˈel/ *noun* **1** [WORKERS] [**plural**] the people who work for an organization *military personnel* **2** [DEPARTMENT] [U] the department of an organization that deals with finding people to work there, keeping records about them, etc *I need to speak to someone in Personnel.* ○ *the personnel manager*

WORD PARTNERS FOR ***perspective***

from sb's perspective • **from** a [historical/political, etc] perspective • perspective **on** sth

perspective /pəˈspektɪv/ *noun* **1** [C] the way you think about something *Being unemployed has made me see things* ***from a different perspective.*** **2** **ART** [U] when things are drawn so that they appear to be a realistic size and in a realistic position **3 put sth in/into perspective** If something puts a problem into perspective, it makes you understand how unimportant that problem is.

perspicacious /ˌpɜːspɪˈkeɪʃəs/ *adjective formal* quick in noticing, understanding, or judging things accurately

perspiration /ˌpɜːspərˈeɪʃən/ *noun* [U] *formal* **BIOLOGY** the liquid that comes out of your skin when you get hot

perspire /pəˈspaɪər/ *verb* [I] *formal* **BIOLOGY** to produce liquid through your skin because you are hot or nervous

O-**persuade** /pəˈsweɪd/ *verb* [T] to make someone agree to do something by talking to them a lot about it [**+ to do sth**] *We managed to persuade him to come with us.* [**+ (that)**] *I persuaded her that it was the right thing to do.* ➲Opposite **dissuade**

persuasion /pəˈsweɪʒən/ *noun* **1** [PERSUADE] [U] when you persuade someone *I'm sure she'll agree, she just needs a little* ***gentle persuasion.*** **2** [BELIEF] [C] *formal* a political, religious, or moral belief *There were people of all persuasions there.*

persuasive /pəˈsweɪsɪv/ *adjective* able to make people agree to do something *It's a very* ***persuasive argument.*** •**persuasively** *adverb*

pertain /pəˈteɪn/ *verb*

pertain to sth *phrasal verb formal* to relate to something *Some important evidence pertaining to the case has been overlooked.*

pertinent /ˈpɜːtɪnənt/ *adjective formal* relating directly to a subject *a* ***pertinent question***

perturbed /pəˈtɜːbd/ *adjective* worried or upset *He seemed slightly perturbed by the news.* •**perturb** *verb* [T]

peruse /pəˈruːz/ *verb* [T] *formal* to look at or read something in order to find what interests you

pervade /pəˈveɪd/ *verb* [T] *formal* to move gradually through every part of something *Cheap perfume and tobacco pervaded the room.*

pervasive /pəˈveɪsɪv/ *adjective formal* moving into or through everywhere or everything *a pervasive smell* ○ *the* ***pervasive influence*** *of television*

perverse /pəˈvɜːs/ *adjective* strange and not what most people would expect or enjoy *In a perverse way, I enjoy going to the dentist.* •**perversely** *adverb*

perversion /pəˈvɜːʃən/ *noun* [C, U] **1** [SEX] getting sexual pleasure in a way that seems strange or unpleasant **2** [WRONG] when something that is right is changed into something that is wrong *the perversion of justice*

pervert[1] /ˈpɜːvɜːt/ *noun* [C] someone who gets sexual pleasure in a strange or unpleasant way

pervert[2] /pəˈvɜːt/ *verb* [T] to change something that is right into something that is wrong *They were charged with conspiracy to* ***pervert the course of justice.***

perverted /pəˈvɜːtɪd/ *adjective* relating to getting sexual pleasure in a strange or unpleasant way

pessimism /ˈpesɪmɪzəm/ *noun* [U] when you believe bad things will happen ➲Opposite **optimism**

pessimist /ˈpesɪmɪst/ *noun* [C] someone who always believes that bad things will happen *Don't be such a pessimist!*

pessimistic /ˌpesɪˈmɪstɪk/ *adjective* always believing that bad things will happen *He was feeling* ***pessimistic about*** *the future.* ➲Opposite **optimistic**

pest /pest/ *noun* [C] **1** **FARMING** an animal that causes damage to plants, food, etc *Most farmers think foxes are pests.* **2** *informal* an annoying person

PEST analysis /ˈpestəˌnæləsɪs/ *noun* [C] **ECONOMICS** a document that shows how the political, economic, social and technological situation will affect a business

pester /ˈpestər/ *verb* [T] to annoy someone by asking them something again and again [**+ to do sth**] *He's been pestering me to go out with him all week.*

pesticide /ˈpestɪsaɪd/ *noun* [C, U] **FARMING** a chemical that is used to kill insects which damage plants

pet¹ /pet/ *noun* [C] an animal that someone keeps in their home *my pet rabbit*

pet² /pet/ *verb* [T] **petting**, *past* **petted** ANIMAL to touch an animal because you feel affection for it

petal /ˈpetᵊl/ *noun* [C] **BIOLOGY** one of the thin, flat, coloured parts on the outside of a flower *rose petals* ➲See picture at **flower**

peter /ˈpiːtəʳ/ *verb*
peter out *phrasal verb* to gradually stop or disappear *The track petered out after a mile or so.*

ˌpet ˈhate *UK* (*US* **ˌpet ˈpeeve**) *noun* [C] something that annoys you a lot *That's one of my pet hates - people who smoke while other people are eating.*

petite /pəˈtiːt/ *adjective* A petite woman is small and thin in an attractive way.

petition¹ /pəˈtɪʃᵊn/ *verb* [I, T] **POLITICS** to officially ask someone in authority to do something [+ **to do sth**] *They are petitioning the government to increase funding for the project.*

WORD PARTNERS FOR ***petition***

launch/organize/sign a petition • a petition **against/(calling) for** sth

petition² /pəˈtɪʃᵊn/ *noun* [C] **POLITICS** a document that has been signed by a lot of people officially asking someone in authority to do something *Will you sign this* ***petition against*** *experiments on animals?*

Petri dish /ˈpetriˌdɪʃ/ *noun* [C] **BIOLOGY, CHEMISTRY** a small clear round dish with a cover, which is used in scientific tests, especially for growing bacteria

petrified /ˈpetrɪfaɪd/ *adjective* extremely frightened *I'm* ***petrified of*** *spiders.*

O-■ **petrol** /ˈpetrᵊl/ *UK* (*US* **gas**) *noun* [U] a liquid fuel used in cars *unleaded petrol*

petroleum /pəˈtrəʊliəm/ *noun* [U] **GEOLOGY** thick oil found under the Earth's surface which is used to produce petrol and other substances

ˈpetrol ˌstation *UK* (*US* **gas station**) *noun* [C] a place where you can buy petrol

petticoat /ˈpetɪkəʊt/ *noun* [C] a thin piece of women's clothing worn under a dress or skirt

petty /ˈpeti/ *adjective* **1** UNIMPORTANT [**always before noun**] unimportant or not serious *petty crime* **2** COMPLAINING [**never before noun**] complaining too much about unimportant things *You can be so petty sometimes!*

ˌpetty ˈcash *noun* [U] **FINANCE** a small amount of money that you keep in an office and use for buying small things for the company *Take the money for stamps out of petty cash.*

petty ˈcash ˌvoucher *noun* [C] **FINANCE** a piece of paper on which an employee writes what they have bought and how much it cost so that the employee can take that amount of money from petty cash

petulant /ˈpetʃələnt/ *adjective* behaving in an angry, silly way like a child

pew /pjuː/ *noun* [C] **RELIGION** a long seat in a church

pewter /ˈpjuːtəʳ/ *noun* [U] a blue-grey metal

pH /ˌpiːˈeɪtʃ/ *noun* [**C usually singular**] **CHEMISTRY, MEASURES** a number which shows how strongly acid or alkaline a substance is, in a range from 0 to 14 *Below pH 6.5 is acid, above pH 7.5 is alkaline.*

phage /feɪdʒ/ (*also* **bacteriophage**) *noun* [C] **BIOLOGY** a virus (= organism that causes disease) that grows and divides inside a bacterium

phagocyte /ˈfægəʊsaɪt/ *noun* [C] **BIOLOGY** a cell that gets rid of bacteria and other cells that cause harm by absorbing them ➲See picture at **blood cells**

phantom¹ /ˈfæntəm/ *noun* [C] the spirit of a dead person

phantom² /ˈfæntəm/ *adjective* [**always before noun**] imagined, not real *phantom pains*

pharaoh /ˈfeərəʊ/ *noun* [C] a king of ancient Egypt

pharmaceutical /ˌfɑːməˈsjuːtɪkᵊl/ *adjective* **HEALTH** relating to the production of medicines *a* ***pharmaceutical company*** ○ *the* ***pharmaceutical industry*** •**pharmaceuticals** *noun* [**plural**] medicines

pharmacist /ˈfɑːməsɪst/ *noun* [C] **HEALTH** someone who is trained to prepare or sell medicines

pharmacy /ˈfɑːməsi/ *noun* **HEALTH** **1** [C] a shop or part of a shop that prepares and sells medicines **2** [U] the study of the preparation of medicines

pharynx /ˈfærɪŋks/ *noun* [C] **ANATOMY** the soft part at the top of the throat which connects the mouth and nose to the throat ➲See picture at **respiratory system**

WORD PARTNERS FOR ***phase***

enter/go through a phase • a **passing** phase • a phase **of** sth

phase¹ /feɪz/ *noun* [C] a stage or period which is part of a longer period *The first phase of the project is scheduled for completion next year.* ○ *My younger daughter is* ***going through*** *a* ***phase*** *of only wearing black.*

phase² /feɪz/ *verb*
phase sth in *phrasal verb* to gradually start using a new system, process, or law *The new tax will be phased in over five years.*
phase sth out *phrasal verb* to gradually stop using something

PhD /ˌpiːeɪtʃˈdiː/ *noun* [C] **EDUCATION** an advanced university qualification, or a person who has this qualification *a PhD course/programme* ○ *Maria has* ***a PhD in*** *mathematics.*

pheasant /ˈfezᵊnt/ *noun* [C] *plural* **pheasants** or **pheasant** **FOOD** a bird with a long tail that is shot for food

phenomenal /fɪˈnɒmɪnᵊl/ *adjective* extremely successful or showing great qualities or abilities *The film has been a phenomenal success.* •**phenomenally** *adverb*

phenomenon /fɪˈnɒmɪnən/ *noun* [C] *plural* **phenomena** something that exists or happens, usually something unusual *storms, lightning, and other* ***natural phenomena*** ○ *Road rage seems to be a fairly recent phenomenon.*

P

phenotype /ˈfiːnəʊtaɪp/ *noun* [C] **BIOLOGY** all the qualities of a living thing, especially the qualities that you can see, for example the colour of the hair and eyes, the weight, etc. ➲Compare **genotype**

pheromone /ˈferəməʊn/ *noun* [C] **BIOLOGY** a chemical that an animal sends into the air or water, whose purpose is to make other animals of the same type do a particular thing, for example to be attracted to them sexually

phew (*also* **whew**) /fjuː/ *exclamation* used when you are happy that something is not going to happen, or when you are tired or hot

philanthropist /fɪˈlænθrəpɪst/ *noun* [C] **FINANCE** someone who gives money to people who need help

-phile /-faɪl/ *suffix* makes a noun meaning 'enjoying or liking something' *a Francophile* (= someone who loves France) ○ *a bibliophile* (= someone who loves books)

philosopher /fɪˈlɒsəfəʳ/ *noun* [C] someone who studies or writes about the meaning of life

philosophical /ˌfɪləˈsɒfɪkəl/ *adjective* **1** PHILOSOPHY relating to the study or writing of philosophy *a philosophical problem/question* **2** CALM accepting unpleasant situations in a calm and wise way *She seems fairly* ***philosophical about*** *the failure of her marriage.* •**philosophically** *adverb*

philosophy /fɪˈlɒsəfi/ *noun* **1** IDEAS [C, U] the study or writing of ideas about the meaning of life, or a particular set of ideas about the meaning of life *Descartes is considered by many to be the father of modern philosophy.* **2** WAY OF THINKING [C] a way of thinking about what you should do in life *My philosophy has always been to give those with ability the chance to progress.*

P

phishing /ˈfɪʃɪŋ/ *noun* [U] **INTERNET** the practice of sending emails to people to trick them into giving information that would let someone take money from their Internet bank account (= an arrangement with your bank to keep your money there and take it out when you need it)

phlegm /flem/ *noun* [U] **BIOLOGY** a thick liquid produced in your lungs, throat, and nose when you have a cold (= common illness that makes you sneeze)

phlegmatic /flegˈmætɪk/ *adjective formal* Someone who is phlegmatic is calm and does not get excited easily.

phloem /ˈfləʊem/ *noun* [U] **BIOLOGY** the part of a plant that carries food from the leaves to other parts where the food is needed ➲Compare **xylem** ➲See picture at **leaf** ➲See picture at **stem**

-phobe /-fəʊb/ *suffix* someone who hates something *a commitment-phobe* (= a person who hates commitment)

phobia /ˈfəʊbiə/ *noun* [C] an extreme fear of something *My mum's got a* ***phobia about*** *birds.*

WORD PARTNERS FOR ***phone***

answer/pick up the phone • **put** the phone **down** • a phone **rings** • **by/over** the phone • a phone **bill/company/conversation**

O-ᵘ**phone¹** /fəʊn/ (*also* **telephone**) *noun* **1** SYSTEM [U] a communication system that is used to talk to someone who is in another place *We'll contact you* ***by phone*** *when we get the results.* **2** EQUIPMENT [C] a piece of equipment that is used to talk to someone who is in another place *Would someone please* ***answer the phone?*** ○ *I could hear the* ***phone ringing.*** **3 on the phone a** USING PHONE using the phone *She's been on the phone all night.* **b** HAVING A PHONE *UK* when you have a phone ➲See also: **cellular phone, mobile phone, pay phone**

O-ᵘ**phone²** /fəʊn/ (*also* **phone up**) *verb* [I, T] to communicate with someone by telephone *I tried to phone her last night, but she was out.* ○ *I'm going to phone for a taxi.* ➲See Common Learner Error at **telephone**

COMMON LEARNER ERROR

phone or **call?**

In British English the verbs **phone** or **call** are used to mean communicate with someone by telephone. You can also use the expressions 'give someone a ring/call' or 'ring (someone)'.

I'll phone you tomorrow.

I'll give you a ring tomorrow.

I'll ring you tomorrow.

In American English **call** is the usual verb which means telephone someone.

Call me later.

I'll call you tomorrow.

ˈphone ˌbook *noun* [C] a book that contains the telephone numbers of people who live in a particular area

ˈphone ˌbox *UK* (*US* **ˈphone ˌbooth**) *noun* [C] a small structure containing a public telephone

ˈphone ˌcall *noun* [C] when you use the telephone *Will you excuse me, I've got to* ***make a phone call.***

ˈphone ˌcard *noun* [C] a small piece of plastic used to pay for the use of some telephones

phone-in /ˈfəʊnɪn/ *UK* (*US* **call-in**) *noun* [C] a television or radio programme in which the public can ask questions or give opinions over the telephone

ˈphone ˌnumber *noun* [C] the number of a particular telephone

phonetic /fəʊˈnetɪk/ *adjective* **LANGUAGE** relating to the sounds you make when you speak *the international phonetic alphabet* •**phonetically** *adverb*

phonetics /fəˈnetɪks/ *noun* [U] **LANGUAGE** the study of the sounds made by the human voice in speech

phoney¹ *UK* (*US* **phony**) /ˈfəʊni/ *adjective informal* not real *He gave the police a phoney number.*

phoney² *UK* (*US* **phony**) /ˈfəʊni/ *noun* [C] *informal* someone who is not sincere •**phoney** *UK* (*US* **phony**) *adjective informal* a phoney smile

ˌphoney ˈwar *noun* [C usually singular] **POLITICS** a period during a war when there is no fighting and the situation appears calm

phosphate /ˈfɒsfeɪt/ *noun* [C, U] **CHEMISTRY** a chemical that is used in cleaning products and to help plants grow

phosphorescent /ˌfɒsfᵊrˈesᵊnt/ *adjective* **PHYSICS** giving off light after radiation has hit it

phosphorus /ˈfɒs.fᵊr.əs/ *noun* [U] **CHEMISTRY** a chemical element, especially a poisonous yellow-white element that shines in the dark and burns when it is in the air (symbol **P**)

O→**photo** /ˈfəʊtəʊ/ *noun* [C] a picture produced with a camera *a* ***black-and-white/colour photo*** ○ *I* ***took a photo*** *of Jack lying on the beach.*

photochemical /ˌfəʊtəʊˈkemɪkᵊl/ *adjective* **PHYSICS, CHEMISTRY** relating to the effect of light on some chemicals

photochemical smog *noun* [U] **ENVIRONMENT** a fog caused by light from the sun shining on chemicals in the air that have been produced by cars and factories

photocopier /ˈfəʊtəʊˌkɒpiəʳ/ *noun* [C] a machine which produces copies of documents by photographing them ➲See colour picture **The Office** on page Centre 5

photocopy /ˈfəʊtəʊˌkɒpi/ *noun* [C] a copy of a document made with a photocopier *I* ***made a photocopy*** *of my letter before sending it.* •**photocopy** *verb* [T]

photoelectric cell /ˌfəʊtəʊɪˌlektrɪkˈsel/ *noun* [C] **PHYSICS** a piece of equipment that reacts if a beam of light is broken, used for example in devices to catch thieves entering buildings

photogenic /ˌfəʊtəʊˈdʒenɪk/ *adjective* Someone who is photogenic has the type of face that looks attractive in a photograph.

O→**photograph¹** /ˈfəʊtəgrɑːf/ *noun* [C] a picture produced with a camera *a* ***black-and-white/colour photograph*** ○ *He* ***took*** *a lovely* ***photograph of*** *the children in the garden.*

photograph² /ˈfəʊtəgrɑːf/ *verb* [T] to take a photograph of someone or something *They were photographed leaving a nightclub together.*

photographer /fəˈtɒgrəfəʳ/ *noun* [C] someone whose job is to take photographs

photographic /ˌfəʊtəˈgræfɪk/ *adjective* [**always before noun**] relating to photographs *photographic equipment/film* ○ ***photographic evidence***

photography /fəˈtɒgrəfi/ *noun* [U] the activity or job of taking photographs

photometer /fəʊˈtɒmɪtəʳ/ *noun* [C] **PHYSICS** a piece of equipment used by scientists to measure the strength of light

photometry /fəʊˈtɒmətri/ *noun* [U] **PHYSICS** the measurement of the strength of light

photosynthesis /ˌfəʊtəʊˈsɪntθəsɪs/ *noun* [U] **BIOLOGY** the process by which a plant uses the energy from the light of the sun to make its own food

phototropism /fəʊtɒˈtrəpɪzᵊm/ *noun* [U] **BIOLOGY** the way that plants grow or move towards light or away from light

photovoltaic cell /ˌfəʊtəʊvɒlteɪkˈsel/ *noun* [C] **PHYSICS** a device that changes light from the sun into electricity

phrasal verb /ˌfreɪzᵊlˈvɜːb/ *noun* [C] **LANGUAGE** a verb together with an adverb or preposition which has a different meaning to the meaning of its separate parts. For example 'look up' and 'carry on' are phrasal verbs. ➲See Extra help page **Phrasal verbs** on page Centre 26. ➲See colour picture **Phrasal Verbs** on page Centre 16

O→**phrase¹** /freɪz/ *noun* [C] **LANGUAGE** a group of words which are often used together and have a particular meaning

phrase² /freɪz/ *verb* [T] **LANGUAGE** to express something by choosing to use particular words *It might have been better if he had phrased it differently.*

phylum /ˈfaɪləm/ *noun* [C] **BIOLOGY** one of the groups into which animals are divided, based generally on the shape of the animal's body and the way that the body is arranged

O→**physical¹** /ˈfɪzɪkᵊl/ *adjective* **1** BODY relating to the body ***physical fitness/strength*** ○ *People put too much emphasis on* ***physical appearance*** (= what you look like). **2** THINGS [**always before noun**] relating to real things that you can see and touch *There was no physical evidence linking Jones to Shaw's murder.*

physical² /ˈfɪzɪkᵊl/ *US* (*UK* **medical**) *noun* [C] **HEALTH** an examination of your body by a doctor to find out if you are healthy

physically /ˈfɪzɪkᵊli/ *adverb* in a way that relates to the body ***physically attractive/fit***

ˌphysical ˈtherapist *US* (*UK/US* **physiotherapist**) *noun* [C] **HEALTH** someone whose job is to give people physical therapy

ˌphysical ˈtherapy *US* (*UK/US* **physiotherapy**) *noun* [U] **HEALTH** treatment for illness or injury in which you practise moving parts of your body

physician /fɪˈzɪʃᵊn/ *noun* [C] **HEALTH** *formal* a doctor

physicist /ˈfɪzɪsɪst/ *noun* [C] **PHYSICS** someone who studies physics

physics /ˈfɪzɪks/ *noun* [U] **PHYSICS** the scientific study of natural forces, such as energy, heat, light, etc

physio /ˈfɪziəʊ/ *noun* [C, U] *UK informal* **HEALTH** *short for* physiotherapy or physiotherapist

physiological /ˌfɪziəˈlɒdʒɪkᵊl/ *adjective* **BIOLOGY** relating to how the bodies of living things work

physiology /ˌfɪziˈɒlədʒi/ *noun* [U] **BIOLOGY** the scientific study of how the bodies of living things work

physiotherapist /ˌfɪziəʊˈθerəpɪst/ (*also US* **physical therapist**) *noun* [C] **HEALTH** someone whose job is to give people physiotherapy

physiotherapy /ˌfɪziəʊˈθerəpi/ (*also US* **physical therapy**) *noun* [U] **HEALTH** treatment for illness or injury in which you practise moving parts of your body

physique /fɪˈziːk/ *noun* [C] the shape and size of your body *He has a very muscular physique.*

pianist /ˈpiːənɪst/ *noun* [C] **MUSIC** someone who plays the piano

P

piano /pi'ænəʊ/ *noun* [C] **MUSIC** a large wooden musical instrument with strings inside and black and white bars that produce sounds when you press them ➲See also: **grand piano**

pick¹ /pɪk/ *verb* [T] **1** [CHOOSE] to choose something or someone *Do you want to help me pick some numbers for my lottery ticket?* ○ *I was never picked for the school football team.* **2** [FLOWERS/FRUIT, ETC] If you pick flowers, fruit, etc, you take them off a tree or out of the ground. *I picked some apples this morning.* **3** [REMOVE] to remove small pieces from something with your fingers *You'll have to let the glue dry and then you can pick it off.* **4 pick a fight/argument** to start a fight or argument with someone **5 pick sb's pocket** to steal something from someone's pocket ➲See also: have a **bone**¹ to pick with sb

pick at sth *phrasal verb* **1 FOOD** to only eat a small amount of your food because you are worried or ill *He picked at his food but had no appetite.* **2** [REMOVE] to remove small pieces from something with your fingers *If you keep picking at that scab it'll never heal.*

pick on sb *phrasal verb* to choose a person and criticize or treat them unfairly *He just started picking on me for no reason.*

pick sth/sb out *phrasal verb* to choose someone or something from a group of people or things *She picked out a red shirt for me to try on.*

pick sth/sb up *phrasal verb* **1** [LIFT] to lift something or someone by using your hands *He picked his coat up off the floor.* ○ *Just pick up the phone and call him.* ➲See colour picture **Phrasal Verbs** on page Centre 16 **2** [COLLECT] to collect someone who is waiting for you, or to collect something that you have left somewhere *Can you pick me up from the airport?*

pick sth up *phrasal verb* **1** [GET] to get something *She picked up some real bargains in the sale.* **2** [LEARN] to learn a new skill or language by practising it and not by being taught it *He hadn't done any skiing before the holiday, but he picked it up really quickly.* **3 HEALTH** to get an illness from someone or something *She picked up a nasty stomach bug while she was on holiday.* **4** [SIGNAL] If a piece of equipment picks up a signal, it receives it. *Antennas around the top of the ship picked up the radar signals.* **5** [NOTICE] to notice something *Police dogs picked up the scent of the two men from clothes they had left behind.*

pick sb up *phrasal verb* **1** [RELATIONSHIP] to start talking to someone in order to try to begin a romantic relationship with them **2** [POLICE] If the police pick someone up, they take that person to the police station.

pick up *phrasal verb* **1** [SITUATION] If a business or social situation picks up, it improves. *Business is really starting to pick up now.* **2** [WIND] If the wind picks up, it becomes stronger.

pick up sth *phrasal verb* If a vehicle picks up speed, it starts to go faster.

pick² /pɪk/ *noun* **1** [C] a sharp metal stick used to break hard ground or rocks **2 the pick of sth** the best of a group of things or people **3 have/take your pick** to choose what you want *We've got tea, coffee, or hot chocolate - take your pick.*

P

picket /'pɪkɪt/ (*also* '**picket,line**) *noun* [C] **POLITICS** a group of people who stand outside a building in order to show their anger about something and to try to stop people going inside •**picket** *verb* [I, T] *Protesters picketed cinemas across the whole country.*

'**picket ,fence** *noun* [C] *US* a low fence made from a row of sticks that are pointed at the top

pickle /'pɪkl/ *noun* **FOOD 1** [C, U] *UK* food which has been put into vinegar or salt water for a long time and has a sour taste *cold meat and pickles* **2** [C] *US* a small cucumber (= a green, cylindrical vegetable) that has been put in vinegar or in a liquid containing salt and spices •**pickled** *adjective pickled onions*

pickpocket /'pɪk,pɒkɪt/ *noun* [C] someone who steals things from people's pockets

pickup /'pɪkʌp/ (*also* '**pickup ,truck**) *noun* [C] *US* a small, open truck

picky /'pɪki/ *adjective informal* Someone who is picky does not like many things. ***a picky eater***

picnic /'pɪknɪk/ *noun* [C] **FOOD** a meal that you make and take with you somewhere to eat outside *We're going to **have a picnic** down by the lake.* •**picnic** *verb* [I] **picnicking**, *past* **picnicked**

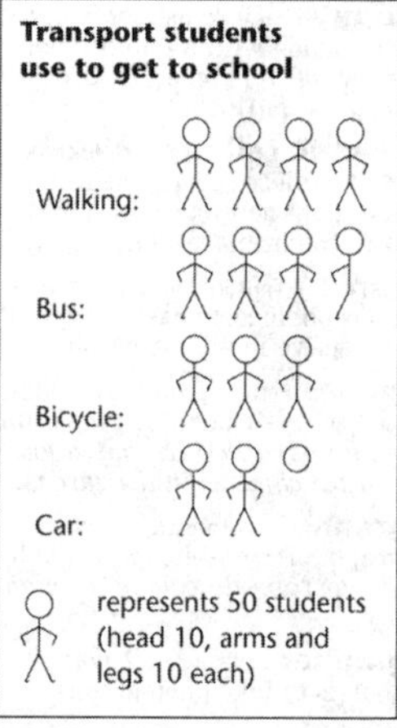

pictogram

pictogram /'pɪktəgræm/ *noun* [C] **MATHEMATICS** a graph that uses simple pictures to show amounts ➲See Extra help page **Graphs and charts** on page Centre 21.

pictorial /pɪk'tɔːriəl/ *adjective* relating to pictures or shown using pictures

WORD PARTNERS FOR ***picture***

draw/paint a picture • **take** a picture • a picture **of** sb/sth • **in** a picture

picture¹ /'pɪktʃəʳ/ *noun* [C] **1 ART** a drawing, painting, or photograph of something or someone *to **draw/paint** a **picture*** ○ *She's got pictures of pop stars all over her bedroom wall.* ○ *Did you **take** many **pictures*** (= photograph many things) *while you were in Sydney?* ➲See colour picture **The Living Room** on page Centre 4

2 IDEA an idea of what something is like [**usually singular**] *I've got a much clearer picture of what's happening now.* **3** TV the image on a television screen *I'm afraid it's not a very good picture.* **4** FILM a film *Could this be the first animated film to win a best picture award?* **5 the pictures** *old-fashioned* the cinema *I really fancy going to the pictures tonight.* **6 get the picture** *informal* used to say that someone understands a situation *Oh right, I get the picture.* **7 paint a bleak/rosy, etc picture of sth** to describe something in a particular way *She paints a rosy* (= happy) *picture of family life.* **8 put/keep sb in the picture** *informal* to explain to someone what is happening *Jim had no idea what was going on till I put him in the picture.*

picture² /ˈpɪktʃəʳ/ *verb* [T] **1** IMAGINE to imagine something in a particular way *The house isn't at all how I had pictured it.* **2** SHOW to show someone or something in a picture [**often passive**] *They were pictured holding hands on the beach.*

ˈpicture ˌmessaging *noun* [C] sending and receiving pictures on a mobile phone

picturesque /ˌpɪktʃəʳˈesk/ *adjective* A picturesque place is attractive to look at. *a picturesque cottage on the edge of the Yorkshire Moors*

pie /paɪ/ *noun* [C, U] **FOOD** a type of food made with meat, vegetables, or fruit which is covered in pastry and baked *apple/meat pie* ➲See also: **mince pie**

O‑ **piece¹** /piːs/ *noun* [C] **1** AMOUNT/PART an amount of something, or a part of something *a **piece of** paper/wood* ○ *She cut the flan into eight pieces.* ○ *Some of the pieces seem to be missing.* ○ *These shoes are **falling to pieces*** (= breaking into pieces). ➲See colour picture **Pieces and Quantities** on page Centre 1 **2** ONE one of a particular type of thing *a useful **piece of equipment*** **3** SOME some of a particular type of thing *a **piece of news/information*** ○ *Can I give you a **piece of advice**?* **4 ART, LITERATURE, MUSIC** an example of artistic, musical, or written work *There was an interesting piece on alternative medicine in the paper yesterday.* **5 FINANCE ten-/twenty-, etc pence piece** a coin with a value of ten/twenty, etc pence (= British money) **6 be a piece of cake** *informal* to be very easy *The test was a piece of cake.* **7 give sb a piece of your mind** *informal* to speak angrily to someone because they have done something wrong **8 go/fall to pieces** If someone goes to pieces, they become so upset that they cannot control their feelings or think clearly. *He went to pieces when his mother died.* ➲See also: **set-piece**

piece² /piːs/ *verb*
piece sth together *phrasal verb* to try to understand something or discover the truth about something by collecting different pieces of information *Police are trying to piece together a profile of the murderer.*

piecemeal /ˈpiːsmiːl/ *adjective, adverb* happening very gradually *The land is being sold in a **piecemeal fashion** over a number of years.*

piecework /ˈpiːswɜːk/ *noun* [U] work for which the amount of money you are paid depends on the number of things you have finished and not the time you have spent working

pier /pɪəʳ/ *noun* [C] a long structure that is built from the land out over the sea and sometimes has entertainments, restaurants, etc on it

pierce /pɪəs/ *verb* [T] **1** HOLE to make a hole in something using a sharp point *I'd like to have my **ears pierced**.* **2** LIGHT/SOUND *literary* If a light or a sound pierces something, it is suddenly seen or heard. *A few rays of sunlight pierced the bedroom shutters.*

piercing /ˈpɪəsɪŋ/ *adjective* **1** STRONG A piercing noise, light, etc is very strong and unpleasant. *I heard a loud, **piercing scream**.* **2** EYES Piercing eyes seem to look at you very closely.

piety /ˈpaɪəti/ *noun* [U] **RELIGION** a strong belief in religious morals

O‑ **pig¹** /pɪg/ *noun* [C] **1 FARMING** a large pink, brown, or black farm animal that is kept for its meat **2** PERSON *informal* someone who is very unpleasant, or someone who eats a lot *He's an ignorant pig.* ➲See also: **guinea pig**

pig² /pɪg/ *verb* **pigging**, *past* **pigged**
pig out *phrasal verb informal* to eat too much *We **pigged out on** the cakes and pastries.*

pigeon /ˈpɪdʒən/ *noun* [C] a grey bird which often lives on buildings in towns

pigeonhole¹ /ˈpɪdʒənhəʊl/ *noun* [C] one of a set of small open boxes in which letters or messages are left, especially in an office or hotel

pigeonhole² /ˈpɪdʒənhəʊl/ *verb* [T] If you pigeonhole someone, you unfairly decide what type of person they are.

piggyback /ˈpɪgibæk/ (*also* **ˈpiggyback ˌride**) *noun* [C] a way of carrying someone on your back in which they put their arms and legs around you

piggy bank /ˈpɪgiˌbæŋk/ *noun* [C] a small container, often in the shape of a pig, used by children to keep money in

pigheaded /ˌpɪgˈhedɪd/ *adjective* refusing to change your opinion or the way you are doing something although it would be better if you did

piglet /ˈpɪglət/ *noun* [C] a baby pig

pigment /ˈpɪgmənt/ *noun* [C, U] a substance that gives something colour •**pigmentation** /ˌpɪgmənˈteɪʃən/ *noun* [U] the natural colour of a living thing

pigsty /ˈpɪgstaɪ/ (*also US* **pigpen** /ˈpɪgpen/) *noun* [C] **FARMING** a place where pigs are kept

pigtail /ˈpɪgteɪl/ *noun* [C] a hairstyle in which the hair is twisted together and tied [**usually plural**] *A little girl in pigtails presented the flowers.*

pike /paɪk/ *noun* [C, U] *plural* **pike** a large river fish with sharp teeth, or the meat of this fish

Pilates /pɪˈlɑːtiːz/ *noun* [U] **SPORT** a system of physical exercise involving controlled movements, stretching and breathing

WORD PARTNERS FOR ***pile***

a pile **of** sth • **be in/put** sth **into** a pile

O‑ **pile¹** /paɪl/ *noun* **1** [C] an amount of a substance in the shape of a small hill or a number of

P

objects on top of each other *a **pile of** books/bricks* ○ *a **pile of** sand/rubbish* ○ *The clothes were arranged **in piles** on the floor.* **2 a pile of sth/piles of sth** *informal* a lot of something *It's all right for him, he's got piles of money.*

pile² /paɪl/ *verb*
pile in/out *phrasal verb informal* to enter/leave a place quickly and not in an organized way *She opened the door and we all piled in.*
pile sth up *phrasal verb* to make a lot of things into a pile by putting them on top of each other *Please cold you just pile those books up over there.*
pile up *phrasal verb* If something unpleasant piles up, you get more of it. *My work's really starting to pile up.*

pile-up /ˈpaɪlʌp/ *noun* **[C]** an accident involving several cars

pilfer /ˈpɪlfəʳ/ *verb* **[I, T]** to steal things that do not have much value

pilgrim /ˈpɪlgrɪm/ *noun* **[C]** **RELIGION** someone who travels to a place which is important in their religion

pilgrimage /ˈpɪlgrɪmɪdʒ/ *noun* **[C, U]** **RELIGION** a journey to a place which has religious importance *to **go on a pilgrimage** to Mecca*

pill /pɪl/ *noun* **HEALTH** **1** **[C]** a small, hard piece of medicine that you swallow *a vitamin pill* ○ *I've **taken** a couple of **pills**, but my headache still hasn't gone.* **2 the pill** a pill which prevents a woman from becoming pregnant ➲See also: **sleeping pill**

pillar /ˈpɪləʳ/ *noun* **1** **[C]** a tall structure made of stone, wood, etc which supports something above it *The new bridge will be supported by 100 concrete pillars.* **2 a pillar of sth** someone or something who is very important to a place, organization, etc *He was a pillar of the local community.*

pillow /ˈpɪləʊ/ *noun* **[C]** a soft object which you rest your head on in bed

pillowcase /ˈpɪləʊkeɪs/ *noun* **[C]** a cloth cover for a pillow

pilot /ˈpaɪlət/ *noun* **[C]** someone who flies an aircraft •**pilot** *verb* **[T]**

pimple /ˈpɪmpl/ *noun* **[C]** a small spot on your skin •**pimply** *adjective* ➲See also: **goose pimples**

pin¹ /pɪn/ *noun* **[C]** **1** FOR CLOTH a thin piece of metal with a sharp point used to fasten pieces of cloth, etc together *She pricked her finger on a pin.* **2** FOR FASTENING a thin piece of metal, wood, plastic, etc that holds or fastens things together *He's had a metal pin put in his leg so that the bones heal properly.* ➲See also: **drawing pin, pins and needles, rolling pin, safety pin**

pin² /pɪn/ *verb* **[T]** **pinning**, *past* **pinned** **1** to fasten something with a pin *We're not allowed to **pin** anything **on** these walls.* ○ *She had a red ribbon **pinned to** her collar.* **2 pin sb to/against/under, etc** to force someone to stay in a position by holding them *They pinned him to the ground.* ➲See also: pin your hopes (**hope²**) on sb/sth
pin sb down *phrasal verb* **1** DETAILS to make someone give you details or a decision about something *I've been trying to get a decision from Jim, but he's very difficult to pin down.* **2** HOLD DOWN to force someone to stay in a horizontal position by holding them *They pinned him down on the floor.*
pin sth down *phrasal verb* to discover exact details about something *Investigators are trying to pin down the cause of the fire.*
pin sth on sb *phrasal verb informal* to blame someone for something they did not do *They tried to pin the murder on the dead woman's husband.*
pin sth up *phrasal verb* to fasten something to a wall using a pin *The exam results have been pinned up on the noticeboard.*

PIN /pɪn/ (*also* **ˈPIN ˌnumber**) *noun* **[C]** **FINANCE** *abbreviation for* Personal Identification Number: the secret number that allows you to use a bank card in a machine

pinafore /ˈpɪnəfɔːʳ/ *UK* (*US* **jumper**) *noun* **[C]** a loose dress with no sleeves that is worn over other clothes such as a shirt

pincer /ˈpɪnsəʳ/ *noun* **[C]** **BIOLOGY** one of a pair of curved hand-like parts of an animal such as a crab (= round, flat sea animal with ten legs)

pinch¹ /pɪnʃ/ *verb* **[T]** **1** PRESS to press someone's skin tightly between your thumb and first finger, sometimes causing pain *One of the kids had been pinching her and she was crying.* **2** STEAL *mainly UK informal* to steal something that does not have much value *Who's pinched my ruler?*

pinch² /pɪnʃ/ *noun* **[C]** **1** SMALL AMOUNT a small amount of a substance that you pick up between your thumb and your first finger *a **pinch of salt*** **2** PRESS when you press part of the body or an area of skin tightly between your thumb and first finger **3 at a pinch** *UK* (*US* **in a pinch**) If something can be done at a pinch, it is possible but it is difficult. *We can fit ten round the table, at a pinch.* **4 feel the pinch** to have problems because you do not have enough money ➲See also: take sth with a pinch of **salt¹**

pinched /pɪnʃt/ *adjective* A pinched face looks thin and ill.

pine¹ /paɪn/ *noun* **1** TREE **[C, U]** (*also* **ˈpine ˌtree**) a tall tree with long, thin leaves shaped like needles **2** WOOD **[U]** the pale coloured wood from this tree

pine² /paɪn/ (*also* **pine away**) *verb* **[I]** to be sad because you want someone or something that has gone away *He's **pining for** his ex-girlfriend.*

pineapple /ˈpaɪnæpl/ *noun* **[C, U]** **FOOD** a large fruit with thick skin and sharp leaves sticking out of the top which is sweet and yellow inside

pinecone /ˈpaɪnˌkəʊn/ *noun* **[C]** **BIOLOGY** a hard, brown, oval object that grows on pine and fir trees (= tall trees which stay green all winter)

ping /pɪŋ/ *verb* **[I]** to make a short, high noise like a bell *They could hear the microwave pinging in the kitchen.* •**ping** *noun* **[C]**

pink /pɪŋk/ *adjective* being a pale red colour *pretty, pink flowers* •**pink** *noun* **[C, U]** ➲See colour picture **Colours** on page Centre 12

pinnacle /ˈpɪnəkl/ *noun* [**no plural**] the highest or best part of something *At 35, she is at the **pinnacle of** her career.*

pinnate /ˈpɪneɪt/ *adjective* **BIOLOGY** describes a type of leaf which has a central stem with small leaves arranged on both sides of it

pinpoint /ˈpɪnpɔɪnt/ *verb* [**T**] to say exactly what or where something is *It is difficult to pinpoint the exact time of death.*

ˌpins and ˈneedles *noun* **have pins and needles** **HEALTH** to feel slight sharp pains in a part of your body when you move it after keeping it still for a period of time

pint /paɪnt/ *noun* [**C**] **1** **MEASURES** (*written abbreviation* **pt**) a unit for measuring liquid, equal to 0.568 litres in the UK and 0.473 litres in the US ➲See Extra help page **Numbers and measurements** on page Centre 24. **2** *UK informal* a pint of beer

pin-up /ˈpɪnʌp/ *noun* [**C**] an attractive, famous person who is often in big photographs which people stick to their walls, or the photograph of that person

pioneer /ˌpaɪəˈnɪəʳ/ *noun* [**C**] someone who is one of the first people to do something *one of the pioneers of modern science* •**pioneer** *verb* [**T**] *He pioneered the use of lasers in surgery.*

pioneering /ˌpaɪəˈnɪərɪŋ/ *adjective* [**always before noun**] starting the development of something important ***pioneering work/research** on atomic energy*

pious /ˈpaɪəs/ *adjective* **RELIGION** having strong religious beliefs, and living or behaving in a way which shows these beliefs

pip¹ /pɪp/ *noun* [**C**] *UK* **BIOLOGY** a small seed inside fruit such as apples and oranges

pip² /pɪp/ *verb* [**T**] **pipping**, *past* **pipped** *UK informal* to beat someone by a very small amount

WORD PARTNERS FOR ***pipe***

a pipe **leads/runs** [from/to, etc] sth • a pipe **bursts/leaks** • **through** a pipe

pipe¹ /paɪp/ *noun* [**C**] **1** TUBE a long tube which liquid or gas can move through *A water **pipe** had **burst**, flooding the basement.* **2** FOR SMOKING a tube with a bowl-shaped part at one end, used to smoke tobacco *to smoke a pipe* ➲See also: **exhaust pipe**

pipe² /paɪp/ *verb* [**T**] to send something through a pipe *Water is piped from a spring to houses in the local area.*
pipe down *phrasal verb informal* to stop making noise and become quieter
pipe up *phrasal verb informal* to suddenly say something *Then Lydia piped up with her view of things.*

pipeline /ˈpaɪplaɪn/ *noun* [**C**] **1** a series of pipes that carry liquid or gas over a long distance **2** **be in the pipeline** If a plan is in the pipeline, it is being developed and will happen in the future. *We have several projects in the pipeline.*

pipette /pɪˈpet/ *noun* [**C**] **CHEMISTRY, BIOLOGY** a thin glass tube used especially in science for measuring or moving a small amount of liquid ➲See picture at **laboratory**

piping /ˈpaɪpɪŋ/ *noun* [**U**] a piece of pipe *copper piping*

ˌpiping ˈhot *adjective* **FOOD** Piping hot food is very hot.

piquant /ˈpiːkənt/ *adjective formal* **FOOD** having a pleasant, spicy taste

pique¹ /piːk/ *noun* [**U**] *formal* when someone is annoyed

pique² /piːk/ *verb* **piquing**, *past* **piqued** **pique sb's curiosity/interest, etc** to make someone interested in something

piqued /piːkt/ *adjective* annoyed

piracy /ˈpaɪərəsi/ *noun* [**U**] **1** SHIPS attacking and stealing from ships **2** MUSIC/FILMS the illegal activity of copying and selling music, films, etc *software/video piracy*

pirate¹ /ˈpaɪərət/ *noun* [**C**] **1** SHIPS someone who attacks ships and steals from them **2** MUSIC/FILMS someone who illegally copies and sells music, films, etc

pirate² /ˈpaɪərət/ *verb* [**T**] **LAW** to illegally copy and sell music, films, etc

pirate³ /ˈpaɪərət/ *adjective* [**always before noun**] **LAW** illegally copied *a pirate CD/DVD*

Pisces /ˈpaɪsiːz/ *noun* [**C, U**] the sign of the zodiac which relates to the period of 20 February - 20 March, or a person born during this period

pistil /ˈpɪstɪl/ *noun* [**C**] **BIOLOGY** the female part of a flower, consisting of one or more carpels (= the female organs which produce seeds)

pistol /ˈpɪstᵊl/ *noun* [**C**] a small gun

piston /ˈpɪstᵊn/ *noun* [**C**] **PHYSICS** a part of an engine that moves up and down and makes other parts of the engine move

pit¹ /pɪt/ *noun* [**C**] **1** HOLE a large hole which has been dug in the ground **2** **BIOLOGY** *US* (*UK* **stone**) a large, hard seed that grows inside some types of fruit and vegetables **3** **GEOLOGY** (*also US* ˈ**pit** ˌ**mine**) a place where coal is dug out from under the ground **4** **the pits** **SPORT** *UK* (*US* **the pit**) the place where racing cars stop to be repaired or filled with fuel during a race **5** **be the pits** *informal* to be very bad *Our hotel was the absolute pits.*

pit² /pɪt/ *verb* **pitting**, *past* **pitted**
pit sb/sth against sb/sth *phrasal verb* to make someone or something compete against someone or something else *Chelsea will be pitted against Manchester United in the fourth round of the tournament.*

pitch¹ /pɪtʃ/ *verb* **1** LEVEL [**T**] to make something suitable for a particular level or group of people [**often passive**] *His talk was **pitched at** slightly too high a level for the audience.* **2** PERSUADE [**I, T**] *mainly US* to try to persuade someone to do something *They are **pitching for** new business at the moment.* **3** **pitch (sb/sth) forward/into, etc** to suddenly move in a particular direction, or to make someone or something suddenly move in a particular direction *He braked too hard and the car pitched forward.* **4** **pitch a tent** to choose a place for a tent and put it there **5** **SPORT** [**I, T**] in baseball, to throw the ball towards the person who is going to hit it *He used to pitch for the Chicago White Sox.* **6** **MUSIC** [**T**] to make sound at a particular level *The tune was pitched much too high for me.*
pitch in *phrasal verb informal* to help a group of people to do some work that needs to be

P

done *If we all pitch in, we'll get this kitchen cleaned up in no time.*

pitch² /pɪtʃ/ *noun* **1 SPORT** [C] *UK* an area of ground where a sport is played *a cricket/football pitch* **2 SPORT** [C] in baseball, a throw towards the person who is going to hit the ball *He struck out two batters with six pitches.* **3 MUSIC** [U] how high or low a sound is **4** [C, U] the things someone says in order to persuade you to do something *I wasn't very impressed by his **sales pitch**.* ➲See also: **fever pitch**

pitch-black /ˌpɪtʃ'blæk/ (*also* **pitch-dark**) *adjective* very dark *Outside it was pitch-black.*

pitcher /'pɪtʃəʳ/ *noun* [C] **1 SPORT** in baseball, someone who throws the ball at the person who is going to hit it ➲See colour picture **Sports 2** on page Centre 15 **2** *US* a container for holding and pouring out liquids *a pitcher of water*

pitfall /'pɪtfɔːl/ *noun* [C] a likely mistake or problem in a situation *the pitfalls of buying a house*

pithy /'pɪθi/ *adjective* A pithy remark expresses something in a very clear and direct way.

pitiful /'pɪtifəl/ *adjective* **1** SAD making you feel pity *I didn't recognize him, he looked so pitiful.* **2** BAD very bad *a pitiful excuse* •**pitifully** *adverb*

pittance /'pɪtəns/ *noun* [**no plural**] a very small amount of money *She works very long hours and yet she **earns a pittance**.*

pituitary gland /pɪ'tjuːɪtəriˌglænd/ *noun* [**C usually singular**] **ANATOMY** a small organ at the bottom of the brain which controls how the body grows and develops by producing hormones ➲See picture at **brain**

WORD PARTNERS FOR ***pity***

feel pity • **take** pity **on** sb • pity **for** sb

O-- **pity¹** /'pɪti/ *noun* **1 It's a pity...** used to say that something is disappointing *It's a pity you're not staying longer.* **2** [U] a feeling of sympathy for someone *I was hoping someone would **take pity on** me* (= help me in a difficult situation) *and give me a lift home.* ➲See also: **self-pity**

pity² /'pɪti/ *verb* [T] to feel sorry for someone *She doesn't want people to pity her.*

pivot /'pɪvət/ *noun* [C] **1 PHYSICS** a fixed point on which something balances or turns **2** the most important part of something •**pivot** *verb* [I, T]

pivotal /'pɪvətəl/ *adjective* having a very important influence on something *He has played a **pivotal role** in the negotiations.*

pixel /'pɪksəl/ *noun* [C] **COMPUTING** a small point that forms part of the image on a computer screen

pixie /'pɪksi/ *noun* [C] a small imaginary person who can do magic things

pizza /'piːtsə/ *noun* [C, U] **FOOD** a food made from a flat, round piece of bread covered with cheese, vegetables, etc and cooked in an oven ➲See colour picture **Food** on page Centre 11

placard /'plækɑːd/ *noun* [C] a large sign with writing that someone carries, often to show that they disagree with something

placate /plə'keɪt/ Ⓤⓢ /'pleɪkeɪt/ *verb* [T] *formal* to make someone less angry about something

O-- **place¹** /pleɪs/ *noun* **1** SOMEWHERE [C] a position, building, town, area, etc *His leg's broken in two places.* ○ *Edinburgh would be a nice place to live.* ○ *What a stupid place to park.* **2 take place** to happen *The meeting will take place next week.* **3 in place a** CORRECT POSITION in the correct position *The chairs are all in place.* **b** EXISTING If a rule, system, etc is in place, it has started to exist. *There are now laws in place to prevent this from happening.* **4 out of place a** WRONG POSITION not in the correct position *Why are my files all out of place?* **b** NOT SUITABLE not right or suitable for a particular situation *Everyone else was wearing jeans and I felt completely out of place in my office clothes.* **5 all over the place** in or to many different places *There was blood all over the place.* **6 in place of sth** instead of something *Try adding fruit to your breakfast cereal in place of sugar.* **7** HOME [C] *informal* someone's home *They've just bought a place in Spain.* **8** OPPORTUNITY [C] an opportunity to take part in something *She's got a place at Liverpool University to do Spanish.* **9 in first/second/third, etc place** If you are in first/second, etc place in a race or competition, that is your position. *He finished in fifth place.* **10 fall into place** When events or details that you did not understand before fall into place, they become easy to understand. **11 in the first place** used to refer to the time when something started *How did this error happen in the first place?* **12 put sb in their place** to let someone know that they are not as important as they think they are ➲See also: **decimal place**, have/take **pride¹** of place

place² /pleɪs/ *verb* **1 place sth in/on, etc** to put something somewhere carefully *She placed a large dish in front of me.* **2** [T] to cause someone to be in a situation *One stupid action has placed us all at risk.* **3 can't place sb** to not be able to remember who someone is or where you have met them *I recognize her face, but I can't quite place her.* **4 place an advertisement/bet/order, etc** to arrange to have an advertisement, bet, order, etc **5 place emphasis/importance, etc on sth** to give something emphasis, importance, etc *They place a lot of importance on qualifications.*

placebo /plə'siːbəʊ/ *noun* [C] **HEALTH** a substance that is not a medicine but which a patient takes, thinking it is a medicine. The purpose of a placebo is either to make a patient feel better because they think they have been treated, or to compare the effect of no medicine with the effect of medicine when it is given to other patients.

placement /'pleɪsmənt/ *noun* **1** WORK [C] *UK* a position that someone has with an organization for a short time in order to learn about the work that is done there *He got a month's placement on a national newspaper.* **2** PUT [U, **no plural**] when you put something or someone somewhere *the placement of additional police on the streets*

placenta /plə'sen.tə/ *noun* [U, C] **BIOLOGY, ANATOMY** the organ that feeds a baby as it is developing inside its mother, or the part that provides food for a seed in a plant ➲See picture at **carpel** ➲See picture at **foetus**

ˈplace ˌvalue *noun* [U] **MATHEMATICS** the value of a number decided by its position, for instance whether it is a one, a ten, a hundred, etc

placid /ˈplæsɪd/ *adjective* A placid person is calm and does not often get angry or excited. •**placidly** *adverb*

plagiarism /ˈpleɪdʒəˈrɪzəm/ *noun* [U] **LAW** when someone copies someone else's work or ideas *He was accused of plagiarism.*

plagiarize (*also UK* **-ise**) /ˈpleɪdʒəraɪz/ *verb* [I, T] **LAW** to copy someone else's work or ideas •**plagiarist** /ˈpleɪdʒəˈrɪst/ *noun* [C] someone who plagiarizes

plague¹ /pleɪg/ *noun* [C] **1 HEALTH** a serious disease that spreads quickly and kills a lot of people **2 a plague of sth** a large number of something unpleasant that causes a lot of damage *a plague of rats*

plague² /pleɪg/ *verb* [T] **plaguing**, *past* **plagued** to make someone suffer for a long time [**often passive**] *He's been plagued by bad luck ever since he bought that house.*

plaice /pleɪs/ *noun* [C, U] **FOOD** a sea fish with a flat circular body, or this fish eaten as food

plaid /plæd/ *noun* [C, U] *US* cloth with a pattern of different coloured squares and crossing lines *a plaid dress*

o→**plain¹** /pleɪn/ *adjective* **1** SIMPLE simple and not complicated *plain food* **2** NOT MIXED not mixed with other colours, substances, etc *a plain blue carpet* ○ *plain yoghurt* **3** PERSON A plain person is not attractive to look at. **4** OBVIOUS obvious and clear [+ (**that**)] *It's quite plain that she doesn't want to talk to me about it.* ➲See also: be plain **sailing**

plain² /pleɪn/ *adverb informal* **plain stupid/wrong, etc** completely stupid/wrong, etc *That's just plain stupid!*

plain³ /pleɪn/ *noun* [C] **GEOGRAPHY** a large area of flat land

plainclothes /ˈpleɪnˌkləʊθz/ *adjective* [**always before noun**] Plainclothes police wear normal clothes and not a uniform.

plainly /ˈpleɪnli/ *adverb* **1** SIMPLY in a simple way that is not complicated *plainly dressed* **2** OBVIOUSLY in a clear and obvious way *This is plainly wrong.*

plaintiff /ˈpleɪntɪf/ *noun* [C] **LAW** someone who takes legal action against someone else in a court of law

plaintive /ˈpleɪntɪv/ *adjective* sounding sad *a plaintive cry*

plait /plæt/ *UK* (*US* **braid**) *verb* [T] to twist three pieces of hair, rope, etc together so that they form one long piece •**plait** *UK* (*US* **braid**) *noun* [C] *She wore her hair in plaits.*

WORD PARTNERS FOR ***plan***

announce/approve/implement/oppose/outline/unveil a plan • an **ambitious/controversial/strategic** plan

o→**plan¹** /plæn/ *noun* [C] **1** ARRANGEMENT an arrangement for what you intend to do or how you intend to do something *the country's economic plan* ○ *Do you have any* ***plans for*** *the weekend?* ○ *The plan is that we'll buy a car once we're there.* ○ *There's been a* ***change of plan*** *and we're going on Wednesday instead.* ○ *Luckily, everything went* ***according to plan*** (= happened the way it was planned). **2** DRAWING a drawing that shows how something appears from above or will appear from above when it is built *a street plan.* ○ *We had a designer draw up a plan for the yard.*

o→**plan²** /plæn/ *verb* **planning**, *past* **planned 1** THINK AND DECIDE to think about and decide what you are going to do or how you are going to do something *We're just planning our holidays.* ○ *As a manager, you've got to* ***plan ahead.*** ○ *I'd* ***planned*** *the meeting* ***for*** *Friday.* **2 plan to do sth** to intend to do something *He plans to go to college next year.* **3** DESIGN [T] to decide how something will be built *We got an architect to help us plan our new kitchen.*

plan on doing sth *phrasal verb* to intend to do something *We're planning on catching the early train.*

plan sth out *phrasal verb* to think about and decide what you are going to do or how you are going to do something *Have you planned out your journey?* ○ *I'm just planning out my day.*

WORD PARTNERS FOR ***plane***

board/catch/get on/get off a plane • a plane **gets in/lands/takes off** • **on** a plane • **by** plane

o→**plane¹** /pleɪn/ *noun* [C] **1** FLYING a vehicle that flies and has an engine and wings *What time does her* ***plane get in*** (= arrive)? ○ *He likes to watch the* ***planes taking off*** *and* ***landing.*** ○ *a plane crash* **2 DT** a tool that you use to make wood smooth **3 MATHEMATICS** in mathematics, a flat surface

plane² /pleɪn/ *verb* [T] **DT** to make a piece of wood smooth using a tool called a plane

planet /ˈplænɪt/ *noun* [C] **ASTRONOMY** a large, round object in space that moves around the sun or another star *Jupiter is the largest planet of our solar system.* •**planetary** *adjective* relating to planets

planetarium /ˌplænɪˈteəriəm/ *noun* [C] *plural* **planetariums** or **planetaria ASTRONOMY** a building that has a machine for showing the positions and movements of the stars and planets

planimeter /plænˈɪmɪtəʳ/ *noun* [C] **MATHEMATICS** a piece of equipment for measuring the area of a flat shape by moving a point around its edge •**planimetric** /ˌplænɪˈmetrɪk/ *adjective*

plank /plæŋk/ *noun* [C] a long, flat piece of wood *wooden planks*

plankton /ˈplæŋktən/ *noun* [U] **BIOLOGY** very small plants and animals in the sea that are eaten by fish and other sea creatures

ˌplanned eˈconomy *noun* [C] **ECONOMICS** an economic system in which industry is controlled by the government and government makes all decisions about what to do with the money made

planner /ˈplænəʳ/ *noun* [C] someone whose job is to plan things, especially which buildings are built in towns *urban planners*

P

planning /'plænɪŋ/ *noun* [U] **1** DECISIONS the activity of thinking about and deciding what you are going to do or how you are going to do something *Events like these take months of careful planning.* **2** BUILDINGS control over which buildings are built in an area *town planning* ➲See also: **family planning**

O⁻ **plant¹** /plɑːnt/ *noun* [C] **1** BIOLOGY a living thing that grows in the soil or water and has leaves and roots, especially one that is smaller than a tree *Have you **watered the plants?*** ○ *tomato plants* **2** FACTORY a large factory where an industrial process happens *a nuclear power plant* ➲See also: **potted plant**

plant² /plɑːnt/ *verb* [T] **1** FARMING to put seeds or plants in the ground so that they will grow *to **plant bulbs/seeds/trees*** **2** SECRETLY to secretly put something in a place that will make someone seem guilty *She insisted that the drugs had been **planted on** her without her knowledge.* **3 plant a bomb** to put a bomb somewhere so that it will explode there **4 plant sth in/next/on, etc** to put something firmly in a particular place *He planted himself next to me on the sofa.* **5** IDEA/DOUBTS to make someone start thinking something *I was confident till you **planted doubts** in my mind.*

plantation /plæn'teɪʃᵊn/ *noun* [C] **1** FARMING an area of land in a hot country where a crop is grown *a banana/cotton/sugar plantation* **2** an area of land where trees are grown to produce wood

plaque /plɑːk/ *noun* **1** [C] a flat piece of metal or stone with writing on it which is fixed to a wall, often in order to make people remember a dead person **2** HEALTH [U] a harmful substance that forms on your teeth

plasma /'plæzmə/ *noun* [U] BIOLOGY the clear liquid part of blood which contains the blood cells

ˈplasma ˌscreen *noun* [C] a screen for showing very clear words or pictures which uses special gases pressed between two flat pieces of glass

plasmolysis /plæz'mɒləsɪs/ *noun* [U] BIOLOGY when protoplasm (= clear liquid in all living cells) shrinks back from cell walls because of lack of water

plaster¹ /'plɑːstəʳ/ *noun* **1** [U] a substance that is spread on walls in order to make them smooth **2** HEALTH [C] *UK* (*US* **Band-Aid** *trademark*) a small piece of sticky material that you put on cuts on your body **3 be in plaster** HEALTH *UK* (*US* **be in a cast**) If your arm or leg is in plaster, it is covered in a hard, white substance to protect a broken bone.

plaster² /'plɑːstəʳ/ *verb* [T] **1** COVER to cover most of a surface with something *My boots were **plastered with** mud.* **2** WALL to cover a wall with a substance in order to make it smooth

plastered /'plɑːstəd/ *adjective informal* very drunk

O⁻ **plastic** /'plæstɪk/ *noun* [C, U] a light, artificial substance that can be made into different shapes when it is soft and is used in a lot of different ways *Most children's toys are made of plastic.* •**plastic** *adjective a **plastic bag***

plasticity /plæs'tɪsəti/ *noun* [U] *formal* the quality of being soft enough to make into many different shapes

ˌplastic ˈsurgery *noun* [U] HEALTH operations on someone's face or body to make them more attractive *to have plastic surgery*

ˈplastic ˌwrap *US* (*UK* **clingfilm**) *noun* [U] thin, transparent plastic used for wrapping or covering food

O⁻ **plate** /pleɪt/ *noun* **1** FOOD [C] a flat, round object which is used for putting food on *a **dinner plate*** ○ *a plate of biscuits* **2** METAL/GLASS [C] a flat piece of metal or glass *I had a metal plate put in my knee after the accident.* **3 gold/silver plate** metal with a thin layer of gold or silver on top **4** PICTURE [C] a picture in a book ➲See also: **L-plate, license plate, number plate** **5** GEOLOGY one of the large pieces of rock that form the surface of the Earth

plateau /'plætəʊ/ Ⓤⓢ /plæ'təʊ/ *noun* [C] *plural UK* **plateaux** or *also US* **plateaus** **1** GEOGRAPHY a large area of high, flat land **2** a period when the level of something stays the same [**usually singular**] *Sales are still good but they've **reached a plateau**.*

platelet /'pleɪtlət/ *noun* [C] BIOLOGY a very small part of a cell in the blood that makes the blood thicker and stops it from flowing when you cut yourself ➲See picture at **blood cells**

plate tectonics /ˌpleɪttek'tɒnɪks/ *noun* [U] GEOLOGY a theory which explains how the Earth's surface formed by the movement of large areas of rock

platform /'plætfɔːm/ *noun* [C] **1** RAISED SURFACE a raised surface for people to stand on, especially when they are speaking to a lot of people *The speakers all stood on a platform.* **2** TRAIN the area in a railway station where you get on and off the train *The train for London, Paddington, will depart from platform 12.* **3** POLITICS all the things that a political party promises to do if they are elected *They campaigned on a platform of low taxation.* **4** FOR OPINIONS a way of telling the public about your opinions *Basically, he uses the newspaper as a **platform for** airing his political views.*

platinum /'plætɪnəm/ Ⓤⓢ /'plætnəm/ *noun* [U] CHEMISTRY a silver-coloured metal that is very valuable (symbol **Pt**)

platitude /'plætɪtjuːd/ *noun* [C] LANGUAGE something that is boring because it has been said many times before

platonic /plə'tɒnɪk/ *adjective* A platonic relationship is friendly and not sexual.

platoon /plə'tuːn/ *noun* [C] a small group of soldiers

platter /'plætəʳ/ *noun* [C] a large plate used for serving food

plaudit /'plɔːdɪt/ *noun* [C] *formal* praise [**usually plural**] *He has **earned/won plaudits*** (= been praised) *for his latest novel.*

plausible /'plɔːzɪbl/ *adjective* If something that someone says or writes is plausible, it could be true. *a **plausible excuse/explanation*** ➲Opposite **implausible** •**plausibility** /ˌplɔːzɪ'bɪləti/ *noun* [U] when something is plausible

O⁻ **play**[1] /pleɪ/ *verb* **1** **SPORT** [I, T] When you play a sport or game, you take part in it. *You play tennis, don't you Sam?* ○ *We often used to play cards.* ○ *I used to* ***play*** *netball* ***for*** *my school.* ○ *I'm playing Tony* (= playing against Tony) *at squash tonight.* ○ *Newcastle are* ***playing against*** *Arsenal tonight.* **2** [CHILDREN] [I, T] When children play, they enjoy themselves with toys and games. *She likes* ***playing with*** *her dolls.* **3** **MUSIC** [I, T] to make music with a musical instrument *Tim was playing the piano.* **4** [RECORD/RADIO] [I, T] If a radio, record, etc plays, it produces sounds, or if you play a radio, record, etc you make it produce sounds. *A radio was playing in the background.* ○ *He plays his records late into the night.* **5** [ACTING] [T] to be a character in a film or play *Morgan played the father in the film version.* **6** **play a joke/trick on sb** to deceive someone as a joke *I played a trick on her and pretended we'd eaten all the food.* ➲See also: play it by **ear**, play games (**game**[1]), play (it) **safe**[1], play for **time**[1], play **truant**

play about/around *phrasal verb* to behave in a silly way *Stop playing around and get on with your homework!*

be playing at sth *phrasal verb UK* If you ask what someone is playing at, you are angry because they are doing something silly. *What do you think you're playing at!*

play sth back *phrasal verb* to listen to sounds or watch pictures that you have just recorded *When I played back our conversation, I realized I hadn't made myself clear.*

play sth down *phrasal verb* to try to make people think that something is less important or bad than it really is *The government have tried to play down the seriousness of the incident.*

play on sth *phrasal verb* to use someone's fears in order to make that person do or believe what you want *A lot of marketing strategies just* ***play on*** *your* ***fears*** *and insecurities.*

play up *phrasal verb UK* **1** [CHILD] If a child plays up, he or she behaves badly. **2** [MACHINE] If a machine plays up, it does not work as it should.

play (about/around) with sth *phrasal verb* **1** [TRY] to think about or try different ways of doing something *We've been playing around with ideas for a new TV show.* **2** [TOUCH] to keep touching or moving something, often when you are bored or nervous *Stop playing with your hair!*

WORD PARTNERS FOR ***play (noun)***

perform/put on/write a play • **in** a play • a play **about** sth

play[2] /pleɪ/ *noun* **1** **LITERATURE** [C] a story that is written for actors to perform, usually in a theatre *We saw a play at the National Theatre.* ○ *Most schools usually* ***put on a play*** (= perform a play) *at Christmas.* **2** **SPORT** [U] the activity of taking part in a sport or a game *Rain stopped play in the Hingis-Davenport match.* **3** [CHILDREN] [U] when children enjoy themselves with toys and games *a* ***play area*** **4** **fair play** behaviour that is fair, honest, and does not take advantage of people **5** **LANGUAGE** **a play on words** a joke using a word or phrase that has two meanings ➲See also: **foul play, role-play**

playboy /ˈpleɪbɔɪ/ *noun* [C] a rich man who spends his time enjoying himself and has relationships with a lot of beautiful women

O⁻ **player** /ˈpleɪəʳ/ *noun* [C] **1** **SPORT** someone who plays a sport or game *football/tennis players* **2** **MUSIC** someone who plays a musical instrument *a piano player* ➲See also: **cassette player, CD player, record player**

playful /ˈpleɪfᵊl/ *adjective* funny and not serious *a* ***playful mood/remark*** •**playfulness** *noun* [U] •**playfully** *adverb*

playground /ˈpleɪgraʊnd/ *noun* [C] **EDUCATION** an area of land where children can play, especially at school

playgroup /ˈpleɪgruːp/ *noun* [C] a place where small children go during the day when they are too young to go to school

ˈ**playing** ˌ**card** *noun* [C] one of a set of 52 small pieces of stiff paper with numbers and pictures on, used for playing games

ˈ**playing** ˌ**field** *noun* [C] **1** **SPORT** an area of land used for sports such as football **2** **a level playing field** a situation in which everyone has the same chance of succeeding

playoff /ˈpleɪɒf/ *noun* [C] **SPORT** a game between two teams that have equal points in order to decide which is the winner

playpen /ˈpleɪpen/ *noun* [C] a small structure with net or bars around the sides that young children are put into so that they can play safely

playroom /ˈpleɪruːm/ *noun* [C] a room in a house for children to play in

PlayStation /ˈpleɪˌsteɪʃᵊn/ *noun* [C] *trademark* a machine that you use to play games on your television

plaything /ˈpleɪθɪŋ/ *noun* [C] someone who is treated without respect and is forced to do things for someone else's enjoyment

playtime /ˈpleɪtaɪm/ *noun* [C, U] *UK* **EDUCATION** a period of time when children at school can play outside

playwright /ˈpleɪraɪt/ *noun* [C] **LITERATURE** someone who writes plays

plaza /ˈplɑːzə/ *noun* [C] *US* **1** [PUBLIC AREA] an open, public area in a city or town *Mexico City's main plaza is called the Zocalo.* **2** [SHOPS] a group of buildings with shops, often including an open, public area *a shopping plaza*

PLC /ˌpiːelˈsiː/ *noun* [C] **ECONOMICS** *abbreviation for* product life cycle: in business, all the stages that a product goes through from being made to being sold

plc, PLC /ˌpiːelˈsiː/ *noun* [C] **ECONOMICS** *abbreviation for* Public Limited Company: used after the name of a large company in Britain whose shares (= equal parts of its total value) can be bought and sold by the public

WORD PARTNERS FOR ***plea***

issue/make/reject a plea • a **desperate/emotional /impassioned** plea • a plea **for** sth • a plea **from** sb

plea /pliː/ *noun* [C] **1** **LAW** when someone says in a court of law if they are guilty or not guilty

P

of the crime they have been accused of *a plea of guilty/not guilty* **2** a strong request *an emotional* ***plea for*** *forgiveness*

plead /pliːd/ *verb past* **pleaded**, *also US* **pled 1 LAW** [T] to say in a court of law if you are guilty or not guilty of the crime you have been accused of *He* ***pleaded*** *not guilty* ***to*** *five felony charges.* **2** ASK [I] to ask for something in a strong and emotional way *He* ***pleaded with*** *her to come back.* ○ *She* ***pleaded for*** *mercy.* **3** EXCUSE [T] to say something as an excuse *You'll just have to* ***plead ignorance*** (= say you did not know). **4 plead sb's case/cause** to say something to try to help someone get what they want or avoid punishment

O-ᵚ**pleasant** /ˈplezᵊnt/ *adjective* **1** ENJOYABLE enjoyable or attractive *pleasant weather/surroundings* ○ *We had a very pleasant evening.* **2** FRIENDLY A pleasant person has a friendly character. ⊃Opposite **unpleasant •pleasantly** *adverb I was* ***pleasantly surprised***.

pleasantry /ˈplezᵊntri/ *noun* [C] a polite thing that you say when you meet someone [**usually plural**] *They* ***exchanged pleasantries*** *about the weather.*

O-ᵚ**please¹** /pliːz/ *exclamation* **1** something that you say to be polite when you are asking for something or asking someone to do something *Could you fill in the form, please?* ○ *Please may I use your telephone?* **2 Yes, please.** used to accept something politely *"Would you like a lift home?" "Oh yes, please."*

please² /pliːz/ *verb* **1** [I, T] to make someone happy *the desire to please* ○ *I only got married to please my parents.* ⊃Opposite **displease 2 anything/as/what/whatever, etc you please** used to say that someone can have or do anything they want *Feel free to talk about anything you please.* ○ *He can come and go as he pleases.* **3 Please yourself.** a slightly rude way of telling someone that you do not care what they choose to do *"I don't want anything to eat." "Please yourself."*

O-ᵚ**pleased** /pliːzd/ *adjective* **1** happy or satisfied *I wasn't very* ***pleased about*** *having to pay.* [**+ to do sth**] *I'm pleased to be back in England.* [**+ (that)**] *He was pleased that she had come back.* ○ *I'm really* ***pleased with*** *the quality of his work.* **2 Pleased to meet you.** a polite way of greeting someone you are meeting for the first time

COMMON LEARNER ERROR

pleased

Be careful to use the correct preposition or verb pattern after this word.

I'm ***pleased with*** *my new computer.*

He wasn't very ***pleased about*** *the news.*

I'm ***pleased to be*** *in London.*

~~*I'm pleased for my new computer.*~~

~~*He wasn't very pleased of the news.*~~

~~*I'm pleased for being in London.*~~

pleasing /ˈpliːzɪŋ/ *adjective* Something that is pleasing gives pleasure. *the most pleasing aspect of her work* ○ *These buildings are very pleasing to the eye.*

pleasurable /ˈpleʒᵊrəbl/ *adjective* enjoyable *a* ***pleasurable experience***

WORD PARTNERS FOR ***pleasure***

derive/express/give pleasure • **take** pleasure **in** sth • **enormous/great/perverse/pure/sheer** pleasure

O-ᵚ**pleasure** /ˈpleʒəʳ/ *noun* **1** HAPPINESS [U] a feeling of happiness or enjoyment *His visits used to give us such* ***pleasure***. ○ *She seemed to* ***take pleasure in*** (= enjoy) *humiliating people.* ○ ***It gives me great pleasure*** *to introduce our next guest.* ⊃Opposite **displeasure 2** ENJOYABLE EXPERIENCE [C, U] an enjoyable activity or experience *Food is one of* ***life's great pleasures***. ○ *I once* ***had the pleasure of*** *sharing a taxi with her.* **3** NOT WORK [U] If you do something for pleasure, you do it because you enjoy it and not because it is your job. *reading* ***for pleasure*** **4 It's a pleasure.; My pleasure.** a polite way of replying to someone who has thanked you *"Thank you for a wonderful evening." "My pleasure."*

pleated /ˈpliːtɪd/ *adjective* A pleated piece of clothing or piece of cloth has regular, vertical folds in it. *a pleated skirt*

plebiscite /ˈplebɪsaɪt/ *noun* [C] *formal* **POLITICS** a referendum (= an occasion when all the people in a country can vote in order to show their opinion about a political question)

pled /pled/ *US past of* plead

WORD PARTNERS FOR ***pledge (noun)***

break/fulfil/make a pledge • a pledge **on** sth

pledge¹ /pledʒ/ *noun* [C] a serious promise [**+ to do sth**] *a pledge to create jobs* ○ *He* ***made a*** *solemn* ***pledge*** *to the American people.*

pledge² /pledʒ/ *verb* [T] to promise seriously to do something or give something *Foreign donors have pledged $550 million.* ○ *He* ***pledged*** *his* ***support*** *to Mandela.* [**+ to do sth**] *He pledged to cut government salaries.*

Pleistocene /ˈplaɪstəʊsiːn/ *adjective* **GEOLOGY** from the period of time between about 1.6 million and 10,000 years ago, in which modern humans first appeared and the northern part of Earth had an ice age *the Pleistocene era*

plentiful /ˈplentɪfᵊl/ *adjective* If something is plentiful, there is a lot of it available. *a* ***plentiful supply*** *of meat*

O-ᵚ**plenty** /ˈplenti/ *quantifier* **1** AS MUCH AS YOU NEED easily as much or as many as you need *Don't bring any food - we've got plenty.* ○ *There is* ***plenty of*** *evidence to support her claims.* ○ *There's plenty of room.* ○ *Help yourself to food - there's plenty more.* **2 plenty big/large/wide, etc enough** easily as big/large/wide, etc as you need something to be *This house is plenty big enough for two families.* **3** A LOT a lot *I know* ***plenty of*** *unemployed musicians.* ○ *There's plenty for you to do.*

plethora /ˈpleθᵊrə/ *noun* **a plethora of sth** *formal* a large number of something *There is a confusing plethora of pension plans.*

pleura /ˈplʊərə/ *noun* [C] *plural* **plurae ANATOMY** the membrane (= thin layer of tissue) that surrounds each lung **•pleural** /ˈplʊərᵊl/ *adjective*

P

pleural membranes ➲See picture at **respiratory system**

pliers /ˈplaɪəz/ *noun* [**plural**] **DT** a tool for holding or pulling small things like nails or for cutting wire *a pair of pliers*

plight /plaɪt/ *noun* [**no plural**] *formal* an unpleasant or difficult situation *the plight of the sick and the poor*

Pliocene /ˈplaɪəʊsiːn/ *adjective* **GEOLOGY** from the period of time between about 5.2 million and 1.6 million years ago, in which the primates (= monkeys, apes, etc.) first appeared which would later become humans *the Pliocene era*

plod /plɒd/ *verb* **plodding**, *past* **plodded plod along/on/through, etc** to walk with slow, heavy steps *We plodded through the mud.*

plonk¹ /plɒŋk/ *verb UK informal* **plonk sth down/in/on, etc** to put something somewhere quickly and without care *She plonked her bag on the floor.*
plonk yourself down *phrasal verb* to sit down quickly and without care

plonk² /plɒŋk/ *noun* [**U**] *UK informal* cheap wine

plop¹ /plɒp/ *noun* [**C**] the sound made by an object when it falls into water

plop² /plɒp/ *verb* **plopping**, *past* **plopped** *US informal* **plop (sth) down/onto, etc** to put something somewhere quickly and without care *She plopped down next to me.*

plot¹ /plɒt/ *noun* [**C**] **1 LITERATURE** the things that happen in a story *I don't like movies with* ***complicated plots.*** **2** [PLAN] a plan to do something bad [**+ to do sth**] *a plot to blow up the embassy* **3** [LAND] a piece of land, often for growing food or for building on *a building plot*

plot² /plɒt/ *verb* **plotting**, *past* **plotted 1** [**I, T**] to plan to do something bad [**+ to do sth**] *They plotted to bring down the government.* ○ *He fired all those accused of* ***plotting against*** *him.* **2 MATHEMATICS** [**T**] to make marks on a map, picture, etc to show the position or development of something *This chart* ***plots*** *the* ***position*** *of all aircraft.*

plotter /ˈplɒtəʳ/ *noun* **1** someone who makes a plan to do something bad **2 COMPUTING** a printing device that is connected to a computer and uses computer information to make graphs (= mathematical pictures showing measurements)

plough¹ *UK* (*US* **plow**) /plaʊ/ *noun* [**C**] **FARMING** a large tool used by farmers to turn over the soil before planting crops

plough² *UK* (*US* **plow**) /plaʊ/ *verb* [**I, T**] **FARMING** to turn over soil with a plough
plough sth back *phrasal verb* to spend the money that a business has earned on improving that business *All profits are* ***ploughed back into*** *the company.*
plough into sth *phrasal verb* to hit something with great force *My car ploughed straight into the car in front.*
plough on *phrasal verb* to continue doing something, although it is difficult or boring
plough through sth *phrasal verb* to finish what you are reading, eating, or working on, although there is a lot of it *I had to plough through the whole report.*

plover /ˈplʌv.əʳ/ *noun* [**C**] a bird with a short tail and long legs, which is found mainly by the sea or in areas covered with grass

plow /plaʊ/ *noun, verb* **FARMING** *US spelling of* plough

WORD PARTNERS FOR ***ploy***

use a ploy • a ploy **backfires/works** • a **clever/cunning/cynical/deliberate** ploy • a ploy **by** sb

ploy /plɔɪ/ *noun* [**C**] a slightly dishonest method used to try to achieve something [**+ to do sth**] *The phone call was just a ploy to get rid of her.*

PLS *informal* **INTERNET** *written abbeviation for* please: used in emails and text messages

pluck /plʌk/ *verb* **1 pluck sth/sb from/out, etc** to quickly pull something or someone from the place where they are *A helicopter plucked him from the sea.* **2 FOOD** [**T**] to pull all the feathers out of a bird before cooking it **3 MUSIC** [**T**] If you pluck the strings of a musical instrument, you pull them with your fingers to make a sound. **4** [PLANT] [**T**] *literary* to pick a flower or part of a plant **5 pluck your eyebrows** to pull hairs out of your eyebrows (= lines of hair above your eyes) to make them look tidy ➲See also: pluck up the **courage** (to do sth)

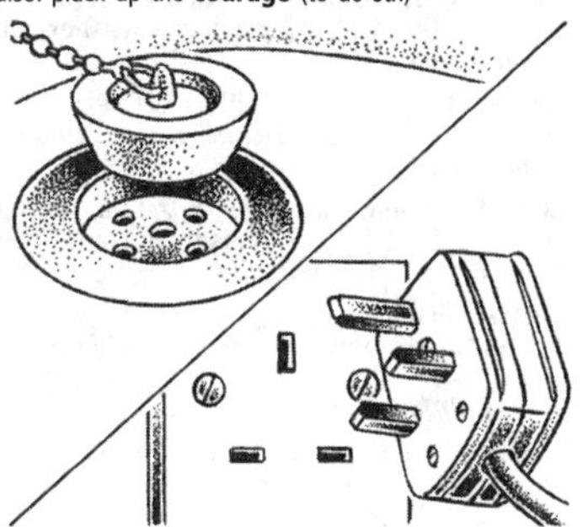

plug

plug¹ /plʌg/ *noun* [**C**] **1 PHYSICS** a plastic or rubber object with metal pins, used to connect electrical equipment to an electricity supply *I need to change the plug on my hairdryer.* **2** [HOLE] something you put in a hole to block it *a* ***bath plug*** **3** [ADVERTISEMENT] when someone talks about a new book, film, etc in public to advertise it *She managed to get in a plug for her new book.* **4 pull the plug** to prevent an activity from continuing *They have pulled the plug on jazz broadcasts.* ➲See also: **spark plug**

plug² /plʌg/ *verb* [**T**] **plugging**, *past* **plugged 1 plug a gap/hole** *mainly UK* to solve a problem by supplying something that is needed *The new computer system will help to plug the gap in the county's ability to collect taxes.* **2** [ADVERTISE] to talk about a new book, film, etc in public in order to advertise it *He was on TV, plugging his new book.* **3** [HOLE] to block a hole
plug away *phrasal verb informal* to work hard at something for a long time *I'm still* ***plugging***

away at my article.
plug sth in *phrasal verb* to connect a piece of electrical equipment to an electricity supply *Could you plug the iron in for me?* ⊃Opposite **unplug**
plug sth into sth *phrasal verb* to connect one piece of electrical equipment to another *You need to plug the speakers into the stereo.*

plughole /ˈplʌghəʊl/ (*also US* **drain**) *noun* [C] the hole in a bath or sink (= place in a kitchen where dishes are washed) where the water flows away

plug-in (*also* **plugin**) /ˈplʌgɪn/ *noun* [C] **COMPUTING** a small computer program that makes a larger one work faster or be able to do more things

plum /plʌm/ *noun* [C] **FOOD** a soft, round fruit with red, yellow, or purple skin and a stone in the middle

plumage /ˈpluːmɪdʒ/ *noun* [U] **BIOLOGY** a bird's feathers

plumber /ˈplʌməʳ/ *noun* [C] someone whose job is to repair or connect water pipes and things like toilets and baths

plumbing /ˈplʌmɪŋ/ *noun* [U] the water pipes in a building

plume /pluːm/ *noun* **1 a plume of dust/smoke, etc** a tall, thin amount of dust/smoke, etc rising into the air. **2** [C] a large feather, often worn for decoration

plummet /ˈplʌmɪt/ *verb* [I] to fall very quickly in amount or value *Temperatures plummeted to minus 20.*

plump¹ /plʌmp/ *adjective* **1** FAT quite fat *a plump child* **2** ROUND pleasantly round or full *nice plump cloves of garlic*

plump² /plʌmp/ *verb*
plump for sth *phrasal verb UK* to choose something, especially after thinking about it for a time *I plumped for the salmon.*

plumule /ˈpluːmjuːl/ *noun* [C] **BIOLOGY** the first shoot (= new branch or stem) that grows from the seed of a plant

plunder /ˈplʌndəʳ/ *verb* [I, T] to steal, especially during a war *Many of the region's churches had been plundered.* •**plunder** *noun* [U]

plunge¹ /plʌndʒ/ *verb* **1 plunge down/into, etc** to fall or move down very quickly and with force *The car came off the road and plunged down the hillside.* **2** [I] to become lower in temperature, value, etc very suddenly and quickly *Temperatures plunged below zero.*
plunge sth into sth *phrasal verb* to push something very hard into something else *He plunged the knife into the man's stomach.*
plunge sb/sth into sth *phrasal verb* to make someone or something suddenly be unhappy or in an unpleasant situation [**often passive**] *The country had been plunged into chaos.*
plunge into sth *phrasal verb* to start doing something with a lot of energy *Trying to forget about her, he plunged into his work.*

WORD PARTNERS FOR ***plunge***
take a plunge • a plunge **in** sth • a **stock market** plunge

plunge² /plʌndʒ/ *noun* **1** [C] a sudden and quick decrease in the value, amount, or level of something *Prices have* ***taken a plunge*** (= suddenly become less). **2 take the plunge** to do something important or difficult, especially after thinking about it for a long time *We're finally going to take the plunge and buy a house.*

the pluperfect /ˌpluːˈpɜːfɪkt/ (*also* **the past perfect**) *noun* **LANGUAGE** the form of the verb that is used to show that an action had already finished when another action happened. In English, the pluperfect is made with 'had' and a past participle.

plural /ˈplʊərᵊl/ *noun* [C] **LANGUAGE** a word or part of a word which shows that you are talking about more than one person or thing. For example 'babies' is the plural of 'baby'. •**plural** *adjective 'cattle' and 'trousers' are plural nouns.*

pluralism /ˈplʊərᵊlɪzᵊm/ *noun* [U] **SOCIETY** the existence in a society of many different types of people with many different beliefs and opinions *political pluralism* •**pluralist** (*also* **pluralistic** /ˌplʊərᵊlˈɪstɪk/) *adjective* relating to pluralism *a pluralist society*

O-ᐧ**plus¹** /plʌs/ *preposition* **1** ADDED added to *Five plus three is eight.* **2** AND and also *You've won their latest CD plus two tickets for their concert.*

plus² /plʌs/ *adjective* **40 plus, 150 plus, etc** more than the amount stated *temperatures of 40 plus*

plus³ /plʌs/ *conjunction informal* and also *That restaurant's too crowded, plus it'll be really expensive.*

plus⁴ /plʌs/ *noun* [C] **1** *informal* an advantage *Well, the apartment has a garden so that's a plus.* **2 MATHEMATICS** (*also* ˈ**plus**ˌ**sign**) the symbol +, used between two numbers to show that they are being added together

plush /plʌʃ/ *adjective* Plush furniture, buildings, rooms, etc are very expensive and comfortable. *a plush red carpet*

Pluto /ˈpluːtəʊ/ *noun* [**no plural**] **ASTRONOMY** a dwarf planet that comes after Neptune in distance from the sun. Pluto was considered to be a proper planet until 2006, when it was officially decided that it was a dwarf planet.

plutonium /pluːˈtəʊniəm/ *noun* [U] **CHEMISTRY** a chemical element that is used in the production of nuclear power and nuclear weapons (symbol **Pu**)

ply /plaɪ/ *verb* **1 ply across/between, etc** *old-fashioned* to often make a particular journey *fishing boats plying across the harbour* **2 ply your trade** to work at your job, especially selling things
ply sb with sth *phrasal verb* **1** GIVE to give someone a lot of something again and again *They plied me with food and drink.* **2** ASK to ask someone a lot of questions *They* ***plied*** *him* ***with questions*** *about where he had been.*

plywood /ˈplaɪwʊd/ *noun* [U] wood that is made by sticking several thin layers of wood together

O-ᐧ**p.m.** (*also* **pm**) /ˌpiːˈem/ used when you are referring to a time after 12 o'clock in the middle of the day, but before 12 o'clock in the middle of the night *Opening hours: 9 a.m. - 6 p.m.*

PM /ˌpiːˈem/ *noun* [C] **POLITICS** *abbreviation for* prime minister: the leader of an elected government in some countries

pneumatic /njuːˈmætɪk/ *adjective* filled with air, or operated using air *pneumatic tyres*

pneumatics /njuːˈmætɪks/ *noun* [U] **DT, PHYSICS** the study of the uses of gases, especially air

pneumonia /njuːˈməʊniə/ *noun* [U] **HEALTH** a serious illness in which your lungs fill with liquid and it is difficult to breathe

poach /pəʊtʃ/ *verb* **1 FOOD** [T] to cook something, especially an egg without its shell, by putting it into liquid that is gently boiling **2** ANIMALS [I, T] to illegally catch or kill animals, especially by going onto land without the permission of the person who owns it **3** PERSON [I, T] to persuade someone to leave a company or team in order to work or play for yours *They can poach experienced people easily because they offer higher salaries.*

poacher /ˈpəʊtʃəʳ/ *noun* [C] someone who illegally catches or kills animals

O⊸**pocket¹** /ˈpɒkɪt/ *noun* [C] **1** BAG a small bag that is sewn or fixed onto or into a piece of clothing, a bag, the back of a seat, etc *a coat/shirt/trouser pocket* ○ *He was asked to* ***empty*** *his* ***pockets****.* ○ *Safety instructions are in the pocket on the seat in front of you.* **2** SMALL AREA/AMOUNT a small area or small amount of something that is different from what is around it *There was real poverty in some* ***pockets of*** *the country.* ○ *small pockets of air trapped inside the glass* **3** MONEY the amount of money that you have for spending *I shouldn't have to pay for travel* ***out of my own pocket*** (= with my own money). **4 be out of pocket** to have less money than you should have because you have paid for something *The holiday company cancelled our trip and we were left hundreds of pounds out of pocket.*

pocket² /ˈpɒkɪt/ *verb* [T] **1** STEAL to take something, especially money, which does not belong to you *His plan was to* ***pocket the money*** *from the sale of the business and leave the country.* **2** PUT IN CLOTHES to put something in your pocket *Juan pocketed the knife and walked away.*

pocket³ /ˈpɒkɪt/ *adjective* [**always before noun**] small enough to fit in your pocket *a pocket dictionary*

pocketbook /ˈpɒkɪtbʊk/ *noun* [C] *US* **1** BAG a woman's bag **2** PAY Someone's pocketbook is their ability to pay for something. *The sales tax hits consumers in the pocketbook.*

pocketful /ˈpɒkɪtfʊl/ *noun* [C] the amount you can fit in a pocket *a pocketful of coins*

pocketknife /ˈpɒkɪtnaɪf/ *noun* [C] *plural* **pocketknives** a small knife that folds into a case

ˈpocket ˌmoney *noun* [U] an amount of money given regularly to a child by its parents

pod /pɒd/ *noun* [C] **BIOLOGY** the long, flat part of some plants that has seeds in it *a pea pod*

podcast /ˈpɒdkɑːst/ *noun* [C] **COMPUTING, INTERNET** a recording that you can listen to on your computer or MP3 player from a website. You can also sign up to (= say that you want to receive) a podcast which is then updated (= new information is added to it) through the Internet when you plug your MP3 player into a computer. ➲See Extra help page **The Web and the Internet** on page Centre 36.

podiatrist /pəʊˈdaɪətrɪst/ *US* (*UK* **chiropodist**) *noun* [C] **HEALTH** someone whose job is to treat problems with people's feet

podium /ˈpəʊdiəm/ *noun* [C] a small, raised area, sometimes with a tall table on it, that someone stands on when they are performing or speaking

WORD PARTNERS FOR ***poem***

read/recite/write a poem • **in** a poem • a poem **about** sth • a poem **by** sb • a **love** poem

O⊸**poem** /ˈpəʊɪm/ *noun* [C] **LITERATURE** a piece of writing, especially one that has short lines and uses words that sound the same *war poems*

poet /ˈpəʊɪt/ *noun* [C] **LITERATURE** someone who writes poems

poetic /pəʊˈetɪk/ *adjective* **1** Something that is poetic makes you feel strong emotions because it is so beautiful. *To him, life seemed poetic.* **2 LITERATURE** relating to poetry *poetic language*

O⊸**poetry** /ˈpəʊɪtri/ *noun* [U] **LITERATURE** poems in general, or the writing of poetry *I enjoy all kinds of poetry, especially love poetry.*

poignant /ˈpɔɪnjənt/ *adjective* making you feel sad *It's a poignant story about a poor family's struggle to survive.* •**poignancy** /ˈpɔɪnjənsi/ *noun* [U] when something is poignant •**poignantly** *adverb*

poikilothermic /ˌpɔɪkɪləʊˈθɜːmɪk/ *adjective* **BIOLOGY** Animals that are poikilothermic have a body temperature that changes with the temperature around them.

WORD PARTNERS FOR ***point***

illustrate/make /prove/raise a point • **take** sb's point • a point **about** sth

O⊸**point¹** /pɔɪnt/ *noun* **1** OPINION [C] an opinion, idea, or fact which someone says or writes *Could I* ***make a point*** *about noise levels?* ○ *I* ***take your point*** (= I agree with you) *about cycling, but I still prefer to walk.* **2** IMPORTANT OPINION [**no plural**] an opinion or fact that deserves to be considered seriously, or which other people agree is true *"She's always complaining that the office is cold." "Well, she's* ***got a point****."* ○ *"How are we going to get there if there are no trains?" "****Good point****."* **3 the point** the most important part of what has been said or written *I thought he was never going to* ***get to the point****.* ○ ***The point is****, if you don't claim the money now you might never get it.* ○ *To say his art is simplistic is* ***missing the point*** (= not understanding the most important thing about it). **4** SHARP [C] the thin, sharp end of something *the point of a needle* **5** PLACE [C] a particular place *a* ***stopping****/fuelling* ***point*** ○ *the point where the pipes enter the building* **6** TIME [C] a particular time in an event or process ***At this point****, people started to leave.* ○ *It has* ***got to***

P

the point where I can hardly bear to speak to him. **7 be at/on the point of doing sth** to be going to do something very soon *Amy was on the point of crying.* **8** REASON [**no plural**] the reason for or purpose of something ***What's the point** of studying if you can't get a job afterwards?* ○ *There's **no point** inviting her - she never comes to parties.* **9 beside the point** not important or not connected with what you are talking about *The fact that he doesn't want to come is beside the point - he should have been invited.* **10 make a point of doing sth** to be certain that you always do a particular thing *He made a point of learning all the names of his staff.* **11 to the point** If something someone says or writes is to the point, it expresses the most important things without extra details. *His report was short and to the point.* **12 up to a point** partly *What he says is true up to a point.* **13 SPORT** [**C**] a unit used for showing who is winning in a game or competition *With 3 games still to play, Manchester United are 5 points ahead.* **14 MEASURES** [**C**] a unit used in some systems of measuring and comparing things *The stock exchange fell by five points.* **15 boiling/freezing/melting point MEASURES** the temperature at which a substance boils, freezes, or melts **16** QUALITY [**C**] a quality which someone has *I know she's bossy, but she has lots of **good points** too.* ○ *Chemistry never was **my strong point*** (= I was never good at it). **17 MATHEMATICS** [**C**] (*also* **decimal point**) the mark (.) that is used to separate the two parts of a decimal *One mile equals one point six* (= 1.6) *kilometres.* **18** DIRECTION [**C**] one of the marks on a compass (= object used for showing directions) **19 MEASURES** [**C**] a unit of measurement of the size of letters, used in printing and on computers ➲See also: **breaking point,** a **case** in point, **decimal point, focal point, moot point, point of view, starting-point, turning point, vantage point**

P

COMMON LEARNER ERROR

point

A **point** (.) is used to separate a whole number from a fraction (= number less than 1).

Normal body temperature is 36.9° celsius.

A **comma** (,) is used to divide large numbers into groups of three so that they are easier to read.

28,071,973

1,378

point² /pɔɪnt/ *verb* **1** SHOW [**I**] to show where someone or something is by holding your finger or a thin object towards it *She **pointed at/to** a bird flying overhead.* **2** AIM [**T**] to hold something so that it faces towards something else *She **pointed** her camera **at** them.* **3** FACE [**I**] to face towards a particular direction *The solar panels were pointing away from the sun.*
point sb/sth out *phrasal verb* to make a person notice someone or something *I didn't think about the disadvantages until you pointed them out to me.*
point sth out *phrasal verb* to tell someone a fact *If he makes a mistake I always think it's best to point it out immediately.*
point to/towards sth *phrasal verb* to show that something probably exists, is happening, or is true *All the evidence points to suicide.*

point-blank /ˌpɔɪnt'blæŋk/ *adjective, adverb* **1** If you refuse point-blank, you refuse completely and will not change your decision. **2 at point-blank range** If someone is shot at point-blank range, they are shot from a very short distance away.

pointed /'pɔɪntɪd/ *adjective* **1** CRITICIZE If someone says something in a pointed way, they intend to criticize someone. *He made some **pointed references** to her history of drug problems.* **2** SHARP A pointed object has a thin, sharp end. *a pointed chin/beard*

pointer /'pɔɪntəʳ/ *noun* [**C**] **1** INFORMATION a piece of information which can help you understand a situation or do something better *I asked for some pointers on applying for jobs.* **2** THIN OBJECT an object that you use to point at something

pointless /'pɔɪntləs/ *adjective* Something that is pointless has no purpose. *pointless arguments/conflict* [**+ to do sth**] *It would be pointless to argue with him.* •**pointlessly** *adverb*

ˌpoint of 'sale (*abbreviation* **PoS**) *noun* [**C usually singular**] **ECONOMICS** the place where a product is sold

WORD PARTNERS FOR ***point of view***

from sb's point of view • **from** a [political/ financial, etc] point of view

ˌpoint of 'view *noun* [**C**] *plural* **points of view** **1** WAY OF THINKING a way of thinking about a situation ***From** a medical **point of view**, there was no need for the operation.* **2** OPINION an opinion *You have to be willing to see other people's points of view.*

COMMON LEARNER ERROR

point of view or **opinion?**

When you want to talk about your own opinion, you should say **In my opinion ...**, not 'In my point of view'.

poise /pɔɪz/ *noun* [**U**] **1** BEHAVIOUR when you behave in a calm and confident way *Recovering his poise, he congratulated his opponent.* **2** MOVEMENT when you move or stand in a careful, pleasant way

poised /pɔɪzd/ *adjective* **1** READY [**never before noun**] ready to do something [**+ to do sth**] *They have three hundred ships, all poised to attack.* **2** POSITION [**never before noun**] in a particular position or situation, ready to move or change *a helicopter poised above the crowd* **3** CALM calm and confident *a **poised performance***

poison¹ /'pɔɪzᵊn/ *noun* [**C, U**] **HEALTH** a substance that can make you ill or kill you if you eat or drink it *Someone had put poison in her drink.*

poison² /'pɔɪzᵊn/ *verb* [**T**] **1 HEALTH** to try to kill someone by giving them a dangerous substance to drink or eat *He tried to poison his wife.* **2 HEALTH** to put poison or a dangerous substance in something *They poisoned the city's water supply.* **3** SPOIL to make something very unpleasant *These arguments were poisoning his life.* **4 poison sb's mind** to make someone think bad things about someone or something *Her father had **poisoned her mind against** me.* •**poisoned** *adjective*

poisoning /ˈpɔɪzᵊnɪŋ/ *noun* [U] **HEALTH** an illness caused by eating, drinking, or breathing a dangerous substance ***alcohol/lead poisoning*** ➲See also: **food poisoning**

poisonous /ˈpɔɪzᵊnəs/ *adjective* **1 HEALTH** containing poison *poisonous gas* **2** ANIMAL A poisonous animal uses poison in order to defend itself. *a poisonous snake*

poke¹ /pəʊk/ *verb* **1** [T] to quickly push your finger or other pointed object into someone or something *Nell kept poking me in the arm.* ○ *He poked the fire with his stick.* **2 poke (sth) round/out/through, etc** to appear through or from behind something, or to make something do this *Grace poked her head round the door.* ➲See also: poke/stick your **nose**¹ into sth

poke about/around *phrasal verb informal* to look for something by moving other things *I was poking around in the garage, looking for a paint brush.*

poke² /pəʊk/ *noun* [C] when you quickly push your finger or other pointed object into someone or something *I gave him a poke in the back.*

poker /ˈpəʊkəʳ/ *noun* **1** GAME [U] a game played with cards in which people try to win money from each other **2** FIRE [C] a long, metal stick used for moving the coal or wood in a fire so that it burns better

poker-faced /ˈpəʊkəˌfeɪst/ *adjective* not showing on your face what you are really thinking or feeling

poky *informal* (*also* **pokey**) /ˈpəʊki/ *adjective* **1** TOO SMALL A room or house that is poky is unpleasant because it is too small. **2** SLOW *US* too slow

polar /ˈpəʊləʳ/ *adjective* **GEOGRAPHY** relating to the North or South Pole

ˈpolar ˌbear *noun* [C] a large, white bear that lives in the North Pole (= most northern part of the Earth)

Polaroid /ˈpəʊlᵊrɔɪd/ *noun* [C] *trademark* a camera that prints a photograph immediately after you have taken it, or a picture taken with this type of camera

pole /pəʊl/ *noun* **1** [C] a long, thin stick made of wood or metal, often used to hold something up *tent poles* **2 GEOGRAPHY the North/South Pole** the part of the Earth that is furthest North/South **3 be poles apart** to be complete opposites

polemic /pəˈlemɪk/ *noun* [C, U] *formal* writing or speech that strongly criticizes or defends an idea, a belief, etc

ˈpole ˌvault *noun* [no plural] **SPORT** a sport in which you use a very long stick to jump over a high bar

WORD PARTNERS FOR ***police***

call the police • **report** sb/sth **to** the police • police **arrest/question** sb

O-ᵚ **police¹** /pəˈliːs/ *noun* [plural] **LAW** the official organization that makes people obey the law and that protects people and places against crime, or the people who work for this organization *I heard a gun shot and decided to **call the police**.* ○ *A 30-year-old taxi driver is being interviewed by police.* ○ *a police investigation*

police² /pəˈliːs/ *verb* [T] **LAW** to make sure that people obey the law in a particular place or when they are doing a particular activity *Clubs have to pay for the cost of policing matches.*

poˌlice ˈconstable *noun* [C] **LAW** in the UK, a police officer of the lowest rank

poˈlice deˌpartment *noun* [C] **LAW** in the US, the police force in an area or city

poˈlice ˌforce *noun* [C] **LAW** the police in a country or area

policeman, policewoman /pəˈliːsmən, pəˈliːsˌwʊmən/ *noun* [C] *plural* **policemen, policewomen LAW** a man/woman who is a member of the police

poˈlice ˌofficer *noun* [C] **LAW** someone who is a member of the police

poˈlice ˌstate *noun* [C] **POLITICS** a country in which the people are not free to do what they want because the government controls them

poˈlice ˌstation *noun* [C] **LAW** the office of the police in a town or part of a city

WORD PARTNERS FOR ***policy***

adopt/formulate/implement/pursue a policy • a policy **on** sth • a policy **of** (doing) sth • **company** policy • **foreign** policy

policy /ˈpɒləsi/ *noun* **1** IDEAS/PLAN [C, U] a set of ideas or a plan of what to do in particular situations that has been agreed by a government, business, etc ***foreign policy*** ○ *It is **company policy** to help staff progress in their careers.* **2** AGREEMENT [C] an agreement that you have with an insurance company (= company that pays the costs if you are injured, etc)

polio /ˈpəʊliəʊ/ *noun* [U] **HEALTH** a serious disease that sometimes makes it impossible for you to move your muscles

polish¹ /ˈpɒlɪʃ/ *noun* **1** SUBSTANCE [C, U] a substance that you rub on something in order to make it clean and shiny **2** RUBBING [no plural] when you rub something in order to make it clean and shiny *Just give the table a polish.* ➲See also: **nail polish**

polish² /ˈpɒlɪʃ/ *verb* [T] to rub something with a cloth in order to make it clean or to make it shine *to polish your shoes*

polish sth off *phrasal verb informal* to finish something quickly *I gave him a bowl of ice cream which he soon polished off.*

polished /ˈpɒlɪʃt/ *adjective* **1** SHINY clean and shiny after polishing *a polished floor* **2** SKILL done with skill and style *He gave a highly **polished performance**.*

O-ᵚ **polite** /pəˈlaɪt/ *adjective* behaving in a way that is not rude and shows that you do not only think about yourself *She was too polite to point out my mistake.* •**politely** *adverb He thanked them politely.* •**politeness** *noun* [U]

OTHER WAYS OF SAYING ***polite***

The adjectives **courteous**, **respectful**, and **well-mannered** are sometimes used when someone is polite and shows respect for other people: *Although she often disagreed with me, she was always* ***courteous***. • *They were quiet,* ***well-mannered*** *children.*

A man who is polite to a woman is sometimes described as **chivalrous**: *He held open the door in that* ***chivalrous*** *way of his.*

The expression **politically-correct** and its abbreviation, **PC**, are regularly used to show that someone is being polite by speaking in a way which does not offend women, people of a particular race, or people who have physical or mental problems: *'Fireman' has been replaced by the* ***politically-correct*** *term 'firefighter'.* • *Calling them 'ladies' - that's not very* ***PC*** *of you!*

Conversation which is polite and calm is sometimes described as **civilized**: *Let's discuss this in a* ***civilized*** *manner.*

O-**political** /pəˈlɪtɪkᵊl/ *adjective* **POLITICS** relating to or involved in politics *There are two main* ***political parties*** *in my country.* ○ *The church has a strong political influence.* •**politically** *adverb*

poˌlitical aˈsylum *noun* [U] **POLITICS** protection given by a government to someone whose political activities have made it too dangerous for them to live in their own country

poˌlitically coˈrrect *adjective* **POLITICS** careful to speak or behave in a way which is not offensive to women, people of a particular race, or people who have physical or mental problems *It's not politically correct to call women 'girls'.* •**political correctness** *noun* [U]

poˌlitical ˈprisoner *noun* [C] **POLITICS** someone who is in prison because their political activities or opinions oppose the government

O-**politician** /ˌpɒlɪˈtɪʃᵊn/ *noun* [C] **POLITICS** someone who works in politics, especially a member of the government

politicize (*also UK* **-ise**) /pəˈlɪtɪsaɪz/ *verb* [T] **POLITICS** to make something or someone become more involved with politics [**often passive**] *The whole issue has been politicized.* ○ *a highly* ***politicized debate***

WORD PARTNERS FOR ***politics***

enter/go into/be involved in politics • **domestic /international/local** politics

O-**politics** /ˈpɒlətɪks/ *noun* **1 POLITICS** [U] ideas and activities relating to how a country or area is governed *He has little interest in* ***local politics***. **2 POLITICS** [U] a job in politics *She's planning to retire from politics next year.* **3 sb's politics** someone's opinions about how a country or area should be governed *I don't know what his politics are, but he strongly disagreed with the decision.* **4** [**plural**] the relationships in a group which allow particular people to have power over others *I try not to get involved in* ***office politics***.

polka /ˈpɒlkə/ *noun* [C] **MUSIC** a type of dance, or a piece of music used for this type of dance

polka-dot /ˈpɒlkəˌdɒt/ *adjective* [**always before noun**] having a regular pattern of small, round spots *a polka-dot bikini*

WORD PARTNERS FOR ***poll***

carry out/conduct a poll • a poll **indicates/reveals/shows/suggests** sth • a poll **of** sb

poll¹ /pəʊl/ (*also* **opinion poll**) *noun* [C] when people are asked questions to discover what they think about a subject *A recent* ***poll indicated*** *that 77 percent of Americans supported the president.*

poll² /pəʊl/ *verb* [T] **1** to ask someone's opinion as part of a study on what people think about a subject [**often passive**] *Most students polled said they preferred the new system.* **2 POLITICS** to receive a particular number of votes in an election *Labour polled only 45 percent of the Scottish vote.*

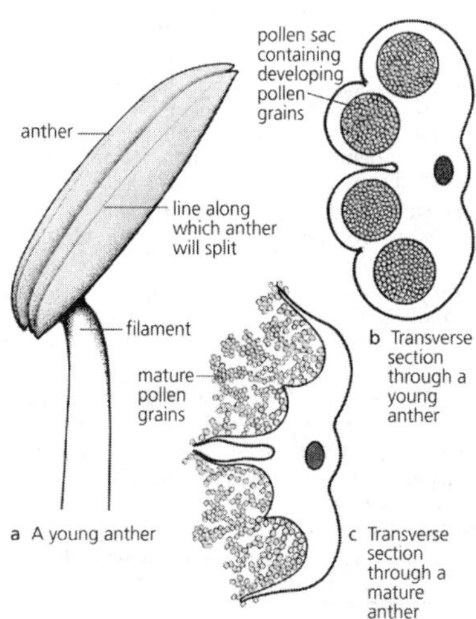

pollen

pollen /ˈpɒlən/ *noun* [U] **BIOLOGY** a powder produced by flowers, which is carried by insects or the wind and makes other flowers produce seeds ➲See picture at **carpel**

ˈpollen ˌcount *noun* [C] **ENVIRONMENT** the measurement of the amount of pollen in the air

pollinate /ˈpɒləneɪt/ *verb* [T] **BIOLOGY** to carry pollen from one plant to another so that they can be fertilized (= made able to produce new plants) •**pollination** /ˌpɒləˈneɪʃᵊn/

ˈpolling ˌday *UK* (*US* **election day**) *noun* [C] **POLITICS** the day when people vote in an election

ˈpolling ˌstation *UK* (*US* **ˈpolling ˌplace**) *noun* [C] **POLITICS** a building where people go to vote in an election

the polls /pəʊlz/ *noun* [**plural**] **POLITICS** voting in an election *The country will* ***go to the polls*** (= vote) *on 13 September.*

pollster /ˈpəʊlstəʳ/ *noun* [C] **POLITICS** someone who tries to discover what most people think about a subject by asking questions

pollute /pəˈluːt/ *verb* [T] **ENVIRONMENT** to make water, air, soil, etc dirty or harmful *We need a fuel that won't pollute the environment.* •**pollutant** *noun* [C] a substance that pollutes water, air, etc

pollution /pəˈluːʃᵊn/ *noun* [U] **ENVIRONMENT** damage caused to water, air, etc by harmful substances or waste *The book shows simple things you can do to reduce pollution from your car.*

polo /ˈpəʊləʊ/ *noun* [U] **SPORT** a game played between two teams who ride horses and hit a ball with long, wooden hammers

ˈpolo ˌneck *UK* (*US* **turtleneck**) *noun* [C] a piece of clothing that covers the top part of the body and has a tube-like part covering the neck *a black polo neck sweater*

ˈpolo ˌshirt *noun* [C] a cotton shirt with short sleeves, a collar, and buttons at the front

poly- /pɒli-/ *prefix* many *polygamy* (= having more than one husband or wife at the same time) ○ *a polygon* (= a shape with many sides)

polyatomic /ˌpɒliəˈtɒmɪk/ *adjective* **PHYSICS, CHEMISTRY** containing more than two atoms

polyester /ˌpɒliˈestəʳ/ *noun* [U] **DT** a type of artificial cloth used for making clothes *a polyester shirt/skirt*

polygon /ˈpɒlɪgɒn/ *noun* [C] **MATHEMATICS** a flat shape with three or more straight sides

polymer /ˈpɒlɪməʳ/ *noun* [C] **CHEMISTRY** a chemical substance consisting of large molecules made from many smaller and simpler molecules

polymerize /ˈpɒlɪməraɪz/ (*mainly UK* **-ise**) *adjective* [I, T] **CHEMISTRY** to form a polymer or to make something form a polymer •**polymerization** /ˌpɒlɪməraɪˈzeɪʃᵊn/ *noun* [U]

polyp /ˈpɒlɪp/ *noun* [C] **1** a small simple water animal shaped like a tube **2 HEALTH** a small mass of cells that grows in the body, and is usually not harmful

polypeptide /ˌpɒlɪˈpeptaɪd/ *noun* [C] **CHEMISTRY** one of a group of polymers (= chemical substance made of large molecules) made from a chain of amino acids (= substance used to make protein)

polypropylene /ˌpɒlɪˈprəʊpəliːn/ *noun* [U] **DT** a type of plastic used for many purposes, such as food packaging, making ropes, and making artificial fabrics

polysaccharide /ˌpɒlɪˈsækᵊraɪd/ *noun* [C] **CHEMISTRY** a type of carbohydrate, such as starch and cellulose, whose molecules are groups of sugar molecules joined together ➲Compare **monosaccharide**

polystyrene /ˌpɒlɪˈstaɪriːn/ *UK* (*US* **Styrofoam**®) *noun* [U] a light plastic material that is wrapped around delicate objects to protect them, and around hot things to keep them hot *polystyrene packaging/polystyrene cups*

polytechnic /ˌpɒlɪˈteknɪk/ *noun* [C] **EDUCATION** a college where students study scientific and technical subjects

polythene /ˈpɒlɪθiːn/ *UK* (*US* **polyethylene** /ˌpɒliˈeθəliːn/) *noun* [U] a thin, soft plastic, often used for making bags

polyunsaturated /ˌpɒl.i.ʌnˈsætʃ.ᵊr.eɪ.tɪd/ *adjective* **CHEMISTRY** describes a fat or oil which is thought to be healthy because it does not seem to cause heart disease *polyunsaturated margarine/vegetable oil* ➲Compare **saturated fat**

polyvinyl chloride /ˌpɒlɪvaɪnᵊlˈklɔːraɪd/ (*abbreviation* **PVC**) *noun* [U] **DT** a type of plastic which is used especially for making clothes, floor coverings and bags

pomp /pɒmp/ *noun* [U] *formal* special clothes, decorations, and music at an official ceremony

pompous /ˈpɒmpəs/ *adjective* Someone who is pompous is too serious and thinks they are more important than they really are. •**pompously** *adverb* •**pomposity** /pɒmˈpɒsəti/ *noun* [U] when someone is pompous

pond /pɒnd/ *noun* [C] a small area of water, especially one that has been made artificially in a park or garden

ponder /ˈpɒndəʳ/ *verb* [I, T] *literary* to think carefully about something [+ **question word**] *He pondered what might have happened if he hadn't gone home.*

ponderous /ˈpɒndᵊrəs/ *adjective* **1** [BORING] Ponderous speech or writing is boring or too serious. **2** [SLOW] slow because of being very heavy or large •**ponderously** *adverb*

pony /ˈpəʊni/ *noun* [C] a small horse

ponytail /ˈpəʊniteɪl/ *noun* [C] hair tied at the back of your head so that it hangs down like a horse's tail

poodle /ˈpuːdl/ *noun* [C] a type of dog with thick, curly hair

pool¹ /puːl/ *noun* **1 SPORT** [C] (*also* **swimming pool**) an area of water that has been made for people to swim in *The hotel has two outdoor pools.* **2** [C] a small area of water or a small amount of liquid on a surface *We dipped our feet in a shallow pool by the rocks.* ○ *a **pool of** blood* **3 SPORT** [U] a game in which two people use long, thin sticks to hit coloured balls into holes around the edge of a table **4 FINANCE** [C] a collection of money, people, or equipment which is shared by a group of people *a **car pool** for company business*

pool² /puːl/ *verb* [T] If a group of people pool their money, knowledge, or equipment, they collect it together so that it can be shared or used for a particular purpose. *Several villages pooled their resources to set up a building project.*

the pools /puːlz/ *noun* [plural] in Britain, a game in which people try to win a lot of money by guessing the results of football matches

O‑ **poor** /pɔːʳ/ (US) /pʊr/ *adjective* **1** [NO MONEY] having very little money or few possessions *Most of these people are desperately poor.* ○ *Modern fertilizers are too expensive for poorer countries to afford.* ○ *housing for the poor* **2** [BAD] of very low quality *poor health* ○ *Last year's exam results were poor.* ○ *a poor harvest* ○ *The meeting went smoothly but attendance was poor* (= not many people came). **3** [NO SKILL] not having much skill at a particular activity *She's always been **poor***

P

at spelling. **4** SYMPATHY **[always before noun]** used to show sympathy for someone *That cold sounds terrible, you* ***poor thing.*** **5 be poor in sth** If something is poor in a particular substance, it has very little of the substance. *Avoid foods which are high in calories but poor in nutrients.*

poorly[1] /ˈpɔːli/ *adverb* badly *poorly educated*

poorly[2] /ˈpɔːli/ *adjective UK informal* ill *Rosie was feeling poorly so I put her to bed.*

pop[1] /pɒp/ *verb* **popping**, *past* **popped 1 [I, T]** to make a short sound like a small explosion, or to make something do this by breaking it *The music played and champagne corks popped.* **2 pop in/out/over, etc** *informal* to go to a particular place *Doug's just popped out for a few minutes.* ○ *I'll pop into the supermarket on my way home.* **3 pop sth in/into/on, etc** *informal* to quickly put something in a particular place *Can you pop the pizza in the oven?* **4 pop out/up** to move quickly and suddenly, especially out of something

pop up *phrasal verb informal* to suddenly appear or happen, often unexpectedly *A message just popped up on my screen.*

pop[2] /pɒp/ *noun* **1 MUSIC [U]** (*also* ˈ**pop** ˌ**music**) modern music with a strong beat which is popular with young people **2** SOUND **[C]** a short sound like a small explosion **3 FOOD [U]** *informal* (*also US* **soda**) a sweet drink with bubbles **4** FATHER **[no plural]** *US informal* father

popcorn /ˈpɒpkɔːn/ *noun* **[U] FOOD** yellow seeds of grain that break open when heated and are eaten with salt, sugar, or butter

Pope /pəʊp/ *noun* **[C] RELIGION** the leader of the Roman Catholic Church *Pope John Paul II* ○ *The Pope was due to visit Paraguay in May.*

P

poplar /ˈpɒpləʳ/ *noun* **[C, U]** a tall tree with branches that grow up to form a thin, pointed shape

popper /ˈpɒpəʳ/ *noun* **[C]** *UK* (*US* **snap**) a metal or plastic object used to fasten clothing, made of two parts which fit together with a short, loud sound

poppy /ˈpɒpi/ *noun* **[C]** a red flower with small, black seeds

populace /ˈpɒpjələs/ *noun* **[group]** *formal* **SOCIETY** all the people who live in a particular country or place

O→**popular** /ˈpɒpjələʳ/ *adjective* **1** LIKED liked by many people *'Jack' was the most popular boy's name.* ○ *The North African coast is becoming increasingly* ***popular with*** *British tourists.* ⊃Opposite **unpopular 2 SOCIETY [always before noun]** for or involving ordinary people and not specialists or people who are very educated *The issue was given full coverage in the popular press.* **3** MANY PEOPLE **[always before noun]** A popular belief, opinion, etc is one that many people have. *The allegations are false, contrary to* ***popular belief.***

WORD PARTNERS FOR ***popularity***

gain popularity • be **growing in/increasing in** popularity • sb's/sth's popularity **increases/soars/wanes** • the popularity **of** sth • sb/sth's popularity **with** sb

popularity /ˌpɒpjəˈlærəti/ *noun* **[U]** the quality of being liked by many people *the increasing popularity of organic produce* ⊃Opposite **unpopularity**

popularize (*also UK* **-ise**) /ˈpɒpjələraɪz/ *verb* **[T]** to make something become known or liked by many people *It was the World Cup which popularized professional soccer in the United States.* •**popularization** /ˌpɒpjələraɪˈzeɪʃən/ *noun* **[U]**

popularly /ˈpɒpjələli/ *adverb* **popularly believed/called/known, etc** believed, called, etc by most people *Los Angeles is popularly known as 'LA'.*

populate /ˈpɒpjəleɪt/ *verb* **be populated GEOGRAPHY** If an area is populated by people or animals, they live in that area. *The countryside is* ***densely/sparsely populated*** (= there are many/few people). ○ *The forest was populated by rare and colourful birds.*

WORD PARTNERS FOR ***population***

have a population **of** [50 million, etc] • population **growth**

O→**population** /ˌpɒpjəˈleɪʃən/ *noun* **1 GEOGRAPHY, SOCIETY [C, U]** the number of people living in a particular area *What's the* ***population of*** *Brazil?* **2 GEOGRAPHY, SOCIETY [group]** all the people living in a particular area, or all the people or animals of a particular type *The government has reported a 9% rise in the prison population.* **3 GEOGRAPHY** all the organisms that belong to a particular species (= group of plants or animals with similar characteristics) ⊃See picture at **ecosystem**

populous /ˈpɒpjələs/ *adjective formal* A populous area has a lot of people living in it. *It's one of the world's most populous cities.*

pop-up /ˈpɒpʌp/ *adjective* **[always before noun]** **1** A pop-up book is a book which has pictures that stand up from the pages when the book is opened. **2 COMPUTING** A pop-up menu is a list of choices on a computer screen which is hidden until you choose to look at it. *Select the option you want from the* ***pop-up menu*** *and then double-click on it.*

porcelain /ˈpɔːsəlɪn/ *noun* **[U]** a hard, shiny, white substance used to make cups, plates, etc, or the cups and plates themselves *a porcelain dish* ○ *a fine collection of porcelain*

porch /pɔːtʃ/ *noun* **[C]** a covered area built onto the entrance to a house *We sat on the front porch sipping iced tea.*

pore[1] /pɔːʳ/ *noun* **[C] ANATOMY** a very small hole in your skin that sweat (= salty liquid) can pass through

pore[2] /pɔːʳ/ *verb*

pore over sth *phrasal verb* to study or look carefully at something, especially a book or document *Jeremy spent the afternoon poring over his exam notes.*

pork /pɔːk/ *noun* **[U] FOOD** meat from a pig *pork chops*

porous /ˈpɔːrəs/ *adjective* **PHYSICS** allowing liquid or air to pass through *porous rock*

porridge /ˈpɒrɪdʒ/ *noun* [U] **FOOD** a soft, white food made of oats (= type of grain) and water or milk

port /pɔːt/ *noun* **1 GEOGRAPHY** [C] a town or an area of a town next to water where ships arrive and leave from *a fishing port* ○ *the Belgian port of Zeebrugge* **2 FOOD** [U] a sweet, strong, red wine which is made in Portugal **3** LEFT [U] the left side of a ship or aircraft *the port side*

portable /ˈpɔːtəbl/ *adjective* able to be carried *a portable computer*

portal /ˈpɔːtəl/ *noun* [C] **INTERNET** a page on the Internet with links to many other pages or websites that people use to start searching the World Wide Web

ˈportal ˌvein (*also* **hepatic portal vein**) *noun* [C usually singular] **ANATOMY** a vein which carries blood to the liver from the stomach and other organs

porter /ˈpɔːtər/ *noun* [C] someone whose job is to carry other people's bags in hotels, stations, etc

portfolio /ˌpɔːtˈfəʊliəʊ/ *noun* [C] **1 ART** a collection of designs, pictures, documents, etc that represents a person's work, or the large, flat container that it is carried in **2 FINANCE** a collection of accounts, money, etc that is owned by a person or organization *a stock portfolio*

porthole /ˈpɔːthəʊl/ *noun* [C] a small, round window in the side of a ship or aircraft

portion /ˈpɔːʃən/ *noun* [C] **1** a part of something *A large portion of their profits go straight back into new projects.* **2 FOOD** the amount of food served to one person, especially in a restaurant

portly /ˈpɔːtli/ *adjective humorous* quite fat *a portly gentleman*

portrait /ˈpɔːtrɪt/ *noun* **1 ART** [C] a painting, drawing, or photograph of someone *a* ***portrait of*** *the princess* ○ *a portrait gallery/painter* **2 a portrait of sb/sth** a film or book which describes someone or something in detail *His latest film is a portrait of life in the 1920s.* ➲See also: **self-portrait**

portray /pɔːˈtreɪ/ *verb* [T] **1** DESCRIBE If a book or film portrays someone or something, it describes or shows them. *Both novels portray the lives of professional athletes.* ○ *In the film he's* ***portrayed as*** *a hero.* **2** ACT to act the part of a character in a film or play •**portrayal** *noun* [C, U] when you portray someone or something *He won several awards for his portrayal of the dictator.*

pose¹ /pəʊz/ *verb* **1 pose a danger/problem/threat, etc** to cause a problem *A lot of these chemicals pose very real threats to our health.* **2 ART** [I] to stay in a particular position so that someone can paint or photograph you *The two leaders* ***posed for*** *photographs outside the White House.* **3** [I] *mainly UK* to try to make people notice and admire you, especially by looking fashionable *Pascal was posing in his new sunglasses.* **4 pose a question** *formal* to ask a question

pose as sb *phrasal verb* to pretend that you are someone else *He got into her house by posing as an electrician.*

pose² /pəʊz/ *noun* **1 ART** [C] the position that you stay in while someone photographs or paints you *an elegant pose* **2** [no plural] when someone pretends to be more clever or interesting than they really are *She's not really interested in art, it's just a pose.*

posh /pɒʃ/ *adjective* **1** EXPENSIVE expensive and used or owned by rich people *a posh hotel/restaurant* **2 SOCIETY** *UK* from a high social class *a posh voice*

O⁻**position¹** /pəˈzɪʃən/ *noun* **1** SITTING/STANDING [C, U] the way someone is sitting, standing, or lying, or if something is pointing up or down, etc *a kneeling position* ○ *I go to sleep on my back but I always wake up* ***in*** *a different* ***position.*** ○ *Make sure your chair is* ***in*** *the upright* ***position.*** **2** SITUATION [C] the situation that someone is in [usually singular] *She's* ***in*** *a very difficult* ***position.*** **3 be in a position to do sth** to be able to do something because of your situation *I'm not in a position to talk about this at the moment.* **4** PLACE [C] the place where someone or something is *I'm trying to find our position on the map.* ○ *You're* ***in*** *a good* ***position*** *next to the window.* **5 be in position** If someone or something is in position, they are in the place that they should be in. **6 in first/second/third, etc position** in first/second/third, etc place in a race or other competition *She finished the race in third position.* **7** JOB [C] *formal* a job *to apply for a position in a company* **8** OPINION [C] *formal* a way of thinking about a subject *What's the company's* ***position on*** *recycling?* **9 SPORT** [C] the part that someone plays in a game such as football *What* ***position*** *does he* ***play?*** **10 SOCIETY** [C] your level of importance in society *the position of women in society*

position² /pəˈzɪʃən/ *verb* [T] to put someone or something in a place for a reason [often reflexive] *I positioned myself as far away from her as possible.*

O⁻**positive** /ˈpɒzətɪv/ *adjective* **1** HAPPY feeling happy about your life and your future *a* ***positive attitude*** ○ *I'm feeling much more positive about things now.* **2** ENCOURAGING Something that is positive makes you feel better about a situation. *We've shown people samples of the product and had a very* ***positive response.*** **3** CERTAIN [never before noun] certain that something is true *"Are you sure you saw him?" "Absolutely positive."* [+ (that)] *I'm positive that I switched it off.* **4** PROOF [always before noun] showing without any doubt that something is true ***positive proof*** **5 HEALTH** If a medical test is positive, it shows that the person being tested has a disease or condition. *She did a pregnancy test and it was positive.* **6 MATHEMATICS** In mathematics, a positive number is greater than zero. **7 PHYSICS** being the type of electrical charge which is carried by protons **8 positive charge PHYSICS** the electrical charge that is carried by protons (= parts of atoms)

positively /ˈpɒzətɪvli/ *adverb* **1** GOOD in a good way that makes you feel happier *Most children* ***respond positively*** *to praise and*

P

encouragement. **2** EMPHASIS used to emphasize something that you say, especially when it is surprising *Our waiter was positively rude.*

positron /ˈpɒzɪtrɒn/ *noun* [C] **PHYSICS** a very small piece of physical substance with a positive electrical charge, and with the same mass as an electron

possess /pəˈzes/ *verb* **1** [T] *formal* to have or own something *He was found guilty of possessing an illegal weapon.* **2 what possessed her/him/you, etc?** something that you say when someone has done something stupid [+ **to do sth**] What possessed you to tell him?

possessed /pəˈzest/ *adjective* controlled by evil spirits

WORD PARTNERS FOR ***possession***

sb's **prized/most treasured** possessions • **material/personal** possessions

possession /pəˈzeʃən/ *noun* **1** THING [C] a thing that you own [**usually plural**] ***personal possessions*** ○ *He woke up to discover that all his possessions had been stolen.* **2** HAVE [U] *formal* when you have or own something *I have* ***in my possession*** *a photograph which may be of interest to you.* ○ *He was caught* ***in possession of*** *explosives.*

possessive /pəˈzesɪv/ *adjective* **1** wanting someone to love and spend time with you and no one else **2 LANGUAGE** In grammar, a possessive word or form of a word shows who or what something belongs to. For example the words 'mine' and 'yours' are possessive pronouns.

WORD PARTNERS FOR ***possibility***

consider/discuss/raise/rule out a possibility • a **distinct/real/strong** possibility • possibility **of** doing sth

P

possibility /ˌpɒsəˈbɪləti/ *noun* **1** CHANCE [C, U] a chance that something may happen or be true *Is there any* ***possibility of*** *changing this ticket?* [+ **(that)**] *There is a* ***strong possibility*** *that she was lying.* **2** CHOICE [C] something that you can choose to do *Have you considered the* ***possibility of*** *flying?* ⊃Opposite **impossibility**

COMMON LEARNER ERROR

possibility, occasion, or **opportunity?**

A **possibility** is a chance that something may happen or be true. **Possibility** cannot be followed by an infinitive.

Is there a possibility of finding a cure for AIDS?

~~*Is there a possibility to find a cure for AIDS?*~~

An **occasion** is an event, or a time when something happens. **Occasion** does not mean 'chance' or 'opportunity'.

Birthdays are always special occasions.

An **opportunity** is a possibility of doing something, or a situation which gives you the possibility of doing something.

The trip to Paris gave me an opportunity to speak French.

Students had the opportunity to ask questions during the lecture.

I have more opportunity to travel than my parents did.

~~*I have more possibility to travel than my parents did.*~~

possible /ˈpɒsəbl/ *adjective* **1** CAN HAPPEN If something is possible, it can happen or be done. [+ **to do sth**] *Is it possible to speak to the manager please?* ○ *The operation will* ***make it possible*** *for her to walk without crutches.* ○ *I'll send it today,* ***if possible.*** ⊃Opposite **impossible** **2** NOT CERTAIN If something is possible, it might or might not exist or be true. *possible safety problems* [+ **(that)**] *It's possible that the tapes were stolen.* **3 as much/quickly/soon, etc as possible** as much/quickly/soon, etc as something can happen or be done *I'll go as soon as possible.* **4 the best/cheapest/worst, etc possible** the best/cheapest/worst, etc that can happen or exist *the shortest possible time*

possibly /ˈpɒsəbli/ *adverb* **1** NOT CERTAIN used when something is not certain *Someone, possibly Tom, had left the window open.* **2** EMPHASIS used with 'can' or 'could' for emphasis *We'll do everything we possibly can to help.* ○ *I couldn't possibly ask you to do that.* **3** QUESTIONS used in polite questions *Could I possibly borrow your bike?*

post[1] /pəʊst/ *noun* **1** SYSTEM [**no plural**] *UK* (*US* **mail**) the system for sending letters, parcels, etc *Your letter is* ***in the post.*** ○ *I'm sending the documents* ***by post.*** **2** LETTERS [U] *UK* (*US* **mail**) letters, parcels, etc that you send or receive *Has the* ***post arrived/come*** *yet?* **3** JOB [C] *formal* a job *a part-time post* ○ *a teaching post* **4** POLE [C] a long, vertical piece of wood or metal fixed into the ground at one end *I found the dog tied to a post.* **5** PLACE [C] a place where someone stands to guard something

post[2] /pəʊst/ *verb* [T] **1** *UK* (*US* **mail**) to send a letter or parcel by post *Did you post my letter?* **2 INTERNET** to leave a message on a website *I posted a query about arthritis treatment.* ⊃See Extra help page **The Web and the Internet** on page Centre 37. **3 be posted to France/London/Singapore, etc** to be sent to France/London/Singapore, etc to work, usually for the government or army **4 post a notice/sign, etc** to put a notice/sign, etc somewhere *He posted the message on the noticeboard.* **5 keep sb posted** to make certain that someone always knows what is happening *Keep me posted if anything happens.*

postage /ˈpəʊstɪdʒ/ *noun* [U] money that you pay to send a letter or parcel *first-class postage* ○ ***postage and packing***

ˌpostage and ˈpacking (*US* **ˌshipping and ˈhandling**) *noun* [U] money that you pay so that a company will send you something through the post

ˈpostage ˌstamp *noun* [C] *formal* a small, official piece of paper that you buy and stick onto a letter or parcel before you post it

postal /ˈpəʊstəl/ *adjective* [**always before noun**] relating to the system of sending letters and parcels *the* ***postal service****/system*

ˈpostal ˌorder *UK* (*US* **money order**) *noun* [C] **FINANCE** an official piece of paper bought at a post office that you can send instead of money

ˈpost ˌbox *UK* (*US* **mailbox**) *noun* [C] a large, metal container in a public place where you can post letters

postcard /ˈpəʊstkɑːd/ *noun* [C] a card with a picture on one side that you send without an envelope *Send me a postcard.*

postcode /ˈpəʊstkəʊd/ *noun* [C] a group of letters and numbers that comes at the end of someone's address in the UK ➲Compare **zip code**

poster /ˈpəʊstəʳ/ *noun* [C] a large, printed picture or notice that you put on a wall, in order to decorate a place or to advertise something

posterity /pɒsˈterəti/ *noun* [U] the people who will be alive in the future *These works of art should be preserved* ***for posterity****.*

postgraduate /ˌpəʊstˈɡrædʒuət/ (*US* **graduate**) (*also* **postgrad**) *noun* [C] **EDUCATION** a student who has one degree and now studies at a university for a more advanced degree •**postgraduate** *adjective a postgraduate degree in mathematics*

posthumous /ˈpɒstjəməs/ *adjective* happening after someone's death *the posthumous publication of her letters* •**posthumously** *adverb*

posting /ˈpəʊstɪŋ/ *noun* [C] *mainly UK* when you are sent to work in another place *a posting to Madrid*

Post-it (note) /ˈpəʊstɪtˌnəʊt/ *noun* [C] *trademark* a small piece of paper that you can write on and then stick to other papers or surfaces

postman /ˈpəʊstmən/ *UK* (*US* **mailman, letter carrier**) *noun* [C] *plural* **postmen** a man who takes and brings letters and parcels as a job

postmark /ˈpəʊstmɑːk/ *noun* [C] an official mark on a letter or parcel, showing the place and time it was sent

post-mortem /ˌpəʊstˈmɔːtəm/ *noun* [C] **HEALTH** a medical examination of a dead body to find out why the person died

ˈpost ˌoffice *noun* [C] a place where you can buy stamps and send letters and parcels

postpone /pəʊstˈpəʊn/ *verb* [T] to arrange for something to happen at a later time *The trip to the museum has been* ***postponed until*** *next week.*

postscript /ˈpəʊstskrɪpt/ *noun* [C] extra information at the end of a letter or email, usually added after writing the letters 'PS'

posture /ˈpɒstʃəʳ/ *noun* [U] the position of your back, shoulders, etc when you are standing or sitting *She has very* ***good posture****.*

postwar /ˈpəʊstwɔːr/ *adjective* happening or existing in the period after a war *postwar Europe*

pot¹ /pɒt/ *noun* **1** [C] a round container, usually used for storing things or cooking *a flower pot* ○ *a pot of coffee/tea* ○ *pots and pans* **2 go to pot** to be damaged or spoilt because no effort has been made *My diet's gone to pot since the holidays.* ➲See also: **melting pot**

pot² /pɒt/ *verb* [T] **potting**, *past* **potted** to put a plant into a pot filled with soil

potassium /pəˈtæsiəm/ *noun* [U] **CHEMISTRY** a chemical element that combines easily with other elements, often used to help plants grow well (symbol **K**)

poˌtassium ˈiodide *noun* [U] **CHEMISTRY** a white chemical compound similar to salt, which is used in photography and in some medical treatments (formula **KI**)

potassium permanganate /pəˌtæsiəmpɜːˈmæŋɡəneɪt/ *noun* [U] **CHEMISTRY** a dark purple chemical, used in industry, for example to kill germs (formula **$KMnO_4$**)

potato /pəˈteɪtəʊ/ *noun* [C, U] *plural* **potatoes** **FOOD** a round vegetable with a brown, yellow, or red skin that grows in the ground *boiled/fried potatoes* ○ *mashed potato* ➲See colour picture **Fruit and Vegetables** on page Centre 10 ➲See also: **couch potato, jacket potato, sweet potato**

poˈtato ˌchip *US* (*UK* **crisp**) *noun* [C] **FOOD** a very thin, dry, fried slice of potato

potent /ˈpəʊtᵊnt/ *adjective* very powerful or very effective *a potent drug/weapon* •**potency** /ˈpəʊtᵊnsi/ *noun* [U] when something is potent

potential¹ /pəʊˈtenʃᵊl/ *adjective* [**always before noun**] A potential problem, employer, partner, etc may become one in the future, although they are not one now. *a* ***potential danger/threat*** ○ *a* ***potential customer*** ○ *A number of* ***potential buyers*** *have expressed interest in the building.* •**potentially** *adverb a* ***potentially fatal*** *condition*

> WORD PARTNERS FOR ***potential***
>
> **have** [enormous/great, etc] potential • **achieve/fulfil/reach/realize** your (full) potential • **see/spot** sb's/sth's potential • sb's/sth's potential **as** sth

potential² /pəʊˈtenʃᵊl/ *noun* **1** SUCCESS [U] qualities or abilities that may develop and allow someone or something to succeed *to* ***achieve your full potential*** **2 potential for sth/doing sth a** the possibility that something may happen *There is the potential for some really interesting research.* **b PHYSICS** the difference in voltage (= how strong an electrical current is) between two points

poˌtential ˈenergy *noun* [U] **PHYSICS** the energy stored by something because of its position compared with other objects, its condition, or its electrical charge

potentiometer /pəʊˌtentʃiˈɒmɪtəʳ/ *noun* [C] **DT, PHYSICS 1** a device for measuring electrical potential (= difference in amount of electrical current between two points) **2** a device for changing the resistance (= how much something prevents the flow of electricity through it), used especially to control volume (= how loud something is)

pothole /ˈpɒthəʊl/ *noun* [C] a hole in the surface of a road

potometer /pəˈtɒmɪtəʳ/ *noun* [C] **BIOLOGY** a device for measuring how much water is taken up into a plant ➲See picture **potometer** on next page

potted /ˈpɒtɪd/ *adjective* **1** planted in a container ***potted plants/flowers*** ○ *a potted palm* **2 potted history/version, etc of sth** *UK* a story or report that has been changed to make it shorter and more simple *a potted version of Shakespeare*

ˌpotted ˈplant (*also UK* **ˈpot ˌplant**) *noun* [C] a plant that is grown in a container, and usually kept inside

P

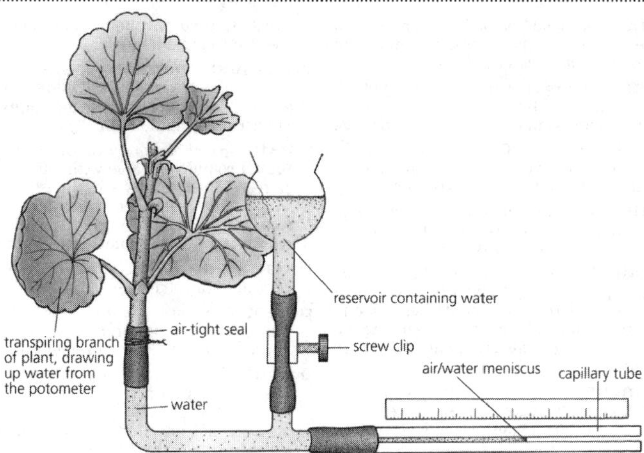

potometer

potter¹ /ˈpɒtəʳ/ *noun* [C] **DT** a person who makes plates, bowls, etc from clay

potter² /ˈpɒtəʳ/ *verb*
potter about/around (sth) *phrasal verb mainly UK* to spend time in a pleasant, relaxed way, often doing small jobs in your house

pottery /ˈpɒtᵊri/ *noun* **1 DT** [U] plates, bowls, etc that are made from clay **2 DT** [U] the activity of making plates, bowls, etc from clay **3** PLACE [C] a place where plates, bowls, etc made from clay are made or sold

potty¹ /ˈpɒti/ *noun* [C] a small toilet that young children use

potty² /ˈpɒti/ *adjective UK informal* crazy or stupid

pouch /paʊtʃ/ *noun* [C] **1** a small, soft bag made of leather or cloth **2 BIOLOGY** a pocket of skin in which some female animals carry their babies

poultry /ˈpəʊltri/ *noun* **1** [plural] **FARMING** chickens and other birds that people breed for meat and eggs **2 FOOD** [U] the meat of chickens and other birds eaten as food

pounce /paʊns/ *verb* [I] to suddenly move towards a person or animal that you want to catch
pounce on sth/sb *phrasal verb* to immediately criticize a mistake

pound¹ /paʊnd/ *noun* [C] **1 ECONOMICS** the unit of money used in the UK and Ireland; £ *a hundred pounds/£100* ○ *a* ***pound coin*** **2 MEASURES** (*written abbreviation* **lb**) a unit for measuring weight, equal to 453.6 grams or 16 ounces *a pound of potatoes* ○ *The baby weighed just four pounds when she was born.* See Extra help page **Numbers and measurements** on page Centre 24.

pound² /paʊnd/ *verb* **1** HIT [I, T] to hit something many times using a lot of force *Someone was* ***pounding on*** *the door.* **2** HEART [I] If your heart pounds, it beats very quickly. *My* ***heart*** *was* ***pounding*** *as I walked out onto the stage.* **3 pound along/down/up, etc** to run somewhere with quick, loud steps *He pounded up the stairs.*

pour /pɔːʳ/ *verb* **1** LIQUID [T] to make a liquid flow from or into a container *I* ***poured*** *the milk* ***into*** *a jug.* [+ two objects] *Can I* ***pour*** *you a* ***drink***? **2** RAIN [I] (*also UK* **pour down**) to rain, producing a lot of water *We can't go out in this weather - it's pouring!* **3 pour into/out/from, etc a** LIQUID to flow quickly and in large amounts *Blood was pouring from my leg.* **b** PEOPLE to enter or leave a place in large numbers *The crowd poured out into the street.*
pour sth out *phrasal verb* If you pour out your feelings or thoughts, you talk very honestly about what is making you sad. *She listened quietly while he* ***poured out*** *his* ***troubles***.

pout /paʊt/ *verb* [I] to push your lips forward because you are annoyed or because you want to look sexually attractive •**pout** *noun* [C]

WORD PARTNERS FOR ***poverty***

die in/live in poverty • **alleviate/fight/tackle** poverty • **abject/extreme** poverty

poverty /ˈpɒvəti/ *noun* [U] when you are very poor *to* ***live in poverty***

poverty-stricken /ˈpɒvətiˌstrɪkᵊn/ *adjective* A poverty-stricken area or person is very poor.

POW /ˌpiːəʊˈdʌbljuː/ *noun* [C] *abbreviation for* prisoner of war: a soldier who is caught by enemy soldiers during a war

powder /ˈpaʊdəʳ/ *noun* [C, U] a dry substance made of many small, loose grains *curry powder* ○ *face powder* •**powdered** *adjective* in the form of a powder *powdered milk/sugar* See also: **talcum powder**

WORD PARTNERS FOR ***power***

come to/devolve/seize/take/wield power • **considerable/enormous** power

O⊸**power**[1] /ˈpaʊəʳ/ *noun* **1** CONTROL [U] control or influence over people and events *He likes to have **power over** people.* **2 POLITICS** [U] political control in a country *They have been **in power** too long.* ○ *When did this government **come to power*** (= start to control the country)*?* **3** ENERGY [U] energy, usually electricity, that is used to provide light, heat, etc *nuclear power* ○ *Turn off the power at the main switch.* **4 POLITICS** [C] a country that has a lot of influence over others *a major world power* **5 LAW** [C, U] an official or legal right to do something [+ **to do sth**] *It's not **in my power** to stop him publishing this book.* **6** STRENGTH [U] strength or force ***economic/military power*** **7** ABILITY [U] a natural ability *to lose the power of speech* **8 MATHEMATICS** the number of times that a number has to be multiplied by itself *2 to the fourth power is 2 times 2 times 2 times 2, which equals 16.* **9 do everything in your power to do sth** to do everything that you are able and allowed to do *I've done everything in my power to help him.* **10 the powers that be** important people who have authority over others ⊃See also: **balance of power**

power[2] /paʊəʳ/ *verb* [T] to supply energy to a machine and make it work [**often passive**] *The clock is powered by two small batteries.*

ˈ**power** ˌ**cut** (*also US* **power outage**) *noun* [C] when the supply of electricity suddenly stops

O⊸**powerful** /ˈpaʊəfəl/ *adjective* **1** CONTROL A powerful person is able to control and influence people and events. *a powerful man/woman* **2** STRENGTH having a lot of strength or force *a powerful engine/weapon* **3** EFFECT having a strong effect on people *a **powerful effect/influence*** •**powerfully** *adverb*

powerless /ˈpaʊələs/ *adjective* not able to control events [+ **to do sth**] *The police were powerless to stop the fighting.*

power outage /ˈpaʊərˌaʊtɪdʒ/ *US* (*UK/US* **power cut**) *noun* [C] when the supply of electricity suddenly stops

ˈ**power** ˌ**station** (*also US* ˈ**power**ˌ**plant**) *noun* [C] a place where electricity is produced

ˈ**power** ˌ**tool** *noun* [C] a tool that uses electricity

pp *written abbreviation for* pages *See pp 10 - 12 for more information.*

PR /ˌpiːˈɑːʳ/ *noun* [U] *abbreviation for* public relations: writing and activities that are intended to make a person, company, or product more popular ***good/bad PR*** ○ ***a PR campaign***

practicable /ˈpræktɪkəbl/ *adjective formal* able to be done successfully *It's just not practicable to travel in this weather.*

O⊸**practical**[1] /ˈpræktɪkəl/ *adjective* **1** REAL relating to real situations or actions and not to thoughts or ideas ***practical experience*** ○ *They can offer **practical help.*** **2** SUITABLE suitable or useful for a situation which may involve some difficulty *practical clothes/shoes* ○ *Pale carpets just aren't practical if you have kids.* **3** POSSIBLE able to be done successfully *a **practical solution*** ○ *The plan is simply not practical.* **4** GOOD AT PLANNING Someone who is practical is good at planning things and dealing with problems. *She has a lot of interesting ideas but she's not very practical.* **5** GOOD WITH HANDS good at repairing and making things

practical[2] /ˈpræktɪkəl/ *noun* [C] **EDUCATION** a lesson or examination in which you do or make something instead of only writing

practicalities /ˌpræktɪˈkælətiz/ *noun* [**plural**] real situations or facts *the **practicalities of** running your own business*

practicality /ˌpræktɪˈkæləti/ *noun* [U] **1** POSSIBLE the possibility that something can be done successfully *I like the idea but I'm not sure about the practicality of it.* **2** SUITABLE how suitable or useful something is for a situation which may involve some difficulty

ˌ**practical** ˈ**joke** *noun* [C] a trick using actions and not words to make people laugh *to **play a practical joke** on someone*

practically /ˈpræktɪkəli/ *adverb* **1** ALMOST almost *It's **practically impossible** to get there.* ○ *We see her practically every day.* **2** SUITABLE in a suitable or useful way *We need to think practically.*

O⊸**practice** /ˈpræktɪs/ *noun* **1** REPEATING [U] when you repeat an activity to improve your ability *We need a bit more practice before the concert.* ○ *I've got basketball practice tonight.* **2** ACTIVITY [C, U] what people do or how they do it ***business/working practices*** [+ **of** + **doing sth**] *the **illegal practice** of copying CDs* [+ **to do sth**] ***It is common practice** to bury waste in landfills.* **3** WORK [C] a business in which several doctors or lawyers work together, or the work that they do *a **legal/medical practice*** **4 in practice** If something is true in practice, this is the real situation. *In practice, the new laws have had little effect.* **5 be out of practice** to not do something well because you have not done it recently **6 put something into practice** to try a plan or idea *Next month we will have a chance to put these ideas into practice.*

O⊸**practise** *UK* (*US* **practice**) /ˈpræktɪs/ *verb* **1** REPEAT [I, T] to repeat something regularly in order to improve your ability *You need to practise your pronunciation.* ○ *They're **practising for** tomorrow's concert.* **2** WORK [I, T] to work as a doctor or a lawyer *to **practise medicine/law*** **3** CUSTOM/RELIGION [T] to do something regularly according to a custom, religion, or a set of rules *to **practise a religion*** **4 practise what you preach** to behave as well as you often tell other people they should behave *I'd have more respect for him if he practised what he preached.*

practised *UK* (*US* **practiced**) /ˈpræktɪst/ *adjective* very good at doing something because you have done it so often *She answered the questions with **practised ease**.*

practising *UK* (*US* **practicing**) /ˈpræktɪsɪŋ/ *adjective* **a practising Catholic/Jew/Muslim, etc RELIGION** someone who follows the rules of a religion

practitioner /prækˈtɪʃənəʳ/ *noun* [C] *formal* someone who works as a doctor or a lawyer *a medical practitioner* ⊃See also: **general practitioner**

pragmatic /prægˈmætɪk/ *adjective* doing things in a practical and realistic way and not using

P

only ideas *a **pragmatic approach** to a problem*

pragmatism /ˈprægmətɪzᵊm/ *noun* [U] when someone is pragmatic •**pragmatist** *noun* [C] someone who is pragmatic

prairie /ˈpreəri/ *noun* [C] **GEOGRAPHY** a large, flat area of land in North America that is usually covered in grass

O‑**praise**[1] /preɪz/ *verb* [T] **1** to say that you admire someone or something, or that they are very good *He praised the team's performance.* ○ *Residents **praised** the firemen **for** their swift action.* **2 RELIGION** to give respect and thanks to a god ***Praise God**, no one was hurt.*

WORD PARTNERS FOR ***praise***

deserve/earn/be singled out for/win praise • **be full of** praise **for/have nothing but** praise **for** sb/ sth • **glowing/high** praise • praise **for** sb/sth • **in** praise **of** sth

praise[2] /preɪz/ *noun* [U] words you say to show that you admire someone or something *They deserve **praise for** their achievements.* ○ *Her first novel **won** a lot of **praise** from the critics.*

praiseworthy /ˈpreɪzˌwɜːði/ *adjective formal* deserving praise

pram /præm/ *noun* [C] *mainly UK* a small vehicle with four wheels for carrying a baby

prance /prɑːns/ *verb* [I] to walk or dance in a proud way, often because you want people to look at you *She was **prancing around** in a bikini.*

prank /præŋk/ *noun* [C] a trick that is intended to be funny

prawn /prɔːn/ *noun* [C] **FOOD** a small sea animal which you can eat, and which has a shell and ten legs

pray /preɪ/ *verb* [I, T] **1 RELIGION** to speak to a god in order to show your feelings or to ask for something *Let us **pray for** all the sick children.* [+ that] *She prayed that God would forgive her.* **2** to hope very much that something will happen *We're just **praying for** rain.*

prayer /preəʳ/ *noun* **1 RELIGION** [C] the words you say to a god *Shall we **say a prayer for** him?* **2 RELIGION** [U] when you say words to a god *They knelt **in prayer**.*

praying mantis /ˌpreɪɪŋˈmæntɪs/ *noun* [C] a large green insect that holds its front legs together when it is waiting to catch another insect

preach /priːtʃ/ *verb* **1 RELIGION** [I, T] to talk to a group of people about a religious subject, usually as a priest in a church *to preach the gospel* **2** [I] to try to persuade people to believe or support something, often in an annoying way ➲See also: **practise** what you preach

preacher /ˈpriːtʃəʳ/ *noun* [C] **RELIGION** someone who speaks in public about a religious subject, especially someone whose job is to do this

preamble /ˈpriːæmbl/ *noun* [C] *formal* an introduction to a speech or piece of writing

Precambrian /ˌpriːˈkæmbriən/ *adjective* **GEOLOGY** from the earliest period of time, between about 4,600 and 570 million years ago, from when the Earth was formed until the first simple forms of life appeared *the Precambrian era* ○ *Precambrian rocks*

precarious /prɪˈkeəriəs/ *adjective* **1** SITUATION A precarious situation is likely to become worse. *Many illegal immigrants are in a **precarious position**.* **2** NOT FIXED not fixed and likely to fall *That shelf looks a bit precarious.* •**precariously** *adverb Her cup was **balanced precariously** on the arm of the chair.*

WORD PARTNERS FOR ***precaution***

take [adequate/extra/necessary, etc] precautions • **as** a precaution • a **sensible/wise** precaution • a **safety** precaution • a precaution **against** sth

precaution /prɪˈkɔːʃᵊn/ *noun* [C] **1** something that you do to prevent bad things happening in the future *Driving alone at night can be dangerous, so always **take precautions**.* ○ *They called the doctor **as a precaution**.* [+ of + doing sth] *He took the precaution of locking the door.* •**precautionary** *adjective* **2 a precautionary measure/step** something that you do in order to prevent something bad from happening

precede /priːˈsiːd/ *verb* [T] *formal* to happen or exist before something else [**often passive**] *The formal ceremony was **preceded by** a parade.* •**preceding** *adjective* [**always before noun**] happening or coming before *the preceding months*

precedence /ˈpresɪdᵊns/ *noun* [U] when someone or something is considered more important than another person or thing *to **give precedence to** something* ○ *Quality should **take precedence** over cost.*

precedent /ˈpresɪdᵊnt/ *noun* [C, U] an action or decision that is used as an example when someone wants to do a similar thing in the future *This decision has **set an** important legal **precedent** for other countries.*

precinct /ˈpriːsɪŋkt/ *noun* **1 a pedestrian/shopping precinct** *UK* an area in a town where there are shops and no cars are allowed **2** [C] *US* an area in a city that a particular group of police are responsible for, or the building in which they work *the 45th precinct*

precincts /ˈpriːsɪŋkts/ *noun* [**plural**] the area of land around a building, especially a large church *the cathedral precincts*

precious[1] /ˈpreʃəs/ *adjective* **1** IMPORTANT very important to you *His books are his most precious possessions.* **2** VALUABLE rare and very valuable *a precious vase* ○ *a precious metal/stone*

precious[2] /ˈpreʃəs/ *adverb* **precious few/little** very little or very few of something *We have precious little money at present.*

ˌprecious ˈmetal *noun* [C] a valuable metal such as gold

precipice /ˈpresɪpɪs/ *noun* [C] **1** SITUATION a dangerous situation that could lead to failure or harm *The two countries stood **on the precipice** of war.* **2 GEOGRAPHY** a steep side of a mountain or high area of land

precipitate[1] /prɪˈsɪpɪteɪt/ *verb* [T] *formal* to make something happen [**often passive**] *The war was precipitated by an invasion.*

precipitate² /prɪˈsɪpɪteɪt/ *noun* [C] **CHEMISTRY** a solid substance found in a liquid during a chemical reaction

precipitation /prɪˌsɪpɪˈteɪʃᵊn/ *noun* [U] **1 GEOGRAPHY** water which falls from the clouds towards the ground, especially as rain or snow *Hail and sleet are types of precipitation.* **2 CHEMISTRY** when a solid substance is formed in a liquid during a chemical reaction

precis /ˈpreɪsiː/ *noun* [C, U] *formal* **LANGUAGE** a report giving the main ideas of a piece of writing or speech

O–ⁿ**precise** /prɪˈsaɪs/ *adjective* **1** EXACT exact and accurate *precise details/instructions* ⊃Opposite **imprecise 2 to be precise** used to give exact details about something *We met in 1994 - October first to be precise.* **3** EMPHASIS [**always before noun**] used to emphasize something that you are referring to *At that* ***precise moment****, the door opened.*

precisely /prɪˈsaɪsli/ *adverb* **1** EXACTLY exactly *at 6 o' clock precisely* **2** EMPHASIS used to emphasize something *This is precisely the kind of thing I was hoping to avoid.* **3** AGREEMENT used to agree with what someone else says *" It's not the shape I dislike, it's the colour. " "Precisely!"*

precision /prɪˈsɪʒᵊn/ *noun* [U] when something is very exact and accurate *She parked the car with great precision.*

preclude /prɪˈkluːd/ *verb* [T] *formal* to prevent something from happening [**+ from + doing sth**] *His illness precludes him from taking part in any sports.*

precocious /prɪˈkəʊʃəs/ *adjective* Children who are precocious have the confidence or skill of an adult. *A precocious child, she went to university at the age of 15.*

preconceived /ˌpriːkənˈsiːvd/ *adjective* Preconceived ideas are decided before the facts of a situation are known. ***preconceived ideas***

preconception /ˌpriːkənˈsepʃᵊn/ *noun* [C] what you believe before you know the facts of a situation *People* ***have*** *so many* ***preconceptions about*** *unmarried mothers.*

precondition /ˌpriːkənˈdɪʃᵊn/ *noun* [C] *formal* what must happen before something else can happen *The ceasefire is a* ***precondition for*** *peace talks.*

precursor /ˌpriːˈkɜːsəʳ/ *noun* [C] *formal* something which happens or exists before something else and influences its development *Infection with HIV is a* ***precursor to*** *AIDS.*

predate /ˌpriːˈdeɪt/ *verb* [T] to exist or happen before something else *The drinking of alcohol predates the Greeks and Romans.*

predator /ˈpredətəʳ/ *noun* [C] an animal that kills and eats other animals

predatory /ˈpredətᵊri/ *adjective* **1** A predatory person tries to get things from other people in a way that is unfair. **2 BIOLOGY** A predatory animal kills and eats other animals.

predecessor /ˈpriːdɪˌsesəʳ/ (US) /ˈpredəsesər/ *noun* [C] **1** PERSON the person who was in a job or position before *He seems a lot better than his predecessor.* **2** THING something that existed before another, similar thing *The predecessors to these computers were much larger and heavier.*

predetermined /ˌpriːdɪˈtɜːmɪnd/ *adjective formal* decided before *They met at a predetermined time and place.*

predeterminer /ˌpriːdɪˈtɒːmɪnəʳ/ *noun* [C] **LANGUAGE** a word that is used before a determiner to give more information about a noun. For example 'all' in 'all these children' is a predeterminer.

WORD PARTNERS FOR ***predicament***

face a predicament • **explain** your predicament • be **in** a predicament

predicament /prɪˈdɪkəmənt/ *noun* [C] a problem or a difficult situation *I sympathize with your predicament.*

predicate /ˈpredɪkət/ *noun* [C] **LANGUAGE** the part of a sentence which gives information about the subject. In the sentence 'We went to the airport.', 'went to the airport' is the predicate.

predicative /prɪˈdɪkətɪv/ *adjective* **LANGUAGE** A predicative adjective comes after a verb. In the sentence 'She is happy.', 'happy' is a predicative adjective. ⊃Compare **attributive**

predict /prɪˈdɪkt/ *verb* [T] to say what you think will happen in the future *Companies are predicting massive profits.* [**+ (that)**] *They predicted that the temperature would reach 80 degrees today.*

predictable /prɪˈdɪktəbl/ *adjective* happening or behaving in a way that you expect and not unusual or interesting *a predictable result* ○ *She's so predictable.* ⊃Opposite **unpredictable** •**predictably** *adverb*

WORD PARTNERS FOR ***prediction***

make a prediction • an **accurate /gloomy** prediction • a prediction **about** sth • a prediction **of** [disaster/an improvement, etc]

prediction /prɪˈdɪkʃᵊn/ *noun* [C, U] when you say what you think will happen in the future *I wouldn't like to* ***make*** *any* ***predictions about*** *the result of this match.*

preˌdictive ˈtexting *noun* [U] when your mobile phone suggests words automatically while you use it to write a text message (= a written message sent from one mobile phone to another)

predilection /ˌpriːdɪˈlekʃᵊn/ *noun* [C] *formal* when you like something very much *She* ***has a predilection for*** *chocolate.*

predisposed /ˌpriːdɪˈspəʊzd/ *adjective* **be predisposed to sth** to be more likely than other people to have a medical problem or to behave in a particular way *Some people are predisposed to addiction.* •**predisposition** /ˌpriːdɪspəˈzɪʃᵊn/ *noun* [C] when you are likely to have a medical problem or to behave in a particular way *people with a* ***predisposition to*** *heart disease*

predominant /prɪˈdɒmɪnənt/ *adjective* more important or noticeable than others *He has played a* ***predominant role*** *in these talks.* •**predominance** /prɪˈdɒmɪnəns/ *noun* [U] when

P

something is more important or noticeable than others *the predominance of English on the Internet*

predominantly /prɪˈdɒmɪnəntli/ *adverb* mostly or mainly *a predominantly Asian community*

predominate /prɪˈdɒmɪneɪt/ *verb* [I] to be the largest in number or the most important *Olive trees predominate in this area.*

pre-eminent /ˌpriːˈemɪnənt/ *adjective* more important or better than others *a pre-eminent artist/scholar* •**pre-eminence** /ˌpriːˈemɪnəns/ *noun* [U] when someone or something is much more important or better than others

pre-empt /ˌpriːˈempt/ *verb* [T] to do something before something else happens in order to prevent it or reduce its effect •**pre-emptive** *adjective* preventing something else from happening *to take **pre-emptive action***

preen /priːn/ *verb* [I, T] **1** BIRD If a bird preens or preens itself, it makes its feathers clean and tidy. **2** PERSON to try to look attractive [**often reflexive**] *The actors preened themselves in the dressing room.*

pre-existing /ˌpriːɪgˈzɪstɪŋ/ *adjective* existing before something else *a pre-existing medical condition*

prefabricated /ˌpriːˈfæbrɪkeɪtɪd/ *adjective* **a prefabricated building/home/house, etc** a building that has already been partly built when it is put together

preface /ˈprefɪs/ *noun* [C] **LITERATURE** a piece of writing at the beginning of a book that explains why it was written

prefect /ˈpriːfekt/ *noun* [C] **EDUCATION** in the UK, an older student in a school who has special duties and some authority

P

O-■ **prefer** /prɪˈfɜːʳ/ *verb* [T] **preferring**, *past* **preferred 1** to like someone or something more than another person or thing *I **prefer** dogs **to** cats.* [+ **doing sth**] *She prefers watching tennis to playing.* **2 would prefer** used to say what you want or ask someone what they want [+ **to do sth**] *I'd prefer to go alone.* ○ *Would you prefer red or white wine?*

COMMON LEARNER ERROR

prefer

Remember that **prefer** is often followed by **to do sth** or **doing sth**.

I prefer to walk.

I prefer walking.

~~*I prefer walk.*~~

preferable /ˈprefᵊrəbl/ *adjective* better or more suitable *Staying at home is **preferable to** going out with someone you don't like.*

preferably /ˈprefᵊrəbli/ *adverb* if possible *Serve the pudding with ice cream, preferably vanilla.*

WORD PARTNERS FOR ***preference***

express/have a preference • a **clear/marked** preference • a **personal** preference • a preference **for** sth

preference /ˈprefᵊrᵊns/ *noun* **1** [C, U] when you like something or someone more than another person or thing ***personal preferences*** ○ *We have white and brown bread. Do you **have a preference**?* ○ *I have a **preference for** dark-haired men.* **2 give preference to sb** to give special treatment to someone *Hospitals must give preference to urgent cases.*

preferential /ˌprefᵊrˈenʃᵊl/ *adjective* **preferential treatment** If you are given preferential treatment, you are treated in a better way than other people. *There were complaints that some guests had been given preferential treatment.*

prefix /ˈpriːfɪks/ *noun* [C] **LANGUAGE** a group of letters that you add to the beginning of a word to make another word. In the word 'unimportant', 'un-' is a prefix. ➲See Extra help page **Word formation** on page Centre 28. ➲Compare **suffix**

pregnancy /ˈpregnənsi/ *noun* [C, U] **BIOLOGY** when a woman is pregnant

O-■ **pregnant** /ˈpregnənt/ *adjective* **1 BIOLOGY** A pregnant woman has a baby developing inside her uterus. *to **get pregnant*** ○ *She's five months pregnant.* **2 a pregnant pause/silence** a pause or silence full of meaning that is not said in words

preheat /priːˈhiːt/ *verb* [T] **FOOD** to heat an oven to a particular temperature before putting food in it *Preheat the oven to 180 degrees.*

prehistoric /ˌpriːhɪˈstɒrɪk/ *adjective* relating to a time in the past before there were written records of events *prehistoric remains*

WORD PARTNERS FOR ***prejudice***

encounter/experience/face prejudice • prejudice **against** sb

prejudice¹ /ˈpredʒədɪs/ *noun* [C, U] when someone dislikes a group of people or treats them unfairly because they are a different race, sex, religion, etc *racial prejudice* ○ ***prejudice against** women*

prejudice² /ˈpredʒədɪs/ *verb* [T] **1** PERSON to influence someone in an unfair way so that they have a bad opinion of someone or something *Her comments may have **prejudiced** the voters **against** him.* **2** SITUATION to have a harmful effect on a situation *Newspaper reports have prejudiced the trial.*

prejudiced /ˈpredʒədɪst/ *adjective* feeling dislike for a group of people or treating them unfairly because they are a different race, sex, religion, etc *Are the police **prejudiced against** black people?*

preliminary /prɪˈlɪmɪnᵊri/ *adjective* [**always before noun**] done or happening in order to prepare for the main event or activity *a preliminary discussion/meeting* •**preliminary** *noun* [C] something that you do at the start of an event or activity

prelude /ˈpreljuːd/ *noun* **1 a prelude to sth** something that happens before another event or activity, usually as an introduction to it *There are hopes that the talks are a prelude to an agreement.* **2 MUSIC** [C] a short piece of music that introduces the main piece

premature /ˈprematʃəʳ/ (US) /ˌpriːməˈtʊr/ *adjective* happening too soon or before the usual time ***premature ageing/death*** ○ *a*

premature baby [**+ to do sth**] *It seems a bit premature to start talking about it already.* •**prematurely** *adverb He died prematurely of cancer.*

premeditated /ˌpriːˈmedɪteɪtɪd/ *adjective* **LAW** If a crime is premeditated, it is planned. ***premeditated murder*** ○ *a* ***premeditated attack***

premenstrual /ˌpriːˈmenstruəl/ *adjective* **HEALTH** related to the time just before a woman's period (= monthly blood from the uterus) ***premenstrual syndrome****/tension*

premier[1] /ˈpremiəʳ/ (US) /prɪˈmɪr/ *noun* [**C**] **POLITICS** the leader of a government *the Chinese premier* •**premiership** *noun* [**U**] the period in which someone is premier

premier[2] /ˈpremiəʳ/ (US) /prɪˈmɪr/ *adjective* [**always before noun**] best or most important *the city's premier hotel*

premiere /ˈpremieəʳ/ (US) /prɪˈmɪr/ *noun* [**C**] the first public performance of a film, play, etc *a* ***film premiere*** ○ *the world premiere* •**premiere** *verb* [**I, T**] [**often passive**] The opera was premiered in Paris.

the Premiership /ˈpremiəˌʃɪp/ *noun* **SPORT** the group of the best English football teams who compete against each other

premise /ˈpremɪs/ *noun* [**C**] *formal* an idea that you use to support another theory

premises /ˈpremɪsɪz/ *noun* [**plural**] the land or buildings used by an organization *We're moving to new premises.* ○ *Smoking is not allowed anywhere* ***on the premises.***

premium[1] /ˈpriːmiəm/ *noun* **1 FINANCE** [**C**] an amount of money you pay for insurance (= payments for an accident or illness) *How much is the monthly premium?* **2** [**C**] an amount or rate that is higher than average *You* ***pay a premium*** *for apartments in the city centre.* **3 be at a premium** If something useful is at a premium, there is not enough of it. *Time is at a premium just before the start of exams.* **4 place/put a premium on sth** to consider a quality or achievement as very important *She puts a premium on honesty.*

premium[2] /ˈpriːmiəm/ *adjective* [**always before noun**] A premium product is of a higher quality or value than others. *premium beer/cigars*

premolar /ˌpriːˈməʊləʳ/ *noun* [**C**] **ANATOMY** one of the two teeth in front of the molars (= large teeth at the back of the mouth) in the mouths of humans and some other animals, used for chewing food ➲See picture at **skull**

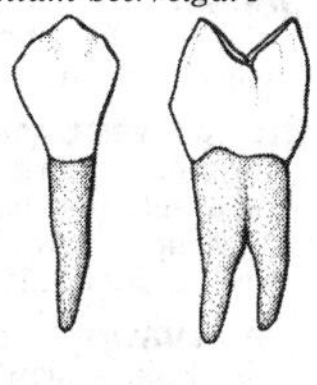

premolar

premonition /ˌpreməˈnɪʃən/ *noun* [**C**] a feeling that something, especially something unpleasant, is going to happen *to* ***have a premonition*** ○ *a* ***premonition of*** *disaster*

prenatal /ˌpriːˈneɪtəl/ *US* (*UK* **antenatal**) *adjective* **HEALTH** relating to pregnant women before their babies are born ***prenatal care***

preoccupation /priːˌɒkjəˈpeɪʃən/ *noun* **1** THINK/WORRY [**C, U**] when you think or worry about something so much that you do not think about other things *a* ***preoccupation with*** *death/food* **2** THING [**C**] something that you think or worry about a lot *His main preoccupations are football and women.*

preoccupied /ˌpriːˈɒkjəpaɪd/ *adjective* thinking or worrying about something a lot *She's been very preoccupied recently.* ○ *He's far too* ***preoccupied with*** *his own problems to notice mine.* •**preoccupy** /ˌpriːˈɒkjəpaɪ/ *verb* [**T**] If something preoccupies you, you think or worry about it a lot.

prepaid /priːˈpeɪd/ *adjective* **FINANCE** If something is prepaid, you pay for it before a particular time. *Susan just got prepaid tickets for the show next weekend.*

O-ᵚ**preparation** /ˌprepəˈreɪʃən/ *noun* [**U**] the things that you do or the time that you spend preparing for something *Did you* ***do*** *much* ***preparation for*** *your interview?* ○ *He's been painting the outside of the house* ***in preparation for*** *winter.* ○ *the preparation of the document*

WORD PARTNERS FOR ***preparations***

begin/finalize/make preparations • **final/last-minute** preparations • preparations are **underway** • preparations **for** sth

preparations /ˌprepərˈeɪʃənz/ *noun* [**plural**] things that you do to get ready for something *wedding preparations* ○ *We've been* ***making preparations for*** *the journey.* ○ *I've been busy with* ***last-minute preparations*** *for our trip.*

preparatory /prɪˈpærətəri/ *adjective* done in order to get ready for something *preparatory work*

preˈparatory ˌschool *noun* [**C**] *formal* **EDUCATION** a prep school *the Perse Prep School, Cambridge*

O-ᵚ**prepare** /prɪˈpeəʳ/ *verb* **1** GET READY [**I, T**] to get someone or something ready for something that will happen in the future *They're* ***preparing for*** *the big match.* ○ *We're preparing the students for their end-of-year exam.* [**+ to do sth**] *I was busy preparing to go on holiday.* **2 prepare yourself** to make yourself ready to deal with a difficult situation *Prepare yourself for a shock.* **3 FOOD** [**T**] to make food ready to be eaten *to prepare lunch*

prepared /prɪˈpeəd/ *adjective* **1** ready to deal with a situation *I wasn't* ***prepared for*** *the cold.* **2 be prepared to do sth** to be willing to do something *You must be prepared to work hard.*

prepayment /ˌpriːˈpeɪmənt/ *noun* [**U**] **FINANCE** payment for goods before they are received

preponderance /prɪˈpɒndərəns/ *noun formal* **a preponderance of sth** when there is a larger amount of one thing than of others *There is a preponderance of older people in this area.*

preposition /ˌprepəˈzɪʃən/ *noun* [**C**] **LANGUAGE** a word or group of words that is used before a noun or pronoun to show place, direction, time, etc. For example 'on' in 'Your keys are on the table.' is a preposition.

preposterous /prɪˈpɒstərəs/ *adjective* extremely stupid *That's a preposterous idea!*

prep school /ˈprepskuːl/ *noun* [**C**] **EDUCATION** **1** in the UK, a private school for children aged

P

between 8 and 13 **2** in the US, a private school which prepares students for college

prerequisite /ˌpriːˈrekwɪzɪt/ *noun* **[C]** *formal* something that is necessary in order for something else to happen or exist *Trust is a* ***prerequisite for*** *any sort of relationship.*

prerogative /prɪˈrɒgətɪv/ *noun* **[C]** *formal* something that you have the right to do because of who you are *Alex makes the decisions - that's his prerogative as company director.*

Presbyterian /ˌprezbɪˈtɪəriən/ *adjective* **RELIGION** belonging or relating to a type of Christian church with elected groups of local members involved in the official organization of local churches •**Presbyterian** *noun* **[C]**

pre-school /ˈpriːskuːl/ *adjective* **[always before noun] EDUCATION** relating to children who are too young to go to school ***pre-school children/education*** •**pre-school** *noun* **[C]** a school for children younger than five years old

prescribe /prɪˈskraɪb/ *verb* **[T] 1 HEALTH** to say what medical treatment someone needs **[often passive]** *Painkillers are the most common drugs prescribed by doctors in Britain.* **2** *formal* to say officially what people must do *rules prescribed by law*

prescription /prɪˈskrɪpʃᵊn/ *noun* **1 HEALTH [C]** a piece of paper saying what medicine someone needs or the medicine itself *a* ***doctor's prescription*** **2 HEALTH on prescription** *UK* (*US* **by prescription**) If you get a medicine on prescription, you only get it if you have a written instruction from your doctor.

prescriptive /prɪˈskrɪptɪv/ *adjective formal* saying exactly what must happen *The government's homework guidelines are too prescriptive.*

P

WORD PARTNERS FOR ***presence***

the presence **of** sb/sth • **in** the presence **of** sb/sth

presence /ˈprezᵊns/ *noun* **1** [IN A PLACE] **[U]** when someone or something is in a place *She signed the document* ***in the presence of*** *two witnesses.* **2** [POLICE/SOLDIERS] **[no plural]** a group of police or soldiers who are watching or controlling a situation *a strong* ***police presence*** **3** [QUALITY] **[U]** a quality that makes people notice and admire you **4 presence of mind** the ability to deal with a difficult situation quickly and effectively *She had the presence of mind to press the alarm.* **5 make your presence felt** to have a strong effect on other people *The new police chief has really made his presence felt.*

present¹ /ˈprezᵊnt/ *adjective* **1 be present** to be in a particular place *The whole family was present.* **2 [always before noun]** happening or existing now *the present situation* ○ *What is your present occupation?* **3 present tense LANGUAGE** the form of the verb which is used to show what happens or exists now

WORD PARTNERS FOR ***present***

buy/get/give sb/**wrap (up)** a present • a present **for/from** sb • a **birthday/wedding** present

present² /ˈprezᵊnt/ *noun* **1 the present a** the period of time that is happening now *The play is set* ***in the present.*** **b LANGUAGE** the form of the verb which is used to show what happens or exists now **2 [C]** something that you give to someone, usually for a particular occasion *a* ***birthday/wedding present*** ○ *to* ***give*** *someone a* ***present*** **3 at present** now *At present she's working abroad.*

present³ /prɪˈzent/ *verb* **[T] 1** [GIVE] to give something to someone, often at a formal ceremony *to* ***present a prize*** ○ *They* ***presented*** *her* ***with*** *a bouquet.* **2** [INFORMATION] to give people information in a formal way *He* ***presented*** *the* ***report to*** *his colleagues.* **3 present a danger/threat/problem, etc** to cause a danger/threat/problem, etc *The final exam may present some problems.* **4** [TV/RADIO] *UK* (*US* **host**) to introduce a television or radio programme *He presents a weekly sports quiz.* **5** [PLAY/FILM] to show a new play or film *The school is presenting 'West Side Story' this term.* **6** [INTRODUCE] to introduce someone formally *May I present my daughters?* **7** [OPPORTUNITY] If an opportunity presents itself, it becomes possible. *I'd be happy to go to New York, if the* ***opportunity presented itself.***

presentable /prɪˈzentəbl/ *adjective* looking clean and tidy enough *He was looking quite presentable in his jacket and tie.*

presentation /ˌprezᵊnˈteɪʃᵊn/ *noun* **1** [SHOW] **[U]** the way something is arranged or shown to people *Presentation is important if you want people to buy your products.* **2** [TALK] **[C]** a talk giving information about something *a* ***sales presentation*** ○ *She* ***gave*** *an excellent* ***presentation.*** **3** [CEREMONY] **[C]** a formal ceremony at which you give someone something *a* ***presentation ceremony***

present-day /ˌprezəntˈdeɪ/ *adjective* existing now *present-day attitudes*

presenter /prɪˈzentəʳ/ *UK* (*US* **host**) *noun* **[C]** someone who introduces a radio or television programme

presently /ˈprezəntli/ *adverb* **1** [NOW] *formal* now *He's presently living with his parents.* **2** [SOON] *old-fashioned* soon or after a short time *I'll be back presently.*

ˌpresent parˈticiple *UK* (*US* **ˌpresent ˈparticiple**) *noun* **[C] LANGUAGE** the form of a verb that ends with '-ing'

the ˌpresent ˈperfect *noun* **LANGUAGE** the form of the verb that is used to show actions or events that have happened in a period of time up to now. The sentence 'I have never been to Australia.' is in the present perfect.

preservation /ˌprezəˈveɪʃᵊn/ *noun* **[U]** when you keep something the same or prevent it from being damaged or destroyed *the preservation of peace* ○ *the preservation of wildlife*

preservative /prɪˈzɜːvətɪv/ *noun* **[C, U] FOOD** a substance used to prevent decay in food or in wood

preserve¹ /prɪˈzɜːv/ *verb* **[T] 1** to keep something the same or prevent it from being damaged or destroyed *to preserve peace* ○ *to preserve the environment* **2 FOOD** to add substances to something so that it stays in good condition for a long time *to preserve food/wood*

preserve² /prɪ'zɜːv/ *noun* **1** **FOOD** [C, U] *UK* (*US* **preserves**) a sweet food made from fruit, sugar, and water *apricot/strawberry preserve* **2** [**no plural**] an activity which only a particular group of people can do *Sport used to be a male preserve.* ○ *Owning racehorses is **the preserve of** the rich.* **3** **ENVIRONMENT** [C] *mainly US* an area where wild animals and plants are protected

preside /prɪ'zaɪd/ *verb* [I] to be officially responsible for a formal meeting or ceremony *An elderly priest **presided at** the marriage ceremony.*

preside over sth *phrasal verb* to be in charge of a situation, especially a formal meeting or legal trial *The case was **presided over by** a senior judge.*

presidency /'prezɪdənsi/ *noun* **POLITICS** **1** [C] the period when someone is president *Her presidency lasted seven years.* **2** **the presidency** the job of being president *He **won the presidency** by a wide margin.*

O⊸**president** /'prezɪdənt/ *noun* [C] **1** **POLITICS** the highest political position in some countries, usually the leader of the government *President Clinton* **2** the person in charge of a company or organization ➲See also: **vice president**

presidential /ˌprezɪ'denʃəl/ *adjective* **POLITICS** relating to the president of a country *a **presidential campaign***

O⊸**press¹** /pres/ *verb* **1** PUSH [I, T] to push something firmly *Press the button to start the machine.* ○ *He pressed his face against the window.* **2** PERSUADE [T] to try hard to persuade someone to do something [+ **to do sth**] *The committee pressed him to reveal more information.* ○ *We **pressed** him **for** an answer but he refused.* **3** **press charges** **LAW** to complain officially about someone in a court of law *The family decided not to **press charges against** him.* **4** MAKE SMOOTH [T] to make clothes smooth by ironing them *I need to press these trousers.* **5** MAKE FLAT [T] to make something flat by putting something heavy on it for a long time *to press fruit/flowers* **6** **press a case/claim** to try to make people accept your demands

press ahead/forward/on *phrasal verb* to continue to do something in a determined way *They're determined to press ahead with their plans despite opposition.*

press² /pres/ *noun* **1** **the press** newspapers and magazines, or the people who write them *the **local/national press*** ○ ***press reports*** **2** **good/bad press** praise or criticism from newspapers, magazines, television, etc *She's had a lot of bad press recently.* **3** BUSINESS [C] a business that prints and sells books *Cambridge University Press* **4** PRINT [C] (*also* **printing press**) a machine used to print books, newspapers, and magazines **5** MAKE FLAT [**no plural**] when you make cloth flat and smooth with a piece of equipment *Can you **give** these trousers **a press**?*

'press ˌconference *noun* [C] a meeting at which someone officially gives information to the newspapers, television, etc *to **call/hold a press conference***

pressed /prest/ *adjective* **be pressed for time/money** to not have much time/money

pressing /'presɪŋ/ *adjective* A pressing problem or situation needs to be dealt with immediately. *a **pressing need** for housing*

'press reˌlease *noun* [C] an official piece of information that is given to newspapers, television, etc

'press ˌstud *noun* [C] a metal or plastic object used to fasten clothes, made of two small round parts which are pressed together

press-up /'presʌp/ *UK* (*US* **push-up**) *noun* [C] **SPORT** a physical exercise in which you lie facing the floor and use your hands to push your body up

WORD PARTNERS FOR ***pressure***

face/feel pressure • **be under/come under** pressure • pressure **on** sb • pressure **from** sb • pressure **for** sth

O⊸**pressure¹** /'preʃəʳ/ *noun* **1** MAKE SOMEONE DO [U] when someone tries to make someone else do something by arguing, persuading, etc ***public/political pressure*** [+ **to do sth**] *Teachers are **under** increasing **pressure** to work longer hours.* ○ *The government is facing **pressure from** environmental campaigners.* **2** PROBLEMS [C, U] difficult situations that make you feel worried or unhappy *the pressures of work* ○ *He's been **under** a lot of **pressure** recently.* **3** **PHYSICS** [C, U] the force that a liquid or gas produces when it presses against an area ***water pressure*** **4** **PHYSICS** [U] the force that you produce when you push something **5** **put pressure on sb** to try to force someone to do something [+ **to do sth**] They're putting pressure on me to make a decision. ➲See also: **blood pressure, peer pressure**

pressure² /'preʃəʳ/ (*also UK* **pressurize, -ise** /'preʃəraɪz/) *verb* [T] to try to force someone to do something [**often passive + into + doing sth**] *We will not be pressured into making a decision.*

'pressure ˌcooker *noun* [C] a pan with a lid which you use to cook food quickly in steam

'pressure ˌgroup *noun* [C] **POLITICS** a group of people who try to influence what the public or the government think about something

pressurize *UK* (*also* **-ise**) /'preʃəraɪz/ *verb* [T] to try to force someone to do something [**often passive + into + doing sth**] *He was pressurized into signing the agreement.*

pressurized (*also UK* **-ised**) /'preʃəraɪzd/ *adjective* **PHYSICS** containing air or gas that is kept at a controlled pressure *a pressurized container*

prestige /pres'tiːʒ/ *noun* [U] when people feel respect and admiration for you, often because you are successful *His company has gained international prestige.* •**prestigious** /pres'tɪdʒəs/ *adjective* respected and admired, usually because of being important *a **prestigious award*** ○ *a prestigious university*

presumably /prɪ'zjuːməbli/ *adverb* used to say what you think is the likely situation *Presumably he just forgot to send the letter.*

presume /prɪ'zjuːm/ *verb* **1** [T] to think that something is likely to be true, although you are not certain [+ **(that)**] *I presume that you've*

P

done your homework. **2 be presumed dead/innocent, etc** If someone is presumed dead/innocent, etc, it seems very likely that they are dead/innocent, etc. **3 presume to do sth** *formal* to do something that you do not have the right or the skills to do *I certainly wouldn't presume to tell you how to do your job.*

presumption /prɪˈzʌmpʃᵊn/ *noun* **1** BELIEF [C] when you believe that something is true without any proof [+ (that)] *I object to the presumption that young people are only interested in pop music.* **2** BEHAVIOUR [U] behaviour that is rude and does not show respect

presumptuous /prɪˈzʌmptʃuəs/ *adjective* Someone who is presumptuous confidently does things that they have no right to do. *It was a bit presumptuous of her to take the car without asking.*

presuppose /ˌpriːsəˈpəʊz/ *verb* [T] *formal* If an idea or situation presupposes something, that thing must be true for the idea or situation to work.

pre-teen /priːˈtiːn/ *noun* [C] **SOCIETY** a boy or girl between the ages of 9 and 12 *a magazine for pre-teens* •**pre-teen** *adjective pre-teen fashions*

pretence *UK* (*US* **pretense**) /prɪˈtens/ *noun* **1** [U] when you make someone believe something that is not true *I can't* ***keep up the pretence*** (= continue pretending) *any longer.* ○ *They* ***made*** *absolutely* ***no pretence of*** *being interested.* **2 under false pretences** If you do something under false pretences, you do it when you have lied about who you are or what you are doing. *The police charged him with obtaining money under false pretences.*

O‑**pretend** /prɪˈtend/ *verb* [I, T] to behave as if something is true when it is not [+ (that)] *I can't pretend that I like him.* [+ to do sth] *Were you just pretending to be interested?*

pretense /prɪˈtens/ *noun US spelling of* pretence

pretension /prɪˈtenʃᵊn/ *noun* [C, U] when you try to seem better or more important than you really are [usually plural] *He seems to be without pretensions of any sort.*

pretentious /prɪˈtenʃəs/ *adjective* trying to seem more important or clever than you really are *a pretentious film*

pretext /ˈpriːtekst/ *noun* [C] a false reason that you use to explain why you are doing something *I called her* ***on the pretext of*** *needing some information.*

O‑**pretty**¹ /ˈprɪti/ *adverb informal* **1** quite, but not extremely *The traffic was pretty bad.* ○ *I'm pretty sure they'll accept.* **2 pretty much/well** almost *We've pretty much finished here.*

O‑**pretty**² /ˈprɪti/ *adjective* **1** WOMAN If a woman or girl is pretty, she is attractive. *Your daughter is very pretty.* **2** OBJECT If a place or an object is pretty, it is pleasant to look at. *a pretty little village*

prevail /prɪˈveɪl/ *verb* [I] *formal* **1** CONTROL to get control or influence *We can only hope that* ***common sense will prevail.*** **2** BE COMMON to be common among a group of people *The use of guns prevails among the gangs in this area.*

prevail on/upon sb to do sth *phrasal verb formal* to persuade someone to do something that they do not want to do *He was eventually prevailed upon to accept the appointment.*

prevailing /prɪˈveɪlɪŋ/ *adjective* [always before noun] **1** existing a lot in a particular group, area, or at a particular time ***a prevailing attitude/mood*** **2 a prevailing wind** a wind that usually blows in a particular place

prevalent /ˈprevᵊlənt/ *adjective* existing a lot in a particular group, area, or at a particular time *These diseases are more prevalent among young children.* •**prevalence** /ˈprevᵊləns/ *noun* [U] when something exists a lot in a particular group, area, or at a particular time *the prevalence of smoking among teenagers*

O‑**prevent** /prɪˈvent/ *verb* [T] to stop something happening or to stop someone doing something *to prevent accidents/crime* [+ from + doing sth] *Members of the public were prevented from entering the building.* •**preventable** *adjective* If something is preventable, it can be prevented.

COMMON LEARNER ERROR

prevent

Prevent should not be followed by 'to do sth'.

We must prevent such a disaster from happening again.

~~*We must prevent such a disaster to happen again.*~~

COMMON LEARNER ERROR

protect or **prevent?**

Protect means to keep someone or something safe from bad things.

You should wear sunscreen to protect your skin.

Prevent means to stop something from happening.

Wearing sunscreen can help prevent skin cancer.

preventative /prɪˈventətɪv/ *adjective another word for* preventive

prevention /prɪˈvenʃᵊn/ *noun* [U] when you stop something happening or stop someone doing something ***crime prevention*** ○ *the* ***prevention of*** *diseases*

preventive /prɪˈventɪv/ (*also* **preventative**) *adjective* Preventive action is intended to stop something before it happens. ***preventive measures*** ○ ***preventive medicine***

preview /ˈpriːvjuː/ *noun* [C] **1** FIRST SHOWING an opportunity to see a film, play, etc before it is shown to the public **2** ADVERTISEMENT a short film that advertises a film or television programme •**preview** *verb* [T]

O‑**previous** /ˈpriːviəs/ *adjective* existing or happening before something or someone else *the previous day/year* ○ *a previous attempt* ○ *his previous marriage* •**previously** *adverb He previously worked as a teacher.*

prey¹ /preɪ/ *noun* **1** [U] an animal that is hunted and killed by another animal **2 fall prey to sth** to be hurt or deceived by something or someone bad ➲See also: **bird of prey**

prey² /preɪ/ *verb*

prey on sth *phrasal verb* If an animal preys on

another animal, it catches it and eats it. *Spiders prey on flies and other small insects.*

prey on/upon sb *phrasal verb* to hurt or deceive people who are weak and easy to deceive *These young thieves prey on the elderly.*

WORD PARTNERS FOR ***price***

charge/increase/pay/put up prices • prices **fall** • an **average/exorbitant/high/low/reasonable** price

O‑ **price¹** /praɪs/ *noun* **1 FINANCE [C]** the amount of money that you pay to buy something ***high/low prices*** ○ *House prices are falling/rising.* ○ *The price of fuel has gone up again.* **2 [no plural]** the unpleasant results that you must accept or experience for getting or doing something *Suspension from the club was **a high/small price to pay*** (= very bad/not very bad thing to experience) *for his mistake.* **3 at a price** If you can get something at a price, you have to pay a lot of money for it. *False passports are available, at a price.* **4 at any price** If you want something at any price, you will do anything to get it. *She wanted the job at any price.*

COMMON LEARNER ERROR

price or **prize?**

These two words sound very similar but have different spellings and very different meanings - be careful not to confuse them.

Price means 'the amount of money that you pay to buy something'.

The price of oil has risen by 20%.

Prize means 'something valuable that is given to someone who wins a competition or who has done good work'.

She won first prize in the competition.

price² /praɪs/ *verb* **[T] FINANCE** to say what the price of something is **[often passive]** *The book **is priced at** $40.*

ˈ**price** ˌ**fixing** *noun* **[U] LAW, FINANCE** an agreement that is usually not legal, where companies all sell goods at a particular price in order to keep prices high

priceless /ˈpraɪsləs/ *adjective* **1** VALUABLE very valuable *a **priceless antique/painting*** **2** IMPORTANT very important or useful *A trip round the world is a priceless opportunity.*

ˈ**price** ˌ**skimming** *noun* **[U] FINANCE, ECONOMICS** the practice of selling a new product at a high price

ˈ**price** ˌ**tag** (also ˈ**price**ˌ**ticket**) *noun* **[C]** a piece of paper attached to a product that shows the amount a product costs

pricey (*also* **pricy**) /ˈpraɪsi/ *adjective informal* expensive *That jacket's a bit pricey!*

prick /prɪk/ *verb* **[T]** to make a very small hole in something with a sharp object *Prick the potatoes all over before baking.* ○ *I pricked my finger on a pin.* •**prick** *noun* **[C]** *The injection won't hurt - you'll just feel a slight prick.*

prickle¹ /ˈprɪkl/ *noun* **[C]** a sharp point on the surface of some plants or the skin of some animals

prickle² /ˈprɪkl/ *verb* **[I]** If part of your body prickles, it feels as if a lot of sharp points are touching it because you are frightened or excited. *a prickling sensation*

prickly /ˈprɪkli/ *adjective* **1** SHARP covered with prickles *a prickly bush* **2** UNFRIENDLY *informal* A prickly person or relationship is unfriendly or difficult to deal with.

pricy /ˈpraɪsi/ *adjective another spelling of* pricey

WORD PARTNERS FOR ***pride***

take pride **in** sth • a **sense/source** of pride • **great** pride • sb's pride **at/in** sth

O‑ **pride¹** /praɪd/ *noun* **[U] 1** SATISFACTION a feeling of satisfaction at your achievements or the achievements of your family or friends *She felt a great **sense of pride** as she watched him accept the award.* ○ *The whole community **takes pride in*** (= feels proud about) *the school.* **2** RESPECT the respect that you feel for yourself *Defeat in the World Cup has badly damaged **national pride**.* **3** IMPORTANCE the belief that you are better or more important than other people *His pride prevented him from asking for help.* **4 sb's pride and joy** something or someone that is very important to you *He spends hours cleaning that motorcycle - it's his pride and joy.* **5 have/take pride of place** If something takes pride of place, you put it in the best position so that it can be seen easily. *A photo of her grandchildren took pride of place on the wall.* **6 swallow your pride** to decide to do something although it will embarrass you *He swallowed his pride and asked if he could have his old job back.*

pride² /praɪd/ *verb*

pride yourself on sth/doing sth *phrasal verb* to feel satisfaction at a quality or skill that you have *The company prides itself on having the latest technology.*

priest /priːst/ *noun* **[C] RELIGION** someone who performs religious duties and ceremonies

the priesthood /ˈpriːsthʊd/ *noun* **RELIGION** the job of being a priest

prim /prɪm/ *adjective* Someone who is prim behaves in a very formal way and is easily shocked by anything rude. *Sarah wouldn't find that funny - she's far too **prim and proper*** (= shocked by anything rude). •**primly** *adverb*

prima donna /ˌpriːməˈdɒnə/ *noun* **[C]** someone who behaves badly and expects to get everything they want because they think that they are very important

primal /ˈpraɪməl/ *adjective formal* very basic, or relating to the time when human life on Earth began ***primal instincts***

primarily /praɪˈmerəli/ *adverb* mainly *She's known primarily as a novelist but she also writes poetry.*

primary¹ /ˈpraɪməri/ *adjective* **[always before noun]** most important *Her primary responsibility is to train new employees.*

primary² /ˈpraɪməri/ *noun* **[C] POLITICS** a vote in which people in a political party in the US choose the person who will represent them in an election

ˌ**primary** ˈ**colour** *UK* (*US* ˈ**primary**ˌ**color**) *noun* **[C] ART, DT** one of the three colours, which in

P

paint, etc are red, blue, and yellow, that can be mixed together to make any other colour

ˌprimary conˈsumer *noun* [C] **BIOLOGY** an animal that eats plants and therefore changes the energy from the sun that is stored in plants into meat that can be eaten by other animals

ˌprimary proˈducer *noun* [C] **BIOLOGY** in the food chain, a plant that produces food from the sun and is then eaten

ˈprimary ˌschool (*also US* **elementary school**) *noun* [C] **EDUCATION** a school for children aged 5 to 11

the ˈprimary ˌsector *noun* **FINANCE, ECONOMICS** industry which involves collecting and selling natural things, for example crops, rock and wood, often in order for them to be made into something else ⊃Compare **the secondary sector**

primate /ˈpraɪmeɪt/ *noun* [C] **BIOLOGY** a member of the group of animals which includes monkeys and people, which have large brains and hands and feet developed for climbing

prime¹ /praɪm/ *adjective* [**always before noun**] **1** MAIN main, or most important *the* ***prime suspect*** *in a murder investigation* **2** BEST of the best quality *The hotel is in a* ***prime location*** *in the city centre.* **3 a prime example** a very good example of something

prime² /praɪm/ *noun* [**no plural**] the period in your life when you are most active or successful *At 35, she's* ***in her prime.*** ○ ***the prime of life***

prime³ /praɪm/ *verb* [T] to prepare someone for an event or situation, often by giving them the information that they need *The president had been well primed before the debate.*

ˌprime ˈcost *noun* [U] **FINANCE** the cost to a business of all the employee's pay, materials and other things that are directly linked to the goods they produce

the ˈprime merˌidian *noun* **GEOGRAPHY** the imaginary line from the North Pole to the South Pole that passes through Greenwich in England and marks 0° longitude

ˌprime ˈminister *noun* [C] **POLITICS** the leader of an elected government in some countries

ˌprime ˈnumber *noun* [C] **MATHEMATICS** a number that cannot be divided by any other number except itself and the number 1 *2, 3 and 7 are prime numbers.*

ˈprime ˌtime *noun* [U] the time in the evening when the largest number of people watch television ***prime-time television***

primeval /praɪˈmiːvəl/ *adjective* belonging to a very early period in the history of the world *primeval forest*

primitive /ˈprɪmɪtɪv/ *adjective* **1 SOCIETY** relating to human society at a very early stage of development, with people living in a simple way without machines or a writing system *primitive man* ○ *primitive societies* **2** BASIC very basic or old-fashioned *The conditions at the campsite were rather primitive.*

primrose /ˈprɪmrəʊz/ *noun* [C] a wild plant with pale yellow flowers

prince /prɪns/ *noun* [C] **1** SON the son of a king or queen, or one of their close male relatives *Prince Edward* **2** RULER the male ruler of a small country

princely /ˈprɪnsli/ *adjective* **a princely sum** a large amount of money *It cost the princely sum of £2 million.*

princess /prɪnˈses/ (US) /ˈprɪnsəs/ *noun* [C] **1** DAUGHTER the daughter of a king or queen, or one of their close female relatives **2** WIFE the wife of a prince

principal¹ /ˈprɪnsəpəl/ *adjective* [**always before noun**] main, or most important *Her principal reason for moving is to be nearer her mother.*

principal² /ˈprɪnsəpəl/ *noun* [C] **EDUCATION** the person in charge of a school or college

principality /ˌprɪnsɪˈpæləti/ *noun* [C] a country ruled by a prince

principally /ˈprɪnsəpəli/ *adverb* mainly *The advertising campaign is aimed principally at women.*

WORD PARTNERS FOR ***principle***

stick to your principles • a **guiding** principle • be **against** sb's principles • be a **matter of** principle

principle /ˈprɪnsəpl/ *noun* **1** MORAL RULE [C, U] a rule or belief which influences your behaviour and which is based on what you think is right *He must be punished - it's a* ***matter of principle.*** **2** BASIC IDEA [C] a basic idea or rule which explains how something happens or works *The organization works* ***on the principle that*** *all members have the same rights.* **3 in principle** If you agree with something in principle, you agree with the idea or plan although you do not know the details or you do not know if it will be possible. *They have approved the changes in principle.* **4 on principle** If you refuse to do something on principle, you refuse to do it because you think it is morally wrong. *She doesn't wear fur on principle.*

principled /ˈprɪnsəpld/ *adjective* showing strong beliefs about what is right and wrong

print¹ /prɪnt/ *verb* **1** WRITING/IMAGES [T] to produce writing or images on paper or other material with a machine *The instructions are printed on the side of the box.* **2** BOOKS/NEWSPAPERS [T] to produce books, newspapers, magazines, etc, usually in large quantities, using machines *Fifty thousand booklets have been printed for the exhibition.* **3** INCLUDE [T] to include a piece of writing in a newspaper or magazine *They printed his letter in Tuesday's paper.* **4** WRITE [I, T] to write words without joining the letters together *Please print your name and address clearly using capitals.* **5** PATTERN [T] to produce a pattern on material or paper

print sth out *phrasal verb* to produce a printed copy of a document that has been written on a computer *Can you print out a copy of that letter for me?*

print² /prɪnt/ *noun* **1** WORDS [U] words, letters, or numbers that are produced on paper by a machine **2 in/out of print** If a book is in print, it is possible to buy a new copy of it, and if it is out of print, it is not now possible. **3 ART** [C] a copy of a picture made using photography or by pressing paper onto a design covered in ink *a print of Van Gogh's 'Sunflowers'* **4** PHOTOGRAPH [C] a photograph that is produced on paper **5 ART** [C] a pattern that is produced on material or paper *a floral print* **6** HAND [C] (*also* **fingerprint**) a mark that is left on a surface where someone has touched it *His prints were found all over the house and he was arrested the next day.* **7** MARK [C] a mark that is left on a surface where someone has walked *The dog left prints all over the kitchen floor.* ➲See also: **small print**

printer /ˈprɪntəʳ/ *noun* [C] **1 COMPUTING** a machine which is connected to a computer and which produces writing or images on paper *a laser printer* **2** a person or company that prints books, newspapers, magazines, etc

printing /ˈprɪntɪŋ/ *noun* [U] when writing or images are produced on paper or other material using a machine

ˈprinting ˌpress *noun* [C] a machine that prints books, newspapers, magazines, etc

printout /ˈprɪntaʊt/ *noun* [C] **COMPUTING** information or a document that is printed from a computer

prior /ˈpraɪəʳ/ *adjective formal* **1** [**always before noun**] existing or happening before something else *The course requires no* ***prior knowledge*** *of Spanish.* **2 prior to sth** before a particular time or event *the weeks prior to her death*

prioritize (*also UK* **-ise**) /praɪˈɒrɪtaɪz/ *verb* [I, T] to decide which of a group of things are the most important so that you can deal with them first *You must learn to* ***prioritize*** *your* ***work***.

priority /praɪˈɒrəti/ *noun* **1** [C] something that is very important and that must be dealt with before other things *My* ***first/top priority*** *is to find somewhere to live.* **2 give priority to sth** to consider that something is more important than other things and deal with it first **3 have/take priority (over sth)** to be more important than other things and to be dealt with first *His job seems to take priority over everything else.*

prise /praɪz/ *verb UK* **prise sth apart/off/open, etc** to use force to move, remove, or open something *I prised the lid off with a spoon.*

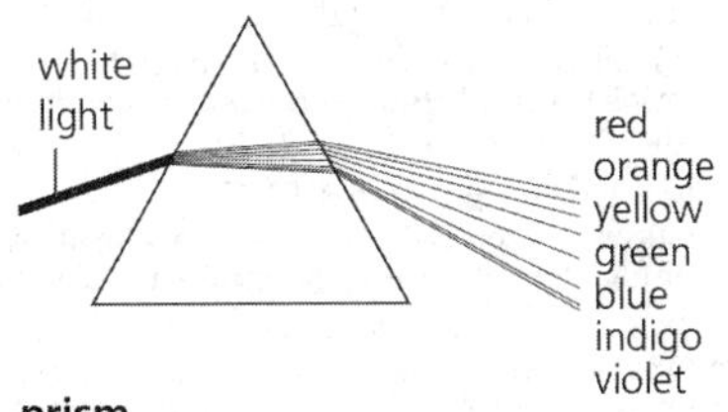

prism

prism /ˈprɪzᵊm/ *noun* [C] **PHYSICS** an object made of clear glass which separates the light that passes through it into different colours

WORD PARTNERS FOR ***prison***

go to/be sent to prison • be released from prison • in/out of prison • a prison sentence

O- **prison** /ˈprɪzᵊn/ *noun* [C, U] **LAW** a place where criminals are kept as a punishment *He's spent most of his life* ***in prison***. ○ *She was* ***sent to prison*** *for two years.*

O- **prisoner** /ˈprɪzᵊnəʳ/ *noun* **1** [C] **LAW** someone who is being kept in prison as a punishment, or because they have been caught by an enemy **2 hold/keep/take sb prisoner** to catch someone and guard them so that they cannot escape ➲See also: **political prisoner**

ˌprisoner of ˈwar *noun* [C] *plural* **prisoners of war POLITICS** a soldier who is caught by enemy soldiers during a war *a prisoner of war camp*

pristine /ˈprɪstiːn/ *adjective* in very good condition, as if new *Her car is in* ***pristine condition***.

privacy /ˈprɪvəsi/ (US) /ˈpraɪvəsi/ *noun* [U] when you are alone and people cannot see or hear what you are doing *I hate sharing a bedroom - I never get any privacy.*

O- **private**[1] /ˈpraɪvɪt/ *adjective* **1** NOT EVERYONE only for one person or group and not for everyone *Each room has a balcony and a private bathroom.* ○ *You can't park here - this is* ***private property***. **2** NOT GOVERNMENT controlled by or paid for by a person or company and not by the government *Charles went to a* ***private school***. **3** SECRET If information or an emotion is private, you do not want other people to know about it. *This is a* ***private matter*** *- it doesn't concern you.* **4 in private** If you do something in private, you do it where other people cannot see or hear you. *I need to talk to you in private.* **5 sb's private life** someone's personal relationships and activities and not their work **6** QUIET A place which is private is quiet and there are no other people there to see or hear what you are doing. *Is there somewhere private where we can talk?* •**privately** *adverb*

private[2] /ˈpraɪvɪt/ *noun* [C] a soldier of the lowest rank in the army

ˌprivate ˈenterprise *noun* [U] **ECONOMICS** industry and businesses owned by ordinary people, not by the government

ˌprivate limited ˈcompany *noun* [C] **ECONOMICS** a company whose shares (= parts that can be bought and sold) cannot be sold to the public

the ˈprivate ˌsector *noun* **ECONOMICS** businesses and industries that are not owned or controlled by the government

privatize (*also UK* **-ise**) /ˈpraɪvɪtaɪz/ *verb* [T] **ECONOMICS, POLITICS** If an industry or organization owned by the government is privatized, it is sold to private companies. •**privatization** /ˌpraɪvɪtaɪˈzeɪʃᵊn/ *noun* [U]

privilege /ˈprɪvᵊlɪdʒ/ *noun* **1** ADVANTAGE [C, U] an advantage that only one person or group has, usually because of their position or because they are rich **2** OPPORTUNITY [**no plural**] an opportunity to do something special or enjoyable [**+ of + doing sth**] *I had the privilege of meeting the Queen.* •**privileged** *adjective* having a privilege *to be in a* ***privileged position***

privy /ˈprɪvi/ *adjective formal* **privy to sth** knowing information that is not known by many people

WORD PARTNERS FOR ***prize***

be awarded/win a prize • **first/second/the runner's-up/the top** prize • a prize **for** sth • a prize **of** [£500/a car, etc] • prize **money/winner**

prize¹ /praɪz/ *noun* [C] something valuable that is given to someone who wins a competition or who has done good work *to **win** a **prize*** ○ ***first/second prize*** ➲See Common Learner Error at **price** ➲See also: **booby prize**

prize² /praɪz/ *adjective* [**always before noun**] A prize animal or vegetable is good enough to win a competition.

prize³ /praɪz/ *verb* [T] to think that something is very valuable or important *His car is his **prized possession**.*

prize-winning /ˈpraɪzˌwɪnɪŋ/ *adjective* [**always before noun**] having won a prize *a prize-winning author*

pro /prəʊ/ *noun* [C] **1 SPORT** *informal* someone who earns money for playing a sport *a golf/tennis pro* **2 the pros and cons** the advantages and disadvantages of something [+ **of** + **doing sth**] We discussed the pros and cons of buying a bigger house.

pro- /prəʊ-/ *prefix* supporting or approving of something *pro-European* ○ *pro-democracy demonstrations* ➲Compare **anti-**

proactive /ˌprəʊˈæktɪv/ *adjective* taking action by causing change and not only reacting to change when it happens

probability /ˌprɒbəˈbɪləti/ *noun* **1** [C, U] how likely it is that something will happen [+ **of** + **doing sth**] *What's the probability of winning?* [+ **(that)**] *There's a **high probability** that he'll get the job.* **2 in all probability** used to mean that something is very likely *She will, in all probability, have left before we arrive.*

P

probable /ˈprɒbəbl/ *adjective* likely to be true or to happen *The **probable cause** of death was heart failure.* [+ **(that)**] *It's **highly probable** that he'll lose his job.*

probably /ˈprɒbəbli/ *adverb* used to mean that something is very likely *I'll probably be home by midnight.*

probation /prəʊˈbeɪʃən/ *noun* [U] **1 LAW** a period of time when a criminal must behave well and not commit any more crimes in order to avoid being sent to prison *to be **on probation*** **2** a period of time at the start of a new job when you are watched and tested to see if you are suitable for the job •**probationary** *adjective* relating to probation *a **probationary** period*

proˈbation ˌofficer *noun* [C] **LAW** someone whose job is to watch and help criminals who have been put on probation

probe¹ /prəʊb/ *verb* [I, T] to ask a lot of questions in order to discover information about something or someone *The interviewer **probed** deep **into** her private life.* ○ ***probing questions***

probe² /prəʊb/ *noun* [C] **1** when you try to discover information about something by asking a lot of questions *an FBI **probe into** corruption* **2 HEALTH** a long, thin, metal tool used by doctors to examine parts of the body

OTHER WAYS OF SAYING ***problem***

The noun **difficulty** is a common alternative to 'problem': *The company is having some financial **difficulties** at the moment.*

A small, temporary problem may be described informally as a **hitch** or a **hiccup**: *The ceremony went without a **hitch**.* • *I'm afraid there's been a slight **hiccup** with the arrangements.*

A **glitch** is a problem that stops something from working properly: *We've had a few technical **glitches**, but I'm confident we'll be ready on time.*

A **hurdle** or **obstacle** is a problem that you need to deal with so that you can continue to make progress: *Getting a work permit is the first **hurdle/obstacle**.*

A **pitfall** is a problem that is likely to happen in a particular situation: *It's just one of the **pitfalls** of buying a house.*

A **setback** is a problem that makes something happen less quickly than it should: *The project has suffered a series of **setbacks** this year.*

WORD PARTNERS FOR ***problem***

cause/face/have/tackle/pose a problem • a problem **arises** • a **big/major/real/serious** problem

problem /ˈprɒbləm/ *noun* **1** DIFFICULT SITUATION [C] a situation that causes difficulties and that needs to be dealt with *health problems* ○ *I'm **having problems with** my computer.* ○ *Drugs have become a serious problem in the area.* ➲See Common Learner Error at **trouble** **2 MATHEMATICS** [C] a question that you use mathematics to solve **3 have a problem with sth/sb** to find something or someone annoying or offensive *Yes, she can smoke in the house - I don't have a problem with that.* **4 No problem. a** AFTER QUESTION something that you say to mean you can or will do what someone has asked you to do *"Can you get me to the airport by 11.30?" "No problem."* **b** AFTER THANKS something that you say when someone has thanked you for something *"Thanks for taking me home." "No problem."*

problematic /ˌprɒbləˈmætɪk/ *adjective* full of problems or difficulties *He has a very problematic relationship with his father.*

WORD PARTNERS FOR ***procedure***

follow a procedure • **correct/proper/standard** procedure • a procedure **for** (doing) sth

procedure /prəʊˈsiːdʒəʳ/ *noun* [C, U] the official or usual way of doing something *The company has new **procedures for** dealing with complaints.*

proceed /prəʊˈsiːd/ *verb* [I] *formal* **1** to continue as planned *His lawyers have decided not to **proceed with** the case.* **2 proceed to do sth** to do something after you have done something else *She sat down and proceeded to tell me about her skiing trip.* **3 proceed along/down/to, etc** *formal* to move or travel in a particular direction *Passengers for Sydney should proceed to gate 21.*

proceedings /prəˈsiːdɪŋz/ *noun* [**plural**] **1 LAW** legal action against someone *The bank is threatening to start **legal proceedings** against him.* **2** a series of organized events or actions *The chairman opened the proceedings with a short speech.*

proceeds /ˈprəʊsiːdz/ *noun* [**plural**] **FINANCE** the money that is earned from an event or activity *All proceeds from the concert will go to charity.*

O⁻**process**¹ /ˈprəʊses/ (US) /ˈprɑːses/ *noun* [**C**] **1** [ACTIONS] a series of actions that you take in order to achieve a result *Buying a house can be a long and complicated process.* **2** [CHANGES] [**C**] a series of changes that happen naturally *the **ageing process*** **3 in the process** If you are doing something, and you do something else in the process, the second thing happens as a result of doing the first thing. *She stood up to say hello and spilled her drink in the process.* **4 be in the process of doing sth** to have started doing something *We're in the process of painting our apartment.*

process² /ˈprəʊses/ (US) /ˈprɑːses/ *verb* [**T**] **1** to add chemicals to a substance, especially food, in order to change it or make it last longer ***processed food*** **2 COMPUTING** to deal with information or documents in an official way *Visa applications take 28 days to process.* **3 COMPUTING** When a computer processes data (= information), it does things to it so that it can be used and understood •**processing** *noun* [**U**] *data processing*

procession /prəˈseʃᵊn/ *noun* [**C**] a line of people or vehicles that moves forward slowly as part of a ceremony or public event *a funeral procession*

processor /ˈprəʊsesəʳ/ *noun* [**C**] **COMPUTING** the main part of a computer that controls all the other parts ➲See also: **food processor, word processor**

proclaim /prəʊˈkleɪm/ *verb* [**T**] *formal* to announce something officially or in public •**proclamation** /ˌprɒkləˈmeɪʃᵊn/ *noun* [**C**] an official announcement about something important

procrastinate /prəʊˈkræstɪneɪt/ *verb* [**I**] *formal* to wait a long time before doing something that you must do *I know I've got to deal with the problem at some point - I'm just procrastinating.*

procure /prəˈkjʊəʳ/ *verb* [**T**] *formal* to obtain something that is difficult to get

prod /prɒd/ *verb* **prodding**, *past* **prodded** **1** [PUSH] [**I, T**] to push someone or something with your finger or with a pointed object *He prodded me in the back and told me to hurry up.* **2** [ENCOURAGE] [**T**] to encourage someone to do something [**+ into + doing sth**] *We need to prod him into making a decision.* •**prod** *noun* [**C**] [**usually singular**] to ***give someone a prod***

prodigious /prəˈdɪdʒəs/ *adjective formal* extremely great in size or ability *a prodigious talent ○ a prodigious appetite*

prodigy /ˈprɒdɪdʒi/ *noun* [**C**] a young person who is very good at something *A **child prodigy**, she entered university at the age of eleven.*

O⁻**produce**¹ /prəˈdjuːs/ *verb* [**T**] **1** [MAKE] to make or grow something *The factory produces about 900 cars a year. ○ This plant will produce small yellow flowers in the spring.* **2** [CAUSE] to cause a particular reaction or result *Nuts produce an allergic reaction in some people.* **3** [SHOW] to take an object from somewhere so that people can see it *One of the men suddenly produced a gun from his pocket.* **4** [FILM/PLAY] to control how a film, play, programme, or musical recording is made *He's produced some of the top Broadway shows.* ➲See also: **mass-produce**

produce² /ˈprɒdjuːs/ *noun* [**U**] **FARMING** food that is grown or made in large quantities to be sold *dairy produce*

producer /prəˈdjuːsəʳ/ *noun* [**C**] **1** [GOODS/FOOD] a company, country, or person that makes goods or grows food *Australia is one of the world's main producers of wool.* **2** [FILM/PLAY] someone who controls how a film, play, programme, or musical recording is made *a **film producer*** **3 BIOLOGY** in the food chain, a plant that can make food from the sun and is then eaten itself

O⁻**product** /ˈprɒdʌkt/ *noun* [**C**] **1** something that is made or grown to be sold *a new range of skin-care products ○ Does she eat **dairy products*** (= things made from milk)? **2 product of sth** someone or something that is the result of a particular experience or process *His lack of confidence is the product of an unhappy childhood.* ➲See also: **by-product, end-product** **3 CHEMISTRY** a substance formed by a chemical reaction **4 MATHEMATICS** the number you get when you multiply one number by another

WORD PARTNERS FOR ***production***

sth **goes into** production • production **of** sth

O⁻**production** /prəˈdʌkʃᵊn/ *noun* **1** [MAKING] [**U**] when you make or grow something *Sand is used in the **production of** glass. ○ The new model **goes into production*** (= starts being made) *next year.* **2** [AMOUNT] [**U**] the amount of something that is made or grown *We need to increase production by 20%.* **3** [PERFORMANCE] [**C**] a performance or series of performances of a play or show *a school production of 'Romeo and Juliet'* **4** [ORGANIZING FILM/PLAY] [**U**] when someone controls how a film, play, programme, or musical recording is made

productive /prəˈdʌktɪv/ *adjective* **1** [USEFUL] producing a good or useful result *We had a very productive meeting and sorted out a lot of problems.* **2** [LARGE AMOUNT] producing a large amount of goods, food, work, etc *productive land ○ a productive worker*

productivity /ˌprɒdʌkˈtɪvəti/ *noun* [**U**] the rate at which goods are produced *We need to increase productivity by 50%.*

ˌ**product** ˈ**life** ˌ**cycle** (*abbreviation* **PLC**) *noun* [**C**] **ECONOMICS** in business, all the stages that a product goes through from being made to being sold

ˈ**product** ˌ**lining** *noun* [**U**] **FINANCE, ECONOMICS** when a business sells several similar or connected products

ˈ**product** ˌ**mix** *noun* [**C usually singular**] **FINANCE, ECONOMICS** the number of different products sold by a business

Prof /prɒf/ *noun* [**C**] **EDUCATION** *short for* professor *Prof Susan Nishio*

P

profane /prəˈfeɪn/ *adjective formal* **RELIGION** showing no respect for God or for religious or moral rules ***profane language*** •**profanity** /prəˈfænəti/ *noun* [U] *formal*

profess /prəˈfes/ *verb* [T] *formal* to express a quality or belief, often when it is not true [+ **to do sth**] *She professes to hate shopping, but she's always buying new things.*

profession /prəˈfeʃən/ *noun* **1** WORK [C] a type of work that needs special training or education *He's working in a restaurant, but he's a teacher* ***by profession*** (= he trained to be a teacher). ➲See Common Learner Error at **work** **2** PEOPLE [**group**] the people who do a type of work considered as a group *The medical profession has expressed concern about the new drug.*

professional¹ /prəˈfeʃənəl/ *adjective* **1** JOB [**always before noun**] relating to a job that needs special training or education *You should get some* ***professional advice*** *about your finances.* **2** EARNING MONEY Someone is professional if they earn money for a sport or activity which most people do as a hobby. *a professional athlete/musician* ➲Opposite **amateur** **3** SKILL showing skill and careful attention *a professional attitude* ○ *He looks very professional in that suit.* ➲Opposite **unprofessional**

professional² /prəˈfeʃənəl/ *noun* [C] **1** TRAINED someone who does a job that needs special training or education **2** WITH EXPERIENCE someone who has done a job for a long time and who does it with a lot of skill *She dealt with the problem like a true professional.* **3** **SPORT** someone who earns money for doing a sport or activity which most other people do as a hobby *a rugby professional* ➲Opposite **amateur**

professionalism /prəˈfeʃənəlɪzəm/ *noun* [U] the skill and careful attention which trained people are expected to have *He complained about the lack of professionalism in the company.*

professionally /prəˈfeʃənəli/ *adverb* **1** WORK in a way that relates to your work *I know him professionally, but he's not a close friend.* **2** WITH TRAINING Work that is done professionally is done by someone who has had special training. *Their house has been professionally decorated.* **3** HIGH STANDARDS in a way that shows high standards or skill *He dealt with the situation very professionally.* **4** **SPORT** If someone does an activity or sport professionally, they earn money for doing it. *He's good enough at football to* ***play professionally****.*

professor /prəˈfesəʳ/ *noun* [C] **EDUCATION** the highest rank of teacher in a British university, or a teacher in an American university or college *a professor of history at Oxford* ○ *Professor Blackman.*

proffer /ˈprɒfəʳ/ *verb* [T] *formal* to offer something to someone *to* ***proffer advice***

proficiency /prəˈfɪʃənsi/ *noun* [U] when you can do something very well *The job requires* ***proficiency in*** *written and spoken English.*

proficient /prəˈfɪʃənt/ *adjective* very good at something *She's* ***proficient in*** *two languages.* ○ *I've become quite* ***proficient at*** *repairing bicycles.*

WORD PARTNERS FOR ***profile***

build up/create a profile • a profile **of** sb/sth

profile¹ /ˈprəʊfaɪl/ *noun* [C] **1** DESCRIPTION a short description of someone's life, character, work, etc **2** HEAD a side view of someone's face or head *The picture shows him* ***in profile****.* **3** ATTENTION the amount of attention that something receives *We need to increase our company's profile in Asia.* **4** **high profile** important and noticeable *a high profile job* **5** **INTERNET** a description of yourself and your interests on a website **6** **keep a low profile** to try not to be noticed

profile² /ˈprəʊfaɪl/ *verb* [T] to describe someone's life, character, work, etc

WORD PARTNERS FOR ***profit***

boost/increase profits • **make** a profit • profits **fall/rise** • an **annual/big/gross/healthy/large/small** profit

profit¹ /ˈprɒfɪt/ *noun* [C, U] **FINANCE** money that you get from selling goods or services for more than they cost to produce or provide *a profit of $4.5 million* ○ *It's very hard for a new business to* ***make a profit*** *in its first year.*

profit² /ˈprɒfɪt/ *verb*

profit from sth *phrasal verb* **FINANCE** to earn a profit or get an advantage from something *Investors have profited from a rise in interest rates.*

profitable /ˈprɒfɪtəbl/ *adjective* **1** **FINANCE** making or likely to make a profit *a profitable business* **2** useful or likely to give you an advantage *a profitable discussion* •**profitability** /ˌprɒfɪtəˈbɪlɪti/ *noun* [U] •**profitably** *adverb*

ˌprofit and ˈloss account *noun* [C] **FINANCE** a record of the money a business or organization has spent and received

ˈprofit ˌmargin *noun* [C] **FINANCE** the amount of money that you get when you sell a thing or a service, not including the money that it costs to make or provide that thing or service *Many small companies operate on very narrow profit margins.*

ˈprofit ˌsharing *noun* [U] **FINANCE** the system of sharing the money that a company makes between all the people who work for it

profound /prəˈfaʊnd/ *adjective* **1** EFFECT If an effect is profound, it is extreme. *The war had a* ***profound impact*** *on people's lives.* **2** FEELING If a feeling is profound, you feel it very strongly. *a* ***profound sense of*** *sadness* **3** UNDERSTANDING If an idea or piece of work is profound, it shows intelligence or a great ability to understand. *a profound question* ○ *His theories were simple, but profound.* •**profoundly** *adverb*

profusely /prəˈfjuːsli/ *adverb* a lot *He* ***apologized profusely*** *for being late.*

profusion /prəˈfjuːʒən/ *noun* [U, **no plural**] *formal* an extremely large amount of something *a profusion of wild flowers* ○ *Bacteria grow* ***in profusion*** *in the warm, wet soil.*

progesterone /prəˈdʒestərəʊn/ *noun* [U] **BIOLOGY** a female hormone (= chemical that influences growth and development) which causes the womb to prepare for pregnancy

prognosis /prɒɡˈnəʊsɪs/ *noun* [C] *plural* **prognoses** /prɒɡˈnəʊsiːz/ *formal* **1** HEALTH a judgment that a doctor makes about an ill person's chance of becoming healthy **2** an opinion about the future of someone or something *The prognosis for economic growth is good.*

O⁻**program¹** /ˈprəʊɡræm/ *noun* [C] **1** COMPUTING a set of instructions that you put into a computer to make it do something *to write a **computer program*** **2** *US spelling of* programme

program² /ˈprəʊɡræm/ *verb* [T] **programming**, *past* **programmed** COMPUTING **1** If you program a computer, you give it a set of instructions to do something. **2** *US spelling of* programme

O⁻**programme¹** *UK* (*US* **program**) /ˈprəʊɡræm/ *noun* [C] **1** [TELEVISION/RADIO] a show on television or radio *a **TV programme** ○ Did you see that programme about spiders last night?* **2** [PLAN] a plan of events or activities with a particular purpose *a health education programme* **3** [THIN BOOK] a thin book that you buy at a theatre, sports event, etc which tells you who or what you are going to see

programme² *UK* (*US* **program**) /ˈprəʊɡræm/ *verb* [T] COMPUTING If you programme a machine, you give it a set of instructions to do something. [+ **to do sth**] *I've programmed the video to start recording at 10 o'clock.*

programmer /ˈprəʊɡræməʳ/ *noun* [C] COMPUTING someone who writes computer programs as a job •**programming** *noun* [U] when someone writes computer programs

WORD PARTNERS FOR ***progress***

halt / impede / make / monitor progress • **rapid / real / significant / slow / steady** progress • progress **on/toward** sth

O⁻**progress¹** /ˈprəʊɡres/ (US) /ˈprɒɡres/ *noun* [U] **1** [DEVELOPMENT] development and improvement of skills, knowledge, etc ***slow/rapid progress*** *○ technological progress ○ He has **made** good **progress** in French this year.* **2 in progress** *formal* happening or being done now *Quiet please - Exams in progress.* **3** [MOVEMENT] movement towards a place

progress² /prəʊˈɡres/ *verb* [I] **1** [IMPROVE] to improve or develop in skills, knowledge, etc *Technology has progressed rapidly in the last 100 years.* **2** [CONTINUE] to continue gradually *I began to feel more relaxed as the evening progressed.*

progression /prəʊˈɡreʃᵊn/ *noun* [C, U] when something or someone changes to the next stage of development *a **logical/natural progression** ○ Drugs can stop the progression of the disease.*

progressive /prəʊˈɡresɪv/ *adjective* **1** [MODERN] thinking or behaving in a new or modern way ***progressive ideas/attitudes*** **2** [GRADUAL] developing or happening gradually *a progressive disease* •**progressively** *adverb* gradually *My headaches are getting **progressively worse**.*

the progressive /prəʊˈɡresɪv/ *noun* LANGUAGE the form of the verb that is used to show that an action is continuing. In English, the progressive is made with 'be' and the present participle.

prohibit /prəʊˈhɪbɪt/ *verb* [T] *formal* to officially forbid something [**often passive**] *Smoking is prohibited on most international flights.* [+ **from** + **doing sth**] *The new law prohibits people from drinking alcohol in the street. ○ a **prohibited substance*** •**prohibition** /ˌprəʊhɪˈbɪʃᵊn/ *noun* [U] when something is prohibited

prohibitive /prəʊˈhɪbətɪv/ *adjective* If the cost of something is prohibitive, it is too expensive for many people. *The cost of flying first class is prohibitive for most people.* •**prohibitively** *adverb* ***prohibitively expensive***

O⁻**project¹** /ˈprɒdʒekt/ *noun* [C] **1** a carefully planned piece of work that has a particular purpose *a research project ○ The new building project will cost $45 million.* **2** EDUCATION a piece of school work that involves detailed study of a subject *We're **doing** a class **project on** the environment.*

project² /prəʊˈdʒekt/ *verb* **1** [CALCULATE] [T] to calculate an amount or make a guess about the future based on information that you have [**often passive + to do sth**] *As people live longer, the demand for health care is projected to increase dramatically. ○ **projected costs/growth*** **2** [IMAGE] [T] to show a film or other image on a screen or a wall *Laser images were **projected onto** a screen.* **3** [QUALITY] [T] If you project a particular quality, that quality is what most people notice about you. *She **projected an image** of strong leadership.* **4 project from/into/out, etc** *formal* to stick out

projection /prəʊˈdʒekʃᵊn/ *noun* **1** [CALCULATION] [C] a calculation or guess about the future based on information that you have *government projections of population growth* **2** [IMAGE] [U] when a film or an image is projected onto a screen or wall

projector /prəʊˈdʒektəʳ/ *noun* [C] a machine that projects films, pictures or words onto a screen or a wall

proletariat /ˌprəʊlɪˈteəriət/ *noun* [**no plural**] SOCIETY the social class of people who have little money and who usually do physical work

proliferate /prəʊˈlɪfᵊreɪt/ *verb* [I] *formal* to increase in number very quickly

proliferation /prəʊˌlɪfᵊrˈeɪʃᵊn/ *noun* [U] when something increases in number very quickly *the proliferation of new TV channels*

prolific /prəʊˈlɪfɪk/ *adjective* producing a lot of something *a **prolific writer**/composer*

prologue /ˈprəʊlɒɡ/ *noun* [C] LITERATURE an introduction to a book, film, or play

prolong /prəʊˈlɒŋ/ *verb* [T] to make something last longer *Eating a good diet can prolong your life.*

prolonged /prəʊˈlɒŋd/ *adjective* continuing for a long time *a prolonged illness*

prom /prɒm/ *noun* [C] in the US, a formal dance party for older students held at the end of the school year *a school prom*

promenade /ˌprɒməˈnɑːd/ *noun* [C] a wide path by the sea

prominence /ˈprɒmɪnəns/ *noun* [U] when someone or something is important or famous *He first **came to prominence** as a singer in the 1980s.*

P

prominent /ˈprɒmɪnənt/ *adjective* **1** IMPORTANT important or famous *a **prominent figure*** **2** NOTICEABLE very easy to see or notice *a **prominent feature*** •**prominently** *adverb*

promiscuous /prəˈmɪskjuəs/ *adjective* Someone who is promiscuous has sex with a lot of people. •**promiscuity** /ˌprɒmɪˈskjuːəti/ *noun* [**U**] when someone is promiscuous

promise¹ /ˈprɒmɪs/ *verb* **1** SAY [**I, T**] to say that you will certainly do something or that something will certainly happen [+ **to do sth**] *She promised to write to me every week.* [+ (**that**)] *Paul promised me that he'd cook dinner tonight.* **2** GIVE [+ **two objects**] to say that you will certainly give something to someone *They promised us a reward.* **3 promise to be sth** If something promises to be good, exciting, etc, people expect that it will be good, exciting, etc.

COMMON LEARNER ERROR

promise

When you use the expression **promise someone something**, no preposition is needed after the verb.

He promised his mum that he would clean his room.

~~*He promised to his mum that he would clean his room.*~~

WORD PARTNERS FOR ***promise***

break/keep/make/renege on a promise • a **broken/rash/solemn/vague** promise

promise² /ˈprɒmɪs/ *noun* **1** [**C**] when you say that you will certainly do something *I'm not sure I can do it so I won't **make** any **promises**.* **2 keep/break a promise** to do/not do what you said that you would do **3 show promise** If someone or something shows promise, they are likely to be successful. *As a child, he showed great promise as an athlete.*

promising /ˈprɒmɪsɪŋ/ *adjective* likely to be very good or successful in the future *a promising student* ○ *a **promising start** to the game*

promo /ˈprəʊməʊ/ *noun* [**C**] *informal* an advertisement, especially a short film

promote /prəˈməʊt/ *verb* [**T**] **1** ENCOURAGE to encourage something to happen or develop *to **promote** good **health/peace*** **2** ADVERTISE to advertise something *The band is promoting their new album.* **3** JOB to give someone a more important job in the same organization [**often passive**] *She's just been **promoted to** manager.*

promoter /prəˈməʊtər/ *noun* [**C**] **1** ORGANIZE someone who organizes a large event *a concert promoter* **2** ENCOURAGE someone who tries to encourage something to happen or develop *a promoter of sexual equality*

WORD PARTNERS FOR ***promotion***

gain/get/be given a promotion • promotion **to** sth

promotion /prəˈməʊʃən/ *noun* **1** ADVERTISEMENT [**C, U**] activities to advertise something *a **sales promotion*** ○ *They're giving away free T-shirts as a special promotion.* **2** JOB [**C, U**] when someone is given a more important job in the same organization *She was **given a promotion** in her first month with the company.* **3** ENCOURAGE [**U, no plural**] when you encourage something to happen or develop *the promotion of a healthy lifestyle*

promotional /prəˈməʊʃənəl/ *adjective* Promotional items or activities are used to advertise something. *a **promotional campaign***

prompt¹ /prɒmpt/ *verb* [**T**] **1** CAUSE to cause something *His remarks prompted a lot of discussion.* **2 prompt sb to do sth** to cause someone to do sth *What prompted him to leave?* **3** HELP REMEMBER to help someone, often an actor, remember what they were going to say or do

prompt² /prɒmpt/ *adjective* done or acting quickly and without waiting, or arriving at the correct time *a **prompt reply*** ○ ***prompt payment*** •**promptly** *adverb*

prone /prəʊn/ *adjective* **1 be prone to sth/doing sth** to often do something or suffer from something, especially something bad *I'm prone to headaches.* **2 accident/injury, etc prone** often having accidents/injuries, etc ➲See also: **accident-prone**

pronoun /ˈprəʊnaʊn/ *noun* [**C**] **LANGUAGE** a word that is used instead of a noun which has usually already been talked about. For example the words 'she', 'it', and 'mine' are pronouns. ➲See also: **personal pronoun, relative pronoun**

pronounce /prəˈnaʊns/ *verb* [**T**] **1 LANGUAGE** to make the sound of a letter or word *How do you pronounce his name?* **2 pronounce sb/sth dead/a success, etc** *formal* to state that something is true in an official or formal way *Doctors pronounced him dead at 12.23 a.m.*

pronounced /prəˈnaʊnst/ *adjective* very easy to notice *She spoke with a pronounced American accent.*

pronouncement /prəʊˈnaʊnsmənt/ *noun* [**C**] *formal* an official announcement *to **make** a **pronouncement***

pronunciation /prəˌnʌnsiˈeɪʃən/ *noun* [**C, U**] **LANGUAGE** how words are pronounced *There are two different pronunciations of this word.*

WORD PARTNERS FOR ***proof***

have/provide proof • **conclusive/positive/scientific** proof • proof **of** sth

proof /pruːf/ *noun* [**U**] a fact or a piece of information that shows something exists or is true *She showed us her passport as **proof of** her identity.* [+ (**that**)] *My landlord has asked for proof that I'm employed.*

-proof /pruːf/ *suffix* used at the end of words to mean 'protecting against' or 'not damaged by' *a bulletproof vest* ○ *a waterproof jacket*

prop¹ /prɒp/ *verb* **propping**, *past* **propped prop sth against/on, etc** to put something somewhere so that it is supported on or against something *He propped the ladder against the wall.*

prop sth up *phrasal verb* **1** LIFT to lift and give support to something by putting something under it *We had to prop up the bed with some bricks.* **2** HELP to help something to continue *For years the industry was propped up by the government.*

prop² /prɒp/ *noun* [**C**] an object used in a film or play *a **stage prop***

propaganda /ˌprɒpəˈgændə/ *noun* [U] information or ideas, which are often false, that an organization prints or broadcasts to make people agree with what it is saying ***political propaganda*** •**propagandist** *noun* [C] someone who creates, prints, or broadcasts propaganda

propagate /ˈprɒpəgeɪt/ *verb formal* **1** **BIOLOGY** [I, T] If you propagate plants, you help them to produce new plants, and if plants propagate, they produce new plants. **2** [T] to tell your ideas or opinions to a lot of people in order to make them agree with what you are saying *to **propagate lies/rumours*** •**propagation** /ˌprɒpəˈgeɪʃən/ *noun* [U] *formal*

propane /ˈprəʊpeɪn/ *noun* [U] **CHEMISTRY** a colourless gas used as fuel, especially in cooking and heating (formula C_3H_8)

propel /prəˈpel/ *verb* [T] **propelling**, *past* **propelled** **1 propel sb into/to sth** to cause someone to do an activity or be in a situation *The film propelled him to international stardom.* **2** to push or move something somewhere, often with a lot of force *a rocket propelled through space*

propeller /prəˈpeləʳ/ *noun* [C] a piece of equipment made of two or more flat metal pieces that turn around and cause a ship or aircraft to move

propensity /prəʊˈpensəti/ *noun* [C] *formal* If someone has a propensity for something or to do something, they often do it. *to have a **propensity for** violence ○ a propensity to talk too much*

O-★**proper** /ˈprɒpəʳ/ *adjective* **1** CORRECT [**always before noun**] correct or suitable *the **proper way** to do something ○ Please put those books back in the **proper place**.* **2** REAL [**always before noun**] *mainly UK* real and satisfactory *his first **proper job*** **3** ACCEPTABLE socially acceptable *It's not proper to interrupt someone when they're speaking.* **4** MAIN [**always after noun**] referring to the main or most important part of something *I live outside Cambridge - I don't live in the city proper.*

ˌproper ˈfraction *noun* [C] **MATHEMATICS** a fraction in which the number under the line is larger than the number above it *3/4 and 5/8 are proper fractions.* ➲Compare **improper fraction**

O-★**properly** /ˈprɒpəli/ *adverb* correctly, or in a satisfactory way *She doesn't eat properly.*

ˌproper ˈnoun *noun* [C] **LANGUAGE** a word or group of words that is the name of a person or place and always begins with a capital letter. For example 'Tony' and 'London' are proper nouns.

WORD PARTNERS FOR ***property***

private property • property **prices** • a property **developer**

O-★**property** /ˈprɒpəti/ *noun* **1** BUILDING [C, U] a building or area of land *There are several properties for sale in this area. ○ **Private property** - no parking. ○ a **property developer*** **2** OBJECT [U] objects that belong to someone *The police recovered a large amount of **stolen property**.* **3** QUALITY [C] a quality of something *the **medicinal properties** of wild plants* ➲See also: **lost property**

the ˈproperty ˌladder *noun* **ECONOMICS** a process in which you buy a small house and then sell it to buy a bigger house when you have more money *When house prices are high, it is hard for buyers to **move up the property ladder**.*

prophecy /ˈprɒfəsi/ *noun* [C, U] when someone says that something will happen in the future •**prophesy** /ˈprɒfəsaɪ/ *verb* [I, T] to say that you believe something will happen in the future

prophet /ˈprɒfɪt/ *noun* [C] **RELIGION** someone sent by God to tell people what to do, or to say what will happen in the future

prophetic /prəʊˈfetɪk/ *adjective* saying what will happen in the future *a **prophetic dream/vision** ○ Her warnings **proved prophetic**.*

proponent /prəʊˈpəʊnənt/ *noun* [C] *formal* someone who supports a particular idea or plan of action *a proponent of nuclear energy*

proportion /prəˈpɔːʃən/ *noun* **1** [C] a part of a total number or amount *Children make up a large **proportion of** the world's population. ○ The class consists of both men and women **in** roughly **equal proportions**.* **2 out of proportion** If something is out of proportion, it is much bigger or smaller than it should be, when compared to other things. *The punishment is completely out of proportion to the crime.* **3 in proportion** If something is in proportion, it is the right size or shape when compared to other things. **4 in proportion to** If something changes in proportion to another thing, it changes to the same degree as that thing. *Your tax payment increases in proportion to your salary.* **5 blow/get sth out of proportion** to behave as if something that has happened is much worse than it really is

proportional /prəˈpɔːʃənəl/ *adjective* **MATHEMATICS** If two amounts are proportional, they change at the same rate so that the relationship between them does not change. *Weight is **proportional to** size.*

proˌportional ˌrepresenˈtation *noun* [U] **POLITICS** a system of voting in which the number of a political party's elected representatives is related to the number of votes the party gets

proportionate /prəˈpɔːʃənət/ *adjective* **MATHEMATICS** If two amounts are proportionate, they change at the same rate so that the relationship between them does not change. *His success was **proportionate to** his efforts.* ➲Opposite **disproportionate** •**proportionately** *adverb*

proportions /prəˈpɔːʃənz/ *noun* [**plural**] the size, shape, or level of something *Crime has increased to **alarming proportions**.*

proposal /prəˈpəʊzəl/ *noun* [C] **1** PLAN a suggestion for a plan [+ **to do sth**] *a proposal to raise taxes ○ The **proposal for** a new sports hall has been rejected.* **2** MARRY when someone asks someone to marry them

propose /prəˈpəʊz/ *verb* **1** SUGGEST [T] to suggest a plan or action [+ **(that)**] *I propose that we delay our decision until we have more information. ○ **proposed changes*** **2 propose to do sth** to intend to do something *They propose to*

P

cycle across Europe. **3** MARRY [I] to ask someone to marry you *He* ***proposed to*** *me on my birthday.*

proposition /ˌprɒpəˈzɪʃən/ *noun* [C] **1** OFFER an offer or suggestion, usually in business *an* ***attractive/interesting proposition*** **2** IDEA an idea or opinion [+ **that**] *the proposition that all people are created equal* **3** PLAN in the US, a formal plan that people accept or refuse by voting

proprietary /prəˈpraɪətəri/ *adjective* [**always before noun**] *formal* owned or controlled by a company

proprietor /prəˈpraɪətər/ *noun* [C] *formal* the owner of a business such as a hotel, shop, newspaper, etc

propriety /prəˈpraɪəti/ *noun* [U] *formal* socially acceptable behaviour

propulsion /prəˈpʌlʃən/ *noun* [U] **PHYSICS** a force that pushes something forward *jet propulsion*

prosaic /prəʊˈzeɪɪk/ *adjective formal* ordinary and not interesting

prose /prəʊz/ *noun* [U] **LANGUAGE, LITERATURE** ordinary written language that is not poetry *He's a wonderful writer - readers love his clear and lively prose.*

prosecute /ˈprɒsɪkjuːt/ *verb* [I, T] **LAW** to accuse someone of a crime in a law court *No one has been* ***prosecuted for*** *the murders.*

prosecution /ˌprɒsɪˈkjuːʃən/ *noun* **LAW** **1 the prosecution** [**group**] the lawyers who are prosecuting someone in a court of law *The prosecution will begin presenting evidence today.* **2** [C, U] when someone is prosecuted

prosecutor /ˈprɒsɪkjuːtər/ *noun* [C] **LAW** a lawyer who prosecutes people

WORD PARTNERS FOR ***prospect***

face the prospect **of** sth • **with** the prospect **of** sth • **at** the prospect **of** sth

prospect /ˈprɒspekt/ *noun* **1** POSSIBILITY [C, U] the possibility that something good might happen in the future *Is there any* ***prospect of*** *the weather improving?* **2** IDEA [**no plural**] the idea of something that will happen in the future [+ **of + doing sth**] *We* ***face the prospect of*** *having to start all over again.* ○ *I'm very excited* ***at the prospect*** *of seeing her again.* **3 sb's prospects** the possibility of being successful at work *He's hoping the course will improve his* ***career prospects.***

prospective /prəˈspektɪv/ *adjective* **prospective buyers/employers/parents, etc** Prospective buyers, employers, parents, etc are not yet buyers, employers, parents, etc but are expected to be in the future.

prospectus /prəˈspektəs/ *noun* [C] a book or magazine which gives information about a school, college, or business for future students or customers

prosper /ˈprɒspər/ *verb* [I] to be successful, usually by earning a lot of money

prosperity /prɒsˈperəti/ *noun* [U] when someone is successful, usually by earning a lot of money

prosperous /ˈprɒspərəs/ *adjective* successful, usually by earning a lot of money

prostate gland /ˈprɒsteɪtˌglænd/ *noun* [C] **ANATOMY** a small organ in a man's body near to the penis, which produces a liquid that carries the sperm (= small cells, one of which joins a woman's egg to make a baby)

prostitute /ˈprɒstɪtjuːt/ *noun* [C] someone whose job is having sex with people •**prostitution** /ˌprɒstɪˈtjuːʃən/ *noun* [U]

prostrate /ˈprɒstreɪt/ *adjective* lying flat on the ground with your face pointing down

protagonist /prəʊˈtægənɪst/ *noun* [C] *formal* **LITERATURE** the main character in a play, film, or story

protease /ˈprəʊtiːeɪz/ *noun* [U] **BIOLOGY** an enzyme (= substance made by living cells) which causes proteins to break into smaller pieces

O⁻ **protect** /prəˈtekt/ *verb* [I, T] to keep someone or something safe from something dangerous or bad *It's important to* ***protect*** *your skin* ***from*** *the harmful effects of the sun.* ○ *Vitamin C may help* ***protect against*** *cancer.* ➲See Common Learner Error at **prevent** •**protection** /prəˈtekʃən/ *noun* [U] *This coat doesn't provide any* ***protection against*** *the rain.*

protectionism /prəˈtekʃənɪzəm/ *noun* [U] **ECONOMICS, POLITICS** when a government tries to help its country's trade or industry by making things that are from other countries more expensive to buy

protective /prəˈtektɪv/ *adjective* **1** PROTECTING giving protection ***protective clothing*** ○ *a protective mask* **2** CARING wanting to protect someone from criticism, hurt, danger, etc because you like them *She's fiercely* ***protective of*** *her children.*

protector /prəˈtektər/ *noun* [C] someone or something that protects

protein /ˈprəʊtiːn/ *noun* [U] **BIOLOGY, FOOD** food such as meat, cheese, fish, or eggs that is necessary for the body to grow and be strong

WORD PARTNERS FOR ***protest***

hold/stage a protest • do sth **as** a protest • **in** protest **at** sth • a protest **against/over** sth • a protest **by/from** sb

protest¹ /ˈprəʊtest/ *noun* [C, U] when people show that they disagree with something by standing somewhere, shouting, carrying signs, etc *a* ***protest against*** *the war* ○ *a* ***peaceful/violent protest***

protest² /prəʊˈtest/ *verb* **1 protest (about/against/at sth)** to show that you disagree with something by standing somewhere, shouting, carrying signs, etc *Students were protesting about cuts to the education budget.* **2 protest sth** *US* to show that you disagree with something by standing somewhere, shouting, carrying signs, etc *Thousands gathered to protest the plan.* **3** [I, T] to say something forcefully or complain about something [+ **that**] *The girl was crying, protesting that she didn't want to leave her mother.*

Protestant /ˈprɒtɪstənt/ *adjective* **RELIGION** belonging or relating to the part of the Christian religion that separated from the Roman

P

Catholic Church in the 1500s •**Protestant** *noun* [C] •**Protestantism** *noun* [U] the beliefs of the Protestant Churches

protestation /ˌprɒtesˈteɪʃᵊn/ *noun* [C] *formal* when someone says something forcefully or complains about something *He was arrested despite his protestations of innocence.*

protester (*also* **protestor**) /prəˈtestəʳ/ *noun* [C] someone who shows that they disagree with something by standing somewhere, shouting, carrying signs, etc

protégé /ˈprɒtəʒeɪ/ *noun* [C] a young person who is helped and taught by an older and usually famous person

protium /ˈprəʊtiəm/ *noun* [U] **CHEMISTRY** the most common isotope (= form of an atom with the same chemical structure but different weight) of hydrogen

protocol /ˈprəʊtəkɒl/ *noun* [C, U] the rules about what you must do and how you must behave in official or very formal situations *royal protocol*

proton /ˈprəʊtɒn/ *noun* [C] **PHYSICS, CHEMISTRY** a part of an atom with a positive electrical charge

protoplasm /ˈprəʊtəplæzᵊm/ *noun* [U] **BIOLOGY** the clear liquid which is inside all living cells

prototype /ˈprəʊtəʊtaɪp/ *noun* [C] the first model or example of something new that can be developed or copied in the future *a **prototype for** a new car*

protozoan /ˌprəʊtəʊˈzəʊən/ *noun* [C] **BIOLOGY** *plural* **protozoans** or **protozoa** a very small animal with only one cell

protracted /prəˈtræktɪd/ *adjective* If an unpleasant situation is protracted, it lasts a long time. *a **protracted dispute/struggle***

protractor /prəˈtræktəʳ/ *noun* [C] **MATHEMATICS** a device used for measuring and drawing angles, usually a half circle made from clear plastic with degrees (°) on it

protrude /prəʊˈtruːd/ *verb* [I] If something such as a part of the body protrudes, it comes out from the surface more than usual. *protruding ears/teeth*

WORD PARTNERS FOR ***proud***

fiercely/immensely/rightly proud • proud of sth/sb

O‑ **proud** /praʊd/ *adjective* **1** [PLEASED] feeling very pleased about something you have done, something you own, or someone you know *She was so **proud of** her son.* [+ **to do sth**] *I'm very proud to be involved in this project.* **2 be too proud to do sth** to not be able to do something, especially ask for help, because you are too embarrassed *He's too proud to ask you for any money.* **3** [IMPORTANT] feeling that you are more important than you really are

proudly /ˈpraʊdli/ *adverb* in a way that shows you are pleased about something you have done, something you own, or someone you know *He proudly showed us a photo of his grandchildren.*

O‑ **prove** /pruːv/ *verb* [T] *past tense* **proved**, *past participle mainly US* **proven 1** to show that something is true *They knew who had stolen the money, but they couldn't prove it.* [+ **(that)**] *Can you prove that you weren't there?* ⊃Opposite **disprove 2 prove sth/to be sth** to show a particular quality after a period of time *The new treatment has proved to be very effective.* **3 prove yourself** to show that you are good at something *I wish he'd stop trying to prove himself all the time.*

proven /ˈpruːvᵊn/ *adjective* If something is proven, it has been shown to be true. ***proven ability/skills***

proverb /ˈprɒvɜːb/ *noun* [C] **LANGUAGE** a famous phrase or sentence which gives you advice *an ancient Chinese proverb* •**proverbial** /prəʊˈvɜːbiəl/ *adjective* relating to a proverb

O‑ **provide** /prəʊˈvaɪd/ *verb* [T] to supply something to someone *This booklet provides useful information about local services.* ○ *It's a new scheme to **provide** schools **with** free computers.* •**provider** *noun* [C] someone who provides something *an Internet service provider*

provide for sb *phrasal verb* to give someone the things they need such as money, food, or clothes *He has a wife and two young children to provide for.*

provided (that) /prəˈvaɪdɪd/ (*also* **providing (that)**) *conjunction* only if *He's welcome to come along, provided that he behaves himself.*

province /ˈprɒvɪns/ *noun* **1** [C] **GEOGRAPHY** one of the large areas which some countries are divided into because of the type of government they have *the Canadian province of Alberta* **2 the provinces** the areas of a country that are not the capital city and so are not considered exciting or fashionable

provincial /prəˈvɪnʃᵊl/ *adjective* **1 GEOGRAPHY** relating to a province **2** [NOT CAPITAL] relating to or typical of the provinces *a provincial town* ○ *provincial attitudes*

provision /prəˈvɪʒᵊn/ *noun* **1** [PROVIDING] [**U, no plural**] when something is provided for someone *We need to increase **the provision of** health care for the elderly.* **2 make provision for sth** to make arrangements to deal with something *He hasn't made any provision for his retirement yet.* **3** [RULE] [C] **LAW** a rule that is part of a law or an agreement

provisional /prəˈvɪʒᵊnᵊl/ *adjective* If a situation or arrangement is provisional, it is not certain and might change in the future. *These dates are only provisional at the moment.* •**provisionally** *adverb*

provisions /prəˈvɪʒᵊnz/ *noun* [**plural**] **FOOD** supplies of food and other necessary items

proviso /prəˈvaɪzəʊ/ *noun* [C] *formal* something that must happen as part of an agreement *He was released from prison **with the proviso that** he doesn't leave the country.*

provocation /ˌprɒvəˈkeɪʃᵊn/ *noun* [C, U] when someone makes you angry *He'll start a fight **at the slightest provocation**.*

provocative /prəˈvɒkətɪv/ *adjective* **1** [CAUSING REACTION] causing an angry reaction, usually intentionally *a provocative question/remark* **2** [SEXUAL] Provocative clothes, images, etc are sexually exciting. •**provocatively** *adverb She dresses very provocatively.*

P

provoke /prəˈvəʊk/ *verb* [T] **1** CAUSE REACTION to cause a strong and usually angry reaction *to **provoke** an **argument*** ○ *Her statement has **provoked** a public **outcry**.* **2** MAKE ANGRY to intentionally make someone angry so that they react in an angry or violent way *He claimed he was provoked by the victim.*

prowess /ˈpraʊɪs/ *noun* [U] *formal* when you are good at doing something ***athletic/sporting prowess***

prowl[1] /praʊl/ *verb* [I, T] to walk around somewhere slowly as if hunting someone or something *to prowl the streets*

prowl[2] /praʊl/ *noun* **be on the prowl** to be hunting for someone or something

proximity /prɒkˈsɪməti/ *noun* [U] *formal* when something is near to something else *What's good about this hotel is its **proximity to** the airport.*

proxy /ˈprɒksi/ *noun* **by proxy** using another person to do something instead of doing something yourself *to vote by proxy*

Prozac /ˈprəʊzæk/ *noun* [U] *trademark* **HEALTH** a drug that is used to make people feel happier and less worried *She's **on Prozac** because of her depression.*

prude /pruːd/ *noun* [C] someone who does not like to hear or see things relating to sex *Don't be such a prude.* •**prudish** *adjective a prudish woman*

prudent /ˈpruːdənt/ *adjective formal* wise and careful [**+ to do sth**] *I think it would be prudent to leave now before it starts raining.* •**prudence** /ˈpruːdəns/ *noun* [U] *formal* •**prudently** *adverb*

prune[1] /pruːn/ *verb* [T] **FARMING** If you prune a tree or bush, you cut off some of the branches or flowers to help it grow better.

prune[2] /pruːn/ *noun* [C] **FOOD** a dried plum (= type of fruit)

pry /praɪ/ *verb* **1** [I] to try to discover private things about people *to **pry into** someone's personal life.* ○ *She wanted a private holiday away from **prying eyes**.* **2 pry sth apart/loose/open, etc** to open something with difficulty *She managed to pry open a window and escape.*

PS /ˌpiːˈes/ used when you want to add extra information at the end of a letter or email *PS Give my love to Emma.*

psalm /sɑːm/ *noun* [C] **LITERATURE, MUSIC, RELIGION** a song or poem from the Bible (= holy book)

pseudo- /sjuːdəʊ-/ *prefix* false *a pseudonym* (= a false name, especially by a writer) ○ *pseudo-academic*

pseudonym /ˈsjuːdənɪm/ *noun* [C] a name used by a writer instead of their own name *He writes **under a pseudonym**.*

PSNCR /ˌpiːesensiːˈɑːr/ *noun* [**C usually singular**] **ECONOMICS, FINANCE** public sector net cash requirement: the difference between how much money the UK government spends and how much it receives

psych /saɪk/ *verb*
psych yourself up *phrasal verb informal* to try to make yourself feel confident and ready to do something difficult

psyche /ˈsaɪki/ *noun* [C] the human mind and feelings *the male psyche*

psychedelic /ˌsaɪkɪˈdelɪk/ *adjective* **1** **HEALTH** Psychedelic drugs make you see things that are not really there. **2** Psychedelic colours or patterns are very strong, bright, and strange.

psychiatrist /saɪˈkaɪətrɪst/ *noun* [C] **HEALTH** a doctor who is trained in psychiatry

psychiatry /saɪˈkaɪətri/ *noun* [U] **HEALTH** the study and treatment of mental illness •**psychiatric** /ˌsaɪkiˈætrɪk/ *adjective* relating to psychiatry *a psychiatric disorder* ○ *a psychiatric nurse*

psychic /ˈsaɪkɪk/ *adjective* having a special mental ability, for example so that you are able to know what will happen in the future or know what people are thinking ***psychic powers***

psycho /ˈsaɪkəʊ/ *noun* [C] *informal* someone who is crazy and frightening

psychoanalysis /ˌsaɪkəʊəˈnæləsɪs/ *noun* [U] **HEALTH** the treatment of mental problems by studying and talking about people's dreams, fears, and experiences •**psychoanalytic** /ˌsaɪkəʊˌænəlˈɪtɪk/ *adjective* relating to psychoanalysis

psychoanalyst /ˌsaɪkəʊˈænəlɪst/ *noun* [C] **HEALTH** someone who treats people using psychoanalysis

psychological /ˌsaɪkəlˈɒdʒɪkəl/ *adjective* **HEALTH** relating to the human mind and feelings *psychological problems* •**psychologically** *adverb*

psychologist /saɪˈkɒlədʒɪst/ *noun* [C] **HEALTH** someone who has studied the human mind and feelings

psychology /saɪˈkɒlədʒi/ *noun* [U] **1 HEALTH** the study of the human mind and feelings ***child psychology*** ○ *He's studying psychology and philosophy.* **2** BEHAVIOUR the way someone thinks and behaves *the psychology of serial killers*

psychopath /ˈsaɪkəʊpæθ/ *noun* [C] **HEALTH** someone who is very mentally ill and usually dangerous •**psychopathic** /ˌsaɪkəʊˈpæθɪk/ *adjective a psychopathic killer*

psychosis /saɪˈkəʊsɪs/ *noun* [C] *plural* **psychoses** /saɪˈkəʊsiːz/ **HEALTH** a mental illness that makes you believe things that are not real

psychotherapy /ˌsaɪkəʊˈθerəpi/ *noun* [U] **HEALTH** the treatment of mental problems by talking about your feelings instead of taking medicine •**psychotherapist** *noun* [C] someone who gives people psychotherapy

psychotic /saɪˈkɒtɪk/ *adjective* **HEALTH** suffering from a mental illness that makes you believe things that are not true

pâté /ˈpæteɪ/ (US) /pætˈeɪ/ *noun* [U] **FOOD** a soft food, usually made of meat or fish, that you spread on bread, etc *liver pâté*

pt *noun* [C] **1 SPORT** *written abbreviation for* point (=a unit used for showing who is winning in a game or competition) *Hill 81 pts, Villeneuve 68 pts* **2 MEASURES** *written abbreviation for* pint (= a unit for measuring liquid)

PTO /ˌpiːtiːˈəʊ/ *UK abbreviation for* please turn over: used at the bottom of a page of writing to show that there is more information on the other side

pub /pʌb/ *noun* [C] a place where you can get drinks such as beer and usually food *We're all going to the pub after work.*

puberty /ˈpjuːbəti/ *noun* [U] **HEALTH** the time when children's bodies change and become like adults' bodies *to reach puberty*

pubic hair /ˌpjuːbɪkˈheəʳ/ *noun* [U] the hair that grows around the sexual organs

O-ᵘ**public¹** /ˈpʌblɪk/ *adjective* **1 public awareness/health/support, etc SOCIETY** the awareness/health/support, etc of all ordinary people ***Public opinion** has turned against him.* ○ *Is it really **in the public interest** (= useful for people) to publish this information?* **2 public parks/toilets/transport, etc SOCIETY** parks/toilets/transport, etc that are for everyone to use and are not private *Smoking should be banned in public places.* **3 a public announcement/appearance/statement, etc** an announcement/appearance/statement, etc that can be seen or heard or known by everyone *The Prime Minister is due to make a public statement later today.* **4 make sth public** to allow everyone to know about something *The government does not plan to make its findings public.* **5 ECONOMICS, POLITICSpublic funds/services/spending, etc** funds/services/spending, etc controlled or supplied by the government and not by a private company

O-ᵘ**public²** /ˈpʌblɪk/ *noun* [group] **1 the (general) public SOCIETY** all ordinary people *a member of the public* ○ *The public has a right to know about this.* ○ *The house is only open to the general public on Sundays.* **2 in public** where everyone can see you *He shouldn't behave like that in public.*

ˌpublic adˈdress system (*also UK* **tannoy**) *noun* [C] a system of equipment used in public places that someone speaks into in order to make their voice loud enough to hear

publication /ˌpʌblɪˈkeɪʃᵊn/ *noun* **1** PRINTING [U] when a book, newspaper, etc is printed and sold **2** BOOK [C] a book, newspaper, or magazine *a monthly/weekly publication*

publicist /ˈpʌblɪsɪst/ *noun* [C] someone whose job is to make people know about someone or something by advertising or giving information in the newspaper, on television, etc

WORD PARTNERS FOR ***publicity***

attract/get/receive/seek publicity • **adverse/bad/good/negative** publicity • publicity **about/for** sth • publicity **surrounding** sth • a publicity **campaign/stunt**

publicity /pʌbˈlɪsəti/ *noun* [U] advertising or information about someone or something in the newspaper, on television, etc *Their publicity campaign was very successful.* ○ *to get **bad/good publicity***

publicize (*also UK* **-ise**) /ˈpʌblɪsaɪz/ *verb* [T] to make people know about something by advertising or giving information in newspapers, on television, etc *a highly/widely publicized event*

ˌpublic limited ˈcompany *noun* [C] **ECONOMICS** a company whose shares (= parts that can be bought and sold) can be sold to the public

publicly /ˈpʌblɪkli/ *adverb* If you do something publicly, everyone can see it, hear it, or know about it.

ˌpublic reˈlations *noun* [U] *formal* PR (=writing and activities that are intended to make a person, company, or product more popular)

ˌpublic ˈschool (*US* **ˈpublic ˌschool**) *noun* [C] **EDUCATION 1** in the UK, a school that you pay to go to **2** (*UK* **state school**) in the US, a school that is free to go to because the government provides the money for it

the ˌpublic ˈsector *noun* [usually singular] **FINANCE** businesses and industries that are owned or controlled by the government *public sector workers*

ˌpublic ˈtransport *noun* [U] a system of vehicles such as buses and trains which operate at regular times and that the public use

ˌpublic uˈtility *noun* [C] an organization that supplies the public with water, gas, or electricity

O-ᵘ**publish** /ˈpʌblɪʃ/ *verb* [T] **1** PRINT to prepare and print a book, newspaper, magazine, article, etc so that people can buy it [**often passive**] *This book is published by Cambridge University Press.* **2** WRITE to write something that is then printed in a book, newspaper, magazine, etc *He's published several short stories in national magazines.* **3** MAKE PUBLIC to make information available to the public

publisher /ˈpʌblɪʃəʳ/ *noun* [C] a company or person who prepares and prints books, newspapers, magazines, etc

publishing /ˈpʌblɪʃɪŋ/ *noun* [U] the business of preparing and printing books, newspapers, magazines, etc *a career in publishing*

puck /pʌk/ *noun* [C] **SPORT** in ice hockey (= a sport), a small, hard disc that players hit with a stick ⊃See colour picture **Sports 1** on page Centre 14

pudding /ˈpʊdɪŋ/ *noun* **FOOD 1** [C, U] in the UK, a sweet dish that is usually eaten as the last part of a meal *We've got apple pie for pudding.* **2** [U] in the US, a soft, sweet food made from milk, sugar, eggs, and sometimes flour *chocolate/vanilla pudding*

puddle /ˈpʌdl/ *noun* [C] a pool of liquid on the ground, usually from rain

puerile /ˈpjʊəraɪl/ (US) /ˈpjuːərɪl/ *adjective formal* behaving in a silly way like a child

puff¹ /pʌf/ *verb* **1** BREATHE [I] to breathe fast and with difficulty, usually because you have been doing exercise **2** SMOKE [I, T] to smoke something *to puff on a cigarette*

puff sth out *phrasal verb* to make your chest or your face become bigger by filling them with air

puff up *phrasal verb* If part of your body puffs up, it becomes larger because it is infected or injured.

puff² /pʌf/ *noun* [C] **1** AMOUNT a small amount of smoke, gas, powder, etc *a puff of smoke/air* **2** BREATH when someone breathes in smoke from a cigarette *to take a puff on a cigarette*

puffin /ˈpʌfɪn/ *noun* [C] a black and white sea bird with a large head and brightly coloured beak

P

puffy /ˈpʌfi/ *adjective* If the skin around your eyes is puffy, it is slightly swollen. *His eyes were still **puffy** with sleep.*

puke /pjuːk/ (*also* **puke up**) *verb* [I, T] *informal* to vomit

O→**pull**[1] /pʊl/ *verb* **1** [I, T] to take hold of something and move it somewhere *If you keep pulling his tail, he'll bite you.* ○ *No wonder it's not working, someone's **pulled** the plug **out**.* ○ *He **pulled off** his boots.* ○ *She bent down and **pulled up** her socks.* **2 pull a muscle** **HEALTH** to injure a muscle by stretching it too much **3 pull a gun/knife, etc on sb** to suddenly take out a weapon *He pulled a gun on us and demanded money.* ➲See also: pull/tear your **hair** out, pull the **plug**[1], not pull any punches (**punch**[2]), pull out all the stops (**stop**[2]), pull strings (**string**[1]), pull your **weight**

pull sth apart *phrasal verb* **1** DESTROY to destroy something by tearing it into pieces **2** CRITICIZE to say that something, usually a piece of work, is very bad

pull sb/sth apart *phrasal verb* to separate two things or people

pull at sth *phrasal verb* to pull something several times, usually with quick, light movements *Stop pulling at my sleeve.*

pull away *phrasal verb* **1** START MOVING If a vehicle pulls away, it starts moving. *I just managed to get on the bus before it pulled away.* **2** MOVE BACKWARDS If you pull away from someone who is holding you, you suddenly move your body backwards, away from them.

pull sth down *phrasal verb* to destroy a building because it is not wanted any more. *They've started pulling down the old cinema.*

pull in/into sth *phrasal verb* If a vehicle pulls in or pulls into somewhere, it moves in that direction and stops there. *They pulled in at the side of the road.*

pull sth off *phrasal verb* to succeed in doing or achieving something difficult *He is about to pull off his biggest deal yet.*

pull off *phrasal verb UK* If a vehicle pulls off, it starts moving. *The car pulled off and sped up the road.*

pull on sth *phrasal verb* to put on clothes quickly *I pulled on my jeans and ran downstairs.*

pull out *phrasal verb* If a vehicle pulls out, it starts moving onto a road or onto a different part of the road. *That car pulled out right in front of me.*

pull over *phrasal verb* If a vehicle pulls over, it moves to the side of the road and stops.

pull through *phrasal verb* to continue to live after you have been badly injured or very ill

pull yourself together *phrasal verb informal* to become calm and behave normally again after being angry or upset

pull up *phrasal verb* **1** If a vehicle pulls up, it stops, often for a short time. *A car pulled up outside the bank and two men got out.* **2 pull up a chair** to move a chair nearer to something or someone *Why don't you pull up a chair and join us?*

pull[2] /pʊl/ *noun* [no plural] **PHYSICS** a strong force that causes something to move somewhere or be attracted to something

P

pull-down /ˈpʊldaʊn/ *adjective* [always before noun] **COMPUTING** A pull-down menu is a list of choices on a computer screen which is hidden until you choose to look at it.

pulley /ˈpʊli/ *noun* [C] a wheel with a rope going round it which is used to lift things

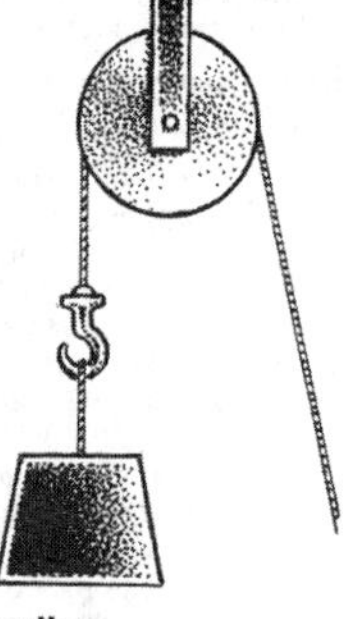
pulley

pullover /ˈpʊləʊvəʳ/ *noun* [C] a warm piece of clothing which covers the top of your body and is pulled on over your head *a black woolly pullover*

pulmonary /ˈpʊlmənᵊri/ *adjective* **ANATOMY, BIOLOGY** relating to the lungs (= organs used for breathing) ➲See picture at **alveoli** ➲See picture at **heart**

pulp /pʌlp/ *noun* [U] **1** a soft, wet substance made from wood, which is used to make paper **2 BIOLOGY, FOOD** the soft part inside a fruit or vegetable

ˌ**pulp** ˈ**cavity** *noun* [C] **ANATOMY** the soft part inside a tooth that contains nerves and blood vessels ➲See picture at **tooth**

pulpit /ˈpʊlpɪt/ *noun* [C] **RELIGION** the raised structure in a church where the priest stands when he speaks to everyone

pulsate /pʌlˈseɪt/ (US) /ˈpʌlseɪt/ *verb* [I] to beat or move with a strong, regular rhythm *The whole room was pulsating with music.*

pulse /pʌls/ *noun* [C] **BIOLOGY, HEALTH** the regular movement of blood through your body when your heart is beating *She put her fingers on my wrist to **take my pulse*** (= count the number of beats per minute). ○ *My **pulse rate** is 70.*

pulses /ˈpʌlsɪz/ *noun* [plural] **FOOD** *UK* seeds such as beans or peas which are cooked and eaten as food

pump[1] /pʌmp/ *noun* [C] a piece of equipment which forces liquid or gas to move somewhere *a **gas/petrol pump*** ○ *a **water pump***

pump[2] /pʌmp/ *verb* [T] to force liquid or gas to move somewhere *Your heart pumps blood around your body.* ○ *Firemen used powerful hoses to **pump** water **into** the building.*

pump sth into sth *phrasal verb* to give a lot of money to a plan or organization *They've pumped millions of pounds into the economy.*

pump sth out *phrasal verb informal* to continuously produce a lot of something *a radio pumping out music*

pump sth up *phrasal verb* to fill something with air using a pump *You should pump your tyres up.*

pumpkin /ˈpʌmpkɪn/ *noun* [C, U] **FOOD** a large, round vegetable with thick, orange skin

pun /pʌn/ *noun* [C] **LANGUAGE** a joke that you make by using a word that has two meanings

punch[1] /pʌnʃ/ *verb* [T] **1** to hit someone or something with your fist (= closed hand) *He punched me twice in the stomach.* **2 punch a hole**

in sth to make a hole in something with a special piece of equipment

WORD PARTNERS FOR ***punch***

aim a punch at sb • **deliver/land/swing/throw** a punch

punch² /pʌnʃ/ *noun* **1** HIT [C] when you hit someone or something with your fist (= closed hand) *a punch on the nose* **2 FOOD** [U] a sweet, mixed drink made from fruit juice, spices, and usually alcohol **3** HOLE [C] a piece of equipment that makes a hole in something **4 not pull any punches** to speak in an honest way without trying to be kind

punchline /ˈpʌntʃlaɪn/ *noun* [C] the last part of a joke that makes it funny

punch-up /ˈpʌntʃʌp/ *noun* [C] *UK informal* a fight in which people hit each other with their fists (= closed hands)

punctual /ˈpʌŋktʃuəl/ *adjective* arriving at the right time and not too late •**punctuality** /ˌpʌnktʃuˈæləti/ *noun* [U] when you are punctual •**punctually** *adverb*

punctuate /ˈpʌŋktʃueɪt/ *verb* [T] **LANGUAGE** to add punctuation marks to written words so that people can see when a sentence begins and finishes, that something is a question, etc

punctuation /ˌpʌŋktʃuˈeɪʃən/ *noun* [U] **LANGUAGE** the use of punctuation marks in writing so that people can see when a sentence begins and finishes, that something is a question, etc ➲See Extra help page **Punctuation** on page Centre 18.

punctuˈation ˌmark *noun* [C] **LANGUAGE** a symbol such as a full stop (.) or a question mark (?) used in writing to show where a sentence begins and finishes, etc.

puncture¹ /ˈpʌŋktʃər/ *noun* [C] **1** HOLE a small hole made by a sharp object **2** TYRE *UK* a hole in a tyre that makes the air come out *to have a puncture*

puncture² /ˈpʌŋktʃər/ *verb* [T] to make a hole in something *The knife punctured his lung.*

pundit /ˈpʌndɪt/ *noun* [C] someone who is an expert in a subject and often gives their opinions on television, radio, etc *a **political pundit***

pungent /ˈpʌndʒənt/ *adjective* A pungent smell is very strong. *the **pungent smell** of vinegar*

O‑**punish** /ˈpʌnɪʃ/ *verb* [T] to make someone suffer because they have done something bad [**often passive**] *They must be severely **punished for** these crimes.*

punishable /ˈpʌnɪʃəbl/ *adjective* **LAW** A crime that is punishable is one that you can be punished for. *Drug dealing is **punishable by death** in some countries.*

punishing /ˈpʌnɪʃɪŋ/ *adjective* very difficult and making you tired *a **punishing schedule***

WORD PARTNERS FOR ***punishment***

capital/corporal punishment • an **appropriate/cruel/harsh/severe** punishment • **deserve/escape/impose/inflict/receive** punishment

O‑**punishment** /ˈpʌnɪʃmənt/ *noun* [C, U] when someone is punished *He had to stay in his bedroom as a punishment for fighting.* ➲See also: **capital punishment, corporal punishment,** be a **glutton** for punishment

punitive /ˈpjuːnətɪv/ *adjective formal* given as a punishment or seeming like a punishment *punitive action*

punk /pʌŋk/ *noun* **1 MUSIC** [U] (*also* ˌ**punk** ˈ**rock**) a style of music and fashion in the 1970s which was wild, loud, and violent **2** PERSON [C] someone who wears punk clothes and likes punk music **3** BAD MAN [C] *US informal* a bad young man

punt¹ /pʌnt/ *noun* [C] **1** a long boat with a flat bottom that you push along the river with a long pole **2 SPORT** in some sports, a powerful kick which causes the ball to go very far

punt² /pʌnt/ *verb* **1** [I, T] to go or take someone along a river in a punt **2 SPORT** [T] in some sports, to kick a ball after you have dropped it from your hands and before it touches the ground

punter /ˈpʌntər/ *noun* [C] *UK informal* someone who is buying something or making a bet (= risking money on a competition)

puny /ˈpjuːni/ *adjective* very small and weak

pup /pʌp/ *noun* [C] **BIOLOGY** a young dog or other particular type of baby mammal *a seal pup*

pupa /ˈpjuːpə/ *noun* [C] **BIOLOGY** *plural* **pupas** or **pupae** an insect in the stage of development which happens before it is completely developed, during which it is inside a cocoon (= cover that protects it) and does not move ➲Compare **chrysalis**

pupil /ˈpjuːpəl/ *noun* [C] **1 EDUCATION** a student at school *The school has 1,100 pupils aged 11 to 18.* ➲See colour picture **The Classroom** on page Centre 6 **2 ANATOMY** the black, round part in the centre of your eye

puppet /ˈpʌpɪt/ *noun* [C] **1** TOY a toy in the shape of a person or animal that you can move with strings or by putting your hand inside *a **glove puppet*** **2** PERSON someone who is controlled by someone else *a political puppet*

puppy /ˈpʌpi/ *noun* [C] a young dog

purchase¹ /ˈpɜːtʃəs/ *verb* [T] *formal* to buy something *Tickets must be purchased two weeks in advance.*

purchase² /ˈpɜːtʃəs/ *noun formal* **1** BUYING [C, U] when you buy something *the illegal purchase of guns* **2** THING [C] something that you buy *a major purchase*

ˈ**purchases acˌcount** *noun* [C] **FINANCE** a record that a business keeps of the goods it has bought in order to sell

ˈ**purchases ˌjournal** (*also* **purchases book, purchases day book**) *noun* [C] **FINANCE** a document that a business keeps of the dates on which it bought things, the names of the companies it bought them from and how much they cost

ˈ**purchases ˌledger** (*also* **creditors ledger**) *noun* [C] **FINANCE** a record that a business keeps of how much it owes to each business that has supplied goods or services to it

ˈ**purchases reˌturns** (*also* **returns outward**) *noun* **ECONOMICS** [plural] goods that are

P

returned to the company that supplied them, for example because they are damaged or not needed

O╍**pure** /pjʊəʳ/ *adjective* **1** NOT MIXED A pure substance is not mixed with anything else. *pure gold ○ pure wool* **2** EMPHASIS **[always before noun]** used to emphasize that a feeling, quality, or state is completely and only that thing ***pure coincidence*** *○ Her face had a look of pure delight.* **3** CLEAN clean and healthy ***pure air/water*** **4 pure mathematics/physics, etc** the study of mathematics/physics, etc based only on ideas and not on practical use **5** GOOD completely good and not having any bad qualities or bad morals

puree /ˈpjʊəreɪ/ (US) /pjʊəˈreɪ/ *noun* **[U]** **FOOD** a thick, smooth, liquid food made by crushing and mixing fruit or vegetables *tomato puree*

purely /ˈpjʊəli/ *adverb* only *She married him* ***purely for*** *his money.*

purgatory /ˈpɜːɡətᵊri/ *noun* **[U]** **1 RELIGION** in the Catholic religion, a very unpleasant place where you have to go and suffer before you go to heaven **2** a very unpleasant situation *This diet is purgatory.*

purge /pɜːdʒ/ *verb* **[T]** **1** FEELINGS to get rid of bad feelings that you do not want **[often reflexive]** *She wanted to* ***purge*** *herself* ***of*** *guilt.* **2** PEOPLE to get rid of people from an organization because you do not agree with them •**purge** *noun* **[C]**

purify /ˈpjʊərɪfaɪ/ *verb* **[T]** to remove bad substances from something to make it pure *Plants help to purify the air. ○ purified water* •**purification** /ˌpjʊərɪfɪˈkeɪʃᵊn/ *noun* **[U]**

purist /ˈpjʊərɪst/ *noun* **[C]** someone who believes in and follows very traditional rules or ideas in a subject

P

puritanical /ˌpjʊərɪˈtænɪkᵊl/ *adjective* having severe religious morals and not wanting people to enjoy themselves •**puritan** /ˈpjʊərɪtᵊn/ *noun* **[C]** a puritanical person

purity /ˈpjʊərəti/ *noun* **[U]** the quality of being pure *air purity*

purple /ˈpɜːpl/ *adjective* being a colour that is a mixture of red and blue *purple pansies* •**purple** *noun* **[C, U]** ➲See colour picture **Colours** on page Centre 12

purport /pəˈpɔːt/ *verb*

purport to be/do sth *phrasal verb formal* to pretend to be or do something *a man purporting to be a police officer*

WORD PARTNERS FOR ***purpose***

defeat/have/fulfil/serve a purpose • a **clear/good/primary/practical/useful** purpose • the purpose **of** sth

O╍**purpose** /ˈpɜːpəs/ *noun* **1** REASON **[C]** why you do something or why something exists *The main* ***purpose of*** *the meeting is to discuss the future of the company. ○ The drug may be legalized for medical purposes.* **2** INTENTION **[U]** the feeling of knowing what you want to do *He seems to have lost all* ***sense of purpose.*** **3 on purpose** intentionally *I didn't do it on purpose, it was an accident.* **4 serve a purpose** to have a use *These small village shops serve a very useful purpose.* ➲See also: **cross purposes**, to/for all intents (**intent**[1]) (and purposes)

purpose-built /ˌpɜːpəsˈbɪlt/ *adjective mainly UK* A purpose-built building has been specially designed for the way it will be used.

purposeful /ˈpɜːpəsfᵊl/ *adjective* showing that you know what you want to do *He has a quiet, purposeful air.* •**purposefully** *adverb*

purposely /ˈpɜːpəsli/ *adverb* intentionally *I wasn't purposely trying to hurt you.*

purr /pɜːʳ/ *verb* **[I]** **1** CAT If a cat purrs, it makes a soft sound in its throat to show pleasure. **2** PERSON to talk in a soft, low voice **3** CAR If a car purrs, its engine is very smooth and makes a soft sound.

purse[1] /pɜːs/ *noun* **[C]** **1** MONEY *UK* a small container for money, usually used by a woman *a leather purse* **2** BAG *mainly US* (*mainly UK* **handbag**) a bag, usually carried by a woman *I always carry aspirin in my purse.*

purse[2] /pɜːs/ *verb* **purse your lips** to press your lips tightly together, often to show that you are angry

pursue /pəˈsjuː/ (US) /pərˈsuː/ *verb* **[T]** **pursuing**, *past* **pursued** **1** TRY If you pursue a plan, activity, or situation, you try to do it or achieve it, usually over a long period of time. *She decided to pursue a career in television.* **2** FOLLOW to follow someone or something, usually to try to catch them *The car was pursued by helicopters.* **3 pursue a matter** to try to discover information about something *We will not be pursuing this matter any further.*

pursuit /pəˈsjuːt/ (US) /pərˈsuːt/ *noun* **[U]** **1** TRY when you try to achieve a plan, activity, or situation, usually over a long period of time *the pursuit of pleasure ○ He left his native country* ***in pursuit of*** *freedom.* **2** FOLLOWING when you follow someone or something to try to catch them *The police are* ***in pursuit of*** *a 25-year-old murder suspect.*

pursuits /pəˈsjuːts/ (US) /pərˈsuːts/ *noun* **[plural]** *formal* activities or hobbies *He enjoys climbing and other* ***outdoor pursuits.***

purveyor /pəˈveɪəʳ/ *noun* **[C]** *formal* someone who sells or provides something *a purveyor of antiques*

pus /pʌs/ *noun* **[U]** **HEALTH** a yellow substance that is produced when part of your body is infected

O╍**push**[1] /pʊʃ/ *verb* **1** MOVE SOMETHING **[I, T]** to move someone or something by pressing them with your hands or body *She* ***pushed*** *the books* ***aside*** *and sat down on my desk. ○ We* ***pushed*** *the children* ***down*** *the slide. ○ He* ***pushed*** *me violently* ***out*** *of the door. ○ Someone* ***pushed*** *him* ***into*** *the river.* **2** MOVE YOURSELF **[I, T]** to move somewhere by moving someone or something away from you *He pushed past me. ○ He* ***pushed his way*** *to the front of the crowd.* **3** PRESS **[T]** to press something *If you push this button, your seat goes back.* **4 push (sb) for sth/to do sth** to try hard to achieve something or to make someone else do something *Local residents are pushing for the road to be made safer.* **5** ENCOURAGE **[T]** to try to make someone do something that they do not want to do

[+ into + doing sth] *My mother pushed me into having ballet lessons.* **6 push yourself** to make yourself work very hard to achieve something ➲See also: push the **boat** out

push sb about/around *phrasal verb* to tell someone what to do in a rude way *I'm fed up with being pushed around.*

push ahead/forward *phrasal verb* to continue doing something, especially when this is difficult *They have decided to* ***push ahead with*** *legal action.*

push sth/sb aside *phrasal verb* to decide to forget about or ignore something or someone *We can't just push these problems aside - we have to deal with them.*

push in *phrasal verb UK informal* to rudely join a line of people who are waiting for something by moving in front of some of the people who are already there

push on *phrasal verb* to continue doing something, especially when this is difficult

push sb/sth over *phrasal verb* to push someone or something so that they fall to the ground

push sth through *phrasal verb* to make a plan or suggestion be officially accepted *We're trying to push this deal through as quickly as possible.*

push sth up *phrasal verb* to increase the amount, number, or value of something *If you want to travel on Saturday, it will push the price up a bit.*

push[2] /pʊʃ/ *noun* **1 a push for sth/to do sth** a big effort to achieve something or make someone do something *a push for higher standards in education* **2** MOVEMENT [C] when you move someone or something by pressing them with your hands or body [usually singular] *She* ***gave*** *him a little* ***push*** *towards the door.* **3 give sb the push** *UK informal* to get rid of someone from a job or relationship **4** ENCOURAGEMENT [C] encouragement to make someone do something [usually singular] *I'm sure he'll go, he just needs a little push that's all.* **5 at a push** *UK* If you can do something at a push, you can do it but it will be difficult. **6 if/when push comes to shove** If you say that something can be done if push comes to shove, you mean that it can be done if the situation becomes so bad that you have to do it. *If push comes to shove, we'll just have to sell the car.*

pushchair /ˈpʊʃtʃeəʳ/ *UK* (*US* **stroller**) *noun* [C] a chair on wheels which is used to move small children

pushed /pʊʃt/ *adjective UK informal* **be pushed for sth** to not have much of something *I can't stop, I'm a bit pushed for time.*

pusher /ˈpʊʃəʳ/ *noun* [C] someone who sells illegal drugs

push-up /ˈpʊʃʌp/ *US* (*UK* **press-up**) *noun* [C] **SPORT** a physical exercise in which you lie facing the floor and use your hands to push your body up *I did forty push-ups yesterday.*

pushy /ˈpʊʃi/ *adjective* behaving in an unpleasant way by trying too much to get something or to make someone do something *a pushy salesman*

O→**put** /pʊt/ *verb* [T] **putting**, *past* **put 1 put sth down/in/on, etc** to move something to a place or position *Where have you put the keys?* ○ *She put her bag on the floor.* ○ *You can put your coat in the car.* ○ *He put his arm around her.* **2 put sb in a mood/position, etc** to cause someone or something to be in a particular situation *They'd had an argument and it had put her in a bad mood.* ○ *This puts me in a very difficult position.* **3** SAY to say something using particular words *I don't know quite* ***how to put this****, but I'm leaving.* **4** WRITE to write something *Please put your name on the list by Monday evening.*

put sth across *phrasal verb* to explain or express something clearly so that people understand it easily

put sth aside *phrasal verb* to save something so that you can use it later *I've been putting a bit of money aside every month.*

put sth away *phrasal verb* to put something in the place where you usually keep it *She folded the towels and put them away in the cupboard.* ➲See colour picture **Phrasal Verbs** on page Centre 16

put sth back *phrasal verb* to put something where it was before it was moved *I put the book back on the shelf.*

O→**put sth down** *phrasal verb* **1** STOP HOLDING to put something that you are holding onto the floor or onto another surface *I'll just put my bag down for a minute, it's rather heavy.* ➲See colour picture **Phrasal Verbs** on page Centre 16 **2** TELEPHONE *UK* If you put the phone down, you put the part of the telephone that you speak into back to its usual position. **3** ANIMAL to kill an animal, usually because it is suffering

put sb down *phrasal verb* **1** CRITICIZE to make someone feel stupid or unimportant by criticizing them *I'm tired of him putting me down all the time.* **2** WRITE to write someone's name on a list or document, usually in order to arrange for them to do something *I've* ***put*** *you* ***down for*** *the trip to Rome next week.*

put sth down to sth *phrasal verb UK* to think that a problem or situation is caused by a particular thing

put sth forward *phrasal verb* to state an idea or opinion, or to suggest a plan, so that it can be considered or discussed

put sb/sth in sth *phrasal verb* to arrange for someone or something to go somewhere *to put someone in prison* ○ *to put some money in the bank* ○ *I'd never put my mother in an old people's home.*

put sth in *phrasal verb* to fix something into a room or building *I've just had a new kitchen put in.*

put sth into sth/doing sth *phrasal verb* If you put time, work, or effort into something, you spend a lot of time or effort doing it. *We've put a lot of effort into this project and we want it to succeed.*

put sth off *phrasal verb* to decide or arrange to do something at a later time *I must talk to her about this, I can't put it off any longer.*

put sb off (sth) *phrasal verb* to make someone not like someone or something, or not want to do something *Jan was talking about her operation and it put me off my food.*

put sth on *phrasal verb* **1** CLOTHES to put clothes or shoes onto your body *You'd better put your coat on, it's cold outside.* ➲See colour picture **Phrasal Verbs** on page Centre 16

P

2 EQUIPMENT *mainly UK* to make a piece of equipment work by pressing a switch *Can you put the light on please?* **3** BEHAVIOUR to pretend to have a particular feeling, or to behave in a way which is not real or natural for you *He's not really upset, he's just putting it on.* **4** MUSIC/FILM to put a CD or other recording into a machine so that you can see or hear it *Why don't you put on some music?* **5 put on weight** *UK* to become fatter and heavier

put sth out *phrasal verb* **1** STOP SHINING *mainly UK* to make a light stop shining by pressing a switch *Please put the lights out when you leave.* **2** STOP BURNING to make something that is burning stop burning *to put out a fire* **3** PUT OUTSIDE to put something outside the house *to put out the rubbish/trash*

put sb out *phrasal verb* to cause trouble or extra work for someone *It would be great if you could help, but I don't want to put you out.*

be put out *phrasal verb* to be annoyed, often because of something that someone has done or said to you *He seemed a bit* ***put out at*** *not having been invited.*

put sb through sth *phrasal verb* to make someone experience or do something unpleasant or difficult *Why did they put themselves through this ordeal?*

put sb through *phrasal verb* to connect someone using a telephone to the person they want to speak to *Can you put me through to customer services, please?*

put sth to sb *phrasal verb* **1** SUGGEST to suggest an idea or plan to someone so that they can consider it or discuss it **2** ASK to ask someone a question *to put a question to someone*

put sth together *phrasal verb* **1** JOIN PARTS to put the parts of something in the correct place and join them to each other *You buy it in a kit and then put it together yourself.* **2** PREPARE WORK to prepare a piece of work by collecting several ideas and suggestions and organizing them *to put together a plan/proposal*

put sth up *phrasal verb* **1** BUILD to build something *to put up a tent* ○ *We spent the weekend putting up a fence in the backyard.* **2** FASTEN to fasten something to a wall or ceiling *to put up shelves* ○ *I need to put up some curtains in the back bedroom.* **3** INCREASE *mainly UK* to increase the price or value of something *They're going to* ***put up the price*** *of fuel.*

put sb up *phrasal verb* to let someone stay in your home for a short period *If you need somewhere to stay, we can put you up for the night.*

put up with sb/sth *phrasal verb* to accept unpleasant behaviour or an unpleasant situation, although you do not like it *He's so rude, I don't know how you put up with him.*

putrid /ˈpjuːtrɪd/ *adjective* decaying and smelling bad *a putrid smell*

putt /pʌt/ *verb* [I, T] **SPORT** in golf, to hit the ball gently when you are near the hole •**putt** *noun* [C]

putty /ˈpʌti/ *noun* [U] **DT** a soft, grey substance that becomes hard when it is dry and is used to fasten glass into windows or to fill small holes in wood

WORD PARTNERS FOR ***puzzle***

resolve/solve a puzzle • the puzzle **of** sth

puzzle¹ /ˈpʌzl/ *noun* [C] **1** GAME a game or activity in which you have to put pieces together or answer questions using skill *to do/solve a puzzle* ○ *a crossword puzzle* ○ *a jigsaw puzzle* **2** SITUATION a situation which is very difficult to understand *Scientists have been trying to* ***solve this puzzle*** *for years.*

puzzle² /ˈpʌzl/ *verb* [T] to make someone confused because they do not understand something [**often passive**] *I was puzzled by what he said.*

puzzle over sth *phrasal verb* to try to solve a problem or understand a situation by thinking carefully about it

puzzled /ˈpʌzld/ *adjective* confused because you do not understand something *He had a puzzled look on his face.*

puzzling /ˈpʌzlɪŋ/ *adjective* If something is puzzling, it confuses you because you do not understand it.

PVC /ˌpiːviːˈsiː/ *noun* [U] **DT** a strong material similar to thick plastic

pyjamas *UK* (*US* **pajamas**) /pɪˈdʒɑːməz/ *noun* [**plural**] shirt and trousers that you wear in bed *a pair of blue pyjamas* ➲See colour picture **Clothes** on page Centre 8

pylon /ˈpaɪlɒn/ *noun* [C] a tall structure which supports electrical wires above the ground

pyramid /ˈpɪrəmɪd/ *noun* [C] a shape with a square base and four triangular sides that meet to form a point at the top

pyre /paɪəʳ/ *noun* [C] a pile of wood on which a dead person is burned in some countries

pyrites /paɪˈraɪtiːz/ *noun* [U] **GEOLOGY** a shiny yellow mineral (= substance that is found in the ground) that contains sulphur and a metal, usually iron

Pythagoras' theorem /paɪˌθægərəsˈθɪərəm/ *noun* [C] **MATHEMATICS** a rule for working out the length of the sides of a right angled triangle (= triangle with one angle of 90°)

python /ˈpaɪθən/ *noun* [C] a large snake that kills other animals by putting itself tightly around them

P

Qq

Q, q /kjuː/ the seventeenth letter of the alphabet

QC /ˌkjuːˈsiː/ *noun* [C] **LAW** *abbreviation for* Queen's Counsel: a lawyer of high rank in the UK *Horace Rumpole QC*

qt **MEASURES** *written abbreviation for* quart (= a unit for measuring liquid)

quack /kwæk/ *noun* [C] the sound made by a duck (= water bird) •**quack** *verb* [I]

quadratic equation /kwɒdˌrætɪkɪˈkweɪʒən/ *noun* [C] **MATHEMATICS** an equation (= mathematical statement) which includes an unknown value that is multiplied by itself only once, and which does not include an unknown value multiplied by itself more than once

quadrilateral /ˌkwɒdrɪˈlætərəl/ *noun* [C] **MATHEMATICS** a flat shape with four straight sides

quadruple /kwɒdˈruːpl/ *verb* [I, T] If an amount quadruples, it becomes multiplied by four, or if you quadruple it, you multiply it by four.

quagmire /ˈkwɒgmaɪəʳ/ *noun* [C] **1** a difficult and unpleasant situation *a* ***legal quagmire*** **2** **GEOGRAPHY** an area of wet ground that you can sink into

quail /kweɪl/ *noun* [C] *plural* **quail** or **quails** **FOOD** a small bird which is shot for food

quaint /kweɪnt/ *adjective* attractive or unusual in an old-fashioned way *a quaint little village*

quake¹ /kweɪk/ *noun* [C] **GEOLOGY, GEOGRAPHY** *US short for* earthquake (= when the Earth shakes)

quake² /kweɪk/ *verb* [I] to shake because you are frightened

WORD PARTNERS FOR ***qualification***

an **academic / basic / formal / recognised** qualification • **gain/get/have/need** a qualification • a qualification **in** sth

qualification /ˌkwɒlɪfɪˈkeɪʃən/ *noun* **1** **EDUCATION** [C] *mainly UK* what you get when you pass an exam or a course [**usually plural**] *legal/medical qualifications* ○ *What qualifications do you need to be a nanny?* **2** [SKILLS] [C] the skills, qualities, or experience that you need in order to do something *The only qualification needed for this job is an eye for detail.* **3** [COMPETITION] [U] success in getting into a competition **4** [ADDITION] [C, U] an addition to something that is said that makes its meaning less certain

qualified /ˈkwɒlɪfaɪd/ *adjective* **1** **EDUCATION** having passed exams or courses *a* ***newly qualified*** *teacher* **2** **qualified to do sth** having the skills, qualities, or experience that you need in order to do something *I think John is the best qualified to make that decision.* **3** [NOT CERTAIN] If something someone says is qualified, they have added something to it to make it less certain. *The answer was a qualified yes.* ➲Opposite **unqualified**

qualifier /ˈkwɒlɪfaɪəʳ/ *noun* [C] **SPORT** **1** a game or competition which decides whether you can enter another competition **2** someone who has succeeded in getting into a competition

qualify /ˈkwɒlɪfaɪ/ *verb* **1** [BE ALLOWED] [I, T] If you qualify for something, you are allowed to do it or have it, and if something qualifies you for something, it allows you to do it or have it. *Foreign students no longer* ***qualify for*** *grants in the UK.* ○ *To qualify for the competition, you must be over 18.* ➲Opposite **disqualify** **2** **EDUCATION** [I] *mainly UK* to pass exams so that you are able to do a job *He's recently* ***qualified as*** *a doctor.* **3** **SPORT** [I] to succeed in getting into a competition *Nigeria were the first team to* ***qualify for*** *the World Cup.* **4** [ADD] [T] to add something to what you say to make its meaning less certain

qualitative /ˈkwɒlɪtətɪv/ Ⓤⓢ /ˈkwɑːlɪteɪtɪv/ *adjective formal* relating to how good something is and not how much of it there is •**qualitatively** *adverb*

WORD PARTNERS FOR ***quality***

affect/enhance/improve/maintain quality • **good/high/inferior/low/poor** quality

O‑‑**quality¹** /ˈkwɒləti/ *noun* **1** [GOOD OR BAD] [U] how good or bad something is ***good/high quality*** ○ ***poor/low quality*** ○ *The air quality in this area is terrible.* ○ *All we are asking for is a decent* ***quality of life.*** ○ *The spokeswoman says a* ***quality control*** *system is being developed for next year.* **2** [GOOD] [U] when something is very good or well made *A designer label isn't necessarily a guarantee of quality.* **3** [CHARACTER] [C] part of the character or personality of someone or something *leadership qualities*

quality² /ˈkwɒləti/ *adjective* [**always before noun**] very good *We only sell quality products in this store.*

ˈquality asˌsurance *noun* [U] the things a company does to make sure that its products and services are as good as they should be

ˈquality conˌtrol *noun* [U] the process of looking at goods when they are being produced to make certain that they are of the intended standard

ˈquality ˌtime *noun* [U] time that you spend with someone when you can give them all of your attention *We've been too busy to give the children much quality time this week.*

qualm /kwɑːm/ *noun* [C] a worry or doubt about something *She* ***has no qualms about*** *taking her clothes off in public.*

quandary /ˈkwɒndəri/ *noun* [**no plural**] a situation in which you are trying to make a difficult choice *We're* ***in a quandary over*** *which school to send her to.*

quantifier /ˈkwɒntɪfaɪəʳ/ *noun* [C] **LANGUAGE** a word or group of words that is used before a noun to show an amount of that noun. For example the words 'many', 'some', and 'a lot of' are quantifiers.

quantify /ˈkwɒntɪfaɪ/ *verb* [T] **MEASURES** to measure or state the amount of something *It is difficult to quantify the damage that this storm has caused.*

Q

quantitative /ˈkwɒntɪtətɪv/ (US) /ˈkwɑːntəteɪtɪv/ *adjective* relating to quantity

WORD PARTNERS FOR ***quantity***

a **huge/large/small/sufficient/vast** quantity • **in** [big/large, etc] quantities

O‐ **quantity** /ˈkwɒntəti/ *noun* **1** [C, U] the amount or number of something *A **vast quantity** of information is available on the Internet.* ○ *They are now developing ways to produce the vaccine **in large quantities** and cheaply.* ➲See colour picture **Pieces and Quantities** on page Centre 1 **2 an unknown quantity** someone or something that you do not know and so you cannot be certain about

quantum leap /ˌkwɒntʌmˈliːp/ *noun* [C] a sudden, large increase or improvement in something [**usually singular**] *a quantum leap in information technology*

quarantine /ˈkwɒrᵊntiːn/ *noun* [U] **HEALTH** If an animal or person is put into quarantine, they are kept away from other animals or people because they have or might have a disease.

quark /kwɑːk/ *noun* [C] **PHYSICS** one of the most basic forms of matter that make up the particles of an atom

WORD PARTNERS FOR ***quarrel***

have a quarrel • a quarrel **about/over** sth • a quarrel **with** sb • a quarrel **between** sb **and** sb

quarrel¹ /ˈkwɒrᵊl/ *noun* **1** [C] an argument *She walked out after **having a quarrel with** her boss.* **2 have no quarrel with sb/sth** to not disagree with someone or something *We have no quarrel with either of those ideas.*

quarrel² /ˈkwɒrᵊl/ *verb* [I] *UK* **quarrelling**, *past* **quarrelled**, *US* **quarreling**, *past* **quarreled** to have an argument with someone *She'd been **quarrelling with** her mother all morning.*

quarry /ˈkwɒri/ *noun* [C] **GEOLOGY** a place where stone is dug out of a large hole in the ground *a marble quarry* •**quarry** *verb* [T] to dig stone out of a quarry

Q

quart /kwɔːt/ (*written abbreviation* **qt**) *noun* [C] **MEASURES** a unit for measuring liquid, equal to 1.14 litres in the UK and 0.95 litres in the US

O‐ **quarter** /ˈkwɔːtəʳ/ *noun* **1 MATHEMATICS** [C] (*also US* **fourth**) one of four equal parts of something; ¹/₄ *Three quarters of the island's residents speak English.* ○ *My house is one and three-quarter miles/a mile and three-quarters from here.* ○ *I waited a quarter of an hour for her.* **2** BEFORE/AFTER HOUR [**no plural**] a period of 15 minutes before or after the hour *It's (a) **quarter to** three* (= 2.45). ○ *also US* It's ***a quarter of** three* (= 2.45). ○ *We're leaving at (a) **quarter past** six* (= 6.15). ○ *also US* We're leaving at (a) ***quarter after** six* (= 6.15). **3 FINANCE** [C] one of four periods of time into which a year is divided for financial calculations such as profits or bills (= orders for payment) *I get an electricity bill every quarter.* **4 EDUCATION** [C] *US* one of four periods of time into which a year at college or university is divided **5 SPORT** [C] *US* one of four periods of time into which some sports games are divided **6** PART OF TOWN [C] a part of a town, often where people from a particular country or religion live *the Jewish quarter* **7 FINANCE** [C] a US or Canadian coin with a value of 25 cents, which is a quarter of a dollar

quarterback /ˈkwɔːtəbæk/ *noun* [C] **SPORT** a player in American football who controls the attack

quarter-final /ˌkwɔːtəˈfaɪnᵊl/ *noun* [C] **SPORT** the part of a competition when eight people or teams are left and there are four games to decide who will reach the semi-final (= when only four people or teams are left) *She was knocked out of the competition **in the quarter-finals**.*

quarterly /ˈkwɔːtᵊli/ *adjective, adverb* produced or happening every three months *Water and electricity bills are paid quarterly.* ○ *a quarterly magazine/report*

quarters /ˈkwɔːtəz/ *noun* [**plural**] rooms to live in or sleep in, usually for people in a military organization

quartet /kwɔːˈtet/ *noun* [C] **MUSIC** four people singing or playing music in a group

quartile /ˈkwɔːtaɪl/ *noun* [C] **MATHEMATICS** one of four equal measurements that a set of things can be divided into *He is in the top quartile for weight.*

quartz /ˈkwɔːts/ *noun* [U] **GEOLOGY** a mineral used to make watches and clocks accurate

quash /kwɒʃ/ *verb* [T] **1 LAW** *formal* to officially change a legal decision so that it stops existing *His **conviction** was **quashed** last month.* **2** to stop something that you do not want to happen *He appeared on television to **quash rumours** that he was seriously ill.*

quasi- /kweɪzaɪ-/ *prefix* partly *quasi-religious ideas*

quay /kiː/ *noun* [C] a structure built next to water where ships stop and goods are taken on and off

queasy /ˈkwiːzi/ *adjective* **HEALTH** If you feel queasy, you feel slightly ill as if you might vomit.

O‐ **queen** /kwiːn/ *noun* [C] **1** FEMALE RULER a female ruler in some countries *Queen Elizabeth II* ○ *God save the Queen!* **2** KING'S WIFE the wife of a king when he is the main ruler in a country **3** PLAYING CARD a playing card with a picture of a queen on it *the queen of diamonds* **4 BIOLOGY** a large female insect which is the most important in a group and which produces all the eggs *queen bee*

queer /kwɪəʳ/ *adjective* **1** HOMOSEXUAL *informal* homosexual **2** STRANGE strange

quell /kwel/ *verb* [T] *formal* to stop something that you do not want to happen *to **quell** a riot* ○ *to **quell** rumours*

quench /kwenʃ/ *verb* **quench your thirst** to drink liquid so that you stop being thirsty

query¹ /ˈkwɪəri/ *noun* [C] a question *His job is to answer telephone **queries about** airline schedules.*

query² /ˈkwɪəri/ *verb* [T] to ask questions in order to check that something is true or correct [+ **question word**] *A few students have* *queried whether exam marks were added up correctly.*

quest /kwest/ *noun* [C] *formal* an attempt to get something or do something difficult *the **quest** for truth* [+ to do sth] *He has begun his quest to become the Conservative Party's first Asian MP.*

WORD PARTNERS FOR ***question***

ask/answer/pose/raise/reply to a question • a question **arises** • an **awkward/fundamental/important/interesting/hypothetical** question • a question **about** sth

O⁻ **question¹** /ˈkwestʃən/ *noun* **1** SENTENCE [C] a sentence or phrase that asks you for information *Is it OK if I **ask** you a few **questions**?* ○ *He refused to **answer** my **question**.* ○ *If you have any **questions about** the scheme, do ask me.* ○ *"So where's the money coming from?" "**That's a good question**"* (= I do not know). **2** SITUATION [C] a situation or problem that needs to be considered *This documentary **raises** important **questions** about the American legal system.* ○ *Two important **questions arise** from this debate.* **3** DOUBT [U] doubt [+ that] *There is **no question** that this was an accidental fire.* ○ *His ability as a chef has never been **in question**.* ○ *"So you agree she's the right person for the job." "Yes, absolutely, **without question**."* ○ *The report **brings/calls into question*** (= causes doubts about) *the safety of this drug.* **4 sb/sth in question** the person or thing that is being discussed *He claims that he was in the pub with his girlfriend on the night in question.* **5 be out of the question** If something is out of the question, it is not possible or not allowed. ➲See also: **loaded question, rhetorical question**

COMMON LEARNER ERROR

ask a question

Remember to use the verb **ask** with **question**.

We weren't allowed to ask any questions.

~~*We weren't allowed to make any questions.*~~

question² /ˈkwestʃən/ *verb* [T] **1** ASK QUESTIONS to ask someone questions *Detectives were **questioning** a boy **about** the murder.* [often passive] *Two out of three people questioned in the survey were non-smokers.* **2** DOUBT to show or feel doubt about something *I'm not for a moment questioning your decision.* [+ question word] *I'm just **questioning whether** we need the extra staff.*

questionable /ˈkwestʃənəbl/ *adjective* **1** NOT CERTAIN possibly not true or correct [+ question word] *It is highly **questionable whether** this drug has any benefits at all.* **2** NOT HONEST not honest or not legal *He's being investigated for questionable business practices.*

questioning /ˈkwestʃənɪŋ/ *noun* [U] when the police ask someone questions about a crime *She was taken in **for questioning** by police yesterday morning.*

ˈ**question** ˌ**mark** *noun* [C] **LANGUAGE** a mark (?) used at the end of a question ➲See Extra help page **Punctuation** on page Centre 18.

WORD PARTNERS FOR ***questionnaire***

complete/fill in a questionnaire • **draw up** a questionnaire • a questionnaire **asks** sth • a questionnaire **about/on** sth

questionnaire /ˌkwestʃəˈneəʳ/ *noun* [C] a set of questions asked of a large number of people to discover information about a subject *Residents have been sent **questionnaires about** their homes and energy use.*

ˈ**question** ˌ**tag** *noun* [C] **LANGUAGE** a short phrase such as 'isn't it' or 'don't you' that is added to the end of a sentence to check information or to ask if someone agrees with you. In the sentence, 'It's hot, isn't it?', 'isn't it' is a question tag.

WORD PARTNERS FOR ***queue***

form/be in/join a queue • a queue **stretches** [for miles/around sth, etc] • a **big/long/short/small** queue • a queue **of** [cars/people, etc] • a queue **for** sth

queue /kjuː/ *UK* (*US* **line**) *noun* [C] **1** a row of people waiting for something, one behind the other *to **join the queue*** ○ *Are you **in the queue**?* **2 jump the queue** to move in front of people who have been waiting longer for something than you •**queue (up)** *UK* (*US* **line up**) *verb* [I] to stand in a row in order to wait for something [+ to do sth] They're queueing up to get tickets.

quibble /ˈkwɪbl/ *verb* **quibble about/over/with sth** to argue about something that is not important *They spend far too much time quibbling over details.* •**quibble** *noun* [C]

quiche /kiːʃ/ *noun* [C, U] **FOOD** a dish made of a pastry base filled with a mixture of egg and milk and usually cheese, vegetables, or meat

O⁻ **quick¹** /kwɪk/ *adjective* **1** FAST doing something fast or taking only a short time *I tried to catch him but he was too quick for me.* [+ to do sth] *Publishers were quick to realize that a profit could be made.* **2** LASTING A SHORT TIME lasting a short time *Can I ask you a quick question?*

quick² /kwɪk/ *adverb informal* fast *Come here, quick!*

quicken /ˈkwɪkᵊn/ *verb* [I, T] to become faster or to cause something to become faster *His breathing quickened.*

O⁻ **quickly** /ˈkwɪkli/ *adverb* fast or in a short time *I quickly shut the door.* ○ *These people need to be treated as quickly as possible.*

ˈ**quick** ˌ**ratio** (*also* **acid test ratio**) *noun* [C usually singular] **FINANCE** a calculation that compares the assets (= things owned) of a business that are in the form of money or can be quickly changed into money with payments that need to be made soon

quid /kwɪd/ *noun* [C] *plural* **quid** *UK informal* a pound (= UK unit of money) *This bike's not bad for twenty quid.*

O⁻ **quiet¹** /kwaɪət/ *adjective* **1** NOT NOISY making little or no noise *Can you **be quiet**, please?* ○ *The children are very quiet.* **2** NOT BUSY without much noise or activity *I fancy a **quiet night in** tonight.* ○ *They found a table in a quiet corner of the restaurant.* **3** NOT TALKING MUCH If someone is quiet, they do not talk very much. *He was a shy, quiet man.* **4 keep (sth) quiet** to

Q

not talk about something that is secret *It might be wise to keep this quiet for a while.*

COMMON LEARNER ERROR

quiet or **quite?**

Be careful, these two words look very similar, but they are spelled differently and have completely different meanings.

Quiet means making little or no noise.

The house was very quiet without the children around.

Quite means a little or a lot but not completely.

It's quite cold today.

quiet² /kwaɪət/ *noun* [U] when there is little or no noise *She needs a bit of* ***peace and quiet.***

quieten /'kwaɪətᵊn/ *UK* (*US* **quiet**) *verb* [T] to make someone or something quiet

quieten (sb/sth) down *phrasal verb UK* (*US* **quiet (sb/sth) down**) to become quieter or calmer, or to make a person or animal become quieter or calmer

O-ᵚ**quietly** /'kwaɪətli/ *adverb* **1** WITHOUT NOISE making little or no noise *"Don't worry," she said quietly.* **2** WITHOUT ACTIVITY doing something without much noise or activity *He sat quietly on the sofa, waiting for her to come home.*

quilt /kwɪlt/ *noun* [C] a cover for a bed which is filled with feathers or other warm material

quilting /'kwɪltɪŋ/ *noun* [U] **ART, DT** the activity of making quilts or the material used for making quilts

quinine /'kwiniːn/ *noun* [U] **HEALTH** a drug used to treat fevers such as malaria (= a serious illness spread by flies)

quip /kwɪp/ *verb* [I, T] **quipping**, *past* **quipped** to say something in a funny and clever way •**quip** *noun* [C]

Q

quirk /kwɜːk/ *noun* **1** [C] a strange habit *My aunt has a few odd quirks.* **2 quirk of fate** a strange and unexpected event ***By some quirk of fate****, we came to live in the same town.* •**quirky** *adjective* strange *a quirky sense of humour*

quit /kwɪt/ *verb* **quitting**, *past* **quit 1** NOT WORK [I, T] to leave your job or school permanently *She recently* ***quit*** *her* ***job*** *to spend more time with her family.* **2** NOT DO [T] to stop doing something *I quit smoking and put on weight.*

O-ᵚ**quite** /kwaɪt/ *adverb* **1** NOT COMPLETELY *UK* a little or a lot but not completely *I'm quite tired, but I'm happy to walk a little further.* ○ *He's quite attractive but not what I'd call gorgeous.* **2** VERY *US* very *My sister and I are quite different.* **3** COMPLETELY completely *The two situations are quite different.* ○ *Are you quite sure you want to go?* **4 not quite** almost but not completely *I'm not quite sure that I understand this.* ○ *He didn't get quite enough votes to win.* **5 quite a bit/a few/a lot, etc** a large amount or number *There are quite a few letters for you here.* ○ *He's changed quite a bit.*

quiver /'kwɪvəʳ/ *verb* [I] to shake slightly •**quiver** *noun* [C]

quiz¹ /kwɪz/ *noun* [C] *plural* **quizzes 1** GAME a game in which you answer questions *a television quiz show* **2 EDUCATION** *US* a short test on a subject in school

quiz² /kwɪz/ *verb* [T] **quizzing**, *past* **quizzed** to ask someone questions about something *A group of journalists* ***quizzed*** *them* ***about/on*** *the day's events.*

quizzical /'kwɪzɪkᵊl/ *adjective* A quizzical expression or look seems to ask a question without words.

quota /'kwəʊtə/ *noun* [C] a limited amount of something that is officially allowed *an import quota*

quotation /kwəʊ'teɪʃᵊn/ *noun* [C] **1 LITERATURE** a sentence or phrase that is taken out of a book, poem, or play *a* ***quotation from*** *Shakespeare/the Bible* **2 FINANCE** the amount that a piece of work will probably cost *Make sure you* ***get a quotation*** *for all the work before they start.*

quot'ation ˌmarks *noun* [plural] **LANGUAGE** a pair of marks (" ") or (' ') used before and after a group of words to show that they are spoken or that someone else originally wrote them ➲See Extra help page **Punctuation** on page Centre 19.

quote¹ /kwəʊt/ *verb* **1** REPEAT [I, T] to repeat what someone has said or written *I was* ***quoting from*** *Marx.* ○ *Witnesses were* ***quoted as saying*** *there were two gunmen.* **2** GIVE EXAMPLE [T] to give a fact or example in order to support what you are saying *The minister quoted recent unemployment figures.* **3 FINANCE** [T] to say how much a piece of work will cost before you do it

quote² /kwəʊt/ *noun* [C] *short for* quotation

quotes /kwəʊts/ *noun* [plural] **LANGUAGE** *short for* quotation marks

the Qur'an /kɒr'ɑːn/ *noun* **RELIGION** *another spelling of* the Koran (= the holy book of Islam)

qwerty /'kwɜːti/ *adjective* **COMPUTING** using or referring to a keyboard on which the letters are arranged so that the top line begins with q,w,e,r,t and y

Rr

R, r /ɑːʳ/ the eighteenth letter of the alphabet

R *informal* **INTERNET** *written abbeviation for* are: used in emails and text messages

rabbi /ˈræbaɪ/ *noun* [C] **RELIGION** a leader and teacher in the Jewish religion *Rabbi Hugo Gryn*

rabbit /ˈræbɪt/ *noun* [C] a small animal with fur and long ears that lives in a hole in the ground

rabble /ˈræbl/ *noun* [no plural] a group of noisy, uncontrolled people

rabies /ˈreɪbiːz/ *noun* [U] **HEALTH** a serious disease that people can get if they are bitten by an infected animal

WORD PARTNERS FOR ***race***

drop out of/lose/win a race • **in** a race

O⊷**race¹** /reɪs/ *noun* **1 SPORT** [C] a competition in which people run, ride, drive, etc against each other in order to see who is the fastest *a horse race* **2 SOCIETY** [C, U] one of the groups that people are divided into according to their physical characteristics *people of many different races* **3** [C] a situation in which people compete against each other for power or control *the **race for** governor* **4 the races SPORT** an event when horses race against each other **5 a race against time/the clock** a situation in which something has to be done very quickly ➲See also: **the human race, the rat race**

COMMON LEARNER ERROR

race or **species?**

Race is used to talk about one of the groups that people are divided into according to their physical characteristics.

the human race

People of all races and religions live in America.

Species is used to talk about types of animals and plants.

eagles, vultures and other species of bird

race² /reɪs/ *verb* **1 SPORT** [I, T] to compete in a race *I'll race you to the end of the road.* ○ *I used to **race against** him at school.* **2 race along/down/over, etc** to move somewhere very quickly *I raced over to see what was the matter.* **3 race sb to/back, etc** to take someone somewhere very quickly *Ambulances raced the injured to a nearby hospital.* **4 SPORT** [T] to put a horse, dog, etc in a race

racecourse /ˈreɪskɔːs/ *noun* [C] **SPORT** *UK* the place where horses, cars, etc race

racehorse /ˈreɪshɔːs/ *noun* [C] **SPORT** a horse that has been trained to run in races

ˌrace reˈlations *noun* [plural] **SOCIETY** the relationship between people from different races who live together in the same place

racetrack /ˈreɪstræk/ *noun* [C] **SPORT** the place where horses, cars, etc race

racial /ˈreɪʃəl/ *adjective* **SOCIETY** relating to people's race *a racial minority* ○ ***racial discrimination/tension*** •**racially** *adverb a **racially motivated** crime*

racing /ˈreɪsɪŋ/ *noun* [U] **SPORT** the activity or sport in which people, animals, or vehicles race against each other *motor racing* ➲See also: **horse racing**

WORD PARTNERS FOR ***racism***

combat/encounter/face/tackle racism • **a form of** racism • racism **against** sb

racism /ˈreɪsɪzəm/ *noun* [U] **SOCIETY** the belief that other races of people are not as good as your own, or the unfair treatment of people because they belong to a particular race

racist /ˈreɪsɪst/ *noun* [C] **SOCIETY** someone who believes that other races of people are not as good as their own •**racist** *adjective a **racist attack***

rack¹ /ræk/ *noun* [C] a type of shelf that you can put things on or hang things from *a **magazine/luggage rack***

rack² /ræk/ *verb* **1 be racked with pain/guilt, etc** If someone is racked with pain or an emotion, they suffer a lot because of it. **2 rack your brain/brains** *informal* to think very hard, usually to try to remember something or solve a problem

rack up sth *phrasal verb informal* to get or achieve a lot of something *He's racked up debts of over thirty thousand pounds.*

rack and pinion /ˌrækəndˈpɪnjən/ *adjective* [always before noun] **DT** using a system where a cog (= round metal part with small pieces sticking out of the edge) turns against a long bar that also has small pieces sticking up, and makes it move *rack and pinion gears*

racket /ˈrækɪt/ *noun* **1 SPORT** [C] (*also* **racquet**) a piece of equipment that you use to hit a ball in sports such as tennis ➲See colour picture **Sports 2** on page Centre 15 **2** ILLEGAL [C] *informal* an illegal activity that is used to make money *a drugs smuggling racket* **3** NOISE [no plural] *informal* a loud noise *The neighbours were **making such a racket**.*

radar /ˈreɪdɑːʳ/ *noun* [U] **PHYSICS** a system that uses radio waves to find out the position of something you cannot see

radiant /ˈreɪdiənt/ *adjective* **1** HAPPY showing that you are very happy *a radiant smile* **2** BRIGHT very bright •**radiance** /ˈreɪdiəns/ *noun* [U]

radiate /ˈreɪdieɪt/ *verb* **1 radiate from/out, etc** to spread out in all directions from a particular point *A number of roads radiate out from the centre.* **2** [T] to show an emotion or quality in your face or behaviour *His face just radiates happiness.* **3 PHYSICS** [T] to send out heat or light

radiation /ˌreɪdiˈeɪʃən/ *noun* [U] **PHYSICS 1** a form of energy that comes from a nuclear reaction and that in large amounts can be very dangerous *dangerously high **levels of radiation*** ○ *radiation sickness* **2** energy from heat or light that you cannot see *solar/microwave radiation*

radiator /ˈreɪdieɪtəʳ/ *noun* [C] **1** HEATER a metal piece of equipment that is filled with hot water and is used to heat a room ➲See colour picture **The Living Room** on page Centre 4 **2** ENGINE PART a part

R

of a vehicle engine that is used to make the engine cool

radical[1] /ˈrædɪkəl/ *adjective* **1** A radical change is very big and important. *a **radical reform*** **2 POLITICS** believing that there should be big social and political changes *a radical group/movement* ○ *a **radical proposal*** •**radically** *adverb The company has **changed radically** in recent years.*

radical[2] /ˈrædɪkəl/ *noun* [C] **POLITICS** someone who supports the idea that there should be big social and political changes

radicle /ˈrædɪkl/ *noun* [C] **BIOLOGY** the first part that comes out of a plant's seed, and later forms the root

O-■ **radio**[1] /ˈreɪdiəʊ/ *noun* **1** BROADCASTS [C] a piece of equipment used for listening to radio broadcasts *a car radio* **2 the radio** the programmes that you hear when you listen to the radio *We heard him speaking **on the radio** this morning.* **3** SYSTEM [U] a system of sending and receiving sound through the air ***local radio*** ○ *a **radio station*** **4** MESSAGES [C] a piece of equipment for sending and receiving messages by sound

radio[2] /ˈreɪdiəʊ/ *verb* [I, T] **radioing**, *past* **radioed** to send a message to someone by radio *They radioed for help.*

radioactive /ˌreɪdiəʊˈæktɪv/ *adjective* **PHYSICS** containing harmful radiation (= energy from a nuclear reaction) ***radioactive waste***

radioactivity /ˌreɪdiəʊækˈtɪvəti/ *noun* [U] **PHYSICS** when something is radioactive

radiocarbon dating /ˌreɪdiəʊkɑːbənˈdeɪtɪŋ/ *noun* [U] **BIOLOGY** a method of calculating the age of extremely old objects by measuring the amount of a particular type of carbon in them

radioisotope /ˌreɪdiəʊˈaɪsətəʊp/ *noun* [C] **CHEMISTRY** an isotope (= form of an atom with a different atomic weight but the same chemical structure) that gives off radiation

radiotherapy /ˌreɪdiəʊˈθerəpi/ *noun* [U] **HEALTH** the use of controlled amounts of radiation to treat disease

R

ˈradio ˌwave *noun* [C] **PHYSICS** an electromagnetic wave that is used to send radio signals

radish /ˈrædɪʃ/ *noun* [C] **FOOD** a small, round, white or red vegetable with a slightly hot taste that you eat in salad

radius /ˈreɪdiəs/ *noun* [C] *plural* **radii** **1 MEASURES** a certain distance from a particular point in any direction *Most facilities lie **within** a two-mile **radius** of the house.* **2 MATHEMATICS** the distance from the centre of a circle to its edge ➲See picture at **circle** **3 ANATOMY** the shorter of the two long thin bones in the lower half of the arm, between the wrist and the elbow

radon /ˈreɪdɒn/ *noun* [U] **CHEMISTRY** a colourless radioactive gas that is formed when radium and some other substances decay (symbol **Rn**)

raffle /ˈræfl/ *noun* [C] a competition in which people buy tickets with numbers on them and win a prize if any of their numbers are chosen ***raffle tickets*** •**raffle** *verb* [T] to offer something as a prize in a raffle

raft /rɑːft/ *noun* **1** [C] a small, flat boat made by tying pieces of wood together **2 a raft of sth/sb** a lot of things or people *a raft of data*

rafter /ˈrɑːftər/ *noun* [C] one of the long pieces of wood that supports a roof

rag /ræg/ *noun* [C] **1** a piece of old cloth that you use to clean things **2 be like a red rag to a bull** *UK* If a particular subject is like a red rag to a bull, it always makes someone angry.

rage[1] /reɪdʒ/ *noun* **1** [C, U] strong anger that you cannot control *a jealous rage* ○ *He **flew into a rage** (= suddenly became angry) over the smallest mistake.* **2 be all the rage** *informal old-fashioned* to be very popular ➲See also: **road rage**

rage[2] /reɪdʒ/ *verb* [I] **1** CONTINUE to continue with great force or violence *The battle raged well into the night.* **2** SPEAK to speak or behave in a very angry way

ragged /ˈrægɪd/ *adjective* **1** CLOTHES old and torn *ragged jeans* **2** PERSON wearing clothes that are old and torn *a ragged child* **3** ROUGH rough and not smooth *a **ragged edge***

rags /rægz/ *noun* [plural] **1** clothes that are old and torn *an old man dressed **in rags*** **2 go from rags to riches** to start your life very poor and then later in life become very rich

WORD PARTNERS FOR ***raid***

carry out a raid • a raid **on** sth • an **air** raid • a **dawn** raid

raid[1] /reɪd/ *noun* [C] **1** SOLDIERS a sudden attack on a place by soldiers *an **air raid*** ○ *a **dawn raid*** **2** POLICE a sudden visit to a place by police in order to find someone or something *a **police raid** to recover illegal weapons* **3** STEAL when people enter a place by force in order to steal from it *a **bank raid*** ➲See also: **air raid**

raid[2] /reɪd/ *verb* [T] **1** SOLDIERS If soldiers raid a place, they suddenly attack it. **2** POLICE If the police raid a place, they suddenly visit it in order to find someone or something. *Police raided nine properties in search of the documents.* **3** STEAL to steal many things from somewhere *to **raid** the **fridge***

rail /reɪl/ *noun* **1** FOR HANGING [C] *UK* a horizontal bar on the wall that you hang things on *a curtain rail* **2** FOR SUPPORTING [C] a bar around or along something which you can hold to stop you from falling *a hand rail* **3** TRAIN SYSTEM [U] trains as a method of transport ***rail travel*** ○ *a **rail link*** ○ *They sent the shipment **by rail**.* **4** TRAIN [C] the metal tracks that trains run on ➲See also: **towel rail**

railing /ˈreɪlɪŋ/ *noun* [C] a fence made from posts and bars *an iron railing*

ˈrailroad ˌtie *US* (*UK* **sleeper**) *noun* [C] a piece of wood that is used to support a railway track

railway /ˈreɪlweɪ/ *noun* **1** [C] (*also US* **railroad** /ˈreɪlrəʊd/) the metal tracks that trains travel on *Repairs are being carried out on the railway.* **2 the railway(s)** (*also US* **the railroad(s)**) the organizations connected with trains *He worked on the railways all his life.*

WORD PARTNERS FOR *rain*

rain falls • **heavy/light/pouring/torrential** rain • be **pouring with** rain • a **drop of/spot** of rain • **in** the rain

O-- **rain¹** /reɪn/ *noun* **1** [U] water that falls from the sky in small drops *heavy rain* ○ *It looks like rain* (= as if it will rain). **2 GEOGRAPHY the rains** in tropical countries, the time of year when there is a lot of rain *They were waiting for the rains to come.* ➲See also: **acid rain**

O-- **rain²** /reɪn/ *verb* **it rains** If it rains, water falls from the sky in small drops. *It was raining all weekend.*
be rained off *phrasal verb UK* (*US* **be rained out**) If a sport or outside activity is rained off, it cannot start or continue because it is raining.

rainbow /ˈreɪnbəʊ/ *noun* [C] a half circle with seven colours that sometimes appears in the sky when the sun shines through rain

ˈrain ˌcheck *noun* [C] **1 FINANCE** *US* a piece of paper which allows you to buy something at a low price although that thing is now being sold at a higher price **2** *US* a ticket that allows you to see an event at a later time if bad weather stops that event from happening **3 take a rain check on sth** something you say when you cannot accept someone's invitation, but would like to do it at a later time

raincoat /ˈreɪnkəʊt/ *noun* [C] a coat that you wear when it is raining ➲See colour picture **Clothes** on page Centre 8

raindrop /ˈreɪndrɒp/ *noun* [C] a single drop of rain

rainfall /ˈreɪnfɔːl/ *noun* [U] **RAIN** the amount of rain that falls in a particular place at a particular time ***monthly rainfall*** ○ ***heavy rainfall***

rainforest /ˈreɪnˌfɒrɪst/ *noun* [C] **ENVIRONMENT, GEOGRAPHY** a forest with a lot of tall trees where it rains a lot *a **tropical rainforest***

ˈrain ˌgauge *noun* [C] **GEOGRAPHY** a device for measuring how much rain falls

rainy /ˈreɪni/ *adjective* raining a lot *a rainy afternoon*

O-- **raise¹** /reɪz/ *verb* [T] **1** LIFT to lift something to a higher position *to raise your hand* **2** INCREASE to increase an amount or level *to **raise prices/taxes*** **3** IMPROVE to improve something *to **raise standards*** **4** MONEY to collect money from other people *They're **raising money** for charity.* **5 raise your voice** to speak loudly and angrily to someone **6 raise hopes/fears/doubts, etc** to cause emotions or thoughts *Her answers raised doubts in my mind.* **7 raise a question/subject, etc** to start talking about a subject that you want other people to consider **8** CHILD to look after and educate a child until they have become an adult *Their ideas on how to **raise children** didn't always agree.* **9 FARMING** to make an animal or crop grow *to raise chickens/sheep* ➲See Common Learner Error at **rise** ➲See also: raise the **alarm**¹

raise² /reɪz/ *US* (*UK* **rise**) *noun* [C] an increase in the amount of money that you earn *We usually get a raise at the start of a year.*

raisin /ˈreɪzᵊn/ *noun* [C] **FOOD** a dried grape (= small round fruit)

rake¹ /reɪk/ *noun* [C] **FARMING** a garden tool with a long handle that is used for moving dead leaves, grass, etc

rake² /reɪk/ *verb* [I, T] to use a rake to move dead leaves, grass, etc
rake sth in *phrasal verb informal* to earn a large amount of money. *He's **raking it in**.*

WORD PARTNERS FOR *rally*

hold/organize/stage a rally • a **mass** rally • **at** a rally

rally¹ /ˈræli/ *noun* [C] **1** a large public meeting in support of something *an **election/campaign rally*** **2 SPORT** a car or motorcycle race *a rally driver*

rally² /ˈræli/ *verb* **1** GIVE SUPPORT [I, T] to come together or bring people together to support something *Her fans **rallied behind** her from the start.* **2** GET BETTER [I] to get stronger or better after being weak *The stock market rallied late in the day.*
rally around/round (sb) *phrasal verb* to help or give support to someone *If one of the family has a crisis we rally round them.*

ram¹ /ræm/ *verb* [T] **ramming**, *past* **rammed** to hit something or push something into something with great force *He had to stop suddenly and a car **rammed into** him.*

ram² /ræm/ *noun* [C] a male sheep

RAM /ræm/ *noun* [U] **COMPUTING** *abbreviation for* random access memory: a computer's ability to immediately store information ➲Compare **ROM**

Ramadan /ˈræmədæn/ *noun* [U] **RELIGION** the Muslim religious period in which Muslims do not eat or drink during the part of the day when it is light

ramble¹ /ˈræmbl/ *verb* **1 ramble along/through, etc** to walk for a long time, especially in the countryside **2** (*also* **ramble on**) to talk for a long time in a boring and often confused way *The old general rambled on for hours about his time in the army.*

ramble² /ˈræmbl/ *noun* [C] a long walk in the countryside

rambler /ˈræmbləʳ/ *noun* [C] someone who walks in the countryside

rambling /ˈræmblɪŋ/ *adjective* **1** SPEECH/LETTER A rambling speech, letter, etc is very long and confused. **2** BUILDING A rambling building is big and without a regular shape.

ramifications /ˌræmɪfɪˈkeɪʃᵊnz/ *noun* [plural] the possible results of an action

ramp /ræmp/ *noun* [C] **1** SURFACE a sloping surface that joins two places that are at different heights *a wheelchair ramp* **2** ROAD *US* (*UK* **slip road**) a short road that is used to drive onto or off a large, fast road

rampage¹ /ræmˈpeɪdʒ/ *verb* [I] to run around or through an area, making a lot of noise and causing damage *Angry citizens **rampaged through** the city.*

R

rampage² /ˈræmpeɪdʒ/ *noun* [**no plural**] when a group of people rampage *Rioters **went on a rampage** through the city.*

rampant /ˈræmpənt/ *adjective* growing or spreading quickly, in a way that cannot be controlled ***rampant corruption/inflation***

ramshackle /ˈræmˌʃækl/ *adjective* A ramshackle building is in very bad condition.

ran /ræn/ *past tense of* run

ranch /rɑːnʃ/ *noun* [**C**] **FARMING** a large farm where animals are kept *a cattle/sheep ranch*

rancher /ˈrɑːnʃəʳ/ *noun* [**C**] **FARMING** someone who owns or works on a ranch

rancid /ˈrænsɪd/ *adjective* **FOOD** Rancid fat, such as oil or butter, smells and tastes bad because it is not fresh.

ˌR and ˈD *noun* [**U**] *abbreviation for* research and development: the part of a business that tries to find ways to improve existing products, and to develop new ones

random /ˈrændəm/ *adjective* **1** done or chosen without any plan or system ***random testing*** ○ *a **random selection*** **2 at random** chosen by chance *Winners will be chosen at random.* •**randomly** *adverb*

ˌrandom ˈsampling *noun* [**U**] choosing items to test without using any pattern to how they are chosen

rang /ræŋ/ *past tense of* ring²

WORD PARTNERS FOR ***range***

a **full/wide** range • a range **of** sth

range¹ /reɪndʒ/ *noun* **1** OF THINGS [**C**] a group of different things of the same general type *a **range of** colours/patterns* ○ *We discussed a **wide range** of subjects.* **2** AMOUNT [**C**] the amount or number between a particular set of limits [**usually singular**] *The **price range** is from $100 to $200.* ○ *The product is aimed at young people in the 18-25 **age range**.* **3** DISTANCE [**U**] the distance from which things can be seen, heard, or reached *The soldiers came **within** firing **range**.* ○ *He was shot **at close range*** (= from very near). **4 GEOGRAPHY** [**C**] a line of hills or mountains **5** SHOOTING [**C**] a place where you can practise shooting a gun *a **rifle/shooting range***

range² /reɪndʒ/ *verb* **1 range from sth to sth** to have several different amounts or types *Tickets range from $12 to $35.* ○ *Choose from 13 colours, ranging from classic white to antique blue.* **2** [**I**] to deal with a large number of subjects *The discussion **ranged over** many topics.*

ranger /ˈreɪndʒəʳ/ *noun* [**C**] someone whose job is to look after a forest or a park *a forest ranger*

rank¹ /ræŋk/ *noun* **1 SOCIETY** [**C, U**] a position in society or in an organization, for example the army *He holds the rank of colonel.* **2 the ranks** the ordinary members of an organization, especially the army **3 break ranks** to publicly show that you disagree with a group that you belong to **4 the rank and file** the ordinary members of an organization and not its leaders ➲See also: **taxi rank**

rank² /ræŋk/ *verb* [**I, T**] to have a position in a list which shows things or people in order of importance, or to give someone or something a position on such a list *He ranked number one in the world at the start of the competition.* ○ *The city's canals now **rank among** the world's dirtiest.*

ransom /ˈrænsəm/ *noun* [**C, U**] the money that is demanded for the return of someone who is being kept as a prisoner *a **ransom note/letter***

rant /rænt/ *verb* [**I**] to talk a lot about something in an excited or angry way *He was **ranting and raving** about the injustice of the situation.*

rap¹ /ræp/ *noun* **1 MUSIC** [**U**] a type of music in which the words are spoken and there is a strong beat *a **rap artist*** **2** [**C**] a sudden, short sound made when someone or something hits a hard surface *There was a **rap on** the window.* **3 a rap on/across/over the knuckles** a punishment that is not severe

rap² /ræp/ *verb* **rapping**, *past* **rapped 1** [**I, T**] to hit a hard surface to make a sudden, short noise *He **rapped on** the door.* **2 MUSIC** [**I**] to perform rap music

rape /reɪp/ *verb* [**T**] to force someone to have sex when they do not want to •**rape** *noun* [**C, U**]

rapid /ˈræpɪd/ *adjective* happening or moving very quickly ***rapid change/growth*** •**rapidity** /rəˈpɪdəti/ *noun* [**U**] •**rapidly** *adverb*

rapids /ˈræpɪdz/ *noun* [**plural**] **GEOGRAPHY** a part of a river where the water moves very fast

rapist /ˈreɪpɪst/ *noun* [**C**] someone who forces another person to have sex when they do not want to

rapper /ˈræpəʳ/ *noun* [**C**] **MUSIC** someone who performs rap music (= a type of music in which the words are spoken and there is a strong beat)

rapport /ræpˈɔːʳ/ *noun* [**U, no plural**] a good understanding of someone and ability to communicate with them *She has a good **rapport with** her staff.*

rapture /ˈræptʃəʳ/ *noun* [**U**] a feeling of extreme pleasure and excitement

O‑ **rare** /reəʳ/ *adjective* **1** very unusual *a **rare disease/species*** [**+ to do sth**] *It's very rare to see these birds in England.* **2 FOOD** If meat is rare, it is still red because it has only been cooked for a short time. *a rare steak*

rarely /ˈreəli/ *adverb* not often *I rarely see her these days.*

raring /ˈreərɪŋ/ *adjective* **be raring to do sth** *informal* to be very enthusiastic about starting something

rarity /ˈreərəti/ *noun* **1 be a rarity** to be unusual *Genuine enthusiasm is a rarity.* **2** [**U**] the fact that something is not common *Precious stones are valued for their rarity.*

rascal /ˈrɑːskəl/ *noun* [**C**] **1** PERSON *humorous* a person who behaves badly, but who you still like **2** DISHONEST *old-fashioned* a dishonest man

rash¹ /ræʃ/ *noun* **1 HEALTH** [**C**] a group of small, red spots on the skin *an **itchy rash*** ○ *Certain foods give him a rash.* **2 a rash of sth** a group of unpleasant events of the same type, happening at the same time *There has been a rash of burglaries in the area.*

rash² /ræʃ/ *adjective* done suddenly and without thinking carefully *a **rash decision/promise***

rasher /ˈræʃəʳ/ *noun* [C] *UK* **FOOD** a slice of bacon (= meat from a pig)

raspberry /ˈrɑːzbᵊri/ *noun* [C] **FOOD** a small, soft, red fruit that grows on bushes

rat /ræt/ *noun* [C] **1** [ANIMAL] an animal that looks like a large mouse and has a long tail *Rats carry disease.* **2** [PERSON] *informal* an unpleasant, dishonest person

WORD PARTNERS FOR ***rate***

a **cut in/drop in/increase in/rise in** the rate • **at** a rate (of) • the rate **for/of**

O-▪**rate¹** /reɪt/ *noun* [C] **1** [HOW MANY] how often something happens, or how many people something happens to *the **birth rate*** ○ *the **rate of** unemployment* **2** **FINANCE** a fixed amount of money given for something *the **interest/exchange rate*** ○ *rates of pay* **3** [SPEED] the speed at which something happens *the rate of progress* **4** **at this rate** used before saying what will happen if a situation continues in the same way *At this rate we're not going to be there till midnight.* **5** **at any rate** used before saying one fact that is certain in a situation that you are generally not certain about *Well, at any rate we need her to be there.* **6** **first-/second-/third-rate** very good, bad, or very bad *a first-rate hotel* ➲See also: **birth rate, exchange rate**

rate² /reɪt/ *verb* [T] **1** [JUDGE] to judge the quality or ability of someone or something *How do you **rate** her **as** a singer?* **2** [DESERVE] to deserve something *The incident didn't even **rate a mention*** (= was not written about) *in the local newspaper.*

O-▪**rather** /ˈrɑːðəʳ/ *adverb* **1** [SLIGHTLY] slightly or to a degree *I rather like it.* ○ *I find her books rather dull.* **2** **rather than** instead of *He saw his music as a hobby rather than a career.* **3** **would rather** If you would rather do something, you would prefer to do that thing. *I'd much rather go out for a meal than stay in and watch TV.* **4** [CORRECT] used to change something you have just said and make it more correct *I tried writing some drama, or rather comedy-drama, but it wasn't very good.*

ratify /ˈrætɪfaɪ/ *verb* [T] **POLITICS** to make an agreement official *Sixty-five nations need to **ratify** the **treaty**.*

WORD PARTNERS FOR ***rating***

give sb/sth **/have a rating** • sb's/sth's rating **drops/falls/improves/increases** • a **high/low** rating • a rating **of** [5/28%, etc]

rating /ˈreɪtɪŋ/ *noun* **1** [C] a measurement of how good or popular something or someone is *A high percentage of Americans gave the President a positive rating.* **2** **the ratings** a list of television and radio programmes showing how popular they are

ratio /ˈreɪʃiəʊ/ *noun* [C] **MATHEMATICS** the relationship between two things expressed in numbers to show how much bigger one is than the other *The female to male ratio at the college is 2 to 1.*

ration¹ /ˈræʃᵊn/ *noun* [C] the amount of something that you are allowed to have when there is little of it available *a **food/petrol ration***

ration² /ˈræʃᵊn/ *verb* [T] to give people only a small amount of something because there is little of it available *They might have to start rationing water.*

rational /ˈræʃᵊnᵊl/ *adjective* **1** [BASED ON FACTS] based on facts and not affected by someone's emotions or imagination *a **rational argument/debate/explanation*** **2** [WITHOUT EMOTION] able to make decisions based on facts and not be influenced by your emotions or imagination *Look, we've got to try to be rational about this.* ➲Opposite **irrational** •**rationally** *adverb*

rationale /ˌræʃəˈnɑːl/ *noun* [C] a group of reasons for a decision or belief *I don't understand **the rationale behind** the policy.*

rationalize (*also UK* **-ise**) /ˈræʃᵊnᵊlaɪz/ *verb* **1** [FIND REASONS] [I, T] to try to find reasons to explain your behaviour or emotions *I can't rationalize the way I feel towards him.* **2** [ORGANIZE] [T] *mainly UK* to improve the way a business is organized, usually by getting rid of people •**rationalization** /ˌræʃᵊnᵊlaɪˈzeɪʃᵊn/ *noun* [C, U]

ˌrational ˈnumber *noun* [C] **MATHEMATICS** a number that can be expressed as the ratio (= relationship expressed in numbers showing how much bigger one thing is than the other) of two whole numbers

the ˈrat ˌrace *noun informal* the unpleasant way that people compete against each other at work in order to succeed

rattle¹ /ˈrætl/ *verb* **1** [NOISE] [I, T] to make a noise like something knocking repeatedly, or to cause something to make this noise *The wind blew hard, rattling the doors and windows.* **2** [PERSON] [T] to make someone nervous [**often passive**] *He was clearly rattled by their angry reaction.*

rattle sth off *phrasal verb* to quickly say a list or something that you have learned *She can rattle off the names of all the players.*

rattle² /ˈrætl/ *noun* [C] a toy that a baby shakes to make a noise

rattlesnake /ˈrætlsneɪk/ *noun* [C] a poisonous snake found in southern parts of the US which makes a loud noise by shaking its tail

raucous /ˈrɔːkəs/ *adjective* loud and unpleasant ***raucous laughter***

ravage /ˈrævɪdʒ/ *verb* [T] to damage or destroy something [**often passive**] *The whole area has been ravaged by war.*

ravages /ˈrævɪdʒɪz/ *noun* [**plural**] **the ravages of disease/time/war, etc** the damaging effects of disease/time/war, etc

rave¹ /reɪv/ *verb* [I] **1** [EXCITED] to talk about something that you think is very good in an excited way *He went there last year and he's been **raving about** it ever since.* **2** [ANGRY] to talk in an angry, uncontrolled way

rave² /reɪv/ *noun* [C] **MUSIC** an event where people dance to modern, electronic music

raven /ˈreɪvᵊn/ *noun* [C] a large, black bird

ravenous /ˈrævᵊnəs/ *adjective* very hungry •**ravenously** *adverb*

R

ravine /rə'viːn/ *noun* [C] **GEOGRAPHY** a narrow, deep valley with very steep sides

raving /'reɪvɪŋ/ *adjective informal* completely uncontrolled *He was acting like a **raving lunatic**.*

ravings /'reɪvɪŋz/ *noun* [**plural**] the strange things that a crazy person says *the ravings of a madman*

ravishing /'rævɪʃɪŋ/ *adjective* very beautiful

raw /rɔː/ *adjective* **1 FOOD** not cooked ***raw meat**/vegetables* **2** in the natural state *raw materials* ○ *raw sugar* **3 HEALTH** If a part of the body is raw, the skin has come off and it is red and painful. •**rawness** *noun* [U] ➲See also: hit/touch a (raw) **nerve**

ray /reɪ/ *noun* **1 PHYSICS** [C] a narrow beam of light, heat, or energy *an ultraviolet ray* ○ *the rays of the sun* **2 a ray of hope/comfort, etc** a small amount of hope, etc ➲See also: **X-ray**

razor /'reɪzəʳ/ *noun* [C] a piece of equipment with a sharp blade used for removing hair from the face, legs, etc ➲See colour picture **The Bathroom** on page Centre 3

'razor ,blade *noun* [C] a very thin, sharp blade that you put in a razor

Rd *written abbreviation for* road *17, Lynton Rd*

re- /riː-/ *prefix* again *to remarry* ○ *a reusable container*

reach[1] /riːtʃ/ *verb* **1** ARRIVE [T] to arrive somewhere *We won't reach Miami till five or six o'clock.* **2** STRETCH [I, T] to stretch your arm and hand to touch or take something *She **reached for** a cigarette.* ○ *She **reached down** to stroke the dog's head.* ○ *He **reached out** and grabbed her arm.* **3 can reach (sth)** to be able to touch or take something with your hand *Could you get that book down for me - I can't reach.* **4** BE LONG ENOUGH [I, T] If something reaches, or reaches something, it is long enough to touch something. *The rope won't be long enough to reach the ground.* **5** LEVEL [T] to get to a particular level, situation, etc *We hope to reach our goal by May next year.* ○ *I've **reached the point** where I'm about to give up.* **6 reach a decision/agreement/conclusion, etc** to make a decision, agreement, etc about something **7** TELEPHONE [T] to speak to someone on the telephone *You can reach him at home.*

COMMON LEARNER ERROR

reach

When **reach** means 'arrive somewhere' or 'get to a particular level' it is not normally followed by a preposition.

We finally reached the hotel just after midnight.

The project has now reached the final stage.

~~*The project has now reached to the final stage.*~~

reach[2] /riːtʃ/ *noun* **1 out of/beyond (sb's) reach** too far away for someone to take hold of *I keep the medicines up here, out of the kids' reach.* **2 beyond (sb's) reach** not possible for someone to have *With all this money we can buy things previously beyond our reach.* **3 be within reach (of sth)** to be close enough to travel to *You'll be within easy reach of London.* **4 be within (sb's) reach a** to be close enough for someone to take hold of *The gun lay within reach.* **b** possible for someone to achieve *Winning the championship suddenly seemed within their reach.*

react /ri'ækt/ *verb* [I] **1** SAY/DO to say, do, or feel something because of something else that has been said or done *He **reacted** angrily **to** her comments.* **2** BAD EFFECT to become ill because something that you have eaten or used on your body has had a bad effect on you *My skin **reacts to** most perfumes.* **3 CHEMISTRY** In science, if a substance reacts with another substance, it changes. *Carbon **reacts with** oxygen to produce carbon dioxide.*

react against sth *phrasal verb* to do the opposite of what someone wants you to do because you do not like their rules or ideas

reactant /ri'æktənt/ *noun* [C] **CHEMISTRY** a chemical substance that reacts with another

WORD PARTNERS FOR ***reaction***

an **adverse / angry / immediate / initial / instinctive/negative/rapid** reaction • **gauge/produce/provoke** a reaction • a reaction **to/towards** sth

reaction /ri'ækʃᵊn/ *noun* **1** CAUSED BY SOMETHING [C, U] something you say, feel, or do because of something that has happened *What was his **reaction to** the news?* **2 reactions** *mainly UK* the ability to move quickly when something suddenly happens *Drivers need to have quick reactions.* **3** CHANGE [**no plural**] a change in the way people behave or think because they do not agree with the way people behaved or thought in the past *In art, there was a **reaction against** Realism.* **4 HEALTH** [C] an unpleasant feeling or illness caused by something you have eaten or used on your body *A number of people have **had a** bad **reaction to** this drug.* **5 CHEMISTRY** [C] a change which happens when two substances are put together *a **chemical reaction*** ➲See also: **chain reaction**

reactionary /ri'ækʃᵊnᵊri/ *adjective* **POLITICS** being against political or social progress •**reactionary** *noun* [C] someone who is against political or social progress

reactive /ri'æktɪv/ *adjective* **CHEMISTRY** reactive substances have a strong chemical change when they are mixed with other substances

reactivity /ˌriæk'tɪvəti/ *noun* [U] **CHEMISTRY** a measure of how much a substance reacts when it is mixed with another substance

reactor /ri'æktəʳ/ (*also* **nuclear reactor**) *noun* [C] **PHYSICS** a large machine which uses nuclear fuel to produce power

read[1] /riːd/ *verb past* **read** /red/ **1** WORDS [I, T] to look at words and understand what they mean *What was the last **book** you **read**?* ○ *I've been **reading about** John F Kennedy.* [+ **that**] *I've read that the economy is going to improve by the end of the year.* **2** SAY [I, T] to look at words that are written and say them aloud for other people to listen to *Do you want me to **read** it **to** you?* [+ **two objects**] *I **read** him a **story** at bedtime.* **3** SIGNS [T] to look at signs and be able to understand them *Can you **read** music?* **4 MEASURES** [T] to show the temperature, time, etc on a piece of measuring equipment *The thermometer read 20 degrees this* *morning.* ➲See also: **lip-read**

read sth into sth *phrasal verb* to believe that an action, remark, etc has a particular meaning when it has not *Don't read too much into anything he says.*

read sth out *phrasal verb* to read something and say the words aloud so that other people can hear *He read out the names of all the winners.*

read sth over/through *phrasal verb* to read something from the beginning to the end, especially to find mistakes *I read over my essay to check for errors.*

read² /riːd/ *noun* [**no plural**] **1** the act of reading something *It's not brilliant but it's worth a read.* **2 a good/easy, etc read** something that is enjoyable, easy, etc to read

readable /ˈriːdəbl/ *adjective* enjoyable and easy to read

reader /ˈriːdəʳ/ *noun* [**C**] someone who reads *She's a slow reader.*

readership /ˈriːdəʃɪp/ *noun* [**no plural**] the number and type of people who read a particular newspaper, magazine, etc *These magazines have a very young readership.*

readily /ˈredɪli/ *adverb* **1** EASILY quickly and easily *Information is **readily available** on the Internet.* **2** WILLINGLY willingly and without stopping to think *He **readily admits** to having problems himself.*

readiness /ˈredɪnəs/ *noun* [**U**] **1** WILLING when someone is willing to do something [**+ to do sth**] *They expressed a readiness to accept our demands.* **2** PREPARED when someone is prepared for something *It was time to repair their shelters **in readiness for** the winter.*

O→**reading** /ˈriːdɪŋ/ *noun* **1** ACTIVITY [**U**] the activity or skill of reading books *I **did** a lot of **reading** on holiday.* **2** EVENT [**C**] an event at which someone reads something to an audience *a **poetry reading*** **3 MEASURES** [**C**] the measurement that is shown on a piece of measuring equipment *It's best to **take** a meter **reading** as soon as you move in.*

readjust /ˌriːəˈdʒʌst/ *verb* **1** CHANGE BEHAVIOUR [**I**] to change in order to deal with a new situation, such as a new job or home *The children will have to **readjust to** a new school.* **2** SMALL CHANGE [**T**] to move something slightly or make a small change to something *He readjusted his tie.*

O→**ready** /ˈredi/ *adjective* **1** PREPARED [**never before noun**] prepared for doing something *Give me a call when you're ready.* [**+ to do sth**] *Are you ready to go yet?* ○ *We're going at eight, so you've got an hour to **get ready**.* ○ *The army was **ready for** action.* **2** AVAILABLE [**never before noun**] prepared and available to be eaten, drunk, used, etc *Is dinner ready?* ○ *When will the book be **ready for** publication?* **3 be ready to do sth** to be willing to do something *We are ready to die for our country.* ➲See also: **rough¹** and ready

ready-made /ˌrediˈmeɪd/ *adjective* made and ready to use ***ready-made meals***

ˈready ˌmeal *noun* [**C**] **FOOD** a meal that has already been cooked, that is bought at a shop but taken home to be heated and eaten

reagent /ˌriːˈeɪdʒənt/ *noun* [**C**] **CHEMISTRY** a substance which acts on another in a chemical reaction

O→**real¹** /rɪəl/ *adjective* **1** NOT IMAGINED existing and not imagined *Romance is never like that **in real life**.* **2** TRUE true and not pretended *What was the **real reason** she didn't come?* ○ *Is that your **real name**?* **3** NOT ARTIFICIAL not artificial or false *real fur/leather* ○ *It's not a toy gun, it's **the real thing**.* **4** FOR EMPHASIS [**always before noun**] used to emphasize a noun *She was a real help.* **5 Get real!** *informal* used to tell someone that they are hoping for something that will never happen, or that they believe something that is not true ➲See also: the real **McCoy**

real² /rɪəl/ *adverb US informal* very *It's real easy to get there from here.*

ˈreal esˌtate *noun* [**U**] *US* buildings and land

ˈreal estate ˌagent *US* (*UK* **estate agent**) *noun* [**C**] someone who sells buildings and land as their job

realism /ˈrɪəlɪzᵊm/ *noun* [**U**] **1 ART, LITERATURE** when things and people in art, literature, etc are shown as they are in real life **2** ACCEPTING when you accept and deal with the true facts of a situation and do not hope for things that will not happen

realist /ˈrɪəlɪst/ *noun* [**C**] **1** PERSON someone who accepts the true facts of a situation and does not hope for things that will not happen **2** ARTIST ETC an artist or writer who shows people and things in their work as they are in real life

realistic /ˌrɪəˈlɪstɪk/ *adjective* **1** ACCEPTING accepting the true facts of a situation and not basing decisions on things that will not happen *Let's be realistic - we're not going to finish this by Friday.* **2** SHOWING showing things and people as they really are, or making them seem to be real *realistic special effects in a film* ➲Opposite **unrealistic** •**realistically** *adverb*

WORD PARTNERS FOR ***reality***

face up to reality • **turn** [an idea/dream, etc] **into** reality • **lose touch with** reality • **in** reality

reality /riˈæləti/ *noun* **1** [**U**] the way things or situations really are and not the way you would like them to be *Sooner or later you have to **face up to reality**.* ○ *He may seem charming but **in reality** he's actually quite unpleasant.* **2 the reality/realities of sth** the truth about an unpleasant situation *the harsh realities of life* **3 become a reality** to start to happen or exist *New jobs could become a reality by next month.* ➲See also: **virtual reality**

reˌality TˈV *noun* [**U**] television programmes about ordinary people who are filmed in real situations

realizable (*also UK* **-isable**) /ˈrɪəlaɪzəbᵊl/ *adjective* **1** possible to do or make happen **2 FINANCE** able to be sold for money

ˌrealizable ˈvalue (*also UK* **-isable**) *noun* [**U**] **FINANCE** in a business, the amount that something is worth if it was sold

realization (*also UK* **-isation**) /ˌrɪəlaɪˈzeɪʃᵊn/ *noun* **1** NOTICING [**U, no plural**] when you notice or understand something that you did not notice or understand before [**+ that**] *There is a*

R

growing realization that education has benefits at many levels. **2** ACHIEVING [U] when you achieve something that you wanted *the* ***realization of*** *an* ***ambition***

O-m **realize** (*also UK* **-ise**) /'rɪəlaɪz/ *verb* [T] **1** to notice or understand something that you did not notice or understand before [+ **question word**] *I didn't realize how unhappy she was.* ○ *I suddenly realized I'd met him before.* [+ **(that)**] *Some people just don't seem to realize that the world has changed.* **2 realize an ambition/dream/goal, etc** to achieve something that you have wanted for a long time *He had realized all his ambitions by the age of 30.* **3 FINANCE** to sell things that you own *to realize your assets* **4 FINANCE** to be sold for a particular amount of money *The shares realized £1.4 million.*

O-m **really** /'rɪəli/ *adverb* **1** VERY very or very much *She's really nice.* ○ *I really don't want to go.* ○ *"Did you like it then?" "Er,* ***not really****"* (= no). **2** TRUTH used when you are saying what is the truth of a situation *She tried to hide what she was really thinking.* **3 Really?** used when you are surprised at what someone has just said *"Apparently, he's leaving." "Really?"*

realm /relm/ *noun* [C] **1** AREA *formal* an area of knowledge or activity *successes in the realm of foreign policy* **2 POLITICS** *literary* a country that has a king or queen

ˌreal ˈnumber *noun* [C] **MATHEMATICS** any number that is not an imaginary number ➲Compare **complex number, imaginary number**

real-time /'rɪəltaɪm/ *adjective* **COMPUTING** describes computing systems that are able to deal with and use new information immediately

realtor /'riːltəʳ/ *US* (*UK* **estate agent**) *noun* [C] someone who sells buildings or land as their job

reap /riːp/ *verb* **1 reap the benefits/profits/rewards** to get something good by working hard for it *Sometimes, this approach can reap tremendous rewards.* **2 FARMING** [I, T] to cut and collect a crop of grain

reappear /ˌriːə'pɪəʳ/ *verb* [I] to appear again or return after a period of time *He reappeared later that day.* •**reappearance** /ˌriːə'pɪərᵊns/ *noun* [C, U]

rear¹ /rɪəʳ/ *noun* **1 the rear** the back part of something *First class accommodation is towards the rear of the train.* **2 bring up the rear** to be at the back of a group of people who are walking or running •**rear** *adjective* [**always before noun**] *a rear window/wheel*

rear² /rɪəʳ/ *verb* **1 FARMING** [T] If you rear children or young animals, you care for them until they are adults. *In these waters they breed and rear their young.* **2** [I] (*also* **rear up**) If a horse rears, it stands on its back legs. ➲See also: raise/rear its ugly **head¹**

rearm /ˌriː'ɑːm/ *verb* [I, T] to supply yourself or others with new weapons •**rearmament** /ri'ɑːməmənt/ *noun* [U]

rearrange /ˌriːə'reɪndʒ/ *verb* [T] **1** POSITION to change the order or position of things *I've* ***rearranged the furniture.*** **2** EVENT to change the time of an event or meeting *I've* ***rearranged the meeting*** *for Monday.*

ˌrear-view ˈmirror *noun* [C] a small mirror inside a car which the driver looks in to see what is happening behind the car ➲See colour picture **Car** on page Centre 7

WORD PARTNERS FOR ***reason***

a **compelling/good/obvious/simple** reason • **have/give/understand** a reason • the reason **for** sth • the reason **why** sth happens

O-m **reason¹** /'riːzᵊn/ *noun* **1** WHY [C] the facts about why something happens or why someone does something *Is there any particular* ***reason why*** *he doesn't want to come?* ○ *He left without* ***giving a reason.*** ○ *That was the* ***reason for*** *telling her.* **2** RIGHT [C, U] something that makes it right for you to do something [+ **to do sth**] *There is* ***every reason*** *to believe the project will be finished on time.* **3** ABILITY [U] the ability to think and make good decisions *By this time he'd lost his powers of reason.* **4 within reason** If something is within reason, it is acceptable and possible. *You can have as much as you like, within reason.* **5 it stands to reason** If it stands to reason that something happens or is true, it is what you would expect. *It stands to reason that a child who is constantly criticized will have little self-confidence.*

COMMON LEARNER ERROR

reason

Be careful to choose the correct preposition.

That was the main ***reason for*** *the trip.*

~~*That was the main reason of the trip.*~~

reason² /'riːzᵊn/ *verb* [T] to decide that something is true after considering the facts [+ **that**] *We reasoned that it was unlikely he would be a serious threat to the public.*

reason with sb *phrasal verb* to persuade someone not to do something stupid by giving them good reasons not to

reasonable /'riːzᵊnəbl/ *adjective* **1** FAIR fair and showing good judgment [+ **to do sth**] *It's not reasonable to expect people to work those hours.* ➲Opposite **unreasonable** **2** BIG ENOUGH big enough or large enough in number, although not big or not many *There were a reasonable number of people there.* **3** GOOD ENOUGH good enough but not the best *I'd say her work is of a reasonable standard.* **4** CHEAP not expensive *reasonable prices*

reasonably /'riːzᵊnəbli/ *adverb* **1** in a fair way, showing good judgment *Why can't we discuss this reasonably, like adults?* **2 reasonably good/successful/well, etc** good/successful/well, etc enough but not very good or very well *I did reasonably well at school but not as well as my sister.* **3 reasonably priced** not expensive

reasoning /'riːzᵊnɪŋ/ *noun* [U] the process of thinking about something in order to make a decision *I don't understand the* ***reasoning behind*** *this decision.*

reassure /ˌriːə'ʃʊəʳ/ *verb* [T] to say something to stop someone from worrying [+ **that**] *He reassured me that I would be paid soon.* •**reassurance** /ˌriːə'ʃʊərᵊns/ *noun* [C, U] something that you say to make someone stop worrying *Despite my repeated reassurances that she was welcome, she wouldn't come.*

reassuring /ˌriːə'ʃʊərɪŋ/ *adjective* making you feel less worried *a reassuring smile/voice* •**reassuringly** *adverb*

R

rebate /ˈriːbeɪt/ *noun* [C] **FINANCE** an amount of money that is given back to you because you have paid too much *a **tax/rent rebate***

rebel[1] /ˈrebᵊl/ *noun* [C] **1 POLITICS** someone who fights against the government in their country, especially a soldier *Rebels seized control of the airport.* **2** someone who does not like authority and refuses to obey rules

rebel[2] /rɪˈbel/ *verb* [I] **rebelling**, *past* **rebelled 1 POLITICS** to fight against the government **2** to refuse to obey rules because you do not like authority *She **rebelled against** her family.*

WORD PARTNERS FOR ***rebellion***

launch/lead/quash/stage a rebellion • a rebellion **against** sb/sth • a rebellion **by** sb

rebellion /rɪˈbeliən/ *noun* [C, U] **POLITICS** when people fight against the government in their country

rebellious /rɪˈbeliəs/ *adjective* refusing to obey rules because you do not like authority *a rebellious teenager*

rebirth /ˈriːbɜːθ/ *noun* [no plural] when something becomes popular or active for the second time *the rebirth of the women's movement*

reboot /ˌriːˈbuːt/ *verb* [T, I] **COMPUTING** When a computer reboots, it switches off and then starts again immediately, and when you reboot a computer, you make it do this

rebound[1] /rɪˈbaʊnd/ *verb* [I] to move back through the air after hitting something *The ball **rebounded off** the post.*

rebound[2] /ˈriːbaʊnd/ *noun* **be on the rebound** to be unhappy because your romantic relationship has ended *She was on the rebound when she met her second husband.*

rebuff /rɪˈbʌf/ *verb* [T] *formal* to refuse someone's suggestion or offer, especially in an unfriendly way *The company has rebuffed several buyout offers.* •**rebuff** *noun* [C]

rebuild /ˌriːˈbɪld/ *verb* [T] *past* **rebuilt 1** [BUILD AGAIN] to build something again after it has been damaged *The cathedral was rebuilt after being destroyed by fire.* **2** [IMPROVE] to make a situation succeed again after something bad caused it to fail *The country is still struggling to rebuild its economy.*

rebuke /rɪˈbjuːk/ *verb* [T] *formal* to speak angrily to someone because they have done something wrong •**rebuke** *noun* [C] *formal*

recalcitrant /rɪˈkælsɪtrᵊnt/ *adjective formal* not willing to obey or help someone *recalcitrant schoolchildren*

recall /rɪˈkɔːl/ *verb* [T] **1** [REMEMBER] to remember something *I don't recall arranging a time to meet.* **2** [RETURN] to order the return of someone or something [**often passive**] *The ambassador was recalled to London.* •**recall** /ˈriːkɔːl/ *noun* [U]

recap /ˈriːkæp/ *verb* [I] **recapping**, *past* **recapped** to repeat the most important parts of what you have just said •**recap** /ˈriːkæp/ *noun* [C]

recapture /ˌriːˈkæptʃəʳ/ *verb* [T] **1** [CATCH] to catch a person or animal that has escaped **2** [EXPERIENCE] to experience or feel something from the past again *Some men try to **recapture** their **youth** by going out with younger women.*

recede /rɪˈsiːd/ *verb* [I] **1** [MOVE AWAY] to become further and further away *The coastline receded into the distance.* **2** [LESS STRONG] If a memory or feeling recedes, it becomes less clear or strong. **3** [HAIR] If a man's hair recedes, it stops growing at the front of his head. *a **receding hairline***

receipt /rɪˈsiːt/ *noun* **1 FINANCE** [C] a piece of paper that proves that you have received goods or money *Could I have a receipt?* ○ *Remember to keep **receipts for** any work done.* **2** [U] *formal* the act of receiving something *Items must be returned within fourteen days of receipt.*

receipts /rɪˈsiːts/ *US* (*UK* **takings**) *noun* [**plural**] **FINANCE** the amount of money that a business gets from selling things *box-office receipts*

O‑**receive** /rɪˈsiːv/ *verb* [T] **1** [GET] to get something that someone has given or sent to you *Occasionally, he **receives** letters **from** fans.* **2** [REACT] to react to a suggestion or piece of work in a particular way [**often passive**] *His first book was not **well received*** (= people did not like it). **3** [WELCOME] to formally welcome guests ➲See also: be on/at the receiving **end**[1] of sth

receiver /rɪˈsiːvəʳ/ *noun* [C] **1** [TELEPHONE] the part of a telephone that you hold in your hand and use for listening and speaking **2** [RADIO/TV] the part of a radio or television that receives signals from the air **3** [PERSON] someone who officially deals with a company when it has to stop business because it cannot pay the money it owes

O‑**recent** /ˈriːsᵊnt/ *adjective* happening or starting from a short time ago *a recent photo* ○ *In recent years, sales have decreased quite markedly.*

O‑**recently** /ˈriːsᵊntli/ *adverb* not long ago *Have you seen any good films recently?* ○ *Until recently he worked as a teacher.*

receptacle /rɪˈseptəkᵊl/ *noun* [C] **1** *formal* a container *Please put any waste in the receptacle provided.* **2 BIOLOGY** the part of a flower's stalk that the petals are attached to ➲See picture at **flower**

WORD PARTNERS FOR ***reception***

get/be given/receive a [cool/good, etc] reception • a **cool/chilly/frosty/hostile** reception • a **good/great/rapturous/warm** reception • a **lukewarm/mixed** reception • reception **from** sb

reception /rɪˈsepʃᵊn/ *noun* **1** [HOTEL/OFFICE] [**no plural**] the place in a hotel or office building where people go when they arrive *Ask for me **at reception**.* ○ *a reception area/desk* **2** [PARTY] [C] a formal party that is given to celebrate a special event or to welcome someone *a **wedding reception*** **3** [REACTION] [**no plural**] the way people react to something or someone *We were given a very **warm reception**.* **4** [RADIO/TV] [U] the quality of a radio or television signal

receptionist /rɪˈsepʃᵊnɪst/ *noun* [C] someone who works in a hotel or office building, answering the telephone and dealing with guests *a **hotel receptionist***

receptive /rɪˈseptɪv/ *adjective* willing to think about and accept new ideas *She's generally very **receptive to** ideas and suggestions.*

R

receptor /rɪ'septəʳ/ *noun* [C] **BIOLOGY** a nerve ending that reacts to a change, such as heat or cold, in the body by sending a message to the central nervous system

recess /rɪ'ses/ *noun* **1** NOT WORKING [C, U] a time in the day or in the year when a parliament or law court is not working *a parliamentary/congressional recess* ○ *The court is* ***in recess*** *for thirty minutes.* **2** **EDUCATION** [C, U] *US* (*UK* **break**) a period of free time between classes at school *At recess the boys would fight.* **3** WALL [C] a part of a wall in a room that is further back than the rest of the wall

recession /rɪ'seʃᵊn/ *noun* [C, U] **ECONOMICS** a time when the economy of a country is not successful *The latest report confirms that the economy is* ***in recession.***

recessive /rɪ'sesɪv/ *adjective* **BIOLOGY** A recessive gene causes a particular characteristic only when it is passed on by both parents. ➲Compare **dominant**

recharge /ˌriː'tʃɑːdʒ/ *verb* [T] to fill a battery (= object that provides a machine with power) with electricity so that it can work again

recipe /'resɪpi/ *noun* **1** [C] **FOOD** a list of foods and a set of instructions telling you how to cook something *a* ***recipe for*** *carrot cake* **2 be a recipe for disaster/trouble/success, etc** to be likely to become a disaster, a success, etc

recipient /rɪ'sɪpiənt/ *noun* [C] someone who receives something *a recipient of an award*

reciprocal¹ /rɪ'sɪprəkᵊl/ *adjective* involving two people or groups that agree to help each other in a similar way *a* ***reciprocal arrangement***

reciprocal² /rɪ'sɪprəkᵊl/ *noun* [C] **MATHEMATICS** a number that when multiplied with another particular number give the answer 1 *The reciprocal of 2 is 0.5.*

reciprocate /rɪ'sɪprəkeɪt/ *verb* [I, T] to do something for someone because they have done something similar for you

recital /rɪ'saɪtᵊl/ *noun* [C] **MUSIC** a performance of music or poetry *a piano recital*

R

recite /rɪ'saɪt/ *verb* [I, T] to say something aloud from memory *She can recite the whole poem.*

reckless /'rekləs/ *adjective* doing something dangerous and not caring about what might happen ***reckless driving*** •**recklessly** *adverb*

reckon /'rekᵊn/ *verb* [T] **1** THINK to think that something is probably true *I reckon he likes her.* [+ (that)] *He reckons that he earns more in a week than I do in a month.* **2** NUMBER to guess that a particular number is correct *His fortune is* ***reckoned at*** *$5 million.* ➲See also: a **force¹** to be reckoned with

reckon on sth/doing sth *phrasal verb* to think that something is going to happen and make it part of your plans

reckon with sb/sth *phrasal verb* to deal with someone or something difficult

reclaim /rɪ'kleɪm/ *verb* [T] **1** to get something back from someone *You can reclaim the tax at the airport.* **2** **FARMING** to make land good enough to be used for growing crops

recline /rɪ'klaɪn/ *verb* **1** PERSON [I] to lie back with the upper part of your body in a horizontal position *I found him* ***reclining on*** *the sofa.* **2** CHAIR [I, T] If a chair reclines, you can lower the back part so that you can lie in it, and if you recline a chair, you put it in this position. ***a reclining chair/seat***

recluse /rɪ'kluːs/ *noun* [C] someone who lives alone and does not like being with other people •**reclusive** *adjective* living alone and avoiding other people

WORD PARTNERS FOR ***recognition***

achieve/deserve/gain recognition • **in** recognition **of** sth • recognition **for** sth

recognition /ˌrekəg'nɪʃᵊn/ *noun* **1** ACCEPT [U, no plural] when you accept that something is true or real *There is a growing* ***recognition of*** *the scale of the problem.* [+ that] *There is a general recognition that she's the best person for the job.* **2** HONOUR [U] when someone is publicly thanked for something good that they have done *Ellen* ***gained recognition for*** *her outstanding work.* ○ *He was given a medal* ***in recognition of*** *his bravery.* **3** KNOW [U] when you know something or someone because you have seen or experienced them before *I waved at her, but she showed no sign of recognition.*

recognizable (*also UK* **-isable**) /'rekəgnaɪzəbl/ *adjective* able to be recognized (= able to be known) *Megan's voice is instantly recognizable.* •**recognizably** *adverb*

O- **recognize** (*also UK* **-ise**) /'rekəgnaɪz/ *verb* [T] **1** KNOW to know someone or something because you have seen or experienced them before *I recognized her from her picture.* ○ *Doctors are trained to recognize the symptoms of disease.* **2** ACCEPT to accept that something is true or real [+ (that)] *She recognized that she had been partly to blame.* ○ *Smoking is* ***recognized as*** *a leading cause of lung cancer.* **3** SHOW RESPECT to officially show respect for someone for an achievement *He was recognized by the governor for his work with teenagers.*

recoil /rɪ'kɔɪl/ *verb* [I] to react to something with fear or hate *She* ***recoiled in*** *horror at the thought of touching a snake.*

recollect /ˌrekᵊl'ekt/ *verb* [T] to remember something *I didn't recollect having seen him.*

recollection /ˌrekᵊl'ekʃᵊn/ *noun* [C, U] when you remember something *He* ***had*** *no* ***recollection*** *of the incident.*

O- **recommend** /ˌrekə'mend/ *verb* [T] **1** SUITABLE to say that someone or something is good or suitable for a particular purpose *Can you recommend a good wine to go with this dish?* ○ *She has been* ***recommended for*** *promotion.* **2** ADVISE to advise someone that something should be done *The judge is likely to recommend a long jail sentence.* [+ that] *The report recommended that tourists avoid the region.*

WORD PARTNERS FOR ***recommendation***

accept/follow/implement/make a recommendation • a recommendation **for/on** sth

recommendation /ˌrekəmen'deɪʃᵊn/ *noun* **1** ADVICE [C] a piece of advice about what to do in a particular situation *The marketing department* ***made*** *several* ***recommendations*** *to improve sales.* [+ that] *It's my recommendation that this factory be closed immediately.*

2 SUITABLE [C, U] a suggestion that someone or something is good or suitable for a particular purpose *I bought this book* ***on*** *Andy's* ***recommendation.***

recompense /'rekəmpens/ *noun* [U] *formal* payment that you give to someone when you have caused them difficulty or an injury *Angry soccer fans sought* ***recompense for*** *the cancelled match.* •**recompense** *verb* [T] *formal He was* ***recompensed for*** *loss of earnings.*

reconcile /'rekᵊnsaɪl/ *verb* [T] **1** to make two different ideas, beliefs, or situations agree or able to exist together *It is sometimes difficult to reconcile science and religion.* ○ *How can you* ***reconcile*** *your love of animals* ***with*** *your habit of eating them?* **2 be reconciled (with sb)** to become friendly with someone after you have argued with them

reconcile yourself to sth *phrasal verb* to accept a situation although you do not like it *Eventually he reconciled himself to living without her.*

reconciliation /ˌrekᵊnˌsɪli'eɪʃᵊn/ *noun* **1** BECOME FRIENDLY [C, U] when two people or groups become friendly again after they have argued *to* ***seek a reconciliation*** **2** AGREE [U, no plural] the process of making two opposite ideas, beliefs, or situations agree *the reconciliation of facts with theory*

reconnaissance /rɪ'kɒnɪsᵊns/ *noun* [U] the process of getting information about a place or an area for military use

reconsider /ˌriːkᵊn'sɪdəʳ/ *verb* [I, T] to think again about a decision or opinion and decide if you want to change it *We've been asked to reconsider the proposal.* •**reconsideration** /ˌriːkᵊnˌsɪdᵊr'eɪʃᵊn/ *noun* [U]

reconstruct /ˌriːkᵊn'strʌkt/ *verb* [T] **1** PAST EVENT to create a description of a past event using all the information that you have *The police tried to reconstruct the crime using evidence found at the scene.* **2** BUILD AGAIN to build something again after it has been damaged or destroyed

reconstruction /ˌriːkᵊn'strʌkʃᵊn/ *noun* [C, U] **1** PAST EVENT when you create a description of a past event using all the information that you have *A reconstruction of the crime was shown on TV.* **2** BUILD AGAIN when you build something again after it has been damaged or destroyed

WORD PARTNERS FOR ***record***

have/keep a record • records **indicate/reveal/show** sth • a record **of** sth • [the hottest/the lowest, etc] **on** record

O━**record¹** /'rekɔːd/ *noun* **1** STORED INFORMATION [C, U] information that is written on paper or stored on computer so that it can be used in the future ***medical/dental records*** ○ *My teacher* ***keeps a record of*** *my absences.* ○ *This has been the hottest summer* ***on record*** (= the hottest summer known about). **2** BEHAVIOUR [C] A person's or company's record is their behaviour or achievements. [**usually singular**] *She has an outstanding academic record* (= has done very well in school). ○ *Of all airlines they have the best* ***safety record.*** **3** BEST [C] the best, biggest, longest, tallest, etc *to* ***set/break a record*** ○ *He* ***holds the*** *world* ***record*** *for 100 metres.* **4 MUSIC** [C] a flat, round, plastic disc that music is stored on, used especially in the past *to play a record* **5 off the record** If you say something off the record, you do not want the public to know about it. **6 put/set the record straight** to tell people the true facts about a situation **7 COMPUTING** a collection of pieces of information in a computer database that is treated as one unit *You can sort the records on any field.* ➲See also: **track record**

O━**record²** /rɪ'kɔːd/ *verb* **1** STORE INFORMATION [T] to write down information or store it on a computer so that it can be used in the future *He* ***recorded details of*** *their conversation in his diary.* **2** STORE SOUNDS/PICTURES [I, T] to store sounds or pictures using electronic equipment, a camera, etc so that you can listen to them or see them again *to record a new album* ○ *a* ***recorded message***

record-breaking /'rekɔːdˌbreɪkɪŋ/ *adjective* [**always before noun**] better, bigger, longer, etc than anything else before *record-breaking sales of the new video*

recorder /rɪ'kɔːdəʳ/ *noun* [C] **1** a machine for storing sounds or pictures *a video recorder* **2 MUSIC** a long, thin, hollow instrument that you play by blowing into it ➲See also: **cassette recorder, tape recorder**

recording /rɪ'kɔːdɪŋ/ *noun* [C, U] sounds or moving pictures that have been recorded, or the process of recording *a recording of classical music* ○ *a new system of digital recording*

'record ˌlabel *noun* [C] **MUSIC** a company that records and sells music

'record ˌplayer *noun* [C] **MUSIC** a machine that makes it possible to hear the music on a record (= a flat, round disc)

recount¹ /rɪ'kaʊnt/ *verb* [T] *formal* to tell a story or describe an event *He was* ***recounting*** *a* ***story*** *about a woman he'd met on a train.*

recount² /ˌriː'kaʊnt/ *verb* [T] to count something again

recount³ /'riːkaʊnt/ *noun* [C] **POLITICS** a second count of votes in an election *They* ***demanded a recount.***

recoup /rɪ'kuːp/ *verb* [T] to get back money that you have lost or spent *to* ***recoup*** *your* ***losses***

recourse /rɪ'kɔːs/ *noun* [U] *formal* someone or something that can help you in a difficult situation *For many cancer patients, surgery is the* ***only recourse.*** ○ *They solved their problem* ***without recourse to*** (= without using) *violence.*

O━**recover** /rɪ'kʌvəʳ/ *verb* **1 HEALTH** [I] to become healthy or happy again after an illness, injury, or period of sadness *It takes a long time to* ***recover from*** *surgery.* ○ *She never* ***recovered from*** *the death of her husband.* **2** SITUATION [I] If a system or situation recovers, it returns to the way it was before something bad happened. *The economy was quick to recover after the election.* **3** BODY [T] to be able to use or feel again part of your body which has been damaged *He never fully recovered the use of his legs.* **4** GET BACK [T] to get something back that has been lost or stolen *Police recovered the stolen money.*

R

WORD PARTNERS FOR *recovery*

make a recovery • a **full/miraculous/slow/speedy** recovery • recovery **from** sth

recovery /rɪˈkʌvəri/ *noun* **1 HEALTH [U, no plural]** when you feel better or happier again after an illness, injury, or period of sadness *She only had the operation last month but she's* ***made a*** *good* ***recovery***. **2** SITUATION **[U, no plural]** when a system or situation returns to the way it was before something bad happened ***economic recovery*** ○ *The housing industry has* ***made a*** *remarkable* ***recovery***. **3** GET BACK **[U]** when you get back something that was lost or stolen *the recovery of stolen jewels*

recreate /ˌriːkriˈeɪt/ *verb* **[T]** to make something exist or happen again *They plan to recreate a typical English village in Japan.*

recreation /ˌrekriˈeɪʃən/ *noun* **[C, U]** activities that you do for enjoyment when you are not working *Shopping seems to be her only form of recreation.* **•recreational** *adjective*

recrimination /rɪˌkrɪmɪˈneɪʃən/ *noun* **[C, U]** *formal* the things you say when you blame someone for something, or the act of blaming someone for something

recruit¹ /rɪˈkruːt/ *verb* **[I, T]** to try to persuade someone to work for a company or to join an organization **•recruitment** *noun* **[U]** when you recruit people *graduate recruitment*

WORD PARTNERS FOR *recruit*

a **new** recruit • a recruit **to** sth

recruit² /rɪˈkruːt/ *noun* **[C]** someone who has recently joined an organization *a* ***new recruit***

rectangle /ˈrektæŋgl/ *noun* **[C]** a shape with four 90° angles and four sides, with opposite sides of equal length and two sides longer than the other two ➲See picture at **shape** ➲See picture at **shape** ➲See picture at **parallelogram •rectangular** /rekˈtæŋgjələr/ *adjective* shaped like a rectangle *a rectangular room*

rectify /ˈrektɪfaɪ/ *verb* **[T]** *formal* to correct something or change it so that it is acceptable *The government has promised to* ***rectify*** *the* ***situation***.

rector /ˈrektər/ *noun* **[C] RELIGION** a priest in some Christian churches

rectum /ˈrektəm/ *noun* **[C] ANATOMY** the last part of the body that solid waste travels through before coming out of the bottom ➲See picture at **alimentary canal**

recuperate /rɪˈkuːpəreɪt/ *verb* **[I] HEALTH** to become healthy again after an illness or injury *She's still* ***recuperating from*** *her injuries.* **•recuperation** /rɪˌkjuːpərˈeɪʃən/ *noun* **[U]**

recur /rɪˈkɜːr/ *verb* **[I] recurring**, *past* **recurred** to happen again or many times *The same ideas recur throughout her books.* **•recurrence** /rɪˈkʌrəns/ *noun* **[C, U]** when something recurs *a recurrence of the disease*

recurring /rɪˈkɜːrɪŋ/ (*also* **recurrent**) *adjective* happening again or many times *a* ***recurring dream***

reˌcurring ˈnumber *noun* **[C] MATHEMATICS** a number that repeats itself forever following a decimal point, such as 7.143333...

recycle /ˌriːˈsaɪkl/ *verb* **[I, T] ENVIRONMENT** to put used paper, glass, plastic, etc through a process so that it can be used again *We recycle all our newspapers and bottles.* **•recyclable** /ˌriːˈsaɪkləbl/ *adjective* able to be recycled *Glass is recyclable.*

recycled /ˌriːˈsaɪkld/ *adjective* **ENVIRONMENT** Recycled paper, glass, plastic, etc has been used before and put through a process so that it can be used again.

recycling /ˌriːˈsaɪklɪŋ/ *noun* **[U] ENVIRONMENT** when paper, glass, plastic, etc is put through a process so that it can be used again *ways to encourage recycling* ○ *a recycling centre*

O-ꟷ**red¹** /red/ *adjective* **redder, reddest 1** COLOUR being the same colour as blood *a red shirt* ➲See colour picture **Colours** on page Centre 12 **2** HAIR Red hair is an orange-brown colour. **3 go red** *UK* (*US* **turn red**) If someone goes red, their face becomes red because they are embarrassed or angry. **4 FOOD** Red wine is made from black grapes (= small, round, purple fruits). ➲See also: be like a red **rag** to a bull

O-ꟷ**red²** /red/ *noun* **1 [C, U]** the colour of blood ➲See colour picture **Colours** on page Centre 12 **2 in the red FINANCE** If your bank account is in the red, you have spent more money than there was in it. **3 see red** to become very angry

ˌred ˈblood ˌcell *noun* **[C] BIOLOGY** any of the cells that carry oxygen around the body ➲Compare **white blood cell**

ˌred ˈcard *noun* **[C] SPORT** in football, a small red card which the referee (= someone who makes sure the players follow the rules) shows to a player to make him stop playing because he has broken a rule

the ˌred ˈcarpet *noun* special treatment that is given to an important person when they go somewhere *She's given* ***the red carpet treatment*** *wherever she goes.*

redden /ˈredən/ *verb* **[I, T]** to become red or to make something become red *His face reddened with anger.*

redeem /rɪˈdiːm/ *verb* **[T] 1** IMPROVE to make something seem less bad *He tried to* ***redeem his reputation*** *by working extra hard.* ○ ***a redeeming feature*** **2 redeem yourself** to do something that makes people have a better opinion of you after you have done something bad *He was two hours late, but he redeemed himself by bringing presents.* **3** GET SOMETHING to exchange something for something else **4 RELIGION** to save someone from evil, especially according to the Christian religion

redemption /rɪˈdemʃən/ *noun* **1 RELIGION [U]** when someone is saved from evil, especially according to the Christian religion **2 be beyond redemption** to be too bad to be improved or saved

redeploy /ˌriːdɪˈplɔɪ/ *verb* **[T]** to move employees, soldiers, equipment, etc to a different place or use them in a more effective way **•redeployment** *noun* **[C, U]** when you redeploy someone or something

redevelop /ˌriːdɪˈveləp/ *verb* **[T]** to make a place more modern by improving old buildings or building new ones *There are plans to redevelop*

R

the city's waterfront area. •**redevelopment** *noun* [C, U] when a place is redeveloped

ˌ**red ˈgiant** *noun* [C] **ASTRONOMY** a large star with a low surface temperature

red-handed /ˌredˈhændɪd/ *adverb* **catch sb red-handed** *informal* to discover someone doing something wrong *He was caught red-handed trying to steal a car.*

redhead /ˈredhed/ *noun* [C] someone who has red hair

ˌ**red ˈherring** *noun* [C] a fact or idea that takes your attention away from something that is important

red-hot /ˌredˈhɒt/ *adjective* extremely hot

redirect /ˌriːdɪˈrekt/ *verb* [T] **1** CHANGE DIRECTION to send something in a different direction *Traffic should be redirected away from the city centre.* **2** USE DIFFERENTLY to use money, energy, etc for a different purpose *Money spent on weapons could be* ***redirected to*** *hospitals and schools.*

redistribute /ˌriːdɪˈstrɪbjuːt/ *verb* [T] to share money, land, power, etc between people in a different way from before *to* ***redistribute wealth*** •**redistribution** /ˌriːdɪstrɪˈbjuːʃᵊn/ *noun* [U] the process of redistributing something

ˌ**red ˈmeat** *noun* [U] **FOOD** meat from animals and not birds or fish

redo /ˌriːˈduː/ *verb* [T] to do something again *I'm going to have to redo that report.*

redox /ˈriːdɒks/ *noun* [U] **CHEMISTRY** a chemical process where an atom, molecule, etc. either gains or loses electrons *a redox reaction*

redress¹ /rɪˈdres/ *verb* [T] *formal* to correct something that is wrong, unfair, or not equal *laws aimed at redressing racial inequality*

redress² /rɪˈdres/ (US) /ˈriːdres/ *noun* [U] *formal* payment for an action or situation that is wrong or unfair

ˌ**red ˈtape** *noun* [U] official rules that do not seem necessary and make things happen very slowly

O⁻**reduce** /rɪˈdjuːs/ *verb* [T] **1** to make something less *to reduce air pollution* ○ *The number of employees was* ***reduced from*** *500* ***to*** *300.* **2** **CHEMISTRY** to add one or more electrons to a substance or to remove oxygen from a substance

reduce sb to sth/doing sth *phrasal verb* to make someone unhappy or cause them to be in a bad situation *She was* ***reduced to tears*** *by his comments.*

reduce sth to sth *phrasal verb* to destroy something, especially something that has been built *The earthquake reduced the city to rubble.*

reˈducing ˌagent *noun* [C] **CHEMISTRY** a substance that reduces (= adds one or more electrons to) another substance

WORD PARTNERS FOR ***reduction***

a **dramatic/drastic/sharp/significant** reduction • a reduction **in** sth

reduction /rɪˈdʌkʃᵊn/ *noun* [C, U] **1** when something is reduced *She refused to accept a* ***reduction in*** *wages.* ○ *price reductions* **2** **CHEMISTRY** the process of adding one or more electrons to a substance or removing oxygen from a substance

redundancy /rɪˈdʌndənsi/ *noun* **1** **ECONOMICS** [C, U] *UK* when your employer makes you stop working because there is not enough work *There have been a lot of redundancies in the mining industry.* **2** EXTRA [U] when something is not needed or used because there are other similar or more modern things

redundant /rɪˈdʌndənt/ *adjective* **1** **ECONOMICS** *UK* not working because your employer has told you there is not enough work *Eight thousand people have been* ***made redundant*** *in Britain this year.* **2** NOT NEEDED *UK* not needed or used any more because there are other similar or more modern things *redundant weapons* **3** TOO MUCH more than is needed, especially extra words that mean the same thing

redwood /ˈredwʊd/ *noun* [C, U] a very tall tree that grows on the west coast of the US, or the wood of this tree

reed /riːd/ *noun* [C] a tall, stiff plant like grass that grows near water

reef /riːf/ *noun* [C] **GEOGRAPHY** a line of rocks or sand near the surface of the sea *a* ***coral reef***

reek /riːk/ *verb* [I] to have a very unpleasant smell *The whole room* ***reeked of*** *sweat.* •**reek** *noun* [**no plural**]

reel¹ /riːl/ *verb* [I] **1** FEEL SHOCK to feel very shocked *She was still* ***reeling from*** *the news of his death.* **2** WALK to walk in a way that looks as if you are going to fall over *He came reeling down the street like a drunk.*

reel sth off *phrasal verb* to say a long list of things quickly and without stopping *She* ***reeled off*** *a* ***list*** *of all the countries she'd been to.*

reel² /riːl/ *noun* [C] an object shaped like a wheel that you can roll film, thread, etc around

re-elect /ˌriːɪˈlekt/ *verb* [T] **POLITICS** to elect someone again to a particular position

re-election /ˌriːɪˈlekʃᵊn/ *noun* [C, U] **POLITICS** when someone is elected again to the same position *She's (UK)* ***standing for****/ (US)* ***running for*** *re-election* (= she wants to be re-elected).

ref /ref/ *noun* [C] **SPORT** *informal short for* referee

refer /rɪˈfɜːʳ/ *verb* **referring**, *past* **referred**

refer to sb/sth *phrasal verb* **1** SAY to talk or write about someone or something, especially briefly *She didn't once refer to her son.* ○ *He always* ***referred to*** *his father* ***as*** *'the old man'.* **2** RELATE TO If writing or information refers to someone or something, it relates to that person or thing. *The sales figures refer to UK sales only.*

refer to sth *phrasal verb* to read something in order to get information *Please refer to your owner's manual for more information.*

refer sb/sth to sb/sth *phrasal verb* to send someone or something to a different place or person for information or help *My doctor referred me to a specialist.*

referee¹ /ˌrefᵊrˈiː/ *noun* [C] **SPORT** someone who makes sure that players follow the rules

R

during a sports game ⊃See colour picture **Sports 2** on page Centre 15

referee² /ˌrefᵊr'iː/ *verb* [I, T] **refereeing**, *past* **refereed** SPORT to be the referee in a sports game

reference /'refᵊrᵊns/ *noun* **1** [SAY] [C, U] when you briefly talk or write about someone or something *In his book, he* ***makes*** *several* ***references to*** *his time in France.* **2 with/in reference to sth** *formal* relating to something *I am writing to you with reference to the job advertised in yesterday's newspaper.* **3** [LOOK AT] [C, U] when you look at information, or the thing that you look at for information *Please keep this handout for* ***future reference*** (= to look at in the future). **4** [LETTER] [C] a letter that is written by someone who knows you, to say if you are suitable for a job or course ⊃See also: **cross reference**

'reference ˌbook *noun* [C] a book that you look at in order to find information

referendum /ˌrefᵊr'endəm/ *noun* [C] **POLITICS** an occasion when all the people in a country can vote in order to show their opinion about a political question

referral /rɪ'fɜːrᵊl/ *noun* [C, U] **HEALTH** when someone or something is sent to a different place or person for information or help

refill /ˌriː'fɪl/ *verb* [T] to fill something again *He got up and* ***refilled*** *their* ***glasses.*** •**refill** /'riːfɪl/ *noun* [C]

refine /rɪ'faɪn/ *verb* [T] **1** [MAKE PURE] to make a substance pure by removing other substances from it **2** [IMPROVE] to improve an idea, method, system, etc by making small changes *The engineers spent months refining the software.*

refined /rɪ'faɪnd/ *adjective* **1** [PURE] A refined substance has been made more pure by removing other substances from it. *refined sugar* **2** [POLITE] very polite and showing knowledge of social rules **3** [IMPROVED] improved by many small changes *a refined method*

refinement /rɪ'faɪnmənt/ *noun* **1** [IMPROVEMENT] [C, U] a small change that improves something *Several* ***refinements*** *have been* ***made*** *to improve the car's performance.* **2** [POLITE] [U] polite behaviour and knowledge of social rules *a woman of refinement* **3** [PURE] [U] the process of making a substance pure

refinery /rɪ'faɪnᵊri/ *noun* [C] a factory where substances, such as sugar, oil, etc are made pure

reflect /rɪ'flekt/ *verb* **1** [SHOW] [T] to show or be a sign of something *The statistics reflect a change in people's spending habits.* **2 PHYSICS** [T] If a surface reflects heat, light, sound, etc, it sends the light, etc back and does not absorb it. **3 PHYSICS** [I, T] If a surface such as a mirror or water reflects something, you can see the image of that thing in the mirror, water, etc. *He saw himself* ***reflected in*** *the shop window.* **4** [THINK] [I] *formal* to think in a serious and careful way *In prison, he had plenty of time to* ***reflect on*** *the crimes he had committed.*

reflect on sb/sth *phrasal verb* If something reflects on someone or something, it affects other people's opinion of them, especially in a bad way. *The whole affair* ***reflects badly*** *on the government.*

re'flected ˌray *noun* [C] **PHYSICS** a ray of light that is reflected from a surface ⊃Compare **incident ray**

reflection /rɪ'flekʃᵊn/ *noun* **1 PHYSICS** [C] the image of something in a mirror, on a shiny surface, etc *I saw my reflection in the window.* **2** [C, U] *formal* when you think in a serious and careful way *He paused for reflection before answering my question.* ○ ***On reflection*** (= after thinking again), *I think I was wrong.* **3 a reflection of sth** something that is a sign or result of a particular situation *His poor job performance is a reflection of his lack of training.* **4 a reflection on sb/sth** something that makes people have a particular opinion about someone or something, especially a bad opinion *Low test scores are a sad reflection on our school system.*

reflective /rɪ'flektɪv/ *adjective* **1** [THINK] thinking carefully and quietly *a reflective mood* **2** [SEE] A reflective surface is one that you can see easily when a light shines on it. *a jacket made of reflective material*

reflex /'riːfleks/ *noun* [C] **BIOLOGY** a physical reaction that you cannot control *Shivering and blushing are reflexes.*

'reflex ˌaction *noun* [C] **1** something that you do without thinking about it because of something that happens to you or near you *I don't know what made me protect my face - it was just a reflex action.* **2 BIOLOGY** an action of the muscles that is caused by something outside the body, and for which the nerve signals do not go through the brain but to a point in the back

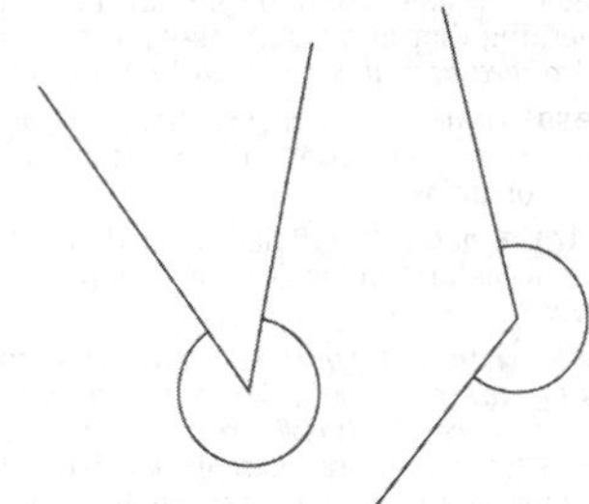

reflex angles

'reflex ˌangle *noun* [C] **MATHEMATICS** an angle that is more than 180° and less than 360°

'reflex ˌarc *noun* [C] **BIOLOGY** the way nerve signals move to a point in a person's back in order to produce a reflex action

re'flexes /'riːfleksɪz/ *noun* [plural] your ability to react quickly *A boxer needs to have* ***good reflexes.***

reflexive /rɪ'fleksɪv/ *adjective* **LANGUAGE** A reflexive verb or pronoun is used to show that the person who does the action is also the person who is affected by it. In the sentence 'I looked at myself in the mirror.', 'myself' is a reflexive pronoun.

reflexology /ˌriːflek'sɒlədʒi/ *noun* [U] **HEALTH** the treatment of your feet by rubbing and pressing them in a special way in order to make the blood flow and help you relax

WORD PARTNERS FOR ***reform***

introduce/propose a reform • a **major/radical/sweeping** reform • reform **in/of** sth • **economic/political** reform

reform¹ /rɪˈfɔːm/ *noun* [C, U] when changes are made to improve a system, organization, or law, or a change that is made ***economic/political reform***

reform² /rɪˈfɔːm/ *verb* **1** IMPROVE [T] to change a system, organization, or law in order to improve it *efforts to reform the education system* **2** BEHAVIOUR [I, T] to change your behaviour and stop doing bad things, or to make someone else do this *a programme to reform criminals* ○ *a reformed drug addict*

reformer /rɪˈfɔːməʳ/ *noun* [C] someone who tries to improve a system or law by changing it *a **social reformer***

refract /rɪˈfrækt/ *verb* [T] **PHYSICS** When water or glass, etc. refracts light or sound, etc., it causes it to change direction or to separate when it travels through it.

refraction /rɪˈfrækʃᵊn/ *noun* [U] **1 PHYSICS** when the direction of light, sound, etc. is changed by moving through water, glass, etc **2 BIOLOGY** when the lens (= curved part at the front of the eye) of the eye bends light so that the retina (= back part of the eye that sends messages to the brain) gets the correct image

refrain¹ /rɪˈfreɪn/ *verb* [I] *formal* to stop yourself from doing something [+ **from** + **doing sth**] *Please **refrain from** talking during the performance.*

refrain² /rɪˈfreɪn/ *noun* [C] **1** *formal* a phrase or idea that you repeat often *'Every vote counts' is a familiar refrain in politics.* **2 LITERATURE, MUSIC** a part of a song that you repeat

refresh /rɪˈfreʃ/ *verb* **1** [T] to make you feel less hot or tired *A cool drink should refresh you.* **2 COMPUTING, INTERNET** [I, T] to make the most recent information on an Internet page appear on your computer **3 refresh sb's memory** to help someone remember something

refreshing /rɪˈfreʃɪŋ/ *adjective* **1** DIFFERENT different and interesting *a **refreshing change*** [+ **to do sth**] *It's refreshing to see a film that's so original.* **2** FEEL BETTER making you feel less hot or tired *a refreshing shower/swim* •**refreshingly** *adverb*

refreshments /rɪˈfreʃmənts/ *noun* [plural] **FOOD** food and drinks that are available at a meeting, event, on a journey, etc *Refreshments are available in the lobby.*

refrigerate /rɪˈfrɪdʒᵊreɪt/ *verb* [T] to make or keep food cold so that it stays fresh *You should refrigerate any leftover food immediately.* •**refrigeration** /rɪˌfrɪdʒᵊrˈeɪʃᵊn/ *noun* [U]

refrigerated /rɪˈfrɪdʒəreɪtɪd/ *adjective* **1** CONTAINER/VEHICLE A refrigerated container or vehicle keeps the things inside it cold. **2** FOOD/DRINK Refrigerated food or drink is cold because it has been kept in a refrigerator.

refrigerator /rɪˈfrɪdʒᵊreɪtəʳ/ *noun* [C] a large container that uses electricity to keep food cold ➲See colour picture **The Kitchen** on page Centre 2

refuel /ˌriːˈfjuːəl/ *verb* [I, T] to put more fuel into an aircraft, ship, etc so that it can continue its journey

refuge /ˈrefjuːdʒ/ *noun* **1** PROTECTION [U] protection from danger or unpleasant conditions *We **took refuge from** the storm in an old barn.* **2** PLACE [C] a place where you are protected from danger *a refuge for homeless people*

refugee /ˌrefjʊˈdʒiː/ *noun* [C] **POLITICS** someone who has been forced to leave their country, especially because of a war *a refugee camp*

WORD PARTNERS FOR ***refund***

claim/give sb /**get** a refund • a **full** refund • a refund **of** sth

refund¹ /ˈriːfʌnd/ *noun* [C] **FINANCE** an amount of money that is given back to you, especially because you are not happy with something you have bought *The holiday company apologized and gave us a **full refund**.*

refund² /ˌriːˈfʌnd/ *verb* [T] **FINANCE** to give back money that someone has paid to you

refurbish /ˌriːˈfɜːbɪʃ/ *verb* [T] *formal* to repair or improve a building •**refurbishment** *noun* [C, U] the process of refurbishing a building *The library was **closed for refurbishment**.*

refusal /rɪˈfjuːzᵊl/ *noun* [C, U] when someone refuses to do or accept something [+ **to do sth**] *his refusal to admit his mistake*

O-ᵜ**refuse¹** /rɪˈfjuːz/ *verb* [I, T] to say that you will not do or accept something *I asked him to leave but he refused.* [+ **to do sth**] *Cathy refuses to admit that she was wrong.*

refuse² /ˈrefjuːs/ *noun* [U] *formal* waste *a pile of refuse*

refute /rɪˈfjuːt/ *verb* [T] *formal* to say or prove that something is not true or correct *attempts to **refute** his **theory*** ○ *She angrily **refuted** their **claims**.*

regain /rɪˈgeɪn/ *verb* [T] to get something back again *Armed troops have **regained control** of the capital.* ○ *It was several hours before he **regained consciousness**.*

regal /ˈriːgᵊl/ *adjective* very special and suitable for a king or queen *a regal dress*

regard¹ /rɪˈgɑːd/ *verb* [T] **1** THINK OF to think of someone or something in a particular way *She is generally **regarded as** one of the greatest singers this century.* ○ *The plans were **regarded with** suspicion.* **2** LOOK *formal* to look carefully at someone or something

regard² /rɪˈgɑːd/ *noun* **1** [U] respect or admiration for someone or something *I **have** the greatest **regard for** her.* ➲Opposite **disregard** **2 in/with regard to sth** *formal* relating to something *I am writing in regard to your letter of 24 June.*

regarding /rɪˈgɑːdɪŋ/ *preposition formal* about or relating to *I am writing to you regarding your application dated 29 April.*

regardless /rɪˈgɑːdləs/ *adverb* **1 regardless of sth** despite something *She'll make a decision*

R

regardless of what we think. **2** without thinking about problems or difficulties *Mr Redwood claimed he would carry on with his campaign regardless.*

regards /rɪ'gɑːdz/ *noun* [**plural**] friendly greetings ***Give/send my regards*** *to your mother when you see her.*

regeneration /rɪˌdʒenᵊr'eɪʃᵊn/ *noun* [**U**] the process of improving a place or system, especially to make it more active or successful *a programme of* ***urban regeneration*** •**regenerate** /rɪ'dʒenᵊreɪt/ *verb* [**T**] to improve a place or system

reggae /'regeɪ/ *noun* [**U**] **MUSIC** a type of popular music from Jamaica with a strong beat

regime /reɪ'ʒiːm/ *noun* [**C**] **POLITICS** a system of government or other control, especially one that people do not approve of *the former Communist regime*

regiment /'redʒɪmənt/ *noun* [**group**] a large group of soldiers •**regimental** /ˌredʒɪ'mentᵊl/ *adjective* relating to a regiment

regimented /'redʒɪmentɪd/ *adjective* too controlled or organized *a regimented lifestyle*

O‑**region** /'riːdʒᵊn/ *noun* **1 GEOGRAPHY** [**C**] a particular area in a country or the world *China's coastal region* **2** [**C**] an area of the body *pain in the lower abdominal region* **3 in the region of sth** approximately *It probably cost somewhere in the region of £900.*

regional /'riːdʒᵊnᵊl/ *adjective* **GEOGRAPHY** relating to a region (= particular area in a country) *a regional dialect/newspaper*

WORD PARTNERS FOR ***register***

compile a register • **on** a register • a register **of** sth

register¹ /'redʒɪstəʳ/ *noun* **1** [**C**] an official list of names *a* ***register of*** *approved builders* ○ *the* ***electoral register*** **2 LANGUAGE** [**C, U**] the style of language, grammar, and words used in particular situations *a formal/informal register* ➲See also: **cash register**

register² /'redʒɪstəʳ/ *verb* **1** [ON A LIST] [**I, T**] to put information about someone or something, especially a name, on an official list *Is he* ***registered with*** *the authorities to sell alcohol?* ○ *Students need to* ***register for*** *the course by the end of April.* ○ *a registered nurse* **2** [SHOW A FEELING] [**T**] to show an opinion or feeling *People gathered to* ***register*** *their* ***opposition*** *to the plans.* **3** [SHOW AMOUNT] [**I, T**] to show an amount on an instrument that measures something *The earthquake registered 7.3 on the Richter scale.*

registered /'redʒɪstəd/ *adjective* **registered mail/post** a special service that records when a letter or parcel is sent and received

ˈregister ˌoffice *noun* [**C**] in Britain, a place where births, deaths, and marriages are officially recorded and where you can get married

registrar /ˌredʒɪ'strɑːʳ/ *noun* [**C**] **1 LAW** someone whose job is to keep official records, especially of births, deaths, and marriages, or of students at a university **2 HEALTH** *UK* a type of hospital doctor

registration /ˌredʒɪ'streɪʃᵊn/ *noun* **1** [OFFICIAL LIST] [**U**] when a name or information is recorded on an official list **2** [VEHICLE] [**C**] (*also* **reɡisˈtration ˌnumber**) *mainly UK* the official set of numbers and letters on the front and back of a vehicle

registry /'redʒɪstri/ *noun* [**C**] a place where official records are kept *the land registry*

ˈregistry ˌoffice *noun* [**C**] in Britain, a place where births, deaths, and marriages are officially recorded and where you can get married

regress /rɪ'gres/ *verb* [**I**] *formal* to go back to an earlier, less advanced state •**regression** /rɪ'greʃᵊn/ *noun* [**U**] *formal* when someone or something regresses

O‑**regret¹** /rɪ'gret/ *verb* [**T**] **regretting**, *past* **regretted** **1** [BAD DECISION] to feel sorry about a situation, especially something that you wish you had not done [**+ doing sth**] *I really regret leaving school so young.* [**+ (that)**] *He began to regret that he hadn't paid more attention in class.* **2** [SORRY TO SAY] *formal* used to say that you are sorry that you have to tell someone about a situation [**+ to do sth**] *We regret to inform you that the application has been refused.*

WORD PARTNERS FOR ***regret***

express regret • **have (no)** regrets • sb's **biggest/only** regret • **with** regret • regret **about/at/over** sth

O‑**regret²** /rɪ'gret/ *noun* [**C, U**] a feeling of sadness about a situation, especially something that you wish you had not done *We married very young but we've been really happy and I've* ***no regrets***. ○ *It is* ***with great regret*** *that I announce Steve Adam's resignation.* •**regretful** *adjective* expressing regret •**regretfully** *adverb*

regrettable /rɪ'gretəbl/ *adjective* If something is regrettable, you wish it had not happened and you feel sorry about it. *a deeply regrettable incident* •**regrettably** *adverb*

O‑**regular¹** /'regjələʳ/ *adjective* **1** [SAME TIME/SPACE] repeated with the same amount of time or space between one thing and the next *a regular pulse* ○ *Plant the seedlings at regular intervals.* **2** [OFTEN] happening or doing something often, especially at the same time every week, year, etc *a* ***regular occurrence*** ○ *We arranged to meet* ***on a regular basis***. **3** [USUAL] *US* usual or normal *I couldn't see my regular dentist.* **4** [SIZE] *informal* being a standard size *a burger and regular fries* **5** [SHAPE] Something that has a regular shape is the same on both or all sides. *She's got lovely, regular teeth.* **6 LANGUAGE** following the usual rules or patterns in grammar *'Talk' is a regular verb but 'go' is not.* ➲Opposite **irregular** •**regularity** /ˌregjə'lærəti/ *noun* [**U**] when something is regular

regular² /'regjələʳ/ *noun* [**C**] *informal* someone who often goes to a particular shop, restaurant, etc *Mick was one of the regulars at the local pub.*

O‑**regularly** /'regjələli/ *adverb* **1** [OFTEN] often *Accidents occur regularly on this stretch of the road.* **2** [SAME TIME] at the same time each day, week, month, etc *They meet regularly - usually once a week.*

regulate /ˈregjəleɪt/ *verb* [T] **1** ACTIVITY/PROCESS to control an activity or process, especially by using rules *laws regulating advertising* **2** SPEED/TEMPERATURE to control the speed, temperature, etc of something *Babies find it difficult to regulate their body temperature.*

WORD PARTNERS FOR ***regulation***

breach / comply with / enforce / introduce regulations • regulations **governing** sth • **strict/stringent/tough** regulations • **under** a regulation

regulation /ˌregjəˈleɪʃən/ *noun* **1** RULE [C] an official rule that controls how something is done [**usually plural**] *building regulations* **2** CONTROL [U] when a process or activity is controlled *government regulation of interest rates*

regulator /ˈregjəleɪtəʳ/ *noun* [C] **1** OFFICIAL someone whose job is to make sure that a system works in a fair way *the water industry regulator* **2** EQUIPMENT a piece of equipment that is used to control the temperature, speed, etc of something

regulatory /ˈregjələtəri/ *adjective* controlling an activity or process, especially by using rules

rehab /ˈriːhæb/ *noun* [U] *informal* treatment to help someone stop drinking too much alcohol or taking drugs *He spent six months **in rehab**.*

rehabilitate /ˌriːhəˈbɪlɪteɪt/ *verb* [T] **HEALTH** to help someone live a normal life again after they have had a serious illness or been in prison *a programme to rehabilitate young offenders* •**rehabilitation** /ˌriːhəˌbɪlɪˈteɪʃən/ *noun* [U]

rehearsal /rɪˈhɜːsəl/ *noun* [C, U] a time when all the people involved in a play, dance, etc practise in order to prepare for a performance

rehearse /rɪˈhɜːs/ *verb* [I, T] to practise a play, dance, etc in order to prepare for a performance

reign¹ /reɪn/ *noun* **1 POLITICS** [C] a period of time when a king or queen rules a country *the reign of Henry VIII* **2** IMPORTANT JOB [**no plural**] a period of time when someone controls a sports team, an organization, etc *Christie's reign as captain of the British athletics team* **3 reign of terror** a period of time when someone uses violence to control people

reign² /reɪn/ *verb* [I] **1 POLITICS** to be the king or queen of a country *Queen Victoria reigned for 64 years.* **2** MAIN FEELING/QUALITY *formal* to be the main feeling or quality in a situation ***Chaos reigned** as angry protesters hammered on the doors.*

ˌreigning ˈchampion *noun* [C] **SPORT** the most recent winner of a competition

reimburse /ˌriːɪmˈbɜːs/ *verb* [T] *formal* **FINANCE** to pay money back to someone, especially money that they have spent because of their work *Employees will no longer be **reimbursed for** taxi fares.* •**reimbursement** *noun* [U] *formal* when you reimburse someone

rein /reɪn/ *noun* **1 SPORT** [C] a long, thin piece of leather that helps you to control a horse [**usually plural**] *Hold the reins in your left hand.* ➲See colour picture **Sports 1** on page Centre 14 **2 free rein** the freedom to do or say what you want [**+ to do sth**] The school gives teachers free rein to try out new teaching methods. **3 keep a tight rein on sb/sth** to have a lot of control over someone or something *We've been told to keep a tight rein on spending.*

reincarnation /ˌriːɪnkɑːˈneɪʃən/ *noun* [U] **RELIGION** the belief that a dead person's spirit returns to life in another body

reindeer /ˈreɪndɪəʳ/ *noun* [C] *plural* **reindeer** a type of deer with large horns that lives in northern parts of Europe, Asia, and America

reinforce /ˌriːɪnˈfɔːs/ *verb* [T] **1** OPINION to make an existing opinion or idea stronger *to reinforce a view/feeling* **2** OBJECT to make something stronger *a security door reinforced by steel bars* ○ *reinforced concrete* •**reinforcement** *noun* [C, U] when you reinforce something

reinforcements /ˌriːɪnˈfɔːsmənts/ *noun* [**plural**] soldiers who are sent to make an army stronger

reinstate /ˌriːɪnˈsteɪt/ *verb* [T] **1** PERSON to give someone the job or position that they had before **2** RULE to cause a rule, law, etc to exist again •**reinstatement** *noun* [C, U] when you reinstate someone or something

reinvent /ˌriːɪnˈvent/ *verb* **1** [T] to produce something new that is based on something that already exists *The story of Romeo and Juliet was **reinvented as** a Los Angeles gangster movie.* **2 reinvent yourself** to change the way you look and behave so that you seem very different ➲See also: reinvent the **wheel**¹

reiterate /riˈɪtəreɪt/ *verb* [T] *formal* to say something again so that people take notice of it [**+ that**] *I must reiterate that we have no intention of signing this contract.* •**reiteration** /riˌɪtərˈeɪʃən/ *noun* [C, U]

O→**reject¹** /rɪˈdʒekt/ *verb* [T] **1** NOT ACCEPT to refuse to accept or agree with something *The United States government **rejected** the **proposal**.* **2** JOB/COURSE to refuse to accept someone for a job, course, etc *I applied to Cambridge University but I was rejected.* **3** PERSON to not give someone the love or attention they were expecting *She felt rejected by her husband.*

reject² /ˈriːdʒekt/ *noun* [C] a product that is damaged or not perfect in some way

rejection /rɪˈdʒekʃən/ *noun* **1** NOT ACCEPT [C, U] when you refuse to accept or agree with something *Their **rejection of** the peace plan is very disappointing for the government.* **2** JOB/COLLEGE [C] a letter that says you have not been successful in getting a job, a place at college, etc **3** PERSON [U] when someone does not give someone else the love or attention they were expecting *a feeling of rejection*

rejoice /rɪˈdʒɔɪs/ *verb* [I] *literary* to feel very happy because something good has happened

rejoicing /rɪˈdʒɔɪsɪŋ/ *noun* [U] when people show that they are very happy because something good has happened

rejoin /rɪˈdʒɔɪn/ *verb* [T] to return to a person or place *I was feeling better, so I rejoined the party.*

R

rejuvenate /rɪˈdʒuːvəneɪt/ *verb* [T] to make someone look or feel young and energetic again *You're supposed to come back from a holiday feeling rejuvenated.* •**rejuvenation** /rɪˌdʒuːvənˈeɪʃən/ *noun* [U]

rekindle /ˌriːˈkɪndl/ *verb* [T] to make someone have a feeling that they had in the past *The trip seemed to rekindle their love for each other.*

relapse /rɪˈlæps, ˈriːlæps/ *noun* [C, U] **1 HEALTH** when someone becomes ill again after a period of feeling better *I **had a relapse** last year and was off work for a month.* **2** when something or someone gets worse again after being better *The company's share prices have **suffered a relapse** this week.* •**relapse** /rɪˈlæps/ *verb* [I]

relate /rɪˈleɪt/ *verb* **1** CONNECT [I, T] to be connected, or to find or show the connection between two or more things *How do the two proposals relate?* **2** TELL [T] *formal* to tell a story or describe a series of events

relate to sb/sth *phrasal verb* to be connected to, or to be about someone or something *Please provide all information relating to the claim.*

relate to sb *phrasal verb* to understand how someone feels *Most teenagers find it hard to relate to their parents.*

related /rɪˈleɪtɪd/ *adjective* **1** connected *There's been an increase in criminal activity **related to** drugs.* **2 SOCIETY** If two or more people are related, they belong to the same family. *Did you know that I'm **related to** Jackie?* ➲Opposite **unrelated**

relation /rɪˈleɪʃən/ *noun* **1** CONNECTION [C, U] a connection between two or more things *the **relation between** smoking and lung cancer* **2 SOCIETY** [C] someone who belongs to the same family as you *He's called Ken Russell, **no relation to*** (= he is not from the same family as) *the film director.* ➲See Common Learner Error at **parent** **3 in relation to sth a** COMPARED WITH when compared with something *Salaries are low in relation to the cost of living.* **b** ABOUT about or relating to something *I'd like to ask you something in relation to what you said earlier.*

relational database /rɪˌleɪʃənəlˈdeɪtəbeɪs/ *noun* [C] **COMPUTING** a database (= organized store of information on a computer) in which many connections are made between the tables in the database

relations /rɪˈleɪʃənz/ *noun* [plural] the way two people or groups feel and behave towards each other *It was an attempt to restore diplomatic **relations between** the two countries.* ➲See also: **public relations, race relations**

WORD PARTNERS FOR ***relationship***

a **close/intimate/personal/loving/stormy** relationship • **end/forge/form/have** a relationship • a relationship **between** sb

O‑ **relationship** /rɪˈleɪʃənʃɪp/ *noun* **1 SOCIETY** [C] the way two people or groups feel and behave towards each other *He has a very good **relationship with** his older sister.* **2 SOCIETY** [C] a sexual or romantic friendship *I don't feel ready for a relationship at the moment.* **3** [C, U] a connection between two or more things *the **relationship between** sunburn and skin cancer*

COMMON LEARNER ERROR

have a relationship with someone

Be careful to use the correct preposition in this expression.

I have a good relationship with my parents.

~~*I have a good relationship to my parents.*~~

O‑ **relative**[1] /ˈrelətɪv/ *noun* [C] **SOCIETY** a member of your family *a party for friends and relatives* ➲See Common Learner Error at **parent**

relative[2] /ˈrelətɪv/ *adjective* **1** [always before noun] compared to other similar things or people *the relative prosperity of the West* **2 relative to sth** when compared to something else *The economy has been declining relative to other countries.*

ˌrelative aˌtomic ˈmass *noun* [U] **MEASURES** the mass of an atom of a particular chemical element, usually expressed in atomic mass units

ˌrelative ˈclause *noun* [C] **LANGUAGE** a part of a sentence that is used to describe the noun which comes just before it. In the sentence, 'The woman who I saw yesterday wasn't his wife.', 'who I saw yesterday' is a relative clause.

relatively /ˈrelətɪvli/ *adverb* quite, when compared to other things or people *Eating out is relatively cheap.*

ˌrelative moˌlecular ˈmass *noun* [U] **MEASURES** the total of the relative atomic masses of the atoms in a particular molecule

ˌrelative ˈpronoun *noun* [C] **LANGUAGE** a word such as 'that', 'which', or 'who' that is used to begin a relative clause

OTHER WAYS OF SAYING ***relax***

The verb **chill** and the phrasal verb **chill out** are very common, informal ways of saying 'relax': *We spent the whole week **chilling out** on the beach.*

The phrasal verb **wind down** and the verb **unwind** mean 'to start to relax after working or doing something difficult': *It takes me a while to **wind down** when I get back from work.* • *Music helps me to **unwind**.*

If a person relaxes so that they don't use up too much energy, the fixed expression **take it easy/take things easy** is often used: *You'll need to spend a few days **taking it easy/taking things easy** after the operation.*

The fixed expression **put your feet up** is also often used to mean 'sit down and relax': *I'm going to make myself a cup of coffee and **put my feet up** for half an hour.*

O‑ **relax** /rɪˈlæks/ *verb* **1** PERSON [I, T] to become happy and comfortable because nothing is worrying you, or to make someone do this *I find it difficult to relax.* ○ *The wine had relaxed him and he began to talk.* **2** LESS STIFF [I, T] If a part of your body relaxes, it becomes less stiff, and if you relax it, you make it become less stiff. *Try these exercises to relax your neck muscles.* **3** RULES [T] to make laws or rules less severe *The government has recently* ***relaxed laws*** *on bringing animals into Britain.* **•relaxation** /ˌriːlækˈseɪʃᵊn/ *noun* [U]

O-■ **relaxed** /rɪˈlækst/ *adjective* **1** PERSON feeling happy and comfortable because nothing is worrying you *She seemed relaxed and in control of the situation.* **2** SITUATION A relaxed situation is comfortable and informal. *There was a very relaxed atmosphere at the party.*

O-■ **relaxing** /rɪˈlæksɪŋ/ *adjective* making you feel relaxed *a relaxing bath*

relay¹ /ˌriːˈleɪ/ *verb* [T] **1** TELL to send a message from one person to another *Cory had an idea which he relayed to his friend immediately.* **2** BROADCAST to broadcast radio or television signals

relay² /ˈriːleɪ/ (*also* **ˈrelay ˌrace**) *noun* [C] **SPORT** a race in which each member of a team runs or swims part of the race

O-■ **release¹** /rɪˈliːs/ *verb* [T] **1** PRISONER to allow a prisoner to be free *Six hostages were released shortly before midday.* **2** STOP HOLDING to stop holding someone or something *Release the handle.* **3** INFORMATION to let the public have news or information about something *Police have not released the dead woman's name.* **4** RECORD/FILM to make a record or film available for people to buy or see *The album is due to be released in time for Christmas.* **5** SUBSTANCE to let a substance flow out from somewhere *Dangerous chemicals were accidentally* ***released into*** *the river.*

WORD PARTNERS FOR ***release***

demand/secure sb's release • release **from** sth

release² /rɪˈliːs/ *noun* **1** FROM PRISON [C] when someone is allowed to leave prison *After his release from jail, Jackson found it difficult to find work.* **2** FILM/RECORD [C] a new film or record that you can buy *Have you heard the group's latest release?* **3** SUBSTANCE [C, U] when a substance is allowed to flow out of somewhere *a release of toxic gas from the factory* ➲See also: **press release**

relegate /ˈrelɪgeɪt/ *verb* [T] to put someone or something in a less important position [**often passive**] *He'd been* ***relegated to*** *the B team.* **•relegation** /ˌrelɪˈgeɪʃᵊn/ *noun* [U]

relent /rɪˈlent/ *verb* [I] to allow something that you refused to allow before *The security guard relented and let them through.*

relentless /rɪˈlentləs/ *adjective* never stopping or getting any less extreme *relentless criticism* **•relentlessly** *adverb*

relevance /ˈreləvəns/ (*also US* **relevancy** /ˈreləvəntsi/) *noun* [U] the degree to which something is related or useful to what is happening or being talked about *This point has no* ***relevance to*** *the discussion.*

relevant /ˈreləvənt/ *adjective* related or useful to what is happening or being talked about ***relevant information*** ○ *Education should be* ***relevant to*** *children's needs.* ➲Opposite **irrelevant**

reliable /rɪˈlaɪəbl/ *adjective* able to be trusted or believed *a reliable car* ○ *reliable information* ○ *Andy's very reliable - if he says he'll do something, he'll do it.* ➲Opposite **unreliable** **•reliability** /rɪˌlaɪəˈbɪləti/ *noun* [U] how reliable someone or something is **•reliably** *adverb I am* ***reliably informed*** *that the concert has been cancelled.*

reliance /rɪˈlaɪəns/ *noun* **reliance on sb/sth** when someone or something depends on someone or something else *our increasing reliance on computers*

reliant /rɪˈlaɪənt/ *adjective* **be reliant on sb/sth** to depend on someone or something *I don't want to be reliant on anybody.* ➲See also: **self-reliant**

relic /ˈrelɪk/ *noun* [C] a very old thing from the past *an Egyptian relic*

WORD PARTNERS FOR ***relief***

a big/great/tremendous relief • **a sense of** relief • **to** sb's relief

O-■ **relief** /rɪˈliːf/ *noun* **1** EMOTION [U, **no plural**] the good feeling that you have when something unpleasant stops or does not happen *It'll be such a relief when these exams are over.* ○ *"James can't come tonight." "Well, that's a relief!"* **2** HELP [U] money, food, or clothes that are given to people because they need help *an international* ***relief operation*** **3** PHYSICAL FEELING [U] when something stops hurting you *I'd been trying to sleep to find* ***relief from*** *the pain.*

reˈlief ˌmap *noun* [C] **GEOGRAPHY** a map that shows the hills, valleys and mountains of a particular area or country

relieve /rɪˈliːv/ *verb* [T] **1** FROM PAIN to make pain or a bad feeling less severe *Breathing exercises can help to relieve stress.* **2** FROM WORK to allow someone to stop working by taking their place *The 7 a.m. team arrived to relieve the night workers.*

relieve sb of sth *phrasal verb formal* to take something away from someone *Let me relieve you of your luggage.*

relieved /rɪˈliːvd/ *adjective* feeling happy because something unpleasant did not happen or you are not worried about something any more [+ **(that)**] *I'm just relieved that she's safe and well.* [+ **to do sth**] *I heard a noise and was relieved to find that it was only a cat.*

WORD PARTNERS FOR ***religion***

believe in/practise a religion • **a major** religion • be **against** sb's religion

O-■ **religion** /rɪˈlɪdʒᵊn/ *noun* [C, U] **RELIGION** the belief in a god or gods, or a particular system of belief in a god or gods *the Christian religion*

O-■ **religious** /rɪˈlɪdʒəs/ *adjective* **RELIGION** **1** relating to religion *religious paintings* **2** having a strong belief in a religion *He's a very religious man.*

religiously /rɪˈlɪdʒəsli/ *adverb* **1** regularly *He visited the old woman religiously every weekend.* **2** **RELIGION** in a religious way

relinquish /rɪˈlɪŋkwɪʃ/ *verb* [T] *formal* to allow something to be taken away from you *At 80 he still refuses to relinquish control of the company.*

R

relish¹ /ˈrelɪʃ/ *verb* [T] to enjoy something *I don't* ***relish the thought*** *of a twelve-hour flight.*

relish² /ˈrelɪʃ/ *noun* **1** [U] enjoyment *He had baked a cake which the children now ate* ***with relish.*** **2** FOOD [C] a sauce that you put on food to give it more taste

relive /ˌriːˈlɪv/ *verb* [T] to remember something so clearly that you feel as if it is happening now

relocate /ˌriːləʊˈkeɪt/ (US) /riːˈləʊˌkeɪt/ *verb* [I, T] to move to another place *The company* ***relocated to*** *Tokyo.* •**relocation** /ˌriːləʊˈkeɪʃᵊn/ *noun* [U] ***relocation costs***

reluctant /rɪˈlʌktᵊnt/ *adjective* not wanting to do something [+ **to do sth**] *Many victims of crime are reluctant to go to the police.* •**reluctance** /rɪˈlʌktᵊns/ *noun* [U] when someone does not want to do something [+ **to do sth**] *a reluctance to accept changes* •**reluctantly** *adverb*

rely /rɪˈlaɪ/ *verb*
rely on sb/sth *phrasal verb* **1** NEED to need someone or something in order to be successful, work correctly, etc *Families rely more on wives' earnings than before.* **2** TRUST to trust someone or something [+ **to do sth**] I know I ***can rely on*** *you to help me.*

remain /rɪˈmeɪn/ *verb* **1** [I] to continue to exist when everything or everyone else has gone *Only a few hundred of these animals remain today.* ➲See Common Learner Error at **rest 2 remain calm/open, etc; remain a secret/mystery/prisoner, etc** to continue to be in the same state *The exact date of the wedding remains a secret.* **3 remain at/in/with, etc** *formal* to stay in the same place *She will remain at her mother's until I return.*

remainder /rɪˈmeɪndəʳ/ *noun* **1** [**no plural**] the things or people that are left when everything or everyone else has gone or been dealt with *He drank* ***the remainder of*** *his coffee and got up to leave.* **2** MATHEMATICS [U] the amount that is left when one number cannot be exactly divided by another

R

remaining /rɪˈmeɪnɪŋ/ *adjective* [**always before noun**] continuing to exist when everything or everyone else has gone or been dealt with *Mix in half the butter and keep the remaining 50g for later.*

remains /rɪˈmeɪnz/ *noun* [**plural**] **1** PARTS OF SOMETHING the parts of something, especially a building, that continue to exist when the rest of it has been destroyed *the remains of a Buddhist temple* **2** PARTS OF BODY *formal* someone's body after they have died

remake /ˈriːmeɪk/ *noun* [C] a film that is the same as one that has been made before *a remake of 'King Kong'* •**remake** /ˌriːˈmeɪk/ *verb* [T] *past* **remade**

remand¹ /rɪˈmɑːnd/ *noun* **on remand** LAW *UK* in prison before your trial (= when a law court decides if you are guilty or not) *He spent two weeks on remand in Bullingdon prison.*

remand² /rɪˈmɑːnd/ *verb* **be remanded in custody** LAW *UK* to be kept in prison on remand *He was charged with murder and remanded in custody.*

WORD PARTNERS FOR ***remark***

make a remark • a remark **about/on** sth

remark¹ /rɪˈmɑːk/ *noun* [C] something that you say *He* ***made a remark*** *about her clothes.*

remark² /rɪˈmɑːk/ *verb* [I] to say something [+ **that**] *He remarked that she was looking thin.*
remark on/upon sth *phrasal verb* to say something about something that you have just noticed *He remarked on how well you were looking.*

remarkable /rɪˈmɑːkəbl/ *adjective* very unusual or noticeable in a way that you admire *a remarkable woman* ○ *He has a remarkable memory.* ➲Opposite **unremarkable**

remarkably /rɪˈmɑːkəbli/ *adverb* in a way that makes you feel surprised *She has remarkably good skin for her age.*

remarry /ˌriːˈmæri/ *verb* [I] SOCIETY to get married again *His wife died in 1970 and he never remarried.*

remedial /rɪˈmiːdiəl/ *adjective* [**always before noun**] **1** EDUCATION intended to help people who are having difficulty learning something *remedial English classes* **2** *formal* intended to improve something ***Remedial action*** *is needed.*

remedy¹ /ˈremədi/ *noun* [C] **1** HEALTH something that makes you better when you are ill *a flu remedy* **2** something that solves a problem *The* ***remedy for*** *the traffic problem is to encourage people to use public transport.*

remedy² /ˈremədi/ *verb* [T] to solve a problem, or to improve a bad situation *They were able* ***to remedy*** *the* ***problem*** *very easily.*

OTHER WAYS OF SAYING ***remember***

More formal alternatives are verbs such as **recall** and (*UK*) **recollect**: *I don't* ***recall*** *arranging a time to meet.* • *I didn't* ***recollect*** *having seen him.*

Remind means 'to make someone remember something', or 'to make someone remember to do something': *Every time we meet he* ***reminds*** *me about the money he lent me.* • *Will you* ***remind*** *me to buy some eggs?*

The phrasal verbs **come back to** and **come to** are often used when someone suddenly remembers something: *I'd forgotten his name but it's just* ***come (back) to*** *me.*

To **reminisce** is to remember and talk about pleasant things that happened in the past: *We were just* ***reminiscing*** *about our school days.*

To **bear** something **in mind** is to remember someone or something that may be useful in the future: *When you book,* ***bear in mind*** *that Christmas is the busiest period.*

remember /rɪˈmembəʳ/ *verb* [I, T] **1** IN YOUR MIND If you remember a fact or something from the past, you keep it in your mind, or bring it back into your mind. *I can't remember his name.* [+ **doing sth**] *I don't remember signing a contract.* [+ **(that)**] *Just as the door closed he remembered that his keys were inside the room.* **2** TO DO SOMETHING to not forget to do something

[+ to do sth] *I must remember to send Carol a birthday card.*

COMMON LEARNER ERROR

remember or **memory?**

Remember is a verb. Use **remember** when you think about or bring thoughts into your mind about a person, place, or event from the past.

I can remember when I was at school.

Memory is a noun. Use **memory** to talk about the person, place, or event from the past that you think about.

I have good memories of when I was at school.

remembrance /rɪˈmembrᵊns/ *noun* [U] when you remember and show respect for someone who has died *They erected a statue* ***in remembrance of*** *him.*

O-- **remind** /rɪˈmaɪnd/ *verb* [T] to make someone remember something, or remember to do something *Every time we meet he* ***reminds*** *me* ***about*** *the money he lent me.* [+ to do sth] *Will you remind me to buy some eggs?*
remind sb of sth/sb *phrasal verb* to make someone think of something or someone else *Harry reminds me of my father.* ○ *This song reminds me of our trip to Spain.*

COMMON LEARNER ERROR

remind or **remember?**

If you **remember** a fact or something from the past, you keep it in your mind, or bring it back into your mind.

I can't remember the name of the film.

Did you remember to bring your passport?

When you **remind** someone to do something, you make them remember it.

Can you remind me to phone Anna tomorrow?

~~*Can you remember me to phone Anna tomorrow?*~~

WORD PARTNERS FOR ***reminder***

need/serve as a reminder • a **constant/gentle/timely** reminder • a **grim/poignant/sharp/stark** reminder • a reminder **of** sth

reminder /rɪˈmaɪndəʳ/ *noun* [C] something that makes you remember something else *For me, ice cream is* ***a reminder of*** *happy childhood holidays at the seaside.*

reminisce /ˌremɪˈnɪs/ *verb* [I] to talk about pleasant things that happened in the past *We were just* ***reminiscing about*** *our school days.* •**reminiscence** *noun* [C, U] when you reminisce

reminiscent /ˌremɪˈnɪsᵊnt/ *adjective* **reminiscent of sth/sb** making you think of someone or something that is similar *a smell reminiscent of an old church*

remission /rɪˈmɪʃᵊn/ *noun* **be in remission** HEALTH to be in a period of time when a serious illness is better *He is in remission at the moment.*

remit[1] /ˈriːmɪt/ *noun* [no plural] *UK* the things that you are responsible for in your job

remit[2] /rɪˈmɪt/ *verb* [T] **remitting**, *past* **remitted** *formal* to send money to someone

remix[1] /ˌriːˈmɪks/ *verb* [T] **MUSIC** to use a machine or computer to change or improve the different parts of an existing music recording to make a new recording

remix[2] /ˈriː.mɪks/ *noun* [C] **MUSIC** a piece of music that has been remixed

remnant /ˈremnənt/ *noun* [C] a piece of something that continues to exist when the rest of that thing has gone *the remnants of last night's meal*

remora /ˈremərə/ *noun* [C] a fish that attaches itself to other fish or objects by sucking on them

remorse /rɪˈmɔːs/ *noun* [U] the feeling that you are sorry for something bad that you have done *He has* ***shown*** *no* ***remorse for*** *his actions.* •**remorseful** *adjective* feeling remorse

remorseless /rɪˈmɔːsləs/ *adjective* **1** NOT STOPPING *UK* never stopping *remorseless pressure to succeed* **2** CRUEL cruel •**remorselessly** *adverb*

remote /rɪˈməʊt/ *adjective* **1** PLACE far away *It was a remote mountain village with no electricity supply.* **2** TIME far in time *in the remote past* **3** SLIGHT slight *There is a* ***remote possibility*** *that it could be cancer.* •**remoteness** *noun* [U]

reˌmote conˈtrol *noun* **1** EQUIPMENT [C] (*also* **remote**) a piece of equipment that is used to control something such as a television from a distance ⊃See colour picture **The Living Room** on page Centre 4 **2** RADIO WAVES [U] the use of radio waves to control something such as a television from a distance

remotely /rɪˈməʊtli/ *adverb* **not remotely interested/surprised/possible, etc** not at all interested, surprised, etc *I'm not remotely interested in football.*

removal /rɪˈmuːvᵊl/ *noun* **1** TAKE AWAY [U] when you remove something *stain removal* **2** HOUSE [C, U] *UK* when you remove everything from one house to take to another *a removals firm*

O-- **remove** /rɪˈmuːv/ *verb* [T] **1** TAKE AWAY to take something away *An operation was needed to* ***remove*** *the bullets* ***from*** *his chest.* **2** TAKE OFF to take something off *Carefully remove the lid, then stir the paint.* **3** JOB *formal* to make someone stop doing their job [often passive] *He had been* ***removed from*** *his job on medical grounds.* **4 be far removed from sth** to be very different from something *The princess's world was far removed from reality.*

remuneration /rɪˌmjuːnᵊrˈeɪʃᵊn/ *noun* [U] *formal* **FINANCE** when someone is paid for work they have done

renaissance /rəˈneɪsᵊns/ (US) /ˌrenəˈsɑːns/ *noun* [no plural] a time when something becomes popular or fashionable again *The British film industry is* ***enjoying a renaissance.***

the Renaissance /rəˈneɪsᵊns/ (US) /ˌrenəˈsɑːns/ *noun* **ART, LITERATURE, MUSIC** the period during the 14th, 15th, and 16th centuries in Europe when there was a lot of interest and activity in art, literature, ideas, etc

rename /ˌriːˈneɪm/ *verb* [T] to give something a new name [+ two objects] *Siam was renamed Thailand in 1939.*

render /ˈrendəʳ/ *verb* [T] *formal* **1** CAUSE TO BE to cause something or someone to be in a particular state or condition *She was rendered*

R

speechless upon hearing the news. **2** GIVE to give someone a decision, opinion, help, etc *payment for **services rendered*** **3** DT to put a first layer of plaster or cement on a wall

rendering /ˈrendərɪŋ/ *noun* [C] the way that something is performed, written, drawn, etc *a child's rendering of a house*

rendezvous /ˈrɒndɪvuː/ *noun* [C] *plural* **rendezvous** an arrangement to meet someone, or the place you have arranged to meet them •**rendezvous** *verb* [I]

rendition /renˈdɪʃən/ *noun* [C] MUSIC the way in which a song, piece of music, etc is performed

renegade /ˈrenɪɡeɪd/ *noun* [C] someone who changes and joins a group that is against their own group *a group of renegade soldiers*

renege /rəˈneɪɡ/ (US) /rəˈnɪɡ/ *verb*
renege on sth *phrasal verb formal* to not do what you said you were going to do *to renege on a promise*

renew /rɪˈnjuː/ *verb* [T] **1** OFFICIAL AGREEMENT to arrange to continue an official agreement that was going to end soon *I've decided not to **renew** my golf club **membership** this year.* **2** BUY UK to get a new one of something that is old *A car isn't the sort of thing you renew every year.* **3** DO AGAIN to start to do something again *The next morning enemy war planes renewed their bombing.* •**renewal** *noun* [C, U] when you renew something

renewable /rɪˈnjuːəbl/ *adjective* **1** ENVIRONMENT A renewable form of energy can be produced as quickly as it is used. *a **renewable energy** source such as wind power* **2** OFFICIAL AGREEMENT A renewable official agreement is one that you can arrange to continue when the time limit is reached. *a 6-month **renewable contract***

renewables /rɪˈnjuːəblz/ *noun* [plural] ENVIRONMENT types of energy such as wind power and power from the sun that can be replaced as quickly as they are used

R

renewed /rɪˈnjuːd/ *adjective* starting again in a stronger way than before *He sang now with renewed confidence.*

renounce /rɪˈnaʊns/ *verb* [T] to officially say that you do not have the right to something any more, or that you do not want to be involved in something any more *They had renounced all rights to ownership of the land.*

renovate /ˈrenəveɪt/ *verb* [T] to repair and decorate a building that is old and in bad condition •**renovation** /ˌrenəˈveɪʃən/ *noun* [C, U]

renowned /rɪˈnaʊnd/ *adjective* famous *The Lake District is **renowned for** its beauty.*

rent¹ /rent/ *verb* FINANCE **1** [I, T] to pay money to live in a building that someone else owns *He'll be renting an apartment until he can find a house to buy.* **2** [T] US (UK **hire**) to pay money to use something for a short time *We could rent a car for the weekend.* **3** [T] (*also* **rent out**) to allow someone to pay you money to live in your building *I rented out my house and went travelling for a year.*

COMMON LEARNER ERROR

rent and hire

In British English you **rent** something for a long time.

I rent a 2-bedroom flat.

In British English you **hire** something for a short time.

We hired a car for the weekend.

In American English the word **rent** is used in both situations.

I rent a 2-bedroom apartment.

We rented a car for the weekend.

WORD PARTNERS FOR ***rent***

pay the rent • the rent **on** sth

rent² /rent/ *noun* [C, U] FINANCE the amount of money that you pay to live in a building that someone else owns *They couldn't afford the rent.*

rental /ˈrentəl/ *noun* [C, U] FINANCE an arrangement to rent something, or the amount of money that you pay to rent something *The price includes flights and car rental.*

rented /ˈrentɪd/ *adjective* FINANCE describes something that you rent ***rented accommodation***

renter /ˈrentər/ *noun* [C] FINANCE US someone who pays money to live in a house or an apartment that someone else owns

renunciation /rɪˌnʌnsiˈeɪʃən/ *noun* [U, no plural] when you say that you do not want something or believe in something any more *a renunciation of violence*

reorganize (*also* UK **-ise**) /ˌriːˈɔːɡənaɪz/ *verb* [I, T] to organize something again in order to improve it *He's completely reorganized his schedule for the week.* •**reorganization** /riːˌɔːɡənaɪˈzeɪʃən/ *noun* [C, U]

rep /rep/ *noun* [C] *informal* someone whose job is to sell things for a company *the UK **sales rep***

repaid /ˌriːˈpeɪd/ *past of* repay

OTHER WAYS OF SAYING ***repair***

The verbs **fix** and **mend** are common alternatives: *I must get my bike **fixed**.* • *Can you **mend** that hole in my trousers?*

The phrasal verbs **do up** (*UK*) and **fix up** are often used when someone repairs something and improves it: *Nick loves **fixing up** old cars.* • *They're planning to buy an old cottage and **do it up**.*

The verb **service** (*UK*) is often used when examining and repairing cars or other machines: *I'm taking the car to the garage to have it **serviced** this afternoon.*

repair¹ /rɪˈpeər/ *verb* [T] **1** FIX to fix something that is broken or damaged *I must **get** my bike **repaired**.* **2** IMPROVE to improve a bad situation *It will take a long time to repair relations between the two countries.*

WORD PARTNERS FOR ***repair (noun)***

carry out/do repairs • be **in need of** repair • **extensive/major/minor** repairs • the repair **of** sth

repair² /rɪˈpeər/ *noun* **1** [C, U] something that you do to fix something that is broken or damaged [**usually plural**] *The repairs cost me £150.* **2 be in good/bad repair** to be in good/bad condition

reparations /ˌrepəˈreɪʃᵊn/ *noun* [**plural**] **POLITICS** payment for harm or damage *The country was forced to pay reparations after the war.*

repatriate /riːˈpætrieɪt/ (US) /riːˈpeɪtrieɪt/ *verb* [**T**] to send someone back to their own country •**repatriation** /ˌriːpætriˈeɪʃᵊn/ (US) /rɪˌpeɪtriˈeɪʃᵊn/ *noun* [**U**]

repay /ˌriːˈpeɪ/ *verb* [**T**] *past* **repaid 1 FINANCE** to pay back money that you have borrowed *to **repay a loan*** **2** to do something kind for someone who has done something to help you *What can I do to repay you for your kindness?* •**repayment** /rɪˈpeɪmənt/ *noun* [**C, U**] when you repay someone or the money that you pay back

repeal /rɪˈpiːl/ *verb* [**T**] **LAW** to officially make a law end

O⁃**repeat**[1] /rɪˈpiːt/ *verb* [**T**] **1** [SAY/DO AGAIN] to say or do something more than once *He repeated the number.* ○ *The test must be repeated several times.* **2** [TELL] to tell someone something that someone else has told you *I've got some news for you but you mustn't **repeat** it **to** anyone.*

repeat[2] /rɪˈpiːt/ *noun* **1** [HAPPEN/DO AGAIN] [**no plural**] when something happens or is done more than once *Everything is being done to avoid **a repeat of** the tragedy.* **2** [TELEVISION/RADIO] [**C**] *UK* (*US* **rerun**) a television or radio programme that is broadcast again

repeated /rɪˈpiːtɪd/ *adjective* [**always before noun**] done or happening more than once *He has refused repeated requests to be interviewed.* •**repeatedly** *adverb The victim was stabbed repeatedly.*

repel /rɪˈpel/ *verb* [**T**] **repelling**, *past* **repelled 1** [MOVE AWAY] to make someone or something move away or stop attacking you *a smell that repels insects* **2** [UNPLEASANT] If someone or something repels you, you think they are extremely unpleasant.

repellent[1] /rɪˈpelᵊnt/ *adjective* extremely unpleasant *I find his views utterly repellent.*

repellent[2] /rɪˈpelᵊnt/ *noun* [**C, U**] **insect/mosquito repellent** a substance that you use to keep insects away

repent /rɪˈpent/ *verb* [**I, T**] *formal* to say that you are sorry for doing something bad •**repentance** *noun* [**U**] *formal* when someone repents

repentant /rɪˈpentənt/ *adjective formal* feeling sorry about something bad that you have done ➲Opposite **unrepentant**

repercussions /ˌriːpəˈkʌʃᵊnz/ *noun* [**plural**] the effects that an action or event has on something, especially bad effects *Any decrease in tourism could have serious **repercussions for** the local economy.*

repertoire /ˈrepətwɑːʳ/ *noun* [**C**] all the songs, plays, etc that someone can perform

repertory /ˈrepətᵊri/ *noun* **1** [GROUP OF ACTORS] [**C, U**] when a group of actors performs several different plays during a period of time *They have four plays **in repertory** this season.* ○ *a **repertory company/theatre*** **2** [ALL THE SONGS ETC] [**C**] all the songs, plays, etc that someone can perform

repetition /ˌrepɪˈtɪʃᵊn/ *noun* [**C, U**] when something is repeated *We don't want a repetition of last year's disaster.*

repetitive /rɪˈpetətɪv/ (*also* **repetitious** /ˌrepɪˈtɪʃəs/) *adjective* doing or saying the same thing several times, especially in a way that is boring *a repetitive job* •**repetitively** *adverb*

reˌpetitive ˈstrain ˌinjury ➲See: **RSI**

O⁃**replace** /rɪˈpleɪs/ *verb* [**T**] **1** [USE INSTEAD] to start using another thing or person instead of the one that you are using now *We're thinking of **replacing** our old TV **with** a fancy new one.* **2** [BE USED INSTEAD] to start to be used instead of the thing or person that is being used now *This system will replace the old one.* **3** [GET SOMETHING NEW] to get something new because the one you had before has been lost or damaged *We'll have to replace this carpet soon.* **4** [PUT BACK] *formal* to put something back in the place where it usually is *She picked up the books and carefully replaced them on the shelf.*

replacement /rɪˈpleɪsmənt/ *noun* **1** [THING OR PERSON] [**C**] the thing or person that replaces something or someone *It's not going to be easy to **find a replacement** for you.* **2** [ACT OF REPLACING] [**U**] when something or someone is replaced

replay /ˈriːpleɪ/ *noun* [**C**] **SPORT 1** an important part of a sports game or other event on television that is shown again immediately after it has happened **2** *UK* a game of sport that is played again •**replay** /ˌriːˈpleɪ/ *verb* [**T**] ➲See also: **action replay** *UK*, **instant replay** *US*

replenish /rɪˈplenɪʃ/ *verb* [**T**] *formal* to fill something or make it complete again *to replenish supplies* •**replenishment** *noun* [**U**] *formal* when you fill something or make it complete again

replica /ˈreplɪkə/ *noun* [**C**] something that is made to look almost exactly the same as something else *a replica of the White House*

replicate /ˈreplɪkeɪt/ *verb* [**T**] *formal* to make or do something again in exactly the same way •**replication** /ˌreplɪˈkeɪʃᵊn/ *noun* [**C, U**]

O⁃**reply**[1] /rɪˈplaɪ/ *verb* [**I, T**] to answer *"I don't understand," she replied.* ○ *He didn't **reply to** my email.* [**+ that**] *Henry replied that he had no idea what I was talking about.*

WORD PARTNERS FOR ***reply (noun)***

give/make/send a reply • **get/have/receive** a reply • a reply **to** sth • **in** reply

O⁃**reply**[2] /rɪˈplaɪ/ *noun* [**C, U**] an answer *Her reply was short and unfriendly.* ○ *Have you had a **reply to** your letter?* ○ *She sent me an email **in reply*** (= as an answer).

O⁃**report**[1] /rɪˈpɔːt/ *noun* [**C**] **1** a description of an event or situation *a police report* ○ *an annual report on the economy* **2 EDUCATION** *UK* (*US* **reˈport ˌcard**) when teachers write about a child's progress at school for their parents

O⁃**report**[2] /rɪˈpɔːt/ *verb* **1** [DESCRIBE] [**I, T**] to describe a recent event or situation, especially on television, radio, or in a newspaper *Jo Smith **reports on** recent developments.* [**+ that**] *She reported that the situation had changed dramatically.* [**+ doing sth**] *A woman outside the*

R

shop reported seeing the gun. **2** TELL [T] to tell someone in authority that something has happened, especially an accident or crime *He should have **reported** the **accident** immediately.* ○ *Have you **reported** the fault **to** a technician?* **3** COMPLAIN [T] to complain about someone's behaviour to someone in authority. *I'm going to **report** him **to** the police.* ○ *Duncan's been **reported for** smoking.*
report to sb/sth *phrasal verb* to go to someone or a place and say that you have arrived *All visitors please report to reception.*

reportedly /rɪˈpɔːtɪdli/ *adverb* If something has reportedly happened or is reportedly a fact, people say it has happened or is true. *Two students were reportedly killed and several wounded.*

reˌported ˈspeech *noun* [U] **LANGUAGE** speech or writing that is used to report what someone has said, but not using exactly the same words

reporter /rɪˈpɔːtəʳ/ *noun* [C] someone whose job is to discover information about news events and describe them on television, radio, or in a newspaper

repossess /ˌriːpəˈzes/ *verb* [T] **FINANCE** to take back someone's house, car, furniture, etc because they cannot finish paying for them •**repossession** /ˌriːpəˈzeʃən/ *noun* [C, U] when someone repossesses something, or the thing that
is repossessed

reprehensible /ˌreprɪˈhensəbl/ *adjective formal* Reprehensible behaviour is extremely bad.

represent /ˌreprɪˈzent/ *verb* [T] **1** BE to be equal to something *In practice the figure represents a 10% pay cut.* ○ *The cancellation of the new road project represents a victory for protesters.* **2** SPEAK FOR to officially speak or do something for someone else because they have asked you to *The union represents over 200 employees.* **3** COMPETITION to be the person from a country, school, etc that is in a competition **4** SIGN to be a sign or symbol of something *The crosses on the map represent churches.* **5** SHOW to show someone or something in a particular way

representation /ˌreprɪzenˈteɪʃən/ *noun* **1** SPEAKING FOR [U] speaking or doing something officially for another person *Can he afford **legal representation**?* **2** SHOWING [C, U] the way someone or something is shown *an accurate representation of country life* ⊃See also: **proportional representation**

representative¹ /ˌreprɪˈzentətɪv/ *noun* [C] someone who speaks or does something officially for another person ⊃See also: **House of Representatives**

representative² /ˌreprɪˈzentətɪv/ *adjective* the same as other people or things in a particular group *Are his views **representative of** the rest of the department?*

repress /rɪˈpres/ *verb* [T] **1** FEELINGS to stop yourself from showing your true feelings *Brigitta repressed a sudden desire to cry.* **2** CONTROL PEOPLE to control what people do, especially by using force •**repression** /rɪˈpreʃən/ *noun* [U] when you repress someone or something

repressed /rɪˈprest/ *adjective* **1** PERSON unable to show your true feelings and emotions *a lonely, repressed man* **2** EMOTION A repressed feeling or emotion is one that you do not show. *repressed anger*

repressive /rɪˈpresɪv/ *adjective* cruel and not allowing people to have freedom ***a repressive** military **regime***

reprieve /rɪˈpriːv/ *noun* [C] **1** PUNISHMENT an official order that stops a prisoner from being killed as a punishment **2** SOMETHING UNPLEASANT when something happens to stop a bad situation •**reprieve** *verb* [T]

reprimand /ˈreprɪmɑːnd/ *verb* [T] to tell someone in an official way that they have done something wrong [+ **for** + **doing sth**] *Watts has already been reprimanded for disclosing confidential information.* •**reprimand** *noun* [C]

reprint /riːˈprɪnt/ *verb* [T, I] to print a book again

WORD PARTNERS FOR ***reprisal***

fear reprisals • **in** reprisal **for** sth • **a** reprisal **against/from** sb

reprisal /rɪˈpraɪzəl/ *noun* [C, U] something violent or unpleasant that is done to punish an enemy for something they have done *The attack was **in reprisal for** police raids.* ○ *He did not wish to be filmed because he **feared reprisals**.*

reproach¹ /rɪˈprəʊtʃ/ *noun* [C, U] criticism of someone, especially for not being successful or not doing what is expected *There was a hint of reproach in his voice.* ○ *The article gave the impression that the teachers were **above/beyond reproach*** (= could not be criticized). •**reproachful** *adjective* showing criticism *a **reproachful look*** •**reproachfully** *adverb*

reproach² /rɪˈprəʊtʃ/ *verb* [T] to criticize someone for not being successful or not doing what is expected [**often reflexive**] *You've no reason to reproach yourself.*

reproduce /ˌriːprəˈdjuːs/ *verb* **1** [T] to make a copy of something *The diagram is reproduced by permission of the original author.* **2** **BIOLOGY** [I] *formal* If people, animals, or plants reproduce, they produce babies or young animals or plants.

reproduction /ˌriːprəˈdʌkʃən/ *noun* **1** **BIOLOGY** [U] the process of producing babies or young animals and plants **2** [C] a copy of something, especially a painting

reproductive /ˌriːprəˈdʌktɪv/ *adjective* [**always before noun**] **BIOLOGY** relating to the process of producing babies or young animals and plants *the **reproductive organs***

reptile /ˈreptaɪl/ *noun* [C] **BIOLOGY** an animal whose body is covered with scales (= pieces of hard skin), and whose blood changes temperature, for example a snake ⊃See picture **reptiles** on next page •**reptilian** /repˈtɪliən/ *adjective* like a reptile, or relating to reptiles

republic /rɪˈpʌblɪk/ *noun* [C] **POLITICS** a country with no king or queen but with an elected government

republican /rɪˈpʌblɪkən/ *noun* [C] **POLITICS** **1** someone who supports the principles of a republic **2** **Republican** someone who supports the Republican Party in the

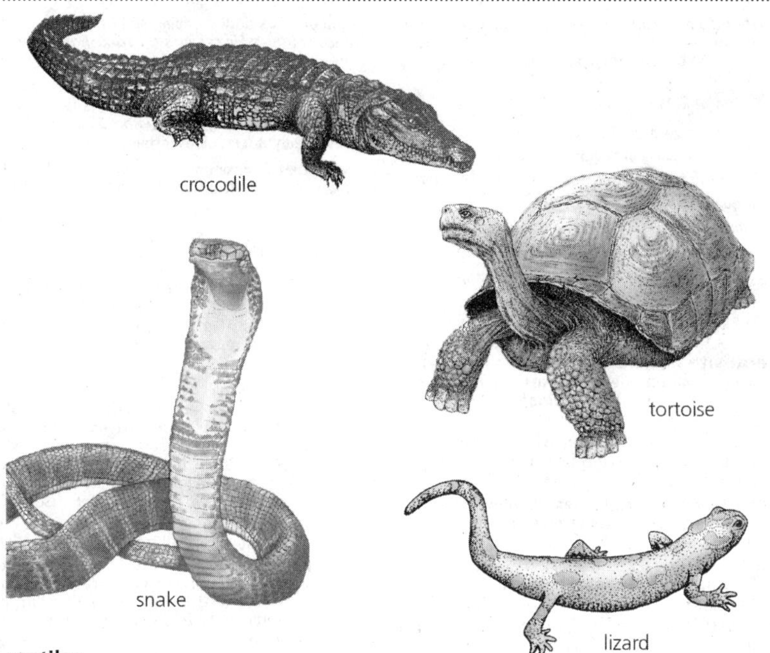

reptiles

US *the Republican candidate* •**republican** *adjective* relating to a republic

the Re'publican ˌParty *noun* [**group**] **POLITICS** one of the two main political parties in the US

repudiate /rɪ'pjuːdieɪt/ *verb* [**T**] *formal* to refuse to accept or agree with something *Cousteau* ***repudiated*** *the* ***criticism/claims****.* •**repudiation** /rɪˌpjuːdi'eɪʃᵊn/ *noun* [**U**] *formal*

repugnant /rɪ'pʌgnənt/ *adjective formal* extremely unpleasant *She thought the idea* ***morally repugnant****.* •**repugnance** /rɪ'pʌgnəns/ *noun* [**U**] *formal* when something or someone is repugnant

repulse /rɪ'pʌls/ *verb* [**T**] **1** UNPLEASANT If someone or something repulses you, you think they are extremely unpleasant. *The smell of him repulsed her.* **2** DEFEAT to successfully stop a military attack [**often passive**] *The enemy attack was quickly repulsed.* **3 PHYSICS** If something repulses a substance or object, it causes it to move away from it

repulsion /rɪ'pʌlʃᵊn/ *noun* [**U, no plural**] **1** a strong feeling that someone or something is extremely unpleasant **2** when something causes an object or substance to move away from it ➲See picture at **magnet**

repulsive /rɪ'pʌlsɪv/ *adjective* extremely unpleasant, especially to look at *a repulsive man with long, greasy hair*

reputable /'repjətəbl/ *adjective* known to be good and honest *a reputable organization* ➲Opposite **disreputable**

WORD PARTNERS FOR ***reputation***

have a reputation • a reputation **for** sth • a **bad/good** reputation • **acquire/establish/get** a reputation • **damage/destroy/ruin** sb's reputation

O-ᵏ**reputation** /ˌrepjə'teɪʃᵊn/ *noun* [**C**] the opinion that people have about someone or something based on their behaviour or character in the past *Both hotels* ***have a good reputation****.* ○ *He has a* ***reputation for*** *efficiency.*

reputed /rɪ'pjuːtɪd/ *adjective formal* believed by most people to be true [**+ to do sth**] *The ghost of a young woman is reputed to haunt the building.* •**reputedly** *adverb*

O-ᵏ**request¹** /rɪ'kwest/ *noun* [**C, U**] when you politely or officially ask for something *His doctor* ***made*** *an urgent* ***request for*** *a copy of the report.* ○ *An application form is available* ***on request*** (= if you ask for it). ○ *A clause was added to the contract* ***at his request*** (= because he asked).

O-ᵏ**request²** /rɪ'kwest/ *verb* [**T**] to politely or officially ask for something *We've requested a further two computers.* [**+ that**] *They requested that no photographs be taken in the church.*

requiem /'rekwiəm/ *noun* [**C**] **MUSIC, RELIGION** a Christian ceremony where people pray for someone who has died, or a piece of music written for this ceremony

O-ᵏ**require** /rɪ'kwaɪəʳ/ *verb* [**T**] **1** to need or demand something *Training to be a doctor requires a lot of hard work.* [**+ that**] *A recent law requires*

R

that all programmes are censored. **2 require sb to do sth** to officially demand that someone does something [**often passive**] *You are required by law to produce a valid passport.*

COMMON LEARNER ERROR

require or **request?**

The main meaning of **require** is 'need'.

Learning a language requires time and effort.

Request means 'ask for'.

I wrote a letter to request more information.

~~*I wrote a letter to require more information.*~~

requirement /rɪˈkwaɪəmənt/ *noun* [**C**] something that is needed or demanded *college **entrance requirements*** ○ *Valid insurance is a **legal requirement**.*

requisite /ˈrekwɪzɪt/ *adjective* [**always before noun**] *formal* needed for a particular purpose *I felt that he lacked the **requisite skills** for the job.*

re-release /ˌriːrɪˈliːs/ *verb* [**T**] to make a record or film available for people to buy or see for a second time

rerun /ˈriːrʌn/ *US* (*UK* **repeat**) *noun* [**C**] a television or radio programme or film that is broadcast again

reschedule /riːˈʃedjuːl/ (US) /riːˈskedʒuːl/ *verb* [**T**] to agree a new and later date for something to happen

rescue[1] /ˈreskjuː/ *verb* [**T**] **rescuing**, *past* **rescued** to save someone from a dangerous or unpleasant situation *Fifty passengers had to be rescued from a sinking ship.* •**rescuer** *noun* [**C**]

rescue[2] /ˈreskjuː/ *noun* **1** [**C, U**] when someone is saved from a dangerous or unpleasant situation *an unsuccessful **rescue attempt*** **2 come to the/sb's rescue** to help someone who is in a difficult situation *I forgot my purse but Anna came to the rescue and lent me some money.*

WORD PARTNERS FOR ***research***

carry out/conduct/do research • research **indicates/proves/reveals/suggests** sth • research **into** sth • a research **assistant/institute/programme/project**

research[1] /rɪˈsɜːtʃ/ *noun* [**U**] when someone studies a subject in detail in order to discover new information ***research into** language development* ○ *They are **doing research** into the effects of passive smoking.* ○ *a **research project*** ➲See also: **market research**

research[2] /rɪˈsɜːtʃ/ *verb* [**I, T**] to study a subject in detail in order to discover new information about it *He spent several years researching a rare African dialect.* •**researcher** *noun* [**C**]

resemblance /rɪˈzembləns/ *noun* [**C, U**] a similarity between two people or things, especially in their appearance *There's a striking **resemblance between** Diane and her mother.* ○ *He **bears a resemblance to*** (= looks like) *someone I used to know.*

resemble /rɪˈzembl/ *verb* [**T**] to look like or be like someone or something *She resembles her father.*

resent /rɪˈzent/ *verb* [**T**] to feel angry and upset about a situation or about something that someone has done [**+ doing sth**] *I resent having to work late.* ○ *He **resents the fact** that she gets more money than he does.*

resentful /rɪˈzentfəl/ *adjective* angry and upset about a situation that you think is unfair *He was bitterly **resentful of** his brother's success.* •**resentfully** *adverb* •**resentfulness** *noun* [**U**]

resentment /rɪˈzentmənt/ *noun* [**U**] a feeling of anger about a situation that you think is unfair

reservation /ˌrezəˈveɪʃən/ *noun* **1** ARRANGEMENT [**C**] an arrangement that you make to have a seat on an aircraft, a room in a hotel, etc *I'd like to **make a reservation** for Friday evening.* **2** DOUBT [**C, U**] a doubt or a feeling that you do not agree with something completely *I still **have reservations** about her ability to do the job.*

reserve[1] /rɪˈzɜːv/ *verb* [**T**] **1** ARRANGE to arrange to have a seat on an aircraft, a room in a hotel, etc *I'd like to reserve two seats on the 9:15 to Birmingham.* **2** PARTICULAR USE to not allow people to use something because it is only for a particular person or for a particular purpose *This seat is **reserved for** elderly or disabled passengers.*

reserve[2] /rɪˈzɜːv/ *noun* **1** SUPPLY [**C**] a supply of something that you keep until it is needed *emergency cash reserves* **2 in reserve** ready to be used if you need it *I always keep a little money in reserve.* **3** QUALITY [**U**] when someone does not show what they are thinking or feeling **4 SPORT** [**C**] in sport, an extra player who is ready to play if one of the other players has an injury **5 ENVIRONMENT** [**C**] an area of land where animals and plants are protected ➲See also: **nature reserve**

reserved /rɪˈzɜːvd/ *adjective* not wanting to show what you are thinking or feeling *a quiet, reserved woman*

reservoir /ˈrezəvwɑːʳ/ *noun* [**C**] **GEOGRAPHY** an artificial lake where water is stored before it goes to people's houses ➲See picture at **hydro-electric power station**

ˈreset ˌ(button) *noun* [**C**] **COMPUTING** a button or switch on a computer that allows the user to turn the computer off and then on again when a program does not work correctly

reshuffle /ˌriːˈʃʌfl/ *noun* [**C**] **POLITICS** when people in an organization, especially a government are given different jobs to do ***a government reshuffle*** •**reshuffle** *verb* [**T**]

reside /rɪˈzaɪd/ *verb formal* **reside in/with, etc** to live somewhere *My sister currently resides in Seattle.*

residence /ˈrezɪdəns/ *noun formal* **1** HOME [**C**] a building where someone lives *the Queen's official residence* **2** LIVE [**U**] when someone lives somewhere *He **took up residence*** (= started to live) *in St. Louis.* **3 in residence** living or working somewhere *He was writer in residence with a professional theatre company.* ➲See also: **hall of residence**

resident[1] /ˈrezɪdənt/ *noun* [**C**] **1** someone who lives in a particular place *complaints from **local residents*** **2 HEALTH** *US* a doctor who is working in a hospital to get extra training in a particular area of medicine

resident² /ˈrezɪdᵊnt/ *adjective* living in a place *She has been resident in Britain for most of her life.*

residential /ˌrezɪˈdenʃᵊl/ *adjective* **1** **GEOGRAPHY** A residential area has only houses and not offices or factories. **2** **EDUCATION** *UK* A residential job or course is one where you live at the same place as you work or study.

residual /rɪˈzɪdjuəl/ *adjective* remaining ***residual value***

residue /ˈrezɪdjuː/ *noun* [C] something that remains after most of a substance has gone or been removed

resign /rɪˈzaɪn/ *verb* [I, T] to officially tell your employer that you are leaving your job *She **resigned as** headteacher.* ○ *Mr Aitken has **resigned from** the company.*
resign yourself to sth *phrasal verb* to make yourself accept something that you do not like because you cannot easily change it *He resigned himself to living alone.*

WORD PARTNERS FOR ***resignation***

accept/call for sb's resignation • **announce/hand in/tender** your resignation • the resignation **of** sb • sb's resignation **as** [manager/chairman, etc] • a **letter of** resignation

resignation /ˌrezɪgˈneɪʃᵊn/ *noun* **1** [LEAVE JOB] [C, U] when someone tells their employer that they are leaving their job *a **letter of resignation*** ○ *I **handed in** my **resignation** yesterday.* **2** [ACCEPT] [U] when you accept something that you do not like because you cannot easily change it

resilient /rɪˈzɪliənt/ *adjective* strong enough to get better quickly after damage, illness, shock, etc *The economy has been fairly resilient.* •**resilience** /rɪˈzɪliəns/ *noun* [U]

resin /ˈrezɪn/ *noun* [C, U] **1** **BIOLOGY** a thick, sticky substance that is produced by some trees **2** a substance that is used for making plastics

resist /rɪˈzɪst/ *verb* [I, T] **1** [AVOID] to stop yourself from doing something that you want to do *I can't resist chocolate.* [+ **doing sth**] *I just can't resist reading other people's mail.* **2** [NOT ACCEPT] to refuse to accept something and try to stop it from happening *The President is resisting calls for him to resign.* **3** [FIGHT] to fight against someone or something that is attacking you *British troops resisted the attack for two days.*

resistance /rɪˈzɪstᵊns/ *noun* [U, no plural] **1** [DISAGREE] when people disagree with a change, idea, etc and refuse to accept it ***resistance to** political change* **2** [FIGHT] when someone fights against someone who is attacking them *She didn't **put up** much **resistance*** (= fight). **3** **HEALTH** the ability of your body to not be affected by illnesses *Cold weather may lower the body's **resistance to** infection.* **4** **PHYSICS** the degree to which a substance prevents the flow of an electric current through it **5** [FORCE] **PHYSICS** a force that makes something move slowly or stop

resistant /rɪˈzɪstᵊnt/ *adjective* **1** [NOT ACCEPTING] not wanting to accept something, especially changes or new ideas *They're **resistant to** change.* **2** [NOT AFFECTED] not harmed or affected by something *a water-resistant cover* ○ *Bacteria can become **resistant to** antibiotics.*

resistor /rɪˈzɪstəʳ/ *noun* [C] **PHYSICS** a device, often a piece of wire, that controls how much electricity goes through a piece of electronic equipment

resolute /ˈrezᵊluːt/ *adjective formal* determined not to change what you do or believe because you think that you are right *a resolute opponent of the war* •**resolutely** *adverb*

resolution /ˌrezᵊlˈuːʃᵊn/ *noun* **1** [DECISION] [C] an official decision that is made after a group or organization have voted *Congress **passed a resolution** in support of the plan* (= voted to support it). **2** [PROMISE] [C] a promise to yourself to do something *My **New Year's resolution** is to do more exercise.* **3** [SOLUTION] [U, no plural] *formal* the solution to a problem *a successful **resolution to** the crisis* **4** [DETERMINATION] [U] *formal* the quality of being determined **5** **PHYSICS** [no plural] the ability of a microscope, or a television or computer screen, to show things clearly and with a lot of detail *a **high/low** resolution image*

resolve¹ /rɪˈzɒlv/ *verb* **1** [SOLVE] [T] to solve or end a problem or difficulty *an attempt to resolve the dispute* **2** [DECIDE] [I, T] *formal* to decide that you will do something and be determined to do it [+ **to do sth**] *I have resolved to keep my bedroom tidy.*

resolve² /rɪˈzɒlv/ *noun* [U] *formal* when you are very determined to do something

resonant /ˈrezᵊnənt/ *adjective* A resonant sound is loud and clear. *a deep, resonant voice* •**resonance** /ˈrezᵊnəns/ *noun* [U]

resonate /ˈrezᵊneɪt/ *verb* [I] to make a loud, clear sound

resort¹ /rɪˈzɔːt/ *noun* **1** [C] a place where many people go for a holiday *a ski resort* **2** **a last resort** something that you do because everything else has failed *Soldiers were given the authority to shoot, but only as a last resort.*

resort² /rɪˈzɔːt/ *verb*
resort to sth/doing sth *phrasal verb* to do something that you do not want to do because you cannot find any other way of achieving something *They should be able to control the riots without resorting to violence.*

resound /rɪˈzaʊnd/ *verb* [I] to make a loud sound, or to be filled with a loud sound *The whole hall **resounded with** applause.*

resounding /rɪˈzaʊndɪŋ/ *adjective* [always before noun] **1** very loud *resounding applause* **2** **a resounding success/victory/failure, etc** a very great success, victory, etc

resource /rɪˈzɔːs, ˈriːsɔːrs/ *noun* [C] something that a country, person, or organization has which they can use [usually plural] ***natural resources*** ⊃See also: **human resources**

resourceful /rɪˈzɔːsfᵊl/ *adjective* good at finding ways to solve problems •**resourcefulness** *noun* [U]

R

WORD PARTNERS FOR ***respect***

command respect • **have/show** (great/no, etc) respect **for** sb • **treat** sb/sth **with** respect

respect[1] /rɪˈspekt/ *noun* **1** POLITE [U] when you are polite to someone, especially because they are older or more important than you *You should show more **respect for** your parents.* **2** ADMIRATION [U] when you admire someone because of their knowledge, skill, or achievements *She's an excellent teacher and I have the greatest **respect for** her.* **3** SHOW IMPORTANCE [U] when you show by your behaviour that you think something is important or needs to be dealt with carefully *Electricity can be dangerous and should always be **treated with respect**.* **4 in this respect/many respects** in a particular way, or in many ways *The school has changed in many respects.* **5 with respect to sth; in respect of sth** *formal* relating to a particular thing *I am writing with respect to your letter of 24 June.* **6 pay your respects a** VISIT SOMEONE *formal* to visit someone or go to talk to them **b** GO TO FUNERAL (*also* **pay your last respects**) to go to someone's funeral ➲See also: **self-respect**

respect[2] /rɪˈspekt/ *verb* [T] **1** ADMIRE to admire someone because of their knowledge, achievements, etc *I **respect** him **for** his honesty.* **2** ACCEPT IMPORTANCE If you respect someone's rights, customs, wishes, etc you accept their importance and are careful not to do anything they would not want.

respectable /rɪˈspektəbl/ *adjective* **1** SOCIALLY ACCEPTABLE behaving in a socially acceptable way or looking socially acceptable *a respectable family* ○ *a respectable hotel* **2** ENOUGH large enough or good enough *a respectable income* •**respectably** *adverb* •**respectability** /rɪˌspektəˈbɪləti/ *noun* [U]

respected /rɪˈspektɪd/ *adjective* admired by people because of your knowledge, achievements, etc *a highly respected doctor*

respectful /rɪˈspektfᵊl/ *adjective* showing respect for someone or something •**respectfully** *adverb*

respective /rɪˈspektɪv/ *adjective* [**always before noun**] relating to each of the people or things that you have just talked about *Members of staff and their respective partners are invited to the reception.*

respectively /rɪˈspektɪvli/ *adverb* in the same order as the people or things you have just talked about *Mr Ewing and Mr Campbell gave £2000 and £250 respectively.*

respiration /ˌrespᵊrˈeɪʃᵊn/ *noun* [U] **BIOLOGY** **1** the process of breathing **2** the process by which living things produce energy from food

respiratory /rɪˈspɪrətᵊri/ (US) /ˈrespərətɔːri/ *adjective* [**always before noun**] **BIOLOGY** relating to the process of breathing *respiratory illnesses* ➲See picture **respiratory system** on next page

respite /ˈrespaɪt/ (US) /ˈrespɪt/ *noun* [**U, no plural**] a short period of rest from something difficult or unpleasant *The weekend was a brief **respite from** the pressures of work.*

respond /rɪˈspɒnd/ *verb* [I] **1** ANSWER to say or do something as an answer or reaction to something that has been said or done [**+ by + doing sth**] *The government has responded by sending food and medical supplies to the region.* ○ *How quickly did the police **respond to** the call?* **2 HEALTH** to improve as the result of a particular medical treatment *She's **responding** well **to** drug treatment.*

respondent /rɪˈspɒndənt/ *noun* [C] someone who has answered a request for information [**usually plural**] *More than half the respondents were opposed to the new tax.*

WORD PARTNERS FOR ***response***

in response **to** sth • sb's response **to** sth • **draw/elicit/provoke** a response • sb's **immediate/initial/instinctive** response

response /rɪˈspɒns/ *noun* [C, U] an answer or reaction to something that has been said or done *The President's comments provoked an **angry response** from students.* ○ *I'm writing **in response to** your letter of 14 February.*

WORD PARTNERS FOR ***responsibility***

abdicate/accept/assume/claim/take/shirk responsibility • **collective/heavy/huge/total** responsibility • responsibility **for** sth

responsibility /rɪˌspɒnsəˈbɪləti/ *noun* **1** [C, U] something that it is your job or duty to deal with *The head of the department has various additional responsibilities.* [**+ to do sth**] *It is your responsibility to make sure that your homework is done on time.* **2 take/accept/claim responsibility for sth** to say that you have done something or caused something to happen, especially something bad *No one has yet claimed responsibility for yesterday's bomb attack.*

responsible /rɪˈspɒnsəbl/ *adjective* **1 be responsible for sb/sth/doing sth** to be the person whose duty is to deal with someone or something *I'm responsible for looking after the children in the evenings.* **2 be responsible for sth/doing sth** to be the person who caused something to happen, especially something bad *Who was responsible for the accident?* **3** BEHAVING CORRECTLY showing good judgment and able to be trusted *a responsible attitude* ➲Opposite **irresponsible** **4** JOB A responsible job is important because you have to make decisions that affect other people. **5 be responsible to sb** If you are responsible to someone at work, they are in a higher position than you and you have to tell them what you have done.

responsibly /rɪˈspɒnsəbli/ *adverb* in a way that shows you have good judgment and can be trusted *to **behave/act responsibly***

responsive /rɪˈspɒnsɪv/ *adjective* listening to someone or something and having a positive and quick reaction to them *a wonderfully responsive audience* ○ *They have not been very **responsive to** the needs of disabled customers.* •**responsiveness** *noun* [U]

rest[1] /rest/ *noun* **1 the rest** the part of something that remains, or the others that remain *I'm not sure I want to spend **the rest of** my life with him.* ○ *She was slightly older than the rest of us.* **2** [C, U] a period of time when you relax

R

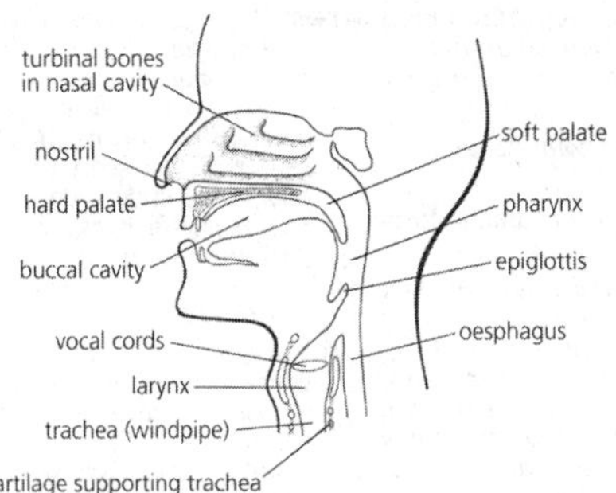

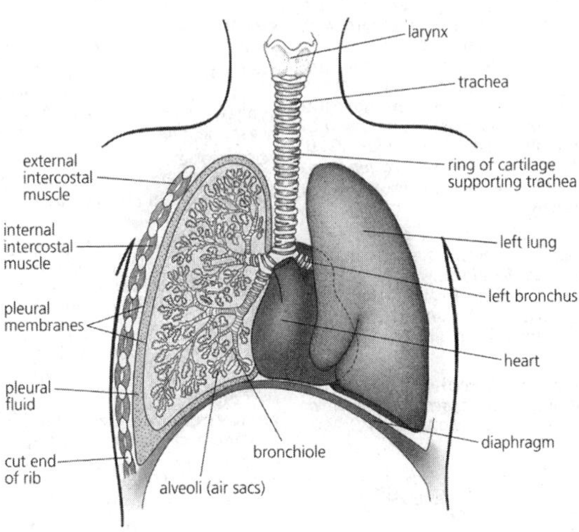

respiratory system

or sleep *Why don't you **have a rest**?* ○ *I must **get** some **rest**.* **3 come to rest** to stop moving ➲See also: put/set sb's **mind**[1] at rest

O-ᵚ**rest²** /rest/ *verb* **1** [I] to relax or sleep because you are tired after doing an activity or because you are ill *Pete's resting after his long drive.* **2 rest your eyes/feet/legs, etc** to stop using your eyes/feet, etc for a while because they are tired **3 rest (sth) on/against, etc** If something rests somewhere, or if you rest it somewhere, it is supported by something else. *She rested her elbows on the table.* ➲See also: rest on your **laurels**

rest on/upon sth *phrasal verb formal* to depend on something *The whole future of the team rests on his decision.*

COMMON LEARNER ERROR

rest, stay, or **remain?**

Rest means to relax or sleep because you are tired or ill.

The doctor told him to rest.

Stay means to continue to be in the same place, job, or particular state.

It was raining, so we stayed at home.

~~*It was raining, so we rested at home.*~~

Remain means to continue to be in the same state, or to continue to exist when everything or everyone else has gone.

He remained unconscious for a week after the accident.

After the earthquake, nothing remained of the village.

restart /ˌriːˈstɑːt/ *verb* [T] **1** to start something again that had stopped *They want to restart the talks.* **2 COMPUTING** If you restart a computer, you turn it off and then on again

WORD PARTNERS FOR ***restaurant***

go to a restaurant • **manage/own/run** a restaurant • a restaurant **offers/serves/specializes in** sth • **at/in** a restaurant

restaurant /ˈrestərɒnt/ *noun* [C] **FOOD** a place where you can buy and eat a meal *an Italian/vegetarian restaurant* ○ *We had lunch* ***at/in a restaurant*** *near the station.*

restaurateur /ˌrestɒrəˈtɜːʳ/ *noun* [C] someone who owns a restaurant

restive /ˈrestɪv/ *adjective formal* unable to be quiet and calm

restless /ˈrestləs/ *adjective* **1** NOT STILL unable to be still or relax because you are bored or nervous *The audience was getting restless.* **2** NOT SATISFIED not satisfied with what you are doing now and wanting something new *After a while in the same relationship I start to get restless.* •**restlessly** *adverb* •**restlessness** *noun* [U]

restore /rɪˈstɔːʳ/ *verb* [T] **1** MAKE EXIST to make something good exist again *Three wins in a row helped* ***restore*** *the team's* ***confidence.*** ○ ***Peace*** *has now been* ***restored*** *in the region.* **2** REPAIR to repair something old *to* ***restore antiques*** **3** RETURN *formal* to give something back to the person it was stolen from or who lost it *The painting was* ***restored to*** *its rightful owner.* •**restoration** /ˌrestəʳˈreɪʃən/ *noun* [C, U] *The building is now closed for restoration* (= repair work). ○ the restoration (= return) of the former government

restrain /rɪˈstreɪn/ *verb* [T] **1** CONTROL SOMEONE to stop someone doing something, sometimes by using force *He became violent and had to be* ***physically restrained.*** [+ **from** + **doing sth**] *I had to restrain myself from shouting at him.* **2** LIMIT to limit something *to restrain arms sales*

restrained /rɪˈstreɪnd/ *adjective* calm and not showing emotions *I was expecting him to be furious but he was very restrained.* ➲Opposite **unrestrained**

restraint /rɪˈstreɪnt/ *noun* **1** CALM [U] showing control over your feelings **2** CONTROL [C] control over something *wage restraints*

restrict /rɪˈstrɪkt/ *verb* [T] to limit something *They've brought in new laws to restrict the sale of cigarettes.* ○ *I* ***restrict*** *myself* ***to*** *one cup of coffee a day.*

restricted /rɪˈstrɪktɪd/ *adjective* controlled or limited *They do good food but the choice is fairly restricted.*

restriction /rɪˈstrɪkʃən/ *noun* [C, U] a rule or law that limits what people can do *There are* ***restrictions on*** *how many goods you can bring into the country.* ○ *parking restrictions*

restrictive /rɪˈstrɪktɪv/ *adjective* limiting activities too much *restrictive practices*

restroom /ˈrestruːm/ *noun* [C] *US* a room with toilets that is in a public place, for example in a restaurant ➲See Common Learner Error at **toilet**

restructure /ˌriːˈstrʌktʃəʳ/ *verb* [I, T] to organize a system or organization in a new way •**restructuring** *noun* [U]

WORD PARTNERS FOR ***result***

the result **of** sth • **as a** result **of** sth • **with** the result **that** • **with** [catastrophic/disastrous, etc.] results • **excellent/good/disappointing/disastrous** results

result¹ /rɪˈzʌlt/ *noun* **1** HAPPEN [C, U] something that happens or exists because something else has happened *Unemployment has risen* ***as a*** *direct* ***result of*** *new economic policies.* ○ *Most accidents are* ***the result of*** *human error.* **2** COMPETITION [C] the score or number of votes at the end of a competition or election *The election results will be known by Sunday.* **3** INFORMATION [C] information that you get from something such as an exam, a scientific experiment, or a medical test

result² /rɪˈzʌlt/ *verb* [I] to happen or exist because something else has happened *There was a food shortage* ***resulting from*** *the lack of rainfall.*

result in sth *phrasal verb* to be the reason something happens *The improvements in training resulted in increased wins.*

resultant /rɪˈzʌltənt/ *adjective formal* happening as a result of something else

resume /rɪˈzjuːm/ *verb* [I, T] *formal* If an activity resumes, or if you resume it, it starts again. *The talks are due to resume today.* •**resumption** /rɪˈzʌmʃən/ *noun* [**no plural**]

resurface /ˌriːˈsɜːfɪs/ *verb* [I] to appear again after having been lost or forgotten *The story resurfaced in the news again last week.*

resurgence /rɪˈsɜːdʒəns/ *noun* [**no plural**] when something starts to happen again or people become interested in something again *There has been a resurgence of interest in the game.* •**resurgent** /rɪˈsɜːdʒənt/ *adjective* happening again

resurrect /ˌrezəʳˈekt/ *verb* [T] to make something exist again which has not existed for a long time *With this film Dykes hopes to resurrect his career.*

resurrection /ˌrezəʳˈekʃən/ *noun* [U] **1** when something starts to exist again which has not existed for a long period *the resurrection of a fashion* **2 RELIGION** in the Christian religion, Jesus Christ's return to life after he was killed

resuscitate /rɪˈsʌsɪteɪt/ *verb* [T] **HEALTH** to make someone breathe again when they have stopped breathing •**resuscitation** /rɪˌsʌsɪˈteɪʃən/ *noun* [U]

retail¹ /ˈriːteɪl/ *noun* [U] **ECONOMICS** when products are sold to customers from shops *jobs in retail*

retail² /ˈriːteɪl/ *verb* **ECONOMICS retail at/for £50/$100, etc** to be sold to the public for a particular price *This computer retails at $2,000.*

retailer /ˈriːteɪləʳ/ *noun* [C] **ECONOMICS** someone who sells products to the public

retailing /ˈriːteɪlɪŋ/ *noun* [U] **ECONOMICS** the business of selling products to customers in shops

ˌretail ˈprice ˌindex (*abbreviation* **RPI**) *noun* [**C usually singular**] **ECONOMICS** a measurement of the changes in the cost of basic goods and services

retain /rɪˈteɪn/ *verb* [T] to continue to keep something *The council will* ***retain control*** *of the school.*

retaliate /rɪˈtælieɪt/ *verb* [I] to do something bad to someone because they have done something bad to you *They have threatened to* ***retaliate against*** *any troops that attack.*

•**retaliation** /rɪˌtæliˈeɪʃᵊn/ *noun* [U] *They bombed the hotel* ***in retaliation for*** *the arrests.* •**retaliatory** /rɪˈtæliəᵊri/ *adjective retaliatory measures*

retention /rɪˈtenʃᵊn/ *noun* [U] when something continues to be kept

rethink /ˌriːˈθɪŋk/ *verb* [I, T] *past* **rethought** to change what you think about something or what you plan to do *We've had to* ***rethink*** *our* ***strategy.*** •**rethink** /ˈriːθɪŋk/ *noun* [no plural] *The whole issue of moving to new offices needs a fundamental rethink.*

reticent /ˈretɪsᵊnt/ *adjective* saying little about what you think or feel *He was reticent about his private life.* •**reticence** /ˈretɪsᵊns/ *noun* [U]

retina /ˈretɪnə/ *noun* [C] **ANATOMY** a part at the back of the eye, which is affected by light and sends messages to the brain ➲See picture at **eye**

O⊸**retire** /rɪˈtaɪəʳ/ *verb* [I] **1** [STOP WORK] to leave your job and stop working, usually because you are old *She* ***retired from*** *the company in 1990.* **2** [GO] *formal* to go to another place where you can be alone or more private *After dinner, he* ***retired to*** *his bedroom.*

retired /rɪˈtaɪəd/ *adjective* having stopped working, often because you are old *a retired farmer/teacher*

retiree /rɪˈtaɪriː/ *noun* [C] *US* someone who has stopped working, usually because they are old

WORD PARTNERS FOR ***retirement***

take early retirement • **in** retirement • retirement **from** sth • retirement **age**

retirement /rɪˈtaɪəmənt/ *noun* [C, U] **1** [STOP WORKING] when you leave your job and stop working, usually because you are old *He's* ***taking early retirement.*** **2** [TIME] the period of your life after you have stopped working *We wish you a long and happy retirement.*

retiring /rɪˈtaɪərɪŋ/ *adjective* shy and quiet

retort /rɪˈtɔːt/ *verb* [T] *formal* to answer someone quickly in an angry or funny way *"That doesn't concern you," she retorted sharply.* •**retort** *noun* [C] *formal*

retrace /rɪˈtreɪs/ *verb* **retrace your steps** to go back somewhere the same way that you came *I was lost so I retraced my steps.*

retract /rɪˈtrækt/ *verb* [I, T] *formal* to admit that something you said before was not true *Several key witnesses have* ***retracted*** *their* ***statements/claims/allegations.***

retrain /riːˈtreɪn/ *verb* [T] to learn a new skill so you can do a different job *Owen used to be an actor but now he's* ***retraining as*** *a teacher.*

retraining /ˌriːˈtreɪnɪŋ/ *noun* [U] when someone learns new skills so they can do a different job

retreat¹ /rɪˈtriːt/ *verb* [I] **1** When soldiers retreat, they move away from the enemy, especially to avoid fighting. *The army was forced to retreat.* **2 retreat to/into, etc** to go away to a place or situation which is safer or quieter *She retreated into the bathroom for some peace and quiet.*

retreat² /rɪˈtriːt/ *noun* **1** [MOVE] [U, no plural] a move away, especially to a place or situation which is safer or quieter *He saw the dog coming towards him and* ***beat a hasty retreat*** (= moved quickly away). **2** [MILITARY] [C, U] a move back by soldiers or an army, especially to avoid fighting *a strategic retreat* **3** [PLACE] [C] a quiet place where you can go to rest or be alone *a mountain retreat*

retrial /ˌriːˈtraɪəl/ *noun* [C] **LAW** a new trial for a crime that has already been judged in a law court *The judge* ***ordered*** *a* ***retrial.***

retribution /ˌretrɪˈbjuːʃᵊn/ *noun* [U] *formal* punishment for something morally wrong that was done *They're seeking* ***retribution for*** *the killings.*

retrieve /rɪˈtriːv/ *verb* [T] to get something after first finding it *I've just* ***retrieved*** *the ball* ***from*** *the bottom of the pond.* ○ *computer tools for* ***retrieving information*** •**retrieval** *noun* [U] when something is retrieved

retriever /rɪˈtriːvəʳ/ *noun* [C] a large dog with thick black or light brown hair

retro /ˈretrəʊ/ *adjective* looking or sounding like something from the past *His clothes had a retro look.*

retrospect /ˈretrəʊspekt/ *noun* **in retrospect** thinking now about something in the past *In retrospect, I should probably have told her.*

retrospective¹ /ˌretrəʊˈspektɪv/ *noun* [C] **ART** a show of work done by an artist over many years

retrospective² /ˌretrəʊˈspektɪv/ *adjective* If a law or decision is retrospective, it affects situations in the past as well as in the future. •**retrospectively** *adverb*

O⊸**return¹** /rɪˈtɜːn/ *verb* **1** [GO BACK] [I] to go or come back to a place where you were before *She* ***returned to*** *America in 1954.* ○ *I won't* ***return from*** *my holiday till May.* **2** [GIVE BACK] [T] to give, send, or put something back where it came from *He immediately* ***returned*** *the records* ***to*** *the files.* **3 return to sth a** [START AGAIN] to start doing an activity again or talking about something again *I returned to work three months after Susie was born.* **b** [AS BEFORE] to go back to a previous condition *Life has begun to* ***return to normal*** *now that the war is over.* **4** [HAPPEN AGAIN] [I] If something returns, it happens again. *If the pains return phone the doctor.* **5** [DO THE SAME] [T] to react to something that someone does or says by doing or saying the same *I must* ***return*** *Michael's* ***call*** (= telephone him because he telephoned me earlier). **6 return a verdict/sentence** to announce if someone is guilty or not guilty or what punishment the person will be given in a law court *The jury returned a verdict of guilty.* **7 SPORT** [T] to hit or throw a ball back to someone when playing a sport

return² /rɪˈtɜːn/ *noun* **1** [GOING BACK] [no plural] when someone goes or comes back to a place where they were before ***On*** *his* ***return*** *to Sydney, he started up a business.* **2** [GIVING BACK] [no plural] when something is given back, put back, or sent back *the return of the stolen goods* **3** [ACTIVITY] [no plural] when someone starts an activity again *This film marks his* ***return to*** *acting.* **4** [HAPPENING AGAIN] [no plural] when something starts to happen or be present again

R

What we are seeing here is ***a return to*** *traditional values.* **5** TICKET [C] *UK* (*US* **round-trip ticket**) a ticket that lets you travel to a place and back again, for example on a train **6** **FINANCE** [C, U] the profit that you get from an investment *This fund has shown* ***high returns*** *for the last five years.* **7** **in return** in exchange for something or as a reaction to something *I'd like to give them something* ***in return for*** *everything they've done for us.* **8** **SPORT** [C] when a ball is thrown or hit back to another player in a sports match **9** **COMPUTING** [U] a key on a computer keyboard that is used to make the computer accept information or to start a new line in a document *Type in the password and* ***press return.*** ➲See also: **day return**

returnable /rɪ'tɜːnəbl/ *adjective* If something is returnable, it can be taken or given back. *a* ***returnable deposit***

reˌturns ˈinward (*also* **sales returns**) *noun* [plural] **ECONOMICS** goods that are returned to the company that supplied them, for example because they are damaged or not needed

reˌturns ˈoutward (*also* **purchases returns**) *noun* [plural] **ECONOMICS** goods that are returned to the company that supplied them, for example because they are damaged or not needed

reunification /ˌriːjuːnɪfɪ'keɪʃən/ *noun* [U] **POLITICS** when a country that was divided into smaller countries is joined together again as one country *the reunification of Germany*

WORD PARTNERS FOR ***reunion***

have/go to a reunion • an **emotional** reunion • a reunion **of** sb • sb's reunion **with** sb • a **family/school** reunion

reunion /ˌriː'juːniən/ *noun* [C] an occasion when people who have not met each other for a long time meet again *a* ***family/school reunion***

reunite /ˌriːjuː'naɪt/ *verb* [I, T] to meet again after being apart for a long time, or to bring people together who have been apart for a long time [often passive] *Years later, he was* ***reunited with*** *his brother.*

reuse /ˌriː'juːz/ *verb* [T] **ENVIRONMENT** to find a new use for something so that it does not have to be thrown away *Businesses are finding new ways to reuse materials.* •**reusable** *adjective*

Rev **RELIGION** *written abbreviation for* Reverend (= title of Christian official) *Rev Jo Harding*

rev /rev/ (*also* **rev up**) *verb* [I, T] **revving**, *past* **revved** to increase the engine speed of a vehicle *He revved the engine and drove off.*

revalue /riː'væljuː/ *verb* [T] **1** **FINANCE** to decide the value of something again because the value has changed **2** **ECONOMICS** If a government revalues its currency (= the money the country uses), it makes it worth more •**revaluation** /riːˌvæljuː'eɪʃən/ *noun* [U]

revamp /ˌriː'væmp/ *verb* [T] to change something in order to make it better *They're revamping the restaurant.*

Revd **RELIGION** *written abbreviation for* Reverend (= title of Christian official) *the Revd Laurie Clow*

O⊸**reveal** /rɪ'viːl/ *verb* [T] **1** TELL to give someone a piece of information that is surprising or that was previously secret [+ **that**] *It was revealed in this morning's papers that the couple intend to marry.* **2** SEE to allow something to be seen that, until then, had been hidden *His shirt came up at the back, revealing an expanse of white skin.*

revealing /rɪ'viːlɪŋ/ *adjective* **1** SHOWING showing someone's true character or the true facts about someone or something *a revealing biography/remark* **2** CLOTHES If clothes are revealing, they show a lot of your body.

revel /'revəl/ *verb UK* **revelling**, *past* **revelled**, *US* **reveling**, *past* **reveled**

revel in sth *phrasal verb* to enjoy a situation or activity very much *He revelled in his role as team manager.*

revelation /ˌrevəl'eɪʃən/ *noun* **1** [C] a piece of information that is discovered although it was intended to be kept secret *He resigned following* ***revelations about*** *his private life.* **2** **be a revelation** to be an extremely pleasant surprise *Anna's boyfriend was a revelation.*

WORD PARTNERS FOR ***revenge***

get/plot/seek/take revenge • **in** revenge for sth • revenge **against/on** sb • an **act of** revenge

revenge /rɪ'vendʒ/ *noun* [U] something that you do to punish someone who has done something bad to you *He's made life very difficult for me but I'll* ***get/take*** *my* ***revenge.*** ○ *He was shot* ***in revenge*** *for the murder.*

revenue /'revənjuː/ (*also* **revenues**) *noun* [U] **ECONOMICS** large amounts of money received by a government as tax, or by a company

reverberate /rɪ'vɜːbəreɪt/ *verb* [I] If a sound reverberates, it is heard for a long time as it is sent back from different surfaces. *The sound of the shots reverberated around the building.*

revere /rɪ'vɪər/ *verb* [T] *formal* to respect and admire someone very much *a revered religious leader*

reverence /'revərəns/ *noun* [U] *formal* a strong feeling of respect and admiration

Reverend /'revərənd/ *adjective* **RELIGION** used as a title before the name of some Christian officials *the Reverend Alan Pringle*

reverie /'revəri/ *noun* [C] *formal* a pleasant state in which you are thinking of something else, not what is happening around you

reversal /rɪ'vɜːsəl/ *noun* [C] when something changes to its opposite *In a reversal of traditional roles, Paul stayed at home to look after the baby and Clare went out to work.*

reverse[1] /rɪ'vɜːs/ *verb* **1** DRIVE [I, T] to drive a vehicle backwards *I hate reversing into parking spaces.* **2** CHANGE [T] to change a situation or change the order of things so that it becomes the opposite *It is unlikely that the judge will* ***reverse*** *his* ***decision.***

reverse[2] /rɪ'vɜːs/ *noun* **1** **the reverse** the opposite of what has been suggested *"So, is he happier?" "Quite the reverse - I've never seen him look so miserable."* **2** [U] (*also* **reˌverse ˈgear**) the method of controlling a vehicle that makes it go backwards *Put the car* ***into reverse***. **3 in reverse** in the opposite order or way *Do the same steps but this time in reverse.*

reverse³ /rɪ'vɜːs/ *adjective* [**always before noun**] opposite to the usual way or to the way you have just described *I'm going to read out the names of the winners in reverse order.*

reversible /rɪ'vɜːsəbl/ *adjective* **1** CAN BE CHANGED If something is reversible, it can be changed back to what it was before. *Most of the damage done to the cells is reversible.* ➲Opposite **irreversible 2** CLOTHES Reversible clothes can be worn so that the inside is the outside. *a reversible jacket*

revert /rɪ'vɜːt/ *verb*
revert to sth/doing sth *phrasal verb* to go back to how something was before *For a while I ate low-fat food but then I reverted to my old eating habits.* •**reversion** /rɪ'vɜːʃᵊn/ *noun* [**U, no plural**]

WORD PARTNERS FOR ***review***

carry out a review • a review **of** sth • be **under** review

review¹ /rɪ'vjuː/ *noun* **1** CONSIDERING [**C, U**] the process of considering something again in order to make changes to it ***a review of*** *teachers' pay* ○ *The policy is now* ***under review*** (= being considered). **2** REPORT [**C**] a report in a newspaper, magazine, or programme that gives an opinion about a new book, film, etc *a book review* ○ *The film has had* ***mixed reviews*** (= some good, some bad).

review² /rɪ'vjuː/ *verb* **1** CONSIDER [**T**] to consider something again in order to decide if changes should be made *The courts will review her case.* **2** REPORT [**T**] to give your opinion in a report about a film, book, television programme, etc *He reviews films for the Times.* **3 EDUCATION** [**I, T**] *US* (*UK* **revise**) to study a subject before you take a test

reviewer /rɪ'vjuːəʳ/ *noun* [**C**] someone who writes reviews of a book, film, etc

reviled /rɪ'vaɪld/ *adjective* hated *He is possibly the most reviled man in Britain.*

revise /rɪ'vaɪz/ *verb* **1** [**T**] to change something so that it is more accurate *a revised edition of the book* **2 EDUCATION** [**I, T**] *UK* (*US* **review**) to study a subject before you take a test

revision /rɪ'vɪʒᵊn/ *noun* **1** [**C, U**] when you change something so that it is more accurate *a downward revision of prices* **2 EDUCATION** [**U**] *UK* when you study a subject before taking a test

revitalize (*also UK* **-ise**) /ˌriː'vaɪtᵊlaɪz/ *verb* [**T**] to make something more active or exciting *attempts to revitalize the city*

revival /rɪ'vaɪvᵊl/ *noun* **1** POPULAR [**C, U**] when something becomes more active or popular again ***a revival in*** *folk music* ○ *Yoga is* ***enjoying a revival***. **2** PERFORMANCE [**C**] a performance of a play, opera, etc that has not been performed for a long time

revive /rɪ'vaɪv/ *verb* **1** EXIST AGAIN [**T**] to make something from the past exist again *to revive memories* ○ *A lot of traditional skills are currently being revived.* **2** CONSCIOUS [**I, T**] to become conscious again or make someone conscious again *A police officer tried unsuccessfully to revive her.* **3** FEEL BETTER [**I, T**] to start to feel healthier and more active again, or to make someone feel this way *A cup of tea and something to eat might revive you.*

revoke /rɪ'vəʊk/ *verb* [**T**] *formal* to stop someone having official permission to do something, or to change an official decision *His work permit was revoked after six months.*

revolt¹ /rɪ'vəʊlt/ *noun* [**C, U**] **POLITICS** when people try to change a government, often using violence, or when they refuse to accept someone's authority *a slave/peasant revolt*

revolt² /rɪ'vəʊlt/ *verb* **1 POLITICS** [**I**] to try to change a government, often using violence, or to refuse to accept someone's authority *Many were killed when nationalists* ***revolted against*** *the new government.* **2 be revolted by sth** to think that something is extremely unpleasant

revolting /rɪ'vəʊltɪŋ/ *adjective* extremely unpleasant

revolution /ˌrevᵊl'uːʃᵊn/ *noun* **1 POLITICS** [**C, U**] a change in the way a country is governed, usually to a different political system and often using violence or war *the French Revolution* **2** CHANGE [**C**] a very important change in the way people think or do things *the technological revolution* ○ *This discovery caused a* ***revolution in*** *medicine.* **3** CIRCLE [**C, U**] one whole circular movement around a central point, for example one whole movement of a wheel

revolutionary¹ /ˌrevᵊl'uːʃᵊnᵊri/ *adjective* **1** completely different from what was done before *The twentieth century has brought about* ***revolutionary changes*** *in our lifestyles.* **2 POLITICS** relating to a political revolution *a* ***revolutionary movement***

revolutionary² /ˌrevᵊl'uːʃᵊnᵊri/ *noun* [**C**] **POLITICS** someone who tries to cause or take part in a political revolution

revolutionize (*also UK* **-ise**) /ˌrevᵊl'uːʃᵊnaɪz/ *verb* [**T**] to change something in every way so that it is much better *This will revolutionize the way we do business.*

revolve /rɪ'vɒlv/ *verb* [**I**] to move in a circle around a central point *A fan was revolving slowly.* •**revolving** *adjective* [**always before noun**] *a revolving door*
revolve around/round sth/sb *phrasal verb* to have as the only interest or subject *Her whole life revolves around her children.*

revolver /rɪ'vɒlvəʳ/ *noun* [**C**] a small gun

revue /rɪ'vjuː/ *noun* [**C**] a show in a theatre with jokes, songs, and dancing

revulsion /rɪ'vʌlʃᵊn/ *noun* [**U**] a strong feeling that something is very unpleasant

WORD PARTNERS FOR ***reward***

get/receive a reward • a **big/handsome/substantial** reward • a reward **for** sb/sth • a reward **of** [$500/$300, etc]

O➡**reward¹** /rɪ'wɔːd/ *noun* **1** GOOD WORK [**C, U**] something good that you get or experience because you have worked hard, behaved well, etc *There'll be a* ***reward for*** *whoever finishes first.* **2** MONEY [**C**] money that the police give to

R

someone who gives them information about a crime

reward² /rɪˈwɔːd/ *verb* [T] to give a reward to someone *She was* ***rewarded for*** *her bravery.*

rewarding /rɪˈwɔːdɪŋ/ *adjective* making you feel satisfied that you have done something well *Teaching is hard work but it's very rewarding.*

rewind /ˈriːwaɪnd/ *verb* [I, T] *past* **rewound** to make a sound or television recording go back to the beginning

rework /ˌriːˈwɜːk/ *verb* [T] to change a piece of music or writing in order to improve it or make it more suitable *Elton John reworked his 1974 hit, 'Candle in the Wind', for Princess Diana's funeral.*

rewrite /ˌriːˈraɪt/ *verb* [T] *past tense* **rewrote**, *past participle* **rewritten** to write something again in order to improve it *I had to rewrite my essay.*

rhapsody /ˈræpsədi/ *noun* [C] **MUSIC** a piece of music for instruments

rhetoric /ˈretərɪk/ *noun* [U] **LANGUAGE** language that is intended to make people believe things, often language that is not sincere *It was the usual political speech, full of* ***empty rhetoric****.* •**rhetorical** /rɪˈtɒrɪkəl/ *adjective* •**rhetorically** *adverb*

rheˌtorical ˈquestion /rɪˌtɒrɪkəlˈkwestʃən/ *noun* [C] **LANGUAGE** a question that is not intended as a real question because you do not expect anyone to answer it

rheumatism /ˈruːmətɪzəm/ *noun* [U] **HEALTH** a disease in which there is swelling and pain in the joints (= parts of the body where bones join)

rhino /ˈraɪnəʊ/ *noun* [C] *short for* rhinoceros

rhinoceros /raɪˈnɒsərəs/ *noun* [C] a large animal from Africa or Asia that has thick skin and one or two horns on its nose

rhizome /ˈraɪzəʊm/ *noun* [C] **BIOLOGY** a stem of some plants which grows horizontally along or under the ground and which produces roots and leaves

rhomboid /ˈrɒmbɔɪd/ *noun* [C] **MATHEMATICS** a flat shape with four sides and opposite sides of equal length, in which the sides next to each other are not of equal length ➲See picture at **parallelogram**

rhombus /ˈrɒmbəs/ *noun* [C] *plural* **rhombuses** or **rhombi** **MATHEMATICS** a flat shape which has four sides that are all of equal length ➲See picture at **parallelogram**

rhubarb /ˈruːbɑːb/ *noun* [U] **FOOD** a plant that has long, red stems that can be cooked and eaten as a fruit

rhyme¹ /raɪm/ *verb* [I] **LITERATURE** If a word rhymes with another word, the end part of the words sound the same. *'Moon' rhymes with 'June'.*

rhyme² /raɪm/ *noun* **LITERATURE** **1** [C] a short poem that has words that rhyme at the end of each line **2** [U] a style of writing or speaking that uses words which rhyme *The story was written entirely in rhyme.* **3** [C] a word that rhymes with another word ➲See also: **nursery rhyme**

rhythm /ˈrɪðəm/ *noun* [C, U] **MUSIC** a regular, repeating pattern of sound *You need a* ***sense of rhythm*** *to be a good dancer.* •**rhythmic** /ˈrɪðmɪk/ *adjective* with rhythm •**rhythmically** *adverb*

rib /rɪb/ *noun* [C] **ANATOMY** one of the curved bones in the chest ➲See picture at **rib cage**

ribbon /ˈrɪbən/ *noun* [C] a long, narrow piece of cloth that is used for tying things or used for decoration

ˈribbon ˌlake *noun* [C] **GEOGRAPHY** a long, narrow lake

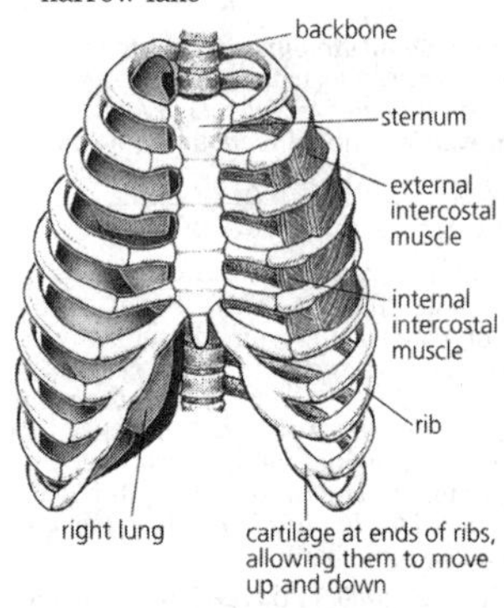

rib cage

ˈrib ˌcage *noun* [C] **ANATOMY** the structure of ribs (= curved bones) in the chest

ribonucleic acid /ˌraɪbəʊnjuːkliːɪkˈæsɪd/ (*abbreviation* **RNA**) *noun* [U] **CHEMISTRY** an important chemical present in all living cells

O‑ **rice** /raɪs/ *noun* [U] **FOOD** small grains from a plant that are cooked and eaten ➲See colour picture **Food** on page Centre 11

ˈrice ˌpaddy (*also UK* **paddy field**) *noun* [C] **FARMING** a field in which rice is grown

OTHER WAYS OF SAYING *rich*

The adjectives **wealthy** and **well-off** are common alternatives to 'rich': *Oliver's parents are very* ***wealthy/well-off****.*

If someone is very rich, in informal situations you can use the adjective **loaded** or the expression **be rolling in it**: *They don't have any money worries - they're* ***loaded****.* • *If he can afford a yacht, he must* ***be rolling in it****.*

If someone is richer than they were previously, the adjective **better-off** is often used: *We're a lot* ***better-off*** *now that Jane's working again.*

The adjectives **affluent** and **prosperous** are sometimes used to describe areas where people are rich: *It's a very* ***affluent*** *neighbourhood.* • *In a* ***prosperous*** *country like this, no-one should go hungry.*

O‑ **rich** /rɪtʃ/ *adjective* **1** MONEY having much more money than most people, or owning things that could be sold for a lot of money *She's the third richest woman in Britain.* ○ *These cars are only for **the rich**.* **2** CONTAINING A LOT containing a lot of something that is important or valuable *rich soil* ○ *Both foods are **rich in** Vitamin C.* **3** FOOD Rich food has a lot of butter, cream, or eggs in it. *a rich sauce* **4** STRONG A rich sound is low and strong, and a rich colour is bright and strong. •**richness** *noun* [U]

riches /ˈrɪtʃɪz/ *noun* [**plural**] *literary* a lot of money or valuable objects ⊃See also: go from **rags** to riches

richly /ˈrɪtʃli/ *adverb* **1 be richly decorated/furnished, etc** to have a lot of beautiful or expensive decoration, furniture, etc *a richly decorated church* **2 be richly rewarded** to be paid a lot of money **3 richly deserve** to very much deserve something *Later that year he received the award he so richly deserved.*

the Richter scale /ðəˈrɪktəskeɪl/ *noun* **GEOLOGY** a system used to measure the strength of an earthquake (= sudden movement of the Earth's surface)

rickets /ˈrɪkɪts/ *noun* [U] **HEALTH** a disease in which the bones become soft and not shaped correctly, caused by not having enough vitamin D

rickety /ˈrɪkəti/ *adjective* likely to break soon *a rickety wooden chair*

ricochet /ˈrɪkəʃeɪ/ *verb* [I] to hit a surface and then be sent back through the air *The bullet **ricocheted off** the wall.*

O→**rid¹** /rɪd/ *adjective* **1 get rid of sth a** to throw something away or give something to someone because you do not want it now *We must get rid of some of those old books.* **b** to end something unpleasant *I can't seem to get rid of this headache.* **2 get rid of sb** to make someone leave *She was useless at her job so we had to get rid of her.* **3 be rid of sb/sth** to be without someone or something that you do not like or want *I'd do anything to be rid of him.*

rid² /rɪd/ *verb* **ridding**, *past* **rid**
rid sth of sth *phrasal verb* to remove something unpleasant from somewhere *to rid the world of nuclear weapons*
rid yourself of sth *phrasal verb* to remove something that you do not want *to rid yourself of a reputation*

riddance /ˈrɪdᵊns/ *noun* **Good riddance!** used to express pleasure when you have got rid of something or someone that you do not want

ridden /ˈrɪdᵊn/ *past participle of* ride

riddle /ˈrɪdl/ *noun* [C] **1** QUESTION a strange and difficult question that has a clever and often funny answer **2** NOT UNDERSTAND a situation or event that you cannot understand *Scientists may have **solved the riddle** of Saturn's rings.*

riddled /ˈrɪdld/ *adjective* **be riddled with sth** to contain a large number of something bad *The wall was riddled with bullets.*

O→**ride¹** /raɪd/ *verb past tense* **rode**, *past participle* **ridden 1 SPORT** [I, T] to travel by sitting on a horse, bicycle, or motorcycle and controlling it *I ride my bike to work.* ○ *She taught me to ride* (= to ride a horse). ⊃See Common Learner Error at **drive 2** [T] *US* to travel in a vehicle as a passenger *I've told her not to ride the subway at night.*
ride on sth *phrasal verb* If something important rides on a situation, it will succeed or fail depending on the situation. *There was $600,000 riding on the outcome of the deal.*
ride out sth *phrasal verb* to continue to exist during a bad situation *to ride out a recession*

WORD PARTNERS FOR ***ride (noun)***

go for/hitch a ride • a ride **in/on** sth • **give** sb a ride

ride² /raɪd/ *noun* [C] **1** VEHICLE a journey in a vehicle or train *Can I **give** you **a ride** to the station?* **2** BICYCLE a journey riding a bicycle, motorcycle, or horse *He's gone out for a ride on his bike.* **3** PLAYING a machine at a fair (= event outdoors) which moves people up and down, round in circles, etc as they sit in it

rider /ˈraɪdəʳ/ *noun* [C] **SPORT** someone who rides a horse, bicycle, or motorcycle ⊃See colour picture **Sports 1** on page Centre 14

ridge /rɪdʒ/ *noun* [C] **1 GEOGRAPHY** a long, narrow piece of high land, especially along the top of a mountain *a mountain ridge* **2** a narrow, raised line on a flat surface

ridicule¹ /ˈrɪdɪkjuːl/ *verb* [T] to make people laugh at someone in an unkind way *I was **ridiculed for** saying they might win.*

ridicule² /ˈrɪdɪkjuːl/ *noun* [U] when people laugh at someone in an unkind way

ridiculous /rɪˈdɪkjələs/ *adjective* very silly *I've never heard anything so ridiculous.* •**ridiculously** *adverb ridiculously expensive*

riding /ˈraɪdɪŋ/ *noun* [U] **SPORT** the sport or activity of riding horses

rife /raɪf/ *adjective* [**never before noun**] Something unpleasant that is rife is very common. *Rumours were rife that the band would split up.*

rifle¹ /ˈraɪfl/ *noun* [C] a long gun that you hold against your shoulder when you shoot

rifle² /ˈraɪfl/ (*also* **rifle through**) *verb* [T] to quickly search through things, often in order to steal something *I caught him rifling through my drawers.*

WORD PARTNERS FOR ***rift***

create/heal a rift • a **deep/growing/huge/serious** rift • a rift **with** sb • a rift **between** sb **and** sb • a rift **over** sth

rift /rɪft/ *noun* [C] **1** a serious disagreement *the deepening **rift between** the government and the unions* **2 GEOGRAPHY** a very large hole that separates parts of the Earth's surface

rig¹ /rɪg/ *verb* [T] **rigging**, *past* **rigged POLITICS** to arrange an election, competition, etc so that the results are not fair or true *He accused the government of rigging the elections.*
rig sth up *phrasal verb* to quickly make a piece of equipment from any materials you can find

rig² /rɪg/ *noun* [C] a large structure for removing gas or oil from the ground or the sea *an **oil rig***

rigging /ˈrɪgɪŋ/ *noun* [U] a system of ropes and chains used to support a ship's masts (= poles)

R

O⁻ **right¹** /raɪt/ *adjective* **1** CORRECT correct or true *He only got half the answers right.* ○ *You're **right about** Alison - she's incredible!* ○ *"You came here in 1979, didn't you?" **"That's right."*** **2** DIRECTION [**always before noun**] on or towards the side of your body that is to the east when you are facing north *your right hand* ○ *There's a tree on the **right side** of the house.* **3** SUITABLE suitable or best in a particular situation *I'm not sure she's the right person for the job.* ○ *Are we going in the right direction?* **4** ACCEPTABLE fair or morally acceptable ***It's not right** to criticize him behind his back.* **5 put sth right** to solve a problem **6** COMPLETE [**always before noun**] *UK informal* used for emphasizing when something is bad *His house is a right mess.* ➲See also: **all right**

COMMON LEARNER ERROR

right or **true?**

Right is usually used to say something is correct or to agree with something someone has said.

He gave the right answer.

"That's right, they live in central London."

True is usually used to say something is based on facts.

Is it true that she's leaving?

Everything I've told you is true.

O⁻ **right²** /raɪt/ *adverb* **1** EXACTLY exactly in a place or time *He's right here with me.* ○ *I fell asleep right in the middle of her speech.* **2** CORRECTLY correctly *He guessed right most of the time.* **3** DIRECTION to the right side ***Turn right** after the bridge.* **4 right away/now/after** immediately *Do you want to start right away?* **5** ALL all the way *Did you read it right through to the end?* **6** IN SPEECH *UK* used at the beginning of a sentence to get someone's attention or to show you have understood someone *Right, who's turn is it to tidy up?* ○ *Right, so Helen's coming tomorrow and Trevor on Thursday.* **7 Right** **POLITICS, RELIGION** used in the UK as part of the title of some politicians and Christian officials *Right Honourable/Reverend* **8 It serves her/him/you right!** *informal* something you say about a bad thing which has happened to a person and which they deserve *So she left him, did she? Serves him right!* •**rightness** *noun* [**U**] ➲See also: be right up sb's **alley**, be right up sb's **street**

R

O⁻ **right³** /raɪt/ *noun* **1 LAW** [**C**] something that the law allows you to do ***the right to** free speech* [**+ to do sth**] *the right to vote* **2** DIRECTION [**U**] the right side of your body, or the direction towards this side *You'll find her in the second room **on the right**.* **3** BEHAVIOUR [**U**] morally correct behaviour *I've tried to teach them the difference between **right and wrong**.* **4 have a/no right to do sth** to have, or not have, a good reason for something *He has a right to be angry.* ○ *She had no right to speak to me like that.* **5 the Right/right POLITICS** political groups which support capitalism (= a system in which industries and companies are owned by people and not the government) *The right campaigned against the president.*

right⁴ /raɪt/ *verb* [**T**] **1** to put something back in a vertical position, or to return to a vertical position [**often reflexive**] *The boat righted itself and I rowed us back to the shore.* **2 right a wrong** to do something good to make an unfair situation seem better *How can we right the wrongs of the past?*

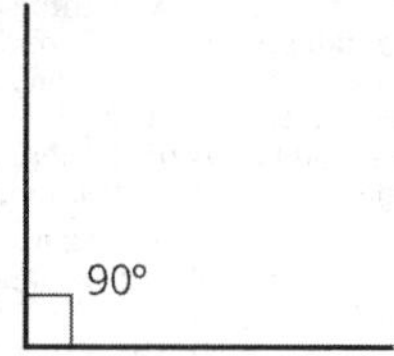

right angle

ˈ**right ˌangle** *noun* [**C**] **MATHEMATICS** a 90 degree angle of the type that is in a square

right-angled triangle /ˌraɪtæŋgldˈtraɪæŋgl/ *UK* (*US* **right triangle**) *noun* [**C**] **MATHEMATICS** a triangle which has one angle of 90°

ˌ**right ˈclick** *verb* [**I**] **COMPUTING** to press the button on the right of a computer mouse (= a small piece of equipment that you move with your hand to control what the computer does)

righteous /ˈraɪtʃəs/ *adjective* morally right and for good moral reasons ***righteous anger/indignation*** •**righteousness** *noun* [**U**] ➲See also: **self-righteous**

rightful /ˈraɪtfᵊl/ *adjective* [**always before noun**] legally or morally correct *The wallet was returned to its **rightful owner**.*

right-hand /ˌraɪtˈhænd/ *adjective* [**always before noun**] **1** on the right of something *On **the right-hand side** you'll see a sign.* **2 sb's right-hand man/woman** the person that you most trust and depend on, especially at work

right-handed /ˌraɪtˈhændɪd/ *adjective* Someone who is right-handed uses their right hand to do most things.

rightly /ˈraɪtli/ *adverb* in a correct way *He is **rightly concerned** about the situation.*

rights /raɪts/ *noun* [**plural**] **SOCIETY** freedom to do and say things without fear of punishment ➲See also: **civil rights, human rights**

right-wing /ˌraɪtˈwɪŋ/ *adjective* **POLITICS** supporting the ideas of parties on the political right *a right-wing newspaper* •**right-winger** *noun* [**C**]

rigid /ˈrɪdʒɪd/ *adjective* **1** NOT CHANGING not able to change or be changed easily *I found the rules a little too rigid.* **2** STIFF not able to bend or move easily *a rigid structure* •**rigidly** *adverb* •**rigidity** /rɪˈdʒɪdəti/ *noun* [**U**] being unable to bend or change easily

rigorous /ˈrɪgᵊrəs/ *adjective* careful to look at or consider every part of something to make sure it is correct or safe *rigorous testing* ○ *a rigorous medical examination* •**rigorously** *adverb*

rigour *UK* (*US* **rigor**) /ˈrɪgəʳ/ *noun* [**U**] when you look at or consider every part of something to make sure it is correct or safe *His arguments lack **intellectual rigour**.*

rigours *UK* (*US* **rigors**) /ˈrɪgəz/ *noun* **the rigours of sth** the difficult conditions of a particular situation *the rigours of a harsh winter*

rim /rɪm/ *noun* [C] the edge of something round *the rim of a wheel*

rind /raɪnd/ *noun* [C, U] **FOOD** the thick skin of fruits such as oranges and lemons and other foods, for example cheese

O‒**ring¹** /rɪŋ/ *noun* [C] **1** JEWELLERY a round piece of jewellery that you wear on your finger *a **wedding ring** ○ a gold ring* **2** CIRCLE something that is the shape of a circle *The children sat in a ring around the teacher.* **3** SOUND the sound a bell makes *The ring of the doorbell woke him up.* **4 a crime/drug/spy, etc ring** a group of people who are involved in an illegal activity together **5 a boxing/circus ring SPORT** an area with seats around it where boxers (= people fighting) or people in a circus (= show) perform **6 give sb a ring** *UK* to telephone someone *If you want anything, just give me a ring.* ➲See also: **key ring**

O‒**ring²** /rɪŋ/ *verb past tense* **rang**, *past participle* **rung 1** SOUND [I, T] If something rings, it makes the sound of a bell, and if you ring a bell, you cause it to make a sound. *The **phone's ringing**. ○ I **rang** the **doorbell**.* **2** TELEPHONE [I, T] *UK* (*UK/US* **call**) to telephone someone *Have you rung your mother? ○ I've **rung for** a taxi.* **3** EARS [I] If your ears are ringing, you can hear a loud sound after the sound has stopped. ➲See also: ring a **bell**, ring **true**
ring (sb) back *phrasal verb UK* (*UK/US* **call (sb) back**) to telephone someone a second time, or to telephone someone who rang you earlier *I'm a bit busy - can I ring you back later?*
ring off *phrasal verb UK* (*UK/US* **hang up**) to end a telephone conversation and put down the part of the telephone that you speak into *She'd rung off before I could say goodbye.*

ring³ /rɪŋ/ *verb* [T] to make a circle around something *Dozens of armed police ringed the building.*

ringleader /ˈrɪŋˌliːdəʳ/ *noun* [C] the leader of a group who are doing something harmful or illegal *the ringleader of a gang of drug smugglers*

ˈring ˌroad *noun* [C] *UK* a road built to take traffic around the outside of a city

ringtone /ˈrɪŋtəʊn/ *noun* [C] the sound that a telephone makes, especially a mobile phone, when someone is calling it

rink /rɪŋk/ *noun* [C] **SPORT** a large, flat surface made of ice or wood where you can skate (= move wearing boots with wheels or a piece of metal) *a roller skating rink* ➲See also: **ice rink**

rinse¹ /rɪns/ *verb* [T] to wash something in clean water in order to remove dirt or soap *Rinse the beans with cold water.*
rinse sth out *phrasal verb* to quickly wash the inside of something with clean water *I'll just rinse these glasses out and leave them to dry.*

rinse² /rɪns/ *noun* [C] **1** WASH when you wash something in clean water to remove dirt or soap ***Give it a quick rinse**, then squeeze it dry.* **2** HAIR a liquid that is used for changing the colour of someone's hair *a dark brown rinse*

WORD PARTNERS FOR ***riot***

quell/spark a riot • a riot **breaks out**

riot¹ /raɪət/ *noun* **1** [C] angry, violent behaviour by a crowd of people *a race riot ○ Riots started in several cities.* **2 run riot** to behave in a noisy, violent, or wild way without being controlled *They allow their kids to run riot.*

riot² /raɪət/ *verb* [I] to take part in a riot *People were rioting in the streets.* •**rioter** *noun* [C]

rioting /ˈraɪətɪŋ/ *noun* [U] when a crowd of people riots *There was **widespread rioting**.*

riotous /ˈraɪətəs/ *adjective* **1** WILD wild and not controlled by anyone *a riotous party* **2** VIOLENT *formal* violent and not controlled *He was charged with riotous behaviour and jailed for six months.*

rip¹ /rɪp/ *verb* **ripping**, *past* **ripped 1** [I, T] to tear quickly and suddenly, or to tear something quickly and suddenly *She ripped her dress getting off her bike. ○ He **ripped open** the parcel.* **2 rip sth out/off/from, etc** to remove something by pulling it away quickly *Hedges had been ripped out to make larger fields.* **3** [T] to copy information from a CD onto an MP3 player (= a piece of electronic equipment or a computer program for storing music)
rip sb off *phrasal verb informal* to cheat someone by making them pay too much money for something *We were ripped off by the first taxi driver.*
rip sth off *phrasal verb* to remove a piece of clothing very quickly and carelessly *I ripped off my clothes and jumped in the shower.*
rip through sth *phrasal verb* to move through a place or building, destroying it quickly *The bomb ripped through the building, killing six people.*
rip sth up *phrasal verb* to tear something into small pieces *He ripped up all her letters.*

rip² /rɪp/ *noun* [C] a hole in the shape of a line when cloth or paper has been torn

ripe /raɪp/ *adjective* **1 FOOD** developed enough and ready to be eaten *ripe bananas* **2 ripe for sth** developed enough to be ready for something *The country is ripe for change. ○ **The time is ripe for*** (= It is the right time for) investing in new technology.

ripen /ˈraɪpᵊn/ *verb* [I, T] **FOOD** to become ripe, or to make something become ripe *The peaches had ripened in the sun.*

rip-off /ˈrɪpɒf/ *noun* [C] *informal* something that costs far too much money *The drinks here are a complete rip-off.*

ripple¹ /ˈrɪpl/ *verb* [I, T] to move in small waves, or to make something move in small waves *A field of wheat rippled in the breeze.*

ripple² /ˈrɪpl/ *noun* [C] **1** WAVE a small wave or series of small waves on the surface of water *She dived in, sending ripples across the pool.* **2** SOUND something that spreads through a place in a gentle way *a **ripple of applause**/laughter*

O‒**rise¹** /raɪz/ *verb* [I] *past tense* **rose**, *past participle* **risen 1** INCREASE to increase in level *rising temperatures ○ Prices **rose by** 10 percent.* **2** GO UP to move up *The balloon rose slowly into the air.* **3** STAND to stand, especially after sitting *He rose from his seat.* **4 rise to/through, etc** to become important, successful, or rich *He quickly rose to stardom.* **5** STRENGTH to become stronger

R

or louder *The wind is rising.* **6** HIGH to be high above something *The bridge rose almost 600 feet above the water.* **7** APPEAR When the sun or moon rises, it appears in the sky. *The sun rises in the East.* **8 rise to the occasion/challenge, etc** to deal with a difficult job or opportunity successfully

COMMON LEARNER ERROR

rise or **raise?**

Be careful not to confuse these two verbs. **Rise** means to increase or move up. This verb cannot be followed by an object.

The price of petrol is rising.

~~*The price of petrol is raising.*~~

Raise means to lift something to a higher position or to increase an amount or level. This verb must always be followed by an object.

The government has raised the price of petrol.

~~*The government has rised the price of petrol.*~~

rise above sth *phrasal verb* to succeed in not allowing something harmful or bad to affect or hurt you

rise up *phrasal verb* to try to defeat and change a government

WORD PARTNERS FOR ***rise***

a big/dramatic/massive/sudden rise • a rise **in** sth • be **on the** rise • the rise **and fall** of sb/sth • a **pay/price** rise

rise² /raɪz/ *noun* **1** [C] an increase in the level of something *a tax rise* ○ *a **rise in** interest rates* **2 sb's rise to fame/power, etc** when someone becomes very famous or powerful **3 give rise to sth** to cause something *The bacteria live in the human body but do not give rise to any symptoms.* **4 FINANCE** [C] *UK* (*US* **raise**) an increase in the amount of money that you earn ***a pay rise***

WORD PARTNERS FOR ***risk***

carry/increase/pose/minimize/reduce/take a risk • **run** the risk **of** sth • a **great/high/serious/slight/small** risk • the risk **of** sth • **at** risk

risk¹ /rɪsk/ *noun* **1** POSSIBILITY [C, U] the possibility of something bad happening *the **risk of** heart disease* ○ *People in the Northeast face the **highest risk** of being burgled.* [+ **(that)**] *There is a slight risk that the blood could have become infected.* **2** SOMETHING BAD [C] something bad that might happen *There are more **health risks** when older women get pregnant.* **3 at risk** being in a situation where something bad is likely to happen *Releasing these prisoners into the community **puts** the public **at risk**.* **4 at your own risk** If you do something at your own risk, you are completely responsible for anything bad that might happen because of it. **5 run the risk of sth** to do something although something bad might happen because of it *I think I'll run the risk of hurting her feelings, and tell her the truth.* **6 take a risk** to do something although something bad might happen because of it *This time I'm not taking any risks - I'm going to get insured.*

risk² /rɪsk/ *verb* [T] **1** MIGHT HAPPEN If you risk something bad, you do something although that bad thing might happen. [+ **doing sth**] *I'd like to help you, but I can't risk losing my job.* **2** MIGHT LOSE If you risk something important, you cause it to be in a dangerous situation where you might lose it. *He risked his life to save me.*

risky /ˈrɪski/ *adjective* dangerous because something bad might happen *Investing in shares is always a **risky business**.*

rite /raɪt/ *noun* [C] **RELIGION, SOCIETY** a traditional ceremony in a particular religion or culture ***initiation/funeral rites***

ritual /ˈrɪtʃuəl/ *noun* [C] an activity or a set of actions that are always done in the same way or at the same time, sometimes as part of a religion *Coffee and the paper are part of my morning ritual.* •**ritualistic** /ˌrɪtjuəlˈɪstɪk/ *adjective* done as a ritual

rival¹ /ˈraɪvəl/ *noun* [C] someone or something that is competing with another person or thing *business/political rivals* •**rival** *adjective* [**always before noun**] *a rival company/gang* •**rivalry** *noun* [C, U] when two people or things are rivals *There is intense **rivalry between** the two teams.*

rival² /ˈraɪvəl/ *verb* [T] *UK* **rivalling**, *past* **rivalled**, *US* **rivaling**, *past* **rivaled** to be good enough to compete with someone or something else *Australian wine can now rival the best from France.*

river /ˈrɪvər/ *noun* [C] **GEOGRAPHY** a long, natural area of water that flows across the land and into a sea, lake, or another river *the River Thames*

riverside /ˈrɪvəsaɪd/ *noun* [**no plural**] **GEOGRAPHY** the area of land at the side of a river *a riverside path*

rivet¹ /ˈrɪvɪt/ *verb* **be riveted** to give something all of your attention because it is so interesting or important *Her eyes were **riveted on/to** his face.*

rivet² /ˈrɪvɪt/ *noun* [C] **DT** a metal pin used to fasten pieces of metal together

riveting /ˈrɪvɪtɪŋ/ *adjective* extremely interesting or exciting *I found the film absolutely riveting.*

RNA /ˌɑːrenˈeɪ/ *noun* [U] **BIOLOGY, CHEMISTRY** *abbreviation for* ribonucleic acid; an important chemical present in all living cells

roach /rəʊtʃ/ *noun* [C] *plural* **roach** or **roaches** *US* a cockroach (= large insect that sometimes breeds in houses)

road /rəʊd/ *noun* **1** [C, U] a long, hard surface built for vehicles to drive on *Be careful when you **cross the road**.* ○ *The journey takes about three hours **by road*** (= in a car, bus, etc). ○ *Follow the **main road*** (= large road) *till you come to a church.* **2 Road** (*written abbreviation* **Rd**) used in the name of a road as part of an address *142 Park Road* **3 along/down/up the road** a distance away on the same road *There's a supermarket just down the road.* **4 over the road** *UK* (*UK/US* **across the road**) on the other side of the road *Who lives in that big house over the road?* **5 on the road** driving or travelling, usually over a long distance *We'd been on the road for 48 hours.* **6 down the road** If an event is a particular period of time down the road, it will not happen until that period has passed. *Why worry about something that's 10 years down the road?* **7 go down that road** to decide to do something in a particular way *I don't think we want to go down that road.* ⊃See also: **ring road, slip road, trunk road**

roadblock /ˈrəʊdblɒk/ *noun* [C] something that is put across a road to stop people who are driving down it *The police had* ***set up a roadblock*** *and were checking identity papers.*

ˈroad ˌmap *noun* [C] a plan for achieving something *the road map for peace in the Middle East*

ˈroad ˌrage *noun* [U] anger and violence between drivers *a* ***road rage incident***

roadshow /ˈrəʊdʃəʊ/ *noun* [C] a radio or television programme broadcast from a public place

roadside /ˈrəʊdsaɪd/ *noun* [C] the area next to a road [**usually singular**] *They found an injured cat lying* ***by the roadside.***

roadway /ˈrəʊdweɪ/ *noun* [C] the part of the road that the traffic drives on

roadworks /ˈrəʊdwɜːks/ *noun* [**plural**] *UK* repairs being done to the road

roadworthy /ˈrəʊdˌwɜːði/ *adjective* If a car is roadworthy, it is in good enough condition to be safe to drive.

roam /rəʊm/ *verb* [**I, T**] to move around a place without any purpose *gangs of youths* ***roaming the street*** *at night*

roar¹ /rɔːʳ/ *verb* **1** MAKE NOISE [**I**] to make a loud, deep sound *We could hear a* ***lion roaring*** *from the other side of the zoo.* ○ *She* ***roared with laughter.*** **2 roar past/down, etc** If a vehicle roars somewhere, it moves fast making a loud noise. *A huge motorcycle roared past.* **3** SHOUT [**I, T**] to say something in a very loud voice *"Stop that!" he roared.*

roar² /rɔːʳ/ *noun* [C] a loud, deep sound *a lion's roar* ○ *the roar of a jet engine*

roaring /ˈrɔːrɪŋ/ *adjective* [**always before noun**] **1** POWERFUL A roaring fire or wind is very powerful. **2** VERY *informal* used to emphasize a situation or state *The party was a* ***roaring success.***

roast¹ /rəʊst/ *verb* [**I, T**] **FOOD** If you roast food, you cook it in an oven or over a fire, and if food roasts, it is cooked in an oven or over a fire. *Roast the lamb in a hot oven for 35 minutes.* •**roast** *adjective* [**always before noun**] *roast beef/pork* ⊃See picture at **cook**

roast² /rəʊst/ *noun* [C] **FOOD** a piece of roasted meat

rob /rɒb/ *verb* [T] **robbing**, *past* **robbed 1** to steal from someone or somewhere, often using violence *to* ***rob a bank*** ○ *Two tourists were robbed at gunpoint in the city centre last night.* **2 rob sb of sth** to take something important away from someone *The war had robbed them of their innocence.*

robber /ˈrɒbəʳ/ *noun* [C] someone who steals *a* ***bank robber*** ○ *a gang of* ***armed robbers***

WORD PARTNERS FOR ***robbery***

commit/take part in a robbery • an **armed/attempted** robbery • a **bank** robbery

robbery /ˈrɒbᵊri/ *noun* [C] the crime of stealing from someone or somewhere *a* ***bank robbery*** ○ *an* ***armed robbery*** ○ *to* ***commit a robbery***

robe /rəʊb/ *noun* [C] a long, loose piece of clothing, often something that is worn for ceremonies or special occasions

robin /ˈrɒbɪn/ *noun* [C] a small, brown bird with a red chest

robot /ˈrəʊbɒt/ *noun* [C] a machine controlled by a computer, which can move and do other things that people can do •**robotic** /rəʊˈbɒtɪk/ *adjective* relating to or like a robot

robust /rəʊˈbʌst/ *adjective* strong and healthy *He looks robust enough.* ○ *a robust economy*

O⊸**rock¹** /rɒk/ *noun* **1 GEOLOGY** [**U**] the hard, natural substance which forms part of the Earth's surface *a layer of volcanic rock* **2 GEOLOGY** [**C**] a large piece of rock or stone *Huge waves were crashing against the rocks.* **3 MUSIC** [**U**] loud, modern music with a strong beat, often played with electric guitars and drums ***hard/soft rock*** ○ ***rock music*** ○ *a* ***rock band/singer*** **4 on the rocks a** RELATIONSHIP If a relationship is on the rocks, it has problems and is likely to end soon. **b** DRINK If a drink is on the rocks, it is served with ice in it.

rock² /rɒk/ *verb* **1** MOVE [**I, T**] to move backwards and forwards or from side to side, or to make someone or something do this *She* ***rocked back and forth*** *on her chair.* ○ *He gently* ***rocked*** *the baby to sleep.* **2** SHOCK [**T**] to shock a large number of people [**often passive**] *The country has been rocked by a series of drug scandals.* ⊃See also: rock the **boat**

ˌrock ˈbottom *noun informal* **hit/reach rock bottom** to reach the lowest level possible *The president's popularity has hit rock bottom.*

the ˈrock ˌcycle *noun* **GEOLOGY** the way that rock is broken down by erosion, then the pieces are carried by wind and water until they are pressed together to form rock again

rocket¹ /ˈrɒkɪt/ *noun* [C] **1** VEHICLE a tube-shaped vehicle for travelling in space **2** WEAPON a tube-shaped weapon that carries a bomb

rocket² /ˈrɒkɪt/ *verb* [**I**] **1** INCREASE to quickly increase in value or amount *House prices have rocketed this year.* **2** PROGRESS to make quick progress *She* ***rocketed to*** *stardom after modelling for Vogue last year.*

rock 'n' roll /ˌrɒkənˈrəʊl/ *noun* [**U**] **1 MUSIC** (*also* **ˌrock and ˈroll**) a type of dance music that was especially popular in the 1950s **2 be the new rock 'n' roll** to now be the most fashionable and popular activity

ˈrock ˌstar *noun* [C] **MUSIC** a famous rock musician

rocky /ˈrɒki/ *adjective* **GEOLOGY** with lots of rocks *a rocky beach*

rod /rɒd/ *noun* [C] a thin, straight pole *a* ***fishing rod*** ○ *The concrete is strengthened with steel rods.*

rode /rəʊd/ *past tense of* ride

R

rodent /ˈrəʊdənt/ *noun* [C] an animal with long, sharp teeth, such as a mouse or rabbit

rodeo /ˈrəʊdiəʊ/ *noun* [C] **SPORT** a competition in which people show their skill at riding wild horses and catching cows

roe /rəʊ/ *noun* [U] **FOOD** fish eggs

rogue /rəʊg/ *adjective* [**always before noun**] not behaving in the way that is expected or wanted *a **rogue state*** ○ ***rogue cells***

WORD PARTNERS FOR ***role***

play a role • an **active/central/key/leading/major** role • **in** a role • sb's role **as** sth • sb/sth's role **in** (doing) sth

⊶**role** /rəʊl/ *noun* [C] **1** PURPOSE the job someone or something has in a particular situation *This part of the brain **plays an** important **role in** learning.* **2** PLAY/FILM a part in a play or film *In his latest film, he **plays the role of** a violent gangster.* ➲See also: **title role**

ˈ**role** ˌ**model** *noun* [C] someone you try to behave like because you admire them *Jane is such a good role model for her younger sister.*

role-play /ˈrəʊlˌpleɪ/ *noun* [C, U] **EDUCATION** pretending to be someone else, especially as part of learning a new skill

roll¹ /rəʊl/ *verb* **1 roll (sth) across/around/over, etc** to move somewhere by turning in a circular direction, or to make something move this way *The ball rolled through the goalkeeper's legs.* ○ *She rolled over onto her side.* **2 roll down/in/off, etc** to move somewhere smoothly *Tears rolled down her face.* **3** [T] to turn something around itself to make the shape of a ball or tube *to roll a cigarette* **4 roll your eyes** to move your eyes so that they are looking up, usually to show surprise or disapproval **5 be rolling in it** *informal* to be very rich ➲See also: **set/start the ball** rolling

roll in *phrasal verb* to arrive in large numbers *She only set up the business last year and already the money's rolling in.*

roll sth up *phrasal verb* to fold something around itself to make the shape of a ball or tube, or to make a piece of clothing shorter *to **roll up** your **sleeves**/trouser legs* ○ *to roll up a carpet* ➲Opposite **unroll**

roll up *phrasal verb informal* to arrive somewhere, usually late *By the time Jim rolled up, the party had almost finished.*

roll² /rəʊl/ *noun* [C] **1** ROUND OBJECT something that has been turned around itself into a round shape like a tube *a roll of film* ○ *a roll of toilet paper* **2 FOOD** a small loaf of bread for one person *Would you like a roll and butter with your soup?* **3** LIST a list of names *the **electoral roll*** **4** SOUND a long, deep sound *a **roll of thunder*** ○ *a **drum roll*** **5 be on a roll** *informal* to be having a successful period *We were on a roll, winning our fourth game in a row.* ➲See also: **rock 'n' roll, toilet roll**

roller /ˈrəʊləʳ/ *noun* [C] a piece of equipment in the shape of a tube which is rolled around or over something *She uses rollers to curl her hair.*

Rollerblades /ˈrəʊləbleɪdz/ *noun* [**plural**] *trademark* (*also* **in-line skates**) **SPORT** boots with a single line of wheels on the bottom, used for moving across the ground •**rollerblading** *noun* [U] *Lots of people **go rollerblading** in Central Park.* ➲See colour picture **Sports 1** on page Centre 14

roller coaster /ˌrəʊləˈkəʊstəʳ/ *noun* [C] an exciting entertainment which is like a fast train that goes up and down very steep slopes

ˈ**roller** ˌ**skate** *noun* [C] **SPORT** a boot with wheels on the bottom, used for moving across the ground •**roller skating** *noun* [U]

ˈ**rolling** ˌ**pin** *noun* [C] a kitchen tool shaped like a tube that you roll over pastry to make it thinner before cooking ➲See colour picture **The Kitchen** on page Centre 2

ROM /rɒm/ *noun* [U] **COMPUTING** *abbreviation for* read only memory: a type of computer memory which holds information that can be used but not changed or added to ➲Compare **RAM**

Roman¹ /ˈrəʊmən/ *adjective* relating to ancient Rome or its empire *Roman remains*

roman³ /ˈrəʊ.mən/ *adjective* **LANGUAGE** describes the ordinary style of printed writing in which the letters are vertical

Roman² /ˈrəʊmən/ *noun* [C] someone who lived in ancient Rome or its empire

ˌ**Roman** ˈ**Catholic** *adjective* **RELIGION** related to the part of the Christian religion that has the Pope (= a very important priest) as its leader •**Roman Catholic** *noun* [C] •**Roman Catholicism** *noun* [U] the beliefs of the Roman Catholic religion

WORD PARTNERS FOR ***romance***

find/look for romance • a romance **blossoms** • a **whirlwind** romance • a **holiday** romance • the romance **between** sb and sb • sb's romance **with** sb

romance /rəʊˈmæns/ *noun* **1** LOVE [C, U] an exciting relationship of love between two people, often a short one *They got married last September after a **whirlwind romance**.* **2 LITERATURE** [C] a story about love **3** EXCITEMENT [U] a feeling of excitement or exciting danger *the romance of the sea*

ˌ**Roman** ˈ**numeral** *noun* [C] **MATHEMATICS** a letter that represents a number in the Roman system in which I is 1, II is 2, V is 5, etc *My watch has Roman numerals.*

romantic¹ /rəʊˈmæntɪk/ *adjective* **1** LOVE relating to exciting feelings of love *a romantic dinner for two* **2 LITERATURE** relating to a story about love ***romantic fiction*** ○ *a **romantic comedy*** **3** IDEAS thinking that things are better than they really are, and that things are possible which are not *a romantic view of the world*
•**romantically** *adverb*

romantic² /rəʊˈmæntɪk/ *noun* [C] someone who thinks that things are better than they really are, and that things are possible which are not

romanticize (*also UK* **-ise**) /rəʊˈmæntɪsaɪz/ *verb* [T] to make something seem much better or exciting than it really is *a romanticized image of married life*

romp /rɒmp/ *verb* **romp around/in/through, etc** to run around in a happy, energetic way *The children were romping around in the garden.* •**romp** *noun* [C]

O⁻ **roof** /ruːf/ *noun* **1** [C] the surface that covers the top of a building or vehicle *a flat/sloping roof* ○ *He climbed onto the roof.* **2 the roof of your mouth** the top part of the inside of your mouth **3 a roof over your head** somewhere to live **4 go through the roof** If the level of something, especially a price, goes through the roof, it increases very quickly. **5 hit the roof** *informal* to become very angry and start shouting *If I'm late again he'll hit the roof.*

roofing /ˈruːfɪŋ/ *noun* [U] material used to make a roof

rooftop /ˈruːftɒp/ *noun* [C] the top of a roof *a view across the city rooftops*

rook /rʊk/ *noun* [C] a large, black bird that lives in Europe

rookie /ˈrʊki/ *noun* [C] *mainly US* someone who has only recently started doing a job or activity and so has no experience *a rookie cop*

WORD PARTNERS FOR ***room***

leave/make room • **take up** room • room **for** sb/sth

O⁻ **room¹** /ruːm, rʊm/ *noun* **1** BUILDING [C] a part of the inside of a building, which is separated from other parts by walls, floors, and ceilings *a hotel room* **2** SPACE [U] space for things to fit into *Is there enough **room for** all of us in your car?* ○ *Can everyone move up a bit to **make room for** these people?* [+ **to do** sth] *There's hardly enough room to move in here.* **3 room for sth** a possibility for something to happen *His work isn't bad but there's still some **room for improvement**.* ⊃See also: **changing room, chat room, dining room, drawing room, dressing room, elbow room, emergency room, living room, locker room, men's room, operating room, sitting room, waiting room**

room² /ruːm, rʊm/ *verb* **room with sb** *US* to share a bedroom with someone, usually at college

roommate /ˈruːmmeɪt/ *noun* [C] **1** ROOM someone who you share a room with **2** HOME *US* (*UK* **housemate/flatmate**) someone who you share your home with

ˌ**room ˌservice** *noun* [U] in a hotel, room service is when someone serves you food and drink in your room

roomy /ˈruːmi/ *adjective* having a lot of space *It looks small, but it's really quite roomy inside.*

roost /ruːst/ *noun* [C] **1** a place where birds go to rest or sleep **2 rule the roost** to be the person who makes all the decisions in a group

rooster /ˈruːstəʳ/ *noun* [C] a male chicken

O⁻ **root¹** /ruːt/ *noun* [C] **1** BIOLOGY the part of a plant that grows under the ground and gets water and food from the soil **2** ANATOMY, BIOLOGY the part of a hair or tooth that is under the skin ⊃See picture at **tooth** **3 the root of sth** the cause of something, usually something bad *the root of all evil* ⊃See also: **grass roots** **4** MATHEMATICS The root of a particular number is another number which, when multiplied by itself one or more times, equals the first number. ⊃See: **square root, cube root**

root² /ruːt/ *verb*

root about/around (sth) *phrasal verb* to search for something, especially by looking through other things *She was rooting around in her drawer for a pencil.*

root for sb *phrasal verb informal* to show support for someone who is in a competition or who is doing something difficult *Good luck! We're all rooting for you.*

be rooted in sth *phrasal verb* to be based on something or caused by something *Most prejudices are rooted in ignorance.*

root sth/sb out *phrasal verb* to find and get rid of the thing or person that is causing a problem *It is our aim to root out corruption.*

ˈ**root ˌhair** *noun* [C] BIOLOGY a thin part like a hair that grows from the roots of plants and takes in water and food

roots /ruːts/ *noun* [plural] where someone or something originally comes from *the roots of modern jazz*

rope¹ /rəʊp/ *noun* [C, U] **1** very thick string made from twisted thread **2 be on the ropes** *mainly US* to be doing badly and likely to fail *His career is on the ropes.* **3 learn/know the ropes** to learn/know how to do a job or activity ⊃See also: at the **end¹** of your tether, **jump rope, skipping rope**

rope² /rəʊp/ *verb* [T] to tie things together with rope

rope sb in *phrasal verb informal* to persuade someone to help you with something, especially when they do not want to

rosé /ˈrəʊzeɪ/ (US) /rəʊˈzeɪ/ *noun* [U] FOOD pink wine

rosary /ˈrəʊzᵊri/ *noun* [C] RELIGION a string of beads (= small, round balls) that is used to count prayers in the Catholic religion

rose¹ /rəʊz/ *noun* [C] a flower with a pleasant smell and thorns (= sharp points on the stem), that grows on a bush

rose² /rəʊz/ *past tense of* rise

rosemary /ˈrəʊzmᵊri/ *noun* [U] FOOD a herb that grows as a bush with thin, pointed leaves

rosette /rəʊˈzet/ *noun* [C] **1** PRIZE *UK* (*US* **ribbon**) a decoration made of coloured cloth, which is given as a prize **2** POLITICS *UK* a decoration made of coloured cloth in the shape of a rose, worn to show political support for someone

WORD PARTNERS FOR ***roster***

draw up/organize a roster • a roster **of** sth • **on** a roster

roster /ˈrɒstəʳ/ *noun* [C] **1** PLAN a plan which shows who must do which jobs and when they must do them *a staff roster* **2** LIST a list of names of people who belong to a team or organization

rostrum /ˈrɒstrəm/ *noun* [C] a raised surface which someone stands on to make a speech or receive a prize

rosy /ˈrəʊzi/ *adjective* **1** PINK Rosy faces are a healthy pink colour. *rosy cheeks* **2** POSITIVE very positive and happy *The future looks rosy.*

rot¹ /rɒt/ *verb* [I, T] **rotting**, *past* **rotted** If vegetable or animal substances rot, they decay, and if something rots them, it makes them decay. *Sugar rots your teeth.* ○ *the smell of rotting fish*

rot² /rɒt/ *noun* [U] **1** decay *There was rot in the woodwork.* **2 the rot sets in** *UK* If the rot sets in, a situation starts to get worse. **3 stop the rot** *UK* to do something to prevent a situation from continuing to get worse

rota /ˈrəʊtə/ *noun* [C] *UK* (*UK/US* **roster**) a plan which shows who must do which jobs and when they must do them

rotary /ˈrəʊtᵊri/ *adjective* [**always before noun**] moving in a circular direction

rotate /rəʊˈteɪt/ *verb* [I, T] **1** TURN to turn in a circular direction, or to make something turn in a circular direction *The television rotates for viewing at any angle.* **2** CHANGE to change from one person or thing to another in a regular order *Farmers usually rotate their crops to improve the soil.* •**rotation** /rəʊˈteɪʃᵊn/ *noun* [C, U] *the rotation of the Earth* ○ *crop rotation*

rotten /ˈrɒtᵊn/ *adjective* **1** **FOOD** Rotten vegetable or animal substances are decaying. *rotten eggs* **2** *informal* very bad *rotten weather*

rottweiler /ˈrɒtwaɪləʳ/ *noun* [C] a type of large, powerful dog

O-- **rough¹** /rʌf/ *adjective* **1** NOT SMOOTH A rough surface is not smooth. *rough hands* ○ *rough ground* **2** APPROXIMATE approximate *a **rough estimate*** ○ *Can you give me a **rough idea** of the cost?* **3** FORCEFUL If the sea or weather is rough, there is a lot of strong wind and sometimes rain. *The boat sank in **rough seas** off the Swedish coast.* **4** ILL [**never before noun**] *UK* ill *I **feel** a bit **rough** after last night.* **5** DIFFICULT difficult or unpleasant *She's having a **rough time** at work.* **6** DANGEROUS dangerous or violent *a rough part of town* ○ *Hockey can be quite a **rough game**.* **7** NOT PERFECT quickly done and not perfect *These are just **rough sketches**.* **8 rough and ready a** NOT PREPARED produced quickly without preparation **b** NOT POLITE not very polite or well-educated •**roughness** *noun* [U]

rough² /rʌf/ *noun* **take the rough with the smooth** *UK* to accept the unpleasant parts of a situation as well as the pleasant parts

R

rough³ /rʌf/ *adverb* **live/sleep rough** *UK* to live and sleep outside because you have nowhere else to live

rough⁴ /rʌf/ *verb* **rough it** to live in a way that is simple and not comfortable

roughage /ˈrʌfɪdʒ/ *noun* [U] **FOOD** a substance in fruit and vegetables that helps you to get rid of waste from the body

roughen /ˈrʌfᵊn/ *verb* [I, T] to become rough or to make something become rough *Years of housework had roughened her hands.*

roughly /ˈrʌfli/ *adverb* **1** APPROXIMATELY approximately *There's been an increase of roughly 30% since last year.* **2** FORCEFULLY forcefully or violently *He pushed us roughly out of the door.*

roulette /ruːˈlet/ *noun* [U] a game in which a small ball moves around a dish with numbers on it, and people try to win money by guessing where the ball will stop

O-- **round¹** /raʊnd/ *adjective* **1** in the shape of a circle or ball *a round table/window* ○ *round eyes* ○ *a round face* **2 round figures/numbers** numbers given to the nearest 10, 100, 1000, etc and not as the exact amounts

O-- **round²** /raʊnd/ *UK* (*UK/US* **around**) *adverb, preposition* **1** IN A CIRCLE on all sides of something *We sat round the table.* ○ *She had a scarf round her neck.* **2** DIRECTION to the opposite direction *She looked round.* ○ ***Turn** the car **round** and let's go home.* **3** TO A PLACE to or in different parts of a place *He showed me round the flat.* **4** SEVERAL PLACES from one place or person to another *Could you pass these forms round, please?* **5** VISIT to someone's home *Wendy's coming round this afternoon.* **6** NEAR near an area *Do you live round here?* **7 round about** at approximately a time or approximately an amount *We'll be there round about 10 o'clock.* **8 round and round** moving in a circle without stopping *We drove round and round trying to find the hotel.*

round³ /raʊnd/ *noun* [C] **1 first/second/third/etc, round** a part of a competition *He was beaten in the first round.* **2** EVENTS a group of events that is part of a series *a **round of interviews*** ○ *a new **round of talks** between the two countries* **3** VISITS *UK* regular visits to a group of people or houses to give them something or to see them *a milk/newspaper round* **4** DRINKS drinks that you buy for a group of people *It's your turn to buy the next round.* **5 round of applause** when people clap *The crowd gave him a huge round of applause.* **6** BULLETS a bullet or a set of bullets to be fired at one time from a gun **7 round of golf SPORT** a game of golf

round⁴ /raʊnd/ *verb* [T] to go around something *They **rounded** the **corner** at high speed.*

round sth down *phrasal verb* **MATHEMATICS** to reduce a number to the nearest whole or simple number

round sth off *phrasal verb* to end an activity in a pleasant way *We rounded off the lesson with a quiz.*

round sb/sth up *phrasal verb* to find and bring together a group of people or animals *The police are rounding up the usual suspects.*

round sth up *phrasal verb* **MATHEMATICS** to increase a number to the nearest whole or simple number

roundabout¹ /ˈraʊndəˌbaʊt/ *noun* [C] **1** ROADS *UK* (*US* **traffic circle**) a circular place where roads meet and where cars drive around until they arrive at the road that they want to turn into *to go round a roundabout* **2** ENTERTAINMENT *UK* an entertainment which goes round and round while children sit on it

roundabout² /ˈraʊndəˌbaʊt/ *adjective* [**always before noun**] A roundabout way of doing something or going somewhere is not the direct way.

rounded /ˈraʊndɪd/ *adjective* smooth and curved *a table with rounded corners*

rounders /ˈraʊndəz/ *noun* [U] **SPORT** a British game in which you try to hit a small ball and then run round all four sides of a large square

rounding /ˈraʊndɪŋ/ *noun* [U] **MATHEMATICS** when a number is put up or down to the nearest whole number or the nearest hundred, thousand, etc

roundly /ˈraʊndli/ *adverb* If you criticize someone or something roundly, you do it very strongly. *The action was* ***roundly condemned*** *by French and German leaders.*

round-the-clock /ˌraʊndðəˈklɒk/ *adjective* all day and all night *round-the-clock nursing care*

ˌround ˈtrip *noun* [C] a journey from one place to another and back to where you started

ˌround-trip ˈticket *US* (*UK* **return**) *noun* [C] a ticket that lets you travel to a place and back again, for example on a train

round-up /ˈraʊndʌp/ *noun* [C] **1** GROUP when a group of people or animals are found and brought together *a police round-up* **2** REPORT a short report of all the facts or events relating to a subject *a* ***news round-up***

rouse /raʊz/ *verb* [T] **1** CAUSE FEELING to cause a feeling or emotion in someone *This issue is rousing a lot of public interest.* **2** WAKE UP *formal* to wake someone up *He was roused from a deep sleep.*

rousing /ˈraʊzɪŋ/ *adjective* making people feel excited and proud or ready to take action *a* ***rousing speech***

rout /raʊt/ *verb* [T] to defeat someone completely •**rout** *noun* [C] *an election rout*

WORD PARTNERS FOR ***route***

follow/take a route • **plan/work out** a route • **along/on** a route • a route **between/from/to**

O⁻**route** /ruːt/ (US) /ruːt, raʊt/ *noun* [C] **1** ROADS the roads or paths you follow to get from one place to another place *an escape route* ○ *Crowds gathered all* ***along the route*** *to watch the race.* **2** METHOD a method of achieving something *A university education is seen by many as the best route to a good job.* ➲See also: **en route**

WORD PARTNERS FOR ***routine***

get into/have/settle into a routine • sb's **daily/normal** routine • a routine **of** doing sth

routine¹ /ruːˈtiːn/ *noun* **1** REGULAR ACTIVITY [C, U] the things you regularly do and how and when you do them *a* ***daily routine*** ○ *He longed to escape the routine of an office job.* **2** PERFORMANCE [C] a regular series of movements, jokes, etc used in a performance *a dance routine*

routine² /ruːˈtiːn/ *adjective* **1** REGULAR done regularly and not unusual *a* ***routine procedure*** ○ ***routine checks*** **2** BORING done regularly and very boring *His job is very routine.*

routinely /ruːˈtiːnli/ *adverb* regularly or often

roving /ˈrəʊvɪŋ/ *adjective* [**always before noun**] moving around from one place to another place *a* ***roving reporter***

O⁻**row¹** /rəʊ/ *noun* **1** LINE [C] a straight line of people or things *a row of chairs/houses* ○ *My students sit at desks* ***in rows*** *for most of the time.* **2** SEATS [C] a line of seats *to sit on the* ***back/front row*** ○ *Isn't that Sophie sitting in the row behind us?* **3 in a row** one after another without a break *He's just won the tournament for the fifth year in a row.* ➲See also: **death row**

row² /rəʊ/ *verb* [**I, T**] to move a boat or move someone in a boat through the water using oars (= poles with flat ends) •**rowing** *noun* [U]

WORD PARTNERS FOR ***row*** (= argument)

have a row • an **almighty/blazing/heated** row • a row **about/over** sth • a row **with** sb • a row **between** sb and sb

row³ /raʊ/ *noun UK* **1** LOUD ARGUMENT [C] a loud, angry argument *a* ***blazing row*** ○ *The couple next door are always* ***having rows.*** **2** DISAGREEMENT [C] a disagreement about a political or public situation *A* ***row*** *has erupted* ***over*** *defence policy.* **3** NOISE [**no plural**] very loud noise *The kids were* ***making*** *a terrible* ***row*** *upstairs.*

rowdy /ˈraʊdi/ *adjective* loud and uncontrolled ***rowdy behaviour*** ○ *rowdy football fans*

ˈrow ˌhouse *US* (*UK* **terraced house**) *noun* [C] one of a row of houses that are joined together

ˈrowing ˌboat *UK* (*US* **rowboat** /ˈrəʊbəʊt/) *noun* [C] a small boat moved by oars (= poles with flat ends)

O⁻**royal¹** /ˈrɔɪəl/ *adjective* **1** relating to a queen or king and their family *the British* ***royal family*** ○ *a* ***royal visit*** **2 Royal** used in the UK as part of the title of a royal person *His Royal Highness, the Duke of York*

royal² /ˈrɔɪəl/ *noun* [C] *informal* a member of a royal family *a book about the royals*

royalist /ˈrɔɪəlɪst/ *noun* [C] **POLITICS** someone who supports the principle of having a King or Queen •**royalist** *adjective*

royalties /ˈrɔɪəltiz/ *noun* [**plural**] **FINANCE** money that is paid to a writer, actor, etc each time their work is sold or performed *He could receive as much as $1 million* ***in royalties*** *over the next six years.*

royalty /ˈrɔɪəlti/ *noun* [U] **POLITICS** the members of the royal family

RPI /ˌɑːpiːˈaɪ/ *noun* [**C usually singular**] **ECONOMICS, FINANCE** *abbreviation for* retail price index

RSI /ˌɑːresˈaɪ/ *noun* [C] **HEALTH** *abbreviation for* repetitive strain injury: a painful medical condition which can damage the hands, arms and backs of people, especially people who use computers

résumé /ˈrezəmeɪ/ *US* (*UK* **CV**) *noun* [C] a document which describes your qualifications and the jobs that you have done, which you send to an employer that you want to work for

RSVP /ˌɑːresviːˈpiː/ used at the end of a written invitation to mean 'please answer' *RSVP by October 9th*

rub¹ /rʌb/ *verb* **rubbing**, *past* **rubbed 1** PRESS YOUR HANDS [T] to press your hand or a cloth on a surface and move it backwards and forwards *She rubbed her hands together to warm them.* ○ *Rub the stain with a damp cloth.* **2 rub sth into/on, etc** to move a substance backwards and forwards over a surface so that it covers it and goes into it *I rubbed some suntan oil on her back.* ○ *Rub the butter into the flour.* **3** TOUCH [**I, T**] to touch and move against something, often causing pain or damage *My new boots are rubbing against my toes.* **4 rub it in** *informal* to upset someone by talking to them about something which you know they want to forget ➲See also: rub shoulders (**shoulder¹**) with sb, rub sb up the wrong **way¹**

R

rub off *phrasal verb* If a quality or characteristic of a particular person rubs off, other people begin to have it because they have been with that person. *His enthusiasm is starting to **rub off on** the rest of us.*
rub sth out *phrasal verb UK* to remove writing from something by rubbing it with a piece of rubber or a cloth

rub² /rʌb/ *noun* [C] when you rub something [usually singular] *Give it a rub and it'll feel better.*

rubber /ˈrʌbəʳ/ *noun* **1** SUBSTANCE [U] a strong material that bends easily, originally produced from the juice of a tropical tree, and used to make tyres, boots, etc **2** PENCIL [C] *UK* (*US* **eraser**) a small object which is used to remove pencil marks from paper ➲See colour picture **The Classroom** on page Centre 6

ˌrubber ˈband (*also UK* **elastic band**) *noun* [C] a thin circle of rubber used to hold things together

ˌrubber ˈboot *noun* [C] *US* (*UK* **wellies** [plural]) a large shoe made of rubber that covers your foot and part of your leg

rubber-stamp /ˌrʌbəˈstæmp/ *verb* [T] to officially approve a decision or plan without thinking very much about it

rubbery /ˈrʌbəri/ *adjective* feeling or bending like rubber *a rubbery piece of meat*

O→**rubbish¹** /ˈrʌbɪʃ/ *noun* [U] *mainly UK* **1** WASTE things that you throw away because you do not want them *Our rubbish gets collected on Thursdays.* ○ *a rubbish dump/bin* **2** NONSENSE something that is nonsense or wrong *Ignore him, he's talking rubbish.* **3** BAD QUALITY *informal* something that is of bad quality *There's so much rubbish on TV.*

rubbish² /ˈrʌbɪʃ/ *verb* [T] to criticize someone or something *I wish you wouldn't rubbish everything about the concert - I really enjoyed it!*

rubbish³ /ˈrʌbɪʃ/ *adjective informal* disappointing or of very bad quality *I got a rubbish mark for chemistry.*

rubble /ˈrʌbl/ *noun* [U] pieces of broken bricks from a building that has been destroyed *a pile of rubble*

rubella /ruːˈbelə/ (*also* **German measles**) *noun* [U] **HEALTH** a disease which causes red spots on your skin

rubric /ˈruːbrɪk/ *noun* [C] a set of instructions or an explanation, especially in an examination paper or book

ruby /ˈruːbi/ *noun* [C] **GEOLOGY** a valuable red stone which is used in jewellery

rucksack /ˈrʌksæk/ *noun* [C] *UK* a bag that you carry on your back ➲See picture at **bag**

rudder /ˈrʌdəʳ/ *noun* [C] a piece of equipment that changes the direction of a boat or aircraft

ruddy /ˈrʌdi/ *adjective* A ruddy face is red. *ruddy cheeks*

OTHER WAYS OF SAYING ***rude***

If someone is slightly rude or behaves without respect in a way that is funny, you might describe them as **cheeky** (*UK*): *You asked your teacher how old she was? That was a bit **cheeky**!*

A more formal alternative to 'rude' is the world **impolite**: *She asks direct questions without being in any way **impolite**.*

If someone is rude or does not show respect to a person who is older or has more authority than they do, they might be described as **impertinent** or **insolent**: *It was clear that they found his questions **impertinent**.*

The adjective **abrasive** describes someone's manner when they are rude and unfriendly: *I found him rather **abrasive**.*

A person who is rude and unpleasant is sometimes described as **uncouth**: *She found him loud-mouthed and **uncouth**.*

Language which is rude, referring to the body in an unpleasant way can be described as **vulgar** or **crude**: *He told a rather **vulgar** joke over dinner.*

O→**rude** /ruːd/ *adjective* **1** OFFENSIVE behaving in a way which is not polite and upsets other people *a rude remark* ○ *He complained that a member of staff had been **rude to** him.* [+ to do sth] *It would be rude to leave without saying goodbye.* **2** SEXUAL/TOILET Rude words or jokes relate to sex or going to the toilet. •**rudely** *adverb* •**rudeness** *noun* [U] ➲See also: a rude **awakening**

rudiments /ˈruːdɪmənts/ *noun formal* **the rudiments of sth** the most basic parts or principles of something •**rudimentary** /ˌruːdɪˈmentᵊri/ *adjective formal* very basic

rueful /ˈruːfᵊl/ *adjective* showing slight sadness about something but not in a serious way *a **rueful smile*** •**ruefully** *adverb*

ruffle /ˈrʌfl/ *verb* [T] If someone ruffles your hair, they rub it gently. *He **ruffled** my **hair** and kissed me.*

rug /rʌg/ *noun* [C] **1** FLOOR a soft piece of material used to cover the floor *The dog was lying on the rug in front of the fire.* ➲See colour picture **The Living Room** on page Centre 4 **2** COVER *UK* a soft cover that keeps you warm or comfortable

rugby /ˈrʌgbi/ *noun* [U] **SPORT** a sport played by two teams with an oval ball and H-shaped goals *a rugby player* ➲See colour picture **Sports 2** on page Centre 15

rugged /ˈrʌgɪd/ *adjective* **1** LAND If an area of land is rugged, it looks rough and has lots of rocks. *a **rugged coastline*** **2** MAN If a man looks rugged, his face looks strong and attractive. *a rugged face*

ruin¹ /ˈruːɪn/ *verb* [T] **1** SPOIL to spoil or destroy something [often passive] *They were late and the dinner was ruined.* **2** LOSING to cause someone to lose all their money or their job *If the newspapers get hold of this story they'll ruin him.*

ruin² /ˈruːɪn/ *noun* **1** DESTRUCTION [U] the destruction of something *Fonthill Abbey **fell into ruin** 10 years after it was built.* **2** BROKEN BUILDING [C] the broken parts that are left from an

R

old building or town *Thousand of tourists wander around these **ancient ruins** every year.* **3** [LOSING EVERYTHING] [U] when someone loses everything such as all their money or their job *The collapse of the bank has left many people **in financial ruin**.* **4 be/lie in ruins** to be in a very bad state *The war left one million people dead and the country in ruins.*

WORD PARTNERS FOR ***rule***

apply/break/enforce/establish a rule • a rule **forbids/prohibits** sth • a **strict/unwritten** rule • a rule **against** sth

O-**rule¹** /ruːl/ *noun* **1** [INSTRUCTION] [C] an official instruction about what you must or must not do *to **break*** (= not obey) *the **rules**.* ○ *to **obey/follow** the **rules*** ○ *You can't smoke at school, it's **against the rules*** (= not allowed). **2** [LEADER] [U] when someone is in control of a country *military rule* ○ *There have been reports of immense human suffering **under his rule**.* **3** [USUAL WAY] [no plural] the usual way something is *an exception to the rule* ○ *Workers in the North are, **as a rule**, paid less than those in the South.* **4** [PRINCIPLE] [C] a principle of a system, such as a language or science *the rules of grammar* **5 a rule of thumb** a way of calculating something, which is not exact but which will help you to be correct enough **6 bend/stretch the rules** to allow someone to do something which is not usually allowed *We don't usually let students take books home, but I'll bend the rules on this occasion.* ➲See also: **ground rules**

rule² /ruːl/ *verb* [I, T] **1 LAW** to make an official legal decision [+ (that)] *The judge ruled that it was wrong for a 16-year-old girl to be held in an adult prison.* **2 POLITICS** to be in control of somewhere, usually a country [often passive] *They were ruled for many years by a dictator.* ○ *the ruling party* ➲See also: rule the **roost**

rule sb/sth out *phrasal verb* to decide that something or someone is not suitable for a particular purpose, or to decide that something is impossible *The police have not ruled him out as a suspect.*

ruler /ˈruːləʳ/ *noun* [C] **1** [LEADER] the leader of a country **2** [MEASURING] a flat, straight stick which is used to measure things ➲See colour picture **The Classroom** on page Centre 6

ruling /ˈruːlɪŋ/ *noun* [C] **LAW** an official legal decision, usually made by a judge

rum /rʌm/ *noun* [C, U] **FOOD** a strong, alcoholic drink made from sugar

rumble /ˈrʌmbl/ *verb* [I] to make a deep, long sound *The smell of cooking made his **stomach rumble**.* •**rumble** *noun* [no plural] *the distant **rumble of thunder***

rumbling /ˈrʌmblɪŋ/ *noun* [C] a deep, long sound *the rumbling of a train passing by*

rumblings /ˈrʌmblɪŋz/ *noun* [plural] signs that people are angry about something *rumblings of discontent*

rummage /ˈrʌmɪdʒ/ *verb* **rummage around/in/through, etc** to search inside something and move things around *I found him rummaging through my drawers.*

ˈ**rummage** ˌ**sale** *US* (*UK* **jumble sale**) *noun* [C] a sale of old items, especially clothes, usually to make money for an organization

WORD PARTNERS FOR ***rumour***

fuel/spark/spread/start rumours • **deny/dismiss/hear** rumours • a rumour **circulates/goes around** • a **persistent/strong/unconfirmed** rumour • a rumour **about/of** sth

rumour¹ *UK* (*US* **rumor**) /ˈruːməʳ/ *noun* [C] a fact that a lot of people are talking about although they do not know if it is true *to **spread rumours*** ○ *to **deny rumours*** [+ (that)] *I **heard a rumour** that you were leaving.*

rumour² *UK* (*US* **rumor**) /ˈruːməʳ/ *verb* **be rumoured** If a fact is rumoured, people are talking about it although they do not know if it is true. [+ (that)] *It's rumoured that the company director is about to resign.* [+ **to do sth**] *The company is rumoured to be in financial difficulty.*

rump /rʌmp/ *noun* [C] the area above an animal's back legs

rumpled /ˈrʌmpld/ *adjective* Rumpled clothes or sheets are untidy because they have folds in them.

O-**run¹** /rʌn/ *verb* **running**, *past tense* **ran**, *past participle* **run** **1** [MOVE FAST] [I, T] to move on your feet at a faster speed than walking *He **ran away** when I tried to pick him up.* [+ **to do sth**] *We had to run to catch up with him.* ○ *I run about three miles every morning.* **2** [ORGANIZE] [T] to organize or control something *She ran her own restaurant for five years.* **3 run sb/sth to/down, etc** to take someone or something somewhere, usually by car *Could you run me to the station this afternoon?* **4** [WORKING] [I, T] If a piece of equipment is running, it is switched on and working, and if you run it, you switch it on and make it work. *The engine is running more smoothly now.* **5 COMPUTING** [T] If you run a computer program, you use it on your computer. *Did you run a virus check this morning?* **6** [TRAVELLING] [I] If trains or buses are running, they are available to travel on. *The buses only run until 11 p.m.* **7** [LIQUID] [I] If liquid runs somewhere, it flows. *Tears ran down her face.* **8** [PUBLISH] [T] to publish something in a newspaper or magazine *All the papers are **running this story** on the front page.* **9 run a bath** *UK* to fill a bath with water so that it is ready to use **10 run sth along/over/through, etc sth** to move something along, over, or through something else *She ran her fingers through her hair.* **11 run through/down/along, etc** If something long and narrow runs somewhere, it is in that position. *There are wires running across the floor.* **12** [CONTINUE] [I] If a play, film, etc runs for a period of time, it continues that long. **13 run in sb's/the family** If a quality, ability, disease, etc runs in the family, many members of the family have it. *A love of animals runs in our family.* **14** [COLOUR] [I] If a colour runs, it comes out of some material when it is washed. **15 be running at sth** to be at a particular level *Inflation is now running at 5.8%.* ➲See also: cast/run your/an **eye¹** over sth, run the **gauntlet**, run **riot¹**, run out of **steam¹**, run **wild¹**

run across sb *phrasal verb* to meet someone

R

you know when you are not expecting to *I ran across Jim in town the other day.*

run after sb/sth *phrasal verb* to chase someone or something that is moving away from you

run around *phrasal verb* to be very busy doing a lot of different things *I'm exhausted, I've been running around all morning.*

run away *phrasal verb* to secretly leave a place because you are unhappy there *to* ***run away from home***

run sth by sb *phrasal verb* to tell someone about something so that they can give their opinion about it *Can I run something by you, Sam?*

run sb/sth down *phrasal verb informal* to criticize someone or something, often unfairly

run for sth *phrasal verb* **POLITICS** to compete in an election *He's running for mayor again this year.*

run into sb *phrasal verb* to meet someone you know when you are not expecting to *I ran into Emma on my way home.*

run into sth *phrasal verb* **1** HIT to hit something while you are driving a vehicle *He skidded and ran into a tree.* **2** REACH A LEVEL If an amount runs into thousands, millions, etc, it reaches that level. **3** PROBLEMS If you run into difficulties, you begin to experience them. *to run into trouble*

run off *phrasal verb informal* to leave somewhere unexpectedly *He* ***ran off with*** *all my money.*

run on sth *phrasal verb* If a machine runs on a supply of power, it uses that power to work. *The scanner runs on mains electricity and batteries.*

run out *phrasal verb* **1** USE to use all of something so that there is none left *I've nearly* ***run out of*** *money.* **2** BE USED If a supply of something runs out, there is none left because it has all been used. *Come on, time is running out.*

run sb/sth over *phrasal verb* to hit someone or something with a vehicle and drive over them, injuring or killing them *He was run over by a bus as he crossed the road.*

run through sth *phrasal verb* to repeat something in order to practise it or to make sure that it is correct *I just need to run through my speech one more time.*

run sth up *phrasal verb* If you run up a debt, you do things which cause you to owe a large amount of money.

run up against sth *phrasal verb* If you run up against problems or difficulties, you begin to experience them.

run² /rʌn/ *noun* **1 SPORT** [C] when you move on your feet at a speed faster than walking as a sport [**usually singular**] *to* ***go for a run*** **2 SPORT** [C] in cricket or baseball, a single point *to score a run* **3 a dummy/practice/trial run** when you do something to practise it before the real time **4 a run of sth** when something happens several times without something different happening during that period *a run of 10 games without a win* ○ *a* ***run of good/bad luck*** **5** [C] a period of performances of a play, film, etc **6 be on the run** to be trying to avoid being caught, especially by the police **7 make a run for it** *informal* to suddenly run fast in order to escape from somewhere **8 in the long/short run** at a time that is far away or near in the future

runaway¹ /ˈrʌnəˌweɪ/ *adjective* [**always before noun**] **1 a runaway success/victory/winner, etc** something good that happens very quickly or easily **2** A runaway vehicle is moving away from somewhere without anyone controlling it. *a runaway car/train*

runaway² /ˈrʌnəˌweɪ/ *noun* [C] someone who has secretly left a place because they are unhappy there *teenage runaways*

run-down /ˌrʌnˈdaʊn/ *adjective* Run-down buildings or areas are in very bad condition. *a run-down housing estate*

rundown /ˈrʌndaʊn/ *noun* [**no plural**] a report of the main facts relating to a subject *He* ***gave*** *us* ***a rundown on*** *what happened at the meeting.*

rung¹ /rʌŋ/ *noun* **1** [C] one of the horizontal parts across a ladder (= structure for climbing up) **2 the first/highest/next, etc rung of the ladder** the first, highest, next, etc position, especially in society or in a job *She's on the bottom rung of the management ladder.*

rung² /rʌŋ/ *past participle of* ring²

run-in /ˈrʌnɪn/ *noun* [C] *informal* an argument *to have a run-in with someone*

runner /ˈrʌnəʳ/ *noun* **1 SPORT** [C] someone who runs, usually in competitions *a long-distance runner* **2 drug/gun runner** someone who takes drugs or guns illegally from one place to another ⇨See also: **front-runner**

ˌrunner ˈbean *UK* (*US* **ˈrunner ˌbean**) *noun* [C] **FOOD** a long, flat, green bean

runner-up /ˌrʌnərˈʌp/ *noun* [C] *plural* **runners-up SPORT** someone who finishes in second position in a competition

running¹ /ˈrʌnɪŋ/ *noun* [U] **1 SPORT** the sport of moving on your feet at a speed faster than walking *I* ***go running*** *three times a week.* ○ *running shoes* ⇨See colour picture **Sports 1** on page Centre 14 **2** the activity of controlling or looking after something *He has recently handed over the* ***day-to-day running*** *of the museum to his daughter.* ○ ***running costs***

running² /ˈrʌnɪŋ/ *adjective* **1** [**always before noun**] continuing for a long time *a* ***running battle*** ○ *a* ***running joke*** **2 second/third, etc day/week, etc running** If something happens for the second/third, etc day/week, etc running, it happens on that number of regular occasions without changing. *He's won the Championship for the fifth year running.* **3 running water** If a place has running water, it has a working water system.

runny /ˈrʌni/ *adjective* **1** A runny substance is more liquid than usual. *runny egg* **2 runny nose HEALTH** If you have a runny nose, your nose is producing liquid all the time.

run-of-the-mill /ˌrʌnəvðəˈmɪl/ *adjective* ordinary and not special or exciting in any way *He gave a fairly run-of-the-mill speech.*

run-up /ˈrʌnʌp/ *noun* **the run-up to sth** *UK* the period of time before an event *Sales increased by 15% in the run-up to Christmas.*

runway /ˈrʌnweɪ/ *noun* [C] a large road that aircraft use to land on or to start flying from

rupture /ˈrʌptʃəʳ/ *verb* [I, T] If you rupture something, you break or tear it, and if something ruptures, it breaks or tears. *He fell and ruptured a ligament in his knee.* •**rupture** *noun* [C]

rural /ˈrʊərəl/ *adjective* relating to the countryside and not to towns *a rural area*

ruse /ruːz/ *noun* [C] a way of deceiving someone so that they do something that you want them to do [+ **to do sth**] *The story was just a ruse to get her out of the house.*

O⁻**rush**[1] /rʌʃ/ *verb* **1** HURRY [I, T] to hurry or move quickly somewhere, or to make someone or something hurry or move quickly somewhere *We **rushed out** into the street to see what all the noise was.* ○ *The UN has **rushed** medical supplies **to** the war zone.* [+ **to do sth**] *We had to rush to catch the bus.* **2 rush to do sth** to do something quickly and enthusiastically *His friends rushed to congratulate him after the ceremony.* **3** FORCE ACTION [T] to make someone do something more quickly than they want to do it [+ **into** + **doing sth**] *I refuse to be rushed into making a decision.*

WORD PARTNERS FOR ***rush***

a **frantic/headlong/last-minute/mad** rush • a rush **for** sth

rush[2] /rʌʃ/ *noun* [no plural] **1** MOVEMENT when something suddenly moves somewhere quickly *a rush of air* **2** ACTIVITY a lot of things happening or a lot of people trying to do something [+ **to do sth**] *There was a **mad rush** to get tickets for the concert.* **3** HURRY when you have to hurry or move somewhere quickly *I'm sorry I can't talk now, I'm **in a rush**.*

rushes /rʌʃɪz/ *noun* [plural] tall plants that grow near water

ˈ**rush** ˌ**hour** *noun* [C, U] the time when a lot of people are travelling to or from work and so roads and trains are very busy ***the morning/evening rush hour***

rust /rʌst/ *noun* [U] **CHEMISTRY** a dark orange substance that you get on metal when it has been damaged by air and water •**rust** *verb* [I, T]

rustic /ˈrʌstɪk/ *adjective* simple and old-fashioned in style in a way that is typical of the countryside

rustle /ˈrʌsl/ *verb* [I, T] If things such as paper or leaves rustle, or if you rustle them, they move about and make a soft, dry sound. *Outside, the trees rustled in the wind.*

rustle up sth *phrasal verb* to produce something very quickly *I managed to rustle up a meal from the bits and pieces I found in his fridge.*

rusty /ˈrʌsti/ *adjective* **1** METAL Rusty metal has rust (= an orange substance) on its surface. *rusty nails* **2** SKILL If a skill you had is now rusty, it is not now good because you have forgotten it. *My French is a bit rusty.*

rut /rʌt/ *noun* **1 in a rut** in a bad situation where you do the same things all the time, or where it is impossible to make progress *He seems to be **stuck in a rut** at the moment.* **2** [C] a deep, narrow mark in the ground made by a wheel

ruthless /ˈruːθləs/ *adjective* not caring if you hurt or upset other people when you try to get what you want *ruthless ambition* ○ *a ruthless dictator* •**ruthlessly** *adverb* •**ruthlessness** *noun* [U]

rye /raɪ/ *noun* [U] **FOOD** a plant that has grains which are used to make things such as bread and whisky (= strong alcoholic drink) *rye bread*

R

Ss

S, s /es/ the nineteenth letter of the alphabet

the Sabbath /ˈsæbəθ/ *noun* **RELIGION** a day of the week that many religious groups use for prayer and rest

sabbatical /səˈbætɪkəl/ *noun* [**C, U**] **EDUCATION** a period when a university teacher does not do their usual work and instead travels or studies *He was* ***on sabbatical*** *last year.*

sabotage /ˈsæbətɑːʒ/ *verb* [**T**] **1** [DAMAGE] to damage or destroy something in order to prevent an enemy from using it *Rebels sabotaged the roads and bridges.* **2** [PREVENT SUCCESS] to spoil someone's plans or efforts in order to prevent them from being successful *She tried to sabotage my chances of getting the job.* •**sabotage** *noun* [**U**] *an act of sabotage*

sac /sæk/ *noun* [**C**] **BIOLOGY** a part in an animal or plant that is like a small bag

saccharin /ˈsækərɪn/ *noun* [**U**] **FOOD** a sweet, chemical substance that is used in food instead of sugar

sachet /ˈsæʃeɪ/ (US) /sæˈʃeɪ/ *noun* [**C**] a small bag containing a small amount of something *sachets of sugar and coffee powder*

sack¹ /sæk/ *noun* **1** [**C**] a large bag made of paper, plastic, or cloth and used to carry or store things **2 the sack** *UK* When someone gets the sack or is given the sack, they are told to leave their job. *He got the sack from his last job.*

sack² /sæk/ *verb* [**T**] *UK* to tell someone to leave their job, usually because they have done something wrong *He was sacked for being late.*

sacrament /ˈsækrəmənt/ *noun* [**C**] **RELIGION** an important religious ceremony in the Christian Church *the sacrament of marriage*

sacred /ˈseɪkrɪd/ *adjective* **1 RELIGION** relating to a religion or considered to be holy *sacred music* ○ *a sacred object* **2** too important to be changed or destroyed *I don't work at weekends - my private time is sacred.*

WORD PARTNERS FOR ***sacrifice***

make (great/huge) sacrifices • sacrifices **for** sb/sth • the sacrifice **of** sth

sacrifice¹ /ˈsækrɪfaɪs/ *noun* [**C, U**] **1** something valuable that you give up in order to achieve something, or the act of giving it up *Sometimes you have to* ***make sacrifices*** *to succeed.* **2 RELIGION** something offered to a god in a religious ceremony, especially an animal that is killed, or the act of offering it ➲See also: **self-sacrifice**

sacrifice² /ˈsækrɪfaɪs/ *verb* [**T**] **1** to give up something that is valuable to you in order to achieve something *There are thousands of men ready to* ***sacrifice*** *their lives* ***for*** *their country.* **2 RELIGION** to kill an animal and offer it to a god in a religious ceremony

sacrilege /ˈsækrɪlɪdʒ/ *noun* [**U, no plural**] when you treat something that is holy or important without respect

sacrosanct /ˈsækrəʊsæŋkt/ *adjective formal* too important to be changed or destroyed *Human life is sacrosanct.*

OTHER WAYS OF SAYING ***sad***

Unhappy and **miserable** mean the same as 'sad': *She'd had a very* ***unhappy*** *childhood.* • *I just woke up feeling* ***miserable.***

If someone is **upset**, they are unhappy because something bad has happened: *They'd had an argument and she was still* ***upset*** *about it.* • *Mike got very* ***upset*** *when I told him the news.*

If someone is **broken-hearted** or **heartbroken** they are very sad because someone they love has ended a relationship with them: *She was* ***broken-hearted*** *when Richard left.*

If someone is **devastated** or **distraught**, they are extremely upset: *She was* ***devastated*** *when he died.* • *The missing child's* ***distraught*** *parents made an emotional appeal for information on TV.*

The adjective **depressed** is often used when someone is very unhappy for a long time: *She became deeply* ***depressed*** *after her husband died.*

O-**sad** /sæd/ *adjective* **sadder, saddest 1** [NOT HAPPY] unhappy or making you feel unhappy *I was very sad when our cat died.* ○ *a sad book/movie* [**+ that**] *It's a bit sad that you'll miss our wedding.* [**+ to do sth**] *I was sad to see him go.* **2** [NOT SATISFACTORY] [**always before noun**] not pleasant or satisfactory *The sad truth is that we've failed.* **3** [NOT FASHIONABLE] *UK informal* boring or not fashionable *You enjoy reading timetables? You sad man!* •**sadness** *noun* [**U**]

sadden /ˈsædən/ *verb* [**T**] *formal* to make someone feel sad or disappointed [**often passive**] *We were saddened by his death.*

saddle¹ /ˈsædl/ *noun* [**C**] **1 SPORT** a leather seat that you put on a horse so that you can ride it ➲See colour picture **Sports 1** on page Centre 14 **2** a seat on a bicycle or motorcycle

saddle² /ˈsædl/ (*also* **saddle up**) *verb* [**I, T**] **SPORT** to put a saddle on a horse

saddle sb with sth *phrasal verb* to give someone a job or problem which will cause them a lot of work or difficulty

saddo /ˈsædəʊ/ *noun* [**C**] *UK informal* someone, especially a man, who is boring and not fashionable and has no friends

sadistic /səˈdɪstɪk/ *adjective* getting pleasure from being cruel or violent *sadistic behaviour* ○ *a sadistic murderer* •**sadist** /ˈseɪdɪst/ *noun* [**C**] someone who gets pleasure from being cruel or violent •**sadism** /ˈseɪdɪzəm/ *noun* [**U**]

sadly /ˈsædli/ *adverb* **1** [NOT HAPPY] in a sad way *She shook her head sadly.* **2** [NOT SATISFACTORY] in a way that is not satisfactory *Enthusiasm has been* ***sadly lacking*** *these past few months at work.* **3** [SORRY] used to say that you are sorry something is true *Sadly, the marriage did not last.*

sae, SAE /ˌeseɪˈiː/ *noun* [C] *UK abbreviation for* stamped addressed envelope or self-addressed envelope: an envelope that you put a stamp and your own address on and send to someone so that they can send you something back

safari /səˈfɑːri/ *noun* [C, U] a journey, usually to Africa, to see or hunt wild animals *She is* ***on safari*** *in Kenya.*

O-ᵡ **safe**[1] /seɪf/ *adjective* **1** NOT DANGEROUS not dangerous or likely to cause harm *a safe driver* ○ *Air travel is generally quite safe.* ○ *We live in a safe neighbourhood.* [+ **to do sth**] *Is it safe to drink the water here?* ⊃Opposite **unsafe** **2** NOT HARMED not harmed or damaged *She returned* ***safe and sound*** (= not harmed in any way). **3** NOT IN DANGER not in danger or likely to be harmed *During the daylight hours we're* ***safe from*** *attack.* **4 safe to say** If it is safe to say something, you are sure it is correct. *I think it's safe to say that he'll be the next president.* **5 a safe place; somewhere safe** a place where something will not be lost or stolen *It's very valuable so put it somewhere safe.* **6 play (it) safe** *informal* to be careful and not take risks •**safely** *adverb Make sure you drive safely.* • *I can safely say* (= I am certain) I have never met anyone as rude as him. ⊃See also: a safe **bet**[2]

safe[2] /seɪf/ *noun* [C] a strong metal box or cupboard with locks where you keep money, jewellery, and other valuable things

safeguard[1] /ˈseɪfgɑːd/ *verb* [T] to protect something from harm *a plan to safeguard public health*

safeguard against sth *phrasal verb* to do things that you hope will stop something unpleasant from happening *A good diet will safeguard against disease.*

safeguard[2] /ˈseɪfgɑːd/ *noun* [C] a law, rule, or system that protects people or things from being harmed or lost

ˌsafe ˈhaven *noun* [C] a place where someone is safe from danger

ˌsafe ˈsex *noun* [U] **HEALTH** when people have sex using a condom (= a thin rubber covering that a man wears on his penis) so that they do not catch a disease

WORD PARTNERS FOR ***safety***

ensure/guarantee sb's safety • safety is **paramount**

O-ᵡ **safety** /ˈseɪfti/ *noun* [U] **1** BEING SAFE when you are safe *food/road safety* ○ *The hostages were led to safety* (= to a safe place). ○ *a safety valve* **2** HOW SAFE SOMETHING IS how safe something is *Safety at the factory has been improved.* ⊃See Common Learner Error at **security**

ˈsafety ˌbelt *noun* [C] a piece of equipment that keeps you fastened to your seat when you are travelling in a vehicle *Please* ***fasten*** *your* ***safety belt*** *for take-off.*

ˈsafety ˌnet *noun* [C] **1** SYSTEM a plan or system that will help you if you get into a difficult situation *Legal aid provides a safety net for people who can't afford a lawyer.* **2** NET a net that will catch someone if they fall from a high place

ˈsafety ˌpin *noun* [C] a pin with a round cover that fits over the sharp end

saffron /ˈsæfrən/ *noun* [U] **FOOD** a yellow powder that is used as a spice

sag /sæg/ *verb* [I] **sagging**, *past* **sagged** **1** SINK to sink or bend down *Our mattress sags in the middle.* **2** BECOME WEAKER *informal* to become weaker or less successful *a sagging economy*

saga /ˈsɑːgə/ *noun* [C] **LITERATURE** a long story about a lot of people or events

sagacious /səˈgeɪʃəs/ *adjective literary* having or showing understanding and the ability to make good decisions and judgments

sage /seɪdʒ/ *noun* **1 FOOD** [U] a herb whose leaves are used to give flavour to food **2** [C] *literary* a wise person

Sagittarius /ˌsædʒɪˈteəriəs/ *noun* [C, U] the sign of the zodiac which relates to the period of 22 November - 22 December, or a person born during this period

said /sed/ *past of* say

sail[1] /seɪl/ *verb* **1** TRAVEL [I] to travel in a boat or a ship *We sailed to Malta.* **2** CONTROL BOAT [I, T] to control a boat that has no engine and is pushed by the wind *She sailed the small boat through the storm.* **3** START JOURNEY [I] When a ship sails, it starts its journey, and if people sail from a particular place or at a particular time, they start their journey. *This ship sails weekly from Florida to the Bahamas.* **4 sail over/past/through, etc** to move quickly through the air *The ball sailed past me.*

sail through (sth) *phrasal verb* to succeed very easily, especially in a test or competition *She sailed through her exams.*

sail[2] /seɪl/ *noun* **1** [C] a large piece of material that is fixed to a pole on a boat to catch the wind and make the boat move **2 set sail** to start a journey by boat or ship

sailboat /ˈseɪlbəʊt/ *noun* [C] *US* a small boat with sails

sailing /ˈseɪlɪŋ/ *noun* **1** [U] **SPORT** a sport using boats with sails *(UK) a sailing boat* **2 be plain sailing** to be very easy

sailor /ˈseɪləʳ/ *noun* [C] someone who sails ships or boats as their job or as a sport

saint /seɪnt/ *noun* [C] **1 RELIGION** a dead person who has been officially respected by the Christian church for living their life in a holy way *Catherine of Siena was* ***made a saint*** *in 1461.* **2** a very kind or helpful person ⊃See also: **patron saint**

saintly /ˈseɪntli/ *adjective* very good and kind

sake /seɪk/ *noun* **1 for the sake of sth** for this reason or purpose *For the sake of convenience, they combined the two departments.* **2 for the sake of sb** in order to help or please someone *He begged her to stay for the sake of the children.* **3 for God's/goodness/heaven's, etc sake** something you say when you are angry about something *For heaven's sake, stop moaning!*

O-ᵡ **salad** /ˈsæləd/ *noun* [C, U] **FOOD** a cold mixture of vegetables that have not been cooked, usually eaten with meat, cheese, etc *I made a big salad for lunch.* ⊃See colour picture **Food** on page Centre 11

S

salami /sə'lɑːmi/ *noun* [C, U] **FOOD** a spicy sausage (= tube of meat and spices) that is usually eaten cold in slices

salaried /'sælᵊrid/ *adjective* **FINANCE** receiving a fixed amount of money from your employer, usually every month

WORD PARTNERS FOR ***salary***

earn a salary • a **good/high/top** salary • an **annual** salary • a salary **cut/increase/rise**

O-**salary** /'sælᵊri/ *noun* [C, U] **FINANCE** a fixed amount of money that you receive from your employer, usually every month ➲See Common Learner Error at **pay**

O-**sale** /seɪl/ *noun* **FINANCE** **1** [U, no plural] the act of selling something, or the time when something is sold *The sale of alcohol is now banned.* ○ *to **make a sale*** **2 (up) for sale** available to buy *For sale: ladies bicycle - good condition.* ○ *The house next to mine is up for sale.* **3 on sale a** *UK* available to buy in a shop *The video and book are now on sale.* **b** available for a lower price than usual *This album was on sale for half price.* **4** [C] an event where things are sold *a sale of used books* **5** [C] a time when a shop sells goods at a lower price than usual *UK I bought this dress **in the sale**.* ➲See also: **car boot sale, jumble sale**

saleable /'seɪləbl/ *adjective* Something that is saleable can be sold easily. *He's painted some very saleable landscapes.*

sales /seɪlz/ *noun* [plural] **FINANCE** **1** the number of items sold *Our sales have doubled this year.* **2** the part of a company that deals with selling things *I used to work **in sales**.* ○ *a **sales department***

'sales ac,count *noun* [C] **FINANCE** a record that a business keeps of the goods it has sold

'sales as,sistant (*also US* **'sales ,clerk**) *noun* [C] someone whose job is selling things in a shop

'sales ,journal (*also* **sales book, sales day book**) *noun* [C] **FINANCE** a record that a business keeps of the dates on which sales were made, the names of the customers and the amounts of the sales

'sales ,ledger (*also* **debtors ledger**) *noun* [C] **FINANCE** a record that a business keeps of how much each customer owes

salesman, saleswoman /'seɪlzmən, 'seɪlz,wʊmən/ *noun* [C] *plural* **salesmen, saleswomen** someone whose job is selling things

salesperson /'seɪlz,pɜːsᵊn/ *noun* [C] *plural* **salespeople** someone whose job is selling things

'sales ,rep (*formal* **sales representative**) *noun* [C] someone who travels to different places trying to persuade people to buy their company's products or services

'sales re,turns (*also* **returns inward**) *noun* [plural] **ECONOMICS** when a customer returns goods to your company, for example because they are damaged or not needed

salient /'seɪliənt/ *adjective formal* The salient facts about something or qualities of something are the most important things about them.

saline /'seɪlaɪn/ (US) /'seɪliːn/ *adjective formal* **CHEMISTRY** containing salt *saline solution*

saliva /sə'laɪvə/ *noun* [U] **BIOLOGY** the liquid that is made in your mouth

salivary duct /sə'laɪvəri,dʌkt/ *noun* [C] **ANATOMY** a small tube that takes saliva into the mouth ➲See picture at **alimentary canal**

salivary gland /sə'laɪvəri,glænd/ *noun* [C] **ANATOMY** one of the body parts that produce saliva (= liquid in the mouth) ➲See picture at **alimentary canal**

sallow /'sæləʊ/ *adjective* Sallow skin is slightly yellow and does not look healthy.

salmon /'sæmən/ *noun* [C, U] *plural* **salmon** **FOOD** a large, silver fish, or the pink meat of this fish *fresh/smoked salmon*

salmonella /,sælmə'nelə/ *noun* [U] **HEALTH** a type of bacteria which can make you very ill, sometimes found in food that is not cooked enough

salon /'sælɒn/ *noun* [C] a shop where you can have your hair cut or have your appearance improved *a **hair salon*** ➲See also: **beauty salon**

saloon /sə'luːn/ *noun* [C] **1** CAR *UK* (*US* **sedan**) a large car with a separate, closed area for bags **2** BAR *US old-fashioned* a public bar

salsa /'sælsə/ *noun* [U] **1 FOOD** a cold, spicy sauce **2 MUSIC** a type of dance and music from Latin America *a salsa club*

O-**salt**[1] /sɔːlt, sɒlt/ *noun* [U] **1 FOOD** a white substance used to add flavour to food *salt and pepper* **2 take sth with a pinch of salt** *UK* (*US* **take sth with a grain of salt**) to not completely believe something that someone tells you

salt[2] /sɔːlt, sɒlt/ *verb* [T] **FOOD** to add salt to food

'salt ,cellar *UK* (*US* **'salt,shaker**) *noun* [C] a small container with holes in for shaking salt on food

saltwater /'sɔːlt,wɔːtəʳ/ *adjective* [always before noun] living in or containing water that has salt in it *a saltwater fish*

salty /'sɔːlti/ *adjective* **FOOD** tasting of or containing salt *Is the soup too salty?*

salute[1] /sə'luːt/ *noun* [C] a sign of respect to someone of a higher rank in a military organization, often made by raising the right hand to the side of the head *to give a **salute***

salute[2] /sə'luːt/ *verb* [I, T] to give a salute to someone of a higher rank in a military organization

salvage[1] /'sælvɪdʒ/ *verb* [T] **1** FROM PLACE to save things from a place where other things have been damaged or lost *gold coins salvaged from a shipwreck* **2** FROM SITUATION to try to make a bad situation better *an attempt to salvage her reputation*

salvage[2] /'sælvɪdʒ/ *noun* [U] when things are saved from being damaged, or the things that are saved *a salvage company*

salvation /sæl'veɪʃᵊn/ *noun* [U] **1 RELIGION** in the Christian religion, when God saves someone from the bad effects of evil **2** something or someone that saves you from harm or a very unpleasant situation *Getting a dog was Dad's salvation after Mum died.*

S

salwar kameez (*also* **shalwar kameez** /sal͵waːkə'miːz/) *noun* [C] a type of suit, worn especially by women in India, with loose trousers and a long shirt ➲See colour picture **Clothes** on page Centre 8

O‑**same¹** /seɪm/ *adjective, pronoun* **1 the same a** exactly alike *He's **the same** age **as** me.* ○ *We work at the same speed.* ○ *Cars cost **the same** here **as** they do in Europe.* **b** not another different thing or situation *They met at the same place every week.* ○ *You meet the same people at all these events.* **c** not changed *She's the same lively person she's always been.* ○ *He looks exactly **the same as** he did ten years ago.* **2 all/just the same** despite what has just been said *He doesn't earn much. All the same, he ought to pay for some of his own drinks.* **3 Same here.** *informal* something that you say when something another person has said is also true for you *"I think she's awful." "Same here."* **4 the same old arguments/faces/story, etc** *informal* something or someone you have seen or heard many times before **5 same old same old** *informal* used to say that a situation or someone's behaviour remains the same, especially when it it boring or annoying *Most people just keep on doing the same old same old every day.* ➲See also: be in the same **boat**, in the same **vein**, be on the same **wavelength**

O‑**same²** /seɪm/ *adverb* **the same** in the same way *We treat all our children the same.*

same-sex /͵seɪm'seks/ *adjective* **SOCIETY** A same-sex relationship, marriage, etc. is a romantic relationship between two men or two women.

WORD PARTNERS FOR ***sample***

analyse/collect/take/test a sample • a sample **of** sth

sample¹ /'sɑːmpl/ *noun* [C] **1** SHOW a small amount of something that shows you what it is like *a **free sample** of chocolate* ○ *She brought in some **samples of** her work.* **2** EXAMINE a small amount of a substance that a doctor or scientist collects in order to examine it *a **blood/urine sample*** **3** NUMBER a small number of people from a larger group that is being tested *a sample of 500 male drivers*

sample² /'sɑːmpl/ *verb* [T] **1** TASTE to taste a small amount of food or drink to decide if you like it *We sampled eight different cheeses.* **2** EXPERIENCE to experience a place or an activity, often for the first time *an opportunity to sample the local night life*

sanatorium (*also US* **sanitarium**) /͵sænə'tɔːriəm/ *noun* [C] *plural* **sanatoriums** or **sanatoria HEALTH** a hospital where people go to rest and get well after a long illness

WORD PARTNERS FOR ***sanction***

impose/lift sanctions • **tough** sanctions • sanctions **against/on** sb • **economic/trade** sanctions

sanction¹ /'sæŋkʃᵊn/ *noun* **1 POLITICS, LAW** [C] a punishment for not obeying a rule or a law ***economic/trade sanctions** against a country* **2** APPROVAL [U] official approval or permission

sanction² /'sæŋkʃᵊn/ *verb* [T] to formally approve of something *He refused to sanction the publication of his private letters.*

sanctity /'sæŋktəti/ *noun formal* **the sanctity of life/marriage, etc** when something is very important and deserves respect

sanctuary /'sæŋktʃuəri/ *noun* **1** QUIET [C, U] a quiet and peaceful place *After a busy day, I like to escape to the sanctuary of my garden.* **2** PROTECTION [C, U] a place that provides protection *to **seek sanctuary*** **3 ENVIRONMENT** [C] a place where animals are protected and cannot be hunted *a **bird/wildlife sanctuary***

O‑**sand¹** /sænd/ *noun* [U] **GEOLOGY** a substance that is found on beaches and in deserts, which is made from very small grains of rock *a grain of sand*

sand² /sænd/ *verb* [T] to make wood smooth by rubbing it with sandpaper (= strong paper with a rough surface)

sandal /'sændᵊl/ *noun* [C] a light shoe with straps that you wear in warm weather ➲See colour picture **Clothes** on page Centre 9

sand-cast /'sændkɑːst/ *verb* [T] **DT** to make something by pouring liquid metal, plastic, etc. into a mould (= hollow container) made of sand •**sand-cast** *adjective*

sandcastle /'sænd͵kɑːsl/ *noun* [C] a model of a castle made of wet sand, usually built by children on a beach

'sand ͵dune *noun* [C] **GEOGRAPHY** a hill of sand in the desert or on the coast

sandpaper /'sænd͵peɪpəʳ/ *noun* [U] strong paper with a rough surface that is rubbed against wood to make it smooth

sands /sændz/ *noun* [**plural**] a large area of sand

sandstone /'sændstəʊn/ *noun* [U] **GEOLOGY** rock made of sand

sandstorm /'sændstɔːm/ *noun* [C] a strong wind in a desert carrying a large amount of sand

O‑**sandwich¹** /'sænwɪdʒ/ *noun* [C] **FOOD** two slices of bread with meat, cheese, etc between them *a cheese/tuna sandwich* ➲See colour picture **Food** on page Centre 11

sandwich² /'sænwɪdʒ/ *verb*

be sandwiched between sth/sb *phrasal verb informal* to be in a small space between two people or things *Andorra is a small country sandwiched between Spain and France.*

sandy /'sændi/ *adjective* covered with or containing sand *a **sandy beach***

sane /seɪn/ *adjective* **1** NOT ILL not suffering from mental illness **2** GOOD JUDGMENT [**always before noun**] showing good judgment *a sane attitude/decision* ➲Opposite **insane**

sang /sæŋ/ *past tense of* sing

sanguine /'sæŋgwɪn/ *adjective formal* positive and full of hope *The director is sanguine about the company's prospects.*

sanitarium /͵sænɪ'teəriəm/ *noun* [C] *plural* **sanitariums** or **sanitaria HEALTH** *another US spelling of* sanatorium (= a hospital where people rest and get well after a long illness)

S

sanitary /ˈsænɪtᵊri/ *adjective* **HEALTH** relating to preventing disease by removing dirt and waste *sanitary conditions*

ˈsanitary ˌtowel *UK* (*US* **ˌsanitary ˈnapkin**) *noun* [C] a thick piece of soft paper that a woman wears to absorb blood from her period (= monthly blood from the uterus)

sanitation /ˌsænɪˈteɪʃᵊn/ *noun* [U] **HEALTH** a system for protecting people's health by removing dirt and waste

sanity /ˈsænəti/ *noun* [U] **1** JUDGMENT the quality of behaving calmly and showing good judgment *Jogging helps me **keep my sanity**.* **2** NOT ILL when you have a healthy mind and are not mentally ill ➲Opposite **insanity**

sank /sæŋk/ *past tense of* sink

sans serif /ˌsænˈserɪf/ *adjective* Sans serif letters have no serifs (= very small lines at the ends of the letters in some styles of printing). ➲Compare **serif**

Santa /ˈsæntə/ (*also* **Santa Claus** /ˈsæntəklɔːz/) *noun* [**no plural**] a kind, fat, old man in red clothes who people say brings presents to children at Christmas

sap¹ /sæp/ *verb* [T] **sapping**, *past* **sapped** to gradually make something weak *Ten years of war had **sapped** the country's **strength**.*

sap² /sæp/ *noun* [U] **BIOLOGY** the liquid inside plants and trees

sapling /ˈsæplɪŋ/ *noun* [C] **BIOLOGY** a young tree

sapphire /ˈsæfaɪəʳ/ *noun* [C] **GEOLOGY** a bright blue, transparent stone

saprophyte /ˈsæprəʊfaɪt/ *noun* [C] **BIOLOGY** an organism that lives and feeds on dead and decaying plant and animal matter

sarcasm /ˈsɑːkæzᵊm/ *noun* [U] when you say the opposite of what you mean to insult someone or show them that you are annoyed *"Oh, I am sorry," she said, her voice heavy with sarcasm.*

sarcastic /sɑːˈkæstɪk/ *adjective* using sarcasm *a sarcastic comment/remark* ○ *Are you being sarcastic?* •**sarcastically** *adverb*

sardine /sɑːˈdiːn/ *noun* [C] **FOOD** a small sea fish that you can eat

S

sari (*also* **saree**) /ˈsɑːri/ *noun* [C] a dress, worn especially by women from India and Pakistan, made from a very long piece of thin cloth

SARS /sɑːz/ *noun* [U] **HEALTH** *abbreviation for* Severe Acute Respiratory Syndrome: a serious disease that makes it difficult to breathe

SASE /ˌeseɪesˈiː/ *noun* [C] *US abbreviation for* self-addressed stamped envelope: an envelope that you put a stamp and your own address on and send to someone so that they can send you something back

sash /sæʃ/ *noun* [C] a long, narrow piece of cloth that is worn around the waist or over the shoulder, often as part of a uniform

sassy /ˈsæsi/ *adjective US informal* **1** ENERGETIC very energetic and confident *a smart, sassy young woman* **2** RUDE slightly rude, but not offensive *a sassy remark*

sat /sæt/ *past of* sit

Sat *written abbreviation for* Saturday

Satan /ˈseɪtᵊn/ *noun* [**no plural**] **RELIGION** the Devil (= the enemy of God)

satanic /səˈtænɪk/ *adjective* **RELIGION** relating to the Devil (= the enemy of God) *a satanic cult/ritual*

satchel /ˈsætʃᵊl/ *noun* [C] a large bag with a strap that goes over your shoulder, often used for carrying school books ➲See colour picture **The Classroom** on page Centre 6

satellite /ˈsætᵊlaɪt/ *noun* [C] **1** a piece of equipment that is sent into space around the Earth to receive and send signals or to collect information *a spy/weather satellite* **2 ASTRONOMY** a natural object that moves around a planet in space *The moon is the Earth's satellite.*

ˈsatellite ˌdish *noun* [C] a round piece of equipment that receives television and radio signals broadcast from satellites

ˌsatellite ˈtelevision (*also* **ˌsatellite TˈV**) *noun* [U] television programmes that are broadcast using a satellite

satin /ˈsætɪn/ *noun* [U] a smooth, shiny cloth

satire /ˈsætaɪəʳ/ *noun* **1** HUMOUR [U] when you use jokes and humour to criticize people or ideas ***political satire*** **2** STORY [C] a story, film, etc that uses satire •**satirist** /ˈsætᵊrɪst/ *noun* [C] someone who uses satire

satirical /səˈtɪrɪkᵊl/ *adjective* using satire *a satirical magazine/novel*

WORD PARTNERS FOR ***satisfaction***

derive/get satisfaction **from** sth • sth **gives** sb satisfaction • **deep/immense** satisfaction • a **sense of** satisfaction • **job** satisfaction

satisfaction /ˌsætɪsˈfækʃᵊn/ *noun* [U] **1** the pleasant feeling you have when you get something that you wanted or do something that you wanted to do ***job satisfaction*** ○ *She smiled **with satisfaction**.* [+ **of** + **doing sth**] *I had the satisfaction of knowing that I'd done everything I could.* **2 to sb's satisfaction** as well as someone wants *He won't get paid until he completes the job to my satisfaction.* ➲Opposite **dissatisfaction**

satisfactory /ˌsætɪsˈfæktᵊri/ *adjective* good enough *We hope very much to find a **satisfactory solution** to the problem.* ➲Opposite **unsatisfactory** •**satisfactorily** *adverb*

satisfied /ˈsætɪsfaɪd/ *adjective* **1** pleased because you have got what you wanted, or because something has happened in the way that you wanted *Are you **satisfied with** the new arrangement?* ➲Opposite **dissatisfied** **2 be satisfied that** If you are satisfied that something is true, you believe it. *The judge was satisfied that she was telling the truth.* ➲See also: **self-satisfied**

satisfy /ˈsætɪsfaɪ/ *verb* **1** [T] to please someone by giving them what they want or need *They sell 31 flavours of ice cream - enough to satisfy everyone!* **2 satisfy conditions/needs/requirements, etc** to have or provide something that is needed or wanted *She satisfies all the requirements for the job.* **3 satisfy sb that** to make someone believe that something is true *I satisfied myself that I had locked the door.*

satisfying /ˈsætɪsfaɪɪŋ/ *adjective* making you feel pleased by providing what you need or want *a satisfying meal* ○ *My work is very satisfying.*

SATNAV /ˈsætnæv/ *noun* [U] *abbreviation for* satellite navigation: a system of computers and satellites (= equipment that is sent into space around the Earth to receive and send signals), used in cars and other places to tell a user where they are or where something is

saturate /ˈsætʃəreɪt/ *verb* [T] **1 be saturated with sth** to be filled with a lot or too much of something *The city is saturated with cheap restaurants.* **2** to make something completely wet *Heavy rain had saturated the playing field.* **3 saturate the market** ECONOMICS to provide so much of a product to be sold that no more can be sold **4** to put as much of a substance that dissolves into a solution as is possible •**saturation** /ˌsætʃərˈeɪʃən/ *noun* [U]

ˌsaturated ˈfat *noun* [C, U] CHEMISTRY, FOOD a fat found in meat, milk, and eggs, which is thought to be bad for your health ➲Compare **unsaturated fat**

O‒ **Saturday** /ˈsætədeɪ/ (*written abbreviation* **Sat**) *noun* [C, U] the day of the week after Friday and before Sunday

Saturn /ˈsætən/ *noun* [no plural] ASTRONOMY the planet that is sixth from the Sun, after Jupiter and before Uranus ➲See picture at **solar system**

O‒ **sauce** /sɔːs/ *noun* [C, U] FOOD a hot or cold liquid that you put on food to add flavour *pasta with tomato sauce* ➲See also: **soy sauce**

saucepan /ˈsɔːspən/ *noun* [C] a deep, metal pan, usually with a long handle and a lid, that is used to cook food in ➲See colour picture **The Kitchen** on page Centre 2

saucer /ˈsɔːsər/ *noun* [C] a small plate that you put under a cup *a cup and saucer*

saucy /ˈsɔːsi/ *adjective* slightly rude, or referring to sex in a funny way *a saucy postcard/joke*

sauna /ˈsɔːnə/ *noun* [C] **1** a room that is hot and filled with steam where people sit to relax or feel healthy *a gym with a pool and a sauna* **2 have a sauna** to spend time inside a sauna

saunter /ˈsɔːntər/ *verb* **saunter into/over/through, etc** to walk in a slow and relaxed way *He sauntered through the door two hours late.*

sausage /ˈsɒsɪdʒ/ *noun* [C, U] FOOD a mixture of meat and spices pressed into a long tube

sauté /ˈsəʊteɪ, səʊˈteɪ/ *verb* [T] FOOD to fry food quickly in a small amount of hot oil

savage[1] /ˈsævɪdʒ/ *adjective* **1** VIOLENT extremely violent *a savage attack* **2** SEVERE severe *savage criticism* •**savagely** *adverb*

savage[2] /ˈsævɪdʒ/ *verb* [T] **1** ATTACK to attack violently [often passive] *A sheep had been savaged by a dog.* **2** CRITICIZE to severely criticize someone or something [often passive] *Her performance was savaged by the critics.*

savage[3] /ˈsævɪdʒ/ *noun* [C] *old-fashioned* an offensive word for a person from a country at an early stage of development

savannah (*also* **savanna**) /səˈvænə/ *noun* [C, U] GEOGRAPHY a large flat area of land covered with grass, usually with few trees, which is found in hot countries, especially in Africa

O‒ **save**[1] /seɪv/ *verb* **1** MAKE SAFE [T] to stop someone or something from being killed or destroyed *He was badly injured, but the doctors **saved** his **life**.* ○ *She **saved** the children **from** drowning.* ○ *He had to borrow money to save his business.* **2** FINANCE [I, T] (*also* **save up**) to keep money so that you can buy something with it in the future *We've **saved** almost $900 **for** our wedding.* ○ *Michael's **saving up for** a new computer.* **3** KEEP [T] to keep something to use in the future *I've **saved** some food **for** you.* **4 save money/space/time, etc** to reduce the amount of money/space/time, etc that you have to use **5 save sb (from) doing sth** to help someone avoid having to do something *We'll eat in a restaurant - it'll save you having to cook.* **6 save files/work, etc** COMPUTING to store work or information electronically on or from a computer **7 save a goal** SPORT to prevent a player from scoring a goal *He saved two goals in the last minute of the game.* ➲See also: save the **day**, lose/save **face**[1]

save on sth *phrasal verb* to avoid using something so that you do not have to pay for it *She walks to work to save on bus fares.*

save[2] /seɪv/ *noun* [C] SPORT when someone prevents a goal from being scored in a sport *The goalkeeper **made** a great **save**.*

saver /ˈseɪvər/ *noun* [C] FINANCE someone who saves money in a bank

saving /ˈseɪvɪŋ/ *noun* [C] *UK* (*US* **savings**) FINANCE when you pay less money than you would usually have to [usually singular] *a saving of £20.*

savings /ˈseɪvɪŋz/ *noun* [plural] FINANCE money that you have saved, usually in a bank *I spent all my savings on a new kitchen.* ○ *a **savings account***

ˈsavings acˌcount *noun* [C] *US* FINANCE a bank account where you keep money that you want to save

savings and ˈloan associˌation *US* (*UK* **building society**) *noun* [C] FINANCE a bank that is owned by the people who keep their money in it and that lets them borrow money to buy a house

saviour *UK* (*US* **savior**) /ˈseɪvjər/ *noun* **1** [C] someone who saves someone or something from harm or difficulty **2 the Saviour** RELIGION in Christianity, Jesus Christ

savour *UK* (*US* **savor**) /ˈseɪvər/ *verb* [T] to enjoy food or a pleasant experience as much and as slowly as possible *to savour a meal* ○ *We savoured our moment of victory.*

savoury *UK* (*US* **savory**) /ˈseɪvəri/ *adjective* FOOD Savoury food is not sweet. *savoury biscuits*

savvy /ˈsævi/ *noun* [U] *informal* practical knowledge and ability ***business/political savvy*** •**savvy** *adjective informal* having knowledge and ability *a savvy consumer*

saw[1] /sɔː/ *noun* [C] a tool with a sharp edge that you use to cut wood or other hard material •**saw** *verb* [I, T] *past tense* **sawed**, *past participle* **sawn**, *mainly US* **sawed** to use a saw *They sawed the door in half.*

saw[2] /sɔː/ *past tense of* see

S

sawdust /ˈsɔːdʌst/ *noun* [U] very small pieces of wood and powder that are produced when you cut wood with a saw

saxophone /ˈsæksəfəʊn/ (*also* **sax** *informal*) *noun* [C] **MUSIC** a metal musical instrument that you play by blowing into it and pressing keys to produce different notes •**saxophonist** /sækˈsɒfənɪst/ (US) /ˈsæksəfəʊnɪst/ *noun* [C] someone who plays the saxophone

O-ᵚ**say**[1] /seɪ/ *verb* [T] **says** *past* **said** **1** WORDS to speak words *"I'd like to go home," she said.* ○ *I couldn't hear what they were saying.* ○ *How do you say this word?* **2** TELL to tell someone about a fact, thought, or opinion [+ **question word**] *Did she say where she was going?* [+ **(that)**] *The jury said that he was guilty.* **3** INFORMATION to give information in writing, numbers, or signs *My watch says one o'clock.* ○ *What do the papers say about the election?* **4** **say sth to yourself** to think something but not speak *"I hope she likes me," he said to himself.* **5** SHOW to show what you think without using words *His smile seemed to say that I was forgiven.* **6** **(let's) say...** used to introduce a suggestion or possible example of something *Say you were offered a better job in another city - would you take it?* **7** **You can say that again!** *informal* used to show that you completely agree with something that someone has just said *"That was a very bad movie!" "You can say that again!"* **8** **it goes without saying** If something goes without saying, it is generally accepted or understood. *It goes without saying that smoking is harmful to your health.* ⊃See also: Say **cheese**!, easier (**easy**[2]) said than done

COMMON LEARNER ERROR

say or **tell?**

Say can refer to any type of speech.

"Good night," she said.

She said she was unhappy.

Jim said to meet him here.

Tell is used to report that someone has given information or an order. The verb **tell** is always followed by the person that the information or order is given to.

Simon told me about his new job.

Say is never followed by the person that the information or order is given to.

He told us to stay here.

~~*He said us to stay here.*~~

WORD PARTNERS FOR ***say (noun)***

be given/have [a/no/some, etc] say • the **final** say • say **in/on** sth

say[2] /seɪ/ *noun* [U] **1** when you are involved in making a decision about something *We **had some say in** how our jobs would develop.* **2** **have your say** to give your opinion about something *We can't vote yet - Christina hasn't had her say.*

saying /ˈseɪɪŋ/ *noun* [C] a famous phrase that people use to give advice about life *Have you heard the saying, "misery loves company"?*

sb *written abbreviation for* somebody •**sb's** *written abbreviation for* somebody's

scab /skæb/ *noun* [C] **HEALTH** a layer of dried blood that forms to cover a cut in the skin

scaffolding /ˈskæfəldɪŋ/ *noun* [U] a temporary structure made of flat boards and metal poles used to work on a tall building

scalar /ˈskeɪlər/ *noun* [C] something that has size but no direction, such as a quantity, distance, speed or temperature ⊃Compare **vector** •**scalar** *adjective*

scald /skɔːld/ *verb* [T] to burn something or someone with very hot liquid or steam *She scalded her mouth on the hot soup.*

WORD PARTNERS FOR ***scale***

on a [grand/large/massive/small, etc] scale • the scale **of** sth

scale[1] /skeɪl/ *noun* **1** SIZE [**no plural**] the size or level of something *We don't yet know the scale of the problem.* ○ *Nuclear weapons cause destruction **on a massive scale*** (= cause a lot of destruction). **2** **large-/small-scale** A large-/small-scale event or activity is large/small in size. *a large-scale investigation* **3** MEASURING SYSTEM [C] the set of numbers, amounts, etc used to measure or compare the level of something *How would you rate her work **on a scale of** 1-10?* **4** EQUIPMENT [C] *US* (*UK* **scales** [**plural**]) a piece of equipment for measuring weight *a bathroom/kitchen scale* ⊃See colour picture **The Kitchen** on page Centre 2, **The Bathroom** on page Centre 3 **5** **ART** [C, U] how the size of things on a map, model, etc relates to the same things in real life *a map with a scale of one centimetre per ten kilometres* **6** **MUSIC** [C] a series of musical notes that is always played in order and that rises gradually from the first note **7** **BIOLOGY** [C] one of the flat pieces of hard material that covers the skin of fish and snakes **8** **CHEMISTRY** (*also* **limescale**) a hard, white layer that forms on the sides of pipes or containers that heat water

scale[2] /skeɪl/ *verb* [T] to climb something that is high or steep *to scale a wall*

scale sth back *phrasal verb mainly US* (*UK/US* **scale sth down**) to make something smaller than it was or smaller than it was planned to be

scalene triangle /ˌskeɪliːnˈtraɪæŋgl/ *noun* [C] **MATHEMATICS** a triangle with three sides all of different lengths ⊃Compare **equilateral, isosceles triangle**

scales /skeɪlz/ *noun* [**plural**] *UK* (*US* **scale** [C]) a piece of equipment for measuring weight *bathroom/kitchen scales* ⊃See colour picture **The Kitchen** on page Centre 2, **The Bathroom** on page Centre 3

scallion /ˈskæliən/ *US* (*UK* **spring onion**) *noun* [C] **FOOD** a small onion with a white part at the bottom and long, green leaves which is eaten in salads

scallop /ˈskæləp/ *noun* [C] **FOOD** a small sea creature that lives in a shell and is eaten as food

scalp /skælp/ *noun* [C] **ANATOMY** the skin on the top of your head under your hair

scalpel /ˈskælpəl/ *noun* [C] **HEALTH** a small, sharp knife that doctors use to cut through skin during an operation

S

scalper /ˈskælpəʳ/ US (UK **tout**) *noun* [C] someone who unofficially sells tickets outside theatres, sports grounds, etc

scaly /ˈskeɪli/ *adjective* **HEALTH** If your skin is scaly, it is rough and falls off in small, dry pieces.

scam /skæm/ *noun* [C] *informal* an illegal plan for making money

scamper /ˈskæmpəʳ/ *verb* **scamper away/down/off, etc** to run quickly and with small steps, like a child or a small animal

scampi /ˈskæmpi/ *noun* [U] **FOOD** prawns (= small sea creatures) that have been fried

scan¹ /skæn/ *verb* **scanning**, *past* **scanned 1 HEALTH** [T] to examine something with a machine that can see inside an object or body *Airports use X-ray machines to scan luggage for weapons.* **2 COMPUTING** [T] to use a piece of equipment that copies words or pictures from paper into a computer *to scan photos into a computer* **3** LOOK [T] to look around an area quickly to try to find a person or thing *She* ***scanned*** *the crowd* ***for*** *a familiar face.* **4** READ [T] (*also* **scan through**) to quickly read a piece of writing to understand the main meaning or to find a particular piece of information *I scanned the travel brochures looking for a cheap holiday.*

scan² /skæn/ *noun* [C] **HEALTH** a medical examination in which an image of the inside of the body is made using a special machine *a brain scan*

WORD PARTNERS FOR ***scandal***

a scandal **breaks/erupts** • be **at the centre of/involved in** a scandal • a scandal **surrounding** sth • a **sex** scandal

scandal /ˈskændəl/ *noun* [C, U] something that shocks people because they think it is morally wrong *a* ***sex scandal***

scandalous /ˈskændələs/ *adjective* shocking or morally wrong *a* ***scandalous waste*** *of money*

Scandinavian /ˌskændɪˈneɪviən/ *adjective* from or relating to the countries of Sweden, Denmark, Norway, and sometimes Finland and Iceland •**Scandinavian** *noun* [C]

scanner /ˈskænəʳ/ *noun* [C] **1 COMPUTING** a piece of equipment that copies words or pictures from paper into a computer **2 HEALTH** a piece of medical equipment used to examine images of the inside of someone's body

scansion /ˈskænʃən/ *noun* [U] **LANGUAGE, LITERATURE** the rhythm of a line of poetry

scant /skænt/ *adjective* [**always before noun**] very little and not enough *His work has received only scant attention outside this country.*

scantily /ˈskæntɪli/ *adverb* **scantily clad/dressed** not wearing many clothes and showing a lot of the body

scanty /ˈskænti/ *adjective* very small in size or quantity *scanty clothing*

scapegoat /ˈskeɪpgəʊt/ *noun* [C] someone who is blamed for a bad situation, although they have not caused it *He was* ***made a scapegoat*** *for the disaster.*

scapula /ˈskæpjələ/ *noun* [C] **ANATOMY** one of the two bones shaped like triangles in a person's shoulders

scar /skɑːʳ/ *noun* [C] **1 HEALTH** a permanent mark left on the body from a cut or other injury **2** damage done to a person's mind by a very unpleasant event or situation *a* ***psychological scar*** •**scar** *verb* [T] **scarring**, *past* **scarred** to cause a scar [**often passive**] He was ***scarred for life*** *by the accident.*

scarce /skeəs/ *adjective* rare or not available in large amounts ***scarce resources***

scarcely /ˈskeəsli/ *adverb* **1** only just *They had scarcely finished eating when the doorbell rang.* **2 can scarcely do sth** If you say you can scarcely do something, you mean it would be wrong to do it. *He's only two - you can scarcely blame him for behaving badly.*

scarcity /ˈskeəsəti/ *noun* [C, U] when there is not enough of something *a scarcity of food/affordable housing*

scare¹ /skeəʳ/ *verb* [T] **1** to frighten a person or animal *Sudden, loud noises scare me.* **2 scare the hell/life/living daylights, etc out of sb** *informal* to make someone feel very frightened ➲See also: scare/frighten sb out of their **wits**

scare sb/sth away/off *phrasal verb* to make a person or an animal so frightened that they go away *She scared off her attacker by screaming.*

scare sb away/off *phrasal verb* to make someone worried about doing something so that they decide not to do it *The recent bomb attacks have scared away the tourists.*

WORD PARTNERS FOR ***scare***

give sb **/have/suffer** a scare • a **food/health** scare

scare² /skeəʳ/ *noun* [C] **1** FEELING a sudden feeling of fear or worry *The earthquake* ***gave us a scare***. **2** SITUATION a situation that worries or frightens people *a* ***food/health scare***

scarecrow /ˈskeəkrəʊ/ *noun* [C] **FARMING** a model of a person that is put in a field to frighten birds and stop them from eating the plants

OTHER WAYS OF SAYING ***scared***

The adjectives **afraid** and **frightened** are common alternatives to 'scared': *Don't be* ***frightened***. *The dog won't hurt you.* • *Gerry has always been* ***afraid*** *of heights.*

If someone is extremely scared, then you can use the adjectives **petrified**, **terrified**, **panic-stricken**, or the informal phrase **scared to death**: *I'm* ***petrified/terrified*** *of spiders.* • *She was* ***panic-stricken*** *when her little boy disappeared.* • *He's* ***scared to death*** *of having the operation.*

If someone is scared because they are worrying about something, then you can use adjectives like **afraid** or **worried**: *I'm* ***afraid/worried*** *that something will go wrong.*

O⁻ **scared** /skeəd/ *adjective* frightened or worried *Robert's* ***scared of*** *heights.* ○ *I was* ***scared to death*** (= very frightened). [**+ (that)**] *We were scared that we'd be killed.*

scarf¹ /skɑːf/ *noun* [C] *plural* **scarves** /skɑːvz/ or **scarfs** a piece of cloth that you wear around your neck, head, or shoulders to keep warm or for decoration See colour picture **Clothes** on page Centre 9

scarf² /skɑːf/ (*also* **scarf down**) *verb* [T] *US informal* (*UK* **scoff**) to eat a lot of something quickly *Who scarfed all the cookies?*

scarlet /'skɑːlət/ *noun* [U] a bright red colour •**scarlet** *adjective*

scarp /skɑːp/ *noun* [C] **GEOGRAPHY** a steep slope or cliff formed by folded or eroded (= washed or blown away) layers of rock

scary /'skeəri/ *adjective informal* frightening *a scary place/woman*

scathing /'skeɪðɪŋ/ *adjective* criticizing very strongly *He was* ***scathing about*** *the report.*

scatter /'skætəʳ/ *verb* **1** THROW [T] to throw objects over an area so that they land apart from each other *He scattered some flower seeds in the garden.* **2** MOVE [I] to suddenly move apart in different directions *The crowd scattered at the sound of gunshots.*

'scatter ˌdiagram *noun* [C] **MATHEMATICS** a graph with points representing amounts of numbers on it, often with a line drawn through the points to show the pattern of the data

scattered /'skætəd/ *adjective* covering a wide area *His toys were scattered all over the floor.* ○ *There will be* ***scattered showers*** (= separate areas of rain) *today.*

scattering /'skætərɪŋ/ *noun* [**no plural**] a small number of separate things, especially in a large area *a scattering of houses*

scatty /'skæti/ *adjective informal* silly and often forgetting things

scavenge /'skævɪndʒ/ *verb* [**I, T**] to search for food or for useful things that have been thrown away •**scavenger** *noun* [C] a person or animal who scavenges

scenario /sɪ'nɑːriəʊ/ *noun* **1** [C] a description of a situation, or of a situation that may develop in the future **2 worst-case scenario** the worst situation that you can imagine

scene /siːn/ *noun* **1 LITERATURE** [C] a short part of a film, play, or book in which the events happen in one place *a* ***love scene*** ○ *the final scene* **2** VIEW [C] a view or picture of a place, event, or activity *scenes of everyday life* **3** PLACE [C] a place where an unpleasant event has happened *the scene of the crime* **4 the club/gay/music, etc scene** all the things connected with a particular way of life or activity **5** ARGUMENT [C] when people have a loud argument or show strong emotions in a public place [**usually singular**] *She* ***made a scene*** *when I told her she couldn't come with us.* **6 behind the scenes** If something happens behind the scenes, it happens secretly. **7 set the scene for sth** to make an event or situation possible or likely to happen

scenery /'siːnᵊri/ *noun* [U] **1** COUNTRYSIDE the attractive, natural things that you see in the countryside *The Grand Canyon is famous for its spectacular scenery.* **2** THEATRE the large pictures of buildings, countryside, etc used on a theatre stage

scenic /'siːnɪk/ *adjective* having views of the attractive, natural things in the countryside *a* ***scenic route*** ○ *an area of great* ***scenic beauty***

scent /sent/ *noun* **1** SMELL [C] a pleasant smell *the sweet scent of orange blossoms* **2** LIQUID [C, U] a pleasant smelling liquid that people put on their skin **3** ANIMAL [C, U] the smell of an animal or a person that is left somewhere

scented /'sentɪd/ *adjective* having a pleasant smell *a scented candle*

sceptic *UK* (*US* **skeptic**) /'skeptɪk/ *noun* [C] someone who doubts that a belief or an idea is true or useful

sceptical *UK* (*US* **skeptical**) /'skeptɪkᵊl/ *adjective* doubting that something is true or useful *Scientists remain* ***sceptical about*** *astrology.* ○ *She was* ***sceptical of*** *the new arrangement.*

scepticism *UK* (*US* **skepticism**) /'skeptɪsɪzᵊm/ *noun* [U] when you doubt that something is true or useful *There was some* ***scepticism about*** *her ability to do the job.*

schedule¹ /'ʃedjuːl/ (US) /'skedʒuːl/ *noun* **1** PLAN [C, U] a plan that gives events or activities and the times that they will happen or be done *I have a very* ***busy schedule*** *today.* ○ *Will the work be completed* ***on schedule*** (= at the expected time)? ○ *The project was finished* ***ahead of schedule*** (= earlier than planned). **2** TRAVEL [C] *mainly US* a list of times when buses, trains, etc arrive and leave

schedule² /'ʃedjuːl/ (US) /'skedʒuːl/ *verb* [T] to arrange that an event or an activity will happen at a particular time [**often passive**] *Your appointment has been* ***scheduled for*** *next Tuesday.* ○ *a scheduled flight*

WORD PARTNERS FOR ***scheme***

come up with/devise a scheme • **implement/introduce/launch/unveil** a scheme • a scheme **for** doing sth

scheme¹ /skiːm/ *noun* [C] **1** OFFICIAL *mainly UK* an official plan or system *an insurance/savings scheme* ○ *a training scheme for teenagers* **2** DISHONEST a plan for making money, especially in a dishonest way *a scheme to steal money from investors*

scheme² /skiːm/ *verb* [I] to make a secret plan in order to get an advantage, usually by deceiving people

schist /ʃɪst/ *noun* [U] **GEOLOGY** a type of rock that breaks easily into thin layers

schizophrenia /ˌskɪtsəʊ'friːniə/ *noun* [U] **HEALTH** a serious mental illness in which someone cannot understand what is real and what is imaginary •**schizophrenic** /ˌskɪtsəʊ'frenɪk/ *noun* [C] someone who suffers from schizophrenia

schizophrenic /ˌskɪtsəʊ'frenɪk/ *adjective* **HEALTH** relating to schizophrenia *schizophrenic patients/symptoms*

schmooze /ʃmuːz/ *verb* [**I, T**] *informal* to talk to someone in a friendly, informal way so that they will like you or do something for you *politicians* ***schmoozing with*** *journalists*

scholar /ˈskɒləʳ/ *noun* [C] **EDUCATION** someone who has studied a subject and knows a lot about it *a legal scholar*

scholarly /ˈskɒləli/ *adjective* **1** WRITING A scholarly article or book is a formal piece of writing by a scholar about a particular subject. **2** PERSON If someone is scholarly, they study a lot and know a lot about what they study.

scholarship /ˈskɒləʃɪp/ *noun* **1 EDUCATION** [C] an amount of money given to a person by an organization to pay for their education, usually at a college or university **2 EDUCATION** [U] when you study a subject for a long time

scholastic /skəˈlæstɪk/ *adjective* **EDUCATION** [**always before noun**] relating to school and education *scholastic achievements*

WORD PARTNERS FOR ***school***

go to school • **at** school • a school **holiday** • a school **year** • school **children/kids**

O-* **school** /skuːl/ *noun* **1 EDUCATION** [C] a place where children go to be educated *Which* ***school*** *do you* ***go*** *to?* ○ *I ride my bike to school.* **2 EDUCATION** [U] the time that you spend at school *I like school.* ○ *We're going shopping after school.* **3 EDUCATION** [**no plural**] all the students and teachers at a school *The whole school took part in the project.* **4 a dance/language/riding, etc school EDUCATION** a place where you can study a particular subject **5 EDUCATION** [C] a part of a college or university *the University of Cambridge Medical School* **6 EDUCATION** [C, U] *US informal* in the US, any college or university, or the time you spend there *Which schools did you apply for?* **7** [C] a group of fish or other sea animals **8 school of thought** the ideas and beliefs shared by a group of people ⊃See also: **boarding school, elementary school, grade school, grammar school, high school, junior high school, junior school, middle school, night school, nursery school, prep school, preparatory school, primary school, public school, secondary school, state school**

schoolboy /ˈskuːlbɔɪ/ *noun* [C] **EDUCATION** a boy who goes to school

schoolchild /ˈskuːltʃaɪld/ *noun* [C] *plural* **schoolchildren EDUCATION** a child who goes to school

schooldays /ˈskuːldeɪz/ *noun* [**plural**] *UK* **EDUCATION** the period in your life when you go to school

schoolgirl /ˈskuːlgɜːl/ *noun* [C] **EDUCATION** a girl who goes to school

schooling /ˈskuːlɪŋ/ *noun* [U] **EDUCATION** education at school

schoolteacher /ˈskuːlˌtiːtʃəʳ/ *noun* [C] **EDUCATION** someone who teaches children in a school

O-* **science** /saɪəns/ *noun* **1 EDUCATION** [U] the study and knowledge of the structure and behaviour of natural things in an organized way **2 EDUCATION** [C, U] a particular type of science *computer science* ○ *Chemistry, physics, and biology are all sciences.* ⊃See also: **natural sciences, social science**

ˌscience ˈfiction *noun* [U] **LITERATURE** stories about life in the future or in other parts of the universe

O-* **scientific** /ˌsaɪənˈtɪfɪk/ *adjective* relating to science, or using the organized methods of science ***scientific experiments/research*** •**scientifically** *adverb a scientifically proven fact*

scienˌtific noˈtation *noun* [U] **MATHEMATICS** a way of writing very large or very small numbers by putting one number before the decimal point, then multiplying by a power of 10, e.g. 3.6 x 103

O-* **scientist** /ˈsaɪəntɪst/ *noun* [C] someone who studies science or works in science

sci-fi /ˈsaɪˌfaɪ/ *noun* [U] **LITERATURE** *informal short for* science fiction

scintillating /ˈsɪntɪleɪtɪŋ/ *adjective* very interesting or exciting *a scintillating performance*

scissors /ˈsɪzəz/ *noun* [**plural**] a tool for cutting paper, hair, cloth, etc that you hold in your hand and that has two blades that move against each other *a pair of scissors*

sclera /ˈsklɪərə/ *noun* [**C usually singular**] **ANATOMY** the strong white layer that covers the outside of the eye

scoff /skɒf/ *verb* **1** CRITICIZE [I] to laugh at someone or something, or criticize them in a way that shows you do not respect them *The critics* ***scoffed at*** *his work.* **2** EAT [I, T] *UK informal* (*US* **scarf**) to eat a lot of something quickly *Who scoffed all the chocolates?*

scold /skəʊld/ *verb* [T] *old-fashioned* to speak angrily to someone because they have done something wrong

scone /skɒn, skəʊn/ *noun* [C] **FOOD** a small, round cake *tea and buttered scones*

scoop¹ /skuːp/ *verb* [T] to remove something from a container using a spoon, your curved hands, etc *She scooped the ice cream into the dishes.*

scoop sth/sb up *phrasal verb* to lift something or someone with your hands

scoop² /skuːp/ *noun* [C] **1** SPOON a large, deep spoon for lifting and moving an amount of something, or the amount that can be held in it *an* ***ice cream scoop*** ○ *a scoop of ice cream* **2** NEWS a piece of news discovered and printed by one newspaper before it appears anywhere else

scoot /skuːt/ *verb informal* **scoot along/down/over, etc** to go somewhere quickly

scooter /ˈskuːtəʳ/ *noun* [C] **1** MOTORCYCLE a small motorcycle **2** TOY a child's vehicle that has two wheels fixed to the ends of a long board and a long handle

WORD PARTNERS FOR ***scope***

expand/extend/limit/widen the scope of sth • be **beyond/outside/within** the scope of sth

scope /skəʊp/ *noun* **1** AMOUNT [**no plural**] how much a subject or situation relates to *Do we know the full* ***scope of*** *the problem yet?* **2** OPPORTUNITY [U] the opportunity to do something *There is plenty of* ***scope for*** *improvement.*

scorch /skɔːtʃ/ *verb* [T] to damage something with fire or heat

scorched /skɔːtʃt/ *adjective* slightly burnt, or damaged by fire or heat *scorched earth/fields*

ˌscorched ˈearth ˌpolicy *noun* [no plural] when an army destroys everything in an area such as food, buildings or equipment which could be useful to an enemy

scorching /ˈskɔːtʃɪŋ/ *adjective* very hot *a* ***scorching hot*** *day*

WORD PARTNERS FOR ***score***

keep score • **even/level** the score • the **final/ latest** score • a score **of** sth • a **high/low** score

O‑ **score**[1] /skɔːʳ/ *noun* **1 SPORT** [C] the number of points someone gets in a game or test *a* ***high/ low score*** ○ *What's the score?* **2 scores of sth** a large number of people or things *Scores of teenage girls were waiting to get his autograph.* **3 MUSIC** [C] a printed piece of music **4 on that/this score** about the thing or subject which you have just discussed *The company will pay your travel expenses, so don't worry on that score.*

O‑ **score**[2] /skɔːʳ/ *verb* [I, T] **SPORT** to get points in a game or test *He scored just before half-time to put Liverpool 2-1 ahead.*

scoreboard /ˈskɔːbɔːd/ *noun* [C] **SPORT** a large board which shows the score of a game

scorer /ˈskɔːrəʳ/ *noun* [C] **SPORT** a player who scores points in a game *Domingo was Italy's* ***top scorer.***

scorn /skɔːn/ *noun* [U] *formal* the feeling that something is stupid and does not deserve your respect •**scorn** *verb* [T] *formal* to show scorn for someone or something *You scorned all my suggestions.*

scornful /ˈskɔːnfᵊl/ *adjective formal* showing that you think something is stupid and does not deserve your respect *I'm very* ***scornful of*** *any findings that lack proper scientific data.* •**scornfully** *adverb*

Scorpio /ˈskɔːpiəʊ/ *noun* [C, U] the sign of the zodiac which relates to the period of 23 October - 21 November, or a person born during this period

scorpion /ˈskɔːpiən/ *noun* [C] a small, insect-like creature with a curved, poisonous tail

S

Scotch /skɒtʃ/ (*also* ˌ**Scotch** ˈ**whisky**) *noun* [C, U] **FOOD** a type of whisky (= strong alcoholic drink)

ˌScotch ˈtape *US trademark* (*UK trademark* **Sellotape**) *noun* [U] clear, thin tape used for sticking things, especially paper, together ➲See colour picture **The Classroom** on page Centre 6

the Scots /skɒts/ *noun* [plural] the people of Scotland

Scottish /ˈskɒtɪʃ/ *adjective* relating to Scotland *Scottish history*

scour /skaʊəʳ/ *verb* [T] **1** [SEARCH] to search for something very carefully, often over a large area *The police* ***scoured*** *the surrounding countryside* ***for*** *possible clues.* **2** [CLEAN] to clean something by rubbing it with something rough

scourge /skɜːdʒ/ *noun formal* **the scourge of sth** something which causes a lot of suffering or trouble *Drug-related crime is the scourge of modern society.*

scout[1] /skaʊt/ *noun* **1** [MEMBER] [C] (*also* **Boy Scout**) a member of an organization for young people which teaches them practical skills and encourages them to be good members of society **2 the Scouts** an organization for young people which teaches them practical skills and encourages them to be good members of society **3** [MUSIC/SPORT] [C] someone whose job is to find good musicians, sports people, etc to join an organization *a* ***talent scout***

scout[2] /skaʊt/ (*also* **scout around**) *verb* [I] to try to find something by looking in different places *I'm* ***scouting around for*** *somewhere to park.*

scowl /skaʊl/ *verb* [I] to look at someone angrily *He* ***scowled at*** *me from behind his paper.* •**scowl** *noun* [C]

scrabble /ˈskræbl/ *verb*

scrabble about/around *phrasal verb* to use your fingers to quickly find something that you cannot see *She scrabbled around in her bag, trying to find her keys.*

scramble /ˈskræmbl/ *verb* **1 scramble down/out/ up, etc** to move or climb quickly but with difficulty, often using your hands *We scrambled up the hill.* **2** [I] to compete with other people for something which there is very little of [+ **to do sth**] *New teachers scramble to get jobs in the best schools.* •**scramble** *noun* [no plural] *There was a* ***mad scramble*** *for places near the front.*

ˌscrambled ˈeggs *noun* [plural] **FOOD** eggs which are mixed together and then cooked

scrap[1] /skræp/ *noun* **1** [SMALL PIECE] [C] a small piece or amount of something *He wrote his phone number on* ***a scrap of*** *paper.* ○ *I've read every* ***scrap of information*** *I can find on the subject.* **2** [OLD] [U] old cars and machines that are not now needed but have parts which can be used to make other things ***scrap metal*** ○ *The car was so badly damaged we could only sell it as scrap.* **3** [FIGHT] [C] *informal* a fight or an argument, usually not very serious *He was always* ***getting into scraps*** *at school.*

scrap[2] /skræp/ *verb* [T] **scrapping**, *past* **scrapped** **1** [STOP] *informal* to not continue with a plan or idea *That project has now been scrapped.* **2** [GET RID OF] to get rid of something which you do not now want

scrapbook /ˈskræpbʊk/ *noun* [C] a book with empty pages where you can stick newspaper articles, pictures, etc, that you have collected and want to keep

scrape[1] /skreɪp/ *verb* [T] **1** [DAMAGE] to damage the surface of something by rubbing it against something rough *Jamie fell over and* ***scraped*** *his* ***knee.*** **2** [REMOVE] to remove something from a surface using a sharp edge *The next morning I had to scrape the ice off the car.* **3 scrape a win/draw/pass** *UK* to succeed in a test or competition but with difficulty *France scraped a 3-2 win over Norway.*

scrape by *phrasal verb* to manage to live when you do not have enough money

scrape through (sth) *phrasal verb* to succeed in something but with a lot of difficulty *I scraped through my exams* (= just passed).

scrape sth together *phrasal verb* to manage

with a lot of difficulty to get enough of something, often money *I finally **scraped together** enough **money** for a flight home.*

scrape² /skreɪp/ *noun* [C] **1** [DAMAGE] the slight damage caused when you rub a surface with something rough *He suffered a few cuts and scrapes but nothing serious.* **2** [SITUATION] *informal* a difficult or dangerous situation which you cause yourself *She's always **getting into scrapes**.*

scrappy /ˈskræpi/ *adjective* **1** [UNTIDY] *UK* untidy or organized badly *They won but it was a scrappy match.* **2** [DETERMINED] *US* determined to win or achieve something *a scrappy competitor*

scratch¹ /skrætʃ/ *verb* **1** [RUB SKIN] [I, T] to rub your skin with your nails, often to stop it itching (= feeling unpleasant) *He scratched his head.* **2** [HURT/DAMAGE] [T] to make a slight cut or long, thin mark with a sharp object *The surface was all scratched.* ○ *I scratched myself on the roses.* **3** [RUB SURFACE] [I, T] to rub a hard surface with a sharp object, often making a noise *I could hear the cat scratching at the door.*

scratch² /skrætʃ/ *noun* **1** [HURT/DAMAGE] [C] a slight cut or a long, thin mark made with a sharp object *I've got all these scratches on my arm from the cat.* **2** [RUB SKIN] [no plural] when you rub your skin with your nails, often to stop it itching (= feeling unpleasant) *Could you give my back a scratch?* **3 from scratch** If you do something from scratch, you do it from the beginning. **4 not be/come up to scratch** *informal* to not be good enough *She told me my work wasn't up to scratch.*

scrawl /skrɔːl/ *verb* [T] to write something quickly so that it is untidy *She scrawled a note, but I couldn't read it.* •**scrawl** *noun* [C, U]

scrawny /ˈskrɔːni/ *adjective* too thin *a scrawny neck*

O-- **scream¹** /skriːm/ *verb* [I, T] to make a loud, high noise with your voice, or to shout something in a loud, high voice because you are afraid, hurt, or angry *She screamed for help.* ○ *I could hear a woman screaming, "Get me out of here!"*

WORD PARTNERS FOR ***scream***

let out a scream • a **blood-curdling/piercing/shrill** scream • a scream **of** [horror/pain/shock, etc]

scream² /skriːm/ *noun* **1** [C] when someone screams *We heard screams coming from their apartment.* ○ *We heard a **blood curdling** scream.* **2 be a scream** *informal* to be very funny *You'd love Amanda - she's a scream.*

scree /skriː/ *noun* [U] **GEOGRAPHY** an area on the side of a mountain covered with large loose broken stones

screech /skriːtʃ/ *verb* **1** [I, T] to make an unpleasant, high, loud sound *A car came screeching around the corner.* ○ *She was screeching at him at the top of her voice.* **2 screech to a halt/stop** If a vehicle screeches to a halt, it suddenly stops, making an unpleasant, high sound. •**screech** *noun* [C] *We could hear the **screech of brakes**.*

O-- **screen¹** /skriːn/ *noun* **1 COMPUTING** [C] the part of a television or computer which shows images or writing *I spend most of my day working in front of a **computer screen**.* **2 on screen COMPUTING** using a computer *Do you work on screen?* **3** [FILM SURFACE] [C] a large, flat surface where a film or an image is shown **4** [CINEMA] [U, no plural] cinema films *an actor of **stage and screen*** (= theatre and films) ○ *She first **appeared on screen** in 1965.* **5** [NET] [C] a wire net which covers a window or door and is used to stop insects coming in **6** [SEPARATE] [C] a vertical structure which is used to separate one area from another

screen² /skriːn/ *verb* [T] **1 HEALTH** to find out if people have an illness by doing medical tests on them *Babies are routinely **screened for** the condition.* **2** [GET INFORMATION] to find out information about someone in order to decide if they are suitable for a particular job *Applicants are screened to ensure that none of them is a security risk.* **3** [SHOW] to show something on television or at a cinema [often passive] *The first episode will be screened tonight.*

screen sth off *phrasal verb* to separate one area from another using a vertical structure *Part of the room is screened off and used as an office.*

screenplay /ˈskriːnpleɪ/ *noun* [C] a story that is written for television or for a film

ˈscreen ˌprinting *noun* [U] **DT, ART** a method of printing by forcing ink through a pattern cut into a piece of cloth stretched across a frame

ˈscreen ˌsaver (*also* **screensaver**) *noun* [C] **COMPUTING** a program to protect a computer screen that automatically shows a moving image if the computer is not used for a few minutes

screw¹ /skruː/ *noun* [C] a small, pointed piece of metal that you turn round and round to fix things together, especially pieces of wood

screw² /skruː/ *verb* **1 screw sth down/to/onto, etc** to fasten something with a screw *You need to screw the cabinet to the wall.* **2 screw sth on/down/together, etc** to fasten something by turning it round until it is tight, or to be fastened this way *The lid is **screwed on** so tight I can't get it off.* ➲Opposite **unscrew 3 screw up your eyes/face** to move the muscles of your face so that your eyes become narrow *He screwed up his eyes in the bright sunlight.*

screw (sth) up *phrasal verb informal* to make a mistake, or to spoil something *I screwed up my exams last year.*

screw sth up *phrasal verb* to twist and crush a piece of paper with your hands *She screwed the letter up and threw it in the bin.*

screwdriver /ˈskruːˌdraɪvəʳ/ *noun* [C] a tool for turning screws

screwed-up /ˌskruːdˈʌp/ *adjective informal* If someone is screwed-up, they are unhappy and anxious because they have had a lot of bad experiences.

scribble /ˈskrɪbl/ *verb* [I, T] to write or draw something quickly and carelessly *She **scribbled** some **notes** in her book.* •**scribble** *noun* [C, U] something that has been scribbled

script /skrɪpt/ *noun* **1** [C] the words in a film, play, etc *He wrote a number of **film scripts**.* **2 LANGUAGE** [C, U] a set of letters used for writing a particular language *Arabic/Roman script*

S

scripted /ˈskrɪptɪd/ *adjective* A scripted speech or broadcast has been written before it is read or performed.

scripture /ˈskrɪptʃəʳ/ (*also* **the scriptures**) *noun* [U] **RELIGION** the holy books of a religion

scriptwriter /ˈskrɪptˌraɪtəʳ/ *noun* [C] someone who writes the words for films or radio or television programmes

scroll¹ /skrəʊl/ *noun* [C] a long roll of paper with writing on it, used especially in the past

scroll² /skrəʊl/ *verb* **scroll up/down/through, etc COMPUTING** to move text or an image on a computer screen so that you can look at the part that you want

scrollbar /ˈskrəʊlbɑːʳ/ *noun* [C] **COMPUTING** on a computer screen, a thin rectangle on the side or bottom that you use to move text or an image

scrooge /skruːdʒ/ *noun* [C] *informal* someone who spends very little money

scrotum /ˈskrəʊtəm/ *noun* [C] *plural* **scrotums** or **scrota ANATOMY** in most male mammals, a bag of skin near the penis which contains the testicles

scrounge /skraʊndʒ/ *verb* [I, T] *informal* to get something from someone else instead of paying for it yourself *He's always* ***scrounging*** *money* ***off*** *you.*

scrub¹ /skrʌb/ *verb* [I, T] **scrubbing**, *past* **scrubbed** to clean something by rubbing it hard with a brush *to scrub the floor*

scrub² /skrʌb/ *noun* **1 GEOGRAPHY** [U] bushes and small trees that grow in a dry area **2** [**no plural**] when you clean something by rubbing it with a brush *I* ***gave*** *my hands* ***a scrub.***

scruff /skrʌf/ *noun* **by the scruff of the/your neck** by the back of the neck *She picked the cat up by the scruff of its neck.*

scruffy /ˈskrʌfi/ *adjective* dirty and untidy *scruffy jeans* ○ *I don't like to look scruffy.*

scruple /ˈskruːpl/ *noun* [C] a belief that something is wrong which stops you from doing that thing [**usually plural**] *She* ***has no scruples*** *about accepting bribes.*

S

scrupulous /ˈskruːpjələs/ *adjective* **1** CAREFUL very careful and giving great attention to details *He's very scrupulous about making sure that all the facts are checked.* **2** HONEST always honest and fair ➲Opposite **unscrupulous**

scrutinize (*also UK* **-ise**) /ˈskruːtɪnaɪz/ *verb* [T] to examine something very carefully *The evidence was carefully scrutinized.*

WORD PARTNERS FOR ***scrutiny***

be under/come under scrutiny • **careful/close/rigorous** scrutiny • **public** scrutiny

scrutiny /ˈskruːtɪni/ *noun* [U] when you examine something carefully *Every aspect of her life* ***came under*** *public* ***scrutiny.***

scuba diving /ˈskuːbəˌdaɪvɪŋ/ *noun* [U] **SPORT** a sport in which you swim under water using special equipment for breathing

scuff /skʌf/ *verb* [T] to make a mark on your shoes by rubbing them against something rough

scuffle /ˈskʌfl/ *noun* [C] a short fight in which people push each other *A* ***scuffle broke out*** (= started) *behind the courtroom.*

sculptor /ˈskʌlptəʳ/ *noun* [C] **ART** someone who makes sculpture

sculpture /ˈskʌlptʃəʳ/ *noun* **1 ART** [C, U] a piece of art that is made from stone, wood, clay, etc *a wooden sculpture* ○ *modern sculpture* **2 ART** [U] the art of making objects from stone, wood, clay, etc *She teaches sculpture at an art school.*

scum /skʌm/ *noun* **1** SUBSTANCE [**U, no plural**] an unpleasant, thick substance on the surface of a liquid **2** PERSON [U] *informal* an offensive way of referring to a very bad person

scurry /ˈskʌri/ *verb* **scurry along/around/away, etc** to walk quickly or run because you are in a hurry

scuttle /ˈskʌtl/ *verb* **scuttle across/along/away, etc** to run quickly using short steps *A beetle scuttled across the floor.*

scythe /saɪð/ *noun* [C] **FARMING** a tool with a long handle and a curved blade that is used to cut tall grass and crops

sea /siː/ *noun* **1** [C, U] **GEOGRAPHY** a large area of salt water *I'd like to live by* ***the sea.*** ○ *It was our third day* ***at sea*** (= travelling on the sea). ○ *It's cheaper to send parcels* ***by sea*** (= on a ship). **2 GEOGRAPHY Sea** a particular area of salt water *the North Sea* ○ *the Black Sea* **3 a sea of sth** a large number of something *He looked across the room and saw a sea of faces.*

seabed /ˈsiːbed/ *noun* [**no plural**] **GEOGRAPHY** the floor of the sea

ˈsea deˌfence *noun* [U, C] **ENVIRONMENT** ways of protecting land from being flooded or worn away by the sea

seafood /ˈsiːfuːd/ *noun* [U] **FOOD** animals from the sea that are eaten as food, especially animals that live in shells

seafront /ˈsiːfrʌnt/ *noun* [C] *UK* a part of a town that is next to the sea [**usually singular**] *We walked* ***along*** *the* ***seafront.***

seagull /ˈsiːgʌl/ *noun* [C] a grey and white bird that lives near the sea

seahorse /ˈsiːhɔːs/ *noun* [C] a small fish that has a head and neck the same shape as a horse's

seal¹ /siːl/ *noun* [C] **1** ANIMAL an animal with smooth fur that eats fish and lives near the sea **2** ON A CONTAINER a piece of paper or plastic on a container that you break in order to open it **3** OFFICIAL MARK an official mark made of wax, paper, or metal that is put on important documents **4** STOP LIQUID/AIR an object or substance that stops liquid or air from leaving or entering a container

seal² /siːl/ *verb* [T] **1** CLOSE ENTRANCE (*also* **seal up**) to close an entrance or container so that air or liquid cannot enter or leave it *She quickly sealed up the bottle.* **2** CLOSE LETTER to close a letter or parcel by sticking the edges together *to seal an envelope*

seal sth off *phrasal verb* to prevent people from entering an area or building, often because it is dangerous *Police immediately sealed off the streets.*

ˈsea ˌlevel *noun* [U] **GEOGRAPHY** the level of the sea's surface, used to measure the height of an area of land

ˈsea ˌlion *noun* [C] a large seal (= sea animal)

seam /siːm/ *noun* [C] **1** a line of sewing where two pieces of cloth have been joined together **2 GEOLOGY** a long, thin layer of coal under the ground

seaman /ˈsiːmən/ *noun* [C] *plural* **seamen** a sailor

seance /ˈseɪɒns/ *noun* [C] a meeting at which people try to communicate with spirits of dead people

O‑ **search¹** /sɜːtʃ/ *verb* **1** TRY TO FIND [**I, T**] to try to find someone or something *I've searched my bedroom but I can't find my watch.* ○ *Police are still* ***searching*** *the woods* ***for*** *the missing girl.* **2** POLICE [T] If the police search someone, they look in their clothes and bags to see if they are hiding anything illegal, such as drugs. *They were searched at the airport.* **3** FIND ANSWER [**I**] to try to find an answer to a problem *Doctors are still* ***searching for*** *a cure.*

COMMON LEARNER ERROR

search or **search for?**

If you **search** a place or person, you are looking for something in that place or on that person.

The police searched the man (= looked in his clothes) *for drugs.*

I searched the kitchen (= looked in the kitchen) *for my watch.*

If you **search for** something or someone, you are looking for that thing or that person.

I searched for my watch.

~~*I searched my watch.*~~

WORD PARTNERS FOR ***search*** (noun)

carry out/conduct/make/mount a search • a **frantic/painstaking/thorough** search • a search **for** sb/sth • **in search of** sb/sth

O‑ **search²** /sɜːtʃ/ *noun* **1** TRY TO FIND [C] when you try to find someone or something [**usually singular**] *Police are continuing their* ***search for*** *the missing girl.* ○ *They went off* ***in search of*** (= to find) *a bar.* **2** FIND ANSWER [**no plural**] when you try to find an answer to a problem *the search for happiness*

ˈsearch ˌengine *noun* [C] **INTERNET** a computer program which finds information on the Internet by looking for words which you have typed in ⊃See Extra help page **The Web and the Internet** on page Centre 36.

searching /ˈsɜːtʃɪŋ/ *adjective* A searching question or look is intended to discover the truth about something.

ˈsearch ˌparty *noun* [C] a group of people who look for someone who is lost

ˈsearch ˌwarrant *noun* [C] **LAW** an official document that allows the police to search a building

searing /ˈsɪərɪŋ/ *adjective* [**always before noun**] extreme and unpleasant ***searing pain/heat***

ˈsea ˌshell *noun* [C] the empty shell of some types of sea animals

the seashore /ˈsiːʃɔːʳ/ *noun* **GEOGRAPHY** the area of land along the edge of the sea

seasick /ˈsiːsɪk/ *adjective* **HEALTH** feeling ill because of the way a boat is moving

the seaside /ˈsiːsaɪd/ *noun* an area or town next to the sea *We had a picnic* ***at the seaside.*** ○ *a seaside resort/community*

O‑ **season¹** /ˈsiːzᵊn/ *noun* [C] **1 GEOGRAPHY** one of the four periods of the year; winter, spring, summer, or autumn **2** SPECIAL TIME a period of the year when a particular thing happens [**usually singular**] *the holiday season* ○ *the rainy/dry season* ○ *the football season* **3 in season a FOOD** If vegetables or fruit are in season, they are available and ready to eat. **b BIOLOGY** If a female animal is in season, she is ready to mate. **4 out of season a** FRUIT/VEGETABLES If vegetables or fruit are out of season, they are not usually available at that time. **b** FEW PEOPLE If you go somewhere out of season, you go during a period of the year when few people are there.

season² /ˈsiːzᵊn/ *verb* [T] **FOOD** to add salt or spices to food that you are cooking

seasonal /ˈsiːzᵊnᵊl/ *adjective* happening or existing only at a particular time of the year *a seasonal worker* ○ *the seasonal migration of birds*

seasoned /ˈsiːzᵊnd/ *adjective* [**always before noun**] having a lot of experience of doing something *a* ***seasoned traveller***

seasoning /ˈsiːzᵊnɪŋ/ *noun* [C, U] **FOOD** salt or spices that you add to food

ˈseason ˌticket *UK* (*US* **ˌseason ˈticket**) *noun* [C] a ticket that you can use many times without having to pay each time

WORD PARTNERS FOR ***seat***

have/take a seat • **in/on** a seat • the **back/driver's/front/passenger** seat

seat¹ /siːt/ *noun* [C] **1** SIT something that you sit on *Please,* ***have/take a seat*** (= sit down). ○ *I've booked three seats for the cinema tonight.* ○ *the* ***back/front seat*** *of a car* **2** PART the flat part of a chair, bicycle, etc that you sit on **3 POLITICS** a position in a parliament or other group that makes official decisions *a seat in parliament* ○ *a congressional seat*

seat² /siːt/ *verb* **1 seat yourself in/on/next to, etc** to sit somewhere *I seated myself next to the fire.* **2 be seated a** to be sitting down *The director was seated on his right.* **b** used to politely ask a group of people to sit down *Would the people at the back please be seated.* **3 seat 4/12/200, etc** If a building, room, or vehicle seats a particular number of people, that many people can sit in it.

ˈseat ˌbelt *noun* [C] a strap that you fasten across your body when travelling in a vehicle *to fasten your seat belt* ⊃See colour picture **Car** on page Centre 7

seating /ˈsiːtɪŋ/ *noun* [U] the seats in a public place, or the way that they are arranged

ˌsea ˈwall *noun* [C] **ENVIRONMENT** a wall that protects land from being covered or damaged by the sea

S

seaweed /'siːwiːd/ *noun* [U] a plant that you find on the beach and that grows in the sea

sebaceous gland /sɪ'beɪʃəs,glænd/ *noun* [C] **ANATOMY, BIOLOGY** one of the many small glands (= parts of the body that produce chemical substances) that produce an oily substance on the hair and skin

sebum /'siːbəm/ *noun* [U] **BIOLOGY** an oily substance that makes hair shiny and prevents skin from becoming dry

sec /sek/ *noun* [C] *informal* a very short time *Just a sec - I'm nearly ready.*

secluded /sɪ'kluːdɪd/ *adjective* If a place is secluded, it is quiet and not near people. *a secluded beach/garden*

seclusion /sɪ'kluːʒən/ *noun* [U] when someone lives alone, away from other people *He lived **in seclusion** for the rest of his life.*

O‑**second**[1] /'sekənd/ *adjective, pronoun* **1** AFTER FIRST referring to the person, thing, or event that comes immediately after the first *You're second on the list.* ○ *This is my second piece of chocolate cake.* ○ *She didn't win but she did **come second*** (= was the one after the winner) *in one race.* **2** NUMBER 2nd written as a word ➲See also: **second best, second-hand, second language, second nature, the second person, second-rate, second thought, second wind**

O‑**second**[2] /'sekənd/ *noun* [C] **1 MEASURES** one of the 60 parts a minute is divided into **2** SHORT TIME *informal* a very short period of time *I'll be back in just a second.* **3** PRODUCT something that is sold cheaply because it is damaged or not in perfect condition [**usually plural**] *Some of those towels are seconds.*

second[3] /'sekənd/ *verb* [T] to formally support an idea at a meeting [**often passive**] *The chairperson's proposal was seconded by Ms Jones.*

second[4] /sɪ'kɒnd/ *verb* [T] *UK* to send someone to another job for a fixed period of time [**often passive**] *He was seconded from the police to the Department of Transport.*

secondary /'sekəndəri/ *adjective* **1 EDUCATION** relating to the education of students aged between 11 and 18 *secondary education* **2** less important than something else *What matters is the size of the office. The location is of secondary importance.*

,secondary con'sumer *noun* [C] **BIOLOGY** an animal that eats other animals

'secondary ,school *noun* [C] *mainly UK* **EDUCATION** a school for students aged between 11 and 18

the 'secondary ,sector *noun* **ECONOMICS** industry where finished items are made ➲Compare **the primary sector**

,second 'best *adjective* not the best but the next best *the second best candidate* •**second best** *noun* [U]

second-class /,sekənd'klɑːs/ *adjective* **1** TRAVEL relating to the less expensive way of travelling in a train, aircraft, etc, that most people use *a second-class carriage/ticket* **2** NOT IMPORTANT less important than other people *Women are still treated as **second-class citizens**.* **3 EDUCATION** A second-class university degree is a good degree but not the best possible. •**second class** *adverb We always travel second class.*

second-guess /,sekənd'ges/ *verb* [T] to guess what someone will do in the future

second-hand /,sekənd'hænd/ *adjective, adverb* If something is second-hand, someone else owned or used it before you. ***second-hand books/clothes*** ○ *She buys a lot of clothes second-hand.*

,second 'language *noun* [C] **LANGUAGE** a language that you speak that is not the first language you learned as a child

secondly /'sekəndli/ *adverb* used for introducing the second reason, idea, etc *I want two things: firstly, more money, and secondly, better working hours.*

,second 'nature *noun* [U] something that you can do easily because you have done it many times before *After a few years, teaching became second nature to me.*

the ,second 'person *noun* **LANGUAGE** the form of a verb or pronoun that is used when referring to the person being spoken or written to. For example 'you' is a second person pronoun

second-rate /,sekənd'reɪt/ *adjective* of bad quality *a second-rate writer*

,second 'thought *noun* **1 on second thoughts** *UK* used when you want to change a decision you have made *I'll have tea, please - on second thoughts, make that coffee.* **2 without a second thought** If you do something without a second thought, you do it without first considering if you should do it or not. *She'll spend a hundred pounds on a dress without a second thought.* **3 have second thoughts** to change your opinion about something or start to doubt it [**+ about + doing sth**] I've been having second thoughts about doing the course.

,second 'wind *noun* [**no plural**] a return of energy that makes it possible to continue an activity *I was feeling tired, but **I got my second wind** after lunch.*

WORD PARTNERS FOR ***secrecy***

be **shrouded in** secrecy • do sth **in** secrecy • **absolute/strict** secrecy • the secrecy **of/surrounding** sth

secrecy /'siːkrəsi/ *noun* [U] when something is kept secret *Politicians criticized **the secrecy surrounding** the air attack.*

O‑**secret**[1] /'siːkrət/ *adjective* **1** If something is secret, other people are not allowed to know about it. *a secret affair/meeting* ○ *I'll tell you but you must **keep it secret**.* **2 secret admirer/drinker, etc** someone who does something or feels something without telling other people about it •**secretly** *adverb He secretly taped their conversation.* ➲See also: **top-secret**

WORD PARTNERS FOR ***secret***

keep a secret • **let sb in on/reveal/tell sb** a secret • a **big/closely-guarded/well-kept** secret

O‑**secret**[2] /'siːkrət/ *noun* [C] **1** something that you tell no one about or only a few people *I'm having a party for him but it's a secret.* ○ *Can you* *keep a secret?* **2 the secret** the best way of achieving something *So what's the secret of your success?* **3 in secret** without telling other people *For years they met in secret.*

ˌsecret ˈagent *noun* [C] someone who tries to find out secret information, especially about another country

secretarial /ˌsekrəˈteəriəl/ *adjective* relating to the work of a secretary (= office worker who types letters, etc) ***secretarial skills***

O-- **secretary** /ˈsekrətəri/ *noun* [C] **1** someone who works in an office, typing letters, answering the telephone, and arranging meetings, etc **2** **POLITICS** (*also* **Secretary**) an official who is in charge of a large department of the government *the Secretary of State*

secrete /sɪˈkriːt/ *verb* [T] **BIOLOGY** to produce a substance *A mixture of substances are secreted by cells within the stomach.* •**secretion** /sɪˈkriːʃən/ *noun* [C, U]

secretive /ˈsiːkrətɪv/ *adjective* not willing to tell people what you know or what you are doing *He's very **secretive about** his relationships.* •**secretively** *adverb*

ˌSecret ˈService *noun* [no plural] **1 POLITICS** in the UK, a department of the government that tries to find out secret information about foreign countries **2 POLITICS** in the US, a government organization that protects the president

sect /sekt/ *noun* [C] **RELIGION, POLITICS** a group of people with a set of religious or political beliefs, often extreme beliefs

sectarian /sekˈteəriən/ *adjective* **RELIGION** relating to the differences between religious groups ***sectarian violence***

O-- **section** /ˈsekʃən/ *noun* [C] **1** PART one of the parts that something is divided into *a non-smoking section in a restaurant* ○ *the business section of a newspaper* ○ *the tail section of an aircraft* **2 DT** a model or drawing of something that shows how it would look if it were cut from top to bottom and seen from the side ➲See also: **cross-section**

sector /ˈsektər/ *noun* [C] **1 ECONOMICS** one part of a country's economy *the **private/public sector*** ○ *the financial/manufacturing sector* **2 GEOGRAPHY** one of the parts that an area is divided into *the British sector of the North Sea*

secular /ˈsekjələr/ *adjective* **RELIGION** not religious or not controlled by a religious group *secular education* ○ *a **secular state***

secure¹ /sɪˈkjʊər/ *adjective* **1** NOT FAIL not likely to fail or be lost *a secure investment/job* **2** SAFE safe from danger *I don't feel that the house is secure.* **3** CONFIDENT confident about yourself and the situation that you are in *I need to feel secure in a relationship.* **4** FIXED firmly fastened and not likely to fall or break *Check that all windows and doors are secure.* ➲Opposite **insecure**

secure² /sɪˈkjʊər/ *verb* [T] **1** ACHIEVE to achieve something, after a lot of effort *to secure the release of hostages* **2** FASTEN to fasten something firmly *He **secured** the bike **to** the gate.* **3** MAKE SAFE to make something safe

securely /sɪˈkjʊəli/ *adverb* If something is securely fastened, it will not fall or become loose.

WORD PARTNERS FOR ***security***

lax/tight security • security **arrangements/checks** • a security **breach/guard/lapse/operation/risk** • **national** security

security /sɪˈkjʊərəti/ *noun* [U] **1** BEING SAFE the things that are done to keep someone or something safe *airport/**national security*** ○ *a security alarm* **2** SAFE SITUATION when something is not likely to fail or be lost ***financial security*** ○ ***job security*** **3** CONFIDENCE confidence about yourself and the situation that you are in *the security of a long-term relationship* ➲Opposite **insecurity** **4 FINANCE** something valuable that you offer to give someone when you borrow money if you cannot pay the money back ➲See also: **social security**

COMMON LEARNER ERROR

security or **safety?**

Security means activities or people that protect you from harm, or that try to stop crime.

He works as a security guard.

airport security

Safety is when you are safe or how safe something is.

Remember to wear your safety belt in the car.

Children should have lessons in road safety.

sedan /sɪˈdæn/ *US* (*UK* **saloon**) *noun* [C] a large car with a separate, closed area for bags

sedate¹ /sɪˈdeɪt/ *adjective* calm and slow *walking at a **sedate pace***

sedate² /sɪˈdeɪt/ *verb* [T] **HEALTH** to give a person or animal a drug to make them feel calm •**sedation** /sɪˈdeɪʃən/ *noun* [U] *She had to be put **under sedation**.*

sedative /ˈsedətɪv/ *noun* [C] **HEALTH** a drug used to sedate a person or an animal

sedentary /ˈsedəntəri/ *adjective* spending a lot of time sitting down or not being active *a **sedentary job/lifestyle***

sediment /ˈsedɪmənt/ *noun* [C, U] a solid substance that forms a layer at the bottom of a liquid

sedimentary /ˌsedɪˈmentəri/ *adjective* **GEOLOGY** (of rock) made from sediment left by the action of water, ice or wind ➲Compare **igneous, metamorphic**

sedimentation tank /ˌsedɪmenˈteɪʃənˌtæŋk/ *noun* [C] a large container in which dirty or waste water is stored until all the solid material in it is lying on the bottom

seduce /sɪˈdjuːs/ *verb* [T] **1** SEX to persuade someone to have sex with you, especially someone young **2** PERSUADE to persuade someone to do something they would not normally do *I wouldn't have bought it but I was seduced by the low prices.*

seductive /sɪˈdʌktɪv/ *adjective* **1** SEX sexually attractive *a seductive smile/voice* **2** WANT making you want to have or do something *the seductive power of money*

S

O‑ **see** /siː/ *verb* **seeing**, *past tense* **saw**, *past participle* **seen** **1** EYES [I, T] to notice people and things with your eyes *Have you seen Jo?* ○ *Turn the light on so I can see.* ⊃See Common Learner Error at **look** **2** UNDERSTAND [I, T] to understand something *I see what you mean.* ○ *I don't see why I should go.* **3** MEET [T] to meet or visit someone *I'm seeing Peter tonight.* ○ *You should see a doctor.* **4** WATCH [T] to watch a film, television programme, etc *Did you see that film last night?* **5** INFORMATION [T] to find out information [+ **question word**] *I'll just see what time the train gets in.* **6** IMAGINE [T] to imagine or think about something or someone in a particular way *I just can't* ***see*** *him* ***as*** *a father.* **7** BELIEVE [T] to believe that something will happen *I can't see us finishing on time.* **8** HAPPEN [T] to be the time or place where something happens *This decade has seen huge technological advances.* **9 see that** If you ask someone to see that something happens, you want them to make sure it happens. *Could you see that everyone gets a copy of this letter?* **10 see sb home/to the station, etc** to go somewhere with someone, especially to make sure they are safe *Let me see you home.* **11 I'll/we'll see** used to say that you will make a decision about something later *"Dad, can I have a guitar?" "We'll see."* **12 see you** *informal* used for saying goodbye ⊃See also: be glad/happy, etc to see the **back**[2] of sb/sth, see **eye**[1] to eye (with sb), see **red**[2]

see about sth/doing sth *phrasal verb* to deal with something, or arrange for something to be done

see sth in sb/sth *phrasal verb* to believe that someone or something has a particular quality *I can't understand what you see in her* (= why you like her).

see sb off *phrasal verb* to go to the place that someone is leaving from in order to say goodbye to them *My parents came to the airport to see me off.*

see sb out *phrasal verb* to take someone to the door of a room or building when they are leaving *Don't worry, I'll see myself out* (= leave the room/building by myself).

see through sb/sth *phrasal verb* to understand that someone is trying to deceive you *I saw through him at once.*

see to sth *phrasal verb* to deal with something *Don't worry, I'll see to everything while you're away.*

seed[1] /siːd/ *noun* **1** BIOLOGY [C, U] a small round or oval object produced by a plant that a new plant can grow from ***Sow the seeds*** (= plant them) *near the surface.* **2 (the) seeds of sth** the beginning of something *the seeds of hope/change* ⊃See also: **sesame seed**

seed[2] /siːd/ *verb* **1** FARMING [T] to plant seeds in the ground **2 be seeded first/second, etc** SPORT in tennis, to be the first/second, etc on a list of players expected to succeed in a competition

seedless /ˈsiːdləs/ *adjective* FOOD without seeds *seedless grapes*

seedling /ˈsiːdlɪŋ/ *noun* [C] BIOLOGY a young plant that has been grown from a seed

seedy /ˈsiːdi/ *adjective informal* looking dirty or in bad condition and likely to be involved in immoral activities *a seedy bar/hotel*

ˌseeing ˈeye dog *US* (*UK/US* **guide dog**) *noun* [C] a dog that is trained to help blind people

seek /siːk/ *verb* [T] *past* **sought** **1** TO FIND/GET to try to find or get something *to* ***seek advice****/a solution* **2** TO DO to try to do something [+ **to do sth**] *They are seeking to change the rules.* ○ *to seek re-election* ⊃See also: **hide-and-seek**

O‑ **seem** /siːm/ *verb* **seem happy/a nice person, etc; seem like/as if, etc** to appear to be a particular thing or to have a particular quality *She seemed happy enough.* ○ *It seemed like a good idea at the time.* ○ *There doesn't* ***seem to be*** *any real solution.* [+ **(that)**] *It seems that the bars close early here.* ○ ***It seems to me*** (= I think) *that she's in the wrong job.*

seemingly /ˈsiːmɪŋli/ *adverb* appearing to be something without really being that thing *a seemingly harmless comment*

seen /siːn/ *past participle of* see

seep /siːp/ *verb* **seep from/into/through, etc** to flow very slowly through something *Water was seeping through the walls.*

seesaw /ˈsiːsɔː/ (*also US* **teeter-totter**) *noun* [C] a long board that children play on by sitting at each end and using their feet on the ground to push the board up and down

seethe /siːð/ *verb* [I] to be very angry, often without showing it *I left him* ***seething with*** *anger.*

segment /ˈsegmənt/ *noun* [C] one of the parts that something can be divided into *a segment of the population/market* ○ *an orange segment*

segregate /ˈsegrɪgeɪt/ *verb* [T] SOCIETY to separate one group of people from another, especially one sex or race from another *At school the girls were* ***segregated from*** *the boys.* •**segregation** /ˌsegrɪˈgeɪʃən/ *noun* [U] *racial segregation*

seismic /ˈsaɪzmɪk/ *adjective* GEOLOGY relating to or caused by an earthquake (= when the earth shakes) ***seismic activity***

seismograph /ˈsaɪzməgrɑːf/ *noun* [C] GEOLOGY a piece of equipment which measures and records the strength of an earthquake (= sudden movement of the Earth's surface)

seize /siːz/ *verb* [T] **1** HOLD to take hold of something quickly and firmly *She seized my arm and pulled me towards her.* **2** OPPORTUNITY to do something quickly when you have the opportunity *You need to* ***seize*** *every* ***opportunity****.* **3** PLACE to take control of a place suddenly by using military force *Troops* ***seized control*** *in the early hours of the morning.* **4** DRUGS ETC to take away something that is illegal, for example drugs *Officials seized 2.7 tons of cocaine from the ship.*

seize on/upon sth *phrasal verb* to quickly use something that will give you an advantage *Her story was seized upon by the press.*

seize up *phrasal verb* If part of your body or a machine seizes up, it stops moving or working in the normal way. *His right leg suddenly seized up during the race.*

seizure /ˈsiːʒəʳ/ *noun* **1** CONTROL [U] when someone takes control of a country, government,

S

etc *a seizure of power* **2 LAW** [C] when someone in authority takes away something that is illegal, for example drugs *a seizure of heroin* **3 HEALTH** [C] a sudden attack of an illness *an epileptic seizure*

seldom /ˈseldəm/ *adverb* not often *We seldom go out in the evenings.*

select[1] /sɪˈlekt/ *verb* [T] to choose someone or something *We've selected three candidates.*

select[2] /sɪˈlekt/ *adjective* consisting of only a small group of people who have been specially chosen *a **select group***

WORD PARTNERS FOR ***selection***

a **good/wide** selection • a selection **of** sth

selection /sɪˈlekʃᵊn/ *noun* **1** CHOOSING [U] when someone or something is chosen *the **selection process*** **2** PEOPLE/THINGS [C] a group of people or things that has been chosen *We have a **wide selection of** imported furniture.* ⊃See also: **natural selection**

selective /sɪˈlektɪv/ *adjective* **1** CAREFUL careful about what you choose *He's very selective about the people he spends time with.* **2** CHOSEN involving only people or things that have been specially chosen *selective breeding*

selenium /səˈliːniəm/ *noun* [U] **CHEMISTRY** a chemical element used in photography and also necessary in small amounts in the body (symbol **Se**)

self /self/ *noun* [C, U] *plural* **selves** /selvz/ your characteristics, including your personality, your abilities, etc *his true self*

self-assured /ˌselfəˈʃʊəd/ *adjective* confident about yourself

self-catering /ˌselfˈkeɪtᵊrɪŋ/ *adjective UK* describes a holiday in which you have a kitchen so that you can cook meals for yourself *We decided to stay in self-catering accommodation rather than in a hotel.*

self-centred *UK* (*US* **self-centered**) /ˌselfˈsentəd/ *adjective* interested only in yourself

self-confident /ˌselfˈkɒnfɪdᵊnt/ *adjective* feeling sure about yourself and your abilities •**self-confidence** *noun* [U] being self-confident

self-conscious /ˌselfˈkɒnʃəs/ *adjective* too aware of what other people are thinking about you and your appearance •**self-consciously** *adverb* •**self-consciousness** *noun* [U]

self-contained /ˌselfkənˈteɪnd/ *adjective UK* If a flat is self-contained, it has its own kitchen, bathroom, and entrance.

self-control /ˌselfkənˈtrəʊl/ *noun* [U] the ability to control your emotions and actions although you are very angry, upset, etc

self-defence *UK* (*US* **self-defense**) /ˌselfdɪˈfens/ *noun* [U] when you protect yourself from someone who is attacking you by fighting *He claimed he had acted **in self-defence**.*

self-destructive /ˌselfdɪˈstrʌktɪv/ *adjective* A self-destructive action harms the person who is doing it.

self-discipline /ˌselfˈdɪsɪplɪn/ *noun* [U] the ability to make yourself do things that you do not want to do

self-employed /ˌselfɪmˈplɔɪd/ *adjective* working for yourself and not for a company or other organization •**self-employment** /ˌselfɪmˈplɔɪmənt/ *noun* [U]

WORD PARTNERS FOR ***self-esteem***

boost/build/damage/raise self-esteem • **high/low** self-esteem

self-esteem /ˌselfɪˈstiːm/ *noun* [U] confidence in yourself and a belief in your qualities and abilities *She suffers from **low self-esteem**.*

self-evident /ˌselfˈevɪdᵊnt/ *adjective* obviously true and not needing to be explained

self-explanatory /ˌselfɪkˈsplænətᵊri/ *adjective* easy to understand and not needing to be explained

self-help /ˌselfˈhelp/ *adjective* A self-help book, activity, organization, etc is designed to help you deal with your problems on your own. *a self-help group for alcoholics*

self-indulgent /ˌselfɪnˈdʌldʒᵊnt/ *adjective* doing or having things that you like although they are not necessary or are bad for you •**self-indulgence** /ˌselfɪnˈdʌldʒᵊns/ *noun* [C, U]

self-inflicted /ˌselfɪnˈflɪktɪd/ *adjective* If an injury or a problem is self-inflicted, you have caused it yourself.

self-interest /ˌselfˈɪntrəst/ *noun* [U] interest in what will help you and not what will help other people

selfish /ˈselfɪʃ/ *adjective* caring only about yourself and not other people *It's very selfish of him.* •**selfishly** *adverb* •**selfishness** *noun* [U]

selfless /ˈselfləs/ *adjective* caring about other people and not about yourself

self-made /ˌselfˈmeɪd/ *adjective* rich because you have earned a lot of money yourself *a self-made millionaire*

self-pity /ˌselfˈpɪti/ *noun* [U] sadness for yourself because you think you have suffered so much, especially when this is not true

self-portrait /ˌselfˈpɔːtreɪt/ *noun* [C] **ART** a picture that you draw or paint of yourself

self-reliant /ˌselfrɪˈlaɪənt/ *adjective* able to do things yourself without depending on other people

self-respect /ˌselfrɪˈspekt/ *noun* [U] the feeling of pride in yourself and your character •**self-respecting** *adjective*

self-righteous /ˌselfˈraɪtʃəs/ *adjective* believing that you are morally better than other people

self-sacrifice /ˌselfˈsækrɪfaɪs/ *noun* [U] when you do not have or do something so that you can help other people

self-satisfied /ˌselfˈsætɪsfaɪd/ *adjective* too pleased with yourself and what you have achieved

self-service /ˌselfˈsɜːvɪs/ *adjective* A self-service restaurant or shop is one in which you serve yourself and are not served by the people who work there.

self-sufficient /ˌselfsəˈfɪʃᵊnt/ *adjective* having everything that you need yourself and not needing help from others

S

O⊸**sell** /sel/ *verb past* **sold 1 FINANCE** [I, T] to give something to someone who gives you money for it *He* ***sold*** *his guitar* ***for*** *£50.* ○ *I* ***sold*** *my bike* ***to*** *Claire.* [+ **two objects**] *I'm hoping she'll sell me her car.* **2 FINANCE** [T] to offer something for people to buy *Excuse me, do you sell newspapers?* **3 FINANCE sell for/at sth** to be available for sale at a particular price *The shirts are selling for £30 each.* **4 FINANCE** [I, T] to be bought in large numbers *His last book sold eight million copies.* **5** MAKE YOU WANT [T] to make someone want to buy something *Scandal sells newspapers.* **6** IDEA/PLAN [T] to persuade someone that an idea or plan is good *I'm currently trying to sell the idea to my boss.*

sell sth off *phrasal verb* to sell all or part of a business

sell out *phrasal verb* If a shop sells out of something, it sells all of that thing. *They'd* ***sold out of*** *bread by the time I got there.*

sell up *phrasal verb UK* to sell your house or company in order to go somewhere else or do something else

ˈ**sell-by** ˌ**date** *noun* [C] *UK* the date printed on a food or drink container after which it should not be sold

seller /ˈseləʳ/ *noun* [C] **FINANCE 1** someone who sells something *a flower seller* **2** a product that a company sells

Sellotape® /ˈseləʊteɪp/ *UK* (*US* **Scotch® tape**) *noun* [U] clear, thin material with glue on it, used to stick things together, especially paper ➲See colour picture **The Classroom** on page Centre 6

sellout /ˈselaʊt/ *noun* [**no plural**] **1** EVENT a performance or event where all of the tickets have been sold **2** FOR MONEY/POWER *informal* when someone does something that is against their beliefs in order to get money or power

selves /selvz/ *plural of* self

semantic /sɪˈmæntɪk/ *adjective* **LANGUAGE** connected with the meaning of language

semblance /ˈsembləns/ *noun* **semblance of normality/order, etc** a small amount of a quality, but not as much as you would like *Our lives have now returned to some semblance of normality.*

semen /ˈsiːmən/ *noun* [U] **BIOLOGY** the liquid that is produced by the male sex organs, that contains sperm (= cells that join with female eggs to make new life)

semester /sɪˈmestəʳ/ *noun* [C] *mainly US* **EDUCATION** one of the two time periods that a school or college year is divided into

semi- /semi-/ *prefix* half or partly *a semicircle* ○ *semifrozen*

semi-arid /ˌsemiˈærɪd/ *adjective* **GEOGRAPHY, ENVIRONMENT** describes an area or climate with little rain but not completely dry

semicircle /ˈsemɪˌsɜːkl/ *noun* [C] half a circle

semicolon /ˌsemɪˈkəʊlən/ (US) /ˈsemɪˌkəʊlən/ *noun* [C] **LANGUAGE** a mark (;) used to separate parts of a sentence, or items in a list which already has commas ➲See Extra help page **Punctuation** on page Centre 19.

semiconductor /ˌsemikənˈdʌktəʳ/ *noun* [C] **PHYSICS** a material, such as silicon, which allows electricity to move through it more easily when its temperature increases, or an electronic device made from this material

semi-detached /ˌsemɪdɪˈtætʃt/ *adjective UK* A semi-detached house has one wall that is joined to another house.

semifinal /ˌsemɪˈfaɪnəl/ *noun* [C] **SPORT** one of the two games in a sports competition that are played to decide who will play in the final game

semilunar valve /ˌsemiluːnəˈvælv/ *noun* [C] **ANATOMY** one of the valves (= structures that open and close) which stop blood from returning into the ventricles (= lower spaces) of the heart from the aorta or the pulmonary artery ➲See picture at **heart**

semi-metal /ˈsemiːˌmetəl/ (*also* **metalloid**) *noun* [C] **CHEMISTRY** a chemical element with some of the properties of a metal and some of a non-metal, for example silicon and arsenic

seminar /ˈsemɪnɑːʳ/ *noun* [C] **EDUCATION** a meeting of a group of people with a teacher or expert for training, discussion, or study of a subject

semipermeable /ˌsemiˈpɜːmiəbl/ *adjective* **PHYSICS,BIOLOGY,GEOLOGY** describes something that allows some liquids and gases to pass through it, but not others

Semitic /sɪˈmɪtɪk/ *adjective* **LANGUAGE, SOCIETY** relating to the Jewish or Arab races, or their languages

the Senate /ˈsenɪt/ *noun* [**group**] **POLITICS** a part of a government in some countries

senator /ˈsenətəʳ/ *noun* [C] **POLITICS** someone who has been elected to the Senate *Senator Moynihan*

O⊸**send** /send/ *verb* [T] *past* **sent 1** SOMETHING to arrange for something to go or be taken somewhere, especially by post [+ **two objects**] *I sent him a letter last week.* ○ *Do you think we should send flowers?* **2** SOMEONE to make someone go somewhere *I sent him into the house to fetch some glasses.* **3 send sb to sleep** to cause someone to start sleeping ➲See also: drive/send sb round the **bend**[2]

send sth back *phrasal verb* to return something to the person who sent it to you, especially because it is damaged or not suitable *I had to send the shirt back because it didn't fit me.*

send for sb *phrasal verb* to send someone a message asking them to come to see you *Do you think we should send for a doctor?*

send (off/away) for sth *phrasal verb* to write to an organization to ask them to send you something *I've sent off for a catalogue.*

send sth in *phrasal verb* to send something to an organization *Viewers were asked to send in photographs of their pets.*

send sb in *phrasal verb* to send soldiers, police, etc to a place in order to deal with a dangerous situation

send sth off *phrasal verb* to send a letter, document, or parcel by post

send sb off *phrasal verb UK* **SPORT** to order a sports player to leave the playing area because they have done something wrong

send sth out *phrasal verb* **1** SEND to send something to a lot of different people *to send out*

invitations **2** [LIGHT/SOUND] to produce light, sound, etc
send sb/sth up *phrasal verb UK* to make someone or something seem stupid by copying them in a funny way

send-off /'sendɒf/ *noun* [C] when a group of people say goodbye to someone at the same time *I got a good* ***send-off*** *at the station.*

senile /'siːnaɪl/ *adjective* **HEALTH** confused and unable to remember things because of old age •**senility** /sɪ'nɪləti/ *noun* [U] the state of being senile

senior¹ /'siːniəʳ/ *adjective* **1** [MORE IMPORTANT] having a more important job or position than someone else *a* ***senior executive*** ○ *We work in the same team but she's* ***senior to*** *me.* **2** [OLDER] older *senior students* **3** [NAME] *mainly US (written abbreviation* **Sr***)* used at the end of a man's name to show that he is the older of two men in the same family who have the same name *Hello, may I speak to Ken Griffey Senior, please?*

senior² /'siːniəʳ/ *noun* **1 be 20/30, etc years sb's senior** to be 20/30, etc years older than someone *She married a man 20 years her senior.* **2 EDUCATION** [C] *US* a student who is in the last year of high school or college

ˌsenior ˈcitizen *noun* [C] **SOCIETY** an old person

seniority /ˌsiːni'ɒrəti/ *noun* [U] **SOCIETY** the state of being older or of having a more important position in an organization

sensation /sen'seɪʃən/ *noun* **1 BIOLOGY** [C, U] a physical feeling, or the ability to physically feel things *a burning sensation* ○ *Three months after the accident she still has no sensation in her right foot.* **2** [FEELING] [C] a strange feeling or idea that you can not explain *I had the strangest sensation that I had met him before.* **3** [EXCITEMENT] [**no plural**] a lot of excitement, surprise, or interest, or the person or event that causes these feelings *Their affair* ***caused a sensation.***

sensational /sen'seɪʃənəl/ *adjective* **1** [SHOCKING] done in a way that is intended to shock people *sensational journalism* **2** [EXCITING] very exciting or extremely good *a sensational performance*

sensationalism /sen'seɪʃənəlɪzəm/ *noun* [U] when a story is told in a way that is intended to shock people

WORD PARTNERS FOR ***sense***

have the sense to do sth • **good** sense

⊸**sense¹** /sens/ *noun* **1** [GOOD JUDGMENT] [U] good judgment, especially about practical things *He had the* ***good sense*** *to book a seat in advance.* **2** [ABILITY] [**no plural**] the ability to do something *a* ***sense of*** *direction* ○ *good* ***business sense*** **3 BIOLOGY** [C] one of the five natural abilities of sight, hearing, touch, smell, and taste *I have a very poor sense of smell.* **4 a sense of humour** *UK (US* **sense of humor***)* the ability to understand funny things and to be funny yourself **5 a sense of loyalty/responsibility/security, etc** the quality or feeling of being loyal, responsible, safe, etc *He has absolutely no sense of loyalty.* **6 LANGUAGE** [C] the meaning of a word, phrase, or sentence **7 in a sense/in some senses** thinking about something in a particular way *In a sense, he's right.* **8 make sense a** [CLEAR MEANING] to have a meaning or reason that you can understand *He's written me this note but it doesn't make any sense.* **b** [SHOULD DO] to be a good thing to do [**+ to do sth**] It makes sense to buy now while prices are low. **9 make sense of sth** to understand something that is difficult to understand *I'm trying to make sense of this document.* **10 come to your senses** to start to understand that you have been behaving stupidly ➲See also: **common sense**

sense² /sens/ *verb* [T] to understand what someone is thinking or feeling without being told about it [**+ (that)**] *I sensed that you weren't happy about this.*

senseless /'sensləs/ *adjective* **1** [NO REASON] happening or done without a good reason ***senseless violence*** **2** [NOT CONSCIOUS] not conscious *He was beaten senseless.*

sensibility /ˌsensɪ'bɪləti/ *noun* [C, U] *formal* someone's feelings, or the ability to understand what other people feel

sensible /'sensɪbl/ *adjective* **1** [JUDGMENT] showing good judgment *a sensible decision* [**+ to do sth**] *Wouldn't it be more sensible to leave before the traffic gets bad?* **2** [PRACTICAL] having a practical purpose *sensible shoes/clothes* •**sensibly** *adverb to eat/behave sensibly*

sensitive /'sensɪtɪv/ *adjective* **1** [KIND] able to understand what people are feeling and deal with them in a way that does not upset them *I want a man who's kind and sensitive.* **2** [EASILY UPSET] easily upset by the things people say or do *He was always* ***sensitive to*** *criticism.* ○ *She's very* ***sensitive about*** *her weight.* **3** [SUBJECT] A sensitive subject or situation needs to be dealt with carefully in order to avoid upsetting people. *Gender is a very sensitive subject.* **4** [EASILY DAMAGED] easily damaged or hurt *sensitive eyes/skin* **5** [EQUIPMENT] Sensitive equipment is able to measure very small changes. ➲Opposite **insensitive** •**sensitively** *adverb I think she dealt with the problem very sensitively.* •**sensitivity** /ˌsensɪ'tɪvəti/ *noun* [U] when someone or something is sensitive

COMMON LEARNER ERROR

sensitive or **sensible?**

Remember that **sensible** does not mean 'easily upset' or 'able to understand what people are feeling'. The word you need to express that is **sensitive**.

Don't criticize her too much. She's very sensitive.

sensor /'sensəʳ/ *noun* [C] a piece of equipment that can find heat, light, etc *Sensors detect movement in the room.*

sensual /'sensjuəl/ *adjective* relating to physical pleasure, often sexual pleasure *a sensual experience* ○ *a sensual mouth* •**sensuality** /ˌsensju'æləti/ *noun* [U] being sensual

sensuous /'sensjuəs/ *adjective* giving physical pleasure *the sensuous feel of silk sheets*

sent /sent/ *past of* send

WORD PARTNERS FOR ***sentence***

impose/receive/serve a sentence • a **jail/prison** sentence • a sentence **for** sth

S

sentence¹ /ˈsentəns/ *noun* **1** LANGUAGE [C] a group of words, usually containing a verb, that expresses a complete idea **2** LAW [C, U] a punishment that a judge gives to someone who has committed a crime *a 30-year sentence*

sentence² /ˈsentəns/ *verb* [T] LAW to give a punishment to someone who has committed a crime [often passive] *She was **sentenced to** six months in prison.*

sentiment /ˈsentɪmənt/ *noun* **1** OPINION [C, U] an opinion that you have because of the way you feel about something *nationalist/religious sentiments* **2** EMOTION [U] emotional feelings such as sympathy, love, etc, especially when they are not considered to be suitable for a situation *I find her writing full of sentiment.*

sentimental /ˌsentɪˈmentᵊl/ *adjective* **1** FEELING showing kind feelings such as sympathy, love, etc, especially in a silly way *a sentimental song* ○ *The British are very sentimental about animals.* **2** VALUE related to feelings and memories and not related to how much money something costs *It wasn't an expensive ring but it had great **sentimental value**.* •**sentimentality** /ˌsentɪmenˈtæləti/ *noun* [U]

sentry /ˈsentri/ *noun* [C] a soldier who stands outside a building in order to guard it

sepal /ˈsepəl/ *noun* [C] BIOLOGY one of the parts that form the outer part of a flower which surrounds the petals and which are usually small and green

separable /ˈsepᵊrəbl/ *adjective* able to be separated ➲Opposite **inseparable**

separate¹ /ˈsepᵊrət/ *adjective* **1** NOT JOINED not joined or touching anything else *a separate compartment* ○ *I try to keep meat **separate from** other food.* **2** NOT AFFECTING not affecting or related to each other *I've asked him to turn his music down on three **separate occasions**.* ○ *I have my professional life and my private life and I try to **keep** them **separate**.* **3** DIFFERENT different *Use a separate sheet of paper.* •**separately** *adverb*

separate² /ˈsepᵊreɪt/ *verb* **1** DIVIDE [I, T] to divide into parts, or to make something divide into parts *I **separated** the class **into** three groups.* **2** MOVE APART [I, T] to move apart, or to make people move apart *I shall separate you two if you don't stop talking.* **3** HUSBAND/WIFE [I] to start to live in a different place from your husband or wife because the relationship has ended *My parents separated when I was four.* ➲See Common Learner Error at **married**

separation /ˌsepᵊrˈeɪʃᵊn/ *noun* **1** WHEN SEPARATE [C, U] when people or things are separate or become separate from other people or things *the separation of church and state* ○ *Their working in different countries meant long periods of separation.* **2** AGREEMENT [C] a legal agreement when two people stay married but stop living together

September /sepˈtembəʳ/ (*written abbreviation* **Sept**) *noun* [C, U] the ninth month of the year

septic /ˈseptɪk/ *adjective* HEALTH infected by poisonous bacteria (= small living things which cause disease)

septum /ˈseptəm/ *noun* [C] ANATOMY, BIOLOGY a part of the body that divides two hollow parts, for example in the heart ➲See picture at **heart**

sequel /ˈsiːkwᵊl/ *noun* [C] a film, book, etc that continues the story from an earlier one

WORD PARTNERS FOR ***sequence***

in a sequence • a sequence **of** sth • be **out of** sequence • a **logical** sequence

sequence /ˈsiːkwəns/ *noun* **1** SERIES [C] a series of related events or things that have a particular order *the **sequence of events** that led to his death* **2** ORDER [U] the order that events or things should happen or be arranged in *I got my slides mixed up and they appeared **out of sequence**.*

sequential /sɪˈkwenʃᵊl/ *adjective* following a particular order •**sequentially** /sɪˈkwenʃᵊli/ *adverb*

sequin /ˈsiːkwɪn/ *noun* [C] a small, flat, shiny circle that is sewn onto clothes for decoration

serenade /ˌserəˈneɪd/ *noun* [C] MUSIC a song, usually about love

serendipity /ˌserᵊnˈdɪpəti/ *noun* [U] *literary* when you are lucky and find something interesting or valuable by chance

serene /sɪˈriːn/ *adjective* calm and quiet *a serene face/smile* •**serenely** *adverb*

serf /sɜːf/ *noun* [C] SOCIETY in the past, a member of a low social class who worked on the land and was the property of the person who owned that land

serfdom /ˈsɜːfdəm/ *noun* [U] SOCIETY the state of being a serf

sergeant /ˈsɑːdʒᵊnt/ *noun* [C] **1** POLICE an officer of low rank in the police **2** ARMY a soldier of middle rank in the army or air force

serial /ˈsɪəriəl/ *noun* [C] a story in a magazine or on television or radio that is told in separate parts over a period of time

ˈserial ˌkiller *noun* [C] someone who has murdered several people over a period of time

ˈserial ˌnumber *noun* [C] one of a set of numbers that is put on an item that is made in large quantities, such as computers, televisions, paper money, etc., so that you can tell one item from another

ˈserial ˌport *noun* [C] COMPUTING a part of a computer where wires from other pieces of equipment can be connected to it, sending through information one bit (= unit of information) at a time ➲Compare **parallel port**

series /ˈsɪəriːz/ *noun* [C] *plural* **series** **1** SAME THINGS several things or events of the same type that come one after the other *a series of lectures* **2** TELEVISION/RADIO a group of television or radio programmes that have the same main characters or deal with the same subject *a four-part drama series*

ˈseries ˌcircuit *noun* [C] PHYSICS a circuit (= closed system of wires) in which the electric current passes through one part after another ➲Compare **parallel circuit**

serif /ˈserɪf/ *noun* the very small lines at the ends of the letters in some styles of printing *a serif font* ➲Compare **sans serif**

O-‒**serious** /ˈsɪəriəs/ *adjective* **1** [BAD] A serious problem or situation is bad and makes people worry. *a serious accident/illness* ○ *This is a serious matter.* **2** [NOT JOKING] thinking or speaking sincerely about something and not joking *I'm being serious now - this is a very real problem.* ○ *Are you* ***serious about*** *changing your job?* **3** [QUIET] A serious person is quiet and does not laugh often. *a serious child* •**seriousness** *noun* [U]

O-‒**seriously** /ˈsɪəriəsli/ *adverb* **1** [SERIOUS WAY] in a serious way *seriously injured* ○ *Smoking can* ***seriously damage*** *your health.* **2** [NOT A JOKE] used to show that what you are going to say is not a joke *Seriously though, you mustn't say that.* **3 take sb/sth seriously** to believe that someone or something is important and that you should pay attention to them *The police have to take any terrorist threat seriously.*

sermon /ˈsɜːmən/ *noun* [C] **RELIGION** a religious speech given by a priest in church *to* ***deliver/give a sermon***

serotonin /ˌserəˈtəʊnɪn/ *noun* [U] **BIOLOGY** a chemical in your brain which controls your moods

serpent /ˈsɜːpᵊnt/ *noun* [C] *literary* a snake

serrated /sɪˈreɪtɪd/ *adjective* A serrated edge, usually of a knife, has sharp triangular points along it.

serum /ˈsɪərəm/ *noun* [U] **ANATOMY, BIOLOGY** a clear liquid in blood that contains substances that stop infection

servant /ˈsɜːvᵊnt/ *noun* [C] someone who works and lives in someone else's house doing their cooking and cleaning, especially in the past ➲See also: **civil servant**

O-‒**serve**[1] /sɜːv/ *verb* **1** [FOOD/DRINK] [I, T] to give someone food or drink, especially guests or customers in a restaurant or bar *We're not allowed to serve alcohol to anyone under 18.* **2** [SHOP] [I, T] to help customers and sell things to them in a shop *Are you being served?* **3** [WORK] [I, T] to do work that helps society, for example in an organization such as the army or the government *to serve in the army* ○ *to serve on a committee/jury* ○ *He* ***served as*** *mayor for 5 years.* **4** [BE USEFUL] [I, T] to be useful as something *It's a very entertaining film but it also* ***serves*** *an educational* ***purpose.*** ○ *The spare bedroom also* ***serves as*** *a study.* [+ **to do sth**] *He hopes his son's death will serve to warn others about the dangers of owning a gun.* **5 LAW** [T] to be in prison for a period of time *Williams, 42, is serving a four-year jail sentence.* **6 SPORT** [I] in a sport such as tennis, to throw the ball up into the air and then hit it towards the other player **7 serves one/two/four, etc** If an amount of food serves a particular number, it is enough for that number of people. ➲See also: It serves her/him/you **right**[2]!

serve[2] /sɜːv/ *noun* [C] **SPORT** in sports such as tennis, when you throw the ball up into the air and hit it towards the other player

server /ˈsɜːvəʳ/ *noun* [C] **COMPUTING** a computer that is used only for storing and managing programs and information used by other computers *an email/Internet server*

WORD PARTNERS FOR ***service***

offer/provide/use a service

O-‒**service**[1] /ˈsɜːvɪs/ *noun* **1** [SHOP] [U] when people help you and bring you things in a place such as a shop, restaurant, or hotel *The food was nice, but the service wasn't very good.* **2 ECONOMICS** [C] a system that supplies something that people need *financial/medical services* ○ *electricity/water services* ○ *They* ***provide*** *a free bus* ***service*** *from the station.* **3** [WORK] [U] the time you spend working for an organization *He retired last week after 25 years' service.* **4 RELIGION** [C] a religious ceremony *They* ***held*** *a memorial* ***service*** *for the victims of the bombing.* **5** [CAR/MACHINE] [C] when a car or machine is examined for faults and repaired **6 SPORT** [C] when you throw a ball up into the air and hit it towards the other player in sports such as tennis ➲See also: **the Civil Service, community service, lip-service, the National Health Service, national service, secret service**

service[2] /ˈsɜːvɪs/ *verb* [T] to examine and repair a car or machine

serviceable /ˈsɜːvɪsəbl/ *adjective* able to be used, but not very good or attractive *I have some old but serviceable chairs.*

ˈservice ˌcharge *noun* [C] **FINANCE** an amount of money that is added to what you pay in a restaurant for being helped and brought things *a 10% service charge*

serviceman /ˈsɜːvɪsmən/ *noun* [C] *plural* **servicemen** a man who is in the army or navy

ˈservice proˌvider *noun* [C] **COMPUTING, INTERNET** a company that connects your computer to the Internet, and lets you use email and other services

the services /ˈsɜːvɪsɪz/ *noun* [**plural**] the military forces such as the army or navy

ˈservice ˌstation *noun* [C] a place at the side of a road where you can buy fuel for cars, and food

serviette /ˌsɜːviˈet/ *UK* (*UK/US* **napkin**) *noun* [C] a piece of cloth or paper used when you eat, to keep your clothes clean and to clean your mouth and hands

servile /ˈsɜːvaɪl/ (US) /ˈsɜːrvᵊl/ *adjective* too willing to do things for other people

serving /ˈsɜːvɪŋ/ *noun* [C] **FOOD** an amount of food for one person to eat *a large serving of rice*

sesame seed /ˈsesəmiˌsiːd/ *noun* [C] **FOOD** a small seed that is used to add a taste to food

session /ˈseʃᵊn/ *noun* **1** [PERIOD OF TIME] [C] a period during which you do one activity *a weekly aerobics session* ○ *We're having a training session this afternoon.* **2** [MEETING] [C, U] a meeting of an official group of people such as in a court or in the government *The court is now* ***in session.***

O-‒**set**[1] /set/ *verb* **setting**, *past* **set 1** [A TIME] [T] to arrange a time when something will happen [**often passive**] *The next meeting is* ***set for*** *6 February.* **2** [LEVEL] [T] to decide the level of something *The interest rate has been* ***set at*** *5%.* **3**-

S

MACHINE [T] to press switches on a machine so that it will start when you want it to *I've **set** the alarm **for** 6.30.* [+ to do sth] *Can you set the video to record 'Neighbours' please?* **4 set an example/a record/a standard, etc** to do something in a way that people will copy or try to improve on *She's set a new world record with that jump.* **5 set fire to sth; set sth on fire** to make something start burning **6 set sb free** to allow someone to leave prison, or to allow a person or animal to escape **7 set sth alight** to make something start burning **8 set the table** to put plates, knives, forks, etc on the table before you have a meal **9** SUN [I] When the sun sets, it moves down in the sky so that it cannot be seen. *The sun rises in the East and sets in the West.* **10** BECOME SOLID [I] If a liquid substance sets, it becomes solid. **11 EDUCATION** [T] *UK* If you set work or an exam at a school or college, you ask the students to do it. [+ **two objects**] *Mr Harley forgot to set us any maths homework.* **12 set sth down/on, etc** to put something somewhere *She set the vase down on the table.* **13** BOOK/FILM/PLAY [T] If a book, play, or film is set in a place or period of time, the story happens there or at that time. [**often passive**] *It's a historical adventure set in India in the 1940s.* **14 set to work** to start working

set about sth/doing sth *phrasal verb* to start doing something, especially something that uses a lot of time or energy *I got home and immediately set about cleaning the house.*

be set against sth/doing sth *phrasal verb* to not want to do or have something *He is **dead set against** the move.*

set sb/sth apart *phrasal verb* If a quality sets someone or something apart, it makes them different from and usually better than others of the same type. *It's their intelligence which **sets them apart from** other rock bands.*

set sth aside *phrasal verb* to save something, usually time or money, for a special purpose

set sb/sth back *phrasal verb* to make something happen more slowly or later than it should *The heavy traffic set us back about half an hour.*

set sb back (sth) *phrasal verb informal* to cost someone a large amount of money *A car like that will probably set you back about £12,000.*

set in *phrasal verb* If something unpleasant sets in, it begins and seems likely to continue. *This rain looks as if it has set in for the rest of the day.*

set off *phrasal verb* to start a journey *What time are you setting off tomorrow morning?*

set sth off *phrasal verb* to cause something to begin or happen, especially a loud noise or a lot of activity *He's always burning the toast and setting off the smoke alarm.*

set sb/sth on/upon sb *phrasal verb* to make a person or animal attack someone *If you come any closer, I'll set the dog on you.*

set out *phrasal verb* **1** INTEND to start doing something when you have already decided what you want to achieve [+ **to do sth**] *I'd done what I set out to do.* **2** START JOURNEY to start a journey

set sth out *phrasal verb* to give all the details of something, or to explain something clearly, especially in writing *Your contract will set out the terms of your employment.*

set sth up *phrasal verb* **1** COMPANY to start a company or organization *A committee has been set up to investigate the problem.* **2** ARRANGE to arrange for something to happen *I've set up a meeting with him for next week.*

set sb up *phrasal verb* to trick someone in order to make them do something, or in order to make them seem guilty of something that they have not done

set (sth) up *phrasal verb* to get all the necessary equipment ready for an activity *I need one or two people to help me set up the display.*

set² /set/ *noun* [C] **1** GROUP a group of things which belong together *a set of instructions/rules* ○ *a **set of** keys/tools* **2** FILM/PLAY the place where a film or play is performed or recorded, and the pictures, furniture, etc that are used *They first met **on the set of** 'Star Wars'.* **3 SPORT** one part of a tennis match *Agassi is leading by four games to one in the third set.* **4** TV/RADIO a television or radio *a TV set* **5 MUSIC** a group of songs or tunes that go together to make a musical performance **6 MATHEMATICS** a group of numbers or things

set³ /set/ *adjective* **1** fixed and never changing *Most people work for a **set number of hours** each week.* ○ *I have no **set routine**.* **2 be all set** to be ready [+ **to do sth**] *We were all set to go when the phone rang.* ➲See also: On your marks (**mark**[1]). Get set. Go!

WORD PARTNERS FOR ***setback***

suffer a setback • a **major/serious** setback • a setback **for** sb • a setback **in/to** sth

setback /ˈsetbæk/ *noun* [C] a problem that makes something happen later or more slowly than it should *The project has **suffered** a series **of setbacks** this year.*

set-piece /ˌsetˈpiːs/ *noun* [C] a speech or set of actions that has been carefully planned and practised

settee /setˈiː/ *UK* (*UK/US* **sofa**) *noun* [C] a large, comfortable seat for more than one person

setting /ˈsetɪŋ/ *noun* [C] **1** PLACE the place where something is or where something happens, often in a book, play, or film *The house provided the **setting for** the TV series 'Pride and Prejudice'.* **2** LEVEL a position on the controls of a piece of equipment *Set the oven at the lowest setting.*

settle /ˈsetl/ *verb* **1** ARGUMENT [T] If you settle an argument, you solve the problem and stop arguing. *to **settle a dispute*** **2** LIVE [I] to start living somewhere that you are going to live for a long time *He travelled around Europe for years before finally settling in Vienna.* **3** DECIDE [T] to decide or arrange something [**often passive**] *Right, that's settled. We're going to Spain.* **4** RELAX [I, T] to relax into a comfortable position [**often reflexive**] *She settled herself into the chair opposite.* **5 FINANCE** [T] If you settle a bill or a debt, you pay the money that you owe. **6** MOVE DOWN [I] to move down towards the ground or the bottom of something and then stay there *Do you think the snow will settle?* ➲See also: the **dust**[1] settles

settle down *phrasal verb* **1** STAY to start living in a place where you intend to stay for a long time, usually with a partner *Do you think*

he'll ever settle down and have a family? **2** FEEL HAPPY to start to feel happy and confident with a new situation *Has she settled down in her new job?*
settle (sb) down *phrasal verb* to become quiet and calm, or to make someone become quiet and calm *Come on children, stop chatting and settle down please!*
settle for sth *phrasal verb* to accept something, especially something that is not exactly what you want *He wants a full refund and he won't settle for anything less.*
settle in *phrasal verb* to begin to feel relaxed and happy in a new home or job *Are you settling in OK?*
settle on/upon sth *phrasal verb* to agree on a decision *We still haven't settled on a place to meet.*
settle up *phrasal verb* **FINANCE** to pay someone the money that you owe them *I need to **settle up** with you for the tickets.*

settled /ˈsetld/ *adjective* **1 be settled** to feel happy and relaxed in a place or situation *He seems quite settled now.* **2** regular and not often changing *The weather's a lot more settled at this time of year.* ➲Opposite **unsettled**

WORD PARTNERS FOR ***settlement***

agree/negotiate/reach a settlement • a settlement **between** sb and sb • a settlement **over** sth • a **peace** settlement

settlement /ˈsetlmənt/ *noun* [C] **1** AGREEMENT an official agreement that finishes an argument *a **peace settlement*** **2 SOCIETY** a town or village which people built to live in after arriving from somewhere else *a Jewish settlement*

settler /ˈsetləʳ/ *noun* [C] **SOCIETY** someone who moves to a new place where there were not many people before *The first European settlers arrived in Virginia in 1607.*

set-top box /ˈsettɒpˌbɒks/ *noun* [C] a piece of electronic equipment that allows you to watch digital broadcasts (= television sounds and pictures sent as signals in the form of numbers) on an ordinary television

set-up /ˈsetʌp/ *noun* [C] *informal* **1** ARRANGEMENT the way that something is arranged or organized *It took me a while to get used to the set-up in my new job.* **2** TRICK a plan that is dishonest and is intended to trick someone

O→**seven** /ˈsevᵊn/ the number 7

O→**seventeen** /ˌsevᵊnˈtiːn/ the number 17 •**seventeenth** 17th written as a word

seventh¹ /ˈsevᵊnθ/ 7th written as a word

seventh² /ˈsevᵊnθ/ *noun* [C] one of seven equal parts of something; ¹/₇

O→**seventy** /ˈsevᵊnti/ **1** the number 70 **2 the seventies** the years from 1970 to 1979 **3 be in your seventies** to be aged between 70 and 79 •**seventieth** 70th written as a word

sever /ˈsevəʳ/ *verb* [T] **1** to cut through something, especially a part of the body *to sever an artery* [**often passive**] *Two of her fingers were severed in the accident.* **2 sever links/ties, etc with sb** to end a relationship with someone

O→**several** /ˈsevᵊrᵊl/ *pronoun, determiner* some, but not a lot *Several people have complained about the scheme.* ○ ***Several of** my friends studied in Manchester.*

severance /ˈsevᵊrəns/ *noun* [U] when an employer forces an employee to leave a job ***severance pay***

severe /sɪˈvɪəʳ/ *adjective* **1** BAD extremely bad *a severe headache* ○ *severe weather conditions* **2** NOT KIND not kind or gentle *a severe punishment* **3** PERSON A severe person looks unfriendly or very strict. •**severely** *adverb to be severely injured* ○ *She has been severely criticized for the speech.*

severity /sɪˈverəti/ *noun* [U] how severe something is

sew /səʊ/ *verb* [I, T] *past tense* **sewed**, *past participle* **sewn** or **sewed** to join things together with a needle and thread
sew sth up *phrasal verb* **1** to close or repair something by sewing the edges together **2 have sth sewn up** *informal* to be certain to win or succeed at something

sewage /ˈsuːɪdʒ/ *noun* [U] waste water and waste from toilets *a sewage treatment plant*

sewer /sʊəʳ/ *noun* [C] a large underground system of pipes that carries away sewage

sewing /ˈsəʊɪŋ/ *noun* [U] **1** ACTIVITY the activity of joining pieces of cloth together or repairing them with a needle and thread **2** CLOTH the pieces of cloth that you are joining together or repairing with a needle and thread

ˈsewing maˌchine *noun* [C] a machine that joins pieces of cloth together with a needle and thread

sewn /səʊn/ *past participle of* sew

O→**sex**¹ /seks/ *noun* **1** [U] **BIOLOGY** sexual activity between people *to **have sex with someone*** ○ ***sex education*** **2 BIOLOGY** [U] the fact of being male or female *Do you know what sex the baby is?* ○ ***sex discrimination*** **3 the female/male/opposite, etc sex** people who are female/male/the other sex from you, etc

ˈsex ˌchromosome *noun* [C] **BIOLOGY** a chromosome that controls what sex an organism will be

sexism /ˈseksɪzᵊm/ *noun* [U] **SOCIETY** when someone is treated unfairly because they are a woman or because they are a man •**sexist** *adjective sexist attitudes/jokes*

ˈsex ˌlife *noun* [C] a person's sexual activities and relationships

O→**sexual** /ˈsekʃʊəl/ *adjective* **1 BIOLOGY** relating to the activity of sex *sexual experiences* ○ *sexual organs* **2 SOCIETY** relating to being male or female ***sexual discrimination*** ○ ***sexual equality***

ˌsexual ˈintercourse *noun* [U] **BIOLOGY** *formal* when a man puts his penis into a woman's vagina

sexuality /ˌsekʃuˈæləti/ *noun* [U] the way you feel about sexual activity and the type of sex you prefer

sexually /ˈsekʃʊəli/ *adverb* in a way that relates to the activity of sex *sexually attractive* ○ *a **sexually transmitted disease***

S

ˌsexual reproˈduction *noun* [U] **BIOLOGY** a method of producing babies where a male seed and a female egg join together

sexy /ˈseksi/ *adjective* attractive or exciting in a sexual way *sexy underwear* ○ *He's very sexy.*

SGML /esdʒiːemˈel/ *noun* [U] **COMPUTING** *abbreviation for* standard generalized markup language: a system for organizing information on computers

sh (*also* **shh**) /ʃ/ *exclamation* used to tell someone to be quiet

shabby /ˈʃæbi/ *adjective* **1** [UNTIDY] looking untidy and in bad condition *shabby clothes/furniture* **2** [UNFAIR] Shabby behaviour or treatment is bad and unfair. •**shabbily** *adverb shabbily dressed* ○ *shabbily treated*

shack¹ /ʃæk/ *noun* [C] a small simple building that has been badly built

shackle /ˈʃækl/ *verb* [T] **1** to fasten a prisoner's arms or legs together with chains **2 be shackled by sth** to be prevented from doing what you want to do by something

shackles /ˈʃæklz/ *noun* [**plural**] chains used to fasten together prisoners' arms or legs

shade¹ /ʃeɪd/ *noun* **1** [NO SUN] [U] an area where there is no light from the sun and so it is darker and not as hot *I'd prefer to sit* ***in the shade***. **2 ART** [C] a colour, especially when referring to how dark or light it is *a pale/dark shade of grey* ○ *pastel shades* **3** [COVER] [C] a cover that stops too much light coming from the sun or from an electric light *a lamp shade* **4 a shade** a small amount *He's perhaps a shade taller.* **5 a shade of meaning/opinion, etc** a slight difference in the meaning of something

shade² /ʃeɪd/ *verb* [T] to cover something in order to protect it from the sun *He shaded his eyes with his hand.*

shades /ʃeɪdz/ *noun* [**plural**] *informal* sunglasses (= dark glasses that protect your eyes from the sun)

WORD PARTNERS FOR ***shadow***

sth **casts** a shadow • a shadow **crosses/falls across** sth • sth is **in** shadow • the shadow **of** sth

S

O-- **shadow¹** /ˈʃædəʊ/ *noun* **1** [C, U] a dark area made by something that is stopping the light *The tree had* ***cast*** (= made) *a long* ***shadow***. **2 beyond/without a shadow of a doubt** If something is true beyond a shadow of a doubt, it is certainly true. **3 cast a shadow over sth** to spoil a good situation with something unpleasant *The bombing has cast a shadow over the Queen's visit.*

shadow² /ˈʃædəʊ/ *verb* [T] to follow someone secretly in order to see where they go and what they do [**often passive**] *He was being shadowed by a private detective.*

shadowy /ˈʃædəʊi/ *adjective* **1** [DARK] dark and full of shadows *in a shadowy corner* **2** [SECRET] secret and mysterious *the* ***shadowy world*** *of espionage*

shady /ˈʃeɪdi/ *adjective* **1** [NOT SUNNY] A shady place is protected from the sun and so it is darker and cooler. *We found a* ***shady spot*** *to sit in.* **2** [DISHONEST] *informal* dishonest and illegal ***shady deals***

shaft /ʃɑːft/ *noun* [C] **1** [HOLE] a long, vertical hole that people or things can move through, either inside a building or in the ground *a mine shaft* ○ *a ventilation shaft* **2** [HANDLE] the handle of a tool or weapon **3 a shaft of light** a beam of light

shake¹ /ʃeɪk/ *verb past tense* **shook**, *past participle* **shaken** **1** [MOVE] [**I, T**] to make quick, short movements from side to side or up and down, or to make something or someone do this *He was shaking with nerves.* ○ *Shake the bottle.* **2 shake hands** to hold someone's hand and move it up and down when you meet them for the first time, or when you make an agreement with them *The two leaders smiled and shook hands for the photographers.* ○ *I* ***shook hands with*** *him.* **3 shake your head** to move your head from side to side to mean 'no' **4** [SHOCK] [T] to shock or upset someone [**often passive**] *No one was injured in the crash, but the driver was badly shaken.* **5** [VOICE] [**I**] If your voice shakes, you sound very nervous or frightened.

shake sth off *phrasal verb* to get rid of an illness or something that is causing you problems *I hope I can shake off this cold before the weekend.*

shake sb off *phrasal verb* to succeed in escaping from someone who is following you

shake sth out *phrasal verb* to hold something that is made of cloth at one end and move it up and down in order to get rid of dirt

shake sb up *phrasal verb* If an unpleasant experience shakes someone up, it makes them feel shocked and upset. *The accident really shook him up.*

shake² /ʃeɪk/ *noun* [C] **1** when you shake something ***Give it a*** *good* ***shake*** *before you open it.* **2 FOOD** (*also* **milkshake**) a sweet drink made of milk and chocolate or fruit

shake-up /ˈʃeɪkʌp/ *noun* [C] when big changes are made to a system or an organization *This is the biggest shake-up in the legal system for fifty years.*

shaky /ˈʃeɪki/ *adjective* **1** [MOVING] making quick, short movements from side to side or up and down *shaky hands* **2** [NOT STRONG] not physically strong because you are nervous, old, or ill *I felt a bit shaky when I stood up.* **3** [LIKELY TO FAIL] not working well and likely to fail *They managed to win the game, despite a very* ***shaky start***.

O-- **shall** *strong form* /ʃæl/ *weak form* /ʃᵊl/ *modal verb* **1 shall I/we...? a** used to make an offer or suggestion *Shall I cook dinner tonight?* ○ *We'll ask him later, shall we?* **b** used to ask someone what to do *Who shall I ask?* **2 I/we shall...** *formal* used to say what you are going to do in the future *I shall be talking to her tomorrow.* ○ *I shan't forget to tell them.* ➲See Extra help page **Modal verbs** on page Centre 34.

COMMON LEARNER ERROR

shall and will

Shall and **will** are both used to talk about what you are going to do in the future. **Shall** is usually used with 'I' or 'we' and is more formal than **will**.

shallot /ʃə'lɒt/ *noun* [C] **FOOD** a vegetable like a small onion

O-**shallow** /'ʃæləʊ/ *adjective* **1** NOT DEEP not deep *shallow water* ○ *a shallow dish* ➲See picture at **deep** **2** NOT SERIOUS not showing any interest in serious ideas

the shallows /'ʃæləʊz/ *noun* [**plural**] areas of shallow water

sham /ʃæm/ *noun* [**no plural**] something that is not what it seems to be and is intended to deceive people *Newspapers have described their marriage as a sham.*

shambles /'ʃæmblz/ *noun* **be a shambles** *informal* to be very badly organized *The performance was a complete shambles.*

WORD PARTNERS FOR ***shame***

bring shame **on** sb/sth • a **sense of** shame • the shame **of** (doing) sth

shame¹ /ʃeɪm/ *noun* **1 a shame** If you describe something as a shame, you are disappointed that it has happened. [**+ to do sth**] ***It's a*** *real* ***shame*** *to waste all this food.* [**+ (that)**] ***What a shame*** *that they had to destroy such a beautiful building.* **2** [**U**] when you feel embarrassed and guilty about something bad that you have done *to be filled with shame* **3 have no shame** to not feel embarrassed or guilty about doing bad or embarrassing things **4 put sb/sth to shame** to be much better than someone or something else *Your cooking puts mine to shame.*

shame² /ʃeɪm/ *verb* [**T**] to make someone feel embarrassed and guilty about something [**+ into + doing sth**] *His children are trying to shame him into giving up smoking.*

shameful /'ʃeɪmfᵊl/ *adjective* Something shameful is bad and should make you feel embarrassed and guilty. *shameful scenes* •**shamefully** *adverb*

shameless /'ʃeɪmləs/ *adjective* without feeling embarrassed or guilty although you should *shameless behaviour/lies* •**shamelessly** *adverb*

shampoo /ʃæm'puː/ *noun* [**C, U**] a liquid substance that you use to wash your hair *a bottle of shampoo* •**shampoo** *verb* [**T**] **shampooing**, *past* **shampooed**

O-**shan't** /ʃɑːnt/ *mainly UK short for* shall not *I was invited to the party, but I shan't be going.*

shanty town /'ʃænti,taʊn/ *noun* [**C**] an area on the edge of a town where poor people live in very simply built houses

WORD PARTNERS FOR ***shape***

an **irregular/pleasing/strange/unusual** shape • **change** shape • **in** the shape **of** sth

O-**shape¹** /ʃeɪp/ *noun* **1** [**C, U**] the physical form of something made by the line around its outer edge *a circular/rectangular shape* ○ *You can recognize trees by the shape of their leaves.* **2 in good/bad/great, etc shape** in good/bad, etc health or condition *She runs every day so she's in pretty good shape.* **3 out of shape HEALTH** not healthy or physically strong **4 keep in shape** to stay healthy and physically strong **5 take shape** to start to develop and become more clear or certain *The project is slowly beginning to take shape.* **6 all shapes and sizes** many different types of people or things *We saw people there of all shapes and sizes.*

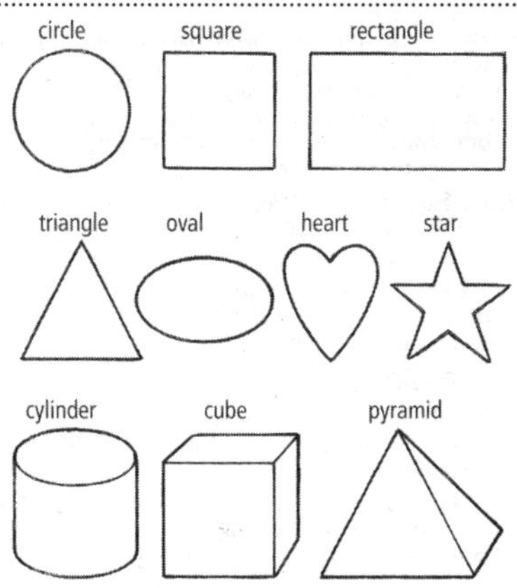

shapes

shape² /ʃeɪp/ *verb* [**T**] **1** INFLUENCE to influence the way that something develops [**often passive**] *Their attitudes were shaped during the war.* **2** MAKE A SHAPE to make something become a particular shape *Combine the meat and egg and shape the mixture into small balls.*
shape up *phrasal verb informal* to develop or improve *Things at work seem to be shaping up quite nicely.*

-shaped /ʃeɪpt/ *suffix* used after nouns to mean 'having a particular shape' *a heart-shaped cake* ➲See also: **pear-shaped**

shapeless /'ʃeɪpləs/ *adjective* not having a clear or well designed shape *a shapeless dress*

shapely /'ʃeɪpli/ *adjective* having an attractive shape *shapely legs*

O-**share¹** /ʃeəʳ/ *verb* **1** AT SAME TIME [**I, T**] to have or use something at the same time as someone else *She* ***shares*** *a house* ***with*** *Paul.* **2** DIVIDE [**I, T**] to divide something between two or more people *We shared a pizza and a bottle of wine.* ○ *We* ***shared*** *the cost of the wedding* ***between*** *us.* **3 share an interest/opinion, etc** to have the same interest/opinion, etc as someone else *They share a love of gardening.* **4 share your problems/thoughts/ideas, etc** to tell someone your problems/thoughts, etc
share sth out *phrasal verb* to divide something into smaller amounts and give one amount to each person in a group *Profits are* ***shared out*** *equally* ***among*** *members of the group.*

WORD PARTNERS FOR ***share*** (noun)

buy/have/sell shares • shares **in** sth • share **prices**

share² /ʃeəʳ/ *noun* [**C**] **1 ECONOMICS** one of the equal parts that the value of a company is divided into when it is owned by a group of people *to* ***buy/sell shares*** ○ *We own shares in a number of companies.* ○ ***Share prices*** *have fallen for the third day running.* **2** a part of

S

something that has been divided [**usually no plural**] *When am I going to get my share of the money?* **3 have your (fair) share of sth** to have a lot of something and enough of it, usually something bad *We've had our fair share of rain already this summer.*

shareholder /ˈʃeəˌhəʊldəʳ/ *noun* [**C**] **ECONOMICS** someone who owns shares in a company *a shareholders' meeting*

shareware /ˈʃeəweəʳ/ *noun* [**U**] **COMPUTING** software that can be used by anyone without having to pay for it

Sharia /ʃəˈriːə/ *noun* [**U**] **RELIGION** the holy law of Islam

shark /ʃɑːk/ *noun* [**C**] a large fish with very sharp teeth

O‒ **sharp¹** /ʃɑːp/ *adjective* **1** [ABLE TO CUT] having a very thin or pointed edge that can cut things *a sharp knife* ○ *sharp claws/teeth* **2 a sharp rise/increase/drop, etc** a sudden and very large increase or reduction in something **3 a sharp contrast/difference/distinction, etc** a very big and noticeable difference between two things **4** [QUICK] quick to notice and understand things *a sharp mind* **5 a sharp pain HEALTH** a sudden, short, strong pain **6** [SEVERE] severe and not gentle *sharp criticism* ○ *She can be a bit sharp with people sometimes.* **7 a sharp bend/turn, etc** a sudden large change in the direction you are travelling **8 FOOD** A sharp taste is slightly sour. **9** [CLEAR] A sharp image is very clear. *a photograph in sharp focus* **10 a sharp wit** the ability to say things that are funny and clever **11 a sharp tongue** If you have a sharp tongue, you often upset people by saying unkind things to them. **12** [FASHIONABLE] If a piece of clothing or a style is sharp, it is fashionable and tidy. *young men in sharp suits* **13 C sharp/F sharp, etc MUSIC** the musical note that is between the note C, F, etc and the note above it **14 MUSIC** A sharp musical note sounds unpleasant because it is slightly higher than it should be. •**sharply** *adverb* •**sharpness** *noun* [**U**]

sharp² /ʃɑːp/ *adverb* **3 o'clock/8.30 p.m., etc sharp** at exactly 3 o'clock, 8.30 p.m., etc

sharp³ /ʃɑːp/ *noun* [**C**] **MUSIC** a musical note that is between one note and the note above it

S

sharpen /ˈʃɑːpᵊn/ *verb* [**T**] to make something sharper *to sharpen a knife/pencil*

shatter /ˈʃætəʳ/ *verb* **1** [BREAK] [**I, T**] to break into very small pieces, or to make something break into very small pieces *Someone threw a stone at the car, shattering the windscreen.* **2** [DESTROY] [**T**] to destroy something good, such as your confidence, hopes, or belief in something *The accident completely shattered her confidence.*

shattered /ˈʃætəd/ *adjective* **1** [UPSET] very upset **2** [TIRED] *UK informal* very tired

shave¹ /ʃeɪv/ *verb* [**I, T**] to cut hair off your face or body *to shave your head/legs* ○ *shaving cream/foam*

shave sth off *phrasal verb* to cut a very thin piece off a surface

shave² /ʃeɪv/ *noun* **1** [**C**] when a man shaves the hair growing on his face **2 a close shave** a situation when something unpleasant or dangerous almost happens

shaven /ˈʃeɪvᵊn/ *adjective* A shaven part of the body has had the hair cut off it. *a gang of youths with **shaven heads***

shaver /ˈʃeɪvəʳ/ *noun* [**C**] a piece of electrical equipment used to cut hair off the head or body

shavings /ˈʃeɪvɪŋz/ *noun* [**plural**] very thin pieces that have been cut off something ***wood shavings***

shawl /ʃɔːl/ *noun* [**C**] a piece of cloth that is worn by a woman around her shoulders or used to cover a baby

O‒ **she** *strong form* /ʃiː/ *weak form* /ʃi/ *pronoun* used as the subject of the verb when referring to someone female who has already been talked about *"When is Ruth coming?" "She'll be here soon."*

sheaf /ʃiːf/ *noun* [**C**] *plural* **sheaves** /ʃiːvz/ **1** several pieces of paper held together *a sheaf of papers* **2 FARMING** several pieces of wheat or corn (= plant for grain) tied together

shear /ʃɪəʳ/ *verb* [**T**] *past tense* **sheared**, *past participle* **sheared** or **shorn FARMING** to cut the wool off a sheep

shears /ʃɪəz/ *noun* [**plural**] a cutting tool with two large blades, like a large pair of scissors *a pair of garden shears*

sheath /ʃiːθ/ *noun* [**C**] a cover for the sharp blade of a knife

O‒ **she'd** /ʃiːd/ **1** [SHE HAD] *short for* she had *By the time I got there, she'd fallen asleep.* **2** [SHE WOULD] *short for* she would *She knew that she'd be late.*

shed¹ /ʃed/ *noun* [**C**] a small building used to store things such as tools *a garden shed*

shed² /ʃed/ *verb* [**T**] **shedding**, *past* **shed 1 shed leaves/skin/hair, etc** to lose something because it falls off *A lot of trees shed their leaves in the autumn.* **2** to get rid of something that you do not want or need *A lot of companies are shedding jobs.* **3 shed tears** to cry **4 shed blood** to kill or injure someone ⊃See also: cast/shed **light**¹ on sth

shedload /ˈʃedləʊd/ *noun* [**C**] *informal* a large amount *They spent shedloads of money on that car.*

sheen /ʃiːn/ *noun* [**no plural**] a smooth shine on a surface

sheep /ʃiːp/ *noun* [**C**] *plural* **sheep FARMING** a farm animal whose skin is covered with wool *a flock of sheep*

sheepish /ˈʃiːpɪʃ/ *adjective* slightly embarrassed, usually because you have done something stupid *a **sheepish grin**/look* •**sheepishly** *adverb*

sheer /ʃɪəʳ/ *adjective* **1** [EXTREME] [**always before noun**] used to emphasize how strong a feeling or quality is *a look of sheer delight/joy* ○ *sheer determination/hard work* **2** [LARGE] [**always before noun**] used to emphasize the large size or amount of something *The delays are due to the sheer volume of traffic.* **3** [STEEP] very steep *a sheer cliff face* **4** [CLOTH] Sheer cloth is very thin and you can see through it. *sheer tights/nylons*

sheet /ʃiːt/ *noun* [C] **1** a large piece of cloth put on a bed to lie on or under *a double fitted sheet* ○ *to change the sheets* **2 a sheet of paper/glass/metal, etc** a flat piece of paper/glass, etc *a sheet of yellow paper* ➲See also: **balance sheet**

sheeting /ˈʃiːtɪŋ/ *noun* [U] a large flat piece of material, usually used as a cover *plastic sheeting*

Sheikh (*also* **Sheik**) /ʃeɪk/ *noun* [C] an Arab leader

shelf /ʃelf/ *noun* [C] *plural* **shelves** /ʃelvz/ a flat, horizontal board used to put things on, often fixed to a wall or inside a cupboard *a book shelf* ○ *on the top/bottom shelf*

ˈshelf ˌlife *noun* [C] *plural* **shelf lives** A product's shelf life is the length of time it stays in good condition and can be used. [**usually singular**] *Fresh fruit has a very short shelf life.*

O-■ **she'll** /ʃiːl/ *short for* she will *She'll be away until Tuesday.*

shell¹ /ʃel/ *noun* [C] **1** BIOLOGY the hard outer covering of some creatures and of eggs, nuts, or seeds *a snail's shell* ○ *an egg shell* **2** a bomb fired from a large gun ➲See also: **sea shell**

shell

shell² /ʃel/ *verb* [T] to attack a place with bombs

shell out (sth) *phrasal verb informal* to pay or give money for something, especially when you do not want to

shellfish /ˈʃelfɪʃ/ *noun* [U] FOOD sea creatures that live in shells and are eaten as food

WORD PARTNERS FOR ***shelter***

find/provide/seek/take shelter • shelter **from** sth • **under** the shelter **of** sth

shelter¹ /ˈʃeltəʳ/ *noun* **1** [PLACE] [C] a place that protects you from bad weather or danger *a bomb shelter* **2** [PROTECTION] [U] protection from bad weather or danger *We **took shelter** from the rain in a doorway.*

shelter² /ˈʃeltəʳ/ *verb* **1 shelter from/in/under, etc** to go under a cover or inside a building to be protected from bad weather or danger *They went under a tree to shelter from the rain.* **2** [T] to provide cover or protection for someone *Many households are already sheltering refugees.*

sheltered /ˈʃeltəd/ *adjective* **1** covered or protected from bad weather or danger *a sheltered spot by the wall* **2 a sheltered existence/life/upbringing, etc** If you have a sheltered life, you are protected too much and experience very little danger or excitement. **3 sheltered accommodation/housing** *UK* houses for old and ill people in a place where help can be given if it is needed

shelve /ʃelv/ *verb* [T] to decide not to continue with a plan [**often passive**] *The project had to be shelved when they ran out of money.*

shelves /ʃelvz/ *plural of* shelf

shenanigans /ʃɪˈnænɪgənz/ *noun* [**plural**] *informal* secret or dishonest behaviour ***political/sexual shenanigans***

shepherd¹ /ˈʃepəd/ *noun* [C] FARMING someone whose job is to look after sheep

shepherd² /ˈʃepəd/ *verb* [T] to go somewhere with someone in order to guide them or protect them *children shepherded to school by their parents*

sheriff /ˈʃerɪf/ *noun* [C] LAW an elected law officer in the US

sherry /ˈʃeri/ *noun* [C, U] FOOD a strong Spanish wine that is drunk before a meal

O-■ **she's** /ʃiːz/ **1** [SHE IS] *short for* she is *She's a very good student.* **2** [SHE HAS] *short for* she has *She's been working very hard.*

shh /ʃ/ *exclamation* used to tell someone to be quiet

Shia /ˈʃiːə/ *noun* [C] RELIGION a Shiite

shield¹ /ʃiːld/ *noun* [C] **1** [METAL OBJECT] a large, flat object that police officers and soldiers hold in front of their bodies to protect themselves **2** [PROTECTION] a person or thing used as protection *The hostages are being used as **human shields**.*

shield² /ʃiːld/ *verb* [T] to protect someone or something from something dangerous or unpleasant *to **shield** your **eyes** from the sun*

WORD PARTNERS FOR ***shift***

a **dramatic/fundamental/gradual/major** shift • a shift **(away) from/towards** sth • a shift **in** sth

shift¹ /ʃɪft/ *noun* [C] **1** [CHANGE] a change in something *There has been a dramatic **shift in** public opinion on this matter.* **2** [WORK] a period of work in a place such as a factory or hospital *afternoon/**night shift*** ○ *He works an eight-hour shift.*

shift² /ʃɪft/ *verb* **1** [CHANGE] [I, T] to change something *We are trying to **shift** the emphasis **from** curing illness **to** preventing it.* **2** [MOVE STH] [T] to move something to another place *We need to shift all these boxes into the other room.* **3** [MOVE YOURSELF] [I, T] to move into a different position *He shifted uncomfortably in his seat.* **4** [CHANGE SPEED] [T] (*also* **shift into**) *US* to change the position of the gears (= parts that control how fast the wheels turn) in a vehicle *to **shift gears***

ˈshift ˌkey *noun* [C] COMPUTING the key on a computer keyboard which allows you to create a capital letter (= a large letter of the alphabet used at the beginning of sentences and names)

shifty /ˈʃɪfti/ *adjective informal* Someone who looks shifty looks dishonest.

Shiite (*also* **Shi'ite**) /ˈʃiːaɪt/ *noun* [C] RELIGION a member of a large group within the Islamic religion •**Shiite** (*also* **Shi'ite**) *adjective* describing the Shiites or their type of Islam

shilling /ˈʃɪlɪŋ/ *noun* [C] a unit of money used in the past in the UK

S

shimmer /ˈʃɪməʳ/ *verb* [I] to shine gently and seem to be moving slightly *The trees shimmered in the moonlight.*

shin /ʃɪn/ *noun* [C] **ANATOMY** the front part of a leg between the knee and the foot ➲See colour picture **The Body** on page Centre 13

shine¹ /ʃaɪn/ *verb past* **shone** or **shined** **1** [PRODUCE LIGHT] [I] to produce bright light *The* ***sun*** *was* ***shining*** *brightly through the window.* **2** [POINT LIGHT] [I, T] to point a light somewhere *The car's headlights shone right into my eyes.* **3** [REFLECT] [I, T] If a surface shines, it reflects light, and if you shine it, you make it reflect light. *She polished her shoes until they shone.* **4** [EYES/FACE] [I] If your eyes or face shine, you look happy, healthy, or excited. *His* ***eyes*** *were* ***shining*** *with excitement.* **5** [DO WELL] [I] to do something very well, usually better than other people.

shine² /ʃaɪn/ *noun* **1** [**no plural**] when something is bright from reflected light on its surface *hair with body and shine* **2 take a shine to sb** *informal* to like someone immediately *I think he's taken a bit of a shine to you.* **3 take the shine off sth** to spoil something pleasant

shingle /ˈʃɪŋgl/ *noun* **GEOLOGY** [U] *UK* a lot of very small pieces of stone on a beach

shiny /ˈʃaɪni/ *adjective* A shiny surface is bright because it reflects light. *shiny hair*

O⊸**ship¹** /ʃɪp/ *noun* [C] a large boat that carries people or goods by sea *a cargo ship*

ship² /ʃɪp/ *verb* [T] **shipping**, *past* **shipped** to send something from one place to another [**often passive**] *These vegetables have been shipped halfway around the world.*

shipbuilder /ˈʃɪpˌbɪldəʳ/ *noun* [C] a person or company that builds ships •**shipbuilding** /ˈʃɪpˌbɪldɪŋ/ *noun* [U]

shipment /ˈʃɪpmənt/ *noun* **1** [AMOUNT] [C] an amount of goods sent from one place to another *The first shipments of food arrived this month.* **2** [SEND SOMEWHERE] [U] when something is sent from one place to another *the shipment of nuclear waste*

S

ˌshipping and ˈhandling *noun* [U] *US* postage and packing

shipwreck¹ /ˈʃɪprek/ *noun* [C] an accident in which a ship is destroyed at sea

shipwreck² /ˈʃɪprek/ *verb* **be shipwrecked** If someone is shipwrecked, the ship they are in is destroyed in an accident.

shipyard /ˈʃɪpjɑːd/ *noun* [C] a place where ships are built or repaired

shirk /ʃɜːk/ *verb* [I, T] to avoid doing something because it is difficult or unpleasant *to* ***shirk*** *your* ***duties/responsibilities***

O⊸**shirt** /ʃɜːt/ *noun* [C] a piece of clothing worn on the top part of the body, often made of thin material like cotton and fastened with buttons down the front ➲See colour picture **Clothes** on page Centre 9 ➲See also: **polo shirt, T-shirt**

shish kebab /ˈʃɪʃkəˌbæb/ *noun* [C] **FOOD** small pieces of meat or vegetables cooked on a long, thin stick

shiver /ˈʃɪvəʳ/ *verb* [I] to shake because you are cold or frightened *She* ***shivered with*** *cold.* •**shiver** *noun* [C] *He felt a shiver run down his spine* (= He felt afraid).

shoal /ʃəʊl/ *noun* [C] a large group of fish swimming together

WORD PARTNERS FOR ***shock***

come as a shock • **get/have** a shock • a **big/nasty/real** shock • a shock **to** sb • be **in** shock

shock¹ /ʃɒk/ *noun* **1** [SURPRISE] [C, U] a big, unpleasant surprise *We* ***got a*** *nasty* ***shock*** *when he gave us the bill.* ○ *Her death* ***came as a*** *terrible* ***shock*** *to him.* ○ *They are still* ***in shock*** (= feeling the effect of a shock) *from the accident.* **2 HEALTH** [U] a medical condition when someone is extremely weak because of damage to their body *He* ***went into shock*** *and nearly died.* **3** [ELECTRICITY] [C] (*also* **electric shock**) a sudden, painful feeling that you get when electricity flows through your body **4** [MOVEMENT] [C] a sudden movement caused by an explosion, accident, etc ➲See also: **culture shock**

shock² /ʃɒk/ *verb* [I, T] to surprise and upset someone [**often passive**] *Many people were shocked by the violent scenes in the film.* •**shocked** *adjective* [+ **to do sth**] *We were shocked to find rat poison in our hotel room.*

shocking /ˈʃɒkɪŋ/ *adjective* **1** [UPSETTING] very surprising and upsetting or immoral *shocking news* ○ *This report contains scenes that some people may find shocking.* **2** [BAD] *UK* very bad *My memory is shocking.* •**shockingly** *adverb*

shoddy /ˈʃɒdi/ *adjective* very bad quality *shoddy goods* ○ ***shoddy work/workmanship/treatment***

O⊸**shoe** /ʃuː/ *noun* [C] **1** a strong covering for the foot, often made of leather *a pair of shoes* ○ *to put your shoes on/take your shoes off* **2 be in sb's shoes** *informal* to be in the same situation as someone else, especially an unpleasant situation *What would you do if you were in my shoes?*

shoelace /ˈʃuːleɪs/ *noun* [C] a long, thin piece of material used to fasten shoes

shoeshine boy /ˈʃuːʃaɪnˌbɔɪ/ *noun* [C] a boy or man who is paid to clean people's shoes

shoestring /ˈʃuːstrɪŋ/ *noun* **on a shoestring** If you do something on a shoestring, you do it using very little money.

shone /ʃɒn/ (US) /ʃəʊn/ *past of* shine

shoo /ʃuː/ *verb* **shooing**, *past* **shooed shoo sb away/off/out, etc** to make a person or animal leave a place by chasing them or shouting 'shoo' at them •**shoo** *exclamation*

shook /ʃʊk/ *past tense of* shake

O⊸**shoot¹** /ʃuːt/ *verb past* **shot** **1** [INJURE] [T] to injure or kill a person or animal by firing a bullet from a gun at them [**often passive**] *He was robbed and then* ***shot in*** *the stomach.* ○ *An innocent bystander was* ***shot dead*** *in the incident.* **2** [FIRE BULLET] [I, T] to fire a bullet from a gun *Don't shoot!* **3 SPORT** [I] to try to score points in sports such as football by hitting,

kicking, or throwing the ball towards the goal **4 shoot across/out/up, etc** to move somewhere very quickly *She shot across the road without looking.* **5** FILM [T] to use a camera to record a film or take a photograph [**often passive**] *Most of the film was shot in Italy.*
shoot sb/sth down *phrasal verb* to destroy an aircraft or make it fall to the ground by firing bullets or weapons at it
shoot up *phrasal verb* If a number or amount shoots up, it increases very quickly. *Prices have shot up by 25%.*

shoot² /ʃuːt/ *noun* [C] **1 BIOLOGY** a new branch or stem growing on a plant *bamboo shoots* **2** when someone takes photographs or makes a film *a* ***fashion shoot***

shooting /ˈʃuːtɪŋ/ *noun* **1** [C] when someone is injured or killed by a bullet from a gun *a fatal shooting* **2 SPORT** [U] the sport of firing bullets from guns, sometimes to kill animals

O-ᵚ**shop¹** /ʃɒp/ (*also US* **store**) *noun* [C] a building or part of a building where you can buy things *a book shop* ○ *a shoe shop* ○ *to go to the shops* ○ *a shop window* ➲See also: **charity shop**

COMMON LEARNER ERROR

shop or **store?**

In **American English** the usual word for shop is **store**.

He went to the store to buy some cookies.

In **British English** the word **store** is only used to mean a very large shop where you can buy many different things.

Harrods is a famous department store.

O-ᵚ**shop²** /ʃɒp/ *verb* [I] **shopping**, *past* **shopped** to buy things in shops *I'm* ***shopping for*** *baby clothes.* ○ *I usually* ***go shopping*** *on Saturday.*
shop around *phrasal verb* to compare the price and quality of the same thing from different places before deciding which one to buy *to shop around for a computer*

ˈshop asˌsistant *UK* (*US* **sales clerk**) *noun* [C] someone whose job is selling things in a shop

ˌshop ˈfloor *noun* [**no plural**] the part of a factory where things are made and not the part where the managers' offices are

shopkeeper /ˈʃɒpˌkiːpəʳ/ *noun* [C] someone who owns or manages a small shop

shoplifting /ˈʃɒplɪftɪŋ/ *noun* [U] **LAW** stealing things from a shop •**shoplifter** *noun* [C] •**shoplift** *verb* [I]

shopper /ˈʃɒpəʳ/ *noun* [C] someone who is buying things from shops

WORD PARTNERS FOR ***shopping***

a shopping **spree/trip** • **to go** shopping

O-ᵚ**shopping** /ˈʃɒpɪŋ/ *noun* [U] **1** BUYING when you buy things from shops *I love shopping.* ○ *a shopping basket/trolley* **2** GOODS the things that you buy from a shop or shops *Can you help me unpack the shopping?* ○ *a shopping bag* ➲See also: **window shopping**

ˈshopping ˌbasket *noun* [C] **INTERNET** a place on a website where you collect things that you plan to buy from the website ➲See: **basket**

ˈshopping ˌcentre *UK* (*US* **shopping center**) *noun* [C] a place where a lot of shops have been built close together

ˈshopping ˌmall *noun* [C] a large, covered shopping area

ˌshop ˈsteward *noun* [C] **POLITICS** a worker chosen by workers in a factory or business to represent them in discussions with the management, usually a member of a trade union

shore¹ /ʃɔːʳ/ *noun* [C, U] **GEOGRAPHY** the area of land along the edge of the sea or a lake *They had to abandon the boat and swim back to shore.*

shore² /ʃɔːʳ/ *verb*
shore sth up *phrasal verb* to help or improve something that is likely to fail

shorn /ʃɔːn/ *past participle of* shear

O-ᵚ**short¹** /ʃɔːt/ *adjective* **1** DISTANCE having a small distance from one end to the other *short, brown hair* ○ *short legs* ○ *a short skirt* **2** TIME continuing for a small amount of time *a short visit* ○ *There's a short break for coffee between classes.* **3** BOOK A short book or other piece of writing has few pages or words. *a short article/story* **4** PERSON A short person is not as tall as most people. *She's short and slim with dark hair.* **5** NOT HAVING ENOUGH not having enough of something *I'm a bit* ***short of*** *money at the moment.* ○ *Would you like to play? We're a couple of people short.* ○ *He seemed a bit* ***short of breath*** (= having difficulty breathing). **6 be short for sth** to be a shorter way of saying the same thing *'Mick' is short for 'Michael'.* **7 be short with sb** to talk to someone quickly in an angry or rude way •**shortness** *noun* [U] ➲See also: in the long/short **run²**

short² /ʃɔːt/ *adverb* **1 short of doing sth** without doing something *He did everything he could to get the money, short of robbing a bank.* **2 stop short of sth/doing sth** to almost do something but decide not to do it *She stopped short of accusing him of lying.* **3 fall short of sth** to not reach a particular level, but only by a small amount *Sales for the first half of this year fell just short of the target.* **4 cut sth short** to have to stop doing something before it is finished *They had to cut the holiday short when her mother was taken ill.*

short³ /ʃɔːt/ *noun* **1 in short** in a few words *In short, we need more staff.* **2** [C] a short film **3 FOOD** [C] *UK* a small amount of a strong alcoholic drink like whisky

WORD PARTNERS FOR ***shortage***

an **acute/chronic/desperate/serious** shortage • a shortage **of** sth

shortage /ˈʃɔːtɪdʒ/ *noun* [C] when there is not enough of something *a* ***shortage of*** *nurses* ○ *food shortages*

shortbread /ˈʃɔːtbred/ *noun* [U] **FOOD** a hard, sweet cake

short-circuit /ˌʃɔːtˈsɜːkɪt/ *noun* [C] **PHYSICS** a fault in an electrical connection •**short-circuit** *verb* [I, T]

shortcoming /ˈʃɔːtˌkʌmɪŋ/ *noun* [C] a fault [**usually plural**] *I like him despite his shortcomings.*

S

shortcut (*also UK* ˌ**short** ˈ**cut**) /ˈʃɔːtkʌt/ *noun* [C] **1** a quicker and more direct way of getting somewhere or doing something *I took **a shortcut** through the car park.* **2 COMPUTING** In computing, a shortcut is a quick way to start or use a computer program. *a shortcut key*

shorten /ˈʃɔːtᵊn/ *verb* [I, T] to become shorter or to make something shorter *Smoking shortens your life.*

shortfall /ˈʃɔːtfɔːl/ *noun* [C] the difference between the amount that is needed and the smaller amount that is available *a shortfall in government spending*

shorthand /ˈʃɔːthænd/ *noun* [U] a fast way of writing using abbreviations and symbols

short-haul /ˈʃɔːthɔːl/ *adjective* travelling a short distance *a **short-haul flight***

shortlist /ˈʃɔːtlɪst/ *noun* [C] *UK* a list of people who are competing for a prize, job, etc, who have already been chosen from a larger list *to be **on the shortlist*** •**shortlist** *verb* [T] *UK shortlisted candidates*

short-lived /ˌʃɔːtˈlɪvd/ *adjective* only lasting for a short time

shortly /ˈʃɔːtli/ *adverb* **1** If something is going to happen shortly, it will happen soon. *Our plans for the next year will be announced shortly.* **2 shortly after/before sth** a short time after or before something *He left here shortly after midnight.*

short-range /ˌʃɔːtˈreɪndʒ/ *adjective* intended to go a short distance *a short-range missile*

shorts /ʃɔːts/ *noun* [plural] **1** [SHORT TROUSERS] a very short pair of trousers that stop above the knees *T-shirt and shorts* ○ *cycling shorts* **2** [UNDERWEAR] *US* men's underwear to wear under trousers ➲See also: **boxers**

short-sighted /ˌʃɔːtˈsaɪtɪd/ *adjective* **1 HEALTH** not able to see far without wearing glasses **2** not thinking enough about how an action will affect the future *a short-sighted policy*

short-term /ˌʃɔːtˈtɜːm/ *adjective* lasting a short time ***short-term memory***

short-wave /ˈʃɔːtweɪv/ *noun* [U] **PHYSICS** a system used to broadcast radio signals around the world *short-wave radio*

shot¹ /ʃɒt/ *noun* [C] **1** [GUN] when a bullet is fired from a gun *Three **shots** were **fired**.* **2 SPORT** when someone tries to score points in sports such as football by hitting or throwing the ball *Good shot!* **3** [PHOTOGRAPH] a photograph *I got a good shot of them leaving the hotel together.* **4 give sth a shot; have/take a shot at sth** *informal* to try to do something, often for the first time *I've never played football, but I'll give it a shot.* **5 HEALTH** an amount of medicine put into the body with a special needle **6 FOOD** a small amount of a strong alcoholic drink *a shot of whisky* **7 like a shot** If someone does something like a shot, they do it quickly and enthusiastically. **8 a shot in the dark** an attempt to guess something when you have no information or knowledge about it ➲See also: **long shot**

shot² /ʃɒt/ *past of* shoot

shotgun /ˈʃɒtgʌn/ *noun* [C] a long gun that fires small, metal balls

O━ **should** *strong form* /ʃʊd/ *weak form* /ʃəd/ *modal verb* **1** [BEST] used to say or ask what is the correct or best thing to do *He should have gone to the doctor.* ○ *Should I apologize to her?* **2** [EXPECT] used to say that you expect something to be true or that you expect something to happen *She should be feeling better by now.* ○ *The letter should arrive by Friday.* **3** [POSSIBLE] *formal* used to refer to a possible event in the future *Should you have any further queries, please do not hesitate to contact me.* **4 why should/shouldn't...?** used to ask or give the reason for something, especially when you are surprised or angry about it *He told me to forgive her, but why should I?* ➲See Extra help page **Modal verbs** on page Centre 34.

O━ **shoulder¹** /ˈʃəʊldəʳ/ *noun* **1 ANATOMY** [C] where your arm joins your body next to your neck *He put his arm around my shoulder.* ➲See colour picture **The Body** on page Centre 13 **2** [C] *US* (*UK* **hard shoulder**) the area on the edge of a main road, where a car can stop in an emergency **3 rub shoulders with sb** to spend time with famous people **4 a shoulder to cry on** someone who gives you sympathy when you are upset ➲See also: have a **chip¹** on your shoulder

shoulder² /ˈʃəʊldəʳ/ *verb* **shoulder the blame/burden/responsibility, etc** to accept that you are responsible for something difficult or bad

ˈ**shoulder** ˌ**bag** *noun* [C] a bag with a long strap that you hang from your shoulder

ˈ**shoulder** ˌ**blade** *noun* [C] **ANATOMY** a large, flat bone on each side of your back below your shoulder

shoulder-length /ˈʃəʊldəleŋθ/ *adjective* If your hair is shoulder-length, it goes down as far as your shoulders.

O━ **shouldn't** /ˈʃʊdᵊnt/ *short for* should not *I shouldn't have said that.*

O━ **should've** /ˈʃʊdəv/ *short for* should have *She should've finished by now.*

O━ **shout¹** /ʃaʊt/ *verb* [I, T] to say something very loudly *"Look out!" she shouted.* ○ *I was angry and I **shouted at** him.* ○ *I **shouted out** her name but she didn't hear me.*

WORD PARTNERS FOR ***shout*** *(noun)*

give a shout • a shout **of** [anger, etc] • an **angry** shout

shout² /ʃaʊt/ *noun* [C] when you say something very loudly or make a very loud sound with your voice *He was woken by a loud shout.*

shouty /ˈʃaʊti/ *adjective informal* Someone who is shouty shouts a lot because they get angry very easily.

shove /ʃʌv/ *verb* [I, T] **1** to push someone or something in a rough way *He wouldn't move, so I shoved him out of the way.* **2 shove sth into/in/under, etc** to put something somewhere in a quick, careless way *She shoved the suitcase under the bed.* •**shove** *noun* [C] *to give someone a shove* ➲See also: if/when **push²** comes to shove

shovel /ˈʃʌvᵊl/ *noun* [C] a tool with a long handle, used for digging or moving things such as soil or snow •**shovel** *verb* [I, T] *UK* **shovelling**, *past* **shovelled**, *US* **shoveling**, *past* **shoveled**

S

O- **show**[1] /ʃəʊ/ *verb past tense* **showed**, *past participle* **shown** **1** PROVE [T] If numbers, results, facts, etc show something, they prove that it is true. [+ (that)] *Research shows that 40% of the programme's viewers are aged over 55.* ○ *Sales figures showed a significant increase last month.* **2** LET SOMEONE SEE [T] to let someone look at something [+ two objects] *Show me your photos.* ○ *Show your passport to the officer.* **3 show sb what to do/how to do sth** to teach someone how to do something by explaining it or by doing it yourself while they watch *She showed me how to use the new computer system.* ○ *Have you shown him what to do?* **4** EXPRESS [T] to express a feeling so that other people are able to notice it *He hasn't shown any interest so far.* ○ *If she was upset, she certainly didn't show it.* **5** EASY TO SEE [I, T] to be easy to see, or to make something easy to see *The sadness really shows on her face.* ○ *Light-coloured carpets show the dirt.* **6 show sb into/around/round, etc** to take someone to or round a place *She showed me round the factory.* **7** IMAGE [T] If a picture, film, map, etc shows something, that thing can be seen in the picture, film, etc. *A diagram shows the levels of rainfall in different parts of the country.* **8** FILM [I, T] If a cinema shows a film or a film is showing somewhere, you can go and see it there.

show off *phrasal verb* to try to make people admire your abilities or achievements in a way which other people find annoying *He was the kind of kid who was always showing off to his classmates.*

show sb/sth off *phrasal verb* to show something or someone you are proud of to other people *I couldn't wait to show off my new ring.*

show up *phrasal verb informal* to arrive somewhere *I waited for nearly half an hour, but he didn't show up.*

show sb up *phrasal verb* to behave in a way that makes someone you are with feel embarrassed *I didn't want my parents there, showing me up in front of all my friends.*

WORD PARTNERS FOR ***show*** *(noun)*

host/present a show • a show is **broadcast/screened** • be **on** a show

show[2] /ʃəʊ/ *noun* **1** ENTERTAINMENT [C] a television or radio programme or a theatre performance *He's got his own show on Channel 5.* **2** PUBLIC EVENT [C] an event at which a group of similar things are brought together for the public to see *a fashion show* **3 a show of sth** an expression of a feeling which can be clearly seen by other people *Crowds gathered in the central square in a show of support for the government.* **4 for show** for looking at only, and not for using *The cakes are just for show - you can't eat them.* **5 on show** being shown to the public *Her designs are currently on show at the Museum of Modern Art.* ⊃See also: **chat show, game show, talk show**

ˈ**show ˌbusiness** (*also* **show biz** *informal*) *noun* [U] the entertainment industry, including films, television, theatre, etc

showcase /ˈʃəʊkeɪs/ *noun* [C] an event which is intended to show the best qualities of something *The exhibition acts as **a showcase for** British design.*

WORD PARTNERS FOR ***showdown***

face/be heading for a showdown • a showdown **between** sb and sb • a showdown **with** sb

showdown /ˈʃəʊdaʊn/ *noun* [C] an argument or fight that is intended to end a period of disagreement *Opponents of the changes are heading for **a showdown with** party leaders.*

O- **shower**[1] /ʃaʊəʳ/ *noun* [C] **1** WASH If you have or take a shower, you wash your whole body while standing under a flow of water. *I got up, **had a shower** and got dressed.* **2** BATHROOM EQUIPMENT a piece of bathroom equipment that you stand under to wash your whole body *He likes to sing **in the shower**.* ⊃See colour picture **The Bathroom** on page Centre 3 **3** RAIN a short period of rain **4 a shower of sth** a lot of small things in the air, especially falling through the air *a shower of glass*

shower[2] /ʃaʊəʳ/ *verb* [I] to wash standing under a shower

shower sb with sth *phrasal verb* to give a lot of something to someone *I was showered with gifts.*

showing /ˈʃəʊɪŋ/ *noun* **1** [C] a broadcast of a television programme at a particular time or of a film at a cinema *There's a repeat showing of Wednesday's episode on Saturday morning.* **2 a good/poor/strong, etc showing** how successful someone is in a competition, election, etc *She **made** a good **showing** in the world championships.*

showman /ˈʃəʊmən/ *noun* [C] *plural* **showmen** someone who is very good at entertaining people

shown /ʃəʊn/ *past participle of* show

show-off /ˈʃəʊɒf/ *noun* [C] someone who tries to make other people admire their abilities or achievements in a way which is annoying

showroom /ˈʃəʊruːm/ *noun* [C] a large room where you can look at large items for sale, such as cars or furniture

ˈ**show ˌtrial** *noun* [C] POLITICS a trial organized by a government for political reasons, not for real justice

shrank /ʃræŋk/ *past tense of* shrink

shrapnel /ˈʃræpnᵊl/ *noun* [U] small, sharp pieces of metal which fly through the air when a bomb explodes

shred[1] /ʃred/ *noun* [C] **1** a very small piece that has been torn from something [usually plural] *She tore the letter **to shreds**.* **2 not a shred of sth** not the smallest amount of something *There is not a shred of evidence to support his story.*

shred[2] /ʃred/ *verb* [T] **shredding**, *past* **shredded** to tear or cut something into small, thin pieces *shredded cabbage*

shrewd /ʃruːd/ *adjective* good at judging situations and making decisions which give you an advantage *a shrewd businessman* ○ *a shrewd investment* •**shrewdly** *adverb*

shriek /ʃriːk/ *verb* [I, T] to make a sudden, loud, high noise because you are afraid, surprised, excited, etc *to shriek with laughter* ○ *"It's about to explode!" she shrieked.* •**shriek** *noun* [C]

S

shrill /ʃrɪl/ *adjective* A shrill sound is very high, loud, and often unpleasant. *a shrill voice*

shrimp /ʃrɪmp/ *noun* [C] **FOOD** a small, pink, sea animal that you can eat, with a curved body and a shell

shrine /ʃraɪn/ *noun* [C] **RELIGION** a place where people go to pray because it is connected with a holy person or event

shrink[1] /ʃrɪŋk/ *verb* [I, T] *past tense* **shrank**, *past participle* **shrunk** to become smaller, or to make something smaller *My shirt shrank in the wash.* ○ *Its forests have shrunk to almost half the size they were 10 years ago.*
shrink from sth/doing sth *phrasal verb* to avoid doing something that is difficult or unpleasant *We will not shrink from using force.*

shrink[2] /ʃrɪŋk/ *noun* [C] *informal* a doctor trained to help people with mental or emotional problems

shrivel /ˈʃrɪvᵊl/ *verb* [I] *UK* **shrivelling**, *past* **shrivelled**, *US* **shriveling**, *past* **shriveled** If something shrivels, it becomes smaller, dryer, and covered in lines, often because it is old. •**shrivelled** *adjective There were a few shrivelled apples at the bottom of the bowl.*

shroud[1] /ʃraʊd/ *noun* [C] a cloth used to cover the body of a dead person

shroud[2] /ʃraʊd/ *verb* **1 be shrouded in darkness/fog/mist** to be hidden or covered by the dark/fog, etc *The island was shrouded in sea mist.* **2 be shrouded in mystery/secrecy** to be difficult to find out about or to know the truth about *Details of the president's trip remain shrouded in secrecy.*

shrub /ʃrʌb/ *noun* [C] a large plant, smaller than a tree, that has several main stems

shrubbery /ˈʃrʌbᵊri/ *noun* **1** AREA [C, U] an area of a garden with shrubs in it **2** GROUP [U] *US* shrubs considered as a group

shrug /ʃrʌg/ *verb* [I, T] **shrugging**, *past* **shrugged** to move your shoulders up and down to show that you do not care about something or that you do not know something *I told him we weren't happy with it but he just* ***shrugged*** *his* ***shoulders***. •**shrug** *noun* [C]
shrug sth off *phrasal verb* to not worry about something and treat it as not important *The team manager shrugged off criticism.*

shrunk /ʃrʌŋk/ *past participle of* shrink

shrunken /ˈʃrʌŋkən/ *adjective* having become smaller or having been made smaller *a shrunken old man*

shudder /ˈʃʌdəʳ/ *verb* [I] to shake, usually because you are thinking of something unpleasant *I still* ***shudder at*** *the thought of the risks we took.* ○ *She* ***shuddered with*** *horror.* •**shudder** *noun* [C]

shuffle /ˈʃʌfl/ *verb* **1** WALK [I] to walk slowly without lifting your feet off the floor *I heard him shuffling around downstairs.* **2** ARRANGE [I, T] If you shuffle papers or cards, you mix them or arrange them in a different order. **3** MOVE [I, T] to move your body or feet a little because you feel nervous or uncomfortable. *People starting* ***shuffling*** *their* ***feet*** *and looking at their watches.*

shun /ʃʌn/ *verb* [T] **shunning**, *past* **shunned** to avoid or ignore someone or something *He was shunned by colleagues and family alike.* ○ *She has always* ***shunned publicity***.

shunt /ʃʌnt/ *verb* [T] to move someone or something from one place to another, usually because they are not wanted *As a teenager he was shunted between different children's homes.*

O⁻**shut[1]** /ʃʌt/ *verb* [I, T] **shutting**, *past* **shut 1** CLOSE to close something, or to become closed *Shut the door.* ○ *He lay back and shut his eyes.* ○ *The lid shut with a bang.* **2** STOP SERVING *UK* (*UK/US* **close**) When a shop, restaurant, etc shuts, it stops serving customers and does not allow people to enter. *The museum shuts at 4 o'clock on a Friday.* ○ *Several schools were shut because of the bad weather.*
shut sb/sth away *phrasal verb* to put someone or something in a place from which they cannot leave or be taken away
shut (sth) down *phrasal verb* If a business or a large piece of equipment shuts down or someone shuts it down, it stops operating. *Many factories have been forced to shut down.*
shut sb/sth in (sth) *phrasal verb* to prevent someone or something from leaving a place by shutting a door or gate *We normally shut the dog in the kitchen when we go out.*
shut sth off *phrasal verb* to stop a machine working, or to stop the supply of something *Shut the engine off.* ○ *Oil supplies have been shut off.*
shut sth/sb out *phrasal verb* to stop someone or something from entering a place or from being included in something *The curtains shut out most of the light from the street.*
shut (sb) up *phrasal verb informal* to stop talking or making a noise, or to make someone do this *Just shut up and get on with your work!*
shut sb/sth up *phrasal verb* to keep a person or animal somewhere and prevent them from leaving *You can't keep it shut up in a cage all day.*

shut[2] /ʃʌt/ *adjective* [never before noun] **1** CLOSED closed *Her eyes were shut and I thought she was asleep.* **2** NOT SERVING *UK* (*UK/US* **closed**) When a shop, restaurant, etc is shut, it has stopped serving customers and does not allow people to enter it.

shutdown /ˈʃʌtdaʊn/ *noun* [C] when a business or a large piece of equipment stops operating, usually for a temporary period

shutter /ˈʃʌtəʳ/ *noun* [C] **1** WINDOW a wooden or metal cover on the outside of a window **2** CAMERA the part at the front of a camera which opens quickly to let in light when you take a photograph

shuttle[1] /ˈʃʌtl/ *noun* [C] **1** TRAVEL a bus, train, plane etc which travels regularly between two places, usually a short distance *the London-Glasgow shuttle* ○ *There's a* ***shuttle service*** *between the airport and the city centre.* **2** SPACE (*also* ˈ**space** ˌ**shuttle**) a spacecraft which can go into space and return to Earth more than once

shuttle[2] /ˈʃʌtl/ *verb* [I, T] to travel or take people regularly between the same two places *He* ***shuttles between*** *Ireland and England.*

shuttlecock /ˈʃʌtlkɒk/ *(also US* **birdie***) noun* [C] **SPORT** a small object with feathers that is used like a ball in badminton (= sport like tennis)

shy[1] /ʃaɪ/ *adjective* **shyer**, **shyest** not confident, especially about meeting or talking to new people *He was too shy to say anything to her.* •**shyly** *adverb She smiled shyly.* •**shyness** *noun* [U]

shy[2] /ʃaɪ/ *verb* [I] If a horse shies, it moves backwards suddenly because it has been frightened by something.

shy away from sth *phrasal verb* to avoid doing something, usually because you are not confident enough to do it *He tends to shy away from public speaking.*

SI /ˌesˈaɪ/ *noun* [U] **MEASURES** *abbreviation for* Système International: the international system of units used for scientific measurements

sibling /ˈsɪblɪŋ/ *noun* [C] *formal* a sister or brother

sic /sɪk/ *adverb* **(sic) LANGUAGE** used in writing after a word that you have copied to show that you know it has been spelt or used wrongly

O‒**sick**[1] /sɪk/ *adjective* **1 HEALTH** ill *He was off work sick for most of last week.* ○ *They provide care for* ***the sick***. **2 be sick HEALTH** If you are sick, food and drink comes up from your stomach and out of your mouth. *The baby was sick all down his shirt.* **3 feel sick HEALTH** to feel that the food or drink in your stomach might soon come up through your mouth *I was so nervous I felt quite sick.* **4 be sick of sth** *informal* to be bored with or annoyed about something that has been happening for a long time *I'm sick of people telling me how to run my life.* **5 It makes me sick.** *informal* something you say when you are jealous of someone *She looks fantastic whatever she wears - it makes me sick.* **6** [CRUEL] cruel and unpleasant *He's got a sick mind.* ○ *a* ***sick joke***

COMMON LEARNER ERROR

sick, ill, and **be sick**

In British English **ill** is the word that is usually used to mean 'not well'. In American English the word for this is **sick**.

He went home early because he felt ill/sick.

In British English to **be sick** is to bring food up from the stomach. Another way of saying this is the word **vomit**, which is used both in British and American English.

sick[2] /sɪk/ *noun* [U] *UK informal* food or liquid that has come up from someone's stomach and out of their mouth

sicken /ˈsɪkᵊn/ *verb* [T] to shock someone and make them very angry *Sickened by the violence, she left.*

sickening /ˈsɪkᵊnɪŋ/ *adjective* causing shock and anger *a sickening act of violence*

sickle /ˈsɪkl/ *noun* [C] **FARMING** a tool with a round blade used to cut long grass or grain crops

ˈsick ˌleave *noun* [U] **HEALTH** when you are away from your work because you are ill

sickly /ˈsɪkli/ *adjective* **1 HEALTH** weak and often ill *a sickly child* **2** unpleasant and making you feel slightly ill *a sickly smell*

sickness /ˈsɪknəs/ *noun* **1 HEALTH** [U] when you are ill *She's had three weeks off for sickness this year.* **2 HEALTH** [U] when the food or drink in your stomach come up through your mouth, or a feeling that this might happen ***morning/travel sickness*** **3 HEALTH** [C, U] a particular illness *radiation sickness*

WORD PARTNERS FOR ***side***

on the [right/left] side • the side **of** sth

O‒**side**[1] /saɪd/ *noun* [C] **1** [PART OF SOMETHING] one of the two parts that something would divide into if you drew a line down the middle *In most countries people drive* ***on*** *the right* ***side*** *of the road.* ○ *Which* ***side of*** *the bed do you sleep on?* **2** [SURFACE] a flat, outer surface of an object, especially one that is not its top, bottom, front, or back *The ingredients are listed on the side of the box.* ○ *The side of the car was badly scratched.* **3** [EDGE] one edge of something *A square has four sides.* ○ *There were chairs round the sides of the room.* **4** [NEXT TO SOMETHING] the area next to something *trees growing by the side of the road* **5** [PAPER/COIN ETC] either of the two surfaces of a thin, flat object such as a piece of paper or a coin *Write on both sides of the paper.* **6** [ARGUMENT] one of the people or groups who are arguing, fighting, or competing *Whose* ***side*** *is he* ***on?*** ○ *Whenever we argue he always* ***takes*** *Alice's* ***side*** (= gives support to Alice). **7 SPORT** *UK* the players in a sports team *He's been selected for the national side.* **8** [PART OF A SITUATION] part of a situation that can be considered or dealt with separately *She looks after the financial* ***side of things***. **9** [CHARACTER] a part of someone's character *She has a very practical side.* **10 ANATOMY** the two areas of your body from under your arms to the tops of your legs *Stand with your arms by your sides.* ○ *She lay on her side.* **11** [STORY] Someone's side of a story is the way in which they explain how something happened. *I thought I'd better listen to Clare's* ***side of the story***. ○ *So far they'd only heard the story from the wife's side.* **12** [TELEVISION/RADIO] *UK* a number on a television or radio that you can choose in order to receive a broadcast *Which side is the film on?* **13 from side to side** If something moves from side to side, it moves from left to right and back again repeatedly. *swinging from side to side* **14 side-by-side** If two things or people are side-by-side, they are next to each other. *sitting side-by-side on the sofa* **15** [RELATIVES] the part of your family who are either your mother's relatives or your father's relatives *They tend to be tall on my mother's side of the family.* **16 err on the side of caution** to be very careful instead of taking a risk or making a mistake **17 on the side** in addition to your main job *She does a bit of bar work on the side.* **18 put sth to one side** to not use or deal with something now, but keep it for a later time ➲See also: **the flip side**

side[2] /saɪd/ *verb*

side with sb *phrasal verb* to support one person or group in an argument *If ever there was any sort of argument, she'd always side with my father.*

sideboard /ˈsaɪdbɔːd/ *noun* [C] a piece of furniture with a flat top and low cupboards and

S

drawers, used for storing dishes and glasses, etc in the room you eat in

sideburns /'saɪdbɜːnz/ *noun* [**plural**] hair that grows on the sides of a man's face in front of the ear

side effect /'saɪdɪfekt/ *noun* [**C**] **1** **HEALTH** another effect that a drug has on your body in addition to the main effect for which the doctor has given you the drug *Headaches are one side effect of this drug.* **2** an unexpected result of a situation

sidekick /'saɪdkɪk/ *noun* [**C**] someone who helps, or is friends with, a more powerful and important person

sideline¹ /'saɪdlaɪn/ *noun* [**C**] a job or business in addition to your main job or business *He works in a bank but teaches English **as a sideline**.*

sideline² /'saɪdlaɪn/ *verb* [**T**] to stop someone from being included in an activity that they usually do, especially a sport [**often passive**] *He's broken his ankle and could be sidelined for weeks.*

sidelines /'saɪdlaɪnz/ *noun* [**plural**] **1** **SPORT** the outside edge of the playing area of a sport such as football *The coach was shouting instructions **from the sidelines**.* **2 on the sidelines** not really involved in something

sidelong /'saɪdlɒŋ/ *adjective* **a sidelong glance/look** a very short look at someone, moving your eyes to the side, and not looking at them directly

'side ˌmirror *US* (*UK* **wing mirror**) *noun* [**C**] a small mirror on the side of a car or truck ➲See colour picture **Car** at page Centre 7

sideshow /'saɪdʃəʊ/ *noun* [**C**] an event or activity that is considered less important than another event or activity

sidestep /'saɪdstep/ *verb* [**T**] **sidestepping**, *past* **sidestepped** to avoid talking about a subject, especially by starting to talk about something else *She neatly **sidestepped questions** about her recent divorce.*

S

sidetrack /'saɪdtræk/ *verb* [**T**] to make someone forget what they were doing or speaking about and start doing or speaking about something different [**often passive**] *Sorry, I was talking about staffing and I got sidetracked.*

sidewalk /'saɪdwɔːk/ *US* (*UK* **pavement**) *noun* [**C**] a path with a hard surface by the side of a road that people walk on

sideways /'saɪdweɪz/ *adverb* in a direction to the left or right, not forwards or backwards *He glanced sideways.*

siding /'saɪdɪŋ/ *noun* **1** RAILWAY [**C**] a short railway track, connected to a main track, where trains are kept when they are not being used **2** WALL [**U**] *US* material which covers the outside walls of a building, usually in layers

sidle /'saɪdl/ *verb* **sidle along/over/up, etc** to walk towards someone, trying not to be noticed *He sidled up to her and whispered something in her ear.*

SIDS /sɪdz/ *noun* [**U**] *US* **HEALTH** *abbreviation for* sudden infant death syndrome: the sudden death of a sleeping baby for no obvious reason ➲See: **cot death**

siege /siːdʒ/ *noun* [**C, U**] when an army or the police stand around a building or city to stop supplies from entering it, in order to force the people inside to stop fighting *The city is **under siege** from rebel forces.*

siesta /si'estə/ *noun* [**C**] a short period of rest or sleep in the afternoon

sieve /sɪv/ *noun* [**C**] a piece of kitchen equipment with a wire or plastic net which separates large pieces of food from liquids or powders *Pass the sauce through a sieve to remove any lumps.* ➲See colour picture **The Kitchen** on page Centre 2 •**sieve** *verb* [**T**]

sift /sɪft/ *verb* [**T**] **1** **FOOD** to put flour, sugar, etc through a sieve (= wire net shaped like a bowl) to break up large pieces *Sift the flour into a large bowl.* **2** (*also* **sift through**) to carefully look at every part of something in order to find something *to **sift through** evidence*

sigh /saɪ/ *verb* [**I, T**] to breathe out slowly and noisily, often because you are annoyed or unhappy *He sighed deeply and sat down.* •**sigh** *noun* [**C**] *a **sigh of relief***

O⁼**sight¹** /saɪt/ *noun* **1** **BIOLOGY** [**U**] the ability to use your eyes to see *Doctors managed to save his sight.* **2 the sight of sb/sth** when you see someone or something *The sight of so much blood had shocked him.* ○ *informal* I ***can't stand the sight of*** *her* (= I hate her). ➲See Common Learner Error at **view** **3** AREA SEEN [**U**] the area that it is possible for you to see *I looked for her but she was nowhere **in sight**.* ○ *I was able to park **within sight of** the house.* ○ *Security guards were waiting **out of sight*** (= where they could not be seen). **4** VIEW [**C**] something which you see, especially something interesting *the **sights and sounds** of the market* **5 at first sight** when you first see or hear about something or someone *It may, at first sight, seem a surprising choice.* **6 the sights** the beautiful or interesting places in a city or country, that a lot of people visit *He took me around New York and showed me the sights.* **7 lose sight of sth** to forget about an important idea or fact because you are thinking too much about other, less important things *We mustn't lose sight of the original aims of this project.* **8 set your sights on sth** to decide to achieve something *She's set her sights on becoming an actress.*

sight² /saɪt/ *verb* [**T**] to see something that it is difficult to see or that you have been looking for [**often passive**] *The ship was last sighted off the French coast at 8 o'clock yesterday evening.*

-sighted /'saɪtɪd/ **HEALTH** used after a word describing a person's ability to see ***long-/short-sighted*** ○ ***partially-sighted***

sighted /'saɪtɪd/ *adjective* **HEALTH** A sighted person is able to see.

sighting /'saɪtɪŋ/ *noun* [**C**] when you see something that is rare or unusual *UFO sightings*

WORD PARTNERS FOR ***sightseeing***

do some/go sightseeing • a sightseeing **tour/trip**

sightseeing /ˈsaɪtsiːɪŋ/ *noun* [U] the activity of visiting places which are interesting because they are historical, famous, etc *a **sightseeing tour** of London* •**sightseer** /ˈsaɪtˌsiːəʳ/ *noun* [C] a person who goes sightseeing

WORD PARTNERS FOR ***sign***

see/take sth as a sign • **show** (no) signs of sth • a **clear/sure** sign • a sign **of** sth

O⊶**sign¹** /saɪn/ *noun* [C] **1** [PROOF] something which shows that something is happening *Flowers are the first **sign of** Spring.* [+ **(that)**] *It's a sign that things are improving.* ○ *Staff are **showing signs of** strain.* **2** [NOTICE] a symbol or message in a public place which gives information or instructions *a **road sign*** ○ *a 'no-smoking' sign* **3** [SYMBOL] a symbol which has a particular meaning *a dollar/pound sign* ○ *the sign of the cross* **4** [MOVEMENT] a movement you make to give someone information or tell them what to do ➲See also: **star sign**

O⊶**sign²** /saɪn/ *verb* [I, T] to write your name on something to show that you wrote/painted, etc it or to show that you agree to it *He signs his letters 'Prof. James D. Nelson'.* ○ *to **sign a contract/treaty***

sign for sth *phrasal verb UK* **SPORT** If a player signs for a football team, he signs a formal agreement saying that he will play for that team.

sign (sb) in *phrasal verb* to write your name or someone else's name in a book when you arrive at a building such as an office or hotel

sign on *phrasal verb* **1** [START WORK] to sign a document saying that you will work for someone *She's **signed on with** a temp agency.* **2** [NOT IN WORK] *UK* to sign a form at a government office to say that you do not have a job and that you want to receive money from the government

sign (sb) out *phrasal verb* to write your name or someone else's name in a book when leaving a building such as an office or factory

sign up *phrasal verb* to arrange to do an organized activity *I've **signed up for** evening classes at the local college.*

signal¹ /ˈsɪgnᵊl/ *noun* [C] **1** [ACTION] a movement, light, or sound which gives information, or tells people what to do *Don't move until I **give the signal**.* **2** [WAVE] a series of light waves or sound waves which are sent to a radio or television **3** [PROOF] something which shows that something else exists or is likely to happen *The changing colour of the leaves on the trees is a signal that it will soon be autumn.* **4** [TRAINS] a piece of equipment which tells trains to stop or to continue **5** [VEHICLES/PEOPLE] *US* a piece of equipment that shows people or vehicles when to stop, go, or move carefully *a **traffic signal***

signal² /ˈsɪgnᵊl/ *verb* [I, T] *UK* **signalling**, *past* **signalled**, *US* **signaling**, *past* **signaled** **1** [ACTION] to make a movement which gives information or tells people what to do *He **signalled for** them to be quiet.* [+ **to do sth**] *He signalled the driver to stop.* **2** [INTENTION] to show that you intend or are ready to do something [+ **(that)**] *The US signalled that they were ready to enter talks.*

signatory /ˈsɪgnətᵊri/ *noun* [C] **POLITICS** *formal* a person or country that signs an official document

signature /ˈsɪgnətʃəʳ/ *noun* [C] your name written in your own way which is difficult for someone else to copy

WORD PARTNERS FOR ***significance***

play down /realize/understand the significance of sth • **have** significance for sb • be **of** [great/little/major/no] significance

significance /sɪgˈnɪfɪkᵊns/ *noun* [U] the importance or meaning of something *I still don't understand **the significance of** his remark.*

O⊶**significant** /sɪgˈnɪfɪkᵊnt/ *adjective* important or noticeable *These measures will save a significant amount of money.* ○ *It is significant that Falkner did not attend the meeting himself.* ➲Opposite **insignificant** •**significantly** *adverb*

sigˌnificant ˈfigures *UK* (*US* **sigˌnificant ˈdigits**) *noun* [plural] **MATHEMATICS** the numbers used to write a number to be as exact as is needed *2.3945 to two significant figures is 2.4.*

signify /ˈsɪgnɪfaɪ/ *verb* [T] to be a sign of something *Red signifies danger.*

signing /ˈsaɪnɪŋ/ *noun* [C] **1** **SPORT** *UK* a player who has joined a sports team or a musician who has joined a record company **2** the act of signing something [**usually singular**] *the signing of the declaration*

ˈsign ˌlanguage *noun* [C, U] **LANGUAGE** a system of communication using hand movements, used by people who are deaf (= cannot hear)

signpost /ˈsaɪnpəʊst/ *noun* [C] a sign by the side of the road that gives information about routes and distances

Sikh /siːk/ *noun* [C] **RELIGION** someone who believes in an Indian religion based on belief in a single god and on the teachings of Guru Nanak •**Sikh** *adjective a Sikh temple* •**Sikhism** *noun* [U]

WORD PARTNERS FOR ***silence***

in silence • **deafening/stunned** silence • **break** the silence • **lapse into** silence • silence **falls/descends/ensues**

O⊶**silence¹** /ˈsaɪləns/ *noun* **1** [NO SOUND] [U] when there is no sound *The three men ate **in silence**.* ○ *No sound **broke the silence** of the wintry landscape.* **2** [NO TALKING] [U] when someone says nothing about a particular subject *She **ended** her **silence** yesterday and spoke to a TV reporter about the affair.* **3** [PERIOD OF TIME] [C] a period of time when there is no sound or no talking *an awkward/embarrassed silence*

silence² /ˈsaɪləns/ *verb* [T] **1** [STOP SOUND] to stop something making a sound or stop someone from talking, often about a particular subject *He silenced the alarm.* ○ *Opponents of the government would be silenced or thrown into prison.* **2** [STOP CRITICISM] to stop people from criticizing you by giving a good argument to support your opinion *He seems to have **silenced his critics**.*

S

silencer /ˈsaɪlənsəʳ/ *noun* [C] **1** VEHICLE UK (*US* **muffler**) a part of a vehicle that reduces noise **2** GUN a piece of equipment that you use on a gun to reduce the sound of it firing

silent /ˈsaɪlənt/ *adjective* **1** NO SOUND without any sound *The building was dark and silent.* ○ *At last the guns **fell silent**.* **2** NO TALKING without talking *He remains silent about his plans.* **3** LETTER If a letter in a word is silent, it is not pronounced. *The 'p' in 'receipt' is silent.* •**silently** *adverb*

silhouette /ˌsɪluˈet/ *noun* [C, U] the shape of something when the light is behind it so that you cannot see any details *He saw a woman **in silhouette**.* •**silhouetted** *adjective the roofs **silhouetted against** the night sky*

silica /ˈsɪlɪkə/ *noun* [U] **GEOLOGY** a mineral which exists in various forms, including sand, quartz and flint, and which is used to make glass and cement

silicon /ˈsɪlɪkən/ *noun* [U] **CHEMISTRY** a chemical element used in making electronic equipment such as computers, and materials such as glass and concrete (symbol **Si**) *a **silicon chip***

silk /sɪlk/ *noun* [U] a type of cloth which is light and smooth *a silk dress/shirt*

silken /ˈsɪlkᵊn/ *adjective literary* soft and smooth, like silk *her silken skin*

silky /ˈsɪlki/ *adjective* soft and smooth, like silk *a large, silky, grey cat*

silly /ˈsɪli/ *adjective* **1** STUPID stupid *silly games/hats* ○ *I feel silly in this hat.* ○ *It's a bit silly spending all that money on something we don't need.* **2** UNIMPORTANT small and not important *She gets upset over such silly things.* •**silliness** *noun* [U]

silt /sɪlt/ *noun* [U] **GEOLOGY** sand and clay that has been carried along by a river and is left on land

silver¹ /ˈsɪlvəʳ/ *noun* **1** **CHEMISTRY** [U] a valuable, shiny, grey-white metal used to make coins and jewellery (symbol **Ag**) *silver and gold* ○ *a solid silver ring* **2** OBJECTS [U] objects made of silver **3** PRIZE [C] a silver medal (= a small, round disc given to someone for finishing second in a race or competition)

silver² /ˈsɪlvəʳ/ *adjective* **1** OBJECT made of silver *a silver coin* ○ *a silver necklace* **2** COLOUR being the colour of silver *a silver sports car*

ˌsilver ˈmedal *noun* [C] a small, round disc given to someone for finishing second in a race or competition

silverware /ˈsɪlvəweəʳ/ *noun* [U] *US* (*UK* **cutlery**) knives, forks, spoons, etc that are used for eating

ˌsilver ˈwedding anniversary *noun* [C] the date that is 25 years after the day that two people married

silvery /ˈsɪlvᵊri/ *adjective* shiny and pale like silver *a silvery light*

sim card /ˈsɪmkɑːd/ *noun* [C] a plastic card in a mobile phone that contains information about you and makes you able to use the phone

similar /ˈsɪmɪləʳ/ *adjective* Something which is similar to something else has many things the same, although it is not exactly the same. *The two houses are remarkably similar.* ○ *The style of cooking is **similar to** that of Northern India.* ➲Opposite **dissimilar**

similarity /ˌsɪmɪˈlærəti/ *noun* [C, U] when two things or people are similar, or a way in which they are similar *There are a number of **similarities between** the two systems.* ○ *He bears a striking **similarity to** his grandfather.*

similarly /ˈsɪmɪləli/ *adverb* in a similar way

simile /ˈsɪmɪli/ *noun* [C] **LANGUAGE** a phrase which compares one thing to something else, using the words 'like' or 'as', for example 'as white as snow'

simmer /ˈsɪməʳ/ *verb* [I, T] **FOOD** to gently cook a liquid or something with liquid in it so that it is very hot, but does not boil

simple /ˈsɪmpl/ *adjective* **1** EASY not difficult to do or to understand [+ **to do sth**] *It's very simple to use.* ○ *Just mix all the ingredients together - it's as simple as that.* **2** NOT COMPLICATED not complicated or containing details which are not necessary *a simple life* ○ *a simple black dress* (= dress without decoration) **3** IMPORTANT used to describe the one important fact, truth, etc *We chose her for the simple reason that she's the best person for the job.*

ˌsimple ˈeye *noun* [C] **BIOLOGY** a basic type of eye with only one lens, found in some insects ➲Compare **compound eye**

ˌsimple ˈleaf *noun* [C] **BIOLOGY** a type of leaf which is formed of one leaf on a leaf stalk ➲Compare **compound leaf**

ˌsimple ˈsugar *noun* [C] **CHEMISTRY** a monosaccharide (= type of carbohydrate, such as glucose and fructose, formed of molecules that cannot be broken down into any simpler form)

simplicity /sɪmˈplɪsəti/ *noun* [U] **1** NOT COMPLICATED when something is not complicated and has few details or little decoration *I admire the simplicity of his designs.* **2** EASY when something is easy to understand

simplify /ˈsɪmplɪfaɪ/ *verb* [T] to make something less complicated or easier to do or to understand *We need to simplify the instructions.* •**simplification** /ˌsɪmplɪfɪˈkeɪʃᵊn/ *noun* [C, U]

simplistic /sɪmˈplɪstɪk/ *adjective* making something complicated seem simple by ignoring many of the details *a simplistic explanation*

simply /ˈsɪmpli/ *adverb* **1** EMPHASIS used to emphasize what you are saying *We simply don't have the time.* **2** ONLY only *A lot of people miss out on this opportunity simply because they don't know about it.* **3** NOT COMPLICATED in a way which is not complicated or difficult to understand *simply prepared food*

simulate /ˈsɪmjəleɪt/ *verb* [T] to do or make something which behaves or looks like something real but which is not real *The company uses a computer to simulate crash tests of its new cars.* •**simulation** /ˌsɪmjəˈleɪʃᵊn/ *noun* [C, U]

simulator /ˈsɪmjəleɪtəʳ/ *noun* [C] a machine on which people can practise operating a vehicle or an aircraft without having to drive or fly *a **flight simulator***

simultaneous /ˌsɪmᵊl'teɪniəs/ *adjective* If two or more things are simultaneous, they happen or exist at the same time. *simultaneous translation* •**simultaneously** *adverb It was broadcast simultaneously in Britain and France.*

WORD PARTNERS FOR ***sin***

commit a sin • the sin **of** [pride/greed, etc

sin¹ /sɪn/ *noun* **1 RELIGION** [C, U] something which is against the rules of a religion ***the sin of pride*** **2** [no plural] *informal* something that you should not do because it is morally wrong *You've only got one life and it's a sin to waste it.*

sin² /sɪn/ *verb* [I] **sinning**, *past* **sinned RELIGION** to do something that is against the rules of a religion •**sinner** *noun* [C] someone who does something against the rules of a religion

O-■ **since¹** /sɪns/ *adverb, preposition* from a time in the past until a later time or until now *They've been waiting since March.* ○ *The factory had been closed since the explosion.* ○ *I've felt fine ever since.*

COMMON LEARNER ERROR

since or **for?**

When you talk about the beginning of a period of time, use **since**.

I have lived here since 1997.

When you talk about the whole period of time, use **for**.

I have lived here for five years.

~~*I have lived here since five years.*~~

O-■ **since²** /sɪns/ *conjunction* **1** TIME from a time in the past until a later time or until now *He's been much happier since he started his new job.* ○ *I've known Tim since he was seven.* **2** BECAUSE because *He drove quite slowly since we had plenty of time.*

sincere /sɪn'sɪəʳ/ *adjective* **1** honest and saying or showing what you really feel or believe *He seems to be sincere.* ➲Opposite **insincere 2 sincere apologies/thanks, etc** *formal* used to add emphasis when you are expressing a feeling *The family wishes to express their sincere thanks to all the staff at the hospital.* •**sincerity** /sɪn'serəti/ *noun* [U] *No one doubted his sincerity.*

sincerely /sɪn'sɪəli/ *adverb* **1** in a sincere way *I **sincerely hope** that this never happens again.* **2 Yours sincerely** *formal* used at the end of formal letters where you know the name of the person you are writing to

sine /saɪn/ *noun* [C] **MATHEMATICS** in a triangle that has one angle of 90°, the ratio of the length of the side opposite an angle less than 90° divided by the length of the hypotenuse (= the side opposite the 90° angle) ➲Compare **cosine**

sinful /'sɪnfᵊl/ *adjective* **RELIGION** against the rules of a religion or morally wrong *sinful thoughts*

O-■ **sing** /sɪŋ/ *verb* [I, T] *past tense* **sang**, *past participle* **sung MUSIC** to make musical sounds with your voice *They all sang 'Happy Birthday' to him.* ○ *She sings in the church choir.*

singer /'sɪŋəʳ/ *noun* [C] **MUSIC** someone who sings *a jazz singer*

singing /'sɪŋɪŋ/ *noun* [U] **MUSIC** the activity of singing

O-■ **single¹** /'sɪŋgl/ *adjective* **1** ONE [**always before noun**] only one *There was a single light in the corner of the room.* **2 every single** used to emphasize that you are talking about each one of a group or series *I call him every single day.* **3 SOCIETY** not married *He's young and single.* ➲See Common Learner Error at **married 4 SOCIETY** [**always before noun**] looking after your children alone without a partner or the children's other parent *a **single mother*** ○ *a **single-parent family*** **5** FOR ONE [**always before noun**] for only one person *a **single bed***

single² /'sɪŋgl/ *noun* [C] **1 MUSIC** a record or CD which includes only one main song **2** TICKET *UK* (*US* **one-way ticket**) a ticket for a journey that is from one place to another but not back again *Could I have a single to London, please?*

single³ /'sɪŋgl/ *verb*

single sb/sth out *phrasal verb* to choose one person or thing from a group to criticize or praise them *The report **singled** him **out for** special criticism.*

single-handedly /ˌsɪŋgl'hændɪdli/ (*also* **single-handed**) *adverb* on your own, without anyone's help *After his partner left, he kept the business going single-handedly.* •**single-handed** /ˌsɪŋgl'hændɪd/ *adjective* [**always before noun**] *a single-handed round-the-world yacht race*

single-minded /ˌsɪŋgl'maɪndɪd/ *adjective* very determined to achieve something *She had a single-minded determination to succeed in her career.*

ˌsingle 'parent (*UK* **lone parent**) *noun* [C] **SOCIETY** someone who has a child or children but no husband, wife or partner that lives with them

singles /'sɪŋglz/ *noun* [U] **SPORT** a game in sports such as tennis, in which one person plays against another *He won the men's singles title two years running.*

singly /'sɪŋgli/ *adverb* separately or one at a time *We don't sell them singly, only in packs of four or ten.*

singular /'sɪŋgjələʳ/ *adjective* **1 LANGUAGE** The singular form of a word is used to talk about one person or thing. For example 'woman' is the singular form of 'women'. **2** *formal* very special, or found only in one person or situation *a landscape of singular beauty*

the singular /'sɪŋgjələʳ/ *noun* **LANGUAGE** the singular form of a word

singularly /'sɪŋgjələli/ *adverb formal* very *Fulbright was singularly uninterested in his comments.*

sinister /'sɪnɪstəʳ/ *adjective* making you feel that something bad or evil might happen *a sinister figure dressed in black*

O-■ **sink¹** /sɪŋk/ *verb past* **sank**, *also US* **sunk**, *past participle* **sunk 1** WATER [I, T] to go down or make something go down below the surface of water and not come back up *The Titanic sank after hitting an iceberg.* **2** SOFT SUBSTANCE [I, T] to go down, or make something go down, into something soft *My feet keep sinking into the*

S

sand. **3** [MOVE DOWN] [I] to move down slowly *The sun sank below the horizon.*

sink in *phrasal verb* If an unpleasant or surprising fact sinks in, you gradually start to believe it and understand what effect it will have on you. *It still hasn't sunk in that I'll never see her again.*

sink sth into sth *phrasal verb* to spend a large amount of money in a business or other piece of work *Millisat has already sunk $25 million into the Hong Kong project.*

sink into sth *phrasal verb* to slowly move into a sitting or lying position, in a relaxed or tired way *I just want to go home and sink into a hot bath.*

sink² /sɪŋk/ *noun* [C] a bowl that is fixed to the wall in a kitchen or bathroom that you wash dishes or your hands, etc in ➲See colour picture **The Kitchen** on page Centre 2, **The Bathroom** on page Centre 3

sinus /ˈsaɪnəs/ *noun* [C] **ANATOMY** one of the spaces inside the head that are connected to the back of the nose

sip /sɪp/ *verb* [I, T] **sipping**, *past* **sipped** to drink, taking only a small amount at a time *She sipped her champagne.* •**sip** *noun* [C] *He **took a sip of** his coffee and then continued.*

siphon¹ /ˈsaɪfᵊn/ *noun* [C] a piece of equipment for moving liquid from one place to another

siphon² /ˈsaɪfᵊn/ *verb* [T] **1** [LIQUID] to remove liquid from a container using a siphon **2** [TAKE] (*also* **siphon off**) to dishonestly take money from an organization or other supply over a period of time

sir /sɜːʳ/ *noun* **1** [POLITE NAME] (*also* **Sir**) You call a man 'sir' when you are speaking to him politely. *Excuse me, sir, is this seat taken?* **2** [FORMAL LETTER] You write 'Sir' at the beginning of a formal letter to a man when you do not know his name. *Dear Sir, I am writing to...* **3** **Sir** a title used in the UK before the name of a man who has been officially respected or who has a high social rank *Sir Cliff Richard*

WORD PARTNERS FOR ***siren***

a siren **goes off/sounds** • a siren **blares/wails** • a **police** siren

siren /ˈsaɪərən/ *noun* [C] a piece of equipment that makes a loud sound as a warning *a police siren*

sister /ˈsɪstəʳ/ *noun* [C] **1** **SOCIETY** a girl or woman who has the same parents as you *an older/younger sister* ○ *my big/little sister* **2** **RELIGION** (*also* **Sister**) a nun (= woman who lives in a female religious group) *Sister Bridget* **3** **HEALTH** (*also* **Sister**) a female nurse in the UK who is responsible for a hospital ward (= an area of a hospital containing beds for ill people) **4** a woman who is a member of the same race, religious group, organization, etc

sister-in-law /ˈsɪstᵊrɪnlɔː/ *noun* [C] *plural* **sisters-in-law** the woman married to your brother, or the sister of your husband or wife

sisterly /ˈsɪstəli/ *adjective* experienced by or for a sister *sisterly love*

sit /sɪt/ *verb* **sitting**, *past* **sat** **1** [BODY POSITION] [I] to be in a position with the weight of your body on your bottom and the top part of your body up, for example, on a chair *Emma was **sitting on** a stool.* ○ *The children **sat at** the table by the window.* ○ *We **sat by** the river and had a picnic.* **2** [MOVE BODY] [I] (*also* **sit down**) to move your body into a sitting position after you have been standing *She came over and **sat beside** him.* ○ *She **sat down on** the grass.* ➲See colour picture **Phrasal Verbs** on page Centre 16 **3** **sit sb down/at/in, etc** to make someone sit somewhere *She sat me down and told me the bad news.* ○ *I thought we'd sit the children at the end of the table.* **4** [STAY] [I] to stay in one place for a long time and not be used *He hardly ever drives the car. It just sits in the garage.* **5** [MEETING] [I] If a court, parliament, etc sits, it has a meeting to do its work. *The board will be sitting next week.* **6** **EDUCATION** [T] *UK* to take a test or exam *The changes will affect many students sitting their exams this summer.* ➲See also: sit on the **fence**¹

sit about/around *phrasal verb* to spend time sitting down and doing very little [+ **doing sth**] *He just sits around all day watching television.*

sit back *phrasal verb* **1** [RELAX] to relax in a chair so that your back is against the back of the chair *Just sit back and enjoy the show.* **2** [DO NOTHING] to wait for something to happen without making any effort to do anything yourself *You can't just sit back and expect someone else to deal with the problem.*

sit in *phrasal verb* to go to a meeting or class to watch *I **sat in on** a couple of classes before choosing a course.*

sit sth out *phrasal verb* **1** [NOT DO] to not do an activity such as a game or dance because you are tired or have an injury *I think I'll sit out the next dance.* **2** [WAIT] to wait for something unpleasant to finish before you do anything *The government is prepared to sit out the strike rather than agree to union demands.*

sit through sth *phrasal verb* to stay until the end of a meeting, performance, etc that is very long or boring *We had to sit through two hours of speeches.*

sit up *phrasal verb* **1** [MOVEMENT] to move your body to a sitting position after you have been lying down *I sat up and opened my eyes.* **2** [STAY AWAKE] to stay awake and not go to bed although it is late [+ **doing sth**] *We sat up talking all night.*

sitar /ˈsɪtɑːʳ/ *noun* [C] **MUSIC** a South Asian musical instrument with a round body, a long neck and two sets of strings

sitcom /ˈsɪtkɒm/ *noun* [C, U] a funny television programme that is about the same group of people every week in different situations

site¹ /saɪt/ *noun* **1** [HISTORY] [C] the place where something important happened in the past *a **historic site*** ○ *the site of a battle* **2** [AREA] [C] an area that is used for something or where something happens *a **building site*** **3** **on site** inside a factory, office building, etc *There are two restaurants on site.* ○ *They provide on-site childcare facilities for employees.* **4** **INTERNET** [C] *short for* website (= an area on the Internet where information about a particular subject, organization, etc can be found)

site² /saɪt/ *verb formal* **site sth in/on, etc** to build something in a particular place [**often passive**] *The company's head office is sited in Geneva.*

sitter /ˈsɪtəʳ/ *noun* [C] *mainly US* a babysitter (= someone who looks after children when their parents go out)

sitting /ˈsɪtɪŋ/ *noun* [C] **1** MEETING a meeting of a parliament, court, etc *a late-night sitting of parliament* **2** MEAL one of the times when a meal is served to a large group of people who cannot all eat at the same time

ˈsitting ˌroom *noun* [C] *UK* the room in a house where people sit to relax and, for example, watch television

situated /ˈsɪtjueɪtɪd/ *adjective formal* **be situated in/on/by, etc** to be in a particular place *a hotel situated by Lake Garda*

WORD PARTNERS FOR ***situation***

bring about/rectify/improve a situation • a situation **arises/deteriorates/worsens** • a **complicated/dangerous/difficult/stressful** situation • **in a** situation

O⌐ **situation** /ˌsɪtjuˈeɪʃᵊn/ *noun* [C] **1** SOMETHING HAPPENING/EXISTING the set of things that are happening and the conditions that exist at a particular time and place *the economic/political situation* ○ *He's **in a** difficult **situation**.* **2** POSITION *formal* the position of a town, building, etc *The park's situation was perfect.*

O⌐ **six** /sɪks/ the number 6

O⌐ **sixteen** /ˌsɪkˈstiːn/ the number 16 •**sixteenth** 16th written as a word

sixth¹ /sɪksθ/ 6th written as a word

sixth² /sɪksθ/ *noun* [C] one of six equal parts of something; 1/6

ˈsixth ˌform *noun* [C] EDUCATION in Britain, the part of a school for students between the ages of 16 and 18

O⌐ **sixty** /ˈsɪksti/ **1** the number 60 **2 the sixties** the years from 1960 to 1969 **3 be in your sixties** to be aged between 60 and 69 •**sixtieth** 60th written as a word

sizable /ˈsaɪzəbl/ *adjective another spelling of* sizeable

WORD PARTNERS FOR ***size***

take/wear a size [10/39, etc] • **come in** [all/different/various, etc sizes]

O⌐ **size¹** /saɪz/ *noun* **1** HOW BIG [C, U] how big or small something is *It's an area about the size of Oxford.* ○ *The size of some of those trees is incredible* (= they are very large). **2** MEASURES [C] one of the different measurements in which things, for example clothes, food containers, etc are made *a size 10 skirt* ○ ***What size** shoes do you **take**?* ○ *I usually buy the 1.5 litre size.* ➲See also: all shapes (**shape**¹) and sizes

size² /saɪz/ *verb*

size sb/sth up *phrasal verb* to look at someone or think about something carefully before making a judgment *I could see her trying to size me up.*

sizeable (*also* **sizable**) /ˈsaɪzəbl/ *adjective* quite large *a sizeable crowd*

-sized /saɪzd/ *suffix* used at the end of a word to mean 'of a particular size' *a medium-sized pizza* ○ *a good-sized bedroom*

sizzle /ˈsɪzl/ *verb* [I] to make the sound of food cooking in hot oil

skanky /ˈskæŋki/ *adjective informal* very unpleasant or dirty

skate¹ /skeɪt/ *noun* [C] **1** SPORT (*also* **roller skate**) a boot with wheels on the bottom, used for moving across the ground *a pair of skates* **2** SPORT (*also* **ice skate**) a boot with a metal part on the bottom, used for moving across ice ➲See colour picture **Sports 1** on page Centre 14 **3 get/put your skates on** *UK informal* used to tell someone to hurry

skate² /skeɪt/ *verb* [I] SPORT to move using skates •**skater** *noun* [C] •**skating** *noun* [U]

skateboard /ˈskeɪtbɔːd/ *noun* [C] SPORT a board with wheels on the bottom, that you stand on and move forward by pushing one foot on the ground ➲See colour picture **Sports 1** on page Centre 14

skateboarding /ˈskeɪtbɔːdɪŋ/ *noun* [U] SPORT the activity of moving using a skateboard ➲See colour picture **Sports 1** on page Centre 14

skeletal /ˈskelɪtᵊl/ *adjective* like a skeleton, or relating to skeletons

skeleton /ˈskelɪtᵊn/ *noun* **1** ANATOMY, BIOLOGY [C] the structure made of all the bones in the body of a person or animal **2 a skeleton crew/staff/service** the smallest number of people that you need to keep an organization working **3 have a skeleton in the cupboard** *UK* (*US* **have a skeleton in the closet**) to have an embarrassing or unpleasant secret about something that happened in the past

skeptic /ˈskeptɪk/ *noun* [C] *US spelling of* sceptic

skeptical /ˈskeptɪkᵊl/ *adjective US spelling of* sceptical

skepticism /ˈskeptɪsɪzᵊm/ *noun* [U] *US spelling of* scepticism

sketch¹ /sketʃ/ *noun* [C] **1** ART a picture that you draw quickly and with few details *He **did** a quick **sketch** of the cat.* **2** ACTING a short piece of acting about a funny situation **3** DESCRIPTION a short description of something without many details

sketch² /sketʃ/ *verb* [T] ART to draw a sketch *I sketched a map for him on a scrap of paper.*

sketch sth out *phrasal verb* to give a short description with few details, especially of an idea or plan *I've sketched out some ideas for my new book.*

sketchy /ˈsketʃi/ *adjective* with few details *Reports about the accident are still sketchy.*

ski¹ /skiː/ *noun* [C] *plural* **skis** SPORT one of a pair of long, thin pieces of wood or plastic that you wear on the bottom of boots to move over snow ➲See colour picture **Sports 1** on page Centre 14

ski² /skiː/ *verb* [I] **skiing**, *past* **skied** SPORT to move over snow wearing skis •**skier** *noun* [C] •**skiing** *noun* [U] *I'd like to **go skiing** in Switzerland.* ➲See also: **water-skiing** ➲See colour picture **Sports 1** on page Centre 14

skid /skɪd/ *verb* [I] **skidding**, *past* **skidded** If a vehicle skids, it slides along a surface and you cannot control it. *The car skidded on ice and hit a tree.* •**skid** *noun* [C]

S

skies /skaɪz/ *noun* [**plural**] the sky in a particular place or in a particular state *beautiful, clear, blue skies*

skilful *UK* (*US* **skillful**) /ˈskɪlfəl/ *adjective* **1** SOMEONE good at doing something *a skilful artist* **2** SOMETHING done or made very well *skilful use of language* •**skilfully** *adverb UK*

WORD PARTNERS FOR ***skill***

acquire/develop/learn/master/require a skill • **consummate/great** skill • a **basic/necessary/useful** skill • skill **at/in** sth

O⊸**skill** /skɪl/ *noun* [**C, U**] the ability to do an activity or job well, especially because you have practised it *You need good communication skills to be a teacher.*

skilled /skɪld/ *adjective* **1** PERSON having the abilities needed to do an activity or job well *a **highly skilled** (= very skilled) photographer* ○ *He has become **skilled in** dealing with the media.* **2** WORK/JOB Skilled work needs someone who has had special training to do it. ⊃Opposite **unskilled**

skillet /ˈskɪlɪt/ *noun* [**C**] *mainly US* a large, heavy pan with a long handle, used for frying food

skillful /ˈskɪlfʊl/ *adjective US spelling of* skilful

skim /skɪm/ *verb* **skimming**, *past* **skimmed** **1** MOVE OVER [**I, T**] to move quickly, and almost or just touch the surface of something *Birds skimmed the surface of the pond.* **2** REMOVE [**T**] (*also* **skim off**) to remove something from the surface of a liquid *Skim off any excess fat before serving.* **3** READ QUICKLY [**T**] (*also* **skim through**) to read or look at something quickly without looking at the details *She began skimming through the reports on her desk.*

ˌskimmed ˈmilk (*also US* **ˈskim ˌmilk**) *noun* [**U**] **FOOD** milk that has had the fat removed from it

skimp /skɪmp/ *verb*
skimp on sth *phrasal verb* to not spend enough time or money on something, or not use enough of something *We've got plenty of cheese so don't skimp on it.*

S

skimpy /ˈskɪmpi/ *adjective* Skimpy clothes show a lot of your body. *a skimpy bikini/dress*

WORD PARTNERS FOR ***skin***

dark/fair/olive skin • **dry/oily/sensitive** skin

O⊸**skin**[1] /skɪn/ *noun* [**C, U**] **1 ANATOMY, BIOLOGY** the outer layer of a person or animal's body ***dark/fair skin*** **2** ANIMAL the outer layer of a dead animal used as leather, fur, etc *a leopard skin rug* **3 BIOLOGY, FOOD** the outer layer of a fruit or vegetable *a banana/potato skin* **4** LIQUID a thin, solid layer that forms on the top of a liquid *A skin had formed on the top of the milk.* **5 COMPUTING** the particular way that information is arranged and shown on a computer screen **6 do sth by the skin of your teeth** *informal* to only just succeed in doing something *They held on by the skin of their teeth to win 1-0.* **7 have (a) thick skin** to not care if someone criticizes you

skin[2] /skɪn/ *verb* [**T**] **skinning**, *past* **skinned** **1 FOOD** to remove the skin from something **2** (*also UK* **graze**) to injure your skin by rubbing it against something rough *Mary fell and skinned her knees.*

skinhead /ˈskɪnhed/ *noun* [**C**] a man who has extremely short hair, especially one who behaves in a violent way

skinny /ˈskɪni/ *adjective* Someone who is skinny is too thin.

skip[1] /skɪp/ *verb* **skipping**, *past* **skipped** **1** MOVE FORWARD [**I**] to move forward, jumping quickly from one foot to the other *She watched her daughter skipping down the street.* **2 SPORT** [**I**] (*US* **ˌskip ˈrope**) to jump over a rope while you or two other people move it over and then under your body again and again *I skip for ten minutes every day to keep fit.* **3** NOT DO [**T**] to not do something that you usually do or that you should do *I think I'll skip lunch today - I'm not very hungry.* **4** AVOID [**T**] (*also* **skip over**) to avoid reading or talking about something by starting to read or talk about the next thing instead *I usually skip the boring bits.*

skip[2] /skɪp/ *noun* [**C**] **1** CONTAINER *UK* (*US* **Dumpster** *trademark*) a very large, metal container for big pieces of rubbish **2** MOVE when you jump quickly from one foot to the other

skipper /ˈskɪpər/ *noun* [**C**] *informal* the leader of a team, an aircraft, a ship, etc

ˈskipping ˌrope *UK* (*US* **jump rope**) *noun* [**C**] **SPORT** a rope that you move over your head and then jump over as you move it under your feet

skirmish /ˈskɜːmɪʃ/ *noun* [**C**] a small fight

skirt[1] /skɜːt/ *noun* [**C**] a piece of women's clothing that hangs from the waist and has no legs ⊃See colour picture **Clothes** on page Centre 8

skirt[2] /skɜːt/ (*also* **skirt around**) *verb* [**T**] **1** AVOID to avoid talking about something *I deliberately skirted the question of money.* **2** MOVE to move around the edge of something *We skirted around the edge of the field.*

skittle /ˈskɪtl/ *noun* **1** [**C**] one of a set of bottle-shaped objects that you try to knock down with a ball as a game **2 skittles** [**U**] a game in which you try to knock down bottle-shaped objects with a ball

skive /skaɪv/ (*also* **skive off**) *verb* [**I, T**] *UK* to not go to school or work when you should, or to leave school or work earlier than you should •**skiver** *noun* [**C**] *UK informal* someone who skives

skulk /skʌlk/ *verb* **skulk about/behind/in, etc** to hide somewhere or move around quietly in a way that makes people think you are going to do something bad *I saw a man skulking behind the shed.*

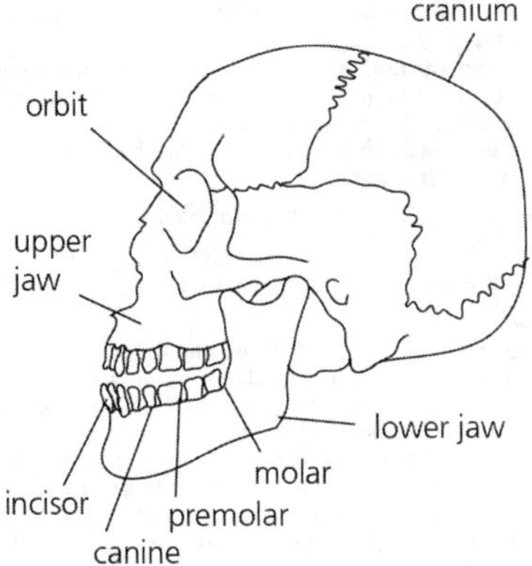

skull

skull /skʌl/ *noun* [C] **ANATOMY** the part of your head that is made of bone and which protects your brain

ˈskull ˌcap *noun* [C] a small round hat worn especially by some religious men

skunk /skʌŋk/ *noun* [C] a black and white animal that produces a very unpleasant smell in order to defend itself

WORD PARTNERS FOR ***sky***

the sky **darkens/lightens** • **in** the sky • a **clear/cloudy/overcast** sky

O⊸**sky** /skaɪ/ *noun* [U, no plural] the area above the Earth where you can see clouds, the sun, the moon, etc *a beautiful, blue sky* ○ *The sky suddenly went dark.* ⊃See also: **skies**

skydiving /ˈskaɪˌdaɪvɪŋ/ *noun* [U] **SPORT** the sport of jumping out of an aircraft with a parachute (= large piece of cloth that allows you to fall slowly to the ground)

skylight /ˈskaɪlaɪt/ *noun* [C] a window in the roof of a building

skyline /ˈskaɪlaɪn/ *noun* [C] the pattern that is made against the sky by tall buildings *the New York skyline*

ˈsky ˌmarshal *noun* [C] a person whose job is to carry a gun and protect the passengers on an aircraft

skyscraper /ˈskaɪˌskreɪpəʳ/ *noun* [C] a very tall building

ˈsky ˌsurfing *noun* [U] the imaginary activity of surfing (= riding on a wave standing on a special board) in the air

slab /slæb/ *noun* [C] a thick, flat piece of something, especially stone *a slab of concrete*

slack¹ /slæk/ *adjective* **1** LOOSE loose or not tight *Suddenly the rope became slack.* **2** BUSINESS If business is slack, there are not many customers. **3** LAZY not trying hard enough in your work *slack management*

slack² /slæk/ *informal* (*also US* **slack off**) *verb* [I] to work less hard than usual *I'm afraid I haven't been to the gym recently - I've been slacking.*

slacken /ˈslækᵊn/ *verb* [I, T] **1** SLOW to become slower or less active, or to make something become slower or less active *Economic growth is slackening.* **2** LOOSE to become loose, or to make something become loose *As you get older your muscles slacken.*

slacks /slæks/ *noun* [plural] *mainly US* trousers

slag /slæg/ *verb* **slagging**, *past* **slagged**
slag sb/sth off *phrasal verb UK informal* to criticize someone or something in an unpleasant way

slain /sleɪn/ *past participle of* slay

slalom /ˈslɑːləm/ *noun* [C] **SPORT** a race in which you go forwards by moving from side to side between poles

slam /slæm/ *verb* **slamming**, *past* **slammed** **1** [I, T] to close with great force, or to make something close with great force *Kate heard the front door slam.* **2** **slam sth down/onto/into, etc** to put something somewhere with great force ***She slammed the phone down.*** •**slam** *noun* [C] [usually singular] the slam of a car door

slander /ˈslɑːndəʳ/ *noun* [C, U] **LAW** the crime of saying bad things about someone that are not true •**slander** *verb* [T] •**slanderous** /ˈslɑːndᵊrəs/ *adjective* saying bad things about someone that are not true

slang /slæŋ/ *noun* [U] **LANGUAGE** informal language, often language that is only used by people who belong to a particular group *prison slang*

slant¹ /slɑːnt/ *verb* [I, T] to slope in a particular direction, or to make something slope in a particular direction *Pale sunlight **slanted through** the curtain.*

slant² /slɑːnt/ *noun* [no plural] **1** POSITION a position that is sloping *The road is **on/at a slant**.* **2** WRITING a way of writing about something that shows who or what you support *a political slant* ○ *It's certainly a new **slant on** the subject.*

slap¹ /slæp/ *verb* [T] **slapping**, *past* **slapped** to hit someone with the flat, inside part of your hand *She slapped him across the face.*
slap sth on *phrasal verb* to quickly put or spread something on a surface *I'll just slap some make-up on.*

slap² /slæp/ *noun* [C] **1** a hit with the flat, inside part of your hand **2** **a slap in the face** something someone does that insults or upsets you *After all that hard work, losing my job was a real slap in the face.*

slapdash /ˈslæpdæʃ/ *adjective* done quickly and without being careful *Her work has been a bit slapdash recently.*

slapstick /ˈslæpstɪk/ *noun* [U] when actors do funny things like falling down, hitting each other, etc to make people laugh

slap-up /ˈslæpˌʌp/ *adjective* **slap-up meal/dinner, etc** *UK informal* **FOOD** a large and very good meal

slash¹ /slæʃ/ *verb* [T] **1** CUT to cut something by making a quick, long cut with something very sharp *His throat had been slashed.* **2** REDUCE to reduce the amount of something by a lot *to **slash prices***

S

slash² /slæʃ/ *noun* [C] **1** a long, deep cut **2** LANGUAGE a mark (/) used in writing to separate words or numbers, often to show a choice or connection

slate¹ /sleɪt/ *noun* [C, U] **GEOLOGY** a dark grey rock that can easily be cut into thin pieces, or a small, flat piece of this used to cover a roof

slate² /sleɪt/ *verb* **1** [T] *UK* to criticize someone or something severely [**often passive**] *The film had been slated by critics.* **2 be slated** *US* to be expected to happen in the future, or to be expected to be or do something in the future [+ **to do sth**] Filming is slated to begin next spring.

slaughter¹ /ˈslɔːtəʳ/ *verb* [T] **1 FARMING** to kill an animal for meat **2** PEOPLE to kill a lot of people in a very cruel way **3** DEFEAT *informal* to defeat someone very easily

slaughter² /ˈslɔːtəʳ/ *noun* [U] when a lot of people or animals are killed in a cruel way

slaughterhouse /ˈslɔːtəhaʊs/ *noun* [C] *plural* **slaughterhouses** /ˈslɔːtəhaʊzɪz/ **FARMING** a place where animals are killed for meat

slave¹ /sleɪv/ *noun* **1 SOCIETY** [C] someone who is owned by someone else and has to work for them *He treats his mother like a slave.* **2 be a slave to sth** to be completely controlled or influenced by something *You're a slave to fashion.*

slave² /sleɪv/ (*also* **slave away**) *verb* [I] *informal* to work very hard *Giorgio was* ***slaving away*** *at his homework.*

slavery /ˈsleɪvᵊri/ *noun* [U] **SOCIETY** the system of owning slaves, or the condition of being a slave

slay /sleɪ/ *verb* [T] *past tense* **slew**, *past participle* **slain** *literary* to kill someone in a very violent way

sleaze /sliːz/ *noun* [U] political or business activities that are morally wrong

sleazy /ˈsliːzi/ *adjective* unpleasant and morally wrong, often in a way that relates to sex *He spent the night drinking in a sleazy bar.*

sledge¹ /sledʒ/ *UK* (*US* **sled** /sled/) *noun* [C] **SPORT** a vehicle that is used for travelling on snow

S

sledge² /sledʒ/ *UK* (*US* **sled** /sled/) *verb* [I] **SPORT** to travel on snow using a sledge

sleek /sliːk/ *adjective* **1** HAIR Sleek hair is smooth and very shiny. **2** CAR A sleek car is attractive and looks expensive.

O-- **sleep¹** /sliːp/ *verb past* **slept 1** [I] to be in the state of rest when your eyes are closed, your body is not active, and your mind is unconscious *Did you sleep well?* **2 sleep four/six, etc** If a place sleeps four, six, etc, it is big enough for that number of people to sleep in. **3 sleep on it** to wait until the next day before making a decision about something important so that you can think about it carefully ⊃See also: not sleep a **wink²**

sleep in *phrasal verb* to sleep longer in the morning than you usually do

sleep sth off *phrasal verb* to sleep until you feel better, especially after drinking too much alcohol

sleep over *phrasal verb* to sleep in someone else's home for a night *After the party, I slept over at Tom's house.*

sleep through sth *phrasal verb* to continue to sleep although there is noise *I don't know how you slept through the storm.*

sleep with sb *phrasal verb informal* to have sex with someone

WORD PARTNERS FOR ***sleep (noun)***

get [no/some, etc] sleep • **get to/go to** sleep • **have** a sleep • a **good night's** sleep • **in** your sleep

O-- **sleep²** /sliːp/ *noun* **1** [U, no plural] the state you are in when you are sleeping, or a period of time when you are sleeping *I haven't had* ***a good night's sleep*** (= a long sleep at night) *for weeks.* ○ *You need to go home and* ***get some sleep.*** ○ *It took me ages to* ***get to sleep*** (= to succeed in sleeping). ○ *He died peacefully* ***in his sleep.*** **2 go to sleep a** to begin to sleep *Babies often go to sleep after a feed.* **b HEALTH** *informal* If part of your body goes to sleep, you cannot feel it. *I'd been sitting on my feet and they'd gone to sleep.* **3 put sth to sleep** to kill an animal that is very old or ill **4 could do sth in your sleep** to be able to do something very easily **5 lose sleep over sth** to worry about something

sleeper /ˈsliːpəʳ/ *noun* **1 a light/heavy sleeper** someone who wakes up easily/does not wake up easily **2** TRAIN [C] a train or a part of a train that has beds in it **3** SUPPORT [C] *UK* (*US* **railroad tie**) a piece of wood that is used to support a railway track (= the thing a train moves along on) **4** JEWELLERY [C] *UK* a small gold or silver ring worn in the ear

ˈsleeping ˌbag *noun* [C] a long bag made of thick material that you sleep inside

ˈsleeping ˌpill *noun* [C] **HEALTH** a medicine that you take to help you sleep

sleepless /ˈsliːpləs/ *adjective* **sleepless night** a night when you are not able to sleep *He'd spent a sleepless night worrying about his exam.* •**sleeplessness** *noun* [U]

sleep-over /ˈsliːpəʊvəʳ/ *noun* [C] a party when a group of young people stay at a friend's house for the night

sleepwalk /ˈsliːpˌwɔːk/ *verb* [I] to get out of bed and walk around while you are sleeping •**sleepwalker** *noun* [C]

sleepy /ˈsliːpi/ *adjective* **1** PERSON feeling tired and wanting to go to sleep *The heat had made me sleepy.* **2** PLACE quiet and with little activity *a sleepy little town* •**sleepily** *adverb* •**sleepiness** *noun* [U]

sleet /sliːt/ *noun* [U] a mixture of snow and rain •**sleet** *verb* [I] ***It was sleeting*** *when I looked outside.*

WORD PARTNERS FOR ***sleeve***

long/short sleeves • **roll up** your sleeves

sleeve /sliːv/ *noun* **1** [C] the part of a jacket, shirt, etc that covers your arm *He* ***rolled up his sleeves*** *to do the dishes.* **2 have sth up your sleeve** *informal* to have a secret plan *They were worried he might have another nasty surprise up his sleeve.*

-sleeved /sliːvd/ *suffix* **short-sleeved/long-sleeved** having short/long sleeves *a short-sleeved shirt*

sleeveless /ˈsliːvləs/ *adjective* describes a piece of clothing with no sleeves *a sleeveless dress*

sleigh /sleɪ/ *noun* [C] a large vehicle that is pulled by animals and used for travelling on snow

slender /ˈslendəʳ/ *adjective* thin in an attractive way *a slender woman with long, red hair*

slept /slept/ *past of* sleep

sleuth /sluːθ/ *noun* [C] *old-fashioned* a police officer whose job is to discover who has committed a crime

slew /sluː/ *past tense of* slay

slice¹ /slaɪs/ *noun* **1** [C] a flat piece of food that has been cut from a larger piece *a slice of bread/cake/meat* ➲See colour picture **Pieces and Quantities** on page Centre 1 **2 a slice of sth** a part of something that is being divided *a large slice of the profits* ➲See also: **fish slice**

slice² /slaɪs/ *verb* **1** FOOD [T] (*also* **slice up**) to cut food into thin, flat pieces *Could you slice the tomatoes?* **2 slice into/off/through, etc** CUT [I, T] to cut into or through something with a knife or something sharp *I almost sliced my finger off.* ➲See also: the best/greatest **thing** since sliced bread

slick /slɪk/ *adjective* **1** WITH SKILL done with a lot of skill *a slick presentation* **2** NOT SINCERE attractive but in a way that is not sincere or honest *He was a bit slick - I didn't trust him.*

slide¹ /slaɪd/ *verb past* **slid 1 slide (sth) across/down/along, etc** to move smoothly over a surface, or to make something move smoothly over a surface *He slid the letter into his pocket.* **2 slide (sth) into/out of/through, etc** to move somewhere quietly, or to make something move quietly *She slid out of the room, being careful not to wake Alan.*

slide² /slaɪd/ *noun* **1** PHOTOGRAPH [C] a small piece of film that you shine light through in order to see a photograph **2** GAME [C] a large object that children climb and slide down as a game **3 CHEMISTRY, BIOLOGY** [C] a small piece of glass that you put something on when you want to look at it under a microscope (= equipment used to make things look bigger) **4** LESS/WORSE [**no plural**] when the level or quality of something gets less or worse *a price slide*

O-- **slight¹** /slaɪt/ *adjective* **1** SMALL small and not important *slight differences in colour* ○ *We're having a slight problem with our computer system.* **2** PERSON Someone who is slight is thin.

slight² /slaɪt/ *noun* [C] an action or remark that insults someone

slighted /ˈslaɪtɪd/ *adjective* **be/feel slighted** to feel insulted because someone has done or said something which shows that they think you are not important *Annie felt slighted because she hadn't been invited to the meeting.*

slightest /ˈslaɪtɪst/ *adjective* **1 the slightest** [**always before noun**] the smallest *The slightest movement will disturb these shy animals.* **2 not in the slightest** not at all *"Do you mind if I open the window?" "Not in the slightest."*

O-- **slightly** /ˈslaɪtli/ *adverb* a little *I think I did slightly better in my exams this time.* ○ *I find it slightly worrying.*

slim¹ /slɪm/ *adjective* **slimmer, slimmest 1** PERSON Someone who is slim is thin in an attractive way. **2** SLIGHT small and not as much as you would like *There's a **slim chance** he'll succeed.*

slim² /slɪm/ *verb* [I] **slimming**, *past* **slimmed** *UK* to eat less in order to become thinner

slim down *phrasal verb* to become thinner

slim sth down *phrasal verb* to reduce the size of something *It is not our intention to slim down the workforce.*

slime /slaɪm/ *noun* [U] a thick, sticky liquid that is unpleasant to touch

slimy /ˈslaɪmi/ *adjective* **1** SLIME covered in slime **2** PERSON *informal* too friendly in a way that is not sincere

sling¹ /slɪŋ/ *noun* [C] **1 HEALTH** a piece of cloth that you wear around your neck and put your arm into to support it when it is injured **2** a piece of cloth or a strap that you tie around your body to carry things in *She had her baby in a sling.*

sling² /slɪŋ/ *verb past* **slung 1 sling sth over/around/on, etc** to put something in a position where it hangs loosely *He slung his bag over his shoulder.* **2 sling sth into/onto/under, etc** to throw something somewhere in a careless way *She slung her coat onto the bed.*

slingshot /ˈslɪŋʃɒt/ *US* (*UK* **catapult**) *noun* [C] a Y-shaped object with a piece of elastic across it used by children to shoot small stones

slink /slɪŋk/ *verb past* **slunk slink away/off/out, etc** to move somewhere quietly so that no one will notice you *I caught him slinking out of the meeting.*

slip¹ /slɪp/ *verb* **slipping**, *past* **slipped 1** FALL [I] to slide by accident and fall or almost fall *She slipped on the ice and broke her ankle.* **2** OUT OF POSITION [I] to slide out of the correct position *The photo had slipped from the frame.* **3 slip away/out/through, etc** to go somewhere quietly or quickly *I'll slip out of the room if I get bored.* **4 slip sth into/through, etc** to put something somewhere quickly or secretly *She slipped the letter into an envelope and sealed it.* **5** GIVE SECRETLY [+ **two objects**] *informal* to give something to someone secretly *I slipped her a five pound note.* **6** GET LESS/WORSE [I] to get less or worse in level or quality *His school grades have slipped recently.* **7 let sth slip** to forget that something is a secret and tell someone about it ➲See also: slip your **mind**¹

slip into sth *phrasal verb* to quickly put on a piece of clothing

slip sth off *phrasal verb* to quickly take off a piece of clothing *Slip your shirt off and I'll listen to your heart.*

slip sth on *phrasal verb* to quickly put on a piece of clothing *I'll just slip my shoes on.*

slip out *phrasal verb* If a remark slips out, you say it without intending to. *I didn't mean to tell anyone you were getting married - it just slipped out.*

slip out of sth *phrasal verb* to quickly take off a piece of clothing

slip up *phrasal verb* to make a mistake

S

slip² /slɪp/ *noun* [C] **1** PAPER a small piece of paper *He wrote the number on a **slip of paper**.* **2** FALL when you slide by accident and fall or almost fall **3** WOMEN'S CLOTHING a piece of clothing that a woman wears under a dress or skirt **4** MISTAKE a small mistake **5 give sb the slip** *informal* to escape from someone you do not want to be with **6 a slip of the tongue** a mistake made by using the wrong word

slipper /ˈslɪpəʳ/ *noun* [C] a soft, comfortable shoe that you wear in the house ⊃See colour picture **Clothes** on page Centre 8

slippery /ˈslɪpᵊri/ *adjective* **1** smooth and wet and difficult to hold or walk on *Be careful - the floor's slippery.* **2 a slippery slope** a bad situation that is likely to get worse

ˈslip ˌroad *UK* (*US* **ramp**) *noun* [C] a short road that is used to drive onto or off a motorway (= wide, fast road)

slit¹ /slɪt/ *noun* [C] a long, narrow cut or hole in something *Make a slit in the pastry to allow the steam to escape.*

slit² /slɪt/ *verb* [T] **slitting**, *past* **slit** to make a long, narrow cut in something *She **slit** her **wrists**.*

slither /ˈslɪðəʳ/ *verb* [I] to move smoothly by twisting and sliding

sliver /ˈslɪvəʳ/ *noun* [C] a thin piece of something that has come off a larger piece ***slivers** of glass*

slob /slɒb/ *noun* [C] *informal* a lazy or dirty person

slog¹ /slɒg/ *verb* **slogging**, *past* **slogged** *informal* **slog up/down/through, etc** to move forward with difficulty *We slogged up the hill in silence.*
slog away *phrasal verb informal* to work very hard for a long time *I've been **slogging away at** this for hours and I'm exhausted.*

slog² /slɒg/ *noun* [U no plural] *UK informal* a period of hard work *Studying for all the exams was a **hard slog**.*

WORD PARTNERS FOR ***slogan***

sth **bears/carries** a slogan • a slogan **of** sth • an **advertising** slogan

slogan /ˈsləʊgən/ *noun* [C] **LANGUAGE** a short phrase that is easy to remember and is used to make people notice something *an **advertising slogan***

slop /slɒp/ *verb* **slopping**, *past* **slopped slop (sth) about/around/into, etc** If liquid slops about, it moves around or over the edge of its container, and if you slop it about, you make it move around or over the edge of its container. *Her hand shook, making her tea slop into the saucer.*

slope¹ /sləʊp/ *noun* [C] a surface or piece of land that is high at one end and low at the other *There's a **steep slope** to climb before we're at the top.* ⊃See also: a **slippery** slope

slope² /sləʊp/ *verb* [I] to be high at one end and low at the other *The field **slopes down** to the river.*

sloppy /ˈslɒpi/ *adjective* **1** CARELESS not done carefully *His work was sloppy and full of spelling mistakes.* **2** CLOTHES Sloppy clothes are loose and untidy. *a girl wearing a sloppy sweater and torn jeans* **3** TOO WET A sloppy substance has too much liquid in it. •**sloppily** *adverb* •**sloppiness** *noun* [U]

slosh /slɒʃ/ *verb* **slosh against/over/around, etc** If liquid sloshes, it moves against or over the edge of its container. *Water sloshed over the edge of the pool as the swimmers dived in.*

sloshed /slɒʃt/ *adjective informal* drunk

slot¹ /slɒt/ *noun* [C] **1** HOLE a long, narrow hole that you put something into, especially money **2** TIME a period of time that you allow for something in a plan *The programme is being moved to a later slot.*

slot² /slɒt/ *verb* [I, T] **slotting**, *past* **slotted** to fit into a slot, or to make something fit into a slot
slot sb/sth in *phrasal verb* to find time for someone or something in a period of time that has already been planned *Dr O'Neil can slot you in around 9.30.*

sloth /sləʊθ/ *noun* **1** ANIMAL [C] an animal that moves very slowly and lives in Central and South America **2** LAZY [U] *literary* when someone is lazy

ˈslot maˌchine *noun* [C] a machine that you put money into in order to try to win money

slouch¹ /slaʊtʃ/ *verb* [I] to stand, sit, or walk with your shoulders forward so that your body is not straight *Stop slouching and stand up straight.*

slouch² /slaʊtʃ/ *noun* **1** [no plural] the position your body is in when you slouch **2 be no slouch** *informal* to work very hard and be good at something *He's no slouch when it comes to cooking.*

slovenly /ˈslʌvᵊnli/ *adjective* lazy, untidy, and dirty *slovenly habits* •**slovenliness** *noun* [U]

O‑ **slow¹** /sləʊ/ *adjective* **1** NOT FAST moving, happening, or doing something without much speed *I'm making slow progress with the painting.* ○ *He's a very slow reader.* **2 be slow to do sth; be slow in doing sth** to take a long time to do something *The government has been slow to react to the problem.* ○ *The ambulance was very slow in coming.* **3** CLOCK If a clock is slow, it shows a time that is earlier than the correct time. **4** BUSINESS If business is slow, there are few customers. **5** NOT CLEVER not quick at learning and understanding things **6** NOT EXCITING not exciting *I find his films very slow.*

slow² /sləʊ/ *verb* [I, T] to become slower or to make something become slower *The car **slowed to a halt** (= moved more and more slowly until it stopped).*
slow (sth) down *phrasal verb* to become slower or to make something become slower *Slow down, Claire, you're walking too fast!*
slow down *phrasal verb* If someone slows down, they become less active. *The doctor told me I should slow down and not work so hard.*

slowdown /ˈsləʊdaʊn/ *noun* [C] **ECONOMICS** when business activity becomes slower *an **economic slowdown*** ○ *The figures show a **slowdown in** retail sales.*

O‑ **slowly** /ˈsləʊli/ *adverb* at a slow speed *Could you speak more slowly, please?*

ˌslow ˈmotion *noun* [U] a way of showing pictures from a film or television programme at a slower speed than normal *They showed a replay of the goal* ***in slow motion***.

sludge /slʌdʒ/ *noun* [U] soft, wet soil, or a substance that looks like this

slug¹ /slʌg/ *noun* [C] **1** ANIMAL a small, soft creature with no legs that moves slowly and eats plants **2** DRINK a small amount of a drink, especially an alcoholic drink *He* ***took a slug*** *of whisky from the bottle.*

slug² /slʌg/ *verb* [T] **slugging**, *past* **slugged** *informal* to hit someone with your fist (= closed hand)
slug it out *phrasal verb informal* to fight, argue, or compete with someone until one person wins *Federer and Hewitt slugged it out for a place in the final.*

sluggish /ˈslʌgɪʃ/ *adjective* moving or working more slowly than usual *a sluggish economy* ○ *I felt really sluggish after lunch.*

slum /slʌm/ *noun* [C] **SOCIETY** a poor and crowded area of a city where the buildings are in a very bad condition *He grew up in the slums of Mexico City.* ○ *slum areas*

slumber /ˈslʌmbəʳ/ *noun* [C, U] *literary* sleep *She lay down on the bed and fell into a deep slumber.* •**slumber** *verb* [I] *literary*

ˈslumber ˌparty *noun* [C] *US* a party when a group of children spend the night at one child's house

slump¹ /slʌmp/ *verb* **1 ECONOMICS** [I] If a price, value, or amount slumps, it goes down suddenly. *Sales have slumped by 50%.* **2 slump back/down/over, etc** to fall or sit down suddenly because you feel tired or weak *She slumped back in her chair, exhausted.*

WORD PARTNERS FOR ***slump (noun)***

a **dramatic/severe** slump • a slump **in** sth

slump² /slʌmp/ *noun* [C] **1 ECONOMICS** a sudden fall in prices or sales *a* ***slump in*** *world oil prices* **2 ECONOMICS** a period when there is very little business activity and not many jobs *It's been the worst* ***economic slump*** *for 25 years.*

slung /slʌŋ/ *past of* sling

slunk /slʌŋk/ *past of* slink

slur¹ /slɜːʳ/ *verb* [I, T] **slurring**, *past* **slurred** to speak without separating your words clearly, often because you are tired or drunk *He'd drunk too much and was slurring his words.*

WORD PARTNERS FOR ***slur***

cast slurs • a slur **against/on** sb/sth

slur² /slɜːʳ/ *noun* [C] a criticism that will make people have a bad opinion of someone or something *a racial slur* ○ *She regarded it as a* ***slur on*** *her character.*

slurp /slɜːp/ *verb* [I, T] *informal* to drink in a noisy way *He slurped his tea.* •**slurp** *noun* [C] *informal*

slush /slʌʃ/ *noun* [U] snow that has started to melt

sly /slaɪ/ *adjective* **slyer**, **slyest 1** deceiving people in a clever way to get what you want **2 sly smile** a smile that shows you know something that other people do not *"I know why Chris didn't come home yesterday," she said with a sly smile.* •**slyly** *adverb*

smack¹ /smæk/ *verb* **1** [T] to hit someone with the flat, inside part of your hand *Do you think it's right to smack children when they're naughty?* **2 smack sth against/onto/down, etc** to hit something hard against something else *Ray smacked the ball into the net.*
smack of sth *phrasal verb* If something smacks of an unpleasant quality, it seems to have that quality. *a policy that smacks of racism*

smack² /smæk/ *noun* [C] a hit with the flat, inside part of your hand *Stop shouting or I'll* ***give you a smack!***

smack³ /smæk/ *informal* (*also UK* **ˈsmack ˌbang**) (*also US* **ˌsmack ˈdab**) *adverb* **1** EXACTLY exactly in a particular place *She lives smack in the middle of Edinburgh.* **2** SUDDENLY suddenly and with a lot of force *He braked too late and ran smack into the car in front.*

OTHER WAYS OF SAYING ***small***

Little is a very common alternative to 'small', and can describe things or people: *I'll just have a* ***little*** *piece of cake.* • *She's so* ***little***.

If someone is extremely small, you can say that they are **tiny** or **minute**, and if something is extremely small, you can say that it is **minute**, **tiny**, or, in more formal contexts, **microscopic** or **minuscule**: *Inside the pram was a* ***tiny*** *baby.* • *The phone he pulled out of his pocket was* ***minute***. • *The cost of vaccination is* ***minuscule*** *compared to the cost of treatment.*

The adjectives **dwarf** and **miniature** are sometimes used to describe things that are smaller than the normal size: *There were* ***dwarf*** *fir trees in pots on the patio.* • *It's a* ***miniature*** *bath for the doll's house.*

If a woman or girl is small in an attractive way, you can use the adjectives **dainty** or **petite**: *She had* ***dainty*** *feet.* • *Like all his girlfriends, Emma was dark and* ***petite***.

You can use the informal adjective **poky** to describe a room or other area that is too small: *They live in a* ***poky*** *little flat in south London.*

The adjective **slight** is sometimes used with abstract nouns to describe things that are small and not important: *There was a* ***slight*** *difference in colour.*

O⁻ **small¹** /smɔːl/ *adjective* **1** LITTLE little in size or amount *They live in a small apartment near Times Square.* ○ *We teach the children in small groups.* **2** YOUNG A small child is very young. *a woman with three small children* **3** NOT IMPORTANT not important or serious *a small mistake* **4 feel small** to feel stupid or unimportant *Simon was always trying to make me feel small.*

S

COMMON LEARNER ERROR

small or little?

Small refers to size and is the usual opposite of 'big' or 'large'.

Could I have a hamburger and a small Coke please?

Our house is quite small.

Little refers to size but also expresses the speaker's feelings. For example, it can suggest that the speaker likes or dislikes something.

They live in a beautiful little village.

Rats are horrible little animals.

The comparative and superlative forms of **little** are not usually used in British English. Use **smaller** or **smallest** instead.

My car is smaller than yours.

~~*My car is littler than yours.*~~

small² /smɔːl/ *adverb* in a small size *Emma knitted the sweater far too small.*

ˈsmall ˌad *noun* [C] *UK* a small advertisement that you put in a newspaper if you want to buy or sell something

ˌsmall ˈbusiness *noun* [C] **ECONOMICS** a business with a small number of employees

ˌsmall ˈchange *noun* [U] **FINANCE** coins that have little value

ˈsmall ˌfry *noun* [U] *informal* people or activities that are not considered important *Compared to companies that size we're just small fry.*

ˌsmall inˈtestine *noun* [C] **ANATOMY** the upper part of the bowels between the stomach and the large intestine ➲Compare **large intestine** ➲See picture at **alimentary canal**

ˌsmall ˈprint *noun* [U] **LAW** the part of a written agreement that is printed smaller than the rest and that contains important information *Make sure you read the small print before you sign.*

small-scale /ˌsmɔːlˈskeɪl/ *adjective* A small-scale activity or organization is not big and involves few people.

ˈsmall ˌtalk *noun* [U] polite conversation between people at social events *He's not very good at **making small talk**.*

small-time /ˈsmɔːlˌtaɪm/ *adjective* [**always before noun**] *informal* not important or successful *a small-time criminal*

smart¹ /smɑːt/ *adjective* **1** INTELLIGENT intelligent *Rachel's one of the smartest kids in the class.* **2** TIDY If you look smart or your clothes are smart, you look clean and tidy. *a smart, blue suit* ○ *I need to look a bit smarter for my interview.* **3** FASHIONABLE fashionable and expensive *a smart, new restaurant* **4 COMPUTING** A smart machine, weapon, etc uses computers to make it work. *smart bombs* •**smartly** *adverb*

smart² /smɑːt/ *verb* [I] **1** to feel upset because someone has said or done something unpleasant to you *The team are still **smarting from** last week's defeat.* **2 HEALTH** If part of your body smarts, it hurts with a sharp, burning pain. *The smoke from the fire made her **eyes smart**.*

ˈsmart ˌcard *noun* [C] **COMPUTING** a small, plastic card that contains a very small computer and can be used to pay for things or to store personal information

smarten /ˈsmɑːtᵊn/ *verb*

smarten (sb/sth) up *phrasal verb* to make a person or place look more clean and tidy *plans to smarten up the city centre*

ˈsmart ˌfibre *UK* (*US* **smart fiber**) *noun* [C] **DT** a type of material that can react, for example to temperature or light

smash¹ /smæʃ/ *verb* **1** BREAK [I, T] to break into a lot of pieces with a loud noise, or to make something break into a lot of pieces with a loud noise *Thieves smashed the shop window and stole $50,000 worth of computer equipment.* **2 smash (sth) against/into/through, etc** to hit a hard object or surface with a lot of force, or to make something do this *The car skidded and smashed into a tree.* ○ *He smashed the glass against the wall.* **3** DESTROY [T] to destroy a political or criminal organization *attempts to smash a drug smuggling ring*

smash sth up *phrasal verb* to damage or destroy something *They were arrested for smashing up a hotel bar.*

smash² /smæʃ/ (*also* ˌ**smash ˈhit**) *noun* [C] a very successful film, song, play, etc *the smash hit movie 'Titanic'*

smashing /ˈsmæʃɪŋ/ *adjective UK old-fashioned* extremely good or attractive *We had a smashing time at Bob and Vera's party.*

smear¹ /smɪəʳ/ *verb* [T] **1** SPREAD to spread a thick liquid or sticky substance over something *His shirt was **smeared with** paint.* ○ *He **smeared** sun cream **over** his face and neck.* **2** SAY to say unpleasant and untrue things about someone in order to harm them, especially in politics

smear² /smɪəʳ/ *noun* [C] **1** MARK a dirty mark *There was a smear of oil on his cheek.* **2** STORY an unpleasant and untrue story about someone that is meant to harm them, especially in politics *a **smear campaign***

O- **smell¹** /smel/ *verb past* **smelled**, *also UK* **smelt** **1 smell of/like; smell delicious/horrible, etc** to have a particular quality that people notice by using their nose *I've been cooking, so my hands smell of garlic.* ○ *That soup smells delicious - what's in it?* **2** NOTICE [T] to notice something by using your nose *I think I can smell something burning.* **3** UNPLEASANT [I] to have an unpleasant smell *Your running shoes really smell!* **4** PUT YOUR NOSE NEAR [T] to put your nose near something and breathe in so that you can notice its smell *Come and smell these flowers.* **5** ABILITY [I] to have the ability to notice smells *Dogs can smell much better than humans.*

O- **smell²** /smel/ *noun* **1** QUALITY [C] the quality that something has which you notice by using your nose *The **smell of** roses filled the room.* ○ *There was a delicious smell coming from the kitchen.* **2** UNPLEASANT [C] an unpleasant smell *I wish I could get rid of that smell in the bathroom.* **3** ABILITY [U] the ability to notice smells *Smoking can affect your **sense of smell**.*

smelly /ˈsmeli/ *adjective* having an unpleasant smell *smelly feet*

S

smelt /smelt/ *UK past of* smell

smile¹ /smaɪl/ *verb* [I] to make a happy or friendly expression in which the corners of your mouth curve up *She **smiled at** me.*

COMMON LEARNER ERROR

smile at someone/something

Be careful to choose the right preposition after the verb **smile**.

*She **smiled at** the little girl.*

~~*She smiled to the little girl.*~~

smile² /smaɪl/ *noun* [C] a happy or friendly expression in which the corners of your mouth curve up *"I passed my driving test," she said with a smile.*

WORD PARTNERS FOR ***smile (noun)***

a **beaming/faint/radiant/rueful/wry** smile • **break into/force/give/wear** a smile • a smile **broadens/flickers across sb's face/fades**

smiley /ˈsmaɪli/ *noun* [C] **INTERNET** an image such as :-) which looks like a face when you look at it from the side, made using keyboard symbols and used in emails to express emotions

smirk /smɜːk/ *verb* [I] to smile in an annoying or unkind way *What are you smirking at?* •**smirk** *noun* [C]

smitten /ˈsmɪtᵊn/ *adjective* [**never before noun**] loving someone or liking something very much *He's absolutely **smitten with** this Carla woman.*

smog /smɒg/ *noun* [U] **ENVIRONMENT** air pollution in a city that is a mixture of smoke, gases, and chemicals

smoke¹ /sməʊk/ *noun* **1** [GAS] [U] the grey or black gas that is produced when something burns **2** [CIGARETTE] [**no plural**] when someone smokes a cigarette *I'm just going outside for a smoke.*

smoke² /sməʊk/ *verb* **1** [CIGARETTE] [I, T] to breathe smoke into your mouth from a cigarette *Do you mind if I smoke?* ○ *She smokes thirty cigarettes a day.* **2** [MEAT/FISH] [T] to give meat or fish a special taste by hanging it over burning wood *smoked ham/salmon* **3** [PRODUCE SMOKE] [I] to produce or send out smoke *smoking chimneys* ➲See also: **chain-smoke**

smoker /ˈsməʊkəʳ/ *noun* [C] someone who smokes cigarettes regularly *He used to be a **heavy smoker*** (= someone who smokes a lot). ➲Opposite **non-smoker**

WORD PARTNERS FOR ***smoking***

give up/stop/quit smoking • **ban** smoking • **heavy** smoking • the **dangers/effects** of smoking

smoking /ˈsməʊkɪŋ/ *noun* [U] when someone smokes a cigarette or regularly smokes cigarettes *The new law will restrict smoking in public places.* ➲See also: **passive smoking**

smoky /ˈsməʊki/ *adjective* **1** [PLACE] filled with smoke *a smoky bar/room* **2** [TASTE] having the smell, taste, or appearance of smoke *That ham has a delicious, smoky flavour.*

smolder /ˈsməʊldəʳ/ *verb* [I] *US spelling of* smoulder

smooth¹ /smuːð/ *adjective* **1** [SURFACE] having a regular surface that has no holes or lumps in it *soft, smooth skin* ○ *a smooth wooden table* **2** [SUBSTANCE] A substance that is smooth has no lumps in it. *Mix the butter and sugar together until smooth.* **3** [MOVEMENT] happening without any sudden movements or changes *The plane made a smooth landing.* **4** [PROCESS] happening without problems or difficulties *Her job is to help students make a smooth transition from high school to college.* **5** [PERSON] too polite and confident in a way that people do not trust *a smooth salesman* •**smoothness** *noun* [U] ➲See also: take the **rough²** with the smooth

smooth² /smuːð/ (*also* **smooth down/out, etc**) *verb* [T] to move your hands across something in order to make it flat *He straightened his tie and smoothed down his hair.*

smooth sth over *phrasal verb* to make a disagreement or problem seem less serious, especially by talking to the people involved in it *Would you like me to smooth things over between you and Nick?*

smoothie /ˈsmuːði/ *noun* [C, U] **FOOD** a thick cold drink made mainly from fruit, sometimes with milk, cream or ice cream (= cold, sweet food)

smoothly /ˈsmuːðli/ *adverb* **1 go smoothly** to happen without any problems or difficulties *Everything was going smoothly until Darren arrived.* **2** without any sudden movements or changes *The car accelerated smoothly.*

smother /ˈsmʌðəʳ/ *verb* [T] **1** [KILL] to kill someone by covering their face with something so that they cannot breathe **2** [LOVE] to give someone too much love and attention so that they feel they have lost their freedom *I try not to smother him.* **3** [PREVENT] to prevent something from happening *I tried to smother my cough.* **4** [FIRE] to make a fire stop burning by covering it with something

smother sth in/with sth *phrasal verb* to cover something completely with a substance *She took a slice of chocolate cake and smothered it in cream.*

smoulder *UK* (*US* **smolder**) /ˈsməʊldəʳ/ *verb* [I] **1** [FIRE] to burn slowly, producing smoke but no flames *a smouldering bonfire* **2** [EMOTION] to have a strong feeling, especially anger, but not express it *I could see he was **smouldering** with anger.*

SMS /esemˈes/ *noun* [U] *abbreviation for* short message service: a system for sending written messages from one mobile phone to another •**SMS** *verb* [T, I]

smudge¹ /smʌdʒ/ *noun* [C] a dirty mark *a smudge of ink*

smudge² /smʌdʒ/ *verb* [I, T] If ink, paint, etc smudges, or if it is smudged, it becomes dirty or not clear because someone has touched it. *Be careful you don't smudge the drawing.*

smug /smʌg/ *adjective* too pleased with your skill or success in a way that annoys other people *a smug smile* •**smugly** *adverb "I've never lost a match yet," she said smugly.*

smuggle /ˈsmʌgl/ *verb* [T] **LAW** to take something into or out of a place in an illegal or secret way *He was arrested for smuggling cocaine into Britain.* •**smuggler** *noun* [C] ***drug smugglers*** •**smuggling** *noun* [U]

WORD PARTNERS FOR ***snack***

have a snack • a **light** snack

snack[1] /snæk/ *noun* [C] **FOOD** a small amount of food that you eat between meals *Do you want a quick snack before you go out?* ○ ***snack food***

snack[2] /snæk/ *verb* [I] *informal* to eat a snack *I've been* ***snacking on*** *chocolate and biscuits all afternoon.*

WORD PARTNERS FOR ***snag***

hit a snag • **the (only)** snag is • a snag **in/with** sth

snag[1] /snæg/ *noun* [C] *informal* a problem or difficulty *I'd love to come -* ***the only snag is*** *I have to be home by 3 o'clock.*

snag[2] /snæg/ *verb* [T] **snagging**, *past* **snagged** **1** [TEAR] If you snag something, it becomes stuck on a sharp object and tears. *I* ***snagged*** *my coat* ***on*** *the wire.* **2** [WIN] *US informal* to get, catch, or win something *She managed to snag a seat in the front row.*

snail /sneɪl/ *noun* [C] **1** a small creature with a long, soft body and a round shell **2 at a snail's pace** very slowly *There was so much traffic that we were travelling at a snail's pace.*

ˈsnail ˌmail *noun* [U] *humorous informal* letters or messages that are not sent by email but by post

snake[1] /sneɪk/ *noun* [C] a long, thin creature with no legs that slides along the ground ➲See picture at **reptile**

snake[2] /sneɪk/ *verb* **snake across/around/through, etc** to follow a route that has a lot of bends *The river snakes through some of the most spectacular countryside in France.*

snap[1] /snæp/ *verb* **snapping**, *past* **snapped** **1** [BREAK] [I, T] If something long and thin snaps, it breaks making a short, loud sound, and if you snap it, you break it, making a short, loud sound. *The twigs snapped as we walked on them.* **2 snap (sth) open/shut/together, etc** to suddenly move to a particular position, making a short, loud noise, or to make something do this *The suitcase snapped open and everything fell out.* **3** [SPEAK ANGRILY] [I, T] to say something suddenly in an angry way *I was* ***snapping at*** *the children because I was tired.* **4** [LOSE CONTROL] [I] to suddenly be unable to control a strong feeling, especially anger *She asked me to do the work again and I just snapped.* **5** [PHOTOGRAPH] [T] *informal* to take a photograph of someone or something *Photographers snapped the Princess everywhere she went.* **6** [ANIMAL] [I] If an animal snaps, it tries to bite someone. *The dog was barking and* ***snapping at*** *my ankles.* ➲See also: snap your fingers (**finger**[1])

snap out of sth *phrasal verb informal* to force yourself to stop feeling sad, angry, upset, etc *He's in a bad mood now but he'll soon snap out of it.*

snap sth up *phrasal verb informal* to buy or get something quickly because it is cheap or exactly what you want *The dress was perfect, so I snapped it up.*

snap sb up *phrasal verb informal* to immediately accept someone's offer to join your company or team because you want them very much *She was snapped up by a large law firm.*

snap[2] /snæp/ *noun* **1** [SOUND] [**no plural**] a sudden, short, loud sound like something breaking or closing *I heard a snap as I sat on the pencil.* **2** [PHOTOGRAPH] [C] *UK informal* (*UK/US* **snapshot**) a photograph ***holiday snaps*** **3** [FASTENING] [C] *US* (*UK* **popper**) a metal or plastic object made of two parts which fit together with a short, loud sound, used to fasten clothing **4** [GAME] [U] a card game in which you say "snap" when you see two cards that are the same **5 be a snap** *US informal* to be very easy *The French test was a snap.*

snap[3] /snæp/ *adjective* **snap decision/judgment** A snap decision or judgment is made very quickly and without careful thought.

snappy /ˈsnæpi/ *adjective* **1** [WRITING/SPEECH] written or spoken in a short and interesting way *a snappy title* **2** [CLOTHES] Snappy clothes are fashionable. *a snappy new suit* **3 make it snappy** *informal* used to tell someone to hurry

snapshot /ˈsnæpʃɒt/ *noun* [C] a photograph that you take quickly without thinking

snare[1] /sneəʳ/ *noun* [C] a piece of equipment used to catch animals

snare[2] /sneəʳ/ *verb* [T] **1** [ANIMAL] to catch an animal using a snare **2** [PERSON] to trick someone so that they cannot escape from a situation *She's trying to snare a rich husband.*

snarl /snɑːl/ *verb* **1** [PERSON] [I, T] to speak angrily *"Go away!" he snarled.* ○ *She* ***snarled at*** *me.* **2** [ANIMAL] [I] If an animal snarls, it shows its teeth and makes an angry sound. •**snarl** *noun* [C]

snatch[1] /snætʃ/ *verb* [T] **1** [TAKE] to take something or someone quickly and suddenly *Bill snatched the telephone from my hand.* ○ *The child was snatched from his bed.* **2** [DO QUICKLY] to do or get something quickly because you only have a short amount of time *I managed to snatch some lunch.*

snatch[2] /snætʃ/ *noun* [C] a short part of a conversation, song, etc that you hear *I keep hearing* ***snatches of*** *that song on the radio.*

sneak[1] /sniːk/ *verb past* **sneaked**, *also US* **snuck** **1 sneak into/out/around, etc** to go somewhere quietly because you do not want anyone to hear you *I sneaked into his bedroom while he was asleep.* **2 sneak sth into/out of/through, etc** to take something somewhere without anyone seeing you *We tried to sneak the dog into the hotel.* **3 sneak a look/glance at sb/sth** to look at someone or something quickly and secretly *I sneaked a look at the answers.*

sneak up *phrasal verb* to move close to someone without them seeing or hearing you *Don't* ***sneak up on*** *me like that - you scared me!*

sneak[2] /sniːk/ *noun* [C] *informal UK* someone who you do not like because they tell people when someone else has done something bad

S

sneaker /ˈsniːkəʳ/ US (UK **trainer**) *noun* [C] a soft sports shoe ➲See colour picture **Clothes** on page Centre 9

sneaking /ˈsniːkɪŋ/ *adjective* **1 have a sneaking feeling/suspicion** to think that something is true but not be sure [+ (that)] *I have a sneaking feeling that the English test is going to be very difficult.* **2 have a sneaking admiration/fondness for sb** UK to like someone secretly, especially when you do not want to

sneaky /ˈsniːki/ *adjective* doing things in a secret and unfair way

sneer /snɪəʳ/ *verb* [I] to talk about, or look at someone or something in a way that shows you do not approve of them *Carlos **sneered at** my attempts to put the tent up.* •**sneer** *noun* [C]

sneeze /sniːz/ *verb* [I] **HEALTH** When you sneeze, air suddenly comes out through your nose and mouth. *He had a cold and was sneezing a lot.* •**sneeze** *noun* [C]

snicker /ˈsnɪkəʳ/ US (UK **snigger**) *verb* [I] to laugh quietly in a rude way •**snicker** *noun* [C]

snide /snaɪd/ *adjective* A snide remark criticizes someone in an unpleasant way.

sniff /snɪf/ *verb* **1** BREATHE [I] to breathe air in through your nose in a way that makes a noise *Sam had a cold and she kept sniffing.* **2** SMELL [I, T] to breathe air in through your nose in order to smell something *She sniffed the flowers.* •**sniff** *noun* [C]

snigger /ˈsnɪgəʳ/ UK (US **snicker**) *verb* [I] to laugh quietly in a rude way *The boys were **sniggering at** the teacher.* •**snigger** *noun* [C]

snip[1] /snɪp/ *verb* [I, T] **snipping**, *past* **snipped** to cut something using scissors (= tool with two flat blades) with quick, small cuts *She snipped the article out of the magazine.*

snip[2] /snɪp/ *noun* **1** [C] a small, quick cut with scissors (= tool with two flat blades) **2 be a snip** UK *informal* to be very cheap

snipe /snaɪp/ *verb* [I] **1** CRITICIZE to criticize someone in an unpleasant way *I hate the way politicians **snipe at** each other.* **2** SHOOT to shoot people from a place that they cannot see *Rebels were indiscriminately **sniping at** civilians.* •**sniping** *noun* [U]

sniper /ˈsnaɪpəʳ/ *noun* [C] **1** someone who shoots at people from a place they cannot see **2** **INTERNET** on a website, someone who makes an offer for an item just before the end of an auction (= a sale in which things are sold to the person who offers the most money)

snippet /ˈsnɪpɪt/ *noun* [C] a small piece of information, news, conversation, etc *I kept hearing **snippets of** conversation.*

snob /snɒb/ *noun* [C] someone who thinks they are better than other people because they are in a higher social position •**snobbery** /ˈsnɒbᵊri/ *noun* [U] behaviour and opinions that are typical of a snob

snobbish /ˈsnɒbɪʃ/ (*also* **snobby**) *adjective* like a snob *a snobbish attitude*

snog /snɒg/ *verb* [I, T] **snogging**, *past* **snogged** UK *informal* If two people snog, they kiss each other for a long time. •**snog** *noun* [C] UK *informal*

snooker /ˈsnuːkəʳ/ *noun* [U] **SPORT** a game in which two people use long sticks to hit coloured balls into holes at the edge of a table

snoop /snuːp/ *verb* [I] to look around a place secretly in order to find out information about someone *I found her **snooping around** in my bedroom.* •**snoop** *noun* [no plural]

snooty /ˈsnuːti/ *adjective* Someone who is snooty behaves in an unfriendly way because they think they are better than other people.

snooze /snuːz/ *verb* [I] *informal* to sleep for a short time, especially during the day *Grandpa was snoozing in his chair.* •**snooze** *noun* [C] *informal Why don't you **have a snooze**?*

snore /snɔːʳ/ *verb* [I] to breathe in a very noisy way while you are sleeping *I couldn't sleep because my brother was snoring.* •**snore** *noun* [C]

snorkel[1] /ˈsnɔːkᵊl/ *noun* [C] **SPORT** a tube that you use to help you breathe if you are swimming with your face under water

snorkel[2] /ˈsnɔːkᵊl/ *verb* [I] UK **snorkelling**, *past* **snorkelled**, US **snorkeling**, *past* **snorkeled** **SPORT** to swim using a snorkel

snort /snɔːt/ *verb* [I, T] to breathe out noisily through your nose, especially to show that you are annoyed or think something is funny *"Stupid man!" he snorted.* ○ *Rosie started **snorting with** laughter.* •**snort** *noun* [C]

snot /snɒt/ *noun* [U] *informal* the thick liquid that is produced in your nose

snout /snaʊt/ *noun* [C] the long nose of some animals, such as pigs

WORD PARTNERS FOR ***snow*** *(noun)*

snow **falls/melts** • a snow **flurry/shower** • **deep/heavy** snow • [walk/tramp, etc] **through** the snow

O- **snow**[1] /snəʊ/ *noun* [U] soft white pieces of frozen water that fall from the sky when the weather is cold *children playing in the snow*

O- **snow**[2] /snəʊ/ *verb* **1 it snows** If it snows, snow falls from the sky. *It snowed all day yesterday.* **2 be snowed in** to be unable to leave a place because there is too much snow *We were snowed in for two days.* **3 be snowed under** to have too much work *I'm snowed under with homework.*

snowball[1] /ˈsnəʊbɔːl/ *noun* [C] a ball made from snow that children throw at each other

snowball[2] /ˈsnəʊbɔːl/ *verb* [I] If a problem, idea, or situation snowballs, it quickly grows bigger or more important. *The whole business idea snowballed from one phone call.*

snowboard /ˈsnəʊbɔːd/ *noun* [C] **SPORT** a large board that you stand on to move over snow ➲See colour picture **Sports 1** on page Centre 14

snowboarding /ˈsnəʊbɔːdɪŋ/ *noun* [U] **SPORT** a sport in which you stand on a large board and move over snow •**snowboarder** *noun* [C] ➲See colour picture **Sports 1** on page Centre 14

snowdrift /ˈsnəʊdrɪft/ *noun* [C] a deep pile of snow that the wind has blown

snowdrop /ˈsnəʊdrɒp/ *noun* [C] a small, white flower that you can see at the end of winter

S

snowfall /ˈsnəʊfɔːl/ *noun* [C, U] the snow that falls at one time, or the amount of snow that falls *a heavy snowfall* (= a lot of snow)

snowflake /ˈsnəʊfleɪk/ *noun* [C] a small piece of snow that falls from the sky

snowman /ˈsnəʊmæn/ *noun* [C] *plural* **snowmen** something that looks like a person and is made from snow *The kids made a snowman in the garden.*

snowplough *UK* (*US* **snowplow**) /ˈsnəʊplaʊ/ *noun* [C] a vehicle used for moving snow off roads and railways

snowstorm /ˈsnəʊstɔːm/ *noun* [C] a storm when a lot of snow falls

snowy /ˈsnəʊi/ *adjective* snowing or covered with snow *a cold, snowy day*

Snr *UK* (*UK/US* **Sr**) *written abbreviation for* senior (= the older of two men in a family with the same name) *Thomas Smith, Snr*

snub /snʌb/ *verb* [T] **snubbing**, *past* **snubbed** to be rude to someone, especially by not speaking to them •**snub** *noun* [C]

snuck /snʌk/ *US past of* sneak

snuff¹ /snʌf/ *noun* [U] tobacco powder that people breathe in through their noses, especially in the past

snuff² /snʌf/ *verb*
snuff sth out *phrasal verb* **1** [END] *informal* to suddenly end something *England's chances were snuffed out by three brilliant goals from the Italians.* **2** [FLAME] to stop a candle flame from burning by covering it or pressing it with your fingers

snug /snʌg/ *adjective* **1** [PLACE/PERSON] warm and comfortable *a snug little house* **2** [CLOTHES] Snug clothes fit tightly. *a pair of snug brown shoes* •**snugly** *adverb*

snuggle /ˈsnʌgl/ *verb* **snuggle up/down/into, etc** to move into a warm, comfortable position *I **snuggled up to** him on the sofa.*

O→**so¹** /səʊ/ *adverb* **1** [VERY] used before an adjective or adverb to emphasize what you are saying, especially when there is a particular result *I was so tired when I got home.* [+ (that)] *I was so upset that I couldn't speak.* **2** [ANSWER] used to give a short answer to a question to avoid repeating a phrase *"Is Ben coming to the party?" "I hope so."* **3 so did we/so have I/so is mine, etc** used to say that someone else also does something or that the same thing is true about someone or something else *"We saw the new Star Trek movie last night." "Oh, so did we."* **4** [GET ATTENTION] used to get someone's attention when you are going to ask them a question or when you are going to start talking *So, when are you two going to get married?* **5** [SHOW SOMETHING] used with a movement of your hand to show someone how to do something or show them the size of something *The box was so big.* ○ *For this exercise, you have to put your hands **like so**.* **6 so it is/so they are, etc** used to agree with something that you had not noticed before *"The cat's hiding under the chair." "So it is."* **7 or so** used after a number or amount to show that it is not exact *"How many people were at the party?" "Fifty or so, I guess."* **8 I told you so** used to say that you were right and that someone should have believed you **9 So (what)?** used to say that you do not think something is important, especially in a rude way *"She might tell Emily." "So what?"* **10 and so on/forth** used after a list of things to show that you could have added other similar things *She plays a lot of tennis and squash and so on.* **11 so as (not) to do sth** used to give the reason for doing something *He went in very quietly so as not to wake the baby.* **12 only so much/many** used to say that there are limits to something *There's only so much help you can give someone.* **13 so much for...** *informal* used to say that something has not been useful or successful *"The computer's crashed again." "So much for modern technology."*

O→**so²** /səʊ/ *conjunction* **1** [REASON] used to say that something is the reason why something else happens *I was tired so I went to bed.* ○ *Greg had some money so he bought a bike.* **2 so (that)** in order to make something happen or be possible *He put his glasses on so that he could see the television better.* **3** [CONNECT] used at the beginning of a sentence to connect it with something that was said or happened previously *So we're not going away this weekend after all?*

so³ /səʊ/ *adjective* **be so** to be correct or true *"Apparently, she's moving to Canada." "Is that so?"*

soak /səʊk/ *verb* [I, T] **1** [PUT IN LIQUID] If you soak something, or let it soak, you put it in a liquid for a period of time. *He left the pan in the sink to soak.* ○ *Soak the bread in the milk.* **2** [MAKE WET] If liquid soaks somewhere or soaks something, it makes something very wet. *The rain soaked my clothes.* ○ *The ink **soaked through** the paper onto the table.*
soak sth up *phrasal verb* If a dry substance soaks up a liquid, the liquid goes into the substance. *Fry the potatoes until they soak up all the oil.*

soaked /səʊkt/ *adjective* completely wet *My shirt was soaked.*

soaking /ˈsəʊkɪŋ/ *adjective* completely wet *You're soaking - why didn't you take an umbrella?* ○ *The dog was **soaking wet**.*

so-and-so /ˈsəʊəndsəʊ/ *noun* [C] **1** [NO NAME] used to talk about someone or something without saying a particular name *It was the usual village news - so-and-so got married to so-and-so, and so-and-so's having a baby.* **2** [BAD PERSON] *informal* someone who you do not like *He's a lazy so-and-so.*

O→**soap** /səʊp/ *noun* **1** [FOR WASHING] [U] a substance that you use for washing *a **bar of soap*** ○ *soap powder* ➲See colour picture **The Bathroom** on page Centre 3 **2** [TELEVISION PROGRAMME] [C] (*also* ˈ**soap** ˌ**opera**) a television programme about the lives of a group of people that is broadcast several times every week

ˈ**soap** ˌ**opera** (*informal* **soap**) *noun* [C] a series of television or radio programmes that continues over a long period and is about the lives of a group of characters

soapy /ˈsəʊpi/ *adjective* containing soap, or covered with soap *soapy hands*

soar /sɔːʳ/ *verb* [I] **1** [INCREASE] to increase to a high level very quickly *House prices have* *soared.* **2** IN THE SKY to move quickly and smoothly in the sky, or to move quickly up into the sky *The birds were soaring high above.* •**soaring** *adjective*

sob /sɒb/ *verb* [I] **sobbing**, *past* **sobbed** to cry in a noisy way •**sob** *noun* [C]

sober[1] /ˈsəʊbəʳ/ *adjective* **1** NOT DRUNK Someone who is sober is not drunk. **2** SERIOUS Someone who is sober is serious and thinks a lot. *He was in a sober mood.* **3** NOT BRIGHT *UK* Clothes or colours that are sober are plain and not bright. *a sober, grey dress* •**soberly** *adverb*

sober[2] /ˈsəʊbəʳ/ *verb*
sober (sb) up *phrasal verb* to become less drunk or to make someone become less drunk

sobering /ˈsəʊbərɪŋ/ *adjective* making you feel serious *a* ***sobering thought***

so-called /ˌsəʊˈkɔːld/ *adjective* [always before noun] used to show that you think a word that is used to describe someone or something is wrong *My so-called friend has stolen my girlfriend.*

soccer /ˈsɒkəʳ/ (*also UK* **football**) *noun* [U] SPORT a game in which two teams of eleven people kick a ball and try to score goals ➲See colour picture **Sports 2** on page Centre 15

sociable /ˈsəʊʃəbl/ *adjective* Someone who is sociable enjoys being with people and meeting new people.

O- **social** /ˈsəʊʃəl/ *adjective* **1** SOCIETY relating to society and the way people live *social problems* ○ *social and political changes* **2** relating to the things you do with other people for enjoyment when you are not working *I have a very good* ***social life***. •**socially** *adverb* ➲Compare **anti-social**

socialism /ˈsəʊʃəlɪzəm/ *noun* [U] POLITICS a political system in which the government owns important businesses and industries, and which allows the people to share the money and opportunities equally

socialist /ˈsəʊʃəlɪst/ *noun* [C] POLITICS someone who supports socialism •**socialist** *adjective socialist principles*

socialize (*also UK* **-ise**) /ˈsəʊʃəlaɪz/ *verb* [I] to spend time enjoying yourself with other people *The cafe is a place where students can* ***socialize with*** *teachers.*

ˌsocial ˈnetworking *noun* [U] INTERNET using a website to communicate with friends and to meet other people ➲See Extra help page **The Web and the Internet** on page Centre 37.

ˌsocial ˈscience *noun* [C, U] SOCIETY the study of society and the way people live

ˌsocial seˈcurity *noun* [U] SOCIETY, FINANCE money that the government gives to people who are old, ill, or not working

ˈsocial ˌworker *noun* [C] SOCIETY someone whose job is to help people who have problems because they are poor, old, have difficulties with their family, etc •**social work** *noun* [U]

WORD PARTNERS FOR ***society***

a **democratic/free/modern/multicultural/secular** society

O- **society** /səˈsaɪəti/ *noun* **1** SOCIETY [C, U] a large group of people who live in the same country or area and have the same laws, traditions, etc *The US is a multicultural society.* **2** [C] an organization for people who have the same interest or aim *the London Zoological Society* ➲See also: **building society**

socio- /səʊʃiəʊ-/ *prefix* SOCIETY relating to society *socio-economic*

sociology /ˌsəʊʃiˈɒlədʒi/ *noun* [U] SOCIETY the study of society and the relationship between people in society •**sociologist** /ˌsəʊʃiˈɒlədʒɪst/ *noun* [C] someone who studies sociology

sociopath /ˈsəʊʃiəʊpæθ/ *noun* [C] someone who is completely unable to behave in a way that is acceptable to society

sock /sɒk/ *noun* [C] *plural* **socks**, *also US* **sox** something that you wear on your foot inside your shoe [**usually plural**] *a pair of black socks* ➲See colour picture **Clothes** on page Centre 9

socket /ˈsɒkɪt/ *noun* [C] **1** ELECTRICITY the place on a wall where you connect electrical equipment to the electricity supply **2** HOLLOW PLACE a hollow place where one thing fits inside another thing *Your eyeball is in your eye socket.*

soda /ˈsəʊdə/ *noun* **1** FOOD [U] (*also* **ˈsoda ˌwater**) water with bubbles in it that you mix with other drinks **2** FOOD [C, U] *US* (*also* **ˈsoda ˌpop**) a sweet drink with bubbles *a can of soda*

sodden /ˈsɒdən/ *adjective* extremely wet

sodium /ˈsəʊdiəm/ *noun* [U] CHEMISTRY a chemical element that is found in salt and food (symbol **Na**) *a low-sodium diet*

sodium carbonate /ˌsəʊdiəmˈkɑːbəneɪt/ *noun* [U] CHEMISTRY a chemical compound used to make water soft, and in foods and producing goods, in the form of white powder or crystals (formula Na_2CO_3) ➲See picture at **sodium chloride**

ˌsodium ˈchloride *noun* [U] CHEMISTRY salt (formula NaCl) ➲See picture **sodium chloride** on next page

sodium hydroxide /ˌsəʊdiəmhaɪˈdrɒksaɪd/ *noun* [U] CHEMISTRY a chemical compound used in soap and paper production and in powerful cleaning substances; caustic soda (formula NaOH) ➲See picture at **sodium chloride**

ˌsodium ˈnitrate *noun* [U] CHEMISTRY a chemical compound used to make explosives, fireworks and fertilizers, and to keep meat in good condition (formula $NaNO_3$)

O- **sofa** /ˈsəʊfə/ *noun* [C] a large, comfortable seat for more than one person ➲See colour picture **The Living Room** on page Centre 4

O- **soft** /sɒft/ *adjective* **1** NOT HARD not hard, and easy to press *a soft cushion* ○ *Cook the onion until it's soft.* **2** SMOOTH smooth and pleasant to touch *soft hair/skin* **3** SOUND A soft sound is very quiet. *He spoke in a soft voice.* **4** COLOUR/LIGHT A soft colour or light is not bright. *soft lilac paint* **5** PERSON too kind and not angry enough when someone does something wrong *The kids are naughty because she's too* ***soft on*** *them.* **6** DRUGS Soft drugs are illegal drugs that some people think are not dangerous. •**softness** *noun* [U] ➲See also: have a soft **spot**[1] for sb

softball /ˈsɒftbɔːl/ *noun* [U] SPORT a game that is like baseball but played with a larger and softer ball

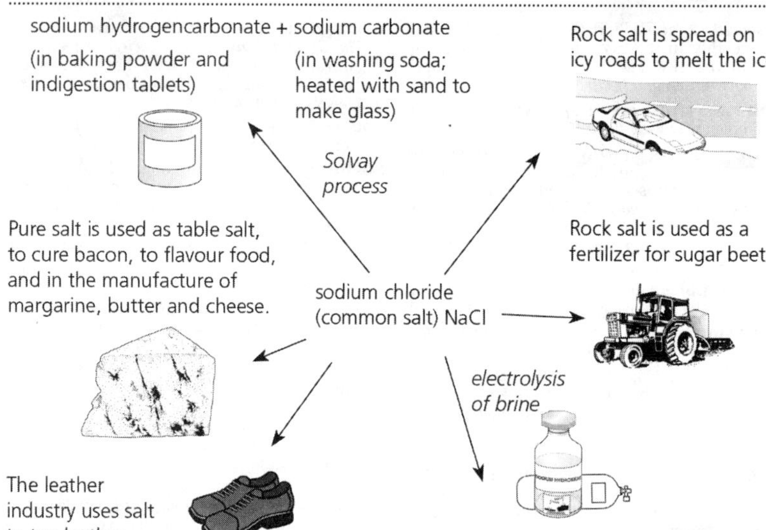
sodium hydrogencarbonate + sodium carbonate
(in baking powder and indigestion tablets)
(in washing soda; heated with sand to make glass)
Solvay process
Rock salt is spread on icy roads to melt the ice.
Pure salt is used as table salt, to cure bacon, to flavour food, and in the manufacture of margarine, butter and cheese.
sodium chloride (common salt) NaCl
Rock salt is used as a fertilizer for sugar beet.
electrolysis of brine
The leather industry uses salt to tan leather.
chlorine + hydrogen + sodium hydroxide

sodium chloride

ˌsoft ˈdrink *UK* (*US* **ˈsoftˌdrink**) *noun* [C] **FOOD** a cold, sweet drink that does not have alcohol in it

soften /ˈsɒfᵊn/ *verb* [I, T] **1** BECOME SOFTER to become softer or to make something become softer *Heat the butter until it softens.* **2** BECOME GENTLE to become more gentle or to make someone or something become more gentle *Her voice softened.*

softly /ˈsɒftli/ *adverb* in a quiet or gentle way *"Are you OK?" she said softly.*

ˌsoft ˈoption *noun* [C] *UK* a choice that is easier than other choices *The cookery course is not a soft option.*

ˌsoft ˈpalate *noun* [C] **ANATOMY** the soft part that forms the top of the mouth at the back, separating the nose from the throat ➲Compare **hard palate** ➲See picture at **respiratory system**

soft-spoken /ˌsɒftˈspəʊkᵊn/ *adjective* having a quiet, gentle voice *a small, soft-spoken man*

software /ˈsɒftweəʳ/ *noun* [U] **COMPUTING** programs that you use to make a computer do different things *educational software*

softwood /ˈsɒftwʊd/ *noun* [U] **DT** wood from evergreen (= never losing their leaves) trees which grow quickly

soggy /ˈsɒgi/ *adjective* very wet and soft *soggy ground*

soil[1] /sɔɪl/ *noun* [C, U] **FARMING** the top layer of earth that plants grow in *clay/sandy soil*

soil[2] /sɔɪl/ *verb* [T] *formal* to make something dirty •**soiled** *adjective* dirty *soiled clothes*

solace /ˈsɒləs/ *noun* [U no plural] *formal* comfort when you are feeling sad *Music was a great solace to me.*

solar /ˈsəʊləʳ/ *adjective* **ASTRONOMY** relating to, or involving the sun ***solar panels***

ˌsolar ˈenergy *noun* [U] **PHYSICS, ENVIRONMENT** energy that uses the power of the sun

ˌsolar ˈpanel *noun* [C] **ENVIRONMENT** a piece of equipment that changes light from the sun into electricity

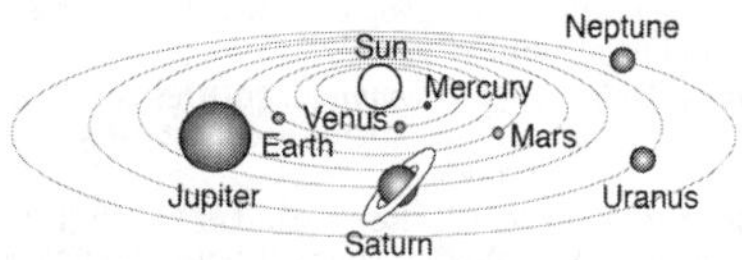
Neptune
Sun
Mercury
Venus
Earth
Mars
Jupiter
Uranus
Saturn

solar system

the ˈsolar ˌsystem *noun* **ASTRONOMY** the sun and planets that move around it

sold /səʊld/ *past of* sell

solder /ˈsəʊl.dəʳ/ *verb* [T] **DT** to join pieces of metal together using melted metal to stick them •**solder** *noun* [U] *I used a small amount of solder to join the pieces.*

O‑‑**soldier** /ˈsəʊldʒəʳ/ *noun* [C] a member of an army

sole[1] /səʊl/ *adjective* [**always before noun**] **1** ONLY only *the sole survivor* **2** NOT SHARED not shared with anyone else *She has **sole responsibility** for the project.*

sole[2] /səʊl/ *noun* **1** **ANATOMY** [C] the bottom part of your foot that you walk on **2** [C] the part of a shoe that is under your foot **3** **FOOD** [C, U] a small, flat fish that you can eat

solely /ˈsəʊlli/ *adverb* only, and not involving anyone or anything else *I bought it solely for that purpose.*

solemn /ˈsɒləm/ *adjective* **1** [SERIOUS] serious or sad *solemn music* **2** [PROMISE/WARNING ETC] A solemn promise, warning, etc is serious and sincere. •**solemnly** *adverb* •**solemnity** /səˈlemnəti/ *noun* [U]

ˌ**sole** ˈ**trader** *noun* [C] **ECONOMICS** a person who has a business on their own, with no business partners

solicit /səˈlɪsɪt/ *verb* **1** [ASK FOR SOMETHING] [T] *formal* to ask someone for money, information, or help *to solicit donations for a charity* **2** [SEX] [I] to offer sex for money, usually in a public place

soliciting /səˈlɪsɪtɪŋ/ *noun* [U] when someone offers to have sex for money

solicitor /səˈlɪsɪtəʳ/ *noun* [C] **LAW** in Britain, a lawyer who gives legal advice and help, and who works in the lower courts of law ⊃See Common Learner Error at **lawyer**

O⁻ **solid**[1] /ˈsɒlɪd/ *adjective* **1** [HARD/FIRM] hard and firm without holes or spaces, and not liquid or gas *solid ground* ○ *solid food* **2** [STRONG] strong and not easily broken or damaged *solid furniture* **3 solid gold/silver/wood, etc** gold/silver/wood, etc with nothing added *a solid silver bracelet* **4** [TIME] continuing for a period of time without stopping *The noise continued for two solid hours/two hours solid.* **5** [INFORMATION] [**always before noun**] Solid information, proof, etc is based on facts and you are certain that it is correct. *This provides **solid evidence** that he committed the crime.* **6** [PERSON] honest and able to be trusted •**solidity** /səˈlɪdəti/ *noun* [U] •**solidly** *adverb*

solid[2] /ˈsɒlɪd/ *noun* [C] **1 PHYSICS** a substance or object that is not a liquid or a gas **2** a shape that has length, width, and height, and is not flat

solidarity /ˌsɒlɪˈdærəti/ *noun* [U] agreement and support between people in a group who have similar aims or beliefs

solidify /səˈlɪdɪfaɪ/ *verb* [I] **PHYSICS** If a liquid solidifies, it becomes solid.

solids /ˈsɒlɪdz/ *noun* [plural] **FOOD** food that is not liquid *Three weeks after the operation he still couldn't eat solids.*

solipsism /ˈsɒlɪpsɪzᵊm/ *noun* [U] the belief that in life you can only really know yourself and your own experiences

solitaire /ˌsɒlɪˈteəʳ/ (US) /ˈsɒləteər/ *US* (*UK* **patience**) *noun* [U] a card game for one person

solitary /ˈsɒlɪtᵊri/ *adjective* **1** [ONLY] A solitary person or thing is the only person or thing in a place. *a solitary figure/walker* **2** [DONE ALONE] A solitary activity is done alone. *solitary walks*

ˌ**solitary con**ˈ**finement** *noun* [U] when a prisoner is kept in a room alone as a punishment

solitude /ˈsɒlɪtjuːd/ *noun* [U] being alone *He went upstairs to read the letter **in solitude**.*

solo[1] /ˈsəʊləʊ/ *adjective, adverb* done alone by one person only *a **solo performance*** ○ *to **perform solo***

solo[2] /ˈsəʊləʊ/ *noun* [C] **MUSIC** a piece of music for one person or one instrument

soloist /ˈsəʊləʊɪst/ *noun* [C] **MUSIC** a musician who performs a solo

solstice /ˈsɒlstɪs/ *noun* [C] **ASTRONOMY** the longest day or the longest night of the year *the **summer/winter solstice***

soluble /ˈsɒljəbl/ *adjective* **CHEMISTRY** If a substance is soluble, it will dissolve in water. *soluble vitamins* ○ *These tablets are soluble in water.*

solute /ˈsɒljuːt/ *noun* [C, U] **CHEMISTRY** a substance that has been dissolved in another substance

WORD PARTNERS FOR ***solution***

find/offer/provide/seek a solution • a **diplomatic/good/long-term/peaceful/simple/workable** solution • a solution **to** sth

O⁻ **solution** /səˈluːʃᵊn/ *noun* [C] **1** [ANSWER] the answer to a problem *There's no easy **solution to** this problem.* **2 CHEMISTRY** a liquid which a substance has been dissolved into

COMMON LEARNER ERROR

solution to a problem

Be careful to choose the correct preposition after **solution**.

This could be one solution to the problem.

~~*This could be one solution of the problem.*~~

the Solvay process /ˈsɒlveɪˌprəʊses/ *noun* **CHEMISTRY** a method used in industry to produce sodium carbonate ⊃See picture at **sodium chloride**

O⁻ **solve** /sɒlv/ *verb* [T] to find the answer to something *to **solve a problem*** ○ *to **solve a mystery/puzzle*** ○ *Police are still no nearer to **solving the crime**.*

solvent[1] /ˈsɒlvənt/ *noun* [C] **CHEMISTRY** a liquid which is used to dissolve other substances

solvent[2] /ˈsɒlvənt/ *adjective* **FINANCE** having enough money to pay your debts

sombre *UK* (*US* **somber**) /ˈsɒmbəʳ/ *adjective* **1** [SAD] sad and serious *a **sombre expression/mood*** **2** [DARK] dark and without bright colours *a **sombre colour***

O⁻ **some**[1] *strong form* /sʌm/ *weak form* /sᵊm/ *pronoun, quantifier* **1** [UNKNOWN AMOUNT] used to refer to an amount of something without saying exactly how much or how many *You'll need a pair of scissors and some glue.* ○ *I can't eat all this chocolate, would you like some?* ○ *Could I have **some more** (= an extra amount of) paper, please?* **2** [NOT ALL] used to refer to part of a larger amount or number of something and not all of it *In some cases it's possible to fix the problem right away.* ○ ***Some of** the children were frightened.* **3** [UNKNOWN NAME] used to refer to someone or something when you do not know the name of it or exact details about it *Some girl phoned for you, but she didn't leave a message.* **4 some time/distance, etc** a large

S

amount of time, distance, etc *I'm afraid it'll be some time before it's ready.*

COMMON LEARNER ERROR

some or **any?**

Be careful not to confuse these two words. **Any** is used in questions and negative sentences.

Have you got any friends in America?

I haven't got any money.

Some is used in positive sentences.

I've got some friends in America.

Sometimes **some** is used in questions, especially when the speaker thinks that the answer will be 'yes'.

Have you got some money I could borrow?

The same rules are true for 'something/anything' and 'someone/anyone'.

I didn't see anyone I knew.

I saw someone I knew at the party.

some² *strong form* /sʌm/ *weak form* /sᵊm/ *adverb* used before a number to show that it is not the exact amount *He died some ten years ago.*

O-- **somebody** /ˈsʌmbədi/ *pronoun another word for* someone

someday /ˈsʌmdeɪ/ *adverb US* at an unknown time in the future *We plan to get married someday.*

O-- **somehow** /ˈsʌmhaʊ/ *adverb* in a way which you do not know or do not understand *Don't worry, we'll fix it somehow.* ○ ***Somehow or other*** (= I do not know how) *they managed to get in.*

O-- **someone** /ˈsʌmwʌn/ (*also* **somebody**) *pronoun* **1** used to refer to a person when you do not know who they are or when it is not important who they are *There's someone at the door.* ○ *Will someone please answer the phone?* **2 someone else** a different person *Sorry, I thought you were talking to someone else.*

someplace /ˈsʌmpleɪs/ *adverb US* used to refer to a place when you do not know where it is or when it is not important where it is *They live someplace in the South.* ○ *If they don't like it here, they can go* ***someplace else*** (= to a different place).

somersault /ˈsʌməsɔːlt/ *noun* [C] when you roll your body forwards or backwards so that your feet go over your head and come back down to the ground again •**somersault** *verb* [I]

O-- **something** /ˈsʌmθɪŋ/ *pronoun* **1** used to refer to a thing when you do not know what it is or when it is not important what it is *As soon as I walked in, I noticed that something was missing.* ○ *We know about the problem and we're trying to do something about it.* ○ *It's not something that will be easy to change.* ○ *There's* ***something else*** (= another thing) *I wanted to tell you.* **2 or something (like that)** used to show that what you have just said is only an example or you are not certain about it *Why don't you go to a movie or something?* **3 something like** similar to or approximately *He paid something like $2000 for his car.* **4 be something** *informal* to be a thing which is important, special, or useful *The President visiting our hotel - that would really be something.* **5 something of a sth** used to describe a person or thing in a way which is partly true but not completely or exactly *It came as something of a surprise.* **6 be/have something to do with sth/sb** to be related to something or a cause of something but not in a way which you know about or understand exactly *It might have something to do with the way it's made.*

sometime /ˈsʌmtaɪm/ *adverb* used to refer to a time when you do not know exactly what it is or when it is not important what it is *sometime before June* ○ *You must come over and visit sometime.*

O-- **sometimes** /ˈsʌmtaɪmz/ *adverb* on some occasions but not always or often *He does cook sometimes, but not very often.* ○ *Sometimes I feel like no one understands me.*

somewhat /ˈsʌmwɒt/ *adverb formal* slightly *We were somewhat disappointed with the food.*

O-- **somewhere** /ˈsʌmweəʳ/ *adverb* **1** used to refer to a place when you do not know exactly where it is or when it is not important exactly where it is *They had difficulties finding somewhere to live.* ○ *He comes from somewhere near London.* ○ *Can you think of* ***somewhere else*** (= a different place) *we could go?* **2 somewhere around/between, etc** approximately *He earns somewhere around £50,000 a year.* **3 get somewhere** to achieve something or to make progress *Right, that's the printer working. Now we're getting somewhere!*

O-- **son** /sʌn/ *noun* [C] **SOCIETY** your male child

sonar /ˈsəʊnɑːʳ/ *noun* [U] **PHYSICS** a system, used especially on ships, which uses sound waves to find the position of things in the water

sonata /səˈnɑːtə/ *noun* [C] **MUSIC** a piece of music written to be played on a piano or on another instrument and the piano together

WORD PARTNERS FOR ***song***

sing/write a song • a song **about** sth • a **love** song

O-- **song** /sɒŋ/ *noun* [C] **MUSIC** words that go with a short piece of music *a folk/****love song*** ○ *to* ***sing*** *a* ***song***

songwriter /ˈʃɒŋˌraɪtəʳ/ *noun* [C] **MUSIC** someone who writes songs

sonic /ˈsɒnɪk/ *adjective* **PHYSICS** relating to sound

son-in-law /ˈsʌnɪnlɔː/ *noun* [C] *plural* **sons-in-law** your daughter's husband

sonnet /ˈsɒnɪt/ *noun* [C] **LITERATURE** a poem with 14 lines, written in a particular pattern *Shakespeare's sonnets*

O-- **soon** /suːn/ *adverb* **1** after a short period of time *I've got to leave quite soon.* ○ *It's too soon to make a decision.* ○ *He joined the company soon after leaving college.* **2 as soon as** at the same time or a very short time after *As soon as I saw her, I knew there was something wrong.* ○ *They want it as soon as possible.* **3 sooner or later** used to say that you do not know exactly when something will happen, but you are sure that it will happen *Sooner or later they'll realize that it's not going to work.* **4 would sooner** would prefer *I'd sooner spend* *a bit more money than take chances with safety.* **5 no sooner ... than** used to show that something happens immediately after something else *No sooner had we got home than the phone rang.*

soot /sʊt/ *noun* [U] a black powder produced when coal, wood, etc is burnt

soothe /suːð/ *verb* [T] **1** MAKE LESS PAINFUL to make something feel less painful *I had a long, hot bath to soothe my aching muscles.* **2** MAKE CALM to make someone feel calm or less worried *to soothe a crying baby* •**soothing** *adjective* making you feel calm or in less pain ***soothing music*** ○ *a* ***soothing effect/voice***

sophisticated /səˈfɪstɪkeɪtɪd/ *adjective* **1** PERSON well-educated and having experience of the world or knowledge of culture **2** SYSTEM A sophisticated machine or system is very advanced and works in a clever way. *a sophisticated computer system* •**sophistication** /səˌfɪstɪˈkeɪʃᵊn/ *noun* [U]

sophomore /ˈsɒfəmɔːʳ/ *noun* [C] *US* **EDUCATION** a student studying in the second year of a course at a US university or high school (= school for students aged 15 to 18)

soprano /səˈprɑːnəʊ/ *noun* [C] **MUSIC** a female singer who sings the highest notes

sordid /ˈsɔːdɪd/ *adjective* unpleasant, dirty, or immoral *a sordid affair*

sore¹ /sɔːʳ/ *adjective* **1** **HEALTH** painful, especially when touched *a* ***sore throat****/knee* ○ *Her eyes were red and sore.* **2 sore point/spot/subject** a subject which causes disagreement or makes people angry when it is discussed *Money is a bit of a sore point with him at the moment.* ➲See also: stick/stand out like a sore **thumb**¹

sore² /sɔːʳ/ *noun* [C] **HEALTH** an area of skin which is red and painful because of an infection

sorely /ˈsɔːli/ *adverb formal* very much *to be* ***sorely disappointed/tempted*** ○ *He will be* ***sorely missed*** *by everyone.*

sorrow /ˈsɒrəʊ/ *noun* [C, U] *formal* when someone feels very sad •**sorrowful** *adjective formal*

O‑**sorry** /ˈsɒri/ *adjective* **1 (I'm) sorry** something that you say to be polite when you have done something wrong, or when you cannot agree with someone or accept something *Sorry I'm late.* ○ *Oh, I'm sorry. I didn't see you there.* ○ *Tom, I'm so* ***sorry about*** *last night - it was all my fault.* ○ *I'm sorry, but I just don't think it's a good idea.* **2** SYMPATHY used to show sympathy or sadness for a person or situation *I* ***feel sorry for*** *the children - it must be very hard for them.* ○ *I was* ***sorry to hear*** *about your brother's accident.* [+ **(that)**] *I'm sorry that things didn't work out for you.* **3 Sorry?** *mainly UK* used as a polite way to say that you did not hear what someone has just said *Sorry? What was that?* **4** WISH SOMETHING WAS DIFFERENT used to say that you wish something in the past had not happened or had been different [+ **(that)**] *I'm sorry that I ever met him.* **5 a sorry sight/state/tale** a bad condition or situation *Her car was in a sorry state after the accident.*

O‑**sort¹** /sɔːt/ *noun* **1** [C] a type of something *We both like the same* ***sort of*** *music.* ○ *What sort of shoes does she wear?* ○ *I'm going to have a salad* ***of some sort.*** **2 all sorts of sth** many different types of something **3 sort of** *informal* used to describe a situation approximately *It's a sort of pale orange colour.* **4 (and) that sort of thing** *informal* used to show that what you have just said is only an example from a larger group of things *They sell souvenirs, postcards, that sort of thing.* **5 of sorts** *informal* used to describe something which is not a typical example *He managed to make a curtain of sorts out of an old sheet.*

O‑**sort²** /sɔːt/ *verb* **1** [T] to arrange things into different groups or types or into an order *They* ***sort*** *the paper* ***into*** *white and coloured for recycling.* ○ *The names are sorted alphabetically.* **2 be sorted/get sth sorted** *UK informal* If something is sorted or you get something sorted, you successfully deal with it and find a solution or agreement. *Did you manage to get everything sorted?*

sort sth out *phrasal verb* to successfully deal with something, such as a problem or difficult situation *Have you sorted out your schedule yet?*

sort through sth *phrasal verb* to look at a number of things to organize them or to find something *I had the sad task of sorting through her papers after she died.*

so-so /ˈsəʊsəʊ/ *adjective informal* not very good, but not bad *"Are you feeling better today?" "So-so."*

soufflé /ˈsuːfleɪ/ (US) /suːfˈleɪ/ *noun* [C, U] **FOOD** a light food made by baking the white part of eggs *chocolate/cheese soufflé*

sought /sɔːt/ *past of* seek

sought-after /ˈsɔːtˌɑːftəʳ/ *adjective* wanted by lots of people, but difficult to get *a house in a sought-after location*

soul /səʊl/ *noun* **1** **RELIGION** [C] the part of a person which is not their body, which some people believe continues to exist after they die **2** **MUSIC** [U] (*also* ˈ**soul** ˌ**music**) popular music which expresses deep feelings, originally performed by Black Americans **3** PERSON [C] *informal* a person *I didn't see a soul when I went out.* ➲See also: **heart** and soul

soulful /ˈsəʊlfᵊl/ *adjective* expressing deep feelings, often sadness ***soulful eyes***

soulless /ˈsəʊlləs/ *adjective* without any interesting or attractive characteristics *a soulless housing estate*

soul-searching /ˈsəʊlˌsɜːtʃɪŋ/ *noun* [U] when you think very carefully about something to decide if it is the right thing to do *After much soul-searching, he decided to leave his job.*

WORD PARTNERS FOR ***sound***

emit/make/produce a sound • **hear/listen** to a sound • the sound **of** sth

O‑**sound¹** /saʊnd/ *noun* **1** [C, U] something that you hear or that can be heard *I could* ***hear*** *the* ***sounds*** *of the city through the open window.* ○ *She stood completely still, not* ***making a sound.*** ○ *Can you turn the sound up* (= make a radio, television, etc louder)*?* **2 the sound of sth** *informal* how something seems to be, from what you have been told or heard *I like the*

S

sound of the beef in red wine sauce. ○ *He's really enjoying college, **by the sound of it**.*

O━**sound²** /saʊnd/ *verb* **1 sound good/interesting/strange, etc** to seem good/interesting/strange, etc, from what you have heard or read *Your job sounds really interesting.* **2 sound like/as if/as though** to seem like something, from what you have heard or read *That sounds like a really good idea.* **3 sound angry/happy/rude, etc** to seem angry/happy/rude, etc when you speak *You don't sound too sure about it.* **4** [I, T] to make a noise *It looks and **sounds like** a real bird.* ○ *If the alarm sounds, you must leave the building immediately.*

sound³ /saʊnd/ *adjective* good or safe and able to be trusted ***sound advice/judgment*** ○ *The building is quite old, but still **structurally sound**.* ➲Opposite **unsound**

sound⁴ /saʊnd/ *adverb* **sound asleep** in a deep sleep

soundbite /ˈsaʊndbaɪt/ *noun* [C] **LANGUAGE** a short statement which is easy to remember, usually used by a politician to get attention on television, in newspapers, etc

ˈsound ˌcard *noun* [C] **COMPUTING** a small piece of electronic equipment inside a computer that makes it able to record and play sound

soundly /ˈsaʊndli/ *adverb* **1 sleep soundly** to sleep well **2 soundly beaten/defeated** beaten/defeated easily and by a large amount

soundtrack /ˈsaʊndtræk/ *noun* [C] **MUSIC** the music used in a film

O━**soup** /suːp/ *noun* [U] **FOOD** a hot, liquid food, made from vegetables, meat, or fish *chicken/tomato soup* ➲See colour picture **Food** on page Centre 11

sour¹ /saʊəʳ/ *adjective* **1 FOOD** having a sharp, sometimes unpleasant, taste or smell, like a lemon, and not sweet *These plums are a bit sour.* **2** very unfriendly or unpleasant *Their relationship suddenly **turned sour**.*

sour² /saʊəʳ/ *verb* [T] to make something unpleasant or unfriendly *This affair has **soured relations** between the two countries.*

WORD PARTNERS FOR ***source***

a [good/important/major, etc] source **of** sth

source /sɔːs/ *noun* [C] **1** ORIGIN where something comes from *a source of income/information* ○ *Oranges are a good **source of** vitamin C.* **2** PERSON someone who gives information to the police, newspapers, etc

ˈsource ˌcode *noun* [U] **COMPUTING** computer instructions written in a form that humans can understand, that must be changed into machine code (= a set of numbers that gives instructions to a computer)

O━**south, South** /saʊθ/ *noun* [U] **1** the direction that is on your right when you face towards the rising sun **2 the south** the part of an area that is further towards the south than the rest •**south** *adjective the south side of the house* •**south** *adverb* towards the south *Birds fly south in winter.*

southbound /ˈsaʊθbaʊnd/ *adjective* going or leading towards the south

southeast, Southeast /ˌsaʊθˈiːst/ *noun* [U] **1** the direction between south and east **2 the southeast** the southeast part of a country •**southeast, Southeast** *adjective, adverb*

southeastern, Southeastern /ˌsaʊθˈiːstən/ *adjective* in or from the southeast

southerly /ˈsʌðᵊli/ *adjective* **1** DIRECTION towards or in the south *We continued in a southerly direction.* **2** WIND A southerly wind comes from the south.

O━**southern, Southern** /ˈsʌðən/ *adjective* in or from the south part of an area *the southern half of the country*

southerner, Southerner /ˈsʌðᵊnəʳ/ *noun* [C] someone from the south part of a country

southernmost /ˈsʌðənməʊst/ *adjective* The southernmost part of an area is the part furthest to the south.

south-facing /ˈsaʊθˌfeɪsɪŋ/ *adjective* [**always before noun**] positioned towards the south *a south-facing garden/window*

the ˌSouth ˈPole *noun* **GEOGRAPHY** a point on the Earth's surface which is furthest south

southward, southwards /ˈsaʊθwəd, ˈsaʊθwədz/ *adverb* towards the south •**southward** *adjective a southward direction*

southwest, Southwest /ˌsaʊθˈwest/ *noun* [U] **1** the direction between south and west **2 the southwest** the southwest part of the country •**southwest, Southwest** *adjective, adverb*

southwestern, Southwestern /ˌsaʊθˈwestən/ *adjective* in or from the southwest

souvenir /ˌsuːvᵊnˈɪəʳ/ *noun* [C] something which you buy or keep to remember a special event or holiday *a **souvenir shop*** ○ *I kept the ticket as a **souvenir of** my trip.*

sovereign¹ /ˈsɒvᵊrɪn/ *adjective* **POLITICS** A sovereign country or state is completely independent. •**sovereignty** /ˈsɒvrᵊnti/ *noun* [U] the power of a country to control its own government

sovereign, Sovereign² /ˈsɒvᵊrɪn/ *noun* [C] *formal* a king or queen

sow¹ /səʊ/ *verb* [T] *past tense* **sowed**, *past participle* **sown** or **sowed FARMING** to put seeds into the ground *to **sow seeds/crops***

sow² /saʊ/ *noun* [C] a female pig

soya bean /ˈsɔɪəˌbiːn/ *UK* (*US* **soybean** /ˈsɔɪbiːn/) *noun* [C] **FOOD** a bean used to produce oil, and which is used in many foods

soy sauce /ˌsɔɪˈsɔːs/ *noun* [U] **FOOD** a dark brown sauce made from soya beans, used in Chinese and Japanese cooking

spa /spɑː/ *noun* [C] **HEALTH** a place where people go to improve their health by exercising or by having baths in special water *a **health spa*** ○ *a **spa town***

WORD PARTNERS FOR ***space***

create/make space • **fill a/occupy a/take up** space • space **for** sb/sth • an **open** space

O━**space¹** /speɪs/ *noun* **1** EMPTY AREA [C, U] an empty area which is available to be used *a **parking space*** ○ *We need more **open spaces** for children to play in.* ○ *There wasn't enough **space for*** everyone. [+ **to do sth**] *We don't have the space to store it all.* **2 ASTRONOMY** [U] the area outside the Earth *They plan to send another satellite into space.* ○ *space travel* **3 in the space of six weeks/three hours, etc** during a period of six weeks/three hours, etc *It all happened in the space of 10 minutes.* ➲See also: **breathing space, outer space**

space² /speɪs/ *verb* [T] to arrange things so that there is some distance or time between them [**often passive**] *They will have to be spaced at least two metres apart.*

spacecraft /ˈspeɪskrɑːft/ *noun* [C] *plural* **spacecraft ASTRONOMY** a vehicle which can travel outside the Earth and into space

spaceship /ˈspeɪsʃɪp/ *noun* [C] **ASTRONOMY** a vehicle which can travel outside the Earth and into space, especially one which is carrying people

ˈspace ˌshuttle *noun* [C] **ASTRONOMY** a vehicle in which people travel into space (= the area outside the Earth) and back again

spacesuit /ˈspeɪssuːt/ *noun* [C] **ASTRONOMY** a piece of clothing worn by a person who travels in space to protect the body when outside a spacecraft

spacious /ˈspeɪʃəs/ *adjective* large and with a lot of space *a spacious apartment/office*

spade /speɪd/ *noun* [C] **1 FARMING** a tool with a long handle and a flat, metal part at one end used for digging **2 spades** playing cards with black leaf shapes on them *the ace of spades*

spaghetti /spəˈgeti/ *noun* [U] **FOOD** long, thin pieces of pasta

spam /spæm/ *noun* [U] **INTERNET** emails that you do not want, usually advertisements •**spam** *verb* [T] •**spammer** *noun* [C] a person who sends spam

span /spæn/ *noun* [C] **1** TIME the period of time that something exists or happens *a short **attention span*** ○ *an average **life span** of seventy years* **2** DISTANCE the length of something from one end to the other *a **wing span** of five metres* •**span** *verb* [T] **spanning**, *past* **spanned** to exist or continue for a particular distance or length of time *Her acting **career spanned** almost forty years.*

spaniel /ˈspænjəl/ *noun* [C] a dog with long hair and long ears

spank /spæŋk/ *verb* [T] to hit someone, usually a child, on their bottom

spanner /ˈspænəʳ/ *UK* (*US* **wrench**) *noun* [C] a tool with a round end that is used to turn nuts and bolts (= metal objects used to fasten things together)

spar /spɑːʳ/ *verb* [I] **sparring**, *past* **sparred** to fight or argue with someone in a friendly way

O- **spare¹** /speəʳ/ *adjective* **1** If something is spare, it is available to use, because it is extra and not being used. *a spare bedroom* ○ *spare cash* ○ ***spare parts*** **2 spare time** time when you are not working *I enjoy gardening **in my spare time**.*

spare² /speəʳ/ *noun* [C] an extra thing which is not being used and which can be used instead of a part which is broken, lost, etc

spare³ /speəʳ/ *verb* **1** GIVE [T] to give time or money to someone *I have to go soon, but I can spare a few minutes.* [+ **two objects**] *Can you spare me some change?* **2** PREVENT [+ **two objects**] to prevent someone from having to experience something unpleasant [**often passive**] *I was spared the embarrassment of having to sing in front of everybody.* **3 to spare** If you have time, money, etc to spare, you have more than you need. *I arrived at the station with more than an hour to spare.* **4 spare no effort/expense, etc** to use a lot of effort/expense, etc to do something [+ **to do sth**] We will spare no effort to find out who did this. **5 spare sb's life** to not kill someone ➲See also: spare a **thought¹** for sb

sparingly /ˈspeərɪŋli/ *adverb* carefully using only a very small amount of something *to eat/drink sparingly* •**sparing** *adjective*

spark¹ /spɑːk/ *noun* [C] **1** FIRE a very small, bright piece of burning material *The fire was caused by a spark from a cigarette.* **2** ELECTRICITY a small flash of light caused by electricity **3** START a small idea or event which causes something bigger to start

spark² /spɑːk/ (*also* **spark off**) *verb* [T] to cause an argument, fight, etc to start happening *to **spark** a **debate/protest*** ○ *to **spark criticism/fears***

sparkle¹ /ˈspɑːkl/ *verb* [I] **1** LIGHT to shine brightly because of reflected light *water sparkling in the sun* ○ *Her **eyes sparkled** with excitement.* **2** SPECIAL to do something in a special or exciting way *The concert gave her an opportunity to sparkle.*

sparkle² /ˈspɑːkl/ *noun* **1** LIGHT [C, U] the light from something reflecting on a shiny surface **2** SPECIAL [U] the quality of being special or exciting *The performance lacked a bit of sparkle.*

sparkling /ˈspɑːklɪŋ/ *adjective* **1** LIGHT shining brightly because of reflected light **2** SPECIAL special or exciting *a **sparkling performance*** ○ ***sparkling conversation*** **3 sparkling water/wine FOOD** water/wine with bubbles in it

ˈspark ˌplug *noun* [C] a part in an engine that makes the fuel burn

sparrow /ˈspærəʊ/ *noun* [C] a small, brown bird which is common in towns and cities

sparse /spɑːs/ *adjective* **1** SMALL AMOUNT existing only in small amounts over a large area ***sparse population/vegetation*** **2** ROOM A room that is sparse contains little furniture and does not seem very comfortable. •**sparsely** *adverb **sparsely populated/furnished***

spartan /ˈspɑːtən/ *adjective* very simple and not comfortable or luxurious *The rooms were clean but spartan.*

spasm /ˈspæzᵊm/ *noun* [C, U] **HEALTH** when a muscle suddenly gets tight in a way that you cannot control *a back/muscle spasm* ○ ***to go into spasm***

spasmodic /spæzˈmɒdɪk/ *adjective* happening suddenly for short periods of time and not in a regular way

spat /spæt/ *past of* spit

spate /speɪt/ *noun* **a spate of accidents/crimes/thefts, etc** a large number of bad things which happen at about the same time

S

spatial /ˈspeɪʃəl/ *adjective* relating to the position, area, and size of things •**spatially** *adverb*

spatter /ˈspætəʳ/ *verb* [T] to cover someone or something with small drops of liquid without intending to [**often passive**] *His shirt was* ***spattered with*** *blood.*

spatula /ˈspætjələ/ *noun* [C] a tool with a wide flat blade, used in cooking for mixing, spreading, or lifting food ⊃See colour picture **The Kitchen** on page Centre 2

spawn /spɔːn/ *verb* [T] to cause a lot of other things to be produced or to exist *Her death spawned several films and books.*

O‑**speak** /spiːk/ *verb past tense* **spoke**, *past participle* **spoken 1** SAY WORDS [I] to say something using your voice *to speak loudly/quietly* ○ *There was complete silence - nobody spoke.* **2 speak to sb** *mainly UK* (*mainly US* **speak with sb**) to talk to someone *Could I speak to Mr Davis, please?* ○ *Have you spoken with your new neighbors yet?* **3 speak about/of sth** to talk about something *He refused to speak about the matter in public.* **4 speak English/French/German, etc** LANGUAGE to be able to communicate in English/French/German, etc *Do you speak English?* **5** IN PUBLIC [I] to make a speech to a large group of people *She was invited to speak at a conference in Madrid.* **6 speak for/on behalf of sb** to express the feelings, opinions, etc of another person or of a group of people *I've been chosen to speak on behalf of the whole class.* **7 generally/personally, etc speaking** used to explain that you are talking about something in a general/personal, etc way *Personally speaking, I don't like cats.* **8 so to speak** used to explain that the words you are using do not have their usual meaning ⊃See also: speak/talk of the **devil**, speak your **mind**[1]

speak out *phrasal verb* to give your opinion about something in public, especially on a subject which you have strong feelings about *He decided to speak out against the bombing.*

speak up *phrasal verb* **1** TALK LOUDER to say something in a louder voice so that people can hear you *Could you speak up a bit? I can't hear you.* **2** OPINION to give your opinion about something, especially about a problem or to support someone else *It's getting bad - it's time someone spoke up about it.*

COMMON LEARNER ERROR

speak or **talk?**

Remember that you **speak** a language. You do not 'talk' it.

She speaks French.

~~*She talks French.*~~

speaker /ˈspiːkəʳ/ *noun* [C] **1** EQUIPMENT the part of a radio, CD player, etc which the sound comes out of ⊃See colour picture **The Living Room** on page Centre 4 ⊃See picture at **computer 2 an English/French/German, etc speaker** someone who can speak English/French, etc **3** SPEECH someone who makes a speech to a group of people *a* ***guest speaker***

spear /spɪəʳ/ *noun* [C] a long weapon with a sharp point at one end used for hunting

spearhead /ˈspɪəhed/ *verb* [T] to lead an attack or series of actions *to spearhead a campaign*

spearmint /ˈspɪəmɪnt/ *noun* [U] **FOOD** a type of mint (= a herb used as a flavour for sweets) *spearmint chewing gum*

OTHER WAYS OF SAYING ***special***

If someone or something is special because they are better than usual, you can describe them as **exceptional** or **outstanding**: *Their standard of acting was very high but there was one* ***exceptional/outstanding*** *performance.*

The adjective **extraordinary** is sometimes used to describe someone or something that is special in a surprising way: *Her capacity to remember things is* ***extraordinary***. • *She has an* ***extraordinary*** *talent.*

The adjectives **deluxe** and **superior** are sometimes used to describe things which you can buy which are special because they are particularly good quality: *The shop assistant tried to sell us the* ***deluxe/superior*** *model.*

The adjectives **rare** and **unique** are sometimes used instead of special when it means 'unusual': *This is a* ***rare/unique*** *opportunity to see inside the building.*

If something is special because it is of extremely good quality, you can describe it as **out of this world**: *Their chocolate cake is just* ***out of this world***.

O‑**special¹** /ˈspeʃəl/ *adjective* **1** VERY GOOD better or more important than usual things *a special friend* ○ *I'm cooking* ***something special*** *for her birthday.* **2 special attention/care/treatment** treatment that is better than usual **3 special offer** *UK* a price which is lower than usual *I bought them because they were* ***on special offer***. **4** DIFFERENT different from normal things, or used for a particular purpose *You need to use a special kind of paint.*

special² /ˈspeʃəl/ *noun* [C] **1** TELEVISION a television programme made for a particular reason or occasion and not part of a series *The Christmas special had 24.3 million viewers.* **2 FOOD** a dish in a restaurant which is not usually available ***Today's specials*** *are written on the board.*

ˌ**special efˈfects** *noun* an unusual type of action in a film, or an entertainment on stage, created by using special equipment *The new Harry Potter film includes some very frightening special effects.*

WORD PARTNERS FOR ***specialist***

a **leading** specialist • a specialist **in** sth • specialist **knowledge**

specialist /ˈspeʃəlɪst/ *noun* [C] someone who has a lot of experience, knowledge, or skill in a particular subject *a cancer/software specialist* ○ *He's* ***a specialist in*** *childhood illnesses.*

speciality /ˌspeʃiˈæləti/ *UK* (*US* **specialty** /ˈspeʃəlti/) *noun* [C] a product, skill, etc that a person or place is especially known for *We tasted a local speciality made from goat's cheese.*

specialize (*also UK* **-ise**) /ˈspeʃəlaɪz/ *verb* [I] to spend most of your time studying one particular subject or doing one type of business *She* *works for a company **specializing in** business law.* •**specialization** /ˌspeʃᵊlaɪˈzeɪʃᵊn/ *noun* [U]

specialized (*also UK* **-ised**) /ˈspeʃəlaɪzd/ *adjective* relating to a particular subject or activity and not general *specialized equipment/language*

O─ **specially** /ˈspeʃəli/ *adverb* for a particular purpose *They searched the building with specially trained dogs.* ○ *I made this **specially for** you.*

COMMON LEARNER ERROR

specially or **especially?**

Sometimes these two words both mean 'for a particular purpose'.

I cooked this meal specially/especially for you.

Specially is often used before an adjective made from a past participle, e.g. specially prepared, specially trained.

He uses a specially adapted wheelchair.

Especially is used to give emphasis to a person or thing. This word is not usually used at the beginning of a sentence.

I like all kinds of films, especially horror films.

ˌspecial ˈneeds *adjective* **HEALTH, EDUCATION** describes something that is intended for people who have an illness or condition that makes it difficult for them to do the things that other people do *a special needs school*

species /ˈspiːʃiːz/ *noun* [C] *plural* **species BIOLOGY** a group of plants or animals which share similar characteristics *a rare species of bird* ➲See Common Learner Error at **race**

specific /spəˈsɪfɪk/ *adjective* **1** PARTICULAR used to refer to a particular thing and not something general *a **specific purpose/reason*** ○ *Could we arrange a specific time to meet?* **2** EXACT exact or containing details *Could you **be more specific about** the problem?*

specifically /spəˈsɪfɪkᵊli/ *adverb* **1** PARTICULAR PURPOSE for a particular reason, purpose, etc *They're designed **specifically for** children.* [+ **to do sth**] *She bought it specifically to wear at the wedding.* **2** EXACTLY exactly or in detail *I specifically told them that she doesn't eat meat.*

specification /ˌspesɪfɪˈkeɪʃᵊn/ *noun* [C] *formal* a detailed description of how something should be done, made, etc *They are made exactly **to the customer's specifications**.*

speˌcific ˈheat (caˌpacity) *noun* [U] **PHYSICS** the amount of energy from heat that is needed to raise the temperature of a particular substance by a particular amount

specifics /spəˈsɪfɪks/ *noun* [**plural**] exact details about something *I can't comment on the specifics of the case.*

specify /ˈspesɪfaɪ/ *verb* [T] to say or describe something in a detailed way [+ **question word**] *They didn't specify what colour they wanted.*

specimen /ˈspesəmɪn/ *noun* [C] **1** EXAMPLE an animal, plant, etc used as an example of its type, especially for scientific study *This is one of the museum's finest specimens.* **2** SMALL AMOUNT a small amount of a substance, such as blood, that is used for a test

speck /spek/ *noun* [C] a very small spot or a very small amount of something *a **speck of dirt/dust*** ○ *I watched the car until it was just a tiny speck in the distance.*

speckled /ˈspekld/ *adjective* covered in a pattern of very small spots *a speckled egg*

specs /speks/ *noun* [**plural**] *informal short for* spectacles

spectacle /ˈspektəkl/ *noun* [C] **1** an event that is exciting or unusual to watch **2 make a spectacle of yourself** to do something that makes you look stupid and that makes other people look at you *He got drunk and made a real spectacle of himself.*

spectacles /ˈspektəklz/ *noun* [**plural**] *old-fashioned* glasses *a pair of spectacles*

spectacular /spekˈtækjələʳ/ *adjective* extremely good, exciting, or surprising *a **spectacular success*** ○ *a **spectacular view*** ○ ***spectacular scenery*** •**spectacularly** *adverb a spectacularly beautiful country*

spectator /spekˈteɪtəʳ/ *noun* [C] someone who watches an event, sport, etc *They won 4-0 in front of over 40,000 cheering spectators.* •**spectate** /spekˈteɪt/ *verb* [I] to watch an event, sport, etc

spectre *UK* (*US* **specter**) /ˈspektəʳ/ *noun* **1 the spectre of sth** the idea of something unpleasant that might happen in the future *This attack **raises the spectre of** a return to racial violence.* **2** [C] *literary* a ghost (= dead person's spirit)

spectroscope /ˈspektrəskəʊp/ (*also* **mass spectrometer**) *noun* [C] **PHYSICS** a piece of equipment used by scientists to separate ions into groups to measure and compare their mass and charge (= amount of electricity)

spectrum /ˈspektrəm/ *noun* [C] *plural* **spectra** **1** all the different ideas, opinions, possibilities, etc that exist *He has support from **across the** whole political **spectrum**.* **2 PHYSICS** the set of colours into which light can be separated

speculate /ˈspekjəleɪt/ *verb* [I, T] to guess possible answers to a question when you do not have enough information to be certain *The police refused to **speculate about** the cause of the accident.* [+ **that**] *The newspapers have speculated that they will get married next year.*

speculation /ˌspekjəˈleɪʃᵊn/ *noun* [U] when people guess about something without having enough information to be certain [+ **that**] *She has dismissed the claims as **pure speculation**.*

speculative /ˈspekjələtɪv/ *adjective* based on a guess and not on information *The article was dismissed as **highly/purely speculative**.* •**speculatively** *adverb*

sped /sped/ *past of* speed

WORD PARTNERS FOR ***speech***

careful/continuous/human/normal speech • **slur** your speech

O─ **speech** /spiːtʃ/ *noun* **1 LANGUAGE** [U] someone's ability to talk, or an example of someone talking *His speech was very slow and difficult to understand.* ○ *These changes can be seen in both speech and writing.* **2** [C] a formal talk that someone gives to a group of people *I had to **make a speech** at my brother's wedding.* **3 free speech/freedom of speech** the right to say or

S

write what you want ➲See also: **figure of speech, reported speech**

COMMON LEARNER ERROR

make/give a speech

Be careful to choose the correct verb.

I have to make a speech.

~~*I have to do a speech.*~~

He gave a speech at the conference.

~~*He said a speech at the conference.*~~

speechless /ˈspiːtʃləs/ *adjective* unable to speak because you are so angry, shocked, surprised, etc *I couldn't believe what he was telling me - I was speechless.*

ˈspeech recogˌnition (*also* **voice recognition**) *noun* [U] **COMPUTING** the process of changing the sound of people speaking into instructions that a computer can understand

WORD PARTNERS FOR ***speed***

gain/gather/pick up speed • **lower /reduce** sb's/sth's speed • **reach** a speed **of** [100kph/70mph, etc] • **at** a speed **of** [100kph/70mph, etc]

O-■**speed¹** /spiːd/ *noun* **1** HOW FAST [C, U] how fast something moves or happens ***high/low speed*** ○ *He was travelling* ***at a speed of*** *90 mph.* **2** FAST MOVEMENT [U] very fast movement *He put on a sudden burst of speed.* **3 up to speed** having all the most recent information about a subject or activity *The course should bring you up to speed with the latest techniques.*

speed² /spiːd/ *verb past* **sped** or **speeded 1 speed along/down/past, etc** to move somewhere or happen very fast *The three men jumped into a car and sped away.* **2 be speeding** to be driving faster than you are allowed to

speed (sth) up *phrasal verb* to move or happen faster, or to make something move or happen faster *Can you try to speed up a bit please?*

speedboat /ˈspiːdbəʊt/ *noun* [C] a small, fast boat with an engine

ˈspeed ˌdating *noun* [U] a way to meet people for possible romantic relationships, in which you talk with lots of people for a short amount of time to see if you like them

S

ˈspeed ˌdial *noun* [U] a feature on a telephone that makes it possible for you to call a number by pressing only one button •**speed dial** *verb* [I, T]

speeding /ˈspiːdɪŋ/ *noun* [U] driving faster than you are allowed to *They were stopped by the police for speeding.*

ˈspeed ˌlimit *noun* [C] the fastest speed that a vehicle is allowed to travel on a particular road *to* ***break the speed limit***

speedometer /spiːˈdɒmɪtəʳ/ *noun* [C] a piece of equipment in a vehicle that shows how fast it is moving ➲See colour picture **Car** on page Centre 7

speedy /ˈspiːdi/ *adjective* done quickly *a* ***speedy recovery*** •**speedily** *adverb*

O-■**spell¹** /spel/ *verb past* **spelled**, *also UK* **spelt 1 LANGUAGE** [T] to write down or tell someone the letters which are used to make a word *How do you spell that?* ○ *Her name's spelt S-I-A-N.* **2 LANGUAGE** [I] If you can spell, you know how to write the words of a language correctly. *My grammar's all right, but I can't spell.* **3 spell disaster/trouble, etc** If something spells disaster, trouble, etc, you think it will cause something bad to happen in the future. *The new regulations could spell disaster for small businesses.*

spell sth out *phrasal verb* to explain something in a very clear way with details *They sent me a letter,* ***spelling out the details*** *of the agreement.*

spell² /spel/ *noun* [C] **1** TIME a period of time *a short spell in Australia* ○ *a spell of dry weather* **2** MAGIC a magic instruction *The witch* ***cast a spell*** *over him and he turned into a frog.*

spell-check (*also* **spellcheck**) /ˈspeltʃek/ *verb* [T] **COMPUTING** to use a computer program to make certain that the words in a document have the correct letters in the correct order •**spell-check** *noun* [C] *to run a spell-check*

O-■**spelling** /ˈspelɪŋ/ *noun* **1 LANGUAGE** [C] how a particular word is spelt *There are two possible spellings of this word.* ○ ***spelling mistakes*** **2 LANGUAGE** [U] someone's ability to spell words *My spelling is terrible.*

spelt /spelt/ *UK past of* spell

OTHER WAYS OF SAYING ***spend***

The most common alternative is the verb **pay**: *When you booked the tickets, how much did you* ***pay?*** • *I* ***paid*** *an extra £30 to get a double room.*

The verb **invest** is used when someone spends money on something because they hope to get a profit: *She's* ***invested*** *all her savings in the business.*

If someone spends a lot of money on something, the phrasal verb **pay out** is sometimes used: *I've just* ***paid out*** *£700 to get the car fixed.*

If someone spends a lot of money on something that they want but do not need, you can use the phrasal verb **splash out**: *We've just* ***splashed out*** *£12,000 on a new kitchen.*

The phrasal verb **dip into** is sometimes used when someone spends part of a supply of money that they have been keeping: *We had to* ***dip into*** *our savings to pay for the repairs.*

If someone spends money on something when they do not want to, the phrasal verbs **fork out** and **shell out** are often used: *We had to* ***shell out*** *two thousand pounds to get the roof fixed.* • *I'm not going to* ***fork out*** *another five hundred quid for their tickets.*

O-■**spend** /spend/ *verb* [T] *past* **spent 1 FINANCE** to use money to buy or pay for something *The company has* ***spent*** *£1.9 million* ***on*** *improving its computer network.* ○ *She* ***spends*** *too much* ***money*** *on clothes.* ○ *How much did you spend?* **2** to use time doing something or being somewhere *He spent 18 months working on the project.* ○ *He's planning to* ***spend*** *some* ***time*** *at home with his family.* ○ *How long did you spend in Edinburgh?*

spending /ˈspendɪŋ/ *noun* [U] **ECONOMICS** the money which is used for a particular purpose, especially by a government or organization *government spending on health* ○ ***spending cuts***

spent[1] /spent/ *adjective* already used, so not useful or effective any more *spent bullets*

spent[2] /spent/ *past of* spend

sperm /spɜːm/ *noun* [C] *plural* **sperm BIOLOGY** a small cell produced by a male animal which joins an egg from a female animal to create a baby

spermatozoon /ˌspɜːmətəˈzəʊɒn/ *noun* [C] *plural* **spermatozoa BIOLOGY** a sperm (= cell from a male animal that joins a female's egg to make a baby)

spew /spjuː/ (*also* **spew out**) *verb* [I, T] If something spews liquid or gas, or liquid or gas spews from something, it flows out in large amounts. *The factory spews out clouds of black smoke.*

SPF /ˌespiːˈef/ *noun* [C] **MEASURES** *abbreviation for* sun protection factor: the letters and numbers on a bottle of sunscreen (= a substance which protects your skin in the sun) which shows how effective the sunscreen is

WORD PARTNERS FOR ***sphere***

in a sphere • a sphere of **activity/influence/life**

sphere /sfɪəʳ/ *noun* [C] **1** [SUBJECT] a subject or area of knowledge, work, etc *the political sphere* **2** [SHAPE] a round object shaped like a ball

spherical /ˈsferɪkᵊl/ *adjective* round, like a ball

sphincter /ˈsfɪŋktəʳ/ *noun* [C] **ANATOMY, BIOLOGY** a muscle that surrounds an opening in the body and can tighten to close it *a sphincter muscle* ➲See picture at **alimentary canal**

spice[1] /spaɪs/ *noun* **1 FOOD** [C, U] a substance made from a plant, which is used to give a special taste to food ***herbs and spices*** **2** [U] something that makes something else more exciting *A scandal or two **adds a little spice to** office life.*

spice[2] /spaɪs/ *verb* [T] **FOOD** to add spice to something [**often passive**] *The apples were **spiced with** nutmeg and cinnamon.*
spice sth up *phrasal verb* to make something more interesting or exciting *You can always spice up a talk with a few pictures.*

spicy /ˈspaɪsi/ *adjective* **FOOD** containing strong flavours from spice ***spicy food*** ○ *a spicy sauce*

spider /ˈspaɪdəʳ/ *noun* [C] a small creature with eight long legs which catches insects in a web (= structure like a net)

spidery /ˈspaɪdəri/ *adjective* thin and often untidy, looking like a spider ***spidery handwriting***

spike /spaɪk/ *noun* [C] a long, thin piece of metal, wood, etc with a sharp point at one end •**spiky** *adjective* covered with spikes or having that appearance ***spiky hair***

O- **spill** /spɪl/ *verb* [T] *past* **spilled**, *also UK* **spilt** to pour liquid somewhere without intending to *Someone at the party spilled red wine on the carpet.* •**spill** *noun* [C] *an oil spill*
spill out *phrasal verb* **1** [FALL] to flow or fall out of a container *The contents of the truck spilled out across the road.* **2** [MOVE] If people spill out of a place, large numbers of them move out of it. *The crowd spilled out onto the street.*
spill over *phrasal verb* If a bad situation spills over, it begins to have an unpleasant effect on another situation or group of people. *There are fears that the war could spill over into neighbouring countries.*

O- **spin**[1] /spɪn/ *verb* [I, T] **spinning**, *past* **spun 1** [TURN] If something spins or you spin something, it turns around and around quickly. *The car **spun across** the road.* **2** [MAKE THREAD] to make thread by twisting together cotton, wool, etc
spin (sb) around/round *phrasal verb* If you spin around, or someone spins you around, your body turns quickly to face the opposite direction.
spin sth out *phrasal verb* to make something such as a story or an activity last as long as possible

spin[2] /spɪn/ *noun* **1** [TURN] [C, U] the movement of something turning round very quickly *The skater did a series of amazing spins and jumps.* **2** [IDEA] [**no plural**] when an idea is expressed in a clever way that makes it seem better than it really is, especially in politics *This report **puts** a different **spin on** the issue.* **3** [CAR] [**no plural**] *informal* a short journey by car

spinach /ˈspɪnɪtʃ/ *noun* [U] **FOOD** a vegetable with large, dark green leaves and a strong taste

spinal /ˈspaɪnᵊl/ *adjective* **ANATOMY** relating to the spine *a spinal injury*

ˌspinal ˈcord *noun* **ANATOMY** the set of nerves inside the spine that connect the brain to other nerves in the body ➲See picture at **brain**

spin-chilling /ˈspaɪnˌtʃɪlɪŋ/ *adjective* very frightening

ˈspin ˌdoctor *noun* [C] *informal* **POLITICS** someone whose job is to make ideas, events, etc seem better than they really are, especially in politics

spine /spaɪn/ *noun* [C] **1 ANATOMY** the long structure of bones down the centre of your back, which supports your body **2** the narrow part of a book cover where the pages are joined together and which you can see when it is on a shelf

spineless /ˈspaɪnləs/ *adjective* A spineless person has a weak personality and is frightened easily.

spinneret /spɪnəˈret/ *noun* [C] **BIOLOGY** the part of a spider or caterpillar that makes thin, sticky thread

spin-off /ˈspɪnɒf/ *noun* [C] a product that develops from another more important product

spinster /ˈspɪnstəʳ/ *noun* [C] *old-fashioned* a woman who has never married

spiracle /ˈspaɪrəkᵊl/ *noun* [C] **1 BIOLOGY** in an insect or spider, one of the small holes that allow air in and out through the surface of the

S

body **2 BIOLOGY** in some fish, a small hole behind each eye used for breathing

spiral /ˈspaɪərᵊl/ *noun* **[C] 1** a shape made by a curve turning around and around a central point *a spiral staircase* **2 a downward spiral** a situation which is getting worse very quickly, and which is difficult to control

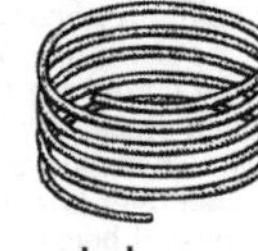
spiral

spire /spaɪəʳ/ *noun* **[C]** a tall, pointed tower on the top of a building such as a church

spirit¹ /ˈspɪrɪt/ *noun* **1** FEELING **[no plural]** the way people think and feel about something *a spirit of optimism* ○ *Everyone soon* ***got into the spirit of*** (= started to enjoy) *the carnival - singing, dancing, and having fun.* **2 community/team, etc spirit** when you feel enthusiasm about being part of a group **3 in good/high/low spirits** feeling good/excited/unhappy **4** NOT BODY **[C]** the part of a person which is not their body, which some people believe continues to exist after they die **5** NOT ALIVE **[C]** something which people believe exists but does not have a physical body, such as a ghost *evil spirits* **6 the spirit of the law/an agreement, etc** the intended meaning of the law/an agreement, etc and not just the written details **7 FOOD [C]** a strong alcoholic drink, such as whisky or vodka **[usually plural]** *I don't often drink spirits.*

spirit² /ˈspɪrɪt/ *verb* **be spirited away/out/to, etc** to be moved somewhere secretly *He was spirited away to a secret hide-out in Mexico.*

spirited /ˈspɪrɪtɪd/ *adjective* enthusiastic and determined, often in a difficult situation *a spirited performance*

spiritual /ˈspɪrɪtʃuəl/ *adjective* **RELIGION** relating to deep feelings and beliefs, especially religious beliefs *a spiritual leader*

spiritualism /ˈspɪrɪtʃuᵊlɪzᵊm/ *noun* **[U]** the belief that living people can communicate with people who are dead •**spiritualist** *noun* **[C]** someone who is involved with spiritualism

S

spirogyra /ˌspaɪərəʊˈdʒaɪərə/ *noun* **[U] BIOLOGY** a type of algae (= very simple plant found in water) formed of cells that contain a green spiral of chloroplast

spit¹ /spɪt/ *verb* **[I, T] spitting**, *past* **spat**, *also US* **spit 1** to force out the liquid in your mouth *I don't like to see people spitting in public.* ○ *He took a mouthful of coffee and then* ***spat*** *it* ***out***. **2 Spit it out!** *informal* used to tell someone to say more quickly what it is they want to say *Come on, spit it out!*

spit² /spɪt/ *noun* **1** LIQUID **[U]** *informal* the liquid that is made in your mouth **2** COOKING **[C]** a long, thin stick used for cooking meat over a fire **3 GEOGRAPHY** a long, thin beach (= area of sand) that goes out into the sea

spite /spaɪt/ *noun* **1 in spite of sth** although something exists or happens *He still smokes, in spite of all the health warnings.* **2 [U]** a feeling of anger towards someone which makes you want to hurt or upset them *He hid my new jacket* ***out of spite***.

spiteful /ˈspaɪtfᵊl/ *adjective* intentionally hurting or upsetting someone *That was a very spiteful thing to do.* •**spitefully** *adverb*

splash¹ /splæʃ/ *verb* **[I, T] 1** If a liquid splashes or you splash a liquid, drops of it hit or fall on something. *The paint splashed onto his new shirt.* ○ *She splashed some cold water on her face.* **2 splash about/around/through, etc** to move in water so that drops of it go in all directions *The children splashed about in the puddles.* **3 be splashed across/all over sth** to be the main story in a newspaper, usually on the front page, which many people will see *His picture was splashed across the front pages of all the newspapers the next morning.*

splash out (sth) *phrasal verb UK* to spend a lot of money on something which you want but do not need *He* ***splashed out on*** *the best champagne for the party.*

splash² /splæʃ/ *noun* **[C] 1** DROP OF LIQUID a drop of liquid which has fallen on something, or the mark made by it *There were several small splashes of paint on the carpet.* **2** NOISE the sound of something falling into or moving in water *They sat listening to the splash of raindrops on the lake.* **3 a splash of colour** a small area of colour which makes something look brighter *The flowers added a splash of colour to the room.* **4 make a splash** *informal* to get a lot of public attention *The film made quite a splash in the US.*

splatter /ˈsplætəʳ/ *verb* **[I, T]** If a liquid splatters or you splatter it, it falls onto a surface, often in many small drops. **[often passive]** *His clothes were* ***splattered with*** *blood.*

splendid /ˈsplendɪd/ *adjective* very good or very beautiful, special, etc *a splendid idea* ○ *a splendid view* •**splendidly** *adverb*

splendour *UK* (*US* **splendor**) /ˈsplendəʳ/ *noun* **[C, U]** when something is extremely beautiful or luxurious *Tourists marvelled at the splendour of the medieval cathedral.*

splinter /ˈsplɪntəʳ/ *noun* **[C] 1** a small, sharp piece of wood, glass, etc which has broken from a large piece *I've got a splinter in my finger.* **2 a splinter group POLITICS** a small group of people that forms after leaving a larger organization, such as a political party •**splinter** *verb* **[I]** to break into small, sharp pieces

O⁻ **split¹** /splɪt/ *verb* **splitting**, *past* **split 1** BREAK **[I, T]** If something splits or if you split it, it tears so that there is a long, thin hole in it. *He split his trousers when he bent over.* ○ *Her shoes were* ***splitting apart*** *at the sides.* **2** DIVIDE **[I, T]** (*also* **split up**) to divide into smaller parts or groups, or to divide something into smaller parts or groups *The children* ***split up into*** *three groups.* **3** SHARE **[T]** to share something by dividing it into smaller parts *The cost of the wedding will be* ***split between*** *the two families.* **4** DISAGREE **[I, T]** If a group of people splits, or something splits them, they disagree and form smaller groups. **[often passive]** *The government is* ***split on*** *the issue of hunting.* ➲See also: split hairs (**hair**)

split up *phrasal verb* If two people split up, they end their relationship. *She* ***split up with*** *her boyfriend.*

WORD PARTNERS FOR *split (noun)*

2 **cause/create** a split • a split **develops** • a split **between** sb and sb • a split **in** sth • a split **on/over** sth

split² /splɪt/ *noun* [C] **1** BREAK a long, thin hole in something where it has broken apart *There's a **split in** my trousers.* **2** DISAGREEMENT when a group of people divides into smaller groups because they disagree about something *This issue is likely to cause a major **split in** the party.* **3** RELATIONSHIP when a marriage or relationship ends *Very few of their friends were surprised when they announced their split last week.*

split³ /splɪt/ *adjective* **a split second** a very short period of time *It was all over in a split second.* ○ *a **split second decision***

ˌsplitting ˈheadache *noun* [C] **HEALTH** a very bad pain in your head *I've got a splitting headache.*

splurge /splɜːdʒ/ *verb* [I, T] to spend a lot of money on something which you want but do not need *We could either save the money or **splurge on** a new car.* •**splurge** *noun* [C]

OTHER WAYS OF SAYING *spoil*

Ruin is a very common alternative to 'spoil': *I put too much salt in the sauce and **ruined** it.*

The verb **deface** is sometimes used when someone spoils the appearance of something by writing or drawing on it: *Many of the library books had been **defaced**.*

The verb **disfigure** is sometimes used when a person's physical appearance has been spoilt: *Her face was **disfigured** by the scar.*

If something spoils a friendship or other relationship, you can use the verbs **sour** or **poison**: *The long dispute has **poisoned/ soured** relations between the two countries.*

In informal situations you can use the phrasal verbs **mess up** and **screw up** to say that something has been spoilt: *Laurie's illness has completely **messed up** all our holiday plans.* • *That new software has really **screwed up** my computer.*

spoil /spɔɪl/ *verb past* **spoiled** or **spoilt** **1** MAKE BAD [T] to stop something from being enjoyable or successful *The picnic was spoiled by the bad weather.* **2** CHILD [T] If you spoil a child, you let them have anything they want or do anything they want, usually making them badly behaved. **3** TREAT WELL [T] to treat someone very well, buying them things or doing things for them *He's always sending flowers - he absolutely spoils me!* **4** FOOD [I] *formal* If food spoils, it starts to decay and you cannot eat it.

spoils /spɔɪlz/ *noun* [plural] *formal* things which are taken by the winners of a war ***the spoils of war***

spoilt /spɔɪlt/ *adjective UK* (*US* **spoiled** /spɔɪld/) badly behaved because you are always given what you want or allowed to do what you want *He was behaving like a **spoilt child**.*

spoke¹ /spəʊk/ *noun* [C] one of the thin pieces of metal which connects the middle of a wheel to the outside edge, for example, on a bicycle

spoke² /spəʊk/ *past tense of* speak

spoken /ˈspəʊkən/ *past participle of* speak

spokesman, spokeswoman /ˈspəʊksmən, ˈspəʊksˌwʊmən/ *noun* [C] *plural* **spokesmen, spokeswomen** a man/woman who is chosen to speak officially for a group or organization *A spokesman for the company refused to comment on the reports.*

spokesperson /ˈspəʊksˌpɜːsən/ *noun* [C] *plural* **spokespeople** someone who is chosen to speak officially for a group or organization

spondee /ˈspɒndiː/ *noun* [C] **LITERATURE** in poetry, a rhythm of two long or strong syllables

sponge /spʌndʒ/ *noun* [C, U] **1** a soft substance full of small holes, which absorbs liquid very easily and is used for washing things **2** **FOOD** (*also* **ˈsponge ˌcake**) a soft, light cake

spongy /ˈspʌnðʒi/ *adjective* soft and full of small holes

sponsor¹ /ˈspɒnsər/ *verb* [T] **SPORT** to give money to someone to support an activity, event, or organization, sometimes as a way to advertise your company or product *The event is sponsored by First National Bank. UK* ○ *a sponsored walk* (= a walk for charity) •**sponsorship** *noun* [U] when someone gives money to support something

sponsor² /ˈspɒnsər/ *noun* [C] **SPORT** a person or organization that gives money to support an activity, event, etc

spontaneous /spɒnˈteɪniəs/ *adjective* happening naturally and suddenly and without being planned *a spontaneous reaction* ○ *The crowd broke into spontaneous applause.* •**spontaneity** /ˌspɒntəˈneɪəti/ *noun* [U] when something is spontaneous •**spontaneously** *adverb*

spoof /spuːf/ *noun* [C] a funny television programme, film, article, etc that copies the style of a real programme, film, article, etc *They did a **spoof of** the Oscars, giving awards for the worst films of the year.*

spooky /ˈspuːki/ *adjective informal* strange and frightening *There's something spooky about that place.*

spoon /spuːn/ *noun* [C] an object with a handle and a round, curved part at one end, used for eating and serving food *knives, forks, and spoons* •**spoon** *verb* [T] to move or serve food using a spoon *Spoon the sauce over the fish.*

spoonful /ˈspuːnfʊl/ *noun* [C] the amount of something which can be held on a spoon *Then add a spoonful of yoghurt.*

sporadic /spəˈrædɪk/ *adjective* not happening regularly or happening in different places *sporadic violence* •**sporadically** *adverb*

sporangium /spəˈrændʒiəm/ *noun* [C] **BIOLOGY** the part of a plant, especially a fungus (= plant like a mushroom) that produces spores (= cells from which new plants grow)

spore /spɔːr/ *noun* [C] **BIOLOGY** a single cell produced by some plants and simple organisms, for example fungus or ferns, from which new plants and organisms grow

S

WORD PARTNERS FOR ***sport***

do/play a sport • **spectator/team** sports

sport[1] /spɔːt/ *noun* **SPORT 1** [C] a game or activity which people do to keep healthy or for enjoyment, often competing against each other *winter sports* ○ ***team sports*** See colour picture **Sports 1 & 2** on pages Centre 14, 15 **2** [U] *UK* all types of physical activity which people do to keep healthy or for enjoyment See also: **blood sport**

sport[2] /spɔːt/ *verb* [T] *humorous* to wear something, especially something which people notice *He turned up sporting a bright red baseball cap and sunglasses.*

sporting /ˈspɔːtɪŋ/ *adjective* **SPORT** relating to sports *a **sporting hero***

ˈ**sports** ˌ**car** *noun* [C] a car designed to go very fast, often with only two seats and an open roof

ˈ**sports** ˌ**centre** *UK* (*US* **sports center**) *noun* [C] **SPORT** a building with places where you can play different sports

sportsmanship /ˈspɔːtsmənʃɪp/ *noun* [U] **SPORT** behaviour in sport which is fair and shows respect for other players *We hope to teach children **good sportsmanship**.*

sportsman, sportswoman /ˈspɔːtsmən, ˈspɔːtsˌwʊmən/ *noun* [C] *plural* **sportsmen, sportswomen SPORT** a man/woman who is good at sport

sportswear /ˈspɔːtsweəʳ/ *noun* [U] **SPORT** clothes, shoes, etc for people to wear when they play sports *a sportswear shop*

sporty /ˈspɔːti/ *adjective* **1** ATTRACTIVE Sporty cars, clothes, etc are attractive, comfortable, and stylish. **2 SPORT** Sporty people are good at sports.

spot[1] /spɒt/ *noun* [C] **1** ROUND MARK a small, round mark which is a different colour to the surface it is on *a blue shirt with white spots* ○ *I noticed a small spot of oil on my jacket.* **2 HEALTH** *UK* (*US* **pimple**) an unpleasant, small, red mark on your skin *He suffered badly with spots as a teenager.* **3** PLACE a place *We found a good spot to sit and have our picnic.* **4 a spot of sth** *UK old-fashioned* a small amount of something *a spot of lunch/shopping* **5 on the spot a** TIME immediately *I accepted the job on the spot.* **b** PLACE in the place where something happens *The police were called and they were on the spot within three minutes.* **6 have a soft spot for sb** to like someone a lot *I've always had a soft spot for her.* **7 put sb on the spot** to ask someone a question which is difficult or embarrassing to answer at that time See also: **beauty spot, blind spot**

spot[2] /spɒt/ *verb* [T] **spotting,** *past* **spotted** to see or notice something or someone *They were spotted together in London last week.* ○ *She soon **spotted** the **mistake**.*

spotless /ˈspɒtləs/ *adjective* completely clean *By the time I'd finished, the whole room was spotless.* •**spotlessly** *adverb **spotlessly clean***

WORD PARTNERS FOR ***spotlight***

2 be under/come under the spotlight • the spotlight **falls on/is on** sb/sth • **put/turn** the spotlight on sb/sth • **in/out of** the spotlight • the **media/public** spotlight

spotlight /ˈspɒtlaɪt/ *noun* **1** [C] a strong light which can be pointed in different directions **2 the spotlight** when someone gets public attention by being on television, in the newspapers, etc *to be **in the spotlight*** ○ *She's rarely **out of the** media **spotlight** these days.* •**spotlight** *verb* [T] *past* **spotlighted** or **spotlit**

ˌ**spot** ˈ**on** *adjective* [**never before noun**] *UK* exactly correct *Her imitation of Ann was spot on.*

spotty /ˈspɒti/ *adjective* **1 HEALTH** *UK* having a lot of unpleasant, small, red marks on your skin *a spotty young man with greasy hair* **2** PATTERN *UK* with a pattern of round marks *a spotty dress* **3** NOT GOOD/REGULAR *US* (*UK* **patchy**) If an action, quality, supply, etc is spotty, it is not all good or regular. *Sales of tickets for the concert have been spotty.*

spouse /spaʊs/ *noun* [C] *formal* **SOCIETY** your husband or wife

spout[1] /spaʊt/ *noun* [C] an opening of a container, in the shape of a tube which liquid flows out through *the spout of a teapot*

spout[2] /spaʊt/ *verb* [I, T] **1** LIQUID If a liquid spouts or if something makes it spout, it flows out of something with force. **2** SPEAK *informal* to talk a lot about something, often when other people are not interested *He was spouting his usual rubbish about politics.*

sprain /spreɪn/ *verb* [T] **HEALTH** to injure part of your body by twisting it, but not so badly that it breaks *I slipped on the ice and sprained my ankle.* •**sprain** *noun* [C]

sprang /spræŋ/ *past tense of* spring

sprawl /sprɔːl/ *verb* [I] **1** PERSON (*also* **sprawl out**) to sit or lie in a relaxed, untidy position with your arms and legs stretched out *He sprawled out on the sofa.* **2** BUILDINGS to cover a large area, often in a way which is not tidy or not planned ***sprawling suburbs*** •**sprawl** *noun* [U] *urban sprawl*

spray[1] /spreɪ/ *noun* **1** LIQUID CONTAINER [C, U] liquid in a container which forces it out in small drops *hair spray* ○ *spray paint* **2** DROPS [U] many small drops of liquid blown through the air *sea spray*

spray[2] /spreɪ/ *verb* **1** LIQUID [T] to force liquid out of a container in many small drops *The fields are **sprayed with** pesticides.* ○ *She sprayed a little perfume on her wrists.* **2** PIECES [I, T] If small pieces of something spray somewhere or if something sprays them, they are sent through the air in all directions. *A brick shattered the window, **spraying** the room **with** pieces of broken glass.*

spread[1] /spred/ *verb past* **spread 1 spread sth across/over/through, etc** to arrange something so that it covers a large area *He **spread** the cards **out** on the table.* **2** TIME [T] (*also* **spread out**) to arrange for something to happen over a period of time and not at once *The **payments** will be **spread** over two years.* **3** INCREASE [I] to increase, or move to cover a larger area or affect a larger number of people *The virus is spread by rats.* **4** SURFACE [T] to move a soft substance across a surface so that it covers it *What I really like is hot buttered toast **spread with** strawberry jam.* ○ *He **spread** a thin layer of glue **on** the paper.* **5** INFORMATION [I, T] If information spreads or if someone spreads it, it is communicated from one person to another. *News of his death **spread** quickly.*

spread out *phrasal verb* If people spread out, they move from being close together in a group to being in different places across a larger area. *They spread out to search the whole area.*

WORD PARTNERS FOR ***spread (noun)***

the spread **of** sth • **control/halt/limit/prevent** the spread of sth

spread[2] /spred/ *noun* **1** MOVEMENT [U] when something moves to cover a larger area or affect a larger number of people *They are looking for ways to slow down **the spread of** the disease.* **2** FOOD [C, U] a soft food which you put on bread *cheese spread* **3** NEWSPAPER [C] an article which covers one or more pages of a newspaper or magazine *a double-page spread*

spreadsheet /ˈspredʃiːt/ *noun* [C] **COMPUTING** a computer program which helps you to do business calculations and planning

spree /spriː/ *noun* **a shopping/spending, etc spree** a short period when someone does a lot of shopping/spending, etc

sprig /sprɪg/ *noun* [C] a small piece of a plant with leaves *a sprig of parsley*

sprightly /ˈspraɪtli/ *adjective* A sprightly person is able to move about easily and quickly although they are old.

WORD PARTNERS FOR ***spring***

in (the) spring • **early/late** spring • **last/next** spring

O-ᵐ**spring[1]** /sprɪŋ/ *noun* **1** SEASON [C, U] the season of the year between winter and summer, when the weather becomes warmer and plants start to grow again *I'm starting a new course **in the spring**.* ○ *spring flowers/weather* **2** METAL [C] a piece of metal which curves round and round and which returns to its original shape after being pushed or pulled *bed springs* **3** **GEOGRAPHY** [C] a place where water comes out of the ground *hot springs* **4** MOVEMENT [C, U] when someone or something suddenly moves or jumps somewhere

spring[2] /sprɪŋ/ *verb past* **sprang**, *also US* **sprung**, *past participle* **sprung** **1 spring back/forward/out, etc** to jump or move somewhere suddenly *The cat sprang onto the sofa.* ○ *I tried to shut the door, but it kept springing open.* **2 spring to life** to suddenly become very active *After about 8 o'clock, the city springs to life.* **3 spring to mind** If a word or idea springs to mind, you suddenly think of it. *He asked if I knew any good places to go, but nothing sprang to mind.*

spring from sth *phrasal verb* to come from or be the result of something *Many of his problems spring from his strict religious upbringing.*

spring sth on sb *phrasal verb* to suddenly tell or ask someone something when they do not expect it *I'm sorry to spring this on you, but could you give a talk at tomorrow's meeting?*

spring up *phrasal verb* to appear suddenly *A lot of new hotels have sprung up along the coast recently.*

ˌspring ˈclean *UK* (*UK/US* **ˌspring ˈcleaning**) *noun* [**no plural**] when you clean a place more carefully and using more effort than usual *I gave the kitchen a spring clean at the weekend.* •**spring clean** *verb* [I, T] *UK*

ˌspring ˈonion *UK* (*US* **scallion**) *noun* [C, U] **FOOD** a small onion with a white part at the bottom and long, green leaves, which is eaten in salads

sprinkle /ˈsprɪŋkl/ *verb* [T] to gently drop small pieces of something over a surface *Sprinkle the cake with sugar before serving.* •**sprinkling** *noun* [**no plural**] a small amount of a powder or liquid that has been sprinkled on a surface *a sprinkling of pepper/snow*

sprinkler /ˈsprɪŋkləʳ/ *noun* [C] a piece of garden equipment which automatically spreads drops of water over grass and plants

sprint /sprɪnt/ *verb* [I] **SPORT** to run very fast for a short distance *She sprinted along the road to the bus stop.* •**sprinter** *noun* [C] someone who runs short distances in competitions •**sprint** *noun* [C] *a 100m sprint*

sprocket /ˈsprɒkɪt/ *noun* [C] **DT** a device like a wheel with small parts sticking out which keeps a chain moving on a bicycle or pulls film, paper, etc. through a machine

sprout[1] /spraʊt/ *verb* [I, T] **BIOLOGY** If a plant sprouts, or if it sprouts something, it begins to produce leaves, flowers, etc. *The seeds I planted are just beginning to sprout.*

sprout up *phrasal verb* If a large number of things sprout up, they suddenly appear or begin to exist. *New buildings are sprouting up all over the city.*

sprout[2] /spraʊt/ *noun* [C] **1 FOOD** (*also* **brussel sprout**) a small, green vegetable which is round and made of leaves **2** a part of a plant that is just beginning to grow

spruce /spruːs/ *verb*

spruce sb/sth up *phrasal verb* to make someone or something cleaner or more tidy [**often reflexive**] *I'd like to spruce myself up a bit before we go out.*

sprung /sprʌŋ/ **1** PAST PARTICIPLE *past participle of* spring **2** PAST TENSE *US past tense of* spring

spun /spʌn/ *past tense of* spin

spur[1] /spɜːʳ/ (*also* **spur on**) *verb* [T] **spurring**, *past* **spurred** to encourage someone to do something or something to happen *Spurred on by his fans, he won the next three games easily.*

spur[2] /spɜːʳ/ *noun* [C] **1** a sharp, pointed piece of metal fixed to the boot of someone riding a horse **2 on the spur of the moment** If you do something on the spur of the moment, you do it suddenly, without planning it.

spurious /ˈspjʊəriəs/ *adjective formal* false and not based on the truth

spurn /spɜːn/ *verb* [T] *formal* to not accept someone or something *He **spurned** my **offer/suggestion**.* ○ *a **spurned** lover*

S

spurt[1] /spɜːt/ *verb* **1** [I, T] (*also* **spurt out**) If something spurts liquid or fire, or if liquid or fire spurts from somewhere, it flows out suddenly with force. *Blood was spurting out of his stomach.* **2 spurt ahead/into/past, etc** to increase your speed, effort, or activity *She spurted ahead in the final lap.*

spurt[2] /spɜːt/ *noun* [C] **1** INCREASE a sudden, short increase in speed, effort, or activity *He works in short spurts.* **2** FLOW a sudden, powerful flow of liquid *The water came out of the tap* ***in spurts.***

sputter /ˈspʌtəʳ/ *verb* [I] to make several quick, explosive sounds *The car sputtered to a halt.*

spy[1] /spaɪ/ *noun* [C] someone who secretly tries to discover information about a person, country, etc

spy[2] /spaɪ/ *verb* **1** INFORMATION [I] to secretly try to discover information about a person, country, etc **2** SEE [T] *literary* to see someone or something, often from a distance *I spied him on the dance floor.*
spy on sb *phrasal verb* to secretly watch someone *He spied on her through the keyhole.*

sq **MEASURES** *written abbreviation for* square in measurements *an area of 70 sq km* (= square kilometres)

squabble /ˈskwɒbl/ *verb* [I] to argue about something that is not important *They're always* ***squabbling over*** *money.* •**squabble** *noun* [C]

squad /skwɒd/ *noun* [C] **1 bomb/drug/fraud, etc squad** a group of police officers who have special skills to deal with particular problems **2 death/firing/hit, etc squad** a group of people who are trained to kill, usually with guns **3** **SPORT** a sports team *the England rugby squad*

squadron /ˈskwɒdrᵊn/ *noun* [C] a group of soldiers, ships, aircraft, etc in a military organization *a squadron of fighter jets*

squalid /ˈskwɒlɪd/ *adjective* **1** DIRTY very dirty and unpleasant *squalid conditions* **2** NOT MORAL morally bad *a squalid affair*

squall /skwɔːl/ *noun* [C] a sudden storm with strong winds

squalor /ˈskwɒləʳ/ *noun* [U] extremely dirty and unpleasant conditions *They live in squalor.*

squander /ˈskwɒndəʳ/ *verb* [T] to waste time, money, etc *He* ***squandered*** *all his money* ***on*** *alcohol and drugs.*

O-* **square**[1] /skweəʳ/ *noun* [C] **1** SHAPE a shape with four equal sides and four 90° angles ➲See picture at **shape** ➲See picture at **parallelogram** **2** PLACE an open area with buildings around it, often in the centre of a town *Trafalgar Square* **3** **MATHEMATICS** a number that results from multiplying a number by itself *The square of 3 is 9.* **4 back to square one** back to the beginning of a long process or piece of work *None of the applicants were suitable, so we had to go back to square one and advertise the job again.* ➲See also: **fair**[3] and square

O-* **square**[2] /skweəʳ/ *adjective* **1** having the shape of a square *a square room* ○ *He has broad shoulders and a square jaw.* **2 square centimetre/metre/mile, etc** **MEASURES** the area of a square with sides that are a centimetre/metre/mile, etc long *3000 square feet of office space* **3 a square meal** a big, healthy meal *You need three square meals a day.*

square[3] /skweəʳ/ *verb* **2/3/4, etc squared** **MATHEMATICS** 2/3/4, etc multiplied by itself *Four squared is sixteen.*
square off *phrasal verb US* to prepare to fight, compete, or argue with someone *The two teams will square off in the finals next Saturday.*
square up *phrasal verb UK* **1** FIGHT to prepare to fight, compete, or argue with someone *The players squared up to each other and started shouting.* **2** PAY *informal* to pay someone the money that you owe them *If you pay for it now, I'll* ***square up with*** *you later.*
square with sth *phrasal verb* to match or to agree with something *Her story doesn't quite square with the evidence.*

squarely /ˈskweəli/ *adverb* directly *I looked him squarely in the eye.* ○ *The report put the blame squarely on the police.*

ˌsquare ˈroot *noun* **the square root of 16/64/144, etc** **MATHEMATICS** the number you multiply by itself to get 16/64/144, etc *The square root of 144 is 12.*

squash[1] /skwɒʃ/ *noun* **1** **SPORT** [U] a sport in which two people hit a small rubber ball against the four walls of a room *a game of squash* ○ *a squash court/racket* **2 it's a squash** *UK* used to say that there are too many people or things in a small space *We managed to get in but it was a squash.* **3** **FOOD** [U] *UK* a sweet drink that tastes like fruit **4** **FOOD** [C, U] a fruit with hard skin, a soft inside, and large seeds, that you cook and eat as a vegetable

squash[2] /skwɒʃ/ *verb* **1** CRUSH [T] to crush something into a flat shape *I stepped on a spider and squashed it.* **2** PUSH [I, T] to push someone or something into a small space [**often passive**] *The kids were all* ***squashed into*** *the back seat.*

squat[1] /skwɒt/ *verb* [I] **squatting**, *past* **squatted** **1** SIT (*also* **squat down**) to bend your legs so that you are sitting with your bottom very close to the ground *He squatted down beside me.* **2** LIVE to live in an empty building without the owner's permission

squat[2] /skwɒt/ *adjective* short and wide *a squat little man*

squat[3] /skwɒt/ *noun* [C] a building that people are living in without the owner's permission

squatter /ˈskwɒtəʳ/ *noun* [C] someone who lives in a building without the owner's permission

squawk /skwɔːk/ *verb* [I] If a bird squawks, it makes a loud, unpleasant noise. •**squawk** *noun* [C]

squeak /skwiːk/ *verb* [I] to make a short, high sound *His shoes squeaked loudly as he walked.* •**squeak** *noun* [C]

squeaky /ˈskwiːki/ *adjective* **1** making short, high sounds *a* ***squeaky voice*** **2 squeaky clean** very clean

squeal /skwiːl/ *verb* [I] to make a loud, high sound, often because of fear or excitement *She* ***squealed with*** *delight.* •**squeal** *noun* [C] *squeals of laughter*

S

squeamish /ˈskwiːmɪʃ/ *adjective* If you are squeamish about something such as blood, you find it very unpleasant and it makes you feel ill.

O━ **squeeze¹** /skwiːz/ *verb* **1** [T] to press something firmly *She squeezed his hand and said goodbye.* **2 squeeze into/through/past, etc** to move somewhere where there is very little space *She squeezed through a narrow gap in the wall.* **3 squeeze a lemon/orange, etc FOOD** to press a lemon/orange, etc to get juice from it ***freshly squeezed** orange juice*
squeeze sth/sb in *phrasal verb* to manage to do something or see someone when you are very busy *The doctor will try to squeeze you in this afternoon.*

squeeze² /skwiːz/ *noun* **1** [C] when you press something firmly *He **gave** her hand a little **squeeze**.* **2 it's a squeeze** used to say that there are too many people or things in a small space *We all got in, but it was a **tight squeeze**.* **3 a squeeze of lemon/orange, etc** a small amount of juice from a lemon/orange, etc

squid /skwɪd/ *noun* [C] *plural* **squid** a sea creature with a long body and ten long arms

squiggle /ˈskwɪgl/ *noun* [C] *informal* a short, curly line *Her signature just looks like a squiggle.*

squint /skwɪnt/ *verb* [I] to look at something with your eyes partly closed *She was **squinting at** her computer screen.*

squirm /skwɜːm/ *verb* [I] to twist your body because you are embarrassed, nervous, etc

squirrel /ˈskwɪrᵊl/ (US) /ˈskwɜːrᵊl/ *noun* [C] a small animal with a big, fur tail that climbs trees and eats nuts

squirt /skwɜːt/ *verb* **1** [I, T] If liquid squirts, it comes out suddenly and with force, and if you squirt liquid, you make it come out suddenly and with force. *Water **squirted out** all over the floor.* **2 squirt sb with sth** to hit someone with a liquid

Sr (*also UK* **Snr**) *written abbreviation for* senior (= the older of two men in a family with the same name) *Joseph Kennedy, Sr.*

St 1 *written abbreviation for* street (= a road in a town or city that has houses or other buildings) *42 Oxford St* **2 RELIGION** *written abbreviation for* saint (= a dead person who has been officially respected by the Christian Church for living their life in a holy way) *St Patrick*

stab¹ /stæb/ *verb* [T] **stabbing**, *past* **stabbed** to push a knife into someone *He was stabbed several times in the chest.*

stab² /stæb/ *noun* [C] **1** the act of pushing a knife into someone *He had a deep **stab wound** in his neck.* **2 a stab of guilt/jealousy/regret, etc** a sudden, unpleasant emotion *She felt a stab of guilt.* **3 have a stab at sth/doing sth** *informal* to try to do something, or to try an activity that you have not done before *She had a stab at solving the problem.*

stabbing /ˈstæbɪŋ/ *noun* [C] when someone stabs someone *Where were you on the night of the stabbing? US* ○ *a stabbing death*

ˈstabbing ˌpain *noun* [C] **HEALTH** a sudden, strong pain

stability /stəˈbɪləti/ *noun* [U] when something is not likely to change or move ***political/financial stability*** ➲Opposite **instability**

stabilize (*also UK* **-ise**) /ˈsteɪbᵊlaɪz/ *verb* [I, T] If you stabilize something, or if something stabilizes, it stops changing or moving. *The economy has finally stabilized.* •**stabilization** /ˌsteɪbᵊlaɪˈzeɪʃᵊn/ *noun* [U]

stable¹ /ˈsteɪbl/ *adjective* **1** SITUATION not likely to change or end suddenly *a stable relationship* ○ *The doctor said his **condition** was **stable**.* **2** OBJECT fixed or safe and not likely to move *Be careful! That chair isn't very stable.* **3** PERSON mentally calm and not easily upset ➲Opposite **unstable**

stable² /ˈsteɪbl/ *noun* [C] a building where horses are kept

stack¹ /stæk/ *noun* [C] **1** a tidy pile of things *a stack of books/CDs* **2 stacks of sth** *informal* a lot of something *There are stacks of studies linking salt to high blood pressure.*

stack² /stæk/ (*also* **stack up**) *verb* [T] to arrange things in a tidy pile *Can you help me **stack** these **chairs**?*

stadium /ˈsteɪdiəm/ *noun* [C] **SPORT** a large, open area with seats around it, used for playing and watching sports *a football/baseball stadium*

WORD PARTNERS FOR ***staff***

administrative/experienced/extra/full-time/senior staff • **employ/lay off/train** staff • **join** the staff • **on** the staff

O━ **staff¹** /stɑːf/ *noun* [group] the people who work for an organization *The company has a staff of over 500 employees.* ○ *Please talk to a **member of staff**.*

staff² /stɑːf/ *verb* [T] to provide workers for an organization [often passive] *The charity was staffed by volunteers.*

stag /stæg/ *noun* [C] a male deer

WORD PARTNERS FOR ***stage***

reach a stage • **at** [one/some/this/that] stage • the **closing/early/final** stages • a stage **in/of** sth

O━ **stage¹** /steɪdʒ/ *noun* **1** TIME [C] a period of development, or a particular time in a process *an **early stage** in his career* ○ *Our project is in its **final stages**.* ○ *I'm not prepared to comment **at this stage**.* **2** THEATRE [C] the raised area in a theatre where actors perform *He's **on stage** for most of the play.* **3 the stage** performances in theatres *He's written plays for television and the stage.* **4 set the stage for sth** to make something possible or likely to happen *The meeting set the stage for cooperation between the men.*

stage² /steɪdʒ/ *verb* **1 POLITICS stage a demonstration/protest, etc** to organize and take part in a public meeting to complain about something **2 stage a concert/show, etc** to organize and produce a performance of music or a play, etc *They staged a free concert in Central Park.*

stagger /ˈstægəʳ/ *verb* **1** MOVE [I] to walk as if you might fall *He staggered drunkenly towards the door.* **2** ARRANGE [T] to arrange events so that

S

they do not happen at the same time *We stagger our lunch breaks at work.*

staggered /'stægəd/ *adjective* [**never before noun**] very shocked or surprised *I was staggered at the prices.*

staggering /'stægərɪŋ/ *adjective* very shocking and surprising *He earns a staggering amount of money.*

stagnant /'stægnənt/ *adjective* **1** NO FLOW Stagnant water or air does not flow and becomes dirty and smells unpleasant. *a stagnant pond* **2 ECONOMICS** A stagnant economy, society, or organization does not develop or grow.

stagnate /stæg'neɪt/ (US) /'stægneɪt/ *verb* [**I**] to stay the same and not grow or develop *He expects the economy to stagnate and unemployment to rise.* •**stagnation** /stæg'neɪʃən/ *noun* [**U**]

'stag ˌnight *noun* [**C**] a night when a group of men go out just before one of them gets married ⊃Compare **hen night**

staid /steɪd/ *adjective* serious and old-fashioned *a staid, middle-aged man*

stain¹ /steɪn/ *noun* **1** MARK [**C**] a dirty mark on something that is difficult to remove *a blood/grass stain* ○ *a stain on the carpet* **2** PAINT [**C, U**] a thin, clear paint that you put on wood to make it darker *wood stain*

stain² /steɪn/ *verb* **1** MARK [**I, T**] to leave a dirty mark on something which is difficult to remove, or to become dirty in this way *That wine I spilt has stained my shirt.* **2 DT** [**T**] to paint a wooden surface with a thin paint in order to change its colour *She stained the bookcase to match the desk.*

ˌstained 'glass *noun* [**U**] **DT** coloured glass that is used to make pictures in windows *a stained-glass window*

stainless steel /ˌsteɪnləs'sti:l/ *noun* [**U**] a type of steel (= strong metal) that is not damaged by water

stair /steəʳ/ *noun* [**C**] one of the steps in a set of steps

staircase /'steəkeɪs/ *noun* [**C**] a set of stairs and the structure around them *a spiral staircase*

WORD PARTNERS FOR ***stairs***

climb/fall down/go down/go up the stairs • the **bottom of/foot of** the stairs • the **head of/top of** the stairs • **on** the stairs • a **flight of** stairs

⊶**stairs** /steəz/ *noun* [**plural**] a set of steps from one level in a building to another *to **climb** the stairs* ○ *a **flight** (= set) **of** stairs*

stairway /'steəweɪ/ *noun* [**C**] a set of stairs and the structure around them

stake¹ /steɪk/ *noun* **1 be at stake** If something is at stake, it is in a situation where it might be lost or damaged. *We have to act quickly - people's lives are at stake.* **2 FINANCE** [**C**] a part of a business that you own, or an amount of money that you have invested in a business *He has a 30 percent **stake in** the company.* **3** [**C**] a strong stick with a pointed end that you push into the ground *a wooden stake*

stake² /steɪk/ *verb* **stake a/your claim** to say that you want something and that you should have it

stake sth on sth *phrasal verb* to risk something on the result of a competition or situation *He has staked his reputation on the film's success.*

stake sth out *phrasal verb* to watch a place in order to catch criminals or to see a famous person *The police are staking out the house where the terrorists are hiding.*

stakeholder /'steɪkˌhəʊldəʳ/ *noun* [**C**] **FINANCE** a person or group of people who own a share in a business

stakes /steɪks/ *noun* [**plural**] money or other advantages that you may get or lose in a competition or situation *People get very competitive because the **stakes** are so **high**.*

stalactite /'stæləktaɪt/ *noun* [**C**] **GEOLOGY** a column of rock that hangs from the roof of a cave

stalagmite /'stæləgmaɪt/ *noun* [**C**] **GEOLOGY** a column of rock which rises from the floor of a cave

stale /steɪl/ *adjective* **1 FOOD** old and not fresh *stale bread* ○ *Cake **goes stale** quickly if it's not covered.* **2** boring or bored, and not producing or feeling excitement or enthusiasm like before *I'd been too long in the same job and was getting stale.*

stalemate /'steɪlmeɪt/ *noun* [**C, U**] a situation in which neither side in an argument can win *The talks **ended in a stalemate**.*

stalk¹ /stɔ:k/ *verb* **1** [**T**] to follow a person or animal closely and secretly, often to try to catch or attack them *She claimed that the man had been stalking her for a month.* **2 stalk out/off, etc** to walk in an angry or proud way *She stalked out of the restaurant.*

stalk² /stɔ:k/ *noun* [**C**] **BIOLOGY** the main stem of a plant

stalker /'stɔ:kəʳ/ *noun* [**C**] someone who follows a person or animal closely and secretly, often to try to catch or attack them

stall¹ /stɔ:l/ *noun* [**C**] **1** SHOP *mainly UK* a small shop with an open front or a table from which goods are sold *a **market stall*** **2** ROOM *US* a small area in a room for washing or using the toilet *a shower stall*

stall² /stɔ:l/ *verb* **1** ENGINE [**I, T**] If an engine stalls, or if you stall it, it stops working suddenly. *The car stalled when I stopped at the traffic lights.* **2** STOP [**I**] to stop making progress *The peace talks have stalled over the issue of nuclear weapons.* **3** MORE TIME [**T**] to intentionally make someone wait or make something happen later so that you have more time *She wanted an answer immediately, but I managed to stall her.*

stallion /'stæljən/ *noun* [**C**] an adult male horse

the stalls /stɔ:lz/ *UK* (*US* **orchestra**) *noun* [**plural**] the seats on the main floor near the front of a theatre or cinema *a seat in the stalls*

stalwart /'stɔ:lwət/ *noun* [**C**] someone who supports an organization, team, etc in a very loyal way •**stalwart** *adjective*

stamen /'steɪmən/ *noun* [C] **BIOLOGY** the male part of a flower that produces pollen ➲See picture at **flower**

WORD PARTNERS FOR ***stamina***

have stamina • **build up/improve/increase** stamina • **mental/physical** stamina • stamina **for** sth • a **test of** stamina

stamina /'stæmɪnə/ *noun* [U] **HEALTH** the physical or mental energy that allows you to do something for a long time *Marathon runners need a lot of stamina.*

stammer /'stæmər/ *verb* [I] to pause a lot and repeat sounds because of a speech problem or because you are nervous *He blushed and began to stammer.* •**stammer** *noun* [C] *He has a stammer.*

O-■**stamp**[1] /stæmp/ *noun* [C] **1** PAPER (*also* **postage stamp**) a small, official piece of paper that you buy and stick onto a letter or parcel before you post it **2** MARK a tool for putting a special ink mark on something, or the mark made by it *a stamp in a passport* **3 stamp of approval** official, public approval *The president has put his stamp of approval on the proposal.*

stamp[2] /stæmp/ *verb* **1** MARK [T] to make a mark on something with a tool that you put ink on and press down *She stamped the date on the invoice.* **2** FOOT [I, T] to put your foot down on the ground hard and quickly, often to show anger *"No!" she shouted, stamping her foot.* ➲See also: **rubber-stamp**

stamp sth out *phrasal verb* to get rid of something that is wrong or harmful *a campaign to stamp out racism*

stampede /stæm'piːd/ *noun* [C] when a large group of animals or people suddenly move in an uncontrolled way, often in the same direction *Gunfire caused a stampede in the marketplace.* •**stampede** *verb* [I]

WORD PARTNERS FOR ***stance***

take a stance • **change** your stance • a **hard-line/tough** stance • a stance **against** sb/sth • sb's stance **on** sth

stance /stæns/ *noun* [C] **1** OPINION an opinion or belief about something, especially if you say it in public [**usually singular**] *What's their **stance on** nuclear energy?* ○ *They are **taking** a very tough **stance against** drugs.* **2** STAND *formal* the way that someone stands [**usually singular**] *an awkward stance*

O-■**stand**[1] /stænd/ *verb past* **stood 1** ON FEET [I] to be in a vertical position on your feet *We'd been standing for hours.* **2** RISE [I] (*also* **stand up**) to rise to a vertical position on your feet from sitting or lying down *I get dizzy if I stand up too quickly.* ○ *Please stand when the bride arrives.* ➲See colour picture **Phrasal Verbs** on page Centre 16 **3 stand in line** *US* (*UK* **queue**) to wait for something as part of a line of people *We stood in line all afternoon.* **4 stand (sth) in/against/by, etc sth** to be in or to put something in a particular place or position *His walking stick stood by the door.* ○ *You'll have to stand the sofa on its end to get it through the door.* **5 can't stand sb/sth** *informal* to hate someone or something *I can't stand him.* [+ **doing sth**] *She can't stand doing housework.* **6** ACCEPT [T] to be able to accept or deal with a difficult situation *She couldn't stand the pressures of the job.* **7 stand at sth** to be at a particular level, amount, height, etc *Inflation currently stands at 3 percent.* **8 where you stand on sth** what your opinion is about something *We asked the senator where she stood on gun control.* **9 where you stand (with sb)** what someone thinks about you, how they expect you to behave, and how they are likely to behave *She said she will never leave her husband, so now at least I know where I stand.* **10** OFFER [I] If an offer still stands, it still exists. *You're welcome to visit any time - my invitation still stands.* **11 as it stands** as something is now, without changes in it *The law as it stands is very unclear.* **12 stand trial** If someone stands trial, they appear in a law court where people decide if they are guilty of a crime. *to stand trial for murder* **13 stand to gain/lose sth** to be in a situation where you can get/lose money or an advantage *He stands to gain a fortune if the company is sold.* **14 POLITICS** [I] *UK* (*US* **run**) to compete in an election for an official position *to stand for office* ➲See also: stand your **ground**[1], not have a **leg** to stand on, it stands to **reason**[1], stand on your own two feet (**foot**[1]), stand sb in good **stead**

stand about/around *phrasal verb* to spend time standing somewhere and doing very little *They stood around waiting for the store to open.*

stand aside *phrasal verb* to leave a job or position so that someone else can do it instead

stand back *phrasal verb* to move a short distance away from something or someone *Stand back while I light the fire.*

stand by *phrasal verb* **1** BE READY to be ready to do something or to help *Doctors were standing by to treat the injured passengers.* **2** DO NOTHING to do nothing to prevent something unpleasant from happening *We can't stand by while millions of people starve.*

stand by sb *phrasal verb* to continue to support someone when they are in a difficult situation *She stood by him throughout his troubled career.*

stand by sth *phrasal verb* If you stand by an agreement, decision, etc, you do not change it. *The government stood by its promise to improve education.*

stand down *phrasal verb UK* to leave a job or position so that someone else can do it instead *He stood down as party leader.*

stand for sth *phrasal verb* **1** LETTER If a letter stands for a word, it is used to represent it. *UFO stands for 'unidentified flying object'.* **2** SUPPORT If a group of people stand for a set of ideas, they support those ideas. *The party stands for low taxes and individual freedom.* **3 not stand for sth** If you will not stand for something, you will not accept a situation or someone's behaviour. *He can't speak to me like that - I won't stand for it!*

stand in *phrasal verb* to do something that someone else was going to do because they cannot be there *She **stood in for** me when I was sick.*

stand out *phrasal verb* **1** NOTICE to be very easy to see or notice *The bright blue letters really stand out on the page.* **2** BETTER to be better than other similar things or people *His application **stood out from** all the rest.*

S

⊃See also: stick/stand out like a sore **thumb**[1]
stand up *phrasal verb* If an idea or some information stands up, it is proved to be correct.
stand sb up *phrasal verb* to fail to meet someone when you said you would *He's stood me up twice now.*
stand up for sth/sb *phrasal verb* to support an idea or a person who is being criticized [**often reflexive**] *Never be afraid to stand up for yourself.*

stand² /stænd/ *noun* **1** SHOP [C] a small shop with an open front or a table from which goods are sold *a hot dog stand* ○ *Visit our stand at the trade fair.* **2 SPORT** [C] *UK* (*US* **stands**) a structure in a sports ground where people can stand or sit to watch an event **3** FURNITURE [C] a piece of furniture for holding things *a music/hat stand* **4 the (witness) stand LAW** (*UK also* **the dock**) the place in a law court where people sit or stand when they are being asked questions *The judge asked her to* ***take the stand*** (= go into the witness stand). **5** OPINION [C] an opinion or belief about something, especially if you say it in public [**usually singular**] *What's the President's* ***stand on*** *gun control?* **6 take a stand** to express your opinion about something publicly *He refuses to take a stand on this issue.* **7 make a stand** to publicly defend something or stop something from happening

standalone /ˈstændəˌləʊn/ *adjective* [**always before noun**] **COMPUTING** a standalone computer can operate without any other equipment or programs

WORD PARTNERS FOR ***standard***

come up to standard • **below/(not) up to** standard • **set** standards • **comply with/conform to/meet** standards • **exacting/high/low/rigorous** standards • standards **of** sth

O-- **standard**¹ /ˈstændəd/ *noun* [C] **1** QUALITY a level of quality, especially a level that is acceptable *a* ***high standard*** *of service* ○ *low* ***safety standards*** ○ *His work was* ***below standard*** (= not acceptable). ○ *She* ***sets*** *very high* ***standards*** *for herself.* **2** BEHAVIOUR a level of behaviour, especially a level that is acceptable [**usually plural**] *high moral standards* ⊃See also: **double standard**

standard² /ˈstændəd/ *adjective* usual and not special ***standard procedure/practice***

ˈ**standard** ˌ**form** *noun* [U] **MATHEMATICS** (*also* **standard index form**) a way of writing a very large number with one number before the decimal point, multiplied by a power of 10. For example, 280,000 is 2.8 x 10^5

standardize (*also UK* **-ise**) /ˈstændədaɪz/ *verb* [T] to change things so that they are all the same *I wish someone would standardize clothing sizes.* •**standardization** /ˌstændədaɪˈzeɪʃᵊn/ *noun* [U] *the standardization of computer terms*

ˌ**standard of** ˈ**living** *noun* [C] *plural* **standards of living SOCIETY, ECONOMICS** how much money and comfort someone has *a high standard of living*

standby /ˈstændbaɪ/ *noun* [C] *plural* **standbys** **1** someone or something extra that is ready to be used if needed *We kept our old TV as a standby in case the new one broke.* **2 be on standby** to be ready to do something or to be used if needed *Police were on standby in case there was any trouble after the game.*

stand-in /ˈstændɪn/ *noun* [C] someone who does what another person was going to do because the other person cannot be there

standing¹ /ˈstændɪŋ/ *noun* [U] Your standing is the opinion that other people have of you. *Last week's speech has improved the Prime Minister's standing in the polls.*

standing² /ˈstændɪŋ/ *adjective* [**always before noun**] **1** permanent and not only created when necessary *a standing committee* ○ *He has a* ***standing invitation*** *to stay at our house.* **2 a standing joke** a situation that a group of people often make jokes about *The poor quality of his work has become a standing joke in the office.* ⊃See also: **long-standing**

ˌ**standing** ˈ**order** *noun* [C] *UK* **FINANCE** an instruction to a bank to pay someone a fixed amount of money at regular times from your account

ˌ**standing o**ˈ**vation** *noun* [C] when people stand while clapping to show that they have enjoyed a performance very much *She* ***got a standing ovation*** *for her speech.*

stand-off *UK* (*US* **standoff**) /ˈstændɒf/ *noun* [C] when an argument or fight stops for a period of time because no one can win or get an advantage

standpoint /ˈstændpɔɪnt/ *noun* [C] a particular way of thinking about a situation or problem *to look at something* ***from*** *a political/religious* ***standpoint***

standstill /ˈstændstɪl/ *noun* [**no plural**] a situation in which all movement or activity has stopped *The traffic* ***came to a standstill*** *in the thick fog.*

stand-up /ˈstændʌp/ *adjective* [**always before noun**] A stand-up comedian is someone who stands in front of a group of people and tells jokes as a performance. ***stand-up comedy***

stank /stæŋk/ *past tense of* stink

stanza /ˈstænzə/ *noun* [C] **LITERATURE** a group of lines of poetry

stapes /ˈsteɪpiːz/ *noun* [**C usually singular**] *plural* **stapes ANATOMY** one of three very small bones that carry sound into the inner ear ⊃Compare **incus, malleus**

staple¹ /ˈsteɪpl/ *adjective* [**always before noun**] A staple food, product, etc is basic and very important. *a* ***staple diet*** *of rice and fish*

staple² /ˈsteɪpl/ *noun* [C] a small piece of wire that you put through pieces of paper to join them together •**staple** *verb* [T] to join pieces of paper together with staples

stapler /ˈsteɪpləʳ/ *noun* [C] a piece of equipment used for putting staples through paper

WORD PARTNERS FOR ***star***

become/make sb a star • a **big** star • a **pop** star

O-- **star**¹ /stɑːʳ/ *noun* [C] **1 ASTRONOMY** a ball of burning gases that you see as a small point of light in the sky at night **2** FAMOUS PERSON a famous singer, actor, sports person, etc *a* ***pop star*** **3** BEST PERSON someone in a group of people who is the best at doing something *Baggio is one of our **star players**.* **4** SHAPE a shape that has five or more points ➲See picture at **shape** **5 two-star/three-star, etc** used to show how good a restaurant or hotel is *a five-star hotel* **6 sb's stars/the stars** *UK informal* something you read that tells you what will happen to you based on the position of the stars in the sky *My stars said it would be a good month for romance.* ➲See also: **co-star, film star, rock star**

star² /stɑːʳ/ *verb* [I, T] **starring**, *past* **starred** If a film, play, etc stars someone, or if someone stars in a film, play, etc, they are the main person in it. *a film starring Meg Ryan* ○ *Tom Hanks **starred in** 'Sleepless in Seattle'.* ➲See also: **co-star**

starboard /ˈstɑːbəd/ *noun* [U] the right side of a ship or aircraft

starch /stɑːtʃ/ *noun* **1 CHEMISTRY, FOOD** [C, U] a substance in foods such as rice, bread, and potatoes **2** [U] a substance used to make cloth stiff •**starchy** *adjective* containing a lot of starch

stardom /ˈstɑːdəm/ *noun* [U] when someone is very famous for acting, singing, etc

stare /steəʳ/ *verb* [I] to look at someone or something for a long time and not move your eyes *Sean was **staring at** me.* •**stare** *noun* [C]

stark¹ /stɑːk/ *adjective* **1** CLEAR unpleasantly clear and obvious *His death is a **stark warning** to other people about the dangers of drugs.* **2 stark difference/contrast** a total difference *Jerry is very lazy, in stark contrast to his sister who works very hard.* **3** PLAIN with a very plain and simple appearance and not very attractive *a stark, snowy landscape* •**starkly** *adverb*

stark² /stɑːk/ *adverb* **stark naked** wearing no clothes

starry /ˈstɑːri/ *adjective* A starry sky or night is one in which you can see a lot of stars.

ˈstar ˌsign *UK* (*US* **sign**) *noun* [C] one of the twelve signs that are based on star positions when you are born, which some people believe shows what type of person you are *"What star sign are you?" "I'm Capricorn."*

O━**start¹** /stɑːt/ *verb* **1** BEGIN DOING [I, T] to begin doing something [+ **doing sth**] *He started smoking when he was eighteen.* [+ **to do sth**] *Maria started to laugh.* ○ *We start work at nine o'clock.* **2** BEGIN HAPPENING [I, T] to begin to happen or to make something begin to happen *The programme starts at seven o'clock.* ○ *Police believe the fire started in the kitchen.* **3** BUSINESS [I, T] (*also* **start up**) If a business, organization, etc starts, it begins to exist, and if you start it, you make it begin to exist. *She started her own computer business.* ○ *A lot of new restaurants have started up in the area.* **4** CAR [I, T] (*also* **start up**) If a car or engine starts, it begins to work, and if you start it, you make it begin to work. *The car won't start.* ○ *Start up the engine.* **5 to start with a** SITUATION used to talk about what a situation was like at the beginning before it changed *I was happy at school to start with, but later I hated it.* **b** LIST used before saying the first thing in a list of things *To start with, we need better computers. Then we need more training.* **6** MOVE SUDDENLY [I] to move suddenly because you are frightened or surprised ➲See also: set/start the **ball** rolling, get/start off on the wrong **foot¹**

start (sth) off *phrasal verb* to begin by doing something, or to make something begin by doing something *She started off the meeting with the monthly sales report.*

start on sth *phrasal verb* to begin doing something *Have you started on your homework yet?*

start out *phrasal verb* to begin your life or the part of your life when you work, in a particular way *My dad started out as a sales assistant in a shop.*

start over *phrasal verb US* to begin something again *If you make a mistake, you'll have to start over.*

WORD PARTNERS FOR ***start***

at the start • **from** the start • the start **of** sth

O━**start²** /stɑːt/ *noun* **1** BEGINNING [C] the beginning of something [**usually singular**] *Our teacher checks who is in class **at the start of** each day.* ○ *Ivan has been involved in the project **from the start**.* ○ *The meeting **got off to a bad start*** (= began badly). **2 make a start** *mainly UK* to begin doing something *I'll **make a start on** the washing-up.* **3 for a start** *UK* used when you are giving the first in a list of reasons or things *I won't be going - I've got too much homework for a start.* **4** ADVANTAGE [C] an advantage that you have over someone else when you begin something [**usually singular**] *I'm grateful for the start I had in life.* **5 the start SPORT** the place where a race begins **6** SUDDEN MOVEMENT [**no plural**] a sudden movement that you make because you are frightened or surprised *Kate sat up **with a start**.* ➲See also: **false start**

starter /ˈstɑːtəʳ/ *noun* **1 FOOD** [C] *UK* (*US* **appetizer**) something that you eat as the first part of a meal **2 SPORT** [C] *US* in sports, a member of a team who is involved in a competition from the beginning *At only 20, he's the team's youngest starter.* **3 for starters** *informal* used to say that something is the first in a list of things *Try this exercise for starters.* ➲See also: **non-starter**

starting-point /ˈstɑːtɪŋˌpɔɪnt/ *noun* [C] an idea, subject, etc that you use to begin a discussion or process

startle /ˈstɑːtl/ *verb* [T] to suddenly surprise or frighten someone *The sound startled me.* •**startled** *adjective a **startled expression***

startling /ˈstɑːtlɪŋ/ *adjective* making you feel very surprised *startling news*

start-up /ˈstɑːtʌp/ *adjective* [**always before noun**] **ECONOMICS, FINANCE** relating to starting a business ***start-up costs***

starve /stɑːv/ *verb* [I, T] **HEALTH** to become ill or die because you do not have enough food, or to make someone ill or die because they do not have enough food *Many people have **starved to death** in parts of Africa.* •**starvation** /stɑːˈveɪʃᵊn/ *noun* [U] *Children were dying of starvation.*

starved /stɑːvd/ *adjective* **1 be starved of sth** *UK* (*US* **be starved for sth**) to not have enough of something that you need very much *a child starved of love* **2** *mainly US informal* very hungry

S

starving /ˈstɑːvɪŋ/ *adjective* **1 HEALTH** dying because there is not enough food *starving people* **2** *informal* very hungry *I'm absolutely starving.*

stash¹ /stæʃ/ (*also* **stash away**) *verb* [T] *informal* to keep a lot of something in a safe, secret place *His money was stashed away in a cupboard.*

stash² /stæʃ/ *noun* [C] *informal* a lot of something that you keep in a safe, secret place *He had a stash of whisky under the bed.*

O→**state¹** /steɪt/ *noun* **1** CONDITION [C] the condition that something or someone is in *the state of the economy* ○ *The building is in a terrible state.* **2 in/into a state** *informal* very upset or nervous *Ben was in a real state before the exam.* **3 GEOGRAPHY** [C] (*also* **State**) one of the parts that some countries such as the US are divided into *Washington State* ○ *Alaska is the largest state in the US.* **4 GEOGRAPHY, POLITICS** [C] a country *a union of European states* ➲See Common Learner Error at **country** **5 the state POLITICS** the government of a country *financial help from the state* **6 POLITICS state visit/occasion, etc** an important visit/occasion, etc involving the leader of a government **7 the States** the United States of America ➲See also: **police state, welfare state**

state² /steɪt/ *verb* [T] to officially say or write something [+ **(that)**] *Two medical reports stated that he was mentally ill.*

stately /ˈsteɪtli/ *adjective* formal and slow *a **stately procession** through the streets*

ˌstately ˈhome *noun* [C] a big, old house in the countryside that people pay to visit in Britain

WORD PARTNERS FOR ***statement***

issue/make/prepare/release a statement • a **false/joint/public/sworn** statement • a statement **about/on** sth

O→**statement** /ˈsteɪtmənt/ *noun* [C] **1** something that someone says or writes officially *The pop star is expected to **make a statement** about his involvement with drugs.* **2 FINANCE** (*also* **bank statement**) a piece of paper that shows how much money you have put into your bank account and how much you have taken out

ˌstatement of acˈcount *noun* [C] **FINANCE** a document that a business sends to regular customers that is a record of what they have bought and how much they owe

ˌstate of aˈffairs *noun* [**no plural**] a situation *a sad state of affairs*

ˌstate of ˈmind *noun* [C] *plural* **states of mind** how you are feeling at a particular time *to be in a positive state of mind*

state-of-the-art /ˌsteɪtəvðiˈɑːt/ *adjective* using the newest ideas, designs, and materials *a computer system that uses **state-of-the-art** **technology***

ˌstate ˈschool *UK* (*US* **public school**) *noun* [C] **EDUCATION** a school that is free to go to because the government provides the money for it

statesman /ˈsteɪtsmən/ *noun* [C] *plural* **statesmen POLITICS** an important politician, especially one who people respect

static¹ /ˈstætɪk/ *adjective* not moving or changing *The number of students on the course has remained static.*

static² /ˈstætɪk/ *noun* [U] **1 PHYSICS** (*also* **ˌstatic elecˈtricity**) electricity that you get when two surfaces rub together **2** NOISE noise on a radio or television that is caused by electricity in the air

O→**station¹** /ˈsteɪʃən/ *noun* [C] **1** TRAINS a building where trains stop so that you can get on or off them *Dad met me at the station.* **2 bus station** (*also UK* **coach station**) a building where a bus starts or ends its journey **3** SERVICE a building where a particular service is based *(UK) a petrol station/ (US) a gas station* **4** RADIO/TV a company that broadcasts television or radio programmes *a classical music station* ➲See also: **filling station, fire station, police station, polling station, power station, service station**

COMMON LEARNER ERROR

station or stop?

Station is used for trains.

the train/railway station

the underground/tube station

Stop or **bus stop** is used for buses.

I stood at the bus stop for over half an hour.

Get off at the third stop.

A **bus station** is a place where many buses start or end their journeys.

station² /ˈsteɪʃən/ *verb* **be stationed at/in, etc** If someone such as a soldier is stationed somewhere, they are sent there to work for a period of time. *US soldiers stationed in Germany*

stationary /ˈsteɪʃənəri/ *adjective* not moving *stationary cars*

stationer's /ˈsteɪʃənəz/ *noun* [C] *UK* a shop where you can buy pens, paper, and other things for writing

stationery /ˈsteɪʃənəri/ *noun* [U] things that you use for writing, such as pens and paper

ˈstation ˌwagon *US* (*UK* **estate car**) *noun* [C] a big car with a large space for bags behind the back seat

WORD PARTNERS FOR ***statistic***

collect/gather statistics • statistics **confirm/indicate/reveal/show** sth • **according to** statistics • statistics **on** sth

statistic /stəˈtɪstɪk/ *noun* [C] **MATHEMATICS** a fact in the form of a number that shows information about something [**usually plural**] ***Statistics show** that skin cancer is becoming more common.* •**statistical** *adjective* relating to statistics ***statistical evidence*** •**statistically** *adverb*

statistics /stəˈtɪstɪks/ *noun* [U] **MATHEMATICS** the subject that involves collecting and studying numbers to show information about something

statue /ˈstætʃuː/ *noun* [C] **ART** a model that looks like a person or animal, usually made from stone or metal

stature /ˈstætʃər/ *noun* [U] *formal* **1** IMPORTANCE the importance that someone has because of

S

their work *a scientist of international stature* **2** HEIGHT your height *a man of small stature*

status /ˈsteɪtəs/ *noun* [U] **1** **SOCIETY** the position that you have in relation to other people because of your job or social position *The pay and status of nurses has improved.* **2** **LAW** the legal position of someone or something *What's your **marital status** (= are you married or not)?*

the status quo /ˌsteɪtəsˈkwəʊ/ *noun formal* the situation that exists now, without any changes *They only want to **maintain** the **status quo**.*

ˈstatus ˌsymbol *noun* [C] something that someone owns that shows they have a high position in society

statute /ˈstætʃuːt/ *noun* [C] *formal* **LAW** a law or rule

statutory /ˈstætjətəri/ *adjective formal* **LAW** decided or controlled by law *a statutory minimum wage*

staunch /stɔːnʃ/ *adjective* [**always before noun**] very loyal in your support for someone or your belief in something *a **staunch supporter** of the Communist party*

stave /steɪv/ *verb*

stave sth off *phrasal verb* to stop something bad from happening now although it may happen later *He had a bar of chocolate to **stave off** his **hunger**.*

O━**stay¹** /steɪ/ *verb* **1** NOT LEAVE [I] to continue to be in a place, job, etc and not leave *The weather was bad so we stayed at home.* ○ *Do you want to stay in teaching?* **2** IN A STATE [T] to continue to be in a particular state *The supermarket stays open late.* ○ *I was tired and couldn't stay awake.* **3** VISIT [I, T] to spend a short period of time in a place *We **stayed in** a hotel.* ○ *We're going to **stay with** my grandmother.* **4** **stay put** *informal* to continue to be in the same place *He told me to stay put while he fetched the car.* ➲See Common Learner Error at **rest**

stay behind *phrasal verb* to not leave a place when other people leave *I stayed behind after class to speak to the teacher.*

stay in *phrasal verb* to stay in your home *Let's stay in tonight and watch a video.*

stay on *phrasal verb* to continue to be in a place, job, or school after other people have left *I stayed on an extra two years at school.*

stay out *phrasal verb* to not go home at night, or to go home late *He stayed out all night.*

stay out of sth *phrasal verb* to not become involved in an argument or discussion *It's better to stay out of their arguments.*

stay up *phrasal verb* to go to bed later than usual [**+ to do sth**] *She stayed up to watch a film.*

stay² /steɪ/ *noun* [C] a period of time that you spend in a place *Did you enjoy your stay in Tokyo?*

stead /sted/ *noun* **stand sb in good stead** to be useful to someone in the future *The course will stand you in good stead.*

steadfast /ˈstedfɑːst/ *adjective formal* refusing to change your beliefs or what you are doing *He is **steadfast in** his support for political change.* •**steadfastly** *adverb*

steady¹ /ˈstedi/ *adjective* **1** GRADUAL happening at a gradual, regular rate ***steady** economic **growth*** ○ *He has had a **steady flow/stream** of visitors.* **2** STILL still and not shaking *You need steady hands to be a dentist.* ➲Opposite **unsteady** **3** NOT CHANGING not changing *She drove at a **steady speed**.* **4** **steady job/work** a job that is likely to continue for a long time and pay you regular money •**steadily** *adverb* •**steadiness** *noun* [U]

steady² /ˈstedi/ *verb* **1** [T] to make something stop shaking or moving *He managed to steady the plane.* **2** **steady yourself** to stop yourself from falling *She grabbed hold of the rail to steady herself.*

steak /steɪk/ *noun* [C, U] **FOOD** a thick, flat piece of meat or fish *steak and chips*

O━**steal** /stiːl/ *verb past tense* **stole**, *past participle* **stolen** **1** [I, T] **LAW** to take something that does not belong to you, without intending to return it *Burglars broke into the house and stole a computer.* ○ *stolen cars* **2** **steal away/in/out, etc** to move somewhere quietly and secretly

stealth /stelθ/ *noun* [U] secret, quiet behaviour •**stealthy** *adjective* behaving in a secret, quiet way •**stealthily** *adverb*

O━**steam¹** /stiːm/ *noun* **1** [U] **PHYSICS, CHEMISTRY** the gas that water produces when you heat it **2** **let off steam** to get rid of your anger, excitement, etc by being noisy or using a lot of energy **3** **run out of steam** to not have enough energy to finish doing something

steam² /stiːm/ *verb* **1** **FOOD** [T] to cook something using steam *steamed rice* **2** [I] to produce steam *a steaming bowl of soup*

steam (sth) up *phrasal verb* If glass steams up, or if you steam it up, it becomes covered in steam.

steamer /ˈstiːmər/ *noun* [C] **1** **FOOD** a pan used for cooking food using steam **2** BOAT a ship that uses steam power

steamy /ˈstiːmi/ *adjective* **1** WATER hot and full of steam *a steamy kitchen* **2** SEX sexually exciting *a steamy love story*

stearic acid /stiˌærɪkˈæsɪd/ *noun* [U] **CHEMISTRY** a substance like wax that is used for making candles and for some medicines

steel¹ /stiːl/ *noun* [U] a very strong metal made from iron, used for making knives, machines, etc ➲See also: **stainless steel**

steel² /stiːl/ *verb* **steel yourself** to prepare yourself to do something difficult or unpleasant *He was steeling himself for an argument.*

ˌsteel ˈband *noun* [C] **MUSIC** a group of musicians who play steel drums

ˌsteel ˈdrum *noun* [C] **MUSIC** large oil container which has been made into a musical instrument and is played like a drum

steely /ˈstiːli/ *adjective* [**always before noun**] very strong and determined *a **steely determination** to succeed*

O━**steep¹** /stiːp/ *adjective* **1** SLOPE A steep slope, hill, etc goes up or down very quickly. *The **hill** was too **steep** to cycle up.* **2** CHANGE A steep increase or fall in something is very big and quick. *a **steep rise** in prices* **3** PRICE *informal*

S

very expensive *Hotel prices are steep at $300 for a room.* •**steeply** *adverb Food prices have **risen steeply**.* •**steepness** *noun* [U]

steep² /stiːp/ *verb* **be steeped in sth** to have a lot of something around or to be strongly influenced by something *The town is steeped in history.*

steeple /ˈstiːpl/ *noun* [C] a church tower that has a point at the top

steer /stɪəʳ/ *verb* **1** VEHICLE [I, T] to control the direction of a vehicle *I tried to steer the boat away from the bank.* **2** SITUATION [T] to influence the way a situation develops *I managed to **steer the conversation** away from my exam results.* **3 steer sb into/out of/towards, etc** to guide someone somewhere, especially by putting your hand on their back *He steered me towards the door.* ➲See also: steer **clear³** of sb/sth

steering /ˈstɪərɪŋ/ *noun* [U] the parts of a vehicle that control its direction

ˈsteering ˌwheel *noun* [C] a wheel that you turn to control the direction of a vehicle ➲See colour picture **Car** at page Centre 7

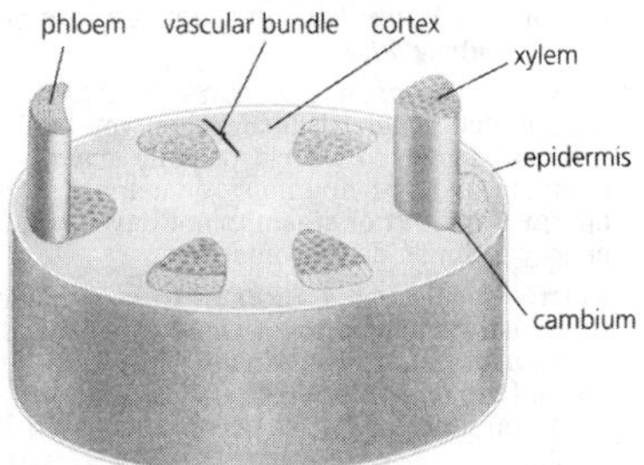

stem: transverse section

stem¹ /stem/ *noun* [C] **BIOLOGY** the long, thin part of a plant that the leaves and flowers grow on

stem² /stem/ *verb* [T] **stemming**, *past* **stemmed** to stop something from continuing or increasing *The new procedures are intended to **stem the flow** of drugs into the country.*

stem from sth *phrasal verb* to develop as the result of something *Her problems stem from childhood.*

ˈstem ˌcell *noun* [C] **BIOLOGY** a cell, especially one taken from a person or animal in a very early stage of development, that can develop into any other type of cell

stench /stenʃ/ *noun* [C] a very unpleasant smell *the stench of rotten fruit*

stencil /ˈstensəl/ *noun* [C] **ART, DT** a piece of paper or plastic with patterns cut into it, that you use to paint patterns onto a surface •**stencil** *verb* [I, T] *UK* **stencilling**, *past* **stencilled**, *US* **stenciling**, *past* **stenciled** to use a stencil to paint patterns onto a surface

WORD PARTNERS FOR ***step (noun)***

take steps to do sth • a **big/important/major** step • the **first/next** step • a step **towards** sth • a step **in** (doing) sth

step¹ /step/ *noun* [C] **1** MOVEMENT one of the movements you make with your feet when you walk *She **took** a few **steps** forward and then started to speak.* **2** METHOD one of the things that you do to achieve something *This meeting is the **first step** towards a peace agreement.* ○ *The company has **taken steps** to improve its customer service.* **3** STAIR one of the surfaces that you walk on when you go up or down stairs **4 in step (with sb/sth)** having the same ideas, opinions, etc as other people *This time, Britain is in step with the rest of Europe.* **5 out of step (with sb/sth)** having different ideas, opinions, etc from other people *Her views are out of step with government policy.* **6 be one step ahead (of sb)** to have done something before someone else **7 watch your step a** WALKING used to tell someone to be careful about where they are walking **b** BEHAVIOUR to be careful about what you say and do

step² /step/ *verb* **stepping**, *past* **stepped 1 step back/forward/over, etc** to move somewhere by lifting your foot and putting it down in a different place *She stepped carefully over the dog.* **2 step on/in sth** to put your foot on or in something *I accidentally stepped on her foot.*

step down *phrasal verb* to leave an important job *He stepped down as manager of the Italian team.*

step in *phrasal verb* to become involved in a difficult situation in order to help [+ **to do sth**] *A Japanese bank stepped in to provide financial help.*

step sth up *phrasal verb* to increase what you are doing to try to achieve something *Police have stepped up their efforts to find the man.*

stepbrother /ˈstepˌbrʌðəʳ/ *noun* [C] not your parent's son but the son of the person your parent has married

step-by-step /ˌstepbaɪˈstep/ *adjective* [**always before noun**] A step-by-step method, plan, etc, deals with one thing and then another thing in a fixed order. *a **step-by-step guide** to buying a house*

ˈstep ˌchange *noun* [C] when a very big change happens *There is a step change taking place in communications technology.*

stepchild /ˈsteptʃaɪld/ *noun* [C] *plural* **stepchildren** the child of your husband or wife from an earlier marriage

stepdaughter /ˈstepˌdɔːtəʳ/ *noun* [C] the daughter of your husband or wife from an earlier marriage

stepfather /ˈstepˌfɑːðəʳ/ *noun* [C] the man who has married your mother but is not your father

stepmother /ˈstepˌmʌðəʳ/ *noun* [C] the woman who has married your father but is not your mother

stepping-stone /ˈstepɪŋstəʊn/ *noun* [C] **1** METHOD an event or experience that helps you achieve something else *Education is a **stepping-stone to** a good job.* **2** STONE one of several stones that you walk on to cross a stream

stepsister /ˈstepˌsɪstəʳ/ *noun* [C] not your parent's daughter but the daughter of the person your parent has married

stepson /ˈstepsʌn/ *noun* [C] the son of your husband or wife from an earlier marriage

stereo /ˈsteriəʊ/ *noun* **1 MUSIC** [C] a piece of equipment for playing CDs, listening to the radio, etc that has two speakers (= parts where sound comes out) *a car stereo* ➲See colour picture **The Living Room** on page Centre 4 **2** SYSTEM [U] a system for hearing music, speech, etc through two speakers (= parts where sound comes out) *The concert was broadcast **in stereo**.* ○ *stereo sound*

WORD PARTNERS FOR ***stereotype***

challenge/fit a stereotype • a **negative** stereotype • a stereotype **of** sth • a **racial** stereotype

stereotype¹ /ˈsteriəʊtaɪp/ *noun* [C] **SOCIETY** a fixed idea that people have about what a particular type of person is like, especially an idea that is wrong ***racial stereotypes*** •**stereotypical** /ˌsteriəʊˈtɪpɪkəl/ *adjective* having the qualities that you expect a particular type of person to have *a stereotypical student*

stereotype² /ˈsteriəʊtaɪp/ *verb* [T] to have a fixed idea about what a particular type of person is like, especially an idea that is wrong [**often passive**] *Young people are often **stereotyped as** being lazy.*

sterile /ˈsteraɪl/ *adjective* **1 BIOLOGY, HEALTH** completely clean and without any bacteria *a sterile needle* **2 BIOLOGY** unable to produce children **3** not having enough new ideas *a sterile discussion* •**sterility** /stəˈrɪləti/ *noun* [U]

sterilize (*also UK* **-ise**) /ˈsterəlaɪz/ *verb* [T] **1 BIOLOGY** to make something clean and without bacteria *a sterilized needle* **2 HEALTH** to perform a medical operation on someone to make them unable to have children •**sterilization** /ˌsterəlaɪˈzeɪʃən/ *noun* [U]

sterling /ˈstɜːlɪŋ/ *noun* [U] **ECONOMICS** British money

stern¹ /stɜːn/ *adjective* very serious and without any humour *a **stern expression/face*** ○ *stern criticism* •**sternly** *adverb*

stern² /stɜːn/ *noun* [C] the back part of a ship

sternum /ˈstɜːnəm/ *noun* [C] *plural* **sternums** or **sterna ANATOMY** the long, flat vertical bone in the centre of your chest; breastbone ➲See picture at **rib cage**

steroid /ˈsterɔɪd/ *noun* [C] **HEALTH** a drug for treating injuries that some people use illegally in sport to make their muscles stronger

stethoscope /ˈsteθəskəʊp/ *noun* [C] **HEALTH** a piece of equipment that a doctor uses to listen to your heart and breathing

stew /stjuː/ *noun* [C, U] **FOOD** a dish made of vegetables and meat cooked together slowly in liquid *beef/lamb stew* •**stew** *verb* [T] to cook food slowly in liquid *stewed fruit*

steward /ˈstjuːəd/ *noun* [C] **1** TRANSPORT a man who looks after people on an aircraft, boat, or train *an air steward* **2** EVENT someone who helps to organize a race or big event

stewardess /ˈstjuːədɪs/ *noun* [C] a woman who looks after people on an aircraft, boat, or train *an air stewardess*

sth *written abbreviation for* something •**sth's** *written abbreviation for* something's

O━ **stick¹** /stɪk/ *verb past* **stuck 1** JOIN [I, T] to become joined to something else or to make something become joined to something else, usually with a substance like glue *Anne stuck a picture of her boyfriend on the wall.* ○ *The stamp wouldn't **stick to** the envelope.* **2 stick sth in/on/under, etc** *informal* to put something somewhere *Just stick your bag under the table.* **3 stick (sth) in/into/through, etc** If something sharp sticks into something, it goes into it, and if you stick something sharp somewhere, you push it into something. *She stuck the needle into his arm.* **4** NOT MOVE [I] to become fixed in one position and not be able to move *This drawer has stuck - I can't open it.* **5 can't stick sb/sth** *UK informal* to not like someone or something *I can't stick her.* ➲See also: stick to your guns (**gun**¹), poke/stick your **nose**¹ into sth, stick/put your **oar** in

stick around *phrasal verb informal* to stay somewhere for a period of time *Stick around after the concert and you might meet the band.*

stick at sth *phrasal verb* to continue trying hard to do something difficult *I know it's hard learning to drive but stick at it.*

stick by sb *phrasal verb* to continue to support someone when they are having problems

stick out *phrasal verb* **1** COME OUT If part of something sticks out, it comes out further than the edge or surface. *His ears stick out a bit.* **2** NOTICEABLE to be very easy to notice *She certainly sticks out in a crowd.* ➲See also: stick/stand out like a sore **thumb**¹

stick sth out *phrasal verb* to make part of your body come forward from the rest of your body *The little boy stuck his tongue out.*

stick it out *phrasal verb informal* to continue doing something that is boring, difficult, or unpleasant

stick to sth *phrasal verb* to continue doing or using something and not change to anything else *I'll stick to lemonade - I'm driving.*

stick together *phrasal verb* If people stick together, they support and help each other.

stick up *phrasal verb* to point up above a surface and not lie flat *I can't go out with my hair sticking up like this.*

stick up for sb/sth *phrasal verb informal* to support someone or something when they are being criticized

stick with sb/sth *phrasal verb* to continue using someone or doing something and not change to anyone or anything else *He's a good builder - I think we should stick with him.*

O━ **stick²** /stɪk/ *noun* [C] **1** WOOD a long, thin piece of wood, usually broken or fallen from a tree **2 walking/hockey, etc stick SPORT** a long, thin piece of wood that you use when you are walking/playing hockey, etc **3** PIECE a long, thin piece of something *a stick of candy/celery* ➲See also: **carrot** and stick, get (hold of) the wrong **end**¹ of the stick

sticker /ˈstɪkər/ *noun* [C] a piece of paper or plastic with writing or a picture on it that you stick onto a surface *a car sticker* ➲See also: **bumper sticker**

sticky /ˈstɪki/ *adjective* **1** LIKE GLUE made of or covered with a substance that can stick to

S

other things ***sticky fingers*** ○ ***sticky tape*** **2** WEATHER Sticky weather is unpleasantly hot. **3 a sticky moment/problem/situation, etc** *informal* a moment/problem/situation, etc that is difficult or embarrasses you

O‒**stiff¹** /stɪf/ *adjective* **1** HARD hard and difficult to bend *stiff material* **2** NOT MOVING A door, drawer, etc that is stiff does not move as easily as it should. **3 HEALTH** If a part of your body is stiff, it hurts and is difficult to move. *I've got **a stiff neck**.* **4** SEVERE very severe or difficult ***stiff competition/opposition*** ○ *We need **stiffer penalties** for drink driving.* **5** FORMAL behaving in a way that is formal and not relaxed **6** THICK A stiff substance is thick and does not move around easily. *Whip the cream until it is stiff.* **7 stiff drink/whisky/vodka, etc FOOD** a strong alcoholic drink *I need a stiff brandy.* **8 stiff wind/breeze** a wind that is quite strong •**stiffly** *adverb* •**stiffness** *noun* [U]

stiff² /stɪf/ *adverb* **bored/scared/worried, etc stiff** extremely bored, worried, etc *The lecture was awful - I was bored stiff.*

stiffen /ˈstɪfᵊn/ *verb* **1** BECOME STIFF [I, T] to become stiff or to make something become stiff **2** STOP MOVING [I] to suddenly stop moving because you are frightened or angry *She stiffened at the sound of the doorbell.*

stifle /ˈstaɪfl/ *verb* [T] to stop something from happening or continuing *to **stifle** a **sneeze/yawn*** ○ *Large supermarkets **stifle competition**.*

stifling /ˈstaɪflɪŋ/ *adjective* extremely hot *a stifling summer in Rome*

WORD PARTNERS FOR ***stigma***

sth **carries** a stigma • the stigma **attached to/surrounding** sth • sth **loses** its stigma • a **social** stigma • the stigma **of** (doing) sth

stigma /ˈstɪgmə/ *noun* **1** [C, U] **SOCIETY** when people disapprove of something, especially when this is unfair *There is still **a stigma attached** to being mentally ill.* **2 BIOLOGY** [C] the top of the central female part of a flower, where pollen is received ⊃See picture at **carpel** ⊃See picture at **flower** •**stigmatize** (*also UK* **-ise**) *verb* [T] to treat someone or something unfairly by disapproving of them [**often passive**] *Unmarried mothers are stigmatized by society.*

stiletto /stɪˈletəʊ/ *noun* [C] a shoe with a very high, pointed heel (= part at the bottom and back of a shoe) *a pair of stilettos*

O‒**still¹** /stɪl/ *adverb* **1** CONTINUING used to say that something is continuing to happen now or that someone is continuing to do something now *He's still here if you want to speak to him.* ○ *Do you still play basketball?* **2** POSSIBLE used to say that something continues to be possible *We could still catch the train if we leave now.* **3** EMPHASIS used to emphasize that you did not expect something to happen because something else makes it surprising *He didn't do much work but still came top of the class.* ○ *The weather was terrible. Still, we had a good holiday.* **4 better/harder/worse, etc still** better/harder/worse, etc than something else

O‒**still²** /stɪl/ *adjective* **1 stand/stay/sit, etc still** to stand, stay, sit, etc without moving *Sit still so I can brush your hair.* **2** A still place is calm and quiet. *It was night and the whole village was still.* **3 FOOD** *UK* A still drink does not have any bubbles in it. •**stillness** *noun* [U]

still³ /stɪl/ *noun* [C] a photograph from one moment in a film

stillborn /ˌstɪlˈbɔːn/ (US) /ˈstɪlˌbɔːn/ *adjective* **HEALTH** born dead *a **stillborn baby***

stilt /stɪlt/ *noun* [C] **1** WALKING one of two long poles that you can stand on and use to walk above the ground [**usually plural**] *a clown on stilts* **2** BUILDING one of several poles that support a building above the ground [**usually plural**] *a house on stilts*

stilted /ˈstɪltɪd/ *adjective* talking or writing in a formal way that does not sound natural *a **stilted conversation***

stimulant /ˈstɪmjələnt/ *noun* [C] **HEALTH** a drug that makes you feel more active and awake *Coffee contains caffeine which is a stimulant.*

stimulate /ˈstɪmjəleɪt/ *verb* [T] **1** MAKE HAPPEN to make something happen or develop more *It stimulates the production of red blood cells.* **2** EXCITED to make someone feel interested and excited *Colourful pictures can stimulate a child.* •**stimulation** /ˌstɪmjəˈleɪʃᵊn/ *noun* [U]

stimulating /ˈstɪmjəleɪtɪŋ/ *adjective* interesting and making you think *a **stimulating discussion***

WORD PARTNERS FOR ***stimulus***

act as/provide a stimulus • a stimulus **for/to** sth

stimulus /ˈstɪmjələs/ *noun* [C, U] *plural* **stimuli** /ˈstɪmjəlaɪ/ something that makes something else happen, grow, or develop more *The report **provided the stimulus** for more studies.*

sting¹ /stɪŋ/ *verb past* **stung** **1 HEALTH** [T] If an insect, plant, etc stings you, it causes pain by putting poison into your skin. *He was stung by a wasp.* **2 HEALTH** [I, T] If your eyes, skin, etc sting, or if something makes them sting, you feel a sudden, burning pain. *That shampoo really made my **eyes sting**.* **3** [T] to upset someone [**often passive**] *She was clearly stung by his criticism.*

sting² /stɪŋ/ *noun* **1 HEALTH** [C] a painful wound that you get when an insect, plant, etc puts poison into your skin *a **wasp/bee sting*** **2 HEALTH** [**no plural**] a sudden, burning pain in your eyes, skin, etc **3** [**no plural**] the feeling of being upset by something *the sting of defeat*

stingy /ˈstɪndʒi/ *adjective informal* not generous *He's too stingy to buy any drinks.*

stink¹ /stɪŋk/ *verb* [I] *past* **stank**, *also US* **stunk**, *past participle* **stunk** **1** SMELL to smell very bad *The kitchen **stinks of** fish.* **2** BAD *informal* to be very bad and dishonest *If you ask me, the whole affair stinks.*

stink² /stɪŋk/ *noun* **1 make/cause/create, etc a stink** *informal* to complain about something in a forceful way **2** [**no plural**] a very bad smell

stint /stɪnt/ *noun* [C] a period of time spent doing something *He had a two-year stint as a teacher in Spain.*

stipulate /ˈstɪpjəleɪt/ *verb* [T] *formal* to say exactly what must be done [+ **(that)**] *The rules*

S

stipulate that smoking is not allowed. •**stipulation** /ˌstɪpjəˈleɪʃᵊn/ *noun* [C]

⊸**stir¹** /stɜːʳ/ *verb* **stirring**, *past* **stirred** **1** **FOOD** [T] to mix food or liquid by moving a spoon round and round in it *Stir the mixture until it is smooth.* **2** MOVE [I, T] to move slightly or make someone move slightly *The baby stirred in its sleep.* **3** FEEL [T] to make someone feel a strong emotion *The case has **stirred** great **anger** among the public.*

stir sth up *phrasal verb* **1** ARGUE to cause arguments or bad feelings between people, often intentionally *I think she just likes to **stir up trouble**.* **2** REMEMBER If something stirs up memories, it makes you remember events in the past. *The photographs **stirred up** some painful **memories**.*

stir² /stɜːʳ/ *noun* **1** **cause/create a stir** to make people excited or surprised *Her new book has caused quite a stir.* **2** **FOOD** [no plural] when you mix food or liquid with a spoon *Could you give the soup a stir?*

stir-fry /ˈstɜːˌfraɪ/ *verb* [T] **FOOD** to fry small pieces of vegetable, meat, etc very quickly while mixing them around •**stir-fry** *noun* [C]

stirring /ˈstɜːrɪŋ/ *adjective* making people feel excitement or other strong emotions *a stirring performance/speech*

stirrup /ˈstɪrəp/ *noun* [C] **SPORT** one of the two metal parts that support your feet when you are riding a horse

stitch¹ /stɪtʃ/ *noun* **1** **DT** [C] a short line of thread that is sewn through a piece of material **2** **HEALTH** [C] one of the small pieces of thread that is used to sew together a cut *She needed 50 stitches in her head.* **3** **DT** [C] one of the small circles of wool that you make when you are knitting (= making something from wool) **4** **HEALTH** [no plural] a sudden pain that you get in the side of your body when you exercise too much *to get a stitch* **5** **in stitches** laughing a lot *He had the whole audience in stitches.*

stitch² /stɪtʃ/ *verb* [I, T] **DT** to sew two things together or to repair something by sewing *I need to get my shoes stitched.*

stitch sth up *phrasal verb* to sew together the two parts of something that have come apart *The nurse stitched up my finger.*

stock¹ /stɒk/ *noun* **1** SHOP [U] all the goods that are available in a shop *We're expecting some new stock in this afternoon.* **2** **be in stock/out of stock** to be available/not available in a shop **3** SUPPLY [C] a supply of something that is ready to be used [usually plural] *stocks of food/weapons* **4** **ECONOMICS, FINANCE** [C, U] the value of a company, or a share in its value *to buy/sell stock* ○ *falling/rising **stock prices*** **5** **FOOD** [U] a liquid made by boiling meat, bones, or vegetables and used to make soups, sauces, etc *chicken/vegetable stock* **6** **take stock (of sth)** to think carefully about a situation before making a decision ➲See also: **laughing stock**

stock² /stɒk/ *verb* [T] to have something available for people to buy *They stock a wide range of books and magazines.*

stock up *phrasal verb* to buy a lot of something *We'd better **stock up on** food for the holiday.*

stock³ /stɒk/ *adjective* **stock answer/phrase, etc** an answer/phrase, etc that is always used and so is not really useful

ˈ**stock acˌcount** *noun* [C] **FINANCE** a record that a business makes, usually at the end of each year, of the value of its stock (= products it has not yet sold)

stockbroker /ˈstɒkˌbrəʊkəʳ/ *noun* [C] **ECONOMICS** someone whose job is to buy and sell stocks and shares in companies for other people

ˈ**stock conˌtrol** *noun* [U] **ECONOMICS** the system of making certain that new supplies are ordered for a business and that goods have not been stolen

the ˈ**stock exˌchange** (*also* **the** ˈ**stock**ˌ**market**) *noun* **1** **ECONOMICS** the place where stocks and shares in companies are bought and sold **2** **ECONOMICS** the value of stocks and shares being bought and sold

stocking /ˈstɒkɪŋ/ *noun* [C] a very thin piece of clothing that covers a woman's foot and leg *a pair of stockings*

stockpile /ˈstɒkpaɪl/ *verb* [T] to collect a lot of something, usually so that it can be used in the future *to stockpile food* •**stockpile** *noun* [C] *a **stockpile of weapons***

stockturn /ˈstɒktɜːn/ *noun* [U] **FINANCE** a measurement of how fast a business is selling its goods

stocky /ˈstɒki/ *adjective* having a wide, strong, body *a short, stocky man*

stoic /ˈstəʊɪk/ *adjective formal* dealing with pain, problems, etc, but never complaining •**stoically** *adverb* •**stoicism** /ˈstəʊɪsɪzᵊm/ *noun* [U]

stole /stəʊl/ *past tense of* steal

stolen /ˈstəʊlᵊn/ *past participle of* steal

stolid /ˈstɒlɪd/ *adjective* calm and not showing emotion or excitement

stoma /ˈstəʊmə/ *noun* [C] *plural* **stomata** **BIOLOGY** one of the many very small holes in the surface of a leaf or stem of a plant through which gases pass in and out ➲See picture at **leaf** ➲See picture at **photosynthesis**

O⊸**stomach¹** /ˈstʌmək/ *noun* [C] *plural* **stomachs** **1** **ANATOMY** the organ inside your body where food goes after it has been eaten and where it starts to be digested ➲See picture at **alimentary canal** **2** **ANATOMY** the front part of your body just below your chest ➲See colour picture **The Body** on page Centre 13 **3** **have no stomach for sth** to not feel brave enough to do something unpleasant ➲See also: have butterflies (**butterfly**) (in your stomach)

stomach² /ˈstʌmək/ *verb informal* **can't stomach sth** to be unable to deal with, watch, etc something unpleasant *I can't stomach horror movies.*

ˈ**stomach** ˌ**ache** *noun* [C, U] **HEALTH** pain in your stomach *I've got terrible stomach ache.*

stomp /stɒmp/ *verb* [I] to put your foot down on the ground hard and quickly, or to walk with heavy steps, usually because you are angry *He stomped off to his room.*

O⊸**stone¹** /stəʊn/ *noun* **1** **GEOLOGY** [U] a hard, natural substance that is found in the ground *a stone wall* **2** **GEOLOGY** [C] a small rock or piece

S

of rock **3** **GEOLOGY** [C] a hard, valuable substance that is often used in jewellery *precious stones* **4** **MEASURES** [C] *plural* **stone** *UK* a unit for measuring weight, equal to 6.35 kilograms or 14 pounds *I gained two stone when I was pregnant.* ➲See Extra help page **Numbers and measurements** on page Centre 24. **5** **BIOLOGY** [C] the hard seed that is at the centre of some fruits *a cherry stone* ➲See also: **stepping-stone**

stone² /stəʊn/ *verb* [T] to kill or hurt someone by throwing stones (= small rocks) at them, usually as a punishment [**often passive**] *Two men were **stoned to death** by the crowd.*

stoned /stəʊnd/ *adjective informal* **1** **HEALTH** relaxed or excited because of the effect of drugs **2** drunk

stonemason /ˈstəʊnˌmeɪsᵊn/ *noun* [C] someone who makes things from stone

stony /ˈstəʊni/ *adjective* **1** **GEOLOGY** covered with or containing stones (= small rocks) *a stony path/road* **2** not friendly, usually because you are angry *a **stony silence***

stood /stʊd/ *past of* stand

stool /stuːl/ *noun* [C] a seat that does not have a back or arms *a piano/bar stool*

stoop¹ /stuːp/ *verb* [I] to bend the top half of your body forward and down *He stooped to pick up the letter.*

stoop to sth/doing sth *phrasal verb* to do something bad that will give you an advantage *I can't believe he would stoop to blackmail.*

stoop² /stuːp/ *noun* **1** BODY [**no plural**] when the upper part of your body is bent forwards *He has a slight stoop.* **2** STEPS [C] *US* a raised area in front of the door of a house, with steps leading up to it

O→ **stop¹** /stɒp/ *verb* **stopping**, *past* **stopped** **1** FINISH [I, T] to finish doing something that you were doing [+ **doing sth**] *Stop laughing - it's not funny.* ○ *He started to say something and then stopped.* ○ *I'm trying to work but I keep having to stop to answer the phone* (= stop so that I can answer the telephone). **2** FOR A SHORT TIME [I] to stop a journey or an activity for a short time *He stopped at a pub for lunch.* **3** NOT OPERATE [I, T] to not continue to operate, or to make something not continue to operate *My watch has stopped.* ○ *Can you stop the video for a minute?* **4** FINISH MOVING [I, T] to not move any more, or make someone or something not move any more *A car stopped outside the house.* ○ *I stopped someone in the street to ask for directions.* **5** BUS/TRAIN [I] If a bus, train, etc stops at a particular place, it pauses at that place so that people can get on and off. *Does this train **stop at** Cambridge?* **6** END [T] to make something end *We must find a way to stop the war.* **7** PREVENT [T] to prevent something from happening or someone from doing something [+ **from** + **doing sth**] *Health workers are trying to stop the disease from spreading.* **8** **Stop it/that!** used to tell someone to finish doing something, usually something annoying **9** **stop a cheque** **FINANCE** *UK* (*US* **stop a check**) to prevent money from being paid from a cheque (= a piece of paper that you sign to pay for things) ➲See also: stop at **nothing**, stop the **rot**²

stop by (sth) *phrasal verb* to visit a person or place for a short time *If you're passing our house, why don't you stop by sometime?*

stop off *phrasal verb* to visit a place for a short time when you are going somewhere else *We stopped off in Paris for a couple of days before heading south.*

COMMON LEARNER ERROR

stop doing something or **stop to do something?**

Stop doing something means 'not continue with an activity'.

Suddenly, everyone stopped talking.

~~*Suddenly, everyone stopped to talk.*~~

Stop to do something means 'stop one activity so that you can do something else'.

We stopped to look at the map.

O→ **stop²** /stɒp/ *noun* [C] **1** BUS/TRAIN a place where a bus or train stops so that people can get on or off *We need to get off at the next stop.* ➲See Common Learner Error at **station** **2** **put a stop to sth** to end something unpleasant *We must put a stop to the violence.* **3** JOURNEY a place where you stop on a journey, or the time that you spend there *We had an overnight stop in Singapore.* **4** **come to a stop** to stop moving *The car came to a stop in front of an old cottage.* **5** **pull out all the stops** to do everything you can to make something succeed ➲See also: **bus stop, full stop**

stoplight /ˈstɒplaɪt/ *noun* [C] *US* a set of red, green, and yellow lights that is used to stop and start traffic

stopover /ˈstɒpˌəʊvəʳ/ *noun* [C] a short stop between parts of a journey, especially a plane journey

stoppage /ˈstɒpɪdʒ/ *noun* [C] **POLITICS** when people stop working because they are angry about something their employers have done

stopwatch /ˈstɒpwɒtʃ/ *noun* [C] a watch that can measure exactly how long it takes to do something and is often used in sports activities

storage /ˈstɔːrɪdʒ/ *noun* [U] **1** when you put things in a safe place until they are needed *We had to put our furniture into storage.* **2** **COMPUTING** the amount of space a computer has for keeping information

O→ **store¹** /stɔːʳ/ *noun* [C] **1** SHOP *mainly US* a shop *a book store* ○ *She works at a men's clothing store.* ➲See Common Learner Error at **shop** **2** SUPPLY a supply of something that you are keeping to use later *a store of grain* **3** **be in store (for sb)** If something is in store for you, it will happen to you in the future. *There's a surprise in store for you!* **4** **set great store by sth** *UK* to believe that something is very important *Martina sets great store by physical strength and fitness.* ➲See also: **chain store, convenience store, department store, liquor store**

O→ **store²** /stɔːʳ/ *verb* [T] **1** KEEP SOMETHING (*also* **store away**) to put something somewhere and not use it until you need it *We have a lot of old clothes stored in the attic.* **2** **COMPUTING** to keep information on a computer *All the data is stored on diskettes.*

S

ˌ**stored** ˈ**energy** *noun* [U] **PHYSICS** in physics, the energy stored by something; potential energy

storeroom /ˈstɔːrruːm/ *noun* [C] a room where goods are kept until they are needed

storey *UK* (*US* **story**) /ˈstɔːri/ *noun* [C] a level of a building *a three-storey house*

stork /stɔːk/ *noun* [C] a large, white bird with very long legs which walks around in water to find its food

WORD PARTNERS FOR ***storm***

an **approaching/gathering** storm • a **fierce/ severe/violent** storm • a storm **breaks** • a storm **abates/passes**

O→**storm¹** /stɔːm/ *noun* [C] **1** very bad weather with a lot of rain, snow, wind, etc *a snow/ thunder storm* **2 a storm of controversy/protest, etc** a strong, negative reaction to something that has been said or done

storm² /stɔːm/ *verb* **1** [T] to attack a building, town, etc, using violence *Armed police stormed the embassy and arrested hundreds of protesters.* **2 storm into/out of, etc** to enter or leave a place in a very noisy way because you are angry *He stormed out of the meeting.*

ˈ**storm** ˌ**surge** *noun* [C] **GEOGRAPHY** when a lot of water is pushed from the sea onto the land, usually caused by a hurricane (= a violent storm with very strong winds)

stormy /ˈstɔːmi/ *adjective* **1** WEATHER If it is stormy, the weather is bad with a lot of wind and rain. *a **stormy night*** ○ ***stormy seas*** **2** ARGUING A stormy relationship or situation involves a lot of anger and arguments. *a **stormy relationship*** ○ *a stormy meeting/debate*

WORD PARTNERS FOR ***story***

read/listen to a story • **tell** sb a story • a story **about/of** sth

O→**story** /ˈstɔːri/ *noun* [C] **1 LITERATURE** a description of a series of real or imaginary events which is intended to entertain people *a horror/detective story* ○ *the story of the revolution* ○ ***Tell** us **a story**, Mum.* ○ *She **reads stories** to the children every night.* **2** REPORT a report in a newspaper, magazine, or news programme *Today's main story is the hurricane in Texas.* **3** EXPLANATION an explanation of why something happened, which may not be true *Did he tell you the same story about why he was late?* **4** BUILDING *US spelling of* storey

stout¹ /staʊt/ *adjective* **1** FAT quite fat *a short, stout man* **2** STRONG If shoes or other objects are stout, they are strong and thick.

stout² /staʊt/ *noun* [C, U] **FOOD** a very dark beer

stove /stəʊv/ *noun* [C] **1 FOOD** a piece of equipment that you cook on *I've left some soup **on the stove** for you.* ➲See colour picture **The Kitchen** on page Centre 2 **2** HEATING a piece of equipment that burns coal, gas, wood, etc and is used for heating a room

stow /stəʊ/ (*also* **stow away**) *verb* [T] to put something in a particular place until it is needed *Our camping equipment is stowed away in the loft.*

stowaway /ˈstəʊəˌweɪ/ *noun* [C] someone who hides on a ship or aircraft so that they can travel without paying

straddle /ˈstrædl/ *verb* [T] **1** SIT to sit or stand with one leg on either side of something *He straddled the chair.* **2** ON BOTH SIDES to be on both sides of a place *Niagara Falls straddles the Canadian border.*

straggle /ˈstrægl/ *verb* [I] **1** MOVE SLOWLY to move more slowly than other members of a group *Some runners are straggling a long way behind.* **2** GROW to grow or spread out in an untidy way *I could see a line of straggling bushes.*

straggly /ˈstrægli/ *adjective* growing or spreading out in an untidy way *a **straggly beard***

O→**straight¹** /streɪt/ *adjective* **1** NOT CURVED not curved or bent *a straight road* ○ *straight hair* **2** LEVEL in a position that is level or vertical *That shelf's not straight.* **3** IN A SERIES [**always before noun**] one after another *They've won five straight games so far.* **4** HONEST honest *a **straight answer*** **5 FOOD** An alcoholic drink that is straight is not mixed with water, ice, etc. **6 get sth straight** to make sure that you completely understand a situation *Let me get this straight - am I paying for this?* **7** NOT HOMOSEXUAL *informal* not homosexual ➲See also: keep a straight **face**¹

O→**straight²** /streɪt/ *adverb* **1** DIRECTION in a straight line *It's **straight ahead**.* ○ *He was looking straight at me.* **2** IMMEDIATELY immediately *I went straight back to sleep.* **3 sit up/stand up straight** to sit or stand with your body vertical **4 not think straight** If you cannot think straight, you are not thinking clearly about something. *I was so tired, I couldn't think straight.* **5 tell sb straight (out)** to tell someone the truth in a clear way *I told him straight that he wasn't getting a pay increase.* **6 straight away** immediately *Go there straight away.*

ˌ**straight** ˈ**angle** *noun* [C] **MATHEMATICS** an angle of 180 degrees

straighten /ˈstreɪtᵊn/ *verb* [I, T] to become straight or to make something straight

straighten sth out *phrasal verb* to successfully deal with a problem or a confusing situation *We need to straighten a few things out.*

straighten sth up *phrasal verb* to make a place tidy *Could you straighten up your room?*

straighten up *phrasal verb* to stand so that your back is straight

straightforward /ˌstreɪtˈfɔːwəd/ *adjective* **1** EASY easy to do or understand *The task looked fairly straightforward.* **2** HONEST saying clearly and honestly what you think *She's very straightforward.*

WORD PARTNERS FOR ***strain***

feel the strain • be **under** strain • the strain **of** doing sth

strain¹ /streɪn/ *noun* **1** FEELING [C, U] when you feel worried and nervous about something *The strain of the last few months had exhausted her.* **2 put a strain on sb/sth** to cause problems for someone or to make a situation difficult *Children put tremendous strains on a marriage.* **3 HEALTH** [C, U] an injury to part of your

S

body that is caused by using it too much *back strain* **4** STRETCH [U] when something is pulled or stretched too tightly *The rope broke* ***under the strain***. **5** **BIOLOGY** [C] a type of disease or plant *a new strain of virus*

strain² /streɪn/ *verb* **1** TRY HARD [I, T] to try hard to do something, usually to see or hear something [+ **to do sth**] *I had to strain to hear the music.* **2** **HEALTH** [T] to injure part of your body by using it too much *I think I've strained a muscle.* **3** CAUSE PROBLEMS [T] to cause problems for a situation or relationship *The incident has strained relations between the two countries.* **4** MONEY [T] to cause too much of something to be used, especially money *The war is straining the defence budget.* **5** **FOOD** [T] to separate solids from a liquid by pouring the mixture into a container with small holes in it *Strain the sauce to remove the seeds and skins.*

strained /streɪnd/ *adjective* **1** NOT RELAXED showing that someone is nervous or anxious *We had a rather* ***strained conversation***. **2** DIFFICULT If a relationship is strained, problems are spoiling that relationship. ***Relations*** *are still* ***strained*** *between the two countries.* ○ *They have a rather* ***strained relationship***.

strait /streɪt/ *noun* [C] **GEOGRAPHY** a narrow area of sea that connects two large areas of sea [**usually plural**] *the straits of Florida*

strait-jacket /ˈstreɪtˌdʒækɪt/ *noun* [C] a special jacket used for mentally ill people that prevents them from moving their arms

strand /strænd/ *noun* [C] **1** THREAD a thin piece of hair, thread, rope, etc *She tucked a* ***strand of hair*** *behind her ear.* **2** PART OF STORY one part of a story, situation, idea, etc *There are a number of different strands to the plot.*

stranded /ˈstrændɪd/ *adjective* unable to leave a place *We were stranded at the airport for ten hours.*

OTHER WAYS OF SAYING ***strange***

Other ways of saying 'strange' are **odd**, **bizarre**, and **weird**: *I always thought there was something a bit* ***odd*** *about her.* • *I had a really* ***bizarre/weird*** *dream last night.*

If something is strange because it is not what you usually expect, you can use the adjectives **curious**, **funny**, or **peculiar**: *This lemonade tastes* ***funny***. • *The chicken had a* ***peculiar*** *smell.* • *A* ***curious*** *thing happened to me yesterday.*

If someone always behaves strangely, you might describe them as **eccentric**: *The whole family are* ***eccentric***.

O-ʷ**strange** /streɪndʒ/ *adjective* **1** UNEXPECTED If something is strange, it is surprising because it is unusual or unexpected. [+ **(that)**] *It's strange that she hasn't called.* ○ *It's midnight and he's still at work - that's strange.* ○ *What a strange-looking man.* **2** NOT FAMILIAR A strange person or place is one that you are not familiar with. *I was stuck in a strange town with no money.* •**strangely** *adverb She's been behaving very strangely* (= in an unusual way) recently.

stranger /ˈstreɪndʒəʳ/ *noun* [C] **1** someone you have never met before *I can't just walk up to a complete stranger and start speaking to them.* **2** **be no stranger to sth** to have a lot of experience of something *He's no stranger to hard work himself.*

strangle /ˈstræŋgl/ *verb* [T] **1** KILL to kill someone by pressing their throat with your hands, a rope, wire, etc [**often passive**] *Police believe the victim was strangled.* **2** PREVENT to prevent something from developing *High-level corruption is strangling the economy.*

stranglehold /ˈstræŋglhəʊld/ *noun* [**no plural**] a position of complete control that prevents something from developing *Two major companies have a* ***stranglehold on*** *the market.*

strap /stræp/ *noun* [C] a narrow piece of material used to fasten two things together or to carry something *a watch strap* ○ *a bra strap* ○ *I want a bag with a shoulder strap.* •**strap** *verb* [T] **strapping**, *past* **strapped** to fasten something using a strap

strategic /strəˈtiːdʒɪk/ *adjective* **1** PLAN helping to achieve a plan, usually in business or politics ***strategic planning*** **2** WAR related to fighting a war ***strategic weapons*** **3** POSITION If something is in a strategic position, it is in a useful place for achieving something. •**strategically** *adverb*

WORD PARTNERS FOR ***strategy***

adopt/develop/have a strategy • a strategy **for** doing sth • the strategy **of** doing sth • an **economic** strategy • a **long-term/short-term** strategy • a **sales** strategy

strategy /ˈstrætədʒi/ *noun* **1** PLAN [C] a plan that you use to achieve something *a* ***an economic strategy*** ○ *a long-term strategy* **2** ACT [U] the act of planning how to achieve something *a* ***military strategy***

the stratosphere /ˈstrætəsfɪəʳ/ *noun* [**no plural**] **GEOGRAPHY** the layer of gases surrounding the Earth at a height of between 15 and 50 kilometres, above the troposphere and below the mesosphere

stratus /ˈstreɪtəs/ *noun* **GEOGRAPHY** a type of flat grey cloud found at the lowest level

straw /strɔː/ *noun* **1** **FARMING** [U] the long, dried stems of plants such as wheat (= plant for grain), often given to animals for sleeping on and eating *a straw hat* **2** [C] a thin plastic or paper tube that you use for drinking through **3** **the final/last straw** the last in a series of unpleasant events which finally makes you stop accepting a bad situation *Last week he came home drunk at five in the morning, and that was the last straw.*

strawberry /ˈstrɔːbᵊri/ *noun* [C] **FOOD** a small, red fruit with a green leaf at the top and small, brown seeds on its surface

stray¹ /streɪ/ *verb* [I] **1** MOVE AWAY to move away from the place where you should be, without intending to *I suddenly realized that I had* ***strayed*** *far* ***from*** *the village.* **2** CHANGE THOUGHTS to start thinking or talking about a different subject from the one you should be giving attention to *We seem to have* ***strayed from*** *the original* ***subject***.

stray² /streɪ/ *adjective* [**always before noun**] **1** LOST A stray animal is lost or has no home.

S

a stray dog **2** SEPARATED A stray piece of something has become separated from the main part. *a stray hair*

stray³ /streɪ/ *noun* [C] an animal that is lost or has no home

streak¹ /striːk/ *noun* [C] **1** MARK a thin line or mark *She has a streak of white hair.* **2** QUALITY a quality in someone's character, especially a bad one *Tom has a* ***mean/ruthless streak.*** **3 a winning/losing streak** a period of always winning/losing a game *I'm* ***on a winning streak.***

streak² /striːk/ *verb* **1 streak across/down/through, etc** to move quickly *The plane streaked across the sky.* **2 be streaked with sth** to have thin lines of a different colour *His dark hair was lightly streaked with grey.*

stream¹ /striːm/ *noun* [C] **1 GEOGRAPHY** a small river **2 a stream of sth a** a line of people or vehicles moving in the same direction *a constant stream of traffic* **b** a large number of similar things that happen or appear one after another *He has produced a steady stream of books.* **c** a moving line of liquid, gas, smoke, etc *A stream of smoke was coming from the chimney.*

stream² /striːm/ *verb* **1 stream down/in/through, etc** to move or flow continuously in one direction *Tears were streaming down her face.* **2 INTERNET** [T] to listen to or watch something on a computer directly from the Internet

streamer /ˈstriːməʳ/ *noun* [C] a long, narrow piece of coloured paper that you use to decorate a room or place for a party

streamline /ˈstriːmlaɪn/ *verb* [T] **1** MAKE SIMPLE to make an organization or process simpler and more effective *We need to streamline our production procedures.* **2** GIVE SHAPE to give a vehicle a smooth shape so that it moves easily through air or water

O-ᵗ **street** /striːt/ *noun* [C] **1** a road in a town or city that has houses or other buildings *We live on the same street.* ○ *a street map* **2 the man/person, etc in the street** a typical, ordinary person **3 be right up sb's street** *UK informal* (*US* **be right up sb's alley**) to be exactly the type of thing that someone knows about or likes to do *I've got a little job here which should be right up your street.* **4 be streets ahead (of sb/sth)** *UK* to be much better or more advanced than someone or something else *American film companies are streets ahead of their European rivals.* ➲See also: **high street, Wall Street**

streetcar /ˈstriːtkɑːʳ/ *US* (*UK/US* **tram**) *noun* [C] an electric vehicle for carrying passengers, mostly in cities, which runs along metal tracks in the road

ˈstreet ˌlight (*also* **ˈstreet ˌlamp**) *noun* [C] a light on a tall post next to a street

streetwise /ˈstriːtwaɪz/ (US *also* **street-smart**) *adjective* Someone who is streetwise knows how to manage dangerous or difficult situations in big towns or cities.

WORD PARTNERS FOR ***strength***

full/great/superhuman strength • **draw/have/muster/regain/sap** strength

O-ᵗ **strength** /streŋθ/ *noun* **1** STRONG [U] when someone or something is strong *upper-body strength* ○ *A good boxer needs skill as well as strength.* **2** INFLUENCE [U] the power or influence that an organization, country, etc has *economic strength* **3** BEING BRAVE [U] when you are brave or determined in difficult situations *I think she showed great* ***strength of character.*** **4** GOOD QUALITIES [C] a good quality or ability that makes someone or something effective *We all have our* ***strengths and weaknesses.*** ○ *The great strength of this arrangement is its simplicity.* **5** STRONG FEELING [U] how strong a feeling or opinion is *There is great* ***strength of feeling*** *against tax increases.* **6 ECONOMICS** [U] the value of a country's money *The strength of the dollar has traders worried.* **7 at full strength** with the necessary number of people *Our team is now at full strength.* **8 on the strength of sth** If you do something on the strength of facts or advice, you do it because of them. *On the strength of this year's sales figures, we've decided to expand the business.* **9 go from strength to strength** *UK* to continue to become more successful ➲See also: a **tower¹** of strength

strengthen /ˈstreŋθᵊn/ *verb* [I, T] to become stronger or make something become stronger *exercises to strengthen the leg muscles*

strenuous /ˈstrenjuəs/ *adjective* using or needing a lot of effort ***strenuous exercise***

WORD PARTNERS FOR ***stress***

be **under** stress • **cope with/deal with/handle** stress • **alleviate/combat/reduce/relieve** stress • stress **levels**

O-ᵗ **stress¹** /stres/ *noun* **1 HEALTH** [C, U] feelings of worry caused by difficult situations such as problems at work *work-related stress* ○ *She's been* ***under*** *a lot of* ***stress*** *recently.* **2** IMPORTANCE [U] special importance that you give to something *At school, they* ***laid*** *great* ***stress*** *on academic achievement.* **3 PHYSICS** [C, U] physical force on something *Jogging* ***puts*** *a lot of* ***stress on*** *your knee joints.* **4 LANGUAGE** [U] when you say one part of a word more strongly *In the word 'blanket', the* ***stress*** *is* ***on*** *the first syllable.*

stress² /stres/ *verb* **1** EMPHASIZE [T] to emphasize something in order to show that it is important [+ **(that)**] *I stressed that this was our policy.* **2** WORRY [I] *US informal* to be worried *Stop stressing about tonight - it'll be fine.*

stressed /strest/ (*also* **stressed out**) *adjective* **HEALTH** worried and not able to relax *Tanya's really stressed out about her exams.*

stressful /ˈstresfᵊl/ *adjective* making you stressed *a* ***stressful*** *job*

O-ᵗ **stretch¹** /stretʃ/ *verb* **1** PULL [I, T] to become longer or wider, or to pull something so that it becomes longer or wider *Don't pull my sweater - you'll stretch it.* **2** MAKE STRAIGHT [I, T] to make your body or part of your body straighter and longer *Stretch your arms above your head.* **3 stretch away/into, etc** to cover a large area *The fields stretched away into the distance.* **4 stretch into/over, etc** to continue for a long period of time *The discussions will probably stretch into next month.* ➲See also: stretch your legs (**leg**), bend/stretch the rules (**rule¹**)

S

stretch out *phrasal verb* to lie with your legs and arms spread out in a relaxed way

stretch² /stretʃ/ *noun* [C] **1 GEOGRAPHY** an area of land or water *a stretch of coastline* **2** TIME a continuous period of time *He often worked ten hours* ***at a stretch.*** **3** BODY when you stretch part of your body *I always* ***do a few stretches*** *before I go jogging.* **4 not by any stretch of the imagination** used to say that something, often a description, is certainly not true *She was never a great player, not by any stretch of the imagination.*

stretcher /ˈstretʃəʳ/ *noun* [C] **HEALTH** a flat structure covered with cloth which is used to carry someone who is ill or injured

stricken /ˈstrɪkᵊn/ *adjective* suffering from the effects of something bad, such as illness, sadness, etc *a child stricken by fear* ➲See also: **panic-stricken, poverty-stricken**

O-- **strict** /strɪkt/ *adjective* **1** PERSON A strict person makes sure that children or people working for them behave well and does not allow them to break any rules. *a strict teacher* ○ *My parents were very* ***strict with*** *us.* **2** RULE If a rule, law, etc is strict, it must be obeyed. *She gave me* ***strict instructions*** *to be there by ten.* **3** BEHAVIOUR [**always before noun**] always behaving in a particular way because of your beliefs *a strict Muslim* **4** EXACT exactly correct *a strict translation of a text*

strictly /ˈstrɪktli/ *adverb* **1** EXACTLY exactly or correctly *That's not* ***strictly*** *true.* ○ ***Strictly speaking*** (= The rules say), *we're not allowed to give you any advice.* **2** ONLY done or existing for a particular person or purpose *Her visit is strictly business.* **3 strictly forbidden/prohibited** used to emphasize that something is not allowed

stride¹ /straɪd/ *verb past* **strode stride across/down/into, etc** to walk somewhere with long steps *She strode across the stage.*

stride² /straɪd/ *noun* [C] **1** a long step when walking or running **2 get into your stride** *UK* (*US* **hit your stride**) to start to do something well and with confidence because you have been doing it for a period *Once I get into my stride, I'm sure I'll work much faster.* **3 take sth in your stride** *UK* (*US* **take sth in stride**) to calmly deal with something that is unpleasant and not let it affect what you are doing *There are often problems at work but she seems to take it all in her stride.*

strident /ˈstraɪdᵊnt/ *adjective* **1** STRONG expressed in a strong way ***strident criticism*** **2** LOUD loud and unpleasant *a* ***strident voice***

strife /straɪf/ *noun* [U] *formal* trouble or disagreement between people

O-- **strike¹** /straɪk/ *verb past* **struck 1** HIT [T] to hit someone or something *His car went out of control and struck a tree.* ○ *I've never heard of anyone being* ***struck by lightning.*** **2** THINK [T] If a thought or idea strikes you, you suddenly think of it. [+ **(that)**] ***It struck me*** *that I'd forgotten to order the champagne.* **3 strike sb as sth** If someone strikes you as having a particular quality, they seem to have that quality. *He didn't strike me as a passionate man.* **4 POLITICS** [I] to stop working for a period of time because you want more money, etc *Bus drivers are threatening to strike.* **5** EFFECT [T] If something bad strikes something or someone, it affects them strongly and quickly. *The hurricane struck the coast at about eight in the morning.* **6** ATTACK [I] to attack suddenly *The marines will strike at dawn.* **7** CLOCK [I, T] If a clock strikes, a bell rings to show what the time is. **8 strike gold, oil, etc** to find a supply of gold, oil, etc in the ground **9 strike a match** to light a match in order to produce fire **10 strike a balance** to give two things the same amount of attention *It's important to* ***strike a balance between*** *spending and saving.* **11 strike a deal** If two people strike a deal, they promise to do something for each other which will give them both an advantage. *The book's author has struck a deal with a major film company.* ➲See also: strike a **chord** (with sb), be struck **dumb**

strike back *phrasal verb* to attack someone who has attacked you

strike out *phrasal verb* **1** START MOVING to start moving towards somewhere in a determined way *She* ***struck out for*** *the opposite bank.* **2** FAIL *US informal* to fail at something *I really struck out with her - she wouldn't even let me kiss her goodbye.*

strike sth out *phrasal verb* to draw a line through something wrong that you have written

strike up sth *phrasal verb* to start a conversation or relationship with someone *I* ***struck up a conversation*** *with a guy who worked behind the bar.*

WORD PARTNERS FOR ***strike*** *(noun)*

be on/go on strike • a strike **over** sth • strike **action**

strike² /straɪk/ *noun* **1 POLITICS** [C, U] a period of time when people are not working because they want more money, etc *Teachers are planning* ***to go on strike*** *next month.* **2** ATTACK [C] a sudden military attack *an air strike* ➲See also: **hunger strike**

striker /ˈstraɪkəʳ/ *noun* [C] **1** someone who is on strike **2 SPORT** a football player whose job is to try to score goals

striking /ˈstraɪkɪŋ/ *adjective* **1** NOTICEABLE easily noticed *There's a* ***striking resemblance*** *between them.* **2** ATTRACTIVE very attractive *She's very striking.*

string¹ /strɪŋ/ *noun* **1** [C, U] very thin rope used for tying things *a ball of string* **2 MUSIC** [C] a piece of wire that is part of a musical instrument *guitar strings* **3 a string of beads/pearls** a set of decorative things joined together on a thread, worn as jewellery **4 a string of sth** a number of similar things *a string of questions* ○ *As a writer, she's enjoyed a string of successes.* **5 no strings (attached)** If there are no strings attached to an offer or arrangement, there is nothing that is unpleasant that you have to accept. *I'll drive you home - no strings attached.* **6 pull strings** to secretly use the influence that you have over important people to get something or to help someone

string² /strɪŋ/ *verb* [T] *past* **strung** to hang something somewhere with string *They had strung flags across the entrance to welcome us home.*

S

string sb along *phrasal verb* to deceive someone for a long time about what you are intending to do

be strung out *phrasal verb* If a group of things or people are strung out somewhere, they are in a line with spaces between them. *There were chairs strung out across the room.*

stringent /ˈstrɪndʒənt/ *adjective* Stringent controls, rules, etc are very strict or extreme.

the strings /strɪŋz/ *noun* [**plural**] **MUSIC** the people in a musical group who play instruments with strings on them such as the violin

strip[1] /strɪp/ *verb* **stripping**, *past* **stripped** **1** CLOTHES [**I, T**] (*also UK* **strip off**) to remove all your clothes, or to remove all someone else's clothes *She was stripped and searched by the guards.* ○ *He stripped off his clothes and ran into the sea.* **2** COVERING [**T**] (*also* **strip off**) to remove a covering from the surface of something *to strip paint/wallpaper off the wall*

strip sb of sth *phrasal verb* to take something important away from someone as a punishment *He was **stripped of** his gold **medal**.*

strip[2] /strɪp/ *noun* [**C**] **1** PIECE a long, narrow piece of something *a strip of paper/plastic* **2** AREA a long, narrow area of land or water *A narrow strip of land separated the lake from the sea.* ➲See also: **comic strip**

stripe /straɪp/ *noun* [**C**] a long, straight area of colour *white with blue stripes*

striped /straɪpt/ *adjective* with a pattern of stripes *a striped shirt*

stripey /ˈstraɪpi/ *adjective another spelling of* stripy

stripy (*also* **stripey**) /ˈstraɪpi/ *adjective* with a pattern of stripes *stripy trousers*

strive /straɪv/ *verb* [**I**] *past* **strove** *or* **strived**, *past participle* **striven** *or* **strived** *formal* to try very hard to do or achieve something *to **strive for** happiness/peace* [**+ to do sth**] *We are constantly striving to improve our service in order to keep up with our rivals.*

strode /strəʊd/ *past of* stride

stroke[1] /strəʊk/ *noun* **1** **HEALTH** [**C**] a sudden problem in your brain that changes the flow of blood and makes you unable to move part of your body *to **have/suffer** a **stroke*** **2** [**C**] a movement that you make against something with your hand, a pen, brush, etc *a **brush stroke*** **3** **SPORT** [**C**] a style of swimming **4** **SPORT** [**C**] when you move your arm and hit the ball in sports such as tennis, golf, etc **5** **a stroke of luck** something good that happens to you by chance *He had exactly the part that I needed so that was a stroke of luck.*

stroke[2] /strəʊk/ *verb* [**T**] to gently move your hand over a surface *to stroke a cat/dog* ○ *He stroked her hair.*

stroll /strəʊl/ *verb* **stroll along/down/through, etc** to walk somewhere in a slow and relaxed way *They strolled along the beach.* •**stroll** *noun* [**C**] *Shall we **go for a stroll** around the garden before lunch?*

stroller /ˈstrəʊləʳ/ *US* (*UK* **pushchair**) *noun* [**C**] a chair on wheels which is used to move small children

O-→**strong** /strɒŋ/ *adjective* **1** PHYSICALLY POWERFUL A strong person or animal is physically powerful. *Are you strong enough to lift this table on your own?* **2** NOT BREAK A strong object does not break easily or can support heavy things. *a strong box/chair* **3** QUALITY of a good quality or level and likely to be successful *a strong competitor/team* ○ *a strong economy* **4** FEELING A strong feeling, belief, or opinion is felt in a very deep and serious way. *a strong sense of pride* **5** NOTICEABLE If a taste, smell, etc is strong, it is very noticeable. *There's a strong smell of burning.* **6** PERSONALITY If a person or their personality is strong, they are confident and able to deal with problems well. **7** ALCOHOL containing a lot of alcohol *a strong drink* **8** RELATIONSHIP If a friendship, relationship, etc is strong, it is likely to last for a long time. **9** **strong chance/possibility, etc** something that is very likely to happen *There's a strong possibility of rain this afternoon.* **10** **strong opposition/support, etc** a lot of opposition/support, etc **11** **strong language** words that some people might consider to be offensive **12** **sb's strong point** something that someone is very good at *Cooking is not my strong point.* **13** **be still going strong** continuing to be successful after a long time *Fran's grandfather is well into his eighties and still going strong.*

ˌstrong ˈacid *noun* [**C**] **CHEMISTRY** an acid with a pH of between 1 and 3, whose ionic compounds separate or divide into smaller molecules completely in a solution containing water

strongly /ˈstrɒŋli/ *adverb* very much or in a very serious way *He is **strongly opposed** to violence of any sort.* ○ *I **strongly believe** that we should take action.*

strong-willed /ˌstrɒŋˈwɪld/ *adjective* very determined to do what you want to do *A strong-willed toddler can be quite difficult to deal with.*

strontium /ˈstrɒntiəm/ *noun* [**U**] **CHEMISTRY** a soft metallic silver-white chemical element that burns easily with a bright red flame, used in fireworks and some colour televisions (symbol **Sr**)

stroppy /ˈstrɒpi/ *adjective UK informal* angry or arguing a lot *He used to be so cute – all of a sudden he's turned into a stroppy teenager.*

strove /strəʊv/ *past tense of* strive

struck /strʌk/ *past of* strike

structural /ˈstrʌktʃərəl/ *adjective* relating to the structure of something ***structural damage*** ○ *The last five years have seen big **structural changes** in the company.* •**structurally** *adverb*

O-→**structure[1]** /ˈstrʌktʃəʳ/ *noun* **1** WAY [**C, U**] the way that parts of something are arranged or put together *cell structure* ○ *grammatical structure* **2** BUILDING [**C**] a building or something that has been built

structure[2] /ˈstrʌktʃəʳ/ *verb* [**T**] to arrange something in an organized way *How is the course structured?*

O-→**struggle[1]** /ˈstrʌgl/ *verb* [**I**] **1** TRY to try very hard to do something difficult [**+ to do sth**] *He's*

S

struggling to pay off his debts. **2** FIGHT to fight someone when they are holding you *She struggled but couldn't break free.*
struggle on *phrasal verb* to continue doing something that is difficult

WORD PARTNERS FOR ***struggle (noun)***

a **constant/ongoing/uphill** struggle • a struggle **for** [justice/survival, etc]

O→**struggle²** /ˈstrʌgl/ *noun* [C] **1** TRY when you try very hard to do something difficult *It was a real struggle to stay awake during the film.* **2** FIGHT a fight between people

strum /strʌm/ *verb* [I, T] **strumming**, *past* **strummed MUSIC** to move your fingers across the strings of a guitar

strung /strʌŋ/ *past of* string

strut /strʌt/ *verb* **strutting**, *past* **strutted strut along/around/down, etc** to walk somewhere with big steps in a proud way ➲See also: strut your **stuff**[1]

stub¹ /stʌb/ *noun* [C] the short, end piece of something such as a cigarette or pencil that is left after it has been used *There were **cigarette stubs** all over the floor.*

stub² /stʌb/ *verb* **stubbing**, *past* **stubbed stub your toe** to hit your toe against a hard surface by accident
stub sth out *phrasal verb* to stop a cigarette from burning by pressing the burning end against a hard surface

stubble /ˈstʌbl/ *noun* [U] **1** HAIRS very short, stiff hairs, usually on a man's face **2 FARMING** the short bits of dried plant stems left in a field after it has been cut

stubborn /ˈstʌbən/ *adjective* determined not to change your ideas, plans, etc, although other people want you to •**stubbornly** *adverb* •**stubbornness** *noun* [U]

stubby /ˈstʌbi/ *adjective* short and thick ***stubby legs/fingers***

stuck¹ /stʌk/ *adjective* [**never before noun**] **1** NOT MOVE not able to move anywhere *My car **got stuck in** a ditch.* ○ *We were stuck at the airport for twelve hours.* **2** NOT CONTINUE not able to continue reading, answering questions, etc because something is too difficult *I keep **getting stuck** on difficult words.* **3 be stuck with sb/sth** to have to deal with someone or something unpleasant because no one else wants to *Whenever we eat out, I always get stuck with the bill.*

stuck² /stʌk/ *past of* stick

stud /stʌd/ *noun* [C] **1** JEWELLERY a small, metal piece of jewellery that is put through a part of your body such as your ear or nose **2** DECORATION a small piece of metal that is fixed to the surface of something, usually for decoration **3 FARMING** (*also* ˈ**stud ˌfarm**) a place where horses are kept for breeding

O→**student** /ˈstjuːdᵊnt/ *noun* [C] **EDUCATION** someone who is studying at a school or university *a law student* ○ *a foreign student* ➲See also: **mature student**

studio /ˈstjuːdiəʊ/ *noun* [C] **1 ART** a room where an artist or photographer works **2** TV/RADIO a room where television/radio programmes or musical recordings are made **3** FILMS a film company or a place where films are made

studious /ˈstjuːdiəs/ *adjective* spending a lot of time studying •**studiously** *adverb*

O→**study¹** /ˈstʌdi/ *verb* **1 EDUCATION** [I, T] to learn about a subject, usually at school or university *I studied biology before going into medicine.* ➲See Common Learner Error at **learn 2** LOOK [T] to look at something very carefully *He studied his face in the mirror.*

WORD PARTNERS FOR ***study (noun)***

carry out/conduct/undertake a study • a study **examines/focuses on** sth • a study **concludes/finds/shows/suggests** sth • a study **into** sth

study² /ˈstʌdi/ *noun* **1** FINDING OUT INFORMATION [C] when someone studies a subject in detail in order to discover new information *For years, **studies have shown** the link between smoking and cancer.* **2 EDUCATION** [U] when you learn about a subject, usually at school or university *the study of English literature* **3** ROOM [C] a room in a house where you can read, write, etc ➲See also: **case study**

O→**stuff¹** /stʌf/ *noun* [U] *informal* **1** used to refer to a substance or a group of things or ideas, etc without saying exactly what they are *There's some sticky stuff on the carpet.* ○ *They sell bread and cakes and stuff like that.* ○ *Can I leave my stuff at your house?* **2 know your stuff** *informal* to know a lot about a subject, or to be very good at doing something *She's an excellent teacher - she really knows her stuff.* **3 strut your stuff** *humorous informal* to dance

stuff² /stʌf/ *verb* [T] **1 stuff sth in/into/behind, etc** to push something into a small space, often quickly or in a careless way *He stuffed the papers into his briefcase and left.* **2** FILL to completely fill a container with something *an envelope stuffed with money* **3 FOOD** to fill meat, vegetables, etc with a mixture of food before you cook them *stuffed peppers* **4** DEAD ANIMAL to fill the body of a dead animal with special material so that it looks as if it is still alive

stuffing /ˈstʌfɪŋ/ *noun* [U] **1 FOOD** a mixture of food which is put into meat, vegetables, etc before they are cooked **2** material which is used to fill the inside of things such as soft chairs, beds, toys, etc

stuffy /ˈstʌfi/ *adjective* **1** AIR If a room or a building is stuffy, it is hot and unpleasant and the air is not fresh. **2** FORMAL old-fashioned, formal and boring *a stuffy club for wealthy old men*

stumble /ˈstʌmbl/ *verb* [I] **1** FALL to step badly and almost fall over *Mary stumbled on the loose rocks.* **2** PAUSE to make a mistake, such as pausing or repeating a word, while speaking or performing *He kept **stumbling over** the same word.*
stumble across/on/upon sth/sb *phrasal verb* to discover something by chance, or to meet someone by chance *I stumbled across these photographs while I was cleaning out my desk.*

ˈ**stumbling ˌblock** *noun* [C] a problem which makes it very difficult to do something *Lack of money has been the main stumbling block.*

stump[1] /stʌmp/ *noun* [C] **1** the short part of something that is left after most of it has been removed *a **tree stump*** **2 SPORT** one of the three vertical wooden sticks that you throw a ball at in the game of cricket ➲See colour picture **Sports 2** on page Centre 15

stump[2] /stʌmp/ *verb* **1 be stumped by sth** *informal* to not be able to answer a question or solve a problem because it is too difficult *Scientists are completely stumped by this virus.* **2 POLITICS** [I] *US* to travel to different places to get political support

stump (sth) up *phrasal verb UK informal* to provide money for something, especially when you do not want to

stun /stʌn/ *verb* [T] **stunning**, *past* **stunned** **1** SHOCK to shock or surprise someone very much [**often passive**] *Friends and family were stunned by her sudden death.* **2** MAKE UNCONSCIOUS to make a person or animal unconscious, usually by hitting them on the head

stung /stʌŋ/ *past of* sting

stunk /stʌŋk/ **1** PAST PARTICIPLE *past participle of* stink **2** PAST TENSE *US past tense of* stink

stunning /ˈstʌnɪŋ/ *adjective* very beautiful *stunning views over the city* ○ *She's stunning.* •**stunningly** *adverb a **stunningly beautiful** woman*

stunt[1] /stʌnt/ *noun* [C] **1** DANGER when someone does something dangerous that needs great skill, usually in a film *He always **does** his own **stunts**.* **2** ATTENTION something that is done to get people's attention *Their marriage was just a cheap **publicity stunt**.*

stunt[2] /stʌnt/ *verb* [T] to stop the normal growth or development of something *They say that smoking **stunts** your **growth**.*

stupefied /ˈstjuːpɪfaɪd/ *adjective* so shocked, tired, etc that you cannot think •**stupefying** *adjective* making you stupefied •**stupefy** *verb* [T]

stupendous /stjuːˈpendəs/ *adjective* extremely good or large *a stupendous performance* •**stupendously** *adverb stupendously successful*

O‑ **stupid** /ˈstjuːpɪd/ *adjective* **1** SILLY silly or not intelligent *That was a really stupid thing to do.* ○ *How could you be so stupid?* **2** ANNOYING [**always before noun**] *informal* used to show that you are annoyed about something which is causing a problem *I can never get this stupid machine to work!* •**stupidity** /stjuːˈpɪdəti/ *noun* [U] •**stupidly** *adverb*

stupor /ˈstjuːpəʳ/ *noun* [**no plural**] when someone is almost unconscious and cannot think clearly, especially because they have drunk too much alcohol *He staggered into the room in a **drunken stupor**.*

sturdy /ˈstɜːdi/ *adjective* very strong and solid *sturdy walking boots*

stutter /ˈstʌtəʳ/ *verb* [I, T] to repeat the first sound of a word several times when you talk, usually because you have a speech problem *"C-c-can we g-go now?" she stuttered.* •**stutter** *noun* [**no plural**] *He has a really bad stutter.*

WORD PARTNERS FOR ***style***

a **distinctive** style • **in** a style • a style **of** doing sth

O‑ **style**[1] /staɪl/ *noun* **1** WAY [C, U] a way of doing something that is typical of a particular person, group, place, or period *a **style of** painting/writing* **2** DESIGN [C, U] a way of designing hair, clothes, furniture, etc *She's had her hair cut in a really nice style.* **3** QUALITY [U] the quality of being attractive and fashionable or behaving in a way which makes people admire you *She's got style.* **4 BIOLOGY** [C] the middle section of the female part of a flower ➲See picture at **carpel** ➲See picture at **flower** **5 do sth in style** to do something in a way that people admire, usually because it involves spending a lot of money *If we ever get married we'll do it in style.* **6 cramp sb's style** to prevent someone from enjoying themselves, especially by going somewhere with them

style[2] /staɪl/ *verb* [T] to shape or design hair, clothes, furniture, etc in a particular way *He spends hours in the bathroom styling his hair.*

-style /staɪl/ *suffix* used at the end of words to mean 'looking or behaving like something or someone' *antique-style furniture* ○ *Japanese-style management* ➲See also: **old-style**

stylish /ˈstaɪlɪʃ/ *adjective* fashionable and attractive *a stylish, black suit* •**stylishly** *adverb stylishly dressed*

stylus /ˈstaɪləs/ *noun* [C] **1** a small point that touches a record (= flat, round, plastic disc that music is stored on) in order to play it **2 COMPUTING** a device shaped like a pen that is used for getting information or images into a computer

Styrofoam /ˈstaɪrəfəʊm/ *noun* [U] *trademark* **DT** polystyrene (= light plastic material used to protect objects when they are packed)

suave /swɑːv/ *adjective* If someone, especially a man, is suave, they are polite and confident in a way that is attractive but may be false. *suave and sophisticated*

sub- /sʌb-/ *prefix* **1** under or below *substandard workmanship* **2** less important or a smaller part of a larger whole *a subsection*

subarctic /sʌbˈɑːktɪk/ *adjective* **GEOGRAPHY** relating to the regions of the world just south of the Arctic Circle

subatomic /ˌsʌbəˈtɒmɪk/ *adjective* **PHYSICS, CHEMISTRY** smaller than or within an atom *a subatomic particle*

subconscious[1] /sʌbˈkɒnʃəs/ *adjective* Subconscious thoughts and feelings influence your behaviour without you being aware of them. *a subconscious fear* •**subconsciously** *adverb*

subconscious[2] /sʌbˈkɒnʃəs/ *noun* [**no plural**] the part of your mind which contains thoughts and feelings that you are not aware of but which influence your behaviour *The memory was buried deep within my subconscious.*

subcontract /ˌsʌbkənˈtrækt/ *verb* [T] to pay someone else to do part of a job that you have agreed to do

subculture /ˈsʌbˌkʌltʃəʳ/ *noun* [C] **SOCIETY** a group of people with beliefs, interests, etc that are different from the rest of society

subdirectory /ˈsʌbdɪˌrektəri/ *noun* [C] **COMPUTING** a directory (= place on a computer for

S

putting files and folders together) that is inside another directory

subdivide /ˌsʌbdɪˈvaɪd/ *verb* [T] to divide something into smaller parts [**often passive**] *Each chapter is* ***subdivided into*** *smaller sections.* •**subdivision** /ˌsʌbdɪˈvɪʒən/ *noun* [C, U]

subduction zone /sʌbˈdʌkʃənˌzəʊn/ *noun* [C] **GEOLOGY** an area where two continental plates (= large layers of rock that form the Earth's surface) meet and where there are often earthquakes

subdue /səbˈdjuː/ *verb* [T] **subduing**, *past* **subdued** to start to control someone or something, especially by using force

subdued /səbˈdjuːd/ *adjective* **1** PERSON quiet because you are feeling sad or worried *She seemed a bit subdued.* **2** LIGHT/COLOUR Subdued lights or colours are not bright. ***subdued lighting***

WORD PARTNERS FOR ***subject***

bring up/broach/raise a subject • **get onto** a subject • **change/drop/get off** a subject • **on** the subject (of sth)

O━**subject**[1] /ˈsʌbdʒɪkt/ *noun* [C] **1** WHAT what someone is writing or talking about *a series of programmes* ***on the subject of*** *homelessness* **2** **EDUCATION** an area of knowledge studied in school or university *Chemistry is my favourite subject.* **3** **LANGUAGE** the person or thing which performs the action described by the verb. In the sentence 'Bob phoned me yesterday.', 'Bob' is the subject. **4** **SOCIETY** someone who is from a particular country, especially a country with a king or queen *a British subject*

subject[2] /ˈsʌbdʒɪkt/ *adjective* **subject to sth a** often affected by something, especially something unpleasant *Departure times are subject to alteration.* **b** only able to happen if something else happens *The pay rise is subject to approval by management.*

subject[3] /səbˈdʒekt/ *verb*
subject sb/sth to sth *phrasal verb* to make someone or something experience something unpleasant *In prison, he was subjected to beatings and interrogations.*

S

subjective /səbˈdʒektɪv/ *adjective* influenced by someone's beliefs or feelings, instead of facts *a subjective judgment* •**subjectively** *adverb* •**subjectivity** /ˌsʌbdʒekˈtɪvəti/ *noun* [U] when someone or something is influenced by beliefs or feelings instead of facts

ˈ**subject** ˌ**matter** *noun* [U] what is being talked or written about *I'm not sure whether the subject matter is suitable for children.*

subjunctive /səbˈdʒʌŋktɪv/ *noun* [**no plural**] **LANGUAGE** the form of the verb which is used to express doubt, possibility, or wish. In the sentence 'I wish I were rich.', 'were' is in the subjunctive. •**subjunctive** *adjective*

sublime /səˈblaɪm/ *adjective* extremely good, beautiful, or enjoyable *sublime scenery* •**sublimely** *adverb*

sublime /səˈblaɪm/ *verb* [T, I] **PHYSICS, CHEMISTRY** to change a substance directly from a solid to a gas, or to change in this way •**sublimation** /ˌsʌblɪˈmeɪʃən/ *noun* [U]

submarine /ˌsʌbmərˈiːn/ *noun* [C] a boat that travels under water

submerge /səbˈmɜːdʒ/ *verb* [I, T] to cause something to be under the surface of water, or to move below the surface of water *The floods destroyed farmland and submerged whole villages.* •**submerged** *adjective*

submission /səbˈmɪʃən/ *noun* **1** CONTROL [U] when you accept that someone has complete control over you *They tried to starve her* ***into submission.*** **2** DOCUMENT [C, U] when you send a document, plan, etc to someone so that they can consider it, or the document, plan, etc that you send *The deadline for submissions is 29 April.*

submissive /səbˈmɪsɪv/ *adjective* always doing what other people tell you to do *a quiet, submissive wife*

submit /səbˈmɪt/ *verb* **submitting**, *past* **submitted 1** DOCUMENT [T] to send a document, plan, etc to someone so that they can consider it *Applications must be submitted before 31 January.* **2** OBEY [I] to accept that someone has control over you and do what they tell you to do *He was forced to* ***submit to*** *a full body search.*

submultiple /ˌsʌbˈmʌltɪpəl/ *noun* [C] **MATHEMATICS** a number that divides into another number an exact number of times

subordinate[1] /səˈbɔːdənət/ *adjective* less important or lower in rank *a* ***subordinate position/role*** ○ *An individual's needs are* ***subordinate to*** *those of the group.*

subordinate[2] /səˈbɔːdənət/ *noun* [C] someone who has a less important position than someone else in an organization

subordinate[3] /səˈbɔːdɪneɪt/ *verb* [T] *formal* to put someone or something into a less important position •**subordination** /səˌbɔːdɪˈneɪʃən/ *noun* [U]

subˌ**ordinate** ˈ**clause** *noun* [C] **LANGUAGE** in grammar, a clause which cannot form a separate sentence but adds information to the main clause

subpoena /səbˈpiːnə/ *noun* [C] **LAW** a legal document ordering someone to go to court •**subpoena** *verb* [T] to give someone a subpoena

subscribe /səbˈskraɪb/ *verb* [I] **FINANCE** to pay money to an organization so that you regularly receive a service or product, such as a magazine or newspaper *to* ***subscribe to*** *a magazine/an internet service* •**subscriber** *noun* [C]
subscribe to sth *phrasal verb formal* to agree with an opinion, belief, etc *I certainly don't subscribe to the view that women are morally superior to men.*

subscript /ˈsʌbskrɪpt/ *adjective* subscript numbers or letters are written just below the rest of the words or numbers, often in a smaller size •**subscript** *noun* [U] ➲Compare **superscript**

WORD PARTNERS FOR ***subscription***

cancel/pay/take out a subscription • a subscription **to** sth • an **annual** subscription

subscription /səbˈskrɪpʃən/ *noun* [C] **FINANCE** an amount of money that you pay regularly to receive a product or service or to be a member of an organization *an* ***annual subscription***

subsequent /ˈsʌbsɪkwənt/ *adjective* [**always before noun**] happening after something else *The mistakes were corrected in a subsequent edition of the book.* •**subsequently** *adverb*

subservient /səbˈsɜːviənt/ *adjective* always doing what other people want you to do

subset /ˈsʌbset/ *noun* [**C**] **MATHEMATICS** a set (= group of similar numbers, objects or people) that is part of another, larger set

subside /səbˈsaɪd/ *verb* [**I**] **1** LESS STRONG to become less strong or extreme *The violence seems to be subsiding at last.* **2** BUILDING If a building subsides, it sinks down to a lower level.

subsidence /səbˈsaɪdᵊns/ *noun* [**U**] when buildings subside or land sinks down to a lower level

subsidiary /səbˈsɪdiᵊri/ *noun* [**C**] a company which is owned by another larger company

subsidize (*also UK* **-ise**) /ˈsʌbsɪdaɪz/ *verb* [**T**] **FINANCE** If a government or other organization subsidizes something, it pays part of the cost of it, so that prices are reduced. *We have a subsidized restaurant at work.*

subsidy /ˈsʌbsɪdi/ *noun* [**C**] **FINANCE** money given by a government or other organization to pay part of the cost of something *housing subsidies for the poor*

subsist /səbˈsɪst/ *verb* [**I**] to manage to live when you only have a very small amount of food or money •**subsistence** *noun* [**U**]

WORD PARTNERS FOR ***substance***

a **dangerous/hazardous/toxic** substance • a **powdery/sticky/waxy** substance

O⁻ **substance** /ˈsʌbstᵊns/ *noun* **1** MATERIAL [**C**] a solid, liquid, or gas *a* ***dangerous substance*** ○ *illegal substances* (= illegal drugs) **2** TRUTH [**U**] truth or importance *There's no* ***substance to*** *the allegations.* **3 the substance of sth** the most important part of what someone has said or written

substandard /sʌbˈstændəd/ *adjective* Something that is substandard is not as good as it should be. *substandard conditions/housing*

substantial /səbˈstænʃᵊl/ *adjective* **1** AMOUNT large in amount *a substantial change/increase* ○ *a substantial amount of money/time* **2** STRENGTH large and strong *a substantial building* ⊃Opposite **insubstantial**

substantially /səbˈstænʃᵊli/ *adverb* by a large amount *House prices are substantially higher in the south.*

substantiate /səbˈstænʃieɪt/ *verb* [**T**] *formal* to provide facts which prove that something is true *His* ***claims*** *have never been* ***substantiated.***

substantive /ˈsʌbstᵊntɪv/ *adjective formal* important or serious *a* ***substantive issue***

substitute¹ /ˈsʌbstɪtjuːt/ *noun* [**C**] someone or something that is used instead of another person or thing *Margarine can be used as* ***a substitute for*** *butter.* ○ *a substitute teacher*

substitute² /ˈsʌbstɪtjuːt/ *verb* **1** [**T**] to use someone or something instead of another person or thing *You can* ***substitute*** *pasta* ***for*** *the rice, if you prefer.* **2 substitute for sb** to do someone's job because they are not there *I'm substituting for her while she's on holiday.* •**substitution** /ˌsʌbstɪˈtjuːʃᵊn/ *noun* [**C, U**]

substrate /ˈsʌbstreɪt/ *noun* [**C**] **1 BIOLOGY** a substance or surface which an organism grows and lives on and uses as food **2 CHEMISTRY** a substance which an enzyme acts on to produce a chemical reaction

subsume /səbˈsjuːm/ *verb* [**T**] *formal* to include someone or something as part of a larger group [**often passive**] *The company has been subsumed by a large US bank.*

subterfuge /ˈsʌbtəfjuːdʒ/ *noun* [**C, U**] *formal* a trick or a dishonest way of achieving something *They obtained the information by subterfuge.*

subterranean /ˌsʌbtᵊrˈeɪniən/ *adjective* under the ground *subterranean passages*

subtitles /ˈsʌbˌtaɪtlz/ *noun* [**plural**] words shown at the bottom of a cinema or television screen to explain what is being said *It's a French film with English subtitles.*

subtle /ˈsʌtl/ *adjective* **1** NOT OBVIOUS not obvious or easy to notice *a subtle change/difference* ○ *a* ***subtle hint*** **2** NOT STRONG A subtle flavour, colour, etc is delicate and not strong or bright. **3** CLEVER clever in a way that does not attract attention *a subtle way of solving the problem* •**subtly** *adverb*

subtlety /ˈsʌtlti/ *noun* **1** QUALITY [**U**] the quality of being subtle **2** THING [**C**] something that is subtle

subtract /səbˈtrækt/ *verb* [**T**] **MATHEMATICS** to take a number or amount away from another number or amount *You need to* ***subtract*** *25%* ***from*** *the final figure.* •**subtraction** /səbˈtrækʃᵊn/ *noun* [**C, U**]

subtropical /ˌsʌbˈtrɒpɪkᵊl/ *adjective* **GEOGRAPHY** relating to parts of the world that are immediately south or north of the tropics (= the hottest areas) *a subtropical climate* •**the subtropics** /ˌsʌbˈtrɒpɪks/ *noun* [**plural**]

suburb /ˈsʌbɜːb/ *noun* [**C**] **GEOGRAPHY** an area where people live outside the centre of a city *a suburb of New York* •**suburban** /səˈbɜːbᵊn/ *adjective* relating to a suburb *a suburban area/home*

suburbia /səˈbɜːbiə/ *noun* [**U**] **GEOGRAPHY** the suburbs of towns and cities generally

subversive /səbˈvɜːsɪv/ *adjective* **POLITICS** trying to destroy the authority of a government, religion, etc *subversive literature* •**subversive** *noun* [**C**] someone who is subversive

subvert /sʌbˈvɜːt/ *verb* [**T**] **POLITICS** *formal* to try to destroy the authority of a government, religion, etc *a plot to subvert the government* •**subversion** /səbˈvɜːʃᵊn/ *noun* [**U**] *formal*

subway /ˈsʌbweɪ/ *noun* [**C**] **1** PASSAGE *UK* (*UK/US* **underpass**) a passage under a road or railway for people to walk through **2** TRAIN *US* (*UK* **underground**) a system of trains that travel underground *We can* ***take the subway*** *to Grand Central Station.* ⊃See Common Learner Error at **metro**

S

sub-zero /ˌsʌbˈzɪərəʊ/ *adjective* Sub-zero temperatures are temperatures below zero degrees.

O⊸**succeed** /səkˈsiːd/ *verb* **1** ACHIEVE [I] to achieve what you are trying to achieve *She has the skill and determination to succeed.* [+ **in** + **doing sth**] *He has finally succeeded in passing his exams.* **2** TAKE POSITION [T] to take an official job or position after someone else *The Queen was succeeded by her eldest son when she died.*

COMMON LEARNER ERROR

succeed

Remember that **succeed** is often followed by the preposition **in + doing sth**. It is not used with 'to do sth'.

Two prisoners succeeded in escaping.

~~*Two prisoners succeeded to escape.*~~

WORD PARTNERS FOR ***success***

achieve/have success • the **key to/secret of** success • success **in** (doing) sth • **without** success

O⊸**success** /səkˈses/ *noun* **1** ACHIEVEMENT [U] when you achieve what you want to achieve *Her success is due to hard work and determination.* **2** GOOD RESULT [C] something that has a good result or that is very popular *His first film was a great success.*

COMMON LEARNER ERROR

success

Be careful to choose the correct verb with this noun.

*The evening **was** a great success.*

*They tried for weeks but **had** little success.*

*They are determined to **make** a success of the scheme.*

~~*She reached success as a writer.*~~

O⊸**successful** /səkˈsesfəl/ *adjective* **1** ACHIEVEMENT achieving what you want to achieve *If the operation is successful, she should be walking within a few months.* **2** WORK having achieved a lot or made a lot of money through your work *a successful businessman* **3** POPULAR very popular *a successful book/film* ➲Opposite **unsuccessful** •**successfully** *adverb*

succession /səkˈseʃən/ *noun* **1** EVENTS [**no plural**] a number of similar events or people that happen, exist, etc after each other *to suffer a **succession of** injuries* ○ *a succession of boyfriends* **2 in quick/rapid succession** If several things happen in quick/rapid succession, they happen very quickly after each other. *She had her first three children in quick succession.* **3** POSITION [U] when someone takes an official position or job after someone else

successive /səkˈsesɪv/ *adjective* happening after each other *He has just won the World Championship for the third **successive year**.*

WORD PARTNERS FOR ***successor***

appoint/choose/find a successor • a **natural/worthy** successor • a successor **to** sb

successor /səkˈsesər/ *noun* [C] **1** PERSON someone who has a position or job after someone else *He is her most likely successor.* **2** THING an organization, product, etc that follows and takes the place of an earlier one

succinct /səkˈsɪŋkt/ *adjective* said in a very clear way using only a few words *a succinct explanation* •**succinctly** *adverb*

succulent /ˈsʌkjələnt/ *adjective* **FOOD** If food is succulent, it is good to eat because it has a lot of juice. *a succulent piece of meat*

succumb /səˈkʌm/ *verb* [I] *formal* **1** to not be able to stop yourself doing something *I **succumbed to** temptation and had some cheesecake.* **2** **HEALTH** to die or suffer badly from an illness

O⊸**such** /sʌtʃ/ *pronoun, determiner* **1** REFER TO used to refer to something or someone that you were just talking about, or something or someone of that type *It's difficult to know how to treat such cases.* **2** FOR EMPHASIS used to emphasize a quality of someone or something *She's such a nice person.* ○ *It's such a shame that he's leaving.* **3 such as** for example *She can't eat dairy products, such as milk and cheese.* **4 as such** used after a word or phrase in negative statements to mean in the exact meaning of that word or phrase *There are no rules as such, just a few guidelines.* **5 such...that** used to talk about the result of something *The whole thing was such a worry that I began to lose sleep over it.* **6 there's no such thing/person (as)...** used to say that something or someone does not exist *There's no such thing as ghosts.*

such-and-such /ˈsʌtʃənsʌtʃ/ *determiner informal* used instead of referring to a particular or exact thing *If they tell you to arrive at such-and-such a time, get there a couple of minutes before.*

suck /sʌk/ *verb* **1** [**I, T**] to have something in your mouth and use your tongue, lips, etc to pull on it or to get liquid, air, etc out of it *to suck a sweet/lollipop* ○ *to suck your thumb* **2 suck sth in/under/up, etc** to pull something somewhere using the force of moving air, water, etc *He was sucked under the boat and drowned.* **3 be sucked into sth** to become involved in something bad when you do not want to **4 he/it/this, etc sucks!** *US very informal* If someone or something sucks, they are bad or unpleasant.

suck up to sb *phrasal verb very informal* to try to make someone who is in authority like you by doing and saying things that will please them

sucker /ˈsʌkər/ *noun* [C] **1** *informal* someone who believes everything that you tell them and is easy to deceive **2** **BIOLOGY** something that helps an animal or object stick to a surface

sucrase /ˈsuːkreɪz/ (*also* **invertase**) *noun* [U] **BIOLOGY** an enzyme (= substance in the body that makes chemical reactions happen) found in the intestines that breaks down sucrose to fructose and glucose

sucrose /ˈsuːkrəʊz/ *noun* [U] **BIOLOGY** a type of sugar that exists naturally in many plants

suction /ˈsʌkʃən/ *noun* [U] **PHYSICS** when something is forced into a container or space by removing air

O‐ **sudden** /ˈsʌdᵊn/ *adjective* **1** done or happening quickly and unexpectedly *a sudden change/increase* ○ *His sudden death was a great shock to us all.* **2 all of a sudden** unexpectedly *All of a sudden she got up and walked out.* •**suddenness** *noun* [U]

ˌsudden ˌinfant ˈdeath ˌsyndrome *noun* [U] **HEALTH** SIDS

O‐ **suddenly** /ˈsʌdᵊnli/ *adverb* quickly and unexpectedly *I suddenly realized who she was.* ○ *It all happened so suddenly that I can't remember much about it.*

Sudoku (also **Su Doku**) /ˌsuːˈdɒkuː/ *noun* [C, U] a number game in which you have to write a number between 1 and 9 in each small box of a 9x9 square

suds /sʌdz/ *noun* [**plural**] small bubbles made from soap and water

sue /suː/ *verb* [I, T] **suing**, *past* **sued LAW** to take legal action against someone and try to get money from them because they have harmed you *He **sued** the newspaper **for** slander.*

suede /sweɪd/ *noun* [U] leather that has a slightly rough surface

O‐ **suffer** /ˈsʌfəʳ/ *verb* **1** PAIN [I, T] to experience pain or unpleasant emotions *I can't bear to see animals suffering.* **2 suffer from sth HEALTH** to have an illness or other health problem *She suffers from severe depression.* **3 suffer a broken leg/a heart attack, etc** to experience an injury or other sudden health problem *He suffered a serious neck injury in the accident.* **4 suffer damage/defeat/loss, etc** to experience something bad such as damage/defeat/loss, etc **5** BECOME WORSE [I] to become worse in quality *If you're tired all the time your work tends to suffer.*

sufferer /ˈsʌfərəʳ/ *noun* [C] **HEALTH** someone who suffers from an illness or other health problem *AIDS/cancer sufferers*

WORD PARTNERS FOR ***suffering***

create/endure/relieve suffering • **human** suffering • **unnecessary/unspeakable** suffering • the suffering **of** sb

suffering /ˈsʌfərɪŋ/ *noun* [U] when someone experiences pain or unpleasant emotions ***human suffering***

suffice /səˈfaɪs/ *verb* [I] *formal* to be enough *You don't need to give a long speech - a few sentences will suffice.*

sufficient /səˈfɪʃᵊnt/ *adjective* as much as is necessary *She didn't have sufficient time to answer all the questions.* ➲Opposite **insufficient** •**sufficiently** *adverb I was sufficiently close to hear what they were saying.* ➲See also: **self-sufficient**

suffix /ˈsʌfɪks/ *noun* [C] **LANGUAGE** a group of letters that you add to the end of a word to make another word. In the word 'slowly', '-ly' is a suffix. ➲See Extra help page **Word formation** on page Centre 29. ➲Compare **prefix**

suffocate /ˈsʌfəkeɪt/ *verb* [I, T] to die because you cannot breathe or to kill someone by stopping them from breathing *He suffocated her with a pillow.* •**suffocation** /ˌsʌfəˈkeɪʃᵊn/ *noun* [U]

suffrage /ˈsʌfrɪdʒ/ *noun* [U] **POLITICS** the right to vote in an election *universal suffrage* (= the right of all adults to vote)

suffragette /ˌsʌfrəˈdʒet/ *noun* [C] **POLITICS** a woman in Britain, Australia and the United States in the early 20th century who was a member of a group that fought for the right of women to vote

suffragist /ˈsʌfrədʒɪst/ *noun* [C] **POLITICS** someone who supports the right of people to vote in elections, especially a supporter of the right of women to vote in the early 20th century

O‐ **sugar** /ˈʃʊgəʳ/ *noun* **1 FOOD** [U] a very sweet substance used to give flavour to food and drinks *coffee with milk and sugar* **2 FOOD** [C] a spoon of sugar in a cup of tea or coffee *He likes two sugars in his tea.*

O‐ **suggest** /səˈdʒest/ *verb* [T] **1** IDEA to express an idea or plan for someone to consider [+ **(that)**] *I suggest that we park the car here and walk into town.* [+ **doing sth**] *He suggested having the meeting at his house.* **2** ADVICE to say that someone or something is suitable for something *to suggest someone for a job* ○ *Can you suggest a good hotel?* **3** SEEM TRUE to make something seem likely to be true *All the evidence suggests that she did it.*

OTHER WAYS OF SAYING ***suggestion***

A suggestion about what to do is sometimes described as a **thought** or **idea**: *Rebecca has a few **ideas** about how we could improve things.* • *I've had a **thought** about what we might do this summer.*

If someone suggests a plan or action, especially in business, you can use nouns such as **proposal** or **proposition**: *The **proposal** for a new sports hall has been rejected.* • *He wrote to me with a very interesting business **proposition**.*

WORD PARTNERS FOR ***suggestion***

bristle at/deny/make/reject/welcome a suggestion • an **alternative/constructive/helpful/ridiculous/sensible** suggestion • **at** sb's suggestion

O‐ **suggestion** /səˈdʒestʃᵊn/ *noun* **1** [C] an idea or plan that someone suggests *to **make a suggestion*** ○ *Have you got any suggestions for improvements?* **2 a suggestion of/that sth** something that makes something seem likely to be true *There's no suggestion of any connection between the two men.* **3 at sb's suggestion** following the advice that someone has given you *We went to that restaurant at Paul's suggestion.*

suggestive /səˈdʒestɪv/ *adjective* **1** making you think about sex *suggestive comments/remarks* **2 suggestive of sth** *formal* similar to something and making you think about it *The shapes are suggestive of human forms.* •**suggestively** *adverb*

suicidal /ˌsuːɪˈsaɪdᵊl/ *adjective* **1** UNHAPPY so unhappy that you want to kill yourself *to feel suicidal* **2** DANGEROUS likely to have an extremely bad result *a suicidal decision*

suicide /ˈsuːɪsaɪd/ *noun* **1** DEATH [C, U] when you intentionally kill yourself *He **committed suicide** after a long period of depression.* **2** MISTAKE

S

[U] when you do something that will have an extremely bad result for you ***political suicide***

ˈsuicide ˌbomber *noun* [C] **POLITICS** a person who has a bomb hidden on their body and who kills themselves in the attempt to kill others

O━**suit**[1] /suːt/ *noun* [C] **1** CLOTHES a jacket and trousers or a jacket and skirt that are made from the same material *She wore a dark blue suit.* ➲See colour picture **Clothes** on page Centre 8 **2** CARDS one of the four types of cards with different shapes on them in a set of playing cards **3 follow suit** to do the same as someone else has just done *If other shops lower their prices, we will have to follow suit.* ➲See also: **bathing suit, pant suit, trouser suit, wet suit**

O━**suit**[2] /suːt/ *verb* [T] **1** ATTRACTIVE to make someone look more attractive *Green really suits you.* **2** ACCEPTABLE to be acceptable or right for someone *It would suit me better if we left a bit earlier.* ➲See Common Learner Error at **fit 3 be suited to/for sth** to be right for someone or something *These plants are better suited to a warm climate.* ➲See also: suit sb down to the **ground**[1]

OTHER WAYS OF SAYING ***suitable***

A common alternative to 'suitable' is the adjective **appropriate**: *Is this film **appropriate** for young children?* • *You should bring **appropriate** footwear.*

If an action is suitable for a particular situation, you can use the adjectives **apt** or **fitting**: *'Unusual', yes, that's a very **apt** description.* • *The promotion was a **fitting** reward for all his hard work.*

The adjective **right** can also be used to show that someone or something is suitable for a particular situation: *I'm not sure that she's the **right** person for the job.* • *Is this the **right** way to do it?*

If someone or something is very suitable, you can use the adjective **perfect**: *It's a **perfect** day for a picnic.* • *She'd be **perfect** for the job.*

The expression **in keeping with** is sometimes used when something is suitable for a particular style or tradition: *The antique desk was very much **in keeping with** the rest of the furniture in the room.*

S

O━**suitable** /ˈsuːtəbl/ *adjective* acceptable or right for someone or something *a suitable time to call* ○ *This film is **suitable for** children.* ➲Opposite **unsuitable** •**suitably** *adverb suitably dressed*

suitcase /ˈsuːtkeɪs/ *noun* [C] a rectangular case with a handle that you use for carrying clothes when you are travelling *to **pack** your **suitcase***

suite /swiːt/ *noun* [C] **1** FURNITURE several pieces of furniture which go together *a bedroom suite* **2** ROOMS a set of hotel rooms which are used together ➲See also: **en suite**

suitor /ˈsuːtəʳ/ *noun* [C] *old-fashioned* a man who wants to marry a particular woman

sulfur /ˈsʌlfəʳ/ *noun* [U] **CHEMISTRY** *US spelling of* sulphur

sulk /sʌlk/ *verb* [I] to look unhappy and not speak to anyone because you are angry about something *He's upstairs sulking in his bedroom.* •**sulky** *adjective a sulky teenager*

sullen /ˈsʌlən/ *adjective* in an unpleasant mood and not smiling or speaking to anyone

sulphate *UK* (*US* **sulfate**) /ˈsʌlfeɪt/ *noun* [C, U] **CHEMISTRY** a chemical formed from sulphur, oxygen and another element

sulphide (*US* **sulfide**) /ˈsʌlfaɪd/ *noun* [C, U] **CHEMISTRY** a chemical formed from sulphur and another element

sulphur *UK* (*US* **sulfur**) /ˈsʌlfəʳ/ *noun* [U] **CHEMISTRY** a yellow chemical element that has an unpleasant smell (symbol **S**)

ˌsulphur diˈoxide (*US* **sulfur dioxide**) *noun* [U] **CHEMISTRY** a gas with no colour which has a strong unpleasant smell and dissolves in water. It is used in various industrial processes and for keeping food fresh, and causes serious air pollution (formula SO_2).

sulphuric acid (*US* **sulfuric acid**) /sʌlˌfjʊərɪkˈæsɪd/ *noun* [U] **CHEMISTRY** a strong acid with no colour (formula H_2SO_4)

sultan /ˈsʌltən/ *noun* [C] **POLITICS** a ruler in some Muslim countries

sultana /sʌlˈtɑːnə/ *noun* [C] *UK* **FOOD** a dried grape (= small round fruit) often used in cakes

sultry /ˈsʌltri/ *adjective* **1** SEXUALLY ATTRACTIVE If a woman is sultry, she behaves in a sexually attractive way. *a sultry voice* **2** HOT If the weather is sultry, it is hot and wet. *a sultry summer night*

O━**sum**[1] /sʌm/ *noun* [C] **1 FINANCE** an amount of money *a large/small sum of money* **2 MATHEMATICS** *UK* a simple mathematical calculation such as adding two numbers together *Kids these days can't **do sums** without a calculator.* **3 MATHEMATICS** the total amount that you get when you add two or more numbers together *The sum of six and seven is thirteen.* ➲See also: **lump sum**

sum[2] /sʌm/ *verb* **summing**, *past* **summed**

sum (sth/sb) up *phrasal verb* to describe briefly the important facts or characteristics of something or someone *The purpose of a conclusion is to sum up the main points of an essay.*

sum sth/sb up *phrasal verb* to quickly decide what you think about something or someone *I think she summed up the situation very quickly.*

summarize (*also UK* **-ise**) /ˈsʌmᵊraɪz/ *verb* [I, T] to describe briefly the main facts or ideas of something

WORD PARTNERS FOR ***summary*** *(noun)*

give/produce/provide a summary • **a brief/quick/short** summary • a summary **of** sth

summary[1] /ˈsʌmᵊri/ *noun* [C] a short description that gives the main facts or ideas about something *He **gave a brief summary of** what happened.*

summary[2] /ˈsʌmᵊri/ *adjective* [**always before noun**] *formal* decided or done quickly, without the usual discussions or legal arrangements ***a summary arrest/execution***

WORD PARTNERS FOR ***summer***

in (the) summer • **last/next** summer • **early/late** summer • the summer **months**

O⊸**summer** /ˈsʌməʳ/ *noun* [**C, U**] the season of the year between spring and autumn, when the weather is warmest *We usually go away **in the summer**.* ○ *a long, hot summer* •**summery** *adjective* typical of or suitable for summer

ˌ**summer ˈholiday** (*US* **summer vacation**) *noun* [**C**] **EDUCATION** the time during the summer when you do not have to go to school

ˈ**summer ˌschool** *noun* [**C**] **EDUCATION** an educational course that happens during the summer when other courses have finished

summertime /ˈsʌmətaɪm/ *noun* [**U**] when it is summer ***In the summertime**, we often eat outside.*

summit /ˈsʌmɪt/ *noun* [**C**] **1 POLITICS** an important meeting between the leaders of two or more governments *a two-day summit* ○ *a summit meeting* **2 GEOGRAPHY** the top of a mountain *The climbers hope to **reach the summit** before nightfall.*

summon /ˈsʌmən/ *verb* [**T**] **1** *formal* to officially order someone to come to a place *He was summoned to a meeting.* **2 summon (up) the courage/strength, etc** to make a great effort to do something [**+ to do sth**] *He tried to summon up the courage to speak to her.*

summons /ˈsʌmənz/ *noun* [**C**] **LAW** an official order saying that you must go to a court of law

Sun *written abbreviation for* Sunday

sun² /sʌn/ *verb* **sunning**, *past* **sunned sun yourself** to sit or lie in the sun

O⊸**sun¹** /sʌn/ *noun* **1 the sun ASTRONOMY** the large, bright star that shines in the sky during the day and provides light and heat for the Earth **2** [**U no plural**] the light and heat that comes from the sun *I can't sit **in the sun** for too long.*

sunbathe /ˈsʌnbeɪð/ *verb* [**I**] to sit or lie in the sun so that your skin becomes brown •**sunbathing** *noun* [**U**]

sunbed /ˈsʌnbed/ (*US* **tanning bed**) *noun* [**C**] a piece of equipment with a flat area like a bed and a strong light, which you lie on in order to make your skin go darker

sunblock /ˈsʌnblɒk/ *noun* [**C, U**] sunscreen

sunburn /ˈsʌnbɜːn/ *noun* [**U**] **HEALTH** when your skin becomes painful and red from being in the sun too long •**sunburnt** (*also* **sunburned**) *adjective*

sundae /ˈsʌndeɪ/ *noun* [**C**] **FOOD** a sweet dish made of ice cream with fruit and nuts

O⊸**Sunday** /ˈsʌndeɪ/ (*written abbreviation* **Sun**) *noun* [**C, U**] the day of the week after Saturday and before Monday

sundial /ˈsʌndaɪl/ *noun* [**C**] a device for telling the time by a shadow made by the sun

sundry /ˈsʌndri/ *adjective* **1** [**always before noun**] of different types ***sundry items*** **2 all and sundry** *UK informal* (*US* **various and sundry**) everyone *I don't want all and sundry knowing about my problems.*

sunflower /ˈsʌnflaʊəʳ/ *noun* [**C**] a tall, yellow flower with a large, black centre full of seeds

sung /sʌŋ/ *past participle of* sing

sunglasses /ˈsʌnˌglɑːsɪz/ *noun* [**plural**] dark glasses that you wear to protect your eyes from the sun ➲See colour picture **Clothes** on page Centre 9

sunk /sʌŋk/ **1** PAST PARTICIPLE *past participle of* sink **2** PAST TENSE *US past tense of* sink

sunken /ˈsʌŋkən/ *adjective* [**always before noun**] **1** LOW at a lower level than the surrounding area *a sunken bath* **2** SEA having fallen down to the bottom of the sea *a sunken ship* **3 sunken eyes/cheeks** eyes or cheeks that make you look ill because they go too far into your face

sunlight /ˈsʌnlaɪt/ *noun* [**U**] the light from the sun

sunlit /ˈsʌnlɪt/ *adjective* [**always before noun**] A sunlit place is bright because of light from the sun. *a sunlit room*

ˈ**sun ˌlotion** *noun* [**C, U**] sunscreen

Sunni /ˈsʊni/ *noun* [**C**] **RELIGION** a member of a large group within the Islamic religion •**Sunni** *adjective* describing the Sunni or their type of Islam

sunny /ˈsʌni/ *adjective* **1** BRIGHT bright because of light from the sun *a lovely **sunny day*** **2** HAPPY behaving in a happy way *a sunny smile/personality*

sunrise /ˈsʌnraɪz/ *noun* [**C, U**] when the sun appears in the morning and the sky becomes light

sunroof /ˈsʌnruːf/ *noun* [**C**] part of a roof of a car which you open to allow air and light from the sun to come in

sunscreen /ˈsʌnskriːn/ *noun* [**C, U**] a substance that protects your skin in the sun

sunset /ˈsʌnset/ *noun* [**C, U**] when the sun disappears in the evening and the sky becomes dark

sunshine /ˈsʌnʃaɪn/ *noun* [**U**] the light from the sun *Let's sit over there in the sunshine.*

sunstroke /ˈsʌnstrəʊk/ *noun* [**U**] **HEALTH** an illness caused by spending too much time in the sun

suntan /ˈsʌntæn/ (*also* **tan**) *noun* [**C**] when your skin is brown from being in the sun *suntan oil* •**suntanned** (*also* **tanned**) *adjective*

super /ˈsuːpəʳ/ *adjective, adverb informal old-fashioned* very good *We had a super time.*

super- /suːpəʳ-/ *prefix* extremely or more than usual *a supermodel* ○ *super-rich*

superb /suːˈpɜːb/ *adjective* excellent *a superb performance/restaurant* •**superbly** *adverb*

superbug /ˈsuːpəbʌg/ *noun* [**C**] **HEALTH** a type of bacteria (= very small living things that cause disease) that is very difficult to destroy

supercomputer /ˈsuːpəkəmˌpjuːtəʳ/ *noun* [**C**] **COMPUTING** a very powerful computer

super-cooled /ˌsuːpəˈkuːld/ *adjective* **PHYSICS** Supercooled liquids have been made colder than the temperature at which they would normally freeze without freezing them.

superficial /ˌsuːpəˈfɪʃᵊl/ *adjective* **1** NOT SERIOUS If someone is superficial, they never think about things that are serious or important. **2** NOT COMPLETE not complete and involving

S

only the most obvious things ***superficial knowledge*** ○ ***a superficial resemblance*** **3** [NOT DEEP] only on the surface of something ***superficial damage/injuries*** •**superficially** *adverb*

superfluous /suːˈpɜːfluəs/ *adjective* not needed, or more than is needed ***superfluous details/information***

supergroup /ˈsuːpəˌɡruːp/ *noun* [C] **MUSIC** a very successful pop group

superhuman /ˌsuːpəˈhjuːmən/ *adjective* **superhuman effort/strength, etc** more effort/strength, etc than a normal human being

superimpose /ˌsuːpərɪmˈpəʊz/ *verb* [T] **ART** to put an image, text, etc over something so that the thing under it can still be seen

superintendent /ˌsuːpərɪnˈtendənt/ *noun* [C] **1** **LAW** in Britain, a police officer of high rank **2** [OFFICIAL] in the US, an official responsible for a place, event, etc

superior¹ /suːˈpɪəriəʳ/ *adjective* **1** [BETTER] better than other things *superior quality* ○ *This car is far* ***superior to*** *the others.* **2** [OPINION] thinking that you are better than other people *She has a very superior manner.*

superior² /suːˈpɪəriəʳ/ *noun* [C] someone in a higher position than you at work *I will have to report this to my superiors.*

superiority /suːˌpɪəriˈɒrəti/ *noun* [U] **1** [BETTER] when something is better than other things *the superiority of modern design* **2** [OPINION] when you think that you are better than other people *She has an* ***air of superiority***.

superlative /suːˈpɜːlətɪv/ *noun* [C] **LANGUAGE** the form of an adjective or adverb that is used to show that someone or something has more of a particular quality than anyone or anything else. For example 'best' is the superlative of 'good' and 'slowest' is the superlative of 'slow'. ➲Compare **comparative**

➔ **supermarket** /ˈsuːpəˌmɑːkɪt/ *noun* [C] a large shop that sells food, drink, products for the home, etc

supermodel /ˈsuːpəˌmɒdəl/ *noun* [C] a very famous model (= someone whose job is to wear fashionable clothes for photographs)

the supernatural /ˌsuːpəˈnætʃərəl/ *noun* things that cannot be explained by our knowledge of science or nature •**supernatural** *adjective* ***supernatural forces/powers***

supernova /ˌsuːpəˈnəʊvə/ *noun* [C] *plural* **supernovas** or **supernovae** **ASTRONOMY** a star that becomes very bright for a few days because it is exploding

superpower /ˈsuːpəˌpaʊəʳ/ *noun* [C] **POLITICS** a country that has great military and political power in the world

superscript /ˈsuːpəskrɪpt/ *adjective* superscript numbers or letters are written just above the rest of the words or numbers, often in a smaller size •**superscript** *noun* [U] ➲Compare **subscript**

supersede /ˌsuːpəˈsiːd/ *verb* [T] to take the place of someone or something that went before [**often passive**] *Records were superseded by CDs.*

supersonic /ˌsuːpəˈsɒnɪk/ *adjective* **PHYSICS** faster than the speed of sound *supersonic aircraft*

superstar /ˈsuːpəstɑːʳ/ *noun* [C] a very famous singer, performer, etc

superstition /ˌsuːpəˈstɪʃən/ *noun* [C, U] when someone believes that particular actions or objects are lucky or unlucky

superstitious /ˌsuːpəˈstɪʃəs/ *adjective* believing that particular objects or events are lucky or unlucky *Are you superstitious about the number 13?*

superstore /ˈsuːpəstɔːʳ/ *noun* [C] a very large shop that sells many different things, often outside a town

supervise /ˈsuːpəvaɪz/ *verb* [I, T] to watch a person or activity and make certain that everything is done correctly, safely, etc *Students must be supervised by a teacher at all times.* •**supervisor** *noun* [C] someone who supervises

WORD PARTNERS FOR ***supervision***

be **under** supervision • **close/constant** supervision • the supervision **of** sb/sth

supervision /ˌsuːpəˈvɪʒən/ *noun* [U] when you supervise someone or something *He needs* ***constant supervision.***

supper /ˈsʌpəʳ/ *noun* [C] **FOOD** a meal that you eat in the evening *What are we having for supper?*

supplant /səˈplɑːnt/ *verb* [T] *formal* to take the place of someone or something

supple /ˈsʌpl/ *adjective* able to bend or move easily *a supple body*

supplement /ˈsʌplɪmənt/ *noun* [C] an extra amount or part added to something *to take a* ***vitamin supplement*** ○ *a newspaper with a* ***colour supplement*** •**supplement** /ˈsʌplɪment/ *verb* [T] *She works part-time to supplement her pension.*

supplementary /ˌsʌplɪˈmentəri/ (*also US* **supplemental**) *adjective* added to something ***supplementary materials***

ˌsupplementary ˈangle *noun* [C] **MATHEMATICS** one of two angles which together add up to 180° ➲Compare **complementary angle**

supplier /səˈplaɪəʳ/ *noun* [C] someone who provides things that people want or need, often over a long period of time

supplies /səˈplaɪz/ *noun* [**plural**] the food, equipment, etc that is needed for a particular activity, holiday, etc

➔ **supply¹** /səˈplaɪ/ *verb* [T] to provide things that people want or need, often over a long period of time *to supply food/drugs to people* ○ *This lake* ***supplies*** *the whole town* ***with*** *water.*

WORD PARTNERS FOR ***supply*** *(noun)*

a supply **of** sth • a **constant/endless/plentiful** supply

➔ **supply²** /səˈplaɪ/ *noun* **1** [AMOUNT] [C] an amount of something that is ready to be used ***a supply of water*** ○ *food supplies* **2 in short supply** If something is in short supply, there is little of it available. **3** [SYSTEM] [C] the system of supplying something to people *Someone has turned off the electricity supply.*

O⊸**support¹** /sə'pɔːt/ *verb* [T] **1** AGREE to agree with an idea, group, or person *Do you **support** their **views** on nuclear weapons?* **2** PROVE to help to show that something is true *There's no evidence to **support** his **story**.* **3** HOLD to hold the weight of someone or something *Is this ladder strong enough to support me?* **4** PAY to look after someone by paying for their food, clothes, etc *She has three children to support.* **5** SPORT *mainly UK* to like a particular sports team and want them to win *Who do you support?*

WORD PARTNERS FOR ***support** (noun)*

enlist/express/give/lose/rally support • **overwhelming/public/strong/tacit/widespread** support • support **for** sb/sth

O⊸**support²** /sə'pɔːt/ *noun* **1** AGREEMENT [U] agreement with an idea, group or person *Is there much public **support for** the death penalty?* **2 in support of sb/sth** agreeing with someone or something *The minister spoke in support of military action.* **3** HELP [U] help or encouragement ***emotional/financial support*** **4** OBJECT [C] an object that can hold the weight of something ➲See also: **child support, income support, moral support**

WORD PARTNERS FOR ***supporter***

a **keen/loyal/staunch/strong** supporter • a supporter **of** sth

supporter /sə'pɔːtəʳ/ *noun* [C] **1** IDEA someone who supports a particular idea, group, or person *a **strong supporter of** the government* **2** SPORT *mainly UK* someone who likes a particular sports team and wants them to win *English football supporters*

supportive /sə'pɔːtɪv/ *adjective* giving help or encouragement *a very supportive friend*

O⊸**suppose** /sə'pəʊz/ *verb* **1 be supposed to do sth a** to be expected or intended to do something, especially when this does not happen *These drugs are supposed to reduce the pain.* ○ *He was supposed to be here by nine.* **b** If you are supposed to do something, the rules say that you should do it. *You're supposed to pay by the end of the month.* ○ *You're not supposed to* (= you should not) *smoke in here.* **2 be supposed to be sth** to be considered by many people to be something *The scenery is supposed to be fantastic.* **3** [T] to think that something is likely to be true [+ **(that)**] *I suppose that you've already heard the news?* **4 suppose/supposing (that)** used to introduce an idea for someone to consider *Suppose he phones tonight. What should I say?* **5 I suppose** used to show that you are not certain or not completely happy about something *It was quite interesting, I suppose.* **6 I suppose so** used to show agreement to something when you do not really want to *"Can I come with you?" 'I suppose so."*

supposed /sə'pəʊzɪd/ *adjective* [**always before noun**] used to show that you do not believe that someone or something really is what many people consider them to be *a supposed genius* •**supposedly** /sə'pəʊzɪdli/ *adverb The building is supposedly in good condition.*

supposition /ˌsʌpə'zɪʃən/ *noun* [**C, U**] *formal* when someone believes that something is true although there is no proof

suppress /sə'pres/ *verb* [T] **1** FEELINGS to control feelings so that they do not show *I could barely suppress my anger.* **2** INFORMATION to prevent information from being known *to suppress evidence/news* **3** FIGHT to stop someone or something by using force [**often passive**] *The rebellion was suppressed by government forces.* •**suppression** /sə'preʃən/ *noun* [**U**]

supremacy /suː'preməsi/ *noun* [**U**] when a country or group of people is more powerful, successful, etc than anyone else *a battle/struggle for supremacy*

supreme /suː'priːm/ *adjective* **1** IMPORTANT of the highest rank or greatest importance *the **supreme ruler*** **2** GREAT very great ***supreme confidence/effort*** •**supremely** *adverb* very *supremely confident*

the suˌpreme 'court *noun* **LAW** the court of law that has the most authority in a state or country

surcharge /'sɜːtʃɑːdʒ/ *noun* [C] **FINANCE** an extra amount of money that you have to pay for something *a surcharge for single rooms*

O⊸**sure** /ʃɔːʳ/ *adjective* **1** [**never before noun**] certain [+ **(that)**] *I'm sure that he won't mind.* [+ **question word**] *She's **not sure** what she's going to do next.* ○ *I'm quite **sure about** the second answer.* ➲Opposite **unsure 2 make sure (that)** to take action so that you are certain that something happens, is true, etc *Make sure that you close all the windows before you leave.* **3 be sure of sth** to be confident that something is true *He'll win, I'm sure of it.* **4 for sure** without any doubts *I think he's from Korea but don't know for sure.* **5 be sure of yourself** to be confident of your own abilities, qualities, etc *She's always been very sure of herself.* **6 be sure to do sth a** If you are sure to do something, it is certain that you will do it. *He's sure to go back there again.* **b** used to tell someone what they must remember to do *Be sure to tell her I called.* **7 a sure sign of/that sth** something that makes something seem certain to be true **8 a sure thing** something that is certain to happen *Death is the one sure thing about life.* **9 sure** (*also US* **sure thing**) used to show agreement *"Can I borrow your pen please?" "Sure."* **10 sure enough** as expected *He said the book was on his desk, and sure enough, there it was.*

O⊸**surely** /'ʃɔːli/ *adverb* used to express surprise that something has happened or is going to happen *You surely didn't tell him, did you?* ○ *Surely you're not going to go out dressed like that?*

surf¹ /sɜːf/ *verb* **1** SPORT [I] to ride on a wave in the sea using a special board **2 surf the Internet/Net/Web INTERNET** to look at information on the Internet by moving from one page to another using electronic links (= connections) ➲See Extra help page **The Web and the Internet** on page Centre 36. •**surfer** *noun* [C] someone who surfs •**surfing** *noun* [U]

surf² /sɜːf/ *noun* [U] the top of the waves in the sea as it moves onto the coast

S

WORD PARTNERS FOR *surface*

a flat/hard/level/smooth/uneven surface • **cover** the surface • **above/below/beneath/on** the surface

O→ **surface¹** /ˈsɜːfɪs/ *noun* **1** [TOP] [C] the top or outside part of something *the Earth's surface* ○ *The sun was reflected on the surface of the water.* **2** [APPEARANCE] [**no plural**] what someone or something seems to be like when you do not know much about them ***On the surface** he seemed very pleasant.* ➲See also: **work surface**

surface² /ˈsɜːfɪs/ *verb* **1** [APPEAR] [I] to appear or become public, often after being hidden *This problem **first surfaced** about two weeks ago.* ○ *So when did these **allegations surface**?* **2** [RISE] [I] to rise to the surface of water *The submarine surfaced a few miles off the coast.* **3** [COVER] [T] to cover a road with a hard substance

ˌsurface ˈarea *noun* [**C usually singular**] **MEASURES, MATHEMATICS** the area of a surface or of all of the outer surfaces of something

ˈsurface ˌmail *noun* [U] letters, parcels, etc that are sent by road, sea, or train and not by aircraft

surfboard /ˈsɜːfbɔːd/ *noun* [C] **SPORT** a long piece of wood or plastic that you use to ride on waves in the sea

surfeit /ˈsɜːfɪt/ *noun* [**no plural**] *formal* too much of something *We've had **a surfeit of** applications from women for this job.*

surfing /ˈsɜːfɪŋ/ *noun* [U] **1 SPORT** the sport of riding on a wave on a special board **2 INTERNET** the activity of looking at a lot of different things on the Internet

surge¹ /sɜːdʒ/ *verb* **1 surge forward/into/through, etc** to move somewhere with great strength *The crowd surged against the barriers.* **2** [I] to increase very quickly ***Prices surged** on the stock exchange.*

surge² /sɜːdʒ/ *noun* [C] **1** [INCREASE] a large increase in something *a **surge in** spending* **2** [MOVEMENT] a sudden movement forward

surgeon /ˈsɜːdʒᵊn/ *noun* [C] **HEALTH** a doctor who does medical operations ➲See also: **veterinary surgeon**

surgery /ˈsɜːdʒᵊri/ *noun* **1 HEALTH** [U] when a doctor cuts your body open and repairs or removes something *to **have surgery*** ○ *heart/knee surgery* **2 HEALTH** [C] *UK* a place where doctors or other medical workers treat people ➲See also: **plastic surgery**

surgical /ˈsɜːdʒɪkᵊl/ *adjective* **HEALTH** relating to medical operations *surgical instruments/gloves* •**surgically** *adverb*

surly /ˈsɜːli/ *adjective* unfriendly and rude *a surly teenager*

surmount /səˈmaʊnt/ *verb* [T] *formal* to deal successfully with a problem

surname /ˈsɜːneɪm/ *noun* [C] the name that you and other members of your family all have *His surname is Walker.*

surpass /səˈpɑːs/ *verb* [T] *formal* to be or do better than someone or something else *The book's success **surpassed** everyone's **expectations**.*

surplus /ˈsɜːpləs/ *noun* [C, U] **1** an amount of something that is more than you need *Every year we produce a huge **surplus of** meat.* **2 FINANCE** the amount of money you have left when you sell more than you buy, or spend less than you have •**surplus** *adjective surplus wheat*

WORD PARTNERS FOR *surprise*

come as a surprise • a **big/nice/unpleasant** surprise • a surprise **to** sb • a surprise **party**

O→ **surprise¹** /səˈpraɪz/ *noun* **1** [EVENT] [C] an event that you did not expect to happen *I didn't know that my parents were coming - it was a lovely surprise.* ○ *Her resignation **came as a** complete **surprise*** (= was very surprising). ○ *a **surprise party*** **2** [FEELING] [U] the feeling that you get when something happens that you did not expect *He agreed to everything, much **to my surprise**.* **3 take/catch sb by surprise** to be unexpected and make someone feel surprise *I wasn't expecting her to be so angry - it took me by surprise.*

OTHER WAYS OF SAYING *surprise*

An unpleasant surprise is often described as a **shock**: *We got a nasty **shock** when he gave us the bill.* • *His death came as a terrible **shock**.*

A **blow** is a surprising event that causes someone to feel very sad and disappointed: *Losing his job was a terrible **blow** to him.*

Something which is so surprising that it is almost difficult to believe is sometimes described as a **miracle**: *It's a **miracle** that she survived the accident.* • *If I pass this exam it'll be a **miracle**.*

The expression **a rude awakening** is sometimes used if someone has an unpleasant surprise when they discover the truth about a situation: *She'll be in for **a rude awakening** when she has to pay her own bills.*

If you want to say informally that an event is a surprise to you, you can use the expression **be news to**: *Sarah is leaving? Well that's **news to** me.*

surprise² /səˈpraɪz/ *verb* [T] **1** [FEELING] to make someone feel surprise *I didn't tell her I was coming home early - I thought I'd surprise her.* **2** [CATCH] to find or attack someone when they are not expecting it

O→ **surprised** /səˈpraɪzd/ *adjective* feeling surprise because something has happened that you did not expect [**+ to do sth**] *I'm surprised to see you here.* ○ *She wasn't **surprised at** his decision.* [**+ (that)**] *I'm surprised that you've decided to leave.*

O→ **surprising** /səˈpraɪzɪŋ/ *adjective* not expected and making someone feel surprised *It's not surprising you're putting on weight, the amount you're eating!* •**surprisingly** *adverb surprisingly good*

surreal /səˈrɪəl/ (*also* **surrealistic** /səˌrɪəˈlɪstɪk/) *adjective* strange and not real, like something in a dream *His paintings have a surreal quality.*

surrender /sᵊrˈendəʳ/ *verb* **1** [STOP FIGHTING] [I] to stop fighting and admit that you have been beaten *Rebel troops are refusing to surrender.* **2** GIVE [T] *formal* to give something to someone else because you have been forced or officially asked to give it to them *He was released on the condition that he surrendered his passport.* •**surrender** *noun* [C, U]

surreptitious /ˌsʌrəp'tɪʃəs/ *adjective* done secretly so that other people do not see ***surreptitious glances*** *at the clock* •**surreptitiously** *adverb*

surrogate /'sʌrəgɪt/ *adjective* [**always before noun**] used instead of someone or something else *Twenty years older than her, he effectively became a surrogate father.* •**surrogate** *noun* [C] someone or something that is used instead of someone or something else *He seemed to regard her as a* ***surrogate for*** *his dead mother.*

ˌsurrogate 'mother *noun* [C] **HEALTH** a woman who has a baby for a woman who is not able to have a baby herself

O‑ **surround** /sə'raʊnd/ *verb* [T] **1** AROUND to be or go everywhere around something or someone *The house is surrounded by a large garden.* ○ *The police have surrounded the building.* ○ *the surrounding countryside* **2 be surrounded by sb/sth** to have a lot of people or things near you *She's surrounded by the people she loves.* **3** CONNECTED WITH If a feeling or situation surrounds an event, it is closely connected with it. ***Mystery*** *still* ***surrounds*** *the exact circumstances of his death.*

surroundings /sə'raʊndɪŋz/ *noun* [**plural**] the place where someone or something is and the things that are in it *Have you got used to your new surroundings?*

surveillance /sɜː'veɪləns/ *noun* [U] when someone is watched carefully, especially by the police or army, because they are expected to do something wrong *The police have* ***kept*** *the man* ***under*** *strict* ***surveillance***.

WORD PARTNERS FOR ***survey***

carry out/conduct/take part in a survey • a survey **finds/reveals/shows/suggests** sth • a survey **of** sth • **in** a survey • **according** to a survey • a **recent** survey

survey¹ /'sɜːveɪ/ *noun* [C] **1** QUESTIONS an examination of people's opinions or behaviour made by asking people questions *Holidays in the UK are becoming more popular, according to a* ***recent survey***. **2** BUILDING *UK* an examination of the structure of a building in order to find out if there is anything wrong with it *The bank have refused a loan until we've had a survey done on the property.* **3 GEOGRAPHY** when an area of land is looked at, and its measurements and details recorded, especially in order to make a map

survey² /sə'veɪ/ *verb* [T] **1** EXAMINE to look at or examine something carefully *I got out of the car to* ***survey*** *the* ***damage***. **2** QUESTION to ask people questions in order to find out about their opinions or behaviour *75% of midwives surveyed were in favour of home births.* **3 GEOGRAPHY** to measure and record the details of an area of land **4** BUILDING *UK* to examine the structure of a building in order to find out if there is anything wrong with it

surveyor /sə'veɪə^r/ *noun* [C] **1** BUILDING *UK* someone whose job is to examine the structure of buildings **2 GEOGRAPHY** someone whose job is to measure and record the details of an area of land

survival /sə'vaɪvəl/ *noun* [U] when someone or something continues to live or exist, especially after a difficult or dangerous situation *Flood victims had to fight for survival.*

O‑ **survive** /sə'vaɪv/ *verb* **1** NOT DIE [I, T] to continue to live after almost dying because of an accident, illness, etc *He was born with a heart problem and only survived ten days.* ○ *No one survived the plane crash.* **2** EXIST [I, T] to continue to exist after being in a difficult or dangerous situation *Only two buildings survived the earthquake.* **3** LIVE LONGER [T] If you survive someone, you continue to live after they have died.

survivor /sə'vaɪvə^r/ *noun* [C] someone who continues to live after almost dying because of an accident, illness, etc *Rescuers have given up hope of finding any more survivors.*

susceptible /sə'septəbl/ *adjective* easily influenced or harmed by something *Older people are more* ***susceptible to*** *the virus.* ○ *a susceptible young teenager* •**susceptibility** /səˌseptə'bɪləti/ *noun* [U] when someone is susceptible

sushi /'suːʃi/ *noun* [U] **FOOD** Japanese food made of cold rice and fish which has not been cooked *a sushi bar*

WORD PARTNERS FOR ***suspect***

the **chief/main/prime** suspect • a suspect **for/in** sth

suspect¹ /'sʌspekt/ *noun* [C] **1 LAW** someone who may have committed a crime *He's the* ***prime suspect*** (= the most likely suspect) *in the murder case.* **2 the usual suspects** the people you would expect to be present somewhere or doing a particular thing *"Who was at the party?" "Oh, Adrian, John, Dave - the usual suspects."*

O‑ **suspect²** /sə'spekt/ *verb* [T] **1** CRIME to think that someone may have committed a crime or done something bad *He was* ***suspected of*** *drug dealing.* ○ *suspected terrorists* **2** THINK LIKELY to think that something is probably true, or is likely to happen [+ **(that)**] *They suspected that he was lying.* **3** NOT TRUST to not trust someone or something *She* ***suspected*** *his* ***motives*** *for offering to help.*

suspect³ /'sʌspekt/ *adjective* difficult to trust or believe *His explanation was highly suspect.*

suspend /sə'spend/ *verb* [T] **1** to stop something happening for a short time *The semi-final was suspended because of bad weather.* **2 suspend sth from/between, etc** to hang something from somewhere [**often passive**] *A light bulb was suspended from the ceiling.* **3 EDUCATION** to not allow someone to go to work or school for a period of time because they have done something wrong [**often passive**] *She was* ***suspended from*** *school for fighting.*

suspenders /sə'spendəz/ *noun* [**plural**] **1** FOR WOMEN *UK* (*US* **garters**) pieces of elastic fixed to a belt that hold up a woman's stockings (= very thin pieces of clothing that cover a

S

woman's foot and leg) **2** FOR TROUSERS *US* (*UK* **braces**) two straps fixed to a pair of trousers that go over your shoulders and stop the trousers from falling down

suspense /sə'spens/ *noun* [U] the feeling of excitement that you have when you are waiting for something to happen *What's your answer then? Don't* ***keep*** *me* ***in suspense.***

sus'pense ac,count *noun* [C] **FINANCE** an account where amounts of money are recorded temporarily until it is decided how to record them properly

suspension /sə'spenʃən/ *noun* **1** STOP [U] when someone stops something happening for a period of time *an immediate suspension of all imports and exports* **2** **EDUCATION** [C, U] when someone is not allowed to go to work or school for a period of time **3** VEHICLE [C, U] equipment which is fixed to the wheels of a vehicle in order to make it move more smoothly **4** **CHEMISTRY** a liquid in which small pieces of solid are contained, but not dissolved

sus'pension ,bridge *noun* [C] a bridge which is supported by strong steel ropes hung from a tower at each end of the bridge

suspensory ligament /sə,spentsəri'lɪgəmənt/ *noun* [C] **ANATOMY, BIOLOGY** one of the strong strips of tissue in the body that hold the lens of the eye in position or that another part or organ hangs from

WORD PARTNERS FOR ***suspicion***

have a suspicion • **confirm** sb's suspicion • a **deep/sneaking/strong** suspicion

suspicion /sə'spɪʃən/ *noun* **1** ABOUT SOMEONE [C, U] a feeling or belief that someone has done something wrong *They were arrested* ***on suspicion of*** *drug dealing.* ○ *Several members of staff are* ***under suspicion*** *of stealing money.* **2** ABOUT SOMETHING [C] an idea that something may be true [+ **(that)**] *I had a* ***sneaking suspicion*** *that the two events might be connected.*

suspicious /sə'spɪʃəs/ *adjective* **1** WRONG/BAD making you feel that something is wrong or that something bad or illegal is happening ***suspicious behaviour/circumstances*** ○ *I called airport security after noticing a* ***suspicious package.*** **2** NOT TRUST not trusting someone *Many of them remain* ***suspicious of*** *journalists.* •**suspiciously** *adverb She's been acting very suspiciously lately.*

sustain /sə'steɪn/ *verb* [T] **1** CONTINUE to cause or allow something to continue for a period of time *The team may not be able to sustain this level of performance.* **2** SUPPORT to support someone or something so that they can live or exist *The money he received was hardly enough to sustain a wife and five children.* **3** **sustain damage/injuries/losses** *formal* If someone or something sustains injuries, damage, losses, etc, they are injured, damaged, etc.

sustainable /sə'steɪnəbl/ *adjective* **1** able to continue over a period of time *sustainable development/growth* **2** **ENVIRONMENT** causing little or no damage to the environment and therefore able to continue for a long time

sustained /sə'steɪnd/ *adjective* continuing for a period of time without getting weaker *a sustained attack* ○ *sustained pressure*

SUV /,esju:'vi:/ *noun* [C, U] *abbreviation for* sports utility vehicle: a large vehicle with an engine that supplies power to all four wheels, so that the vehicle can travel easily over rough ground

svelte /svelt/ *adjective* thin in an attractive way

swab /swɒb/ *noun* [C] **HEALTH** a small piece of material used for cleaning an injury or for taking a small amount of a substance from someone's body so that it can be tested

swagger /'swægər/ *verb* [I] to walk in a way that shows that you are confident and think that you are important *A group of young men swaggered around in leather jackets.* •**swagger** *noun* [**no plural**]

O▪ **swallow¹** /'swɒləʊ/ *verb* **1** [T] to move your throat in order to make food or drink go down *The snake swallowed the bird whole.* **2** [I] to make a movement with your throat as if you are eating, sometimes because you are nervous *Claire swallowed hard, opened the door and stepped inside.* **3** ACCEPT [T] to accept something unpleasant *They found the final decision* ***hard to swallow.*** **4** BELIEVE [T] *informal* to believe something, usually something which is not true *I told him we were journalists and he seemed to swallow it.* ➲See also: swallow your **pride**¹

swallow sth up *phrasal verb* to make something disappear *Many small businesses are being swallowed up by large international companies.*

swallow² /'swɒləʊ/ *noun* [C] **1** BIRD a small bird with long, pointed wings and a tail with two points **2** the movement of swallowing

swam /swæm/ *past tense of* swim

swamp¹ /swɒmp/ *noun* [C, U] **GEOGRAPHY** an area of very wet, soft land

swamp² /swɒmp/ *verb* [T] **1** to give someone more of something than they can deal with [**often passive**] *The company was* ***swamped with*** *calls about its new service.* ○ *The market has been* ***swamped by*** *cheap imports.* **2** **GEOGRAPHY** If an area is swamped, it becomes covered with water. *Heavy rain has swamped many villages in the region.*

swan /swɒn/ *noun* [C] a large, white bird with a long neck which lives on lakes and rivers

swap /swɒp/ *verb* [I, T] **swapping**, *past* **swapped** to give something to someone and get something from them in return *Would you mind if Dave* ***swapped*** *places* ***with*** *you for a bit?* •**swap** *noun* [C] *We'll* ***do a swap.***

swarm¹ /swɔ:m/ *noun* [C] a large group of things, usually insects, moving together *a swarm of bees*

swarm² /swɔ:m/ *verb* [I] to move in a large group *TV reporters swarmed outside the pop star's home.*

swarm with sb/sth *phrasal verb* If a place is swarming with people, insects, etc, there are a lot of them moving around it. *The house was swarming with police.*

swarthy /ˈswɔːði/ *adjective* having dark skin

swat /swɒt/ *verb* [T] **swatting**, *past* **swatted** to hit something, especially an insect, with a flat object *He swatted a fly with his newspaper.*

sway /sweɪ/ *verb* **1** MOVE [I] to move slowly from one side to the other *The trees swayed gently in the wind.* **2** PERSUADE [T] to persuade someone to change their opinion or decision *I think I was swayed by what James said.*

O━**swear** /sweəʳ/ *verb past tense* **swore**, *past participle* **sworn** **1** **LANGUAGE** [I] to use language which people think is rude or offensive *He was sent home because he **swore at** the teacher.* **2** PROMISE [I, T] to make a serious promise [+ **to do sth**] *I swear to tell the truth.* [+ **(that)**] *She swore that she was at home at the time of the accident.* **3** TRUE [T] used to say that you are sure something is true [+ **(that)**] ***I could have sworn** that she said she lived in Canterbury* (= I was sure she lived in Canterbury, but now I have found that it is not true).

swear by sth *phrasal verb* to believe strongly that something is useful or effective *Have you tried using vinegar to clean windows? My mum swears by it.*

swear sb in *phrasal verb* **LAW** to make someone such as a president, judge, etc officially promise to be honest and responsible when they start their job [**often passive**] *Mr Stein was sworn in as City Council president yesterday.*

swearing /ˈsweərɪŋ/ *noun* [U] **LANGUAGE** using rude or offensive language *He was always getting into trouble for swearing.*

ˈswear ˌword *noun* [C] **LANGUAGE** a word which people think is rude or offensive

sweat /swet/ *verb* [I] **BIOLOGY** to produce liquid through your skin because you are hot or nervous *I'd been running and I was sweating.* •**sweat** *noun* [U] *The sweat was running down his face.*

sweat it out *phrasal verb informal* to wait nervously for an unpleasant situation to improve or end *I don't get my exam results till the end of June so I'll just have to sweat it out till then.*

sweat over sth *phrasal verb* to work hard at something *She's been sweating over the preparations for the party all weekend.*

sweater /ˈswetəʳ/ (*also UK* **jumper**) *noun* [C] a warm piece of clothing which covers the top of your body and is pulled on over your head ➲See colour picture **Clothes** on page Centre 8

ˈsweat ˌgland *noun* [C] **ANATOMY, BIOLOGY** a gland in the skin that produces sweat

sweats /swets/ *noun* [**plural**] *US* a sweatshirt and sweatpants (= loose, comfortable trousers), often worn for exercising ➲See colour picture **Clothes** on page Centre 9

sweatshirt /ˈswetʃɜːt/ *noun* [C] a piece of clothing made of soft cotton which covers the top of your body and is pulled on over your head ➲See colour picture **Clothes** on page Centre 9

sweatshop /ˈswetʃɒp/ *noun* [C] a small factory where workers are paid very little and work many hours in very bad conditions

sweaty /ˈsweti/ *adjective* covered in sweat *He was hot and sweaty from working in the garden.*

swede /swiːd/ *noun* [C, U] *UK* **FOOD** a round, yellow vegetable which grows in the ground

sweep[1] /swiːp/ *verb past* **swept** **1** CLEAN [I, T] (*also* **sweep up**) to clean the floor using a brush *She's just swept the floor.* ○ *He swept up the pieces of broken glass* (= removed them from the floor with a brush). **2** **be swept along/away, etc** to be pushed or carried along, often by something strong which you cannot control *Many trees were swept away in the flood.* **3** AFFECT [I, T] to quickly affect a large area *The disease is **sweeping the country**.* ○ *Panic **swept through** the crowd.* **4** **sweep along/into/past, etc** to move quickly, especially in a way that shows you think you are important *She swept past me in the corridor.*

sweep[2] /swiːp/ *noun* [C] **1** MOVEMENT a long movement [**usually singular**] *With a sweep of his arm, he gestured towards the garden.* **2** CURVE something shaped in a long curve *a long sweep of sandy beach* ➲See also: **chimney sweep**

sweeping /ˈswiːpɪŋ/ *adjective* **1** [**always before noun**] affecting many things or people *sweeping changes/reforms* **2** **sweeping statement/generalization** when someone says something that is very general and has not been carefully thought about

sweepstake /ˈswiːpsteɪk/ *UK* (*US* **sweepstakes**) *noun* [C] a type of betting (= risking money on a competition) in which the winner receives all the money

O━**sweet**[1] /swiːt/ *adjective* **1** **FOOD** with a taste like sugar *It was covered in a very sweet chocolate sauce.* **2** ATTRACTIVE attractive, often because of being small *Look at that kitten - isn't she sweet?* **3** KIND kind and friendly *It was really sweet of you to come.* **4** SMELL/SOUND A sweet smell or sound is pleasant. •**sweetness** *noun* [U]

sweet[2] /swiːt/ *UK* (*US* **candy**) *noun* [C] **FOOD** a small piece of sweet food, often made of sugar or chocolate *You shouldn't eat so many sweets - they're bad for your teeth.*

sweetcorn /ˈswiːtkɔːn/ *UK* (*US* **corn**) *noun* [U] **FOOD** the sweet, yellow seeds of maize (= a plant) which are eaten as a vegetable ➲See colour picture **Fruit and Vegetables** on page Centre 10

sweeten /ˈswiːtᵊn/ *verb* [T] **FOOD** to make something sweeter, for example by adding more sugar *She gave me a hot lemon drink, sweetened with honey.*

sweetener /ˈswiːtᵊnəʳ/ *noun* [C] **1** **FOOD** something which is used to make something taste sweeter *an **artificial sweetener*** **2** something that is used to persuade someone to do something

sweetheart /ˈswiːthɑːt/ *noun* [C] You call someone 'sweetheart' to show affection or to be friendly. *Come here, sweetheart.*

sweetly /ˈswiːtli/ *adverb* in an attractive or kind way *She smiled sweetly.*

ˌsweet poˈtato *UK* (*US* **ˈsweet poˌtato**) *noun* [C, U] *plural* **sweet potatoes** **FOOD** a long, red vegetable like a potato but that tastes slightly sweet

S

swell[1] /swel/ *verb past tense* **swelled**, *past participle* **swollen** or **swelled** **1** [SIZE] [I] (*also* **swell up**) to increase in size *One side of his face had swollen up where he'd been stung.* **2** [AMOUNT] [I, T] to increase in amount because more things are added *The population of the region was swollen by refugees from across the border.*

swell[2] /swel/ *noun* **1** **GEOGRAPHY** [C, U] the movement of waves in the sea, or the waves themselves *ocean swells* **2** [INCREASE] [C] an increase

swell[3] /swel/ *adjective US old-fashioned* good or pleasant *Everyone's having a swell time.*

swelling /ˈswelɪŋ/ *noun* [C, U] **HEALTH** a part of your body which has become bigger because of illness or injury *The doctor gave me drugs to reduce the swelling in my ankle.*

sweltering /ˈsweltərɪŋ/ *adjective* so hot that you feel uncomfortable *It was a sweltering afternoon in August.*

swept /swept/ *past of* sweep

swerve /swɜːv/ *verb* [I] to change direction suddenly, especially when you are driving a vehicle *He swerved to avoid a cyclist and hit another car.*

swift /swɪft/ *adjective* happening or moving quickly *a swift response* •**swiftly** *adverb*

swig /swɪg/ *verb* [T] **swigging**, *past* **swigged** *informal* to drink something, taking a lot of liquid into your mouth at a time •**swig** *noun* [C] *He* ***took a swig of*** *his beer and carried on with the story.*

swill[1] /swɪl/ *verb* [T] **1** [CLEAN] (*also* **swill out**) to clean something by making liquid move around it *The dentist handed me a glass of water to swill my mouth out.* **2** [DRINK] to quickly drink a large amount of something, especially alcohol

swill[2] /swɪl/ *noun* [U] **FARMING** waste food that is fed to pigs

O-ᵡ**swim**[1] /swɪm/ *verb* **swimming**, *past tense* **swam**, *past participle* **swum** **1** **SPORT** [I, T] to move through water by moving your body *I learnt to swim when I was about 5 years old.* ○ *I swim thirty lengths of the pool most mornings.* ➲See colour picture **Sports 1** on page Centre 14 **2** [HEAD] [I] If your head swims, you feel confused and are unable to see or think clearly. **3** [SEEM TO MOVE] [I] to seem to move about *I got up suddenly and the room started swimming.* •**swimming** *noun* [U] **SPORT** *I usually* ***go swimming*** *about twice a week.* •**swimmer** *noun* [C] *I'm not a very* ***strong swimmer.***

S

swim[2] /swɪm/ *noun* [C] **SPORT** a time when you swim *I* ***went for a swim*** *before breakfast.*

ˈswim ˌbladder *noun* [C] **BIOLOGY** an organ like a bag of air inside a fish that keeps the fish in the correct position

ˈswimming ˌcostume *UK* (*US* **bathing suit**) *noun* [C] **SPORT** a piece of clothing that you wear to go swimming ➲See colour picture **Clothes** on page Centre 9

ˈswimming ˌpool *noun* [C] **SPORT** an area of water that has been made for people to swim in

ˈswimming ˌtrunks *noun* [plural] **SPORT** a piece of clothing that boys and men wear when they swim ➲See colour picture **Clothes** on page Centre 9

swimsuit /ˈswɪmsuːt/ *noun* [C] **SPORT** a piece of clothing that girls and women wear to go swimming ➲See colour picture **Clothes** on page Centre 9

swindle /ˈswɪndl/ *verb* [T] to get money from someone by cheating or deceiving them [**often passive**] *She was* ***swindled out of*** *thousands of dollars.* •**swindle** *noun* [C] *a multi-million-pound swindle* •**swindler** *noun* [C]

swine /swaɪn/ *noun* **1** [PIGS] [**plural**] *formal* pigs **2** [PERSON] [C] *informal* an unpleasant person

swing[1] /swɪŋ/ *verb past* **swung** **1** [BACKWARDS/FORWARDS] [I, T] to move smoothly backwards and forwards, or to make something do this *She really swings her arms when she walks.* **2** [CURVE] [I, T] to move smoothly in a curve, or to make something do this *The door swung shut.* ○ *Watch the ball as you swing the bat.* **3** [CHANGE] [I] If someone's opinion or their feelings swing, they suddenly change. *Her moods swing with absolutely no warning.*

swing around/round *phrasal verb* to turn around quickly

swing at sb *phrasal verb informal* to try to hit someone

swing[2] /swɪŋ/ *noun* [C] **1** [FOR CHILDREN] a chair hanging on two ropes that children sit on and swing backwards and forwards **2** [HIT] an attempt to hit someone *Isn't that the boy Mark* ***took a swing at*** (= tried to hit)*?* **3** [CHANGE] a sudden change *He suffered terrible* ***mood swings.*** **4 be in full swing** If an event is in full swing, everything has started and there is a lot of activity. *By ten o'clock, the party was in full swing.*

swipe[1] /swaɪp/ *verb* [T] **1** [HIT] (*also* **swipe at**) to move your arm in order to try to hit someone or something **2** [STEAL] *informal* to steal something

swipe[2] /swaɪp/ *noun* [C] an attempt to hit someone

ˈswipe ˌcard *noun* [C] *UK* a small piece of plastic that contains electronic information, used to open doors, etc

swirl /swɜːl/ *verb* [I, T] to move around and around quickly, or to make something do this *The mist swirled round the castle.* •**swirl** *noun* [C]

swish /swɪʃ/ *verb* [I, T] to move quickly through the air making a soft sound, or to make something do this •**swish** *noun* [C] *the swish of curtains closing*

O-ᵡ**switch**[1] /swɪtʃ/ *verb* [I, T] **1** [CHANGE] to change from one thing to another *We're trying to encourage people to* ***switch from*** *cars* ***to*** *bicycles.* ○ *He's just switched jobs.* **2** [EXCHANGE] to exchange something with someone else *After a couple of months we switched roles.*

switch (sth) off *phrasal verb* to turn off a light, television, etc by using a switch *Have you switched the computer off?*

switch off *phrasal verb UK* to stop giving your attention to someone or something *I'm afraid I just switch off when she starts telling me about her problems.*

switch (sth) on *phrasal verb* to turn on a light,

television, etc by using a switch
switch over *phrasal verb* **1** TELEVISION *UK* to change from one television or radio station to another **2** CHANGE to change from doing one thing to another *We've decided to* ***switch over*** *to low fat milk.*

WORD PARTNERS FOR ***switch***

flick/press a switch • the **on/off** switch

O-■**switch²** /swɪtʃ/ *noun* [C] **1 PHYSICS** a small object that you push up or down with your finger to turn something electrical on or off **2** CHANGE a change *There has been a switch in policy.*

switchboard /ˈswɪtʃbɔːd/ *noun* [C] a piece of equipment that is used to direct all the telephone calls made from and to a building

swivel /ˈswɪvᵊl/ (*also* **swivel around**) *verb* [I, T] *UK* **swivelling**, *past* **swivelled**, *US* **swiveling**, *past* **swiveled** to turn round, or to make something turn round

swollen¹ /ˈswəʊlən/ *adjective* bigger than usual *a swollen wrist/ankle ○ swollen rivers*

swollen² /ˈswəʊlən/ *past participle of* swell

swoop /swuːp/ *verb* [I] **1** MOVE to suddenly move very quickly down through the air *Huge birds* ***swoop down*** *from the sky.* **2** ATTACK to suddenly attack *The day before police had* ***swooped on*** *his home.* •**swoop** *noun* [C]

swop /swɒp/ *verb* [I, T] **swopping**, *past* **swopped** *another UK spelling of* swap (= to give something to someone and get something from them in return)

sword /sɔːd/ *noun* [C] a weapon with a long, metal blade and a handle, used especially in the past

swordfish /ˈsɔːdfɪʃ/ *noun* [C, U] *plural* **swordfish** a large fish with a long, pointed part at the front of its head, that can be eaten as food

swore /swɔːʳ/ *past tense of* swear

sworn¹ /swɔːn/ *adjective* **1 LAW sworn statement/testimony, etc** something that you have officially said is true **2 sworn enemies** two people, or two groups of people who are completely against each other

sworn² /swɔːn/ *past participle of* swear

swot¹ /swɒt/ *noun* [C] *UK informal* someone who studies too much

SWOT /swɒt/ *noun* [U] **ECONOMICS** *abbreviation for* strength, weaknesses, opportunities, threats; a way of looking at the good and bad parts of a business in order to plan for its future *a SWOT analysis*

swot² /swɒt/ *UK informal* (*US* **cram**) *verb* [I] **swotting**, *past* **swotted** to study a lot *I'm swotting for tomorrow's exam.*
swot up (on sth) *phrasal verb* to learn as much as you can about a subject, especially before an examination

swum /swʌm/ *past participle of* swim

swung /swʌŋ/ *past of* swing

sycamore /ˈsɪkəmɔːʳ/ *noun* [C, U] a tree with leaves that are divided into five parts and with seeds that turn around as they fall

sycophantic /ˌsɪkəʊˈfæntɪk/ *adjective formal* Someone who is sycophantic praises people in authority in a way that is not sincere, especially in order to get an advantage for themselves. •**sycophant** /ˈsɪkəfænt/ *noun* [C]

syllable /ˈsɪləbl/ *noun* [C] **LANGUAGE** a word or part of a word that has one vowel sound *'But' has one syllable and 'apple' has two syllables.*

syllabus /ˈsɪləbəs/ *noun* [C] *plural* **syllabuses** or **syllabi EDUCATION** a list of the subjects that are included in a course of study

symbiosis /ˌsɪmbaɪˈəʊsɪs/ *noun* [U] **BIOLOGY** when two organisms live together and get advantages from each other

O-■**symbol** /ˈsɪmbᵊl/ *noun* [C] **1** SIGN a sign or object that is used to represent something *A heart shape is the symbol of love.* **2 CHEMISTRY** a number, letter, or sign that is used instead of the name of a chemical substance, another number, etc *The symbol for oxygen is O.* ➲See also: **status symbol**

symbolic /sɪmˈbɒlɪk/ *adjective* representing something else *The blue, white and red of the French flag are symbolic of liberty, equality and fraternity.* •**symbolically** *adverb*

symbolism /ˈsɪmbᵊlɪzᵊm/ *noun* [U] **ART, LITERATURE** the use of signs and objects in art, films, etc to represent ideas

symbolize (*also UK* **-ise**) /ˈsɪmbᵊlaɪz/ *verb* [T] to represent something *The lighting of the Olympic torch symbolizes peace and friendship among the nations of the world.*

symmetrical /sɪˈmetrɪkᵊl/ (*also* **symmetric**) *adjective* having the same shape or size on both halves *Faces are roughly symmetrical.*

symmetry /ˈsɪmətri/ *noun* [U] when something is symmetrical

O-■**sympathetic** /ˌsɪmpəˈθetɪk/ *adjective* **1** PROBLEMS showing that you understand and care about someone's problems *My boss is very* ***sympathetic about*** *my situation.* **2** IDEAS agreeing with or supporting someone's ideas or actions *He was* ***sympathetic to*** *their views.* ➲Opposite **unsympathetic** •**sympathetically** *adverb*

COMMON LEARNER ERROR

sympathetic

Be careful not to use **sympathetic** when you simply want to say that someone is **nice**, **friendly**, or **kind**. Remember that if someone is **sympathetic**, they understand your problems.

sympathize (*also UK* **-ise**) /ˈsɪmpəθaɪz/ *verb* [I] **1** PROBLEMS to understand and care about someone's problems *It's a really bad situation - I do* ***sympathize with*** *her.* **2** IDEAS to agree with or support someone's ideas or actions *I* ***sympathize with*** *the general aims of the party.*

sympathizer (*also UK* **-iser**) /ˈsɪmpəθaɪzəʳ/ *noun* [C] someone who supports a particular political organization, or believes in a particular set of ideas *a communist sympathizer*

WORD PARTNERS FOR ***sympathy***

have/express/feel [every/little/no, etc] sympathy **for sb** • **look for** sympathy • **deep/great/heartfelt** sympathy • **words of** sympathy

O⊸**sympathy** /ˈsɪmpəθi/ *noun* [U] **1** PROBLEMS when you show that you understand and care about someone's problems *I **have** no **sympathy for** people who say they can't find work but are really just too lazy to look.* **2** IDEAS agreement with or support for someone's ideas or actions *Scott was **in sympathy with** this view.*

symphony /ˈsɪmfəni/ *noun* [C] **MUSIC** a long piece of music for an orchestra (= large group of different musicians)

symptom /ˈsɪmptəm/ *noun* [C] **1 HEALTH** a physical feeling or problem which shows that you have a particular illness *The inability to sleep is often a **symptom of** some other illness.* **2** a problem that is caused by and shows a more serious problem *The drinking was just a **symptom of** his general unhappiness.* •**symptomatic** /ˌsɪmptəˈmætɪk/ *adjective* relating to a symptom

synagogue /ˈsɪnəgɒg/ *noun* [C] **RELIGION** a building in which Jewish people pray

synapse /ˈsaɪnæps/ *noun* [C] **ANATOMY, BIOLOGY** the point at which electrical signals move from one nerve cell to another •**synaptic** /saɪˈnæptɪk/ *adjective*

sync /sɪŋk/ *noun informal* **1 be in sync** to be happening at the same time **2 be out of sync** to not be happening at the same time

synchronize (*also UK* **-ise**) /ˈsɪŋkrənaɪz/ *verb* [T] **1** to make something happen at the same time as something else *We had a problem synchronizing the music and the images.* **2 synchronize watches** to make two or more watches show exactly the same time •**synchronization** /ˌsɪŋkrənaɪˈzeɪʃən/ *noun* [U]

syncline /ˈsɪŋklaɪn/ *noun* [C] **GEOLOGY** a downward, U-shaped fold in the layers of rock in the Earth's surface ➲Compare **anticline**

syndicate /ˈsɪndɪkət/ *noun* [C] a group of people or companies who join together in order to achieve something *a bank syndicate* ○ *a crime syndicate*

syndrome /ˈsɪndrəʊm/ *noun* [C] **HEALTH** a combination of physical problems that often go together in a particular illness

synergy /ˈsɪnədʒi/ *noun* [C, U] **ECONOMICS** when two companies or groups work together and achieve more success than they would separately *a synergy between the two software companies*

synonym /ˈsɪnənɪm/ *noun* [C] **LANGUAGE** a word or phrase that means the same as another word or phrase

synonymous /sɪˈnɒnɪməs/ *adjective* **1** If one thing is synonymous with another, they are very closely connected with each other in people's minds. *It is a country where wealth is **synonymous with** corruption.* **2 LANGUAGE** If one word is synonymous with another, they have the same meaning.

synopsis /sɪˈnɒpsɪs/ *noun* [C] *plural* **synopses** **LITERATURE** a short description of a book, film, etc

synovial fluid /saɪˌnəʊviəlˈfluːɪd/ *noun* [U] **BIOLOGY** a transparent liquid in our joints (= place where bones join), that helps them to move easily

syntax /ˈsɪntæks/ *noun* [U] **LANGUAGE** the grammatical arrangement of words in a sentence

synthesis /ˈsɪnθəsɪs/ *noun* [C, U] *plural* **syntheses** /ˈsɪnθəsiːz/ *formal* the mixing of several things to make another whole new thing

synthesize (*also UK* **-ise**) /ˈsɪnθəsaɪz/ *verb* [T] to mix several things in order to make something else

synthesizer (*also UK* **-iser**) /ˈsɪnθəsaɪzəʳ/ *noun* [C] **MUSIC** an electronic musical instrument that can copy the sounds made by other musical instruments

synthetic /sɪnˈθetɪk/ *adjective* not made from natural substances *synthetic rubber* •**synthetically** *adverb*

syphilis /ˈsɪfɪlɪs/ *noun* [U] **HEALTH** a serious disease caught during sex that spreads slowly from the sex organs to all parts of the body

syringe /sɪˈrɪndʒ/ *noun* [C] **1 HEALTH** a piece of medical equipment used to push liquid into or take liquid out of someone's body **2** a similar piece of equipment used by scientists for adding or taking small amounts of liquid ➲See picture at **laboratory**

syringe

syrup /ˈsɪrəp/ *noun* [U] **FOOD** a very sweet liquid made from sugar and water

O⊸**system** /ˈsɪstəm/ *noun* [C] **1** METHOD a way or method of doing things *the American **legal system*** ○ *the public transport system* **2** EQUIPMENT a set of connected pieces of equipment that operate together *They've had an alarm system installed at their home.* **3 BIOLOGY** parts of the body that work together in order to make something happen *the body's **immune system*** **4 the system SOCIETY** the laws and rules of a society **5 get sth out of your system** to get rid of a strong feeling or a need to do something, especially by expressing that feeling or doing the thing you want to do *It's not a bad idea to travel before getting a job - that way you get it out of your system.* ➲See also: **immune system, nervous system, operating system, public address system, the solar system**

systematic /ˌsɪstəˈmætɪk/ *adjective* done using a fixed and organized plan *the systematic collection and analysis of information* •**systematically** *adverb*

systemic /sɪˈstemɪk/ *adjective* **HEALTH** A systemic drug, disease or poison reaches and has an effect on the whole of a body or a plant.

ˈsystems ˌanalyst *noun* [C] **COMPUTING** someone who examines businesses and industry in order to find ways of improving the way they work, especially by using computer programs and equipment •**ˈsystems anˌalysis** *noun* [U]

ˈsystem ˌsoftware *noun* [U] **COMPUTING** software that controls computer hardware (= machines and equipment) ➲Compare **application software**

systole /ˈsɪstəli/ *noun* [C] **BIOLOGY** the part of a heart's action where it pushes blood out ➲Compare **diastole** •**systolic** /sɪˈstɒlɪk/ *adjective*

Tt

T, t /tiː/ the twentieth letter of the alphabet

ta /tɑː/ *exclamation UK informal* thank you

tab /tæb/ *noun* [C] **1** a small piece of paper, metal, etc that is fixed to something and that you use to open it or find out information about it *Pull tab to open.* **2 FINANCE** an amount of money that you owe for something you have bought or for a service you have used *Officials said the tab for the new bridge would be $8 million.* **3 pick up the tab** to pay for something, especially a meal in a restaurant **4 keep tabs on sb/sth** *informal* to watch someone or something carefully to check they do nothing wrong

tabby /ˈtæbi/ *noun* [C] a cat that has stripes in its fur

ˈtab ˌkey *noun* [C] **COMPUTING** the key on a computer keyboard which allows you to move the cursor (= a symbol which shows you where you are working) forward a few spaces

tabla /ˈtæblə/ *noun* [C] **MUSIC** two small drums that are played with the hands, used especially in Indian music

O⊸**table¹** /ˈteɪbl/ *noun* [C] **1** FURNITURE a piece of furniture with four legs, used for eating off, putting things on, etc *the kitchen table* **2 lay the table** *UK* (*UK/US* **set the table**) to put plates, knives, forks, etc on the table to prepare for a meal **3** NUMBERS/WORDS a set of numbers or words written in rows that go across and down the page *The table below shows the results of the experiment.* **4 COMPUTING** a collection of a particular kind of information in a database **5 turn the tables on sb** to change a situation so that you have an advantage over someone who before had an advantage over you ⊃See also: put/lay your cards (**card**) on the table, **coffee table, dressing table**

table² /ˈteɪbl/ *verb* [T] **1** SUGGEST *UK* to formally suggest that a particular subject is discussed **2** LATER *US* to decide to discuss something later

tablecloth /ˈteɪblklɒθ/ *noun* [C] a piece of material that covers a table, especially during a meal

tablespoon /ˈteɪblspuːn/ *noun* [C] **MEASURES** a large spoon used for measuring or serving food, or the amount this spoon can hold

WORD PARTNERS FOR ***tablet***

take a tablet • a tablet **for** sth • **sleeping** tablets • **headache** tablets

tablet /ˈtæblət/ *noun* [C] **1 HEALTH** a small, round object containing medicine that you swallow **2** STONE a square piece of stone that has words cut into it **3** PAPER *US* (*UK/US* **pad**) sheets of paper that have been fastened together at one edge, used for writing or drawing **4 COMPUTING** a graphics tablet (= flat device that is connected to a computer that you draw on with a special pen to make an image on the computer screen)

ˈtable ˌtennis *noun* [U] **SPORT** a game in which two or four people hit a small ball over a low net on a large table

tabloid /ˈtæblɔɪd/ *noun* [C] a small newspaper with a lot of pictures and short, simple news stories

taboo /təˈbuː/ *noun* [C, U] **SOCIETY** something that you should not say or do because people generally think it is morally wrong, unpleasant, or embarrassing *Sex is a taboo in this country.* •**taboo** *adjective Suicide is a taboo subject.*

tabulate /ˈtæbjʊleɪt/ *verb* [T] to show information in the form of a table (= an arrangement of facts and numbers in rows or blocks)

ˈT acˌcount *noun* [C] **FINANCE** a method of keeping financial records with debits (= money spent) on one side, credits (= money received) on the other side, and a line down the middle

tacit /ˈtæsɪt/ *adjective formal* understood without being said *a **tacit agreement***

taciturn /ˈtæsɪtɜːn/ *adjective formal* saying very little and not seeming friendly

tack¹ /tæk/ *noun* **1 take/try a different tack** to try to deal with a problem in a different way *I've tried being nice to her and it doesn't work so I might take a different tack.* **2** NAIL [C] a small, sharp nail with a flat top *carpet tacks* **3** PIN [C] *US* (*UK* **drawing pin**) a short pin with a flat, round top, used for fastening pieces of paper to the wall

tack² /tæk/ *verb* [T] **1** FASTEN to fasten something to a wall with a tack **2** SEW to sew something loosely

tack sth on *phrasal verb* to add something that you had not planned to add

tackle¹ /ˈtækl/ *verb* [T] **1** DEAL WITH to try to deal with a problem *new ways to **tackle crime*** **2** SPEAK TO *UK* to speak to someone about something bad that they have done *I decided to tackle him about his absences.* **3 SPORT** to try to get the ball from someone in a game such as football

tackle² /ˈtækl/ *noun* **1 SPORT** [C] an attempt to get the ball from someone in a game such as football **2** [U] all the things you need for a particular activity ***fishing tackle***

tacky /ˈtæki/ *adjective* **1** CHEAP *informal* cheap and of bad quality *tacky holiday souvenirs* **2** STICKY slightly sticky

tact /tækt/ *noun* [U] the ability to talk to people about difficult subjects without upsetting them

tactful /ˈtæktfəl/ *adjective* careful not to say or do anything that could upset someone •**tactfully** *adverb*

WORD PARTNERS FOR ***tactic***

adopt/employ/use tactics • a **change of** tactics • **bullying/underhand** tactics

tactic /ˈtæktɪk/ *noun* [C] a way of doing something that you plan in order to achieve what you want [**usually plural**] *These bomb attacks represent a **change of tactics** by the terrorists.*

tactical /ˈtæktɪkəl/ *adjective* relating to tactics, or done in order to achieve something ***tactical voting*** ○ *a **tactical error*** •**tactically** *adverb*

T

tactless /'tæktləs/ *adjective* not being careful about saying or doing something that could upset someone

tad /tæd/ *noun informal* **a tad** a little *It was a tad expensive, I thought.*

tadpole /'tædpəʊl/ *noun* [C] a small, black animal that lives in water and will become a frog (= green jumping animal)

taffeta /'tæfɪtə/ *noun* [U] a stiff, shiny cloth used in women's formal dresses

TAFN **INTERNET** *internet abbreviation for* that's all for now: used at the end of an email or message

tag¹ /tæg/ *noun* [C] a small piece of paper or plastic with information on it that is fixed to something *a **price tag***

tag² /tæg/ *verb* [T] **tagging**, *past* **tagged** to put a tag on something

tag along *phrasal verb informal* to go somewhere with someone, especially when they have not asked you to

t'ai chi /taɪ'tʃiː/ *noun* [U] **SPORT** a form of Chinese exercise that involves a series of slow movements

tail¹ /teɪl/ *noun* [C] **1 BIOLOGY** the long, narrow part that sticks out at the back of an animal's body *The dog's pleased to see you - he's **wagging his tail**.* **2** the back part of something long, such as a plane **3 the tail end of sth** the last part of something *the tail end of the eighties*

tail² /teɪl/ *verb* [T] to secretly follow someone, especially because you think they have done something wrong

tail off *phrasal verb* to gradually become quieter, smaller, less frequent, etc *His voice tailed off.*

tailback /'teɪlbæk/ *noun* [C] *UK* a line of cars that have stopped or are moving very slowly because of an accident or other problem on the road in front of them

tailcoat /'teɪl,kəʊt/ *noun* [C] a formal coat that has a short front part and a long back part that is divided in two

tailgate /'teɪlgeɪt/ *verb* [I, T] to drive too closely to the car in front of you •**tailgating** *noun* [U]

'tail ,light *noun* [C] *US* one of the two red lights on the back of a car ➲See colour picture **Car** on page Centre 7

tailor¹ /'teɪlər/ *noun* [C] someone whose job is to make or repair clothes, especially men's clothes

tailor² /'teɪlər/ *verb* [T] to make or change something so that it is suitable *The kitchen can then be **tailored** exactly **to** the customer's needs.*

tailor-made /,teɪlə'meɪd/ *adjective* **1** PERFECT perfect for a particular person or purpose *It sounds as if you're **tailor-made for** the job.* **2** CLOTHES Tailor-made clothes are made by a tailor.

tailpipe /'teɪlpaɪp/ *US* (*UK* **exhaust pipe**) *noun* [C] the pipe that waste gas from a vehicle's engine flows through ➲See colour picture **Car** on page Centre 7

tails /teɪlz/ *noun* [plural] **1** COIN the side of a coin that does not have someone's head on it *Let's toss a coin - **heads or tails?*** **2** COAT a formal coat that has a short front part and a long back part that is divided in two

taint /teɪnt/ *verb* [T] **1** OPINION to spoil people's opinion of someone [**often passive**] *a government tainted by scandal* **2** MAKE HARMFUL to spoil something, especially food or blood, by adding a harmful substance

O-▪**take** /teɪk/ *verb* [T] *past tense* **took**, *past participle* **taken** **1** CARRY to get and carry something with you when you go somewhere *I always **take** my mobile phone **with** me.* **2** GO to go somewhere with someone, often paying for them or being responsible for them *I **took** the kids **to** the park.* ➲See Common Learner Error at **bring** **3** WITHOUT PERMISSION to remove something without permission *Someone's taken my coat.* **4** GET HOLD to get hold of something and move it *He reached across and took the glass from her.* **5** ACCEPT to accept something *So, are you going to take the job?* ○ *Do you take credit cards?* **6** NEED If something takes a particular amount of time, or a particular quality, you need that amount of time or that quality in order to be able to do it. [**+ to do sth**] *It's taken me three days to get here.* ○ *It takes a lot of courage to stand up and talk in front of so many people.* **7 HEALTH** to swallow or use medicine *Take two tablets, three times a day.* **8** MEASURE to measure something *Have you taken her temperature?* **9** CLOTHES to wear a particular size of clothes *I take a size 12 in trousers.* **10** SPACE to have enough space for a particular number of people or things *There's six of us and the car only takes five.* **11** TRAVEL to travel somewhere by using a bus, train, car, etc, or by using a particular road *Are you taking the train to Edinburgh?* **12 take a break/rest, etc** to stop working for a period **13 take pleasure/pride/an interest, etc** to have a particular, good feeling about something that you do *I take great pleasure in cooking.* ○ *These women take their jobs very seriously* (= think their jobs are very important). **14 take a look** to look at something *Take a look at these photos.* **15** UNDERSTAND to understand something in a particular way *Whatever I say she'll take it the wrong way.* **16 I take it (that)** used when you think that what you say is probably true *I take it you're not coming with us.* **17 can't take sth** to not be able to deal with an unpleasant situation *We argue all the time - I really can't take it any more.* **18 take it from me** accept that what I say is true, because I know or have experienced it *You could be doing a much less interesting job, take it from me.* **19 take sth as it comes** to deal with something as it happens, without planning for it **20** BY FORCE to get control of something by force *By morning they had taken the city.*

COMMON LEARNER ERROR

take part in or **take place?**

If someone **takes part in** something, they join other people in doing it.

All the children took part in the competition.

If something **takes place**, it happens.

The festival takes place every summer in the castle gardens.

take after sb *phrasal verb* to be similar to an older member of your family *Peter's very tall - he takes after his father.*

take sth apart *phrasal verb* to separate something into its different parts *He spent the whole afternoon taking his bike apart.*

O-m **take sth away** *phrasal verb* **1** REMOVE to remove something *The waitress took our plates away.* ○ *Supermarkets are* ***taking*** *business* ***away from*** *small local shops.* **2** NUMBER to subtract a number ***Take*** *3* ***away from*** *20.*

take sb away *phrasal verb* to make someone leave a place and go with you

take sth back *phrasal verb* **1** THING to return something to the place you borrowed or bought it from **2** WORDS to admit that your opinion was wrong *You're right, he's nice - I take back everything I said about him.*

take sth down *phrasal verb* **1** WRITE to write something *Did you take down the telephone number?* **2** REMOVE to remove something that is on a wall or something that is temporary *I've taken the pictures down.*

take sth in *phrasal verb* **1** UNDERSTAND to understand something *It was an interesting lecture but there was just too much to take in.* **2** FILM/BUILDING ETC to go to see a film, visit an interesting building, etc for enjoyment *I thought we might get something to eat and then take in a movie.* **3** CLOTHES to make a piece of clothing narrower

take sb in *phrasal verb* **1** POLICE If the police take someone in, they take that person to the police station. **2** LET SOMEONE STAY to let someone stay in your house *You could earn some extra cash by taking in foreign students.* **3 be taken in** to be deceived by someone

O-m **take sth off** *phrasal verb* **1** REMOVE to remove something *If you're hot, take your jacket off.* ➲See colour picture **Phrasal Verbs** on page Centre 16 **2** TIME to spend time away from your work *I'm taking Friday off to get some things done around the house.*

take off *phrasal verb* **1** AIRCRAFT If an aircraft takes off, it begins to fly. **2** SUCCESSFUL to suddenly become successful *Her career had just taken off.* **3** LEAVE to suddenly leave without telling anyone where you are going *He took off in the middle of the night.*

take sth on *phrasal verb* to accept a responsibility *I don't want to take on too much work.*

take sb on *phrasal verb* **1** EMPLOY to begin to employ someone *We'll be taking on two new members of staff.* **2** COMPETE to compete against someone *I might* ***take you on at*** *tennis sometime.*

take on sth *phrasal verb* to begin to have a particular quality *Her voice took on a tone of authority.*

take sth out *phrasal verb* to remove something from somewhere *He reached into his bag and took out a book.*

take sb out *phrasal verb* to go somewhere with someone and pay for them *Are you taking her out for her birthday?*

take sth out on sb *phrasal verb* to unfairly treat someone badly because you are upset *Don't take it out on me!*

take (sth) over *phrasal verb* to get control of or responsibility for something *They've recently been taken over by a larger company.* ○ *Who'll be* ***taking over from*** *Cynthia when she retires?*

take sb through sth *phrasal verb* to explain something to someone

take to sb/sth *phrasal verb* to start to like someone or something *For some reason, I just didn't take to him.*

take to sth/doing sth *phrasal verb* to start doing something *Dad's taken to swimming every morning.*

take sth up *phrasal verb* **1** ACTIVITY to start doing a particular job or activity *I thought I might take up cycling.* **2** TIME/SPACE to use an amount of time or space *This desk takes up too much space.*

take sb up on sth *phrasal verb* to accept an offer *Could I take you up on your offer of a ride home?*

take sth up with sb *phrasal verb* to discuss something with someone *You'll have to take the matter up with your manager.*

takeaway /ˈteɪkəweɪ/ *UK* (*US* **takeout** /ˈteɪkaʊt/) *noun* [C] **FOOD** a meal that you buy in a restaurant but eat at home, or a shop that sells this type of meal

take-off /ˈteɪkɒf/ *noun* **1** AIRCRAFT [C, U] when an aircraft leaves the ground and begins to fly **2** COPY [C] a film, book, etc that copies someone else's style in a way that is funny

takeover /ˈteɪkˌəʊvəʳ/ *noun* [C] **ECONOMICS** when a company gets control of another company

takings /ˈteɪkɪŋz/ *UK* (*US* **receipts**) *noun* [plural] **FINANCE** all the money that a business gets from selling things

talcum powder /ˈtælkəmˌpaʊdəʳ/ (*also* **talc**) *noun* [U] white powder that you put on your skin after a bath

tale /teɪl/ *noun* [C] **LITERATURE** a story, especially one which is not true or is difficult to believe *My grandfather used to* ***tell us tales*** *of his time as a pilot during the war.* ➲See also: **fairy tale**

WORD PARTNERS FOR ***talent***

have/show a talent for sth • a **natural** talent • sb's talent **as** sth

O-m **talent** /ˈtælənt/ *noun* [C, U] a natural ability to do something *She showed an early* ***talent for*** *drawing.* •**talented** *adjective* showing natural ability in a particular area *a talented young musician*

talisman /ˈtælɪzmən/ *noun* [C] *plural* **talismans** an object that people think will make them lucky

O-m **talk¹** /tɔːk/ *verb* **1** SAY [I] to say things to someone *We were just* ***talking about*** *Simon's new girlfriend.* ○ *It was nice* ***talking to*** *you. US* ○ *It was nice* ***talking with*** *you.* ➲See Common Learner Error at **speak** **2** DISCUSS [I] to discuss something with someone, often to try to find a solution to a disagreement *The two sides have agreed to talk.* **3 talk about sth/doing sth** to think about or make plans to do something in the future *They're talking about building a new fire station just up the road.* **4 talk business/politics, etc** to discuss a particular subject *I don't like to talk business over lunch.* **5 talking of sth** *UK* (*US* **speaking of sth**) used when you are going

T

to start talking about something that is related to what has just been said *Talking of holidays, did you hear about Lesley's skiing trip?* ➲See also: speak/talk of the **devil**

talk at sb *phrasal verb* to talk to someone without letting them say anything or without listening to them

talk back *phrasal verb* If a child talks back to an adult, they answer them rudely.

talk down to sb *phrasal verb* to talk to someone in a way that shows you think they are not intelligent or not important

talk sb into/out of (doing) sth *phrasal verb* to persuade someone to do or not do something *We managed to talk Lisa into doing the cooking.*

talk sth over *phrasal verb* to discuss something with someone, often to find out their opinion or to get advice before making a decision

OTHER WAYS OF SAYING ***talk***

The most common alternatives are **speak** and **say**: *Could you **speak** more quietly, please?* • *I couldn't hear what they were **saying**.*

The verb **chat** or the expression **have a chat** are often used if a person is talking with someone in a friendly, informal way: *We were just **chatting** about the party on Saturday.* • *Give me a call and we'll **have a chat**.*

If people talk for a long time about things that are not important, verbs such as **chatter**, **natter** (*UK, informal*), and the expression **have a natter** (*UK, informal*) are sometimes used: *She spent the morning **chattering** away to her friends.* • *We **had a** long **natter** over coffee.*

If someone talks about something too much in an annoying way, you can use the phrasal verb **go on** (*UK*): *He's always **going on** about how much he hates his work.*

If someone talks quietly so that their voice is difficult to hear, often because they are complaining about something, then the verbs **mumble** and **mutter** are used: *She walked past me, **muttering** to herself.* • *He **mumbled** something about it being a waste of time.*

The verb **whisper** is used when someone talks extremely quietly so that other people cannot hear: *What are you two girls **whispering** about?*

WORD PARTNERS FOR ***talk (noun)***

have a talk • a talk **with** sb • a talk **about** sth • a **long/serious** talk

O-ꟷ**talk²** /tɔːk/ *noun* **1** [CONVERSATION] [C] a conversation between two people, often about a particular subject *I **had a** long **talk with** Chris at the weekend about going to university.* **2** [PEOPLE] [U] when people talk about what might happen or be true *There's been some **talk of** possible job losses.* **3** [TO A GROUP] [C] when someone speaks to a group of people about a particular subject *Someone's coming to the school to **give a talk about** road safety.* **4 be all talk (and no action)** If someone is all talk, they never do the brave or exciting things they often say they will do. ➲See also: **small talk**

talkative /ˈtɔːkətɪv/ *adjective* A talkative person talks a lot.

WORD PARTNERS FOR ***talks***

attend/have/hold/resume talks • talks **break down/take place** • **lengthy/secret/urgent** talks • talks **about/on** sth

talks /tɔːks/ *noun* [plural] **POLITICS** formal meetings, especially between political leaders, to discuss a problem and to try to reach an agreement *peace talks* ○ *US officials are **holding talks with** EU leaders over trade.*

ˈtalk ˌshow *US* (*UK* **chat show**) *noun* [C] an informal television or radio programme where people are asked questions about themselves and their lives

O-ꟷ**tall** /tɔːl/ *adjective* **1** [BIG] having a greater than average height. *He's tall and thin.* ○ *It's one of the tallest buildings in the city.* **2** [SIZE] used to describe or ask about the height of someone or something *How tall is she?* ○ *He's almost 2 metres tall.*

tally¹ /ˈtæli/ *noun* [C] the number of things you have achieved, used, won, etc until now *This adds to his **tally of** 12 race wins so far this year.*

tally² /ˈtæli/ *verb* **1** [SAME] [I] If two numbers or stories tally, they are the same. **2** [TOTAL] [T] (*also* **tally up**) to find out the total number

the Talmud /ˈtælmʊd/ *noun* **RELIGION** the ancient Jewish written laws and traditions

talon /ˈtælən/ *noun* [C] **BIOLOGY** a sharp nail on the foot of a bird that it uses to catch animals

Tamagotchi /ˌtæməˈgɒtʃi/ *noun* [C] *trademark* a small electronic toy which you pretend to look after by feeding it, playing with it, etc

tambourine /ˌtæmbᵊrˈiːn/ *noun* [C] **MUSIC** a musical instrument with a wooden ring and small metal discs loosely fixed to it which you play by shaking or hitting

tame¹ /teɪm/ *adjective* **1** [ANIMAL] If an animal is tame, it is not wild and not frightened of people. **2** [NOT EXCITING] too controlled and not exciting *His TV show is very tame in comparison with his live performances.*

tame² /teɪm/ *verb* [T] to make a wild animal tame

tamper /ˈtæmpəʳ/ *verb*

tamper with sth *phrasal verb* to touch or make changes to something which you should not, often in order to damage it

tampon /ˈtæmpɒn/ *noun* [C] a small roll of cotton which a woman puts in her vagina to absorb her monthly flow of blood

tan¹ /tæn/ (*also* **suntan**) *noun* [C] when your skin is brown from being in the sun

tan² /tæn/ *verb* [I, T] **tanning**, *past* **tanned** **1** to become brown from the sun, or to make a person or body part become brown *I tan quite easily.* **2** to make the skin of animals into leather (= material for shoes, etc.)

tan³ /tæn/ *adjective* **1** [COLOUR] being a pale yellow-brown colour *a tan jacket* **2** [SKIN] *US* (*UK/*

US **tanned**) having darker skin because you have been in the sun

tandem /ˈtændəm/ *noun* **1 in tandem (with sb)** If someone does something in tandem with someone else, they do it together or at the same time. **2** [C] a bicycle for two people

tangent /ˈtændʒᵊnt/ *noun* [C] **1 MATHEMATICS** a straight line which touches but does not cross a curve **2 MATHEMATICS** in a triangle that has one angle of 90°, the ratio of the length of the side opposite an angle less than 90° divided by the length of the shorter of the two sides that are next to the angle ⊃Compare **cosine, sine 3 go off at/on a tangent** to suddenly start talking about a different subject

tangerine /ˌtændʒᵊrˈiːn/ *noun* [C] **FOOD** a fruit like a small orange

tangible /ˈtændʒəbl/ *adjective* Something which is tangible is real and can be seen, touched, or measured. ***tangible benefits/evidence*** ⊃Opposite **intangible**

tangle¹ /ˈtæŋgl/ *noun* [C] several things which have become twisted together in an untidy way *a tangle of hair/wires*

tangle² /ˈtæŋgl/ *verb* [I, T] to become twisted together, or to make things become twisted together ⊃Opposite **disentangle, untangle**

tangled /ˈtæŋgld/ *adjective* **1** TWISTED (*also* **tangled up**) twisted together in an untidy way *The wires are all tangled.* **2** CONFUSED confused and difficult to understand *tangled finances* **3 be tangled up in/with sth** to be involved in something unpleasant or complicated that is difficult to escape from

tango /ˈtæŋgəʊ/ *noun* [C] a South American dance

tangy /ˈtæŋi/ *adjective* **FOOD** having a strong, sharp but pleasant taste or smell *a tangy lemon drink* •**tang** *noun* [**no plural**]

tank /tæŋk/ *noun* [C] **1** CONTAINER a large container for storing liquid or gas *(UK) a **petrol tank**/ (US) a **gas tank*** ○ *a hot-water tank* **2** MILITARY a large, strong military vehicle with a gun on it which moves on wheels inside large metal belts ⊃See also: **think tank**

tanker /ˈtæŋkəʳ/ *noun* [C] a ship or truck used to carry large amounts of liquid or gas *an oil tanker*

tanned /tænd/ (*also US* **tan**) *adjective* having darker skin because you have been in the sun

ˈtanning ˌbed *noun* [C] *US* a sun bed

tannoy /ˈtænɔɪ/ *UK trademark* (*UK/US* **public address system**) *noun* [**no plural**] a system of equipment used in public places that someone speaks into in order to make their voice loud enough to hear

tantalizing (*also UK* **-ising**) /ˈtæntəlaɪzɪŋ/ *adjective* Something that is tantalizing is very attractive and makes you want it, although often you cannot have it. *a tantalizing glimpse of blue sea*

tantamount /ˈtæntəmaʊnt/ *adjective* **be tantamount to sth** to be almost as bad as something else *Resignation would be tantamount to admitting he was guilty.*

tantrum /ˈtæntrəm/ *noun* [C] when someone, especially a child, suddenly shows that they are very angry, usually because they cannot have something *Tom **threw a tantrum** in the middle of the supermarket.*

WORD PARTNERS FOR ***tap***

turn on/turn off a tap • a tap is **dripping/running** • the **cold/hot** tap • **under** the tap • tap **water**

tap¹ /tæp/ *noun* [C] **1** WATER *mainly UK* (*also US* **faucet**) the part at the end of a pipe which controls the flow of water *the **cold/hot tap*** ○ *to **turn a tap on/off*** ○ *She rinsed the cup **under the tap**.* **2** KNOCK a gentle knock or touch, or the noise made by knocking something gently *I felt a tap on my shoulder.* ○ *There was a tap at the door.* **3** TELEPHONE a small piece of equipment that can be fixed to someone's telephone in order to listen to their telephone calls **4 on tap** easily available *They have all that sort of information on tap.*

tap² /tæp/ *verb* **tapping**, *past* **tapped 1** KNOCK [I, T] to knock or touch something gently *I **tapped on** the window to try and get her attention.* **2** A SUPPLY [T] If you tap a supply of something, you use what is available. *There are immense natural resources here waiting to be tapped.* **3** TELEPHONE [T] to use a special piece of equipment to listen to someone's telephone calls [**often passive**] *I think the phone's been tapped.*

tap into sth *phrasal verb* to use part of a large supply of something for your own advantage

ˈtap ˌdancing *noun* [U] a type of dancing where the dancer wears special shoes with pieces of metal on the bottom which make a noise •**tap dance** *verb* [I] •**tap dancer** *noun* [C]

tape¹ /teɪp/ *noun* **1** RECORDING [C, U] a long, thin piece of plastic which is used to store sound, pictures, or information, or a plastic box containing it *I've got the match **on tape**.* **2** STICKY [U] a thin piece of plastic which has glue on one side and is used for sticking things together ***adhesive/sticky tape*** **3 DT** [C, U] a long, thin piece of material used, for example, in sewing or to tie things together ⊃See also: **red tape, Scotch tape**

tape² /teɪp/ *verb* **1** [T] to record something onto tape *I often tape programmes and watch them later.* **2 tape sth to/onto, etc** to stick something somewhere using tape

ˈtape ˌmeasure *noun* [C] a long, thin piece of cloth, metal, or plastic used to measure lengths

taper /ˈteɪpəʳ/ *verb* [I, T] to become gradually narrower at one end •**tapered** *adjective*

taper off *phrasal verb* to become gradually smaller or less frequent *Sales have gradually tapered off.*

ˈtape reˌcorder *noun* [C] a machine used to record sound onto tape •**tape recording** *noun* [C] something which has been recorded on tape

tapestry /ˈtæpɪstri/ *noun* [C] **ART** a picture or pattern created by sewing different coloured threads onto heavy cloth

taproot /ˈtæpruːt/ *noun* [C] **BIOLOGY** the main thick root found in some plants, such as the

T

carrot, which stores food and grows straight down

ˈtap ˌwater *noun* **[U]** water which comes out of a tap (= part at the end of a pipe)

tar /tɑːʳ/ *noun* **[U]** **1** ROAD a thick, black substance that is sticky when hot and is used to cover roads **2 HEALTH** a black, sticky substance that is produced when tobacco burns •**tar** *verb* **[T]** **tarring**, *past* **tarred** to cover something with tar

tarantula /təˈræntjələ/ *noun* **[C]** a large, hairy spider that is often poisonous

WORD PARTNERS FOR ***target***

attack/hit/miss/strike a target • an **obvious/prime** target • a target **for** sth

target¹ /ˈtɑːgɪt/ *noun* **[C]** **1** ATTACK something or someone that you attack, shoot at, try to hit, etc *It's very difficult to **hit** a moving **target**.* ○ *Foreign businesses in the region have become a **target for** terrorist attacks.* **2** ACHIEVE something that you intend to achieve *I'm hoping to save £3,000 by June - that's my target.* ○ *If you want to lose weight, you have to **set** yourself* (= decide) *a **target**.* **3** BLAME the person or thing that people are criticizing or blaming for something *Such extreme views have recently made him the target of criticism.* **4 be on target** to have made enough progress in order to achieve something that you intended to achieve **[+ to do sth]** *We're on target to finish the project in June.* **5 target audience/market, etc** the group of people that a programme, product, etc is aimed at

target² /ˈtɑːgɪt/ *verb* **[T]** **1** ATTACK to aim an attack at a particular person or place *They mostly targeted military bases.* **2** AIM AT to aim advertising, criticism, or a product at someone **[often passive]** *The products are **targeted at** people in their late twenties.*

tariff /ˈtærɪf/ *noun* **[C]** **1 ECONOMICS, FINANCE** an amount of money that has to be paid for goods that are brought into a country *import tariffs* **2 FINANCE** a list of prices

tarmac /ˈtɑːmæk/ *noun trademark* **1** **[U]** *UK* (*US* **asphalt**) a thick, black substance that is sticky when hot and is used to cover roads **2 the tarmac** the area at an airport where aircraft land and take off

tarnish /ˈtɑːnɪʃ/ *verb* **1** SOMEONE **[T]** to spoil the way in which people think of someone so that they do not respect them *to **tarnish** someone's **image/reputation*** **2** METAL **[I, T]** If a metal tarnishes or something tarnishes it, it becomes less bright and shiny.

tarpaulin /tɑːˈpɔːlɪn/ (*also US* **tarp**) *noun* **[C, U]** a large piece of plastic or cloth that water cannot go through which is used to cover and protect things

tart² /tɑːt/ *adjective* **FOOD** having a sour, bitter taste

tartan /ˈtɑːtᵊn/ *noun* **[C, U]** cloth with a pattern of different coloured squares and crossing lines *a tartan kilt*

O⊸**task** /tɑːsk/ *noun* **[C]** a piece of work, especially something unpleasant or difficult **[+ of + doing sth]** *I was given the task of sorting out all the stuff in the garage.*

taskbar /ˈtɑːskbɑːʳ/ *noun* **[C]** **COMPUTING** on a computer screen, a set of symbols that shows the programs you are using and allows you to change them

ˈtask ˌforce *noun* **[C]** a group of people, often a military group, who are brought together in order to do a particular job

tassel /ˈtæsᵊl/ *noun* **[C]** a decoration made of a group of short threads tied together which is hung on curtains, furniture, etc

WORD PARTNERS FOR ***taste***

disguise/improve/like/spoil a taste • a **bitter/pleasant/strong/unpleasant/unusual** taste

O⊸**taste¹** /teɪst/ *noun* **1 FOOD** **[C, U]** the flavour of a particular food in your mouth *a sweet/**bitter taste*** ○ *It's got quite a **strong taste**.* **2** ABILITY **[U]** the ability to feel different flavours in your mouth *When you've got a cold you often lose your **sense of taste**.* **3 a taste** a small amount of food that you have in order to try it *Could I **have just a taste** of the sauce?* **4** WHAT YOU LIKE **[C, U]** the particular things you like, such as styles of music, clothes, decoration, etc *I don't like his **taste in** music.* ○ *It's okay, but it's not really **to my taste**.* **5** ART/STYLE ETC **[U]** the ability to judge what is attractive or suitable, especially in things related to art, style, beauty, etc *Everything in his house is beautiful - he's got very **good taste**.* **6 be in good taste** to be acceptable in a way that will not upset or anger people **7 be in bad/poor taste** to be unacceptable in a way that will upset or anger people *He told a joke about a plane crash which I thought was in rather poor taste.* **8 a taste for sth** when you like or enjoy something *I've developed a bit of a taste for opera.* **9 taste of sth** when you do or experience something new for a short time *That was my first taste of Mexican culture.*

O⊸**taste²** /teɪst/ *verb* **1 taste funny/nice/sweet, etc** If food tastes a particular way, it has that flavour. *This sauce tastes strange.* ○ *It **tastes of** chocolate.* **2 can taste sth** to be able to experience a particular flavour in a food *You can really taste the garlic in it.* **3** **[T]** to put food or drink in your mouth to find out what its flavour is like *I always taste food while I'm cooking it.*

ˈtaste ˌbuds *noun* **[plural]** **ANATOMY, BIOLOGY** the cells on your tongue that allow you to taste different foods

tasteful /ˈteɪstfᵊl/ *adjective* attractive and chosen for style and quality *a tasteful beige suit* •**tastefully** *adverb tastefully dressed/decorated*

tasteless /ˈteɪstləs/ *adjective* **1** UGLY ugly or without style **2** OFFENSIVE likely to upset or anger people *a **tasteless joke*** **3 FOOD** having no flavour *The meat was dry and tasteless.*

tasty /ˈteɪsti/ *adjective* **FOOD** Food which is tasty has a good flavour and is nice to eat.

tattered /ˈtætəd/ *adjective* old and badly torn ***tattered clothes***

tatters /ˈtætəz/ *noun* **in tatters** badly torn, damaged, or spoilt *The yacht finally made it to the* *harbour, its sails in tatters.* ○ *His reputation is in tatters.*

tattoo /tæt'uː/ *noun* [C] a design on someone's skin that is put on using ink and a needle •**tattoo** *verb* [T] *past* **tattooed**

tatty /'tæti/ *adjective UK informal* untidy and in bad condition *He turned up wearing a pair of tatty old jeans.*

taught /tɔːt/ *past of* teach

taunt /tɔːnt/ *verb* [T] to repeatedly say unkind things to someone in order to upset them or make them angry *He was taunted by his classmates because of his size.* •**taunt** *noun* [C]

Taurus /'tɔːrəs/ *noun* [C, U] the sign of the zodiac which relates to the period of 21 April - 22 May, or a person born during this period

taut /tɔːt/ *adjective* stretched very tight *My skin feels taut.*

tavern /'tævᵊn/ *noun* [C] *mainly US* a place where people go to drink alcohol

tawdry /'tɔːdri/ *adjective* **1** UNPLEASANT unpleasant and immoral **2** BAD QUALITY cheap and of bad quality

tawny /'tɔːni/ *adjective* being a light yellow-brown colour

WORD PARTNERS FOR ***tax***

deduct/increase/pay tax • **high/low** taxes • a tax **on** sth • **after/before** tax

O➡ **tax¹** /tæks/ *noun* [C, U] **ECONOMICS, FINANCE** money that you have to pay to the government from what you earn or when you buy things *They're putting up the **tax on** cigarettes.* ○ *Do you have to **pay tax** on that?* ➲See also: **income tax**

tax² /tæks/ *verb* [T] **1 ECONOMICS, FINANCE** to make someone pay a tax *Goods such as clothes are taxed at 15%.* **2** to need a lot of effort *It's only a short report - it shouldn't tax me too much.*

taxable /'tæksəbl/ *adjective* **ECONOMICS, FINANCE** If something is taxable, you have to pay tax on it. ***taxable income***

taxation /tæk'seɪʃᵊn/ *noun* [U] **ECONOMICS** the system of making people pay taxes

tax-free /ˌtæks'friː/ *adjective* **ECONOMICS, FINANCE** If something is tax-free, you do not pay tax on it.

WORD PARTNERS FOR ***taxi***

call/get/hail/order/take a taxi • a taxi **driver/fare/firm**

O➡ **taxi** /'tæksi/ *noun* [C] a car with a driver who you pay to take you somewhere *a **taxi driver*** ○ *I'll **take a taxi** to the airport.*

taxing /'tæksɪŋ/ *adjective* difficult and needing a lot of thought or effort to do or understand

'taxi ˌrank *UK* (*US* **'taxi ˌstand**) *noun* [C] a place where you can go to get a taxi

taxonomy /tæk'sɒnəmi/ *noun* **1** [U] **BIOLOGY** the process of organizing groups of things which are similar, especially plants and animals, and giving names to those groups **2** [C] one particular system for organizing groups of similar things

taxpayer /'tæksˌpeɪəʳ/ *noun* [C] **ECONOMICS** a person who pays tax

TB /ˌtiː'biː/ *noun* [U] **HEALTH** *abbreviation for* tuberculosis (= a serious infectious disease of the lungs)

tbsp **MEASURES** *written abbreviation for* tablespoonful: the amount that can be held by a large spoon used for measuring food

T-cell /'tiːsel/ *noun* [C] **BIOLOGY** a type of white blood cell that helps to protect the body against diseases

O➡ **tea** /tiː/ *noun* [C, U] **1 FOOD** a hot drink that you make by pouring water onto dried leaves, or the leaves that you use to make this drink ***herbal teas*** ○ *Would you like **a cup of tea** or coffee?* **2 FOOD** *UK* a small afternoon meal of cakes, biscuits, etc and tea to drink *They invited us for **afternoon tea**.* **3 FOOD** *UK* a word used by some people for the meal that is eaten in the evening

teabag /'tiːbæg/ *noun* [C] **FOOD** a small paper bag with dried leaves inside, used for making tea

O➡ **teach** /tiːtʃ/ *verb past* **taught** **1 EDUCATION** [I, T] to give lessons in a particular subject at a school, university, etc *She taught at Harvard University for several years.* ○ *He teaches history.* **2** SHOW HOW TO [T] to show or explain to someone how to do something [**+ to do sth**] *My dad taught me to drive.* ○ *Can you **teach** me **how to** knit?* **3** GET KNOWLEDGE [T] If a situation teaches you something, it gives you new knowledge or helps you to understand something. [**+ to do sth**] *The whole experience taught him to be more careful with money.* ➲See Common Learner Error at **learn** ➲See also: teach sb a **lesson**

O➡ **teacher** /'tiːtʃəʳ/ *noun* [C] **EDUCATION** someone whose job is to teach in a school, college, etc *a history/science teacher* ➲See colour picture **The Classroom** on page Centre 6 ➲See Common Learner Error at **lecturer**

teaching /'tiːtʃɪŋ/ *noun* [U] **EDUCATION** the job of being a teacher *He decided to **go into teaching*** (= become a teacher).

teachings /'tiːtʃɪŋz/ *noun* [**plural**] the ideas or beliefs of someone, such as a political or religious leader *the teachings of Martin Luther King*

teacup /'tiːkʌp/ *noun* [C] a cup that you drink tea from

WORD PARTNERS FOR ***team***

be **in/on** a team • **join/play for** a team • team **captain/coach/member**

O➡ **team¹** /tiːm/ *noun* [**group**] **1 SPORT** a group of people who play a sport or game together against another group of players *a basketball/football team* **2** a group of people who work together to do something *a management team* ○ *a team of advisers*

team² /tiːm/ *verb*

team up *phrasal verb* to join someone else and work together with them to do something *I **teamed up with** Brendan for the doubles tournament.*

T

teammate /ˈtiːmmeɪt/ *noun* [C] **SPORT** a member of your team

teamwork /ˈtiːmwɜːk/ *noun* [U] when a group of people work well together

teapot /ˈtiːpɒt/ *noun* [C] a container used for making and serving tea, which has a lid, a handle, and a spout (= tube that liquid comes out of) ➲See colour picture **The Kitchen** on page Centre 2

tear¹ /teəʳ/ *verb past tense* **tore**, *past participle* **torn 1** DAMAGE SOMETHING [T] to pull paper, cloth, etc into pieces, or to make a hole in it by accident *The nail had **torn a hole in** my skirt.* **2** BECOME DAMAGED [I] If paper, cloth, etc tears, it becomes damaged because it has been pulled. **3 tear sth out of/off/down, etc** to remove something by pulling it quickly and violently *She tore his picture down from the wall.* **4 tear along/about/past, etc** *informal* to move somewhere very quickly *The kids were tearing around the house.* **5 be torn between sth and sth** to be unable to decide between two choices *I'm torn between the apple pie and the chocolate mousse.* ➲See also: pull/tear your **hair** out

tear sth apart *phrasal verb* **1** FIGHT/ARGUE to make a group of people argue or fight with each other *The country was torn apart by 12 years of civil war.* **2** DESTROY to destroy something *The building was torn apart by the bomb blast.*

tear sb apart *phrasal verb* to make someone very unhappy

tear sb away *phrasal verb* to make someone stop doing something that they enjoy, in order to do something else *I'll bring Ian, if I can **tear** him **away from** his computer games.*

tear sth down *phrasal verb* to intentionally destroy a building or structure *They tore down the old hospital and built some offices.*

tear sth off *phrasal verb* to quickly remove your clothes *He tore off his shirt and jumped into the stream.*

tear sth up *phrasal verb* to tear paper into a lot of small pieces *He tore up her photograph.*

tear² /teəʳ/ *noun* [C] a hole in a piece of cloth, paper, etc where it has been torn

tear³ /tɪəʳ/ *noun* [C] a drop of water that comes from your eye when you cry *Suddenly he **burst into tears*** (= started crying). ○ *I was **in tears*** (= crying) *by the end of the film.* •**tearful** *adjective* crying *a tearful goodbye* •**tearfully** *adverb* ➲See also: in floods (**flood²**) of tears

ˈtear ˌgas *noun* [U] a gas that makes people's eyes hurt, used by the police or army to control violent crowds

tease /tiːz/ *verb* [I, T] to laugh at someone or say unkind things to them, either because you are joking or because you want to upset them *They were **teasing** Dara **about** her new haircut.* ○ *Don't get upset, I'm only teasing.*

teaspoon /ˈtiːspuːn/ *noun* [C] a small spoon that is used for mixing drinks and measuring small amounts of food, or the amount this spoon can hold

teatime /ˈtiːtaɪm/ *noun* [C, U] *UK* **FOOD** the time in the evening when people have a meal

ˈtea ˌtowel *UK* (*US* **dishtowel**) *noun* [C] a cloth that is used for drying plates, dishes, etc

tech¹ /tek/ *adjective mainly US short for* technical¹ *online tech support*

tech² /tek/ *noun mainly US* **1** TECHNOLOGY [U] *short for* technology *high/low tech* ○ *tech stocks* **2** PERSON [C] *informal short for* technician *Bill was a lab tech at NYU.*

techie /ˈteki/ *noun* [C] *informal* someone who has a strong interest in technology, usually computers

technical /ˈteknɪkəl/ *adjective* **1** SCIENCE/INDUSTRY relating to the knowledge, machines, or methods used in science and industry *We're having a few **technical problems**.* **2** SPECIALIZED relating to the knowledge and methods of a particular subject or job *There are a few **technical terms** here that I don't understand.* **3** PRACTICAL SKILL relating to practical skills and methods that are used in a particular activity *As a dancer she had great technical skill.*

technicalities /ˌteknɪˈkælətiz/ *noun* [plural] the exact details of a system or process *the technicalities of photography*

technicality /ˌteknɪˈkæləti/ *noun* [C] a small detail of a law or rule

technically /ˈteknɪkəli/ *adverb* **1** SCIENCE/INDUSTRY relating to the knowledge, machines, or methods used in science and industry *technically advanced weapons* **2** DETAIL according to the exact details of a rule, law, or fact *Irvine is technically British but lives in Dublin and races for the Irish team.*

technician /tekˈnɪʃən/ *noun* [C] someone whose job involves practical work with scientific or electrical equipment *a **lab technician***

technique /tekˈniːk/ *noun* [C, U] a particular or special way of doing something [+ **for** + **doing sth**] *Scientists have developed a new technique for taking blood samples.*

techno /ˈteknəʊ/ *noun* [U] *UK* **MUSIC** a type of electronic dance music

techno- /teknəʊ-/ *prefix* relating to technology *a technophile* (= a person who loves technology)

WORD PARTNERS FOR ***technology***

advanced/cutting-edge/modern technology • **develop/harness** technology

technology /tekˈnɒlədʒi/ *noun* [C, U] knowledge, equipment, and methods that are used in science and industry *computer technology* •**technological** /ˌteknəˈlɒdʒɪkəl/ *adjective* relating to, or involving technology *technological developments* •**technologically** *adverb* ➲See also: **information technology**

tectonic /tekˈtɒnɪk/ *adjective* **GEOLOGY** relating to the structure of the Earth's surface and the way that it moves •**tectonics** /tekˈtɒnɪks/ *noun* [**no plural**] the processes which change the structure of the Earth's surface

teddy bear /ˈtediˌbeəʳ/ (*also UK* **teddy**) *noun* [C] a soft, toy bear

tedious /ˈtiːdiəs/ *adjective* boring *a tedious job* •**tediously** *adverb*

tee /tiː/ *noun* [C] **SPORT** a small stick that is used for holding a golf ball

teem /tiːm/ *verb*
be teeming with sb/sth *phrasal verb* to contain large numbers of people or animals *The mall was teeming with shoppers on Saturday afternoon.*

teeming /ˈtiːmɪŋ/ *adjective* full of people *the teeming city*

teen[1] /tiːn/ *noun* [C] **SOCIETY** *mainly US short for* teenager

teen[2] /tiːn/ *adjective* [**always before noun**] *informal* **SOCIETY** relating to, or popular with people who are between 13 and 19 years old *a* ***teen idol***

teenage /ˈtiːneɪdʒ/ *adjective* [**always before noun**] **SOCIETY** aged between 13 and 19 or suitable for people of that age *a teenage daughter* ○ *a teenage disco*

O-- **teenager** /ˈtiːnˌeɪdʒəʳ/ *noun* [C] **SOCIETY** someone who is between 13 and 19 years old

teens /tiːnz/ *noun* [**plural**] **SOCIETY** the part of your life between the age of 13 and 19 *Tony and Sally's youngest daughter is still* ***in her teens.***

ˈ**tee ˌshirt** *noun* [C] *another spelling of* T-shirt (= a piece of cotton clothing for the top part of the body with short sleeves and no collar)

teeter /ˈtiːtəʳ/ *verb* **1 be teetering on the brink/edge of sth** to be in a situation where something bad might happen very soon *The British economy is teetering on the brink of collapse.* **2 teeter about/across/around, etc** to look as if you are going to fall *She teetered around the room in six-inch heels.*

teeter-totter /ˈtiːtəˌtɒtəʳ/ *US* (*UK/US* **seesaw**) *noun* [C] a long board that children play on by sitting at each end and using their feet on the ground to push the board up and down

teeth /tiːθ/ **ANATOMY** *plural of* tooth

teethe /tiːð/ *verb* **1 be teething** If a baby is teething, it is getting its first teeth. **2 teething problems/troubles** problems that happen because something is new and has not been done before

teetotal /ˌtiːˈtəʊtəl/ *adjective* never drinking any alcohol •**teetotaller** *UK* (*US* **teetotaler**) *noun* [C] someone who never drinks alcohol

TEFL /ˈtefl/ *noun* [U] **EDUCATION** *abbreviation for* Teaching English as a Foreign Language

tel *written abbreviation for* telephone number *Tel 0113 246369*

tele- /telɪ-/ *prefix* **1** TELEPHONE done using a telephone *telesales* **2** TELEVISION connected with television *telecast* (= something that is broadcast on television) **3** DISTANCE over a long distance *telephoto lens* (= a camera lens that makes distant objects look nearer)

telecommunications /ˌtelɪkəˌmjuːnɪˈkeɪʃənz/ *noun* [U, group] **ECONOMICS** the process or business of sending information or messages by telephone, radio, etc

telecommuting /ˌtelɪkəˈmjuːtɪŋ/ (US) /ˈtelɪkəˌmjuːtɪŋ/ *US* (*UK* **teleworking**) *noun* [U] working at home, while communicating with your office by computer and telephone •**telecommuter** *noun* [C] *US*

telecoms /ˈtelɪkɒmz/ *noun* [U] *short for* telecommunications

teleconference /ˌtelɪˈkɒnfərəns/ *noun* [C] when people in different places have a meeting using computers, telephones, televisions etc to allow them to talk to each other and see each other

telegram /ˈtelɪgræm/ *noun* [C] a message that is sent by telegraph and printed on paper

telegraph /ˈtelɪgrɑːf/ *noun* [U] an old-fashioned system of sending messages using radio or electrical signals

telemarketing /ˈtelɪˌmɑːkɪtɪŋ/ (*also UK* **telesales**) *noun* [U] the selling of goods or services by telephone

telepathy /tɪˈlepəθi/ *noun* [U] the ability to know what someone is thinking or to communicate thoughts without speaking or writing •**telepathic** /ˌtelɪˈpæθɪk/ *adjective* having or involving telepathy

WORD PARTNERS FOR ***telephone***

answer/pick up/put down the telephone • the telephone **rings** • **on** the telephone • a telephone **call**

O-- **telephone**[1] /ˈtelɪfəʊn/ (*also* **phone**) *noun* **1** COMMUNICATION [U] a communication system that is used to talk to someone who is in another place *a* ***telephone call*** ○ *I'm sorry, he's* ***on the telephone*** (= using the telephone) *at the moment.* **2** EQUIPMENT [C] a piece of equipment that is used to talk to someone who is in another place *The* ***telephone rang*** *and she hurried to pick it up.* ○ *Could you* ***answer*** *the* ***telephone?***

telephone[2] /ˈtelɪfəʊn/ (*also* **phone**) *verb* [I, T] *formal* to communicate with someone by telephone

COMMON LEARNER ERROR

telephone and **phone**

Telephone and **phone** mean the same thing, but we usually use **phone** for both the noun and the verb.

I'll phone you this evening.

Can I use your phone, please?

When the phone rings or when you want to make a phone call, you **pick** it **up**.

I picked up the phone and dialled his number.

When you finish a phone call, you **put** the phone **down** or you **hang up**.

Don't hang up - I can explain everything!

She thanked him and put the phone down.

~~*She thanked him and hung up the phone.*~~

ˈ**telephone diˌrectory** *noun* [C] a book that contains the telephone numbers of people who live in a particular area

ˈ**telephone ˌnumber** (*also* **phone number**) *noun* [C] the number of a particular telephone

telesales /ˈtelɪseɪlz/ *UK* (*UK/US* **telemarketing**) *noun* [U] the selling of goods or services by telephone

T

telescope /ˈtelɪskəʊp/ *noun* [C] **PHYSICS** a piece of equipment, in the shape of a tube, that makes things which are far away look bigger or nearer

telescope

Teletext /ˈtelɪˌtekst/ *noun trademark* a system that gives written information on many subjects, such as news, on a television screen *You can get all the latest football news on Teletext.*

televise /ˈtelɪvaɪz/ *verb* [T] to show something on television *The concert will be televised live around the world.*

WORD PARTNERS FOR ***television***

watch television • **see/watch** sth **on** television • **on** television • a television **channel/presenter/programme/series**

O⁻**television** /ˈtelɪvɪʒᵊn/ *noun* **1** EQUIPMENT [C] a piece of equipment in the shape of a box, with a screen on the front, used for watching programmes **2** PROGRAMMES [U] the programmes that are shown on a television *I mostly* ***watch television*** *in the evening.* ○ *I saw it* ***on television.*** ○ *a* ***television programme*** **3** SYSTEM [U] the system or business of making and broadcasting programmes for television ➲See also: **closed-circuit television, satellite television**

COMMON LEARNER ERROR

watch television

Be careful to choose the correct verb with television.

My children watch too much television.

~~*My children look too much television.*~~

teleworking /ˈtelɪˌwɜːkɪŋ/ *UK* (*US* **telecommuting**) *noun* [U] working at home, while communicating with your office by computer and telephone •**teleworker** *noun* [C] *UK*

O⁻**tell** /tel/ *verb past* **told 1** SAY [T] to say something to someone, usually giving them information *He* ***told*** *me* ***about*** *his new school.* [+ **(that)**] *Sally told me that the play didn't start until 9 o'clock.* [+ **question word**] *Can you tell me what time the next bus leaves?* ➲See Common Learner Error at **say 2 tell sb to do sth** to order someone to do something *I told you to stay here.* **3 can tell** to know or recognize something from what you hear, see, etc [+ **(that)**] *You could tell that he was tired.* [+ **question word**] *You can never tell whether Hajime's being serious or not.* ○ *I can't* ***tell the difference between*** *them.* **4** UNDERSTAND FROM [T] If something tells you something, it gives you information. *What does the survey tell us about the lives of teenagers?* **5 (I'll) tell you what** used to suggest a plan *Tell you what, let's go swimming and then get a pizza.* **6** EFFECT [I] to have a bad effect on someone *The worry of the last few months was starting to* ***tell on*** *him.* **7 (I) told you so!** *informal* used when someone has caused problems for themselves by doing something that you told them not to ➲See also: tell sb's **fortune**

tell sb/sth apart *phrasal verb* to be able to see the difference between two things or people that are very similar *It's impossible to tell the twins apart.*

tell sb off *phrasal verb* to tell someone that they have done something wrong and that you are angry about it [+ **for** + **doing sth**] *Darren* ***got told off*** *for talking in class.* ➲See colour picture **Phrasal Verbs** on page Centre 16

teller /ˈteləʳ/ *noun* [C] *US* someone who works in a bank and gives out or takes in money ➲See also: **fortune-teller**

telling /ˈtelɪŋ/ *adjective* showing the truth about a situation, or showing what someone really thinks *a telling comment*

telltale /ˈtelteɪl/ *adjective* [**always before noun**] showing something that someone is trying to keep secret *She was showing all the* ***telltale signs*** *of pregnancy.*

telly /ˈteli/ *noun* [C, U] *UK informal short for* television

temp /temp/ *noun* [C] someone who works in an office for a short time while someone else is away, ill, etc •**temp** *verb* [I] to work as a temp in an office

temper¹ /ˈtempəʳ/ *noun* **1** [C, U] when someone becomes angry very easily *He's got a really* ***bad temper.*** **2 be in a bad/foul, etc temper** to be feeling angry *I'd avoid her if I were you - she's in a foul temper.* **3 lose your temper (with sb)** to suddenly become very angry *I lost my temper with the children this morning.* **4 keep your temper** to succeed in staying calm and not becoming angry

temper² /ˈtempəʳ/ *verb* [T] *formal* to make something less strong, extreme, etc *I learnt to temper my criticism.*

temperament /ˈtempᵊrəmənt/ *noun* [C, U] the part of your character that affects your moods and the way you behave *I don't think he's got the right temperament to be a teacher.*

temperamental /ˌtempᵊrəˈmentᵊl/ *adjective* **1** PERSON becoming angry or upset very often and suddenly **2** MACHINE A machine, vehicle, etc that is temperamental does not always work correctly.

temperate /ˈtempᵊrət/ *adjective formal* **GEOGRAPHY** having weather that is not very hot and not very cold *Virginia has a* ***temperate climate.***

WORD PARTNERS FOR ***temperature***

average/extreme/high/low temperatures • temperatures **drop/fall/rise/soar**

O⁻**temperature** /ˈtemprətʃəʳ/ *noun* **1 MEASURES** [C, U] how hot or cold something is *The room's kept at* ***a temperature of*** *around 20°C.* **2 sb's temperature HEALTH** how hot or cold someone's body is *The doctor examined him and* ***took*** *his* ***temperature*** (= measured his temperature). **3 have a temperature HEALTH** to be hotter than usual because you are ill

template /ˈtempleɪt/ *noun* [C] **1** a metal, plastic, etc pattern that is used for making many copies of a shape **2 COMPUTING** a system that helps you arrange information on a computer screen

temple /ˈtempl/ *noun* [C] **1 RELIGION** a building where people in some religions go to pray or worship *a Buddhist temple* **2 ANATOMY** the

T

area on each side of your head in front of the top of your ear

tempo /ˈtempəʊ/ *noun* **1** [**U, no plural**] the speed at which an activity happens *The tempo of the game increased in the second half.* **2** **MUSIC** [**C, U**] *formal* the speed of a piece of music

OTHER WAYS OF SAYING ***temporary***

The phrase **for now** can be used to say that something should happen or be done now but can be changed later: *Just put everything on the table **for now** - I'll sort it all out later.*

The adjective **disposable** can be used to describe objects which are intended to be used temporarily and then thrown away: *I bought a **disposable** camera at the airport.*

If something is temporary and low quality, you can say that it is **makeshift**: *We built a **makeshift** shelter under the trees.*

The adjective **short-lived** can be used instead of 'temporary' when it means 'lasting for a short time': *I had a few relationships at college, most of which were fairly **short-lived**.*

The expression **acting manager/chairman**, etc is often used to describe someone who does a job temporarily while the person who usually does it is not there: *He'll be the **acting** director until they appoint a permanent one.*

temporary /ˈtempᵊrᵊri/ *adjective* existing or happening for only a short or limited time *a temporary job* ○ *temporary accommodation/housing* •**temporarily** *adverb*

tempt /tempt/ *verb* [**T**] to make someone want to have or do something, especially something that they do not need or something that is wrong [**+ to do sth**] *She's trying to tempt me to go shopping with her.*

WORD PARTNERS FOR ***temptation***

avoid/resist (the) temptation • **give in to/succumb to** temptation • **a strong** temptation • the temptation **of** doing sth

temptation /tempˈteɪʃᵊn/ *noun* **1** FEELING [**C, U**] a feeling that you want to do or have something, although you know you should not [**+ to do sth**] *I **resisted the temptation** to* (= I did not) *have another piece of chocolate cake.* **2** SOMETHING THAT TEMPTS [**C**] something that makes you want to do or have something although you know you should not *He knew crime was wrong but the money was too great a temptation.*

tempting /ˈtemptɪŋ/ *adjective* Something that is tempting makes you want to have or do it. *a **tempting invitation/offer***

O⁻ **ten** /ten/ the number 10

tenacious /tɪˈneɪʃəs/ *adjective* very determined to do something and not wanting to stop •**tenaciously** *adverb* •**tenacity** /tɪˈnæsəti/ *noun* [**U**]

tenancy /ˈtenənsi/ *noun* [**C, U**] the period of time when someone rents a room, house, etc

tenant /ˈtenənt/ *noun* [**C**] someone who pays rent to live in a room, house, etc

O⁻ **tend** /tend/ *verb* **1** **tend to do sth** to often do a particular thing or be likely to do a particular thing *I tend to wear dark colours.* ○ *July and August tend to be our busiest months.* **2** [**T**] (*also* **tend to**) *formal* to look after someone or something *He spends most afternoons tending his vegetable garden.*

tendency /ˈtendənsi/ *noun* [**C**] something that someone often does, or something that often happens [**+ to do sth**] *She **has a tendency** to talk for too long.* ○ *There is a growing **tendency for** companies to employ people on short contracts.*

tender¹ /ˈtendəʳ/ *adjective* **1** GENTLE kind and gentle *a tender kiss/look* **2** **FOOD** Tender meat or vegetables are soft and easy to cut. **3** **HEALTH** If part of your body is tender, it is painful when you touch it. **4** **at the tender age of 8/17/25 etc** *literary* at the young age of 8/17, etc •**tenderness** *noun* [**U**]

tender² /ˈtendəʳ/ *verb formal* **1** OFFER [**I**] to make a formal offer to do a job or to provide a service **2** IDEA/SUGGESTION [**T**] *formal* to formally offer a suggestion, idea, money etc *He **tendered** his **resignation*** (= offered to leave his job).

tender³ /ˈtendəʳ/ *noun* [**C, U**] a formal offer to do some work *The work has been **put out to tender*** (= people have been asked to make offers to do the work).

tenderly /ˈtendəli/ *adverb* in a kind and gentle way *He looked at her tenderly.*

tendon /ˈtendən/ *noun* [**C**] **ANATOMY** a strong piece of tissue in your body that connects a muscle to a bone

tenement /ˈtenəmənt/ *noun* [**C**] a large building that is divided into apartments, usually in a poor area of a city

tenet /ˈtenɪt/ *noun* [**C**] a principle or belief of a theory or religion *one of the basic tenets of Islam*

tenner /ˈtenəʳ/ *noun* [**C**] *UK informal* a piece of paper money that has a value of £10

tennis /ˈtenɪs/ *noun* [**U**] **SPORT** a sport in which two or four people hit a small ball to each other over a net ⊃See colour picture **Sports 2** on page Centre 15 ⊃See also: **table tennis**

tenor /ˈtenəʳ/ *noun* [**C**] **MUSIC** a male singer with a high voice

tense¹ /tens/ *adjective* **1** FEELING nervous, worried, and not able to relax *The students looked tense as they waited for their exam results.* **2** SITUATION A tense situation makes you feel nervous and worried. *There were some tense moments in the second half of the game.* **3** MUSCLE A tense muscle feels tight and stiff.

tense² /tens/ (*also* **tense up**) *verb* [**I, T**] If your muscles tense, they become tight and stiff, and if you tense them, you make them do this.

tense³ /tens/ *noun* [**C, U**] **LANGUAGE** the form of a verb which shows the time at which an action happened. For example 'I sing' is in the present tense and 'I will sing' is in the future tense.

T

WORD PARTNERS FOR *tension*

create/defuse/ease tension • tension **mounts** • **growing/increased/mounting** tension • tension **between** sb and sb • **ethnic/racial** tensions

tension /ˈtenʃən/ *noun* **1** NO TRUST [C, U] a feeling of fear or anger between two groups of people who do not trust each other ***ethnic/racial tension*** ○ *There are growing* ***tensions between*** *the two countries.* **2** BEING NERVOUS [U] a feeling that you are nervous, worried, and not relaxed *You could feel the tension in the room as we waited for her to arrive.* **3** TIGHT [U] when a muscle, rope, etc, is tight or stiff

tent /tent/ *noun* [C] a structure made of metal poles and cloth which is fixed to the ground with ropes and used as a cover or to sleep under *It only took twenty minutes to* ***put*** *the* ***tent up*** (= make it ready to use).

tentacle /ˈtentəkl/ *noun* [C] **BIOLOGY** one of the long, arm-like parts of some sea creatures

tentative /ˈtentətɪv/ *adjective* **1** NOT CERTAIN A tentative idea, plan, agreement, etc is not certain. *The two companies have announced a tentative deal.* **2** NOT CONFIDENT doing something in a way that shows you are not confident *a child's tentative first steps* •**tentatively** *adverb*

tenth¹ /tenθ/ 10th written as a word

tenth² /tenθ/ *noun* [C] one of ten equal parts of something; 1/10; 0.1

tenuous /ˈtenjuəs/ *adjective* A tenuous connection, idea, or situation is weak and possibly does not exist. *The court is unlikely to accept such tenuous evidence.* •**tenuously** *adverb*

tenure /ˈtenjəʳ/ *noun* [U] **1** BUILDING/LAND the legal right to live in a building or use a piece of land for a period **2** TIME the period of time when someone has an important job *his tenure as president* **3** PERMANENT If you have tenure in your job, your job is permanent.

tepee /ˈtiːpiː/ *noun* [C] a type of tent in the shape of a cone made from animal skins or cloth, used by some Native Americans

tepid /ˈtepɪd/ *adjective* A tepid liquid is slightly warm.

T

terabyte /ˈterəbaɪt/ (*written abbreviation* **Tb**) *noun* **COMPUTING, MEASURES** a unit for measuring the amount of information a computer can store, equal to 1,000,000,000,000 bytes

O-- **term¹** /tɜːm/ *noun* **1 LANGUAGE** [C] a word or phrase that is used to refer to a particular thing, especially in a technical or scientific subject *a* ***legal/technical term*** **2** TIME [C] the fixed period of time when someone does an important job or is in a particular place *a prison term* ○ *The government has been elected for another four-year term.* **3 EDUCATION** [C] one of the periods of time that the school or university year is divided into *We've got a test at the* ***end of term.*** **4 in the long/short, etc term** a long/short, etc period of time from now ➲See also: **half-term**

term² /tɜːm/ *verb* [T] *formal* **LANGUAGE** to use a particular word or phrase to describe something *Critics termed the movie a 'disaster'.*

terminal¹ /ˈtɜːmɪnəl/ *noun* [C] **1** a building where you can get onto an aircraft, bus, or ship *a terminal building* **2 COMPUTING** a screen and keyboard with which you can use a computer

terminal² /ˈtɜːmɪnəl/ *adjective* **HEALTH** A terminal illness will cause death. *terminal cancer* •**terminally** *adverb terminally ill*

terminate /ˈtɜːmɪneɪt/ *verb* [I, T] *formal* If something terminates, it ends, and if you terminate something, you make it end. *His contract has been terminated.* •**termination** /ˌtɜːmɪˈneɪʃən/ *noun* [C, U]

terminology /ˌtɜːmɪˈnɒlədʒi/ *noun* [C, U] **LANGUAGE** the special words and phrases that are used in a particular subject *medical/scientific terminology*

terminus /ˈtɜːmɪnəs/ *noun* [C] the place where a train or bus finishes its journey

WORD PARTNERS FOR *terms*

agree terms • **break/meet** the terms **of** sth • **under** the terms **of** sth

terms /tɜːmz/ *noun* [plural] **1** the rules of an agreement ***Under the terms of*** *their contract, employees must give 3 months notice if they want to leave.* **2 be on good/bad/friendly, etc terms** to have a good/bad, etc relationship with someone **3 not be on speaking terms** to not speak to someone because you have argued with them **4 in ... terms** (*also* **in terms of sth**) used to explain which part of a problem or situation you are referring to *In financial terms, the project was not a success.* **5 in no uncertain terms** in a direct and often angry way *I told him to go away in no uncertain terms.* **6 come to terms with sth** to accept a sad situation *He still hasn't come to terms with his brother's death.* ➲See also: a **contradiction** in terms

terrace /ˈterɪs/ *noun* [C] **1** FLAT AREA a flat area outside a house, restaurant, etc where you can sit **2** HOUSE *UK* a row of houses that are joined together

ˌ**terraced** ˈ**house** *UK* (*US* **row house**) *noun* [C] one of a row of houses that are joined together

the terraces /ˈterɪsɪz/ *noun* [plural] **SPORT** in the UK, wide, concrete steps where people stand to watch a football game

terracotta /ˌterəˈkɒtə/ *noun* [U] **DT** a hard, red-brown clay that is used for making containers for plants, tiles for house roofs, etc. *terracotta pots*

terrain /təˈreɪn/ *noun* [C, U] a particular type of land *rough terrain*

terrestrial /təˈrestriəl/ *adjective formal* relating to the Earth, not space

O-- **terrible** /ˈterəbl/ *adjective* very bad, of low quality, or unpleasant *a terrible accident* ○ *The weather was terrible.*

terribly /ˈterəbli/ *adverb* **1** VERY very *She seemed terribly upset.* **2** BADLY very badly *I slept terribly last night.*

terrier /ˈteriəʳ/ *noun* [C] a type of small dog

terrific /təˈrɪfɪk/ *adjective* **1** EXCELLENT excellent *a terrific opportunity* ○ *I thought she looked terrific.* **2** LARGE/SERIOUS [always before noun] very large, great, or serious *a terrific increase in prices* ○ *a terrific storm* •**terrifically** *adverb*

terrified /ˈterəfaɪd/ *adjective* very frightened *I'm **terrified of** flying.* [+ (**that**)] *Maggie was terrified that her parents would discover the truth.*

terrify /ˈterəfaɪ/ *verb* [T] to make someone feel very frightened *The idea of parachuting out of an aircraft terrifies me.* •**terrifying** *adjective a terrifying experience*

territorial /ˌterɪˈtɔːriəl/ *adjective* **POLITICS** relating to the land that is owned or controlled by a particular country *a territorial dispute*

territory /ˈterɪtᵊri/ *noun* **1 POLITICS** [C, U] land that is owned or controlled by a particular country *Spanish territory* **2** PERSON/ANIMAL [C, U] an area that an animal or person thinks belongs to them *Cats like to protect their territory.* **3** AREA OF KNOWLEDGE [U] an area of knowledge or experience *With this project we'll be moving into unknown territory.*

terror /ˈterəʳ/ *noun* [U] a feeling of being very frightened *There was a look of terror on his face.* ➲See also: **reign**[1] of terror

terrorism /ˈterᵊrɪzᵊm/ *noun* [U] **POLITICS** the use of violence for political purposes, for example putting bombs in public places *an **act of terrorism***

terrorist /ˈterərɪst/ *noun* [C] **POLITICS** someone who is involved in terrorism *a **terrorist attack***

terrorize (*also UK* **-ise**) /ˈterᵊraɪz/ *verb* [T] to make someone feel very frightened by saying that you will hurt or kill them *A gang of young men with knives have been terrorizing local people.*

terse /tɜːs/ *adjective* said or written in a few words, often showing that you are annoyed •**tersely** *adverb*

tertiary /ˈtɜːʃᵊri/ *adjective UK formal* **EDUCATION** Tertiary education is education at university or college level. *a tertiary institution*

the ˈtertiary ˌsector *noun* **ECONOMICS** businesses that provide services but do not make anything, for example banks and shops

TESOL /ˈtiːsɒl/ *noun* [U] **EDUCATION** *abbreviation for* Teaching English to Speakers of Other Languages

tessellate /ˈtesᵊleɪt/ *verb* [I] **DT** If shapes tessellate, they fit together completely, with no spaces between them. •**tessellation** /ˌtesᵊlˈeɪʃᵊn/ *noun* [U]

WORD PARTNERS FOR ***test***

do/sit/take a test • **fail/pass** a test • a test **on** sth

O‑**test**[1] /test/ *noun* [C] **1 EDUCATION** a set of questions to measure someone's knowledge or ability *a driving test* ○ *You have to **take a test**.* ○ *Only two students in the class **failed the test**.* ○ *Did you **pass** the biology **test**?* **2 HEALTH** a short medical examination of part of your body *an eye test* ○ *a pregnancy test* **3** EXPERIMENT something that you do to discover if something is safe, works correctly, etc *a safety test* **4** SITUATION a situation that shows how good something is *This will be a real **test of** his ability.*

O‑**test**[2] /test/ *verb* [T] **1** EXPERIMENT to do something in order to discover if something is safe, works correctly, etc *None of our products are **tested on** animals.* **2 HEALTH** to do a medical examination of part of someone's body *I'm going to get my hearing tested.* **3 EDUCATION** to give someone a set of questions, in order to measure their knowledge or ability *You'll be **tested on** all the things we've studied this term.* **4** SITUATION If a situation tests someone, it proves how good, strong, etc they are.

testa /ˈtestə/ *noun* [C] **BIOLOGY** in plants with flowers, a hard layer that covers and protects the surface of a seed

testament /ˈtestəmənt/ *noun formal* **a testament to sth** *formal* proof of something good *It's a testament to Jane's popularity that so many people are celebrating with her today.* ➲See also: **the New Testament, the Old Testament**

testicle /ˈtestɪkl/ *noun* [C] **ANATOMY, BIOLOGY** one of the two round, male sex organs that produce sperm

testify /ˈtestɪfaɪ/ *verb* [I] **LAW** to say what you know or believe is true in a law court [+ **that**] *Elliott testified that he had met the men in a bar.*

testimony /ˈtestɪməni/ *noun* **1 LAW** [C, U] a formal statement about what someone knows or believes is true, especially in a law court *the testimony of a witness* **2 testimony to sth** *formal* proof of something good *The book's continued popularity is testimony to the power of clever marketing.*

testis /ˈtestɪs/ *noun plural* **testes** /ˈtestiːz/ **ANATOMY, BIOLOGY** a testicle (= round male sex organ which produces sperm)

testosterone /ˌtesˈtɒs.tᵊr.əʊn/ *noun* [U] **CHEMISTRY** a male hormone that makes boys develop into men and causes changes in the male sexual organs

ˈtest ˌplan *noun* [C] **COMPUTING** a document that explains the way that new computer software and systems will be tested

ˈtest ˌtube *noun* [C] a glass tube that is open at one end and used in scientific experiments ➲See picture at **laboratory**

tetanus /ˈtetᵊnəs/ *noun* [U] **HEALTH** a serious disease that makes your muscles stiff and is caused by an infection that gets into the body through a cut

tether /ˈteðəʳ/ *verb* [T] to tie an animal to something so that it cannot move away •**tether** *noun* [C] ➲See also: at the **end**[1] of your tether

tetrahedron /ˌtetrəˈhiːdrᵊn/ *noun* [C] *plural* **tetrahedra** or **tetrahedrons MATHEMATICS** a solid shape that has four flat triangular surfaces

O‑**text**[1] /tekst/ *noun* **1 LANGUAGE** [C, U] the written words in a book, magazine, etc, not the pictures *a page of text* **2 EDUCATION** [C] a book or piece of writing that you study as part of a course **3** a written message, usually containing words with letters left out, sent from one mobile phone to another

text[2] /tekst/ *verb* [I, T] to send a text message (= written message from a mobile phone)

textbook /ˈtekstbʊk/ *noun* [C] **EDUCATION** a book about a particular subject, written for

T

students *a chemistry/French textbook* ➲See colour picture **The Classroom** on page Centre 6

textile /ˈtekstaɪl/ *noun* [C] **DT** any type of cloth that is made by weaving (= crossing threads under and over each other)

WORD PARTNERS FOR ***text message***

get/send a text message • a text message **saying** sth • a text message **from/to** sb

ˈtext ˌmessage *noun* [C] a written message, usually containing words with letters left out, sent from one mobile phone to another •**text messaging** *noun* [U]

texture /ˈtekstʃəʳ/ *noun* [C, U] the way that something feels when you touch it *wood with a rough texture*

O-■ **than** *strong form* /ðæn/ *weak form* /ðən/ *preposition, conjunction* used to compare two different things or amounts *Susannah's car is bigger than mine.* ○ *Tom's a bit taller than Sam.* ○ *It cost less than I expected.*

O-■ **thank** /θæŋk/ *verb* [T] **1** to tell someone that you are grateful for something they have done or given you *I haven't **thanked** her **for** her present yet.* [+ **for** + **doing sth**] *Yu Yin thanked the boys for helping her.* **2 thank God/goodness/Heavens, etc** something that you say when you are happy because something bad did not happen *Thank goodness you're okay - I was really worried.*

thankful /ˈθæŋkfəl/ *adjective* pleased or grateful about something [+ **(that)**] *We were thankful that none of the children saw the accident.*

thankfully /ˈθæŋkfəli/ *adverb* used at the beginning of a sentence to show that you are pleased or grateful about something *Thankfully, nobody was hurt.*

thankless /ˈθæŋkləs/ *adjective* A thankless job is difficult or unpleasant and no one thanks you for doing it. *Nursing can be a **thankless job**.*

thanks¹ /θæŋks/ *exclamation informal* **1** used to tell someone that you are grateful because they have given you something or done something for you *Can you pass me the book? Thanks very much.* ○ ***Thanks for** all your help.* **2 thanks/no, thanks** used to accept or refuse someone's offer *"Would you like a cup of coffee?" "No, thanks."*

O-■ **thanks²** /θæŋks/ *noun* [plural] **1** words that show you are grateful for something someone has given to you or done for you *He sent a message of thanks.* **2 thanks to sb/sth** because of someone or something *I passed my driving test, thanks to the extra help my Dad gave me.*

Thanksgiving /ˌθæŋksˈɡɪvɪŋ/ *noun* [C, U] a holiday in the autumn in the US and Canada, when families have a big meal together

O-■ **ˈthank ˌyou** *exclamation* **1** used to tell someone that you are grateful because they have given you something or done something for you ***Thank you** very much **for** the birthday card.* ○ *"Here's the money I promised you." "Thank you."* **2 thank you/no, thank you** used to accept or refuse someone's offer *"Would you like something to eat?" "No, thank you."*

O-■ **thank-you** /ˈθæŋkju/ *noun* [C] something that you say or do to thank someone for doing something [+ **for** + **doing sth**] *I bought Emma some chocolates as a thank-you for looking after the dog.* ○ *a **thank-you present***

O-■ **that¹** /ðæt/ *determiner plural* **those** **1** ALREADY DISCUSSED/SEEN used to refer to something or someone that has already been talked about or seen *Did you know that woman in the post office?* ○ *How much are those shoes?* **2** NOT NEAR used to refer to something or someone that is not near you *He went through that door.* ○ *Have you seen that man over there?* ➲See Common Learner Error at **this**

O-■ **that²** /ðæt/ *pronoun plural* **those** **1** ALREADY DISCUSSED/SEEN used to refer to something that has already been talked about or seen *That looks heavy.* ○ *You can't possibly wear those!* **2** NOT NEAR used to refer to something that is not near you *What's that in the corner?* **3 that's it a** CORRECT used to say that something is correct *You need to push the two pieces together. That's it.* **b** ENDED used to say that something has ended *Well that's it then, we've finished.* **4 that's that** used to say that something has happened or a decision has been made and there is nothing more to say or do *I won't agree to it and that's that.* **5 that is (to say)** used to correct something you have said or give more information about something *Everybody was at the meeting, well everyone except Jeanne, that is.*

COMMON LEARNER ERROR

this/these or **that/those ?**

Use **this** or **these** to talk about people and things which are close to the speaker.

This is my sister Sarah.

Do you like these earrings I'm wearing?

Use **that** or **those** to talk about people and things which are further away from the speaker.

That girl over there is called Sarah.

I liked those earrings you wore last night.

O-■ **that³** *strong form* /ðæt/ *weak form* /ðət/ *conjunction* **1** AFTER VERB/NOUN/ADJECTIVE used after some verbs, nouns, and adjectives to introduce a new part of a sentence *He said that he'd collect it later.* ○ *Is it true that she's pregnant?* **2** RELATIVE CLAUSE used instead of 'who' or 'which' at the beginning of a relative clause *Have you eaten all the cake that I made yesterday?*

that⁴ /ðæt/ *adverb* **1** used when describing the size, amount, or state of something or someone *I've never seen a fish that big before.* **2 not (all) that big/good/warm, etc** not very big, good, warm, etc *It hasn't been all that cold this winter.*

thatched /θætʃt/ *adjective* A thatched building has a roof that is made of straw (= dried grass-like stems). *a **thatched cottage***

thaw /θɔː/ *verb* **1** FROZEN SUBSTANCE [I, T] (*also* **thaw out**) If something that is frozen thaws, it becomes warmer and softer or changes to liquid, and if you thaw something that is frozen, you make it do this. *Allow the meat to thaw before cooking it.* **2** RELATIONSHIP [I] If a relationship between people thaws, it becomes more friendly after being bad. •**thaw** *noun* [C]

O➡**the** *strong form* /ðiː/ *weak forms* /ði, ðə/ *determiner* **1** ALREADY KNOWN used before nouns to refer to particular things or people that have already been talked about or are already known *Can you pass the salt?* ○ *I'll pick you up at the station.* ○ *That's the new restaurant I told you about.* **2** ONLY ONE used before nouns when only one of something exists *Have you seen the Eiffel Tower?* ○ *I'd love to travel round the world.* **3** SINGULAR NOUN used before a singular noun to refer to all the things or people described by that noun *The tiger has become extinct in many countries.* **4** ADJECTIVE used before some adjectives to make them into nouns *a home for the elderly* ○ *relatives of the deceased* **5** COMPARE used before each of two adjectives or adverbs to show how one thing changes depending on another *The longer we live here, the more we like it.* **6** EACH used with units or measurements to mean each or every *How many Belgian francs to the pound?* **7** BODY used when referring to a part of the body *He held her tightly by the arm.* **8** TIME used before numbers which refer to dates or periods of time *the sixties* ○ *Thursday the 29th of April* **9** MUSIC used with the names of musical instruments or dances to mean the type of instrument or dance in general *Can you play the violin?*

O➡**theatre** *UK* (*US* **theater**) /ˈθɪətəʳ/ *noun* **1** BUILDING WITH STAGE [C] a building with a stage where people go to watch plays *the Arts Theatre* **2** BUILDING FOR FILMS [C] *US* a building where people go to watch films *a movie theater* **3** WORK [U] the work of writing, acting in, and producing plays **4** HEALTH [C, U] *UK* a room in a hospital where doctors do operations

WORD PARTNERS FOR ***theatre***

go to the theatre • **at** the theatre • **musical** theatre • **street** theatre • a theatre **company/director**

theatrical /θiˈætrɪkəl/ *adjective* **1** THEATRE [**always before noun**] relating to the theatre *theatrical make-up* **2** BEHAVIOUR doing and saying things in a very obvious way that is intended to make people notice you

theft /θeft/ *noun* [C, U] the action or crime of stealing something *car theft*

O➡**their** /ðeəʳ/ *determiner* **1** OF A GROUP belonging to or relating to a group of people, animals, or things that have already been talked about *It was their problem, not mine.* **2** HIS/HER used to refer to what belongs to or relates to a person when you want to avoid saying 'his' or 'her' or when you do not know if the person is male or female *Did this person give their name?*

O➡**theirs** /ðeəz/ *pronoun* the things that belong or relate to a group of people, animals, or things that have already been talked about *I think she's a relation of theirs.*

O➡**them** *strong form* /ðem/ *weak form* /ðəm/ *pronoun* **1** GROUP used after a verb or preposition to refer to a group of people, animals, or things that have already been talked about *I'm looking for my keys - have you seen them?* **2** HIM/HER used after a verb or preposition to refer to a person when you want to avoid saying 'him' or 'her' or when you do not know if the person is male or female *When each passenger arrives we ask them to fill in a form.*

WORD PARTNERS FOR ***theme***

a theme **runs through** sth • the **central/main** theme • a **recurring** theme • the theme **of** sth • **on** the theme **of** sth

theme /θiːm/ *noun* **1** [C] the subject of a book, film, speech, etc *The **theme of** loss **runs through** most of his novels.* **2 theme music/song/tune** MUSIC the music that is played at the beginning and end of a particular television or radio programme

ˈtheme ˌpark *noun* [C] a park with entertainments, such as games, machines to ride on, restaurants, etc, that are all based on one idea

O➡**themselves** /ðəmˈselvz/ *pronoun* **1** REFLEXIVE the reflexive form of the pronoun 'they' *They're both 16 - they're old enough to look after themselves.* **2** EMPHASIS used to emphasize the pronoun 'they' or the particular group of people you are referring to *They've decided to run the club themselves.* **3 (all) by themselves** alone or without anyone else's help *The kids arranged the party all by themselves.* **4 (all) to themselves** for their use only *They had the whole campsite to themselves.*

O➡**then¹** /ðen/ *adverb* **1** TIME at that time *Call me tomorrow - I'll have time to speak then.* ○ *Tim and I were at school together, but I haven't seen him **since then**.* **2** NEXT next, or after something has happened *She trained as a teacher and then became a lawyer.* ○ *Let me finish my drink, then we'll go.* **3** SO so or because of that *Have a rest now, then you won't be tired this evening.* ○ *"My interview's at 9 o'clock." "You'll be catching an early train, then?"* **4** IN ADDITION used in order to add something to what you have just said *I've got two essays to write and then my science project to finish.* **5 now then/right then/okay then** used to introduce a question or a suggestion *Right then, what do you want to drink?*

then² /ðen/ *adjective* [**always before noun**] used to refer to something which was true in the past but which is not true now *the then Prime Minister Margaret Thatcher*

thence /ðens/ *adverb formal* from there *The oil is shipped to Panama and thence to Texan refineries.*

theology /θiˈɒlədʒi/ *noun* [U] RELIGION the study of religion and religious belief •**theological** /ˌθiːəˈlɒdʒɪkəl/ *adjective theological college*

theorem /ˈθɪərəm/ *noun* [C] MATHEMATICS (especially in maths) a formal statement that you can show to be true *a mathematical theorem*

theoretical /θɪəˈretɪkəl/ *adjective* **1** IDEAS based on the ideas that relate to a subject, not the practical uses of that subject *theoretical physics* **2** NOT PROVED related to an explanation that has not been proved

theoretically /θɪəˈretɪkəli/ *adverb* in a way that obeys some rules but is not likely *It is theoretically possible.*

T

theorist /ˈθɪərɪst/ *noun* [C] someone who develops ideas about the explanation for events *a political theorist*

theorize (*also UK* **-ise**) /ˈθɪəraɪz/ *verb* [I, T] to develop a set of ideas about something [+ that] *Investigators theorized that the crash was caused by engine failure.*

WORD PARTNERS FOR ***theory***

challenge/formulate/prove/test a theory • a **popular/plausible/new** theory • a theory **about** sth

O→**theory** /ˈθɪəri/ *noun* **1** IDEA [C] an idea or set of ideas that is intended to explain something *Darwin's theory of evolution* **2** PRINCIPLES [U] the set of principles on which a subject is based *economic theory* **3 in theory** If something is possible in theory, it should be possible but often it does not happen this way.

therapeutic /ˌθerəˈpjuːtɪk/ *adjective* **1** **HEALTH** helping to cure a disease or improve your health *the **therapeutic benefits** of massage* **2** helping you to feel happier and more relaxed *I find gardening very therapeutic.*

therapist /ˈθerəpɪst/ *noun* [C] **HEALTH** someone whose job is to treat a particular type of mental or physical illness *a speech therapist*

therapy /ˈθerəpi/ *noun* [C, U] **HEALTH** the work of treating mental or physical illness without using an operation *cancer therapy* ○ *She's now **in therapy** to help her deal with her alcohol problem.* ➲See also: **physical therapy**

O→**there¹** *strong form* /ðeəʳ/ *weak form* /ðəʳ/ *pronoun* **There is/are/was, etc** used to show that something exists or happens *There are three pubs in the village.* ○ *There's not much room in the back of the car.* ○ *There have been a lot of accidents on this road.* ○ *Is there any milk?*

O→**there²** /ðeəʳ/ *adverb* **1** PLACE in or at a particular place *We live in York because my wife works there.* ○ *I went to the party but I didn't know anyone there.* ○ *We'll never **get there*** (= arrive) *in time!* **2** DIRECTION used when you are pointing or looking at something in order to make someone look in the same direction *Put them in that box there.* ○ *Your bag's **over there** by the door.* **3** AVAILABLE present or available *They were all there - Mark, Jill, and the three kids.* ○ *That money is there for you if you need it.* **4** POINT at a particular point in a process or activity *Do you want to play another game or do you want to stop there?* ○ *Keep on trying - you'll **get there*** (= succeed) *in the end.* **5 there and then** If you do something there and then, you do it immediately. *I showed James the ring I liked and he bought it there and then.* **6 There you are/go. a** GIVING used when you are giving something to someone *Do you want a tissue? There you are.* **b** EMPHASIZING used to emphasize that you were right *There you go - I told you you'd win!*

thereabouts /ˈðeərəbaʊts/ *adverb mainly UK* near the number, amount, or time that has just been given *For this recipe you'll need 1kg of tomatoes, **or thereabouts**.*

thereafter /ˌðeəˈrɑːftəʳ/ *adverb formal* after a particular amount, time, or event *Faxes cost $1.20 for the first page, and 60 cents for each page thereafter.*

thereby /ˌðeəˈbaɪ/ *adverb formal* as a result of a particular action or event *The new dam will improve the water supply and thereby reduce hunger and disease.*

O→**therefore** /ˈðeəfɔːʳ/ *adverb* for that reason *The region has suffered severe flooding and tourists are therefore advised not to travel there.*

therein /ˌðeəˈrɪn/ *adverb formal* **1** in a particular document or place *We recommend that you study the report and the proposals contained therein.* **2 therein lies sth** because of the reason that has just been given *But the medicines are expensive, and therein lies the problem.*

thereof /ˌðeəˈrɒv/ *adverb formal* relating to what has just been said *It's gospel music, traditional country, jazz, and some strange combinations thereof.*

thermal /ˈθɜːməl/ *adjective* [always before noun] **1** **PHYSICS** relating to heat *thermal energy* **2** CLOTHES Thermal clothes are made to keep you warm. ***thermal underwear***

thermistor /θɜːˈmɪstəʳ/ *noun* [C] **PHYSICS** a device in which resistance (= the amount of electricity it allows to pass through) gets less as the temperature gets higher

thermo- /ˈθɜːməʊ-/ *prefix* **PHYSICS** relating to heat or temperature *a thermostat* (= a piece of equipment that controls temperature) ○ *a thermometer*

thermodynamics /ˌθɜːməʊdaɪˈnæmɪks/ *noun* [U] **PHYSICS** the part of physics that deals with the relationship between heat and other types of energy

thermometer /θəˈmɒmɪtəʳ/ *noun* [C] **HEALTH** a piece of equipment that measures the temperature of the air or of your body

thermoplastic /ˌθɜːməʊˈplæstɪk/ *adjective* **PHYSICS** Thermoplastic substances can be melted and formed into shapes which become hard, and then can be melted again.

Thermos /ˈθɜːmɒs/ *noun* [C] *trademark* a container that keeps hot liquids hot or cold liquids cold *(UK) a Thermos flask/ (US) a Thermos bottle* ➲See picture at **flask**

thermosetting /ˌθɜːməʊˈsetɪŋ/ *adjective* **PHYSICS** Thermosetting substances can be melted and formed into shapes which become hard and cannot be melted again.

thermostat /ˈθɜːməstæt/ *noun* [C] **PHYSICS** a piece of equipment that controls the temperature of something or of a place

thesaurus /θɪˈsɔːrəs/ *noun* [C] **LANGUAGE** a book in which words with similar meanings are put together in groups

O→**these** /ðiːz/ *pronoun, determiner plural of* this ➲See Common Learner Error at **that, this**

thesis /ˈθiːsɪs/ *noun* [C] *plural* **theses** /ˈθiːsiːz/ **1** **EDUCATION** a long piece of writing that you do as part of an advanced university course *a master's/PhD thesis* **2** *formal* a theory that is suggested and can then be argued with or agreed with *That is the central thesis of the book.*

T

O→ **they** /ðeɪ/ *pronoun* **1** GROUP used as the subject of the verb when referring to a group of people, animals, or things that have already been talked about *I saw Kate and Nigel yesterday - they came over for dinner.* ○ *"Have you seen my car keys?" "They're on the kitchen table."* **2** PERSON used to refer to a person when you want to avoid saying 'he' or 'she' or when you do not know if the person is male or female *Someone I met at a party said they knew you.* **3** PEOPLE people in general *They say that breaking a mirror brings you seven years' bad luck.*

O→ **they'd** /ðeɪd/ **1** THEY HAD *short for* they had *They'd just moved in when I saw them.* **2** THEY WOULD *short for* they would *They'd like to take us out to dinner.*

O→ **they'll** /ðeɪl/ *short for* they will *They'll be in Scotland next week.*

O→ **they're** /ðeəʳ/ *short for* they are *They're both from Washington.*

they've /ðeɪv/ *short for* they have *They've got three children - two girls and a boy.*

O→ **thick¹** /θɪk/ *adjective* **1** DISTANCE Something that is thick is larger than usual between its opposite sides. *a thick slice of meat* ○ *a thick layer of snow* **2 10cm/2m, etc thick** being 10cm/2m, etc thick *a piece of wood 2cm thick* **3** LARGE AMOUNT growing very close together and in large amounts *thick, dark hair* **4** SMOKE Thick smoke, cloud, or fog is difficult to see through. *Thick, black smoke was pouring out of the chimney.* **5** LIQUID A thick substance or liquid has very little water in it and does not flow easily. *Stir the sauce over a low heat until thick.* **6** STUPID *UK informal* not intelligent **7 be thick with sth** If something is thick with a particular substance, it is covered in or full of that substance. *The air was thick with petrol fumes.* **8 thick and fast** quickly and in large numbers *Calls were coming in thick and fast by the end of the programme.* ➲See also: have (a) thick **skin¹**

thick² /θɪk/ *noun* **1 be in the thick of sth** to be involved in a situation at the point where there is most activity *He loves being in the thick of the action.* **2 through thick and thin** If you support or stay with someone through thick and thin, you always support or stay with them in easy and difficult situations. *She'd stuck by* (= stayed with) *Neil through thick and thin.*

thicken /ˈθɪkᵊn/ *verb* [I, T] to become thicker, or to make something thicker *Boil the sauce until it thickens.*

thickly /ˈθɪkli/ *adverb* in thick pieces, or in a thick layer *toast **thickly spread** with butter*

thickness /ˈθɪknəs/ *noun* [C, U] the distance between the opposite sides of something

thick-skinned /ˌθɪkˈskɪnd/ *adjective* If someone is thick-skinned, they do not get upset when other people criticize them.

thief /θiːf/ *noun* [C] *plural* **thieves** /θiːvz/ someone who steals things *a car thief* ○ *Thieves stole $500,000 worth of computer equipment.*

thigh /θaɪ/ *noun* [C] **ANATOMY** the top part of your leg above your knee ➲See colour picture **The Body** on page Centre 13

thimble /ˈθɪmbl/ *noun* [C] **DT** a small metal or plastic object that you use to protect your finger when you are sewing

O→ **thin¹** /θɪn/ *adjective* **thinner, thinnest 1** DISTANCE Something that is thin is smaller than usual between its opposite sides. *a thin slice of ham* ○ *The walls are very thin.* **2** PERSON A thin person or animal has very little fat on their body. **3** LIQUID A thin substance or liquid has a lot of water in it and flows easily. *thin soup* **4** AMOUNT having only a small number of people or a small amount of something *His hair is going thin on top.* **5** AIR Thin air does not have enough oxygen in it. **6 wear thin** ANNOYED If your patience wears thin, you become less and less patient with someone who is annoying you. REPEATED If a joke or explanation wears thin, it becomes less effective because it has been used too much. ➲See also: disappear/vanish into thin **air¹**, be thin on the **ground¹**, through **thick²** and thin

thin² /θɪn/ *verb* [T] **thinning**, *past* **thinned** to make a substance less thick, often by adding a liquid to it

thin out *phrasal verb* If a large number of people or things thin out, they become fewer in number.

O→ **thing** /θɪŋ/ *noun* **1** OBJECT [C] used to refer to an object without saying its name *How do I switch this thing off?* ○ *I need to get a few things in town.* **2** PERSON [C] used to refer to a person or animal when you are expressing your feelings towards them *You look tired, you poor thing.* **3** IDEA [C] used to refer to an idea, event, or activity *I can't believe Nick would say such a thing!* ○ *Meeting Nina was the best thing that's ever happened to me.* **4 for one thing** used to give a reason for something *You can't give Amy that shirt - for one thing it's too small for her.* **5 the thing is** *informal* used to introduce a problem which relates to something that you have just said *I'd love to go out tonight, but the thing is, I've got to finish my report.* **6 a thing** used instead of 'anything' in order to emphasize what you are saying *I haven't got a thing to wear!* **7 have a thing about sth/sb** *informal* to like or dislike something or someone very much *He's got a thing about blonde women.* **8 it's a good thing** *informal* If it is a good thing that something happened, it is lucky that it happened. [+ (that)] *It's a good thing that Jo was there to help you.* **9 first/last thing** *informal* at the beginning/end of the day *I'll phone him first thing and tell him I can't come.* ○ *She likes a glass of milk last thing at night.* **10 be sb's thing** *informal* If an activity or subject is someone's thing, they are very interested in it and like doing it. *Jogging's just not my thing - I prefer team sports.* **11 the best/greatest thing since sliced bread** *humorous* extremely good *When I first got this computer I thought it was the best thing since sliced bread.*

things /θɪŋz/ *noun* [plural] **1** SITUATIONS what is happening in your life *Don't worry - things will get better soon.* **2** OBJECTS the objects that you own *I'll just gather my things and then I'll be ready.* **3 be hearing/seeing things** to imagine that you can hear or see things that do not exist

T

thingy /ˈθɪŋi/ *noun* [C] *UK informal* used to refer to something or someone when you cannot remember their name *We ate that beef thingy for lunch.*

O-**think**[1] /θɪŋk/ *verb past* **thought 1** OPINION [I, T] to have an opinion about something or someone *Do you think it's going to rain?* [+ (that)] *I don't think that Emma will get the job* (= I believe she will not get it). ○ *What did you* ***think of*** *the film?* ○ *What do you* ***think about*** *modern art?* **2** CONSIDER [I] to consider an idea or a problem *He thought for a few seconds before answering.* ○ *You should* ***think about*** *where you want to live.* **3** EXPECT [I, T] to believe that something is true, or to expect that something will happen, although you are not sure *I think she's called Joanna.* ○ *"Does this train stop at Oxford?" "Yes, I* ***think so.****"* [+ (that)] *I never thought that I would see Steven again.* **4 think about/of doing sth** to consider doing something *I'm thinking of moving to Sydney.* ○ *We thought about getting married, but decided not to.* **5 think about/of sb/sth** to use your mind to imagine a situation *I'm sorry I can't be at the wedding, but I'll be thinking of you.* **6 think of sth** to use your imagination and intelligence to produce an idea, a solution to a problem, or an answer to a question *When did you first think of the idea?* **7 think a lot of sb/sth** to admire someone, or to believe that something is good quality *Simon thinks a lot of you, you know.* **8 not think much of sb/sth** to not like someone, or to believe that something is not good quality *I don't think much of the food here.* **9 I think** used to introduce a suggestion or explanation in order to be polite [+ (that)] *It's getting late - I think that we should go.* **10 Who would have thought...?** used to express how surprising something is [+ (that)] *Who would have thought that buying a house could take so long!* ➲See also: think the **world**[1] of sb **11 think outside the box** to use new ideas instead of traditional ideas when you think about something

COMMON LEARNER ERROR

think about or think of?

Think about someone/something means to have thoughts in your mind about a person or thing, or to consider them.

I was thinking about my mother.

I thought about the question before answering.

~~*I thought the question before answering.*~~

Think of/about something/someone also means to have an opinion about something or someone.

What do you think of/about the colour?

~~*What do you think the colour?*~~

Think of doing something means to consider the possibility of doing something.

We are thinking of having a party.

~~*We are thinking to have a party.*~~

think back *phrasal verb* to remember something that happened in the past *I* ***thought back to*** *the time when I was living in Toronto.*

think sth out *phrasal verb* to consider all the possible details of something *The scheme was well thought out.*

think sth over *phrasal verb* to consider an idea or plan carefully before making a decision

think sth through *phrasal verb* to carefully consider the possible results of doing something

think sth up *phrasal verb* to produce a new idea or plan *I don't want to go tonight and I'm trying to think up an excuse.*

think[2] /θɪŋk/ *noun UK* **have a think** to consider something carefully *Have a think about it and then tell me what you've decided.*

thinker /ˈθɪŋkəʳ/ *noun* [C] someone who considers important subjects or produces new ideas *a political/religious thinker*

WORD PARTNERS FOR ***thinking***

the thinking **behind/on** sth • the **current** thinking

thinking /ˈθɪŋkɪŋ/ *noun* [U] **1** CONSIDER when you use your mind to consider something *This problem requires careful thinking.* **2** OPINION someone's ideas or opinions *The book discusses the impact of Christian thinking on western society.* ➲See also: **wishful thinking**

ˈ**think ˌtank** *noun* [C] a group of people who advise the government or an organization about particular subjects and who suggest new ideas

thinly /ˈθɪnli/ *adverb* **1** SIZE in thin pieces, or in a thin layer *She sliced the bread thinly.* **2** AMOUNT with only a small number of people or things *thinly populated areas*

third[1] /θɜːd/ 3rd written as a word

O-**third**[2] /θɜːd/ *noun* [C] **1** one of three equal parts of something; ⅓ **2 a third EDUCATION** in the UK, one of the lowest exam results you can achieve at the end of a university course

thirdly /ˈθɜːdli/ *adverb* used in order to introduce the third thing in a list

ˌ**third ˈparty** *noun* [C] someone who is not one of the two main people or groups that are involved in a situation

the ˌthird ˈperson *noun* **LANGUAGE** the form of a verb or pronoun that is used when referring to the person or thing being spoken about or described. For example 'she' and 'they' are third person pronouns.

the ˌThird ˈWorld *noun* **ECONOMICS** the countries in Africa, Asia, and South America, which do not have well-developed economies

thirst /θɜːst/ *noun* **1** [U, no plural] the feeling that you want to drink something *I had a long, cold drink to* ***quench*** *my* ***thirst*** (= stop me feeling thirsty). **2 a thirst for sth** a strong wish for something *a thirst for adventure*

O-**thirsty** /ˈθɜːsti/ *adjective* wanting or needing a drink *I felt really hot and thirsty after my run.* •**thirstily** *adverb*

O-**thirteen** /θɜːˈtiːn/ the number 13 •**thirteenth** 13th written as a word

O-**thirty** /ˈθɜːti/ **1** the number 30 **2 the thirties** the years from 1930 to 1939 **3 be in your thirties** to be between the ages of 30 and 39 •**thirtieth** 30th written as a word

O-**this**[1] /ðɪs/ *determiner plural* **these 1** ALREADY TALKED ABOUT used to refer to something that you have already talked about *Most people don't agree with this decision.* ○ *How did you* *hear about this course?* **2** [NEAR] used to refer to something or someone that is near you or that you are pointing to *How much does this CD cost?* ○ *David gave me these earrings for my birthday.* **3** [TIME] used to refer to the present week, month, year, etc or the one that comes next *I'll see you this evening.* ○ *Kate and Nigel are getting married this June.* **4** [NOW TALKING ABOUT] *informal* used to refer to a particular person or thing that you are going to talk about *We went to this really great club last night.* ➲See Common Learner Error at **that** ➲See also: be out of this **world**[1]

COMMON LEARNER ERROR

this/that or **these/those?**

Remember **this** and **that** are used before a singular noun. **These** and **those** are used before a plural noun.

Look at this photo.

Look at these photos.

Can you pass me that book please?

Can you pass me those books please?

O‐**this**[2] /ðɪs/ *pronoun plural* **these 1** [ALREADY TALKED ABOUT] used to refer to something that you have already talked about *When did this happen?* ○ *This is the best news I've heard all week!* **2** [NEAR] used to refer to something or someone that is near you or that you are pointing to *Try some of this - it's delicious.* ○ *Are these your keys?* ○ *This is my girlfriend, Beth.* **3** [SAY/ASK WHO] used to say or ask who someone is when speaking on the telephone, radio, etc *"Hello, is this Julie Hawkins?" "Yes, who's this?"* **4 this and that** different things which are not very important *"What are you doing today?" "Oh, just this and that."*

O‐**this**[3] /ðɪs/ *adverb* used when describing the size, amount, or state of something or someone *I need a piece of wood this big.* ○ *I've never seen her this angry.*

thistle /ˈθɪsl/ *noun* [C] a wild plant with purple flowers and sharp points

THNQ *informal* **INTERNET** *written abbeviation for* thank you: used in emails and text messages

thong /θɒŋ/ *noun* [C] **1** [UNDERWEAR] a piece of underwear or the bottom part of a bikini (= a piece of clothing with two parts that women wear for swimming) which does not cover the bottom **2** [SHOE] *US* a flip flop

thorax /ˈθɔːræks/ *noun* [C] **1 ANATOMY, BIOLOGY** in humans and animals, the middle part of the body below the neck and above the waist **2 BIOLOGY** in insects, the middle part of the body, to which its legs and wings are attached •**thoracic** /θɔːˈræsɪk/ *adjective*

thorn /θɔːn/ *noun* [C] **BIOLOGY** a small, sharp point on the stem of a plant

thorny /ˈθɔːni/ *adjective* **1 BIOLOGY** covered in thorns **2** [PROBLEM] A thorny problem, question, subject, etc is difficult to deal with.

thorough /ˈθʌrə/ (US) /ˈθɜːrəʊ/ *adjective* careful and covering every detail *The government has promised a thorough investigation of the matter.* •**thoroughness** *noun* [U]

thoroughbred /ˈθʌrəbred/ *noun* [C] **SPORT** a horse especially bred for racing

thoroughly /ˈθʌrəli/ *adverb* **1** [CAREFULLY] very carefully *Wash the spinach thoroughly before cooking.* **2** [VERY] very, or very much *We thoroughly enjoyed ourselves.*

O‐**those** /ðəʊz/ *pronoun, determiner plural of* that ➲See Common Learner Error at **that, this**

O‐**though**[1] /ðəʊ/ *conjunction* **1** [INTRODUCE FACT] used to introduce a fact or opinion that makes the other part of the sentence seem surprising *And though she's quite small, she's very strong.* ○ *Nina didn't phone,* ***even though*** *she said she would.* **2** [BUT] but *They're coming next week, though I don't know when.* ○ *The restaurant serves good, though extremely expensive, food.*

though[2] /ðəʊ/ *adverb* used to add a new fact or opinion which changes what you have just said *Okay, I'll come to the party - I'm not staying late though.*

WORD PARTNERS FOR ***thought***

give sth some thought • **have** a thought • a **secret/sobering/terrible** thought

O‐**thought**[1] /θɔːt/ *noun* **1** [IDEA] [C] an idea or opinion *Do you have any* ***thoughts about/on*** *where you want to spend Christmas?* [+ **of** + **doing sth**] *The thought of seeing her again filled him with happiness.* ○ *informal* "Why don't we invite Ben?" "***That's a thought*** (= That's a good idea)." **2** [THINKING] [U] the activity of thinking, or when you think about something carefully *She sat staring at the picture,* ***deep in thought.*** ○ *You'll need to* ***give*** *the matter* ***some thought.*** **3** [CARE] [**no plural**] when you do something that shows you care about someone *Thanks for the card - it was a really kind thought.* **4** [SET OF IDEAS] [U] a set of ideas about a particular subject *The book examines his influence on recent political thought.* **5 spare a thought for sb** to think about someone who is in a bad situation *Spare a thought for all the people who have lost their homes.* ➲See also: **school** of thought, **second thought**

thought[2] /θɔːt/ *past of* think

thoughtful /ˈθɔːtfᵊl/ *adjective* **1** [QUIET] quiet because you are thinking about something *You look thoughtful.* **2** [KIND] kind and always thinking about how you can help other people *Thank you for the card - it was very* ***thoughtful of*** *you.* •**thoughtfully** *adverb She gazed thoughtfully into the distance.* •**thoughtfulness** *noun* [U]

thoughtless /ˈθɔːtləs/ *adjective* not considering how your actions and words might upset someone else *I should have called her to say we'd be late - it was a bit thoughtless of me.* •**thoughtlessly** *adverb*

thought-provoking /ˈθɔːtprəˌvəʊkɪŋ/ *adjective* making you think a lot about a subject *a thought-provoking book/film*

O‐**thousand** /ˈθaʊzᵊnd/ **1** the number 1000 **2 thousands** *informal* a lot *She tried on* ***thousands of*** *dresses but didn't like any of them.*

thousandth[1] /ˈθaʊzᵊndθ/ 1000th written as a word

thousandth[2] /ˈθaʊzᵊndθ/ *noun* [C] one of a thousand equal parts of something; $^{1}/_{1000}$; .001 *a thousandth of a second*

T

thrash /θræʃ/ *verb* **1** HIT [T] to hit a person or animal several times as a punishment **2** MOVE [I] to move from side to side in a violent way *He was screaming in pain and* ***thrashing around*** *on the floor.* **3** DEFEAT [T] *informal* to win against someone very easily
thrash sth out *phrasal verb* to discuss a plan or problem in detail until you reach an agreement or find a solution

thrashing /ˈθræʃɪŋ/ *noun* [C] **1** DEFEAT *informal* when you win against someone very easily **2** HIT *old-fashioned* when someone hits a person or animal several times as a punishment

thread¹ /θred/ *noun* **1** MATERIAL [C, U] a long, thin piece of cotton, wool, etc that is used for sewing *a needle and thread* **2** CONNECTION [C] the connection between different events or different parts of a story or discussion *By that point I'd* ***lost the thread*** *of the conversation.* **3** **INTERNET** a group of pieces of writing on the Internet in which people discuss one subject ➲See Extra help page **The Web and the Internet** on page Centre 37.

thread² /θred/ *verb* [T] **1** **DT** **thread a needle** to push thread through the hole in a needle **2** **thread your way through, between, etc** to move carefully through a crowded place, changing direction in order to avoid people or things

threadbare /ˈθredbeəʳ/ *adjective* Threadbare material or clothes are very thin because they have been used too much. *a threadbare carpet*

WORD PARTNERS FOR ***threat***

2 a threat **to** sb/sth • **pose** a threat • a **potential** threat • a **security/terrorist** threat

O→**threat** /θret/ *noun* **1** HARM [C] when someone says they will kill or hurt you, or cause problems for you if you do not do what they want *a* ***death threat*** ○ *I was scared he would* ***carry out*** *his* ***threat*** (= do what he said he would do). **2** DAMAGE [C] someone or something that is likely to cause harm or damage [**usually singular**] *a* ***threat to*** *the environment* ○ *Smoking* ***poses*** (= is) *a serious* ***threat*** *to your health.* **3** POSSIBILITY [**no plural**] the possibility that something bad will happen *the threat of invasion*

O→**threaten** /ˈθretᵊn/ *verb* **1** HARM [T] to tell someone that you will kill or hurt them, or cause problems for them if they do not do what you want *He* ***threatened*** *the staff* ***with*** *a gun and demanded money.* [**+ to do sth**] *He threatened to report her to the police.* **2** DAMAGE [T] to be likely to cause harm or damage to something or someone *His knee problem is threatening his cycling career.* **3** HAPPEN [I] If something bad threatens to happen, it is likely to happen. [**+ to do sth**] *The conflict threatened to spread to neighbouring countries.* •**threatening** *adjective* ***threatening behaviour*** •**threateningly** *adverb*

O→**three** /θriː/ the number 3

three-dimensional /ˌθriːdɪˈmenʃᵊnᵊl/ (*also* **3-D** /θriːˈdiː/) *adjective* **DT, ART** having length, depth, and height *three-dimensional computer graphics*

threshold /ˈθreʃhəʊld/ *noun* **1** LEVEL [C] the level at which something starts to happen *He had a low* ***boredom threshold.*** **2** **on the threshold of sth** at the start of a new and important time or development *We're on the threshold of a new era in European relations.* **3** ENTRANCE [C] the floor of an entrance

threw /θruː/ *past tense of* throw

thrift /θrɪft/ *noun* [U] careful use of money so that you do not spend too much •**thrifty** *adjective*

ˈthrift ˌshop *US* (*UK* **charity shop**) *noun* [C] a shop which sells goods given by the public, especially clothes, to make money for a particular charity

WORD PARTNERS FOR ***thrill***

feel a thrill • **get** a thrill **from/out of** doing sth • a **big/great** thrill • the thrill **of** (doing) sth • a thrill **seeker**

thrill¹ /θrɪl/ *noun* [C] a strong feeling of excitement and pleasure *It was a* ***big thrill*** *meeting the stars of the show.* [**+ of + doing sth**] *the* ***thrill of*** *winning a competition*

thrill² /θrɪl/ *verb* [T] to make someone feel excited and happy *Ballesteros thrilled the golf world with his performance.*

thrilled /θrɪld/ *adjective* very excited and pleased *She was thrilled with your present.*

thriller /ˈθrɪləʳ/ *noun* [C] **LITERATURE** a book or film with an exciting story, often about crime

thrilling /ˈθrɪlɪŋ/ *adjective* very exciting *a thrilling game*

thrive /θraɪv/ *verb* [I] to grow very well, or to become very healthy or successful *The business is thriving.* ○ *He seems to* ***thrive on*** *hard work.* •**thriving** *adjective a* ***thriving economy***

throat /θrəʊt/ *noun* [C] **1** **ANATOMY** the back part of your mouth and the passages inside your neck *a* ***sore throat*** **2** **ANATOMY** the front of your neck *He grabbed her round the throat.* ➲See colour picture **The Body** on page Centre 13 **3** **clear your throat** to cough once so that you can speak more clearly

throb /θrɒb/ *verb* [I] **throbbing**, *past* **throbbed** **1** PART OF THE BODY If a part of your body throbs, you feel pain in it in a series of regular beats. *My head was throbbing.* **2** SOUND OR MOVEMENT to make a strong, regular sound or movement *The whole house* ***throbbed with*** *the music.* •**throb** *noun* [C] *the throb of the engine*

throes /θrəʊz/ *noun* **in the throes of sth** in a difficult or unpleasant situation *a country in the throes of war*

thrombosis /θrɒmˈbəʊsɪs/ *noun* [C] *plural* **thromboses** **HEALTH** when the flow of blood in the body is stopped by a clot (= solid piece) of blood

throne /θrəʊn/ *noun* **1** [C] the special chair that a king or queen sits on **2** **POLITICS** **the throne** the position of being king or queen *He* ***came to the throne*** *in 1936.*

throng¹ /θrɒŋ/ *noun* [C] *literary* a large group of people

throng² /θrɒŋ/ *verb* [I, T] to be or go somewhere in very large numbers *The street was* ***thronged with*** *shoppers and tourists.*

throttle¹ /ˈθrɒtl/ *verb* [T] to press someone's throat tightly so they cannot breathe

throttle² /ˈθrɒtl/ *noun* [C] the part of a vehicle that controls how much fuel or power goes to the engine

O-■ **through¹** /θruː/ *preposition* **1** ONE SIDE TO ANOTHER from one end or side of something to the other *The River Seine flows through Paris.* ○ *The sun was shining through the window.* ○ *She cut through the wire.* **2** START TO END from the start to the end of something *He worked through the night.* ○ *The phone rang halfway through the programme.* **3** BECAUSE OF because of someone or something, or with someone's help *I got the job through my mum's friend.* ○ *He became ill through eating undercooked meat.* **4** UNTIL *US* (*UK* **to**) from a particular time until and including another time *The store is open Monday through Friday.*

O-■ **through²** /θruː/ *adverb* **1** FROM ONE SIDE TO ANOTHER from one end or side to another *He opened the door and walked through.* **2 read/think/talk, etc sth through** to read, think, talk to someone, etc very carefully about something from the start to the end *I've thought it through and decided not to take the job.* **3** TELEPHONE connected to someone by telephone *I tried to phone David but I couldn't* ***get through.*** ○ *Can you* ***put*** *me* ***through*** *to the manager, please?*

through³ /θruː/ *adjective* **1 be through with sth** *informal* to have finished using something or doing something *Let me know when you're through with the iron.* **2 be through (with sb)** *informal* to not have a relationship with someone any more **3** [**always before noun**] *UK* A through train goes all the way from one place to another place without the passenger having to change trains.

O-■ **throughout** /θruˈaʊt/ *adverb, preposition* **1** EVERYWHERE in every part of a place *The same laws apply throughout much of Europe.* ○ *The house was painted pink throughout.* **2** DURING during the whole of a period of time *He yawned throughout the performance.*

O-■ **throw¹** /θrəʊ/ *verb* [T] *past tense* **threw**, *past participle* **thrown** **1** THROUGH THE AIR to make something move through the air by pushing it out of your hand *Amy* ***threw*** *the ball* ***to*** *the dog.* ○ *He* ***threw*** *the book* ***at*** *the wall.* [+ **two objects**] *Throw me a chocolate.* ○ *How far can you throw?* **2 throw sth in/on, etc** to put something somewhere quickly and without thinking about it *He threw his clothes on the floor and got into bed.* **3 throw sth around/down/on, etc** to suddenly and quickly move your body or a part of your body *She threw her arms around the child.* ○ *Gabriela threw herself onto the bed and started to cry.* **4 throw sb from/forward, etc** to make someone move somewhere suddenly or fall down [**often passive**] *The bus suddenly stopped and we were thrown forward.* **5** CONFUSE to make someone feel shocked or confused *It threw me completely when he asked me to marry him.* **6** LIGHT to make light or shadows (= dark shapes) appear on something *The trees threw shadows across the road.* ➲See also: throw **caution**¹ to the wind, throw sb in at the deep **end**¹, throw down the **gauntlet**, throw in the **towel**, throw your **weight** around

throw sth away *phrasal verb* **1** GET RID OF to get rid of something that you do not want any more *He read the magazine and then threw it away.* ➲See colour picture **Phrasal Verbs** on page Centre 16 **2** WASTE OPPORTUNITY to waste a skill or opportunity *You've spent three years studying - don't throw it all away.*

throw sth in *phrasal verb* to add something extra when you sell something and not increase the price *They're selling computers with a free printer thrown in.*

throw sth out *phrasal verb* to get rid of something that you do not want any more *I must throw some of my old clothes out.*

throw sb out *phrasal verb* to force someone to leave *He was thrown out of school for taking drugs.*

throw (sth) up *phrasal verb informal* **HEALTH** to vomit

throw sth up *phrasal verb* to produce new problems or ideas *The meeting threw up some interesting ideas.*

throw² /θrəʊ/ *noun* [C] when you throw something *a throw of the dice*

throwback /ˈθrəʊbæk/ *noun* [C] something that is like something of the same type in the past *Her style of playing is* ***a throwback to*** *the early days of jazz.*

thru /θruː/ *adjective, adverb, preposition mainly US informal another spelling of* through, used in signs and advertisements

thrust¹ /θrʌst/ *verb past* **thrust** **thrust sth behind/into/through, etc** to push something somewhere suddenly and with force *She thrust a letter into my hand and told me to read it.*

thrust sth on/upon sb *phrasal verb* to force someone to accept or deal with something [**often passive**] *Fatherhood had been thrust on him.*

thrust² /θrʌst/ *noun* **1** **PHYSICS** [C, U] a strong push or the power used to push something forward **2 the thrust of sth** the main part or ideas of what someone says or does *The main thrust of our work involves helping victims of crime.*

thud /θʌd/ *noun* [C] the sound that is made when something heavy falls or hits something else *There was a thud as he fell on the floor.* •**thud** *verb* [I] **thudding**, *past* **thudded**

thug /θʌg/ *noun* [C] an unpleasant person who behaves violently

thumb¹ /θʌm/ *noun* [C] **1** **ANATOMY** the short, thick finger on the side of your hand that can touch the top of all your other fingers ➲See colour picture **The Body** on page Centre 13 **2 have a green thumb** *US* (*UK* **have green fingers**) to be good at gardening and making plants grow well **3 be under sb's thumb** If you are under someone's thumb, they control you completely. **4 stick/stand out like a sore thumb** to be very different from all the other people or things around *I was the only one in uniform and I stuck out like a sore thumb.* ➲See also: a **rule**¹ of thumb

thumb² /θʌm/ *verb* ➲See: thumb your **nose**¹ at sth/sb

thumb through sth *phrasal verb* to quickly turn the pages of a book or magazine

T

thumbtack /ˈθʌmtæk/ *US* (*UK* **drawing pin**) *noun* [C] a pin with a wide, flat top, used for fastening pieces of paper to a wall

thump /θʌmp/ *verb* **1** HIT [T] *UK* to hit someone with your fist (= closed hand) **2** NOISE [I, T] to hit something and make a noise *She thumped the tambourine.* **3** HEART [I] If your heart thumps, it beats very quickly because you are excited or frightened. •**thump** *noun* [C]

WORD PARTNERS FOR ***thunder***

a **clap/crack/crash/roll/rumble** of thunder • thunder **rumbles/rolls** • thunder **and lightning**

thunder¹ /ˈθʌndəʳ/ *noun* [U] the loud noise in the sky that you hear during a storm ***thunder and lightning***

thunder² /ˈθʌndəʳ/ *verb* **1 it thunders** When it thunders during a storm, a loud noise comes from the sky. **2 thunder along/down/through, etc** to move in a way that makes a deep, loud, continuous sound *Traffic thunders through the village all day.*

thunderous /ˈθʌndᵊrəs/ *adjective* extremely loud *the* ***thunderous roar*** *of the aircraft's engine*

thunderstorm /ˈθʌndəstɔːm/ *noun* [C] a storm that has thunder (= loud noise) and lightning (= sudden flashes of light in the sky)

Thursday /ˈθɜːzdeɪ/ (*written abbreviation* **Thur, Thurs**) *noun* [C, U] the day of the week after Wednesday and before Friday

thus /ðʌs/ *adverb formal* **1** SHOWING RESULT used after saying a fact to introduce what then happened as a result *The guard fell asleep, thus allowing Bates to escape.* **2** IN THIS WAY in this way *They limit the number of people allowed into the forest, thus preventing damage to the trails.*

thwart /θwɔːt/ *verb* [T] to prevent someone from doing what they have planned to do

thyme /taɪm/ *noun* [U] **FOOD** a herb used in cooking

thyristor /θaɪˈrɪstəʳ/ *noun* [C] **PHYSICS** a device, usually a semiconductor, that is used as a switch to control the amount of electricity passing through a particular point

thyroid /ˈθaɪrɔɪd/ *noun* [C] **ANATOMY, BIOLOGY** an organ in the neck that produces a substance that helps your body to grow and develop

thyroxine /θaɪˈrɒksɪn/ *noun* [U] **BIOLOGY** the main hormone produced by the thyroid gland. It increases metabolism (= the changing of food into energy) and in this way, makes the body grow and develop.

TIA **INTERNET** *internet abbreviation for* thanks in advance: used in an email when you have asked someone for something

tibia /ˈtɪbiə/ *noun* [C] **ANATOMY** the thick inside bone in a person's leg, between the knee and the foot

tick¹ /tɪk/ *noun* [C] **1** CLOCK the sound that some clocks or watches make every second **2** MARK *UK* (*US* **check**) a mark (✓) that shows something is correct or has been done **3** INSECT a small insect that sucks the blood of animals **4** TIME *UK informal* a short time *Wait a tick!*

tick² /tɪk/ *verb* **1** CLOCK [I] If a clock or watch ticks, it makes a sound every second. **2** MARK [T] *UK* to mark something with a tick **3 what makes sb tick** *informal* the reasons for someone's behaviour

tick away/by *phrasal verb* If seconds or minutes tick away or by, they pass. *With the final seconds ticking away, Milan scored a goal.*

tick sth off *phrasal verb UK* (*US* **check sth off**) to put a small mark next to something on a list to show that you have dealt with it

tick sb off *phrasal verb* **1** CRITICIZE *UK informal* to tell someone that they have done something wrong and that you are angry about it *I got ticked off for not going to the meeting.* **2** ANNOY *US informal* to annoy someone

tick over/along *phrasal verb UK* If a business or system ticks over, it continues to work but makes little progress. *Carlton managed to* ***keep the business ticking over.***

WORD PARTNERS FOR ***ticket***

book/buy/get/purchase a ticket • a ticket **for** sth

ticket /ˈtɪkɪt/ *noun* [C] **1** TRAVEL OR ENTERTAINMENT a small piece of paper that shows you have paid to do something, for example travel on a bus, watch a film, etc *a lottery ticket* ○ *plane tickets* **2** **LAW** a piece of paper that orders you to pay money because you have put your car in an illegal place, driven too fast, etc *a parking ticket* ➲See also: **round-trip ticket, season ticket**

tickle /ˈtɪkl/ *verb* **1** TOUCH LIGHTLY [T] to touch someone lightly with your fingers, in order to make them laugh **2** PART OF THE BODY [I, T] If a part of your body tickles, or if something tickles it, it feels uncomfortable and you want to rub it. *My nose is tickling.* **3** AMUSE [T] to make someone smile or laugh *I was very tickled by his comments.* •**tickle** *noun* [C]

tidal /ˈtaɪdᵊl/ *adjective* **GEOGRAPHY** relating to the regular rising and falling of the sea

ˈtidal ˌwave *noun* [C] **GEOGRAPHY** a very large wave that destroys things, often caused by an earthquake (= when the Earth shakes)

tidbit *US* (*UK* **titbit**) /ˈtɪdbɪt/ *noun* [C] a small piece of nice food, or an interesting piece of information

WORD PARTNERS FOR ***tide***

the tide **comes in/goes out** • the tide is **in/out** • **at high/at low** tide

tide¹ /taɪd/ *noun* **1** **GEOGRAPHY** [C] the regular rise and fall in the level of the sea ***high/low tide*** **2** [**no plural**] an increase in something that is developing *the* ***rising tide*** *of drug-related deaths*

tide² /taɪd/ *verb*

tide sb over (sth) *phrasal verb* to help someone through a difficult time, especially by giving them money

tidy¹ /ˈtaɪdi/ *adjective* **1** PLACE having everything in the right place and arranged in a good order *Her room was clean and tidy.* **2** PERSON liking to keep things in the correct place and arranged in a good order *I'm afraid I'm not very tidy.* ➲Opposite **untidy** •**tidily** *adverb* •**tidiness** *noun* [U]

tidy² /'taɪdi/ (*also* **tidy up**) *verb* [I, T] *UK* to make a place tidy *I'm tidying up before our guests arrive.*
tidy sth away *phrasal verb UK* to put things back in drawers, cupboards, etc after you have used them

O-w **tie¹** /taɪ/ *verb* **tying**, *past* **tied 1 tie sth to/together/around, etc** to fasten something with string, rope, etc *The dog was tied to a tree.* **2** [T] to make a knot in a piece of string, rope, etc *She tied the scarf.* ➲Opposite **untie 3 SPORT** [I] to have the same score as someone else at the end of a competition or game *Sweden **tied with** France in the winter sports competition.* ➲See also: tie the **knot**[1]
tie sb down *phrasal verb* to limit someone's freedom *I don't want to be tied down by having children.*
tie in *phrasal verb* If one idea or statement ties in with another one, they have some of the same information in them. *His story **ties in with** what Gemma told me.*
tie sb/sth up *phrasal verb* to tie a part of someone's body with a rope or something similar so they cannot move ➲Opposite **untie**
tie sth up *phrasal verb* to fasten something together using string, rope, etc
be tied up *phrasal verb* to be very busy and unable to speak to anyone, go anywhere, etc

WORD PARTNERS FOR ***tie***

2 **create/forge** ties • **cut/sever** (all) ties • **have** ties **with** sb/sth • **close/strong** ties • ties **between** sb **and** sb • ties **to/with** sb/sth

tie² /taɪ/ *noun* [C] **1** [CLOTHES] a long, thin piece of cloth that a man wears around his neck with a shirt ➲See colour picture **Clothes** on page Centre 9 **2** [CONNECTION] a relationship that connects you with a place, person, etc [**usually plural**] *The two countries have **close ties with** each other.* **3 SPORT** when a game or competition ends with two people or teams having the same score ➲See also: **bow tie**

tie-break /'taɪbreɪk/ *noun* [C] **SPORT** an extra part that is played when a game or competition ends in a tie, to decide who is the winner

tie-dye /'taɪdaɪ/ *verb* [T] **tie-dyeing**, *past tense* **tie-dyed**, *past participle* **tie-dyed DT** to give cloth a pattern of circles by tying it in knots before putting it in a dye (= substance which changes the colour of cloth) *There are pictures of us in the sixties wearing flares and tie-dyed T-shirts.*

tier /tɪəʳ/ *noun* [C] one of several rows or layers *the upper tier of seats in a stadium*

tiger /'taɪgəʳ/ *noun* [C] a large wild cat that has yellow fur with black lines on it

O-w **tight¹** /taɪt/ *adjective* **1** [FIRM] firm and difficult to move *Make sure the knot is tight.* **2** [CLOTHES] fitting your body very closely *a tight skirt* **3** [CONTROLLED] controlled and obeying all rules completely *tight security* ○ *They kept tight control of the school budget.* **4** [STRAIGHT] If cloth, wire, skin, etc is tight, it has been pulled so that it is straight or smooth. **5** [NOT MUCH] If money, time, or space is tight, there is only just enough of it. *We should get six people into the car but it will be tight.* •**tightly** *adverb* •**tightness** *noun* [U] ➲See also: keep a tight **rein** on sb/sth

tight² /taɪt/ *adverb* very firmly or closely *He held her tight.*

tighten /'taɪtᵊn/ *verb* [I, T] to become tighter or to make something become tighter *His hand tightened around her arm.* ➲See also: tighten your **belt**[1]
tighten sth up *phrasal verb* to make something become firmer and less easy to move *Tighten up the screws.*
tighten (sth) up *phrasal verb* to make a rule, system, or law more difficult to avoid *I think they should **tighten up** the laws **on** gun ownership.*

tightrope /'taɪtrəʊp/ *noun* [C] a rope high above the ground that a performer walks along at a circus (= show)

tights /taɪts/ *UK* (*US* **pantyhose**) *noun* [**plural**] a piece of women's clothing made of very thin material that covers the legs and bottom *a pair of black tights* ➲See colour picture **Clothes** on page Centre 9

tile /taɪl/ *noun* [C] one of the flat, square pieces that are used for covering roofs, floors, or walls •**tile** *verb* [T] *a tiled kitchen*

till¹ /tɪl/ *preposition, conjunction* until *The supermarket is open till midnight.* ○ *I lived with my parents till I was twenty.*

till² /tɪl/ *noun* [C] **1** [MACHINE] *UK* a machine that holds the money in a shop and shows how much you have to pay **2** [DRAWER] *US* a drawer where money is kept in a store

tilt /tɪlt/ *verb* [I, T] to move into a position where one end or side is higher than the other, or to make something move into this position *He tilted backwards on his chair.* •**tilt** *noun* [**no plural**]

timber /'tɪmbəʳ/ *noun* **1** [WOOD] [U] *UK* (*US* **lumber**) wood that is used for building **2** [TREE] [U] *US* trees that are grown to provide wood for building **3** [PIECE OF WOOD] [C] *UK* a large piece of wood *The roof was supported by timbers.*

O-w **time¹** /taɪm/ *noun* **1** [HOURS/YEARS ETC] [U] Time is what we measure in minutes, hours, days, etc. *He wants to **spend** more **time** with his family.* ○ ***Time** seems to **pass** so slowly when you're unhappy.* **2** [PARTICULAR POINT] [C, U] a particular point in the day or night ***What time** is it?* ○ ***What time** do you leave for school in the mornings?* ○ *Can you tell me the times of the trains to London, please?* ➲See Common Learner Error at **hour 3 it's time (for/to do sth)** used to say that something should happen or be done now *It's time to get up.* **4 in (good) time** early or at the right time *We arrived in time to catch the train.* **5 on time** not early or late *I got to school on time.* **6 can tell the time** to be able to know what time it is by looking at a clock or watch **7** [PERIOD] [**no plural**] a period of minutes, hours, years, etc *I lived in Switzerland for a **long time**.* ○ ***It takes time*** (= takes a long time) *to make friends at a new school.* **8 have time** to

T

have enough time to do something *Do you have time for a cup of coffee?* [+ **to do sth**] *I never have time to eat breakfast.* **9 in no time** very soon *We'll be home in no time.* **10** OCCASION [C] an occasion when something happens *Give me a call the* ***next time*** *you're in Seattle.* ○ *I can't remember the* ***last time*** *we went away.* ○ ***How many times*** *have you been to Germany?* **11 at the same time** If two things happen at the same time, they happen together. *We arrived at the same time.* **12 one, two, six, etc at a time** one, two, six, etc on one occasion *He carried the chairs, three at a time.* **13 time after time** again and again on repeated occasions **14 all the time a** OFTEN very often *"She's been late twice this week." "It happens all the time."* **b** WHOLE TIME during the whole of a period of time *He was ill all the time we were in Spain.* **15 three/eight/nine, etc times** used to say how much bigger, better, worse, etc one thing is than another thing *Ben earns three times more than me.* **16 in a day's/two months', etc time** a week, two months, etc from now *I have to go to the doctor again in a month's time.* **17 at times** sometimes *At times, I wish I didn't have to go to school.* **18 for the time being** for now but not permanently *I'm living with my parents for the time being.* **19** IN THE PAST [C] a period of time in the past *Did you enjoy your time in Japan?* **20 at one time** at a time in the past *At one time, you could drive without taking a driving test.* **21 before sb's time** before someone was born **22 from time to time** sometimes, but not often *I still see my ex-boyfriend from time to time.* **23 SPORT** [C] the amount of time that someone takes in a race *a winning time of three minutes* **24** IN A PLACE [U] the time in a particular place *The plane arrives at 20.50, New York time.* **25 be ahead of your time** to have new ideas a long time before other people think that way **26 behind the times** not fashionable or modern *Dad's a bit behind the times.* **27 bide your time** to wait for an opportunity to do something *She was biding her time until she could get her revenge.* **28 give sb a hard time** to criticize someone and make them feel guilty about something they have done *Ever since I missed the goal, the other players have been giving me a hard time.* **29 have no time for sb/sth** to have no respect for someone or something *I have no time for people who are racist.* **30 kill time** to do something while you are waiting for something else *I went shopping to kill some time before my job interview.* **31 play for time** *UK* to try to make something happen more slowly because you want more time or because you do not want it to happen **32 take your time** to do something without hurrying ➲See also: **half-time, local time,** in the **nick**[2] of time, **night-time, prime time, a race**[1] against time/the clock

time[2] /taɪm/ *verb* [T] **1** DECIDE A TIME to decide that something will happen at a particular time *They timed production of the CD so it was in the shops just before Christmas.* ○ *Her comment was* ***well timed.*** **2** MEASURE to measure how long it takes for something to happen or for someone to do something *It's a good idea to time yourself while you do the exercises.* ➲See also: **two-time**

time-consuming /ˈtaɪmkənˌsjuːmɪŋ/ *adjective* needing a lot of time *The legal process was time-consuming and expensive.*

ˈtime ˌframe ➲See: **timescale**

time-honoured *UK* (*US* **time-honored**) /ˈtaɪmˌɒnəd/ *adjective* [**always before noun**] A time-honoured tradition or way of doing things is one that has been used for a long time.

ˈtime ˌlag *noun* [C] a period of time between two things happening

timeless /ˈtaɪmləs/ *adjective* not changing because of time or fashion *Her clothes have a* ***timeless quality.*** ○ ***a timeless classic***

timely /ˈtaɪmli/ *adjective* happening or done at exactly the right time ➲Opposite **untimely**

time-out /ˌtaɪmˈaʊt/ *noun* [C] **SPORT** a short period during a sports game in which players can rest

timer /ˈtaɪməʳ/ *noun* [C] a piece of equipment that measures time

times /taɪmz/ *preposition* **MATHEMATICS** used to say that one number is multiplied by another number *Two times three is six.*

timescale /ˈtaɪmskeɪl/ (*also* **time frame**) *noun* [C] the amount of time that something takes or during which something happens

WORD PARTNERS FOR ***timetable***

draw up/give/keep to/set a timetable • a timetable **for** (doing) sth

timetable /ˈtaɪmˌteɪbl/ *noun* [C] **1** BUS/TRAIN ETC (*also US* **schedule**) a list of times when buses, trains, etc arrive and leave **2** PLANNED EVENTS a list of dates and times that shows when things will happen ➲See colour picture **The Classroom** on page Centre 6

ˈtime ˌtraveller *UK* (*US* **ˈtime traveler**) *noun* [C] someone who can move between different times in the past or the future

ˈtime ˌzone *noun* [C] one of the areas of the world that has a different time from all the other areas *London and New York are five time zones apart.*

timid /ˈtɪmɪd/ *adjective* shy and easily frightened *a timid little boy* •**timidly** *adverb* •**timidity** /tɪˈmɪdəti/ *noun* [U]

timing /ˈtaɪmɪŋ/ *noun* [U] **1** TIME the time when something happens *the timing of the announcement* **2** SKILL the ability to do something at exactly the right time *You need great timing to be a good football player.*

tin /tɪn/ *noun* **1** METAL CONTAINER [C] *UK* (*UK/US* **can**) a metal container in which food is sold *a tin of beans/soup* **2** CONTAINER WITH LID [C] *UK* a metal container with a lid that you keep food or other substances in *a biscuit tin* ○ *a paint tin* **3** COOKING EQUIPMENT [C] (*US* **pan**) a flat pan that you cook food in *a roasting tin* **4 CHEMISTRY** [U] a soft, silver metal that is often combined with other metals or used to cover them (symbol **Sn**)

tinfoil /ˈtɪnfɔɪl/ *noun* [U] metal made into very thin sheets like paper and used mainly for covering food

tinge /tɪndʒ/ *noun* [C] a small amount of a sad feeling or colour *"Goodbye," he said, with a tinge of sadness.* •**tinged** *adjective Her dark hair is now **tinged with** grey.*

tingle /ˈtɪŋgl/ *verb* [I] If a part of your body tingles, the skin feels slightly uncomfortable. *My hands are starting to tingle with the cold.* •**tingle** *noun* [C]

tinker /ˈtɪŋkəʳ/ *verb* [I] to make small changes to something in order to improve or repair it *Tim loves **tinkering with** car engines.*

tinkle /ˈtɪŋkl/ *verb* [I] to make a soft, high, ringing sound •**tinkle** *noun* [C]

tinned /tɪnd/ *UK* (*UK/US* **canned**) *adjective* Tinned food is sold in metal containers.

ˈtin ˌopener *UK* (*UK/US* **can opener**) *noun* [C] a piece of kitchen equipment for opening metal food containers ➲See colour picture **The Kitchen** on page Centre 2

tinsel /ˈtɪnsəl/ *noun* [U] long, shiny, coloured string, used as a decoration at Christmas (= a Christian holiday)

tint¹ /tɪnt/ *noun* [C] **ART** a particular colour *the yellow and red tints of autumn*

tint² /tɪnt/ *verb* [T] to add a small amount of a colour to something *Do you think he tints his hair?*

tinted /ˈtɪntɪd/ *adjective* Tinted glass has colour added to it. *tinted sunglasses*

O-■ **tiny** /ˈtaɪni/ *adjective* extremely small *a tiny baby* ○ *a tiny little room*

WORD PARTNERS FOR ***tip***

give/pass on/pick up tips • a **handy/helpful/hot/useful** tip • tips **for/on** sth

tip¹ /tɪp/ *noun* [C] **1** END the end of something long and narrow *the tips of your fingers* **2** ADVICE a piece of useful advice *gardening tips* ○ *Emma was giving me some **tips on** how to grow tomatoes.* **3** MONEY an extra amount of money that you give to a driver, someone working in a restaurant, etc to thank them *We **left a tip** because the waiter was so friendly.* **4** WASTE *UK* (*UK/US* **dump**) a place where people take things that they want to get rid of *We took our old fridge to the tip.* **5** UNTIDY PLACE *UK informal* (*UK/US* **dump**) a place that is dirty and untidy *His bedroom is an absolute tip.* **6 be on the tip of your tongue** If a word is on the tip of your tongue, you want to say it but cannot remember it. **7 be the tip of the iceberg** to be a small part of a very big problem

tip² /tɪp/ *verb* **tipping**, *past* **tipped 1** MOVE [I, T] to move so that one side is higher than the other side, or to make something move in this way *The table tipped and all the drinks fell on the floor.* **2 tip sth into/onto/out of sth** to make the contents of a container fall out by holding the container in a position where this happens *She tipped the contents of her purse onto the table.* **3** GIVE MONEY [I, T] to give an extra amount of money to a driver, someone working in a restaurant, etc to thank them **4 be tipped as/to do/for sth** *UK* If someone is tipped to achieve something, most people say it will happen. *Christie was tipped to win the race.*

tip sb off *phrasal verb* to warn someone secretly about something so that they can take action or prevent it happening •**tip-off** /ˈtɪpɒf/ *noun* [C] a piece of information that you give someone secretly, so that they can take action or prevent something happening

tip (sth) over *phrasal verb* If something tips over, or if you tip it over, it falls onto its side.

tiptoe¹ /ˈtɪptəʊ/ *noun* **on tiptoe** standing on your toes with the rest of your feet off the ground

tiptoe² /ˈtɪptəʊ/ *verb* **tiptoe across/down/through, etc** to walk quietly on your toes

tire¹ /taɪəʳ/ *noun* [C] *US spelling of* tyre ➲See colour picture **Car** on page Centre 7

tire² /taɪəʳ/ *verb* [I, T] to become tired or to make someone become tired *He tires easily.*

tire of sth/doing sth *phrasal verb* to become bored with something *He never tires of playing games on his computer.*

tire sb out *phrasal verb* to make someone very tired

OTHER WAYS OF SAYING ***tired***

If someone is extremely tired, you can say that they are **exhausted**, **worn-out**, or, in informal situations in the UK, **shattered**: *I'm too **exhausted** to take the dog for a walk tonight.* • *By the time I got home, I was absolutely **shattered**.*

You can use the adjectives **burnt-out** and **drained** to describe someone who is tired because they have been working very hard: *He was completely **burnt-out** after a full week of performances.* • *I'd worked a twelve-hour day and was absolutely **drained**.*

If someone is tired and wants to go to sleep, you can describe them as **drowsy** or **sleepy**: *The heat had made me **drowsy/sleepy**.*

O-■ **tired** /taɪəd/ *adjective* **1** feeling that you want to rest or sleep *He was **tired out** (= very tired) by the end of the day.* ○ *She never seems to **get tired**.* **2 tired of doing sth** bored or annoyed by something that has happened too often *I'm tired of listening to her problems.* •**tiredness** *noun* [U]

COMMON LEARNER ERROR

tired of or **tired from?**

If you are **tired of** something or **of doing** something, you are bored or annoyed by it.

I'm tired of hearing his awful jokes.

If you are **tired from** something, you want to rest because of it.

I'm tired from the long journey.

tireless /ˈtaɪələs/ *adjective* working very hard at something and not stopping *He was a **tireless campaigner/worker** for children's organizations.* ○ *I want to thank James for his **tireless efforts** on behalf of the company.*

tiresome /ˈtaɪəsəm/ *adjective formal* making you feel annoyed or bored *a tiresome little boy*

tiring /ˈtaɪərɪŋ/ *adjective* making you feel tired *a long and tiring day*

tissue /ˈtɪʃuː/ *noun* **1 BIOLOGY** [C, U] the material that animals and plants are made of *human*

T

brain tissue **2** FOR YOUR NOSE [C] a soft piece of paper that you use for cleaning your nose **3** FOR WRAPPING [U] (*also* **ˈtissue ˌpaper**) soft, thin paper that you cover things with in order to protect them

ˈtissue ˌculture *noun* **1 BIOLOGY** [U] the scientific process of growing tissue (= cells) taken from a living thing in a special substance **2 BIOLOGY** [C] an amount of tissue (= cells) that has been grown in this way

titbit *UK* (*US* **tidbit**) /ˈtɪtbɪt/ *noun* [C] a small piece of nice food, or an interesting piece of information

WORD PARTNERS FOR ***title***

defend/lose/retain/take/win the title • the **world** title

O⁃**title** /ˈtaɪtl/ *noun* [C] **1** BOOK/FILM ETC the name of a book, film, etc **2 SPORT** what you get if you win an important sports competition *He* ***won*** *the 1999 world motor racing* ***title***. **3** SOMEONE'S NAME a word such as 'Lord', 'Dr', etc that is used before someone's name

ˈtitle ˌbar *noun* [C] **COMPUTING** the long thin part along the top of a computer screen that shows the name of the document or program that is open

titled /ˈtaɪtld/ *adjective* **SOCIETY** having a title such as 'Lord', 'Lady', or 'Duke' that shows you have a high social position

title-holder /ˈtaɪtlˌhəʊldəʳ/ *noun* [C] **SPORT** someone who has won a sports competition

ˈtitle ˌrole *noun* [C] the person in a play or film who has the same name as the play's or film's title

titration /taɪˈtreɪʃᵊn/ *noun* [U] **CHEMISTRY** a way of finding out how much of a substance there is in a liquid by adding to it measured amounts of another substance which reacts to it, for example by making it change colour

titter /ˈtɪtəʳ/ *verb* [I] to laugh in a nervous way •**titter** *noun* [C]

tjanting tool /ˈtjæntɪŋˌtuːl/ *noun* [C] **DT** a tool for putting wax onto cloth before it is dyed (= has had colour put on it) so that that area will not be coloured

T-junction /ˈtiːˌdʒʌnkʃᵊn/ *UK* (*US* **intersection**) *noun* [C] a place where two roads join and make the shape of the letter 'T'

TNT /ˌtiːenˈtiː/ *noun* [U] **CHEMISTRY** *abbreviation for* trinitrotoluene, a powerful explosive substance

O⁃**to¹** /tə/ **1** INFINITIVE used with a verb to make the infinitive *I want to learn Spanish.* ○ *He forgot to feed the cat.* **2** REASON used to give the reason for doing something *I'm just going out to get some milk.*

O⁃**to²** *strong form* /tuː/ *weak forms* /tʊ, tə/ *preposition* **1** DIRECTION in the direction of somewhere *Dimitri is going to Germany next week.* ○ *I ran to the door.* **2** ANOTHER PERSON used to show who receives something or experiences an action *Could you give these keys to Pete?* ○ *Anna was speaking to her mother on the phone.* ○ *I lent my bike to Tom.* **3** POSITION almost touching or facing something *She stood with her back to the window.* **4 from ... to ... a** TIME/DISTANCE used to give information about periods of time and distances *The museum is open from Monday to Saturday.* ○ *The bus goes from London to Cambridge.* **b** INCLUDING including *The book deals with everything from childhood to old age.* **5** BEFORE used to say 'before' the hour when you are saying what time it is *It's five to three.* **6** COMPARE used to compare two things *I prefer football to cricket.* **7** UNTIL until a particular time or state *It's only two weeks to my birthday.* ○ *She nursed him back to health.* **8** SOMEONE'S OPINION used to say what someone's opinion is *Fifty pounds is nothing to Matthew* (= he would not think it was a lot of money). **9 to sb's disappointment/relief/surprise, etc** used to say that someone feels surprised, disappointed, etc by something *To Pierre's disappointment, Monique wasn't at the party.* **10** MEASUREMENT used to say how many parts make up a whole unit of measurement or money *There are 100 pence to the British pound.* **11** BELONGING belonging to or connected with *Can you give me the keys to the car?*

to³ /tuː/ *adverb* **1** *UK* If you push or pull a door to, you close it. **2 to and fro** backwards and forwards *The sign was swinging to and fro in the wind.*

toad /təʊd/ *noun* [C] a small, brown animal with long back legs for swimming and jumping

toadstool /ˈtəʊdstuːl/ *noun* [C] **BIOLOGY** a poisonous fungus (= organism like a plant) with a short stem and a round top

toast¹ /təʊst/ *noun* **1 FOOD** [U] bread that has been heated to make it brown *a slice of toast* **2** [C] a time when people lift their glasses and drink because they want someone to be successful, happy, etc *At the wedding, there was a* ***toast to*** *the happy couple.*

toast² /təʊst/ *verb* [T] **1** DRINK to lift your glass and drink with other people because you want someone to be successful, happy, etc **2** BREAD to heat bread so that it becomes brown

toaster /ˈtəʊstəʳ/ *noun* [C] a machine that heats bread so that it becomes brown ➲See colour picture **The Kitchen** on page Centre 2

toasty /ˈtəʊsti/ *adjective* warm and comfortable *It's nice and toasty near the fire.*

tobacco /təˈbækəʊ/ *noun* [U] dried leaves that are inside cigarettes

toboggan /təˈbɒgᵊn/ *noun* [C] **SPORT** a board that you sit or lie on, used for going down a hill on a surface of snow

O⁃**today** /təˈdeɪ/ *noun* [U], *adverb* **1** THIS DAY this day, or on this day *It's Johann's birthday today.* ○ *Today is Friday.* **2** THIS PERIOD OF TIME the period of time that is happening now or in this period of time *More young people smoke today than in the past.*

toddle /ˈtɒdl/ *verb* **toddle down/off/to, etc** *informal* to walk somewhere *Sophie said goodbye and toddled off towards the station.*

toddler /ˈtɒdləʳ/ *noun* [C] a child who has just learned to walk

toe¹ /təʊ/ *noun* [C] **1 ANATOMY** one of the five separate parts at the end of your foot *your big*

T

toe (= largest toe) ○ *your **little toe*** (= smallest toe) ➲See colour picture **The Body** on page Centre 13 **2** the part of a shoe or sock that covers your toes **3 keep sb on their toes** to make sure that someone gives all their attention to what they are doing and is ready for anything that might happen

toe² /təʊ/ *verb* ➲See: toe the (party) **line¹**

toenail /ˈtəʊneɪl/ *noun* [C] **ANATOMY** one of the hard, flat parts on top of the end of your toes ➲See colour picture **The Body** on page Centre 13

toffee /ˈtɒfi/ *noun* [C, U] **FOOD** a sticky sweet, made by boiling sugar and butter together

tofu /ˈtəʊfuː/ (also **bean curd**) *noun* [U] **FOOD** a soft pale food made from the soya bean plant

O‑ **together¹** /təˈgeðəʳ/ *adverb* **1** WITH SOMEONE with each other *We went shopping together.* ○ *They live together.* **2** CONNECTED used to say that two or more things are joined to each other, mixed with each other, etc *She tied the two pieces of rope together.* **3** SAME PLACE in the same place or close to each other *We all sat together.* **4** SAME TIME at the same time *We'll deal with the next two items on the list together.* **5 together with sth** in addition to something *She sent some flowers together with a card.* ➲See also: get your **act²** together, **get-together**

together² /təˈgeðəʳ/ *adjective informal* Someone who is together thinks clearly and organizes their life well.

togetherness /təˈgeðənəs/ *noun* [U] a feeling of friendship

toil /tɔɪl/ *verb* [I] *literary* to do difficult work for a long time •**toil** *noun* [U] *literary*

WORD PARTNERS FOR ***toilet***

be on/go to/flush/need the toilet • toilet **facilities** • a toilet **seat**

O‑ **toilet** /ˈtɔɪlɪt/ *noun* [C] **1** BOWL a bowl that you sit on or stand near when you get rid of waste substances from your body ➲See colour picture **The Bathroom** on page Centre 3 **2** ROOM *UK* (*US* **bathroom**) a room with a toilet in it

COMMON LEARNER ERROR

toilet

Toilet is the most general word. In **British English** the informal word **loo** is often used. In **American English** the word **bathroom** is often used to mean toilet, especially in the home.

In public places toilets are usually called **the ladies** or **the gents** in Britain and the **men's room**, **ladies' room**, or **restroom** in America.

The **lavatory** is slightly formal and **WC** is only used in **British English**. These two words are not used much today.

ˈtoilet ˌpaper *noun* [U] paper used for cleaning your body after you have used the toilet ➲See colour picture **The Bathroom** on page Centre 3

toiletries /ˈtɔɪlɪtriz/ *noun* [plural] things such as soap, toothpaste (= substance for cleaning teeth), etc that you use for making yourself clean

ˈtoilet ˌroll *noun* [C] *UK* paper for cleaning your body after using the toilet that is folded around a tube ➲See colour picture **The Bathroom** on page Centre 3

token¹ /ˈtəʊkən/ *noun* [C] **1** LOVE/THANKS something that you give to someone in order to show them love, to thank them, etc *I gave Helen some chocolates as **a token of** thanks for all her help.* **2** INSTEAD OF MONEY a round piece of metal or plastic that you put in some machines instead of money *You need a token to get out of the car park.* **3** PAPER *UK* (*US* **gift certificate**) a piece of paper that you give someone which they can exchange for a book, CD, etc *a **book/record/gift token***

token² /ˈtəʊkən/ *adjective* [**always before noun**] **1** PERSON A token person is chosen so that an organization can pretend that they care about that type of person. *a token woman* **2** ACTION A token action is small or unimportant and may show your future intentions or may only pretend to. *He made a **token effort** to find a job.*

told /təʊld/ *past of* tell

tolerable /ˈtɒlərəbl/ *adjective* acceptable but not excellent *The food was just about tolerable but the service was terrible.* ➲Opposite **intolerable** •**tolerably** *adverb*

WORD PARTNERS FOR ***tolerance***

show tolerance • tolerance **of/towards** sb/sth • sb's tolerance **level** • **racial/religious** tolerance

tolerance /ˈtɒlərəns/ *noun* [U] the quality of allowing people to do or believe what they want although you do not agree with it ***religious/racial tolerance*** ➲See also: **zero tolerance**

tolerant /ˈtɒlərənt/ *adjective* allowing people to do what they want especially when you do not agree with it *a tolerant attitude* ○ *I think we're becoming more **tolerant of** children in public places.* ➲Opposite **intolerant**

tolerate /ˈtɒləreɪt/ *verb* [T] **1** ALLOW to accept or allow something although you do not like it *We will not tolerate racism of any sort.* **2** DEAL WITH to be able to deal with something unpleasant and not be harmed by it *These plants can tolerate very low temperatures.* •**toleration** /ˌtɒlərˈeɪʃən/ *noun* [U]

toll¹ /təʊl/ *noun* **1 FINANCE** [C] money that you pay to use a bridge, road, etc **2** [**no plural**] the number of people who are killed or injured **3 take its toll** to have a bad effect on someone or something, especially over a long period of time *The stress was starting to **take its toll on** him.* ➲See also: **death toll**

toll² /təʊl/ *verb* [I] When a bell tolls, it rings slowly, especially because someone has died.

toll-free /ˌtəʊlˈfriː/ *US* (*UK* **freephone**) *adjective* A toll-free number is a telephone number that you can connect to without paying.

O‑ **tomato** /təˈmɑːtəʊ/ (US) /təˈmeɪtəʊ/ *noun* [C, U] *plural* **tomatoes FOOD** a soft, round, red fruit eaten in salad or as a vegetable ➲See colour picture **Fruit and Vegetables** on page Centre 10

tomb /tuːm/ *noun* [C] a place where a dead person is buried, usually with a monument (= stone structure)

tomboy /ˈtɒmbɔɪ/ *noun* [C] a young girl who behaves and dresses like a boy

T

tombstone /ˈtuːmstəʊn/ *noun* [C] a stone that shows the name of a dead person who is buried under it

tomcat /ˈtɒmkæt/ *noun* [C] a male cat

tomorrow /təˈmɒrəʊ/ *noun* [U], *adverb* **1** DAY AFTER TODAY the day after today or on the day after today *It's my birthday tomorrow.* ○ *Tomorrow is Friday.* **2** THE FUTURE the future, or in the future *the children of tomorrow*

ton /tʌn/ *noun* [C] *plural* **tons** or **ton** **1** **MEASURES** a unit for measuring weight, equal to 1016 kilograms in the UK and 907 kilograms in the US ➲See Extra help page **Numbers and measurements** on page Centre 24. ➲Compare **tonne** **2** **tons of sth** *informal* a lot of something *We've got tons of cheese left.* **3** **weigh a ton** *informal* to be very heavy

tone[1] /təʊn/ *noun* **1** **MUSIC** [C, U] the quality of a sound, especially of someone's voice *I knew by her* ***tone of voice*** *that she was serious.* **2** FEELING/STYLE [U, no plural] the general feeling or style that something has *Then the director arrived and the whole tone of the meeting changed.* **3** TELEPHONE [C] an electronic sound made by a telephone *a dialling tone/an engaged tone* **4** **ART** [C] one of the many types of a particular colour

tone[2] /təʊn/ (*also* **tone up**) *verb* [T] **HEALTH** to make your muscles or skin firmer and stronger *These exercises will tone up your stomach muscles.*

tone sth down *phrasal verb* to make a piece of writing, a speech, etc less offensive or rude

tone-deaf /ˌtəʊnˈdef/ (US) /ˈtəʊndef/ *adjective* **MUSIC** unable to sing the correct musical notes or hear the difference between musical notes

toner /ˈtəʊnəʳ/ *noun* [U] a type of ink used for computer printers and photocopiers (= machines that copy documents)

tongs /tɒŋz/ *noun* [plural] a tool used for picking things up, that has two pieces joined together at one end

tongue /tʌŋ/ *noun* **1** **ANATOMY** [C] the soft thing inside your mouth that you move and use for tasting and speaking **2** [C, U] the tongue of some animals that you can eat as meat **3** **LANGUAGE** [C] *formal* a language *Japanese is her* ***native tongue*** (= the language she learnt to speak as a child). ➲See also: **mother tongue**, a **slip**[2] of the tongue, be on the **tip**[1] of your tongue ➲See picture at **alimentary canal**

T

tongue-in-cheek /ˌtʌŋɪnˈtʃiːk/ *adjective, adverb* said or done as a joke

tongue-tied /ˈtʌŋtaɪd/ *adjective* unable to say anything because you are nervous

ˈtongue ˌtwister *noun* [C] **LANGUAGE** a phrase or sentence that is difficult to say quickly because it has many similar sounds in it

tonic /ˈtɒnɪk/ *noun* **1** **FOOD** [C, U] (*also* **ˈtonic ˌwater**) a drink with bubbles in it that has a bitter taste and is often added to alcoholic drinks **2** [no plural] something that makes you feel better *Spending time with Leo is always a tonic.*

tonight /təˈnaɪt/ *noun, adverb* [U] the night of this day, or during the night of this day *What are you doing tonight?*

tonne /tʌn/ *noun* [C] *plural* **tonnes** or **tonne** *UK* **MEASURES** a metric ton (= unit for measuring weight, equal to 1000 kilograms) ➲Compare **ton**

tonsil /ˈtɒnsəl/ *noun* [C] **ANATOMY** one of the two small, soft parts at the back of your mouth

tonsillitis /ˌtɒnsəlˈaɪtɪs/ *noun* [U] **HEALTH** an illness that makes your tonsils very painful

too /tuː/ *adverb* **1** **too small/heavy/much, etc** used before adjectives and adverbs to mean 'more than is allowed, necessary, possible, etc' *The film is also far too long.* ○ *There are too many cars on the roads these days.* [+ **to do sth**] *I decided it was too early to get up and went back to sleep.* **2** also *Do you know Jason too?* ○ *I'll probably go there next year too.* **3** **not too** used before adjectives and adverbs to mean 'not very' *"How was your exam?" "Not too bad, I suppose."* ○ *I didn't play too well today.*

took /tʊk/ *past tense of* take

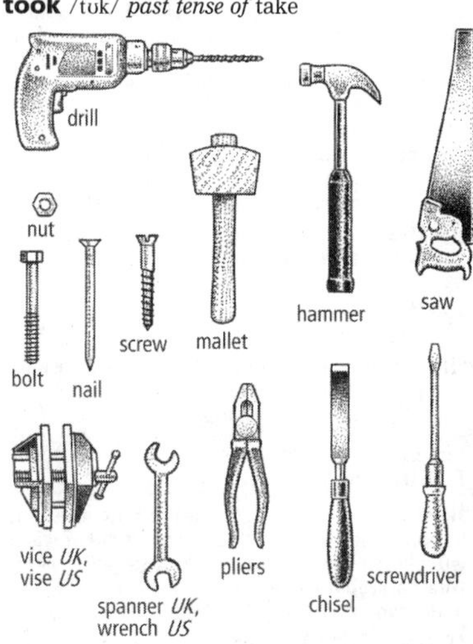

tools

tool /tuːl/ *noun* [C] **1** EQUIPMENT a piece of equipment that you use with your hands in order to help you do something **2** HELP something that helps you to do a particular activity *Computers are an essential tool for modern scientists.* ➲See also: **power tool**

toolbar /ˈtuːlbɑːʳ/ *noun* [C] **COMPUTING** on a computer screen, a row of icons (= small pictures that you choose in order to make the computer do something)

ˈtool ˌbox *noun* [C] a container in which you keep and carry small tools

toot /tuːt/ *UK* (*UK/US* **honk**) *verb* **toot your horn** If a driver toots their horn, they make a short sound with the horn (= thing you press to make a warning noise). •**toot** *noun* [C]

WORD PARTNERS FOR ***tooth***

brush/clean your teeth • your **back/front** teeth • **have** a tooth **removed/taken out** • a **set of** teeth

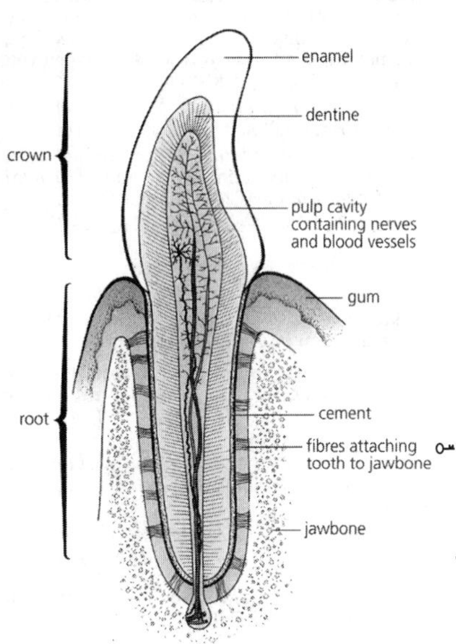

tooth

O➡**tooth** /tuːθ/ *noun* [C] *plural* **teeth** **1** **ANATOMY** one of the hard, white objects in your mouth that you use for biting and crushing food *You should* ***brush*** *your teeth twice a day.* **2** one of the row of metal or plastic points that stick out from a tool such as a comb (= thing used to make your hair tidy), or saw (= thing used to cut wood) **3 grit your teeth** to accept a difficult situation and deal with it in a determined way ➲See also: a **kick**[2] in the teeth, do sth by the **skin**[1] of your teeth, **wisdom tooth**

toothache /ˈtuːθeɪk/ *noun* [U] **HEALTH** a pain in one of your teeth

toothbrush /ˈtuːθbrʌʃ/ *noun* [C] a small brush that you use to clean your teeth

toothpaste /ˈtuːθpeɪst/ *noun* [U] a substance that you use to clean your teeth ➲See colour picture **The Bathroom** on page Centre 3

toothpick /ˈtuːθpɪk/ *noun* [C] a small, thin stick that you use to remove pieces of food from between your teeth

WORD PARTNERS FOR ***top***

reach the top • **at** the top • **on** top • the top **of** sth

O➡**top**[1] /tɒp/ *noun* **1** HIGHEST PART [C] the highest part of something *They were waiting for him* ***at the top of*** *the stairs.* ○ *I want a cake with cherries* ***on top.*** **2** SURFACE [C] the flat, upper surface of something *the table top* **3** LID [C] the lid or cover of a container, pen, etc *Put the top back on the bottle.* **4** CLOTHING [C] a piece of women's clothing worn on the upper part of the body **5** TOY [C] a toy that turns round and round when you move its handle up and down **6 the top** the most important position in a company, team, etc *At forty he was already* ***at the top of*** *his profession.* **7 at the top of your voice** *UK* (*US* **at the top of your lungs**) shouting very loudly **8 from top to bottom** completely *I've searched the house from top to bottom and still can't find it.* **9 get on top of sb** *UK* If a difficult situation gets on top of someone, it upsets them. **10 off the top of your head** *informal* If you say a fact off the top of your head, you say it immediately, from memory. *"What date is their wedding?" "I couldn't tell you off the top of my head."* **11 on top of sth** IN ADDITION in addition to something else that is bad *And then, on top of everything else, her car was stolen.* IN CONTROL able to deal with or in control of something *I'm not at all sure that he's on top of the situation.* **12 be on top of the world** *informal* to be very happy **13 over the top** *mainly UK informal* too extreme and not suitable *I thought her performance was way over the top.*

O➡**top**[2] /tɒp/ *adjective* [**always before noun**] **1** BEST the best, most important, or most successful *He's one of the country's top athletes.* **2** HIGHEST at the highest part of something *I can't reach the top shelf.*

top[3] /tɒp/ *verb* [T] **topping**, *past* **topped** **1** to be better or more than something *I don't think film makers will ever top 'Gone With The Wind'.* **2 be topped with sth** to be covered with something *lemon tart topped with cream*

top sth off *phrasal verb informal* to finish something in an enjoyable or successful way

top sth up *phrasal verb UK* (*US* **top sth off**) **1** to add more liquid to a container in order to make it full **2** to add more of something, especially money, to an existing amount to create the total you need *Can I top up my mobile phone here?*

ˌtop ˈhat *UK* (*US* **ˈtop ˌhat**) *noun* [C] a tall, black or grey hat worn by men on some formal occasions

WORD PARTNERS FOR ***topic***

cover/discuss/raise a topic • a **controversial/hot** topic • the **(main)** topic **of** sth • a topic **of conversation /discussion**

topic /ˈtɒpɪk/ *noun* [C] a subject that you talk or write about

topical /ˈtɒpɪkəl/ *adjective* relating to things that are happening now

topless /ˈtɒpləs/ *adjective* without clothes on the upper part of your body

topmost /ˈtɒpməʊst/ *adjective* [**always before noun**] highest *the topmost branches of a tree*

topography /təˈpɒgrəfi/ *noun* [U] **GEOGRAPHY** the shape and other physical characteristics of a piece of land

topping /ˈtɒpɪŋ/ *noun* [C, U] **FOOD** food that is put on top of other food in order to give it more flavour, or to make it look attractive

topple /ˈtɒpl/ *verb* **1** FALL [I, T] to fall, or to make something or someone fall **2** LEADER [T] to make a leader lose their position of power

top-secret /ˌtɒpˈsiːkrət/ *adjective* Top-secret information is very important and must not be told to anyone.

T

topsy-turvy /ˌtɒpsiˈtɜːvi/ *adjective informal* confused or badly organized

ˈtop-up ˌcard *noun* [C] a card you can buy which gives you a special number so that you can use your mobile phone for longer

the Torah /ˈtɔːrə/ *noun* **RELIGION** the holy books of the Jewish religion, especially the first five books of the Bible

torch¹ /tɔːtʃ/ *noun* [C] **1** [LIGHT] *UK* (*US* **flashlight**) a small electric light that you hold in your hand **2** [STICK] a long stick with material that burns tied to the top of it

torch² /tɔːtʃ/ *verb* [T] *informal* to destroy something by burning it *A number of houses were torched.*

tore /tɔːʳ/ *past tense of* tear

torment¹ /tɔːˈment/ *verb* [T] to make someone suffer or worry a lot *All evening the question tormented her.* •**tormentor** *noun* [C]

torment² /ˈtɔːment/ *noun* [C, U] extreme unhappiness or pain

torn /tɔːn/ *past participle of* tear

tornado /tɔːˈneɪdəʊ/ (*also US* **twister**) *noun* [C] *plural* **tornados** or **tornadoes** an extremely strong and dangerous wind that blows in a circle and destroys buildings as it moves along

torpedo /tɔːˈpiːdəʊ/ *noun* [C] *plural* **torpedoes** a long, thin bomb that is fired from a ship and moves under water to destroy another ship

torrent /ˈtɒrᵊnt/ *noun* [C] **1 a torrent of sth** a lot of something unpleasant ***a torrent of abuse*** **2** a large amount of water that is moving very fast

torrential /təˈrenʃᵊl/ *adjective* Torrential rain is very heavy rain.

torso /ˈtɔːsəʊ/ *noun* [C] **ANATOMY** the main part of a human body without its arms, legs, or head

tortilla /tɔːˈtiːə/ *noun* [C] **FOOD** a type of thin round Mexican bread

tortoise /ˈtɔːtəs/ *noun* [C] an animal with a thick, hard shell that it can move its head and legs into for protection ➲See picture at **reptile**

tortuous /ˈtɔːtʃuəs/ *adjective formal* **1** [DIFFICULT] very complicated or difficult *Gaining permission to build was a long and **tortuous process**.* ○ ***a tortuous path/route*** **2** [ROAD] A tortuous road has many turns in it.

torture¹ /ˈtɔːtʃəʳ/ *verb* [T] to cause someone severe pain, often in order to make them tell you something •**torturer** *noun* [C]

torture² /ˈtɔːtʃəʳ/ *noun* [C, U] **1** [PHYSICAL PAIN] when someone is tortured **2** [BORING/UNPLEASANT] a very unpleasant experience *I had to sit there listening to her for two whole hours - it was torture!*

Tory /ˈtɔːri/ *noun* [C] **POLITICS** someone who supports the Conservative Party in the UK *a Tory voter*

toss¹ /tɒs/ *verb* **1 toss sth away/into/on, etc** to throw something somewhere carelessly *He read the letter quickly, then tossed it into the bin.* **2** [I, T] (*also* **toss up**) to throw a coin in the air and guess which side will land facing upwards as a way of deciding something

toss² /tɒs/ *noun* **1 a toss of a coin** when you throw a coin in the air and guess which side will land facing upwards as a way of deciding something **2 a toss of your head/hair** when you move your head quickly backwards

tot /tɒt/ *noun* [C] *informal* **1** a small child **2** **FOOD** *UK* a small amount of strong alcohol

O⊸**total¹** /ˈtəʊtᵊl/ *adjective* [**always before noun**] **1** [EVERYTHING] including everything *The total cost of the work was $800.* **2** [EXTREME] extreme or complete *The whole evening was a total disaster.*

WORD PARTNERS FOR ***total** (noun)*

sth **brings/takes** the total to [500/4000, etc] • **reach** a total of [500/4000, etc] • the **final/overall/sum** total • [500/4000, etc] **in** total

O⊸**total²** /ˈtəʊtᵊl/ *noun* [C] **MATHEMATICS** the amount you get when you add several smaller amounts together ***In total** we made over £3,000.*

total³ /ˈtəʊtᵊl/ *verb* [T] *UK* **totalling**, *past* **totalled**, *US* **totaling**, *past* **totaled** to add up to a particular amount

totalitarian /təʊˌtælɪˈteəriən/ *adjective* **POLITICS** belonging to a political system in which the people in power have complete control and do not allow anyone to oppose them •**totalitarianism** *noun* [U]

O⊸**totally** /ˈtəʊtᵊli/ *adverb* completely *They look totally different.* ○ *I totally disagree.*

tote bag /ˈtəʊtˌbæg/ *noun* [C] *US* a large bag with handles and an open top

totter /ˈtɒtəʳ/ *verb* [I] to walk in a way that looks as if you are going to fall *She tottered around the dance floor.*

toucan /ˈtuːkən/ *noun* [C] a South American bird that has a brightly coloured beak

O⊸**touch¹** /tʌtʃ/ *verb* **1** [HAND] [T] to put your hand on something *You can look at them but please don't touch them.* **2** [GET CLOSE] [I, T] If two things touch, they are so close to each other that there is no space between them. *These two wires must not touch.* **3** [EMOTION] [T] If something kind that someone says or does touches you, it makes you feel pleased or a little sad. [**often passive**] *I was deeply touched by her letter.* **4 not touch sth** to not eat or drink something **5 not touch sb/sth** to not harm someone or not damage something ➲See also: touch/cover all the bases (**base¹**), hit/touch a (raw) **nerve**

touch down *phrasal verb* When a plane touches down, it lands.

touch on sth *phrasal verb* to briefly talk about something *We only touched on the subject.*

touch sth up *phrasal verb* to improve something by making small changes

touch² /tʌtʃ/ *noun* **1** [HAND] [**no plural**] when you put your hand on something *I felt the touch of his hand on my face.* **2** [ABILITY] [U] the ability to feel things by putting your hand on them *It was cold **to the touch*** (= when I touched it). **3** [DETAIL] [C] a small detail that makes something better *Having flowers on the tables was **a nice touch**.* **4 a touch** a little *Add a little olive oil and **a touch of** vinegar.* **5 be/get/keep, etc in touch** to communicate or continue to communicate with someone by telephoning, or writing to them **6 lose touch** to stop communicating with someone, usually because they do not live near you now **7 be out of touch** to know little about what has recently happened

touchdown /ˈtʌtʃdaʊn/ *noun* **1** [C, U] when an aircraft lands **2** SPORT [C] when the ball is carried or thrown over a line in order to score points in rugby or American football

touched /tʌtʃt/ *adjective* pleased or a little sad because someone has done something kind *She was touched that he had remembered her birthday.*

touching /ˈtʌtʃɪŋ/ *adjective* making you feel sadness or sympathy *a touching performance*

touchpad /ˈtʌtʃpæd/ (**trackpad**) *noun* [C] COMPUTING a flat device, often part of a laptop computer, that you touch with your fingers to move the cursor (= symbol that shows the place on the screen where you are working)

ˈtouch ˌscreen *noun* [C] COMPUTING a screen that works when you touch it

touchstone /ˈtʌtʃstəʊn/ *noun* [**no plural**] something that other things can be judged against

touchy /ˈtʌtʃi/ *adjective* **1** easily upset *Why are you so touchy today?* **2 touchy subject/issue, etc** a subject that you have to talk about carefully because it is likely to upset someone

tough /tʌf/ *adjective* **1** DIFFICULT difficult *He's had a **tough time** at work recently.* ○ *We've had to make some **tough decisions**.* **2** SEVERE Tough rules are severe. ***tough** new **laws** on noise pollution* **3** STRONG THING not easily damaged, cut, etc *Children's shoes have to be tough.* ○ *This meat's very tough.* **4** STRONG PERSON physically strong and not afraid of violence *a **tough guy*** **5** DETERMINED determined and not easily upset *You have to be tough to survive in politics.* **6** UNFAIR unfair or unlucky *It can **be tough on** kids when parents get divorced.*

toughen /ˈtʌfᵊn/ (*also* **toughen up**) *verb* [I, T] to become stronger, or to make something or someone stronger *School tends to toughen kids up.*

toupee /ˈtuːpeɪ, tuːpˈeɪ/ *noun* [C] a piece of artificial (= not natural) hair worn by a man to cover part of his head where there is no hair

WORD PARTNERS FOR ***tour***

be on/go on a tour • a **guided/sightseeing/world** tour • a tour **of** sth

tour¹ /tʊəʳ/ *noun* [C, U] a visit to and around a place, area, or country *a **tour of** Europe* ○ *We went on a **guided tour** of the cathedral.* ○ *The band are **on tour*** (= travelling and performing in different places).

tour² /tʊəʳ/ *verb* [I, T] to travel around a place for pleasure *to tour the States*

tourism /ˈtʊərɪzᵊm/ *noun* [U] the business of providing services for tourists, including organizing their travel, hotels, entertainment, etc

tourist /ˈtʊərɪst/ *noun* [C] someone who visits a place for pleasure and does not live there

WORD PARTNERS FOR ***tournament***

host/play in/pull out of/take part in/win a tournament • **in** a tournament • a **major** tournament • a **round/stage** of a tournament

tournament /ˈtʊənəmənt/ *noun* [C] SPORT a competition with a series of games between many teams or players, with one winner at the end *a golf/tennis tournament*

tourniquet /ˈtʊənɪkeɪ/ (US) /ˈtɜːrnɪkɪt/ *noun* [C] HEALTH a long piece of cloth that you tie tightly around an injured arm or leg to stop the blood coming out

tousled /ˈtaʊsld/ *adjective* Tousled hair is untidy.

tout¹ /taʊt/ *verb* **1** PRAISE [T] to praise someone or something in order to make people think that they are important [**often passive**] *He is being **touted as** the next big star.* **2** SELL [I, T] *mainly UK* to try to persuade people to buy something *Drug dealers were seen **touting for business** outside schools.*

tout² /taʊt/ *UK* (*US* **scalper**) *noun* [C] someone who unofficially sells tickets outside theatres, sporting events, etc

tow¹ /təʊ/ *verb* [T] to pull a car, boat, etc, using a rope or chain connected to another vehicle *His car was **towed away** by the police.*

tow² /təʊ/ *noun informal* **in tow** If you have someone in tow, you have them with you. *Shopping can be very stressful with young children in tow.*

towards /təˈwɔːdz/ *mainly UK* (*mainly US* **toward**) *preposition* **1** DIRECTION in the direction of someone or something *She stood up and walked towards him.* **2** POSITION near to a time or place *Your seats are towards the back of the theatre.* ○ *He only became successful towards the end of his life.* **3** FEELING used when talking about feelings about something or someone *His attitude towards work needs to improve.* **4** PURPOSE for the purpose of buying or achieving something *We're asking people for a contribution towards the cost.* ○ *This piece of work counts towards your final mark.*

towel /taʊəl/ *noun* [C] **1** a soft piece of cloth or paper that you use for drying yourself or for drying something *a **bath/beach towel*** ○ *a paper towel* ⊃See colour picture **The Bathroom** on page Centre 3 **2 throw in the towel** to stop trying to do something because you do not think you can succeed ⊃See also: **sanitary towel, tea towel**

ˈtowel ˌrail *UK* (*US* **ˈtowel ˌrack**) *noun* [C] a horizontal bar on the wall that you hang towels on

tower¹ /taʊəʳ/ *noun* [C] **1** a very tall, narrow building, or part of a building *a church tower* ○ *the Eiffel Tower* **2 a tower of strength** someone who helps you a lot during a difficult time

tower² /taʊəʳ/ *verb* **tower over/above sb/sth** to be much taller or higher than someone or something else *David towers over his mother.*

ˈtower ˌblock *noun* [C] *UK* a very tall building divided into apartments or offices

towering /ˈtaʊərɪŋ/ *adjective* [**always before noun**] very tall *towering mountains/trees*

T

WORD PARTNERS FOR *town*

go into town • **in** town • **a part of/side of** town • (*UK*) the town **centre**

town /taʊn/ *noun* **1** PLACE [C] a place where people live and work, usually larger than a village but smaller than a city *It's a small town in the north of England.* **2** CENTRAL AREA [U] the central area of a town where the shops are *I usually **go into town** on a Saturday.* ○ *Shall I meet you **in town?*** **3 go to town (on sth)** to spend a lot of money or time doing something in order to make it special *They've really gone to town on the decorations.* **4 out on the town** *informal* enjoying yourself in bars, restaurants, etc in the evening ➲See also: **ghost town, shanty town**

ˌ**town** ˈ**hall** *noun* [C] a large building where local government is based

township /ˈtaʊnʃɪp/ *noun* [C] in South Africa, an area where only black people live

townspeople /ˈtaʊnzˌpiːpl/ *noun* [group] **SOCIETY** the people who live in a particular town, considered as a group

toxic /ˈtɒksɪk/ *adjective* **HEALTH, ENVIRONMENT** poisonous ***toxic chemicals/fumes*** ○ ***toxic waste*** (= poisonous waste materials produced by industry) •**toxicity** /tɒkˈsɪsəti/ *noun* [U] *formal* how poisonous a substance is

toxin /ˈtɒksɪn/ *noun* [C] *formal* **HEALTH, ENVIRONMENT** a poisonous substance

toy¹ /tɔɪ/ *noun* [C] an object for children to play with *a toy car/train* ○ *He was happily playing with his toys.*

toy² /tɔɪ/ *verb*
toy with sth *phrasal verb* **1** THINK ABOUT to briefly think about doing something, but not really intend to do it *I've toyed with the idea of going to work abroad.* **2** TOUCH to move something around in your hands without any clear purpose *He sat toying with his empty glass.*

TQM /ˌtiːkjuːˈem/ *noun* [U] *abbreviation for* total quality management: a system used in businesses and other organizations to make sure that every part of the organization is of high quality

trace¹ /treɪs/ *verb* [T] **1** FIND to find someone or something that was lost *Police have so far failed to trace the missing woman.* **2** ORIGIN to find the origin of something *She's **traced** her family **back** to the sixteenth century.* ○ *They were able to **trace the call*** (= find out the number of the telephone used). **3** DEVELOPMENT to describe the way something has developed over time *The book traces the development of women's art since the start of the century.* **4 ART** to copy a picture by putting transparent paper on top and following the outer line of the picture with a pen *tracing paper*

WORD PARTNERS FOR *trace*

find no/leave no trace (of sth) • **disappear without/vanish without** trace

trace² /treɪs/ *noun* **1** PROOF [C, U] proof that someone or something was in a place *There was **no trace** of her anywhere.* ○ *Ships have **disappeared without trace*** (= completely). **2** SMALL AMOUNT [C] a small amount of something *They found traces of blood on his clothing.*

traceable /ˈtreɪsəbl/ *adjective* If something is traceable, it is possible to find out where it came from.

ˈ**trace** ˌ**element** *noun* [C] **CHEMISTRY** one of many types of simple chemical substance that are in animals and plants in small amounts and are necessary for the animal or plant to grow and develop

trachea /trəˈkiːə/ *noun* [C] *plural* **tracheae** or **tracheas ANATOMY** the tube that carries air from your throat to your lungs ➲See picture at **alimentary canal** ➲See picture at **respiratory system**

track¹ /træk/ *noun* **1** PATH [C] a narrow path or road *We followed a dirt track off the main road.* **2** RAILWAY [C] the long metal lines which a train travels along *(UK) a railway track/ (US) a railroad track* **3 SPORT** [C] a path, often circular, used for races *a race track* ○ *track events* **4 SPORT** [U] *US* the sport of running in races around a wide circular path made for this sport **5 MUSIC** [C] one song or piece of music on a CD, record, etc **6 keep track** to continue to know what is happening to someone or something *He changes jobs so often - I find it hard to keep track of what he's doing.* **7 lose track** to not know what is happening to someone or something any more *I've lost track of how much we've spent.* **8 on track** making progress and likely to succeed [+ **to do sth**] *A fighter from Edinburgh is on track to become world heavyweight boxing champion.* **9 a fast track (to sth)** a very quick way of achieving or dealing with something *These intensive courses claim to offer a fast track to wealth and success.* **10 off the beaten track** in a place where few people go

track² /træk/ *verb* [T] **1** FOLLOW to follow a person or animal by looking for proof that they have been somewhere, or by using electronic equipment *The wolves are tracked by using radio collars.* **2** PROGRESS to record the progress or development of something over a period *The project tracks the effects of population growth on the area.*
track sth/sb down *phrasal verb* to find something or someone after looking for them in a lot of different places *The man was finally tracked down by French police.*

ˌ**track and** ˈ**field** *US* (*UK* **athletics**) *noun* [U] **SPORT** the sports which include running, jumping, and throwing ➲See colour picture **Sports 1** on page Centre 14

trackball /ˈtrækbɔːl/ *noun* [C] **COMPUTING** a ball on the keyboard of a computer that you roll with your finger in order to move the cursor (= symbol which shows where you are working) on the screen

trackpad /ˈtrækpæd/ (*also* **touchpad**) *noun* [C] **COMPUTING** a flat device, often part of a laptop computer, that you touch with your fingers to move the cursor (= symbol that shows the place on the screen where you are working)

ˌ**track** ˈ**record** *UK* (*US* ˈ**track** ˌ**record**) *noun* [C] how well or badly you have done in the past *This company has an impressive track record in completing projects on time.*

tracks /træks/ *noun* [**plural**] the marks left on the ground by a person, animal, or vehicle *We followed their tracks in the snow.*

tracksuit /ˈtræksuːt/ *noun* [**C**] *UK* loose, comfortable clothes, usually trousers and a top, especially worn for exercising ➲See colour picture **Clothes** on page Centre 9

tract /trækt/ *noun* [**C**] **1 ANATOMY, BIOLOGY** a system of connected tubes in someone's body which has a particular purpose *the **digestive/respiratory tract*** **2** a large area of land

tractor /ˈtræktəʳ/ *noun* [**C**] **FARMING** a strong vehicle with large back wheels used on farms for pulling things

WORD PARTNERS FOR ***trade (noun)***

trade **agreement/deal/policy** • trade **between** [two countries/regions] • trade **with** [a country] • trade **in** sth • a trade **dispute**

O‑ **trade¹** /treɪd/ *noun* **1** [**U**] **ECONOMICS** the buying and selling of large numbers of goods or services, especially between countries *a **trade agreement/dispute*** ○ *They rely heavily on **trade with** Europe.* ○ *The laws ban the international **trade in** ivory.* **2 ECONOMICS** [**C**] a particular area of business or industry *the building/tourist trade* **3** JOB [**C**] someone's job, especially one which needs skill in using their hands *He's a builder **by trade**.*

trade² /treɪd/ *verb* **1 ECONOMICS** [**I**] to buy and sell goods or services, especially between countries *This will increase costs for companies **trading with** Asia.* **2** EXCHANGE [**T**] *mainly US* to give something to someone and receive something else in exchange *He **traded** his guitar **for** a leather jacket.* •**trading** *noun* [**U**]
trade sth in *phrasal verb* to give something as part of your payment for something else *He traded his old car in for a new model.*

ˈ**trade** ˌ**barrier** *noun* [**C**] **ECONOMICS** anything that makes international trade more difficult, such as taxes

ˌ**trade** ˈ**creditor** *noun* [**C**] **FINANCE** a company that supplies goods to a business that have not yet been paid for

ˌ**trade** ˈ**debtor** *noun* [**C**] **FINANCE** a business that owes money to a company for goods that company has supplied

ˌ**trade** ˈ**deficit** *noun* [**C**] **ECONOMICS** a situation in which the value of goods that a country sells to other countries is lower than the value of goods it buys from other countries, or the size of this difference

the ˌ**Trade Des**ˈ**criptions** ˌ**Act** *noun* **LAW** a law in the UK to make sure that people selling things describe them fairly and accurately

ˌ**trade** ˈ**discount** *noun* [**C, U**] **FINANCE** a lower price that is sometimes given to people who work in the same area of business

ˈ**trade** ˌ**fair** (*also* **trade show**) *noun* [**C**] **ECONOMICS** a large event at which companies show their new products to people who might buy them

trademark /ˈtreɪdmɑːk/ *noun* [**C**] the name of a particular company or product which cannot be used by anyone else

trade-off /ˈtreɪdɒf/ *noun* [**C**] a situation where you accept something bad in order to have something good *There's always **a trade-off between** speed and quality.*

trader /ˈtreɪdəʳ/ *noun* [**C**] **1** a person who buys and sells things *His father was a market trader.* **2** a person who buys and sells company shares or money *a currency/futures trader*

tradesman /ˈtreɪdzmən/ *noun* [**C**] *plural* **tradesmen** *UK* someone who works in trade or in a trade which needs skill in using their hands, usually in the building industry

ˌ**trade** ˈ**surplus** *noun* [**C**] **ECONOMICS** a situation in which the value of goods that a country sells to other countries is bigger than the value of goods it buys from other countries, or the size of this difference

ˌ**trade** ˈ**union** (*also US* **labor union**) *noun* [**C**] **POLITICS** an organization that represents people who do a particular job

WORD PARTNERS FOR ***tradition***

break with/follow/revive/uphold a tradition • an **ancient/old/proud/rich/strong** tradition

O‑ **tradition** /trəˈdɪʃᵊn/ *noun* [**C, U**] **SOCIETY** a custom or way of behaving that has continued for a long time in a group of people or a society *There is a **strong tradition** of dance in St Petersburg.* ○ *We decided to **break with tradition*** (= not behave as usual) *this year and go away for Christmas.*

O‑ **traditional** /trəˈdɪʃᵊnᵊl/ *adjective* **SOCIETY** following the customs or ways of behaving that have continued in a group of people or society for a long time *traditional Hungarian dress* ○ *traditional farming methods* •**traditionally** *adverb*

traditionalist /trəˈdɪʃᵊnᵊlɪst/ *noun* [**C**] someone who believes in traditional ideas and ways of doing things

WORD PARTNERS FOR ***traffic***

reduce/ease/divert/slow down traffic • **bad/heavy** traffic • be **stuck in** traffic • a traffic **accident**

O‑ **traffic** /ˈtræfɪk/ *noun* [**U**] **1** CARS ETC the cars, trucks, etc using a road ***Traffic** is **heavy*** (= there are a lot of cars, etc) *in both directions.* ○ *a **traffic accident*** ○ *Sorry we're late - we got **stuck in traffic**.* **2** PLANES AND SHIPS the planes or ships moving around an area *air traffic control* **3 LAW** the illegal buying and selling of goods, such as drugs, weapons, etc *the **traffic in** illegal drugs*

ˈ**traffic** ˌ**circle** *US* (*UK* **roundabout**) *noun* [**C**] a circular place where roads meet and where cars drive around until they arrive at the road that they want to turn into

ˈ**traffic** ˌ**jam** *noun* [**C**] a line of cars, trucks, etc that are moving slowly or not moving at all *They got stuck in a traffic jam.*

trafficking /ˈtræfɪkɪŋ/ *noun* [**U**] **LAW** the activity of illegally buying and selling goods, such as drugs or weapons ***arms/drug trafficking*** •**trafficker** *noun* [**C**]

ˈ**traffic** ˌ**light** *noun* (*also* **lights** [**plural**]) a set of red, green, and yellow lights that is used to

T

stop and start traffic [**usually plural**] *Turn left at the traffic lights.*

ˈtraffic ˌwarden *noun* [C] *UK* someone whose job is to make sure that people do not leave their cars in illegal places

tragedy /ˈtrædʒədi/ *noun* **1** SAD EVENT [C, U] an event or situation which is very sad, often involving death *the tragedy of their daughter's death* **2 LITERATURE** [C] a play with a sad end *a Greek tragedy*

tragic /ˈtrædʒɪk/ *adjective* very sad, often relating to death and suffering *a* ***tragic accident/death*** •**tragically** *adverb He was tragically killed in a flying accident at the age of 25.*

trail¹ /treɪl/ *noun* [C] **1** SIGNS a line of marks that someone or something leaves behind as they move *He left a trail of muddy footprints across the kitchen floor.* **2** PATH a path through the countryside, often where people walk *a* ***nature trail***

trail² /treɪl/ *verb* **1** FOLLOW [T] to follow someone, especially without them knowing, in order to watch or catch them *He suspected he was being trailed by undercover police.* **2** HANG DOWN [I, T] *UK* to hang down and touch the ground, or to make something do this *Your coat's trailing in the mud.* **3** LOWER SCORE [I, T] to have a lower score than someone else, especially in a sporting event *City were trailing United 2-1 at half time.*
trail away/off *phrasal verb* If someone's voice trails away or off, it gradually becomes quieter until it stops.

trailer /ˈtreɪlər/ *noun* [C] **1** CONTAINER a container with wheels that can be pulled by a car or a truck **2** HOUSE *mainly US* a house on wheels which can be pulled by a car **3** FILM short parts of a film or television programme which are shown in order to advertise it

ˈtrailer ˌpark *noun* [C] *US* a place where trailers (= vehicles that people live in) can park

O-ɯ **train¹** /treɪn/ *noun* **1** [C] a long, thin vehicle which travels along metal tracks and carries people or goods *a train journey* ○ *We could go* ***by train.*** ○ *You'll have to* ***catch/get*** *the next* ***train.*** **2 train of thought/events** a series of connected thoughts, ideas, or events which come or happen one after the other *I was interrupted and lost my train of thought.*

T

O-ɯ **train²** /treɪn/ *verb* **1 EDUCATION** [T] to teach someone how to do something, usually a skill that is needed for a job *We are* ***training*** *all our staff* ***in*** *how to use the new computer system.* [+ **to do sth**] *The aid workers trained local people to give the injections.* **2 EDUCATION** [I] to learn the skills you need to do a job *He* ***trained as*** *a lawyer in Vienna.* ○ *I'm* ***trained in*** *basic first aid.* **3 SPORT** [I, T] to practise a sport or exercise, often in order to prepare for a sporting event, or to help someone to do this *He's been training hard for the race for several weeks now.*

trainee /ˌtreɪˈniː/ *noun* [C] someone who is learning how to do something, especially a job *a trainee accountant/teacher*

trainer /ˈtreɪnər/ *noun* [C] **1** PERSON someone who trains people *a fitness trainer* **2 SPORT** a person who trains animals *a racehorse trainer* **3** SHOE *UK* (*US* **sneaker**) a soft sports shoe *a pair of trainers* ➲See colour picture **Clothes** on page Centre 9

WORD PARTNERS FOR ***training***

have/receive/undergo training • **give** sb / **provide** training • training **in/on** sth • a training **course/day/programme/session**

O-ɯ **training** /ˈtreɪnɪŋ/ *noun* [U] **1 EDUCATION** the process of learning the skills you need to do a particular job or activity *a* ***training course*** ○ *management training* **2 SPORT** preparation for a sport or competition *weight training* ○ *He's* ***in training*** *for the big match next month.*

trait /treɪt/ *noun* [C] a quality, good or bad, in someone's character *a family trait*

traitor /ˈtreɪtər/ *noun* [C] someone who is not loyal to their country or to a group which they are a member of

trajectory /trəˈdʒektəri/ *noun* [C] *formal* **PHYSICS** the curved line that something follows as it moves through the air

tram /træm/ *noun* [C] an electric vehicle for carrying passengers, mostly in cities, which moves along metal lines in the road

tramp¹ /træmp/ *noun* [C] someone who has no home, job, or money and who lives outside

tramp² /træmp/ *verb* [I, T] to walk a long way, or to walk with heavy steps because you are tired *We spent all day tramping around the city looking for somewhere cheap to stay.*

trample /ˈtræmpl/ (*also* **trample on**) *verb* [T] to walk on something, usually damaging or hurting it *She shouted at the boys for trampling on her flowers.* ○ *Two people were* ***trampled to death*** *in the panic.*

trampoline /ˈtræmpəliːn/ *noun* [C] **SPORT** a piece of sports equipment that you jump up and down on, made of a metal structure with a piece of strong material fixed to it

trance /trɑːns/ *noun* [C] a condition in which you are not completely conscious of what is happening around you or able to control what you are doing *He sat staring out of the window as if* ***in a trance.***

tranquil /ˈtræŋkwɪl/ *adjective* calm and quiet *a tranquil garden* •**tranquility** (*also* **tranquillity**) /træŋˈkwɪləti/ *noun* [U] *I love the tranquility of the woods.*

tranquilizer (*also UK* **-iser**) /ˈtræŋkwɪˌlaɪzər/ *noun* [C] **HEALTH** a drug which is used to make people or animals sleep or to make them calm

trans- /træns-, trænz-/ *prefix* **1** ACROSS across *transatlantic flights* **2** CHANGE showing a change *to transform* ○ *to translate*

transaction /trænˈzækʃən/ *noun* [C] *formal* **FINANCE** when someone buys or sells something, or when money is exchanged *a* ***business/financial transaction***

transatlantic /ˌtrænzətˈlæntɪk/ *adjective* crossing the Atlantic *a* ***transatlantic flight****/phone call*

transcend /trænˈsend/ *verb* [T] *formal* to be better or more important than something else *Somehow her appeal transcends class barriers.*

transcribe /trænˈskraɪb/ *verb* [T] **LANGUAGE** to make a written record of something you hear, such as speech or music *I later transcribed the tapes of the interviews.* •**transcription** /træn'skrɪpʃᵊn/ *noun* [C, U] a written record of speech, music, etc, or the process of making it

transcript /'trænskrɪpt/ *noun* [C] **LANGUAGE** an exact written record of speech, music, etc

transducer /trænz'dju:.səʳ/ *noun* [C] **PHYSICS** an electronic device that changes one form of energy into another, such as a microphone, which changes sound waves into electrical signals

transfer /træns'fɜ:ʳ/ *verb* **transferring**, *past* **transferred** **1** MOVE [T] to move someone or something from one place to another *She was later **transferred to** a different hospital.* ○ *I'll **transfer** some money **into** my other account.* **2** **SPORT** [I, T] to change to a different job, team, place of work, etc, or to make someone do this *After a year he **transferred to** University College, Dublin.* **3** CHANGE OWNER [T] to change who owns or controls something *We had all the documents transferred to my name.* •**transfer** /'trænsfɜ:ʳ/ *noun* [C, U] *I'm hoping for a transfer to the Brussels office.*

transfixed /træns'fɪkst/ *adjective* unable to move or stop looking at something because you are so interested, surprised, or frightened *We all sat in silence, transfixed by what we saw on the screen.*

transform /træns'fɔ:m/ *verb* [T] to change something completely, usually to improve it *Within weeks they had **transformed** the area **into** a beautiful garden.* •**transformation** /ˌtrænsfə'meɪʃᵊn/ *noun* [C, U] a complete change *The company has **undergone** a dramatic **transformation** in the past five years.*

transformer /træns'fɔ:məʳ/ *noun* [C] **PHYSICS** a piece of equipment that changes the strength of an electrical current

transfusion /træns'fju:ʒᵊn/ (*also* **blood transfusion**) *noun* [C] **HEALTH** when blood is put into someone's body

transgress /trænz'gres/ *verb* [I, T] *formal* to do something which is against a law or rule •**transgression** /trænz'greʃᵊn/ *noun* [C]

transient[1] /'trænziənt/ *adjective formal* **1** TEMPORARY lasting only for a short time *transient pleasures* **2** **SOCIETY** staying in one place only for a short time

transient[2] /'trænziənt/ *noun* [C] *US* **SOCIETY** someone who has no home and stays in a place for only a short time

transistor /træn'zɪstəʳ/ *noun* [C] **PHYSICS** a small piece of electrical equipment used in radios, televisions, etc

transit /'trænsɪt/ *noun* [U] *formal* the movement of goods or people from one place to another *Some things got damaged **in transit**.*

transition /træn'zɪʃᵊn/ *noun* [C, U] *formal* when something changes from one system or method to another, often gradually *The country is in the process of **making the transition from** military rule **to** democracy.* •**transitional** *adjective a **transitional period/phase*** ○ *a **transitional government***

tran'sition ˌmetal (*also* **tran'sition ˌelement**) *noun* [C] **CHEMISTRY** any of a group of metals, including iron and gold, which are heavy, melt at high temperatures and show more than one valency (= number of hydrogen atoms that can combine with one of its atoms to form a compound)

transitive /'trænsətɪv/ *adjective* **LANGUAGE** A transitive verb always has an object. In the sentence 'I'll make a drink.', 'make' is a transitive verb. ➲See Extra help page **Verb patterns** on page Centre 25. ➲Compare **intransitive**

transitory /'trænsɪtᵊri/ *adjective formal* lasting only for a short time

translate /trænz'leɪt/ *verb* [I, T] **1** **LANGUAGE** to change written or spoken words from one language to another *The book has now been **translated from** Spanish **into** more than ten languages.* **2** *formal* If an idea or plan translates into an action, it makes it happen. *So how does this theory **translate into** practical policy?*

translation /trænz'leɪʃᵊn/ *noun* [C, U] **LANGUAGE** something which has been translated from one language to another, or the process of translating

translator /trænz'leɪtəʳ/ *noun* [C] **LANGUAGE** someone whose job is to change written or spoken words from one language to another

translocation /ˌtrænzləʊ'keɪʃᵊn/ *noun* [U] **1** **BIOLOGY** when one part of a chromosome (= part of a cell that controls what an animal or plant is like) moves to another part of the same chromosome or to a different chromosome **2** **BIOLOGY** the way the substances a plant needs to live and grow are carried through it in a liquid

translucent /trænz'lu:sᵊnt/ *adjective* If something is translucent, light can pass through it and you can almost see through it. *translucent fabric*

transmission /trænz'mɪʃᵊn/ *noun* **1** **PHYSICS** [C, U] the process of broadcasting something by radio, television, etc, or something which is broadcast *radio/satellite transmission* **2** **HEALTH** [U] *formal* the process of passing something from one person or place to another *There is still a risk of transmission of the virus through infected water.* **3** CAR [U] the system in a car that moves power from its engine to its wheels *automatic/manual transmission*

transmit /trænz'mɪt/ *verb* [T] **transmitting**, *past* **transmitted** **1** **PHYSICS** to broadcast something, or to send out signals using radio, television, etc [**often passive**] *The information is transmitted electronically to the central computer.* **2** **HEALTH** *formal* to pass something from one person or place to another *The **disease is transmitted** by mosquitoes.* •**transmitter** *noun* [C] *a radio/television transmitter*

transparency /træn'spærᵊnsi/ *noun* [C] a photograph or picture printed on plastic which you can see on a screen by shining a light through it

transparent /træn'spærᵊnt/ *adjective* If a substance or material is transparent, you can see through it. *transparent plastic*

transpiration /ˌtrænspɪ'reɪʃᵊn/ *noun* [U] **BIOLOGY** the process by which water is lost

T

through the surface of a plant ➲See picture at **potometer** ➲See picture at **water cycle**

transpire /træn'spaɪəʳ/ *verb formal* **1 It transpires that** If it transpires that something has happened, this fact becomes known. *It later transpired that he had known about the plan from the beginning.* **2** [I] to happen **3 BIOLOGY** When a plant transpires, it loses water through its surfaces.

WORD PARTNERS FOR *transplant*

have/perform/undergo a transplant • a transplant **donor/operation/patient/surgeon**

transplant /'trænsplɑːnt/ *noun* [C] **HEALTH** an operation in which a new organ is put into someone's body *a heart/kidney transplant* •**transplant** /træn'splɑːnt/ *verb* [T] to remove an organ or other body part from one person and put it into someone else's body

WORD PARTNERS FOR *transport*

provide/arrange/improve transport • **free/cheap** transport • **public** transport • the transport **system**

transport[1] /'trænspɔːt/ *noun* [U] **1** VEHICLES a vehicle or system of vehicles, such as buses, trains, aircraft, etc for getting from one place to another *He can't drive so he has to rely on* ***public transport****.* ○ *the city's* ***transport system*** **2** PEOPLE/GOODS when people or goods are moved from one place to another *the transport of live animals*

transport[2] /træn'spɔːt/ *verb* [T] to move people or goods from one place to another

transportation /ˌtrænspɔː'teɪʃᵊn/ *noun* [U] **1** VEHICLES *US* (*UK* **transport**) a vehicle or system of vehicles, such as buses, trains, etc for getting from one place to another **2** PEOPLE/GOODS when people or goods are moved from one place to another *transportation costs*

transverse /trænz'vɜːs/ *adjective* **MATHEMATICS** in a position or direction that is at an angle of 90° to something else

ˌtransverse 'wave *noun* [C] **PHYSICS** in physics, a wave moving at a 90° angle to the vibrations (= fast movements backwards and forwards) of the particles of the substance through which it is moving ➲Compare **longitudinal wave**

transvestite /trænz'vestaɪt/ *noun* [C] someone, especially a man, who likes to wear the clothes of someone of the opposite sex

trap[1] /træp/ *noun* [C] **1** CATCHING ANIMALS a piece of equipment for catching animals *a mouse trap* **2** SITUATION a dangerous or unpleasant situation which is difficult to escape from [**usually singular**] *Such families* ***get caught in*** *the poverty* ***trap****.* ➲See also: **booby trap**

trap[2] /træp/ *verb* [T] **trapping**, *past* **trapped 1** CANNOT ESCAPE If someone or something is trapped, they cannot move or escape from a place or situation. *The car turned over, trapping the driver underneath.* **2** ANIMAL to catch an animal using a trap **3** TRICK to trick someone into doing or saying something that they do not want to

ˌtrap 'door *noun* [C] a small door that you cannot see in a floor or ceiling

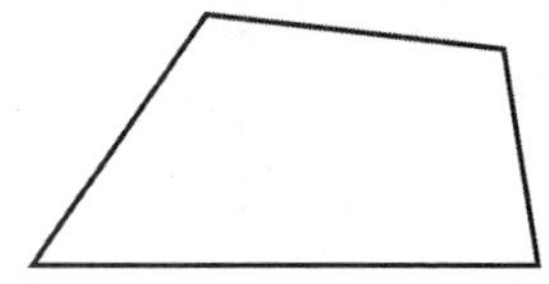

trapezium UK, trapezoid US

trapezium /trə'piːziəm/ *noun* [C] **1 MATHEMATICS** *UK* a flat shape with four sides, where two of the sides are parallel **2 MATHEMATICS** *US* a trapezoid

trapezoid /'træpɪzɔɪd/g *noun* [C] **1 MATHEMATICS** *UK* a shape with four sides of different lengths, none of which are parallel **2 MATHEMATICS** *US* a trapezium

trappings /'træpɪŋz/ *noun* [**plural**] things that you usually get when you are rich and successful, such as a big house and car *the trappings of success/power*

trash[1] /træʃ/ *noun* [U] **1** WASTE *US* (*UK* **rubbish**) things that you throw away because you do not want them **2** BAD *informal* something that is of bad quality *It's better than the trash she usually reads.*

trash[2] /træʃ/ *verb* [T] *informal* to destroy something *Vandals broke in and trashed the place.*

'trash ˌcan *noun* [C] *US* a container for waste, often one that is kept outdoors ➲See colour picture **The Office** on page Centre 5

trashy /'træʃi/ *adjective informal* of very bad quality *a trashy novel/movie*

trauma /'trɔːmə/ *noun* [C, U] severe shock caused by an unpleasant experience, or the experience which causes this feeling *the trauma of marriage breakdown*

traumatic /trɔː'mætɪk/ *adjective* If an experience is traumatic, it makes you feel very shocked and upset. *His parents split up when he was eight, which he found very traumatic.*

traumatized (*also UK* **-ised**) /'trɔːmətaɪzd/ *adjective* **HEALTH** very shocked and upset for a long time *The violence that he witnessed left him traumatized.*

travel[1] /'trævᵊl/ *verb UK* **travelling**, *past* **travelled**, *US* **traveling**, *past* **traveled 1** MAKE A JOURNEY [I, T] to make a journey *I spent a year travelling around Asia.* ○ *He has to travel abroad a lot on business.* **2** MOVE [I] If light, sound, or news travels, it moves from one place to another. *News of the accident travelled fast.* ➲See Common Learner Error at **move**

travel[2] /'trævᵊl/ *noun* **1** [U] the activity of travelling *air/rail travel* ○ ***travel expenses/insurance*** **2 sb's travels** someone's journey *I meet all kinds of interesting people* ***on my travels****.*

COMMON LEARNER ERROR

travel, journey, or **trip?**

The noun **travel** is a general word which means the activity of travelling.

Air travel has become much cheaper.

Use **journey** to talk about when you travel from one place to another.

He fell asleep during the train journey.

Did you have a good journey?

~~*Did you have a good travel?*~~

A **trip** is a journey in which you visit a place for a short time and come back again.

a business trip

a 3-day trip to Spain

ˈtravel ˌagency (*also* **ˈtravel ˌagent's**) *noun* [C] a company or shop that makes travel arrangements for people

ˈtravel ˌagent *noun* [C] someone whose job is making travel arrangements for people

ˈtravel ˌcard *noun* [C] a ticket that can be used for several journeys or for a particular length of time in an area

traveller /ˈtrævᵊləʳ/ *noun* [C] **1** (*also US* **traveler**) someone who is travelling or who often travels *We're doing a survey of business travellers.* **2** **SOCIETY** *UK another word for* gypsy (= a member of a race of people who travel from place to place, especially in Europe)

ˈtraveller's ˌcheque *UK* (*US* **traveler's check**) *noun* [C] **FINANCE** a special piece of paper which you buy at a bank and exchange for local money when you are in another country

traverse /trəˈvɜːs/ *verb* [T] *formal* to move across something

travesty /ˈtrævəsti/ *noun* [C] *formal* If something is a travesty, it is very badly done or unfair and does not represent how that thing should be. *She described the trial as **a travesty of justice**.*

trawl /trɔːl/ *verb*

trawl through sth *phrasal verb mainly UK* to look through a lot of things in order to find something *to trawl through data*

trawler /ˈtrɔːləʳ/ *noun* [C] a large ship which is used for catching fish by pulling a large net through the sea behind it

tray /treɪ/ *noun* [C] a flat object with higher edges, used for carrying food and drinks *She came back carrying a tray of drinks.*

treacherous /ˈtretʃᵊrəs/ *adjective* **1** DANGEROUS very dangerous, especially because of bad weather conditions *Ice had made the roads treacherous.* **2** NOT LOYAL *formal* If someone is treacherous, they deceive people who trust them.

treachery /ˈtretʃᵊri/ *noun* [U] *formal* when a person deceives someone who trusts them

treacle /ˈtriːkl/ *UK* (*UK/US* **molasses**) *noun* [U] **FOOD** a sweet, thick, dark liquid used in sweet dishes

tread¹ /tred/ *verb past tense* **trod**, *past participle* **trodden** **1** [I, T] *mainly UK* to put your foot on something or to press something down with your foot *I **trod on** a piece of broken glass.* ○ *David **trod in** some paint.* ○ *The kids were **treading** cake crumbs **into** the carpet.* **2** **tread carefully/gently/lightly, etc** to be careful what you say so that you do not upset someone **3** **tread water** to float vertically in the water by moving your arms and legs up and down

tread² /tred/ *noun* **1** TYRE [C, U] the pattern of lines on the surface of a tyre **2** STEP [**no plural**] the sound of someone putting their feet down when walking

treadmill /ˈtredmɪl/ *noun* [C] **1** **SPORT** a machine with a moving part which you walk or run on for exercise **2** a job which is boring because you have to repeat the same thing again and again

treason /ˈtriːzᵊn/ *noun* [U] **LAW, POLITICS** the crime of doing something that harms your country or government, especially by helping its enemies

treasure¹ /ˈtreʒəʳ/ *noun* **1** GOLD/JEWELLERY [U] a collection of gold, silver, jewellery and valuable objects, especially in children's stories *buried treasure* **2** VALUABLE OBJECT [C] a very valuable object [**usually plural**] *art treasures*

treasure² /ˈtreʒəʳ/ *verb* [T] If you treasure something, it is very important to you and gives you a lot of pleasure. *I shall treasure those memories of her.*

treasurer /ˈtreʒᵊrəʳ/ *noun* [C] **FINANCE** someone who is responsible for the money of an organization

treasury /ˈtreʒᵊri/ *noun* [C] **POLITICS, ECONOMICS** the government department which controls a country's money supply and economy

O⁻ **treat¹** /triːt/ *verb* [T] **1** DEAL WITH to behave towards or deal with someone in a particular way *He **treats** her really **badly**.* ○ *She felt she'd been **unfairly treated** by her employer.* ○ *They **treat** her **like** one of their own children.* **2** CONSIDER to consider something in a particular way *He **treated** my suggestion **as** a joke.* **3** **HEALTH** to give medical care to someone for an illness or injury *He's being **treated for** cancer at a hospital in Manchester.* **4** SPECIAL to do or buy something special for someone *I'm going to **treat** her **to** dinner at that nice Italian restaurant.* **5** PROTECT to put a substance on something in order to protect it *The wood is then **treated with** a special chemical to protect it from the rain.*

treat² /triːt/ *noun* [C] something special which you buy or do for someone else *a **birthday treat*** ○ *As a **special treat** I'm taking him out for dinner.* ○ *Annie, put your money away, this is **my treat*** (= I am paying). ⊃See also: **Trick or treat!**

treatise /ˈtriːtɪz/ *noun* [C] a formal piece of writing that examines a particular subject

WORD PARTNERS FOR ***treatment***

get/have/receive/undergo treatment • **give/provide** treatment • **respond to** treatment • treatment **for** sth

O⁻ **treatment** /ˈtriːtmənt/ *noun* **1** **HEALTH** [C, U] something which you do to try to cure an illness or injury, especially something suggested or done by a doctor *She's **receiving treatment** for a lung infection.* **2** [U] the way you deal with or behave towards someone or something *There have been complaints about the treatment of prisoners.*

WORD PARTNERS FOR ***treaty***

draw up/ratify/sign a treaty • the **terms of** a treaty • **under** a treaty • a treaty **between** sb and sb • a treaty **on** sth • a **peace** treaty • an **international** treaty

treaty /ˈtriːti/ *noun* [C] **POLITICS** a written agreement between two or more countries *a **peace treaty** ○ an **international treaty***

treble /ˈtrebl/ *verb* [I, T] to increase three times in size or amount, or to make something do this

O⁻**tree** /triː/ *noun* [C] a tall plant with a thick stem which has branches coming from it and leaves ➲See also: **Christmas tree, family tree, palm tree**

trek /trek/ *noun* [C] a long, difficult journey that you make by walking *They started out on the long trek across the mountains.* •**trek** *verb* [I] **trekking**, *past* **trekked**

trellis /ˈtrelɪs/ *noun* [C] a wooden structure fixed to a wall for plants to grow up

tremble /ˈtrembl/ *verb* [I] to shake slightly, especially because you are nervous, frightened, or cold *My hands were trembling so much I could hardly hold the pen.*

tremendous /trɪˈmendəs/ *adjective* **1** GOOD extremely good *I think she's doing a tremendous job.* **2** LARGE very large, great, strong, etc *a tremendous amount of money* •**tremendously** *adverb* very much

tremor /ˈtreməʳ/ *noun* [C] **1 GEOLOGY** a slight earthquake (= when the Earth shakes) **2** a slight shaking of part of your body which you cannot control

trench /trenʃ/ *noun* [C] a long, narrow hole dug into the ground

trenchant /ˈtrenʃənt/ *adjective formal* expressing strong criticism ***trenchant criticism/views***

trenchcoat /ˈtrentʃˌkəʊt/ *noun* [C] a long coat that does not let water through, similar in style to a military coat

trend /trend/ *noun* [C] **SOCIETY** a general development or change in a situation *There's a **trend towards** more locally produced television programmes. ○ I'm not familiar with the latest **trends in** teaching methodology.*

T

trendy /ˈtrendi/ *adjective informal* fashionable at the moment

trepidation /ˌtrepɪˈdeɪʃən/ *noun* [U] *formal* fear or worry about something you are going to do *It was **with trepidation** that I accepted Klein's invitation.*

trespass /ˈtrespəs/ *verb* [I] **LAW** to go on someone's land without their permission •**trespasser** *noun* [C]

tri- /traɪ-/ *prefix* three *a triangle ○ a tripod*

WORD PARTNERS FOR ***trial***

be on/stand trial (for sth) • **be awaiting/be facing** trial • a trial **court/date/judge**

O⁻**trial** /traɪəl/ *noun* [C, U] **1 LAW** a legal process to decide if someone is guilty of a crime *The two men are now **on trial for** attempted murder. ○ He will be taken to the US to **stand trial**.* **2** TEST a test of something new to find out if it is safe, works correctly, etc *The drug is currently undergoing **clinical trials**.* **3 trial and error** a way of learning the best way to do something by trying different methods

ˈ**trial ˌbalance** *noun* **FINANCE** a list of how much a business has in its accounts that is produced on a particular date to check that the business's double entry bookkeeping accounts do not have mistakes

trials /traɪəlz/ *noun* [plural] **1 SPORT** a sports competition to find out how good a player is **2 trials and tribulations** problems and suffering *the trials and tribulations of growing up*

triangle /ˈtraɪæŋgl/ *noun* [C] **1** a flat shape with three sides ➲See picture at shape **2 MUSIC** a small musical instrument made of a piece of metal with three sides which you hit with a metal bar •**triangular** /traɪˈæŋgjələʳ/ *adjective* shaped like a triangle

Triassic /traɪˈæsɪk/ *adjective* **GEOLOGY** from the period of time between around 245 and 208 million years ago, in which dinosaurs first appeared
the Triassic period

triathlon /traɪˈæθlɒn/ *noun* [C] **SPORT** a competition in which you must swim, ride a bicycle and run a particular distance without stopping between these activities

tribe /traɪb/ *noun* [C] **SOCIETY** a group of people who live together, usually in areas far away from cities, and who share the same culture and language and still have a traditional way of life *Native American tribes* •**tribal** *adjective* relating to a tribe *a tribal dance*

tribulations /ˌtrɪbjəˈleɪʃənz/ *noun* [plural] ➲See: **trials** and tribulations

tribunal /traɪˈbjuːnəl/ *noun* [C] **LAW** an official court or group of people whose job is to deal with a particular problem or disagreement ➲See also: **industrial tribunal**

tributary /ˈtrɪbjətəri/ *noun* [C] **GEOGRAPHY** a river or stream which flows into a larger river

tribute /ˈtrɪbjuːt/ *noun* [C, U] **1** something which you do or say to show that you respect and admire someone, especially in a formal situation *The concert was organized as **a tribute to** the singer who died last year. ○ The President **paid tribute to*** (= expressed his admiration for) *the brave soldiers who had defended the country.* **2 be a tribute to sb/sth** to show how good someone or something is *It's a tribute to Mark's hard work that the project is finished.*

ˈ**tribute ˌband** *noun* [C] **MUSIC** a group of musicians who play the music of a famous pop group and pretend to be that group *a Rolling Stones tribute band*

triceps /ˈtraɪseps/ *noun* [C] *plural* **triceps** **ANATOMY** the large muscle at the back of the upper arm

WORD PARTNERS FOR ***trick***

play a trick (on sb) • a **cheap/cruel/dirty/sneaky** trick • a trick **question**

trick[1] /trɪk/ *noun* [C] **1** DECEIVE something you do to deceive or cheat someone, or to make someone look stupid as a joke *a **trick question** ○ I* *wasn't really ill - it was just a trick.* ○ *My little brother liked to* ***play tricks on*** *me* (= do things to deceive me as a joke). **2** METHOD an effective way of doing something *What's the* ***trick to*** *pulling out this sofa bed?* **3** MAGIC something that is done to entertain people and that seems to be magic *a card trick* **4 do the trick** If something does the trick, it solves a problem or has the result you want. *If I've got a headache, a couple of aspirins usually do the trick.* ➲See also: **hat trick**

trick² /trɪk/ *verb* [T] to deceive someone [+ **into** + **doing sth**] *They tricked him into signing the papers.*

trickery /ˈtrɪkəri/ *noun* [U] the use of tricks to deceive or cheat people

trickle /ˈtrɪkl/ *verb* **1 trickle down/from/out of, etc** If liquid trickles somewhere, it flows slowly and in a thin line. *She could feel the sweat trickling down her back.* **2 trickle in/into/out, etc** to go somewhere slowly in small numbers *People began to trickle into the classroom.* •**trickle** *noun* [C] *a trickle of blood*

ˌTrick or ˈtreat! 1 something that children say on Halloween (= a holiday on 31 October), when they dress to look frightening and visit people's houses to ask for sweets **2 go trick or treating** If children go trick or treating, they visit people's houses on Halloween to ask for sweets.

tricky /ˈtrɪki/ *adjective* difficult to deal with or do *a* ***tricky question/situation***

tricuspid valve /traɪˈkʌspɪdˌvælv/ *noun* [**C usually singular**] **ANATOMY** the valve (= part that opens and closes) in the heart which stops blood from returning into the right atrium (= upper space) from the right ventricle (= lower space) ➲Compare **mitral valve** ➲See picture at **heart**

tricycle /ˈtraɪsɪkl/ *noun* [C] a bicycle with one wheel at the front and two at the back

trifle /ˈtraɪfl/ *noun* **1 a trifle** *formal* slightly *It does seem a trifle odd.* **2 FOOD** [C, U] *UK* a cold, sweet dish that has layers of cake, fruit, custard (= sweet, yellow sauce), and cream **3** [C] *formal* something silly or unimportant

trigger¹ /ˈtrɪgəʳ/ (*also* **trigger off**) *verb* [T] to make something begin to happen *His arrest triggered mass protests.*

trigger² /ˈtrɪgəʳ/ *noun* [C] **1** GUN the part of a gun that you pull when you shoot **2** CAUSE an event or situation that makes something else happen *Stress can be a* ***trigger for*** *many illnesses.*

trigonometry /ˌtrɪgəˈnɒmətri/ *noun* [U] **MATHEMATICS** the type of mathematics that deals with the relationship between the angles and sides of triangles, used in measuring the height of buildings, mountains, etc

trillion /ˈtrɪljən/ the number 1,000,000,000,000

trilogy /ˈtrɪlədʒi/ *noun* [C] a series of three books, plays, etc with the same characters or subject

trim¹ /trɪm/ *verb* [T] **trimming**, *past* **trimmed** **1** CUT (*also* **trim off**) to cut a small amount from something to make it tidy or to remove parts that you do not need *I've had my hair trimmed.* ○ *Trim the fat off the meat.* **2** REDUCE to reduce something *to trim costs* **3 be trimmed with sth** to be decorated with something around the edges *a silk dress trimmed with lace*

trim² /trɪm/ *noun* **1** CUT [**no plural**] when you cut something to make it tidy *The hedge needs a trim.* **2** DECORATION [**U, no plural**] decoration that is added to something such as clothes or a car *The car has a stereo, sunroof, and leather trim.*

trim³ /trɪm/ *adjective* looking thin and healthy

trimaran /ˈtraɪməræn/ *noun* [C] a small fast sailing boat with three hulls (= the part of the boat that floats on the water)

trimester /trɪˈmestəʳ/ Ⓤⓢ /traɪˈmestər/ *noun* [C] *mainly US* **EDUCATION** one of the periods of time that the school or university year is divided into

trimming /ˈtrɪmɪŋ/ *noun* [C, U] decoration on the edge of something such as a piece of clothing

trimmings /ˈtrɪmɪŋz/ *noun* [plural] **FOOD** extra dishes that are often eaten with a main dish *a roast dinner* ***with all the trimmings***

trinitrotoluene /ˌtraɪnaɪtrəʊˈtɒljuiːn/ (*abbreviation* **TNT**) *noun* [C] **CHEMISTRY** a powerful explosive substance

the Trinity /ˈtrɪnəti/ *noun* **RELIGION** the existence of God in three forms, Father, Son, and Holy Spirit, in the Christian religion

trio /ˈtriːəʊ/ *noun* [C] **MUSIC** a group of three things or people, especially three musicians who play together

WORD PARTNERS FOR ***trip***

go on/take a trip • a **day/two-day/weekend** trip • **on** a trip • a trip **around/to** sth • a **business** trip

O⁻ **trip¹** /trɪp/ *noun* [C] a journey in which you visit a place for a short time and come back again *a* ***business trip*** ○ *a* ***day trip*** *to Paris* ○ *We might* ***take a trip to*** *Spain later in the summer.* ➲See Common Learner Error at **travel** ➲See also: **round trip**

trip² /trɪp/ *verb* **tripping**, *past* **tripped** **1** FALL [I] to fall or almost fall because you hit your foot on something when you are walking or running *Careful you don't* ***trip over*** *the cat!* ○ *He* ***tripped on*** *a stone and hurt his ankle.* **2** MAKE FALL [T] to make someone fall by putting your foot in front of their foot

trip (sb) up *phrasal verb* **1** FALL *UK* to fall because you hit your foot on something, or to make someone fall by putting your foot in front of their foot **2** MAKE A MISTAKE to make a mistake, or to cause someone to make a mistake *I tripped up on the last question.*

triple¹ /ˈtrɪpl/ *adjective* having three parts of the same type, or happening three times *a triple world champion*

triple² /ˈtrɪpl/ *verb* [I, T] to increase three times in size or amount, or to make something do this *Sales have tripled in the past five years.*

the ˌTriple Alˈliance *noun* **POLITICS** the agreement of Germany, Austria-Hungary and Italy to support each other, that lasted from 1882-1914

T

the Triple Entente /ˌtrɪplɒn'tɒnt/ *noun* **POLITICS** an agreement in 1907 between the UK, France and Russia to support each other

triplet /'trɪplət/ *noun* [C] one of three children who are born to the same mother at the same time

tripod /'traɪpɒd/ *noun* [C] a piece of equipment with three legs, used for supporting a camera or a container in a science laboratory ➲See picture at **laboratory**

trite /traɪt/ *adjective* A trite remark, idea, etc does not seem sincere or true because it has been used so much before or is too simple.

tritik /trɪ'tiːk/ *noun* [U] **DT** a method of dyeing (= putting colour on) cloth in which the cloth is folded and sewn so that the dye does not get onto some areas

tritium /'trɪtiəm/ *noun* [U] **CHEMISTRY** a radioactive isotope (= form of an atom which has a different atomic weight from other forms of the same atom) of hydrogen

triumph¹ /'traɪəmf/ *noun* **1** SUCCESS [C] an important success, achievement, or victory *Barcelona's 2-0 triumph over Manchester United* **2** FEELING [U] the feeling of happiness that you have when you win something or succeed

triumph² /'traɪəmf/ *verb* [I] to win or succeed *The Democrats once again triumphed in recent elections.*

triumphant /traɪ'ʌmfənt/ *adjective* feeling very pleased because you have won something or succeeded *the President's triumphant return to the White House* •**triumphantly** *adverb*

trivia /'trɪviə/ *noun* [U] small facts or details that are not important

trivial /'trɪviəl/ *adjective* small and not important *a* ***trivial matter/offence***

trivialize (*also UK* **-ise**) /'trɪviəlaɪz/ *verb* [T] to make something seem less important or serious than it really is *I don't mean to trivialize the problem.*

trochee /'trəʊkiː/ *noun* [C] **LITERATURE** a rhythm in poetry with one long or strong syllable and one short or weak syllable

T

trod /trɒd/ *past tense of* tread

trodden /'trɒdən/ *past participle of* tread

trojan (horse) /ˌtrəʊdʒən'hɔːs/ *noun* [C] **COMPUTING** a computer program that looks useful but does harm, often by allowing other people to get into a computer system

trolley /'trɒli/ *noun* [C] **1** CARRYING THINGS *UK* (*US* **cart**) a metal structure on wheels that is used for carrying things *a supermarket trolley ○ a luggage trolley* **2** CARRYING PEOPLE *US* (*UK/US* **tram**) an electric vehicle for carrying passengers, mostly in cities, which runs along metal tracks in the road **3 off your trolley** *informal* mad

trombone /trɒm'bəʊn/ *noun* [C] **MUSIC** a metal musical instrument that you play by blowing into it and sliding a tube up and down

troop¹ /truːp/ *noun* [C] a group of people or animals

troop² /truːp/ *verb informal* **troop into/through/out of, etc** to walk somewhere in a large group *We all trooped into the hall in silence.*

trooper /'truːpəʳ/ *noun* [C] **LAW** a police officer in the US state police force

troops /truːps/ *noun* [**plural**] soldiers *UN troops have been sent to help in the rescue effort.*

trophic level /ˌtrɒfɪk'levəl/ *noun* [C] **BIOLOGY** any of the layers of an ecosystem with the same position in the food chain

trophy /'trəʊfi/ *noun* [C] a prize, such as a silver cup, that you get for winning a race or competition

tropical /'trɒpɪkəl/ *adjective* **GEOGRAPHY** from or in the hottest parts of the world

ˌtropical ˈrain ˌforest *noun* [C, U] **GEOGRAPHY** thick forest that grows in hot parts of the world

the tropics /'trɒpɪks/ *noun* [**plural**] **GEOGRAPHY** the hottest parts of the world, near to the Equator (= imaginary line around the Earth's middle)

tropism /'trəʊpɪzəm/ *noun* [U] **BIOLOGY** when living things turn towards or away from something, for example light

the troposphere /'trɒpəsfɪər/ *noun* [**no plural**] **GEOGRAPHY** the layer of gases surrounding the Earth from the surface up to about 10 kilometres

trot¹ /trɒt/ *verb* **trotting**, *past* **trotted 1** [I] If a horse trots, it runs slowly with short steps. **2 trot down/up/along, etc** to walk with quick, short steps *The little boy trotted along behind his father.*

trot sth out *phrasal verb informal* to say something that has been said many times before and does not seem sincere *They always trot out the same old statistics.*

trot² /trɒt/ *noun* **1 SPORT** [**no plural**] the speed that a horse moves when it trots **2 on the trot** If you do several things on the trot, you do them one after the other. *They won three games on the trot.*

WORD PARTNERS FOR ***trouble***

have trouble with sth • **get into/run into** trouble • the trouble **is** • **without** any trouble

trouble¹ /'trʌbl/ *noun* **1** PROBLEMS [C, U] problems, difficulties, or worries [+ **doing sth**] *We* ***had trouble*** *finding somewhere to park. ○ She's been having a lot of* ***trouble with*** *her boss recently. ○ I'd like to go to the party, but* ***the trouble is*** *my parents won't let me.* **2 the trouble with sb/sth** used to say what is wrong with someone or something *The trouble with a white floor is that it gets dirty so quickly.* **3** NOT WORKING [U] a problem that you have with a machine or part of your body *back trouble ○* ***car trouble*** **4** FIGHTING [U] a situation in which people are fighting or arguing *The trouble started after a group of drunken football fans started to throw bottles.* **5** DIFFICULT SITUATION [U] a difficult or dangerous situation *The company was* ***in trouble*** *and had huge debts.* **6** PUNISHMENT [U] when you have done something wrong and are likely to be punished *Her children are always* ***in trouble****. ○ They* ***got***

into trouble with the police. **7** EXTRA WORK [U] when you use extra time or energy to do something [+ to do sth] *He* ***took the trouble*** *to write to each of them personally.*

COMMON LEARNER ERROR

trouble or **problem?**

Problem means 'a situation that causes difficulties and that needs to be dealt with'. You can talk about **a problem** or **problems**.

Tell me what the problem is.

There's a problem with the engine.

He's having a few problems at work.

Trouble means 'problems, difficulties, or worries' and is used to talk about problems in a more general way. **Trouble** is almost always uncountable so do not use the determiner 'a' before it.

We had some trouble while we were on holiday.

He helped me when I was in trouble.

I had trouble with the car last night.

~~*I had a trouble with the car last night.*~~

trouble² /ˈtrʌbl/ *verb* [T] **1** WORRY If something troubles you, you think about it a lot and it makes you worry. *The situation has been troubling me for a while.* **2** FORMAL REQUEST *formal* used to ask someone politely to help you *I'm sorry to trouble you, but could you tell me how to get to the station?*

troubled /ˈtrʌbᵊld/ *adjective* worried or having a lot of problems *You look troubled.*

troublemaker /ˈtrʌblˌmeɪkəʳ/ *noun* [C] someone who intentionally causes problems

troublesome /ˈtrʌblsəm/ *adjective* causing a lot of problems, especially over a long period of time *a troublesome knee injury*

trough /trɒf/ *noun* [C] **1 FARMING** a long, narrow container that animals eat or drink from **2** *formal* a low point in a series of high and low points ***peaks and troughs***

troupe /truːp/ *noun* [C] a group of singers, dancers, etc who perform together

O⁻**trousers** /ˈtraʊzəz/ (*also US* **pants**) *noun* [plural] a piece of clothing that covers the legs and has a separate part for each leg *a* ***pair of trousers*** ➲See colour picture **Clothes** on pages Centre 8, 9

ˈtrouser ˌsuit *UK* (*US* **pant suit**) *noun* [C] a woman's jacket and trousers made of the same material

trout /traʊt/ *noun* [C, U] *plural* **trout FOOD** a type of river fish, or the meat from this fish

truant /ˈtruːənt/ *noun* [C] **1 EDUCATION** a child who stays away from school without permission **2 play truant** *UK* to stay away from school without permission •**truancy** /ˈtruːənsi/ *noun* [U] when children are truants

WORD PARTNERS FOR ***truce***

agree/call/offer a truce • a **fragile/uneasy** truce • a truce **between** sb and sb • a truce **with** sb

truce /truːs/ *noun* [C] an agreement between two enemies to stop fighting for a period of time

O⁻**truck** /trʌk/ (*also UK* **lorry**) *noun* [C] a large road vehicle for carrying goods from place to place

trucker /ˈtrʌkəʳ/ *noun* [C] *mainly US* someone whose job is driving trucks

trudge /trʌdʒ/ *verb* **trudge along/through/up, etc** to walk slowly with heavy steps, especially because you are tired *We trudged back up the hill.*

O⁻**true** /truː/ *adjective* **1** NOT FALSE based on facts and not imagined *a true story* [+ (that)] *Is it true that Martin and Sue are getting married?* ➲Opposite **untrue** ➲See Common Learner Error at **right** **2** REAL [always before noun] real *a true friend* ○ ***true love*** **3 come true** If a dream or hope comes true, it really happens. **4 be true to sb/sth** to be loyal and sincere even in a difficult situation *It's important to be true to your principles.* **5 ring true** to seem to be the truth *Something about the story didn't ring true.*

truffle /ˈtrʌfl/ *noun* [C] **1 FOOD** a soft sweet that is made with chocolate **2 FOOD** a fungus (= organism like a plant) that you can eat, which grows under the ground

truly /ˈtruːli/ *adverb* **1** NOT FALSE used to emphasize that something is true in every way *The project was truly a team effort.* **2** VERY used to emphasize a description of something *It's truly amazing to watch a baby being born.* **3** SINCERE used to emphasize that something is sincere or honest *I truly believe that he is innocent.*

trump /trʌmp/ *noun* **1** [C] a card that has a higher value than other cards in some card games **2 come/turn up trumps** *UK* to be successful, or provide something that is needed, especially when people do not expect you to *He's really come up trumps with this latest book.*

ˈtrump ˌcard *noun* [C] an advantage that will help you succeed, especially one that other people do not know about

trumpet /ˈtrʌmpɪt/ *noun* [C] **MUSIC** a metal musical instrument that you play by blowing into it and pressing buttons to make different notes •**trumpeter** *noun* [C]

truncheon /ˈtrʌnʃᵊn/ *UK* (*US* **nightstick**) *noun* [C] a short stick that police officers carry to use as a weapon

trundle /ˈtrʌndl/ *verb* **trundle (sth) along/down/up, etc** to move slowly on wheels, or to push something slowly on wheels *The bus trundled along the lane.*

trunk /trʌŋk/ *noun* [C] **1 BIOLOGY** the thick stem of a tree that the branches grow from **2** CAR *US* (*UK* **boot**) a closed space at the back of a car for storing things in ➲See colour picture **Car** on page Centre 7 **3 BIOLOGY** the long nose of an elephant (= large, grey animal) **4** CONTAINER a large box with a lid that you store things in **5 ANATOMY** the main part of your body, not your head, legs, or arms

ˈtrunk ˌroad *noun* [C] *UK* a main road across a country or area

trunks /trʌŋks/ *noun* [plural] **1** (*also* **swimming trunks**) a piece of clothing that boys and men wear when they swim **2** underwear worn by men ➲See colour picture **Clothes** on page Centre 9

O⁻**trust¹** /trʌst/ *verb* **1** [T] to believe that someone is good and honest and will not harm you *My sister warned me not to trust him.* ➲Opposite

T

distrust, mistrust 2 trust sb to do sth to be sure that someone will do the right thing or what they should do *I trust them to make the right decision.* **3 trust sb with sb/sth** to allow someone to look after someone or something because you believe they will be careful *I wouldn't trust him with my car.* **4 Trust sb (to do sth)!** *mainly UK informal* used to say that it is typical of someone to do something stupid *Trust Chris to leave the tickets at home!* **5 I trust (that)** *formal* used to say that you hope something is true *I trust that you had an enjoyable stay.*

WORD PARTNERS FOR ***trust (noun)***

have/show trust **in** sb • **earn/gain/win** sb's trust • **betray** sb's trust • trust **between** [two people]

O⁼**trust²** /trʌst/ *noun* **1** BELIEF [U] the belief that you can trust someone or something *a marriage based on love and trust* ○ *They **showed** a lot of **trust in** me right from the beginning.* ➲Opposite **distrust, mistrust 2 FINANCE, LAW** [C, U] a legal arrangement that allows a person or organization to control someone else's money

trustee /trʌs'tiː/ *noun* [C] **LAW** someone who has legal control over someone else's money or possessions

trusting /'trʌstɪŋ/ *adjective* always believing that other people are good or honest and will not harm or deceive you

trustworthy /'trʌstˌwɜːði/ *adjective* Someone who is trustworthy can be trusted.

WORD PARTNERS FOR ***truth***

tell the truth • **discover/find out/learn/uncover** the truth • the truth **comes out/emerges** • the **awful/honest/simple** truth • the truth **about** sb/sth

O⁼**truth** /truːθ/ *noun plural* **truths** /truːðz/ **1 the truth** the real facts about a situation *Do you think he was **telling the truth**?* ○ *I don't think we'll ever know **the truth about** what really happened.* **2** BEING TRUE [U] the quality of being true *There may be some truth in their claim.* **3** TRUE FACT [C] a fact or idea that people accept is true *moral/religious truths* ➲Opposite **untruth**

truthful /'truːθfᵊl/ *adjective* honest and not containing or telling any lies *a truthful answer* •**truthfully** *adverb* •**truthfulness** *noun* [U]

O⁼**try¹** /traɪ/ *verb* **1** ATTEMPT [I] to attempt to do something [**+ to do sth**] *I tried to open the window but couldn't.* ○ *Try not to drop anything this time.* **2** TEST [T] to do, test, taste, etc something to discover if it works or if you like it *I tried that recipe you gave me last night.* [**+ doing sth**] *Why don't you try using a different shampoo?* **3 LAW** [T] to examine facts in a court of law to decide if someone is guilty of a crime [**often passive**] *He was **tried for** attempted murder.*

try sth on *phrasal verb* to put on a piece of clothing to discover if it fits you or if you like it *Could I try this dress on, please?*

try sth out *phrasal verb* to use something to discover if it works or if you like it *We're going to try out that new restaurant tonight.*

try² /traɪ/ *noun* **1** [C] an attempt to do something *She suggested I should **have a try**.* **2 give sth a try** to do something in order to find out if it works or if you like it **3 SPORT** [C] when a team scores points in rugby (= game played with an oval ball) by putting the ball on the ground behind the other team's goal line

trying /traɪɪŋ/ *adjective* annoying and difficult *I've had a very **trying day/time**.*

trypsin /'trɪpsɪn/ *noun* [U] **BIOLOGY** an enzyme (= chemical substance produced by living cells) that breaks down proteins

tsar *UK* (*UK/US* **czar**) /zɑːʳ/ *noun* [C] **POLITICS 1** a male Russian ruler before 1917 **2** a powerful official who makes important decisions for the government about a particular activity

T-shirt (*also* **tee shirt**) /'tiːʃɜːt/ *noun* [C] a piece of cotton clothing for the top part of the body with short sleeves and no collar ➲See colour picture **Clothes** on page Centre 8

tsp MEASURES *written abbreviation for* teaspoonful: the amount that can be held by a small spoon used for measuring food

tsunami /tsuː'nɑːmi/ *noun* [C] **GEOGRAPHY** an extremely large wave from the sea which causes a lot of damage to buildings, etc. on land and is often caused by an earthquake (= sudden movement of the Earth's surface) under the sea

tub /tʌb/ *noun* [C] **1** LARGE CONTAINER a large, round container with a flat base and an open top *Outside was a stone patio with tubs of flowering plants.* **2** FOOD CONTAINER a small, plastic container with a lid, used for storing food *a tub of ice cream/margarine* **3** BATH *US* (*UK* **bath**) a large container that you fill with water and sit in to wash ➲See colour picture **The Bathroom** on page Centre 3

tuba /'tjuːbə/ *noun* [C] **MUSIC** a large, metal musical instrument that produces low notes, and is played by blowing into it

tube /tjuːb/ *noun* **1** PIPE [C] a pipe made of glass, plastic, metal, etc, especially for liquids or gases to flow through **2** CONTAINER [C] a long, thin container for a soft substance, that you press to get the substance out *a tube of toothpaste* **3 the Tube** the system of railways under the ground in London *I got the Tube to Oxford Circus.* ➲See also: **test tube**

tuber /'tjuːbəʳ/ *noun* [C] **BIOLOGY** the round part of a plant such as a potato that grows underground and from which new plants can grow

tuberculosis /tjuːˌbɜːkjə'ləʊsɪs/ (*abbreviation* **TB**) *noun* [U] **HEALTH** a serious infectious disease of the lungs

tubing /'tjuːbɪŋ/ *noun* [U] a long piece of metal, plastic, etc in the shape of a tube *steel tubing*

tubular /'tjuːbjələʳ/ *adjective* in the shape of a tube

tuck /tʌk/ *verb* **1 tuck sth into/behind/under, etc** to push a loose piece of clothing or material somewhere to make it tidy *Tuck your shirt in.* **2 tuck sth behind/under/in, etc** to put something in a small place so that it is safe and cannot move *I found an old letter tucked in the back of the book.*

tuck sth away *phrasal verb* to put something in a safe place *Helen tucked the money away in her purse.*

be tucked away *phrasal verb* to be in a place that is hidden, or in a place that few people go to *He lives in a cottage tucked away in the Suffolk countryside.*

tuck in/tuck into sth *phrasal verb UK informal* to start eating something, especially with enthusiasm *I was just about to tuck into a huge bowl of pasta.*

tuck sb in/up *phrasal verb* to make someone, especially a child, comfortable in bed by putting the covers around them

O‑ **Tuesday** /ˈtjuːzdeɪ/ (*written abbreviation* **Tue, Tues**) *noun* [C, U] the day of the week after Monday and before Wednesday

tuft /tʌft/ *noun* [C] a small group of hairs, grass, etc

tug¹ /tʌg/ *verb* [T] **tugging**, *past* **tugged** to pull something suddenly and strongly *Tom **tugged at** his mother's arm.*

tug² /tʌg/ *noun* [C] **1** PULL a sudden, strong pull on something **2** BOAT (*also* **tugboat** /ˈtʌgbəʊt/) a boat used for pulling larger ships

WORD PARTNERS FOR ***tuition***

get/be given/offer/receive tuition • **expert** tuition • **individual/one-to-one/private** tuition • tuition **in** sth

tuition /tjuˈɪʃən/ *noun* [U] **1** EDUCATION the teaching of one person or of a small group of people *French tuition* **2** EDUCATION *mainly US* money that you pay for being taught, especially at college or university

tulip /ˈtjuːlɪp/ *noun* [C] a brightly coloured spring flower in the shape of a cup

tumble /ˈtʌmbl/ *verb* [I] **1** FALL to suddenly fall *He **tumbled down** the stairs.* **2** BECOME LOWER If the price or value of something tumbles, it suddenly becomes lower. *Share prices tumbled by 20%.* •**tumble** *noun* [C]

ˌtumble ˈdryer *UK* (*US* **dryer**) *noun* [C] a machine that dries clothes

tumbler /ˈtʌmbləʳ/ *noun* [C] a glass that you drink out of, that has straight sides and no handle

tummy /ˈtʌmi/ *noun* [C] *informal* stomach

tumour *UK* (*US* **tumor**) /ˈtjuːməʳ/ *noun* [C] HEALTH a group of cells in someone's body which are not growing normally

tumultuous /tjuːˈmʌltjuəs/ *adjective* full of noise and excitement ***tumultuous applause*** ○ *a **tumultuous reception/welcome***

tuna /ˈtjuːnə/ *noun* [C, U] *plural* **tuna** FOOD a large sea fish, or the meat from this fish

WORD PARTNERS FOR ***tune***

hum/play/sing/whistle a tune • a **catchy** tune

tune¹ /tjuːn/ *noun* **1** MUSIC [C] a series of musical notes that are pleasant to listen to *He was humming a tune as he dried the dishes.* **2 in tune** MUSIC singing or playing the right notes **3 out of tune** MUSIC singing or playing the wrong notes *The piano is out of tune.* **4 change your tune** to suddenly change your opinion about something **5 be in tune with sb** to be able to understand what someone wants or needs *The government is not in tune with the voters.*

tune² /tjuːn/ *verb* [T] **1** MUSIC to make slight changes to a musical instrument so that it plays the right notes **2** to make changes to a television or radio so that it receives programmes from a particular company ***Stay tuned for*** (= continue watching or listening for) *more details.* ○ *The radio is **tuned to** Radio 5.*

tune in *phrasal verb* to watch or listen to a particular television or radio programme *Be sure to **tune in to** next week's show.*

tune (sth) up *phrasal verb* MUSIC to make slight changes to a musical instrument before you play it so that it produces the right notes *The orchestra were tuning up.*

tunic /ˈtjuːnɪk/ *noun* [C] a loose piece of clothing that covers the top part of your body

tunnel¹ /ˈtʌnəl/ *noun* [C] a long passage under the ground or through a mountain *The train went into the tunnel.* ➲See also: **light¹** at the end of the tunnel

tunnel² /ˈtʌnəl/ *verb* [I, T] *UK* **tunnelling**, *past* **tunnelled**, *US* **tunneling**, *past* **tunneled** to dig a tunnel

turban /ˈtɜːbən/ *noun* [C] a long piece of cloth that men from some religions fold around their heads

turbine /ˈtɜːbaɪn/ *noun* [C] PHYSICS a large machine that produces power by using gas, steam, etc to turn a wheel ➲See picture at **hydro-electric power station** ➲See picture at **wind turbine**

turbulent /ˈtɜːbjələnt/ *adjective* **1** SITUATION/TIME A turbulent situation, time, etc is one in which there are a lot of sudden changes, arguments, or violence. *a **turbulent relationship*** **2** AIR/WATER Turbulent air or water moves very strongly and suddenly. •**turbulence** /ˈtɜːbjələns/ *noun* [U]

turf¹ /tɜːf/ *noun* [U] short, thick grass and the soil it is growing in

turf² /tɜːf/ *verb*

turf sb out *phrasal verb UK informal* to make someone leave

turgor /ˈtɜːgəʳ/ *noun* [U] BIOLOGY the normal state of how hard a cell is, caused by its contents pressing against the cell wall

turkey /ˈtɜːki/ *noun* [C, U] FOOD a bird that looks like a large chicken, or the meat of this bird

WORD PARTNERS FOR ***turmoil***

be in/be thrown into turmoil • **a state of** turmoil • **emotional/political** turmoil • the turmoil **of** (doing) sth

turmoil /ˈtɜːmɔɪl/ *noun* [U **no plural**] a situation in which there is a lot of trouble, confusion, or noise *The whole region is **in turmoil**.*

O‑ **turn¹** /tɜːn/ *verb* **1** MOVE YOUR BODY [I] to move your body so that you are facing a different direction *Ricky turned and saw Sue standing in the doorway.* **2** CHANGE DIRECTION [I, T] to change direction when you are moving, or to make a car do this *Turn left at the traffic lights.* **3** CHANGE POSITION [T] to move something round so that it faces a different direction *Ella*

T

turned the cup to hide the crack in it. **4** GO ROUND [I, T] to move around a central point in a circle, or to make something do this *Turn the steering wheel as quickly as you can.* **5 turn blue/cold/sour, etc** to become blue, cold, etc *The sky turned black and it started to rain.* **6 turn 16/21, etc** to become a particular age *He turned 18 last May.* **7 turn a page** to move a page in a book or magazine in order to see the next one ➲See also: turn your **back**[2] on sb/sth, turn/put the **clock**[1] back, turn a blind **eye**[1] (to sth), turn over a new **leaf**[1], turn your **nose**[1] up at sth, turn the tables (**table**[1]) on sb, come/turn up trumps (**trump**), turn sth **upside down**[1]

turn sb away *phrasal verb* to not allow someone to enter a place *By 10 o'clock the club was already full and they were turning people away.*

turn (sb) back *phrasal verb* to return in the direction you have come from, or to make someone do this *They had to turn back because of the bad weather.*

turn sb/sth down *phrasal verb* to refuse an offer or request *They did offer me the job, but I turned it down.*

turn sth down *phrasal verb* to reduce the level of sound or heat that a machine produces *Could you turn the radio down, please?*

turn (sb/sth) into sb/sth *phrasal verb* to change and become someone or something different, or to make someone or something do this *There are plans to turn his latest book into a film.*

turn off (sth) *phrasal verb* to leave the road you are driving along and drive on a different road

turn sth off *phrasal verb* to move the switch on a machine, light, etc so that it stops working, or to stop the supply of water, electricity, etc *How do you turn the computer off?* ➲See colour picture **Phrasal Verbs** on page Centre 16

turn sth on *phrasal verb* to move the switch on a machine, light, etc so that it starts working, or to start the supply of water, electricity, etc *Ben turned the TV on.* ➲See colour picture **Phrasal Verbs** on page Centre 16

turn out *phrasal verb* **1** RESULT to happen in a particular way, or to have a particular result *The bomb warning **turned out to be** a false alarm.* [+ (that)] *I got talking to her and **it turned out** that we'd been to the same school.* **2** GO TO If people turn out for an event, they go to be there or watch. *Over 800 people **turned out for** the protest.*

turn sth out *phrasal verb* **1** PRODUCE to produce something *The factory turns out more than 600 vehicles a month.* **2** LIGHT to move the switch on a light so that it stops working

turn (sth) over *phrasal verb UK* to change to a different television station *Are you watching this or can I turn over?*

turn to sb *phrasal verb* to ask someone for help or advice *Eventually she **turned to** her aunt **for** help.*

turn to sth *phrasal verb* **1** PAGE to find a page in a book *Turn to page 105.* **2** SOMETHING BAD to start to do something bad, especially because you are unhappy *She turned to drugs after the break-up of her marriage.*

turn up *phrasal verb* **1** ARRIVE *informal* to arrive *Fred turned up late again.* **2** APPEAR If something that you have been looking for turns up, you find it.

turn sth up *phrasal verb* to increase the level of sound or heat that a machine produces *I'm cold, could you turn the heating up please?*

turn[2] /tɜːn/ *noun* **1** TIME [C] the time when you can or must do something, usually before or after someone else [+ **to do sth**] *It's your turn to feed the rabbit - I did it yesterday.* ○ *You'll have to be patient and **wait** your **turn**.* **2 take turns** (*also UK* **take it in turns**) If two or more people take turns, one person does something, then another person does something, etc. [+ **doing sth**] *They all took turns carrying the suitcase.* [+ **to do sth**] *The children took it in turns to hold the baby.* **3 in turn** one after another *He spoke to the three boys in turn.* **4** CHANGE DIRECTION [C] a change in the direction in which you are moving or facing ***a right/left turn*** **5** BEND [C] a bend or corner in a road, river, etc *Take the next turn on the right.* **6 turn of events** the way in which a situation develops, especially a sudden or unexpected change **7 take a turn for the better/worse** to become better or worse suddenly **8 do sb a good turn** to do something to help someone **9 the turn of the century** the start of a new century ➲See also: **U-turn**

turnaround /ˈtɜːnəraʊnd/ *noun* [C] when a bad situation changes into a good one

turning /ˈtɜːnɪŋ/ *noun* [C] *UK* a corner where one road meets another *Take the second turning on the left.*

WORD PARTNERS FOR ***turning point***

mark/prove/reach a turning point • the turning point **came** • **be at** a turning point • the turning point **in/of** sth • the turning point **for** sb • a **crucial/important/major/real** turning point

ˈturning ˌpoint *noun* [C] a time when an important change begins to happen *This event **marked** a **turning point** in the country's history.*

turnip /ˈtɜːnɪp/ *noun* [C, U] FOOD a large, round, pale yellow vegetable that grows under the ground

turn-off /ˈtɜːnɒf/ *noun* **1** PLACE [C] a place where you can leave a main road to go onto another road **2** DISLIKE [no plural] *informal* something which you dislike or which makes you feel less interested, especially sexually *Greasy hair is a real turn-off.*

turnout /ˈtɜːnaʊt/ *noun* [C] the number of people at an event, such as a meeting or election [usually singular] *They blamed the **low turnout** on the bad weather.*

turnover /ˈtɜːnˌəʊvər/ *noun* **1** FINANCE [no plural] how much money a business earns in a period of time **2** [U, no plural] the rate at which workers leave an organization and new workers join it *a **high turnover** of staff*

ˈturn ˌsignal *US* (*UK* **indicator**) *noun* [C] a light that flashes on a vehicle to show that the driver intends to turn right or left ➲See colour picture **Car** on page Centre 7

turnstile /ˈtɜːnstaɪl/ *noun* [C] a gate that only allows one person to go through it at a time

turpentine /ˈtɜːpᵊntaɪn/ (*also UK* **turps** /tɜːps/) *noun* [U] **DT** a clear liquid that has a strong smell and is used for removing paint

turquoise /ˈtɜːkwɔɪz/ *noun* [U] a blue-green colour •**turquoise** *adjective*

turret /ˈtʌrɪt/ *noun* [C] a small tower that is part of a building

turtle /ˈtɜːtl/ *noun* [C] an animal with four legs and a hard shell that lives mainly in water

turtleneck /ˈtɜːtlnek/ *US* (*UK* **polo neck**) *noun* [C] a piece of clothing that covers the top part of the body and has a tube-like part covering the neck *a turtleneck sweater*

tusk /tʌsk/ *noun* [C] **BIOLOGY** one of the two long, pointed teeth that come out of the mouth of some animals

tussle /ˈtʌsl/ *noun* [C] a fight or argument, especially between two people who want the same thing

tut /tʌt/ (*also* **tut-tut**) *exclamation* a sound you make when you do not approve of something

tutor /ˈtjuːtəʳ/ *noun* [C] **1 EDUCATION** someone who teaches one person or a very small group of people *a private tutor* **2 EDUCATION** *UK* a university teacher who is responsible for a small group of students •**tutor** *verb* [T]

tutorial /tjuːˈtɔːriəl/ *noun* [C] **1 EDUCATION** a class in which a small group of students talks about a subject with their tutor, especially at a British university **2 EDUCATION** a set of instructions and exercises that teaches you how to use a computer program

tux /tʌks/ *noun* [C] *US short for* tuxedo

tuxedo /tʌkˈsiːdəʊ/ *US* (*UK* **dinner jacket**) *noun* [C] a black or white jacket that a man wears on a very formal occasion

O‑‑ **TV** (*also* **tv**) /ˌtiːˈviː/ *noun* [C, U] *abbreviation for* television *What's **on TV** tonight?* ○ *We could stay in and **watch TV**.* ⊃See colour picture **The Living Room** on page Centre 4

twang /twæŋ/ *noun* [C] the sound that is made by pulling a tight string or wire •**twang** *verb* [I, T]

tweak /twiːk/ *verb* [T] **1** CHANGE to change something slightly to try to improve it **2** PULL to pull or twist something quickly and suddenly *Dad sat there tweaking his beard.* •**tweak** *noun* [C]

tweed /twiːd/ *noun* [U] a thick, rough cloth made of wool

tweezers /ˈtwiːzəz/ *noun* [plural] a small tool with two narrow pieces of metal joined at one end, used for picking up or pulling out very small things

twelfth[1] /twelfθ/ 12th written as a word

twelfth[2] /twelfθ/ *noun* [C] one of twelve equal parts of something; 1/12

O‑‑ **twelve** /twelv/ the number 12

O‑‑ **twenty** /ˈtwenti/ **1** the number 20 **2 the twenties** the years from 1920 to 1929 **3 be in your twenties** to be aged between 20 and 29 •**twentieth** 20th written as a word

O‑‑ **twice** /twaɪs/ *adverb* two times *I've been there twice.* ○ *I have to take the tablets twice a day.*

twiddle /ˈtwɪdl/ *verb* [I, T] to move your fingers around, or turn something around many times, especially because you are bored *Karen just sat there **twiddling with** her hair.*

twig /twɪg/ *noun* [C] **BIOLOGY** a small, thin branch on a tree

twilight /ˈtwaɪlaɪt/ *noun* [U] the time just before it becomes completely dark in the evening

ˈtwilight ˌzone *noun* [C] a state where things are strange and not clear *He is hovering in a twilight zone between life and death.*

WORD PARTNERS FOR ***twin***

a **set of** twins • sb's twin **brother/sister** • **identical** twins

twin[1] /twɪn/ *noun* [C] **SOCIETY** one of two children who are born to the same mother at the same time ⊃See also: **identical twin**

twin[2] /twɪn/ *adjective* [always before noun] used to describe two similar things that are a pair ***twin beds***

twin[3] /twɪn/ *verb UK* **be twinned with sth** If a town in one country is twinned with a town in another country, the two towns have a special relationship. *Leeds in England is twinned with Dortmund in Germany.*

twinge /twɪndʒ/ *noun* [C] **1** a sudden, slight emotion *a **twinge of** guilt* **2 HEALTH** a sudden, slight pain

twinkle /ˈtwɪŋkl/ *verb* [I] **1** LIGHT If light twinkles, it shines and seems to be quickly flashing on and off. *The lights of the town twinkled in the distance.* **2** EYES If someone's eyes twinkle, they look bright and happy. •**twinkle** *noun* [C]

twirl /twɜːl/ *verb* [I, T] to turn around and around quickly, or to make something do this •**twirl** *noun* [C]

twist[1] /twɪst/ *verb* **1** TURN [T] to turn something using your hand *She sat there nervously twisting the ring around on her finger.* **2** BEND [T] to bend and turn something many times and change its shape *The wheels of the bike had been twisted in the accident.* **3** TURN YOUR BODY [I, T] to turn part of your body to face a different direction *She twisted her head so she could see what was happening.* **4** CHANGE DIRECTION [I] If a road, river, etc twists, it has a lot of bends in it. *The path **twisted and turned** up the side of the mountain.* **5 HEALTH** [T] If you twist a part of your body, such as your knee, you injure it by turning it suddenly. **6** CHANGE MEANING [T] to unfairly change the meaning of something that someone has said *Journalists had twisted his remarks.* ⊃See also: twist sb's **arm**[1]

twist[2] /twɪst/ *noun* [C] **1** UNEXPECTED CHANGE a sudden change in a story or situation that you do not expect *The story has an unusual twist at the end.* **2** MOVEMENT when you twist something **3** PART a part of something that is twisted *There's a twist in the wire.* **4** SHAPE a shape that is made by twisting something *Finally, add a twist of lemon for decoration.* **5** RIVER/ROAD a bend in a river, road, etc

twisted /ˈtwɪstɪd/ *adjective* **1** SHAPE Something that is twisted is bent a lot of times and does not have its usual shape. **2** STRANGE strange and slightly unpleasant or cruel *He'd become **bitter and twisted**.*

twister /ˈtwɪstəʳ/ *noun* [C] *US another word for* tornado (= an extremely strong and dangerous wind that blows in a circle) ➲See also: **tongue twister**

twit /twɪt/ *noun* [C] *informal* a silly person

twitch /twɪtʃ/ *verb* [I] **HEALTH** If a part of your body twitches, it suddenly makes a slight movement in a way that you cannot control. *His face twitched nervously.* •**twitch** *noun* [C]

twitter /ˈtwɪtəʳ/ *verb* [I] If a bird twitters, it makes a series of short, high sounds.

O-ᵚ**two** /tuː/ **1** the number 2 **2 in two** into two pieces *She broke the chocolate in two.* **3 put two and two together** to guess the truth from details that you notice about a situation *She didn't tell me she was pregnant - I just put two and two together.* ➲See also: the **lesser** of two evils, be in two minds (**mind**[1]), stand on your own two feet (**foot**[1])

two-dimensional /ˌtuːdaɪˈmentʃənəl/ *adjective* describes a shape which is flat

two-time /ˌtuːˈtaɪm/ *verb* [T] *informal* If someone two-times their partner, they secretly have a romantic relationship with someone else.

two-way /ˈtuːˌweɪ/ *adjective* moving, or allowing something to move or work in two directions *a two-way street*

tycoon /taɪˈkuːn/ *noun* [C] someone who is very successful and powerful in business and has a lot of money *a **media tycoon*** ○ *a **property/shipping tycoon***

tying /ˈtaɪɪŋ/ *present participle of* tie

Tylenol /ˈtaɪlənɒl/ *noun* [C, U] *trademark* **HEALTH** a common drug used to reduce pain and fever

WORD PARTNERS FOR ***type***

of this type • **all types of sth** • **different/various types**

O-ᵚ**type**[1] /taɪp/ *noun* [C] **1** SIMILAR QUALITIES a person or thing that is part of a group of people or things that have similar qualities, or a group of people or things that have similar qualities *They sell over 20 **different types** of cheese.* ○ *Illnesses **of this type** are very common in children.* **2** PERSON someone who has particular qualities or interests *He's the outdoor type* (= enjoys being outside). **3 not be sb's type** *informal* to not be the type of person that someone thinks is attractive *I like Bertrand but he's not really my type.* ➲See also: **blood type**

type[2] /taɪp/ *verb* [I, T] to write something using a keyboard •**typing** *noun* [U]

typeface /ˈtaɪpfeɪs/ *noun* [C] a set of letters and symbols that are printed in a particular design

typewriter /ˈtaɪpˌraɪtəʳ/ *noun* [C] a machine with keys that you press to produce letters and numbers on paper •**typewritten** /ˈtaɪpˌrɪtən/ *adjective* printed using a typewriter *a typewritten letter*

typhoid /ˈtaɪfɔɪd/ *noun* [U] **HEALTH** a serious infectious disease that is caused by dirty water or food

typhoon /taɪˈfuːn/ *noun* [C] a violent storm with very strong winds

O-ᵚ**typical** /ˈtɪpɪkəl/ *adjective* having all the qualities you expect a particular person, object, place, etc to have *typical German food* ○ *This style of painting is **typical of** Monet.*

typically /ˈtɪpɪkəli/ *adverb* **1** TYPICAL used for saying that something is typical of a person, thing, place, etc *behaviour that is typically English* **2** SITUATION used for saying what usually happens *Schools in the area typically start at 8.30.*

typify /ˈtɪpɪfaɪ/ *verb* [T] to be a typical example or quality of something *Emma's opinions typify the attitude of many young people.*

typist /ˈtaɪpɪst/ *noun* [C] *old-fashioned* someone who types (= writes using a machine)

typography /taɪˈpɒgrəfi/ *noun* [U] **DT** the style and size of the letters in a piece of printing

tyranny /ˈtɪrəni/ *noun* [U] **POLITICS** when a leader or government has too much power and uses that power in a cruel and unfair way •**tyrannical** /tɪˈrænɪkəl/ *adjective* using or involving tyranny

tyrant /ˈtaɪərənt/ *noun* [C] someone who has total power and uses it in a cruel and unfair way

tyre *UK* (*US* **tire**) /taɪəʳ/ *noun* [C] a thick, round piece of rubber filled with air, that fits around a wheel *It's got a **flat tyre*** (= tyre with no air in it). ➲See colour picture **Car** on page Centre 7

T

Uu

U, u /juː/ the twenty-first letter of the alphabet

uber- /uːbəʳ-/ *prefix humorous* used before nouns to mean 'extreme' or 'extremely good or successful' *uber-billionaire*

ubiquitous /juːˈbɪkwɪtəs/ *adjective formal* seeming to be in all places *the ubiquitous security cameras*

U-boat /ˈjuːbəʊt/ *noun* [C] a German submarine (= boat that travels under water), used especially in World Wars I and II

udder /ˈʌdəʳ/ *noun* [C] **BIOLOGY** the part of a female cow, goat, etc that hangs under its body and produces milk

UFO /ˌjuːefˈəʊ/ *noun* [C] *abbreviation for* unidentified flying object: something strange that you see in the sky that could be from another part of the universe

ugh /ʌg/ *exclamation* used to show that you think something is very unpleasant *Ugh! What a smell!*

ugly /ˈʌgli/ *adjective* **1** NOT ATTRACTIVE unpleasant to look at *an ugly city* **2** SITUATION An ugly situation is very unpleasant, usually because it involves violence. *There were **ugly scenes** outside the stadium.* •**ugliness** *noun* [U] ⊃See also: raise/rear its ugly **head**[1]

uh *US* (*UK* **er**) /ə/ *exclamation* something that you say when you are thinking what to say next *It's not too far - it's about, uh, five miles from here.*

UK /ˌjuːˈkeɪ/ *noun abbreviation for* United Kingdom

ulcer /ˈʌlsəʳ/ *noun* [C] **HEALTH** a painful, infected area on your skin or inside your body ***a mouth/stomach ulcer***

ulna /ˈʌlnə/ *noun* [C] **ANATOMY** the longer of the two long thin bones in the lower half of the arm, between the wrist and the elbow ⊃Compare **radius, [BONE]**

ulterior /ʌlˈtɪəriəʳ/ *adjective* **ulterior motive/purpose, etc** a secret purpose or reason for doing something

ultimate[1] /ˈʌltɪmət/ *adjective* [**always before noun**] **1** BEST better, worse, or greater than all similar things *Climbing Mount Everest is the ultimate challenge.* ○ *the ultimate insult* **2** FINAL final or most important *the ultimate aim/solution*

ultimate[2] /ˈʌltɪmət/ *noun* **the ultimate in sth** the best or greatest example of something *It describes the hotel as 'the ultimate in luxury'.*

ultimately /ˈʌltɪmətli/ *adverb* **1** FINALLY finally, after a series of things have happened *a disease that ultimately killed him* **2** MOST IMPORTANT used to emphasize the most important fact in a situation *Ultimately, he'll have to decide.*

WORD PARTNERS FOR ***ultimatum***

deliver/give sb **/issue** an ultimatum • an ultimatum **demands** sth • an ultimatum **from/to** sb

ultimatum /ˌʌltɪˈmeɪtəm/ *noun* [C] when someone says they will do something that will affect you badly if you do not do what they want *The children were **given an ultimatum** - finish their work quietly or stay behind after class.*

ultra- /ʌltrə-/ *prefix* extremely *ultra-modern architecture* ○ *ultra-careful*

ultrasonic /ˌʌltrəˈsɒnɪk/ *adjective* **PHYSICS** involving ultrasound

ultrasound /ˈʌltrəsaʊnd/ *noun* **1 HEALTH, PHYSICS** [U] very high sound waves, especially those that are used in medical examinations to produce an image of something inside your body *an **ultrasound scan*** **2 HEALTH** [C] a medical examination which produces an image of something that is inside the body, especially a baby, using sound waves *An ultrasound revealed a perfectly healthy baby.*

ultraviolet /ˌʌltrəˈvaɪələt/ *adjective* **PHYSICS** Ultraviolet light makes your skin become darker.

umbilical cord /ʌmˈbɪlɪklˌkɔːd/ *noun* [C] **ANATOMY, BIOLOGY** the tube that connects a baby to its mother before it is born ⊃See picture at **foetus**

umbrella /ʌmˈbrelə/ *noun* [C] **1** a thing that you hold above your head to keep yourself dry when it is raining **2 umbrella group/organization, etc** a large organization that is made of many smaller organizations

umpire /ˈʌmpaɪəʳ/ *noun* [C] **SPORT** someone whose job is to watch a sports game and make sure that the players obey the rules *a tennis/cricket umpire* •**umpire** *verb* [**I, T**]

umpteen /ʌmˈtiːn/ *quantifier informal* very many *I've been there **umpteen times** and I still can't remember the way.* •**umpteenth** *I drank my umpteenth cup of coffee.*

un- /ʌn-/ *prefix* not or the opposite of *unhappy* ○ *unfair* ○ *to unfasten*

the UN /ˌjuːˈen/ *noun* **POLITICS** *abbreviation for* the United Nations: an international organization that tries to solve world problems in a peaceful way

O-- **unable** /ʌnˈeɪbl/ *adjective* **be unable to do sth** to not be able to do something *Some days he is unable to get out of bed.*

unabridged /ˌʌnəˈbrɪdʒd/ *adjective* **LITERATURE** An unabridged book, play, etc is in its original form and has not been made shorter.

WORD PARTNERS FOR ***unacceptable***

find sth unacceptable • **completely/totally/wholly** unacceptable • unacceptable **to** sb

unacceptable /ˌʌnəkˈseptəbl/ *adjective* too bad to be allowed to continue *The water contains unacceptable levels of pollution.* ○ *I find that sort of behaviour completely unacceptable.* •**unacceptably** *adverb*

unaccompanied /ˌʌnəˈkʌmpənid/ *adjective* not having anyone with you when you go somewhere *Unaccompanied children are not allowed in the museum.*

U

unaccountable /ˌʌnəˈkaʊntəbl/ *adjective* **1** SURPRISING impossible to explain *For some* ***unaccountable reason****, I've got three copies of the same book.* **2** PERSON not having to give reasons for your actions or decisions •**unaccountably** *adverb*

unadulterated /ˌʌnəˈdʌltərеɪtɪd/ *adjective* **1** COMPLETE complete *I've never heard such unadulterated nonsense in all my life!* **2** PURE pure and with nothing extra added *People using drugs can never be sure that they're using unadulterated substances.*

unadventurous /ˌʌnədˈventʃərəs/ *adjective* not willing to take risks or try something new

unaffected /ˌʌnəˈfektɪd/ *adjective* not changed by something *Smaller colleges will* ***be unaffected by*** *the new regulations.*

unaided /ʌnˈeɪdɪd/ *adjective, adverb* without help *He's now well enough to* ***walk unaided****.*

unanimous /juːˈnænɪməs/ *adjective* agreed by everyone *The jury was unanimous in finding him guilty.* •**unanimity** /ˌjuːnəˈnɪməti/ *noun* [U] when everyone agrees about something •**unanimously** *adverb The members* ***unanimously agreed*** *to the proposal.*

unannounced /ˌʌnəˈnaʊnst/ *adjective, adverb* without telling anyone first *an* ***unannounced visit***

unappealing /ˌʌnəˈpiːlɪŋ/ *adjective* not attractive or enjoyable *Five hours on a train with Mike is a fairly* ***unappealing prospect****.* ○ *an* ***unappealing character***

unarmed /ʌnˈɑːmd/ *adjective* not carrying a weapon

unashamedly /ˌʌnəˈʃeɪmɪdli/ *adverb* in a way that shows you are not embarrassed or worried about what other people think of you *Galliano is unashamedly romantic.*

unassuming /ˌʌnəˈsjuːmɪŋ/ *adjective* not wanting to be noticed *a shy, unassuming man*

unattached /ˌʌnəˈtætʃt/ *adjective* not married or having a romantic relationship

unattended /ˌʌnəˈtendɪd/ *adjective* not being watched or looked after *Passengers should not* ***leave*** *bags* ***unattended****.*

unattractive /ˌʌnəˈtræktɪv/ *adjective* **1** NOT BEAUTIFUL not beautiful or nice to look at *I felt old and unattractive.* **2** NOT INTERESTING not interesting or useful *an unattractive proposition*

unauthorized (*also UK* **-ised**) /ʌnˈɔːθəraɪzd/ *adjective* done without official permission *an unauthorized use of company money*

unavailable /ˌʌnəˈveɪləbl/ *adjective* **1** CANNOT DO SOMETHING not able to talk to someone or meet them, especially because you are doing other things *The manager was* ***unavailable for comment****.* **2** CANNOT GET impossible to buy or get *The book is unavailable in Britain.*

unavoidable /ˌʌnəˈvɔɪdəbl/ *adjective* impossible to avoid or prevent *an unavoidable delay*

WORD PARTNERS FOR ***unaware***

blissfully/completely/seemingly/totally unaware • unaware **of** sth

unaware /ˌʌnəˈweər/ *adjective* [**never before noun**] not knowing about something *He seems totally* ***unaware of*** *the problem.*

unawares /ˌʌnəˈweəz/ *adverb* **catch/take sb unawares** If something catches or takes you unawares, it happens when you do not expect it to. *The rain caught me unawares and I didn't have my umbrella.*

unbalanced /ʌnˈbælənst/ *adjective* **1** HEALTH slightly mentally ill **2** NOT FAIR false and not fair *He gave an unbalanced view of the situation.*

unbearable /ʌnˈbeərəbl/ *adjective* too painful or unpleasant for you to continue to experience *The heat was almost unbearable.* •**unbearably** *adverb*

unbeatable /ʌnˈbiːtəbl/ *adjective* much better than everyone or everything else *We aim to sell the best products at unbeatable prices.*

unbeaten /ʌnˈbiːtən/ *adjective* SPORT in sports, having won every game *Manchester United* ***remain unbeaten*** *this season.*

unbelievable /ˌʌnbɪˈliːvəbl/ *adjective* **1** EXTREME extremely bad or good and making you feel surprised *It's unbelievable how lucky she's been.* **2** NOT LIKELY not probable and difficult to believe •**unbelievably** *adverb*

unborn /ʌnˈbɔːn/ *adjective* not yet born *the* ***unborn child***

unbreakable /ˌʌnˈbreɪkəbl/ *adjective* impossible to break *unbreakable glass/plastic*

unbridled /ʌnˈbraɪdld/ *adjective* An unbridled feeling is one that you do not try to hide or control. ***unbridled enthusiasm/passion***

unbroken /ʌnˈbrəʊkən/ *adjective* continuous and with no pauses *unbroken sunshine*

unbutton /ʌnˈbʌtən/ *verb* [T] to open the buttons on a piece of clothing *He unbuttoned his jacket.*

uncalled for /ʌnˈkɔːldfɔːr/ *adjective* If an action or remark is uncalled for, it is unfair or unkind. *That was uncalled for, Tess - apologize to your brother.*

uncanny /ʌnˈkæni/ *adjective* strange and impossible to explain *an* ***uncanny resemblance*** •**uncannily** *adverb*

uncaring /ʌnˈkeərɪŋ/ *adjective* without sympathy for people with problems *victims of an uncaring society*

uncertain /ʌnˈsɜːtən/ *adjective* **1** SOMEONE not sure or not able to decide about something *Bridie was* ***uncertain about*** *meeting him.* **2** SITUATION not known, or not completely certain *The museum faces an* ***uncertain future****.* •**uncertainly** *adverb* •**uncertainty** *noun* [C, U]

WORD PARTNERS FOR ***uncertainty***

face uncertainty • the uncertainty **surrounding** sth • uncertainty **about/as to/over** sth • **continuing/great/growing** uncertainty • the uncertainty **of** sth

uncertainty /ʌnˈsɜːtənti/ *noun* [C, U] when something is uncertain *Life is full of uncertainties.*

U

unchanged /ʌn'tʃeɪndʒd/ *adjective* staying the same *The area has **remained** virtually **unchanged** in fifty years.*

uncharacteristic /ˌʌnkærəktər'ɪstɪk/ *adjective* not typical •**uncharacteristically** *adverb*

unchecked /ʌn'tʃekt/ *adjective* If something bad continues unchecked, it is not stopped.

O-ᵐ**uncle** /'ʌŋkl/ *noun* [C] SOCIETY the brother of your mother or father, or the husband of your aunt

unclean /ʌn'kliːn/ *adjective* RELIGION morally bad, as described by the rules of a religion

unclear /ʌn'klɪəʳ/ *adjective* **1** DIFFICULT TO UNDERSTAND not easy to understand *The situation at the moment is unclear.* [+ question word] *It's unclear what actually happened that night.* **2** NOT SURE If you are unclear about something, you do not understand it exactly. *I'm **unclear about** exactly who's doing what.*

uncomfortable /ʌn'kʌmftəbl/ *adjective* **1** PHYSICAL not feeling comfortable and pleasant, or not making you feel comfortable and pleasant *These shoes are really uncomfortable.* **2** SITUATION slightly embarrassed, or making you feel slightly embarrassed *an uncomfortable silence* •**uncomfortably** *adverb*

uncommon /ʌn'kɒmən/ *adjective* unusual [+ for + to do sth] *It's not uncommon for people to become ill* (= they often become ill) *when they travel.* •**uncommonly** *adverb*

uncompromising /ʌn'kɒmprəmaɪzɪŋ/ *adjective* determined not to change your ideas or decisions *an **uncompromising attitude***

unconcerned /ˌʌnkən'sɜːnd/ *adjective* not worried by something *The baby seemed **unconcerned by** all the noise.*

unconditional /ˌʌnkən'dɪʃənəl/ *adjective* done or given without any limits and without asking for anything for yourself ***unconditional** love* •**unconditionally** *adverb*

unconfirmed /ˌʌnkən'fɜːmd/ *adjective* An unconfirmed report or story may not be true because there is no proof yet.

unconnected /ˌʌnkə'nektɪd/ *adjective* If two or more things are unconnected, there is no connection between them. *The stomach ailment was **unconnected with** his cancer.*

unconscious¹ /ʌn'kɒnʃəs/ *adjective* **1** HEALTH in a state as though you are sleeping, for example because you have been hit on the head *She was **knocked unconscious**.* **2** An unconscious thought or feeling is one that you do not know you have. *an unconscious fear* •**unconsciousness** *noun* [U]

unconscious² /ʌn'kɒnʃəs/ *noun* [no plural] the part of your mind that contains feelings and thoughts that you do not know about, and that influences the way you behave

unconsciously /ʌn'kɒnʃəsli/ *adverb* If you do something unconsciously, you do it without knowing that you are doing it.

unconstitutional /ʌnˌkɒnstɪ'tjuːʃənəl/ *adjective* LAW not allowed by the rules of an organization or political system

uncontrollable /ˌʌnkən'trəʊləbl/ *adjective* unable to be controlled *uncontrollable anger* ○ *an uncontrollable desire to cry* •**uncontrollably** *adverb*

unconventional /ˌʌnkən'venʃənəl/ *adjective* SOCIETY doing things in a way that is different from most people *an unconventional lifestyle*

unconvincing /ˌʌnkən'vɪntsɪŋ/ *adjective* not seeming true or real

uncool /ʌn'kuːl/ *adjective* embarrassing and not stylish or fashionable

uncountable noun /ʌnˌkaʊntəbəl'naʊn/ (*also* **uncount noun**) *noun* [C] LANGUAGE a noun which does not have a plural form and cannot be used with 'a' or 'one'. For example 'music' and 'furniture' are uncountable nouns. ⊃See Extra help page **Countable and uncountable nouns** on page Centre 30.

uncouth /ʌn'kuːθ/ *adjective* behaving in a rude, unpleasant way

WORD PARTNERS FOR ***uncover***

uncover **evidence**/ a **plot**/ a **secret**/the **truth** • an **investigation** uncovers sth

uncover /ʌn'kʌvəʳ/ *verb* [T] **1** DISCOVER to discover something that had been secret or hidden *The inspectors **uncovered evidence** of corruption.* **2** REMOVE COVER to remove a cover from something

undaunted /ʌn'dɔːntɪd/ *adjective* not frightened to do something that is difficult or dangerous *Keiko spoke, **undaunted by** the crowd.*

undecided /ˌʌndɪ'saɪdɪd/ *adjective* If you are undecided about something, you have not made a decision yet.

undefeated /ˌʌndɪ'fiːtɪd/ *adjective* SPORT in sports, having won every game *Both teams **remain undefeated** in the final weeks of the season.*

undelete /ʌndɪ'liːt/ *verb* [T] COMPUTING to make something that has been deleted (= removed from a computer's memory) able to be seen again

undeniable /ˌʌndɪ'naɪəbl/ *adjective* certainly true *an undeniable fact* •**undeniably** *adverb*

O-ᵐ**under¹** /'ʌndəʳ/ *preposition* **1** BELOW below something *She pushed her bag under the table.* ○ *The children were sitting under a tree.* **2** BELOW THE SURFACE below the surface of something *He could only keep his head under the water for a few seconds.* **3** LESS THAN less than a number, amount, or age *You can buy the whole system for just under $2000.* ○ *We don't serve alcohol to anyone under 18.* **4** CONTROLLED BY controlled or governed by a particular person, organization, etc *a country under military rule* ○ *The restaurant is under new management.* **5** RULE/LAW according to a rule, law, etc *Under the new law, all new buildings must be approved by the local government.* **6** IN A PARTICULAR STATE in a particular state or condition *The President is under pressure to resign.* **7** IN PROGRESS used to say that something is happening at the moment but is not finished *A new 16-screen cinema is **under construction**.* ○ *Several different plans are **under discussion**.* **8** NAME using a particular name, especially one that is not your usual name *He also wrote several detective novels under the name, Edgar Sandys.*

U

9 PLACE IN LIST used to say which part of a list, book, library, etc you should look in to find something *Books about health problems are under 'Medicine'.*

under- /ʌndəʳ-/ *prefix* **1** not enough *under-cooked potatoes* **2** below *underwear* ○ *an underpass*

under² /'ʌndəʳ/ *adverb* **1** BELOW THE SURFACE below the surface of something *The child was swimming and suddenly started to go under.* **2** LESS THAN less than a particular number, amount, or age *I want a computer that is £2000 or under.*

under-age /ˌʌndər'eɪdʒ/ *adjective* **LAW** younger than the legal age when you are allowed to do something ***under-age drinking***

undercover /ˌʌndə'kʌvəʳ/ *adjective, adverb* working secretly in order to get information for the police or government *an **undercover** police officer*

undercut /ˌʌndə'kʌt/ *verb* [T] **undercutting**, *past* **undercut FINANCE** to sell something at a lower price than someone else

the underdog /'ʌndədɒg/ *noun* the person or team that is expected to lose a race or competition

underestimate /ˌʌndᵊr'estɪmeɪt/ *verb* [T] **1** SIZE/AMOUNT to not understand how large, strong, or important something is *Many people underestimate the cost of owning a car.* **2** PERSON to not understand how powerful or clever someone is *I thought it would be an easy game but I had underestimated my opponent.* ➲Opposite **overestimate**

underfoot /ˌʌndə'fʊt/ *adverb* under your feet as you walk *Several people were **trampled underfoot** in the rush to escape.*

undergo /ˌʌndə'gəʊ/ *verb* [T] **undergoing**, *past tense* **underwent**, *past participle* **undergone** to experience something, especially a change or medical treatment *The country is currently **undergoing** major political **change**.* ○ *He is **undergoing surgery** for a heart problem.*

undergraduate /ˌʌndə'grædʒuət/ (*also* **undergrad** /'ʌndəgræd/ *informal*) *noun* [C] **EDUCATION** a student who is studying for their first university degree (= qualification)

underground¹ /'ʌndəgraʊnd/ *adjective, adverb* **1** under the surface of the ground *underground caves* ○ *an animal that lives underground* **2 POLITICS** Underground political activities are secret and illegal. *an underground political organization*

> WORD PARTNERS FOR ***underground*** *(noun)*
>
> **take** the underground • **on** the underground • an underground **station /train**

underground² /'ʌndəgraʊnd/ *UK* (*US* **subway**) *noun* [**no plural**] a system of trains that is built under a city *the London Underground* ➲See Common Learner Error at **metro**

undergrowth /'ʌndəgrəʊθ/ *noun* [U] short plants and bushes that grow around trees

underhand /ˌʌndə'hænd/ (*also* **underhanded**) *adjective* secret and not honest ***underhand business deals***

underline /ˌʌndə'laɪn/ *verb* [T] **1** DRAW A LINE to draw a line under a word or sentence **2** EMPHASIZE to emphasize the importance or truth of something *The report **underlines the need** for more teachers in schools.*

underlying /ˌʌndə'laɪɪŋ/ *adjective* [**always before noun**] An underlying reason or problem is the real reason or problem, although it is not obvious. *We need to look at the **underlying reasons** for ill health.*

undermine /ˌʌndə'maɪn/ *verb* [T] to make someone less confident or make something weaker *A series of scandals have **undermined** people's **confidence** in the government.*

underneath¹ /ˌʌndə'niːθ/ *adverb, preposition* under something *Florian was wearing a jacket with a red shirt underneath.* ○ *Deborah pushed her shoes underneath the bed.*

the underneath² /ˌʌndə'niːθ/ *noun* the bottom part of something

underpaid /ˌʌndə'peɪd/ *adjective* not earning enough for your work

underpants /'ʌndəpænts/ *noun* [**plural**] a piece of underwear that covers the area between your waist and the top of your legs ➲See colour picture **Clothes** on page Centre 9 ➲See Common Learner Error at **underwear**

underpass /'ʌndəpɑːs/ *noun* [C] a road or path that goes under another road

underprivileged /ˌʌndə'prɪvᵊlɪdʒd/ *adjective* poor and having fewer opportunities than most people *underprivileged families*

underrate /ˌʌndə'reɪt/ *verb* [T] to think that someone or something is not as good as they really are *Critics have continued to underrate Sampras.* •**underrated** *adjective I think he's really underrated as an actor.* ➲Opposite **overrated**

underscore /ˌʌndə'skɔːʳ/ *verb* [T] *mainly US* to emphasize the importance of something

undersea /ˌʌndə'siː/ *adjective* below the surface of the sea

undershirt /'ʌndəʃɜːt/ *US* (*UK* **vest**) *noun* [C] a piece of underwear that you wear under a shirt

the underside /'ʌndəsaɪd/ *noun* the bottom surface of something *There was some damage to the underside of the car.*

understand /ˌʌndə'stænd/ *verb* [I, T] *past* **understood 1** KNOW MEANING to know the meaning of something that someone says *I don't understand half of what he says.* ○ *She didn't understand so I explained it again.* **2** KNOW WHY/HOW to know why or how something happens or works [+ **question word**] *We still don't fully understand how the brain works.* **3** KNOW FEELINGS to know how someone feels or why they behave in a particular way *I don't understand James sometimes.* [+ **question word**] *I understand why she's so angry.* **4 I/we understand (that)...** *formal* used to say that you believe something is true because someone has told you it is *I understand that the school is due to close next year.* **5 make yourself understood** to say something to someone in a way that they understand *I had a little difficulty making myself understood.*

understandable /ˌʌndəˈstændəbl/ *adjective* An understandable feeling or action is one that you would expect in that particular situation. *It's understandable that he's angry.* •**understandably** *adverb She's understandably upset.*

WORD PARTNERS FOR ***understanding***

develop/gain/have an understanding (of sth) • a **better/clear** understanding • an understanding **of** sth

understanding¹ /ˌʌndəˈstændɪŋ/ *noun* **1** KNOWLEDGE [**U, no plural**] knowledge about a subject, situation, etc or about how something works *We now* ***have a better understanding of*** *this disease.* **2** AGREEMENT [**C**] an informal agreement between two people [**usually singular + that**] *We* ***have*** *an* ***understanding*** *that we don't discuss the subject in front of his mother.* **3** SYMPATHY [**U**] sympathy *Thank you for your understanding.* **4 my/her/his, etc understanding** what you thought to be true *It was my understanding that she was coming alone.* **5** ABILITY [**U**] the ability to learn or think about something

understanding² /ˌʌndəˈstændɪŋ/ *adjective* showing sympathy for someone's problems *Fortunately, my girlfriend is very understanding.*

understated /ˌʌndəˈsteɪtɪd/ *adjective* simple and attractive in style *an understated black dress*

understatement /ˌʌndəˈsteɪtmənt/ *noun* [**C, U**] when you say that something is less extreme than it really is *'Quite big', did you say? That's an understatement - he's enormous!*

understood /ˌʌndəˈstʊd/ *past of* understand

understudy /ˈʌndəˌstʌdi/ *noun* [**C**] an actor in the theatre who learns the words and actions of another character so that they can perform if the usual actor is ill

undertake /ˌʌndəˈteɪk/ *verb past tense* **undertook**, *past participle* **undertaken** *formal* **1** [**T**] to start work on something that will take a long time or be difficult *Max has undertaken the task of restoring an old houseboat.* **2 undertake to do sth** to promise to do something

undertaker /ˈʌndəˌteɪkəʳ/ *noun* [**C**] someone whose job is to organize funerals and prepare dead bodies to be buried or burned

WORD PARTNERS FOR ***undertaking***

give/sign an undertaking • **a written** undertaking • an undertaking **by/from** sb

undertaking /ˈʌndəˌteɪkɪŋ/ *noun* [**C**] **1** WORK a difficult or important piece of work, especially one that takes a long time [**usually singular**] *Building your own house is a* ***major undertaking.*** **2 LAW** *UK* a legal or official promise to do something [**usually singular**] *The newspaper* ***has given an undertaking*** *not to print the story.*

undertone /ˈʌndətəʊn/ *noun* [**C**] a feeling or quality that exists but is not obvious *an article with worrying political undertones*

undertook /ˌʌndəˈtʊk/ *past tense of* undertake

undervalued /ˌʌndəˈvæljuːd/ *adjective* If someone or something is undervalued, they are more important or useful than people think they are.

underwater /ˌʌndəˈwɔːtəʳ/ *adjective, adverb* under the surface of water *an underwater camera* ○ *Seals can hear very well underwater.*

underwear /ˈʌndəweəʳ/ *noun* [**U**] the clothes that you wear next to your skin, under your other clothes

COMMON LEARNER ERROR

types of underwear

Underpants are a piece of underwear that cover the bottom. In British English **underpants** are only worn by men or boys, but in American English they can also be worn by women and girls.

The American English word **panties** is a piece of underwear for women or girls that covers the bottom. The British English word for **panties** is **knickers** or **pants**.

underweight /ˌʌndəˈweɪt/ *adjective* **HEALTH** too light

underwent /ˌʌndəˈwent/ *past tense of* undergo

underworld /ˈʌndəwɜːld/ *noun* [**no plural**] criminals and their activities *the* ***criminal underworld*** ○ *the London underworld*

undesirable /ˌʌndɪˈzaɪərəbl/ *adjective formal* Something that is undesirable is not wanted because it is bad or unpleasant. *an undesirable influence*

undeveloped /ˌʌndɪˈveləpt/ *adjective* Undeveloped land has no buildings on it and is not used for anything.

undid /ʌnˈdɪd/ *past tense of* undo

undisclosed /ˌʌndɪsˈkləʊzd/ *adjective* If official information is undisclosed, it is secret. *The meeting is taking place at an undisclosed location.*

undisputed /ˌʌndɪˈspjuːtɪd/ *adjective* If something is undisputed, everyone agrees about it. *an* ***undisputed fact*** ○ *the* ***undisputed champion/master***

undisturbed /ˌʌndɪˈstɜːbd/ *adjective* not interrupted or changed in any way *undisturbed sleep*

undivided /ˌʌndɪˈvaɪdɪd/ *adjective* **undivided attention/loyalty/support, etc** complete attention, support, etc *There, now you can have my undivided attention.*

undo /ʌnˈduː/ *verb* [**T**] **undoing**, *past tense* **undid**, *past participle* **undone** **1** OPEN to open something that is tied or fastened *I took off my hat and undid my coat.* **2** GET RID OF EFFECTS to get rid of the effects of something that has been done before *Some of the* ***damage*** *caused by pollution cannot be* ***undone.***

undoing /ʌnˈduːɪŋ/ *noun* **be sb's undoing** to be the thing that makes someone fail *It was a policy that proved to be the President's undoing.*

undone /ʌnˈdʌn/ *adjective* **1** NOT FASTENED not fastened or tied *Her coat was undone.* **2** NOT DONE not done *I don't think I've* ***left*** *anything* ***undone.***

undoubted /ʌnˈdaʊtɪd/ *adjective* [**always before noun**] used to emphasize that something is true

U

*The project was an **undoubted success.*** ○ *her **undoubted ability/talent***

undoubtedly /ʌn'daʊtɪdli/ *adverb* used to emphasize that something is true *Stress has undoubtedly contributed to her illness.*

undress /ʌn'dres/ *verb* [I, T] to remove your clothes or someone else's clothes •**undressed** *adjective I **got undressed** and went to bed.*

undue /ʌn'djuː/ *adjective* [always before noun] *formal* more than is necessary *I don't want to cause **undue alarm**.*

undulating /'ʌndjəleɪtɪŋ/ *adjective formal* having slight slopes or curves, or moving slightly up and down *undulating roads*

unduly /ʌn'djuːli/ *adverb formal* more than necessary *She didn't seem **unduly concerned/worried**.*

unearth /ʌn'ɜːθ/ *verb* [T] **1** FIND BY DIGGING to find something in the ground [often passive] *Thousands of dinosaur bones have been unearthed in China.* **2** FIND to find something that has been secret or hidden *Reporters **unearthed evidence** of criminal activity.*

unearthly /ʌn'ɜːθli/ *adjective* strange and frightening *an **unearthly light/beauty***

unease /ʌn'iːz/ *noun* [U] when you feel worried because you think something bad might happen

uneasy /ʌn'iːzi/ *adjective* worried because you think something bad might happen *I feel a bit **uneasy about** her travelling alone.*

uneconomic /ʌnˌiːkə'nɒmɪk/ (*also* **uneconomical**) *adjective* **1** WASTING SOMETHING using too much money, fuel, time, etc *a car that is uneconomic to run* **2** ECONOMICS not making enough profit *plans to close uneconomic factories*

unemployed /ˌʌnɪm'plɔɪd/ *adjective* SOCIETY not having a job *I've been unemployed for six months.* ○ *The government is helping to create jobs for **the unemployed**.*

WORD PARTNERS FOR ***unemployment***

unemployment **drops/falls/increases/rises** • **high/low/rising/soaring** unemployment • the unemployment **rate** • a **drop/fall/increase/rise** in unemployment

unemployment /ˌʌnɪm'plɔɪmənt/ *noun* [U] ECONOMICS, SOCIETY **1** the number of people who are unemployed *a **rise/fall in unemployment*** ○ *The **unemployment rate** has increased to 20 percent.* **2** when you do not have a job

unending /ʌn'endɪŋ/ *adjective* seeming to continue forever *an **unending series** of problems*

unequal /ʌn'iːkwəl/ *adjective* **1** NOT THE SAME different in size, level, amount, etc **2** UNFAIR unfair *the unequal distribution of wealth* •**unequally** *adverb*

unequivocal /ˌʌnɪ'kwɪvəkəl/ *adjective formal* clear and certain *an unequivocal answer* •**unequivocally** *adverb*

unethical /ʌn'eθɪkəl/ *adjective* morally bad *unethical business methods*

uneven /ʌn'iːvən/ *adjective* not level or smooth *an uneven floor* •**unevenly** *adverb*

uneventful /ˌʌnɪ'ventfəl/ *adjective* without problems and without anything exciting happening *The journey itself was fairly uneventful.*

unexpected /ˌʌnɪk'spektɪd/ *adjective* Something that is unexpected surprises you because you did not know it was going to happen. *His death was completely unexpected.* •**unexpectedly** *adverb*

unfailing /ʌn'feɪlɪŋ/ *adjective* An unfailing quality or ability is one that someone always has. ***unfailing support/courtesy*** •**unfailingly** *adverb*

unfair /ʌn'feər/ *adjective* **1** NOT EQUAL not treating people in an equal way *an unfair system* ○ *The test was unfair because some people had seen it before.* **2** NOT RIGHT not true and morally wrong [+ to do sth] *It's unfair to blame Frank for everything.* •**unfairly** *adverb* •**unfairness** *noun* [U]

ˌunfair disˈmissal *noun* [U] when someone is forced to leave their job for a reason that is not fair or legal

unfaithful /ʌn'feɪθfəl/ *adjective* having sex with someone who is not your wife, husband, or usual sexual partner *She was **unfaithful to** me.*

unfamiliar /ˌʌnfə'mɪljər/ *adjective* **1** not known to you *an unfamiliar face* ○ *His name was **unfamiliar to me**.* **2 be unfamiliar with sth** to not have any knowledge or experience of something *Many older people are unfamiliar with computers.*

unfashionable /ʌn'fæʃənəbl/ *adjective* not fashionable or popular at a particular time

unfasten /ʌn'fɑːsən/ *verb* [T] to open something that is closed or fixed together *to unfasten a seat belt*

unfavourable *UK* (*US* **unfavorable**) /ʌn'feɪvərəbl/ *adjective* **1** CRITICIZING negative and showing that you do not like something ***unfavourable publicity*** **2** NOT GOOD not good and likely to cause problems ***unfavourable** weather **conditions*** •**unfavourably** *adverb*

unfeeling /ʌn'fiːlɪŋ/ *adjective* not having sympathy for other people

unfettered /ʌn'fetəd/ *adjective formal* not limited by rules *The UN inspectors were given **unfettered access** to all nuclear sites.*

unfinished /ʌn'fɪnɪʃt/ *adjective* not completed *an unfinished novel/portrait*

unfit /ʌn'fɪt/ *adjective* **1** not suitable or good enough *The food was judged **unfit for** human consumption.* **2** HEALTH *UK* not healthy because you do too little exercise

unflattering /ʌn'flætərɪŋ/ *adjective* making someone look less attractive or seem worse than usual *an unflattering photo/dress/colour*

unfold /ʌn'fəʊld/ *verb* **1** DEVELOP [I] If a situation or story unfolds, it develops or becomes known. *The nation watched on TV as the tragic events unfolded.* **2** OPEN [I, T] to become open and flat, or to make something become open and flat *I unfolded the map.*

unforeseen /ˌʌnfɔː'siːn/ *adjective* not expected *The concert was cancelled due to **unforeseen circumstances**.*

U

unforgettable /ˌʌnfəˈgetəbl/ *adjective* Something that is unforgettable is so good, interesting, etc that you remember it for a long time. *Seeing Niagara Falls was an* ***unforgettable experience.***

unfortunate /ʌnˈfɔːtʃənət/ *adjective* **1** [SHOW FEELING] used to show that you wish something was not true or had not happened *an unfortunate mistake* [+ **(that)**] *It was unfortunate that she lost her job just as her husband became ill.* **2** [NOT LUCKY] unlucky *One unfortunate person failed to see the hole and fell straight into it.*

O‑‑**unfortunately** /ʌnˈfɔːtʃənətli/ *adverb* used to say that you wish something was not true or that something had not happened *I'd love to come, but unfortunately I have to work.*

unfounded /ʌnˈfaʊndɪd/ *adjective* not based on facts ***unfounded allegations/rumours***

unfriendly /ʌnˈfrendli/ *adjective* not friendly

unfulfilled /ˌʌnfʊlˈfɪld/ *adjective* **1** [NOT DONE] An unfulfilled wish, hope, promise, etc is one that has not happened or not been achieved. *an* ***unfulfilled ambition/dream*** ○ ***unfulfilled potential*** **2** [UNHAPPY] unhappy because you think you should be achieving more in your life

ungainly /ʌnˈgeɪnli/ *adjective* moving in a way that is not attractive *an ungainly walk*

ungrateful /ʌnˈgreɪtfəl/ *adjective* not thanking or showing that you are pleased with someone who has done something for you

OTHER WAYS OF SAYING ***unhappy***

Sad and **miserable** mean the same as unhappy: *I felt so* ***sad*** *after he left.* ● *I just woke up feeling* ***miserable.***

If someone is **upset**, they are unhappy because something bad has happened: *They'd had an argument and she was still* ***upset*** *about it.* ● *Mike got very* ***upset*** *when I told him the news.*

If someone is **broken-hearted** or **heart-broken** they are very sad because someone they love has ended a relationship with them: *She was* ***broken-hearted*** *when Richard left.*

If someone is **devastated**, or **distraught**, they are extremely upset: *She was* ***devastated*** *when he died.* ● *The missing child's* ***distraught*** *parents made an emotional appeal for information on TV.*

The adjective **depressed** is often used when someone is very unhappy for a long time: *She became deeply* ***depressed*** *after her husband died.*

O‑‑**unhappy** /ʌnˈhæpi/ *adjective* **1** [SAD] sad *an unhappy childhood* **2** [NOT SATISFIED] not satisfied *Giorgio was* ***unhappy with*** *his test results.* ○ *I'm* ***unhappy about*** *the situation.* ●**unhappily** *adverb* ●**unhappiness** *noun* [U]

unharmed /ʌnˈhɑːmd/ *adjective* [**never before noun**] not harmed or damaged *Both children* ***escaped unharmed*** *from the burning building.*

unhealthy /ʌnˈhelθi/ *adjective* **1** **HEALTH** likely to damage your health *Eating too much is unhealthy.* **2** **HEALTH** not strong, and likely to become ill *She looks pale and unhealthy.* **3** not normal and slightly unpleasant *an* ***unhealthy interest*** *in weapons*

unheard /ʌnˈhɜːd/ *adjective* not listened to or considered *Her cries* ***went unheard.***

unˈheard ˌof *adjective* [**never before noun**] never having happened before *Thirty years ago the disease was unheard of.*

unhelpful /ʌnˈhelpfʊl/ *adjective* **1** [NOT IMPROVE] not improving a situation *an unhelpful remark* **2** [NOT HELP] not wanting to help someone, in a way that seems unfriendly *The taxi driver was rude and unhelpful.*

unhurt /ʌnˈhɜːt/ *adjective* not harmed

unicellular /ˌjuː.nɪˈsel.jə.lər/ *adjective* **BIOLOGY** describes a living thing that is made of only one cell *Most algae are unicellular.*

unicorn /ˈjuːnɪkɔːn/ *noun* [C] an imaginary white horse with a horn growing from the front of its head

unidentified /ˌʌnaɪˈdentɪfaɪd/ *adjective* not recognized *The body of an unidentified woman was found in a field last night.*

unification /ˌjuːnɪfɪˈkeɪʃən/ *noun* [U] **POLITICS** when two or more countries join together and become one country *the unification of East and West Germany*

uniform[1] /ˈjuːnɪfɔːm/ *noun* [C, U] a special set of clothes that are worn by people who do a particular job or people who go to a particular school *a* ***school uniform*** ○ *a nurse's uniform* ○ *Tom looks completely different* ***in uniform*** (= wearing a uniform). ●**uniformed** *adjective uniformed police officers*

uniform[2] /ˈjuːnɪfɔːm/ *adjective* being the same size, shape, amount, etc *a row of houses of uniform height* ●**uniformity** /ˌjuːnɪˈfɔːməti/ *noun* [U] ●**uniformly** *adverb*

unify /ˈjuːnɪfaɪ/ *verb* [T] **POLITICS** to join together two or more countries or groups to make a single one *We need a leader who can unify the party.* ●**unified** *adjective Many people want a more unified Europe.*

unilateral /ˌjuːnɪˈlætərəl/ *adjective* A unilateral action or decision is done or made by one country, group, etc without waiting for others to agree. *unilateral nuclear disarmament* ●**unilaterally** *adverb*

unimaginable /ˌʌnɪˈmædʒɪnəbl/ *adjective* Something that is unimaginable is difficult to imagine because it is so bad, good, big, etc. *unimaginable pain/wealth* ●**unimaginably** *adverb*

unimportant /ˌʌnɪmˈpɔːtənt/ *adjective* not important

unincorporated /ʌnɪnˈkɔːpəreɪtɪd/ *adjective* An unincorporated business is not incorporated (= organized in a particular legal way).

uninhabitable /ˌʌnɪnˈhæbɪtəbl/ *adjective* too cold, dangerous, etc to live in

uninhabited /ˌʌnɪnˈhæbɪtɪd/ *adjective* If a place is uninhabited, no one lives there. *an uninhabited island*

uninhibited /ˌʌnɪnˈhɪbɪtɪd/ *adjective* feeling free to behave in any way that you want without worrying about other people's opinions

U

uninstall /ˌʌnɪnˈstɔːl/ *verb* [T] **COMPUTING** to remove a computer program from a computer

unintelligible /ˌʌnɪnˈtelɪdʒəbl/ *adjective* impossible to understand

unintentional /ˌʌnɪnˈtentʃənəl/ *adjective* not planned or intended *If I did offend her it was entirely unintentional.*

uninterested /ʌnˈɪntrəstɪd/ *adjective* not interested *He's completely* ***uninterested in*** *politics.*

uninterrupted /ʌnˌɪntərˈʌptɪd/ *adjective* continuous *I want a radio station that offers uninterrupted music.*

WORD PARTNERS FOR ***union***

join a union • a union **member/official/leader/representative**

union /ˈjuːnjən/ *noun* **POLITICS 1** [C] (*also* **trade union**) (*also US* **labor union**) an organization that represents people who do a particular job *a teachers'/firefighters' union* **2** [U, no plural] when two or more countries, groups, etc join together to make one country, group, etc *a move towards full economic union of EU countries* ⊃See also: **the European Union**

ˌUnion ˈJack (*also* **Union flag**) *noun* [C] the red, white and blue flag of the United Kingdom

unique /juːˈniːk/ *adjective* **1** NOT THE SAME different from everyone and everything else *Everyone's fingerprints are unique.* **2** SPECIAL unusual and special *a* ***unique opportunity*** **3 be unique to sb/sth** to exist in only one place, or be connected with only one person or thing *It's a method of education that is unique to this school.* •**uniquely** *adverb* •**uniqueness** *noun* [U]

unisex /ˈjuːnɪseks/ *adjective* for both men and women *unisex clothes* ○ *a unisex hairdresser*

unison /ˈjuːnɪsən/ *noun* **in unison** If people do something in unison, they all do it at the same time.

unit /ˈjuːnɪt/ *noun* [C] **1** GROUP a group of people who are responsible for a particular part of an organization *an anti-terrorist unit* **2 MEASURES** a measure used to express an amount or quantity *The kilogram is a* ***unit of*** *weight.* **3** SINGLE a single, complete thing that may be part of a larger thing *a French course book with ten units* **4** FURNITURE a piece of furniture that fits together with other pieces ***kitchen units*** **5** MACHINE a small machine, or part of a machine, that has a particular purpose *a computer's central processing unit* **6** BUILDING a single apartment, office, etc in a larger building

unite /juːˈnaɪt/ *verb* [I, T] to join together as a group, or to make people join together as a group *We need a leader who can unite the party.*

united /juːˈnaɪtɪd/ *adjective* **1** AGREE If people are united, they all agree about something. *On the issue of education the party is united.* **2** JOINED joined together *a united Germany*

the Unˌited ˈNations *noun* [group] **POLITICS** an international organization that tries to solve world problems in a peaceful way

WORD PARTNERS FOR ***unity***

achieve/maintain/restore unity • unity **among/between** sb • **a show of** unity

unity /ˈjuːnəti/ *noun* [U] when everyone agrees with each other or wants to stay together *national unity* ○ *family unity*

universal /ˌjuːnɪˈvɜːsəl/ *adjective* relating to everyone in the world, or to everyone in a particular group *Kittens and puppies have an almost* ***universal appeal.*** •**universally** *adverb* *It's a style of music that is universally popular.*

ˌuniversal ˈindicator *noun* [C] **CHEMISTRY** a substance which changes colour with different pH levels, used to discover how acid or alkaline something is

ˌuniversal ˈset *noun* [C] **MATHEMATICS** a set that contains all the things being considered

the universe /ˈjuːnɪvɜːs/ *noun* **ASTRONOMY** everything that exists, including stars, space, etc *Many people believe that there is life elsewhere in the universe.*

WORD PARTNERS FOR ***university***

go to university • **at** university • **a university course**

O⊸ **university** /ˌjuːnɪˈvɜːsəti/ *noun* [C, U] **EDUCATION** a place where students study at a high level to get a degree (= type of qualification) *the University of Cambridge* ○ *I applied to three universities.* ○ *(mainly UK) Sarah studied chemistry* ***at university.*** ○ *(mainly UK) I want* ***to go to university*** *when I finish school.*

unjust /ʌnˈdʒʌst/ *adjective* not fair ***unjust treatment/laws/sanctions*** •**unjustly** *adverb*

unjustified /ʌnˈdʒʌstɪfaɪd/ *adjective* done without a reason and not deserved ***unjustified criticism***

unkempt /ʌnˈkempt/ *adjective* untidy *Her hair was long and unkempt.*

unkind /ʌnˈkaɪnd/ *adjective* slightly cruel *I didn't tell her the truth because I thought it would be unkind.* •**unkindly** *adverb* •**unkindness** *noun* [U]

unknown[1] /ʌnˈnəʊn/ *adjective* **1** NOT KNOWN not known *The cause of his death is still unknown.* **2** NOT FAMOUS not famous *an unknown actor* ⊃See also: an unknown **quantity**

unknown[2] /ʌnˈnəʊn/ *noun* **1 the unknown** things that you have not experienced and know nothing about *It's normal to fear the unknown.* **2** [C] someone who is not famous *The game was won by a complete unknown.*

unlawful /ʌnˈlɔːfəl/ *adjective formal* **LAW** illegal ***unlawful possession of guns*** •**unlawfully** *adverb*

unleaded /ʌnˈledɪd/ *adjective* **ENVIRONMENT** Unleaded fuel does not contain lead (= a metal).

unleash /ʌnˈliːʃ/ *verb* [T] to suddenly cause a strong reaction *The newspaper report unleashed a storm of protest from readers.*

O⊸ **unless** /ənˈles/ *conjunction* except if *I won't call you unless there are any problems.*

unlike /ʌnˈlaɪk/ *preposition* **1** DIFFERENT different from someone or something *Jackie's really* *clever, unlike her sister.* ○ *The furniture was unlike anything she had ever seen.* **2** NOT TYPICAL not typical of someone or something *It's unlike her to be quiet - was there something wrong?*

O━ **unlikely** /ʌn'laɪkli/ *adjective* **1** NOT HAPPEN not expected to happen [+ **(that)**] *It's unlikely that I'll be able to come to the party.* [+ **to do sth**] *He's unlikely to arrive before midday.* **2** NOT TRUE probably not true *an unlikely explanation*

unlimited /ʌn'lɪmɪtɪd/ *adjective* without any limits *a service that offers unlimited Internet access*

un,limited lia'bility *noun* [U] **ECONOMICS, FINANCE** when the owner or owners of a business are responsible for all its debts

unload /ʌn'ləʊd/ *verb* **1** REMOVE [I, T] to remove things from a vehicle *Can you help me unload the car?* **2** SHIP/AIRCRAFT [I] If a ship, aircraft, etc unloads, goods are taken off it.

unlock /ʌn'lɒk/ *verb* [T] to open something which is locked using a key

unlucky /ʌn'lʌki/ *adjective* having or causing bad luck [+ **to do sth**] *The team played well and was unlucky to lose.* ○ *Some people think it's unlucky to walk under ladders.* •**unluckily** *adverb*

unmarked /ʌn'mɑːkt/ *adjective* having no signs or words that show what something is *The once famous actor was buried in an* ***unmarked grave.***

unmarried /ʌn'mærɪd/ *adjective* not married

unmatched /ʌn'mætʃt/ *adjective* better than anyone or anything else *Horses have an athletic beauty* ***unmatched by*** *any other animal.*

unmistakable /ˌʌnmɪ'steɪkəbl/ *adjective* Something that is unmistakable is very obvious and cannot be confused with anything else. *an unmistakable look of disappointment* •**unmistakably** *adverb*

unmoved /ʌn'muːvd/ *adjective* not feeling any emotion *It's impossible to* ***remain unmoved*** *by pictures of starving children.*

unnamed /ʌn'neɪmd/ *adjective* An unnamed person or thing is talked about but their name is not said. *The money was given by an unnamed businessman.*

unnatural /ʌn'nætʃərəl/ *adjective* not normal or right *an unnatural interest in death* •**unnaturally** *adverb unnaturally thin*

unnecessary /ʌn'nesəsəri/ *adjective* **1** NOT NEEDED not needed *You don't want to make any unnecessary car journeys in this weather.* **2** UNKIND unkind *Why did she say that? That was unnecessary.* •**unnecessarily** /ʌn'nesəsərəli/ *adverb*

unnerve /ʌn'nɜːv/ *verb* [T] to make someone feel nervous or frightened

unnerving /ʌn'nɜːvɪŋ/ *adjective* making you feel nervous or frightened *He kept looking at me which I found unnerving.*

unnoticed /ʌn'nəʊtɪst/ *adjective* without being seen or noticed *We managed to slip away unnoticed.*

unobtrusive /ˌʌnəb'truːsɪv/ *adjective* not attracting attention *He was quiet and unobtrusive.* •**unobtrusively** *adverb*

unoccupied /ʌn'ɒkjəpaɪd/ *adjective* An unoccupied building, room, seat, etc has no one in it.

unofficial /ˌʌnə'fɪʃəl/ *adjective* not said or done by the government or someone in authority ***Unofficial reports*** *suggest the death toll from the earthquake is around 600.* •**unofficially** *adverb*

unorthodox /ʌn'ɔːθədɒks/ *adjective* unusual and different from most people's opinions, methods, etc ***unorthodox ideas/views*** ○ *an* ***unorthodox style*** *of teaching*

unpack /ʌn'pæk/ *verb* [I, T] to take things out of a bag, box, etc *Bella* ***unpacked*** *her* ***suitcase.*** ○ *I haven't had time to unpack yet.*

unpaid /ʌn'peɪd/ *adjective* **1 FINANCE** An unpaid debt, tax, etc has not been paid. **2** working without getting any money ***unpaid work***

unpalatable /ʌn'pælətəbl/ *adjective formal* shocking and difficult to accept *an* ***unpalatable fact***

unparalleled /ʌn'pærəleld/ *adjective formal* better, greater, worse, etc than anything else *an act of unparalleled cruelty*

unplanned /ʌn'plænd/ *adjective* not planned or expected *an* ***unplanned pregnancy***

unpleasant /ʌn'plezənt/ *adjective* **1** NOT ENJOYABLE not enjoyable or pleasant *an unpleasant experience/smell* **2** RUDE rude and angry *The waiter got quite unpleasant with us.* •**unpleasantly** *adverb*

unplug /ʌn'plʌg/ *verb* [T] to stop a piece of electrical equipment being connected to an electricity supply by pulling its plug (= object with pins) out of the wall

unpopular /ʌn'pɒpjələr/ *adjective* disliked by most people *an unpopular idea* ○ *an unpopular teacher* •**unpopularity** /ʌnˌpɒpjə'lærəti/ *noun* [U]

unprecedented /ʌn'presɪdəntɪd/ *adjective* never having happened before *The Internet has given people unprecedented access to information.*

unpredictable /ˌʌnprɪ'dɪktəbl/ *adjective* changing so much that you do not know what will happen next *unpredictable weather conditions* •**unpredictability** /ˌʌnprɪˌdɪktə'bɪlɪti/ *noun* [U]

unprofessional /ˌʌnprə'feʃənəl/ *adjective* behaving badly at work *an unprofessional attitude*

unprovoked /ˌʌnprə'vəʊkt/ *adjective* An unprovoked attack is one in which the person who is attacked has done nothing to cause it.

unqualified /ʌn'kwɒlɪfaɪd/ *adjective* **1** WITHOUT QUALIFICATIONS without the qualifications or knowledge to do something [+ **to do sth**] *She was totally unqualified to look after children.* **2** TOTAL [**always before noun**] *formal* total and not limited in any way *an* ***unqualified success***

U

unquestionably /ʌn'kwestʃənəbli/ *adverb* in a way that is obvious and causes no doubt *She is unquestionably the best person for the job.*

unravel /ʌn'rævᵊl/ *verb* [I, T] *UK* **unravelling**, *past* **unravelled**, *US* **unraveling**, *past* **unraveled** **1** BECOME CLEAR If you unravel a difficult situation or story, or if it unravels, it becomes clear and easier to understand. *No one has yet unravelled the mystery of his death.* **2** THREAD/STRING to stop being twisted together, or to move pieces of string, etc so that they are not twisted together

unreal /ʌn'rɪəl/ *adjective* Something that is unreal seems so strange that it is difficult to believe. *For a while I couldn't believe she was dead - it all seemed unreal.* •**unreality** /ˌʌnri'æləti/ *noun* [U]

unrealistic /ˌʌnrɪə'lɪstɪk/ *adjective* not thinking about what is likely to happen or what you can really do *She has a totally unrealistic view of life.* [+ **to do sth**] *It's unrealistic to expect their decision before Tuesday.*

unreasonable /ʌn'riːzᵊnəbl/ *adjective* not fair ***unreasonable demands/behaviour*** [+ **to do sth**] *It seems unreasonable to expect one person to do both jobs.* •**unreasonably** *adverb*

unrelated /ˌʌnrɪ'leɪtɪd/ *adjective* having no connection *Police said his death was **unrelated to** the attack.*

unrelenting /ˌʌnrɪ'lentɪŋ/ *adjective formal* never stopping or getting any less extreme *unrelenting pressure* ○ *The heat was unrelenting.*

unreliable /ˌʌnrɪ'laɪəbl/ *adjective* not able to be trusted or depended on *an **unreliable witness*** ○ *The trains were noisy, dirty, and unreliable.*

unremarkable /ʌnrɪ'mɑːkəbl/ *adjective* ordinary and not interesting *an unremarkable town*

unremitting /ˌʌnrɪ'mɪtɪŋ/ *adjective formal* never stopping or getting any less extreme ***unremitting hostility/pressure*** ○ *unremitting efforts*

unrepentant /ˌʌnrɪ'pentənt/ *adjective* not feeling sorry about something bad that you have done

unreservedly /ˌʌnrɪ'zɜːvɪdli/ *adverb* completely *The minister has **apologized unreservedly**.*

U

unresolved /ˌʌnrɪ'zɒlvd/ *adjective formal* If a problem or question is unresolved, there is still no solution or answer. *The question of who owns the land **remains unresolved**.*

WORD PARTNERS FOR ***unrest***

cause unrest • **continuing/growing** unrest • unrest **among** sb • unrest **over** sth • **a wave of** unrest • **political/social** unrest

unrest /ʌn'rest/ *noun* [U] when a lot of people are angry about something and are likely to become violent ***political/social unrest***

unrestrained /ˌʌnrɪ'streɪnd/ *adjective* not limited or controlled *unrestrained anger*

unrivalled *UK* (*US* **unrivaled**) /ʌn'raɪvᵊld/ *adjective* better than any other of the same type *The museum has an **unrivalled** collection of modern American paintings.* ○ *an **unrivalled** reputation*

unroll /ʌn'rəʊl/ *verb* [T] to open something that was rolled into a tube shape and make it flat *He unrolled the carpet.*

unruly /ʌn'ruːli/ *adjective* **1** PEOPLE behaving badly and difficult to control ***unruly children*** **2** HAIR Unruly hair is difficult to keep tidy.

unsafe /ʌn'seɪf/ *adjective* **1** DANGEROUS dangerous *The building is unsafe.* [+ **to do sth**] *The water was dirty and unsafe to drink.* **2** IN DANGER If you feel unsafe, you feel that you are in danger. *Many women feel unsafe on the streets at night.*

unsatisfactory /ʌnˌsætɪs'fæktᵊri/ *adjective* not good enough to be acceptable *Many school buildings are in an unsatisfactory condition.*

unsaturated fat /ˌʌnsætʃəreɪtɪd'fæt/ **FOOD** a fat or oil that is found in plants, vegetable oil and fish and thought to be better for your health than saturated fat ⊃Compare **saturated fat**

unsavoury *UK* (*US* **unsavory**) /ʌn'seɪvᵊri/ *adjective* unpleasant and morally offensive *an **unsavoury reputation/incident/character***

unscathed /ʌn'skeɪðd/ *adjective* [**never before noun**] not harmed *The driver of the car was killed but both passengers **escaped unscathed**.*

unscrew /ʌn'skruː/ *verb* [T] **1** TWIST to remove something by twisting it *I can't unscrew the lid.* **2** REMOVE METAL PIECES to remove something by taking the screws (= small, metal pieces) out of it

unscrupulous /ʌn'skruːpjələs/ *adjective* behaving in a way that is dishonest or unfair in order to get what you want *an unscrupulous financial adviser*

unseat /ʌn'siːt/ *verb* [T] **POLITICS** to remove someone from a powerful position *Kennedy has a good chance of unseating the President at the next election.*

unseen /ʌn'siːn/ *adjective, adverb* not seen or noticed *an exhibition of previously unseen photographs*

unsettled /ʌn'setld/ *adjective* **1** CHANGING changing often *The **weather** continues to be **unsettled**.* **2** ANXIOUS anxious and not able to relax or feel happy in a situation *Children tend to get unsettled if you keep changing their routine.*

unsettling /ʌn'setlɪŋ/ *adjective* making you feel anxious *an **unsettling experience/feeling***

unsightly /ʌn'saɪtli/ *adjective* unpleasant to look at *unsightly piles of litter*

unskilled /ʌn'skɪld/ *adjective* **1** PEOPLE without special skills or qualifications *an **unskilled labourer/worker*** **2** WORK Unskilled work does not need people with special skills or qualifications.

unsociable /ʌn'səʊʃəbl/ *adjective* not wanting to be with other people

unsolicited /ˌʌnsə'lɪsɪtɪd/ *adjective* not asked for and often not wanted ***unsolicited advice/offer***

unsolved /ʌn'sɒlvd/ *adjective* having no answer or solution *an **unsolved mystery/murder/crime***

unsound /ʌn'saʊnd/ *adjective* **1** WRONG based on ideas, facts, and reasons that are wrong *an **unsound practice*** **2** BAD CONDITION in a bad condition *The bridge was **structurally unsound**.*

unspeakable /ʌn'spiːkəbl/ *adjective* extremely bad or shocking *unspeakable crimes/suffering* •**unspeakably** *adverb*

unspecified /ʌn'spesɪfaɪd/ *adjective* If something is unspecified, you are not told what it is. *The court awarded her an unspecified amount of money.*

unspoiled (*also UK* **unspoilt**) /ʌn'spɔɪlt/ *adjective* An unspoiled place is beautiful because it has not been changed or damaged by people. *an island with clean, unspoiled beaches*

unspoken /ʌn'spəʊkᵊn/ *adjective* not said, but thought or felt *unspoken doubts*

unstable /ʌn'steɪbl/ *adjective* **1** CHANGE likely to change or end suddenly *an **unstable situation** ○ an unstable economy* **2** PERSON If someone is unstable, their moods and behaviour change suddenly, especially because they are mentally ill. **3** MOVE not fixed or safe and likely to move *That chair looks a bit unstable.*

unsteady /ʌn'stedi/ *adjective* moving slightly from side to side, as if you might fall *The alcohol had made her unsteady on her feet.*

unstuck /ʌn'stʌk/ *adjective* **come unstuck a** *UK* If something comes unstuck, it stops being fixed to something. *One of the photos has come unstuck.* **b** *UK informal* to experience difficulties and fail *The negotiations came unstuck at a crucial stage.*

unsubscribe /ˌʌnsəb'skraɪb/ *verb* [**I, T**] **COMPUTING** to remove your name from an Internet mailing list (= a list of names and addresses that an organization sends information to)

unsuccessful /ˌʌnsək'sesfᵊl/ *adjective* not achieving what was wanted or intended *an unsuccessful attempt/effort* •**unsuccessfully** *adverb*

unsuitable /ʌn'suːtəbl/ *adjective* not acceptable or right for someone or something *My parents considered the programme unsuitable for children.*

unsung /ʌn'sʌŋ/ *adjective* not famous or praised although you have done something very well *He was the **unsung hero** of the match.*

unsure /ʌn'ʃʊəʳ/ *adjective* **1** not certain or having doubts *I'm a bit **unsure about** what to do.* **2 unsure of yourself** without confidence

unsuspecting /ˌʌnsə'spektɪŋ/ *adjective* [**always before noun**] not aware that something bad is happening *In each case the **unsuspecting victim** had been invited into Cooper's home.*

unsustainable /ˌʌnsə'steɪnəbᵊl/ *adjective* **1** Something that is unsustainable cannot continue at the same rate **2 ENVIRONMENT** causing damage to the environment by using more of something than can be replaced naturally *unsustainable fishing methods*

unsympathetic /ˌʌnsɪmpə'θetɪk/ *adjective* **1** WITHOUT SYMPATHY showing that you do not understand or care about someone's problems *I told him I'd got a cold but he was completely unsympathetic.* **2** NOT SUPPORTING not agreeing with or supporting someone's ideas or actions

untangle /ʌn'tæŋgl/ *verb* [**T**] **1** SEPARATE to separate pieces of string, hair, wire, etc that have become twisted together *I'm trying to untangle these wires.* **2** UNDERSTAND to understand the different parts of a situation that has become confused or very complicated *Historians have tried to untangle the complex issues behind the events.*

untapped /ʌn'tæpt/ *adjective* not yet used ***untapped potential***

untenable /ʌn'tenəbl/ *adjective formal* If an argument, action, or situation is untenable, it cannot be supported or defended from criticism. *an **untenable position***

unthinkable /ʌn'θɪŋkəbl/ *adjective* If something is unthinkable, it is so strange that you can not imagine it will ever happen. *Thirty years ago a no-smoking restaurant would have been unthinkable.*

untidy /ʌn'taɪdi/ *adjective* not tidy *an untidy room ○ She's really untidy at home.*

untie /ʌn'taɪ/ *verb* [**T**] **untying**, *past* **untied** to open a knot or something that has been tied with a knot *I untied my shoelaces and kicked off my shoes.*

O→ **until** /ᵊn'tɪl/ (*also* **till**) *preposition, conjunction* **1** HAPPEN THEN STOP continuing to happen before a particular time or event and then stopping *The show will be on until the end of the month. ○ Whisk the egg whites until they look white and fluffy.* **2** AS FAR AS as far as *Carry on until you reach the traffic lights and turn right.* **3 not until** not before a particular time or event *It doesn't open until 7. ○ We won't start until Jeanne arrives.*

untimely /ʌn'taɪmli/ *adjective* happening too soon *her **untimely death** from cancer*

untold /ʌn'təʊld/ *adjective* [**always before noun**] too much to be measured or counted ***untold riches*** ○ ***untold damage***

untouched /ʌn'tʌtʃt/ *adjective* **1** NOT DAMAGED not changed or damaged in any way *Most of the island remains **untouched by** tourism.* **2** NOT EATEN If food is untouched, it has not been eaten.

untoward /ˌʌntə'wɔːd/ *adjective formal* unexpected and causing problems *If nothing **untoward happens** we should be there by midday.*

untrained /ʌn'treɪnd/ *adjective* **1** never having been taught the skills for a particular job *untrained staff* **2 the untrained eye** someone without the skill or knowledge to judge what they see ***To the untrained eye**, most fake diamonds look real.*

untried /ʌn'traɪd/ *adjective* not yet used or tested *new and untried technology*

untrue /ʌn'truː/ *adjective* false

untruth /ʌn'truːθ/ *noun* [**C**] *formal* a lie, or something that is not true

U

unused[1] /ʌn'juːzd/ *adjective* not used now or not used before now *an unused room*

unused[2] /ʌn'juːst/ *adjective* **be unused to sth** to not have experience of something *I was unused to city life.*

unusual /ʌn'juːʒuəl/ *adjective* different and not ordinary, often in a way that is interesting or exciting *an unusual name* [+ **to do sth**] *It's fairly unusual to keep insects as pets.*

unusually /ʌn'juːʒuəli/ *adverb* **1 unusually big/strong/good, etc** bigger, stronger, better, etc than is normal *unusually warm weather* **2 unusually for sb** in a way that is not usual for someone *Unusually for me, I actually couldn't finish my meal.*

unveil /ʌn'veɪl/ *verb* [T] **1** TELL THE PUBLIC to tell the public about an idea or plan that was secret before *The new policy is due to be unveiled later this month.* **2** REMOVE COVER to remove the cover from an object as part of an official ceremony

unwanted /ʌn'wɒntɪd/ *adjective* not wanted *an **unwanted gift***

unwarranted /ʌn'wɒrəntɪd/ *adjective formal* without a good reason ***unwarranted intrusion***

unwary /ʌn'weəri/ *adjective* not aware of possible dangers ***Unwary travellers** can easily get lost in these parts.*

unwelcome /ʌn'welkəm/ *adjective* not wanted *unwelcome publicity* ○ *an unwelcome visitor*

unwell /ʌn'wel/ *adjective* [**never before noun**] *formal* **HEALTH** ill *to feel/look unwell*

unwieldy /ʌn'wiːldi/ *adjective* An unwieldy object is difficult to carry because it is heavy, large, or a strange shape.

unwilling /ʌn'wɪlɪŋ/ *adjective* not wanting to do something [+ **to do sth**] *A lot of people are unwilling to accept change.* •**unwillingly** *adverb* •**unwillingness** *noun* [U]

unwind /ʌn'waɪnd/ *verb past* **unwound 1** RELAX [I] *informal* to relax, especially after working *Music helps me to unwind.* **2** MAKE STRAIGHT [I, T] If you unwind something, or if something unwinds, it stops being curled round or twisted round something else and is made straight. *He unwound the bandage.*

U

unwise /ʌn'waɪz/ *adjective* stupid and likely to cause problems *an unwise decision* •**unwisely** *adverb*

unwittingly /ʌn'wɪtɪŋli/ *adverb* without intending to do something *I apologized for the chaos I had unwittingly caused.*

unworkable /ʌn'wɜːkəbl/ *adjective* A plan that is unworkable is impossible. *The policy has been described as unworkable.*

unwrap /ʌn'ræp/ *verb* [T] **unwrapping**, *past* **unwrapped** to remove the paper, cloth, etc that is covering something *She carefully unwrapped the present.*

unwritten /ʌn'rɪtən/ *adjective* **an unwritten agreement/law/rule** an agreement, law, etc that is accepted and obeyed by most people but is not formally written

unzip /ʌn'zɪp/ *verb* [T] **unzipping**, *past* **unzipped 1** to open something by using its zip (= two rows of metal or plastic points that fasten two sides together) *He unzipped his trousers.* **2 COMPUTING** to make a file bigger again after it has been zipped (= made smaller so that you can send or store it) so that it can easily be used

O⊸**up**[1] /ʌp/ *adverb, preposition* **1** HIGHER PLACE towards or in a higher place *He ran up the stairs.* ○ *Pick up your clothes and put them away.* ○ *She looked up and smiled at me.* **2** VERTICAL vertical or as straight as possible *He stood up.* ○ *She opened her eyes and sat up.* **3** INCREASE to a greater degree, amount, volume, etc *Inflation keeps pushing prices up.* ○ *Can you turn up the heat? I'm freezing!* ○ *Please speak up* (= speak louder), *I can't hear you.* **4** COMPLETELY used to emphasize that someone completes an action or uses all of something *I used up all my money.* ○ *Eat up the rest of your dinner.* **5 up the road/street, etc** along or further along the street/road, etc *My best friend lives up the street from me.* ○ *He ran up the path and hugged her.* **6 go/walk, etc up to sb/sth** to walk directly towards someone or something until you are next to them *He walked straight up to me and introduced himself.* **7** DIRECTION in or towards a particular direction, usually north *We moved from London **up to** Scotland.* ○ *Chris lives up north.* **8 up and down** If something or someone moves up and down, they move repeatedly in one direction and then in the opposite direction. *The children were constantly running up and down the stairs.* **9 up to 10, 20, etc** any amount under 10, 20, etc *We can invite up to 65 people.* **10 up to** until a particular time *You can call me up to midnight.* **11 up to sth** equal in quality or achievement *His work wasn't up to his usual standard.* **12 up to sth/doing sth** able to do something *It'll be a while before I feel up to walking again.* **13 be up to (sth)** *informal* to be doing or planning something, often something secret and bad *Joe, what are you up to?* **14 be up to sb** If an action or decision is up to someone, they are responsible for doing or making it. *I can't decide for you Jack, **it's up to you**.* [+ **to do sth**] *It's up to her to decide whether she wants to enter the competition.* **15 be up against sb/sth** If you are up against a situation or a person, they make it very difficult for you to achieve what you want to achieve. *We were up against some of the best players in the world.*

O⊸**up**[2] /ʌp/ *adjective* [**never before noun**] **1** NOT IN BED not in bed *I was up all night with the baby.* ○ *Is she up yet?* **2 be up and around/about** to be well enough after an illness to get out of bed and move around **3** FINISHED If a period of time is up, it has ended. *My health club membership is up.* **4** INCREASE If a level or amount is up, it has increased. *Profits are up by 26%.* **5** ROAD UK If a road is up, it is being repaired. **6 COMPUTING** If a computer system is up, it is operating. **7 SPORT** *US* In baseball and similar sports, if a player is up, they are taking a turn to play. **8 be up and running** If a system, organization, or machine is up and running, it is operating. **9 be up for sth** *informal* to want to do something *We're going clubbing tonight if you're up for it.*

up³ /ʌp/ *verb* [T] **upping**, *past* **upped** to increase something *Dad's upped my allowance by fifty cents a week.*

up-and-coming /ˌʌpəŋˈkʌmɪŋ/ *adjective* [**always before noun**] becoming popular and likely to achieve success *He's a young, up-and-coming DJ.*

upbeat /ˈʌpˌbiːt/ *adjective informal* positive and expecting a situation to be good or successful *He remains upbeat about the future.*

upbringing /ˈʌpˌbrɪŋɪŋ/ *noun* [**no plural**] **SOCIETY** the way your parents treat you when you are growing up *a middle-class/religious upbringing*

upcoming /ˈʌpˌkʌmɪŋ/ *adjective* [**always before noun**] An upcoming event will happen soon. *the upcoming elections*

update¹ /ʌpˈdeɪt/ *verb* [T] **1** [INFORMATION] to add new information *We've just updated our website.* ○ *I'll **update** you **on*** (= tell you about) *any developments.* **2** [MODERN] to make something more modern *They need to update their image.*

WORD PARTNERS FOR ***update (noun)***

get/give an update • an update **on** sth • an update **from** sb

update² /ˈʌpdeɪt/ *noun* [C] **1** [INFORMATION] new information *I'll need regular **updates on** your progress.* **2** [NEW FORM] a new form of something which existed at an earlier time *It's an **update of** an old 60's movie.*

upfront¹ /ˌʌpˈfrʌnt/ *adjective* **1** [MONEY] paid or obtained before work starts *an **upfront payment/fee*** **2** [BEHAVIOUR] behaving in a way that makes your beliefs and intentions obvious to other people *She's very **upfront about** her dislike of men.*

upfront² /ˌʌpˈfrʌnt/ *adverb* If you pay someone upfront, you pay them before they work for you.

upgrade /ʌpˈgreɪd/ *verb* [T] to improve something so that it is of a higher quality or a newer model *to upgrade a computer* •**upgrade** /ˈʌpgreɪd/ *noun* [C]

upheaval /ʌpˈhiːvəl/ *noun* [**C, U**] a very big change that causes difficulty or confusion ***political/social upheaval***

uphill¹ /ʌpˈhɪl/ *adjective* **an uphill battle/struggle/task** something that is difficult to do and needs a lot of effort *I can lose weight but it's a real uphill struggle.*

uphill² /ʌpˈhɪl/ *adverb* towards the top of a hill *We'd walked half a mile uphill.*

uphold /ʌpˈhəʊld/ *verb* [T] *past* **upheld** **1** [AGREE] to agree with a decision, especially a legal one, and say it was correct *The court **upheld** the **ruling**.* **2** [SUPPORT] to support a decision, principle, or law *Police officers are expected to **uphold the law**.*

upholstery /ʌpˈhəʊlstəri/ *noun* [U] the material that covers chairs and other types of seats

upkeep /ˈʌpkiːp/ *noun* [U] the process of keeping something in good condition, or of keeping a person or animal healthy

upland /ˈʌplənd/ *adjective* [**always before noun**] existing on a hill or mountain *upland areas*

upland /ˈʌplənd/ *adjective* **GEOGRAPHY** describes an area of land that is high up, such as on a hill or mountain •**uplands** *noun* [**plural**]

uplands /ˈʌpləndz/ *noun* [**plural**] **GEOGRAPHY** high areas of land *the uplands of Nepal*

uplifting /ʌpˈlɪftɪŋ/ *adjective* making you feel happy and full of good feelings *an uplifting film*

upload /ʌpˈləʊd/ *verb* [T] **COMPUTING** to copy computer programs or information electronically, usually from a small computer to a larger one or to the Internet ➲See Extra help page **The Web and the Internet** on page Centre 36. ➲Compare **download**

upmarket /ˌʌpˈmɑːkɪt/ *UK* (*US* **upscale**) *adjective* expensive and used by people who are rich and from a high social class *an upmarket hotel/restaurant*

upon /əˈpɒn/ *preposition formal* on

upper /ˈʌpəʳ/ *adjective* [**always before noun**] **1** [POSITION] at a higher position *an upper floor* ○ *the upper lip* ○ *the upper body* **2** [SOCIAL CLASS] of a higher social class **3 the upper limit** the highest amount or level, or the longest time that something is allowed ➲See also: get/gain the upper **hand¹**

ˌ**upper** ˈ**case** *noun* [U] letters written as capitals

ˌ**upper** ˈ**class** *noun* [C] **SOCIETY** the highest social class of people *members of the upper classes* •**upper-class** *adjective an upper-class accent*

uppermost /ˈʌpəməʊst/ *adjective* **1** highest *the building's uppermost floors* **2 be uppermost in sb's mind** to be the most important thing someone is thinking about *The safety of her children was uppermost in her mind.*

upright¹ /ˈʌpraɪt/ *adverb* vertical and as straight as possible *to sit/stand upright* ➲See also: **bolt upright**

upright² /ˈʌpraɪt/ *adjective* **1** [VERTICAL] straight up or vertical *Please return your seat to an upright position and fasten your seat belt.* **2** [MORAL] honest and morally good *an upright citizen*

uprising /ˈʌpˌraɪzɪŋ/ *noun* [C] **POLITICS** when a large group of people try to make political changes or change the government by fighting [**usually singular**] *a **general/popular uprising***

WORD PARTNERS FOR ***uproar***

cause/provoke (an) uproar • be (UK) **in** (US) **in an** uproar • uproar **among** sb • uproar **at/over** sth

uproar /ˈʌprɔːʳ/ *noun* [**U no plural**] when many people complain about something angrily *The book **caused** an **uproar** in the United States.* ○ *Local residents are UK **in uproar**/ US **in an uproar** over plans for the new road.*

uproot /ʌpˈruːt/ *verb* [T] **1** [TREE] to pull a tree or plant out of the ground *Hundreds of trees were uprooted in the storm.* **2** [PERSON] to make someone leave a place where they have been living for a long time *The war has uprooted nearly half the country's population.*

U

ˌ**ups and 'downs** *noun* [**plural**] the mixture of good and bad things that happen to people *Like most married couples, we've* ***had our ups and downs.***

upscale /'ʌpˌskeɪl/ *US* (*UK* **upmarket**) *adjective* expensive and used by people who are rich and from a high social class *an upscale restaurant/neighbourhood*

O→**upset**[1] /ʌp'set/ *adjective* **1** unhappy or worried because something unpleasant has happened *They'd had an argument and she was still* ***upset about it.*** ○ *Mike* ***got*** *very* ***upset*** *when I told him the news.* **2 upset stomach/tummy HEALTH** an illness in the stomach

upset[2] /ʌp'set/ *verb* [**T**] **upsetting**, *past* **upset** **1** WORRY to make someone feel unhappy or worried *The phone call had clearly upset her.* **2** SPOIL to cause problems for something *If I arrived later would that upset your plans?* **3 upset sb's stomach HEALTH** to make someone feel ill in the stomach

upset[3] /'ʌpset/ *noun* [**C**] **1** SPORT when someone beats the player or team that was expected to win *After Harding won the second set, a major upset seemed likely.* **2 a stomach/tummy upset HEALTH** *UK* an illness in the stomach **3** PROBLEM a difficulty or problem *We had the usual upsets but overall the day went well.*

upsetting /ʌp'setɪŋ/ *adjective* making you feel unhappy or worried *I found the programme very upsetting.*

the upshot /'ʌpʃɒt/ *noun* the final result of a discussion or series of events *The upshot is that we've decided to move to Sydney.*

ˌ**upside 'down**[1] *adverb* **1** turned so that the part that is usually at the top is now at the bottom *One of the pictures had been hung upside down.* ○ ***Turn*** *the jar* ***upside down*** *and shake it.* **2 turn sth upside down a** MAKE UNTIDY to make a place very untidy while looking for something **b** CHANGE COMPLETELY to change someone's life or a system completely *Their lives were turned upside down when their son was arrested.*

ˌ**upside 'down**[2] *adjective* turned so that the part that is usually at the top is now at the bottom *Why is this box upside down?*

upstage /ʌp'steɪdʒ/ *verb* [**T**] to do something that takes people's attention away from someone or something and gives it to you instead *You mustn't upstage the bride.*

U

upstairs /ʌp'steəz/ *adverb* on or to a higher level of a building *He ran upstairs to answer the phone.* •**upstairs** *adjective an upstairs bedroom*

upstart /'ʌpstɑːt/ *noun* [**C**] someone who has just started a job but already thinks they are very important

upstate /ˌʌp'steɪt/ *adjective US* in the northern part of a US state (= one of the parts into which the country is divided) *upstate New York* •**upstate** *adverb She's taken a trip upstate with some friends.*

upstream /ʌp'striːm/ *adverb* along a river in the opposite direction to the way that the water is moving

upsurge /'ʌpsɜːdʒ/ *noun* [**C**] a sudden increase *an* ***upsurge in*** *violent crime*

uptake /'ʌpteɪk/ *noun informal* **be slow/quick on the uptake** to be slow/quick to understand something

uptight /ʌp'taɪt/ *adjective informal* worried or nervous and not able to relax

up-to-date /ˌʌptə'deɪt/ *adjective* **1** MODERN modern, and using the most recent technology or knowledge **2** INFORMATION having the most recent information *The Internet* ***keeps*** *us* ***up-to-date.***

up-to-the-minute /ˌʌptəðə'mɪnɪt/ *adjective* most recent *up-to-the-minute news*

uptown /ʌp'taʊn/ *adjective, adverb US* in or to the northern part of a city *She lives uptown.*

upturn /'ʌptɜːn/ *noun* [**C**] **ECONOMICS** an improvement, especially in economic conditions or a business *There's been a sharp* ***upturn in*** *sales.*

upturned /ʌp'tɜːnd/ *adjective* pointing up, or turned so the under side faces up *an upturned boat*

upward /'ʌpwəd/ *adjective* [**always before noun**] moving towards a higher place or level *an upward glance* ○ *an upward trend in sales*

upwards /'ʌpwədz/ *mainly UK* (*mainly US* **upward**) *adverb* **1** towards a higher place or level *House prices have started moving upwards again.* **2 upwards of sth** more than a particular amount *Double rooms cost upwards of £70 a night.*

uranium /jʊə'reɪniəm/ *noun* [**U**] **CHEMISTRY** a heavy, grey metal that is used in the production of nuclear power (symbol **U**)

Uranus /'jʊərᵊnəs/ *noun* [**no plural**] **ASTRONOMY** the planet that is seventh from the Sun, after Saturn and before Neptune ➲See picture at **solar system**

urban /'ɜːbᵊn/ *adjective* **GEOGRAPHY, SOCIETY** belonging or relating to a town or city *urban areas* ○ *urban development*

urbane /ɜː'beɪn/ *adjective* confident, relaxed, and polite *With his good looks and urbane manner, he was very popular.*

urbanization (*also UK* **-isation**) /ˌɜː.bᵊn.aɪ'zeɪ.ʃᵊn/ *noun* [**U**] **GEOGRAPHY** the way in which cities get bigger and more and more people leave the countryside to live in them

urea /jʊᵊ'riːə/ *noun* [**U**] **BIOLOGY** a colourless substance found in urine (= the liquid that comes out of your body when you go to the toilet) ➲See picture at **nitrogen cycle**

ureter /jʊə'riː.təʳ/ *noun* [**C**] **ANATOMY** a tube on each side of the body that takes urine (= liquid waste) from the kidney (= organ that makes urine) to the bladder (= organ that stores urine)

urethra /jʊə'riːθrə/ *noun* [**C**] **ANATOMY** the tube which carries urine (= liquid waste) out of the body. In men and male animals it also carries sperm (= small cells, one of which joins an egg to make a baby).

urge[1] /ɜːdʒ/ *verb* [**T**] **1 urge sb to do sth** to try to persuade someone to do something *His parents urged him to go to university.* **2** *formal* to strongly advise an action *Financial experts are **urging caution**.*

urge sb on *phrasal verb* to encourage someone to do or achieve something

WORD PARTNERS FOR *urge (noun)*

feel/have/resist/satisfy an urge • an **irresistible/overwhelming/strong/sudden/uncontrollable** urge

urge² /ɜːdʒ/ *noun* [C] a strong wish or need [+ **to do sth**] *I **resisted** a powerful **urge** to slap him.*

WORD PARTNERS FOR ***urgency***

a **matter of** urgency • a **sense of** urgency • the urgency **of** sth

urgency /ˈɜːdʒənsi/ *noun* [U] when something is very important and needs you to take action immediately *a **matter of** great **urgency***

urgent /ˈɜːdʒənt/ *adjective* very important and needing you to take action immediately *an urgent message* ○ *The refugees were **in urgent need of** food and water.* •**urgently** *adverb I need to **speak to** you **urgently**.*

urinate /ˈjʊərɪneɪt/ *verb* [I] **BIOLOGY** to get rid of urine from your body

urine /ˈjʊərɪn/ *noun* [U] **BIOLOGY** the liquid that comes out of your body when you go to the toilet

URL /juːɑːrˈel/ **INTERNET** *abbreviation for* uniform resource locator: a website address ➲See Extra help page **The Web and the Internet** on page Centre 36.

urn /ɜːn/ *noun* [C] **1** PLANTS a round container that is used for plants or to store someone's ashes (= the powder that is left after a dead body has been burned) **2** DRINKS a metal container that is used to make a large amount of coffee or tea and to keep it hot

urogenital /ˌjʊərəʊˈdʒenɪtəl/ *adjective* **ANATOMY, BIOLOGY** relating to the parts of the body which make and carry urine (= liquid waste), and also the genitals (= sexual organs)

O—**us** *strong form* /ʌs/ *weak forms* /əs, s/ *pronoun* used after a verb or preposition to refer to the person who is speaking or writing and one or more other people *She gave us all a present.* ○ *Come and have dinner with us tonight.*

USA /ˌjuːesˈeɪ/ *noun abbreviation for* United States of America

usage /ˈjuːsɪdʒ/ *noun* **1 LANGUAGE** [C, U] the way that words are used *a guide to English grammar and usage* **2** [U] the amount of something that is used, or the way that something is used *restrictions on water usage*

USB /ˌjuːesˈbiː/ *noun* [C] **COMPUTING** *abbreviation for* Universal Serial Bus: a part of a computer which allows you to connect extra devices, such as printers and cameras, without stopping and starting the computer again

O—**use¹** /juːz/ *verb* [T] *past* **used 1** PURPOSE If you use something, you do something with it for a particular purpose. *Can I use your pen?* ○ *She **uses** her car **for** work.* [+ **to do sth**] *Nick used the money to buy a CD player.* **2** MAKE LESS to take an amount from a supply of something *A shower uses less water than a bath.* **3** PERSON to treat someone badly in order to get what you want *He was just using me to make his girlfriend jealous.* **4** WORD to say or write a particular word or phrase *'Autumn' is used in British English and 'fall' in American English.* **5 could use sth** *mainly US informal* something that you say when you want or need something *I could use some help with these packages, please.*

use sth up *phrasal verb* to finish a supply of something *Someone's used up all the milk.*

O—**use²** /juːs/ *noun* **1** USING [U] when you use something, or when something is being used *an increase in the use of mobile phones* ○ *Guests have free use of the hotel swimming pool.* ○ *Turn the machine off when it's not **in use*** (= being used). **2** PURPOSE [C] a purpose for which something is used *A food processor has a variety of uses in the kitchen.* ○ *Can you **find a use for** this box?* **3 be (of) any/some use** to be useful *Is this book of any use to you?* **4 be (of) no use** to not be useful *His advice was no use at all.* **5 be no use; be no use doing sth** used to say that trying to do something has no effect *It was no use talking to him - he wouldn't listen.* **6** WORD [C] one of the meanings of a word, or the way that a particular word is used *Can you list all the uses of the verb 'go'?* **7 the use of sth** permission to use something, or the ability to use something *Martin has offered me the use of his car.* **8 make use of sth** to use something that is available *We were encouraged to make use of all the facilities.*

O—**used¹** /juːst/ *adjective* **used to sth/doing sth** If you are used to something, you have done it or experienced it many times before. *He's used to working long hours.* ○ *We've been living here for two years and we've (UK) **got used to**/ (US) **gotten used to** the heat.* ➲Opposite **unused**

used² /juːzd/ *adjective* Something that is used is not new and has been owned by someone else. *a **used car*** ➲Opposite **unused**

O—**used to** /ˈjuːsttuː/ *modal verb* **used to do/be sth** If something used to happen or a situation used to exist, it happened regularly or existed in the past but it does not happen or exist now. *I used to go out every night when I was a student.* ○ *He used to be a lot fatter.*

COMMON LEARNER ERROR

used to and **be used to**

Used to + verb is for talking about a situation or regular activity in the past.

My dad used to smoke when he was younger.

I used to live in Italy, but now I live in England.

When you make **used to + verb** into a question or negative using the verb do, the correct form is **use to**.

My dad didn't use to smoke.

Where did you use to live?

~~*Where did you used to live?*~~

The expression **be used to something/doing something** is for talking about something which you have done or experienced a lot before.

I don't mind the heat. I'm used to hot weather.

He's not used to working long hours.

~~*He's not use to working long hours.*~~

U

OTHER WAYS OF SAYING useful

If something is useful because it helps you do or achieve something, you can describe it as **helpful** or **valuable**: *They gave us some really **helpful** advice.* • *He was able to provide the police with some **valuable** information.*

The adjective **invaluable** means 'extremely useful': *The Internet is an **invaluable** resource for teachers.*

An activity which requires a lot of effort but is useful, is sometimes described as **worthwhile**: *It's a difficult course but it's very **worthwhile**.*

Something which is useful because it is simple to use is often described as **handy**: *That's a **handy** little gadget.*

The expression **come in handy** is often used when you think something will be useful in the future: *Don't throw that away - it'll **come in handy** for the party.*

If speech or writing contains a lot of useful information, you can describe it as **informative** or **instructive**: *It's an interesting and highly **informative** book.*

O-ₓ**useful** /ˈjuːsfəl/ *adjective* **1** helping you to do or achieve something *useful information* **2 come in useful** *UK* to be useful and help someone do or achieve something, especially when there is nothing else to help them *You should keep that paint - it might come in useful.* •**usefully** *adverb* •**usefulness** *noun* [U]

useless /ˈjuːsləs/ *adjective* **1** THING If something is useless, it does not work well or it has no effect. *This umbrella's useless - there's a big hole in it.* [+ **doing sth**] *It's useless arguing with her.* **2** PERSON *UK informal* having no skill in an activity *Dave's **useless at** football.*

user /ˈjuːzəʳ/ *noun* [C] someone who uses a product, machine, or service *Internet users*

user-friendly /ˌjuːzəˈfrendli/ *adjective* A machine or system that is user-friendly is easy to use or understand. *user-friendly software*

ˈuser ˌgroup *noun* [C] **COMPUTING, INTERNET** a group of people who use the Internet to share information about a particular area of computing or a particular product

ˌuser IˈD *noun* [U] **COMPUTING** information that proves who a person using a computer system is

U

ˈuser ˌname (*also* **username**) *noun* [C] **COMPUTING, INTERNET** a name or otherword that you sometimes need to use together with a password (= secret word) before you can use a computer on the Internet ➲See Extra help page **The Web and the Internet** on page Centre 37.

usher¹ /ˈʌʃəʳ/ *verb* **usher sb into/to/across, etc** to show someone where to go or sit *She ushered me into her office.*
usher in sth *phrasal verb formal* to be at the start of a period when important changes happen, or to cause important changes to start happening *His presidency ushered in a new era of democracy.*

usher² /ˈʌʃəʳ/ *noun* [C] someone who shows people where to sit in a theatre or at a formal event

O-ₓ**usual** /ˈjuːʒuəl/ *adjective* **1** normal and happening most often *I went to bed at my usual time.* ○ *This winter has been much colder than usual.* ➲Opposite **unusual 2 as usual** in the way that happens most of the time *As usual, Ben was the last to arrive.*

O-ₓ**usually** /ˈjuːʒəli/ *adverb* in the way that most often happens *I usually get home at about six o'clock.* ○ *Usually I just have a sandwich.*

usurp /juːˈzɜːp/ *verb* [T] *formal* to take someone else's job or power when you should not

utensil /juːˈtensəl/ *noun* [C] a tool that you use for doing jobs in the house, especially cooking *wooden cooking utensils* ➲See colour picture **The Kitchen** on page Centre 2

uterus /ˈjuːtərəs/ *noun* [C] **ANATOMY** the organ inside a woman's body where a baby grows ➲See picture at **foetus**

utilitarian /ˌjuːtɪlɪˈteəriən/ *adjective* designed to be useful and not beautiful *utilitarian furniture*

utility /juːˈtɪləti/ (*also* **public utility**) *noun* [C] an organization that supplies the public with water, gas, or electricity

utilize *formal* (*also UK* **-ise**) /ˈjuːtɪlaɪz/ *verb* [T] to use something in an effective way *The vitamins come in a form that is easily utilized by the body.*

utmost¹ /ˈʌtməʊst/ *adjective* [**always before noun**] *formal* used to emphasize how important or serious something is *a matter of the **utmost importance*** ○ *The situation needs to be handled **with the utmost** care.*

utmost² /ˈʌtməʊst/ *noun* **do your utmost** to try as hard as you can to do something [+ **to do sth**] *We did our utmost to finish the project on time.*

utopia /juːˈtəʊpiə/ *noun* [C, U] **SOCIETY** an imaginary place where everything is perfect

utopian /juːˈtəʊpiən/ *adjective* **SOCIETY** A utopian idea or plan is based on the belief that things can be made perfect. *a **utopian vision** of society*

utter¹ /ˈʌtəʳ/ *adjective* [**always before noun**] used to emphasize something *She dismissed the article as utter nonsense.*

utter² /ˈʌtəʳ/ *verb* [T] *formal* to say something *She left without **uttering a word**.*

utterance /ˈʌtərəns/ *noun* [C] *formal* something that you say

utterly /ˈʌtəli/ *adverb* completely *It's **utterly** ridiculous.*

U-turn /ˈjuːtɜːn/ *noun* [C] **1** VEHICLE a change of direction that you make when driving in order to travel in the opposite direction **2** DECISION a complete change from one opinion or plan to an opposite one *the government's **U-turn on** economic policy*

UV /juːˈviː/ *adjective abbreviation for* ultraviolet (= of the type of light that makes your skin darker) *UV light*

Vv

V, v /viː/ the twenty-second letter of the alphabet

V MEASURES *written abbreviation for* volt (= a unit for measuring an electric current) *a 9V battery*

v *UK* (*UK/US* **vs**) /viː/ *preposition* SPORT *abbreviation for* versus (= used to say that one team or person is competing against another) *Germany v France*

vacancy /ˈveɪkənsi/ *noun* [C] **1** ROOM a room that is not being used in a hotel *Do you have any vacancies?* **2** JOB a job that is available for someone to do *Tell me if you hear of any vacancies for secretaries.*

vacant /ˈveɪkənt/ *adjective* **1** EMPTY Somewhere that is vacant is available because it is not being used. *a vacant building* **2** JOB A vacant job is available for someone to do. **3** EXPRESSION A vacant expression on someone's face shows they are not thinking about anything. •**vacantly** *adverb*

vacate /vəˈkeɪt/ (US) /ˈveɪkeɪt/ *verb* [T] *formal* to leave a room, building, chair, etc so that someone else can use it

O‑ **vacation¹** /vəˈkeɪʃən/ (US) /veɪˈkeɪʃən/ *noun* [C, U] **1** *US* (*UK* **holiday**) a period of time when you are not at home but are staying somewhere else for enjoyment *We're **taking a vacation** in Florida.* ○ *We met Bob and Wendi **on vacation**.* **2** EDUCATION *mainly US* a period of the year when schools or colleges are closed *the summer vacation* ○ *He's **on vacation** for three months.*

vacation² /vəˈkeɪʃən/ (US) /veɪˈkeɪʃən/ *US* (*UK* **holiday**) *verb* **vacation in/on/by, etc** to go on vacation *Sam was vacationing in Guatemala.*

vaccinate /ˈvæksɪneɪt/ *verb* [T] HEALTH to give someone a vaccine to stop them from getting a disease *Have you been **vaccinated against** polio?* •**vaccination** /ˌvæksɪˈneɪʃən/ *noun* [C, U]

vaccine /ˈvæksiːn/ *noun* [C, U] HEALTH a substance that is given to people to stop them from getting a particular disease

vacuole /ˈvækjuəʊl/ *noun* [C] BIOLOGY a space inside a living cell, often containing a liquid ⊃See picture at **cell** ⊃See picture at **leaf**

vacuum¹ /ˈvækjuːm/ *noun* **1** PHYSICS [C] a space that has no air or other gas in it **2** [no plural] when someone or something important is not now in your life and you are unhappy *When her husband died, it left a big vacuum in her life.*

vacuum² /ˈvækjuːm/ *verb* [I, T] to clean somewhere using a vacuum cleaner

ˈvacuum ˌcleaner (*also UK* **Hoover**) *noun* [C] an electric machine that cleans floors by sucking up dirt

ˌvacuum ˈpacked *adjective* packed in a plastic covering with no air inside it

vagaries /ˈveɪgəriz/ *noun* [plural] sudden changes that are not expected or known about before they happen ***the vagaries of the** English weather*

vagina /vəˈdʒaɪnə/ *noun* [C] ANATOMY the part of a woman's body that connects her outer sex organs to the place where a baby grows

vagrant /ˈveɪgrənt/ *noun* [C] *formal* someone who has no job and no home and who lives outside

WORD PARTNERS FOR ***vague***

a vague **feeling/idea/impression/memory/promise**

vague /veɪg/ *adjective* **1** NOT CLEAR not clear or certain *I have a **vague idea** of where the hotel is.* ○ *He was a bit vague about directions.* **2** NOT THINKING showing that someone is not thinking clearly or does not understand *a vague expression* •**vaguely** *adverb I **vaguely** remember* (= slightly remember) meeting her. •**vagueness** *noun* [U]

vain /veɪn/ *adjective* **1 in vain** without any success *I tried in vain to start a conversation.* **2 vain attempt/effort/hope** A vain attempt, effort, etc does not have the result you want. **3** too interested in your own appearance and thinking you are very attractive •**vainly** *adverb*

valency /ˈveɪləntsi/ *noun* [C] CHEMISTRY a measurement of the ability of an atom of a particular chemical element to combine with other hydrogen atoms *Zinc has a valency of 2.*

Valentine /ˈvæləntaɪn/ (*also* **ˈValentine ˌcard**) *noun* [C] a card (= stiff, folded paper with a message inside) that you give someone on Valentine's Day

Valentine's Day /ˈvæləntaɪnzˌdeɪ/ *noun* [C, U] 14 February, a day when you give a Valentine to someone you have a romantic relationship with or want a romantic relationship with

valet /ˈvæleɪ/ *noun* [C] **1** CAR someone who parks your car when you arrive at a restaurant, hotel, or airport **2** SERVANT a male servant who looks after a man's clothes and helps him to dress

valiant /ˈvæliənt/ *adjective formal* very brave *a valiant effort* •**valiantly** *adverb*

valid /ˈvælɪd/ *adjective* **1** GOOD REASONS based on good reasons or facts that are true *a **valid** argument* **2** LAW A valid ticket or document is legally acceptable. *The ticket is valid for three months.* ⊃Opposite **invalid** •**validity** /vəˈlɪdəti/ *noun* [U]

validate /ˈvælɪdeɪt/ *verb* [T] *formal* to prove that something is true •**validation** /ˌvælɪˈdeɪʃən/ *noun* [C, U]

valley /ˈvæli/ *noun* [C] GEOGRAPHY an area of low land between hills or mountains

valour *UK literary* (*US* **valor**) /ˈvæləʳ/ *noun* [U] when someone is very brave, especially during a war

OTHER WAYS OF SAYING *valuable*

If something is valuable because it helps you do or achieve something, you can describe it as **helpful** or **useful**: *They gave us some really **helpful** advice.* • *She made a really **useful** contribution to the project.*

Something which is valuable because it produces useful results may be described as **constructive** or **productive**: *It was a very **constructive** discussion.* • *We had a very **productive** meeting and sorted out a lot of problems.*

An activity which is valuable but requires a lot of effort, is sometimes described as **worthwhile**: *It's a difficult course but it's very **worthwhile**.*

If speech or writing contains a lot of valuable information, you can describe it as **informative** or **instructive**: *It's an interesting and highly **informative** book.*

O-■ **valuable** /'væljuəbl/ *adjective* **1** OBJECT Valuable objects could be sold for a lot of money. *valuable paintings and antiques* **2** USEFUL Valuable information, help, advice, etc is very helpful.

valuables /'væljuəblz/ *noun* [**plural**] small things that you own which could be sold for a lot of money *valuables such as jewellery and watches*

valuation /ˌvælju'eɪʃən/ *noun* [**C, U**] **FINANCE** when someone judges how much money something could be sold for

WORD PARTNERS FOR *value*

the value **of** sth • **of** [any/great/real] value • values **go up/increase** • values **decrease/go down** • a **drop/fall/increase/rise in** value

O-■ **value**[1] /'vælju:/ *noun* **1 FINANCE** [**C, U**] how much money something could be sold for *The new road has affected the **value of** these houses.* ○ *Cars quickly go down in value.* **2** [**U**] how useful or important something is *a document of great historical value* **3 good value (for money)** If something is good value it is of good quality or there is a lot of it so you think the amount of money you spent on it was right. *The meal was very good value.* ⊃See also: **face value**

value[2] /'vælju:/ *verb* [**T**] **valuing**, *past* **valued 1** If you value something or someone, they are very important to you. *I always value his opinion.* **2 FINANCE** to judge how much money something could be sold for *The ring was **valued at** $1000.*

values /'vælju:z/ *noun* [**plural**] your beliefs about what is morally right and wrong and what is most important in life

valve /vælv/ *noun* [**C**] something that opens and closes to control the flow of liquid or gas

vampire /'væmpaɪər/ *noun* [**C**] in stories, a dead person who bites people's necks and drinks their blood

van /væn/ *noun* [**C**] a vehicle that is used for carrying things but which is smaller than a truck

vanadium /və'neɪdiəm/ *noun* [**U**] **CHEMISTRY** a silver-grey metal used to make steel alloys (= metal mixtures) (symbol **V**)

vandal /'vændəl/ *noun* [**C**] someone who intentionally damages things in public places *Vandals had smashed the shop window.*

vandalism /'vændəlɪzəm/ *noun* [**U**] the crime of intentionally damaging things in public places

vandalize (*also UK* **-ise**) /'vændəlaɪz/ *verb* [**T**] to intentionally damage things in public places

vanguard /'vængɑ:d/ *noun* **in the vanguard of sth** involved in the most recent changes in technology and understanding *Libraries are in the vanguard of the electronic revolution.*

vanilla /və'nɪlə/ *noun* [**U**] **FOOD** a substance that is used to give flavour to some sweet foods *vanilla ice cream*

vanish /'vænɪʃ/ *verb* [**I**] to disappear suddenly *The sun vanished behind the trees.* ○ *The report mysteriously vanished from the files.* ⊃See also: disappear/vanish into thin **air**[1]

'vanishing ˌpoint *noun* [**C usually singular**] **ART** in a picture, the point in the distance at which two parallel (= same distance apart) lines look as though they join

vanity /'vænəti/ *noun* [**U**] when someone thinks they are very attractive and is too interested in their own appearance

vantage point /'vɑ:ntɪdʒˌpɔɪnt/ *noun* [**C**] **1** WAY OF THINKING the way you think about a subject when you are in a particular situation *From my vantage point, it is difficult to see how things can improve.* **2** PLACE a place from which you can see something very well

vapour *UK* (*US* **vapor**) /'veɪpər/ *noun* [**U**] **1 PHYSICS, CHEMISTRY** many small drops of liquid in the air which look like a cloud **2 PHYSICS** the form of a liquid when it has become a gas

variable[1] /'veəriəbl/ *adjective* changing often *The sound quality on the recording is variable.* •**variability** /ˌveəriə'bɪləti/ *noun* [**U**]

variable[2] /'veəriəbl/ *noun* [**C**] **MATHEMATICS** a number, amount or situation which can change *A patient's recovery time depends on so many variables, such as age, weight and general health.*

ˌvariable 'costs *noun* [**plural**] **FINANCE** the things that a business must pay for, the amount of which changes according to things such as how much work it is doing ⊃Compare **fixed costs**

variance /'veəriəns/ *noun formal* **at variance with sb/sth** If two things or people are at variance with each other, they do not agree or are very different. *The statement seems to be at variance with government policy.*

variant /'veəriənt/ *noun* [**C**] something that is a slightly different form from the usual one *There are several **variants of** the virus.* ○ *spelling variants*

variation /ˌveəri'eɪʃən/ *noun* **1** DIFFERENCE [**C, U**] a difference in amount or quality ***variations in** price* **2** SOMETHING DIFFERENT [**C**] something that is slightly different from the usual form *It's a **variation on** the standard apple pie.*

varied /ˈveərɪd/ *adjective* consisting of many different types of things *a long and varied career*

WORD PARTNERS FOR ***variety***

a **bewildering/great/infinite/wide** variety • **offer/provide** variety

O→**variety** /vəˈraɪəti/ *noun* **1 a variety of sth/sb** many different types of things or people *Ben has done a variety of jobs.* **2** TYPE [C] a different type of something *a new variety of potato* **3** DIFFERENT THINGS [U] a lot of different activities, situations, people, etc *I need more variety in my life.*

O→**various** /ˈveəriəs/ *adjective* many different *They have offices in various parts of the country.* ○ *I started learning Spanish for various reasons.*

variously /ˈveəriəsli/ *adverb* in many different ways *The event was variously described as "terrible", "shocking", and "unbelievable".*

varnish¹ /ˈvɑːnɪʃ/ *noun* [C, U] a clear liquid that you paint onto wood to protect it and make it shine ➲See also: **nail varnish**

varnish² /ˈvɑːnɪʃ/ *verb* [T] to put varnish on a surface

vary /ˈveəri/ *verb* **1** BE DIFFERENT [I] If things of the same type vary, they are different from each other. *Car prices vary greatly across Europe.* ○ *Roses vary widely in size and shape.* **2** CHANGE [I] to change *Temperatures vary depending on the time of year.* **3** INTENTIONALLY CHANGE [T] to often change something that you do *I try to vary what I eat.*

vascular /ˈvæskjələʳ/ *adjective* **BIOLOGY** containing veins (= thin tubes that carry blood in animals and other liquid in plants)

ˌ**vascular ˈbundle** *noun* [C] **BIOLOGY** the part of a plant's stem or leaves that has veins ➲See picture at **stem**

vas deferens /ˌvæsˈdefərenz/ *noun* [C] *plural* **vasa deferentia** /ˌveɪsədefəˈrentʃiə/ **BIOLOGY, ANATOMY** the tube through which a male's sperm (= seeds that join with the female's egg to make a baby) pass on the way out of the body

vase /vɑːz/ (US) /veɪs/ *noun* [C] a container that you put flowers in

vasectomy /vəˈsektəmi/ *noun* [C] **HEALTH** a medical operation that is done to stop a man having children

vasoconstriction /ˌveɪzəʊkənˈstrɪkʃən/ *noun* [U] **BIOLOGY** when blood vessels (= tubes that carry blood) become more narrow

vasodilation /ˌveɪzəʊdaɪˈleɪʃən/ *noun* [U] **BIOLOGY** when blood vessels (= tubes that carry blood) become wider

vast /vɑːst/ *adjective* extremely big *a vast amount of money* ○ *vast forest areas*

vastly /ˈvɑːstli/ *adverb* very much *Life now is vastly different from 100 years ago.*

VAT /ˌviːeɪˈtiː/ *noun* [U] **ECONOMICS, FINANCE** *abbreviation for* value added tax: a tax on goods and services in the UK

vault¹ /vɔːlt/ *noun* [C] **1** IN A BANK a special room in a bank where money, jewellery, and other valuable objects are kept **2** IN A CHURCH a room under a church where people are buried

vault² /vɔːlt/ *verb* [I, T] to jump over something by first putting your hands on it *Rick vaulted the gate and ran off.* ➲See also: **pole vault**

VCR /ˌviːsiːˈɑːʳ/ *mainly US* (*UK* **video**) *noun* [C] *abbreviation for* video cassette recorder: a machine that you use for recording television programmes and playing videos (= recorded films or programmes) ➲See colour picture **The Living Room** on page Centre 4

VDU /ˌviːdiːˈjuː/ *noun* [C] *UK* **COMPUTING** *abbreviation for* visual display unit: a machine with a screen that shows information from a computer

've /v/ *short for* have *I've already eaten.*

veal /viːl/ *noun* [U] **FOOD** meat from a very young cow

vector /ˈvektəʳ/ *noun* [C] **1 PHYSICS** something physical such as a force which has size and direction ➲Compare **scalar 2 BIOLOGY** an insect or animal which carries a disease from one animal or plant to another

vee belt /ˈviːˌbelt/ *noun* [C] **DT** a strip of material that is used to connect two turning parts in a machine

veer /vɪəʳ/ *verb* **veer across/off/towards, etc** to suddenly change direction *The car veered off the road and hit a tree.*

veg /vedʒ/ *noun* [C, U] *plural* **veg** *UK informal* **FOOD** *short for* vegetables ***fruit and veg***

vegan /ˈviːgən/ *noun* [C] **FOOD** someone who does not eat meat, fish, eggs, milk, or cheese •**vegan** *adjective*

O→**vegetable** /ˈvedʒtəbl/ *noun* [C] **FOOD** a plant that you eat, for example potatoes, onions, beans, etc ➲See colour picture **Fruit and Vegetables** on page Centre 10

vegetarian¹ /ˌvedʒɪˈteəriən/ *noun* [C] **FOOD** someone who does not eat meat or fish

vegetarian² /ˌvedʒɪˈteəriən/ *adjective* **FOOD** not eating, containing, or using meat or fish *All her children are vegetarian.* ○ *a vegetarian restaurant/pizza*

vegetation /ˌvedʒɪˈteɪʃən/ *noun* [U] **BIOLOGY, GEOGRAPHY** the plants and trees that grow in a particular area

veggie /ˈvedʒi/ *noun* [C] *UK informal* a vegetarian •**veggie** *adjective*

veggie burger /ˈvedʒiˌbɜːgəʳ/ *noun* [C] **FOOD** a flat round piece of food, made of vegetables, nuts, etc. and no meat, usually eaten inside two pieces of bread

vehement /ˈviːəmənt/ *adjective formal* showing strong, often negative, feelings about something *vehement criticism/opposition* •**vehemently** *adverb*

O→**vehicle** /ˈviːɪkl/ *noun* **1** [C] *formal* something such as a car or bus that takes people from one place to another, especially using roads **2 a vehicle for sth/doing sth** something that you use as a way of telling people your ideas or opinions *The paper was merely a vehicle for his political beliefs.*

V

men with blue eyes

men with blue eyes and beards

men with beards

Venn diagram

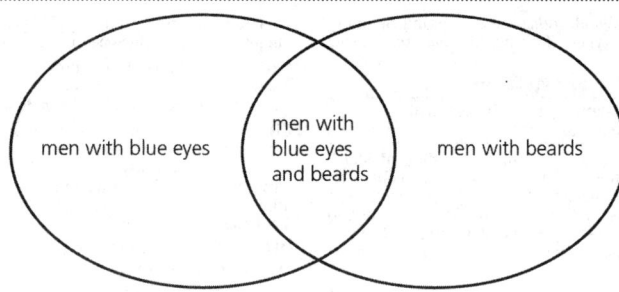

veil /veɪl/ *noun* **1** [C] a thin piece of material that covers a woman's face **2 draw a veil over sth** *UK* to not talk any more about a subject because it could cause trouble or embarrassment

veiled /veɪld/ *adjective* said so that the true meaning or purpose is not clear ***veiled criticism***

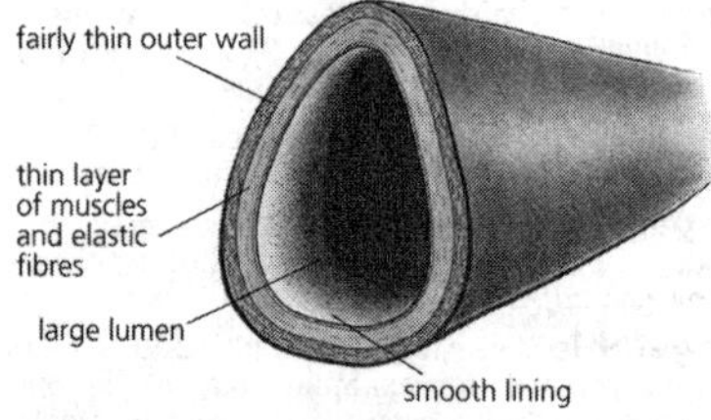

vein

vein /veɪn/ *noun* [C] **1 ANATOMY, BIOLOGY** one of the tubes in your body that carries blood to your heart **2 BIOLOGY** one of the thin lines on a leaf ➲See picture at **leaf** **3 in the same vein** in the same style of speaking or writing

Velcro /ˈvelkrəʊ/ *noun* [U] *trademark* **DT** material that consists of two pieces of cloth that stick together, used to fasten clothes

velocity /vɪˈlɒsəti/ *noun* [C, U] **PHYSICS** the speed at which something moves

velvet /ˈvelvɪt/ *noun* [U] cloth that has a thick, soft surface on one side *a black velvet jacket*

V

vena cava /ˌviːnəˈkeɪvə/ *noun* [C] *plural* **venae cavae** /ˌviːniːˈkeɪviː/ **BIOLOGY, ANATOMY** one of the two very large veins (= tubes that carry blood) which take blood without oxygen to the heart ➲See picture at **heart**

vendetta /venˈdetə/ *noun* [C] when someone tries to do something bad to someone over a period of time because they have been treated badly by them *He had a **vendetta against** the company after he lost his job.*

vending machine /ˈvendɪŋməˌʃiːn/ *noun* [C] a machine that sells drinks, cigarettes, etc

vendor /ˈvendɔːʳ/ *noun* [C] **1** SELL OUTSIDE someone who sells something outside *an ice cream vendor* **2** COMPANY *formal* a company that sells goods or services

veneer /vəˈnɪəʳ/ *noun* **1** [C, U] **DT** a thin layer of wood that covers a piece of furniture that is made of a cheaper material **2 a veneer of sth** *formal* a way of behaving that is not sincere and hides someone's real character or emotions *a thin veneer of calm/respectability*

venerable /ˈvenᵊrəbl/ *adjective* old and very much respected *a **venerable institution**/tradition*

venetian blind /vəˌniːʃᵊnˈblaɪnd/ *noun* [C] a covering for a window that is made from long, flat, horizontal pieces of metal or wood which you can move to let in light

vengeance /ˈvendʒᵊns/ *noun* **1** [U] when you do something bad to someone who has done something bad to you, or the feeling of wanting to do this *an act of vengeance* **2 with a vengeance** If something happens with a vengeance, it happens a lot or in a very strong way. *The disease swept across the country with a vengeance.*

vengeful /ˈvendʒfᵊl/ *adjective formal* wanting vengeance

venison /ˈvenɪsᵊn/ *noun* [U] **FOOD** meat from a deer

Venn diagram /ˌvenˈdaɪəgræm/ *noun* [C] **MATHEMATICS** a drawing in which mathematical sets are shown inside a group of circles, parts of which cover each other. Numbers which belong to more than one set are shown in these parts of the circles.

venom /ˈvenəm/ *noun* [U] **1** POISON poison that some snakes and insects produce **2** ANGER/HATE a feeling of extreme anger or hate *Much of his venom was directed at his boss.* •**venomous** *adjective* containing or involving venom

vent¹ /vent/ *noun* [C] a hole in a wall or machine that lets air in and allows smoke or smells to go out

vent² /vent/ *verb* **vent your anger/frustration, etc** to do or say something to show your anger or another strong, bad feeling

ventilate /ˈventɪleɪt/ *verb* [T] to let air come into and go out of a room or building •**ventilation** /ˌventɪˈleɪʃᵊn/ *noun* [U] *a ventilation system*

ventricle /ˈventrɪkl/ *noun* [C] **ANATOMY** each of the two main spaces in the heart, left and right ➲See picture at **heart**

venture[1] /ˈventʃər/ *noun* [C] a new activity that may not be successful *a* ***business venture*** ➲See also: **joint venture**

venture[2] /ˈventʃər/ *verb formal* **1 venture into/out/outside, etc** to leave a safe place and go somewhere that may involve risks *If the snow stops I might venture out.* **2** [T] to be brave enough to say something that might be criticized *I didn't dare* ***venture*** *an* ***opinion****.*

ˈventure ˌcapital *noun* [U] **ECONOMICS, FINANCE** money that is spent on a new activity or company, especially when there is a chance that the activity or company will not be successful

venue /ˈvenjuː/ *noun* [C] a place where a sports game, musical performance, or special event happens

venule /ˈviːnjuːl/ *noun* [C] **ANATOMY, BIOLOGY** a very small vein ➲See picture at **capillary**

Venus /ˈviːnəs/ *noun* [**no plural**] **ASTRONOMY** the planet that is second from the Sun, after Mercury and before the Earth ➲See picture at **solar system**

veranda (*also* **verandah**) /vəˈrændə/ *noun* [C] a room that is joined to the outside of a house and has a roof and floor but no outside wall

O- **verb** /vɜːb/ *noun* **LANGUAGE** a word that is used to say that someone does something or that something happens. For example the words 'arrive', 'make', 'be', and 'feel' are verbs. ➲See also: **auxiliary verb, modal verb, phrasal verb**

verbal /ˈvɜːbəl/ *adjective* **LANGUAGE 1** spoken and not written *a verbal promise* **2** relating to words or the use of words *verbal ability/skills* •**verbally** *adverb*

verbatim /vɜːˈbeɪtɪm/ *adjective, adverb* using the exact words that were originally used

WORD PARTNERS FOR ***verdict***

deliver/reach/return a verdict • a **guilty/not guilty** verdict

verdict /ˈvɜːdɪkt/ *noun* [C] **1 LAW** a decision in a court of law saying if someone is guilty or not *a* ***guilty verdict*** ○ *The jury took nine hours to* ***reach*** *a* ***verdict****.* **2** [DECISION] someone's opinion about something after experiencing it, often for the first time *You tried out that Italian restaurant? What was the verdict?*

verge[1] /vɜːdʒ/ *noun* [C] **1** *UK* the edge of a road or path that is usually covered in grass **2 be on the verge of sth/doing sth** to be going to happen or to do something very soon *a company on the verge of financial disaster*

verge[2] /vɜːdʒ/ *verb*
verge on sth *phrasal verb* to almost be a particular state or quality *His constant questions verged on rudeness.*

verify /ˈverɪfaɪ/ *verb* [T] to prove that something is true, or do something to discover if it is true *It was impossible to verify her statement.* •**verification** /ˌverɪfɪˈkeɪʃən/ *noun* [U]

veritable /ˈverɪtəbl/ *adjective* [**always before noun**] *formal* used to emphasize how extreme something is *Their house was a veritable palace* (= was very large).

vermin /ˈvɜːmɪn/ *noun* [**plural**] small animals that damage crops and can cause disease

versatile /ˈvɜːsətaɪl/ (US) /ˈvɜːrsətəl/ *adjective* **1** [PERSON] having many different skills *a versatile player/performer* **2** [THING] useful for doing a lot of different things *a versatile tool* •**versatility** /ˌvɜːsəˈtɪləti/ *noun* [U]

verse /vɜːs/ *noun* **1 LITERATURE, MUSIC** [C] one of the parts that a song or poem is divided into *I only know the first verse.* **2 LITERATURE** [U] words that are in the form of poetry *The story was told in verse.*

WORD PARTNERS FOR ***version***

a new/the latest version • a version **of** sth • **in** a version

O- **version** /ˈvɜːʃən/ *noun* [C] **1** [FORM] one form of something that is slightly different to other forms of the same thing *I saw the original version of the film.* **2** [DESCRIPTION] someone's description of what has happened *Bates gave his version of events to the police.*

versus /ˈvɜːsəs/ *preposition* **1 SPORT** used to say that one team or person is competing against another *Tomorrow's game is Newcastle versus Arsenal.* **2** used to compare two things or ideas, especially when you have to choose between them *private education versus state education*

vertebra /ˈvɜːtɪbrə/ *noun* [C] *plural* **vertebrae** /ˈvɜːtɪbriː/ **ANATOMY** any of the small bones that form the spine (= bones that go up the back) •**vertebral** /ˈvɜːtɪbrəl/ *adjective* ➲See picture at **brain**

vertebrate /ˈvɜːtɪbrət/ *noun* [C] **BIOLOGY** an animal that has a spine (= bone in the back) *Birds, fish, mammals, amphibians and reptiles are all vertebrates.* •**vertebrate** *adjective* ➲Compare **invertebrate**

vertical /ˈvɜːtɪkəl/ *adjective* pointing straight up from a surface *a vertical line* •**vertically** *adverb* ➲See picture at **horizontal**

ˈvertical ˌaxis *noun* [**no plural**] **MATHEMATICS** the line of figures or letters along the side of a graph or map; the y-axis ➲See Extra help page **Graphs and charts** on page Centre 20. ➲Compare **horizontal axis**

ˌvertical ˈmerger *noun* [C] **ECONOMICS** when two companies that work on different stages in the production of the same product join together

vertigo /ˈvɜːtɪgəʊ/ *noun* [U] when you feel slightly ill because you are in a high place and feel as if you might fall

verve /vɜːv/ *noun* [U] *formal* energy and enthusiasm

O- **very[1]** /ˈveri/ *adverb* **1** used to emphasize an adjective or adverb *She was very pleased.* ○ *Marie speaks very slowly.* ○ *Thank you very much.* **2 not very good/tall/happy, etc** not good, happy, etc *The film wasn't very good.*

very[2] /ˈveri/ *adjective* [**always before noun**] used to emphasize a noun *This is the very house where we stayed.*

vesicle /ˈvesɪkəl/ *noun* [C] **BIOLOGY** a small hollow part in the body of a plant or animal

V

vessel /ˈvesᵊl/ *noun* [C] **1** SHIP *formal* a ship or large boat **2** CONTAINER *old-fashioned* a container for liquids ➲See also: **blood vessel**

vest /vest/ *noun* [C] **1** UNDERWEAR *UK* (*US* **undershirt**) a piece of underwear that you wear under a shirt **2** WORN OVER A SHIRT *US* (*UK* **waistcoat**) a piece of clothing with buttons at the front and no sleeves, that you wear over a shirt ➲See colour picture **Clothes** on page Centre 9

vested interest /ˌvestɪdˈɪntrest/ *noun* [C] If you have a vested interest in something, you want it to happen because it will give you advantages.

vestige /ˈvestɪdʒ/ *noun* [C] a very small amount of something that still exists after most of it has gone *There is still a vestige of hope that she might be found alive.*

vet¹ /vet/ *noun* [C] someone whose job is to give medical care to animals that are ill or hurt

vet² /vet/ *verb* [T] **vetting**, *past* **vetted** to look at details of someone's life, in order to make sure that they are suitable for a particular job [**often passive**] *Applicants for the job are carefully vetted.*

veteran /ˈvetᵊrᵊn/ *noun* [C] **1** MILITARY PERSON someone who has been in an army or navy during a war *a veteran of World War Two* **2** A LONG TIME someone who has done a job or activity for a long time *a 20-year veteran of BBC news*

veterinarian /ˌvetᵊrɪˈneəriən/ *noun* [C] *US* a vet

veterinary /ˈvetᵊrɪnᵊri/ *adjective formal* relating to medical care given to animals that are ill or hurt

ˈveterinary ˌsurgeon *noun* [C] *UK formal* a vet

veto¹ /ˈviːtəʊ/ *verb* [T] **vetoing**, *past* **vetoed** **POLITICS** If someone in authority vetoes something, they do not allow it to happen, although other people have agreed to it. *The plan was vetoed by the President.*

veto² /ˈviːtəʊ/ *noun* [C, U] *plural* **vetoes** **POLITICS** when someone in authority does not allow something to happen

vexed /vekst/ *adjective* **vexed question/issue, etc** a situation that causes problems and is difficult to deal with *the vexed issue of unemployment*

via /vaɪə/ *preposition* **1** GOING THROUGH going through or stopping at a place on the way to another place *The train to Utrecht goes via Amsterdam.* **2** USING using a particular machine, system, or person to send or receive something *I receive all my work via e-mail.*

V

viable /ˈvaɪəbl/ *adjective* effective and able to be successful *a **viable alternative** to nuclear power* ○ *an economically viable plan* •**viability** /ˌvaɪəˈbɪləti/ *noun* [U]

viaduct /ˈvaɪədʌkt/ *noun* [C] a long, high bridge across a valley

vibes /vaɪbz/ *noun* [**plural**] *informal* the way a person or place makes you feel *I get **bad/good vibes** from her.*

vibrant /ˈvaɪbrənt/ *adjective* **1** EXCITING full of excitement and energy *a vibrant city* ○ *a vibrant, young performer* **2** COLOUR A vibrant colour is very bright.

vibrate /vaɪˈbreɪt/ Ⓤⓢ /ˈvaɪbreɪt/ *verb* [**I, T**] to shake with small, quick movements or to make something shake this way *The music was so loud that the floor was vibrating.* •**vibration** /vaɪˈbreɪʃᵊn/ *noun* [**C, U**]

vicar /ˈvɪkəʳ/ *noun* [C] **RELIGION** a priest in some Christian churches

vicarage /ˈvɪkᵊrɪdʒ/ *noun* [C] **RELIGION** the house where a vicar lives

vicarious /vɪˈkeəriəs/ *adjective* [**always before noun**] A vicarious feeling is one you get from seeing or hearing about another person's experiences. *It gives me **vicarious pleasure** to watch him eat.*

vice /vaɪs/ *noun* **1** BAD HABIT [C] something bad that someone often does *Smoking is his only vice.* **2** CRIME [U] crime that involves sex or drugs **3 DT** [C] *UK* (*US* **vise**) a tool used for holding something tightly while you cut it, make it smooth, etc

ˌvice ˈpresident *noun* [C] **1 POLITICS** the person who is a rank lower than the president of a country **2** *US* someone who is responsible for part of a company *She's vice president of sales and marketing.*

vice versa /ˌvaɪsˈvɜːsə/ *adverb* used for referring to the opposite of what you have just said *Never use indoor lights outside and vice versa.*

vicinity /vɪˈsɪnəti/ *noun* **in the vicinity (of sth)** *formal* in the area near a place *A number of buildings in the vicinity of the fire were damaged.*

vicious /ˈvɪʃəs/ *adjective* **1** VIOLENT violent and dangerous *a vicious attack on a child* ○ *a vicious dog* **2** UPSETTING intended to upset someone *a **vicious rumour*** •**viciously** *adverb*

ˌvicious ˈcircle (*also* **ˌvicious ˈcycle**) *noun* [**no plural**] when one problem causes another problem which then makes the first problem worse

O-ᵚ**victim** /ˈvɪktɪm/ *noun* [C] someone who has suffered the effects of violence, illness, or bad luck *victims of crime* ○ *hurricane/flood victims*

victimize (*also UK* **-ise**) /ˈvɪktɪmaɪz/ *verb* [T] to treat someone unfairly because you do not like or approve of them *Ben feels he has been victimized by his teacher.*

victor /ˈvɪktəʳ/ *noun* [C] *formal* the person who wins a fight or competition

Victorian /vɪkˈtɔːriən/ *adjective* from or relating to the period between 1837 and 1901 in Britain *a Victorian house*

victorious /vɪkˈtɔːriəs/ *adjective* having won a fight or competition *a victorious army*

WORD PARTNERS FOR ***victory***

claim/secure victory • a **comfortable/easy/impressive** victory • a victory **for/over** sb

victory /ˈvɪktᵊri/ *noun* [**C, U**] when you win a fight or competition *Phoenix managed a 135-114 **victory over** Denver.*

O-ᵚ**video¹** /ˈvɪdiəʊ/ *noun* **1** TAPE [U] a film or television programme recorded on videotape *'Pride and Prejudice' has just come out **on video**.* **2** RECORDING [C] something that you have recorded on videotape using a video camera *Caroline and Yann showed us their wedding video last night.* **3** [C] (*also* **VCR**) (*also* **video recorder**) a machine that you use for recording a television programme or watching a video ➲See colour picture **The Living Room** on page Centre 4

video² /ˈvɪdiəʊ/ *verb* [T] **videoing**, *past* **videoed** **1** to record a television program using a video recorder **2** to film something using a video camera

ˈvideo ˌcamera *noun* [C] a piece of equipment used to record something onto videotape

ˈvideo ˌclip *noun* [C] a short video recording

video conferencing /ˈvɪdiəʊˌkɒnfərəntsɪŋ/ *noun* [U] when two or more people who are in different parts of the world talk to each other and see each other on television screens

ˈvideo ˌgame *noun* [C] **COMPUTING** a game in which you make pictures move on a screen

videophone /ˈvɪdiəʊfəʊn/ *noun* [C] a telephone with a small screen so that you can see the person you are talking to

ˈvideo recˌorder *noun* [C] a video machine

videotape /ˈvɪdiəʊteɪp/ *noun* [C, U] a thin strip of material inside a plastic box that is used for recording television programmes and films

vie /vaɪ/ *verb* [I] **vying**, *past* **vied** to try hard to do something more successfully than someone else *The children were* ***vying for*** *attention.* [+ **to do sth**] *Film crews were* ***vying with*** *each other to get the best pictures.*

WORD PARTNERS FOR ***view***

express/have/hold a view • **strong** views • **in** sb's view • sb's views **about/on** sth • an **exchange of** views

O-ᵥ **view¹** /vjuː/ *noun* **1** OPINION [C] your opinion *We have different* ***views about/on*** *education.* ○ ***In*** *her* ***view*** *this is wrong.* **2** THINGS YOU SEE [C] the things that you can see from a place *There was a lovely view of the lake from the bedroom window.* **3** ABILITY TO SEE [**no plural**] how well you can see something from a particular place *We had a great view of the procession.* **4** POSITION [U] a position from which something can be seen *The house was hidden from view behind a wall.* ○ *He turned the corner and the harbour* ***came into view.*** **5 in full view of sb** happening where someone can easily see *All this happened in full view of the cameras.* **6 in view of sth** *formal* because of *In view of recent events, we have decided to cancel the meeting.* **7 with a view to doing sth** *formal* so that you can do something *He's doing some improvements on the house with a view to selling it.* ➲See also: **point of view**

COMMON LEARNER ERROR

view or **sight?**

View means the countryside, buildings, things, etc which you can see from a place, or how well you can see something. A **view** is usually pleasant.

We had a wonderful view from the aircraft.

~~*We had a wonderful sight from the aircraft.*~~

Sight means when you see something, or the ability to see.

The sight of blood makes me feel sick.

~~*The view of blood makes me feel sick.*~~

view² /vjuː/ *verb* [T] *formal* **1** OPINION to have a particular opinion about someone or something *In all three countries he is* ***viewed as*** *a terrorist.* **2** WATCH to watch something *They were able to view the city from a helicopter.*

viewer /ˈvjuːəʳ/ *noun* [C] someone who watches a television programme

viewpoint /ˈvjuːpɔɪnt/ *noun* [C] a way of thinking about a situation ***From his viewpoint*** *the action seemed entirely justified.*

vigil /ˈvɪdʒɪl/ *noun* [C, U] when people stay somewhere quietly in order to show that they support someone, disagree with someone, etc *an all-night vigil for peace*

vigilant /ˈvɪdʒɪlənt/ *adjective* watching carefully and always ready to notice anything dangerous or illegal *Police have asked people to be vigilant after yesterday's bomb attack.* •**vigilance** /ˈvɪdʒɪləns/ *noun* [U]

vigilante /ˌvɪdʒɪˈlænti/ *noun* [C] a member of a group of people who try to catch criminals and punish them without having any legal authority

vigor /ˈvɪgəʳ/ *noun* [U] *US spelling of* vigour

vigorous /ˈvɪgərəs/ *adjective* **1** ENERGETIC showing or needing a lot of physical energy ***vigorous exercise*** **2** FORCEFUL showing strong, often negative, feelings about something *a vigorous debate* ○ *He was a* ***vigorous opponent*** *of the government.* •**vigorously** *adverb Bates* ***vigorously denies*** (= strongly denies) *murdering his wife.*

vigour *UK* (*US* **vigor**) /ˈvɪgəʳ/ *noun* [U] strength and energy *She set about her work* ***with*** *great* ***vigour.***

vile /vaɪl/ *adjective* extremely unpleasant *a vile attack* ○ *The bathroom was vile.*

vilify /ˈvɪlɪfaɪ/ *verb* [T] *formal* to say bad things about someone so that other people will not like or approve of them

villa /ˈvɪlə/ *noun* [C] a large house, especially one used for holidays in a warm country

O-ᵥ **village** /ˈvɪlɪdʒ/ *noun* [C] a place where people live in the countryside that includes buildings such as shops and a school but which is smaller than a town *She lives in a small village outside Oxford.* ○ *a village shop*

villager /ˈvɪlɪdʒəʳ/ *noun* [C] someone who lives in a village

villain /ˈvɪlən/ *noun* [C] a bad person in a film, book, etc

villus /ˈvɪləs/ *noun* [**C usually plural**] *plural* **villi** /ˈvɪlaɪ/ **ANATOMY, BIOLOGY** one of many small finger-like parts on the inside surface of the small intestine (= part of body where food goes after the stomach), through which the food is absorbed

vindicate /ˈvɪndɪkeɪt/ *verb* [T] *formal* to prove that what someone said or did was right after people generally thought it was wrong •**vindication** /ˌvɪndɪˈkeɪʃən/ *noun* [C, U] *formal*

vindictive /vɪnˈdɪktɪv/ *adjective* intending to harm or upset someone who has harmed or upset you

V

vine /vaɪn/ *noun* [C] a plant that grapes (= small, green or purple fruit used for making wine) grow on

vinegar /ˈvɪnɪgəʳ/ *noun* [U] **FOOD** a sour liquid that is used in cooking, often made from wine

vineyard /ˈvɪnjəd/ *noun* [C] **FARMING** an area of land where someone grows grapes (= small, green or purple fruit) for making wine

vintage¹ /ˈvɪntɪdʒ/ *adjective* **1 FOOD** Vintage wine is wine of a good quality that was made in a particular year. **2** VERY GOOD having all the best or most typical qualities of something, especially from the past *a vintage Hollywood movie* **3** CAR A vintage car was made between 1919 and 1930.

vintage² /ˈvɪntɪdʒ/ *noun* [C] **FOOD** the wine that was made in a particular year *The 1993 vintage is one of the best.*

vinyl /ˈvaɪnəl/ *noun* [U] **DT** a type of very strong plastic

viola /viˈəʊlə/ *noun* [C] **MUSIC** a wooden instrument, larger than a violin, that you hold against your neck and play by moving a special stick across strings

violate /ˈvaɪəleɪt/ *verb* [T] *formal* **1** NOT OBEY to not obey a law, rule, or agreement *Countries that violate international law will be dealt with severely.* **2** NOT ALLOW to not allow someone something that they should morally be allowed to have *They were accused of violating human rights.* •**violation** /ˌvaɪəˈleɪʃən/ *noun* [C, U] *a violation of privacy*

WORD PARTNERS FOR ***violence***

erupt into/renounce/use violence • **escalating/extreme/gratuitous** violence • violence **against/towards** sb

O-ᵘ **violence** /ˈvaɪələns/ *noun* [U] **1** CAUSING HURT when someone tries to hurt or kill someone else *an act of violence* ○ *A number of people were killed in the violence.* ○ ***Violence against*** *women has increased in recent years.* **2** EXTREME FORCE extreme force and energy, especially of something causing damage *Such was the violence of the explosion that three buildings collapsed.*

O-ᵘ **violent** /ˈvaɪələnt/ *adjective* **1** ACTION involving violence *a victim of* ***violent crime*** ○ *a violent protest* ○ *I don't like violent films* (= films that show violence). **2** PERSON likely to hurt or kill someone else *a violent criminal* **3** DAMAGE sudden and causing damage *a violent explosion/storm* **4** EMOTIONS showing very strong feelings, especially anger *violent emotions* •**violently** *adverb* ➲See also: **non-violent**

V

violet /ˈvaɪələt/ *noun* **1** FLOWER [C] a small plant with a small, purple flower **2** COLOUR [U] a pale purple colour

violin /ˌvaɪəˈlɪn/ *noun* [C] **MUSIC** a wooden musical instrument that you hold against your neck and play by moving a bow (= special stick) across strings •**violinist** /vaɪəˈlɪnɪst/ *noun* [C] someone who plays a violin

VIP /ˌviːaɪˈpiː/ *noun* [C] *abbreviation for* very important person: someone who is famous or powerful and is treated in a special way *The airport has a separate lounge for VIPs.*

viper /ˈvaɪpəʳ/ *noun* [C] a small, poisonous snake

viral /ˈvaɪrəl/ *adjective* **HEALTH** caused by or relating to a virus (= infectious organism) *a viral infection*

virgin¹ /ˈvɜːdʒɪn/ *noun* [C] someone who has never had sex

virgin² /ˈvɜːdʒɪn/ *adjective* Virgin land, forest, etc has not been used or damaged by people.

virginity /vəˈdʒɪnəti/ *noun* [U] when someone has never had sex *Emma* ***lost her virginity*** (= had sex for the first time) *at sixteen.*

Virgo /ˈvɜːgəʊ/ *noun* [C, U] the sign of the zodiac which relates to the period of 23 August - 22 September, or a person born during this period

virile /ˈvɪraɪl/ (US) /ˈvɪrəl/ *adjective* A virile man is strong and has sexual energy. •**virility** /vɪˈrɪləti/ *noun* [U]

virtual /ˈvɜːtʃuəl/ *adjective* [**always before noun**] **1** almost a particular thing or quality *They played the game in virtual silence.* **2 COMPUTING** using computer images and sounds that make you think an imagined situation is real *a virtual art gallery*

virtually /ˈvɜːtʃuəli/ *adverb* almost *They're virtually the same.* ○ *I've virtually finished.*

ˌvirtual ˈmemory *noun* [U] **COMPUTING** on a computer, space that software can use to store information for a short time

ˌvirtual reˈality *noun* [U] **COMPUTING** when a computer produces images and sounds that make you feel an imagined situation is real

virtue /ˈvɜːtjuː/ *noun* **1** ADVANTAGE [C, U] an advantage or useful quality *The great* ***virtue of*** *having a small car is that you can park it easily.* **2** GOOD QUALITY [C] a good quality that someone has *Patience is not among his virtues.* **3** MORAL BEHAVIOUR [U] behaviour that is morally good **4 by virtue of sth** *formal* because of something *She succeeded by virtue of hard work rather than talent.*

virtuoso /ˌvɜːtjuˈəʊsəʊ/ *noun* [C] **MUSIC** someone who is extremely good at doing something, especially playing a musical instrument

virtuous /ˈvɜːtʃuəs/ *adjective* behaving in a good and moral way •**virtuously** *adverb*

virulent /ˈvɪrʊlənt/ *adjective* **1 HEALTH** A virulent disease or poison causes severe illness very quickly. **2** HATE *formal* criticizing or hating someone or something very much *a virulent attack on the government*

WORD PARTNERS FOR ***virus***

carry/contract/have/transmit a virus • a **deadly/rare** virus

O-ᵘ **virus** /ˈvaɪərəs/ *noun* [C] **1 BIOLOGY, HEALTH** an infectious organism too small to be seen that causes disease, or an illness that it causes *The doctor says I've got a virus.* **2 COMPUTING** a program that is secretly put onto a computer in order to destroy the information that is stored on it

visa /ˈviːzə/ *noun* [C] an official mark in your passport (= document which proves your nationality) that allows you to enter or leave a particular country *She went to Miami* ***on a tourist visa.***

viscous /ˈvɪskəs/ *adjective* describes a liquid that is thick and sticky and does not flow easily •**viscosity** /vɪˈskɒsɪti/ *noun* [U]

vise /vaɪs/ *noun* [C] *US spelling of* vice (= a tool used for holding something tightly while you cut it, make it smooth, etc)

visibility /ˌvɪzəˈbɪləti/ *noun* [U] how far or how well you can see because of weather conditions *good/poor visibility* ○ *It was foggy and visibility was down to 50 metres.*

visible /ˈvɪzəbl/ *adjective* able to be seen *The fire was* ***visible from*** *five kilometres away.* ➲Opposite **invisible** •**visibly** *adverb She was visibly upset.*

vision /ˈvɪʒᵊn/ *noun* **1** IDEA [C] an idea or image in your mind of what something could be like in the future *a vision of a better society* **2** **BIOLOGY** [U] the ability to see *He has poor vision in his left eye.* **3** ABILITY TO PLAN [U] the ability to make plans for the future that are imaginative and wise *As a leader, he lacked vision.* **4** **RELIGION** [C] when you see someone or something that no one else can see as part of a religious experience

visionary /ˈvɪʒᵊnᵊri/ *adjective* able to make plans for the future that are imaginative and wise *a visionary leader* •**visionary** *noun* [C]

O-ʷ **visit¹** /ˈvɪzɪt/ *verb* [I, T] **1** SEE A PERSON to go to someone's home and spend time with them *We have friends coming to visit this weekend.* **2** SEE A PLACE to go to a place and spend a short amount of time there *Did you visit St Petersburg while you were in Russia?* **3** **INTERNET** to look at a website

visit with sb *phrasal verb US* to spend time talking with someone who you know *Mom was visiting with our neighbor.*

WORD PARTNERS FOR ***visit***

a visit **to** sth • a visit **from** sb • **on** a visit • **pay** sb a visit • **have** a visit **from** sb • **a brief/flying** visit

O-ʷ **visit²** /ˈvɪzɪt/ *noun* [C] when you visit a place or a person *the President's* ***visit to*** *Hong Kong* ○ *Why don't you* ***pay*** *him* ***a visit*** (= visit him)*?*

O-ʷ **visitor** /ˈvɪzɪtəʳ/ *noun* [C] someone who visits a person or place *The museum attracts large numbers of visitors.*

visor /ˈvaɪzəʳ/ *noun* [C] **1** PART OF HAT the part of a helmet (= hard hat that protects your head) that you can pull down to cover your face **2** HAT (*also* ˈ**sun** ˌ**visor**) a hat that has a curved part above your eyes to protect them from the sun ➲See colour picture **Clothes** on page Centre 9 **3** CAR the parts in the front window of a car that you pull down to protect your eyes from the sun ➲See colour picture **Car** on page Centre 7

vista /ˈvɪstə/ *noun* [C] a view, especially a beautiful view that you look at from a high place

visual /ˈvɪʒuəl/ *adjective* relating to seeing *The film has some powerful* ***visual effects.*** •**visually** *adverb visually appealing*

ˌ**visual** ˈ**aid** *noun* [C] **EDUCATION** something that helps you understand or remember information, such as a picture or film

visualize (*also UK* **-ise**) /ˈvɪʒuᵊlaɪz/ *verb* [T] to create a picture in your mind of someone or something *I was very surprised when I met Geoff - I'd visualized someone much older.* •**visualization** /ˌvɪʒuᵊlaɪˈzeɪʃᵊn/ *noun* [U]

vis-à-vis /ˌviːzəˈviː/ *preposition* relating to something, or in comparison with something *I have to speak to James vis-à-vis the conference arrangements.*

vital /ˈvaɪtᵊl/ *adjective* **1** IMPORTANT necessary *Tourism is* ***vital to*** *the country's economy.* [+ **(that)**] *It's vital that you send off this form today.* **2** ENERGY *formal* full of energy

vitality /vaɪˈtæləti/ *noun* [U] energy and strength *At 48, he still projects an image of youth and vitality.*

vitally /ˈvaɪtəli/ *adverb* in a very important way *Safety at work is* ***vitally important.***

vitamin /ˈvɪtəmɪn/ (US) /ˈvaɪtəmɪn/ *noun* [C] **HEALTH** one of a group of natural substances in food that you need to be healthy *Oranges are full of vitamin C.*

ˌ**vitreous** ˈ**humour** *noun* [U] **ANATOMY, BIOLOGY** the thick clear substance inside the eye behind the lens (= part that you see through) ➲Compare **aqueous humour**

vitriolic /ˌvɪtriˈɒlɪk/ *adjective formal* criticizing someone in a very severe and unpleasant way

viva /ˈvaɪvə/ *noun* [C] *UK* **EDUCATION** a spoken examination at university

vivacious /vɪˈveɪʃəs/ *adjective* A vivacious person, especially a woman, is full of energy and enthusiasm.

vivid /ˈvɪvɪd/ *adjective* **1** IMAGE Vivid descriptions or memories produce strong, clear images in your mind. *He gave a very* ***vivid description*** *of life in Caracas.* **2** COLOUR A vivid colour is very bright. •**vividly** *adverb I remember my first day at school very vividly.*

vivisection /ˌvɪvɪˈsekʃᵊn/ *noun* [U] when living animals are used in scientific experiments, especially in order to discover the effects of new drugs

vixen /ˈvɪksᵊn/ *noun* [C] a female fox (= wild dog with red-brown fur)

V-neck /ˈviːnek/ *noun* [C] a V-shaped opening for your neck on a piece of clothing, or a sweater, dress, etc with this opening *a V-neck jumper* •**V-necked** /viːˈnekt/ *adjective a V-necked dress*

WORD PARTNERS FOR ***vocabulary***

a **limited/wide** vocabulary • be **in** sb's vocabulary • **widen** your vocabulary

vocabulary /vəʊˈkæbjəlᵊri/ *noun* **1** **LANGUAGE** [C, U] all the words you know in a particular language *Reading helps to widen your vocabulary.* **2** **LANGUAGE** [**no plural**] all the words that exist in a language, or that are used when discussing a particular subject *Computing has its own specialist vocabulary.* **3** **LANGUAGE** [**no plural**] a list of words and their meanings

vocal /ˈvəʊkᵊl/ *adjective* **1** expressing your opinions in a strong way *She is a* ***vocal supporter*** *of women's rights.* **2** **MUSIC** involving or relating to the voice, especially singing *vocal music*

V

ˈvocal ˌcords (*also* **vocal chords**) *noun* [**plural**] **ANATOMY** folds of skin at the top of your throat that make sounds when air from your lungs moves over them ➲See picture at **respiratory system**

vocalist /ˈvəʊkəlɪst/ *noun* [**C**] **MUSIC** the person who sings in a group of people who play popular music

vocals /ˈvəʊkəlz/ *noun* [**plural**] **MUSIC** the part of a piece of music that is sung

vocation /vəʊˈkeɪʃən/ *noun* [**C, U**] a strong feeling that you are right for a particular type of work, or a job that gives you this feeling *He knew that teaching was his true vocation.*

vocational /vəʊˈkeɪʃənəl/ *adjective* **EDUCATION** Vocational education and skills prepare you for a particular type of work.

vociferous /vəʊˈsɪfərəs/ *adjective formal* expressing your opinions in a loud and strong way *She has become increasingly **vociferous in** her opposition to the scheme.*

vodka /ˈvɒdkə/ *noun* [**C, U**] **FOOD** a strong alcoholic drink that is popular in Russia and Poland

vogue /vəʊg/ *noun* [**U no plural**] If there is a vogue for something, it is very fashionable. *This period saw a **vogue for** Japanese painting.* ○ *Flat shoes are **in vogue*** (= fashionable) *this spring.*

WORD PARTNERS FOR ***voice***

a deep/husky/low voice • **lose** your voice • **lower/raise** your voice • **in** a [bored/stern, etc.] voice • your **tone of** voice

voice¹ /vɔɪs/ *noun* **1** SOUNDS [**C**] the sounds that you make when you speak or sing *I could hear voices in the next room.* ○ *Jessie has a beautiful singing voice.* ○ *Could you please **keep your voices down*** (= speak more quietly)*?* ○ *He **raised his voice*** (= spoke more loudly) *so that everyone could hear.* **2 lose your voice HEALTH** to become unable to speak, often because of an illness *She had a bad cold and was losing her voice.* **3** OPINION [**C**] someone's opinion about a particular subject *The programme gives people the opportunity to make their voices heard.* **4** PERSON [**no plural**] someone who expresses the opinions or wishes of a group of people *It's important that students have a voice on the committee.* ➲See also: **the passive voice**

voice² /vɔɪs/ *verb* [**T**] to say what you think about a particular subject *He has voiced concern about the new proposals.*

V

voice-activated /ˌvɔɪsˈæktɪveɪtɪd/ *adjective* A machine that is voice-activated can recognize and follow spoken instructions.

ˈvoice ˌbox *noun* [**C**] **ANATOMY** *informal* the larynx

ˈvoice ˌmail *noun* [**U**] an electronic telephone answering system

ˈvoice recogˌnition (*also* **speech recognition**) *noun* [**U**] **COMPUTING** the process of changing the sound of people speaking into instructions that a computer can understand

void¹ /vɔɪd/ *adjective* **1** [**never before noun**] not legally or officially acceptable *The contracts were **declared void**.* **2 be void of sth** *formal* to be without something *His last statement was entirely void of meaning.*

void² /vɔɪd/ *noun* [**no plural**] **1** FEELING when someone or something important is not now in your life and you are unhappy *Her husband's death **left a void** in her life.* **2** SPACE a large hole or empty space

vol MEASURES *written abbreviation for* volume

volatile /ˈvɒlətaɪl/ (US) /ˈvɑːlətəl/ *adjective* **1** PERSON A volatile person can suddenly become angry or violent. **2** SITUATION A volatile situation might suddenly change. *a volatile political situation* •**volatility** /ˌvɒləˈtɪləti/ *noun* [**U**]

volcano /vɒlˈkeɪnəʊ/ *noun* [**C**] *plural* **volcanoes** or **volcanos GEOGRAPHY, GEOLOGY** a mountain with a large hole at the top which sometimes explodes and produces hot, melted rock and smoke ➲See picture **volcano** on next page •**volcanic** /vɒlˈkænɪk/ *adjective* relating to a volcano *volcanic ash*

vole /vəʊl/ *noun* [**C**] a small animal like a mouse

volition /vəʊˈlɪʃən/ *noun* [**U**] *formal* the power to make your own decisions *He left the firm **of his own volition*** (= because he decided to).

volley¹ /ˈvɒli/ *noun* **1 SPORT** [**C**] in sports, a kick or hit in which a player returns a ball before it touches the ground **2 a volley of shots/gunfire, etc** when a lot of bullets are shot at the same time *A volley of bullets ripped through the floorboards.* **3 a volley of abuse/complaints, etc** a lot of insults/complaints, etc said at the same time

volley² /ˈvɒli/ *verb* [**I, T**] **SPORT** in sports, to return a ball by kicking or hitting it before it touches the ground

volleyball /ˈvɒlibɔːl/ *noun* [**U**] **SPORT** a game in which two teams use their hands to hit a ball over a net without allowing it to touch the ground ➲See colour picture **Sports 2** on page Centre 15

volt /vɒlt/ (*written abbreviation* **V**) *noun* [**C**] **MEASURES** a unit for measuring the force of an electric current

voltage /ˈvəʊltɪdʒ/ *noun* [**C, U**] **MEASURES** the force of an electric current, measured in volts

voltmeter /ˈvəʊltˌmiːtər/ *noun* [**C**] **PHYSICS** a device used for measuring voltage

volume /ˈvɒljuːm/ *noun* **1** SOUND [**U**] the level of sound produced by a television, radio, etc *to turn the volume up/down* **2** AMOUNT [**U**] the number or amount of something, especially when it is large *the volume of work involved* **3 MEASURES** [**U**] the amount of space inside an object *Which of the bottles has the larger volume?* **4** BOOK [**C**] a book, especially one of a set *a new dictionary in two volumes*

voluminous /vəˈluːmɪnəs/ *adjective formal* very large *voluminous trousers*

voluntary /ˈvɒləntəri/ *adjective* **1** WORK Voluntary work is done without being paid and usually involves helping people. *She does **voluntary work** for the Red Cross.* ○ ***voluntary organizations*** **2** NOT FORCED done or given because you want to and not because you have been forced to ***voluntary contributions*** ➲Opposite **involuntary** •**voluntarily** /ˌvɒlənˈteərəli/ *adverb She left voluntarily.*

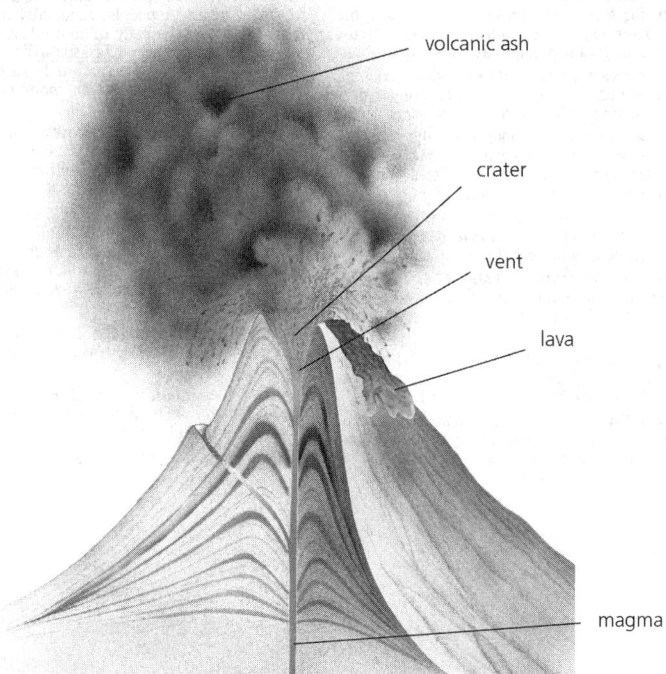

volcano

volunteer¹ /ˌvɒlən'tɪər/ *verb* **1** OFFER [I, T] to offer to do something without being asked or told to do it [+ **to do sth**] *Rob volunteered to look after the kids.* **2** ARMY [I] to join the army, navy, etc without being officially told to join *In 1939 he* ***volunteered for*** *active service.* **3** INFORMATION [T] to give information without being asked *No one volunteered the truth.*

volunteer² /ˌvɒlən'tɪər/ *noun* [C] **1** NOT PAID someone who does work without being paid, especially work that involves helping people *a Red Cross volunteer* **2** NOT FORCED someone who does or gives something because they want to and not because they have been forced to *Any volunteers to help me move these books?*

voluptuous /və'lʌptʃuəs/ *adjective* A voluptuous woman has a sexually attractive body, often with large breasts.

vomit¹ /'vɒmɪt/ *verb* [I, T] **HEALTH** If someone vomits, the food or liquid that was in their stomach comes up and out of their mouth. *She was vomiting blood.*

vomit² /'vɒmɪt/ *noun* [U] **HEALTH** the food or liquid that comes from your mouth when you vomit

voodoo /'vu:du:/ *noun* [U] **RELIGION** a religion involving magic and praying to spirits

voracious /və'reɪʃəs/ *adjective* wanting to do something a lot, especially wanting to eat a lot of food *She has a* ***voracious appetite.*** ○ *a voracious reader of historical novels* •**voraciously** *adverb* •**voracity** /və'ræsəti/ *noun* [U]

O→**vote¹** /vəʊt/ *verb* [I, T] **POLITICS** to show your choice or opinion in an election or meeting by writing a cross on an official piece of paper or putting your hand up *Who did you* ***vote for?*** ○ *The unions* ***voted against*** *strike action.* [+ **to do sth**] *Staff have voted to accept the pay offer.*

WORD PARTNERS FOR ***vote***

cast your vote • a vote **against/for** sb/sth • a vote **on** sth

O→**vote²** /vəʊt/ *noun* [C] **1 POLITICS** when someone shows their choice or opinion in an election or meeting by writing a cross on an official piece of paper or putting their hand up *He lost the election by twenty votes.* **2** a way of making a decision by asking a group of people to vote *We called a meeting in order to* ***take a vote on*** *the proposal.* **3 the vote a POLITICS** the total number of votes given or received in an election *The Green party got 10% of the vote.* **b POLITICS** when someone is officially allowed to vote *In some countries women still don't have the vote.*

voter /'vəʊtər/ *noun* [C] **POLITICS** someone who votes or who is officially allowed to vote

V

vouch /vaʊtʃ/ *verb*
vouch for sb/sth *phrasal verb* to say that you know from experience that something is true or good, or that someone has a good character

voucher /ˈvaʊtʃəʳ/ *noun* [C] **FINANCE** a piece of paper that can be used instead of money to pay for goods or services *a discount voucher*

vow[1] /vaʊ/ *verb* [T] to make a serious promise or decision [+ **(that)**] *She vowed that she would never leave the children again.* [+ **to do sth**] *I've vowed never to go there again.*

vow[2] /vaʊ/ *noun* [C] a serious promise or decision *marriage vows* ○ *I **made a vow** that I would write to him once a week.*

vowel /vaʊəl/ *noun* [C] **LANGUAGE** a speech sound that you make with your lips and teeth open, shown in English by the letters 'a', 'e', 'i', 'o' or 'u'

voyage /ˈvɔɪɪdʒ/ *noun* [C] a long journey, especially by ship, or in space *The ship sank on its **maiden voyage*** (= first journey).

vs (*also UK* **v**) *preposition* **SPORT** *written abbreviation for* versus (= used to say that one team or person is competing against another)

vulgar /ˈvʌlgəʳ/ *adjective* **1** RUDE rude and likely to upset or anger people, especially by referring to sex and the body in an unpleasant way *vulgar jokes/language* **2** NOT SUITABLE not showing good judgment about what is suitable or pleasant to look at *a vulgar shade of yellow* •**vulgarity** /vʌlˈgærəti/ *noun* [U]

ˌvulgar ˈfraction *noun* [C] **MATHEMATICS** a fraction written with one number above and one number below the line, not written as a number with a decimal point in it

vulnerable /ˈvʌlnᵊrəbl/ *adjective* easy to hurt or attack physically or emotionally *She was a vulnerable sixteen-year-old.* ○ *The troops are in a vulnerable position.* ○ *He's more **vulnerable to** infection because of his injuries.* •**vulnerability** /ˌvʌlnᵊrəˈbɪləti/ *noun* [U]

vulture /ˈvʌltʃəʳ/ *noun* [C] a large bird with no feathers on its head or neck that eats dead animals

vulva /ˈvʌlvə/ *noun* [C] *plural* **vulvas** or **vulvae** **ANATOMY** the parts of the female sex organs which are outside the body, between the legs

vying /ˈvaɪɪŋ/ *present participle of* vie

V

Ww

W, w /ˈdʌbljuː/ the twenty-third letter of the alphabet

W **MEASURES** *written abbreviation for* watt (= a unit for measuring electrical power) *a 40W light bulb*

wacky /ˈwæki/ *adjective informal* unusual in a funny or surprising way *a wacky sense of humour*

wad /wɒd/ *noun* [C] **1** PILE a thick pile of pieces of paper, especially paper money *a wad of cash* **2** BALL a piece of soft material in the shape of a ball *a wad of (UK) cotton wool/ (US) cotton*

waddle /ˈwɒdl/ *verb* [I] A duck (= water bird) or fat person that waddles walks with short steps, moving from side to side.

wade /weɪd/ *verb* **wade across/through, etc** to walk through water *He waded across the river.* **wade through sth** *phrasal verb* to read a lot of boring or difficult information

wafer /ˈweɪfəʳ/ *noun* [C] **FOOD** a light, thin biscuit

waffle[1] /ˈwɒfl/ *noun* **1** [U] *informal* speech or writing that says nothing important **2** **FOOD** [C] a square, flat cake with a pattern of holes in it, eaten especially in the US

waffle[2] /ˈwɒfl/ (*also* **waffle on**) *verb* [I] *informal* to talk or write a lot and say nothing important

waft /wɒft/ *verb* **waft from/through, etc** to gradually move through the air *The smell of coffee wafted through the room.*

wag /wæg/ *verb* [I, T] **wagging**, *past* **wagged** **1** DOG If a dog wags its tail, it moves it from side to side. **2** FINGER If you wag your finger, you move it from side to side, often to tell someone not to do something.

WORD PARTNERS FOR ***wage***

earn a wage • a **decent** wage • a wage **increase/rise** • the **minimum** wage

wage[1] /weɪdʒ/ *noun* [**no plural**] **FINANCE** (*also* **wages** [**plural**]) the amount of money a person regularly receives for their job *weekly wages* ○ *the **minimum wage*** ➲See Common Learner Error at **pay**

wage[2] /weɪdʒ/ *verb* **wage a battle/campaign/war, etc** to fight or organize a series of activities in order to achieve something *They're currently waging a campaign to change the law.*

wager /ˈweɪdʒəʳ/ *verb* [T] to risk money on the result of a game, race, competition, etc •**wager** *noun* [C]

wagon /ˈwægən/ *noun* [C] a large vehicle with four large wheels pulled by horses

wail /weɪl/ *verb* [I, T] **1** PERSON to cry loudly because you are very unhappy *"I've lost my mummy," she wailed.* **2** DANGER If a siren (= loud noise to warn of danger) wails, it makes a noise. *Somewhere in the distance a police siren was wailing.* •**wail** *noun* [C]

waist /weɪst/ *noun* [C] **1** **ANATOMY** the part around the middle of your body where you wear a belt *She had a 26 inch waist.* ➲See colour picture **The Body** on page Centre 13 **2** the part of a piece of clothing that fits round the waist

waistband /ˈweɪstbænd/ *noun* [C] the strip of material at the top of a pair of trousers or a skirt that goes around the waist

waistcoat /ˈweɪstkəʊt/ *UK* (*US* **vest**) *noun* [C] a piece of clothing with buttons at the front and no sleeves, that you wear over a shirt ➲See colour picture **Clothes** on page Centre 9

waistline /ˈweɪstlaɪn/ *noun* [C] how big or small your waist is, or the part of a piece of clothing that goes around the waist

O┅**wait**[1] /weɪt/ *verb* [I] **1** STAY to stay in a place until someone or something arrives or someone or something is ready for you *I'm **waiting for** Clive.* ○ *How long did you wait for a taxi?* [**+ to do sth**] *I'm still waiting to use the phone.* **2** NOT DO SOMETHING to not do something until something else happens *We'll wait till Jane gets here before we start eating.* **3** **can't wait** *informal* used to say how excited you are about something that you are going to do [**+ to do sth**] *I can't wait to see him.* **4** **keep sb waiting** to be late so that someone has to wait for you *I'm sorry to have kept you waiting.* **5** **wait and see** to wait to discover what will happen *We'll wait and see what she says.* ➲See also: be waiting in **the wings**

COMMON LEARNER ERROR

wait or **expect?**

When you **wait**, you stay somewhere until a person or thing arrives or is ready.

I waited twenty minutes for the bus.

She's waiting for her exam results.

When you **expect** something, you think that it will happen.

I'm expecting the bus to arrive in about 5 minutes.

She expected to do well in the exam.

~~*She waited to do well in the exam.*~~

COMMON LEARNER ERROR

wait

Wait must always be followed by **for** or **to do sth**. It cannot be followed by the thing you are waiting for.

I am waiting for my mother.

~~*I am waiting my mother.*~~

wait about/around *phrasal verb* to stay in a place and do nothing while you wait for someone to arrive or something to happen

wait in *phrasal verb UK* to stay at home because you are expecting someone to visit or telephone you

wait on sb *phrasal verb* to bring a meal to someone, especially in a restaurant

wait up *phrasal verb* to not go to bed at night until someone has come home *I'll be quite late, so don't **wait up for** me.*

W

WORD PARTNERS FOR ***wait***

face/have a wait • an **agonizing/anxious/long** wait • the wait **for** sth • sth is **(well) worth the wait**

wait² /weɪt/ *noun* [**no plural**] when you stay in a place until someone or something arrives or someone or something is ready for you *We **had a long wait** at the airport.*

waiter /ˈweɪtəʳ/ *noun* [**C**] a man who works in a restaurant, bringing food to customers

ˈwaiting ˌlist *noun* [**C**] a list of people who are waiting until it is their time to have or do something *a hospital waiting list*

ˈwaiting ˌroom *noun* [**C**] a room in which people wait for something, for example to see a doctor or take a train

waitress /ˈweɪtrəs/ *noun* [**C**] a woman who works in a restaurant, bringing food to customers

waive /weɪv/ *verb* [**T**] **1** ALLOW UNUSUAL ACTION to allow someone not to obey the usual rule or not to pay the usual amount of money *He agreed to waive his fee to help us.* **2** **LAW** to decide not to have something that you are allowed by law to have *She **waived** her **right** to have a lawyer representing her.*

O-■ **wake¹** /weɪk/ (*also* **wake up**) *verb* [**I, T**] *past tense* **woke**, *past participle* **woken** to stop sleeping or to make someone else stop sleeping *I've only just woken up.* ○ *Could you wake me up before you go?* ○ *You woke me up making so much noise.* ⊃See colour picture **Phrasal Verbs** on page Centre 16

wake up to sth *phrasal verb* to start to understand something that is important *We need to wake up to the fact that the Earth's resources are limited.*

wake² /weɪk/ *noun* **1 in the wake of sth** after something has happened, and often because it has happened *Airport security was extra tight in the wake of last week's bomb attacks.* **2** SHIP [**C**] the waves behind a moving ship **3** FUNERAL [**C**] when people come together to remember someone who has recently died

ˈwake-up ˌcall *noun* [**C**] **1** TELEPHONE a telephone call to wake you in the morning, especially when you are staying in a hotel **2** EVENT something bad that happens and shows you that you need to take action to change a situation

O-■ **walk¹** /wɔːk/ *verb* **1** [**I, T**] to move forward by putting one foot in front of the other and then repeating the action *She walks to school.* ○ *We walked twenty miles in all.* **2 walk sb home/to sth** to walk with someone in order to guide them or keep them safe *He walked me to my house.* **3 walk the dog** to walk with a dog to give the dog exercise **4 walk all over sb** *informal* to treat someone badly

COMMON LEARNER ERROR

walk or **go on foot?**

The expression **go on foot** means **walk**, usually when you are describing how you get somewhere.

How do you get to school? I go on foot/I walk.

walk into sth *phrasal verb* to get a job easily

walk off with sth *phrasal verb* to win something easily *She walked off with the top prize.*

walk out *phrasal verb* to leave a job, meeting, or performance because you are angry or do not approve of something *He was so disgusted by the film he walked out.*

walk out on sb *phrasal verb* to suddenly leave your husband, wife, or partner and end your relationship with them *He walked out on his wife and kids.*

WORD PARTNERS FOR ***walk***

go for/take a walk • a **brisk** walk • a **long/short** walk

O-■ **walk²** /wɔːk/ *noun* **1** JOURNEY [**C**] a journey that you make by walking, often for enjoyment *We usually **go for a walk** on Sunday afternoons.* ○ *He took the dog for a walk.* **2 a short/ten-minute, etc walk** a journey that takes a short time/ten minutes, etc when you walk *The station is just a five-minute walk from the house.* **3** PATH [**C**] a path or route where people can walk for enjoyment *There are some lovely walks in the forest.* **4 walk of life** People from different walks of life have different jobs and different experiences in life.

walker /ˈwɔːkəʳ/ *noun* [**C**] **SPORT** someone who walks for exercise or enjoyment

walkie talkie /ˌwɔːkiˈtɔːki/ *noun* [**C**] a radio that you carry with you and that lets you talk to someone else with a similar radio

Walkman /ˈwɔːkmən/ *noun* [**C**] *trademark* **MUSIC** a small piece of equipment with parts that you put in your ears which allows you to listen to music that no one else can hear

O-■ **wall** /wɔːl/ *noun* [**C**] **1** PART OF BUILDING one of the vertical sides of a room or building *There were several large paintings on the wall.* **2** DIVIDE AREA a vertical structure made of brick or stone that divides areas that are owned by different people *a garden wall* **3 drive sb up the wall** *informal* to make someone very angry *She drives me up the wall.* ⊃See also: **fly²** on the wall, be banging your **head¹** against a brick wall

wallaby /ˈwɒləbi/ *noun* [**C**] an animal like a small kangaroo, with strong back legs for jumping with and a long tail

walled /wɔːld/ *adjective* **walled garden/city** a garden/city with walls around it

wallet /ˈwɒlɪt/ (*also US* **billfold**) *noun* [**C**] a small, flat container for paper money and credit cards (= plastic cards used for paying with), usually used by a man

wallop /ˈwɒləp/ *verb* [**T**] *informal* to hit someone or something hard •**wallop** *noun* [**no plural**] *informal*

wallow /ˈwɒləʊ/ *verb* [**I**] **1** EMOTION to allow yourself to feel too much sadness in a way that stops people respecting you *There's no use **wallowing in** self-pity.* **2** LIE AROUND to lie or move around in soil or water, especially for pleasure

wallpaper /ˈwɔːlˌpeɪpəʳ/ *noun* [**C, U**] **1** paper, usually with a pattern, that you decorate walls with **2** **COMPUTING** a design or image that you choose to appear on the screen of your computer •**wallpaper** *verb* [**T**]

W

ˈWall ˌStreet *noun* **ECONOMICS** the financial area of New York where shares (= small, equal parts of the value of a company) are bought and sold *The company's shares rose **on Wall Street** yesterday.*

wally /ˈwɒli/ *noun* [C] *UK informal* a silly person

walnut /ˈwɔːlnʌt/ *noun* **1 FOOD** [C] a nut that is in two halves inside a brown shell, and whose surface has curves and folds in it **2** [U] the hard wood of the tree that produces walnuts, used to make furniture

walrus /ˈwɔːlrəs/ *noun* [C] a large sea animal that has two tusks (= long, pointed teeth that come out of the mouth)

waltz¹ /wɒls/ *noun* [C] **MUSIC** a dance for two partners performed to music that has a rhythm of three beats, or the music for the dance

waltz² /wɒls/ *verb* [I] **1** to dance a waltz **2 waltz in/off, etc** to walk somewhere quickly and confidently, often in a way that annoys other people *You can't just waltz into my bedroom - it's private!*

wan /wɒn/ *adjective* pale and looking ill or tired

WAN /wæn/ *noun* [C] *abbreviation for* **COMPUTING** wide area network: a computer network that connects separate machines over a wide area, for example in different countries ⊃Compare **LAN**

wand /wɒnd/ *noun* [C] a thin stick that someone who performs magic tricks holds in their hand

wander /ˈwɒndəʳ/ *verb* **1** [WALK] [I, T] to walk slowly about a place without any purpose *They wandered aimlessly around the town.* **2** [LEAVE PLACE] [I] (*also* **wander off**) to walk away from the place where you should be *He was here a moment ago - he must have wandered off.* **3 sb's attention/mind/thoughts, etc wander** If someone's attention/mind, etc wanders, they start thinking about one subject when they should be thinking about a different subject. *I was bored and my thoughts started to wander.*

wane /weɪn/ *verb* [I] to become less powerful, important, or popular *Interest in the product is starting to wane.*

wangle /ˈwæŋgl/ *verb* [T] *informal* to succeed in getting something that a lot of people want, by being clever or tricking someone *He managed to wangle an invitation to the party.*

O-■ **want¹** /wɒnt/ *verb* [T] **1** [HOPE] to hope to have or do something, or to wish for something *He wants a new car.* [+ **to do sth**] *I don't want to talk about it.* ○ *You can't always do what you want.* ○ *We can go later if you want.* ○ *I want him to explain why.* **2** [NEED] to need something *This soup wants more salt.* **3 want to do sth** *UK informal* used to give advice to someone *You want to go to bed earlier and then you won't be so tired.* **4 be wanted** to be needed for a particular activity or in a particular place *You're wanted on the phone.*

COMMON LEARNER ERROR

want something/someone to do something

Be careful to use the correct form after this expression. You cannot say 'that' after **want**.

I just want him to enjoy himself.

~~*I just want that he enjoy himself.*~~

They don't want the school holidays to end.

~~*They don't want that the school holidays end.*~~

want² /wɒnt/ *noun* **want of sth** when there is not enough of something *If we fail, it won't be **for want of** effort* (= it is not because we have not tried).

wanted /ˈwɒntɪd/ *adjective* **LAW** If someone is wanted, the police think they have committed a serious crime and are trying to find them. *He is **wanted for** murder.*

wanton /ˈwɒntən/ *adjective formal* done in order to cause suffering or destruction but with no other reason *wanton cruelty/violence*

wants /wɒnts/ *noun* [**plural**] the things you want or need

WORD PARTNERS FOR ***war***

all-out/full-scale war • **declare/go to** war • **wage** war on sb • war **breaks out** • war **against** sb

O-■ **war** /wɔːʳ/ *noun* **1** [FIGHTING] [C, U] fighting, using soldiers and weapons, between two or more countries, or two or more groups inside a country *They've been **at war** for the past five years.* ○ *He was only a child when the **war broke out*** (= started). ○ *If this country **goes to war*** (= starts to fight in a war), *thousands of people will die.* **2** [COMPETING] [C, U] when two or more groups are trying to be more successful than each other *a **price war** between supermarkets* **3** [TO STOP] [**no plural**] an attempt to stop something bad or illegal *the **war against** crime/drugs* ⊃See also: **civil war, prisoner of war, world war**

ˈwar ˌcrime *noun* [C] **LAW** a crime during a war that breaks the international rules of war •**war criminal** *noun* [C] someone guilty of a war crime

ward¹ /wɔːd/ *noun* [C] **HEALTH** a room in a hospital where people receiving treatment stay, often for the same type of illness *the maternity ward*

ward² /wɔːd/ *verb*

ward sth off *phrasal verb* to prevent something unpleasant happening *I take vitamin C to ward off colds.*

warden /ˈwɔːdᵊn/ *noun* [C] **1** [PRISON] *US* (*UK* **governor**) someone who is responsible for controlling a prison **2** [BUILDING] *UK* someone who is responsible for looking after a particular building or the people in it ⊃See also: **traffic warden**

warder /ˈwɔːdəʳ/ *noun* [C] *UK* a prison guard

wardrobe /ˈwɔːdrəʊb/ *noun* **1** [CUPBOARD] [C] *UK* (*US* **closet**) a large cupboard for keeping clothes in **2** [CLOTHES] [**no plural**] all the clothes that you own

-ward, wards /-wəd, -wədz/ *suffix* makes an adverb meaning 'towards a direction or place' *inward* ○ *forward* ○ *homeward*

warehouse /ˈweəhaʊs/ *noun* [C] *plural* **warehouses** /ˈweəhaʊzɪz/ a large building for storing goods that are going to be sold

W

wares /weəz/ *noun* [**plural**] *literary* goods that are for sale, especially not in a shop *People were selling their wares at the side of the road.*

warfare /ˈwɔːfeəʳ/ *noun* [**U**] fighting in a war, especially using a particular type of weapon ***chemical/modern warfare***

warhead /ˈwɔːhed/ *noun* [**C**] the part of a missile (= weapon) that explodes when it reaches the place it is aimed at *a **nuclear warhead***

warlord /ˈwɔːlɔːd/ *noun* [**C**] **POLITICS** a military leader who controls a particular area of a country

O⁻**warm**[1] /wɔːm/ *adjective* **1** TEMPERATURE having a temperature between cool and hot *It's nice and warm in here.* ○ *Are you warm enough?* ○ *Make sure you **keep warm**.* **2** CLOTHES Warm clothes or covers keep your body warm. *a warm sweater* **3** FRIENDLY friendly and showing affection *a warm smile/welcome*

warm[2] /wɔːm/ *verb* [**I, T**] to become warm or to make something become warm *She warmed her feet against his.* ○ *I'll warm the soup.*

warm to sb/sth *phrasal verb* to start to like a person or idea

warm up *phrasal verb* **SPORT** to do gentle exercises in order to prepare yourself for more energetic exercise *They were warming up before the match.* •**warm-up** /ˈwɔːmʌp/ *noun* [**C**]

warm (sb/sth) up *phrasal verb* to become warmer or to make someone or something warmer *The house soon warms up with the heating on.*

warmly /ˈwɔːmli/ *adverb* in a friendly way

warmth /wɔːmθ/ *noun* [**U**] **1** HEAT the heat that is produced by something *the warmth of the fire* **2** FRIENDLY when someone is friendly and shows affection *There was no warmth in his eyes.*

O⁻**warn** /wɔːn/ *verb* [**T**] **1** OF DANGER to tell someone that something bad may happen in the future, so that they can prevent it [**+ that**] *I warned you that it would be cold but you still wouldn't wear a coat.* ○ *I've been warning him for months.* **2** ADVISE to advise someone not to do something that could cause danger or trouble [**+ to do sth**] *I **warned** you **not** to tell her.*

WORD PARTNERS FOR ***warning***

deliver/give/heed/ignore/issue a warning • a **blunt/final/stern** warning • **without** warning

O⁻**warning** /ˈwɔːnɪŋ/ *noun* [**C, U**] something that tells or shows you that something bad may happen *All cigarette packets carry a warning.* ○ *The bombs fell completely **without warning**.*

W

warp /wɔːp/ *verb* **1** TWIST [**I, T**] to become bent into the wrong shape or to make something do this *The window frames had warped.* **2** MIND [**T**] If something warps your mind, it makes you strange and cruel.

the warp /wɔːp/ *noun* **DT** the threads that go from one end to the other in a piece of cloth and which the other threads are twisted over and under

warpath /ˈwɔːpɑːθ/ *noun* **be on the warpath** *informal* to be trying to find someone in order to be angry with them

warped /wɔːpt/ *adjective* strange and cruel *You've got a warped mind!*

warplane /ˈwɔːˌpleɪn/ *noun* [**C**] an aircraft for carrying bombs

warrant[1] /ˈwɒrᵊnt/ *noun* [**C**] an official document that allows someone to do something, for example that allows a police officer to search a building *The police have a **warrant for** his arrest.* ➲See also: **search warrant**

warrant[2] /ˈwɒrᵊnt/ *verb* [**T**] **LAW** to make something necessary *None of her crimes is serious enough to warrant punishment.*

warranty /ˈwɒrᵊnti/ *noun* [**C, U**] **LAW** a written promise made by a company to change or repair one of its products if it has a fault *a five-year warranty*

warren /ˈwɒrᵊn/ (*also* ˈ**rabbit ˌwarren**) *noun* [**C**] a group of connected underground holes where rabbits live

warring /ˈwɔːrɪŋ/ *adjective* **warring factions/parties/sides, etc** groups that are fighting against each other

warrior /ˈwɒriəʳ/ *noun* [**C**] a person who has experience and skill in fighting in a war, especially in the past

warship /ˈwɔːʃɪp/ *noun* [**C**] a ship with weapons, used in war

wart /wɔːt/ *noun* [**C**] **HEALTH** a small, hard lump that grows on the skin

wartime /ˈwɔːtaɪm/ *noun* [**U**] a period when a country is fighting a war

war-torn /ˈwɔːˌtɔːn/ *adjective* damaged by war *a war-torn country*

wary /ˈweəri/ *adjective* If you are wary of someone or something, you do not trust them completely. *She's still **wary of** strangers.* •**warily** *adverb* •**wariness** *noun* [**U**]

was /wɒz/ *past simple I/he/she/it of* be

O⁻**wash**[1] /wɒʃ/ *verb* **1** CLEAN SOMETHING [**T**] to make something clean using water, or water and soap *Dad was washing the dishes.* **2** CLEAN YOURSELF [**I, T**] to clean part of your body with water and soap *Have you washed your hands?* ○ ***I got washed** and dressed.* **3 be washed away/out/up, etc** If something is washed away/out, etc, it is moved there by water. *A lot of the waste is washed out to sea.* **4 wash against/on, etc** If water washes somewhere, it flows there. *Waves washed against the base of the cliff.*

wash sth away *phrasal verb* If water washes something away, it removes that thing. *Floods washed away much of the soil.*

wash sth down *phrasal verb* to drink something with food or medicine to make it easier to swallow *I had a plate of sandwiches, washed down with a glass of cool beer.*

wash out *phrasal verb* If a colour or dirty mark washes out, it disappears when you wash something. *Most hair dye washes out after a few weeks.*

wash (sth) up *phrasal verb UK* to wash the dishes, pans, and other things you have used for cooking and eating a meal ➲See colour picture **Phrasal Verbs** on page Centre 16

wash up *phrasal verb US* to wash your hands, especially before a meal *Go and wash up - your dinner's ready.*

wash² /wɒʃ/ *noun* **1 a wash a** when you wash a part of your body *Have you **had a wash**?* **b** *mainly UK* when you wash something *Could you **give** the car **a wash**?* **2** [C, U] clothes, sheets, etc that are being washed together *Your jeans are **in the wash**.*

washable /ˈwɒʃəbl/ *adjective* Something that is washable will not be damaged by being washed.

washbasin /ˈwɒʃˌbeɪsᵊn/ *UK* (*UK/US* **sink**) *noun* [C] a bowl in a bathroom that water can flow into, used for washing your face or hands

washcloth /ˈwɒʃklɒθ/ *US* (*UK* **flannel**) *noun* [C] a small cloth that you use to wash your face and body ➲See colour picture **The Bathroom** on page Centre 3

washed-out /ˌwɒʃtˈaʊt/ *adjective* looking pale and tired

washer /ˈwɒʃəʳ/ *noun* [C] **1** RING a thin, flat ring that is put between a nut and a bolt (= metal objects used to fasten things together) **2** MACHINE a machine that washes clothes

washing /ˈwɒʃɪŋ/ *noun* [U] clothes, sheets, and similar things that are being washed or have been washed, or when you wash these *I'm **doing the washing** this morning.* ○ *He does his own washing and ironing.*

ˈwashing maˌchine *noun* [C] a machine that washes clothes

ˈwashing ˌpowder *UK* (*US* **laundry detergent**) *noun* [C] a soap in the form of a powder that is used to wash clothes

washing-up /ˌwɒʃɪŋˈʌp/ *noun* [U] *UK* when you wash the dishes, pans, and other things you have used for cooking and eating a meal *He was **doing the washing-up**.*

ˌwashing-ˈup ˌliquid *UK* (*US* **dish soap**) *noun* [C, U] a thick liquid soap used to wash pans, plates, knives and forks, etc

washout /ˈwɒʃaʊt/ *noun* [no plural] *informal* an event that fails badly *No one came to the fete - it was a complete washout.*

washroom /ˈwɒʃruːm/ *noun* [C] *mainly US* a room where you can go to the toilet or wash your hands and face

wasn't /ˈwɒzᵊnt/ *short for* was not *I wasn't hungry this morning.*

wasp /wɒsp/ *noun* [C] a flying insect with a thin, black and yellow body *a wasp sting* ➲See picture at **insect**

wastage /ˈweɪstɪdʒ/ *noun* [U] when you waste something *fuel wastage*

WORD PARTNERS FOR ***waste***

a waste **of** sth • a waste **of effort/money/time** • **household/nuclear/toxic** waste • waste **disposal** • **go to** waste

O-m **waste¹** /weɪst/ *noun* **1** BAD USE [U, no plural] a bad use of something useful, such as time or money, when there is a limited amount of it *Meetings are a **waste of time**.* ○ *They throw away loads of food - it's such a waste.* ○ *a waste of energy/resources* **2** REMAINING MATERIAL [U] things that are not wanted, especially what remains after you have used something ***household/nuclear waste*** **3 go to waste** to not be used *I hate to see good food go to waste.*

O-m **waste²** /weɪst/ *verb* [T] **1** to use too much of something or use something badly when there is a limited amount of it *I don't want to waste any more time so let's start.* ○ *Why waste your money on things you don't need?* **2 be wasted on sb** to be clever or of high quality in a way that someone will not understand or enjoy *Good coffee is wasted on Joe - he prefers instant.*
waste away *phrasal verb* to become thinner and weaker

waste³ /weɪst/ *adjective* [always before noun] Waste material is not now needed and can be got rid of. ***waste paper***

wasteful /ˈweɪstfᵊl/ *adjective* using too much of something, or using something badly when there is a limited amount of it

wasteland /ˈweɪstlænd/ *noun* [C, U] an area of land that cannot be used in any way

ˈwastepaper ˌbasket *UK* (*US* **wastebasket**) *noun* [C] a container that is used inside buildings for putting rubbish such as paper into

O-m **watch¹** /wɒtʃ/ *verb* **1** LOOK AT [I, T] to look at something for a period of time *I watched him as he arrived.* ○ *The kids are watching TV.* ○ *I want to watch the news* (= programme on television). ➲See Common Learner Error at **look 2** BE CAREFUL [T] to be careful about something *She has to watch what she eats.* ○ *Watch how you cross the road!* **3** GIVE ATTENTION TO [T] to give attention to a situation which is changing *We'll be watching the case with interest.* ➲See also: **bird-watching,** watch your **step**¹
watch out *phrasal verb* used to tell someone to be careful because they are in danger *Watch out! There's a car coming!* ○ *Drivers were told to **watch out for** black ice on the road.*
watch over sb *phrasal verb* to look after someone and protect them if it is necessary

WORD PARTNERS FOR ***watch (noun)***

wear a watch • **glance at/look at** your watch

O-m **watch²** /wɒtʃ/ *noun* **1** CLOCK [C] a small clock on a strap that you fasten round your wrist (= lower arm) *I don't **wear a watch**.* **2** ATTENTION [U, no plural] when you watch or give attention to something or someone, especially to make sure nothing bad happens *We're **keeping a** close **watch** on the situation.*

watchdog /ˈwɒtʃdɒg/ *noun* [C] an organization whose job is to make sure that companies behave legally and provide good services

watchful /ˈwɒtʃfᵊl/ *adjective* careful to notice things and ready to deal with problems *They were playing outside under the **watchful eye** of a teacher.*

watchword /ˈwɒtʃwɜːd/ *noun* [no plural] a word or phrase that describes the main ideas or most important part of something *As regards fashion, the watchword this season is simplicity.*

O-m **water¹** /ˈwɔːtəʳ/ *noun* [U] **1** LIQUID the clear liquid that falls from the sky as rain and that is in seas, lakes, and rivers ***hot/cold water*** ○ *a drink of water* **2 GEOGRAPHY** (*also* **waters**) an area in the sea or in a river or lake *coastal*

W

waters **3 be in deep water** to be in a difficult situation which is hard to deal with *They tried to adopt a baby illegally and ended up in very deep water.* **4 be (like) water off a duck's back** If criticisms, insults, etc are like water off a duck's back to you, they do not affect you at all. *She calls him lazy and useless, but it's like water off a duck's back.* ⊃See also: **drinking water, mineral water, tap water**

water² /ˈwɔːtəʳ/ *verb* **1** PLANTS [T] to pour water over plants **2** MOUTH [I] If food makes your mouth water, it makes you want to eat it, sometimes making your mouth produce liquid. *The smells from the kitchen are making my mouth water.* **3** EYES [I] If your eyes water, they produce liquid because something is hurting them. *The smoke was making my eyes water.*
water sth down *phrasal verb* **1** DRINK to add water to a drink, especially an alcoholic drink **2** MAKE WEAKER to make a plan or idea less extreme, usually so that people will accept it

watercolour *UK* (*US* **watercolor**) /ˈwɔːtəˌkʌləʳ/ *noun* [C] **ART** a type of paint that is mixed with water, or a picture made with this paint

ˈwater ˌcooler *noun* [C] a machine for providing cool drinking water, usually in an office or other public place

watercress /ˈwɔːtəkres/ *noun* [U] **FOOD** a small, strong-tasting plant that is eaten in salads

the ˈwater ˌcycle *noun* **BIOLOGY, GEOGRAPHY** the way that water is taken up from the sea, rivers, soil, etc and then comes back down as rain or snow

waterfall /ˈwɔːtəfɔːl/ *noun* [C] **GEOGRAPHY** a stream of water that flows from a high place, often to a pool below

waterfront /ˈwɔːtəfrʌnt/ *noun* [C] a part of a town which is next to the sea, a lake, or a river *waterfront restaurants*

waterhole /ˈwɔːtəhəʊl/ *noun* [C] a small pool of water in a dry area where animals go to drink

ˈwatering ˌcan *noun* [C] a container used for watering plants in the garden

waterlogged /ˈwɔːtəlɒgd/ *adjective* Waterlogged land is too wet.

watermark /ˈwɔːtəmɑːk/ *noun* [C] a pattern or picture on paper, especially paper money, which you can only see when a strong light is behind it

watermelon /ˈwɔːtəˌmelən/ *noun* [C, U] **FOOD** a large, round, green fruit that is pink inside with a lot of black seeds

waterproof /ˈwɔːtəpruːf/ *adjective* Waterproof material or clothing does not let water through. *a waterproof sleeping bag*

waters /ˈwɔːtəz/ *noun* [plural] **GEOGRAPHY** the part of a sea around the coast of a country that legally belongs to that country

watershed /ˈwɔːtəʃed/ *noun* [no plural] an important event after which a situation completely changes *The discovery marked **a watershed in the history of medicine.***

water-skiing /ˈwɔːtəskiːɪŋ/ *noun* [U] **SPORT** a sport in which someone is pulled behind a

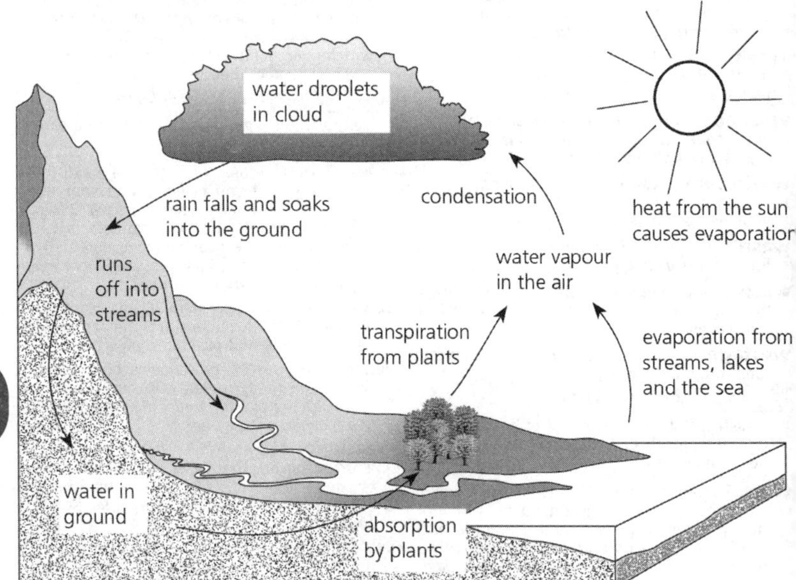

water cycle

boat while standing on skis (= long, narrow pieces of wood or plastic fastened to the feet)

ˈwater ˌtable *noun* [C] **GEOLOGY** the layer below the Earth's surface where water is found

watertight /ˈwɔːtətaɪt/ *adjective* **1** [WATER] Something that is watertight prevents any water from entering it. **2** [REASON/EXCUSE] A watertight reason or excuse is one that no one can prove is false. *a watertight alibi*

waterway /ˈwɔːtəweɪ/ *noun* [C] a river or canal (= river made by people, not nature) which people can use to travel along

watery /ˈwɔːtᵊri/ *adjective* **1** [FOOD] made with too much water *watery soup* **2** [EYES] Watery eyes are wet with tears.

watt /wɒt/ (*written abbreviation* **W**) *noun* [C] **MEASURES, PHYSICS** a unit for measuring electrical power *a 60 watt light bulb*

O⁻**wave¹** /weɪv/ *verb* **1** [WITH HAND] [I] to raise your hand and move it from side to side in order to attract someone's attention or to say goodbye ***Wave goodbye*** *to Grandma.* ○ *She* ***waved at*** *him.* **2 wave sb in/on/through, etc** to show which way you want someone to go by moving your hand in that direction *The police waved him on.* **3** [MOVE SIDE TO SIDE] [I, T] (*also* **wave about/around**) to move from side to side in the air or make something move this way *The long grass waved in the breeze.* ○ *He started waving his arms about wildly.*

wave sth aside *phrasal verb* to refuse to consider what someone says *She waved aside all my objections.*

wave sb off *phrasal verb* to wave your hand to someone as they are leaving in order to say goodbye *We went to the station to wave him off.*

O⁻**wave²** /weɪv/ *noun* [C] **1 GEOGRAPHY** a line of higher water that moves across the surface of the sea or a lake *I could hear the waves crashing against the rocks.* **2** [GROUP] a group of people or things that arrive or happen together or in a short period of time *There has been a* ***wave of*** *kidnappings in the region.* ○ *Another wave of refugees is arriving at the border.* **3 a wave of hatred/enthusiasm/sadness, etc** when you suddenly feel an emotion *She felt a sudden wave of sadness.* **4** [HAND] when you raise your hand and move it from side to side in order to attract someone's attention or say goodbye *She* ***gave a*** *little* ***wave*** *as the train left.* **5 PHYSICS** a piece of sound, light, or other energy that travels up and down in a curved pattern *a radio wave* ➲See also: **new wave, tidal wave**

wavelength /ˈweɪvleŋθ/ *noun* [C] **1 PHYSICS** the length of radio wave used by a radio company for broadcasting its programmes **2 PHYSICS** the distance between one sound or light wave, etc and the next **3 be on the same wavelength** If two people are on the same wavelength, they have the same way of thinking and it is easy for them to understand each other.

waver /ˈweɪvəʳ/ *verb* [I] **1** [NOT SURE] to start to be uncertain about a belief or decision *Her support for him never wavered.* ○ *I'm* ***wavering between*** *the blue shirt and the red.* **2** [SHAKE] to shake slightly or lose strength *His voice wavered and I thought he was going to cry.*

wavy /ˈweɪvi/ *adjective* with slight curves *wavy hair*

wax¹ /wæks/ *noun* [U] a solid substance that becomes soft when warm and melts easily, often used to make candles

wax² /wæks/ *verb* [T] **1** [WAX] to put wax on something, especially to make it shiny *They cleaned and waxed my car.* **2** [HAIR] If you wax your legs, you remove the hair from them by using wax.

O⁻**way¹** /weɪ/ *noun* **1** [METHOD] [C] how you do something [**+ to do sth**] *I must* ***find a way*** *to help him.* [**+ of + doing sth**] *We looked at various ways of solving the problem.* [**+ (that)**] *It was the way that she told me that I didn't like.* **2** [ROUTE] [C] the route you take to get from one place to another [**usually singular**] *Is there another way out of here?* ○ *I must buy a paper* ***on the way*** *home.* ○ *Can you* ***find your way*** *back to my house?* ○ *I took the wrong road and* ***lost my way*** (= got lost). **3 make your way to/through/towards, etc** to move somewhere, often with difficulty *We made our way through the shop to the main entrance.* **4 be on her/my/its, etc way** to be arriving soon *Apparently she's on her way.* **5 in/out of the/sb's way** in/not in the area in front of someone that they need to pass or see through *I couldn't see because Bill was in the way.* ○ *Sorry, am I in your way?* ○ *Could you move out of the way, please?* **6 a third of the way/most of the way, etc** used to say how much of something is completed *A third of the way through the film she dies.* **7 get in the way of sth/sb** to prevent someone from doing or continuing with something *Don't let your new friends get in the way of your studies.* **8 be under way** to be already happening *Building work is already under way.* **9 give way (to sb/sth) a** [ALLOW] to allow someone to get what they want, or to allow something to happen after trying to prevent it *The boss finally gave way when they threatened to stop work.* **b** [TRAFFIC] (*US* **yield**) *UK* to allow other vehicles to go past before you move onto a road **10 give way to sth** to change into something else *Her excitement quickly gave way to horror.* **11 give way** If something gives way, it falls because it is not strong enough to support the weight on top of it. *Suddenly the ground gave way under me.* **12 get sth out of the way** to finish something *I'll go shopping when I've got this essay out of the way.* **13** [DIRECTION] [C] a direction something faces or travels *This bus is going the* ***wrong way.*** ○ *Which* ***way up*** *does this picture go* (= which side should be at the top)? ○ *UK He always wears his baseball cap* ***the wrong way round*** (= backwards). **14** [SPACE/TIME] [**no plural**] an amount of space or time *We're* ***a long way*** *from home.* ○ *The exams are still* ***a long way away/off.*** **15 make way** to move away so that someone or something can pass **16 make way for sth** If you move or get rid of something to make way for something new, you do so in order to make a space for the new thing. *They knocked down the old houses to make way for a new hotel.* **17 in a way/in many ways** used to say that you think something is partly true *In a way his behaviour is understandable.* **18 in no way** not at all *This is in no way your fault.* **19 there's no way** *informal* If there is no way that something will happen, it is certainly not

W

allowed or not possible. *There's no way that dog's coming in the house.* **20 No way!** *informal* certainly not *"Would you invite him to a party?" "No way!"* **21 get/have your (own) way** to get what you want, although it might upset other people *She always gets her own way in the end.* **22 in a big/small way** *informal* used to describe how much or little you do a particular thing *They celebrate birthdays in a big way.* **23 a/sb's way of life** the way someone lives *Violence has become a way of life there.* **24 by the way** used when you say something that does not relate to what is being discussed *Oh, by the way, my name's Julie.* **25 go out of your way to do sth** to try very hard to do something pleasant for someone *He went out of his way to make us feel welcome.* **26 rub sb up the wrong way** *UK* (*US* **rub sb the wrong way**) *informal* to annoy someone without intending to ➲See also: **the Milky Way**

way² /weɪ/ *adverb informal* used to emphasize how extreme something is *The room was* ***way*** *too hot.* ○ *He's in second place but he's* ***way behind/off***.

ˌway ˈout *noun* [C] **1** DOOR *UK* (*UK/US* **exit**) a door that takes you out of a building **2** SITUATION a way of avoiding doing something unpleasant *I'm supposed to be going to this meeting at 2.00 and I'm looking for a way out.*

wayside /ˈweɪsaɪd/ *noun* **fall by the wayside** to fail to complete something or be completed *Many students fall by the wayside during their first year at college.*

wayward /ˈweɪwəd/ *adjective literary* behaving badly in a way that causes trouble for other people

WC /ˌdʌbljuːˈsiː/ *noun* [C] *UK abbreviation for* water closet: a toilet, especially in a public place ➲See Common Learner Error at **toilet**

we *strong form* /wiː/ *weak form* /wi/ *pronoun* **1** used as the subject of the verb when the person speaking or writing is referring to themselves and one or more other people *My wife and I both play golf and we love it.* **2** people generally *The world in which we live is very different.*

weak /wiːk/ *adjective* **1** BODY not physically strong *He felt too weak to sit up.* ○ *The children were* ***weak with/from*** *hunger.* **2** CHARACTER not powerful, or not having a strong character *a weak government/leader* **3** LIKELY TO FAIL likely to fail *a weak economy* ○ *a weak team* **4** LIKELY TO BREAK likely to break and not able to support heavy things *a weak bridge* **5 FOOD** A weak drink has little taste or contains little alcohol. *weak coffee/beer* **6** REASON A weak reason or excuse is one that you cannot believe because there is not enough proof to support it. **7** NOT GOOD not good at something *She reads well but her spelling is weak.* **8** SLIGHT difficult to see or hear *He spoke in a weak voice.* ○ *a weak light* **9 CHEMISTRY** describes an acid, alkali or chemical base that does not produce many ions (= atoms with an electrical charge) when it is dissolved in water •**weakly** *adverb*

ˌweak ˈacid *noun* [C] **CHEMISTRY** an acid with a pH of 5 or 6 whose ionic compounds do not completely separate or divide into smaller molecules in a solution containing water

weaken /ˈwiːkᵊn/ *verb* [I, T] **1** LOSE POWER to become less strong or powerful, or to make someone or something less strong or powerful *A number of factors have weakened the economy.* **2** LOSE CONFIDENCE to become less certain or determined about a decision, or to make someone less determined *I told him he wasn't having any more money but then I weakened.*

weakling /ˈwiːklɪŋ/ *noun* [C] someone who is physically weak

weakness /ˈwiːknəs/ *noun* **1** FEELING WEAK [U] when someone or something is not strong or powerful *Asking for help is not a* ***sign of weakness.*** **2** FAULT [C] a particular part or quality of something or someone that is not good *What do you think are your weaknesses as a manager?* ○ *There are a number of weaknesses in this proposal.* **3 have a weakness for sth/sb** to like a particular thing or person very much *She has a real weakness for ice cream.*

wealth /welθ/ *noun* **1** [U] when someone has a lot of money or valuable possessions *He enjoyed his new wealth and status.* **2 a wealth of sth** a large amount of something good *a wealth of experience/information*

wealthy /ˈwelθi/ *adjective* rich *a wealthy businessman/nation* ○ *Only* ***the*** *very* ***wealthy*** *can afford to live here.*

wean /wiːn/ *verb* [T] **FOOD** to start to give a baby food to eat instead of its mother's milk

wean sb off sth *phrasal verb* to make someone gradually stop using something that is bad for them *I'm trying to wean myself off fatty food generally.*

WORD PARTNERS FOR ***weapon***

biological /chemical/nuclear weapons • **deadly/lethal/offensive** weapons • **carry/possess** a weapon

weapon /ˈwepən/ *noun* [C] a gun, knife, or other object used to kill or hurt someone ***nuclear weapons*** ○ *Police have found the murder weapon.* •**weaponry** *noun* [U] weapons

wear¹ /weəʳ/ *verb past tense* **wore**, *past participle* **worn** **1** DRESS [T] to have a piece of clothing, jewellery, etc on your body *I wear jeans a lot of the time.* ○ *She wears glasses.* ○ *I don't usually wear make-up for work.* **2** FACE [T] to show a particular emotion on your face. *He was wearing a smile/frown.* **3** HAIR [T] to arrange or grow your hair in a particular way *She usually wears her hair in a ponytail.* **4** SPOIL [I, T] to become thin and damaged after being used a lot, or to make this happen *The carpet is already starting to wear in places.* ○ *He keeps* ***wearing holes in*** *his socks.* ➲See also: wear **thin¹**

wear (sth) away *phrasal verb* to disappear after a lot of time or use, or to make something disappear in this way *The words on the gravestone had worn away completely.*

wear sb down *phrasal verb* to make someone feel tired and less able to argue *Their continual nagging just wears me down.*

wear off *phrasal verb* If a feeling or the effect of something wears off, it gradually disappears. *The anaesthetic is starting to wear off.*

wear on *phrasal verb* If a period of time wears on, it passes, especially slowly. *As time wore on she became more and more unhappy.*

W

wear sb out *phrasal verb* to make someone extremely tired
wear (sth) out *phrasal verb* to use something so much that it is damaged and cannot be used any more, or to become damaged in this way

wear² /weəʳ/ *noun* [U] **1** DAMAGE (*also* **wear and tear**) damage that happens to something when it is used a lot *The furniture is already showing signs of wear.* **2** USE how much you wear a piece of clothing *These clothes are not for everyday wear.* **3 be the worse for wear** to be in a bad state or condition

-wear /weəʳ/ *suffix* used at the end of words that describe a particular type of clothes *menswear/swimwear*

wearing /ˈweərɪŋ/ *adjective* making you tired or annoyed

weary /ˈwɪəri/ *adjective* **1** tired *You look weary, my love.* **2 weary of sth/sb** bored with something or someone *She **grew weary of** the children and their games.* •**wearily** *adverb* •**weariness** *noun* [U]

weasel /ˈwiːzəl/ *noun* [C] a small animal with a long body that kills and eats other small animals

WORD PARTNERS FOR ***weather***

bad/cold/good/hot/stormy/warm/wet weather • weather **brightens up/improves/worsens**

O-ꟷ **weather¹** /ˈweðəʳ/ *noun* [U] **1** the temperature or conditions outside, for example if it is hot, cold, sunny, etc *The flight was delayed because of **bad weather**.* **2 be/feel under the weather** to feel ill

weather² /ˈweðəʳ/ *verb* [T] to deal with a difficult situation or difficult conditions *to weather criticism/a recession*

weathered /ˈweðəd/ *adjective* looking rough and old *a weathered face*

ˈ**weather** ˌ**forecast** *noun* [C] a description of what the weather will be like

weathering /ˈweðərɪŋ/ *noun* [U] **ENVIRONMENT, GEOLOGY** when rocks are broken into small pieces by the action of the weather

weave /wiːv/ *verb* **1 weave in and out; weave through** *past* **weaved** to go somewhere by moving around a lot of things *to weave in and out of the traffic* **2** [I, T] *past tense* **wove**, *past participle* **woven DT** to make cloth on a machine by crossing threads under and over each other

O-ꟷ **web** /web/ *noun* [C] **1** a type of net made by a spider (= small creature with eight legs) to catch other insects *a spider's web* **2 the Web INTERNET** (*also* **the World Wide Web**) part of the Internet that consists of all the connected websites (= pages of text and pictures) ➲See Extra help page **The Web and the Internet** on page Centre 36.

ˈ**web** adˌ**dress** (*US* ˈ**web** ˌ**address**) *noun* [C] **INTERNET** an email or website address ➲See Extra help page **The Web and the Internet** on page Centre 36.

ˈ**web** ˌ**browser** *noun* [C] **INTERNET** a computer program which allows you to look at pages on the Internet

webcam /ˈwebkæm/ *noun* [C] **COMPUTING, INTERNET** a camera which records moving pictures and sound and allows these to be shown on the Internet as they happen ➲See picture at **computer**

webcast /ˈwebkɑːst/ *noun* [C] **INTERNET** a broadcast made on the Internet

ˈ**web** ˌ**page** *noun* [C] **INTERNET** a part of a website that can be read on a computer screen ➲See Extra help page **The Web and the Internet** on page Centre 36.

ˈ**web** ˌ**server** *noun* [C] **INTERNET** a computer system or program that finds and sends web pages when Internet users ask for them

O-ꟷ **website** /ˈwebsaɪt/ *noun* [C] **INTERNET** an area on the Web (= computer information system) where information about a particular subject, organization, etc can be found ➲See Extra help page **The Web and the Internet** on page Centre 36.

O-ꟷ **we'd** /wiːd/ **1** WE HAD *short for* we had *By the time she arrived we'd eaten.* **2** WE WOULD *short for* we would *We'd like two tickets for the three o'clock show, please.*

Wed (*also* **Weds**) *written abbreviation for* Wednesday

WORD PARTNERS FOR ***wedding***

go to/be invited to/plan a wedding • **at** a wedding • sb's wedding **day** • a wedding **dress/guest/present/reception/ring**

O-ꟷ **wedding** /ˈwedɪŋ/ *noun* [C] an official ceremony at which a man and woman get married *We're **going to a wedding** on Saturday afternoon.* ○ ***a wedding dress/ring*** ➲See also: **golden wedding**

wedge¹ /wedʒ/ *noun* [C] a piece of something that is thin at one end and thicker at the other *a big wedge of cheese*

wedge² /wedʒ/ *verb* [T] **1 wedge sth open/shut** to use a wedge or similar shaped object to keep a door or window firmly open or closed *I wedged the door open.* **2** to push something into a narrow space *I was wedged between Andy and Pete in the back of the car.*

O-ꟷ **Wednesday** /ˈwenzdeɪ/ (*written abbreviation* **Wed, Weds**) *noun* [C, U] the day of the week after Tuesday and before Thursday

wee¹ /wiː/ *noun* [**no plural**] *mainly UK informal* when you urinate *to have a wee* ○ *I need a wee.* •**wee** *verb* [I] **weeing**, *past* **weed**

wee² /wiː/ *adjective* small, usually used by Scottish speakers *a wee girl*

weed¹ /wiːd/ *noun* [C] a wild plant that you do not want to grow in your garden

weed² /wiːd/ *verb* [I, T] to remove wild plants from a garden where they are not wanted
weed sb/sth out *phrasal verb* to get rid of people or things that you do not want from a group *The government plans to weed out bad teachers.*

weedy /ˈwiːdi/ *adjective UK informal* thin and weak *He looks too weedy to be an athlete.*

O-ꟷ **week** /wiːk/ *noun* **1** [C] a period of seven days *last week/next week* ○ *I've got three exams this week.* ○ *We get paid every week.* **2 the week** the five days from Monday to Friday when people

W

usually go to work or school *I don't go out much during the week.*

weekday /ˈwiːkdeɪ/ *noun* [C] one of the five days from Monday to Friday, when people usually go to work or school

weekend /ˌwiːkˈend/ (US) /ˈwiːkend/ *noun* [C] **1** Saturday and Sunday, the two days in the week when many people do not work *Are you doing anything this weekend?* ○ *I'm going home for the weekend.* **2 at the weekend** *UK* (*US* **on the weekend**) on Saturday or Sunday *He's going to a football match at the weekend.*

weekly /ˈwiːkli/ *adjective, adverb* happening once a week or every week *a weekly newspaper* ○ *We're paid weekly.*

weep /wiːp/ *verb* [I, T] *past* **wept** *literary* to cry, usually because you are sad

the weft /weft/ *noun* **DT** the threads in a piece of cloth that go from side to side and are twisted over and under threads going from end to end

weigh /weɪ/ *verb* **1 weigh 200g/75 kg/10 stone, etc** to have a weight of 200g/75 kg/10 stone, etc *How much do you weigh?* **2** MEASURE [T] to measure how heavy someone or something is *Can you weigh that piece of cheese for me?* ○ *She weighs herself every day.* **3** CONSIDER [T] (*also UK* **weigh up**) to consider something carefully, especially in order to make a decision *The jury must weigh the evidence.* ○ *He needs to weigh up the pros and cons of going to college.*

weigh sth against sth *phrasal verb* to judge which of two things is more important before making a decision *The advantages have to be weighed against the possible disadvantages.*

be weighed down by/with sth *phrasal verb* **1** CARRYING to be carrying or holding too much *She was weighed down with shopping bags.* **2** WORRIED to be very worried about something *be weighed down by problems/debts*

weigh on/upon sb/sth *phrasal verb* If a problem or responsibility weighs on you, it makes you worried or unhappy. *Problems at work are weighing on me.*

weigh sth out *phrasal verb* to measure an amount of something *Weigh out 8 ounces of flour.*

WORD PARTNERS FOR ***weight***

gain/lose/put on weight • **carry/lift/support** a weight • **average/excess/heavy/ideal/light** weight

weight /weɪt/ *noun* **1** AMOUNT [U] how heavy someone or something is *He's about **average** height and **weight**.* **2 lose weight** If someone loses weight, they become lighter and thinner. *I need to **lose a bit of weight**.* **3 put on/gain weight** If someone puts on weight or gains weight, they become heavier and fatter. **4** HEAVINESS [U, no plural] the quality of being heavy *The shelf collapsed under the weight of the books.* **5** OBJECT [C] something that is heavy *You're not supposed to lift heavy weights after an operation.* **6 carry weight** to be considered important and effective in influencing someone *His opinions carry a lot of weight with the scientific community.* **7 pull your weight** to work as hard as other people in a group *The rest of the team complained that Sarah wasn't pulling her weight.* **8 throw your weight around** to behave as if you are more important or powerful than other people **9 a weight off your mind** when a problem which has been worrying you stops or is dealt with *Finally selling that house was a weight off my mind.* ➲See also: **paper weight**

weighted /ˈweɪtɪd/ *adjective* **be weighted in favour of/towards/against sth** to give one group an advantage or disadvantage over other people *The system is weighted in favour of families with young children.*

weights /weɪts/ *noun* [plural] **SPORT** heavy pieces of metal that you lift up and down to make your muscles stronger

weighty /ˈweɪti/ *adjective* very serious and important *The film deals with the **weighty issues** of religion and morality.*

weir /wɪəʳ/ *noun* [C] *UK* a low wall built across a river to control the flow of water

weird /wɪəd/ *adjective* very strange *I had a really weird dream last night.*

weirdo /ˈwɪədəʊ/ *noun* [C] *informal* a person who behaves strangely

welcome[1] /ˈwelkəm/ *exclamation* used to greet someone who has just arrived somewhere *Welcome home!* ○ *Welcome to the UK.*

welcome[2] /ˈwelkəm/ *verb* [T] **1** GREET to greet someone who has arrived in a place *Both families were there to welcome us.* **2** LIKE to be pleased about something and want it to happen *The decision was welcomed by everybody.* ○ *I would welcome your advice.*

welcome[3] /ˈwelkəm/ *adjective* **1** If something is welcome, people are pleased about it and want it to happen. *a **welcome change*** ○ *Your comments are very welcome.* ➲Opposite **unwelcome** **2 You're welcome.** used to be polite to someone who has thanked you *"Thank you." "You're welcome."* **3 make sb (feel) welcome** to make a visitor feel happy and comfortable in a place by being kind and friendly to them *They made me very welcome in their home.* **4 be welcome to do sth** used to tell someone that they can certainly do something, if they want to *Anyone who is interested is welcome to come along.* **5 be welcome to sth** used to tell someone that they can certainly have something, if they want it, because you do not

WORD PARTNERS FOR ***welcome*** *(noun)*

get/be given a [big/friendly/warm, etc] welcome

welcome[4] /ˈwelkəm/ *noun* [no plural] **1** when someone is greeted when they arrive somewhere *He was **given a warm** (= friendly) **welcome** by his fans.* **2 outstay/overstay your welcome** to stay somewhere too long so that people want you to leave

weld /weld/ *verb* [T] **DT** to join pieces of metal together by heating them until they almost melt and then pressing them together

welfare /ˈwelfeəʳ/ *noun* [U] **1** Someone's welfare is their health and happiness. *He is concerned about the welfare of young men in prison.* **2 SOCIETY** *US* (*UK* **social security**) money paid by a government to people who are poor, ill, or who do not have jobs *to be **on welfare*** (= getting welfare)

ˌwelfare ˈstate *UK* (*US* **ˈwelfareˌstate**) *noun* [**no plural**] **SOCIETY** a system in which the government looks after and pays for people who are ill, old, or who cannot get a job

O-■ **we'll** /wiːl/ *short for* we shall or we will *We'll be home on Friday.*

O-■ **well**[1] /wel/ *adjective* [**never before noun**] **better, best 1 HEALTH** healthy *to feel/look well* ○ *I'm not very well.* ○ *Are you feeling better now?* ➲Opposite **unwell 2 all is well** everything is in a good or acceptable state *I hope all is well with Jack.* **3 be all very well** used to show that you do not agree with something or that you are annoyed about something *It's all very well for her to say everything's fine, she doesn't have to live here.* **4 be (just) as well** used to say that something might be a good thing to do or happen [+ **(that)**] *It was just as well that you left when you did.* ➲See also: be **alive** and kicking/well

O-■ **well**[2] /wel/ *adverb* **better, best 1** SUCCESSFULLY in a successful or satisfactory way *I thought they played well.* ○ *He's **doing well** at school/work.* **2** COMPLETELY in a complete way or as much as possible *I know him quite well.* ○ *Stir the mixture well.* ➲See Common Learner Error at **good 3 as well** also *Are you going to invite Steve as well?* **4 as well as sth** in addition to something *They have lived in the United States as well as Britain.* **5 may/might as well do sth** If you may/might as well do something, it will not spoil the situation if you do that thing. *If we're not waiting for Karen, we might as well go now.* **6 may/might/could well** used to say that something is likely to be true *He could well be at Michelle's house.* **7 well above/ahead/below, etc** above/ahead/below, etc by a large amount *It was well after seven o'clock when we got home.* **8 can't/couldn't very well do sth** used to say that something is not a suitable or practical thing to do *I couldn't very well tell her while he was there.* **9 Well done!** used to tell someone how pleased you are about their success *"I passed my exams." "Well done!"*

O-■ **well**[3] /wel/ *exclamation* **1** PAUSE used at the beginning of a sentence to pause slightly or to express doubt or disagreement *"You'll go, won't you?" "Well, I'm not sure."* ○ *"You said the food was bad." "Well, I didn't exactly say that."* **2** SURPRISE (*also* **well, well**) used to express surprise *Well, well, I never expected that to happen.* **3 oh well** used to say that a situation cannot be changed although it might be disappointing *Oh well, it doesn't matter, I can always buy another one.*

well[4] /wel/ *noun* [**C**] a deep hole in the ground from which you can get water, oil, or gas

well-balanced /ˌwelˈbælənst/ *adjective* **1 FOOD, HEALTH a well-balanced diet/meal** food which includes all the different types of food that the body needs to be healthy **2** Well-balanced people are calm and have good judgment.

well-behaved /ˌwelbɪˈheɪvd/ *adjective* behaving in a polite and quiet way *a well-behaved child*

well-being /ˈwelˌbiːɪŋ/ *noun* [**U**] when someone is healthy, happy, and comfortable

well-built /ˌwelˈbɪlt/ *adjective* having a large, strong body

well-connected /ˌwelkəˈnektɪd/ *adjective* having important or powerful friends

well-done /ˌwelˈdʌn/ *adjective* Meat that is well-done has been cooked completely and is not pink inside.

well-dressed /ˌwelˈdrest/ *adjective* wearing attractive, good quality clothes

well-earned /ˌwelˈɜːnd/ *adjective* **well-earned break/holiday/rest, etc** a rest that you deserve because you have been working hard

well-educated /ˌwelˈedʒʊkeɪtɪd/ *adjective* having had a good education

well-established /ˌwelɪˈstæblɪʃt/ *adjective* having existed for a long time *a well-established tradition*

well-fed /ˌwelˈfed/ *adjective* having eaten enough good food *a well-fed cat*

well-heeled /ˌwelˈhiːld/ *adjective* having a lot of money, expensive clothes, etc

wellies /ˈweliz/ *UK informal* (*US* **rubber boots**) *noun* [**plural**] large rubber boots that you wear outside when the ground is wet and dirty *a pair of wellies*

well-informed /ˌwelɪnˈfɔːmd/ *adjective* knowing a lot of useful information

wellingtons /ˈwelɪŋtənz/ *noun* [**plural**] *UK* wellies

well-intentioned /ˌwelɪnˈtenʃənd/ *adjective* trying to be helpful and kind but not improving a situation

well-kept /ˌwelˈkept/ *adjective* **1 a well-kept secret** something that has been carefully and successfully kept secret *The recipe is a well-kept secret.* **2** tidy and organized *a well-kept kitchen*

well-known /ˌwelˈnəʊn/ *adjective* famous *a well-known actor*

well-meaning /ˌwelˈmiːnɪŋ/ *adjective* trying to be helpful and kind but not improving a situation *well-meaning friends*

well-off /ˌwelˈɒf/ *adjective* having a lot of money *His parents are very well-off.*

well-organized (*also UK* **-ised**) /ˌwelˈɔːgənaɪzd/ *adjective* working in an effective and successful way because of good organization

well-paid /ˌwelˈpeɪd/ *adjective* earning a lot of money

well-placed /ˌwelˈpleɪst/ *adjective* in a very convenient position or in a position that gives someone an advantage [+ **to do sth**] *She's very well-placed to find out what's going on.*

well-read /ˌwelˈred/ *adjective* having read a lot of books on different subjects

well-to-do /ˌweltəˈduː/ *adjective old-fashioned* having a lot of money *a well-to-do family*

well-wisher /ˈwelˌwɪʃər/ *noun* [**C**] someone who wants another person to be happy, successful, or healthy *A crowd of well-wishers gathered outside the hospital.*

W

Welsh /welʃ/ *noun* [U] **1** a language that is spoken in some parts of Wales **2 the Welsh** the people of Wales

went /went/ *past tense of* go

wept /wept/ *past of* weep

we're /wɪəʳ/ *short for* we are *Hurry! We're late!*

were /wɜːʳ/ *past simple you/we/they of* be

weren't /wɜːnt/ *short for* were not *They weren't there.*

west, West¹ /west/ *noun* [U] **1** the direction that you face to see the sun go down **2 the west** the part of an area that is further towards the west than the rest **3 GEOGRAPHY, POLITICS the West** the countries of North America and western Europe •**west** *adjective the west coast of Ireland* •**west** *adverb* towards the west *They lived in a village four miles west of Oxford.*

the ˌWest ˈEnd *noun* a part of central London that has a lot of shops, theatres, restaurants, etc

westerly /ˈwestᵊli/ *adjective* **1** DIRECTION towards or in the west *Senegal is the most westerly country in Africa.* **2** WIND A westerly wind comes from the west. *westerly breezes*

western, Western¹ /ˈwestən/ *adjective* [**always before noun**] **1** AREA in or from the west part of an area *western France* **2** COUNTRIES related to the countries of North America and western Europe *a Western diplomat*

western² /ˈwestən/ *noun* [C] a film or story that happens in the west of the US at the time when Europeans started living there

westerner, Westerner /ˈwestənəʳ/ *noun* [C] **SOCIETY** someone who is from a country in North America or western Europe

westernized (*also UK* **-ised**) /ˈwestənaɪzd/ *adjective* having a culture like North America and western Europe *Some Asian countries are becoming increasingly westernized.*

ˌWest ˈIndian *adjective* belonging or relating to the West Indies *a West Indian island* •**West Indian** *noun* [C] someone from the West Indies

the ˌWest ˈIndies *noun* [**plural**] a group of islands in the Caribbean Sea

westward, westwards /ˈwestwəd, ˈwestwədz/ *adverb* towards the west *They were travelling westward.* •**westward** *adjective*

wet¹ /wet/ *adjective* **wetter, wettest 1** WATER covered in water or another liquid *a wet towel* ○ *We* ***got soaking wet*** *in the rain.* ○ *UK Look at you - you're* ***wet through*** (= very wet)! **2** RAIN raining *a wet and windy day* **3** NOT DRY not dry yet *wet paint* **4** PERSON *UK informal* Someone who is wet has a weak personality.

W

wet² /wet/ *verb* [T] **wetting**, *past* **wet** or **wetted 1 wet the bed/your pants/yourself, etc** to urinate in your bed or in your underwear without intending to **2** to make something wet

ˈwet ˌsuit *noun* [C] **SPORT** a piece of clothing covering the whole body that keeps you warm and dry when you are under water

we've /wiːv/ *short for* we have *We've bought a house.*

whack /wæk/ *verb* [T] *informal* to hit someone or something in a quick, strong way *She whacked him on the head with her book.* •**whack** *noun* [C] *informal*

whale /weɪl/ *noun* [C] a very large animal that looks like a large fish, lives in the sea and breathes air through a hole at the top of its head

whaling /ˈweɪlɪŋ/ *noun* [U] hunting whales

wharf /wɔːf/ *noun* [C] *plural* **wharves** /wɔːvz/ an area next to the sea or a river where goods can be put on or taken off ships

what /wɒt/ *pronoun, determiner* **1** INFORMATION used to ask for information about something *What's this?* ○ *What time is it?* ○ *What happened?* ➲See Common Learner Error at **how 2** THE THING used to refer to something without naming it *I heard what he said.* ○ *Do you know what I mean?* ○ *What I like most about her is her honesty.* **3** NOT HEARD *informal* used when you have not heard what someone has said and you want them to repeat it. Some people think this use is not very polite. *"Do you want a drink Tom?" "What?"* **4** REPLY *informal* used to ask what someone wants when they call you *"Hey Jenny?" "Yes, what?"* **5 what a/an ...** used to give your opinion, especially when you have strong feelings about something *What a mess!* ○ *What an awful day!* **6 what about...?** used to suggest something *What about asking Martin to help?* **7 what ... for?** used to ask about the reason for something *What are you doing that for?* ○ *"We really need a bigger car." "What for?"* **8 what if...?** used to ask about something that could happen in the future, especially something bad *What if I don't pass my exams?* **9 what's up (with sb)** *informal* used to ask why someone is unhappy or angry *What's up, Angie? You look troubled.* **10 what with** *informal* used to talk about the reasons for a particular situation, especially a bad or difficult situation *I'm tired, what with travelling all day yesterday and sleeping badly.* **11 what's more** used to add something surprising or interesting to what you have just said

COMMON LEARNER ERROR

what

When you have not heard what someone has said and you want them to repeat it, you can say **what?**, but this is not polite. It is better to say **sorry?** or **pardon?**.

"It's 10 o'clock." "Sorry/Pardon?" "I said it's 10 o'clock."

whatever /wɒtˈevəʳ/ *adverb, pronoun, determiner* **1** ANYTHING anything or everything *Do whatever you want.* ○ *He eats whatever I put in front of him.* **2** NO DIFFERENCE used to say that what happens is not important because it does not change a situation *Whatever happens I'll still love you.* ○ *We'll support you, whatever you decide.* **3** QUESTION used to ask for information when you are surprised or angry about something *Whatever do you mean?* **4** ANGRY *informal* something that you say when you are angry with someone who is asking you something *'Isabel, will you just listen when I'm talking to you?' 'Whatever.'* **5 or whatever** or something similar *The children are usually outside playing football or whatever.*

whatnot /ˈwɒtnɒt/ **and whatnot** *informal* and other things of a similar type *They sell cards and wrapping paper and whatnot.*

whatsoever /ˌwɒtsəʊˈevəʳ/ (*also* **whatever**) *adverb* **no...whatsoever** none at all *There's no evidence whatsoever that she was involved.*

wheat /wiːt/ *noun* [U] **FOOD** a plant whose grain is used for making flour, or the grain itself

O-ᵚ**wheel¹** /wiːl/ *noun* **1** [C] a circular object fixed under a vehicle so that it moves smoothly over the ground *My bike needs a new front wheel.* **2 the wheel** a steering wheel (= circular object you turn to direct a vehicle) *You should drive with both hands on the wheel.* ○ *He fell asleep **at the wheel*** (= while driving). **3 reinvent the wheel** to waste time trying to create something that has been done before ⊃See also: **Ferris wheel**

wheel² /wiːl/ *verb* **wheel sth around/into/to, etc** to push something that has wheels somewhere *He wheeled his bicycle into the garden.*
wheel around/round *phrasal verb* to quickly turn around *She wheeled around to face him.*

wheelbarrow /ˈwiːlˌbærəʊ/ *noun* [C] a big, open container with a wheel at the front and handles that is used to move things, especially around in a garden

wheelchair /ˈwiːltʃeəʳ/ *noun* [C] a chair with wheels used by someone who cannot walk

wheeze /wiːz/ *verb* [I] **HEALTH** to make a noisy sound when breathing because of a problem in your lungs

O-ᵚ**when¹** /wen/ *adverb* used to ask at what time something happened or will happen *When's your birthday?* ○ *When did he leave?* ○ *When are you going away?*

O-ᵚ**when²** /wen/ *conjunction* **1** TIME used to say at what time something happened or will happen *I found it when I was cleaning out the cupboards.* ○ *We'll go when you're ready.* **2** ALTHOUGH although *Why are you doing this when I've asked you not to?*

whenever /wenˈevəʳ/ *conjunction* every time or at any time *You can go whenever you want.* ○ *I try to help them out whenever possible.*

O-ᵚ**where¹** /weəʳ/ *adverb* used to ask about the place or position of someone or something *Where does she live?* ○ *Where are my car keys?*

O-ᵚ**where²** /weəʳ/ *conjunction* **1** PLACE/POSITION at, in, or to a place or position *He's not sure where they are.* ○ *I know where to go.* **2** PART OF PROCESS/SITUATION relating to a particular part of a process or situation *We've now reached the point where we can make a decision.*

whereabouts¹ /ˌweərəˈbaʊts/ *adverb* used to ask in what place or area someone or something is *Whereabouts does he live?*

whereabouts² /ˈweərəbaʊts/ *noun* **sb's whereabouts** the place where someone or something is *His whereabouts are unknown.*

whereas /weəˈræz/ *conjunction* compared with the fact that *His parents were rich, whereas mine had to struggle.*

whereby /weəˈbaɪ/ *adverb formal* by which *They've introduced a system whereby people share cars.*

wherein /weəˈrɪn/ *adverb formal* in which

whereupon /ˈweərəpɒn/ *conjunction formal* after which *We decided to have a picnic, whereupon it started to rain.*

wherever¹ /weəˈrevəʳ/ *conjunction* **1** in or to any place or every place *You can sit wherever you like.* **2 wherever possible** every time it is possible *We try to use natural fabrics wherever possible.*

wherever² /weəˈrevəʳ/ *adverb* used to ask in what situation or place something happened, especially when the person asking feels surprised *Wherever did you get that idea?*

wherewithal /ˈweəwɪðɔːl/ *noun* **the wherewithal to do sth** the money, skills, or other things that are needed to do something

O-ᵚ**whether** /ˈweðəʳ/ *conjunction* **1** CHOICE used to talk about a choice between two or more possibilities *Someone's got to tell her, **whether** it's you **or** me.* ○ *I didn't know **whether or not** to go.* **2** IF if *I wasn't sure whether you'd like it.*

whew /fjuː/ *exclamation* used when you are happy that something is not going to happen, or when you are tired or hot

O-ᵚ**which** /wɪtʃ/ *pronoun, determiner* **1** CHOICE used to ask or talk about a choice between two or more things *Which of these do you like best?* ○ *Which way is it to the station?* ○ *I just don't know which one to choose.* **2** REFERRING TO SOMETHING used at the beginning of a relative clause to show what thing is being referred to *These are principles which we all believe in.* **3** EXTRA INFORMATION used to give more information about something *The book, which includes a map, gives you all the information you need about Venice.* **4** GIVING OPINION used when you give an opinion about what you have just said *He took us both out for lunch, which I thought was very kind of him.*

COMMON LEARNER ERROR

which or who?

Use **which** to refer to a thing.

The restaurant which is next to the pub is good.

~~*The restaurant who is next to the pub is good.*~~

Use **who** to refer to a person.

The boy who is wearing the red coat is called Paul.

~~*The boy which is wearing the red coat is called Paul.*~~

Sometimes it is possible to use 'that' or no word instead of **which** or **who**.

He's the man (that) I saw in the bar.

This is the shirt (that) I bought yesterday.

whichever /wɪˈtʃevəʳ/ *pronoun, determiner* **1** NO DIFFERENCE used to say that what happens is not important because it does not change a situation *Whichever option we choose there'll be disadvantages.* ○ *It's a sad situation whichever way you look at it.* **2** ANY any of a group of similar things *Choose whichever bedroom you want.*

whiff /wɪf/ *noun* [**no plural**] a smell which you only smell for a short time *I just caught **a whiff of** garlic from the kitchen.*

W

O-ꟷ **while**[1] /waɪl/ (*also UK* **whilst** /waɪlst/) *conjunction* **1** DURING during the time that *I read a magazine while I was waiting.* ○ *I can't talk to anyone while I'm driving.* ○ *While you're away, I might decorate the bathroom.* **2** ALTHOUGH although *And while I like my job, I wouldn't want to do it forever.* **3** COMPARING used to compare two different facts or situations *Tom is very confident while Katy is shy and quiet.*

WORD PARTNERS FOR ***while*** *(noun)*

take/wait a while • **after/for/in** a while • **quite** a while • a **short** while • a while **ago**

O-ꟷ **while**[2] /waɪl/ *noun* **a while** a period of time *a long/short while* ○ *I'm going out* ***for a while.***

while[3] /waɪl/ *verb*

while sth away *phrasal verb* to spend time in a relaxed way because you are waiting for something or because you have nothing to do *We played a few games to while away the time.*

whim /wɪm/ *noun* [C] when you suddenly want to do something without having a reason *We booked the holiday* ***on a whim.***

whimper /ˈwɪmpəʳ/ *verb* [I] to make quiet crying sounds because of fear or pain *The dog was whimpering with pain.*

whimsical /ˈwɪmzɪkəl/ *adjective* unusual in a way that is slightly funny *a whimsical tale*

whine /waɪn/ *verb* [I] **1** COMPLAIN to complain in an annoying way *She's always whining about something.* **2** CRY to make a long, high, sad sound *The dog whined and scratched at the door.* •**whine** *noun* [C]

whinge /wɪndʒ/ *verb* [I] **whingeing** or **whinging** *UK informal* to complain in an annoying way *Oh, stop whingeing!* •**whinge** *noun* [C] *UK He was just* ***having a whinge.***

whip[1] /wɪp/ *noun* [C] a long piece of leather fixed to a handle and used to hit an animal or person

whip[2] /wɪp/ *verb* **whipping**, *past* **whipped 1** HIT [T] to hit a person or animal with a whip **2** FOOD [T] to make a food such as cream more solid by mixing it hard with a kitchen tool **3 whip (sth) away/off/out, etc** *informal* to move or make something move in a fast, sudden way *She opened the bag and whipped out her camera.*

whip up sth *phrasal verb* **1** FEELINGS to try to make people have strong feelings about something *to whip up enthusiasm/hatred* **2** FOOD to prepare food very quickly *I could whip up a plate of spaghetti if you like.*

whir /wɜːʳ/ *noun, verb* **whirring**, *past* **whirred** *US spelling of* whirr

whirl[1] /wɜːl/ *verb* [I, T] to move or make something move quickly round and round

whirl[2] /wɜːl/ *noun* [no plural] **1** ACTIVITY when a lot of exciting or confusing things happen at the same time *a whirl of activity* **2** TURN a sudden turning movement **3 give sth a whirl** *informal* to try to do something, often for the first time *I've never danced salsa before but I'll give it a whirl.*

whirlpool /ˈwɜːlpuːl/ *noun* [C] an area of water that moves round and round very quickly

whirlwind[1] /ˈwɜːlwɪnd/ *adjective* **a whirlwind romance/visit/tour, etc** a relationship/visit, etc that only lasts a short time

whirlwind[2] /ˈwɜːlwɪnd/ *noun* **1 a whirlwind of sth** a lot of sudden activity, emotion, etc *a whirlwind of activity* **2** [C] a strong wind that moves round and round very quickly

whirr *UK* (*US* **whir**) /wɜːʳ/ *noun* [no plural] a low, continuous sound *the whirr of machinery* •**whirr** *UK* (*US* **whir**) *verb* [I]

whisk[1] /wɪsk/ *verb* [T] **1 whisk sb away/off/into, etc** *informal* to take someone somewhere quickly *They whisked him off to the police station.* **2 FOOD** to mix food such as eggs, cream, etc very quickly using a fork or whisk *Whisk the mixture until smooth.*

whisk[2] /wɪsk/ *noun* [C] a kitchen tool made of wire that is used to mix eggs, cream, etc, or to make such food thicker ➲See colour picture **The Kitchen** on page Centre 2

whisker /ˈwɪskəʳ/ *noun* [C] one of the long, stiff hairs that grows around the mouths of animals such as cats

whiskers /ˈwɪskəz/ *noun* [plural] *old-fashioned* hairs growing on a man's face

whiskey /ˈwɪski/ *noun* [C, U] **FOOD** whisky in Ireland or the United States

whisky /ˈwɪski/ *noun* [C, U] **FOOD** a strong, alcoholic drink made from grain

O-ꟷ **whisper** /ˈwɪspəʳ/ *verb* [I, T] to speak extremely quietly so that other people cannot hear *She whispered something to the girl sitting next to her.* •**whisper** *noun* [C]

whistle[1] /ˈwɪsl/ *verb* **1** MOUTH [I, T] to make a sound by breathing air out through a small hole made with your lips or through a whistle *Someone whistled at her as she walked past.* **2** WIND [I] to produce a sound when air passes through a narrow space *He could hear the wind whistling through the trees.*

whistle[2] /ˈwɪsl/ *noun* [C] **1 MUSIC** a small, simple instrument that makes a high sound when you blow through it *The referee* ***blew the whistle*** *to end the game.* **2** the sound made by someone or something whistling

O-ꟷ **white**[1] /waɪt/ *adjective* **1** COLOUR being the colour of snow or milk *a white T-shirt* ○ *white walls* ➲See colour picture **Colours** on page Centre 12 **2** PERSON Someone who is white has skin that is pale in colour. *He's described as a white man in his early thirties.* **3** OF WHITE PEOPLE relating to white people *the white community* **4** FACE having a pale face because you are ill or you are feeling shocked *He was white with shock.* **5 FOOD** *UK* White coffee has milk or cream added to it. *Two coffees please, one black and one white.* **6 FOOD** White wine is a pale yellow colour. •**whiteness** *noun* [U] ➲See also: **black**[1] and white

O-ꟷ **white**[2] /waɪt/ *noun* **1** COLOUR [C, U] the colour of snow or milk ➲See colour picture **Colours** on page Centre 12 **2** PERSON [C] a white person *For a long time, whites controlled the economy here.* **3 FOOD** [C] the part of an egg that is white when it is cooked *Mix the egg whites with the sugar.* ➲See also: in **black**[2] and white

W

ˌ**white ˈblood ˌcell** *noun* [C] **BIOLOGY** a cell in the blood that has no red colour and is involved in the fight against infection ⊃Compare **red blood cell**

whiteboard /ˈwaɪtbɔːd/ *noun* [C] **1 COMPUTING** (*also* **interactive whiteboard**) a white screen on which you can write with a special pen and which allows other people with computers to see what you have written **2 EDUCATION** a large board with a white surface that teachers write on ⊃See colour picture **The Classroom** on page Centre 6

white-collar /ˌwaɪtˌkɒləʳ/ *adjective* **SOCIETY** relating to work in an office or in a job that needs special knowledge and education *white-collar jobs/workers*

ˌ**white ˈdwarf** *noun* [C] **ASTRONOMY** a small star that is not very bright, but is very dense (= contains a lot of matter)

the ˈWhite ˌHouse *noun* **1 POLITICS** the US president and government **2 POLITICS** the building that is the official home and offices of the US president •**White House** *adjective a White House spokesman*

ˌ**white ˈlie** *noun* [C] a lie which is not important and is usually said to avoid upsetting someone

ˈ**white ˌmatter** *noun* [U] **BIOLOGY** the part of the brain and spinal cord (= nerves inside the backbone) which is light in colour

ˌ**white ˈmeat** *noun* [U] **FOOD** a meat that is pale in colour, such as chicken

whiten /ˈwaɪtᵊn/ *verb* [**I, T**] to become white or to make something become white

ˌ**White ˈPaper** *noun* [C] **POLITICS** a government report in the UK giving information or suggestions on a subject *a White Paper on employment*

whitewash /ˈwaɪtwɒʃ/ *noun* [**no plural**] when the truth about a serious mistake, crime, etc is hidden from the public *The newspaper accused the government of a whitewash.* •**whitewash** *verb* [T]

whizz (*also* **whiz**) /wɪz/ *verb* **whizz by/past/through, etc** *informal* to move somewhere very quickly *She whizzed down the street in her new sports car.*

whizzkid (*also* **whizkid**) /ˈwɪzˌkɪd/ *noun* [C] a young person who is very successful or good at doing something *a computer whizzkid*

O⁻**who** /huː/ *pronoun* **1** NAME used to ask about someone's name or which person or group someone is talking about *Who told you?* ○ *Who's that?* **2** WHICH PERSON used at the beginning of a relative clause to show which person or group of people you are talking about *That's the man who I saw in the bank.* **3** ADD INFORMATION used to give more information about someone *My brother, who's only just seventeen, has already passed his driving test.* ⊃See Common Learner Error at **which**

O⁻**who'd** /huːd/ **1** WHO HAD *short for* who had *I was reading about a man who'd sailed around the world.* **2** WHO WOULD *short for* who would *Who'd have thought we'd still be friends?*

whoever /huːˈevəʳ/ *pronoun* **1** WHICH PERSON the person who *Whoever broke the window will have to pay for it.* ○ *Could I speak to whoever is in charge please?* **2** ANY PERSON used to say that it is not important which person or group does something *Can whoever leaves last lock up, please?* **3** SURPRISE used to ask who a person is when expressing surprise *Whoever could that be phoning at this time?* ○ *Whoever would believe such a ridiculous story?*

O⁻**whole¹** /həʊl/ *adjective* **1** COMPLETE [**always before noun**] complete, including every part *She spent the whole afternoon studying.* ○ *The whole family went to the show.* **2** NOT IN PIECES [**never before noun**] as a single object and not in pieces *The chick swallowed the worm whole.* ⊃See also: a whole new **ball game**, the whole **world**¹

O⁻**whole²** /həʊl/ *noun* **1 the whole of sth** all of something *His behaviour affects the whole of the class.* **2 as a whole** when considered as a group and not in parts *The population as a whole is getting healthier.* **3 on the whole** generally *We've had a few problems, but on the whole we're very happy.*

wholefood /ˈhəʊlfuːd/ *noun* [U] *UK* **FOOD** food that is as natural as possible, without artificial things added to it *a wholefood shop*

wholehearted /ˌhəʊlˈhɑːtɪd/ *adjective* **wholehearted agreement/approval/support, etc** complete agreement/approval/support, etc without any doubts •**wholeheartedly** *adverb I agree wholeheartedly.*

wholemeal /ˈhəʊlmiːl/ *UK* (*UK/US* **whole wheat**) *adjective* **FOOD** made using whole grains, or made from flour that contains whole grains ***wholemeal bread/flour***

wholesale /ˈhəʊlseɪl/ *adjective* **1 FINANCE** relating to products which are sold in large amounts, usually at a cheaper price ***wholesale prices*** **2** [**always before noun**] complete or affecting a lot of things, people, places, etc ***wholesale changes*** •**wholesale** *adverb*

wholesaler /ˈhəʊlˌseɪləʳ/ *noun* [C] a company that sells products in large amounts to shops which then sell them to customers

wholesome /ˈhəʊlsᵊm/ *adjective* **1 FOOD** Wholesome food is good for your health. **2** GOOD morally good *wholesome family entertainment*

ˈ**whole ˌwheat** (*also UK* **wholemeal**) *adjective* **FOOD** made using whole grains, or made from flour that contains whole grains ***whole wheat bread/flour***

O⁻**who'll** /huːl/ *short for* who will *Who'll be at your party?*

wholly /ˈhəʊlli/ *adverb* completely *His behaviour is wholly unacceptable.*

whom /huːm/ *pronoun formal* used instead of 'who' as the object of a verb or preposition *I met a man with whom I used to work.*

COMMON LEARNER ERROR

whom or **who?**

Whom is very formal and most people use **who** instead.

Whom did you see at the party?

Who did you see at the party?

Whom should be used after a preposition but most people avoid this by putting the preposition at the end of the sentence and using **who**.

W

With whom did you go to the party?
Who did you go to the party with?

whoop /wuːp/ *noun* [C] a loud, excited shout *He gave a loud whoop of delight.*

whooping cough /ˈhuːpɪŋˌkɒf/ *noun* [U] **HEALTH** a serious children's disease in which a cough is followed by a 'whoop' noise

whoops /wʊps/ *exclamation* used when you make a mistake or have a small accident

whopping /ˈwɒpɪŋ/ *adjective* [**always before noun**] *informal* extremely large *a whopping 50 percent increase*

who're /ˈhuːəʳ/ *short for* who are *Who're the people we're going to see?*

whore /hɔːʳ/ *noun* [C] an offensive word for someone whose job is having sex with people

O- **who's** /huːz/ **1** WHO IS *short for* who is *Who's your new friend?* **2** WHO HAS *short for* who has *Who's been using my computer?*

O- **whose** /huːz/ *pronoun, determiner* **1** QUESTIONS used to ask who something belongs to or who someone or something is connected with *Whose gloves are these?* ○ *Whose car shall we use?* **2** CONNECTED WITH used to say that something or someone is connected with or belongs to a person *She has a brother whose name I can't remember.*

O- **who've** /huːv/ *short for* who have *I know people who've bought their homes on the Internet.*

O- **why** /waɪ/ *adverb* **1** used to ask or talk about the reasons for something *Why didn't you call me?* ○ *I wonder why he didn't come.* ○ *So that's **the reason why** he asked her!* **2 Why don't you?/Why not do sth?** used to make a suggestion *Why don't you come with us?* ○ *Why not give it a try?* **3 why not?** *informal* used to agree with something that someone has suggested *"Let's have an ice cream." "Yes, why not?"*

wicker /ˈwɪkəʳ/ *adjective* **DT** made from thin branches crossed over and under each other *a wicker basket*

wicket /ˈwɪkɪt/ *noun* [C] **SPORT** in cricket, an arrangement of three long, vertical poles with two short poles across the top

O- **wide**[1] /waɪd/ *adjective* **1** LONG DISTANCE measuring a long distance or longer than usual from one side to the other *a wide river/road* ○ *I have very wide feet.* ⊃See picture at **narrow 2 5 miles/3 inches/6 metres, etc wide** having a distance of 5 miles/3 inches/6 metres, etc from one side to the other *The swimming pool is five metres wide.* **3 a wide range/selection/variety, etc** a lot of different types of thing *The library is a good source of a wide range of information.* **4** EYES If your eyes are wide, they are completely open. *Her eyes were wide with fear.* **5 SPORT** If a ball, shot, etc is wide, it does not go near enough to where it was intended to go. ⊃See also: be wide of the **mark**[1]

O- **wide**[2] /waɪd/ *adverb* **1 wide apart/open** as far apart/open as possible *The window was wide open.* **2 wide awake** completely awake

wide-eyed /ˌwaɪdˈaɪd/ *adjective* with your eyes completely open because of surprise, fear, happiness, etc *The children looked on, wide-eyed with wonder.*

O- **widely** /waɪdli/ *adverb* **1** including a lot of different places, people, subjects, etc *widely known* ○ *He has travelled widely in Europe.* **2 differ/vary widely** to be very different *Prices vary widely from shop to shop.*

widen /ˈwaɪdᵊn/ *verb* [I, T] **1** DISTANCE to become wider or make something become wider *The road is being widened to two lanes.* **2** INCREASE to increase or make something increase in number or degree *to widen choice*

wide-ranging /ˌwaɪdˈreɪndʒɪŋ/ *adjective* including a lot of subjects *a **wide-ranging discussion/interview***

widescreen /ˈwaɪdskriːn/ *adjective* describes a very wide cinema or television screen which shows very clear pictures ***widescreen TV***

widespread /ˈwaɪdspred/ *adjective* affecting or including a lot of places, people, etc *a **widespread problem.*** ○ *widespread support*

widow /ˈwɪdəʊ/ *noun* [C] **1** a woman whose husband has died **2** in printing, the last line of a paragraph, separated from the rest which is on the page before

widowed /ˈwɪdəʊd/ *adjective* If someone is widowed, their husband or wife has died.

widower /ˈwɪdəʊəʳ/ *noun* [C] **SOCIETY** a man whose wife has died

WORD PARTNERS FOR ***width***

the width **of** sth • [1 metre/5 feet, etc] **in** width • the **full** width of sth

width /wɪtθ/ *noun* **1 MEASURES** [C, U] the distance from one side of something to the other side *a **width of** 2 metres* ○ *height, length, and width* ⊃See picture at **length 2 SPORT** [C] the distance across the shorter side of a swimming pool when you swim across it

wield /wiːld/ *verb* [T] **1** to hold a weapon or tool and look as if you are going to use it *They were confronted by a man wielding a knife.* **2 wield influence/power, etc** to have a lot of influence or power over other people

wiener /ˈwiːnəʳ/ *noun* [C] *US* **FOOD** a long thin sausage (= tube of meat and spices) that is usually eaten in bread

O- **wife** /waɪf/ *noun* [C] *plural* **wives** /waɪvz/ the woman that a man is married to *I've never met William's wife.*

wi-fi /ˈwaɪfaɪ/ *noun* [U] **COMPUTING** a system for connecting electronic equipment such as computers and electronic organizers to the Internet without using wires

wig /wɪg/ *noun* [C] a covering of real or artificial hair that you wear on your head *She was **wearing** a blonde **wig**.*

wiggle /ˈwɪgl/ *verb* [I, T] to make small movements from side to side or to make something else move from side to side *He was wiggling his hips to the music.* •**wiggle** *noun* [**no plural**]

O- **wild**[1] /waɪld/ *adjective* **1 BIOLOGY, ENVIRONMENT** A wild animal or plant lives or grows in its natural environment and not where people live. *a wild dog* ○ ***wild flowers*** **2** LAND Wild land is in a completely natural state. *a wild garden* **3** ENERGETIC very energetic and not controlled *a wild party* ○ *wild dancing* **4** WEATHER with a lot of wind, rain, etc *a wild and stormy*

W

night **5 a wild accusation/guess/rumour, etc** something that you say which is not based on facts and is probably wrong **6 be wild about sth** *informal* to be very enthusiastic about something *He's wild about jazz.* **7 run wild** If someone, especially a child, runs wild, they behave as they want to and no one controls them. •**wildness** *noun* [U] ⊃See also: beyond your wildest dreams (**dream**[1])

wild² /waɪld/ *noun* **1 in the wild** in a natural environment *Animals are better off in the wild than in a zoo.* **2 the wilds** an area which is far from where people usually live *the wilds of Alaska*

ˌwild ˈboar *noun* [C] a wild pig

ˈwild ˌcard *noun* [C] someone or something that you know nothing about *a **wild-card candidate** in the election*

wildcard /ˈwaɪldˌkɑːd/ *noun* [C] **COMPUTING** a sign that is used to represent any letters, numbers or symbols *a **wildcard search***

wilderness /ˈwɪldənəs/ *noun* [C] **GEOGRAPHY** a place that is in a completely natural state without houses, industry, roads, etc [**usually singular**] *a beautiful mountain wilderness*

wildlife /ˈwaɪldlaɪf/ *noun* [U] **ENVIRONMENT, BIOLOGY** animals, birds, and plants living in their natural environment *a wildlife park*

wildly /ˈwaɪldli/ *adverb* **1** [ENERGETICALLY] in a very energetic way and without control *They cheered wildly.* **2** [EXTREMELY] extremely *It hasn't been wildly successful.*

wiles /waɪlz/ *noun* [**plural**] tricks or clever ways of making other people do what you want *I'll use my **womanly wiles**.*

wilful *UK* (*US* **willful**) /ˈwɪlfəl/ *adjective* doing what you want to do, although you are not allowed to or other people tell you not to *wilful disobedience* •**wilfully** *adverb*

O━ **will¹** *strong form* /wɪl/ *weak forms* /wəl, əl/ *modal verb* **1** [FUTURE] used to talk about what is going to happen in the future, especially things that you are certain about *Claire will be five next month.* ○ *I'll see him on Saturday.* ○ *She'll have a great time.* ⊃See Common Learner Error at **shall 2** [ABLE/WILLING] used to talk about what someone or something is willing or able to do *Ask Susie if she'll take them.* ○ *I've asked her but she won't come.* ○ *The car won't start.* **3** [ASK] used to ask someone to do something or to politely offer something to someone *Will you give me her address?* ○ *Will you have a drink with us, Phil?* **4** [IF] used in conditional sentences that start with 'if' and use the present tense *If he's late again I'll be very angry.* **5** [HAPPENING OFTEN] used to talk about something that often happens, especially something annoying *Accidents will happen.* ○ *He will keep talking when I'm trying to concentrate.* **6 it/that will be** *mainly UK* used to talk about what is probably true *That will be his mother with him.* ⊃See Extra help page **Modal verbs** on page Centre 34.

WORD PARTNERS FOR ***will***

make/write a will • **in** sb's will • **leave** sb sth in your will

will² /wɪl/ *noun* **1** [MENTAL POWER] [**C, U**] the mental power to control your thoughts and actions or to succeed in doing something difficult *She has a very strong will.* [**+ to do sth**] *He lacks the will to win.* **2** [WANT] [**no plural**] what someone wants *She was forced to marry him **against** her **will**.* **3** [DOCUMENT] [**C**] a legal document that gives instructions about what should happen to your money and possessions after you die *She left me some money **in** her **will**.* ⊃See also: **free will, ill will**

willful /ˈwɪlfəl/ *adjective US spelling of* wilful

O━ **willing** /ˈwɪlɪŋ/ *adjective* **1 be willing to do sth** to be happy to do something, if you need to *He's willing to pay a lot of money for that house.* **2** wanting to do something *He is a very willing assistant.* ⊃Opposite **unwilling** •**willingly** *adverb He would willingly risk his life for her.* •**willingness** *noun* [U]

willow /ˈwɪləʊ/ *noun* [C] a tree with long, thin leaves that grows near water

willowy /ˈwɪləʊi/ *adjective* tall and attractively thin *a willowy blonde*

willpower /ˈwɪlpaʊəʳ/ *noun* [U] the ability to make yourself do difficult things or to stop yourself from doing enjoyable things that are bad for you *It takes great willpower to lose weight.*

wilt /wɪlt/ *verb* [I] If a plant wilts, it starts to bend because it is dying or needs water.

wily /ˈwaɪli/ *adjective* good at getting what you want, especially by deceiving people

wimp /wɪmp/ *noun* [C] *informal* someone who is not brave and tries to avoid dangerous or difficult situations *I'm too much of a wimp to go rock climbing.* •**wimpy** *adjective informal*

WORD PARTNERS FOR ***win (noun)***

a **comfortable/convincing/emphatic** win • a win **against/over** sb • a win **for** sb

O━ **win¹** /wɪn/ *verb* **winning**, *past* **won 1** [COMPETITION] [**I, T**] to get the most points in a competition or game, or the most votes in an election *Barcelona won the game 6-0.* ○ *Who do you think will win the election?* **2** [ARGUMENT] [**I, T**] to be successful in a war, fight, or argument *Protesters have won their battle to stop the road being built.* **3** [PRIZE] [**T**] to get a prize in a game or competition *He won $500.* ○ *She won a gold medal at the Olympics.* **4 win approval/respect/support, etc** to get approval/respect/support, etc because of your skill and hard work *Her plans have won the support of many local people.* **5 sb can't win** *informal* used to say that nothing someone does in a situation will succeed or please people *Whatever I do seems to annoy her - I just can't win.*

win sb over *phrasal verb* to persuade someone to support you or agree with you

COMMON LEARNER ERROR

win or **beat?**

You **win** a game or competition.

Who do you think will win the football game?

You **beat** someone, or a team you are playing against.

We beat both teams.

~~*We won both teams.*~~

W

win² /wɪn/ *noun* [C] when someone wins a game or competition *The Jets have only had three wins this season.*

wince /wɪns/ *verb* [I] to suddenly look as if you are suffering because you feel pain or because you see or think about something unpleasant *It makes me wince just to think about eye operations.*

winch /wɪnʃ/ *noun* [C] a machine with a thick chain, used for lifting heavy things •**winch** *verb* [T] to lift someone or something with a winch *The injured climber was **winched to safety** by a helicopter.*

WORD PARTNERS FOR ***wind***

the wind **blows** • a **gust of** wind • a **biting/light/strong** wind • **high** winds • **in** the wind

wind¹ /wɪnd/ *noun* **1** [C, U] a natural, fast movement of air *The weather forecast said there would be **strong winds** and rain.* **2 HEALTH** [U] *UK* (*US* **gas**) gas or air in your stomach that makes you feel uncomfortable and sometimes makes noises **3 get wind of sth** to discover something that is intended to be a secret *Dad got wind of our plans for a party.* **4 get your wind (back)** to breathe easily again, for example after you have been running ➲See also: throw **caution**¹ to the wind, **second wind**

wind² /wɪnd/ *verb* [T] to make someone have difficulty breathing, often by hitting them in the stomach

wind³ /waɪnd/ *verb past* **wound 1 wind sth around/round, etc sth** to turn or twist something long and thin around something else several times *She wound the rope around the tree.* ➲Opposite **unwind 2 wind (up) a clock/toy/watch, etc** to make a clock/toy/watch, etc work by turning a small handle or button several times *Did you remember to wind the alarm clock?* **3 wind along/down/through, etc** If a river, road, etc winds somewhere, it bends a lot and is not straight. *The path winds along the edge of the bay.*

wind (sth) down *phrasal verb* to gradually end, or to make something gradually end *to wind down a business*

wind down *phrasal verb* (*also* **unwind**) to gradually relax after doing something that has made you tired or worried

wind up *phrasal verb* to finally be somewhere or do something, especially without having planned it *If he carries on like this, he'll wind up in prison.* [+ **doing sth**] *I wound up having to start the course from the beginning again.*

wind (sth) up *phrasal verb* to end, or to make something end *It's time to wind up the game now.*

wind sb up *phrasal verb UK informal* **1** JOKE to tell someone something that is not true, as a joke *Have I really won or are you winding me up?* **2** ANNOY to annoy someone *He keeps complaining and it really winds me up.*

windfall /ˈwɪndfɔːl/ *noun* [C] **FINANCE** an amount of money that you get that you did not expect *Investors each received a windfall of £1000.*

winding /ˈwaɪndɪŋ/ *adjective* **a winding path/road/street, etc** a path/road, etc that bends a lot and is not straight

ˈwind ˌinstrument *noun* [C] **MUSIC** a musical instrument that you play by blowing into it *A flute is a wind instrument.*

windmill /ˈwɪndmɪl/ *noun* [C] a building with long parts at the top that turn in the wind, used for producing power or crushing grain

window /ˈwɪndəʊ/ *noun* [C] **1** a space in the wall of a building or vehicle that has glass in it, used for letting light and air inside and for looking through ***Open the window*** *if you're too hot.* ○ *I could see the children's faces **at the window**.* ○ *a **window frame/ledge*** ➲See colour picture **The Living Room** on page Centre 4 **2 COMPUTING** a separate area on a computer screen showing information and which you can move around *to minimize/maximize a window* ➲See also: **French windows**

windowpane /ˈwɪndəʊpeɪn/ *noun* [C] a piece of glass in a window

ˈwindow ˌshopping *noun* [U] when you look at things in shops but do not buy anything

windowsill /ˈwɪndəʊsɪl/ *noun* [C] a shelf at the bottom of a window ➲See colour picture **The Living Room** on page Centre 4

windpipe /ˈwɪndpaɪp/ *noun* [C] **ANATOMY** the tube that carries air from your throat to your lungs

windscreen /ˈwɪndskriːn/ *UK* (*US* **windshield** /ˈwɪndʃiːld/) *noun* [C] the window at the front end of a car, bus, etc ➲See colour picture **Car** on page Centre 7

ˈwindscreen ˌwiper *UK* (*US* **ˈwindshieldˌwiper**) *noun* [C] one of two long, metal and rubber parts that move against a windscreen to remove rain ➲See colour picture **Car** on page Centre 7

windsurfing /ˈwɪndsɜːfɪŋ/ *noun* [U] **SPORT** a sport in which you sail across water by standing on a board and holding onto a large sail •**windsurfer** *noun* [C]

windswept /ˈwɪndswept/ *adjective* **1** PLACE A windswept place often has strong winds. *a remote, windswept hill* **2** PERSON looking untidy because you have been in the wind *windswept hair*

ˈwind ˌturbine *noun* [C] **ENVIRONMENT, PHYSICS** a machine with long parts at the top that are turned by the wind, used to make electricity ➲See picture **wind turbine** on next page

windy /ˈwɪndi/ *adjective* with a lot of wind *a windy day* ○ *Outside it was cold and windy.*

wine /waɪn/ *noun* [C, U] **FOOD** an alcoholic drink that is made from the juice of grapes (= small, green or purple fruit), or sometimes other fruit *a **glass of wine*** ○ ***red/white wine***

WORD PARTNERS FOR ***wine***

a **bottle of/glass of** wine • **dry/red/sparkling/sweet/white** wine

wing /wɪŋ/ *noun* [C] **1 BIOLOGY** one of the two parts that a bird or insect uses to fly **2** AIRCRAFT one of the two long, flat parts at the sides of an aircraft that make it stay in the sky **3** CAR *UK* (*US* **fender**) one of the parts at each corner of a car above the wheels **4** BUILDING a part of a large building that is joined to the side of the main part *Their offices are in the West wing.* **5 POLITICS** a group of people in an organization

W

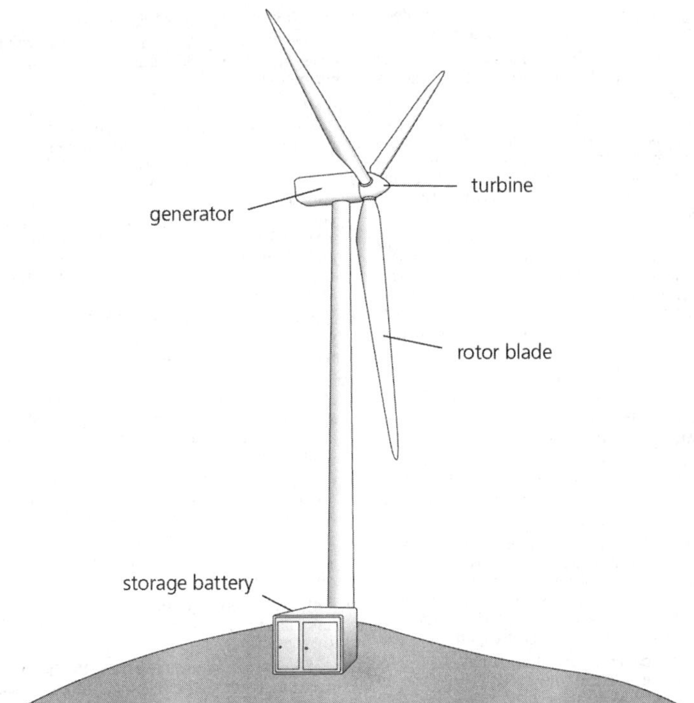

wind turbine

or political party who have the same beliefs *the nationalist wing of the party* **6 take sb under your wing** to help and protect someone who is younger than you or who has less experience than you

winged /wɪŋd/ *adjective* **BIOLOGY** with wings *a winged insect*

ˈwing ˌmirror *UK* (*US* **side mirror**) *noun* [**C**] a small mirror on the side of a car or truck ➲See colour picture **Car** on page Centre 7

the wings /wɪŋz/ *noun* [**plural**] **1** the area behind the sides of a stage where actors wait just before they perform **2 be waiting in the wings** to be ready to do something or be used at any time

wink¹ /wɪŋk/ *verb* [**I**] to quickly close and then open one eye, in order to be friendly or to show that something is a joke *She smiled and **winked at** me.*

wink² /wɪŋk/ *noun* [**C**] **1** when you wink at someone *He gave me a friendly wink.* **2 not sleep a wink** to not have any sleep *I was so excited last night - I didn't sleep a wink.*

O-- **winner** /ˈwɪnəʳ/ *noun* [**C**] someone who wins a game, competition, or election *the winners of the World Cup*

winnings /ˈwɪnɪŋz/ *noun* [**plural**] money that you win in a competition

WORD PARTNERS FOR ***winter***

in (the) winter • a **cold/severe** winter • a **mild** winter • **last/next** winter • the winter **months**

O-- **winter** /ˈwɪntəʳ/ *noun* [**C, U**] the coldest season of the year, between autumn and spring *We went skiing **last winter**.* ○ *a **mild winter***
•**wintry** /ˈwɪntri/ *adjective* cold and typical of winter ***wintry showers*** (= snow mixed with rain) ➲See also: the **dead³** of night/winter

win-win /ˈwɪnwɪn/ *adjective* A win-win situation is one in which something good happens to everyone.

wipe¹ /waɪp/ *verb* [**T**] **1** to clean or dry something by moving a cloth across it *I had a job wiping tables in a cafe.* ○ *She wiped her hands on the towel.* **2 wipe sth from/away/off, etc** to remove dirt, water, a mark, etc from something with a cloth or your hand *He wiped a tear from his eye.*

wipe sth out *phrasal verb* to destroy something completely *The earthquake wiped out many villages.*

wipe sth up *phrasal verb* to remove a substance, usually liquid, with a cloth *Have you got something I could wipe this mess up with?*

wipe² /waɪp/ *noun* [**C**] **1** CLEAN/DRY when you clean or dry something with a cloth *I'll give*

W

the table ***a wipe.*** **2** CLOTH a thin cloth or piece of paper used for cleaning ***baby wipes***

wiper /ˈwaɪpəʳ/ (*also* **windscreen wiper**) *noun* [C] a long, metal and rubber part that removes rain from the front window of a vehicle

wire¹ /waɪəʳ/ *noun* **1** METAL [C, U] thin, metal thread, used to fasten things or to make fences, cages, etc **2** ELECTRICITY [C] a long, thin piece of metal thread, usually covered in plastic, that carries electricity *electrical wires* ➲See also: **barbed wire**

wire² /waɪəʳ/ *verb* [T] **1** ELECTRICITY (*also* **wire up**) to connect wires so that a piece of electrical equipment will work *Do you know how to wire a burglar alarm?* **2** JOIN to join two things together using wire **3** SEND *US* to send a message or money using an electrical communication system

wireless /ˈwaɪələs/ *adjective* without a cable

wiring /ˈwaɪərɪŋ/ *noun* [U] the system of wires that carry electricity around a building *The fire was caused by* ***faulty wiring.***

wiry /ˈwaɪəri/ *adjective* **1** PERSON Someone who is wiry is strong but quite thin. **2** HAIR Wiry hair is thick and stiff, like wire. *a wiry beard*

wisdom /ˈwɪzdəm/ *noun* **1** [U] the ability to use your knowledge and experience to make good decisions and judgments **2 the wisdom of sth/doing sth** If you doubt the wisdom of something, you think it is probably not a good plan. *Many people have questioned the wisdom of spending so much money on weapons.*

ˈwisdom ˌtooth *noun* [C] *plural* **wisdom teeth** **ANATOMY** one of the four teeth at the back of your mouth that are the last to grow

wise¹ /waɪz/ *adjective* **1** DECISION A wise decision or action shows good judgment and is the right thing to do. *I think we've made a wise choice.* [+ **to do sth**] *It's always wise to see a doctor if you're worried about your health.* ➲Opposite **unwise** **2** PERSON A wise person is able to use their knowledge and experience to make good decisions and give good advice. **3 be none the wiser** *informal* to still not understand something after someone has tried to explain it to you •**wisely** *adverb*

-wise /-waɪz/ *suffix* changes a noun into an adverb meaning 'relating to this subject' *Weather-wise, the holiday was great.* ○ *How are we doing time-wise?*

wise² /waɪz/ *verb*

wise up *phrasal verb informal* to start to understand the truth about a situation *Employers are starting to* ***wise up to*** *the fact that people want flexible working hours.*

W

wish¹ /wɪʃ/ *verb* **1 wish (that)** to want a situation that is different from the one that exists *I wish that I didn't have to go to work.* ○ *I* ***wish*** *he* ***would*** *leave.* ○ *I* ***wish*** *I* ***had*** *been there.* **2 wish to do sth** *formal* to want to do something *I wish to speak to the manager.* **3 wish sb luck/success, etc** to say that you hope someone will be lucky, successful, etc *I wished him luck for his test.* **4 I/you wish!** *informal* used to say that you would like something to be true although you know it is not true *"Have your exams finished yet?" "I wish!"*

WORD PARTNERS FOR ***wish*** *(noun)*

ignore/respect sb's wishes • **get your wish** • **have no** wish to do sth • **according to/against** sb's wishes

wish² /wɪʃ/ *noun* [C] **1** WANT what you want to do or what you want to happen *The hospital always tries to* ***respect*** *the* ***wishes*** *of its patients.* ○ *I* ***have no wish*** *to travel the world.* **2** SECRET something that you say secretly to yourself about what you want to have or happen *She closed her eyes and* ***made a wish.*** **3 best wishes** something you say or write at the end of a letter, to show that you hope someone is happy and has good luck *Please give her my best wishes when you see her.*

wishful thinking /ˌwɪʃfəlˈθɪŋkɪŋ/ *noun* [U] when you want something to happen or be true but it is impossible

wisp /wɪsp/ *noun* [C] **1 a wisp of cloud/smoke/steam** a small, thin line of cloud/smoke/steam **2 a wisp of hair/grass, etc** a thin piece of hair/grass, etc •**wispy** *adjective* in the form of wisps ***wispy hair*** ○ *a* ***wispy cloud***

wistful /ˈwɪstfəl/ *adjective* slightly sad because you are thinking about something you cannot have *a* ***wistful look/smile*** •**wistfully** *adverb*

wit /wɪt/ *noun* [U] the ability to say things that are funny and clever *a woman of great intelligence and wit*

witch /wɪtʃ/ *noun* [C] in stories, a woman who has magical powers that she uses to do bad or strange things

witchcraft /ˈwɪtʃkrɑːft/ *noun* [U] the use of magic to make bad or strange things happen

witch-hunt /ˈwɪtʃhʌnt/ *noun* [C] when a group of people try to blame someone and punish them for something, in a way that is unfair

with /wɪð/ *preposition* **1** TOGETHER used to say that people or things are in a place together or are doing something together *Emma lives with her boyfriend.* ○ *Hang your coat with the others.* **2** HAVING having or including something *a house with a swimming pool* ○ *a woman with brown eyes* **3** USING using something *She hit him over the head with a tennis racket.* **4** HOW used to describe the way someone does something *He plays with great enthusiasm.* ○ *She shut the drawer with a bang.* **5** WHAT used to say what fills, covers, etc something *a bucket filled with water* ○ *shoes covered with mud* **6** CAUSE because of something *She was trembling with fear.* **7** RELATING TO relating to something or someone *There's something wrong with the car.* ○ *The doctors are very pleased with his progress.* **8** POSITION used to describe the position of someone's body *She sat with her legs crossed.* **9 be with me/you** *informal* to understand what someone is saying *Sorry, I'm not with you - can you say that again?*

withdraw /wɪðˈdrɔː/ *verb past tense* **withdrew**, *past participle* **withdrawn** **1 FINANCE** [T] to take money out of a bank account *She withdrew $50.* **2** REMOVE [T] to remove something, especially because of an official decision *This product has been* ***withdrawn from*** *sale.* ○ *He has threatened to withdraw his support.* **3** MILITARY [I, T] If a military force withdraws, or if someone withdraws it, it leaves the place where it is fighting. *The President has ordered troops to be **withdrawn from** the area.* **4** COMPETITION **[I]** to decide that you will not now be in a race, competition, etc *Christie was forced to **withdraw from** the race because of injury.* **5** SOMETHING SAID **[T]** *formal* to say that you want people to ignore something you said before because it was not true *He admitted taking the money, but later **withdrew** his **confession**.*

withdrawal /wɪð'drɔːəl/ *noun* **1** FINANCE **[C]** when you take money out of a bank account *This account allows you to **make withdrawals** whenever you want to.* **2** STOP **[C, U]** when someone stops doing something, for example helping someone or giving money **[usually singular]** *the withdrawal of financial support* **3** MILITARY **[C, U]** when a military force moves out of an area **[usually singular]** *the withdrawal of troops* **4** HEALTH **[U]** the unpleasant feelings that someone gets when they stop taking a drug that they have taken for a long time ***withdrawal symptoms*** **5** ALONE **[U]** when someone prefers to be alone and does not want to talk to other people *Withdrawal can be a symptom of depression.*

withdrawn /wɪð'drɔːn/ *adjective* **[never before noun]** quiet and not talking to other people

wither /'wɪðəʳ/ (*also* **wither away**) *verb* **[I]** If a plant withers, it becomes dry and starts to die.

withering /'wɪðərɪŋ/ *adjective* **withering attack/contempt/look** criticism or an expression that shows that someone strongly disapproves of someone or something *He published a withering attack on the government's policies.*

withhold /wɪð'həʊld/ *verb* **[T]** *past* **withheld** to not give someone the information, money, etc that they want *The company has decided to **withhold payment** until the job has been finished.*

O— **within¹** /wɪ'ðɪn/ *preposition* **1** TIME before a particular period of time has finished *The ambulance arrived within 10 minutes.* ○ *Consume within two days of purchase.* **2** DISTANCE less than a particular distance from something *She was born within 20 miles of New York.* ○ *The hotel is **within easy reach of*** (= near) *the airport.* **3** INSIDE inside an area, group or system *a dispute within the department* ○ *There's a pharmacy within the hospital building.* **4** LIMIT not outside the limits of something *The project was completed well within budget.* **5 within the law/the rules/your rights, etc** allowed according to the law/the rules/your rights, etc *You're perfectly within your rights to complain.*

within² /wɪ'ðɪn/ *adverb* inside someone or something *The organization needs to change from within.*

O— **without** /wɪ'ðaʊt/ *preposition* **1** NOT HAVING not having, using, or doing something *I did the test without any problems.* ○ *I can't see without my glasses.* ○ *He went to school without eating any breakfast.* **2** NOT PRESENT when someone is not with someone else *You can start the meeting without me.* **3 go/do without (sth)** to not have something important *They went without sleep for three days.*

withstand /wɪð'stænd/ *verb* **[T]** *past* **withstood** to not be damaged or broken by something *a bridge designed to withstand earthquakes*

WORD PARTNERS FOR ***witness***

appeal for a witness • a witness **to sth** • a **character/key** witness • a witness **account/testimony**

O— **witness¹** /'wɪtnəs/ *noun* **[C]** **1** COURT someone in a court of law who says what they have seen and what they know about a crime *The witness was called to the stand.* **2** SEE someone who sees an accident or crime *Police are appealing for **witnesses to** the shooting.* **3** LAW someone who signs their name on an official document to say that they were present when someone else signed it

witness² /'wɪtnəs/ *verb* **[T]** LAW **1** to see something happen, especially an accident or crime *Did anyone witness the attack?* **2** to sign your name on an official document to say that you were present when someone else signed it

'witness ˌbox *UK* (*UK/US* **'witness ˌstand**) *noun* **[C]** LAW the place in a court of law where a witness stands or sits when they are answering questions

wits /wɪts/ *noun* **[plural]** **1** intelligence and the ability to think quickly **2 keep/have your wits about you** to be ready to think quickly in a situation and react to things that you are not expecting *You have to keep your wits about you when you're cycling.* **3 be at your wits' end** to be very worried about something and not know what you should do next **4 scare/frighten sb out of their wits** to make someone very frightened

witty /'wɪti/ *adjective* using words in a funny and clever way *a witty comment* ○ *He was witty and charming.*

wives /waɪvz/ *plural of* wife

wizard /'wɪzəd/ *noun* **[C]** **1** MAGIC in stories, a man who has magical powers **2** SKILL *informal* someone who is very good at something or knows a lot about something *a computer wizard* **3** COMPUTING a computer program that gives the user a series of questions or instructions to help them use a particular system

WMD /ˌdʌbəljuːem'diː/ *noun* **[plural]** *abbreviation for* weapons of mass destruction: weapons, such as nuclear bombs, which cause a lot of damage and death when used

wobble /'wɒbl/ *verb* **[I, T]** If something wobbles or you make something wobble, it moves from side to side, often because it is not on a flat surface. *The ladder started to wobble.* ○ *Stop wobbling the table.* •**wobbly** *adjective* likely to wobble *a **wobbly chair***

woe /wəʊ/ *noun* **[U]** *literary* sadness *full of woe*

woeful /'wəʊfəl/ *adjective* very bad and showing no skill *a woeful attempt/performance* •**woefully** *adverb*

woes /wəʊz/ *noun* **[plural]** *formal* **your woes** your problems and worries

wok /wɒk/ *noun* **[C]** a large, bowl-shaped pan that is used for frying Chinese food

woke /wəʊk/ *past tense of* wake

woken /'wəʊkən/ *past participle of* wake

W

wolf¹ /wʊlf/ *noun* [C] *plural* **wolves** /wʊlvz/ a wild animal like a large dog

wolf² /wʊlf/ (*also* **wolf down**) *verb* [T] *informal* to eat something very quickly *I gave her a plate of pasta and she wolfed it down.*

woman /ˈwʊmən/ *noun* [C] *plural* **women** /ˈwɪmɪn/ an adult female person *a 30-year-old woman* ○ *There were two women at the bus stop.* •**womanhood** *noun* [U] the state of being a woman

womanly /ˈwʊmənli/ *adjective* having the qualities and appearance that people think a woman should have *womanly charms*

womb /wuːm/ *noun* [C] **ANATOMY** the organ inside a woman's body where a baby grows

women /ˈwɪmɪn/ *plural of* woman

won /wɒn/ *past of* win

wonder¹ /ˈwʌndəʳ/ *verb* **1** [I, T] to want to know something or to try to understand the reason for something [+ **question word**] *I wonder what he's making for dinner.* ○ *I wonder why she left so suddenly.* **2 I/we wonder if/whether ...** used to politely ask someone for something or to suggest something *I wonder if you could help me?* ○ *We were wondering if you'd like to come over for a meal sometime.*

wonder² /ˈwʌndəʳ/ *noun* **1** ADMIRATION [U] surprise and admiration *The boys gazed **in wonder** at the shiny, red Ferrari.* **2** THING [C] something that makes you feel surprise or admiration [**usually plural**] ***the wonders of** modern medicine* **3 no wonder** used to say that you are not surprised about something *No wonder she failed the test if she didn't do any work.* **4 it's a wonder (that)** used to say that you are surprised about something *It's a wonder he's still alive.*

wonderful /ˈwʌndəfəl/ *adjective* very good *a wonderful idea* ○ *We had a wonderful time in Spain.* •**wonderfully** *adverb*

won't /wəʊnt/ *short for* will not *I won't be home before midnight.*

woo /wuː/ *verb* [T] **wooing**, *past* **wooed** to try to persuade someone to support you or to use your business *a political party trying to woo young voters*

wood /wʊd/ *noun* **1** MATERIAL [C, U] the hard material that trees are made of *a piece of wood* **2** AREA [C] (*also* **woods**) a large area of trees growing near each other *We went for a walk in the woods.*

wooded /ˈwʊdɪd/ *adjective* covered with trees *a wooded area*

wooden /ˈwʊdən/ *adjective* made of wood *a wooden chair*

woodland /ˈwʊdlənd/ *noun* [C, U] **GEOGRAPHY** an area of land with a lot of trees

woodwind /ˈwʊdwɪnd/ *noun* [U] **MUSIC** the group of musical instruments that you play by blowing into them ***woodwind instruments***

woodwork /ˈwʊdwɜːk/ *noun* [U] **1** PARTS the parts of a building that are made from wood **2** **DT** the activity of making things from wood

woof /wʊf/ *noun* [C] the sound made by a dog

wool /wʊl/ *noun* [U] **1** SHEEP the soft, thick hair on a sheep **2** **DT** thick thread or material that is made from the hair of a sheep *a wool suit* ○ *a ball of wool* ➲See also: **cotton wool**

woollen *UK* (*US* **woolen**) /ˈwʊlən/ *adjective* made of wool *woollen gloves*

woolly *UK* (*US* **wooly**) /ˈwʊli/ *adjective* made of wool, or made of something that looks like wool *a green woolly hat*

word¹ /wɜːd/ *noun* **1** **LANGUAGE** [C] a group of letters or sounds that mean something, or a single letter or sound that means something *'Hund' is the German word for 'dog'.* ○ *He has difficulty spelling long words.* **2 not believe/understand/hear, etc a word** to not believe/understand/hear, etc anything *I don't believe a word he says.* **3 a word of warning/advice/thanks, etc** something that you say to warn someone, give them advice, thank them, etc *Just a word of warning - he doesn't like people being late.* **4 have a word with sb** to talk to someone for a short time *I'll have a word with Ted and see if he wants to come.* **5 put in a good word for sb** to praise someone, often to someone who might be able to employ them **6 give sb your word** to promise someone something *He gave me his word that he wouldn't tell anyone.* **7 take sb's word for it** to believe what someone says without any proof **8 in other words** used to explain what something means in a different way *He said he's too busy, in other words, he isn't interested.* **9 in sb's words** used when you repeat what someone said *In the manager's words, the game was 'a total disaster'.* **10 word for word** using the exact words that were originally used *She repeated word for word what he had told her.* **11 have the last word** to say the last thing in a discussion or argument or make the final decision about something **12 not breathe a word** to not tell people a secret *Don't breathe a word about this to anyone.* **13 not get a word in edgeways** *UK* (*US* **not get a word in edgewise**) to be unable to say anything because someone else is talking so much ➲See also: a **play²** on words, **swear word**

word² /wɜːd/ *verb* [T] to choose the words you use when you are saying or writing something *How should I word this letter?*

> WORD PARTNERS FOR ***wording***
>
> **change** the wording • the **exact** wording • the wording **of** sth • a **form of** wording

wording /ˈwɜːdɪŋ/ *noun* [U] **LANGUAGE** the words that are used when someone says or writes something

ˌword ˈprocessor *noun* [C] **COMPUTING** a computer or computer program that you use for writing letters, reports, etc •**word processing** *noun* [U]

wore /wɔːʳ/ *past tense of* wear

work¹ /wɜːk/ *verb* **1** JOB [I, T] to do a job, especially the job you do to earn money *Helen **works for** a computer company.* ○ *He **works as** a waiter in an Italian restaurant.* ○ *My dad works very long hours* (= he works a lot of hours). **2** MACHINE [I] If a machine or piece of equipment works, it is not broken. *Does this radio work?* ○ *The washing machine isn't working.* **3** SUCCEED [I] If something works, it is

W

effective and successful. *Her plan to get rid of me didn't work.* **4 can work sth; know how to work sth** to know how to use a machine or piece of equipment *Do you know how to work the video recorder?* **5** EFFORT [I, T] to do something that needs a lot of time or effort, or to make someone do this [+ **to do sth**] *He's been working to improve his speed.* ○ *Our teacher works us very hard.* **6 work your way around/through/up, etc sth** to achieve something gradually *I have a pile of homework to work my way through.*

work against sb *phrasal verb* to make it more difficult for someone to achieve something *Age can work against you when you are looking for a job.*

work at sth *phrasal verb* to try hard to achieve something [+ **doing sth**] You need to work at improving your writing.

work on sth *phrasal verb* to spend time repairing or improving something *Tim loves working on old cars.*

work sth out *phrasal verb* **1 MATHEMATICS** to calculate an amount *I'm trying to work out the total cost.* **2** THINK to understand something or decide something after thinking very carefully [+ **question word**] *I haven't worked out what to do yet.*

work out *phrasal verb* **1** PROBLEM If a problem or difficult situation works out, it gradually becomes better. *Don't worry - everything will work out in the end.* **2 SPORT** to do exercises to make your body stronger ➲See colour picture **Phrasal Verbs** on page Centre 16 **3 work out badly/well, etc** to happen or develop in a particular way *Changing schools worked out really well for me.* **4 work out at sth** to be the result when you calculate something *If we share the costs, it works out at $10 per person.*

work sb out *phrasal verb UK* to understand the reasons for someone's behaviour *I can't work him out at all.*

work up to sth *phrasal verb* to gradually prepare yourself for something difficult

WORD PARTNERS FOR ***work***

do/find/finish/have work • **clerical/dirty/hard/part-time/pioneering** work • **at** work

O‑ **work²** /wɜːk/ *noun* **1** EFFORT [U] when you use physical or mental effort to do something *Decorating that room was **hard work**.* **2** PLACE [U] the place where you go to do your job *He had an accident **at work**.* **3** JOB [U] something you do as a job to earn money *Has she got any work yet?* ○ *Many young people are **out of work*** (= they do not have a job). **4** ACTIVITY [U] the activities that you have to do at school, for your job, etc *Have you got a lot of work to do?* ○ *The teacher said she was pleased with my work.* **5 get/set to work (on sth)** to start doing something **6 ART, LITERATURE, MUSIC** [C, U] a painting, book, piece of music, etc *The exhibition includes works by Picasso and Klee.* ○ *the **complete works** of Shakespeare* **7 do sb's dirty work** to do something unpleasant or difficult for someone else because they do not want to do it themselves **8 have your work cut out** to have something very difficult to do *It's a demanding job - she's going to have her work cut out for her.* ➲See also: **donkey work, work of art**

COMMON LEARNER ERROR

work, job or **occupation?**

Work is something you do to earn money. Remember that this noun is uncountable.

She enjoys her work in the hospital.

He's looking for work.

~~*He's looking for a work.*~~

Job is used to talk about the particular work activity which you do.

He's looking for a job in computer programming.

Teaching must be an interesting job.

~~*Teaching must be an interesting work.*~~

Occupation is a formal word which means the job that you do. It is often used on forms. See also: **career** and **profession**.

workable /ˈwɜːkəbl/ *adjective* A workable plan or system can be used or done easily and is effective. ➲Opposite **unworkable**

workaholic /ˌwɜːkəˈhɒlɪk/ *noun* [C] *informal* someone who works too much and does not have time to do anything else

workbook /ˈwɜːkbʊk/ *noun* [C] **EDUCATION** a book with questions and exercises in it that you use when you are learning something

ˌworked ˈup *adjective* very nervous, angry, or excited

worker /ˈwɜːkəʳ/ *noun* **1** [C] someone who works for a company or organization but does not have a powerful position *an office worker* **2 a quick/slow/good, etc worker** someone who works quickly/slowly/well, etc ➲See also: **social worker**

workforce /ˈwɜːkfɔːs/ *noun* [**group**] **1** COMPANY all the people who work for a company or organization **2** COUNTRY all the people in a country who are able to do a job *10% of the workforce are unemployed.*

working /ˈwɜːkɪŋ/ *adjective* [**always before noun**] **1** relating to your job *good working conditions* **2 a working man/woman, etc** someone who has a job *a working mother* **3 a working knowledge of sth** knowledge about something which is good enough to be useful *She has a working knowledge of German and Russian.* ➲See also: **hard-working**

ˌworking ˈcapital *noun* [U] **FINANCE** the amount of money that a company has available to run its business

ˌworking ˈcapital ˌratio *noun* [C **usually singular**] **FINANCE** a calculation that compares the assets (= things owned) of a business that will be changed into money within 12 months with the payments that have to be made in that time

ˌworking ˈclass *noun* [C] **SOCIETY** the social class of people who have little money and who usually do physical work •**working-class** /ˌwɜːkɪŋˈklɑːs/ *adjective a working-class family*

workings /ˈwɜːkɪŋz/ *noun* **the workings of sth** how something works *the workings of the mind*

W

workload /ˈwɜːkləʊd/ *noun* [C] the amount of work that you have to do *Nurses have a very* ***heavy workload*** (= they work hard).

workman /ˈwɜːkmən/ *noun* [C] *plural* **workmen** someone who does a physical job such as building

workmanship /ˈwɜːkmənʃɪp/ *noun* [U] the skill that is used in making something

ˌwork of ˈart *noun* [C] *plural* **works of art** **1** **ART** a very beautiful and important painting, drawing, etc *They stole several valuable works of art.* **2 be a work of art** to be something which is beautiful or needed a lot of skill to create *Have you seen the wedding cake? It's a work of art.*

workout /ˈwɜːkaʊt/ *noun* [C] **SPORT** when you do a series of exercises to make your body strong and healthy *a daily workout at the gym*

workplace /ˈwɜːkpleɪs/ *noun* [C] the place where you work *We are trying to get rid of bullying* ***in the workplace****.*

worksheet /ˈwɜːkˌʃiːt/ *noun* [C] **EDUCATION** a piece of paper with questions and exercises for students

workshop /ˈwɜːkʃɒp/ *noun* [C] **1** **EDUCATION** when a group of people meet to learn more about something by discussing it and doing practical exercises *a workshop on crime prevention* **2** a place where people use tools and machines to make or repair things

workstation /ˈwɜːkˌsteɪʃən/ *noun* [C] **COMPUTING** a computer and the area around it where you work in an office

ˈwork ˌsurface (*also* **worktop** /ˈwɜːktɒp/) *noun* [C] a flat surface for preparing food in a kitchen ⊃See colour picture **The Kitchen** on page Centre 2

work-to-rule /ˌwɜːktəˈruːl/ *noun* [C **usually singular**] **POLITICS** a situation at work in which people do only the work that they agreed to do and nothing extra in order to show that they disagree with something, such as the amount of money they are paid or the hours that they work

WORD PARTNERS FOR ***world***

travel the world • **in** the world • **across/all over** the world

world¹ /wɜːld/ *noun* **1 the world GEOGRAPHY** the Earth and all the people, places, and things on it *Everest is the highest mountain* ***in the world****.* **2** [C] the people and things that are involved in a particular activity or subject [**usually singular**] *the entertainment world* ○ *the world of politics* **3 the developing/industrialized/Western, etc world** a particular area of the Earth **4 the plant/animal, etc world** plants/animals, etc as a group **5 your world** your life and experiences *His whole world fell apart when she left.* **6 do sb a/the world of good** *informal* to make someone feel much happier or healthier *That swim has done me a world of good.* **7 be out of this world** *informal* to be of extremely good quality *Their chocolate cake is just out of this world!* **8 think the world of sb** to like and admire someone very much **9 the whole world** *informal* everyone *The whole world knew she was getting married before I did.* ⊃See also: have the **best³** of both worlds, not be the **end¹** of the world, **the Old World, the outside world, the Third World,** be on **top¹** of the world

world² /wɜːld/ *adjective* [**always before noun**] relating to the whole world *world peace* ○ *the world championships*

the ˌWorld ˈBank *noun* **ECONOMICS** an international organization that lends money to countries that need it

world-class /ˌwɜːldˈklɑːs/ *adjective* one of the best in the world *a world-class swimmer*

world-famous /ˌwɜːldˈfeɪməs/ *adjective* known by people everywhere in the world *The Eiffel Tower is a world-famous landmark.*

worldly /ˈwɜːldli/ *adjective* **1 sb's worldly goods/possessions** everything that someone owns **2** having had a lot of experience of life *a worldly woman*

the ˌWorld ˈTrade Organiˌzation (*abbreviation* **WTO**) *noun* **ECONOMICS** an organization that tries to control international trade and make it easier

ˌworld ˈwar *noun* [C] a war in which several large or important countries fight

worldwide /ˌwɜːldˈwaɪd/ *adjective, adverb* in all parts of the world *10 million copies have been sold worldwide.*

the ˌWorld Wide ˈWeb *noun* **INTERNET** all the websites (= pages of text and pictures) on the Internet ⊃See Extra help page **The Web and the Internet** on page Centre 36.

worm¹ /wɜːm/ *noun* [C] a small creature with a long, thin, soft body and no legs ⊃See also: a **can²** of worms

worm² /wɜːm/ *verb* **worm your way into sth** to gradually get into a situation by making people like you and trust you, especially by deceiving them *He wormed his way into the family.*

worn¹ /wɔːn/ *adjective* Worn clothing or objects have been used a lot and show damage. *a worn leather chair*

worn² /wɔːn/ *past participle of* wear

worn-out /ˌwɔːnˈaʊt/ *adjective* **1** TIRED extremely tired *I was absolutely worn-out after all that dancing.* **2** DAMAGED Something that is worn-out is so old or has been used so much that it is damaged too much to repair. *a worn-out carpet*

worried /ˈwʌrid/ *adjective* anxious because you are thinking about problems or unpleasant things that might happen *She's really* ***worried about*** *her son.* [+ **(that)**] *I'm worried that she'll tell Maria.*

worry¹ /ˈwʌri/ *verb* **1** BE ANXIOUS [I] to think about problems or unpleasant things that might happen in a way that makes you feel anxious ***Don't worry*** *- she'll be all right.* ○ *She's always* ***worrying about*** *something.* [+ **(that)**] *I worry that he might run away.* **2** MAKE ANXIOUS [T] to make someone feel anxious because of problems or unpleasant things that might happen *It worries me that he hasn't phoned yet.*

COMMON LEARNER ERROR

worry about something or **someone**

Be careful to use the correct preposition after this verb.

They were worried about the weather.

~~*They were worried for the weather.*~~

WORD PARTNERS FOR ***worry** (noun)*

allay/ease/express a worry • a **constant/lingering/nagging/real** worry • a worry **about/over** sth

worry² /ˈwʌri/ *noun* **1** PROBLEM [C] a problem that makes you feel anxious *health worries* **2** FEELING [U] when you are anxious about something *She's been sick with worry.*

worrying /ˈwʌriɪŋ/ *adjective* making you feel anxious *a worrying situation* •**worryingly** *adverb She's worryingly thin.*

O→**worse¹** /wɜːs/ *adjective* (*comparative of* bad) **1** LESS GOOD more unpleasant or difficult than something else that is also bad *The exam was **worse than** I expected.* ○ *We'll have to stop the game if the rain **gets** any **worse**.* **2** MORE ILL more ill *The drugs aren't working, he just seems to be **getting worse**.* **3 be none the worse for sth** to not be harmed or damaged by something *He seemed none the worse for the experience.* **4 worse luck** *UK informal* used to show that you are annoyed or unhappy about something *I've got to work on Saturday, worse luck!*

worse² /wɜːs/ *noun* [U] **1** something that is more unpleasant or difficult *It was a nasty accident, although I've seen worse.* **2 for the worse** If a situation changes for the worse, it becomes worse.

worse³ /wɜːs/ *adverb* (*comparative of* badly) less well *He was treated much worse than I was.*

worsen /ˈwɜːsᵊn/ *verb* [I, T] to become worse or to make something become worse *His condition suddenly worsened last week.*

ˌworse ˈoff *adjective* [never before noun] poorer or in a more difficult situation *If Rick loses his job we'll be even worse off.*

worship /ˈwɜːʃɪp/ *verb* **worshipping**, *past* **worshipped**, *also US* **worshiping**, *past* **worshiped** **1** RELIGION [I, T] to show respect for a god by saying prayers or performing religious ceremonies **2** [T] to love and respect someone very much *She worshipped her mother.* •**worship** *noun* [U] *a **place of worship*** (= a religious building) •**worshipper** *noun* [C]

O→**worst¹** /wɜːst/ *adjective* (*superlative of* bad) **the worst** the most unpleasant or difficult *What's the worst job you've ever had?*

worst² /wɜːst/ *noun* **1 the worst** the most unpleasant or difficult thing, person, or situation *I've made some mistakes in the past, but this is definitely the worst.* **2 at worst** used to say what the most unpleasant or difficult situation could possibly be *At worst, we might lose our money.* **3 if the worst comes to the worst** *UK* (*US* **if worse/worst comes to worst**) if a situation develops in the most unpleasant or difficult way

worst³ /wɜːst/ *adverb* (*superlative of* badly) the most badly *the **worst affected** area*

O→**worth¹** /wɜːθ/ *adjective* **1 be worth sth** to have a particular value, especially in money *Our house is worth about £600,000.* **2 be worth doing/seeing/trying, etc** to be useful or enjoyable to do/see/try, etc *It's not as good as his last book but it's definitely worth reading.* **3 be worth it** to be useful or enjoyable despite needing a lot of effort *It was a long climb up the mountain but the view was worth it.* ○ *Don't bother complaining - it's really not worth it.* **4 be worth your while** If it is worth your while doing something, it is useful or enjoyable despite needing a lot of effort. *It isn't worth my while going all that way just for one day.*

COMMON LEARNER ERROR

be worth doing something

When **worth** is followed by a verb, the verb is always in the **-ing** form.

Do you think it's worth asking Patrick first?

~~*Do you think it's worth to ask Patrick first?*~~

O→**worth²** /wɜːθ/ *noun* **1 £20/$100, etc worth of sth** the amount of something that you can buy for £20/$100, etc *I've put £2 worth of stamps on the letter.* **2 a month's/year's, etc worth of sth** the amount of something that can be done or used in a month/year, etc *an hour's worth of free phone calls* **3** [U] how important or useful someone or something is *She's finally proved her worth.*

worthless /ˈwɜːθləs/ *adjective* **1** NOT IMPORTANT not important or useful *He made me feel stupid and worthless.* **2** MONEY having no value in money *The painting's a fake - it's completely worthless.*

worthwhile /ˌwɜːθˈwaɪl/ *adjective* useful and enjoyable, despite needing a lot of effort *It's a difficult course but it's very worthwhile.*

worthy /ˈwɜːði/ *adjective* **1** deserving respect, admiration, or support *a worthy cause* ○ *a worthy champion* **2 be worthy of attention/respect, etc** to deserve attention/respect, etc

O→**would** *strong form* /wʊd/ *weak form* /wəd/ *modal verb* **1** IF used to say what might happen if something else happens *What would you do if you lost your job?* **2** SAID/THOUGHT used as the past form of 'will' to talk about what someone has said or thought *Sue promised that she would help.* ○ *They thought that she would never recover.* **3** WILLING used as the past form of 'will' to talk about what someone was willing to do or what something was able to do *I asked her to talk to him, but she wouldn't.* ○ *The car wouldn't start this morning.* **4 would like/love sth** used to say politely that you want something *I'd* (= I would) *like a cup of coffee, please.* **5 would you** used to politely ask someone something *Would you like a drink?* ○ *Would you come with me, please?* **6** IMAGINE used to talk about a situation that you can imagine happening *It would be lovely to go to New York.* **7 I would imagine/think, etc** used to give an opinion in a polite way *I would imagine she'll discuss it with her husband first.* **8** OFTEN used to talk about things that happened often in the past *He would always turn and wave at the end of the street.* **9 She/he/you would!** *mainly UK* used to show that you are

W

not surprised by someone's annoying behaviour *Margot spent £200 on a dress for the occasion but she would, wouldn't she?* ⊃See Extra help page **Modal verbs** on page Centre 34.

O→**wouldn't** /ˈwʊdᵊnt/ *short for* would not *She wouldn't let us watch TV.*

WORD PARTNERS FOR ***wound (noun)***

inflict/sustain a wound • a wound **heals (up)** • **bullet/gunshot/stab** wounds • a wound **on/to** [sb's arm/back, etc] • an **open** wound

wound¹ /wuːnd/ *noun* [C] **HEALTH** an injury, especially one that is made by a knife or bullet

wound² /wuːnd/ *verb* [T] **1** INJURE to injure someone, especially with a knife or gun [**often passive**] *He was badly wounded in the attack.* **2** UPSET to upset someone [**often passive**] *She was deeply wounded by his rejection.*

wound³ /waʊnd/ *past of* wind³

ˌ**wound** ˈ**up** *adjective* very nervous, worried, or angry *He gets very wound up before an important match.*

wove /wəʊv/ *past tense of* weave²

woven /ˈwəʊvᵊn/ *past participle of* weave²

wow /waʊ/ *exclamation informal* something that you say to show surprise, excitement, admiration, etc *Wow! Look at that car!*

WORD PARTNERS FOR ***wrangle***

be involved in/get into a wrangle • a **bitter/legal** wrangle • a wrangle **over** sth • a wrangle **between** sb and sb • a wrangle **with** sb

wrangle¹ /ˈræŋgl/ *noun* [C] a long and complicated argument *a **legal wrangle***

wrangle² /ˈræŋgl/ *verb* [I] to argue with someone for a long time *They're still **wrangling over** money.*

wrap /ræp/ *verb* [T] **wrapping**, *past* **wrapped** **1** (*also* **wrap up**) to cover something or someone with paper, cloth, etc *to wrap a present* ○ *They wrapped him in a blanket.* ⊃Opposite **unwrap** **2 wrap sth around sb/sth** to fold paper, cloth, etc around something to cover it *He wrapped a towel around his waist.* **3 wrap your arms/fingers, etc around sb/sth** to put your arms/fingers, etc around someone or something *She wrapped her arms around my neck.*

wrap sth up *phrasal verb* **1** COVER to fold paper, cloth, etc around something to cover it *Have you wrapped up Jenny's present?* **2** FINISH to finish an activity successfully *We hope to have this deal wrapped up by Monday.*

wrap up *phrasal verb* to dress in warm clothes *Wrap up well - it's cold outside.*

be wrapped up in sth *phrasal verb* to give so much of your attention to something that you do not have time for other things or people *She's so wrapped up in her work that she hardly sees her kids.*

wrapper /ˈræpəʳ/ *noun* [C] a piece of paper or plastic that covers something that you buy, especially food *(UK) sweet wrappers/ (US)* candy wrappers

wrapping /ˈræpɪŋ/ *noun* [C, U] paper or plastic that is used to cover and protect something

ˈ**wrapping** ˌ**paper** *noun* [U] decorated paper that is used to cover presents

wrath /rɒθ/ *noun* [U] *literary* extreme anger

wreak /riːk/ *verb past* **wrought**, **wreaked** **wreak havoc** to cause a lot of damage or harm *Floods have wreaked havoc in central Europe.*

wreath /riːθ/ *noun* [C] *plural* **wreaths** /riːðz/ a large ring of leaves and flowers used as a decoration or to show respect for someone who has died

wreck¹ /rek/ *verb* [T] to destroy something completely *The explosion wrecked several cars and damaged nearby buildings.*

wreck² /rek/ *noun* [C] **1** VEHICLE a car, ship, or aircraft that has been very badly damaged **2** PERSON *informal* someone who is in a bad physical or mental condition [**usually singular**] *I was a complete wreck by the end of my exams.* **3** ACCIDENT *mainly US* a bad accident involving a car or train *a car/train wreck*

WORD PARTNERS FOR ***wreckage***

be **cut (free) from/pulled from/recovered from** the wreckage • be **trapped in** the wreckage • a **piece of** wreckage • the **tangled** wreckage of sth

wreckage /ˈrekɪdʒ/ *noun* [U] the parts that remain of a car, ship, or aircraft that has been destroyed *Two survivors were **pulled from the wreckage**.*

wren /ren/ *noun* [C] a very small, brown bird

wrench¹ /renʃ/ *verb* [T] **1 wrench sth from/off, etc sb/sth** to pull something violently away from a fixed position *The phone had been wrenched off the wall.* **2 HEALTH** to injure part of your body by turning it suddenly *I wrenched my right shoulder playing tennis.*

wrench² /renʃ/ *noun* **1** SADNESS [**no plural**] when you are very sad because you have to leave someone or something *She found leaving home a real wrench.* **2 DT** [C] *US* (*UK* **spanner**) a tool with a round end that is used to turn nuts and bolts (= metal objects used to fasten things together)

wrestle /ˈresl/ *verb* [I] **SPORT** to fight with someone by holding them and trying to push them to the ground

wrestle with sth *phrasal verb* to try very hard to deal with a difficult problem or decision *He's still wrestling with his conscience.*

wrestling /ˈreslɪŋ/ *noun* [U] **SPORT** a sport in which two people fight and try to push each other to the ground •**wrestler** *noun* [C]

wretched /ˈretʃɪd/ *adjective* **1** UNHAPPY very unhappy or ill *I'd been feeling wretched all day so I went to bed early.* **2** BAD very bad or of poor quality *The refugees were living in **wretched conditions**.* **3** ANNOYED [**always before noun**] used to show that something or someone makes you angry *This wretched phone won't work!*

wriggle /ˈrɪgl/ *verb* [I, T] **1** to twist your body or move part of your body with short, quick movements *She wriggled her toes in the warm sand.* **2 wriggle out of sth/doing sth** to avoid doing something that you have agreed to do *Are you trying to wriggle out of going to the meeting?*

W

wring /rɪŋ/ (*also* **wring out**) *verb* [T] *past* **wrung** to twist a cloth or piece of clothing with your hands to remove water from it *He wrung out his socks and hung them up to dry.* ➲See also: wring your hands (**hand**[1])

wrinkle /ˈrɪŋkl/ *noun* [C] **1** SKIN a small line on your face that you get when you grow old **2** CLOTH a small fold in a piece of cloth •**wrinkle** *verb* [I, T] *a wrinkled face*

wrist /rɪst/ *noun* [C] **ANATOMY** the part of your body between your hand and your arm

wristband /ˈrɪstbænd/ *noun* [C] **1** ATTACH a piece of material which goes around the wrist (= the part of your body between your hand and your arm), for example to hold a watch **2** SHOW SUPPORT a piece of material in a particular colour which goes around the wrist and shows that the person wearing it supports a certain charity

wristwatch /ˈrɪstwɒtʃ/ *noun* [C] a watch which you wear on your wrist (= the part of your body between your hand and your arm)

writ /rɪt/ *noun* [C] **LAW** a legal document that orders someone to do something

write /raɪt/ *verb past tense* **wrote**, *past participle* **written** **1** WORDS [I, T] to produce words, letters, or numbers on a surface using a pen or pencil *Write your name at the top of the page.* ○ *She can't read or write.* **2** BOOK [I, T] to create a book, story, article, etc or a piece of music *He's writing a book on Russian literature.* ○ *She writes for Time magazine.* **3** LETTER [I, T] to send someone a letter [+ two objects] *I wrote her a letter last week.* ○ *Has Bill* ***written to*** *you recently?* **4** DOCUMENT [T] (*also* **write out**) to put all the information that is needed on a document *He wrote out a cheque for £250.*

COMMON LEARNER ERROR

write

Remember to use the correct grammar after **write**.

write to someone

Rachel wrote to me last week.

write someone **a letter**

Rachel wrote me a letter last week.

write someone (American English)

Rachel wrote me last week.

write back *phrasal verb* to reply to someone's letter

write sth down *phrasal verb* to write something on a piece of paper so that you do not forget it *Did you write Jo's phone number down?*

write in *phrasal verb* to write a letter to a newspaper, television company, etc *Lots of people have written in to complain about the show.*

write off *phrasal verb* to write a letter to an organization asking them to send you something *I've* ***written off for*** *an information pack.*

write sth off *phrasal verb* **1 FINANCE** to accept that an amount of money has been lost or will never be paid to you *to write off debts* **2** VEHICLE *UK* to damage a vehicle so badly that it cannot be repaired

write sb/sth off *phrasal verb* to decide that someone or something is not useful or important *They had written him off before they even met him.*

write sth up *phrasal verb* to write something in a complete form, usually using notes that you made earlier *Have you written up that report yet?*

write-off /ˈraɪtɒf/ *noun* [C] *UK* a vehicle that is damaged so badly in an accident that it cannot be repaired *I wasn't hurt, but the car was a complete write-off.*

writer /ˈraɪtəʳ/ *noun* [C] **LITERATURE** someone whose job is writing books, stories, articles, etc

write-up /ˈraɪtʌp/ *noun* [C] an article in a newspaper or magazine in which someone gives their opinion about a performance, product, etc *The film* ***got*** *a very good* ***write-up*** *in yesterday's paper.*

writhe /raɪð/ *verb* [I] to twist your body in a violent way, often because you are in pain *She lay on her bed, writhing in agony.*

writing /ˈraɪtɪŋ/ *noun* [U] **1** SKILL the skill or activity of producing words on a surface *Teachers focus on reading and writing in the first year.* **2** WORDS words that have been written or printed *The writing was too small to read.* **3** STYLE the way that someone writes *You've got very neat writing.* **4 LITERATURE** the books, stories, articles, etc written by a particular person or group of people *She's studying women's writing of the 1930s.* **5 LITERATURE** the activity or job of creating books, stories, or articles **6 in writing** An agreement that is in writing is official because it has been written and not only spoken. *Please confirm your reservation in writing.*

written[1] /ˈrɪtᵊn/ *adjective* [**always before noun**] presented as a document on paper *a* ***written statement/warning***

written[2] /ˈrɪtᵊn/ *past participle of* write

wrong[1] /rɒŋ/ *adjective* **1** NOT CORRECT not correct *the* ***wrong answer*** ○ *We're going the* ***wrong way***. **2 be wrong** to think or say something that is not correct *You were* ***wrong about*** *the party - it's today, not tomorrow.* **3 get sth wrong** to produce an answer or result that is not correct *I got most of the answers wrong.* **4** PROBLEM [**never before noun**] If something is wrong, there is a problem. *There's something* ***wrong with*** *my computer.* ○ ***What's wrong?*** **5** NOT MORAL [**never before noun**] morally bad [+ **to do sth**] *It's wrong to tell lies.* **6** NOT SUITABLE not suitable *I think she's* ***wrong for*** *this job.* ➲See also: get (hold of) the wrong **end**[1] of the stick , get/start off on the wrong **foot**[1], not put a **foot**[1] wrong, rub sb up the wrong **way**[1]

wrong[2] /rɒŋ/ *adverb* **1** in a way that is not correct *He always says my name wrong.* **2 go wrong** to develop problems *Something's gone wrong with my computer.* **3 Don't get me wrong.** *informal* used when you do not want someone to think that you do not like someone or something *Don't get me wrong, I like her, but she can be very annoying.*

wrong[3] /rɒŋ/ *noun* **1** [C, U] when something is not morally right *She's old enough to know the difference between* ***right and wrong***. **2 be in the wrong** to be responsible for a mistake or something bad that has happened

W

wrong[4] /rɒŋ/ *verb* [T] *formal* to treat someone unfairly *a wronged man*

wrongdoing /ˈrɒŋˌduːɪŋ/ *noun* [C, U] *formal* when someone does something that is illegal or not honest

wrongful /ˈrɒŋfəl/ *adjective* **wrongful arrest/ conviction/imprisonment, etc** when someone is accused of something or punished for something unfairly or illegally •**wrongfully** *adverb* ***wrongfully arrested***

wrongly /ˈrɒŋli/ *adverb* **1** in a way that is not correct *The letter was wrongly addressed.* **2 wrongly accused/convicted/imprisoned, etc** accused or punished unfairly or illegally *She was wrongly convicted of drug smuggling.*

wrote /rəʊt/ *past tense of* write

wrought /rɔːt/ *past of* wreak

ˌ**wrought ˈiron** *noun* [U] iron that can be bent into shapes and used to make gates, furniture, etc

wrung /rʌŋ/ *past of* wring

wry /raɪ/ *adjective* A wry expression or remark shows your humour despite being in a difficult or disappointing situation. *a **wry smile*** •**wryly** *adverb*

WTO /ˌdʌbljuːtiːˈəʊ/ *noun* **ECONOMICS** *abbreviation for* World Trade Organisation: an organization that tries to control international trade and make it easier

www /ˌdʌbljuːˌdʌbljuːˈdʌbljuː/ *noun* **INTERNET** *abbreviation for* World Wide Web (= part of the Internet that consists of all the connected websites) ⊃See Extra help page **The Web and the Internet** on page Centre 36

W

X, x /eks/ **1** [LETTER] the twenty-fourth letter of the alphabet **2** [WRONG] used to show that an answer is wrong **3** [KISS] used to represent a kiss at the end of a letter **4** [UNKNOWN] used to represent an unknown person or thing

x-axis /'eks,æksɪs/ *noun* [**no plural**] **MATHEMATICS** the line of figures or letters along the bottom of a graph or map; the horizontal axis ➲Compare **y-axis**

X-chromosome /'eks,krəʊməsəʊm/ **BIOLOGY** a sex chromosome (= part of a cell that controls the appearance, characteristics, etc. of an animal or plant). In the cells of female humans and most mammals there are two of these and in the cells of males there is one X-chromosome and there is also a Y-chromosome. ➲Compare **Y-chromosome**

xenon /'zenɒn/ *noun* [**U**] **CHEMISTRY** a gas that is found in the air and used in some electric lights (symbol **Xe**)

xenophobia /ˌzenəʊ'fəʊbiə/ *noun* [**U**] extreme dislike or fear of people from other countries •**xenophobic** /ˌzenəʊ'fəʊbɪk/ *adjective*

XL /ˌeks'el/ *abbreviation for* extra large: the largest size of clothes

Xmas /'krɪstməs/ *noun* [**U**] *informal* used as a short way of writing 'Christmas' (= a Christian holiday), mainly on signs or cards *Happy Xmas!*

XML /eksem'el/ *noun trademark abbreviation for* **COMPUTING** extensible mark up language: a system of organizing information on computers

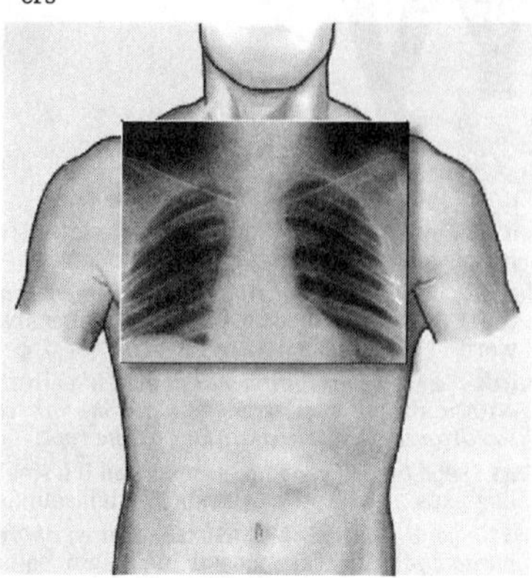

X-ray

X-ray /'eksreɪ/ *noun* [**C**] **1 HEALTH** a photograph that shows the inside of your body *They took an X-ray of his leg.* **2 PHYSICS** a wave of energy that can pass through solid materials •**X-ray** *verb* [**T**] to take a photograph that shows the inside of something

xylem /'zaɪləm/ *noun* [**U**] **BIOLOGY** the part of a plant that carries water from the roots to the leaves and gives support to the stem or trunk ➲Compare **phloem** ➲See picture at **leaf** ➲See picture at **photosynthesis** ➲See picture at **stem**

xylophone /'zaɪləfəʊn/ *noun* [**C**] **MUSIC** a musical instrument consisting of a row of flat, metal bars that you hit with sticks

X

Y, y /waɪ/ the twenty-fifth letter of the alphabet

ya /jə/ *pronoun informal* you *See ya later.*

yacht /jɒt/ *noun* [C] a large boat with sails used for pleasure or in races *a luxury yacht*

Yank /jæŋk/ *noun* [C] *informal* someone from the US, sometimes considered an offensive word

yank /jæŋk/ *verb* [T] *informal* to pull something with a strong, sudden movement *She yanked the drawer open.* ○ *He* ***yanked at*** *the rope.*

yap /jæp/ *verb* [I] **yapping**, *past* **yapped** If a small dog yaps, it makes a lot of short, high sounds.

yard /jɑːd/ *noun* [C] **1 MEASURES** (*written abbreviation* **yd**) a unit for measuring length, equal to 0.9144 metres or 3 feet *There's a bus stop a few hundred yards up the road.* ➲See Extra help page **Numbers and measurements** on page Centre 24 **2** [HOUSE] *US* (*UK* **garden**) an area of land in front of or behind a house **3** [AREA] a small area of ground next to a building, often with a fence or wall around it *a school yard*

yardstick /ˈjɑːdstɪk/ *noun* [C] something that you use to judge how good or successful something else is *If popularity is the yardstick of success, he's done very well.*

yarn /jɑːn/ *noun* **1 DT** [U] thread used for making cloth **2** [STORY] [C] *informal* a long story that is probably not true

yawn /jɔːn/ *verb* [I] to take a deep breath with your mouth wide open, because you are tired or bored *She yawned and looked at her watch.* •**yawn** *noun* [C]

yawning /ˈjɔːnɪŋ/ *adjective* **a yawning gap** a very big gap (= space or difference)

y-axis /ˈwaɪˌæksɪs/ *noun* [**no plural**] **MATHEMATICS** the line of figures or letters along the side of a graph or map; the vertical axis ➲Compare **x-axis**

Y-chromosome /ˈwaɪˌkrəʊməsəʊm/ *noun* [C] **BIOLOGY** a sex chromosome (= part of a cell that controls the appearance, characteristics, etc. of an animal or plant) that exists only in male cells of humans and most mammals ➲Compare **X-chromosome**

yd MEASURES *written abbreviation for* yard (= a unit for measuring length)

yeah /jeə/ *exclamation informal spoken* yes *Yeah, I agree.*

WORD PARTNERS FOR ***year***

each/every/last/next year • the **past** year • [2/5, etc] years **ago**

year /jɪəʳ/ *noun* [C] **1** a period of 12 months, or 365 or 366 days, especially from 1 January to 31 December ***last year/next year*** ○ *He joined the company a year ago.* **2 the academic/financial, etc year** the period of a year that is used by universities/businesses, etc to organize their activities **3 be two/twelve/37, etc years old** to be a particular age *Her son is six years old.* **4 a two-/twelve-/37-, etc year-old** someone who is a particular age **5 EDUCATION** *UK* a group of students who start college or a course together *He was* ***in my year*** *at school.* **6 years** a long time *I haven't seen Linda* ***for years.*** ➲See also: for **donkey**'s years, **leap year, new year**

COMMON LEARNER ERROR

describing age

If you describe someone's age by saying 'Tom is 8 years old', you always write the age as three separate words.

My son is 8 years old.

You can use also use 8-year-old, etc. as an adjective. When you do this, the words are written together using hyphens (-).

I've got a 12-year-old son.

You can also do the same with days, weeks, and months.

I've got a 10-week-old rabbit.

The baby is three months old.

a three-month-old baby

yearbook /ˈjɪəbʊk/ *noun* [C] a book produced every year by a school or organization, containing information about its activities, members, etc

yearly /ˈjɪəli/ *adjective, adverb* happening once a year or every year *a yearly fee* ○ *Interest is paid yearly.*

yearn /jɜːn/ *verb* **yearn for sth; yearn to do sth** to want something very much with a feeling of sadness *They yearned for peace.* ○ *She yearned to get away.* •**yearning** *noun* [C, U]

yeast /jiːst/ *noun* [U] **FOOD** a substance used to make bread rise and to make beer and wine

yell /jel/ *verb* [I, T] to shout something very loudly *The policeman* ***yelled at*** *them to stop.* •**yell** *noun* [C]

yellow /ˈjeləʊ/ *adjective* being the same colour as a lemon or the sun *a bright yellow tablecloth* •**yellow** *noun* [C, U] the colour yellow ➲See colour picture **Colours** on page Centre 12

ˌyellow ˈcard *noun* [C] **SPORT** in football, a small card shown to a player as a warning that the player has not obeyed a rule ➲Compare **red card**

the ˌYellow ˈPages *UK trademark* (*US* **the ˈYellow ˌPages**) *noun* [**plural**] a big, yellow book containing telephone numbers of shops and businesses

yelp /jelp/ *verb* [I] If a dog yelps, it gives a sudden cry because of pain or shock.

yep /jep/ *exclamation informal spoken* yes

yes¹ /jes/ *exclamation* **1** [AGREE] used to agree with something, or to give a positive answer to something *"Can I borrow your pencil?" "Yes, of course."* ○ *"Are you feeling better?" "Yes, thanks."* ○ *"Coffee?" " Yes, please."* **2** [ANSWER] used as an answer when someone calls you *"Jack!" "Yes?"* **3** [DISAGREE] used to disagree with a negative announcement *"He's not here yet." "Yes he is, I've just seen him."*

yes² /jes/ *noun* [C] a positive reaction or agreement with something *Was that a yes or a no?*

yesterday /ˈjestədeɪ/ *noun* [U], *adverb* the day before today *I went to see the doctor yesterday.* ○ *yesterday morning/afternoon*

O-w **yet**[1] /jet/ *adverb* **1** BEFORE before now or before that time *Have you read his book yet?* ○ *"Has he called?" "No, not yet."* **2** NOW now or as early as this time *I don't want to go home yet.* **3 the best/worst, etc yet** the best or worst, etc until now *That was my worst exam yet.* **4 be/have yet to do sth** to not have done something that was expected before this time *They have yet to make a decision.* **5 yet again/another/more, etc** used to show that you are surprised or annoyed that something is being repeated or increased *He's given us yet more work to do.* **6 could/may/might, etc yet** used to say there is still a possibility that something will happen *He may win yet.*

yet[2] /jet/ *conjunction* used to add something that seems surprising because of what you have just said *simple yet effective*

yew /juː/ *noun* [**C, U**] a tree with dark, needle-shaped leaves, or the wood of this tree

WORD PARTNERS FOR *yield*

yield **clues/information/** a **profit/** a **result**

yield[1] /jiːld/ *verb* **1** PRODUCE [**T**] to produce or provide something *to* ***yield a profit*** ○ *The investigation* ***yielded*** *some unexpected* ***results***. **2 yield to demands/pressure, etc** to be forced to do something **3** TRAFFIC [**I**] *US* (*UK* **give way**) to stop in order to allow other vehicles to go past before you drive onto a bigger road

yield[2] /jiːld/ *noun* [**C**] the amount of something that is produced

yo /jəʊ/ *exclamation mainly US informal* used as a greeting

yob /jɒb/ *noun* [**C**] *UK informal* a rude or violent young man

yoga /ˈjəʊgə/ *noun* [**U**] **SPORT** a set of exercises for the mind and body, based on the Hindu religion *She does yoga three times a week.*

yoghurt (*also* **yogurt**) /ˈjɒgət/ (US) /ˈjəʊgərt/ *noun* [**C, U**] **FOOD** a thick, liquid food with a slightly sour taste which is made from milk *a low-fat strawberry yoghurt* ➲See colour picture **Food** on page Centre 11

yolk /jəʊk/ *noun* [**C**] **1 FOOD** the round, yellow part in the middle of an egg **2 BIOLOGY** the substance in the eggs of all animals and birds, that provides food for the growing baby ➲See picture at **egg**

Yom Kippur /ˌjɒmkɪˈpʊəʳ/ *noun* [**U**] **RELIGION** a Jewish holy day in September or October

yonder /ˈjɒndəʳ/ *adverb, determiner literary* in that place or direction

O-w **you** *strong form* /juː/ *weak forms* /ju, jə/ *pronoun* **1** PERSON SPOKEN TO used to refer to the person or people you are talking to *I love you.* ○ *You said I could go with you.* **2** PEOPLE GENERALLY people generally *You learn to accept these things as you get older.*

O-w **you'd** /juːd/ **1** YOU HAD *short for* you had *You'd better go home now.* **2** YOU WOULD *short for* you would *I expect you'd like some lunch.*

O-w **you'll** /juːl/ *short for* you will *I hope you'll come again.*

O-w **young**[1] /jʌŋ/ *adjective* having lived or existed for only a short time and not old *young children/people* ○ *We were very young when we met.*

young[2] /jʌŋ/ *noun* [**plural**] **1 the young** young people generally *It's the sort of music that appeals mainly to the young.* **2 sth's young BIOLOGY** an animal's babies

youngster /ˈjʌŋstəʳ/ *noun* [**C**] a young person, especially an older child *He talked to the youngsters about the dangers of drugs.*

O-w **your** *strong form* /jɔːʳ/ *weak form* /jəʳ/ *determiner* **1** OF PERSON SPOKEN TO belonging or relating to the person or people you are talking to *Can I borrow your pen?* ○ *It's not your fault.* **2** OF PEOPLE IN GENERAL belonging or relating to people in general *You never stop loving your children.*

O-w **you're** /jɔːʳ/ *short for* you are *You're my best friend.*

O-w **yours** /jɔːz/ *pronoun* **1** the things that belong or relate to the person or people you are talking to *Is this pen yours?* ○ *Our tent's smaller than yours.* **2 Yours faithfully/sincerely, etc** used just before your name at the end of a polite or formal letter **3 yours truly** *humorous* I or me

O-w **yourself** /jɔːˈself/ *pronoun plural* **yourselves** **1** REFLEXIVE the reflexive form of the pronoun 'you' *Don't cut yourself with that sharp knife.* **2** EMPHASIZE used to emphasize the pronoun 'you' when talking about the actions of the person you are speaking to *Did you make the dress yourself?* **3 (all) by yourself/yourselves** alone or without anyone else's help *I'm amazed you managed to move those boxes all by yourself.* **4 (all) to yourself** for your use only *So you've got the whole house to yourself this weekend?*

WORD PARTNERS FOR *youth*

recapture/relive your youth • **in** sb's youth

youth /juːθ/ *noun* **1 SOCIETY** [**C**] a young man *gangs of youths* **2 SOCIETY** [**group**] young people generally *the youth of today* ○ *a youth club* **3 sb's youth** the period of time when someone is young *I was very shy* ***in*** *my* ***youth***. **4** [**U**] the quality of being young

youthful /ˈjuːθfəl/ *adjective* typical of a young person *youthful energy/good looks*

ˈyouth ˌhostel *noun* [**C**] a cheap, simple hotel, especially for young people who are travelling around

O-w **you've** /juːv/ *short for* you have *If you've finished your work, you can go.*

yo-yo /ˈjəʊjəʊ/ *noun* [**C**] a small, round toy that you make go up and down on a string that you hang from your finger

yuck /jʌk/ *exclamation informal* used to say that something looks or tastes very unpleasant

yum /jʌm/ (*also* **ˌyum ˈyum**) *exclamation informal* used to say that something tastes very good

yummy /ˈjʌmi/ *adjective informal* If food or drink is yummy, it tastes very good.

yuppie /ˈjʌpi/ *noun* [**C**] **SOCIETY** a young person who earns a lot of money and likes expensive things

Y

Zz

Z, z /zed/ the twenty-sixth and last letter of the alphabet

zany /ˈzeɪni/ *adjective* funny in a strange way ***zany humour***

zap /zæp/ *verb* [T] **zapping**, *past* **zapped** *informal* to attack or destroy something in a fast and powerful way

zeal /ziːl/ *noun* [U] extreme enthusiasm *religious zeal*

zealous /ˈzeləs/ *adjective* extremely enthusiastic •**zealously** *adverb*

zebra /ˈzebrə/ (US) /ˈziːbrə/ *noun* [C] an animal like a horse with black and white lines

ˌzebra ˈcrossing *noun* [C] *UK* a part of the road painted with black and white lines where people can cross over safely

Zen /zen/ *noun* [U] **RELIGION** a religion that developed from Buddhism

zenith /ˈzenɪθ/ (US) /ˈziːnɪθ/ *noun* [**no plural**] *literary* the highest or most successful point of something *The city **reached its zenith** in the 1980s.*

WORD PARTNERS FOR ***zero***

sth **drops to/falls to** zero • **above/below** zero

zero /ˈzɪərəʊ/ the number 0

ˌzero ˈtolerance *noun* [U] **LAW, SOCIETY** when you do not accept any bad behaviour, often by using laws to prevent it *zero tolerance of crime*

zest /zest/ *noun* [U] **1** [FEELING] excitement and enthusiasm *a zest for life* **2** [FRUIT] the outer skin of a lemon or orange used to give flavour to food

zigzag /ˈzɪgzæg/ *noun* [C] a line that changes direction from left to right and back again at sharp angles •**zigzag** *verb* [I] **zigzagging**, *past* **zigzagged** to make a movement or pattern like a zigzag

zillion /ˈzɪljən/ *quantifier informal* a very large number *a zillion times*

zinc /zɪŋk/ *noun* [U] **CHEMISTRY** a blue-white metal that is used to make or cover other metals (symbol **Zn**)

zip¹ /zɪp/ *UK* (*US* **zipper**) *noun* [C] a thing for fastening clothes, bags, etc consisting of two rows of very small parts that connect together *Your zip's undone.*

zip² /zɪp/ *verb* **zipping**, *past* **zipped** **1** [T] (*also* **zip up**) to fasten something with a zip *He zipped up his jacket.* **2 COMPUTING** (*also* **zip up**) to reduce the size of a computer file (= collection of information) so that it uses less space and can be sent or stored more easily **3 zip along/around/past, etc** *informal* to move somewhere very quickly

ˈzip ˌcode *noun* [C] a set of numbers that go after someone's address in the US ➲Compare **postcode**

ˈzip ˌdrive *noun* [C] **COMPUTING** a device used for copying large documents onto special disks ➲See: **memory stick**

ˈzip ˌfile *noun* [C] **COMPUTING** a computer file (= collection of information) that has been made smaller so that it uses less space

zipper /ˈzɪpəʳ/ *noun* [C] *US* a zip¹

the zodiac /ˈzəʊdiæk/ *noun* the twelve signs representing groups of stars which are thought by some people to influence your life and personality *What sign of the zodiac are you?*

zombie /ˈzɒmbi/ *noun* [C] **1** a dead body that walks around because of magic **2 like a zombie** *informal* in a very tired, slow way *The day after the party I was walking around like a zombie.*

zone /zəʊn/ *noun* [C] an area where a particular thing happens *a **war zone*** ○ *a nuclear-free zone* ➲See also: **buffer zone**

zoo /zuː/ *noun* [C] a place where wild animals are kept and people come to look at them

zoological /ˌzəʊəʊˈlɒdʒɪkəl/ *adjective* **BIOLOGY** relating to the scientific study of animals

zoology /zuˈɒlədʒi/ (US) /zəʊˈɒlədʒi/ *noun* [U] **BIOLOGY** the scientific study of animals and how they behave •**zoologist** *noun* [C] someone who studies zoology

zoom /zuːm/ *verb informal* **zoom along/down/past, etc** to travel somewhere very fast, especially with a loud noise

zoom in *phrasal verb* to make something appear much closer and larger when using a camera or computer *The TV cameras zoomed in on her face.*

ˈzoom ˌlens *noun* [C] a lens (= part of a camera) that can make something appear much closer and larger

zorbing /ˈzɔːbɪŋ/ *noun* [U] **SPORT** the sport of rolling down a hill inside a plastic ball

zucchini /zʊˈkiːni/ *US* (*UK* **courgette**) *noun* [C, U] *plural* **zucchini** or **zucchinis** **FOOD** a long, green vegetable which is white inside

zygote /ˈzaɪgəʊt/ *noun* [C] **BIOLOGY** the cell which will develop into a baby person or animal and which is made by the combining of a male and female gamete (= cell from each parent)

Z

Appendices

Popular first names

These two lists give you the most common names for males and females in English-speaking countries, along with their pronunciation. The names in brackets are common short forms or different forms of the name.

Male names

Adam /ˈædəm/
Alan /ˈælən/
Alexander /ˌælɪgˈzɑːndər/
(Alex) /ˈælɪks/
Andrew /ˈændruː/
(Andy) /ˈændi/
Anthony
UK /ˈæntəni/
US /ˈænθəni/
(Tony) /ˈtəʊni/
Benjamin /ˈbendʒəmɪn/
(Ben) /ben/
Charles /tʃɑːlz/
(Charlie) /ˈtʃɑːli/
Christopher /ˈkrɪstəfər/
(Chris) /krɪs/
Daniel /ˈdænjəl/
(Dan) /dæn/
Darren /ˈdærən/
David /ˈdeɪvɪd/
(Dave) /deɪv/
Edward /ˈedwəd/
(Ed) /ed/
(Ted) /ted/
Ethan /ˈiːθən/
Gareth /ˈgærəθ/
Gary /ˈgæri/
Gene /dʒiːn/
Geoffrey /ˈdʒefri/
(Geoff) / (Jeff) /dʒef/
George /dʒɔːdʒ/
Harry /ˈhæri/
Ian /ˈiːən/
Jack /dʒæk/
Jacob /ˈdʒeɪkəb/
(Jake) /dʒeɪk/
James /dʒeɪmz/
(Jim) /dʒɪm/
Jamie /ˈdʒeɪmi/
John /dʒɒn/
Jonathan /ˈdʒɒnəθən/
Joseph /ˈdʒəʊzɪf/
(Joe) /dʒəʊ/
Joshua /ˈdʒɒʃjuə/
(Josh) /dʒɒʃ/
Kevin /ˈkevɪn/
Liam /ˈliːəm/
Louis /ˈluːi/
Luke /luːk/
Mark /mɑːk/
Martin /ˈmɑːtɪn/
Matthew /ˈmæθjuː/
(Matt) /mæt/
Max /mæks/
Michael /ˈmaɪkəl/
(Mike) /maɪk/
(Mick) /mɪk/
Nathan /ˈneɪθən/
Nicholas /ˈnɪkələs/
(Nick) /nɪk/
Oliver /ˈɒlɪvə/
(Ollie) /ˈɒli/
Oscar /ˈɒskə/
Patrick /ˈpætrɪk/
(Pat) /pæt/
(Paddy) /ˈpædi/
Paul /pɔːl/
Peter /ˈpiːtə/
(Pete) /piːt/
Philip /ˈfɪlɪp/
(Phil) /fɪl/
Richard /ˈrɪtʃəd/
(Ricky) /ˈrɪki/
(Dick) /dɪk/
(Rick) /rɪk/
Robert /ˈrɒbət/
(Bob) /bɒb/
(Rob) /rɒb/
(Bobby) /bɒbi/
Samuel /ˈsæmjʊəl/
(Sam) /sæm/
Scott /skɒt/
Simon /ˈsaɪmən/
Steven /ˈstiːvən/
(Steve) /stiːv/
Thomas /ˈtɒməs/
(Tom) /tɒm/
(Tommy) /ˈtɒmi/
Timothy /ˈtɪməθi/
(Tim) /tɪm/
Tyler /ˈtailə/
William /ˈwɪljəm/
(Billy) /ˈbɪli/
(Bill) /bɪl/
(Will) /wɪl/

Female names

Alice /ˈælɪs/
Alison /ˈælɪsən/
Amanda /əˈmændə/
(Mandy) /ˈmændi/
Amy /ˈeɪmi/
Ann/Anne /æn/
Anna /ˈænə/
Ashley /ˈæʃli/
Bridget /ˈbrɪdʒɪt/
Carol /ˈkærəl/
Caroline /ˈkærəlaɪn/
Catherine/Katherine/
Kathryn /ˈkæθrɪn/
(Kate) /keɪt/
(Katie) /ˈkeɪti/
(Cath) /kæθ/
Charlotte /ˈʃɑːlət/
Chloe /ˈkləʊi/
Christine /ˈkrɪstiːn/
(Chris) /krɪs/
Clare/Claire /kleər/
Daisy /ˈdeɪzi/
Deborah /ˈdebrə/
(Debbie) /ˈdebi/
Diane /daɪˈæn/
Elizabeth /ɪˈlɪzəbəθ/
(Beth) /beθ/
(Liz) /lɪz/
Ella /ˈelə/
Emily /ˈemɪli/
Emma /ˈemə/
Georgia /ˈdʒɔːdʒə/
Grace /greɪs/
Hannah /ˈhænə/
Helen /ˈhelən/
Isabel/Isobel /ˈɪzəbel/
(Izzie) /ˈɪzi/
Jane /dʒeɪn/
Jennifer /ˈdʒenɪfə/
(Jenny) /ˈdʒeni/
Jessica /ˈdʒesɪkə/
Joanne /dʒəʊˈæn/
(Jo) /dʒəʊ/
Julie /ˈdʒuːli/
Karen /ˈkærən/
Laura /ˈlɔːrə/
Lauren /ˈlɪrən/
Lily /ˈlɪli/
Linda /ˈlɪndə/
Lucy /ˈluːsi/
Margaret /ˈmɑːgərət/
(Maggie) /ˈmægi/
Mary /ˈmeəri/
Megan /ˈmegən/
Molly /ˈmɒli/
Olivia /əˈlɪviə/
Rachel /ˈreɪtʃəl/
Rebecca /rɪˈbekə/
(Becky) /ˈbeki/
Rosie /ˈrəʊzi/
Ruth /ruːθ/
Sarah /ˈseərə/
Sharon /ˈʃærən/
Sophie /ˈsəʊfi/
Susan /ˈsuːzən/
(Sue) /suː/
Tracy /ˈtreɪsi/
Valerie /ˈvæləri/
Zoe /ˈzəʊi/

Geographical names

This list shows the spellings and pronunciations of countries, regions, and continents. Each name is followed by its related adjective. Most of the time you can use the adjective to talk about a person who comes from each place. However, in some cases you must use a special word, which is listed in the column labelled 'Person' (for example, **Finland**, **Finnish**, **Finn**).

To talk about more than one person from a particular place, add '**s**', except for:

- words ending in '**ese**' or '**s**', which remain the same (**Chinese**, **Swiss**)
- words ending in '**man**' or '**woman**', which change to '**men**' and '**women**' (**Irishman**).

This list is for reference only. Inclusion does not imply or suggest status as a sovereign nation.

Name	Adjective	Person (if different from adj)
Afghanistan /æf'gænɪstæn/	**Afghan** /'æfgæn/	
Africa /'æfrikə/	**African** /'æfrikən/	
Albania /æl'beɪniə/	**Albanian** /æl'beɪniən/	
Algeria /æl'dʒɪəriə/	**Algerian** /æl'dʒɪəriən/	
Central America /ˌsentrəl ə'merɪkə/	**Central American** /ˌsentrəl ə'merɪkən/	
North America /ˌnɔːθ ə'merɪkə/	**North American** /ˌnɔːθ ə'merɪkən/	
South America /ˌsaʊθ ə'merɪkə/	**South American** /ˌsaʊθ ə'merɪkən/	
Andorra /æn'dɔːrə/	**Andorran** /æn'dɔːrən/	
Angola /æŋ'gəʊlə/	**Angolan** /æŋ'gəʊlən/	
Antigua and Barbuda /æn'tiːgə æn bɑː'bjuːdə/	**Antiguan** /æn'tiːgən/	
Argentina /ˌɑːdʒən'tiːnə/	**Argentine** /'ɑːdʒəntaɪn/	
Armenia /ɑː'miːniə/	**Armenian** /ɑː'miːniən/	
Asia /'eɪʒə/	**Asian** /'eɪʒən/	
Australia /ɒs'treɪliə/	**Australian** /ɒs'treɪliən/	
Austria /'ɒstriə/	**Austrian** /'ɒstriən/	
Azerbaijan /ˌæzəbaɪ'dʒɑːn/	**Azerbaijani** /ˌæzəbaɪ'dʒɑːni/	**Azeri** /ə'zeəri/
The Bahamas /ðə bə'hɑːməz/	**Bahamian** /bə'heɪmiən/	
Bahrain /bɑː'reɪn/	**Bahraini** /bɑː'reɪni/	
Bangladesh /ˌbæŋglə'deʃ/	**Bangladeshi** /ˌbæŋglə'deʃi/	
Barbados /bɑː'beɪdɒs/	**Barbadian** /bɑː'beɪdiən/	
Belarus /ˌbelə'ruːs/	**Belorussian** /ˌbelə'rʌʃən/	
Belgium /'beldʒəm/	**Belgian** /'beldʒən/	
Belize /be'liːz/	**Belizian** /bə'liːziən/	
Benin /be'niːn/	**Beninese** /ˌbenɪ'niːz/	
Bhutan /buː'tɑːn/	**Bhutanese** /ˌbuːtə'niːz/	
Bolivia /bə'lɪviə/	**Bolivian** /bə'lɪviən/	
Bosnia-Herzegovina /ˌbɒzniəˌhɜːzəgɒ'vɪnə/	**Bosnian** /'bɒzniən/	
Botswana /bɒt'swɑːnə/	**Botswanan** /bɒt'swɑːnən/	**Motswana** /mɒt'swɑːnə/
Brazil /brə'zɪl/	**Brazilian** /brə'zɪliən/	
Brunei /bruː'naɪ/	**Bruneian** /bruː'naɪən/	
Bulgaria /bʌl'geəriə/	**Bulgarian** /bʌl'geəriən/	

Name	Adjective	Person
Burkina Faso /bɜːˈkiːnə ˈfæseʊ/	**Burkinabe** /bɜːˈkiːnəˌbei/	
Burundi /bʊˈrʊndi/	**Burundi** /bʊˈrʊndi/	**Burundian** /bʊˈrʊndiən/
Cambodia /ˌkæmˈbəʊdiə/	**Cambodian** /ˌkæmˈbəʊdiən/	
Cameroon /ˌkæməˈruːn/	**Cameroonian** /ˌkæməˈruːniən/	
Canada /ˈkænədə/	**Canadian** /kəˈneɪdiən/	
Cape Verde /ˌkeɪp ˈvɜːd/	**Cape Verdean** /ˌkeɪp ˈvɜːdiən/	
The Central African Republic /ðə ˈsentrəl ˈæfrɪkən rɪˈpʌblɪk/	**Central African** /ˌsentrəl ˈæfrɪkən/	
Chad /tʃæd/	**Chadian** /ˈtʃædiən/	
Chile /ˈtʃɪli/	**Chilean** /ˈtʃɪliən/	
China /ˈtʃaɪnə/	**Chinese** /tʃaɪˈniːz/	
Colombia /kəˈlʌmbiə/	**Colombian** /kəˈlʌmbiən/	
Comoros /ˈkɒmərəʊz/	**Comoran** /kəˈmɔːrən/	
The Democratic Republic of the Congo /ðə ˌdeməˈkrætɪk rɪˈpʌblɪk əv ðə ˈkɒŋgəʊ/	**Congolese** /ˌkɒŋgəˈliːz/	
The Republic of the Congo /ðə rɪˈpʌblɪk əv ðə ˈkɒŋgəʊ/	**Congolese** /ˌkɒŋgəˈliːz/	
Costa Rica /ˌkɒstəˈriːkə/	**Costa Rican** /ˌkɒstəˈriːkən/	
Côte d'Ivoire /ˌkəʊt diːˈvwɑː/	**Ivorian** /aɪˈvɔːriən/	
Croatia /krəʊˈeɪʃə/	**Croatian** /krəʊˈeɪʃən/	**Croat** /ˈkrəʊæt/
Cuba /ˈkjuːbə/	**Cuban** /ˈkjuːbən/	
Cyprus /ˈsaɪprəs/	**Cypriot** /ˈsɪpriət/	
The Czech Republic /ðə tʃek rɪˈpʌblɪk/	**Czech** /tʃek/	
Denmark /ˈdenmɑːk/	**Danish** /ˈdeɪnɪʃ/	**Dane** /deɪn/
Djibouti /dʒɪˈbuːti/	**Djiboutian** /dʒɪˈbuːtiən/	
Dominica /ˌdəˈmɪnɪkə/	**Dominican** /dəˈmɪnɪkən/	
The Dominican Republic /ðə dəˈmɪnɪkən rɪˈpʌblɪk/	**Dominican** /dəˈmɪnɪkən/	
East Timor /iːst ˈtiːmɔːʳ/	**East Timorese** /iːst ˌtiːmɔːˈriːz/	
Ecuador /ˈekwədɔːʳ/	**Ecuadorian** /ˌekwəˈdɔːriən/	
Egypt /ˈiːdʒɪpt/	**Egyptian** /ɪˈdʒɪpʃən/	
El Salvador /ˌelˈsælvədɔːʳ/	**Salvadoran** /ˌsælvəˈdɔːrən/	
Equatorial Guinea /ˌekwətɔːriəl ˈgɪni/	**Equatorial Guinean** /ˌekwətɔːriəl ˈgɪniən/	
Eritrea /ˌerɪˈtreɪə/	**Eritrean** /ˌerɪˈtreɪən/	
Estonia /esˈtəʊniə/	**Estonian** /esˈtəʊniən/	
Ethiopia /ˌiːθiˈəʊpiə/	**Ethiopian** /ˌiːθiˈəʊpiən/	
Europe /ˈjʊərəp/	**European** /ˌjʊərəˈpiːən/	
Fiji /ˈfiːdʒiː/	**Fijian** /fɪˈdʒiːən/	
Finland /ˈfɪnlənd/	**Finnish** /ˈfɪnɪʃ/	**Finn** /fɪn/
France /frɑːnts/	**French** /frentʃ/	**Frenchman** /ˈfrentʃmən/
Gabon /gæbˈɒn/	**Gabonese** /ˌgæbənˈiːz/	
The Gambia /ðəˈgæmbiə/	**Gambian** /ˈgæmbiən/	
Georgia /ˈdʒɔːdʒə/	**Georgian** /ˈdʒɔːdʒən/	
Germany /ˈdʒɜːməni/	**German** /ˈdʒɜːmən/	
Ghana /ˈgɑːnə/	**Ghanaian** /gɑːˈneɪən/	
Greece /griːs/	**Greek** /griːk/	
Greenland /ˈgriːnlənd/	**Greenland** /ˈgriːnlənd/	**Greenlander** /ˈgriːnləndəʳ/
Grenada /grəˈneɪdə/	**Grenadian** /grəˈneɪdiən/	
Guatemala /ˌgwɑːtəˈmɑːlə/	**Guatemalan** /ˌgwɑːtəˈmɑːlən/	
Guinea /ˈgɪni/	**Guinean** /ˈgɪniən/	

Name	Adjective	Person
Guinea-Bissau /ˌɡɪnibɪˈsaʊ/	Guinea-Bissauan /ˌɡɪnibɪˈsaʊən/	
Guyana /ɡaɪˈænə/	Guyanese /ˌɡaɪəˈniːz/	
Haiti /ˈheɪti/	Haitian /ˈheɪʃən/	
Honduras /hɒnˈdjʊərəs/	Honduran /hɒnˈdjʊərən/	
Hungary /ˈhʌŋɡəri/	Hungarian /hʌŋˈɡeəriən/	
Iceland /ˈaɪslənd/	Icelandic /aɪsˈlændɪk/	Icelander /ˈaɪsləndəʳ/
India /ˈɪndiə/	Indian /ˈɪndiən/	
Indonesia /ˌɪndəˈniːʒə/	Indonesian /ˌɪndəˈniːʒən/	
Iran /ɪˈrɑːn/	Iranian /ɪˈreɪniən/	
Iraq /ɪˈrɑːk/	Iraqi /ɪˈrɑːki/	
Ireland /ˈaɪələnd/	Irish /ˈaɪrɪʃ/	Irishman /ˈaɪrɪʃmən/
Israel /ˈɪzreɪl/	Israeli /ɪzˈreɪli/	
Italy /ˈɪtəli/	Italian /ɪˈtæliən/	
Jamaica /dʒəˈmeɪkə/	Jamaican /dʒəˈmeɪkən/	
Japan /dʒəˈpæn/	Japanese /ˌdʒæpəˈniːz/	
Jordan /ˈdʒɔːdn/	Jordanian /dʒɔːˈdeɪniən/	
Kazakhstan /ˌkæzækˈstɑːn/	Kazakh /kæˈzæk/	
Kenya /ˈkenjə/	Kenyan /ˈkenjən/	
Kiribati /ˌkɪrəˈbæs/	Kiribati /ˌkɪrəˈbæs/	
North Korea /ˌnɔːθ kəˈriːə/	North Korean /ˌnɔːθ kəˈriːən/	
South Korea /ˌsaʊθ kəˈriːə/	South Korean /ˌsaʊθ kəˈriːən/	
Kuwait /kuːˈweɪt/	Kuwaiti /kuːˈweɪti/	
Kyrgyzstan /ˌkɜːɡɪˈstɑːn/	Kyrgyz /ˈkɜːɡɪz/	
Laos /laʊs/	Laotian /ˈlaʊʃən/	
Latvia /ˈlætviə/	Latvian /ˈlætviən/	
Lebanon /ˈlebənən/	Lebanese /ˌlebəˈniːz/	
Lesotho /ləˈsuːtuː/	Basotho /bəˈsuːtuː/	Mosotho /məˈsuːtuː/
Liberia /laɪˈbɪəriə/	Liberian /laɪˈbɪəriən/	
Libya /ˈlɪbiə/	Libyan /ˈlɪbiən/	
Liechtenstein /ˈlɪktənstaɪn/	Liechtenstein /ˈlɪktənstaɪn/	Liechtensteiner /ˈlɪktənstaɪnəʳ/
Lithuania /ˌlɪθjuˈeɪniə/	Lithuanian /ˌlɪθjuˈeɪniən/	
Luxembourg /ˈlʌksəmbɜːɡ/	Luxembourg /ˈlʌksəmbɜːɡ/	Luxembourger /ˈlʌksəmbɜːɡəʳ/
Madagascar /ˌmædəˈɡæskəʳ/	Malagasy /ˌmæləˈɡæsi/	
Malawi /məˈlɑːwi/	Malawian /məˈlɑːwiən/	
Malaysia /məˈleɪziə/	Malaysian /məˈleɪziən/	
The Maldives /ðə ˈmɔːldiːvz/	Maldivian /mɔːlˈdɪviən/	
Mali /ˈmɑːli/	Malian /ˈmɑːliən/	
Malta /ˈmɔːltə/	Maltese /mɔːlˈtiːz/	
The Marshall Islands /ðə ˈmɑːʃəl ˈaɪləndz/	Marshallese /ˌmɑːʃəˈliːz/	
Mauritania /ˌmɒrɪˈteɪniə/	Mauritanian /ˈmɒrɪˈteɪniən/	
Mauritius /məˈrɪʃəs/	Mauritian /məˈrɪʃən/	
Mexico /ˈmeksɪkəʊ/	Mexican /ˈmeksɪkən/	
Micronesia /ˌmaɪkrəˈniːziə/	Micronesian /ˌmaɪkrəˈniːziən/	
Moldova /mɒlˈdəʊvə/	Moldovan /mɒlˈdəʊvən/	
Monaco /ˈmɒnəkəʊ/	Monégasque /mɒneɪˈɡæsk/	
Mongolia /mɒŋˈɡəʊliə/	Mongolian /mɒŋˈɡəʊliən/	
Montenegro /ˌmɒntɪˈniːˌɡrəʊ/	Montenegrin /ˌmɒntɪˈniːˌɡrən/	
Morocco /məˈrɒkəʊ/	Moroccan /məˈrɒkən/	
Mozambique /ˌməʊzæmˈbiːk/	Mozambican /ˌməʊzæmˈbiːkən/	

Name	Adjective	Person
Myanmar /ˈmjænmɑːʳ/	Burmese /bɜːˈmiːz/	
Namibia /nəˈmɪbiə/	Namibian /nəˈmɪbiən/	
Nauru /nɑːˈuːruː/	Nauruan /nɑːuːˈruːən/	
Nepal /nəˈpɔːl/	Nepalese /ˌnepəlˈiːz/	
The Netherlands /ðə ˈneðələnz/	Dutch /dʌtʃ/	Dutchman /ˈdʌtʃmən/
New Zealand /ˌnjuːˈziːlənd/	New Zealand /ˌnjuːˈziːlənd/	New Zealander /ˌnjuːˈziːləndəʳ/
Nicaragua /ˌnɪkəˈrɑːgwə/	Nicaraguan /ˌnɪkəˈrɑːgwən/	
Niger /niːˈʒeə/	Nigerien /niːˈʒeəriən/	
Nigeria /naɪˈdʒɪəriə/	Nigerian /naɪˈdʒɪəriən/	
Norway /ˈnɔːweɪ/	Norwegian /nɔːˈwiːdʒən/	
Oman /əʊˈmɑːn/	Omani /əʊˈmɑːni/	
Pakistan /ˌpɑːkɪˈstɑːn/	Pakistani /ˌpɑːkɪˈstɑːni/	
Palestine /ˈpæləstaɪn/	Palestinian /ˌpæləˈstɪniən/	
Panama /ˈpænəmɑː/	Panamanian /ˌpænəˈmeɪniən/	
Papua New Guinea /ˈpæpuə njuː ˈgɪni/	Papua New Guinean /ˈpæpuə njuː ˈgɪniən/	
Paraguay /ˈpærəgwaɪ/	Paraguayan /ˌpærəˈgwaɪən/	
Peru /pəˈruː/	Peruvian /pəˈruːviən/	
The Philippines /ðə ˈfɪlɪpiːnz/	Philippine /ˈfɪlɪpiːn/	Filipino /ˌfɪlɪˈpiːnəʊ/
Poland /ˈpəʊlənd/	Polish /ˈpəʊlɪʃ/	Pole /pəʊl/
Portugal /ˈpɔːtʃəgəl/	Portuguese /ˌpɔːtʃəˈgiːz/	
Qatar /ˈkʌtɑːʳ/	Qatari /kʌˈtɑːri/	
Romania /rʊˈmeɪniə/	Romanian /rʊˈmeɪniən/	
Russia /ˈrʌʃə/	Russian /ˈrʌʃən/	
Rwanda /ruˈændə/	Rwandan /ruˈændən/	
Saint Kitts and Nevis /seɪnt kɪts ən ˈnevɪs/	Kittsian /ˈkɪtsiən/	
Saint Lucia /seɪnt ˈluːʃə/	Saint Lucian /seɪnt ˈluːʃən/	
Saint Vincent and the Grenadines /seɪnt ˈvɪntsənt ən ðə ˌgrenəˈdiːnz/	Vincentian /vɪnˈsɪntiən/	
Samoa /səˈməʊə/	Samoan /səˈməʊən/	
San Marino /ˌsænməˈriːnəʊ/	Sanmarinese /ˌsænmærɪˈniːz/	
São Tomé and Príncipe /ˌsaʊ təˈmeɪ ən ˈprɪnsɪpəɪ/	Sao Tomean /ˌsaʊ təˈmeɪən/	
Saudi Arabia /ˌsaʊdi əˈreɪbiə/	Saudi /ˈsaʊdi/	
Scandinavia /ˌskændɪˌneɪviə/	Scandinavian /ˌskændɪˌneɪviən/	
Senegal /ˌsenɪˈgɔːl/	Senegalese /ˌsenɪgəˈliːz/	
Serbia /ˌsɜɣbiə/	Serbian /ˈsɜɣbiən/	
The Seychelles /ðə seɪˈʃelz/	Seychelles /seɪˈʃelz/	Seychellois /seɪʃelˈwɑː/
Sierra Leone /siˌerəliˈəʊn/	Sierra Leonean /siˈerə liˈəʊniən/	
Singapore /ˌsɪŋəˈpɔːʳ/	Singaporean /ˌsɪŋəˈpɔːriən/	
Slovakia /sləˈvækiə/	Slovak /ˈsləʊvæk/	
Slovenia /sləˈviːniə/	Slovenian /sləˈviːniən/	Slovene /ˈsləʊviːn/
The Solomon Islands /ðə ˈsɒləmən ˈaɪləndz/	Solomon Islander /ˈsɒləmən ˈaɪləndəʳ/	
Somalia /səˈmɑːliə/	Somali /səˈmɑːli/	
South Africa /ˌsaʊθ ˈæfrɪkə/	South African /ˌsaʊθ ˈæfrɪkən/	
Spain /speɪn/	Spanish /ˈspænɪʃ/	Spaniard /ˈspænjəd/
Sri Lanka /ˌsriːˈlæŋkə/	Sri Lankan /ˌsriːˈlæŋkən/	

Name	Adjective	Person
Sudan /suː'dɑːn/	**Sudanese** /ˌsuːdə'niːz/	
Suriname /ˌsʊərɪ'næm/	**Surinamese** /ˌsʊərɪnæm'iːz/	
Swaziland /'swɑːzilænd/	**Swazi** /'swɑːzi/	
Sweden /'swiːdn/	**Swedish** /'swiːdɪʃ/	**Swede** /swiːd/
Switzerland /'swɪtsələnd/	**Swiss** /swɪs/	
Syria /'sɪriə/	**Syrian** /'sɪriən/	
Taiwan /ˌtaɪ'wɑːn/	**Taiwanese** /ˌtaɪwə'niːz/	
Tajikistan /tɑː'dʒiːkɪˌstɑːn/	**Tajik** /tɑː'dʒiːk/	
Tanzania /ˌtænzə'niːə/	**Tanzanian** /ˌtænzə'niːən/	
Thailand /'taɪlænd/	**Thai** /taɪ/	
Tibet /tɪ'bet/	**Tibetan** /tɪ'betn/	
Togo /'təʊgəʊ/	**Togolese** /ˌtəʊgə'liːz/	
Tonga /'tɒŋə/	**Tongan** /'tɒŋən/	
Trinidad and Tobago /'trɪnɪdæd ən tə'beɪgəʊ/	**Trinidadian** /ˌtrɪnɪ'dædiən/	
Tunisia /tjuː'nɪziə/	**Tunisian** /tjuː'nɪziən/	
Turkey /'tɜːki/	**Turkish** /'tɜːkɪʃ/	**Turk** /tɜːk/
Turkmenistan /tɜːkˌmenɪ'stɑːn/	**Turkmen** /'tɜːkmen/	
Tuvalu /tuː'vɑːluː/	**Tuvaluan** /ˌtuːvɑː'luːən/	
Uganda /juː'gændə/	**Ugandan** /juː'gændən/	
Ukraine /juː'kreɪn/	**Ukrainian** /juː'kreɪniən/	
The United Arab Emirates /ðə juː'naɪtɪd 'ærəb 'emɪrəts/	**Emirian** /e'mɪriən/	
The United Kingdom /ðə juː'naɪtɪd 'kɪŋdəm/	**British** /'brɪtɪʃ/	**Briton** /'brɪtən/
The United States of America /ðə juː'naɪtɪd steɪts əv ə'merɪkə/	**American** /ə'merɪkən/	
Uruguay /'jʊərəgwaɪ/	**Uruguayan** /ˌjʊərə'gwaɪən/	
Uzbekistan /ʊzˌbekɪ'stɑːn/	**Uzbek** /'ʊzbek/	
Vanuatu /ˌvænu'ɑːtuː/	**Vanuatuan** /ˌvænuɑː'tuːən/	
Vatican City /'vætɪkən 'sɪti/	**Vatican** /'vætɪkən/	
Venezuela /ˌvenɪ'zweɪlə/	**Venezuelan** /ˌvenɪ'zweɪlən/	
Vietnam /ˌviːet'næm/	**Vietnamese** /ˌviːetnə'miːz/	
Western Sahara /ˌwestən ˌsə'hɑːrə/	**Sahrawian** /sɑː'rɑːwɪən/	
Yemen /'jemən/	**Yemeni** /'jeməni/	
Yugoslavia /ˌjuːgəʊ'slɑːviə/	**Yugoslav** /'juːgəʊslɑːv/	
Zambia /'zæmbiə/	**Zambian** /'zæmbiən/	
Zimbabwe /zɪm'bɑːbweɪ/	**Zimbabwean** /zɪm'bɑːbwiən/	

Regular verb tenses

The simple tenses

Present Simple

used for action in the present, for things that are always true or that happen regularly, and for opinions and beliefs

I/we/you/they arrive (**do not** arrive)
he/she/it arrive**s** (**does not** arrive)

Past Simple

used for completed actions and events in the past

I/we/you/they arrive**d** (**did not** arrive)
he/she/it arrive**d** (**did not** arrive)

Future Simple

used for actions and events in the future

I/we/you/they **will** arrive (**will not** arrive)
he/she/it **will** arrive (**will not** arrive)

Present Perfect

used to show that an event happened or an action was completed at some time before the present

I/we/you/they **have** arrive**d** (**have not** arrive**d**)
he/she/it **has** arrive**d** (**has not** arrive**d**)

Past Perfect

used to show that an event happened or an action was completed before a particular time in the past

I/we/you/they **had** arrive**d** (**had not** arrive**d**)
he/she/it **had** arrive**d** (**had not** arrive**d**)

Future Perfect

used to show that something will be completed before a particular time in the future

I/we/you/they **will have** arrive**d** (**will not have** arrive**d**)
he/she/it **will have** arrive**d** (**will not have** arrive**d**)

The continuous/progressive tenses

Present Continuous/Progressive

used for actions or events that are happening or developing now, for future plans, or to show that an event is repeated

I	**am** arriving (**am not** arriving)
we/you/they	**are** arriving (**are not** arriving)
he/she/it	**is** arriving (**is not** arriving)

Past Continuous/Progressive

used for actions or events in the past that were not yet finished or that were interrupted

I	**was** arriving (**was not** arriving)
we/you/they	**were** arriving (**were not** arriving)
he/she/it	**was** arriving (**was not** arriving)

Future Continuous/Progressive

used for actions or events in the future that will continue into the future

I/we/you/they	**will be** arriving (**will not be** arriving)
he/she/it	**will be** arriving (**will not be** arriving)

Present Perfect Continuous/Progressive

used for actions or events that started in the past but are still happening now, or for past actions which only recently finished and their effects are seen now

I/we/you/they	**have been** arriving (**have not been** arriving)
he/she/it	**has been** arriving (**has not been** arriving)

Past Perfect Continuous/Progressive

used for actions or events that happened for a period of time but were completed before a particular time in the past

I/we/you/they	**had been** arriving (**had not been** arriving)
he/she/it	**had been** arriving (**had not been** arriving)

Future Perfect Continuous/Progressive

used for actions or events that will already be happening at a particular time in the future

I/we/you/they	**will have been** arriving (**will not have been** arriving)
he/she/it	**will have been** arriving (**will not have been** arriving)

Irregular verbs

This list gives the infinitive form of the verb, its past tense, and then the past participle. If two forms are given, look the verb up in the dictionary to see whether they have a different meaning.

Infinitive	Past Tense	Past Participle
arise	arose	arisen
awake	awoke	awoken
be	was/were	been
bear	bore	borne
beat	beat	beaten (*also US*) beat
become	became	become
befall	befell	befallen
begin	began	begun
bend	bent	bent
bet	bet, betted	bet, betted
bid	bid, bade	bid, bidden
bind	bound	bound
bite	bit	bitten
bleed	bled	bled
blow	blew	blown
break	broke	broken
breed	bred	bred
bring	brought	brought
broadcast	broadcast (*also US*) broadcasted	broadcast (*also US*) broadcasted
build	built	built
burn	burnt, burned	burnt, burned
burst	burst	burst
bust	(*UK*) bust, (*US*) busted	(*UK*) bust, (*US*) busted
buy	bought	bought
cast	cast	cast
catch	caught	caught
choose	chose	chosen
cling	clung	clung
come	came	come
cost	cost	cost
creep	crept	crept
cut	cut	cut
deal	dealt	dealt
dig	dug	dug
dive	dived (*also US*) dove	dived
draw	drew	drawn
dream	dreamed, (*also UK*) dreamt	dreamed, (*also UK*) dreamt
drink	drank	drunk
drive	drove	driven
dwell	dwelled, (*also UK*) dwelt	dwelled, (*also UK*) dwelt
eat	ate	eaten
fall	fell	fallen
feed	fed	fed
feel	felt	felt
fight	fought	fought
find	found	found
flee	fled	fled
fling	flung	flung
fly	flew	flown
forbid	forbade	forbidden
forecast	forecast, forecasted	forecast, forecasted
foresee	foresaw	foreseen
forget	forgot	forgotten
forgive	forgave	forgiven
forgo	forwent	forgone
forsake	forsook	forsaken
freeze	froze	frozen
get	got	got (*also US*) gotten
give	gave	given
go	went	gone
grind	ground	ground
grow	grew	grown
hang	hung, hanged	hung, hanged
have	had	had
hear	heard	heard
hide	hid	hidden
hit	hit	hit
hold	held	held
hurt	hurt	hurt
input	inputted, input	inputted, input
keep	kept	kept
kneel	knelt, kneeled	knelt, kneeled
know	knew	known

Infinitive	Past Tense	Past Participle
lay	laid	laid
lead	led	led
lean	leaned (*also UK*) leant	leaned (*also UK*) leant
leap	leapt, leaped	leapt, leaped
learn	learned (*also UK*) learnt	learned (*also UK*) learnt
leave	left	left
lend	lent	lent
let	let	let
lie	lay, lied	lain, lied
light	lit, lighted	lit, lighted
lose	lost	lost
make	made	made
mean	meant	meant
meet	met	met
mislay	mislaid	mislaid
mislead	misled	misled
misread	misread	misread
misspell	misspelled (*also UK*) misspelt	misspelled (*also UK*) misspelt
mistake	mistook	mistaken
misunderstand	misunderstood	misunderstood
mow	mowed	mown, mowed
outdo	outdid	outdone
outgrow	outgrew	outgrown
overcome	overcame	overcome
overdo	overdid	overdone
overhang	overhung	overhung
overhear	overheard	overheard
override	overrode	overridden
overrun	overran	overrun
oversee	oversaw	overseen
oversleep	overslept	overslept
overtake	overtook	overtaken
overthrow	overthrew	overthrown
pay	paid	paid
plead	pleaded (*also US*) pled	pleaded (*also US*) pled
prove	proved (*also US*) proven	proved,
put	put	put
quit	quit	quit
read	read	read
rebuild	rebuilt	rebuilt
repay	repaid	repaid
rethink	rethought	rethought
rewind	rewound	rewound
rewrite	rewrote	rewritten
rid	rid	rid
ride	rode	ridden
ring	rang	rung
rise	rose	risen
run	ran	run
saw	sawed	sawn (*also US*) sawed
say	said	said
see	saw	seen
seek	sought	sought
sell	sold	sold
send	sent	sent
set	set	set
sew	sewed	sewn, sewed
shake	shook	shaken
shear	sheared	sheared, shorn
shed	shed	shed
shine	shone	shone
shoot	shot	shot
show	showed	shown, showed
shrink	shrank	shrunk
shut	shut	shut
sing	sang	sung
sink	sank	sunk
sit	sat	sat
slay	slew	slain
sleep	slept	slept
slide	slid	slid
sling	slung	slung
slink	slunk	slunk
slit	slit	slit
smell	smelled (*also UK*) smelt	smelled (*also UK*) smelt
sow	sowed	sown, sowed
speak	spoke	spoken
speed	sped, speeded	sped, speeded
spell	spelled (*also UK*) spelt	spelled (*also UK*) spelt
spend	spent	spent
spill	spilled (*also UK*) spilt	spilled (*also UK*) spilt
spin	spun	spun
spit	spat (*also US*) spit	spat (*also US*) spit
split	split	split
spoil	spoiled, spoilt	spoiled, spoilt
spread	spread	spread

Infinitive	Past Tense	Past Participle
spring	sprang	sprung
stand	stood	stood
steal	stole	stolen
stick	stuck	stuck
sting	stung	stung
stink	stank (*also US*) stunk	stunk
stride	strode	strode
strike	struck	struck
string	strung	strung
strive	strove,strived	striven, strived
swear	swore	sworn
sweep	swept	swept
swell	swelled	swollen, swelled
swim	swam	swum
swing	swung	swung
take	took	taken
teach	taught	taught
tear	tore	torn
tell	told	told
think	thought	thought
throw	threw	thrown
thrust	thrust	thrust

Infinitive	Past Tense	Past Participle
tread	trod	trodden
undercut	undercut	undercut
undergo	underwent	undergone
understand	understood	understood
undertake	undertook	undertaken
undo	undid	undone
unwind	unwound	unwound
uphold	upheld	upheld
upset	upset	upset
wake	woke	woken
wear	wore	worn
weave	wove, weaved	woven, weaved
weep	wept	wept
wet	wet, wetted	wet, wetted
win	won	won
wind	wound	wound
withdraw	withdrew	withdrawn
withhold	withheld	withheld
withstand	withstood	withstood
wring	wrung	wrung
write	wrote	written

Word beginnings and endings

You can change the meaning of many English words simply by adding a group of letters to the beginning or the ending of a word.

Prefixes

A group of letters added to the beginning of a word is called a **prefix**. Here is a list of the most common prefixes and examples of how they are used.

Anglo- relating to the UK or England *an Anglophile* (= someone who loves England)
anti- **1** opposed to or against *anti-racist laws* **2** preventing or destroying *an anti-aircraft missile*
astro- relating to stars or outer space *astronomer* • *astrophysics*
audio- relating to hearing or sound *audiotape*
auto- **1** operating without being controlled by humans *autopilot* (= a computer that directs an aircraft) **2** self *an autobiography* (= a book that someone writes about their own life)
bi- two *bilingual* (= speaking two languages) • *bimonthly* (= happening twice in a month or once every two months)
bio- relating to living things or human life *biodiversity* • *bioethics*
centi-, cent- hundred *a centimetre* • *a century*
co- with or together *a co-author* • *to coexist*
contra- against or opposite *to contradict* (= say the opposite) • *contraception* (= something that is used to prevent pregnancy)
counter- opposing or as a reaction to *a counter-attack* (= an attack on someone who has attacked you)
cross- **1** across *cross-border* **2** including different groups or subjects *a cross-party committee* (= one formed from many political parties) • *cross-cultural*
cyber- relating to electronic communications, especially the Internet *cyberspace*
de- to take something away *deforestation* (= when the trees in an area are cut down)
deca- ten *decade*
demi- half, partly *demitasse* (=a small coffee cup) • *demigod* (=a creature that is part god and part human)
dis- not or the opposite of *dishonest* • *disbelief* • *to disagree*
e- electronic, usually relating to the Internet *email* • *e-commerce*
eco- relating to the environment *eco-friendly tourism* (= tourism which does not damage the environment)
equi- equal, equally *equidistant* (=the same distance from two or more places)
Euro- relating to Europe *Europop* (= modern, young people's music from Europe)
ex- from before *an ex-boyfriend* • *an ex-boss*
extra- outside of or in addition to *extracurricular activities* (= activities that are in addition to the usual school work)
geo- of the earth *geothermal* (=of or connected with the heat inside the earth)
hydro- relating to water *hydroponic* (=a method of growing plants in water)
hyper- having a lot of or too much of a quality *hyperactive* • *hypersensitive* (= more than normally sensitive)
ill- in a way which is bad or not suitable *ill-prepared* • *an ill-judged remark*
in-, il-, im-, ir- not *incorrect* • *illegal* • *impossible* • *irregular*
inter- between or among *international* • *an interdepartmental meeting*
intra- within *an intranet*
kilo- a thousand *a kilometre* • *a kilogram*
macro- on a large scale *macroeconomics* (= the study of economics at a national or international level)
maxi- most, very large *maximum*
mega- **1** *informal* extremely *megarich* (= extremely rich) **2** one million *40 megabytes*
micro- very small *a microchip* • *microscopic* (= extremely small)
mid- in the middle of *mid-July* • *a man in his mid-forties* • *mid-afternoon/-morning*
milli- a thousandth *a millisecond*
mini- small *a miniskirt* (= very short skirt) • *a minibus*
mis- not or badly *mistrust* • *to misbehave*
mono- one or single *monolingual* • *a monologue*
multi- many *a multi-millionaire* • *a multi-storey car park*
nano- **1** one billionth *nanometre* **2** extremely small *nanotechnology*
neo- new *neo-fascists*
non- not or the opposite of *non-alcoholic drinks* • *non-smokers*
out- more than or better than *to outgrow* • *to outnumber* • *to outdo someone* (= to show that you are better than someone)
over- too much *to overeat* • *overpopulated*
poly- many *polygamy* (= having more than one husband or wife at the same time) • *a polygon* (= shape with many sides)
post- after or later than *postwar* • *a postgraduate*
pre- before or earlier than *pre-tax profits* • *pre-school*

pro- supporting *pro-democracy demonstrations*

pseudo- false *a pseudonym* (= false name used especially by a writer) • *pseudo-academic*

quasi- partly *quasi-religious ideas*

re- again *to remarry* • *a reusable container*

semi- half or partly *a semicircle* • *semi-frozen*

socio- relating to society *socio-economic*

sub- **1** under or below *subzero temperatures* **2** less important or a smaller part of a larger whole *a subsection*

super- extremely or more than usual *a supermodel* • *super-rich*

techno- relating to technology *technophile* (=a person who loves technology)

tele- 1 done using a telephone *telesales* 2 connected with television *telecast* (=something that is broadcast on television) 3 over a long distance *telephoto lens* (=a camera lens that makes distant objects look nearer)

thermo- relating to heat or temperature *a thermostat* (= piece of equipment that controls temperature) • *a thermometer*

trans- **1** across *transatlantic flights* **2** showing a change *to transform* • *to translate*

tri- three *a triangle* • *a tripod*

ultra- extremely *ultra-modern architecture* • *ultra-careful*

uber- *humorous* used before nouns to mean 'extreme' or 'extremely good or successful' *uber-successful*

un- not or the opposite of *unhappy* • *unfair* • *to unfasten*

under- **1** not enough *undercooked potatoes* • *underprivileged children* **2** below *underwear* • *an underpass*

Suffixes

A **suffix** is a group of letters at the end of a word which changes the word's meaning and often its part of speech. Here is a list of the most common suffixes and examples of how they are used.

-able,-ible changes a verb into an adjective meaning 'able to be' *avoid → avoidable* • *admire → admirable* • *like → likeable*

-age changes a verb into a noun meaning 'the action described by the verb or the result of that action' *marry → marriage* • *break → breakage* • *spill → spillage*

-aholic unable to stop doing or taking something *chocaholic* (=someone who cannot stop eating chocolate)

-al **1** changes a noun into an adjective meaning 'relating to' *culture → cultural* • *nation → national* • *nature → natural* **2** changes a verb into a noun meaning 'the action described by the verb' *approve → approval* • *remove → removal*

-an, -ian **1** makes a noun meaning 'a person who does something' *historian* • *politician* **2** makes an adjective meaning 'belonging somewhere' *American*

-ance, -ence, -ancy, -ency makes a noun meaning 'an action, state, or quality' *performance* • *independence* • *preference*

-athon an event or activity that lasts a long time, usually to raise money for charity *a walkathon* (=a long walk)

-ation, -ion changes a verb into a noun meaning 'the process of the action described by the verb, or the result of that action' *educate → education* • *explain → explanation* • *connect → connection*

-ed makes an adjective meaning, 'having this thing or quality' *bearded* • *coloured* • *surprised*

-ee changes a verb into a noun meaning 'someone that something is done to' *employ → employee* • *interview → interviewee* • *train → trainee*

-en changes an adjective into a verb meaning 'to become or make something become' *thick → thicken* • *fat → fatten* • *soft → soften*

-ence, -ency See **-ance**

-er, -or changes a verb into a noun meaning 'the person or thing that does the activity' *dance → dancer* • *employ → employer* • *act → actor* • *cook → cooker* (= a machine for cooking) • *time → timer*

-ese of a place, the language spoken there *Lebanese* • *Chinese*

-esque in the style of *Kafka-esque* (= in the style of writer Franz Kafka)

-est makes superlative adjectives and adverbs *bravest* • *latest*

-ful changes a noun into an adjective meaning, 'having a particular quality' *beauty → beautiful* • *power → powerful* • *use → useful*

-hood makes a noun meaning 'the state of being something and the time when someone is something' *childhood* • *motherhood*

-ian See **-an**

-ible See **-able**

-ical changes a noun ending in **-y** or **-ics** into an adjective meaning 'relating to' *history → historical* • *politics → political*

-ify to produce a state or quality *simplify*

-in an activity in which many people take part *a sit-in*

-ing makes an adjective meaning 'making someone feel something' *interest → interesting* • *surprise → surprising* • *shock → shocking*

-ion See **-ation**

-ise See **-ize**

-ish makes an adjective meaning **1** slightly *a greyish colour* • *a smallish* (= quite small) *house* **2** typical of or similar to *a childish remark* **3** approximately *fiftyish* (= about fifty)

-ist **1** makes a noun meaning 'a person who does a particular activity' *artist* • *novelist* • *scientist* **2** makes a noun and an adjective meaning 'someone with a particular set of beliefs' *communist* • *feminist*

-ive changes a verb into an adjective meaning 'having a particular quality or effect' *attract* → *attractive* • *create* → *creative* • *explode* → *explosive*

-ize, -ise *UK* changes an adjective into a verb meaning 'to make something become' *modern* → *modernize* • *commercial* → *commercialize*

-less changes a noun into an adjective meaning 'without' *homeless people* • *a meaningless statement* • *a hopeless situation*

-let small, *piglet*

-like changes a noun into an adjective meaning 'typical of or similar to' *childlike trust* • *a cabbage-like vegetable*

-ly **1** changes an adjective into an adverb describing the way that something is done *She spoke slowly.* • *Drive safely.* **2** makes an adjective and an adverb meaning 'happening every day, night, week, etc' *a daily newspaper* • *We hold the meeting weekly.* **3** changes a noun into an adjective meaning 'like that person or thing' *mother* → *motherly* • *coward* → *cowardly*

-ment changes a verb into a noun meaning 'the action or process described by a verb, or its result' *develop* → *development* • *disappoint* → *disappointment*

-ness changes an adjective into a noun meaning 'the quality or condition described by the adjective' *sweet* → *sweetness* • *happy* → *happiness* • *dark* → *darkness* • *ill* → *illness*

-ology makes a noun meaning 'the study of something' *psychology* (= the study of the mind) • *sociology* (= the study of society)

-or See **-er**

-ous changes a noun into an adjective meaning 'having that quality' *danger* → *dangerous* • *ambition* → *ambitious*

-phile makes a noun meaning 'enjoying or liking something' *a Francophile* (= someone who loves France) • *a bibliophile* (= someone who loves books)

-phobe someone who hates something or someone *commitment-phobe* (= a person who hates commitment)

-ship makes a noun showing involvement between people *friendship* • *a relationship* • *partnership*

-ster a person who is associated with something *gangster*

-ward, -wards makes an adverb meaning 'towards a direction or place' *inward* • *forward* • *homeward*

-wise changes a noun into an adverb meaning 'relating to this subject' *Weather-wise, the holiday was great.* • *How are we doing time-wise?*

-y changes a noun into an adjective meaning 'having a lot of something, *noise* → *noisy* • *dirt* → *dirty* • *smell* → *smelly*

Word building

It is useful to know how to build up word families, and for some exams you need to know these word families. In the list below, words in **bold** type are words which have the symbol o━ by them in the dictionary, meaning that they are very common and important to learn. The other words on each line are words in the same family, often formed with prefixes and suffixes, or sometimes just a different part of speech (e.g. **anger**, which is a noun and a verb). All the words in this list have entries in the dictionary except for some beginning with 'un-', 'im-', 'in-' or 'ir-', or ending with '-ly' or '-ily', where the meaning is always regular. Sometimes words in a word family can have meanings which are quite different from others in the group, so you should always check in the dictionary if you are not sure of the meaning.

Nouns	Verbs	Adjectives	Adverbs
ability, disability, inability	enable, disable	**able**, unable, disabled	ably
acceptance	**accept**	**acceptable**, unacceptable, accepted	acceptably, unacceptably
accident		accidental	accidentally
accuracy, inaccuracy		**accurate**, inaccurate	accurately, inaccurately
accusation, the accused, accuser	**accuse**	accusing	accusingly
achievement, achiever	**achieve**	achievable	
act, **action**, inaction, interaction, reaction, transaction	**act**	acting	
activity, inactivity	activate	**active**, inactive, interactive, proactive	actively
addition	**add**	additional	additionally
admiration, admirer	**admire**	admirable	admirably
advantage, disadvantage		advantageous, disadvantaged	advantageously
advertisement, advertiser, **advertising**	advertise		advertise
advice, adviser	**advise**	advisable, inadvisable, advisory	advisedly
agreement, disagreement	**agree**, disagree	agreeable	agreeably
aim	**aim**	aimless	aimlessly
amazement	amaze	amazed, **amazing**	amazingly
anger	anger	**angry**	angrily
announcement, announcer	**announce**	unannounced	unannounced
appearance, disappearance, reappearance	**appear**, disappear, reappear		
applicant, application	**apply**	applicable, applied	
appreciation	**appreciate**	appreciable, appreciative	appreciatively
approval, disapproval	**approve**, disapprove	approving, disapproving	approvingly
approximation	approximate	approximate	**approximately**
argument	**argue**	arguable, argumentative	arguably
arrangement	**arrange**, rearrange		
art, **artist**, artistry		artistic, arty	artistically
shame	shame	**ashamed**, unashamed, shameful, shameless	shamefully, shamelessly
attachment	**attach**, detach	attached, unattached, detachable, detached	

Nouns	Verbs	Adjectives	Adverbs
attack, counter-attack, attacker	**attack**, counter-attack		
attention	attend	attentive, inattentive	attentively
attraction, attractiveness	attract	**attractive**, unattractive	attractively
authority, authorization	authorize	authoritarian, authoritative, authorized, unauthorized	
availability		**available**, unavailable	
avoidance	**avoid**	avoidable, unavoidable	
awareness		**aware**, unaware	unawares
base, the basics, basis	**base**	baseless, **basic**	**basically**
bearer	**bear**	bearable, unbearable	
beat, beating	**beat**	unbeatable, unbeaten	
beautician, **beauty**		**beautiful**	beautifully
beginner, **beginning**	**begin**		
behaviour/US **behavior**, misbehaviour/US misbehavior	**behave**, misbehave	behavioural/US behavioral	
belief, disbelief	**believe**, disbelieve	believable, unbelievable	unbelievably
block, blockage	**block**, unblock	blocked, unblocked	
blood, bleeding	bleed	bloodless, bloody	
the boil, boiler	**boil**	boiling	
bore, boredom	bore	**bored**, **boring**	boringly
break, breakage, outbreak	**break**	**broken**, unbreakable, unbroken	
breath, breather, breathing	**breathe**	breathless	breathlessly
brother, brotherhood		brotherly	
build, builder, **building**	**build**, rebuild		
burn, burner	**burn**	burning, burnt	
burial	**bury**	buried	
calculation, calculator	**calculate**	incalculable, calculated, calculating	
calm, calmness	calm	**calm**	calmly
capability		**capable**, incapable	capably
care, carer	**care**	careful, careless, caring, uncaring	carefully, carelessly
celebration, celebrity	**celebrate**	celebrated, celebratory	
centre/US **center**, centralization, decentralization	centre/US center, centralize, decentralize	**central**, centralized	centrally
certainty, uncertainty	ascertain	**certain**, uncertain	certainly, uncertainly
challenge, challenger	challenge	challenging	
change	**change**	changeable, interchangeable, unchanged, changing	
character, characteristic, characterization	characterize	characteristic, uncharacteristic	characteristically
chemical, chemist, chemistry		chemical	chemically
circle, semicircle, circulation	circle, circulate	circular	
cleaner, cleaning, cleanliness	**clean**	**clean**, unclean	clean, cleanly
clarity, clearance, clearing	**clear**	**clear**, unclear	clear, **clearly**
close, closure	**close**	closed, closing	
closeness		**close**	**close**, closely
clothes, clothing	clothe	clothed, unclothed	
collection, collector	**collect**	collected, collective	collectively
colour/US **color**, colorfully colouring/US coloring	colour/US color	coloured/US colored, discoloured/US discolored, colourful/US colorful, colourless/US colorless	colourfully/US
combination	**combine**	combined	

Nouns	Verbs	Adjectives	Adverbs
comfort, discomfort	comfort	**comfortable**, uncomfortable, comforting	comfortably
commitment	**commit**	noncommittal, committed	
communication, communicator	**communicate**	communicative, uncommunicative	
comparison	**compare**	comparable, incomparable, comparative	comparatively
competition, competitor	**compete**	competitive, uncompetitive	competitively
completion, incompleteness	**complete**	**complete**, incomplete	**completely**, incompletely
complication	complicate	**complicated**, uncomplicated	
computer, computing, computerization	computerize		
concentration	**concentrate**	concentrated	
concern	**concern**	**concerned**, unconcerned	
conclusion	conclude	concluding, conclusive, inconclusive	conclusively
condition, precondition, conditioner, conditioning	condition	conditional, unconditional	conditionally, unconditionally
confidence	confide	**confident**, confidential	confidently, confidentially
confirmation	**confirm**	confirmed, unconfirmed	
confusion	**confuse**	confused, confusing	confusingly
connection	**connect**, disconnect	connected, disconnected, unconnected	
subconscious, unconscious, consciousness, unconsciousness		**conscious**, subconscious, unconscious	consciously, unconsciously
consequence		consequent, inconsequential	consequently
consideration	**consider**, reconsider	considerable, considerate, inconsiderate, considered	considerably, considerately
continent		continental, intercontinental	
continuation, continuity	**continue**, discontinue	continual, continued, **continuous**	continually, continuously
contribution, contributor	**contribute**	contributory	
control, controller	**control**	controlling, uncontrollable	uncontrollably
convenience, inconvenience	inconvenience	**convenient**, inconvenient	conveniently
	convince	convinced, convincing, unconvincing	convincingly
cook, cooker, cookery, **cooking**	**cook**	cooked, uncooked	
cool, coolness	cool	**cool**	coolly
correction, correctness	**correct**	**correct**, incorrect, corrective	correctly, incorrectly
count, recount	**count**, recount	countable, uncountable, countless	
cover, coverage, covering	**cover**, uncover	undercover, uncovered	undercover
creation, creativity, creator	**create**, recreate	creative, uncreative	creatively
crime, **criminal**, criminologist	incriminate	criminal, incriminating	criminally
critic, **criticism**	**criticize**	**critical**, uncritical	critically
crowd, overcrowding	crowd	**crowded**, overcrowded	
cruelty		**cruel**	cruelly
cry, outcry	cry	crying	
culture, subculture		cultural, cultured	culturally
cure	**cure**	cured, incurable	
custom, **customer**, customs	accustom	customary	customarily
cut, cutting	**cut**, undercut	cutting	
damage, damages	**damage**	damaging, undamaged	
danger	endanger	endangered, **dangerous**	dangerously

Nouns	Verbs	Adjectives	Adverbs
dare, daring	**dare**	daring	daringly
dark, darkness	darken	**dark**, darkened, darkening	darkly
date	date, predate	dated, outdated	
day, midday		daily	daily
dead, **death**	deaden	**dead**, deadly, deathly	deadly, deathly
deal, dealer, dealings	**deal**		
deceit, deceiver, deception	**deceive**	deceitful, deceptive	deceptively
decision, indecision	**decide**	decided, undecided, decisive, indecisive	decidedly, decisively, indecisively
decoration, decorator	**decorate**	decorative	decoratively
deep, **depth**	deepen	**deep**, deepening	deeply
defeat, defeatism, defeatist	**defeat**	undefeated, defeatist	
defence/US **defense**, defendant, defender	**defend**	defenceless/US defenseless, indefensible, defensive	defensively
definition	define	**definite**, indefinite	**definitely**, indefinitely
demand, demands	**demand**	demanding, undemanding	
democracy, democrat		democratic, undemocratic	democratically
demonstration, demonstrator	**demonstrate**	demonstrable, demonstrative	demonstrably
denial	**deny**	undeniable	undeniably
dependant, dependence, independence, dependency	**depend**	dependable, dependent, independent	dependably, independently
description	**describe**	describable, indescribable, descriptive, nondescript	descriptively
desire	desire	desirable, undesirable, desired, undesired	
destroyer, destruction	**destroy**	indestructible, destructive	destructively
determination, determiner	determine	**determined**, predetermined indeterminate	determinedly
developer, **development**, redevelopment	**develop**, redevelop	developed, undeveloped, developing	
difference, indifference, differentiation	differ, differentiate	**different**, indifferent	differently
directness, **direction**, directions, **director**	**direct**, redirect	**direct**, indirect	directly, indirectly
disagreement	**disagree**	disagreeable	disagreeably
disappointment	disappoint	**disappointed**, disappointing	disappointingly
disaster		disastrous	disastrously
disciplinarian, **discipline**	discipline	disciplinary, disciplined, undisciplined	
discoverer, **discovery**	**discover**		
distance	distance	**distant**	distantly
disturbance	**disturb**	disturbed, undisturbed, disturbing	disturbingly
divide, division, subdivision	**divide**, subdivide	divided, undivided, divisible, divisive	
divorce, divorcee	divorce	divorced	
do, doing	**do**, outdo, overdo, redo, undo	done, overdone, undone	
doubt, doubter	**doubt**	undoubted, doubtful, doubtless	undoubtedly, doubtfully
dream, dreamer	**dream**	dream, dreamless, dreamy	dreamily
dress, dresser, dressing	**dress**, redress, undress	dressed, undressed, dressy	
drink, drinker, drinking, drunk, drunkenness	**drink**	**drunk**, drunken	drunkenly
drive, **driver**, driving	**drive**	driving	
due, dues		**due**, undue	due, duly, unduly
earner, earnings	**earn**		
earth	unearth	earthy, earthly, unearthly	
ease, unease, easiness	ease	**easy**, uneasy	**easily**, uneasily, easy

Nouns	Verbs	Adjectives	Adverbs
east, easterner		east, easterly, eastern	east, eastward(s)
economics, economist, **economy**	economize	**economic**, economical, uneconomic(al)	economically
education	educate	educated, uneducated, educational	educationally
effect, effectiveness, ineffectiveness	effect	**effective**, ineffective, ineffectual	effectively, ineffectively
effort		effortless	effortlessly
election, re-election, elector, electorate	elect, re-elect	unelected, electoral	
electrician, **electricity**	electrify	**electric**, **electrical**	electrically
electronics		**electronic**	electronically
embarrassment	embarrass	**embarrassed**, **embarrassing**	embarrassingly
emotion		emotional, emotive	emotionally
emphasis	**emphasize**	emphatic	emphatically
employee, **employer**, **employment**, unemployment	**employ**	unemployed	
encouragement, discouragement	**encourage**, discourage	encouraged, encouraging, discouraging	encouragingly
end, ending	**end**	unending, endless	endlessly
energy	energize	energetic	energetically
enjoyment	**enjoy**	enjoyable	enjoyably
enormity		**enormous**	enormously
entrance, entrant, **entry**	**enter**		
entertainer, **entertainment**	entertain	entertaining	entertainingly
enthusiasm, enthusiast	enthuse	**enthusiastic**, unenthusiastic	enthusiastically, unenthusiastically
environment, environmentalist		environmental	environmentally
equality, inequality	equalize	**equal**, unequal	**equally**, unequally
escape, escapism	**escape**	escaped, inescapable	inescapably
essence, essentials		**essential**	essentially
estimate, estimation	**estimate**, overestimate underestimate	estimated	,
event, non-event		eventful, uneventful, eventual	eventfully, eventually
exam, examination, cross-examination, examiner	examine, cross-examine		
excellence	excel	**excellent**	excellently
excitement	excite	excitable, **excited**, **exciting**, unexciting	excitedly, excitingly
excuse	**excuse**	excusable, inexcusable	inexcusably
existence	**exist**, coexist	non-existent, existing, pre-existing	
expectancy, expectation	**expect**	expectant, unexpected	expectantly, unexpectedly
expense, expenditure, expenses	expend	**expensive**, inexpensive	expensively, inexpensively
experience, inexperience	experience	**experienced**, inexperienced	
experiment	experiment	experimental	experimentally
expert, expertise		expert, inexpert	expertly
explaining, **explanation**	**explain**	unexplained, explanatory, explicable, inexplicable	inexplicably
explosion, explosive	**explode**	exploding, explosive	explosively
exploration, explorer	**explore**	exploratory	
expression	**express**	expressive	expressively
extreme, extremism, extremist, extremity		**extreme**, extremist	**extremely**

Nouns	Verbs	Adjectives	Adverbs
fact		factual	factually
fail, failure	**fail**	unfailing	unfailingly
fairness		**fair**, unfair	**fairly**, unfairly
faith, faithfulness		faithful, unfaithful	faithfully
familiarity, **family**	familiarize	**familiar**, unfamiliar	familiarly
fame		famed, **famous**, infamous	famously, infamously
fashion	fashion	fashionable, unfashionable	fashionably, unfashionably
fat	fatten	**fat**, fattening, fatty	
fastener	**fasten**, unfasten		
fault	fault	faultless, faulty	faultlessly
fear	fear	fearful, fearless, fearsome	fearfully, fearlessly
feel, **feeling**, feelings	**feel**	unfeeling	
fiction, nonfiction		fictional	
fill, refill, filling	**fill**, refill	filling	
final, finalist, semifinal	finalize	**final**	**finally**
finish	**finish**	finished, unfinished	
firmness, infirmity		**firm**, infirm	firmly
fish, fishing	fish	fishy	fishily
fit, fittings	**fit**	fitted, fitting	fittingly
fix, fixation, fixture	**fix**	fixed, transfixed, unfixed	fixedly
flat	flatten	**flat**	flat, flatly
flower	flower	flowered/flowery, flowering	
fold, folder	**fold**, unfold	folded, folding	
follower, following	**follow**	following	
force	**force**	forceful, forcible	forcefully, forcibly
forest, deforestation, forestry		forested	
forgetfulness	**forget**	forgetful, unforgettable	forgetfully
forgiveness	**forgive**	forgiving, unforgiving	
form, formation, transformation, reformer, transformer	**form**, reform, transform	reformed	
formality	formalize	**formal**, informal	formally, informally
fortune		fortunate, unfortunate	**fortunately**, unfortunately
freedom, freebie	**free**	**free**	free, freely
freeze, freezer, freezing	**freeze**	freezing, frozen	
frequency, infrequency	frequent	**frequent**, infrequent	**frequently**, infrequently
freshness, refreshments	freshen, refresh	**fresh**, refreshing	freshly, refreshingly
friend, friendliness	befriend	friendly, unfriendly	
fright	**frighten**	**frightened**, **frightening**, frightful	frighteningly, frightfully
fruit, fruition		fruitful, fruitless, fruity	fruitfully, fruitlessly
fund, refund, funding	fund, refund	funded	
furnishings, **furniture**	furnish	furnished, unfurnished	
garden, gardener, gardening	garden		
generalization	generalize	**general**	**generally**
generosity		**generous**	generously
gentleness		**gentle**	gently
gladness	gladden	**glad**	gladly
glass, glasses		glassy	
good, goodies, goodness, goods		**good**	
government, governor	govern	governmental, governing	governmentally
gratitude, ingratitude		**grateful**, ungrateful	gratefully
greatness		**great**	greatly

Nouns	Verbs	Adjectives	Adverbs
green, greenery, greens		**green**	
ground, underground, grounding, grounds	ground	groundless, underground	underground
grower, **growth**, undergrowth	**grow**, outgrow	growing, grown, overgrown	
guilt, guiltiness		**guilty**	guiltily
habit		habitual	habitually
hair, hairiness		hairless, hairy	
hand, handful	**hand**	underhand, handy	
handle, handler, handling	**handle**		
hanger	**hang**, overhang	hanging	
happiness, unhappiness		**happy**, unhappy	happily, unhappily
hardship	harden	**hard**	**hard**, hardly
harm	**harm**	harmful, harmless, unharmed	harmlessly
head, heading, overheads	head, behead	overhead, heady	overhead
health		**healthy**, unhealthy	healthily, unhealthily
hearing	**hear**, overhear	unheard, unheard of	
heart		heartened, heartening, heartless, hearty	heartily, heartlessly
heat, heater, heating	heat, overheat	heated, unheated	heatedly
height, heights	heighten	heightened	
help, helper, helpfulness, helping	**help**	helpful, unhelpful, helpless	helpfully, helplessly
height	**high**	high, highly	
historian, **history**		historic, prehistoric, historical	historically
hold, holder, holding	**hold**		
home	home	homeless, homely	**home**
honesty, dishonesty		**honest**, dishonest	honestly, dishonestly
hope, hopefulness, hopelessness	**hope**	hopeful, hopeless	**hopefully**, hopelessly
human, humanism, humanity, inhumanity	humanize	**human**, inhuman, superhuman, humane	humanly, humanely
hunger		**hungry**	hungrily
hurry	**hurry**	hurried, unhurried	hurriedly
hurt	**hurt**	unhurt, hurtful	hurtfully
ice, icicle, icing	ice	icy	icily
identification, identity	**identify**	identifiable, unidentified	
imagination	**imagine**	imaginable, unimaginable, imaginary, imaginative	imaginatively, unimaginably
importance		**important**, unimportant	importantly
impression	impress	impressionable, impressive	impressively
improvement	**improve**	improved	
increase	**increase**	increased	increasingly
credibility, incredulity		**incredible**, credible, incredulous	incredibly, incredulously
independence, independent		**independent**	independently
industrialist, industrialization, **industry**		**industrial**, industrialized, industrious	industrially, industriously
infection, disinfectant	infect, disinfect	infectious	infectiously
inflation	inflate, deflate	inflatable, inflated, inflationary	
information, informant, informer	inform, misinform	informative, uninformative, informed, uninformed	
injury	**injure**	injured, uninjured	
innocence		**innocent**	innocently
insistence	**insist**	insistent	insistently
instance, instant		**instant**, instantaneous	instantly, instantaneously
instruction, instructor	instruct	instructive	instructively

Nouns	Verbs	Adjectives	Adverbs
intelligence		**intelligent**, unintelligent, intelligible, unintelligible	intelligently
intent, **intention**	**intend**	intended, unintended, intentional, unintentional	intentionally, unintentionally
interest	interest	**interested**, **interesting**, disinterested, uninterested	interestingly
interruption	**interrupt**	uninterrupted	
interview, interviewee	interview		
introduction	**introduce**	introductory	
invention, inventiveness, inventor	**invent**, reinvent	inventive	inventively
invitation, invite	**invite**	uninvited, inviting	invitingly
involvement	**involve**	**involved**, uninvolved	
item	itemize	itemized	
joke, joker	joke	jokingly	
journal, journalism, **journalist**		journalistic	
judge, **judg(e)ment**	**judge**	judgmental	
juice, juices		juicy	
keenness		**keen**	keenly
keep, keeper, keeping	**keep**	kept	
kill, overkill, killer, killing	**kill**		
kindness, unkindness		**kind**, unkind	kindly, unkindly
knowledge	**know**	knowing, knowledgeable, known, unknown	knowingly, unknowingly, knowledgeably
enlargement	enlarge	**large**	largely
laugh, **laughter**	**laugh**	laughable	laughably
law, **lawyer**, outlaw	outlaw	lawful, unlawful	lawfully, unlawfully
laziness		**lazy**	lazily
lead, **leader**, leadership	**lead**	lead, leading	
learner, learning	**learn**, unlearn	learned, unlearned	
legality, illegality, legalization	legalize	**legal**, illegal	legally, illegally
length	lengthen	lengthening, lengthy	lengthily
liar, **lie**	lie	lying	
life		lifeless, lifelike, lifelong	lifelessly
light, lighter, lighting, lightness	light, lighten	**light**	lightly
dislike, liking	**like**, dislike	likeable	
likelihood		**likely**, unlikely	likely
limit, limitation, limitations	**limit**	limited, unlimited	
literature, literacy		literary, literate, illiterate	
liveliness, living	**live**, outlive, relive	**live**, lively, living	live
local, location, relocation	dislocate, relocate	**local**	locally
loser, **loss**	**lose**	lost	
		loud	aloud, loud/loudly
love, lover	**love**	lovable, unlovable, loveless, lovely, loving	lovingly
low	lower	**low**, lower, lowly	low
luck		**lucky**, unlucky	luckily, unluckily
machine, machinery, mechanic, mechanics, mechanism		mechanical, mechanized	mechanically
magic, magician		magic, magical	magically
make, remake, maker, making	**make**, remake	unmade	
man, manhood, mankind	man	manly, manned, unmanned	
management, manager	**manage**	manageable, unmanageable, managerial	
mark, marker, markings	**mark**	marked, unmarked	markedly

Nouns	Verbs	Adjectives	Adverbs
market, marketing, marketer	market	marketable	
marriage	**marry**, remarry	**married**, unmarried	
match	**match**	matching, unmatched	
material, materialism, materialist, materials	materialize	material, immaterial, materialistic	
meaning	**mean**	meaningful, meaningless	meaningfully
measure, **measurement**	**measure**	measurable, immeasurable	immeasurably
medical, medication, **medicine**		**medical**, medicated, medicinal	medically, medicinally
memorial, **memory**	memorize	memorable	memorably
mentality		**mental**	mentally
method, methodology		methodical, methodological	methodically
militancy, militant, the military, militia		**military**, militant	militantly, militarily
mind, minder, reminder	**mind**, remind	mindless	mindlessly
minimum	minimize	minimal, **minimum**, minimalist	minimally
miss	**miss**	**missing**	
mistake	mistake	mistaken, unmistakable	unmistakably, mistakenly
mix, mixer, **mixture**	**mix**	mixed	
modernity, modernization	modernize	**modern**	
moment		momentary, momentous	momentarily
mood, moodiness		moody	moodily
moral, morals, morality, immorality		**moral**, amoral, immoral	morally
mother, motherhood		motherly	
move, **movement**, removal, remover	**move**, remove	movable, unmoved, moving	movingly
murder, murderer	**murder**	murderous	murderously
music, musical, musician		musical, unmusical	musically
name	**name**, rename	named, unnamed, nameless	namely
nation, national, multinational, nationalism, nationalist, nationality, nationalization	nationalize	**national**, international, multinational, nationalistic	nationally, internationally
nature, naturalist, naturalization, naturalness the supernatural	naturalize	**natural**, unnatural, supernatural, naturalistic	naturally, unnaturally
necessity, unnecessarily	necessitate	**necessary**, unnecessary	necessarily, unnecessarily
need, needs	**need**	needless, needy	needlessly
nerve, nerves, nervousness	unnerve	**nervous**, unnerving	nervously, unnervingly
news, renewal	renew	**new**, renewable, renewed	newly, anew
night, midnight			overnight, nightly
noise		noisy	noisily
normality/US normalcy, abnormality, norm		**normal**, abnormal	**normally**, abnormally
north, northerner		north, northerly, northern	north, northward(s)
notice	**notice**	noticeable, unnoticed	noticeably
number, numeral	number, outnumber, enumerate	innumerable, numerical, numerous	
nurse, nursery, nursing	nurse		
obedience, disobedience	**obey**, disobey	obedient, disobedient	obediently, disobediently
occasion		occasional	occasionally
offence/US **offense**, offender, offensive	**offend**	offensive, inoffensive	offensively
office, officer, official		**official**, unofficial	officially, unofficially
the open, opener, opening, openness	**open**	**open**, opening	openly

Nouns	Verbs	Adjectives	Adverbs
operation, cooperation, operative, cooperative operator	**operate**, cooperate	operational, operative, cooperative	operationally
opposition, opposite	**oppose**	opposed, opposing, **opposite**	opposite
option	opt	optional	optionally
order, disorder	**order**	disordered, orderly, disorderly	
organization, disorganization, reorganization, organizer	**organize**, disorganize, reorganize	organizational, organized, disorganized	
origin, original, originality, originator	originate	**original**, unoriginal	**originally**
owner, ownership	**own**, disown		
pack, package, packaging, packet, packing	**pack**, unpack, package	packed	
pain	pain	pained, **painful**, painless	painfully, painlessly
paint, painter, **painting**	**paint**		
part, counterpart, parting, partition	part, partition	partial, parting	part, partially, **partly**
pass, overpass, underpass, passage, passing	**pass**	passing	
patience, impatience, **patient**		**patient**, impatient	patiently, impatiently
pay, **payment**, repayment	**pay**, repay	unpaid, underpaid	
peace		**peaceful**	peacefully
perfection, imperfection, perfectionist	perfect	**perfect**, imperfect	**perfectly**
performance, performer	**perform**		
permission, permit	permit	permissible, impermissible, permissive	
person, **personality**	personalize, personify	**personal**, impersonal, personalized	personally
persuasion	**persuade**, dissuade	persuasive	persuasively
photo, **photograph**, photographer, photography	photograph	photogenic, photographic	
picture	picture	pictorial, picturesque	
place, placement, displacement, replacement	place, displace, replace	misplaced	
plan, planner, planning	**plan**	unplanned	
plant, transplant, plantation	plant, transplant		
play, **player**, interplay, replay, playfulness	**play**, outplay, replay	playful	playfully
pleasure, pleasantry, displeasure	please, displease	**pleasant**, unpleasant, **pleased**, displeased, pleasing, pleasurable	pleasantly, unpleasantly
poem, **poetry**, poet		poetic	
point, pointer	**point**	pointed, pointless	pointlessly
politeness		**polite**, impolite	politely, impolitely
politician, **politics**	politicize	**political**, politicized	politically
popularity, unpopularity, popularization	popularize	**popular**, unpopular	popularly
population	populate	populated, unpopulated, populous	
possibility, impossibility, the impossible		**possible**, impossible	**possibly**, impossibly
post, postage	**post**	postal	
power, superpower	power, empower, overpower	**powerful**, overpowering, powerless	powerfully
practical, practicalities, practicality		practicable, **practical**, impractical	practically

Nouns	Verbs	Adjectives	Adverbs
practice, practitioner	**practise**/US **practice**	practised/US practiced, practising/US practicing	
precision		**precise**, imprecise	precisely
preference	**prefer**	preferable, preferential	preferably
preparation, preparations	**prepare**	prepared, unprepared, preparatory	
present, presence, presentation, presenter	present, represent	**present**, presentable	presently
pressure, press	**press**, pressure/pressurize	pressed, pressing, pressurized	
prevention	**prevent**	preventable, preventive/preventative	
price	price	overpriced, priceless, pricey/pricy	
print, printer, printing	**print**	printed	
prison, **prisoner**, imprisonment	imprison		
privacy, private, privatization	privatize	**private**	privately
probability		probable, improbable	**probably**, improbably
process, processing, procession, processor	process	processed	
produce, producer, **product**, **production**, reproduction, productivity	**produce**, reproduce	productive, counterproductive, reproductive, unproductive	
profession, professional, professionalism		**professional**, unprofessional	professionally
profit, profitability	profit	profitable, unprofitable	profitably
progress, progression	progress	progressive	progressively
proof	prove, disprove	proven, unproven	
protection, protector	**protect**	protected, unprotected, protective	protectively
provider, provision, provisions	**provide**	provisional	provisionally
public, publication, publicist, publicity	publicize	**public**	publicly
publisher, publishing	**publish**	published, unpublished	
punishment	**punish**	punishable, punishing, punitive	
purification, purist, purity, impurity	purify	**pure**, impure	purely
purpose		purposeful	purposefully, purposely
push, pusher	**push**	pushed, pushy	
qualification, disqualification, qualifier	qualify, disqualify	qualified, unqualified	
quarter, quarters	quarter	quarterly	quarterly
question, questioning, questionnaire	question	questionable, unquestionable	unquestionably
quiet, disquiet	quieten/quiet	**quiet**	quietly
race, racism, racist		racial, multiracial, racist	racially
rarity		**rare**	rarely
rate, rating, ratings	rate, underrate	overrated, underrated	
reaction, reactor	**react**, overreact	reactionary	
read, reader, readership, **reading**	**read**	readable, unreadable	
readiness		**ready**	readily
realism, realist, reality, unreality, realization	**realize**	**real**, unreal, realistic, unrealistic	real, **really**, realistically
reason, reasoning	reason	reasonable, unreasonable	reasonably, unreasonably
receipt, receipts, receiver, reception, recipient	**receive**	receptive	
recognition	**recognize**	recognizable, unrecognizable	recognizably

Nouns	Verbs	Adjectives	Adverbs
record, recorder, recording	recorded, unrecorded	**record**	
referee, reference, referral	**refer**, referee		
reflection	**reflect**	reflective	
regret	**regret**	regrettable, regretful	regrettably, regretfully
regular, regularity, irregularity, irregularly	regulate	**regular**, irregular	**regularly**
relation, relations, **relationship**, **relative**	relate	**related**, unrelated, relative	relatively
relaxation	**relax**	**relaxed**, relaxing	
reliability, reliance	**rely**	**reliable**, unreliable, reliant	reliably
religion		**religious**, irreligious	religiously
the remainder, remains	**remain**	remaining	
remark	remark	remarkable, unremarkable	remarkably
repair, disrepair	**repair**	irreparable	irreparably
repeat, repetition	**repeat**	repeated, repetitive/repetitious	repeatedly, repetitively
report, reporter	**report**	unreported	reportedly
representation, representative	**represent**	representative, unrepresentative	
reputation, disrepute		reputable, disreputable, reputed	reputedly
respect, disrespect, respectability	**respect**	respectable, respected, respectful, disrespectful, respective	respectably, respectfully, disrespectfully, respectively
respondent, **response**, responsiveness	**respond**	responsive, unresponsive	responsively
responsibility, irresponsibility		**responsible**, irresponsible	responsibly, irresponsibly
rest, unrest, restlessness	**rest**	restless	restlessly
retiree, retirement	**retire**	retired, retiring	
reward	reward	rewarding, unrewarding	
riches, richness, enrichment	enrich	**rich**	richly
ride, rider, riding	**ride**, override	overriding	
right, rights, rightness, righteousness	right	right, righteous, rightful	**right**, rightly, rightfully
roll, roller	**roll**, unroll	rolling	
romance, romantic	romance, romanticize	**romantic**, unromantic, romanticized	romantically
rough, roughage, roughness	rough, roughen	**rough**	rough, **roughly**
round, rounders, roundness	round	**round**, rounded	**round**, roundly
royal, royalist, royalty		**royal**, royalist	royally
rudeness		**rude**	rudely
rule, ruler, ruling	rule, overrule	ruling, unruly	
run, rerun, runner, running, rundown	**run**, outrun, overrun	running, runny	
sadness	sadden	**sad**	sadly
safe, **safety**		**safe**, unsafe	safely
satisfaction, dissatisfaction	satisfy	**satisfactory**, unsatisfactory, **satisfied**, dissatisfied, unsatisfied, satisfying	satisfactorily, unsatisfactorily
save, saver, saving, savings, saviour/US savior	**save**		
scare	scare	**scared**, scary	
school, pre-school, schooling		pre-school	
science, **scientist**		**scientific**, unscientific	scientifically
score, scorer	**score**, outscore, underscore		
search, research, researcher	**search**, research	searching	
seat, seating	seat, unseat	seated	
secrecy, secret		**secret**, secretive	secretly, secretively

Nouns	Verbs	Adjectives	Adverbs
sense, nonsense, sensibility, sensitivity, insensitivity, sensor	sense	**sensible**, senseless, sensitive, insensitive	sensibly, sensitively, insensitively
separation	**separate**	separable, inseparable, **separate**	inseparably, separately
seriousness		**serious**	**seriously**
servant, serve, server, **service**, disservice, services, serving	**serve**, service	serviceable, servile	
sex, sexism, sexuality, sexist		sexist, **sexual**, bisexual, sexy	sexually
shadow	shadow, overshadow	shadowy	
shake	**shake**	shaky	shakily
shape	shape	shapeless, shapely	
(pencil) sharpener, sharpness	sharpen	**sharp**	sharp, sharply
shine	**shine**, outshine	shiny	
shock	**shock**	shocked, shocking	shockingly
shop, shopper, **shopping**	shop		
short, shortage, shortness, shorts	shorten	**short**	short, shortly
shyness	shy	**shy**	shyly
sick, sickness	sicken	**sick**, sickening, sickly	sickeningly
sight, insight, oversight, sighting	sight	sighted, unsightly	
sign, **signal**, signatory, signature, signing	**sign**, signal	signed, unsigned	
significance, insignificance	signify	**significant**, insignificant	significantly, insignificantly
silence, silencer	silence	**silent**	silently
similarity		**similar**, dissimilar	similarly
simplicity, simplification	simplify	**simple**, simplistic	simply
singer, singing	**sing**	unsung	
single, singles	single	**single**, singular	singly
skill		skilful/US skillful, skilled, unskilled	skilfully/US skillfully
sleep, sleeper, sleepiness, sleeplessness	**sleep**	asleep, sleepless, sleepy	sleepily
slight		**slight**, slighted, slightest	**slightly**
slip, slipper	**slip**	slippery	
smoke, smoker, non-smoker, smoking	**smoke**	smoked, smoking, non-smoking, smoky	
smoothness, smoothie	**smooth**	smooth	smoothly
society, sociologist, sociology	socialize	sociable, unsociable, **social**, anti-social, unsocial	socially
softness	soften	**soft**	softly
solid, solidarity, solidity, solids	solidify	**solid**	solidly
solution, solvent	**solve**	soluble, insoluble, unsolved, solvent	
south, southerner		south, southerly, southern	south, southward(s)
speaker, **speech**	**speak**	unspeakable, speechless, outspoken, unspoken	unspeakably
special, specialist, speciality/US specialty, specialization	specialize	**special**, specialized	**specially**
speed, speeding	speed	speedy	speedily
spelling, speller	**spell**, misspell		
spoils	**spoil**	spoilt/spoiled, unspoiled/unspoilt	
sport	sport	sporting, sporty	
spot	spot	spotted, spotless, spotty	spotlessly
stand, standing, standoff, standstill	**stand**, withstand	standing, outstanding	outstandingly

Nouns	Verbs	Adjectives	Adverbs
standard, standardization	standardize	standard, substandard	
start, starter, non-starter	**start**, restart		
statement, understatement	state, overstate	understated	
steam, steamer	steam	steamy	
steepness		**steep**	steeply
sticker	**stick**	sticky, stuck, unstuck	
stiffness	stiffen	**stiff**	stiff, stiffly
stone	stone	stoned, stony	
stop, stoppage	**stop**	non-stop	non-stop
storm	storm	stormy	
	straighten	**straight**	**straight**
stranger		**strange**, estranged	strangely
strength	strengthen	**strong**	strongly
stress	stress	stressed, stressful	
strike, striker	**strike**	striking	
structure, restructuring	structure, restructure	structural	structurally
student, **study**	**study**	studious	studiously
stupidity		**stupid**	stupidly
style	style	stylish	stylishly
substance	substantiate	substantial, insubstantial, substantive	substantially
success, succession, unsuccessfully	**succeed**	**successful**, unsuccessful, successor	successfully, successive
suddenness		**sudden**	**suddenly**
sufferer, suffering	**suffer**	insufferable	insufferably
suggestion	**suggest**	suggestive	suggestively
summer, midsummer		summery	
supplier, supplies, **supply**	**supply**		
support, supporter	**support**	supportive	
supposition	**suppose**, presuppose	supposed	supposedly
surface	surface, resurface	surface	
surprise	surprise	**surprised**, surprising	surprisingly
surroundings	**surround**	surrounding	
survival, survivor	**survive**		
suspect, suspicion	**suspect**	suspect, suspected, unsuspecting, suspicious	suspiciously
swearing	**swear**	sworn	
sweet, sweetener, sweetness	sweeten	**sweet**	sweetly
swim, swimmer, swimming	**swim**		
symbol, symbolism	symbolize	symbolic	symbolically
sympathy, sympathizer	sympathize	**sympathetic**, unsympathetic	sympathetically
system		systematic	systematically
takings, undertaking	**take**, overtake, undertake		
talk, talks	**talk**	talkative	
taste, distaste	**taste**	tasteful, distasteful, tasteless, tasty	tastefully, distastefully
tax, taxation	tax	taxable, taxing	
teacher, teaching, teachings	**teach**		
tear		tearful	tearfully
technicalities, technicality, technician, technique		**technical**	technically
technology		technological	technologically
thanks	**thank**	thankful, thankless	thankfully
theorist, **theory**	theorize	theoretical	theoretically
thickness	thicken	**thick**	thickly
thinness	thin	**thin**	thinly
think, rethink, thinker, thinking	**think**, rethink	unthinkable	

Nouns	Verbs	Adjectives	Adverbs
thirst		**thirsty**	thirstily
thought, thoughtfulness		thoughtful, thoughtless	thoughtfully, thoughtlessly
threat	**threaten**	threatening	threateningly
tightness	tighten	**tight**	tight, tightly
time, overtime, timer, timing	time	timeless, timely, untimely	
tiredness	tire	**tired**, tireless, tiresome, tiring	tirelessly
title, subtitles	entitle	titled	
top, topping	top	**top**, topless, topmost	
touch	**touch**	touched, untouched, touching, touchy	touchingly
	toughen	**tough**	toughly
trade, trader, trading	trade		
tradition, traditionalist		**traditional**	traditionally
trainee, trainer, **training**, retraining	**train**	trained, untrained	
transport, transportation	transport		
treat, **treatment**, mistreatment	**treat**, mistreat	untreated	
trick, trickery	trick	tricky	
trouble	trouble	troubled, troublesome	
trust, distrust, mistrust, trustee	**trust**, distrust, mistrust	trusting, trustworthy	
truth, untruth, truthfulness		**true**, untrue, truthful	truly, truthfully
try	**try**	trying, untried	
turn, upturn, turning	**turn**, overturn	upturned	
twist, twister	**twist**	twisted	
type, typist	typify	**typical**	typically
understanding, misunderstanding	**understand**	understandable, understanding, misunderstood	understandably, misunderstand
upset	upset	**upset**, upsetting	
urgency, urge	urge	**urgent**	urgently
usage, **use**, disuse, misuse, usefulness, user	**use**, misuse, reuse	reusable, **used**, disused, unused, **useful**, **useless**	usefully
valuables, **value**, values	value, devalue	**valuable**, invaluable, undervalued	
variable, variance, variant, **variety**	vary	variable, varied, **various**	invariably, variously
view, overview, preview, review, viewer	view, preview, review		
violence	violate	**violent**, non-violent	violently
visit, **visitor**	**visit**, revisit		
vote, voter	**vote**		
want, wants	**want**	wanted, unwanted	
war, warfare, warrior		postwar, warring	
warmth	warm	**warm**	warmly
wash, washer, washing	**wash**	washable, unwashed	
waste, wastage	**waste**	waste, wasteful	wastefully
watch	**watch**	watchful	
water, waters	water	underwater, waterproof, watery	underwater
way, subway		wayward	midway
weakling, weakness	weaken	**weak**	weakly
wear, underwear	**wear**	wearing, worn	
week, midweek		weekly, midweek	weekly, midweek
weight, weights	**weigh**, outweigh	overweight, underweight, weighted, weighty	
welcome	**welcome**	welcome, unwelcome	

Nouns	Verbs	Adjectives	Adverbs
west, western, westerner		westerly, western	west, westward(s)
white, whiteness	whiten	**white**	
whole		**whole**, wholesome, unwholesome	
width	widen	**wide**	**wide**, **widely**
wild, wildness		**wild**	wildly
willingness, unwillingness		**willing**, unwilling	willingly, unwillingly
win, **winner**, winnings	**win**		
winter, midwinter		wintry	
wire, wireless, wiring	wire	wiry	
woman, womanhood		womanly	
wonder	**wonder**	**wonderful**	wonderfully
wood		wooded, wooden	
wool		woollen/US woolen, woolly/US wooly	
word, wording	word		
work, workaholic, worker, workings	**work**, rework	workable, unworkable, overworked, working	
world, underworld		world, worldly, unworldly, worldwide	worldwide
worry	**worry**	**worried**, unworried, worrying	worryingly
worth		**worth**, worthless, worthwhile, worthy, unworthy	
writer, **writing**	**write**, rewrite	written, unwritten	
wrong	wrong	**wrong**, wrongful	**wrong**, wrongly, wrongfully
year		yearly	yearly
young, youngster, youth		**young**, youthful